PROCEEDINGS OF THE 2013 INTERNATIONAL CONFERENCE ON PARALLEL AND DISTRIBUTED PROCESSING TECHNIQUES AND APPLICATIONS

PDPTA 2013

Volume I & II

Editors

Hamid R. Arabnia, Hiroshi Ishii
Minoru Ito, Kazuki Joe
Hiroaki Nishikawa, Fernando G. Tinetti

Associate Editors

George A. Gravvanis
George Jandieri
Ashu M. G. Solo

(An Imprint of Laxmi Publications Pvt. Ltd.)
An ISO 9001:2008 Company

BENGALURU • CHENNAI • COCHIN • GUWAHATI • HYDERABAD
JALANDHAR • KOLKATA • LUCKNOW • MUMBAI • RANCHI • NEW DELHI
BOSTON (USA) • ACCRA (GHANA) • NAIROBI (KENYA)

This set of volumes contains papers presented at The 2013 International Conference on Parallel and Distributed Processing Techniques and Applications (PDPTA'13). Their inclusion in this publication does not necessarily constitute endorsements by editors or by the publisher.

Branches

Branch	Telephone	
Bengaluru	080-26 75 69 30	
Chennai	044-24 34 47 26,	24 35 95 07
Cochin	0484-237 70 04,	405 13 03
Guwahati	0361-254 36 69,	251 38 81
Hyderabad	040-27 55 53 83,	27 55 53 93
Jalandhar	0181-222 12 72	
Kolkata	033-22 27 43 84	
Lucknow	0522-220 99 16	
Mumbai	022-24 91 54 15,	24 92 78 69
Ranchi	0651-220 44 64	

PUBLISHED IN INDIA BY

An ISO 9001:2008 Company
113, GOLDEN HOUSE, DARYAGANJ,
NEW DELHI - 110002, INDIA
Telephone : 91-11-4353 2500, 4353 2501
Fax : 91-11-2325 2572, 4353 2528
www.laxmipublications.com info@laxmipublications.com

C—
Printed at:

Foreword

It gives us great pleasure to introduce this collection of papers to be presented at the 2013 International Conference on Parallel and Distributed Processing Techniques and Applications (PDPTA'13), July 22 through 25, 2013, at The New Tropicana Hotel, Las Vegas, USA.

An important mission of the World Congress in Computer Science, Computer Engineering, and Applied Computing (a federated congress to which this conference is affiliated with) includes *"Providing a unique platform for a diverse community of constituents composed of scholars, researchers, developers, educators, and practitioners. The Congress makes concerted effort to reach out to participants affiliated with diverse entities (such as: universities, institutions, corporations, government agencies, and research centers/labs) from all over the world. The congress also attempts to connect participants from institutions that have* ***teaching*** *as their main mission with those who are affiliated with institutions that have* ***research*** *as their main mission. The congress uses a quota system to achieve its institution and geography diversity objectives."* By any definition of diversity, this congress is among the most diverse scientific meeting in USA. We are proud to report that this federated congress has authors and participants from 82 different nations representing variety of personal and scientific experiences that arise from differences in culture and values. As can be seen (see below), the program committee of this conference as well as the program committee of all other tracks of the federated congress are as diverse as its authors and participants.

The program committee would like to thank all those who submitted papers for consideration. About 52% of the submissions were from outside the United States. Each submitted paper was peer-reviewed by two experts in the field for originality, significance, clarity, impact, and soundness. In cases of contradictory recommendations, a member of the conference program committee was charged to make the final decision; often, this involved seeking help from additional referees. In addition, papers whose authors included a member of the conference program committee were evaluated using the double-blinded review process. One exception to the above evaluation process was for papers that were submitted directly to chairs/organizers of pre-approved sessions/workshops; in these cases, the chairs/organizers were responsible for the evaluation of such submissions. The overall paper acceptance rate for regular papers was 29%; 8% of the remaining papers were accepted as poster papers (at the time of this writing, we had not yet received the acceptance rate for a few individual tracks.)

We are very grateful to the many colleagues who offered their services in organizing the conference. In particular, we would like to thank the members of the Program Committee of PDPTA'13, members of the congress Steering Committee, and members of the committees of federated congress tracks that have topics within the scope of PDPTA. Many individuals listed below, will be requested after the conference to provide their expertise and services for selecting papers for publication (extended versions) in journal special issues as well as for publication in a set of research books (to be prepared for publishers including: Springer, Elsevier, BMC, and others).

- *Dr. Alireza Abbasi; School of Engineering and Information Technology, University of New South Wales (UNSW), Canberra, Australia*
- *Dr. Selim Aissi (World Congress Steering Committee); formerly, Chief Strategist - Security, Intel Corporation, USA; Senior Business Leader & Head of Global Enterprise Security Architecture, Visa Corporation, USA*
- *Prof. Babak Akhgar (World Congress Steering Committee); Fellow of the British Computer Society, CITP; Professor of Informatics; Co-Director of CENTRIC (Centre of Excellence in Terrorism, Resilience, Intelligence & organised Crime research), Sheffield Hallam University, Sheffield, UK*
- *Prof. Hussain Al-Asaad; Senior Member, IEEE; University of California at Davis, Davis, California, USA*
- *Prof. Nizar Al-Holou (World Congress Steering Committee + ICWN); Professor and Chair, Electrical and Computer Engineering Department; Vice Chair, IEEE/SEM-Computer Chapter; University of Detroit Mercy, Detroit, Michigan, USA*
- *Prof. Hideharu Amano (ERSA); Keio University, Japan; Head, technical group of computer systems of IEICE; Editor, Journal of Parallel and Distributed Computing; Japan*
- *Prof. Hamid R. Arabnia (World Congress Steering Committee); Professor, Computer Science; Editor-in-Chief, The Journal of Supercomputing (Springer); Co-Editor/Board, Journal of Computational Science*

- *Dr. Jong Kwan (Jake) Lee; Department of Computer Science, Bowling Green State University, Ohio, USA*
- *Prof. Kun Chang Lee (World Congress Steering Committee); Professor of MIS and WCU Professor of Creativity Science, Business School and Department of Interaction Science, Sungkyunkwan University, Seoul, South Korea*
- *Prof. Zhongyu (Joan) Lu (CSC + IPCV); University of Huddersfield, Huddersfield, UK*
- *Dr. Bala Krishna Maddali; University School of Information Technology, GGS Indraprastha University, New Delhi, India*
- *Muhammad Naufal Bin Mansor; Intelligent Signal Processing Group (ISP), University Malaysia Perlis, Kangar, Perlis, Malaysia*
- *Prof. Gevorg Margarov; Head of Information Security and Software Development Department, State Engineering University of Armenia, Armenia*
- *Prof. George Markowsky (World Congress Steering Committee and SAM Session Chair); Professor and Associate Director, School of Computing and Information Science; Chair International Advisory Board of IEEE IDAACS; Director 2013 Northeast Collegiate Cyber Defense Competition; University of Maine, Orono, Maine, USA*
- *Dr. Sara Moein; Editorial Board, International Journal of Science and Technology; Faculty of Engineering, MultiMedia University, Malaysia*
- *Dr. Ali Mostafaeipour; Industrial Engineering Department, Yazd University, Iran*
- *Dr. Saurabh Mukherjee; Associate Professor, Department of Computer Science, Banasthali University, Banasthali, Rajasthan, India*
- *Dr. Asoke Nath (SAM + BIOCOMP); Department of Computer Science, St. Xavier's College, India*
- *Daniel Nenni (ERSA Advisory Board); Founder at The Semiconductor Wiki Project, USA*
- *Prof. Hiroaki Nishikawa (Session Chair, PDPTA); University of Tsukuba, Ibaraki, Japan*
- *Prof. Noel De Palma; Associate Vice President for Research, Computer Science; Leader, ERODS Research, LIG Labs.; Board of Directors, OW2 Consortium; Department of Computer Science; University Joseph Fourier (UJF), Grenoble, France*
- *Prof. G. N. Pandey (World Congress Steering Committee); Vice-Chancellor, Arunachal University of Studies, Arunachal Pradesh, India; Adjunct Professor, Indian Institute of Information Technology, Allahabad, India*
- *Prof. James J. (Jong Hyuk) Park (World Congress Steering Committee); Professor of Computer Science and Engineering, Seoul National University of Science and Technology (SeoulTech), Korea; President, KITCS; President, FTRA; Editor-in-Chiefs: HCIS, JoC and IJITCC Journals*
- *Dr. Satish Penmatsa; Assistant Professor, Computer Science, University of Maryland - Eastern Shore, Maryland, USA*
- *Dr. Toomas Plaks (Chair, ERSA); WEBestSOL and Webest Solutions Ltd, UK*
- *Prof. R. Ponalagusamy; Department of Mathematics, National Institute of Technology, Tiruchirappalli, India*
- *Prof. Junfeng Qu; Clayton State University, Morrow, Georgia, USA*
- *Dr. Salva Sebastien (SERP); Fellow, Limos laboratory (CNRS), France; Associate Professor, University of Auvergne (UdA), LIMOS Complexe scientifique des Cezeaux, Aubiere, France*
- *Dr. Liang Shi; Senior Researcher, McAfee, USA*
- *Dr. Zhefu Shi; Microsoft Corporation, Redmond, Washington, USA*
- *Dr. Kok Swee Sim; Faculty of Engineering and Technology, Jalan Ayer Keroh Lama, Melaka, Malaysia*
- *Ashu M. G. Solo, (Publicity Chair); Fellow of British Computer Society, Principal/R&D Engineer, Maverick Technologies America Inc., USA*
- *Prof. K. Subramani; West Virginia University, USA*
- *Dr. Alain Tchana (GCA); Grenoble University, France*
- *Prof. Fernando G. Tinetti (World Congress Steering Committee); School of Computer Science, Universidad Nacional de La Plata, La Plata, Argentina; Co-editor, Journal of Computer Science and Technology (JCS&T)*
- *Dr. Predrag Tosic (World Congress Steering Committee); Microsoft, Washington, USA*
- *Prof. Quoc-Nam Tran, Ph.D. (Vice-Chair of BIOCOMP); Professor and Chair of Computer Science, The University of Texas at Tyler, Tyler, Texas, USA*
- *Dr. Vinay Vaidya (IPCV); CTO and Vice President, Center for Research in Engineering Sciences and Technology (CREST), KPIT Cummins Infosystems Limited, Pune, India*
- *Prof. Vladimir Volkov (World Congress Steering Committee & Vice-Chair of IPCV); The Bonch-Bruevich State University of Telecommunications, Saint-Petersburg, Russia*
- *Dr. Alexander Wohrer (ICOMP + GCA); Program Manager ICT at Vienna Science and Technology Fund, Schlickgasse, Vienna, Austria*
- *Prof. Dr. Bernd E. Wolfinger; Telecommunications and Computer Networks Division, Computer Science Department, University of Hamburg, Germany*

- *Prof. Jongwook Woo; Director, High-Performance Information Computing Center (HiPiC), Computer Information Systems Department, California State University, Los Angeles, California, USA*
- *Prof. Jane You (Vice-Chair of IPCV); The Hong Kong Polytechnic University, Hong Kong*

As Sponsors-at-large, partners, and/or organizers each of the followings (separated by semicolons) provided help for at least one track of the World Congress: Aldebaran Robotics Inc., USA (http://www.aldebaran-robotics.com); Altera Corporation, USA (http://www.altera.com/); Computer Science Research, Education, and Applications Press (CSREA); Impulse Accelerated Technologies, Inc., USA (http://www.impulseaccelerated.com/); NVIDIA Corporation, USA (http://www.nvidia.com/object/about-nvidia.html); Parallella Community, Supercomputing for Everyone, USA (http://forums.parallella.org/); Pico Computing, Inc., USA (http://picocomputing.com/); SemiWiki.com, The Semiconductor Wiki Project, USA (http://www.semiwiki.com/); Solarflare Communications, Inc., USA (http://www.solarflare.com/); Stream Computing, Performance Engineers, The Netherlands (http://streamcomputing.eu/); Taylor & Francis, UK (http://www.taylorandfrancis.com/); US Chapter of World Academy of Science (http://www.world-academy-of-science.org/) ; and WEBestSOL & Webest Solutions Ltd, UK (http://webestsol.com/). In addition, a number of university faculty members and their staff (names appear on the cover of the set of proceedings), several publishers of computer science and computer engineering books and journals, chapters and/or task forces of computer science associations/organizations from 5 countries, and developers of high-performance machines and systems provided significant help in organizing the conference as well as providing some resources. We are grateful to them all.

We express our gratitude to keynote, invited, and individual conference/tracks and tutorial speakers - the list of speakers appears on the conference web site. We would also like to thank the followings: UCMSS (Universal Conference Management Systems & Support, California, USA) for managing all aspects of the conference; Dr. Tim Field of APC for managing the printing of the proceedings; and the staff of the New Tropicana Hotel in Las Vegas for the professional service they provided. Last but not least, we would like to thank the Co-Editors and Associate Co-Editors of PDPTA'13: Prof. Hamid R. Arabnia, Dr. George A. Gravvanis, Prof. Hiroshi Ishii, Prof. Minoru Ito, Prof. George Jandieri, Prof. Kazuki Joe, Prof. Hiroaki Nishikawa, Ashu M. G. Solo, and Prof. Fernando G. Tinetti.

We present the proceedings of PDPTA'13.

Steering Committee, 2013
http://www.world-academy-of-science.org/

Contents

SESSION: RESOURCE ALLOCATION, SCHEDULING, ENERGY-AWARE COMPUTING + LOAD-BALANCING + FAULT-TOLERANT SYSTEMS

SESSION: PARALLEL AND DISTRIBUTED ALGORITHMS AND APPLICATIONS

SESSION: WORKSHOP: MATHEMATICAL MODELING AND PROBLEM SOLVING - MPS

SESSION: GRID + CLOUD COMPUTING AND SUPPORTING TOOLS + APPLICATIONS

SESSION: SYSTEMS SOFTWARE + PROGRAMMING MODELS + THREADS + CACHING + FILE SYSTEMS + TESTING AND MONITORING METHODS

SESSION: PERFORMANCE EVALUATION, ESTIMATION, AND RELATED ISSUES

SESSION: COMMUNICATION SYSTEMS + NETWORKS AND INTERCONNECTION NETWORKS + PEER-TO-PEER NETWORKS AD-HOC NETWORKS + SENSOR NETWORKS AND APPLICATIONS

SESSION: CLUSTER COMPUTING + MULTI-CORE, GPU, FPGA PROCESSING AND APPLICATIONS

SESSION: DATA-DRIVEN NETWORKING SYSTEMS WITH HIGH TOLERANCE FOR DISASTER, FAULT AND CONGESTION

SESSION: POSTERS AND SHORT RESEARCH PAPERS

SESSION: POSITION AND REGULAR - COMMUNICATION SYSTEMS, CLOUD COMPUTING, RECONFIGURABLE SYSTEMS, PARALLEL AND DISTRIBUTED COMPUTING, SCHEDULING, ARCHITECTURES, AND APPLICATIONS

SESSION: LATE BREAKING PAPER - cloud computing, optimization, sensor networks, scheduling, and applications

SESSION

RESOURCE ALLOCATION, SCHEDULING, ENERGY-AWARE COMPUTING + LOAD-BALANCING + FAULT-TOLERANT SYSTEMS

Chair(s)

TBA

A Machine-by-Machine Analysis of a Bi-Objective Resource Allocation Problem

Ryan Friese[1], **Tyler Brinks**[1,2], **Curt Oliver**[1]
Anthony A. Maciejewski[1], **Howard Jay Siegel**[1,2], **and Sudeep Pasricha**[1,2]
[1]Department of Electrical and Computer Engineering
[2]Department of Computer Science
Colorado State University
Fort Collins, CO, 80523

Abstract—*As high performance computing systems continually become faster, the operating cost to run these systems has increased. A significant portion of the operating costs can be attributed to the amount of energy required for these systems to operate. To reduce these costs it is important for system administrators to operate these systems in an energy-efficient manner. To help facilitate a transition to energy-efficient computing, the trade-offs between system performance and system energy consumption must be analyzed and understood. We analyze these trade-offs through bi-objective resource allocation techniques, and in this paper we explore an analysis approach to help system administrators investigate these trade-offs. Additionally, we show how system administrators can perform "what-if" analyses to evaluate the effects of adding or removing machines from their high performance computing systems. We perform our study using three environments based on data collected from real machines and real applications. We show that by utilizing different resource allocations we are able to significantly change the performance and energy consumption of a given system, providing a system administrator with the means to examine these trade-offs to help make intelligent decisions regarding the scheduling and composition of their systems.*

Keywords: bi-objective optimization; energy-aware computing; heterogeneous computing; resource allocation

1. Introduction

As large computing systems (e.g., supercomputers, clusters, datacenters) have increased in size and performance, the costs of operating these systems have increased as well. A significant portion of these costs can be attributed to the amount of energy that is required to run these systems. Between the years 2000 and 2006 the energy consumption more than doubled for high performance computing (HPC) systems, resulting in servers and datacenters accounting for approximately 1.5% of the total United States energy consumption for that year [1]. This amounts to approximately 61 billion kWh, or $4.5 billion in electricity costs. Energy consumption by HPC systems has continued to increase; from 2005 - 2011 the electricity consumption of these systems has increased by 56% worldwide [2].

Due to the increased electricity use and costs, some system administrators are now faced with the challenge of operating under limitations on electricity usage. To operate efficiently under these limitations, it is important to understand the trade-offs between system performance and system energy consumption. In [3] and [4] it was shown that increasing the energy consumption of a system often leads to an increase in the performance of the system, and vice-versa. Based on these studies, it is imperative for system administrators to analyze the trade-offs between energy consumption and performance of their systems to operate at a desirable level.

In this research, we examine how utilizing different resource allocations (i.e., mapping of tasks to machines) on a given system can allow us to analyze the trade-offs between energy consumption and performance for that system. The current state of the art resource managers, such as MOAB, are unable to reasonably determine the trade-offs between performance and energy based on our experience with it in cluster computing environments.

We model a heterogeneous distributed computing environment used to execute a workload consisting of a bag of tasks. In such an environment, a task may have different execution and power consumption characteristics when executed on different machines. This behavior requires one to explore different resource allocations to optimally manage the energy consumption and performance of the system. We define a resource allocation to be a complete mapping of all the tasks in the bag to the machines. The competing nature of minimizing energy consumption and increasing system performance allows this problem to be modeled as a bi-objective optimization problem.

Many bi-objective optimization algorithms exist, such as those found in [5], that can be adapted and used to produce resource allocations for our problem. We take the solutions produced by such algorithms and create graphical representations that allow us to analyze the performance and energy trade-offs. We produce plots that show general trends between performance and energy consumption, as well as more detailed graphs that allow us to analyze how different allocations use the system on a machine-by-machine basis. Analysis of these graphs can help system administrators find allocations that will allow the system to run at a specified energy/performance level as well as identify inefficiencies in their systems. Additionally, system administrators may desire to simulate the effect and observe the performance and energy consumption implications of adding or removing machines to the system. This could lead to the design of more efficient and cost effective computing systems.

We examine the trade-offs between energy consumption and performance for three different environments. Each environment is based on a set of real machines and real tasks. By analyzing numerous resource allocations, we show that for each environment the behavior of the systems can differ greatly, allowing system administrators to select a resource allocation that best fits the needs of their system.

In this paper we make the following contributions:

1) Perform a machine-by-machine analysis of how different resource allocations can affect the perfomance and energy consumption of a given system.
2) Provide an analysis approach that can identify both energy efficient and energy-inefficient machines, allowing system administrators to use this knowledge to help build and manage their systems.
3) Demonstrate the versatility of our analysis technique using three different heterogeneous environments.

The remainder of the paper is organized as follows. Related work is discussed in Section 2. We explain the system model in Section 3. In Section 4, we describe our bi-objective optimization problem. Our experimental setup is detailed in Section 5. Section 6 analyzes our simulation results. Finally, our conclusion and future work is given in Section 7.

2. Related Work

Several prior efforts have examined bi-objective resource allocation problems in large computing environments.

The bi-objective genetic algorithm NSGAII [6] is adapted for use within the resource allocation domain in [3] and [4]. System-level analyses are performed, specifically looking at the trade-offs of energy and makespan [3] or energy and utility [4]. Our current work performs an in-depth analysis on a machine-by-machine level with a realistic system model.

A bi-objective heterogeneous task scheduling problem between makespan and reliability is presented in [7] and [8]. Instead of reliability, our work investigates the trade-offs between makespan and energy consumption with a machine-by-machine allocation analysis.

In [9], the authors solve a bi-objective optimization between makespan and robustness for a heterogeneous scheduling problem. Solutions are created using a weighted sum simulated annealing heuristic, where one run of the heuristic produces a single solution. In our work we are concerned with multiple solutions, and analyzing how their allocations change based on their location in the search space.

A bi-objective flowshop scheduling problem between makespan and total tardiness is modeled in [10]. Solutions are created using a Pareto-ant colony optimization approach. While we could use methods such as this Pareto-ant approach, the focus of our paper is on the resulting allocations, not how they are created.

The authors of [11] model a homogeneous job-shop scheduling problem between makespan and energy consumption. We are interested in analyzing the behavior of systems that consist of heterogeneous machines, which significantly changes the problem and solution space.

An energy-constrained heterogeneous task scheduling problem is examined in [12]. In this environment, the energy constraint is realized by modeling devices with limited battery capacity in an ad-hoc wireless network. In our work, we are not directly concerned with an energy constraint, though by analyzing different solutions from a Pareto front, a solution could be picked that meets an energy constraint if it was needed.

In [13], the authors try to minimize energy consumption while trying to meet a makespan robustness constraint. Because there is a constraint on the makespan robustness, this is not a bi-objective optimization problem, and does not involve the type of machine-by-machine analysis that we preform.

There are many environments that can be modeled as dynamic resource allocation problems. One such environment is [14], where the system must complete as many tasks as possible by their individual deadlines while staying within the energy budget of the system. This environment does not perform a machine-by-machine analysis to to investigate the trade-offs between energy and makespan.

3. System Model

3.1 Machines

We model a heterogeneous suite of $\underline{M}$ machines, where each machine is one of $\underline{MT}$ machine types. Because we are modeling a heterogeneous system, machine type A may be faster for some tasks than machine type B, but may be slower for other tasks [15]. Machines are also heterogeneous in power consumption. We assume that each machine can only execute a single task at a time, similar to the Colorado State University ISTeC Cray [16]. Once a machine finishes executing all of its assigned tasks it shuts down, and no longer consumes any energy.

3.2 Workload

We model a workload environment where we have a bag of $\underline{T}$ tasks, and each task belongs to a given task type. Every task is known before the schedule is created. Due to the heterogenous nature of the system, each task type

i executing on machine type j will have known execution (Estimated Time to Compute (ETC)) and power consumption (Estimated Power Consumption (EPC)) characteristics denoted as ETC(i,j) and EPC(i,j). Tasks of the same task type have the same ETC and EPC characteristics. In resource allocation, it is common to assume the availability of such characteristics (e.g. [17], [18], [19], [20], [21]). These values may be taken from historical sources ([20], [19]) or may be constructed synthetically for simulation purposes ([22], [15]).

4. Bi-Objective Optimization

4.1 Overview

Many interesting engineering problems deal with multiple objectives. It is often the case that these objectives are competing with one another, and optimizing for one objective may cause the performance of another objective to decrease. It therefore becomes important for one to analyze the behavior (trade-offs) between these objectives. In our research we are trying minimize system makespan (Section 4.2.1) while trying to minimize system energy consumption (Section 4.2.2).

4.2 Objective Functions

4.2.1 Minimizing Makespan

One objective is to minimize makespan, which is defined as the time when all tasks have finished executing. Makespan is used to measure the performance of the system.

The makespan for a specific resource allocation, denoted μ, is the maximum machine finishing time in the system. The finishing time of a machine is the time at which all tasks $\underline{T_m}$ assigned to machine m have finished executing. Let $t_m \in T_m$, $\Upsilon(t_m)$ be the task type of t_m, $\Omega(m)$ be the machine type of m, and

$$F_m = \sum_{\forall t_m \in T_m} ETC(\Upsilon(t_m), \Omega(m)). \quad (1)$$

Makespan is given as

$$\mu = \max_{\forall m \in M} F_m. \quad (2)$$

4.2.2 Minimizing Energy Consumed

The other objective is to minimize total energy consumed. This is defined as the total amount of energy consumed by the machines to execute all tasks. The Expected Energy Consumption (EEC) of a given task t on a given machine m is

$$EEC[\Upsilon(t),\Omega(m)]=ETC[\Upsilon(t),\Omega(m)]\times EPC[\Upsilon(t),\Omega(m)]. \quad (3)$$

The total energy consumption for the system is

$$E = \sum_{\forall m \in M} \sum_{\forall t_m \in T_m} EEC[\Upsilon(t_m), \Omega(m)]. \quad (4)$$

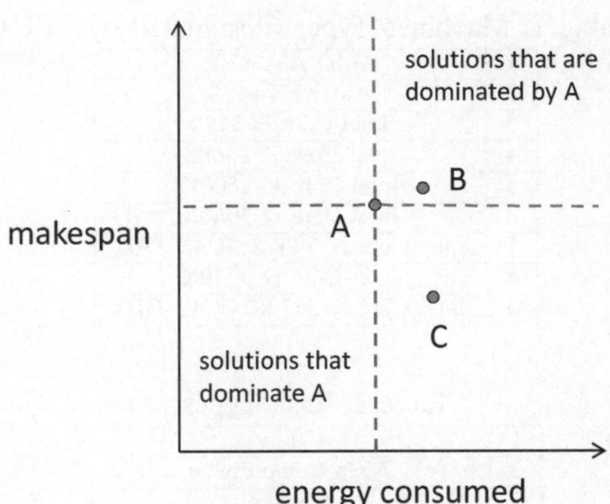

Fig. 1: Illustration of solution dominance for three solutions: A, B, and C. Solution A dominates solution B because A has lower energy consumption as well as a lower makespan. Neither solution A nor C dominate each other because A uses less energy, while C has a lower makespan.

4.3 Generating Solutions

In general, bi-objective optimization problems have a *set* of optimal solutions (not a single solution). This set of solutions is known as the Pareto optimal set, represented as the Pareto front in objective space, defined as the set of known solutions for which no better solutions in any objective have been found [23]. Pareto fronts are useful for analyzing the trade-offs between two objectives. A Pareto front is calculated from existing solutions, but it is not known where the true optimal set lies.

For a solution to exist within the Pareto optimal set, it must not be dominated by any other solution. Domination is defined as one solution being better than another solution in at least one objective, and better than or equal to in the other objective. A simple illustration of dominance is shown in Fig. 1. We have three solutions: A, B, and C. B is dominated by A because A has a lower makespan as well as a lower energy consumption. Thus any solution located in the upper right quadrant would be dominated by A, while any solution located in the lower left quadrant would dominate A. Neither solution A nor C dominate each other because A has a lower energy consumption, and C has a lower makespan. Both of these solutions would then be a part of the Pareto optimal set.

Pareto fronts can be generated using any number of algorithms, such as those found in [5]. The Pareto fronts found in this paper were created using the Non-Dominating Sorted Genetic Algorithm II (NSGAII) [6] adapted for use within the scheduling domain as described in [3]. Note that The method for generating the Pareto fronts are not the focus of this paper, rather it is the analysis of the resource allocations on the Pareto front.

Table 1: Machines Types (designated by CPU)

1	AMD A8-3870k
2	AMD FX-8159
3	Intel Core i3 2120
4	Intel Core i5 2400S
5	Intel Core i5 2500K
6	Intel Core i7 3960X
7	Intel Core i7 3960X @ 4.2 GHz
8	Intel Core i7 3770K
9	Intel Core i7 3770K @ 4.3 GHz

Table 2: Task Types

1	C-Ray
2	7-Zip Compression
3	Warsow
4	Unigine Heaven
5	Timed Linux Kernel Compilation

5. Experimental Setup

5.1 Datasets

To accurately model the relationships between machine performance and energy consumption in the ETC and EPC matrices, we used the method outlined in [4] where a dataset consisting of five applications executed on nine machines [24] is used to create a larger synthetic dataset. The synthetic data set resembles the original data set in terms of heterogeneity characteristics, such as the coefficient of variation, skewness, and kurtosis [25]. The original machine types (designated by CPU) are listed in Table 1 and the original task types are listed in Table 2. The original data contained both execution times and total system power consumption (measured at the outlet) for each task on each machine. Each machine used 16GB of memory, a 240GB SSD, and ran Ubuntu 12.04 (but had different processors).

5.2 Experiments

We considered three test environments each with 36 machines. The first test environment only used machine types 1 and 2 and there were 18 machines of each type in the system. The second test environment utilized machine types 1-6, and there existed six machines per type. Finally the third test environment consisted of the full set of nine machine types with four machines belonging to each type. The bag of tasks for each test environment was identical and consisted of 1000 tasks distributed among 30 task types (the five original task types and 25 synthetic task types).

6. Results

In Figs. 2- 4 we present the results of our experiments for the two machine type, six machine type, and nine machine type environments, respectively. In each fig., the subfig. "F" shows the Pareto front for each environment, where the x-axis is the total system energy consumption measured in megajoules(smaller is better) and the y-axis is the makespan of the system measured in minutes (smaller is better). Each individual marker in these plots represents a complete resource allocation. In each of these Pareto fronts, we see that makespan decreases (e.g. system performance increases) as the energy consumption of the system increases. This is consistent with the results from [3] and [4]. To better understand why this trend occurs, we analyzed five separate resource allocations from the Pareto front (the square markers in each of the Figs. 2F, 3F, and 4F).

For each of our selected resource allocations for each environment, we plotted the completion time and energy consumption of each machine, and grouped the machines by machine type as seen in subfigs. A-E for each environment. Subfigs. A-E range from illustrating the minimum energy consumption allocation in subfig. A to the minimum makespan allocation in subfig. E. For the minimum energy allocations (subfig. A), each task ends up being assigned to a machine that is part of the machine type that executes that task with the least amount of energy.

In the A subfigs. (in all three environments), we find that for each environment there is one machine type that has a longer finishing time than the other machine types (the left graph in the subfig.), and thus determines the makespan for this solution. This occurs because that machine type has more tasks for which it is the minimum energy machine type (implying it is a more energy-efficient machine type), thus those tasks will prefer to run on machines of that type, forcing the completion time for those machines to increase. There can exist many allocations that minimize energy consumption, therefore to be in the Pareto front, a minimum energy allocation must dominate by lowering the makespan of the system. The resource allocation heuristic accomplishes this by decreasing the finishing times of machines in the longest finishing time machine type. This results in balanced finishing times for machines of that type as can be seen in the subfigs. The other machine types have unbalanced finishing times among their machines because they do not have any effect on the makespan of the system. Another interesting observation is that in the environments with six and nine machine types (Subfigs. 3A and 4A) there exist machines that do not execute even a single task. This is because these machine types are not the minimum energy machines for any task.

Examining the subfigs. from A to E, we find the completion times of all the machines start to become balanced. This is because to lower the system makespan, a resource allocation must distribute the tasks to all the machines so that one machine (or machines in a machine type) is not forced to execute significantly more tasks than the other machines. Hence, working through the Pareto front (from left to right) the machine completion times become more balanced (lower makespan) by forcing tasks to run on machine types that consume higher amounts of energy. This becomes most apparent in the E subfigs., where the machines have balanced

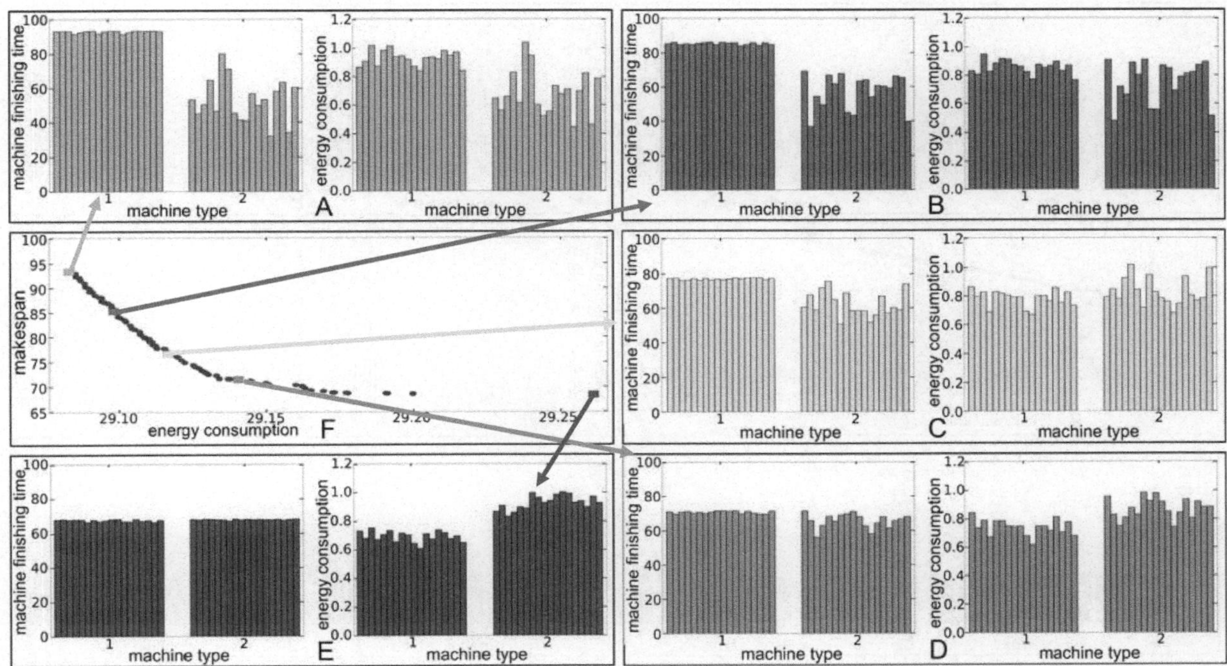

Fig. 2: Pareto front (F) and five resource allocations (A-E) for an environment with two machine types. The Pareto front illustrates the trade-offs between energy consumption in megajoules (x-axis) and makespan in minutes (y-axis). In A-E, the left graph shows the completion of each machine in minutes (y-axis) in the system. The right graph shows the energy consumption of each machine in megajoules (y-axis). In both graphs the machines are grouped by machine type (x-axis).

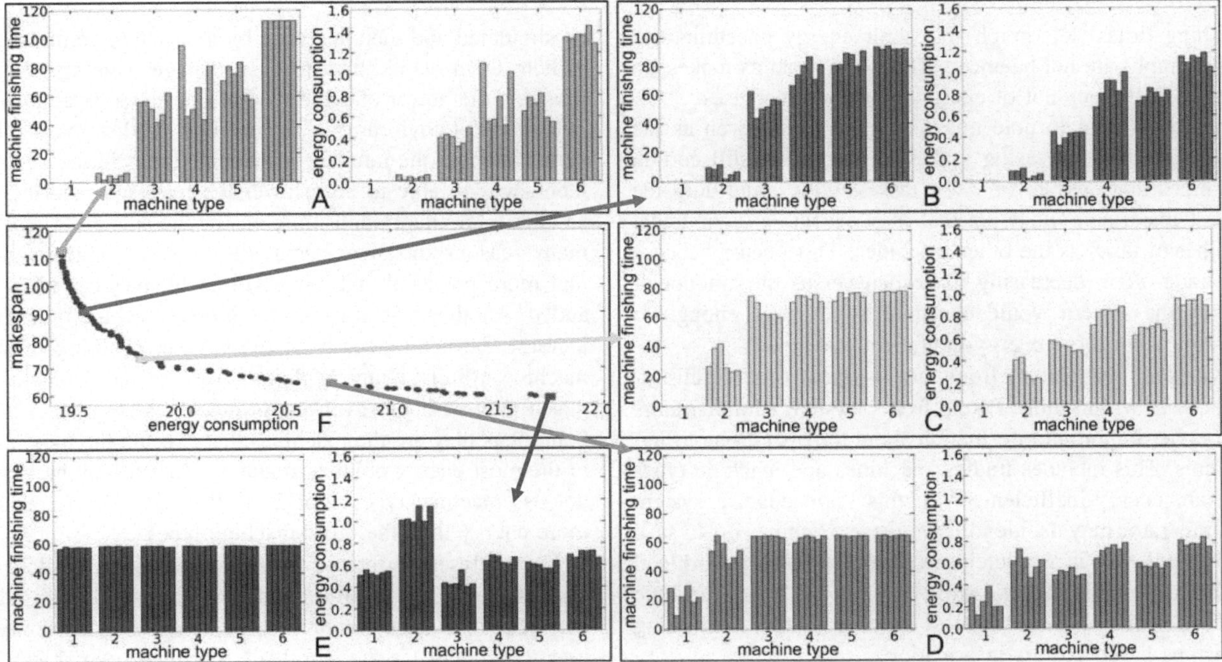

Fig. 3: Pareto front (F) and five resource allocations (A-E) for an environment with six machine types. The Pareto front illustrates the trade-offs between energy consumption in megajoules (x-axis) and makespan in minutes (y-axis). In A-E, the left graph shows the completion of each machine in minutes (y-axis) in the system. The right graph shows the energy consumption of each machine in megajoules (y-axis). In both graphs the machines are grouped by machine type (x-axis).

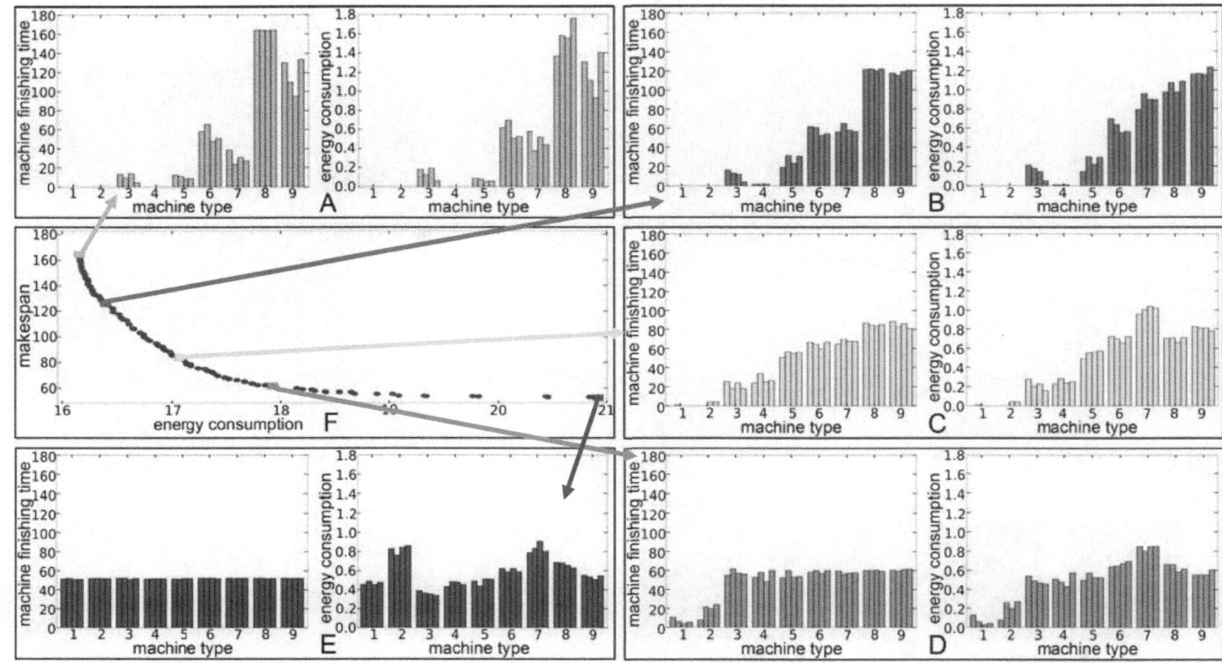

Fig. 4: Pareto front (F) and five resource allocations (A-E) for an environment with nine machine types. The Pareto front illustrates the trade-offs between energy consumption in megajoules (x-axis) and makespan in minutes (y-axis). In A-E, the left graph shows the completion of each machine in minutes (y-axis) in the system. The right graph shows the energy consumption of each machine in megajoules (y-axis). In both graphs the machines are grouped by machine type (x-axis).

finishing times (left graph) but their energy consumptions (right graph) are not balanced. This shows that as makespan decreases, the amount of energy consumed increases.

It is important to note in Figs. 3 and 4 that even as the allocations are decreasing makespan, there are still certain machines that execute very few tasks, and it is not until the lowest makespan allocation that they execute a comparable number of tasks as the other machines. This occurs because the trade-off in decreasing makespan versus the amount of energy the system would consume is not large enough to warrant using these energy-inefficient machines.

By examining Pareto fronts and various resource allocations from within those Pareto fronts, system administrators can gather important information about the operation of their systems. This includes finding machines and machine types that are energy-inefficient. With this knowledge, a system administrator may decide to leave these machines off to save energy unless it is absolutely necessary to finish a workload as fast as possible. Additionally, they can see which machine types are being utilized the most and make future purchasing decisions based on this information.

Finally, this study provides and example of how system administrators can perform "what-if" analyses. For example, what if we add more machine types to the system, what if we add more machines of a specific machine type, or what if we turn off certain machines? All of these scenarios could be simulated and then analyzed by the system administrator to help them decide how to best manage their system. We illustrate the power of these type of questions by comparing our three test environments against one another. We see that as we increase the number of machine types in the environment, we are able to both lower the makespan and have a smaller total energy consumption for the system. There are many reasons this may occur, the most straightforward is that more powerful and energy efficient machine types are added. Another reason is that additional machine types may increase the heterogeneity of the system, resulting in task-machine affinity being exploited. We are also able to see that it may be better to invest in machines that are of types 8 and 9 as they are the machines that execute the most tasks in the most energy efficient manner, while it may be best to not use machine types 1 or 2 at all as they both consume more energy than the other machine types.

The analyses performed in this work cannot be done by evaluation of only the ETC and EPC characteristics, rather, they require a more comprehensive analysis of the complex interaction between the workload, machines, two objectives.

7. Conclusions and Future Work

Energy-efficient computing is becoming very important due to the need for greater performance and the rising costs of energy consumption. System administrators must have tools that will allow them to evaluate the energy and performance characteristics of their systems. In this work, we provide a tool that allows system administrators to study the trade-offs between system performance and system energy consumption. We show that by analyzing individual resource allocations we can examine how a given system is distributing and executing tasks depending on the performance and energy consumption desired. This investigation can help identify the degree of energy-inefficiency of the machines, as well as allow system administrators to perform "what-if" analyses to determine the effect of adding or removing machines from their systems.

There are many directions for future work. These include examining different performance and cost objectives such as: maximizing robustness, minimizing temperature, maximizing utility, and minimizing monetary costs. We would like to enhance our power model by utilizing dynamic voltage and frequency scaling techniques to save additional energy.

8. Acknowledgements

This work was supported by the National Science Foundation (NSF) under grant number CNS-0905399, the NSF Graduate Research Fellowship, and by the Colorado State University George T. Abell Endowment. Any opinion, findings, and conclusions or recommendations expressed in this material are those of the authors and do not necessarily reflect the views of the NSF. This research also used the CSU ISTeC Cray System supported by NSF Grant CNS-0923386. The authors thank M. Oxley and T. Hansen for their valuable comments.

References

[1] Environmental Protection Agency, "Report to congress on server and data center energy efficency," http://www.energystar.gov/ia/partners/prod_development/downloads/EPA_Datacenter_Report_Congress_Final1.pdf, Aug. 2007.

[2] J. Koomey, "Growth in data center electricity use 2005 to 2010," *Analytics Press*, Aug. 2011.

[3] R. Friese, T. Brinks, C. Oliver, H. J. Siegel, and A. A. Maciejewski, "Analyzing the trade-offs between minimizing makespan and minimizing energy consumption in a heterogeneous resource allocation problem," in *2nd Int'l Conf. on Advanced Communications and Computation (INFOCOMP 2012)*, Oct. 2012, p. 9.

[4] R. Friese, B. Khemka, A. A. Maciejewski, H. J. Siegel, G. A. Koenig, S. Powers, M. Hilton, J. Rambharos, G. Okonski, and S. W. Poole, "An analysis framework for investigating the trade-offs between system performance and energy consumption in a heterogeneous computing environment," in *IEEE 22nd Heterogeneity in Computing Workshop (HCW 2013)*, May 2013.

[5] A. Konak, D. W. Coit, and A. E. Smith, "Multi-objective optimization using genetic algorithms: A tutorial," *Journal of Reliability Engineering ans System Safety*, vol. 91, pp. 992–1007, Sept. 2006.

[6] K. Deb, A. Pratap, S. Agarwal, and T. Meyarivan, "A fast and elitist multiobjective genetic algorithm: NSGA-II," *IEEE Evolutionary Computation*, vol. 6, no. 2, pp. 182–197, Apr. 2002.

[7] J. J. Dongarra, E. Jeannot, E. Saule, and Z. Shi, "Bi-objective scheduling algorithms for optimizing makespan and reliability on heterogeneous systems," in *19th Annual ACM Symp. on Parallel Algorithms and Architectures (SPAA '07)*, 2007, pp. 280–288.

[8] E. Jeannot, E. Saule, and D. Trystram, "Bi-objective approximation scheme for makespan and reliability optimization on uniform parallel machines," in *14th Int'l Euro-Par Conf on Parallel Processing (Euro-Par '08)*, 2008, vol. 5168, pp. 877–886.

[9] B. Abbasi, S. Shadrokh, and J. Arkat, "Bi-objective resource-constrained project scheduling with robustness and makespan criteria," *Applied Mathematics and Computation*, vol. 180, no. 1, pp. 146–152, 2006.

[10] J. Pasia, R. Hartl, and K. Doerner, "Solving a bi-objective flowshop scheduling problem by Pareto-ant colony optimization," in *Ant Colony Optimization and Swarm Intelligence*, 2006, vol. 4150, pp. 294–305.

[11] Y. He, F. Liu, H.-j. Cao, and C.-b. Li, "A bi-objective model for job-shop scheduling problem to minimize both energy consumption and makespan," *Journal of Central South University of Technology*, vol. 12, pp. 167–171, Oct. 2005.

[12] J.-K. Kim, H. J. Siegel, A. A. Maciejewski, and R. Eigenmann, "Dynamic resource management in energy constraind heterogeneous computing systems using voltage scaling," *IEEE Parallel and Distrubted Systems*, vol. 19, no. 11, pp. 1445–1457, Nov. 2008.

[13] J. Apodaca, B. D. Young, L. Briceno, J. Smith, S. Pasricha, A. A. Maciejewski, H. J. Siegel, S. Bahirat, B. Khemka, A. Ramirez, and Y. Zou, "Stochastically robust static resource allocation for energy minimization with a makespan constraint in a heterogeneous computing environment," in *9th IEEE/ACS Int'l Conf. on Computer Systems and Applications (AICCSA '11)*, Dec. 2011, pp. 22–31.

[14] B. D. Young, J. Apodaca, L. D. Briceno, J. Smith, S. Pasricha, A. A. Maciejewski, H. J. Siegel, B. Khemka, S. Bahirat, A. Ramirez, and Y. Zou, "Deadline and energy constrained dynamic resource allocation in a heterogeneous computing environment," *Journal of Supercomputing*, vol. 63, Feb. 2013.

[15] S. Ali, H. J. Siegel, M. Maheswaran, D. Hensgen, and S. Ali, "Representing task and machine heterogeneities for heterogeneous computing systems," *Tamkang Journal of Science and Engineering*, vol. 3, no. 3, pp. 195–207, 2000.

[16] (2013, Mar.) ISTeC Cray high performance computing (HPC) system. http://istec.colostate.edu/istec_cray/.

[17] P. Chitra, R. Rajaram, and P. Venkatesh, "Application and comparison of hybrid evolutionary multiobjective optimization algorithms for solving task scheduling problem on heterogeneous systems," *Applied Soft Computing*, vol. 11, no. 2, pp. 2725–2734, Mar. 2011.

[18] M. K. Dhodhi, I. Ahmad, A. Yatama, and I. Ahmad, "An integrated technique for task matching and scheduling onto distributed heterogeneous computing systems," *Journal of Parallel and Distributed Computing*, vol. 62, no. 9, pp. 1338–1361, Sept. 2002.

[19] A. Khokhar, V. Prasanna, M. Shaaban, and C.-L. Wang, "Heterogeneous computing: Challenges and opportunities," *IEEE Computer*, vol. 26, no. 6, pp. 18–27, June 1993.

[20] A. Ghafoor and J. Yang, "A distributed heterogeneous supercomputing management system," *IEEE Computer*, vol. 26, no. 6, pp. 78–86, June 1993.

[21] M. Kafil and I. Ahmad, "Optimal task assignment in heterogeneous distributed computing systems," *IEEE Concurrency*, vol. 6, no. 3, pp. 42–50, Jul.-Sep. 1998.

[22] P. Lindberg, J. Leingang, D. Lysaker, S. U. Khan, and J. Li, "Comparison and analysis of eight scheduling heuristics for the optimization of energy consumption and makespan in large-scale distributed systems," *Supercomputing*, vol. 59, no. 1, pp. 323–360, Jan. 2012.

[23] V. Pareto, *Cours D'economie Politique*. Lausanne: F. Rouge, 1896.

[24] "Intel core i7 3770k power consumption, thermal," http://openbenchmarking.org/result/1204229-SU-CPUMONITO81#system_table, Jul. 2012, accessed: 07/24/2012.

[25] A. M. Al-Qawasmeh, A. A. Maciejewski, H. Wang, J. Smith, H. J. Siegel, and J. Potter, "Statistical measures for quantifying task and machine heterogeneities," *Journal of Supercomputing*, vol. 57, no. 1, pp. 34–50, Jul. 2011.

A Load Balancing Schema for Agent-based SPMD Applications

Claudio Márquez, Eduardo César, and Joan Sorribes
Computer Architecture and Operating Systems Department (CAOS),
Universitat Autònoma de Barcelona, 08193 Bellaterra, Spain
Email: claudio.marquez@caos.uab.es, {eduardo.cesar,joan.sorribes}@uab.cat

Abstract— *Agent based applications are used for large simulations of complex systems. When large number of agents and complex interaction rules are required, an HPC infrastructure can be helpful for executing such simulations in a reasonable time. However, complex interaction rules usually cause workload imbalances that negatively affect the simulation time. In this paper, we propose a load balancing schema that tries to find a reduced combination of exchanges to balance the computing time of the processes. The method adjusts the computational load within a certain range of tolerance, computing the global reconfiguration of the workload using computing time, and the number of agents. Experiments show gains between 15 and 30 percent of the Execution time. In addition, we propose a modification of the agent-based simulation framework named FLAME that provides the automatic generation of the routines needed to dynamically migrate agents among different computational units.*

Keywords: Agent-based Simulation, FLAME, Load Balancing, Application Tuning, SPMD.

1. Introduction

Agent-Based Modeling and Simulations (ABMS) can take advantage of High Performance Computing (HPC) systems. Generally, HPC systems facilitate the execution of more realistic scenarios with many agents and complex interaction rules. Moreover, when the simulation requires more computational scalability, SPMD paradigm is commonly used. These SPMD applications execute the same program in all processes, but with a different set of the domain.

ABMS show significant variations in amount of computing and communication times. During the simulation process load imbalances are likely to appear due to the high-level of interaction between agents and the different rules of behavior exhibited by most of these models. In addition, an unequal distribution of agents causes load imbalances that negatively affect the execution time of the simulation.

In order to solve such problems, the parallel SPMD simulation environments should include a dynamic load balancing mechanisms that allows the migration of agents between different computational units.

This paper is addressed to the PDPTA'13 Conference

Currently, few parallel ABMS environment oriented to HPC environments can be found. Ecolab [1] is an object oriented environment written in C++ and MPI. Repast HPC [2] was recently released in 2012, it is also written in C++ using MPI for parallel operations. Contrary to Ecolab, Repast HPC was created from the beginning for large-scale distributed computing platforms. Although both Ecolab and Repast HPC argue that agents should be migrated; they do not include generic migration routines, so the developer should implement the whole migration code. Finally, FLAME [3] allows the production of automatic parallelizable code to run on large HPC system.

Dynamic load balancing strategies are commonly developed using centralized or hierarchical approaches. Unfortunately, these approaches report a high computational cost and scalability problems. In other hand, decentralized approaches can present problems regarding the quality of the balance because the neighboring processes exchange incomplete information. In [4] is proposed a centralized load balancing based on space repartitioning. In [5] a hierarchical multi-level load balancing strategy is presented, and centralized and hierarchical schemas are compared. In [6] three algorithms using recursive domain decomposition in a binary tree structure are compared using balance speed and communication costs. In [7] a complex partitioning approach based on irregular spatial decompositions is presented. In [8] and [9] distributed cluster-based partitioning and load balancing schema for problems of flocking behaviors are defined.

In general, most of ABMS platforms do not include a load balancing mechanism, and usually the strategy depends on the nature of the agent model. Moreover, the load balancing studies take place usually in non-SPMD platforms, and most of them use applications created with integrated strategies. Consequently, we decided to develop a strategy independent platform, and integrate it in FLAME as a plugging. This platform has been continuously developed from 2006. FLAME is written in C using MPI and is aimed principally at the economical, medical, biological and social science domains. The code generated by FLAME lacks the necessary routines to allow the migration of agents. Therefore, before using any Load Balancing schema, a migration mechanism should be implemented.

This paper describes a Load Balancing schema and a modification of the FLAME framework that provides the automatic generation of the routines needed to migrate agents between different computational units. Using these routines, our Load Balancing schema allows automatic and dynamic tuning decisions in terms of computational load.

The rest of this document is organized into five sections. First, Section 2 briefly describes FLAME. Next, the proposed load balancing schema is discussed (3), then the migration routines are presented (4). The results section presents a comparison of the schema for two scenarios (5). The final section includes the conclusions (6).

2. FLAME

FLAME was developed at the University of Sheffield in collaborations with the Science and Technology Facilities Council (STFC) in the United Kingdom. FLAME can be used to solve problems involving multiple domains such as economical, medical, biological and social sciences. This framework allows writing several agents and non-agent models using a common simulation environment, and then performs simulations in a simple way on different parallel architectures, including GPUs.

2.1 General Overview

FLAME is not a simulator in itself, but a tool able to generate the necessary source code for the simulation. It automatically generates the simulation code in C through a template engine. FLAME provides a set of template files that the template engine uses to generate the simulation code getting information from the model specification. In the same way, the migration routines are automatically generated from a set of extra template files. The model specification is described by two types of files, XMML (X-Machine Markup Language) files, which is a dialect of XML, and the implementation of the agent functions contained in C files. Figure 1 shows the files required by FLAME to create the simulation code.

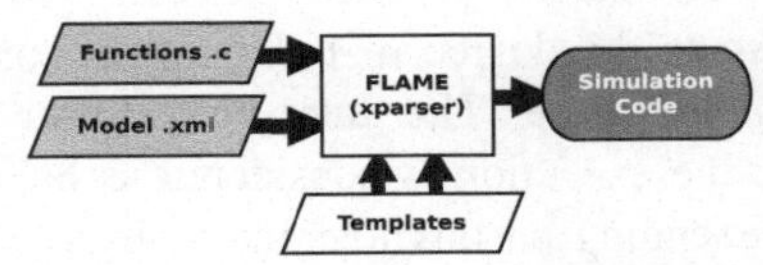

Fig. 1: Diagram of the FLAME framework.

The functionality of FLAME is based on finite state machines called X-machines, which consists of a finite set of states, transitions between states, and actions. To perform the simulation, FLAME holds each agent as an X-machine data structure, whose state is changed via a set of transition functions. Furthermore, the transition functions perform message exchanges between agents if necessary. Then, the simulation environment is composed mainly of a set of X-machines defined through their state transitions, internal memory, and agent messages.

The transitions between the states of the agents are accomplished by keeping the X-machines in linked lists. The simulation environment has one linked list for each state of a specific agent. During the simulation, the X-machines are inserted into the list related to the initial state, later the corresponding transition function is applied to each X-machine. Afterwards, these X-machines are inserted in the list related to the next state. This process is repeated until the last state, which determines the end of the iteration.

2.2 Parallelization

In HPC environments, FLAME communications are managed by the Message Board Library *libmboard*, which uses MPI to communicate between processes. *Libmboard* handles the agents messages through message managing mechanisms and filtering before being sent to local agents and agents belonging to external processes. FLAME handles deadlocks through synchronization points, which ensure that all the data is coordinated among agents using a Single Program Multiple Data (SPMD) pattern.

Figure 2(a) shows the communication between local agents and external agents using *libmboard* library. Hence, this library sends all messages to the agents through a coordinated communication between different MPI processes.

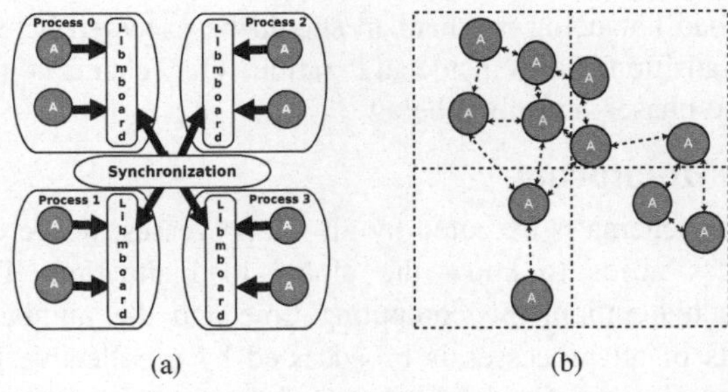

Fig. 2: Parallel communication and synchronization via libmboard (a). Workload problems associated with distribution of agents (b).

2.3 Distribution of the Agents

The parallel distribution of the agents in FLAME is based on two static partitioning methods: geometric partitioning and round-robin partitioning. Currently, FLAME does not include mechanisms to enable the movement of agents between processes. Thus, the workload in each process will rely on the evolution of the model from its initial population of agents. Consequently, evolution of the simulation may trigger computing problems causing overhead, and also may produce excessive external communications due to the interaction among agents (as shown in Figure 2(b)). Therefore, the time required to complete the simulation will be negatively affected.

3. Load Balancing Schema

In agent-based SPMD applications, estimation of performance is a difficult task. In many instances, the performance can vary by issues such as: amount of computation, interaction pattern between agents, and environmental influences. These issues depend on the complexity of the model, and whether the simulation model has different kinds of agents or not. In the same way, depending on the internal state of the agents, these issues can change during the simulation process. For this reason, this schema dynamically decides the global reconfiguration of the workload using an imbalance threshold, computing time, and the number of agents. The threshold is a value between 0 and 1 that represents the acceptable imbalance degree. Computing times and number of agents are monitored in each iteration during the simulation. This approach is executed by all the processes without a central unit of decision. Therefore, each process knows the global load situation and executes the algorithm with the same input. Consequently, all processes calculate the same reconfiguration of the workload.

The mechanism is triggered when an imbalance factor is detected outside the tolerance range. This factor indicates the percentage of imbalance in respect to the mean, and the tolerance range defines the permissible degree of imbalance (see algorithm 1). Moreover, it does not need to perform after an iteration has been finished. In order to get a better result, the load balancing mechanism should be executed between the transition phases inside an iteration. Our schema consists of the phases described below.

3.1 Monitoring

The schema is executed by all the processes; hence each process needs to know the global load situation. Thus, in each iteration, the computing time and the number of agents of all processes is broadcasted by a collective MPI communication. Our load balancing schema can be executed in each iteration of the simulation. However, depending on the complexity of the agent model, the migration process would have better result if used between the transition phases of the simulation. For this reason, before sharing the workload information, we have to determine the current computing time. Based on the results of a previous iteration, the current computing time predicts the computing time for the current number of agents before finalizing the current iteration. As described in Equation 1, the current computing time is predicted based on the current number of agents and the information of the previous iteration.

$$comp\_time_{iter} = \frac{comp\_time_{iter-1} * num\_agents_{iter}}{num\_agents_{iter-1}} \quad (1)$$

This information is exchanged using a collective MPI call. Once all processes have the global workload information, the activation mechanism is checked.

Algorithm 1 Global overview of the Load Balancing schema

collect all computing times for each process
$avg\_time \leftarrow \sum comp\_time_i / nprocs$
$ib\_factor_i \leftarrow comp\_time_i / avg\_time$
$tolerance \leftarrow threshold * avg\_time$
if $\forall i \in procs, \exists\ proc_i / \ |imbalance(proc_i)| \geqslant tolerance$ **then**
  sort computing times in descending order
  $center \leftarrow$ index of the less overloaded process
  $i \leftarrow$ index of the first process in the $sorted\ list$
  $j \leftarrow$ index of the last process in the $sorted\ list$
end if
while $|imbalance(proc_i \wedge proc_j)| \geqslant tolerance$ **do**
  calculate $contribution\_range_i$
  $j \leftarrow$ index of the last process in the $sorted\ list$
  while $|imbalance(proc_i \wedge proc_j)| \geqslant tolerance$ **do**
    calculate $acquisition\_range_j$
    calculate expected migration for $proc_i | proc_j$
    sort underloaded computing times from $center$
    if $|imbalance(proc_i)| \leqslant tolerance$ **then**
      break
    end if
    $j--$
  end while
  sort overloaded computing times until $center$
  $i \leftarrow$ index of the first process in the $sorted\ list$
  if $|imbalance(proc_i)| \leqslant tolerance$ **then**
    break
  end if
end while
Execute the asynchronous exchanges

3.2 Activation Mechanism

In this phase, with the purpose of detecting imbalances, the imbalance factor and the permitted tolerance of imbalance are calculated for each process. The imbalance factor represents the degree of imbalance according to the mean computing time. The tolerance allows setting the range where the execution is considered as balanced. Consequently, depending on this tolerance range, an imbalance can be detected (respectively, Equations 2 and 3 show the imbalance factor, tolerance and the tolerance range).

$$ib\_factor_i = \frac{comp\_time_i}{avg\_time} \quad (2)$$

$$tolerance = avg\_time * threshold$$
$$tolerance\_range = avg\_time \pm tolerance \quad (3)$$

The Load Balancing mechanisms is triggered if a computing time is detected outside of this tolerance range. Furthermore, as every process executes this analysis with

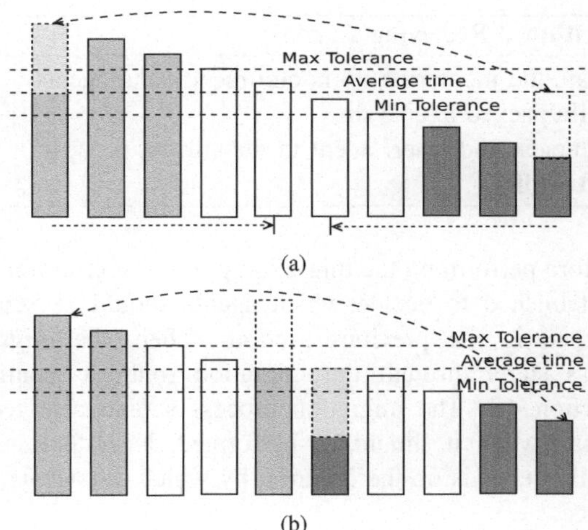

Fig. 3: Comparison and resorting in pairs.

the same inputs (times and agents of all processes), every process have same balanced and imbalanced processes.

3.3 Comparison procedure

In this step, the schema should decide how many agents need to be reallocated. This phase consists of performing comparisons between the most overloaded and the most underloaded processes. In order to reduce communication cost, the criterion of migration is defined by adjusting these processes inside the tolerance range during one exchange. This is explained in the next subsection.

First, our algorithm sorts the computing times per node by descending imbalance factor (Figure 3(a)). Then, following the criterion described in the next subsection, the number of agents that should be migrated for the first and the last process is determined. Therefore, the computing time of these processes will change by the expected time, which corresponds to the time for the expected configuration of agents. Once this is done, the next step consists of reordering by the expected imbalance factors after the migration. Then, first and last process will be changed as shown in Figures 3(a) and 3(b).

The load balancing procedure is repeated until all processes are in the tolerance range of balance.

3.4 Load Balancing Criterion

In this section, the criterion for calculating the expected migration agents between two processes is depicted. Due to the complex interaction rules of the agents, the computing time of one agent is not fixed. Therefore, doing a speculation of this time based on the current total of the agents in the simulation can be inaccurate. In order to ensure the balancing of the overloaded process, we consider calculating the number of agents to migrate according to the average time per agent of the sender process (overloaded process).

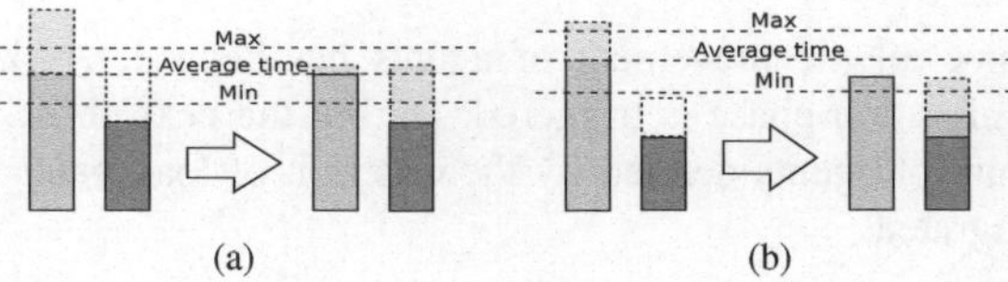

Fig. 4: Examples of the expected migration.

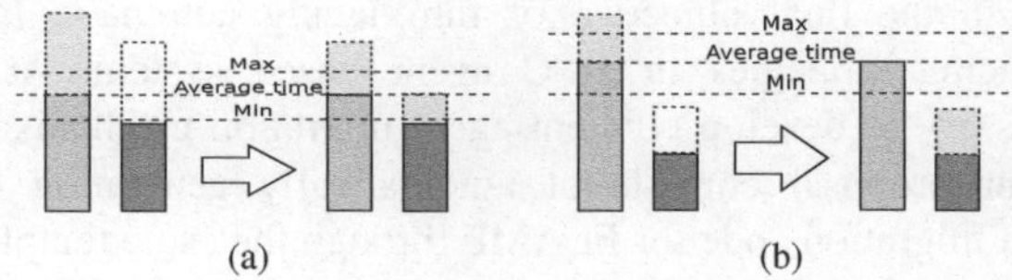

Fig. 5: Examples of the expected migration.

This algorithm tries to find a reduced combination of exchanges to balance the computing time of the processes. To begin with, the time required to reach the tolerance range of balancing is calculated by Equations 4 and 5 (i and j represent the most overloaded and underloaded process, respectively).

$$exceeded\_time_i = comp\_time_i - avg\_time$$
$$contribution\_range_i = exceeded\_time_i \pm tolerance \quad (4)$$

$$required\_time_j = avg\_time - comp\_time_j$$
$$acquisition\_range_j = required\_time_j \pm tolerance \quad (5)$$

In order to minimize the migration exchanges, the expected number of agents to migrate should make both processes go If the sender process has more exceeded time than the required time for the receiver, then as shown in Figure 5(a), the exceeded time is split according to the ideal required time by the receiver. Subsequently, this procedure should be repeated over the next underloaded process until the entire exceeded time of the sender is reduced. In the other hand, if the sender process has not enough exceeded time to fill the required time of the receiver, then as shown in Figure 5(b), the full exceeded time of the sender is migrated. Likewise, this procedure should be repeated over the next overloaded process until the entire required time of the receiver is completed.

Consequently, based on the total time to be reallocated, the number of agents for the migration should be calculated. As noted above, we use the number of agents to migrate according to the average time per agent of the overloaded process because we consider that the overloaded process has priority for the global reduction of the computing time. This time is determined by the Equation 6 (i means the number rank of the overloaded process).

$$time\_per\_agent_i = \frac{comp\_time_i}{num\_agent_i} \quad (6)$$

Once all the movement of agents has been determined, the migration phase is triggered. During the next phase, the amount of agents defined by the criterion of load balancing is migrated.

4. Migration of Agents

With the final objective of introducing automatic load balancing strategies in HPC agent based systems, it is necessary to develop efficient agent migration mechanisms.

Our proposal consists of automatically generating the agent migration code for FLAME through the same template structure used for generating the simulation code. In order to achieve this new feature, new templates for generating the migration routines are required. Then, the template engine processes these templates to obtain the information about the model and generates migration routines together with the simulation code (as shown in Figure 6).

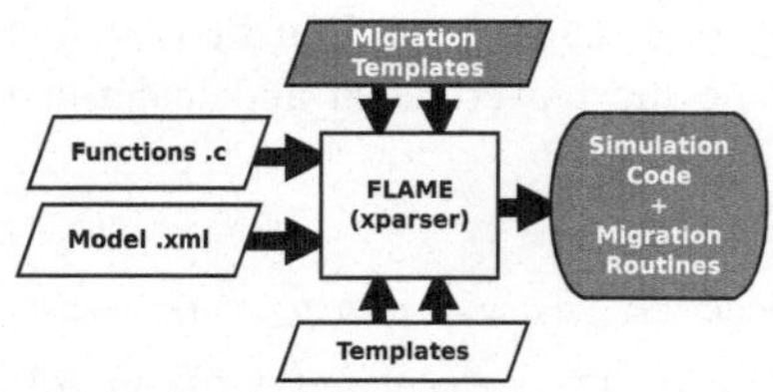

Fig. 6: Diagram of the FLAME framework with the enhancing.

Once the information about the agent has been obtained by the new templates, the migration routines can automatically add and remove agents in the migration process. This agents are held in *output lists* identified by the *id* of the target process. Later, the agents in the *output lists* are packed to be sent out. The received data is unpacked and later inserted with the others agents in the recipient process. Algorithms 2 and 3 show the procedures involved during the migration of agents.

With the purpose of sending the agents to a recipient process in a single communication, the agents in the lists need to be stored in contiguous memory.This migration is accomplished by packing and unpacking data using MPI functions. These MPI functions require memory buffers before being used, which sizes depend on the type and amount of agents. Consequently, the generated migration routines automate calculations of the buffer sizes required during the migration process.

Algorithm 2 Sending Agents

```
while agents to be sent do
  insert in the recipient list
end while
calculate the sizes and create the buffers
pack the agents and send the packages
```

Algorithm 3 Receiving Agents

```
create the memory buffers and receive the agents
while packed agents do
  unpack and insert agent in the current process
end while
```

Before performing the migration process, a criterion must be established to decide which agents should be sent (as discussed in the previous section). Then, the migration process starts through the migration routines mentioned in section 4.1. The migration process should also require deciding when it should be performed. Nevertheless, this partially depends on the criterion by which the agents were selected.

4.1 Migration Routines

The migration routines are specifically generated for each type of agent in the model. In consequence, it is possible to perform migrations after any transition.

The following list introduces the main migration routines. In addition, the prefix NAME indicates the name of a specific type of agent.

- *Init_movement*: Initializes global variables and data structures involved in the migration.
- *prepare_to_move_NAME*: Moves agents to a specific *output linked list* and removes them from the current process.
- *Pack_NAME_agent_list*: Packs all agents kept in the *output linked lists* in contiguous memory (MPI_PACKED datatype), one for each recipient.
- *UnPack_NAME_agent_list*: Unpacks the packed agents received as MPI_PACKED. Then, inserts the received agents in the X-machine list of the current process.

5. Experimental Results

The main objective of this section is to demonstrate that using the proposed load balancing schema and migration routines, it is possible to correct imbalance problems in an agent based SPMD application.

The example is a SIR epidemic model on a 2D toroidal space. The SIR model describes the spread of an epidemic within a population. The population is divided into three groups: the Susceptible (S), the Infectious (I), and the Recovered (R). For this reason, this model is called SIR. Summarizing, a susceptible individual is who is not infected and not immune, the infectious are those who are infected and can transmit the disease, and the recovered are those who have been infected and are immune. Additionally, natural births and deaths during the epidemic are included in this SIR model, so individuals might die from the disease or by natural death due to aging. Consequently, births and deaths represent a dynamic creation and elimination of agents. Therefore, the workload can change as the simulation proceeds.

Table 1: Initial parameters for both scenarios.

Parameters	values	Parameters	values
infected	10	infectiousness	65
lifespan	100	chance recovery	50
average offspring	4	disease duration	20

In this section, two scenarios are presented. Table 1 depicts the environmental configurations of the simulations. Both simulations are started with an initial population (see Table 2), and 10 of these are infected. The experiments were performed during 200 simulation steps and, the agents were distributed doing a round-robin distribution. Thus, depending on the number of processes and the initial agents, the initial number of agents per process can be equal or similar.

Table 2: Scenarios of the experiments.

scenario	agents	carrying capacity	space dimensions
A	30000	30000	650X650
B	50000	50000	1000x1000

The Load Balancing schema is activated after the fifth simulation step. Given that the computing measurements vary when the migration process has been triggered, the activation mechanism is blocked during the next iteration. After this, the activation mechanism will be enabled again. Sending and receiving of the agents has been deployed using MPI asynchronous functions to overlap the costs of communication and computation.

The experiments were run using the FLAME Framework 0.16.2, libmboard 0.2.1 and OpenMPI 1.4.1. All experiments were executed on a Cluster IBM with the following features: 32 IBM x3550 Nodes, 2xDual-Core Intel(R) Xeon(R) CPU 5160 @ 3.00GHz 4MB L2 (2x2), 12 GB Fully Buffered DIMM 667 MHz, Hot-swap SAS Controller 160GB SATA Disk and Integrated dual Gigabit Ethernet. Additionally, we tested our schema using a case without Load Balancing schema, and three imbalance tolerances: 0.3(30%) , 0.15(15%) and 0.05(5%). Moreover, for both scenarios, 16, 32, 64 and 128 cores were used.

Figures 7(a) and 7(b) compare the execution time with varying number of processes by comparing different values of tolerance with the original simulation without the load balancing schema. Here, both scenarios have better results using our load balancing schema. Moreover, in most cases if the imbalance tolerance is reduced the improvement is better. In Figure 7(a), when the number of processes is increased, a larger value for the imbalance tolerance result in a worse execution time. Due to the amount of agents per process decrease for 128 processes, the communication time grows versus the computing time.

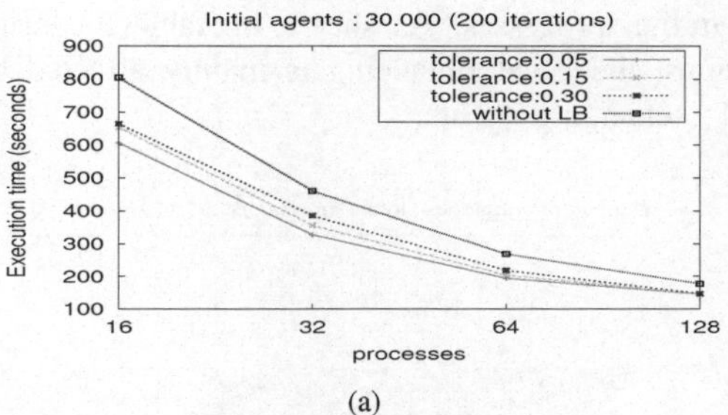

(a)

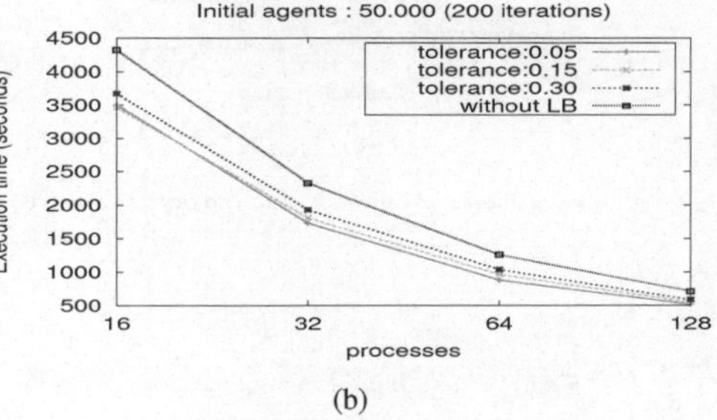

(b)

Fig. 7: Executions times in both scenarios.

Table 3: Execution time of scenarios A on 128 processes.

tolerance	comp.(sec)	gain(%)	LB time	agents - bytes mig.
0.05	69.4678	17.76	0.2860	11927 - 584546
0.15	74.2281	17.74	0.2386	9613 - 466639
0.30	81.9558	16.97	0.2108	8201 - 396513
original	117.5274	-	-	-

Table 4: Execution time of scenarios B on 128 processes.

tolerance	comp.(sec)	gain(%)	LB time	agents - bytes mig.
0.05	340.9736	27.62	0.3472	26581 - 1282533
0.15	369.3261	22.88	0.1620	14675 - 705725
0.30	405.1615	17.75	0.1301	11589 - 556842
original	534.8094	-	-	-

Table 5: Overhead of the Load Balancing schema of both scenarios on 128 processes.

scenario	A			B		
tolerance	pack	comm	unpack	pack	comm	unpack
0.05	0.0028	0.280	0.0017	0.0064	0.324	0.0047
0.15	0.0035	0.233	0.0021	0.0073	0.153	0.0059
0.30	0.0039	0.205	0.0027	0.0054	0.125	0.0043
original	-	-	-	-	-	-

Tables 3, 4 and 5 summarizes the execution time for different values of tolerances. Packing, Communication, Unpacking and Load Balancing times were calculated by the sum of the maximum times per iteration. Migrated and Bytes consist of the sum of all agents exchanged during all migration processes. As shown in Table 5, during the migrations, the Load Balancing is mainly affected by the cost of exchanging agents.

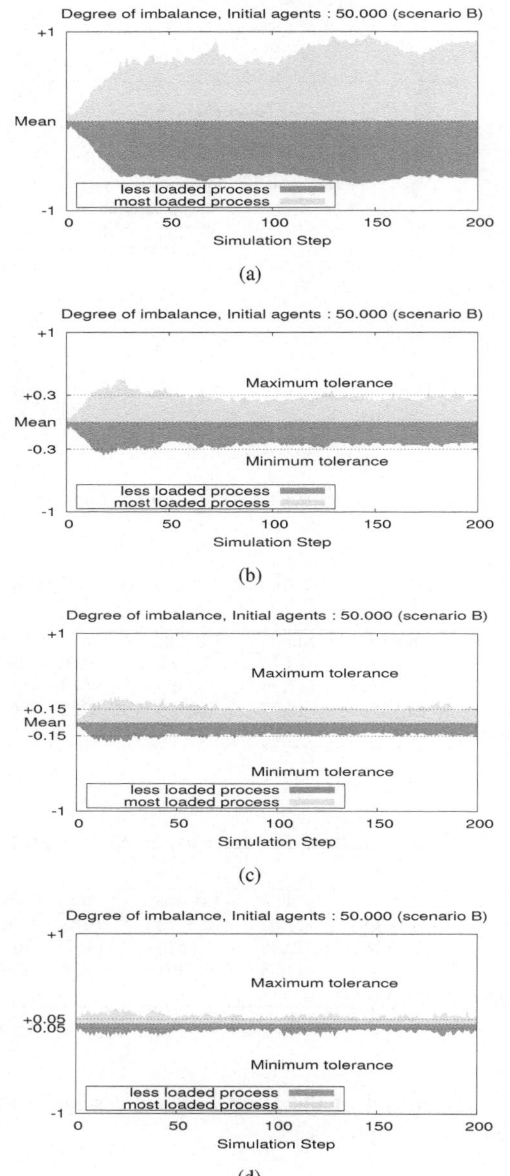

Fig. 8: Degree of computing imbalance varying the tolerance factor, for the scenario B on 128 processes.

Figure 8 shows the variability of the degree of imbalance for different values of tolerance factor. This Figure shows the degree of imbalance that decreases when the tolerance factor is increased, but the Load Balancing schema is triggered more frequently. Consequently, values of Table 5 expose that the overhead of our schema is greater when reducing the tolerance factor. For this reason, better results in terms of execution time are related to finding a tolerance value which does not imply an excessive overhead for exchanging agents.

6. Conclusion

Due to the different rules of behavior and the high levels of interaction between agents, the ABMS applications may present computational and communicational imbalances during the simulation process. Therefore, to solve this problem, the simulation environment should be equipped with migration mechanisms to move agents between overloaded and underloaded processes.

In this paper, we have presented a Dynamic Load Balancing schema is proven in a model with high-level workload variability. For both scenarios, our schema obtains good results improving simulation execution time, and keeps a quite stable overhead. This overhead is caused by the amount of exchanges during the load balancing process. In addition, our modification of the FLAME framework for automatically generating agent migration functions. In this manner, the workload among the different processes can be adjusted dynamically during the simulation. In future work, we will aim our research on balancing communication times.

Acknowledgment

This work was funded by MICINN Spain, under the project TIN2011-28689-C02-01.

References

[1] R. K. Standish and R. Leow, "Ecolab: Agent based modeling for c++ programmers," *CoRR*, vol. cs.MA/0401026, 2004.

[2] N. Collier and M. North, "Repast sc++: A platform for large-scale agent-based modeling," *Large-Scale Computing Techniques for Complex System Simulations*, 2011.

[3] M. Kiran, P. Richmond, M. Holcombe, L. S. Chin, D. Worth, and C. Greenough, "Flame: simulating large populations of agents on parallel hardware architectures," in *AAMAS*, 2010, pp. 1633–1636.

[4] B. Zhou and S. Zhou, "Parallel simulation of group behaviors," in *Proceedings of the 36th conference on Winter simulation*, ser. WSC '04. Winter Simulation Conference, 2004, pp. 364–370.

[5] G. Zheng, E. Meneses, A. Bhatele, and L. V. Kale, "Hierarchical load balancing for charm++ applications on large supercomputers," in *Proceedings of the 2010 39th International Conference on Parallel Processing Workshops*, ser. ICPPW '10. Washington, DC, USA: IEEE Computer Society, 2010, pp. 436–444.

[6] D. Zhang, C. Jiang, and S. Li, "A fast adaptive load balancing method for parallel particle-based simulations," *Simulation Modelling Practice and Theory*, vol. 17, no. 6, pp. 1032–1042, 2009.

[7] G. Vigueras, M. Lozano, and J. M. Orduña, "Workload balancing in distributed crowd simulations: the partitioning method," *J. Supercomput.*, vol. 58, no. 2, pp. 261–269, Nov. 2011.

[8] B. Cosenza, G. Cordasco, R. De Chiara, and V. Scarano, "Distributed load balancing for parallel agent-based simulations," in *Proceedings of the 2011 19th International Euromicro Conference on Parallel, Distributed and Network-Based Processing*, ser. PDP '11. Washington, DC, USA: IEEE Computer Society, 2011, pp. 62–69.

[9] R. Solar, R. Suppi, and E. Luque, "Proximity load balancing for distributed cluster-based individual-oriented fish school simulations," *Procedia Computer Science*, vol. 9, no. 0, pp. 328 – 337, 2012, proceedings of the International Conference on Computational Science, ICCS 2012.

Towards an Operating System Based Framework for Energy-Efficient Scheduling of Parallel Workloads

Shwetha Shankar[1], **Dan Tamir**[1], **and Apan Qasem**[1]
[1]Department of Computer Science, Texas State University, San Marcos, TX, USA

Abstract— *Power is a dominant obstacle for significant cost performance improvements of VLSI technology. Excessive and unbalanced power consumption affects device reliability, requires expensive packaging, and causes irreversible damage to semiconductor devices. Hence, power monitoring and thermal hot-spot elimination is a major concern of the semiconductor industry. This research addresses multicore power monitoring, management, and control via power-aware task scheduling and load balancing; supporting hot-spot elimination as well as overall power balancing and reduction. The paper concentrates on the scheduling aspects of efficient power management schemes in the context of multicore systems. We utilize an in-house scheduling simulator and incorporate power and execution metrics in several* classic *scheduling algorithms. Results show a potential for scheduling with high level of power efficiency and tolerable degradation in execution time.*

Keywords: task scheduling, energy-efficiency, optimization

1. Introduction

The need for achieving high performance without a commensurate increase in power consumption has lead chip manufactures to adopt the multicore design. The multicore shift, however, is not an end-all solution to the power dissipation problem, in fact it has made the problem of energy efficient computing more complex. With multicore systems becoming mainstream, power and thermal density are no longer just a concern for large data centers and embedded processors but for all types of computers. In recent years, because of this need, there has been a plethora of work in making computation more energy efficient, without sacrificing performance. Among the many different methods proposed, task scheduling has emerged as one of the most promising techniques in this area.

The strategies proposed for power-aware scheduling span architectural, compiler, runtime and operating system (OS) based approaches. Although diverse, most strategies use some form of dynamic voltage and frequency scaling (DVFS) [1], [2], [3]. The central idea is to alert the system to environmental changes, such as an increase in temperature and then reduce the frequency of the processor with DVFS, so as to consume less power. Although DVFS-based techniques prove useful for reducing power consumption, it has been shown that this strategy does incur a performance penalty. This happens in two situations. First, some architectures do not allow core-level scaling which implies that slowing down an idle core, slows down all cores on the chip, leading to overall lower performance. Another issue arises, when the workload is dominated by parallel applications. In this case, reducing the frequency of one core (or thread) by 50% can cause the entire application to run 50% slower because of inter-thread dependencies. Thus, for a scheduling strategy that aims to optimize for both power and performance it is imperative that we devise a technique that does not rely on DVFS as the primary mechanism for controlling power consumption

A second issue with power-aware schedulers that has surfaced in the last few years is that they have diverged in two separate but related directions. Scheduling methods have been proposed that aim to schedule single parallel applications on to large clusters [4], [5], [6]. These techniques usually operate as runtime schedulers in the user-space and tend to do much of the work statically, based on a priori information (e.g., dependence DAG). On the other hand, there has been some work that attacks the problem from the OS-perspective and aim to dynamically schedule a workload consisting of many different programs both parallel and sequential. The latter approach has focused mostly on real-time systems and often do not consider communication or synchronization among parallel tasks [1]. Given current architectural trends, it is clear that systems of all ranges, will have to deal with an increasingly parallel workload. Hence, for power-aware scheduling of current and future architectures, it is crucial that we consider a marriage of these two divergent strategies.

This paper describes the design and some of the challenges of a scheduling framework that addresses the two issues mentioned above. We propose a framework that uses DVFS only as a secondary technique, and instead relies primarily on smart thread placement and migration at the software-level. Furthermore, we propose the deployment of a user-space runtime scheduler that provides support and works in tandem with the OS-scheduler allowing us to leverage the complementary strengths of the two units into a single unified framework. The proposed framework emphasizes aspects of scheduling that we believe are critical to power-aware scheduling of parallel workloads.

1. Resource sharing: Thread executing on current

architectures contend for resources at multiple levels. Since cores waiting on a resource dissipate power without making progress, contention of shared resources becomes a principal bottleneck for parallel applications both in terms of performance and energy efficiency. On the other hand, situations that cause favorable sharing of resources lead to better power utilization. This occurs when two threads sharing a cache exhibit a high degree of locality, which reduces offchip memory access, resulting in saved energy. Thus, it is essential for a scheduler to not only consider when to schedule a thread but where to schedule it as well. In parallel to the work reported here, we are extending current work in resource-conscious schedulers by constructing hierarchical sharing information, derived through analytical models and HW performance counter measurements.

2. Multi-objective scheduling algorithms: Power-aware scheduling is a truly multi-dimensional problem since many different factors can impact overall power consumption of a parallel workload. Further, the objective might vary depending on context. For a real-time system the goal might be to minimize power consumption while meeting task deadlines, whereas a data center might exclusively focus on operating under a thermal threshold. Regardless of the end goal, there are many issues in intelligent scheduling that are overlapping. Thus, in our framework, we propose the inclusion of scheduling heuristics, that provide *Pareto-normal* solutions, allowing us to schedule for multiple objectives such as performance and power.

3. Extensibility and Adaptability: Given the changing landscape of computer architecture it is important, that new scheduling algorithms be both extensible and adaptable. For this reason. we support a variety of scheduling techniques including work-stealing (WS) [7], [8], complete fair share (CFS), and multilevel feedback-queue scheduling (MFQ). The software infrasturcture extends Linsched [9] and enables fast implementation and evaluation of scheduling algorithms. Furthermore, our simulator includes hooks for machine learning algorithms [10] to make scheduling heuristics more intelligent.

The rest of the paper is organized as follows : in Section 2 we review related work in power-aware scheduling, in Section 3 we describe the proposed framework and highlight its key features, in Section 4 we present preliminary evaluation results of different scheduling algorithms with power constraints; finally, we conclude and discuss future plans in Section 5

2. Related Work

Much of the work in scheduling for power, has focused on developing runtime strategies that aim to find an optimal schedule for a single parallel application [4], [5], [6], [11]. General OS-based strategies for power-aware scheduling are less common [12], [3].

The main approach to energy efficient scheduling has been to use the technique of dynamic voltage and frequency scaling (DVFS) to control the peak CPU temperature. Kim et al. describe a DVFS-based scheduler for real-time parallel applications running on large clusters [1]. In their model they assume that no synchronizations are required between concurrent threads but all sub-tasks must complete execution before a job is considered complete. In addition, each job must finish within a certain deadline. They use two heuristic algorithms : earlier-deadline-first (EDF) and proportional sharing and demonstrate through simulation results that their techniques are effective in reducing power dissipation, while maintaining the deadline constraints. Bautista et al. present a power-aware scheduler for real-time applications that aims to minimize power consumption while respecting task deadlines. [2]. Wierman et al. provide theoretical bounds on DVFS-based scheduling techniques [13]. They show that in terms of performance and power, a static DVFS scheduling strategy works as well as a dynamic strategy. However, a dynamic strategy can yield benefits when the objective is to make the system more reliable. Their simulator models a web server and tasks in their framework represent network requests. Tasks are picked from a Poisson distribution and arrive and leave at fixed intervals. Kashif et al. propose a Priority-based Muti-level Feedback Queue Scheduler (PMLFQS) for mobile devices. PMLFQS is a work-conserving algorithm that uses different CPU speeds for queues to minimize the overall energy consumed by the CPU for each task. The paper, however, focuses on changes to CPU speed to reflect energy efficiency on single core processors. In contrast, we propose changes at the software level, enabling a multicore operating system to incorporate energy efficiency considerations into the scheduling algorithm [14].

Recently Zong et al. have proposed two scheduling algorithms for scheduling parallel applications on large clusters. Their framework takes as input a precedence-constrained task graph of the application to be scheduled and emits a schedule that is predicted to be most energy-efficient [6]. Teodorescu and Torellas present a power management algorithm that takes into account variations in voltage and frequency among cores and attempt to improve performance within a given power envelope. The algorithm uses linear programming and is intended to complement the existing OS-scheduling policies [15].

Banikazemi et al. present a user-space meta scheduler that provides hints to the OS scheduler based on resource congestion in cores. Resource congestion is estimated through HW performance counter measurements. Their strategy shows a 14% overall improvement on the SPEC CPU workload [16]. One limitation of their approach is that they do not consider memory affinity. Merkel et al. develop heuristics that schedule threads based on resource sharing. They combine these algorithms with DVFS based techniques. They evaluate their strategy on a workload with homogeneous sharing patterns and show that their strategy is able to reduce the Energy Delay Product (EDP) significantly [3]. The EDP is computed based on the following formula

$$\text{EDP} = (\text{Turnaround Time})^2 \times \text{Energy Consumed}$$

Boyd-Wickizer et al. propose a technique that operates at the level of objects. The idea is to migrate threads from core-to-core based on the data structures they access. bringing threads closer to their data and thereby reducing memory latency [12]. Tam et al. also propose a scheduler that considers resource sharing on CMPs and SMTs[17]. However, their strategy does not take power into consideration. Wu et al. propose LTEDF (Low Thermal Early Deadline First), a temperature-aware task scheduling algorithm for realtime multi-core systems. In LTEDF, a History Coolest Neighborhood First (HCNF) task allocation algorithm is employed to balance the temperature loads. When cores are thermally saturated, task migration is performed to alleviate thermal saturation. Zhou et al. proposes an algorithm that is based on the observation that, given two tasks, one that is hot (i.e., a high power consuming task) and one that is cool (a low power consuming task), executing the hot task before the cool one results in a lower final temperature than the reversed order as long as executing the hot task itself does not violate the thermal threshold [18]. Yang et al. maximize performance by scheduling workloads to keep the temperature below a given threshold. This threshold can be the manufacturer-defined temperature threshold for the physical chip, or an OS-defined threshold for a system to stay within a thermal envelope [19]. Tang et al. propose a combined hardware-software approach for thermal-aware scheduling of applications in data centers [4].

3. Scheduling Framework

3.1 Overview

Fig. 1 outlines our proposed framework. A user-space scheduler is combined with the OS-scheduler to handle workloads that consist of both parallel and sequential tasks. Performance monitors are used to extract information about resource sharing from the platform. This resource sharing information is fed into both the user-space scheduler and the OS-scheduler. The user-space scheduler uses this information to provide hints to the OS scheduler for scheduling tasks on the next time slice. In our framework, we have two representations of a task : one for the user-space and one for the OS scheduler. In user-space a multithreaded program is represented as a directed acyclic graph (DAG) of dynamic instructions connected with dependency edges. The set of dynamic instructions make a up a task node, which are in turn connected by spawn edges to create the final dependence DAG.

3.2 Capturing Resource Sharing

The processing units on scalable multicore systems are organized in a hierarchy of nodes, chips, cores and thread contexts and a variety of resources are shared at different levels. For example, TLBs may be shared by hardware threads running on the same core, an L2 cache may be shared by two cores on a quad-core chip, and memory bandwidth is generally shared by all cores on a chip. Favorable and non-favorable sharing of these resources has significant impact on power consumption. The need for incorporating resource sharing into scheduling decisions has been recognized by the OS community [12], [20], [21], [3]. However, the key challenge in this regard has been the collection, extraction and efficient delivery of this information to the operating system. To address this issue, we take advantage of HW performance counters. We probe a range of counters and use analytical models to derive resource sharing information at multiple levels. This includes information about inter-thread data locality, cache conflicts and bandwidth congestion. Cost estimates is assigned to each metric and the hierarchical resource sharing information is stored as a persistent tree structure. To utilize this information in scheduling we introduce the notion of *inter-thread affinity*, which represents the cost (or benefit) of coscheduling two threads on the same chip (or node), where coscheduling implies the execution of the two threads will overlap during some time slice. Inter-thread affinity is computed by a runtime system that consolidates and summarizes the RST information. This data is stored in a power affinity graph (PAG) which is a weighted undirected graph where vertices represent schedulable tasks. An edge between two vertices denotes the impact of scheduling the tasks on the same unit (e.g., chip) on power consumption. Positive weights represent favorable impact, whereas negative weights represent negative impact on power efficiency. The PAG is probed by the OS scheduler at the beginning of each time slice during scheduling. The maintenance of this information entails some overhead and hence we allow this option to be disabled.

3.3 Fine-grain Performance Monitoring

For power-aware scheduling on emerging multicore systems, it is evident that continuing with performance metrics currently used by Linux systems (e.g., completion time, waiting time, or single-core metrics like IPC) will not be sufficient. Threads may behave differently based on what other threads have been scheduled on the same chip, or what threads were scheduled on the same core prior. Thus, scheduling techniques need to extend the set of metrics that are considered for making scheduling decisions. Modern microprocessors provide a wealth of information on application performance through a large set of HW performance counters. For example, AMD Phenom exposes 119 major native counter events, while Intel Nehalem exposes over

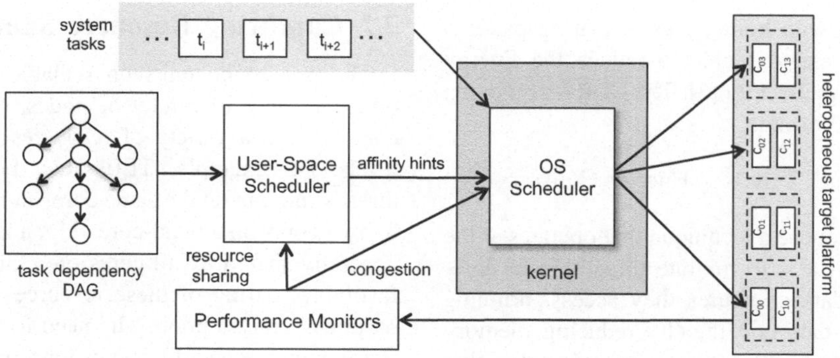

Fig. 1: Scheduling Framework Overview

130. Software for probing these counters has matured significantly and the use of performance counters has grown in popularity in performance tuning and even compiler optimizations[22]. Their role in scheduling has not been explored to that great an extent, however. We propose to include HW performance counters in our framework to capture dynamic performance characteristics. They are used to measure resource sharing and congestion (see Section 3.2) and also get power estimates on a per-thread basis [23]. We intend to use the perfmon interface on Linux to collect counter values and instrument the scheduler with calls to the API so that it can take decision on the fly.

3.4 Scheduling Algorithms

We have performed a detailed analysis of several scheduling policies. Following this analysis we are currently extending a range of scheduling algorithms to make them energyconscious. We distinguish between two types of scheduling policies, inter-core and intra-core, and augment both types using a combination of execution metrics and power consumption considerations. To further explain, consider a multicore system. Each core is implementing an internal scheduling policy (intra-core) such as *first-in, first-out* (FIFO), *round robin* (RR), or *highest response ratio next* (HRRN). In addition, an inter-core scheduling policy such as *work stealing* (WS), *Multi-level feedback queue (MFQ)*, or *complete fair sharing (CFS)* may be used to balance load among cores and eliminate core 'starvation'. We have selected HRRN as the intra-core policy. Work stealing has been selected as the inter-processor scheduling policy. We have implemented several basic intra-processor policies such as round robin, shortest remaining time as well as the CFS and MFQ. Additionally, we are implementing four different variants of the work-stealing scheduler (WS). Although WS has proven effective in scheduling parallel applications onto multicore systems, their role in power-aware scheduling has not been explored. We believe that by providing resource sharing information, extracted from HW performance counter values, the scheduler can be made effective in this context.

4. Preliminary Evaluation

4.1 Experimental Setup

As described in Section 3, we are extending the Linsched simulator to include a multitude of intra-core and inter-core scheduling policies. Each policy is implemented in two ways. First, a 'classical' power-agnostic method is implemented. Next, a power-aware version of the policy is utilized. In both cases, we measure execution and power metrics and compare the power-agnostic performance (execution and power consumption) to the performance of the power-aware policy. We define 'success' as the case where the power-aware significantly improves the power consumption, e.g., by a factor of 2, while maintaining low impact on execution performance, e.g., less than 10 percent performance degradation. While the work on extending Linsched is ongoing, we have performed an initial set of experiments utilizing an in-house simple scheduling simulator and incorporated basic intra-processor policies including *round robin* (RR), *shortest remaining time first* (SRTF), and the *highest response ratio next* (HRRN) scheduling policies. In each case, we run the simulation ten times with different seeds for random selection of parameters such as task arrival rate, task service time (the amount of time a task is expected to spend on the system), and task power consumption. We run each simulation with 50,000 tasks generated over the span of 1000 seconds. An average arrival time of 5 tasks per second with ah average service time of 0.1 seconds and average power consumption of 5 'power units' are utilized. Wherever applicable, we used a time slice of 0.1 seconds and an eviction threshold of 0.5 power units which enforces a large number of evictions in preemptive policies such as round robin.

4.2 Overall Performance

Table 1 summarizes the performance of the three scheduling strategies. For each scheduling policy, we present data on three metrics : total energy consumed, turnaround time and EDP. Each metric is a ratio of the power-agnostic policy over the power-aware version. Thus, a value of less than one

Table 1: Power-aware vs. power-agnostic performance comparison

	RR	SRTF	HRRN
Energy Consumed Ratio	0.93	0.51	0.72
Turnaround Ratio	0.97	1.46	0.97
EDP Ratio	0.88	1.07	0.67

indicates that the power-aware version was able to improve performance or energy consumption.

From the results in Table 1, we observe that overall the power-aware heuristic in *HRRN* shows the most marked improvement over the power-agnostic version. This policy causes a significant reduction in energy consumed, coupled with a small improvement in turnaround time. As a result, this strategy obtains the lowest EDP ratio. *SRTF* is most-effective in reducing overall energy consumption but it pays a significant penalty in terms of wait time. The power-aware version of *RR* yields a better EDP ratio than *SRTF*. Although *RR* is not able to have a significant effect on energy consumption, it has no negative effect on turnaround time.

4.3 Impact of Eviction Threshold

The power consumption difference between power-aware and power-agnostic policies of *RR* is quite small. This insignicant change can be attributed to the values of the eviction threshold. In our simulations, an eviction threshold is the amount of energy a task is allowed to consume before it is evicted from the CPU. The eviction thresholds are user-defined values, randomly chosen at the beginning of a simulation. We speculate that larger values for the eviction threshold caused tasks to be switched at the time slice rather than when the task has consumed too much energy. To verify this claim, we ran a set of simulations with different eviction thresholds. Results from these runs are presented in Fig. 2. As we can see, with an RR policy there is a direct correlation between energy consumed and eviction threshold. For larger values of the eviction threshold, tasks are allowed to spend more time on the CPU, leading to overall higher energy consumption. Thus, the *RR* policy can be made more effective by reducing the eviction threshold. However, this may lead to an increase in turnaround time.

4.4 Impact of Power Dissipation

The *SRTF* power-aware policy is most successful in reducing overall energy consumption of the workload. *SRTF* prioritizes tasks based on the following heuristic:

$$task \leftarrow t : min(t_p \times t_s)$$

where, t_p is the power consumeed and t_s is the remaining service time of the task in question. Thus, tasks that get to run first are the ones with smaller energy demands. In the power-agnostic version, tasks that get to execute first are tasks with least service time, even if they have higher power demands. To measure the impact of power demands

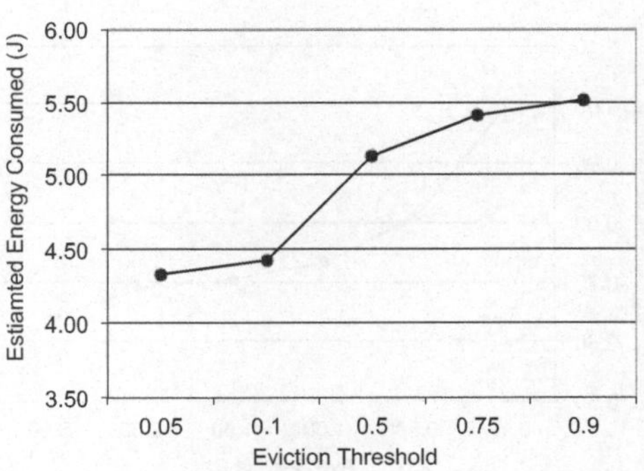

Fig. 2: Round Robin Efficiency with Variations in Eviction Threshold

on *SRTF*, we ran simulations where the power demands of individual tasks in the workload are varied. The results of these experiments are shown in Fig. 3. We notice that when there are many tasks in the workload with lower demands it leads to a significant reduction in energy consumption than when we have many tasks with higher power and wait time demands.

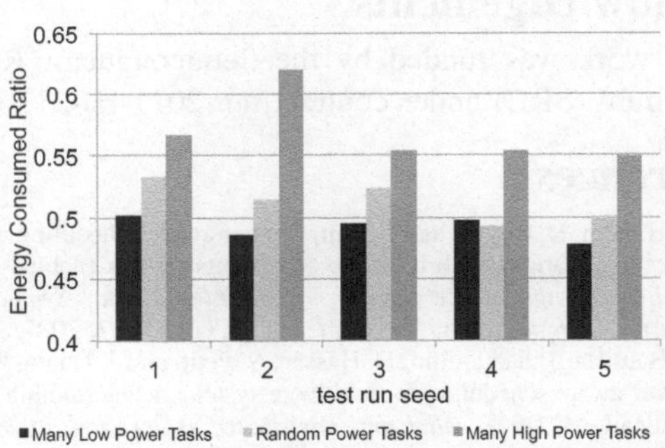

Fig. 3: SRTF efficiency with power variations in workload

4.5 Impact of Service Time

Service time is another important parameter for scheduling policies. The HRRN policy considers both the energy demands and the remaining service time in prioritizing tasks for execution. Because of this it outperforms both RR and SRTF. As the service times are increased (i.e., there are more long-running tasks in the workload), the efficiency of *HRRN* also improves, as can be seen in Fig. 4

5. Conclusions and Future Work

Maintaining a homogeneous multicore system within an allowable power envelope and balancing the power without drastically affecting performance is the problem addressed in this paper. For this end, we are developing scheduling policies that integrate power metrics with performance metrics.

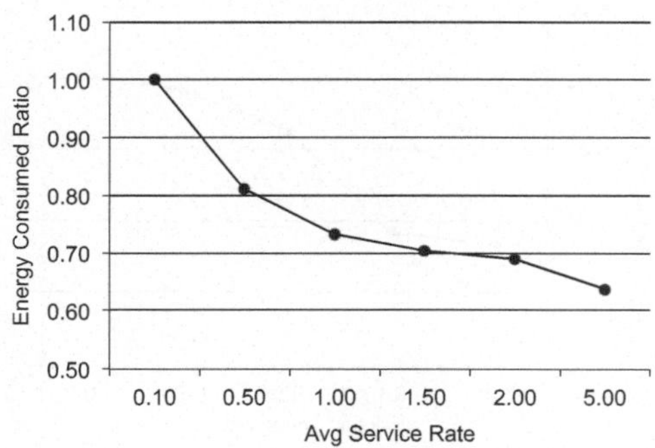

Fig. 4: HRRN performance with variations in average service rate

As a first step towards the evaluation of the utility of power-aware policies, we have implemented several basic intra-core policies using a simple scheduling simulator and performed experiments with EDP based power-aware policies. The experiments show that a power-aware policy has potential for noticeable improvement in power consumption with minor degradation in turnaround time.

Acknowledgements

This work was funded by the Semiconductor Research Consortium (SRC) under contract no. 2011-HJ-2156.

References

[1] K. H. Kim, R. Buyya, and J. Kim, "Power aware scheduling of bag-of-tasks applications with deadline constraints on dvs-enabled clusters," in *Proceedings of the Seventh IEEE International Symposium on Cluster Computing and the Grid*, ser. CCGRID '07, 2007.

[2] D. Bautista, J. Sahuquillo, H. Hassan, S. Petit, and J. Duato, "A simple power-aware scheduling for multicore systems when running real-time applications," in *Parallel and Distributed Processing, 2008. IPDPS 2008. IEEE International Symposium on*, 2008.

[3] A. Merkel, J. Stoess, and F. Bellosa, "Resource-conscious scheduling for energy efficiency on multicore processors," in *Proceedings of the 5th European conference on Computer systems*, ser. EuroSys '10, 2010.

[4] Q. Tang, S. K. S. Gupta, and G. Varsamopoulos, "Energy-efficient thermal-aware task scheduling for homogeneous high-performance computing data centers: A cyber-physical approach," *IEEE Trans. Parallel Distrib. Syst.*, vol. 19, pp. 1458–1472, November 2008.

[5] Y. Guo, J. Zhao, V. Cave, and V. Sarkar, "Slaw: A scalable locality-aware adaptive work-stealing scheduler," in *Parallel Distributed Processing (IPDPS), 2010 IEEE International Symposium on*, 2010.

[6] Z. Zong, A. Manzanares, X. Ruan, and X. Qin, "EAD and PEBD: Two energy-aware duplication scheduling algorithms for parallel tasks on homogeneous clusters," *Computers, IEEE Transactions on*, 2011.

[7] M. Frigo, C. E. Leiserson, and K. H. Randall, "The implementation of the cilk-5 multithreaded language," in *Proceedings of the ACM SIGPLAN 1998 conference on Programming language design and implementation*, 1998.

[8] A. Robison, M. Voss, and A. Kukanov, "Optimization via reflection on work stealing in tbb," in *Parallel and Distributed Processing, 2008. IPDPS 2008. IEEE International Symposium on*, 2008.

[9] J. M. Calandrino, D. P. Baumberger, T. Li, J. C. Young, and S. Hahn, "Linsched: The linux scheduler simulator," in *ISCA 21st International Conference on Parallel and Distributed Computing and Communication Systems, PDCCS 2008, September 24-26, 2008, Holiday Inn Downtown-Superdome, New Orleans, Louisiana, USA*, 2008.

[10] S. Sarangkar and A. Qasem, "Intelligent feedback for fast and effective autotuning," in *23rd International Conference for High Performance Computing, Networking, Storage and Analysis, (SC10)*, 2010.

[11] I. Ahmad, R. Arora, D. White, V. Metsis, and R. Ingram, "Energy-constrained scheduling of dags on multi-core processors," in *Contemporary Computing*, ser. Communications in Computer and Information Science, S. Ranka, S. Aluru, R. Buyya, Y.-C. Chung, S. Dua, A. Grama, S. K. S. Gupta, R. Kumar, and V. V. Phoha, Eds. Springer Berlin Heidelberg, 2009, vol. 40, pp. 592–603.

[12] S. Boyd-Wickizer, R. Morris, and M. F. Kaashoek, "Reinventing scheduling for multicore systems," in *Proceedings of the 12th conference on Hot topics in operating systems*, ser. HotOS'09, 2009.

[13] A. Wierman, L. Andrew, and A. Tang, "Stochastic analysis of power-aware scheduling," in *Communication, Control, and Computing, 2008 46th Annual Allerton Conference on*, 2008.

[14] M. Kashif, T. Helmy, and E. El-Sebakhy, "A priority-based mlfq scheduler for CPU power saving," in *Proceedings of the IEEE International Conference on Computer Systems and Applications*, 2006.

[15] R. Teodorescu and J. Torrellas, "Variation-aware application scheduling and power management for chip multiprocessors," in *Proceedings of the 35th Annual International Symposium on Computer Architecture*, ser. ISCA '08, 2008.

[16] M. Banikazemi, D. Poff, and B. Abali, "Pam: a novel performance/power aware meta-scheduler for multi-core systems," in *Proceedings of the 2008 ACM/IEEE conference on Supercomputing*, ser. SC '08, 2008.

[17] D. Tam, R. Azimi, and M. Stumm, "Thread clustering: sharing-aware scheduling on smp-cmp-smt multiprocessors," in *Proceedings of the 2nd ACM SIGOPS/EuroSys European Conference on Computer Systems 2007*, 2007.

[18] X. Zhou, J. Young, M. Chrobak, and Y. Zhang, "Manycore work stealing," in *Proceedings of the 2010 IEEE/ACM IntâĂŹl Conference on Green Computing and Communications*, 2010.

[19] J. Yang, X. Zhou, M. Chrobak, Y. Zhang, and L. Jin, "Dynamic thermal management through task scheduling," in *Performance Analysis of Systems and software, 2008. ISPASS 2008. IEEE International Symposium on*, 2008.

[20] M. Rajagopalan, B. T. Lewis, and T. A. Anderson, "Thread scheduling for multi-core platforms," in *Proceedings of the 11th USENIX workshop on Hot topics in operating systems*, 2007.

[21] S. Chen, P. B. Gibbons, M. Kozuch, V. Liaskovitis, A. Ailamaki, G. E. Blelloch, B. Falsafi, L. Fix, N. Hardavellas, T. C. Mowry, and C. Wilkerson, "Scheduling threads for constructive cache sharing on cmps," in *Proceedings of the nineteenth annual ACM symposium on Parallel algorithms and architectures*, ser. SPAA '07, 2007, pp. 105–115.

[22] S. Eranian, "What can performance counters do for memory subsystem analysis?" in *MSPC '08: Proceedings of the 2008 ACM SIGPLAN workshop on Memory systems performance and correctness*, 2008, pp. 26–30.

[23] K. Singh, M. Bhadauria, and S. A. McKee, "Real time power estimation and thread scheduling via performance counters," *SIGARCH Comput. Archit. News*, vol. 37, no. 2, pp. 46–55, 2009.

A Fault-Tolerant Approach to Distributed Applications

T. Nguyen[1], J-A. Desideri[2], and L. Trifan[1]
[1]INRIA, Grenoble Rhône-Alpes, Montbonnot, Saint-Ismier, France
[2]INRIA, Sophia-Antipolis Méditerranée, Sophia-Antipolis, France

Abstract *- Distributed computing infrastructures support system and network fault-tolerance, e.g., grids and clouds. They transparently repair and prevent communication and system software errors. They also allow duplication and migration of jobs and data to prevent hardware failures. However, only limited work has been done so far on application resilience, i.e., the ability to resume normal execution after errors and abnormal executions in distributed environments. This paper addresses issues in application resilience, i.e., fault-tolerance to algorithmic errors and to resource allocation failures. It addresses solutions for error detection and management. It also overviews a platform used to deploy, execute, monitor, restart and resume distributed applications on grids and cloud infrastructures in case of unexpected behavior.*

Keywords: Resilience, fault-tolerance, distributed computing, e-Science applications, high-performance computing, workflows.

1 Introduction

This paper overviews some solutions for application errors detection and management when running on distributed infrastructures. A platform is presented relying on a workflow system interfaced with a grid infrastructure to model cloud environments. Section 2 gives some definitions of terms. Section 3 goes into details concerning a platform based on a workflow management system to support application resilience on distributed infrastructures, e.g., grids and clouds. Ttwo testcases illustrating resilience to hardware and sysem errors, and resilience to application errors respectively are described in Section 4, where an algorithm-based fault-tolerant approach is illusrated. Section 5 is a conclusion.

2 Definitions

This section provides some definitions of terms used in this paper in order to make clear some commonly used words, and ultimately avoid confusion related to the complex computer systems ecosystems [17].

The generic term *error* is used to characterize abnormal behavior, originating from hardware, operating systems and applications that do not follow prescribed protocols and algorithms. Errors can be fatal, transient and warnings, depending on their criticity level. Because sophisticated hardware and software stacks are operating on all production systems, there is a need to classify the corresponding concepts.

A *failure* is different from a process *fault*, e.g., computing a bad expression. Indeed, a system failure does not impact the correct logics of the application process at work, and should not be handled by it, but by the system error-handling software instead: "failures are non-terminal error conditions that do not affect the normal flow of the process" [11].
However, an activity can be programmed to throw a *fault* following a system failure, and the user can choose in such a case to implement a specific application behavior, e.g., a predefined number of activity retries or a termination.
Application and system software can raise *exceptions* when faults and failures occur. The exception handling software then handles the faults and failures. This is the case for the YAWL workflow management system [19][20], where so-called dedicated *exlets* can be defined by the users [21] . They are components dedicated to the management of abnormal application or system behavior. The extensive use of these exlets allows the users to modify the behavior of the applications on-line, without stopping the running processes. Further, the new behavior is stored as a new component of the application workflow, which incrementally modifies its specifications. It can therefore be modified dynamically to handle changes in the user and application requirements.
Fault-tolerance is a generic term that has long been used to name the ability of systems and applications to cope with errors. Transactional systems and real-time software for example need to be fault-tolerant [1]. Fault-tolerance is usually implemented using periodic *checkpoints* that store the current state of the applications and the corresponding data.
However, this checkpoint definition does not usually include the tasks execution states or contexts, e.g., internal loop counters, current array indices, etc. This means that interrupted tasks, whatever the causes of errors, cannot be restarted from their exact execution state immediately prior to the errors.
We assume therefore that the *recovery* procedure must restart the failed tasks from previously stored elements in the set of existing checkpoints. A consequence is that failed tasks cannot

be restarted on the fly, following for example a transient non-fatal error. They must be restarted exclusively from previously stored checkpoints.

Application *robustness* is the property of software that are able to survive consistently from data and code errors. This area is a major concern for complex numeric software that deal with data uncertainties. This is particularly the case for simulation applications [7].

Resilience is also a primary concern for the applications faced to system and hardware errors. In the following, we include both application (external) fault-tolerance and (internal) robustness in the generic term resilience [9]. This is fully compatible with the following definition of resilience: "Resilience is a measure of the ability of a computing system and its applications to continue working in the presence of system degradations and failures" [30].

In the following section, a platform for high-performance distributed computing is described (Section 3.2). Examples of application resilience are then given. They address system faults (Section 4.1), application failures (Section 4.2) and algorithm-based fault-tolerance (ABFT) (Section 4.3).

3 Application Resilience

3.1 Overview

Several proposals have emerged recently dedicated to resilience and fault management in HPC systems [14][15][16]. The main components of such sub-systems are dedicated to the management of error, ranging from early error detections to error assessment, impact characterization, healing procedures concerning infected codes and data, choice of appropriate steps backwards and effective low overhead restart procedures.

General approaches which encompass all these aspects are proposed for Linux systems, e.g., CIFTS [5]. More dedicated proposals focus on multi-level checkpointing and restart procedures to cope with memory hierarchy (RAM, SSD, HDD), hybrid CPU-GPU hardware, multi-core hardware topology and data encoding to optimize the overhead of checkpointing strategies, e.g., FTI [22]. Also, new approaches take benefit of virtualization technologies to optimize checkpointing mechanisms using virtual disks images on cloud computing infrastructures [23], and checkpoint on failure approaches [32]. The goal is to design and implement low overhead, high frequency and compact checkpointing schemes.

Two complementary aspects are considered here:

• The detection and management of failures inherent to the hardware and software systems used

• The detection and management of faults emanating from the application code itself

Both aspects are different and imply different system components to react. However, unforeseen or incorrectly handled application errors may have undesirable effects on the execution of system components. The system and hardware fault management components might then have drastic procedure to confine the errors, which can lead to the application aborting. This is the case for out of bound parameter and data values, incorrect service invocations, if not correctly taken care of in the application codes.

This raises an important issue in algorithms design. Parallelization of numeric codes on HPC platforms is today taken into account in an expanding move towards petascale and future exascale computers. But so far, only limited algorithmic approaches take into account fault-tolerance from the start.

Generic system components have been designed and tested for fault-tolerance. They include fault-tolerance backpanes [5] and fault-tolerance interfaces [22]. Both target general procedures to cope with systematic monitoring of hardware, system and applications behaviors. Performance consideration limit the design options of such systems where incremental and multi-level checkpoints become the norm, in order to alleviate the overhead incurred by checkpoints storage and CPU usage. These can indeed exceed 25% of the total wall time requirements for scientific applications [22]. Other proposals take advantage of virtual machines technologies to optimize checkpoints storage using incremental ("shadowed" and "cloned") virtual disks images on virtual machines snapshots [23] or checkpoint on failures protocols [32].

3.2 Distributed Platform

The distributed platform is built by the connection of two components:

• workflow management system for application definition, deployment, execution and monitoring [1][2];

• middleware allowing for distributed resource reservation, and execution of the applications on a wide-area network.

This forms the basis for the cloud infrastructure.

3.2.1 Distributed workflow

The applications are defined using a workflow management system, i.e., YAWL [20]. This allows for dataflow and control flow specifications. It allows parameter definition and passing between application tasks. The tasks are defined incrementally and hierarchically. They can bear constraints that trigger appropriate code to cope with exceptions, i.e., exlets, and user-defined real-time runtime branchings. This allows for situational awareness at runtime and supports user interventions, when required. This is a powerful tool to deal with fault-tolerance and application resilience at runtime [9].

3.2.2 Middleware

The distribution of the platform is designed using an open-source middleware, i.e., Grid5000 [1]. This allows for reservation, deployment and execution of customized systems and application configurations. The Grid5000 nationwide infrastructure currently includes 12 sites in France and abroad, 19 research labs, 15 clusters, 1500 nodes, 8600 cores, connected by a 10Gb/s network. The resource reservations, deployment and execution of the applications are made through standardized calls to specific system libraries. Because the infrastructure is shared between many research labs, resource reservation and job executions, i.e., applications, are queued with specific priority considerations.

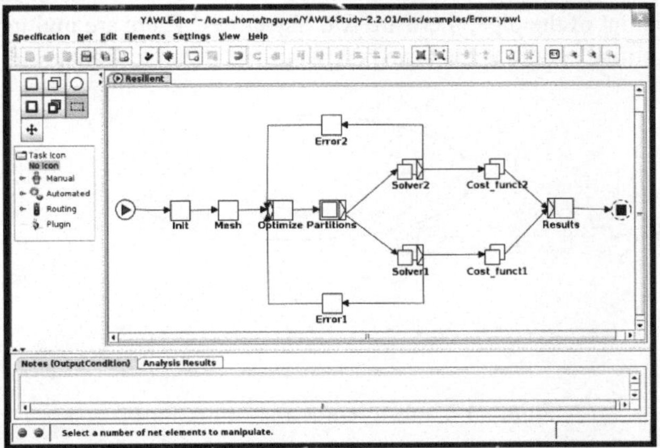

Figure 1. Distributed application workflow.

4 Experiments

Experiments are defined, run and monitored using the standard YAWL workflow system interface [6][19]. They invoke automatically or manually the tasks, as defined in the application specification interface. Tasks in turn invoke the various executable components tranparently through the middleware, using Web services [21]. They are standard in YAWL and used to invoke remote executable codes specific to each task. The codes are written in any programming language, ranging from Python to Java and C++. Remote script invocations with parameters are also possible. Parameter passing and data exchange, including files, between the executable codes are standardized in the workflow interface. Data structures are extendible user-defined templates to cope with all potential applications. As mentioned in the previous sections (Section "Workflow", above), constraints are defined and rules trigger component tasks based on data values conditional checks at runtime. The testcases are distributed on a network of HPC clusters using the Grid5000 infrastructure. The hardware characteristics of the clusters are different. The application performance when running on various clusters are therefore different.

Two complementary testcases are described in the following sections. The first one focuses on resilience to hardware and systems failures, e.g., memory overflow (Section 4.1). The second one is focused on resilience to application faults, e.g., runtime error of a particular application component (Section 4.2). It is supported by a fault-tolerant algorithm (Section 4.3).

4.1 Resilience to hardware or system failures

We use the infrastructure to deploy the application tasks on the various clusters and take advantage of the different cluster performance characteristics to benefit from load-balancing techniques combined with error management. This approach therefore combines optimal resource allocation with the management of specific hardware and system errors, e.g., memory overflow, disk quota exceeded.

The automotive testcase presented in this section includes 17 different rear-mirror models tested for aerodynamics optimization. They are attached to a vehicle mesh of 22 million cells. A reference simulation was performed in 2 days on a 48 CPU non-distributed cluster with a total of 144 GB RAM. The result was a 2% drag reduction for the complete vehicle. The mesh will be eventually refined to include up to 35 million cells. A DES (Detached Eddy Simulation) flow simulation model is used.

The tasks include, from left to right in Figure 1:

• An initialization task for configuring the application (data files, optimization codes among which to choose…)

• A mesh generator producing the input data to the optimizer from a CAD file

• An optimizer producing the optimized data files (e.g., variable vectors)

• A partitioner that decomposes the input mesh into several sub-meshes for parallelization

• Each partition is input to a solver, several instances of which work on particular partitions

• A cost function evaluator, e.g., aerodynamic drag

• A result gathering task for output and data visualization

• Error handlers in order to process the errors raised by the solvers

The optimizer and solvers are implemented using MPI. This allows highly parallel software executions. Combined with the parallelization made possible by the various mesh partitions, and the different geometry configurations of the testcase, it follows that there are three complementary parallelization levels in this testcase, which allow to fully benefit from the HPC clusters infrastructure.

Should a system failure occur during the solver processes, an exception is raised by the tasks and they transfer the control to the corresponding error handler. This one will process the failures and trigger the appropriate actions, including:

• Migrate the solver task and data to another cluster, in case of CPU time limit or memory overflow: this is a load-balancing approach

• Retry the optimizer task with new input parameters requested from the user, if necessary (number of iterations, switch optimizer code…)

• Ignore the failure, if applicable, and resume the solver task

This approach merges two different and complementary techniques:

• Application-level error handling

• A load-balancing approach to take full benefit of the various cluster characteristics, for best resources utilization and application performance

Finally, the testbed implements the combination of a user-friendly workflow system with a grid computing infrastructure. It includes automatic load-balancing and resilience techniques. It therefore provides a powerful cloud infrastructure, compliant with the "Infrastructure as a Service" approach (IaaS).

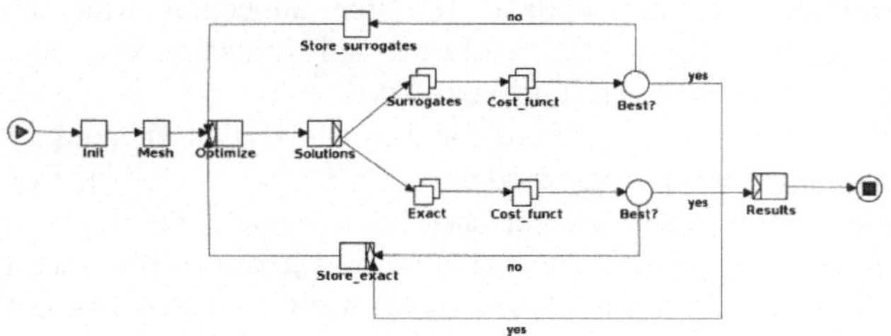

Figure 2. Distributed parallel application.

4.2 Resilience to application faults

An important issue in achieving resilient applications is to implement fault-tolerant algorithms. Programming error-aware codes is a key feature that supports runtime checks, including plausibility tests on variables values at runtime and quick tests to monitor the application behavior. Should unexpected values occur, the users can then pause the applications, analyzes the data and take appropriate actions at runtime, without aborting the applications and restarting them all over again.

It is also important that faults occurring in a particular part of the application code do not impair other running parts that behave correctly. This is fundamental to distributed and parallel applications, particularly for e-Science application running for days and weeks on petabytes of data. Thus, the correct parts can run to completion and wait for the erroneous part to restart and resume, so that the whole application can be run to satisfactory results. This is mentioned as *local recovery* in [30].

This section details an approach to design and implement a fault-tolerant optimization algorithm which is robust to runtime faults on data values, e.g., out of bounds values, infinite loops, fatal exceptions.

In contrast with the previous experiment (Section 3.3.1), where the application code was duplicated on each computing node and data migrated for effective resources utilization and robustness with respect to hardware and system failures, this new experiment is based on a fully distributed and parallel optimization application which is inherently resilient to application faults.

It is based on several parallel branches that run asynchronously and store their results in different files, providing the inherent resilience capability. This is complemented by a fault-tolerant algorithm described in the next section (Section 3.3.3).

The application is designed to optimize the geometry of an air-conditioner [24]. It uses both a genetic algorithm and a surrogate approach that run in parallel and collaborate to produce pipe geometries fitting best with two optimization objectives: minimization of the pressure loss at the output of the pipe and minimization of the flow distribution at the output (Figures 2). The complete formal definition and a detailed description of the application are given in [24].

Solutions to the optimization goals are formed by several related elements corresponding to the different optimization criteria. In case of multi-objective optimization, as is the case here with the minimization of pressure loss throughout the air-conditioner pipe and minimization of speed variations at the output of the pipe, there are two objectives. There are multiple optimal solutions than can be vizualised as Pareto fronts.

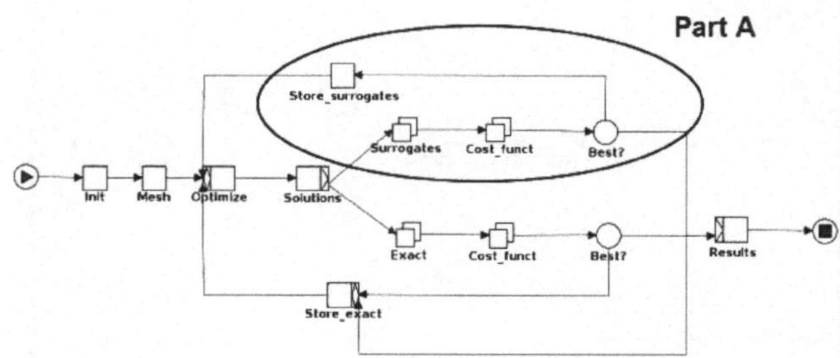

Figure 3. Fault-tolerant algorithm: Part A.

Approximate solutions using the surrogates (Figure 3: Part A) and exact solutions using the genetic algorithm (Figure 4: Part B) run asynchronously in parallel to evaluate temporary partial solutions.

When a surrogate is deemed correct, i.e., its accuracy is below-user defined thresholds with respect to the fitness criteria, it is stored in the exact file and tagged "provisional". Future evaluations by the exact genetic algorithm will use it together with the other exact values to improve the future exact solutions (Figure 4, Part B). The genetic algorithm will eventually supersede the provisional solutions. In contrast, surrogates values are computed as long as "better" exact values are not produced.

Each part stores its results in a specific file (Figure 7: Part E and Part F). When the exact solutions satisfy predefined accuracy criteria with respect to the optimization objectives, they are stored in the final results file (Figure 7, Part G).

Each part in the application workflow implements an asynchronous parallel loop that is driven by the optimizer. Each loop runs independently of the other. Each loop is itself parallelized by multiple instances of the Surrogates (Figure 5: Part C) and Exact (Figure 6: Part D) evaluation codes that compute potential solution in parallel. Each solution is a candidate geometry for the air-conditioner pipe optimizing the fitness criteria, e.g., pressure loss and flow speed variations at the output of the pipe.

The final results file stores the combined values for the optimal solutions (Figure 7: Part G). There are multiple optimal solutions, hence the need for a specific file to store them.

4.3 Fault-tolerant algorithm

The solution to resilience for the application described in the previous section (Section 4.2) is the fault-tolerant algorithm implemented to compute the solutions to the multi-objective optimization problem. This illustrates the algorithm-based fault-tolerance approach (ABFT) used here.

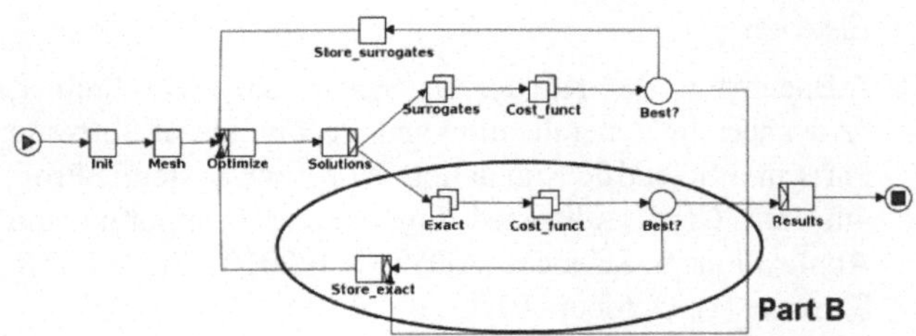

Figure 4. Fault-tolerant algorithm: Part B.

As mentioned above, the implementation of the application is distributed, parallel and asynchronous. It is distributed because the tasks are deployed on the various sites where the application codes run. It is parallel because these tasks can run multiple instances simultaneously for the computations of the surrogates and the exact solutions. It is asynchronous because the surrogates and exact solutions are computed in two distinct parallel loops and produce their results whatever the state of the other loop. This paves the way to implement an inherently fault-tolerant algorithm which is described in more details in this section.

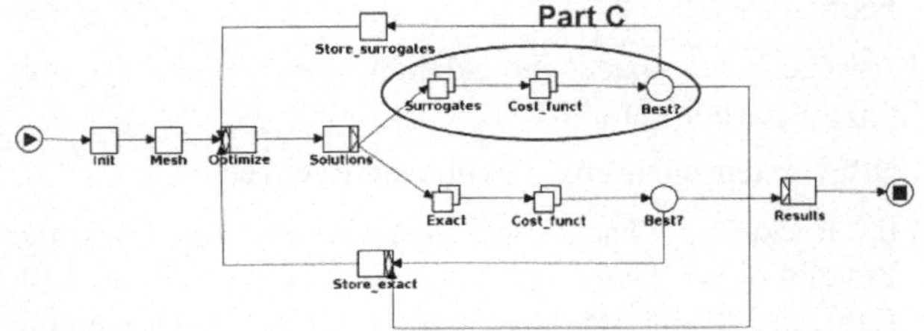

Figure 5. Fault-tolerant algorithm: surrogate branch.

There are four complementary levels of parallelism running concurrently: the surrogate (Part A) and exact (Part B) parts and inside each part, the multiple instances of approximate (Part C) and exact solutions (Part D) that are computed in parallel.

Faults in either part A and B do not stop the other part. Further, faults in particular instances of the approximate and exact solutions computations do not stop the other instances computing the other solutions in parallel.

Indeed, surrogates and exact solutions are computed in parallel using multiple instances of the task "Surrogates" and "Exact" in part C and Part D of the workflow (Figures 5 and 6). Also, the faults in a particular instance inside parts C and D do not stop the computation of the other solutions running in parallel inside those parts.

Further, the three independent files used to store the surrogates, the exact solutions and the final solutions respectively allow for the restart of whatever part has failed without impacting any other file (Figure 7). The content of the three files are indeed the checkpoints where the failed parts can restart from. This allows for effective checkpointing and restart mechanisms. Errors need not the whole applications to be restarted from scratch. They can be resumed using the most recent surrogates and exact solutions already computed.

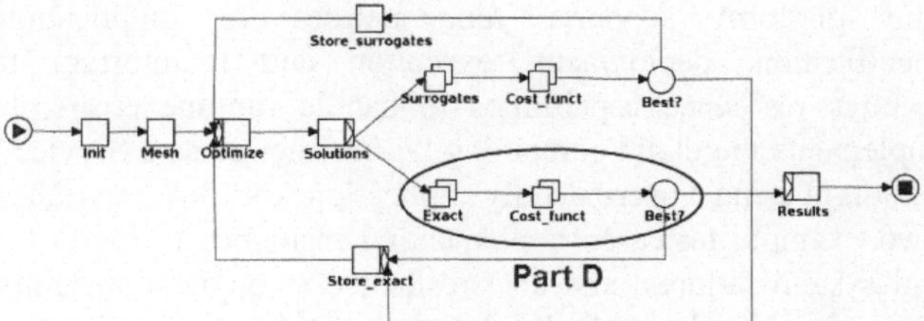

Figure 6. Fault-tolerant algorithm: exact branch.

The vulnerability of the files to faults and failures is also a critical issue for application resilience. Most file management systems provide transaction and back-up capabilities to support this. Faults and failures impacting the Part E and Part F files will have little impact since the lost data they contained is automatically recomputed by the Part C and Part D loops respectively, which take into account the current provisional and exact solutions stored. Lost data in either file after a restart will therefore be recomputed seamlessly. The overhead is therefore only the recalculation of the lost data, without the need for a specific recovery procedure.

The most critical part is the Part G file which stores the final optimal solutions. It should be duplicated on the fly to another location for best availability after errors. But the final results already stored in the Part G file are not impacted by faults and failures in either Part A, B, E and F. They need not be computed again.

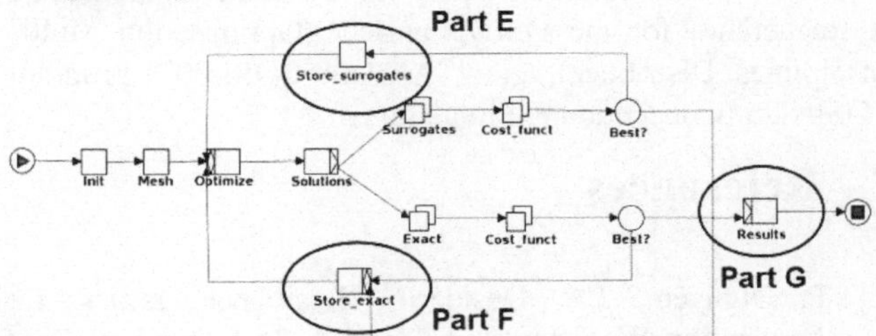

Figure 7. Fault-tolerant algorithm: result files .

5 Conclusion

High-performance computing and cloud infrastructures are today commonly used for running large-scale e-Science applications.

This has raised concerns about system fault-tolerance and application resilience. Because exascale computers are emerging and cloud computing is commonly used today, the need for supporting resilience becomes even more stringent.

New sophisticated and low-overhead functionalities are therefore required in the hardware, systems and application layers to support effectively error detection and recovery.

This paper defines concepts, details current issues and sketches solutions to support application resilience. Our approach is currently implemented and tested on simulation testcases using a distributed platform that operates a workflow management system interfaced with a grid infrastructure, providng a seamless cloud computing environment.

The platform supports functionalities for application specification, deployment, execution and monitoring. It features resilience capabilities to handle runtime errors. It implements the cloud computing "Infrastructure as a Service" paradigm using a user-friendly application workflow interface. Two example testcases implementing resilience to hardware and system failures, and also resilience to application faults using algorithm-based fault-tolerance (ABFT) are described. Future work is still needed concerning the recovery of unforeseen errors occuring simultaneously in the applications, system and hardware layers of the platform, which raise open and challenging problems [31].

6 Acknowledgments

The authors wish to thank Piotr Breitkopf, Head of Laboratoire Roberval at the University of Compiègne (France), Alain Viari and Frederic Desprez, Directeurs de Recherche with INRIA, and Balaji Raghavan (PhD) for many fruitful discussions concerning the testcases design and deployment. This work is supported by the European Commission FP7 Cooperation Program "Transport (incl. aeronautics)", for the GRAIN Coordination and Support Action ("Greener Aeronautics International Networking"), grant ACS0-GA-2010-266184. It is also supported by the French National Research Agency ANR (Agence Nationale de la Recherche) for the OMD2 project (Optimisation Multi-Disciplines Distribuée), grant ANR-08-COSI-007, program COSINUS (Conception et Simulation).

7 References

[1] T. Nguyên, J.A Désidéri. "Resilience Issues for Application Workflows on Clouds". Proc. 8th Intl. Conf on Networking and Services (ICNS2012). pp. 375-382. Sint-Maarten (NL). March 2012.

[2] E. Deelman et Y. Gil., "Managing Large-Scale Scientific Workflows in Distributed Environments: Experiences and Challenges", Proc. of the 2nd IEEE Intl. Conf. on e-Science and the Grid. pp. 165-172. Amsterdam (NL). December 2006.

[3] H. Simon. "Future directions in High-Performance Computing 2009- 2018". Lecture given at the ParCFD 2009 Conference. Moffett Field (Ca). May 2009.

[4] Dongarra, P. Beckman et al. "The International Exascale Software Roadmap". Volume 25, Number 1, 2011, International Journal of High Performance Computer Applications, pp. 77-83. Available at: http://www.exascale.org/

[5] R. Gupta, P. Beckman et al. "CIFTS: a Coordinated Infrastructure for Fault-Tolerant Systems", Proc. 38th Intl. Conf. Parallel Processing Systems. pp. 145-156. Vienna (Au). September 2009.

[6] D. Abramson, B. Bethwaite et al. "Embedding Optimization in Computational Science Workflows", Journal of Computational Science 1 (2010). Pp 41-47. Elsevier.

[7] A.Bachmann, M. Kunde, D. Seider and A. Schreiber, "Advances in Generalization and Decoupling of Software Parts in a Scientific Simulation Workflow System", Proc. 4th Intl. Conf. Advanced Engineering Computing and Applications in Sciences (ADVCOMP2010). Pp 247-258. Florence (I). October 2010.

[8] E.C. Joseph, et al. "A Strategic Agenda for European Leadership in Supercomputing: HPC 2020", IDC Final Report of the HPC Study for the DG Information Society of the EC. July 2010. http://www.hpcuserforum.com/EU/

[9] T. Nguyên, J.A. Désidéri. "A Distributed Workflow Platform for High-Performance Simulation", Intl. Journal on Advances in Intelligent Systems. 4(3&4). pp 82-101. IARIA. 2012.

[10] E. Sindrilaru, A. Costan and V. Cristea. "Fault-Tolerance and Recovery in Grid Workflow Mangement Systems", Proc. 4th Intl. Conf. on Complex, Intelligent and Software Intensive Systems. pp. 162-173. Krakow (PL). February 2010.

[11] Apache. The Apache Foundation. http://ode.apache.org/bpel-extensions.html#

BPELExtensionsActivityFailureandRecovery

[12] P. Beckman. "Facts and Speculations on Exascale: Revolution or Evolution?", Keynote Lecture. Proc. 17th European Conf. Parallel and Distributed Computing (Euro-Par 2011). pp. 135-142. Bordeaux (F). August 2011.

[13] P. Kovatch, M. Ezell, R. Braby. "The Malthusian Catastrophe is Upon Us! Are the Largest HPC Machines Ever Up?", Proc. Resilience Workshop at 17th European Conf. Parallel and Distributed Computing (Euro-Par 2011). pp. 255-262. Bordeaux (F). August 2011.

[14] R. Riesen, K. Ferreira, M. Ruiz Varela, M. Taufer, A. Rodrigues. "Simulating Application Resilience at Exascale", Proc. Resilience Workshop at 17th European Conf. Parallel and Distributed Computing (Euro-Par 2011). pp. 417-425. Bordeaux (F). August 2011.

[15] P. Bridges, et al. "Cooperative Application/OS DRAM Fault Recovery", Proc. Resilience Workshop at 17th European Conf. Parallel and Distributed Computing (Euro-Par 2011). pp. 213-222. Bordeaux (F). August 2011.

[16] IJLP. Proc. 5th Workshop INRIA-Illinois Joint Laboratory on Petascale Computing. Grenoble (F). June 2011. http://jointlab.ncsa.illinois.edu/events/workshop5/

[17] F. Capello, et al. "Toward Exascale Resilience", Technical Report TR-JLPC-09-01. INRIA-Illinois Joint Laboratory on PetaScale Computing. Chicago (Il.). 2009. http://jointlab.ncsa.illinois.edu/

[18] Moody A., G.Bronevetsky, K. Mohror, B. de Supinski. Design, "Modeling and evaluation of a Scalable Multi-level checkpointing System", Proc. ACM/IEEE Intl. Conf. for High Performance Computing, Networking, Storage and Analysis (SC10). pp. 73-86. New Orleans (La.). Nov. 2010. http://library-ext.llnl.gov Also Tech. Report LLNL-TR-440491. July 2010.

[19] Adams M., ter Hofstede A., La Rosa M. "Open source software for workflow management: the case of YAWL", IEEE Software. 28(3): 16-19. pp. 211-219. May/June 2011.

[20] Russell N., ter Hofstede A. "Surmounting BPM challenges: the YAWL story.", Special Issue Paper on Research and Development on Flexible Process Aware Information Systems. Computer Science. 23(2): 67-79. pp. 123-132. March 2009. Springer 2009.

[21] Lachlan A., van der Aalst W., Dumas M., ter Hofstede A. "Dimensions of coupling in middleware", Concurrency and Computation: Practice and Experience. 21(18):233-2269. pp. 75-82. J. Wiley & Sons 2009.

[22] Bautista-Gomez L., et al., "FTI: high-performance Fault Tolerance Interface for hybrid systems", Proc. ACM/IEEE Intl. Conf. for High Performance Computing, Networking, Storage and Analysis (SC11), pp. 239-248, Seattle (Wa.)., November 2011.

[23] Nicolae B. and Capello F., "BlobCR: Efficient Checkpoint-Restart for HPC Applications on IaaS Clouds using Virtual Disk Image Snapshots", Proc. ACM/IEEE Intl. Conf. High Performance Computing, Networking, Storage and Analysis (SC11), pp. 145-156, Seattle (Wa.)., November 2011.

[24] Raghavan B., Breitkopf P. "Asynchronous evolutionary shape optimization based on high-quality surrogates: application to an air-conditioning duct". In: Engineering with Computers. Springer. April 2012. http://www.springerlink.com/content/bk83876427381p3w/fulltext.pdf

[25] Jeffrey K., Neidecker-Lutz B. "The Future of Cloud Computing". Expert Group Report. European Commission. Information Society & Media Directorate-General. Software & Service Architectures, Infrastructures and Engineering Unit. Jannuary 2010.

[26] Latchoumy P., Sheik Abdul Khader P. "Survey on Fault-Tolerance in Grid Computing". Intl. Journal of Computer Science & Engineering Survey. Vol. 2. No. 4. November 2011.

[27] Garg R., Singh A. K.. "Fault Tolerance in Grid Computing: State of the Art and Open Issues". Intl. Journal of Computer Science & Engineering Survey. Vol. 2. No. 1. February 2011.

[28] Heien E., et al. "Modeling and Tolerating Heterogeneous Failures in Large Parallel Systems". Proc. ACM/IEEE Intl. Conf. High Performance Computing, Networking, Storage and Analysis (SC11), pp. 45:1-45:11, Seattle (Wa.)., November 2011.

[29] Bougeret M., et al. "Checkpointing Strategies for Parallel Jobs". Proc. ACM/IEEE Intl. Conf. High Performance Computing, Networking, Storage and Analysis (SC11), pp. 33:1-11, Seattle (Wa.), November 2011.

[30] LLNL. "FastForward R&D Draft Statement of Work". Lawrence Liverrmore National Lab. US Department of Energy. Office of Science and National Nuclear Security Administration. LLNL-PROP-540791-DRAFT. March 2012.

[31] SC. LLNL-SC "The opportunities and Challenges of Exascale Computing". Summary Report of the Advanced Scientific Computing Advisory Subcommittee. US Department of Energy. Office of Science. Fall 2010.

[32] Xiao Liu, et al. "The Design of Cloud Workflow Systems". Springer Briefs in Computer Science. Springer 2012.

Two-Phase Atomic Commitment Protocol in Asynchronous Distributed Systems with Crash Failure

Yong-Hwan Cho, Sung-Hoon Park and Seon-Hyong Lee
School of Electrical and Computer Engineering, Chungbuk National Unvi. Cheongju ChungBuk 361-763
E-mail: [yhcho,spark]@chungbuk.ac.kr

Abstract

This paper defines the Non-Blocking Atomic Commitment problem in a message-passing asynchronous system and determines a failure detector to solve the problem. This failure detector, which we call the modal failure detector star, and which we denote by M, is strictly weaker than the perfect failure detector P but strictly stronger than the eventually perfect failure detector ◇P. The paper shows that at any environment, the problem is solvable with M*.*

1. Introduction

1.1 Background

We address the fault-tolerant *Non-Blocking Atomic Commitment* problem, simply NB-AC, in an asynchronous distributed system where the communication between a pair of processes is by a message-passing primitive, channels are reliable and processes can fail by crashing. In distributed systems, to ensure transaction failure atomicity in a distributed system, an agreement problem must be solved among a set of participating processes. This problem, called the Atomic Commitment problem (AC) requires the participants to agree on an outcome for the transaction: commit or abort [5,11,12,17]. When it is required that every correct participant eventually reach an outcome despite the failure of other participants, the problem is called Non-Blocking Atomic Commitment (NB-AC) [2,6].

The problem of Non-Blocking Atomic Commitment becomes much more complex in distributed systems (as compared to single-computer systems) due to the lack of both a shared memory and a common physical clock and because of unpredictable message delays. Evidently, the problem cannot be solved deterministically in a crash-prone asynchronous system without any information about failures. There is no way to determine that a process is crashed or just slow. Clearly, no deterministic algorithm can guarantee Non-Blocking Atomic Commitment simultaneously. In this sense, the problem stems from the famous impossibility result that consensus cannot be solved deterministically in an asynchronous system that is subject to even a single crash failure [7].

1.2 Failure Detectors

In this paper, we introduced a *modal failure detector M** and showed that the Non-Blocking Atomic Commitment problem is solvable with it in the environment with majority correct processes. The concept of (unreliable) failure detectors was introduced by Chandra and Toueg [3,4], and they characterized failure detectors by two properties: completeness and accuracy. Based on the properties, they defined several failure detector classes: perfect failure detectors *P*, weak failure detectors W, eventually weak failure detectors ◊W and so on. In [3] and [4] they studied what is the "weakest" failure detector to solve Consensus. They showed that the weakest failure detector to solve Consensus with any number of faulty processes is $\Omega+\Sigma$ and the one with faulty processes bounded by $\lceil n/2 \rceil$ (i.e., less than $\lceil n/2 \rceil$ faulty processes) is ◊W. After the work of [8], several studies followed. For example, the weakest failure detector for stable leader election is the perfect failure detector *P* [4], and the one for Terminating Reliable Broadcast is also P [1,3].

Recently, as the closest one from our work, Guerraoui and Kouznetsov showed a failure detector class for mutual exclusion problems that is different from the above weakest failure detectors. The failure detector, called the Trusting failure detector, satisfies the three properties, i.e., strong completeness, eventual strong accuracy and trusting accuracy so that it can solve the mutual exclusion problem in asynchronous distributed systems with crash failure. And they used the bakery algorithm to solve the mutual exclusion problem with the trusting failure detector.

1.3 Contributions

How about the Non-Blocking Atomic Commitment problem? More precisely, what is the *weakest* failure detector to solve the Non-Blocking Atomic Commitment problem? The mutual exclusion algorithm is completely different from the NB-AC in which the order of getting the critical section is decided based on a ticket order. In contrast to the mutual exclusion algorithm, the NB-AC algorithm should receive the messages from all members of a group to make a decision.

In general, Non-Blocking Atomic Commitment algorithms assume that the system is either a failure-free model [13,14,16] or a synchronous model in which (1) if a process crash, it is eventually detected by every correct process and (2) no correct process is suspected before crash [13,16]: with the conjunction of (1) and (2), the system is assumed to equipped with the capability of the *perfect* failure detector *P* [3]. In other words, the perfect failure detector *P* is *sufficient* to solve the Non-Blocking Atomic Commitment problem. But is *P necessary*? For the answer to the question, we present a *modal failure detector star M**, that is a new failure detector we introduce here, which is strictly weaker than *P* (but strictly stronger than ◇*P*, the *eventually perfect* failure detector of [3]). We show that the answer is "no" and we can solve the problem using the *modal* failure detector star *M**.

Roughly speaking, failure detector *M** satisfies (1) eventual strong accuracy and (2) strong completeness together with (3) modal accuracy, i.e., initially, every process is suspected, after that, any process that is once confirmed to be correct is not suspected before crash. If *M** suspects the confirmed process again, then the process has crashed. However, *M** might suspect temporarily every correct process before confirming it's alive as well as might not suspect temporarily a crashed process before confirming it's crash. Intuitively, *M** can thus make at least one mistake per every correct process and algorithms using *M** are, in terms of a practical distributed system view, more useful than those using *P*.

We here present the algorithm to show that *M** is sufficient to solve Non-Blocking Atomic Commitment and it is inspired by the well-known Non Blocking Atomic Commit Protocols of D. Skeen [4,7].

1.4 Road Map

The rest of the paper is organized as follows. Section 2 addresses motivations and related works and Section 3 overviews the system model. Section 4 introduces the Modal failure detector star *M**. Section 5 shows that *M** is sufficient to solve the problem, respectively. Section 6 concludes the paper with some practical remarks.

2. Motivations and Related Works

Actually, the main difficulty in solving the Non-Blocking Atomic Commitment problem in presence of process crashes lies in the detection of crashes. As a way of getting around the impossibility of Consensus, Chandra and Toug extended the asynchronous model of computation with unreliable *failure detectors* and showed in [4] that the FLP impossibility can be circumvented using failure detectors. More precisely, they have shown that Consensus can be solved (deterministically) in an asynchronous system augmented with the failure detector ◊*S (Eventually Strong)* and the assumption of a majority of correct processes. Failure detector ◊*S* guarantees *Strong Completeness*, i.e., eventually, every process that crashes is permanently suspected by every process, and *Eventual Weak Accuracy*, i.e., eventually, some correct process is never suspected. Failure detector ◊*S* can however make an arbitrary number of mistakes, i.e., false suspicions.

A Non-Blocking Atomic Commitment problem, simply NB-AC, is an agreement problem so that it is impossible to solve in asynchronous distributed systems with crash failures. This stems from the FLP result which mentioning the consensus problem can't be solved in asynchronous systems. Can we also circumvent the impossibility of solving NB-AC using some failure detector? The answer is of course "yes". The NB-AC algorithm of D. Skeen [16] solves the NB-AC problem with assuming that it has the capability of the failure detector *P* (*Perfect*) in asynchronous distributed systems. This failure detector ensures *Strong Completeness* (recalled above) and *Strong Accuracy*, i.e., no process is suspected before it crashes [2]. Failure detector *P* does never make any mistake and obviously provides more knowledge about failures than ◊*S*.

But it is stated in [7] that Failure detector ◊*S* cannot solve the NB-AC problem, even if only one process may crash. This means that NB-AC is strictly harder than Consensus, i.e., NB-AC requires more knowledge about failures than Consensus. An interesting question is then "What is the weakest failure detector for solving the NB-AC problem in asynchronous systems with unreliable failure detectors?" In this paper, as the answer to this question, we show that there is a failure detector that solves NB-AC weaker than the Perfect Failure Detector. This means that the weakest failure detector for NB-AC is not a Perfect Failure Detector *P*.

3. Model

We consider in this paper a crash-prone asynchronous message passing system model augmented with the failure detector abstraction [3].

3.1 The Non-Blocking Atomic Commitment problem

Atomic commitment problems are at the heart of distributed transactional systems. A transaction originates at a process called the Transaction Manager (abbreviated TM) which accesses data by interacting with various processes called Data Managers abbreviated DM. The TM initially performs a begin transaction operation, then various write and read operations by translating writes and reads into messages sent to the DM and initially an end-transaction operation. To ensure the so-called failure atomicity property of the transaction, all DMs on which write operations have been performed, must resolve an Atomic Commitment problem as part of the end-transaction operation. These DMs are called participants in the problem. In this paper we assume that the participants know each other and know about the transactions.

The atomic commitment problem requires the participants to reach a common outcome for the transaction among two possible values: *commit* and *abort*. We will say that a participant AC-decides commit (respectively AC-decides abort). The write operations performed by the DMs become permanent if and only if participants AC-decide commit. The outcome AC-decided by a participant depends on votes (*yes* or *no*) provided by the participants. We will say that a participant votes *yes* (respectively votes *no*). Each vote reflects the ability of the participant to ensure that its data updates can be made permanent.

We do not make any assumption on how votes are defined except that they are not predetermined. For example, a participant votes *yes* if and only if no concurrency control conflict has been locally detected and the updates have been written to stable storage. Otherwise the participant votes no. A participant can AC-decide commit only if all participants vote yes. In order to exclude trivial situations where participants always AC-decide abort, it is generally required that commit must be decided if all votes are yes and no participant crashes. We consider the Non-Blocking Atomic Commitment problem, NB-AC, in which a correct participant AC-decides even if some participants have crashed, NB-AC is specified by the following conditions:

- Uniform-Agreement: No two participants AC-decide different outcomes.
- Uniform-Validity: If a participant AC-decides commit, then all participants have voted yes.
- Termination: Every correct participant eventually AC-decides.
- Non-Triviality: If all participants vote yes and there is no failure, then every correct participant eventually AC-decides commit.

Uniform-Agreement and Uniform-Validity are safety conditions. They ensure the failure atomicity property of transactions. Termination is a liveness condition which guarantees non-blocking. Non-Triviality excludes trivial solutions to the problem where participants always AC-decide abort. This condition can be viewed as a liveness condition from the application point of view since it ensures progress, i.e. transaction commit under reasonable expectations when no crash and no participant votes no.

4. The modal failure detector star M*

Each module of failure detector *M** outputs a subset of the range 2^{Π}. Initially, every process is suspected. However, if any process is once confirmed to be correct by any correct process, then the confirmed process *id* is removed from the failure detector list of *M**. If the confirmed process is suspected again, the suspected process *id* is inserted into the failure detector list of *M**. The most important property of *M**, denoted by *Modal Accuracy*, is that a process that was once confirmed to be correct is not suspected before crash. Let H_M be any history of such a failure detector *M**. Then $H_M(i,t)$ represents the set of processes that process *i* suspects at time *t*. For each failure pattern *F*, *M(F)* is defined by the set of all failure detector histories H_M that satisfy the following properties:

- *Strong Completeness:* There is a time after which every process that crashes is permanently suspected by every correct process:
  - $\forall i,j \in \Omega,\ \forall i \in correct(F),\ \forall j \in F(t),\ \exists\ t'': \forall t' > t'',$

$j \in H(i, t')$.

- *Eventual Strong Accuracy:* There is a time after which every correct process is never suspected by any correct process. More precisely:

- $\forall i,j \in \Omega, \forall i \in correct(F), \exists\, t{:}\forall t'>t, \forall j \in correct(F), j \notin H(i, t')$.

- *Modal Accuracy:* Initially, every process is suspected. After that, any process that is once confirmed to be correct is not suspected before crash. More precisely:
  - $\forall i,j \in \Omega{:}\ j \in H(i,t_0),\ t_0 < t < t',\ j \notin H(i,t) \wedge j \in \Omega\text{-}F(t') \Rightarrow j \notin H(i, t')$

Note that *Modal Accuracy* does not require that failure detector *M** keeps the Strong Accuracy property over every process all the time *t*. However, it only requires that failure detector *M** never makes a mistake before crash about the process that was confirmed at least once to be correct.

If process *M** outputs some crashed processes, then *M** accurately knows that they have crashed, since they had already been confirmed to be correct before crash. However, concerning those processes that had never been confirmed, *M** does not necessarily know whether they crashed (or which processes crashed).

5. Solving NB-AC Problem with *M**

We give in Figure 1 an algorithm solving NB-AC using *M** in any environment of group where at least one node is available. The algorithm uses the fact that eventual strong accuracy property of *M**. More precisely, with such a property of *M** and the assumption of at least one node being available, we can implement our algorithm of Figure 1.

```
Var status: {rem, try, ready } initially rem
Var coordinator : initially NULL
Var token : initially empty list
Var group_i : set of processes

  Periodically(τ) do
     request M* for H_M

1.   Upon received (trying, upper_ layer)
2.     if not (status = try) then
3.         wait until ∀j ∈ group_i : j ∉ H_M
4.         status_i := try
5.         send (ready, i) to ∀j ∈ group_i

6.   Upon received (ok, j)
7.     token := token ∪ { j }
8.     If group = token then
9.         send (commit, i) to ∀j ∈ Q_k
10.        status:= rem

11. Upon received (ready, j )
12.   if status = rem then  send (ok, i ) to j
13.       coordinator:=i
14.       status:= ready
15.   else send (no, i) to j

16. Upon received (no, j )
17.   if status=try then send (abort, i) to∀j∈group
18.   status:= rem

19. Upon received (abort, j )
20.   if status=ready then  do abort()
21.           status:= rem

22. Upon received (commit, j )
23.   if status=ready then  commit-transaction()
24.       status:= rem

25. Upon received H_M from M_i
26.   if (status=try and ∃i ∈ my_group and H_M )
        then send (abort, i) to to ∀j ∈my_group
          abort-transaction()
27.       status:= rem
28.   if (status=ready and coordinator ∈ H_M )
        then coordinator:=NULL
          abort-transaction()
29.       status:= rem
```

Figure 1: NB-AC algorithm using *M** : process ***i***.

We give in Figure 1 an algorithm solving NB-AC using *M** in any environment *E of a group* with any number of correct processes ($f < n$). Our algorithm of Figure 1 assumes:

- Each process *i* has access to the output of its modal failure detector module M_i*;
- At least one process is available;

In our algorithm of Figure 1, each process *i* has the following variables:

1. A variable status, initially rem, represents one of the following states {*rem, try, ready*};
2. A variable *coordinator$_i$*, initially NULL, which denotes the coordinator when *i* send its *ok* message to other node;
3. A list *token$_i$*, initially empty, keeping the ok messages that *i* has received from each member of the group.

Description of [Line 1-5] in Figure 1; the idea of our algorithm is inspired by the well-known NB-AC algorithm of D. Skeen[4,7]. That is, the processes that wish to try their Atomic Commitment first wait for the group whose members are all alive based on the information H_M from its failure detector *M**. Those processes eventually know the group by the eventual strong accuracy property of *M** in line 3 of Figure 1 and then sets its *status* to "*try*", meaning that it is try to commit. It sets the variable *group* with all members and send the message "(*ready*, *i*)" to all nodes in the group.

Description of [Line 6-10] in Figure 1; the coordinator asking for a ready to proceed an atomic commitment from every process of the group does not take steps until the all "ok messages" are received from the group. But it eventually received ok or no messages from the group, and it will commits or aborts the transaction.

Description of [11-15] in Figure 1; On received "ready message from the coordinator, the node sends "*ok*" to the coordinator and it set its status with "*ready*" meaning that it is in ready state to wait a decision that is "commit" or "abort".

Description of [16-18] in Figure 1; If the coordinator received the message "*no*" from a node of group, it sends the "abort" message to every member of the group and after that it remains in "rem" state again.

Description of [19-21] in Figure 1; The node *i*, received "*abort*" from coordinator *j*, if it is in ready state, aborts the transaction.

Description of [22-24] in Figure 1; The node *i*, received "*commit*" from coordinator *j*, if it is in ready state, commits the transaction.

Description of [25-27] in Figure 1; When the node *i* received the failure detector history H_M from *M**, if it is a coordinator and knows that a node of group died, it sends the abort message to all members of group.

Description of [28-29] in Figure 1; Upon received the failure detector history H_M from *M**. If it is a node waiting a decision from the coordinator and it knows that the coordinator died, it aborts the transaction.

Now we prove the correctness of the algorithm of Figure 1 in terms of two properties: *Uniform-Agreement* and *Uniform-Validity*. Let *R* be an arbitrary run of the algorithm for some failure pattern $F \in E$ (f<n). Therefore we prove Lemma 1 and 2 for *R* respectively.

Lemma 1. (*Uniform-Agreement*) *No two participants atomic-commit decide different outcomes.*

Proof: By contradiction, assume that *i* and *j* ($i \neq j$) have made a different decision, one is commit and other is abort at time *t'*. According to the line 7-9 of the algorithm 1, the process *i* sends "ok" message and *j* sends "no" message to the coordinator. Without loss of generality, one of the following events occurred before *t''* at every member of a group:

(1) Assume the event that *i* received "commit" message from the coordinator. Then all participants of group eventually received the "commit" message" from the coordinator: a contradiction.

(2) Assume the event that *j* received "abort" message from the coordinator. Then all participants of group eventually received the "abort" message" from the coordinator: a contradiction.

Hence, Uniform-Agreement is guaranteed.

Lemma 2. *(Uniform-Validity) If a participant atomic decides commit, then all participants have voted yes.*

Proof: Assume that a correct process *i* sends "no" message but commits the transaction at time *t'*, and all correct processes except *i* send "ok" message to the coordinator after *t'*. According to the algorithm, after *t'*, the coordinator eventually receives the messages from the group including process *i* and make a decision: *commit* or *abort*. But the coordinator received at least one "no" message from the participant of group. It would send "abort" message to all member of group. So it is contradiction.

Theorem 1 *The algorithm of Figure 1 solves NB-AC using M*, in any environment E of a group with* $f < n$, *combining with two lemmas 1 and 2.*

6. Concluding remarks

Is it beneficial in practice to use a Non-Blocking Atomic Commitment algorithm based on *M**, instead of a traditional algorithm assuming *P*? The answer is "yes". Indeed, if we translate the very fact of not trusting a correct process into a *mistake*, then *M** clearly tolerates mistakes whereas *P* does not. More precisely, *M** is allowed to make up to n^2 mistakes (up to *n* mistakes for each module M_i, $i \in \Pi$). As a result, *M**'s implementation has certain advantages comparing to *P*'s (given synchrony assumptions).

For example, in a possible implementation of *M**, every process *i* can gradually increase the timeout corresponding to a heart-beat message sent to a process *j* until a response from *j* is received. Thus, every such timeout can be flexibly adapted to the current network conditions. In contrast, *P* does not allow this kind of "fine-tuning" of timeout: there exists a maximal possible timeout, such that *i* starts suspecting *j* as soon as timeout exceeds. In order to minimize the probability of mistakes, it is normally chosen sufficiently large, and the choice is based on some a priori assumptions about current network conditions.

This might exclude some remote sites from the group and violate the properties of the failure detector.

Thus, we can *implement* M^* in a more effective manner, and an algorithm that solves NB-AC using M^* exhibits a smaller probability to violate the requirements of the problem, than one using P, i.e., the use of M^* provides more resilience.

7. References

[1] T. D. Chandra, V. Hadzilacos, and S. Toueg. The weakest failure detector for solving consensus. Journal of the ACM, 43(4):685.722, March 1996.

[2] T. D. Chandra and S. Toueg. Unreliable failure detectors for reliable distributed systems. Journal of the ACM, 43(2):225.267, March 1996.

[3] G. Chockler, D. Malkhi, and M. K. Reiter. Backo. protocols for distributed Non-Blocking Atomic Commitment and ordering. In Proceedings of the 21st International Conference on Distributed Computing Systems (ICDCS-21), April 2001.

[4] D. Skeen. Non-Blocking Commit Protocols. In Proceedings of the ACM SIGMOD International Conference on Management of Data, pages 133-142, ACM Press, 1981

[5] M. J. Fischer, N. A. Lynch, and M. S. Paterson. Impossibility of distributed consensus with one faulty process. Journal of the ACM, 32(3):374.382, April 1985.

[6] E. Gafni and M. Mitzenmacher. Analysis of timing-based Non-Blocking Atomic Commitment with random times. SIAM Journal on Computing, 31(3):816.837, 2001.

[7] V. Hadzilacos. A note on group Non-Blocking Atomic Commitment. In 20th ACM SIGACTSIGOPS Symposium on Principles of Distributed Computing, August 2001.

[8] Y.-J. Joung. Asynchronous group Non-Blocking Atomic Commitment. In 17th ACM SIGACT-SIGOPS Symposium on Principles of Distributed Computing, pages 51.60, June 1998.

[9] P. Keane and M. Moir. A simple local-spin group Non-Blocking Atomic Commitment algorithm. IEEE Transactions on Parallel and Distributed Systems, 12(7):673. 685, July 2001.

[10] L. Lamport. A new solution of Dijkstra's concurrent programming problem. Communications of the ACM, 17(8):453.455, August 1974.

[11] L. Lamport. The Non-Blocking Atomic Commitment problem. Parts I&II. Journal of the ACM, 33(2):313.348, April 1986.

[12] S. Lodha and A. D. Kshemkalyan. A fair distributed Non-Blocking Atomic Commitment algorithm. IEEE Transactions on Parallel and Distributed Systems, 11(6):537. 549, June 2000. 24

[13] N. A. Lynch. Distributed Algorithms. Morgan Kaufmann Publishers, 1996.

[14] J. Gray. A Comparison of the Byzantine Agreement Problem and the Transaction Commit Problem. In Fault-Tolerant Distributed Computing, pages 10-17, B. Simons and A. Spector ed., Springer-Verlag LNCS 487, 1987.

[15] D. Manivannan and M. Singhal. An efficient fault-tolerant Non-Blocking Atomic Commitment algorithm for distributed systems. In Proceedings of the ISCA International Conference on Parallel and Distributed Computing Systems, pages 525.530, October 1994.

[16] M. Raynal. Algorithms for Non-Blocking Atomic Commitment. MIT Press, Cambridge, Massachusetts, 1986.

[17] G. Ricart and A. K. Agrawala. An optimal algorithm for Non-Blocking Atomic Commitment in computer networks. Communications of the ACM, 24(1):9.17, January 1981.

[18] M. Singhal. A taxonomy of distributed Non-Blocking Atomic Commitment. Journal of Parallel and Distributed Computing, 18(1):94.101, May 1993.

[19] M.J. Fischer, N.A. Lynch, M.S. Paterson, Impossibility of distributed consensus with one faulty process, J. ACM 32 (3) (1985) 374–382.

Load Balancing in Heterogeneous Distributed Computing Systems using Approximation Algorithm

Bibhudatta Sahoo
Department of Computer Science and Engineering
NIT Rourkela, Odisha, India
Email: bdsahu@nitrkl.ac.in

Sanjay Kumar Jena
Department of Computer Science and Engineering
NIT Rourkela, Odisha, India
Email: skjena@nitrkl.ac.in

Sudipta Mahapatra
Department of Electronics and Electrical Communication
IIT Kharagpur, India
Email: sudipta@ece.iitkgp.ernet.in

***Abstract*—Approximation algorithms have been used to design polynomial time algorithms for intractable problems that provide solutions within the bounded proximity of the optimal solution. Load balancing problem on Heterogeneous Distributed Computing System (HDCS) deals with allocation of tasks to computing nodes, so that computing nodes are evenly loaded. Load-balancing algorithms are attempts to compute the assignment with smallest possible makespan(i.e. the completion time at the maximum loaded computing node). Load balancing problem is a NP hard problem. This paper presents an analysis of approximation algorithms based on task and machine heterogeneity through ETC matrix on Heterogeneous Distributed Computing Systems with makespan as performance metric.**

I. Introduction

Heterogeneous Distributed Computing platforms are widely used to process various jobs from different field of scientific applications. The potential of distributed computing system are related to the management and allocation of computing resources relative to the computational load of the system [1][2][3][4][5][6]. These computational environments are consists of multiple heterogeneous computing modules, these modules interact with each other to solve the problem. In a Heterogeneous distributed computing system (HDCS), processing loads arrive from many users at random time instants. A proper scheduling policy attempts to assign these loads to available computing nodes so as to complete the processing of all loads in the shortest possible time. Modern distributed computing technology includes clusters, the grid, service-oriented architecture, massively parallel processors, pear-to-pear networking, and cloud computing [7].

Balancing the computing loads among the computing nodes in a Heterogeneous Distributed Computing system (HDCS) are carried out by the central server that assigns the jobs to the nodes so as to optimize the makespan. Load balancing has been studied by various researchers as a problem to minimize the makespan [4][5][8][9][10][11][12][13].The central or serial scheduler schedules the processes in a distributed system to make use of the system resources in such a manner that resource usage, response time, network congestion, and scheduling overhead are optimized. There are number of techniques and methodologies for scheduling processes of a distributed system. These are task assignment, load-balancing, load-sharing approaches [1]. Due to heterogeneity of computing nodes, jobs encounter different execution times on different processors. Therefore, research should address scheduling in heterogeneous environment. The *load balancing* problem is to compute the assigned task with the smallest possible makespan. The load balancing problem is NP-hard and proved in [14] by reduction from partition problem.Approximation algorithms has been used by the researchers for attacking NP-hard optimization problems.

An optimization problem is NP-hard (intractable), if the associated decision problem is NP-complete. The load balancing problem is a minimization problem, to minimize the makespan of n tasks on m computing nodes [4][14][15]. The problem of finding an assignment of minimum makespan is NP-hard [16]. The most common approach used by the researchers to find solutions to NP-hard problems were treating them with *integer programming tools* or *heuristics* or *approximation algorithm*[14][15]. Heuristic algorithms may produce good solutions against the quality of the solution. Where as approximation algorithm have the capability to produce solution, that are guaranteed to be within some constant. An approximation algorithm is characterised by a factor ρ called *the approximation factor* or *approximation ratio*; for some $\rho < 1$ for optimization problem and named as $\rho - approximation\, algorithm$. A $\rho - approximation\, algorithm$ guaranteed to produce a solution with objective function value at most ρ times the optimal solution[17]. To prove an *algorithm* to be $\rho - approximation\ algorithm$, it is required to know optimal solution to the problem, as optimal solution to the load-balancing problem (minimization problem) is not known, lower bound of the problem is to be used, to compare with the proposed algorithm.

Here, the load balancing is a job scheduling policy which takes a job as a whole and assign it to the computing node [1]. This paper reviews the scope of applying approximation algorithms for finding sub-optimal solution to load balancing problem in heterogeneous distributed system. The rest of the paper is organized as follows. *Section 2* defines the system model of Heterogeneous distributed computing system structure and the load-balancing problem. *Section 3* discusses how the approximation algorithms are used by various researchers to solve load balancing problems using different approximation schemes. *Section 4* presents describes the different approximation schemes and their applicability to solve dynamic load balancing problem. Finally, conclusions and directions for future research are discussed in *Section 5*.

II. Load Balancing for Heterogeneous Distributed System

A. Heterogeneous distributed computing system

Heterogeneous distributed computing system (HDCS) utilizes a distributed suite of different high-performance nodes, interconnected with high-speed links, to perform different computationally intensive applications that have diverse computational requirements [1][7][18][19][20]. Distributed computing provides the capability for the utilization of remote computing resources and allows for increased levels of flexibility, reliability, and modularity. In heterogeneous distributed computing system the computational power of the computing entities are possibly different for each processor as shown in figure 1. A large heterogeneous distributed computing system consists of potentially millions of heterogeneous computing nodes connected by the global Internet [14][21][22]. The applicability and strength of HDCS are derived from their ability to meet computing needs to appropriate resources [1][23][[24]. Heterogeneity in Distributed computing system (DCS) can be expressed by considering three systems attributes (i) Processor with computing node, (ii) memory, and (iii) networking [29]. The metrics used to quantify the processor or node processing power by means of processing speed and represented with FLOPS (Floating point Operations per Second) and can be measured through LINPACK. Memory attributes are measured as the available memory capacity to support the process. The networking attributes are the link capacity associated with transmission medium, propagation delay and available communication resources can also contributes to the system heterogeneity[25]. In general, load-balancing algorithms can be broadly categorized as centralized or decentralized, dynamic or static, periodic or non-periodic, and those with thresholds or without thresholds [1][24]. We have used a centralized load-balancing algorithm framework as it imposes fewer overheads on the system than the decentralized algorithm [1][4]. Centralized load balancing algorithms requires the global information on computing nodes at a single location and the load balancing policy is initiated from the central location. Heterogeneity of architecture and configuration complicates the load balancing problem [1]. Heterogeneity can arise due to the difference in task arrival rate at homogeneous processors or processors having different task processing rates.

We have assumed that all computational tasks are capable of executed on any computing nodes of DCS. A single computing node that acts as a central scheduler or resource manager of the DCS collects the global load information of other computing nodes. Resource management sub systems of the HDCS are designated to schedule the execution of the tasks dynamically as that arrives for the service. HDCS environments are well suited to meet the computational demands of large, diverse groups of tasks. The problem of optimally mapping also defined as matching and scheduling. A basic assumption is that all computing nodes are always available for processing.

B. Load balancing problem in Heterogeneous distributed computing system

We consider a heterogeneous distributed computing system consists of a set of $M = \{M_1, M_2, ..., M_m\}$, m independent heterogeneous, uniquely addressable computing entity (computing nodes). Let there are $T = \{t_1, t_2, ..., t_n\}$ n number of tasks with each task t_i has an expected time to compute t_{ij} on node M_j. The tasks are arriving from the different users or nodes to the central scheduler or or serial scheduler have the probability to be allocated to any of the m computing nodes. Hence the tasks are characterized by expected time to compute(ETC)as on table I, where all m computing nodes, can be represented in first row. In ETC matrix, the elements along a row indicate the execution time of a given task on different nodes [20] in particular t_{ij} represent expected time to compute i^{th} task on machine M_j.

TABLE I. Expected Time to Compute: ETC

$Task/Node$	M_1	$\cdots$	M_j	$\cdots$	M_m
t_1	t_{11}	$\cdots$	t_{1j}	$\cdots$	t_{1m}
$\vdots$	$\vdots$	$\cdots$	$\vdots$	$\vdots$	$\vdots$
t_i	t_{i1}	$\cdots$	t_{ij}	$\cdots$	t_{im}
$\vdots$	$\vdots$	$\cdots$	$\vdots$	$\vdots$	$\vdots$
t_n	t_{n1}	$\cdots$	t_{nj}	$\cdots$	t_{nm}

The ETC model presented in [20] are characterized by three parameters (i) machine heterogeneity, (ii) task heterogeneity and (iii) consistency. The task heterogeneity can be represented with two categories (i) consistent and (ii) inconsistent, here a consistent ETC matrix the computing nodes are arranged in the order of their processing capability or may be arranged as decreasing order of FLOPS. In particular a node M_i has a lower execution time than node M_j for task t_k , then $t_{ki} < t_{kj}$. Inconsistent ETC matrix is resulted in practice, when HDCS includes different type of machine architectures (HPC clusters, Multi-core processor based workstations, parallel computers, work station with GPU units). In literature most of the researchers used the $task\ execution\ times$ as uniformly distributed [18][20][26][27].Impact of heterogeneity with greedy resource allocation algorithms for dynamic load balancing in heterogeneous distributed computing system using simulation is presented in [28]. The entire task has expected time to compute on m nodes of HDCS. Hence the generalized load-balancing problem is to assign each task to one of the node M_j so that the loads placed on all nodes are as "balanced" as possible [14].

Let $A(j)$ be the set of jobs assigned to node M_j; and T_j be the total time machine M_j have to work to finish all the task in $A(j)$. Hence $T_j = \sum_{t_i \in A(j)} t_{ij}$; for all task in $A(j)$. This is otherwise denoted as L_j and defined as load on node M_j. The basic objective of load balancing is to minimize make span, which is defined as maximum loads on any node $(T = max_{j:1:m} T_j)$. Let x_{ij} correspond to each pair (i, j) of node $M_j \in M$ and task $t_i \in T$.

$$x_{ij} = 0;\ when\ the\ task\ i\ not\ assign\ to\ node\ M_j. \quad (1)$$

$$x_{ij} = t_{ij};\ when\ the\ load\ of\ task\ i\ on\ node\ M_j. \quad (2)$$

For each task t_i, we need $\sum_{j=1}^{m} x_{ij} = t_{ij}$;for all task $t_i \in T$. The load on node M_j can be represented as $L_j = \sum_{j=1}^{m} x_{ij}$, where $x_{ij} = 0$ whenever task $t_i \notin A(j)$). The load balancing problem aims to find an assignment that minimizes the maximum load. Let L be the load of a HDCS with m nodes.

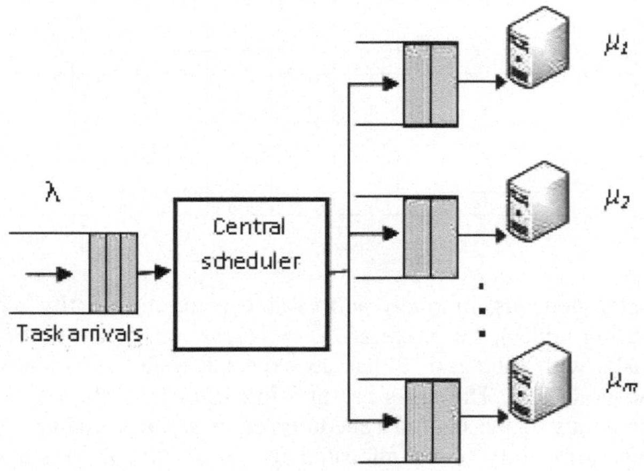

Fig. 1. Heterogeneous Distributed Computing System with central scheduler

Hence the generalized load balancing problem on HDCS can be formulated as

$$Minimize\, L = \sum_{j=1}^{m} x_{ij} = t_{ij}, \forall\, t_i \in T \tag{3}$$

$$\sum_{j=1}^{n} x_{ij} \leq L, \forall\, M_j \in M \tag{4}$$

$$where\, x_{ij} \in \{0, t_{ij}\}, \forall t_i\, \in T, and\, M_j \in M \tag{5}$$

$$x_{ij} = 0, \forall\, t_i \notin A(j) \tag{6}$$

Feasible assignments are one-to-one correspondence with x_{ij} satisfying the constraints in equation 4. Hence an optimal solution to this problem is the load L_i on a machine (corresponding assignment). The problem of finding an assignment of minimum makespan is NP-hard [14][16][23]. The problem is therefore untractable with number tasks or computing nodes (processors) exceeds a few units. The solutions to load balancing problem can be obtained using a dynamic programming algorithm with time complexity $\bigcirc(nL_m)$, where L is the minimum makespan [14]. Queuing models are used as the key model for performance analysis and optimization of parallel and distributed system [27]. The HDCS can be modeled as $M/M/m/n$ (Markovian arrivals, Markovian distributed service times, m computing nodes as server, and space for $n \geq m$ tasks in the system) multi-server queuing system with m servers as computing nodes.

In this HDCS model the node M_1 is the fastest computing node and M_m is the slowest computing node. Assume that service time follow exponential distribution with service rate μ_j,so that $\mu_1 \geq \mu_2 \geq ...\mu_j \geq ... \geq \mu_m$, where μ_j is the service rate of node M_j. The arrivals of the tasks at the central server or resource manager are modeled as Poisson with arrival rate λ. Each computing nodes can be modeled as shown in figure 2. The tasks that are to be executed at a node are under the control of local scheduler and the scheduling policy of the node is responsible for the execution of the assigned task. We have assumed First Come First Serve(FCFS) policy is being used

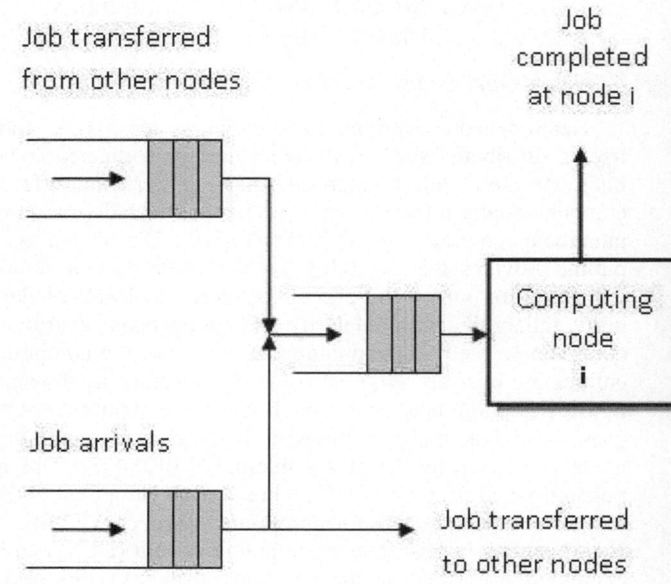

Fig. 2. Heterogeneous Distributed Computing System with central scheduler

at the computing nodes, which can be modelled as $M/M/1$ queuing system [29][30].

The load balancing problem has been evenly treated, in both the fields of computer science and operation research. The algorithm approaches used for load balancing problem are roughly classified as (i) exact algorithms,(ii) heuristic algorithms,and (iii) approximation algorithm [23][15]. The lower bound of the minimization problem in equation 3 can be calculated with the observation that, if it is possible to allocate the tasks over all the m computing nodes equally, the load on each node will be $(\sum_{1 \leq j \leq m} L_j)/m$. More over if a task to be assigned to the slowest machine M_m, the completion time of that task can be decisive for the lower bound. The lower bound can be obtained as,the maximum time taken by a task to complete processing on node M_m, i.e: $max_{1 \leq\, i \leq\, n} t_{im}$. If L_{max} denotes the optimal solution for the load balancing problem, then following equation 7 holds for HDCS with m computing nodes.

$$L_{max} \geq max\,((\sum_{1 \leq j \leq m} L_j)/m,\, max_{1 \leq\, i \leq\, n} t_{im}) \tag{7}$$

Hence the lower bound of load balancing problem is defined to be $L_{min} = max((\sum_{1 \leq j \leq m} L_j)/m, max_{1 \leq\, i \leq\, n} t_{im})$. This lower bound is used to characterize the approximation algorithm in this paper.

III. Related work

Load balancing for distributed computing system is a problem that has been deeply studied for a long time. Different heuristic algorithms are used by researcher to find suboptimal solutions for homogeneous and heterogeneous distributed system. Dandamudi[22]addressed dynamic load sharing in distributed systems and established that load sharing improves performance by moving work from heavily loaded nodes to lightly loaded nodes. An algorithmic approach to load balancing problem is presented in [14]. Techniques for mapping tasks to machines in HDCS, considering task and machine heterogeneity is reported in [19] for static and dynamic heuristics. Gopal and et al. in[6] presented a simulation study for four load balancing algorithm on heterogeneous distributed system with central job dispatcher. Different form of linear programming formulation of the load balancing problem has been discussed along with greedy, randomized and approximation algorithm to produce sub-optimal solutions to the problem. The solution to this intractable problem was discussed under different algorithm paradigm. Modeling of optimal load balancing strategy using queuing theory was proposed by Francois Spies(1996)[31]. This is one of the pioneer works reported in the literature that presents an analytical model of dynamic load balancing techniques as $M/M/k$ queue and simulate with fundamental parameters like load, number of nodes, transfer speed and overload rate [31].

A review is presented in [13] considering the ten most open questions in the area of polynomial time approximation algorithms for NP-hard deterministic machine scheduling problems. Approximation algorithm for scheduling problem for n jobs on m identical machine has been presented by Graham(1966)[15]. A polynomial-time 2-approximation algorithm was presented by Shmoys and Tardos, that minimizes the *makespan of the schedule* and the *mean job completion time* for generalized assignment problem for n independent task on m unrelated parallel machine[32]. A polynomial time 2-approximation algorithm for the single criterion problem of minimizing the makespan was given by Lenstra, Shmoys and Tardos[17]. An approximation algorithm for minimizing cost and makespan is presented in [15] is based on the [32].Fast approximation algorithms for resource allocation is suggested in [33] that applicable to very large linear programming problems with packing and covering constraints. Alon and et al. presented an $\varepsilon-$approximation scheme for the general load balancing problem on m identical machines[34].An efficient approximation algorithm for solving the generalized assignment problem presented in [35] with $(1+\alpha)$ approximation ratio, where α as approximation ratio of knapsack algorithm. Chen and Choi [36] presented a 2-approximation algorithm for data distribution with load balancing of Web Servers. An improved 1/3-approximation algorithm for resource allocation presented in [37] for reusable resources for the set of n tasks.An efficient approximation algorithm for load balancing with resource migration in distributed system is suggest in [38], by partitioning the system into regions.Chudak and Shmoys presented an $\bigcirc(log\ m)$ approximation algorithm for n jobs on m machine heterogeneous machine [39]. The results are based upon the new linear programming formulation [39] using the speed at which job has to be processed on the computing nodes.

IV. Approximation Schemes for Load Balancing

Approximation algorithms are being used an approach to tackle NP-hard optimization problems. Since it is unlikely that there can ever be efficient exact algorithms solving NP-hard problems, one settles for non-optimal solutions, but requires them to be found in polynomial time[14][16]. A simple load balancing approximation algorithm for HDCS based on greedy paradigm is shown in algorithm 1. Each task are assigned one by one,to the computing nodes by selecting the node with minimum load. Selecting the minimum load from the m nodes can be possible in $\bigcirc(1)$ time with the use of a binary min-heap. A min-heap with m nodes can be used maintain the current load of m computing nodes in HDCS. The heap can be updated in $\bigcirc(log\ m)$ time for each T_j. As n number of task to be assigned the running time of the algorithm 1 is $\bigcirc(n\ log\ m)$.

Algorithm 1 `Greedy resource allocation`

Require: $ETC(MaxTask, MaxNode)$
Ensure: $makespan$

$T_j \longleftarrow 0\ forall$ node M_j
$A(j) \longleftarrow \phi\ forall$ node M_j
for $i = 1$ to MaxTask **do**
Let M_j be a node with minimum T_j
Allocate task t_i to Node M_j
$A(j) \longleftarrow A(j) \cup \{t_i\}$
$T_j \longleftarrow T_j + t_{ij}$
end for
$T \longleftarrow max_j T_j$

Theorem 1: Algorithm *Greedy resource allocation* is a 2-approximation algorithm.

Proof: Let L_{max} be the optimal solution to the load balancing problem on HDCS. It has to be prove that *Greedy resource allocation* always completes as assignment of n tasks to the computing nodes such that the makespan T satisfies $T \leq 2\,L_{max}$.
Let M_k be the machine with load $A(k)$that determines the makespan of an assignment with ETC matrix(Table I) using algorithm 1 on m computing node. On successful execution of the algorithm 1 we have $T_k = max_{1\leq j\leq m} T_j$. Let t_{i*} be the last task that assigned to node M_k, where at the time of assignment of t_{i*}, the computing node M_k is smallest load among all m nodes. Let $T_k^{'}$ be the load of machine M_k just before the assignment of task t_{i*}, then $T_k = T_k^{'} + t_{i*k}$ and $T_k^{'} \leq T_j^{'} forall 1 \leq j \leq m$ .That leads to

$$m.T_k^{'} \leq \sum_{1\leq j\leq m} T_j^{'} = \sum_{1\leq i<i*} t_{ik} < \sum_{1\leq i\leq n} t_{ik} \leq m.L_{min} \quad (8)$$

As $T_k^{'} < L_{min}$, we can have

$$\begin{aligned} T_k &= t_{i*k} + T_k^{'} \\ &\leq t_{i*k} + L_{min} \\ &\leq max_{1\leq i\leq n} t_{im} + L_{min} \\ &\leq 2.L_{min} \\ &\leq 2.L_{max} \quad \text{by using equation 7} \end{aligned}$$

■

So the algorithm 1 is never more than a factor 2 from optimal solution for load balancing problem. The *Greedy resource allocation* leads to a larger makespan, when we have large number of tasks with small expected time to compute , followed by a single very very large task. Then greedy algorithm 1 will assign the small task evenly on computing nodes followed by the large task to one of the computing node. A better allocation can be possible by assigning large

TABLE II. SORTED EXPECTED TIME TO COMPUTE: ETC'

$Task/Node$	M_m	M_{m-1}	$\cdots$	M_1
t_1	t_{1m}	$t_{1(m-1)}$	$\cdots$	t_{11}
t_2	t_{2m}	$t_{2(m-1)}$	$\cdots$	t_{21}
$\vdots$	$\vdots$	$\vdots$	$\vdots$	$\vdots$
t_n	t_{nm}	$t_{n(m-1)}$	$\cdots$	t_{n1}

task to machine with lest ETC value, followed by allocation of small tasks among $m-1$ nodes. Hence a better greedy algorithm can be possible using the ETC matrix, where task are arranged according to increasing expected time to compute on m computing nodes. Let the computing node M_1 is the fastest computing node and M_m is the slowest computing node in the HDCS. Assume that service time follow exponential distribution with service rate μ_j of node M_j. Considering the ETC matrix for n number task on m nodes, so that $t_{ij} \le t_{ik}$ for task t_i on machine M_j and M_k, with $\mu_j \ge \mu_k$. Hence for task t_i, we have $t_{i1} \le t_{i2} \le \ldots \le t_{im}$.

Lemma 2: Let there are $T = \{t_1, t_2, ..., t_n\}$ be the n number of tasks with each task t_i has an expected time to compute t_{ij} on node M_j, to be scheduled on m machines,where $t_{im} \ge t_{i(m-1)} \ge \cdots \ge t_{i1}$, then $L_{max} \ge t_{m1} + t_{(m+1)1}$

Proof: Suppose there are $m+1$ task to be assigned to m heterogeneous machines, then at least two of the task from $t_1, t_2, ..., t_m, t_{m+1}$ to be assigned on the same machine. As M_1 is the fastest machine, if those two task are to assigned to the fastest machine say, then load of the machine can be at least $t_{m1} + t_{(m+1)1}$.Hence makespan of the system can be $L_{max} \ge t_{m1} + t_{(m+1)1}$. ■

Let table II ETC' represents sorted matrix in descending order of $expected\, time\, to\, compute$ for task in every row.

Algorithm 2 `Sorted Greedy resource allocation`

Require: $ETC'(MaxTask, MaxNode)$
Ensure: $makespan$

$T_j \longleftarrow 0\, forall$ node M_j
$A(j) \longleftarrow \phi\, forall$ node M_j
for $i = 1$ to MaxTask **do**
  Let M_j be a node with maximum $t_{ij}; max_{1 \le j \le m}(t_{ij})$
  Allocate task t_i to Node M_j
  $A(j) \longleftarrow A(j) \cup \{t_i\}$
  $T_j \longleftarrow T_j + t_{ij}$
end for
$T \longleftarrow max_j T_j$

Theorem 3: Algorithm *Sorted Greedy resource allocation* is a 3/2 approximation algorithm.

Proof: Let machine M_k be the machine with maximum load As first m task are to assigned on different machine, When we are suppose to assign task t_{m+1}, we have the information on $m$node that is with maximum load. We have also assumed that the task t_{i*} allotted to the node M_k. If $i* \le m$, then t_{i*} is the only task to be assigned to M_k. This is feasible because first m tasks are assigned to different nodes using greedy resource allocation algorithm. Hence, allocation algorithm is optimal as every node gets a single task, and second, If $i* > m$, then by using Theorem 1, we can have

$$T_k \le t_{i*k} + \frac{1}{m} \sum_{1 \le j \le m} L_j.$$

where L_j is the total load on node M_j and $\frac{1}{m} \sum_{1 \le j \le m} L_j$ is the average load of the system. hence:

$$\frac{1}{m} \sum_{1 \le j \le m} L_j \le max(max_{1 \le j \le m} L_j, \frac{1}{m} \sum_{1 \le j \le m} L_j) \le L_{max} \tag{9}$$

since the tasks are ordered by ETC on subjected for allocation, for any computing node M_j, $t_{1j} \ge t_{2j} \ge \cdots \ge t_{nj}$ holds. Hence for $i* > m$, for any arbitrary computing node M_j; we have $t_{i*j} \le t_{(m+1)j} \le t_{mj}$ .Then by using Lemma 2 we have

$$t_{i*j} \le (t_{mj} + t_{(m+1)j})/2 \le L_{max}/2 \tag{10}$$

hence the total load on node M_k is at most $(3/2).L_{max}$ ■

V. CONCLUSION

In this paper, the dynamic load balancing problem is modeled as an minimization problem. Load balancing is being performed during runtime at various stages to keep the workload balance on different computing nodes of a HDCS. This paper presents approximation algorithm to solve load balancing problem on HDCS with central scheduler with defined lower bound.The approximation schemes are based on task and machine heterogeneity through ETC matrix. This work can be further enhanced to design approximation algorithms considering four category of ETC matrix [20] based upon task heterogeneity,machine heterogeneity, and consistency. Some of the application on HDCS restricts a task to be executed on the set of nodes $H \subseteq M$ with specific resource dependability. Scope of designing approximation load balancing algorithm for such systems can also be explored.

ACKNOWLEDGMENT

This Research is supported by Professional Development Assistance(PDA) program of National Institute of Technology Rourkela, India.

REFERENCES

[1] J. Wu, *Distributed System Design.* CRC press, 1999.

[2] V. K. Garg, *Elements of Distributed Computing.* Wiley-Interscience: John Wiley and Sons, Inc. Publication, 2006.

[3] H. Attiya and J. Welch, *Distributed Computing: Fundamentals, simulations, and Advanced Topics*, ser. Wiley Series on Parallel and Distributed Computing. John Wiley and Sons Inc., 2000.

[4] A. Zomaya and Y. Teh, "Observations on using genetic algorithms for dynamic load-balancing," *Parallel and Distributed Systems, IEEE Transactions on*, vol. 12, no. 9, pp. 899–911, 2001.

[5] H. Siegel, H. Dietz, and J. Antonio, "Software support for heterogeneous computing," *ACM Computing Surveys (CSUR)*, vol. 28, no. 1, pp. 237–239, 1996.

[6] T. Gopal, N. Nataraj, C. Ramamurthy, and V. Sankaranarayanan, "Load balancing in heterogenous distributed systems," *Microelectronics Reliability*, vol. 36, no. 9, pp. 1279–1286, 1996.

[7] K. Hwang, G. Fox, and J. Dongarra, *Distributed and Cloud Computing: From Parallel Processing to the Internet of Things.* Morgan Kaufmann, 2012.

[8] S. Dhakal, B. Paskaleva, M. Hayat, E. Schamiloglu, and C. Abdallah, "Dynamical discrete-time load balancing in distributed systems in the presence of time delays," in *Decision and Control, 2003. Proceedings. 42nd IEEE Conference on*, vol. 5. IEEE, 2003, pp. 5128–5134.

[9] E. Altman, U. Ayesta, and B. Prabhu, "Load balancing in processor sharing systems," *Telecommunication Systems*, vol. 47, no. 1, pp. 35–48, 2011.

[10] T. Braun, H. Siegel, A. Maciejewski, and Y. Hong, "Static resource allocation for heterogeneous computing environments with tasks having dependencies, priorities, deadlines, and multiple versions," *Journal of Parallel and Distributed Computing*, vol. 68, no. 11, pp. 1504–1516, 2008.

[11] J. Chen, G. Liao, J. Hsie, and C. Liao, "A study of the contribution made by evolutionary learning on dynamic load-balancing problems in distributed computing systems," *Expert Systems with Applications*, vol. 34, no. 1, pp. 357–365, 2008.

[12] R. Friese, T. Brinks, C. Oliver, H. Siegel, and A. Maciejewski, "Analyzing the trade-offs between minimizing makespan and minimizing energy consumption in a heterogeneous resource allocation problem," in *INFOCOMP 2012, The Second International Conference on Advanced Communications and Computation*, 2012, pp. 81–89.

[13] P. Schuurman and G. J. Woeginger, "Polynomial time approximation algorithms for machine scheduling: Ten open problems," *Journal of Scheduling*, vol. 2, no. 5, pp. 203–213, 1999.

[14] J. Kleinberg and E. Tardos, *Algorithm Design*. Pearson Education Inc., 2006.

[15] D. S. Hochbaum, *Approximation Algorithms for NP-Hard Problems*. Thomson Asia Pte Ltd., 2003.

[16] M. Garey and D. Johnson, *Computing and Intractability, A Guide to the Theory of NP-Completeness*. New York: W.H. Freeman and Company, 1979.

[17] J. Lenstra, D. Shmoys, and É. Tardos, "Approximation algorithms for scheduling unrelated parallel machines," *Mathematical programming*, vol. 46, no. 1, pp. 259–271, 1990.

[18] H. Karatza and R. Hilzer, "Load sharing in heterogeneous distributed systems," in *Simulation Conference, 2002. Proceedings of the Winter*, vol. 1. IEEE, 2002, pp. 489–496.

[19] H. J. Siegel and S. Ali, "Techniques for mapping tasks to machines in heterogeneous computing systems," *Journal of Systems Architecture*, vol. 46, no. 8, pp. 627–639, 2000.

[20] M. M. S. Ali, H.J. Siegel and D. Hensgen, "Task execution time modeling for heterogeneous computing systems," in *Heterogeneous Computing Workshop, 2000. (HCW 2000) Proceedings. 9th*, 2000, pp. 185–199.

[21] G. Attiya and Y. Hamam, "Task allocation for maximizing reliability of distributed systems: a simulated annealing approach," *Journal of Parallel and Distributed Computing*, vol. 66, no. 10, pp. 1259–1266, 2006.

[22] S. Dandamudi, "Sensitivity evaluation of dynamic load sharing in distributed systems," *Concurrency, IEEE*, vol. 6, no. 3, pp. 62–72, 1998.

[23] G. Attiya and Y. Hamam, "Two phase algorithm for load balancing in heterogeneous distributed systems," in *Parallel, Distributed and Network-Based Processing, 2004. Proceedings. 12th Euromicro Conference on*. IEEE, 2004, pp. 434–439.

[24] J. Li and H. Kameda, "Load balancing problems for multiclass jobs in distributed/parallel computer systems," *Computers, IEEE Transactions on*, vol. 47, no. 3, pp. 322–332, 1998.

[25] R. Subrata, A. Y. Zomaya, and B. Landfeldt, "Artificial life techniques for load balancing in computational grids," *Journal of Computer and System Sciences*, vol. 73, no. 8, pp. 1176–1190, 2007.

[26] S. Ali, T. D. Braun, H. J. Siegel, and A. A. Maciejewski, "Heterogeneous computing," 2002.

[27] T. Braun, H. Siegel, N. Beck, L. Bölöni, M. Maheswaran, A. Reuther, J. Robertson, M. Theys, B. Yao, D. Hensgen *et al.*, "A comparison of eleven static heuristics for mapping a class of independent tasks onto heterogeneous distributed computing systems," *Journal of Parallel and Distributed computing*, vol. 61, no. 6, pp. 810–837, 2001.

[28] B. Sahoo, D. Kumar, and S. K. Jena, "Analysing the impact of heterogeneity with greedy resource allocation algorithms for dynamic load balancing in heterogeneous distributed computing system," *International Journal of Computer Applications*, vol. 62, no. 19, pp. 25–34, January 2013, published by Foundation of Computer Science, New York, USA.

[29] K. S. Trivedi, *Probability and Statistics with Reliability, Queuing and Computer Science Applications*. Prentice Hall of India, 2001.

[30] D. Grosu and A. Chronopoulos, "Algorithmic mechanism design for load balancing in distributed systems," *Systems, Man, and Cybernetics, Part B: Cybernetics, IEEE Transactions on*, vol. 34, no. 1, pp. 77–84, 2004.

[31] F. Spies, "Modeling of optimal load balancing strategy using queueing theory," *Microprocessing and microprogramming*, vol. 41, no. 8, pp. 555–570, 1996.

[32] D. Shmoys and É. Tardos, "An approximation algorithm for the generalized assignment problem," *Mathematical Programming*, vol. 62, no. 1, pp. 461–474, 1993.

[33] N. R. Devanur, K. Jain, B. Sivan, and C. A. Wilkens, "Near optimal online algorithms and fast approximation algorithms for resource allocation problems," in *Proceedings of the 12th ACM conference on Electronic commerce*. ACM, 2011, pp. 29–38.

[34] N. Alon, Y. Azar, G. Woeginger, and T. Yadid, "Approximation schemes for scheduling on parallel machines," *Journal of Scheduling*, vol. 1, no. 1, pp. 55–66, 1998.

[35] R. Cohen, L. Katzir, and D. Raz, "An efficient approximation for the generalized assignment problem," *Information Processing Letters*, vol. 100, no. 4, pp. 162–166, 2006.

[36] L.-C. Chen and H.-A. Choi, "Approximation algorithms for data distribution with load balancing of web servers," in *Proc. Intl Conf. on Cluster Computing (CLUSTER 2001)*, 2001.

[37] G. Calinescu, A. Chakrabarti, H. Karloff, and Y. Rabani, "Improved approximation algorithms for resource allocation," *Integer Programming and Combinatorial Optimization*, pp. 401–414, 2006.

[38] R. Varadarajan, "An efficient approximation algorithm for load balancing with resource migration in distributed systems," *manuscript. University of Florida*, 1992.

[39] F. A. Chudak and D. B. Shmoys, "Approximation algorithms for precedence-constrained scheduling problems on parallel machines that run at different speeds," in *Proceedings of the eighth annual ACM-SIAM symposium on Discrete algorithms*. Society for Industrial and Applied Mathematics, 1997, pp. 581–590.

SESSION

PARALLEL AND DISTRIBUTED ALGORITHMS AND APPLICATIONS

Chair(s)

TBA

Parallel Algorithms for Hybrid Multi-core CPU-GPU Implementations of Component Labelling in Critical Phase Models

K.A. Hawick and D.P. Playne
Computer Science, Massey University, North Shore 102-904, Auckland, New Zealand
k.a.hawick@massey.ac.nz, d.p.playne@massey.ac.nz
Tel: +64 9 414 0800 Fax: +64 9 441 8181

April 2013

Abstract

Optimising the use of all the cores of a hybrid multi-core CPU and its accelerating GPUs is becoming increasingly important as such combined systems become widely available. We show how a complex interplay of cross-calling kernels and host components can be used to support good throughput performance on hybrid simulation tasks that have inherently serial analysis calculations that must be run alongside more easily parallelisable simulation time-stepping calculations. We present results for a cluster component-labelling analysis performed during simulation of a Potts lattice simulation model. We discuss how these hybrid techniques can be more broadly applied to this class of numerical simulation experiments in computational science.

Keywords: hybrid CPU/GPU; component labelling, phase transitions; Potts model; heterogeneous system; multi-core.

1 Introduction

Graphical Processing Units have become widely used for a range of scientific computational problems and they have been shown useful for accelerating the performance of a CPU core. Many problems fit neatly onto the large number of cores typically available on modern GPUs. However, CPUs themselves have also been developing and it is now routine to find 6, 8 or even 16 cores on a CPU. These are not the lighter-weight cores of a GPU - it is therefore incumbent on programmers to find ways to keep both their CPU heavyweight cores and their GPU lighter-weight cores busy on a computation to make optimal use of the devices [22].

In this paper we explore how a many-cored CPU can participate more fully in computations for a simulation problem and how work can be interleaved between the CPU cores and calls to GPU kernels to keep the combined CPU/GPU busy and fully contributing towards the problem. We use the general class of problem based around simulation of critical phenomena and the associated analysis of the simulated system to investigate how to program and schedule useful work across the

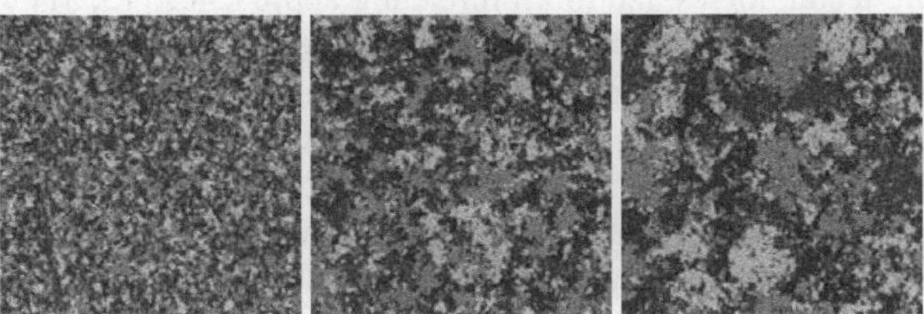

Figure 1: Potts system at the critical temperature with Q=4 for simulation steps $\{512, 4096, 32768\}$.

many-cored [3] CPU/GPU hybrid. We report on work based on both Intel and AMD multi-cored CPUs and accelerated by a range of different NVidia GPU models [17, 21].

We focus on simulations of the Q-state Potts model [23, 34] in two dimensions. This is an interesting system that exhibits a critical temperature that shifts when an increasing number Q of states are present in the model. We combine this simulation with algorithms to analyse the number of component clusters present in the system [10] and show a relationship between the cluster size distribution histograms and the intrinsic phase transitional behaviour changes when Q is explored between $Q = 2, 3, ...9$. The Potts model has been studied using conventional methods for some years and it has a number of interesting known properties, many of which have been obtained using numerical methods [1]. It is a potential basis for other new models [8, 18] however and our work in exploring the cluster size properties is motivated by this as well as the model's convenience as a size-parameterised parallel benchmarking tool.

Figure 1 shows some typical screen snapshots of a Potts model system. We explain the model further in Section 2 below. Essentially it is an extension of the well-known Ising model [12, 16] of magnetic spins. The Potts system allows each spin to take on any of a discrete number Q of possible states. Each spin site can change to a different spin value subject to available energy and thermal fluctuations. The energy behaviour is driven by a coupling between local neighbouring sites so that for a ferromagnetic Potts system like-like spin values are favoured energetically. The consequence is that a hot random system will gradually equilibrate to the chosen finite temperature and if it is around or just below the critical temperature it will form droplets [27] which later coarsen to form large and growing domains [7] of like-like spin values. If the system is too cold then the formation of domains slows down and the spatial structure becomes stuck or frozen in. If it is too hot then randomness prevails and there is no long range spatial order. The Potts system therefore exhibits a particular critical temperature T_c corresponding to this change in collective behaviour and it transpires that T_c depends upon the allowed number of possible states Q. Increasing the number of states lowers the critical temperature at which long-range order can be sustained.

There are a number of concurrency techniques [4,29] and software technologies and multi threading approaches [13, 31] to parallelising models such as the Potts system. One approach is running the entire model on the GPU as a parallel kernel with parts of the system geometrically split across different GPU cores [6, 11, 32] . Another is to use a more conventional CPU threading library to split the decomposition across threads running on the available CPU cores. There are various threading solutions possible, some of which are reliant on special features of the hardware or operating system [14, 26], and some of which are relatively platform independent [28]. As far as we are aware no one has employed the combined interleaving of work across both CPU and GPU cores that we describe in this present paper.

Our article is structured as follows: In Section 2 we describe the Potts simulation model and its computational algorithm. We summarise the typical CPU/GPU architectural arrangement in Section 3 before describing details of our implementation in Section 4, including the component-labelling aspect of the computation in Section 5 and the unusual hybrid cpu/GPU interleaving approach we adopted in Section 6. We report on the performance scalability we obtained in Section 7 but also record some observations on the Potts cluster size distribution we were able to study in Section 8. We comment on the implications of this hybrid CPU/GPU approach in and offer some conclusions and areas for further work in Section 9.

2 Potts Model

The Potts model is usually formulated on a rectilinear lattice with a coupling parameter J that aligns nearest neighbouring spins to the same value. The Potts system is an extension of the Ising model – the Ising system has only two possible spin values - sometimes known as "up" and "down" and hence Q=2 for the Ising system. A simulation of the Potts model can be formulated in terms of the Metropolis Monte Carlo method [19].

The system geometry is fixed so there are $N = L^d$ spin sites arranged on the lattice. For the work reported here we fixed dimension $d = 2$ and varied $Q = 2, 3, 4, ...9$ although the ideas discussed would extend to higher dimensional simulations.

$$H = -J \sum_{<i,j>} \delta(s_i, s_j) \quad (1)$$

The energy function or Hamiltonian is given in equation 1 where the summation is over the nearest neighbouring sites i, j only and the spin variables s_i take on any of the Q allowed values. The Dirac delta function δ yields 1 when the spin variables s_i, s_j are equal and zero otherwise.

At each time step each spin site is "hit" in a random order and the energy consequences of flipping the site to one of the other $Q - 1$ possible states is computed using the coupling term. If the hit leads to a lowering of energy the change is accepted, but even if the change would lead to a higher energy, then the change might still be accepted - and this is done by comparing a random number with the thermal probability $\exp -\delta k_B T$ where the exponent is the change or delta in energy of the system and k_B is Boltzmann;'s constant. As is commonly reported in the research literature [2], we work in physical units where $k_B \equiv 1$ and so we can take temperature T as the reciprocal of the coupling J.

In the work we report here, we first explore how much computational work is required to take a randomly initialised "hot" Potts configuration to thermal equilibrium, then run the system for a further number of update steps, recording the then averaged properties. The novel property we focus on in this present work is the component cluster size distribution. We obtain this by first labelling all the connected spin sites and then building up appropriate histograms of the component cluster sizes present in the system at that step.

Since the critical temperature of the Potts system is known to vary for different numbers of allowed spin states we carry out our investigation at the known $T_c(Q)$ values published by Monroe [20] for the square lattice. This allows us to focus on the interesting cluster sizes produced at large length scales at or around the critical temperatures for all the Q values sampled. There is likely to be a measurable finite size effect deviation from these theoretical values but we minimise this by using relatively large simulated lattice sizes of $N = 1024^2$. Other algorithms such as that of Swendsen and Wang [15] or Wolff [9, 33] could be applied to minimise spurious simulation effects further but we believe the Metropolis algorithm is adequate for the work we report in this present article.

3 Background on Architecture

During the rise of GPU computing, most CPU processors had two- or four-cores. For applications such as the Potts model, a CUDA program could achieve speeds of approximately 100x faster than a CPU core [11]. With this kind of performance difference the CPU was often forgotten and simply used as a host to launch kernels on the GPU. At the time of writing, almost all modern CPUs contain at least four cores and may contain up to sixteen cores in the case of the AMD Opteron 6274 and twelve virtual cores (six hyper threaded cores) in the case of the Intel Xeon X5675 or i7-970. These CPUs now represent a significant computing resource that would be wasted being used as just a host for the GPU.

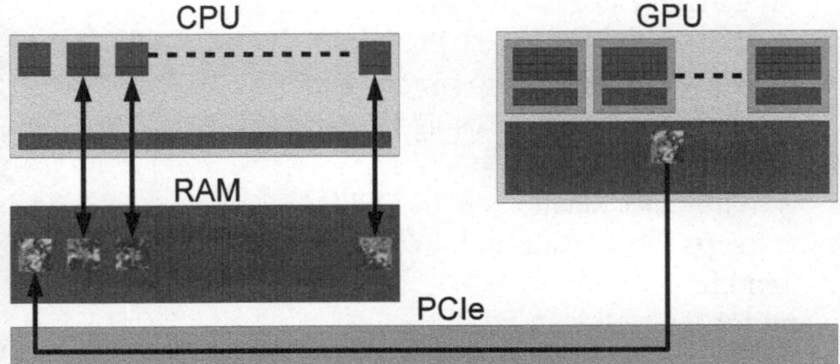

Figure 2: Architecture of typical CPU/GPU hybrid system showing thread relationships and data transfer bottleneck.

Figure 2 shows a typical architectural arrangement of the cores of a CPU and a GPU, this diagram shows a CPU with a number of cores and a GPU with many cores grouped into multiprocessors. All communication between the CPU and GPU takes place through the PCI Express Bus, this communication may be the CPU launching kernels on the GPU or copying data between the host system memory and the GPU device memory.

These separate memory areas and the limited communication between them have traditionally made developing hybrid application difficult. Splitting computation between the host and the GPU device if often not efficient for simulations such as the Potts model because the data transfer outweighs the benefit of making use of the CPU. In this application however, there are two separate tasks that can be computed simultaneously - the Potts simulation and the Connected Component Labelling.

4 Potts Simulation Implementation

In this work, the simulation of the Potts model itself is computed entirely on the CUDA capable NVIDIA GPU devices. The regular data structure of a Potts system and the local nature of the memory access required lends itself very well to computation on the GPU architecture. The hybrid part of the algorithm involves computing the Potts model on the GPU which the Connected Component Labelling is performed on the CPU. This is discussed further in Section 6.

The Potts system is stored using an array of `unsigned char` in global memory. This limits the maximum Q value for this simulation to $Q = 256$, this work explores the range of $Q = 2..9$ so this limit is entirely sufficient. In the unusual case that a system with $Q > 256$ is required, it would be a minor change to change this type to an `unsigned int` which would allow a value of Q up to 2^{32}. Because there is a random component in the update of the Potts model, a random number generator is required. The storage requirement for the selected random number generator is three arrays of `long int`. The last storage requirement is the labels of the field. Because the number and size of the components are being counted, the clusters of each system must be labelled, an array of `unsigned int` is used to store these labels.

The Potts simulation is performed on the GPU by creating on thread for each cell in the system. Updating the system consists of a two-step process using the checkerboard method. By splitting the cells into the two colours of a checkerboard, it can be guaranteed that all the cells of the same colour can be updated without any of their neighbouring cells values changing during the process. This means that two separate kernel calls are required to update the Potts system, one for each set of cells.

Algorithm 1 The algorithm for the RAN random number generator.

$u = u * 2862933555777941757 + 7046029254386353087$
$v\wedge = v >> 17; v\wedge = v << 31; v\wedge = v >> 8$
$w = 4294957665 * (w\&0\text{xffffffff}) + (w >> 32)$
$r = u \wedge (u << 21); r\wedge = r >> 35; r\wedge = r << 4$
$r = (r + v) \wedge w$

The **random number generator** used by this simulation is the Ran algorithm described in Numerical Recipes [25]. Previous research [24] has showed that this algorithm is sufficient for our purposes and can be implemented effectively on a GPU. In this implementation a separate random number generator is used by each thread on the GPU. Each of these random number generators is initialised on the host (using a completely separate random number generation process) and copied onto the GPU. This way each thread can execute independently from every other thread and doesn't have to synchronise or share random number generators.

Algorithm 1 summarises the random number generator algorithm. It is noteworthy that it is based on integer operations and is therefore useful for GPUs, when not all models have equally good balance and distribution of floating point units across the cores.

5 Connected Component Labelling

Component labeling is a complex problem in its own right and often poses challenges for labelling large systems on parallel systems [10]. In addition to the main labelling activity, for the cluster-size analysis we discuss in this paper, we also require to histogram the sizes which involves an additional pass over the labelled component cells. The connected component labelling algorithm used in this work is a multi-pass algorithm based on the one presented in [30]. This particular algorithm is used because it can be implemented as a parallel algorithm on the GPU and was shown to label a system $\approx$ 10x faster than a single CPU core [10]. This algorithm can be seen in Algorithm 2.

Although this is a multi-pass algorithm, in our experiments is has been found to label most system with 6-7 iterations through the data and its performance is comparable to other common algorithms. In fact for this type of complex cluster

Algorithm 2 The Connected Component Labelling algorithm.

initialise labels using position as label
while labels have changed **do**
  find the lowest neighbouring value for each label
  resolve label equivalences
  set all labels using equivalence list
end while

it can often outperform other popular algorithms such as the Contour Tracing algorithm [5].

This algorithm is implemented on the CPU as a single-threaded function as the hybrid update algorithm allows different system states to be labelled at the same time. In this type of situation we have found it is better to give a different system state to each core rather than all the cores attempting to work on the same data at the same time. The GPU labelling method used in the work is a CUDA implementation of this algorithm, it follows the same high-level process but each step of the labelling algorithm is parallelised. The details of how this algorithm can be implemented for a GPU can be found in [10].

6 Hybrid CPU/GPU Implementation

The simple approach to simulating the Potts model on a GPU would be to run the entire simulation and analysis on the device to minimise the overhead of communication. This would be suitable approach when the time taken to perform the analysis is small compared to the runtime of the simulation. However, in this case where the number of components in the Potts system is counted every update, the analysis process takes considerably longer than the simulation itself; $\approx$ 4-10x longer depending on the system size of the simulation, see Section 7 for more details. In this case it makes sense to use the cores of the CPU (which would otherwise be sitting idle) to analyse the clusters while the GPU runs the simulation.

Unfortunately offloading the analysis to the CPU does not have the desired effect, in fact it can slow down the simulation. Because the GPU is able to compute the simulation so fast, the CPU is not able to keep up with all of the systems that get copied off the GPU for analysis. The options to overcoming this problem are to slow down the simulation and make the GPU wait for an available CPU thread to label the latest system, create a large buffer to store all of the systems and allow the CPU to label them later or the solution used in this research where the analysis of the systems is split between the CPU and the GPU.

This hybrid approach allows the GPU to offload as much of the analysis as possible but does not have to wait for the CPU to catch up. Rather than attempt to model the comparative computational throughput of different GPUs and CPUs this method simply checks to see if there are any unoccupied CPU threads every time a new system state is ready to be analysed. If thread is available the system will be copied off the GPU

Algorithm 3 The algorithm for the Hybrid Update & Analysis method.

for all *steps* **do**
  call *potts* function on the GPU
  if CPU thread available **then**
    thread $\leftarrow$ available CPU thread
    copy Potts system to *thread* buffer
    call *label* Function using *thread*
  else
    call *label* function on the GPU
    copy label results to host
  end if
end for

into that thread's buffer and leave it to label it. If all the CPU threads are currently occupied it will analyse the system using the GPU and copy the results into the host memory. This process is shown in Algorithm 3

7 Performance Results

CPU Model	Cores	Cache (MBytes)	Clock Speed (GHz)
i7-2700K	4 (8)	8	3.50
i7-970	6 (12)	12	3.20
Xeon E5-2640	6 (12)	16	2.50
Xeon X5675	6 (12)	12	3.06
Opteron 6274	16	16	2.20

Table 1: CPU relevant Properties.

To test the performance of the hybrid labelling method, the simulation has been run on a range of different machines containing different processors and graphics cards. The CPUs tested include Intel i7, Intel Xeon and AMD Opteron processors. These CPUs differ in terms of number of cores, clock speeds and cache sizes, the specifications of the processors tested are shown in Table 1. The Intel processors support hyper threading and for each physical core have two virtual cores, the number of virtual cores are shown in brackets in the table. The machines containing Intel Xeon and Opteron processors are dual CPU machines with two processors, this increases the ratio of CPU/GPU computational power. The purpose of testing these different configurations is to determine how well the hybrid labelling method performs for a range of different CPU and GPU architectures and relative performances.

GPU Model	Cores	Memory Bandwith (GB/sec)	Clock Speed (GHz)
GTX580	512	192.4	1.54
GTX590	512	163.85	1.22
GTX680	1536	192.2	1.01
M2075	448	150 (ECC off)	1.15
M2090	512	177 (ECC off)	1.30

Table 2: GPU relevant Properties.

The different GPU models tested include the gamer-level GeForce range and the compute-card Tesla range. All these cards are Fermi or Kepler architecture devices which have L1 and shared L2 cache. All the GPUs tested are high performance cards as this experiment is designed to determine whether using the CPU can accelerate an optimised simulation on a high-end graphics card. The specifications of the GPU devices used for this research are given in Table: 2. Please note that although the GTX590 is a dual-GPU card, the specifications given here are for only a single GPU.

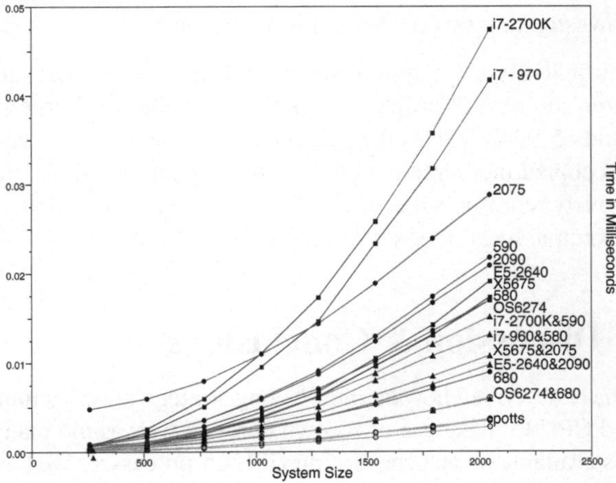

Figure 3: The performance results of the GPU Potts simulation as well as the CPU, GPU and Hybrid labelling methods. Results are shown in milliseconds per step.

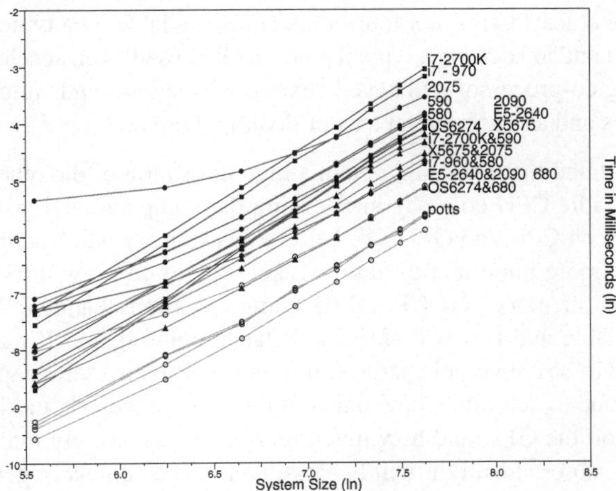

Figure 4: The same information as Figure 3 but plotted on a log-log scale to emphasise the power law relationship.

Figures 3 and 4 show the average time per step for the Potts simulation executed on the GPUs as well as the CPU, GPU and Hybrid labelling methods. The machines tested in these experiments have a number of different configurations: an i7-2700K and a GTX GTX590 (using one GPU), an i7-970 and a GTX580, two Xeon E5-2640s and an M2090, two Xeon X5675s and an M2075 and finally two Opteron 6274s and a GTX680. The GPUs tested are the GTX580, GTX 590 (using one GPU), GTX680, M2075 (hosted in a PCIe chassis) and M2090.

The performance analysis show some interesting results, in all test cases using the hybrid algorithm provided the best results performing $\approx$ 20-50% faster than using just the GPU. For the GPUs the relative performance was as expected with the GTX680 being the fastest followed by the GTX580, M2090, GTX 590 and the M2075. In all cases the GPU could compute the Potts simulation significantly faster than it could label the system.

The CPU results showed an interesting comparison between the machine equipped with two Xeon X5675s and the one with two Opteron 6274s. Although the two Opterons have a combined total of 32 cores its performance was very close to the two Xeons which have a combined total of 12 physical hyperthreaded cores or 24 virtual cores. This shows that the Xeon 5675s can make better use of their resources. The performance of the Opteron machine was still the overall fastest though due to its higher performance GTX680 graphics card.

8 Potts Model Results

In addition to the speed and performance results presented in Section 7 we also observe some interesting behaviours of the component population sizes for the Potts system as we systematically vary the allowable number of states Q.

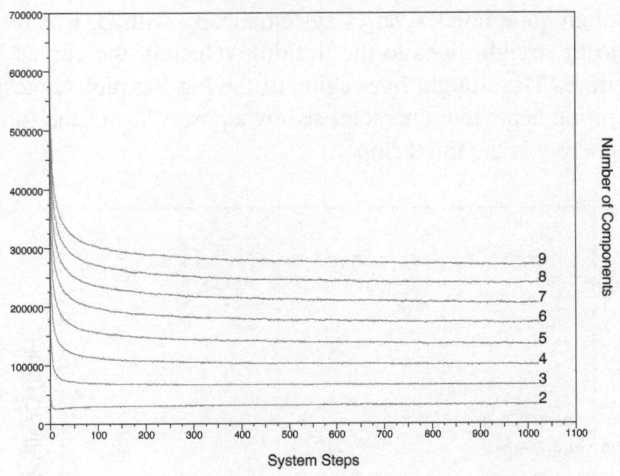

Figure 5: The number of clusters over time for Potts systems at the critical temperature for Q = {2,3..9}.

Our first concern is to determine how long the randomized Potts model system must be equilibrated to attain reasonable measurements that are truly representative of the critical temperature at each of eight Q values that we studied. Figure 5 shows the number of clusters as it progresses exponentially towards a representative average value. We observe that generally the system will approach a representative value after approximately $L = 1024$ steps. This is likely related to the effective speed limitation on the propagation of any information across the system. The periodic boundary conditions mean that phenomena require at least $L/2$ on average to reach across any of the geometric lengths in the system. We appear to be justified in starting our measurements after at least L time steps.

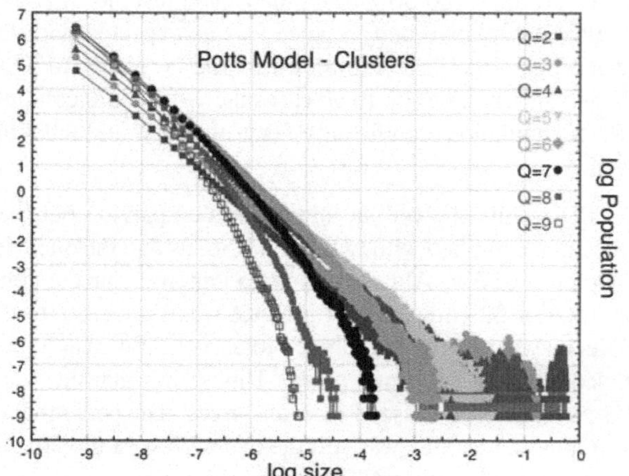

Figure 6: Log-log scale plot of the cluster size populations measured over many samples and for each of the separate Q values.

Figure 6 shows a log-log scale plot of the cluster size distribution, based upon many averaged samples for the different Q values. We observe that the upper cluster size cutoff value - although quite noisy - varies systematically with Q. It is useful to fit straight lines to the limiting values of the curves in Figure 6. The straight line region of the log-log plot suggests a limiting behaviour characterised by a power law of the form s^{ν} where ν is the fitted slope.

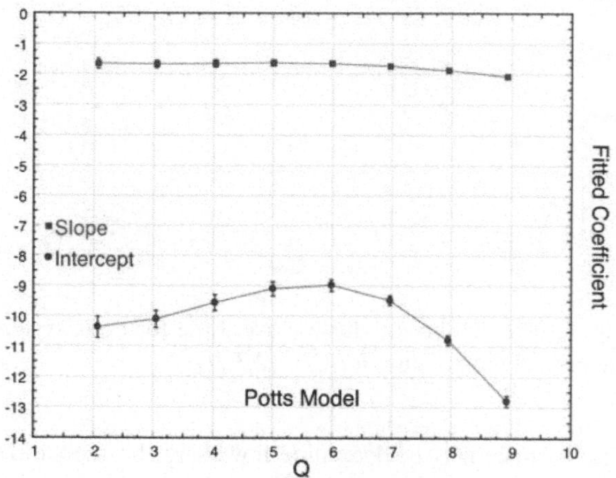

Figure 7: Fitted slopes and intercepts for the cluster size population data.

Figure 7 shows these fitted slopes and there is a perceptible change in behaviour over the range of Q and a possible irregularity around $Q \approx 4, 5$. The fitted intercepts however showed a quite remarkable sensitivity to the different behavioural regimes however. the Potts system is known to have continuous phase transition for $Q <= 4$, and an inter-facial wetting behaviour for $Q >= 3$ leading to a first-order phase transition for $Q >= 5$. The fitted intercepts shown in the lower curve of Figure 7 shows corresponding points of inflection between $Q = 2, 3$ and also around $Q \approx 4, 5$, subject to the experimental uncertainties, which we used for the error bars on the plots. This suggests that the cluster size distribution is a worthwhile metric to compute and that there is scope for investigating this further in higher dimensions.

On sufficiently large system sized problems ($N \approx 512^2$) and greater, the overall utilisation efficiency of the CPU cores is around 85-90%. This is the percentage of time that all threads are occupied measured over the entire program duration. This obviously represents a considerable improvement over having for example five out of six Xeon CPU cores idle.

9 Discussion & Conclusions

We have described how an interleaving strategy allows a multi cored CPU to make use of its own cores as well as the many-cores available on an accelerating GPU co-processor. We have demonstrated this strategy with a scientific simulation problem involving the application of a Monte Carlo update procedure to a Potts model system alongside an analysis of the growing domains in the simulation using a component labelling algorithm.

At the time of writing it is becoming increasingly common to have at least two if not four or six cores available on a typical CPU and in addition a typical modern GPU used as an accelerating co-processor will have in excess of one thousand simple cores and at least several tens of floating point units.

We found that we could obtain a high utilisation of the otherwise idle CPU cores by interleaving the computational tasks between CPU and GPU. We believe this strategy will become even more important in future. Likely future GPUs will have better memory and CPU/GPU communications bandwidths available and this will shift the balance point again. It may need to be a tune-able parameter or possibly even a self adapting one to determine how much of the computation should be run on the GPU and how much on one of increasingly many CPU cores. Ideally it will be possible to have kernels or generated software that can perform the same task on both.

More sophisticated systems may have multiple GPUs supporting a single CPU and it is also common to have clusters with one or two CPUs supported by two to four GPUs at each node. These numbers are likely to develop in future although for computational problems like the one we discuss in this present paper, it is desirable to ensure and maintain a close balance of the number of GPU accelerators to CPU handling cores in hardware and with the appropriate threading support available in software. There is scope for investigating how our approach would scale up to handle multiple GPU accelerators, handled by a many-cored CPU.

There is also scope for applying this interleaving approach to other scientific simulation problems. similar strategy but with a different loading/decomposition approach might also be useful for future co-processors such as the Intel Xeon Phi and its likely ancestors which will have uniform floating-point capable cores that are more coarse grained and more powerful that the typical (more numerous) but finer cores on a GPU.

References

[1] G. Barkema and J. de Boer. Numerical study of phase transitions in potts models. *Phys.Rev.A*, 44(12):8000–8005, dec 1991.

[2] K. Binder, editor. *Monte Carlo Methods in Statistical Physics*. Topics in Current Physics. Springer-Verlag, 2 edition, 1986. Number 7.

[3] S. Bokhari and J. Saltz. Exploring the Performance of Massively Multithreaded Architectures. *Concurrency and Computation: Practice and Experience*, 22(5):588–616, April 2010.

[4] B. Cantrill and J. Bonwick. Real-world concurrency. *Communications of the ACM*, 51(11):34–39, November 2008.

[5] F. Chang and C.-J. Chen. A component-labeling algorithm using contour tracing technique. *Computer Vision and Image Understanding*, 93:206–220, 2004. Proc. Int. Conf. on Document Analysis and Recogntion 2003.

[6] B. R. Gaster and L. Howes. Can gpgpu programming be liberated from the data-parallel bottleneck? *IEEE Computer*, August:42–52, 2012.

[7] K. A. Hawick. *Domain Growth in Alloys*. PhD thesis, Edinburgh University, 1991.

[8] K. A. Hawick and M. G. B. Johnson. Bit-packed damaged lattice potts model simulations with cuda and gpus. In *Proc. Int. Conf. on Modelling, Simulation and Identification (MSI 2011)*, pages 371–378, Pittsburgh, USA, 7-9 November 2011. IASTED.

[9] K. A. Hawick, A. Leist, and D. P. Playne. Cluster and fast update lattice simulations using graphical processing units. Technical Report CSTN-104, Computer Science, Massey University, Albany, North Shore 102-904, Auckland, New Zealand, August 2010.

[10] K. A. Hawick, A. Leist, and D. P. Playne. Parallel Graph Component Labelling with GPUs and CUDA. *Parallel Computing*, 36(12):655–678, December 2010.

[11] K. A. Hawick, A. Leist, and D. P. Playne. Regular Lattice and Small-World Spin Model Simulations using CUDA and GPUs. *Int. J. Parallel Prog.*, 39(CSTN-093):183–201, 2011.

[12] E. Ising. Beitrag zur Theorie des Ferromagnetismus. *Zeitschrift fuer Physik*, 31:253–258, 1925.

[13] S. W. Keckler and S. K. Reinhardt. Massively multithreaded computing systems. *IEEE Computer*, August:24–25, 2012.

[14] R. Knauerhase, R. Cledat, and J. Teller. For extreme parallelism, your os is sooooo last-millennium. In *Proceedings of the 4th USENIX conference on Hot Topics in Parallelism*, HotPar'12, pages 3–3, Berkeley, CA, USA, 2012. USENIX Association.

[15] Y. Komura and Y. Okabe. Gpu-based swendsen-wang multi-cluster algorithm for the simulation of two-dimensional classical spin systems. *Computer Physics Communications*, 183:1155–1161, 2012.

[16] A. Leist, K. A. Hawick, and D. P. Playne. Hybrid update algorithms for regular lattice and small-world ising models on graphical processing units. In *Proc. Int. Conf. on Scientific Computing (CSC'12)*, pages 228–234, Las Vegas, USA, 16-19 July 2012. CSREA.

[17] E. Lindholm, J. Nickolls, S. Oberman, and J. Montrym. NVIDIA Tesla: A Unified Graphics and Computing Architecture. *IEEE Micro*, 28(2):39–55, March-April 2008.

[18] J. Machta, Y. S. Choi, A. Lucke, and T. Schweizer. Invaded cluster algorithm for potts models. *Phys. Rev. E*, 54:1332–1345, 1996.

[19] N. Metropolis, A. W. Rosenbluth, M. N. Rosenbluth, A. H. Teller, and E. Teller. Equation of state calculations by fast computing machines. *J. Chem. Phys.*, 21(6):1087–1092, Jun 1953.

[20] J. L. Monroe. Critical temperature estimates for higher-spin ising and potts models. *Phys. Rev. E*, 66:066129–1–5, 2002.

[21] NVIDIA® Corporation. *NVIDIA CUDA C Programming Guide Version 4.1*, 2011. `http://www.nvidia.com/` (last accessed April 2012).

[22] M. Oskin. The revolution inside the box. *Communications of the ACM*, 51(7):70–78, 2008.

[23] R. B. Potts. Some generalised order-disorder transformations. *Proc. Roy. Soc*, pages 106–109, 1951. received July.

[24] V. D. Preez, M. G. B.Johnson, A. Leist, and K. A. Hawick. Performance and quality of random number generators. In *International Conference on Foundations of Computer Science (FCS'11)*, number FCS4818, pages 16–21, Las Vegas, USA, 18-21 July 2011. CSREA.

[25] W. H. Press, S. A. Teukolsky, W. T. Vetterling, and B. P. Flannery. *Numerical Recipes - The Art of Scientific Computing*. Cambridge, third edition, 2007. ISBN 978-0-521-88407-5.

[26] J. Reinders. *Intel Threading Building Blocks: outfitting C++ for multi-core processor parallelism*. Number ISBN 978-0596514808. O'Reilly, 1st edition, 2007.

[27] W. Selke. Droplets in Two-dimensional Ising and Potts models. *J.Stat.Phys*, 56(5):609–620, 1989.

[28] J. A. Stretton, C. Rodrigues, I.-J. R. Sung, L.-W. Chang, N. Anssari, G. D. Liu, W. mei W. Hwu, and N. Obeid. Algorithm and data optimization techniques for scaling to massively threaded systems. *IEEE Computer*, August:26–32, 2012.

[29] H. Sutter and J. Larus. Software and the concurrency revolution. *Queue*, 3(7):54–62, September 2005.

[30] K. Suzuki, I. Horiba, and N. Sugie. Fast connected-component labeling based on sequential local operations in the course of forward raster scan followed by backward raster scan. In *Proc. 15th International Conference on Pattern Recognition (ICPR'00)*, volume 2, pages 434–437, 2000.

[31] A. Tumeo, S. Secchi, and O. Villa. Designing next-generation massively multithreaded architectures for irregular applications. *IEEE Computer*, August:53–61, 2012.

[32] S. Tzeng, B. Lloyd, and J. D. Owens. A gpu task-parallel model with dependency resolution. *IEEE Computer*, August:34–41, 2012.

[33] U. Wolff. Comparison Between Cluster Monte Carlo Algorithms in the Ising Model. *Physics Letters B*, 228(3):379–382, September 1989.

[34] F. Y. Wu. The Potts model. *Rev. Mod. Phys.*, 54(1):235–268, Jan 1982.

Parallel Asynchronous Modelization and Execution of Cholesky Algorithm using Petri Nets

Gustavo Wolfmann
Laboratorio de Computación
Fac. Cs. Exactas Físicas y Naturales
Universidad Nacional de Córdoba
Av. Vélez Sársfield 1611 - Córdoba - Argentina
gwolfmann@efn.uncor.edu

Armando De Giusti
III LIDI
Fac. Informática
Universidad Nacional de La Plata
50 y 120 - La Plata - Argentina
degiusti@lidi.info.unlp.edu.ar

***Abstract*—PDPTA 2013 - Parallelization of algorithms with hard data dependency has a need of task synchronization. Synchronous parallel versions are simple to model and program, but inefficient in terms of scalability and processors use rate. The same problem for Asynchronous versions with elemental static task scheduling. Efficient Asynchronous algorithms implement out-of-order execution and are complex to model and execute. In this paper we introduce Petri Nets as a tool for simplifying the modeling and execution of parallel asynchronous versions of this kind of algorithms, while using an efficient dynamic task scheduling implementation. The Cholesky factorization algorithm was used as testbed. Simulations were carried out as a proof of concept, based on real execution times on GPGPU's, and have shown excellent performances.**

Keywords*—Petri Net Modelization - Asynchronous Parallel Execution - Dynamic Task Scheduling - Cholesky Factorization Algorithm.

I. Introduction

The fork-join parallelization model is a natural step from a sequential to a parallel version of an algorithm. An important drawback is the insertion of synchronization points in the algorithm which compels all the processors involved in the execution to wait in idle state, the slowest. This causes poor performance and scalability in those algorithms in which the task loads of each parallel thread differ, which is typical of algorithms with data dependency [1]. QR, LU and Cholesky factorizations are algorithms with this type of problem.

Tiled algorithms emerge as a solution to the problem of load balance for dense linear algebra algorithms on multicore processors [2]. This type of algorithms are an evolution from rectangular block-based algorithms, in which data reusability was the concept to optimize. Tiled algorithms presents, as many LAPACK algorithms do, two fundamentals steps of the algorithm: panel factorization and trailing submatrix update. However, now the key concepts are fine granularity and asynchronicity to achieve better thread level parallelism.

Tiled algorithms divide data in square blocks that allow to computing "out of order", thus increasing the number of tasks that can run in parallel. As with block based algorithms, factorizations and updates consist in applying the proper routines ("kernels") among the operations defined in the BLAS [3] and LAPACK libraries [4]. Block sizes are tuned to achieve good performance in the execution of the kernels involved in the algorithm.

The major difference between block and tiled algorithms is that the former are synchronous, whereas the later are asynchronous. The difference is well shown graphically in [5]. Asynchronicity and fine granularity make it possible for many tasks to run in parallel. "Out of order" means that while one processor computes a factorization, the others can simultaneously compute updates.

Since the number of tasks available to run in parallel exceeds the number of processors, it is possible to do different selection of tasks, in order to define the scheduling of the parallel algorithm. Static scheduling are those defined prior the algorithm execution. Common examples are the left looking (LL) or right looking (RL), which differ according to whether priority updates are on the left or on the right of the current factorization panel [1], [6]. Both algorithms are shown inf Fig. 1 and 2, and have in common that they are fork-join synchronized.

Another known technique of static scheduling is *look ahead*. As LL and RL, it is based on performing panel factorization in one thread while the remaining update sub-matrix from previous stages is done by others threads. It has been observed that LL and RL are the extreme points of a wide spectrum of possibilities of task selection, acting in a parametrized way *look ahead* as a path for going from one point to another [1]. All alternatives generate bubbles of idleness in the algorithm due their static nature.

Directed Acyclic Graphs (DAG) have been used to model

```
do step=1:bl_nu
  do i=1:step-1
    syrk step,i
  end
  potr step
  do j=step+1:bl_nu
    do k=1:step-1
      gemm step,k,j,k
    end
    trsm j,step
  end
end
```

Fig. 1. Left looking Cholesky

```
do step=1:bl_nu
  potr step
  do i=step+1:bl_nu
    trsm i,step
    syrk i,step
  end
  do j=step+1:bl_nu-1
    do k=j+1:bl_nu
      gemm j,step,k,step
    end
  end
end
```

Fig. 2. Right looking Cholesky

the algorithms, with the vertex representing the tasks and the edges, the dependency among them. The graph is also known as Dependency Graph. Asynchronous execution is helped by the use of DAG's to control the dependency of tasks. The DAG is mainlly used by the scheduler to select the next task [2].

Dynamic scheduling is introduced to improve static scheduling, by selecting the task on run time according the availability of free processors and enabled tasks. This type of scheduling are aimed at preventing the existence of the stalled points of static schedulers. However, they are complex and cause overhead in the algorithm execution [6].

Hogg's research shows no significant advantage in using dynamic or static schedulers [7]. He also uses a DAG to model the algorithm and the scheduling control. Concurrency control and DAG implementation generate an overhead that seems to consume the improvements of the dynamic scheduler.

Also in the line of dynamic scheduling, LAWN 243 [6] introduces the use of the "locality" parameter to help the scheduler dynamically select the next task to be assigned to a processor, according the previously used data. Improvements in parallel execution depend on the type of algorithm (LL or RL), the size of the DAG's window resident in memory and the number of tiles into which the matrix is divided.

At the best of our knowledge, all dynamic attemps are based on DAG, which are good to represent the structure of the algorithm, but not for the execution and the scheduler. Both are implemented in an ad-hoc, sophisticated style, without parallel execution modelization.

A key factor to achieve a performing parallel algorithm, is to minimize processor idle time due to synchronization. Asynchronous execution is a big step in this path. Scheduling is another. Tiled algorithms improve the parallelism of an algorithm by increasing the number of tasks. The drawback lies in the complexity of managing a large number of parallel asynchronous tasks. The lack of a model for this results in complex or pre-developed libraries implementations [6], [8].

Our research has two main objectives:

- To model the structure and parallel execution of dense linear algebra algorithms with a simple tool.
- To improve performance by minimizing processor idle time through the use of dynamic scheduler

The second objective follows the first: with a simple model, dynamic overheads decrease and the scheduler can perform an adequate selection without loss of performance.

Petri Net is the formalism chosen to represent the algorithm. Its capability to represent parallel processes is known. A few additions to this well-known formalism are enough to achieve our objectives. As a "proof of concept" we develop a simulation tool to represent and execute the Petri Nets, which simulates different running parameters.

Cholesky factorization was chosen as a testbed algorithm. We follow the kernels and DAG representation used in tiled algorithm as defined in [9]. These kernels are xPOTRF, xGEMM, xTRSM and xSYRK, where x can be 's' or 'd' depending on whether single or double precision data are used.

II. Petri Net Model of Parallel Algorithms

A Petri Net (PN) is a bipartite directed graph consisting of Places and Transition nodes. Usually, Places represent "states" and Transitions "actions". Arcs always link a Place to a Transition (acting as input) or vice versa (acting as output). There are tokens, which only exist in Places, and represents "facts". The overall state evolves when a transition is "fired", moving tokens from input places to output places. A transition can be fired when all input places have enough tokens [10]. This net is also known as Token Petri Net (TPN).

Petri Nets are used to model the algorithm, with operations (kernels to execute) represented by Transitions and data represented by Places. Input parameters are represented by arcs that go from Places to Transitions, and operations results, by arcs from Transitions to Places.

Petri Nets can model the algorithm dependencies, and can also describe the execution by means of the firing of Transitions. The following subsections explain how the net is used for both purposes.

A. *Coloured Petri Net*

Coloured Petri Nets (CPN) are one type of the many defined as "High Level Petri Nets". The major difference with TPN is that tokens have different values ("colours") from a domain. This permits to model with a high level of abstraction. Here, transitions are enabled by having not only enough tokens in their input places but also from the "color" defined. CPN definition is taken from from [10], [11].

Coloured Petri Nets permit to model complex nets at high level in a simple manner. DAGs of task dependencies with many blocks divisions are difficult to understand due to their large number of nodes (see Fig. 10 of LAWN 243 [6]). To model tiled algorithms with CPN, the main domain used to define tokens is tile position, represented by the row-column pair.

The strategy to model the algorithm is:

1) Each operation is represented by one transition
2) For each transition, there are as many input Places as data blocks parameters are involved in the operation.
3) No more places or transitions are used.
4) Output arcs represent data dependency.

To specify conditions in places, we extend or restrict the tile-block domain. Also, multisets are used to represent repetitions of blocks, and function arc expressions, to limit token flowing [11].

Fig. 3 shows the CPN that represents the Cholesky algorithm. It has only four transitions and eight places, according to the strategy suggested. The name of the places follow the number of the block used in each operation. Color token is represented by $< x,y >$, multiset repetitions by braces $\{x\}$, and functions arcs are only booleans of the form $if(cond)$.

In each place, the domains used are:

For potr1 and trsm2, the domain is $< i, i >, i = 1 \dots n$.

For trsm1, syrk1, and gemm1, the domain is $< j, i > j = 2 \dots n, i = 1 \dots j-1, j > i$

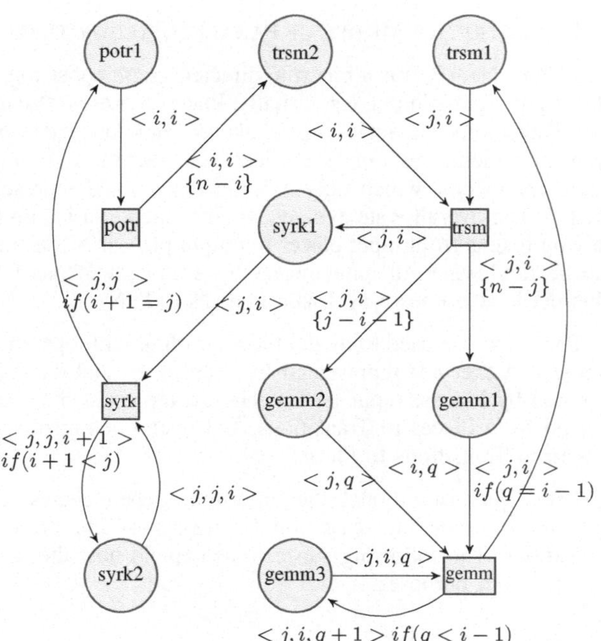

Fig. 3. Coloured Petri Net that represents Cholesky factorization algorithm.

For gemm2 the domain is $< j,i >, j = 3 \dots n, i = 1 \dots j-2, j > i$

For syrk2 the domain is $< j,j,i >, j = 2 \dots n \wedge i = 1 \dots j-1 \wedge j > i$

For gemm3 the domain is $< j,i,q >, j = 3 \dots n, i = 2 \dots n-1, q = 1 \dots i-1 \wedge j > i \wedge i > q$

The inital places mark is:

- In potr1: $< 1,1 >$
- In trsm1: $< i,1 >, i = 2..n$
- In syrk2: $< i,i,1 >, i = 2..n$
- In gemm3: $< j,i,1 >, j = 3..n, i = 2..j-1$

In this way, a tiled algorithm is generically defined by a CPN, and any consideration in the number of tiles is dispensed with, it being only a parameter for domain definition. Its simplicity and facility to analyze the parallel algorithm are highlighted.

Nevertheless, CPNs are not used to execute the algorithm. The overhead necessary to abstractly represent domains and function arcs is expensive in terms of high performance computing. On the other hand, the CPN developed in this way fulfill the definition of well-formed CPNs [10]. This type of nets are easily transformed to a TPN, which have a computational implementation that is simple and light to execute.

B. Token Petri Net

The previous section shows the facility to model a parallel algorithm with a CPN and the procedure used to define places and transitions. The resulting net is easily unfolded to a TPN.

To unfold a CPN we follow the steps defined in Diaz [10]. Each Place P_j in a CPN has a Domain $D(P_j)$ associated with it, and is unfolded to generate as many Places in TPN as is the cardinality of $D(P_j)$ in the colored Place. The repetitions from the bag that represent the Place must be respected. Thus, each Place in TPN is associated with an unique value from the pairs (color, place) in CPN and repeated according the bag pair cardinal.

The unfolding for Transitions is similar: for each Transition in CPN there will be generated as many Transitions in TPN as the cardinal of the Cartesian Product of all its input Places in the CPN, respecting the cardinal of the bag in each Place. Each Transition in TPN is associated with a unique value from tuples of the Cartesian Product, repeated as the respective cardinal of the bags of each input place.

Input Arcs in CPN is unfolded to TPN from the corresponding unfolded Place / Transition in TPN. The same occurs for output arcs, with reference to the condition of the guard function.

Table in Fig. 4 show an unfolding example for Places from CPN to TPN, for the case of 3×3 tiles divisions. The names of Places in TPN follow the respective name in CPN, concatenate with the color of the token that is represented. For example, syrk132, is the Place in TPN, that came from Place syrk1 with color $< 3,2 >$ in CPN, and represents the first argument in syrk operation of the tile in third row, second column. Graphically, the unfolded TPN of the example is shown in Fig. 5.

It is not difficult to see how fast the number of Places and Transitions in TPN grow with an incresing number of tile divisions. It is practically impossible to show and understand its graphical representation. However, the matricial representation is elementary and easy to use. The importance of unfolding is that a TPN can be represented with two matrices and one vector of natural numbers, and that elementary matrix - vector operations models the execution of the net.

The structure of TPN net can be represented by Negative and Positive Incidence Matrix (NIM / PIM). Both have dimension $p \times t$, where p is the number of Places and t is the number of Transitions. Each position in the matrix represents the relation between a pair place/transition, which is the equivalent of an arc between them in terms of graph theory. A position with zero represents absence of arc. A positive value represents the number of tokens that will be absorbed / injected by the transition depending on Negative or Positive case, if the transition is fired.

Token existence in Places is represented by a Mark Vector (MV). It has dimension $1 \times p$, and values are also naturals numbers. Values represents the number of tokens that exists in the respective Place.

The matricial representation highlights the facility to compute enabled transitions and to fire them. We call NI_j^- and PI_j^+ the j-th column (transition) in NIM and PIM respectively. By computing $MV - NI_j^-$, if the result has no negative values, MV has enough tokens in the input Places of j-transition, and thus can be fired.

Computing the difference for all the columns, determines all the transitions that are enabled to fire. By construction,

Place in CPN	Domain in CPN	Places in TPN
potr1	$< i, i >$ $i = 1 \ldots n$	potr111 potr122 potr133
trsm1	$< j, i >$ $j = 2 \ldots n$ $i = 1 \ldots j-1$ $j > i$	trsm121 trsm131 trsm132
trsm2	$< i, i >$ $\{n-1\}$ repetitions	trsm211 {2} trsm222 {1}
syrk1	$< j, i >$ $j = 2 \ldots n$ $i = 1 \ldots j-1$ $j > i$	syrk121 syrk131 syrk132
syrk2	$< j, j, i >$ $j = 2 \ldots n$ $i = 1 \ldots j-1$ $j > i$	syrk2221 syrk2331 syrk2332
gemm1	$< j, i >$ $j = 2 \ldots n$ $i = 1 \ldots j-1, j > i$ $\{n-j\}$ repetitions	gemm121 {1}
gemm2	$< j, i >$ $j = 3 \ldots n$ $i = 1 \ldots j-2, j > i$ $\{j-i-1\}$ repetitions	gemm231 {1}
gemm3	$< j, i, q >$ $j = 3 \ldots n$ $i = 2 \ldots n-1$ $q = 1 \ldots i-1$ $j > i > q$	gemm3321

Fig. 4. Unfold example for Places for the Coloured Petri Net in Fig.3 supousing only 3 × 3 tiles divisions.

Places of the unfolded TPN have only one transition to act as input. That guarantees the no competition of enabled transitions for input tokens, and that all enabled transitions can be fired simultaneusly.

To modelize the net execution, an additional function is defined in order to compute the set of transitions enabled to be fired. The function is $h : \mathbb{N}^{1\times p} \times \mathbb{N}^{p\times t} \rightarrow \mathbb{N}^{1\times t}$, which has parameters M y NI^-, and its result values are:

$$h(j) = \begin{cases} 0 & \text{if } (M - NI_j^-) \text{ has negatives values} \\ 1 & \text{if } (M - NI_j^-) \text{ else} \end{cases} \qquad j = 1 \ldots t$$

then h positions with value 1 reference to transitions enabled to be fired.

Firing all enabled transitions defines a new mark for Mark Vector (MV'):

$$MV' = MV - h \times NIM^t + h \times PIM^t \tag{1a}$$

III. Execution Model

DAGs can model dependencies of tasks in a parallel algorithm, but they do not modelize the execution. Petri Nets have implicit modelization of execution: by representing tasks as Transitions, all enabled Transitions are those that can be executed.

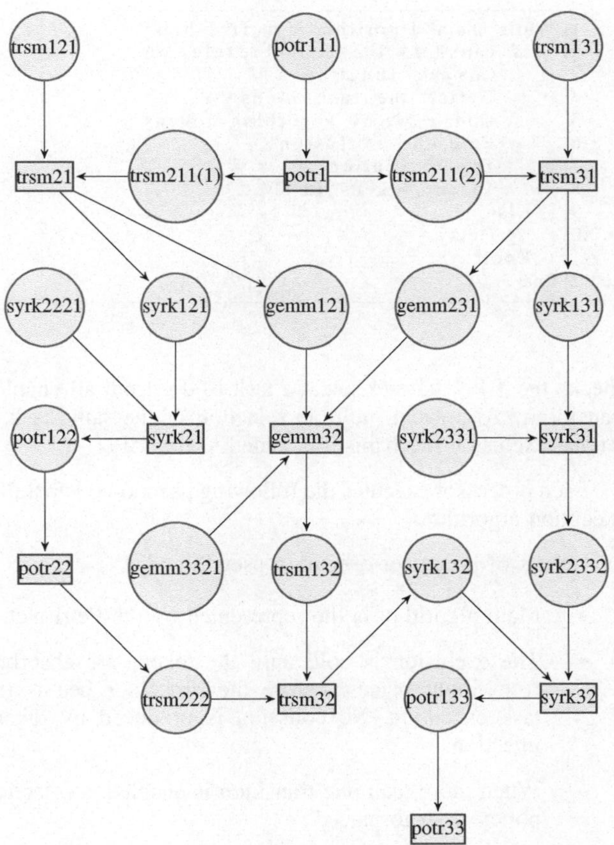

Fig. 5. Token Petri Net unfolded from the Coloured Petri Net in Fig.3 suposing only 3 x 3 tiles divisions.

Nevertheless, TPN is not sufficient to model the execution of a parallel algorithm. It has no information about the running time of a task, and has no limit about the number of processors that execute the task.

To solve the problem of execution time, we use Timed Petri Nets (TiPN) [10]. They have an important feature, the representation of the time in Transitions. By adding a delay between the time in which tokens are absorbed from input places and the time in which tokens are injected in output places, transitions can represent the notion of execution time.

Firing a transition k in TiPN implies an MV update in two times:

$$MV' = MV - NI_k^- \qquad \text{in } t_{ini} \tag{2a}$$

$$MV'' = MV' + PI_k^+ \qquad \text{in } t_{ini} + \Delta(T_k) \tag{2b}$$

where t_{ini} is the initial firing time, and $\Delta(T_k)$ is the execution time of task T_k.

To solve the problem of the availability of many processors, we define an execution model. The model consists of a set of processors and one TiPN that represent the algorithm and its dependencies as we have used along this paper. Each processor knows how to do the task that each transition represents. The TiPN is shared by all the processors. Each processor

```
While main algorithm not finished
   If can hold the mutual exclusion
      Compute function h
      Define the task to do
      Update MV by absorbing tokens
      Free the exclusion
      Task execution
      Inject tokens in MV
   Else
      Delay
   Endif
End
```

checks the TiPN state to select a task to do, from all enabled transitions. To prevent multiple selection of the same task, a mutual exclusion mechanism is added to the TiPN.

Each processor executes the following pseudo-code parallel execution algorithm:

Details of processor execution pseudo-code:

- Main algorithm is the represented by the Petri Net.
- The exclusion is hold until the tokens are absorbed from input places, before the processor begins the task execution. No colission is produced by tokens injection.
- When more than one transition is enabled, a selection policy must to placed.
- A delay is introduced if the processor can't hold the exclusion to avoid starvation.

The overhead introduced by the parallel execution is defined by three factors. First, the mutual exclusion mechanism, the execution of which uses few clocks cycles. Second, the integer matrix and vector operations, which are highly optimized to run in milliseconds in today processors. Third, the selection policy must be guided by balancing between selection algorithm and overall algorithm performance. In fact, the sum of the three factors is several orders of magnitude smaller than the kernels execution time, which means a minimum overhead.

IV. Dynamic Scheduling

Task selection between all the enabled tasks is a key factor in the execution model. In the model implementation, Patterns from Object Oriented Design was chosen as a design tool. The design has three basic objects: one Petri Net, many Processors that interact with the PN, and Selectors that colaborate with the Processors, to select the next executable task.

Each Processor has a link to the Petri Net Object and a link to one Selector. The Selector object is responsible for defining the task that the Processor will do. It is a method that, taking as input parameters the state of the PN and the processor, returns the next task to the Processor. The design principle is to decouple processing from selecting tasks.

Different selecting policies are implemented by simply implementing the selecting method of Selector accordingly. This is a way to modelize homogeneous or even heterogeneous processors with different scheduling policies. Also, static or dynamic scheduling can be easily implemented using the appropriate Selector collaborator.

Simulation tests were developed to run static and dynamic tasks schedulers. In both cases, task assignation to a processor is dynamic, i.e. static or dynamic refers to the execution sequence, not the execution processor.

Two static schedulers are tested, following LL and RL algorithms. They were implemented easily by defining the order of tasks that Selector must follow. The sequence was defined from the algorithms shown in Fig. 1 and Fig. 2.

Two dynamic schedulers are tested. Both are based on DAGs, but differ in the selection metric applied. The first, called *height tree (HT)*, selects the enabled task that is higher in the dependency tree. The second, called *inverse tree (IT)*, select the enabled task that has a longer path to finish in the graph. By longer path we mean that it has a bigger number of steps in the longest path from the current to the end task. Non deterministic selection is done in case of equal height.

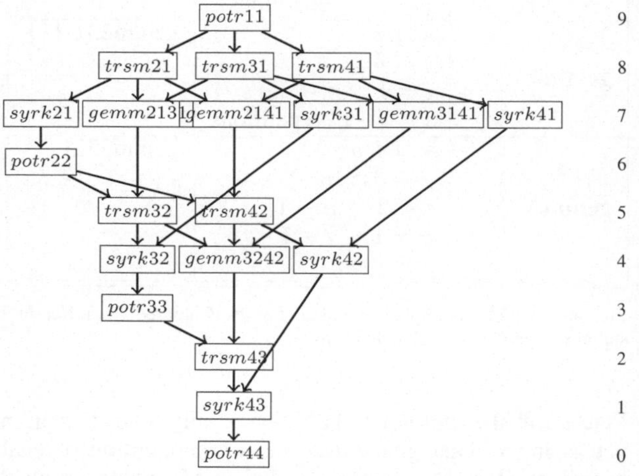

Fig. 6. Dependency graph of Cholesky algorithm, 4×4 tiles. Right values references to the stage number in which the task is enabled to fire (bigger value is earlier).

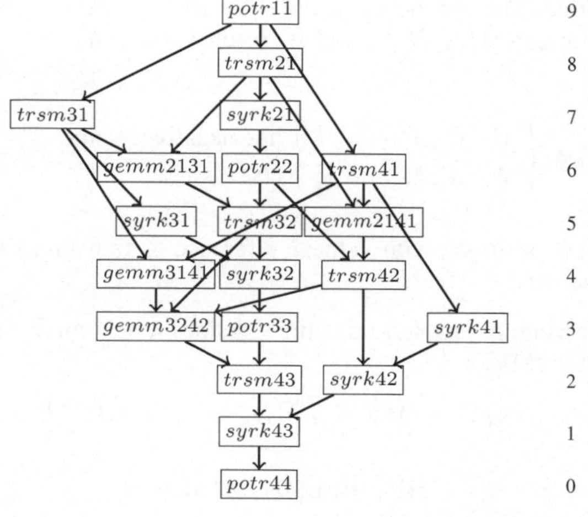

Fig. 7. Dependency graph of Cholesky algorithm, 4×4 tiles. Right values references to the latest stage number in which a task must to be fired (bigger value is earlier).

Figures 6 and 7 show examples of DAGs of dynamic schedulers used in tests. In *height tree* the level of a task is assigned according the step in which the task is enabled. In *inverse tree*, the level is assigned according to number of steps in the longest path to the end. For example, task *trsm41* has level 8 in the first graph and level 6 in the second.

Differences between both schedulers are exposed in the next example. Suppose you have three processors. Following the dynamic schedulers previously shown, the first step is compute *potr11*, and then compute *trsm21, trsm31* and *trsm41*. In the third step, scheduler *height tree*, must select any task from all those that have level 7 assigned, but scheduler *inverse tree* will select exactly *syrk21, gemm2131* and *gemm2141*. Is easy to see in Fig. 7 that *syrk21* is a priority tasks in the path to the end because it enables *potr22*. Scheduler *height tree*, due to its non determination, may delay it selection.

V. Simulation Results

Simulations of parallel algorithm were tested with different values for four parameters: matrix size, number of processors, number of block division and scheduler used. To test performance, a simulation tool was developed using a high level language (Smalltalk). The tool takes the number of blocks and defines all the tasks to be executed; then take matrix size and decides the block size, and finally it takes the number of processors and creates the same number of Processor objects and one thread for each of them to execute in parallel. According the scheduler, the respective Selector object is linked to each Processor. The execution of each kernel is simulated by throwing a time delay according the task.

In order to run simulations, it was used the time of running of each kernel, obtained for different block sizes, single precision, from a NVIDIA GTX 470 GPU. CUDA was used for BLAS kernels and MAGMA for LAPACK kernel xPOTRF. The results are shown in Table I. In all cases, the time of communication of all data from main memory to GPU and vice versa is considered. It was assumed that the main processor uses one thread to control each GPGPU.

Table II shows results of simulations with only four processors and block range of 6000 and 8000, single precision. Due to space limitations, only these results are presented, but they are representative of other combination of execution parameters. The metric of performance used is the idleness of processors, which is calculated as a difference between total execution time and total of processing time.

For Cholesky factorization algorithm, RL algorithm brings the best results for static scheduling, which are consistent with previous work [9]. For dynamic scheduling, *inverse tree* brings results which are near the optimum. A timeline for both schedulers is shown in Figures 8 and 9. Two things are noted:

Kernel	Single pres. 6000	Double pres. 6000	Single pres. 8000	Double pres. 8000
potr	0.249	0.882	0.509	1.895
trsm	0.568	2.018	1.122	N/A
syrk	0.465	1.907	1.001	N/A
gemm	0.755	3.506	1.678	N/A

TABLE I. Observed time for the kernels executed over an NVIDIA GTX 470 GPU, in seconds.

Block Size	# Blocks	# Procs.	Algor.	Time (sec)	% idle time
6000	6	4	LL	17.50	53.66
6000	6	4	RL	13.26	38.77
6000	6	4	HT	10.16	20.56
6000	6	4	IT	9.51	14.97
6000	8	4	LL	40.59	53.45
6000	8	4	RL	26.33	28.47
6000	8	4	HT	20.98	10.95
6000	8	4	IT	20.69	9.65
8000	6	4	LL	36.89	53.35
8000	6	4	RL	27.79	38.08
8000	6	4	HT	21.37	19.64
8000	6	4	IT	19.95	13.96
8000	8	4	LL	85.34	53.16
8000	8	4	RL	55.05	25.37
8000	8	4	HT	44.30	10.21
8000	8	4	IT	43.71	8.97

TABLE II. Observed values of simulations.

the idle time of processors in synchronization points in RL and the practical absence of idle time in IT.

The nature of the Cholesky algorithm imposes no parallelism in the beginning and in the end of the execution, which sum four serial tasks. Beyond those points, and also at the end of execution, there is a limited number of parallel tasks which produce idle state for some processors. For the rest of the execution, all processors are always working.

VI. Conclusion and Future Research

We have developed a model of parallel programming starting from CPN, unfolding them to TPN and executed by a set of distributed processors that share in a memory area the representation of the state of the algorithm, and decouple the execution from the selection of the next task to do.

The model was used as a simulation tool, but it is easy to adapt it to running real algorithms. We hope to get performance improvements, due to the minimal overhead of the scheduling policy and its almost optimal "idleness" rate of processors.

The simulations were based on times taken from a currently usual multicore - multiGPU machine. Its results show that important improvements in performance can be obtained with respect to static scheduler algorithms, using a dynamic scheduler based on Petri Nets, which is easy to implement.

The model is adaptable to different numbers of processors and data block partitions: the unfolding of the CPN capture the number of partitions by generating the respective incidence matrix. Data dependencies are automatically generated. Besides, the execution model only needs as parameter the matricial information; thus, to execute different algorithms, no programming is necessary, it is enough to change the matrix.

Dynamic scheduling can be executed without need of previous time execution of each kernel. That information is necessary to achieve an optimal scheduling, at the cost of more complex schedulers. Our simulations show a result that is near the optimal, with a very light overload. Others dynamic scheduling policies may achieve optimal or sub-optimal results, but they are complex to understand and implement.

Execution on a set of asymmetric processors can be implemented by changing the Selector of task in each processor.

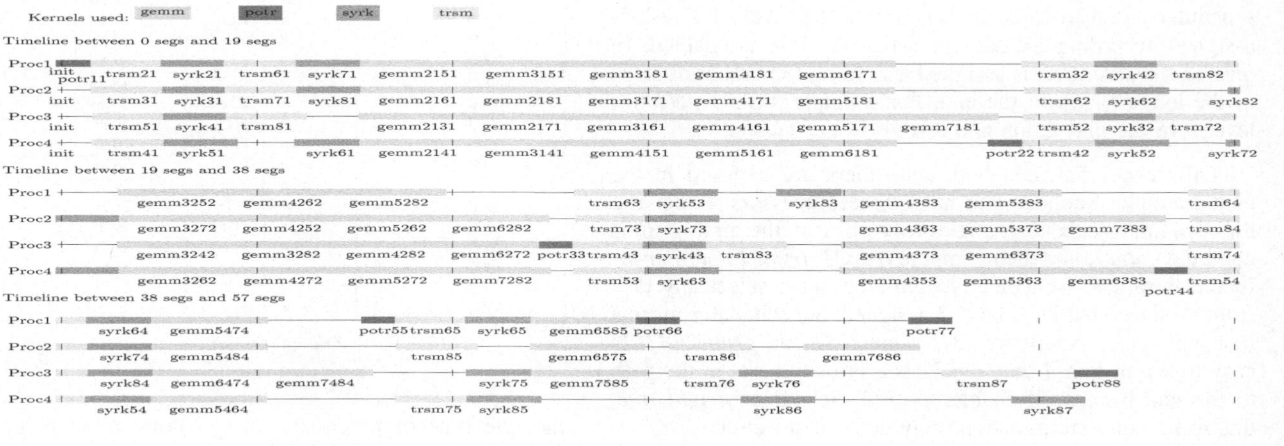

Fig. 8. Simulation timeline, RL scheduler, 8 blocks, 8000 range each, 4 processors

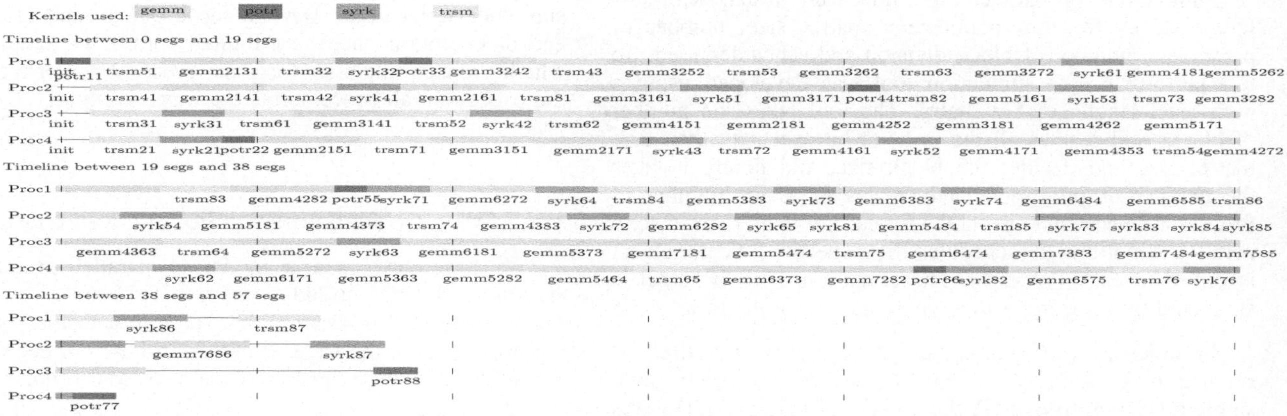

Fig. 9. Simulation timeline, IT scheduler, 8 blocks, 8000 range each, 4 processors

By restricting the execution of tasks that have forwarding dependencies in a non critical path to slower processors, those processors can help in the overall parallel execution.

Future work will implement the effective execution with this model, not only for linear algebra factorizations, but for others algorithms as well. An implementation in a distributed memory parallel architecture will also be researched.

ACKNOWLEDGMENT

The authors would like to thank to Profesor Orlando Micolini for his continuos sugestions and contributions.

REFERENCES

[1] J. Kurzak and J. J. Dongarra, "Implementing linear algebra routines on multi-core processors with pipelining and a look ahead," LAPACK Working Note, Tech. Rep. 178, Sep. 2006.

[2] A. Buttari, J. Langou, J. Kurzak, and J. J. Dongarra, "A class of parallel tiled linear algebra algorithms for multicore architectures," LAPACK Working Note, Tech. Rep. 191, Sep. 2007.

[3] "Basic Linear Algebra Subprograms Technical Forum Standard," University of Tennessee, Tech. Rep., 2001. [Online]. Available: http://www.netlib.org/blas/

[4] E. Anderson, Z. Bai, C. Bischof, L. S. Blackford, J. Demmel, J. J. Dongarra, J. Du Croz, S. Hammarling, A. Greenbaum, A. McKenney, and D. Sorensen, *LAPACK Users' guide (third ed.)*. Philadelphia, PA, USA: Society for Industrial and Applied Mathematics, 1999.

[5] J. Kurzak, A. Buttari, and J. J. Dongarra, "Solving systems of linear equations on the CELL processor using cholesky factorization," LAPACK Working Note, Tech. Rep. 184, May 2007.

[6] A. Haidar, H. Ltaief, A. YarKhan, and J. Dongarra, "Analysis of dynamically scheduled tile algorithms for dense linear algebra on multicore architectures." LAPACK Working Note, Tech. Rep. 243, Mar. 2011.

[7] J. Hogg, "A dag-based parallel cholesky factorization for multicore systems," Technical Report RAL-TR-2008-029, Rutherford Appleton Laboratory, Chilton, Oxfordshire, England, Tech. Rep., 2008.

[8] J. Kurzak, P. Luszczek, M. Faverge, and J. Dongarra, "Lu factorization with partial pivoting for a multi-cpu, multi-gpu shared memory system." LAPACK Working Note, Tech. Rep. 266, Apr. 2012.

[9] H. Ltaief, S. Tomov, R. Nath, P. Du, , and J. Dongarra, "A scalable high performant cholesky factorization for multicore with gpu accelerators." LAPACK Working Note, Tech. Rep. 223, Nov. 2009.

[10] M. Diaz, *Petri Nets: Fundamental Models, Verification and Applications*. London, Hoboken: ISTE Ltd - John Wiley & Sons, Inc., 2009.

[11] K. Jensen and L. M. Kristensen, *Coloured Petri Nets - Modelling and Validation of Concurrent Systems*. Springer, 2009.

Parallel Implementation of GRAph Aligner (GRAAL) Algorithm for Network Alignment

Si Li[1], **Shengai Jin**[1], **Jonathan Z. Sun**[1], **Chaoyang Zhang**[1]

[1]School of Computing, University of Southern Mississippi, Hattiesburg, MS, 39406, USA

Abstract - *Network alignment is one of the most commonly used biological network comparison methods since determining protein functions shifted the focus from targeting specific proteins based solely on sequence homology to analyses of the whole proteome based on protein-protein interactions (PPI). Aligning PPI networks of different species is of great importance when detecting evolutionary conserved pathways, or protein complexes. However, when it comes to large biological network data, the improved serial algorithms still take a long time. In this paper, a parallel algorithm for network alignment, which is based on the serial implementation of the GRAph Aligner Algorithm (GRAAL), is designed to improve the efficiency of network alignment. This algorithm is implemented in parallel with C++ and the Message Passing Interface (MPI) library. The results show that the parallel implementation of GRAph Aligner improves significantly in efficiency without losing accuracy, compared to the serial GRAph Aligner algorithm.*

Keywords: GRAAL, network alignment, PPI, parallel implementation

1 Introduction

1.1 Network alignment

Network alignment is considered to be one of the most common methods to analyze and compare biological networks. It is mainly about finding structure or topology similarities between two or more networks. Similar to sequence alignments, network alignments have two main instances: local network alignment and global network alignment. Based on the hypothesis that aligned sub-graphs are conserved through evolution, the goal of local alignment is to search for evolutionary conserved building blocks of the cellular machinery, disregarding the overall similarity between networks. A global network alignment gives a unique and one-to-one alignment from every node in a smaller network to exactly one node in the other network. Hence, the goal of global network alignment is to search the maximal overall match between two or more networks.

1.2 PPI datasets

PPI networks are usually obtained by two high-throughput experimental bio-techniques. They are yeast two-hybrid screening, resulting in binary interaction data and protein complex purification methods using mass-spectrometry, resulting in co-complex data. Many databases containing PPI networks are also available online. These include Biological General Repository for Interaction Datasets (BioGRID), IntAct, Database of Interacting Proteins (DIP), Mammalian Protein-Protein Interaction Database (MIPS), and many others. The datasets that we use in this thesis are mainly from BioGRID and DIP databases.

1.3 Background

Recently, large amounts of experimental biological network data are becoming available due to the advanced techniques used in the biological field. These biological networks include protein-protein interaction (PPI) networks, transcriptional-regulation networks, brain functional networks, and metabolic networks. We mainly focus on analyzing PPI networks, which are probably the most commonly studied type of biological networks. In PPI networks, nodes represent proteins and edges among nodes stand for the interactions between proteins. It is generally represented as an undirected graph with no self-loops. PPI networks are of particular importance because proteins play a crucial role in all cell functions. Instead of acting in isolation, proteins always cooperate with other proteins to perform many biological functions and create large complicated networks. We learn protein-protein interaction (PPI) networks and apply network alignment as the biological network comparison method to focus on the analysis of the entire proteome. Comparative analyzing of PPI networks can give valuable insight into biological mechanisms, evolutionary changes, and provide deeper understanding of complex diseases. Exploring the inner relationship of PPI network topology and biological functions are a big challenge given the scale of biological network data. Therefore, an efficient algorithm is essential to be implemented.

The GRAph Aligner Algorithm (GRAAL), which is a global network alignment method, works well in network alignment. However, when it comes to large scale biological network data, the computational costs are increased significantly. In this work, we develop a parallel implementation based on the GRAph Aligner Algorithm (GRAAL).

In this paper, we first give a brief introduction to the serial GRAAL algorithm in Section 2. Then, the parallel GRAAL algorithm including design and implementation are presented in Section 3. In the Section 4, we introduce the implementation environment. Section 5 analyzes the performance of the parallel algorithm. Finally, we conclude the work in section

2 Serial GRAAL algorithm

Kuchaiev et al. recently proposed a topological method of the global alignment of biological networks based on graphlet degree signatures, GRAph Aligner (GRAAL) [1]. Since this method does not use protein information, it can be used to align any two networks, not just biological ones. It mainly contains four steps given as follows:

Step 1: Compute the vector of graphlet degrees of a node and signature similarities, which provide a novel method to measure the local topology in a node's vicinity and similarity between nodes from two networks (this vector is a matrix, also called a signature, that describes the node's neighborhood topology).

$$D_i(u,v) = \frac{w_i \times |\log(u_i+1) - \log(v_i+1)|}{\log(\max\{u_i, v_i\}+2)} \quad (1)$$

Step 2: Compute the cost matrix of aligning each node of the first network with each node in the second network.

$$C(u,v) = 2 - \left((1-\alpha) \times \frac{\deg(u)+\deg(v)}{\max\_\deg(G)+\max\_\deg(H)} + \alpha \times S(u,v)\right) \quad (2)$$

Step 3: Choose a pair of nodes (u, v) from the two networks respectively as an initial seed with minimal cost, then build 'spheres' of all possible radii around nodes u and v. Spheres of the same radius in the two networks are then greedily aligned.

Step 4: Calculate the edge correctness (EC) which is the percentage of edges in the first graph that are aligned to edges in the second graph.

$$EC = \frac{|\{(u,v)\} \in E_1 \wedge (f(u),f(v)) \in E_2|}{|E_1|} \times 100\% \quad (3)$$

3 Parallel GRAAL algorithm

Based on the analysis of the four steps of the serial algorithm introduced in the Section 2, we see that there are two main parts in this algorithm that can be implemented in parallel. The first part is the vector matrix calculation which describes the node's neighborhood topology. The second part is the cost matrix calculation which is the foundation to choose the initial seeds of two networks. Considering cost matrix calculation is just a formula based on previous result, it costs little time which we can skip. So we are focus on the parallel implementation of vector matrix calculation. The Implementation in [1] uses 73 different orbits across all graphlets of size 2 to 5. The vector of 73 coordinates is the signature of a node that describes the topology of its neighborhood and captures its interconnectivities.

Therefore, the vector of 73 coordinates must be calculated for each node in the network. Note that the calculation of the vector matrix of a large network is a time consuming task. In order to reduce the running time and improve the performance, we can calculate the vector matrix and cost matrix using parallel computing technology. In order to do matrix calculations, we implement a block-row decomposition technology to partition both the data and the computational operations.

3.1 Data decomposition

The vector calculation contains a matrix-vector multiplication operation. So, we use a block-row decomposition technology to partition data into equal-size sub-matrix, which are sent to each processor. Figure 1 shows the data decomposition.

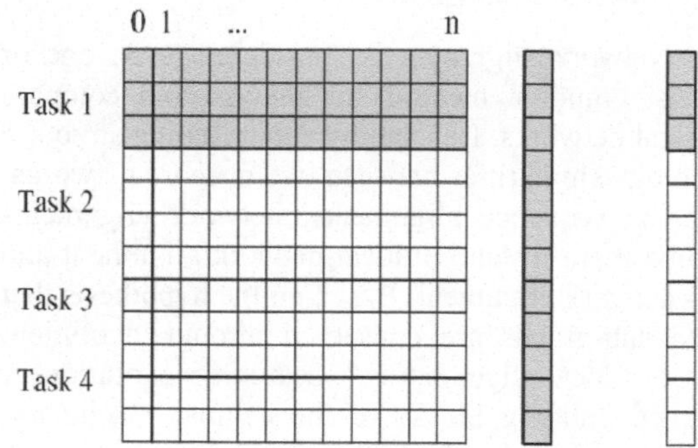

Figure 1: Data block-row decomposition

3.2 Task decomposition

Step 1: We use one processor to read adjacency matrix from two network files.

Step 2: Scatter the adjacency matrix to each processor to compute local vector matrix.

Step 3: Gather those local vector matrix from each processor.

3.3 Parallel algorithm implementation

3.3.1 Degree matrix calculation

For each node in each network, its degree must be calculated. We use several processors to calculate the fixed number of many different nodes' degrees simultaneously, and then combine these results to get the final degree matrix at a single destination process.

3.3.2 Vector matrix calculation

According to the number of graphlets we choose, there are related number of orbits among those graphlets. For every node in the two networks, we count the number of graphlets connecting to a node for all graphlets through different orbits. This is the node's signature vector. For example, if there are 73 different orbits between 30 graphlets consisting of 2 to 5 nodes, then the signature vector of a node has 73 coordinates. Calculating the matrix of this vector can also be parallelized in the same way as in Step 1.

3.3.3 Distance matrix calculation

$D_i(u, v)$ denotes the distance between the ith orbits of nodes u and v from the two networks. $D_i(u, v)$ for all node pairs from a matrix. The total distance D(u, v) between nodes u and v is calculated as

$$D(u, v) = \frac{\sum_{i=0}^{72} D_i(u,v)}{\sum_{i=0}^{72} w_i} \quad (4)$$

and D(u, v) for all node pairs from a matrix, too. We can calculate both matrices in parallel.

3.3.4 Construction of spheres and alignment of spheres

Once the seed is found, GRAAL builds 'spheres' of all possible radii around nodes u and v. Spheres of the same radius in two networks are then greedily aligned. These two tasks are independent on different nodes and can be easily parallelized.

4 Implementation Environment

The parallel algorithm was implemented using C++ and MPI. It was tested on the platform of Albacore Linux cluster in the School of Computing at the University of Southern Mississippi [8]. The cluster consists of 256 processor cores, 300GB of RAM and a 1-Gigabit Ethernet interconnects. Albacore is a hybrid, distributed-shared memory cluster, consisting primarily of Intel Xeon 56xx processors and Intel Xeon 55xx processors.

5 Results and Performance Analysis

The parallel GRAAL algorithm was compiled and executed on the Albacore cluster. Both the serial and the parallel GRAAL algorithms resulted in the same aligned networks, which verify the correctness of the parallel implementation.

We downloaded four datasets from the Database of Interacting Proteins (DIP) online database [9] and BioGRID websites [10], and created four synthetic networks. Then we aligned these synthetic networks using both serial and parallel codes to verify the results and analyze the performance of the parallel algorithm. The parallel code is executed with different numbers of processors, e.g. 2, 4, 8 and 16 in the Albacore Linux cluster.

We further tested the parallel code using three different datasets: the Fruit fly PPI network with 96 nodes from DIP database, the Human Herpes Virus PPI network with 152 nodes, and the Human Immunodeficiency Virus PPI network with 321 nodes from BioGRID website. As described in the Section 3, the vector matrix calculation is the most time consuming part in the parallel GRAAL algorithm, so we only analyze the performance of the vector matrix calculation in this paper. Table 1, Table 2, and Table 3 give the computation time T for calculating the vector matrix in the serial and parallel GRAAL algorithms for Fruit fly PPI network dataset, the Human Herpes Virus PPI network dataset and the Human Immunodeficiency Virus PPI network dataset with respect to different number of processors P. Table 4 shows the corresponding speedup that is defined as the ratio of serial computation time to the parallel computation time (We denote the serial and parallel execution times as T_P and T_S, speedup is defined as $S = T_S / T_P$). Table 5 shows the corresponding efficiency that is defined as the ratio of speedup to the number of processors (Efficiency is defined as E = S / p, which S is the speedup and p is the number of processors). The reasons why the speedup and efficiency are chosen are that, for speedup, it delineates how much performance gain is achieved via a parallel design over serial design; and for efficiency, it describes how much time is spent on the computation. For convenience of performance analysis, the speedup and efficiency are shown in Figure 5 and 6.

From Table 1, through Table 5, P is the number of processors and T is the average execution time (in seconds). For Table 4 and Table 5, H.Immu is short for Human Immunodeficiency Virus PPI network, H.Herp is short for Human Herpes Virus PPI network, F.Fly is short for Fruit Fly PPI network.

Table 1: The execution times with different number of processors for the Fruit Fly dataset

P	1	2	4	8	16
T	1.41	0.75	0.39	0.21	0.12

Table 2: The execution times with different number of processors for the Human Herpes Virus dataset

P	1	2	4	8	16
T	39.64	22.26	11.97	6.58	3.97

Table 3: The execution times with different number of processors for the Human Immunodeficiency Virus dataset

P	1	2	4	8	16
T	219.69	126.53	77.52	50.63	33.29

Table 4: The speedup (S) of the three datasets

	P=1	P=2	P=4	P=8	P=16
H.Immu	1.00	1.74	2.83	4.34	6.60
H.Herp	1.00	1.78	3.31	6.02	9.98
F.Fly	1.00	1.88	3.62	6.71	11.75

Table 5: The efficiency (E) of the three datasets

	P=1	P=2	P=4	P=8	P=16
H.Immu	1.00	0.87	0.71	0.54	0.41
H.Herp	1.00	0.89	0.83	0.75	0.62
F.Fly	1.00	0.94	0.91	0.84	0.73

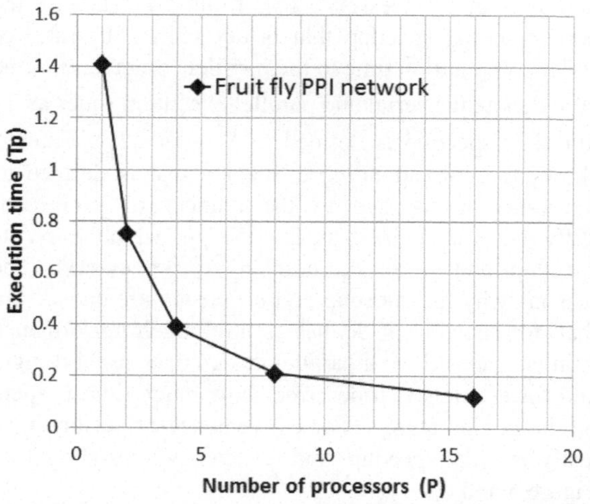

Figure 2: Execution time for Fruit Fly dataset

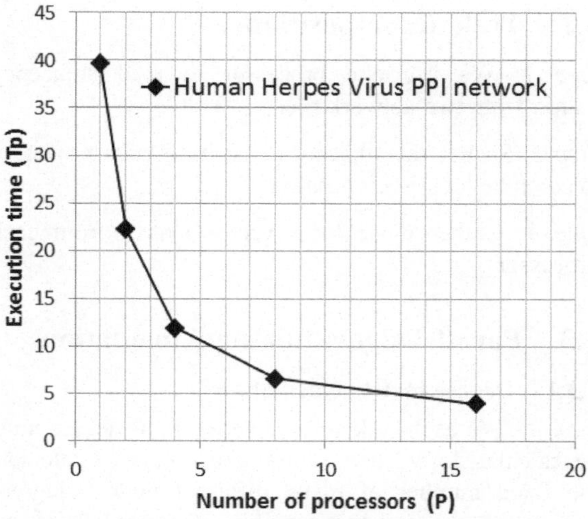

Figure 3: Execution time for Human Herpes virus dataset

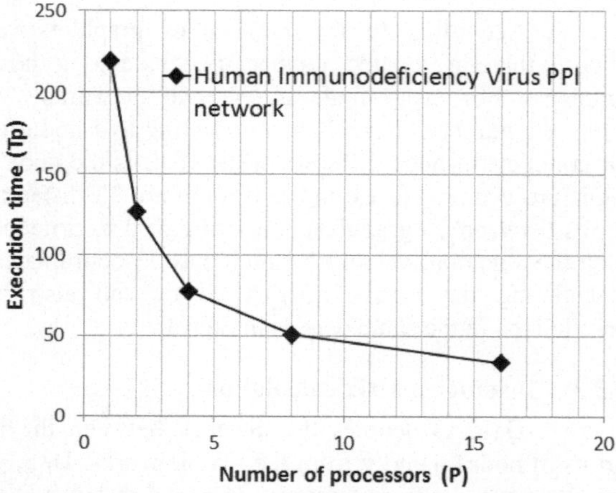

Figure 4: Execution time for Human Immunodeficiency virus dataset

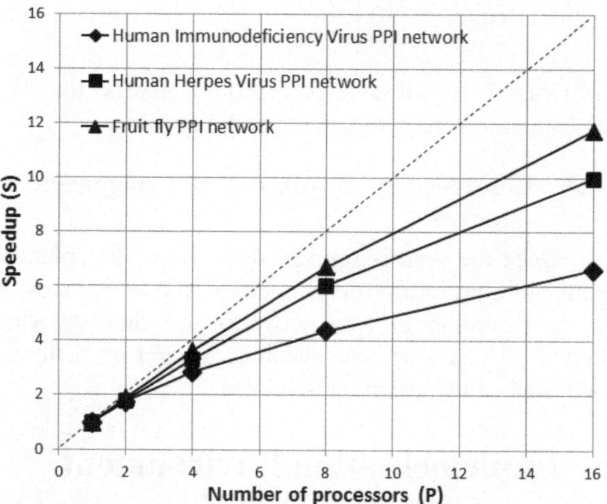

Figure 5: The speedup with different processors on Albacore

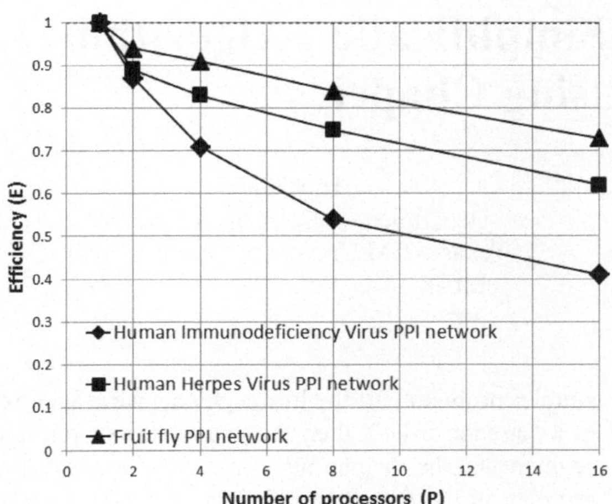

Figure 6: The efficiency with different processors on Albacore

The results show that the computation time decreases significantly and the speedup increases when the number of processors increases. It is noted that the speedup curve is below the ideal speedup denoted by the dashed line in the Figure 5 because the parallel GRAAL algorithm needs to complete extra tasks and communication between processors. Since most parallel tasks are independent in the parallel algorithm, the communication cost is not significant. In summary, the parallel implementation of the GRAAL algorithm can significantly improve the computational performance of network alignment.

6 Conclusion

A parallel implementation of vector matrix and cost matrix calculations in the GRAAL algorithm is presented, which uses a block-row decomposition technique. The adjacency matrices of two networks are distributed onto p processes, with each process solving a sub-problem. This preliminary study shows that the parallel GRAAL implementation can significantly improve the computational performance, which provides an efficient way for aligning large networks, especially biological networks.

7 Acknowledgement

This work was partially supported by the NSF EPSCoR project "Modeling and Simulation of Complex Systems" (NSF #EPS-0903787). School of Computing at the University of Southern Mississippi provided high performance computing facilities, and Dr. Glover George provided technical support.

8 References

[1] Kuchaiev O, Milenkovic T, Memisevic V, Hayes W, Przulj N. Topological network alignment uncovers biological function and phylogeny. Journal of the Royal Society Interface. 2010. doi: 10.1098/ rsif.2010.0063.

[2] Kuchaiev O, Stevanovi c A, Przulj N: GraphCrunch 2: Software tool for network modeling, alignment and clustering.

[3] Kuchaiev O, Przulj N: Integrative Network Alignment Reveals Large Regions of Global Network Similarity in Yeast and Human. Bioinformatics 2011, 27(10):1390-1396.

[4] Kuchaiev O, Milenkovic T, Memisevic V, Hayes W, Przulj N. Topological network alignment uncovers biological function and phylogeny. Journal of the Royal Society Interface. 2010. doi: 10.1098/ rsif.2010.0063.

[5] Milenkovic T, Pržulj N. Uncovering biological network function via graphlet degree signatures. Cancer Informatics. 2008;6:257–73.

[6] Milenkovic, T., Leong Ng, W., Hayes, W., and Przulj, N. (2010). Optimal network alignment with graphlet degree vectors. Cancer Informatics, 9, 121–137.

[7] Memisevic V, Przulj N. C-GRAAL: common-neighbors-based global graph alignment of biological networks. Integr Biol 2012;4:10.

[8] http://albacore.st.usm.edu:8080/platform.

[9] http://www.ncbi.nlm.nih.gov/pmc/articles/PMC102387/

[10] http://thebiogrid.org/download.php

A Massively Parallel Line Simplification Algorithm Implemented Using Chapel

Michael Scherger
Department of Computer Science
Texas Christian University
Email: m.scherger@tcu.edu

Huy Tran
Department of Computing Sciences
Texas A&M University Corpus Christi
Email: *htran@islander.tamucc.edu*

Abstract - *Line simplification is a process of reducing the number of line segments to represent a polyline. This reduction in the number of line segments and vertices can improve the performance of spatial analysis applications. The classic Douglas-Peucker algorithm developed in 1973 has a complexity of O(mn), where n denotes the number of vertices and m the number of line segments. An enhanced version of this algorithm was developed in in 1992 and has a complexity of O(n log n). In this paper, we present a parallel line simplification algorithm and discuss the implementation results using only one instruction stream of the parallel Multiple-instruction-stream Associative Computing model (MASC). The parallel algorithm is implemented in Chapel, a parallel programming language developed by Cray Inc., has parallel complexity of O(n) on n processors. The performance of the parallel program was then evaluated on different parallel computers.*

Keywords: *Parallel algorithms, associative computing, SIMD algorithms, line simplification, vertex elimination, level curve*

1. Introduction

2D planar level curves are the polylines where mathematical functions take on constant values. An example of a level curve in AutoCAD is shown in Figure 1. The number of digitized line segments collected is far more than necessary [2]. Due to the high complexity of often-irregular geospatial functions, the number of line segments to represent the planar level curve can be very large, which may cause inefficiencies in visual performance. Therefore, the polyline needs to be represented with fewer segments and vertices. It is necessary to perform a polyline simplification algorithm on a 2D planar level curve.

In this problem, the line segments of polylines are digitized in a raster scan order (left-to-right, top-to-bottom). The raster scan ordering of the line segments requires intensive searching on the remaining set of line segments to reconstruct the 2D planar curve polylines ($O(n^2)$ searches). A much simpler problem is if the line segments were acquired in a "stream order", then the end vertex of one line segment is the beginning vertex of the next line segment in the file. It would then be straightforward to apply a polyline simplification algorithm.

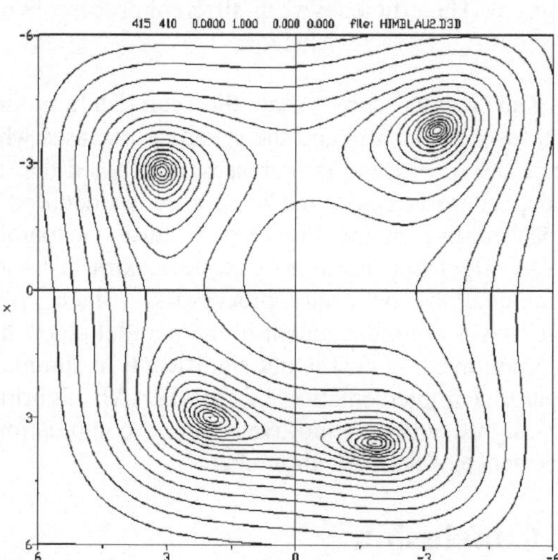

Figure 1: An example of a level curve.

The Douglas-Peucker line simplification algorithm is considered an effective line simplification algorithm [2, 13]. The algorithm uses the *closeness* of a vertex to a segment as a rejection condition. Its worst-case complexity is *O(mn)*, where *n* denotes the number of vertices and *m* the number of segments. Furthermore, in 1992 Hershberger and Snoeyink introduced an improvement for Douglas-Peucker algorithm to gain an enhanced *O(n log n)* time complexity [4]. The speed up is achieved by using binary search to maintain the path hulls of subchains. Different approaches to this issue have also been discussed in [5, 10, and 12]. However, even the worst-case complexities *O(mn)* and *O(nlogn)* are considered computationally expensive when it comes to work with significantly large visualizations.

In a previous paper [12] we presented a polyline simplification algorithm using the Multiple-instruction-stream Associative Computing model (MASC) [6, 8] to reduce the number of vertices required to represent polylines. MASC is an enhanced SIMD model with associative properties. By using the constant global operations of the MASC model, our algorithm has a parallel complexity of linear time O(*n*) in the worst case using n processing elements.

For this research we present the results of an initial implementation, benchmarking, and performance analysis for the aforementioned algorithm.

This paper is organized as follows. Section 2 will briefly discuss the MASC model of parallel computation that the algorithm is grounded upon. Section 3 will discuss the sequential and parallel polyline simplification algorithms in more detail. Section 4 will briefly discuss the implementation of the algorithm using Chapel. Section 5 will present the results of our implementation and Section 6 will provide the discussions on future work and conclusion.

2. The MASC Model of Parallel Computation

The following is a description of the Multiple Associative Computing (MASC) model of parallel computation. As shown in Figure 2, the MASC model consists of an array of processor-memory pairs called *cells* and an array of instruction streams.

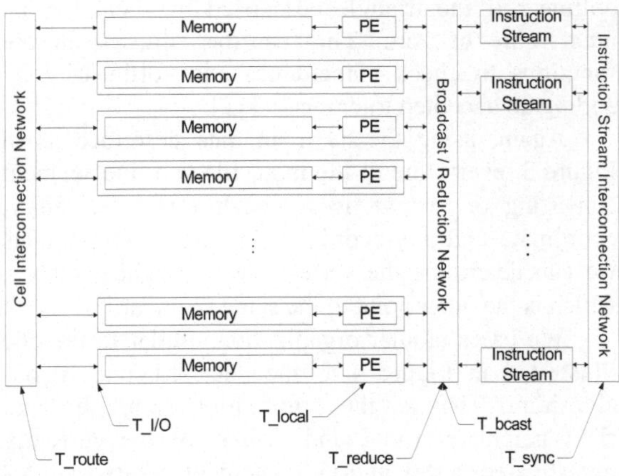

Figure 2: Conceptual view of MASC.

A MASC machine with *n* cells and *j* instruction streams is denoted as *MASC(n, j)*. It is expected that the number of instruction stream processors be much less than the number of cells.

Cells can receive their next set of instructions to execute from the instruction stream broadcast network. Cells can be instructed from their current instruction stream to send and receive messages to other cells in the same partition using some communication pattern via the cell network. Each instruction stream processor is also connected to two interconnection networks. An instruction stream processor broadcasts instructions to the cells using the instruction stream broadcast network. The instruction streams also may need to communicate and may do so using the instruction stream network. Any of these networks may be virtual and be simulated by whatever network is present.

MASC provides one or more instruction streams. Each active instruction stream is assigned to a unique dynamic partition of cells. This allows a task that is being executed in a data parallel fashion to be partitioned into two or more data parallel tasks using control parallelism. The multiple IS's supported by the MASC model allows for greater efficiency, flexibility, and re-configurability than is possible with only one instruction stream. While SIMD architectures can execute data parallel programs very efficiently and normally can obtain near linear speedup, data parallel programs in many applications are not completely data parallel and contain several non-trivial regions where significant branching occurs [3]. In these parallel programming regions, only a subset of traditional SIMD processors can be active at the same time. With MASC, control parallelism can be used to execute these different branches simultaneously. Other MASC properties are described in [6, 7, 8, 9, 11].

3. Polyline Simplification Algorithms

In order to perform the polyline simplification, the raster scan digitized line segments in the input stream need to be re-arranged. The random nature of the digitized line segments necessitates a massive number of search operations to determine coincident points. For example, as shown in Figure 3, five line segments have been digitized.

After rearrangement, the stream order would be: [B2 A2 A1 B1 B3 A3 A4 B4 A5 B5]. Then, each vertex will be checked with its next vertex for coincidence and eliminated accordingly. In this example, points [A1, B1, A3, B4] will be eliminated due to coincidence, and points [A4, B3] will be deleted due to collinearity. The procedure for accomplishing these results is mentioned in the next two sub-sections.

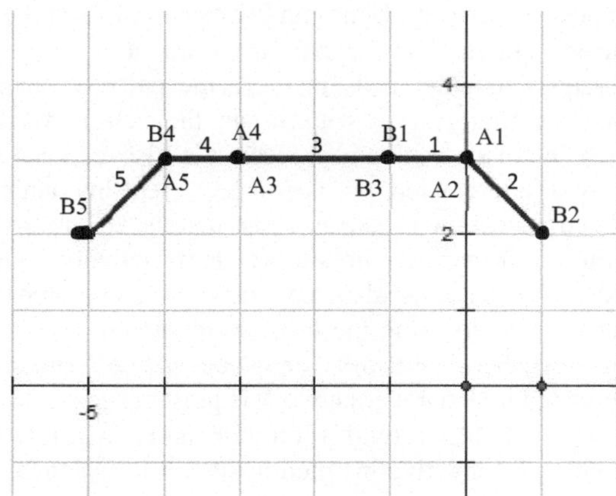

A1(0, 3) B1(-1, 3)

A2(0, 3) B2(1, 2)

A3(-3, 3) B3(-1, 3)

A4(-3, 3) B4(-4,3)

A5(-4, 3) B5(-5, 2)

Segments Example

Figure 3: Example of line segments with integer coordinates.

3.1. A sequential algorithm

An algorithm to simplify line segments is constructing polylines from coincident and collinear vertices. This can be obtained by eliminating vertices whose distances to the prior initial vertex are less than a maximum accepted tolerance α. The vertices having further distance to the initial vertex ($> \alpha$) could be considered as part of a different polyline. However, finding the coincident and collinear vertices is expensive in this problem.

Sequential Line Simplification Algorithm
Begin

1. Set pointer *current* to the first segment in *segArray* (*current=0*)
2. While *current* does not reach the end of *segArray*
   2.1. Set pointer *next* to the next segment of *current* segment (*next=current+1)*
   2.2. While *next* does not reach the end of *segArray*
      a. Check if the segment in *next* has coincident vertices with *current* segment
      b. If yes, invert *next* segment if needed
      c. Move the *next* segment closed to the *current* segment in the array
      d. Move pointer *current* to the next segment (*current+=1)*
      e. Repeat step 2.2
   2.3. Move pointer *current* to the next segment of *current* segment (*current+=1*)
   2.4. Repeat step 2

End

The sequential algorithm above is to re-arrange line segments into a stream order. The mechanism is similar to the selection sort. The algorithm requires searching all line segments for every investigated line segment to look for the line segment having coincident vertex and move it to the right place. This ineffective searching and sorting can be noticed by the usage of two *while* loops in step 2 and 2.2. Consequently, the complexity of this algorithm is $O(n^2)$, where n is the number of vertices.

3.2. Parallel Line Simplification Algorithm

Using the MASC model to counter the inefficiencies of the search and sorting discussed earlier, we adopt global constant time search operations of the MASC model to avoid such inefficiencies.

Consider the simple example with five segments having integer-coordinate vertices as shown in Figure 3. In the example, coincident vertices have the same value of coordinates, and three vertices are called collinear if the triangle composed by them has an area value of zero. This can be adjusted in the functions to check coincidence and collinearity by adding an accepted tolerance α [12].

Again, using the he input data described as in Figure 3, every line of the input file is a line segment consisting of two vertices. Each vertex has an x-coordinate and a y-coordinate. Using cross products we can determine the vertex's left or right neighbor, which is the other point in the same segment.

We use a tabular organization similar to the one illustrated in Figure 4 as the data structure in our algorithm. That is, the information about left and right neighbors (*left$* and *right$*) of the currently investigated vertex and its coincident vertex (*coin$* - if any) are stored in each PE. Vertex A is called on the left of vertex B if A's x-coordinate is less than B's or if A's y-coordinate is less than B's when A and B have the same x value. Vertex A is called on the right of vertex B if A's x-coordinate is greater than B's or if A's y-coordinate is greater than B's when A and B have the same x value. In addition to those location variables, two more variables are defined: visited$ for tracking if the vertex has been visited and delete$ for showing if the vertex should be eliminated or not. Furthermore, every vertex is assigned to one PE in the MASC model, which results in a massive number of processing elements.

MASC_LINE_SIMPLIFICATION Algorithm
Begin

1. Set all PEs to active
2. Set del$ = 'No', visited$ = 'No'
3. Set left$/right$ to the other vertex of the segment
4. For all PEs, repeat until no visited$ = 'No'
   4.1. Find the coincident vertex
   4.2. If there is no responder (no coincident vertex)
      4.2.1. Set visited$ = 'Yes'
   4.3. Get the vertex from the responder (if any)
   4.4. Set empty left$/right$ of the two coincident vertices to its coincident vertex
   4.5. Check if left$/right$ of the two coincident vertices and themselves are collinear
      4.5.1. If not:
         a) Set the current PE's del$ = 'Yes', del$ = 'No'
         b) Update field having the deleted vertex as neighbor to its coincident vertex (responders)
         c) Set visited$ of both vertices = 'Yes'
         d) Clear coin$ of both vertices
      4.5.2. Else if they are collinear:
         a) Set both vertices' del$ to 'Yes'
         b) Set the current PE's visited$ = 'Yes'
         c) Update fields that have the deleted vertices (responders) as neighbor
            i. If the deleted vertex is in left$, update left$ of the deleted vertices
            ii. Else if the deleted vertex is in right$, update right$ of the deleted vertices
         d) Clear coin$ of both vertices

End

Using the MASC model, our algorithm does not have to re-arrange the line segments because it takes advantage of associative searching. The operations "Find its coincident vertex" in step 4.1 and "Find vertices that have it as neighbor" in step 4.5.1b and 4.5.2c return values in constant time. After the program finishes (all visited$ are 'Yes'), there would be vertices whose del$ is 'No'. Those remaining vertices belong to the simplified polylines of the level curve's visual representation. The directions of remaining vertices are maintained with their left$ and right$ neighbors.

Figure 4 illustrates the initial table representing the original digitized vertices. During each iteration, a vertex is used in an associative search for its coincident vertex. Then, it checks their neighbors if they are collinear points. Appropriate actions are executed to guarantee that after every round of iteration, there is no deleted vertex in the table, and all vertices will be visited after the program finishes. Figure 5 demonstrates the table after one iteration. The associative searching capabilities of the MASC model helps each round of iteration take constant time. Figure 6 shows the final state of the table after all vertices are visited. Figure 7 is the resultant polyline constructed by fewer segments and vertices. The running time of the algorithm is $O(n)$ in the worst case when there is no coincidence between vertices.

	vertex	left$	right$	coin$	visited$	del$
PE	A1	B1			No	No
PE	B1		A1		No	No
PE	A2		B2		No	No
PE	B2	A2			No	No
PE	A3		B3		No	No
PE	B3	A3			No	No
PE	A4	B4			No	No
PE	B4		A4		No	No
PE	A5	B5			No	No
PE	B5		A5		No	No

Figure 4: The initial table for the parallel algorithm

	vertex	left$	right$	coin$	visited$	del$
PE	A1	B1	A2		Yes	Yes
PE	B1		A2		No	No
PE	A2	A2	B2		Yes	No
PE	B2	A2			No	No
PE	A3		B3		No	No
PE	B3	A3			No	No
PE	A4	B4			No	No
PE	B4		A4		No	No
PE	A5	B5			No	No
PE	B5		A5		No	No

Figure 5: The table after one iteration.

	vertex	left$	right$	coin$	visited$	del$
PE	A1	B5	A2		Yes	Yes
PE	B1	B5	A2		Yes	Yes
PE	A2	A2	B2		Yes	No
PE	B2	A2			Yes	No
PE	A3	B5	A2		Yes	Yes
PE	B3	B5	A2		Yes	Yes
PE	A4	B5	A2		Yes	Yes
PE	B4	A5	A2		Yes	Yes
PE	A5	B5	A2		Yes	No
PE	B5		A5		Yes	No

Figure 6: The table after all nodes are visited

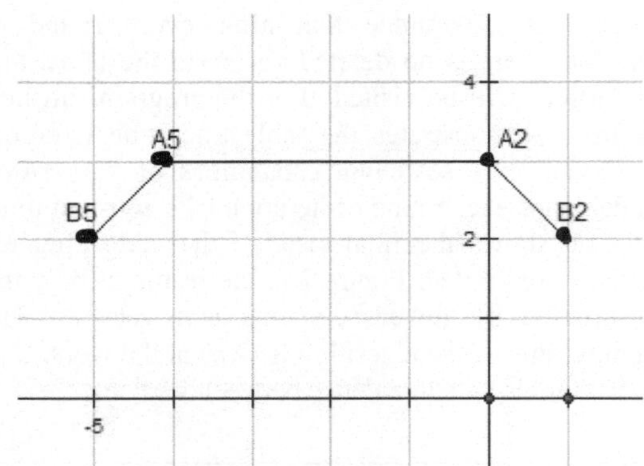

Figure 7: The resultant polyline

4. Implementation Using Chapel

While many parallel programming tools exist that could be used to implement the parallel algorithm as described in Section 3, the language Chapel was selected because it can implement many (if not all) of the features of the MASC model of parallel computation efficiently using SMP's or clusters. Chapel is a parallel programming language that has been in development (and currently being used) by Cray Inc. since 2007. Chapel was selected as the language of choice because of its language features in data parallelism, task parallelism, concurrency and nested parallelism via high-level abstractions. The major features of Chapel used in this research are parallel domains and arrays and parallel iteration.

4.1. Parallel Domains and Arrays

A domain is a language construct to define the size and shape of arrays. Domains support parallel iteration. Chapel has two main classes of domains: arithmetic domains and indefinite domains. Arithmetic domains are represented using multidimensional integer coordinates. They are similar to traditional arrays. Arithmetic domains could be dynamic allocated. An example to create a simple 2D arithmetic domain and array is as follows:

var D: domain(2) = [1..m, 1..n];
var A: [D] float; // an m x n array of floating point values

Indefinite domains represent a set of special type that is specified by users. Indefinite domains are mostly used to implement associative arrays. The following example creates an array of integers indexed using strings:

var People: domain(string);
var Age: [People] int;
People += "Mike";
Age("Mike") = 21;

4.2. Parallel Iteration

Parallel iteration is specified in Chapel using *forall loops*. The *forall loops* iterate over domains and arrays. The *forall loops* provide a high-level of data parallelism or associative searching to users. If there are enough number of processors, all of the elements in the domains/arrays could be accessed in parallel. An example of *forall loops* is as follows:

forall point in Points:
{
NeighborOf(point) = ...;
}

5. Results and Analysis

The parallel program was tested on various parallel computing machinery (SMPs and clusters) that supported Chapel. Test data from the level curves in Figure 1 was used for benchmarking this algorithm. There are 20 level curves in the figure with a total of 15,530 points. The parallel program will gradually take all of 20 level curves as input and will measure the time it takes to get the results. The results are compared to the same parallel program but only use one processing element.

5.1. Results: Symmetric Multiprocessors

The first test was conducted on a Dell workstation in 8 processors at 3.0 GHz and has 16 GB of RAM. The following graph (Figure 8) is the execution times collected from the test run. The unit in the number of processors column is microseconds.

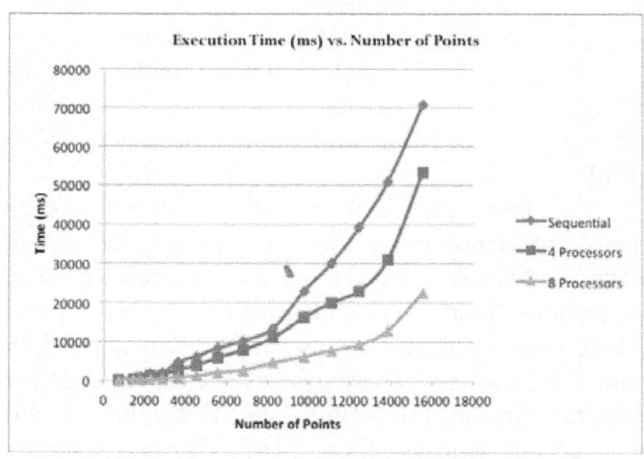

Figure 8: Execution time (microseconds) vs. number of data points (SMP).

5.2. Results: Clusters

The cluster machines used in this research include 8 computing nodes, each of which has 2 processors running at 3.0 GHz with 4 GB of RAM. Therefore, there are 16 processors in total. A 1 Gbps network connects these computing nodes. The parallel program is tested from using 1 computing node to using all 8 computing nodes with the data size of 15530 points. The following graph (figure 9) shows the execution times vs. the number of processor cores for a fixed (maximum) number of points.

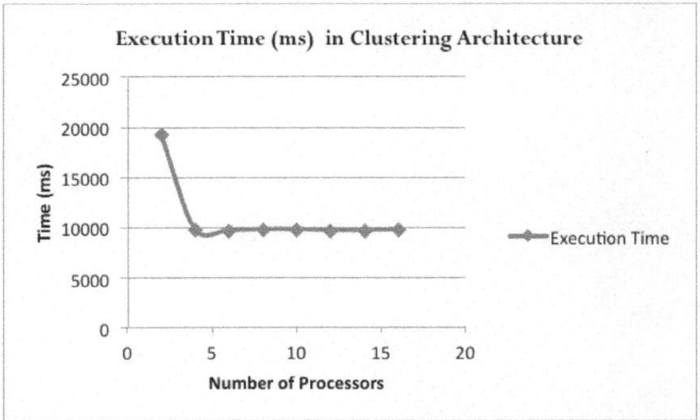

Figure 9: Execution time (ms) vs. number of processors (cluster).

5.3. Analysis

The communication between the computing nodes on the physical network really affects the performance of the parallel algorithm. Reviewing the conceptual model of the MASC model (Figure 2) in we can clearly see that the broadcast/reduction network is an important factor deciding the performance of the parallel program. Since each subset of points is located on different computing nodes, the parallel program has to go through the physical network in order to get the coincident points. This can be observed on the graph of execution time when the number of points is increasing in the clustering architecture. Running with 4 processors on two computing nodes can reduce the amount of execution nearly 50%. Nevertheless, when more computing nodes are added, the program's execution time is not improved. From this observation, we can conclude that clustering architecture is not suitable for this research problem MASC model until we can have a really fast network (close to the speed of SMP machine's bus).

6. Conclusion and Future Work

This report has reviewed the importance of polyline simplification process on geometric applications such as visualizations of level curves or geographic map boundaries. The reduction in the number of points and segments can help improve the efficiency of these applications but still maintain the important geometric characteristics of the visualizations.

Douglas-Peucker's algorithm has a time complexity of *O(mn),* and its enhanced version has the time complexity of *O(n log n)*. After investigating the sequential algorithms, we have developed a massively parallel algorithm on this polyline simplification problem. The developed parallel algorithm takes advantage of the associative operations of the Multiple-instruction-stream Associative Computing Model. The theoretical parallel complexity of the parallel algorithm is *O(n)*.

The MASC model's architecture and properties were also studied in this report. A significant aspect in the MASC model is data parallelism. Chapel, a parallel language developed by Cray Inc., was chosen as the language to implement the parallel polyline simplification algorithm because of its support for data parallelism.

A parallel polyline simplification algorithm was implemented using Chapel and the program was tested on different parallel architectures. The evaluations have shown that the symmetric multiprocessing architecture is appropriate to support the parallel polyline simplification algorithm. On the other hand, the communication over the network of the clustering architecture adversely affected the performance of the parallel program.

One interesting study to extend this work would be to consider using hardware accelerators such as CUDA or Intel Phi. The ability to efficiently manage a massive number of threads provides a potential capability on the parallel polyline simplification algorithm when each thread in hardware accelerator can be considered a processing element in the conceptual MASC model. The performance would be increased significantly.

References

[1] B. L. Chamberlain, D. Callahan, H. P. Zima, "Parallel Programmability and the Chapel Language", Int'l Journal of High Performance Computing Applications, 21(3), pp. 291-312, August 2007.

[2] D. Douglas, T. Peucker, "Algorithms for the Reduction of the Number of Points Required to Represent a Digitized Line or Its Caricature", Canada Cartographer, Univ. of Toronto Press, 10(2), pp. 112-122, December 1973.

[3] G. Fox, "What Have We Learnt from Using Real Parallel Machines to Solve Real Problems", Proc. of the 3rd Conf. on Hypercube Concurrent Computers and Applications, vol. 2, ACM Press, pp. 897-955, 1988.

[4] J.Hershberger, J. Snoeyink, "Speeding Up the Douglas-Peucker line-simplification algorithm", Proc. of the 5th Symposium. on Data Handlings, pp. 134-143, 1992.

[5] G.F. Jenks, "Lines, Computers and Human Frailties", Annuals of the Association of American Geographers, pp. 1-10, 1981.

[6] M. Jin, J. Baker, "Two Graph Algorithms On an Associative Computing Model", Proc. of the Int'l Conf. on Parallel and Distributed Processing Techniques (PDPTA), Las Vegas, June 2007.

[7] M. Jin, J. Baker, and K. Batcher, "Timing of Associative Operations on the MASC model", Proc. of the 15th IPDPS (Workshop in Massively Parallel Processing), CD-ROM, April 2011.

[8] J. Potter, "Associative Computing: A Programming Paradigm for Massively Parallel Computers", Plenum Press, New York, NY, 1992.

[9] J. Potter, J. Baker, S. Scott, A. Bansal, C. Leangsuksun, and C. Asthgiri, "ASC: An Associative-Computing Paradigm", Computer, 27(11), 19-25, 1994.

[10] K. Reumann, A.P.M Witkam, "Optimizing curve segmentation in computer graphics", Proc. of the Int'l Computing Symposium, pp. 467-472, 1974.

[11] M. Scherger, "On Using the UML to Describe the MASC Model of Parallel Computation", Proc. of the Int' Conf. on PDPTA, pp. 2639-2645, Las Vegas, June 2000.

[12] M. Scherger, H. Tran, "A Massively Parallel Algorithm for Polyline Simplification Using and Associative Computing Model", Proc. Of the Int'l Conf. on PDPTA, Las Vegas, July, 2011.

[13] M. Visvalingam, J.D. Whyatt, "Line Generalization by Repeated Elimination of Points", Cartographic Journal, 30(1):46-52, 1993.

[14] S.T. Wu, R.G. Marquez, "A Non-self-intersection Douglas-Peucker Algorithm", Computer Graphics and Image Processing, pp. 60-66, Oct 2003.

A Parallel Ford-Fulkerson Algorithm For Maximum Flow Problem

Zhipeng Jiang[1], Xiaodong Hu[1], and Suixiang Gao[2]
[1]Academy of Mathematics and Systems Science, Chinese Academy of Sciences, Beijing, China
[2]School of Mathematical Sciences, University of Chinese Academy of Sciences, Beijing, China

Abstract— *The maximum flow problem is one of the most fundamental problems in network flow theory and has been investigated extensively. The Ford-Fulkerson algorithm is a simple algorithm to solve the maximum flow problem based on the idea of augmenting path. But its time complexity is high and it's a pseudo-polynomial time algorithm. In this paper, a parallel Ford-Fulkerson algorithm is given. The idea of this algorithm is not intuitive. All the arcs in the computed flow network are processed simultaneously in the parallel steps in every iteration. We execute the algorithm in CUDA and the simulation result shows that this parallel algorithm has a good performance.*

Keywords: Flow network, Maximum flow problem, Ford-Fulkerson algorithm, Parallel Algorithm, CUDA

1. Flow network

In graph theory, a flow network (also known as a transportation network) is a directed graph where each edge has a capacity and each edge receives a flow. The amount of flow on an edge cannot exceed the capacity of the edge. Often in Operations Research, a directed graph is called a network, the vertices are called nodes and the edges are called arcs. A flow must satisfy the restriction that the amount of flow into a node equals the amount of flow out of it, except when it is a source, which has more outgoing flow, or sink, which has more incoming flow. A network can be used to model traffic in a road system, fluids in pipes, currents in an electrical circuit, or anything similar in which something travels through a network of nodes.

$G(V, E)$ is a finite directed graph in which every edge $e = (u, v) \in E$ has a non-negative, real-valued capacity $c(u, v)$. Two special kinds of vertices are distinguished: a source S and a sink T. A flow network is a real function $f : V \times V \to R$ with the following three properties for all nodes u and v:

- Capacity constraints: $f(u, v) \le c(u, v)$. The flow along an edge cannot exceed its capacity.
- Skew symmetry: $f(u, v) = -f(v, u)$. The flow from u to v must be the opposite of the net flow from v to u.
- Flow conservation: $\sum_{w \in V} f(u, w) = 0$. unless $u = s$ or $u = t$. The flow to a node is zero, except for the source, which "produces" flow, and the sink, which "consumes" flow.

Notice that $f(u, v)$ is the net flow from u to v. If the graph represents a physical network, and if there is a real flow of, for example, 4 units from u to v , and a real flow of 3 units from v to u, we have $f(u, v) = 1$ and $f(v, u) = -1$.

The residual capacity of an edge is $c_f(u, v) = c(u, v) - f(u, v) = 1$. This defines a residual network denoted $G_f(V, E_f)$, giving the amount of available capacity. See that there can be a path from u to v in the residual network, even though there is no path from u to v in the original network. Since flows in opposite directions cancel out, decreasing the flow from v to u is the same as increasing the flow from u to v. An augmenting path is a path $(u_1, u_2, \cdots, u_k)$ in the residual network, where $u_1 = s$, $u_k = t$, and $c_f(u_i, u_{i+1}) > 0$. A network is at maximum flow if and only if there is no augmenting path in the residual network.

Should one need to model a network with more than one source, a super source is introduced to the graph. This consists of a vertex connected to each of the sources with edges of infinite capacity, so as to act as a global source. A similar construct for sinks is called a super sink. An example of flow network is shown in Fig.1

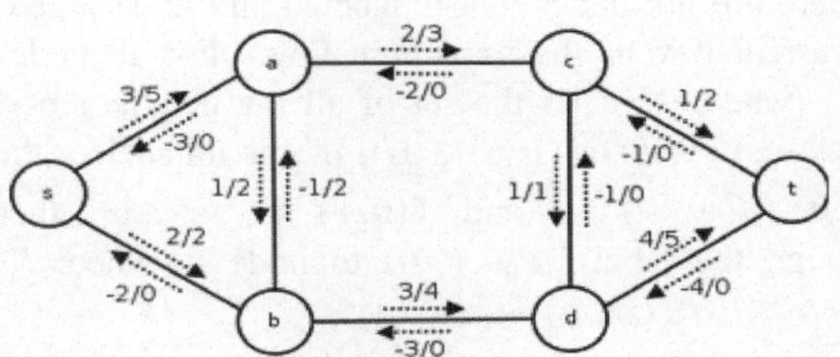

Fig. 1: An example of flow network

2. Maximum flow problem

The maximum flow problems involve finding a feasible flow through a single-source, single-sink flow network that is maximum. The maximum flow problem can be seen as a special case of more complex network flow problems, such as the circulation problem.

Let $G = (V, E)$ be a network with $s, t \in V$ being the source and the sink of N respectively. The value of flow of N is defined by $|f| = \sum_{v:(s,v) \in E} f(s, v)$, where s is the source of G. It represents the amount of flow passing from the source to the sink. The maximum flow problem is to maximize $|f|$, that is, to route as much flow as possible from s to t.

3. Ford-Fulkerson algorithm

The Ford-Fulkerson method[1] (named for L. R. Ford, Jr. and D. R. Fulkerson) is an algorithm which computes the maximum flow in a flow network. The name "Ford-Fulkerson" is often also used for the Edmonds-Karp algorithm, which is a specialization of Ford-Fulkerson. The idea behind the algorithm is simple. As long as there is a path from the source (start node) to the sink (end node), with available capacity on all edges in the path, we send flow along one of these paths. Then we find another path, and so on. A path with available capacity is called an augmenting path.

Let $G(V, E)$ be a graph, and for the arc $e = (u, v)$, let $c(u, v)$ be the capacity and $f(u, v)$ be the flow. We want to find the maximum flow from the source s to the sink t.

The Ford-Fulkerson algorithm has two main steps. The first is a labeling process that searches for a flow augmenting path i.e., a path from s to t for which $f < c$ along all forward arcs and $f > 0$ along all backward arcs. If this step finds a flow augmenting path, the second step changes the flow accordingly. Otherwise, no augmenting path exists, then we get the maximum flow. The detail step is as follows:

The algorithm begin with any feasible flow (e.g., $f = 0$). In general, a node is in one of three states:unlabeled, labeled and scanned, or labeled and un-scanned. Upon entering Step 1, all nodes areunlabeled. The first step renders the source labeled and un-scanned.

Step 1. Initially, label the source $(s, l(s) = \infty)$;

Step 2. Select any node u, that is labeled and un-scanned (If there are not nodes that is labeled and un-scanned, then the current flow is the maximum flow). For all nodes $v \in N(u)$ (where $N(u)$ is the set of all the neighbor nodes of u, i.e. $(u, v) \in E$ or $(v, u) \in E$). If v is unlabeled, then:

- If $(u, v) \in E$ and $f(u, v) < c(u, v)$, then assign the label $(u, +, l(v))$ to node v. where $l(v) = min(l(u), c(u, v) - f(u, v))$;
- If $(v, u) \in E$ and $f(v, u) > 0$, then assign the label $(u, -, l(v))$ to node v. where $l(v) = min(l(u), f(v, u))$;

Then let u be labeled and scanned, meanwhile let v be labeled and un-scanned. If the sink node t is labeled then go to step 3, else return to step 2.

Step 3. let $x = t$, then do the following work until $x = s$.

- If the label of x is $(y, +, l(x))$, then let $f(y, x) = f(y, x) + l(t)$
- If the label of x is $(y, -, l(x))$, then let $f(x, y) = f(x, y) - l(t)$
- Let $x = y$

Then go to step 1.

The Ford-Fulkerson algorithmis simple to implement but its time complexity is high and it's a pseudo-polynomial time algorithm. By adding the flow augmenting path to the flow already established in the graph, the maximum flow will be reached when no more flow augmenting paths can be found in the graph. However, there is no certainty that this situation will ever be reached, so the best that can be guaranteed is that the answer will be correct if the algorithm terminates. In the case that the algorithm runs forever, the flow might not even converge towards the maximum flow. However, this situation only occurs with irrational flow values. When the capacities are integers, the runtime of Ford-Fulkerson is bounded by $O(|E|f)$, where $|E|$ is the number of edges in the graph and f is the maximum flow in the graph. This is because each augmenting path can be found in $O(|E|)$ time and increases the flow by an integer amount which is at least 1.

In order to decrease the computational time, many researches gave different algorithms. Edmonds and Karp[2] showed that the Ford and Fulkerson algorithm runs in time $O(|V||E|^2)$if flows are augmented along shortest paths from source to sink. Independently, Dinic [3] introduced the concept of shortest path networks, called layered networks, and obtained an $O(|V|^2|E|)$ algorithm. This bound was improved to O(V3)by Karzanov[4], who introduced the concept of preflows in a layered network. Since then, researchers have improved the complexity of Dinic's algorithm for sparse networks by devising sophisticated data structures. Among these contributions, Sleator and Tarjan's[5] dynamic tree data structure is the most attractive from a worst-case point of view. The algorithms of Goldberg[6] and of Goldberg and Tarjan[7] are a novel departure from these approaches in that they do not construct layered networks. Their method maintains a preflow, as per Karzanov, and proceeds by pushing flows to nodes estimated to be closer to the sink.

All the works above and some other works gave algorithms that have good computational performance, i.e. the time complexity is lower than the Ford-Fulkerson algorithm. But the algorithms in these works are very complicated and some of them are only suitable for the flow networks with specific structure. In this paper, an parallel based on the Ford-Fulkerson label algorithm is given which is not complicated and the computational performance is good when there are enough processers.

4. Parallel Ford-Fulkerson algorithm

The parallel work is executed on the step 2. But our parallel method is different from the intuitive idea that processing all the nodes which is labeled and un-scanned with all their neighbor nodes synchronous. For example:

Let $L = u_1, u_2, \cdots, u_m$ is the set of all the nodes which is labeled and un-scanned. Let $P = (u, v)|u \in Landv \in N(u)$, then all the elements in P is processed synchronous in step 2.

The method above has a drawback that in every iteration of the algorithm, the set P must be constructed before step 2 and this work can't be processed by a parallel mode.

The effect of the parallel process is terrible because of this drawback.

The parallel mode in our algorithm can avoid this drawback and the basic idea is that all the arcs in E are processed simultaneously in step 2. The detail of this parallel method is as follows:

Step 1. Initially, label the source $(s, l(s) = \infty)$;

Step 2. For every arc $(u, v) \in E$, only one of the two possible situations may occur:

- **u is labeled and un-scanned, v is unlabeled and** $f(u,v) < c(u,v)$. If this situation occurs, then assign the label $(u, +, l(v))$ to node v. Where $l(v) = min(l(u), c(u,v) - f(u,v))$. Let u be labeled and scanned and v is labeled and un-scanned
- **v is labeled and un-scanned, u is unlabeled and** $f(u,v) > 0$. If this situation occurs, then assign the label $(v, -, l(u))$ to node u. Where $l(u) = min(l(v), f(u,v))$. Let v be labeled and scanned and u is labeled and un-scanned

If the sink node t is labeled then go to step 3, else return to step 2.

Step 3. let $x = t$, then do the following work until $x = s$.

- If the label of x is $(y, +, l(x))$, then let $f(y,x) = f(y,x) + l(t)$
- If the label of x is $(y, -, l(x))$, then let $f(x,y) = f(x,y) - l(t)$
- Let $x = y$

Then go to step 1.

5. Simulation Result

We execute our work and do the experiments on Dell Work Station with 8 CPUs.

First, we execute our parallel algorithm to a flow network with 100 nodes and 896 arcs. The flow network is shown in Fig.2. We compare our parallel algorithm with the Edmonds-Karp algorithm which is an improvement version of the Ford-Fulkerson algorithm. As the run time of both the two algorithm are lower than 1ms, we run each algorithm 100 times and get the total run time. The total run time of the Edmonds-Karp algorithm is 63ms. The total run time of our parallel algorithm is 94 ms.

Then we execute our parallel algorithm to a flow network with 1000 nodes and 94522 arcs. As there are too many arcs and nodes, the flow network can't be shown as figure. And in this flow network, the run time of both the two algorithm are long enough, so we run each algorithm only one time and get the run time. The run time of the Edmonds-Karp algorithm is 265ms and the run time of our parallel algorithm is 141ms.

From the simulation results, we can see that our algorithm can get a better performance of run time than the Edmonds-Karp algorithm in the situation with more nodes and arcs even if there are only 8 processors on our experiment platform. But there can't be a large number of CPUs in a PC (even a Work Station), so we can't get the effect of our algorithm presented in this paper. For this reason, we use GPU (graphics processing units) instead of CPU to compute. CUDA (formerly Compute Unified Device Architecture) is a parallel computing platform and programming model created by NVIDIA and implemented by the graphics processing units (GPUs) that they produce. CUDA gives developers access to the virtual instruction set and memory of the parallel computational elements in CUDA GPUs. Using CUDA, the latest Nvidia GPUs become accessible for computation like CPUs. Unlike CPUs, however, GPUs have a parallel throughput architecture that emphasizes executing many concurrent threads slowly, rather than executing a single thread very quickly. This approach of solving general-purpose (i.e., not exclusively graphics) problems on GPUs is known as GPGPU.

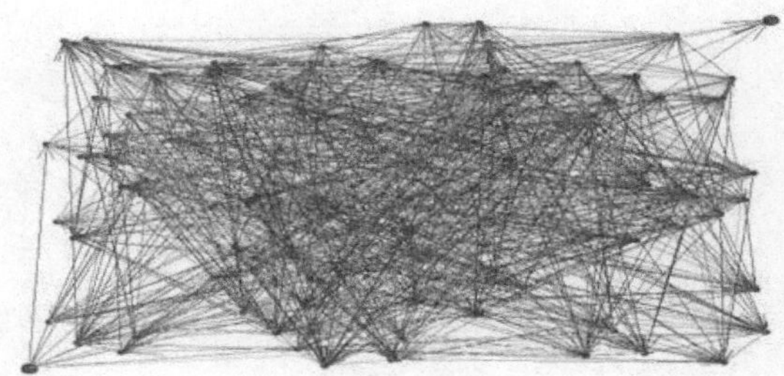

Fig. 2: A flow network with 100 nodes and 896 arcs

For the reason that the computing performance and frequency of GPU and CPU are different, we implement both the Edmonds-Karp algorithm and the parallel algorithm on GPUs. We use 256 GPUs for the parallel algorithm and only one of the GPUs is used when we implement the Edmonds-Karp algorithm. The simulation results are shown in Fig.3 and Fig.4. In Fig.3, the number of nodes is fixed as 500 and the mean degree of the flow network is increased from 25 to 250. The dotted line is the result of the Edmonds-Karp algorithm and the solid line is the result of the parallel algorithm. From Fig.3, we can see that with the mean degree increasing, the effect of the parallel algorithm is get more evident. The similar result is shown in Fig.4. The mean degree of the network is fixed as half of the number of the nodes, and the number of the nodes is increased from 50 to 500. With the number of nodes increasing, the effect of the parallel algorithm is get more evident.

6. Conclusion

The maximum flow problem is one of the most fundamental problems in network flow theory and has been investigated extensively. In this paper, we give a parallel Ford-Fulkerson algorithm, which is simple to implementation. Different from the intuitive idea, the basic idea of our algorithm is processing all the arcs simultaneously in the

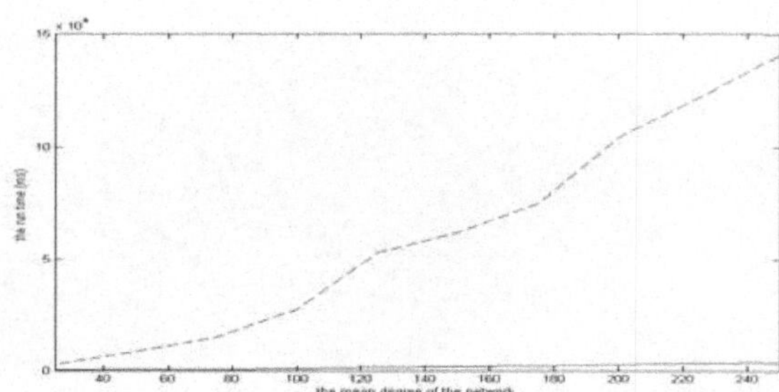

Fig. 3: Run time and the the mean degree of the flow network

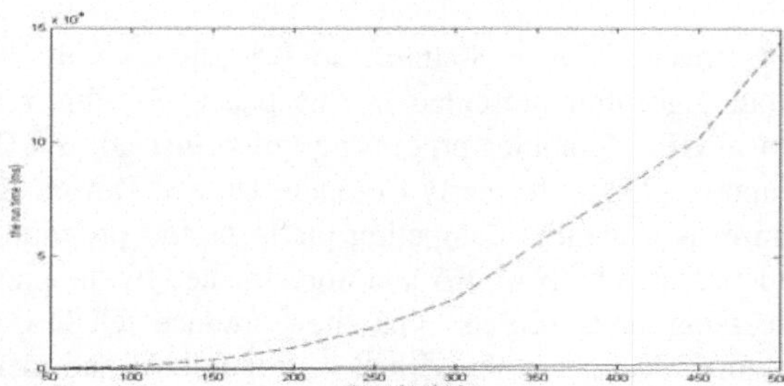

Fig. 4: Run time and number of nodes

step of searching for a flow augmenting path. The simulation result show that the given parallel algorithm have a great improvement of the computing time.

References

[1] FORD.L.R. AND D. R. FULKERSON 1956. Maximal Flow Through a Network. Can. J. Math. 8,399-404.

[2] EDMONDS.J.AND R.M.KARP 1972. Theoretical Improvements in Algorithmic Efficiency for Network Flow Problems. J. Assoc. Comput. Mach. 19, 248-264.

[3] DINICE.A. 1970. Algorithm for Solution of a Problem of Maximum Flow in Networks With Power Estimation.Soviet Math. Dokl. 11, 1277-1280.

[4] KARZANOVA.V. 1974. Determining the Maximal Row in a Network by the Method of Preflows. Soviet Math.Dokl.15,434-437.

[5] SLEATOR.D.D.AND R.E.TARJAN. 1983. A Data Structure for Dynamic Trees, J. Comput. Syst. Sci. 24,362-391.

[6] GOLDBERGA.V. 1985. A New Max-Flow Algorithm. Technical Report MIT/LCS/TM-291, Laboratory for Computer Science, MIT, Cambridge, Mass.

[7] GOLDBERGA.V. AND R.E.TARJAN1.1986.A New Approach to the Maximum Flow Problem.Proc. of the 18th Annual ACM Symposium on the Theory of Computing, 136-146.

Model Checking Prioritized Token-Based Mutual Exclusion Algorithms

Mitchell L. Neilsen
Department of Computing and Information Sciences
Kansas State University
Manhattan, KS, USA
{neilsen@ksu.edu}

Abstract - *Many existing token-based, distributed mutual exclusion algorithms can be generalized by a single algorithm. The number of messages required to provide mutual exclusion is dependent upon the logical topology imposed on the nodes and the policy used to forward requests.*

This paper extends the generalized algorithm to support prioritized requests and presents models that can be used to analyze the performance and verify the correctness of the prioritized algorithm. Both safety and liveness properties are verified. Model checking can also be used to analyze performance. Using the best topology, the generalized algorithm attains the same worst-case performance as a centralized algorithm; that is, three messages per critical section. In the average case, the generalized algorithm performs better than a centralized one when the star topology is used.

Keywords: distributed algorithm, model checking, mutual exclusion, real-time, token-based

1 Introduction

Many distributed mutual exclusion algorithms have been proposed [1, 4, 5, 6, 8, 12, 13, 16, 17, 18, 19]. These algorithms can be classified into two groups [14, 17]. The algorithms in the first group are called *permission-based* [1, 5, 6, 16]. A node enters its critical section only after receiving permission from a set of nodes. The algorithms in the second group are called *token-based* [4, 8, 12, 17, 18, 19]. The possession of a system-wide unique token gives a node the right to enter its critical section.

Lamport proposed one of the first distributed mutual exclusion algorithms [5]. Lamport's algorithm is permission-based and requires $3*(N-1)$ messages to provide mutual exclusion. Another permission-based algorithm, proposed by Ricart and Agrawala, reduces the number of required messages to $2*(N-1)$ messages per critical section entry [15]. Maekawa proposed a permission-based algorithm in which the number of messages required is $O(\sqrt{N})$ [6]. Sanders generalized permission-based algorithms [16].

Ricart and Agrawala proposed a token-based algorithm which is essentially the same as Suzuki and Kasami's algorithm [18]. Based on Suzuki and Kasami's algorithm, Singhal proposed a heuristically-aided algorithm that uses state information to more accurately guess the location of the token [17]. The maximum number of messages required by these three algorithms is N.

By imposing a tree-based logical structure on the nodes, another class of token-based algorithms has been obtained. In this class of algorithms, all of the nodes, except for the root node, are on a path to the root node (a sink node) in the logical structure. The logical structure determines the path along which a request message travels. There are two different types of logical structures: dynamic and static.

An algorithm, based on a dynamic logical structure, was proposed by Trehel and Naimi [19]. The basic notion underlying this algorithm is path reversal. *Path reversal* at each node is performed as a request from node x travels along the path from node x to the root node. As the request travels, node x becomes the new parent of each node on the path, except for node x. Thus, node x becomes the new root node. A complete analysis of path reversal has been given by Ginat [3]. The average number of messages required per critical section is $O(log(N))$.

If a static logical structure is used, the basic notion underlying the algorithm is what we call edge reversal [11]. *Edge reversal* at each node is performed as the request from node x travels along the path from node x to the root node. At each node, the direction of each edge on the path is changed to point towards node x; that is, to the neighboring node who sent the request on behalf of node x. However, the shape of the logical structure never changes. Suprisingly, this small change results in algorithms which have a small fixed upper bound on the number of messages required per critical section, and the upper bound only depends on the logical structure. Algorithms based on edge-reversal were proposed by Neilsen and Mizuno [10] and Raymond [12]. Raymond's algorithm assumes that the static logical structure is an unrooted tree. If the radiating star topology is used, the average number of messages required is $O(logN)$. However, this is not optimal, using a simple star topology with one root node only requires 4 messages per critical section, two messages to pass the request, and two for the token.

Neilsen and Mizuno introduced a token-based algorithm that achieves optimal performance with respect to worst-case performance [11]; i.e., 3 messages per critical section. They also proposed another algorithm that generalizes all existing token-based algorithms that impose a logical structure on the nodes [9]. Both algorithms assume a fully-connected physical network and a directed acyclic graph (dag) structured logical network. A node or a token does not need to maintain a queue of outstanding requests for mutual exclusion. Instead, the queue is maintained implicitly in a distributed manner and may be deduced by observing the states of the nodes. The algorithms require very simple data structures; each node maintains a few simple variables, and the token carries no (or a very simple) data structure. Furthermore, the algorithms can adapt to changes in the network.

More recently, the notion of prioritized mutual exclusion algorithms have been proposed [7]. Mueller's algorithm extends Trehel and Naimi's algorithm by incorporating a priority queue at each node. Our generalized algorithm can also be easily adapted to operate much like a priority-based scheduler which schedules tasks based on their priority, and schedules tasks at the same priority level using round robin scheduling. The basic single-priority, generalized algorithm can be used to provide round robin scheduling. To support prioritized requests, the generalized algorithm is easily extended to pass the token between priority levels.

Section 2 introduces the generalized algorithm. Section 3 presents models that can be used to verify correctness with respect to guaranteed mutual exclusion, deadlock freedom, and starvation freedom for the highest priority tasks. Section 4 analyzes the performance of the algorithm using these models.

2 Overview

We assume that the system consists of N nodes, which are uniquely numbered from 0 to $N-1$. At any given time, each node can have at most one outstanding request to enter its critical section. Physically, the nodes are fully connected by a reliable network, but logically, the nodes at each priority level are organized in a directed acyclic graph (dag). Nodes can be assigned different priorities. We start by describing the basic generalized algorithm for each priority level.

Two types of messages, called REQUEST and TOKEN, are exchanged among nodes. When a node requests to enter its critical section, it initiates a REQUEST message. A TOKEN message represents the token; when a node receives a TOKEN message, it may enter its critical section.

Each node maintains three simple variables: integer variables LAST and NEXT, and a boolean variable HOLDING or SINK. The logical directed acyclic graph (dag) structure indicates the path along which a REQUEST message travels and is imposed by the LAST variables in the nodes. When a node initiates or receives a REQUEST message, the node forwards the request to the neighboring node pointed at by its LAST variable (unless the node is a sink, in which case its LAST variable is -1).

The NEXT variable indicates the node which will be granted mutual exclusion after this node. If the node is currently the last node to be granted mutual exclusion, its NEXT variable is -1. Thus, by following the NEXT variables from the token holder to the node whose NEXT variable is -1, the implicit waiting queue of the system can be deduced. When a node leaves its critical section, it forwards the token to the node at the front of the waiting queue and also performs a *dequeue* operation. That is, it sends a TOKEN message to the node indicated by its NEXT variable (this is the node at the front of the queue) and clears the variable (this corresponds to the dequeue operation), unless NEXT is -1. If NEXT is -1, the node continues to hold the token if it is at the highest priority level by setting HOLDING to true, otherwise the token is returned to the highest priority level as described below.

Semantically, a sink node in the system is (1) the last node in the implicit waiting queue (i.e., its NEXT variable is -1), and (2) the last node on the path along which a request travels within a given priority level (i.e., its LAST variable is -1). When a sink node receives a REQUEST message, it *enqueues* the request into the implicit waiting queue and becomes a non-sink. The node initiating the request becomes the new sink since it is now the last node in the queue. Each edge in the path must change direction to point in the direction of the new sink. This is done by the nodes along the path in a distributed manner as follows:

- When a node initiates a new REQUEST message, it forwards the message to its neighboring node indicated by its LAST variable and sets its LAST variable to -1 to become a new sink. It remains a sink until it receives a subsequent request.

- When an intermediate (non-sink) node receives a REQUEST message from a neighboring node X, it passes the message to the neighboring node indicated by its LAST variable. Then, the node sets its LAST variable to *any* node on the path traveled by the REQUEST message. Thus, if it receives a subsequent request, it forwards the request in the direction of the new sink. In Trehel and Naimi's algorithm, the LAST variable is set to the node that initiated the request; this is called *path reversal.* In Neilsen and Mizuno's algorithm, the LAST variable is set to point to the neighboring node from which it received the REQUEST message; this is called *edge reversal.*

- When a sink node receives a REQUEST message from a node X, it sets its NEXT variable to the identifier of the node initiating the request. This corresponds to an *enqueue* operation. The node also sets its LAST variable to *any* node on the path traveled by the REQUEST message. Note that if a sink node holds the token, but is not in its critical section (this state is indicated by a boolean variable HOLDING) when it receives a request, it immediately forwards the token to the node initiating the request.

Because of message delay, there may be several sink nodes in the system while requests are in transit. The system is initialized so that only one node at the highest priority level possesses the token. Initially, there is only one sink node at each priority level, and its LAST variable is initialized to -1. In all other nodes, LAST is set to point to the neighbor which is on a path to the node holding the token at the highest priority level (or the sink at all lower priority levels indicated by setting SINK to true).

```
const
   I = node identifier
var
   HOLDING          : boolean;
   LAST, NEXT       : integer;

proc ProcessWork;
   begin
      if (not HOLDING) then
         begin
            send REQUEST(< I >) to LAST;
            LAST := -1;
            wait until a TOKEN
               message is received;
         end;
      HOLDING := false;

            critical section (CS)

      if (NEXT ≠ -1) then
         begin
            send TOKEN message to NEXT;
            NEXT := -1;
         end;
      else HOLDING := true;
   end;
```

```
proc ProcessRequest; (receive REQUEST(X1, ···, Xk))
   begin
      if (LAST = -1) then
         begin
            if HOLDING then
               begin
                  send TOKEN
                     message to X1;
                  HOLDING := false;
               end;
            else NEXT := X1;
         end;
      else send REQUEST(X1, X2, ···, Xk, I)
         to LAST;
      LAST := Xi for some 1 ≤ i ≤ k;
   end;
```

Figure 1. Single Priority Algorithm

The complete generalized algorithm for a single priority level is shown in Figure 1. There are two procedures at each node: ProcessWork and ProcessRequest. Procedure ProcessWork is executed when a high priority node I requests for entry into its critical section, and procedure ProcessRequest is executed when a high priority node I receives a request from some other high priority node. In the algorithm, REQUEST messages are of form REQUEST$(X_1, X_2, \cdots, X_k)$ where $X_1, X_2, \cdots, X_k$ denotes the path on which the request traveled and X_1 denotes the node where the request originated. Each node executes procedures ProcessWork and ProcessRequest in local mutual exclusion. The only exception is that a node does not have to execute in mutual exclusion while waiting for a TOKEN message to arrive or while in its critical section.

The prioritized algorithm for low priorty nodes is similar, except that the boolean variable HOLDING is replaced with SINK. Initially, a node in the highest priority level holds the token, and HOLDING for that node is set to true. Likewise, the root node at each lower priorty level has its SINK variable set to true. When a request from a low priority node reaches the sink node, a PROXY REQUEST is sent up to a node at the highest priority level, called the *proxy,* and eventually the PROXY REQUEST reaches a node that holds the token or will receive the token in the future. Low priority requests are eventually enqueued in the token. Also, proxy requests are forwarded, at the highest priority level, just like a regular requests, except that the edges are not reversed; i.e., higher priority nodes never request the token from lower priority nodes so there is no need to dynamically adjust the edges. When a node that is holding the token passes the token to a low priority node, a PROXY TOKEN message is used to pass the token, and the token is returned to the high priority node who sent the token using a PROXY RETURN message.

3 Verification Model

In this section we provide models that can be used to verify the correctness of the generalized algorithm with respect to guaranteed mutual exclusion, deadlock freedom, and starvation freedom using UPPAAL [2]. The model for a single priority level consists of two templates, **ProcessWork** and **ProcessRequest**, corresponding to **proc** ProcessWork and **proc** ProcessRequest, respectively, in the algorithm shown above in Figure 1. Channels are used to model the exchange of request messages and the token. Global arrays are used to model the state at each node using the arrays `Holding`, `Sink`, `Next`, and `Last` as defined above. Initially, one node will hold the token, so `Holding[i] = true` at that node. Also, the topology is defined by the initial values assigned to `Last`.

The first UPPAAL template, **ProcessWork**, is shown below in Figure 2. It models the work performed at each node. Initially, all nodes are in the Idle state. The template is parameterized using `id` to identify each node where `id` $\in \{0, 1, \cdots, N-1\}$. At node 0, `id = 0`, etc. Also, `Holding[id]` is set to true at the node currently holding, but not using, the token. This node can enter its critical section immediately after setting `Holding[id]` to false to indicate that the token is in use.

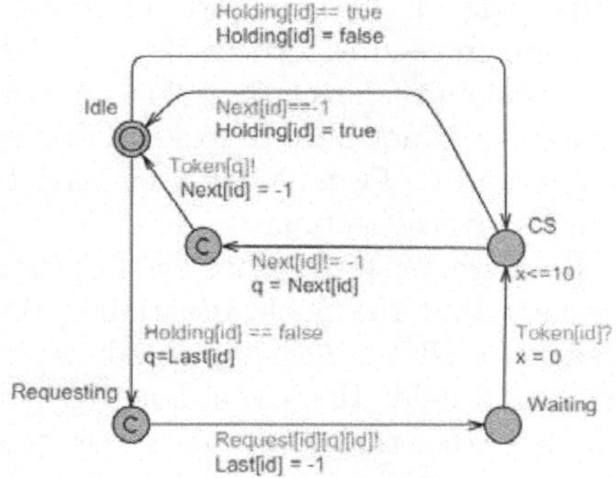

Figure 2. ProcessWork Template

All other nodes must send a request message to the node identified by `LAST[id]`, and set `LAST[id] = -1`. Upon receipt of the token via a `Token` message, the requesting node may enter its critical section.

A local clock, x, is used to prevent a node from remaining in it's critical section forever. The model limits critical sections to be at most 10 time units through the location invariant $x \leq 10$.

To process requests, the **ProcessRequest** template is used as shown in Figure 3. When a request message is received, at node `id` from node `p`, using `Request[p][id][s]?`, the source node requesting to enter its critical section is node `s`.

If the node receiving the request is a sink node, `Last[id] == -1`, the request can be satisfied immediately if the node receiving the request is holding, but not using, the token; that is, if `Holding[id] == true`. In which case, the `Token` message can be sent immediately. On the other hand, if the token is currently in use, then the request is simply enqueued by setting `Next[id] = t` which is a local meta variable assigned to `s` when the request is received.

If the node receiving the request is not a sink node, `Last[id]`$\geq$`0`, then the request is forwarded on to the node indicated by `Last[id]`.

In all cases, `Last[id]` is set to the identifier of the neighboring node which sent the request; that is, *edge reversal* is used.

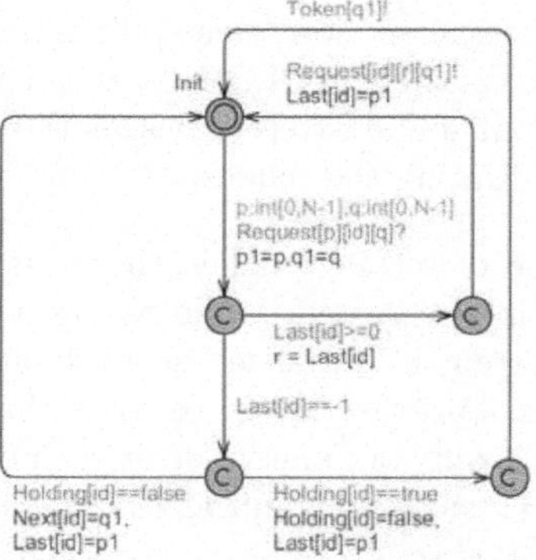

Figure 3. ProcessRequest Template

The generalized algorithm is slightly more complex because each node can set it's `Last[id]` value to be any node visited from the requesting node to the sink. Consequently, a list or queue of visited node numbers must be carried with the `Request` message. This is modeled with a set of global queues that get updated as the `Request` travels. One queue is assigned to each node and used to enqueue the nodes on the path from the given requesting node to a sink. Since each node can have at most one outstanding request to enter its critical section, the queues can be initialized when a request is first initiated, and each requesting node can be associated with a single queue. The nodes can be initialized to impose any logical topology. For example, to impose the star topology, with node 0 as the root, each node could execute the following code:

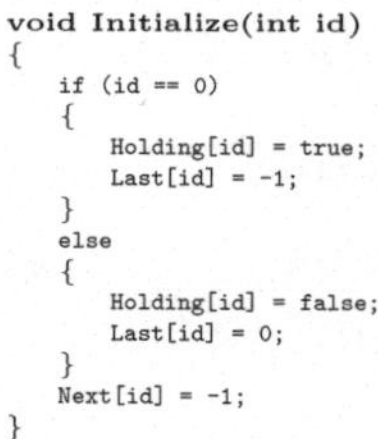

```
void Initialize(int id)
{
    if (id == 0)
    {
        Holding[id] = true;
        Last[id] = -1;
    }
    else
    {
        Holding[id] = false;
        Last[id] = 0;
    }
    Next[id] = -1;
}
```

Figure 4. Initialization Routine

The generalized **ProcessWork** template is shown in Figure 5. By making Init a committed state, all nodes will enter the Ready state before any nodes start requesting. The only other change required is to add a function, `initRequest(id)`, that is used to initialize the queue passed with the `Request` message to contain a single element `<id>`.

The generalized **ProcessRequest** template is shown in Figure 6. As the `Request` message travels from a requesting node to a sink node, the identifier of each node receiving the request must be enqueued in the request message. Since UPPAAL messages have zero capacity, this is modeled using a set of global queues and a function call `enQueue(t,id)` to enqueue `id` on the queue for the requesting node `t`. Also, each node on the path sets `Last[id]` to be some element in the queue. Recall that if it is set to the node at the front of the queue (the requesting source node), then this is just path reversal; at the other extreme, setting `Last[id]` to the neighboring node sending the request, namely node `p`, then this results in edge reversal.

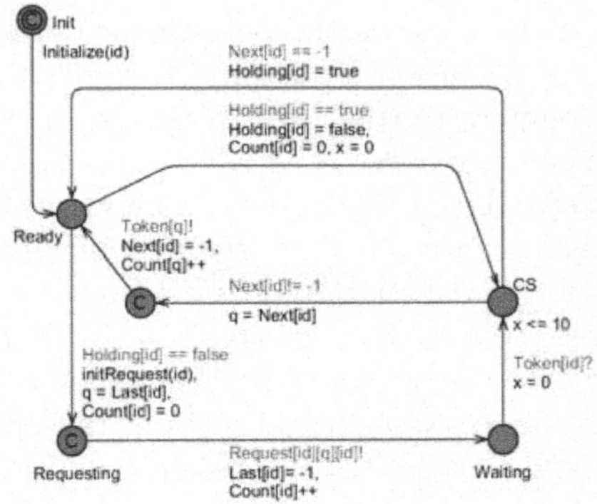

Figure 5. Generalized ProcessWork

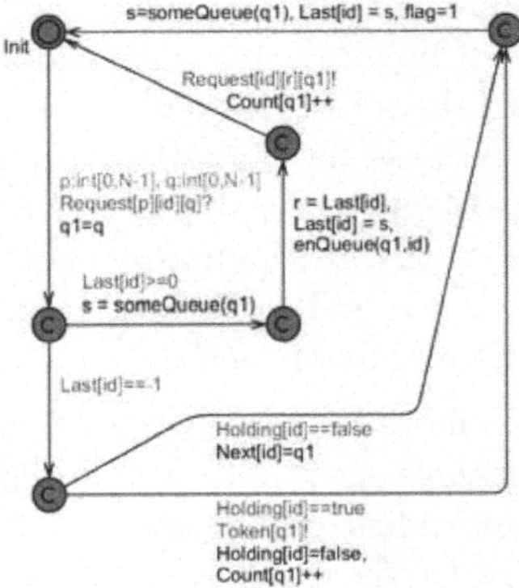

Figure 6. Generalized ProcessRequest

The function, `someQueue()`, relies on a random number generator, modeled by the RandomValue template shown below, to randomly select a random element from the queue carried with the request.

Figure 7. RandomValue

Finally, to support different priority levels, we can add the notion of a proxy node at the highest priority level, and use algorithms similar to the above to request the token.

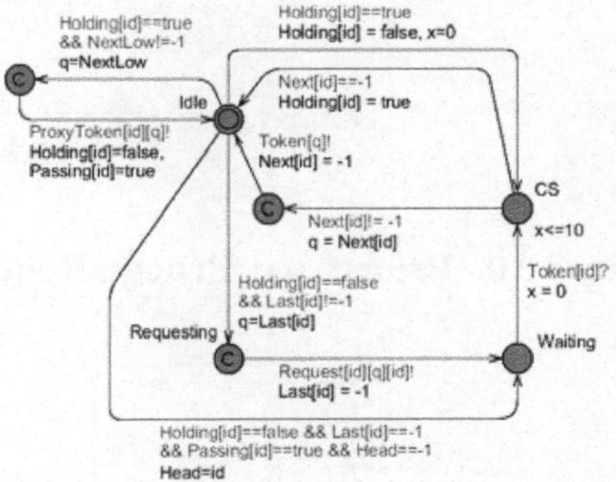

Figure 8. Prioritized ProcessWork

When no requests are pending at the highest priority level, and a request is pending at some lower priority level, the token is passed to allow a node at a lower priority level to obtain the token. The first pending request at each lower priority level is enqueued in priority order in the token. Of course, this may lead to starvation; if there is always a pending request at the highest priority level, then lower priority requests will not be satisfied.

For the prioritized case, four templates are used, nodes at the highest priority level use **ProcessWork** and **ProcessRequest** as shown in Figures 8 and 10, and the lower priority nodes use **ProcessWorkLow** and **ProcessRequestLow** as shown in Figures 9 and 11. Due to space constraints, we only include the prioritized models for edge reversal (extending the templates shown in Figures 2 and 3), but the generalized case is similar.

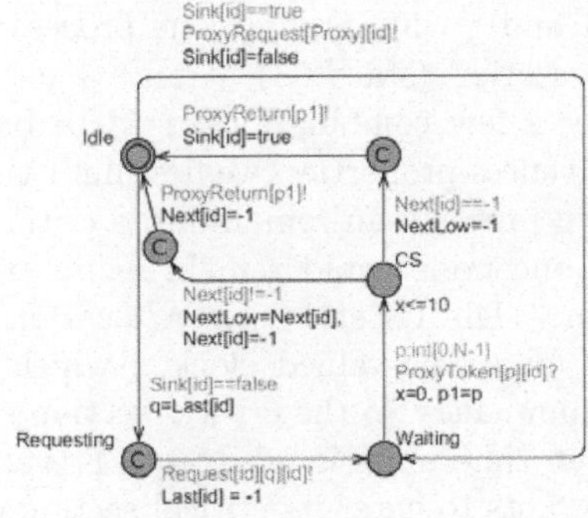

Figure 9. Prioritized ProcessWorkLow

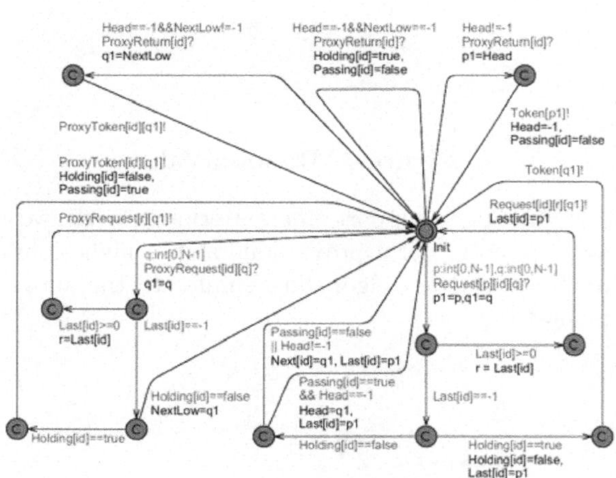

Figure 10. Prioritized ProcessRequest

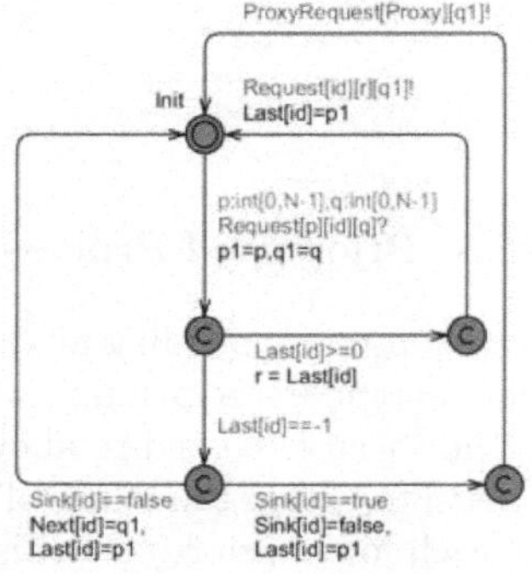

Figure 11. Prioritized ProcessRequestLow

4 Performance Analysis

To verify the correctness of the algorithm we have developed analytical proofs of correctness. We have also verified both safety and liveness properties using UPPAAL [2]. To verify that the algorithm satisfies mutual exclusion, the property: `A[](not (ProcessWork(i).CS and ProcessWork(j).CS))` must be verified for different values of `i` and `j`; that is, only one process can be in its critical section (state `CS`) at any time. By symmetry, only a few combinations need to be checked. To verify liveness properties, we first limit the amount of time each process can remain in its critical section; otherwise, one node could remain in its critical section forever. The `CS` state has a location invariant of $x \leq 10$ for a real-valued clock x which is initialized to 0 upon entry to the critical section state. The choice of ten time units is arbitrary. To verify that a node that wants to enter its critical section can enter, we verify the property `ProcessWork(1).Requesting --> ProcessWork(1).CS`; that is, requesting the critical section "leads to" entry. Formally, a process, at the highest priority level, in the `Requesting` state eventually reaches the `CS` state. Starvation freedom is not satisfied by lower priority processes.

The performance of the algorithm depends on the topology of the logical structure. The best topology is the star topology, with one node in the center and all other nodes as leaf nodes. For the analysis, we define the *diameter* D of a logical structure to be the length of the longest path in the structure. As the logical structure evolves, the value of D may also change.

First, we consider a single priority level. The *upper bound* is equal to $(D+1)$ messages per critical section entry. This occurs when a requesting node and a sink node are at opposite ends of the longest path: D messages for the request to travel to the sink node and one message for the token to be sent back to the requesting node. Thus, using the straight line topology, the upper bound is N, where N is the number of nodes in the system. Using the best topology, the upper bound is 3, since the diameter of a star is 2. This is the same as the performance of a centralized mutual exclusion algorithm. To verify this upper bound, counters can be used, as shown in Figures 4 and 5. Once a request is satisfied, the counter is set back to zero. Then, the model can be verified to see if there exists a path on which the number of messages required for a request from a given node to be satisfied is possible; e.g., E<>(Count[1]==3). For the star topology with *edge reversal*, each leaf node can require up to 3 messages per critical section; thus, the property E<>(Count[1]==3) is satisfied if node 1 is a leaf node, and the property E<>(Count[1]==4) is never satisfied. Likewise, the central node requires at most two messages per critical section. Not suprisingly, for the worst topology – a straight line – the worst-case for path reversal and the generalized algorithm is N messages, $N-1$ `Request` messages and a `Token` message to forward the token. However, this is not true for edge reversal because the underlying topology doesn't change. Consequently, the number of `Request` messages required is the maximum distance from the requesting node to the end of the line. Roughly, $N/2$ for the node in the middle of the line.

If there is more than one priority level, then the number of messages required at the highest priority level is only dependent on the number of nodes in the highest level with the same analysis as above. For lower priority messages, after the request reaches a sink node, by traversing at most the diameter of the topology used for the given priority level, a proxy request may need to be forwarded up to the highest priority level, and to a sink node – again, at most the diameter of the nodes at the highest priority level. The token is passed to the lower priority node with a single message, and returned with a single message. Thus, the worst-case message complexity is $D_H + D_L + 2$ for low priority requests, where D_H is the diameter of high priority nodes, and D_L is the diameter of low priority nodes. If the low priority level consists of a single node, then $D_L = 0$. For the star topology, and the *proxy* node set as the root, at most 3 messages are required per critical section.

5 Summary

This paper presented a prioritized token-based algorithm for distributed mutual exclusion. The algorithm imposes very little storage overhead on each node and in each message. Furthermore, the algorithm generalizes several existing token-based algorithms and shows how they can be extended for prioritized systems. Using the best topology and edge reversal, the algorithm attains comparable performance to a centralized mutual exclusion algorithm; that is, three messages per critical section entry. In the average case, the algorithm attains the best performance of any known algorithm.

References

[1] D. Agrawal and A. El Abbadi. An efficient solution to the distributed mutual exclusion problem. In *Proc. 8th ACM Symposium on Principles of Distributed Computing*, pages 193–200, 1989.

[2] G. Behrmann, A. David, K.G. Larsen, J. Håkansson, P. Pettersson, W. Yi, and M. Hendriks. UPPAAL 4.0. In *Proceedings of the 3rd International Conference on the Quantitative Evaluation of SysTems (QEST) 2006*, IEEE Computer Society, pages 125–126, 2006.

[3] D. Ginat, D.D. Sleator, and R.E. Tarjan. A tight amortized bound for path reversal. *Information Processing Letters*, 31:3–5, 1989.

[4] J.M. Helary, N. Plouzeau, and M. Raynal. A distributed algorithm for mutual exclusion in an arbitrary network. *The Computer Journal*, 31(4):289–295, 1988.

[5] L. Lamport. Time, clocks, and the ordering of events in a distributed system. *Communications of the ACM*, 21(7):558–565, 1978.

[6] M. Maekawa. A $\sqrt{N}$ algorithm for mutual exclusion in decentralized systems. *ACM Transactions on Computer Systems*, 3(2):145–159, 1985.

[7] F. Mueller. Prioritized token-based mutual exclusion for distributed systems. In *International Parallel and Processing Symposium (IPPS)*, pages 791–795, 1998.

[8] M. Naimi and M. Trehel. How to detect a failure and regenerate the token in the log(n) distributed algorithm for mutual exclusion. *Lecture Notes in Computer Science*, 312:155–166, 1987.

[9] M.L. Neilsen. A generalized token-based mutual exclusion algorithm for wireless networks. In *Proceedings of the 20th Int'l Conference on Parallel and Distributed Computing Systems (PDCS-2007), Las Vegas, Nevada, USA*, ISCA, 2007.

[10] M.L. Neilsen and M. Mizuno. A dag-based algorithm for distributed mutual exclusion. Technical Report TR-CS-89-12, Kansas State University, Manhattan, Kansas, 1989.

[11] M.L. Neilsen and M. Mizuno. A dag-based algorithm for distributed mutual exclusion. In *IEEE 11th International Conference on Distributed Computing Systems*, pages 354–360, 1991.

[12] K. Raymond. A tree-based algorithm for distributed mutual exclusion. *ACM Transactions on Computer Systems*, 7(1):61–77, 1989.

[13] M. Raynal. *Algorithms for Mutual Exclusion*. MIT Press, 1986.

[14] M. Raynal. A simple taxonomy for distributed mutual exclusion algorithms. Technical Report 560, INRIA, 78153 Le Chesnay Cedex, France, 1990.

[15] G. Ricart and A. K. Agrawala. An optimal algorithm for mutual exclusion in computer networks. *Communications of the ACM*, 24(1):9–17, 1981.

[16] B.A. Sanders. The information structure of distributed mutual exclusion algorithms. *ACM Transactions on Computer Systems*, 5(3):284–299, 1987.

[17] M. Singhal. A heuristically-aided algorithm for mutual exclusion in distributed systems. *IEEE Transactions on Computers*, 38(5):651–662, 1989.

[18] I. Suzuki and T. Kasami. A distributed mutual exclusion algorithm. *ACM Transactions on Computer Systems*, 3(4):344–349, 1985.

[19] M. Trehel and M. Naimi. A distributed algorithm for mutual exclusion based on data structures and fault tolerance. In *Proc. IEEE 6th International Conference on Computers and Communications*, pages 35–39, 1987.

A Parallel Implementation of the Modus Ponens Inference Rule in a DNA Strand-Displacement System

Jack K. Horner
P.O. Box 266
Los Alamos NM 87544 USA

PDPTA 2013

Abstract

Computation implemented in DNA reactions promises to advance high-performance computing (HPC) for at least three reasons. It (1) is inherently Amdahl-scalable by reactor-volume, (2) has a power/operations-per-second(OPS) ratio that is potentially orders of magnitude smaller than that of silicon circuits, and (3) can provide a natural access-interface to DNA-based high-density information storage. In order to serve as general-purpose computing regime, DNA computing will have to support Boolean operations. Here, I describe an implementation of the modus ponens inference rule (commonly used in Boolean logic) in a DNA strand-displacement (DSD) system.

Keywords: DNA computing, DNA strand displacement, modus ponens

1.0 Introduction

Computing implemented in DNA reactions promises to advance high-performance computing (HPC) for at least three reasons. It:

- Is inherently Amdahl-scalable ([6]; [7], p. 39) by reactor-volume
- Has a power/operations-per-second(OPS) ratio that is potentially orders of magnitude smaller than that of silicon circuits ([7], pp. 18-19; [8])
- Provides a natural access-interface to DNA-based high-density information storage ([2]).

DNA strand displacement

A variety of information-processing circuits, including a catalytic gate ([3], an implementation of which has been tested *in vitro*), have recently been implemented in DNA strand displacement (DSD) reactions. In a DSD reaction, portions of a strand of DNA in one reactant displace portions of a strand in another DNA reactant.

A DSD simulation system is described in [4] and [5]. Some examples of DNA molecules represented in the language defined in [5] follow. (A "stroke" (|) denotes the juxtaposition of multiple molecules.)

1 2 1 2 1 2 1 2 3 4 1 2 3 4 5

1:2 | <1 2> | [1 2] | [1 2]:[3 4] | [1 2]:3:[4 5]

Figure 1. Some examples of DNA molecules expressed in the language of [5].

In Figure 1, the notation 1:2 represents a lower strand of DNA, where the 3' end of the strand is on the left, denoted by an arrowhead. The strand is divided into *domains*, which correspond to short DNA sequences. In the leftmost element of Figure 1, the domains are represented by numbers 1 and 2, where each number represents a distinct domain.

In Figure 1, the red domain 1 represents a *toehold* domain, while the black domain 2 represents an ordinary *specificity* domain. Toehold domains are very short sequences, generally between 4 and 10 nucleotides in length, that enable one DNA strand to bind to another. Since toehold domains are short, two strands bound to one another will quickly unbind in the absence of further interaction along neighboring domains.

In Figure 1, the notation <1 2> represents an upper strand of DNA, where the 3' end of the strand is assumed to be on the right. The strand consists of two domains that are *complementary* to domains 1 and 2 of the leftmost element of Figure 1, where two domains are complementary if their respective sequences are Watson-Crick complementary. Two complementary strands, 1:2 and <1 2>, can hybridize along their complementary domains to form a double-stranded molecule, denoted by [1 2], as shown in the third element from the left in Figure 1. A molecule can also consist of multiple upper strands bound to a single lower strand. For example, [1 2]:[3 4] denotes a DNA molecule that consists of upper strands <1 2>and <3 4> bound to a single lower strand 1:2:3:4.

There can also be gaps between bound upper strands as in the molecule [1 2]:3:[4 5], where domain 3 of the lower strand is unoccupied (see rightmost element of Figure 1).

Bound upper strands can also overhang to the left or right, as shown in Figure 2.

Figure 2. Three examples of overhanging strands, expressed in the notation of [5].

In Figure 2, the molecule <1>[2 3]<4> consists of an upper strand<1 2 3 4> bound to a lower strand 2:3. The region[2 3] of the molecule is double-stranded, while <1>and <4> represent single-stranded regions overhanging to the left and right. The molecule [1]<2>:[3] consists of an upper strand <1 2> bound to a molecule1:[3], where the single-stranded region <2> is overhanging the double-stranded region [3]. Multiple overhanging strands can be bound simultaneously along different regions, as in the case of the molecule<1>[2 3]<4>:<5>[6 7]<8>, which represents two upper strands, <1 2 3 4> and <5 6 7 8>, bound along regions [2 3] and [6 7], respectively. Notice that the colon is used to separate the two bound upper strands.

A given strand can also be displaced by another strand as a result of binding, as shown in Figure 3.

<1 2> | 1:[2]<3>   [1]<2>:[2]<3>   [1 2] | <2 3>

Figure 3. An example of a strand displacement reaction in the notation of [5].

Although toehold domains are short enough to unbind rapidly in the absence of additional specificity domains, they are still long enough to greatly accelerate the initiation of strand displacement when additional specificity domains are present. In Figure 3, when the strand <1 2> becomes bound it initiates the displacement of its neighboring strand by a process of *branch migration*. Although this process involves a random walk of multiple elementary steps, these are relatively fast at experimental concentrations and can be omitted ([3]). This means that the unbinding reaction on toehold domain 1 in Figure 3 can be effectively ignored and the two consecutive reactions can be approximated by a single displacement reaction.

In general, the DNA molecules are assumed to have no additional secondary structure. This can be achieved by careful selection of appropriate DNA sequences ([3],[4]). In addition, DNA sequences of distinct domains are assumed to be sufficiently different that they do not interfere with each other. For further detail, see [4] and [5].

Modus ponens

Modus ponens, sometimes called the "rule of detachment"([9], p. 47), is an inference rule widely used in Boolean logic ([1]). It allows us to infer a proposition ψ from a conjunction of propositions of the form φ -> ψ and φ, where φ and ψ range over propositions and -> denotes Boolean implication ([1]). Implementing modus ponens in [4] requires mapping the elements of the rule (i.e., φ, φ -> ψ, and ψ) to elements of DNA circuits that are implementable in [4].

2.0 Method

Figure 4 shows a mapping of "φ" and " φ -> ψ" to the DSD strand-definition language of [5].

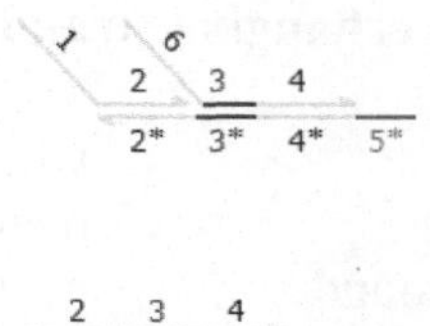

Figure 4. Mapping of φ and φ -> ψ to input species of [4]. The top species (the "substrate", in catalyst-gate nomenclature) represents the proposition φ -> ψ. The bottom species (the "fuel", in catalyst-gate nomenclature) represents the proposition φ.

Figure 5 shows the DSD script for the catalytic gate described in [3] (without the "reporter" molecules of [3]), implemented in the language described in [5], using the input descriptors shown in Figure 4.

The reaction product of interest is the sequence <1 2>, which represents ψ.

```
(*  DIRECTIVES AND DOMAIN-DEFINITION SEGMENT *)
directive duration 7000.0 points 1000  (* run sim for 7000 sec, save 1000 points *)
(* directive leak 1.0E-9,   default leakage rate /nM/s *)
(* directive tau 0.1126,  default merged rate /s *)
(* directive migrate 8000.0, default nucleotide migration rate /s *)
(* directive lengths 6 20, default toehold and normal domain lengths *)
(* directive tolerance 1.0E-6, default ODE tolerance for deterministic simulator *)
(* directive time s, default time units *)
(* directive concentration nM, default concentration units *)
directive plot <2 3^ 4>; <1>[2]:<6>[3^ 4]:5^*; <1 2> (* plot a subset of strands *)
directive scale 500.0 (* multiply concentrations, divide binding and leak rates *)
new 3@ 4.2E-4 , 4.0E-2 (* initialize *)
new 5@ 6.5E-4 , 4.0E-3 (* initialize *)


(* PROGRAM SEGMENT *)
( 13 * <2 3^ 4>
| 10 * <4 5^>
| 10 * <1>[2]:<6>[3^ 4]:5^**
)
```

Figure 5. DSD code used in this study (adapted from [4]).

The script shown in Figure 5 was executed as a "deterministic" system under [4] on a Dell Inspiron 545 with an Intel Core2 Quad CPU Q8200 clocked at 2.33 GHz, with 8.00 GB RAM, under *Windows Vista Home Premium/SP2.*

3.0 Results

Figure 6 shows the reaction graph produced by the method described in Section 2.0.

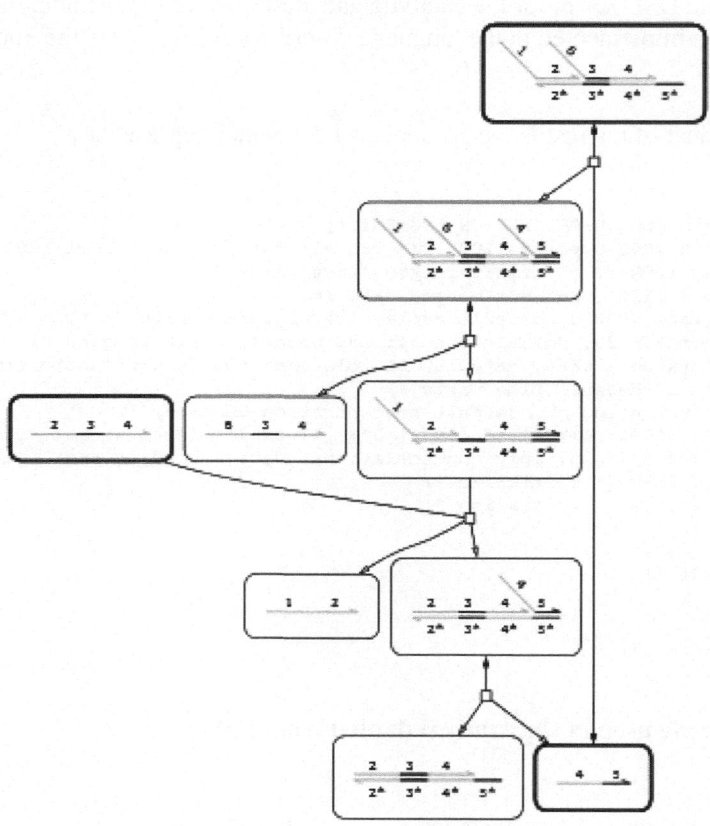

Figure 6. The reaction graph produced by the method described in Section 2.0. Rectangles with darker borders represent inputs; all other rectangles represent intermediates. Arrows represent reaction direction. The output of interest is the strand <1 2>, which represents ψ. ψ is "detached" by the system from the main reactant of the system, `<1>[2]:<6>[3^ 4]:5^*` (modus ponens is sometimes called the "rule of detachment"). Strand <4 5> is the catalyst of the system. (See Figure 7 for concrete realizations of the sequences in the diagram.)

Figure 7 shows a concrete DNA segment-description realization, generated by [4], of the species in Figure 6.

```
3^ --> (5') TATTCC (3')
5^ --> (5') GCTA (3')
1 --> (5') CCCTTTACATTACATAACAA (3')
2 --> (5') CCCAAAACAAAACAAAACAA (3')
4 --> (5') CCCTTTTCTAAACTAAACAA (3')
6 --> (5') CCCTTATCATATCAATACAA (3')
```

Figure 7. A concrete DNA segment-description realization of the DNA species in Figure 6.

Figure 8 shows part of the output of DSD simulation of modus ponens under the conditions described in Section 2.0.

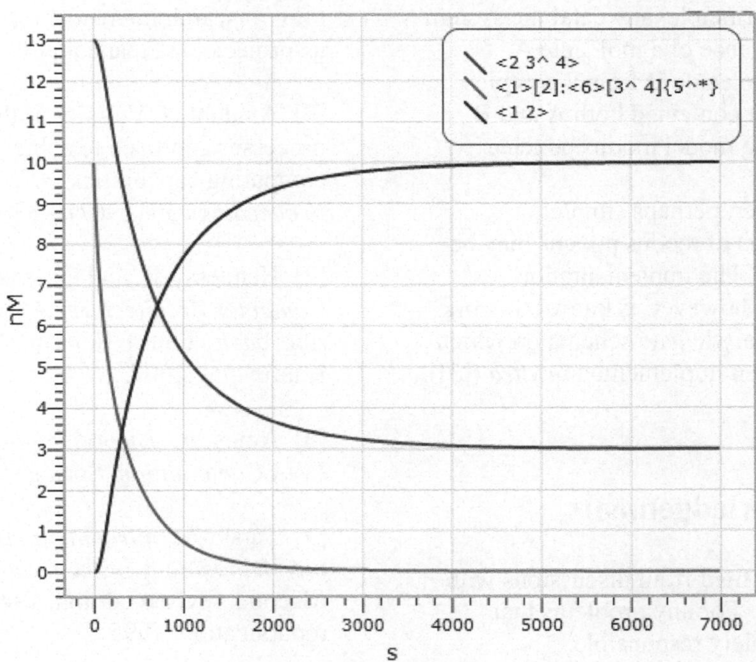

Figure 8. Output of the simulation described in Section 2.0. The green line represents the proposition φ -> ψ (the "substrate", in catalytic-gate nomenclature) . The red line represents φ (the "fuel", in catalytic-system nomenclature). The blue line represents the production of ψ (= " <1 2>") from modus ponens ("(φ and φ -> ψ) implies ψ "). The system is Amdahl-scalable by reactor-volume. In actual practice, a "reporter" species (typically, a dye) would be used to visualize the production of ψ.

Compilation of the system described in Section 2.0 took ~3 seconds. The subsequent simulation utilized ~25% of the CPU and ~0.5 GB memory on the platform described in Section 2.0, as measured on the system monitor, and executed in ~0.1 second.

4.0 Conclusions and discussion

The method described in Section 2.0 and the results described in Section 3.0 motivate several observations.:

1. Modus ponens can be implemented in a DSD system.

2. The implementation is Amdahl-scalable by reactor-volume.

3. The implementation shown here could be easily abstracted to a DSD *module* ([5]) which would hide the representation internals of the implementation.

4. In principle, any catalytic system that, in the presence of a molecule A, "detached" a molecule B from a complex molecule C that contained both A and B, could be used to model modus ponens.

5. Other, perhaps simpler, implementations of modus ponens may be possible in [4]. The implementation described here, however, is known to work because the catalytic gate schema on which it trades has been implemented *in vitro* ([3]).

5.0 Acknowledgements

This work benefited from discussions with Tony Pawlicki. For any problems that remain, I am solely responsible.

6.0 References

[1] Church A. *An Introduction to Mathematical Logic.* Volume I. Princeton. 1956.

[2] Goldman N, Bertone P, Chen S, Dessimoz C, LeProust EM, Sipos B, and Birney E. Towards practical, high-capacity, low-maintenance information storage in synthesized DNA. *Nature* 494 (7 February 2013), 77-80.

[3] Zhang DY, Turberfield, AJ, Yurke B, and Winfree E. Engineering entropy-driven reactions and networks catalyzed by DNA. *Science* 318 (2007). 1121–1125.

[4] Phillips A. The DNA strand displacement simulator, *DSD v0.14-20130214-28315.* Software is available for Windows (and other operating systems) at http://research.microsoft.com/en-us/projects/dna/. 2013.

[5] Lankin MR, Petersen R, and Phillips A. *Visual DSD user manual v0.14 beta.* http://research.microsoft.com/en-us/projects/dna/manual.pdf. 2012.

[6] Amdahl G. Validity of the single processor approach to achieving large-scale computing capabilities. *AFIPS Conference Proceedings* 30 (1967), 483-485.

[7] Hennessy JL and Patterson D. *Computer Architecture: A Quantitative Approach.* Fourth Edition. Morgan Kaufmann. 2007.

[8] Amos M. *Theoretical and Experimental DNA Computation*. Springer. 2005.

[9] Tarski A. *Introduction to Logic and to the Methodology of the Deductive Sciences* (Second, revised edition, 1946). Dover republication, 1995.

Hadoop-Collaborative Caching in Real Time HDFS

Meenakshi Shrivastava [1], **Dr. Hans-Peter Bischof** [2]
Computer Science, Rochester Institute of Technology, Rochester, NY, USA

Abstract—*Massive amounts of data is being produced in everyday activities hence it is necessary to store and analyze such data. Hadoop is a popular distributed system used to store this data and MapReduce is used for performing analysis on it. Detail study and experiments led to conclusion that MapReduce job's execution times can be lowered. A cost-effective mechanism known as collaborative caching has been proposed for efficient use of resources and system. This mechanism helps in improving the performance, reducing access latency and increasing the throughput. A new architecture called Hadoop-Collaborative Caching is proposed in order to lower the execution times. It incorporates collaborative caching, reference caching and Modified-ARC algorithm. Each of the DataNodes have their own dedicated Cache Manager that manages caching, replacement, collaborative caching and eviction. Cache is organized in to recent, frequent, recent history and frequent history. To evaluate, results obtained were compared with default configuration of Hadoop.*

Keywords: Hadoop Collaborative Caching, Distributed Computing, MapReduce

1. Introduction

Data is being generated at an enormous rate, due to online activities and use of resources related to computing. To access and handle such enormous amount of data spread, distributed systems is an efficient mechanism. Hadoop is a widely used distributed system, follows clustered approach, highly scalable and it allows massive amounts of data to be stored. Hadoop follows the master/slave architecture decoupling system metadata and application data where metadata is stored on dedicated server NameNode and application data on DataNodes. Over the years, Hadoop has gained importance because of its scalability, reliability, high throughput and performing analysis and large computations on these massive amounts of data. Currently, Hadoop is being used by all the leading industries like the Amazon, Google, Facebook, Yahoo etc. Hadoop's filesystem architecture and data computational paradigm has been inspired by Google File System and Google's MapReduce[3]. At Yahoo, there is a of span 25,000 servers, and stores 25 petabytes of application data, with the largest cluster being 3500 servers[11]. In a paper presented at Sigmod [2], describes how Facebook is using Hadoop in real time, with only few modifications made to it, it provides high throughput and low latency.

1.1 MapReduce

Hadoop uses MapReduce paradigm [20] to perform analysis, transformations and parallel computations on the data stored. MapReduce is a parallel processing framework which divides the input into smaller inputs and execute tasks on it simultaneously hence achieving higher performance[10]. But according to PACMan [7], the initial phase which is map phase in MapReduce involves reading raw data from the disk and this task is I/O intensive. According to recent summit by Cloudera in June 2012, Optimizing MapReduce Job Performance [4], explains that certain optimizations can be made in order to improve the processing of MapReduce task. Also in paper "Optimizing Hadoop for the cluster" by Christer [5], mentions that the default configuration is slow and optimizations are needed. In a paper, "The Performance of MapReduce: An In-depth Study" [6] clearly mentions that MapReduce is slow, the processing execution time can be improved by adding more nodes to the cluster, but that is not a cost effective solution. There were two observed facts after the initial analysis of MapReduce experiments; the data during the initial phase was being read from disk and there were more Rack-Local tasks scheduled.

1.2 New Approach

It is known that accessing data from cache is much faster as compared to disk access. Hence to lower the job execution time of MapReduce jobs and improve the overall cluster efficiency of Hadoop system, improvements and architectural changes were incorporated in Hadoop Distributed filesystem which led to new system, Hadoop-Collaborative Caching. The new approach followed in order to lower job execution times was *collaborative caching* on DataNode. Collaborative caching is one such mechanism in which the cache distributed over the clients or dedicated servers or storage devices form a single cache to serve the requests. This technique led to more data-local jobs. Not only local data was cached on DataNodes and served as an input to MapReduce jobs but information about data cached on remote caches was stored on DataNodes, introducing a new layer to hierarchy resulting in NameNode cache, DataNode's cache, Remote DataNode's cache and the disk. Caches of all the participating DataNode's machines taken together formed a single cache or global cache. NameNode is the central co-ordinator of this global cache, but allowing the decisions of remote caching to be taken by Cache Manager on DataNodes. New DataNode protocols have been introduced. New Approach allows efficient use of resources where instead of increasing the number of nodes, more slots can be added in order to improve performance.

Caching of data was made faster and easier by the reference caching technique. A HDFS block is composed of two files which is meta file and the block file. Meta file refers to checksum value of the data and block file refers to actual data. If these file references are cached, it helps in locating the meta files faster for checksum checks, faster caching of data from disk to memory since not much time is spent in searching for files when data stored is about petabytes. This mechanism provides an additional method of reducing the overall time.

Modified-ARC cache replacement policy was used in order to maximize cache hit ratio and to improve efficiency.

The organization of the paper is as follows; Section 2 explains the Related Work, Section 3 New Architecture, Section 4 Modified-ARC, Section 5 Data Flow between the different components of the newly proposed system, Section 6 Factors leading to improvement in the system, Section 7 Evaluations and Section 8 Concludes.

2. Related Work

According to PACMan, when multiple jobs are run in parallel, job's running time can be decreased only when all the inputs related to running a job are cached. So according to Dhruba[7] *et.al*, either cache all the inputs related to that particular job or do not cache the inputs at all. Caching only part of the inputs will not help in improving the performance. These massive distributed clustered systems have large memories and job execution performance can be improved if these memories can be utilized to the fullest. PACMan is a caching service that coordinates access to the distributed caches[7]. This service aims at minimizing total execution time of job by evicting those items whose inputs are not completely cached. For evicting the inputs which have been minimally used, LFU-F algorithm, LIFE sticky policy have been proposed. They define a new parameter wave-width of the job which refers to total tasks which can be executed in parallel at a time. They have used MapReduce and Dyrad as examples to illustrate their algorithm and hypothesis. According to them reading the raw input from filesystem is IO intensive and forms 79% of the phase[7]. They conducted experiments on Hadoop and observed improvement in job execution time. They emphasize on memory-locality tasks which is an important factor contributing to cluster efficiency.

Dhruba[7] *et.al* proposes an architecture called the PACMan which coordinates the caches globally and it takes care of two things which is support queries where block is cached and coordinating the cache replacement[7]. Its architecture includes a coordinator service and PACManClients are located on nodes where data lies. Blocks are cached on these clients. The coordinator includes the information regarding this block belonging to which file and wave-width of the file. This overall structure of the coordinator is used for scheduling tasks which are memory local, in implementing sticky policy[7] and to check on the incomplete files. If the data is not cached then it accesses disk. Also it emphasizes to schedule a data local job. For replacement policies they go for global cache replacement policies which are LIFE and LFU-F[7]. The overall job execution time is reduced attempting to schedule jobs of smaller-wave widths. This system does not take into account the remote caching.

The main aim defined in paper Dynamic Caching [16] is caching mechanism allowing concurrent access to data and proposes algorithms relating to locality of data which focuses on the decrease in the overall job completion time. For implementing Dynamic caching they are using Hadoop and their caching mechanism is based on Memcached[16] which are a set servers storing the mapping of block-id to datanode-ids. These servers also serve the remote cache requests. The caching of blocks is carried out on DataNodes.

The paper mentions about two different design architectures, First architecture defines; to serve the request of DataNode, simultaneous requests are sent to NameNode and Memcached servers. DataNode receives reply from both of them, but it checks if true from Memcache then access block from Memacache else access the block from disk whose location as indicated by NameNode. In second design architecture, again simultaneous request is sent to Memcache and NameNode, but NameNode does not reply back untill indicated by Memcache about unavailability of block where in such a case NameNode sends block locations to DataNode. The design includes prefetching where whenever request is seen by Memcache, neighbouring blocks are also looked up. If neighbouring blocks are missing then Memcache requests NameNode to look for replicas and if available, requests are sent to DataNode to cache blocks and Memcache updates it's locations. The caching system designed is not distributed and for lookups it is always required to contact the single set of Memcache servers. Also there incurs an extra delay with respect to second architecture when Memcache does not contain the blocks in cache.

3. Hadoop-Collaborative Caching: Architecture

Following section explains in detail the Hadoop-Collaborative Caching architecture; added functionalities to already existing components and newly added components. Fig.1, shows diagram of Hadoop-Collaborative Caching system architecture.

3.1 Cache Manager

Each of the DataNodes have their dedicated CacheManagers who have responsibilities of managing caches, lookup in local as well as global cache image upon request, replacement policy for cache and eviction policy for cache when cache is fully utilized. A buffer is maintained to cache the file references which are meta file and block file. Blocks in the cache will be replaced when the cache is fully utilized and eviction in either of the caches will take place in LRU manner. Cache is divided into recent, frequent, recent history and frequent history.

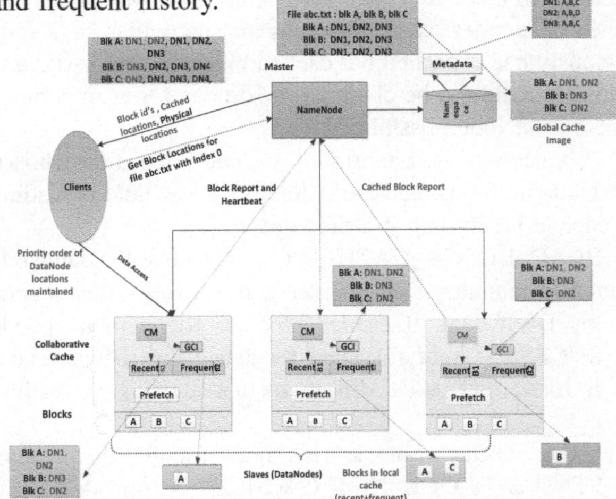

Fig. 1: Proposed Architecture

3.2 Global Cache Image

Global Cache image is a mapping of block to DataNode, denoting that this block is cached on which DataNodes in the cluster. This mapping is maintained by NameNode and copy of it is sent to all the DataNodes as a response to cache block report. Each of the DataNodes maintain a copy of Global Cache Image as well. Global Cache Image lookup is done by Cache Manager upon local cache miss.

3.3 NameNode

NameNode is the central co-ordinator for maintaining the Global Cache Image. It builds its global cache image when it obtains the cached block report from the DataNodes. As soon as it obtains its report, it updates the mapping of cachedblock to DataNode. Upon updation of the Global Cache Image, as a response to cached block report it sends a copy of Global Cache Image to the DataNode via DNA_UPDATE_GCI command.

3.4 DataNode

DataNode provides a cached block report of its local cache to NameNode after periodic interval. As a response to this report NameNode commands DataNode to update global cache image.

3.5 DFSClient

DFSClient receives set of caching DataNodes along with non caching DataNodes from NameNode as response to its request to read a particular file.

3.6 New DataNodeProtocols

These OP Codes have been introduced as part of the collaborative caching mechanism and as DataNode transfer protocol. The receipt of these OP Codes help in determining the next set of steps to be taken by DFSClient or DataNode.

- OP_READ_BLOCK_CACHED: To indicate that DFSClient is attempting to read the data from cache.
- OP_STATUS_BLOCK_CACHED_ELSEWHERE: DataNode sends this to DFSClient to signify that this block is cached on a different node.
- OP_STATUS_BLOCK_NOT_CACHED: DataNode sends this to DFSClient to signify that this block is not cached at all.
- DNA_UPDATE_GCI: This is the instruction sent by NameNode to DataNode in response to the cached block report.

4. Modified-ARC algorithm

The following section explains the Modified-ARC algorithm in detail. Fig 2 shows the diagram of Modified-ARC. A variant of this algorithm is implemented. Basic idea is to divide the caches into two different sections namely cached objects and history objects. Cached section contains the actual data and History section contains the references of evicted items. Hence the cached section is further divided into Recent Cache and its Recent History and Frequent Cache and its Frequent History. The size of recent and frequent together is fixed. The idea derived from actual ARC algorithm[9].

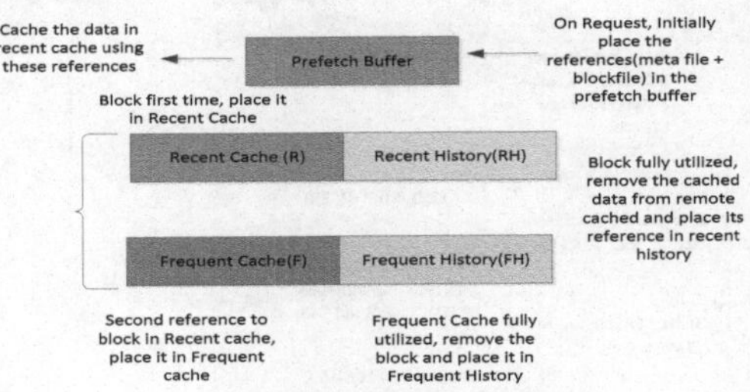

Fig. 2: Modified-ARC

- Recent Cache: A cache where the block seen for the first time is placed.
- Frequent Cache: A second reference to the same block will cause the block to be placed in this cache.

The basic idea behind is:

- Initially on a request for block, check for references in either of the history caches, if present then place their blocks in recent or frequent cache, else cache references and serve request from either of the history caches which helps in faster caching as well as locating the files for initial checks.
- If references are found in the recent history then it is used to cache the block and place it in recent cache. If block is found in recent cache, then place it in frequent

cache, hence hit in either of the history caches removes the references and places the corresponding block in either of the caches (recent or frequent). Caching of block involves caching metadata as well data.

- When either of the caches are fully utilized then block is evicted from recent or frequent cache but its reference is placed into its corresponding history. When either of the history caches are fully utilized causes the references to just drop out of the cache.

5. Data Flow

In the following section, detailed explanation is provided of interaction between the components DataNode, DFSClient and NameNode with respect to new functionalities implemented.

5.1 NameNode and DFSClient Data Flow

DFSClient requests NameNode for blocks locations depending on the file and offset. Upon the request, NameNode returns block's id and set of locations where these blocks are located along with replicated blocks locations. If the blocks are cached, then it returns set of caching DataNodes as well as non caching DataNodes. DFSClient tries to connect to best possible node by sorting in the order such that caching DataNodes are first in the list and then Non Caching DataNodes.

5.2 DFSClient and DataNode Data Flow

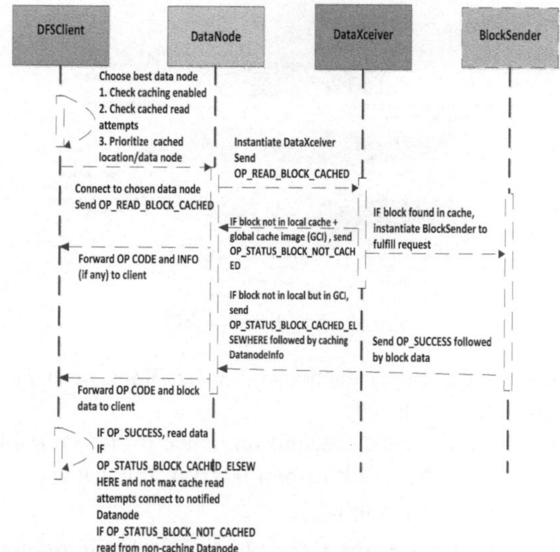

Fig. 3: DFSClient and DataNode Interaction Sequence Diagram

Fig3. shows the sequence diagram of data flow between DataNode and DFSClient. After obtaining locations of the blocks and their block ids from NameNode, DFSClient sorts them in the order such that caching DataNodes are first in the list. It checks for total cached read attempts, if maxed then connect directly to non caching DataNode. It checks if the DataNode it is trying to connect was previously declared dead. A dead DataNode is a node when the client tried to read earlier and after maxed attempts, the DFSClient failed to connect to DataNode. Similar to deadnodes are cached deadnodes which indicates that particular DataNode previously had it cached but cached block was removed and the block could not be obtained. It sorts and tries to connect to best DataNode possible.

A connection is established between the first chosen DataNode in the list and DFSClient. If DFSClient is reading the cached block then it writes opcode OP_READ_BLOCK_CACHED to the DataNode. DataNode in turn instantiates DataXceiver and forwards the opcode sent by DFSClient. If cached block is found then opcode OP_SUCESS is sent followed by data using BlockSender and is forwarded to DFSClient so that it can start reading data.

If the cached block is not found then send OP_STATUS_BLOCK_NOT_CACHED opcode or OP_STATUS_BLOCK_CACHED_ELSEWHERE to DFSClient. Opcode OP_STATUS_BLOCK_NOT_CACHED indicates no cached block can be found and opcode OP_STATUS_BLOCK_CACHED_ELSEWHERE indicates this block can be obtained in remote cache. This opcode is followed by the socket address of the DataNode to connect to. This is where collaborative caching helps, attempting to read from neighboring cache.

After receiving the opcode OP_STATUS_BLOCK_CACHED_ELSEWHERE, it again checks for cache read attempts, if not maxed out then try reading from cache specified by other DataNode, if caching DataNode is available. If opcode OP_READ, then read the data from non caching DataNode. If the read is for the first time, DataNode indicates CacheManager to cache the block's metadata as well data.

5.3 NameNode and DataNode Data Flow

DataNode sends NameNode cached block report about its locally cached blocks after a certain configured interval. This is sent in the form of CachedBlocksCommand. Accordingly Global Cache Image in the namesystem is updated. As a response to this command NameNode sends DataNode instruction to updates its Global Cache Image with the help of DNA_UPDATE_GCI command.

6. Improvements in Hadoop

The proposal to implement collaborative caching and integrating with Hadoop works. It proved to be successful resulting in a considerable lower job execution times which led to improvement and enhancement in the overall system.

Reading data from cache is always faster as compared to reading data from the disk. On the DataNode side, the data was being streamed from disk hence the overall performance of a MapReduce job was considerably slow and had a overall high I/O rate. An attempt has been made to cache this data and stream from cache. Moreover, collaborative caching allows us to stream the data from remote caches which proves to be an added advantage. In Hadoop, it was also observed that caching references added to the overall improvement of the system performance. There are three main reasons that contribute to improvement in the system.

a) Remote Memory Caching: Caching of input data at the DataNode level helps in improving job execution time. A distributed cache structure is followed where each of the DataNodes have their own caches maintained by Cache Managers. We are utilizing the memories of all the participating DataNodes thus reducing the no. of disk accesses. If the data is not found in requested node's cache but found in other node's cache, so instead of serving from disk we are serving from cache and which saves us execution time. This approach not only reduces job execution time, but also helps us to utilize the resources efficiently. To improve the performance, instead of adding more nodes, we can focus on adding more slots causing more map and reduce tasks to be scheduled at once parallely and with the technique of collaborative caching, data is available in cache causing in overall lowering of the job execution timing.

b) More data-local Tasks: The second reason is, whenever JobClient submits the Job, JobTracker tries to schedule the job on the same node as the input. More the data-local tasks, better the execution time. So as soon as TaskTracker contacts JobTracker either with slot available or no, if the slot is available then schedule a task. If the input required for the task resides on a different node, then it is rack-local and in such a case the data is streamed from other node to the node where the task is scheduled and then the task is carried out. This results in added extra time to complete the task resulting in increasing the overall job execution time. But with caching, the tasks scheduled get completed earlier and slots become available faster which provides room for tasks to be scheduled as data-local, hence improving the overall execution time. Also in terms of collaborative caching, the data is streamed from neighbouring node's cache, although there is n/w I/O involved, but minimal and moreover, it is from cache hence it reduces the overall time.

c) Reference Caching: The third reason was, initial request served by the references which were cached during the request contributed to the improvement as well. This is because, these references help the system to obtain the data into cache faster since disk lookup with large number of files stored incurs extra time and with reference caching, this lookup is saved. Hence, the effect of caching was visible the first time itself. When first time a request is encountered and a cache check is made for the request, if data is not found in cache causes the data to be cached with the help of reference caching. The main advantage here is that with the initial request, only certain number of bytes are read and not the actual data. The same request for the same block comes again and this time it is already cached, so the data is streamed from cache. But with first time requests, there incurs extra time to cache the block although difference in timings due to reference caching can be observed during initial execution. The second time, a request for the same block and with data available and streamed from cache, a considerable decrease in the timing can be observed.

With the Modified-ARC cache replacement algorithm, better cache hit ratios were observed, a factor leading to overall improvement.

d) Collaborative Caching Works: The overall improvement is also result of the caching algorithm. DFSClient always attempts to sort so as to have caching DataNode first in the list indicates that attempt is made to always stream from cache. Moreover, if DFSClient cannot find the block in the local cache of this DataNode, it can connect to next location provided by DataNode for streaming from cache.

7. Evaluation

This is a preliminary work. The experiments were conducted with limited number of nodes and hardware. Experiments were performed on default configuration of Hadoop and compared with results obtained on execution of jobs on Hadoop-Collaborative Caching.

The following section explains the configurable parameters used, metrics used and the different experiments conducted in order to test the new functionality and improvements.

7.1 Configurable Parameters

Following are the list configurable parameters used while conducting experiments:

- Local Cache Size: To calculate the cache hit and miss rates, recent cache size and frequent cache capacity, parameters were configured from 6 - 24 blocks depending on the block size.
- Block Size: To perform experiments on cluster, the block sizes used 32 MB, 64 MB, 128 MB.
- Minimum Block Size For Caching: Block size >1 MB
- History Cache Size: This size was configured to 100.
- Max Read Cached Attempts: This number is set to 2.
- Caching Enable: To enable or disable caching.
- Cache Block Report Interval: Configured as 10 secs.

7.2 Metrics

Following section explains the metrics used while conducting the experiments:

- **Average Block Access Time**: Hadoop has large block size (default 64MB), it does not read all the data at once, instead it streams the data in the form of packets

and then sends over the network to recipient. Hence for Hadoop the total average block access time is
Total Average Block Access Time = Time to read from disk or cache + Time to transmit the data over the network.

- **Cache Hit / Miss Rate**: It is used to measure how many times a block was read from the cache. The higher the number, the better it is. Cache hit rate is calculated :
  Hit Rate (%) : Total no. hits / Total number of requests for blocks.
  Total Hits (%) : Total no. hits in local cache(recent + frequent) and global cache
- **Local Cache Size**: Local Cache size is a combination of Recent cache size and Frequent cache size.
  Local Cache Size: Recent Cache Size + Frequent Cache Size.
- **Max Read Cached Attempts**: This number indicates the maximum number of times we connect to DataNode to read from cache before we finally read from the disk.
- **Cache Block Report**: It is a report send by all the DataNodes regarding information about their local caches to NameNode. This helps NameNode construct the Global Cache Image.

7.3 Experiments and Results

The experiments described below uses WordCount application, in order to test the new improvements incorporated, The WordCount application counts the frequency of words for a given input. Inbuilt *"time"* command of linux was used to compare the results. The cluster was restarted when files of greater data size was run due to memory limitations.

e) MapReduce: Following explains in detail of how the MapReduce experiment was conducted, results obtained and explanation about the observations made.

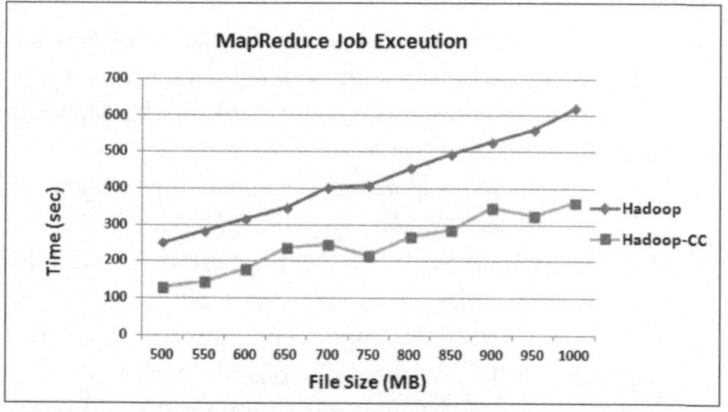

Fig. 4: MapReduce Job Execution (Block Size 64 MB)

Experiment Conducted: For MapReduce experiments, MapReduce Job was run on datasets ranging from 500 MB - 1 GB on default as well Hadoop-Collaborative Caching in cluster mode. It was conducted for block sizes 32MB, 64MB and 128 MB. Cluster was restarted for Hadoop-Collaborative Caching when MapReduce Job was run for data files greater than 650MB, due to memory limitations. Fig 4 depicts graph for MapReduce Job Execution for block size 64MB.

The results varies depending on the distribution of blocks across the cluster and the way the jobs are scheduled across the cluster

Observations and Results: It can be observed that Hadoop-Collaborative Caching results obtained showed a considerable improvement. From Fig.4 graph, it can be seen that with increase in file size, the map reduce timings have decreased. It can also be observed that there are drop in timings when file size is 750 MB and 950 MB. Also it is observed that with increase in file size, difference in the job execution time of default Hadoop and Hadoop-Collaborative Caching increases. Hence collaborative caching shows a significant improvement in MapReduce job execution times.

Explanation: This is due to the fact that streaming from cache is faster as compared to from disk which is combined with serving requests from references. With increase in file size, no. of blocks that make up the block increases and if the blocks are found in cache (local or remote) instead of accessing from disk, the overall execution time decreases resulting in a larger gap between Hadoop and Hadoop-Collaborative Caching. The another major factor leading to decrease in overall job execution time is job being executed as data-local tasks. Job can be executed as data-local and rack-local. When jobs are executed on the same node as the input, it is data-local task whereas when the job is executed on node other than the input it is rack-local job. Execution of data-local jobs are faster as compared to rack-local. In Rack-Local jobs, when job is executed data is streamed from other node hence increasing the overall timing. So more the rack-local jobs, more time required to complete the job. The reason for execution of rack-local jobs is; as number of slots are fixed, for slots are being used by TaskTrackers, if JobTracker receives a request from TaskTracker and it has an empty slot, an attempt is been made to schedule a data-local task. But if that is not possible then rack-local task is scheduled. In case of collaborative caching because of the raw data in memory, jobs are executed and completed earlier and hence slots become available earlier leading to more of data-local tasks. The next factor which acts as an advantage is during the first run with Hadoop-Collaborative Caching implemented, the caching effect is seen. This is because Hadoop initially reads 516 bytes and then the whole data. When the initial bytes are read, with the help of reference caching block is cached and when the data is to be read, it is read from cache. Although there incurs extra time when the block is cached for the first time and successive requests for the same blocks results in higher decrease in timings. A drop in timings from file size 900 MB to 950 MB, which is due to fact the way jobs are scheduled and the data distribution of the blocks when the input files are loaded into HDFS. The overall decrease in timings was also due to reference caching and Modified-ARC algorithm.

There seemed to be overall high n/w I/O so caching results can be improved to a larger extent with higher network speed of 1 Gbps.With increase in file size, the MapReduce job execution time decreases.More data-local tasks lead to better execution time

f) Multiple Clients Execution: Following explains in detail of how the Multiple Client Execution experiment was conducted, results obtained and explanation about the observed results.

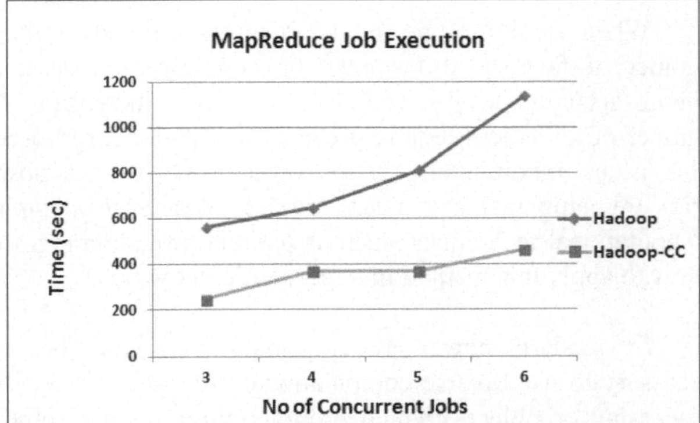

Fig. 5: Multiple Job Execution (File Size 500 MB)

Experiment: This experiment was conducted to run jobs parallely such that each of them are run in background. The maximum jobs which could be run was 6 due to memory limitations. Fig 5 shows graph for Multiple Job Execution time for multiple clients. This experiment was carried out for file size 500 MB, where multiple clients are trying to run MapReduce task for file size 500 MB.

Observations and Results: Above graph shows simultaneous clients submitting the job. It can be clearly observed that Hadoop-Collaborative Caching shows better results as compared to default Hadoop configuration. It can also be observed that execution time of Hadoop-Collaborative Caching is consistently low.

Explanation: The reason for only having 6 max jobs in parallel is due to infrastructure and memory limitations. The machines could not launch more than 6 JVMs limiting the experiment to run only 6 jobs at a time. The execution time is low for Hadoop-Collaborative Caching due to the reason that data is available in cache causes more data-local tasks which causes overall decrease in the job execution time.

8. Conclusions

Our next steps would be to expand this preliminary set of experiments to larger cluster. A new architecture has been proposed named as Hadoop-Collaborative Caching.The architecture aimed at improving the overall MapReduce job execution time by lowering it and increasing the efficiency of the system. This was done through the mechanism of collaborative caching where data is served from local caches as well as remote caching. This was combined with caching references and Modified-ARC algorithm. NameNode's response to client was modified to send cached locations as well to the non cached locations of DataNode. NameNode maintains the Global Cache Image which is image of location of all the cached blocks on the cluster. This is mapping of cached block to DataNodes indicating this block is cached on these DataNodes. On the DataNode side, each of them have their dedicated Cache Managers which have responsibilities of caching data, replacement policy which is Modified-ARC and caching of references. Caching of the references also improved the overall system execution. The cache was divided into four sections recent, recent history, frequent and frequent history instead of maintaining just a single cache. This mechanism helped in better caching replacement. Hence overall, the job execution time decreased by a considerable amount, efficiency of the system increased and there were more data-local jobs scheduled.

References

[1] http://hadoop.apache.org/docs/r0.20.2/hdfs_design.html
[2] Dhruba Borthakur, et.al "Apache Hadoop Goes Realtime at FacebookâĂİ, Proceedings of the 2011 International conference on Management of Data, SIGMOD'11. ACM, pp. 1071-1080.
[3] http://en.wikipedia.org/wiki/Apache_Hadoop
[4] http://www.slideshare.net/cloudera/mr-perf
[5] Christer A. Hansen. "Optimizing Hadoop for the cluster". University of TromsΦ, Norway
[6] Dawei Jiang, Beng Chin Ooi, Lei Shi Sai Wu, "The Performance of MapReduce: An In-depth Study", Proceedings of the VLDB Endowment, Vol. 3, No. 1, 36th International Conference on Very Large Data Bases, September 13-17, 2010, Singapore.
[7] G. Ananthanarayanan, A. Ghodsi, A.Wang, D.Borthakur, S.Kandula and I. Stoica. "PACMan: Coordinated memory caching for parallel jobs", In NSDI, 2012.
[8] David Leong, "Collaborative Object Caching for Heterogenous OSD Clusters, Proceedings of the 2007 Computer Science and IT Education Conference, pp.425-436.
[9] Megiddo, N. et.al "Outperforming LRU with an Adaptive Replacement Cache", Computer, IEEE, April 2004, pp.58-65
[10] Tom White, Hadoop: The Definitive Guide, O'Reilly Media, Inc., June 2009.
[11] Konstantin Shvachko, Hairong Kuan, Sanjay Radia and Robert Chansler, The Hadoop Distributed File System Mass Storage Systems and Technologies (MSST), IEEE 26th Symposium, May 2010 , pp. 1-10.
[12] http://kazman.shidler.hawaii.edu/ArchDoc.html
[13] http://developer.yahoo.com/hadoop/tutorial/module4.html
[14] http://www.gutenberg.org/
[15] ftp://ftp.uni-duisburg.de/linux/filesys/Lustre/whitepaper.pdf
[16] "Gurmeet Singh", "Puneet Chandra", "Rashid Tahir", "A Dynamic Caching Mechanism for Hadoop using Memcached", https://wiki.engr.illinois.edu/download/attachments/197297260/ClouData-1st.pdf?version=1&modificationDate=1330747624000
[17] http://hadoop.apache.org/releases.html
[18] Eric Anderson et.al. "New Algorithms for File System Cooperative Caching", Modeling, Analysis & Simulation of Computer and Telecommunication Systems (MASCOTS), 2010 IEEE International Symposium, pp.437-440.
[19] http://bradhedlund.com/2011/09/10/understanding-hadoop-clusters-and-the-network/
[20] Jeffrey Dean and Sanjay Ghemawat,: Simplified Data Processing on Large Clusters," Google, 2004.
[21] http://hadoop.apache.org/docs/r0.20.2/quickstart.html#Local
[22] http://www.aosabook.org/en/hdfs.html

Stochastic Assessment of Voltage Sags by Applying a Parallelized Method

C. Ceja-Espinosa, A. Ramos-Paz, E. Espinosa-Juárez
Faculty of Electrical Engineering, Universidad Michoacana de San Nicolás de Hidalgo
Morelia, México

Abstract - *In this paper, the parallelization of the Fault Position Method for the stochastic assessment of voltage sags is presented. The parallelization of this stochastic method is made by using multi-thread programming in an algorithm written in C programming language, including functions defined by the POSIX threads header and library in order to perform the parallel calculations desired. All tests were performed using the GNU/Linux operating system. The proposed parallelized method is applied to two electrical systems: a small 5-bus test system and the IEEE 57-bus test system, in order to demonstrate its proper operation. A comparative analysis of the parallelized Fault Position Method with respect to the traditional method is presented, and the reduction in computational time is shown.*

Keywords: Voltage sags; fault position method; parallel processing; multi-threading

1 Introduction

A voltage sag is defined as a decrease in RMS voltage at the power frequency for durations from 0.5 cycles to 1 minute, usually reported as the remaining voltage [1]. Short circuits are the main cause of their appearance in electrical systems, but they can also be caused by the starting of large motors, overloads or the disconnection of capacitor banks [1][2].

A voltage sag is a phenomenon of power quality that significantly affects energy users, especially in the industrial sector, where considerable economic losses are originated by this disturbance [2][3]. Furthermore, within the scope of smart grids, an important goal is to design electrical systems that operate in a more automated, secure and efficient way, providing power quality in the range of need [4][5].

In recent decades, several methods have been proposed for evaluating a power system in terms of voltage sags [6][10]. One of the most widely used methods is the well-known Fault Position Method (FPM) [7][11], which allows to estimate the occurrence of sags based on statistical data of faults in the elements and parameters of the electrical network under study.

When applying the Fault Position Method, a large number of fault positions must be considered in order to obtain accurate results [10][12], however, increasing the number of faults will require greater computational resources. This is an important aspect to consider when large power grids are being analyzed. Therefore, it is of interest to employ computational techniques, such as parallel programming, that allow to apply this method in a more efficient way.

In modern power system analysis, it has become necessary to use diverse computational tools such as parallel processing or object-oriented programming, amongst others. Parallel processing is defined as a method of data processing in which two or more processing elements perform calculations to solve a problem working simultaneously together. Parallel processing has been applied in the solution of several problems in the field of power system analysis and industrial applications. For example, in [13], an algorithm for fault detection in DC motor drivers using parallel programming is presented; in [14], parallel processing is employed in the study of electromagnetic transients; in [15], a method for the harmonic power flow analysis is developed; in [16], this technique is applied to the fast steady-state solution of power systems. Recently, fine-grained parallel processing techniques have been applied to the fast steady-state solution of large-scale electric power systems [17]. In previous works, parallel processing has allowed to reduce the computational time required to perform a study, which, in consequence, makes it possible to perform power system analyses in less time and improve the system operation, thus reducing economic losses associated with electrical faults.

In this paper, the Fault Position Method for the stochastic assessment of voltage sags in electrical power systems is implemented employing parallel processing techniques based on multi-thread programming. The proposed method is applied to IEEE test systems in order to demonstrate its performance

2 Parallelized Fault Position Method

In order to illustrate the procedure to parallelize the Fault Position Method, a brief description of the method is presented first, and then the steps for its parallelization are exposed.

2.1 Fault Position Method Basis

The Fault Position Method is based on the classic short circuit calculation, combined with data of fault probability in nodes and lines, in order to estimate the occurrence of sags in a given period of time. The procedure followed to apply this method is described next [7][11].

Consider the generic system with n buses shown in Fig. 1. When a fault occurs at a generic bus i of the electrical system, according to the classic short circuit calculation, the impedance matrix of the system, Z_{bus}, is of order ($n \times n$), and the voltage at bus m can be calculated by [18]

$$V_m = V_m^{pf} - Z_{mi} I_i \tag{1}$$

where:

V_m^{pf} is the pre-fault voltage at bus m;

Z_{mi} is the transfer bus impedance between busbar m of the system and the faulted bus i;

I_i is the fault-current phasor at bus i that can be calculated as

$$I_i = \frac{V_i^{pf}}{Z_{ii}} \tag{2}$$

where:

V_i^{pf} is the pre-fault voltage at bus i;

Z_{ii} is the transfer bus impedance of the faulted bus i.

Then,

$$V_m = V_m^{pf} - \frac{Z_{mi}}{Z_{ii}} V_i^{pf} \tag{3}$$

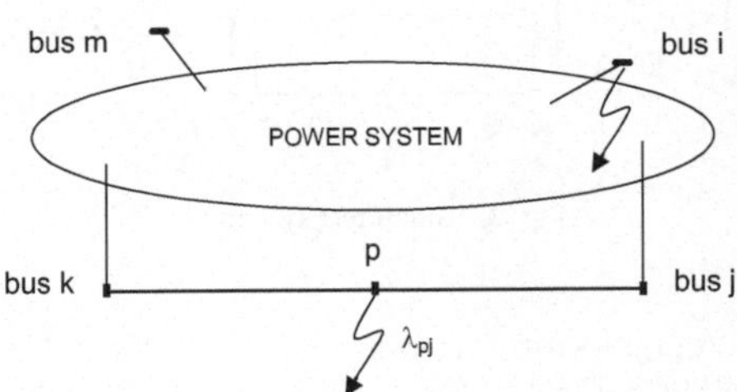

Fig. 1. Electrical system

In order to estimate the frequency of voltage sags, short circuit calculations must be performed throughout the system, i.e., the magnitudes of voltage sag due to faults at each bus of the system are obtained, considering all fault positions, both at lines and buses.

For the calculation of voltage magnitudes due to line faults, fictitious buses along the lines must be considered. For example, in the generic system shown in Fig. 1, one fault position in the middle of the line connecting buses k and j is considered. Then, according to the classic short circuit calculation, the voltage at bus k can be calculated by

$$V_k = V_k^{pf} - \frac{Z_{kp}^*}{Z_{pp}^*} V_p^{pf} \tag{4}$$

where:

Z_{kp}^* is the modified transfer bus impedance between busbar k and the faulted bus p;

Z_{pp}^* is the modified transfer bus impedance of the faulted bus p.

It is important to notice that in equation (4) the order of the correspondent bus impedance matrix, Z^*_{bus}, is $((n+1)\times(n+1))$, due to the addition of the fictitious bus p.

Then, considering that the fault at the generic position p (real or fictitious bus) has an associated value of fault rate, λ_p (usually faults/year), the accumulated frequency of voltage sags for a magnitude threshold between V_{low} and V_{up}, at a generic bus k, can be calculated by [2][7]

$$P_k = \sum \lambda_p \; : \; V_{low} < V_p \le V_{up} \tag{5}$$

where:

P_k is the voltage sags probability at bus k (voltage sag/year)

2.2 Parallelization of the Method

From the previous description of the Fault Position Method, it is clear that in order to achieve an acceptable level of precision, a large number of fault positions must be included in the calculations. Furthermore, if a fictitious bus is added in each calculation, the dimension of the problem grows significantly when several fault positions in the electrical system are simultaneously analyzed.

For example, for the IEEE 57-bus test system that consists of 63 lines [19], if 10 fault positions are included in the lines, 687 fault calculations are required, with a (57×57) order impedance matrix, or a new (687×687) order impedance matrix must be created, which would include all the fault positions of the system (assuming fictitious buses). Obviously, when large systems are being analyzed, the computational requirements become a more relevant aspect, and it results interesting to apply techniques such as parallel processing in order to perform calculations more efficiently.

In the designed algorithm for the parallelization of the Fault Position Method, each processing element divides the line in a specified number of parts. Then, a fault position is set in each one of these parts and the bus admittance matrix is re-calculated for every part. As it was previously mentioned, the dimension of the admittance matrix for each calculation is $((n+1)(n+1)))$, due to the addition of the fictitious bus that represents the fault position. Once the bus admittance matrices are obtained, they must be inverted in order to find the impedance matrices and calculate the voltage magnitudes at buses for each assumed fault. Then, based upon these values, the probability of voltage sags occurrence in each bus will be obtained according to specific voltage ranges. To perform this task, parallel processing based on multi-threading was applied.

In multi-threading [20], multiple control threads can solve a large portioned problem; lightweight sub-processes executed within a process share code and data segments, but with their own program counter, machine registers and stack. Global and static variables are common to all threads.

The efficiency of the parallel algorithm is measured in terms of the time it takes to complete the calculations with one processing element in comparison to the time it takes to complete the calculations with p processing elements; this relation is known as *Speed-Up* (S) [21].

$$S = \frac{T_1}{T_p} \tag{6}$$

where:

T_1 is the execution time with one processing element;

T_p is the execution time with p processing elements.

Using this metric of performance ensures that the reduction of execution time is independent of the computer characteristics.

In this work, the parallelization algorithm was written in C programming language, including functions defined by the POSIX threads header and library in order to perform the parallel calculations desired. All tests were performed using the GNU/Linux operating system, in particular the Xubuntu 12.10 distribution, and using an Intel (R) Xeon (R) CPU ES40S with two quad-core processors running at 2.0 GHz.

3 Case Studies

Two case studies are presented, which allow to verify the operation and efficiency of the method implemented using multi-thread programming.

3.1 Studies in a small test system

In order to analyze in detail the performance of the proposed method, a 5-bus test network (Fig. 2) is adopted. Impedances of the network elements are indicated in Fig. 2 in per-unit values. In this example, uniform distribution of faults along the transmission lines has been assumed. Balanced three-phase faults have been considered with the following statistical rates of faults/year for the different lines: line 2–4, λ=16; line 2–5, λ=8; and line 4–5, λ=4.

In order to demonstrate the performance of the proposed parallelized Fault Position Method, the results are compared to the results obtained from the application of an analytical method [10], in which the accuracy does not depend on discrete values, as is the case of the Fault Position Method.

In Table 1, the voltage sags per year calculated using the parallelized Fault Position Method, considering different number of fault positions, are presented. It can be clearly seen that as the number of fault positions considered increases, the obtained result is closer to the analytical solution. The results obtained using a small number of fault positions are significantly different to the analytical solution, however, when a large number of fault positions is considered, there is no appreciable difference between the results yielded by the Fault Position Method and the analytical method. A similar behavior would be observed when this calculation is made for the rest of the buses.

In Table 2, the speedup results using the proposed technique for different number of fault positions are shown. The efficiency of the parallel algorithm is more evident when the number of fault positions increases. The maximum speedup factor in this case is 2.984 (columns S in Table 2), which means that the calculations are performed almost three times faster than they would be if a sequential algorithm was used.

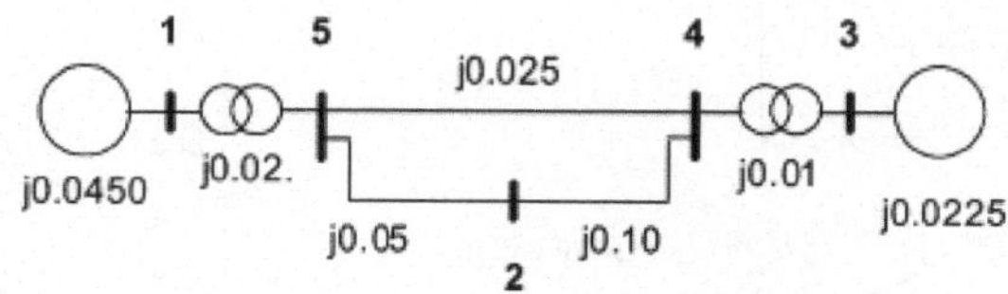

Fig. 2. Small test system

TABLE 1. VOLTAGE SAGS/YEAR AT BUS 2 USING THE FAULT POSITION METHOD WITH DIFFERENT NUMBER OF FAULT POSITIONS

Voltage sag range	Analytical method	Fault position method (voltage sags/year)				
		Fault positions				
		1	50	100	1000	10000
0.0<V≤0.1	4.74	0.0	4.64	4.64	4.74	4.74
0.1<V≤0.2	10.37	8.0	10.24	10.48	10.45	10.46
0.2<V≤0.3	7.12	4.0	7.04	7.12	7.12	7.12
0.3<V≤0.4	5.77	16.0	6.08	5.76	5.77	5.77

TABLE 2. SPEEDUP OF THE PARALLEL SOLUTION OF THE 5-BUS TEST CASE USING THREADS AND DIFFERENT NUMBER OF FAULT POSITIONS

	100 faults	**1,000 faults**	**10,000 faults**	**100,000 faults**	**1,000,000 faults**
Threads	**S**	**S**	**S**	**S**	**S**
1	1.000	1.000	1.000	1.000	1.000
2	1.588	1.404	1.499	1.493	1.506
3	1.588	2.314	2.837	2.946	2.989
4	1.500	2.403	2.870	2.938	2.984

3.2 Studies in the IEEE-57 buses test system

The IEEE 57-bus test system consists of 57 buses (see Fig. 3) which are interconnected by means of 63 lines, 15 transformers and 7 generating units [15]. Balanced three-phase faults have been considered and a fault rate of 1.0 for all lines; fault rates at buses have been neglected.

Fig. 4 shows the results of voltage sags for the voltage range from 0.5 to 0.6 p.u. when different number of fault positions at lines are considered. In order to visualize the differences more clearly, graphs are shown for 1, 10 and 100 fault positions. It is observed that as one increases the number of fault positions, results tend to values that would be obtained without the discretization of fault positions. Similarly, Fig. 5 shows the results for the voltage sags range of 0.6 to 0.7, and once again it can be observed that the results with 10 positions are closer to the obtained with 100 positions than the obtained with one fault position.

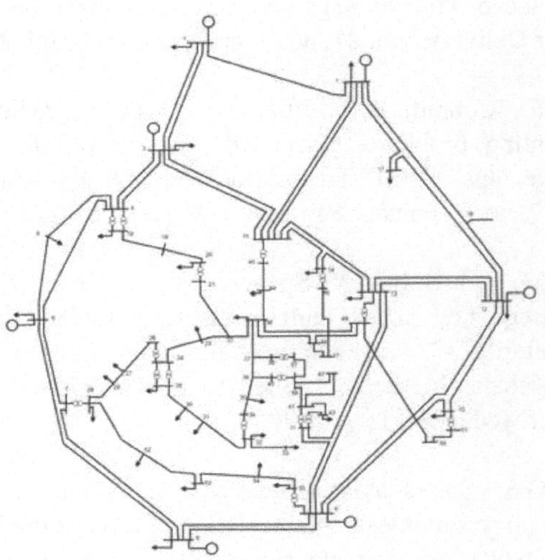

Fig. 3. IEEE-57 buses test system

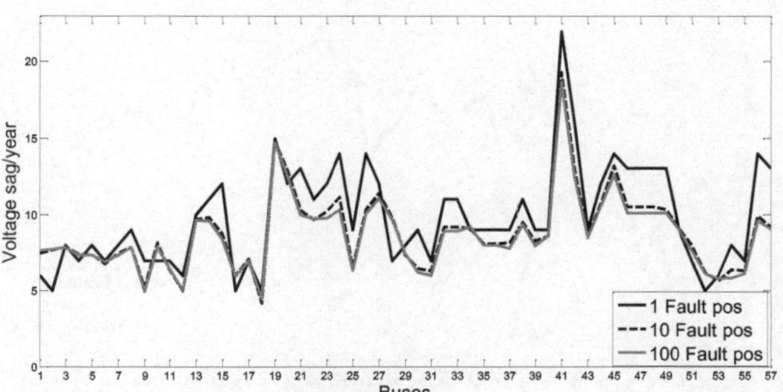

Fig. 4. Voltage sags/year considering a voltage sags range from 0.6 to 0.7 p.u.

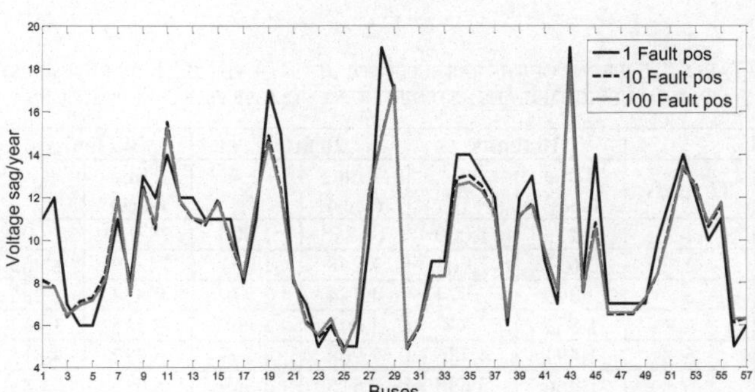

Fig. 5. Voltage sags/year considering a voltage sags range from 0.6 to 0.8 p.u.

In Fig. 6 and Fig. 7, the number of voltage sags/year for a voltage range up to 0.7 p.u. and 0.8 p.u. are shown, respectively. It can be seen that the differences are smaller for the more widely voltage sags range.

In Table 3, the execution times considering different number of fault positions for the 57-bus system are shown. It can be seen that when the number of threads used to perform parallel calculations is increased, a significant reduction in execution time is achieved. The speedup obtained with 8 threads and 40 faults indicates that the problem is solved approximately 7.8 times faster than when a single processing element is used.

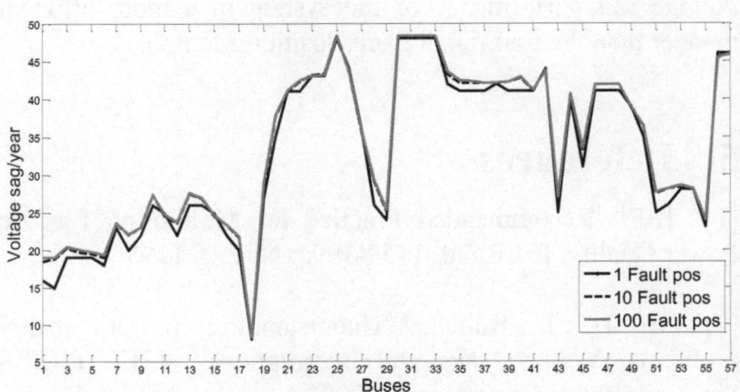

Fig. 6. Voltage sags/year considering a voltage sags range from 0.1 to 0.7 p.u.

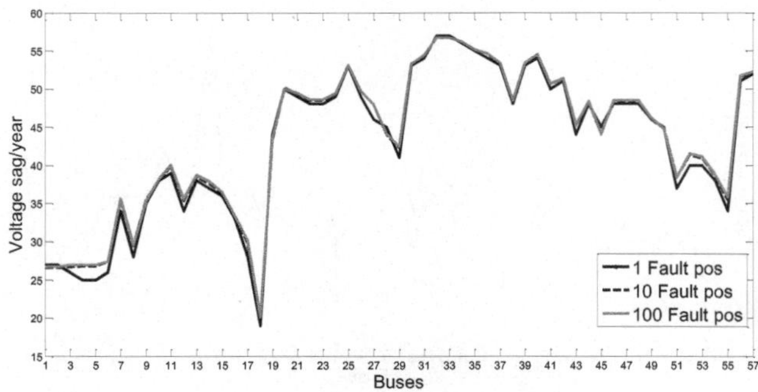

Fig. 7. Voltage sags/year considering a voltage sags range from 0.1 to 0.8 p.u.

TABLE 3. SPEEDUP OF THE PARALLEL SOLUTION OF THE IEEE-57 BUSES TEST SYSTEM USING THREADS AND DIFFERENT NUMBER OF FAULT POSITIONS

Threads	10 faults		20 faults		40 faults	
	Time (secs)	S	Time (secs)	S	Time (secs)	S
1	7.136	1.000	14.258	1.000	28.520	1.000
2	3.637	1.961	7.268	1.961	14.528	1.963
3	2.399	2.974	4.784	2.979	9.554	2.985
4	1.831	3.897	3.647	3.909	7.285	3.914
5	1.491	4.786	2.968	4.803	5.922	4.815
6	1.266	5.635	2.515	5.669	5.015	5.686
7	1.041	6.852	2.062	6.914	4.112	6.935
8	0.941	7.583	1.847	7.718	3.666	7.779

4 Conclusions

In this paper, parallel processing techniques have been applied to the parallelization of the Fault Position Method for the stochastic assessment of voltage sags. The applied parallelization is based on multi-thread programming, which allows to divide the task of short circuit calculations for the assumed faults in the electrical system.

The proposed parallelized method was applied to a small 5-bus test system and to the IEEE 57-bus test system. In the case studies performed, it is demonstrated that the proposed parallelized method can be a helpful tool to estimate the voltage sag performance of the system in a more efficient manner than the traditional Fault Position Method.

5 References

[1] IEEE Recommended Practice for Monitoring Electric Power Quality, IEEE Std. 1159-1995, Nov. 2, 1195

[2] M. H. J. Bollen, "Understanding power quality problems. Voltage sags and interruptions", IEEE PRESS Series on Power Engineering, 2000.

[3] J. Mason, R. Targosz, "European power quality survey report", Leonardo Energy Initiative, Nov. 2008. Available in: http://www.leonardo-energy.org/ european-power-quality-survey-report

[4] A. F. Vojdani, "Smart Integration", IEEE Power and Energy Magazine, IEEE, vol. 6, Issue 6, pp. 71-79.

[5] United States Department of Energy, "2010 Smart Grid System Report", U. S. Department of Energy, February 2012.

[6] M. H. J. Bollen, "Method of critical distances for stochastic assessment of voltage sags", IEEE Proc. Generation, Transmission and Distribution, vol. 145, no. 1, pp. 70-76, Jan. 1998.

[7] M. R. Qader, M. H. J. Bollen, "Stochastic prediction of voltage sags in a large transmission system", IEEE Trans. Industry Application, vol. 35, no. 1, pp. 152-162, Jan. 1999.

[8] Y. S. Lim, G. Strbac, "Analytical approach to probabilistic prediction of voltage sags on transmission networks", IEE Proc. Generation, Transmission and Distribution, vol. 149, no. 1, pp. 7-14, Jan. 2002.

[9] S. Quaia, F. Tosato, "A method for analytical voltage sags prediction", IEEE Bologna Power Tech 2003, Jun. 2003.

[10] E. Espinosa-Juárez, A. Hernández., "An analytical approach for stochastic assessment of balanced and unbalanced voltage sags in large systems", IEEE Trans. Power Delivery, vol. 21, no. 3, pp. 1493-1500, Jul. 2006.

[11] L. Conrad, K. Little, C. Grigg, "Predicting and preventing problems associated with remote fault-clearing voltage dips", IEEE Transactions on Industry Applications, vol. 27, no. 1, January/February 1991, pp, 167-172.

[12] M. H. J. Bollen, M. Speychal, K. Lindén, "Estimation of dip frequency from fault statistics-including three-phase characteristics", Proceedings of the International Conference Probabilistic Methods Applied to Power Systems, PMAPS 2006, Sweden, 11-15 June 2006.

[13] G.S. Stavrakakis, C. Lefas, A. Pouliezos, "Parallel processing computer implementation of a real time DC motor drive fault detection algorithm", IEE Proceedings Electric Power Applications, Vol. 137, No. 5 September 1990, pp 309-313.

[14] K. Werler, H. Glavitsch, "Computation of transients by parallel processing", IEEE Transactions on Power Delivery, Vol. 8, No. 3, July 1993.

[15] Z.A. Mariños, J.L.R. Pereira, Jr. Carneiro, "Fast harmonic power flow calculation using parallel processing",

IEE Proc.-Gener. Transm. Distrib., Vol. 141, No. 1 January 1994, pp 27-32.

[16] N. Garcia, A. Medina, "Swift time domain solution of electric systems including SVSs". IEEE Transactions on Power Delivery, Vol. 18, No. 3, July 2003, pp 921-927.

[17] O.A. Rico-Hernández, A. Ramos-Paz, "Analysis of electrical networks using fine-grained techniques of parallel processing based on OpenMP", Proceedings of the 2011 8th International Conference on Electrical Engineering Computing Science and Automatic Control (CCE).

[18] J. J. Grainger, W. D. Stevenson, “Power system analysis”, Ed. McGraw-Hill, Inc., U.S.A., 1994.

[19] R. Christie, "Power Flow Test Cases, 57 Bus Power Flow Test Case", University of Washington, College of Engineering, Electrical Engineering, May 1993. Available: http://www.ee.washington.edu/research/pstca/.

[20] S. Kleiman, B. Smaalders, D. Stein, D. Shah, "Writing multithreading code in solaris", Thirty-Seventh IEEE Computer Society International Conference, 1992.

[21] I. Foster, "Designing and building parallel programs", Addison Wesley, 1994

Large scale 3D shape retrieval by exploiting multi-core and GPU

M. BENJELLOUN[1], E.W. DADI[2], and E.M. DAOUDI[2]
[1]University of Mons, Faculty of Engineering. Dept of Computer Science
Mons, BELGIUM
[2]University of Mohammed First, Faculty of Sciences, LaRi Laboratory,
Oujda, Morocco

Abstract - *this paper addresses the problem of 3D shape retrieval in large databases of 3D objects (large retrieval). While this problem is emerging and interesting as the size of 3D object databases grows rapidly, the main two issues the community has to focus on are: computational efficiency of 3D object retrieval and the quality of retrieved results. In this work we deal with the first consideration, namely the computational efficiency of 3D object retrieval by exploiting new implementations based on parallel computing by exploiting multi-core and GPU architectures. Experimental results, show that the large scale retrieval can be achieved using the multi-core environment.*

Keywords: 3D Content-based Shape Retrieval, Large Scale Retrieval, GPU, multi-core architecture, CMBOF method, OpenMP

1 Introduction

Currently, there are an increasing number of 3D objects on the web, leading to large databases, thanks to recent digitizing and modeling technologies. The need of efficient methods for 3D shape-content based retrieval, in order to ease navigation into related large databases, and also to structure, organize and manage this new multimedia type of data, has become an active topic in various research communities such as computer vision, computer graphics, mechanical CAD, and pattern recognition. The 3D shape retrieval is the processing of retrieving visual similar objects to given 3D object query.

Various 3D shape retrieval methods have been proposed in the literature [3,4,5,6,7]. All recent methods are based on the shape descriptors; that consists in designing an efficient canonical characterization of the objects. This characterization is referred as a descriptor or a signature. Since the descriptor serves as a key in the search process, it is a critical kernel with a strong influence on the searching performances (i.e. computational efficiency and relevance of the results). Designing an efficient canonical characterization of the objects was become a major challenge in 3D objects indexation. A good 3D shape retrieval method must satisfy at least the two following conditions simultaneously [3]:

- The relevance and the quality of retrieval results: the first 3D objects returned by the method must be the most similar to the query.
- Computational efficiency of 3D object retrieval: the retrieval results should be fast.

Most existing methods do not satisfy the above conditions simultaneously. Moreover, for the large database, the retrieval process needs more computational time which does not permit the large scale retrieval. In order to achieve faster retrieval of 3D object, we propose in this work, new implementations based on parallel computing by exploiting multi-core and GPU architectures. For the tests, we use the CMBOF method proposed by Lian et al. [8], since it gives the best result comparing to many other methods in particular the view based methods [9,10,11,12].

Generally, the retrieval process is performed into two essentials stages: indexation and shape matching. Our contribution in this paper is to study the problem of retrieval in large database in particular the stage of matching, since this stage needs more computational times regarding to the size of 3D object databases which grows rapidly.

The rest of the paper is organized as follows. In section 2 we give a brief description of the CMBOF method. The parallelization on multi-core is presented in section 3. We conclude the paper in section 4.

2 Description of the CMBOF method

The CM-BOF (Clock Matching Bag-Of-Features) is a 3D retrieval method, proposed by Lian et al [8], this method gives the best result comparing to many other methods in particular the view based methods [9,10,11,12].

The two essential stages of the 3D shape retrieval are: indexation and shape matching. In the following we give a brief description of the two stages of the CMBOF method.

2.1 Shape indexing

The indexation is the process for computing the descriptor of a given 3D object. It is based on the following steps:

- *Normalization and alignment*: 3D objects are given in arbitrary position, orientation and scale. So, a step of normalization and alignment of the 3D shape is necessary in order to assure the invariance of affine transformations (scaling, translation rotation and reflection). To compare two 3D objects using multi-view methods, these objects must have the same length, orientation and position. Actually there is no efficient method of normalization and alignment which satisfies at the same time the following constraints: rotation invariance, best alignment and computational time.
- *Multi-view rendering*: in this step, a set of depth-buffer views (2D images) are uniformly captured around the 3D object. CMBOF method uses vertices of a given unit geodesic sphere which is obtained by subdividing the unit regular octahedron. The number of views to be captured is 6, 18, 66 or 258. Lian et al [8] showed that 66 is the best number of views.
- *SIFT feature extraction:* a 3D object can be approximately represented by a set of depth-buffer views. In the CMBOF method, each view is described as a word Histogram (descriptor of the view) using SIFT (Scale Invariant Feature Transform) algorithm [13]. This algorithm is used to extract salient local features from each 2D view. In this case, a 3D object is characterized by several descriptors depending on the number of the views captured around this object instead one descriptor as proposed in other multi-view methods [9,10,11,12].
- *Vector quantization and histogram generation:* Each SIFT feature extracted from 2D view is quantized as a vector or visual word (descriptor) by using a global visual codebook. The quantized local features are accumulated into a histogram which becomes the feature vector (descriptor) of the corresponding 2D view.

2.2 Shape matching

To retrieve visual similar 3D objects to a given 3D object-query, the descriptor of the query is compared with the descriptors of objects in the database. Instead of completely solving the problem of normalization and alignment, Lian et al [8] are proposed the Clock Matching approach. The basic idea of this approach is to consider 24 matching pairs when comparing two 3D Objects, by placing one object in the original orientation while the second one may appears in 24 different poses. The dissimilarity between the two 3D objects is measured by the minimum distance of their all (24) possible matching pairs. After the query is compared with each object in the database, the obtained distances are sorted according to query; the top k results returned should be the most similar to the query.

3 Parallelization of the retrieval process

Current machines offer microprocessors composed of multiple cores (processors) and Graphical Processing Units (GPU). The major challenge is to exploit efficiently the potential of these architectures at their maximum performance. The aim of this work is to propose new implementations based on parallel computing to achieve faster retrieval of 3D object and therefore allows the large scale retrieval (the retrieval in large databases) by exploiting the potential of GPU and multi-core architectures. Recall that the retrieval process, using the CMBOF method, is performed into the following two essential phases that are performed online:

- Indexation of the 3D query-object: computing the descriptor of the query shape
- Shape matching: comparing the descriptor of the query-object with the descriptor of each 3D objects of the database.

Note that a few works have been proposed in the literature to implement the 3D shape retrieval under HPC environments. These works are partial, since they only concern indexation phase (particularly the SIFT Quantization [1,2]) and not the shape matching phase. On the other hand, several works have been proposed in the literature based on sequential solutions to allow the large scale of 3D shape retrieval [14,15].

Experimental are performed as follow:

- Tests on GPU (Graphics Card Units) are performed on GeForce GT610, 2048 MB of global memory, L2 Cache size 6,6 MB.
- For the GPU programming we have used CUDA5.0.
- Tests on multi-core are performed on a Dell PowerEdge R910 Server Intel® Xeon® Processor E7-4850 2GHz of 10 cores, 32GB RAM.
- For multi-core programming we have used OpenMP
- For the 3D-object data base, we have used Princeton 3D Shape Benchmark database [17] composed of 1800 - 3D Objects. In order to make tests in large database, we have increased the size of the data base by duplication of the 3D-objects.
- To capture 66 views around a 3D object, we have used the executable provided by Lian [8].

3.1 Indexing phase

To compute the descriptor of a given 3D object, the CMBOF method [8] proposes to describe the 3D-object by several word histograms (descriptors) where each descriptor corresponds to a 2D view (2D image) captured around the shape of this object. To compute the descriptor of a given 2D view, the following steps are performed:

- Extraction of the SIFT salient local features from this 2D view.
- Vector quantization and histogram generation.

For the first step, the extraction of SIFT salient local features using SIFT algorithm executed on CPU is very time consuming; especially if it is necessary to extract SIFT features from several 2D views as in case of CM-BOF method.

In this work, we extracted the local features of each 2D view using the SIFT-GPU version proposed by Changchang Wu [18], since it gives a higher computing performance compared to the CPU version [16]. For 66 views, the SIFT is performed in 1,8s on GPU compared to 10,8s on CPU.

3.2 Shape matching phase

In this phase, the descriptor of the query is compared with descriptors of each 3D object belonging to the database. Note that the descriptors of objects in the database are computed offline.

Sequentially shape matching in a large database is time consuming. The advantage of using multi-core is to compare simultaneously the query-object with p objects; where p is the number of cores. After the comparison of the query with each 3D object in the database is completed, the obtained distances will be sorted.

Assume that the database is composed of m 3D objects. To exploit the potential of the multi-core architecture at their maximum performance and improve the load balancing between different cores we use a dynamic data distribution as follows:

- Each core deals with an initial workload (a number k of objects with k≤m/p). The remaining block of objects will be shared between all cores.
- All cores execute simultaneously the comparison process between the query object with their own objects.
- As soon as a processor (core) completes its work, it takes one objects from the shared block (the remaining objects). This process is repeated as long as it remains untreated objects.

Figure 1 presents the evolution of the execution time of the shape matching process by various cores using the clause "dynamic schedule" of OpenMP. Tests are performed on 3D-objects of a database composed of 10800 3D-objects. Thus the Figure 1 states that, the execution time is significantly reduced in proportion to the number of cores.

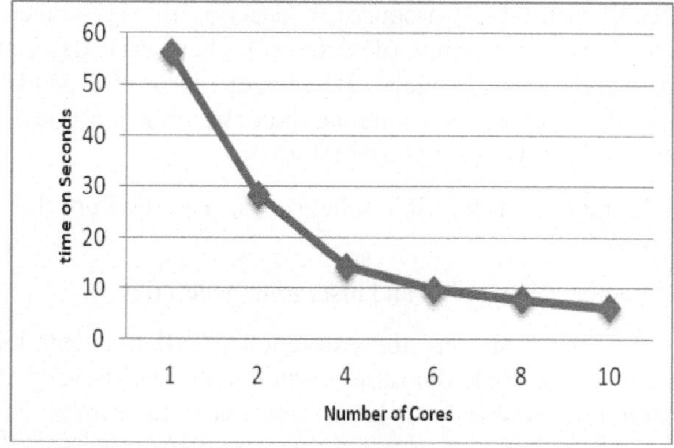

Figure 1 . Execution time for the shape matching process

In Figure 2, we report the results of the measured speed up (sequential_time/parallel_time) of the shape matching process compared to the ideal one. The obtained speed (up to 90%) shows that the proposed implementation is scalable, which means that; if we increase the number of cores, the parallel time remains close to the sequential time divided by the number of cores.

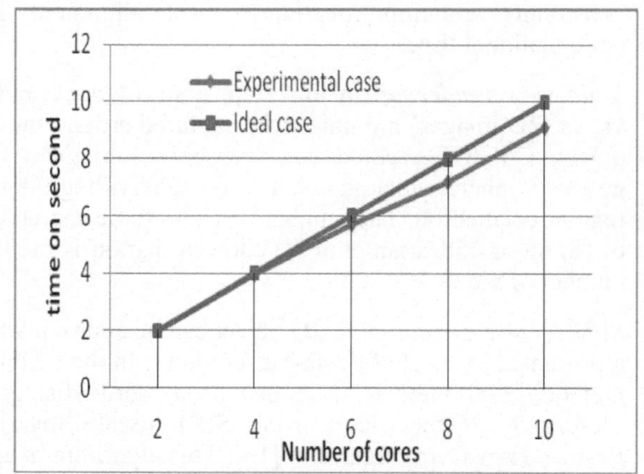

Figure 2 . Mesured speed up compared to the ideal one

In Figure 3, we measure the efficiency (the percentage of the using processor performance when increasing the number of cores)

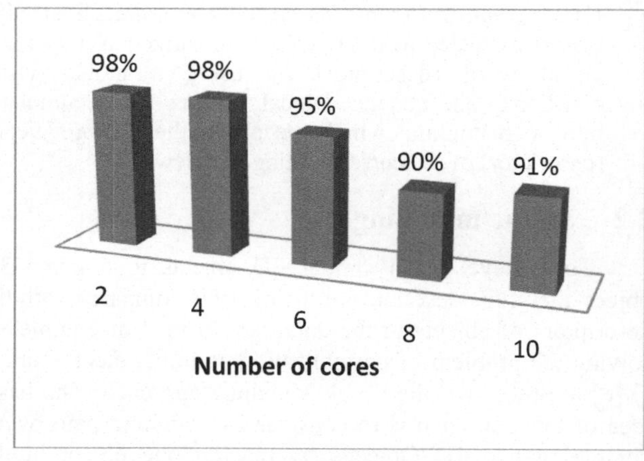

Figure 3 . Efficiency

In Figure 4, we compare the execution time of the matching process for different sizes of databases. In this test we report the evolution of the parallel time on 10 cores versus sequential time. The results show that the size of the database does not affect the speed up. If we use large databases on p cores, the parallel time remains close to the sequential time divided by p. We conclude that the large scale can be achieved by using a great number of cores.

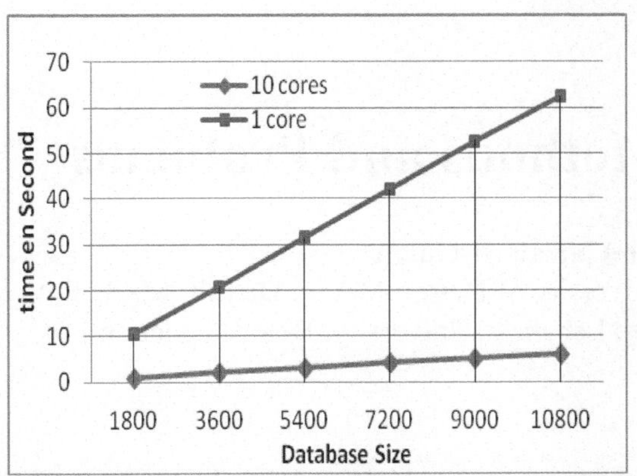

Figure 4 . Execution time of the retrieval process on databases with different sizes

4 Conclusion

In this paper we are interested by the computational efficiency of 3D objects retrieval. We have proposed new implementations of the retrieval process based on parallel computing by exploiting the multi-core environment and GPU accelerators. The proposed implementations, for the matching process, are independent of the 3D object algorithm. So that, for our tests, we have used the CMBOF method proposed by Lian et al. [8], since it gives the best results compared to many other methods, proposed in the literature, in particular the view based methods.

First, we have compared the SIFT algorithm both on CPU and GPU. For the version on GPU, we have used the algorithm proposed in [18].

Then, we have proposed parallel implementations on multi-core environment. The experimental results show that the execution time is significantly reduced as the number of cores grows. On the other hand, for fixed number of cores, the execution time grows linearly (almost linear) as the size of the database grows. We conclude that the large scale can be achieved using parallel computing.

5 Acknowledgment

We thank TNAC team "Théorie des Nombres et Applications en Cryptographie" for the use of their machine Dell PowerEdge R910 Server

6 References

[1]. Ryutarou Ohbuchi, Takahiko Furuya, "Accelerating Bag-of-Features SIFT Algorithm for 3D Model Retrieval", SAMT09

[2].Quansheng Kuang, and Lei Zhao, "A Practical GPU Based KNN Algorithm", Proceedings of the Second Symposium International Computer Science and Computational Technology(ISCSCT '09) , Huangshan, P. R. China, , pp. 151-155, 26-28,Dec. 2009

[3].J.W.H. Tangelder and R.C. Veltkamp, "A survey of content based 3D shape retrieval methods," Multimedia Tools and Applications, vol. 39, no. 3, pp. 441–471, Sept. 2008.

[4].Shilane P, Kazhdan M, Min P, Funkhouser T, "The princeton shape benchmark". In: Proc. shape modeling international 2004, pp 157–166

[5].T. Zaharia and F. Preteux, "3D versus 2D/3D shape descriptors: A comparative study," in SPIE Conf. on Image Processing: Algorithms and Systems III - IS & T/ SPIE Symposium on Electronic Imaging, Science and Technology '03, San Jose, CA, Jan. 2004, vol. 5298

[6].B. Bustos, D. A. Keim, T. Schreck, and D. Vranic, "An experimental comparison of feature-based 3D retrieval methods," in 2nd Int. Symp. on 3D Data Processing, Visualization, and Transmission (3DPVT'04), Thessaloniki, Greece, Sept. 2004.

[7].A. Del Bimbo and P. Pala, "Content-based retrieval of 3D models," ACM Trans. Multimedia Com

[8].Zhouhui Lian, AfzalGodil, Xianfang Sun: "Visual Similarity based 3D Shape Retrieval", IEEE International Conference on Shape Modeling and Applications (SMI) 2010

[9].Ding-Yun Chen, Xiao-Pei Tian, Yu-TeShen et Ming Ouhyoung :"On visual similarity based 3d model retrieval". In EUROGRAPHICS, Granada, Spain, sep 2003.

[10]. R. Ohbuchi, K. Osada, T. Furuya, T. Banno, "Salient Local Visual Features for Shape Based 3D Model Retrieval", Proc. IEEE International Conference on Shape Modeling and Applications (SMI'08), Stony Brook University, June 4 - 6, 2008.

[11]. P. Daras and A. Axenopoulos, "A 3D shape retrieval framework supporting multimodal queries", Int'l Journal of Computer Vision (IJCV).

[12]. M. Chaouch and A. Verroust-Blondet, "A new descriptor for 2D depth image indexing and 3D model retrieval," in Proc. ICIP'07,vol. 6, 2007, pp. 373–376.

[13]. D.G. Lowe, "Distinctive Image Features from Scale-Invariant Keypoints", Int'l Journal of Computer Vision, 60(2), November 2004.

[14]. El Wardani Dadi , El Mostafa Daoudi, Claude Tadonki, "Fast 3D shape retrieval method for classified databases",IEEE International Conference on Complex Systems (ICCS) 2012

[15]. Remco C. Veltkamp, Geert-Jan Giezeman, Hannah Bast, Thomas Baumbach, Takahiko Furuya, Joachim Giesen, AfzalGodil, Zhouhui Lian, RyutarouOhbuchi, WaqarSaleem, SHREC'10 Track: Large Scale Retrieval, Eurographics Workshop on 3D Object Retrieval (2010)

[16]. A. Vedaldi, SIFT++ A lightweight C++ implementation of SIFT, http://vision.ucla.edu/~vedaldi/code/siftpp/siftpp.html

[17]. P. Shilane, P. Min, M. Kazhdan, and T. Funkhouser, "The Princeton shape benchmark," in Shape Modeling and Applications Conference, SMI'2004, Genova, Italy, June 2004, IEEE, pp. 167–178

[18]. A GPU Implementation of Scale Invariant Feature Transform (SIFT) http://cs.unc.edu/~ccwu/siftgpu

Multi Sensor Data Fusion, Methods and Problems

Rawa Adla[1], Youssef Bazzi[2], and Nizar Al-Holou[1]
[1]Department of Electrical and Computer Engineering, University of Detroit Mercy, Detroit, MI, U.S.A
[2]Department of Electrical and Computer Engineering, Lebanese University, Beirut, Lebanon

Abstract - *Sensors, which monitor the surrounding environment in order to enhance our decisions, play a major role in our lives and contribute to our actions. A single sensor, however, is not capable of providing enough information; therefore, multiple sensors have to be integrated in a way to perform the additional task of interpretation, which may be more helpful and informative than what can be observed using a single sensor. Since the nature of sensor's functional characteristics can lead to output that contains erroneous measurement readings due to noise, measurement errors, and delays, multiple sensors are needed to confirm the certainty of desired actions. For sensors to work properly, a computational system is required in order to fuse sensor data in a process called multi-sensor-data fusion.*

This paper presents an overview of multi-sensor-data fusion, using two techniques (Bayes and Dempster-Shafer), with highlights of the techniques' shortcomings.

Keywords: sensor fusion; Bayes' theory; Dempster-Shafer; fusion model.

1 Introduction

Sensor-data fusion refers to the integration of data from multiple sensors of identical or different technical characteristics. The merits of the sensor fusion methods are to provide a better estimate of the feature of interest and to provide a result represented by hypothesis that is more accurate than would be obtained when using a single sensor. There are many problems considered when designing a system with a single sensor [1], such as loss of data when a sensor failure occurs, individual sensors providing data only from its own field of view, the frequency of measurements being limited to the time needed for a sensor to process its data, which is limited in accuracy due to the precision of the sensing system of the sensor, and the uncertainty in sensor measurement about objects which have been detected.

In order to enhance the certainty measure of the observed data, a multi-sensor-data fusion system is required. Countless benefits can be derived from using sensor-data fusion methods, depending on the system and the application nature, since each system expects at least one of the following features to exist [2][3]: redundancy, which enables the whole system to be active even when a sensor failure or breakdown channel occurs; improved coverage area, which therefore makes complementary data available; increased confidence in the results and the certainty of information; enhancement of spatial resolution; extended temporal coverage; and improvement in the detection rate of objects.

In the past few decades, sensor-data fusion has been researched and has appended developments for many fields such as science, technology, and engineering. In order to build a multi-sensor-data fusion system, deep understanding of the application characteristics is required. This can help in choosing the suitable data-fusion architecture, and in setting the data transmission facets. Then, determining the optimal fusion technique and acquiring a reliable algorithm for estimation and prediction are required [4].

This paper has been organized as follows: Section II presents types of sensors, and section III defines the levels of data fusion. In section IV the architecture of fusion has been proposed and an overview of multi-sensor fusion models is presented in section V. In Section VI we discuss two methods of combining data which are (Bayes' and Theory of Evidence). The paper concludes with an evaluation of these two fusion techniques and a declaration of their shortcomings.

2 Types of Sensors

There are two types of sensors: active and passive [5]. In active sensors, the output is generated as a result of stimulation that causes an alteration in the electrical amplitude. This type of sensor requires a power source for excitation and data security because it uses a direct transfer of data. Such examples: sonar, radar, or an ultra-wide band sensor. Alternatively, passive sensors do not require an electrical power source to work; they generate a voltage output using the temperature of the energy they are sensing. Also, passive sensor-data is considered more secure than active sensor-data. As an example of such sensors, a camera senses the amount of light it receives from the environment, and converts it into voltage levels. The variations in these voltages are stored as different pixel values in the computer.

Each of these types of sensors can be further sub-divided depending on whether the targets identify themselves or not; that is, whether they are cooperative or uncooperative sensors [5].

3 Sensor-Data Fusion Levels

In general, the process of sensor-data fusion can be categorized into three levels: low, intermediate, and high-level [4].

- Low-level: Also referred to as raw-data fusion. Raw-data is fused from multi sensors of the same type to generate a new raw data set which is more annotative than the original raw-data, as collected by sensors.
- Intermediate-level: This level of fusion also called feature fusion. It combines different features into a feature map, which is usually used for detection of objects.
- High-level: This level of fusion, known as decision fusion, requires a fusion method to be applied, such as the statistical or fuzzy logic method, to compute a hypothesis value representing the decision.

4 Fusion Architecture

Three different multi-sensor-data fusion architectures exist: centralized, pre-processed, and hybrid [6] [7].

- Centralized fusion: This architecture is employed when sensors of the same type are selected. The fusion process combines raw data from all sensors in a central processor. This process requires a time synchronization of all sensors' data. The decision resulting from this type of fusion is based on the amount of data collected by sensors. The advantage of centralizing fusion is secured data, and there is no data loss in the preprocessing. On the other hand, centralizing fusion requires sending all the collected data to the central processor, which is not acceptable in some applications.
- Pre-processed fusion: known as distributed fusion. Used for sensors of the same or different types. In this architecture, the central processor is relieved from preprocessing the raw data from the individual sensors.
- Hybrid fusion: This fusion architecture involves a mix of centralized and pre-processed fusion schemes. In practice, this is the best set-up of fusion architecture.

5 Fusion Models

There are several fusion models to consider when designing a multi-sensor-data fusion system. They will be reviewed in this section.

5.1 Joint Directors of Laboratories- JDL Model:

The JDL model was proposed by the US. Department of Defense (DoD) in 1986 [8]. The JDL model consists of: five levels of data processing, as follows [8]: Level 0 is Source Preprocessing, which determines the time, type, and identity of the collected data. Level 1 is Object Refinement, a level that combines information received from Level 0, in order to generate a representation of individual objects. Level 2 is a Situation Refinement, which defines the relationship between objects and detected targets and incorporates environmental information and observations. Level 2 is Threat Refinement, in which inferences are constructed about the target to have a solid base for decisions and actions. These inferences are based on a priori information and prediction about the next state. Level 4 is a Processing, which consists of three processes: monitoring data fusion efficiency, defining the missing information needed to enhance multi-level data fusion, and allocating sensors in order to accomplish the aim of the fusion process. At the same time, the JDL model has a database management system responsible for controlling data fusion processes, and a bus for interconnection between levels [3] [8].

5.2 Waterfall Model

This model assigns the priority of processing to the lower levels first. The fusion process is based on six levels of processing [9]; these levels can be matched to the JDL model levels: The first two levels, Sensing and Signal Processing, are similar to the first level in the JDL model (Level 0). The next two levels, Levels 3 and 4; are Feature Extraction and Pattern Processing, and these levels relate to Level 1 of the JDL model. Level 5 is a Situation Assessment that can be matched to Level 2 in the JDL model. Level 6 is Decision Making that is equivalent to the Threat Refinement level in the JDL model (Level 3).

The advantage of the Waterfall model is the simplicity in understanding and applying, but it has a major limitation, as there is no feedback loop between levels.

5.3 Intelligence Cycle–Based Model

The Intelligence Cycle–Based model is a cyclic model that captures some inherent processing behaviors among stages. It consists of five stages: planning, collection, collation, evaluation, and the dissemination stage [1] [10].

Stage-1 is the Planning and Direction stage, where determinations of the requirements take place; Stage-2 is the Collection stage, which collects required information; and Stage-3 is a Collation stage, that streamlines the collected information. Stage-4 is Evaluation stage, where the fusion process occurs, and the last, Stage-5 is the Dissemination stage, that distributes the fused inferences.

5.4 Boyd Model

The Boyd model is considered a cyclical model [11]. Its cycle has four stages of processing: observation, orientation, decision, and action. Each stage can be matched to a specific level of the JDL model [3]:

The Observation stage is similar to Source Preprocessing in the JDL model and to the Collection stage of the Intelligence Cycle model. The Orientation stage is comparable to Levels 1, 2, and 3 of the JDL model, and it can be considered similar to the Collection and Collation stages of Intelligence cycle model. The Decision stage is comparable to the processing level in the JDL model and equivalent to the "evaluation and dissemination stages" of the Intelligence cycle model. While the Action stage has no match to any level in the JDL model, it can be considered as the Dissemination stage of the Intelligence cycle model. A better fusion process model can be obtained by a combination of the intelligence cycle and Boyd models, such as the Omnibus Model.

5.5 Omnibus Model

This model is based on a combination of the Intelligence cycle and Boyd models. The cyclic structure of this model can be compared to the Boyd loop, with more enhancements to the structure of the processing levels [12].

The observation step of the Boyd model has been modeled as a sensing and signal processing. While the orientation step of the Boyd model is conducted as feature extraction and pattern processing. The decision step of the Boyd model has been replaced in Omnibus by two phases: context processing and decision making. The action step of the Boyd model is divided into control and resource tasking.

The Omnibus model is considered more efficient and generalized than other fusion models, such as Waterfall, Intelligence cycle, or Boyd models. The Omnibus model employs the strengths of other previous models and at the same time is considered very easy to employ in a sensor fusion system.

5.6 Thomopoulos Model

The architecture of this model is based on three levels of data processing: signal level, evidence level, and dynamic level [13].

The signal level is a correlation and learning process that integrates sensor data. The evidence level is used to describe the statistical model that processes data from different sensors in some form of local inference. The dynamic level combines different observations in a centralized or decentralized fashion, assuming that a mathematical model that describes the process from which data is collected is known [13].

6 Fusion Techniques

Once the fusion architecture is designed, one or more fusion techniques should be implemented to fuse the data at different levels, keeping in mind that uncertainty exists in all descriptions of the sensing and data fusion process. Then, an explicit measurement of this uncertainty must be provided, in order to fuse the sensory information in an efficient and predictable manner [14]. However, there are many methods used for representing uncertainty; almost all of the theoretical developments are based on the use of probabilistic models [14].

Probabilistic models have an important aspect when developing data fusion methods. It is an essential requirement to obtain a well understanding of probabilistic modeling techniques when a data fusion is required in any coherent manner [14]. This section discusses two approaches used in sensor fusion systems, Bayesian network 'Posteriori' as a probabilistic model technique and an alternative method to the probability; theory of evidence by Dempster-Shafer. The Bayes' approach deals with probability values in which incomplete information which leads to uncertainty is not accounted for, that is: $P_A + P_{\bar{A}} = 1$. Where Dempsetr-Shafer accounts for incomplete information in the mass function: $m(A, \bar{A}, \theta) = 1$.

6.1 Multi Sensor Data Fusion Using Bayes' Tachnique

The main objective when developing a sensor fusion system is to integrate data from multiple sensors, whether identical or different, active or passive, in order to generate reliable estimation about the object of interest, as depicted in Fig.1. Several methods are modeled when multi-sensor fusion is required, such as: Deciding, Guiding, Averaging, Bayesian statistics, and Integration [15].

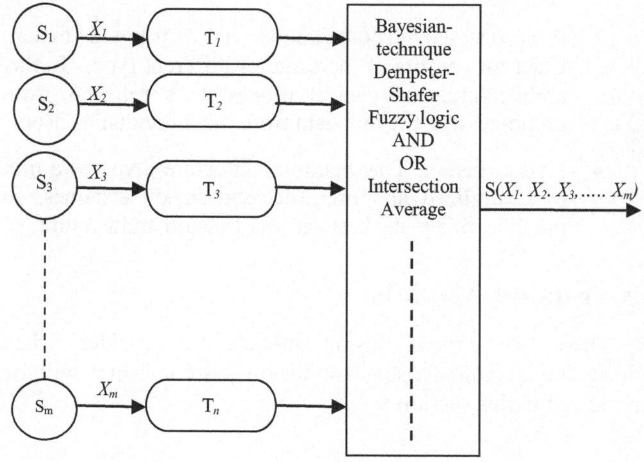

Fig. 1. General model of multi-sensor data fusion

In general, the model of sensor fusion consists of a set of sensors $S_j = \{s_1, s_2, s_3, \ldots, s_m\}$ where each sensor's output is represented by an array of likelihood values; that is, the conditional probabilities. This array represents the environment of interest, which could be modeled by a single state T represented by finite types of targets, $T_i = \{t_1, t_2, t_3, \ldots, t_n\}$. A single sensor S observes targets t_n and returns a single value for each type T. These values form the Likelihood Probability array, $P(s|t_i)$, which are illustrated in Table I .

When more than one sensor is employed in the system, a sensor fusion method must be applied to integrate the various observations in order to make an assessment of each target type being detected. In the case of another sensor S_2 is introduced to detect or observe the same target types, namely $t_1, t_2, t_3, t_4, \ldots t_n$, a second likelihood array is generated as in Table I. For every sensor in the system, a likelihood vector is generated.

TABLE I. LIKLIHOOD VECTORS FROM SENSOR1(S_1) AND SENSOR2 (S_2)

Target type	t_1	t_2	t_3	----------	t_n
Sensor S_1	$P(s_1\|t_1)$	$P(s_1\|t_2)$	$P(s_1\|t_3)$	----------	$P(s_1\|t_n)$
Sensor S_2	$P(s_2\|t_1)$	$P(s_2\|t_2)$	$P(s_2\|t_3)$	------------	$P(s_2\|t_n)$

6.1.1 Bayes' Theorem

Bayes' rule is based on the joint and the conditional probability [16].

$$P(T_i|S) = \frac{P(S|T_i)P(T_i)}{\sum_i P(S|T_i)\,P(T_i)} \quad (1)$$

Where,
P (T_i): The prior beliefs about the values of T_i.
P $(S|T_i)$: The observation S about the state T_i, which is the conditional probability describing each state of nature T_i. This is called the likelihood that observation *S* will be made.
P $(T_i|S)$: It is computed from the original prior information and the information gained by observation. It represents the posterior probability value describing the likelihoods associated with T_i, given the observation *S*.
The Bayesian posterior probability represents our confidence in the hypothesis, which is based on the prior data and current observation values, which enable the user to make a decision based on the application type. Table II represents the joint likelihood probability values JLV, and the posteriori probability values. JLV is generated for a target type t_i from S1 and S2; $P(S1,S2 \mid t_i)$, based on (2)

$$P(S|t_i) = P(S_1|t_i) \cdot P(S_2|t_i) \quad (2)$$

Then by applying Bayes' theory, the hypotheses values for each target type are computed by applying the posterior probability values using (1).

On the other hand, Bayes' theory still suffers a few disadvantages; one disadvantage when using a Bayes' theorem that is acquiring accurate a priori probabilities values *P(T)* or $P(T_i)$. In many cases all the a priori probabilities are assigned equal values that would affect the precision in the posteriori probability, which differs from case to case, based on the number of targets, as in (3).

$$P(t_1) = P(t_2) = P(t_3) = \text{-------} = P(t_n) = 1/n \quad (3)$$

Where,
n: is the number of targets.

TABLE II. GENERATING THE CONDITIONAL AND POSTERIOR PROBABILITY

JLV $P(s\|t_i)$	$P(s\|t_1) = P(s_1\|t_1).P(s_2\|t_1)$	$P(s\|t_2) = P(s_1\|t_2).P(s_2\|t_2)$	$P(s\|t_3) = P(s_1\|t_3).P(s_2\|t_3)$	------------	$P(s\|t_n) = P(s_1\|t_n).P(s_2\|t_n)$
Posteriori $P(t_i\|s)$	$P(t_1\|s) = \frac{P(s\|t_1)P(t_1)}{\sum_i P(s\|t_i)\,P(t_i)}$	$P(t_2\|s) = \frac{P(s\|t_2)P(t_2)}{\sum_i P(s\|t_i)\,P(t_i)}$	$P(t_3\|s) = \frac{P(s\|t_3)P(t_3)}{\sum_i P(s\|t_i)\,P(t_i)}$	-------------	$P(t_n\|s) = \frac{P(s\|t_n)P(t_n)}{\sum_i P(s\|t_i)\,P(t_i)}$

6.2 Multi Sensor Date Fusion Using Theory of Evidences

This theory was developed by Dempster and Shafer [17] [18], as a mathematical method that generalizes Bayesian theory, which allows the representation of ignorance. The Bayesian theory assigns for each evidence only one possible event, while Dempster-Shafer associates evidence with multiple possible events. The Dempster-Shafer theory assumes that the states for which we have probabilities are independent with respect to our subjective probability judgments. The implementation of this method to a specific problem normally involves two steps [18]. The first step is to solve the uncertainties into a priori independent items of evidence. The second is a computation using the Dempster-Shafer method, as illustrated in Table III.

Three functions in Dempster-Shafer theory must be noted due to their importance [16]:

1) *The Basic Probability Assignment function or Mass function (bpa or m):* This is the fundamental of Dempster/Shafer theory. It presented by a mass function m and defined as follows in (4):

$$m: P(x) \rightarrow [0,1]$$

$$m(\emptyset) = 0$$

$$\sum_{A \in P(x)} m(A) = 1 \qquad (4)$$

Where,
P *(x)* is the power set of *x*
$\emptyset$ is the null set
A is a set in the power set ($A \in$ P (x)). [19]

2) *The Belief function (Bel):* represents the lower boundary of the pba interval. Where the Belief for a set A is defined in (5):

$$Bel(A) = \sum_{B|B \subseteq A} m(B) \qquad (5)$$

Where,
(*B*) is a proper subset of set (*A*).

3) *The Plausibility function (Pl):* Is the upper boundary of the pba interval. The plausibility for a set A is defined in (6):

$$Pl(A) = \sum_{B|B \cap A \neq \emptyset} m(B) \qquad (6)$$

Based on the basis that all assignments should be added up to one, we can derive these two measures from each other in (7):

$$Pl(A) = 1 - Bel(\bar{A}) \qquad (7)$$

Where,
$\bar{A}$ is the classical complement of *A*.

6.2.1 Dempster –Shafer Method of Fusion

Since the Dempster-Shafer method of integration of two events is a conjunctive relation (AND), then the integration of two masses m_1 and m_2 is performed as in (8) [20]:

$$m_{12}(A) = \sum_{B \cap C = A} m_1(B).m_2(C) \Big/ 1 - k \qquad (8)$$

Where,
$A \neq \emptyset$,
$m_{12}(\emptyset) = 0$
$K = \sum_{B \cap C = \emptyset} m_1(B).m_2(C)$

K is the conflict degree between evidences, and (1-K) is used as a normalization factor.

TABLE III. INTEGRATION OF SENSOR$_1$ (S$_1$) AND SENSOR$_2$(S$_2$) USING DEMPSTER/SHAFER

Sensor$_1$ (S$_1$)

Sensor$_2$ (S$_2$)		$m_1(A_1)$	$m_1(A_2)$	------	$m_1(A_n)$
	$m_2(B_1)$	$m_1(A_1).m_2(B_1)$	$m_1(A_2).m_2(B_1)$	------	$m_1(A_n).m_2(B_1)$
	$m_2(B_2)$	$m_1(A_1).m_2(B_2)$	$m_1(A_2).m_2(B_2)$	------	$m_1(A_n).m_2(B_2)$
	$m_2(B_3)$	$m_1(A_1).m_2(B_3)$	$m_1(A_2).m_2(B_3)$	-----	$m_1(A_n).m_2(B_3)$
	⋮	⋮	⋮	⋮	⋮
	$m_2(B_m)$	$m_1(A_1).m_2(B_m)$	$m_1(A_2).m_2(B_m)$	-----	$m_1(A_n).m_2(B_m)$

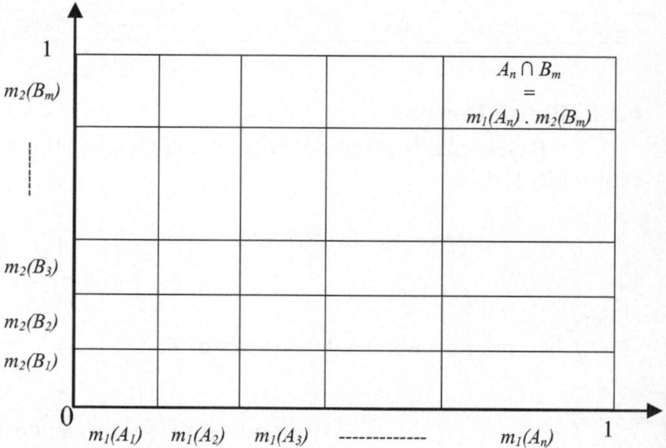

Dempster/Shafer theory is considered as a forward straight method to express pieces of evidence with different levels of abstraction, and it can be used to combine pieces of evidence, which is not always available when using other methods of fusion.

7 Conclusion

This paper presents a review of multi-sensor fusion and the requirement for building a data fusion system. Two fusion techniques were proposed: Bayes and Dempster/Shafer's theories. While Bayes' theory does not account for incomplete information, it is the sum of a probability, and its complement in a sample space is one. Dempster/Shafer accounts for ignorance or incomplete information, so the sum of the probability and its complement with ignorance is equal to one.

Both methods represent the hypothesis with a single value (posteriori or support). Dempster/Shafer introduces an upper boundary called plausibility; therefore, it gives more room for the decision making process. However, both theories require a prior knowledge of the state; Bayes' theory requires a priori probability, and Dempster/Shafer requires a mass function. Based on the prior information available, one method has an advantage over the other.

One of the major problems when using both techniques is that both assume independency in their computation process between events, and this assumption leads to uncertainty in the hypothesis, sometimes adding or taking away part of the value associated with the hypothesis. In our ongoing research we were able to show that when we quantified dependency between two sensors' events (outputs), we accounted for uncertainty, but the assumption of independence does not control the performance of the system.

8 References

[1] W. Elmenreich, "An introduction to sensor fusion. Research report 47/2001," Institute fur Technische Informatik, Vienna University of Technology, Austria, 2002.

[2] P. Grossmann, "Multisensor data fusion," GEC J Technol 15:27–37, 1998.

[3] D. L. Hall, and S. H. Mcmullen, "Mathematical techniques in multi-sensor data fusion," MA: Artech House, London, 1992.

[4] J. R. Raol, G. Girija, and N. Shanthakumar, "Theory of data fusion and kinematic-level fusion," CRC Press book, 2009

[5] R. C. Luo, and M. G. Kay, "Data fusion in robotics and machine intelligence," Academic press, 1992.

[6] P. Lytrivis, G. Thomaidis, and A. Amditis, "Sensor data fusion in automotive applications," Sensor and Data Fusion, Nada Milisavljevic (Ed.), ISBN: 978-3-902613-52-3, InTech, DOI: 10.5772/6574, 2009.

[7] A. G. O. Mutambra, "Decentralized estimation and control for multisensory systems," Florida, USA: CRC Press, 1998.

[8] J. Llinas, and D. L. Hall, "An introduction to multi-sensor data fusion," Proc. IEEE International Symposium on Circuits and Systems 1998, 6: 537-540.

[9] C. J. Harris, A. Bailey and T. J. Dodd, "Multi-sensor data fusion in defence and aerospace," Aeronautical Journal, 102 (1015): 229-244.

[10] A. N. Shulsky, "Silent warfare: Understanding the world of intelligence," New York: Brassey's.

[11] . J. R. Boyd, " A discourse on winning and losing," Jhon R Boyd, 1987.

[12] M. Bedworth, and J. O'Brien. "The omnibus model: A new model for data fusion?," 2nd International Conference on Information Fusion (FUSION'99), 1999.

[13] S. C. Thomopoulos, "Sensor integration and data fusion," Proc. SPIE 1198, Sensor Fusion II: Human and Machine Strategies, 1989.

[14] H. D. Whyte, "Multi Sensor Data Fusion," Australian Centre for Field Robotics, 2006

[15] J. K. Hackett,M. Shah, "Multi-sensor fusion: a perspective," Robotics and Automation, 1990. Proceedings., 1990 IEEE International Conference on , vol., no., pp.1324,1330 vol.2, 13-18 May 1990

[16] D. Koks, and S. Challa, " An Introduction to Bayesian and Dempster-Shafer Data Fusion," Sadhana 29(2):145–76, 2004.

[17] G. Shafer, "A Mathematical Theory of Evidence," 1976, Princeton University Pres

[18] K. Sentz, S. Ferson, "Combination of Evidence in Dempster-Shafer Theory," Sandia National Laboratories, 2002.

[19] G. J. Klir, and M. J. Wierman "Uncertainty-Based Information: Elements of Generalized Information Theory," Heidelberg, Physica-Verlag,1998.

[20] G. M. Provan, "The validity of Dempster–Shafer belief functions," Int J Approx Reason, 1992, 6:389–99.

Lighting Control Algorithm using Linear Programming for An Intelligent Lighting System and Dealing with Disturbance using Kalman Filter

Miki Mitsunori[1], Ikegami Hisanori[2], Azuma Yohei[2], Sakakibara Yuki[2], and Motoya Yo[2]
[1]Department of Science and Engineering, Doshisha University, Kyoto, Japan
[2]Graduate School of Science and Engineering, Doshisha University, Kyoto, Japan

Abstract— *We propose a new control algorithm using Linear Progamming in the Intelligent Lighting System. The Intelligent Lighting System is a lighting control system that provides desired illuminance distributions at minimum electrical power. Parameter tuning in the current control algorithm is generally expensive, because the current control algorithm bases on Hill Climbing Method. So to reduce loads by parameter tuning, We study on applying Linear Progamming to the Intelligent Lighting System. We can treat object problem in the Intelligent Lighting System as linear programming problem. And so, Simplex Method is derived optimized solution, and lighting fixtures are controled. As a result of verification, it was confirmed that proposed method is superior to conventional algorithm on parameter tuning and dealing with changing required illuminance.*

Keywords: Lighting Control, Lenear Programming, Simplex Method, Kalman Filter

1. Introduction

In recent years, continuing research into the office environment has identified that the office environment has a major influence on workers. Previous research has reported that improving the office environment can increase workers' intellectual productivity and comfort[1], [2]. With regard to the lighting environment, it has also been reported that providing each worker's desired brightness can raise intellectual productivity[3]. However, at present, the standard lighting design of Japanese offices features a desktop illuminance of 750 lx or greater in Japan. Consequently, this cannot be considered a lighting environment suited to each worker. Furthermore, it is also believed that desired illuminance differs by race and culture. For all these reasons, we have been researching into an intelligent lighting system in order to provide individual illuminance environments in our laboratory[4], [5]. An intelligent lighting system provides each user's desired illuminance, and also gives energy saving. And we have shown an effective control algorithm ANA/RC[4], [6], [7] based on hill climbing method.

Since ANA/RC, based on the hill-climbing method, is a heuristic method, preset parameters strongly influence the search efficiency of the optimal solution. If search efficiency is poor, convergence to the target value also becomes poor, so improving search efficiency is an important issue to consider. A tuning system has not yet been proposed for intelligent lighting systems, so further experience and experiments are needed in order to sustain search efficiency. Tuning costs are expected to increase in the future when intelligent lighting systems are introduced to large-scale offices. Therefore, in this study we propose a control algorithm using linear programming, as a method that facilitates tuning by decreasing the number of parameters from the previous algorithm (ANA/RC). In addition, for practical use, we propose a disturbance detection method that uses a Kalman filter.

2. Intelligent lighting system

2.1 Overview of the intelligent lighting system

The intelligent lighting system, as indicated in Fig 1, is composed of lights equipped with microprocessors, portable illuminance sensors, and electrical power meters, with each element connected via a network.Individual users set the illuminance constraint on the illuminance sensors. At this time, each light repeats autonomous changes in luminance to converge to an optimum ligthing pattern. Also, with the intelligent lighting system, positional information for the lights and illuminance sensors is unnecessary. This is because the lights learn the factor of influence to the illuminance sensors, based on illuminance data sent from illuminance sensors. In this fashion, each user's target illuminance can be provided rapidly.

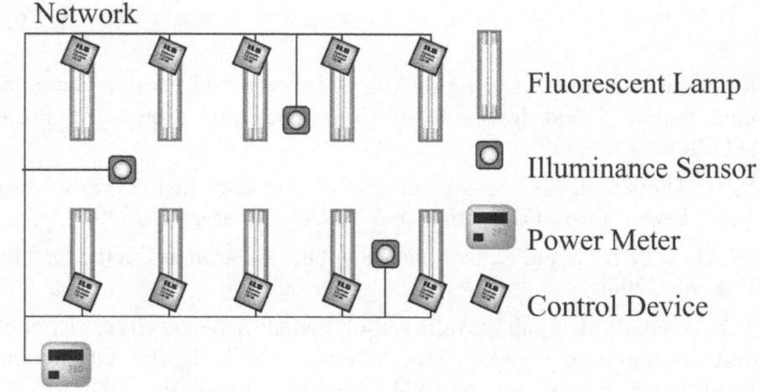

Fig. 1: Configuration of the Intelligent Lighting System

2.2 Illuminance control algorithm

we have shown an effective control algorithm ANA/RC (Adaptive Neighborhood Algorithm using Regression Coefficiet) [4], [6], [7] based on hill climbing method.

The hill-climbing method is an algorithm where the optimal solution is derived by generating the solution of the next step based on the solution of the current step. Solutions are accepted based on the changes in the objective function value, and the transition process is repeated until an optimal solution is derived. Control is performed by taking the lightness of lighting (the luminous intensity) to be the design variable, and taking the sum of the difference between current and target illuminance and electric power consumption to be the objective function. Furthermore, in ANA/RC, differences in lightness that a light exerts on the illuminance meter are learned by regression analysis, and luminous intensity is appropriately changed in response to the degree of exertion [4], [6], [7]. By using this process, solutions can be quickly derived. Hereafter, the lightness difference a light exerts on an illuminance meter will be called 'influence.'

$$f = P + w \sum_{i=1}^{n} g_i \tag{1}$$

$$g_i = \begin{cases} (Ic_i - It_i)^2 & (Ic_i - It_i) \leq 0 \\ 0 & otherwise \end{cases} \tag{2}$$

P:electric power consumption[W]
Ic:current illuminancelx
It:target illuminancelx
w:weight, n:the number of illuminance sensors

The objective function was derived from amount of electric power P and illuminance constraint g_i . Also, changing weighting factor w enables changes in the order of priority for electrical energy and illuminance constraint. The illuminance constraint brings current illuminance to target illuminance or greater, as indicated by formula (2).

2.3 Requirements for control algorithm

Because the hill-climbing method, which is the control algorithm the intelligent lighting systems are based in, is a heuristic method, parameter tuning heavily influences the search efficiency. If search efficiency is poor, conversion to the target also becomes poor, which is why search efficiency is an important issue. However, efficient techniques for the parameter tuning of intelligent lighting systems have yet to be proposed. For this reason, tuning based on experience is needed, and personnel cost is incurred. In particular, due to the largeness of scale and the complexity that is foreseen for future environments, further complexities are predicted for parameters. Thus, we propose a method for reducing costs through parameter tuning by effective tuning methods. In this paper, we propose a control algorithm using linear programming, as a method for facilitating tuning by reducing the number of parameters. Also, in terms of practical use, handling disturbances/faults such as noise from measuring equipment, effects from daylight, or malfunctioning of equipment, becomes important. We therefore propose a disturbance and fault response method that uses a Kalman filter.

3. Object problem for the Intelligent Lighting System

There are three points required, as below

1) Minimize electric power consumption
2) Realize illuminance required by worker
3) Be in lighting controlable range

These are formulized Eq (3)∼Eq (5)

$$min \quad f(\overline{L}) = P \tag{3}$$

$$subjectto \quad Ic_j \geq It_j \tag{4}$$

$$\overline{L} \in \{l | m \leq L_i \leq M\} \tag{5}$$

P:electric power consumption[W]
Ic:current illuminancelx
It:target illuminancelx
m:lower limit of luminous intensity[cd]
L:luminous intensity of lighting fixture[cd]
M:upper limit of luminous intensity[cd]

As shown in Equation 3, the design variable is the luminous intensity of lighting. Therefore, in cases where optimization methods are used that are not heuristic searches (e.g., quasi-Newton method), it is necessary for the objective function and constraints to be operable in terms of the design variable.

4. Formulization of objective function

The objective function is the electric power consumption shown in Equation 3. It is expressed as a function of the design variable (luminous intensity). Luminance and electric power consumption have a proportional relationship. For example, luminous efficiency [lm/W] is used as an index for evaluating light-source efficiency. A preliminary experiment was conducted to formulize this; in this experiment, the relationship between vertically downward luminance from lighting and electric power consumption was examined. The result is shown in Figure 2. The vertical axis is electric power consumption [W] and the horizontal axis is percentage of luminance compared to the luminance when the lights are lit to their maximum luminous intensity.

Figure 2 shows luminance and electric power consumption to have a relationship that can be approximated by a linear equation. This means that, for an intelligent lighting system

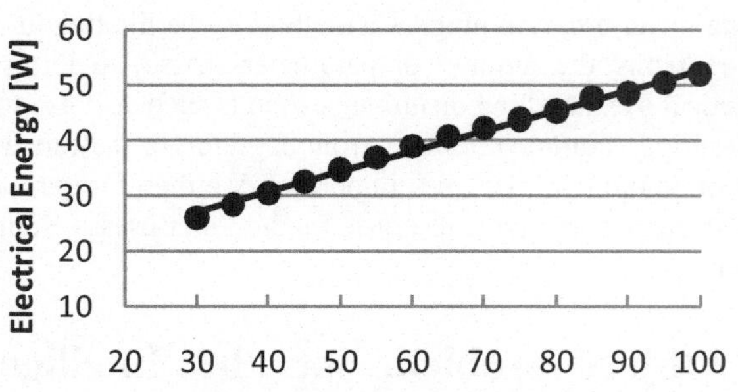

Fig. 2: Relation between luminance and electric power consumption

comprised of multiple luminaires, electric power consumption can be expressed as in Equation 6.

$$P = f_1(\overline{L}) = \sum_{i=1}^{n}(\alpha_i \times L_i) + \beta \quad (6)$$

P: electric power consumption[W]
α : main coefficient[W/cd]
β : constant term[W]
L : luminous intensity[cd]

The main coefficient α and constant term β in Figure 6 are values particular to each luminaire. Preliminary experiments are therefore necessary to find main coefficient α and constant term β for each luminaire. However, the precision of the objective function would be sufficient if is enough to evaluate this. Therefore, Equation 7 is used for the objective function, so that the preliminary experiment can be abridged.

$$P \doteqdot f_2(\mathbf{L}) = \alpha \sum_{i=1}^{n} L_i \quad (7)$$

P : electric power consumption[W], L : luminance intensity[cd], α is an arbitrary value

Equation 7 enables the expression of the target function as a linear function of the design variable.

5. Formulization of penalty condition

5.1 Relation between luminance and illuminance

The constraints are the current illuminance Ic and target It, and are expressed as illuminance values. This can be expressed as a function of the design variable (luminous intensity). Luminance and illuminance have a causal relationship; for example, when a light is strongly lit, a place becomes brighter. The relationship between luminance and illuminance is shown in Equation 8, using the point-by-point method.

$$I = \frac{L}{A \times \cos\theta} \oint_{S_e} \frac{dS_e \cos\theta \cos\delta}{p^2} \quad (8)$$

I:illuminance [lx], L:luminance intensity [cd]
S_e:surface of light sources A:size of the surface $[m^2]$
p:distance to light sources [m]
θ:degree from points of illumination to the surface of light sources. [rad]
δ:angle of elevation from plane of illumination to light sources [rad]

From Equation 8, it can be understood that illuminance and luminance have a linear relationship. Furthermore, each of the terms in Equation 8, with the exception of luminance, are values that change in response to the shape of the light source, or the positional relation to the light source. Due to this, these terms can be treated as constants in an environment where neither the shape of the light source, nor the positional relation to the light source, change. In such an environment, Equation 8 can be expressed in the form of Equation 9. Hereafter, we call this numerical constant the 'influence factor.'

$$I = R \times L \quad (9)$$

I:illuminance [lx], R:influence factor [lx/cd]
L:luminous intensity of lighting fixture [cd]

Equation 9 shows that, by calculating influence factor R, the relationship between luminance and illuminance can be digitized. This makes it possible to express the illuminance constraint as a function of design variable. Hereafter, the set of influence factor R will be called the 'model of the lighting environment.'

5.2 Estimate influence factor

In order to express the illuminance constraint as a function of design variable, it becomes necessary to estimate the influence factor, which digitizes the relationship between lighting and the illuminance meter. Because the relationship between luminance and illuminance can be expressed in the form of Equation 9, the model equation for the lighting environment in terms of an intelligent lighting system comprised of multiple lights and illuminance meters, becomes Equation 10.

$$I_j = \sum_{i=1}^{n}(R_{ij} \times L_i) + D_j \quad (10)$$

I:illuminance [lx], R:influence factor[lx/cd]
L:luminous intensity of lighting fixture[cd]
D:illuminance from daylight [lx]

In ANA/RC, an estimation of the influence factor is conducted. In this method, the intelligent lighting system randomly increases and decreases the luminance of lighting in a range undetectable by humans. In other words, in the process of optimization, the illuminance changes in various ways in response to the changes in luminance. Taking these changes as a basis, the state estimation method is used to digitize the relationship between luminance and illuminance. However, in ANA/RC the least squares method is used as the state estimation method, so it cannot respond to changes in environment. In addition, because single regression analysis is done independently for each light, as a model for predicting illuminance from luminance, as in Equation 10, its precision is low. Therefore, in this paper, the Kalman filter is used as the state estimation method, and state estimation is conducted, integrating all lighting information.

5.3 Estimation using Kalman filter

5.3.1 Kalman filter

The Kalman filter is a method where observed values with error are used to estimate the state variables of linear systems. Provided that the noise conforms to normal distribution, the Kalman filter is the most suitable filter among all filters, including those that are nonlinear. Furthermore, because it is a sequential estimation method, calculations only use recent data rather than using all data. Due of this, an increase in calculations due to an increase in transition history data is limited. For this reason, it is thought to be suitable for long-term system operations.

5.3.2 Dealing with Disturbance

In the illuminance information obtained by the illuminance meters, effects from light sources that the intelligent lighting system holds no luminance information on (e.g. daylight or task-lights) can take up a large part. These effects are called disturbance, and there are four main types.

1) Noise of illuminance sensors
2) Noise of lighting fixture
3) Disturbance to sensors (shadow of a person, paper or partition and so on)
4) Changing of Daylight intensity

Items 1 and 2 are disturbances that conform to normal distribution. Thus, as is characteristic of Kalman filters, as the updating process of the Kalman filter progresses, their influence becomes minimized. Item 3, however, does not conform to normal distribution, so it is necessary to reject it as an unexpected observed value so that its effect on the current model is minimized. Here, an acceptance decision is conducted on the observed values. If the Kalman filter is effective, then observation prediction error ν should comply with normal distribution. Statistic Φ, comprised of observation prediction error ν and error covariance S, is used to conduct a chi-square test. Statistic Φ is shown in Equation 11.

$$\begin{aligned} \Phi &= {\nu_k}^T S_k^{-1} \nu_k \quad (11) \\ \nu_k &= Z_k - H_k \hat{x}_{k/k-1} \end{aligned}$$

Φ:statistic, ν:observation prediction error, k:steps
S:error covariance, Z:observed value
H:observation model, $\hat{x}$:state space

As a result of chi-square test, if observation prediction error ν does not occur with significant probability, the observed value is accepted and the Kalman filter is updated. If observation prediction error ν does occur with significant probability, the observed value is rejected and the Kalman filter is not updated. From this, the disturbance item 3 exerts on the model can be minimized. The disturbance of item 4 is an environmental change, for which it becomes necessary to correct the model. However, for the meter, the only difference between it and item 3, is in whether the effect disturbance exists over a mid-long period rather than a short period, so it is difficult to make a decision at the point when the disturbance occurs. Because of this, item 4 disturbances are rejected in the same way as item 3 disturbances, and the influence they have on the model becomes minimized. As a result, a lot of data would be necessary in order to correct the model. Therefore, we propose a method where a new Kalman filter is constructed at the moment the environmental change occurs, and then after a set amount of time, the filter is compared with the previous filter.

5.4 Making and selecting Kalman filter

To correct the model in response to the item 4 disturbance mentioned in the previous section, a Kalman filter is newly constructed in response to the environmental change, and then the filter that better suits the environment is selected. First, a Kalman filter constructed during operation of the intelligent lighting system. We will call this filter the 'main filter.' While updating the main filter, an acceptance decision for observed values is performed that is based on Equation 11. If an unexpected observed value is detected as a result of this, then it is assumed that an item 4 disturbance has occurred, and in that moment, a new Kalman filter is constructed that is independent of the main filter. This new filter is updated in the same way as the main filter. Hereafter, we will call this new constructed filter ' the main candidate filter.' After a set amount of time has passed, the main filter and main candidate filter are compared. The filter with the smaller value for evaluation norm Ψ, in Equation 12, is chosen to become the new main filter.

$$\begin{aligned} \Psi &= {\nu_k}^T \nu_k \quad (12) \\ \nu_k &= Z_k - H_k \hat{x}_{k/k-1} \end{aligned}$$

Ψ:evaluation norm, ν:observation prediction error, k:steps
Z:observed value, H:observation model, $\hat{x}$:state space

To summarize the above process, for a short-term effect (item 3 disturbance), where the original environment is restored after a set amount of time, the main filter is updated without change, and for a mid-long term effect (item 4 disturbance), where the environment remains changed after a set amount of time, the main candidate filter, which has taken into account the effect of the disturbance, is chosen to be the new main filter. In other words, this means that the set length of time until the evaluation comparison will determine which disturbances are rejected and which disturbances are incorporated and reflected. By using Equation 10, it has become possible to express illumination constrictions as linear functions of design variables.

6. Control algorithm using linear programming

6.1 Linear programming

By the methods described in Chapter 4 and Chapter 5, it has become possible to express objective functions and constraints in an object problem as functions of design variables. Particularly, because both can be expressed as a linear function of a design variable, it is possible now to treat the object problem as a problem in linear programming. In linear programming problems, with some exceptions (e.g., when constraints are contradictory), it is possible to derive a global optimal solution. For this reason, it is advantageous from both the perspective of tuning simplification and in the accuracy of solutions. This is especially true in comparison to the previous algorithm, in which the accuracy of solutions is not necessarily guaranteed. Therefore, we will derive the solution by using a linear programming method. Two representative linear programming methods are the simplex method and the interior point method. In this paper we chose to use the simplex method.

6.2 Simplex method

The simplex method is an iterative method, where executable base solutions with the smaller objective function values are generated in succession. The simplex method, by following Bland 's smallest subscript rule, is guaranteed to be finitely convergent. In other words, either an optimal solution is derived through a finite amount of repetitions, or it is discriminated that a no solution exists. Because of this, a precondition is that the model mentioned in Chapter 5 is of high precision. However, by this method, an optimal solution can be derived while only using the internal processing of the computer, without synchronization with hardware. The simplex method, however, is an exponential time algorithm, and is inferior in terms of search efficiency when compared to the interior point method (a polynomial time algorithm). Generally, however, it is known to be capable of deriving optimal solutions in the number of occurrences ranging from 1.5n to 3n, with regard to number of constraints n. Therefore, in practical use, it is thought to be sufficiently quick. Because of this, we use the simplex method, as it is easy to implement.

6.3 Control algorithm using simplex method

The processing of our proposed method consists of two phases: the modeling phase, where modeling of the lighting environment is performed (described in Chapter 5), and the optimization phase, where a solution is sought by the simplex method. In the modeling phase, Equation 10 is derived by first changing the luminance of the lighting in minute increments that stay within a range undetectable by the human eye, and then, using the illuminance changes that occur, state estimation is conducted using the Kalman filter. The process is conducted persistently, the precision of the Kalman filter is improved, and Equation 10 is accurately derived. Each time Equation 10 is updated by the modeling phase, the optimization phase is conducted. In the optimization phase, Equation 7 and Equation 10 are used for formulizing the object problem as Equations 13-15. The optimal solution is then derived using the simplex method.

$$min \qquad f(\overline{L}) = P = \alpha \sum_{i=1}^{n} L_i \tag{13}$$

$$subjectto \qquad Ic_j \geq It_j = \sum_{j=1}^{n} (R_{ij} L_i) + D_j \tag{14}$$

$$\overline{L} \in \{l | m \leq L_i \leq M\} \tag{15}$$

L : luminous intensity of lighting fixture [cd]
P : electric power consumption [W]
Ic : current illuminance [lx], It : target illuminance [lx]
R : influence factor [lx/cd], D : illuminance from daylight [lx]
m : lower limit of luminous intensity[cd]
M : upper limit of luminous intensity[cd]

In addition, when model precision in the modeling phase cannot be guaranteed, or in other words, if the Kalman filter' s estimated error covariance exceeds the threshold value, the modeling phase is not conducted. The process above enables the derivation of a level of luminance that actualizes the user' s desired brightness of room-environment while consuming as little electric power as possible.

7. Verification of proposed method

7.1 Overview of Experiment

A simulation was conducted, in which a real office was simulated. The simulation environment used is shown in Figure 3.

In the simulation, illumination was calculated from the luminance of lighting, by using the point-by-point method. Furthermore, in order to simulate observational noise of the illuminance meter, random numbers from the normal distribution of average value 0 lx, variance 5 lx2 were added to the illuminance information. The values used were obtained empirically from actual meter information. In addition, the time until the comparison of the main filter with the main candidate filter was set to 300 seconds. This means that the effects from disturbance lasting less than 300 seconds were rejected as faults (item 3 disturbance), and the effect from

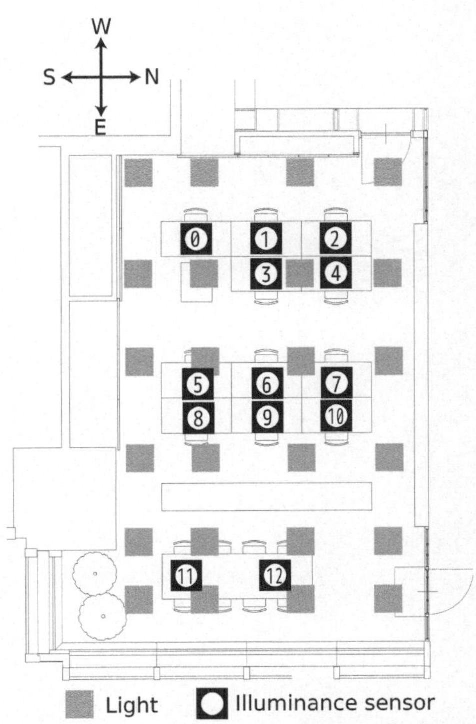

Fig. 3: Simulation environment in ground plan

disturbance lasting 300 seconds or longer was reflected in the model as a change in environment (item 4 disturbance).

7.2 Result of Estimating Daylight illuminance

For 3000 seconds, luminance was varied in a range undetectable by the human eye, and the lighting pattern satisfying the required illuminance was sought. Based on the luminance information and illuminance information obtained during operation, the transition state of the estimated illuminance-from-daylight value, estimated using the Kalman filter, was verified. In addition, to set up a situation of environmental change, for illuminance meter 7, influence from daylight was set to 0 lx until 1000 seconds and to 500 lx after 1000 seconds. Figure 4 shows the estimated illuminance-from-daylight values and the actual illuminance-from-daylight values for illuminance meter 7.

As Figure 4 shows, the estimated illuminance-from-daylight value stabilized at around 60 seconds, and with the exception of the time between 1000-1300 seconds, the estimated illuminance-from-daylight value closely matched the actual illuminance-from-daylight value. The process is conducted in the way described in Section 5.4, where, any time a change in environment is detected, a new Kalman filter is generated, and the filter better suited to the environment is chosen after a set amount of time has passed. This means the change in environment is not reflected until the set amount of time passes. In the verification experiment, this time was set at 300 seconds, so an error compared to the

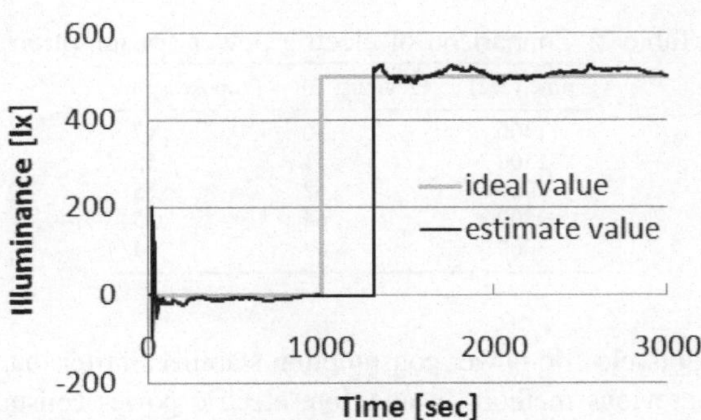

Fig. 4: History of estimating daylight illuminance on sensor 7

predicted illuminance-from-daylight value is expected from the timeframe of 1000 seconds to 300 seconds. The result in Figure 4 matched this expectation, confirming that the above process was conducted correctly. Furthermore, in the span of 60 seconds (where the estimated value was stabilized) to 1000 seconds (where the environmental change occurred), the average error was 9 lx and the maximum error was 23 lx. On the other hand, in the timeframe after 1300 seconds (the point where environmental adaption was completed), the average error was 10 lx and the maximum error was 30 lx. The human eye cannot sense illuminance differences of around 50 lx [8], so the error of the estimated illuminance-from-daylight value was sufficiently small.

7.3 Changing required illuminance

Setting up a situation where target illuminance changes, a comparison was performed between the previous method and proposed method. Target-setting was the same as for the previous section, but at 1500 seconds, the target illuminance value of illuminance meter 8 was shifted to 800 lx. In Table 1, the error in terms of target illuminance after the targets were changed is shown for the previous method and the proposed method.

Table 1: Differences between required illuminance and proposed illuminance

time (sec)	Previous (lx)	Propose (lx)
1400	62	8
1500	134	6
2000	90	9
2500	58	1
3000	50	6

As Table 1 shows, the proposed method converges to the target illuminance more quickly than the previous method. Electric power consumption of each of the previous and proposed methods is shown in Table 2. The values in Table 2 are percentages where the electric power consumption from having all lights switched on at maximum luminance is considered to be 100%. Table 2 shows that in the proposed

Table 2: Conparison of electric power consumption

time (sec)	Previous(%)	Propose (%)
1400	50	47
1500	51	55
2000	62	55
2500	64	55
3000	63	54

method, electric power consumption stabilizes faster than in the previous method. In addition, electric power consumption after stabilization is lower than in the previous method.

8. Conclusion

In this paper, we proposed a new control algorithm for intelligent lighting systems. The proposed method consists of two phases: a phase where the lighting environment is modeled using the Kalman filter, and a phase where the simplex method is used to find a solution. Through a verification experiment, we showed that the proposed method was superior to the previous method in terms of quick-response to changes of target illuminance. Furthermore, using the proposed method enables lighting control where target illuminance can be responded to without requiring complex parameter tuning. Through the modeling phase described in this paper, it is also possible to use as an optimization method other than the simplex method as the control algorithm for the intelligent lighting system.

References

[1] Olli Seppanen, William J. Fisk: A Model to Estimate the Cost-Effectiveness of Improving Office Work through Indoor Environmental Control, Proceedings of ASHRAE, 2005

[2] M. J. Mendell, and G. A. Heath: Do indoor pollutants and thermal conditions in schools influence student performance A critical review of the literature, Indoor Air, Vol.15, No.1, pp.27-52, 2005

[3] Peter R. Boyce, Neil H. Eklund, S. Noel Simpson, Individual Lighting Control: Task Performance, Mood and Illuminance JOURNAL of the Illuminating Engineering Society, pp.131-142, 2000

[4] Miki M, Hiroyasu T, Imazato K, Proposal for an intelligent lighting system, and verification of control method effectiveness, Proc IEEE CIS, pp. 520 - 525, 2004

[5] M.Miki, An Intelligent Lighting System and the Consortium for Smart Office Environment, Journal of Japanese Society for Artif icial Intelligence, Vol.85 No.5, pp.346-351, 2001

[6] K.Ono,M.Miki,Y.Motoi,Autonomous Distributed Optimization Algorithm for Intelligent Lighting System, The transactions of the Institute of Electrical Engineers of Japan. C, A publication of Electronics, Information and System Society Vol.130 No.5, pp.750-757, 2010

[7] S.Tanaka,M.Miki,T.Hiroyasu,M.Yoshikata,An Evolutional Optimization Algorithm to Provide Individual Illuminance in Workplaces,Proc IEEE Int Conf Syst Man Cybern,Vol.2, pp.941-947, 2009

[8] S.Tomoaki,M.Hiroyuki,N.Yoshiki, Research on the Perception of Lighting Fluctuation in a Luminous Offices Environment, Journal of the Illuminationg Engineering Institute of Japan, Vol.85 No.5, pp.346-351, 2001

Issues in Building Parallel Multimedia Systems: A Survey

SeongKi Kim[1], and SangYong Han[2]
[1]S. LSI, Samsung Electronics, Yongin, Korea
[2]School of CSE, Seoul National University, Seoul, Korea

Abstract - *As streaming services have become increasingly popular, the use of multimedia systems has become widespread. However, research has shown that multimedia systems based on a single supercomputer are limited in scalability, capability, fault tolerance, and cost efficiency. Owing to these limitations, much research on building parallel multimedia systems has been conducted. Here, to provide an overview of this research, we classify existing studies and describe representative examples of the different issues under investigation.*

Keywords: multimedia system, video server, parallel processing, content delivery network

1 Introduction

As the number of people playing multimedia content on personal internet-connectable mobile devices such as smart phones and tablet PCs has grown in recent years, multimedia delivery through the internet has increased. When delivering content, a multimedia system is required for streaming services to clients. However, building a multimedia system with a single supercomputer is difficult owing to its limitations in capacity, scalability, fault tolerance, and cost efficiency. For example, if the supercomputer is shut down by a problem, all of its services will be terminated because no other servers are available.

A parallel multimedia system, which consists of video servers that provide streaming services and a load balancer that provides a request-routing service, can overcome these limitations. Adding other affordable servers extends total delivery capability by increasing the total network bandwidth or CPU performance. This also improves the availability, fault tolerance, and cost efficiency of the system.

Extensive research has been conducted to build parallel multimedia systems, including numerous studies on disk scheduling, data placement, buffer management within a disk, and admission control in the storage system, as well as on geographical server placement, movie allocation to individual servers, server selection among available servers, and request routings in delivery systems. In this paper, we introduce various investigations on future parallel multimedia systems and describe the differences between parallel multimedia systems and parallel web server systems.

We present background knowledge in Section 2 and describe research on storage and delivery systems in Sections 3 and 4, respectively. We then summarize the research in Section 5.

2 Related works

In this section, we describe background knowledge on topics such as parallel multimedia systems, content delivery networks (CDNs), and differences between parallel web and parallel multimedia systems.

2.1 Parallel multimedia system

In a parallel multimedia system, many servers simultaneously deliver movies through a network after receiving requests from users. Figure 1 shows the general architecture of such a system.

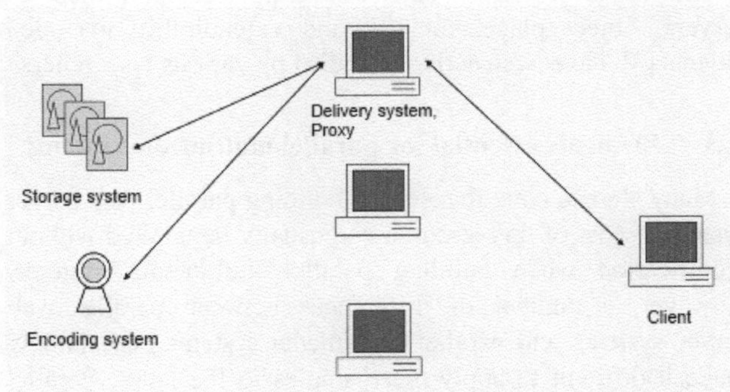

Figure 1. General architecture of a parallel multimedia system

When an author wishes to broadcast a movie, the author delivers it to the appropriate publishing point of a delivery system. The delivery system may be a cluster of PCs or a single supercomputer; the storage system may be a disk set or computers that share their storage capacities with the delivery system. The encoding system may be camcorder or any other device that outputs content. Recently, PC clusters are widely used as delivery systems and storage systems for their fault tolerance and affordability.

A client can view a movie at the publishing point through a unicast or multicast delivery method according to the server setting. In unicast methods, the delivery system maintains and manages all streams and connections to the clients, whereas in multicast methods, a server sends movies to a group, after which a router distributes them to the clients.

2.2 Content Delivery Networks

CDNs place surrogates (replicas) in selected regions and distribute content to each surrogate. To select a surrogate to serve the requesting client, network proximity, geographical proximity, or response time can be used.

CDNs consist of origin servers, surrogates, distribution systems, request-routing systems, and accounting systems. Content providers create and deliver content to the origin servers. To actually serve the clients, the content is delivered to the surrogates. Distribution systems have the role of distributing the created content to surrogates by one of two methods: push or pull. In the push method, content is distributed when a surrogate anticipates a client to make a content request; in the pull method, content is distributed immediately when a surrogate receives a request from a user. Request-routing systems directly receive requests from users, select surrogates, and redirect clients to the selected surrogates. Accounting systems record both the content distribution to surrogates and the content delivery to clients [1].

The issues of CDNs, such as the physical placement of servers, object placement [2], and extendibility to video objects [3], have been actively studied by various researchers.

2.3 Elements essential for parallel multimedia systems

Many studies have focused on building parallel web server systems. Most of this research can usually be applied without modification when building parallel multimedia systems. However, a number of differences between parallel web server systems and parallel multimedia systems occasionally make it difficult to apply these studies to the latter. Parallel multimedia systems place greater emphasis on the following elements than do parallel web server systems.

2.3.1 Content allocation

Although storage capacity has increased, storing the same content on all servers wastes storage space because the content size is enormous, especially in the case of multimedia systems. Therefore, the content stored in one video server is usually different from that in another video server. In addition to saving storage space, efficient content allocation minimizes delay and jitter because the client makes a request to the fastest video server and the allocation can utilize both the temporal and spatial localities [4].

2.3.2 Content awareness

Owing to the allocation of content differing on every video server, the load balancer must investigate the requested content, find the server on which it is stored, and redirect the requesting client to this server. Such routing based on the requested content is called content-aware routing. Storage scalability can be also achieved through content awareness. For example, when new storage is added to a multimedia system and a content-aware multimedia system has the content information in this newly added storage, the former can immediately begin streaming the content. Content awareness can also support session integrity, sophisticated load balancing, and differentiated services [5]. Content awareness is actively studied in parallel web systems [6], and most of this research can also be applied to building parallel multimedia systems.

2.3.3 Support to heterogeneous servers

Numerous servers such as Windows media, Helix universal, and Darwin streaming have been developed as video servers. However, various video servers do not operate together and are thus mutually incompatible. If heterogeneous servers could operate simultaneously for a multimedia system, the total building cost could be significantly reduced owing to the freedom of selection and use of already existing video servers.

3 Storage systems

The storage system is an important component of a multimedia system. In this section, we review the numerous requirements of a multimedia storage system and the extensive research to support efficient streaming to clients.

3.1 Requirements of a multimedia storage system

Although a storage system may take various forms, including a single hard disk, a single computer, or multiple computers, every storage system, in addition to meeting the performance and fairness requirements in the traditional system, must satisfy the following requirements for the multimedia system.

3.1.1 Real-time characteristics

Storage systems must deliver movies to the delivery system within the given time so that the latter can successfully deliver the requested movies to the clients, who can then view the movies with minimal interference or jitter [7].

3.1.2 Large file sizes and high data rate

Given the large file size of movies, storage systems must store large movies efficiently. In addition, movies must be continuously read at a high data rate from the storage systems. For example, a 2-h MPEG-1 video stream requires a streaming rate of approximately 1.2 Mbps for appropriate display and a storage size of 1.2 GB [8].

3.1.3 Multiple data streams

Storage systems must consider the fact that clients may make many requests for different movies [7]. As such requests make a disk head move significantly forward or backward, disk scheduling must be designed efficiently.

3.1.4 Continuous access

If a movie is accessed by a user request, the access has a greater likelihood of continuing for a longer time than general file, text file access, or a graphic file access.

3.2 Research on multimedia storage systems

For the abovementioned requirements, research has been conducted on the following aspects.

3.2.1 Disk scheduling

This must be improved because traditional systems do not support real-time characteristics although they support performance and fairness. In addition, multiple data streams make the disk head take large forward or backward jumps in multi-user environments. Efficient disk scheduling for multimedia storage systems must minimize this overhead and support real-time characteristics.

Traditional scheduling schemes include First Come First Served (FCFS), Shortest Seek Time First (SSTF), Elevator (SCAN), and C-SCAN algorithms [9]. As an example of a disk-scheduling algorithm for multimedia storage systems, Earliest Deadline First (EDF) [10] is an algorithm that processes the request closest to the deadline first, and can support real-time characteristics. However, EDF has the limitation that it has a long seek time and rotational delay, which in turn lead to poor performance. Hence, many researchers have attempted to improve EDF or SCAN with other algorithms [11, 12]. Although SCAN-EDF [11] operates like EDF in cases of requests with different deadlines, it operates like SCAN with identical deadline requests. WRR-SCAN [12] combines WRR (Weighted-Round-Robin) with SCAN. A weight is assigned to each real-time task, and the disk head provides service based on this weight.

3.2.2 Data placement

Either contiguous or scattered block placement can be used for storing movies. If the requested movie is placed on physically contiguous blocks in a single disk, the response time can be significantly reduced, especially for multimedia systems, because the seek time and rotational delay are reduced. However, this continuous placement is likely to cause a fragmentation problem. In contrast, this problem does not occur when scattered physical blocks are used for placing movies. However, the reading overheads are greater for scattered placement than for contiguous placement owing to the greater number of intra-file seeks relative to the physical blocks during numerous requests [13].

Extent-based, cylinder-based, or constrained placement [7] attempts to minimize the seek time by placing the physical blocks of a movie within an extent, a cylinder, or an average distance, respectively. Log-structured placement attempts to minimize writing time instead of the seek time; it writes all modifications to the physical blocks after collecting them in a large contiguous area of free space on a disk. Consequently, this placement scheme is suitable for storage systems with numerous movie updates.

Data striping and data interleaving are both technologies that scatter movies across a set of disks.

3.2.3 Buffer management

Both caching and replacement algorithms are critical for buffer management because a buffer is a restricted resource. Replacement algorithms can be classified into block-based and stream-based algorithms [7]. In block-based algorithms, a block in the disk is cached and replaced using algorithms such as Least Recently Used (LRU) and Least Frequently Used (LFU), similar to caching algorithms at the CPU level. Least/Most Relevant for Presentation (L/MRP) was proposed as a block-based algorithm for multimedia systems [7]. L/MRP considers a presentation mode and a presentation point as parameters.

Stream-based algorithms assume that if many requests for the same movie are issued, then the same requests will be issued. Interval caching, which is among the stream-based algorithms [7], selects the smallest intervals as to-be-cached objects in order to maximally utilize the temporal locality [14].

The prefetching strategy is especially efficient for a multimedia system because it exploits the continuous access pattern of the multimedia system.

3.2.4 Admission control

These algorithms determine whether to admit a new request to the storage system after considering the deadlines of existing requests. There are cases in which new sequential requests must be denied because the deadlines of existing requests must be met first. There are also cases in which a client application can reward missed deadlines or tolerate some missed deadlines. These various requirements of deadlines can be classified into the following three categories [13].

- **Deterministic**: All deadlines must be met. In this category, requests that may violate the deadline must be denied.

- **Statistical**: A certain probability of deadlines may be met. In this category, for example, a client application can view a movie even if only 80% of the deadlines are guaranteed. Admission control algorithms determine admission according to the statistics.

- **Best effort**: There is no guarantee in this category. The storage systems simply attempt their best to meet the deadlines.

4 Delivery systems

The delivery system delivers movies to clients after receiving them from the storage systems. In this section, we describe the geographical placement of servers, movie allocation to delivery systems, server selection, and request routings that deliver a request to one of the delivery systems and serve the clients.

4.1 Server placement

The geographical placement of delivery systems is important because the optimal placement enables movies to be delivered with minimal delay and jitter. Studies on finding the optimal placement have been conducted with extra servers in distributed systems [15] and with replica placement [16] in the web environment. Wua et al. [15] propose a dynamic programming algorithm and a heuristic in the case that the server can serve unlimited requests and three different heuristics in the case that the server has some limitations. Qiu et al. [16] suggest that the greedy algorithm is the best among the algorithms mentioned in their paper for this placement problem. Balázs et al. [17] show that the other algorithms can be better than the greedy algorithm. Qiu et al. and Balázs et al. show that this problem can be addressed by using many algorithms that address the Facility Location Problem or K-median problem.

Although the initial placement can be determined by using one of these algorithms when the client requests and network topologies are given, dynamically changing the initial placement is difficult. Thus, movie allocation and server selection, described in the following subsections, are more widely investigated for optimal streaming.

4.2 Movie allocation

The file sizes of movies in a multimedia system are enormous. Hence, storing the same movies in all of the delivery systems is a waste. However, allocation of movies to all of the delivery systems can guarantee minimum network delays owing to the close distance between a client and a system. The frequency of movie duplication in delivery systems may be another problem because frequent duplication may cause serious performance deterioration because of the excessive time consumed to copy movies. Simple cache replacement algorithms such as FIFO, MRU, LRU, and LFU are difficult to use owing to the enormous file sizes of movies. Another issue worth considering is that user access to movies has temporal and spatial localities like those of a CPU-level cache [18]. In other words, a movie that is once accessed is more likely to be accessed in the near future and in nearby locations. Movies should be allocated to the delivery systems after considering these complex factors, such as the storage capacity, network delay, frequency of movie duplication, temporal locality, and spatial locality.

The problem of optimal allocation, which maximally saves storage capacity and minimizes communication overheads between clients and the delivery systems, was known as the File Allocation Problem and shown to be NP-complete [19]. This problem has been investigated in [20 - 22]. Bisdikian et al. [20] describe their cost model and many issues regarding movie allocation for future studies, and Akiko et al. [21] describe their cost model and propose an approximate algorithm for movie allocation. Takeshita et al. [22] propose a new algorithm that runs on a dynamically reconfigurable processor.

When designing movie allocation algorithms, the following three different processes are considered.

- **Movie selection**: This process determines the to-be-duplicated movie. The movie is usually chosen by the predictive load [23], by ascending order [24], by descending order [20], by alternating order according to popularity, or at random [25]. The sequentially ascending or descending method selects a movie based on popularity in ascending or descending order. In the alternation method, movies are alternatively selected. For example, movies may be selected in the following order: the most popular movie first, the least popular movie next, the next most popular movie third, the next least popular movie fourth, and so on. In the random method, a movie is randomly selected.

- **Count selection**: This process determines the number of duplications of a movie. For example, a highly popular movie can be duplicated to numerous delivery systems. The duplication number has been determined by solving the apportionment problem [26]. The predictive load [23] and popularity [20, 24] have been investigated for this determination. Furthermore, Wolf et al. [27] used Webster's monotone divisor based on popularity.

- **Selection of movie-duplicating server**: This process determines the server on which the selected movie is duplicated. If the movie and number of duplications are selected, the delivery system with the movie will be chosen. The delivery systems were determined based on the round-robin [24] or circular first fit [25] methods. In addition, the first fit or best fit can be used. The round-robin method simply selects one of the delivery systems from a list in a round-robin manner; the first fit method selects the first delivery system with sufficient network bandwidth and storage capacity; the best fit method selects the best delivery system among them; and the circular first fit (the next fit) is the same as the first fit, except that the delivery system is found from the next delivery system that is previously selected.

4.3 Server selection

Server selection in web systems, which has been actively investigated, can be applied to multimedia systems. One of the servers can be selected after considering the factors that are classified into the following three classes [28].

- **Static**: One of the video servers is statically selected by using static data such as geographical proximity [24], the number of hops between a client and a server [25], bandwidth of network interfaces, speed of the CPU, and disk speed.

- **Statistical**: One of the video servers is statistically selected by using the past performance data, such as network latencies and network bandwidth.

- **Dynamic**: One of the video servers is dynamically selected after probing the current CPU usage, disk usage, or round-trip time through the Ping.

Dynamic approaches show the best results in many studies [28]. However, dynamic approaches have additional probing overheads, and most of the tests were conducted for parallel web server systems instead of parallel multimedia systems.

In addition, random selection and round-robin selection can be used without considering any of the factors mentioned above.

4.4 Request routings

Request routing redirects the requesting client to one of the selected servers by using one of the methods introduced in the previous sub-section. For the purpose of distributing a request transparently to clients, many request routings such as Linux Virtual Server (LVS) and DNS have been developed. We refer the interested reader to [29] for request routings.

5 Conclusions

In this paper, we classified studies on parallel multimedia systems largely into two categories: those on storage systems and those on delivery systems. We also classified the research on storage systems into the following four categories: disk scheduling, data placement, buffer management, and admission control. Furthermore, we classified the research on delivery systems into studies on server placement, movie allocation, server selection, and request routing. We describe each sub-category and introduce some existing research within it for the future researches.

We believe that this paper is valuable in providing a summary of research on parallel multimedia systems thus far. To the best of our knowledge, this paper describes the broadest fields on parallel multimedia systems.

6 References

[1] George Pallis, Athena Vakali. "Insight and perspectives for content delivery networks"; Communications of the ACM, 49, 1, 101—106, 2006.

[2] Jussi Kangasharju, James Roberts, Keith W. Ross. "Object replication strategies in content distribution networks"; Computer Communications, 25, 4, 376—383, 2002.

[3] Adrian J. Cahill, Cormac J. Sreenan. "VCDN: A content distribution network for high quality video distribution"; Proceedings of Information Technology & Telecommunications, Letterkenny, Ireland, 2003.

[4] Michael Kozuch, Wayne Wolf, Andrew Wolfe. "Network caching resource allocation for multimedia objects"; Proceedings of IEEE Real-Time Systems Symposium Workshop on Resource Allocation Problems in Multimedia Systems, 1996.

[5] Chu-Sing Yang, Mon-Yen Luo. "Efficient support for content-based routing in web server clusters"; Proceedings of 2nd USENIX Symposium on Internet Technologies and Systems, 1999.

[6] Mon-Yen Luo, Chu-Sing Yang, Chun-Wei Tseng. "Analysis and improvement of content-aware routing mechanism"; IEICE Trans. Commun, E88-B, 1, 227-238, 2005.

[7] Pål Halvorsen, Carsten Griwodz, Ketil Lund, Vera Goebel, Thomas Plagemann. "Storage system support for multimedia applications"; Research Report No. 307, 2003.

[8] Xiaofei Liao, Hai Jin. "A new distributed storage scheme for cluster video server, Journal of Systems Architecture" ; 51, 2, 79—94, 2005.

[9] Andrew S. Tanenbaum. "Modern Operating Systems". Prentice Hall, 2001.

[10] Ishan Khera, Ajay Kakkar. "Comparative study of scheduling algorithms for real time environment"; International Journal of Computer Applications, 44, 2, 5—8, 2012.

[11] A. L. N. Reddy, Jim Wyllie, K. B. R. Wijayaratne. "Disk scheduling in a multimedia I/O system"; Proceedings of ACM Multimedia Conference, Anaheim, CA, USA, 225—233, 1993.

[12] Cheng-Han Tsai, Edward T.-H. Chu, Tai-Yi Huang. "WRR-SCAN: A rate-based real-time disk-scheduling algorithm"; Proceedings of the 4th ACM international conference on Embedded software, 86—94, 2004.

[13] D. James Gemmell, Harrick M. Vin, Dilip D. Kandlur, P. Venkat. "Multimedia storage servers: A tutorial and survey"; IEEE Computer, 1995.

[14] Sudhir N. Dhage, B.B. Meshram. "Buffer management scheme for video-on-demand (VoD) system"; Proceedings of International Conference on Information and Computer Networks, 2012.

[15] Jan-Jan Wua, Shu-Fan Shiha, Pangfeng Liuc, Yi-Min Chung. "Optimizing server placement in distributed systems in the presence of competition"; Journal of Parallel and Distributed Computting, 71, 1, 62—76, 2012.

[16] Lili Qiu, Venkata N. Padmanabhan, Geoffrey M. Voelker. "On the placement of web server replicas"; Proceedings of the 20th IEEE INFOCOM, 2001.

[17] Balázs Goldschmidt, Tibor Szkaliczki, László Böszörményi. "Placement of nodes in an adaptive distributed multimedia server"; Proceedings of Euro-Par, 776—783, 2004.

[18] Soam Acharya, Brian Smith, Peter Parnes. "Characterizing user access to videos on the world wide web"; Proceedings of ACM/SPIE Multimedia Computing and Networking, 2000.

[19] Samee Ullah Khan, Ishfaq Ahmad. "Data replication in large distributed computing systems using discriminatory game theoretic mechanism design"; Proceedings of International Conference on Parallel Computing Technologies, 2005.

[20] C. C. Bisdikian, B. V. Patel. "Issues on movie allocation in distributed video-on-demand systems"; Proceedings of IEEE Int. Conf. on Communications, 250—255, 1995.

[21] Akiko Nakaniwa, Masaki Ohnishi, Hiroyuki Ebara, Hiromi Okada. "File allocation in distributed multimedia information networks"; Proceedings of Global Telecommunications Conference, 740—745, 1998.

[22] Hidetoshi Takeshita, Sho Shimizu, Hiroyuki Ishikawa, Akifumi Watanabe, Yutaka Arakawa, Naoaki Yamanaka, Kosuke Shiba. "Fast optimal replica placement with exhaustive search using dynamically reconfigurable processor"; Journal Computer Networks and Communications, 1—11, 2011.

[23] K. F. Tsang, S. H. Kwok. "Video management in commercial distributed video on demand (VoD) systems"; Proceedings of PACIS, 2000.

[24] Dimitrios N. Serpanos, Leonidas Georgiadis, Tasos Bouloutas. "MMPacking: A load and storage balancing algorithm for distributed multimedia servers"; IEEE Transactions on Circuits and Systems for Video Technology", 8, 1, 13—17, 1998.

[25] Ming-Syan Chen, Hui-I Hsiao, Chung-Sheng Li, Philip S. Yu. "Using rotational mirrored declustering for replica placement in a disk-array-based video server"; Proceedings of the Third ACM Conference on Multimedia, 121—130, 1995.

[26] A. Karve, T. Kimbrel, G. Pacifici, M. Spreitzer, M. Steinder, M. Sviridenko, A. Tantawi. "Dynamic placement for clustered web applications"; Proceedings of the 15th International Conference on World Wide Web, 595—604, 2006.

[27] Joel L. Wolf, Philip S. Yu, Hadas Shachnai. "DASD dancing: A disk load balancing optimization scheme for video-on-demand computer systems"; Proceedings of the ACM International Conference on Measurement and Modeling of Computer Systems (SIGMETRICS), 157—166, 1995.

[28] Sandra G. Dykesz, Clinton L. Jeffery, Kay A. Robbins. "An empirical evaluation of client-side server selection algorithms"; Proceedings of IEEE Infocom, 1361—1370, 2000.

[29] Kim SeongKi, Han SangYong. "MediaFrame: Parallel multimedia system architecture through HTTP redirection"; KIPS Transactions Part A, 14, 1, 15—24, 2007.

From Sequence of Tumor Liberated Protein (TLP) to Function and Potential Targets for Diagnosis and Therapy

Giulio Tarro, MD, PhD
Department of Biology, Center for Biotechnology, Sbarro institute for Cancer Research and Molecular Medicine, Temple University, Philadelphia, PA, USA.
Committee on Biotechnologies and VirusSphere, World Academy of Biomedical Technologies, UNESCO, Paris, France.
Correspondence to: Prof. Dr. Giulio Tarro, Via Posillipo 286, 80123 Naples, Italy
e-mail: gitarro@tin.it giuliotarro@gmail.com

Abstract *- From the first analysis of immuneprecipitation followed by Western Blotting (WB) Corin and TLP seem to precipitate at the same height (approximately 50KDa) and are recognized by the same antibodies. In parallel we are improving the tests of immunoprecipitation by the use of cell extracts derived from lung cancer cells A549 and NCI-H23 with the aim to be able of obtaining a precipitate containing only the TLP. In fact the partial aminoacid sequence of TLP showes a high homology with the sequence of human Corin (only one aminoacid is different) and is present in lung cancer under different isoforms. It is known that human Corin is expressed mostly outside the cells and the protein extract derived from the extracellular medium and from the cells transfected with the plasmid, which overexpresses Corin, showes many more bands analyzed on SDS-PAGE that are equivalent to the bands (about 50-100 KDa) observed in the WB analyzed with anti-TLP.*

Keywords: *TLP, NSCL, Corin, Immunotherapy, Vaccine*

1 Introduction

While surgery, radiotherapy and chemotherapy are able to cure many cancers, new approaches are required to improve radical curative therapy. A possible route is to utilize the latest achievements made in research on the immunology and genetics of cancer [1]. Cancer immunotherapy [2], or the manipulation of the naturally occurring oncolytic immune reaction, is based on the observation that both in animals and humans neoplastic cell antigens stimulate the onset of specific humoral and cellular antibodies [3]. Certain difficulties that have been encountered reflect the lack of well-purified antigens and/or their ability to unblock cell immunity in the cancer patient.

Two ways are known to enhance the host's immunity: aspecific activation (BCG in primis) and specific activation (to stimulate oncolytic circulating and cell antibodies). Moreover, some researchers have performed therapeutic trials with antigens, from autologous and homologous human cancer cells, obtained by various purification procedures [4]; [5].

The first observation by Tarro et al [6] demonstrated that when TLP is extracted from a tumor, purified in the laboratory, and reintroduced into the patients body, it boosts the immune system's cancer responsive capabilities [7]. As lung cancer accounts for the largest number of cancer deaths in the Western world, TLP may have the potential to greatly improve the cure rate and or serve as a lung cancer vaccine (Table 1) [8].

Corin is a cardic serine protease that activates natriuretic peptides. It consists of an N-terminal cytoplasmic tail, a transmembrane domain, and an extracellular region with a C-terminal trypsin-like protease domain. The transmembrane domain anchors corin on the surface of cardiomycytes. To date, the function of the corin cytoplasmic tail remains unknown [9]. Corin shows high homology with TLP and is present in various isoforms in the lung [10]. If the fragments from cutting with thrombin proved to be the same, the data would support the hypothesis that TLP and Corin are the same protein. At the same time we are arranging to use a plasmid that allows us to transfect and over-express human corin with the purpose to assess by Western blotting (with anti-TLP and anti-Corin antibodies) whether the two proteins are actually the same protein or are different.

2 Material and Methods

1. Antigens, Ac-RTNKEASI-Ahx-C-amide,Ac-Ahx-C-amide-NQRNRD, Corin
2. Antibodies, Anti-Corin antibody, Anti-TLP antibody
3. Cell Lines, Cancer cell lines : A549, H23, H82, H187
Control cell lines : MET-SA, NL-20, Primary line of fibroblasts
4. Tests, a) Immunoblotting, b) Immunoprecipitation,
c) Peptide competions assay, d) Western blotting
5. Other reagents, Thrombin to cut protein, Plasmid to transfect Corin

3 Results

From the first analysis of immuneprecititation followed by Western blotting Corin and TLP seem to precipitate at the same height (approximately 50KDa) and are recognized by the same antibodies, Concurrently we obtained a plasmid from Prof, Qingyu (Cleveland, Ohio) that let us transfect HEK-293 cells and overexpressthe human Corin with the purpose to evaluate by Western blotting (with anti- TLP and anti-Corin) whether the two proteins are really the same protein. In parallel we are improving the tests of immunoprecipitation by the use of cell extracts derived from lung cancer cells A549 and NCI-H23 with the aim to be able of obtaining a precipitate containing only the TLP. This result would allow a better sequence of the aminoterminal fragment of TLP and furthermore would allow to look in details the homologies between TLP and Corin.

From a careful analysis of bibliography conceming both TLP and Human Corin, and from our data achieved during the present time, it seems that is coming out that Corin and TLP are really the same protein.

In fact the partial aminoacid sequence of TLP showes a high homology with the sequence of human Corin (only one aminoacid is different) and is present in lung cancer under different isoforms. From the references it is known that human Corin is expressed mostly outside the cells and the protein extract derived from the extracellular medium and from the cells transfected with the plasmid, which overexpresses Corin, showes many more bands analyzed on SDS-PAGE that are equivalent to the bands (about 50-100 KDa) observed in the Western blots analyzed with anti- TLP.

3.1 Tables

TLP AS A TUMOR – ASSOCIATED ANTIGEN
• 50 KD PROTEIN OVEREXPRESSED IN LUNG TUMORS AND OTHERS EPITHELIAL ADENOCARCINOMAS
• IMMUNIGENIC IN HUMANS AS EVIDENCED BY SERUM ANTIBODIES

Table 1. Tumor Liberated Protein from Lung Cancer and Perspectives for Immunotherapy

TISSUE MICROARRAY PROFILE (a)		
NSCLC STAGE I	POSITIVITY (%)	NEGATIVITY (%)
TISSUE		
400	56.3 (225/400)	43.7 (175/400)
NORMAL LUNG TISSUE	POSITIVITY (%)	NEGATIVITY (%)
400	0 (0/400)	100 (400/400)
(a) Carried out by William C. Hyun, Ph.D., at the University of California San Francisco, Cancer Center, Laboratory Cell Analysis.		

Table 2. Sensitivity and Specificity of TLP for Antibodies

3.2 Figures

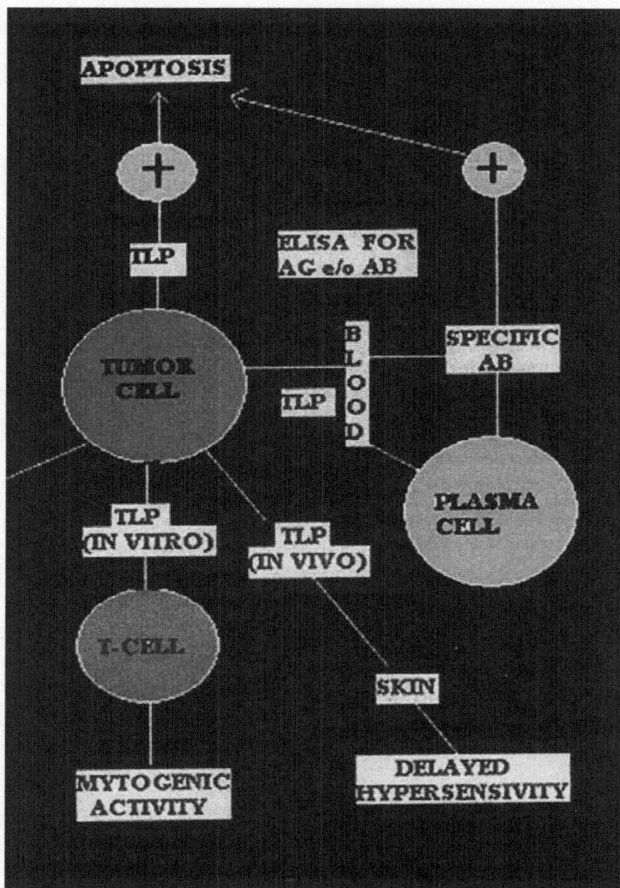

Fig 1. In *vitro* and in *vivo* Functions of TLP

4 Conclusions

Tumor Liberated Protein (TLP) is a new protein extracted from tumors in *vivo* and transformed cells in *vitro* (Fig. 1)[8]. TLP is detectable in blood as well as in cancer tissue [11];

[12].
TLP is a tumor associated antigen of 50 KD monomer [13]; [14].
TLP is overexpressed in lung tumor [13]; [14] and other epithelial adenocarcinomas [15]; [16].
TLP is immunogenic in humans as evidenced by serum antibodies [17].
Preliminary information on lung tissue microarray is shown in table 2.
<Research is ongoing to obtain the complete sequence of TLP, by proteomics approaches, in order to achieve adequate antigen preparations that might be used to generate assays for early diagnosis and, possibly, a specific anticancer vaccine> [18].
The perspectives of TLP are the following:

– Since its sequences stimulate cytotoxic immunoresponse in humans and animal models, it is possible to design potential active and passive immunotherapies for NSCL cancer and colorectal cancers (CRC) based on TLP epitopes and humanized antibodies [19]; [20].
– Fragments of TLP can be used to stimulate immune response to attack existing tumors [9]; [21].
– At risk populations could be inoculated with TLP fragments to stimulate immune response to undetected or newly developing tumors [22]; [23].
– Therefore the ability of the immune system to recognize TLP, represents a main target for diagnosis and therapy in this field of research.

5 References

[1]OJ. Finn. Molecular origins of cancer: Cancer immunology. N Engl J Med 358: 2704-2715, 2008.

[2] BE. Rennik. Cancer immunotherapy: facts and fancy. J Clin 29: 362-365, 1979.

[3] DW. Weiss. Tumor antigenicity and approches to tumor immunotherapy. An outline In: current topics in microbiology and immunology. Berlin, Heidelberg, New York: Springer Verlag, 1980.

[4] A. Hollinshed et al. Immunogenecity of a soluble transplantation antigen from adenovirus 12 - induced tumor cells demostrated in inbred hamsters (PD-4). Can. J. Microbiol 18;1365-1369, 1972.

[5] MD. Prager et al. Immunity induction by multiple methods, including soluble membrane fractions to a mouse lymphoma. J Natl Cancer Inst 51: 1607, 1973.

[6] G. Tarro, A. Pederzini, G. Flaminio, S. Maturo. Human tumor antigens inducing in vivo delayed hypersensitivity and in vitro mitogenic activity. Oncology 40: 248-254. 1983.

[7] G. Tarro. Present and future of cancer immunotherapy: A. Sagripanti, C. Gagliardi, A. Carpi. G. Tarro. , editors. Progress in Medicine and Surgery, Proc. Nat. Meeting, San Romano (Pisa) 13 April 1991, 181-186 ETS, Publisher, Pisa. 1991.

[8] G. Tarro. Tumor liberated protein from lung cancer and perspectives for immunotherapy. J Cell Physiol 221:26-30. 2009.

[9] F. Wu, Q. Wu. Corin-mediated processing of pro-atrial natriuretic Peptide in human small cell lung cancer. 63: 8318-8322, 2003.

[10] X. Qi, J. Jiang, M. Zhu, Q. Wu. Human corin isoforms with different cytoplasmic tails that alter cell surface targeting. The Journal of Biological Chemistry 286: 20963-20969. 2011.

[11] G. Tarro, C. Esposito. Progress and new hope in the fight against cancer: novel developments in early detection of lung cancer. Int Med 10: 7-11. 2002.

[12] G. Tarro, A. Perna, C. Esposito. Early diagnosis of lung cancer by detection of tumor liberated protein. J Cell Physiol. 203: 1-5. 2005.

[13] G. Tarro, DR. Marshak, A. Perna, C. Esposito. Antigenic regions of tumor liberated protein complexes and antibodies against the same. In: A. Carpi, A. Sagripanti, B. Grassi, editors. Third International Congress. Advances in Management of Malignancies. Pisa, Italy: 6/10 December 1993. Biomed & Pharmacother 47: 237-240. 1993.

[14] G. Tarro, C. Esposito, A. Perna, PP. Claudio, A. Giordano, Immunoistochemical characterization of tumor liberated particles (TLP) expression pattern in lung cancer. Anticancer Res 18: 2365-2370. 1998.

[15] F. Guadagni, P. Graziano, M. Roselli, S. Mariotti, P. Bernard, P. Sinibalsi-Vallebona, G. Rasi, E. Garaci. Differential expression of a new tumor-associated-antigen TLP during human colorectal cancer tumorigenesis. Am J Pathol 154:993-999. 2000.]

[16] G. Rasi, P. Sinibaldi-Vallebona, A. Serafino, P. Bernard, P. Pierimarchi, E. Guarino, L. Faticanti-Scucchi, P. Graziano, F. Guadagni, E. Garaci. A new human tumor-associated antigen (TLP) is naturally espressed in rat DHD-K12 colorectal tumor cells. Int J Cancer 85: 540-544. 2000.

[17] C. Esposito, G. Tarro, N. Cuomo, F. Morelli. Anti-TLP antibodies in lung cancer patients. Int Med 5: 191-194. 1997.

[18] P. Indovina, E. Marcelli, P. Maranta, G. Tarro. Lung cancer proteomics: recent advances in biomarker discovery. Int Journal of Proteomics. 10.1155, 2011.

[19] RB. Herberman. Immunotherapy: where we are and how to proceed. In: Croce CM Doctor's Acta pp 14-15, 1997,

[20] G.Tarro. Tumor liberated protein (TLP). Its potential for diagnosis and therapy. Anticancer Res 19: 1755-1758. 1999.

[21] P. Bernard, P. Sinibaldi-Vallebona, G. Rasi, E. Guarino, F. Guadagni, E. Garaci. Immunisation with TLP (A new Tumor Associated Antigen) induces CTL activity in syngeneic rats. Anticancer Res 18: 4990-4994. 1998.

[22] G. Tarro. An overview of the lung tumor liberated protein (TLP).Characterization of the genetic immunologic profile. Int Med 8:5-8. 2000.

[23] G. Tarro. Characterization of a fragment containing a putative TLP cDNA sequence. Anticancer Res 22: 2693-2696. 2002.

The author declares no conflict of interests.

SESSION

WORKSHOP: MATHEMATICAL MODELING AND PROBLEM SOLVING - MPS

Chair(s)

Prof. Minoru Ito

Inferring Strengths of Protein-Protein Interactions Using Support Vector Regression

Yusuke Sakuma, Mayumi Kamada, Morihiro Hayashida, and Tatsuya Akutsu
Bioinformatics Center
Institute for Chemical Research
Kyoto University
Gokasho, Uji, Kyoto 611–0011, Japan
Email: {sakuma, kamada, morihiro, takutsu}@kuicr.kyoto-u.ac.jp

Abstract— *Protein-protein interactions (PPIs) play various important roles in living organisms. Hence, many efforts have been made to investigate and predict PPIs. Analysis of strengths of PPIs is important as well as PPIs because such strengths are involved in functionality of proteins. In this paper, we propose several feature space mappings from protein pairs, which make use of protein domain information, and perform five-fold cross-validation for data obtained from biological experiments. The result of average root mean square error (RMSE) using support vector regression (SVR) with our proposed feature was better than that by the best existing method, APM proposed by Chen et al.*

Keywords: protein-protein interaction strength, support vector regression, protein domain

1. Introduction

Many investigations and analyses have been done for protein-protein interactions (PPIs) due to their importance in cellular systems. In addition, many prediction methods have been developed. As well as studies of PPIs, analyses of *strengths* of PPIs are important because such strengths are involved in functionality of proteins. In terms of transcription factor complexes, if a member protein has a weak binding affinity, target genes may not be transcribed depending on intracellular circumstance. For example, it is known that multi-subunit complex NuA3 in *Saccharomyces Cerevisiae* consists of five proteins, Sas3, Nto1, Yng1, Eaf6, and Taf30, acetylates lysine 14 of histone H3, and activates gene transcription. However, Yng1 and Nto1 are often found in the complex, and interactions with other member proteins are difficult to be observed by biological experiments. Hence, Byrum et al. proposed a biological methodology for identifying transient and unstable protein interactions recently [1].

Although many biological experiments have been conducted for protein-protein interactions [2], [3], strengths of PPIs have not been always provided. Ito et al. conducted large-scale yeast two-hybrid experiments for whole yeast proteins. In their experiments, yeast two-hybrid experiments were conducted for each protein pair multiple times, and the number of experiments that interactions were observed, or the number of interaction sequence tags (ISTs), was counted. Consequently, they decided that protein pairs having three or more ISTs should interact, and reported interacting protein pairs.

The ratio of the number of ISTs to the total number of experiments for a protein pair can be regarded as the interaction strength between their proteins. On the basis of this consideration, several prediction methods for strengths of PPIs have been developed. LPNM [4] is a linear programming-based method, and ASNM [4] is a modified method from the association method [5] for predicting PPIs. Chen et al. proposed association probabilistic method (APM) [6], which is the best existing method for predicting strengths of PPIs as far as we know. These methods make use of protein domain information. Domains are known as structural and functional units in proteins, and are stored in several databases such as Pfam [7] and InterPro [8]. The same domain can be identified in several different proteins. In these prediction methods, interaction strengths between domains are estimated from known interaction strengths between proteins, and interaction strengths for target protein pairs are predicted from estimated strengths of domain-domain interactions.

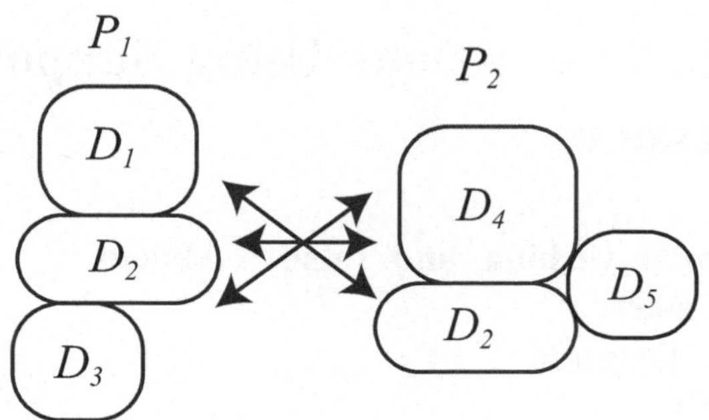

Fig. 1: Illustration of protein-protein interaction model based on domain-domain interactions

In this paper, we also make use of domain information, and propose several feature space mappings from protein pairs. We use support vector regression (SVR), perform five-fold cross-validation for data from biological experiments by Ito et al. [3] and WI-PHI dataset [9], and take the average root mean square error (RMSE). The average RMSE by our proposed method was smaller than that by the best existing method, APM [6].

2. Method

In this section, we briefly review a probabilistic model and related methods, the association method [5], ASNM (association method for numerical interaction data) [4], APM (association probabilistic method) [6], and propose several feature space mappings using domain information.

2.1 Probabilistic Model of Protein-Protein Interactions Based on Domain-Domain Interactions

Many strength prediction methods are based on the probabilistic model of protein-protein interactions proposed by Deng et al. [10]. This model utilizes domain-domain interactions, and assumes that two proteins interact with each other if and only if at least one pair of domains contained in the respective proteins interacts. Fig. 1 illustrates this interaction model between two proteins P_1 and P_2, which consist of domains D_1, D_2, D_3, and domains D_2, D_4, D_5, respectively. As in this case, two proteins can contain the same domain. According to this model, if P_1 and P_2 interact, at least one pair among (D_1, D_2), (D_1, D_4), (D_1, D_5), (D_2, D_2), (D_2, D_4), (D_2, D_5), (D_3, D_2), (D_3, D_4), and (D_3, D_5) interacts. Conversely, if a pair, for instance (D_3, D_4), interacts, P_1 and P_2 interact.

From the assumption of this model, we can derive the following simple probability that two proteins P_i and P_j interact with each other.

$$Pr(P_{ij} = 1) = 1 - \prod_{D_m \in P_i, D_n \in P_j} (1 - Pr(D_{mn} = 1)), \quad (1)$$

where $P_{ij} = 1$ indicates the event that proteins P_i and P_j interact (otherwise $P_{ij} = 0$), $D_{mn} = 1$ indicates the event that domains D_m and D_n interact (otherwise $D_{mn} = 0$), P_i and P_j also represent the sets of domains contained in P_i and P_j, respectively. Deng et al. applied the EM (expectation maximization) algorithm to the problem of maximizing log-likelihood functions, estimated probabilities that two domains interact, $Pr(D_{mn} = 1)$, and proposed a method for predicting PPIs using the estimated probabilities of domain-domain interactions [10]. Actually, they calculated $Pr(P_{ij} = 1)$ using Eq. (1), and determined whether or not P_i and P_j interact by introducing a threshold θ, that is, P_i and P_j interact if $Pr(P_{ij} = 1) \geq \theta$, otherwise the proteins do not interact. Since interacting sites may not be always included in some known domain region, it can cause the decrease of prediction accuracy in this framework.

2.2 Association Method

Let $\mathcal{P}$ be a set of protein pairs that have been observed to interact or not to interact. The association method [5] gives the following simple score for two domains D_m and D_n using proteins that include the domains.

$$ASSOC(D_m, D_n) = \frac{|\{(P_i, P_j) \in \mathcal{P} | D_m \in P_i, D_n \in P_j, P_{ij} = 1\}|}{|\{(P_i, P_j) \in \mathcal{P} | D_m \in P_i, D_n \in P_j\}|}, \quad (2)$$

where $|S|$ indicates the number of elements contained in the set S. This score represents the ratio of the number of interacting protein pairs including D_m and D_n to the total number of protein pairs including D_m and D_n. Hence, it can be considered as the probability that D_m and D_n interact.

2.3 Association Method for Numerical Interaction Data (ASNM)

The association method for numerical interaction data (ASNM) [4] is a modified method for predicting strengths of PPIs from the original association method [5]. This method takes strengths of PPIs as input data. Let ρ_{ij} represent the interaction strength between P_i and P_j, and we suppose that ρ_{ij} is defined for all $(P_i, P_j) \in \mathcal{P}$. Then, the ASNM score for domains D_m and D_n is defined as the average strength over protein pairs including D_m and D_n by

$$ASNM(D_m, D_n) = \frac{\sum_{\{(P_i,P_j)\in\mathcal{P}|D_m\in P_i, D_n\in P_j\}} \rho_{ij}}{|\{(P_i, P_j) \in \mathcal{P}|D_m \in P_i, D_n \in P_j\}|}. \quad (3)$$

If ρ_{ij} always takes only 0 or 1, $ASNM(D_m, D_n)$ becomes $ASSOC(D_m, D_n)$.

2.4 Association Probabilistic Method (APM)

Although ASNM is a simple average of strengths of PPIs, Chen et al. proposed the association probabilistic method (APM) by replacing the strength with an improved strength [6]. It is based on the idea that the contribution of one domain pair to the strength of a PPI should vary depending on the number of domain pairs included in a protein pair. They assumed that the interaction probability of each domain pair is equivalent in a protein pair, and transformed Eq. (1) as follows:

$$Pr(D_{mn} = 1) = 1 - (1 - Pr(P_{ij} = 1))^{\frac{1}{|P_i||P_j|}}. \quad (4)$$

Thus, by substituting the numerator of ASNM, APM is defined by

$$APM(D_m, D_n) = \frac{\sum_{\{(P_i,P_j)\in\mathcal{P}|D_m\in P_i, D_n\in P_j\}} (1 - (1 - \rho_{ij})^{\frac{1}{|P_i||P_j|}})}{|\{(P_i, P_j) \in \mathcal{P}|D_m \in P_i, D_n \in P_j\}|}. \quad (5)$$

They conducted some computational experiments, and reported that APM outperforms existing prediction methods such as ASNM and LPNM.

2.5 Feature Based on Number of Domains (DN)

We propose a feature space mapping based on the number of domains (DN) from two proteins. It can be considered that the probability that two proteins interact increases with a larger number of domains included in the proteins. Thus, the feature vector of

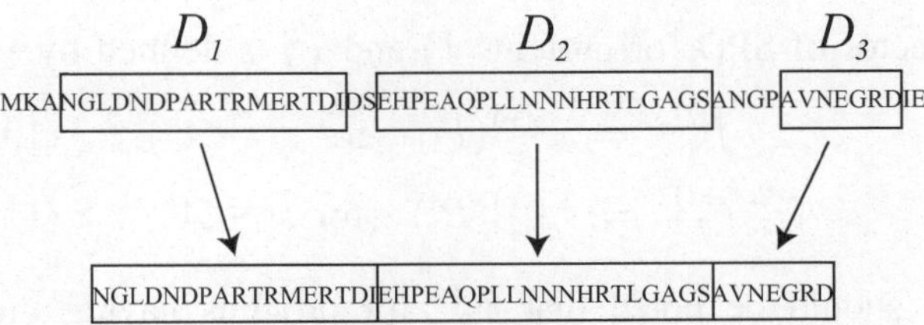

Fig. 2: Illustration of restricting an amino acid sequence to which the spectrum kernel is applied to the domain regions

DN for two proteins P_i and P_j is defined by

$$f_{ij}^{(m)} = M(D_m, P_i) \text{ (for } D_m \in P_i), \quad (6)$$
$$f_{ij}^{(T+n)} = M(D_n, P_j) \text{ (for } D_n \in P_j), \quad (7)$$
$$f_{ij}^{(l)} = 0 \text{ (for } D_l \notin P_i \cup P_j), \quad (8)$$

where T indicates the total number of domains over all proteins, and $M(D_m, P_i)$ indicates the number of domains identified as D_m in protein P_i.

2.6 Feature by Restriction of Spectrum Kernel to Domain Region (SPD)

Furthermore, we propose a feature space mapping by restricting the application of the spectrum kernel [11] to domain regions (SPD). Let $\mathcal{A}$ be the set of alphabets representing twenty types of amino acids. Then, $\mathcal{A}^k$ ($k \geq 1$) means the set of all strings with length k generated from $\mathcal{A}$. The k-spectrum kernel for sequences x and y is defined by

$$K_k(x, y) = \langle \Phi_k(x), \Phi_k(y) \rangle, \quad (9)$$

where $\Phi_k(x) = (\phi_s(x))_{s\in\mathcal{A}^k}$ and $\phi_s(x)$ indicates the number of times that s occurs in x.

To make use of domain information, we restrict an amino acid sequence to which the k-spectrum kernel is applied to the domain regions. Fig. 2 illustrates the restriction. In this example, the protein consists of domains D_1, D_2, D_3, and each domain region is surrounded by a square. Then, the subsequence in each domain is extracted, and all the subsequences in the protein are concatenated in the same order as domains. We apply the k-spectrum kernel to the concatenated sequence. Let $\phi_s^{(r)}(x)$ be the number of times that string s occurs in the sequence restricted to the domain regions in protein x in the above manner. The feature vector of SPD for proteins P_i and P_j is defined by

$$f_{ij}^{(l)} = \phi_{s_l}^{(r)}(P_i) \quad (\text{for } s_l \in \mathcal{A}^k), \quad (10)$$
$$f_{ij}^{(20^k+l)} = \phi_{s_l}^{(r)}(P_j) \quad (\text{for } s_l \in \mathcal{A}^k). \quad (11)$$

It should be noted that $\phi_s^{(r)}$ for proteins having the same composition of domains can vary depending on the amino acid sequences of their proteins. That is, even if P_i and P_j have the same compositions as P_k and P_l, respectively, and the feature vector of DN for P_i and P_j is the same as that for P_k and P_l, then the feature vector of SPD for P_i and P_j can be different from that for P_k and P_l.

2.7 Support Vector Regression (SVR)

We employ support vector regression (SVR) [12] with our proposed features to predict strengths of PPIs. In the case of linear functions, SVR finds parameters w and b for $f(x) = \langle w, x\rangle + b$ by solving the following optimization problem.

$$\begin{aligned} \text{minimize} \quad & \tfrac{1}{2}||w||^2 + C\textstyle\sum_i(\xi_i + \xi_i'), \\ \text{subject to} \quad & y_i - \langle w, x_i\rangle - b \le \epsilon + \xi_i, \\ & y_i - \langle w, x_i\rangle - b \ge -\epsilon - \xi_i', \\ & \xi_i \ge 0, \quad \xi_i' \ge 0, \end{aligned}$$

where C and ϵ are positive constants, and (x_i, y_i) is a training data. Here, the penalty is added only if the difference between $f(x_i)$ and y_i is larger than ϵ. In our problem, x_i means a protein pair, and y_i means the corresponding interaction strength.

3. Computational Experiments

To evaluate our proposed features, DN and SPD, we conducted computational experiments, and compared them with the existing method, APM.

3.1 Data and Implementation

It is difficult to directly measure actual strengths of PPIs for many protein pairs by biological and physical experiments. Hence, we used Ito's yeast two-hybrid data with 1586 interacting protein pairs [3] and WI-PHI dataset with 50000 protein pairs [9]. For each protein-protein interaction, WI-PHI contains a weight that is considered to represent some reliability of the PPI, and is calculated from several different kinds of PPI datasets in some statistical manner. As strengths of PPIs, we used the value dividing the number of ISTs by the total number of yeast two-hybrid experiments for Ito's data, and used the value dividing the weight of PPI by the maximum weight for WI-PHI. Since these datasets do not include protein pairs with interaction strength 0, we randomly selected 100 protein pairs that were not included in the datasets, and added them as protein pairs with strength 0. We used UniProt database [13] to get amino acid sequences and information of domain compositions and domain regions in proteins. We used SVM light [14] for executing support vector regression, and used the polynomial kernel $K(x, y) = (s\langle x, y\rangle + c)^d$.

Table 1: Results of the average RMSE by SVR with our proposed features, DN and SPD ($k = 1, 2$), and by the existing method, APM, for training and test data

method	RMSE for training	RMSE for test
SVR with DN	0.0927	0.0831
SVR with SPD (k=1)	0.0289	0.0516
SVR with SPD (k=2)	**0.0242**	**0.0282**
APM	0.0265	0.0331

3.2 Root Mean Square Error (RMSE)

The root mean square error (RMSE) is a measure of differences between predicted values $\hat{y}_i$ and actually observed values y_i, and is defined by

$$RMSE = \sqrt{\frac{1}{N}\sum_{i=1}^{N}(\hat{y}_i - y_i)^2}, \quad (12)$$

where N is the number of test data.

3.3 Result

We conducted five-fold cross-validation, and calculated the average RMSE. We examined various values of parameters of the polynomial kernel in the range of $1 \le s, c, d \le 50$. Table 1 shows the results of the average RMSE by SVR with our proposed features, DN and SPD of $k = 1, 2$, and by APM [6], for training and test data, where parameters (s, c, d) for the polynomial kernel were $(1, 1, 3)$ in DN, $(28, 7, 17)$ in SPD of $k = 1$, and $(19, 4, 23)$ in SPD of $k = 2$. Although the average RMSEs by SVR with DN and by SVR with SPD of $k = 1$ were larger than those by APM for both training and test data, those by SVR with SPD of $k = 2$ were smaller than those by APM.

4. Conclusion

We proposed feature space mappings, DN and SPD, for predicting strengths of protein-protein interactions.

DN is based on the number of domains in a protein. SPD is based on the spectrum kernel, and is defined using the amino acid subsequences in domain regions. We employed support vector regression (SVR) with polynomial kernel, and conducted five-fold cross-validation using Ito's yeast two-hybrid data and WI-PHI dataset. For both training and test data, the average RMSEs by SVR with SPD of $k = 2$ were smaller than those by APM, which is the best existing method. It implies that the use of amino acid sequences in domain regions enhanced the prediction accuracy comparing with only information of domain compositions.

It is desired that additional datasets of accurate interaction strengths for many proteins are provided. However, to further enhance the prediction accuracy, we can improve kernel functions combining physical characteristics of domains and amino acids.

Acknowledgment

This work was partially supported by Grants-in-Aid #22240009 and #24500361 from MEXT, Japan.

References

[1] S. Byrum, S. Smart, S. Larson, and A. Tackett, "Analysis of stable and transient protein-protein interactions," *Methods in Molecular Biology*, vol. 833, pp. 143–152, 2012.

[2] P. Uetz, L. Giot, G. Cagney, T. Mansfield, R. Judson, J. Knight, D. Lockshon, V. Narayan, M. Srinivasan, P. Pochart, A. Qureshi-Emili, Y. Li, B. Godwin, D. Conover, T. Kalbfleisch, G. Vijayadamodar, M. Yang, M. Johnston, S. Fields, and J. Rothberg, "A comprehensive two-hybrid analysis to explore the yeast protein interactome," *Nature*, vol. 403, pp. 623–627, 2000.

[3] T. Ito, T. Chiba, R. Ozawa, M. Yoshida, M. Hattori, and Y. Sakaki, "A comprehensive two-hybrid analysis to explore the yeast protein interactome," *Proceedings of the National Academy of Sciences of USA*, vol. 98, pp. 4569–4574, 2001.

[4] M. Hayashida, N. Ueda, and T. Akutsu, "Inferring strengths of protein-protein interactions from experimental data using linear programming," *Bioinformatics*, vol. 19, pp. ii58–ii65, 2003.

[5] E. Sprinzak and H. Margalit, "Correlated sequence-signatures as markets of protein-protein interaction," *Journal of Molecular Biology*, vol. 311, pp. 681–692, 2001.

[6] L. Chen, L.-Y. Wu, Y. Wang, and X.-S. Zhang, "Inferring protein interactions from experimental data by association probabilistic method," *Proteins: Structure, Function, and Bioinformatics*, vol. 62, pp. 833–837, 2006.

[7] R. Finn, J. Mistry, J. Tate, P. Coggill, A. Heger, J. Pollington, O. Gavin, P. Gunesekaran, G. Ceric, K. Forslund, L. Holm, E. Sonnhammer, S. Eddy, and A. Bateman, "The Pfam protein families database," *Nucleic Acids Research*, vol. 38, pp. D211–D222, 2010.

[8] S. Hunter, P. Jones, A. Mitchell, R. Apweiler, T. K. Attwood, A. Bateman, T. Bernard, D. Binns, P. Bork, S. Burge, E. de Castro, P. Coggill, M. Corbett, U. Das, L. Daugherty, L. Duquenne, R. D. Finn, M. Fraser, J. Gough, D. Haft, N. Hulo, D. Kahn, E. Kelly, I. Letunic, D. Lonsdale, R. Lopez, M. Madera, J. Maslen, C. McAnulla, J. McDowall, C. McMenamin, H. Mi, P. Mutowo-Muellenet, N. Mulder, D. Natale, C. Orengo, S. Pesseat, M. Punta, A. F. Quinn, C. Rivoire, A. Sangrador-Vegas, J. D. Selengut, C. J. A. Sigrist, M. Scheremetjew, J. Tate, M. Thimmajanarthanan, P. D. Thomas, C. H. Wu, C. Yeats, and S.-Y. Yong, "InterPro in 2011: new developments in the family and domain prediction database," *Nucleic Acids Research*, vol. 40, pp. D306–D312, 2012.

[9] L. Kiemer, S. Costa, M. Ueffing, and G. Cesareni, "WI-PHI: A weighted yeast interactome enriched for direct physical interactions," *Proteomics*, vol. 7, pp. 932–943, 2007.

[10] M. Deng, S. Mehta, F. Sun, and T. Chen, "Inferring domain-domain interactions from protein-protein interactions," *Genome Research*, vol. 12, pp. 1540–1548, 2002.

[11] C. Leslie, E. Eskin, and W. Noble, "The spectrum kernel: a string kernel for SVM protein classification," in *Proceedings of Pacific Symposium on Biocomputing 2002*, 2002, pp. 564–575.

[12] V. Vapnik, *The Nature of Statistical Learning Theory*. Springer, New York, 1995.

[13] The UniProt Consortium, "Reorganizing the protein space at the Universal Protein Resource (UniProt)," *Nucleic Acids Research*, vol. 40, pp. D71–D75, 2012.

[14] T. Joachims, *Advances in Kernel Methods – Support Vector Learning*. MIT-Press, 1999, ch. Making large-scale SVM learning practical.

Mining Infrequent Patterns of Two Frequent Substrings from a Single Set of Biological Sequences

Daisuke Ikeda
Department of Informatics, Kyushu University
744 Moto-oka, Fukuoka 819-0395, Japan.
daisuke@inf.kyushu-u.ac.jp

Abstract— *This paper is devoted to considering mining infrequent patterns from biological sequences. Two typical approaches to find infrequent patterns are* model-driven *and* data-driven, *and each of them has advantages and disadvantages. As a mixed approach, FPCS (Finding Peculiar Composite Strings) was proposed in a literature, where two substrings x and y are decided by given data and their concatenation xy is evaluated in a model-driven manner. Although its effectiveness has already shown, it requires the background set of sequences, in addition to the target set. In this paper, we propose another approach for infrequent patterns, which, given a single set of sequences, finds string patterns of two substrings frequent in the set. Therefore, the proposed approach is simpler than FPCS. Using biological features, such as RNA, of popular bacterial DNA sequences, the effectiveness of the proposed approach is evaluated. For B. subtilis and C. perfringens, the proposed approach can find RNA regions as well as FPCS while it fails to do that for E. coli and S. enterica because FPCS is more finely granular than the proposed approach.*

Keywords: Under-represented patterns, Infrequent patterns, Text mining, Bioinformatics

1. Introduction

With plenty of biological sequences, it is becoming much more important to develop mining algorithms for such sequences. As one of such mining algorithms, those for frequent or infrequent patterns, called *over-represented* or *under-represented* ones, respectively, have been attracted in bioinformatics [2].

Compared to frequent patterns, it is more difficult for mining algorithms to find infrequent ones from biological sequences because of data sparseness. That is, there exist a huge number of infrequent subsequences due to the sparseness, and thus it is critical to select useful patterns out of the huge number of infrequent candidate patterns.

We can see existing methods as two basic approaches for infrequent pattern mining: one is *model-driven* in which a probabilistic model is assumed for being normal and a candidate pattern is under- or over-represented if its frequency is far from the expected frequency estimated from the model; the other is *data-driven* in which, given two sets of sequences, an algorithm outputs a pattern if it frequently appears in one of the sets while it rarely does in the other.

A typical approach of the former types is the z-score [2]. The score for a pattern w is defined as

$$z(w) = \frac{f(w) - E(w)}{N(w)},$$

where $f(w)$ is the frequency of w in a given set of sequences, $E(w)$ its expected value of w under an assumed probabilistic model, and $N(w)$ a normalization factor of w. As a probabilistic model, the Bernoulli model is assumed in [3], [4] and the Markov model is considered in [5], [6]. However, a simple model can not describe the given sequences well while a complicated one requires huge computational resources, and thus it is difficult to decide an appropriate model in advance.

A typical approach for the latter types is the contrast or distinguish pattern. In this case, a background set is assumed to define being normal, in addition to a target set [7], [8]. However, this approach is basically for frequent patterns by eliminating useless candidate patterns which are both frequent in two sets.

In [9], the algorithm called *FPCS* (Finding Peculiar Compositions) were proposed, where, given a target set T and a background set B of sequences, a pattern w is extracted as the form of $w = xy$ if each of x and y is more frequent in B than in T and conversely $w = xy$ is more frequent in T. More precisely, given two parameters $\theta_T, \theta_B (\geq 1)$, a candidate pattern w is extracted if

$$\mathrm{P}(x|B) > \theta_B \mathrm{P}(x|T),$$
$$\mathrm{P}(y|B) > \theta_B \mathrm{P}(y|T), \text{ and}$$
$$\mathrm{P}(xy|T) > \theta_T \mathrm{P}(xy|B),$$

where $\mathrm{P}(w|S)$ denotes the empirical probability of w in S. This means that we estimate $P(xy)$ by $\mathrm{P}(x|B) \cdot \mathrm{P}(y|B)$ and, if the observed probability $\mathrm{P}(xy|T)$ is larger than the estimated probability $P(xy) = \mathrm{P}(x|B) \cdot \mathrm{P}(y|B)$, we say xy is quite unusual in T.

In this framework, the estimation of probabilities is done like z-score with a probabilistic model, but the unit of *words*, such as x and y, is defined automatically using the given background set of data. In this sense, we can say that FPCS is a mixed approach of model- and data-driven approaches.

In [9], it is shown that, given bacterial sequences as the target and background sets, many of found peculiar compositions are exceptional by a z-score criteria, and some peculiar compositions are not [9]. This implies that we can find peculiar compositions which can not be found by z-score. In [10], it is shown that many peculiar compositions are found in biological features, such as rRNA and transposase, using DNA sequences of 7 popular bacteria, such as *Escherichia coli K-12* (*E. coli*) and *Bacillus subtilis* (*B. subtilis*).

Although FPCS's effectiveness has shown, it requires the background set of sequences, in addition to the target set. Of course, it seems to be natural in bioinformatics to compare the target sequences with some other sequences. However, it is much more useful when we can use an infrequent mining algorithm for a single set of sequences. In this paper, we proposed another approach for under-represented patterns, inspired by FPCS.

The proposed method requires a set of sequences and outputs infrequent patterns of the form $w = xy$, where x and y are frequent in the input set and $P(xy)$ is much more frequent than its estimated value $P(x)P(y)$. Using biological features, such as RNA, of popular bacterial DNA sequences, the effectiveness of the proposed method is evaluated.

2. Finding Peculiar Compositions

According to [9], [10], we briefly explain the *peculiar composition discovery problem* and its significance on DNA sequences of popular bacteria.

2.1 Problem Definition

Let Σ be an *alphabet* and an element of Σ is called a *letter*. In case of nucleotide sequences, $\Sigma = \{A, C, G, T\}$. The set of all the finite sequences of one or more letters is denoted by Σ^+, and an element of Σ^+ is called a *string*. The length of a string x, denoted by $|x|$, is the number of letters of x.

Consider a string $x = a_1 \cdots a_n$ ($a_i \in \Sigma$). A letter a_i in x is denoted by $x[i]$, and $a_i a_{i+1} \ldots a_j$ ($i < j$) is called a *substring*[1].

For two strings $x, y \in \Sigma^+$, the concatenation of x and y is denoted by xy. We call xy the *composition* of x and y. Conversely, a pair of two strings (x, y) is called a *division* of w if $w = xy$. There exist $O(|w|)$ divisions. For instance, if $x = AAC$ and $y = GC$ then $xy = AACGC$, and $(A, ACGC), (AA, CGC), \ldots (AACG, C)$ are divisions of $AACGC$.

Let $x, y \in \Sigma^+$. An occurrence of x in y is an integer i such that $x[j] = y[i+j]$ ($1 \leq j \leq |x|$). The *frequency* of x in y is the number of occurrences of x in y. We extend this notion in case of a set D of strings, instead of a string y, as follows: $f_D(x)$ to denote the sum of the frequencies of x in all strings in D. Since the frequency is affected by the absolute size of D, we introduce the *empirical probability* of x in D as the relative frequencies $\mathrm{P}(x|D) = f_D(x)/\#_D$, where $\#_D$ is the sum of frequencies.

We define a set of *positions* of x in y as follows:

$$\mathrm{Pos}_y(x) = \{i + j \mid x[j] = y[i+j], 1 \leq j \leq |x|\}.$$

For example, $\mathrm{Pos}_{babbab}(ab) = \{2, 3, 5, 6\}$. In other words, $\mathrm{Pos}_y(x)$ is a set of all positions on y covered by x. It is naturally extended for a set D of substrings in y by $\mathrm{Pos}_y(D) = \cup_{x \in D} \mathrm{Pos}_y(x)$. Note that we count only one time even if two substrings x and x' share some positions in y since $\mathrm{Pos}_y(D)$ is defined as a set.

The peculiar composition discovery problem is defined as follows.

Definition 1: The peculiar composition discovery problem is, given two sets T and B of strings and threshold values $\theta_T > 1$, $\theta_B > 1$ and $\eta \geq 2$, to find all peculiar compositions of the form xy such that

$$\mathrm{P}(x|B) > \theta_B \mathrm{P}(x|T),$$
$$\mathrm{P}(y|B) > \theta_B \mathrm{P}(y|T),$$
$$\mathrm{P}(xy|T) > \theta_T \mathrm{P}(xy|B), \text{ and}$$
$$f_T(xy) \geq \eta.$$

From the first two conditions, both frequencies of x and y are much larger in B than those in T. Therefore, we can expect that the composition xy appear frequently in B than in T. From the third condition, however, a found peculiar composition xy appear more frequently in T than in B. In this sense, xy is exceptional.

2.2 Peculiar Compositions in Biological Sequences

Fig. 1 provides found peculiar compositions on a genetic map of the whole target sequence *B. subtilis* from 1bp at the top-left to 4,214,630bp at the bottom-right, where *E. coli* is used as the background sequence. A map contains two tracks. The above one is for biological features, where a feature is displayed above (resp. below) of the track line if it is in the normal strand (resp. its complement); the below track is for found peculiar compositions, where they are drawn at both strands because if a peculiar composition is found at the normal strand then its corresponding composition is also found at the corresponding position of the complement, and vice versa.

Fig. 1 includes rRNA colored by blue, tRNA lightblue, and other RNA related features navyblue as biological features, where we say that a feature is RNA related if its feature key includes "RNA" as a substring. A "gene" or "CDS" whose function, product, or note record contains "transposon" and "phage" is colored in green and yellow, respectively. We exclude other "gene" and "CDS" from the map because it is known that genes prevail in bacterial DNA sequences.

[1] In this paper, we do not consider the empty string, that is the case $i = j$.

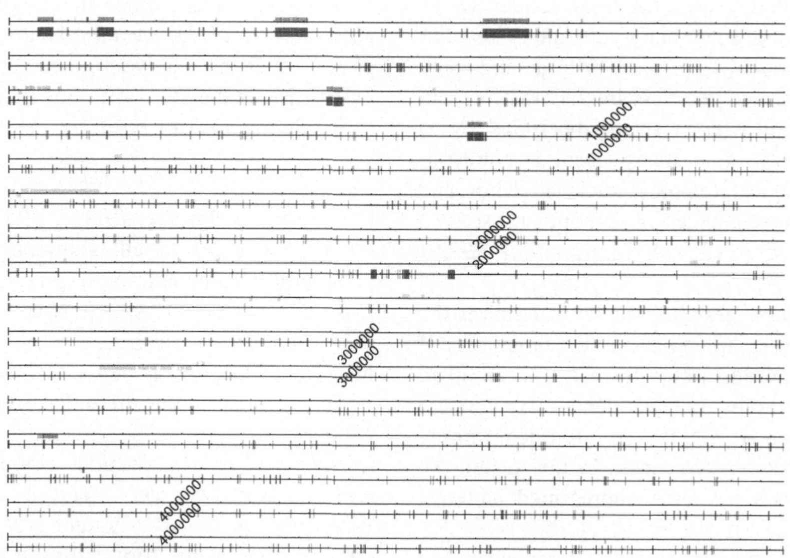

Fig. 1: A genetic map of the whole DNA sequence of *B. subtilis* with two tracks, where rRNA, tRNA, other RNAs, transposon, and phage are colored in blue, lightblue, navyblue, green and yellow, respectively, on the above track, and found peculiar compositions are colored in red on the below track.

We see that peculiar compositions found in case that $\theta_T = 2.0, \theta_B = 2.0$ and $\eta = 3$ densely appear at biological features, especially RNAs. It is known that RNAs are well preserved among species, and transposons and phages are external, and thus we can say that found peculiar compositions are useful.

Fig. 2 shows three enlarged maps of *B. subtilis* from 1bp to around 1Mbp, where parameter values for η are changed. From these maps, we see that found peculiar compositions are densely appear at biological features, even if we use a larger value for a parameter.

In [10], it is also shown that patterns extracted by the z-score and contrast patterns appearing infrequently in the target sequence can not match well to biological features.

Peculiar compositions in Table 1 are found in *B. subtilis*, where *E. coli* is used as the background set, and $\theta_T = \theta_B = 2.0$ and $\eta = 10$. They are found in rRNA (rrnO-16S).

3. Peculiar Compositions of Frequent Substrings

In this section, we introduce the *peculiar composition of frequent substrings* discovery problem.

First of all, we assume a single set of sequences. To define frequent x and y, we have used T and B in the peculiar composition discovery problem. However, now we do not have B and thus we define frequent x and y by a minimum support threshold. Once we obtain frequent x and y, all we have to do is to find xy whose probability is much larger than its estimation value, $P(x)P(y)$.

The peculiar composition of frequent substrings discovery problem is defined as follows.

Definition 2: The peculiar composition of frequent substrings discovery problem is, given a set T of strings and threshold values $\theta > 1$, $\text{minsup}_f \geq 2$ and $\text{minsup}_{xy} \geq 2$, to find all peculiar compositions of frequent substring of the form xy such that

$$f_T(x) \geq \text{minsup}_f$$
$$f_T(y) \geq \text{minsup}_f$$
$$\text{P}(xy|T) > \theta\text{P}(x|T)\text{P}(y|T), \text{ and}$$
$$f_T(xy) \geq \eta.$$

From the first two conditions, both x and y must be frequent, and the probability of xy must be larger than its expectation value $\text{P}(x|T)\text{P}(y|T)$. The last condition is for the minimum support of found patterns.

4. Experiments

In this section, after describing data sets and how to evaluate, we show both qualitative and quantitative evaluation of the proposed method.

4.1 Setting

The data sets used in our experiments are whole DNA sequences of four bacteria, *E. coli*, *B. subtilis*, *Clostridium perfringens* (*C. perfringens* for short), and *Salmonella enterica* (*S. enterica* for short), whose statistics are shown in

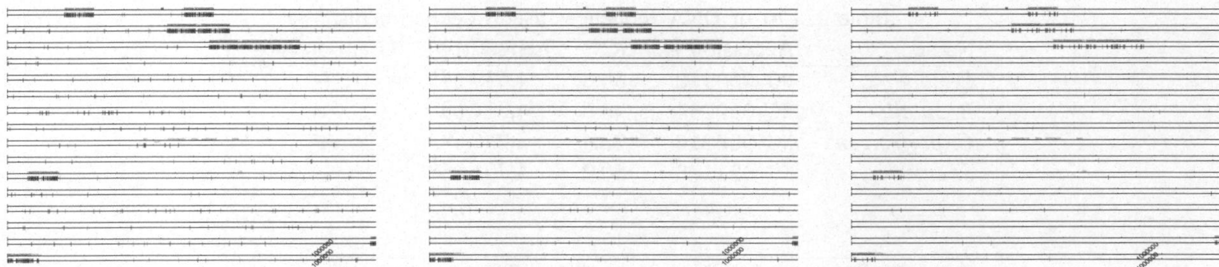

Fig. 2: Three maps in case $\eta = 3, 5$ and 10 from left to right, where the target set, the background one, and the other parameters θ_T, θ_B are fixed to *B. subitilis*, *E. coli*, 2 and 2, respectively.

Table 1: Some peculiar compositions found in *B. subtilis*, where *E. coli* is used as the background set.

(x, y)	$(f_T(xy), f_B(xy))$	$(f_T(x), f_B(x))$	$(f_T(y), f_B(y))$
$(AACGCTGG, CGGCGTG)$	(9, 1)	(92, 389)	(399, 1217)
$(ACGCTG, GCGGCGT)$	(9, 3)	(1532, 4008)	(584, 1838)
$CGCTGGCG, GCGTG)$	(9, 2)	(104, 895)	(4009, 11412)
$(CGCTG, GCGGCGT)$	(10, 6)	(6718, 17434)	(584, 1838)

Fig. 3: A gene map of *B. subtilis* from 1bp to around 20Kbp.

Table 2. We have chosen *E. coli* and *B. subtilis* since they are typical model bacterium with different properties: the former is Gram-negative while the latter is Gram-positive. We have chosen *C. perfringens* (resp. *S. enterica*) since it is gram-positive (resp. gram-negative).

As qualitative evaluation, we use genetic maps as shown above, and as qualitative evaluation we caluculate a popular evaluation value used in information retrieval, F-masure, which is defined as

$$F_\beta = \frac{(1+\beta^2)\cdot P \cdot R}{\beta^2 \cdot P + R},$$

where P and R denote precision and recall, respectively. We choose $\beta = 1/4$ for F_β although F-measure typically means F_1, which puts weight on precision and recall equally. However, our goal is not to find these features but to show that found peculiar compositions match biological features. Although found patterns seem to fully cover RNAs (see Fig. 1), they are sparse in an enlarged map of Fig. 3, where only about 20Kbp are described. From the viewpoint of our goal, we do not need high recall values since we are trying to find useful, infrequent patterns and we can't expect that infrequent patterns cover all occurrences of some features. Thus, we choose $\beta = 1/4$, which weighs precision four times as much as recall.

4.2 Genetic Maps

As qualitative evaluation, we show genetic maps, like Fig. 1.

First, we show a map obtained from *B. subtilis* with parameter values $\theta = 1 \times 10^7$, $\mathrm{minsup}_f = 1000$, and $\mathrm{minsup}_{xy} = 20$ (see Fig. 4). We see that dense regions of peculiar compositions of frequent substrings match to blue regions, that is, rRNA and tRNA.

Next, we show a map obtained from *E. coli* with parameter values $\theta = 2 \times 10^7$, $\mathrm{minsup}_f = 3000$, and $\mathrm{minsup}_{xy} = 20$ (see Fig. 5). In this case, we can't find dense regions even when we change parameter values. To compare FPCS, we show a genetic map of *E. coli*, where *B. subtilis* is used as the background set, $\theta_T = \theta_B = 2$, and $\eta = 5$ (Fig. 6). Unlike Fig. 5, we can clearly see dense regions and most of these regions correspond to some biological features.

Fig. 7 shows genetic maps of *C. perfringens* and *S. enterica*. From the map of *C. perfringens*, we see dense regions at rRNA and tRNA while we can't see such regions at designated features from the map of *S. enterica* although there exist dense regions.

4.3 F-measures

In this section, we quantitatively evaluate the proposed method by the F-measure. Table 3 shows the results, where "feature" column shows features we consider as correct ones. For *E. coli*, we use RNA and transposon as target features

Table 2: List of DNA sequences used in experiments.

Name	Accession #	GC%	Length (bp)	Gram-pos/neg
E. coli	NC_000913	50.8	4,639,675	–
B. subtilis	NC_000964	43.6	4,214,630	+
C. perfringens	NC_008216	28.4	3,256,683	+
S. enterica	NC_021176	50.2	4,791,958	–

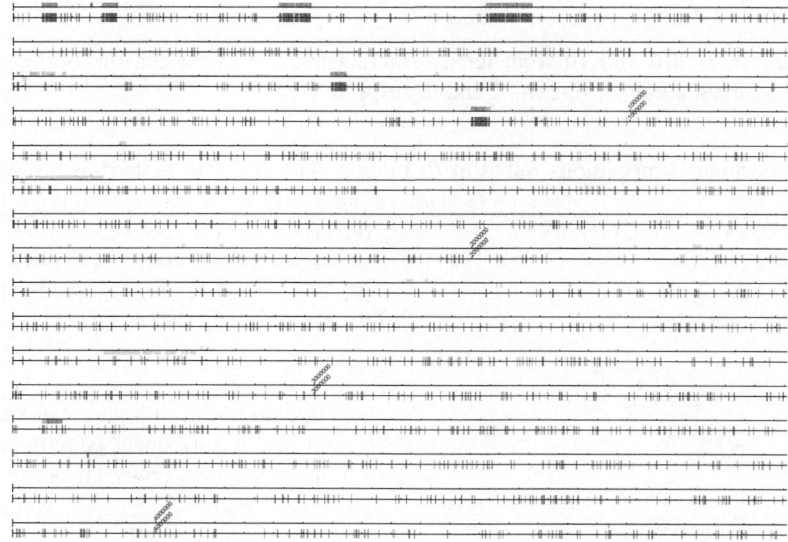

Fig. 4: A genetic maps of the whole DNA sequences of *B. subtilis*, where $\theta = 1 \times 10^7$, $\text{minsup}_f = 1000$, and $\text{minsup}_{xy} = 20$.

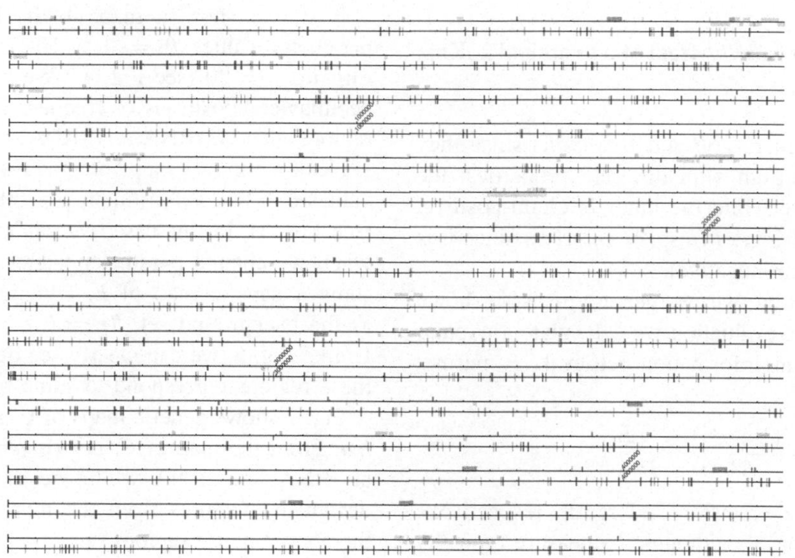

Fig. 5: A genetic map of the whole DNA sequences of *E. coli*, where $\theta = 2 \times 10^7$, $\text{minsup}_f = 3000$, and $\text{minsup}_{xy} = 20$.

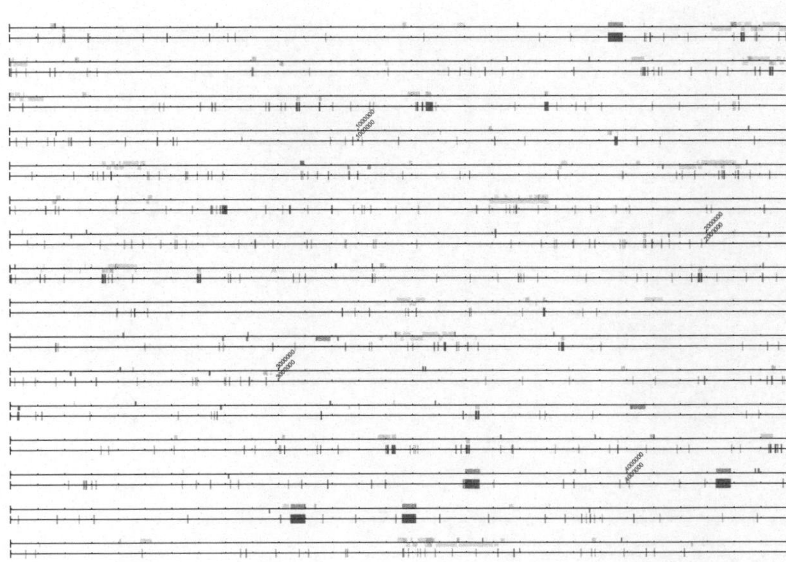

Fig. 6: A genetic map of the whole DNA sequence of *E. coli*, where *B. subtilis* is used as the background set, $\theta_T = \theta_B = 2.0$ and $\eta = 5$.

Table 3: Precisions, recalls, and $F_{1/4}$ values *E. coli* and *B. subtilis*, where features in "feature" column are assumed to be correct.

NC#	feature	θ	minsup$_f$	minsup$_{xy}$	precision	recall	$F_{1/4}$
NC_000913	RNA, Transposon	1.5×10^7	1000	20	0.0559	0.2819	0.0586
NC_000913	RNA, Transposon	1.5×10^7	1000	20	0.0306	0.0567	0.0314
NC_000913	RNA, Transposon	1.5×10^7	2000	20	0.0316	0.0126	0.0290
NC_000913	RNA, Transposon	1.5×10^7	3000	20	0.0241	0.0082	0.0217
NC_000964	RNA	1×10^7	1000	20	0.1869	0.0755	0.1720
NC_000964	RNA	1×10^7	2000	20	0.1949	0.0596	0.1720
NC_000964	RNA	2×10^7	1000	20	0.6032	0.0071	0.1011

and, for *B. subtilis*, we use only RNA.

First of all, F-measure values for *B. subtilis* are much better than those for *E. coli* as we have seen from genetic maps.

Next, we compare these results with those of FPCS [10]. F-measures obtained by FPCS are much larger than those of the proposed method. In case of *E. coli*, $F_{1/4} = 0.2116$ for RNA and transposon, where precision is 0.7161 and recall is 0.0172, and when *B. subtilis* is given, and $F_{1/4} = 0.3230$ for only RNA, where precision is 0.6319 and recall is 0.0366.

5. Conclusion

We have proposed a peculiar composition of frequent substrings which requires only a single set of sequences, and evaluated both quantitatively and qualitatively. The proposed method only requires a single set and thus it is simpler than FPCS. However, F-measure values of the proposed method are much smaller than those of FPCS.

The reason for this may be due to the definitions of x's and y's being frequent for final output patterns of the form xy. In FPCS, x and y are defined independently using two ratios, θ_T and θ_B, and thus the frequencies for them can be quite different. In fact, we see quite different frequencies of x and y in Table 1. On the other hand, being frequent is defined absolutely by one parameter value, minsup$_f$, in the proposed method. Therefore, frequencies of x and y must be similar. Thus, FPCS is more finely granular than the proposed approach.

From maps of 4, 5, 7, it seems that peculiar compositions of frequent substrings appear at RNA given gram-negative bacteria while they do not given gram-positive bacteria. It is important to validate this hypothesis with more experiments.

References

[1] L. Parida, *Pattern Discovery in Bioinformatics: Theory & Algorithms*. Chapman & Hall/CRC, July 2007.

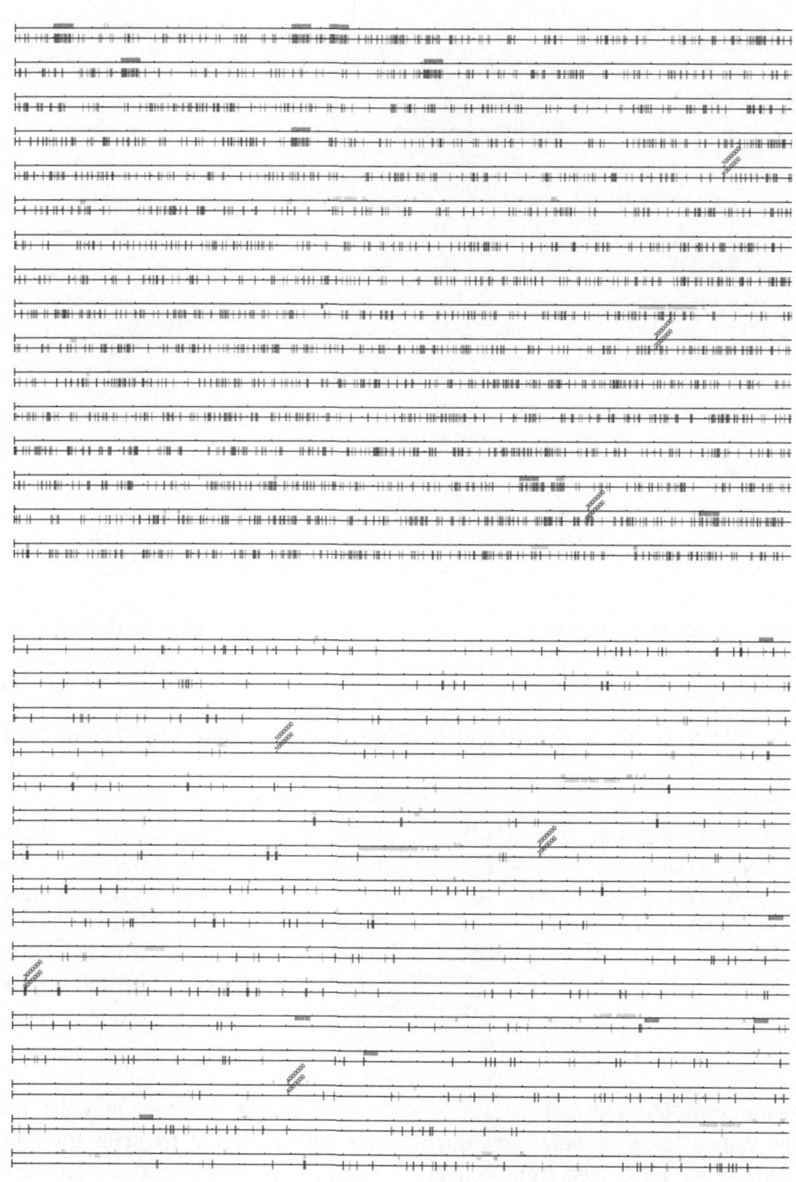

Fig. 7: Genetic maps of the whole DNA sequence of *C. perfringens* (upper side) and *S. enterica* (lower side), where 2×10^7, $\text{minsup}_f 3000$, and $\text{minsup}_{xy} 10$ are used for *C. perfringens* and mytheta57, $\text{minsup}_f 2000$, and $\text{minsup}_{xy} 10$ for *S. enterica*.

[2] A. Apostolico, M. E. Bock, S. Lonardi, and X. Xu, "Efficient Detection of Unusual Words," *J. of Comput. Biol.*, vol. 7, no. 1/2, pp. 71–94, Jan. 2000.

[3] M.-Y. Leung, G. M. Marsh, and T. P. Speed, "Over- and Underrepresentation of Short DNA Words in Herpesvirus Genomes," *J. of Comput. Biol.*, vol. 3, no. 3, pp. 345–360, 1996.

[4] S. Schbath, "An Efficient Statistic to Detect Over- and Underrepresented Words in DNA Sequences," *J. of Comput. Biol.*, vol. 4, no. 2, pp. 189–192, 1997.

[5] T. Marschall and S. Rahmann, "Efficient Exact Motif Discovery," *Bioinformatics*, vol. 25, no. 12, pp. i356–i364, 2009.

[6] D. Ikeda, "Characteristic Sets of Strings Common to Semi-structured Documents," in *Proceedings of the Second International Conference on Discovery Science*, ser. Lecture Notes in Artificial Intelligence 1721, December 1999, pp. 139–147.

[7] X. Ji, J. Bailey, and G. Dong, "Mining Minimal Distinguishing Subsequence Patterns with Gap Constraints," *Knowledge and Information Systems*, vol. 11, no. 3, pp. 259–286, 2007.

[8] D. Ikeda and E. Suzuki, "Mining Peculiar Compositions of Frequent Substrings from Sparse Text Data Using Background Texts," in *Proc. of ECML PKDD*, September 2009, pp. 596–611.

[9] D. Ikeda, O. Maruyama, and S. Kuhara, "Infrequent, Unexpected, and Contrast Pattern Discovery from Bacterial Genomes by Genome-wide Comparative Analysis," in *Proceedings of the 4th International Conference on Bioinformatics Models, Methods and Algorithms*, February 2013, pp. 308–311.

SDBP: An easy-to-use R program package for assessing reliability of estimated phylogenetic trees based on the speedy double bootstrap method

Aizhen Ren[1], Takashi Ishida[2], and Yutaka Akiyama[2]
[1]Department of Mathematical and Computing Science, Tokyo Institute of Technology, W8-76, 2-12-1 Ookayama, Meguro-ku, Tokyo 152-8550, JAPAN
[2]Department of Computer Science, Graduate School of Information Science and Engineering, Tokyo Institute of Technology, W8-76, 2-12-1 Ookayama, Meguro-ku, Tokyo 152-8550, JAPAN

Abstract— *Evaluating the reliability of estimated phylogenetic trees is of critical importance in the field of molecular phylogenetics, and for other endeavors that depend on accurate phylogenetic reconstruction. The bootstrap method is a well-known computational approach to assessing phylogenetic trees, and more generally for assessing the reliability of statistical models. However, it is known to be biased under certain circumstances, calling into question the accuracy of the method. Therefore, several advanced bootstrap methods have been developed to achieve higher accuracy, one of which is the speedy double bootstrap approach (sDBP-method). In the phylogenetic tree selection problem, it has been shown that the sDBP-method has comparable accuracy to the double bootstrap approach and is much more computationally efficient. In this study, we thus develop an R package named SDBP, which is an implementation of our sDBP-method on a statistical software R to assesse the reliability of phylogenetic trees. We are confident that biologists will benefit from our sDBP-method and SDBP package.*

Keywords: SDBP, Speedy double bootstrap method, Phylogenetic trees, Reliability, Rapid computation, R package

1. Introduction

The analytical methods used in the field of molecular phylogenetics are important basic tools for reconstructing the evolutionary history (phylogenetic relationships) of molecules and organisms. Molecular phylogenetic methods are primarily used in the context of biological systematics, but they also find applications in a wide variety of other fields as diverse as community ecology [1], biogeography [2] and proteomics, including inference of the similarity of protein-protein interactions [3]. Many methods for phylogenetic reconstruction have been developed and are in regular use [4]. However, those based on maximum likelihood estimation have proved most effective for reconstructing phylogenies using molecular sequence data (DNA, protein, etc.). Early work on this application of maximum likelihood was conducted by [5], whose approach involved computing the maximum likelihood value for many topologies and selecting the topology with the highest likelihood (the maximum likelihood (ML) tree) as the most probable candidate for the true topology.

It must be noted that maximum likelihood values are dependent on the particular characteristics of a random variable; that is, the molecular sequences that constitute the underlying data for phylogenetic reconstruction. Thus, some analysis of the statistical reliability of the estimated ML tree or multiple alternative trees should be undertaken. Statistical hypothesis testing is commonly used for this purpose, and the 'bootstrapping' technique is a well-known computational method for calculating reliability when a simple mathematical formula is difficult to derive. Bootstrapping is a resampling method that approximates a random sample by creating a bootstrap sample, generated by random sampling with replacement from the original single data set. In the context of phylogenetic tree selection, Felsenstein [6] proposed the use of bootstrapping to place confidence intervals on phylogenies. He defined the p-value of a tree according to a frequency called the bootstrap probability (BP); the proportion of bootstrap pseudoreplicates of the original data set in which the tree is found to be optimal. However, it is known that under some circumstances the naive bootstrap probability can be biased [7], [8]. Thus, some advanced bootstrap methods have been proposed, to achieve higher accuracy [9], [10], [11].

Among these, the double bootstrap method (DBP-method) [9], [10] has been shown to be third-order accurate and is potentially a useful measure of phylogenetic tree support. However, the method has a huge computational cost. To overcome the computational burden in the phylogenetic tree selection problem, we have previously proposed a 'speedy' double bootstrap (sDBP-method) method to compute the reliability of phylogenetic trees [12]. In the phylogenetic tree selection problem, our previous work [12] has been shown that the sDBP-method has comparable accuracy to the DBP-method and is much more computationally efficient. Because, it is well known that a good statistical method is not in itself sufficient, we also need to develop an easy-to-use computer tool. We thus develop the R package named SDBP, which is an implementation of our sDBP-method on a statistical software R to assess the reliability of phylogenetic trees. We are confident that biologists, who may not have advanced computer skills, will benefit from our sDBP-method and SDBP package.

R is a language and environment for statistical computing and graphics. It is an open-source GNU project based on the S language and environment developed at Bell Laboratories (formerly AT&T, now Lucent Technologies) by John Chambers and colleagues. We can summarize why we implemented our method in R as follows. At first, R provides a wide variety of statistical (linear and non-linear modeling, classical statistical tests, time-series analysis, classification, clustering, $\cdots$) and graphical techniques, and is highly extensible. In addition, it is important that R is not only applicable to statistical fields of research, but also to the biological field. Genome analysis, including GneABEL [13], and areas related to biotechnology also have a great many applicable R packages. Finally, R is available under the terms of the Free Software Foundation's GNU General Public License in source code form. It can be compiled and run on a wide variety of UNIX platforms and similar systems (including FreeBSD and Linux), Windows, and MacOS.

This paper is organized as follows. We first give some background, and then briefly introduce the mathematical theory of the sDBP-method and its algorithm for assessing the reliability of phylogenetic trees. Next, we describe the basic usage of our package `SDBP` using the mammalian mitochondrial data from [14]. Finally, we describe the results.

2. Theory and Algorithm

2.1 The reliability of a phylogenetic tree

In this study, homologous sites of aligned molecular sequence data are regarded as the units for sampling, and we use DNA data as our example for the following methodological descriptions. Suppose we have m homologous sequences, each with n nucleotide sites. These data can be represented as an $m \times n$ matrix $\mathbf{X} = \{x_{jh}\} = \{\mathbf{x_1}, \cdots, \mathbf{x_n}\}$, where $\mathbf{x}_h$ is the value of the h-th site and x_{jh} is one of the four deoxyribonucleotides (T, C, A, or G).

$$\begin{array}{lcllcl} Species\ 1 & : & x_{11} & x_{12} & \cdots & x_{1n} \\ Species\ 2 & : & x_{21} & x_{22} & \cdots & x_{2n} \\ \vdots & & & & \vdots & \\ Species\ m & : & x_{m1} & x_{m2} & \cdots & x_{mn} \end{array} \qquad (1)$$

The log-likelihood can be expressed as

$$l(\theta; \mathbf{X}) = \sum_{h=1}^{n} log f(\mathbf{x}_h; \theta), \qquad (2)$$

where $f(\mathbf{x}_h; \theta) = f(x_{1h}, x_{2h}, \cdots, x_{mh}; \theta)$ is the probability that at a particular homologous site, species 1 has base x_{1h}, species 2 has x_{2h} and species m has x_{mh}. The vector θ denotes unknown parameters such as the edge lengths (branch lengths) of a tree, and the base substitution rates along these branches. Here we assume that the base substitution rates have already been estimated, so θ denotes only the unknown edge lengths. For a given tree topology, θ is estimated by maximizing the log-likelihood, and the maximum log-likelihood of any tree topology i is given by

$$l_i(\hat{\theta}_i; \mathbf{X}) = \sum_{h=1}^{n} log f_i(\mathbf{x}_h; \hat{\theta}_i). \qquad (3)$$

The topology with the highest value of $l(\hat{\theta}; \mathbf{X})$ is the maximum likelihood phylogeny (T_{ML}) for the data set $\mathbf{X}$, and is thus the most likely candidate for the true topology. To define null hypotheses for performing model comparisons, we must consider the true distribution for a random variable $\mathbf{x}$ can be expressed as

$$q(\mathbf{x}) \qquad (4)$$

And the expectation of $l_i(\hat{\theta}_i; \mathbf{X}), i = 1, \cdots, K$ with respect to

$$(\mathbf{x_1}, \cdots, \mathbf{x_n}) \overset{i.i.d.}{\sim} q(\cdot) \qquad (5)$$

can be expressed as

$$\mu_i = E_q[l_i(\hat{\theta}_i; \mathbf{X})] \qquad (6)$$

If we assume that tree T_1 is the best topology, the null and alternative hypotheses will then be

$$H_1 : \mu_1 = max_{i=1,\cdots,K}\ \mu_i \quad vs. \quad H_1^A : \ others, \qquad (7)$$

and we must continue performing these comparisons as many times as is necessary, assuming in turn that tree $T_i, i = 2, \cdots, K$ is the best topology. Note that the null hypothesis H_1 involves multiple comparisons with the "best" topology [15]. As can be seen from equation (7), the null contains $K-1$ hypotheses such that

$$H_{1j} : \mu_1 \geq \mu_j, j = 2, \cdots, K. \qquad (8)$$

The null hypothesis H_1 is a polyhedral convex cone and $B(h_1)$, which is the boundary of H_1, is nonsmooth at the vertex as well as on the faces of dimension less than $K-1$. Shimodaira and Hasegawa [14] proposed a multiple comparisons procedure (the SH-test) to test H_1, but this was shown to be overly conservative because they assumed that the parameter configuration is $\mu_1 = \mu_2 = \cdots = \mu_K$, that is, the least favorable configuration or the vertex of $B(h_1)$ [16]. A different method (the AU-test), which uses a multiscale bootstrap technique to obtain third-order accurate p-values for testing the null hypothesis, has also been proposed [11]. In our previous work [12], we developed an algorithm using an advanced bootstrap method [10] that was also able to provide third-order accurate p-values to assess statistical reliability of phylogenetic trees. We call it the speedy double bootstrap method, which will be considered in the following subsection.

2.2 The theory of speedy double bootstrap method

In this subsection, it is necessary to review the theory of the speedy double bootstrap method. For this, we start by explaining the third-order accurate p-value. It was first proposed by [17] for the multivariate normal model, which can be represented as

$$\mathbf{Y} \overset{i.i.d.}{\sim} N_t(\eta, I_t). \tag{9}$$

This normal model is a simplification of reality. Let $\mathcal{H} \subset R^t$ be an arbitrarily-shaped region with smooth boundaries denoted by $B(h)$. We want to calculate a p-value $p(y)$ for testing the null hypothesis $\eta \in \mathcal{H}$. According to [17], when the true parameter η is on the boundary surface $B(h)$, the third-order accurate p-value can be expressed as

$$p(y) = 1 - \Phi(d - c), \tag{10}$$

where d is the signed distance from y to $\hat{\eta}(y)$, with a positive or negative sign when y is outside or inside $\mathcal{H}$, respectively. The point $\hat{\eta}(y)$ is the closest point to y (in Euclidean distance) on the surface $B(h)$, and c in equation (10) is a quantity related to the curvature of $B(h)$ at the point $\hat{\eta}(y)$. The speedy double bootstrap method of [10] (named later by [12]) begins with a bootstrap resampling from the multivariate normal model with distribution

$$\mathbf{Y}^* \overset{i.i.d.}{\sim} N_t(\hat{\eta}(y), I_t). \tag{11}$$

It then uses Y^* to calculate d^*, which is the signed distance from Y^* to $B(h)$. According to [10], the third-order accurate p-value obtained by the sDBP-method can be expressed as

$$1 - \Phi(d - c) = P(d^* > d; \hat{\eta}(y)) + O(n^{-3/2}). \tag{12}$$

2.3 The algorithm for the speedy double bootstrap method for phylogenetic trees

We now return to the problem of phylogenetic trees, as seen in H_1 and the vector $(l_1, \cdots, l_K)$. We describe the algorithm using the sDBP-method to calculate the p-value of H_1. First, we find a vector corresponding to $\hat{\eta}(y)$ in equation (11). According to [18], the maximum log-likelihood vector

$$\mathbf{l} = (l_1(\hat{\theta}_1), \cdots, l_K(\hat{\theta}_K)) \tag{13}$$

asymptotically follows a multivariate normal distribution, the mean vector of which is

$$\mu = (\mu_1, \cdots, \mu_K). \tag{14}$$

Note that the vector $\mathbf{l}$ in equation (13) is an unrestricted maximum likelihood estimate for μ. Because we assumed that $\mu_1 = max_{i=1,\cdots,K}\ \mu_i$ in H_1, under this restriction the restricted estimator for μ can be estimated using the PAVA (pool adjacent violators algorithm) [19] method, and is expressed as

$$\hat{\mu} = (\hat{\mu}_1, \cdots, \hat{\mu}_K). \tag{15}$$

We then excise a subset $W \in \{1, \cdots, K\}$, including the element 1, so that

$$\begin{aligned} \hat{\mu}_1 &= \frac{\sum_{j \in W} l_j(\hat{\theta}_j)}{\#W}, \\ \hat{\mu}_j &= min(\hat{\mu}_1, l_j(\hat{\theta}_j)), \quad j \in \{2, \cdots, K\}. \end{aligned} \tag{16}$$

The vector $\hat{\mu} = (\hat{\mu}_1, \cdots, \hat{\mu}_K)$ corresponds to $\hat{\eta}(y)$. Also, the covariance matrix of the vector $(l_1, l_2, \cdots, l_K)$ can be estimated by $\Sigma = (\sigma_{ij})$, with σ_{ij} given as

$$\frac{n}{n-1}\sum_{h=1}^{n}\left[logf_i(\mathbf{x_h}; \hat{\theta}_\mathrm{i}) - \frac{1}{n}\sum_{h=1}^{n} logf_i(\mathbf{x_h}; \hat{\theta}_\mathrm{i})\right] \tag{17}$$
$$\times \left[logf_j(\mathbf{x_h}; \hat{\theta}_\mathrm{j}) - \frac{1}{n}\sum_{h=1}^{n} logf_j(\mathbf{x_h}; \hat{\theta}_\mathrm{j})\right].$$

We then need to calculate two other quantities corresponding to d^* and d in equation (12). To do this, we generate $B1$, for example 10000 bootstrap pseudoreplicates of the vector $(\hat{\mu}_1, \hat{\mu}_2, \cdots, \hat{\mu}_K)$ in equation (15). The pseudoreplicates $(\hat{\mu}_1^{*(b1)}, \cdots, \hat{\mu}_K^{*(b1)}), b1 = 1, \cdots, B1$ are sampled from

$$(\hat{\mu}_1^{*(b1)}, \cdots, \hat{\mu}_K^{*(b1)})^T \overset{i.i.d.}{\sim} N_K((\hat{\mu}_1, \hat{\mu}_2, \cdots, \hat{\mu}_K)^T, \Sigma), \tag{18}$$

where T represents the transpose, and Σ is used as above. The vectors $(\hat{\mu}_1^{*(b1)}, \cdots, \hat{\mu}_K^{*(b1)})$ constitute the first-order (first-tier) bootstrap pseudoreplicates. Now, d^* and d in equation (12) can be written as

$$\begin{aligned} d^{*(b1)} &= max_{j=2,\cdots,K}\hat{\mu}_j^{*(b1)} - \hat{\mu}_1^{*(b1)}, \\ d &= max_{j=2,\cdots,K} l_j - l_1. \end{aligned} \tag{19}$$

Next, we calculate the p-value for H_1, defined below and also denoted by $sDBP$:

$$sDBP = \frac{\#(d^{*(b1)} > d)}{B1}. \tag{20}$$

In exactly the same way as shown for H_1, we can apply the sDBP method to all other hypotheses $H_k, k = 2, \cdots, K$.

3. Implementation

3.1 Implementation in R

We have implemented the sDBP algorithm for phylogenetic inference as a R package. Our package is named `SDBP`, and calculates p-values for phylogenetic trees. It can be used in combination with several other functions or packages in R.

The package was written in the S language using the S3 object system, and consists of a number of user-level objects:

sdbp, sdbpk, bpk, bp, dbpk, and mam20. The following subsections describe how to use these user-level objects. The SDBP provides three types of p-value: the sDBP (speedy double bootstrap probability), the DBP (double bootstrap probability), and the BP (bootstrap probability).

3.2 Usage – Using the mammalian mitochondrial protein sequences

In this subsection, we explain how to use SDBP with the mammalian mitochondrial protein sequences data from [14]. This data set included in file mam15-files, which can be download from scaleboot Home Page.
http://www.is.titech.ac.jp/~shimo/prog/scaleboot/index.html
Scaleboot also is an R package. The mammalian protein data set includes sequences of n = 3414 amino acids from six mammalian species (human, seal, cow, rabbit, mouse, and opossum). The proteins coded for in the mammalian mitochondrial genome are ND1, ND2, COX1, COX2, ATP8, ATP6, COX3, ND3, ND4L, ND4, ND5, and CYTB. The clade $\{seal, cow\}$ was significantly supported in preliminary analyses, so only the 15 unrooted trees (see Table 1) that included this clade were considered in our comparisons (the opossum is the outgroup). Now, the number of trees K is 15, and the sample size n is 3414. Hypothesis H_1 denotes that $\mu_1 = max_{i=1,\cdots,15}\ \mu_i$. Our aim is to calculate the p-values for hypothesis H_1 as well as $H_i, i = 2, \cdots, 15$.

In advance, we used the software package PAML [20], to calculate the site-wise log-likelihood for each tree. The output file is file mam15.lnf. The format of mam15.lnf is not available for our package, so the format was changed using CONSEL [21] by executing the command "seqmt −−paml mam15.lnf". Thus we obtain the site-wise log-likelihood matrix saved in the file mam15.mt for each tree. The file mam15.mt obtained by CONSEL should be placed in the R work directory. The 15 tree topologies is in the file mam15.tpl, that can be found in mam15-files.

Our SDBP package is built under R version 3.0.0. Therefore, this R version (or later) is needed to install our package. For Windows OS, after booting R, choose the tab **Packages** in the upper tool-bar and select the tab **Install Package(s) from zip files** option, then choose the **SDBP_1.0.zip** file downloaded from CRAN, the official R package archive.

For using the command line on UNIX platforms to install the source version package **SDBP_1.0.tar.gz** downloaded from CRAN, just write the following command:

```
R CMD INSTALL SDBP_1.0.tar.gz
```

and boot R via the command line using the command.

```
R
```

Then, the following on the **R console** command line to load our package (the following command can be typed on both Unix and regular Windows machines):

```
> library("SDBP")# load our package
```

And then, read the data named mam15.mt.

```
# read scaleboot for reading .mt files
> library(scaleboot)
> dat<-read.mt(mam15.mt)
> dim(dat)# dat matrix demation
[1] 3414   15
```

Calculating the sDBP-value for each tree requires the following line. Thus our package is as easy-to-use as R package.

```
> result <- sdbp.default(dat)
> result
```

We performed this on a personal computer with the following specifications: 2.50 GHz CPU (Core (TM) i5-2520M CPU) and 8.00 GB RAM. The results are output in decreasing order of log-likelihood.

```
Call:
sdbp.default(dat = dat)

Speedy double bootstrap probabilities:
t1     t3     t2     t5     t6     t7
0.5828 0.3905 0.2237 0.1191 0.1109 0.0681 ...
```

Calculating the stand error for each value, we can use the command summary.

```
> summary(result)
```

The output is

```
Call:
speedy.default(dat = dat)


   stdErr p.value
t1 0.0049  0.5717
t3 0.0049  0.3928
t2 0.0041  0.2173
t5 0.0032  0.1136
...
attr(,"class")
[1] "summary.sdbp"
```

This command is for testing hypothesis H_1 in equation (7) for tree 1 in the topology file mam15.tpl, using the algorithm in subsection 2.3. Also, for testing hypotheses $H_i : \mu_i = max_{k=1,\cdots,15}\mu_k, i = 2, \cdots, 15$ for tree 2, $\cdots$, tree 15 in the topology file mam15.tpl, we repeatedly use the algorithm in subsection 2.3. However, the algorithm for testing one of the hypothesis H_i of $H_i, i = 2, \cdots, 15$ is a little different from the algorithm for testing hypothesis H_1. The difference is that we calculate the projection $\hat{\mu}$ of the maximum log-likelihood vector $\mathbf{l} = (l_1, \cdots, l_{15})$ for each hypothesis and the signed distances. For example, the projection vector $\hat{\mu}$ of the maximum log-likelihood vector $\mathbf{l} = (l_1, \cdots, l_{15})$ under hypothesis H_2 is obtained using the following equations.

$$\hat{\mu}_2 = \frac{\sum_{j\in W_2} l_j(\hat{\theta}_j)}{\#W_2}, \hat{\mu}_j = min(\hat{\mu}_2, l_j(\hat{\theta}_j)), \quad j \in \{1, 3, \cdots, 15\},$$

where W_2 is subset of the numbers $\{1, \cdots, 15\}$ including the element 2. For details of the implementation of the PAVA method, see our R source code in sdbp.R in SDBP. The signed distances are

$$d^{*(b1)} = max_{j=1,3,\cdots,15}\hat{\mu}_j^{*(b1)} - \hat{\mu}_2^{*(b1)}, d = max_{j=1,3,\cdots,15}l_j - l_2.$$

The similarity between testing $H_i, i = 2, \cdots, 15$ and H_1 is the covariance matrix Σ in equation (17).

When we want to calculate the reliability for one tree, for example tree 2, we can use the command `sdbpk`, with the output shown below. This command corresponds to testing hypothesis $H_2 : \mu_2 = max_{k=1,2,\cdots,15}\mu_k$ for tree 2 in the topology file mam15.tpl.

```
> result1 <- sdbpk(dat,2)
> result1

Call:
sdbpk(dat = dat, k = 2)

t2
0.2237
```

Then, calculating the bootstrap probability can use the command bp, again shown with the output.

```
> result2 <- bp(dat)
> result2

Call:
bp(dat = dat)

Bootstrap probabilities:
t1     t3     t2     t5     t6     t7
0.5794 0.3213 0.0342 0.0124 0.0279 0.0057 ...
```

4. Result

4.1 Analysis of mammalian mitochondrial protein sequences

Table 1 presents the results of our sDBP value calculations for the 15 phylogenetic trees analyzed in this study, along with values reported by [11] for traditional BP analyses and the AU-test. We also developed an algorithm for the regular double bootstrap approach for phylogenetic trees [12], although in this paper we have omitted the description of how the DBP were calculated. In Table 1, the original tree number in the file mam15.tpl is renamed in decreasing order of log-likelihood. The confidence sets of trees obtained by the sDBP algorithm and the DBP algorithm at $\alpha = 0.05$ were $\{1, 2, 3, 4, 5, 6, 7\}$ and $\{1, 2, 3, 5, 7\}$, respectively (Table 1). The sDBP tree set was thus slightly larger than the set selected by DBP. Tree 7 is the most strongly supported as T_{ML} by recent analyses incorporating additional sequence data [22], [23], [24], and our results for this tree indicate that sDBP=0.084>0.05 and DBP=0.056 $>$ 0.05. Our conclusions are thus not in contradiction with the latest data. For a confidence set of models, our sDBP algorithm gives a confidence set of candidate trees, and includes the "best" topology $\max_{i=1,\cdots,15}\mu_i$, with an error rate below the 0.05 level. Thus, our sDBP tree set does not immediately give the work for straightly gives the "best" topology.

4.2 Comparison of computational speed

For the sDBP algorithm, the DBP algorithm, the AU-test and the BP-test, we measured the time taken to calculate a p-value for tree 7 (see Table 1), based on the site-wise log-likelihood data. We used the RELL approximation method [18] with the BP-test, and conducted two separate sets of analyses. In the first set, we applied the sDBP algorithm with $B1 = 10^3$ pseudoreplicates, the DBP algorithm with $B1 = 10^3$ and $B2 = 10^3$ pseudoreplicates, and the BP-test with 10^3 pseudoreplicates. In the second set, we applied the sDBP algorithm with $B1 = 5 \times 10^3$ pseudoreplicates, the DBP algorithm with $B1 = 5 \times 10^3$ and $B2 = 5 \times 10^3$ pseudoreplicates, and the BP-test with 5×10^3 pseudoreplicates. The results of the two sets are shown in Table 2. This time, we used the command `sdbpk`, `bpk` and `dbpk` to measure the time. For measuring time of AU-test, we used the command `relltest` from R package scaleboot. For both sets, the BP-test was the fastest, followed by the sDBP algorithm, the AU-test then the DBP algorithm. For the first set of calculations (lower numbers of pseudoreplicates) the sDBP algorithm was 1021-fold faster than the DBP algorithm, and this advantage improved substantially for the second set (higher pseudoreplication), with the sDBP algorithm being 5076-fold faster than the DBP algorithm.

Table 1 Comparison of four different p-values from analyses of fifteen mammalian trees, based on protein sequence data from [14]. The p-values that are NOT significant at $\alpha = 0.05$ are emphasized in bold type.

Tree[a]	$\triangle l_i$	BP_i^b	DBP_i^c	$sDBP_i^d$	AU_i^e	Tree form[f]
1	-2.7	**0.579**	**0.607**	**0.576**	**0.789**	(((1(23))4)56)
2	2.7	**0.312**	**0.458**	**0.401**	**0.516**	((1((23)4))56)
3	7.4	0.036	**0.167**	**0.235**	**0.114**	(((14)(23))56)
4	17.6	0.013	0.041	**0.116**	**0.075**	((1(23))(45)6)
5	18.9	0.035	**0.082**	**0.110**	**0.128**	(1((23)(45))6)
6	20.1	0.005	0.031	**0.069**	0.029	(1(((23)4)5)6)
7	20.6	0.017	**0.056**	**0.084**	**0.101**	((1(45))(23)6)
8	22.2	0.001	0.007	0.042	0.009	((15)((23)4)6)
9	25.4	0.000	0.002	0.022	0.000	(((1(23))5)46)
10	26.3	0.003	0.011	0.023	0.028	(((15)4)(23)6)
11	28.9	0.000	0.003	0.013	0.003	(((14)5)(23)6)
12	31.6	0.000	0.001	0.004	0.001	(((15)(23))46)
13	31.7	0.000	0.002	0.005	0.001	(1(((23)5)4)6)
14	34.7	0.000	0.003	0.001	0.005	((14)((23)5)6)
15	36.2	0.000	0.001	0.000	0.002	((1((23)5))46)

[a]Trees are numbered by increasing order of $\triangle l_i = max_{j\neq i} l_j - l_i$, the difference between the log-likelihood value for a given tree and the largest value among all other trees.
[b]Bootstrap probability, calculated from 10000 pseudoreplicates (from Shimodaira (2002)).
[c]Double bootstrap probability, calculated from 25 million pseudoreplicates (B1 = 5 ×1000, $B2 = 5 \times 1000$).
[d]Speedy double bootstrap probability, calculated from 10000 pseudoreplicates (B1 = 10000).
[e]Multiscale bootstrap probability, calculated from 100000 pseudoreplicates (AU-test; from Shimodaira (2002)).
[f]Taxon labels: 1 = human, 2 = seal, 3 = cow, 4 = rabbit, 5 = mouse, 6 = opossum.

Table 2 Comparison of the BP, DBP, sDBP and AU methods, regarding their speed for computing a p-value for tree-7.

	BP	DBP	sDBP	AU	Speed increase (sDBP/DBP)
Time (secs)[a]	0.69	715	0.73	3.72	1021-fold
Time (secs)[b]	3.52	17921	3.53	14.39	5076-fold

[a] Case of $B1 = 10^3$, $B2 = 10^3$ pseudoreplicates
[b] Case of $B1 = 5 \times 10^3$, $B2 = 5 \times 10^3$ pseudoreplicates

5. Conclusion

As shown in the result section, the sDBP algorithm has comparable accuracy to the DBP algorithm and is much more computationally efficient for phylogenetic tree selection problem. For allowing researchers to apply the sDBP algorithm easily, we have developed an easy to use R package. We think this implementation of sDBP algorithm will be of further utilities to assessing the reliability of phylogenetic trees.

Availablity

The program is freely distributed under GNU General Public License (GPL) and can directly installed from CRAN,
http://cran.r.-project.org/
the official R package archive. The instruction and program source code are avaliable at
http://www.bi.cs.titech.ac.jp/sdbp/

References

[1] C. Webb, D. Ackerly, M. McPeek, and M. Donoghue, "Phylogenies and community ecology," *Annual Review of Ecology and Systematics*, pp. 475–505, 2002.

[2] E. Wiley, *Phylogenetics: The Theory and Practice of Phylogenetic Systematics*. Wiley-Interscience, New York, 1981.

[3] F. Pazos and A. Valencia, "Similarity of phylogenetic trees as indicator of protein–protein interaction," *Protein Engineering*, vol. 14, no. 9, pp. 609–614, 2001.

[4] J. Felsenstein, *Inferring Phylogenies*. Sinauer Associates, Sunderland, Massachusetts, 2004.

[5] ——, "Evolutionary trees from dna sequences: A maximum likelihood approach," *Journal of Molecular Evolution*, vol. 17, no. 6, pp. 368–376, 1981.

[6] ——, "Confidence limits on phylogenies: An approach using the bootstrap," *Evolution*, pp. 783–791, 1985.

[7] D. Hillis and J. Bull, "An empirical test of bootstrapping as a method for assessing confidence in phylogenetic analysis," *Systematic Biology*, vol. 42, no. 2, pp. 182–192, 1993.

[8] M. Sanderson and M. Wojciechowski, "Improved bootstrap confidence limits in large-scale phylogenies, with an example from neo-astragalus (leguminosae)," *Systematic Biology*, vol. 49, no. 4, pp. 671–685, 2000.

[9] P. Hall, *The bootstrap and Edgeworth expansion*. Springer Verlag, New York, 1992.

[10] B. Efron and R. Tibshirani, "The problem of regions," *Stanford Technical Report*, vol. 192, 1996. [Online]. Available: ftp://utstat.toronto.edu/pub/tibs/regions.ps.

[11] H. Shimodaira, "An approximately unbiased test of phylogenetic tree selection," *Systematic Biology*, vol. 51, no. 3, pp. 492–508, 2002.

[12] A. Ren, T. Ishida, and Y. Akiyama, "Assessing statistical reliability of phylogenetic trees via a speedy double bootstrap method," *Molecular Phylogenetics and Evolution*, vol. 67, pp. 429–435, 2013.

[13] Y. S. Aulchenko, S. Ripke, A. Isaacs, and C. M. van Duijn, "Genabel: an r library for genome-wide association analysis," *Bioinformatics*, vol. 23, no. 10, pp. 1294–1296, 2007.

[14] H. Shimodaira and M. Hasegawa, "Multiple comparisons of log-likelihoods with applications to phylogenetic inference," *Molecular Biology and Evolution*, vol. 16, pp. 1114–1116, 1999.

[15] J. Hsu, "Simultaneous confidence intervals for all distances from the " best "," *The Annals of Statistics*, pp. 1026–1034, 1981.

[16] H. Shimodaira, "Testing regions with nonsmooth boundaries via multiscale bootstrap," *Journal of Statistical Planning and Inference*, vol. 138, no. 5, pp. 1227–1241, 2008.

[17] B. Efron, "Bootstrap confidence intervals for a class of parametric problems," *Biometrika*, vol. 72, no. 1, pp. 45–58, 1985.

[18] H. Kishino, T. Miyata, and M. Hasegawa, "Maximum likelihood inference of protein phylogeny and the origin of chloroplasts," *Journal of Molecular Evolution*, vol. 31, no. 2, pp. 151–160, 1990.

[19] M. Ayer, H. Brunk, G. Ewing, W. Reid, and E. Silverman, "An empirical distribution function for sampling with incomplete information," *The Annals of Mathematical Statistics*, pp. 641–647, 1955.

[20] Z. Yang, "Paml: a program package for phylogenetic analysis by maximum likelihood," *Computer Applications in the Biosciences*, vol. 13, no. 5, pp. 555–556, 1997.

[21] H. Shimodaira and M. Hasegawa, "Consel: for assessing the confidence of phylogenetic tree selection," *Bioinformatics*, vol. 17, no. 12, pp. 1246–1247, 2001.

[22] Y. Cao, M. Fujiwara, M. Nikaido, N. Okada, and M. Hasegawa, "Interordinal relationships and timescale of eutherian evolution as inferred from mitochondrial genome data," *Gene*, vol. 259, no. 1, pp. 149–158, 2000.

[23] O. Madsen, M. Scally, C. Douady, D. Kao, R. DeBry, R. Adkins, H. Amrine, M. Stanhope, W. de Jong, and M. Springer, "Parallel adaptive radiations in two major clades of placental mammals," *Nature*, vol. 409, no. 6820, pp. 610–614, 2001.

[24] W. Murphy, E. Eizirik, W. Johnson, Y. Zhang, O. Ryder, and S. O'Brien, "Molecular phylogenetics and the origins of placental mammals," *Nature*, vol. 409, no. 6820, pp. 614–618, 2001.

Acceleration of Tandem Mass Spectrometry Analysis Software CoCoozo using Multi-core CPUs and Graphics Processing Units

Yasufumi Obata[1], Takashi Ishida[2], Tohru Natsume[3], and Yutaka Akiyama[2]
[1]Department of Computer Science, Faculty of Engineering, Tokyo Institute of Technology, W8-76, 2-12-1 Ookayama, Meguro-ku, Tokyo 152-8550, JAPAN
[2]Department of Computer Science, Graduate School of Information Science and Engineering, Tokyo Institute of Technology, W8-76, 2-12-1 Ookayama, Meguro-ku, Tokyo 152-8550, JAPAN
[3]Molecular Profiling Research Center for Drug Discovery, National Institute of Advanced Industrial Science and Technology, 2-4-7 Aomi, Koto-ku, Tokyo 135-0064, JAPAN

Abstract— *Tandem mass spectrometry, a method involving multiple steps of mass spectral selection, is widely used in various biological fields. In recent years, steady improvements have been made with respect to speed, and the number of protein databases available for analysis has rapidly increased. Consequently, computational analysis has become the bottleneck in tandem mass spectrometry.*

To overcome this problem, we attempted to improve the tandem mass spectrometry analysis software CoCoozo. To accelerate the program, we improved the algorithm and also incorporated utilization of multi-core CPU and GPGPU. As a result of algorithm improvements, when all mass spectral data files had precursor data, we achieved 8.9-fold speedups compared with the original software. In addition, in the case of no precursor data, by using a 12-core CPU and a GPU card we achieved 18.1-fold speedups compared with the original software.

Keywords: Mass Spectrometry, MS/MS, CoCoozo, Multi-threading, GPGPU.

1. Introduction

Mass spectrometry is currently commonly used in proteomics research, a field of study in which the entire set of proteins expressed by a genome, cell tissue, or organism is examined [1]. Although various mass spectrometry methods have been developed, tandem mass spectrometry (MS/MS, MS^2) is the primary technique now used in many biological investigations, including research on cancer biomarkers [2], Alzheimer's disease [3], and protein-protein interactions [4].

In mass spectrometry analysis, target sample proteins or peptides are divided into several fragments whose masses are measured by a mass analyzer, with an analyzer outputting their spectra. Mass spectrometry analysis software is then used to identify the sample peptides or proteins based on these spectra. Tandem mass spectrometry, in which sample masses are measured in two or more steps, is currently in wide use. The advantage of tandem mass spectrometry is enabling the analysis of mixed protein samples. In two-step tandem mass spectrometry, the peptide ions fragmented from sample proteins during the first step are called precursors, and those fragmented from precursors during the second step are called fragments. Two-step tandem mass spectrometry generates mass spectral data for both precursors and fragments, and identifies sample proteins using both spectra. The mass spectral data contain mass-to-charge ratios (m/z) and collateral intensities of fragments and, in most cases, the precursor that is the source of the fragments.

Various software programs have been developed to analyze mass spectra from tandem mass spectrometry. To identify proteins in a sample, the software calculates the similarity between the spectral data and that of a protein in a database. MASCOT [5] is well known and widely used, but other software programs, such as SEQUEST [6], SpectraST [7], and CoCoozo have also been developed. Each program employs a different algorithm for database searching and similarity measurement, with each algorithm having different advantages and disadvantages with respect to speed and sensitivity. MASCOT, for example, uses a statistical evaluation algorithm [5], whereas SEQUEST uses a cross-correlation scoring algorithm [6]. For similarity measurement, SpectraST utilizes an inner product algorithm between measured and database mass spectral vectors [7].

CoCoozo is a mass spectrometry analysis software package developed at the National Institute of Advanced Industrial Science and Technology (AIST) of Japan and the Tokyo Institute of Technology. It features a unique error correction function for analyzing mass spectra with high precision. CoCoozo has performed consistently over the past several years of use in AIST projects.

In recent years, the speed and sensitivity of tandem mass spectrometry analyzers have steadily improved, with their throughput continually increasing. In addition, the number

Correspondence to: Yutaka Akiyama

of reference protein databases has steadily increased. Consequently, computational analysis is more time intensive than ever, and has become a bottleneck in mass spectrometry.

During the same time period, computer system performance has also been materially improved. Current computer systems have been enhanced by various acceleration technologies, including "multi-core CPU" and "General-Purpose computing on Graphics Processing Units" (GPGPUs). A graphics processing unit (GPU) was originally developed for processing graphics in the 1980s. GPU computational performance has increased dramatically over time, eventually overtaking that of CPUs. Consequently, GPUs have come to be used for general-purpose calculations rather than graphics processing, and this technique is now called "GPGPU". A GPU has dozens or hundreds of streaming processors that are activated in parallel for calculations. GPGPU programing is difficult, requiring high parallel computing skills. To overcome this problem, several platforms have been developed to facilitate computational use of GPGPUs. At present, NVIDIA's CUDA is the most substantial platform, and is widely used. Through the CUDA platform, programmers can make use of GPUs without having knowledge of GPU low-level instructions. As a result, GPGPU techniques have already been used in various applications, such as for astronomical calculations [8] and Fast Fourier Transform (FFT) [9].

In this paper, we report attempted enhancement of the computational speed of the tandem mass spectrometry analysis software package CoCoozo. To achieve this goal, we improved the algorithm and also incorporated multi-threading and the above-mentioned GPGPU-based acceleration technology at parts of similarity evaluation. As a result, when all mass spectral data files had precursor data, we achieved 8.9-fold speedups compared with the original software. In addition, in the case of no precursor data, by using a 12-core CPU we achieved 15.9-fold speedups with the original software. Moreover, by using a 12-core CPU and a GPU card we achieved 18.1-fold speedups compared with the original software.

2. CoCoozo

CoCoozo, which is mass spectrometry analysis software, has been already developed and used in several research fields. In this section, we briefly describe the algorithm of CoCoozo and discuss about its bottlenecks.

A flowchart of CoCoozo main processes is shown in Figure 1. For each precursor in a database, CoCoozo first checks whether or not a query data file includes precursor spectral data. If the query data file contains precursor spectral data, CoCoozo then performs a "precursor matching" process, which checks whether query precursor spectral data correspond to database precursor spectral data. If so, a "fragment matching" process is subsequently performed. If a query data file does not include precursor spectral data,

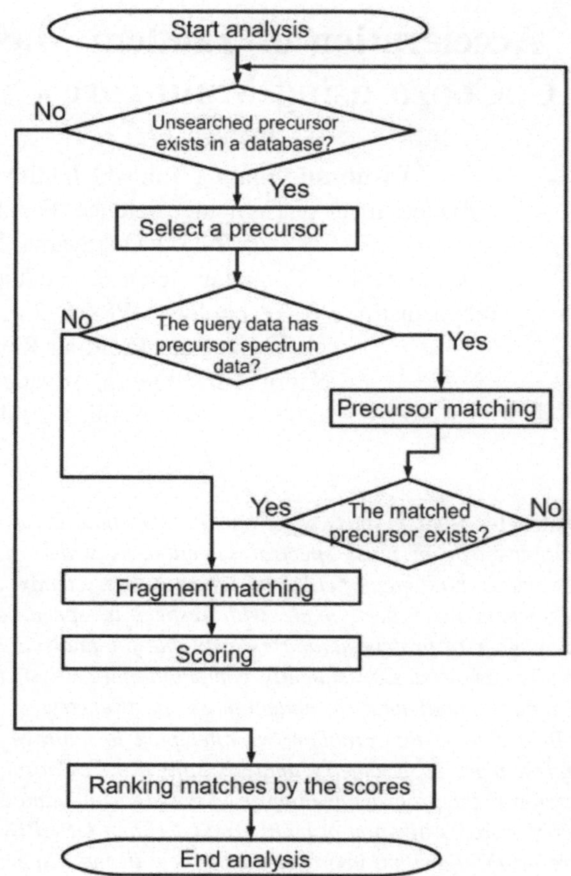

Fig. 1: CoCoozo Main Process Flowchart (for a mass spectral data)

the process goes directly to "fragment matching", which calculates a similarity score between query fragment spectral data and fragment spectral data in a database. After fragment matching, a database precursor data entry has an assigned score based on the results of fragment matching. Finally, all precursors are ranked by their scores, with the highest-scoring precursors outputted as the analysis results.

During precursor and fragment matching processes, the matching algorithm judges whether m/z of a precursor or a fragment in a database matches, within a given tolerance, that of a query. Because the measured data sometimes includes error, the tolerance value is set based on the m/z value and a tolerance ratio parameter. One of the differences between precursor matching and fragment matching is the tolerance ratio parameter. In precursor matching, the ratio is fixed. In contrast, in fragment matching, the ratio varies depending on query spectrum intensity. When there are multiple spectra within a tolerance during fragment matching, the spectrum with the strongest intensity is judged as a "match". The precursor matching process is therefore faster than fragment matching.

If a data file has no precursor spectrum, the matching process takes much longer. This is because a large number of fragment matchings are needed in proportion to the number of precursor spectra in a database if a data file has no precursor spectrum. If, however, a data file contains a precursor spectrum, only a few fragment matchings are required because most of the precursors have already been filtered out based on the results of the precursor matching process.

2.1 Bottlenecks in CoCoozo

We profiled CoCoozo to locate the bottlenecks for two cases. The first case was one in which all mass spectral files included precursor spectral data (case of complete precursor data); the other case was one in which about 10% of mass spectral files were lacking precursor spectral data (case of incomplete precursor data).

The comparison between queries and database was found to be the dominant process in the entire execution time profile. This "matching" process targeting both precursors and fragments is the main process of the CoCoozo search algorithm. In addition, execution time was about 13 times longer in the case of incomplete precursor data compared with the case of complete precursor data. In the case of complete precursor data, the precursor matching comparison was the most dominant process in the entire execution time profile. On the other hand, fragment matching comparison was the most dominant process in the case of incomplete precursor data.

3. Methods

In this section, we introduce our newly proposed to accelerate the CoCoozo software using Multi-core CPUs and Graphics Processing Units.

3.1 Improvement of Matching Algorithm and Initialization Process

A similar matching algorithm is used for both precursors and fragments. To improve the process, the data is sorted that is replaced every comparison by m/z. In other words, we sort the data that is compared with the tolerance. Proteins are often diversely denatured, however, by post-translational modification (PTM), leading to a change in their masses. The way in which CoCoozo handles this PTM complicates sorting by m/z. We thus modified the program structure to improve the sorting. The new sorting algorithm allows matching to terminate when the sorted data exceed the tolerance upper limit. Because fragment matching has variable tolerance, the sort termination is based on a predefined maximum tolerance. In addition to early termination, the number of comparisons is decreased during precursor matching by skipping the data below the lower tolerance limit. This skip is especially effective in precursor matching because the number of comparisons with a given tolerance range is larger than in fragment matching. On the other hand, the skip is less effective in fragment matching because the number of comparisons with a given tolerance range is small.

In addition, we improved initialization of the variable for storing the score for each query. In the original initialization process, all of the scores are initialized regardless of whether or not they have changed. This guarantees that all scores are initialized when an analysis begins. Because initialization of all scores is redundant, scores that are unchanged since the last initialization are omitted.

3.2 Multithreading

When mass spectral files without precursor spectral data are included, the execution time materially increases. Based on profiling, fragment matching occupies about 85% of the entire execution time for the case of incomplete precursor data. Consequently, we apply a multithreading technique to fragment matching and scoring after fragment matching in cases in which an analysis target mass spectral data file lacks precursor spectral data. The two processes are consecutive. The one-time process targets database fragments created from the same precursor, and the consecutive process independence from other continuative processes, so the application of multithreading is relatively easy. In the multithreading part, each thread is in charge of matching fragments created from the same precursor and their scoring.

For multithreading implementation, we used the POSIX threads (pthread) library, a part of POSIX.1 [10] standardized by IEEE.

3.3 Acceleration by GPGPU

Even after improving the matching algorithm, fragment matching in the case of incomplete precursor data still occupied about 70% of the entire execution time. We therefore tried to introduce GPGPU to the fragment matching calculation. Each comparison between a fragment spectrum and one of the database entries in the fragment matching process is independent of the other comparisons, and each comparison is computationally not very intensive. The processes that follow the comparison are not independent, however, and the results of these processes depend on the results of other comparisons between database fragments created from the same precursor and query fragments. These should therefore be processed in serial, but serial processes are difficult to effectively execute on a GPU.

Consequently, we only applied the GPGPU technique to m/z and intensity comparisons. We parallelized each comparison on GPUs. Variable tolerance is inefficient on GPUs, however, because implementation of variable tolerance requires conditional statements, which results in CPU utilization scarcely decreasing. Because of this, a fixed tolerance based on maximum width ratio is used on the GPUs. In other words, preliminary selection is performed on the GPU, with remaining matching executed on the CPU using results from the GPU.

In addition, we applied multithreading to the CPU processing that follows the GPU processing. The CPU processing corresponds to the original fragment matching and scoring. The one-time process targets database fragments created from the same precursor and the consecutive process independence from other continuative processes, so the application of multithreading is relatively easy.

For the GPGPU implementation, we used CUDA (Compute Unified Device Architecture), a platform for GPGPU provided by NVIDIA. Our software requires CUDA version higher than 2.3, and we used CUDA version 4.1 for the following experiments.

4. Results

4.1 Datasets and Database

We used 1,486 mass spectral data files as input queries. The files were in PKL format and had already been filtered. Because all of the files contained precursor spectrum data, we also prepared another dataset for checking the performance in the case of incomplete precursor data. In the second dataset, precursor spectral data was deleted from 149 randomly selected files, with the remaining 1,337 files identical to those in the original dataset. We used a database containing 38,415 proteins, 857,298 precursors, and 26,489,468 fragments, with lysyl endopeptidase (Lys-C) used for dividing a protein into precursors.

We allowed CoCoozo to search monovalent and divalent fragment ions, and to consider N-terminal acetylation.

4.2 Computing Environment

For this research, we used the TSUBAME2.0 supercomputer system at Tokyo Institute of Technology. Programs were executed on a thin node of TSUBAME2.0 with 12 CPU cores. Node specifications are shown in Table 1.

Table 1: Computing Environment

CPU	Intel Xeon 2.93 [GHz] (6 cores) x 2
Memory	54 [GB]
OS	SUSE Linux Enterprise Server 11 SP1
GPU	NVIDIA Tesla M2050
Compiler	gcc 4.3.4
MPI	OpenMPI 1.4.2
CUDA	CUDA 4.1 (64bit)
Profiler	Intel VTune Amplifier XE 2011

We used the UNIX "time" command to measure execution times and Intel VTune Amplifier XE 2011 for more detailed profiling.

4.3 Improvement of Matching Algorithm and Initialization Process

Figure 2 shows execution time results when all of the mass spectral data files include precursor spectral data (case of complete precursor data). CoCoozo with the improved algorithm is approximately 8.9-fold faster than the original version. In particular, a precursor-matching step is about 65.3-fold faster than that of the original, and a fragment-matching step is approximately 2.5-fold faster. With respect to score initialization, the improved version is approximately 483.1-fold faster than the original, equivalent to other short processes.

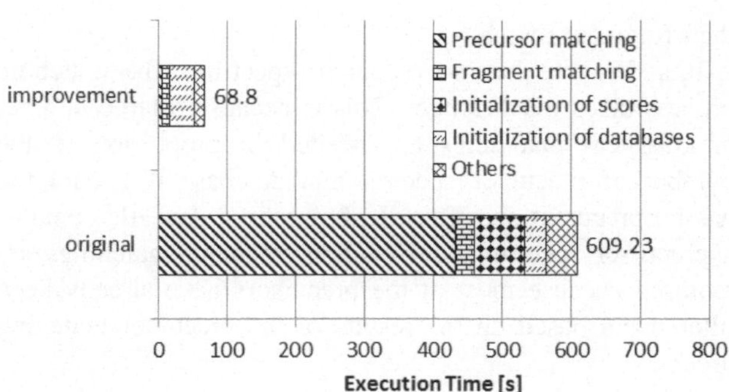

Fig. 2: Result of "Improvement of Matching Algorithm and Initialization Process" (execution time) in the case of complete precursor data.

Table 2: Results of Improvements in the case of complete precursor data

	times [sec]	speedup
Original	609.23	
- Precursor-matching	443.0	
- Fragment-matching	27.61	
- Score Initialization	72.46	
Improvement of Algorithm	68.80	8.9-fold
- Precursor-matching	6.63	65.3-fold
- Fragment-matching	11.08	2.5-fold
- Score Initialization	0.15	483.1-fold

These results demonstrate the magnitude of the improvements arising from the revised algorithm in the case of complete precursor data. Table 2 summarizes the results of improvements in the case of complete precursor data.

4.4 Multithreading

Figure 3 shows execution time as a function of number of threads when about 10% of mass spectral data files lack precursor spectra (case of incomplete precursor data). As seen in the figure, even in the one-thread case, execution is much faster than in the original version, because the multi-threaded version used an improved matching algorithm. CoCoozo with 12 threads is approximately 5.3-fold faster than CoCoozo with 1 thread; the increased speed is less than 12-fold because multi-threaded processing is only applicable to certain parts of the entire program. Another reason is concurrency of threads. As measured by Intel Vtune Amplifier, the peak concurrency is 6 threads even on

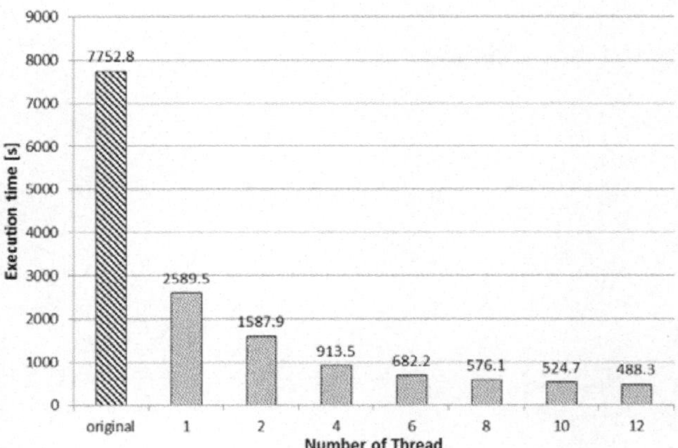

Fig. 3: Result of "Multithreading" (execution time) in the case of incomplete precursor data.

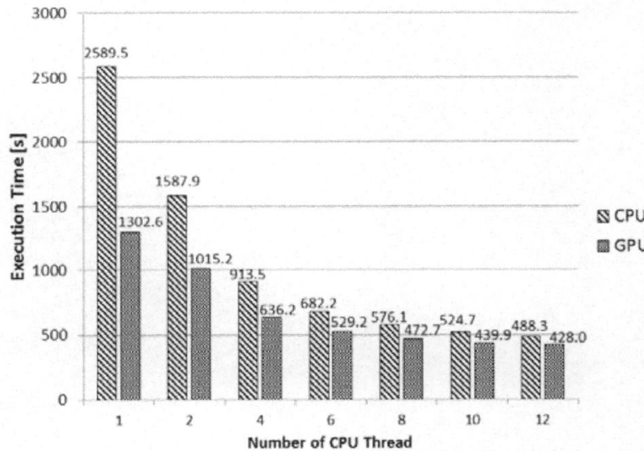

Fig. 4: Result of "Acceleration by GPGPU" (execution time) in the case of incomplete precursor data.

a 12 CPU core system: 12 threads cannot be simultaneously used, and several threads are often idle.

Finally, compared with the original version, CoCoozo with the improved matching algorithm and running with 12 threads is approximately 15.9-fold faster.

4.5 Acceleration by GPGPU

Figure 4 shows CoCoozo execution time with GPGPU for the case of incomplete precursor data. In the figure, the data represented by bars labeled "CPU" is the same as in Figure 3. CoCoozo with GPGPU is approximately 2.0-fold faster than CoCoozo with the improved algorithm but without GPGPU, and approximately 6.0-fold faster than the original version. In particular, a fragment-matching step with GPGPU is approximately 13.8-fold faster than that with the improved matching algorithm. CoCoozo with GPGPU and 12 threads is approximately 3.0-fold faster than CoCoozo with GPGPU and 1 thread. The reason for the low efficiency gain is the same as above. When concurrency is measured with Vtune Amplifier, peak concurrency is 3 threads, and with parallel execution is scarcely over 9 threads. The deterioration of concurrency is caused by the use of GPGPU, as it assists in fragment matching comparisons. Because there is less opportunity for multithreading processes when using GPGPU, more threads are idle. Finally, CoCoozo with GPGPU and 12 threads is about 18.1-fold faster than the original version.

Table 3 summarizes the results of improvements in the case of incomplete precursor data.

Table 3: Results of Improvements in the case of incomplete precursor data

	times [sec]	speedup
Original	7752.82	
Improvement of Algorithm	2589.52	3.0-fold
Multithreading (12-thread)	488.30	15.9-fold
GPGPU	1302.57	6.0-fold
Multithreading (12-thread) & GPGPU	427.97	18.1-fold

5. Discussion

Although analysis results are almost unchanged following improvements, a subtle difference was noted: the values of some scores are different. This difference does not affect the substance of the results, and thus the results after implementation of improvements are not distinguishable from the original ones. The difference is caused by results from fragment matching changing slightly because of data sorting, but this only appears when some peaks having the exactly same intensities are sorted and the matching order of the peaks change from the original order. We believe this change seldom occurs and has little or no effect.

In the case of complete precursor data, database initialization dominates program execution time, representing over 50% of the entire elapsed time. Because initialization is only executed once at the beginning of the program, however, it is not a very serious problem, even when very large query data files are inputted.

6. Conclusions

We have enhanced the tandem mass spectrometry analysis software CoCoozo in three ways: through improved matching and initialization algorithms, multithreading, and GPGPU. When mass spectral data files all contain precursor spectrum data, CoCoozo with the improved algorithm achieves an 8.9-fold speedup compared with the original version. In cases where 10% of mass spectral data files lack precursor spectrum data, CoCoozo with the improved algorithm is 3.0-fold faster than the original. In addition, the multithreading version of CoCoozo with 12 CPU cores achieves a 15.9-fold speedup, and the GPGPU version of

CoCoozo with 1 GPU and 12 CPU cores is 18.1-fold faster than the original.

In this research, we applied multithreading programming and GPGPU only to the case of incomplete precursor data. The case of incomplete precursor data does not often occur in practice, however. Consequently, the application of multithreading programing and GPGPU to the case of complete precursor data is an important focus of future work.

Acknowledgements

We are deeply grateful to Mr. Katsuyuki Koike, Mr. Hideo Kusano, Mr. Tomohisa Hatta, the members of the developing team of original version of CoCoozo, for their insightful comments and suggestions. We also thank Mr. Yasuhiro Fujihara, a main programming staff of the original version of CoCoozo, for his generous support.

References

[1] W. P. Blackstock, M. P. Weir, "Proteomics: quantitative and physical mapping of cellular proteins.", *Trends Biotechnol.*, vol. 17, No. 3, pp. 121-127, 1999.

[2] E. P. Diamandis, "Mass spectrometry as a diagnostic and a cancer biomarker discovery tool: opportunities and potential limitations.", *Mol Cell Proteomics.*, vol. 3, no. 4, pp. 367-378, 2004.

[3] D. C. German, P. Gurnani, A. Nandi, H. R. Garner, W. Fisher, R. Diaz-Arrastia, P. O'Suilleabhain, K. P. Rosenblatt: "Serum biomarkers for Alzheimer's disease: proteomic discovery.", *Biomed Pharmacother.*, vol. 61 no. 7, pp. 383-389, 2007.

[4] A. C. Gavin, K. Maeda, S. Kühner, "Recent advances in charting protein-protein interaction: mass spectrometry-based approaches.", *Curr Opin Biotechnol.*, vol. 22 no. 1, pp. 42-49, 2011.

[5] D. N. Perkins, D. J. Pappin, D. M. Creasy, J. S. Cottrell, "Probability-based protein identification by searching sequence databases using mass spectrometry data", *Electrophoresis.*, vol. 20, no. 18, pp. 3551-3567, 1999.

[6] J. K. Eng, A. L. McCormack, J. R. Yates, III, "An Approach to Correlate Tandem Mass Spectral Data of Peptides with Amono Acid Sequences in a Protein Database", *J. Am. Soc. Mass Spectrom*, vol. 5, no. 11, pp. 976-989, 1994.

[7] H. Lam, E. W. Deutsch, J. S. Eddes, J. K. Eng, N. King, S. E. Stein, R. Aebersold, "Development and validation of a spectral library searching method for peptide identification from MS/MS", *Proteomics*, vol. 7, no. 5, pp. 655-667, 2007.

[8] Hubert Nguyen, *GPU Gems 3*, Boston, U.S.A.: Addison-Wesley Professional, 2007.

[9] N. K. Govindaraju, B. Lloyed, Y. Dotsenko, B. Smith, J. Manferdelli, "High Performance Discrete Fourier Transforms on Graphics Processors", *the 2008 ACM/IEEE conference on supercomputing*, pp. 1-12, 2008.

[10] *Information Technology - Portable Operating System Interface (POSIX) - Part1 : System Application Program Interface (API) [C Language]*, IEEE, Inc., 1996.

A Case Study of Calculation of Source Code Module Importance

Takaaki Goto[1], Setsuo Yamada[2], Tetsuro Nishino[1], and Kensei Tsuchida[3]
[1]Graduate School of Informatics and Engineering, The University of Electro-Communications, Chofu, Tokyo, Japan
[2]Nippon Telegraph and Telephone Corporation
[3]Faculty of Information Science and Arts, Toyo University, Kawagoe, Saitama, Japan

Abstract— *Open Source Software (OSS) has been widely used in software development. However, OSS often lacks adequate documentation and as a result developers cannot obtain enough information to develop software with OSS. The popularization of OSS, or free software, has enabled developers to more easily obtain source codes to improve their coding skills. Developers read source codes in order to understand the architecture and behavior of OSS. However, it is difficult for developers to find the information they need due to the lack of documentation .*

In this paper, we propose a method for calculating the importance of source code modules based on the dependency of the source codes. We target Java language, and we calculate the degrees from class dependency.

Keywords: open source software, software maintenance, source code reading

1. Introduction

As a result of the short-term nature of software development and the creation of large software programs, creating and managing many software documents poses problems. In recent years, software development using Open Source Software (OSS) has increased; however, developers find it difficult to obtain information about OSS due to the lack of documentation. Therefore, developers have to read OSS source code that offers them less information.

On the other hand, developers have found it easier to obtain source codes with the popularization of OSS or free software. They use this information to either revise the OSS or improve their coding skills. However, it is difficult for developers to determine the order of reading source codes; and this is especially true for primary developers.

Many research studies targeting source code summarization [1], [2], [3] and source code mining [4], [5], [6] have been done. Source code summarization helps developers to quickly understand software. However, methods for reading source code modules are also important.

In this paper, we propose a method to calculate the importance of source code modules, using the dependency of source codes. Here we target Java programming, and calculate the importance degree using class dependency.

2. Source Code Reading

Developers develop various methods to read source codes. Generalized methods for source code reading are as follows [7]:

1) First, developers find the focus point for reading by keyword searching, and then start reading the source code from the located point.
2) Developers start reading from the main function or the main method.
3) Developers use a debugger when they read source code. They set break points to focus areas, after which the debugger is executed. Developers can read source code with various debugging information such as a variable's value.

In addition to the methods listed above, it has been shown to be effective for developers to read the source code module, which is primarily obtained from other modules. Frequently accessed source code may have an important function. As such, it is considered to be an effective method for reading and understanding source code. Developers can detect the reading points from the dependency of the source codes.

3. Class Dependency

In the Java program, each part of the source code refers to various classes. For instance, one class uses another class. If class A uses class B, a relationship between class A and class B is established, which is identified as "class A refers to class B". Figure 1 illustrates the relationship.

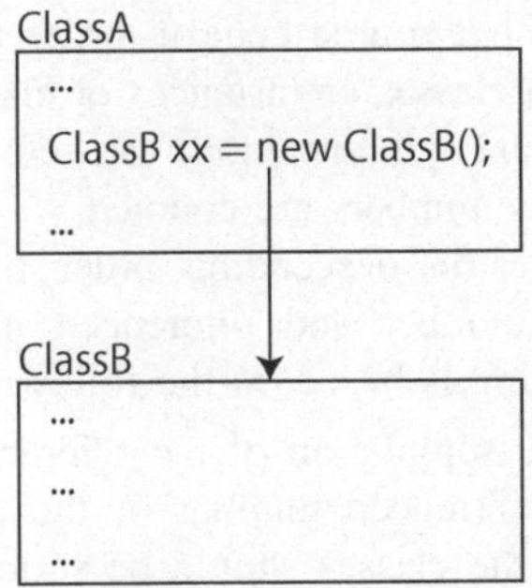

Fig. 1: Class dependency relationship: "Class A refers to Class B"

In our method, dependency is computed by using other classes in one class. However we do not consider usage frequency. For example, if class A uses class B many times in one class, we only count one relation between class A and class B.

Because some class dependencies arise from these referring relationships among classes, developers can understand the links in the source code.

Some open source software have functions that enable developers to analyze class dependency. "ispace" [8] is one example of such software. "ispace"" is a plug-in software for eclipse, and it provides a function that enables users to draw a class dependency graph. Users can gain an understanding of class dependency in source codes.

However, when users describe a large software program using such tools, it is hard for users to understand dependency intuitively because of its complexity. For example, Figure 2 shows a class dependency of JUnit [9] Version 4.10.

In this way, it is important for developers to have a function that provides a guide for source code reading. Calculation of the source code module importance is required. We propose such a method in the next section.

4. Module Importance

When developers try to read source codes without software documentation, they find it difficult to decide where to start reading the source code when they have to refer to complicated class dependency diagrams (Figure 2). Here, we propose a method that defines the importance of source code modules using information obtained from source code analysis. In this paper, we apply our source code analysis method to Java.

Module importance is calculated by analyzing strings in source codes. After the analysis, the reference and referenced relationships are obtained. In this context, we refer to classes with a large value of importance as "frequently-used" classes and these are treated as important classes in the source code. Here, we show an algorithm for obtaining module importance.

1) Analyze input source code in order to collect tokens relevant to classes or instances of classes.
2) From obtained information, the reference and referenced class numbers are counted.
3) Sort classes in descending order of summation of reference number and referenced number for each class. Sorting is based on the following rules:
   a) If the summation of the reference numbers and the referenced number of the classes is equal, then the classes should be sorted in descending order based on the referenced number.
   b) If the summation of the reference numbers and the referenced number is equal, and also the referenced number is equal, then the classes should be sorted in descending order based on the reference number.
   c) If the summation of the reference number and the referenced number is equal, and also the reference number and the referenced number are equal, then the classes should be sorted in descending order based on the sum of the reference number and the referenced number of the neighboring class.
   d) If neighboring class values are equal, then it does not matter which number (the reference number or the referenced number) you choose. Here neighbor means classes that are connected to a focus class.
   e) If it is not possible to decide upon the precedence order of the classes, then the antecedence classes are given priority in the ordering.

Module importance serves as a guide for source code reading. We defined it as, "frequently used classes are important." Therefore we designed the above algorithm. In order to sort the importance in detail in the case in which the summation of the reference number and the referenced number is equal, the algorithm uses the neighbor class's value for sorting.

5. Case Study

Here, we show a case study of our method using a small Java source code. The intended software is a template of image processing software, which can be used by students in a practical software development class to modify the software in order to develop a more sophisticated program. The name of the template software is "SimColorBase" [10], which can process file filtering for images such as "brighten up" or "darken up". Figure 3 shows a SimColorBase screen shot.

Fig. 3: SimColorBase screen shot

In this case study, we target classes included in SimColorBase and do not cover classes provided by Java.

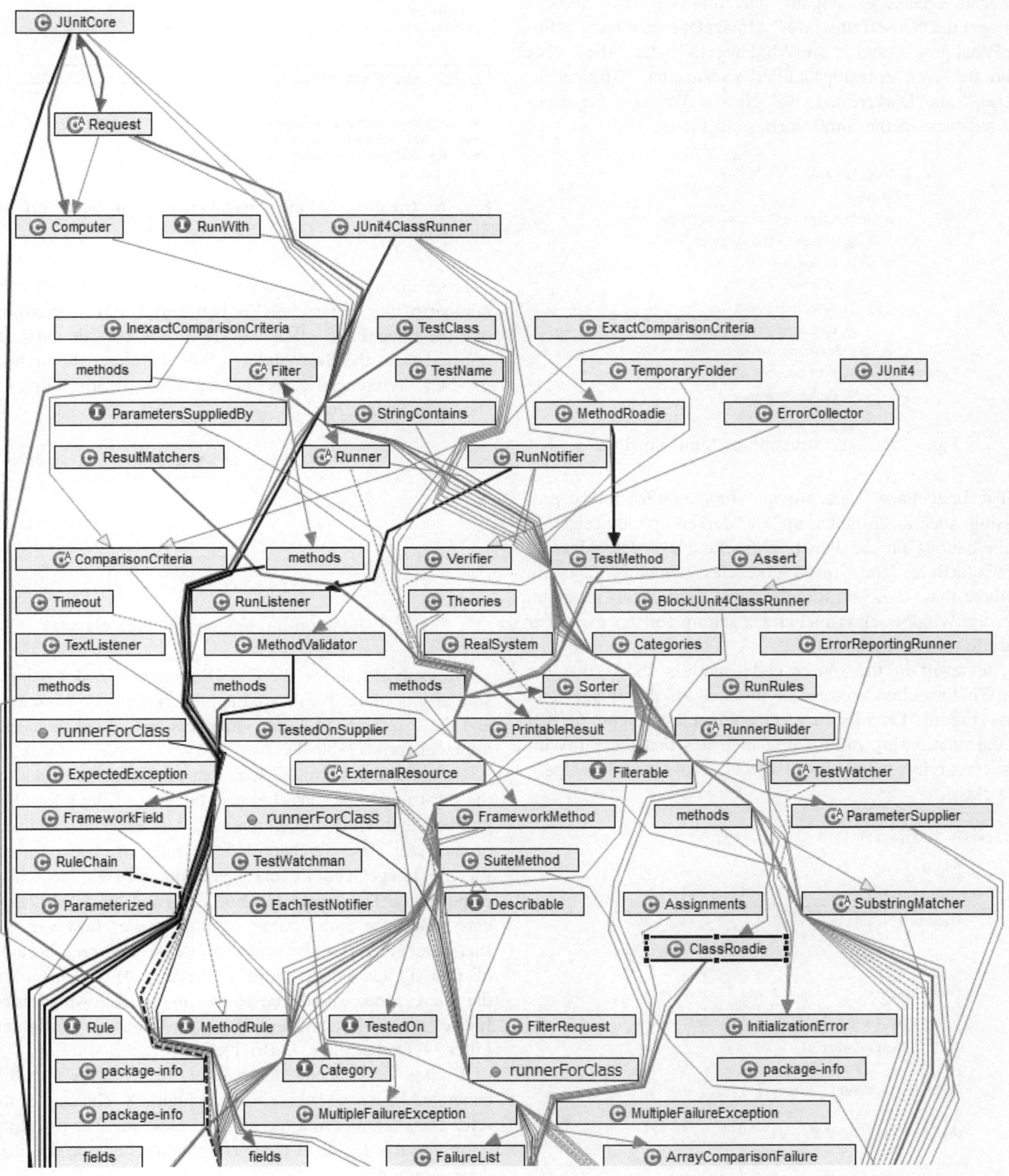

Fig. 2: Class dependency schematic for JUnit Ver. 4.10

This software consists of two packages "dyschromatopsia" and "dyschromatopsia.filter". The "dyschromatopsia" package contains the following four classes: "ImageFileChooserFilter.java," "ImageOpenFile.java," "ImagePanel.java," and "SimWindow.java". On the other hand, the "dyschromatopsia.filter" package has "BrighterFilter.java" and"DarkerFilter.java" classes. We show the package structure of the SimColorBase in Figure 4.

```
SimColorBase
  src
    jp.ac.uec.psd3.dyschromatopsia
      ImageFileChooserFilter.java
      ImageOpenFile.java
      ImagePanel.java
      SimWindow.java
      tune1.jpg
    jp.ac.uec.psd3.dyschromatopsia.filter
      BrighterFilter.java
      DarkerFilter.java
```

Fig. 4: Package structure of SimColorBase

The ImagePanel class provides functions for image processing, such as "brighten up" or "darken up", by selecting radio buttons on the Panel. This class is a core class of SimColorBase. The SimWindow class contains the main method; that is, this class is the entry point of this program. The SimWindow class includes a setting for the menu bar and file processing codes.

The result of the source code analysis shows that the SimWindow class creates an instance of the ImagePanel class (Figure 5) and the ImageOpenFile class (Figure 6); that is, the relationship information indicates that the SimWindow class refers to the ImagePanel class and the ImageOpenFile class.

```
public SimWindow()
{
    URL url;
    try {
        url = this.getClass().getResource("tune1.jpg");
        img = ImageIO.read(url);
    } catch (Exception e2) {
        e2.printStackTrace();
    }

    WindowListener listtener = new WindowAdapter()
    {
        public void windowClosing( WindowEvent e )
        {
            System.exit(0);
        }
    };
    addWindowListener( listtener );

    this.setTitle("画像変換");

    imgPnl = new ImagePanel(img);
    add(imgPnl);
```

Fig. 5: Creation of the ImagePanel instance on the SimWindow class

```
private final ImagePanel imgPnl;

private JMenuBar menubar;
private JMenu fileMenu;
private JMenu viewMenu;

private static ImageOpenFile imageOpenFile = new ImageOpenFile();

static BufferedImage bimage;
static BufferedImage bufImg;
private BufferedImage img;
```

Fig. 6: Creation of the ImageOpenFile instance on the SimWindow class

From the above the analysis, we can determine that the number of the "refer class" is two. We can also determine that the ImagePanel class and the ImageOpenFile class are referred from the SimWindow class; therefore, the number for each "referenced class" is one. Those relationships are shown in Figure 7.

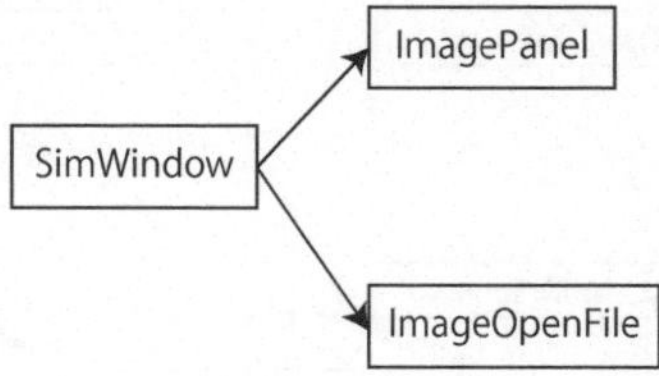

Fig. 7: Relationship among the three classes

We analyzed all the SimColorBase source codes using a similar procedure. We then tallied the "refer class" numbers and the " referenced class " numbers and sorted them into a tabular form (Table 1).

From Table 1, it can be seen that the ImagePanel class is the most important class because the sum of the refer class numbers and referred class numbers was larger than the sum of the refer class numbers and the referred class numbers for the ImageOpenFile class and the SimWindow class, respectively. The ImageOpenFile class and the SimWindow class have the same value of importance; however, the ImageOpenFile class is located on the second rank because of rule 3b (as noted above in Section 4). In this case, the source code should be shown in the following order: ImagePanel $\rightarrow$ ImageOpenFile $\rightarrow$ SimWindow $\rightarrow$ BrighterFilter $\rightarrow$ DarkerFilter $\rightarrow$ BrighterFilter.

A class dependency diagram of SimColorBase that is generated by ispace [8] is shown in Figure 8. The sum of the refer class number and the referred class number conforms closely to the degree of the corresponding node on the class dependency diagram.

Here, we discuss the validity of our method using the result of the case study. In the case study, the ImagePanel class was evaluated as the most important class. The ImagePanel class is the core class of the SimColorBase application and

Table 1: Class dependency data for the SimColorBase class

Importance	Class name	Referenced class	Refer class	total
1	ImagePanel	1	2	3
2	ImageOpenFile	1	1	2
3	SimWindow	0	2	2
4	BrighterFilter	1	0	1
5	DarkerFilter	1	0	1
6	ImageFileChooserFilter	1	0	1

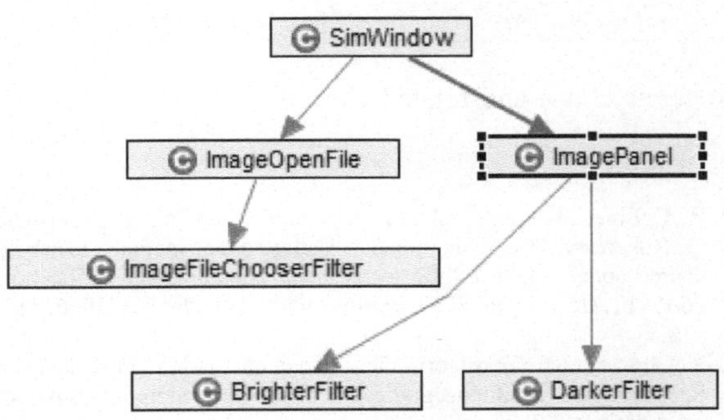

Fig. 8: Class dependency for the SimColor Base class

defines the graphical user interface of the SimColorBase. For practical purposes, the ImagePanel class is the class for reading first if a developer wants to understand the SimColorBase. Therefore, we find that our method works in practice.

On the other hand, SimColorBase is an application for filtering image files. However the importance of BrighterFilter and DarkerFilter classes that process filtering are low. Such frequently performed classes can not be judged as important in our method. In order to calculate importance in consideration of frequently performed classes, dynamic analysis is required.

In this case study, we analyzed a small software program; however, when targeting large software programs, it is difficult to find points for reading the source code due to the size of the source code or the dependency graph. Our method can reduce the challenges developers face when analyzing source codes by enabling them to calculate the importance of the source code modules. We are also considering other methods for calculating the importance of the dependency using natural language processing methods.

6. Presentation of important class

After calculating the importance of the source code module, the source code is shown according to its order of importance. The importance of the source code can be presented in two different ways. First, the source code can be identified by its appropriate class. Second, the source code's appropriate class can be shown with its related classes. In order to understand the program, it is also important to understand the context of a class; therefore, it is important to also identify the refer class and referred class for each class.

Figure 9 illustrates a case showing the ImagePanel class and its related classes. As can be seen, the ImagePanel class is the focus class. Figure 9 also includes information about the SimWindow class , the BrighterFilter class and the DarkerFilter class. The point of instantiation for the ImagePanel class in the SimWindow class is also focused on.

7. Related works

To date, only research that has targeted supporting source code reading has been done.

Karrer et al. [11] propose a method that presents a focus method centered around a call graph. DeLine et al. [12] propose a source code navigation method. In that method, the source code is displayed with a thumbnail and users can understand the source code using the spatial memory of the entire code. In these research studies, users move the focus point manually; on the other hand, the focus points we propose are presented automatically. Therefore, differences exist between the method we use for detecting the focus class and the methods used by other researchers.

Inoue et al. [13] proposed a component ranking model. In the model, rank is computed using class inheritance, interface implementation, abstract class implementation, variable declaration, instance creation, field access, and method invocation. Moreover the ranking model also considers similarity between the two components. In our method, we restricted use to the appearance of class names that can be obtained from the source code, we do not consider similarity among classes.

8. Conclusion

In this paper, we proposed a method for calculating the importance of a source code module that supports a developer's ability to read source code. Moreover, we conducted a substantive experiment using a small software program. In future works, we have a plan to develop a

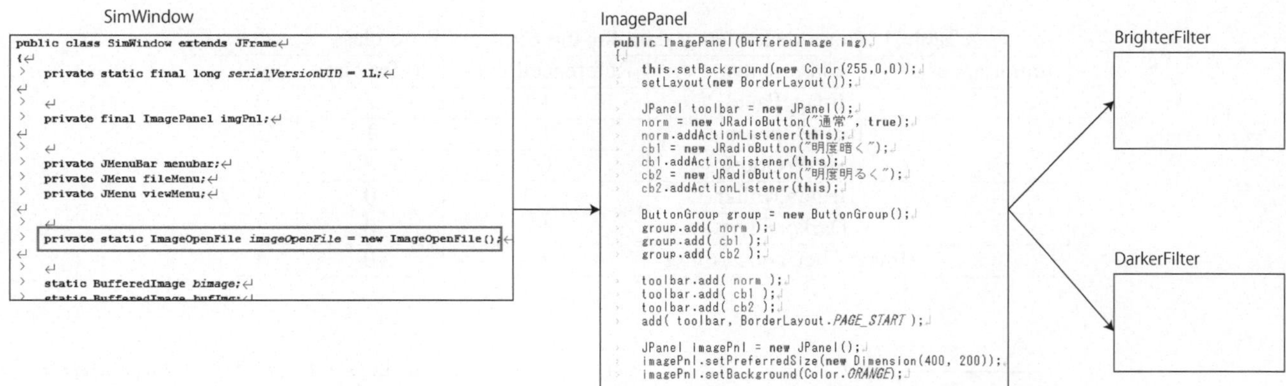

Fig. 9: Presentation of the ImagePanel class (focus class) and related classes

system based on the proposed method. Moreover, we will construct a source code reading support environment and conduct a survey of software developers. A source code reading support environment requires a supporting function that shows the focus points which software developers are currently reading. As such, the Focus+Context presentation of the source code must also be considered.

References

[1] S. Haiduc, J. Aponte, and A. Marcus, "Supporting program comprehension with source code summarization," in *Proceedings of the 32nd ACM/IEEE International Conference on Software Engineering - Volume 2*. New York, NY, USA: ACM, 2010, pp. 223–226. [Online]. Available: http://doi.acm.org/10.1145/1810295.1810335

[2] S. Haiduc, J. Aponte, L. Moreno, and A. Marcus, "On the use of automated text summarization techniques for summarizing source code," in *Proceedings of 2010 17th Working Conference on Reverse Engineering (WCRE)*, October 2010, pp. 35 –44.

[3] S. Rastkar, G. C. Murphy, and A. W. Bradley, "Generating natural language summaries for crosscutting source code concerns," in *Proceedings of 2011 27th IEEE International Conference on Software Maintenance (ICSM)*, September 2011, pp. 103 –112.

[4] D. Poshyvanyk, A. Marcus, and Y. Dong, "Jiriss - an eclipse plug-in for source code exploration," in *Proceedings of 14th IEEE International Conference on Program Comprehension, 2006. ICPC 2006*, 2006, pp. 252 –255.

[5] E. Enslen, E. Hill, L. Pollock, and K. Vijay-Shanker, "Mining source code to automatically split identifiers for software analysis," in *Proceedings of 6th IEEE International Working Conference on Mining Software Repositories, 2009. MSR '09*, May 2009, pp. 71 –80.

[6] T. Kobayashi and S. Hayashi, "Recent researches for supporting software construction and maintenance with data mining," *Computer Software*, vol. 27, no. 3, pp. 3_13–3_23, 2010, (in Japanese).

[7] Y. Matsumoto, *How to read source code*. Nikkei BP, 2007, no. Nikkei Software 2007, January, (in Japanese).

[8] "ispace," http://ispace.stribor.de/index.php?n=Ispace.Home.

[9] "Junit," http://junit.sourceforge.net/.

[10] U. S. Repository, "Software development material image processing program simcolorbase," https://www.repository.uec.ac.jp/.

[11] T. Karrer, J.-P. Krämer, J. Diehl, B. Hartmann, and J. Borchers, "Stacksplorer: call graph navigation helps increasing code maintenance efficiency," in *Proceedings of the 24th annual ACM symposium on User interface software and technology*. New York, NY, USA: ACM, 2011, pp. 217–224. [Online]. Available: http://doi.acm.org/10.1145/2047196.2047225

[12] R. DeLine, M. Czerwinski, B. Meyers, G. Venolia, S. Drucker, and G. Robertson, "Code thumbnails: Using spatial memory to navigate source code," in *Visual Languages and Human-Centric Computing, 2006. VL/HCC 2006. IEEE Symposium on*, September 2006, pp. 11 –18.

[13] K. Inoue, R. Yokomori, T. Yamamoto, M. Matsushita, and S. Kusumoto, "Ranking significance of software components based on use relations," *Software Engineering, IEEE Transactions on*, vol. 31, no. 3, pp. 213–225, 2005.

Implementation of the Orthogonal QD Algorithm for Lower Tridiagonal Matrices

Sho ARAKI[*1], Hiroki TANAKA[*2], Kinji KIMURA[*3] and Yoshimasa NAKAMURA[*4]

[*]Graduate School of Informatics, Kyoto University, Yoshidahonmachi, Sakyo-ku, Kyoto 606-8501, JAPAN
[1]contact author:araki@amp.i.kyoto-u.ac.jp
[2]hirotnk@amp.i.kyoto-u.ac.jp
[3]kkimur@i.kyoto-u.ac.jp
[4]ynaka@i.kyoto-u.ac.jp

Abstract— *The orthogonal qd algorithm with shifts (oqds algorithm), proposed by von Matt, is an algorithm for computing the singular values of bidiagonal matrices. This algorithm is accurate in terms of relative error, and it is also applicable to general triangular matrices. In particular, for lower tridiagonal matrices, BLAS Level 2.5 routines are available in preprocessing stage for this algorithm. BLAS Level 2.5 routines are faster than BLAS Level 2 routines widely used in preprocessing for bidiagonalization. Generally, it takes $O(n^3)$ operations to reduce a full n-by-n matrix to a band matrix such as bidiagonal or lower tridiagonal matrix. On the other hand, computing the singular values of a bidiagonal or lower tridiagonal matrices takes only $O(n^2)$ operations. Consequently, if we have an algorithm for computing the singular values of lower tridiagonal matrices, we can expect that the total computation time including preprocessing to obtain the singular values is reduced.*

In this paper, we consider the oqds algorithm for lower tridiagonal matrices. We propose a shift strategy for lower tridiagonal matrices to accelerate convergence and derive criteria for deflation or splitting.

(This paper is submitted to PDPTA'13)

Keywords

singular value computation, orthogonal qd algorithm, lower tridiagonal matrix, shift strategy, deflation, splitting.

1. Introduction

In 1997, von Matt proposed an algorithm, based on Rutishauser's qd algorithm [1], called orthogonal qd algorithm with shifts (oqds algorithm) for computing the singular values of bidiagonal matrices in which all the transformations consist of Givens rotations [2]. It is shown that the oqds algorithm is also applicable to general triangular matrices [3].

In this paper, we shall consider the application of the oqds algorithm to lower tridiagonal matrices. It allows us to use lower-tridiagonalization as pre-processing instead of bidiagonalization. The lower-tridiagonalization is less computational complexity than the bidiagonalization. Further, we can adopt BLAS Level 2.5 routines with efficient cache reuse which are faster than BLAS Level 2 routines for implementation of the lower-tridiagonalization. The oqds algorithm for lower tridiagonal matrices thus enables us to reduce the total computation time to obtain the singular values of general triangular matrices.

For practical use, we should design good shift strategies for convergence acceleration and good convergence criteria for accurate computation. However, appropriate shift strategies and convergence criteria for lower tridiagonal matrices have not been proposed yet. In this paper, we propose a shift strategy consisting of the generalized Newton shift and associated two methods, Laguerre shift and Kato-Temple shift, and the well known Gerschgorin shift. Moreover, we design new convergence criteria for deflation and splitting required for the implementation of the oqds algorithm. By the criteria, we can do the convergence test for lower tridiagonal matrices. At the end, we show some results of numerical experiments to compare the oqds algorithms for bidiagonal matrices and for lower tridiagonal matrices.

2. Orthogonal QD Algorithm for Lower Tridiagonal Matrix

Let

$$L = \begin{bmatrix} \alpha_1 & & & & \\ \beta_1 & \alpha_2 & & & \\ \gamma_1 & \beta_2 & \alpha_3 & & \\ & \ddots & \ddots & \ddots & \\ & & \gamma_{n-2} & \beta_{n-1} & \alpha_n \end{bmatrix} \quad (1)$$

be an n-by-n lower tridiagonal matrix. One step of Cholesky LR method [4] with shift σ^2 transforms the lower tridiagonal matrix L into the upper tridiagonal matrix U by

$$L^T L - \sigma^2 I = U^T U. \quad (2)$$

Then, we set $L := U^T$. By repeating this procedure iteratively, the diagonal elements of the matrix L converge to the singular values of the matrix L and the non-diagonal elements get into zero. It is known that the Cholesky decomposition is numerically unstable; the Cholesky decomposition may collapse even if the shift value σ is zero. For resolving this problem, we use the *implicit* Cholesky decomposition [2]. The implicit Cholesky decomposition is designed by using

Algorithm 1 Generalized Givens transformation (rotg2(x_1, x_2, σ, c, s))

```
scale := max (|x1| , |x2|)
if scale = 0 then
    c := 1
    s := 0
else
    x1 := x1/scale
    x2 := x2/scale
    sig := σ/scale
    norm2 := x1^2 + x2^2
    r := sqrt(norm2 − sig^2)
    c := (x1 × r + x2 × sig) /norm2
    s := (x2 × r − x1 × sig) /norm2
    x1 := scale × r
    x2 := σ
end if
```

the generalized Givens transformation which is numerically stable. The oqds algorithm is formulated as the iteration of the implicit Cholesky LR step.

2.1 Implicit Cholesky decomposition

The implicit Cholesky decomposition computes an upper tridiagonal matrix U from L and σ by an orthogonal transformation

$$Q\begin{bmatrix} L \\ 0 \end{bmatrix} = \begin{bmatrix} U \\ \sigma I \end{bmatrix}, \tag{3}$$

where Q is a $2n$-by-$2n$ orthogonal matrix. It is readily verified that, for the same L and σ, the same U is obtained by (3) as by the Cholesky LR method (2). The orthogonal matrix Q is given by superposition of the Givens and the generalized Givens transformations on $\mathbb{R}^2$.

Definition 2.1 (Generalized Givens transformation [2]). Let σ be a real. The transformation on $\mathbb{R}^2$

$$G\begin{bmatrix} x_1 \\ x_2 \end{bmatrix} = \begin{bmatrix} r \\ \sigma \end{bmatrix} \tag{4}$$

by a 2-by-2 orthogonal matrix G is called the generalized Givens transformation if $r = \pm\sqrt{x_1^2 + x_2^2 - \sigma^2}$ and $\sigma^2 < x_1^2+x_2^2$. Such a matrix G is uniquely determined by

$$G = \begin{bmatrix} c & s \\ -s & c \end{bmatrix}, \tag{5}$$

$$\begin{bmatrix} c \\ s \end{bmatrix} = \frac{1}{x_1^2 + x_2^2}\begin{bmatrix} x_1 & x_2 \\ x_2 & -x_1 \end{bmatrix}\begin{bmatrix} r \\ \sigma \end{bmatrix}. \tag{6}$$

It should be noted that the generalized Givens transformation is equal to the ordinary Givens transformation if $\sigma = 0$. The procedure of the generalized Givens transformation is shown in Algorithm 1. The first step of the implicit Cholesky decomposition is a series of three orthogonal transformations:

$$G_1\begin{bmatrix} \alpha_1 & & & & & & \\ \beta_1 & \alpha_2 & & & & & \\ \gamma_1 & \beta_2 & \ddots & & & & \\ & \gamma_2 & \ddots & & & & \\ & & \ddots & & & & \\ 0 & & & & & & \\ & 0 & & & & & \\ & & \ddots & & & & \\ & & & 0 & & & \end{bmatrix} = \begin{bmatrix} \tilde{\alpha}_1 & & & & & & \\ \beta_1 & \alpha_2 & & & & & \\ \gamma_1 & \beta_2 & \ddots & & & & \\ & \gamma_2 & \ddots & & & & \\ & & \ddots & & & & \\ \sigma & & & & & & \\ & 0 & & & & & \\ & & \ddots & & & & \\ & & & 0 & & & \end{bmatrix}, \tag{7}$$

$$G_2\begin{bmatrix} \tilde{\alpha}_1 & & & & & & \\ \beta_1 & \alpha_2 & & & & & \\ \gamma_1 & \beta_2 & \ddots & & & & \\ & \gamma_2 & \ddots & & & & \\ & & \ddots & & & & \\ \sigma & & & & & & \\ & 0 & & & & & \\ & & \ddots & & & & \\ & & & 0 & & & \end{bmatrix} = \begin{bmatrix} \tilde{\tilde{\alpha}}_1 & \tilde{\beta}_1 & 0 & & & & \\ 0 & \tilde{\alpha}_2 & & & & & \\ \gamma_1 & \beta_2 & \ddots & & & & \\ & \gamma_2 & \ddots & & & & \\ & & \ddots & & & & \\ \sigma & & & & & & \\ & 0 & & & & & \\ & & \ddots & & & & \\ & & & 0 & & & \end{bmatrix}, \tag{8}$$

and then

$$G_3\begin{bmatrix} \tilde{\tilde{\alpha}}_1 & \tilde{\beta}_1 & 0 & & & & \\ 0 & \tilde{\alpha}_2 & & & & & \\ \gamma_1 & \beta_2 & \ddots & & & & \\ & \gamma_2 & \ddots & & & & \\ & & \ddots & & & & \\ \sigma & & & & & & \\ & 0 & & & & & \\ & & \ddots & & & & \\ & & & 0 & & & \end{bmatrix} = \begin{bmatrix} \check{\alpha}_1 & \check{\beta}_1 & \check{\gamma}_1 & & & & \\ 0 & \tilde{\alpha}_2 & & & & & \\ 0 & \tilde{\beta}_2 & \ddots & & & & \\ & \gamma_2 & \ddots & & & & \\ & & \ddots & & & & \\ \sigma & & & & & & \\ & 0 & & & & & \\ & & \ddots & & & & \\ & & & 0 & & & \end{bmatrix}. \tag{9}$$

In the first column, the first transformation (7) by G_1 generates the lower diagonal element σ. The second (8), the third (9) by G_2, G_3 vanish β_1, γ_1, respectively. Here, G_1 is the generalized Givens transformation for the first and the $(n+1)$th rows and G_2, G_3 are Givens transformations for the first and the second rows, the first and the third rows, respectively. After the three transformations, we obtain the first column of the matrix on the right hand side of equation (3). Applying similar operations for second to nth columns successively, we obtain the upper tridiagonal matrix U in the equation (3) and let the next L be U^T to continue the algorithm. The operations are numerically stable.

Algorithm 2 summarizes the above procedures. The subroutines "rotg" and "rot" appeared in the Algorithm 2 are basic BLAS routines. If we call the "rotg(x_1, x_2, c, s)", the rotation angle of the Givens transformation is stored in the arguments c and s with cos and sin forms. The subroutine "rot(x_1, x_2, c, s)"

applies the Givens transformation defined by the arguments c and s.

Algorithm 2 Implicit Cholesky Decomposition for an n-by-n lower tridiagonal matrix L (icds(L))

```
U := 0
for i = 1 to n do
  α̌_i := α_i
  rotg2(α̌_i, 0, σ, c, s)

  *eliminate subdiagonal element
  rotg(α̌_i, β_i, c, s)
  rot(β̌_i, β_i, c, s)

  *eliminate subsubdiagonal element
  rotg(α̌_i, γ_i, c, s)
  rot(β̌_i, β_i, c, s)
  rot(γ̌_i, γ_i, c, s)
end for
return Ľ
```

3. Shift Strategy

In the implicit Cholesky decomposition, proper choice of the shift value σ significantly accelerates convergence of the oqds algorithm. The shift value σ must be smaller than the minimum singular value of the matrix L to keep the positive-definiteness of $U^T U$. Therefore, we need a method to estimate the lower bound of the minimum singular value of the lower tridiagonal matrix L or the minimum eigenvalue of $L^T L$.

In this section, we discuss four types of lower bounds of the minimum singular value or eigenvalue and design shift method using them.

3.1 Gerschgorin Shift

Theorem 3.1 (Gerschgorin [5]). *For an n-by-n matrix* $A = (a_{ij})$, *let us define*

$$R_i := \sum_{k \neq i} |a_{ik}|. \tag{10}$$

Then, for any eigenvalue λ *of* A, *there exists an integer* i *such as*

$$|\lambda - a_{ii}| \leq R_i. \tag{11}$$

If the matrix A is positive-definite symmetric, $\min(a_{ii} - R_i)$ gives a lower bound of the eigenvalues since all the eigenvalues of A are positive real number.

3.2 Generalized Newton shift

For a positive-definite symmetric matrix A and an arbitrary positive integer p, the value of $(\mathrm{Tr}(A^{-p}))^{-1/p}$ is a lower bound of the eigenvalues of A. Then, finding the value of $\mathrm{Tr}\{(L^T L)^{-p}\}$, we get a lower bound of the singular values of L. We consider a method of computing the value of $\mathrm{Tr}\{(L^T L)^{-p}\}$ in this subsection.

Algorithm 3 Gerschgorin shift (gerschgorin(L))

```
σ := α²_{n-1} + β²_{n-2} + γ²_{n-3} − |α_{n-3}γ_{n-3}| − |β_{n-3}γ_{n-3} + α_{n-2}β_{n-2}|
if σ ≤ 0 then
  return 0
end if
tmp := α²_{n-2} + β²_{n-3} + γ²_{n-4} − |α_{n-4}γ_{n-4}| − |β_{n-4}γ_{n-4} + α_{n-3}β_{n-3}| −
  |β_{n-3}γ_{n-3} + α_{n-2}β_{n-2}|
if tmp ≤ 0 then
  return 0
else if tmp < σ then
  σ := tmp
end if
for i = N - 2 to 3 do
  tmp := α²_i + β²_{i-1} + γ²_{i-2} − |α_{i-2}γ_{i-2}| − |β_{i-1}γ_{i-1} + α_iβ_i| −
    |β_{i-2}γ_{i-2} + α_{i-1}β_{i-1}| − |α_iγ_i|
  if tmp ≤ 0 then
    return 0
  else if tmp < σ then
    σ := tmp
  end if
end for
tmp := α²_2 + β²_1 − |α_1β_1| − |β_1γ_1 + α_2β_2| − |α_2γ_2|
if tmp ≤ 0 then
  return 0
else if tmp < σ then
  σ := tmp
end if
tmp := α²_1 − |α_1β_1| − |α_1γ_1|
if tmp ≤ 0 then
  return 0
else if tmp < σ then
  σ := tmp
end if
```

Let $\bar{L}$ be an n-by-n lower tridiagonal matrix,

$$\bar{L} = \begin{bmatrix} \bar{\alpha}_1 & & & & \\ \bar{\beta}_1 & \bar{\alpha}_2 & & & \\ \bar{\gamma}_1 & \bar{\beta}_2 & \bar{\alpha}_3 & & \\ & \ddots & \ddots & \ddots & \\ & & \bar{\gamma}_{n-2} & \bar{\beta}_{n-1} & \bar{\alpha}_n \end{bmatrix} \tag{12}$$

determined from L with shift s by

$$\bar{L}\bar{L}^T = LL^T - sI. \tag{13}$$

The relationships among elements are given by

$$\bar{\alpha}_i^2 + \bar{\beta}_{i-1}^2 + \bar{\gamma}_{i-2}^2 = \alpha_i^2 + \beta_{i-1}^2 + \gamma_{i-2}^2 - s, \tag{14}$$

$$\bar{\beta}_{i-2}\bar{\gamma}_{i-2} + \bar{\alpha}_{i-1}\bar{\beta}_{i-1} = \beta_{i-2}\gamma_{i-2} + \alpha_{i-1}\beta_{i-1}, \tag{15}$$

$$\bar{\alpha}_{i-2}\bar{\gamma}_{i-2} = \alpha_{i-2}\gamma_{i-2}. \tag{16}$$

Differentiating equations (14)–(16) with respect to s, we obtain

$$2\bar{\alpha}_i\bar{\alpha}_i' + 2\bar{\beta}_{i-1}\bar{\beta}_{i-1}' + 2\bar{\gamma}_{i-2}\bar{\gamma}_{i-2}' = -1, \tag{17}$$

$$\bar{\beta}_{i-2}'\bar{\gamma}_{i-2} + \bar{\beta}_{i-2}\bar{\gamma}_{i-2}' + \bar{\alpha}_{i-1}'\bar{\beta}_{i-1} + \bar{\alpha}_{i-1}\bar{\beta}_{i-1}' = 0, \tag{18}$$

$$\bar{\alpha}'_{i-2}\bar{\gamma}_{i-2} + \bar{\alpha}_{i-2}\bar{\gamma}'_{i-2} = 0. \tag{19}$$

Note that the α_i, β_i, γ_i are independent of s but the $\bar{\alpha}_i$, $\bar{\beta}_i$, $\bar{\gamma}_i$ are not. Differentiating once more, we get

$$2\bar{\alpha}_i'^2 + 2\bar{\alpha}_i\bar{\alpha}_i'' + 2\bar{\beta}_{i-1}'^2 + 2\bar{\beta}_{i-1}\bar{\beta}''_{i-1} + 2\bar{\gamma}_{i-2}'^2 + 2\bar{\gamma}_{i-2}\bar{\gamma}''_{i-2} = 0, \tag{20}$$

$$\bar{\alpha}''_{i-2}\bar{\gamma}_{i-2} + 2\bar{\alpha}'_{i-2}\bar{\gamma}'_{i-2} + \bar{\alpha}_{i-2}\bar{\gamma}''_{i-2} = 0, \tag{21}$$

$$\bar{\beta}''_{i-2}\bar{\gamma}_{i-2} + 2\bar{\beta}'_{i-2}\bar{\gamma}'_{i-2} + \bar{\beta}_{i-2}\bar{\gamma}''_{i-2} + \bar{\alpha}''_{i-1}\bar{\beta}_{i-1} + 2\bar{\alpha}'_{i-1}\bar{\beta}'_{i-1} + \bar{\alpha}_{i-1}\bar{\beta}''_{i-1} = 0. \tag{22}$$

Let us write the eigenvalues of the matrix LL^T by $\lambda_1, \lambda_2, \cdots, \lambda_n$. Then, the characteristic polynomial of the matrix LL^T

$$f(s) = \det(LL^T - sI) = (\lambda_1 - s)(\lambda_2 - s)\cdots(\lambda_n - s), \tag{23}$$

because of the triangularity of the matrix L, is expressed by

$$f(s) = \bar{\alpha}_1\bar{\alpha}_2\cdots\bar{\alpha}_n. \tag{24}$$

Let us define

$$g(s) := -\frac{f'(s)}{f(s)} = -2\frac{\bar{\alpha}'_1}{\bar{\alpha}_1} - 2\frac{\bar{\alpha}'_2}{\bar{\alpha}_2} - \cdots - 2\frac{\bar{\alpha}'_n}{\bar{\alpha}_n}, \tag{25}$$

$$h(s) := g'(s) = -2\frac{\bar{\alpha}''_1\bar{\alpha}_1 - \bar{\alpha}_1'^2}{\bar{\alpha}_1^2} - \cdots - 2\frac{\bar{\alpha}''_n\bar{\alpha}_n - \bar{\alpha}_n'^2}{\bar{\alpha}_n^2} \tag{26}$$

so that $g(0) = \mathrm{Tr}\{(L^TL)^{-1}\}$ and $h(0) = \mathrm{Tr}\{(L^TL)^{-2}\}$. Each $\bar{\alpha}_i$ tends to α_i as $s \to 0$. Hence, we can calculate the value of $\bar{\alpha}'_i$, $\bar{\beta}'_i$, $\bar{\gamma}'_i$, $\bar{\alpha}''_i$, $\bar{\beta}''_i$, $\bar{\gamma}''_i$ at $s = 0$ from α_i, β_i, γ_i by using (17)–(22), and then $g(0)$ and $h(0)$ by (25) and (26). It is clear by the definition of $g(0)$ and $h(0)$ that the values are always nonnegative without numerical error (in infinite-precision arithmetic). The procedure of computation for the traces of lower tridiagonal matrix L is shown in Algorithm 4. The generalized Newton shift is value of $1/\sqrt{tr2}$.

3.3 Laguerre Shift

If we already have the value of $\mathrm{Tr}\{(LL^T)^{-1}\}$ and $\mathrm{Tr}\{(LL^T)^{-2}\}$, we could improve the sharpness of the shift by $O(1)$ operation. Laguerre shift is one of the methods to improve the shift value.

Theorem 3.2 (Laguerre [7]). *For an n-by-n positive-definite symmetric penta-diagonal matrix $B = LL^T$, let θ be the following value:*

$$\theta := \frac{n}{\mathrm{Tr}(B^{-1}) + \sqrt{(n-1)\left(n\mathrm{Tr}(B^{-2}) - \mathrm{Tr}(B^{-1})^2\right)}}.$$

Then, the θ is a lower bound of the eigenvalues of B which is greater than $\mathrm{Tr}(B^{-1})^{-1}$ and $\mathrm{Tr}(B^{-2})^{-1/2}$.

If the value $n\mathrm{Tr}\left(B^{-2}\right) - \mathrm{Tr}\left(B^{-1}\right)^2$ is negative, Laguerre shift is useless. In that case, we adopt the generalized Newton shift. Algorithm 5 shows a procedure of Laguerre method.

Algorithm 4 Computation for the traces (trace(L))

$\alpha'_1 := -1/(2\alpha_1)$
$\beta'_1 := -\alpha'_1\beta_1/\alpha_1$
$\gamma'_1 := -\alpha'_1\gamma_1/\alpha_1$
$\alpha'_2 := (-\beta_1\beta'_1 - 0.5)/\alpha_2$
$\beta'_2 := -(\gamma'_1\beta_1 + \gamma_1\gamma'_1 + \alpha'_2\beta_2)/\alpha_2$
$\alpha'_3 := -(1 + 2\times\gamma_1\gamma'_1 + 2\beta_2\beta'_2)/(2\alpha_3)$
$\alpha''_1 := -\alpha_1'^2/\alpha_1$
$\beta''_1 := -(\alpha''_1\beta_1 + 2\alpha'_1\beta'_1)/\alpha_1$
$\gamma''_1 := -(\alpha''_1\gamma_1 + 2\alpha'_1\gamma'_1)/\alpha_1$
$\alpha''_2 := -(\beta_1'^2 + \beta_1\beta''_1 + \alpha_2'^2)/\alpha_2$
$\beta''_2 := -(\gamma''_1\beta_1 + 2\gamma'_1\beta'_1 + \gamma_1\beta''_1 + \alpha''_2\beta_2 + 2\alpha'_2\beta'_2)/\alpha_2$
$\alpha''_3 := -(\gamma_1'^2 + \gamma_1\gamma''_1 + \beta_2'^2 + \beta_2\beta''_2 + \alpha_3'^2)/\alpha_3$
for $i = 4$ to N **do**
  $\gamma'_{i-2} := -\alpha'_{i-2}\gamma_{i-2}/\alpha_{i-2}$
  $\beta'_{i-1} := -(\beta'_{i-2}\gamma_{i-2} + \beta_{i-2}\gamma'_{i-2} + \alpha'_{i-1}\beta_{i-1})/\alpha_{i-1}$
  $\alpha'_i := -(1 + 2\beta_{i-1}\beta'_{i-1} + 2\gamma_{i-2}\gamma'_{i-2})/(2\alpha_i)$
  $\gamma''_{i-2} := -(\alpha''_{i-2}\gamma_{i-2} + 2\alpha'_{i-2}\gamma'_{i-2})/\alpha_{i-2}$
  $\beta''_{i-1} := -(\beta''_{i-2}\gamma_{i-2} + 2\beta'_{i-2}\gamma'_{i-2} + \beta_{i-2}\gamma''_{i-2} + \alpha''_{i-1}\beta_{i-1} + 2\alpha'_{i-1}\beta'_{i-1})/\alpha_{i-1}$
  $\alpha''_i := -(\alpha_i'^2 + \beta_{i-1}'^2 + \beta_{i-1}\beta''_{i-1} + \gamma_{i-2}'^2 + \gamma_{i-2}\gamma''_{i-2})/\alpha_i$
end for
$tr1 := 0$
for $i = 1$ to N **do**
  $tr1 := tr1 - (2\alpha'_i/\alpha_i)$
end for
$tr2 := 0$
for $i = 1$ to N **do**
  $tr2 := tr2 - 2(\alpha''_i\alpha_i - \alpha_i'^2)/\alpha_i^2$
end for
return $(tr1, tr2)$

Algorithm 5 Laguerre shift (laguerre($tr1, tr2$))

$(tr1, tr2) :=$ trace(L)
$tmp := n \times tr2 - tr1^2$
if $tmp > 0$ **then**
  return $n/(tr1 + \sqrt{(n-1)\times tmp})$
else
  return 0
end if

3.4 Kato-Temple Shift

There is another lowerbound, Kato-temple shift.

Theorem 3.3 (Kato-Temple [8]). *For an n-by-n symmetric matrix A_n, let A_{n-1} denote the submatrix of A_n obtained by deleting the last row and column. For any lower bound λ^* of the eigenvalues of A_{n-1}, and for any $x \in \mathbb{R}^n$, $\|x\| = 1$, let $\rho = x^TAx$. Then, if $\rho < \lambda^*$, the value*

$$\rho - \frac{\|A_nx - \rho x\|^2}{\lambda^* - \rho} \leq \lambda_{\min}(A_n)$$

gives a lower bound of the eigenvalues of A_n.

We choose $x = (0, \ldots, 0, 1)^T$. The method requires λ^* which is a lower bound for the submatrix A_{n-1}, but the generalized Newton method enables us to find the lower bound of A_{n-1}

in computation of the lower bound of A_n. Consequently, we obtain one more improved shift value by $O(1)$ operation. Algorithm 6 shows a procedure of Kato-Temple method. The

Algorithm 6 Kato-Temple method

```
x := (0, ..., 0, 1)^T
(tr1, tr2) := trace(L_{n-1})
λ* := laguerre(tr1, tr2)
ρ := x^T L_{n-1} x
if ρ < λ* then
    return ρ − ||A_n x − ρx||^2 / (λ* − ρ)
else
    return 0
end if
```

procedure of the proposed shift composed by the generalized Newton, Laguerre and Kato-Temple is shown in Algorithm 7. We adopt the largest value of them.

3.5 Applying Shift

Among the shifts discussed in this section, we cannot determine which is the most effective. The sharpness of each shift depends on the type of matrix, and the type of matrix is unknown before computing. Laguerre shift often gives sharp shift but if the value of $n\mathrm{Tr}\left(B^{-2}\right) - \mathrm{Tr}\left(B^{-1}\right)^2$ is negative, we cannot adopt the shift. Besides, even if a shift value is smaller than minimum singular value, iteration of the oqds algorithm might fail. For example, if $\sigma > x_1^2 + x_2^2$, we could not apply the generalized Givens transformation. Gerschgorin shift gives a sharp value if the subdiagonal and second-subdiagonal elements are small. On the other hand, if non-diagonal elements are too large, Gerschgorin shift gives useless value such as zero or negative value. In such a case, we should choose another shift. Generalized Newton shift always gives usable value in the case other shifts failed.

For those reasons, we should design a proper shift strategy. Generally, non-diagonal elements converge to zero in the oqds algorithm, and after deflation or splitting, the eigenvalues of the matrix A become more clustered. Therefore, we adopt the largest value of generalized Newton, Laguerre, Kato-Temple shift first, and if the generalized Givens transformation failed, then we move to the Gerschgorin shift. Then, one step of the oqds algorithm works as Algorithm 8. The subroutine "gerschgorin(L)" returns the value of Gerschgorin shift of matrix L.

4. Convergence Criteria

It is nontrivial how to assess a series of matrices generated by the iterative process of the oqds algorithm converges sufficiently.Besides, in the implementation of this algorithm, deflation and splitting are required for activating the shift method. In this section, we consider the situation that deflation or splitting is available where the values of subdiagonal and second-subdiagonal elements are so small.

Let us write

$$\hat{L} := L - \beta_k \mathbf{e}_{k+1} \mathbf{e}_k^T$$

Algorithm 7 Proposed shift (algshift(L))

```
α'_1 := −1/(2α_1)
β'_1 := −α'_1 β_1/α_1
γ'_1 := −α'_1 γ_1/α_1
α'_2 := (−β_1 β'_1 − 0.5)/α_2
β'_2 := −(γ'_1 β_1 + γ_1 γ'_1 + α'_2 β_2)/α_2
α'_3 := −(1 + 2 × γ_1 γ'_1 + 2β_2 β'_2)/(2α_3)
α''_1 := −α'_1^2/α_1
β''_1 := −(α''_1 β_1 + 2α'_1 β'_1)/α_1
γ''_1 := −(α''_1 γ_1 + 2α'_1 γ'_1)/α_1
α''_2 := −(β'_1^2 + β_1 β''_1 + α'_2^2)/α_2
β''_2 := −(γ''_1 β_1 + 2γ'_1 β'_1 + γ_1 β''_1 + α''_2 β_2 + 2α'_2 β'_2)/α_2
α''_3 := −(γ'_1^2 + γ_1 γ''_1 + β'_2^2 + β_2 β''_2 + α'_3^2)/α_3
for i = 4 to N do
    γ'_{i−2} := −α'_{i−2} γ_{i−2}/α_{i−2}
    β'_{i−1} := −(β'_{i−2} γ_{i−2} + β_{i−2} γ'_{i−2} + α'_{i−1} β_{i−1})/α_{i−1}
    α'_i := −(1 + 2β_{i−1} β'_{i−1} + 2γ_{i−2} γ'_{i−2})/(2α_i)
    γ''_{i−2} := −(α''_{i−2} γ_{i−2} + 2α'_{i−2} γ'_{i−2})/α_{i−2}
    β''_{i−1} := −(β''_{i−2} γ_{i−2} + 2β'_{i−2} γ'_{i−2}
                 +β_{i−2} γ''_{i−2} + α''_{i−1} β_{i−1} + 2α'_{i−1} β'_{i−1})/α_{i−1}
    α''_i := −(α'_i^2 + β'_{i−1}^2 + β_{i−1} β''_{i−1} + γ'_{i−2}^2 + γ_{i−2} γ''_{i−2})/α_i
end for
tr1 := 0
for i = 1 to N − 1 do
    tr1 := tr1 − (2α'_i/α_i)
end for
tr2 := 0
for i = 1 to N − 1 do
    tr2 := tr2 − 2(α''_i α_i − α'_i^2)/α_i^2
end for
λ* := 1/sqrt(tr2)
tmp := n × tr2 − tr1^2
if tmp > 0 then
    λ* := max(λ*, n/(tr1 + sqrt((n − 1) × tmp)))
end if
tr1 := tr1 − (2α'_N/α_N)
tr2 := tr2 − 2(α''_N α_N − α'_N^2)/α_N^2
shift := 1/sqrt(tr2)
x := (0, ..., 0, 1)^T
ρ := x^T L_{n−1} x
if ρ < λ* then
    shift := max(shift, ρ − ||A_n x − ρx||^2 / (λ* − ρ))
end if
tmp := n × tr2 − tr1^2
if tmp > 0 then
    shift := max(shift, n/(tr1 + sqrt((n − 1) × tmp)))
end if
return shift
```

Algorithm 8 oqds step(oqds(L, $shift$))

```
flag := 0
if flag = 0 then
    σ := algshift(L)
else if flag := 1 then
    σ := gerschgorin(L)
else
    σ := 0
end if
if σ + shift = shift then
    Ľ := icds(L, 0)
    L := Ľ
else
    Ľ := icds(L, σ)
    if α̌ ≠ α̌ then
        flag := flag + 1
    else
        shift := shift + σ
        L := Ľ
    end if
end if
```

which is the matrix equal to L except for zero at $(k+1, k)$-entry. Then

$$L^T L = \hat{L}^T \hat{L} + E_1, \quad (27)$$
$$LL^T = \hat{L}\hat{L}^T + E_2 \quad (28)$$

hold, where

$$E_1 := \beta^2 \mathbf{e}_k \mathbf{e}_k{}^T + \alpha_{k+1}\beta_k \left(\mathbf{e}_k \mathbf{e}_{k+1}^T + \mathbf{e}_{k+1}\mathbf{e}_k^T\right) + \beta_k \gamma_{k-1} \left(\mathbf{e}_{k-1}\mathbf{e}_k^T + \mathbf{e}_k \mathbf{e}_{k-1}^T\right), \quad (29)$$

$$E_2 := \beta^2 \mathbf{e}_{k+1} \mathbf{e}_{k+1}{}^T + \alpha_k\beta_k \left(\mathbf{e}_{k-1} \mathbf{e}_k^T + \mathbf{e}_k\mathbf{e}_{k-1}^T\right) + \beta_k \gamma_k \left(\mathbf{e}_{k+1}\mathbf{e}_k^T + \mathbf{e}_k \mathbf{e}_{k+1}^T\right). \quad (30)$$

Theorem 4.1 (Weyl's monotonicity theorem [9], [10]). *For an n-by-n positive-definite matrix A, let $\lambda_i(A)$ denote the i-th largest eigenvalue of A. Then, there exist reals u_i and v_i such that*

$$\lambda_i\left(L^T L\right) = \lambda_i\left(\hat{L}^T \hat{L}\right) + u_i \|E_1\|_1, \quad (31)$$
$$\lambda_i\left(LL^T\right) = \lambda_i\left(\hat{L}\hat{L}^T\right) + v_i \|E_2\|_1 \quad (32)$$

where $|u_i| \le 1$, $|v_i| \le 1$.

From the definitions (29) and (30) of E_1 and E_2, we have

$$\|E_1\|_1 = \|E_1\|_\infty = |\beta_k| \left(|\alpha_{k+1}| + |\beta_k| + |\gamma_{k-1}|\right), \quad (33)$$
$$\|E_2\|_1 = \|E_2\|_\infty = |\beta_k| \left(|\alpha_k| + |\beta_k| + |\gamma_k|\right). \quad (34)$$

By Weyl's monotonicity theorem, we thus get the numerical deflation or splitting criterion to neglect a subdiagonal element β_k:

$$\sigma^2 + |\beta_k| \left(|\beta_k| + \min\left(|\alpha_{k+1}| + |\gamma_{k-1}|, |\alpha_k| + |\gamma_k|\right)\right) \simeq \sigma^2, \quad (35)$$

where '$\simeq$' means that the left-hand side and the right-hand side are numerically equal. We assume that β_k is so small and negligible provided that (35) holds numerically.

Similarly, we get the numerical criterion for neglecting a second-subdiagonal element γ_k. On the setting of

$$\hat{L} := L - \gamma_k \mathbf{e}_{k+2} \mathbf{e}_k{}^T,$$

the perturbation matrices are given by

$$E_1' := \gamma^2 \mathbf{e}_k \mathbf{e}_k{}^T + \alpha_{k+2}\gamma_k \left(\mathbf{e}_{k+2}\mathbf{e}_k^T + \mathbf{e}_k \mathbf{e}_{k+2}^T\right) + \beta_{k+1}\gamma_k \left(\mathbf{e}_{k+1}\mathbf{e}_k^T + \mathbf{e}_k \mathbf{e}_{k+1}^T\right),$$
$$E_2' := \gamma^2 \mathbf{e}_{k+2} \mathbf{e}_{k+2}{}^T + \alpha_k\gamma_k \left(\mathbf{e}_{k-2}\mathbf{e}_k^T + \mathbf{e}_k \mathbf{e}_{k-2}^T\right) + \beta_k\gamma_k \left(\mathbf{e}_{k-1}\mathbf{e}_k^T + \mathbf{e}_k \mathbf{e}_{k-1}^T\right).$$

Then, by evaluating the 1- and ∞-norms of these matrices, we obtain the criterion for neglecting a second-subdiagonal element γ_k as follows:

$$\sigma^2 + |\gamma_k| \left(|\gamma_k| + \min\left(|\alpha_{k+2}| + |\beta_{k+1}|, |\alpha_k| + |\beta_k|\right)\right) \simeq \sigma^2. \quad (36)$$

For the matrices in iteration, we perform deflation and splitting as follows:

1) If β_{n-1} and γ_{n-2} in the last row satisfy the criteria (35) and (36), then we deflate the matrix by deleting the last row and column.
2) If β_{k-1}, γ_{k-1} and γ_{k-2} satisfy the criteria (35) and (36), then we split the matrix into two submatrices formed by rows and columns 1 to $k-1$ and k to n, respectively.

5. Numerical Experiments

Some numerical experiments were performed for the oqds algorithms for bidiagonal matrices and for lower tridiagonal matrices. The singular values of square random matrices were computed by the oqds algorithm for bidiagonal matrices by von Matt and by the oqds algorithm for lower tridiagonal matrices which we propose. It should be noted that: The oqds for bidiagonal matrices were applied to random bidiagonal matrices and the proposed oqds algorithm for lower tridiagonal matrices were applied to random lower tridiagonal matrix. The numerical experiments were performed on a Linux PC with Intel Core i7 920 (Nehalem) 2.66GHz and DDR3-1066 12GB memory. Table 1 shows the computation time of each algorithm. The first row shows the size of matrices. The second and the third rows show the computation time taken by the oqds algorithm for bidiagonal matrices and for lower tridiagonal matrices, respectively.

Table 1
COMPUTATION TIME (SECONDS)

matrix size	10000	20000	30000
oqds for bidiagonal	11.764	43.243	93.080
proposed oqds for lower tridiagonal	27.089	100.013	210.225

5.1 Discussion

Hence, in order to compute the eigenvalues of matrices of the same size, the oqds algorithm for lower tridiagonal matrices is expected to take a longer computation time than the oqds for bidiagonal matrices. From Table 1, we observe that the computation time in the former algorithm is not extremely longer than the latter algorithm: the former is two or three times slower than the latter.

This observation demonstrates that the oqds algorithm for lower tridiagonal matrices is practically useful for the general dense matrices. Commonly, the computation of the singular values of a dense matrix is twofold:

1) preprocess of reducing into a sparse band matrix.
2) singular computation of the sparse band matrix.

The computation time for preprocess is estimated $O(n^3)$ while for the singular value computation $O(n^2)$. Hence, a vast amount of the computation time is consumed by the preprocess. On the preprocess for dense matrices, it is reported in [11] that the reduction into a lower tridiagonal matrix is about 50% faster than that into bidiagonal matrices. Therefore, the total time of preprocess into a lower tridiagonal matrix and the oqds for lower tridiagonal matrices is much faster than the time of preprocess into bidiagonal matrices and the oqds for bidiagonal matrices.

6. Conclusions

We proposed the oqds algorithm for lower tridiagonal matrices. Though computing singular values of lower tridiagonal matrices takes longer time than bidiagonal matrices, preprocess reducing dense matrices into lower tridiagonal matrices takes less time than into bidiagonal matrices. Not only simple reduction of computational complexity, we can apply the BLAS Level 2.5 routines to lower tridiagonalization. The BLAS Level 2.5 routines are more cache efficient than BLAS Level 2 routines commonly applied to bidiagonalization. A cache efficient algorithm saves a number of memory accesses which waste a big time. The computation time for preprocess is estimated $O(n^3)$ while for the singular value computation $O(n^2)$, hence, a vast amount of the computation time is consumed by the preprocess. Therefore, if we can compute the singular values of lower tridiagonal matrices not so longer than for bidiagonal matrices, it is expected that total computation time decreases extremely.

For an implementation of this algorithm, we proposed a new shift strategy consisting of the generalized Newton shift and associated two methods, Laguerre shift and Kato-Temple shift, and the well known Gerschgorin shift. Moreover, we design new convergence criteria for deflation and splitting required for the implementation of the oqds algorithm. By the criteria, we can do the convergence test for lower tridiagonal matrices.

As a result, the algorithm computes the singular values of a lower tridiagonal matrix within $O(n^2)$ computation time. Although it takes about two or three times as long time for tridiagonal matrices as for bidiagonal matrices, proposed algorithm is expected to be faster than the conventional methods since the preprocessing requires $O(n^3)$ operations and takes much larger time than the oqds algorithm.

As a future work, we have to perform more experiment to compare the computation time including preprocessing. Furthermore, exact error analysis should be made and we ought to check out the accuracy of the algorithm after improving the implementation and setting proper test matrices which have known eigenvalues.

Acknowledgments

The authors would like to express a sincere gratitude to Professor Shuhei Kamioka and Mr. Kazuki Maeda for valuable discussions and comments. This work was supported by JSPS KAKENHI Grant Number 24360038.

References

[1] H. Rutishauser, "Der Quotienten-Differenzen-Algorithms," in *ZAMP*, 5 (1954), pp. 233–251.
[2] U. von Matt, "The orthogonal QD algorithm," *SIAM J. Sci. Comput.*, vol.18, Issue:4, (1997), pp.1163–1186.
[3] U. von Matt, "The orthogonal QD algorithm," *Technical Reports of the Computer Science Department*, University of Maryland, 1994.
[4] H. Rutishauser, "Uber eine kubisch konvergente Variante der LR-Thransformation," *Zeitschrift fur Angewandte Mathematik und Mechanik*, vol. 40 (1960), pp. 49–54.
[5] S. Gerschgorin, "Uber die Abgrenzung der Eigenwerte einer Matrix," *Izv. Akad. Nauk.*, USSR Otd. Fiz.-Mat. Nauk 7,(1931), pp.749–754.
[6] T. Yamashita, Y. Yamamoto and K. Kimura, "A new method for computation of conserved quantities of the discrete finite Toda equation," unpublished.
[7] B. N. Parlett, "Laguerre's Method Applied to the Matrix Eigenvalue Problem," *Math. Comp.*, 18 (1964), pp. 464–485.
[8] F. Chatelin, *Valeurs propres de matrices*, Masson, Paris, 1988, ISBN 2-225-80968-2.
[9] B. N. Parlett, *The Symmetric Eigenvalue Problem*, Prentice-Hall, Englewood Cliffs, 1980.
[10] J. H. Wilkinson, *The Algebraic Eigenvalue Problem*, Clarendon Press, Oxford, 1995.
[11] T. Imamura, S. Yamada and M. Machida, "Narrow-band reduction approach of a DRSM eigensolver on a multicore-based cluster system," *Advances in Parallel Computing*, vol.19, *Parallel Computing: From Multicores and GPU's to Petascale*, IOS Press, 2010, pp.91–98.

Improved Computation of Bounds for Positive Roots of Polynomials

Masami Takata[1], **Takuto Akiyama**[2], **Sho Araki**[3], **Kinji Kimura**[4], **and Yoshimasa Nakamura**[5]
[1]Academic Group of Information and Computer Sciences, Nara Women's University,
Kita-Uoya-Nishi-Machi, Nara 630-8506, JAPAN
[2345]Graduate School of Informatics, Kyoto University,
Yoshidahonmachi, Sakyo-ku, Kyoto 606-8501, JAPAN
[1]takata@ics.nara-wu.ac.jp, [2]akiyama@amp.i.kyoto-u.ac.jp, [3]araki@amp.i.kyoto-u.ac.jp,
[4]kkimur@amp.i.kyoto-u.ac.jp, [5]ynaka@i.kyoto-u.ac.jp

Abstract—*A new lower bound for computing positive roots of polynomial equations is proposed. We discuss a two-stage algorithm for computing positive roots of polynomial equations. In the first stage, we use the continued fraction method based on Vincent's theorem, which employs the lower bound of real roots, for isolating the positive roots into intervals. In the second stage, we apply a bisection method to each interval. In order to compute the proposed lower bound, we follow three steps. First, we compute a candidate for the lower bound generated by Newton's method. Second, by using Laguerre's theorem, we check whether the candidate for the lower bound is suitable. Third, we compare the local-max bound and the proposed lower bound. Then, we employ the larger bound to accelerate the continued fraction method based on Vincent's theorem. Finally, we conduct experiments to evaluate the effectiveness of the proposed lower bound.*

(This paper is submitted to PDPTA'13.)

Keywords: continued fraction method, Vincent's theorem, local-max bound, Newton's method, Laguerre's theorem

1. Introduction

The real roots of univariate polynomial equations are more useful than the imaginary roots for practical applications in various engineering fields. Thus, the objective of this study is the computation of all real roots of polynomial equations. For this purpose, we develop a real-root isolation algorithm. For polynomial equations without multiple roots, each root can be isolated into a numeric interval. Then, the accuracy of the isolated real roots can be easily enhanced by using a bisection method.

The continued fraction method for isolating the positive roots of univariate polynomial equations is based on Vincent's theorem [2], [10]. In this method, each positive root is isolated using Descartes' rule of signs [3], which focuses on the coefficients of the polynomial equations. The execution of Descartes' rule of signs requires origin shifts. Thus, several coefficients of a polynomial equation are transformed into nonzero coefficients, even in the case of sparse polynomial equations, which have many zero coefficients. The Krawczyk method [8], which is based on the numerical verification method, is a technique that has been developed for isolating the positive roots of polynomial equations that have many zero coefficients. In this paper, we investigate the continued fraction method, which is based on Vincent's theorem, for isolating the positive roots of polynomial equations that have many nonzero coefficients.

To accelerate the continued fraction method based on Vincent's theorem, the lower bound of the smallest positive root is required. In general, to obtain the lower bound of positive roots of a polynomial equation, we first substitute $1/x$ for x in the polynomial equation $f(x)$. Second, we compute the upper bound of the positive roots. Third, we obtain the lower bound by computing the inverse of the upper bound. The Cauchy bound [9] and the Kioustelidis bound [6] are known as upper bounds of the positive roots of polynomial equations. Akritas *et al.* introduced a generalized theorem including the Cauchy bound and the Kioustelidis bound [1]ï£¡D Then, by specializing this generalized theorem, they proposed a new upper bound called the local-max bound, which is different from both the Cauchy bound and the Kioustelidis bound.

In this paper, we propose a new lower bound for accelerating the continued fraction method based on Vincent's theorem. The new lower bound is obtained using Newton's method [5] and Laguerre's theorem [7]. The magnitude correlation of the local-max bound and the new lower bound depends on the input polynomial. Thus, after we compare the local-max bound and the new lower bound, the larger lower bound is adopted for the continued fraction method based on Vincent's theorem. Note that computing lower bounds incurs computation time. Therefore, the new lower bound must be sometimes larger than the local-max bound.

To evaluate the new lower bound, we compare the time for computing the lower bound generated by only the local-max bound with that for computing the lower bound generated by both the local-max bound and the new lower bound. If the computation time decreases by virtue of the new lower bound, it is proved that the new lower bound is sometimes larger than the local-max bound.

The remainder of this paper is organized as follows. In Section 2, we describe univariate polynomial equations. In

Section 3, we introduce the continued fraction method based on Vincent's theorem. In Section 4, we propose the new lower bound, which is computed using Newton's method and checked using Laguerre's theorem. In Section 5, we evaluate the effectiveness of the proposed lower bound. Finally, in Section 6, we state our conclusions and briefly describe the scope for further investigation.

2. Positive Roots of Polynomials

To compute the positive roots of a polynomial equation

$$f(x) = a_0x^n + a_1x^{n-1} + \cdots + a_{n-1}x + a_n = 0, \quad x \in \mathbb{R}, a_i \in \mathbb{Z}, \tag{1}$$

in the interval $x \in (0, \infty)$, we first isolate each root into a numeric interval. Second, we improve the accuracy of the real roots by using a bisection method. If a real root is equal to 0, then $a_n = 0$. Thus, we discuss only the problem in $x \in (0, \infty)$. Here, the intervals are defined by,

$$x \in [a, b], \; x \in (a, b] \text{ or } x \in [a, b), a, b \in \mathbb{R}, a \le b, \tag{2}$$

where $[,]$, $(,]$ or $[,)$ denote a closed interval, a left-open right-closed interval, and a left-closed right-open interval, respectively.

A polynomial equation $f(x)$ should have no multiple roots so that the continued fraction method can be employed for isolating its positive roots. If a polynomial equation $g_1(x)$ has multiple roots, then these roots are transformed into simple roots by using the equation

$$f(x) := \frac{g_1(x)}{\text{G.C.D.}(g_1(x), g_1'(x))}, \tag{3}$$

where G.C.D.$(,)$ is the greatest common divisor related to two equations, and $g_1'(x)$ denotes the first derivative of $g_1(x)$. Thus, we can assume that $f(x)$ have no multiple roots.

A polynomial equation $g_2(x)$ with rational coefficients b_i is given by the equation

$$g_2(x) = b_0x^n + b_1x^{n-1} + \cdots + b_{n-1}x + b_n = 0, \quad b_i = \frac{d_{i,2}}{d_{i,1}} \in \mathbb{Q}. \tag{4}$$

By using the least common multiple, or L.C.M., of all $d_{i,1}$, the polynomial equation $g_2(x)$ can be transformed into the equation $f(x)$ with integer coefficients:

$$f(x) := \text{L.C.M.}(d_{i,1})g_2(x). \tag{5}$$

A polynomial equation $g_3(y)$ with integer coefficients and no multiple roots is set to the equation

$$g_3(y) = a_0y^n + a_1y^{n-1} + \cdots + a_{n-1}y + a_n = 0, \quad y \in \mathbb{R}, a_i \in \mathbb{Z}. \tag{6}$$

The real roots of $g_3(y)$ in the interval $[u, v], u, v \in \mathbb{R}$ are isolated through the following procedure. By using the replacement,

$$y \to -\frac{1}{x + \frac{1}{-u+v}} + v, \tag{7}$$

we transform $g_3(y)$ into the equation

$$g_4(x) = g_3\left(-\frac{1}{x + \frac{1}{-u+v}} + v\right), \tag{8}$$

$$f(x) := \text{numerator}\,(g_4(x)), \tag{9}$$

where the function "numerator" implies computation of the numerator of $g_4(x)$. Under eq. (7), $y \in [u, v)$ in $g_3(y)$ corresponds to $x \in [0, \infty)$ in $f(x)$. However, the case that $y = v$ is not included in the interval $[u, v)$. Thus we treat the case that $y = v$ as a special case.

Hence, polynomial equations with rational coefficients and multiple roots in the interval $[u, v]$ can be transformed into eq. (1) by the above operations.

3. Continued Fraction Method based Vincent's Theorem for Isolating Positive Roots

3.1 Concept

In the continued fraction method based on Vincent's theorem, real roots in $(0, \infty)$ can be isolated using the Descartes' rule of signs.

Descartes' rule of signs is derived from the following theorem.

Theorem 1 (The Descartes' rule of signs): In a polynomial equation

$$f(x) = a_0x^n + \cdots + a_{n-1}x + a_n = 0, \quad x \in \mathbb{R},$$

with real coefficients,

W := the number of "changes of sign" in the list of coefficients$\{a_0, a_1, \ldots, a_n\}$ except $a_i = 0$,

N := the number of positive roots in $(0, \infty)$

are defined. Under these definitions, we have,

$$N = W - 2h.$$

Here, h is a non-negative integer.

By using Theorem 1, the number of positive roots of the polynomial equation $f(x)$ is determined in the following conditional branch:

- In the case that $W = 0$, $f(x), x \in (0, \infty)$ does not have any positive roots.

Table 1: Synthetic division in $g_5(x)$.

a_0	a_1	a_2	a_3
	a_0	a_0+a_1	$a_0+a_1+a_2$
a_0	a_0+a_1	$a_0+a_1+a_2$	$a_0+a_1+a_2+a_3$
	a_0	$2a_0+a_1$	
a_0	$2a_0+a_1$	$3a_0+2a_1+a_2$	
	a_0		
a_0	$3a_0+a_1$		

- In the case that $W=1$, $f(x)$ has only one positive root in the interval $x \in (0,\infty)$.
- In the case that $W \geq 2$, the number of positive roots of $f(x)$ cannot be determined.

In the case that $W=1$, the isolated interval should be set to $(0, ub]$, where ub denotes the upper bound of positive roots for a polynomial equation $f(x)$. Computation methods for the upper bound of positive roots of a polynomial equation $f(x)$ are described in Section 3.2.

In the case that $W \geq 2$, we divide the interval $(0,\infty)$ in the two intervals. Then, Descartes' rule of signs is applied in each interval. In the continued fraction method based on Vincent's theorem, the interval $(0,\infty)$ is divided in $(0,1)$ and $(1,\infty)$. The division is performed by the replacement

$$x \to x+1,$$
$$x \to \frac{1}{x+1}.$$

By using the replacement $x \to x+1$, the interval $(0,\infty)$ of the replaced polynomial equation corresponds to the interval $(1,\infty)$ of the original polynomial equation. Similarly, by using the replacement $x \to 1/(x+1)$, the interval $(0,\infty)$ of the replaced polynomial equation corresponds to the interval $(0,1)$ of the original polynomial equation. The intervals $(1,\infty)$ and $(0,1)$ do not include the case that $x=1$. To solve for this case, after either replacement, we check whether the coefficient a_n, which is a constant term, vanishes. If $a_n=0$ in the replaced polynomial equation, then 1 is a root of the original polynomial equation.

In the above replacements, the computation of coefficients of a replaced polynomial equation is required. For example, in the case that the coefficients of

$$g_5(x) = a_0(x+1)^3 + a_1(x+1)^2 + a_3(x+1) + a_4, \quad (10)$$

are computed, the synthetic division, which is shown in Table 1, can be adopted. In Table 1, the coefficients of x^3, x^2, x^1, and x^0 become a_0, $3a_0+a_1$, $3a_0+2a_1+a_2$, and $a_0+a_1+a_2+a_3$, respectively. Thus, by using the synthetic division, the computation cost, which is incurred for obtaining the coefficients of the replaced polynomial equation for a replacement $x \to x+1$, is $O(n^2)$.

3.2 Computation for Upper Bound

To obtain the upper bound, the following theorem [1] can be applied.

Theorem 2 (Akritas, 2006): Let $f(x)$ be a polynomial with real coefficients and we assume $a_0 > 0$ in this section. Let $d(f)$ and $t(f)$ denote its degree and number of terms, respectively.
In addition, assume that $f(x)$ can be reshaped as follows:

$$f(x) = q_1(x) - q_2(x) + \cdots - q_{2m}(x) + g_6(x), \quad (11)$$

where all the polynomials $q_i(x)$, $i = 1, 2, \cdots, 2m$ and $g_6(x)$ have only positive coefficients. Moreover, assume that for $i = 1, 2, \cdots, m$ we obtain,

$$q_{2i-1}(x) = c_{2i-1,1}x^{e_{2i-1,1}} + \cdots + c_{2i-1,t(q_{2i-1})}x^{e_{2i-1,t(q_{2i-1})}} \quad (12)$$

and

$$q_{2i}(x) = b_{2i,1}x^{e_{2i,1}} + \cdots + b_{2i,t(q_{2i})}x^{e_{2i,t(q_{2i})}} \quad (13)$$

where $e_{2i-1,1} = d(q_{2i-1})$ and $e_{2i,1} = d(q_{2i})$, and the exponent of each term in $q_{2i-1}(x)$ is greater than the exponent of each term in $q_{2i}(x)$. If for all indices $i = 1, 2, \cdots, m$, we obtain

$$t(q_{2i-1}) \geq t(q_{2i}), \quad (14)$$

then the upper bound of the positive roots of $f(x)$ is defined by,

$$ub = \max_{i=1,2,\cdots,m} \left\{ \left(\frac{b_{2i,1}}{c_{2i-1,1}}\right)^{\frac{1}{e_{2i-1,1}-e_{2i,1}}}, \cdots, \left(\frac{b_{2i,t(q_{2i})}}{c_{2i-1,t(q_{2i})}}\right)^{\frac{1}{e_{2i-1,t(q_{2i})}-e_{2i,t(q_{2i})}}} \right\}, \quad (15)$$

for any permutation of the positive coefficients $c_{2i-1,j}$, $j = 1, 2, \cdots, t(q_{2i-1})$. Otherwise, for each of the indices i for which we obtain

$$t(q_{2i-1}) < t(q_{2i}), \quad (16)$$

we break up one of the coefficients of $q_{2i-1}(x)$ into $t(q_{2i}) - t(q_{2i-1}) + 1$ parts, so that now $t(q_{2i}) = t(q_{2i-1})$ and we apply the same formula defined in eq. (15).

In general, we can get better bounds if we pair coefficients from non-adjacent polynomials $q_{2l-1}(x)$ and $q_{2i}(x)$, for $1 \leq l < i$. A well-known implementation of this type is the Cauchy rule. In the Cauchy rule, if $f(x)$ is given by eq. (1), of degree $n > 0$, with $a_k < 0$ for at least one k, $1 \leq k \leq n$, and if λ is the number of negative coefficients, then an upper bound of the positive roots of $f(x)$ is defined by,

$$ub_1 = \max_{1 \leq k \leq n : a_k < 0} \sqrt[k]{-\frac{\lambda a_k}{a_0}}. \quad (17)$$

Algorithm 1 Implementation of the "local-max" bound.

```
cl ← {a_n, a_{n-1}, ··· , a_1, a_0}
if n + 1 ≤ 1 then
    return ub_3 = 0
end if
j = n + 1
t = 1
for i = n to 1 step −1 do
    if cl(i) < 0 then
        tempub = (2^t(−cl(i)/cl(j)))^{1/(j−i)}
        if tempub > ub then
            ub = tempub
        end if
        t + +
    else if cl(i) > cl(j) then
        j = i
        t = 1
    end if
end for
ub_3 = ub
```

We have another bound called Kioustelidis' bound [6] as follows:

$$ub_2 = 2 \max_{1 \le k \le n : a_k < 0} \sqrt[k]{-\frac{a_k}{a_0}}. \quad (18)$$

The Kioustelidis bound is closely related to the Cauchy rule. However, the Cauchy bound and the Kioustelidis bound give an overestimation of the upper bound for some cases. Thus, Akritas et al. introduced the local-max pairing strategy (defined in Definition 1) in order to generate a suitable bound.

Definition 1 ("local-max"): For a polynomial equation $f(x)$ given by eq. (1), the coefficient $-a_k$ of the term $-a_k x^{n-k}$ in $f(x)$ is paired with the coefficient $a_m/2^l$ of the term $a_m x^{n-m}$, where a_m is the largest positive coefficient with $0 \le m < k$ and t denotes the number of times the coefficient a_m has been used.

The implementation of the local-max bound is described in Algorithm1, and the output is ub_3.

3.3 Acceleration using Lower Bound

The continued fraction method based on Vincent's theorem requires many replacement operations $x \to x + 1$ and $x \to 1/(x + 1)$. In other words, the origin shift is realized by $x \to x + 1$. Thus, if the positive roots are much larger than 1, then the computation time increases, as we must repeat the replacement operation $x \to x+1$. To decrease the computation time, the lower bound of the smallest positive root of a polynomial equation should be used as a shift.

In general, to obtain the lower bound lb of an original polynomial equation, we first substitute $1/x$ for x in the original polynomial equation. Second, we compute the upper bound ub_3 of the positive roots. Third, we obtain the lower bound lb by computing the inverse of the upper bound as follows:

$$lb = \frac{1}{ub_3}. \quad (19)$$

If $lb > 1$, then the replacement $x \to x+lb$ is adopted, as the computation time for isolating the positive roots decrease. If $lb \le 1$, then we do not adopt the lower bound lb, as the lower bound lb is not sufficiently large to reduce the computation time.

Algorithm 2 shows a continued fraction method based on Vincent's theorem with origin shift using the local-max bound. The computation time for the Algorithm 2 is less than that for the continued fraction method based on Vincent's theorem without the origin shift. The replacements $x \to x+1$ and $x \to 1/(x+1)$ are called Möbius transformations. After the intervals for isolating the positive roots of a polynomial equation are determined, each interval should be replaced by the interval processed by all inverse transformations of Möbius transformations.

4. New Lower Bound

The acceleration of the continued fraction method based on Vincent's theorem employs the origin shift, which adopts the lower bound lb of the smallest positive root of a given polynomial equation. Thus, if the lower bound tends to the smallest positive root, then the computation time of the continued fraction method decreases.

In this paper, we propose a new lower bound generated by Newton's method. Note that in some polynomial equations, a bound generated by Newton's method is not suitable as the lower bound. Hence, by using Laguerre's theorem, it must be checked whether a bound generated by Newton's method is a suitable lower bound.

Newton's method is defined by the following recurrence formula:

$$x_{m+1} = x_m - \frac{f(x_m)}{f'(x_m)}. \quad (20)$$

Here, $f'(x)$ denotes the first derivative of $f(x)$. If Newton's method is adopted at the origin, then a candidate for the lower bound r is computed as follows:

$$r = 0 - \frac{f(0)}{f'(0)} = -\frac{a_n}{a_{n-1}}. \quad (21)$$

The cost for computing r is $O(1)$.

We can check whether a candidate for the lower bound r is suitable by using the following theorem.

Algorithm 2 Continued fraction method based on Vincent's theorem with the local-max shift strategy.

```
R ← φ
S ← {poly}
if 0 is a solution of poly then
    R ← R ∪ [0,0]
    poly ← poly/x
end if
while S ≠ φ do
    poly ← dequeue(S)
    W ← Descartes(poly)
    if W = 1 then
        ub3 ← Algorithm1 with poly
        R ← R ∪ Inverse Möbius trans ((0, ub3])
    else if W ≥ 2 then
        poly2 ← Trans(poly, x → 1/x)
        ub3 ← Algorithm1 with poly2
        lb ← 1/ub3
        if lb > 1 then
            poly ← Trans(poly, x → x + lb)
            if 0 is a solution of poly then
                R ← R ∪ Inverse Möbius trans ([lb, lb])
                poly ← poly/x
            end if
        end if
        poly3 ← Trans(poly, x → x + 1)
        if 0 is a solution of poly3 then
            R ← R ∪ Inverse Möbius trans ([1, 1])
            poly3 ← poly3/x
        end if
        poly4 ← Trans(poly, x → 1/x + 1)
        S ← S ∪ {poly3, poly4}
    end if
end while
```

Theorem 3 (the Laguerre theorem): For a polynomial equation

$$f(x) = a_0x^n + a_1x^{n-1} + \cdots + a_n = 0$$

with real coefficients, let N be the number of positive roots that are larger than a positive value α. The number N is less than or equal to the number of sign changes in the following polynomials $f_k(\alpha)$:

$$f_k(\alpha) = a_0\alpha^k + a_1\alpha^{k-1} + \cdots + a_k, k = 0, 1, \ldots, n.$$

Here, $f(\alpha) \neq 0$ is assumed.

If x in Theorem 3 is replaced by $1/x$, Theorem 3 can be transformed into the following theorem.

Theorem 4: The number of positive roots of a polynomial equation

$$f(x) = a_0 + a_1x + a_2x^2 + \cdots + a_nx^n = 0,$$

in the interval $0 < x < r$ is less than or equal to the number of sign changes in the following polynomials $p_k(r)$:

$$\begin{aligned} p_0(r) &= a_0, \\ p_1(r) &= a_0 + a_1r, \\ p_2(r) &= a_0 + a_1r + a_2r^2, \ldots, \\ p_n(r) &= a_0 + a_1r + \cdots + a_nr^n. \end{aligned}$$

Here, $r > 0$ and $p_n(r) \neq 0$.

Thus, if the number of sign changes in $p_k(r), k = 0, \cdots, n$ is 0, then no positive roots in the interval $0 < x < r$ exist. In such a case, the computation cost is $O(n)$.

To get a candidate for the lower bound r, it is necessary that the signs of a_n and a_{n-1} must be opposite. Moreover, it is needed to check $p_n(r) \neq 0$.

If a candidate for the lower bound r generated by Newton's method is the lower bound of the smallest positive root, then we adopt the lower bound lb as an origin shift defined in the following equation:

$$lb = \max\left(\frac{1}{ub_3}, r\right). \tag{22}$$

If $lb > 1$, then the origin shift $x \to x + lb$ is performed.

The improved algorithm of the continued fraction method based on Vincent's theorem with the shift strategy, including both the local-max bound and the new lower bound generated by Newton's method, is shown in Algorithm 3.

5. Experiment

In this section, we conduct experiments to evaluate the effectiveness of the proposed lower bound.

Here, Algorithm 2 and Algorithm 3 are compared.

As test polynomial equations, we use $f(x)$ with integer coefficients:

$$\begin{aligned} f(x) &= \prod_{i=0}^{r}(x - x_i) \times \\ &\quad \prod_{j=0}^{s}(x - \alpha_j + i\beta_j)(x - \alpha_j - i\beta_j), \\ &\quad x_i, \alpha_j, \beta_j \in \mathbb{R}. \end{aligned} \tag{23}$$

Here, parameters x_i, α_j, and β_j are randomly set as follows:

$$-10000 \leq x_i, \alpha_j, \beta_j \leq 10000, \tag{24}$$

Parameters s and r are set to $s = 490, r = 20$. Then, we generate 100 test polynomial equations.

Table 2 shows the experimental environment. In the continued fraction method based on Vincent's theorem, the multiple-precision arithmetic library GMP [4] is needed to compute all coefficients in replaced polynomial equations.

Figure 1 shows the plots of the computation time in all test polynomial equations. In Figure 1, the computation time for Algorithm 3 is less than that for Algorithm 2, and the

Algorithm 3 Improvement of the continued fraction method based on Vincent's theorem with the shift strategy including both the local-max bound and the new lower bound generated by Newton's method.

```
R ← φ
S ← {poly}
if 0 is a solution of poly then
  R ← R ∪ [0, 0]
  poly ← poly/x
end if
while S ≠ φ do
  poly ← dequeue(S)
  W ← Descartes(poly)
  if W = 1 then
    ub ← Algorithm 1 with poly
    R ← R ∪ Inverse Möbius trans ((0, ub])
  else if W ≥ 2 then
    poly2 ← Trans(poly, x → 1/x)
    ub3 ← Algorithm 1 with poly2
    r ← NewtonLowerbound(poly) which is checked
    by using the Laguerre theorem
    lb ← max(1/ub3, r)
    if lb > 1 then
      poly ← Trans(poly, x → x + lb)
      if 0 is a solution of poly then
        R ← R ∪ Inverse Möbius trans ([lb, lb])
        poly ← poly/x
      end if
    end if
    poly3 ← Trans(poly, x → x + 1)
    if 0 is a solution of poly3 then
      R ← R ∪ Inverse Möbius trans ([1, 1])
      poly3 ← poly3/x
    end if
    poly4 ← Trans(poly, x → 1/x + 1)
    S ← S ∪ {poly3, poly4}
  end if
end while
```

difference among the computation time in Algorithm 3 is small.

Table 3 shows the computation time for the 100 random polynomial equations. The maximum computation time for Algorithm 3 is 1.48 times faster than that for Algorithm 2. The average computation time for Algorithm 3 is 1.09 times faster than that for Algorithm 2. The standard deviations in Algorithm 2 and Algorithm 3 are not considerably large.

The computation cost of the local-max bound, which is used the continued fraction method based on Vincent's theorem described in Section 3.3, is $O(n)$. The computation cost of Newton's method, which can compute a candidate for the lower bound r, is $O(1)$. The computation cost of Laguerre's theorem, which can check whether a candidate for the lower bound r is suitable, is $O(n)$. Thus, the computation cost of Algorithm 3 is equal to that of Algorithm 2. However, from Figure 1 and Table 3, the computation time for Algorithm 3 is less than that for Algorithm 2. This is because some lower bounds generated from Newton's method are more suitable than the local-max bound. Consequently, the continued fraction method based on Vincent's theorem is improved by using the proposed lower bound.

Hence, the improved continued fraction method with the local-max bound and the proposed lower bound generated by Newton's method is efficient.

Table 2: Experimental environment.

CPU	Core i7 3770K 3.5GHz
Memory size	32GB
Compiler	GCC 4.7.2
Library	GMP 5.1.1

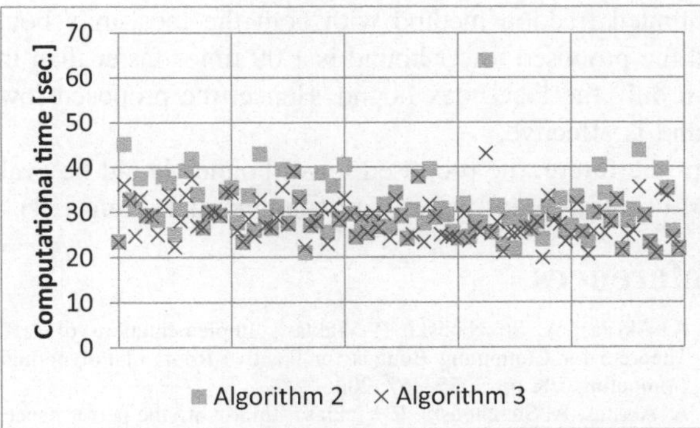

Fig. 1: Computation time in all test polynomial equations. [sec.]

6. Conclusions

In this paper, we proposed a new lower bound for accelerating the continued fraction method based on Vincent's theorem. To accelerate this method, a suitable lower bound should be computed. In the original continued fraction method based on Vincent's theorem, the local-max bound is adopted. In contrast, we used Newton's method to obtain another lower bound. This method can sometimes generate a lower bound larger than the local-max bound. To compute the proposed lower bound, we followed three steps. First, we computed a candidate for the lower bound generated by Newton's method. Second, we used Laguerre's theorem to check whether the candidate is suitable. Third, we compared the local-max bound and the new lower bound. Then, we employed the larger bound to accelerate the continued fraction method based on Vincent's theorem. Experiments were conducted to evaluate the proposed lower bound. The results showed that the average computation time of the

Table 3: Computation time.

	average [sec.]	deviation	max.[sec.]	min.[sec.]
Algorithm 2	30.45	6.45	68.74	20.76
Algorithm 3	28.05	4.46	43.04	19.89

continued fraction method with both the local-max bound and the proposed lower bound is 1.09 times faster than that with only the local-max bound. Hence, the proposed lower bound is effective.

In the future, the proposed lower bound should be evaluated using different types of test polynomials from (24).

References

[1] A. Akritas, A. Strzeboński, P. Vigklas, "Implementations of a New Theorem for Computing Bounds for Positive Roots of Polynomials," *Computing*, 78, pp. 355–367, 2006.

[2] A. Akritas, A. Strzeboński, P. Vigklas, "Improving the performance of the continued fractions method using new bounds of positive roots". *Nonlinear Analysis: Modelling and Control*, 13, pp. 265–279, 2008.

[3] G. Collins, A. Akritas, "Polynomial Real Root Isolation Using Descartes' Rule of Signs", *SYMSAC '76, Proceedings of the third ACM symposium on Symbolic and algebraic computation*, Yorktown Heights, NY, USA, ACM, pp. 272-275, 1976.

[4] (2013) The GNU MP Bignum Library. [Online]. Available: http://gmplib.org/

[5] P. Henrich, "Applied and computational complex analysis", *Wiley Classics Library Edition*, Volume I, 1988.

[6] B. Kioustelidis, "Bounds for positive roots of polynomials,", *J. Comput. Appl. Math.*, 16(2), pp. 241–244, 1986.

[7] E. Laguerre, "On the Theory of Numeric Equations", *Journal de Mathématique pures et appliquées*, 3e série, t. IX, 1883. Translated by Stewart A. Levin, available from http://sepwww.stanford.edu/oldsep/stew/laguerre.pdf

[8] R.E. Moore, "Interval Analysis". Prentice Hall, Englewood Cliffs, N.J., 1966

[9] N. Obreschkoff, "Verteilung und Berechnung der Nullstellen reeller Polynome", Berlin: VEB Deutscher Verlag der Wissenschaften 1963.

[10] A.J.H. Vincent, "Sur la resolution des équations numériques, " *J. Math. Pures Appl.* 1, pp. 341–372, 1836.

Latent Feature Independent Cascade Model for Social Propagation

Yuya Yoshikawa[1], **Tomoharu Iwata**[2], **and Hiroshi Sawada**[3]
[1]Graduate School of Information Science, Nara Institute of Science and Technology, Nara, Japan
[2]NTT Communication Science Laboratories, NTT Corporation, Kyoto, Japan
[3]NTT Service Evolution Laboratories, NTT Corporation, Kanagawa, Japan

Abstract—*People share various types of information including opinions on hot topics, bookmarking activity and rumors via online communities. To make it possible to predict future trends in online communities, it is important that we develop a model of information diffusion through social networks and a method for estimating its parameters. In this paper, we present a latent feature independent cascade model, which can effectively estimate diffusion probabilities by capturing the influences between latent communities. In particular, we incorporate two types of latent features for each node. The first represents the features as a sender and the second represents the features as a receiver. We demonstrate experimentally that the proposed model can estimate the diffusion probabilities more accurately than commonly used methods. We also show the effectiveness of the proposed model for estimating information spread.*

Keywords: information diffusion model, independent cascade, social network, latent feature model

1. Introduction

In online communities, various types of information including opinions on hot topics, bookmarking activity and rumors are shared between individuals by word of mouth. Based on the facts that the user activations in online communities are reflected in the box-office performance of movies [1], market prices [2] and the polling number for elections [3], there is great interest in predicting future trends and discovering instances where information is shared on social networks [4], [5], [6].

Various diffusion models have been proposed for simulating the information diffusion behavior on social networks [7], [8], [9], [10], [11]. The Independent Cascade Model (ICM) proposed by Kempe et al. [7] has been particularly well-studied in recent years, and is used for addressing the influence maximization/minimization problem [7], [12] and finding influential nodes [13], [14], [15]. ICM is a simple probabilistic model that describes processes by which pieces of information spread from node to node on a social network, where the behavior is based on the diffusion probability of each link. Thus, to simulate the real information diffusion behavior, it is important to learn the diffusion probabilities of all links precisely.

Some methods have been developed for estimating the diffusion probability parameters [16], [17], [18], [19]. Saito et al. developed an estimation method based on the EM algorithm under the assumption that continuous time delays occur between the activations [17], while Gruhl et al. assumed discrete time delays [16]. Although their methods provide ways to obtain the diffusion probabilities given the observations of activity, the low generalization performance results when the observations are insufficient. For example, information diffusion does not occur abundantly throughout the network, or often occurs in one portion of the network but not in another. Such cases lead to a poor parameter estimation result.

In realistic social networks, each node has attribute information such as affiliation, age and gender. We can expect the estimation performance regarding diffusion probabilities to improve by using these attributes. However, whether or not the attributes can be observed depends on the target applications.

In this paper, we propose a Latent Feature Independent Cascade Model (LFICM), which is designed to estimate the diffusion probabilities effectively. In the LFICM, we incorporate two types of latent features for each node. The first represents the features as a sender and the second represents the feature as a receiver. The diffusion probabilities are generated based on the latent features between the nodes of each link. By incorporating the latent features, we can estimate the diffusion probabilities with high generalization performance, since the LFICM has a smaller number of parameters than a conventional ICM. For the LFICM, we developed a parameter estimation method based on the EM algorithm. Although a method that estimates the diffusion probabilities based on the observed attribute features of each node has already been developed [18], the proposed model can estimate the ICM parameters without observing additional attribute features by treating the features as latent variables. In our experiments, we show that the proposed model can estimate the diffusion probabilities better than the conventional parameter estimation methods using three real network structures and synthetic activation data. We also show that in a simulation-based influence estimation method, the estimated influence degrees behave in much the same way as the true influence degrees.

2. Proposed Method

In this section, we present our proposed model, the Latent Feature Independent Cascade Model (LFICM), and

Table 1: Notation of LFICM

K	Number of dimensions of latent feature vectors
$\boldsymbol{I}$	Set of pieces of information
$\boldsymbol{x}_u$	Latent feature vector of node u as sender
$\boldsymbol{y}_u$	Latent feature vector of node u as receiver
$\boldsymbol{d}_i$	Diffusion sequence for information i
κ_{uv}	Diffusion probability from node u to node v
r	Time-delay parameter
γ	Bias parameter
σ_X	Standard deviation of $\boldsymbol{x_u}$ (hyperparameter)
σ_Y	Standard deviation of $\boldsymbol{y_u}$ (hyperparameter)

its parameter estimation method.

2.1 Model

Suppose that a set of pieces of information $\boldsymbol{I}$ spreads over a directed social network $\mathcal{G} = (\mathcal{V}, \mathcal{E})$, where $\mathcal{V}$ is a set of nodes corresponding to individuals and $\mathcal{E} \subseteq \mathcal{V} \times \mathcal{V}$ is a set of links corresponding to relationships between individuals. We define $B(v)$ as a set of parents of node $v \in \mathcal{V}$, $B(v) = \{u|(u,v) \in \mathcal{E}\}$, and $F(v)$ as a set of children of node $v \in \mathcal{V}$, $F(v) = \{w|(v,w) \in \mathcal{E}\}$. Table 1 lists the symbols and the descriptions used in LFICM.

For a piece of information $i \in \boldsymbol{I}$, we observe logs showing when each node transmitted the information i. We refer to a status of a node from which information is transmitted as *active*. The logs form a sequence of length L_i of active node-time pairs as follows,

$$\boldsymbol{d}_i = \{(v_{i1}, t_{v_{i1}}), (v_{i2}, t_{v_{i2}}), \cdots (v_{iL_i}, t_{v_{iL_i}})\}.$$

Note that each active node can be affected by any of its parent nodes, but we cannot observe by whom the active nodes are influenced.

LFICM assumes that the pieces of information spread according to the same mechanism as with the Independent Cascade Model (ICM) [7]. ICM provides a process whereby the information spreads from node to node through the links. ICM has two types of model parameters for each link $(u,v) \in \mathcal{E}$, *diffusion probability* κ_{uv} and *time-delay parameter* r_{uv}, where $0 \leq \kappa_{uv} \leq 1$ and $r_{uv} > 0$. For simplicity, we assume $r_{uv} = r$ although it is easy to run.

The diffusion process of the ICM is as follows. We first fix a set of source nodes $\mathcal{S} \subseteq \mathcal{V}$ from which the information diffusion process starts. Thus, node $v \in \mathcal{S}$ becomes active at time $t_v = 0$. Then the process iteratively executes the following two steps until no more activations are possible:

- When node u becomes active, it attempts to transmit information to each inactive child node $v \in F(u)$. This trial succeeds with the diffusion probability κ_{uv}.
- If node v is activated by node u in the above step, then the activated time of node v is $t_u + \Delta$ where Δ is a random variable following an exponential distribution with parameter r given below:

$$\Delta \sim \text{Exponential}(r) \quad (1)$$

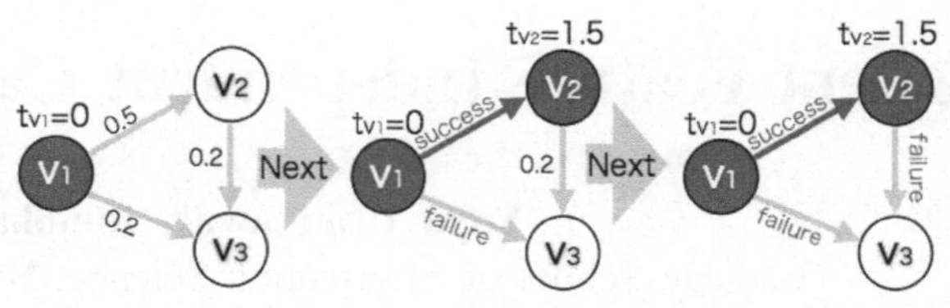

Fig. 1: Step by step procedure of the ICM. **(left)** Initial state. Diffusion probabilities are assigned to each link in advance. Node v_1 is a source node. **(center)** Node v_2 becomes active when affected by node v_1. **(right)** Node v_3 is not affected by node v_1 or v_2.

Figure 1 shows the step-by-step procedure of ICM.

To extend ICM for estimating the diffusion probabilities with high generalization performance, we introduce two types of K-dimension latent feature vectors $\boldsymbol{x}_u \in \mathbb{R}^K$ and $\boldsymbol{y}_u \in \mathbb{R}^K$for each node $u \in \mathcal{V}$. In LFICM, the diffusion probability from node u to node v, κ_{uv}, is calculated as follows:

$$\kappa_{uv} = f(\boldsymbol{x}_u, \boldsymbol{y}_v, \gamma) = \left(1 + \exp(-\boldsymbol{x}_u^\top \boldsymbol{y}_v - \gamma)\right)^{-1}, \quad (2)$$

where γ is a bias parameter that does not depend on the nodes. Function f is a sigmoid function, thus $0 \leq \kappa_{uv} \leq 1$. Here, $\boldsymbol{x}_u$ and $\boldsymbol{y}_u$ represent the features as an information sender and the features as an information receiver, respectively. The diffusion probability κ_{uv} has a high value when $\boldsymbol{x}_u^\top \boldsymbol{y}_v$ is high.

The latent features of node $u \in \mathcal{V}$, $\boldsymbol{x}_u$ and $\boldsymbol{y}_u$ follow a K-dimension normal distribution,

$$\boldsymbol{x}_u \sim \mathcal{N}(\mathbf{x}_u|\mathbf{0}, \sigma_X^2\mathbf{I}), \quad (3)$$
$$\boldsymbol{y}_u \sim \mathcal{N}(\mathbf{y}_u|\mathbf{0}, \sigma_Y^2\mathbf{I}), \quad (4)$$

where $\mathbf{0}$ and $\mathbf{I}$ denote K-dimension zero vector and a unit matrix of size $K \times K$, respectively.

Under the calculated parameters described above, a diffusion sequence $\boldsymbol{d}_i$ is generated based on the ICM diffusion process shown in Algorithm 1 given source nodes $\mathcal{S}_i \subseteq \mathcal{V}$,

$$\boldsymbol{d}_i \sim \text{ICM}\left(\{\kappa_{uv}\}_{(u,v)\in\mathcal{E}}, r, \mathcal{G}, \mathcal{S}_i\right).$$

2.2 Parameter Estimation

We present a parameter estimation algorithm for the LFICM based on the Expectation-Maximization (EM) algorithm [20].

Given a set of diffusion sequences $\boldsymbol{D} = \{\boldsymbol{d}_i\}_{i\in\boldsymbol{I}}$, we can write the posterior probability for LFICM parameters $\boldsymbol{X} = [\boldsymbol{x}_u]_{u\in\mathcal{V}}, \boldsymbol{Y} = [\boldsymbol{y}_u]_{u\in\mathcal{V}}$ as follows,

$$\begin{aligned} &P(\boldsymbol{X}, \boldsymbol{Y} \mid \gamma, r, \boldsymbol{D}, \sigma_X, \sigma_Y, \mathcal{G}) \quad (5)\\ &\quad \propto P(\boldsymbol{D}|\boldsymbol{X}, \boldsymbol{Y}, \gamma, r, \mathcal{G})P(\boldsymbol{X}|\sigma_X)P(\boldsymbol{Y}|\sigma_Y). \end{aligned}$$

The first factor on the right hand side of Eq. (5) is the likelihood of LFICM. Let $\Delta_{uv}^{(i)}$ be the difference between the active times of nodes u and v for information i, i.e.,

$\Delta_{uv}^{(i)} = t_{iv} - t_{iu}$. For convenience, let C_i and $C_i(t)$ be a set of active nodes and a set of active nodes by time t for information i, respectively, that is,

$$C_i = \{v \mid (v,t) \in \boldsymbol{d}_i\}, \;\; C_i(t) = \{v \mid (v,t') \in \boldsymbol{d}_i,\; t' < t\}.$$

Although we omit the detailed derivation of the likelihood due to space limitations, we can obtain the following likelihood,

$$\begin{aligned} & P(\boldsymbol{D}|\boldsymbol{X},\boldsymbol{Y},\gamma,r,\mathcal{G}) \qquad (6) \\ &= \prod_{i\in \boldsymbol{I}} \prod_{v\in C_i} \prod_{u\in B(v)\cap C_i(t_{iv})} p_{u\rightarrow v}^{(i)} \sum_{u\in B(v)\cap C_i(t_{iv})} \frac{p_{u\rightarrow v}^{(i)}}{p_{u\nrightarrow v}^{(i)}} \\ &\times \prod_{w\in F(v)\setminus C_i} (1-\kappa_{vw}), \end{aligned}$$

where $p_{u\rightarrow v}^{(i)}$ represents the probability that node u makes node v active, and $p_{u\nrightarrow v}^{(i)}$ represents the probability that node u fails to affect node v,

$$\begin{aligned} p_{u\rightarrow v}^{(i)} &= \kappa_{uv} r \exp(-r\Delta_{uv}^{(i)}), && (7) \\ p_{u\nrightarrow v}^{(i)} &= \kappa_{uv} \exp(-r\Delta_{uv}^{(i)}) + 1 - \kappa_{uv}. && (8) \end{aligned}$$

The second and third factors are prior distributions for $\boldsymbol{X}$ and $\boldsymbol{Y}$, respectively,

$$\begin{aligned} P(\boldsymbol{X}|\sigma_X) &= \prod_{u=1}^{|\mathcal{V}|} \frac{1}{\sqrt{2\pi\sigma_X^K}} \exp\Big(-\frac{\boldsymbol{x}_u^\top \boldsymbol{x}_u}{2\sigma_X^2}\Big), && (9) \\ P(\boldsymbol{Y}|\sigma_Y) &= \prod_{u=1}^{|\mathcal{V}|} \frac{1}{\sqrt{2\pi\sigma_Y^K}} \exp\Big(-\frac{\boldsymbol{y}_u^\top \boldsymbol{y}_u}{2\sigma_Y^2}\Big). && (10) \end{aligned}$$

With the posterior probability Eq. (5), we find parameters $\hat{\boldsymbol{X}}$, $\hat{\boldsymbol{Y}}$, $\hat{\gamma}$ and $\hat{r}$ based on the maximum a posteriori (MAP) principle. The parameters can be estimated with an EM algorithm that alternates between estimating which active nodes are affected by the E-step, and updating the parameters under the E-step result in the M-step. We use $\bar{x}$ as a current estimate for variable x to avoid confusion.

E-step: In the E-step, we need only to consider the likelihood Eq. (6) in the posterior probability Eq. (5). By employing a similar method to that described in [17], we can derive function Q, which is the expectation of the complete-data likelihood, from the likelihood Eq. (6) as follows,

$$\begin{aligned} & Q(\boldsymbol{X},\boldsymbol{Y},\gamma,r;\bar{\boldsymbol{X}},\bar{\boldsymbol{Y}},\bar{\gamma},\bar{r}) \qquad (11) \\ &= \sum_{i\in\boldsymbol{I}} \sum_{v\in C_i} \Bigg[\sum_{u\in B(v)\cap C_i(t_{iv})} \Big(\bar{\xi}_{uv}^{(i)} \log \kappa_{uv} \\ &\quad + (1-\bar{\xi}_{uv}^{(i)}) \log(1-\kappa_{uv}) + \bar{q}_{uv}^{(i)} \log r + \bar{\xi}_{uv}^{(i)} r \Delta_{uv}^{(i)} \Big) \\ &\quad + \sum_{w\in F(v)\setminus C_i} \log(1-\kappa_{vw}) \Bigg] \\ &\quad + \log P(\boldsymbol{X}|\sigma_X) + \log P(\boldsymbol{Y}|\sigma_Y) \end{aligned}$$

Algorithm 1 ICMGENERATOR

Require: diffusion probability $\{\kappa_{uv}\}_{(u,v)\in\mathcal{E}}$, time-delay parameter r, network $\mathcal{G}$, source nodes $\mathcal{S}$

```
d_i ← {(u, 0) | u ∈ S}
repeat
    (u, t_iu) ← min_{t_ix} {(x, t_mx) | (x, t_mx) ∈ d_i, x ∈ S}
    for v ∈ {inactive nodes in child nodes of u } do
        if u succeeds in propagation to v with κ_uv then
            t_iv ← t_iu + Δ, where Δ follows Eq. (1).
            d_i ← d_i ∪ {(v, t_iv)}
            S ← S ∪ {v}
        end if
    end for
    S ← S \ {u}
until S = ∅
return d_i
```

---

where

$$\begin{aligned} q_{uv}^{(i)} &= \frac{p_{u\rightarrow v}^{(i)}/p_{u\nrightarrow v}^{(i)}}{\sum_{u'\in B(v)\cap C_i(t_{iv})} p_{u\rightarrow v}^{(i)}/p_{u\nrightarrow v}^{(i)}}, && (12) \\ \eta_{uv}^{(i)} &= \frac{\kappa_{uv}\exp(-r\Delta_{uv}^{(i)})}{\kappa_{uv}\exp(-r\Delta_{uv}^{(i)}) + (1-\kappa_{uv})}, && (13) \\ \xi_{uv}^{(i)} &= q_{uv}^{(i)} + (1-q_{uv}^{(i)})\eta_{uv}^{(i)}. && (14) \end{aligned}$$

Here, function Q is guaranteed to be a lower bound for the posterior Eq. (5), that is, $P(\boldsymbol{X},\boldsymbol{Y} \mid \gamma, r, \boldsymbol{D}, \sigma_X, \sigma_Y, \mathcal{G}) \geq Q$. $q_{uv}^{(i)}$ can be regarded as the probability that node u is influenced by node v on information i under the current estimates.

In the M-step, we estimate the parameters by maximizing the function Q.

M-step: Using the current estimates, $\bar{\boldsymbol{X}}, \bar{\boldsymbol{Y}}, \bar{r}, \bar{\gamma}, \bar{q}_{uv}^{(i)}, \bar{\eta}_{uv}^{(i)}$ and $\bar{\xi}_{uv}^{(i)}$, we update the parameters, $\boldsymbol{X}, \boldsymbol{Y}, r$ and γ. The closed form solution for Eq. (11) does not exist for the parameters, $\boldsymbol{X}, \boldsymbol{Y}$ and γ owing to the non-linearity of the sigmoid function. Thus, we need to use a kind of optimization method based on a gradient with respect to each parameter. In this study, we use the quasi-Newton method, which only needs first-order derivations with respect to the parameters.

The first-order derivations of the parameters, $\boldsymbol{x}_u, \boldsymbol{y}_u$ for each $u \in \mathcal{V}$ and γ are derived as follows:

$$\begin{aligned} & \frac{\partial Q(\boldsymbol{X},\boldsymbol{Y},\gamma,r;\bar{\boldsymbol{X}},\bar{\boldsymbol{Y}},\bar{\gamma},\bar{r})}{\partial \boldsymbol{x}_u} \qquad (15) \\ &= \sum_{i\in\boldsymbol{I}} \Big(\sum_{v\in F(u)\cap C_i} (\bar{\xi}_{uv}^{(i)} - f(\boldsymbol{x}_u, \bar{\boldsymbol{y}}_v, \bar{\gamma}))\bar{\boldsymbol{y}}_v \\ &\quad - \sum_{w\in F(u)\setminus C_i} f(\boldsymbol{x}_u, \bar{\boldsymbol{y}}_w, \bar{\gamma})\bar{\boldsymbol{y}}_w \Big) - \frac{1}{\sigma_X^2}\boldsymbol{x}_u \end{aligned}$$

$$\frac{\partial Q(\boldsymbol{X},\boldsymbol{Y},\gamma,r;\bar{\boldsymbol{X}},\bar{\boldsymbol{Y}},\bar{\gamma},\bar{r})}{\partial \boldsymbol{y}_v} = \sum_{i\in \boldsymbol{I}}\Big(\sum_{u\in B(v)\cap C_i(t_{iv})} \big(\bar{\xi}^{(i)}_{uv} - f(\bar{\boldsymbol{x}}_u,\boldsymbol{y}_v,\bar{\gamma})\big)\bar{\boldsymbol{x}}_u - \sum_{s\in B(v)\cap C_i, v\notin C_i} f(\bar{\boldsymbol{x}}_s,\boldsymbol{y}_v,\bar{\gamma})\bar{\boldsymbol{x}}_s\Big) - \frac{1}{\sigma_Y^2}\boldsymbol{y}_v \tag{16}$$

$$\frac{\partial Q(\boldsymbol{X},\boldsymbol{Y},\gamma,r;\bar{\boldsymbol{X}},\bar{\boldsymbol{Y}},\bar{\gamma},\bar{r})}{\partial \gamma} = \sum_{i\in \boldsymbol{I}}\Big(\sum_{v\in C_i}\sum_{u\in B(v)\cap C_i(t_{iv})} \big(\bar{\xi}^{(i)}_{uv} - f(\bar{\boldsymbol{x}}_u,\bar{\boldsymbol{y}}_v,\gamma)\big) - \sum_{v\in C_i}\sum_{s\in F(v)\setminus C_i} f(\bar{\boldsymbol{x}}_u,\bar{\boldsymbol{y}}_s,\gamma)\Big) \tag{17}$$

The time-delay parameter r can be calculated using the following closed form,

$$r = \frac{\sum_{i\in \boldsymbol{I}}\sum_{v\in C_i}\sum_{u\in B(v)\cap C_i(t_{iv})} \bar{q}^{(i)}_{uv}}{\sum_{i\in \boldsymbol{I}}\sum_{v\in C_i}\sum_{u\in B(v)\cap C_i(t_{iv})} \bar{\xi}^{(i)}_{uv}\Delta^{(i)}_{uv}}. \tag{18}$$

In the EM algorithm, the parameters are estimated by alternating E-step and M-step and continuing the procedure until the improvement of the log-likelihood converges. In summary, the parameter estimation procedure is given by Algorithm 2.

Algorithm 2 LFICMESTIMATOR

Require: network $\mathcal{G}$, diffusion sequences $\boldsymbol{D}$, dimension of features K, hyper-parameters σ_X and σ_Y

Initialize $\boldsymbol{X},\boldsymbol{Y},\gamma,r$

repeat

  E-step: update $q_{muv},\eta_{muv},\xi_{muv}$ based on Eqs. (12),(13) and (14)

  M-step: update $\boldsymbol{X},\boldsymbol{Y},\gamma$ using quasi-Newton method based on Eqs. (15) - (17), and r based on Eq. (18)

until convergence of improving the log-likelihood Eq. (5)

return $\boldsymbol{X},\boldsymbol{Y},\gamma,r$

3. Experiments

To evaluate the proposed model with respect to the precision and effectiveness of the estimated diffusion probabilities of the ICM, we ran experiments using real networks and synthetic diffusion sequences.

3.1 Experimental Data and Settings

Three real networks data. In this study, we used three kinds of real network structure datasets. The first is BLOG data, which we obtained by tracing the track-back of posts in the *goo* blog in May 2005 [17]. The network is constructed by putting a link from blog (node) u to blog v if a post on blog u refers to one on blog v through the track-back function. The second dataset is referred to as ENRON data and consists of exchanges of e-mail in Enron Corp. The network regards each sender and receiver as a node and puts a link if node u sends an e-mail to node v. The last dataset is referred to as MIXI data, which is bidirectional (co-link) friendship network data obtained from a well-known social networking service in Japan[1].

Table 2: Parameter settings for generating synthetic diffusion sequences

	K	γ	r	$\mathcal{S}$	σ_X	σ_Y
BLOG	5	-3.5	10.0	Random	1.0	1.0
ENRON	5	-6.5	1.0	Random	1.0	1.0
MIXI	7	-6.5	1.0	Random	1.0	1.0

Table 3: Statistics of network data for evaluation of LFICM

	$\lvert\mathcal{V}\rvert$	$\lvert\mathcal{E}\rvert$	$\lvert\boldsymbol{I}\rvert$	avg. $\lvert\boldsymbol{d}_i\rvert$
BLOG	12,047	79,920	200	207.1
ENRON	36,692	367,662	200	203.4
MIXI	80,608	571,136	1,500	8.6

Synthetic diffusion sequence generation. In our experiments, diffusion sequences are generated artificially based on the proposed model. The procedure for generating the diffusion sequences is as follows. First we generate the latent feature vectors under the parameter settings for each dataset shown in Table 2, and calculate the diffusion probability for each link. Then we generate diffusion sequences $\boldsymbol{d}_i$ based on Algorithm 1. Table 3 shows the statistics of generating diffusion sequences. Note that there are too few diffusion sequences for complete estimation, as suggested by a comparison of the number of links with the volume of the sequences.

Baseline methods. We use two parameter estimation methods as baselines for comparison, which are adopted in [17], [19]. The first method attempts to estimate the parameter directly by the maximum likelihood method [17]. This method is the basis of our model. We refer to it as `SaitoICM`. The second method is identical to `SaitoICM` but estimates a uniform diffusion probability throughout the network, that is, $\kappa_{uv} = \kappa$. We refer to it as `SimpleICM`. This method makes it possible to estimate the parameters robustly, but it is not a flexible model.

3.2 Precision of Parameter Estimation

In the first experiment, we evaluate the proposed method and the baselines by estimating the diffusion probabilities from synthetic diffusion sequences for each dataset. Since the proposed model controls the complexity of the model

[1] https://mixi.jp/

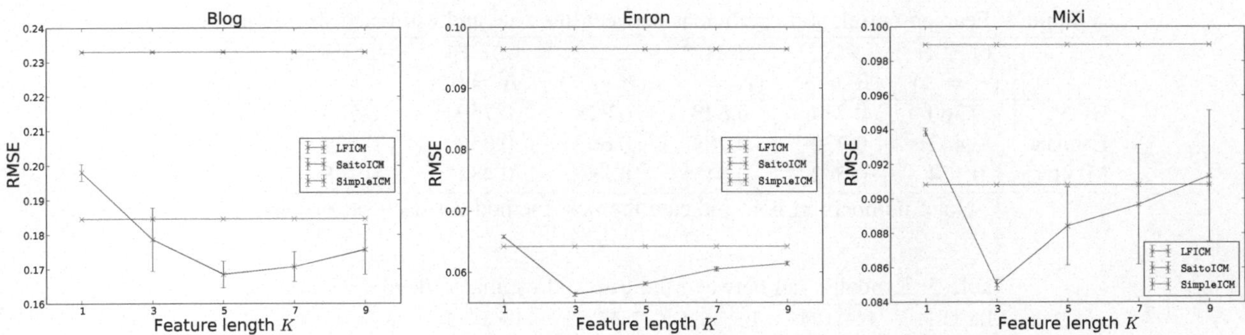

Fig. 2: Average RMSE between true and estimated diffusion probabilities in each dataset

by changing the value of K, we adopt K value of 1, 3, 5, 7 and 9. Note that the true K values, which are used for generating synthetic diffusion sequences for BLOG, ENRON and MIXI, are five, five and seven, respectively.

Figure 2 shows comparison results of the estimation error between the proposed method and each baseline for each dataset. The vertical axis denotes the root mean squared error (RMSE) between the true and estimated diffusion probabilities, while the horizontal axis denotes the dimension of the feature vector, K. In the results using BLOG and ENRON data, respectively, the proposed model outperformed the baselines except for when $K = 1$. The result obtained using MIXI data is characterized by a large standard deviation shown as a vertical bar on the proposed model. Nevertheless, `LFICM` outperformed the baselines when $K = 3, 5, 7$.

To summarize these results, `SaitoICM` seems to be a poor estimator compared with `LFICM` and `SimpleICM`, even though it is the most flexible model. This is because `SaitoICM` poses an over-fitting problem due to a lack of observed data.

3.3 Estimation of degree of influence

Estimation method for degree of influence. Let us define the *degree of influence* of node u as the average number of active nodes affected by source node u. Thus, it consists of the number of nodes that receive information transmitted from node u directly and indirectly. We have studied a method for estimating the degree using the ICM [15]. This method is largely dependent on the performance of a selected parameter estimation method. We simplify the algorithm of [15] into Algorithm 3, and evaluate the estimated degree of influence using the parameters with the proposed model and the baseline values. In this experiment, we fix $T = 50$ in Algorithm 3.

Evaluation method. We evaluate our model according to the following procedure:

1) For each node, we calculate the degree of influence using Algorithm 3 under the true parameter settings shown in Table 2, and we define it as the true degree of influence for each node.
2) We calculate the degree of influence under the parameters estimated in Section 3.2, by `LFICM`, `SaitoICM` and `SimpleICM`, respectively, and we define them as the estimated degree of influence of each method for each node.
3) We calculate the *Pearson correlation coefficient* and *Kendall's tau coefficient* between the true and estimated degrees of influence for each method.

Algorithm 3 INFLUENCEPREDICTOR

Require: network $\mathcal{G}$, source nodes $\mathcal{S}$, time-delay parameter r, diffusion probability $\{\kappa_{uv}\}_{(u,v)\in\mathcal{E}}$, trials T.

$influence \leftarrow 0$
for $i \leftarrow 1, 2, \cdots, T$ **do**
  $d_m \leftarrow$ ICMGENERATOR($\{\kappa_{uv}\}_{(u,v)\in\mathcal{E}}, r, \mathcal{G}, \mathcal{S}$)
  $influence \leftarrow influence + \frac{1}{T}|d_i|$
end for
return $influence$

where, the Pearson correlation coefficient is calculated simply using the degree of influence, while Kendall's tau coefficient uses the rank of degree of influence for each method. The values of these coefficients range from -1 to $+1$, and if the value is close to $+1$, then we can consider that the two compared values behave in the same way.

Experimental results. Tables 4 and 5 show results of an evaluation of the Pearson correlation coefficient and Kendall's tau coefficient between the true and estimated degree of influence, respectively. They are significantly correlated with significant probability $p < 0.01$. As shown in these tables, with any of the proposed methods, `LFICM`, is better than the baseline methods for each dataset.

However, we find that the K value of at which highest correlation is reached does not necessarily coincide with that one of the lowest RMSE. With the evaluation by RMSE of the estimated diffusion probabilities, all the diffusion

Table 4: Pearson correlation coefficient between the true and estimated degree influence .

	LFICM ($K=1$)	LFICM ($K=3$)	LFICM ($K=5$)	LFICM ($K=7$)	LFICM ($K=9$)	SaitoICM	SimpleICM
BLOG	0.360	0.734	**0.848**	0.828	0.769	0.753	0.827
ENRON	0.442	**0.730**	0.703	0.669	0.657	0.539	0.656
MIXI	0.174	0.542	0.545	**0.556**	0.484	0.468	0.382

Note: numbers in bold indicate the best method for each set of data.

Table 5: Kendall's tau between the true and estimated degree of influence.

	LFICM ($K=1$)	LFICM ($K=3$)	LFICM ($K=5$)	LFICM ($K=7$)	LFICM ($K=9$)	SaitoICM	SimpleICM
BLOG	0.424	0.534	**0.599**	0.585	0.553	0.532	0.591
ENRON	0.293	**0.379**	0.371	0.370	0.370	0.372	0.369
MIXI	0.517	0.443	0.441	0.445	**0.445**	0.252	0.441

Note: numbers in bold indicate the best method for each set of data.

probabilities are used only once. Estimating each diffusion probability itself with high generalization performance or without outliers leads to a good result. On the other hand, this experiment might evaluate the diffusion probability of a link many times because the information passes through nodes with a lot of links, i.e, *authorities*, many times in our simulations. This fact makes it especially important in this experiment to learn the probabilities of links extending from the authority nodes to estimate the degrees of influence of all the nodes. The proposed model is useful in complex situations such as that represented by this experiment.

4. Conclusion and Future Work

In this paper, we proposed the Latent Feature Independent Cascade Model (LFICM) for modeling information diffusion phenomena and the predicting future trends to estimate the diffusion probabilities of each link. In particular, we newly incorporated two latent features for each node, which represent the sensitivity to incoming information and the power of influence. We then assumed that each diffusion probability is calculated from the features of both terminating nodes. To estimate the parameters of the LFICM from observations we formulated the posterior probability of the model and derived the parameter estimation method based on the EM algorithm. In the experiments, the proposed model outperformed the conventional estimation methods with respect to the precision of the diffusion probability estimation for four kinds of dataset. Moreover, we showed that estimating the parameters of the ICM with the proposed model allows us to understand precisely the degrees of influence of nodes.

In realistic settings, the influence power and the sensitivity of each individual vary widely and these variations are unknown. To consider this fact, we will attempt to extend the proposed model to a Bayesian model using proper prior distributions so as to estimate standard deviations σ_X and σ_Y along with the other parameters. For K estimation, we can use the cross-validation method and model selection methods such as AIC and BIC.

References

[1] A. S. S. Reddy, A. Siva, P. Kasat, and A. Jain, "Box-Office Opening Prediction of Movies based on Hype Analysis through Data Mining," *International Journal of Computer Applications*, vol. 56, no. 1, pp. 1–5, 2012.

[2] X. Zhang, H. Fuehres, and P. A. Gloor, "Predicting Stock Market Indicators Through Twitter " I hope It Is Not as Bad as I Fear "," *The 2nd Collaborative Innovation Networks Conference*, vol. 26, pp. 55–62, 2011.

[3] F. Franch, "2010 UK Election Prediction with Social Media," *Journal of Information Technology & Politics*, vol. 10, no. 1, pp. 57–71, Jan. 2013.

[4] J. Iribarren and E. Moro, "Impact of Human Activity Patterns on the Dynamics of Information Diffusion," *Physical Review Letters*, vol. 103, no. 3, pp. 8–11, July 2009.

[5] W. Galuba and K. Aberer, "Outtweeting the Twitterers-Predicting Information Cascades in Microblogs," *WOSN'10 Proceedings of the 3rd Conference on Online Social Networks*, 2010.

[6] T.-T. Kuo, S.-C. Hung, W.-S. Lin, S.-D. Lin, T.-C. Peng, and C.-C. Shih, "Assessing the Quality of Diffusion Models Using Real-World Social Network Data," *2011 International Conference on Technologies and Applications of Artificial Intelligence*, pp. 200–205, Nov. 2011.

[7] D. Kempe, J. Kleinberg, and E. Tardos, "Maximizing the Spread of Influence through a Social Network," *Proceedings of the Ninth ACM SIGKDD International Conference on Knowledge Discovery and Data Mining*, p. 137, 2003.

[8] V. Sood and S. Redner, "Voter Model on Heterogeneous Graphs," *Physical Review Letters*, vol. 94, no. 17, pp. 178 701–, May 2005.

[9] D. Trpevski and L. Kocarev, "Model for Rumor Spreading over Networks," *Physical Review E*, vol. 81, no. 5, pp. 1–11, May 2010.

[10] C. Budak, D. Agrawal, and A. El Abbadi, "Limiting the Spread of Misinformation in Social Networks," in *Proceedings of the 20th International Conference on World Wide Web*. New York, New York, USA: ACM Press, Mar. 2011, p. 665.

[11] W. Chen, A. Collins, and R. Cummings, "Influence Maximization in Social Networks When Negative Opinions May Emerge and Propagate," *SIAM International Conference on Data Mining*, 2011.

[12] M. Kimura, K. Saito, and H. Motoda, "Blocking Links to Minimize Contamination Spread in a Social Network," *ACM Transactions on Knowledge Discovery from Data*, vol. 3, no. 2, pp. 1–23, Apr. 2009.

[13] D. Kempe, J. Kleinberg, and E. Tardos, "Influential Nodes in a Diffusion Model for Social Networks," *Automata, Languages and Programming*, vol. 3580, pp. 1127–1138, 2005.

[14] M. Kimura, K. Saito, and R. Nakano, "Extracting Influential Nodes for Information Diffusion on a Social Network," *Proceedings of the National Conference on Artificial Intelligence*, vol. 22, no. 2, p. 1371, 2007.

[15] Y. Yoshikawa, K. Saito, H. Motoda, K. Ohara, and M. Kimura, "Acquiring Expected Influence Curve from Single Diffusion Sequence," *Knowledge Management and Acquisition for Smart Systems and Services*, pp. 273–287, 2010.

[16] D. Gruhl, R. Guha, D. Liben-Nowell, and A. Tomkins, "Information Diffusion through Blogspace," *Proceedings of the 13th International Conference on World Wide Web*, pp. 491–501, 2004.

[17] K. Saito, M. Kimura, K. Ohara, and H. Motoda, "Learning Continuous-Time Information Diffusion Model for Social Behavioral Data Analysis," *First Asian Conference on Machine Learning*, pp. 322–337, 2009.

[18] K. Saito, K. Ohara, Y. Yamagishi, and M. Kimura, "Learning Diffusion Probability Based on Node Attributes in Social Networks," *19th International Symposium, ISMIS 2011*, pp. 153–162, 2011.

[19] L. Dickens, I. Molloy, and J. Lobo, "Learning Stochastic Models of Information Flow," *2012 IEEE 28th International Conference on Data Engineering (ICDE)*, 2012.

[20] A. P. Dempster, N. M. Laird, and D. B. Rubin, "Maximum Likelihood from Incomplete Data via the EM Algorithm," *Journal of the Royal Statistical Society. Series B (Methodological)*, 1977.

Decidability of k-secrecy against inference attacks using functional dependencies on XML databases

Nobuaki Yamazoe[1], **Kenji Hashimoto**[2], **Yasunori Ishihara**[1], **and Toru Fujiwara**[1]
[1]Graduate School of Information Science and Technology, Osaka University, Suita, Japan
[2]Graduate School of Information Science, Nara Institute of Science and Technology, Ikoma, Japan

Abstract—*An inference attack means that a database user tries to identify, or narrow down the candidates for, sensitive information from non-sensitive information such as queries authorized to the user and their results, the schema of a database, functional dependencies satisfied by the database, etc. If the size of the candidate set is at least k, the database is said to be k-secret. In our previous papers, we targeted XML databases and proposed how to determine k-secrecy without functional dependencies. In this paper, we show the decidability of k-secrecy with functional dependencies provided that the functional dependencies satisfy a restriction called the non-prefix restriction. To be specific, we reduce the problem of finding a candidate to the satisfiability problem of functional dependencies. Then, the decision algorithm of k-secrecy is simply designed as an enumeration of candidates.*

Keywords: XML database; inference attack; secrecy

1. Introduction

Direct access to a database is controlled in general. That is, database management systems specify which users can issue which queries. However, by using non-sensitive information such as authorized queries and their results, the schema of the database, and the functional dependencies satisfied by the database, a user may be able to identify, or narrow down the candidates for, the result of some unauthorized query. Such indirect access to the result of an unauthorized query is called an *inference attack*. In order to maintain the secrecy of the database, it is important for database managers to know of possible inference attacks in advance. Below is an example of an inference attack.

Example 1: Consider an XML database containing information on patients in a hospital. Suppose that three queries T_1, T_2, and T_3 are authorized to a user:

- T_1 retrieves all the patients examined by Dr. Abe and the day of the week of the examination;
- T_2 retrieves all the patients in room 101 and the day of the week of the examination; and
- T_3 retrieves all the doctors who examine a patient in room 102.

Also suppose that this XML database satisfies the following two functional dependencies f_1 and f_2:

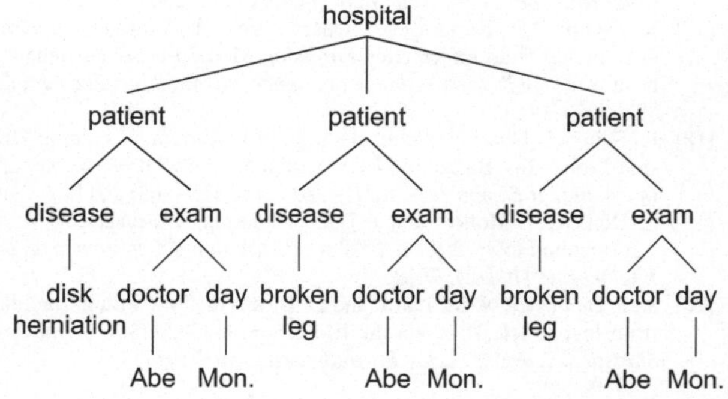

Figure 1: The result of query T_1.

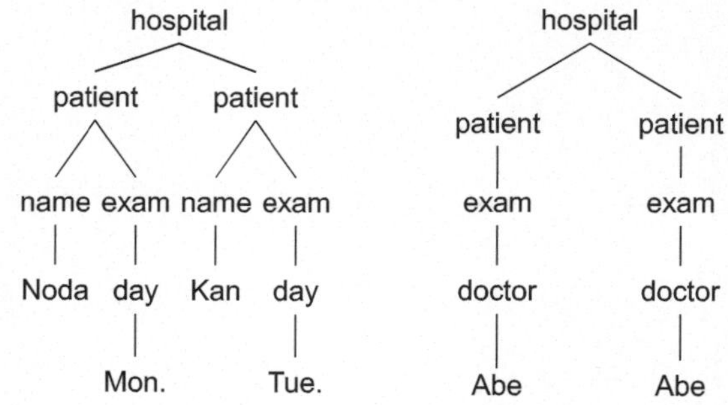

Figure 2: The result of query T_2.

Figure 3: The result of query T_3.

- f_1: the day of the week of the examination uniquely determines the doctor; and
- f_2: the room uniquely determines the disease of the patients in the room.

The user is interested in the result of the following query T_S:

- T_S retrieves the disease of patient Noda.

Suppose that T_S is not authorized to the user, so the user attempts indirect access to the result of T_S.

Now, suppose that the results of T_1, T_2, and T_3 are the trees shown in Figures 1, 2, and 3. We can see in Figure 3 that there are two patients in room 102 examined by Dr. Abe. Moreover, by f_2, these two patients have the same disease. Figure 1 indicates that Dr. Abe examines three patients. Since two of the three patients are in room 102 and have the same disease, the patient with disk herniation is in a room other than 102. By f_1 and Figures 1 and 2, it can be concluded that Dr. Abe examines patient Noda. Moreover, since the patient with disk herniation is the only patient examined by Dr. Abe other than the patients in room 102, it can be inferred that patient Noda has disk herniation.

Note that in this example, if f_2 is unavailable to the user, the disease of patient Noda cannot be identified but the candidates are narrowed down to disk herniation and broken leg. On the other hand, if f_1 is unavailable to the user, it is impossible to even narrow down the candidates.

If the number of candidates narrowed down by the attacker is large, it is hard to identify which candidate is the true value and the database is considered safe. If the size of the candidate set is at least k, the database is said to be *k-secret*, and if the size of the set is not finite, the database is *infinity-secret* [1]. Aiming at XML databases, we previously proposed how to determine infinity-secrecy and k-secrecy without functional dependencies [1]. We also proposed how to determine infinity-secrecy with a single functional dependency [2]. However, it remains an open problem whether k-secrecy with functional dependencies is decidable or not.

In this paper, we show the decidability of k-secrecy with multiple functional dependencies provided that the functional dependencies satisfy a restriction called the *non-prefix restriction*. Roughly speaking, the non-prefix restriction requires the paths constituting the functional dependencies not to be prefixes of each other. Under this restriction, k-secrecy is determined as follows. First, compute a set of databases conforming to the given database schema and for which the results of authorized queries are the same as the target database. Next, enumerate databases in the set that return distinct results for the unauthorized query. Then, determine k-secrecy by checking whether there are any such k databases or not. Technically, the decidability of the *satisfiability of multiple functional dependencies* plays an important role for the enumeration to work. This paper shows that the decidability result of the satisfiability of a single functional dependency [2] can be extended to the multiple case under the non-prefix restriction.

The rest of this paper is organized as follows. Section 2 introduces several definitions. Section 3 shows the decidability of k-secrecy. Section 4 discusses related studies. We summarize the paper and conclude in Section 5.

2. Definitions

2.1 Trees

An XML database instance is represented by an *unranked labeled ordered tree*, where the number of each node of a tree is independent of its label. Let $\mathcal{T}_\Sigma$ denote the set of all unranked labeled ordered trees over Σ.

The *position* of a node of $t \in \mathcal{T}_\Sigma$ is a sequence of positive integers defined as follows: the position of the root node is ϵ; if the position of a node v is p and v_i is the i-th child of v, then the position of v_i is $p \cdot i$. The nodes and their positions have one-to-one correspondence, so hereafter, we use the term position to mean the node itself. Let $Pos(t)$ be the set of the positions of t. Let $t|_p$ denote the subtree of t at the position p.

Let $\lambda_t(p)$ denote the label of the position p of t. Moreover, let $\tilde{\lambda}_t(p)$ denote the label path from the root to the position p in t, and let $\tilde{\lambda}_t^-(p)$ denote the label path obtained from $\tilde{\lambda}_t(p)$ by removing the leading label. These two notations are useful for expressing a concatenation of label paths concisely, i.e.,

$$\tilde{\lambda}_t(p \cdot p') = \tilde{\lambda}_t(p) \cdot \tilde{\lambda}_{t|_p}^-(p').$$

2.2 Tree automata

We use a *finite tree automaton* (TA) to represent a schema or a set of candidates for the value of the sensitive information.

First, we define a regular expression. A regular expression (RE) over an alphabet Σ consists of constants $\emptyset$ (empty set), ϵ (empty sequence), and the symbols in Σ, and operators $\cdot$ (concatenation), $*$ (zero or more occurrences), $+$ (one or more occurrences), | (disjunction), and & (interleaving). The concatenation operator is often omitted as usual. The string language represented by a regular expression e is denoted by $L(e)$.

Next, we define an (unranked) TA over Σ. A TA A is a 4-tuple $(Q, \Sigma, \hat{Q}, R)$, where

- Q is a finite set of states,
- Σ is an alphabet,
- $\hat{Q} \subseteq Q$ is a set of initial states, and
- R is a set of transition rules in the form of (q, a, e), where $q \in Q$, $a \in \Sigma$, and e is an RE over Q.

Example 2: The following is an example TA A_{H} representing the XML schema supposed in Example 1:

- Q contains Ho, Pa, Na, Di, Ro, Ex, Do, Da, PCDATA;
- Σ contains hospital, patient, name, disease, room, exam, doctor, day;
- $\hat{Q} = \{\mathsf{Ho}\}$; and
- R contains the following rules:
  - (Ho, hospital, Pa*),
  - (Pa, patient, Na · Ro · Di · Ex),
  - (Na, name, PCDATA),
  - (Ro, room, PCDATA),
  - (Di, disease, PCDATA),
  - (Ex, exam, Do · Da),
  - (Do, doctor, PCDATA),
  - (Da, day, PCDATA).

The TA also contains states, symbols, and rules for PCDATA, i.e., string data. In this paper we assume that string data are encoded by trees in some appropriate way [1].

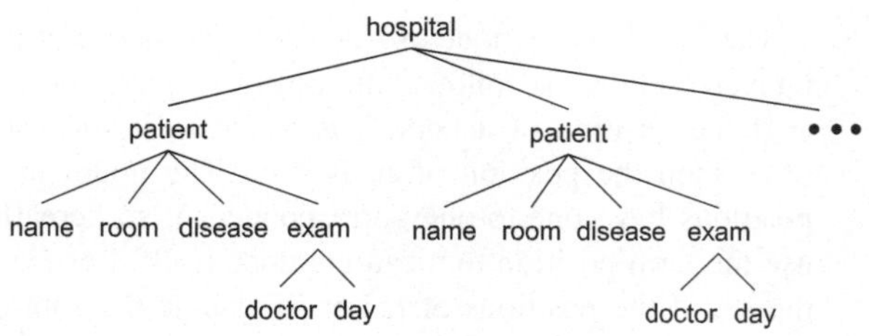

Figure 4: A tree accepted by A_{H}.

A *(successful) run* r_A^t *of* A *on* t is a mapping from $Pos(t)$ to Q with the following properties:

- $r_A^t(\epsilon) \in \hat{Q}$.
- For each position p, if p has n children, there exists a transition rule $(q, a, e) \in R$ such that
  - $r_A^t(p) = q$,
  - $\lambda_t(p) = a$, and
  - $r_A^t(p \cdot 1) r_A^t(p \cdot 2) \cdots r_A^t(p \cdot n) \in L(e)$.

We say that a tree $t \in \mathcal{T}_\Sigma$ is *accepted* by A if there exists a run of A on t. Let $TL(A)$ denote the tree language *recognized* by A, i.e., the set of trees accepted by A. For $q \in Q$, let $TL(A, q)$ be the tree language recognized by A when the initial state is q. We extend the run to a set P of positions, i.e., $r_A^t(P) = \{r_A^t(p) \mid p \in P\}$. For $t \in TL(A)$, we define the state path $\tilde{r}_A^t(p)$ to p on $\tilde{r}_A^t$ as follows: $\tilde{r}_A^t(\epsilon) = r_A^t(\epsilon)$; $\tilde{r}_A^t(p \cdot i) = \tilde{r}_A^t(p) r_A^t(p \cdot i)$. We say A is *unambiguous* if the run r_A^t is unique for each $t \in TL(A)$. We say A is *bottom-up deterministic* if $TL(A, q_1) \cap TL(A, q_2) = \emptyset$ for any two distinct states $q_1, q_2 \in Q$. Note that for any TA, an equivalent bottom-up deterministic TA can be constructed.

Example 3: A tree accepted by A_{H} is shown in Figure 4, where the PCDATA parts are omitted. It is not difficult to see that A_{H} is unambiguous and bottom-up deterministic, provided that so is the PCDATA part of A_{H}.

2.3 Queries

We regard queries as tree-to-tree transformation functions. Our verification method requires a query model which preserves inverse recognizability [3]. That is, given a query T and a TA A, a TA which recognizes $\{t' \mid t \in TL(A), T(t') = t\}$ can be constructed. The construction is called *inverse type inference*. Finite compositions of macro tree transducers [4] is one of the query models satisfying the requirement. It is also known that the model is powerful enough to describe many real-world XML transformations.

In this paper, we do not mention a concrete query model, and just assume that queries preserve inverse recognizability.

2.4 Functional dependencies

A *functional dependency* (FD) f is a triple (H, X, Y) where H, X, Y are simple paths over Σ. For a simple path

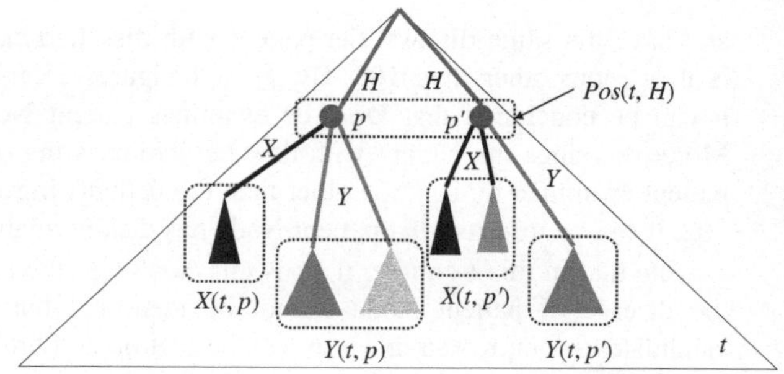

Figure 5: Definition of an FD.

s and a tree $t \in \mathcal{T}_\Sigma$, $Pos(t, s)$ is defined as follows:

$$Pos(t, s) := \{p \in Pos(t) \mid \tilde{\lambda}_t(p) = s\}.$$

$Pos(t, s)$ is the set of positions of t reachable from the root by the path s including the root label. Also, for a position p of t, let $Pos(t, p, s)$ denote the set of positions of t reachable from p by the path s excluding the label of p. Formally,

$$Pos(t, p, s) := \{p \cdot p' \in Pos(t) \mid \tilde{\lambda}^-_{t|_p}(p') = s\}.$$

We write the set of subtrees of t at positions in $Pos(t, s)$ (resp. $Pos(t, p, s)$) as $s(t)$ (resp. $s(t, p)$). Given a tree t and an FD f, t *satisfies* f if and only if for any two positions $p, p' \in Pos(t, H)$, $X(t, p) \cap X(t, p') \neq \emptyset$ implies $Y(t, p) \cap Y(t, p') \neq \emptyset$ (see Figure 5). For an FD f, let $TL(f)$ denote the set of trees which satisfy f. FDs $f_1, \ldots, f_N$ are said to be *satisfiable* under a TA A if $TL(A) \cap \bigcap_{i=1}^N TL(f_i)$ is not empty.

Our verification method handles a finite number of FDs $f_1, \ldots, f_N$ such that, letting $f_i = (H_i, X_i, Y_i)$,

- for each i $(1 \leq i \leq N)$, neither of X_i nor Y_i is a prefix of the other;
- for each i, j $(1 \leq i, j \leq N, i \neq j)$,
  - if $H_i = H_j$, then none of X_i, X_j, Y_i, and Y_j is a prefix of any of the others;
  - if $H_i \neq H_j$, then neither H_i nor H_j is a prefix of the other.

We refer to this restriction as the *non-prefix restriction*.

Example 4: The two FDs f_1 and f_2 in Example 1 can be represented as follows:

$$f_1 = (\mathsf{hospital} \cdot \mathsf{patient} \cdot \mathsf{exam}, \mathsf{day}, \mathsf{doctor}),$$
$$f_2 = (\mathsf{hospital} \cdot \mathsf{patient}, \mathsf{room}, \mathsf{disease}).$$

Unfortunately, the set $\{f_1, f_2\}$ does not satisfy the non-prefix restriction. However, the following FD f_1' is "equivalent" to f_1 under A_{H} in the sense that $TL(A_{\mathsf{H}}) \cap TL(f_1) = TL(A_{\mathsf{H}}) \cap TL(f_1')$:

$$f_1' = (\mathsf{hospital} \cdot \mathsf{patient}, \mathsf{exam} \cdot \mathsf{day}, \mathsf{exam} \cdot \mathsf{doctor}).$$

Note that the set $\{f_1', f_2\}$ satisfies the non-prefix restriction.

2.5 k-secrecy

Let t_G be a target tree to be attacked. We assume that the following information is available to the attackers: the database schema A_G of t_G, authorized queries $T_1, \ldots, T_n$ and their results $T_1(t_G), \ldots, T_n(t_G)$, an unauthorized query T_S, and FDs $f_1, \ldots, f_N$. The sensitive information is $T_S(t_G)$. Suppose that the attacker infers the set L_C of all the candidates for the value of the sensitive information consistent with the above available information. That is,

$$L_C = \{T_S(t') \mid t' \in TL(A_G) \cap \bigcap_{i=1}^{N} TL(f_i), \quad T_1(t') = T_1(t_G), \ldots, T_n(t') = T_n(t_G)\}.$$

For a positive integer k, t_G is *k-secret* (with respect to T_S) if $|L_C| \geq k$.

3. A decision algorithm of k-secrecy

Suppose that a target tree t_G to be attacked, authorized $T_1, \ldots, T_n$, unauthorized query T_S, and FDs $f_1, \ldots, f_N$ with the non-prefix restriction are given. In what follows, we show a decision algorithm of k-secrecy of t_G with respect to T_S.

First, we compute

$$L_{INF} = \{t' \in TL(A_G) \mid T_1(t') = T_1(t_G), \ldots, T_n(t') = T_n(t_G)\}$$

by inverse type inference, i.e., we construct a TA A_{INF} such that $L_{INF} = TL(A_{INF})$. Then, letting $A = A_{INF}$, we enumerate candidates for the value of the sensitive information as follows:

- Decide the satisfiability of the FDs $f_1, \ldots, f_N$ under A. If satisfiable, find a tree $u \in TL(A)$ that satisfies the FDs. Also, by inverse type inference, compute the set of trees t such that $T_S(t) = u$. Let A' be a TA such that $TL(A')$ is the difference of $TL(A)$ and the set.
- Letting $A = A'$, repeat the above process until k trees are found or the satisfiability check fails. The database is k-secret if and only if k trees are found.

In what follows, we explain how to check the satisfiability of FDs, and then, how to enumerate the candidates for the value of sensitive information in detail.

3.1 Checking the satisfiability of functional dependencies

Let A be a TA and $f_1, \ldots, f_N$ be FDs. To check the satisfiability of the FDs under A, construct *path-fixed automata* $A^1_{dv}, \ldots, A^l_{dv}$ as explained in Appendix. It holds that $TL(A^i_{dv}) \cap TL(A^j_{dv}) = \emptyset$ for each i and j ($1 \leq i, j \leq l$, $i \neq j$), and $TL(A) = \bigcup_{1 \leq i \leq l} TL(A^i_{dv})$. Satisfiability check is done for each of these path-fixed automata. That is, FDs $f_1, \ldots, f_N$ are satisfiable under A if and only if there is some TA A^i_{dv} under which FDs $f_1, \ldots, f_N$ are satisfiable.

A TA A is *path fixed* with respect to FDs $f_1, \ldots, f_N$ if A is unambiguous and satisfies the following three conditions for each $f = (H, X, Y) \in \{f_1 \ldots, f_N\}$:

1) $\forall t, t' \in TL(A).r^t_A(Pos(t, H)) = r^{t'}_A(Pos(t', H))$.
2) $\forall t, t' \in TL(A).\forall p \in Pos(t, H).\forall p' \in Pos(t', H).$ $(r^t_A(p) = r^{t'}_A(p') \Rightarrow \forall Z \in \{X, Y\}.$ $r^t_A(Pos(t, p, Z)) = r^{t'}_A(Pos(t', p', Z)))$.
3) $\forall t \in TL(A).\forall Z \in \{X, Y\}.$ $\forall p, p' \in Pos(t, HZ).r^t_A(p) \neq r^t_A(p') \Rightarrow t|_p \neq t|_{p'}$.

This is an extension of the notion of *f-path fixity* introduced in [2] to multiple FDs. The first condition means that for every tree in $TL(A)$, the set of states assigned to the positions in $Pos(t, H)$ is fixed. The fixed set is denoted by Q^A_H. The second condition means that for any tree in $TL(A)$ and any position p in $Pos(t, H)$, the set of states assigned to the positions in $Pos(t, p, X)$ (resp. $Pos(t, p, Y)$) is fixed on the state assigned to the position p. For each $q_h \in Q^A_H$, the fixed sets are denoted by $Q^A_{q_h,X}$ and $Q^A_{q_h,Y}$, respectively. The third condition means that for any tree in $TL(A)$ and any two positions in either of $Pos(t, HX)$ or $Pos(t, HY)$, if the states assigned to the positions are distinct, then so are the subtrees at the positions. Let $Q^A_{HX} = \bigcup_{q_h \in Q^A_H} Q^A_{q_h,X}$ and $Q^A_{HY} = \bigcup_{q_h \in Q^A_H} Q^A_{q_h,Y}$.

For a tree $t \in TL(A)$ and $p_x \in Pos(t, HX)$, let $QP^t_{HX}(p_x)$ denote the pair $(r^t_A(p_h), r^t_A(p_x))$ of states of A such that $p_x = p_h \cdot p$ for some p and $\lambda_t(p_h) = H$. Let QP^t_{HX} denote the set $\{QP^t_{HX}(p_x) \mid p_x \in Pos(t, HX)\}$. Note that QP^t_{HX} is fixed over all $t \in TL(A)$ because of the path fixity of A. The fixed set is also denoted by QP^A_{HX}.

The satisfiability of FDs $f_1, \ldots, f_N$ under a path-fixed TA A is equivalent to the existence of the following mappings M_{HX} and M_{HY} for each $f = (H, X, Y) \in \{f_1 \ldots, f_N\}$:

- The domain of M_{HX} is QP^A_{HX}. For each $(q_h, q_x) \in QP^A_{HX}$, $M_{HX}((q_h, q_x))$ must be an element of $TL(A, q_x)$. Moreover, for $(q_{h1}, q_x), (q_{h2}, q_x) \in QP^A_{HX}$ such that $q_{h1} \neq q_{h2}$ and $Q^A_{q_{h1},HY} \cap Q^A_{q_{h2},HY} = \emptyset$, it must hold that $M_{HX}((q_{h1}, q_x)) \neq M_{HX}((q_{h2}, q_x))$.
- The domain of M_{HY} is Q^A_{HY}. For each $q_y \in Q^A_{HY}$, $M_{HY}(q_y)$ must be an element of $TL(A, q_y)$.

Intuitively, for a tree $t \in TL(A)$ satisfying the FDs, mappings M_{HX} and M_{HY} represent the subtree of t at position in $Pos(t, HX)$ and $Pos(t, HY)$, respectively. Note that for any $q_y \in Q^A_{HY}$, $TL(A, q_y)$ is nonempty because the definition of Q^A_{HY} is based on a successful run. Hence the existence of M_{HY} is always guaranteed, and the key point is the existence of M_{HX}. The next lemma formally states this intuition.

Lemma 1: FDs $f_1, \ldots, f_N$ are satisfiable under a path-fixed TA A with respect to $f_1, \ldots, f_N$ if and only if for each $f = (H, X, Y) \in \{f_1, \ldots, f_N\}$, there exists a mapping M_{HX} satisfying the above condition.

Proof: If part. Consider an arbitrary tree $t' \in TL(A)$. Since A is path fixed with respect to $f_1, \ldots, f_N$, t' has all of the paths $H_1X_1,\ldots, H_NX_N, H_1Y_1,\ldots, H_NY_N$. That is, $Pos(t', HX)$ and $Pos(t', HY)$ are nonempty for all $f = (H,X,Y) \in \{f_1,\ldots,f_N\}$. Let $r_A^{t'}$ be the unique run of A on t'. Let t be a tree obtained from t' by the following replacement:

- for each $p_x \in Pos(t', HX)$, replace the subtree $t'|_{p_x}$ of t' with $M_{HX}(QP_{HX}^{t'}(p_x))$; and
- for each $p_y \in Pos(t', HY)$, replace the subtree $t'|_{p_y}$ of t' with $M_{HY}(r_A^{t'}(p_y))$.

Note that t is well defined because of the non-prefix restriction on FDs. Now, the tree t is obviously in $TL(A)$. Moreover, for all $f = (H,X,Y) \in \{f_1,\ldots,f_N\}$ and for any pairs of positions p_{h1} and p_{h2} in $Pos(t,H)$, if $X(t,p_{h1}) \cap X(t,p_{h2}) \neq \emptyset$, then $Y(t,p_{h1}) \cap Y(t,p_{h2}) \neq \emptyset$.

Only if part. Suppose that for some $f = (H,X,Y) \in \{f_1,\ldots,f_N\}$, there is no mapping M_{HX} satisfying the above condition. Here, for any $(q_h, q_x) \in QP_{HX}^A$, $TL(A,q_x)$ is nonempty because the definition of QP_{HX}^A is based on a successful run. Hence, there are some $(q_{h1},q_x),(q_{h2},q_x) \in QP_{HX}^A$ such that $q_{h1} \neq q_{h2}$, $M_{HX}((q_{h1},q_x)) = M_{HX}((q_{h2},q_x))$, and $Q_{q_{h1},HY}^A \cap Q_{q_{h2},HY}^A = \emptyset$. Now, suppose contrarily that a tree $t' \in TL(A)$ satisfies the FD f. Because A is path fixed, there are $p_{h1}, p_{h2} \in Pos(t',H)$ such that $r_A^{t'}(p_{h1}) = q_{h1}$ and $r_A^{t'}(p_{h2}) = q_{h2}$. Moreover, by the path fixity of A again, $Q_{q_{h1},HY}^A \cap Q_{q_{h2},HY}^A = \emptyset$ implies that $Y(t',p_{h1}) \cap Y(t',p_{h2}) = \emptyset$. Hence, in order for t' to satisfy f, it must hold that $X(t',p_{h1}) \cap X(t',p_{h2}) = \emptyset$. However, this is a contradiction to the assumption that the condition for M_{HX} cannot be satisfied because by choosing $M_{HX}((q_{h1},q_x))$ from $X(t',p_{h1})$ and $M_{HX}((q_{h2},q_x))$ from $X(t',p_{h2})$, it would hold that $M_{HX}((q_{h1},q_x)) \neq M_{HX}((q_{h2},q_x))$. In summary, there is no tree $t' \in TL(A)$ satisfying f. ■

In what follows, we show that existence of the mapping M_{HX} is decidable. Let $q_x \in Q_{HX}^A$. Consider a subset Q' of Q_H^A such that for any distinct q_{h1} and q_{h2} in Q',

- $q_x \in Q_{q_{h1},X}^A \cap Q_{q_{h2},X}^A$, and
- $Q_{q_{h1},Y}^A \cap Q_{q_{h2},Y}^A = \emptyset$.

For q_x, such Q' is not unique. Let $k(q_x)$ denote the maximum size of such Q'.

Lemma 2: Fix $f = (H,X,Y)$ in $\{f_1,\ldots,f_n\}$. Mapping M_{HX} exists if and only if $|TL(A,q_x)| \geq k(q_x)$ for all $q_x \in Q_{HX}^A$.

Proof: If part. Suppose that $|TL(A,q_x)| \geq k(q_x)$ for all $q_x \in Q_{HX}^A$. Recall that the domain of M_{HX} is QP_{HX}^A. Let $QP_{HX}^A(q_x)$ denote the subset of QP_{HX}^A such that the second components of the elements are $q_x \in Q_{HX}^A$. Let QP_{d} be a subset of $QP_{HX}^A(q_x)$ such that

- QP_{d} has $k(q_x)$ elements, and
- for any distinct pair $(q_{h1},q_x),(q_{h2},q_x)$ in QP_{d}, it holds that $Q_{q_{h1},HY}^A \cap Q_{q_{h2},HY}^A = \emptyset$.

By the maximality of $k(q_x)$, for any $(q'_h,q_x) \in QP_{HX}^A(q_x) - QP_{\mathrm{d}}$, there is $(q_h,q_x) \in QP_{\mathrm{d}}$ such that $Q_{q'_h,HY}^A \cap Q_{q_h,HY}^A \neq \emptyset$. Now, define M_{HX} as follows. M_{HX} maps elements in QP_{d} to $k(q_x)$ distinct elements in $TL(A,q_x)$. Also, M_{HX} maps each $(q'_h,q_x) \in QP_{HX}^A(q_x) - QP_{\mathrm{d}}$ to $M_{HX}((q_h,q_x))$ such that $Q_{q'_h,HY}^A \cap Q_{q_h,HY}^A \neq \emptyset$. Then M_{HX} satisfies that for any distinct $(q_{ha},q_x),(q_{hb},q_x) \in QP_{HX}^A(q_x)$, $Q_{q_{ha},HY}^A \cap Q_{q_{hb},HY}^A = \emptyset$ implies $M_{HX}((q_{ha},q_x)) \neq M_{HX}((q_{hb},q_x))$.

Only if part. Suppose that $|TL(A,q_x)| < k(q_x)$ for some $q_x \in Q_{HX}^A$. Define QP_{d} as in the proof of the if part. That is, $|QP_{\mathrm{d}}| = k(q_x)$ and for any distinct $(q_{h1},q_x),(q_{h2},q_x) \in QP_{\mathrm{d}}$, it holds that $Q_{q_{h1},HY}^A \cap Q_{q_{h2},HY}^A = \emptyset$. Hence, M_{HX} must map elements in QP_{d} to distinct elements. However, the image of M_{HX} must be an element of $TL(A,q_x)$ and we have ony $|TL(A,q_x)| < k(q_x) = |QP_{\mathrm{d}}|$ elements. It is concluded that mapping M_{HX} does not exist. ■

Since it is decidable whether $|TL(A,q_x)| \geq k(q_x)$ for all $q_x \in Q_{HX}^A$, the following theorem is immediate.

Theorem 1: Let $f_1,\ldots, f_N$ be FDs satisfying non-prefix restriction, and A be a general TA. Satisfiability of $f_1,\ldots, f_N$ under A is decidable.

3.2 Enumerating candidates for the value of sensitive information

Using the decidability result of satisfiability of FDs, we show the decidability of k-secrecy.

Theorem 2: k-secrecy against inference attacks using FDs is decidable, provided that the FDs satisfy the non-prefix restriction. Moreover, if k-secret, $u_1,\ldots,u_k \in L_{INF}$ such that $T_S(u_i) \neq T_S(u_j)$ for any i and j $(1 \leq i,j \leq k, i \neq j)$ are computable.

Proof: The theorem is shown by induction on k.

Basis. Let $k = 1$. Since L_C always contains $T_S(t_G)$ for the target tree t_G, t_G is always 1-secret. Hence, k-secrecy is decidable when $k = 1$. Moreover, we can choose t_G as $u_1 \in L_{INF}$ because t_G satisfies $f_1,\ldots, f_N$.

Induction. Let $k > 1$. Suppose that $(k-1)$-secrecy is decidable. Suppose also that if $(k-1)$-secret, $u_1,\ldots,u_{k-1} \in L_{INF}$ such that $T_S(u_i) \neq T_S(u_j)$ for any i and j $(1 \leq i,j \leq k-1,\ i \neq j)$ are computable. The decision algorithm of k-secrecy is as follows:

1) Run the $(k-1)$-secrecy decision algorithm.
2) If t_G is not $(k-1)$-secret, then return "t_G is not k-secret." Otherwise, do the following process.
   a) Compute $u_1,\ldots,u_{k-1} \in L_{INF}$ such that $T_S(u_i) \neq T_S(u_j)$ for any i and j $(1 \leq i,j \leq k-1,\ i \neq j)$.
   b) By inverse type inference on T_S, compute a TA A_i^{EQ} such that $TL(A_i^{EQ}) = \{t' \in L_{INF} \mid T_S(t') = T_S(u_i)\}$ for each i $(1 \leq i \leq k-1)$.
   c) Compute a TA A_k such that $TL(A_k) = L_{INF} - \bigcup_{1 \leq i \leq k-1} TL(A_i^{EQ})$.
   d) Check the satisfiability of $f_1,\ldots, f_N$ under A_k. If not satisfiable, then return "t_G is not k-secret." Otherwise, do the following process.

i) Compute a tree $u_k \in TL(A_k)$ satisfying FDs $f_1, \ldots, f_N$. This computation is possible by a naive enumeration of unranked trees followed by checking the membership of $TL(A_k)$ and satisfaction of $f_1, \ldots, f_N$.

ii) Return "t_G is k-secret," with trees $u_1, \ldots, u_k$.

The correctness of the above algorithm is almost obvious. The algorithm returns "t_G is not k-secret" only if t_G is not even $(k-1)$-secret or there is no $u_k \in TL(A_k)$ satisfying FDs $f_1, \ldots, f_N$. On the other hand, the algorithm returns "t_G is k-secret" with trees $u_1, \ldots, u_k$ only if all of $u_1, \ldots$, u_k are in L_{INF}, all of them satisfy the FDs $f_1, \ldots, f_N$, and $T_S(u_1), \ldots, T_S(u_k)$ are all distinct. ■

4. Related Work

Inference attacks have been one of the most well-known threats on databases for the past few decades. On relational databases, aggregate functions can be used for inferring sensitive information [5]. Disclosure Monitor [6] is a part of a relational database management system that monitors information disclosure by inference attacks. Roughly speaking, Disclosure Monitor keeps track of users' knowledge obtained by queries issued so far. When a user issues a query, Disclosure Monitor determines whether the result of the query with the current knowledge of the user disclose the sensitive information. According to the determination result, Disclosure Monitor decides whether the query should be allowed or not. Several stronger security definitions [7], [8] require that authorized views and the answers of them do not change the probability distribution of possible secrets. As for XML databases, there have been a few studies on secure view publishing [9], [10].

Security against inference attacks is often discussed in the context of privacy protection. k-anonymity [11] is one of the most famous security criteria, which assumes *linking attacks* to privacy data in multiple tables. A set of attributes that can be useful for identifying individuals is called a pseudo-identifier. The concept of k-anonymity is based on the idea that a database is safe if it contains many corresponding tuples for each possible value of a pseudo-identifier. Another famous criterion is l-diversity [12]. It is based on the idea that a database is safe if it contains many candidates for values of sensitive information for each possible value of a pseudo-identifier. Our notion of k-secrecy is similar to the notion of l-diversity but differs in that our model assumes attackers infers *all the candidates* for the value of sensitive information *consistent with the information available to the attackers*. That is, it is assumed that attackers can perform more than linking attacks. Our result is therefore useful for guaranteeing higher secrecy than l-diversity.

Research on inference attacks is closely related to research on incomplete information because an attacker's knowledge is considered as incomplete information on the sensitive information. Conditional tables [13] are a simple but powerful representation of incomplete relational databases. In conditional tables, unknown values are represented by variables, and the domains of variables and the existence of tuples are specified by conditional expressions. Actually, to keep track of the user's knowledge, Disclosure Monitor uses a data structure similar to conditional tables. As for XML databases, incomplete trees were proposed [14]. They can handle trees with data values, but only a limited number of tree shapes. In our formulation, data values are assumed to be encoded by trees. Therefore, we can adopt finite tree automata as a representation of incomplete information, which have good closure properties, although comparisons between data values are limited.

5. Conclusion

In this paper, we have shown that k-secrecy against inference attacks using multiple FDs of XML databases is decidable, provided the FDs satisfy the non-prefix restriction. As demonstrated in Example 1, inference using multiple FDs is strictly more powerful than inference using a single FD. Our result shows that the risk by multiple FDs is detectable, while it is not necessarily detected by existing methods.

The non-prefix restriction is critical for our decision procedure to work correctly. For example, consider the following two FDs: $f_1 = (H_1, X_1, Y_1)$ and $f_2 = (H_2, X_2, Y_2)$. Without the restriction, H_2X_2 might be a prefix of H_1. The number of possible subtrees at H_2X_2 could not be independent of the numbers of possible subtrees at H_1X_1 and H_1Y_1. This means that it is impossible to decide the satisfiability for each FD independently. Our future work will include relaxing the non-prefix restriction so that k-secrecy is still decidable.

References

[1] K. Hashimoto, K. Sakano, F. Takasuka, Y. Ishihara, and T. Fujiwara, "Verification of the security against inference attacks on XML databases," *IEICE Transactions on Information and Systems*, vol. E92-D, no. 5, pp. 1022–1032, 2009.

[2] K. Hashimoto, H. Kawai, Y. Ishihara, and T. Fujiwara, "Decidability of the security against inference attacks using a functional dependency on XML databases," *IEICE Transactions on Information and Systems*, vol. E95-D, no. 5, pp. 1365–1374, 2012.

[3] D. Suciu, "The XML typechecking problem," *SIGMOD Record*, vol. 31, no. 1, pp. 89–96, 2002.

[4] S. Maneth, A. Berlea, T. Perst, and H. Seidl, "XML type checking with macro tree transducers," in *Proceedings of the 24th ACM SIGMOD-SIGACT-SIGART Symposium on Principles of Database Systems*, 2005, pp. 283–294.

[5] D. E. R. Denning, *Cryptography and Data Security*. Addison-Wesley, 1982.

[6] A. Brodsky, C. Farkas, and S. Jajodia, "Secure databases: Constraints, inference channels, and monitoring disclosures," *IEEE Transactions on Knowledge and Data Engineering*, vol. 12, no. 6, pp. 900–919, 2000.

[7] A. Deutsch and Y. Papakonstantinou, "Privacy in database publishing," in *Proceedings of the 10th International Conference on Database Theory*, 2005, pp. 230–245.

[8] G. Miklau and D. Suciu, "A formal analysis of information disclosure in data exchange," *Journal of Computer and System Sciences*, vol. 73, no. 3, pp. 507–534, 2007.

[9] W. Fan, C. Y. Chan, and M. N. Garofalakis, "Secure XML querying with security views," in *Proceedings of the 2004 ACM SIGMOD International Conference on Management of Data*, 2004, pp. 587–598.

[10] X. Yang and C. Li, "Secure XML publishing without information leakage in the presence of data inference," in *Proceedings of the 30th International Conference on Very Large Data Bases*, 2004, pp. 96–107.

[11] L. Sweeney, "k-anonymity: A model for protecting privacy," *International Journal on Uncertainty, Fuzziness and Knowledge-based Systems*, vol. 10, no. 5, pp. 557–570, 2002.

[12] A. Machanavajjhala, J. Gehrke, D. Kifer, and M. Venkitasubramaniam, "ℓ-diversity: Privacy beyond k-anonymity," in *Proceedings of the 22nd International Conference on Data Engineering*, 2006, p. 24.

[13] T. Imielinski and W. L. Jr., "Incomplete information in relational databases," *Journal of the ACM*, vol. 31, no. 4, pp. 761–791, 1984.

[14] S. Abiteboul, L. Segoufin, and V. Vianu, "Representing and querying xml with incomplete information," in *Proceedings of the Twentieth ACM SIGACT-SIGMOD-SIGART Symposium on Principles of Database Systems*, 2001.

Appendix

Construction of path-fixed automata with respect to FDs $f_1, \ldots, f_N$ consists of the following two steps: construction of an FD automaton for $f_1, \ldots, f_N$; and division into path-fixed TAs.

A Construction of an FD automaton

Given FDs $f_1, \ldots, f_N$, we construct an FD automaton A_F which is the intersection TA of all the FD automata A_{f_i} for each f_i $(1 \leq i \leq N)$. In what follows, we provide a construction method of the FD automaton A_f with respect to a single FD $f = (H, X, Y)$.

First, construct two TAs A_{HX} and A_{HY} as follows. Let $H = h_1 \cdots h_n$ and $X = x_1 \cdots x_m$. Then, $A_{HX} = (Q_X^H \cup \bar{Q}_X^H, \Sigma, \{q_{h_1}, \bar{q}_{h_1}, q_{\bar{h}_1}\}, R_X^H)$, where

$$\begin{aligned} Q_X^H &= \{q_{h_1}, \ldots, q_{h_n}\} \cup \{q_{x_1}, \ldots, q_{x_m}\}, \\ \bar{Q}_X^H &= \{\bar{q}_{h_1}, \ldots, \bar{q}_{h_{n-1}}\} \cup \{q_{\bar{h}_1}, \ldots, q_{\bar{h}_n}\} \\ &\quad \cup \{\bar{q}_{x_1}, \ldots, \bar{q}_{x_{m-1}}\} \cup \{q_{\bar{x}_1}, \ldots, q_{\bar{x}_m}\} \cup \{q_{any}\}, \end{aligned}$$

and R_X^H consists of the following transition rules:

- for each i $(1 \leq i \leq n-2)$,
  - $(q_{h_i}, h_i, (q_{h_{i+1}}{}^+ \;\&\; \bar{q}_{h_{i+1}}{}^* \;\&\; q_{\bar{h}_{i+1}}{}^*))$,
  - $(\bar{q}_{h_i}, h_i, (\bar{q}_{h_{i+1}}{}^* \;\&\; q_{\bar{h}_{i+1}}{}^*))$,
  - $(q_{\bar{h}_i}, \alpha, q_{any}{}^*)$ for each $\alpha \in \Sigma - \{h_i\}$,
- for $i = n-1$,
  - $(q_{h_i}, h_i, (q_{h_{i+1}}{}^+ \;\&\; q_{\bar{h}_{i+1}}{}^*))$,
  - $(\bar{q}_{h_i}, h_i, q_{\bar{h}_{i+1}}{}^*)$,
  - $(q_{\bar{h}_i}, \alpha, q_{any}{}^*)$ for each $\alpha \in \Sigma - \{h_i\}$,
- for $i = n$,
  - $(q_{h_i}, h_i, (q_{x_1}{}^* \;\&\; \bar{q}_{x_1}{}^* \;\&\; q_{\bar{x}_1}{}^*))$,
  - $(q_{\bar{h}_i}, \alpha, q_{any}{}^*)$ for each $\alpha \in \Sigma - \{h_i\}$,
- for each j $(1 \leq j \leq m-2)$,
  - $(q_{x_j}, x_j, (q_{x_{j+1}}{}^+ \;\&\; \bar{q}_{x_{j+1}}{}^* \;\&\; q_{\bar{x}_{j+1}}{}^*))$,
  - $(\bar{q}_{x_j}, x_j, (\bar{q}_{x_{j+1}}{}^* \;\&\; q_{\bar{x}_{j+1}}{}^*))$,
  - $(q_{\bar{x}_j}, \alpha, q_{any}{}^*)$ for each $\alpha \in \Sigma - \{x_j\}$,
- for $j = m-1$,
  - $(q_{x_j}, x_j, (q_{x_{j+1}}{}^+ \;\&\; q_{\bar{x}_{j+1}}{}^*))$,
  - $(\bar{q}_{x_j}, x_j, q_{\bar{x}_{j+1}}{}^*)$,
  - $(q_{\bar{x}_j}, \alpha, q_{any}{}^*)$ for each $\alpha \in \Sigma - \{x_j\}$,
- for $j = m$,
  - $(q_{x_j}, x_j, q_{any}{}^*)$,
  - $(q_{\bar{x}_j}, \alpha, q_{any}{}^*)$ for each $\alpha \in \Sigma - \{x_j\}$, and
- $(q_{any}, \alpha, q_{any}{}^*)$ for each $\alpha \in \Sigma$.

Construct A_{HY} in the same way.

Then, $A_f = (Q_f \cup \bar{Q}_f, \Sigma, \hat{Q}, R_f)$ is the intersection TA of A_{HX} and A_{HY}, where $Q_f = Q_X^H \times (Q_Y^H \cup \bar{Q}_Y^H) \cup (Q_X^H \cup \bar{Q}_X^H) \times Q_Y^H$ and $\bar{Q}_f = \bar{Q}_X^H \times \bar{Q}_Y^H$. Since A_{HX} and A_{HY} are unambiguous, so is A_f.

B Division into path-fixed TAs

Given a TA $A = (Q, \Sigma, \hat{Q}, R)$ and the FD automaton $A_F = (Q_F, \Sigma, \hat{Q}_F, R_F)$ with respect to FDs $f_1, \ldots, f_N$, we divide A into a finite set of TAs each of which is path fixed with respect to $f_1, \ldots, f_N$. We assume that A is a bottom-up deterministic TA without loss of generality. In what follows, we show a procedure for dividing A into a finite set of path-fixed TAs with respect to $f_1, \ldots, f_N$.

First, construct the intersection TA A_p of A and A_F. Next, let Q'_F be the subset of Q_F such that i-th component of the elements is in Q_{f_i} for some i $(1 \leq i \leq N)$. Consider the following binary relation $\prec$ over $Q \times Q'_F$: $q' \prec q$ if and only if there is some rule (q, a, e) in A_p such that q' appears in e. From the construction of A_F, no state in Q'_F is recursive on A_F, and thus the reflective transitive closure $\prec^*$ of $\prec$ is a partial order. According to a topological ordering of $\prec^*$, starting from the smallest state, for each $q \in Q \times Q'_F$, do the equivalence transformation of A_p as follows: if the rule (q, a, e) exists in A_p, let Q_e be the set of states appearing in e. For each $Q' \subseteq Q_e$, create a new state $q_{Q'}$, and a new rule $(q_{Q'}, a, e')$ such that e' is the intersection RE of e and $(q_1'{}^+ \& \cdots \& q_m'{}^+)$ where $Q' = \{q'_1, \ldots, q'_m\}$. Moreover, for every rule (q', a', e') such that q appears in e', replace q in e' with $q_\emptyset \mid \cdots \mid q_{Q_e}$. The equivalence transformation eventually terminates because $\prec^*$ is a partial order. Let A_{dv} be the TA obtained by the equivalence transformation. By this transformation, for each state appearing on the label path HX or HY, the set of states assigned to their children position is fixed in any tree accepted by A_{dv}. Let $\hat{Q}_{dv} = \{\hat{q}_1, \ldots, \hat{q}_l\}$ be the set of the initial states of A_{dv}. For each initial state $\hat{q}_i \in \hat{Q}_{dv}$, the TA A_{dv}^i obtained by restricting the set of initial states to the singleton $\{\hat{q}_i\}$ is path fixed with respect to $f_1, \ldots, f_N$. We have that $TL(A) = TL(A_{dv}) = \bigcup_{1 \leq i \leq l} TL(A_{dv}^i)$ and $TL(A_{dv}^i) \cap TL(A_{dv}^j) = \emptyset$ for all i, j $(1 \leq i, j \leq l, i \neq j)$.

Implementation of Multiple Classifier System on MapReduce Framework for Intrusion Detection

Masataka Mizukoshi
Graduate School of Information Science and Technology
Hokkaido University Sapporo
Sapporo 060-0811, Japan
Email:m.mizukoshi@ist.hokudai.ac.jp

Bando Shintaro
Graduate School of Information Science and Technology
Hokkaido University Sapporo
Sapporo 060-0811, Japan
Email:dontforget3-7@ec.hokudai.ac.jp

Martin Schlueter
Information Initiative Center
Hokkaido University Sapporo
Sapporo 060-0811, Japan
Email: schlueter@midaco-solver.com

Masaharu Munetomo
Information Initiative Center
Hokkaido University Sapporo
Sapporo 060-0811, Japan
Email: munetomo@iic.hokudai.ac.jp

***Abstract*—Since the data volume from various facilities keeps growing rapidly in recent years, "big data" processing frameworks such as Hadoop have been developed as a scalable architecture to process large amount of data in cloud computing environment. We focus on intrusion detection problems which require large amount of data to be processed in order to detect malicious attacks. In this paper we discuss a Hadoop implementation of a multiple classifier system to enhance performances of the learning process in intrusion detection.**

I. Introduction

Currently, the amount of data that has to be processed by many companies has reached Petabytes and is expected to keep growing in the future. Under these circumstances, it is critical that these large amounts of data be efficiently treated. This requires that useful information be gleaned from such data. To do this, various Machine Learning approaches are being proposed. This is also true in the field of Intrusion Detection Systems (IDS). Many machine learning approaches have been proposed in the field of IDS. These approaches include Support Vector Machines (SVM), Neural Networks (NN), and classifier systems (see [1]-[5]). IDSs need to to analyze large-scale data quickly and respond promptly to any new intrusion detected. However, if machine learning is applied to large scale data, time becomes a critical issue.Here, we suggest an early learning technique by executing multiple classifier systems simultaneously (parallel) on Hadoop MapReduce framework (see [8],[9]). Classifier systems are valid for a variety of input environments. A multiple classifier system extends this concept to facilitate the processing of big data. Recently, classifier systems have been studied extensively as a powerful way to learn large-scale data. In this paper, a proposed implementation of such a multiple classifier system on the Hadoop MapReduce Framework is presented. Hadoop is an open source software for large-scale distributed data processing that enables users to easily perform distributed processing (see [10]).

II. Classifier Systems

Classifier systems are the learning process of rule-based machine learning system. They are composed of a set of rules, called a classifier, which consists of IF/THEN statements. The method by which a classifier system learns is described below (Fig. 1).

A. Flow of learning in a Classifier System

Classifier systems can roughly be divided into five modules: i) action module, ii) renumeration assignment module, iii) discovery module, iv) effector module, and v) detector module. A classifier system first converts the input from the environment to adapt it for use by the system. In the action module, the system determines the classifier that should act on the input data. In the renumeration assignment module, the classifiers chosen in the action module return some rewards for the classifiers. In the discovery module, a Genetic Algorithm (GA) is executed in order to receive a better population of classifiers.

In the action module, the system selects classifiers that match the input from the environment and move them into a message list. Classifiers have their own level of intensity. Classifiers that have a high intensity perform in the message list. When selecting an action classifier, we consider not only intensity but also the number of hashes (#). The method by which classifiers are chosen depends on the nature of the problem to be dealt with.

In the renumeration assignment module, a reward is assigned to the classifier population. The reward allocation method heavily influences learning efficiency. Let us now look at a typical reward allocation algorithm, called the bucket brigade algorithm.

If the reward is only assigned to the classifier that acted, a large deviation appears when learning with many test cases. It is therefore impossible to perform learning by considering the

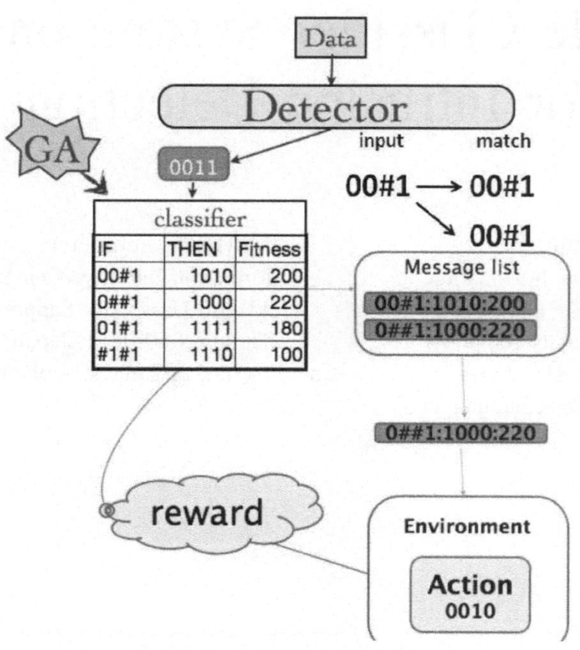

Fig. 1. Structure of a typical Classifier System

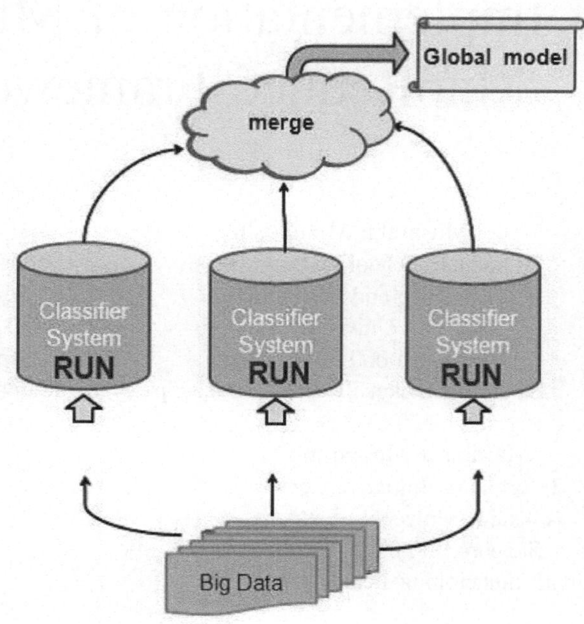

Fig. 2. Structure of a typical Multiple Classifier System

turn in which classifiers acted. The bucket brigade algorithm was proposed as a way to overcome this problem.
With the bucket brigade algorithm, the classifiers perform an auction market using the intensity of the classifiers and acquire their reward in this way. First, those classifiers that match the input from the environment are put in a message list. In this message list, the classifiers that act are chosen and classifiers pay intensity for the classifier leading to a matching. Only those classifiers that acted are kept in the message list, classifiers that did not act are excluded from the list. Therefore, those classifiers that remain in the list cause the next match. Thus, by causing matching continuously, renumeration can also be assigned to the classifier relevant to the classifier outputted to the environment.

In the discovery module, a GA is executed on a classifier population. GAs are approximative optimization algorithms inspired by the process of biological evolution. In GAs, the mechanisms of selection, intersection, and mutation are represented by operations on bit strings. In a classifier system, a classifier is considered to be a gene sequence (represented as a bit string) and a GA is used to manipulate this gene sequence. By performing the GA, a classifier population's flexibility is maintained and refined.

III. Flow of Learning in a Multiple Classifier System

In a multiple classifier system (MCS), input data is distributed to each machine and a classifier system is executed by each machine. One classifier population is made by the classifier from which it is shifted to execution by each machine and is summarized in one place. Although learning big data is attained in a short time using this method, the accuracy of the learning depends on the composition of the population collected in one place. Thus, the method that is used to conduct the merge is very important. The efficiency of learning changes significantly according to which classifier is entered into a population and which classifier is removed.

A. Merge technique

In the merge technique, classifiers, which are sent sequentially, are sorted by the system according to intensity and number of hashes (#) in order to make a high-quality population. The decision as to whether the system leaves a classifier that has a high correspondence power or a classifier that has high intensity is dependent on the learning objective or contents. The performance of the population changes in accordance with the kind of population constituted. There is no absolute way that is good to constitute a population from any kind of technique since many methods have been proposed. Figure 2 ilustrates the system-wide flow in a typical MCS (Fig. 2).

B. Bottlenecks in a multiple classifier system

It is required that an optimal classifier group be generated by a suitable merge method in an MCS, as mentioned above. Moreover, in order to obtain a better classifier and for group flexibility, it is necessary to generate to some extent a large group. In order that a problem does not arise here, a search may be conducted by the merge technique for a group that contains a new classifier. At this point the merge may take time, so that the collective size becomes large.

IV. Intrusion Detection System (IDS)

Intrusion detection is an adversarial classification task. In recent years, it has become necessary to use big data for learning of intrusion detection. To date, many types of machine learning techniques have been proposed for IDS. Nowadays, MCS are used for learning of intrusion detection, which leaves a track record. intrusion detection has two types of detection methods: anomaly detection and misuse detection. Misuse detection is based on a comparison of the current connection pattern with known attack patterns. In contrast to misuse detection, anomaly detection learns from normal patterns of connection. The two types of detection methods also have different respective features. Misuse detection has a low false positive rate and a high detection rate for known attack patterns. However, against new attack patterns it receives it is weak. Anomaly detection can detect new attacks, but it has a high false negative rate. In intrusion detection by machine learning, the anomaly method is used in many cases. The purpose of an IDS is to suppress the false positive rate and keep the false negative rate low. In our proposed system, the two types of detection methods, anomaly detection and misuse detection, are utilized by dividing the gathering as a result of the classifier system.

V. Proposed Implementation

A. Hadoop

Hadoop is an open source large-scale distributed processing software that uses the MapReduce Framework. Hadoop performs Terabyte to Petabyte levels of big data processing that ordinarily takes a lot of time and is not dependent on an expensive computer as the work is distributed over thousands of nodes comprising ordinary servers that can be obtained cheaply. By using the MapReduce Framework, underlying details and troublesome problems, such as data distribution, which must be solved in the usual distributed processing, failure processing, and load balancing are taken care of. Thus, parallel distributed processing can be performed easily. Hadoop comprises MapReduce and HDFS: Data distribution, node management, etc. are enabled by the Hadoop distributed file system (HDFS). Hadoop simplifies the construction of distributed processing programs. The typical layout of the Hadoop MapReduce Frameowork is depicted in Fig. 3.

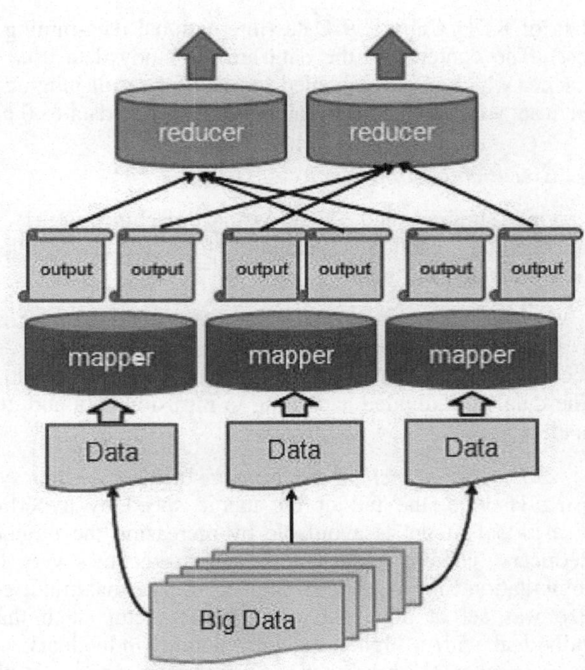

Fig. 3. Typical layout of the Hadoop MapReduce Framework

B. MapReduce Framework

A MapReduce Framework is divided into three phases: Map, Shuffle, and Reduce. By passing data to each phase using the value from the key/value pair, processing is performed by each phase. Users can carry out distributed processing by describing the processing in the Map and Reduce functions. In Map processing, the input data are received as key/value pairs and processing by analyzing the contents generates middle data in the form of key/value pairs. The generated data is gathered by key in Shuffle processing, and is sent to Reduce processing. In Reduce processing, the value processed for every key is generated and output as a result.

C. Mounting of the multiple classifier system on Hadoop

In Hadoop, classifier systems are individually mounted in Map processing and merge is performed in Reduce processing. The contents of mounting within each phase of processing is explained below.

1) Map processing: A classifier system is individually mounted in Map processing. A classifier is tagged by the kind of environment the classifier is matched to by setting this tag to key. The classifier is treated as value and outputted. The processesed classifier is outputted with a parameter such as intensity or others and is then sent to Shuffle processing.

2) Shuffle and Reduce processing: In Shuffle processing, data is classified according to the middle value generated by Shuffle processing for every tag, and the classified classifier is put into Reduce processing. In Reduce processing, merge is performed by each Reducer and a classifier population generated. In Hadoop, Reduce processing is also arranged in parallel by two or more machines. Therefore, if the number of Reducers increases,the computation time in the merging method is reduced.
A group corresponding to the inputs from various environments is generated by two or more groups classified according to the input from environment is generated. If a classification with a tag is increased and the number of Reducers is increased, the system can learn during the merge execution time even if in the whole group the number of individuals becomes large.
A group forms the colony of the classifier, which reacts to similar inputs so it is not subject to or influenced by learning advance of classifiers with a far relation. With this method, learning about rare inputs from which learning is seldom made repeatedly can be performed efficiently.

VI. Experiment

A. Object problem

In our experiment, a classifier system was built to study data for intrusion detection using the network communication data of KDD Cup 1999 Data (international data-mining contest). The contents of the data are the study data used by a teacher which is accompanied by data for result judging. The environment was set up by binary coding this data to 0 and 1.

B. Execution environment

One hundred and thirty virtual machines (VM) were launched on a CloudStack cloud platform and Hadoop version 1.0.4 mounted on them.

1) Key setup: An execution classifier was tagged according to the kind of input data it processes. Keys were setup according to attacks from 22 kinds of intrusion attack data. The data were divided according to intrusion data and groups made.

2) The merge method performed: In the classifier system using Hadoop, the fall of the merge speed by hypertrophy of a global model is avoidable by increasing the number of Reducers. Therefore, even if the group becomes very large, computation time is seldom influenced. The maximum global size was set at 500. The groups were setup such that an individual with a higher specialty nature (individuals with a small number of hashes, '#') might remain since it is highly possible to setup a maximum. In this experiment, classifiers were sorted using conditions 1 and 2:

1) Keep those classifiers with a low number of hashes, #'s, in the system.

2) If two classifiers have an identical number of hashes, #'s, keep the one with the higher intensity in the system.

VII. Experimental results

The system was mounted and two or more Mappers started learning in the multiple classifier system. Learning with a simple classifier system was compared with learning distributed with the MCS using the method outlined in Section IV.

The number of nodes used by the Mapper was varied from

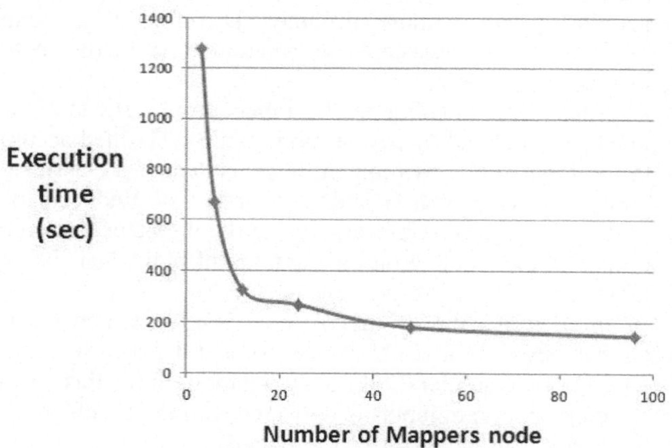

Fig. 4. Execution time versus number of Mappers

3 to 93 and execution time measured. The resulting execution time is depicted in Fig. 4. Block count was also changed in increments of 8 MB, 16 MB, 32 MB,... and so on in Hadoop, when distributing a file. Like the upper graph, it turned out

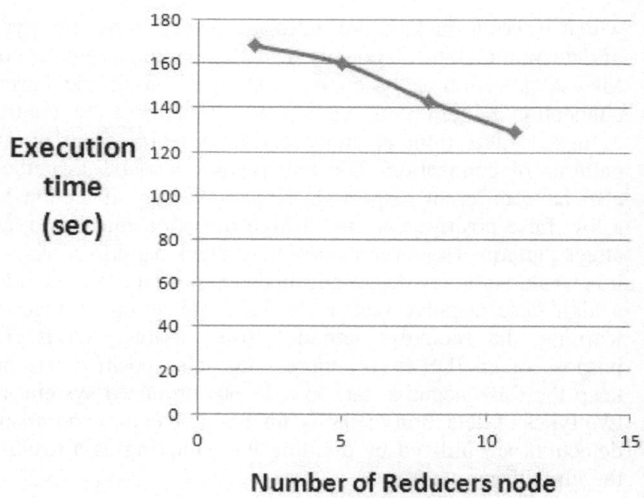

Fig. 5. Execution time versus number of Reducers

that execution time decreased linearly.

As shown in Fig. 5, execution time decreased as the number of Reducers increased. However, the change is not linear because the execution time resulting from the change in the number of Reducers is influenced by the items of learning data.

Next, we examined the change in the accuracy of learning in terms of the change in the number of nodes. Here, the accuracy is determined by the probability of the classifier group generated to learn and judge a result correctly according to the test data.

Figure 6 illustrates learning accuracy with respect to the

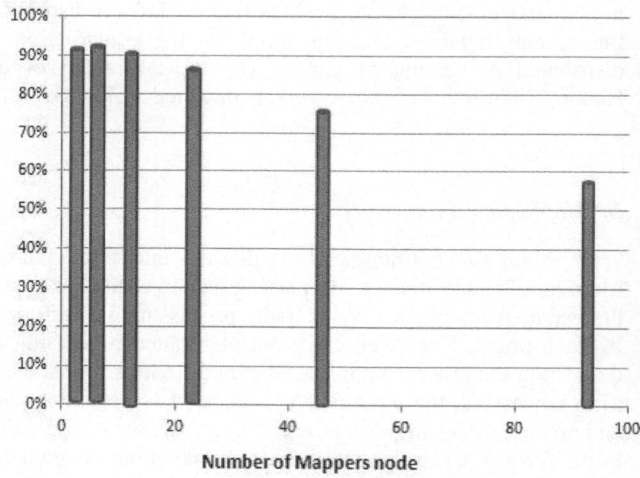

Fig. 6. Accuracy of learning versus number of Mappers.

number of Mappers. If the number of Mappers is increased by too much, a state will be reached where there is hardly any learning. Also, if a file is divided too much, learning by each machine will become insufficient, and as a result, the overall learning rate will fall. In this experiment, the size of the learning data used was 740 MB. The accuracy of the learning became low for sizes smaller than 64 MB. Thus, it was necessary to search the MCS on Hadoop to determine the optimal file assignment size.

Next, learning with a simple classifier system was compared with learning using our proposed MCS technique.

The column on the right of the graph shows learning with

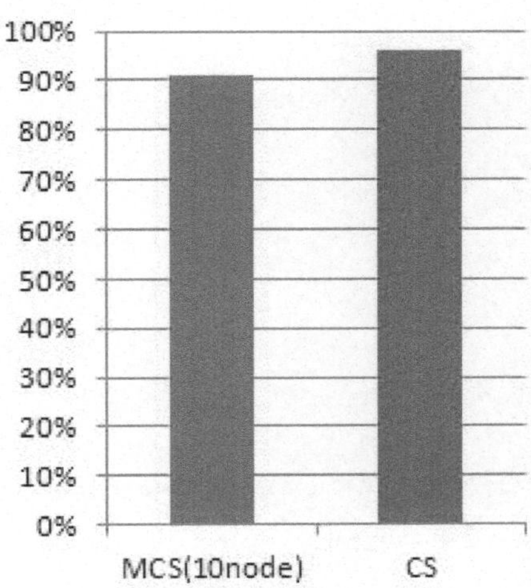

Fig. 7. Accuracy of learning in simple and multiple classifier systems

the simple classifier system, while that on the left represents learning by our proposed MCS. As can be seen in the graph, the accuracy of the overall learning fell in the MCS. Since a classifier system is what is originally risen and learned in one classifier group, when it merges, as the whole group's work, it is inferior to the simple classifier system.

The pie chart depicted in Fig. 8 illustrates the items of learning data used in the experiment. In the learning data used (740 MB), attack intrusion data of a very rare kind comprising only about 20 KB (less than 1 % of the whole), such as guess passed and nmap, was included. Next, we examined how the learning rate varied with the small amount of attack data (Fig. 9). It was difficult for the above data to update the learning

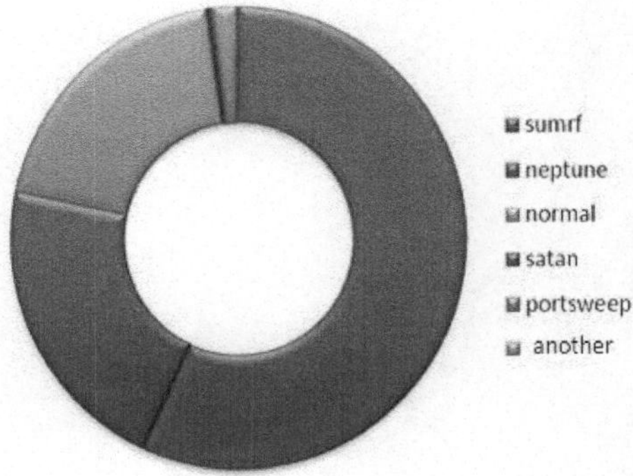

Fig. 8. Learning data items, displayed according to their proportional likelihood to be attacked.

intensity of the simple classifier system. Because there was the possibility of obtaining learning by other inputs, leaking and being removed from a group was high, so there was hardly any learning. However, in our proposed technique, since the classifier was gathered by distributing classifiers that received and reacted to each small input in learning to each Reducer,

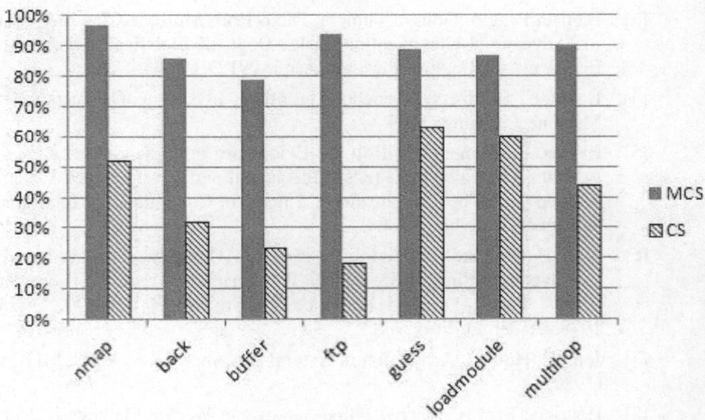

Fig. 9. Left: Learning of multiple classifier system. Right: Learning of simple classifier system

it was possible to keep the learning rate high.

VIII. Conclusion

Learning by a multiple classifier system, compared with learning with a simple classifier system, can significantly reduce the learning time and the effectiveness of the learning method on large-scale problem data sets. Moreover, a time reduction in the merge process was gained when executing the proposed multiplier classifier system on the Hadoop Map Reduce framework. However, it turns out that some accuracy of learning is lost when using a MCS. In order to raise the accuracy of learning, we have to consider a better merging method and to further study the method of classifiers. When learning data was distributed, It turned out, that the optimal distribution of data is problematic. Learning by each machine is inefficient, if the processed data is too small. Also, one has to be careful with splitting data where the distribution of important of data is unknown.To consider that Hadoop divides a data file automatically, it seems that this issue becomes a big subject to the proposed technique.

By the proposed technique, it was possible to learn without leaking small input data. Even in large scale data, the proposed technique was able to learn in a reasonable fast time without leaking small input data.

Recently, an improvement of the MCS technique, such as sharing classifiers and other parameters between individual machines, has been proposed (see [2]). Such improvements seems also to be promising for our proposed technique and should be investigated further in the future.

Acknowledgement

This work is supported by KAKENHI (No.22500196), Japan Society for the Promotion of Science.

References

[1] Igino Corona, Roberto Tronci, Giorgio Giacinto. A Multiple Classifier System for the Protection of Web Services. 21st International Conference on Pattern Recognition (ICPR 2012).

[2] Szymon Sztajer, Michal Wozniak. Untrained Multiple Classifier System for Designing Security Scanner for Web Applications. 5th International Conference on Information and Automation for Sustainability (ICIAFs), 2010.

[3] Battista Biggio, Goirgio Fumera, Fabio Roli. Multiple Classifier System for Adversarial Classification Tasks. Dept. of Electrical and Electronic Eng, Univ. of Cagliari Piazza d'Armi, 09123 Cagliari, Italy.

[4] David E. Goldberg.: Genetic Algorithms in search, Optimization and Machine Learning. 1989

[5] Biggio, B., Fumera, G., Roli, F.: Evide hard multiple classifier systems. In:Okun, O., Valentini,G.(eds.) Supervised and Unsupervised Ensemble Methods and Their Applications. Studies in Computational Intelligence. Springer, Heidelberg. 2009.

[6] John H. Holland and Judith S. Reitman. Cognitive systems based on adaptive algorithms. In Donald A. Waterman and Frederick Hayes-Roth, editors, Pattern-Directed Inference Systems, pages 313-329, Orlando, 1978.Academic Press.

[7] John H. Holand, Adaptation in Natural and Artificial Systems, MIT Press (1989)

[8] Henrique Santos, Manuel Filipe Santos and Wesley Mathew, University of Minho, Portugal, Supervised Learning Classifier System For Grid Data Mining.2009

[9] Tajai Terano, Hasnat Elias Mohammad Abu, Mhd Irvan. Acquiring Plant Operation Knowledge through Learning Classifier Systems. 2011

[10] Tom White. Hadoop. O'Reilly Media, 2010.

[11] Future view: Web navigation based on learning user's browsing patterns. 2003

[12] Apache CloudStack, available at: http://incubator.apache.org/cloudstack/ (2013)

[13] Apache Hadoop, available at: http://hadoop.apache.org (2013)

A Change of Order Balance Implies Intraday Price Trend in Japanese Stock Market

Hwion YOON

CMD Laboratory Inc.
1-3-2, Sendagaya, Shibuya-ku, Tokyo, Japan
yoon@cmdlab.co.jp

***Abstract*— This paper focuses on the relation between order book condition and price movement. The presented model is applicable to making trading strategies during the day and to estimating them in the Japanese stock market. Nevertheless, it is difficult to reveal the absolute mechanism of the financial market. We find that the information on order books are more meaningful in constructing a trading strategy rather than the information from traded prices and volume data. Particularly, a change of the balance on order book implies price trend not only in a moment, but also over a certain period, due to a memory effect. Additionally, it is indicated that thinning out data is still good enough to study intraday market movement, even if there are many HFT order flows. We can recognize that HFT requires algorithmic trade, but algorithmic trade does not require HFT.**

***Keywords*— Order Book, Ita, Stock Market, Market Impact, Algorithmic Trade, High Frequency Trade, Intraday movement.**

I. INTRODUCTION

The price in financial markets seems to be determined when the quantity of demand which buyers wish and the quantity of supply which sellers wish balance. Although the sense that market mechanism balances demand and supply is common in economics, the price is not necessarily determined from the result of demand and supply in real financial markets, particularly in intraday movement. In the Japanese equity market, the price is caused from balancing demand and supply directly at the market opening and closing, but the price is not determined by the excess demand or excess supply during the trading hours.

This paper shows that the methodology that approximates the demand or the supply with a power function during the trading hours in Japanese equity market is effective. Using the approximation model by a power function, we discuss the influence on a subsequent price change from the change of a demand-supply balance on an order book. A change of demand-supply balance on an order book may serve as an information source in an algorithmic trade or HFT. Finally, we refer why order book information is so important for regarding the relation between algorithmic trade and HFT.

II. ORDER BOOK AND INTRADAY PRICE MOVEMENTS IN JAPANESE STOCK MARKET

In the Japanese equity market, opening price and closing price are determined by the Ita-yose methodology. The Ita-yose methodology is a system in which the price and the trading volume are determined by the intersection of a demand curve and a supply curve just before a certain time, such as opening or closing. In Japanese, the order book table is called "Ita" and the matching is called "Yose", so we say Ita-yose for demand-supply matching. On the other hand, a market participant trades for Ita shown as Fig.1 during intraday-trading hours. We call this price and trading volume determinant system "Zaraba". The key issue for the difference between Ita-yose and Zaraba is that the Ita-yose system reflects demand-supply, but Zaraba does not. On the Zaraba system, one market participant watches Ita, then he or she decides to trade at bid or ask. Depending on the order book information, he or she may get aggressive or hesitate to trade. This means intraday movement is caused from the information of demand-supply situation, not from demand-supply condition directly.

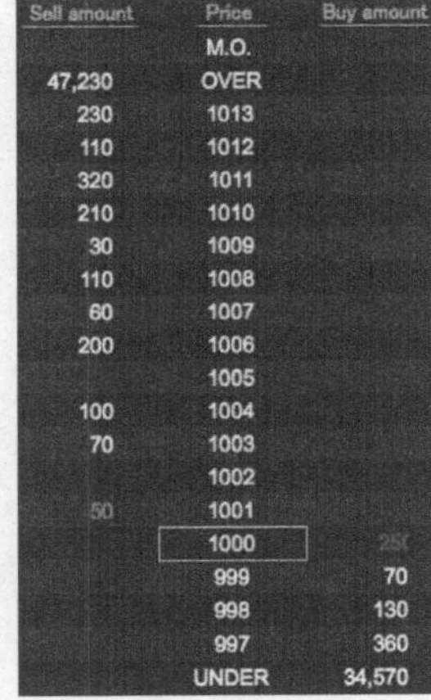

Sell amount	Price	Buy amount
	M.O.	
47,230	OVER	
230	1013	
110	1012	
320	1011	
210	1010	
30	1009	
110	1008	
60	1007	
200	1006	
	1005	
100	1004	
70	1003	
	1002	
50	1001	
	1000	25[illegible]
	999	70
	998	130
	997	360
	UNDER	34,570

Fig. 1 Order book, "Ita" illustrated by Tokyo Stock Exchange

III. THE MODEL OF MARKET IMPACT

In order to recognize the information of demand-supply situation, a real Ita sample is shown in Fig.2. It is a snap shot of the Sony order book at 9:00:01 on Feb 15th, 2012. Buy orders are positioned on the right hand side, and sell orders on the left hand side. The black bar indicates immediate executable price range where one order can make a price push up or down. The range is calculated from the current market price. In case of Fig.2, the current price is 1526, and the range corresponding to it is 80 yen, so one order may trigger to push the price up or down 5.24%.

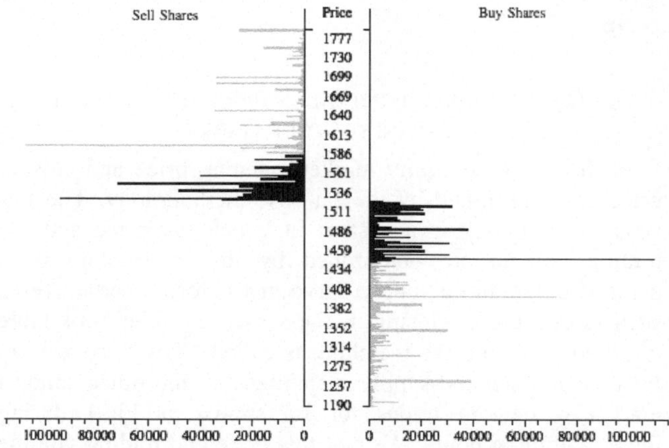

Fig. 2 A snap shot of Sony's Ita at 10:00:02 on Feb. 15th, 2012

Focusing on the range, we can draw a market impact curve that indicates the cost for the number of trading shares. Fig.3 shows two impact curves for the market, one for the buyer and one for the seller. The horizontal axis is the order quantity, and the vertical axis is the trading cost. For example, if you wish to buy 500,000 shares of Sony stock at 10:00:02 on Feb. 15th, 2012, your buying cost should be 1535.99 yen from the Ita condition. It should be noticed that impact curve indicates the cost not market price.

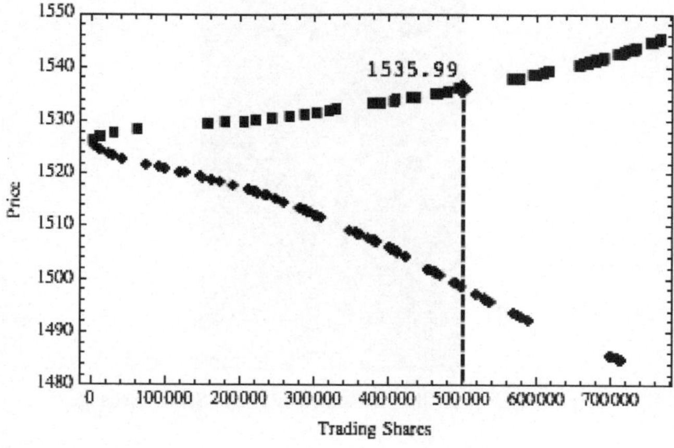

Fig. 3 A snap shot of Sony's Ita curves at 10:00:02 on Feb. 15th, 2012

Observing a snap shot data of Ita, we can approximate the curve, (1) as a liner function, (2) as an exponential function, and (3) as a power function.

$$impact = a \cdot S \quad (1)$$

$$impact = a \cdot \exp(b \cdot S) \quad (2)$$

$$impact = a \cdot S^c \quad (3)$$

In the function, S is trading shares, impact = Abs[executed price – current price], a is a scale coefficient, b is a exponential coefficient, c is a power low coefficient.

Corresponding to curves in Fig.3, these 3 approximated curves are shown in Fig.4. A intraday movement in financial market is so unstable that these coefficient numbers are variable, even triggered by one order.

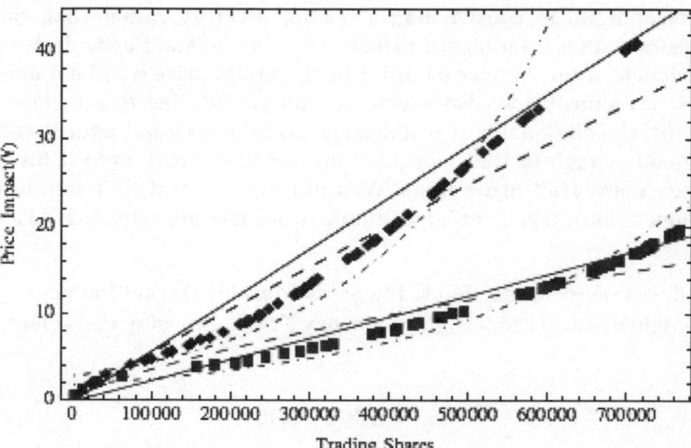

Fig. 4 Approximating function curves for snap shot of Sony's Ita

Here, approximating functions are follows;

A. *Approximating Impact Functions in Buying(Red lines)*
   1) *The liner Approximation (the red line)*
      $impact = 0.0000245 \times S$, R^2=0.97
   2) *The Exponential Approximation(the red dashed lines)*
      $impact = 1.93 \times \exp(0.0000032 \times S)$, R^2=0.91
   3) *The Power Approximation (the red dot-dashed lines)*
      $impact = 0.00105 \times S^{0.711}$, R^2=0.93

B. *Approximating Impact Functions in Selling(Blue lines)*
   4) *The liner Approximation (the blue line)*
      $impact = 0.0000589 \times S$, R^2=0.98
   5) *The Exponential Approximation(the blue dashed lines)*
      $impact = 2.93 \times \exp(0.0000045 \times S)$, R^2=0.87

6) *The Power Approximation (the blue dot-dashed lines)*

$$impact = 0.000137 \times S^{0.923}, \quad R^2=0.97$$

Considering the variable market conditions and mathematical reason that the function should pass through point zero, the exponential function or the power function is better than the liner function. Analyzing for empirical data, the power function seems to be suitable for the approximating function for market impacts. Finally we propose the market impact model as follows;

$$impact_i(S,t) = a_i(t) \cdot S(t)^{C_i(t)} \qquad (4)$$

Here, i is a dummy index for recognizing stock, S is trading shares, t is a time parameter.

IV. The Empirical study for Japanese equity market

A. Data

Tokyo Stock Exchange, Inc. calculates market impact parameters, a_i in buying impact, C_i in buying impact, a_i in selling impact, C_i in selling impact, and publishes them every 5 seconds on the web site "TSE Market Impact View."

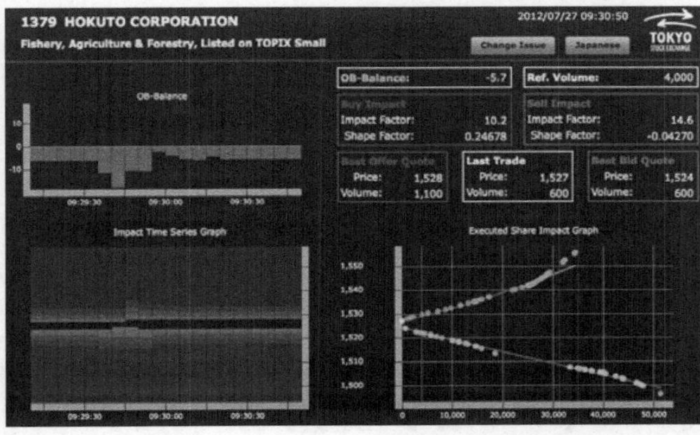

Fig. 5 TSE Market Impact View

TSE also calculates Ita balance data by the following definition.

$$\Delta_B = I_B^{buy} - I_B^{sell} = \log\left(S_B^{buy} S_B^{sell} / (P^{mid})^2\right) \qquad (5)$$

Here, I_B^{buy} is buyer's impact at basic trading shares, I_B^{sell} is seller's impact at basic trading shares, S_B^{buy} is basic trading shares on buyer's, S_B^{sell} is basic trading shares on seller's, P^{mid} is mid price, and basic trading shares are 10% of total shares within the immediate executable range on yesterday's Ita. We show Sony's intraday price movement and Ita balance movement on Feb. 15th, 2012 in Fig.6 as one example. The horizontal axis is time, the left vertical axis is stock price, and the right vertical axis is the degree of Ita balance in which plus values indicate more buyer' s order shares and minus values do more seller's order shares on Ita. The mid dot line separates the morning session and the afternoon session at 11:30 am (the morning session close) or 12:30 pm (the afternoon session open).

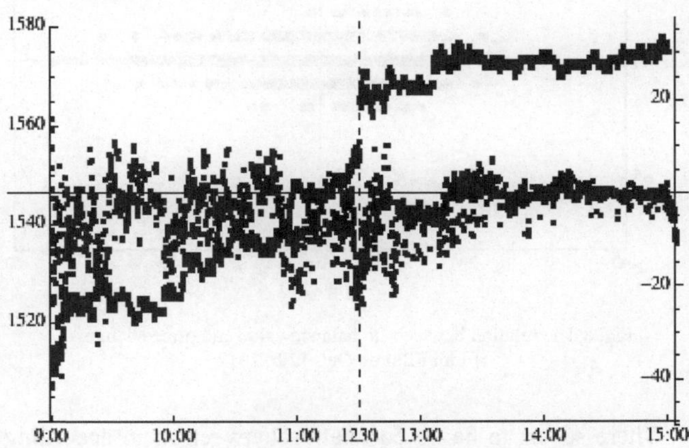

Fig. 6 Intraday price movement and Ita balance movement of Sony on Feb. 15th, 2012

B. Observing the relation between Ita balance value and price movement

First, simply we observe the relation between Ita balance value and price movement of the next 5 seconds.

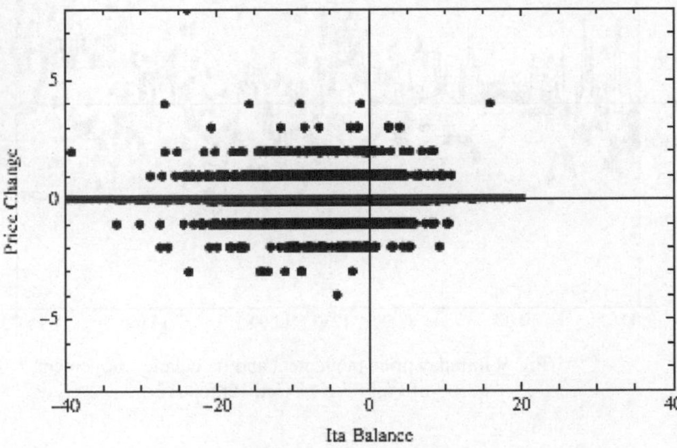

Fig. 7 The relation between Ita balance value and price change of Sony on Feb. 15th, 2012

Fig.7 shows the case of Sony on Feb. 15th, 2012. The red line is the linear regression as follow;

$$PriceChange = 0.000320 \times S + 0.0197, \quad R^2=0.0000072$$

Fig. 8 shows a case of Fuji Film on Oct. 12th, 2012, and Fig.9 shows intraday movement for Fuji Film on the day, which are picked just as an example. The linear regression is;

$$PriceChange = 0.000188 \times S + 0.0018, \quad R^2 = 0.0000140$$

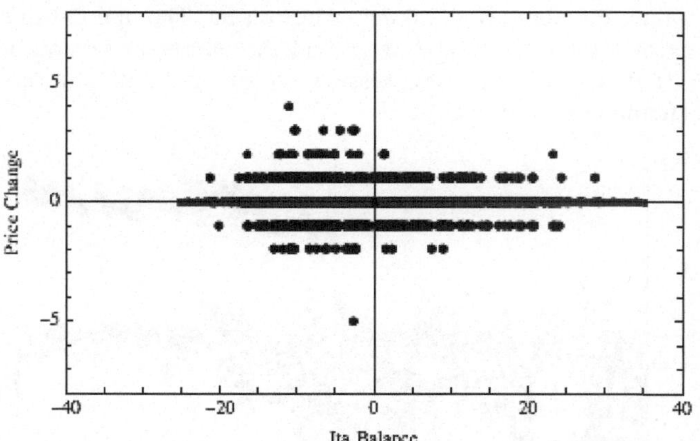

Fig. 8 The relation between Ita balance value and price change of Fuji Film on Oct. 12th, 2012

There seems to be no correlation between them according to Fig.7 and Fig.8. However, the most of market participants strongly believe that some relation exists and that market movement is not random walk. On the next section, we discuss the issue whether the relation between order conditions and price movements exist.

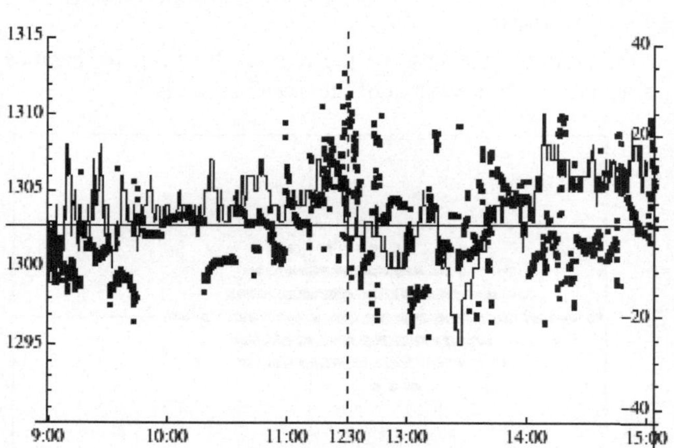

Fig. 9 Intraday price movement and Ita balance movement of Fuji Film on Oct. 12th, 2012

C. *Discussion for Ita balance*

If we accept the above previous pictures, the quantity of demand and supply seems to make no effect on the market. The key point in how we discuss their situations is that we should stand on a market participant's point of view. In case of the situation that there are many big selling orders on Ita, a buyer tends to wait and see the market situation. However in case of the situation that selling orders are decreasing, the buyer changes his or her attitude to pay more tension towards Ita and he ore she may buy immediately. It means the Ita balance value itself is not so important, but the change of the Ita balance value should be more focused on.

Considering the above reaction, we observe the relation between the change of Ita balance value and price movement in Fig. 10 and Fig. 11.

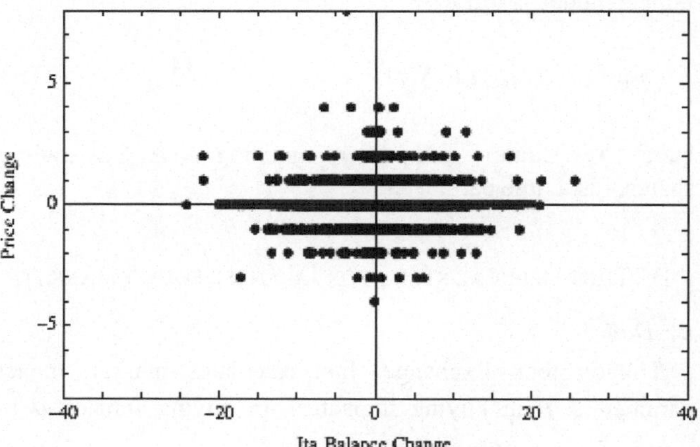

Fig. 10 The relation between the change of Ita balance value and price change of Sony on Feb. 15th, 2012

Here, the red line is the linear regression as follow;

$$PriceChange = -0.000557 \times S + 0.0189, \quad R^2 = 0.0000077$$

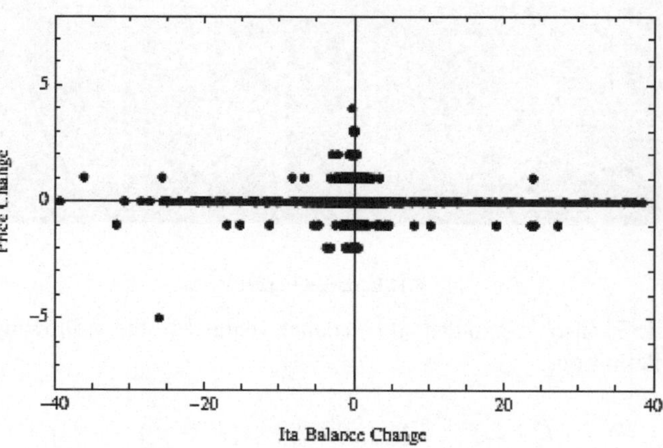

Fig. 11 The relation between the change of Ita balance value and price change of Fuji Film on Oct. 12th, 2012

Here, the red line is the linear regression as follow;

$$PriceChange = 0.000809 \times S + 0.0014, \quad R^2 = 0.0000509$$

Comparing Fig. 7 with Fig.10 and Fig.8 with Fig.11, it is difficult to recognize the obvious correlation between them.

Based on the above results, we try to apply a statistical test on them in order to find out whether the correlation between Ita balance and price movement exists or not.

D. The Kendall rank correlation test

Regarding intraday movement in financial market, price movement is not a random walk, so we should not premise normal distribution for price change. In this case, we should make a non parametric statistical test, then choose the Kendall rank correlation test in order to find out whether there is a correlation between Ita balance and price movement. The test process is as follows;

1) Null Hypothesis H_0: population correlation coefficient is Zero.

2) Alternatives H_1 : population correlation coefficient is not Zero.

3) Test Statistics : $T = \dfrac{|r_k|}{\sqrt{\dfrac{4n+10}{9n(n-1)}}}$

n = sample size (= 3600), r_k is Kendall's rank correlation coefficient.

4) Critical region : $\alpha = 0.05, Z(\alpha/2) = 1.96$

5) Calculate : We calculate 2 pair of Test Statistics T of 10 stocks' intraday data. One is the pair of Ita balance - price change on next 5 seconds, and the other one is the pair of Ita balance change and price change on next 5 seconds just after Ita balance change, for each day from Jan. 4th, 2012 to Dec. 28th, 2012.

V. THE RESULTS OF STATISTICAL TEST

The calculated results are shown as Table.1. There are 248 trading days in 2012, but stock trading may have suspended time due to huge amount of in-balanced order, so available data shown in the mid column is not the same among them.

The results indicate 3 points as follows;

1. The correlation between Ita balance and price movement may be observed only less than 30%, but it seems to exist.
2. The correlation between the change of Ita balance and price movement may be more observable than Ita balance itself on each stock.
3. The change of Ita balance seems to be more useful information to predict intraday price movement, compared to Ita balance value.

TABLE I
THE RESULTS OF STATISTIC TEST

			Ita balance and Price movement	**Ita balance Change and Price movement**
Code	**Stock Name**	**number of data**	**number of Reject H_0**	**number of Reject H_0**
1379	Hokuto	247	41	72
1925	Daiwa House	243	44	89
2801	Kikkoma	246	73	84
3401	Teijin	210	1	50
4901	FujiFilm	230	35	50
6301	Komatsu	210	21	41
6758	Sony	212	13	45
7201	Nissan	217	5	65
8802	Mitsubishi Est.	233	69	49
9432	NTT	203	2	36

VI. DISCISSONS AND CONCLUSIONS

Although market demand and supply seem to influence market price movement, it is difficult to find out the obvious correlation between shares on order book and price movement.

The main reason why it is hard to see the correlation is un-stability on intraday trading circumstances. It is very common to trigger jumps or collapses by one order in the financial market, so the correlation as a linearity measure often disappears.

The other reason is the features of time dependency. Normally a market, just after opening, is more volatile compared to the other time periods. It means market condition is not a homogeneity, particularly during the intraday trading periods. As we calculate the correlation using whole intraday data, statistical figures sometimes eliminate the important property.

Today, information flow in the financial market is numerous and micro second movement occurs. It causes the idea that high-speed responses are necessary to trade. However, it is more important to recognize the current condition in market. Without recognition of the market condition, high-speed is meaningless. The essential matter should be to analyze the market features, and to reflect for trading strategy. A trading strategy is often realized by algorithmic trade, because it is necessary to manage huge information flows. After constructing management framework to trade, HFT technology gives us value-added methodology, not before. HFT is an addition to the last.

This paper concludes that focusing on the change of Ita balance seems to be better than Ita balance value itself. Even the degree of the correlation between Ita information and price information is limited, but the relation exists, and it has a possibility to develop dynamic algorithm trading strategies.

Lastly, we mention Ita information is suitable for HFT. Since Ita information is the current condition data, high-speed response needs the information which imply market conditions. Lastly, executed price and traded volume are data in of the past. HFT should require the current information rather than the past information.

REFERENCES

[1] N. Bershova, and D. Rakhlin, The Non-Linear Market Impact of Large Trades: Evidence from Buy-Side Order Flow, Journal of Investment Strategies, Vol. 2, No. 2, Spring, 2013, p. 25-69
[2] N. Taleb, "The Black Swan," Random House, 2007.
[3] K. Gopal, "100 STATISTICAL TESTS," SAGE Publications, 2006.

Poisson Observed Image Restoration using a Latent Variational Approximation with Gaussian MRF

Hayaru SHOUNO[1] Masato Okada[2]

[1] Graduate School of Informatics and Engineering, University of Electro-Communications, Chofugaoka 1-5-1, Chofu, JAPAN

[2] Graduate School of Frontier Sciences, The University of Tokyo, 5-1-5 Kashiwanoha, Kashiwa, 277-8561, Japan.

[3] RIKEN BSI, 2-1 Hirosawa, Wako, 351-0198, Japan.

Abstract— *We treat an image restoration problem throughout a Poisson noise channel. The Poisson randomness might be appeared in observation of low contrast object, and its variable takes discrete and positive value. The Poisson noise observation is often hard to treat in a theoretical analysis. In our formulation, we interpret the Poisson noise channel observation as a Bernoulli process, and apply a latent variable method to transform the observation as a Gaussian process with single latent variable. We formulate the image restoration problem as a Bayesian approach, and introduce a Gaussian Markov random field as its prior. The latent parameters and Poisson parameters are treated as hyper-parameters, and we infer them in the expectation maximization framework.*

Keywords: Poisson noise, Bayes inference, Image restoration, Latent variational method

1. Introduction

The techniques of the noise reducing, which is called image restoration in the field of digital image processing, is an important in the meaning of the pre-processing.

From the theoretical view of Bayesian image restoration, additive white Gaussian noise (AWGN) was mainly discussed as the image corrupting process. However, in the real world, the noise corruption process could not be described as such Gaussian process. For example, night photograph must treat low contrast object observation as a Poisson process. In this study, we treat image restoration with the Poisson corruption process in the manner of the Bayesian approach.

Assuming Gaussian Markov random field as a prior of Bayes inference, Poisson corruption process makes difficult to derive posterior probability in analytic form, since the Poisson variable take discrete and non-negative value. Thus,

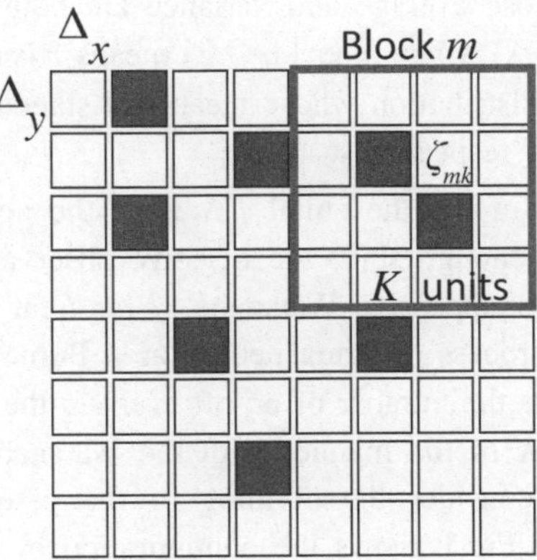

Fig. 1: Schematic diagram of the relationship between Poisson and Bernoulli observation. The large rectangles shows the pixel block and small indicates the minimum event unit which can describe only two-state, that is on-off events.

we introduce a latent variational approximation in the inference derivation [1][2][3]. In this study, we transform the Poisson corruption process as the corresponding Bernoulli process, and introduce the latent variable to approximate the Poisson process as the Gaussian process[3]. Once, we get the corresponding Gaussian process, we can infer the posterior probability easily. In this formulation, we introduce several latent parameters, so that, we should infer them. In order to solve the problem, we introduce a expectation maximization (EM) algorithm as a inference engine.

2. Formulation

2.1 Image Observation process

The digital image is defined by the 2-dimensional array of pixels, and each pixel has some value. Considering Poisson noise corruption means the pixel have some parameter, and the observation is obtained by stochastic process under the parameter. Let us consider to assign the parameter $\rho\Delta$ and derive the Poisson random variable z can be denoted as

$$p(z \mid \rho\Delta) = \frac{(\rho\Delta)^z}{z!} \exp(-\rho\Delta),$$

which means the number of observed photons dropping into the pixel. The Poisson noise corruption process appears in the low contrast object observation such like night photograph, and some kind of computed tomography such like positron emission tomography (PET). Assuming large parameter of $\rho\Delta$, this corruption process can be approximated by the additive white Gaussian noise (AWGN) corruption process, whose average and variance are both $\rho\Delta$, that is $\mathcal{N}(z \mid \rho\Delta, \rho\Delta)$ where $\mathcal{N}(x \mid m, \sigma^2)$ means x is generated by the normal distribution whose mean and standard deviation are m and σ respectively.

However, in the the small $\rho\Delta$ area, the approximation is not good enough since the negative observation value z is sometimes appeared. Watanabe *et al.* treat the Poisson corruption process of firing neuron as a Bernoulli process, which counts the number of on-off event in the proper time bins [3].ãĂĂ In the manner with the Watanabe's method, we should consider the dividing of the pixel area with miniregions. Fig.1 shows the configuration of the dividing system. The thick large rectangle shows the pixel area size. On the other hand, the small rectangles show the miniregions which have $\Delta_x\Delta_y = \Delta$ area sizes, so that one pixel include several miniregions. We assume each miniregion has only information of on-off event which means a photon drop into the miniregion or not. We consider the image have M pixels and denote the pixel index as m. Each pixel has K miniregions whose index is denoted as k. And (m, k)-th miniregion have an event value $\zeta_{mk} = \pm 1$. The $\zeta_{mk} = +1$ means the photon count is on, and $\zeta_{mk} = -1$ is off. Assuming the on-event probability in the pixel m is uniform as $\rho_m\Delta$, we can define the observation probability as

$$p(\zeta_{mk} \mid \rho_m) = (\rho_m\Delta)^{\frac{1+\zeta_{mk}}{2}} (1 - \rho_m\Delta)^{\frac{1-\zeta_{mk}}{2}}. \quad (1)$$

In the observation, each pixel value z_m can be defined as the sum of the whole on-events in the pixel:

$$p(z_m \mid \{\zeta_{mk}\}) = \delta\left(z_m - \sum_k \frac{\zeta_{mk} + 1}{2}\right), \quad (2)$$

where $\delta(\cdot)$ denotes Kronecker's function. Our interest in the causality of the parameter ρ_m for the observed value z_m. Hence, we derive the probability by marginalization:

$$p(z_m \mid \rho_m) = \sum_{\{\zeta_{mk}\}} p(z_m \mid \{\zeta_{mk}\}) \prod_{k=1}^{K} p(\zeta_d mk \mid \rho_m\Delta) \quad (3)$$

$$= \binom{K}{z_m} (\rho_m\Delta)^{z_m} (1 - \rho_m\Delta)^{K - z_m}. \quad (4)$$

In this formulation, we can confirm the eq.(4) converges to the Poisson process,

$$p(z_m \mid \rho_m) = \frac{(\rho_m\Delta)^{z_m}}{z_m!} \exp(-\rho_m\Delta), \quad (5)$$

in the limit of $K \to \infty$ with keeping $\rho_m\Delta \ll 1$.

In the following analysis, the non-negative parameter ρ_m is not enough tractable, so that we apply the logit transform in the manner of the Watanabe *et al.*[3]. The logit transform from ρ_m to x_m is denoted as

$$x_m = \frac{1}{2} \ln \frac{\rho_m\Delta}{1 - \rho_m\Delta}, \quad (6)$$

and we can also denote the inverted transform from x_m to ρ_m as

$$\rho_m\Delta = \frac{e^{x_m}}{2\cosh(x_m)}. \quad (7)$$

Thus, we can rewrite the Poisson noise corruption $p(z_m \mid \rho_m) = \frac{(\rho_m\Delta)^{z_m}}{z_m!} e^{-\rho_m\Delta}$ as the conditional probability

$$p(z_m|x_m) = \sum_{\{\zeta_{mk}\}} p(z_m|\{\zeta_{mk}\}) \prod_k p(\zeta_{mk} \mid x_m) \quad (8)$$

$$= \binom{K}{z_m} \exp((2z_m - K)x_m - K \ln 2\cosh x_m). \quad (9)$$

Thus, the image restoration problem can be interpreted as the inference from the observation z_m to the parameter x_m.

2.2 Prior probability

Introducing the Bayesian inference requires several prior probability for the image. In this study, we assume some kinds of Gaussian Markov random field (GMRF). GMRF, which is defined in collection of the neighborhoods pixel value pairs, can be denoted as the multidimensional Gaussian distribution, so that it can be applied in the theoretic analysis[4]. Usually, GMRF is defined by the sum of neighborhood differential square $\sum \|\rho_m - \rho_n\|^2$ where ρ_m and ρ_n are neighborhood pixel values. Thus, the only difference of these values $\rho_m - \rho_n$ are effective, but the absolute values are not effective in the GMRF. In this study, however, we define the parameter of the prior as $\{x_m\}$, which are logit-transformed values for $\{\rho_m\}$. Hence the absolute value

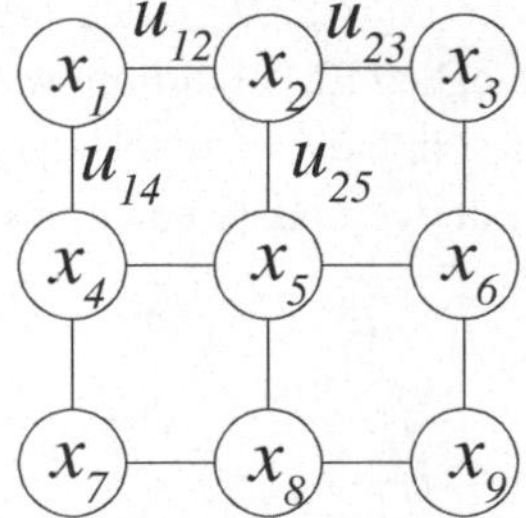

Fig. 2: Prior Probability under a Markov random field (MRF) we introduced. Under the MRF prior, the neighbor units values x_m and x_n are controlled to take similar values. The absolute values of cause different effect since they are defined in the logit-transformed space. Thus, we introduce a compensate value u_{mn} for each bond.

of x_m are effective when we define the GMRF with the difference $x_m - x_n$ where x_m and x_n are neighbor parameter values. Thus we introduce a compensate value u_{mn} for each neighborhood. We define the energy function of the prior as

$$H_{\text{pri}}(\boldsymbol{x}) = \frac{1}{2}\sum_{(m,n)}((x_m - x_n) - u_{mn})^2 \tag{10}$$

$$p(\boldsymbol{x}) = \exp\left(-\alpha H_{\text{pri}}(\boldsymbol{x})\right), \tag{11}$$

where (m, n) means the neighborhood pixel indices. The prior corresponding to the energy function can denote as

$$p(\boldsymbol{x} \mid \alpha, \boldsymbol{\mu}) \propto \exp\left(-\frac{\alpha}{2}(\boldsymbol{x}-\boldsymbol{\mu})^{\mathrm{T}}\Lambda(\boldsymbol{x}-\boldsymbol{\mu})\right), \tag{12}$$

, where $Lambda$ is a correlation matrix, since eq.(11) is a quadratic form of $\{x_m\}$. Fig. 2 shows the simple example of our GMRF configuration in 3×3 pixels image. In this case, the image has 9 pixels, so that, the $Lambda$ in the eq.(12) becomes a constant 9×9 matrix,

$$\Lambda = \begin{pmatrix} 2 & -1 & 0 & -1 & 0 & 0 & 0 & 0 & 0 \\ -1 & 3 & -1 & 0 & -1 & 0 & 0 & 0 & 0 \\ 0 & -1 & 2 & 0 & 0 & -1 & 0 & 0 & 0 \\ -1 & 0 & 0 & 3 & -1 & 0 & -1 & 0 & 0 \\ 0 & -1 & 0 & -1 & 4 & -1 & 0 & -1 & 0 \\ 0 & 0 & -1 & 0 & -1 & 3 & 0 & 0 & -1 \\ 0 & 0 & 0 & -1 & 0 & 0 & 2 & -1 & 0 \\ 0 & 0 & 0 & 0 & -1 & 0 & -1 & 3 & -1 \\ 0 & 0 & 0 & 0 & 0 & -1 & 0 & -1 & 2 \end{pmatrix}. \tag{13}$$

When we denote the edge differential values u_{mn} as $\boldsymbol{u}$, the relationship between $\boldsymbol{\mu}$ and $\boldsymbol{u}$ can be written as

$$\Lambda\boldsymbol{\mu} = \begin{pmatrix} \sum_{n \in B(1)} u_{1n} \\ \vdots \\ \sum_{n \in B(m)} u_{mn} \\ \vdots \\ \sum_{n \in B(9)} u_{9n} \end{pmatrix}, \tag{14}$$

where $B(m)$ means the collection of pixels connected to the m-th pixels. Anyway, inferring the $\boldsymbol{\mu}$ is required and sufficient for image restoration, so that, we only consider the parameter $\boldsymbol{\mu}$ in the following.

Considering the prior eq.(12), the inference sometimes unstable since the determinant of the accuracy matrix $\alpha Lambda$ is 0. So that, we introduce some diagonal matrix hI where $h > 0$ and I means the unit matrix for the accuracy matrix. Thus, we rewrite the prior distribution as

$$p(\boldsymbol{x} \mid \alpha, h, \boldsymbol{\mu}) = \mathcal{N}\left(\boldsymbol{x} \mid \boldsymbol{\mu}, (\alpha\Lambda + hI)^{-1}\right), \tag{15}$$

and add h as inference hyper-parameter as well as α and $\boldsymbol{\mu}$

2.3 Image restoration with Latent variable approximation

Eq.(9) shows an exponential expression and it can be as Gauss distribution family when we can approximate the argument as the quadratic form. In this study, we introduce a latent variable approximation [2][3]. Palmer *et al.* proposed the super-Gaussian distribution can be approximated as multiplied form of the Gaussian distribution and concave parameter function[2], that is, any distribution function, which denote as $p(u) = \exp(-g(u^2))$ where $g(\cdot)$ is a concave, can be described as

$$p(u) = \exp(-g(u^2)) \tag{16}$$

$$= \sup_{\eta>0} \varphi(\eta)\mathcal{N}\left(u \mid 0, \eta^{-1}\right), \tag{17}$$

$$\varphi(\eta) = \sqrt{\frac{2\pi}{\eta}} \exp\left(g^*\left(\frac{\eta}{2}\right)\right). \tag{18}$$

The function pair $g(u)$ and $g^*(\eta)$ is a convex conjugate relationship which is derived from Legendre's transform

$$g(u) = \inf_{\eta>0} \eta u - g^*(\eta), \tag{19}$$

$$g^*(\eta) = \inf_{u>0} \eta u - g(u). \tag{20}$$

In the eq(17), the stochastic value u is included in the Gaussian distribution part, and non-Gaussian part is driven into the $\varphi(\eta)$ with latent-parameter η. Thus, ignoring the $\sup_{\eta>0}$ operator, we can treat eq.(17) as the Gaussian form. Using this approximation form, we derive the observation process defined by eq.(9) as the Gaussian form with latent-parameter. In the eq.(9), the untractable term is $\ln 2\cosh(\cdot)$. When we introduce the latent parameter form, we obtain the upper limit:

$$\ln 2\cosh x \le \frac{\tanh\xi}{2\xi}(x^2 - \xi^2) + \ln 2\cosh\xi. \tag{21}$$

Thus, we introduce it into the eq.(9), we obtain

$$p_{\boldsymbol{\xi}}(\boldsymbol{z} \mid \boldsymbol{x}) = \prod_m \binom{K}{z_m} \exp\left(-\frac{1}{2}\boldsymbol{x}^{\mathrm{T}}\Xi\boldsymbol{x} + \boldsymbol{z}^{\mathrm{T}}\boldsymbol{x}\right)$$
$$\exp\left(\frac{1}{2}\boldsymbol{\xi}^{\mathrm{T}}\Xi\boldsymbol{\xi} - K\sum_m \ln 2\cosh\xi_m\right), \quad (22)$$

where $\boldsymbol{z}$ means observation vector

$$\boldsymbol{z} = (2z_1 - K, \cdots, 2z_m - K, \cdots, 2z_M - K)^{\mathrm{T}}, \quad (23)$$

$\boldsymbol{\xi}$ means the collection of latent parameter $\{\xi_m\}$, and matrix Ξ means a diagonal matrix whose components are $\{\frac{\tanh \xi_m}{\xi_m}\}$.

From the observation (9) and the prior (12), we can derive posterior as

$$p_{\boldsymbol{\xi}}(\boldsymbol{x} \mid \boldsymbol{z}, \alpha, \boldsymbol{\mu}) \propto p_{\boldsymbol{\xi}}(\boldsymbol{z} \mid \boldsymbol{x})\, p(\boldsymbol{x} \mid \alpha, h, \boldsymbol{\mu}), \quad (24)$$

and the observation can be approximated by the latent-valued form:

$$p_{\boldsymbol{\xi}}(\boldsymbol{x} \mid \boldsymbol{z}, \alpha, \boldsymbol{\mu}) \sim \mathcal{N}(\boldsymbol{x} \mid \boldsymbol{m}, (\Xi + \alpha\Lambda + hI)^{-1}), \quad (25)$$
$$\boldsymbol{m} = (\Xi + \alpha\Lambda + hI)^{-1}(\boldsymbol{z} + (\alpha\Lambda + hI)\boldsymbol{\mu}). \quad (26)$$

Considering the inference parameter of $\boldsymbol{x}$ as the posterior mean of the $\boldsymbol{x}$, that is $\hat{\boldsymbol{x}} = \langle \boldsymbol{x} \rangle$, we can obtain the inference parameter explicitly:

$$\langle \boldsymbol{x} \rangle = \sum_{\boldsymbol{x}} \boldsymbol{x}\, p_{\boldsymbol{\xi}}(\boldsymbol{x} \mid \boldsymbol{z}, \alpha, \boldsymbol{\mu}) = \boldsymbol{m}. \quad (27)$$

However, in this form, the variable parameter $\boldsymbol{\xi}$ and the hyper-parameters α and h is undefined, so that, we introduce expectation-maximization (EM) algorithm to infer these parameters. For convenient in the following we derive these inference parameter as $\theta = \{\alpha, h, \boldsymbol{\mu}, \boldsymbol{\xi}\}$. The marginal log-likelihood of $p(\boldsymbol{z}, \boldsymbol{x}; \mid \theta)$ is extracted as

$$\ln p(\boldsymbol{z} \mid \theta) = \ln \sum_{\boldsymbol{x}} p(\boldsymbol{x}, \boldsymbol{z} \mid \theta)$$
$$\geq Q(\theta \mid \theta^{(t)}) + S[p(\boldsymbol{x} \mid \boldsymbol{z}, \theta^{(t)})], \quad (28)$$

where $Q(\theta \mid \theta^{(t)})$ and entropy function $S[p(\boldsymbol{x} \mid \boldsymbol{z}, \theta^{(t)})]$ can be described as

$$Q(\theta \mid \theta^{(t)}) = \sum_{\boldsymbol{x}} p(\boldsymbol{x} \mid \boldsymbol{z}, \theta^{(t)}) \ln p(\boldsymbol{x}, \boldsymbol{z} \mid \theta), \quad (29)$$
$$S[p(\boldsymbol{x} \mid \boldsymbol{z}, \theta^{(t)})] = -\sum_{\boldsymbol{x}} p(\boldsymbol{x} \mid \boldsymbol{z}, \theta^{(t)}) \ln p(\boldsymbol{x} \mid \boldsymbol{z}, \theta^{(t)}). \quad (30)$$

In the marginal log-likelihood (28), the inference parameter is denoted as θ under the some fixed parameter $\theta^{(t)}$. The entropy function $S[p(\boldsymbol{x} \mid \boldsymbol{z}, \theta^{(t)})]$ does not include the inference parameter θ, so that we should find the theta which maximize the function $Q(\theta \mid \theta^{(t)})$. Then, we can consider the iteration algorithm called EM algorithm with substituting the obtained parameter θ into $\theta^{(t+1)}$ in the eq.(28). From the EM algorithm, we can derive update equations as following:

$$\boldsymbol{\mu}^{(t+1)} = \langle \boldsymbol{x} \rangle_{\theta^{(t)}}, \quad (31)$$
$$(\xi_m^2)^{(t+1)} = \langle x_m^2 \rangle_{\theta^{(t)}}, \quad (32)$$
$$\mathrm{Tr}\left((\alpha^{(t+1)}\Lambda + h^{(t+1)}I)^{-1}\Lambda\right) =$$
$$\mathrm{Tr}\Lambda(\Xi^{(t)} + \alpha^{(t)}\Lambda + h^{(t)}I)^{-1}$$
$$+ (\boldsymbol{\mu}^{(t+1)} - \boldsymbol{\mu}^{(t)})^{\mathrm{T}}\Lambda(\boldsymbol{\mu}^{(t+1)} - \boldsymbol{\mu}^{(t)}) \quad (33)$$
$$\mathrm{Tr}\left((\alpha^{(t+1)}\Lambda + h^{(t+1)}I)^{-1}\right) = \|\boldsymbol{\mu}^{(t+1)} - \boldsymbol{\mu}^{(t)}\|^2 \quad (34)$$

In order to obtain the inference parameter θ, we should solve the equation eq.(33) and (34).

3. Computer Simulation

In order to solve the eqs. (33) and (34), we introduce eigenvalue extraction of the determinant. The left hand of the equations come from the partial derivation for the $\ln|\alpha\Lambda + hI|$. Thus, we assume $\{\lambda_i\}$ as the eigenvalues of the matrix Λ and obtain the relationship

$$\ln|\alpha\Lambda + hI| = M\ln\alpha + \sum_i \ln\left(\lambda_i + \frac{h}{\alpha}\right), \quad (35)$$

where M is the size of the matrix Λ. Then, the simultaneous equations (33) and (34) can be denoted as

$$\frac{M}{\alpha} - \sum_i \frac{h}{\alpha\lambda_i + h} = \mathrm{Tr}\Lambda(\Xi^{(t)} + \alpha^{(t)}\Lambda + h^{(t)}I)^{-1}$$
$$+ (\boldsymbol{\mu}^{(t+1)} - \boldsymbol{\mu}^{(t)})^{\mathrm{T}}\Lambda(\boldsymbol{\mu}^{(t+1)} - \boldsymbol{\mu}^{(t)}), \quad (36)$$
$$\sum_i \frac{\alpha}{\lambda_i + h} = \|\boldsymbol{\mu}^{(t+1)} - \boldsymbol{\mu}^{(t)}\|^2. \quad (37)$$

We solve the simultaneous equations for the α and h and assign them as $\alpha^{(t+1)}$ and $h^{(t+1)}$ respectively.

In the computer simulation, we use 32×32 pixels image for evaluation, and assume the original image consists of a spatial frequency. Each pixel is assigned event rate $\rho_m\Delta$, which controls the on-off event described in the eq.(1). We denote the lowest and highest event rates as $L_{\min}$ and $L_{\max}$ respectively, and define the contrast as $L_{\max}/L_{\min}$. In the simulation, each pixel divided into the $K = 10000$ miniregions.

In the initial value of the restoration image $\boldsymbol{\mu}^0$ as the observed image $\boldsymbol{z}$, and the hyper-parameters $\alpha^0 = h^0$ is assumed as K. We use the relative errors of the restoration image and hyper-parameters as the convergence condition of

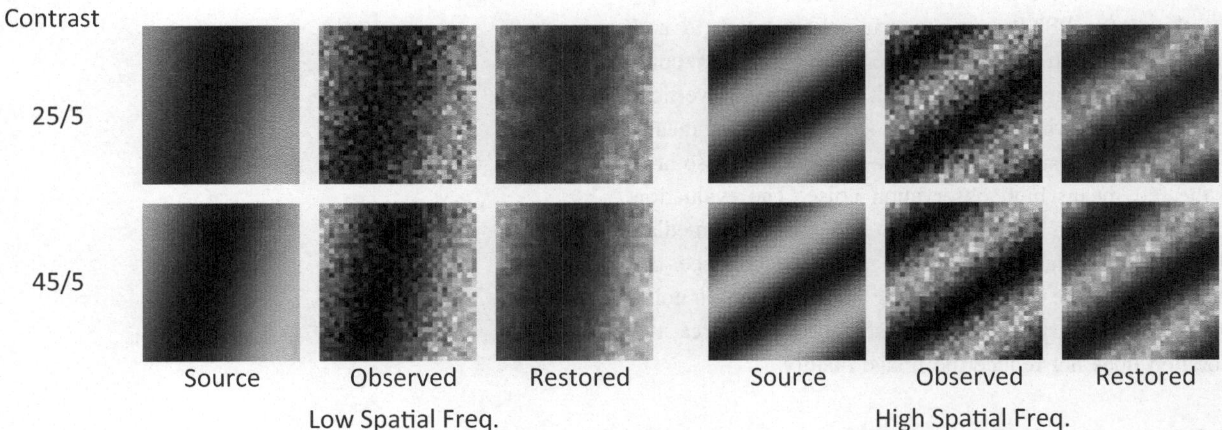

Fig. 3: Reconstruction result: The Left part shows the image with low spatial frequency and the right part shows the high frequency. In each part, the left shows the source image defined by $\rho_m\Delta$, the middle shows the Poisson observed image, and the right shows the restored image. The top row shows the case of low contrast image which means the minimum and the maximum of the $\rho_m\Delta$ is 5 and 25 respectively, which denote as $5/25$. The bottom row shows the high contrast case with $5/45$.

the EM-algorithm, that is, $\frac{\sum_i |\mu_i^{t+1}-\mu_i^t|}{\sum_i |\mu_i|} < 10^{-4}$, $\frac{\alpha^{t+1}-\alpha^t}{\alpha^t} < 10^{-3}$, and $\frac{h^{t+1}-h^t}{h^t} < 10^{-3}$. In typical iteration requires about 200 times for convergence.

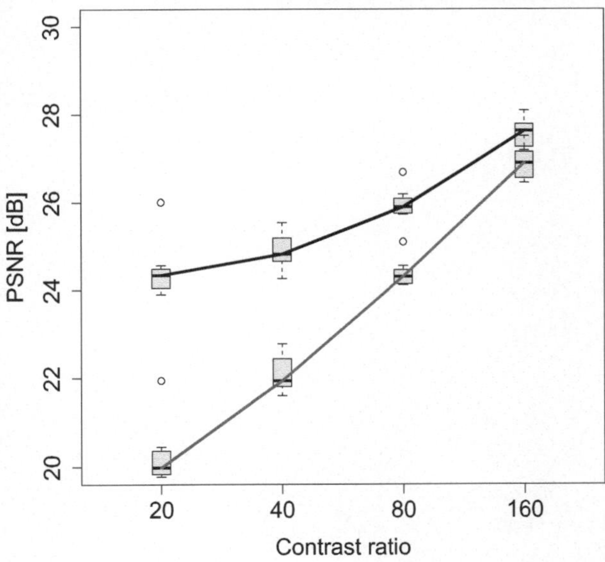

Fig. 4: Quantitative evaluation of image restoration: The horizontal axis shows the contrast ratio, and the vertical shows the peak signal to noise ratio (PSNR). The thick line shows the restoration result and the thin shows the observed one.

4. Results

Fig. 3 shows the restoration result of two spatial frequencies. The left part shows the result for the low spatial frequency image and the right one shows the high spatial frequency. In each part, the left, middle, and right columns show the original image $\{\rho_m\Delta\}$, observed image $\{z_m\}$, and restored image respectively. The top row shows the result for low contrast image which ratio $L_{\max}/L_{\min}$ equals $25/5$. The bottom shows the high contrast image with $45/5$. In the Poisson observation, the image contrast ratio controls the noise strength. Thus, the top row corresponds to the low S/N ratio, and the bottom shows the just higher than the top. Even though the corruption is high in the top row, the restoration image is just smoothed. On the contrary, the bottom row shows just lower corruption, so that the observation and the restoration images looks similar.

In order to evaluate restoration quantitatively, we introduce the peak signal noise to ratio (PSNR). The PSNR is defined as a kind of similarity between the reference image $\boldsymbol{q}^*$ and the test image $\boldsymbol{q}$ as:

$$\mathrm{PSNR}(\boldsymbol{q}, \boldsymbol{q}^*) = 10 \log_{10} \left(\frac{\max \boldsymbol{q}^* - \min \boldsymbol{q}^*}{MSE(\boldsymbol{q}, \boldsymbol{q}^*)} \right)^2, \tag{38}$$

$$\mathrm{MSE}(\boldsymbol{q}, \boldsymbol{q}^*) = \frac{1}{M} \sum_m (q_m - q_m^*)^2 \tag{39}$$

$$\tag{40}$$

Fig.4 shows the PSNR between original image $\rho_m\Delta$ and restored image with inverse logit transform. The horizontal axis shows the image contrast $L_{\max}/L_{\min}$, and the vertical shows the PSNR values. The right side of the plot means the high contrast that means the low observation noise area and the left means high observation noise. The evaluation is carried out with 10 times trials and plot with median with quantile deviation. From the plot, we can see the improvement by the restoration in the high observation noise area. On the contrary, in the low observation noise area, the restoration does not reduce the image quality.

5. Summary & Conclusion

In this study, we propose a image restoration method for the Poisson noised observation. For the inference of the Poisson parameters, we introduce a logit-transform and latent-valued form, and treat the observation process as a Gaussian function with latent-parameters. By this transformation, the observation process becomes tractable in the meaning of the Bayesian approach. By use of the GMRF like prior, obtaining the posterior mean is easy to derive. The induced latent-parameters and hyper-parameters are inferred by the EM algorithm. Thus, our algorithm can infer whole unknown parameters from the observation data.

In the computer simulation, we carry out several contrast ratio examples with two spatial frequencies cases that are defined on the small image plane 32×32 pixels. In the low contrast case that means high observation noise, we confirm the smoothness operation works well by visual comparison. For the quantitative evaluation, we introduce PSNR as the measure for the restoration. We also confirm our restoration algorithm works well within the low contrast area, and does not reduce image quality in within the high contrast area. Thus, we conclude our inference method work well with adapting in the noise strength automatically.

References

[1] M. W. Seeger. Bayesian inference and optimal design for the sparse linear model. *Journal of Machine Learning Research*, 9:759–813, 2008.

[2] J. A. Palmer, K. Kerutz-Delgado, D. P. Wipf, and B.D. Rao. Variational em algorithm for non-gaussian latent variable models. In *Advances in Neural Information Processing Systems 18*, volume 18, pages 1059–1066. MIT Press, 2005.

[3] K. Watanabe and M. Okada. Estimation of varying binomial process using local variational approximation. *IEICE Transactions on Information and Systems*, page to be appeared, 2011.

[4] K. Tanaka. Statistical-mechanical approach to image processing. *Journal of Physics A: Mathematical and General*, 35(37):R81–R150, 2002.

SESSION

GRID + CLOUD COMPUTING AND SUPPORTING TOOLS + APPLICATIONS

Chair(s)

TBA

Configuration challenges when migrating applications to a cloud: the JEE use case

Alain Tchana[1], Noel De Palma[1], Xavier Etchevers[2], and Daniel Hagimont[3]
[1]University Joseph Fourier, LIG Laboratory, Grenoble, France, (alain.tchana, noel.depalma)@imag.fr
[2]Orange Labs, Grenoble, France, xavier.etchevers@orange.com
[3]Toulouse University, IRIT Laboratory, Toulouse, France, daniel.hagimont@enseeiht.fr

Abstract— *Cloud computing brings new opportunities and challenges to run applications' scalability on a per-demand. Migrating an application to the Cloud raises two main questions: (i) which configuration of VM (in terms of resources) is appropriated for the application, while minimizing price? and (ii) what are the appropriated configuration parameters for the application, regarding the type of the VM? In this paper we answer these questions by studying the case of JEE n-tier applications, which are composed of several types of servers, making their configuration very complex. Based on experiments we have conducted in our private cloud on a reference JEE benchmark (RUBiS), we show how to migrate such applications to cloud platforms with their best configurations.*

Keywords: JEE; Cloud Computing; Performance

1. Introduction

Cloud computing brings new opportunities and challenges to run applications' scalability since it provides the capacity to deliver IT resources and services automatically on a per-demand, self-service basis over the network. IT resources can be provisioned in a matter of minutes rather than days or weeks like in traditional enterprises IT. One of the main characteristic of the cloud technology is its pay-for-use pricing model. Indeed, application providers (customers) only pay for the resources they have used, for their uptime. For these reasons, companies are increasingly migrating their infrastructures to the cloud. When migrating to the cloud, customers are faced with several configurations/types of VMs (each with identify by a particular CPU, memory, disk space, and bandwidth resources) provided by the cloud platform. For example, Amazon EC2 defines 14 types of VM and Windows Azure proposes 5. Even if some platforms give some guidelines about the choice VM according to the expected workload of the running server, this diversity of VM configurations increases the difficulty of configuring applications, which depends on their hosting VM. In summary, migrating an application to the Cloud raises two main questions: (i) which type of VM is appropriated for the application, while minimizing price? and (ii) what are the appropriated value for the application configuration parameters, regarding the type of the VM?

In this paper we answer these questions by studying the case of JEE n-tier applications. These applications are composed of several types of servers, making their configuration very complex. A bad configuration of one participant server can lead to a poor application performance (in terms of throughput for example). We conduct several experiments in our private cloud, on a reference JEE benchmark (RUBiS [10]) composed of a Tomcat server linked to a MySQL server. According to the conclusion of [9], we focus on their threads pool configuration parameters: maxThreads parameter for Tomcat and max_connections parameter for MySQL. (1) We observe that the appropriate configuration value of the MySQL max_connections parameter is the number of vcpu of the MySQL VM. (2) We show that even if the bottleneck tier of such applications is the MySQL tier, the Tomcat tier allows the application to maintain its maximum throughput. (3) Finally, we show that replicating Small VMs is more efficient than running Medium or Large VM type, even if the latter have twice or four times the size of the former in terms of resources.

The remainder of this paper is structured as follows. Section 2 presents the motivations of this work. Section 3, 4, 5, and 7 detail experiments we have conducted. Section 8 and 9 present respectively the related work and the conclusion of this paper.

2. Problem Statement and Experimental Context

2.1 Problem Statement: JEE applications in the Cloud

These last years have seen the development of the JAVA technology (JEE) for complex web applications based on the n-tier architecture. With the PHP technology, JEE applications are one the most executed applications in the web. For that reason, most popular cloud platforms provide prepackaged virtual machines (VM for short) including JEE servers ([2], [1], [3]). Deploying such applications to the cloud raises two questions ([6]):

- (Q1) What is the best configuration for each tier of the application?

- (Q2) Which type of VM (e.g. small, medium, large) is appropriated for each tier of the application while avoiding resources waste, and minimizing cost?

2.1.1 Question Q1

As reported by [7], the configuration of a JEE application is very difficult. In the scope of this paper, our considered JEE application (RUBiS) is composed of HAProxy loadbalancer, Tomcat, MySQL-Proxy and MySQL servers. Regarding the number of parameters, it is obviously non feasible to tune all of them. Qingyang shows in [9] that parameters which define thread and database connection pool are very crucial. These parameters correspond to the Tomcat maxThreads and the MySQL max_connections parameters in our considered RUBiS configuration. Therefore, a bad configuration of the Tomcat maxThreads or the MySQL max_connections parameters impacts the overall performance of the application. Fig. 1 (vUsers is the number of emulated Internet clients) shows the behavior of the RUBiS application when the Tomcat maxThreads parameter is set to 1. We observe that the application is unable to maintain a stable throughput (about 180req/s, Fig. 1(a)), whereas the response time is under 10ms (Fig. 1(b)) and the Tomcat server is not saturated (Fig. 1(c)).

2.1.2 Question Q2

Since the configuration of the JEE application depends on the resources of machines housing its servers, this task becomes more difficult in the context of cloud computing. This comes from the diversity of the configurations/types of VM proposed by the cloud platform. Although cloud platforms provide some guidelines to help customers to choose VM configurations according to the expected workload of their applications, these informations are not sufficient. In fact, the cloud platform is not able to provide depth studies about all existing applications.

2.2 Experimental context

2.2.1 The JEE application benchmark: RUBiS

The JEE application we use is provided by RUBiS [10] (servlet version), a JEE benchmark. RUBiS implements an auction web site modeled over eBay. It defines interactions such as registering new users, browsing, buying or selling items. RUBiS is provided with a web client emulator which implements the behavior of one/many e-commerce customers, including human think time. This emulator is equipped with different types of workloads, allowing it to generate browsing and browsing mix traffics. We configure this tool to progressively generate traffics for our experiments. To remain within allowable page length, we only present in this paper experiments results for browsing requests.

2.2.2 Cloud environment

Our experiments were carried out using the Grid'5000 [13] platform, which is composed of clusters in different areas of France. We used two Grid'5000's clusters (Chinqchint and Chicon) to deploy the RUBiS servers and the RUBiS client emulator servers separately. The two clusters run OpenStack [12] and Xen hypervisors (version 3.2) to set up a virtualized cloud providing three types of VM with configurations similar to those defined by Amazon EC2 [2]: Small, Medium and Large. They run the same operating system as the nodes which host them: Linux Ubuntu 10.0.4 distribution with a 2.6.30 kernel, over a gigabit connection.

2.2.3 Experiments workflow

The workflow of experiments we have realized is the following:

- First of all, we identify the first tier that we will begin the experiment with. This corresponds to the bottleneck tier.
- Secondly, we evaluate the appropriate configuration value of Tomcat maxThreads and MySQL max_connections parameters for each type of VM. This experiment results in a guideline we propose concerning the choice of these parameters.
- Thirdly, we determine which type of VM is appropriated for Tomcat and MySQL tiers when they are well configured.
- Finally, we evaluate the limit of each tier when increasing the replication degree of the other tier. This is helpful to implement scalability strategies, which is commonly encountered in JEE applications.

2.2.4 Metrics

For these experiments, we considered the following metrics:

- The CPU and memory loads of VM servers;
- The response time for requests and their throughput;
- The number of vUsers.

We focus on the maximal throughput (given by the RUBiS client emulator) provided by the application in various configurations which all maintain a percentage of requests under a given response time threshold. We consider that the RUBiS application has reached is maximum capacity when the response time for more than 10% of requests exceeds this threshold (set to 5 seconds). This is in line with the conclusion of [11], where a response time longer than 5 seconds was described as likely to make 10% of potential customers navigate away in a e-commerce application. Based on these parameters, we defined the notions of *goodThroughput* (respectively *badThroughput*), which represents the throughput of requests below the threshold (respectively above the threshold). The throughput metric

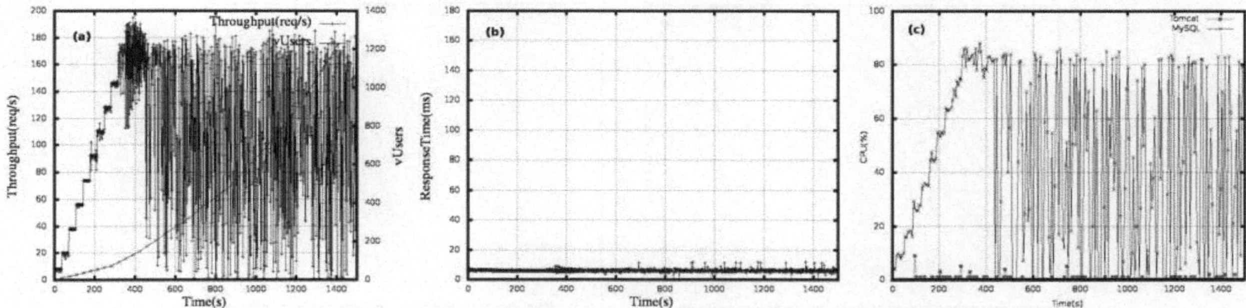

Fig. 1: The consequence of a bad configuration of Tomcat maxThreads parameter (set to 1) on the RUBiS performance: (a) application throughput, (b) response time, and (c) servers CPU and memory loads.

determines the capacity of the RUBiS application while ensuring an SLO response time. In addition to throughput, we considered the number of vUsers (emulated Internet clients) causing application saturation.

3. The bottleneck tier

To prevent skewing the satisfaction results, the beginning tier should be the first bottleneck tier, since its behavior may bias the configuration of other tier if it is not well configured. The first bottleneck tier was the one limiting application performance (maximum throughput in our case). To identify this tier, we tested a RUBiS configuration comprising a Tomcat server linked to a MySQL server, each other runs on Small VM. Their crucial parameters are kept to their default value: maxThreads to 200 and max_connections to 100. The results of this experiment are shown in Fig. 2. It is clear that the MySQL VM CPU reaches 100% at 380 s (Fig. 2(a)), while the Tomcat VM CPU load is negligible (close to 1%). In terms of memory load, neither VM becomes saturated (Fig. 2(b)). The maximum throughput for the application (about 180 req/s) is shown to be achieved when the CPU load of MySQL VM reaches 100%. In fact, the throughput increases until 380 s, and remains constant for the remainder of the experiment, whereas the number of vUsers continues to increase (Fig. 2(c)). For the response time (Fig. 2(d)), there is no badThroughput until the MySQL VM CPU reaches 100% (time 380s, curve "Good SLA"). After this time, some requests take more than 10 s to execute (curve "Bad SLA"). **In conclusion, the bottleneck tier is MySQL and its bottleneck resource is the CPU**. Thus, we start investigating the configuration of the RUBiS application in the cloud by MySQL.

4. Tuning the MySQL max_connections parameter

We tested different values of max_connections from 1 to 500 (1, 20, 40, 60, 80, 100, 200, 300, 400, and 500). These experiments were performed for the three types of VM housing the MySQL server. During these tests, Tomcat was deployed on a Small VM, and its maxThreads parameter was maintained at its default value. This Tomcat configuration does not affect the experimental results since MySQL is the bottleneck tier, as shown above.

Small VM: The application has the same capacity (180 req/s) whatever the value of max_connections. Maximum capacity is reached from 110 vUsers. However, although the response time remains below the defined threshold, its grows with the value of max_connections (Fig. 3). This is due to the fact that the increase in max_connections increases the number of threads running on the MySQL VM. This reduces the server's efficiency since its VM uses CPU time to switch between process contexts.

Medium VM: Once again, the application has the same capacity (210 req/s) whatever the value of max_connections from 2 to 500. Maximum capacity is reached from 130 vUsers. However, a lower capacity (180 req/s) is noted when max_connections is set to 1 because with 1 thread, the Medium VM (2 vcpus) does not use its overall CPU resources. The increase in response time observed is due to the reasons outlined above.

Large VM: The application has a capacity of 240 req/s whatever the value of max_connections from 4 to 500. This throughput is reached from 130 vUsers. When max_connections is set to 1, throughput is 180 req/s; it is 210 req/s with max_connections set to 2 and 3. The response time increases with max_connections as for the other two VM sizes tested.

Conclusion: The results of all these experiments are summarized in Fig. 4. The appropriate value of max_connections appears to be equal to the number of virtual CPUs (vcpus) available on the VM hosting MySQL. Higher max_connections values increase the response time, and multiplying the resources available to the MySQL VM does not result in a proportional increase in application performance.

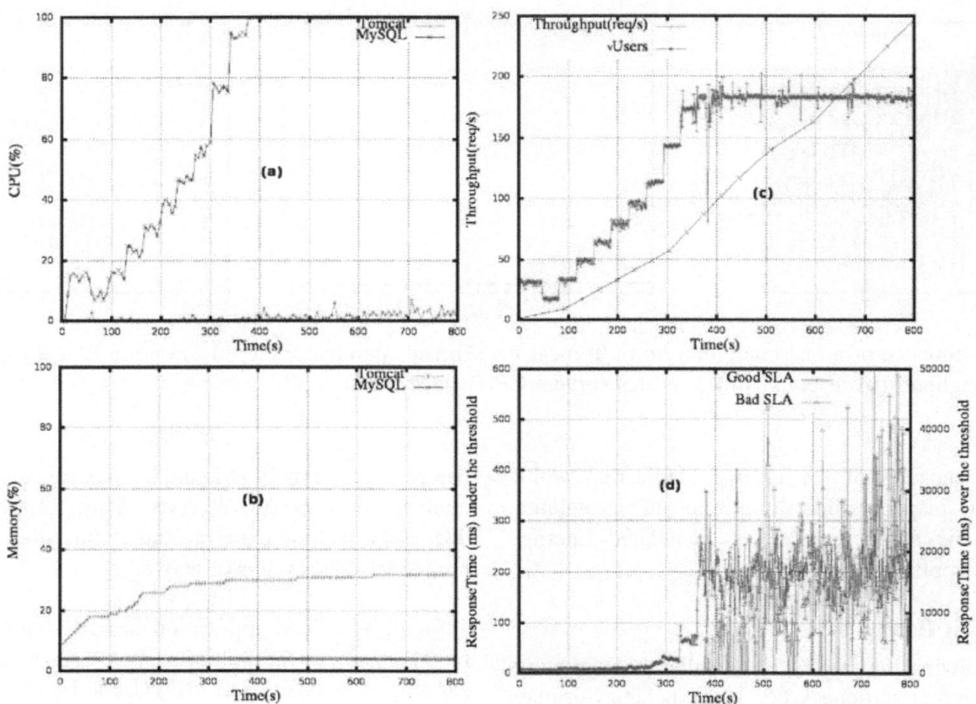

Fig. 2: Bottleneck tier detection: the MySQL server is CPU-bound. (a) Server CPU load, (b) Server memory load, (d) Application throughput, and (d) application response time (below and above the threshold)

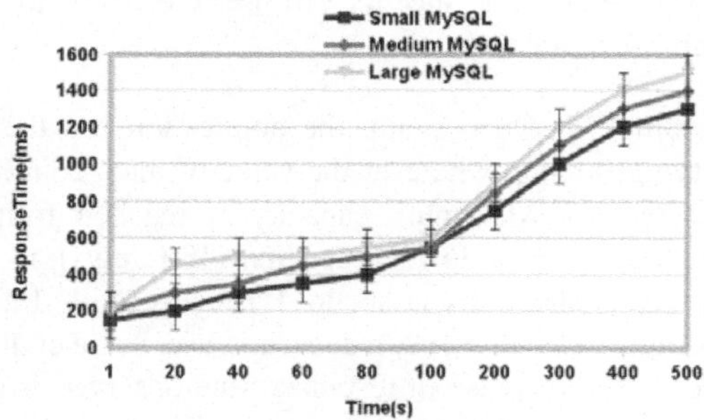

Fig. 3: Tuning the MySQL max_connections parameter does not significantly affect the application's response time

VM type	Maximum throughput (req/s)	vUsers	Recommendation
Small	180	110	any value of max_connections is correct (1 is the best).
Medium	210	130	max_connection=1 is limiting: Choose a value beyond 1.
Large	240	130	max_connection < 4 is limiting: Choose a value beyond 4.

Fig. 4: Recommended settings for the MySQL max_connections parameter

5. Tuning the Tomcat maxThreads parameter

After the MySQL server, the second tunable parameter in the RUBiS application is the Tomcat maxThreads setting. For this experiment, MySQL was run on a Small VM with max_connections set to 1 (its best value). We chose this type of VM for MySQL because the other types only increase the application's throughput. They are therfore equivalent in this second experiment. For the Tomcat server we tested a Small, Medium and Large VM with the maxThreads parameter varying from 1 to 2500 (1, 20, 40, 60, 80, 100, 200, 300, 400, 500, 1000, 1500, 2000, 2500). Because Tomcat is not the first bottleneck tier, the same behavior was observed for all three VMs. The application's capacity is determined by MySQL. The results of this second RUBiS tuning step are shown in Fig. 5 for the Small Tomcat VM. This analysis reveals that the maximum throughput for the application remains unchanged whatever the value of maxThreads: 180 req/s reached from about 110 vUsers. However, with maxThreads set to 1 (Fig. 5(a)), the application cannot maintain this throughput even though the response time remains below the threshold. One thread is obviously insufficient to serve all the injectors' requests. At values between 20 and 400, a constant response time is maintained throughout the experiment (Fig. 5(b)); while the response time declines with maxThreads from 500 to 2500 (Fig. 5(c)). This degradation can be explained by context switching between processes and the higher number of processes overall. Increasing maxThreads results in increases in both CPU and memory loads for Tomcat. However, Tomcat is still not the bottleneck for the application since it saturates after the MySQL server. Nevertheless, its saturation affects the application's ability to maintain throughput. In our experiments, the optimal

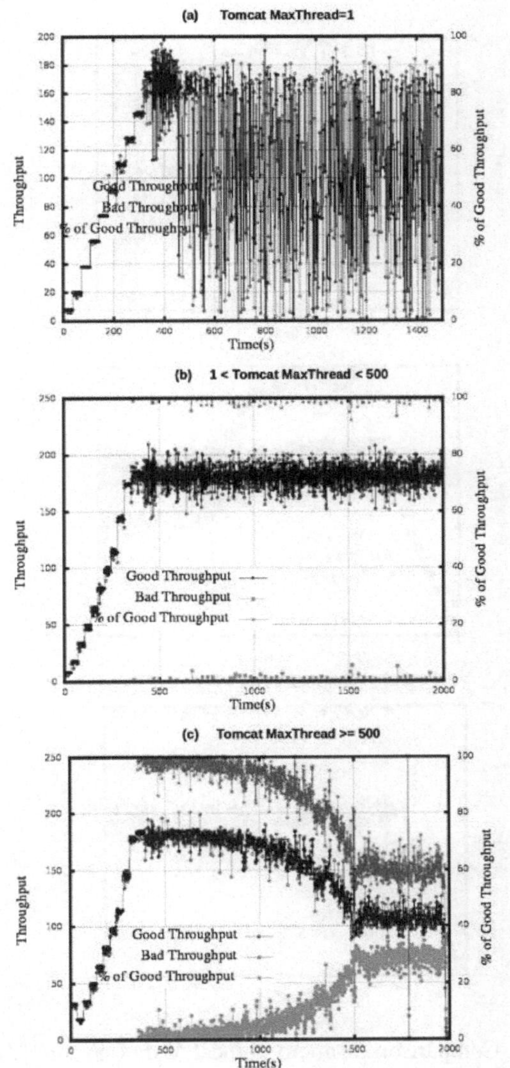

Fig. 5: Impact of the Tomcat maxThreads parameter on application throughput

maxThreads setting is 100.

6. Which type of VM for each tier?

After configuring Tomcat and MySQL servers for each type of VM, let us now investigate what is the best type of VM for each tier. Experiments we presented above show that among the tree type of VM, the Small one is the best candidate. In fact, concerning MySQL tier, Medium VM (respectively Large VM) does not dubbed (respectively quadruple) the performance of the application even if their resources represent twice (respectively four times) the Small VM. About Tomcat, the Small VM is sufficient since it is not the bottleneck tier. Thus, for this tier, we need to know if micro VM type (as also provided by Amazon EC2) can provide the same performance as Small Tomcat VM. We experiment two types of Tomcat micro VM and compare their results with Small VM:

- $[SmallVM]/2$: a half of a Small VM,
- $[SmallVM]/4$: a quarter of a Small VM.

Fig. 6 and 7 show the comparison of the three types of VM in terms of maximum throughput and the ability of the application to maintain this throughput. We observe the same maximum throughput (180req/s) whatever the type of VM (Fig. 6). However, this throughput is not maintainable with $[SmallVM]/4$ (the application is down after 1200vUsers, Fig. 6(a)). This is due to the saturation of Tomcat (CPU and Memory). Regarding $[SmallVM]/2$, it gives about the same performance as Small Tomcat VM. However the application maintains only 60% of goodThroughput in this configuration ("% of Good Throughput" curve in Fig 7(b)). The other requests are performed with at least 20s of response time. In conclusion, the micro VM $[SmallVM]/4$ type is not recommended. If the customer just wants to maintain the maximum throughput, the $[SmallVM]/2$ is sufficient for Tomcat. If he wants both the maximum throughput with good response time, at least the Small VM Tomcat is required.

7. JEE tiers replication/scalability

We have shown in section 5 that MySQL is the first bottleneck tier; in this step, we determined the saturation point for the Tomcat server (i.e., how many replicated MySQL servers are needed to make Tomcat into the bottleneck tier). To do this, the experiment was repeated varying the number of MySQL servers. Experiments were stopped when the application's capacity (maximum throughput) in the current experiment (running n MySQL servers) was the same as in the previous experiment (running n-1 MySQL servers); n-1 MySQL servers are therefore required to saturate the Tomcat tier. This was performed for one (Fig. 8(a)) and two (Fig. 8(b)) Tomcat instances.

With one Tomcat instance (Fig. 8(a)) 18 instances of MySQL fully saturate the Tomcat tier. Plotting the CPU and memory loads for different servers in these experiments reveals Tomcat as the first bottleneck tier, with a CPU load of 100%.

With two Tomcat instances (Fig. 8(b)) the Tomcat tier became saturated with 30 MySQL instances. Note that even when the number of Tomcat instances is doubled, the number of MySQL instances needed to saturate the Tomcat tier does not increase proportionally. Indeed, the application's performance is not doubled either. This is also the case when MySQL instances are doubled.

8. Related work

Few research works are conducted in order to help applications deployers (particularly JEE in our case) to configuration their applications in cloud environments. [6] proposes

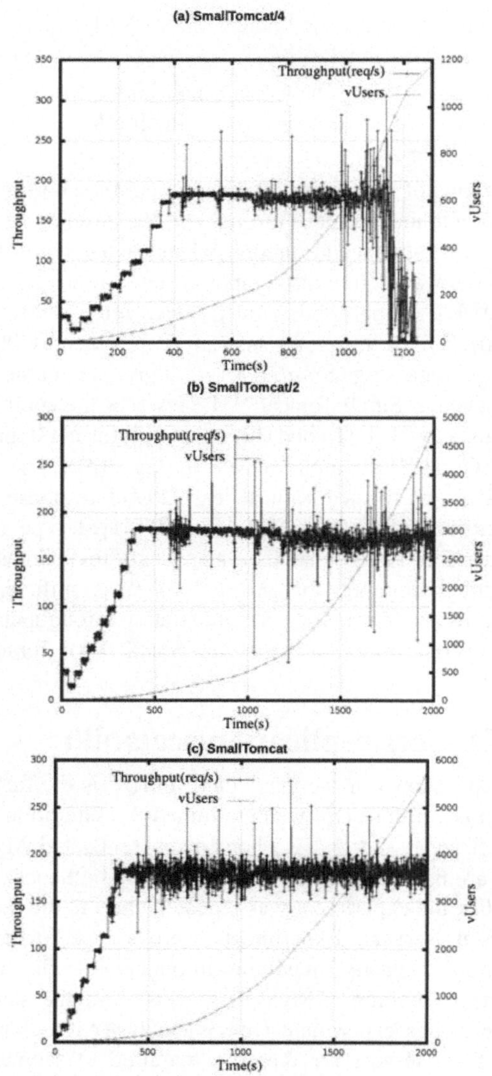

Fig. 6: Comparison of micro Tomcat VMs ($[SmallVM]/2$, $[SmallVM]/4$) with Small VM: the throughput view.

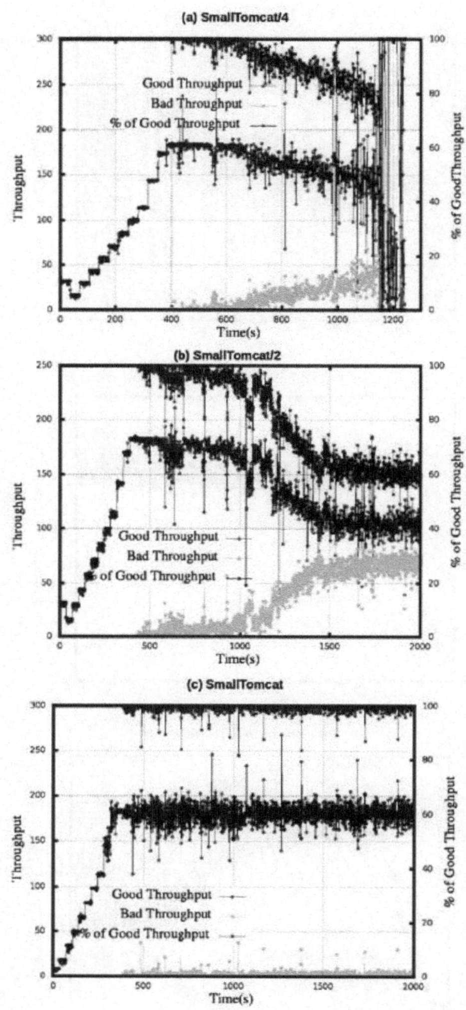

Fig. 7: Comparison of micro Tomcat VMs ($[SmallVM]/2$, $[SmallVM]/4$) with Small VM: the throughput maintainability view.

a self-provisioning system that help applications deployers to choose the appropriate VM configuration according to the workload of the application, considering the cost of the type of VM. Many research works are done about the optimization of resources usage for JEE applications. [14] describes an analytic model for capacity planning of JEE applications deployed in a large scale environment. It identifies the same questions as us about the configuration of a JEE application (bottleneck tier, resources needed, maximum throughput, etc.). However, [14] is concentrated to the analysis of the JEE application performance when receiving different type of workloads. The impact of the configuration of each JEE server is not treated as we have done. [15] is in line with [14]. It proposes a performance prediction model for JEE applications, based on messages exchanged between the JEE components. In comparison with [14], the [15]'s model operates at the application design phase and requires that the JEE components communicate via a message server.

About JEE applications tuning, [16] studies the performance of several implementations of EJB. It analyses the influence of each type of EJB implementation on the overall performance of the JEE application, and also compares an JEE application based on EJB vs JEE application implemented exclusively with servlets. [17] reports the importance of threads pool parameters in JEE application, and proposes a middleware to tune them automatically. [5] identifies 28 configuration parameters for an 3-tier e-commerce application. As [17], it shows that threads pool parameters are the most crucial. It analyzes their impact on the JEE application performance. In comparison to our work, [5] only

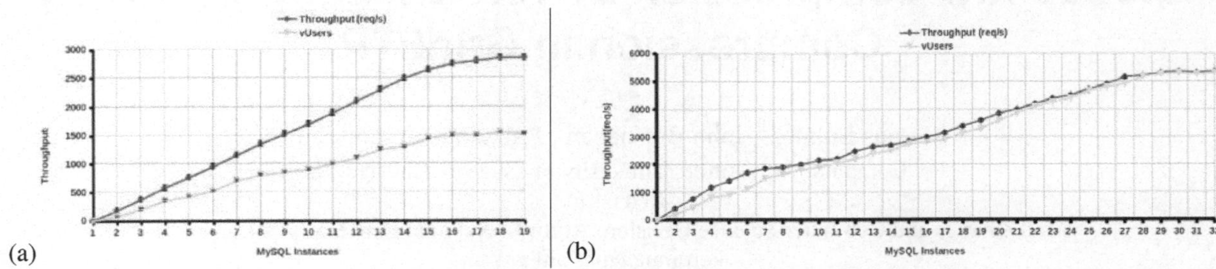

Fig. 8: How many instances of MySQL makes Tomcat the bottleneck tier with one (a) and two (b) Tomcat instances?

experiments lower and higher allocation values. In the same vein, [8] proposes a methodology to help administrators to determine the appropriate configuration of each JEE application layer. This methodology is based on random configuration values for each parameter. The problem of this methodology is that random values are chosen in a range of values identified by authors, but without any justification. [4] automates the generation of configuration files in JEE applications composed of Apache, Tomcat and MySQL servers. More important, [4] proposes a dependency graph of parameters in such applications, which can be used to determine the configuration workflow in such applications.

9. Conclusion

This paper explores the deployment of a JEE applications in the Cloud. As reported by [7], this is a hard task. We have realized several experiments in order to determine the appropriate configuration of each JEE server, regarding cloud provided VM configuration. Our experiments was carried out in our private cloud, with a reference JEE application, RUBiS: composed of Tomcat and MySQL servers. We have explored several configurations of each JEE server, running on thee types of VM (Small, Medium and Large) with comparable characteristics as the Amazon EC2 cloud.

As a future research, we plan to extend this work with browsing mix and write workloads.

Acknowledgment

This work is supported by the French Fonds National pour la Societe Numerique (FSN) and Poles Minalogic, Systematic and SCS, through the FSN Open Cloudware project.

References

[1] *Righscale web site*, in http://www.rightscale.com, visited on 2012, October.

[2] Amazon Web Services, *Amazon EC2 auto-scaling functions*, in http://aws.amazon.com/fr/autoscaling/, visited on 2012, October.

[3] *Windows Azure*, in www.windowsazure.com/, visited on 2012, October.

[4] Wei Zheng, Ricardo Bianchini, and Thu D. Nguyen Automatic configuration of internet services. In *Proceedings of the 2nd ACM SIGOPS/EuroSys European Conference on Computer Systems*, pp. 219-229, Lisbon, Portugal, 2007.

[5] Monchai Sopitkamol, and Daniel A. Menasce A method for evaluating the impact of software configuration parameters on e-commerce sites. In *Proceedings of the 5th international workshop on Software and performance*, pp. 53-64, Palma, Illes Balears, Spain, 2005.

[6] Upendra Sharma, Prashant Shenoy, Sambit Sahu, and Anees Shaikh. A Cost-Aware Elasticity Provisioning System for the Cloud. In *Proceedings of the 2011 31st International Conference on Distributed Computing Systems*, pp. 559-570, Minneapolis, Minnesota, USA, 2011.

[7] Bill Pugh and Jaime Spacco. RUBiS revisited: why J2EE benchmarking is hard In *Proceeding of the Companion to the 19th annual ACM SIGPLAN conference on Object-oriented programming systems, languages, and applications*, pp. 204-205, Vancouver, BC, Canada, October 2004.

[8] Mukund Raghavachari, Darrell Reimer, and Robert D. Johnson The deployer's problem: configuring application servers for performance and reliability. In *Proceedings of the 25th International Conference on Software Engineering*, pp. 484-489, Portland, Oregon, 2003.

[9] Qingyang Wang, Simon Malkowski, Deepal Jayasinghe, Pengcheng Xiong, Calton Pu, Yasuhiko Kanemasa, Motoyuki Kawaba, and Lilian Harada. The impact of soft resource allocation on n-tier application scalability. In *Proceedings of the 2011 IEEE International Parallel & Distributed Processing Symposium*, pp. 1034-1045, Washington, DC, USA, 2011.

[10] C. Amza, E. Cecchet, A. Chanda, A. L. Cox, S. Elnikety, R. Gil, J. Marguerite, K. Rajamani, and W. Zwaenepoel, *Specification and implementation of dynamic web site benchmarks*, in IEEE Annual Workshop on Workload Characterization, Austin, TX, USA, 2002.

[11] Bojan Simic, *The performance of web applications: Customers are won or lost in one second*, A. R. Library, 2008.

[12] *Openstack web site*, in http://openstack.org/, visited on 2012, April.

[13] *Grid'5000: a scientific instrument designed to support experiment-driven research*, in https://www.grid5000.fr/mediawiki/index.php/Grid5000:Home, visited on 2012, April.

[14] Samuel Kounev and Alejandro P. Buchmann, *Performance Modeling and Evaluation of Large-Scale J2EE Applications*, Proceedings of the 29th International Computer Measurement Group Conference, pp. 273-283, Dallas, Texas, USA, December, 2003.

[15] Yan Liu and Ian Gorton, *Performance prediction of J2EE applications using messaging protocols*, Proceedings of the 8th international conference on Component-Based Software Engineering, pp. 1-16, St. Louis, MO, USA, May, 2005.

[16] Emmanuel Cecchet, Julie Marguerite, and Willy Zwaenepoel, *Performance and scalability of EJB applications*, Proceedings of the ACM SIGPLAN Conference on Object-Oriented Programming Systems, Languages and Applications, pp. 4-8, Seattle, Washington, USA, November, 2002.

[17] Yan Zhang, Wei Qu, and Anna Liu, *Automatic performance tuning for J2EE application server systems*, Proceedings of the 6th international conference on Web Information Systems Engineering, pp. 520-527, New York, USA, November, 2005.

Globus XIO Compression Driver: Enabling On-the-fly Compression in GridFTP

Mattias Lidman[1], John Bresnahan[2], Rajkumar Kettimuthu[1,3]
[1]Computation Institute, University of Chicago, Chicago, IL
[2]Redhat Inc.
[3]Mathematics and Computer Science Division, Argonne National Laboratory, Argonne, IL
*kettimut@mcs.anl.gov

***Abstract*—Multicore systems open the door to compression in Grid environments with high-speed networks to enable "faster than network speed" transfers. GridFTP is a data transport protocol that can break up its transfer payload in such a way that streaming it through multiple cores is possible. With the additional parallel processing power added by multicore systems it is possible to pipeline compression and packet switching in such a way that seemingly faster than network speed transfers are possible. In this paper, we present the Globus XIO compression driver, which enables GridFTP to compress data on-the-fly. We also present a detailed performance study of the compression driver using XIOPerf, an Iperf-like tool and GridFTP.**

***Index Terms*— GridFTP, Compression, High-speed transfers**

I. Introduction

The need to move data faster is ever increasing. The use of compression to improve data transfer rates is not a new idea [1]. But this has not been adopted as a standard feature for data movement in Grid [2] environments. Also, for sites connected with by high-speed networks such as ESnet [3] and Internet2 [4], the network was not the bottleneck most of the time. But as host systems with many cores emerge, compression might provide benefits even on these high-speed networks. We have developed a compression driver for the Globus XIO framework [5] that compresses data as it is sent, and decompress, as it is received. The driver can under virtually any circumstances reduce network load by reducing the amount of data actually transferred. Under the right circumstances it can also help individual endpoints achieve higher-than-network speeds. This study will attempt to investigate under which circumstances this occurs, and when the driver is downright harmful. The answer to this question depends primarily on four factors:

- System resources - assuming infinite system resources and finite network bandwidth the driver will virtually always be beneficial or have no effect. In the case where the transferred data is completely random, the amount of data transferred will increase by a few hundreds of a percent. We will not consider this a factor because of the miniscule amount of possible overhead, and because of the relative rarity of transferring completely random data.
- Network bandwidth - assuming infinite bandwidth and finite system resources at the end-points, the driver will virtually always be a bottleneck to some extent.
- Block size - the driver compresses one block at a time and compression algorithms behave differently depending on block size.
- Data type - certain types of data (such as plain text) compresses nicely while others (such as random and already compressed data) do not.

We present a detailed performance study of the compression driver using XIOPerf [6], an Iperf-like tool and GridFTP [7,8], and provide a number of insights. The rest of the paper is organized as follows. In Section II, we provide background on GridFTP and Globus XIO. In Section III, we describe the compression driver. In Section IV, we present the experimental results and describe the conclusions drawn from the experiments in Section V. In Section VI, we discuss future work. We summarize in Section VII.

II. BACKGROUND

In this section we provide details on GridFTP and the Globus eXtensible Input/Output (XIO) framework.

A. GridFTP

The GridFTP protocol is a backward-compatible extension of the legacy RFC959 FTP protocol. It maintains the same command/response semantics introduced by RFC959. It also maintains the two-channel protocol semantics. One channel is for control messaging (the control channel), such as requesting what files to transfer and the other is for streaming the data payload (the data channel). Once a client successfully forms a control channel with a server, it can begin sending commands to the server. In order to transfer a file, the client must first establish a data channel. This task involves sending the server a series of commands on the control channel describing attributes of the desired data channel. Once these commands are successfully sent, a client can request a file transfer. At this point a separate data channel connection is formed using all the agreed-upon attributes, and the requested file is sent across it.

In standard FTP, the data channel can be used to transfer only a single file. Subsequent transfers must repeat the data channel setup process. GridFTP modifies this part of the protocol to allow many files to be transferred across a single data channel. This enhancement is known as data channel caching. GridFTP also introduces other enhancements to improve performance over the standard FTP mode. For example, parallelism and striping allow data to be sent over several independent data connections and reassembled at the destination.

Globus GridFTP is widely used to move large volumes of data over the wide area network. The XIO-based Globus GridFTP framework makes it easy to plug in other transport protocols. The Data Storage Interface [9] allows for easier integration with various storage systems. It supports non-TCP-based protocols such as UDT [10,11] and RDMA [12]. It also provides advanced capabilities such as concurrency [13] multilinking [14] and transfer resource management [15].

B. Globus XIO

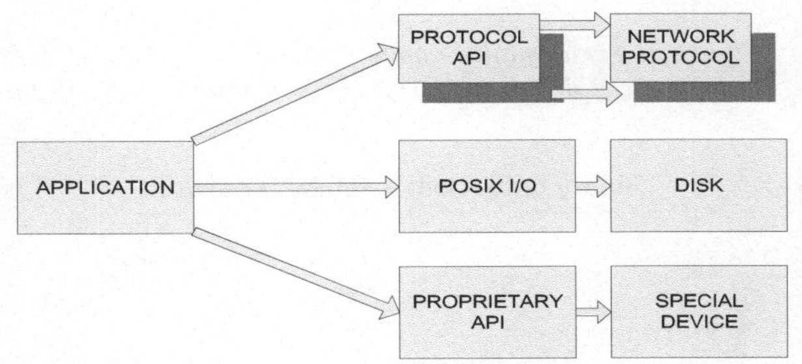

Figure 1. Typical application interaction with various devices.

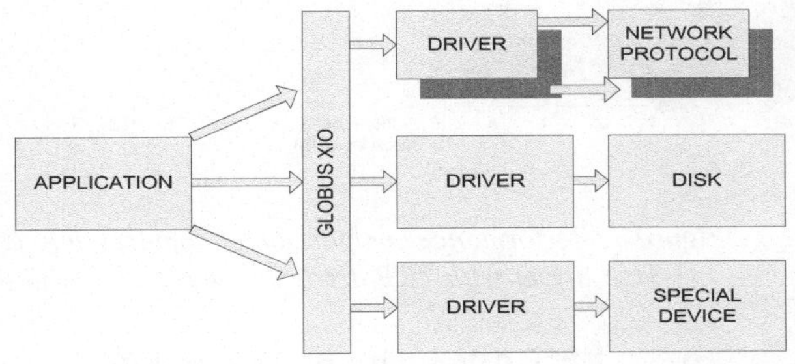

Figure 2. Application interaction with various devices via Globus XIO.

XIO is an extensible and flexible I/O library written for use with the Globus Toolkit. XIO is written in C programming language and provides us with one API that currently supports many different wire protocols. All implementations of these protocols are encapsulated as drivers that are modular.

GridFTP uses the XIO interface for network and disk I/O operations. The XIO framework presents a single, standard open/close, read/write interface to many different protocol implementations. The protocol implementations, called drivers, are responsible for manipulating and transporting the user's data. Drivers are grouped into a stack. When an I/O operation is requested, the XIO framework passes the operation request down the driver stack. An XIO driver can be thought of as a modular protocol interpreter that can be plugged into an I/O stack without concern about the application using it. This modular abstraction is what allowed us to achieve our success here without disturbing the application's tested code base and without forcing endpoints to run new and unfamiliar code.

III. Compression Driver

There are two types of drivers in XIO - transform drivers and transport drivers. Transport drivers are those that actually move data into or out of the process space. Examples of this are TCP and UDP. Transform drivers are those that manipulate, examine, frame, or change the data, or in other words, drivers that take any action other than moving the data across the process boundary. Examples of this are compression and logging.

The compression driver performs compression and decompression of data for XIO. It supports zlib and lzo compression algorithms. It is designed with ease of further development in mind - adding different methods of compressing data is straightforward. Like any XIO driver, the compression driver implements the open, close, read and write functions. The driver is designed in such a way that the code that handles various aspects of the communication with XIO and the code that manipulates the data are clearly abstracted. These are entirely separate entities; the block functionality does not know and does not care what the data handling functions does with the data, as long as they fulfill certain requirements. This separation makes it easier to add new compression strategies.

IV. Experimental Results

The experimental results were obtained using three different hardware configurations. Configuration 1: AMD Athlon 64 X2 3800+, Configuration 2: Intel Core2 Quad Q9300 Configuration 3: 2 Intel XEON 2.0GHz. In all configurations the hosts where connected by a 100Mbps local area network.

We used the following datasets for our experiments:

- ASCII - plain text. Original file consisted of 400MB of US census data. A common file type that is very compressible.
- Binary - consists of various software libraries. A common type of data that is somewhat compressible.
- MPEG - an MPEG encoded movie. This was used as an example of already compressed data, which will therefore be difficult to compress further.
- Random - a file consisting of random data created from /dev/urandom. This is used to establish a lower bound for compressible data.
- Zero - a file consisting entirely of zeros created from /dev/zero. This is used to establish an upper bound for compressible data.

Each file was 1.2GB in size. In the case of the ASCII and binary data, the original files were concatenated to fit this size.

The original files were several hundred MBs in size, which ensures that no unfair advantage was given to the compression algorithms due to the repetition of data.

The tests were performed using both the zlib and LZO compression libraries. In both cases the default compression level was used. The tests where done in a network environment which at times may have been used by others. To ensure that this did not affect the results, the tests where done during a time of year and times of day when the network could be expected to see minimal activity. Further, each test was run ten times and the results were taken as the average of each set of tests. In total, these results are the product of several days of network time.

The results were obtained using XIOPerf and GridFTP. The XIOPerf results were obtained using configuration 1 and 2. Configuration 3 was used for the GridFTP results. A brief description of XIOPerf is given below.

A. XIOPerf

XIOPerf, a network protocol testing and evaluation tool. XIOPerf is a command line program written on top of Globus XIO with a simple and well-defined interface to many different protocol implementations. XIOPerf was created to give users a way to quickly and easily experiment with an open-ended set of protocols over real networks to determine which will best suit their needs. XIOPerf presents a similar interface to that of IPerf. The main difference between IPerf and XIOPerf is that while IPerf is limited to TCP and UDP, XIOPerf is written on a framework that allows the user to plug in arbitrary protocol implementations.

B. Compression Ratios

Tables 1 and 2 show the compressed size of each type of data when transferred at a block size of 16KB for zlib and lzo respectively. In other words, this is the amount of data actually sent across the network when using the Compression Driver to transfer these 1.2GB files.

Table 1: Compression ratio for zlib

Type of data	Compressed size	Percentage of original file
Zero	1.72MB	0.14%
ASCII	97.04MB	8.15%
Binary	465.11MB	38.76%
MPEG	1172.49MB	97.70%
Random	1200.66MB	100.05%

Table 2: Compression ratio for lzo

Type of data	Compressed size	Percentage of original file
Zero	5.11MB	0.43%
ASCII	180.54MB	15.05%
Binary	599.31MB	49.94%
MPEG	1184.65MB	98.72%
Random	1204.99MB	100.42%

C. XIOPerf Results for zlib Compression

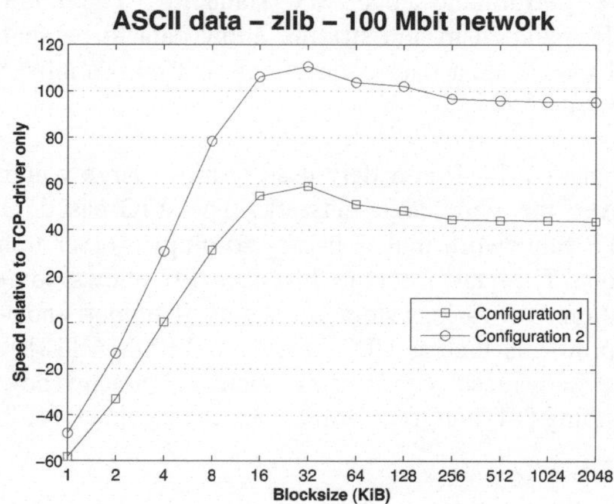

Figure 3: Performance comparison of compression driver (zlib) + TCP driver with TCP driver alone for ASCII data

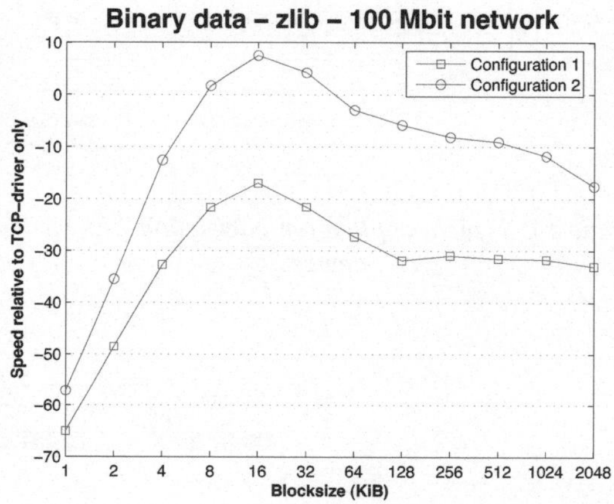

Figure 4: Performance comparison of compression (zlib) + TCP driver with TCP driver alone for Binary data

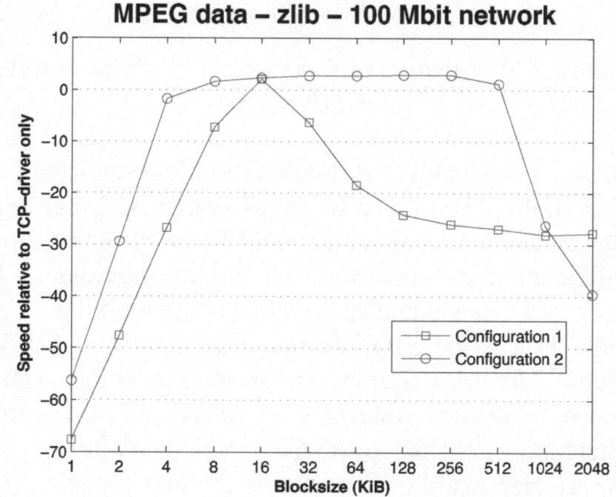

Figure 5: Performance comparison of compression (zlib) + TCP driver with TCP driver alone for MPEG data

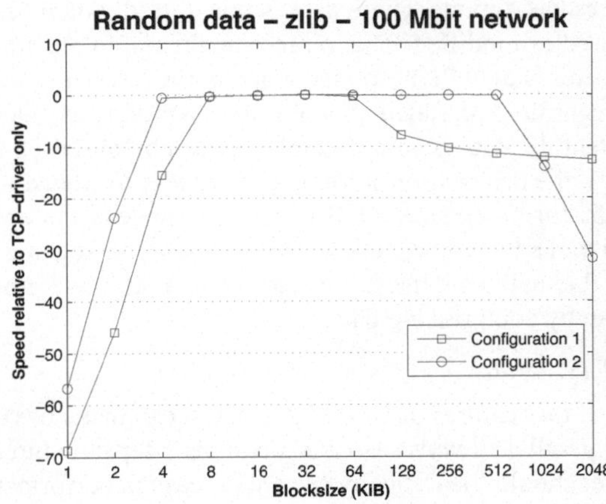

Figure 6: Performance comparison of compression (zlib) + TCP driver with TCP driver alone for Randon data

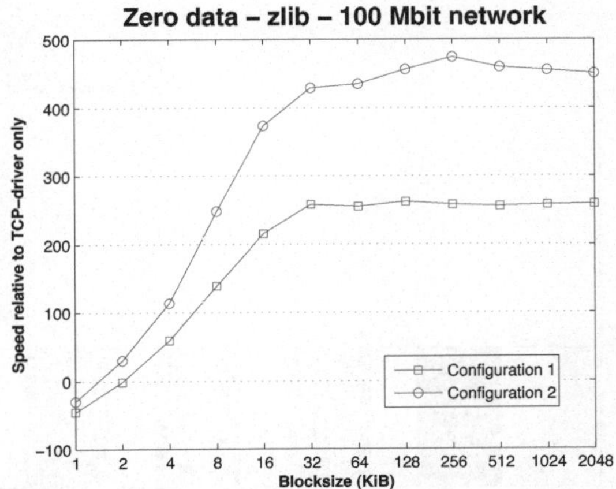

Figure 7: Performance comparison of compression driver (zlib) + TCP driver with TCP driver alone for Zero data

Figures 3 through 7 show the performance of using compression driver using zlib algorithm on top of the TCP driver in Globus XIO relative to that of using TCP driver alone, for various types of datasets. The results are mostly on the expected lines with zero files getting the big performance boost followed by ASCII. Interestingly, the performance for binary data is worse than random data especially for configuration 2.

D. XIOPerf Results for lzo Compression

Figures 8 through 12 show the performance of using compression driver using lzo algorithm on top of the TCP driver in Globus XIO relative to that of using TCP driver alone, for various types of datasets. The results are on the expected lines except that configuration 2 really did produce significantly lower results than configuration 1 at certain block sizes despite having much more powerful hardware.

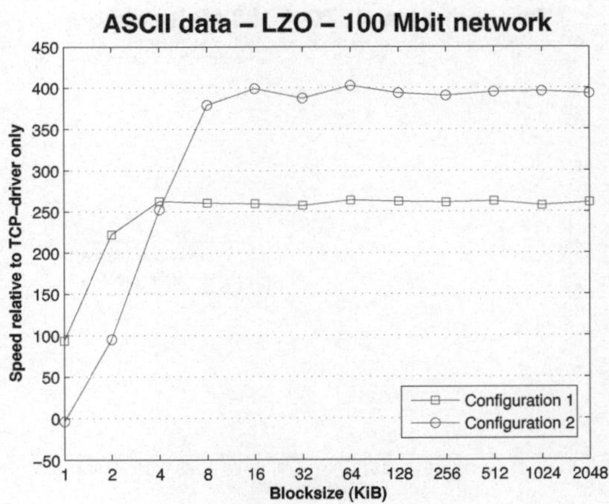

Figure 8: Performance comparison of compression driver (lzo) + TCP driver with TCP driver alone for ASCII data

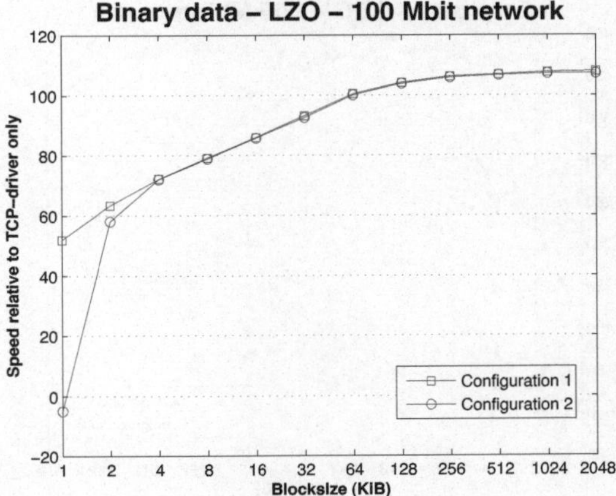

Figure 9: Performance comparison of compression driver (lzo) + TCP driver with TCP driver alone for Binary data

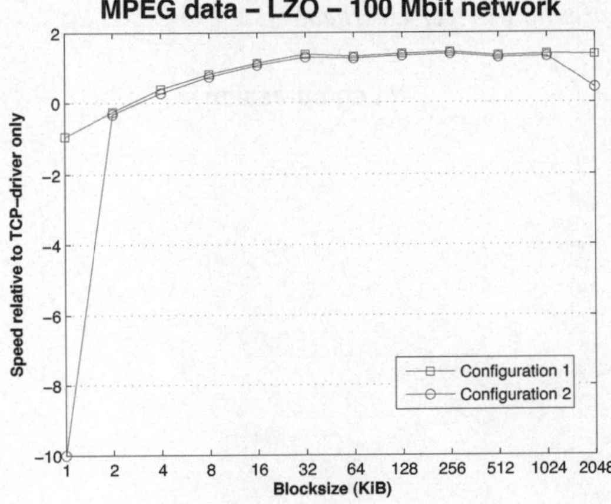

Figure 10: Performance comparison of compression (lzo) + TCP driver with TCP driver alone for MPEG data

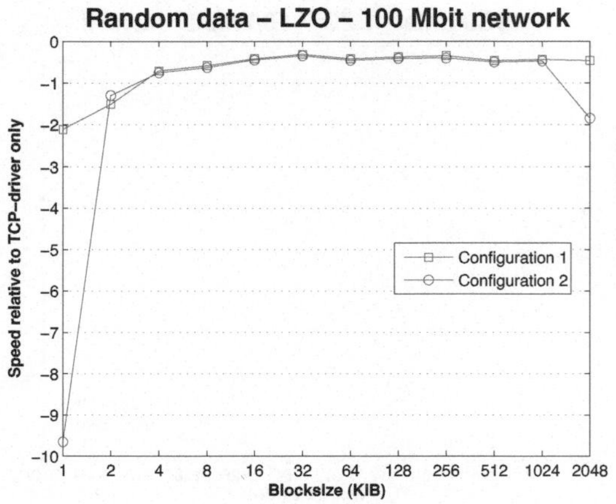

Figure 11: Performance comparison of compression (lzo) + TCP driver with TCP driver alone for Random data

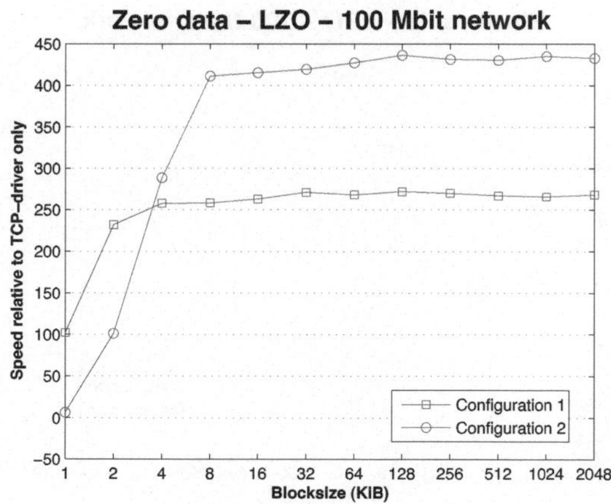

Figure 12: Performance comparison of compression (lzo) + TCP driver with TCP driver alone for Zero data

E. Compression Driver Overhead

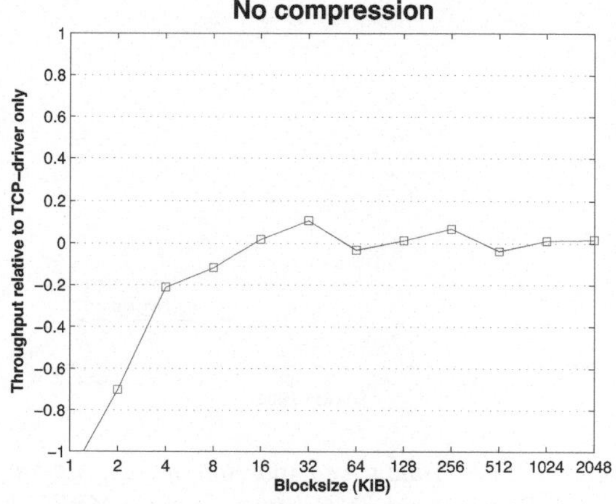

Figure 13: Compression driver overhead

The driver has a mode where data is transferred without being compressed or modified. This represents the minimum amount of overhead that will be added due to the presence of the driver, regardless of which compression method is used and to what extent the data is compressible. As can be observed from Figure 13, the driver itself introduces very less overhead – less than 0.2% for block sizes 4KB or more – exceeds 1% only at block size 1KB. Values above zero should be regarded as random fluctuations - the driver cannot increase performance other than by compressing data.

F. GridFTP results

One of the features of GridFTP is that it can make use of multiple parallel streams. As each stream is a separate thread, this driver should theoretically see an increase in performance when used in a multi-core/multi-CPU setup. To test this theory, these tests were performed with GridFTP using four different degrees of parallelism.

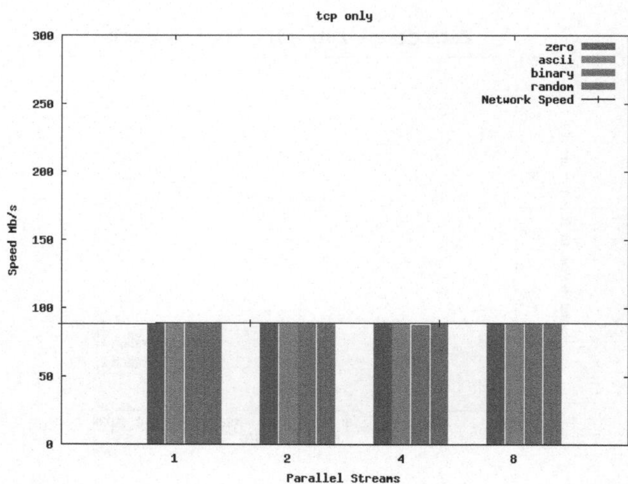

Figure 14: Performance of GridFTP with no compression

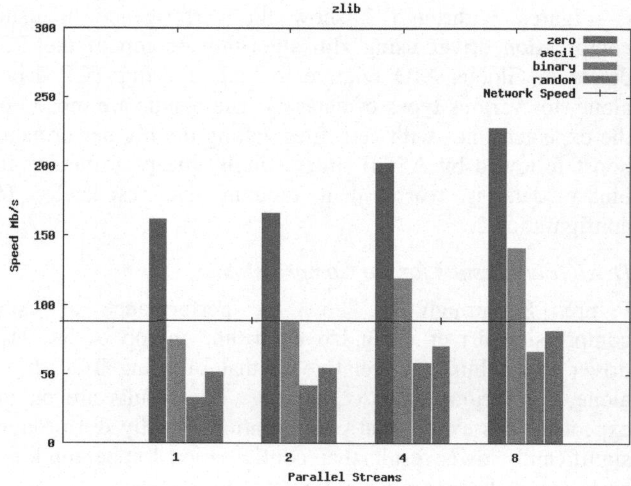

Figure 15: Performance of GridFTP with compression driver (zlib) for different parallelism values

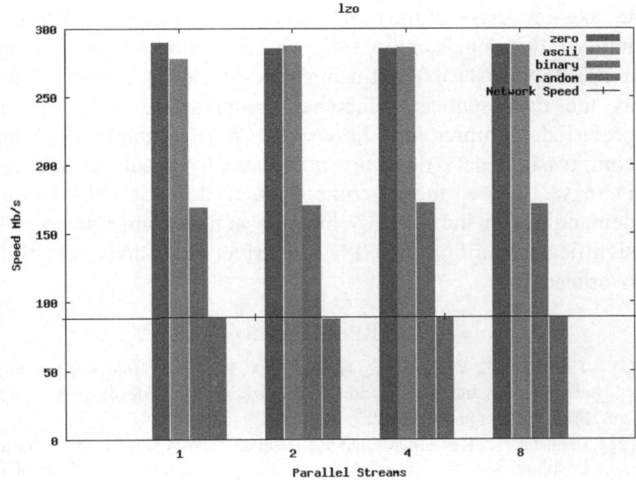

Figure 16: Performance of GridFTP with compression driver (lzo) for different parallelism values

G. Fluctuations in the Results

As noted above, each test was run ten times and the result was taken as the average. A general pattern could be noted that the fluctuations would be greater for highly compressible data. To get a feel for the these fluctuations, Table 3 presents the differences found in the results for ASCII and MPEG data using zlib-compression, at a block size of 16KB.

Table 3: Deviations in the results

	ASCII	MPEG
Mean value	185.10 m/s	91.92 m/s
Median value	187.16 m/s	91.94 m/s
Minimum value	176.03 m/s	91.79 m/s
Maximum value	192.30 m/s	91.95 m/s
Standard deviation	5.35 m/s	0.05 m/s

V. INTERPRETING THE RESULTS

A number of useful conclusions can be drawn by looking at the data that has been collected.

A. Effect on Network Load

The compression ratios measured tells us two important things about the performance of the driver. The first is the impact on network load. For example, when transferring the binary file used in these tests using zlib compression network load is reduced to 38.76%, to 97.70% for the MPEG, and so on. This means that in congested network environments using this driver may have a fortunate side effect – Increase the performance even for other applications and hosts by reducing total network load.

B. Effect on Host-to-Host Throughput

The second thing we learn looking at the compression ratios is the maximum change in speed the driver can achieve. We will refer to this as the optimal speed multiplier and is calculated by 1 / compression ratio.

Consider the following example, which matches the results for configuration 1 using zlib compression at a blocksize of 16KB:

- Throughput sans the compression driver is 90 Mbps.
- Throughput with the compression driver is 139 Mbps.
- Compression ratio is 0.0815.

If we could use hosts with infinite CPU resources, the observed speed would be roughly 90 * (1/0.0815) = 1104 Mbps. Of course, there is no such thing as a host with infinite CPU resources. But this is still useful knowledge, because it gives us an idea of when the local hosts will be the bottleneck, and when the network will. In this case the hosts are clearly bottlenecks by a wide margin since the observed result (about 139 Mbps) is a far cry from the theoretical maximum (1104 Mbps). Second, it let's us derive the average speed at which data is actually sent across the network by the formula 's/opt', where s is the observed speed when using the compression driver, opt is the optimal speed multiplier described above (inverse of the compression ratio). Continuing the above example, this means that the break-even point between the hosts and the network being the bottleneck for ASCII data occurs when the network allows a throughput of 139*0.0815 = 11.33 Mbps. Similarly, we can predict that the speed will remain fairly constant at around 139Mbps so long as network throughput remains above 11.33Mbps.

C. Effect of Data Type

The formula s/opt for describing at which network speed the local hosts ceases to be the bottleneck can also tell us conclusively that the more a particular type of data can be compressed, the more strain it puts on the local hosts: Above we concluded that the host in configuration 1 can only output 11.33 m/s of compressed ASCII data to the network. Consider the following example from the same test setup (configuration 1, 16KB block size, zlib compression), but transferring MPEG data, which is very difficult to compress further:

- Throughput sans the compression driver remains 90Mbps.
- Throughput with the compression driver is 91.70Mbps.
- Compression ratio is 0.977.

The formula s/opt yields that throughput should about 89.29Mbps - meaning that the CPU in this case can output compressed data essentially as fast as the network can transmit it. The results support this conclusion - configuration 2 is not able to exceed these results noticeably despite having a considerably more powerful processor.

D. Choice of the Compression Algorithm

In general, zlib offers the best compression while LZO beats zlib by a wide margin when it comes to speed. Which library is to be preferred depends on the situation - if the network is the bottleneck by a wide margin, zlib will likely be the better choice. If not, LZO will produce better results. LZO can be considered the safer choice, since it is less likely to have a negative impact. Also note that there is no great difference in speed between configuration 1 and 2 at most block sizes when using LZO, except for ASCII and zero data. Identical performance tells us that the host CPUs were not bottlenecks in either case, even without doing the type of calculations described above - if they were, configuration 2 would have showed higher performance than configuration 1 due to the more powerful CPU.

E. Effect of Block Size

As noted above, compression algorithms perform differently depending on how much data they are fed at a time - the block size. Generally, this means that a higher level of compression will be achieved with larger block sizes. But, as we have concluded, higher compression level does not automatically translate into higher speeds. So which block size is to be preferred? When using zlib-compression the optimal block size seems to be 16KB, or possibly 32KB. LZO seems to perform better when the block size is bigger, with the notable exception of the drop in performance for configuration 2 at the highest block size for random and MPEG data. No answer has been found for why this drop takes place. Also note that these results may vary depending on hardware configuration - we cannot conclude from these results that 16KB will be the optimal size for zlib for all configurations.

VI. Future Work

A. Customizing the Driver

Imagine you have a situation that matches that of configuration 1 using zlib compression - the driver is beneficial in some circumstances but detrimental in others. What you would want to do is add rules such as "only compress if block size is 4KB or larger, and if compression ratio is greater than 80%" which would mean that the driver would be detrimental under very few circumstances, if any. We plan to add the capability to allow this type of customization.

B. Dynamically Determine the Compression Strategy

We plan to add the ability to determine compression strategy dynamically. For example, do a test-compression of data using all available strategies and choose the one which gives the best ration. This should probably only be done once each transfer - if the first block compresses nicely, we can probably assume that the rest will also compress nicely.

VII. Summary

We have developed a compression driver for the Globus XIO framework and presented a detailed performance study using different compression techniques for different hardware configurations. We have also showed how this driver can be used to compress the data on-the-fly for GridFTP transfers and how it can be used to speed up the transfers using parallelism to take advantage of the multiple cores in the hosts. Our results indicate that consistently higher speeds can be achieved across a 100Mbps LAN without using state-of-the-art CPUs, as long as the data sent is somewhat compressible. LZO is the preferred compression library in most situations. More compressible data does not automatically result in a speed increase, since more compressible data is also more demanding on the CPU. While the actual compression puts significant strain on the CPU, the driver itself adds very little overhead.

References

[1] T. Chiueh, C. Yang, T. He, H. Pfister, A. Kaufman, "Integrated volume compression and visualization," Visualization '97 proceedings, vol., no., pp.329-336, 24-24 Oct. 1997

[2] I. Foster, C. Kesselman, and S. Tuecke, "The Anatomy of the Grid: Enabling Scalable Virtual Organization," The International Journal of High Performance Computing Applications, vol. 15, no. 3, pp. 200–222, Fall 2001.

[3] Energy Science Network – http://www.es.net

[4] Internet2 - http://www.internet2.edu/

[5] W. Allcock, J. Bresnahan, R. Kettimuthu, and J. Link, "The Globus eXtensible Input/Output System (XIO): A Protocol Independent I/O System for the Grid," in Proceedings of the 19th IEEE International Parallel and Distributed Processing Symposium - Workshop 4, Vol. 5, IEEE Computer Society, Washington, DC, 2005. 179.1. DOI= http://dx.doi.org/10.1109/IPDPS.2005.429.

[6] J. Bresnahan, R. Kettimuthu, and I. Foster, "XIOPerf: A Tool for Evaluating Network Protocols," in Proceedings of the Third International Workshop on Networks for Grid Applications, 2006.

[7] Allcock, B., Bresnahan, J., Kettimuthu, R., Link, M., Dumitrescu, C., Raicu, I. and Foster, I., The Globus Striped GridFTP Framework and Server. SC'2005, 2005.

[8] R. Kettimuthu, L. Lacinski, M. Link, K. Pickett, S. Tuecke and I. Foster, Instant GridFTP. In 9th Workshop on High Performance Grid and Cloud Computing, May 2012.

[9] R. Kettimuthu, M. Link, J. Bresnahan, and W. Allcock, "Globus Data Storage Interface (DSI) – Enabling Easy Access to Grid Datasets," First DIALOGUE Workshop: Applications-Driven Issues in Data Grids, Aug. 2005.

[10] Y. Gu and R. L. Grossman, "UDT: UDP-based Data Transfer for High-Speed Wide Area Networks," Comput. Networks 51, no. 7 (May 2007), 1777–1799.

[11] J. Bresnahan, M. Link, R. Kettimuthu, I. Foster, "UDT as an Alternative Transport Protocol for GridFTP," 7th International Workshop on Protocols for Future, Large-Scale and Diverse Network Transports (PFLDNeT 2009), Tokyo, Japan, May 2009.

[12] H. Subramoni, P. Lai, R. Kettimuthu, D.K. Panda, "High Performance Data Transfer in Grid Environment Using GridFTP over InfiniBand," 10th IEEE/ACM International Symposium on Cluster, Cloud and Grid Computing (CCGrid 2010), May 2010.

[13] R. Kettimuthu, A. Sim, D. Gunter, B. Allcock, P. Bremer, J. Bresnahan, A. Cherry, L. Childers, E. Dart, I. Foster, K. Harms, J. Hick, J. Lee, M. Link, J. Long, K. Miller, V. Natarajan, V. Pascucci, K. Raffenetti, D. Ressman, D. Williams, L. Wilson, L. Winkler, "Lessons Learned from Moving Earth System Grid Data Sets over a 20 Gbps Wide-Area Network", 19th ACM International Symposium on High Performance Distributed Computing (HPDC), 2010.

[14] J. Bresnahan, M. Link, R. Kettimuthu, I. Foster, "GridFTP Multilinking," 2009 TeraGrid Conference, Arlington, VA, June 2009.

[15] J. Bresnahan, M. Link, R. Kettimuthu, and I. Foster, "Managed GridFTP," 8th Workshop on High Performance Grid and Cloud Computing, May 2011

Cost-effective Cloud Services for HPC in the Cloud: The IaaS or The HaaS?

Ifeanyi P. Egwutuoha[1], Shiping Chen[2], David Levy[1], and Rafael Calvo[1]
[1]School of Electrical & Information Engineering, The University of Sydney, Australia
Email: {ifeanyi.egwutuoha, david.levy, rafael.calvo}@sydney.edu.au
[2]Information Engineering Laboratory, CSIRO ICT Centre, Australia
Email: shiping.chen@csiro.au

Abstract—*In the scientific research domain, traditional High Performance Computing (HPC) refers to the use of supercomputers, grid environments and/or clusters of computers to solve computation-intensive and/or data-intensive problems. The traditional HPC systems are expensive and sometimes require huge start-up investment, technical and administrative support and job queuing. With the benefits of cloud computing, cloud services such as Infrastructure as a Service (IaaS) and Hardware as a Service (HaaS), enables scientists and researchers to run their HPC applications in the cloud without upfront investment associated with the traditional HPC infrastructure. In this paper we analyze the computational performance and dollar cost of running HPC applications in the cloud when IaaS or HaaS is leased. We find that HaaS significantly reduces the cost of running HPC application in the cloud by 20% compare to IaaS without significant impact to application's performance. We also found that there is a substantial improvement in computational performance in HaaS compare to IaaS.*

Keywords: HPC, cloud computing, HaaS, computation-intensive applications, computational performance

1. Introduction

In the scientific research domain, traditional High Performance Computing (HPC) refers to the use of supercomputers, grid environments and/or clusters of computers to solve computation-intensive problems. Some common uses of HPC systems include weather forecasting, aircraft crash simulations, computational fluid dynamics for aerodynamics studies and many other computation-intensive applications [14], [20]. Today, HPC systems also offer new opportunities in business. For example, in financial institutions HPC systems are used in real time modelling to make informed investment decisions. The most powerful HPC systems are ranked on top500 [1]. Huge capital is needed to acquire the HPC systems, this makes it difficult for research communities. Until recently, HPC systems would have been out of reach for most research communities.

With the recent advancement in computing technologies, computation-intensive applications are not only executed in the traditional HPC systems but also in HPC system in the cloud. Cloud computing [2], [3], [8] is a revolutionary computing paradigm for storing data and running applications, including computation-intensive applications. It promises numerous benefits, which includes, no upfront investments. Cloud computing also reduces development time, staff (e.g., administrators), and hardware, resulting in better service and significant cost saving. It is expected that more computation-intensive applications will be deployed and run in HPC systems in the cloud [5], [3]. Furthermore, the Amazon Elastic Compute Cloud (Amazon EC2) cluster recently appeared in TOP500 list [1], which shows that there is a great future for HPC systems in the cloud.

With Cloud computing pay-as-you-go pricing model, scientists and researchers can lease cloud services such as Infrastructure as a Service (IaaS) and Hardware as a Service (HaaS) for computation-intensive applications. These services are relinquished when not in use. This avoids the job queuing, which is a common phenomenon in traditional HPC system. The price model is also attractive when compared to traditional HPC systems that require huge investments capital, administrative issues and allocation policies.

However, the cost of running HPC application on the cloud may be high if the cloud services are not well understood and the cost-effective cloud services chosen. If the dollar cost of running HPC applications in the cloud is high comparing to traditional HPC system, then the benefits of running computation-intensive application on the cloud may have been defected. HPC research communities are concerned about the cost and computational performance of different cloud services.

In this paper we analyze the computational performance and dollar cost of running computation-intensive application in HPC systems in the cloud when IaaS and HaaS are leased. We find that the cost of executing computation-intensive application when HaaS is leased is significantly lower compared to the IaaS model. We show that there is significant improvement in computational performance of the application on HaaS if the computation-intensive application is not a network intensive application. Our experimental setup uses the Message Passing Interface (MPI) implementation [4]. We provide our test results, but do not reveal the identify of the cloud providers, to avoid any head-to-head comparisons. However, we do include the relevant technical details of the cloud instances.

In Section 2 we present the overview of Cloud services for HPC systems in the clouds, while Section 3 presents the experimental setup. MPI applications and benchmark are presented in Section 4. Experimental results and Cost analysis are presented in Section 5 and 6 respectively, while Section 7 discusses related work. Finally, some conclusions are presented in Section 8.

2. Overview of Cloud Services for HPC Systems in the cloud

With the advent of cloud computing infrastructures, cloud services providers such as Salesforce.com, Amazon [5], Rackspace, Baremetalcloud [6], Microsoft Azure, SoftLayer [7], Google, IBM offer different cloud services to cloud users. Some of these services offered are Software as a Service (SaaS), Platform as a Service (PaaS), Infrastructure as a Service (IaaS), Hardware as a Service (HaaS), Network as a Service (NaaS) and Storage as a Service (STaaS). Based on the capability provided by the cloud service provider, cloud computing services fall into four major competing categories [8], [9]. *Application as a Service, Platform as a Service, Infrastructure as a Service and Hardware as a Service.* Figure 1 shows the architecture of the cloud computing services.

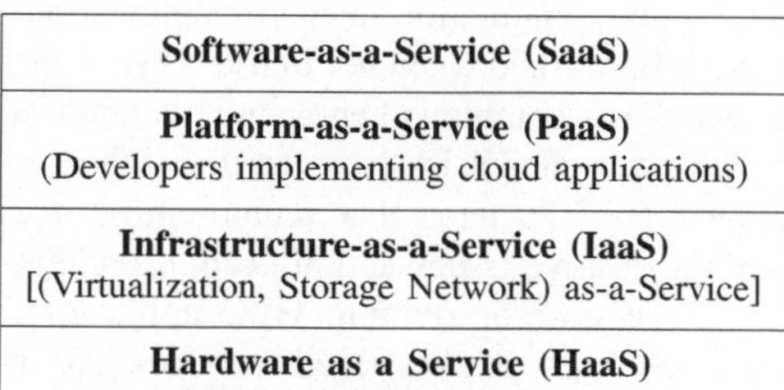

Fig. 1: Cloud layered architecture [8]

Software as a Service (SaaS) is the highest abstraction level in the cloud. It offers cloud users ready-to-use online applications that are already deployed in the cloud. This layer is hidden from the users and managed by the SaaS providers. The users do not know where or how these applications are deployed, but simply use them. SaaS cloud applications can be accessed via the internet with any internet-ready device such as a laptops, smart phones, or iPads. This enables relatively dumb clients to perform complex tasks, by shifting the real work, transparently to the user, into the cloud. A good example of SaaS is the commonly used Gmail (email services) provided by Google.

Platform as a Service (PaaS) provides cloud users with a fully configured and managed computing platform, ready to run custom software developed by the users. Each PaaS platform is targeted to software developed in a specific programming language or software framework (e.g., Java EE) and ready to execute corresponding builds. PaaS cloud users deploy and run their software, without setting up servers and software stacks, without thinking about scalability or clustering, and often even without knowing how many computers or CPUs their application will run on.

Infrastructure as a Service (IaaS) is similar to HaaS, but virtual machines are rented out instead of real hardware. IaaS cloud users have to install, configure, and maintain the virtual machines they rent and are free to choose the operating system and software stack they install in their VMs. Often IaaS users make use of a pre-installed and preconfigured VM image supplied by their provider as base installation. Users do not have root access to the hardware. A good example of cloud provider that offers IaaS for HPC applications is Amazon [5]. The Amazon Elastic Compute Cloud (Amazon EC2) offers cluster compute instances for HPC applications.

Hardware as a Service (HaaS); in this case, the cloud provider basically rents out '*bare-metal*' hardware (e.g., server/host and storage). Notable examples of cloud providers that offer HaaS are Baremetalcloud [6] and SoftLayer [7]. Cloud users connect to HaaS via the Internet, install and configure (e.g., VMs) the server they leased. Cloud users choose HaaS, because it gives them full control of the server, operating system, and software/hardware stack, as well as the number of VMs they execute on it. Research communities do lease HaaS for computation-intensive and/or data-intensive applications and configure HPC systems according to their needs [8], [9]. Consequently, computation-intensive applications that were traditionally run on HPC systems can now be executed in the cloud. Figure 2 shows the HaaS architecture and access level of the provider and user.

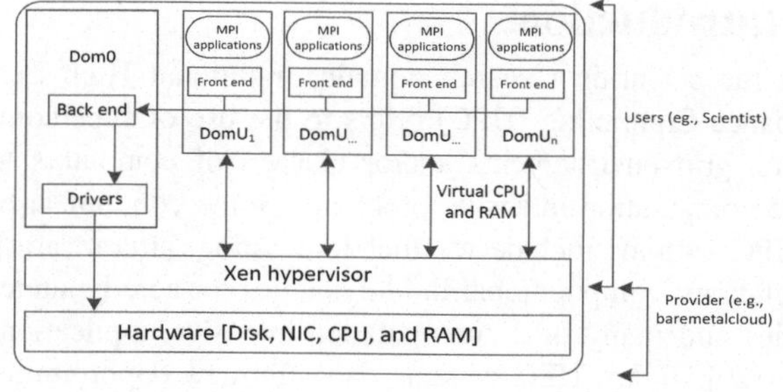

Fig. 2: An example of HaaS architecture with level of involvement of key players

3. Experimental setup

We setup experimental environments to evaluate the computational performance and dollar cost of running computation-intensive application on IaaS and HaaS. Our experimental setup includes two services we have leased from two cloud service providers; for the purpose of avoiding head-to-head comparison of the two cloud providers, we call them Cloud-A and Cloud-B. Cloud-A offers IaaS in different kind of cluster instances for HPC applications: for example, cluster compute instances. Cloud-B offers HaaS which can be configured to run HPC applications.

3.1 Cluster Compute Instances from Cloud-A (IaaS)

Cloud-A is one of the major cloud service providers. They offer IaaS in different instances for HPC applications. Table 1 shows a sample of cluster compute instances with price details of on-demand instances from cloud providers. The clusters compute instances are available with commonly used Operating System (OS) (Windows and Linux) in 32-bit and 64-bit platforms. For our experiments, we choose the Ref-C virtual instance in the Table 1 because it is widely used for HPC applications. The instances use Xen full virtualization. The I/O network communication between the cluster instance is 10 Gigabit Ethernet.

In order to compare the computational performance and dollar cost of running HPC applications when IaaS and HaaS services are leased. We leased a cluster compute instance with a total of 16 processors. The details of the leased cluster compute instance are shown in Table 2. We installed OpenMPI 1.6 [23] on the node. OpenMPI is an open source implementation of the Message Passage Interface (MPI).

Table 1: Virtual and HaaS Instances from Cloud-A and Cloud-B

Instance type	Memory	CPU	Disk	Cost of instance for Linux	Cost of instance Window
Ref-A Virtual instance	30 GB	2x2.0 GHz (sixteen-core)	500 GB	$1.600 per hour	$1.800 per hour
Ref-B Virtual instance	244 GB	2 x Intel Xeon E5-2670 (eight-core)	240 GB	$3.500 per hour	$3.831 per hour
Ref-C Virtual instance	22 GB	2 x Intel Xeon X5570 (quad-core)	1690 GB	$2.100 per hour	$2.600 per hour
Ref-D Virtual instance	23.00 GB	2 x Intel Xeon X5570 (quad-core)	1690 GB	$1.30 per hour	$1.610 per hour
Ref-E Hardware Instance	96 GB DDR3-1333	2x2.13 GHz E5606 (eight-core)	1000.0GB, 7200RPM	0.99 per hour	$1.19 per hour
Ref-F Hardware Instance	48 GB DDR3-1066	2x2.66 GHz X5650 (twelve-core)	300GB, 10000RPM	0.73 per hour	$0.93 per hour
Ref-G Hardware Instance	64 GB	2x2.0 GHz E5-2650-OctoCore (sixteen-core)	500.0GB	1.54 per hour	$1.59 per hour
Ref-H Hardware Instance	32 GB	2x2.0 GHz (eight-core)	250.0GB	1.25 per hour	$1.3 per hour

3.2 HPC system on HaaS in the cloud

As explained in Section II, HaaS allows users to have full control of the system and control environment for measuring system performance and other available experiments. This enables users to determine the number of VMs to be deployed for HPC applications. We have leased an HaaS instance (Ref-G) with 64GB RAM from Cloud-B. Table 1 shows some of the cloud services that the HaaS providers offer that are similar to cluster compute instances that Cloud-A offers. The table also gives a summary of HaaS and price of the service leased. The communication network between each HaaS is a 1 Gigabit Ethernet.

The summary of the VM we provisioned on the HaaS is shown in Table 2. We installed Xen hypervisor [11] on the host. Xen hypervisor is an open source, industry standard virtualization technology. Linux Operating System (Ubuntu 12.4 64-bit) runs on top of the Xen hypervisor. We imported our pre-configured para-virtualised guest OS (Ubuntu 12.4 64-bit) on the HaaS instance. The pre-configured para-virtualised guest reduces the time to setup the HPC system on the HaaS instance. A para-virtualized OS uses a modified kernel, and reduces the size of the image. The VM is configured to have 16 processors with 60GB memory and 200GB hard drive. We installed OpenMPI on the node. This setup is almost equivalent to the cluster compute instances we leased from Cloud-A. The setup also allow us to have a good comparison environment for IaaS and HaaS in terms of computational performance and dollar cost. Table 2 shows both the IaaS and HaaS environments we used.

Table 2: Computational environment for IaaS and HaaS

Cloud-A, VM of IaaS	Cloud-B, VM of HaaS
RAM: 24 GB	RAM: 60 GB
Architecture: x86_64	Architecture: x86_64
CPU op-mode(s): 32-bit, 64-bit	CPU op-mode(s): 64-bit
CPU(s): 16	CPU(s): 16
On-line CPU(s) list: 0-15	Thread(s) per core: 16
Thread(s) per core: 2	Core(s) per socket: 1
Core(s) per socket: 4	CPU socket(s): 1
NUMA node(s): 1	NUMA node(s): 1
Vendor ID: GenuineIntel	Vendor ID: GenuineIntel
CPU family: 6	CPU family: 6
Model: 26	Model: 26
Stepping: 5	Stepping: 5
CPU MHz: 2933.440	CPU MHz: 2266.796
Hypervisor vendor: Xen	Hypervisor vendor: Xen
Virtualization type: full	Virtualization type: para

4. MPI applications and benchmark

We used a commonly used HPC benchmark and real HPC application to analyze and evaluate the MPI applications running on IaaS and HaaS services. The benchmark was the High Performance Linpack (HPL) benchmark [12] and the application was ClustalW-MPI [14]. We desribe them below.

HPL [12] is a benchmark that is commonly used to evaluate the computational performance of HPC systems for example, top500 [1]. It measures the floating execution rate of linear equations based on the problem size. We executed the HPL benchmark with five different problem sizes of 2,000, 4,000, 6,000, 8,000 and 10,000 on the both cloud services on VMs from IaaS and on HaaS. The execution of each the problem sizes was carried twice and the average execution time calculated. The five different problem sizes enable us to obtain different wall clock execution times of HPL. We recorded the wall clock execution time for each problem size. We used the wall clock execution time to analyse the dollar cost and computational performance of the both platforms. Figure 3 show the results obtained on computational-performance.

ClustalW-MPI [14] is a parallel implementation of ClustalW [15] which is based on MPI. ClustalW is a tool that is widely used in bioinformatics for multiple alignments of nucleic acid and protein sequences. It uses three alignments steps: pairwise alignment, guide-tree generation and progressive alignment. We ran a sample of 'A full multiple sequence alignment', 'A guide tree only seqence alignment', and 'A multiple sequence alignment out of an existing' on nodes from IaaS and from HaaS. We recorded the execution time of the three alignment steps to compare time to finish executions with both IaaS and HaaS. The results are shown in figure 4.

5. Results and Discussion

One of the major attractions to the Cloud-A cluster compute instance is that it is relatively easy to set up the clusters compared to setting up a cluster in HaaS. However, some level of technical knowledge is required to setup cluster on Cloud-A that will run HPC applications due to varying needs of HPC applications. In order to reduce the time to set up an HPC system on HaaS instances in the cloud, we uploaded our pre-configured para-virtualized image to the cloud. There are also similar VM images which can be downloaded from different sites. We estimated that this technique reduces the set up time by up to 80%. We did not compare the time to setup HPC system in Cloud-A (IaaS) cloud and in Cloud-B (HaaS) because setup time varies with individuals technical experiences.

From the computational performance result of the HPL benchmark shown in figure 3, we can see that the wall clock execution time of HPL benchmark on a provisioned instance on HaaS is shorter when compared to IaaS provided by Cloud-A. We achieved this because the memory of the virtual instances deployed on HaaS is 60GB. We chose to allocate this amount of memory to our virtual instance because we can predict the memory needed. This option is not available for the IaaS instance (users cannot change the memory of the virtual instance chosen). We also have full control of the Hardware instance and virtual instances.

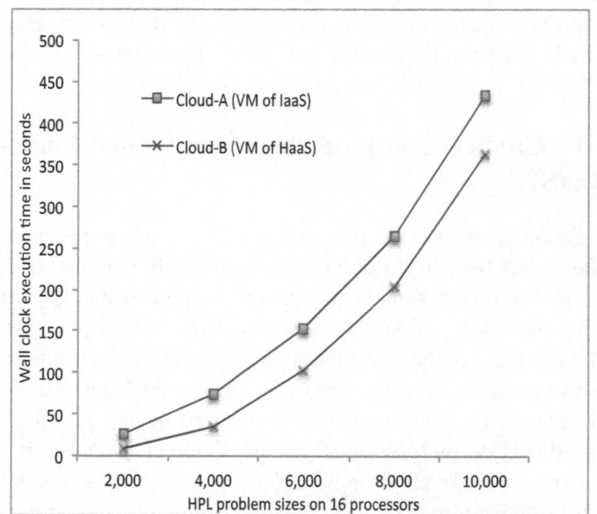

Fig. 3: Computational performance of High Performance Linpack on 1 node with 16 processors

As shown in Figure 3, executing the HPL on 1 node with 16 processor eliminates the bandwidth inequality on both providers. The virtual instances HaaS out performs IaaS. This is because we have full control of the applications running of our HaaS instance and we allocated higher memory to VM on HaaS. On IaaS, other VM instances may have been hosted on the hardware which may have affected the performance of the application running on our lease IaaS instance. As shown in [19], high resource allocations on infrastructure affect applications running on VMs.

The ClustalW-MPI results is shown in Figure 4. Cloud-A IaaS uses 10 Gigabit Ethernet network, whereas HaaS we leased uses a 1 gigabit Ethernet network. We could have benchmarks with the same bandwidths, however the two major providers of HaaS do not have 10 gigabit Ethernet network. The results in Figure 4 show that there is no significant impact on application running on IaaS and on virtual instances on HaaS.

6. Cost Analysis

At the time of writing, Cloud-A offers different price models to their cluster compute instance customers; The primary price model which is widely used is called 'on-demand instances'. The on-demand instances price model allows users to pay hourly without contract while other price models may require up front payments and/or contracts.

Cloud-B offers their customers a pay-as-you-go price model, which is similar to on-demand instance prices offered by Cloud-A. Therefore we use on-demand price instance

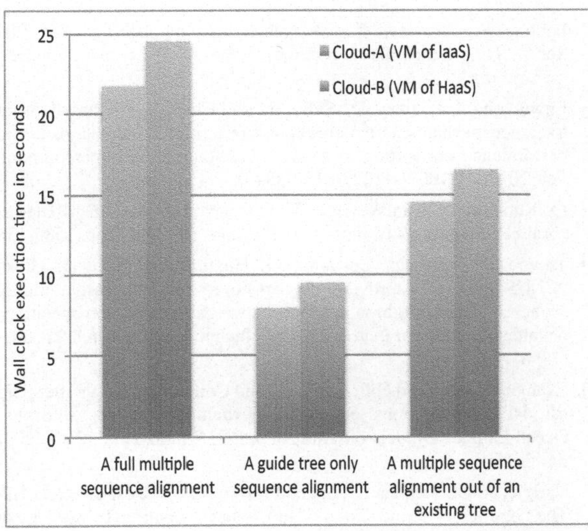

Fig. 4: Performance of ClustalW-MPI application on 16 processors

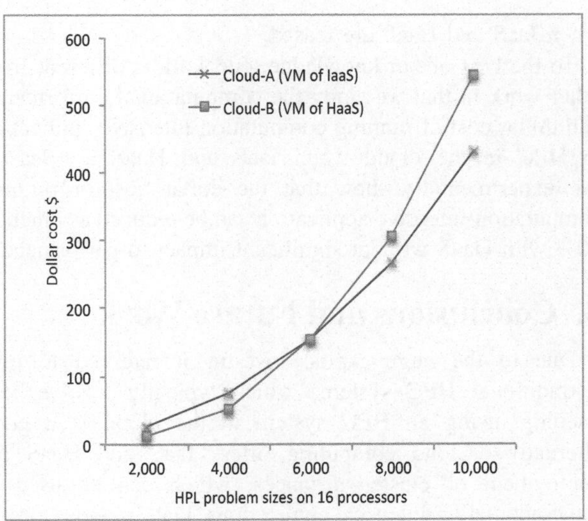

Fig. 5: The cost analysis VM of IaaS and VM of HaaS

to compare the cost of running computation-intensive applications on both cloud services. In addition to the on-demand/pay-as-you-go instances prices, there are charges, which are charged for some cloud services such as network bandwidth and IP addresses which we do not consider to avoid complexity. We used the results obtained from HPL benchmarking to analyse the cost. As previously used in a similarly cost analysis [18], we assume that 1 second is equal to hourly rate which the both cloud providers offer. This also allows us to do the analysis without paying the for hours the experiment would have cost. We used the prices of the leased services as shown in Table 1 and 2. The cost analysis computation of IaaS and HaaS is shown in figure 5.

Based on the computational performance and cost analysis it appears that it is more cost effective to lease HaaS and configure the HPC systems. Cloud service users of HaaS have full control of the hardware as well as the VMs they provisioned. Application performance and other metrics can be easily measured. From the result, it seems that the cost of running HPC applications can be reduced by 20% when HaaS is leased.

7. Related work

Cloud computing is a revolutionary computing paradigm for storing data, running applications, including computation-intensive applications. Cloud computing promises numerous benefits, which includes no up front investments for HPC applications, which is attractive, compared to traditional HPC systems. Many studies have evaluated the suitability of HPC systems in the cloud and showed that it is expected that more computation-intensive HPC applications will be run in the cloud HPC than traditional HPC systems [16]. Furthermore, the Amazon Elastic Compute Cloud (Amazon EC2) cluster recently appeared in TOP500 list [1] in year 2010, which shows that there is a viable future for HPC systems in the cloud.

Many past researches evaluating of HPC applications on HPC systems in the Cloud with emphasis on Amazon EC2 have been carried out. These investigations focus on the performance of Amazon EC2 and Traditional HPC systems [16], [17], [18], [19].

Carlyle *et al.* [17] studied the cost effective HPC System. They show that it is cost effective for institutions like Purdue University to operate a community/traditional cluster than to lease HPC resources from Amazon EC2. This study clearly shows that Amazon on-demand cluster compute instances prices are not cost effective for HPC applications for some institutions. Their work focuses on Amazon EC2 service IaaS and traditional HPC systems.

Deelman *et al.* [18] in their work on 'The Cost of Doing Science on the Cloud: The Montage examples'; show that the cost of cloud services could be significantly reduced without significant impact on application performance, if the right storage and compute resources are provisioned. However, they did not consider different platforms like HaaS. We extended their work, demonstrating that HaaS can significantly reduce the cost of running computation-intensive application on HPC in the cloud.

Ekanayake and Fox [19] compare HPC applications with different needs and showed the performance of applications with latency. However, they did not compare the cost of executing computation-intensive application on different services such as IaaS and HaaS.

Yao *et al.* [21] showed that optimal cost-performance ratio can be achieved with th appropriate cloud instance. However, they did not consider cost and computational performance when IaaS and HaaS are leased.

To the best of our knowledge, our work is different from other work in that we study the computational performance and dollar cost of running computation-intensive application in HPC in the cloud when IaaS and HaaS are leased. We experimentally show that the dollar cost of running computation-intensive application can be reduced as much as 20% with HaaS without significant impact to performance.

8. Conclusions and Future Work

Due to the huge capital investment required to own a traditional HPC systems which typically involves job queuing, using an HPC system in the cloud is a good alternative. Cloud computing offers IaaS and HaaS for deployment of cluster instances, which can be used to run computation-intensive applications. IaaS provides almost ready to use clusters with minimal deployment installation tasks. With HaaS, virtual machines can be provisioned to run computation-intensive application. We have conducted experimental analysis to determine the performance and cost when cloud services IaaS and HaaS are leased to run computation-intensive application. We showed that the dollar cost of running computation-intensive application in the cloud can be reduced by as much as 20% when HaaS is leased. We showed that there is no significant impact in performance of the applications when executed on the leased HaaS.

Acknowledgment

The authors would like to thank Bran Selic for providing valuable comments and suggestions.

References

[1] http://www.top500.org/

[2] Armbrust, M., Fox, A., *et al*, "A view of cloud computing," Communications of the ACM, 53(4), pp. 50-58, 2010.

[3] Mell, P., and Grance, T. "The NIST definition of cloud computing (draft)," NIST special publication, 800, (2011), pp. 145.

[4] Message Passing Interface Forum, "MPI: A message-passing interface standard," International Journal of Supercomputer Applications, 8(3/4):165-414, 1994.

[5] Amazon. (2013), [Online], http://aws.amazon.com/ec2/

[6] Baremetalcloud [Online], http://baremetalcloud.com/index.php/en/

[7] SoftLayer (2013), http://www.softlayer.com/

[8] Rimal, B. P., Choi, E., and Lumb, I., "A taxonomy and survey of cloud computing systems," In INC, IMS and IDC, 2009, NCM'09, Fifth International Joint Conference on (pp. 44-51). IEEE, 2009.

[9] Egwutuoha, I. P., Chen, S., Levy, D., Selic, B. and Calvo, R., "A Proactive Fault Tolerance Approach to High Performance Computing (HPC) in the Cloud," in The 2nd International Conference on Cloud and Green Computing, Xiangtan, Hunan, China, 2012, pp. 268-273.

[10] http://www.mpi-forum.org/

[11] Xen hypervisor, [Online], http://www.xen.org/products/xenhyp.html

[12] Petitet, A., Whaley, C., Dongarra, J., and Cleary, A., (2008, Sept), "HPL Benchmark," [Online], http://www.netlib.org/benchmark/hpl/

[13] Egwutuoha, I. P., Levy, D., Selic, B., and Chen, S., "A survey of fault tolerance mechanisms and checkpoint/restart implementations for high performance computing systems," The Journal of Supercomputing, Feb 2013, 10.1007/s11227-013-0884-0.

[14] Li, Kuo-Bin. "ClustalW-MPI: ClustalW analysis using distributed and parallel computing," Bioinformatics 19, no. 12 (2003): pp. 1585-1586.

[15] Thompson, Julie D., Desmond G. Higgins, and Toby J. Gibson. "CLUSTAL W: improving the sensitivity of progressive multiple sequence alignment through sequence weighting, position-specific gap penalties and weight matrix choice" Nucleic acids research 22, no. 22 (1994): 4673-4680.

[16] Evangelinos, C., and Hill, C. N., "Cloud Computing for parallel Scientific HPC Applications: Feasibility of running Coupled Atmosphere-Ocean Climate Models on Amazon's EC2," ratio 2, no. 2.40 (2008): pp. 2-34.

[17] Carlyle, A. G., Stephen L. H., and Preston M. S., "Cost-effective HPC: The community or the Cloud?," In Cloud Computing Technology and Science (CloudCom), 2010 IEEE Second International Conference on, pp. 169-176. IEEE, 2010

[18] Deelman, E., Singh, G., Livny, M., Berriman, B., and Good, J., "The cost of doing science on the cloud: the montage example," In Proceedings of the 2008 ACM/IEEE conference on Supercomputing, (2008, November), (p. 50), IEEE Press.

[19] Ekanayake, J., and Fox, G., "High performance parallel computing with clouds and cloud technologies" Cloud Computing (2010): 20-38.

[20] Fox, G. C., and Coddington, P. D., "An overview of high performance computing for the physical sciences," In Proceedings of Mardi Gras Conference: High Performance Computing and Its Applications in the Physical Sciences, 1993.

[21] Yao, J., Ng, A., Chen, S. *et al*, "A Performance Evaluation of Public Cloud Using TPC-C Benchmark," The 1st International Workshop on Analytics Services on the Cloud (ASC 2012), in conjunction with ICSOC 2012: 1-7.

[22] Penguin Computing. http://www.penguincomputing.com/services/hpc-cloud/pod/architecture.

[23] OpenMPI, http://www.open-mpi.org/

A Chord-based Architecture for Efficient Dynamic Service Provisioning over Distributed Resources

D. Jaiswal[1], **S. Mistry**[2], **A. Mukherjee**[3] **and N. Mukherjee**[1]
[1]Department of Computer Science and Engineering, Jadavpur University, Kolkata-700032, India
[2]School of Mobile Computing and Communication, Jadavpur University, Kolkata-700098, India
[3]Innovation Labs, Tata Consultancy Services, Kolkata-700091, India

Abstract— *The demand for distributed applications has been increasing since the birth of internet. It has scaled geographical areas in search of information and computational resources for processing. With the advent of Grid computing, ad-hoc Virtual Organizations have added an impetus towards distributed applications by providing on-demand service provisioning. The use of job-based paradigms and strong coupling of current service-based paradigms with static registries such as UDDI hinder the achievement of complete dynamism over volatile resources of the Grid. A possible solution is the use of structured peer to peer overlay networks to keep a check on the resources as well as handle the volatility of the system. In this paper, we present an architecture of a web service based P2P Grid framework for managing the services and resources using the Chord protocol over a de-centralized registry which facilitates demand driven provisioning of web services and enables a virtual market place for computational resources.*

Keywords: Grid Computing, SOA, Dynamic Deployment, P2P, Chord, UDDI.

1. Introduction

In the recent past distributed computing has evolved as a new paradigm where resources are shared among the consumers over the Internet in collaborative manner. With the advent of technologies like Service Oriented Architecture (SOA), Grid Computing and Cloud Computing, a new era of distributed computing has started which is characterised by availability of high-end resources and services over the Internet, access to the resources and services any time anywhere and non-requirement for the consumers of owning the resources - instead using them on demand and on pay-per use basis. However, this era is also marked with challenges like scalability, heterogeneity and dynamism of resources which need to be handled for large-scale adoption of the new technologies by the consumers [1], [2].

As Internet forms the basic communication backbone of all the major distributed computing systems, provisioning web services is a keystone to operating pay-per-use services between businesses. Furthermore, to deal with the inherent dynamic characteristics within a distributed environment, there is a need for dynamic adaptation for provisioned services to accommodate the ever-changing business requirements externally, as well as the computing resource status internally, while maintaining the continuousness of service provisioning. Hence, dynamic web service provisioning has been one of the major research issues for quite some time [3], [4].

In order to deal with the challenges mentioned earlier, we have proposed a fully distributed SOA-oriented framework [5] which offers loose coupling, robustness, scalability, availability and extensibility for large-scale distributed systems. The proposed distributed architecture acts as the basis of a service-oriented system using P2P as its communication backbone, thus allowing more flexibility and dynamism when compared with previous approaches [6], [4] used for dynamic service deployment in distributed environments. The main goals of the new architecture are mentioned below:

- To provide a distributed environment to overcome issues associated with centralized registry based architectures.
- To allow clients and service providers mention specific requirements for a service in order to achieve desired quality of service for clients.
- To provide scalability by load-balancing of deployed instances and re-deploying on demand using a P2P communication model.

One of the key features of this architecture is complete segregation of provider of services and provider of resources. Thus, providers of resources (platforms for service execution), i.e. the *Host Providers* (HPs) are placed in a different layer as compared with the *Web Service Providers* (WSPs), who provide services to the consumer and take care of all the collaboration with hosts. Consumers are placed in the third layer. In this three-layer architecture all the nodes act as peers to each other providing P2P based service publication, discovery, deployment and management. Resource discovery and allocation are done in a heterogeneous environment as per resource availability and metric of the Web Service.

In this paper we focus on the implementation of our proposed architecture on a structured overlay peer-to-peer (P2P) network, Chord [7], with the following goals:

1) de-centralizing the service registry in a structured

manner

2) making the registry adaptable with volatile set of resources
3) deployment cost of a given service incurred by a single WSP is shared among all WSPs.
4) making the registry scalable, having definite time bounds for a service query

In the earlier approaches [5], though the registry is decentralized as multiple single-site registries, a service may become unavailable if the hosting WSP goes down. To increase the service availability, we propose that the service is to be hosted from more than one WSP incurring a separate set of deployments for the same service. The framework presented in this paper provides a robust approach towards dynamically deploying web services, as well as decentralizing the registry to meet the increased availability of the services and maintaining its scalability at the same time.

The rest of the paper is organised as follows: Section 2 discusses the existing technologies and frameworks related to our work, Section 3 explains the proposed architecture and its implementation. The experimental results are presented in the section 4 and section 5 provides a discussion and future scopes of the proposed architecture.

2. Approaches for Dynamic Web Service Discovery and Deployment

With the growth of the Internet and web technologies, more and more complex services have come into existence spreading across organizational boundaries and multi-layered architectures, which has also resulted in complexity of cost-effective service discovery.

In this context, dynamic service discovery and deployment are two of the few most important issues for the Grid/Web framework. The Web Services Resource Framework (WSRF) utilizes tools like Monitoring and Discovery System (MDS) [8] for such purpose. But, an MDS Index Service registries are functionally similar to the centralized UDDI [9] registries with some additional flexibilities, which still are limited in terms of exploiting and reflecting the complete dynamism of a Grid.

2.1 UDDI-based Approaches

Most service oriented architectures use the UDDI standard for creating service registries. Since UDDI is based on XML, platform independence and inter-operability is implicit, but at a syntactic level. As UDDI uses a keyword-based service query, the discovery process is limited to a certain precision. With the increase in number of entries corresponding to services in the registry, the efficiency of the service discovery process and its scalability become a critical issue. The common model of a centralized UDDI is liable to single point of failure when the demand is extremely high. Decentralizing the registry, by having replicas of the service and the service metadata over various sites may be considered as a solution to the problem, but this distributed architecture makes the discovery process even more complex and requires periodic synchronisation to maintain an uniform view.

The concept of dynamic service deployment on available resources using UDDI was introduced by DynaSOAr [3], [4], [10] which was capable of deploying services on-demand, based on consumer requests. The DynaSOAr architecture offered a clear separation between Web Service Providers (WSP) and Host Providers (HP) in order to better manage the simultaneous tasks of service publication and discovery and service execution. In this architecture, the consumers send requests to the WSP, which in turn routes them to an appropriate HP for completion. For an already deployed service, the request is executed on the host and the result is returned back to the consumer. In case of a request for an yet undeployed service, the process involves its discovery from the centralized UDDI registry used by WSP's to publish the available services, locating the repository for service download and thereafter its deployment and the execution of the request. But, due to that static nature of UDDI, there are certain limitations related to service metadata and dynamic nature of resources in the grid environment.

2.2 P2P-based Approaches

As opposed to the UDDI-based approaches, P2P networks accomplish sharing of resources based on the discovery of peers in the network involving various discovery strategies and P2P network topologies. Hence decentralized P2P architectures coupled with Web Services as resources have the potential to be able to exploit the dynamism of the Grid more efficiently.

P2P overlays generally make use of DHT [11] to index and store data items. Unstructured P2P overlays support partial-match and complex queries, which fail to discover rare items as compared to popular ones, within specified time bounds. In contrast, structured P2P networks have some definite algorithms to guide the resource discovery process having an upper bound of the search time required for example such as Chord [7], CAN [12], Pastry [13], Tapestry [14]. Among these structured P2P networks the architecture proposed in this paper is based on Chord. The reason behind this is two-fold - (i) Chord is efficient in terms of tracking the networked resources and (ii) Chord uses an efficient mechanism of key assignment for network nodes as well as the retrieval by locating the node responsible for the key.

In recent years, the developments in decentralized P2P techniques related to resource sharing and discovery have ensured fault tolerance and scalability in the systems. At the same time, researchers have also looked into the possibility of incorporating P2P techniques with web service based architectures to cater to dynamic provisioning of services.

WSPeer [15] emerged as an interesting framework which combines the benefits of P2P's decentralized resource sharing with the XML based web service technologies. One of the major advantages of WSPeer is, consumers and service providers are located in remote places and can use it as an interface. This architecture provides the dynamic deployment facility such a way that anyone can easily deploy their application or part of application as web services. WSPeer has two different approaches towards service publication and discovery by the use of: (a) HTTP and UDDI coupled together, and, (b) a P2PS [16] implementation with a pluggable architecture of nodes. In the case of HTTP/UDDI implementation, the static centralized registry still remains a bottleneck of the infrastructure, which was removed in the P2PS implementation. Since the peer can act as both a service provider as well as service consumer a service endpoint was made available only when the node remains available in the network.

In recent years, there have been a lot of work on efficient ways of service discovery in Grid and SOA based frameworks [17] applying different approaches such as key word based matching, semantics or syntax based matching for the discovery process. Some approaches also use a ranking model to enhance the search procedure. All these approaches differ from each other and it is claimed in [17] that the suitability of the approaches depend on the application requirements, which in turn makes the selection of an appropriate service discovery process difficult. Further, it is desirable that the service discovery process should also be flexible enough for changing requirements. Hence, there is a need for a service discovery mechanism coupled with a registry which also caters to dynamic service provisioning. Frameworks which provide a complete solution for the entire cycle of web service publication to the deployment and management of the resources are rare or are in their initial stages of development.

A comparative study of the architectures mentioned in this section reveals that a static registry such as UDDI is a bottleneck for of any system based on SOA in terms of availability, capability of handling volatile resources in the network and system scalability. Since P2P systems are capable of handling the volatility of networked resources, a merger of the two concepts (P2P and SOA) may have certain advantages. P2P systems make use of *distributed hash tables* (DHTs) to keep track of the resources provided by the peers in the networks. Considering the web services as resources provided by peers in the system, the registry can be decentralized. Making use of a structured P2P overlay network with DHT implementation may further facilitate discovery and retrieval of resources within definite time bounds, making the registry scalable. DHT implementations such as CAN, Pastry, Tapestry, Chord can help achieve the above characteristics for a decentralized registry.

3. Using Chord for Dynamic Service Provisioning

In the context of dynamic web service provisioning, availability of services as well as provisioning based on service requirements to meet its QoS play an important role. The performance of such architectures totally relies on two important factors: firstly, the computational resources on which the web services are deployed and secondly discovery of web services. Hence managing both i.e. web services and computational resources, turns out to be an important issue.

In our previous work [5] we presented an architecture enabling dynamic on-demand service discovery and deployment based on the concepts of P2P computing. It strives to use the idle resources in the network via service deployments among the distributed resources on the basis of their capability and load factors. The services are made available from the provider of services and are deployed on-demand, after a proper matchmaking of the service metrics with the capability of the resources available to provide better performance. Successive deployments are made if the existing deployments get loaded or fail to offer response with some specified QoS. Though this approach could efficiently manage the computational resources for service deployments and their execution, web service discovery was limited to multiple single-site registry, i.e. the web services known to a given service provider were not known to other service providers, hence the service was available from a single service provider only. To increase the availability of a given service, it must be hosted from multiple service providers. In such a case deployment costs of a given service are incurred separately from different service providers. Thus, with an objective to provision web services on-demand, in the proposed architecture we focus on de-centralizing the registry, making it discoverable and thus increasing the service availability and reducing the deployment costs by sharing the current deployments. In the remaining part of this section, we describe the improvements made to our earlier work by decentralizing the registry using Chord after giving a brief overview of the proposed architecture.

3.1 Overview of the Architecture

Figure 1 shows the architectural diagram of the proposed framework. It consists of three loosely coupled entities as follows:

- **Client :** To invoke web services as consumer/client requests, using an interface provided by some WSP.
- **Web Service Provider(WSP) :** It acts as provider of services in the system for establishing and managing the registry of web services and provisioning them on demand.
- **Host Provider(HP) :** It acts as provider of computational resources for deploying the web services and serving client requests.

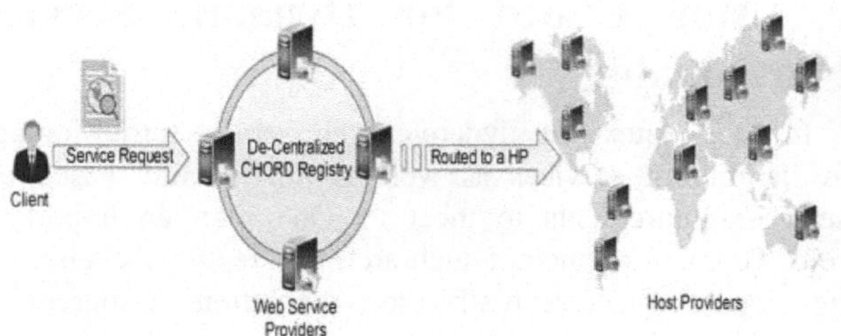

Fig. 1: Basic Architecture Diagram

The Client is the simplest component of the architecture. The clients can make service requests to the system by making a search query to the registry, via the interface provided by any of the WSP/s in the network. Apart from the client, all the nodes contributing to the system are peers to each other. Each peer can functionally act as either a WSP or a HP which is to be determined before a peer joins the network. The peers which aim to host web services, join the network as WSPs, whereas the peers that aim to provide computational resources join the network as HPs. The main role of HPs is to provide a platform for carrying out deployment of web service by WSPs. All the peers share their dynamic load information with all other peers to achieve better functionality and QoS for the clients.

WSP plays the most important role in the system. It is mainly responsible for:

1) Providing an interface for the clients.
2) Establishing and maintaining the service registry.
3) Taking care of new and successive deployments of the web services on the basis of current load information of the peers, on demand basis.
4) Scheduling the incoming consumer requests to the current deployed instances.

Figure 2 shows a snapshot of the interface provided by the WSP to the client. It provides a *list* of services hosted by the WSPs in the network, along with their status and link for making the service requests. A prospective client can choose a service among the available services or can choose to use an already deployed service as per its service requirements, to the WSP, which is then scheduled an appropriate HP as discussed in [5]. If the client is unable to find a service, it can attempt to make search query to the registry with the name of the service via the search space provided by the interface.

3.2 Decentralizing the Registry using Chord

Chord [7] - a DHT [11]-implementation over structured P2P overlay network, is a distributed lookup protocol that helps in efficiently locating a node that stores a particular data item in p2p applications. It can adapt itself with a changing set of resources (nodes) and hence can answer

Dynamic Web Service Provisioning Over De-centralized Registry

Home About Services Administrator Contact

You can Query for a Web Service here :

Name of Service : Submit Query

List of Web Services with Status.

Name of Service	Status	Link
FactorialWS	Available	Make a Request
Node8_FactorialWS	Available	Make a Request
Node8_SpellCheckService	Deployed	Enter Value Here Submit
Node8_FibonacciWS	Available	Make a Request

Fig. 2: The Web Service Provider Interface

search queries even when nodes join and leave the system. Chord uses consistent hashing of the resources over a ring of node identifiers. This is achieved by a single operation: given a key it maps the key onto a node identifier. The registry is composed of a DHT of web services stored as *[key, value]* pairs. It uses a hash function to generate unique keys from the byte version of a service name, that are mapped to node identifiers generated as hash value of nodes' IP address.

Within our framework whenever a node wishes to join the network as a WSP, it may or may not have web services to host. In either case it joins the de-centralized registry within the network and shares the web services as resources with other WSP peers. This sharing and de-centralization of the registry is achieved by use of Chord protocol. Since the resources to be shared here are web services, the value corresponding to a key is service metadata, which consists of:

1) Name of Service
2) Status of the service (Available /Deployed)
3) Owner of the service i.e. WSP hosting the service.
4) List of HPs on which the service is currently deployed.

Such service metadata help in identifying the service, its endpoints and other details necessary for proper execution in SOA framework.

3.3 Workflow of Registry with SOA Framework

In order to maintain and use to the registry for the dynamic set of resources, three basic steps are required. These steps are responsible for *publish-find-bind* notion of the SOA framework that achieves interoperability of web services.

3.3.1 Publishing a Web Service

The first task performed by a WSP as it joins the network is to publish the web services it owns. If a WSP is the first one to join the network, it initializes the service registry by uploading its services to the DHT. It also identifies itself as the bootstrap peer for the chord protocol, so as to facilitate other WSP peers to join the network and contribute to same DHT so formed. As the number of WSPs and the web services hosted by them increases in the network, the entries in the registry are distributed among the WSP peers with respect to the Chord protocol. This is done by mapping the keys to the respective node identifiers and distributing the information over the nodes/WSPs in the network. Each WSP also maintains a *list* of all web services (i.e. [key, value] pairs) locally, assigned by chord along with the web services it owns/hosts.

A WSP publishes a service as its *owner* in the registry, it is now discoverable by clients and other WSPs, until and unless it is explicitly removed by the *owner* itself. No other WSP has the rights to perform administrative tasks for a service such as publishing, deploying, replacing, modifying and removing the service to or from the registry, except the owner itself. Since the registry provides some service metadata (i.e. value), which is sufficient enough to make the service discoverable by different WSP and clients, it does not provide the whole service package in order to maintain the security of the service.

Once the service is published it may so happen that the *owner* undergoes failure or leaves the chord ring, thereby creating uncertainty of the environments. In such a scenario the service still remains discoverable in the network. This is possible because the keys of the services which the owner in concern is responsible for and the services which it owned are shared among the predecessor and successor of the concerned peer in a structured fashion as per the chord protocol. Such a phenomenon of exchanging information and re-mapping the keys provides higher service availability.

3.3.2 Discovery of Web Services from Registry

A client can make a service request only when the service endpoint is made available to the client via the interface. By default the interface enlists all the services with endpoints maintained locally as a list of DHT entries. Depending on the list a client request can be made in two ways:

- **Case 1:** If the service is in the *list* then the service endpoint is made directly available to client by which a service request can be made.
- **Case 2:** If the service is not in the *list* then a service query is made to the registry. As a result an endpoint for the same is returned if the service exists.

Chord uses an efficient routing algorithm for locating a key in the ring with an upper bound of O(log N), where N is the number of nodes taking part in the chord ring [7], thus even with increase in number of web services and WSP's the registry remains scalable as compared to previous approaches.

3.3.3 Binding of Web Services with clients

After the service endpoint is made available to the client, depending on the three parameters i.e. status of the service, the WSP through whom the service request is being made and the WSP who owns the service; a client request is scheduled accordingly among the available HPs. To represent the work flow, the requests are modeled as a tuple of three parameters i.e. [*Name of Service, Request to WSP, Request of WSP*]. For example as shown in Figure 3, a service request tuple [WS2, WSP#1,WSP#2] means a client request for web service WS2, the request is made via WSP#1 and the owner of WS2 is WSP#2. Describing the service request tuple in a generalized manner denoting WSx be the name of the web service owned by a WSP#x and WSy be a name of the web service owned by WSP#y and so on, with respect to these parameters four generic kinds of requests can occur as depicted in Table 1 along with there scheduling criteria.

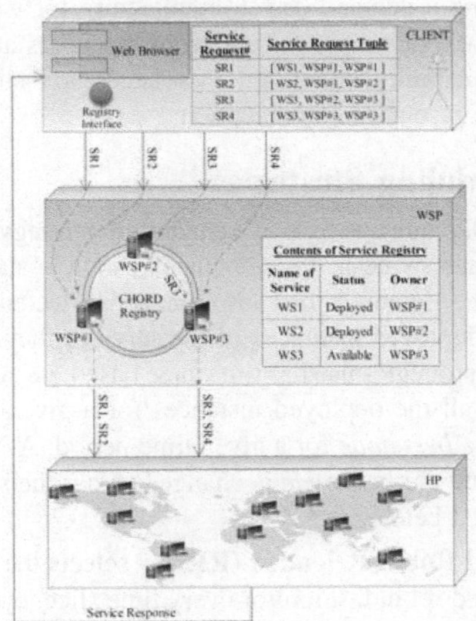

Fig. 3: Basic Architecture Diagram

Table 1: Service Request Types

Request Type	Status	Request Tuple	Scheduling Criteria
SR1	Deployed	[WSx,WSP#x,WSP#x]	Routed to HP using WSP#x's scheduling strategy
SR2	Deployed	[WSx,WSP#y,WSP#x]	Routed to HP using minimum load criteria
SR3	Available	[WSx,WSP#y,WSP#x]	Routed to owner i.e. WSP#x for deployment
SR4	Available	[WSx,WSP#x,WSP#x]	Deployed on an appropriate HP

From the above table it is evident that for a service

which is deployed, a client request made directly to the service owner (SR1) is routed using a default scheduling strategy. A service request made to a WSP other than the owner (SR2) of the service is routed to a minimum loaded HP so that QoS is not compromised. If the service is not deployed yet, a request made to a WSP other than the owner (SR3) first routes the request to the owner for the deployment of the service. After which a normal deployment procedure is carried out similar to deployment request made to same owner (SR4). As mentioned earlier, if the owner of a service goes down, the service still remains discoverable and hence can be used by client via SR2. Since the deployment rights are constrained to the owner of the service, further new deployments will not occur and all the incoming client requests will be serviced from the existing deployments.

Catering the client requests employing the benefits of chord protocol, thereby increasing the service availability by de-centralizing the registry, provides a unique approach for rendering a demand driven architecture for web service provisioning. For proper utilization of resources at the same time the incoming client requests needs to scheduled to appropriate resources for execution.

3.4 Scheduling Strategies

The WSPs always use a scheduling strategy to route the consumer requests for adequate resource management based on the dynamic load information collected from the HPs, with deployed instances of the services they own. The scheduling strategies used as time slice based, i.e. an instance among the all the deployed instances for a given service is selected as a *best node* for a given time period. At the end of the time slice the *best node* is changed as per the scheduling strategy used below:

- **Round Robin Reloaded (RRR)** - selects the *best node* in round robin fashion for every time slice, cycling over the deployed instances.
- **Least Recently Used Reloaded (LRUR)** - selects the least recently used instance as the *best node* if the current instance is loaded, for the next time slice, cycling over the deployed instances.
- **Minimum Loaded First (MLF)** - selects the instance with minimum load as the *best node* for every time slice among the deployed instances.

All the incoming requests of WSx made to WSP#x are scheduled by the use of any one of the above mentioned strategy. Whereas the incoming requests of WSx made to WS#y are always scheduled via MLF strategy, to avoid the overhead of constantly assigning a *best node* for the services which they do not own.

4. Experimental Results

In this section we present the results of the experiments performed for dynamically deploying web services and managing client requests over a distributed registry. The tests were conduct with 3 WSP peers, and 7 HP of different node configuration. A web service for calculating the Nth Fibonacci term is used with value of N=40. Nodes taken into account were of configuration ranging from 1GB-4GB of physical memory, 1.86GHz-3GHz dual-core processors. The test were conducted by making 10000 client requests, made to different WSPs each time, and hence calculating the response times. The graphs are obtained by using different scheduling strategies as discussed earlier and hence plotting the service response times with number of service requests made.

From the graphs we can observe that few requests which incur the deployment costs (shown as red peaks) take higher response times. For rest of the requests, the response time required is comparatively low. Thus it can be concluded that the initial deployment cost is shared over successive consumer requests and the idea of deploy once and use many times is well implemented, proving to be a major advantage over the job-based framework.

Comparing the plots we can observe the cumulative response time for RRR (Figure 4) strategy is high as compared to other two strategies. This is because an instance with a lower capacity is selected as *best node* in every cycle leading to higher response time, which is not the case in other two strategies. Hence RRR strategy implements better utilization of resources at the cost of high response time. In contrast LRUR (Figure 5) strategy achieves lower response times for a longer time, till the current instance does not gets loaded. At the same time it also guarantees to use all the instances in a cyclic fashion, hence provides an approach with lower response time and better utilization of resources as well. Since MLF (Figure 6) does not cycles over the deployed instances and hence provides the best possible response time for every time slice, hence low cumulative response time as compared to other strategies, though is suffers from poor utilization of resources as the instances with lower capacity may have load values higher as compared to instances with higher capacity.

5. Discussion and Future Work

The architecture presented in this paper overcomes the drawbacks of distributed environments by strongly coupling it with the SOA. It uses on-demand web service provisioning frameworks and employs service provisioning on the basis of load balancing and meeting minimum service requirements to achieve better performance with emerging demands of web applications.

Further, incorporation of P2P technologies provides a robust approach towards handling the uncertainty of grid environments. It overcomes the scenario of single point failure as it is devoid of any centralized mechanism of service registry. The architecture not only decentralizes the registry but at the same time dynamically adapts the registry

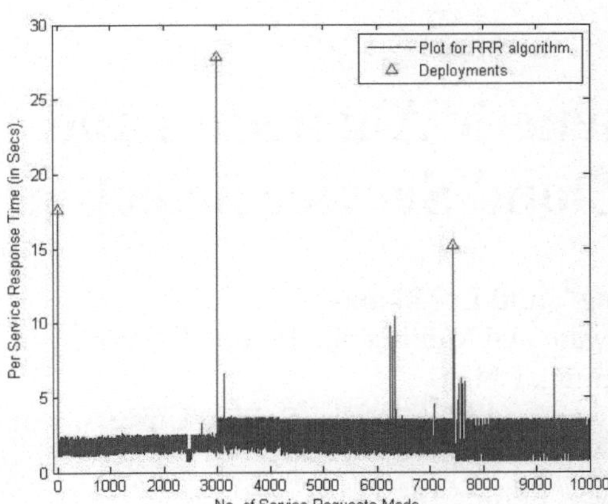

Fig. 4: Plot for RRR

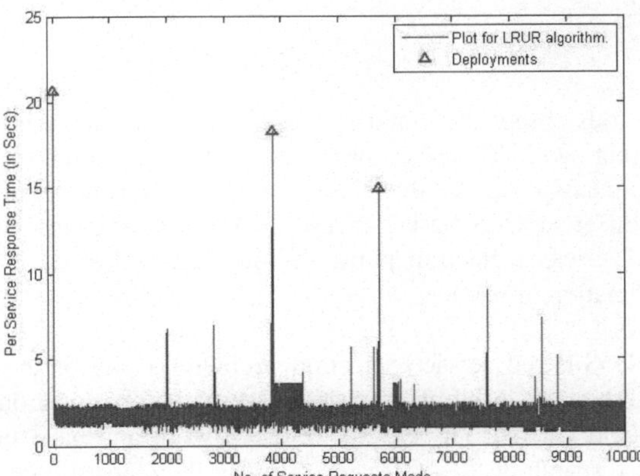

Fig. 5: Plot for LRUR

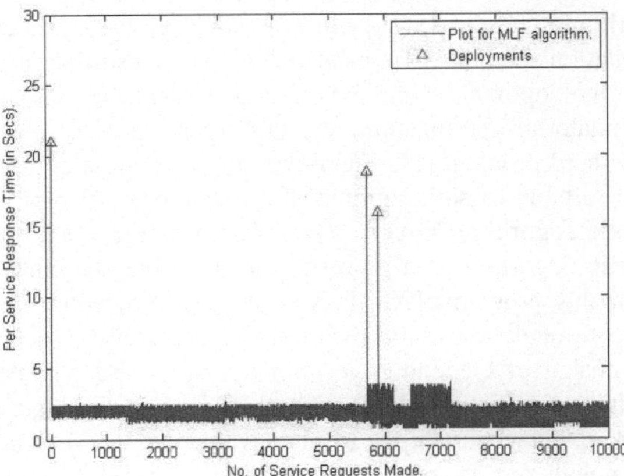

Fig. 6: Plot for MLF

to the volatile changes of the network. Since the service information is distributed over the registry, and not the service itself, this approach restricts WSPs other than the owner of the service to perform any administrative tasks of the service. This is because the security of the service (executable code and service metrics) is an important issue, still to be taken care of. The authors are of believe that the security of the service is a separate research problem focusing on what information and to whom and how the service must be made available.

The framework also establishes new scopes for virtual organizations which can take part as provider of services as well as provider of resources. The approach towards de-centralizing the registry may further enhance business opportunities for cross hosting the web services, agreed on some cost model. Combining SLA for client requests is a future aspect still to be achieved which would provide freedom for client to choose a cost model best suited for them.

References

[1] A. De Sarkar, S. Roy, D. Ghosh, R. Mukhopadhyay, and N. Mukherjee, "An adaptive execution scheme for achieving guaranteed performance in computational grids," *Journal of Grid Computing*, vol. 8, no. 1, pp. 109–131, 2010.

[2] S. Roy and N. Mukherjee, "Efficient resource management for running multiple concurrent jobs in a computational grid environment," *Future Generation Computer Systems*, vol. 27, no. 8, pp. 1070–1082, 2011.

[3] P. Watson and C. Fowler, "Dynasoar: An architecture for the dynamic deployment of web services on a grid or the internet."

[4] P. Watson, C. Fowler, C. Kubicek, A. Mukherjee, J. Colquhoun, M. Hewitt, and S. Parastatidis, "Dynamically deploying web services on a grid using dynasoar," in *Object and Component-Oriented Real-Time Distributed Computing, 2006. ISORC 2006. Ninth IEEE International Symposium on*, april 2006, p. 8 pp.

[5] S. Mistry, D. Jaiswal, S. Virani, A. Mukherjee, and N. Mukherjee, "An architecture for dynamic web service provisioning using peer-to-peer networks," in *Distributed Computing and Internet Technology*, ser. Lecture Notes in Computer Science, C. Hota and P. Srimani, Eds., 2013, vol. 7753.

[6] T. Tannenbaum, D. Wright, K. Miller, and M. Livny, "Condor - a distributed job scheduler," in *Beowulf Cluster Computing with Linux*, T. Sterling, Ed. MIT Press.

[7] I. Stoica, R. Morris, D. Liben-Nowell, D. Karger, M. Kaashoek, F. Dabek, and H. Balakrishnan, "Chord: a scalable peer-to-peer lookup protocol for internet applications," *Networking, IEEE/ACM Transactions on*, vol. 11, no. 1, pp. 17 – 32, feb 2003.

[8] Monitoring and discovery system. [Online]. Available: http://www.globus.org/toolkit/mds/

[9] Universal description, discovery and integration(uddi) v3.0.2. [Online]. Available: http://uddi.org/pubs/uddi-v3.0.2-20041019.htm

[10] S. Cavalieri, F. Scibilia, C. Fowler, S. Parastatidis, and P. Watson, "Web services usage monitoring for dynasoar," in *Telecommunications, 2006. AICT-ICIW '06. International Conference on Internet and Web Applications and Services/Advanced International Conference on*, feb. 2006, p. 183.

[11] F. Dabek, "A distributed hash table," Tech. Rep., 2005.

[12] S. Ratnasamy, P. Francis, M. Handley, R. Karp, and S. Shenker, "A scalable content-addressable network," in *IN PROC. ACM SIGCOMM 2001*, 2001, pp. 161–172.

[13] A. Rowstron and P. Druschel, "Pastry: Scalable, distributed object location and routing for large-scale peer-to-peer systems," 2001.

[14] B. Zhao, J. Kubiatowicz, A. Joseph, *et al.*, "Tapestry: An infrastructure for fault-tolerant wide-area location and routing," 2001.

[15] A. Harrison and I. Taylor, "Dynamic web service deployment using wspeer."

[16] I. Wang, "P2ps (peer-to-peer simplified)," 2003.

[17] D. Mukhopadhyay and A. Chougule, "A survey on web service discovery approaches," Department of Information Technology, Maharashtra Institute of Technology, Pune 411038, India, Tech. Rep.

A Hybrid Algorithm Based on Genetic Algorithm and Simplex Method for QoS-aware Cloud Service Selection

Chengwen Zhang [1], Jiali Bian [2], Bo Cheng [3], and Lei Zhang [4]

[1]Beijing Key Laboratory of Intelligent Telecommunications Software and Multimedia, Beijing University of Posts & Telecommunications, Beijing, China

[2]Beijing Key Laboratory of Intelligent Telecommunications Software and Multimedia, Beijing University of Posts & Telecommunications, Beijing, China

[3]State Key Lab of Networking and Switching Technology, Beijing University of Posts & Telecommunications, Beijing, China

[4]Key Laboratory of Trustworthy Distributed Computing and Service (BUPT), Ministry of Education, Beijing, China

Abstract - *Aiming at the problem of cloud service selection based on global Quality-of-Service (QoS) constraints, this paper provides a hybrid algorithm of Simplex Method (SM) and Genetic Algorithm (GA). In this algorithm, some relevant variables are defined, some Simplex Method operations are proposed and the hybrid algorithm based on GA and SM is provided. The global convergence ability and local convergence capacity of GA can be gotten better. The hybrid algorithm can get more excellent composite service plan from a lot of composite plans on the basis of global QoS constraints because it accords with the characteristics of cloud service selection very well. Passed tests and analyses show that the hybrid algorithm proposed in this paper can be a good choice to solve the QoS-based cloud service selection problem.*

Keywords: Cloud service, Selection, QoS-aware, Genetic algorithms, Simplex method

1 Introduction

Cloud computing [1-3, 31] is an emerging computing technology that allows businesses to implement their own services using on-demand IT infrastructures. These on-demand infrastructures enable end users to access business services without installation, at any computer with Internet access. Cloud computing environments offer three major types of services: infrastructure as a service (IaaS), platform as a service (PaaS), and software as a service(SaaS)[4].These services are called cloud services. Cloud service composition is one of the motive forces of the development of cloud services.

With the rapid development of cloud service technology, as well as intensified competition among cloud service providers, there are inevitably many cloud service providers to provide cloud services with same functionalities and different QoS. These cloud services can combine tens of thousands composite cloud services with same functions and different QoS. Therefore, we need to choose cloud service components from massive cloud services with same functions and different QoS based on user's QoS requirements. QoS-based service selection plays an important role[5-6] in the combination of services.

QoS-based service selection problem is one of the hot research areas. A lot of international research organizations in this field carried out relevant research work and have made some research results [7-25, 29-30]. But there are still certain deficiencies.

Exhaustive methods [7-9, 12, 20-25] and approximate algorithms [10-11, 13-19] are two kinds of QoS properties calculation methods. To meet the global constraints and to find the optimal combination are under the scope of combinatorial optimization, and QoS-based service selection is NP-hard problem [11], therefore, approximate algorithm is more suitable to solve optimization combinatorial problems. Genetic Algorithm (GA) is a kind of approximate algorithm. Genetic Algorithm is a powerful tool to solve combinatorial optimizing problems [26]. It is an iterative procedure on the basis of population where each individual describes a solution. The design of Genetic Algorithm operators and parameters will have significant impact on itself [27]. Genetic Algorithm is not advantageous for the local convergence. Its efficiency is not enough and its speed of convergence is slow. In order to compensate for local search capability of Genetic Algorithm itself, the combination of Genetic Algorithm and some kind of local search algorithms is needed to enhance the local search capabilities of Genetic Algorithm.

Based on the above analysis, this paper presents an improved Genetic Algorithm. To compensate for the local search capabilities of Genetic Algorithm itself, a hybrid algorithm of Genetic Algorithm and Simplex Method (SM) is introduced.

The remaining sections of this paper are as follows. Section two described researches of QoS-based cloud service selection computing. The proposed hybrid algorithm was discussed in detail in section three. Section four presented some simulation works and discussed the simulation results. Section five came to conclusions and noted that the next step in research content.

2 Quality-based cloud service selection

Based on all global QoS constraints, to select the best plan from a large number of cloud service composition plans is in the area of combinatorial optimization. To solve such problems, the calculation methods based on QoS attributes are divided into two categories. One category is exhaustive algorithm. In this kind of algorithm, all of candidate plans are calculated according to certain rules in order to choose the best plan. The methods used in the literatures [7-9, 12, 20-25] fall into this category. The other is approximate algorithm. In this type of algorithm, an ideal composition plan is infinitely close to the best one. At last, a plan that meets all QoS requirements but is not the best one will be gained. The methods in the literatures [10-11, 13-19] fall into this category.

QoS properties calculation through the establishment of QoS matrix is a representative calculation method. The literature [7] presented a run-time services choice method in dynamic service composition. It could select a single better service, but it could not meet the entire QoS requirements. In the literatures [8, 9], a local optimization algorithm and a global optimization algorithm were proposed. The local optimization algorithm could not reach a global optimal solution. When the size of composition services was large, the compution of the global computational algorithm had increased a lot. The literature [12] expanded the methods in the literature[9]. It analysed the conditions of triggering service re-selection in detail, gave the idea of the service re-selection and gave the constraint expression for a stateful cloud service selection.

The service selection problem based on QoS belongs to NP-hard problem[11], so the exhaustive combinatorial optimization method is poor scalability and has large calculation. Heuristics method can be used to obtain an approximate solution.

In the literature [13], a multidimensional 0-1 knapsack problem model was used for multiple QoS constraints selection. A method based on branch-and-branch was proposed for solving MMKP (Multi-dimension Multi-choice Knap sack Problem) optimal solution and heuristic-based method for solving second-best solution. In the field of combinatorial optimization, the solution based on Genetic Algorithm is a novel global optimization one. The literatures [10-11, 14-18] used Genetic Algorithm for the optimization of service composition. The literature [10] used Genetic Algorithm to solve the QoS-based service selection. It used one-dimensional chromosome encoding method to describe the combination of services. The literature [11] also used an one-dimensional chromosome encoding method to describe the combination of services. The literatures [17] and [18] proposed a combination service method based on Genetic Algorithm. Through Genetic Algorithm, it could be ensured that the results of services choice met the restrictive conditions.

To compensate for the local search capability of Genetic Algorithm itself, Genetic Algorithm and some kind of local search algorithms need to be combined to enhance its local search capabilities and to achieve fairly good results.

3 Genetic algorithm with simplex method

In this section, we present a novel genetic algorithm with Simplex Method in order to solve quality-driven selection.

3.1 Definition of relevant variables

Suppose that a composite cloud service includes n tasks. The ith ($1 \le i \le n$) task t_i has N_i candidate services. The sign s_{ij} is used to represent the jth ($1 \le j \le N_i$) candidate cloud service. The sign Q_{ijq} denotes the qth QoS attribute of s_{ij} candidate cloud service. The weight value of Q_{ijq} is W_q.

The symbol y_{ij} denotes a decision variable. In a composite cloud service instance, the value of y_{ij} is 1 only when the cloud service s_{ij} is selected, otherwise its value is 0. For the task t_i, only one decision variable value is 1, the rest values are 0. Its formula is the following formula (1).

$$\sum_{j=1}^{Ni} y_{ij} = 1, \ y_{ij} \in [0,1] \quad (1)$$

In addition, in normal circumstances, the value of N_i of every task is usually not equal one another. Suppose that m is the maximum value in all of N_i, namely, m = Max {N_1, N_2, …, N_n}. Therefore, in order to build a decision variable matrix formed by all decision variables, the number of candidate cloud services of every task needs to be expanded to m. The following is the method. If $N_i < m$ for a task i ($1 \le i \le n$), the value of y_{ij} is 0 in the case of $N_{i+1} \le j \le m$. Accordingly, the total number of the decision variables is expanded to $n \times m$. Since the new expanded candidate cloud services will never be selected, the corresponding decision variable values are always 0.

Based on the above expansion, all of decision variables y_{ij} ($1 \le i \le n, 1 \le j \le m$) can constitute a $n \times m$ class of decision variable matrix that is denoted by Y. Its formula is the following formula (2).

$$Y = \begin{pmatrix} y_{11} & y_{12} & \cdots & y_{1m} \\ y_{21} & y_{22} & & y_{2m} \\ \cdots & & & \cdots \\ y_{n1} & y_{n2} & \cdots & y_{nm} \end{pmatrix} \quad (2)$$

In Y, each row represents the decision variable vector of all candidate cloud services of a task.

3.2 Main steps of the simplex operations

Genetic Algorithm can effectively handle the optimization problem with multi-variable and complex functions. However, local convergence of Genetic Algorithms is not an advantage. Therefore, in order to compensate for Genetic Algorithm itself in lack of local search capability, Genetic Algorithm needs to be integrated with some kind of local search algorithms to enhance its local search capabilities.

Simplex Method is a local optimization approach. A combination of Genetic Algorithm and Simplex Method can form a hybrid algorithm [28] that includes the global optimization algorithm and the local optimization algorithm. The two algorithms complement each other. Genetic Algorithm ensures that the hybrid algorithm has the global search capability and can find the global optimal point. Simplex Method can add a number of parallel searches in many local areas and it can use local search methods to direct the search. It can not only speed up the process of global optimization, but also solve the "premature" problem of Genetic Algorithm to a certain extent. Better convergence speed and search capability can be gotten at the same time.

Based on the research about the combination of simplex method and Genetic Algorithm, this paper presents a hybrid algorithm that is the combination of Genetic Algorithm and Simplex Method. This hybrid algorithm will be used to solve the cloud service choice problem.

The following is the main idea of the hybrid algorithm. After Genetic Algorithm produces a new generation of population, some local initial simplexes are composed by some randomly selected individuals in a certain probability. Individuals with higher fitness values are introduced through continuous reflection operations and they will replace the individuals whose fitness values are lower. So, a number of new better individuals will be included into the next generation of population and will participate in genetic manipulations in the next generation of population. In addition, during the reflection operation, the decision variable matrix will be used.

Some Simplex Method operations are joined between two generations of population. After a series of reproduction, crossover and mutation operators, a number of individuals are randomly selected to form a certain number of initial simplexes. Some local Simplex operations are run in parallel. After all initial simplexes have completed their simplex operations, more excellent individuals are obtained. We can proceed with the next generation of genetic manipulations.

N_s is the number of generated initial simplexes. The formula of N_s is the following formula (3).

$$Ns = floor(Ng / n) \quad (3)$$

In the formula (3), N_g is the population size of Genetic Algorithm, that is, it is the number of individuals in each generation of population. The symbol n is the length of a chromosome.

For each initial simplex, the main steps of the simplex operations are as follows:

3.2.1 To establish an initial simplex

n+1 individuals are selected randomly from the current population and form an initial simplex in a n-dimensional space. Each individual's fitness function value shall be the function value of the corresponding vertex in the simplex.

3.2.2 To select the worst individual

After the function values of n+1 vertices are compared, the vertex with the smallest function value is found and its corresponding individual is denoted by C_{n+1}. The individuals corresponding to the remaining n vertices are indicated respectively by $C_1, C_2, \cdots, C_n$.

3.2.3 To construct the decision variable matrix of every vertex

The decision variable matrixes $Y_1, Y_2, \cdots, Y_n, Y_{n+1}$ are built respectively for the individuals $C_1, C_2, \cdots, C_n, C_{n+1}$. As shown below is the specific method of construction. Only when the jth candidate cloud service of the ith task is selected, the component y_{ij} is 1 in the decision variable matrix Y_k, otherwise the value of y_{ij} is 0.

3.2.4 To calculate the decision variable matrix of reflection center

C_c is the reflection center that is about n individuals except the worst individual C_{n+1}. The decision variable matrix Y_c about C_c can be built according to the following formula (4).

$$Y_c = \frac{1}{n}\left(\sum_{k=1}^{n} Y_k\right) \quad (4)$$

3.2.5 To compute the decision variable matrix about the reflection point

C_0 is the reflection point of the worst individual C_{n+1} on C_c. Its decision variable matrix is Y_0. Its formula is the following formula (5).

$$Y_0 = 2Y_c - Y_{n+1} \quad (5)$$

3.2.6 Boolean the decision variable matrix of the reflection point

Boolean-oriented approach is to reassign 0 or 1 to each component y_{ij} in the decision variable matrix Y_0. The value 1 will be set to the largest component in each row vector Y_k of Y_0 and the remaining components are assigned the value of 0. Thereby, a boolean decision variables matrix Y_0' will be generated. In the Boolean process, if there are multiple components with the same and maximum value in a row vector, the value 1 will be set to random component among them. The remaining components in the row vector are 0.

3.2.7 To generate the new individual corresponding to the reflection point

A new individual C_0 is generated on the basis of the decision variable matrix Y_0'. For each row vector in Y_0', the only component with the value of 1 is used to select its atom service instance. The atom service instance will is assigned to corresponding gene locus on a chromosome. After all of gene loci are set atom service instances, the formation of a new individual C_0 will be done.

3.2.8 To determine whether the new individuals meet the user's global constraints

If the new individual's fitness is greater than the worst individual and the new individual meets the user's global QoS constraints, the new individual will replace the worst one in population and joins the next generation population evolution. Otherwise, if the new individual's fitness is less than the worst individual or the new individual does not meet the user's global QoS constraints, the new individual will also replace the worst one in population and form a new simplex to continue with the next iteration of the simplex algorithm. We can end the operation of the simplex until a new individual's fitness is greater than the worst individual and the new individual meets the user's global QoS constraints.

In accordance with the above steps, simplex operations are done in N_s initial simplexes in turn. After every simplex has gained a new individual whose fitness value is better than the worst individual in the simplex and that is able to meet the global user constraints, these new individuals will be generated and added into the population to participate in the next generation of population genetic manipulations.

On the one hand, because individuals are randomly selected to compose an initial simplex, the randomness of Genetic Algorithm can be ensured. And the opportunities to generate new individuals are increased. On the other hand, Simplex Method can control the evolution direction of Genetic Algorithm to make better solutions. It is parallel searches in a number of local solution spaces not only that enhances the local search ability bus also that accelerates the global convergence and solves the "premature" problem of GA to a certain extent.

3.3 GA with SM

In this section, we present a novel genetic algorithm mixed by SM. This GA is available in figure 1.

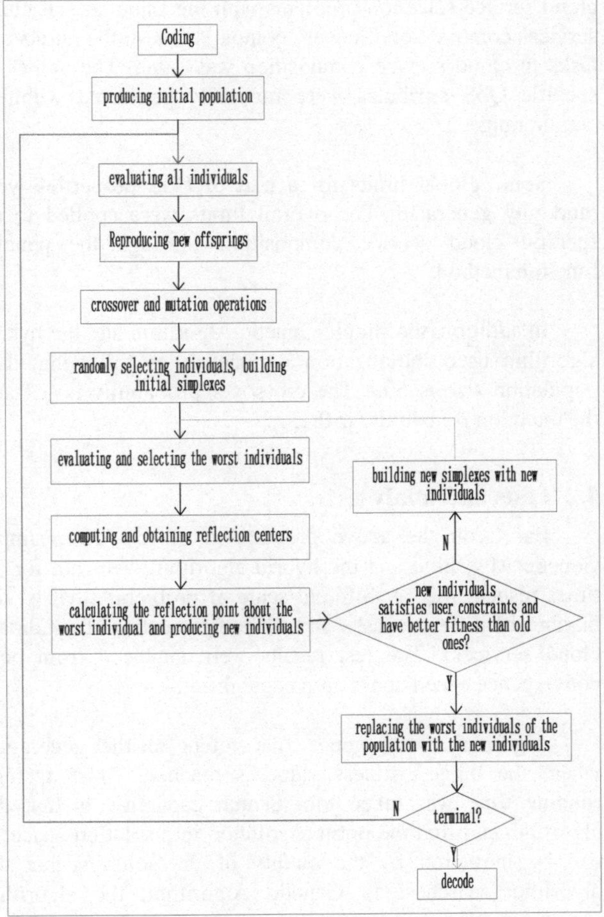

Fig.1. GA with SM operations

The SM operations promote the search ability of GA. The hybrid GA can gain better composition services.

4 Tests and analyses

The proposed cloud service selecting algorithm in this paper improves simple Genetic Algorithm. That is to build a more powerful and efficient hybrid search algorithm that is composed by Genetic Algorithm and Simplex Method. Through the above improvement, this algorithm has better search ability. Here are tests results and test analyses through which the capacity and efficiency of presented hybrid algorithm will be validated.

4.1 Test data preparation

In order to verify the effect of cloud services choice done by the hybrid algorithm, some comparison tests between simple Genetic Algorithm and the hybrid algorithm were made.

In order to fairly test the two algorithms, they would run in the same hardware and software operating environment, including CPU, memory, OS, development language and IDE, etc. In the comparison tests, the two algorithms solved the cloud service selection problems with the same size of cloud services combination. In every comparison test, the number of tasks in cloud service composition was same. The values of specific QoS attributes were randomly generated within a certain range.

Some global limits for a part of QoS properties were randomly generated. The overall limits were applied to all specific cloud service compositions through the penalty function method.

In addition, the simple Genetic Algorithm and the hybrid algorithm used initialization parameters as following. The population size is 500. The crossover probability is 0.7 and the mutation probability is 0.1.

4.2 Tests and analyses

Based on the above preparation of test data, simple Genetic Algorithm and the hybrid algorithm were run for 50 times respectively at different scale of problems (that is, the number of different tasks and different number of candidate cloud services). The test results were analyzed from both convergence speed and search capabilities.

Algorithm convergence rate refers to the generation where the biggest fitness value is reached. The average running time was taken too. Search capability is that the algorithm can find the optimal solution in a solution space. It can be measured by the quality of the solution that the algorithm searches. In Genetic Algorithm, the algorithm search capability can be measured through the fitness value of the final selected individual. In the hybrid algorithm, the bigger the fitness value is, the better the selection result is. The average values of the final fitness values at all running time were taken.

A few of test data are listed in Table 1. SGA is the abbreviation of simple Genetic Algorithm.

Table.1.Comparison data (SGA : Hybrid algorithm).

Tasks Num	Average Maximum Fitness	Average Time	Average Generation
10	0.134:0.139	256:537	343:284
25	0.061:0.173	983:2135	386:297
30	0.031:0.105	2676:5375	352:308

As can be seen from Table 1, when the number of tasks is added, the running time will increase.

The efficiency of simple Genetic Algorithm is still unsatisfactory, although to a certain extent it solved the cloud service selection problem. As described in Table 1, comparison of data can fully verify that the hybrid algorithm has faster convergence than the simple Genetic Algorithm and can get better results of cloud service selection.

When in the face of the selection problem with the same size of combination cloud services, the hybrid algorithm can get higher average final fitness value than the simple Genetic Algorithm. When the scale of the composition problem is small, the advantage of the hybrid algorithm is not clear. But, when there are a larger number of tasks in a combined service flow, the hybrid algorithm can get much better solutions than the simple Genetic Algorithm. In the test conditions of this article, when the number of tasks is more than 25, the hybrid algorithm clearly has stronger search capabilities. This shows that the hybrid algorithm has better search capabilities, especially in the larger scale of cloud service selection, that the search capabilities are more prominent. The reason is that the presented hybrid algorithm in this paper has greatly enhanced the local convergence rate and capability with the combination of Simplex Method and Genetic Algorithm.

But, the average running time of the hybrid algorithm were larger than the SGA. This means that the running of Simplex Method raises the running time of the hybrid algorithm. Some improvement methods should be established in the future.

5 Conclusions

Since cloud services technologies have become more sophisticated, more and more easily used cloud services with the stability characteristics are shared on network. But a single atomic cloud service can provide limited functionalities. In order to more fully utilize the shared cloud services, it is necessary to combine shared cloud services to form a new combination of cloud services to provide more powerful service functions.

With the progressive development of cloud services technology and application, it is inevitable for a task to appear a large number of candidate cloud services with the same function properties and different non-functional attributes (mainly referring to QoS attributes). It has become an urgent problem that how to fast and flexibly select a high-availability, high reliability, high performance and the best cloud service to meet user' needs from massive candidate cloud services. Namely, it is QoS-based cloud service selection problem.

This paper presents a combination cloud services selection algorithm based on a hybrid algorithm. Based on the analyses of composite cloud service selection problem, a simple Genetic Algorithm combines a local optimization algorithm – Simplex Method. In order to compensate the lack of the ability of local search of Genetic Algorithm itself, Genetic Algorithm and Simplex Method are applied to the formation of a new hybrid algorithm. In the result, the search ability and convergence speed can be improved at the same time.

Through the realization of the above-mentioned algorithm, some strong validations of the proposed algorithm in capacity and efficiency effects were done. The hybrid algorithm can be a good solution to QoS-driven cloud services selection.

In the future, some ways should be adopted to decrease the running time of the hybrid algorithm. In the above experiments, the number of individuals in populations is the same in the face of different combination sizes. If the populations with different sizes can be adopted for different composition scales, the efficiency of algorithm will be greatly improved. Therefore, the next study will examine the dynamic adaptive mechanism of population size. An approach of Genetic Algorithm with ant colony algorithm is used to select concrete services in the literature 19. MMAS (Max-Min Ant System) has abilities of parallel processing and global searching. MMAS can put feedback information to Genetic Algorithm. So, another future work is about how Genetic Algorithm works together with MMAS in dynamic cloud service selection environment.

Acknowledgments: This work was supported by NSFC under Grant Nos. 60872042, the Fundamental Research Funds for the Central Universities (2011RC0203) and the Co-construction Special Funds of Beijing.

6 References

[1] B. Rochwerger, D. Breitgand and E. Levy, et al. "The Reservoir model and architecture for open federated cloud computing"; IBM Journal of Research and Development, 53, 4, 1—17, 2009.

[2] M. Armburst, et al. "Above the clouds: a berkeley view of cloud computing". Tech. report UCB/EECS-2009-28, Electrical Eng. and Computer Science Dept., Univ. of California, Berkeley, 2009.

[3] B. Hayes. "Cloud computing. Comm"; ACM, 51, 7, 9—11, 2008.

[4] P. Mell and T. Grance. "The nist definition of cloud computing". Nat'l Inst. of Standards and Technology Computer Security Division, http://csrc.nist.gov/groups/SNS/cloud-computing/cloud-def-v15.doc, 2009.

[5] D. A. Menascé. "QoS issues in web services"; IEEE Internet Computing, 6, 6, 72—75, 2002.

[6] D. A. Menascé. "Composing web services: a QoS view"; IEEE Internet Computing, 8, 6, 88—90, 2004.

[7] Y. Liu, A. H. Ngu and L. Zeng. "QoS computation and policing in dynamic web service selection". In Proceedings of the 13th International Conference on World Wide Web (WWW), ACM Press, New York, USA, 66—73, 2004.

[8] L. Zeng, B. Benatallah and M. Dumas, etc. "Quality driven web services composition". Proc. 12th Int'l Conf. World Wide Web (WWW), ACM Press, Budapest, Hungary, 411—421, 2003.

[9] Liang Zhao Zeng and Boualem Benatallah, etc. "QoS-aware middleware for web services composition"; IEEE Transactions on Software Engineering, 30, 5, 311—327, 2004.

[10] Liang Jie Zhang, Bing Li and Tian Chao, etc. "On demand web services-based business process composition". IEEE International Conference on System, Man, and Cybernetics (SMC'03), Washington, USA, 4057—4064, 2003.

[11] G. Canfora, M. Di Penta and R. Esposito, etc. "A lightweight approach for QoS–aware service composition". In Proc. 2nd International Conference on Service Oriented Computing (ICSOC'04), New York, USA, 36—47, 2004.

[12] Danilo and P. Barbara. "Adaptive service composition in flexible processes"; IEEE Transactions on Software Engineering, 33, 6, 369—384, 2007.

[13] T. Yu, Y. Zhang and K. J. Lin. "Efficient algorithms for web services selection with end-to-end QoS constraints"; ACM Transactions on the Web, 1, 1, 1—26, 2007.

[14] M. Gao, M. L. Cai and Chen Huowang. "QoS-aware service composition based on tree-coded Genetic Algorithm". 31st Annual International Computer Software and Applications Conference, 1, 361—367, 2007.

[15] W. Zhang, S. Su and J. L. Chen. "DiGA: population diversity handling Genetic Algorithm for QoS-Aware web services selection. Computer Communications" ; Elsevier, 30, 5, 1082—1090, 2007.

[16] Y. H. Yan and Y. Liang. "Using genetic algorithms to navigate partial enumerable problem space for web services composition". 3rd International Conference on Natural Computation, 475—479, 2007.

[17] G. Canfora, M. Dipenta, R. Esposito and M. L. Villani. "A light weight approach for QoS-aware service composition". Proceedings of the 2th International Conference on Service Oriented Computing, 232—239, 2004.

[18] G. Canfora, M. Dipenta and R. Esposito. "An approach for QoS-aware service composition based on genetic algorithms". Proceedings of the 2005 Conference on Genetic and Evolutionary Computation, 1069—1075, 2005.

[19] Cang Hong Jin, Ming-hui Wu and Tao Jiang, etc. "Combine automatic and manual process on web service selection and composition to support QoS". 12th International Conference on Computer Supported Cooperative Work in Design, 459—464, 2008.

[20] B. Y. Wu and C. H. Chi, etc. "QoS requirement generation and algorithm selection for composite service based on reference vector" ; Journal of Computer Science and Technology, 24, 2, 357—372, 2009.

[21] P. Wang. "QoS-aware web services selection with intuitionistic fuzzy set under consumer's vague perception". Expert Systems with Applications, 36, 4460—4466, 2009.

[22] P. Xiong and Y. Fan, etc. "Web service configuration under multiple quality-of-service attributes" ; IEEE Transactions on Automation Science and Engineering, 6, 2, 311—321, 2009.

[23] F. Huang and C. W. Lan, etc. "An optimal QoS-based web service selection scheme" ; Information Sciences, 179, 19, 3309—3322, 2009.

[24] H. Chan and T. Chieu. "Ranking and mapping of applications to cloud computing services by SVD". IEEE/IFIP, 362—369, 2010.

[25] S, Pearson and T, Sander. "A mechanism for policy-driven selection of service providers in SOA and cloud environments". IEEE, 333—338, 2010.

[26] M. Srinivas and L. M. Patnaik. "Genetic algorithm: a survey" ; IEEE Computer, 27, 6, 17—26, 1994.

[27] R. Ignacio, G. Jesús and P. Héctor, etc. "Statistical analysis of the main parameters involved in the design of a genetic algorithm" ; IEEE Transactions on Systems, Man, and Cybernetics—Part C: Applications and Reviews, 32, 1, 31—37, 2002.

[28] J. Yen, C. Liao and B. Lee, etc. "A hybrid approach to modeling metabolic systems using a genetic algorithms and simplex method" ; IEEE Trans. on Systems, Man, and Cybernetics-part B: Cybernetics, 28, 2, 173—191, 1998.

[29] Qing Wu, ZhenBang Li, YuYu Yin. "Adaptive service selection method in mobile cloud computing" ; China Communications, 9, 12, 46—55, 2012.

[30] Jun Huang, Yanbing Liu, Ruozhou Yu. "Modeling and algorithms for QoS-aware service composition in virtualization-based cloud computing" ; IEICE Transactions on Communications, E96B, 1, 10—19, 2013.

[31] A. A. Ahson and M. Ilyas (eds.). "Cloud computing and software services". CRC Press, 2010.

Open Source Cloud Computing: Characteristics and an Overview

Naylor G. Bachiega[1], Henrique P. Martins[1], Roberta Spolon[1], Marcos A. Cavenaghi[1], Renata S. Lobato[2], Aleardo Manacero[2]
[1]Computer Science Dept., Paulista State University – UNESP, Bauru, Brazil
[2]Computer Science and Statistics Dept., Paulista State University – UNESP, São José do Rio Preto, Brazil

Abstract - *In an attempt to reduce costs by taking advantage of efficient computing resources, new developed technologies and architectures are gaining wide acceptance in the market. One of such technologies is cloud computing, which uses existing technologies, such as virtualization, trying to solve problems like energy consumption and space allocation in data centers or large companies. This paper presents a study on cloud computing, describing their main characteristics, models of deployment, services, and architectures, including an analysis over its benefits, risks and challenges. It also presents a study over some open-source cloud managers, presenting its advantages and drawbacks. All of this is presented aiming to provide a clear guide for those that are evaluating the possible adoption of cloud technology for their IT problems.*

Keywords: Cloud Computing, Architecture, Virtualization.

INTRODUCTION

With the constant growth in the use of computers problems such as power consumption and storage space for data centers are becoming a commonplace. Several solutions have been launched to solve this problem, including Cloud Computing, as named from IBM in 2007 [1].

Cloud computing is devised as a strong trend nowadays, with most of the organizations using or planning to use it. The advantages brought by cloud computing include the reduction in hardware's acquisition and maintenance cost, accessibility, flexibility, and a highly automated process for software upgrades [2].

The cloud can be defined as a network infrastructure based in the share of computing resources along the Internet. The major differential is that clouds try to make the infrastructure's complexity transparent for users. This is performed through the offering of "services" that deliver clients' requests using the Internet. Such offering is enabled by the use of virtualization technologies throughout datacenter's infrastructure, storing and processing users data outside their local resources [3].

Although the rise in its application, cloud computing is still evolving. Open issues include how clients pay for resources and what resources have to be paid for. Also, there are open problems in its maintenance cost, accessibility, and flexibility.

In this paper we provide a concise review of the main concepts involved with clouds, including virtualization, virtual machines and hypervisors. We also provide a description of some characteristics that must or should be present in clouds. We finish with an evaluation of three open-source cloud managers.

VIRTUALIZATION

Virtualization is an important concept for the cloud architecture. Most of modern processors support native virtualization, with several solutions implementing virtual machines present in the market. This is useful since it is rare to find dedicated servers using most of its processing capacity. Therefore it is costly to maintain several physical hosts with a different operating system in each one, making desirable and viable to have several virtual machines running in a single physical one.

Virtualized environments are designed through the insertion of a virtualization layer between the hardware and the virtual machine (VM), as shown in Figure 1. A VM enable a more efficient use of hardware resources while executing the user's applications running in a given operating system [4].

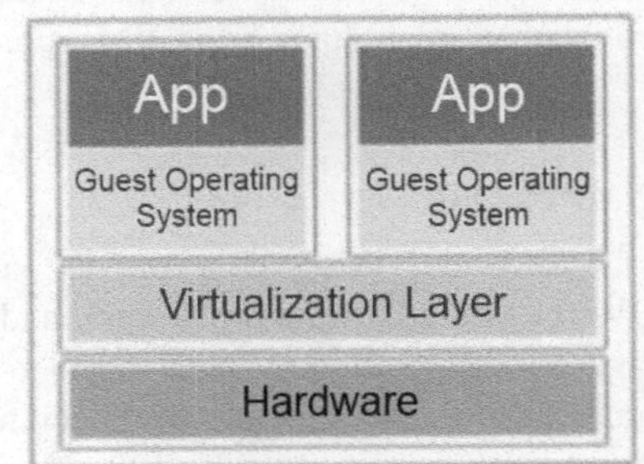

Figure 1. Architecture of hardware virtualization [4].

A. Virtualization Environment

The virtualization layer is the software responsible by the hosting and management of all virtual machines through a VM monitor (VMM). It is a hypervisor running directly over the hardware, with different capabilities for each different architecture. Each VMM executing in the hypervisor implements a hardware's abstraction of the virtual machine and runs a guest operating system. All VM share CPU, memory, and peripherals in order to successfully build a virtualized environment [4].

Unfortunately some hardware instructions cannot be effectively virtualized, since they have different semantics when executed in non-privileged modes. The approaches to circumvent such problems are:

Total virtualization with binary translation: any x86-based operating system can be virtualized by a combination of binary translation and straight execution techniques. This approach translates the kernel to replace non-virtualizable instructions with macros that have the intended effect in the virtual hardware [4].

Assisted Virtualization or Paravirtualization: modifies the guest OS kernel in order to replace non-virtualizable instructions with hypercalls that directly communicate with the hypervisor layer. The hypervisor also provides interfaces (named hypercalls) to other kernel's critical operations, such as memory management, interrupt management, or time management. Paravirtualization differs from total virtualization in the sense that here the unmodified OS does not know that it is being virtualized and sensitive system calls are captured through binary conversion [4].

Hardware Assisted Virtualization: hardware providers are rapidly adopting virtualization, improving the resources to make it easier. Improvements here include Intel's Virtualization Technology (VT-x) and AMD's AMD-V. In both cases the technique is to provide new modes to execute privileged instructions [4].

B. Hypervisor

The hypervisor is a software layer between hardware and operating system, controlling the access of the guest OS to the hardware's resources. In order to work correctly, the hypervisor needs to have control over the real system's resources. It also needs to satisfy certain constraints, such as to provide an exact copy of the real execution environment to the applications running in the virtual machine. There are several hypervisors available, including Xen, VMware, KVM and QEMU [4].

CLOUD COMPUTING

A cloud is a system using concepts as virtualization, emulation, OVF (VM configuration patterns), and Libvirt (an API to manage guest operating systems), and to assemble a new architecture from them. This new architecture basic idea is to provide computing power from demand, where more virtual machines can be added to the cloud when an user needs it. Actual machines can be added in order to increase the computing power and/or storage capacity.

Since hardware virtualization allows the creation of multiple virtual machines over a real machine, cloud computing uses it to create an environment (the cloud), allocating instances (guest operating systems) accordingly to the available resources (physical hosts). These virtual machine instances are allocated to the convenient actual hosts that compose the computing cloud [5].

The key to achieve cloud computing is the "cloud", which is a massive network of hosts (servers or simple machines) connected as a grid. These computers may work independently or in parallel, when resources are combined in order to create a high performance system [6].

As shown in Figure 2, individual users access the cloud from their own computers, or portable devices, using the internet. For these individual users, the cloud can be seen as a single application to share documents or devices. Both hardware and operating system are made transparent for the user, simplifying the cloud's access by the user.

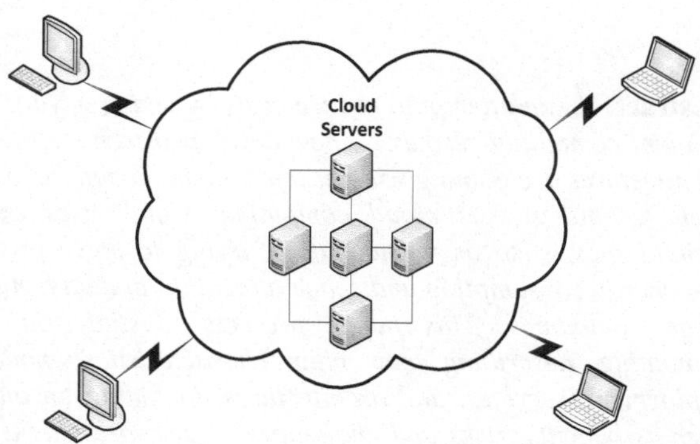

Figure 2 – A typical, simplified, cloud system [7].

A. Classification schemes

According to Sasikala [8], computing clouds can be classified accordingly to the type of users sharing/providing their services/resources. The defined classes are:

Public cloud: the infrastructure is provided to many clients and managed by a third party, that is paid by its usage. In this class several companies may be involved in the same environment.

Private cloud: the infrastructure is built aiming specific clients inside one organization. It can be managed by the own organization or by a third party. In this case, virtualization can be made using proprietary tools.

Community cloud: the infrastructure is shared among several organizations, usually with a common goal. It can be managed by the organizations or by a single service provider.

Hybrid cloud: is composed by two or more of the previous models, demanding transparency in all transfers between them.

B. Architecture

According to Zhang, Cheng and Boutaba [9], the architecture of a cloud computing environment can be divided in four layers: hardware/datacenter, infrastructure, platform and application layers, as shown in Figure 3. The description of these layers follows:

Hardware layer: it is responsible of managing the cloud's physical resources, including servers, network devices, electrical power, and cooling systems. It is usually implemented through datacenters, with hundreds or thousands of servers in order to deal with issues such as fault tolerance and traffic routing.

Infrastructure layer: it is also known as virtualization layer and creates a pool of resources for storage and processing, allocating physical resources through hypervisors such as Xen, KVM or VMware. This layer is essential in the cloud environment since dynamic resource allocation and other important features are provided by hypervisors.

Platform layer: it is built over the infrastructure layer, consisting of the operating systems and frameworks for software applications. It is designed aiming the reduction in the cost of developing applications directly for VM stubs. As an example, the Google App Engine operates in this layer in order to provide a support API for the development of databases, storage and typical businesses rules for web applications.

Application layer: in the top level of this hierarchy, the application layer is composed by actual cloud applications. These applications differ from conventional ones since they can take advantage from automatic resizing in the resources in order to achieve a better performance, availability and operational cost.

This layered architecture resembles the OSI reference model for computer networks, providing modularity, flexibility and independence from changes in each layer. This allows the reduction in costs of management and maintenance, at the same time it can execute a wider range of applications.

In order to achieve such characteristics it is expected that a cloud computing environment would offer the following properties [10], also appearing in Figure 3:

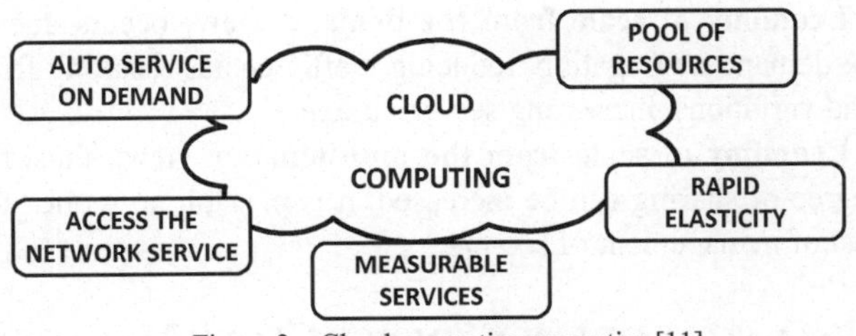

Figure 3 – Cloud computing properties [11].

Automatic service on demand: computational services are provided automatically, without human intervention over the service provider;

Wide access to network services: since computing resources are available through the internet, they must be easily accessible via standard protocols by any kind of device (mobile, handheld, or desktops);

Pool of Resources: provided computing resources (physical or virtual) have to serve multiple users, being allocated and reallocated accordingly to the demand;

Rapid Elasticity: services must be fast and made available whenever necessary. Users of them must feel as they have unlimited resources, which can be acquired in any amount, anytime. The elasticity property appears in three components: linear scalability, use by demand, and payment of what is consumed;

Measurable Services: the management systems used by the cloud must control and monitor each resource, automatically, for each kind of service (storage, processing, and bandwidth). This monitoring must be transparent for both entities involved (service provider and user).

Zhang, Cheng and Boutaba [9] establish that cloud computing provides services in a form that largely differs from the form provided by conventional computing datacenters. The differences include:

Multiple tenants: in a cloud environment services owned by multiple providers can be located in a single data center. With this approach the issues with performance and management of these services can be dealt by all service and the infrastructure providers. The layered architecture offers a natural division of duties, that is, the owner of each layer will have to deal only with the specific goals associated with that layer. Unfortunately, the multiple tenancies also create problems in the understanding and management of the interactions between parts.

Sharing of the pool of resources: the infrastructure provider offers a pool of resources that can be dynamically allocated to the resource consumers. This capability creates a great flexibility to the cost-effective management of resources. As an example, a service provider can take advantage of the technique of VM migration in order to maximize resource utilization, what implies in the reduction of costs associated with cooling and power consumption.

Access through a worldly distributed network: clouds are usually accessible from the Internet, therefore, any device connected to it, either a cell phone or a desktop, is capable of using the cloud services. Even more, in order to achieve a high performance and availability, many of the current clouds are composed by several datacenters distributed over the world.

Service Oriented: cloud computing adopts a service-oriented operational model, putting a strong emphasis in service management. Each provider offers his service trying to guarantee a Service Level Agreement (SLA), which is negotiated with the users of that service.

Dynamic resource provisioning: differently from conventional systems, where resources are fixed, in clouds we have the capability of dynamically adjust the amount of offered resources by the acquisition and publishing of extra resources by the service provider, guided by current demands.

Self-organization: the property of dynamic resource provisioning implies in the ability of providers and clients to adjust their resources upon demand. Resources can be allocated or returned to the pool depending the current needs. This flexibility results in the elasticity property.

Price-based utilities: cloud computing uses an economical model based in "pay what you use". The exact price of processing may be different for different services. For example, a software provider may rent a VM in a by-hour basis, while other may charge the service by the number of clients served. Although services priced by-use may reduce client's costs, they introduce difficulties in the management of the whole operation.

There are also important differences that distinguish the

model of cloud computing from the traditional model of computing. Table I, adapted from [12], summarizes these differences.

TABLE I
DIFFERENCES BETWEEN CONVENTIONAL AND CLOUD MODELS

	Conventional Computing	Cloud Computing
Acquisition Model	Hardware Physical space Infrastructure of installation and operation	Service acquisition
Business Model	Cost and depreciation of assets Administrative overhead (maintenance, support, safety of equipment, refrigeration)	Payment based on demand
Access Model	Internal network Intranet	Internet, through various types of devices (not just desktop computers)
Technical Model	One tenant Without sharing Static	Scalable, Elastic, Dynamic

Additionally it is known that cloud computing and grid computing share some goals, including cost reduction, flexibility and reliability through the use of third party hardware. They differ in the way they allocate resources, where in grids it is attempted a more homogeneous allocation and in a cloud the allocation occurs on demand. Also, the virtualization in cloud computing allows for a greater separation between the resources used by all users.

C. Classes of services

Services in cloud computing have different levels of support, accordingly to what is offered to clients. There are three classes of services, depicted in Figure 4, named IaaS (for infrastructure), SaaS (for software) and PaaS (for platform) [5]. A short description of them follows:

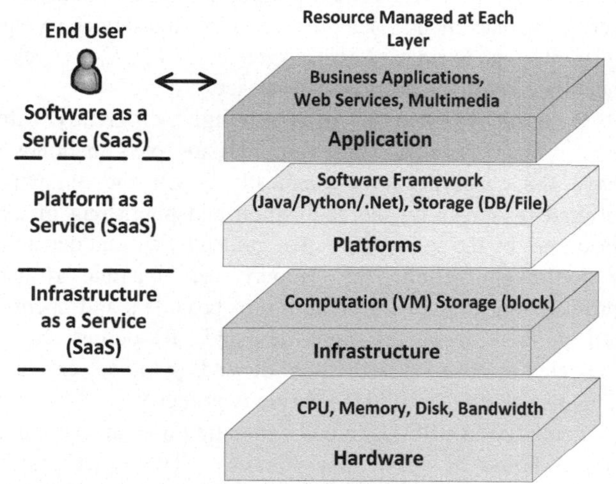

Figure 4 – Cloud computing architecture (Adapted from [9]).

Infrastructure as a Service (IaaS): in this type of service clients are provided with processing, storage, network bandwidth, and other computing resources, being able to reconfigure them as needed. Clients do not manage or control the infrastructure of the remaining cloud, paying only for what is used. Amazon Elastic Compute Cloud (Amazon EC2), Eucalyptus, OpenNebula and OpenStack are examples of providers in this class [8].

Platform as a Service (PaaS): in this class clients get an environment for development, test and deployment of their own applications, disregarding the needs of infrastructure (memory, storage, processors, etc.). Google Apps and Microsoft Azure are examples of services in this class [8].

Software as a Service (SaaS): here the applications are the service provided, with clients demanding the execution of specific programs. The applications can be accessed from several types of devices, usually from a web browser. The client has no control over the infrastructure or even the application [8].

D. Benefits from cloud computing

According to Veras [11], the main benefit brought with the use of cloud computing is scalability. With the resource provisioning provided by the cloud, based on demand, it is easier to scale the system, introducing more resources when they are needed. This allows for reduction in power consumption and management effort, optimizing the use of servers, network and storage space. The economics of clouds involve the following aspects:

Economy of scale from the providers view: it is achieved from big datacenters, minimizing operating costs related to power consumption, personnel, and management. The minimization is a direct result of the assembly of multiple resources in a single domain.

Economy of scale from the demand view: occurs due to the demand aggregation, reducing inefficiencies resulting from load variations, increasing server's usage.

Economy of scale from the multitenancy view: since the degree of sharing can be increased, it is possible to reduce the cost of management of servers.

EVALUATION OF OPEN SOURCE CLOUD MANAGERS

We analyzed three open-source cloud managers, OpenStack, Eucalyptus e OpenNebula, which were chosen because they have better documentation available. In order to perform the evaluation we used six personal computers, configured with 4GB of memory, running 2.66GHz Core 2 Quad processors, linked through a 1 Gbps network and running Ubuntu Server 10.10 64bits. One computer was used as the cluster's manager, while the remaining five were used as computing nodes, using KVM and working as an IaaS model.

A. Eucalyptus manager

As the other managers, Eucalyptus can work in the all-in-one model, where the main services include data storage, VM images server, cluster control and cloud management, and are offered through a single or distributed servers. A single server topology can be seen in Figure 5.

It operates verifying which nodes are part of the cloud and aggregating their resources accordingly to the profiles of the

VM instances present. The cluster uses a round-robin policy to select and execute a VM image in a given node. Once started, that instance can be accessed through its public IP address, attributed by the manager.

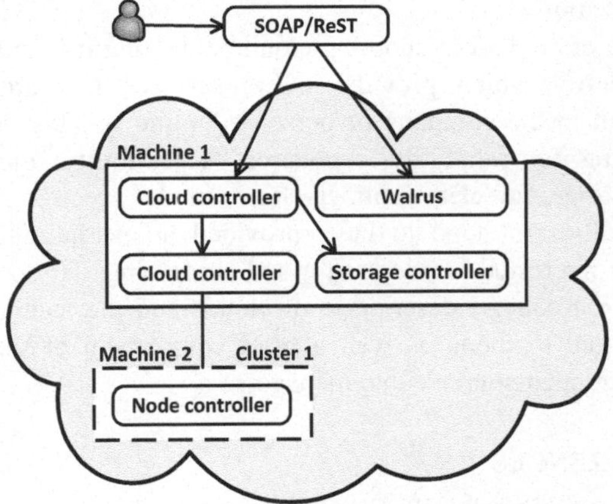

Figure 5 – Eucalyptus topology for a single cluster [13].

As it can be seen from Figure 6, a cluster with 5GB of memory can generate five profiles with different amounts of RAM in each one. They can be selected afterward by the demand needs from each client.

```
Every 2.0s: euca-describe-availability-zones verbose     Sat Jan 14 15:31:48 2012

AVAILABILITYZONE        cluster1         10.10.34.25
AVAILABILITYZONE        |- vm types      free / max   cpu   ram  disk
AVAILABILITYZONE        |- m1.small      0010 / 0010   1    192     8
AVAILABILITYZONE        |- c1.medium     0010 / 0010   1    256     8
AVAILABILITYZONE        |- m1.large      0010 / 0010   1    512    10
AVAILABILITYZONE        |- m1.xlarge     0005 / 0005   1   1024    10
AVAILABILITYZONE        |- c1.xlarge     0000 / 0000   1   2800    10
```

Figure 6 – Profiles of VM instances in Eucalyptus.

B. OpenNebula manager

OpenNebula uses the Ruby language to implement communication among nodes.

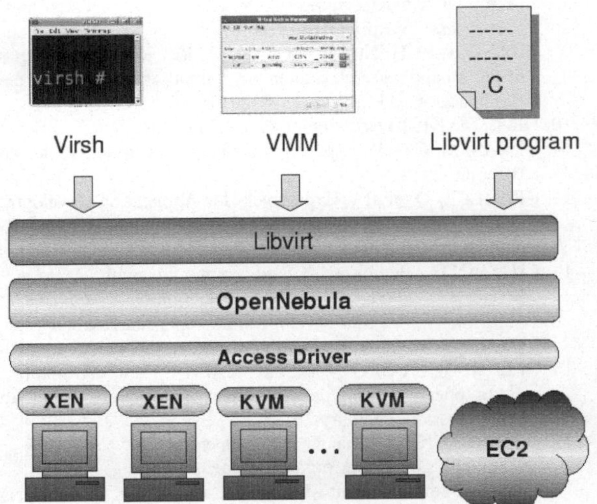

Figure 7 – Libvirt API 1.4 API [14].

It also uses Libvirt (a framework for the creation of VMs), as shown in Figure 7. In OpenNebula the requests for the creation of VM are managed with Libvirt, which translates them to the different hypervisors.

C. OpenStack manager

OpenStack is a collection of open-source projects that can be used, by companies and service providers, to configure and run their storage infrastructure. NASA and Rackspace, among others, contributed massively for its maturation. Rackspace provided a platform for object storage, while NASA contributed with OpenNebula's platform. As it can be seen in Figure 8, there are three main service components in OpenStack:

- Computing node (Nova);
- Storage (Swift);
- Image service (Glance).

The computing node (Nova) is the OpenStack's controller. All activities necessary to support the life cycle of the VM instances are managed on it, using the Libvirt API to interact with the supported hypervisors.

Swift provides a distributed object storage service. It is similar to the Amazon Web Services – Simple Storage Service (S3).

Glance is a search engine and a VM image retrieval system. It can be configured to use any of the storage back-ends available.

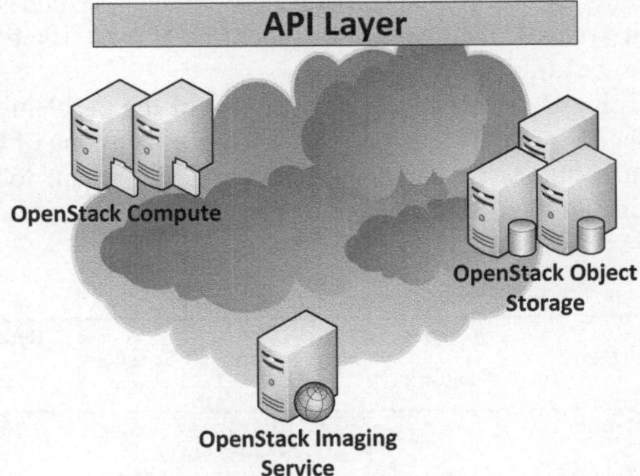

Figure 8 – OpenStack's architecture [15].

OpenStack has also several installation options, being able to be installed in one or more servers, with or without virtualization support. It has to be noted that when there is no virtualization support, it is necessary to emulate it through QEMU.

D. Identified limitations in the managers

With our analysis some flaws, or limitations, were identified in the managers evaluated:

Failover: all tested managers do not have systems against failures, either for the manager or its nodes. For example, if the manager crashes, the remaining nodes can still work normally, but if a node becomes unavailable, that instance is lost, needing a human intervention in order to upload it in another VM.

Scheduler: the choice of which physical node will receive each VM instance is done by the manager's scheduler, what is more effective if dynamic algorithms are in use. Eucalyptus has three algorithms for instance scheduling, round-robin, Greedy (allocates to first found node), and PowerSave (turn off nodes that are not running any VM). OpenNebula and OpenStack have also similar static algorithms. In all cases, the manager is unable to schedule nodes in a dynamic, and more efficient, approach.

Geographical dispersion: for geographically distributed clouds, the manager should be able to reschedule a given VM instance accordingly to the region from which it gets more accesses. However, in many situations, virtualized applications are not ready to be accessed through the network, and do not take location as a parameter in the VM creation.

Power consumption: nodes that are not executing any instance should be turned off or put in a low consumption mode. However, in order to achieve this manager has to have schedulers capable of activating or reactivating nodes as soon the demands requires that. Among the managers evaluated Eucalyptus has the PowerSave algorithm that is capable of this.

Data protection: in all open-source cloud managers there is no a policy or control for data backup. Another issue is that the managers use third party solutions for storage, such as NFS or SAN. These solutions make harder to guarantee data redundancy, especially due to network bandwidth that constrains the speed of data transfers among the nodes. At current systems, this bandwidth should be at least 10Gb/s, in order to be efficient.

In Table II we present a short review of the problems just described. From that it is possible to devise that none of them present solutions for those problems. It is important to note that some of them are managed by proprietary managers.

TABLE II
PROBLEMS WITH OPEN SOURCE CLOUD PROVIDERS

Manager	Storage Virtualization	High Availability	Scheduler	Recovery Data
Eucalyptus	No	No	Static	No
OpenNebula	No	No	Static	No
OpenStack	No	No	Static	No

CONCLUSION

Since cloud computing is becoming more present nowadays, with several companies and organizations adopting this approach, it is very important to understand it. To have this understanding is useful to a better dimensioning of its capabilities, vulnerabilities, and risks. Among the major benefits from clouds there are the minimization of power consumption and physical space, easier provisioning, and easier access to external interfaces (APIs), among others characteristics.

Accordingly to the performed tests, OpenStack presented the best results. This includes a complete documentation, active community, concerns with bug fixes, easy installation, a good quantity of different VM images, allowing assisted instance migration (in the licensed version).

The other two managers presented some deficiencies, such as lack of documentation, obscure architecture, and use of third party solutions in the platform. These problems are an obstacle for a faster adoption of cloud computing by some organizations.

Therefore, before adopting cloud computing it is important to identify which provider offers services that are more relevant to the company or person adopting it. This includes checking for reliability, reputation, accessibility, migration capabilities, and clear contracts, for example.

Finally, we hope to have provided an useful guide for people interested in adopting cloud computing. To do so, we provide a concise description of clouds and the technologies associated to them, as well a brief comparison of the most relevant open-source cloud managers.

REFERENCES

1. HE, Zhonglin; HE, Yuhua. Analysis on the security of cloud computing. Proc. Spie, Qingdao, China, n., p.7752-775204, 2011.
2. BHADAURIA, Rohit; CHAKI, Rituparna. A Survey on Security Issues in Cloud Computing. CORR, P. abs/1109.5388, 2011.
3. SABAHI, F. Cloud computing security threats and responses. Communication Software and Networks (ICCSN), 2011 IEEE 3rd International Conference on May 2011.
4. VMWARE. Understanding Full Virtualization, Paravirtualization, and Hardware Assist. Available at: <http://www.vmware.com/files/pdf/VMware_paravirtualization.pdf>. Last access: 09 July 2012.
5. BUYYA, Rajkumar; BROBERG, James; GOSCISNSKI, Andrzej M. Cloud Computing: Principles and Paradigms. John Wiley and Sons: San Francisco, 2011.
6. CEARLEY, D. et al – Hype Cycle for Application Development – Gartner Group report number G00147982 – Technical Report available at http://www.gartner.com/, 2009.
7. MILLER, M. Cloud Computing: Web-Based Applications That Change the Way You Work and Collaborate Online. Que Publishing Digital, 2008.
8. SASIKALA, P. Cloud computing: present status and future implications. Available at: <http://www.inderscience.com/storage/f123101246118579.pdf>. Last access: 29 April 2012.
9. ZHANG, Q.; CHENG, L.; BOUTABA, R. Cloud computing: state-of-the-art and research challenges. Journal of Internet Services and Applications, v. 1, n. 1, p. 7–18, 2010.
10. NIST. The NIST Definition of Cloud Computing, NIST, 2011.
11. VERAS, M. Cloud computing: new IT architecture. Rio de Janeiro: Brasport, 2012.
12. CEARLEY, D. et al – Hype Cycle for Application Development – Gartner Group report number G00147982 – Technical Report Gartner group. Available at: http://www.gartner.com/, 2009.
13. CHAGANTI, Prabhakar. Cloud computing with Amazon Web Services, Part 1: Introduction, Available at <http://www.ibm.com/developerworks/opensource/library/ar-cloudaws1/index.html>. Last access: 05 April 2013.
14. OPENNEBULA.ORG. Libvirt API 1.4. Available at: <http://opennebula.org/documentation:archives:rel1.4:libvirtapi>. Last access: 24 February 2013.
15. OPENSTACK. What is OpenStack? Available at: <http://docs.openstack.org/cactus/openstack-compute/admin/content/what-is-openstack.html>. Last access: 05 March 2013.

SESSION

SYSTEMS SOFTWARE + PROGRAMMING MODELS + THREADS + CACHING + FILE SYSTEMS + TESTING AND MONITORING METHODS

Chair(s)

TBA

Write Buffer Sharing Control in SMT Processors

Yilin Zhang and Wei-Ming Lin
Department of Electrical and Computer Engineering
The University of Texas at San Antonio
San Antonio, TX 78249-0669, USA

Abstract— *Simultaneous Multi-Threading (SMT) has been widely studied to lend modern-day CPUs a mechanism to improve resource utilization so as to lead to a higher instruction throughput by allowing concurrent execution of multiple independent threads with sharing of key datapath components. The key to a high-performance SMT is to optimize the distribution of shared resources among temporally competing threads. Allowing any of the threads to overwhelm these resources not only leads to unfair thread processing but also may severely degrade overall system throughput. Write buffer is one of the most critical shared resources in SMT systems due to its size constraint and potentially long occupancy latency from its data. In this paper, we show that, by limiting the number of write buffer entries each thread is allowed to occupy in the commit stage, the overall system throughput is enhanced by a substantial margin. An improvement in IPC of up to 26% and 95% is observed when the proposed technique is applied to a 4-threaded and an 8-threaded SMT system, respectively.*

Keywords: Simultaneous Multi-Threading; Superscalar; Write Buffer

1. Introduction

Noting the resource utilization deficiencies in the traditional superscalar processors, Simultaneous Multi-Threading (SMT) offers an improved mechanism by allowing instructions from different threads to be issued in the same clock cycle in order to exploit the full potential of the shared resources. Essentially SMT improves the overall performance by exploiting Thread-Level Parallelism (TLP) among threads to overcome the limitation of Instruction-Level Parallelism (ILP) presented in a single thread [1], [2].

There have been numerous research efforts targeting in improving SMT performance by adopting scheduling algorithms for effective resource allocation, including advanced fetch policies and other resource partitioning methods applied in multiple stages on various buffers such as Instruction Fetching Queue (IFQ), rename registers, Re-Order Buffer (ROB) and Issue Queue (IQ), etc. A significant amount of work has been emphasized in instruction fetching including: in ICOUNT [5] a higher priority in fetching instructions is assigned to a thread with fewer instructions in pre-issue stages; a fetch policy taking L2 cache misses into consideration is adopted in STALL and FLUSH [6]; a dynamical fetch policy based on memory performance of each thread and exploiting parallelism beyond stalled memory operations is presented in DCRA [7]. Advances in other stages of pipeline have also been proposed including: Hill-Climbing [8] is a learning-based algorithm that uses performance feedback to partition the shared hardware resources in the pipeline including rename registers, ROB and IQ; APRA [9] dynamically assigns IFQ, ROB and IQ to threads according to the changes of threads' behavior; IQ-capping in [10] limits each thread's occupancy in IQ to obtain a more effective and fair resource allocation; Instruction-Recalling in [11] further improves IQ utilization by recalling stalling instructions from IQ; Speculative-Control in [12] significantly reduces the amount of flush-out due to miss-speculation to improve threads' overall flow in IQ.

Note that the common resources in an SMT system shared by threads include various machine bandwidths (e.g., inter-stage bandwidth, read/write ports for register files and memory, etc.), inter-stage buffers (e.g., Issue Queue), functional units, write buffer, etc. Our analysis in a later section shows that the write buffer proves to be the most critical shared resources in affecting overall performance No research in the literature so far has investigated issues regarding the sharing of this critical buffer among threads in an SMT system. How to effectively assign the write buffer to competing threads to prevent long-term blocking due to lengthy and dominant occupancy from slower thread(s) is the main theme of this paper.

A new technique is developed in this paper to effectively relieve the pressure of the write buffer in an SMT system so as to achieve better resource utilization. Write operations in a program tend to be bursty in nature and thus a sequence of writes from one program could easily overwhelm the whole write buffer. In order to prevent any single thread from disproportionately occupying the write buffer, a simple capping algorithm is proposed in this paper by limiting the number of buffer entries each thread is allowed to occupy at any given time. Our simulation results show that IPC (Instructions Per Clock-cycle) improvement can be as high as 26% for a 4-threaded workload and a whopping 95% for an 8-threaded workload.

2. Write Buffer

A write buffer (or referred to as "store buffer" in some articles) is designed to hide long write latency when CPU encounters cache misses [3], [4], [13], [14]. A typical two-level cache organization with write-back policy at both levels is shown in Figure 1. Modern-day processors usually have a

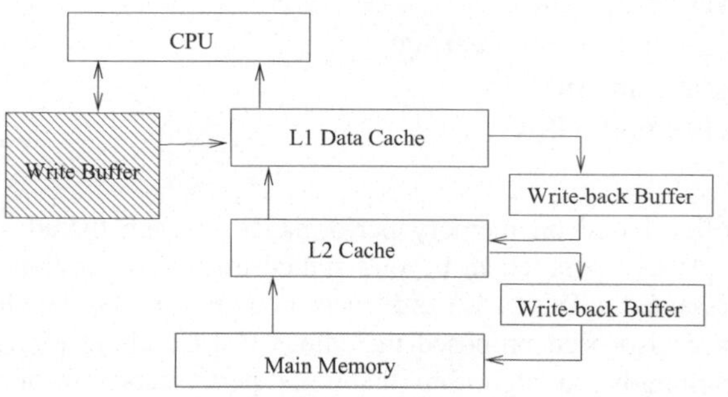

Fig. 1: A Typical Two-Level Cache Organization with a Write Buffer

multi-level cache architecture and may adopt different write policies, write-through and write-back, at different levels, which in turn may require a different design for the write buffer.

Write-merging (also known as write-coalescing) is a technique aggregating writes to the same cache block (line) to reduce miss penalty as well as the buffer size requirement, which is prevalent in most modern processors [4]. In a write-coalescing buffer, a data read operation retrieves its target data from either the L1 data cache or the write buffer (if the target data is still residing in the buffer from a previous write yet to finish); a write operation will be merged into an existing write in the buffer if they belong to the same block (cache line), i.e. they will share the same entry in the buffer until the write operation finishes. When no merging exists, a write will not be allowed to commit if the buffer is full. Some researchers have focused their work on designing more efficient write buffer management for a generic superscalar CPU system including the study of effects from write buffer depths, retirement and load-hazard policies [13], and a new write option update policy in [14], etc.

In a superscalar system, all instructions have to be committed in order to ensure precise exception and correct speculative processing. Thus, if a write instruction cannot commit due to a full write buffer, all subsequent instructions will be blocked as well. In an SMT system where multiple threads are processed concurrently, blocking of one thread due to a full write buffer may very well mean blocking of another thread if it also has a write operation waiting to commit. What makes the difference between superscalar and SMT systems is that in the superscalar one if such a blocking happens it is an inevitable one since the order of committing instructions in the only program cannot be changed. On the other hand, in an SMT system, the order of committing instructions from different threads does not have to be fixed and therefore the order to committing write instructions from different threads may affect the overall system flow dramatically.

Since the write buffer is an on-chip component, to retain a large write buffer can be both cost and clock-timing prohibitive. For example, the 3rd generation of Intel XScale microarchitecture has a write buffer with only 12 entries [15]. Without employing a larger buffer, exploitation of TLP among threads in SMT will be thus severely hampered – contention among threads in this buffer may prevent "faster" threads (with faster writes) from committing their writes. To fully exploit both TLP and ILP, proper intelligence has to be incorporated into this resource sharing mechanism to ensure that threads share this component in an efficient and fair manner.

The cache design shown in Figure 1 will be assumed in our discussion with both levels of cache using the write-back policy. Note that there is very minimal effect on the write buffer performance from adopting a different write policy. In this paper, our proposed algorithm is tested in such a system with the feature of write coalescing.

3. Simulation Environment

The simulation environment adopted by our research, including the simulator and the workloads used are described in this section.

3.1 Simulator

We use the M-Sim [16], a multi-threaded micro-architectural simulation environment model, to estimate performance of the proposed scheme. The detailed configuration is shown in Table 1.

Parameter	Configuration
Machine Width	8 wide fetch/dispatch/issue/commit
L/S Queue size	48-entry Load/Store queue
ROB & IQ size	128-entry ROB, 32-entry IQ
Function Units & Latency (total/issue)	4 Int Add (1/1) 1 Int Mult (3/1) / Div (20/19) 2 Load/Store (1/1), 4 FP Add (2/1) 1 FP Mult (4/1) / Div (12/12) / Sqrt (24/24)
Physical registers	integer and floating point 256 (for 4-thread) / 512 (for 8-thread)
L1 I-cache	64KB, 2-way set-associative 64-byte line
L1 D-cache	64KB, 4-way set-associative 64-byte line write-back, 1 cycle access latency
L2 Cache unified	512KB, 16-way set-associative 64-byte line write-back, 10 cycles access latency
BTB	512 entry, 4-way set-associative
Branch Predictor	bimod: 2K entry
Pipeline Structure	5-stage front-end (fetch-dispatch) scheduling (for register file access: 2 stages, execution, write back, commit)
Memory	32-bit wide, 300 cycles access latency

Table 1: Configuration of the Simulated Processor

3.2 Workloads

Simulation runs for multi-threaded workloads in this paper all use the mixed SPEC CPU2006 benchmark suite [17] with mixtures of various levels of ILP for diversified representation of workloads. ILP classification of each benchmark is obtained by initializing it in accordance with the procedure mentioned in Simpoints tool and simulated individually in a simplescalar environment. Three types of ILPs, low ILP (memory bound), medium ILP and high ILP (execution bound), are so identified. As shown in Table 2 for 4-threaded workloads and Table 3 for 8-thread workloads, a number of multi-threaded workloads are used with threads of various mixtures of ILP types.

Mix	Benchmarks	Classification (ILP)		
		Low	Med	High
Mix 1	libquantum, dealII, gromacs, namd	0	0	4
Mix 2	soplex, leslie3d, povray, milc	0	4	0
Mix 3	hmmer, sjeng, gobmk, gcc	0	4	0
Mix 4	lbm, cactusADM, xalancbmk, bzip2	4	0	0
Mix 5	libquantum, dealII, gobmk, gcc	0	2	2
Mix 6	gromacs, namd, soplex, leslie3d	0	2	2
Mix 7	dealII, gromacs, lbm, cactusADM	2	0	2
Mix 8	libquantum, namd, xalancbmk, bzip2	2	0	2
Mix 9	povray, milc, cactusADM, xalancbmk	2	2	0
Mix 10	hmmer, sjeng, lbm, bzip2	2	2	0

Table 2: 4-threaded Workload for Simulation

Mix	Benchmarks	Classification (ILP)		
		Low	Med	High
Mix 1	libquantum, dealII, gromacs, namd, soplex, leslie3d, povray, milc	0	4	4
Mix 2	libquantum, dealII, gromacs, namd, lbm, cactusADM, xalancbmk, bzip2	4	0	4
Mix 3	hmmer, sjeng, gobmk, gcc, lbm, cactusADM, xalancbmk, bzip2	4	4	0
Mix 4	libquantum, dealII, gromacs, soplex, leslie3d, povray, lbm, cactusADM	2	3	3
Mix 5	dealII, gromacs, namd, xalancbmk, hmmer, cactusADM, milc, bzip2	3	2	3
Mix 6	gromacs, namd, sjeng, gobmk, gcc, lbm, cactusADM, xalancbmk	3	3	2

Table 3: 8-threaded Workload for Simulation

3.3 Metrics

For a multi-threaded workload, total combined IPC is a typical indicator used to measure the overall performance, which is defined as the sum of each thread's IPC:

$$Overall\_IPC = \sum_{i}^{n} IPC_i \quad (1)$$

where n denotes the number of threads per mix in the system. However, in order to preclude starvation effect among threads, the so-called Harmonic IPC is also adopted, which reflects the degree of execution fairness among the threads, namely,

$$Harmonic\_IPC = n / \sum_{i}^{n} \frac{1}{IPC_i} \quad (2)$$

In this paper, these two indicators are used to compare the proposed algorithm to the baseline (default) system. The following metric indicates the improvement percentage averaged over the selected mixes, which is applied to both $Overall\_IPC$ and $Harmonic\_IPC$, namely,

$$Perc\_Improved = (\sum_{j}^{m} \frac{IPC_j^{new} - IPC_j^{baseline}}{IPC_j^{baseline}} \times 100\%)/m \quad (3)$$

where m denotes the number of mixes of the workload in our simulation.

4. Motivation

The technique proposed in this paper is based on the conjectures that a write buffer of limited size tends to be the bottleneck for the pipeline operation, especially in an SMT system. What contributes to this bottleneck is a combination of high buffer occupancy and imbalanced occupancy among the threads. This section is devoted to the discussion to support these conjectures. The simulation results in this section are based on the system configuration with the ten mixes of 4-threaded workload as described in Section 3.

4.1 Write Buffer Size Analysis

We first analyze how critical the size of write buffer is to the overall throughput. Figure 2 shows the average of

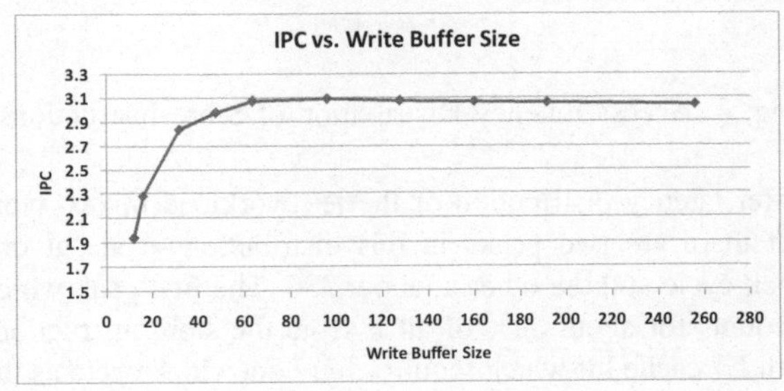

Fig. 2: IPC vs. Write Buffer Size

overall IPC from using different sizes of write buffer. When the size of the buffer (denoted as B) increases from 12 to 64 the overall IPC increases by almost 60%. In order to reach the highest possible IPC, a minimum of 64 entries are required, which is beyond nowadays-acceptable size for such an on-chip buffer. This minimum size becomes even larger when the number of threads further increases. This clearly indicates that the write buffer could easily become the performance bottleneck if its size is kept within the practical range.

4.2 Write Buffer Occupancy

The next analysis is to determine how often the write buffer and how much of it is occupied. Figure 3 shows the percentages of clock cycles during which the given

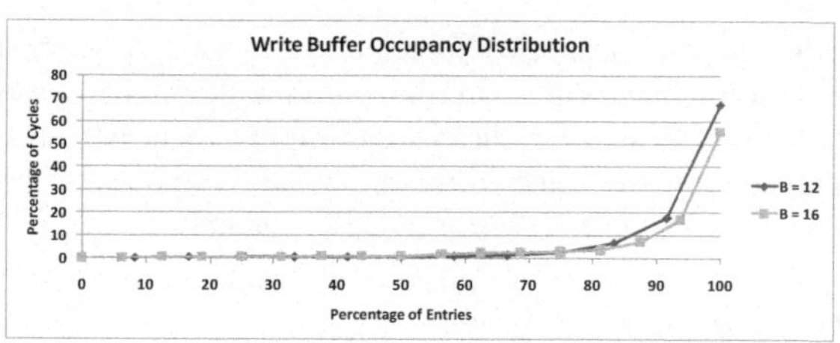

Fig. 3: Write Buffer Occupancy Distribution

percentage of entries are occupied in the write buffers with $B = 12$ and $B = 16$. In almost 70% (55%) of time the buffer is completely occupied for $B = 12$ ($B = 16$), and for 90% of time more than 80% of entries are occupied for either case. An explanation to the write buffer's high-occupancy rate would be the long latency of some write instructions staying in the buffer, which in turn leads to the investigation on this latency. Figure 4 shows the average

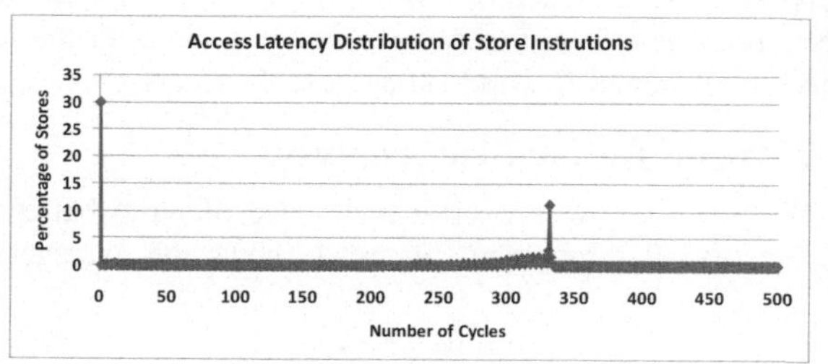

Fig. 4: Access Latency Distribution of Store Instructions

buffer latency distribution of the ten workload mixes. Note that there are two peaks in this distribution – one at one clock cycle and the other at about 330. The first peak which accounts for about 30% of all is from the store instructions with L1 cache hit which requires only one clock cycle as the "default delay" (meaning no waiting for the block that may be in the process of loading from L2). The second peak at 330 obviously corresponds to the instructions that encounter an L2 cache miss which incurs a default delay including the memory access latency (300 clock cycles according to simulator parameter setting) and the access latency to the two levels of cache plus some extra overhead for block transfer. All other occurrences in the distribution are from writes with various levels of hit/miss which, in addition to the corresponding default delay, take on additional delays from bus contention with other read and/or write operations. The delay from the bus contention varies depending on the severity of the competition with other cache misses. Due to this, some of the buffer latency values can go beyond 500.

Another even more intriguing and damaging factor to the SMT's performance is that the write buffer can be completely overwhelmed by a single thread. Figure 5 shows the percentages of time that at least one thread is occupying

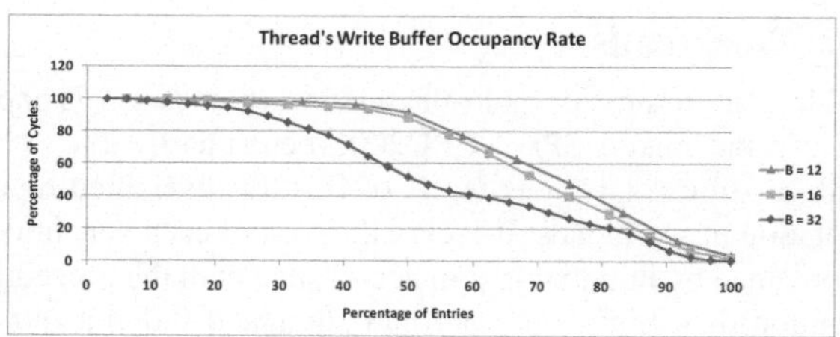

Fig. 5: Write Buffer's Single-Thread Dominance Rate

at least the given percentage of the write buffer entries. As expected, the smaller the write buffer is the more prominent the said dominance becomes. For example for $B = 12$ or $B = 16$, in about 90% of time there is at least one thread occupying half of the write buffer entries, and in over 40% of time at least one thread uses at least three quarters of entries, clearly indicating the imbalance of the resource usage. Even when the write buffer size increases to 32, there is still at least one thread occupying half of entries for over 50% of time. Such a single-thread usage dominance may easily lead to performance degradation when the dominating thread has mostly long-latency write operations, leaving very few precious entries for other threads to compete for.

4.3 A Larger Write Buffer?

As discussed above, the write buffer is obviously a bottleneck in an SMT system, and to retain a larger write buffer does not seem to be an economical or practical solution. Control logic required to support a larger buffer can be difficult to justify or simply becomes infeasible timing-wise. Even if a larger-size buffer is attainable, its utilization can be discouraging due to the intrinsic nature of write operations. Statistics from the benchmark programs employed in this study show that store instructions account for only about 10% to 18% of all instructions and not only their occurrences are mostly bursty in time but the distribution of their buffer latency (i.e. their hit/miss behavior) is also egregiously bursty, which easily leads to a very uneven occupancy level in time. This is clearly illustrated by Figure 6 where, under

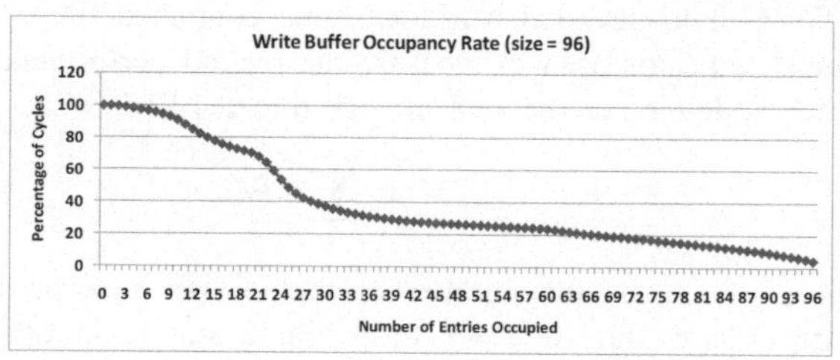

Fig. 6: Write Buffer Occupancy Rate

a large write buffer ($B = 96$), for at least a given number of entries occupied the percentage of cycles is tallied. Very much to our amaze, about three quarters of the buffer entries are actually left unused in 50% of time, a strong testament to the decision in not using a large buffer. Instead, one should resort to developing a better allocation algorithm to utilize the limited buffer space in a more intelligent manner.

5. Proposed Method

The proposed allocation technique is considered a modification to the ***commit*** stage of the default algorithm by imposing a very simple control mechanism on assigning the write buffer entries. This technique is based on a simple intention to prevent the buffer from being overwhelmed by any single thread. In this technique, a "cap" value (denoted as (C) is set to limit the number of write buffer entries any thread is allowed to occupy at any time. In order to have a simpler and more systematic comparison among using different buffer sizes, instead of using the absolute cap value, we adopt the ratio between the cap value and the buffer size (B), denoted as the "cap fraction (F)" for our simulation where $F = C/B$. A thread will stop committing any store instruction (at the head of ROB) once this thread has reached its cap value. The complete commit stage algorithm is shown in Figure 7 modified with the proposed technique (the shaded region in flowchart).

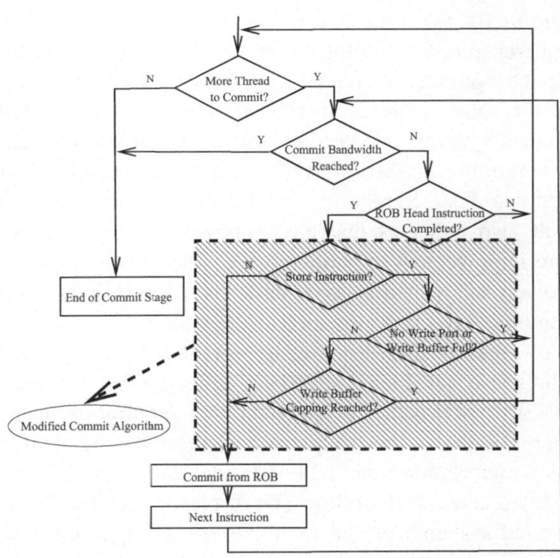

Fig. 7: Flow Chart of Modified Commit Algorithm

A write instruction from a thread when reaching the head of its ROB may come across three separate delays waiting for each of the following shared resources: (1) commit bandwidth (2) write port and (3) write buffer, as depicted in the three condition checking steps in the flowchart. Most of the delays are from the third condition waiting for the write buffer, if left uncontrolled. The newly imposed fourth condition is added to reduce this delay.

Note that any control technique aimed at eliminating the intended overwhelming occupancy problem, no matter how complicated the technique is, will suffer a drawback in compromising the flexibility that the true shared resource offers. The main compromise between the benefits and drawbacks from the techniques depends on the setting of the cap fraction value. If the cap fraction is set too high, the intended function of this technique in suppressing single thread's dominating occupancy will not be effective. On the other hand, if the cap fraction is set too low, overall performance may suffer if concurrent writes from multiple threads do not happen often enough. Our simulation to be presented in the next section will be used to study the effect of this compromise and to lend us a good indication of where a good range of cap fraction should be.

6. Simulation Results

Based on the simulation environment and the workloads described in Section 3, the proposed technique is tested compared to the default system. As aforementioned, throughout the simulation, the notion of cap fraction will be adopted for a systematic comparison when buffer size is varied, and the fraction value is adjusted with a fixed increment of fraction of $1/16$ no matter what value of B is chosen. That is, for each simulation run the cap fraction is set to $d/16$ where d varies from 1 to 16 (the cap fraction value is always rounded down to the next integer).

Figure 8 shows the result of IPC improvement when the

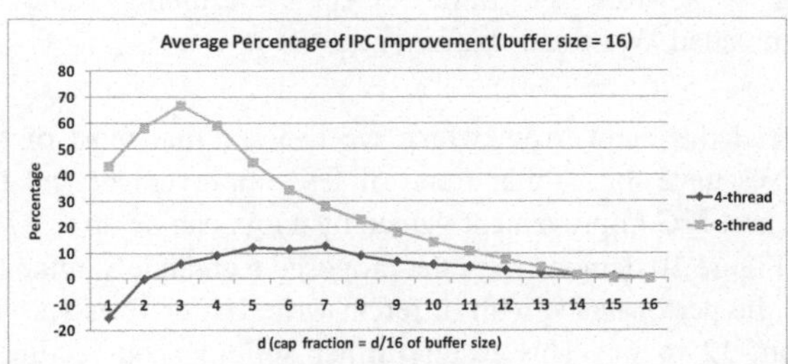

Fig. 8: Average Percentage of IPC Improvement ($B = 16$)

proposed technique is applied to 4-threaded and 8-threaded workloads. Improvement from this technique can go up to 12.5% and 66.4% for the 4-threaded and 8-threaded one, respectively. This result in general solidifies all our aforementioned claims. First of all, the effectiveness of our technique is more prominent for an 8-threaded system than a 4-threaded one due to higher competition. Secondly, optimal setting of the cap fraction is above the point of $1/n$ – the optimal cap fraction happens at $7/16$ for the 4-threaded system and $3/16$ for the 8-threaded system. Thirdly, there exists an obvious compromise between the ensuing benefit and drawback from setting a different cap fraction value. When the cap fraction is set higher than the optimal point, the higher the cap is the less benefit this technique can produce, and there is virtually no more improvement once the cap fraction is set to be at least $14/16$. On the other hand, once the cap fraction is set lower then the optimal value, the tighter (lower) the cap is, the less flexible the buffer allocation becomes and the benefit of sharing becomes less. In the 4-threaded case, when the cap fraction falls below $2/16$ any benefit from the technique is completely offset by its ensuing detrimental effect.

However, in the 8-threaded case, very much to our surprise, there is still a very significant performance improvement (43%) even when the cap fraction is set to the lowest $1/16$ (i.e. a cap of "one" entry). This scenario clearly indicates that, in such a high competition environment: 8 threads for a buffer size of 16, any capping is better than no capping and, if left uncontrolled, constant dominating occupancy situation from one or very few threads.

Figure 9 further shows per-mix IPC improvement in a 4-threaded system, from which we can see that most of the mixes have the similar trend of IPC improvement and the highest IPC improvement gained by a mix can be up to 87%.

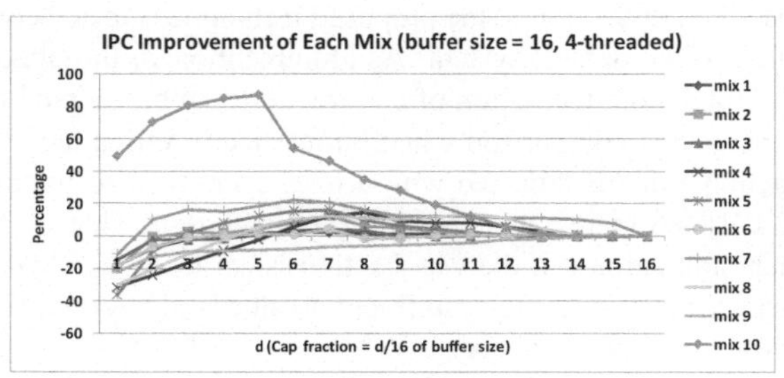

Fig. 9: Per-Mix IPC Improvement vs. Capping Value for 4-threaded Workload (buffer size = 16)

Figure 10 demonstrates the proposed technique's influence on the performance with different write buffer sizes varying from 12 to 64. This result further solidifies our claim in how the effective of our technique can be swayed by the buffer size, achieving a maximum improvement of 26% and 95% with $B = 12$ on 4-threaded and 8-threaded workloads, respectively. On the other hand, in the 4-threaded case, there is minimal gain from this technique when the buffer size exceeds 32. In the 8-threaded case, the technique somehow still maintains a discernible amount of improvement (up to 3.6%) even the buffer is increased to 64.

In order to reflect the degree of execution fairness among the threads when the proposed technique is applied, Figure 11 shows the percentage of improvement of Harmonic IPC for 4-threaded and 8-threaded workloads. As the result shows, when cap fraction is set too small, the harmonic IPC tends to suffer even when the system sees an improved IPC. In a system with more threads, the effect in balancing resource among threads brought by the proposed technique

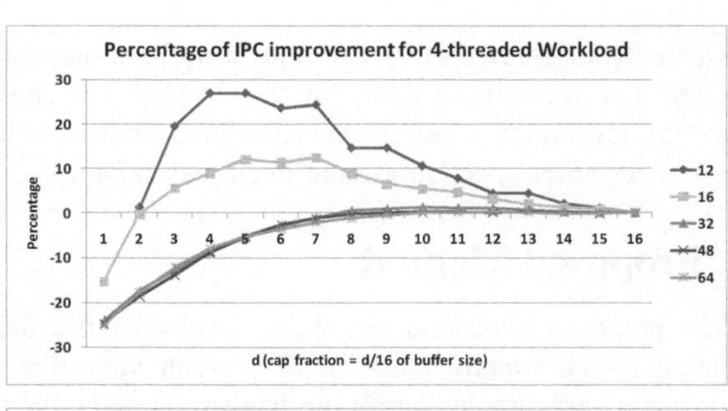

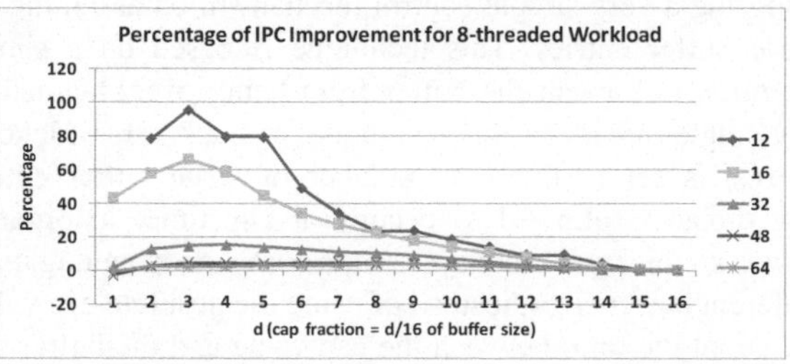

Fig. 10: Performance Comparison with Varying Write Buffer Size for 4-threaded and 8-threaded Workloads

is much more significant. For example, in a 4-threaded system, our algorithm gains a harmonic IPC improvement of up to 10.8%, while in a 8-threaded system, the maximal improvement can be as high as 46.7%. One would also notice that the optimal cap fraction for harmonic IPC usually is not the same value as that of IPC, which means in the practical systems, one needs to choose the best cap fraction by compromising the improvement between overall IPC and harmonic IPC. Similar to the trend in overall IPC, this result also indicates that the proposed technique leads to more improvement in harmonic IPC when more threads are involved and a smaller write buffer is employed, due to the additional fairness it provides to the system.

An analysis that can directly reveal how the proposed technique is capable of effectively relieving the pressure on the write buffer is the comparison on write buffer occupancy. Figure 12 shows the comparison of the write buffer occupancy rate between the default system before and after the modified commit algorithm. The displayed result is for a 4-threaded system with the write buffer size equal to 16 and the capping fraction set at 7/16. With the proposed method applied, the percentage of cycles with a high-occupancy write buffer shrinks dramatically. The percentage of time when the buffer is completely full is reduced from 56% to 14%, a huge improvement leading to the necessary buffer space to sustain a less disrupted write traffic.

7. Conclusion

This paper clearly demonstrated that uncontrolled utilization of resource shared among the threads in an SMT system could significantly affect the overall performance. Due to the

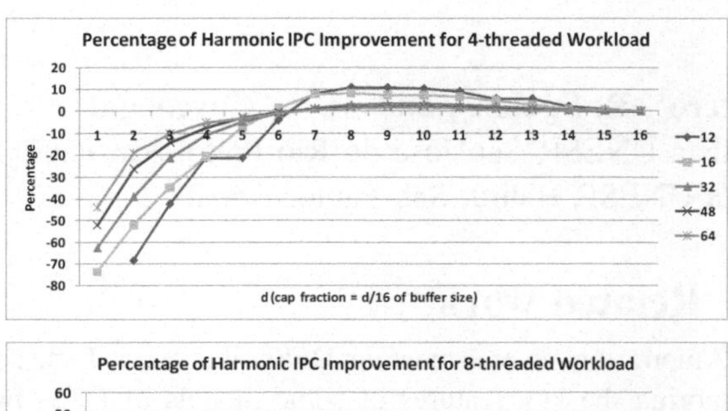

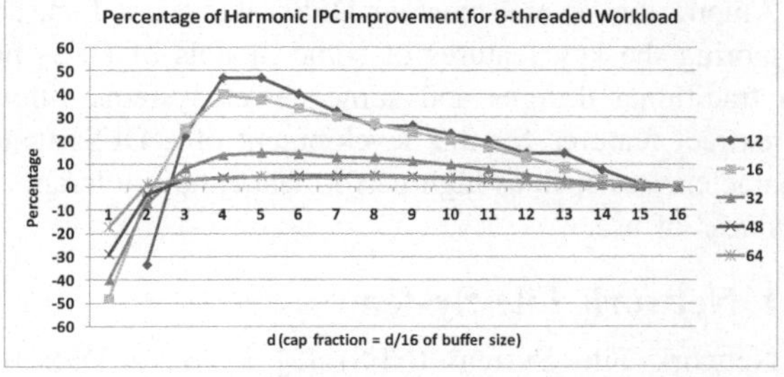

Fig. 11: Harmonic IPC Comparison with Varying Write Buffer Size for 4-threaded and 8-threaded Workloads

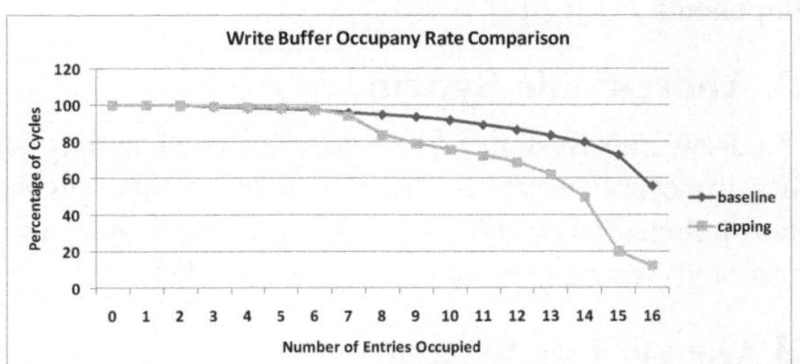

Fig. 12: Write Buffer Occupancy Rate Comparison (buffer size = 16)

limited size of the write buffer and long latency from some write operations, write buffer easily becomes a bottleneck that severely limits performance of an SMT system. By capping the write buffer usage of each thread, utilization of this critically shared resource can be vastly improved and consequently leads to a very considerable performance gain. Another noteworthy aspect in this technique is that such an improvement is achieved without having to invest much extra hardware nor imposing extra constraints on the clock rate and can be incorporated with further intelligence into such a control technique for even more performance improvement.

Acknowledgment

This material is based in part upon work supported by the National Science Foundation under Grant Number HRD 0932339. Any opinions, findings, and conclusions or recommendations expressed in this material are those of the author(s) and do not necessarily reflect the views of the National Science Foundation.

References

[1] H. Hirate, K. Kimura, S. Nagamine, Y. Mochizuki, A. Nishimura, Y. Nakase and T. Nishizawa, "An Elementary Processor Architecture with Simultaneous Instruction Issuing from Multiple Threads", *In the Proceedings of the 19th Annual International Symposium on Computer Architecture*, pp. 136-145, May 1992.

[2] D. Tullsen, S. J. Eggers and H. M. Levy, "Simultaneous Multithreading: Maximizing On-Chip Parallelism", *In the Proceedings of the 22nd Annual International Symposium on Computer Architecture*, pp. 392-403, May 1995.

[3] P. P. Chu and R. Gottipati, "Write Buffer Design for On-Chip Cache", *In the Proceedings of IEEE International Conference on Computer Design: VLSI in Computers and Processors*, pp. 311-316, October 1994.

[4] J. L. Hennessy and D. A. Patterson, "Computer Architecture:A Quantitative Approach", *Morgan Kaufmann Publishers*, 2007.

[5] D. M. Tullsen, S. J. Eggers, J. S. Emer, H. M .Levy, J. L. Lo and R. L. Stamm, "Exploiting Choice: Instruction Fetch and Issue on an Implementable Simultaneous MultiThreading Processor", *In the Proceedings of the 23rd Annual International Symposium on Computer Architecture*, pp. 191-202, May 1996.

[6] D. M. Tullsen and J. A. Brown, "Handling Long-latency Loads in a Simultaneous Multithreading Processor", *In the Proceedings of the 34th International Symposium on Microarchitecture*, pp. 318-327, December 2001.

[7] F. J. Cazorla, A. Ramirez, M. Valero and E. Fernandez, "Dynamically Controlled Resource Allocation in SMT Processors", *In the Proceedings of the 37th International Symposium on Microarchitecture*, pp. 171-182, December 2004.

[8] S. Choi and D. Yeung, "Learning-Based SMT Processor Resource Distribution via Hill-Climbing", *In the Proceedings of the 33rd Annual International Symposium on Computer Architecture*, pp. 239-251, June 2006.

[9] H. Wang, I. Koren and C. M. Krishna, "An Adaptive Resource Partitioning Algorithm for SMT Processors", *In the Proceedings of the 17th international conference on Parallel architectures and compilation techniques*, pp. 230-239, October 2008.

[10] T. K. D. Nagaraju, C. Douglas, W. M. Lin and E. John "Effective Dispatching for Simultaneous Multi-Threading (SMT) Processors by Capping Per-Thread Resource Utilization", *The Computing Science and Technology International Journal*, Vol. 1, No.2, pp. 5-14, December 2011.

[11] Y. Zhang, C. Douglas and W.-M. Lin, "On Maximizing Resource Utilization for Simultaneous (SMT) Processors by Instruction Recalling", *The 18th International Conference on Parallel and Distributed Processing Techniques and Applications (PDPTA'12)*, July 16-19, 2012, Las Vegas, NV.

[12] Y. Zhang and W.-M. Lin, "Capping Speculative Traces to Improve Performance in Simultaneous Multi-Threading CPUs", *The 18th International Conference on Parallel and Distributed Processing Techniques and Applications (PDPTA'13) Workshop on Multithreaded Architectures and Applications*, May 20-24, 2013, Boston, MA.

[13] K. Skadron and D. W. Clark "Design Issues and Tradeoffs for Write Buffers", *In the Proceedings of the 3rd International Symposium on High-Performance Computer Architecture*, pp. 144-155, February 1997.

[14] S. Kim and J. Lee"Write Buffer-Oriented Energy Reduction in the L1 Data Cache of Two-level Caches for the Embedded System", *In the Proceedings of the 20th symposium on Great lakes symposium on VLSI*, pp. 257-262, May 2010.

[15] "3rd Generation Intel XScale Microarchitecture–Developer's Manual", *http://www.intel.com*.

[16] J. Sharkey, "M-Sim: A Flexible, Multi-threaded Simulation Environment", *Tech. Report CS-TR-05-DP1*, Department of Computer Science, SUNY Binghamton, 2005.

[17] Standard Performance Evaluation Corporation (SPEC) website, http://www.spec.org/.

A Flexible and Adaptable Distributed File System

S. E. N. Fernandes[1], R. S. Lobato[1], A. Manacero[1], R. Spolon[2], and M. A. Cavenaghi[2]
[1]Dept. Computer Science and Statistics, Univ. Estadual Paulista UNESP, São José do Rio Preto, São Paulo, Brazil
[2]Dept. Computing, Univ. Estadual Paulista UNESP, Bauru, São Paulo, Brazil

Abstract— *This work describes the development of a flexible and adaptable distributed file system model where the main concepts of distributed computing are intrinsically incorporated. The file system incorporates characteristics such as transparency, scalability, fault-tolerance, cryptography, support for low-cost hardware, easy configuration and file manipulation.*

Keywords: Distributed file systems, fault-tolerance, data storage.

1. Introduction

The amount of stored data increases at an impressive rate, demanding more storage space and compatible processing speeds. Aiming to avoid complete data loss from failures or system overloads, it became usual to adopt the distributed files model [1] [2].

Therefore, a distributed file system (DFS) is a system where files are stored along distinct computers, linked through a communication network. Even though several DFS are capable of attending several characteristics, such as access/location transparency, performance, scalability, concurrency control, fault-tolerance and security, to attend them simultaneously is complex and difficult to manage. Another important aspect to consider is that when one characteristic has its complexity increased, the remaining ones may be negatively affected. This explains why most of the DFS are developed aiming at fulfilling specific scenarios [2] [3] [4].

This paper proposes a novel model for a flexible DFS, named FlexA (**Flex**ible and **A**daptable Distributed File System), that can be adapted to the environment where it is being used. This flexibility allows for DFS features to be adapted or even replaced by other including but not limited to the cryptography algorithm, level of replication, application programming interfaces, move some tasks from servers to clients and several configurations of software and hardware.

In the following sections we start with a brief description of other DFS in use, focusing on ones that are the basis for the model presented here. Then we focus in the description of the proposed model, including its main characteristics and architecture. Results from the model evaluation are presented next, finishing with conclusions drawn from this evaluation and directions for future work.

2. Related work

Among the several existing DFSs, this work focused on exploring the key features of some models of DFSs based on traditional designs and some newer systems, allowing to extract features for the development of a DFSs that has characteristics such as high performance, fault-tolerance and easiness of use.

2.1 Network File System

Network File System (NFS) [2] [3] is a DFS based on remote procedure calls (RPC) providing a convenient medium to applications through a virtual layer (Virtual File System - VFS) that enables a transparent access to NFS components [5] [6] [7].

2.2 Andrew File System

Andrew File System (AFS) was designed aiming scalability to several users. In order to achieve this, aggressive cache policies are implemented on the client side, as well as efficient techniques for consistency [2] [3].

2.3 Google File System

Google File System (GFS) operates on an architecture composed by parallel server clusters. GFS is distinguished by the serialization and file distribution directly to chunk servers that are the actual storage nodes, without the need for additional accesses to the main server, called "master" [1].

2.4 Tahoe - The Least-Authority Filesystem

Tahoe-LAFS is a DFS in the user space, where file sharing occurs through a sequence of characters manipulated by the Uniform Resource Locator (URL). This form of sharing allied to a decentralized security model, based on individual access control, allowed Tahoe-LAFS to manage directories and files as independent objects, which can be referenced by several processes using different names [8].

2.5 Another systems

Besides the systems just presented, other works seek to establish different priorities for their DFS models, such as SPRITE [9], CODA [10], IBM General Parallel File System [11], Ceph [12], XtreemFS [13], HDFS [14], Red Hat Global File System [15] and GlusterFS [16]. Among these DFSs, the choice of NFS, AFS and GFS is justified by extensive documentation available, allowing to explore problems commonly encountered in the development of DFSs. As regards the Tahoe-LAFS, its importance for this project was motivated by his development in an open-source project, providing a model for access to files by *upload/download* and the use of *the Principle of Least Authority* [17] to distribute files.

3. A model for DFS

This work describes a DFS model that incorporates the important characteristics of NFS, AFS, GFS and Tahoe-LAFS. It is expected to work in a controlled environment, offering support to heterogeneity, flexibility, easier file management, fast and secure cryptographic mechanisms, and fault-tolerance tools.

The main characteristics of this model are listed in this section.

3.1 Adaptability and Flexibility

Adaptability allows clients to become part of the server group for helping in the provision of distributed files. Through this feature, resources of the client station such as disk space can be shared. Also, the client can become a host server completely. The concept of flexibility comes from the possibility of making changes in FlexA to adjust the scenario utilized, in other words, providing a means to modify their functionality by replacement or adjustment of the model components. The components that can be modified are designed to be independent of the set, among them can be emphasized the modification or replacement of the cryptographic algorithm, the changing levels of replication and the adaptation interface for other applications such as, for example, using the file system through a web browser.

3.2 Access Control

Our model uses a set of hash sequences to generate the encryption key file and its variations, providing two levels of access: read-write and read-only. The methodology used for this process is adapted from the cryptographic security model of the Tahoe-LAFS, which follows the Principle of Least Authority. With this model, the files and directories are managed directly by the user through independents handlers, which are responsible for identifying and providing the permissions for that type of file/directory, replacing the traditional fields of "login" and "password". As a result, our model enables users to interact with DFS without the need of system administrator privileges [8].

3.3 Low Cost Hardware

The specification of this our model was based on an open language, widely used in operating system implementations. It also expected that the client stations are in charge of most of the process involved on serving files to the distributed system. This inversion of which side does the processing, allows for several gains in the server side, making it more reliable (less failures due to overloads) and less expensive. Moreover, the rapid advances in of-the-shelf hardware for the client has brought better conditions for the user to effectively use these resources.

File storage is managed by the local file systems, making it easier to adapt to individual operating systems. This also makes model implementation, management and manipulation easier [1] [8].

3.4 Fault-Tolerance

Fault-tolerance is achieved through the division of a file into smaller blocks (chunks), which are transferred to a set of servers. This process allows the client to work with distributed chunks, thus avoiding compromising data integrity due to isolated problems in specific servers.

File chunks are stored in two groups of servers: write and replica. The former is composed of a fixed set of three servers in charge of receiving or providing file chunks, and is capable of reading and writing operations. The latter is composed of replicas of the first group and allows only reading operations of file chunks. Consistency is achieved by modifications initiated by servers from the first group [1] [3] [8].

The use of replicas is optional, enabling the control of chunks availability according to the demand for such chunks.

For agreement and consistency purposes, it is necessary for the write group to have two of the three servers active. All transfer operations only occur under this condition.

3.5 Performance

FlexA tries to minimize the number of interactions with the servers, bringing most of the operations to the client side. Accessing a local file improves the overall performance. To achieve this, the DFS uses a load/update model where the client transfers the file chunks to the local file system before executing operations on the file.

The use of a cache in the client prevents future interactions on files already transferred. In the situation where the file's version becomes outdated, the client will be warned about the availability of a newer version in the servers group.

Chunks are transferred in parallel from different servers, using variable sized blocks. The smallest size of a block is 4096 bytes.

4. Project overview

4.1 Architecture

Differently from the conventional client-server model, FlexA, as shown in Figure 1, eliminates the concept of a main server that would be in charge of manage all requests to the files.

This architecture resembles a peer-to-peer architecture, enabling clients to interact with storage groups without the

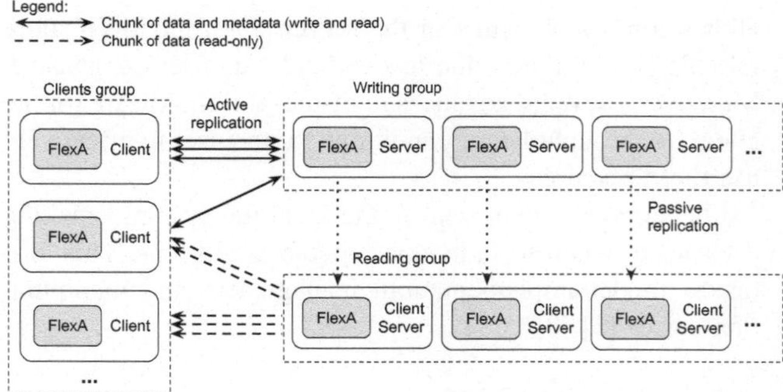

Fig. 1: FlexA architecture

presence of a central manager. Another point is that, due to the access control model, a certification centre is not necessary, since each client is responsible for controlling the access permissions to its own files, without the intervenience of managers or super-users.

In this model, computers belonging to the DFS are administered in specific groups, which can be of three types: reading, writing and clients. The first, called writing group or primary servers, comprises computers with active server process, and it is responsible to manage and store files with their metadata. The second group, called replicas or secondary servers, consists of computers that can be clients and servers at the same time, creating a backup set of primary servers for assistance in case of overload or failures. The third group is formed by the client workstations, which are responsible for encryption and distribution chunks of the file to the primary servers.

Files can be read in parallel from several storage computers, either from the write or the replica group. The transfer of new or update files can only be performed by computers in the write group.

Network latency is minimized by the elimination of intermediary servers and the addition of concurrent access to different sets of servers. These characteristics also allow the prevention of possible bottlenecks in the transfer process.

As stated before, the migration of most of the operations to the client side, including cryptography and file partitioning, also provides gains in the model's performance. Indeed, this also reduces the usage of hardware resources in the storage nodes.

4.2 Security

The access to files is determined by the client's handler, which can be read-write or read-only. Each handler has two keys: one cryptographic and other for validation.

The "write" cryptographic key (WK) is given by *WK = SHA256Trunc(Key)*, where *Key* is a 16 bytes sequence randomly generated, and the function *SHA256Trunc* is the hash 256 bits (32 bytes) with output encoded in Base64 and truncated in 32 bytes. The "read" cryptographic key (RK) is given by *RK=sha256Trunc(WK)*. Each file is encrypted using its RK and the symmetric AES 256 bits algorithm in the CBC (*Cipher Block Chaining*) mode [18]. This allows modifying a *WK* to a *RK*, but not the other way round. These steps are illustrated in Figure 2.

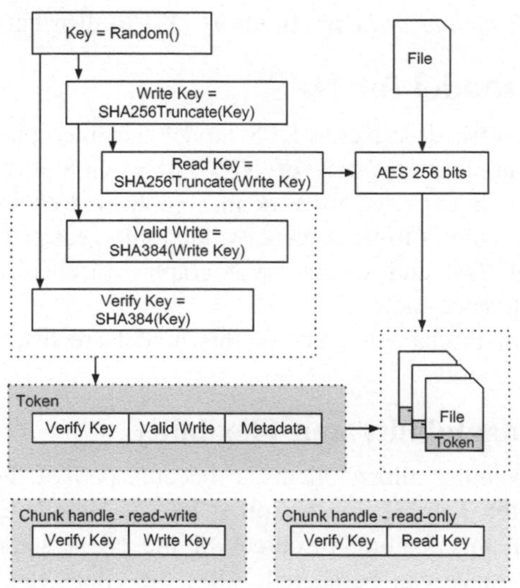

Fig. 2: FlexA security

Two other keys determine the validation process: *Verify Key* (*VK*) and *Valid Write* (*VW*), both in 48 bytes. The *VK* is present in the client handler and in the token sent to the servers. It is used to certify the communication between nodes and it is generated by *VK = SHA384(Key)*. The *VW* is also generated by the client, but only the servers have its copy. It is used to verify the validity of the client's *WK*. This key is given by *VW = SHA384(WK)*. If the result from the client's *VW* is equal to the stored chunk's *VW*, the file modification is executed in the write group.

File decryption can be performed only through the keys generated by the client. This is true independently of the communication channel in use or the server security level. This process produces three chunks, each one with one token containing file attributes, *VK* and *VW* and the handlers that allow the user to change the permissions.

4.3 Client

Three separated modules make up the client process, as shown in Figure 3: *Collector* manages the data input, *Synchronizer* manages outward data transmission, and *Communicator* identifies which hosts are active and which are in the replica group or are clients.

In each client there is a reduced part of the storage server database. This part contains some information about the availability and locality of file chunks. This local database helps for a fast search/recovery of data, without the need of performing these operations in the storage servers.

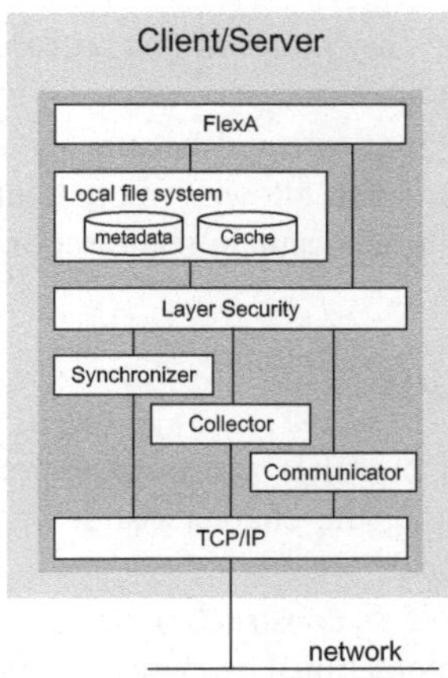

Fig. 3: FlexA structure

4.4 Storage

The servers, in the DFS model proposed here, have the function of store file chunks, validate client requests and execute replication between the groups of servers. Since there is no specific server in charge of the communication management or acting as a central unit, all servers follow architecture close to the client's model.

The chunk organization is performed through the local database, which provides the file properties with its routing table and keys for verification and validation.

4.5 Communication

Communication between the components of FlexA occurs with TCP/IP protocol and persistent connections. Each file chunk is transferred this way.

The *Communicator* module scans the network searching for active hosts and looking at what functions they execute. This operation enables the interaction between clients and storage groups. Periodically, the identified hosts exchange messages in order to keep their status updated.

The user performs the choice between a client or storage station, whilst the definition of the write servers group is made independently. The independent definition of write servers guarantees that the needed number of storage servers is satisfied.

In case of a failure in the servers of the write group, it is possible to relocate stations from the replica group through an election process. Specifically, a Bully algorithm is used to determine a new candidate to the write group through the priority of each member of the replica group. Once the new station is defined, all active process in FlexA are informed of the new member [19].

4.6 Synchronization

Chunk synchronization occurs automatically through client interactions with the write group. These interactions are propagated to the replica group and the active clients are informed about new updates.

Indexers present in each local database are used to identify if the copies in cache are obsolete in relation to the write group. The update of these copies, however, is only performed when a user tries to use them.

Since each station keeps a record of the status of every other station, services can be re-established quickly in case of failures or a host crash.

The consistency of the chunks is determined by its version in the database on each station, which is controlled by write group. All clients and the read group are notified about every operation that modifies a file in a server. Periodically, stations communicate with the write group to update its data base.

The entry of a new station needs a token from the write group, that token contains information about the actual state of all stations.

5. Performance evaluation

5.1 Micro-benchmarks

Performance evaluation used a set of computers with Intel Pentium Dual E2160 - 1,8 GHz processor, 2GB of RAM memory, hard disk of 40GB at 7200RPM, Ubuntu Linux operating system with 64-bit and interconnected by Ethernet 100 Mbps full-duplex using a 3Com switch. To do the performance tests, we used operations of reading and writing (upload/download) of files of 1MB, 5MB, 10MB, 25MB and 50MB. These files seeking include the variation of data found in the academic environment, which can be text files, music, photos, videos and applications.

5.2 Evaluation

The evaluation process considered five cases of access to the servers. Each one contains sequential access of writing and reading for each one the clients simultaneously.

For each test scenario, levels of interactions were used 12 times for each size in each read and write operation, totalising 120 interactions for each client. In tests with more than 1 client, simultaneous interactions followed the same read/write sequences with same sized files.

For evaluation and comparison of performance we used Tahoe-LAFS, because it is precursor of FlexA, and NFS because it is a client-server DFS without additional layers.

For the comparison between DFSs, the tests were considered with 5 concurrent clients using 5 types of files to read and write operation.

For the write operation, as shown in Figure 4, it is possible to verify that the NFS in environment with multiple requests becomes slower, affecting the overall system performance. Even in an environment small-scale, centralized architectures may represent a factor of performance degradation and risks of failure.

The write operation using FlexA and Tahoe-LAFS has similarity, because the logic of this operation (encryption,

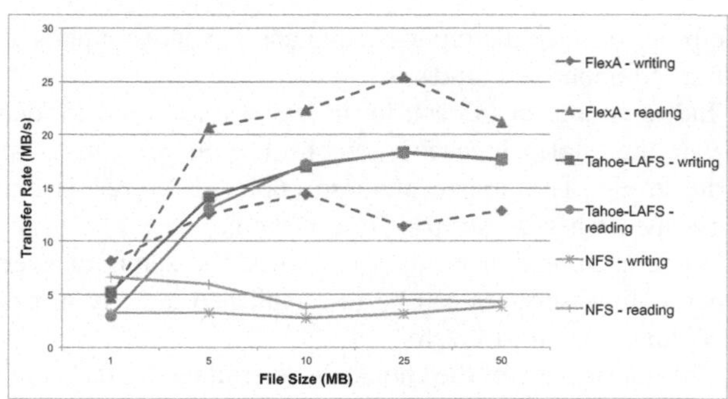

Fig. 4: Rate of reading and writing files

split and distribution) is similar, differing in some aspects such as the encryption without using RSA asymmetric keys in FlexA, in the splitting the file in 66% compared with 50% for Tahoe-LAFS and distribution using TCP/IP compared to the HTTP in Tahoe-LAFS. However, the write operation using Tahoe-LAFS is faster than FlexA during the evolution of files, being less optimized for files smaller than 4MB, to which FlexA is slightly faster than Tahoe-LAFS (8MB/s in FlexA and 5MB/s in Tahoe-LAFS). The reason for FlexA be significantly slower than Tahoe-LAFS for writing files over 5MB is justified by the large number of divisions and distributions of chunks of files that FlexA does for set of three servers, totaling 66% of the file for each computer against 50% of a file in Tahoe-LAFS.

Considering the read operation, showed in Figure 4, FlexA has the highest rate of evolution for the transfer. Because of its number of divisions of the file and the process of choice for distributed chunks, the read operation in FlexA can uses all the available servers of the writing group. This situation does not happen with the Tahoe-LAFS which is limited to a few servers to restore the file again.

The fact that the client station is responsible for data processing (division and cryptography) causes a small part of the consumption of the hardware resources compared with NFS, but much smaller compared to Tahoe-LAFS, as is shown in Figure 5.

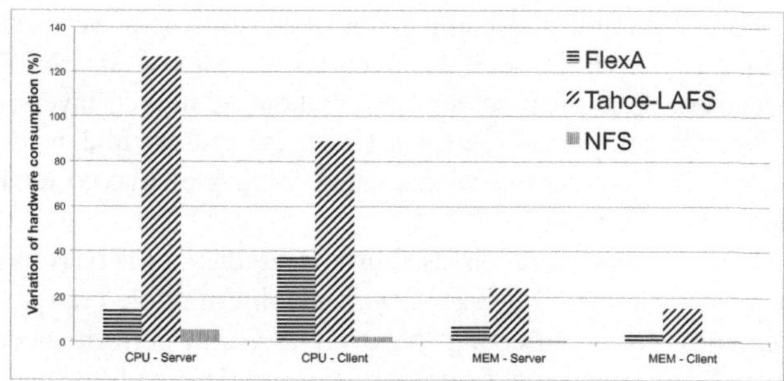

Fig. 5: Variation of hardware consumption

The advantage of our DFS model is to permit a larger quantity of simultaneous operations to big client files, while the storage server only concentrates on receiving and organizing the chunks.

Another point implemented in our model is the direct replication by the client, allowing more control and security for the user if failures occur in some servers.

6. Conclusion

The developed model is a way of expressing the possibility of aggregating the characteristics of others DFS and making it functional.

The simplicity of its construction brought flexibility to the utilization of computational resources, a more efficient use of the client's processing power and less conditions for an overload in the servers.

The adaptation of the model of decentralized permissions allowed more independence for system administrators and a quicker cryptography process. This is due to the smaller number of steps that are used to achieve an acceptable security level.

It brought more data reliability with the use of cryptography directly on the files, avoiding cases where security failure or fault of the storage set compromises data integrity.

The use of storage groups guarantees availability of the files and presents conditions for fault tolerance by distributing data among several nodes.

FlexA model was constructed to create an environment favouring the client, to provide a DFS that is easier to implant and use in normal conditions, and offer some of characteristics that are found in most file systems.

In this evaluation, focusing only on the technical upload/download the files, there is a similarity between FlexA and Tahoe-LAFS. FlexA has better read rate than Tahoel-LAFS, but Tahoe-LAFS has the best writing performance.

The best performance in FlexA in read operation is explained by the division factor of the files in order to simultaneously use 3 servers, which therefore creates greater consumption in the writing process than Tahoe-LAFS.

At this stage, this research work presents the components that are needed for an operational use in a controlled environment. Among the next steps of the research are the enlargement of the model's functionality, aiming at providing a more convenient way of interacting with the operating system, support for efficient chunk compression, optimize cryptography, support mobile devices, and other characteristics.

Acknowledgment

The authors would like to thank Brazilians foundations FAPESP 2012/02926-5, Fundunesp and CAPES for their financial support.

References

[1] S. Ghemawat, H. Gobioff, and S.-T. Leung, "The google file system," in *Proceedings of the nineteenth ACM symposium on Operating systems principles*. ACM, 2003, pp. 29–43.

[2] G. Coulouris, J. Dollimore, and T. Kindberg, *Distributed systems: concepts and design*. Addison-Wesley, 2005.

[3] S. D. Pate, *Unix Filesystems: Evolution, Design, and Implementation*. Wiley Publishing, 2003.

[4] H. H. Huang and A. S. Grimshaw, "Design, implementation and evaluation of a virtual storage system," *Concurr. Comput. : Pract. Exper.*, vol. 23, pp. 311–331, March 2011.

[5] A. Batsakis and R. Burns, "Cluster delegation: high-performance, fault-tolerant data sharing in nfs," in *Proceedings of the High Performance Distributed Computing, HPDC-14*. 14th IEEE International Symposium, 2005, pp. 100–109.

[6] S. Shepler, "Nfs version 4 design considerations, rfc 2624," Tech. Rep., 1999.

[7] S. Shepler, B. Callaghan, D. Robinson, R. Thurlow, C. Beame, M. Eisler, and D. Noveck, "Network file system (nfs) version 4 protocol, rfc 3530," Tech. Rep., 2003.

[8] Z. Wilcox-O'Hearn and B. Warner, "Tahoe: the least-authority filesystem," in *Proceedings of the 4th ACM international workshop on Storage security and survivability*, ser. StorageSS '08.ACM, 2008, pp. 21–26.

[9] M. Nelson, B. Welch, and J. Ousterhout, "Caching in the sprite network file system," *SIGOPS Oper. Syst. Rev.*, vol. 21, pp. 3–4, 1987.

[10] J. J. Kistler and M. Satyanarayanan, "Disconnected operation in the coda file system," *ACM Trans. Comput. Syst.*, vol. 10, pp. 3–25, 1992.

[11] M. R. Barrios, J. Barkes, F. Cougard, P. G. Crumley, D. Marin, H. Reddy, and T. Thitayanun, "Gpfs: A parallel file system." IBM Cor., Tech. Rep., 1998. [Online]. Available: http://www.redbooks.ibm.com/

[12] S. A. Weil, S. A. Brandt, E. L. Miller, D. D. E. Long, and C. Maltzahn, "Ceph: a scalable, high-performance distributed file system," in *Proceedings of the 7th symposium on Operating systems design and implementation*, ser. OSDI '06, 2006, pp. 307–320.

[13] F. Hupfeld, T. Cortes, B. Kolbeck, E. Focht, M. Hess, J. Malo, J. Marti, J. Stender, and E. Cesario, "Xtreemfs - a case for object-based file systems in grids," *Concurrency and Computation: Practice and Experience*, vol. 20, 2008.

[14] K. Shvachko, H. Kuang, S. Radia, and R. Chansler, "The hadoop distributed file system," in *Mass Storage Systems and Technologies (MSST), 2010 IEEE 26th Symposium on*, 2010.

[15] RedHat, "Red hat global file system," 2011. [Online]. Available: http://www.redhat.com/software/rha/gfs/

[16] Gluster, "Glusterfs," 2011. [Online]. Available: http://www.gluster.org

[17] A. H. Karp, "Enforce pola on processes to control viruses," *Commun. ACM*, vol. 46, no. 12, pp. 27–29, 2003.

[18] M. Dworkin, "Special publication 800-38a: Recommendation for block cipher modes of operation: Methods and techniques," NIST - National Institute of Standards and Technology, Tech. Rep., 2001.

[19] A. S. Tanenbaum and M. V. Steen, *Distributed systems: principles and paradigms*. Pearson Prentice Hall, 2007.

Optimizing the use of the Hard Disk in MapReduce Frameworks for Multi-core Architectures*

Tharso Ferreira[1], **Antonio Espinosa**[1], **Juan Carlos Moure**[2] **and Porfidio Hernández**[2]
Computer Architecture and Operating Systems Department, University Autonoma of Barcelona, Bellaterra, Barcelona, Spain
[1]{tsouza, antonio.espinosa}@caos.uab.es [2]{juancarlos.moure, porfidio.hernandez}@uab.es

Abstract—*MapReduce simplifies parallel programming, abstracting the responsibility of the programmer, such as synchronization and task management. The paradigm allows the programmer to write sequential code that is automatically parallelized. The MapReduce Frameworks developed for multi-core architectures provide large processing keys which consequently growth intermediate data structure, which in some environments causes the use of all the available main memory. Recently, with the development of MapReduce frameworks for multi-core architectures that distribute keys through the memory hierarchy, the problem of using the entire main memory, by the data generated was minimized. But in an environment where all threads access the same hard disk, certain situations may lead a competition between the threads, to take keys generated from main memory to the hard disk, thus creating a bottleneck.*

Based on the behavior of threads and the growth of intermediate data structure in multi-core environments, we present an improvement of access to the hard disk in MapReduce frameworks for multi-core architectures. The main objective is to ensure that distinct threads do not compete to take the keys processed, from the memory until the hard disk.

Keywords: MapReduce, Multi-Core, Main Memory, Thread, Virtual memory.

1. Introduction

The massive use of multi-core processors in recent years has opened the possibility of creating new parallel applications. The idea of these new applications is to take advantage of the use of parallel processing offered by the existence of more than one processor or core on the same architecture. These applications force developers to manage a series of low-level details, such as thread creation, synchronization, concurrency, resource management and fault tolerance [1]. Within this context, creating a scalable, and correct parallel application has become a complex task.

MapReduce assumes that the programmer needs to express two functions to develop the application, Map and Reduce [2]. The Map function processes the input file and generates a set of intermediate pairs of key/values. The Reduce function joins these pairs through an intermediate sum or some kind of aggregation, using each key as an index, and the framework takes care of the parallelization details.

The MapReduce frameworks for multi-core architectures have been designed to work on the main memory, avoiding the need to use any type of secondary memory [3]. However, the increase in the number of keys processed, may consume the entire main memory, because of the growth of intermediate data structure. Previous studies [4] have shown the dependence that exists between the execution time and the distribution of keys in the input file. The same dependence is seen in the growth of intermediate data structures in the MapReduce framework, and therefore the use of main memory.

This situation has resulted in implementation of a MapReduce framework that distributes keys through the memory hierarchy, main memory and hard disk, preventing the entire main memory to be consumed [5]. However, we identified that in environments with an increasing number of threads, with a single hard disk, there may be competition between the threads to take the keys generated from main memory to the hard disk.

Our goal is through the administration of limits and priorities among different threads, avoid a situation where multiple threads need to take large amount of keys to the hard disk at the same time.

The objective is to evaluate the system dynamically, define a set of execution parameters, and manage intermediate data structures and access of the framework to hard disk by distinct threads. The focus in this paper is the use of applications involving a relatively large number of unique keys. A word count application represents this scenario, where there may be a large amount of unique keys.

To reach our goal, we developed and implemented an model, which evaluates the use of main memory dynamically. Based on the usage of main memory, determines the moment that a certain amount keys should be moved from main memory to the hard disk at different times by distinct threads.

The rest of this paper is organized as follows. In Section 2 we introduce the MapReduce paradigm, and present an ex-

*This paper is addressed to the PDPTA'13 Conference

tension to Metis that distributes keys between main memory and hard disk, the basis for this work. In Section 3 we present the main issue on which we dedicate ourselves to this work. In the section 4 we show our proposed model. In section 5 we present a summary of the environment, the benchmark application and the evaluation method implemented in this work. Finally in section 6 we present a brief conclusion of this work.

2. Related Work

There are different studies and implementations of the MapReduce model in different types of architectures. Of the model introduced by Google [2], there are implementations for clusters, such as Hadoop [6], or multi-core architectures as Phoenix [1] [3], Metis [7] and Phoenix++ [8], as well as the extension of Metis that distributes keys through the memory hierarchy [5]. This section summarizes the basic principles of the MapReduce model, and the basis for this work.

2.1 MapReduce Programming Model

MapReduce [2] is a paradigm created by Google, to support parallel processing of large data sets. The goal of this paradigm is to make easy the programmer creating parallel applications, where it is only necessary to provide a sequential implementation, expressed by two main functions, Map and Reduce.

MapReduce is able to achieve a high degree of data parallelism because it breaks workloads down into tasks that can be processed independently of each other [9]. In theory MapReduce splits the input file into M parts and sends each Map worker. Each Map worker using the functions provided by the programmer, processes their own part of the input file, generating a list of key/values pairs. When all parts end up to be processed by the Map tasks, the MapReduce framework invokes the function Reduce, which performs data reduction through a sequential implementation provided by the programmer, one task for each distinct key produced by the Map tasks. Each Reduce worker generates an output of key/value, which are usually aggregates to generate a final output.

One problem that MapReduce solves, is to take the output of the Map phase to Reduce phase through an intermediate structure, which receives the keys of Maps tasks [7].

In the multi-core architectures, the structures used are placed in main memory.The entire organization of Map output is critical to the performance of MapReduce applications, since the entire set of intermediate data need to be rearranged between the Map and Reduce phases. In short, the data produced by the Map phase are dumped in the same order they are read from the input file, while the Reduce phase the data are grouped by key. In multi-core architecture, the whole application performance is dominated by the operations performed on the intermediate structure, which is in main memory. To guarantee the performance of MapReduce applications on multi-core architectures, the system should provide enough main memory to run of the application.

2.2 Metis

Using Phoenix [3] as a base, Metis [7] has been developed as a library of MapReduce, an improvement to store intermediate data in a new data structure, to improve the performance with most types of workloads.

To reduce the amount of data stored in intermediate structure, Metis uses a combiner function, as proposed by Google the original idea of MapReduce paradigm. The combiner performs data reduction per Map thread before the Reduce phase starts, in a way to avoid all the main memory be consumed.

Metis uses as an intermediate data structure, a hash table, where each entry contains a B+tree, as shown in figure 1. The idea is to take advantage of the complexity O(1) in search of the hash table, to find the entrance of certain key, and then down in the tree using O(logN) complexity of the B+tree to find the key position. If the key already exists, the framework adds a new value to list of this key. Using the combiner function that list of occurrences is reduced to only one item, which represents the number of occurrences of a given key. If the key does not exist, then the new key is inserted into the tree. To avoid competition between different threads on the same memory region, each thread has its own Hash+tree, which is represented by each row of the matrix shown in figure 1.

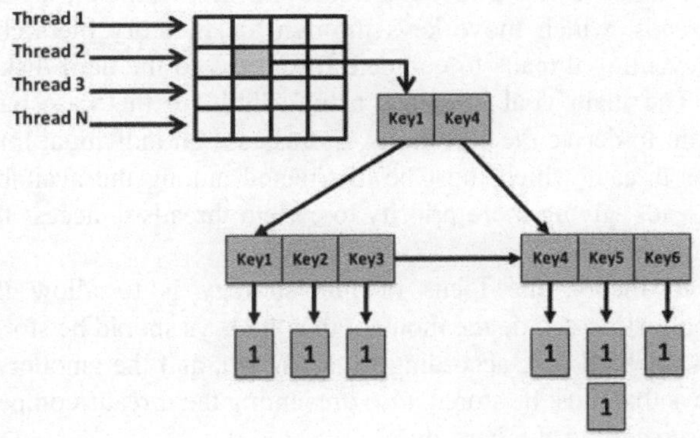

Fig. 1: Metis Data Structure.

All the Map workers share the same hash table size, and the same hash function, which attempts to ensure a good distribution of keys throughout the hash table.

3. The Problem

In Metis, there are two types of memory allocation. The first of these occurs in the prediction phase, when the size of the hash table is set, depending on the number of distinct keys. This size is fixed and is not changed during use of the intermediate structure. The second memory allocation is observed in the creation of trees, which occur dynamically, depending on the number of levels and nodes.

Metis tries to keep an average of 10 distinct keys for each hash entry, however for environments that provide an execution of many threads in parallel, this number is usually lower. For example, for an input of 100 million distinct keys using the standard 10 distinct keys for hash entry, are necessary 10 million of hash entries. In an environment where there are 24 threads for example, this would create a hash table of 24 rows by 10 million of columns, or 240 million hash entries.

Assuming that the framework takes to hard disk only the key and value, where each key is a word of 20 characters and the value is an integer, each line would have a cost around 228 megabytes of data. In the worst case, depending on the memory usage, move all keys from the intermediate data structure to the hard disk in an environment of 24 threads, would cost about 5472 megabytes. Move large set of keys in an environment where all the threads can not access the hard disk at the same time, requires that the operating system serialize the access.

In short, while a thread takes their own keys to the hard disk, all other threads are waiting. With the waiting threads, no more key are processed, resulting in a cost-time.

4. Implementation

Using the extension of Metis that distributes the keys through the memory hierarchy as a base [5], we propose a solution using a model of soft and hard limit on all the threads, which move keys through the memory hierarchy, preventing threads to compete for access to the hard disk.

The main goal is to use a high limit, in this case hard limit to derive the soft limits, in this case an individual limit per thread, which must be distributed among the available threads, giving more priority to certain threads to access the hard disk.

In theory, the focus of this strategy is to allow the application decide the moment that the keys should be stored on the hard disk according to the thread, and the amount of keys that must be stored, also preventing the threads compete for access to the hard disk.

4.1 Map phase

Map phase is where the keys are are inserted in the intermediate data structure, it is essential to manage the growth of this structure, and the consumption of main memory.

As may be seen in figure 2 item 2, when a key is emitted by the Map task in the function `emit_intermediate`, the thread searches the entry in the hash table in which this key corresponds. When the hash entry is found the thread traverses down on the tree contained in the entry, until it finds the key position. Each new key, inserted into the hash entries, has a cost in memory usage. At the end of the Map task, an amount of keys have been generated and stored in main memory, generating main memory consumption. The memory consumed by Map Task is variable, depending on the amount and distribution of unique keys in the hash table. Knowing that the B+tree is a order 3 tree, and may be up to 7 keys per node, each time that a new key is inserted into a new node, is allocated space for seven keys. In short, if the key distribution occurs in different hash entries, the consumption of main memory will occur more rapidly, dominant situation when there is an large amount of different keys.

At the end of the Map task, the same thread executes the function `verify_hard_limit` and `verify_soft_limit`, as may be seen in figure 2 items 3 and 4. The `verify_hard_limit` function returns the maximum memory that can be used in the environment, i.e. the most critical memory usage. This value is the same for all threads, which serves as the basis for determination the soft limit, returned by the function `verify_soft_limit`. The soft limit is unique to each thread, and determines the time that each thread can start to take the keys to the hard disk, i.e., while a thread move keys between main memory and hard disk, another thread can continue processing new keys and inserting on the intermediate data structure.

If the soft limit of the running thread has been reached or exceeded, the same thread copies the keys stored in the last column of its own line of the hash table using `copy_keys`, as is shown in figure 2 item 5, to the buffer through `buffer_keys` on item 6. When the copying of keys is completed, the same thread back to check if the main memory was reduced to below the limit. If memory usage is not reduced sufficiently, the same thread performs the same operation by copying the keys from the last column, in direction to first column. The thread moves to the next task only if the memory is reduced enough or column zero is reached.

The buffer where the keys are copied has a fixed size, and just spills the keys on the hard disk through `spill_keys`, as is shown in figure 2 item 7, when the task is completed or the buffer is full. Each thread running generates a file on the hard disk, where it stores its keys. The goal is that at the end of Phase Map, if the memory is not enough, some of the keys are stored in the main memory through the intermediate data structure, while the other part of the key are stored on the hard disk. The idea is to take the keys that exceed the limit of main memory to the hard disk, providing space in main memory, so that the Map tasks can continue processing keys without the use of swap.

The use of a device such as the hard disk, means inserting overhead in the framework. The objective is hiding the latency of hard disk and minimize the overhead generated, through a set of proposed strategies to prevent the movement of keys be made between main memory and swap.

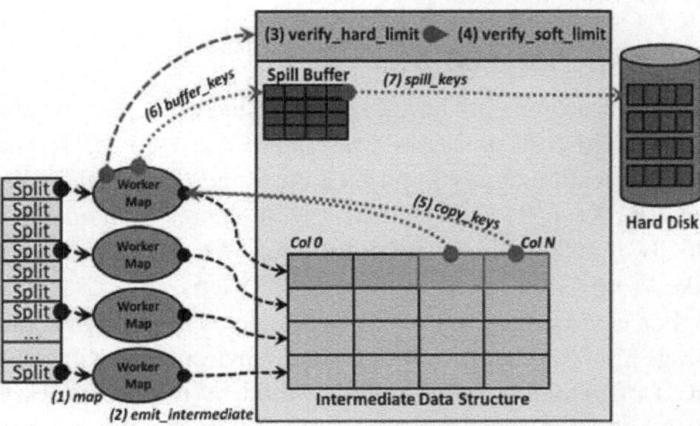

Fig. 2: Map Phase.

4.2 Evaluation of main memory available

To avoid that the amount of keys generated by the Map tasks use the entire main memory, monitor the environment and the amount of available main memory becomes essential. We created a set of functions that aims to evaluate the amount of memory available at the end of each Map task. Each thread at the end of its execution verifies that the limit set has been reached.

4.3 Hard Limit and Soft Limit

To avoid competition between different threads to take the keys to hard disk, we set two parameters to the limits, soft limits and hard limits. The goal is to treat each thread differently, so that disk access is done at different times.

The value of the hard limit, is calculated in percent on the total amount of main memory. To calculate the base of the soft limit, the running thread divides the hard limit by total number of threads. To find the corresponding soft limit, the running thread calculates $(Nt * SoftLimit + SoftLimit)$, where Nt corresponds to the number of the running thread, and $SoftLimit$ corresponds to the base of the soft limit previously calculated. Using as an example an environment with 6 threads, where the total amount of available main memory is 24 gigabytes, and using a hard limit of 50% would result in the following limits soft shown in table 1.

Table 1: Memory Limit.

Thread	Soft Limit(MB)	Hard Limit(MB)
0	2.000	12.000
1	4.000	12.000
2	6.000	12.000
3	8.000	12.000
4	10.000	12.000
5	12.000	12.000

In small environments with few threads, the competence for access to the hard disk becomes small. In this situation the use of soft limit creates a situation of overhead. To avoid adding overhead when the number of threads is less than 4, in this case only the hard limit is checked.

4.4 Spill Buffer

Before spilling the keys on the hard disk, the thread responsible should copy the keys to a buffer. To manage these keys, we create a spill buffer, which has the same number of rows as the original hash table, i.e., the amount of threads that are running, but that does not have hash function, and simply performs sequential storage. Although the keys were removed from the intermediate data structure and taken to spill buffer are in memory, until the spill buffer is full or the task ends. Each key stored in spill buffer occupies less space as opposed to the tree. Since this is only an intermediate buffer, without search purpose, only sequential insertion, each line consists of an array that stores only keys and value. Each B+tree which contains 10 different keys, occupies about 726 bytes in the intermediate structure of Metis, while in our array the same 10 keys occupy 540 bytes. Thus freeing memory until the keys of the Spill buffer has been spilled on the hard disk.

4.5 Reduce phase

Knowing that part of keys that exceed the memory is on the hard disk, and should be brought back to the main memory to be processed by the Reduce workers, we turn to the problem of how to keep all keys in main memory. To avoid the risk of running out of main memory, the keys must be brought from the disk on demand. In this case we took advantage Reduce tasks are performed in sequence, i.e., column 0 to the N column or last column. Before the Reduce phase starts, a certain amount of keys is moved from the hard disk to fill the first group of columns which will be reduced. Until the `read_data_disk` finishes copying the keys to the first group of columns, all the threads stay blocked.

When the copy is complete, the threads are liberated to effect the reduction of keys and store them in the final buffer. To know what the limit is of columns to be reduced before brings the next sets of keys from the hard disk, we maintain a column counter. When the counter reaches the value of the next group, again all threads are blocked waiting for a copy of a new set of keys that are on the hard disk. Before starting to copy the keys from the hard disk into main memory, the thread that is running to make the copy, checks the memory usage using `verify_hard_limit`. If the amount of main memory used reached or exceeded the limit, the running thread makes a copy of the keys stored in the final buffer through the `copy_keys`, and stores it in the spill buffer with `buffer_keys` to be spilled back into the hard disk using `spill_keys`, freeing up space in the main memory.

When all columns of intermediate data structure are reduced by Reduce workers, if there are keys on the hard disk, they are all copied to the buffer for the merge phase through the `read_data_disk_merge`.To start the Merge phase, all the keys that were on the hard disk needs to be brought back to memory. The entire scheme of phase Reduce can be seen from figure 3.

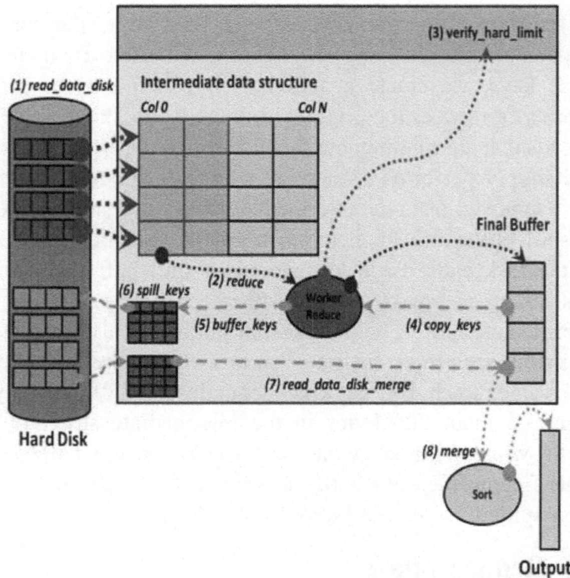

Fig. 3: Reduce Phase.

4.6 Influence of key distribution

Performance optimization is directly linked to key distribution in the hash table entries, i.e., the number of keys stored in each entry when the workers begin to copy them to the hard disk. If workers begin to copy keys to the hard disk too early, it may be that find a few keys stored in the hash entries, occupying the time of the workers, however making little reduction of main memory. The decision to start taking the keys to the hard disk, depends directly on the consumption of main memory, and the memory usage limit set.

If other applications are consuming the main memory, the framework will choose to start store the keys on the hard disk in the execution of the first Map tasks. This scenario is not favorable to our optimization, since many hash entries may still be empty. Each thread executes only one copy of keys from its own line, in short, if a Map task verifies that a given entry in the hash table has no keys stored, this task proceeds to the next hash entry. If the data structure exceeds the available memory, and the framework decides spill keys on the hard disk, just will be copied keys of hash entries that have not been verified by Map tasks. So if the copies of keys, is made by the last Map task, will be copied more keys than if the copy is made by first Map tasks. In the worst case, the Map tasks will take to hard disk few keys, for having started the spill too soon. The result of this is a little reduction in memory usage, consequently the increased use of swap and more page faults.

4.7 Experimental Method

The measurements have been taken in two environments: (1) a multi-core processor with Intel Core Duo 3GHz and 6GB of main memory in 64-bit Linux, and (2) a dual-socket Intel(R) Xeon(R) E5645 2.4GHz with 6 cores each one, and 96GB of main memory in 64-bit Linux. We use a benchmark like Word Count, used in the original Metis.

For environment with 2 cores, we set a limit of memory usage by 70%, because it is a small environment with only 6GB of memory, and this limit would be reached quickly, being possible check for page faults. While the environment of 12 cores, the limit was set at 30%, 12% and 10%, to be a relatively larger environment, with 96GB of main memory, and the inputs used are the same used in the environment of 2 cores. The idea of the experiments in the second environment, is see how much overhead is created by hard disk access, besides the advantage of using the strategy of soft limit and hard limit.

As dataset for this evaluation, we use a key distribution, where all the input files have different keys, which can be seen in Table 2.

Table 2: Workload.

Input Size	Keys	Words
228MB	10.000.000	10.000.000
457MB	20.000.000	20.000.000
686MB	30.000.000	30.000.000
915MB	40.000.000	40.000.000
1100MB	50.000.000	50.000.000
1373MB	60.000.000	60.000.000

Working on the problem described in section 3, we show in Figure 4 and 5, the reduction in the use of main memory, obtained in the Map and Reduce phases for the optimized version. To the input files of 10, 20 and 30 million keys, it can be seen that there is no change from the original, because for these types of workloads, the memory limit is not reached. As the memory consumption does not exceed the limit, there is no change on the way that the MapReduce framework works.

As seen in Figure 4 and 5, for input files of 40, 50 and 60 million of keys, memory usage is exceeded, the framework this way makes the decision to make use of our optimization.

As can be seen in figure 4, to the inputs of 40, 50 and 60 millions of keys, it is possible to note an increase at execution time Map phase observing the columns of optimized version against the main memory reduction observed by line corresponding. This increase in execution time is justified by the spill of keys on the hard disk, each Map task has responsibility to manage it own keys. While the keys do not end up to be taken to the hard disk, the Map task does not resume emitting new keys in main memory. Each keyset brought to hard disk allows the release of new memory space, preventing the main memory to be fully consumed, this would force the system to use the swap, increasing the number of page faults. Also in figure 5 we can observe the same behavior as figure 4, but with a smaller reduction in main memory. This situation is justified by the fact that the Reduce phase needs more data in memory to make the reduction. Unlike the Map phase where the main work consists of producing and storing keys in a intermediate data structure, Reduce phase the data must be read from an intermediate structure, processed and stored in a second structure, forcing the framework to hold more keys a time into memory.

Although the Reduce phase is normally faster than the Map phase, becomes difficult to avoid the increase in execution time, because of the constant interaction with the hard disk. First for keys that have been stored by the Map phase in the hard disk, and must be brought back to main memory for processing. And second, by taking the reduced keys back to the hard disk if the memory is close to the limit, i.e., double of interactions with the hard disk that Map phase

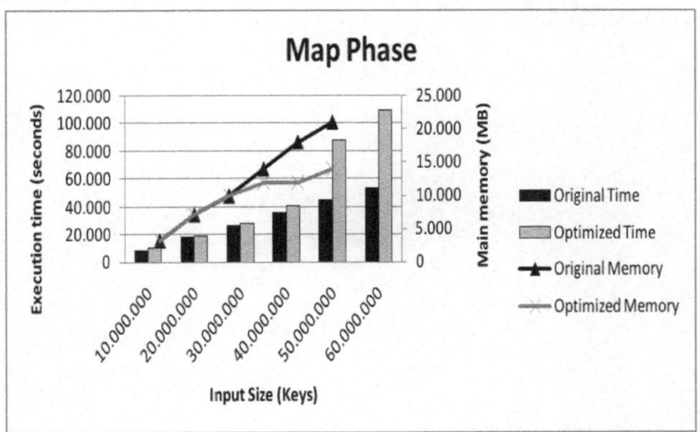

Fig. 4: Execution time and memory usage on Map phase.

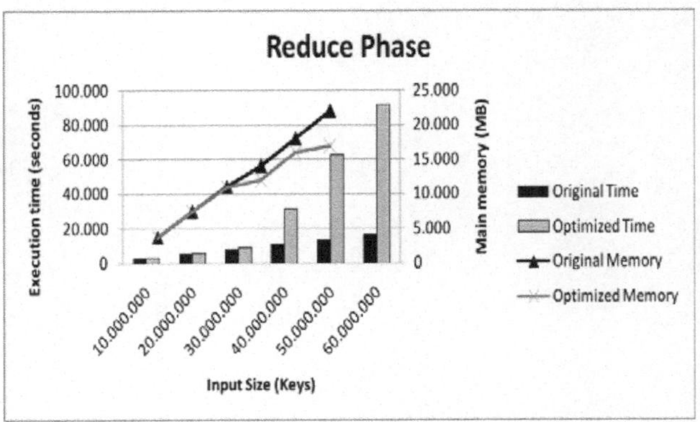

Fig. 5: Execution time and memory usage on Reduce phase.

The system uses the swap as an extension of memory, which normally causes the pages faults. In contrast, we define in this first model, the need to reduce these pages faults, since the constant interaction of the system with the hard disk becomes costly to the execution time. Sending a set of keys to the hard disk before the main memory to be consumed, prevents the system to need use the swap, this way it is possible to decrease the page faults, also reducing the constant and disordered hard disk access. In Figures 6 and 7 is possible to see the decrease of page faults, both in the Map and the Reduce phase. Take the keys to the hard disk in groups, before the memory is fully consumed, reduces the influence of latency of access to hard disk at execution time, effect that can be observed by the use of swap.

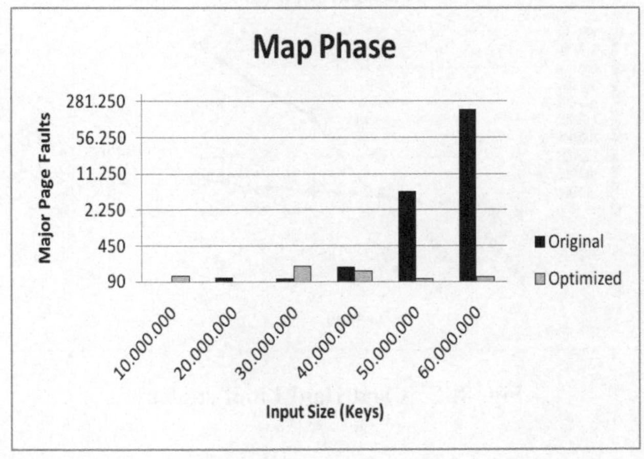

Fig. 6: Map phase major page faults.

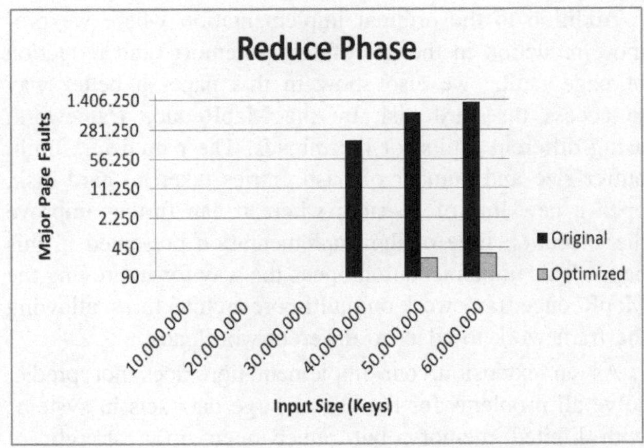

Fig. 7: Reduce phase major page faults.

In the figure 8 it is possible see that for execution with a limit of 10%, where only hard limit is used, there is a significant increase in runtime. This situation is result in the use of the 24 threads available to take large amounts of keys to the hard disk.

Increasing the hard limit, i.e., increasing the difference between the soft limits of threads, can be seen a greater reduction of execution time as is shown in the execution with hard limit of 30%, because fewer threads access the hard disk. The increase in the hard limit, and combining with the type of input and memory usage, reflects in more keys taken to hard disk and a greater reduction of memory, or fewer keys taken to hard disk and a lower memory reduction. The knowledge of type of workload in use, combined with the configuration of these parameters may provide better performance of the framework.

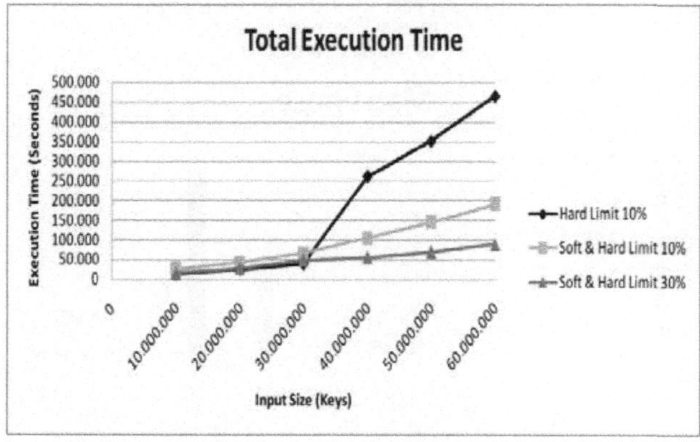

Fig. 8: Soft and Hard Limit strategy.

5. Conclusions

Addition to the original implementation where we promote reduction in the use of main memory, and reduction of page faults, we also show in this paper a better way to access the hard disk by the MapReduce framework, using different limits for the threads. The parameters limit, buffer size and number of hash entries taken to hard disk, open a new line of research where it can further improve the execution time of the implementation presented in this paper. This implementation opens the way for improving the MapReduce framework on multi-core architectures, allowing the framework to adapt to different workloads.

As an extension, our implementation does not predict solve all problems for the use of large data sets in systems with limited memory, but rather open up a straight of research for future solutions.

Acknowledgements

This work was supported by the Ministry of Education of Spain under contract TIN2011-28689-c02-01.

References

[1] C. Ranger, R. Raghuraman, A. Penmetsa, G. Bradski, and C. Kozyrakis, "Evaluating mapreduce for multi-core and multiprocessor systems," In HPCA '07: Proceedings of the 13th International Symposium on High-Performance Computer Architecture. IEEE Computer Society, 2007, pp. 13–24.

[2] J. Dean, S. Ghemawat, and G. Inc, "Mapreduce: simplified data processing on large clusters." In OSDI'04: Proceedings of the 6th conference on Symposium on Opearting Systems Design and Implementation, 2004.

[3] R. M. Yoo, A. Romano, and C. Kozyrakis, "Phoenix rebirth: Scalable mapreduce on a large-scale shared-memory system." IISWC. IEEE, 2009, pp. 198–207.

[4] D. Tiwari and Y. Solihin, "Modeling and analyzing key performance factors of shared memory mapreduce," in *IPDPS*, 2012, pp. 1306–1317.

[5] T. Ferreira, A. Espinosa, J. C. Moure, and P. Hernández, "An optimization for mapreduce frameworks in multi-core architectures," 2013, accepted on International Conference on Computational Science, ICCS'13.

[6] T. White, *Hadoop: The Definitive Guide*, 1st ed. O'Reilly Media, June 2009.

[7] Y. Mao, R. Morris, and M. F. Kaashoek, "Optimizing mapreduce for multicore architectures," *Computer Science and Artificial Intelligence Laboratory, Massachusetts Institute of Technology, Tech. Rep*, 2010.

[8] J. Talbot, R. M. Yoo, and C. Kozyrakis, "Phoenix++: modular mapreduce for shared-memory systems," pp. 9–16, 2011.

[9] N. Backman, K. Pattabiraman, R. Fonseca, and U. Cetintemel, "C-mr: continuously executing mapreduce workflows on multi-core processors," in *Proceedings of third international workshop on MapReduce and its Applications Date*, ser. MapReduce '12. New York, NY, USA: ACM, 2012, pp. 1–8.

Application Characteristics of Many-tasking Execution Models

T. Gilmanov, M. Anderson, M. Brodowicz and T. Sterling
Center for Research in Extreme Scale Technologies, Indiana University, Bloomington, IN, USA

Abstract— *Performance gain for computer systems through Moore's Law is jeopardized by the limitations of clock rate growth due to power considerations and the limitations in instruction-level parallelism improvement from processor core computer architecture experienced over the last decade. High performance computer architectures are addressing this challenge through multicore processors that combine many processing units on a single chip. For this class of machines, conventional programming and execution practices, while still effective for some application algorithms, are suffering in scalability for many others. Multithreaded runtime systems offer convenient many-tasking execution model implementations that show increased efficiency and scalability through exploiting medium-grained thread parallelism. This paper provides an overview of the existing runtime systems and libraries used for many-tasking computation. They are empirically examined in terms of overheads and the potential impact resulting on application performance. Intra-node performance aspects are investigated using synthetic benchmarks.*

Keywords: runtime systems, thread parallelism, benchmarks

1. Introduction

Sustaining performance growth of high performance computing systems through device technology improvements reflected by Moore's Law is becoming increasingly challenging using conventional static programming and execution methods. Due to power limitations, processor core clock rates are constrained and in some cases even reduced. Also, opportunities for instruction level parallelism (ILP) within core architectures have been exhausted as well. Thus, the two principal means of performance growth of microprocessor cores that have served high performance computing (HPC) for more than two decades have ceased to be a significant factor. Alternative architecture strategies based on multi-core processors accelerators to deliver continued performance growth have introduced the need for abundant and continually increasing medium-grained parallelism to achieve scalability.

While the concept of runtime systems is not new, their application to HPC is extremely constrained due to the problems of additional overheads being introduced. But runtimes offer the possibility of dynamic adaptive resource management and task scheduling employing information during time of execution that is not available at time of programming or compilation. It is postulated that access to runtime information may provide the means to dramatically improve operational efficiency while achieving significant increases in scalability. Such runtime systems must reduce typical sources of work starvation, latency effects, overhead, and waiting for contention resolution to shared resources (physical or logical).

In a multiprocessor setting, task schedulers can implicitly load balance computations and more easily enable fine grain computations. Asynchrony management constructs remove global barriers and enable codes to overlap phases of computation to improve performance. In a distributed setting, this introduces the capability to hide network latency and better overlap computation and communication. Both Charm++ [1] and Unified Parallel C (UPC) [2] have for a long time exhibited the major benefits of task parallelism along with a shared address space. Other more recent approaches include the Intel Threading Building Blocks library (TBB) [3], the High Performance ParalleX (HPX) runtime system [4], Cilk plus [5], Chapel [6], Qthreads [7]. Even MPI and OpenMP [8] have been used to accomplish task parallelism.

This paper provides an overview of the existing runtime systems and libraries used for many-tasking computation. They are empirically examined in terms of overheads and the potential impact resulting on application performance. The approach taken starts by characterizing cumulative overhead of task initialization, execution, and end-synchronization for several many-tasking runtime systems and libraries, namely: TBB, Cilk plus (both Intel and gcc versions), OpenMP (both Intel and gcc versions), Charm++, HPX, and Qthreads. We explore the impact of NUMA awareness and the TCMalloc allocator [9] separately for each runtime system and library. Two micro benchmarks are presented: homogeneous task spawn and heterogeneous task spawn.

2. Related Work

In spite of the significant interest in task parallelism, there exists relatively few side by side comparisons of the various overheads in implemented many-tasking execution models. This is partially explained by the fact that the functional capabilities of a fundamental task vary widely from implementation to implementation and depend upon the particular many-tasking execution model that the runtime system intends to implement. This makes direct comparisons difficult. However, some key similarities are shared among the various execution models and some studies have been conducted to compare these overheads.

Burkhart et al. [10] examined Chapel, Unified Parallel C, OpenMP, and MPI using a generic stencil computation as the unified performance test. system. The work by Olivier et al. [11] discusses an approach to compare the performance of a

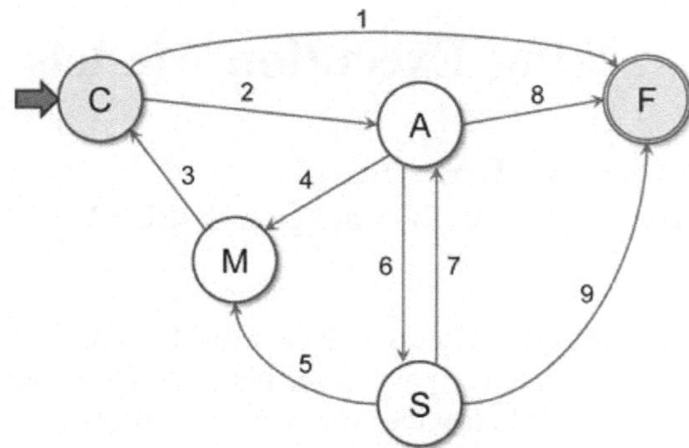

Fig. 1: General task state diagram. The nodes (marked with letters) represent states; the edges (with number labels) signify transitions between the states. The life cycle of a task starts in the creation state C identified by the arrow and ends in finished state F; both are represented by shaded circles to emphasize the transition endpoints. The remaining states include active (or execution) state A, suspended state S, and migration state M.

few runtime systems, including OpenMP, Cilk, Cilk++, and Intel TBB using a highly unbalanced task graph in order to introduce challenges arising in work balancing, scheduling, and termination detection. Other comparison works include comparing Cilk with MPI for finite differencing [12].

3. Task benchmarks

Central to a many-tasking execution model performance quantification is the threading characteristics of a simulation as it scales to larger core counts. Some implementations support thread asynchrony management thereby enabling activation, migration, and suspension of tasks. Other implementations support a much smaller subset of possible thread states. Quantification of these overheads is fundamental to the development of a performance model for design and deployment of many-tasking based applications.

Figure 1, even though substantially simplified, illustrates the significant number of possible task states and transitions, each with an associated latency and implementation overhead, in a many-tasking execution model. Note that while some runtime systems do not explicitly use the notion of tasks, this term is often equivalent to a work unit executed by a user level thread (*cf.* HPX, Qthreads). Among the possible task states are creation and initialization (C), migration (M), active (A), suspended (S), and finished (F). Every task's life cycle begins in the creation state C. The creation state involves a potentially complex sequence of operations, ranging from creating an entry in the runtime system's task table or queue, allocating the memory to hold the necessary description of task state, function to execute and its arguments, hooks to the related runtime system data structures and functions, *etc*. An initialized task typically transitions along edge 2 from the creation state C to the active execution state A. In rare cases when the work in the application has been already completed but an abundance of tasks has been created to increase the parallelism or conditionally explore additional branches of program execution, they will be automatically terminated after moving to state F. The active execution state A is a superposition of internal states in which a task may actively execute on a processor, may await the assignment of a physical execution resource, or be queued in scheduler's run queue. These internal states share a common characteristics: all data dependencies required by the task to perform the next logical operation must be satisfied. If this condition is not true, for example, the task needs data returned by a pending I/O operation or data that has to be conveyed by a message from a remote node, the runtime system places the task in a suspended state S. Similarly to the active state, the suspended state may internally include a number of variants. The efficient utilization of the hardware resources depends on the runtime system's ability to identify tasks blocked due to data dependencies and removing them from the active state; note that this is not always straightforward as such knowledge may be available only at the operating system level. Over the lifetime of a complex task, the transitions 6 and 7 between active and suspended state may happen many times. Other transitions from the active and suspended states lead to either termination F or migration M. Currently, only few runtime systems support migration of task state at a global (distributed machine) scale; moreover, additional restrictions may be placed on which tasks are permitted to migrate to remote execution locales. Most general implementations will support migration for both suspended and executing tasks (although the latter will have to be preempted from the execution resource and removed from the active queue before the state migration sequence is initiated). Since recreation of task structures on the remote end shares many similarities with creation of a new task (with possible differences in initialization phase), transition 3 from migration leads to the initial state C. All tasks entering the finished state F are terminated. Their representation is removed from the runtime system data structures and all related resources are reclaimed. Entering this state may not always cause the immediate release of the resources used by the task. In cases where the final value computed by a task has to be communicated to other tasks (akin to thread join), the related portion of task state may linger long after its execution phase is over. Additionally, other dedicated system entities, such as garbage collectors, may ultimately decide when to reclaim the terminated task's storage.

We first consider the most fundamental task phases in a many-tasking implementation shared by all aforementioned implementations: task initialization, task execution, and final synchronization. They are directly related to the task states described above. The task initialization corresponds to the creation state C, perhaps with the added overhead of an external loop generating the task instances. Task execution is a superposition of active (A) and suspended state (S), since migration was not explored in our tests. Given that the single work grain does not include any blocking operations, once a task is moved to the active state, it will remain there until completion. The synchronization at the end of workload certainly involves transition of individual tasks to the F state, but also includes transition between states A and S of the master task (spawner) that monitors the execution. This may be caused, for example, by the readout of an atomically updated counter representing the number of completed tasks, or by checking the state of a future object which hasn't been updated yet. Note that such updates may be performed either by the code of individual tasks directly, or by a background system thread, depending on the implementation. For the former, additional A↔S transitions (possibly multiple) may occur at the very end of task execution during periods of high contention when competing for access to the shared resource.

The cumulative overhead of these task phases is crucial in determining the optimal task granularity for a specific application simulation. The tests described in the next two subsections analyze the task spawn performance on various systems using two modes of operation; homogeneous and heterogeneous.

3.1 Homogeneous Task Spawn

In the homogeneous task benchmark presented in this section, we spawn a fixed number of tasks, 5×10^5 in this case, where each task has the same work unit defined by a function given in Listing 1. The grain size given the work unit is specified by the number of iterations in the for loop in Listing 1. It is varied across several orders of magnitude from 0, 10, 100, 1000, and 10,000 in order to reflect fine to medium grain application simulations. Code listings for this benchmark are given for OpenMP (Listing 2), HPX (Listing 3), Cilk+ (Listing 4), Charm++ (Listing 5), Qthreads (Listing 6), and TBB (Listing 7).

Listing 1: Work function used in conjunction with the various task spawn tests [13]

```
void worker(){
  double volatile d = 0.;
  for (uint64_t i=0; i<delay; ++i)
    d += 1. / (2. * i + 1.);
}
```

Listing 2: OpenMP task spawn [13]

```
#pragma omp parallel
#pragma omp single
{
  for (uint64_t i=0; i<tasks; ++i)
    #pragma omp task untied
    worker();

  #pragma omp taskwait
}
```

Listing 3: HPX task spawn [13]

```
for (uint64_t i=0; i<tasks; ++i)
  register_work(HPX_STD_BIND(&worker));

do suspend();
while (get_thread_count() > 1);
```

Listing 4: Cilk+ task spawn [14]

```
for (uint64_t i=0; i<tasks; ++i)
  cilk_spawn worker();

cilk_sync;
```

Listing 5: Charm++ task spawn

```
main::main(CkArgMsg *m){
  mainProxy = thishandle;
  count = tasks;

  for (uint64_t i=0; i<tasks; ++i)
    CProxy_worker::ckNew();
}

void main::results(){
  if (0 == --count) CkExit();
}

worker::worker(){
  double volatile d = 0.;
  for (uint64_t i=0; i<delay; ++i)
    d += 1. / (2. * i + 1.);

  mainProxy.results();
}
```

Listing 6: Qthreads task spawn [14]

```
for (uint64_t i=0; i<tasks; i++) {
  qthread_fork(worker_task, NULL, NULL);

  do qthread_yield();
  while (donecount != tasks);
}
```

Listing 7: TBB task spawn [14]

```
// body of worker::execute()
// identical to Listing 1

tbb::task *spawner::execute(){
  set_ref_count(tasks+1);

  for (uint64_t i=0; i<tasks; ++i){
    worker& a =
      *new(tbb::task::allocate_child())
        worker();

    if (i != tasks-1) spawn(a);
    else spawn_and_wait_for_all(a);
  }
}

int tbb_main(){
  spawner& a =
    *new(tbb::task::allocate_root())
      spawner();
  tbb::task::spawn_root_and_wait(a);
  return 0;
}

int main(int argc, char **argv){
  tbb::task_scheduler_init init(tasks);
  return tbb_main();
}
```

The task spawn tests were benchmarked on a computer equipped with dual 8-core E5-2670 Intel processors running at 2.6 GHz and 32 GB of memory. This machine is representative of the type of nodes commonly found in recent supercomputer configurations. The hyper-threading was explicitly disabled in BIOS to avoid issues related to inconsistent enumeration of

Package	Version
Compilers	
GNU binutils	2.23.1
gcc	4.6.3 release
gcc Cilk+ patch	4.8.0 (20121210)
Intel Composer	2013.1.117
Support libraries	
boost	1.52.0
hwloc	1.6
Google Performance Tools	2.0
Runtime systems	
Charm++	6.4.0
HPX	git hash a0786ed (12/12/2012)
Qthreads	git hash f2ae33d (01/02/2013)
TBB	4.1.20121003

Table 1: Versions of software packages used in task spawn tests.

Iterations	0	10	100	1,000	10,000
Duration	2.5 ns	103 ns	1.059 μs	10.61 μs	106.2 μs

Table 2: Actual duration of the work units used in the tests.

logical processors between different libraries used for NUMA affinity management. Red Hat Enterprise Linux version 6.3 provided the basic operating environment. It was augmented with the prerequisite libraries and compilation tools required by runtime systems tested; they are listed in Table 1 for reference.

The work unit durations for various grain sizes collected on a minimally loaded system are listed in Table 2. To obtain them, many runs were performed in sequence to alleviate the effects of finite timer resolution and ensure full cache initialization. Since the E5 Xeon processors feature Turbo Boost technology (temporary increase of clock speed when executing workload on a limited number of cores), the presented numbers are very close to the minimal possible execution times per task on that architecture.

Unless stated otherwise (in particular for Cilk+ and OpenMP tests), all runtime system libraries and test codes were compiled using gcc-4.6.3. Using more recent 4.7 series resulted in unstable code in some instances. Whenever possible, production or release configurations were used, with optimization flag of "-O2" and no debugging information. Since certain implementations exhibit measurable performance improvements when using additional external libraries, separate tests were performed for these configurations. They include NUMA affinity management (typically using `hwloc` library), and thread-aware memory allocation (e.g., `tcmalloc` from Google Performance Tools suite). The impact of these packages in a typical case can be seen in Figure 2. The NUMA-aware thread assignment improves the performance for lower numbers of cores by limiting the degree of freedom in distributing the OS threads across available NUMA domains; these benefits are gone when the number of underlying OS threads matches the core count. Contrariwise, `tcmalloc` effects are greatest for high OS thread counts, as these cases exhibit the highest access contention to shared resources used by conventional memory allocation routines. To avoid excessive clutter in charts comparing the performance of multiple runtime systems, only the best performing configurations were selected, with relevant details embedded in plot labels.

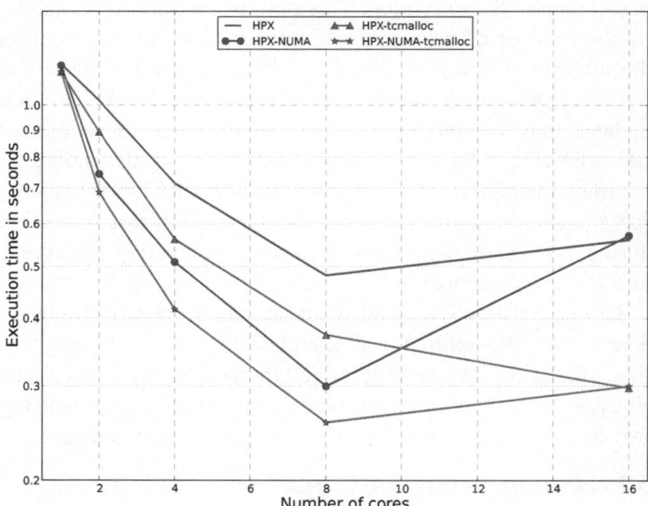

Fig. 2: Impact of NUMA-aware OS thread placement and thread caching memory management on many-tasking performance in HPX using a medium granularity where each tasks performs $\sim 1\mu$s of workload.

Special care was taken to ensure that the simulated work unit is identical between the benchmarks and no unfair optimizations are taking place. For this reason, the work unit function was placed in a separate compilation unit and inter-procedural analysis in the linkage phase was suppressed. The memory management calls, required by several systems to create and release required data structures representing individual tasks were removed outside the timed region, or low-overhead equivalents provided by the runtime systems were used where possible. Similarly, detection of the completion of task execution phase relied on optimized techniques suggested by the programming manuals or was leveraged from code examples distributed with the runtime systems.

Figures 3–7 present the results of homogeneous task spawn for various runtime systems and libraries. The data are generated for the plots using the following methodology: each data point is independently computed ten times; the four largest outliers in the data are then discarded and the remaining six points are averaged to produce the data point. Figure 3 shows the results for the lightest weight tasks with only $\sim 2-3$ ns of work per task. Nearly all problems scale poorly in this test, with Cilk+ showing the best performance. Figure 4 presents comparisons using ~ 103 ns per task resulting in a much closer result between the flavors of Cilk+ and Qthreads. Figures 5 and 6 use $\sim 1\mu$s and $\sim 10\mu$s tasks, respectively. We begin to observe scaling for most systems in these medium grain cases with Qthreads optimal in both the 100 and 1,000 iteration cases and TBB along with HPX closely following the Qthreads performance in the 1,000 iteration case. A peculiar performance drop is observed for OpenMP after 8 cores in Figure 6, which may be attributed to insufficient NUMA support in the OpenMP runtime libraries, coupled with the default affinity policies enforced by the OS. In Figure 7 we explore a medium-heavy grain size with each task taking $\sim 106\mu s$. Here all systems show sustained scaling while the best performance is achieved for Cilk+ and OpenMP using Intel compilers. Many of the remaining runtime systems show very similar performance across the processor counts tested at this granularity.

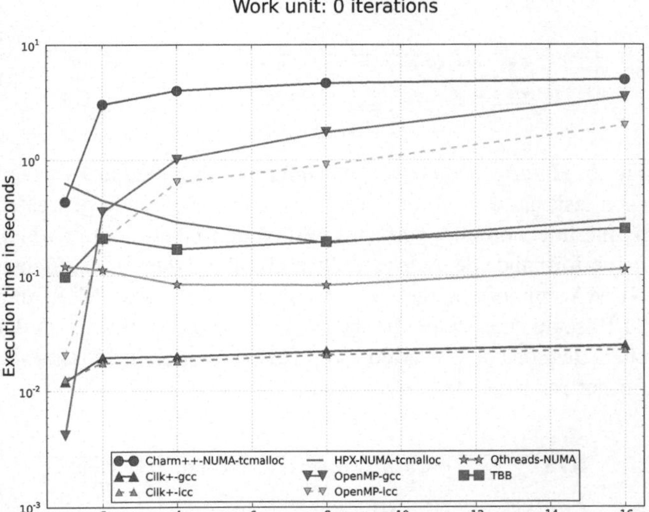

Fig. 3: Homogeneous task spawning with 500,000 tasks where each task has a work unit of approximately 2-3 ns. Poor scaling is generally observed throughout as the task overhead significantly exceeds the amount of work done per task. The two flavors of Cilk+, gcc and icc, significantly outperform the other alternatives in this regime.

In large applications, we do not expect all tasks to have the exact same work unit. This naturally leads us to explore a benchmark where tasks have various sized work units selected from a stable probability distribution.

3.2 Heterogeneous Task Spawn

The heterogeneous task benchmark spawns 5×10^5 tasks just as in the homogeneous task benchmark; however, this time the work unit per task is varied. The code used for heterogeneous tests is almost identical to that of the homogeneous tests (Listing 1- 7), except that each task was assigned a delay parameter (the number of iterations from Listing 1) taken from a probability distribution. The delay parameters in the heterogeneous test were drawn from three stable distributions: the Normal distribution, the CMS distribution, and the Lévy

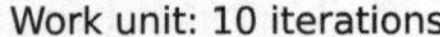

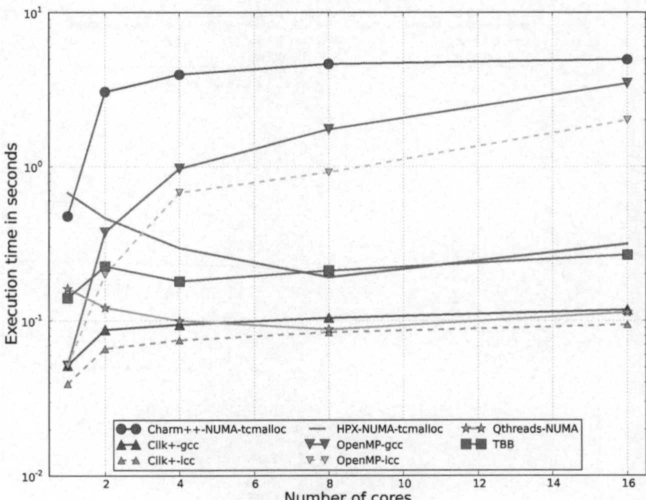

Fig. 4: Homogeneous task spawning with 500,000 tasks where each task has a work unit of ~ 103 ns. The results here share much in common with those of the null tasks in Figure 3 except that the flavors of Cilk+ and Qthreads are much more similar in terms of performance.

distribution. These distributions are stable and are also attractors in probability space making them physically relevant for performance modeling.

The probability density function of a Normal distribution is defined as follows:

$$f(x) = \frac{1}{\sigma\sqrt{2\pi}} \exp\left[-\frac{1}{2}\left(\frac{x-\mu}{\sigma}\right)\right]^2,$$

where μ is the expectation, σ is the standard deviation, and $x \in (-\infty, \infty)$. The standard deviations of $\sigma = 25$ and $\sigma = 75$ were used in the experiments presented in Table 3; an expectation of $\mu = 100$ was selected for the heterogeneous experiments in order to compare with the homogeneous results presented in Figure 5.

The CMS distribution [15] provides much fatter tails than the Normal distribution along with a parameter to control skewness. A generic characteristic function for this distribution is as follows:

$$f(t; \alpha, \beta) = \exp\left[-|t|^\alpha \exp\left(-\frac{1}{2}\pi\beta k(\alpha)\,\mathrm{sign}(t)\right)\right],$$

with $0 < \alpha \leq 2, \alpha \neq 1$, where parameter β controls skewness, function $k(\alpha) = 1 - |1 - \alpha|$, α controls the leptokurtosis, and t is the Fourier transform variable. This formula assumes a location parameter of zero and dispersion parameter of unity. Random variables from this distribution are translated to have a location parameter of 100 in order to better compare results with those in Figure 5. The other parameters selected were skewness $\beta = -1$ and $\alpha = 1.0744$ producing a near-Cauchy distribution. These parameters reflect the observation that tasks

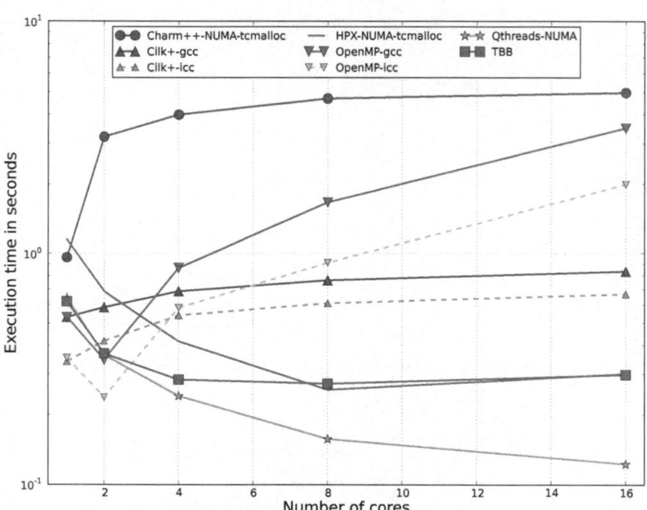

Fig. 5: Homogeneous task spawning with 500,000 tasks where each task has a work unit of $\sim 1\mu$s. The flavors of Cilk+ perform worse at this grain size than they did in Figures 3 and 4. Qthreads substantially outperforms the other packages at this grain size while the flavors of OpenMP still do not show any sustained scaling.

on occasion take minimally faster than the average time but often much longer than that; hence a non symmetric fat tail towards longer work units.

The probability density function of the Lévy stable distribution [16] is given by

$$L(z) = \frac{1}{\pi} \int_0^\infty \exp(-\gamma q^\alpha) \cos(qz) dq,$$

with parameters γ and α, and $z \in (-\infty, \infty)$. Like CMS, the location of the extremum in this probability density function was selected to be 100, with $\alpha = 1.5$ and $\gamma = 1$.

A comparison between the homogeneous and heterogeneous measurements is presented in Table 3. Within each probability distribution, each test used the exact same set of random numbers describing the work unit sizes. The largest work unit sizes in the task set for the CMS and Lévy distributions were 3×10^5 and 1×10^6, respectively. In the table, the largest percentage difference in the heterogeneous run from the comparable homogeneous run is presented when run across 1 - 16 cores. The maximum difference in execution time of heterogeneous vs homogeneous task spawn did not exceed 2% for any of the distributions, runtime systems or libraries, or core counts explored. The runtime systems and libraries tested are fairly robust against variations in task work unit size. The results suggest that Cilk and OpenMP may be slightly more sensitive to both Lévy-distributed and CMS task spawn experiments; in case of Normally-distributed delays, HPX, OpenMP, and Cilk were the most sensitive systems found.

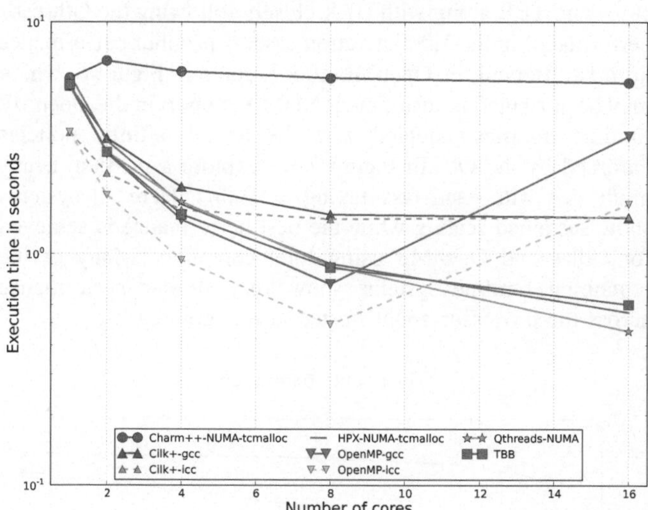

Fig. 6: Homogeneous task spawning with 500,000 tasks where each task has a work unit of $\sim 10\mu$s. OpenMP code generated by the Intel compiler performs best on up to 8 cores after which its performance degrades significantly likely due to insufficient NUMA support in the implementation. Qthreads, HPX, and TBB scale well with the number of cores, showing similar characteristics at this grain size. This similarity increases even further for larger task sizes, as in Figure 7.

RTS	**CMS, 3e5**	**Lévy, 1e6**	**Normal, 25**	**Normal, 75**
Charm++	0.0456	0.9871	0.0260	0.0404
Cilk+-gcc	0.0358	1.2718	0.0355	-0.1197
Cilk+-icc	0.1104	1.2603	0.1452	0.0805
HPX	0.1214	0.8918	0.1955	0.2526
OpenMP-gcc	0.2523	1.2677	0.2977	0.3510
OpenMP-icc	0.0814	1.2440	-0.4012	-0.2708
Qthreads	0.0260	1.1783	-0.0091	0.0272
TBB	0.0995	1.1943	0.0700	0.0599

Table 3: The largest percentage difference in runtime between the heterogeneous and homogeneous benchmarks is presented here for three different probability distributions and eight runtime systems (RTS) or libraries when run on 1 – 16 cores. Within each probability distribution, each test used the exact same set of random numbers describing the work unit sizes. The largest work unit sizes in the task set for the CMS and Lévy distributions were 3×10^5 and 1×10^6, respectively. The standard deviations used in the Normal distribution ($\sigma = 25$ and $\sigma = 75$)) are given in the Normal column header. The largest difference of heterogeneous vs homogeneous runs across all the runtime systems or libraries, probability distributions, and core counts is lower than 2%. These results suggest that the runtime systems explored here are fairly robust in terms of execution times even when there is a broad mix of both lighter and heavier weight tasks in the task scheduler.

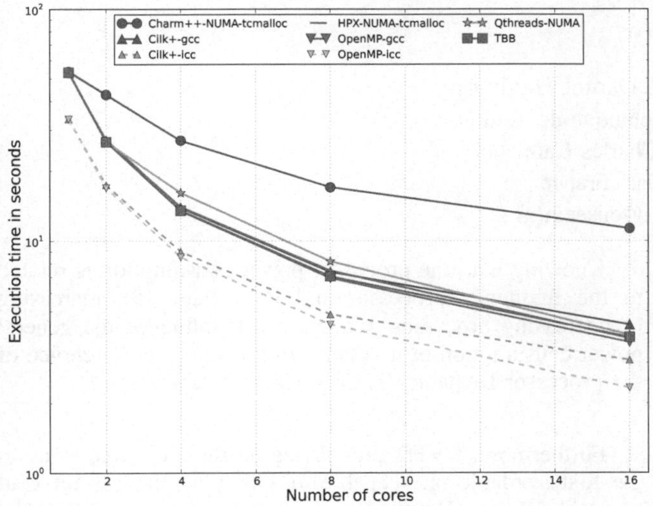

Fig. 7: Homogeneous task spawning with 500,000 tasks where each task has a work unit of $\sim 106\mu s$. The Intel OpenMP and Cilk+ flavors outperform the other runtime systems and libraries at this grain size. The remaining systems, with the exception of Charm++, begin to behave in almost exactly the same way.

4. Conclusions

With the continued dominance of multi-core processors in HPC systems and the emergence of a number of many-tasking capable runtime systems and libraries, some performance comparisons and characterization of overheads are critical in order to better understand and leverage dynamic execution capabilities with balancing overhead costs. These overheads have important implications for determining the grain size at which an application using one of these runtime systems behaves optimally. We have examined a number of many-tasking runtime systems in the context of task initialization, execution and finalization, both for uniform and varying workload sizes in order to better characterize the overheads introduced by the runtime system itself.

In the synthetic benchmarks examined, we found that Cilk plus behaves better at close-to-zero-workload tasks while OpenMP outperforms the other runtime systems for the largest workloads examined. We did not find a significant sensitivity to the fat tails in the heterogeneous task spawn benchmark. The results also revealed a few surprises. The first is that there is no "one size fits all" solution that performs uniformly well for all workload granularities. The second is that despite the old age, some runtime systems still manage to stay competitive to relatively modern implementations in a number of scenarios.

The synthetic benchmarks presented here contain a minimal number of synchronization types compared to what a full application would contain. Such synchronizations would introduce potentially expensive context switches with a different overhead characteristic to each runtime system. Future work in characterizing the runtime system overheads will include context switches and synchronization primitives. Future work will also incorporate these characteristic overheads into a discrete event simulator for application performance modeling.

5. Acknowledgments

The authors wish to thank Hartmut Kaiser, Dylan Stark and Daniel Kogler for their technical assistance.

References

[1] L. Kalé and S. Krishnan, "CHARM++: A Portable Concurrent Object Oriented System Based on C++," in *Proceedings of OOPSLA'93*, A. Paepcke, Ed. ACM Press, September 1993, pp. 91–108.

[2] W. W. Carlson, J. M. Draper, D. E. Culler, K. Yelick, E. Brooks, and K. Warren, "Introduction to UPC and Language Specification," *CCS-TR-99-157*, May 1999.

[3] J. Reinders, *Intel Threading Building Blocks: Outfitting C++ for Multi-Core Processor Parallelism*, 1st ed. O'Reilly Media, July 2007. [Online]. Available: http://www.amazon.com/exec/obidos/redirect?tag=citeulike07-20&path=ASIN/0596514808

[4] C. Dekate, M. Anderson, M. Brodowicz, H. Kaiser, B. Adelstein-Lelbach, and T. Sterling, "Improving the scalability of parallel N-body applications with an event-driven constraint-based execution model," *International Journal of High Performance Computing Applications*, vol. 26, no. 3, pp. 319–332, 2012. [Online]. Available: http://hpc.sagepub.com/content/26/3/319.abstract

[5] "Intel Cilk Plus," http://cilkplus.org/, 2012.

[6] B. Chamberlain, D. Callahan, and H. Zima, "Parallel programmability and the Chapel language," *Int. J. High Perform. Comput. Appl.*, vol. 21, no. 3, pp. 291–312, Aug. 2007. [Online]. Available: http://dx.doi.org/10.1177/1094342007078442

[7] K. Wheeler, R. Murphy, and D. Thain, "Qthreads: An API for Programming with Millions of Lightweight Threads," in *International Parallel and Distributed Processing Symposium. IEEE Press*, 2008.

[8] L. Dagum and R. Menon, "OpenMP: An industry-standard API for shared-memory programming," *IEEE Computational Science and Engineering*, vol. 5, no. 1, pp. 46–55, 1998.

[9] "Tcmalloc: Thread-caching malloc," available from http://goog-perftools.sourceforge.net/doc/tcmalloc.html.

[10] H. Burkhart, M. Christen, M. Rietmann, M. Sathe, and O. Schenk, "Run, Stencil, Run! A Comparison of Modern Parallel Programming Paradigms," in *PARS-Mitteilungen*, 2011.

[11] S. Olivier and J. F. Prins, "Comparison of OpenMP 3.0 and other task parallel frameworks on unbalanced task graphs." *International Journal of Parallel Programming*, vol. 38, no. 5-6, pp. 341–360, 2010. [Online]. Available: http://dblp.uni-trier.de/db/journals/ijpp/ijpp38.html

[12] S. Tham, "Cilk vs MPI: comparing two very different parallel programming styles," in *International Conference on Parallel Processing*, 2003, pp. 143–152.

[13] Stellar group, "HPX GIT repository," 2012, https://github.com/STEllAR-GROUP/hpx.git.

[14] Available from https://code.google.com/p/qthreads/.

[15] J. M. Chambers, C. L. Mallows, and B. W. Stuck, "A method for simulating stable random variables," *Journal of the American Statistical Association*, vol. 71, no. 354, pp. 340–344, 1976. [Online]. Available: http://www.jstor.org/stable/2285309

[16] R. N. Mantegna, "Fast, accurate algorithm for numerical simulation of Lévy stable stochastic processes," *Phys. Rev. E*, vol. 49, no. 5, pp. 4677–4683, May 1994. [Online]. Available: http://dx.doi.org/10.1103/PhysRevE.49.4677

Virtual processor frequency emulation

Christine Mayap and Daniel Hagimont
Institut National Polytechnique de Toulouse
ENSEEIHT, 2 rue Charles Camichel
31000 Toulouse, France
Email: hagimont@enseeiht.fr

***Abstract*—Nowadays, virtualization is present in almost all computing infrastructures. Thanks to VM migration and server consolidation, virtualization helps in reducing power consumption in distributed environments. On another side, Dynamic Voltage and Frequency Scaling (DVFS) allows servers to dynamically modify the processor frequency (according to the CPU load) in order to achieve less energy consumption. We observe that while DVFS is widely used, it still generates a waste of energy. By default and thanks to the ondemand governor, it scales up or down the processor frequency according to the current load and the different predefined threshold (up and down). However, DVFS frequency scaling policies are based on advertised processor frequencies, i.e. the set of frequencies constitutes a discrete range of frequencies. The frequency required for a given load will be set to a frequency higher than necessary; which leads to an energy waste. In this paper, we propose a way to emulate a precise CPU frequency thanks to the DVFS management in virtualized environments. We implemented and evaluated our prototype in the Xen hypervisor.**

Keywords*—*DVFS, frequency, emulation.

I. Introduction

Nowadays, cloud computing is one of the widely used IT solutions for distributed services. Almost 70% of companies are interested in it and 40% of them plan to adopt it within one year [1]. Cloud computing can be defined as a way of sharing hardware or/and software resources with clients according to their needs. The idea of cloud computing is to simulate an unlimited set of resources for users and to guarantee a good Quality of Service(QoS), while optimizing all relevant costs [2].

Cloud computing mainly relies on virtualization. Virtualization consists of providing concurrent and interactive access to hardware devices. Thanks to his live migration properties, it is possible to migrate applications on a few number of computers, while ensuring good QoS and security isolation. This advantage is highly exploited by cloud computing to effectively manage energy consumption and to efficiently manage resources [3].

Recent advances in hardware design have made it possible to decrease energy consumption of computer systems through Dynamic voltage and frequency scaling (DVFS) [4]. DVFS is a hardware technology used to dynamically scale up or down the processor frequency according to the governor policy and the workload demand.

Knowing that, the processor power consumption is related to the frequency processor and its voltage [5], increasing or decreasing processor frequency will influence the general power consumption of a system. In this context, the choice of the processor frequency is of great importance.

Furthermore, DVFS aims at setting the CPU frequency to the first available one capable of satisfying the current load to avoid wastage. However, there may be situations where the selected frequency is still the subject of wastage because it is higher than the required frequency.

In this paper, we explore and propose a way to emulate a precise desired processor frequency in a virtualized and single-core environment. After presenting the context and the motivation of our work in section 2, we will describe our contributions in section 3. In section 4, we present experiments to validate our proposal. After a review of related works in section 5, we conclude the article in Section 6.

II. Context and Motivation

In this section, we present some concepts of virtualization, DVFS and how this later is applied in virtualized systems.

A. Context

1) Virtualization: According to a general observation, the rate of server utilization was around 20% [6]. Thanks to virtualization, the rate has increased and allows efficient server utilization. Indeed, virtualization is a software-based solution for building and running simultaneously many operating systems (called *guest OS* or *Virtual Machine*) on top of a "classic" OS (called *host OS*). A special application, named *Virtual Machine Monitor (VMM)* or *hypervisor* emulates the underlying hardware and interprets communications between guests OS and devices.

Among existing virtualization technologies, we adopt *paravirtualization* as the base of our experience. With paravirtualization, the VMM is placed between the hardware and the host OS. Guest OS is modified to use optimized instructions (named *hypercall*) from VMM to access hardware.

Paravirtualization is used because of its good VM performance and its implementation on all types of processors. In fact, with *full virtualization*, VM performance is more than 30% degraded [7]. Meanwhile *Hardware-assisted virtualization* requires specific processors though the performance of guest OS are close-to-native performance.

Paravirtualization is highly adopted and vulgarized by Xen [8] and VMWare ESX Server [9]. In this context, our work is based on Xen platform because it is prevalent in many computing infrastructures, as well as in the vast majority of our previous work.

2) Dynamic Voltage and Frequency Scaling (DVFS): Today, all processors integrate dynamic frequency/voltage scaling to adjust frequency/voltage during runtime. The decision to change the frequency is commanded by the current processor's *governor*. Each governor has its own strategy to perform frequency scale. According to the configured policy, governor can decide to scale processor speed to a specific frequency, the highest, or the lowest frequency.

Several governors are implemented inside the Linux kernel. *Ondemand* governor changes frequency depending on CPU utilization. It changes frequency from the lowest (whenever CPU utilization is less than a predefined (low_therehold) to the highest and vice-versa. *Performance* governor always keeps the frequency at the highest value while slowest CPU speed is always set by *powersave* governor. *Conservative* governor decreases or increases frequency step-by-step through a range of frequency values supported by the hardware. *Userspace* governor allows user to manually set processor frequency [10]. In order to control CPU frequency, governors use an underlying subsystem inside the kernel called cpufreqq [11]. Cpufreq provides a set of modularized interfaces to allow changing CPU frequency. Cpufreq, in turn, relies on CPU-specific drivers to execute requests from governors.

As aforementioned, effectively usage of DVFS brings the advantage of reducing power consumption by lowering processor frequency. Moreover, almost all computing infrastructures possess multi-core and high frequency processors. Thus, the benefit from using DVFS has been realized and achieved in many different systems.

The next section describes the motivation of this work.

B. Motivation

During the last decade, several efforts have been made in order to find an efficient trade-off between energy consumption/resources management and applications performance. Most of them relies on DVFS, and are highly explored due to the advent of new modern powerful processors integrating this technology.

According to the ondemand governor (the default governor policy implemented by DVFS), the CPU frequency is dynamically changed depending on the CPU utilisation. With this governor, the highest available processor frequency is set when the CPU load is greater than a predefined threshold (up_threshold). When the load decreases below the threshold, the processor frequency is decreased step by step until the one capable of satisfying the current process load is found.

However, in most CPUs, the DVFS technology provides a reduced number of frequency levels (in the order of 5) [12]. This configuration might not be enough for some experiments.

Suppose a virtualized muti-core processor Intel(R) Xeon(R) E5520 with 2.261 GHz and the DVFS technology enable. Consider its six frequencies levels distributed as follows: 1.596 GHz, 1.729 GHz, 1.862 Ghz, 1.995 Ghz, 2.128 GHz and 2.261 GHz. Assume the host OS with a global load which needs 1.9285 Ghz to be satisfied. Knowing that the computation of the best execution time of an application is made on a basis of the maximum frequency of a processor, scheduling it with a lower frequency would end up with a lower than expected performance. From the SLA point of view and because of the non-existence of the expected frequency, the ondemand governor will set the CPU frequency to the first one, higher that the required frequency, capable of satisfying the current load. Precisely in our example, the ondemand governor will set the processor frequency to 1.995 GHz.

However, it would be more beneficial in terms of energy to assign to the processor the exact required frequency. Indeed, the DVFS technology consists of concurrently lowering the CPU voltage and the CPU frequency. By lowering them, the current total energy consumption of the system is globally decreased [13]. To improve this well-known energy management, we will realise some adjustments on the DVFS technology. Hence, instead of setting the CPU frequency to the first higher available frequency, we decided to emulate some of the non-existent CPU frequency according to the system needs.

Concretely, emulating a CPU frequency, in our work, consists of executing the processor successively on the available frequencies around the desired CPU frequency. Our emulation process is essentially based on the conventional operation of the DVFS. The use of the DVFS possesses as asset the fact of generating no overhead while switching between frequencies because it has been done in the hardware.

The next section describes our contributions.

III. CONTRIBUTION

As previously mentioned, the main idea of this paper is to emulate a CPU processor frequency based on periodic oscillations of frequencies between two levels of successive frequencies. This extension will suggest a way of decreasing power consumption in virtualized systems while keeping good VM performance. The next section will expound our approach and the implementation we made.

A. Our appraoch

Our approach is two folds: (1) To determine the exact processor frequency need by the current load and (2) to emulate it if necessary.

Let's assume a host with several VMs running on it. Suppose that they generate a global load of W_{host}. Consider that we need our CPU to be running at processor frequency of f_{host} to satisfy the current load (W_{host}). However, the desired processor frequency f_{host} is not present among the available processor frequencies of our host. This frequency need to be emulated.

A weighted average can be defined as an average in which each quantity to be averaged is assigned a weight. These weightings determine the relative importance of each quantity on the average. Weightings are the equivalent of having that many similar items with the same value involved in the average. Indeed, the emulation of CPU processor is based on weighted average of CPU frequency around the frequency to emulate. Although it is possible to determine in advance the neighboring processor frequencies, the computation of the execution time for each of them is not realistic.

Firstly, we need to determine the required frequency and later the both frequencies around the desired one. Assume that f_{high} and f_{low} are the frequency above and below the desired frequency respectively. To emulate f_{host}, we need to compute our load during t_{high} at f_{high} and during t_{low} at f_{low} so that the required frequency f_{host} is the weighted-average of f_{high} with t_{high} as weight and f_{low} with t_{low} as weight. It means that:

$$f_{host} = \frac{(f_{high} \times t_{high}) + (f_{low} \times t_{low})}{t_{high} + t_{low}} \quad (1)$$

Unfortunately, it is not possible to determine beforehand the exact execution times allowing to fulfill the equation 1. Instead of considering t_{high} and t_{low} as the execution time, we exploited it as the occurrence count. Meaning that to emulate f_{host}, the processor needs to be executed t_{high} times in higher frequency f_{high} and t_{low} times in lower frequency f_{low}.

It is important to note that, the real execution time at each processor frequency level can be computed as follows: $NumberOccur \times TickDuration$. Where $NumberOccur$ represents either t_{high} or t_{low} and $TickDuration$ the duration of each tick of reconfiguration.

To validate this assumption, let's consider the small example of II-B. By executing our processor, once on the lower frequency (that means at 1.862 Ghz) and once on the higher frequency (that means 1.995 Ghz), we will obtain the required frequency (1.9285 Ghz).
It means that: $f_{host} = \frac{1.995 \times 1 + 1.862 \times 1}{1+1} = 1.9285$

As aforementioned, the number of executions at each processor frequency cannot be known at the beginning of the experiments. It must be dynamically computed.

The next section presents our implementation.

B. Implementation

In this section, we address the design and the implementation choices of our frequency emulator, and the conditions of his exploitation.

Our implementation is two folds: (1) checking the appropriate processor frequency for the current load and (2) emulating If it is not existing.

1) Appropriate processor frequency: By default DVFS advertises a discrete range of processor frequencies. It means that, only a fixed and predefined number of processor frequencies are available.

To fulfill the first aspect of our work (determine the adequate frequency), we assume that, on each processor, it is possible to have a continuous range of frequencies. Knowing that the difference between two successive frequencies is practically identical, we virtually subdivided them into 3 (value obtained thanks to analysis and successive experiments). Indeed, this subdivision allowed the obtaining of the more moved closer frequencies. This nearness at the level of the frequencies so allowed to satisfy at best the processor's loads.

Assuming that the frequency range is now continuous, it is then always possible to have a precise processor frequency for a given load. The return of the suitable processor frequency is made according to the frequency ratio presented in our proposal in [8].

Indeed, at each tick of the scheduler, a monitoring module gathers the current CPU load of each VM. It then aggregates the total Absolute load of all the VM and computes the new processor frequency and the frequencies surrounding it, as depicted in the algorithm below (Listing 1) where

- *LFreq[]*: represents a table of 3 processor frequencies classified as follows: the required frequency and the surrounding ones (higher and lower respectively)
- *VFreq*: value obtained after the division of the interval between consecutive frequencies by 3. It is used to obtain some virtual processor frequencies.
- *Freq[]*: represents the available processor frequencies. The table is sorted in descending order.

We iterate on the processor frequencies (line 2). Following our assumption regarding frequencies (it will be validated in section IV-B1), we compute for each frequency the frequency ratio (line 3) and check if the computing capacity of the processor at that frequency can absorb the current absolute load (line 6). If the current frequency can not satisfy the load, we iterate on virtual processor frequencies (line 22 to line 29).

```
1 void computeNewFreq(int LFreq[], int VFreq) {
2 for (i=1; i<=fmin; i++) {
3   int ratio = Freq[i]/Freq[1];
4   int NFreq;
5
6   if(ratio * 100 < Absolute_load){
7     if ((i == 1) || (i == fmin){
8       LFreq[0] = LFreq[1] = LFreq[2] = Freq[i];
9     }
10    else{
11      LFreq[0]= Freq[i] + VFreq;
12      LFreq[1]= Freq[i-1];
13      LFreq[2]= Freq[i];
14    }
15  }
16  else{
17    NFreq= Freq[i] - VFreq;
18    LFreq[1] = Freq[i];
19    LFreq[2] = Freq[i+1];
20    ratio = NFreq/Freq[1];
21
22    while (ratio * 100 > ratio){
23      if (NFreq != Freq[i+1]){
24        NFreq -= VFreq;
25        ratio = NFreq/Freq[1];
26      }
27      else
28        break;
29    }
30    if (ratio * 100 < Absolute_load){
31      NFreq += VFreq;
32      if (NFreq == Freq[i]){
33        LFreq[1] = LFreq[2] = Freq[i];
34      }
35      LFreq[0] = NFreq;
36    }
37    }
38 }
```

Listing 1. Algorithm for computing the adequate processor frequency and the surrounding frequencies

By the end of the algorithm, if the required frequency is not among the known frequency of the processor, it is immediately emulated.

2) Processor frequency emulation: The emulation is based on the cumulative functions principle. It is convenient to describe data flows by means of the cumulative function f(t), defined as the number of elements seen on the flow in time interval [0, t]. By convention, we take f(0) = 0, unless otherwise specified. Function f is always wide-sense increasing, it means that $f(s) \leq f(t)$ for all $s \leq t$.

Suppose 2 wide-sense increasing functions f and g, the notation $f + g$ denotes the point-wise sum of functions f and g.

$$(f + g)(t) = f(t) + g(t) \qquad (2)$$

Notation $f \leq (=, \geq)\ g$ means that $f(t) \leq (=, \geq)\ g(t)$ for all t [14].

To exploit this notion, we defined 3 cumulative frequency functions: $CumF_{high}(t)$, $CumF_{low}(t)$ and $CumF_{host}(t)$. Where $CumF_{high}(t)$, $CumF_{low}(t)$ and $CumF_{host}(t)$ represent the functions for the higher processor frequency , the lower and the required processor frequency respectively. In our case, we defined the cumulative frequency corresponding to a particular value as the sum of all the frequencies up to and including that value. Meaning that: $CumF_{high}(t) = \sum_{k=0}^{t} f_{high}$.

At each tick of the scheduler and for each frequency involved (including the emulated frequency) in the emulation of the frequency, we compute its cumulative frequency (Listing 2). The computation of each cumulative frequency is executed as follow:

- Initially, the cumulative frequencies functions are equal to zero (their initial value). This value is reinitialized when the current load need a different frequency or when the current one is already emulated (line 17),
- At each tick, the cumulative frequency of the emulated frequency ($CumF_{host}(t)$) is incremented by its value: $CumF_{host}(t) += f_{host}$ (line 7 and line13),
- At each tick, only one frequency is set (either f_{high} or f_{low}). The choice of the frequency is carried out as follows:
  - The sum of $CumF_{high}(t)$ and $CumF_{low}$ is computed according to the equation 2 and the result is compared to $CumF_{host}(t)$ (line 3),
  - If the sum is lower than $CumF_{host}(t)$, then the processor frequency is set to f_{high} during the next quantum (line 6),
  - Else, if the sum is higher than $CumF_{host}$, the processor frequency is set to f_{low} during the next quantum (line 12),
  - If both are equal, the desired frequency was emulated and the different cumulative frequencies are reinitialized (line 17).

Through these iterations and these oscillations, we managed to emulate our desired frequency. It should be mentioned that, the emulated frequency and the neighboring frequencies are obtained with the algorithm presented in Listing 1.These later (*table LFreq[]*) are passed as a parameter to the algorithm below.

For instance, if we consider our example of section II-B, the goal was to emulate a processor frequency of 1.9285 Ghz. The surrounding frequencies are 1.995 Ghz and 1.862 Ghz. The execution of the algorithm of Listing 2 is as follows (Table I):

Init.	CumFH = CumFL = CumF = SumFreq = 0 cpuid = 0 ; NumbFH = NumFL = 0 LFreq[0]=1.9285; LFreq[1]=1.995; LFreq[2]=1.862
Step 1	SetFreq(0, LFreq[1]); CumFL = 0 CumFH = 1.995 ; CumF = 1.9285 NumbFH = 1;NumFL = 0 ; SumFreq= 1.995
Step 2	SumFreq ¿ CumF ⇒ SetFreq(0, LFreq[2]); CumFL = 1.862 ; NumFL = 1; CumFH = 1.995 CumF = 3.857 ; NumbFH = 1, SumFreq = 3.857
Step 3	SumFreq = CumF ⇒ Init NumFL = 1 and NumFH = 1

TABLE I. ALGORITHM VALIDATION

This execution validates the number of time needed to emulate 1.9285 Ghz as presented in section III-A.

```
1  void EmulateFrequency(int LFreq[], int CumFH,int CumFL,
       int CumF,int cpuid) {
2    int SumFreq;
3    SumFreq = CumFH + CumFL;
4
5    if (SumFreq < CumF){
6      SetFreq(cpuid,LFreq[1]);
7      CumF += LFreq[0];
8      CumFH += LFreq[1];
9    }
10   else{
11     if (SumFreq > CumF){
12       SetFreq(cpuid,LFreq[2]);
13       CumF += LFreq[0];
14       CumFL += LFreq[2];
15     }
16     else{
17       CumF = CumFH = CumFL = 0;
18     }
19   }
20 }
```

Listing 2. Emulate processor frequency

During this execution, we remind that there is a trigger in charge of the computation of the absolute load and the notification of the current desired frequency. This situation also leads to a reinitialization of all the cumulative frequencies value.

The next section presents some experiments to validate our proposal.

IV. Verification of our Proposal

We previously presented our approach and its implementation in the default Xen credit scheduler. In this section, we will present the experiment environment, the application scenario and some experiments to validate our proposition.

A. Experiment environment and scenario

Our experiments were performed on a DELL Optiplex 755, with an Intel Core 2 Duo 2.66GHz with 4G RAM. We run a Linux Debian Squeeze (with the 2.6.32.27 kernel) in a single processor mode. The Xen hypervisor (in his 4.1.2 version) is used as virtualization solution. The evaluation described below was performed with an application which computes an approximation of π. This application is called π-*app*. In this scenario, we aim at measuring an execution time.

B. Verification

1) Proportionality: In our validation, we rely on one main assumption: proportionality of frequency and performance. This property means that if we modify the frequency of the processor, the impact on performance is proportional to the change of the frequency.

This proportionality is defined by:

$$\frac{F_i}{F_{max}} = \frac{T_{max}}{T_i} \tag{3}$$

which means that if we decrease the frequency from F_{max} down to F_i, the execution time will proportionally increase from T_{max} to T_i. For instance, if F_{max} is 3000 and F_i is 1500, the frequency ratio is 0.5 which means that the processor is running 50% slower at F_i compared to F_{max}. So if we consider an application that runs in 10 mn at F_{max}, the same application will be completed at $\frac{10}{0.5} = 20mn$ at F_i.

To validate this proportionality rule, we conducted the following experiment. We ran different π-app workloads at different processor frequencies and measured the execution times, allowing us to verify the proportionality of frequency ratios and execution time ratios. Figure 1 gives some of the results we obtained, which shows that frequency ratios and execution time ratios are very close, as assumed in equation 3.

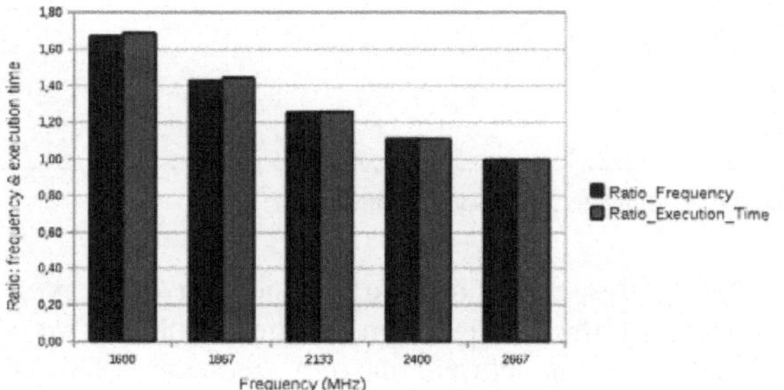

Fig. 1. Proportionality of frequency and execution time

2) Validation: Our textbed advertises the following processor frequency: 2.66GHz, 2.40GHz, 2.13GHz, 1,86GHz and 1.60GHz.

The first part of our validation consists on validate our approach of emulation. For this validation, we executed our π-*app* application initially at 2.4 Ghz. Based on our proposal, we will execute the same computation by emulating the frequency 2.4 Ghz. We started by a well-known frequency for this workshop, but others experiences not presented here emulate the non-existent frequency.

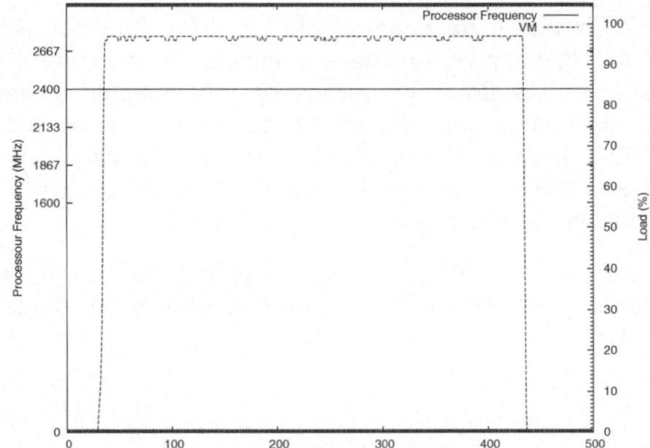

Fig. 2. Execution of π-*app* at 2.4Ghz

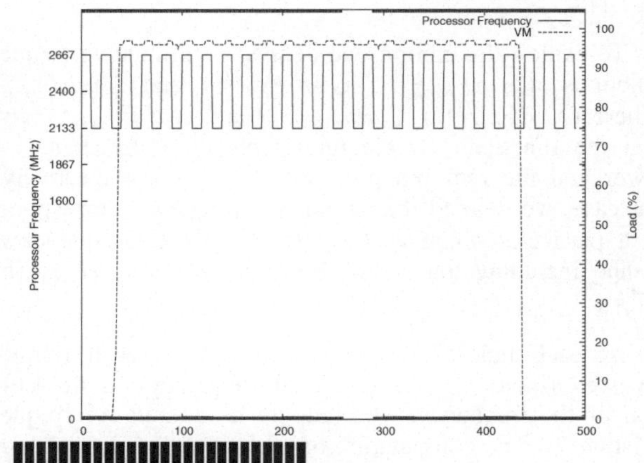

Fig. 3. Emulation of 2.4Ghz with oscillations

According to figure 2, the execution time of the π-*app* is about 410 Units. While emulating the same processor frequency, we obtained an execution time of 415 Units, as depicted by the figure 3. Based on this first use case, we can validate our approach. Furthermore, with similar experiences (not presented here), we have proved that the oscillation of the frequency in non intrusive.

The second part consists of validating the emulation of a non-existent frequency. We executed our π-*app* application of the maximum frequency (figure 4)and we recorded its execution time for future comparisons (*Cf. Table II*). Then, we choose two of our virtual processor frequencies (2.222 Ghz and 2.576 GHz); we have emulated them to execute our application (respectively figure 5 and figure 6). Their execution time is used for comparison with the expected execution time according to our proportionality rule (*Cf. Table II*). The expected time formula is: $T_i = \frac{F_{max} \times T_{max}}{F_i}$

Thanks to this scenario, we can validate our implementation approach. After execution, we can conclude that the real execution time are almost equal to the expected time. Further evaluations are to be done in order to identify the possible weaknesses/advantages of this proposal.

The next section presents the related works.

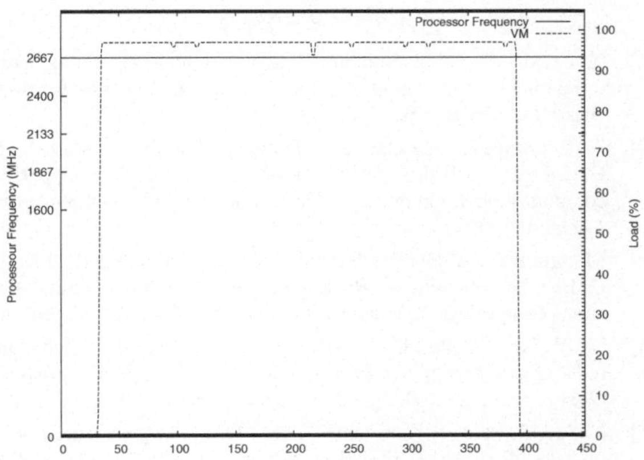

Fig. 4. Execution of π-*app* at maximum frequency

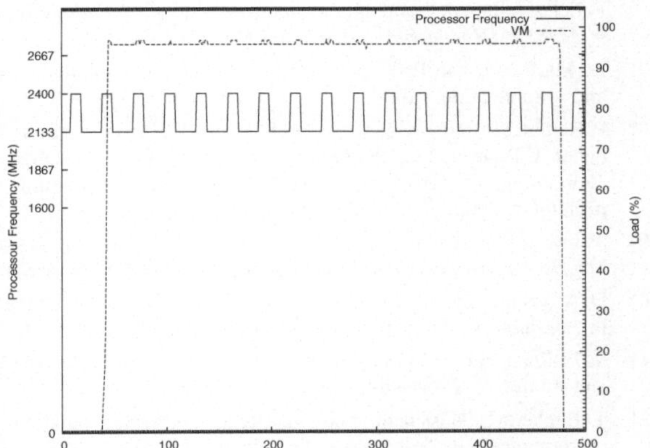

Fig. 5. Execution of π-*app* at emulated frequency 2.22Ghz

V. Related works

Numerous research projects have focused on optimization of the operating cost of data centers and/or cloud computers. Most of them concerned efficient power consumption [15]. Proposed solutions are based on either virtualization or DVFS.

In virtualized environment, power reduction is made possible through servers' consolidation and live migration. Classic

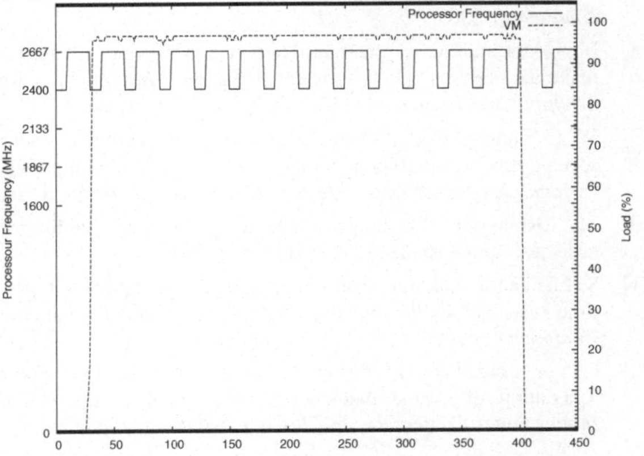

Fig. 6. Execution of π-*app* at 2.578Ghz

Frequency (GHz)	Execution Time (s)	Expected time (s)
2.667	108.65	
2.222	131.52	$T_i = \frac{2.667 \times 108.65}{2.222} = 130.41$
2.578	112.79	$T_i = \frac{2.667 \times 108.65}{2.578} = 112.40$

TABLE II. Execution time results

consolidation consists on gathered multiples VMs (according to their load) on top of a reduced number of physical computers [16].

In [17], Verma et al. aims at minimizing power consumption using consolidation after server workload analysis. They design two new consolidation approaches based respectively on, peak cluster load and correlation between applications before consolidating. Mueen et al. Strategy for power reduction consists in categorizing servers in pools according to their workload and usage. After categorizing, server consolidation is executed on all categories based on their utilization ratio in the data center [18].

As for the live migration, it consists of migrating a VM from a physical host to another without shutting down the VM. Korir et al [19] proposes a secure solution of power reduction based on live migration and server consolidation. Their security constraints are related to VM migration. Indeed, critical challenge of VM live migration appears when VM is still running when migration is in process. Well known attacks, such as Time-of-heck to time-of-use (TOCTTOU) [20] and replay attack, can be launched. In their solution, they design a live migration solution capable of avoiding VM to be exposed to eventual attacks.

One of the most rising approaches in power reduction is *Dynamic voltage and frequency scaling(DVFS)* [21], where voltage/frequency can be dynamically modified according to the CPU load. In [22], the authors design a new scheduling algorithm to allocate VMs in a DVFS-enabled cluster by dynamically scaling the voltage. Precisely, Laszewski et al. minimizes the voltage of each processor of physical machine by scaling down their frequency. In addition, they schedule the VMs on those lower voltage processors while avoiding to scale physical machine to high voltage.

In general, those previous approaches only are focused on well-known processor frequency. In [12], Blucher et al. suggests some approaches of the CPU performance emulator. Precisely, they propose and evaluate three approaches named as : CPU-Hogs, Fracas and CPU-Gov. CPU-Hogs consists of a CPU-burner process which burn and degrades the initial CPU processor according to a predefined percentage. CPU-Hogs has the disadvantage of being responsible for deciding when CPUs will be available for user processes. With Fracas, every decision is made by the scheduler. With Fracas, one CPU-intensive process is started on each core. Their scheduling priorities are then carefully defined so that they run for the desired fraction of time. CPU-Gov is a hardware based solution base. It consists on leveraging the hardware frequency scaling to provide emulation by switching between the two frequencies that are directly lower and higher than the requested emulate.

Although, those approaches are related to the CPU performance, they aim at emulating a predefined known processor frequency. Concretely, their goal is the answer this question: Given a CPU (characterized by its CPU performance for example), how can we emulate another CPU with a precise characteristics? Their emulation is done once and experiments are executed on it. In our case, it consists of a real-time emulation of CPU and it constitutes a base for an energy aware resources management.

VI. Conclusion and perspectives

With the emergence of cloud computing environments, large scale hosting centers are being deployed and the energy consumption of such infrastructures has become a critical issue. In this context, two main orientations have been successfully followed for saving energy:

- Virtualization which allows to safely host several guest operating systems on the same physical machines and more importantly to migrate guest OS between machines, thus implementing server consolidation,
- DVFS which allows adaptation of the processor frequency according to the CPU load, thus reducing power usage.

We observe that DVFS is mainly used, but still generates a waste of energy. In fact, the DVFS frequency scaling policies are based on advertised processor frequency. By default and thanks to the ondemand governor, it scales up or down the processor frequency according to the current load and the different predefined threshold (up and down). However, the set of frequency constitutes a discrete range of frequency. In this case, the frequency required for a specific load will almost be scaled to a frequency higher than expected; which leads to a non-efficient use of energy.

In this paper, we proposed a technique which addresses this issue. With our approach, we are able to determine and allocate a more precise processor frequency according to the current load. We subdivided the interval between two frequencies of the processor into tinier virtual frequencies. This leads to simulate a continuous processor frequency range. With this configuration and the ratio proportionality rule, it is thus almost possible to set the suitable frequency for a given load. Furthermore, thanks to oscillations, made possible through the principle of cumulative frequency, between the frequencies surrounding the desired one, it was possible to emulate a non-existent frequency.

Our proposal was implemented in the Xen hypervisor running with its default Credit scheduler. Different scenarios were used to validate our assumptions and our proposal.

Our main perspective is to sustain this proposal with a real world benchmark before a complete validation. Furthermore, we aim to investigate and address the issue of energy conserving while eventually exploiting this operation.

VII. Acknowledgement

The work presented in this article benefited from the support of ANR (Agence Nationale de la Recherche) through the Ctrl-Green project.

References

[1] Y. Ezaki and H. Matsumoto, "Integrated management of virtualized infrastructure that supports cloud computing: Serverview resource orchestrator," *Fujitsu Sci. Tech. J.*, vol. 47, no. 2, 2011.

[2] A. J. Young, R. Henschel, J. T. Brown., G. von Laszewski, J. Qiu, and G. C. Fox, "Analysis of virtualization technologies for high performance computing environments," in *IEEE International Conference on Cloud Computing*, 2011.

[3] M. Armbrust, A. Fox, R. Griffith, A. D. Joseph, R. Katz, A. Konwinski, G. Lee, D. Patterson, A. Rabkin, I. Stoica, and M. Zaharia, "A view of cloud computing," *Communications of the ACM*, vol. 53, no. 4, 2010.

[4] M. Weiser, B. Welch, A. Demers, and S. Shenker, "Scheduling for reduced cpu energy," in *Proceedings of the 1st USENIX conference on Operating Systems Design and Implementation*, 1994.

[5] E. Seo, S. Park, J. Kim, and J. Lee, "Tsb: A dvs algorithm with quick response for general purpose operating systems," *Journal of Systems Architecture*, vol. 54, no. 1-2, 2008.

[6] D. Gmach, J. Rolia, L. Cherkasova, G. Belrose, T. Turicchi, and A. Kemper, "An integrated approach to resource pool management: Policies, efficiency and quality metrics," in *IEEE International Conference on Dependable Systems and Networks*, 2008.

[7] D. Marinescu and R. Krger, "State of the art in autonomic computing and virtualization," 2007.

[8] P. Barham, B. Dragovic, K. Fraser, S. Hand, T. Harris, A. Ho, R. Neugebauer, I. Pratt, and A. Warfield, "Xen and the art of virtualization," in *Proceedings of the nineteenth ACM symposium on Operating systems principles*, 2003.

[9] "Vmware esx web site." [Online]. Available: http://www.vmware.com/products/vsphere/esxi-and-esx/index.html

[10] D. Miyakawa and Y. Ishikawa, "Process oriented power management," in *International Symposium on Industrial Embedded Systems*, 2007.

[11] V. Pallipadi and A. Starikovskiy, "The ondemand governor: past, present and future," in *Proceedings of Linux Symposium, vol. 2*, 2006.

[12] T. Buchert, L. Nussbaum, and J. Gustedt, "Accurate emulation of CPU performance," in *8th International Workshop on Algorithms, Models and Tools for Parallel Computing on Heterogeneous Platforms*, 2010.

[13] M. F. Dolz, J. C. Fernández, S. Iserte, R. Mayo, and E. S. Quintana-Ortí, "A simulator to assess energy saving strategies and policies in hpc workloads," *ACM SIGOPS Operating Systems Review*, vol. 46, no. 2, 2012.

[14] J.-Y. L. Boudec and P. Thiran, *Network calculus: a theory of deterministic queuing systems for the internet.* LNCS 2050, Springer-Verlag, 2001.

[15] M. Poess and R. O. Nambiar, "Energy cost, the key challenge of today's data centers: a power consumption analysis of tpc-c results," *Proceedings of the VLDB Endowment*, vol. 1, no. 2, 2008.

[16] W. Vogels, "Beyond server consolidation," *ACM Queue magazine*, vol. 6, no. 1, 2008.

[17] A. Verma, G. Dasgupta, T. K. Nayak, P. De, and R. Kothari, "Server workload analysis for power minimization using consolidation," in *Proceedings of the 2009 conference on USENIX Annual technical conference*, 2009.

[18] M. Uddin and A. A. Rahman, "Server consolidation: An approach to make data centers energy efficient and green," *International Journal of Scientific and Engineering Research*, vol. 1, no. 1, 2010.

[19] W. C. Sammy Korir, Shengbing Ren, "Energy efficient security preserving vm live migration in data centers for cloud computing," *International Journal of Computer Science Issues*, vol. 9, no. 3, 2012.

[20] M. Bishop and M. Dilger, "Checking for race conditions in file accesses," in *Computing Systems*, vol. 2, 1996.

[21] S. Lee and T. Sakurai, "Run-time voltage hopping for low-power real-time systems," in *Proceedings of the 37th Annual Design Automation Conference*, 2000.

[22] G. von Laszewski, L. Wang, A. Younge, and X. He, "Power-aware scheduling of virtual machines in dvfs-enabled clusters," in *IEEE International Conference on Cluster Computing*, 2009.

Actions, Objects, and Subjects

Hannu-Matti Järvinen Department of Pervasive Computing, Tampere University of Technology, Finland

Abstract— *This paper proposes an action-oriented computational model to be used as the low-level implementation of programs, hence effectively omitting processes. The benefits of the model are that concurrent execution, mutual exclusion, and synchronisation are automatically provided without explicit programming, messages are not needed between executing bodies, deadlocks do not exist at the action level, and the system uses implicitly as many parallel execution units as possible.*

However, action orientation is not a natural way to think for humans. Therefore, also subjects, which are objects providing liveness, are introduced to make programming sequential, but still making it easy to implement the program as actions, hence getting the benefits listed above.

Keywords: Concurrent languages, concurrent programming, parallel processors

1. Introduction

Concurrent execution has become a more and more important part of software. Many systems are distributed and processors have several cores. Traditionally, each process computes one task, and in some cases, interacts with other processes or threads. This interaction may take place as common variables, causing critical sections to appear, or by message passing, where messages carry data from process to process. Anyway, introducing concurrency causes needs for mutual exclusion and synchronisation mechanisms, and creates problems like starvation and deadlock.

To overcome the problems caused by concurrency, programming languages offer concepts like monitors, message passing, channels, futures, or rendez-vous. However, the basic problems, i.e., mutual exclusion and synchronisation, still exist, and the programmers have to understand them to cope with them. In most cases, concurrency has to be programmed explicitly into programs, the main exception being parallel processing in scientific computing.

The action-oriented execution model used in this paper was independently suggested by Chandy and Misra as Unity [2], by Back and Kurki-Suonio as Joint Actions [1], and by Lamport as Temporal Logic of Actions (TLA) [8]. The model makes critical sections obsolete, and hence also mutual exclusion. The model also has a built-in synchronisation mechanism. These are evident benefits if compared with the traditional process-oriented execution model. However, although this model has been used in several research projects, the models have not been adopted in practical software production. There are probably two main reasons for that. First, humans tend to think causally and find causal relations even if there are none [6]. Using actions is in contradiction to this causality. Second, all these methods are intended for specification and the real implementation still has to be process-oriented. Since changing the program structure from action-oriented to process-oriented is not a trivial task and there are no tools to automatically do it, this may consume all benefits that action orientation can offer. In short, the action-oriented paradigms have been suggested for high-level specification, and the implementation is assumed to be process-oriented.

In this paper, a low-level action-oriented system is introduced with high-level sequential programming bodies, *subjects*. The benefits of the idea are that synchronisation and mutual exclusion is implicitly solved by the action-oriented model, but the programmer will still be able to describe the system as programs where statements have the human-expeced causal relationships.

This paper is organised as follows: First, action system with objects are discussed, then action execution at low level is introduced, and before brief discussion subjects are described through an example.

2. Action-oriented execution model with objects

In action-oriented models, actions can be considered either state transitions from a state to another, or relations between two states. Hence, actions do not contain any memory, but the whole state of the computation is stored in variables. In contrast, in process-oriented systems the state of the computation is in the variables and program counters of the processes or threads. The DisCo specification language uses the same model as [1], [2], and [8], but its variables are collected into objects [4]. The action-oriented approach is discussed in detail by Kurki-Suonio in [7].

2.1 Concurrent Actions

Actions alter the state, but do not consume time ideally. In TLA, an action A can be expressed as a predicate between two states, e.g. $s[[A]]t$, where s and t are states. Starting from a state s_0, we can see a sequence of actions take place, forming a *behaviour*. Formally, a behaviour is an infinite sequence of states $\sigma = s_0, s_1, s_2, s_3...$

There is a non-stuttering[1] action between each state of

[1]Stuttering actions do not alter the interesting set of variables; they can be added anywhere. Altering the set of interesting variables, alters the set of stuttering actions, too, and an alternative behavior is constructed.

a behaviour. If two actions access distinct sets of variables, their order can be changed without violating TLA formulas, since TLA does not have operators *next step* or *previous step*. Hence, behaviours $\sigma_0 = s_0, s_1, s_2, s_3, ...$ and $\sigma_1 = s_0, s_2, s_1, s_3, ...$ are different, but there are no TLA predicates that can distinguish these behaviours from each other (note that if the sets of accessed variables are not distinct, this is probably not the case, but then action guards may prevent either behaviour).

In action-oriented models, therefore, concurrency is modelled by nondeterministic selection of actions to be executed. Further, actions accessing distinct variables can be executed concurrently, since we can serialise them in any order. To be precise, we can execute actions concurrently, if the sets of assigned variables are distinct and action do not refer to variables assigned to by other actions. Formally, if V_{A_a} is the set of variables assigned (and referred) to by action A, and V_{A_r} is the set of variables referred only by action A, then parallel execution is possible for a set of *distinct* actions $\mathbf{S}$, where

$$\forall A, B \in \mathbf{S}, A \neq B :$$
$$V_{A_a} \cap V_{B_a} = \emptyset \wedge V_{A_a} \cap V_{B_r} = \emptyset \wedge V_{B_a} \cap V_{A_r} = \emptyset \quad (1)$$

This means that even if the action models are originally sequential, we can execute actions concurrently, provided that (1) holds for each set of actions executed concurrently. Since actions do consume time in real computation, this might have other consequences as well, but they are not discussed in this paper. When variables are collected into objects, (1) can be used for objects instead of variables. In some cases, this may appear as unnecessarily strict, but this is good enough for many practical purposes.

In this paper, the action-oriented execution model is used as the lowest mechanism in computation instead of processes. Since the model allows concurrent execution of distinct actions, we get a system which can use as many parallel processing units as there are distinct actions enabled. There are huge benefits in this idea: without the concept of processes, programmers do not need to take care of mutual exclusion or synchronisation, deadlocks cannot happen at action level, and there is no need for message passing. All execution takes place in actions that alter the contents of objects that participate in them.

The basic components of the action-oriented execution model are objects and actions. In this paper, we use a model derived from DisCo [5]. Actions, objects, and their properties in this model are briefly introduced.

2.2 Objects

An object may contain any kind of data, data structures, containers, or combination of them. In this paper, objects are unnamed entities that contain data; from the programmer's point of view they can be considered record types.

Objects are usually created by the initialisation of the system. However, the model allows the creation and destruction of objects and actions during execution.

2.3 Actions

An action can be considered a potential state transition between two states determined by the objects of the system. The action has participants (objects) that participate in the action in *roles*, and two parts: a *guard* and a *body*. The guard indicates when the action can be selected for execution, i.e., the action is *enabled*. The body contains a piece of program code that is executed whenever the action is selected for execution. The participants are distinct, i.e., an object may participate in an action in one role only. In contrast to DisCo, syntactic actions are not models that introduce a set of TLA actions whose participants are computed in run-time, but actions have fixed participants and parameters that are given at the creation time.

Action guards and bodies may refer to the data of the action participants only. Any datatype can be part of an object. Since actions may not refer to data outside its participants, referencing through pointers or references is allowed only in those cases where the target data is also either a participant of the action or part of a participant object.

The action guards in Joint actions, Unity, TLA, and DisCo can be divided into three parts:

1) *Global part* that can refer to any variable or object in the system. The reference is possible by quantifications or closures.
2) *Common part* that can refer to the contents of several participants.
3) *Local part* that can refer to the contents of a single participant only.

Although a very powerful expression, global part of the guard is hard to implement and very inefficient if implemented. They are not included in the action model of this paper. Furthermore, action guards are syntactically separated to local and common parts to make the implementation of the scheduler more efficient. For example, the local part of the guard has to be evaluated only, if the contents of the participant are changed, and if any of local parts of the action guard is false, there is no use to evaluate the common part. Once evaluated, the value of the common part can be stored for further use until the contents of an action participant is changed.

2.4 Objects in Action-oriented Systems

In traditional object-oriented systems, classes contain both the data and the methods that access the data. This is illustrated on the left side of Figure 1. Whenever the values of objects are needed or updated, corresponding method is invoked. Method calls are indicated by arrows in Figure 1 to

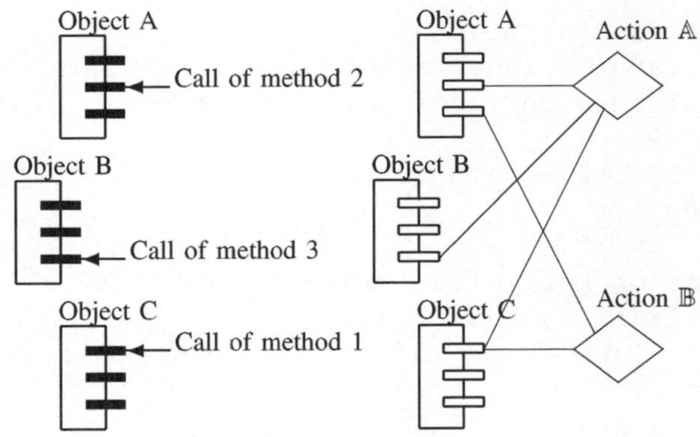

Fig. 1: Classes and methods (left), Classes and actions (right)

emphasise that an external caller is needed. The methods are printed in black, since normally their contents are private.

On the right side of Figure 1, the action 𝔸 (illustrated by a large diamond) contains the calls illustrated on the left side of the picture. Action 𝔹 is another action with two participants; it shares the first method of object C with action 𝔸. Methods are white, since they are programmed as part of the action. Although private implementations of methods could be used also with actions, in any case an action has to contain some code of its own to make the methods interact. An action may be selected for execution if it is *enabled*. Hence, an external caller is not needed and lines are used instead of arrays to emphasise this.

3. Action Execution

This part describes the high-level idea of execution where basic primitives are actions instead of processes. Without going to details, there exists an experimental environment where this model has been tested.

The system consists of a scheduling processor and n processing units that execute the actions. These can be traditional processors. For efficiency, they should be connected to each other by special hardware, but the experimental environment we have is built to run on a normal multiprocessor computer. The overall structure is illustrated in Figure 2.

The model works as follows: First, the scheduler selects a set of enabled actions from the action store to the action queue, remembering that actions to be selected shall be distinct from each other and actions already in the queue or in execution. Second, one of the processing units takes an action description from the queue, loads the action code and accessed objects into its local memory[2], and executes the action. Third, when the execution is finished, altered objects are copied to the common memory, and action is returned to the action store.

[2]Loading is not needed if the processors have access to the common memory.

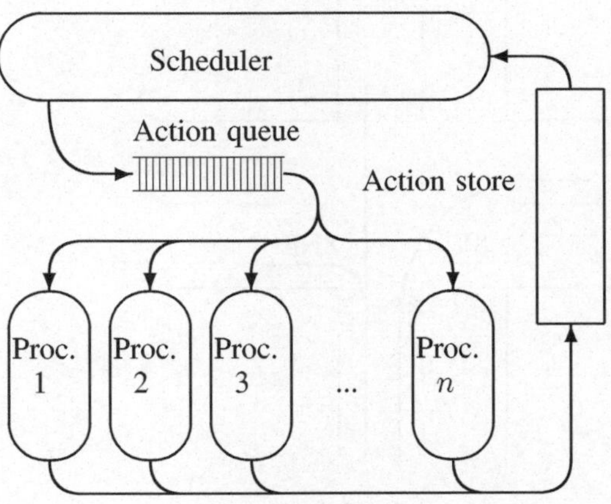

Fig. 2: The overall structure of action execution.

In short, synchronisation conditions are expressed by action guards, and mutual exclusion is automatically taken care of by the scheduler. This means that the basic primitives for concurrent execution are handled by hardware and the scheduler instead of the programmer, much like how the virtual memory is taken care of by hardware and the operating system instead of manual overlay by programmers. Note that the code to be executed is not affected when processors are added or removed.

3.1 Crossing roads

An example of crossing roads is used to show how action-oriented approach works. Consider a crossing of two roads, one north to south and the other west to east.

There is a lane to go forward or turn right and a separate lane of its own to turn left, all of these for each direction. Each lane has a corresponding traffic light, as illustrated in Figure 3.

The lanes are named as follows: the first letter gives the approaching direction, and second and third letters give the destination. So, SW stands for from south to west, and SNE from south to north and east. One possible set of pairs that are safe to have green lights on at the same time is NSW and SNE, WES and EWN, NE and SW, and WN and ES. Running this sequence will eventually give all directions a green light.

There are three classes that can be identified: a traffic light, a lane, and a car. The car is not part of the system but an external object. The lane is an abstraction that is connected to traffic lights: the traffic light can be green or yellow only if the lane is safe, i.e. all lanes crossing the lane have the corresponding traffic light red.

The simplest class is *Lane*. It has to contain a variable indicating if the lane is safe or not. Class *Traf_light* includes

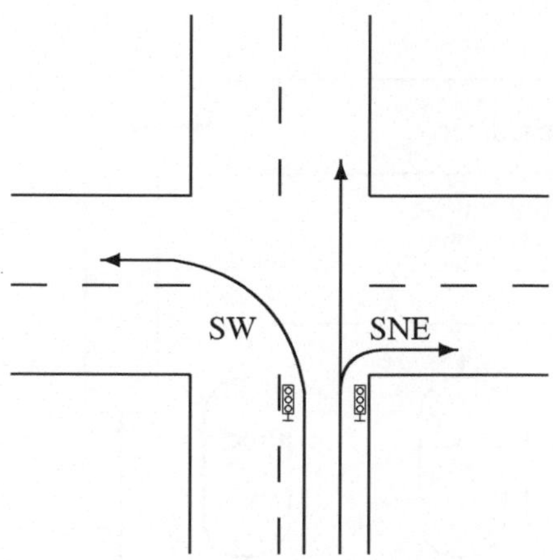

Fig. 3: Crossing with lanes SW and SNE and their signals illustrated.

```
class Lane is
  safe: Boolean:=false;
end;

class Traf_light is
  lamp: (RED, YELLOW, GREEN):=RED;
end;
```

Fig. 4: Classes Lane and Traf_light.

a state variable that corresponds to the colour of the traffic light. Classes *Lane* and *Traf_light* could be combined to one class since they are closely connected, but this would make the objects less intuitive. The classes are given in Figure 4.

Actions *set_red*, *set_green*, *set_yellow*, *free_lane*, and *reserve_lane* are using these classes. The first four actions have participants of the given classes only and they are shown in Figure 5.

Action *set_green* puts the green light on, if the corresponding *Lane* is safe. Action participants are defined between keywords *is* and *body* of the action. Expression after participant name list (after the colon) is the local guard of the participant.

Note that the connection between participants *lane* and *light* could be expressed in the common guard using identities (e.g. lane.id=light.id), but since these relations never change, the condition is left out, and actions are created for only those pairs of lanes and traffic lights that are connected.

Action *set_yellow* is enabled, if the traffic light is green and given time have been elapsed. It has only one participant, *green_on*, indicating the time green light should be on. This value is given when the action is created. Function *timeout* returns true if given time has elapsed since last update of the object. This requires that also the time of the update is stored when updating an object. Action *set_red* is almost

```
action set_green is
  Lane as lane: safe;
  Traf_light as light: lamp=RED;
body
  light.lamp:=GREEN;
end;

action set_yellow(green_on: seconds) is
  Traf_light as light:
    lamp=GREEN and timeout(green_on);
body
  light.lamp:=YELLOW;
end;

action set_red (yellow_on: seconds) is
  Traf_light as light:
    lamp=YELLOW and timeout(yellow_on);
body
  light.lamp:=RED;
end;

action free_lane (margin: seconds) is
  Lane as lane: safe;
  readonly Traf_light as light:
    lamp=RED and timeout(margin);
body
  lane.safe:=false;
end;
```

Fig. 5: Actions set_green, set_yellow, set_red and free_lane.

identical to action *set_yellow*.

Action *free_lane* waits *margin* seconds after the execution of *set_red* to be sure that there are no cars on the lane before freeing it.

To enforce any sequence to go through all lanes, a control object is needed to guide the behaviour of action *reserve_line*. The control class has four states indicating the current phase of the system; this ensures all directions will get green light in a steady basis. The control class, action *reserve_line* are in Figure 6.

3.2 Initialisation

The initialisation code has to create the traffic lights, lanes, and actions. It is intended to be sequential code executed before the action system is invoked. Note that new actions and objects can be created and deleted also in run-time. The code in Figure 7 shows how the participants and parameters of actions are given static values in creation, hence making it possible to omit common parts of guards describing the relations between the objects.

This system will execute forever. In some cases execution will lead to a situation where no actions are enabled and the

```
type Safe_pairs is
  (NSW_SNE, NE_SW, WES_EWN, WN_ES);
class Control is
  state: Safe_pairs:=NSW_SNE;
end;

action reserve_lane
  (current, next: Safe_pairs) is
  Control as cont: state=current;
  readonly Lane as old_1, old_2:
    not safe;
  Lane as new_1, new_2: not safe;
body
  cont.state := next;
  new_1.safe, new_2.safe:=true, true;
end;
```

Fig. 6: Action reserve_line

```
initially
  nsw, sne, ne, sw, wes,
    ewn, wn, es: Lane;   // Creates lanes
  tl_nsw, tl_sne, tl_ne, tl_sw, tl_wes,
    tl_ewn, tl_wn, tl_es: Traf_light;
  control: Control;
  // Some constant values
  green_on, yellow_on: seconds:=20, 5;
  margin: seconds:=8;
  // Create actions for a lane
  create set_red(yellow_on, nse);
  create set_yellow(green_on, nse);
  create set_green(nse, tl_nse);
  create free_lane(margin, nse, tl_nse);
  // etc. for each lane
  create reserve_lane(NSW_SNE, NE_SW,
                      nsw, sne, ne, sw);
  // etc. for each safe pair
end initially;
```

Fig. 7: Initialisation code for the action version

system terminates. This means that deadlocks are possible at the application level although at action level the deadlocks caused by the mutual exclusion of objects as resources are prevented.

4. Subjects

As mentioned in the introduction, the action-oriented view is not close to the way humans think. For example, reading and changing the algorithm that controls which lanes are given turn is not easy. Hence, even if the traditional problems of concurrency and scalability for n processors could be solved by actions, there is no much hope to alter the way

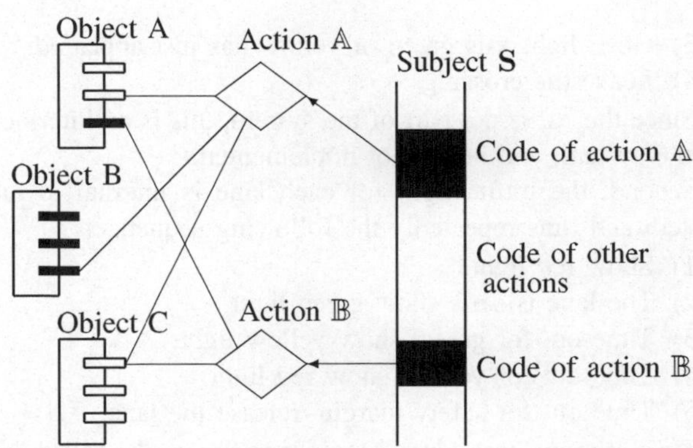

Fig. 8: Subjects versus actions and objects.

of human thinking. Virtual memory was referred to as an analogous example. It also gives a good next goal, since one cannot see from the source code if the application is made for a virtual memory computer or not. Unfortunately, action orientation abandons the basic abstraction of processes and use actions instead and this is too drastic a change to be completely hidden from the programmer.

To make programming for action systems closer to sequential thinking characteristic for humans, a concept of *subjects* is introduced. Note that although term *subject* is used, the model does not follow subject-oriented programming introduced in [3]. However, there are some similarities. In [3] subjects are different views to an object; in this paper, subjects are different views to a set of objects.

On the left side of Figure 8, there are the same actions and objects as were on the right side of Figure 1. On the right side of Figure 8 is a subject code, from which the actions are recognised and implemented. Note that there can be both private and open methods; however, their details are not it the scope of this paper.

In contrast to action-oriented systems, subjects provide an illusion of sequential behaviour; this is maintained by an implicit control object (not shown in Figure 8) and writing the code sequentially. The compiler recognises the boundaries of actions, and transforming this to an action system can be hidden from the programmer. Concurrency is implicit, if there are more than one subject in the system, and the programmer does not need to worry about the mutual exclusion or synchronisation of objects.

The example of crossing roads is revisited to illustrate how subject-oriented approach works. We can observe this example from three points of view. These views are first described informally as follows.

First, the car (or the driver) sees the crossing as the following sequence of events:

1) Approach the crossing and select correct lane x.
2) Arrive at the stop line of lane x. Stop if light x is red or yellow has been on for some time.

3) Go if light x is green or yellow has just appeared.
4) Leave the crossing.

Since the car is not part of the system, this is an interface of the system, and hence not implemented.

Second, the traffic light for each lane is internal to the system and runs repeatedly the following sequence:

1) Show red light.
2) The lane is safe, show green light.
3) Time out for green, show yellow light.
4) Time out for yellow, show red light.
5) Time out for safety margin, release the lane.

Third, the internal control logic may repeat the following sequence:

1) Wait lanes are free and reserve the first pair of lanes.
2) Wait lanes are free and reserve the second pair of lanes.
3) Wait lanes are free and reserve the third pair of lanes.
4) Wait lanes are free and reserve the fourth pair of lanes.

Naturally, the control logic could be much more sophisticated. For example, each step could check if there are cars approaching on the corresponding lane. However, we continue with this simple system.

We can identify the following objects: cars, traffic lights for each lane, and the lanes. Cars are not part of the implementation, and lanes and lights could be united, but since the lights are actually control objects (subjects) and lanes are mostly abstractions within the system, we keep them separate. Using these objects we can write subjects Traf_light and Control (Figure 9) from the informal description (the cars and initialisation of the system have been omitted to save space). Note that although class *Lane* of Figure 4 is used, the introduction of subject *Traf_light* makes separate class for traffic lights obsolete.

Each wait statement on Control and Traf_light can be represented as an action. For example, the first wait of Control could be transformed to the action *Control_1* in Figure 10 that resembles action *reserve_line* in Figure 6.

The detailed semantics of the programming language used for subjects is not in the scope of this paper. Actually, any object-oriented programming language will do, if *subjects* and statements *wait* and *collection* are added.

The *wait* statement means that the execution of the subject in that branch is stopped until the given condition is true. In translating to actions, the condition is used as the guard of an action and its statements form the action body.

The *collection* statement indicates alternatives that may take place; each of them is actually an action of its own, and if they are distinct, they can be executed in parallel. This statement was not needed in this example.

The following rules to transform sequential code of subjects to actions are created from the notes above.

1) Create a control object with a control variable for the subject.
2) The guard of the first action is a test if the control variable is in the initial state.

```
subject Traf_light (lane: Lane,
  green_on, yellow_on, margin: seconds)
is
  lamp: (RED, YELLOW, GREEN);
begin
  lamp:=RED;
  loop
    wait lane.safe then
      lamp:=GREEN;
    end;
    wait timeout(green_on) then
      lamp:=YELLOW;
    end;
    wait timeout(yellow_on) then
      lamp:=RED;
    end;
    wait timeout(margin) then
      lane.safe:=false;
    end;
  end loop;
end Traf_light;

subject Control (
  p1s, p1t, // pair 1: straight and turn
  p2s, p2t, p3s, p3t, p4s, p4t: Lane) is
begin   // Lanes are initially unsafe
  loop
    wait not (p4s.safe or p4t.safe) then
      p1s.safe, p1t.safe:=true, true;
    end;
    wait not (p1s.safe or p1t.safe) then
      p2s.safe, p2t.safe:=true, true;
    end;
    wait not (p2s.safe or p2t.safe) then
      p3s.safe, p3t.safe:=true, true;
    end;
    wait not (p3s.safe or p3t.safe) then
      p4s.safe, p4t.safe:=true, true;
    end;
  end loop;
end Control;
```

Fig. 9: Subjects Traf_light and Control

```
action Control_1 is
  readonly Lane as p4s, p4t: not safe;
  Lane as p1s, p1t;
  Control as cont: status=1;
begin
  p1s.safe, p1t.safe:=true, true;
  cont.status:=2;
end Control_1;
```

Fig. 10: Action Control_1 generated from subject Control

3) The body of the first action starts immediately after *begin*, and ends when a collection, wait, or a loop containing wait(s) is encountered.
4) A loop containing waits introduces a new control object that is used within the loop, applying these same rules. If the loop does not include waits, it is implemented as a traditional loop in the action body.
5) The condition of a wait becomes the guard of the next action.
6) The code until the next collection, wait, or loop containing wait(s) becomes the body of the action.
7) Add update code for the control variables into each action body, and the corresponding tests of the control variables to the action guards.

Actions can be automatically generated from the subject descriptions and directly executed by the action model computer described earlier as illustrated in Figure 8. The objects participating in actions can be resolved relatively easy by the compiler.

Subjects and objects are closely related. Objects provide room for local variables and methods associated with them; so do subjects, but they also make something happen. When methods describe potential things that can happen, i.e., safety properties, subjects also introduce liveness properties for the system, just like processes have implicit liveness properties.

5. Discussion and Conclusions

The action-oriented model can be used on top of a general purpose operating system as was done when the concept was tested by an experimental environment built on Posix threads interface. The experiments show that the action-oriented system is working in principle, but the existence of the operating system and its scheduler makes it impossible to determine if this paradigm is really competitive in comparison with a traditional process-oriented system. The experiments also indicate that action-oriented programs work logically equally well regardless of the number of processors available.

The model is expected to work better in specialised environments having multiple processors. Hence, actual hardware supporting the action orientation as shown in Figure 2 together with measurements are needed—in other words, the idea needs empirical results to support it.

The main difference with action orientation and most other approaches is to completely omit the idea of processes, and gather data to objects that participate in actions. In spite of the benefits of action systems, they are as such not very attractive, since they are in contradiction to the way humans think. Our thinking is based on causality, and we even tend to find causality when there is none. Hence, working with actions requires a lot of effort. Introducing subjects that describe the system from the viewpoints of active interfaces gives the programmer possibility to think causally, and makes it easy to implement the program as actions.

The proposed approach has several benefits:

1) implicit mutual exclusion
2) implicit synchronisation
3) the prevention of most of the potential deadlocks
4) less starvation possibilities
5) still sequential programming
6) power control is implemented easier.

Starvation and high-level deadlocks may still occur. These deadlocks are either programmed (i.e., the computations should terminate anyway) or high-level logical errors. Starvation cannot happen without mutual exclusion. Hence, it is possible, but its possibility can be considerably decreased by a good action scheduler.

The power control has not been mentioned before. Shortly, if a processor finds the queue empty, it can enter a power-saving mode. The scheduler can wake up processors if the queue is longer than the number of active processors.

The proposed subject-oriented programming idea hides the actions of action-oriented models, but does not harm the benefits of action orientation: implicit mutual exclusion and synchronisation, no low-level deadlocks and implicitly parallel execution whenever possible.

Overall, this approach seems to be very attractive especially in environments where computation power and efficient power control is needed. However, although tested in principle, it is still mostly an idea, which requires a lot of further research.

Acknowledgements

I want to thank professors Mikko Tiusanen, Tommi Mikkonen, and Kari Systä for their comments, and especially professor Shmuel Katz from Technion for his inspiring questions that started the way towards subjects.

References

[1] Back, R.J.R., Kurki-Suonio, R., Distributed co-operation with action systems. *ACM Transactions on Programming Languages and Systems 10*, 4 (Oct. 1988), pp. 513–554.

[2] Chandy, K.M., Misra, J., *Parallel Program Design: A Foundation.* Addison-Wesley, 1988.

[3] Harrison, W., Ossher, H. Subject-oriented programming: a critique of pure objects. *Proceedings of the eighth annual conference on Object-oriented programming systems, languages, and applications (OOPSLA '93).* ACM, New York, NY, USA, pp. 411–428. http://doi.acm.org/10.1145/165854.165932

[4] Järvinen, H.-M., Kurki-Suonio, R., DisCo specification language: marriage of actions and objects. *Proc. 11th International Conference on Distributed Computing.* Arlington, Texas, May 1991, IEEE Computer Society Press, 142–151.

[5] Järvinen, H.-M., *The Design of a Specification Language for Reactive Systems.* Doctoral thesis. Tampere University of Technology, 1992. ISBN 951–721–817–6.

[6] Kahneman, D., *Thinking Fast and Slow*, Macmillan, 2011. ISBN 978–1–4299–6935–2.

[7] Kurki-Suonio, R., *A Practical Theory of Reactive Systems*, Springer 2005. ISBN 3–540–23342–3.

[8] Lamport, L., *The temporal logic of actions.* Research Report 71, Digital systems Research Center, 1991.

Efficient Replacement Policy for Sub-Block Cache Architectures

Oluleye Olorode, Mehrdad Nourani
Department of Electrical Engineering, University of Texas, Dallas, TX, USA

Abstract - *In this paper, we present a replacement policy for use in sub-block memory system caches. Sub-block caches aim at reducing area overhead of tag RAMs in cache architectures. By merging multiple cache-lines (sub-blocks) to make up a wider cache-line, these sub-block caches are able to index multiple sub-blocks with a single tag line, thereby reducing the tag hardware overhead. However, this causes all sub-blocks indexed by a tag to be replaced or evicted together, which could degrade the performance of sub-block caches when compared with conventional caches. To address this drawback, we present a replacement policy that considers cache sub-block information in making replacement decisions. For experimentation and evaluation of this policy, we implemented a sub-block cache simulator by modifying the Simplescalar Toolset. Our extensive simulations indicate that sub-block caches using our proposed replacement policy reduce sub-blocking miss rate penalty by up to 34%.*

Keywords: memory; cache; replacement; performance.

1 Introduction

Increase in Microprocessor speed has exceeded the rate of improvement in Dynamic Random Access Memory (DRAM) speed in recent years [1]. Although there is a continued drive for better processor performance, memory systems have to be carried along to enable this improved performance. The widening performance gap between processors and Memories [2] created several challenges for computer designers. To solve this problem, designers turn to memory performance improvements which ultimately dictate the performance and power consumption of a processor. Caching is a common approach used to achieve memory system speed up, by storing data that has been recently used in a local memory. Using a large cache could increase the access hit rate, which in turn improves processor speed but this approach comes with a cost of increased hardware and higher energy consumption. As a result, there is always a trade-off in memory system design since not all accessed memory locations can be stored in faster memories such as caches. Current memory systems designed with SRAMs, DRAMs and/or CAMs [3,4], have not been able to catch up with processor performance. Attempting to cover this shortfall by just memory size increments incur significant hardware and power overhead as memory sizes increase.

Several architectures have been proposed [5] that attempt to increase cache performance without paying a huge price in hardware/energy overhead. One approach is requesting wider cache lines than needed from farther memories. Only the desired bytes are then selected using enable bits while the other bytes are cached for future usage. This approach requires wider buses at the different memory hierarchies. Alternatively, the wider block could be made up of smaller blocks that are allocated independent of each other. This approach, known as sub-blocking, allows the interfaces to retain smaller cache-block width and is completely transparent to software. For example, a cache with block size of 256-bytes could request only 64-bytes from next level cache at a time. These 64-byte sub-blocks (SB) can be allocated independently to the 256-byte cache block with individual valid bits to differentiate between the different fetched/allocated blocks. This is very similar to a conventional 4-way cache with 64-byte cache blocks except that the two (2) LSBs of the tag are not stored in the tag RAMs and fewer tag lines are required for indexing. These two LSB bits from an incoming cache access are used as index to the specific sub-block in the wider cache block. This process of grouping multiple sub-blocks to a single wider block is referred to as aggregation throughout this paper. Therefore, aggregates share a common tag. Figure 1 shows a simple example of a single cache way with four cache lines and four sub-blocks per cache line along with the corresponding valid bits.

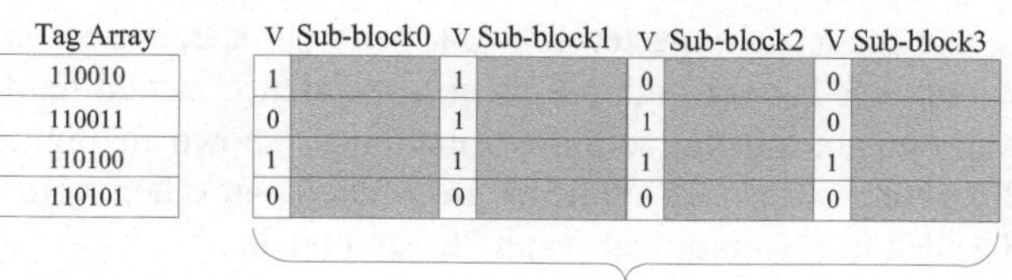

Figure 1: A Sub-block Cache with four cache lines

1.1 Motivation

Using additional DRAM cells to implement a large cache may appear as a simple solution to the memory bottleneck problem, but this would lead to other setbacks in the design, like large tag array sizes. For example, a 48-bit byte-addressable physical address access, to a 16-way set associative 1MB cache with 64-byte line size and 1024 sets requires 30 bit (i.e. approximately four bytes) per tag entry. This tag entry may require extra metadata (e.g., replacement bits, coherence state, and shared information) which could add up to 2 bytes in tag overhead. Therefore, at 6-bytes of tag overhead and 64-byte cache-lines, about 9.3% of the total on-chip storage is used for tag storage. This overhead could be significant in larger caches. For example a 1GB DRAM would have 96MB tag overhead. This large tag overhead has been observed by other researchers, and a common approach to reduce this overhead is cache line increase [24,25]. For example, using 4KB instead of 64-byte cache lines reduces the tag overhead by about 98%. This is because a single 6-byte tag used to index a 64-byte line can now be used as index to a 4KB line (i.e. 64*64-byte line). Very large cache lines are known to suffer from fragmentation problems; in the worst case, only a 64-byte sub-block will be used from each 4KB cache-line allocated. Also, moving 4KB data chunks at a time could cause significant bus contention off-chip, leading to substantial performance degradation throughout the cache hierarchy. Similarly, large cache-lines can cause severe false-sharing in multi-threaded applications [26] although the fragmentation problem is usually of a greater concern [27]. Moving unused blocks back and forth also wastes power and uses up bandwidth [28]. Supporting large cache-lines also has other challenges like mapping data across more than one physical DRAM row and timing constraints.

Sub-blocking has been shown to alleviate fragmentation and false sharing problems [29] and it is achieved by breaking a large cache-line/super-block (e.g. 4KB) to multiple smaller cache-lines/sub-blocks (e.g., 64 chunks of 64-byte). The entire cache-line is still indexed by a single tag entry, but additional valid and coherence bits are added for each sub-block. For example, using 3-bits for coherence and 1 valid bit in our previous example of 4KB line (64-byte sub-lines) leads to 64*4 (256) bits. This increases the overhead of the tag array compared to a single large cache-line approach, but offers about 92% tag array reduction when compared to a conventional cache with 64-byte lines. The sub-block cache consumes bandwidth and power to fetch only requested sub-blocks, compared to a large cache-line approach that transfers the entire cache-line. Sub-blocking still does not address the problem of tracking only a limited number of cache-lines. For workloads with low spatial locality, the large cache-lines can result in high miss rates. Selective caching of the most frequently used cache-lines can alleviate some of this effect [24, 30], but applications with large active working sets will still suffer. Therefore we explore a new replacement policy that uses sub-line information in addition to existing replacement policies to determine cache-line replacement.

Whenever a tag is present in the cache tag RAM and satisfies a new request, it is called a "Cache Hit". When this occurs, data is read directly from the indexed location in cache and is therefore faster than the case of a "Cache Miss", where the request must be forwarded to a slower (secondary) memory. The most common caching algorithms include First In First Out (FIFO), Last In First Out (LIFO), Least Recently Used (LRU), Most Recently Used (MRU), Least Frequently Used (LFU) and Most Frequently Used (MFU) [6]. Of the several replacement policies available, LRU is often regarded as the most efficient [7][8] and therefore the basis of the different replacement policies discussed in this paper. For ease of hardware implementation, Pseudo-LRU is often considered the best choice [31].

Since sub-block (SB) caches are capable of using a single tag to index multiple data blocks, conventional replacement (also called eviction) policies may significantly degrade the performance of SB caches, depending on the number of sub-blocks in each cache block. This is because replacement decision is at the cache-block/super-block granularity and such replacements do not consider the individual state of the sub-blocks that make up the larger/wider cache block. For example, the LRU cache-block of a set may contain four valid sub-blocks and another non LRU block of the same set may contain only one valid sub-block. Replacing one of the four sub-blocks in the LRU entry will require evicting or invalidating the other three valid entries because the tag has to be updated with the new entry which will render the existing tag entry invalid. This multiple sub-block evictions, based in LRU, could be more detrimental to cache performance than evicting a non LRU cache-block that contains a single valid sub-block. In this paper, we introduce a replacement policy that factors the degree of aggregation of a super-block in replacement, and we run simulation on CPU2006 benchmarks to show this new replacement policy outperforms existing policies in sub-block caches. Implementation details are summarized in Section 2.

For evaluating different cache eviction policies presented in this paper, we use existing LRU policy as reference. Firstly, we simulate a conventional LRU cache configuration with 64-byte lines, then with wider cache-lines and sub-blocking with full cache line/super-block evictions, and finally a sub-block cache using our newly proposed replacement policy. This approach enables us to quantify the performance degradation due to sub-blocking and compare with the performance regained by our proposed replacement policy. Further details of these policies are given in Section 3 of this paper.

1.2 Key Contributions

The major contribution of this work is twofold. Firstly, we describe an eviction policy that is specific to sub-block cache architectures. Secondly, we describe both the hardware and our implementation of a modified simulator that allows for the seamless simulation of different cache configurations and replacement policies. We specifically focus on partial eviction of sub-blocks to minimize the miss rate. To achieve this, a few additional bits are used to track the different sub-blocks indexed by a single tag. For simulation/evaluation of this architecture, we implement a cache simulator based on the Simplescalar Toolset [9] to mimic the behavior of memory systems designed with sub-block caches. We finally test our new architecture by running SPEC2006 benchmarks on the modified Simplescalar simulator.

1.3 Prior Work

The three main principles that influence the design of memory systems are: (i) making frequent accesses fast, (ii) the concept of temporal and spatial localities and (iii) achieving maximum speed with minimal size. The above principles suggest that recently accessed items should be placed in the fastest memory available which is the basis of cache architectures. These fast memories often come with a cost. TCAMs were introduced by memory system designers to reduce hardware cost because of their ability to store don't care value. However, TCAMs are known for high power consumption. Some methods for reducing TCAM power have been proposed, including routing-table compaction and partitioning techniques with current solutions mainly using a two-level architecture [18][19]. Other common power reduction solutions involve the use of binary search trees, B-trees, ASICs, and so on. Several other strategies - e.g., [20], [21], [22], and [23] - have been proposed to reduce TCAM power by taking advantage of a feature in contemporary TCAMs which allows the selection of a portion of the TCAM array for search. However, these methods have not completely removed the power and area overhead due to TCAMs.

Another approach for reducing power consumption in memory is by reducing the tag area of an on-chip cache. Hong Wang et al. [10] studied the locality property of memory references and after extensive simulation experiments, observed that address tags of cached data are usually clustered at a given time frame during program execution. The spatial/temporal locality property of references causes many tags to be identical during a period of time, effectively making the working set of unique tags much smaller than the working set of data references. This suggests that tag area can be significantly reduced by grouping multiple blocks into a single larger cache-line. This larger cache-line/super-block is then indexed by a single tag which yields smaller tag array but with the possibility of several unwanted replacements.

Modern processor designs employ various replacement policies such as Random [2], LRU (Least Recently Used) [11], Round-robin (or FIFO – First-In-First-Out) [12], and PLRU (Pseudo LRU) [13] indicating there is no single optimal cache replacement policy. All these policies except the random replacement policy rely on access history to predict the entries to be replaced and therefore require additional hardware which increases with associativity. The Random policy however, suffers from performance degradation. Across different SPEC2000 benchmarks, LRU policy gives the best performance on the average [14]. Therefore, multiple flavors of LRU policy have been proposed over the years to improve cache hit rate. The detection of temporal locality coupled with existing LRU policy have been used [15] in level two caches to improve the cache miss rate over pure LRU policy. Other replacement policies based on the LRU include the Early Eviction LRU [16], which adapts to reference patterns at all scales and has been shown to give 10-30% improvement over pure LRU. An LRU Insertion Policy (LIP) has also been proposed [8] which protects the cache from thrashing and gives close to optimal hit rate for applications that have a cyclic reference pattern. Bimodal Insertion Policy (BIP) which is an enhancement of LIP [8] adapts to changes in the working set while maintaining the thrashing protection of LIP. Another policy is the Dynamic Insertion Policy (DIP) [8] which dynamically chooses between BIP and the traditional LRU policy depending on which policy incurs fewer misses. All these policies act on individual cache entries and are still not efficient for SB caches where multiple sub-blocks have been combined to a super-block indexed by a single tag entry.

2 SB Cache Architecture

In sub-block cache architectures, a single tag entry is capable of indexing multiple sub-blocks depending on the level of sub-blocking desired. Since, a single tag now indexes multiple aggregated sub-blocks, a few of the tag LSBs are not stored in the tag array but rather used as index to the accessed sub-block of a cache-line. For the ease of indexing, we store sub-blocks in specific locations given by the tag LSBs not stored. For example, suppose we have a 32 bit address request to a cache-line with four sub-blocks as shown in figure 2, with bits "[9:2]" reserved for set indexing. The SB cache uses only bits [9:4] for set indexing, reserving the $\log_2 4$ (i.e. 2) LSBs for sub-block indexing. This reduces the number of tag lines by 75%, from $2^{(9-2+1)}=256$ to $2^{(9-4+1)}=64$, and removes the need to store $2*2^{(9-4+1)}$ bits for the dropped LSBs. Individual valid bits are added for each sub-block, making it possible to both allocate and de-allocate a sub-block entry independent of the other sub-blocks. They also give the additional information used to implement the replacement policy presented in this paper. The overhead due to valid bits is the same as in an equivalent conventional cache with cache-line equal to the sub-block size (i.e. $2^{(9-2+1)} *1 = 2^{(9-4+1)} *4$). Significant tag array reduction is therefore the major benefit of sub-blocking.

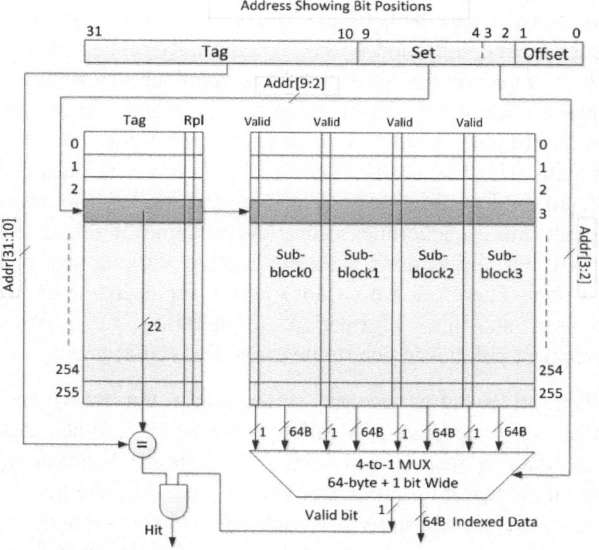

Figure 2: A Single Way of a Sub-block Cache

3 Sub-Block Replacement Policies

Given that multiple sub-blocks are indexed by a single tag in sub-block caches, replacements need to be handled differently than in a conventional cache to minimize unwanted evictions or invalidations of aggregate sub-blocks. For example, if eight sub-blocks have been allocated to a single super-block that is to be evicted but there exists another way with only one (1) valid sub-block in its super-block, existing replacement policies will still replace the super-block with eight valid sub-blocks if that superblock has been chosen by the replacement policy. This could lead to significant cache performance degradation.

In this section, we present different eviction schemes based on the LRU policy because it is considered the most efficient of the different replacement policies [16]. In what follows, we will provide detailed description of two replacement policies along with the architectural implementation in our simulator. The first policy in Section 3.1 is used as a reference for comparison with our newly proposed policy. All cache accesses in this work are at the sub-block granularity to minimize the bus width at the different interfaces and maintain consistency across the whole architecture.

3.1 Full Eviction of LRU Super-Block (FE)

The FE replacement policy based on the Least Recently Used – "LRU" replacement policy and is included here specifically as a reference policy for comparing the performance of our new sub-block replacement policy described later in Subsection 3.2. Since the LRU replacement policy is already implemented in the Simplescalar toolset, we added logic to enable sub-blocking. The FE policy causes replacement of an individual sub-block of an LRU super-block, in addition to invalidating all other sub-blocks that were aggregated to make the super-block entry. For example, in a four sub-block cache with 8-bit wide address tag, only the 6 MSBs are stored, such that if the following four tag accesses - 11111100, 11111101, 11111110 and 11111111 occur to the same set, they are all stored in the same super-block and indexed by "111111" tag. If a single new request with tag "11001101" is determined by LRU to be allocated to the same superblock currently indexed by tag – "111111", then the sub-block allocated to the second location (i.e. entry 11111101 indexed by the same two LSBs - 01) is replaced and the other sub-blocks are invalidated. This implies sub-blocks are marked valid individually but sub-blocks belonging to the same way are all marked invalid as a super-block to enable grouped replacement. In this policy, the MRU entry takes priority if both the LRU and MRU sub-blocks belong to the same super-block or cache way. This causes both the LRU and MRU sub-blocks to be retained, along with all other sub-blocks that belong to the same super-block. The effect of this is degradation in the hit rate of a SB cache when compared with an equivalent sized conventional cache with cache-lines equal to that of the SB cache sub-block. The advantage, however, is significant savings in tag array hardware.

3.2 Least Aggregated Entry Eviction

Our LA replacement policy aims at keeping the most entries possible in the cache. It does this by tracking the total valid sub-blocks in each super-block of a set and elects the least aggregated super-block for replacement. This requires keeping a count of all sub-blocks that have been allocated to a super-block and evicting the entry with the lowest count. In a scenario where multiple super-blocks contain equal valid sub-blocks, we use LRU as tie breaker. This approach obviously places priority on keeping maximum entries in the cache rather than the most recently used entry. The advantage of this scheme becomes more pronounced as we increase the number of sub-blocks per cache-line/super-block. It is obvious that SB caches benefit more in terms of performance from replacement schemes that keep more entries in the cache after replacements because these policies retain the maximum possible entries after allocation of sub-blocks. This also minimizes contention with other memory accesses off chip.

To implement this replacement policy in hardware, an n-bit counter is used to track valid sub-blocks of each super-block where $n = \log_2 N$ and N is the number of sub-blocks in a cache-line. It is worth noting that "n" is also the number of tag LSBs that are not stored in the tag array. These n bits of the tag array are instead used to store the current counter value for each super-block. On a miss with tag match but invalid sub-block, the accessed super-block count value is incremented while the miss is being fetched. On the other hand, a miss with tag mismatch causes the current count value for all super-blocks of the accessed set to be compared and the super-block with minimum count is elected for eviction/replacement. Since allocation only occurs on a miss, it is expected that this counter comparison or increment operation is completed in the background while the missed entry is being fetched from a higher level memory location. Also, since only one miss is processed in any given cycle, a single comparator and adder pair is sufficient to support this replacement policy, thereby minimizing extra hardware overhead.

4 Modified Simplescalar Simulator

Our sub-block cache simulator builds on the Simplescalar toolset. We extended the existing interface to allow SB cache configuration inputs to be easily fed into the simulator. Most of the changes were implemented in the "sim-cache", "sim-outorder" and "cache" Simplescalar codes. The approach used was to keep the existing implementation of the cache architecture and adding command line control to enable the use of the existing simulator code or switch to any of the other configurations we added to the simulator. Most modifications were made to the behavioral code that models the behavior of the cache whenever there is a hit, miss or replacement in the cache. This allows for easy comparison of the new architecture with the existing as reference.

The simulator was implemented and validated through extensive experimentations by leveraging the existing cache way model to implement the sub-block cache simulator.

Firstly, we developed a mechanism for linking multiple cache lines to form a super-block. This was achieved by adding extra logic that links multiple tag entries to form a single aggregated tag entry. We ensure the total number of ways is equal to those of an equivalent conventional cache. Then, we link *"n"* of the ways together based on the degree of sub-block aggregation desired, to form a single way/super-block, where *"n"* is the number of sub-blocks in a super-block. Secondly, we implemented comparator and adder as previously described in Section 3.2. Since replacement decisions only occur on a miss and in the background while a miss is being fetched, we used a non time consuming routine. Finally, we added code segments to mimic the two replacement policies described in this paper. Eviction is allowed to take place normally, followed by additional sub-block evictions/invalidations depending on the chosen replacement policy.

5 Experimental Results

5.1 Configuration and Simulation setup

For the purpose of simulations, we populated five different configurations as follows. The conventional configuration (conv) which represents the default non sub-block 4-way conventional cache, two sub-block configurations for the LA and FE replacement policies using only two sub-block per super-block, and finally, two sub-block configurations for the LA and FE replacement schemes that use four sub-blocks per super-block. All these were configured to have the same cache size for accurate comparisons. Our measurements were taken for L1I miss rate, L1D miss rate and L2 miss rate across different SPEC 2006 benchmarks. We chose 8KB L1 caches and 32KB L2 unified cache to create multiple replacements and therefore stress the replacement policies.

5.2 Simulation Results

As expected, there is a miss rate increase as we move from conventional cache to the sub-block cache when using the FE replacement policy. This is a result of evicting all entries of a super-block whenever it is the LRU entry. It becomes more pronounced as we increase the number of sub-blocks used per super-block since this increases the possible number of unwanted sub-block invalidations. We use FE as a reference for comparison with our newly proposed replacement policy – LA. The simulation results below show that we can close a significant amount of the gap in performance between a conventional cache and an equivalent tag array saving sub-block cache by using our LA replacement policy. These results also reveal that the different replacement policies do not perform consistently across all benchmarks. This is expected because sub-block aggregation is heavily dependent on locality of reference and this varies across different programs [17]. However, overall average results improve by up to 33% for LA. Figure 3 shows the comparison of L1I miss rate across the different benchmarks, with sub-block caches having higher miss-rate due to super-block evictions. 2SB and 4SB represent two and four sub-blocks per super-block respectively. Dynamic selection between different replacement policies is being deferred for future work.

Figures 4 and 5 capture the Level 1 Data (L1D) and Level 2 (L2) unified cache hit rate across different SPEC2000 benchmarks. It is obvious from the Miss Rate plots that sub-block caches using existing replacement policy (FE) suffer performance degradation due to eviction of aggregates during sub-block replacement. Although the LA policy did not completely close the gap between the performances of the conventional cache and SB cache, it did give a significant improvement over FE across most of the SPEC2006 benchmarks. This is even more pronounced in the Level 1 instruction cache results shown in Figure 3. The "soplex" benchmark shows LA policy outperforms the conventional cache in unified L2 miss rate. Dynamically choosing between the two replacement policies could benefit from the different policies but is outside the scope of this paper. In a few cases, the LA policy did not perform better than the reference FE policy. This shows that keeping the most aggregated entry is not always the best decision in SB cache replacement, especially when using fewer sub-blocks per super-block.

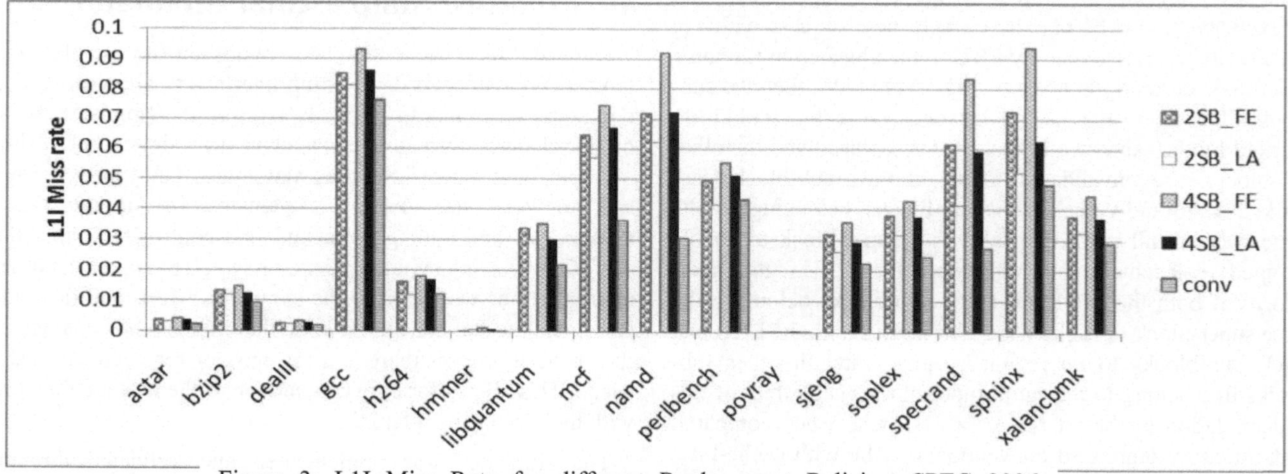

Figure 3: L1I Miss Rate for different Replacement Policies -SPEC 2006

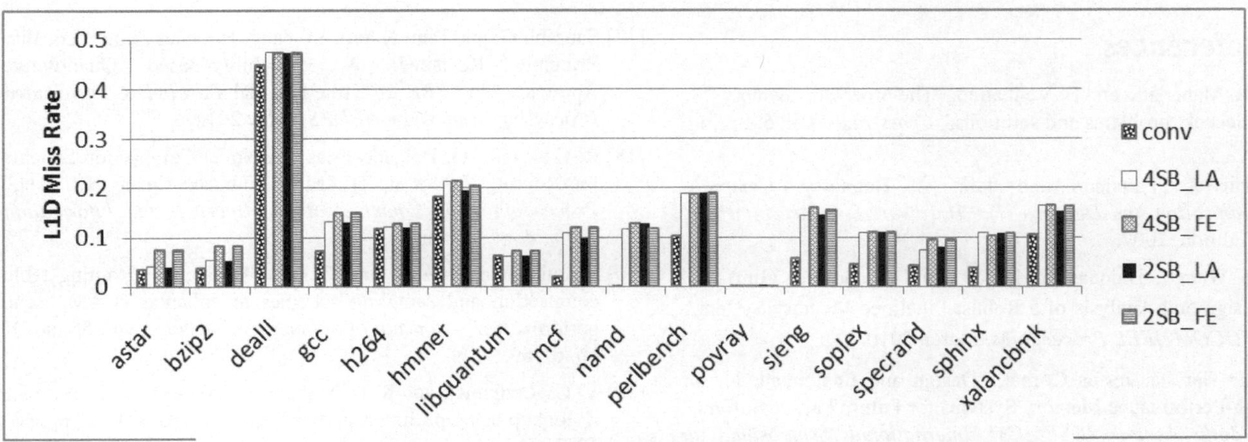

Figure 4: L1D Miss Rate for different Replacement Policies -SPEC 2006

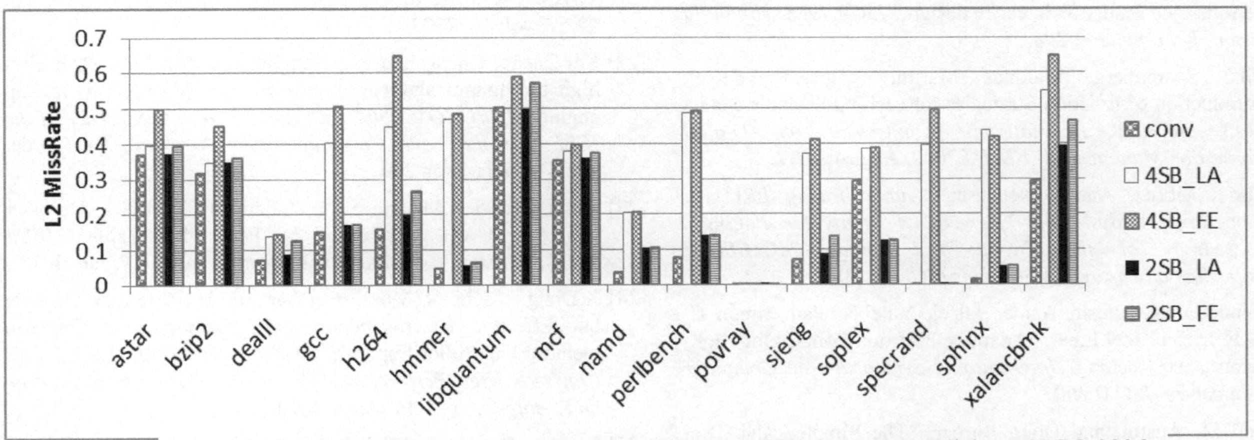

Figure 5: L2 Unified Cache Miss Rate for different and Replacement Policies - SPEC 2006

Table II gives a summary of the performance improvement achieved by our newly proposed eviction policy when compared with the reference replacement policy – FE. We specifically measured the improvement given by the LA replacement policy and normalized it over the difference between the conventional cache using LRU replacement policy and a SB cache using the FE replacement policy. On the average, the LA gave the best performance improvement in the L1I cache as expected because of the temporal nature of program accesses. The hit rate regained by LA policy in the unified L2 cache serving the two L1 caches is not exactly the average of the L1I and L1D cache hit rate improvements because the effective traffic pattern from both streams, independently contribute to the overall performance.

Table II: Performance Improvement Summary

	Hit Rate Percentage gain		
	L1I	**L1D**	**L2 Unified**
FE→LA (% Gain)	33.38	27.58	30.34

6 Conclusions

The use of sub-blocks in the design of a cache allowed us to use a smaller number of tags to index cache data entries, depending on the degree of sub-blocking. The penalty incurred is degradation in hit rate due to multiple evictions of aggregate sub-blocks. We proposed a new replacement policy LA that minimizes the hit penalties associated with sub-block caches. A second replacement policy – FE was used as a reference for comparison.

The LA replacement policy presented in this paper is novel to SB cache architectures since existing replacement schemes make decisions at the super-block level. The simulation results show that the performance of this new eviction scheme varies across the different SPEC2006 benchmarks but outperform the default FE replacement policy Our results also show that our LA policy is capable of gaining back some of the performance lost to multiple evictions of aggregated sub-blocks.

7 References

[1] N. R. Mahapatra and B. Venkatrao, "The processor-memory bottleneck: problems and solutions," *Crossroads*, vol. 5, Spring 1999.

[2] David A. Patterson and John L. Hennessy, *Computer Organization and Design – The Hardware/Software Interface,* 3rd Edition, 2007.

[3] Hao Wang , Haiquan C. Zhao, Bill Lin and Jun (Jim) Xu, "Design and Analysis of a Robust Pipelined Memory System," *INFOCOM, IEEE Proceedings*, March 2010.

[4] Jorge Garc´ıa, Jes´us Corbal, "Design and Implementation of High-Performance Memory Systems for Future Packet Buffers," In *36th Annual IEEE/ACM International Symposium on Microarchitecture, (MICRO-42,)* 2003.

[5] Steven Przybylski, Mark Horowitz, John L. Hennessy "Performance Tradeoffs in cache design," *ISCA 1988: Honolulu Hawaii, USA, pp. 290-298.*

[6] Heiko Sparenberg, Matthias Martin, Siegfried Foessel, "Introduction of Eviction Strategies for caching Scalable Media Files," *Seventh International Conference on Digital Information Management, ICDIM 2012*, August, 2012.

[7] Gabriel Moruz, Andrei Negoescu, "*Outperforming LRU via Competitive Analysis on Parametrized Inputs for Paging". Proceedings of the Twenty-Third Annual ACM-SIAM Symposium on Discrete Algorithms (SODA),* 2012.

[8] Moinuddin K.Qureshi, Aamer Jaleel, Yale N. Patt, Simon C. Steely Jr., and Joel Emer, "Adaptive Insertion Policies for High-Performance Caching" *International Symposium on Computer Architecture (ISCA) 2007.*

[9] Todd M. Austin, and Doug Burger, "The SimpleScalar Tool Set, Version 2.0," *University of Wisconsin-Madison Computer Sciences Technical Report #1342*, June 1997.

[10] Hong Wang, Tong Sun and Qing Yang, "Minimizing Area Cost of On-Chip Cache Memories by Caching Address Tags," *IEEE Transactions on Computers*, vol. 46, no. 11, Nov., 1997.

[11] Ackland B., Anesko D., Brinthaupt D., Daubert S.J, Kalavade A.., Knoblock J., Micca E., Moturi M., Nicol C.J., O'Neill J.H., Othmer J., Sackinger E., Singh K. J., Sweet J., Terman C. J., and Williams J., "A Single-Chip, 1.6 Billion, 16-b MAC/s Multiprocessor DSP," *IEEE Journal of Solid-state circuits, vol. 35, no. 3,* pp. 412-423, March 2000.

[12] Intel ® Xscale ™ Core – Developer's Manual, December 2000, http://developer.intel.com

[13] Intel ® Pentium ® 4 and Intel ® Xeon Processor Optimization –Reference Manual ™ - Reference Manual, http://developer.intel.com.

[14] Hussein Al-Zoubi, Aleksandar Milenkovic, Milena Milenkovic, "Performance Evaluation of Cache Replacement Policies for the SPEC CPU2000 Benchmark Suite" *In Proc. of 42nd ACM Southeast Conf.,* April 2004.

[15] W. A. Wong and J.-L. Baer, "Modified LRU policies for improving second-level cache behavior," In *HPCA-6*, 2000.

[16] Yannis Smaragdakis, Scott Kaplan and Paul Wilson, "The EELRU adaptive replacement algorithm" *Performance Evaluation*, vol. 53, no. 2, pp. 93–123, 2003.

[17] Saurabh Gupta, Ping Xiang, Yi Yang, Huiyang Zhou, "Locality Principle Revisited: A Probability-Based Quantitative Approach" In *IEEE 26th* International *Parallel & Distributed Processing Symposium (IPDPS),* May 2012.

[18] R. Guo and J.G. Delgado-Frias, "A Novel Compaction Scheme for Routing Tables in TCAM to Enhance Cache Hit Rate," *Proceeding (575) Communications, Internet, and Information Technology,* 2007.

[19] Ruirui Guoa, José G. and Delgado-Friasb, "IP Routing table compaction and sampling schemes to enhance TCAM cache performance," - *Journal of Systems Architecture*, vol. 55, no. 1, pp. 61-69, 2009.

[20] V. C. Ravikumar and R. N. Mahapatra, "TCAM architecture for IP lookup using prefix properties," *IEEE Micro*, vol. 24, pp. 60-69, 2004.

[21] F. Zane , G. Narlikar and A. Basu "CoolCAMs: Power-efficient TCAMs for forwarding engines," *Proc. IEEE INFOCOM*, pp. 42-52, vol. 1, 2003.

[22] Kai Zheng, Chengchen Hu, Hongbin Liu, Bin Liu, , "An ultra high throughput and power efficient TCAM-based IP lookup engine," *INFOCOM 2004. 23rd Annual Joint Conference of the IEEE Computer and Communications Societies*, vol.3, pp. 1984-1994 , March 2004.

[23] Tania Banerjee Mishra, Sartaj Sahni, "PETCAM - A Power Efficient TCAM Architecture for Forwarding Tables," *IEEE Transactions on Computers*, vol. 61, no. 1, pp. 3-17, Jan. 2012.

[24] X.Dong, Y.Xie, N. Muralimanohar, and N. P. Jouppi," Simple but Effective Heterogeneous Main Memory with On-Chip memory Controller Support," *In Proc. Of the ACM/IEEE Int'l Conf. for High Performance Computing, Networking, Storage and Analysis,* pp. 1-11, Nov., 2010.

[25] L. Zhao, R. Iyer, R. Illikkal, and D. Newell, "Exploring DRAM cache architectures for CMP server platforms," *In Proc. of the 25th Intl. Conf. on Computer Design*, pp 55–62, October 2007.

[26] M. Kadiyala, L.N. Bhuyan, "A dynamic cache sub-block design to reduce false sharing," *In IEEE International Conference on Computer Design: VLSI in Computers and Processors,* pp. 313-318, Oct 1995.

[27] J. Torrellas, M. S. Lam, and J. L. Hennessy, "False Sharing and Locality in Multiprocessor Caches," *IEEE Transactions on Computers,* pp. 651–663, 1994.

[28] J. Jalminger and P. Stenström, "Improvement of Energy-Efficiency in Chip Caches by Selective Prefetching," *Microprocessors and Microsystems*, pp. 107–121, Apr. 2002.

[29] J. S. Liptay, "Structural Aspects of the System/360 Model 85, Part II: The Cache," *IBM Systems Journal,* pp. 15–21, 1968.

[30] X. Jiang, N. Madan, L. Zhao, M. Upton, R. Iyer, S. Makineni, D. Newell, Y. Solihin, and R. Balasubramanian, "CHOP: Adaptive filter-based dram caching for CMP server platforms," In *Proc. of the 16th Intl. Symp. on High Performance Computer Architecture,* pp. 1–12, Jan. 2010.

[31] Hassan Ghasemzadeh, S. Mazrouee, M.R. Kakoee, "Modified pseudo LRU replacement algorithm," *13th Annual IEEE Int'l Symposium and Workshop on Engineering of Computer Based Systems,* pp. 376-381, March 2006.

Locality Analysis for Characterizing Applications Based on Sparse Matrices

Noboru Tanabe[1], **Sonoko Tomimori**[2], **Masami Takata**[2], **and Kazuki Joe**[2]
[1] Research and Development Center, Toshiba corporation, Kanagawa, Japan
[2] Department of Advanced Information and Computer Sciences, Nara Women's University, Nara, Japan

Abstract - *We propose an adaptability judging method applied to sparse matrices and the target cache memory using two metrics based on spatial locality and temporal locality. For indirect access sequences of sparse matrix-vector multiplications, one metric is the number of valid data within a cache line, and another metric is average reference interval. We also develop a set of analysis tools to generate the above performance metrics, histograms of reference intervals and theoretical cache hit rates. As an experimental result, a cache memory behavior which was difficult to explain from the view point of spatial locality becomes explicable from that of temporal locality. Outputs of the tool show that return on investment is too thin to increase the cache memory capacity unless all the elements of a column vector with the same size as the number of columns of the sparse matrix are stored in the cache memory.*

Keywords: Sparse matrix; Cache memory; Spatial locality; Temporal locality; Workload characterization.

1 Introduction

Recently there are serious considerations [1] in Japan in order to put exascale machines to practical use in 2018. We make a prediction that the exascale machines will adopt a complicated memory system because of inevitable memory bandwidth problems. A very high demand for memory bandwidth includes applications of simultaneous linear equations (sparse matrix-vector multiplication) with large sparse matrix coefficient. Since such simultaneous linear equations are used in calculations for important scientific theme in Japan, there is a great need for them.

In the meantime, big data processing such as large-scale graph processing draws global attention. In general, large-scale graphs are represented as large and complicated sparse matrices with small number of non-zero elements. Recommendations/preferences of information retrieval or large-scale ad hoc information search[2] such as PageRank, which gives an importance of the website, needs that a sparse matrix processing expanding the scale and speeding up.

The K-computer that is the world's third fastest supercomputer in the Top 500 list of Nov 2012 has a relatively simple memory system based on two levels of cache memory. However, it is not easy to optimize in spite of its present simplicity. Optimization experts work only for a few selected applications and they do their best of optimization using the specific characteristics of the applications[3]. On the other hand, users of scientists can not take enough time and give any hands for performance tuning for the other applications without optimization experts and the applications with a short life cycle. Just looking at the applications formed with sparse matrices, there is a great variety of placements for non-zero elements as the University of Florida sparse matrix collection [4] shows. For such applications, parallelizing compilers and/or pre-optimized libraries are very important. In the exascale machines with complicated memory systems, the importance of automatic optimization mechanism is widely informed.

The above consideration leads us to start the development of a sparse matrix library that provides a universal adjustment function without the application-specific optimization techniques and auto-tuning new methods for sparse matrices by selecting the access mechanism. As a first step of the development, we propose a characteristic metric about spatial locality of sparse matrices. Furthermore, we propose a characteristic metric about temporal locality as well as spatial locality for their combinatory use. We develop a set of tools to calculate the metrics which measure the characteristics of various sparse matrices and investigate the correlation between the proposed metrics and L1 cache hit rates that have a strong correlation with the GPU processing speed.

The paper is organized as follows. In section 2 we marshal the locality of data accesses. We propose a combination of a characteristic metric based on spatial locality and another characteristic metric based on temporal locality, which compensates the spatial index, for sparse matrices in section 3. We explain the overview of analysis programs based on the proposed metrics and the application of the programs to optimize in section 4 and 5, respectively. In section 6, we describe some experiments using the proposed indices. Related works are given in section 7.

2 Locality of references

This section is organized in terms of locality of reference that cache memory is used to increase the speed of memory accesses.

2.1 Spatial locality

If a particular memory location is referenced at a particular time, then it is likely that the other memory locations around the particular memory will be referenced in the near future. Usually, in order to make effective use of the locality reference characteristic, a block (a cache line) of data addressed near the memory is able to judge cache hit or miss, move the cache line in the case of cache miss, or access the external memory by cache line. A lot of processors including the K-computer and GPUs are equipped with 128 bytes line size caches. The reason of the 128 bytes line size is that data transfer efficiency can be improved by making the burst length longer than a certain length. Furthermore many benchmarks evaluate the trade-off between the magnitude of the penalty per cache miss and the advantage of having the number of lines fitting into the limited cache memory capacity, which is described later as making use of temporal locality. It may be greater in the future because there is a tendency that the larger cache memory capacity is, the larger cache line size is.

However, the Graph500 benchmark and applications with strong random accesses of several sparse matrix-vector multiplications exhibit a lack of spatial locality. Even when just 4 bytes of a cache line is used, the whole 128 bytes including other 124 bytes in the cache line must be transferred from the external memory, and the transferred cache line causes a very inefficient performance as the result. Therefore, it is very important to control the spatial locality in sparse matrix accesses in order to speed up sparse matrix processing.

In particular, it is very difficult for software to control the spatial locality within a cache line. Solving this problem requires the memory system of vector supercomputers without cache memory, some hardware level supports such as the gather function of DIMMnet-2 combined with a cache-based system[5], or Hybrid memory Cube with gather function[6]. When sparse matrices with low temporal locality and low spatial locality are to be processed, the above hardware level supports are a promising solution.

2.2 Temporal locality

If a particular memory location is referenced, then it is likely that the same location will be referenced again in the near future. Usually, in order to make effective use of the locality reference characteristic, cache memory is composed of many lines so that it increases the probability of hitting cache by the accesses except the last access. Theoretical study of temporal locality has a long history. Denning et al. have proposed the concept [11] of working set (t, T) which is defined with the current time t and the window size T in 1968, and a new algorithm [12] to calculate the average working set size from the set of references within one pass.

A tiling method, which divides a matrix into smaller parts of matrices, may be a useful technique to improve the temporal locality of memory references in matrix processing such as dense matrices multiplication. However, the tiling method is not valid for most sparse matrix processing because sparse matrices have various non-zero elemental locations. In this case, by performing the replacement of the row and column numbers to change the order of memory references, the sparse matrix can improve its own temporal locality. That means temporal locality is controllable by software to some extent.

3 Matrix characteristic metrics based on reference locality

3.1 Matrix characteristic metrics based on spatial locality of references

We propose the "spatial locality of column-index sequences" as a new metric on the characteristics of sparse matrix that contributes to the classification of sparse matrix adaptability for cache memory. Fig. 1 shows the conceptual diagram.

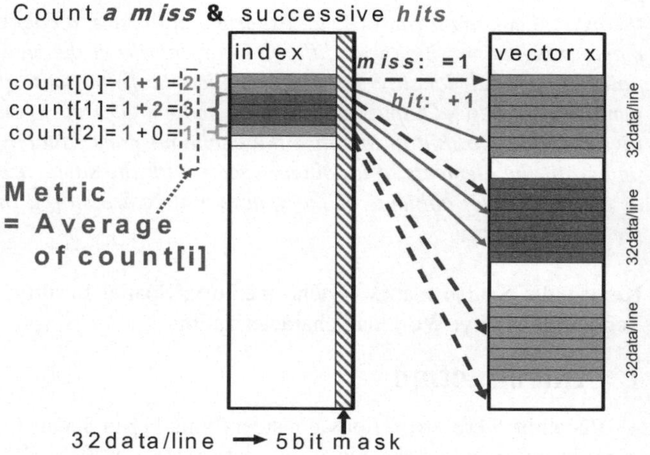

Fig. 1. The proposed metric 1 (spatial locality of column-index sequences)

The following are the definitions used to represent the characteristic value of sparse matrix.

1. Store just the non-zero elements of a sparse matrix in CRS (Compressed Row Storage) format.
2. When read the index array from the top used to load column vectors, count the number of indexes they match except lower 5 bits which come from 32 data per line.
3. If upper bits of the new index do not match with them of the last index, it means cache-miss. Record the counter to count[line_ID], reset the counter to 1, increment the line_ID and continue reading the index array (i.e., go to step2).
4. The spatial locality of column-index sequences is defined as the average of the count numbers recorded in 3.

Measuring the spatial locality of column-index sequences of sparse matrices with various formats and memory reference orders, we can find the impracticability of a sparse matrix to the target cache memory architecture which is not controllable by software. Namely, when the metric is not improved by just changing the orders and/or formats, it requires some hardware support to get better performance.

3.2 Matrix characteristic metrics based on temporal locality of references

In the previous subsection, we explain the spatial locality of references within a cache line and propose a metric for spatial locality of column-index sequences. In this subsection, we propose a combinatorial use of the temporal locality of references within the same cache line in addition to the spatial locality. To measure the temporal locality by cache line, we use a line identifier *line_ID[t]*, which is obtained by right-shifting the number of column-index sequences by the number of bits corresponding to the number of items (5 bits, which represent 128/4=32, in the case of 128 byte cache line and single-precision floating point) in the cache line, as input address sequences.

The temporal locality is concretely calculated as follows. We apply the Denning's algorithm [12] that generates a histogram of reference intervals for cache lines, and we measure the resultant temporal locality for each column-index sequence of a sparse matrix to obtain the adaptability of the sparse matrix to the target cache memory. Figure 2 shows the conceptual diagram of reference intervals for cache lines used as the temporal locality of column-index sequences. The reference interval for a cache line is the time interval between time t which is the time when the cache line is accessed and time *TIME[line_ID[t]]* which means that the last time the cache line has been accessed. In the above algorithm, it records the current time *t* into *TIME [line_ID [t]]* before updating the time *t*.

As a metric about the temporal locality of references for cache lines, we use average reference interval or average working set size that is calculated by multiplying the average reference interval with the cache line size. There is no need to generate a histogram as necessarily in Denning's algorithm for those calculations. So the histogram should not be generated by default since the calculation time for temporal locality must be short as the front-end part of our target sparse matrix library.

The performance metrics about spatial locality and temporal locality are computable within one pass since they use the same column-index sequences. In particular, it is better to calculate them within one pass when the column-index sequences are in a file rather than calculate them separately to shorten the whole processing time. In the above algorithm to calculate the reference intervals, the cache hit ratio can be obtained by dividing the access numbers where the reference interval does not exceed the number of the cache line by the total access numbers. Since the calculation of the cache hit rate requires an assumption of the FIFO cache line replacement algorithm, the calculation may have some error with different replacement algorithms or different way numbers of set associability.

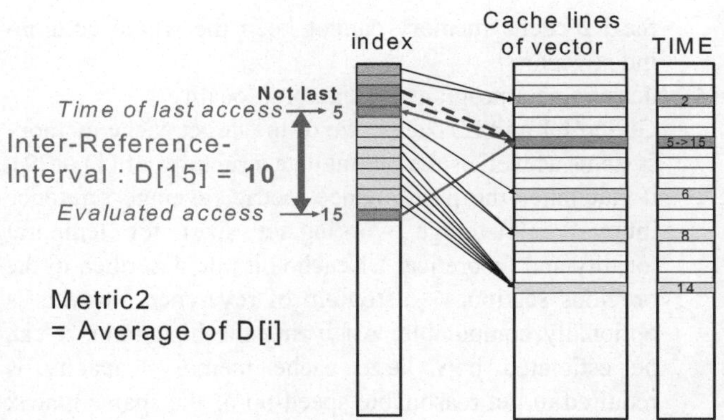

Fig. 2. The proposed metric 2 (temporal locality of column-index sequences)

4 Overview of the programs based on the proposed metrics

4.1 Input

One of the most parts of the calculation time of user applications is sparse matrix-vector multiplications. The access patterns of them are given by index array of sparse matrix. Our programs require sparse matrix files as their inputs to be given by users. These files represent the characteristics of applications for analyzing memory access properties. At this time, the programs accept the format of MatrixMarcket. It is one of the most popular formats, and it is also valid for University of Florida Sparse Matrix Collection.

4.2 Output and Component

The outputs and components of the programs are listed below.

(1) Translator for CRS format
It reads sparse matrix files with the MatrixMarket format to save the data structure with the CRS format in memory.

(2) Translator for GPU related formats
It converts sparse matrices with the CRS format generated in (1) into the data structure with applying a pre-processing for GPUs, the Fold method [7], which consists of 0-padding, folding and transposition. The pre-processing tends to generate the data structures with completely different access patterns from the CRS format. As a result, a sparse matrix with the CRS format having low access performance is converted to a data structure having high access performance using the pre-processing, and vice versa.

(3) Measurement program for spatial locality
Giving the output data structures of (1) or (2), it calculates the performance metric for spatial locality proposed in the previous section. In either case, sparse matrices with low (close to 1) calculated values for spatial locality are considered as having low adaptability to the cache memory because the practically available memory bandwidth decreases so much in the case that

the L2 cache memory cannot keep the whole column-index vectors.

(4) Measurement program for temporal locality
Giving L1 and L2 cache size of the target cache memory systems as well as the output data structures of (1) or (2), it calculates the performance metric (average reference interval or average working-set size) for temporal locality and theoretical L1 cache hit rate described in the previous section. A histogram of reverence intervals is optionally computable. Analyzing the histogram, it can be estimated how large cache memory capacity is required to get reasonable speed-up of the sparse matrix processing.

5 Qualitative optimization strategy

The average working set size, which is expressed in byte, indicates how much cache capacity it needs in order to be stable for the cache hit rate. Comparing the average working set size with the cache memory capacity of the target platform, it is expected that we know how the cache memory works from the view point of temporal locality and whether the cache memory should be used aggressively or not with automatic optimization. Table 1 qualitatively summarizes the optimization strategy with the performance metrics of spatial locality and temporal locality.

Table 1. Optimization strategy based on dual properties of access locality

	Low temporal locality	High temporal locality
High spatial locality	Explore the other ordering.	Use cache.
Low spatial locality	Use hardwired gather.	Within L1 : Use cache.
		Overflow from L1 : Use hardwired gather.

From the view point of high spatial locality, a high cache hit rate is expected while extremely low temporal locality may cancel out the performance effect. In this case, since the spatial locality is already high, a memory system with gather functions may not work well and the cache memory benefit is very limited. However, it is possible for the temporal locality to be improved by changing memory reference orders, so the automatic optimization should be performed with ordering changes. Since changing ordering tends to induce the changes of temporal and spatial locality, it is possible to be included in a different category in Table 1.

On the other hand, from the view point of high spatial locality (a high cache hit rate), when the average working-set size is sufficiently-small compared with the cache memory capacity, the temporal locality is extremely high and it cancels out the effect. In this case, the use of cache memory does not really degrade the execution efficiency. Therefore, the automatic optimization should be performed using the cache memory.

In the case of low spatial locality and not extremely high temporal locality, the effect of a memory system with gather functions is very promising, and the automatic optimization should adopt it.

6 Evaluation

6.1 Environments and matrices for experiments

Table 2 and 3 shows the computing environment and matrices used in the experiment, respectively. These matrices are selected from the University of Florida sparse matrix collection, which is a collection of sparse matrices found in real-world applications. These sparse matrices are often used by researchers in numerical linear algebra for the development and performance evaluation of sparse matrix algorithms. In this experiment we chose the sparse matrices to focus on the non-zero elements that look like scattered in irregular shapes (the optimization is difficult for cache memory) on the matrix diagram. They are derived from the sparse matrices of structural analysis, electronic circuit analysis, web analysis, and road network analysis.

Table 2. Experimental environment

CPU	Intel®Xeon®* X5670 @ 2.93GHz
GPU	Nvidia Tesla C2050 (# of core : 448)
Device memory	144GB/s, 3GB
Host I/F	PCI express x16 Gen.2 (8GB/s)
OS	RedHat Enterprise Linux Client release5.5
CUDA	Cuda3.2

Table 3. Experimented matrices

Name	# of non 0 elements	# of rows
crankseg_2	7,106,348	63,838
nd24k	14,393,817	72,000
thermal2	3,489,300	147,900
hood	5,494,489	220,542
F1	13,590,452	343,791
msdoor	10,328,399	415,863
rajat29	4,866,270	643,994
ASIC_680ks	12,329,176	682,712
apache2	2,766,523	715,176
ldoor	23,737,339	952,203
webbase-1M	3,105,536	1,000,005
delaunay_n20	2,097,124	1,048,576
roadNET-TX	1,281,106	1,393,383
Hamrle3	5,514,242	1,447,360
G3_circuit	4,623,152	1,585,478
roadNET-CA	1,844,404	1,971,281

* Intel, Xeon are trademarks of Intel Corporation in the U.S. and/or other countries.

6.2 Experiments

We measure the proposed performance metrics of sparse matrices with the CRS format and pre-processed sparse matrices as well as the L1 cache hit rates for the pre-processed sparse matrices. We use the fold method [7] as the pre-process, which converts the access order of index arrays of CRS format sparse matrices into the transposed order for GPUs. The change of the access order affects the cache hit rate. Namely, the converted access order has better compatibility to cache memory rather than the CRS format, the effect of the pre-processing is easily observed.

We examine the correlation between the L1 cache hit rate of a GPU and the proposed metrics for spatial locality. The results are shown in Fig.3. Figure 3 clearly shows that there is a majority group showing positive correlation between the L1 cache hit rate of the GPU and the proposed metrics (the sparse matrices group surrounded by a green ellipse), a minor group showing no correlation (surrounded by a blue ellipse), and an isolated sparse matrix (surrounded by a red circle). It means that only the metric for spatial locality is insufficient for judging the adaptability of a given sparse matrix to cache memory in advance.

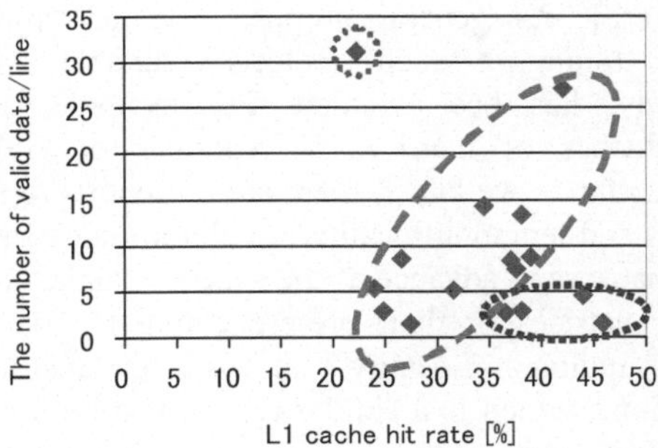

Fig. 3. The relation between L1 cache hit rate of GPU(C2050) and the number of valid data/line (Pre-processed by Fold-method)

Table 4 shows the average inter-reference interval and the average working set size of each sparse matrix. Thermal2 and roadNET-TX obviously have small average working set sizes, and they are less than or equal to the GPU L1 cache size (16KB in the case of Fermi). We think this is the reason why our experiments described in the previous subsection show the relatively high cache hit rates in spite of low spatial locality. This is the notable effect that becomes obvious with the combinatorial use of temporal locality as well as spatial locality. Considering the cases of thermal2 and roadNET-TX from the view point of automatic optimization, they have low spatial locality as well as high temporal locality where most working sets are cacheable in the L1 cache memory, so we conclude the cache memory first strategy is appropriate. L1 cache may overflow in case of the kernel implementation in which both the index parts and data part of sparse matrices go through L1 cache. In the case with cache-overflow, the memory system should have gather functions.

Table 4. Outputs about temporal locality from tools

Name	Ave. inter-reference distance [line]	Ave. working set size [B]
crankseg_2	41.8	5,344
nd24k	73.6	9,418
thermal2	103.2	13,206
hood	335.9	42,989
F1	135.7	17,370
msdoor	135.0	17,281
rajat29	463.3	59,306
ASIC_680ks	442.6	56,647
apache2	1,088.5	139,323
ldoor	97.3	12,448
webbase-1M	360.5	46,141
delaunay_n20	403.8	51,681
roadNET-TX	130.7	16,730
Hamrle3	345.9	44,277
G3_circuit	499.1	63,886
roadNET-CA	652.5	83,526

On the other hand, *apache2* has a larger average working set size than the other four applications in the blue group from the view point of temporal locality. From the fact that it is significantly larger than the L1 cache memory size, we can explain that the L1 hit rate is observed low in apache2 in spite of the high spatial locality. This is also the notable effect that becomes obvious with the combinatorial use of temporal locality.

Figure 4 shows the relationship between the average reference intervals measured in the experiments and the L1 cache hit rate of a GPU (C2050). The correlation coefficient is -0.682, and any abnormal samples deviating significantly as shown in Fig.3 in the spatial locality are not found although the variance is slightly loosened. A linear approximation formula is expressed as $hit = -0.018d + 41.267$.

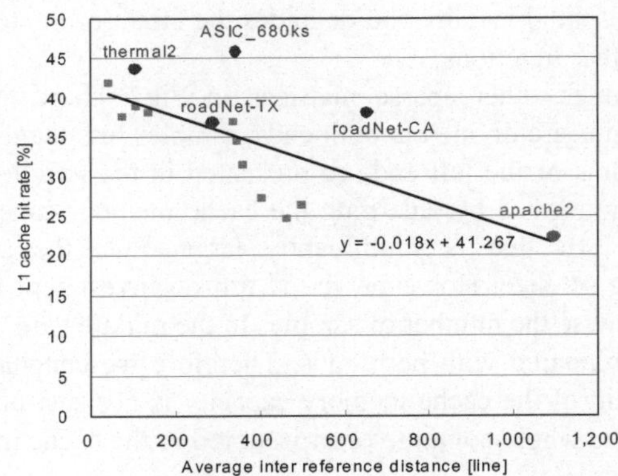

Fig. 4. The relation between average inter reference distance and L1 cache hit rate of GPU(C2050)

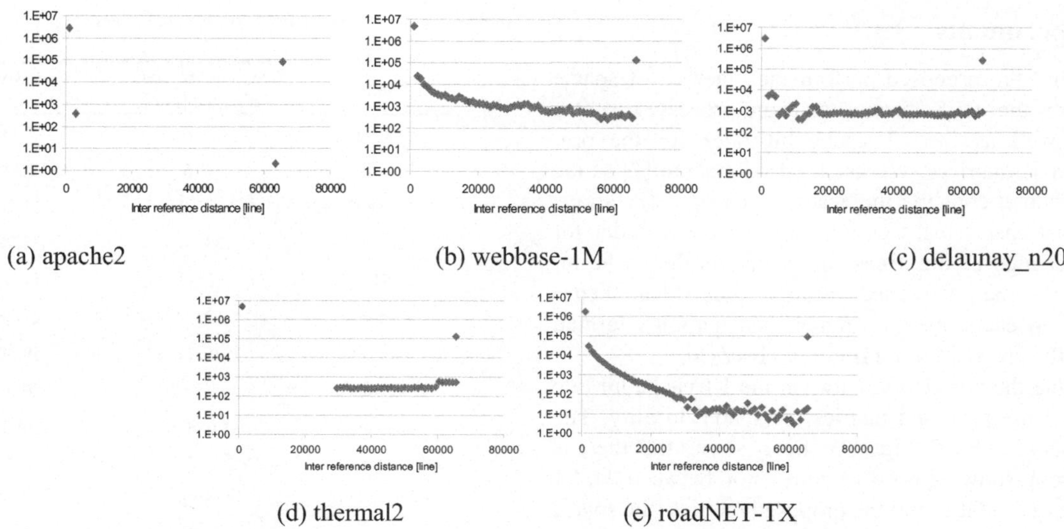

(a) apache2 (b) webbase-1M (c) delaunay_n20

(d) thermal2 (e) roadNET-TX

Fig. 5. The histogram of inter-reference interval for sparse matrices

Figure 5 shows the histograms of reference intervals for each sparse matrix. The right end of each histogram is the sum of the number of reference intervals that are larger than *L* and the number of the initial cache misses. In this measurement we measure the average interval to assume the window size L corresponding to the L2 cache memory size of 8MB, which is one of the largest ones at this point. The histograms of reference intervals of sparse matrices in Fig.5 show the properties about the adaptability of the sparse matrices to the target cache memory. For example, in the case of *apche2* of which cache hit rate is low, there are no sample points but both ends and the cache misses in the right end are not improved by the cache memory with insufficient capacity. Since the spatial locality in this state is extremely high, the effect of the memory system with gather functions is not expected at all. There are two possible optimization for speed-up. One is to change the memory reference orders to improve the cache hit rate and another is to change folded point of pre-proccessing in order to reduce padded zero which improves inflated spatial locality and degrades the effect of the memory with gather functions .

Although other sparse matrices in Fig.5 show that the histograms are divided in both ends, samples less than several hundredths of the left end are presented in the middle. They can be improved by enlarging the cache memory capacity to several MB that is significantly larger than the average working set size. However, the return on investment is very thin because the number of samples in the middle parts is very small compared with both ends. Therefore we conclude that increment of the cache memory capacity is not cost-effective unless the whole column vector is stored in the cache memory.

7 Related work

On the K-computer, optimization with specific character of two applications of which main calculation is for sparse matrix is performed by human hands. For example, the applications are optimized provided that the maximum number of nonzero elements in a row of the sparse matrix is set to 27 [3]. As general purpose oriented approaches, automatic tuning, which selects suitable software automatically, has been studied. For example, selecting storage schemes of matrices is reported for GPUs [8]. However, as far as we know, there are no reports to measure both spatial and temporal locality of column-index sequences of sparse matrices in advance as the specific characteristics of the sparse matrices or their pre-processing to be used for automatic tuning. Locality in sparse matrix-vector multiplications, which is a similar research to be focused on sparse matrix and memory reference locality, has been investigated by Heras [9]. In this research, three distance functions are proposed as metrics. Since the selection of suitable window size or indices is given by experimental results, it cannot be used for automatic tuning. Our research and Perarnau's research [10] are focused on the locality of sparse matrix. The target of Perarnau's research is the AMG method, which makes use of trace data from real machines. On the other hand, the target of our research is sparse matrix-vector multiplication. We use the column-index sequences, which is placement pattern of nonzero elements of the sparse matrix. As for temporal locality, Denning's working set is widely known [11][12], and we measure performance metrics based on inter-reference interval, which is derived from Denning's working set. There are many existing researches [14-16] that uses the Reuse distance (Stack distance) proposed by Matson [13]. They are using only the metric for temporal locality. On the other side, we calculate the spatial locality, we can know the efficiency of memory bus and cache and can judge which sparse matrix should be located on the memory with gather functions.

8 Conclusions

We guess that the exascale machines adopt a complicated memory system. Toward the implementation of a sparse matrix library to be possibly used for the exascale machines, in this paper we proposed an adaptability judging method applied to sparse matrices and the target cache memory using metrics of spatial locality within a cache line and temporal locality among cache lines. For indirect access sequences of sparse matrix-vector multiplications, the former metric is the number of valid data within a cache line, and the latter metric is average reference interval and average working set size. We also developed a set of analysis programs to generate the above metrics, histograms of reference intervals and theoretical cache hit rates. We evaluated the proposed metrics based on the analysis programs and the University of Florida sparse matrix collection. As a result, a case that a cache memory behavior was difficult to explain from the view point of spatial locality becomes explicable from the view point of temporal locality. Thus, we could strengthen the basis for deriving more appropriate optimization strategies just by the placement patterns of non-zero elements of sparse matrices.

Now we can estimate how much the cache memory capacity should be increased to reasonably optimize the sparse matrix processing using the reference interval histogram generated by the program. The access characteristics to sparse matrices in the experiments are classified into two groups; small reference intervals where most accesses hit the L1 cache memory and long reference intervals where considerable numbers of accesses do not hit any cache memory. It means that return on investment is too thin to increase the cache memory capacity unless all the elements in a dense column vector are stored in the cache memory.

As described above, just generating a sparse matrix for the target application, the proposed programs make scientists with a poor knowledge of computer architecture judge in advance whether it works efficiently on a cache memory based processor or a special library for sparse matrices judge it at runtime. In addition, we can obtain useful information for future computer designers to investigate appropriate and possible cache memory capacity or consider the use of the memory system with gather functions.

Our future work includes comprehensive survey of sparse matrices and sparse matrix library with auto-tuning mechanisms using the proposed metrics.

Acknowledgements

A part of this work is supported by the Ministry of Internal Affairs and Communications (Soumu-sho).

References

[1] K. Hiraki "[Invited talk] Architecture for Future HPC", HPCS'12, pp.163-167, (In Japanese) Jan.2012.

[2] X. Yang, S. Parthasarathy, P. Sadayappan "Fast sparse matrix-vector multiplication on GPUs: implications for graph mining", Proc. VLDB Endowment, Vol.4, No.4, pp.231-242, 2011.

[3] K. Minami, S. Inoue, S. Tsutsumi, T. Maeda, Y. Hasegawa, A. Kuroda, M. Terai, M. Yokokawa. "Performance Tuning and Evaluation of Sparse matrix-vector multiplication on the K computer", HPCS'12, pp.32-41, (In Japanese) Jan.2012.

[4] Tim Davis " The University of Florida Sparse Matrix Collection", http://www.cise.ufl.edu/research/sparse/matrices/.

[5] N. Tanabe, H. Hakozaki, Y. Dohi, Z. Luo, H. Nakajo : " An enhancer of memory and network for applications with large-capacity data and non-continuous data accessing", The Journal of Supercomputing, Vol. 51, No. 3, pp. 279-309, Mar. 2010.

[6] N. Tanabe, B. Nuttapon, H. Nakajo, Y. Ogawa, J. Kogou, M. Takata, K. Joe : "A memory accelerator with gather functions for bandwidth-bound irregular applications", Proceedings of the first workshop on Irregular applications: architectures and algorithm (IAAA'11),pp.35-42, 2011

[7] N. Tanabe , Y. Ogawa , M. Takata , K. Joe "Scaleable Sparse Matrix-Vector Multiplication with Functional Memory and GPUs", Euromicro PDP2011, 2011.

[8] Y. Kubota, D. Takahashi "Optimization of sparse matrix-vector multiplication by auto selecting storage schemes on GPU", ICCSA'11 Proceedings of the 2011 international conference on Computational science and its applications - Vol. II, pp.547-561, 2011.

[9] D. B. Heras, J. C. Cabaleiro, F. F. Rivera "Modelng data locality for the sparse matrix-vector product using deistance measures", Parallel computing, Vol.27, pp.897-912, 2001.

[10] S. Perarnau "Toward Automated Cache Partitioning for the K Computer", IPSJ SIG-HPC Oct. 2012.

[11] P. J. Denning "The Working Set Model for Program Behavior", Comm. ACM, 1968, Vol.11,No.5, pp323-333.

[12] P. J. Denning , S.C.Schwartz "Properties of the Working-Set Model", Comm . ACM , Vol.15, No.3 , pp.191-198, 1972.

[13] R. L. Mattson, J. Gecsei, D. Slutz, I. L. Traiger. "Evaluation techniques for storage hierarchies", IBM System Journal, Vol.9, No.2, pp.78-117, 1970.

[14] K. Beyls and E. D'Hollander "Reuse distance as a metric for cache behavior", In Proceedings of the IASTED Conference on Parallel and Distributed Computing and Systems, 2001.

[15] Ding, Zhong "Predicitind Whole-Program Locality through Reuse Distance Analysis", Proceedings of the ACM SIGPLAN 2003 conference on Programming language design and implementation (PLDI'03) pp.245-257, 2003.

[16] C. Fang, S. Carr, S. Onder, Z. Wang. "Reuse-distance-based miss-rate prediction on a per instruction basis", Proceedings of the 2004 workshop on Memory system performance (MSP '04), pp.60-68, 2004.

Design and implementation of an In-Network Cache Coherence protocol

Christian Bernard[1], **Huy-Nam Nguyen**[2], **Eric Guthmuller**[1] **and Yves Durand**[1]
[1]CEA LETI Minatec, Grenoble, France
[2]Bull S.A.S., Les Clayes sous bois, France

Abstract: *Manycore processor bring new programmability challenges. Shared memory with cache coherency greatly simplifies their programmability but faces scalability and cost issues. Eisley et als. proposed an original In-Network Cache Coherence (IN-CC) protocol with linear scalability. In this paper we extend Eisley's protocol with many improvements : deadlock prevention mechanisms for both message routing cycles and resource reservation, support of MOESI states and acceleration of data transfers by splitting the network in two parallel parts. Eventually, we realize an implementation of the improved protocol on FPGA for the purpose of functional validation and performance measurements.*

Keywords: *Manycore processor, Cache Coherency, Memory Consistency, Protocol, Distributed Directory*

1 Introduction and related works

Manycore architecture has been recognized as an efficient solution for exploiting the available silicon resource on a single chip. On one hand, the limitation of bus-based communication leads to the necessity to consider the more scalable network-based interconnection. On the other hand, programmers still require shared memory as programming model, and hence cache coherence still represents a highly preferred hardware feature. Since snooping does not scale on a network, directory-based solutions are preferred in manycore architectures. But then, both the cost of storage required for the directories and the amount of coherency-related messaging become critical constraints.

Various scalable directory-based cache coherency protocols have been proposed. Authors of [4] proposed a distributed directory scheme based on the Scalable Coherent Interface (SCI). The directory is implemented as a history-ordered list linking nodes sharing common cache lines (sharers). The major drawback with this organisation is the ordering of the list that does not match the topological proximity of sharers, thus leading to high latency and bandwidth overheads. The same drawbacks apply to the singly linked list directory proposed in [3]. Furthermore, a deadlock-free implementation of such algorithms becomes highly complex, particularly for the resolution of conflicts.

Authors of [2] proposed hierarchical directory schemes to reduce the size of the directory. However the introduction of a hierarchy in a regular 2D-mesh CMP architecture leads to sub-optimal behaviours when a sharer is located near the requester but is not in the same region.

In [5], the directory is centralized in the home directory with a fixed cost thanks to dynamic tracking of sharers. The list of sharers is stored in a centralized linked list and when the memory containing the list is full, a sharer is invalidated to free the corresponding list entry. The cost of the directory scales logarithmically well with the number of processors in the system. The European Catrene/TSAR [7] project proposes a more flexible scheme: when the heap of the memory is full, the system can switch to a source snooping scheme. The major drawback with centralized directories is the serialisation point of the home directory which can be overwhelmed by requests when a data is shared by too many processors.

Eisley and al. proposed a new in-network cache coherence protocol (IN-CC) in [1] combining both scalability and sharer's proximity exploitation. By linking nodes of the network to build trees of sharers, each entry in the directory costs only five bits, one for each direction, and read requests can be routed in the tree to a nearby sharer. Thus 20% of average read latency reduction is observed. The major drawback of the IN-CC implementation resides in its complexity which leads to a relative weak performance and *a posteriori* resolution of deadlock configurations.

Recently, authors of [6] proposed a virtual tree directory scheme by storing sharers identification at a coarser granularity than IN-CC. This granularity may exceed the cache line size. Moreover, multiple memory regions may be mapped into the same tree, thus reducing the number of trees in the system and so the cost of tree management. In this approach, the home node is a synchronization point for operations on cache lines. It simplifies acknowledgements and thus the whole protocol, but since all requests go to the home node, this protocol does not benefit from data replication in sharers.

Contribution : our works target the implementation and extensive analysis and validation of a MOESI cache coherence protocol distributed in the network. Our implementation has been adapted from the IN-CC protocol proposed in [1]. For the purpose of verification, the protocol has been designed with an optimally simplified architecture and implemented in a FPGA technology, thus providing the ability to validate at RT level, thus taking into account potential link level deadlocks, inconsistencies due to the dynamic evolution of the context and micro-architecture issues due to resource sharing. In addition, such implementation provides accurate area and performance estimation.

Outline : in the first part, we briefly review the original protocol. Then we introduce the NoC-based macro architecture and the node micro architecture. Next, we describe the main issues encountered during protocol analysis and validation phases. Afterwards, we present our validation methodology and the results of logic synthesis and performance measurements in simulation. At the end, we discuss these results, and suggest perspectives for future works.

2 IN-CC implementation

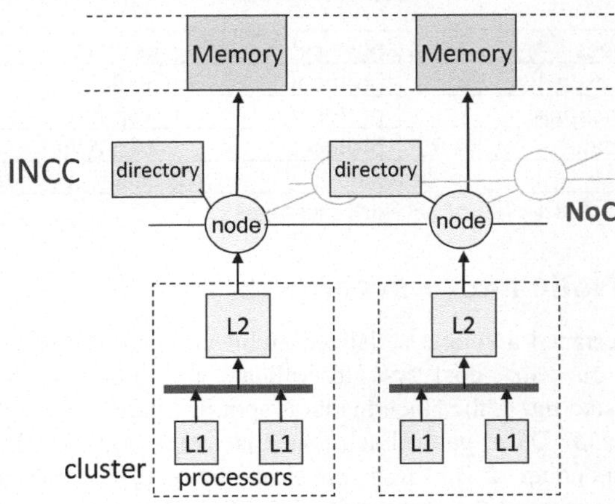

Figure 1: IN-CC System on Chip

2.1 Context

Our context is a system made of nodes to which can be attached either clusters of processing elements, memory interface or both. Nodes are physically linked via a 2D-mesh NoC (Network on Chip). We consider a single L2 cache per cluster, and all clusters see the distributed memory as a unique address space. The memory is logically partitioned into segments that are further divided into cache lines. The memory interface to each segment (either a L3 cache or DDR controller) is handled by a node, called the Home for this segment. For each cache line, the system must be able to identify all the sharers, i.e. L2 caches holding a copy, in order to insure cache coherency. In IN-CC, this information is organized as a dynamic pointer tree called Virtual Tree whose vertices are mapped onto directory entries, contained in the nodes. Nodes exchange messages. Those messages, such as *read* request, *acknowledge, cleanup,* used for data access, change the structure of the tree or the internal state of its vertices.

2.2 Tree building

When a processor reads a cache line not present in the L2 cache, the node attached to this L2 cache emits a *read* request message which is routed towards the Home node. Whenever the request message reaches a node holding a directory entry which matches the cache line, the request is rerouted through the tree to a node containing a copy of the line.

If no copy is already present in the network, the Home node is in charge of fetching the data from the memory interface, and building a new tree, i.e. a branch from the Home to the requester considered then as the Root of the tree. The tree is oriented towards the Root, so insuring that any request propagating through the tree will eventually reach a copy. Each time a new sharer is added in the tree, a new branch may be built up to this sharer along with the *response* message.

So, each node directory entry contains the address tag, the list of the links to the neighbouring nodes of the tree (by means of a short bit vector), a flag "Copy" (the cluster owns a copy), the direction (link number) to the root and other pieces of information that will be detailed further. An entry is valid when at least one link is valid. An example of virtual tree implementation into the system is shown in fig. 2

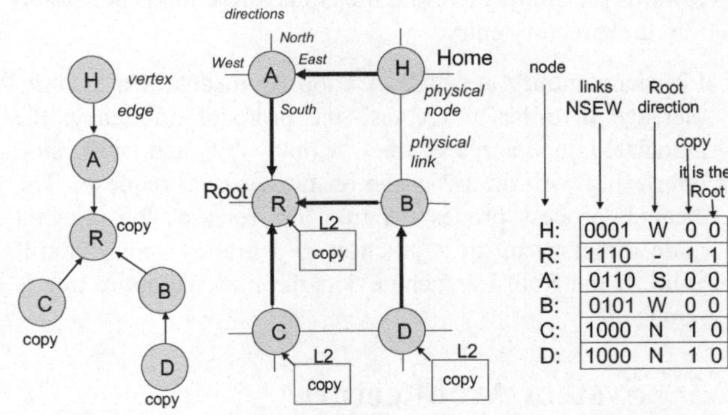

Figure 2: Tree implementation

2.3 Tree teardown

A tree is removed on a L2-cache *exclusive read* request, Root cache eviction or Node directory eviction. When a processor attempts to write into a line, the L2 cache must get its exclusive ownership first. So it sends an *exclusive read* request to the Home. If a valid tree already exists for this line, it must be removed; this process called "teardown" is described in next paragraph. Then, a new tree is built with the exclusive owner as the Root of the tree. However, the Root may share the modified line with other nodes further, but it can no more change its value (Owner state). Our policy is write-back; therefore the memory is updated only on the next tree invalidation.

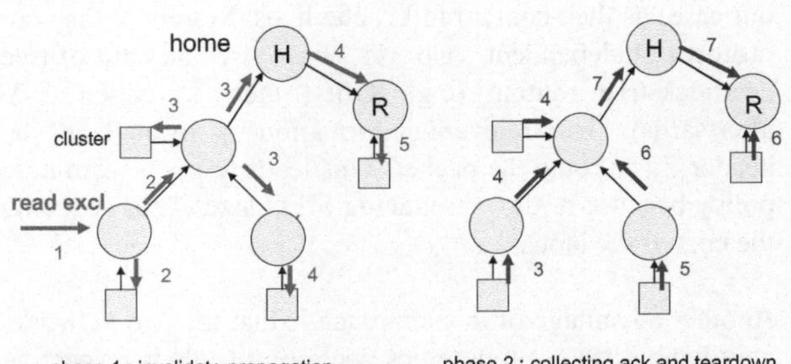

Figure 3: Teardown process

As shown in fig. 3, a smart process, called teardown, is used to invalidate the tree by propagating *invalidate* requests through the tree from any starting node of the tree, and then collecting acknowledgement responses (called *ack* afterwards) from the sharer nodes, gradually removing the branches of the tree down to the Home: as a node receives an *ack* from a link, it removes this link, and when only one link remains, it is the home direction. Then the node sends its *ack* and invalidates itself in turn. If the Root cluster modified the line, the data are returned to Home node in order to update the Memory. The teardown has the following properties:

1) Several *invalidate* messages can propagate concurrently through the tree. Each directory entry has a flag "Touched"; the first *invalidate* processed at a node sets this flag in the corresponding entry and is propagated on other links of the tree, the following are ignored.

2) *Invalidate* requester identity is not relevant.

3) After return of all *acks*, the last remaining link is oriented towards the Home therefore the Home direction is not stored into the directory entry.

L2 caches notify any line eviction by means of a *cleanup* message in order to increase the protocol efficiency: the associated node resets the "Copy" bit and will stop interfering with the L2 cache on further *read* requests. The cleanup process prunes the tree, i.e. releases the relevant node directory up to a junction to a branch which is still valid. If the Root L2 cache evicts the line, the entire tree is removed.

3 System Architecture

We introduced 2 physical NoCs: one for protocol messages, the other for data packets that have different properties and constraints. Synchronization mechanisms between them must be added due to side effects of some messages.

3.1 Two networks

Protocol messages are routed through arbitrary virtual trees, so deadlocks are unavoidable, as demonstrated further in section V. Messages have reduced size (1 or 2 flits according to the link width). For efficiency purpose, the node processes the message only once it is integrally received, so avoiding to hold a critical resource. This leads to use rather a store and forward or virtual cut through routing policy.

Data packets have larger size (1 header flit and 8 data flits in our case) as they contain full cache lines. Moreover they are protocol independent and so may use an out-of-tree deadlock-free routing (e.g. X-first then Y, called X-Y afterwards). The relevant information is located in the header flit to route the packet. This leads to use a wormhole policy because it allows reducing FIFO sizes, thus reducing the cost of the NoC.

Another advantage of this approach is that the two networks may have different topologies according to their respective needs. Nevertheless, in our implementation we used the same 2D-mesh topology for both networks.

3.2 Synchronization

However this organization brings extra cost. The separation between both networks requires extra synchronization: 1) *read response* messages must be added on protocol side, in order to build new branches of the trees. This leads to add a new virtual channel on protocol side and consequent buffers. 2) The two networks need to synchronize each other at Home and requester nodes: a requester node must wait for data if protocol *response* arrives first, and a Home node must be aware of data change if the tree is torn down before data arrival. We added only one bit "Wait Data" in the node directory entry for the two situations although they may occur simultaneously, leading to a more complex state machine but less costly solution.

Finally we defined 3 virtual channels in protocol network and only one channel in data network :

messages	physical	virtual
read / exclusive read	protocol	read
read response	protocol	response
invalidate/ ack/	protocol	teardown
data	data	data

Table 1 : list of network messages

4 Node micro-architecture

We designed a simple serialized architecture for the node, since our first goal was to validate the protocol. As illustrated fig. 4, the Node model is split in 2 parts: Protocol part and Data part. Each one is connected to the corresponding 2-D Mesh physical network, i.e. to 4 neighbouring nodes (except for the side nodes) in addition to the local processor cluster.

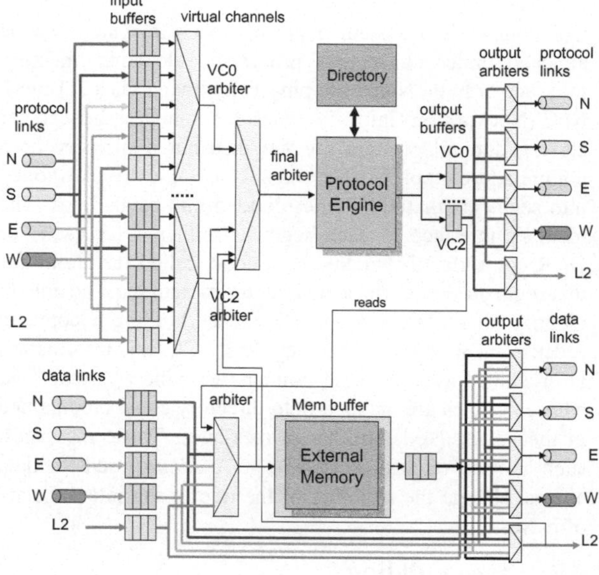

Figure 4: Node micro-architecture

The data channel transfers data packets using the X-Y routing strategy, which is known as deadlock-free. Arbitration to go from input buffer to outputs is made in a clock cycle. This part also accesses to the piece of external memory, associated to the node that is modelled as a local

RAM with immediate access. *The protocol pa*rt receives all protocol messages, competing to access to a single directory, which contains the description of the virtual tree nodes. So the protocol part has to arbitrate to access this directory, and only one request is processed at a time.

A 3-stage pipeline (arbitration, directory consultation, decision) is able to process a new request every clock cycle (unless dependency detection). The request arbitration is executed in one clock cycle, with two stages: 1) round robin arbitration between source directions for each virtual channel, 2) fixed priority arbitration between virtual channels. The second clock cycle is fully dedicated to the single port SRAM directory read, and tag comparison. At the third clock cycle, the *Protocol Engine* decodes the request and the directory state, in order to generate a list of actions (output requests, directory update, etc.) that is registered into output buffers. Furthermore, conflicts between requests to the same address are detected by using address comparison in most input and output buffer entries. There is one output buffer per output virtual channel and per direction. Therefore the output buffers compete to access to each output direction and a round robin arbitration per direction is used. The Protocol Engine was generated automatically from a table of the 140 identified elementary rules of the protocol expressed as an AND of elementary conditions.

Three other objects are not displayed in fig. 4: 1) the Directory Update FIFO, to give priority to requests over updates, 2) the Pending request buffer, to wait teardown completion before re-scheduling conflicting *reads*, 3) the Eviction Buffer, to process evicted entries, allowing re-use of the directory entry before the eviction is achieved

5 issues

From the protocol analysis, 3 transaction processes appear 1) *read* request downto *response* reception 2) teardown or cleanup process 3) an *exclusive read* request may combine the 2 preceding ones. Our analysis methodology was 1) to analyze each transaction individually, 2) then to considerer the evolution of trees on atomic transaction sequences: the identified issue is the cycle forming inside a tree 3) to consider atomicity at node/microarchitecture level, i.e. situations where transactions occur simultaneously, or message concurrence during a teardown. Races create inconsistencies and deadlocks inside a same tree since the only interaction with another tree is to initiate a teardown by cache or directory eviction. Issues involving different trees are deadlocks due to resource access competition. Finally, we classify these issues into 3 categories: 1) cycles, 2) deadlocks, 3) races. Most interesting issues are highlighted hereafter.

5.1 Cycles

The dynamic construction of the virtual trees is likely to create cycles. Indeed we did not find routing strategy that avoids cycle forming in the trees. The cycles must be broken because they are fatal for the tree teardown.

5.1.1 Cycle forming

We chose an adaptive routing for *read responses* in order to reduce the number of nodes of a tree. So we reuse the already existing branches as far as possible while coming closer to the requester (choosing as a priority X direction if both X and Y are possible), and use non adaptive X-Y routing once out of the tree. The figure 5 shows an example of cycle forming in a tree, which is described hereafter.

First, the L2 cache of node R sends a *read* request to the home node H going up the path R-A-H. Once the Home has processed the request, it sends back a protocol *read response* to R and concurrently reads the line data onto memory, data are then returned to R on separate data network. The *read response* progression creates the first branch H-A-R of the tree. Let us note that the *read response* has a flag "init" to indicate that the *response* is creating a new tree and the requester will become the Root. If the flag "init" is set, the Root direction for the current node is the output link of the *response*, else it is the source link. Then node B transmits the *read* request of its L2 cache towards the Home, the request goes to node A according to the X-Y routing strategy. As A is in the tree, A transmits the request to R (according to root orientation). Node R requires data to its own L2-cache, and sends a *read response* to B, using first Y direction, as it comes closer to B while remaining in the tree. Then the link A-B is created. When C requests data in turn, the request goes directly to R, and the *response* creates the branch R-C. Then D sends its request to H that transmits it to R following the tree orientation. At node R, as X and Y directions remain in the tree, X direction is chosen to send the *response* to C, that proceeds propagating the *response* to B and a cycle is formed.

5.1.2 Effect of a cycle on tree teardown

In this example, when the node D sends its *ack*, it has no more link and becomes invalid. A, B, C and R nodes are in deadlock, because each one of these nodes remains with two links, once its cache returned its *ack*, preventing the node from sending its own *ack* in turn.

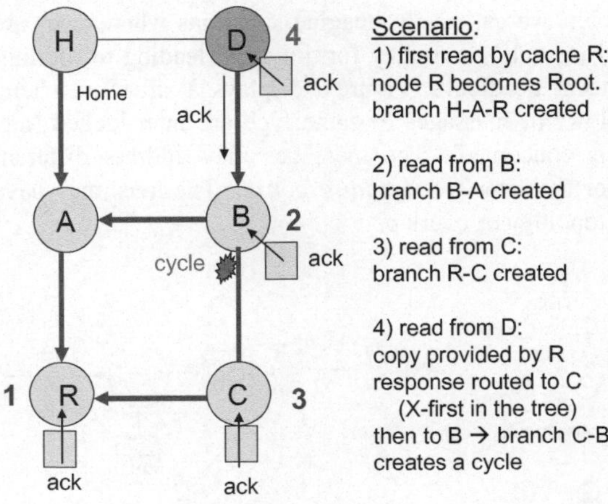

Figure 5: Cycle forming

5.1.3 Cycle breaking

As a *read response,* once it has left the tree, is not allowed to come back into the tree, we added in the *response* message a flag "exit" indicating that the message exited the tree at the previous node output. Initially a *read response* is produced by a Node in the tree (exit=0). When the node C of the fig. 5 decides to propagate the *response* out of tree, i.e. to a direction that is not an edge of the tree, the node sets the exit flag of the *response*, and adds the direction in the link list of the directory entry corresponding to the tree. As the node B is a vertex of the tree, B detects that a cycle is being formed when it processes the *response* with flag exit=1. Then node B sends a *cleanup* to the *response* source direction (e.g. to C), in order to remove the unwanted new branch. The *response* can proceed from the current node B to D (with exit=1). A new branch B-D is created and the branch B-C is removed.

5.2 Deadlocks

Our implementation of the INCC protocol obeys to different tradeoffs with a constant concern for reducing hardware complexity. Unfortunately, our realization of the messaging protocol cannot avoid the occurrence of deadlocks. In other words, we cannot relax any of the four Coffman characteristic conditions for deadlocks [8]: Only one message can hold a node input buffer at a time, thus the *mutual exclusion* condition is fulfilled. This is inherent to the underlying NoC transport protocol used. The message transfers may hold one output finite size buffer while requesting an input buffer, which is the *resource holding* condition. However we partially relaxed this condition by routing different message types into independent virtual channels. By using several virtual channels, we avoid message-dependent deadlocks between *reads* and *responses*, *read* or *response* and teardown messages [9]. We do not separate *invalidates, acks* and *cleanup* because the tree teardown is a complex process itself implying message concurrence. Therefore a single channel avoids buffers and extra logic to solve race issues. However, this channel virtualization reduces the probability of resource conflicts but does not suppress it. Next, there is no provision for *preemption* in the transport infrastructure, which implements a strict FIFO order in the routers. Finally, *circular wait* is possible: we can easily imagine situations where trees are nested in such a way they form a cycle leading to routing-dependent deadlocks. Figure 6 displays a situation where two flows of messages of same type are inter-locked (any type is concerned). The messages may address different trees or the same tree (*read/response*). The trees may have same topology or overlap.

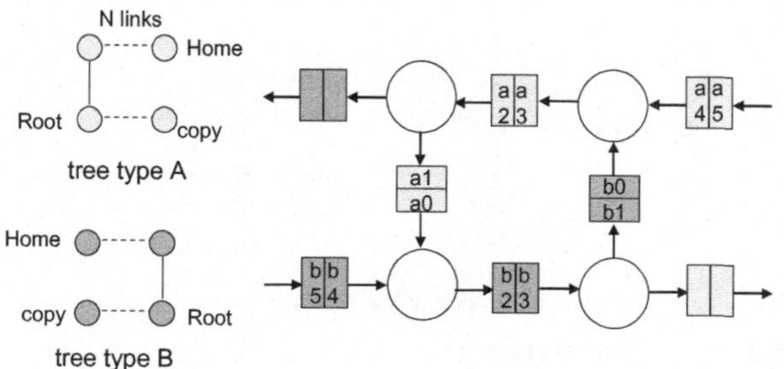

Figure 6: Routing-dependant deadlock.

As a consequence, since we cannot prevent the deadlocks, we implement detection and correction for them. A deadlock of any virtual channel is detected with a timeout on the next request waiting to go out in the output buffer.

Deadlock correction of read and response channels : the output request is cancelled and a *retry response* is sent to the requester. However for the response channel, all the responses of the output buffer at the same address are retried and if the first outcoming response has the flag "exit" set, then a *cleanup* is processed by the Protocol Engine in order to remove the branch being added.

Retry messages are used to help solving conflicting situations. This *response* indicates to the requester that its *read* request did not succeed and it has to retry later. Retry messages specify if the requester must wait for data (retried *response*) or not (the request was retried before reaching the data). As the *retry* has no more interaction with the tree, it is routed through the data channel with a deadlock free (X-Y) routing strategy.

The teardown messages are not retryable because the emitter of the message is probably removed from the tree when the conflict is detected. Furthermore, the teardown of a tree cannot be aborted without creating incoherent situation.

Our deadlock solution for teardown channel is to free the input buffers. So the deadlocked nodes will progressively enable the service of next output requests, which unlocks the situation. As an input request (*invalidate/ack/cleanup*) is propagated inside the tree, the Protocol Engine updates the line state in the directory and notifies in this entry that a teardown must be resumed. In order to do that, our minimal solution adds only one flag "Pending teardown" in the directory entry, and pending *invalidates* are not differentiated from pending *acks*. Therefore, *invalidates* may be repeated wrongly, but *invalidates* can be repeated without violating the protocol. Cases where an *ack* must be output are non ambiguous because they occur when only one link remains.

Therefore, when the situation is unlocked, an independent process resumes the pending requests. This process scans the directory by sending resume requests to the Protocol Engine. It competes with the input buffers with low priority. Once a directory entry is processed, the "Pending" flag is reset. Each time the resume process is stalled by a successive deadlock, the process fairly restarts from the stalled address, and proceeds circularly until it succeeds to make a complete turn without interruption.

5.3 Inconsistencies inside a tree due to races

As we cannot implement protocol transactions in an atomic way, races between transactions for the same tree may occur and cause inconsistencies. This phenomenon is worsened considerably by the distributed aspect of the protocol. Tree construction and teardown may occur simultaneously; new branches may be created by *responses* while other parts of the tree are removed partially by *cleanup* or completely by *invalidates*. The concurrent requests progress at different speeds according to the arbitration contentions and FIFO occupations. Multiple conflicting situations were identified, adding even more detection logic and sophistications to basic mechanisms. We distinguish different types of race issues:

1) **a *read* request** encountering a teardown is stalled at Home node. A *read* request is retried when it comes into a L2-cache that is sending a *cleanup* message to its node, or is still invalid because the data have not been received yet.

2) **races during edge construction:**
Atomicity: the building of a new branch cannot be atomic due to the distributed aspect of the protocol: several nodes may decide to propagate *responses* concurrently. Particularly, edge building between 2 vertices is not atomic. In a first time, only the edge initiator node has a link towards the target node. The edge is entirely built when both initiator and target nodes have a link towards the other node, as shown fig. 6. Therefore different situations may occur at a node: they are detected by using flag "exit" of the *response*, valid state of the node and source link of the *response*. In a cycle free situation, when a *response* exited the tree, it comes into a node from a direction that is not a link of the tree. The following table summarizes the different situations and the reactions of the Protocol Engine: when the situations are considered as too problematic, the *response* is changed into a *retry response*. The case where a *response* crosses a *cleanup* will be detailed in following paragraph V-3.

	invalid node	valid node invalid src link	valid node valid source link
response exit =1	normal situation: resp. proceeds	cycle forming: cleanup to src resp. proceeds	resp. crossing: cleanup to src resp. proceeds
exit=0	cleanup cross: retry response	cycle series: retry response	normal : resp. proceeds

Table 2: response processing by the Protocol Engine

Cycle series occurs when a further *response* is propagated through a link that creates a cycle, before the *cleanup* removes this link. This case is easily drawn by adding a node E at the North at node D in the fig. 5. Node E may send a *read* request just after D. Then the 2 *responses* follow the same path.

Response crossing: a case where 2 *responses* cross on a link and form a cycle is given is given by Fig. 6, and illustrates how unexpected situations may occur when concurrent branch constructions progress at different speeds. Starting from an initial tree H-A-R, branches of the tree are successively built by *responses*: R-D at t7, R-B at t9, B-E at t11. We assume that request from C proceeds towards the Home before the link D-R is registered in the directory of node D, and stays at the input of node E, until node E gets a copy of the line. The *response* to F exits the node R at t8, before branch R-B is created, but as the branch R-D already exits, it follows this link, and stays for a long time at the input of the node D (due to FIFO saturation, dependencies, etc). At clock cycle t14, node E sends its *response* to C, and node D sends its *response* to F. The two *responses* cross on the same link at the same time, each one coming from the opposite node, just after adding the link in the tree list. By applying the rule given in Table 2, both nodes D & E detect the situation and send back a *cleanup* to the other node.

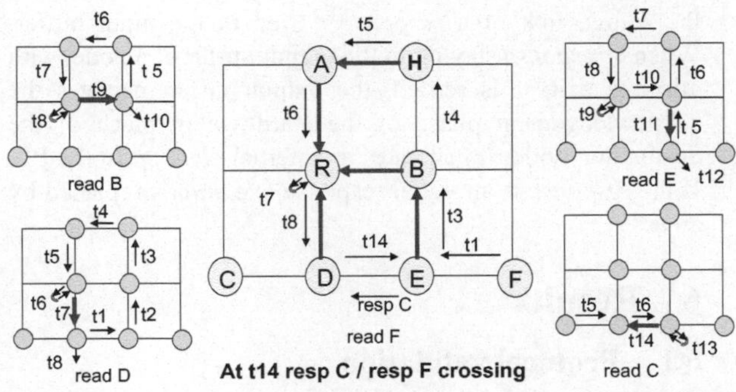

Figure 6: cycle forming by response crossing

3) **races occurring during a teardown** may :a) create an incoherent branch , b) insulate an *invalidate* message that will kill further the tree, c) block a teardown due to ack mismatch.

a) **avoiding the creation of an incoherent branch:**
The *read responses* in progress during a teardown are retried because they are creating new branches to be deleted. It is necessary to prevent the creation of a separate branch disconnected from the tree being deleted. So *read responses* are changed into *retry responses* by a Protocol Engine when the Node is already "Touched". But as *invalidates* and *responses* are in different virtual channels, they may be processed by a PE in any order. For example, an *invalidate* may pass beyond a *response* : it finds an invalid state if this *response* is building a new edge, so the *invalidate* is ineffective and the *response* will build a separate branch. In order to remedy such situations, when an *invalidate/ack/cleanup* message is processed by a node Protocol Engine, all the *responses* to the same address, staying inside input or output buffers of the node, are transformed into *retry response*. But in some cases, the conflict cannot be detected because the *response* is hidden to the other requests while crossing through the physical link. To solve this issue, we created a new request called *cleanback*, and an associated virtual channel. Each time a PE processes an *invalidate* or *cleanup*, it firstly sends a *cleanback* onto the source link of this request with a high priority. As soon as it is received by the source node, the *cleanback* cancels the *invalidate* and retries the *responses* at the same address, arrived before in the input buffer from the same link. The drawback of the *cleanback* solution is to bring non negligible traffic on the links in case of teardown.

b) **insulation of an invalidate message:**
An *invalidate* request must be cancelled itself by a *cleanback* when it is staying in the input buffer of a node. If this node already completed the teardown while the *invalidate* crossed through the link, the *invalidate* may be processed after, while a new tree is being built, therefore this tree is removed wrongly.

c) **acknowledge mismatch:**

A teardown is blocked if a node waits in vain for an *ack* which will never be generated. The rules to avoid such situations are the following. A *cleanup* request is interpreted as an *ack*, when it is received by a Node already marked as "Touched". The Protocol Engine propagates a *cleanup* to the source link of a *response* retried in the input buffer. When a *response* staying in the output buffer of a node, with attribute exit=1, is retried, the output buffer manages the acknowledgement phase of the teardown in place of the destination node: it generates an internal *cleanup* to the PE. If the *response* is an initial response, *cleanup* is replaced by an *ack*.

6 Results

6.1 Protocol validation

A model of the system was written in Verilog in order to make reliability tests on a FPGA platform. The model is reduced in order to put more nodes onto the FPGA. However the reduction of address space and directory sizes favours the occurrences of conflicts and critical situations for the protocol. Each cluster is replaced by a transactor in charge of generating requests to the network, and to provide responses to the requests coming from the network. The transactor detects output request timeout and non-consistent data or responses using a system reference memory. Requests are generated in a pseudo random way under constraints and the transactor holds 8 outstanding requests. The external memory or L3 level is modelled by a local FPGA RAM with rapid access.

Software simulations were performed on several NoC configurations of up to 16x16 nodes, each one during around 1M clock cycles. Executions on FPGA board (Altera/ Stratix III EP3SL150) DE3 of Terasic were done on configurations 2x2, 4x4 and 16x1, each one during 100 Gcycles @ 40MHz without error.

6.2 evaluation of performances and cost

Although we use a reduced node architecture (32-bit addresses, 1K-entry directory), we get a total area of 0,7mm2 from a logic synthesis of the node, in a 65nm CMOS LP technology from STMicroelectronics (with 70% cell area ratio). For a 4x4 network , throughput per node is about 30K (29334) *reads* for 1M clock cycles (3%) , e.g. a 33-cycle average delay between 2 *reads*. Directories of central nodes are clearly the bottleneck since they are busy up to 98% of time, due to uniform addressing and X-Y routing. For a 8x8 network, optimum insertion delay is about 75 cycles and resulting throughput per node is about 1080 *reads* for 1M cycle (0,1%), i.e. a 93-cycle average delay between 2 *reads*. Furthermore, the system is also auto-limited by the number of possible outstanding requests of each L2-cache.

Unsurprisingly, the performances of the reduced architecture are insufficient, even if uniform request address distribution is a worst case. Node directory access is the first bottleneck to solve. In [1], it is claimed that "the virtual tree cache is assumed to be maximally ported; there is a read and write port for each of the 5 router ports", but such memories cannot be implemented on real hardware. In order to draw near this ideal, we could use 1) dual port RAM to read/update status simultaneously, 2) adopt a multi-bank architecture (minimum 4 banks) for the directory, that leads to multiply the number of buffers and to increase the stage number of arbitration, having strong impact on area and consumption.

7 Conclusion

This paper addresses many issues found in the implementation of the IN-CC [1] protocol, most of them are related to the handling of concurrent requests resulted in building and/or removing simultaneously branches of virtual trees. This work illustrates the implementation complexity of a distributed protocol *versus* a centralised protocol. Efficient solutions have been proposed to avoid the creation of loops during virtual tree expansion and to recover from deadlocks during the teardown process. Specific corrective action has been founded for each race issue, increasing however the protocol complexity. Finally, our experiences demonstrate that the IN-CC protocol necessitates a more sophisticated switch architecture in order to provide better performances. Those considerations are parts of our present and future works.

Acknowledgment : we would like to thank Patrice Bulot (Bull) who contributed to the design of cache transactor and implemented the model in the FPGA platform. This work was achieved within the frame of the European CATRENE TSAR project and supported by the French Public Authority.

8 References

[1] N. Eisley, L.-S. Peh, et L. Shang, "In-Network Cache Coherence," in 39th Annual IEEE/ACM International Symposium on Microarchitecture, 2006. MICRO-39, 2006, p. 321 -332.

[2] Y.-C. Maa, D. K. Pradhan, et D. Thiebaut, "A hierarchical directory scheme for large-scale cache-coherent multiprocessors," in Parallel Processing Symposium, 1992. Proceedings., Sixth International, 1992, p. 43 -46.

[3] M. Thapar, B. Delagi, et M. J. Flynn, "Linked list cache coherence for scalable shared memory multiprocessors," in Parallel Processing Symposium, 1993., Proceedings of Seventh International, 1993, p. 34 -43.

[4] Q. Li et S. Vlaovic, "Redundant linked list based cache coherence protocol," in Proceedings of IEEE Workshop on Fault-Tolerant Parallel and Distributed Systems, 1994, 1994, p. 43 -50.

[5] R. Simoni et M. Horowitz, "Dynamic Pointer Allocation for Scalable Cache Coherence Directories," in International Symposium on Shared Memory Multiprocessing, 1991, p. 72–81.

[6] N. D. Enright Jerger, L.-S. Peh, et M. H. Lipasti, "Virtual tree coherence: Leveraging regions and in-network multicast trees for scalable cache coherence," in Proceedings of the 41st annual IEEE/ACM International Symposium on Microarchitecture, Washington, DC, USA, 2008, p. 35–46.

[7] "TSAR project website" [Online]. Available: https://wwwsoc.lip6.fr/trac/tsar/

[8] Coffman, E., & Elphick, M. J. (1971). System Deadlocks. *Computing Surveys*, 67--78.

[9] A.Hansson, K.Goossens, A.Radulescu "Avoiding Message-Dependant Deadlock in Network-Based Systems on Chip" Research Article in VLSI Design January 1, Introduction

A Visualization System and Monitoring Tool to Measure Concurrency in MPICH Programs

Michael Scherger
Department of Computer Science
Texas Christian University
Email: m.scherger@tcu.edu

Zakir Hussain Syed
Department of Computing Sciences
Texas A&M University - Corpus Christi
Email: zsyed@islander.tamucc.edu

Abstract – *Distributed algorithms implemented using MPI are often concerned with time and message complexities. These measures mainly address the quantitative aspect of the distributed programs. The qualitative aspect, which is the performance of the distributed program, can be ascertained only by measuring the concurrency of the distributed program. Raynal, in 1992, developed a method of computing concurrency of distributed computations based on the volumetric abstractions of cones and cylinders. Both cone and cylinder abstractions make use of the values: weight, volume and height. With the help of these 3 values, the measure of concurrency can be calculated for both cone and cylinder abstraction. In this research, a visualization system was developed that measures and analyzes the concurrency of a distributed program by making use MPICH event clog2 event trace files and the above cone and cylinder abstractions. This paper will discuss the development of this visualization system and the accuracy and efficiency of the visualization tool.*

Keywords: Concurrency measurements, distributed systems, software visualization tools, MPI, vector clocks.

1. Introduction

In distributed algorithms, time and message complexities are the two measures that are used to identify the efficiency of a distributed program. However, these two measurements are quantitative and do not answer address any concerns regarding the quality of the distributed program, or amount of concurrency in a program. Without a measure to calculate the quality of the distributed program, it is not certain to know if the execution is well distributed and if the execution will have delays due to synchronization constraints [8].

These questions can be answered by finding the amount of concurrency in the distributed computation. The underlying theoretical approach, used in this research and visualization system, is quoted in [8]. According to this approach, the degree of concurrency can be calculated by quantifying the synchronization delay. Synchronization delay is a delay that might exist between two successive events in the same process.

In order to measure the concurrency, this research makes use of two abstractions, a cone and a cylinder. These geometric shapes are used to quantify the synchronization delay and to find the concurrency measure. The cone abstraction is associated with individual events, whereas the cylinder abstraction is associated with the whole program computation. Three values are associated with both the abstractions: *weight*, *volume* and *height*.

Cone and cylinder abstraction will be discussed further in section 2. The design of the visualization system that automates the calculation of concurrency by making use of the said approach will be discussed in section 3. The evaluation of the visualization system is tested on a sample program as is discussed in section 4. Section 5 will present future work and conclusions.

2. Background and Related Research

To implement the concept to causality relation in distributed system, Lamport proposed logical clocks in 1978 [6]. He proposed the concept of causality relation (also known as happen before relation) denoted by "→" which described the causal ordering of events.

In [5] and [7], Fidge and Mattern independently proposed vector clocks that overcame the limitation of logical clocks. A vector clock of a system of *N* processes is a vector of *N* logical clocks, one clock per process. In vector clocks, a local copy of the global clock array is kept in each process. However, a vector clock only provides the timestamp of the event. The use of these timestamp values to find the interval between 2 events but the concurrency of the distributed computation cannot be known from the vector clock elements.

2.1. Concurrency Measures

While calculating a concurrency measure, it is assumed that the message passing is instantaneous. It is also assumed that each event consumes approximately the same amount of computing time. This computing time is known as time unit.

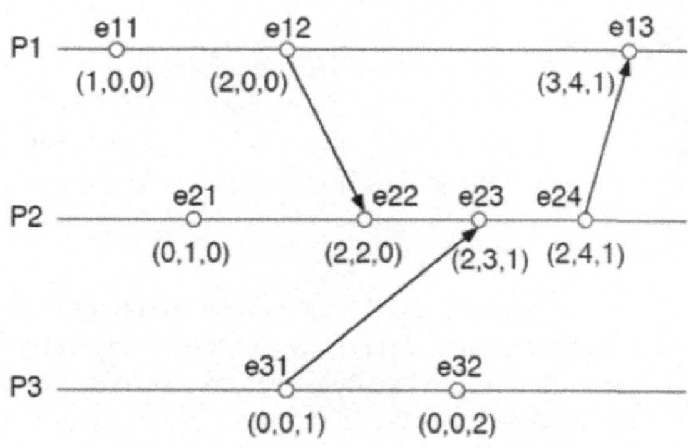

Figure 1: Sample time-event diagram.

The time-event diagram shown in Figure 1 has 3 processes and each process contains some events. Vector timestamps are shown on each event. The delay between two events is known as synchronization delay. The purpose of concurrency measure is to effectively measure the number of synchronization delay. This idea was first introduced in [3].

2.2. Cone and cylinder abstractions

In order to effectively measure synchronization delay, cone and cylinder abstractions were introduced. Cone abstraction deals with the concurrency measure of the individual event. Cylinder abstraction deals with the concurrency measure of the entire computation.

From [8], with cone and cylinder abstractions, three values are associated: *volume*, *weight* and *height*. Weight, denoted by *wt*, in a cone abstraction is the exact number of events that causally precede an event *e*. Weight in a cylinder abstraction is the number of events that are produced in the total computation. Volume, denoted by *vol*, in a cone abstraction is the maximum number of events that could possibly precede an event *e*. Volume in a cylinder abstraction is the maximum number of events that can be produced in the entire computation. Height, denoted by *ht*, in a cone abstraction is the number of events that could come before the event *e* but it has to be on the longest causal path ending with event *e*. Height in a cylinder abstraction is the largest logical time associated with an event *e*.

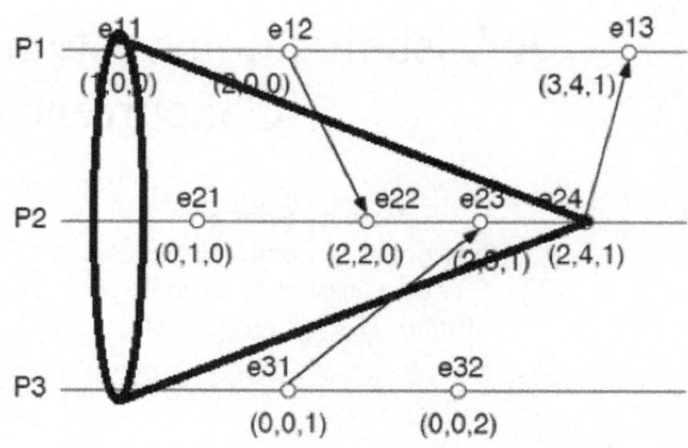

Figure 2: Cone abstraction on time-event diagram.

Note: a similar analysis can be constructed for a cylinder abstraction on a time-event diagram.

2.3. Calculating Concurrency

From [8], the concurrency measure is calculated for cone and cylinder abstraction using the following formulas,

For cone abstraction:

$$\alpha'_e(e) = \frac{vol(CON(e)) - wt(CON(e))}{vol(CON(e)) - ht(CON(e))}$$

For cylinder abstraction:

$$\alpha'(C) = \frac{vol(CYL(C)) - wt(CYL(C))}{vol(CYL(C)) - ht(CYL(C))}$$

In the above equations the numerator denote the total number of synchronization delay which have actually occurred and the denominator denotes the maximum number of synchronization delay which could have possibly occurred.

Once the value of $\alpha'_e(e)$ and $\alpha'(C)$ are calculated, it is subtracted from 1 in order to get the concurrency measure. The reason it has to be subtracted from 1 is because as it is seen in both [3] and [4], when $\alpha = 1$, the computation is said to be maximally concurrent and when $\alpha = 0$, the computation is said to be sequential. Hence by subtracting by 1, the concurrency measure calculated in [8] can be made compatible with [3] and [4].

3. System Design

The input to the visualization system is a clog2 trace file that is generated by the program written using MPICH2. The clog2 is a default log format of Multi-Processing Environment (MPE), which is a suite of performance analysis tools for programs written for MPI. The visualization system was written solely in Java and supporting tools. The concurrency measure database was created using a MySQL database and the bridge between Java and MySQL was made with the help of Hibernate. Third-party Java libraries such as JFreeChart were used to display graphs and Jssh was used to establish connection with the Linux server.

As shown in Figure 3, the user would initiate the application by giving authorization to make a connection to the Linux server by entering the hostname, username and password.

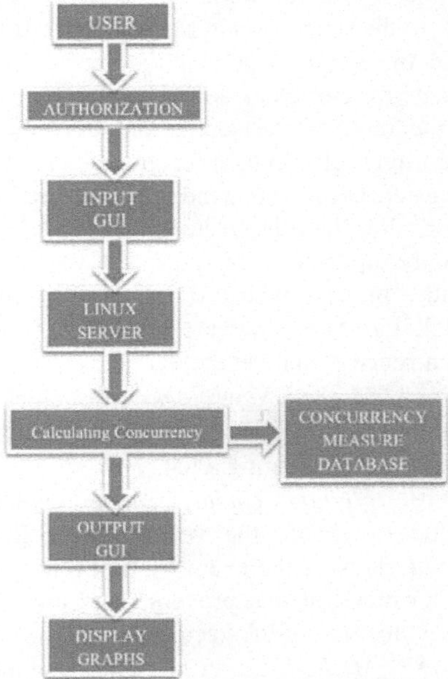

Figure 3: Concurrency visualization system design.

Once the connection is established with the server, Figure 3 shows the GUI that is displayed prompting the user to enter the name of the MPI program, number of processes and a command line argument, which is optional. The application can access the MPI program file on the server written in C/C++ only when it is stored in a folder called "Project" and has a makefile. The application then executes the MPI program on the server multiple times and each time the MPI program executes, the clog2 file will be converted from binary to text format using the "clog2_print" UNIX command and then the contents of clog2 file will be written and stored in a text file on the client machine. With the help of these clog2 files, the visualization system can measure the concurrency of the distributed computation and it stores the concurrency measures in the concurrency measure database. When all the concurrency measure values have been calculated, the output GUI is displayed. From the output GUI, the user can select a graph to view.

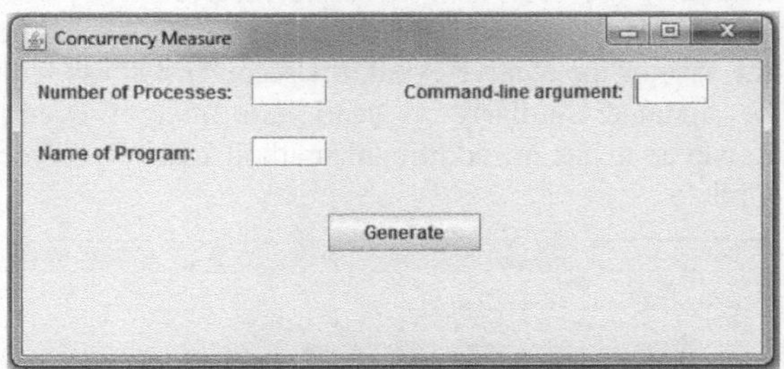

Figure 4: System input GUI screen.

Once the generate button is pressed, the user's input would be used to generate several script files to control the execution of the program. The program will then generate a series of clog2 files which are then parsed and imported into a database for further analysis.

One of the challenges of this research was to determine the structure of the clog2 file generated by the MPE environment when an MPI program is executed. The original clog2 file is passed through this parser to find the size of the communicator and the number assigned to the starting and ending event of the internal event. Scanning each line of the clog2 file searching for some specific words does this. The first word is "max_comm_word_size", the variable assigned to this word will be the size of the communicator. The size of the communicator is extracted and stored in the variable "size". The words "s_et" and "e_et" corresponds to start event and end event respectively and the number assigned to both start and end event are extracted, as shown in Figure 5.

Once the have the size, start event and end event are determined, the document can be searched for only the required information. The parser scans each sentence, searching for the occurrence of "send", "recv" (start event, and end event). The lines that contain these words will be written to another text file. This text file will be named as the name of the program entered by the user in the input GUI followed by "_required info". The newly created text file will be used by the application to measure the concurrency of the distributed computation.

The text file created in the previous section will be passed through this parser, which is known as "InfoParser". This parser would first scan the text file line by line determining which event is occurring on each line.

If the event is a send event then the "Send Event" method is called which will update the vector clock of the sender process. It first checks if the clock has been initialized, if the clock has already been initialized it will call the "Update Clock" method otherwise it will call the "New Clock" method.

Similarly the vector clock of the receiver process is updated if the type of the event is internal event. In the case of the receive event, the receiver process will be updated similarly to send and internal event, however it has an additional method call "Receiver Update".

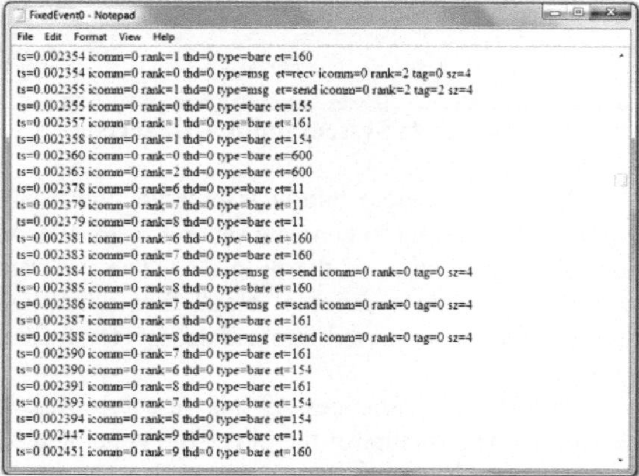

```
FixedEvent0 - Notepad
File Edit Format View Help
ts=0.002354 icomm=0 rank=1 thd=0 type=bare et=160
ts=0.002354 icomm=0 rank=0 thd=0 type=msg  et=recv icomm=0 rank=2 tag=0 sz=4
ts=0.002355 icomm=0 rank=1 thd=0 type=msg  et=send icomm=0 rank=2 tag=2 sz=4
ts=0.002355 icomm=0 rank=0 thd=0 type=bare et=155
ts=0.002357 icomm=0 rank=1 thd=0 type=bare et=161
ts=0.002358 icomm=0 rank=1 thd=0 type=bare et=154
ts=0.002360 icomm=0 rank=0 thd=0 type=bare et=600
ts=0.002363 icomm=0 rank=2 thd=0 type=bare et=600
ts=0.002378 icomm=0 rank=6 thd=0 type=bare et=11
ts=0.002379 icomm=0 rank=7 thd=0 type=bare et=11
ts=0.002379 icomm=0 rank=8 thd=0 type=bare et=11
ts=0.002381 icomm=0 rank=6 thd=0 type=bare et=160
ts=0.002383 icomm=0 rank=7 thd=0 type=bare et=160
ts=0.002384 icomm=0 rank=6 thd=0 type=msg  et=send icomm=0 rank=0 tag=0 sz=4
ts=0.002385 icomm=0 rank=8 thd=0 type=bare et=160
ts=0.002386 icomm=0 rank=7 thd=0 type=msg  et=send icomm=0 rank=0 tag=0 sz=4
ts=0.002387 icomm=0 rank=6 thd=0 type=bare et=161
ts=0.002388 icomm=0 rank=8 thd=0 type=msg  et=send icomm=0 rank=0 tag=0 sz=4
ts=0.002390 icomm=0 rank=7 thd=0 type=bare et=161
ts=0.002390 icomm=0 rank=6 thd=0 type=bare et=154
ts=0.002391 icomm=0 rank=8 thd=0 type=bare et=161
ts=0.002393 icomm=0 rank=7 thd=0 type=bare et=154
ts=0.002394 icomm=0 rank=8 thd=0 type=bare et=154
ts=0.002447 icomm=0 rank=9 thd=0 type=bare et=11
ts=0.002451 icomm=0 rank=9 thd=0 type=bare et=160
```

Figure 5: Sample clog2 file.

The parser will create two new vector clocks for each event in the distributed computation. The first vector clock is known as "LocalClock", this vector clock is like any other vector clock. However, the second vector clock, which is known as "WeightClock", is a special vector clock, as it keeps tracks of the synchronization delays between the events.

Summaries of methods created for this visualization system are described here.

- *Method Line separator:* When a line is read from the text file, the parser will determine if the event is a send, receive or internal event by looking at the type of the message and call the appropriate subordinate method.
- *Method Internal event:* If the event is an internal event then it will either call the "New Clock" method (first call) or the "Update Clock" method.
- *Method Send event:* If the event is a send event then it will either call the "New Clock" method (first call) or the "Update Clock" method.
- *Method Receive event:* If the event is a receive event then it will either call the "New Clock" method (first call) or the "Update Clock" method. After updating the vector clock of the receiver process, receive event will call "Receiver update" to update its value by comparing with the vector clock of the corresponding send event.
- *Method Receiver update:* Receiver update is called to update the vector clock of the receiver process by comparing it with the vector clock of the sender process. In the case of multiple send events as seen in *send event,* receiver update will first retrieve the corresponding vector clock of the send event from the array list and then each position of the vector clock in receiver process is compared with the corresponding position in the vector clock of the sender process. The maximum of the two values is then updated in the vector clock of the receiver process. The above procedure only works when a corresponding send event has already occurred before this receive event. In some cases, it was noticed that the clog2 text file had receive events occurring before send events. Simulating a send event solved this problem. For example, if receive event occurred before the send event at the very start of the clog2 file then the vector clock of the receive event will be updated vector clock with 1 in the ith position, where i is the rank of the sender process and keeping the remaining elements as zero. If the receive event occurred before the send event in the middle of the clog2 file, then the vector clock of the receive event will be updated with the latest vector clock of the sender process where the ith position of the vector clock has been incremented by 1 to simulate the occurrence of send event.
- *Method New clock:* New clock is called to initialize the vector clock. It initializes the vector clock by first creating a list.
- *Method Update clock:* Update clock is called to update the vector clock. It updates the vector clock of the event by first retrieving the latest vector clock of that process i and then it increments the ith position of the vector clock.
- *Method ConcCal:* This method calculates the measure of concurrency. This method takes the weight, volume and height as arguments. After receiving the values, it computes in the formula to calculate the measure of concurrency [8].
- *Method Cylinder abstraction:* After all the values have been calculated for "LocalClock" and "WeightClock", the method "CylinderCal" is called. This method first takes the ith position of each process i and stores it in an array. It then adds the elements of the array to find the weight of the cylinder. The height of the cylinder is calculated by taking the "WeightClock" of the last event of the distributed computation and finding the maximum value among them. Volume is calculated by simply multiplying the height with the number of processes. Once the value is known for weight, volume and height, the concurrency can be easily calculated by sending the 3 values as arguments to ConcCal method, which after calculating the concurrency of the cylinder returns it back to "CylinderCal".
- *Method Cone abstraction:* Since the cone abstraction is associated with individual events, its concurrency must be calculated after completion of each event. This can be achieved by having 3 methods for weight, volume and height.

Once the value of weight, volume and height is known for each event, the method "ConeCal" is called. This method will remove the first element from the lists "Weight", "Volume" and "Height" and then it sends the 3 values as arguments to the method "ConcCal", which after calculating concurrency returns it backs to "ConeCal". This is repeated until the 3 lists are empty and the measure of concurrency for each event in the distributed computation.

The output GUI consists of 6 buttons, 5 of the 6 buttons corresponds to a type of graph and the 6th is the exit button, as shown in Figure 6.

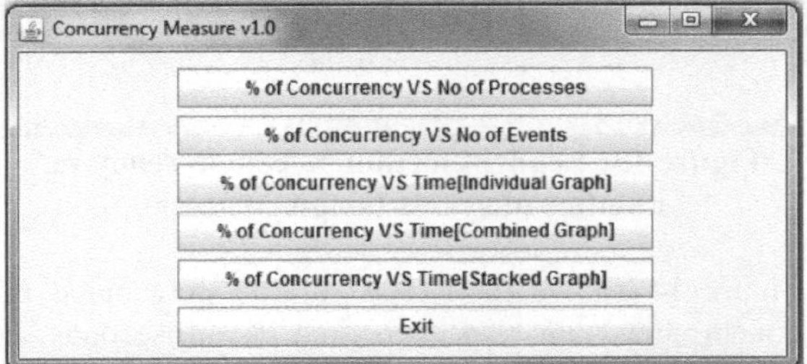

Figure 6: Output graph selection GUI screen.

The 1st button when clicked would display the graph plotted with percentage of concurrency measure on the y-axis and the number of processes on the x-axis as shown in Figure 7. The 2nd button when clicked would display the graph plotted with percentage of concurrency measure on the y-axis and the number of events on the x-axis as shown in Figure 8.

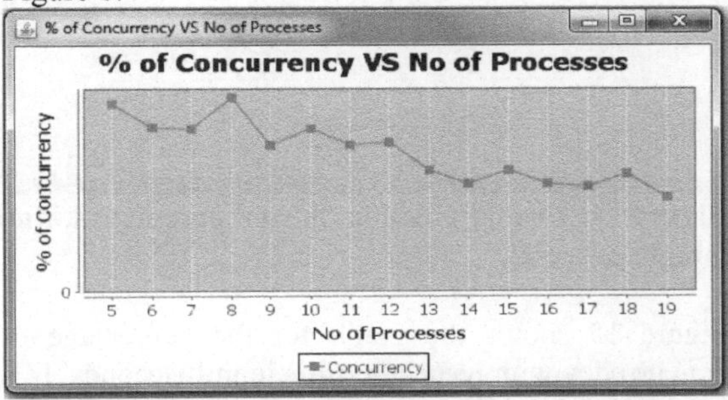

Figure 7: Sample graph of % concurrency vs. number of processes.

The 3rd button when clicked would display the graph plotted with percentage of concurrency measure on the y-axis and time (in milliseconds) on the x-axis as shown in Figure 9. The 4th button when clicked would display the graph plotted with percentage of concurrency measure on the y-axis and time (in milliseconds) on the x-axis, however the concurrency measure of each process is displayed separately as shown in Figure 10. The 5th button when clicked would display the graph plotted with percentage of concurrency measure on the y-axis and time (in milliseconds) on the x-axis, however this graph is a collection of smaller graphs stacked one over the other, where each graph corresponds to a process as shown in Figure 11.

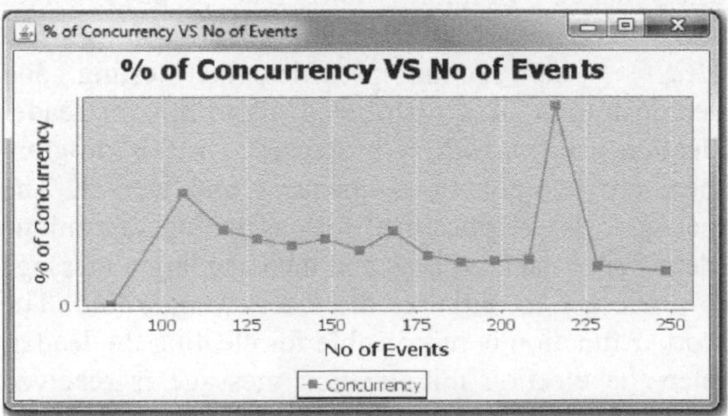

Figure 8: Sample graph of % concurrency vs. number of events.

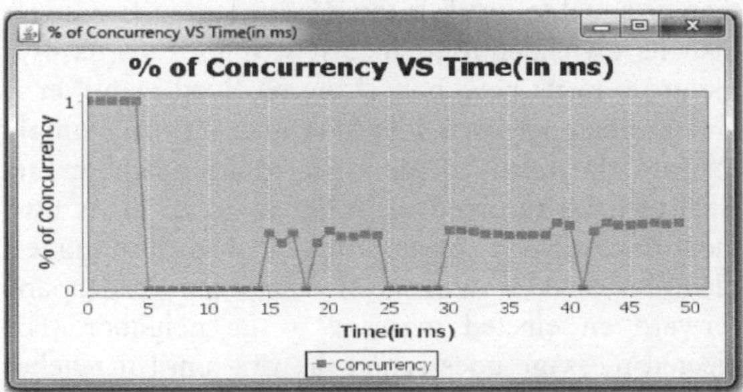

Figure 9: Sample graph of % concurrency vs. time (individual process).

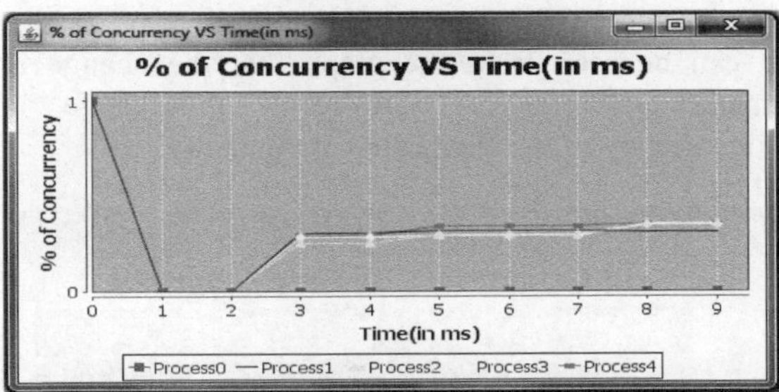

Figure 10: Sample graph of % concurrency vs. time (combined processes).

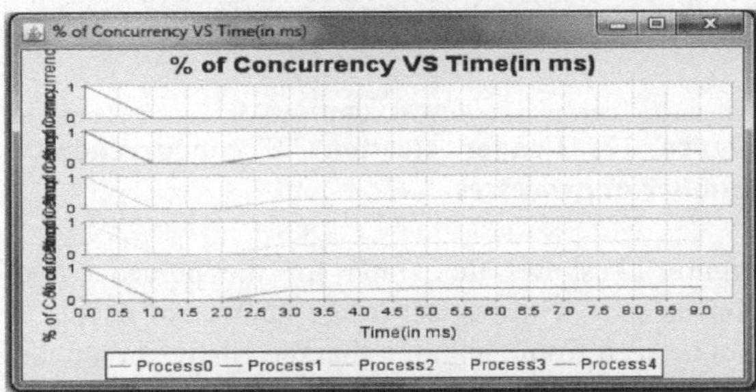

Figure 11: Sample graph of % concurrency vs. time (stacked processes).

4. Experimental Results

The visualization system was tested on several benchmark and sample student-programming assignments. (*Author's note: Due to page length limitations only one such program is discussed.- MCS*) This section provides the testing and demonstration of a distributed algorithm for leader election using a ring of processes. In this program there are two functions, manager and worker. The manager is responsible for assigning a unique identifier to each process and then sending a message to process 1 to initialize the election algorithm. The worker function is responsible for electing the leader, once the election initialization message is received from the manager, it will start the election algorithm. In the election algorithm it performs 3 checks, it checks if the received identifier is less than, greater than or equal to itself. If the received identifier is less than its own identifier, then it will forward its own identifier to its neighbor. If the received identifier is greater than its own identifier than it will simply forward the received identifier to its neighbor and finally if the received identifier is equal to its own identifier then it means that it has the highest identifier and it will elect itself the leader and forward an elected message to its neighbor. The elected message goes round the ring until it reaches back to the process which was elected the leader and the program terminates.

Figure 12 shows the graph for the percentage of concurrency with respect to the number of processes. It can be seen from the graph that the change in number of process will result in change in concurrency of the distributed computation.

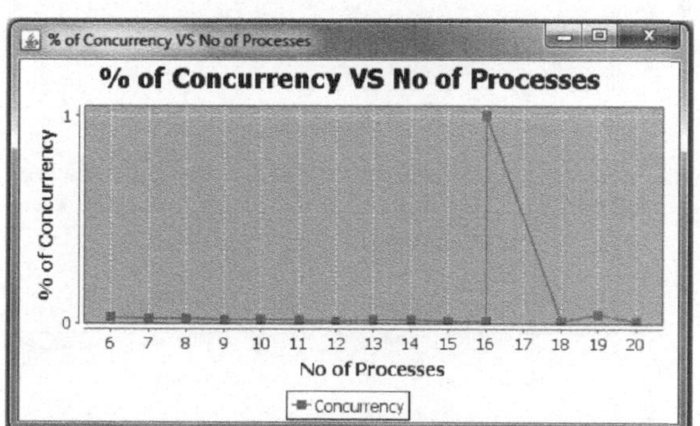

Figure 12: Leader election % concurrency vs. number of processes.

Figure 13 shows the graph for the percentage of concurrency with respect to the number of events. It can be seen from the graph that the change in number of events will result in change in concurrency of the distributed computation. Since this program does not take any command line arguments, the graph would be plotted by counting the events occurring in the program and finding the concurrency, so in some of the cases the number of events can be same for two or more programs.

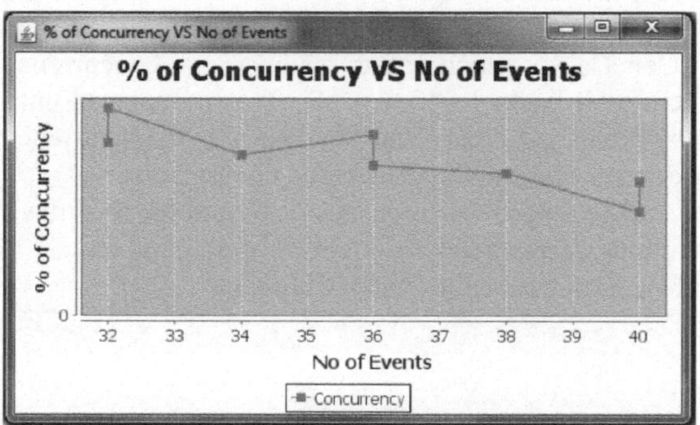

Figure 13: Leader election % concurrency vs. number of events (single process).

Figure 14 shows the graph for the percentage of concurrency with respect to time in milliseconds. It can be seen from the graph that the concurrency of this program oscillates between 0 and 1 in the beginning and then it slowly reduces with time.

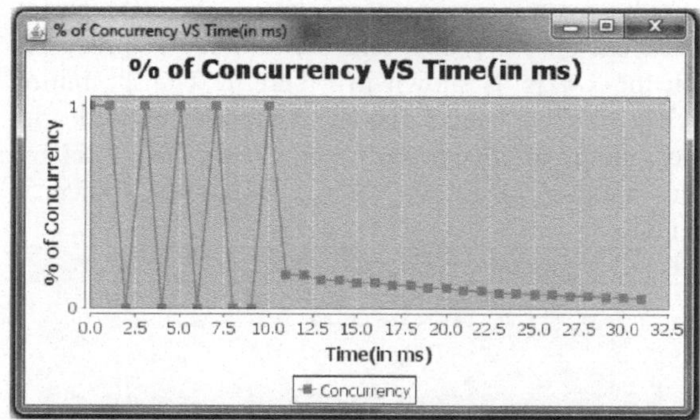

Figure 14: Leader election % concurrency vs. time (single process).

Figure 15 shows the graph for the percentage of concurrency with respect to time in milliseconds. It is interesting to see in the graph that one process 0 had concurrency of 100% while the concurrency of other processes was in the range of 0 to 10%.

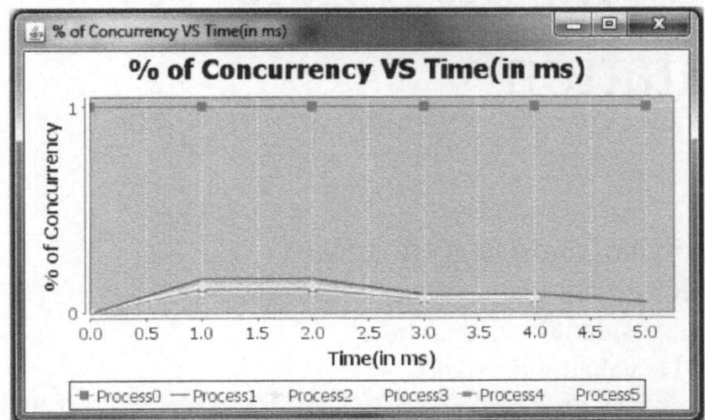

Figure 15: Leader election % concurrency vs. number of events (all processes).

Figure 16 shows the graph for the percentage of concurrency with respect to time in milliseconds. It can be seen from the graph that the concurrency of process 0 was 100% and the remaining processes had maximum concurrency of 10%.

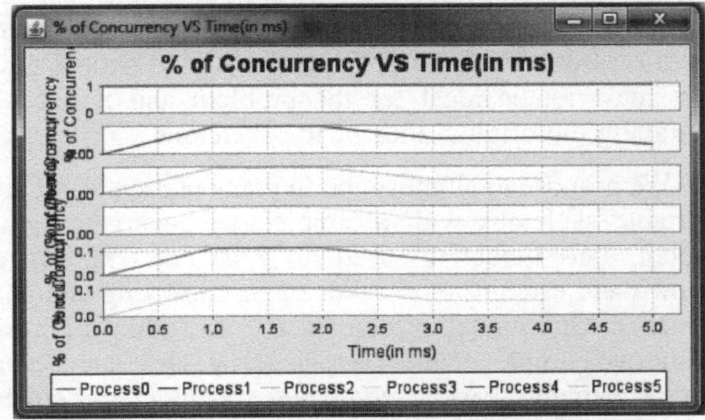

Figure 16: Leader election % concurrency vs. time (stacked processes).

5. Future Work and Conclusions

In this research, a visualization system to measure the concurrency of a distributed computation is implemented. The visualization system is based on the approach proposed in [8].

The proposed visualization system is designed to be very user friendly. The user can enter the input values in the user interface and the tool does all the necessary calculations to compute and visualize the concurrency of a program.

This tool was able to accurately measure the concurrency for both cylinder and cone abstraction. By looking at the graphs generated by this tool, we were able to easily differentiate between a sequential program and a program that was written concurrently.

The visualization system can be further improved by implementing a scanner at the very start of the program. The function of this scanner would be to scan the clog2 file and find any inconsistencies and try to rectify them.

It is known that sometimes the test programs can be large and may take a lot of time to measure the concurrency. In the future, having a proper database to store the concurrency values of each program can solve this problem. The GUI could be modified where the user can select the name of the program that has already run through the tool and the tool will just load the values from the database and display them instead of calculating them again.

References

1. D.P. Bertsekaa and J.N. Tsitsiklis., *Parallel and Distributed Computation, Numerical Methods.* Prentice-Hall, Inc., 1989.
2. Chandy, K.M and Lamport, L., "Distributed Snapshots: Determining Global States of Distributed Systems", *ACM Transactions on Computer Systems*, Vol. 3, No. 1, February 1985, Pages 63-75.
3. Charron-Bost, B. Measure of Parallelism of Distributed Computations", In B. Monien, editor, *Proceedings of the 6th Annual Symposium onTheoretical Aspects of Computer Science (STACS 89),* pages 434-445, 1989.
4. Fidge, C.J., "A Simple Run-Time Concurrency Measure". *3rd Australian Transputer and OCCAM User Group Conference*, 1990.
5. Fidge, C.J., "Logical Time in Distributed Computing Systems", *Computer*, vol.24, no.8, pp.28-33, Aug, 1991.
6. Lamport, L., "Time, Clocks, and the Ordering of Events in a Distributed System", *Communications of the ACM*, Vol. 21, no.7, July 1978.
7. Mattern, F., "Virtual Time and Global States of Distributed Systems", *Proceedings of the International Workshop on Parallel and Distributed Algorithms*, 1988.
8. Raynal, M.; Mizuno, M.; Neilsen, M.L.; "Synchronization and concurrency measures for distributed computations", *Proceedings of the 12th International Conference on Distributed Computing Systems,* pp.700-707, 1992.

Runtime Support for Dynamic Skeletons Implementation

Javier Fresno, Arturo Gonzalez-Escribano, and Diego R. Llanos
Departamento de Informática
Edif. Tecn. de la Información, Universidad de Valladolid,
Campus Miguel Delibes, 47011 Valladolid, Spain
E-mail: {jfresno, arturo, diego}@infor.uva.es

Abstract—**Algorithmic skeletons have proved to be a good solution to the problem of implementing parallel applications with specify communication structures. They define the overall structure of the computation, hiding the complex communication details. Nowadays, the different frameworks available offer a fixed set of skeletons. The programmer can implement efficient programs if the computation and communication patterns match the available skeletons. Because of that, the usage of skeleton frameworks has been limited to an important but relative small set of patterns featuring the most common parallel structures, such as map, pipeline, farm, or wavefront.**

In this paper, we present a programming model that can be used to implement efficient and portable parallel skeletons. We also discuss its implementation and integration into Hitmap, a tool for hierarchical tiling and mapping. This combined proposal allows to develop tailored static and dynamic skeletons while still hiding implementation and communication details. The performance of the implementation is measured against a well-known skeleton framework.

Keywords*—*Algorithm skeletons, Parallel programming models, Dynamic computation

I. Introduction

Development of parallel software is a quite complicated task. Typically, programming for parallel machines is based on message passing libraries such as MPI [1] or shared memory APIs like OpenMP [2]. These solutions allow to write portable code for different machine architectures. However, the programmer has to deal with several non-trivial issues such as problem decomposition, data distribution across processes, local computation, data exchanges, load balancing, or synchronization. Consequently, implementing and debugging a parallel application can be a tedious and error-prone task.

Algorithm skeletons [3], [4] offer the programmer a different view, based on the fact that many parallel algorithms share common computation patterns. Skeletons are a high-level parallel programming model that aims to encapsulate the overall structure of computation, hiding the complex details of parallel applications. With skeletons, programmers do not have to write the code to perform the coordination or communication. They only have to provide the specific code to solve the problem, using the skeleton as a template.

The skeletons could be classified in two groups depending on the nature of their computation structure. A skeleton with a static computation structure (i.e. based on a stencil) can be implemented with coarse-grain partition techniques, using a static scheduling that can be pre-calculated at compilation or initialization time. However, in a dynamic computation structure (i.e. a farm), where data dependent tasks flow through diverse computation stages, dynamic load-balancing solutions are needed to develop efficient programs.

Due to the advantages provided by the use of algorithmic skeletons, a significant number of frameworks and libraries have been developed so far. However, each one of them offers a limited set of skeletons focused on particular techniques or architectures. Thus, the programmer has to choose a solution that may not be ideal for the problem and/or not portable, betraying the original idea of the skeletons.

We propose to simplify the implementation of efficient and portable skeletons with a simple and generic programming model. This model is based on Petri nets [5], [6], a well-known and established formalism for modeling and analyzing systems. Our model represents the task flow of a skeleton with two simple element types (processes and containers). These elements can be combined to model the structure of any skeleton. The model supports both static and dynamic structures. However, we focus on dynamic skeletons since the static ones can be more easily implemented with static scheduling techniques.

This paper also shows how to efficiently implement the proposed model. We have developed an implementation integrated into Hitmap, a tool for hierarchical tiling and mapping of dense arrays and sparse structures. Hitmap already offers solutions to automatize programs with static computation structures. It incorporates data partition techniques that automatically adapt the program to the current data size and current available computational units. Our extension adds support for dynamic skeletons in Hitmap.

Experimental work has been conducted to prove that the implementation achieves good performance with a case of study. Any framework using the proposed abstraction layer can take advantage of this generic model to design skeletons while obtaining efficient implementations.

The rest of the paper is organized as follows. Section II describes some related work in the field. A list of common skeletons and related concepts is given in Sect. III. Section IV discusses the design of our solution model. Section V provides an overview of the Hitmap library, while Sect. VI shows the implementation of our solution in Hitmap. Section VII presents experimental work conducted to test this implementation. Finally, Section VIII concludes our paper.

II. Related work

This section describes some related skeleton frameworks. Each one of them has a different approach, offering a set of skeletons, or focusing on a particular architecture. A more exhaustive survey can be found in [7].

Some skeleton frameworks are designed with a distributed memory model in mind. For example, the Edinburgh Skeleton Library (eSkel) [8] is a C library that uses the standard message passing interface (MPI). It defines several data and task skeletons that are presented as collective operations involving groups of processes.

Another distributed skeleton framework is the Münster Skeleton Library Muesli [9]. It also uses MPI for communications. Muesli follows a two-tier model, where data parallel skeletons can be nested inside task parallel ones. This library is implemented with C++ and takes advantage of object-oriented features, such as polymorphic types.

A successful solution for shared-memory multi-core architectures is Threading Building Blocks (TBB) [10], a library developed by Intel. TBB provides a portable implementation of parallel patterns, thread-safe containers, and synchronization primitives. The core of the library is a thread pool managed by a task scheduler. This scheduler efficiently maps tasks onto threads, balancing the computational load using a work-stealing algorithm.

A well-known model for processing large data sets is MapReduce [11]. It is a two-stage model and it is used to process pairs of key/value elements. There are several implementations of this model, for example the open-source project Apache Hadoop.

Finally, SkelCL [12] is a GPU skeleton library based on data-parallel algorithmic skeletons. It generates OpenCL code, that is compiled by OpenCL at runtime.

III. A Skeleton Taxonomy

Skeletons are generally classified as *data parallel* and *task parallel*. Previous surveys add an extra category with part of the task skeletons class, named *resolution skeletons* [7], [9]. Data parallel skeletons work with data structures and manipulate their elements according with computation patterns in a fine grain. Task parallel skeletons compute workflows of tasks. Resolution skeletons solve a family of problems with iterative phases of computation, communication, and control.

We propose to classify the skeletons in *static* or *dynamic*. depending on the nature of their computation structure. Static skeletons maintain the same structure during all their execution, whereas dynamic skeletons have a mutable computation structure. Static skeletons can take advantage of static scheduling methods pre-calculated during the initialization phase. While dynamic skeletons need dynamic scheduling and load balancing techniques.

Table I shows the relation between both classifications. Data parallel skeletons are static. On the other hand, resolutions skeletons are dynamic because their computation structure depend on the particular data being processed. Finally, we find in the task-parallel skeletons class both static and dynamic examples.

	Static	**Dynamic**
Data parallel	map, fork, zip, reduce, scan, stencil	-
Task parallel	pipeline, wavefront	farm
Resolution	-	divide and conquer (D&C), branch and bound (B&B), mapreduce

TABLE I. Algorithm taxonomy.

A. *Summary of skeleton solutions*

There are several design concepts that have to be taken into account when developing a new skeleton framework. This section collects the details introduced previously in the literature.

a) Nesting mode: If a skeleton uses internally another one, there are two possible nesting modes: transient or persistent [8], [13]. In a transient nesting, the outer skeleton calls an inner one to process some internal data. The inner skeleton only exists during the invocation of the external stage. A new instance is created each time. In a persistent nesting, the input and output of the outer skeleton is mapped to the inner one. The instance is persistent between invocations.

b) Interaction mode: This concept defines the relationship between the skeleton input and output. There are two possible interaction modes: implicit and explicit [8]. In an implicit interaction mode, a skeleton produces an output for each consumed input. In an explicit interaction mode, a stage in the skeleton can produce an output arbitrarily without a previous input. Moreover, a skeleton can process an input without producing a result.

c) Task scheduler: Several skeletons such as Farm or Divide&Conquer are composed of a set of workers. This kind of skeleton needs a mechanism to send the tasks to workers and to collect the results. The use of a dispatcher and a collector is one of the possible solutions. However, it has been proved that this solution does not achieve a good performance [14]. Instead, distributed solutions, such as the TBB scheduler [10] or a distributed work pool [15], are preferred because they avoid the contention and bottleneck that may arise with the use of a centralized scheme.

d) Task distribution: A work pool requires a distribution scheme to assign task to workers. Since the time required to process a particular task is usually not known, many work pools assume that each one requires the same time. Under these conditions, there are two independent distribution schemes: Random and cyclic. Both schemes lead to similar performance when there are a big number of tasks. However, a cyclic distribution performs a fairer distribution when the number of tasks is small [14]. More complex schemes with load balancing can be applied if there is information about the actual load of each task and worker.

IV. Uniform model for skeleton implementation

In this section we present our proposed model to represent algorithm skeletons. The model is based on Petri nets [6], [5], a mathematical modeling language for the description of systems. A Petri net is a particular kind of directed bipartite graph, whose nodes represent transitions. We will add new

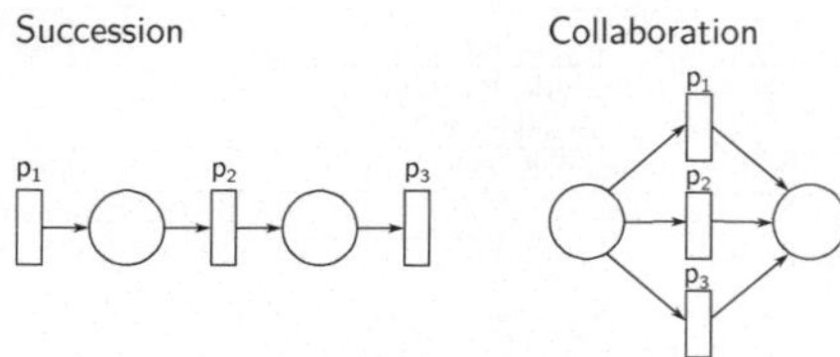

Fig. 1. Representation of the composition operators.

concepts to the original Petri nets definition to describe the tasks involved in the computational patterns of skeletons.

The top level element of the model is an *Application*. It corresponds to a Petri net, and it is defined as a 3-tuple, $A = (C, P, F)$ where:

- $C = \{c_1, c_2, \ldots, c_n\}$ is a finite set of *Task Containers*. This is one of the partitions of the bipartite graph. The task containers correspond to the Petri net *places*, although task containers are typed and store tasks instead of tokens. The task type has to agree with the container type.
- $P = \{p_1, p_2, \ldots, p_m\}$ is a finite set of *Processes*. They are the equivalent to the Petri net *transitions*. This set of process is the other partition of the bipartite graph. A process executes a function with state, they are defined by the user to implement the particular skeleton application. The function has r inputs and s outputs: $f_i : x_1, x_2, \ldots, x_r \rightarrow y_1, y_2, \ldots, y_s$
- The last element of the application $F \subseteq (P \times T) \cup (T \times P)$, is a set of *Flow Relationships* (Petri arcs) between task containers and processes, and vice versa, defining the edges of the bipartite graph.

Based upon the arcs, we can define the input containers. A container is called an *Input Container* for a process if there is an arc from it to the process. *Output Containers* can be defined analogously.

An application net can be nested inside a process node. Transient and persistent nesting modes can be represented with this model. In transient nesting, a process will execute another Application as part of the function, while in persistent mode a process can be replaced by another net, keeping its inputs and outputs.

A. Composition operators

We define two operators that help to define the structure of the application: *succession* and *collaboration*. The succession operator links several processes one after the other using containers and creating the flow relationships between them. The collaboration operator creates a different structure where the processes share the input and output containers. Fig. 1 shows the representation of the composition operators.

B. Execution semantics

Once created, the structure of an application is fixed, although its state (the distribution of tasks in the containers) can change. The behavior of the application is described in

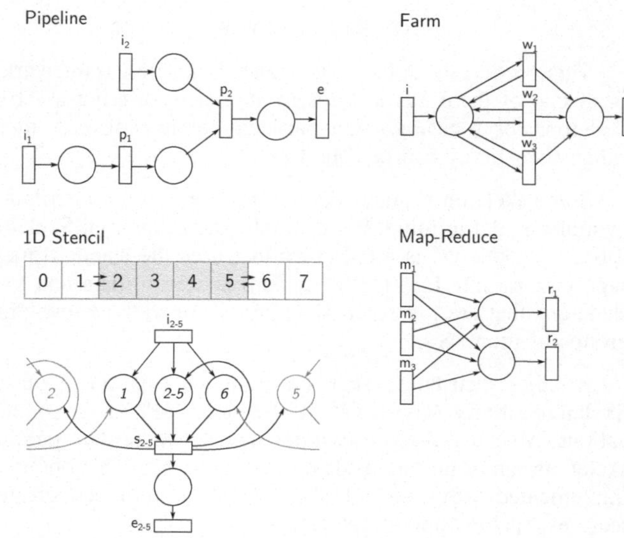

Fig. 2. Common skeletons using the model. A circle represents a container and a rectangle indicates a process.

term of those states. The tasks in the containers are consumed/-generated by the processes based on the following rules:

- At the initial state, the containers are empty.
- When a process is executed, it consumes tasks from each of its input containers. There have to be at least one task at each of them.
- The retrieved tasks are fed to the process function. The result tasks are sent to the output containers. The process function may do not produce tasks for all the output containers.
- The evolution of the application is not deterministic. When more than one process could be executed, we can not tell which one will be executed first.
- The execution finishes when all tasks have been processed.

C. Representing skeletons with this model

We discuss in this section how the algorithm skeletons can be represented using processes and containers. We have selected one representative example from each group defined in the taxonomy of secction III. Fig. 2 shows the structure for each example. The figure uses the standard Petri net representation, where a circle indicates a container, a process is shown as a rectangle, and the flow relationships are arrows from/to elements.

e) Pipeline: A Pipe skeleton is composed of a set of connected stages. The output of one stage is the input of the following one. The structure of this skeletons is just a set of processes (one for each stage) that exchanges tasks using containers. As shown in Fig. 2, a process can receive tasks from several stages using different containers, leading to a more complex pipeline structure. In the same way, a process can feed tasks to more than one output container.

f) Farm: A Farm skeleton, also known as master-slave/worker, consists of a farmer and several workers. The farmer receives a sequence of independent tasks and schedules them across the workers. In a farm skeleton structure, the farmer and the workers are independent processes. There exist two tasks containers. The first one is shared by all the workers and it keeps the tasks that are scheduled to them. The other one is used to store the output results. In some farm configurations, the workers can add more tasks to the input container.

g) Stencil: Although the model is more useful to represent dynamic structure skeletons, it can also represent static ones. A Stencil skeleton updates the value of each element of a data structure applying an operation with the values of their neighbor elements. Fig. 2 shows an example of an 1D stencil. The structure to represent this skeleton has a container for its local elements and containers for the values of the neighbors. Each process updates its local part and inserts the values needed by its neighbors in the appropriate containers.

h) Map-Reduce: This is a distributed programming model used by Google for efficient large-scale computations [11]. The model proposes two steps: map and reduce. The computation in the map step takes a set of input key/value pairs and processes them in parallel. The result for each pair is another set of intermediate output key/value pairs. The reduce step merges together all the intermediate pair associated with the same key, returning a smaller set of output key/value pairs. A Map-Reduce structure has a pair of process sets, one with the processes performing the map operation and the other performing the reduction. They are connected by several task containers that hold the intermediate key/value pairs.

V. The Hitmap library

Before describing the implementation of this model in Hitmap, we will briefly show the main features of the Hitmap library.

Hitmap [16] is a library for hierarchical tiling and mapping, with support for dense and sparse data structures [17]. It is based on a distributed SPMD programming model, using abstractions to declare data structures with a global view, automatizing the partition, mapping, and communication of hierarchies of tiles, while still delivering good performance.

Hitmap was designed with an object-oriented approach, although it is implemented in C language. The classes are implemented as C structures with associated functions.

Hitmap abstractions allow to represent different data domains with a single interface. This interface has currently implementations for dense arrays, subspaces of array indexes with regular jumps, and sparse domains, such as Compressed Sparse Row (CSR) or Bitmaps. Hitmap also has functionalities to modify the domains, make selections, allocate memory for an index subspace, or make efficient data copies.

Hitmap has a runtime plug-in system to distribute the data domains. Plug-ins with different partition methods can be selected. They divide the domains according to the actual processors arranged in a virtual topology. Hitmap has different partitioning and load-balancing techniques implemented. Moreover, programmers may include their own new techniques. It also allows to define communication patterns in terms of the mapping results and neighbor relationships, that automatically adapt the data distribution and communication scheme at execution time.

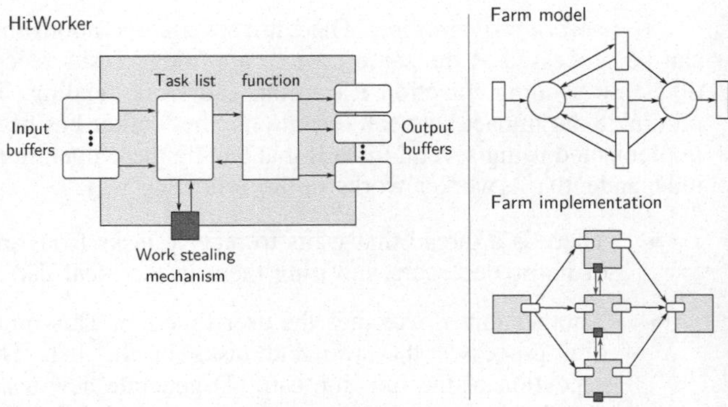

Fig. 3. Implementation of the HitWorker class, and an example of the farm skeleton.

The library is built on top of the MPI communication library, for portability across different architectures. Hitmap internally exploits several MPI techniques that increase performance, such as MPI derived data-types and asynchronous communications. The Hitmap library is publicly available [18].

VI. Skeleton Model Implementation using Hitmap

This section explains how we have extended the Hitmap library to implement the proposed model.

This extension constitutes another step in the development of Hitmap. The library has functionalities to deal with static computation structures, being able to partition different kinds of data structures at initialization time. This proposal adds support for load balancing, and dynamic distribution of tasks.

i) Implementation of the model elements: The current implementation of the model adds two new classes to the architecture: a *HitTask*, and a *HitWorker*. A HitTask class, an abstract datatype, is used to encapsulate the data that flows between application stages. This HitTask class has a weight attribute that is used in load-balancing decisions. A HitWorker is a generic worker that runs over a process, executing a user function.

The containers of the model are implemented as lists of tasks inside the workers. When a worker generates a task for another process, the task is sent using MPI communications, and it is inserted in the worker task list. If several processes share an input container, for example in a farm structure, it is implemented as a distributed list. Each worker has a local list and the tasks are communicated using a work stealing mechanism to balance the load.

The arcs of the bipartite graph are task channels between workers, creating successor-predecessor relations. This allows them to be arbitrarily nested. Fig. 3 shows the internal details of an example HitWorker object with two input and three output channels. It also shows how several workers can be linked to implement a farm skeleton structure defined using the model.

j) Worker operations: There are several operations that can be processed at the same time in a worker: Tasks reception, task sending, function execution, and work stealing. To minimize the impact between operations, the worker has been implemented using several threads that handle these operations independently. A worker works in the following way:

- There is a thread that waits to receive tasks from any of its predecessors, inserting them in the local list.
- Another thread executes the user function. This function processes the available tasks in the list. The execution of the function can: (1) generate new tasks for the local list, (2) generate new tasks for the successors, or (3) produce no output.
- If the list is a distributed one, a work-staling mechanism runs in the background. When the local list is going to be emptied, it tries to get tasks from the other workers that share the virtual container.

A. Optimization details

This section describes the most relevant optimization details of the implementation described above. Using MPI to communicate a single task is not efficient in a generic case, due to the time and memory overhead of the communication operations. To avoid this, we have implemented input and output tasks buffers that group tasks before communication. The granularity of the buffers can be modified in terms of task weights. These buffers use asynchronous blocking MPI calls managed by different threads. In this way, communication operations can overlap. In addition, MPI Communicators are used to isolate message contexts for the work-stealing mechanism, also allowing skeleton nesting.

Special care has been taken to design the worker's internal list of tasks. The different threads of the worker can modify this list, so mutual exclusion should be ensured to avoid inconsistent states. Moreover, the task in the list can be originated from different sources: predecessors workers, work stealing exchanges, and locally generated tasks. The user function extracts and inserts tasks using one end of the list while the input buffers and worker stealing mechanism use the other one. This improves task locality for the applications that can exploit it.

Our tool allows to change different parameters in order to test which configurations are better for a given program. We can change the list and buffers sizes, change the task grouping policy, or disable the work-stealing mechanism.

To allow explicit, as well as implicit interaction modes, the required user function is executed once. This allows to declare and free internal data structures to keep state, wrapping the task management loop. The implementation offers to the programmer of the function an API of methods to retrieve tasks from the list, access the data of the tasks, create new tasks, or send tasks to the output buffers. The input and output are not limited to the one to one relation of the implicit interaction mode. The programmer is free to combine the functions of this API to created any skeleton stage.

Support for both transient and persistent nesting modes has been considered. Persistent mode is achieved just by linking workers. The transient mode poses a bigger challenge, it implies that sub-skeletons could be created during the execution of the upper one. This is solved with a pile of execution contexts.

B. Implementation examples

This section exemplifies how to create skeletons with our implementation of the model. Fig. 4 shows an example of a pipeline. The function in line 5 creates a three stage pipeline. It receives three function pointers as parameters, one for each stage. These user functions must receive a HitWorker structure as defined in the typedef of their prototype on line 2. The *pipe3* function creates three workers with the corresponding user function and defines the number and types of the inputs and outputs. Then, it combines the workers with the succession operator to create the relationships. The result is another worker that encapsulates the previous ones. We can use it to execute the whole pipe with a single call in the main function (line 19).

Creating a farm is a similar process but uses the collaborator operator instead. More complex computation structures can be created manually defining how the inputs and outputs of the different workers are linked.

VII. Experimental Results

Experimental work has been conducted to show that the implementation developed achieves good performance with different configurations, and compared with another skeleton framework. We use two different experimental platforms with different architectures: A multicore shared-memory machine and a distributed cluster of commodity PCs. The shared-memory system, Geopar, is an Intel S7000FC4URE server with four quad-core Intel Xeon MPE7310 processors at 1.6GHz and 32GB of RAM. The distributed system is a homogeneous Beowulf cluster composed by 20 AMD Athlon 3000+ single-core processors at 1.8GHz and 1Gb of RAM each. The cluster is interconnected by a 100Mbit Ethernet network. The MPI implementation used is MPICH2.

A. Mandelbrot set benchmark

We have chosen a simple benchmark with no complex application interactions, to focus on the efficiency of the implementation. The selected benchmark calculates the Mandelbrot set [19], one of the best-known examples of mathematical visualization. It has become popular as a benchmark in parallel computing since it is easily parallelizable but introduces a load-balancing problem [1]. Several skeleton frameworks use it as a case study [4], [12].

The Mandelbrot set is defined in the following way. Given a complex number $c \in \mathbb{C}$ and the sequence $z_{n+1} = z_n + c$, starting with $z_0 = 0$, c belongs to the Mandelbrot set if, when applying the iteration repeatedly, the sequence remains bounded regardless of how big n gets.

The benchmark computes the iterative equation for each point to calculate whether the sequence tends to infinity. If this sequence does not cross a given threshold before reaching a given number of iterations, it is considered that the sequence will converge. This problem is straightforwardly parallelizable

```
// Typedef for the user function pointer.
typedef void (*HitWorkerFunc) (HitWorker*);

// Three-stage pipeline
HitWorker pipe3(HitWorkerFunc f_ini, HitWorkerFunc f_mid, HitWorkerFunc f_end) {
    HitWorker pipe;
    HitWorker * workers = malloc(3 * sizeof(HitWorker));

    hit_workerCreate(&workers[0], f_ini, 0, 1, HIT_DOUBLE);
    hit_workerCreate(&workers[1], f_mid, 1, 1, HIT_DOUBLE, HIT_DOUBLE);
    hit_workerCreate(&workers[2], f_end, 1, 0, HIT_DOUBLE);

    hit_workerOpSuccession(&pipe,3,&workers[0],&workers[1],&workers[2]);

    return pipe;
}

// Main function
int main(int argc, char ** argv) {

    hit_comInit(&argc,&argv);
    HitWorker pipe = pipe3(init,process,end);
    hit_workerExecute(&pipe);
    hit_comFinalize();
}
```

Fig. 4. Fragment of code showing the creation of a pipe and a farm.

because the calculation of the equation on a particular point is independent on the result from any other point. However, it can present significant load imbalances, because some points reach the threshold after only a few iterations, others could take longer, and the points that belong to the set require the maximum number of iterations.

B. Performance

To test the performance obtained by the implementation of the model, we measure and compare the run-time of several implementations of the Mandelbrot benchmark: (1) the Hitmap implementation; (2) the Hitmap implementation with the work stealing mechanism disabled, (3) a code using the Muesli skeleton framework [9] forced to use only MPI processes, and (4) the Muesli code forced to use OpenMP threads instead of MPI processes.

The two plots in Fig. 5 show the results of the previously-described implementations of the benchmark for both architectures considered. The programs have been run with a square matrix of 4 000 × 4 000 elements, a limit of 2 000 iterations, and task grain of 16 × 16 elements. Hitmap obtains a good scalability in the shared-memory machine. In the cluster, the results are not as good because the selected task grain is not enough, and the communications drag down the scalability. The difference of using work stealing in Hitmap is not noticeable for this application. The Muesli implementations do not scale as good as Hitmap. It is specially noticeable in the Beowulf cluster. As expected, in the shared-memory machine, the experiment with the Muesli code using only OpenMP threads has slightly better performance than using MPI processes. It is remarkable than Hitmap performs better in both cases.

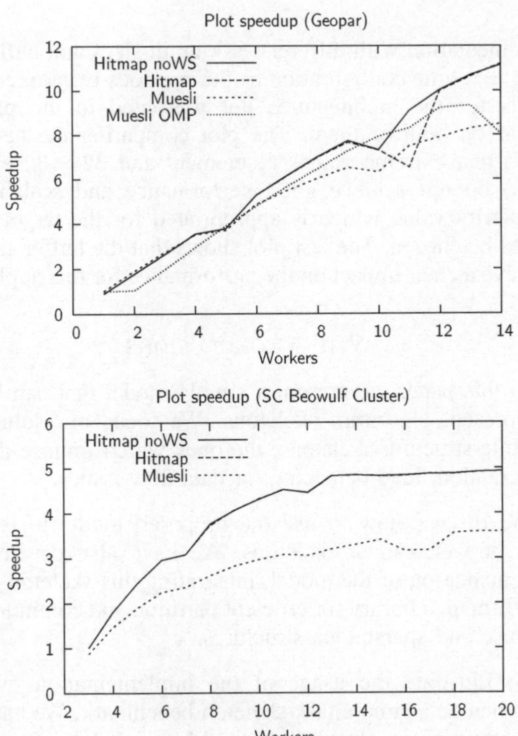

Fig. 5. Speedup comparison for Hitmap, Hitmap without work stealing, and Muesli implementations of the Mandelbrot benchmark.

The plots in Fig. 6 show the performance of the Hitmap

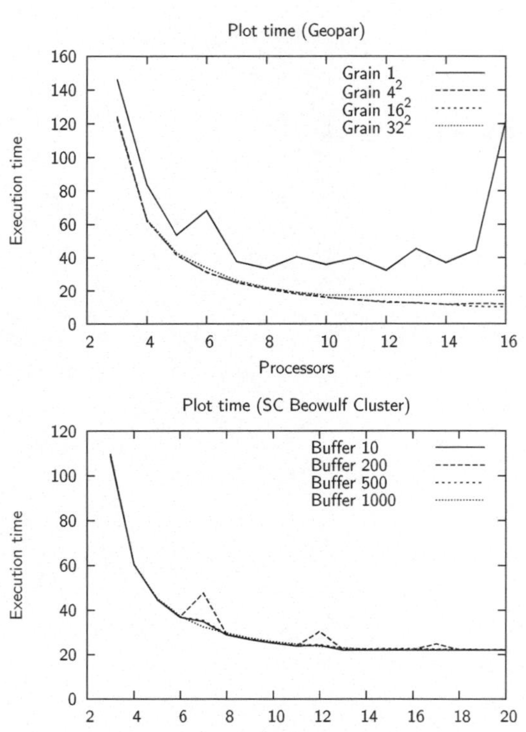

Fig. 6. Execution time comparison for different task grain sizes and communication buffer sizes of the Hitmap implementation.

implementation with different task grain sizes and buffer sizes using the same configuration as the previous experiments. The results for the architectures not presented in the plots are similar on both of them. The plot comparing the task grain shows that extreme values (1 element and 32×32 elements block) do not achieve good performance and scalability. A granularity value which is appropriated for the target system should be chosen. The last plot shows that the buffer size does not have a clear impact on the performance for this application.

VIII. Conclusions

In this paper we present a simple model that can be used to represent algorithm skeletons. We focus our solution on dynamic-structure skeletons, the ones which impose dynamic task-creation, load-balancing, or data-flow issues.

We discuss how to use the proposed model to represent a set of well-known skeletons. We have also developed an implementation of the model, integrating this skeleton support into Hitmap, a library for efficient partition and communication of dense and sparse data structures.

To illustrate the usage of the implementation, we have implemented a simple task skeleton benchmark. We have used it to compare our solution with the Muesli skeleton framework. Our experimental results show that the implementation is highly efficient and configurable.

Our ongoing work includes the creation and encapsulation of more complex skeletons using this model to show its applicability for production parallel applications.

Acknowledgments

The authors would like to thank Prof. Murray Cole for many fruitful discussions. This research is partly supported by the Castilla-Leon Regional Government (VA172A12-2); Ministerio de Industria, Spain (CENIT OCEANLIDER); MICINN (Spain) and the European Union FEDER (Mogecopp project TIN2011-25639, CAPAP-H3 network TIN2010-12011-E, CAPAP-H4 network TIN2011-15734-E); and the HPC-EUROPA2 project (project number: 228398) with the support of the European Commission - Capacities Area - Research Infrastructures Initiative.

References

[1] W. Gropp, E. Lusk, and A. Skjellum, *Using MPI : Portable Parallel Programming With the Message-passing Interface*. MIT Press, 1999.

[2] R. Chandra, L. Dagum, D. Kohr, D. Maydan, J. McDonald, and R. Menon, *Parallel programming in OpenMP*, 1st ed. Morgan Kaufmann, 2001.

[3] M. Cole, *Algorithmic Skeletons: Structured Management of Parallel Computation*. MIT Press, 1989.

[4] ——, "Bringing skeletons out of the closet: a pragmatic manifesto for skeletal parallel programming," *Parallel Computing*, vol. 30, no. 3, pp. 389–406, Mar. 2004.

[5] T. Murata, "Petri nets: Properties, analysis and applications," *Proceedings of the IEEE*, vol. 77, no. 4, pp. 541–580, 1989.

[6] W. M. P. van der Aalst and K. van Hee, *Workflow Management: Models, Methods, and Systems*. The MIT Press, 2002.

[7] H. González-Vélez and M. Leyton, "A survey of algorithmic skeleton frameworks: high-level structured parallel programming enablers," *Software: Practice and Experience*, vol. 40, no. 12, pp. 1135–1160, 2010.

[8] A. Benoit, M. Cole, S. Gilmore, and J. Hillston, "Flexible skeletal programming with eSkel," in *Proceedings of the 11th international Euro-Par conference on Parallel Processing*, Lisbon, Portugal, 2005, pp. 761–770.

[9] P. Ciechanowicz, M. Poldner, and H. Kuchen, "The Münster Skeleton Library Muesli – A Comprehensive Overview," Westfälsche Wilhelms-Universität Münster (WWU) - European Research Center for Information Systems (ERCIS), Tech. Rep. 7, 2009.

[10] J. Reinders, *Intel® threading building blocks: Outfitting C++ for Multi-Core Processor Parallelism*, 1st ed. O'Reilly Media, 2007.

[11] J. Dean and S. Ghemawat, "MapReduce: Simplified data processing on large clusters," in *Proceedings of the 6th conference on Symposium on Opearting Systems Design & Implementation (OSDI'04)*. USENIX Association, 2004.

[12] M. Steuwer, P. Kegel, and S. Gorlatch, "SkelCL – A Portable Skeleton Library for High-Level GPU Programming," in *Proc. 2011 IEEE International Symposium on Parallel and Distributed Processing Workshops and Phd Forum (IPDPSW)*, 2011, pp. 1176–1182.

[13] A. Benoit and M. Cole, "Two Fundamental Concepts in Skeletal Parallel Programming," in *The International Conference on Computational Science (ICCS)*, 2005, pp. 764–771.

[14] M. Poldner and H. Kuchen, "On Implementing the Farm Skeleton," *Parallel Processing Letters*, vol. 18, no. 1, pp. 117–131, 2008.

[15] ——, "Algorithmic Skeletons for Branch and Bound," *Software and Data Technologies*, pp. 204–219, 2008.

[16] A. Gonzalez-Escribano, Y. Torres, J. Fresno, and D. R. Llanos, "An extensible system for multilevel automatic data partition and mapping," *IEEE Transactions on Parallel and Distributed Systems*, 2013, to appear.

[17] J. Fresno, A. Gonzalez-Escribano, and D. R. Llanos, "Extending a hierarchical tiling arrays library to support sparse data partitioning," *The Journal of Supercomputing*, vol. 64, no. 1, pp. 59–68, Apr. 2013.

[18] Trasgo Group, "Hitmap Repository," 2013, http://trasgo.dcs.fi.uva.es/hitmap.

[19] B. B. Mandelbrot, "Fractal aspects of the iteration of $z \mapsto \lambda z(1-z)$," *Annals of the New York Academy of Sciences*, vol. 357, pp. 249–259, 1980.

Fully Automatic Parallel Programming

Bryant Nelson and Nelson Rushton(contact author)
(bryant.nelson | nelson.rushton) @ ttu.edu
Dept. of Computer Science, Texas Tech University
Box 43104 Lubbock, TX 79409-3104

Abstract - *SequenceL is a small, statically typed, purely functional programming language, whose semantics enable compilation to parallel executables from function definitions. This paper reports the results of experiments on the performance of parallel programs automatically generated by the SequenceL compiler. In particular we examine the parallel speedups obtained in running SequenceL programs on multicore hardware.*

Keywords: SequenceL, Functional Programming, Parallel Programming

1 SequenceL

SequenceL is a simple, general purpose, purely functional programming language [Cooke et.al. 2008]. By *simple*, we mean that the entire syntax and semantics of the language can be described in about 20 pages, including examples. By *general purpose*, we mean the language is not specific to any domain; and by *purely functional* we mean that SequenceL programs consist of equations defining functions, without any I/O or assignment. To be part of a working executable program, SequenceL programs are compiled to C++ and linked with so-called "driver code" that orchestrates I/O operations.

The original aim of SequenceL was to give programmers a way to describe computations in terms of the relation between input and output data, without direct reference to a particular procedure for obtaining them [Cooke et. al. 2009]. On its surface, this sounds like the aim of functional languages in general, but in reality almost all functional languages act as shorthand for known procedures. For example, the author of a Haskell or Lisp program does not necessarily have to think about how his program will be executed (say, left to right lazy evaluation, or left to right eager evaluation, respectively), but if he *does* think about it, he may know exactly how it will execute because the language semantics make guarantees about the order. The semantics of SequenceL make no such guarantees.

Because SequenceL makes no guarantees about the order of evaluation, it is not possible for a SequenceL programmer to optimize their code in a compiler-independent way. On the other hand, this means the compiler may perform optimizations in ways that are not constrained as in other languages. In particular, since the language makes no guarantees about the order of evaluation, evaluations may be done in parallel. SequenceL's Normalize-Transpose semantic (see Section 2) is particularly amenable to parallelisms being automatically discovered and exploited by the compiler. This automated parallelism was first pointed out in [Cooke/Andersen 2000], and implemented as a prototype with encouraging results reported by Nemanich [Nemanich et. al. 2010]. In 2009 the patent on SequenceL's semantics was licensed to Texas Multicore Technologies (TMT), who have since been engaged in commercial scale development of the compiler.

2 Parallelizations by SequenceL

2.1 Normalize-Transpose

The parameters of a SequenceL function are explicitly typed according to their *depth*. *Depth* can be thought of as the dimensionality of an expression. For example, scalars have depth 0, lists have depth 1, matrices have depth 2, etc. One way in which SequenceL alleviates the need for iterative or recursive algorithms is with Normalize-Transpose (NT). NT is a method of function application that applies some operation on every element in a list. A function defined on

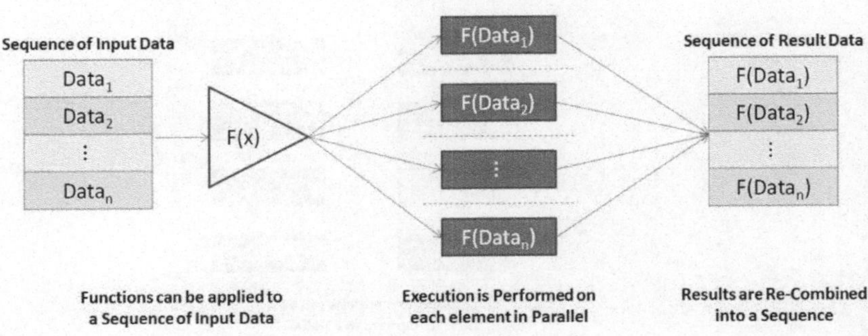

Figure 1: NT Illustration

arguments of depth D can be applied to a list of arguments of depth D. The result is the function applied element-wise.

For example, since the scalar addition function (+) is declared with scalars (depth 0) for both arguments, the expression [10,20,30] + 1, where the first argument is a list, triggers an NT and has a value of [11,21,31]. Similarly because of NT, the value of the SequenceL expression [10,20,30] + [1,2,3] is [11,22,33]. The NT semantic is one device that allows SequenceL to automatically extract parallelizations. It can be proven that the parallelisms generated are free of race conditions and other parallel anomalies.

2.2 Indexed Functions

Another way SequenceL avoids the use of recursion is through a construct called indexed functions. Using indexed functions a programmer can specify a nonscalar data structure element-wise, a function of the parameters of the function. This is very similar to the way vector and matrix valued functions are often defined in informal mathematics. Take for example the *Identity* function defined below -- where for each nonnegative integer *N*, *Identity(N)* is the *NxN* identity matrix:

```
Identity(N(0))[i, j] :=
        1 when i = j
    else
        0
    foreach i within 1 ... N,
            j within 1 ... N;
```

Figure 2: Identity Matrix as Indexed Function

2.3 Consume-Simplify-Produce

The third source of automatic parallelizations in SequenceL is that parameters of a function call may be evaluated in parallel. This is known as Consume-Simplify-Produce, or CSP.

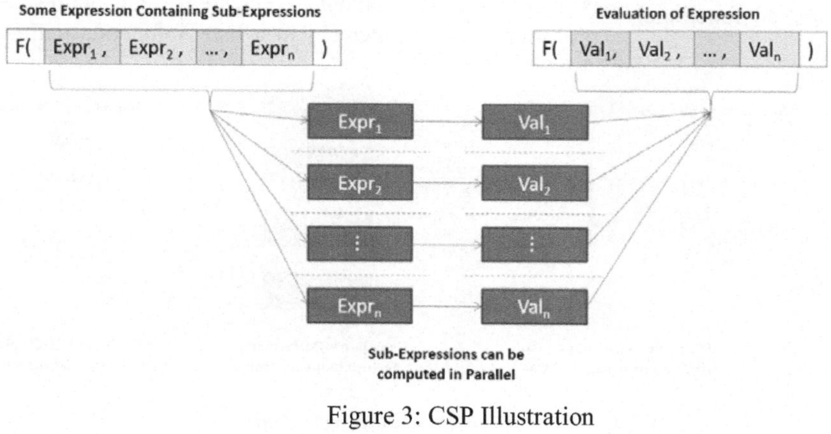

Figure 3: CSP Illustration

When SequenceL is compiled to C++ CSPs, indexed functions, and NTs are compiled into highly parallel programs, capable of running on an arbitrary number of processor cores. The number of cores can be specified at runtime.

3 Heat Map and its Explanation

A set of benchmarks informally known as a heat map is periodically run to test the performance of compiled SequenceL. The heat map problems have been chosen essentially at random from modules that have been written for commercial TMT customers over the past three years. Tables 1 and 2 list all of the heat map problems that are at least 70 lines of SequenceL code. The cut-off at 70 lines of code was chosen to represent problems that cannot be trivially parallelized by hand.

The problems in Table 1 (LU factorization, 2D Fourier Transform, and the Barnes-Hut N-body problem) have well known specifications and can be considered repeatable experiments, which can be used for performance comparison between SequenceL and other methods including by-hand parallelization. The problems in Table 2 (Semblance, Compare Predicates, Speech Filter, and WirelessHART) are not repeatable in the sense that they contain algorithms proprietary to TMT customers. They are listed here as anecdotal observations.

The heat map reports the average run time over 10 executions of several different programs and compares the performance of the SequenceL on 1, 2, 4, 8, 12, 16, 20 and 24 cores. The following table shows the average run times over 10 executions when run on a Centos 6.3 machine with 16GB of memory, and a 1333MHz / E5-2620, running at 2.0 GHz.

Table 1: Standard Algorithms

Cores	LU Factorization	2D Fourier Transform	Barnes-Hut N-Body
1	12.426	2.690	29.850
2	6.335	1.347	15.976
4	4.130	0.674	8.830
8	2.973	0.338	4.765
16	2.494	0.245	3.483
12	2.400	0.218	3.297
20	2.425	0.215	3.174
24	2.511	0.203	3.007

Table 2: Proprietary Algorithms

Cores	Semblance	Compare Predicates	Speech Filter	WirelessHART
1	20.993	3.341	108.742	21.996
2	11.335	2.167	54.364	18.000
4	5.962	1.129	29.324	14.668
8	4.038	0.654	20.021	13.194
12	3.100	0.593	14.353	12.993
16	2.542	0.608	16.185	13.196
20	2.902	0.607	11.142	13.484
24	3.371	0.559	9.979	13.770

4 Conclusions and Future Work

The SequenceL compiler generated parallel algorithms automatically, without human intervention between the functional description of the solution and the parallel executable. Parallel speedups were obtained in every case. In most cases the speedups continued nearly linearly up to around 8 cores. Above 8 cores, performance either increased slightly or decreased slightly as more cores were added, with the exception of *speech filter* in which substantial speedups were obtained up to 24 cores.

This "core ceiling" phenomenon for linear speedups is not unexpected in general, since any parallel program running on a physical machine will eventually reach such a threshold due both to communication overhead and to the theoretical limits of parallelization for the algorithm. The fact that the threshold (of 8 cores) was consistent across problems indicates that in this case the ceiling may have been hardware dependent. This is especially plausible here, because the machine used in this experiment has only 12 distinct physical processors, with up to 24 simulated through hyper-threading.

In our experience this performance is competitive with the performance of hand coded parallel algorithms -- though of course the reader with similar or greater experience may draw their own conclusions. Future work includes a comparison of this performance with hand coded parallel implementations of the same algorithms, comparison with the performance of hand coded sequential algorithms, and running the experiment on different hardware.

5 References

[Cooke/Andersen 2000] Daniel E. Cooke, Per Andersen: Automatic parallel control structures in SequenceL. Softw., Pract. Exper. 30(14): 1541-1570 (2000)

[Cooke et.al. 2008] Daniel E. Cooke, J. Nelson Rushton, Brad Nemanich, Robert G. Watson, Per Andersen: Normalize, transpose, and distribute: An automatic approach for handling nonscalars. ACM Trans. Program. Lang. Syst. 30(2) (2008)

[Cooke et. al. 2009] Daniel E. Cooke, J. Nelson Rushton: Taking Parnas's Principles to the Next Level: Declarative Language Design. IEEE Computer 42(9): 56-63 (2009)

[Nemanich et. al. 2010] Brad Nemanich, Daniel E. Cooke, J. Nelson Rushton: SequenceL: transparency and multi-core parallelisms. DAMP 2010: 45-52
[1] 06).

An Efficient Mixed-Mode BIST Scheme for Test-Per-Clock Testing

Tieqiao Liu[1], Jishun Kuang[1], Shuo Cai[1, 2], Yinbo Zhou[1], and Zhiqiang You[1]
[1] College of Information Science & Engineering, Hunan University, China
[2] School of Computer & Communication Engineering, Changsha University of Science & Technology, China

Abstract - *A new design methodology for a pattern generator based on build-in self-test (BIST) scheme is proposed. The phase of pattern generation consists of two components: a pseudo-random test sequence followed by a deterministic one generated by a controlled linear-feedback shift-register (LFSR). Based on theoretical analysis of the proposed test architecture, a controlled linear shift test generation method for deterministic test is proposed. Simulation results for benchmark circuits show that the proposed method can obtain complete fault coverage for the single stuck-at fault, while deriving lower overhead of test generation and shorter test application time compared with other recently-published methods.*

Keywords: Designs for Testability, Test-Per-Clock Testing, Test-Per-Scan Testing, Build-In Self-Test, Test Generation

1 Introduction

With the complexity of VLSI designs growing, huge amount of necessary test data prolongs the testing time and demands complicated and expensive Automatic Test Equipment (ATE). In order to alleviate these testing problems, Build-in Self-Test (BIST) has been widely adopted in the industry [1], which enables the chip to test itself and evaluate the responses within an acceptable cost. Moreover, an efficient BIST should possess three properties, including high fault coverage, low hardware overhead, and short test application time.

Many recent BIST methods have been proposed to find some trade-off among these three aspects that are mutually antipodal. In LFSR-ROM test scheme [2], Linear-feedback shift-register (LFSR) is used to detect easy-to-detect faults with an acceptable test length, while the ROM provides a small number of test patterns for remaining random-pattern-resistant faults. Another mixed BIST technique [3] used a combinational block to produce the deterministic test patterns, which needs no memory elements. Weighted random testing [4] is also one of the most known approaches for reducing both test application time and LFSR size, in which the LFSR code words are modified by a weighting logic. However, the main drawbacks of these techniques are that they are only suitable for small size circuit testing, and a surfeit of additional logics may enlarge the delay of the circuit. With the growth of the size of the circuit, the rapid increase in test length of the pseudo-random pattern generation and the overhead of extra logic blocks will be unacceptable. Reference [5] used control bits to skip irrelevant pseudo-random test patterns, and reference [6] proposed a scan disabling technique to block irrelevant pseudo-random patterns slices. They achieve a high compression gain by storing the control signals instead of the test set. Another technique that can be used to achieve high fault coverage while reduce the size of the ROM is the LFSR reseeding techniques [7-8]. In these techniques some selected seeds are stored in ROM instead of full test patterns. Seeds are serially loaded into LFSR as different initial states to generate the deterministic test patterns.

By transforming the CUT from a sequential one into its combinational parts in test mode, as the most popular designs for testability (DFT) technique, the full-scan based method significantly improves the CUT's testability. However, in conventional test-per-scan schemes, test patterns are shifted into the chain of scan registers (scan chain) and the test response is shifted out to the Response Analyzer through a serial interface. With the test data volume increasing ceaselessly, test-per-scan schemes expose drawback of long test application time during the shift process.

This paper presents an efficient test-per-clock BIST design using LFSR-ROM architecture. The design employs an LFSR to generate pseudo-random patterns first, and then adopts a controlled linear shift test generation method to target the remaining faults, where the control bits are stored in a ROM. Experimental results demonstrate that the proposed method can achieve a complete stuck-at fault coverage, with a less test data storage and a short application time.

This paper is organized as follows. Section 2 presents the proposed test architecture. Determination of the length of pseudo-random test sequence followed by a deterministic test generation algorithm is described in section 3. Simulation results are shown in Section 4. Section 5 concludes this paper.

2 Proposed Hybrid BIST Architecture

The proposed BIST architecture shown in Fig. 1 is composed of a Test Pattern Generator (TPG) and a Response Analyzer (RA). The TPG consists of an LFSR and a control bit stream provider. The LFSR plays two roles during the mixed-mode test: a free one and a controlled one. First, the

LFSR generates pseudo-random test patterns freely to detect easy-to-detect faults (the input 0 of MUX is selected), where the Counter records the length of pseudo-random test sequence. Then the LFSR is controlled by the bits stream from the ROM to generate deterministic test patterns for the remained faults. The internal scan chain constructed by all internal flip-flops is serially fed by the rightmost bit of the LFSR. In every test clock, a new test pattern is generated and applied to the CUT.

As a test-per-clock BIST architecture, the hardware overhead of response analyzer may be considerably high. Zero-error-aliasing linear space compactor [9] has been employed in BIST schemes to compress the test responses from a k-output circuit to q signature streams, where $q<<k$. Thus, the test responses appearing at the end of outputs can be compacted by a zero-aliasing space compactor and a Multiple-input Signature Register (MISR). In this paper, we no longer address the problem of Response Analyzer.

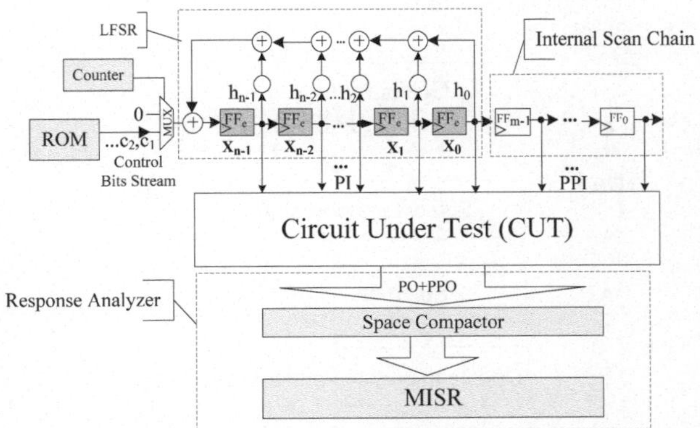

Figure 1. Controlled Shift BIST Architecture.

It can be seen from the above, the total test application time is the sum of the time of pseudo-random test and the time of deterministic test. During the deterministic test sequence generation, the control bits stream stored in the ROM determines the patterns in next clocks, as well as the hardware overhead of test data store and the total time of test application. The key issues of the shown test scheme lie on how to determine the appropriate length of pseudo-random test and how to specify the control bits stream to complete test generation in efficiency. The next section will describe them in detail.

3 Test Generation

The proposed test patterns generation includes a pseudo-random test sequence using free LFSR and a deterministic one using controlled LFSR. The determination of free LFSR test sequence length and deterministic test generation algorithm are presented in this section, respectively.

3.1 Determination of Pseudo-random Test Sequence Length

The length of pseudo-random test sequence affects the total test application time and the followed deterministic test generation. By means of statistical testing, we found that the number of faults newly detected falls sharply as the pseudo-random test generation continues. Furthermore, LFSRs using different initial values have a similar characteristic. Fault detection scatter diagram statistics for circuit S5378 are shown in Figure 2. 10000 pseudo-random patterns are applied 50 times with different initial values, 3 of 50 random samples and the average are shown in the figure. It can be seen that the fault number newly detected by each new generated pattern is rather rare after 5000 patterns, and the average value tends to 0. In this paper, we take advantage of this phenomenon to determine the length of pseudo-random test sequence.

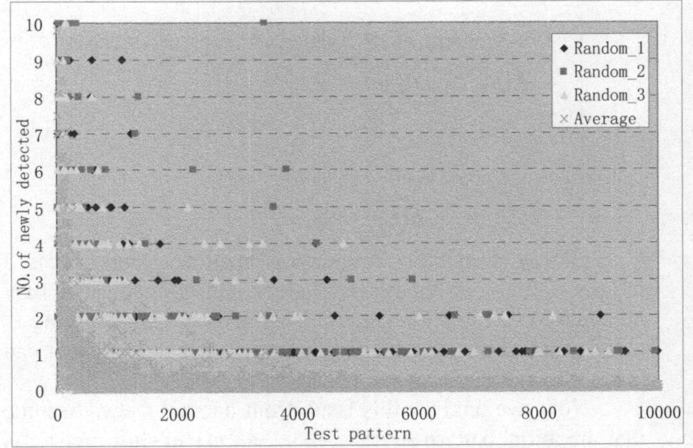

Figure 2. Fault Detection Statistics For S5378.

3.2 Deterministic Test Generation Algorithm

Before the description of our deterministic test generation algorithm, theoretical analysis on the proposed test architecture is discussed.

Definition 1: As shown in Fig. 1, n-stage LFSR and m-stage internal scan chain compose an L-stage shift register ($L=n+m$).

Theorem 1: For an L-stage shift register (n-stage LFSR+m-stage internal scan chain), it will certainly be able to shift the current pattern to any other targeted pattern by applying L' ($L'\leq L$) control bits to the input of the LFSR.

Proof: Assume the current pattern: A={ x_{n-1}, x_{n-2} ... x_1, x_0, a_{m-1}, a_{m-2} ... a_1, a_0}, the targeted pattern: B={ y_{n-1}, y_{n-2} ... y_1, y_0, b_{m-1}, b_{m-2} ... b_1, b_0 }, the control bits stream: C={c_1, c_2 ... c_i ... c_L }.

At the first clock, control bit c_1 is shifted into the shift register, and the pattern in the shift register turns into:

$$A^1=\{ c_1 + \sum_{i=0}^{n-1} h_i x_i, x_{n-1}, x_{n-2} \dots x_1, x_0, a_{m-1}, a_{m-2} \dots a_1 \} \quad (1)$$

where $c_1 + \sum_{i=0}^{n-1} h_i x_i$ is modulo 2 add operation, and h_i denotes a feedback network. Since c_1 is the only unknown variable in $c_1 + \sum_{i=0}^{n-1} h_i x_i$, it is denoted by $f(c_1)$.

In the same way, at the second clock, when control bit c_2 is shifted into the shift register, the pattern turns into:

$$A^2=\{ c_2 + \sum_{i=0}^{n-2} h_i x_{i+1} + h_{n-1} f(c_1), f(c_1), x_{n-1} \ldots x_0, a_{m-1}, \ldots a_2 \} \quad (2)$$

we also take $f(c_1, c_2)$ substituting for $c_2 + \sum_{i=0}^{n-2} h_i x_{i+1} + h_{n-1} f(c_1)$.

Deduced by analogy, when c_L is shifted into the shift register, the pattern turns into:

$$A^L=\{ f(c_1,c_2 \ldots c_L), f(c_1,c_2 \ldots c_{L-1}) \ \ldots \ f(c_1,c_2), f(c_1) \} \quad (3)$$

The description above is equivalent to the problem of solving a set of linear equations as follows:

$$\begin{cases} f(c_1,c_2 \ldots c_{L-1},c_L) = y_{n-1} \\ f(c_1,c_2 \ldots c_{L-1}) = y_{n-2} \\ \ldots \\ f(c_1,c_2) = b_1 \\ f(c_1) = b_0 \end{cases} \quad (4)$$

This is a modulo 2 operator equations, and it has a unique solution. At the ith ($i \le L$) clock, current pattern A^i may be equal to the targeted pattern. That is to say, by applying L' ($L' \le L$) control bits, the existing pattern in the shift register can turn into any other targeted pattern.

Now, we analyze this issue from another view. Assume that the initial pattern A={a_{L-1}, a_{L-2} ... a_1, a_0} in shift register is specified with random values (every bit is 1 or 0), and the targeted pattern B has a probability λ ($0 \leqslant \lambda \leqslant 1$) of don't care bits (Xs) for each bit. The probability that the initial pattern A is compatible to B is:

$$p_0 = (\lambda \times 1 + (1-\lambda) \times \frac{1}{2})^L = (\frac{1+\lambda}{2})^L \quad (5)$$

At every test clock, the shift-in bit can be temporarily regarded as an X. After L' test clock cycles, the current pattern in the shift register turns into {$X_{L'}$, ..., X_1, a_{L-1}, a_{L-2} ... $a_{L'}$}. Now, the probability that current pattern A' is compatible to B is:

$$P_{L'} = (\frac{1+\lambda}{2})^{L-L'} \quad (6)$$

As we known, $P_{L'}$ increases with the decrement of $L-L'$ and the increment of λ. In other words, higher λ of a test set will deduce a shorter control shift time L'.

The flow of the proposed deterministic test generation algorithm is shown in Figure 3. After the pseudo-random test generation, the remained faults are obtained. In order to obtain a high λ for each pattern, one corresponding pattern with X bits is generated for each remained fault, and these patterns constitute the original test repository *ORG_T*. We use the modified ATPG tool ATALANTA [10] as the basic pattern generator. As Figure 3 shows, the algorithm is mainly divided into three steps. Step 1 is the process to find the targeted pattern with the minimal shift. If there exists more than one satisfied pattern, the pattern that has the least number of Xs is selected. As mentioned before, higher λ patterns left may enhance the matching possibility later. Step 2 is the process of solving equations. The related patterns are updated with solved control bits and added to the new test set *T*. In order to accelerated the fault detecting, when the last bit of current pattern is X, it is specified with a random value, while its related patterns also need to be updated. Step 3 is the process of fault simulation. When a fault is detected, it is deleted from the fault list *F*, and its corresponding pattern is deleted from test repository *ORG_T* simultaneously. When the fault list *F* is empty, the algorithm is finished; otherwise it continues to find the next optimal targeted pattern.

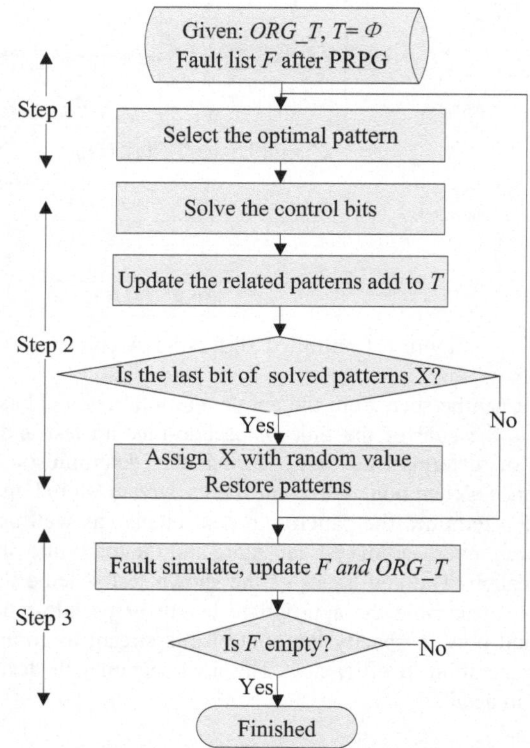

Figure 3. Flow of Deterministic Test Generation Algorithm.

. The time complexity of the deterministic test generation algorithm is $O(L^2 \cdot NoF^2)$, where L and NoF denote the number of bits of a pattern and the number of initial remained faults after pseudo-random test generation, respectively.

4 Experimental Results

In this section, we evaluate the effectiveness of the proposed method for the larger ISCAS'89 benchmark circuits. The performance results are implemented in the C language on a PC (Intel Core i3 550, 2.0GB RAM). The fault simulation tool is based on HOPE [11].

Table 1 shows the results of the proposed test generation. The first three columns give the circuit name, the size of LFSR and the number of redundant faults. Consideration for layout constraints and wiring overhead, the LFSR is usually constructed only by additional flip-flops added at each primary input (PI), but somtimes by the whole scan chain when the number of PIs is very small, such as S9234, S38584, etc. The pseudo-random test length of LFSR is shown in the column "Ran_TL", which is determined by the method described in section 3.1. The following two columns show the minimal and the average control bits storage of the deterministic test generation. In all the cases the algorithm runs 20 times. The average total Test Application Time (TAT) and computation time (in seconds) of our proposed test generation algorithm is shown in the last two columns, respectively.

Note that the CPU time includes the time of pseudo-random test generation and fault simulation. For every circuit, the fault coverage achieves 100% for detectable faults. As shown in Table 1, the proposed test generation method shows high performance. It takes tolerable computation time, deriving a less test storage and short test application time.

Table 2 compares the proposed method with previous work including scan disabling-based test scheme [6], test-per-clock based LFSR Reseeding [7] and test-per-scan based LFSR Reseeding [8]. Column "TAT" and column "Store" still give the test application time and the volume of test data of each approach. As can be seen from the table, our proposed method represents efficiency both in test application time and test data storage. The average TAT reduction and ROM reduction are shown in the last row, where the "Ave. Red(%)" is calculated as:

$$\text{Ave. Red}(\%) = \text{Average}(\frac{\#\text{Reference}[] - \#\text{Proposed}}{\#\text{Reference}[]} * 100) \quad (7)$$

Table 1. Experimental Results of Proposed Approach.

Circuit	*N*	#Red	Ran_TL	Min_Store	Ave_Store	TAT	CPU(s)
S5378	35	40	5000	711	754	5754	1.35
S9234	247	452	10000	6023	6658	16658	18.52
S13207	31	151	5000	2899	3033	8033	31.04
S15850	611	389	5000	3038	3451	8451	22.55
S35932	35	3984	1500	202	204	1704	15.67
S38417	1664	165	10000	13256	14568	24568	1335.58
S38584	1464	1506	5000	3922	4023	9023	225.25

Table 2. Results for Comparisons with Previous work.

Circuit	Proposed		[6]		[7]		[8]	
	TAT	*Store*	*TAT*	*Store*	*TAT*	*Store*	*TAT*	*Store*
s5378	5754	754	11014	11014	23112	11440	13182	5040
s9234	16658	6658	20543	20543	11808	1935	19957	7931
s13207	8033	3033	16472	16472	21731	6696	47600	7723
s15850	8451	3451	17739	17739	8550	3505	45947	9423
s35932	1704	204	1295	1295	12180	5508	N/A	N/A
s38417	24568	14568	96645	96645	34510	34965	210329	36884
s38584	9023	4023	25685	25685	8052	8790	139372	15622
Ave.Red(%)			39.7	82.3	28.7	16.3	69.9	60.0

5 Conclusions

In this paper we propose a BIST scheme using LFSR-ROM architecture for full-scan circuits. In addition to using the LFSR to generate pseudo-random test patterns, a ROM is used to store the control bits stream to generate deterministic test patterns. Through theoretical analysis of the proposed test architecture, an efficient controlled linear shift feedback test generation method for the following deterministic test is proposed. Experimental results show that the proposed scheme shows high advantages on short test application time and low overhead of test data storage. The drawback of the proposed method is that, as a test-per-clock test, the proposed scheme needs to capture the responses in every test clock, which leads to an expensive Response Analyzer. However, this can be alleviated by the Space Compactor as mentioned before, moreover, when this test scheme is applied to Register-transfer Level (RTL) testing, where the method of partitioning testing is utilized, the Response Analyzer can be partially or totally constructed by internal resources of the CUT [12]. In addition, the control bits are directly stored in

ROM which needs no extra decode logics, the area overhead of the TPG is less.

6 Acknowledgements

This paper was supported by the National Natural Science Foundation of China (NSFC) under grant No. 60673085, 60773207 and the Students' Innovative Experiment Foundation of Hunan Province under grant No.2010-224-114.

7 References

[1] Chatterjee, M., Pradhan, D.K. "A BIST Pattern Generator Design for Near-Perfect Fault Coverage", IEEE Transactions on Computers, vol. 52, no. 12, 2003, pp. 1543-1558.

[2] L. Li and Y. Min, "An Efficient BIST Design Using LFSR-ROM Architecture," Proc. Ninth Asian Test Symp., Nov.2000, pp. 386-390.

[3] P. Fišer, H. Kubátová, "An Efficient Mixed-Mode BIST Technique", Proc. 7th IEEE Design and Diagnostics of Electronic Circuits and Systems Workshop 2004, Tatranská Lomnica, SK, 18.-21.4.2004, pp. 227-230.

[4] A. Jas, C. V. Krishna, and N. A. Touba, "Weighted pseudo-random hybrid BIST," IEEE Trans. Very Large Scale Integr. (VLSI) Syst., vol. 12, no. 12, pp. 1277–1283, Dec. 2004.

[5] Hu Chen, Xu Gefu, Zhang Zhe, "A BIST structure and test pattern generation method based on controlled LFSR", Journal of Circuits and Systems, 7(3): 13-16, 2002.

[6] Zhiqiang You, Weizheng Wang, Zhiping Dou, Peng Liu, Jishun Kuang. "A Scan Disabling-Based BAST Scheme for Test Cost Reduction". IEICE Electronics Express, 2011, 8(16), pp. 1367-1373.

[7] E. Kalligeros, D. Bakalis, X. Kavousianos and D. Nikolos, "Reseeding-based test set embedding with reduced test sequences," in Proc. Int'l Symp. on Quality Electronic Design, pp. 226-231, 2005.

[8] Seongmoon Wang, Wenlong Wei, Zhanglei Wang, "A Low Overhead High Test Compression Technique Using Pattern Clustering With N-Detection Test Support", Journal of IEEE Transactions on Very Large Scale Integration (VLSI) Systems, 18(12): 1672-1685, 2010.

[9] Chakrabarty, K., "Zero-Aliasing Space Compaction Using Linear Compactors with Bounded Overhead", Journal of IEEE Transactions on Computer-Aided Design of Integrated Circuits and Systems, 17(5), Page(s): 452-457, 1998.

[10] H. K. Lee, D. S. Ha, "Atalanta: an Efficient ATPG for Combinational Circuits", Technical Report, 93-12, Dep't of Electrical Eng., Virginia Polytechnic Institute and State University, Blacksburg, Virginia, 1993.

[11] H. K. Lee and D. S. Ha, "HOPE: An Efficient Parallel Fault Simulator for Synchronous Sequential Circuits", Journal of IEEE Transactions on Computer-Aided Design of Integrated Circuits and Systems, 15(9): 1048-1058, 1996.

[12] Z. You, M. Inoue and H. Fujiwara, "On the Non-Scan BIST Schemes under Power Constraints for RTL Data Paths", Digest of papers 4th Int'l Workshop on RTL and High Level Testing. (WRTLT'2003), pp. 14-21, 2003.

SESSION

PERFORMANCE EVALUATION, ESTIMATION, AND RELATED ISSUES

Chair(s)

TBA

Tuning Master/Worker Applications: A Practical Use Case with MATE

Andrea Martínez, Anna Sikora, Eduardo César and Joan Sorribes
Computer Architecture and Operating Systems Department, Universitat Autònoma de Barcelona,
08193 Bellaterra, Barcelona, Spain
{amartinez, ania}@caos.uab.es, {eduardo.cesar, joan.sorribes}@uab.cat

Abstract— *Programming parallel/distributed applications is a difficult task that requires a high degree of knowledge and expertise, especially to achieve the potential performance offered by HPC. Analysis and tuning tools can be helpful for automatically improving applications performance. In particular, dynamic analysis and tuning tools are necessary for applications that vary their behaviour at execution time. MATE is a tool that, employing performance models, can automatically and dynamically tune parallel applications. This work presents how a theoretical performance model has been integrated into MATE for dynamically tune the data distribution and the number of workers of Master/Worker applications. The results show the effectiveness of using performance models for dynamically tuning parallel applications, and the achieved reduction in time when the application modifies its behaviour during its execution.*

Keywords: dynamic performance analysis; dynamic and automatic tuning; performance models; parallel/distributed computing

1. Introduction

Currently, software applications are used to solve complex problems in several areas of science and engineering. Many of these problems have very high computing requirements that can only be addressed through parallel/distributed processing. Therefore, performance is usually the most important issue related to parallel applications. In this work, we apply a methodology, based on performance models, for automatically and dynamically tuning the performance of parallel applications. In particular, we focus on the implementation and integration of a performance model for Master/Worker applications in MATE [1].

When a programmer develops a parallel application, he or she wishes to achieve a level of performance close to the expected theoretical performance. Unfortunately, this is not usually the case because the development of this type of applications is a difficult task. So, with the aim of increasing the performance of their applications, developers must undertake a performance improvement process. This process includes 3 successive phases: monitoring, analysis and tuning. First, during the monitoring phase, information about the application behaviour is captured. Then, by studying this information, the analysis phase looks for bottlenecks, deduces their causes, and tries to determine what the correct actions to eliminate the problems are. Finally, in the tuning phase these actions are applied to the application to solve the problems and improve its performance. As a result, developers must be familiar with the application, the software layers involved, and the behaviour of the system on which it is executed.

This paper is addressed to the **PDPTA'13** Conference

Various approaches and tools have been developed to support the performance improvement process [2] [3]. In particular, one of these approaches is the automatic and dynamic tuning of the application without stopping, recompiling, or rerunning it. This type of performance tuning approach is especially recommended for applications that behave differently depending on input data, or may even change their behaviour during each execution. In such cases, it is not worth carrying out a post-mortem performance analysis and tuning because conclusions based on one execution may be invalid for another. MATE (Monitoring Analysis and Tuning Environment) is a tool that implements this approach. It is able to automatically and dynamically tune a parallel/distributed application using the knowledge provided by a performance model.

The remainder of this work is organised as follows. Section 2 briefly describes MATE. In Section 3, we present an overview of the performance model developed for dynamically tuning Master/Worker applications. Section 4 explains the integration of the performance model into MATE. In Section 5 we present the results of the experiments conducted using MATE to improve the performance of a Master/Worker application. Section 6 presents the related work in automatic and dynamic tuning. And finally, Section 7 details the conclusions of this study.

2. MATE

MATE is a tool that performs monitoring, analysis, and tuning of MPI parallel applications. Its objective is to improve the performance of a parallel application at runtime, by adapting it to the variable conditions of the system.

First, at run-time MATE instruments the application to gather information about its behaviour. During the analysis phase MATE receives events, searches for bottlenecks and specifies solutions for solving the performance problems encountered. Finally, the application is dynamically modified by applying the given solutions. MATE uses dynamic instrumentation [4] to modify the application at run-time, so it does not need to be recompiled or restarted.

MATE is composed of the following modules which cooperate to control and improve the application's performance [5]:

- The **Application Controller** (AC) is a daemon that controls the execution and the dynamic instrumentation of each individual MPI task.
- The **Analyzer** is a centralised process that carries out the application performance analysis, and decides on monitoring and tuning. It automatically detects existing performance problems on the fly and requests appropriate changes to improve the application's performance.
- The **Dynamic Monitoring Library** (DMLib) is a shared library that is dynamically loaded by the AC in the application tasks to facilitate collecting data and delivering it to the Analyzer.

Performance models constitute the knowledge used by MATE to conduct the performance analysis process. Each performance model is encapsulated in MATE in a piece of software called a tunlet. Each tunlet implements the logic to overcome a particular performance problem by encapsulating information concerning to the measurement points to insert instrumentation in the target application to gather performance information, the performance functions, which are a set of expressions that mjodel the application's behaviour, and the tuning points, which are the points of the applications that can be changed by a tuning action to improve its performance.

3. Master/Worker Performance Model

The goal of performance analysis is to identify and solve the application performance problems. This process may be supported by a performance model that can be a combination of analytical expressions and heuristics. The parameters needed for evaluating the model correspond to the measurements gathered during the application execution. We have implemented and integrated into MATE a tunlet with the Master/Worker performance model described in [6]. It is designed for Master/Worker iterative applications, where all process repeatedly performs all operations. The condition of the iteration-based application behaviour implies the existence of a significant number of iterations and persistent performance problems between iterations.

This performance model includes two phases to solve Master/Worker application performance problems: a load balancing strategy, and an analytical model to evaluate and predict the appropriate number of workers for the application. In the following subsections we summarise both phases, and how to represent them in terms of the knowledge organisation required by MATE.

3.1 Load Balancing

Load balancing techniques try to avoid that some processes complete their processing before others. Some of these techniques are based on distributing the tasks in portions of decreasing size called batches.

In particular, we have implemented the strategy called *Dynamic Adjusting Factoring* (DAF) [7]. This technique divides the task set into different sized batches using a partition factor x_i whose value is dynamically adapted to the current load conditions of the application through expressions (1) and (2) located at Table 1. This factor depends on the mean μ_C and standard deviation σ_C of task processing C, and the number of workers N. Table 1 shows the Dynamic Adjusting Factoring strategy definition, represented according to the MATE knowledge requirements.

Table 1: Definition of the load balancing strategy

Parameters	- N, number of workers - C, task processing time, ms
Performance functions	Partition factor of the first batch of the iteration: $x_0 = 1 + \left(\sigma_C \sqrt{N/2}\right) / \mu_C$ (1) Partition factor of the remaining batches of the iteration: $x_i = 2 + \left(\sigma_C \sqrt{N/2}\right) / \mu_C$ (2)
Tuning points/actions	Partition factor. Its value can be modified throughout the iteration.

3.2 Adapting the Number of Workers

For determining the appropriate number of workers of the application, we have used the performance index *Pi* proposed in [6]. This index relates the execution time to the efficient use of resources in order to maximise the performance without wasting resources. Following the requirements of knowledge representation in MATE, the definition of this tuning strategy is presented in Table 2.

The parameters m_0 and λ are statically configured taking into account the characteristics of the computing platform. α is calculated as the sum of task sizes sent to workers while the total communication volume, V, is the sum of task sizes sent/receive to/from workers. Finally the total computation time, T_c, is obtained by adding the computation time of workers in an iteration.

Table 2: Definition of the adjust number of workers strategy

Parameters	- m_0, start up time per message, in ms - λ, communication cost per byte, in ms/byte. - V, total communication volume, in bytes. - α, portion of V sent to workers, in bytes. - T_c, total computation time, in ms.
Performance functions	Performance index for different number of workers x: $Pi(x) = \frac{xT_t(x)^2}{T_c}/\mu_C$ (3) Execution time of one iteration for x workers: $T_t(x) = 2m_0 + \frac{\lfloor((x-1)\alpha+1)\lambda V T_c\rfloor}{x}/\mu_C$ (4)
Tuning points/actions	The number of workers. Its value can be modified at the beginning of each iteration.

4. Tunlet Implementation

To dynamically tune the performance of Master/Worker applications, we have developed a tunlet that integrates the tuning strategies presented in Section 3. A tunlet is a library that encapsulates the information about a performance problem, implementing a particular tuning technique. Its implementation must use the Dynamic Tuning API [1] provided by the MATE's Analyzer module.

Earlier works featuring MATE show applying separate tuning techniques to load balancing [8] or to adapting the number of workers [9]. It is worth noting the complexity of the developed tunlet as it encapsulates two tuning phases, taking into account the interactions between them. In particular, the phase for adapting the number of worker considers that the application is balanced.

For the proper development of the tunlet, its definition should include the identification and interpretation of a set of elements related to the performance model and the type of the applications under study. From the point of view of the performance model, the following must be defined: measurement points, analytic performance functions and tuning points/actions. With respect to the application, in our work we have taken into consideration:

- The programming model followed by the applications.
- The variables or values that can be manipulated, with the aim of locating variables to tune.
- The functions whose execution must be detected to gather behavioural information.

In order to implement the tunlet based on the presented Master/Worker performance model, we have followed a tunlet design and development process [10] consisting of four steps which are explained in the following subsections.

4.1 Identify Application Actors

The designed tunlet needs information about the different types of application processes that cooperate to solve a concrete problem. This knowledge is required because each type of process should be instrumented depending on the role that it plays in the application. The application to be tuned follows a Master/Worker paradigm, so, two types of process can be identified: the master and N workers.

4.2 Identify Measurement Points

Performance model evaluation requires determination of which points in the application execution - measurement points - must be monitored in order to collect behavioural information about the application to calculate the parameters of the model's analytical expressions, which are shown in Tables 1 and 2.

The measurement points are located in either the entry to or exit from a function. One value is extracted of each of these points. However some parameters require multiple values and multiple measurement points for being calculated.

4.3 Identify Events

Events are messages in which the values extracted at the measurement point are sent to MATE's Analyzer module. These events are explicitly defined within the tunlet. Multiple values obtained at the same measurement point can be encapsulated in a single event and these values will be used by the Analyzer module for calculating the parameters for evaluating the performance model.

Table 3 presents the relationship between events and measurement points required by the analysis process. For each measurement point the table shows the actor, the function where it is situated, whether it is the entry to or exit from this function and the value which will be obtained.

4.4 Identify the Tuning Points and Actions

The last step consists of identifying the specific variables that will be modified by MATE at runtime. Consequently, a Master/Worker application must include a variable indicating the partition factor to be applied to the set of tasks for the load balancing strategy, and a variable indicating the current number of workers. Once MATE has taken all measurements to calculate the parameters of the analytical expressions, the performance model can be evaluated, and depending on the results of this evaluation, the adequate point to modify the associated variable should be determined.

For the load balancing strategy, the evaluation of the expressions is triggered when two separate events are received by the Analyzer: *Start Iteration* and *End computing worker*. At the beginning of the iteration, the tunlet has gathered all the information for calculating the mean μ_C and standard deviation σ_C of the task processing time for the previous iteration. This allows the calculation of the partition factor values for the first and second batch of the current iteration. On the other hand, when a worker has ended computing, the tunlet can verify if the information about the processing time of each worker that has participated in the computation

Table 3: Relationship between events and the required measurement point by the analysis process.

Parameters	Measurement Points				Events
	Actor	Function	Location	Value obtained	
Number of workers N	Master	Global send to workers	Entry	#workers	Start iteration
Task processing time, C	Worker	Receive tasks from master	Entry	Clock time, #tasks from master	Start computing
	Worker	Send tasks to master	Exit	Clock time	End computing
Total communication volume, V	Master	Send to worker i	Entry	#tasks to worker i	Master sends to worker
	Master	Receive tasks from worker i	Exit	#tasks from worker i	Master receives from worker
Total computation time, T_c	Worker	Receive tasks from master	Entry	Clock time	Start computing
	Worker	Send tasks to master	Exit	Clock time	End computing

of a particular batch has been collected. If so, the tunlet can calculate the partition factor for the following batches taking into account the current load balancing conditions.

Then, the tuning action can be invoked and the partition factor modified at any time during the iteration. On the other hand, for adjusting the number of workers, the evaluation of the expressions is triggered when the Start iteration event arrives to the Analyzer. At this moment, the tunlet has all the required information from the previous iteration (T_c, V, λ, and m_0). If the number of workers calculated by the Analyzer differs from the current number of workers, the tuning action is invoked between two iterations, and the predicted number of workers will be used in the next iteration.

5. Experimental Results

In this section, we present the experimental results obtained to validate the efficiency of the developed tunlet when it is integrated into MATE for dynamically tuning of Master/Worker applications. To conduct the experiments, we selected a computationally intensive Forest Fire Propagation parallel application called Xfire [11]. It is a Master/Worker MPI application that simulates fire line propagation following the Andre-Viegas model [12]. It iteratively calculates the next position of the fire line considering the current fire line position and environment aspects, such as weather, wind, vegetation, topology, etc. In each iteration, the master distributes the fire line among the workers and waits for the results. Then, it composes the new fire line and starts the next iteration. Workers calculate the evolution of the received fire line and send it back to the master. The application presents computational imbalance, with processing time differences between 20% and 100% among workers.

Experiments were conducted on a 33 node homogenous cluster running 3.00 GHz Intel Xeon Dual-Core processors, SuSE Linux 10, and connected by dual Gigabit Ethernet. The experiments were performed using 2, 4, 8, 16 and 31 workers. Each worker, the master, and the Analyzer were executed on a dedicated node. We have conducted our experiments using four scenarios:

1) Xfire was executed for different numbers of workers without tuning.
2) Xfire was executed with MATE, but only tuning the load balancing following the DAF algorithm. The initial partition factor was 0.5, and during the execution this value was adjusted to the load balancing conditions.
3) Xfire was executed with MATE, but only tuning the number of workers. The application started with two workers, and during the execution this number was changed according to the model described in Section 3.
4) Xfire was executed with MATE applying the entire developed tunlet, i.e., Xfire was tuned using the load balancing strategy and adjusting the number of workers.

Table 4 summarises the results obtained. The comparison of the execution times obtained for scenario 1 and 2 shows that dynamic tuning of the partition factor improves the Xfire performance because MATE is able to detect the load imbalance and correct the factor to reduce the execution time.

Table 4: Execution time (seconds) of Xfire in the different scenarios

Scenario	#Workers				
	2	4	8	16	31
1	48.08	24.38	13.67	8.75	6.08
2	37.19	18.10	10.54	7.38	6.68
3	Starting with two workers 7.49				
4	Starting with two workers 6.48				

Regarding scenario 3, MATE starts with two workers and then, upon receiving data from each iteration it adjusts the number of workers being employed. As it can be seen in Figure 1, as time passes, computational load variations cause changes in the number of workers in the application in order to achieve an optimal performance, making efficient use of the available resources. These changes in the computational load are due to varying condition in the weather, wind, vegetation or topology as the fire line progresses, and consequently the calculation of the new fire front may have a greater or lesser complexity. It can be observed that the execution time of Xfire with MATE is close to the best execution time obtained by different fixed number of workers, however with a better user of resources.

Figure 2 shows the execution time of Xfire application considering different number of workers and in the last column the execution time of Xfire under MATE applying the entire developed tunlet. It can be seen that tuning both the partition factor and the number of workers gives a lower execution time than when applying just one of the tuning policies, while at the same time making efficient use of the available resources.

6. Related Work

MATE presents an approach that automatically and dynamically improves the performance of parallel applications. This approach is based on the use of dynamic instrumentation and performance models as the intelligence engine of the analysis process. Currently, there are other tools which perform dynamic tuning processes.

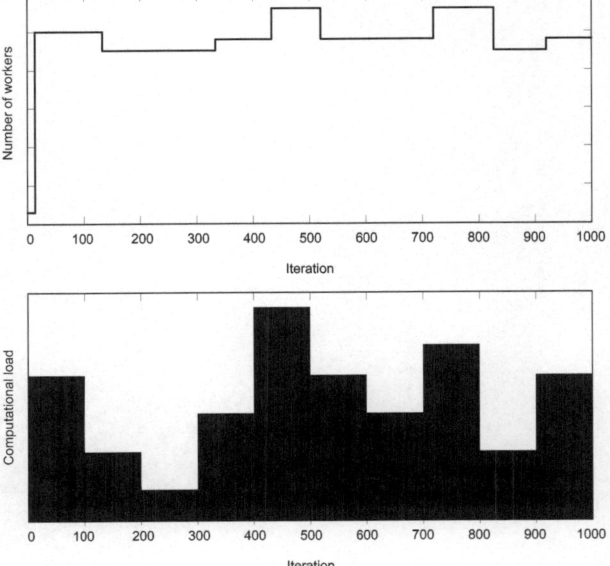

Fig. 1: Evolution of the number of workers with a variable computational load.

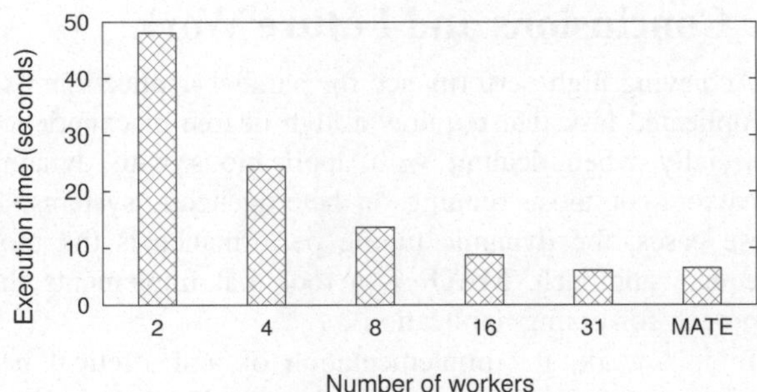

Fig. 2: Execution time of Xfire with different number of workers and under MATE applying the entire tunlet.

Autopilot [13] is a project for dynamic performance tuning in heterogeneous environments. It is based on the use of real-time techniques, which dynamically adapt the system to different demands and resource availability. Similar to MATE, Autopilot monitoring process is based on dynamic integration of sensors, which extract information about the application. The information analysis and decision procedures are performed using fuzzy logic. The application tuning is done by dynamically inserting actuator processes that adjust the application behaviour. This requires knowledge about the application.

Active Harmony [14] is a framework, which allows dynamic adaptation of an application to the network and available resources using automatic adjustment of algorithms, data distribution and load balancing. Its structure is based on a client-server model. The client is the harmonised application, which sends performance information to the server. The server performs the tuning based on this information. In this tool, the monitoring process gathers measures for various libraries with the same functionality. Then, it uses heuristic techniques to explore the application optimisation space and to adjust the tuning values.The tuning process is based on choosing the best implementation among the libraries.

PerCo [15] is a framework for performance monitoring in heterogeneous environments. It is able to manage the distributed execution of applications using migrations, for example, in response to changes in the runtime environment. PerCo monitors execution times and reacts according to a control strategy to adapt the performance when significant changes occur in the application behaviour. The performance analysis and tuning process is performed using historical data, and combining time series and data adjustment methods.

The main difference between MATE and presented tools is in the analysis phase. In MATE, the analysis is based on performance models, whereas Autopilot, Active Harmony and PerCo use fuzzy logic, heuristic techniques, and historical data and time series respectively.

7. Conclusions and Future Work

Achieving high performance for parallel applications is a complicated task that requires a high degree of experience, especially when dealing with applications with dynamic behaviour, or those running on heterogeneous systems. In these cases, the dynamic tuning performance is the most adequate approach. MATE is a tool that implements this approach for tuning applications.

In this work, the implementation of a theoretical performance model for Master/Worker applications and its integration into MATE has been presented. MATE has been extended to improve application performance by balancing the load and determining the appropriate number of workers. The performance model has been encapsulated in a MATE component called a tunlet. To correctly design and develop the tunlet, it has been necessary to identify and interpret the relation between the performance model, the type of tuned application, and the tuning tool. The developed tunlet can be used to tune other applications based, as in the case of Xfire, on iterations and a Master/Worker paradigm. It would only be necessary to adapt the application to the tuning process, adjusting the names of certain functions and tuning variables.

The experimental results present the applicability of the MATE dynamic tuning environment and performance models to reduce the execution time significantly adapting the application to changing conditions and using the resources efficiently.

Acknowledgment

This research has been supported by the MICINN-Spain under contract TIN2011-28689.

References

[1] A. Morajko, "Dynamic Tuning of Parallel/Distributed Applications," Ph.D. dissertation, Universitat Autònoma de Barcelona, 2004.

[2] M. Geimer, F. Wolf, B. Wylie, E. ÃĄbrahÃąm, D. Becker, and B. Mohr, "The SCALASCA Performance Toolset Architecture," in *Int. Workshop on Scalable Tools for High-End Computing*, Kos, Greece, 2008, pp. 51–65.

[3] S. Benedict, V. Petkov, and M. Gerndt, "PERISCOPE: An Online-based Distributed Performance Analysis Tool," in *Workshop on Parallel Tools for HPC*, 2009, pp. 1–16.

[4] B. Buck and J. Hollingsworth, "An API for Runtime Code Patching," *The Int. Journal of High Performance Computing Applications*, vol. 14, pp. 317–329, 2000.

[5] A. Morajko, T. Margalef, and E. Luque, "Design and Implementation of a Dynamic Tuning Environment," *J. Parallel Distrib. Comput.*, vol. 67, pp. 474–490, 2007. [Online]. Available: http://portal.acm.org/citation.cfm?id=1232942.1233008

[6] E. César, A. Moreno, J. Sorribes, and E. Luque, "Modeling Master/Worker Applications for Automatic Performance Tuning," *Parallel Comput.*, vol. 32, no. 7, pp. 568–589, 2006.

[7] I. Banicescu and V. Velusamy, "Load Balancing Highly Irregular Computations with the Adaptive Factoring," in *Proc. of IPDPS Conference*, 2002.

[8] A. Morajko, P. Caymes-Scutari, T. Margalef, and E. Luque, "Automatic Tuning of Data Distribution Using Factoring in Master/Worker Applications," in *Int. Conference on Computational Science*, 2005, pp. 132–139.

[9] A. Morajko, E. César, P. Caymes-Scutari, T. Margalef, J. Sorribes, and E. Luque, "Automatic Tuning of Master/Worker Applications," in *Euro-Par*, 2005, pp. 95–103.

[10] P. Caymes-Scutari, A. Morajko, T. Margalef, and E. Luque, "A Methodology for Transparent Knowledge Specification in a Dynamic Tuning Environment," *Software: Practice and Experience*, 2011.

[11] J. Jorba, T. Margalef, E. Luque, J. Andre, and D. Viegas, "Application of Parallel Processing to the Simulation of Forest Fire Propagation," in *Proc. of ICFFR*, vol. II, Coimbra, Portugal, 1998.

[12] J. André and D. Viegas, "A Strategy to Model the Average Fireline Movement of a light-to-medium Intensity Surface Forest Fire," in *Proc. of ICFFR*, Coimbra, Portugal, 1994, pp. 221–242.

[13] R. Ribler, J. Vetter, H. Simitci, and D. A. Reed, "Autopilot: Adaptive Control of Distributed Applications," in *Proc. of IEEE Symp. on HPDC*, 1998, pp. 172–179.

[14] C. Tapus, I.-H. Chung, and J. Hollingsworth, "Active Harmony: Towards Automated Performance Tuning," in *Proc. from the Conference on High Performance Networking and Computing*, 2003, pp. 1–11.

[15] K. Mayes, M. LujÃąn, G. D. Riley, J. Chin, P. V. Coveney, and J. R. Gurd, "Towards Performance Control on the Grid," *Philosophical Transactions: Mathematical, Physical and Engineering Sciences*, vol. 363, no. 1833, pp. 1793–1805, 2005.

Performance Model for the Impact of Hardware Characteristics in Accelerated Processing Units

Mario A. Chapa M.[1] **and Hiroyuki Sato**[1,2]
[1]Department of Electrical Engineering and Information Science, The University of Tokyo, Tokyo, Japan
[2]Information Technology Center, The University of Tokyo, Tokyo, Japan

Abstract— *The importance of Graphic Processing Units (GPU) as high performance accelerators has been increasing since the late 90's. However, a limiting factor of the peak performance that a GPU can achieve lies in the bandwidth limitations of the interface used to connect the GPU to the rest of the system. The Accelerated Processing Unit (APU) was developed as an attempt to deal with this limiting factor. Aiming to provide insights of the behavior of memory-bound kernels in APU systems, we develop a performance model for the Matrix-Matrix Multiplication (MMM) algorithm as it is executed in the APU. The model is elaborated from the analysis of a tiling MMM kernel. By studying the different aspects of the execution in the APU hardware and utilizing a statistical approach we developed a model to estimate the impact of hardware characteristics in the performance and attempt to explain the nature of the experimental results. The formula consist of a linear combination of three terms, global memory accesses, local memory accesses and floating-point operations times. These three factors are integrated into a performance model formula by applying the Least Squares Method (LMS). We show that the estimation obtained by this formula closely matches the experimental results.*

Keywords: GPU, APU, Performance Modeling,

1. Introduction

Since the late 90's, the GPUs has successfully been used as accelerator hardware in addition to their original purpose as graphics processors. The reason behind this success is the price to performance ratio they offer and being a massively-parallel computing engine widely available. It has been demonstrated that the raw floating-point performance of even a low-end GPU is higher than the most sophisticated CPU available [2]. However, because the system's memory and the GPU memory are physically separated, the data that is processed by the GPU must be copied to the GPU memory, typically using the PCIe port. Due to its limited bandwidth, this port becomes a performance bottleneck. A great amount of effort has been made to overcome this limitation and a number of algorithmic as well as hardware solutions have been developed. A system where the GPU is closely coupled within the same chip as the CPU is one of the proposed solutions. One of such hybrid systems is the Accelerated Processing Unit (APU). In an APU, the GPU processing cores and shared memory are integrated into the same silicon die as the CPU cores. Including the CPU and GPU in the same chip eliminates the need of communicating data through the PCI port. This is opposed to traditional discrete GPUs in which the GPU hardware resides in a separate card that is attached to the system via an I/O port.

Because GPU hardware is so complex and different from the CPU and even though modern GPUs have a more and more general purpose computation-oriented architecture, a programmer still has to spend certain time to write a program that produce the desired results, and even more time to optimize that program. GPUs are a special kind of accelerators with a very particular architecture. This is because the original purpose of including a GPU engine in a system was to handle graphic tasks that slowed down the CPU. Computations on graphics are easy to perform concurrently and exhibit predictable memory access patterns, programming tools are mature and well developed in the graphics processing area. However in General Purpose GPU development, the amount of effort centered around developing and supporting tools for performance analysis has been minimal compared to that devoted to application development. For example, even though proprietary tools and academy-developed tools are advocated to provide program execution statistics (e.g. executed instructions counters, memory requests counters, etc.), these tools do not provide insights about how the statistics relate to program performance. In our research we develop a performance model of kernel execution for the APU. The has been build by analyzing the kernel execution flow and considering GPU hardware characteristics such as the number of compute units and the size of the shared memory space. The model breaks-down the time costs of the three major operations: floating-point computations, global memory transfers, and shared memory transfers. The model also takes into consideration how the chosen thread-group size affects the kernel execution time.

The rest of this paper is organized as follows. A brief description of the OpenCL programing model and an overview of the APU hardware necessary to understand the GPU program execution flow appears in section 2. Section 3 describes the methodology followed to develop the model. Section 4 presents the performance analysis of a Matrix-Matrix Multiplication algorithm. The experiments and results used to validate the model are presented in section 5. Section 6 features the related work. Finally section 7 summarizes the paper with the conclusions and the future work.

2. Programming Model and APU Hardware

In order to understand how GPU are constituted and the performance implications of different programming techniques and hardware configurations, it is necessary to know the programming models and the hardware characteristics used in the design of the APU. The APU was developed by AMD and the programming model available to program it is OpenCL. OpenCL is based on the Single Program Multiple Data (*SPMD*) programming. To enable the use of a GPU in a program, it is necessary to employ an API. For this purpose, the non-profit organization Kronus Group have developed the OpenCL libraries. Using the OpenCL libraries enables the use of a wide range of special accelerator hardware and this includes GPUs from all vendors. In order to make use of the GPU programmers must write at least two source code files that includes the appropriate calls to the OpenCL libraries. One of them is the *Host program*, that is the program that will be compiled an run in the CPU, and a *Kernel program*, that will contain the functions that will execute in the GPU.The host initialize and prepare the system to execute kernels in the devices. When a kernel is submitted for execution a index space containing a defined number of software threads is defined. Because the GPU operates with the SPMD model, the index space purpose is to provide a mean for processing threads to know which data elements they operate on. In OpenCL terms, a processing thread is referred as work-item and as in the traditional sense of software threads, a work-item represents a light-weight process that is running a set of computer instructions and has allocated resources. Work-items are grouped unto a larger logical instance called Work-group. The most important aspect of work-groups, is that communication is enabled across work-items only if they belong to the same work-group. In the next paragraph we briefly describe the main hardware components of a GPU and how they relate to the concepts in the OpenCL programming model.

In general, GPUs are throughput-oriented devices made up of hundreds of processing cores that allow a high level of concurrency. Figure 3 shows a block diagram that includes the general components of all GPU devices. In modern GPUs architectures, the processing elements have a two-level hierarchical architecture. The top level is made of vector processors, called Compute Units (*CU*) that operate in a Single Instruction Multiple Data (*SIMD*) fashion. In the next level, each vector unit contains an array of processing elements (*PE*). All the PEs inside a CU are able to communicate through an on-chip, user-managed memory known as shared memory. When a work-group is created within a program, all wok-items in that work-group are assigned to the same CU. The purpose is to ensure scalability, allowing a program to run across different generations of GPUs with different number of CUs. Although the vector processors can process an arbitrary number of work-items within some constraints, the scheduler always arrange work-items in groups of 64 or 32 depending on the vendor. Such group of work-items is known as a *Wave-front* and it is the smallest scheduling unit. This means that if some number smaller than 64 work-items need to be executed, the schedulers in the CU will still create 64 work-items and since not all the theads have useful work to do, some of them will be idling. The performance impact of this idling is a reduced computational throughput.

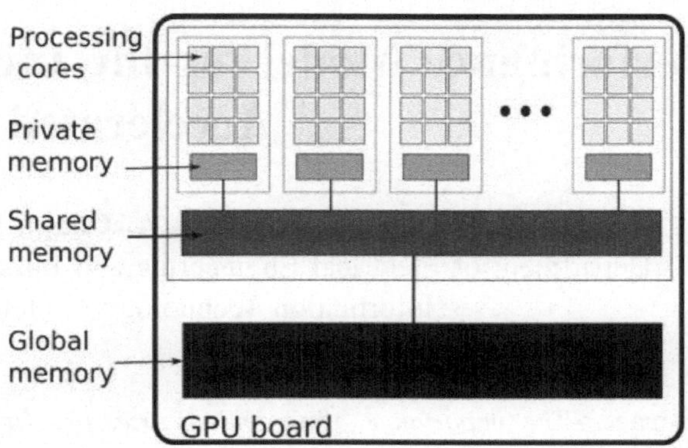

Fig. 1: General block diagram of a GPU device. The different levels of the memory hierarchy are show. It is important to notice that the global memory is separated from the system's memory

3. Model Design

In this section we first briefly discuss how the total execution time of a kernel time is measured for an APU device; then we describe how the model was developed and the characteristics of the GPU hardware that have a major impact on the behavior of the performance curve.

3.1 Calculating Kernel Execution Time

A simple formula for modeling the execution time of any given algorithm in a computer system can be obtained by dividing the number of clock cycles required by the algorithm and the duration of one clock cycle. For simplicity, we measure elapsed time instead of clock cycles. Taking one step ahead in the analysis of computation time, The time required to complete an algorithm can be divided into the time spend into performing numerical computations and time spend copying data from one level of the memory hierarchy to another as shown in equation 1.

$$RunningTime = ComputationTime + DataTransferTime \quad (1)$$

A more refined model suited for GPU computations considers that the data transfer inside a GPU is divided into two categories. The First category refers to the data transfers from global memory to shared memory inside the GPU, then from the shared memory to the registers of the processing cores. In our model we do not consider transfers between system memory and global memory because we assume zero-copy data buffers, the main advantage of an APU system [5]. An important observation is that it is not possible to measure with perfect accuracy the time elapsed for either the floating point operations or the memory transfers. Taking this into consideration, we obtain equation 2 that its a linear combination of three terms.

$$\begin{aligned} \mathit{RunningTime} =& \alpha_1 \cdot \mathit{ComputationTime} + \\ & \alpha_2 \cdot \mathit{LocalMem.TransferTime} + \\ & \alpha_3 \cdot \mathit{GlobalMem.TransferTime} \end{aligned} \quad (2)$$

We will refer to the proposed model as Linear Performance Breakdown Model (**LPBM**). The α parameters in the equation define the weight of each individual term of the equation. They also help to interpret the breakdown of the performance, indicating which component represents a greater contribution to the total processing time so that optimization effort can be applied in the correct direction.

3.2 Linear Performance Breakdown Model

In the present subsection we first describe how we developed each of the components of the LPBM based on the hardware characteristics of the APU. To determine how the kernel execution parameters affect the performance, it is necessary to consider the characteristics of the APU, and how kernels are scheduled for execution in the hardware resources of the device. When using the GPU for non-graphic related algorithms, the achievable amount of parallelism is an important parameter that will define the execution time of an algorithm. It is linked to the mapping of work-groups to the Compute Units (CU) and to the scheduling of wave-fronts. All GPU devices are massively parallel processors, it is important to understand the source of parallelism in GPU hardware. As an example, in a multi-core CPU environment a parallel task can be partitioned in n sub-tasks, where n is the number of cores in that particular CPU. The source of parallelism then is well defined as the number of cores. On the other hand, even the low-end GPUs count with several hundreds of cores and the attainable parallelism is dependent on factors like the resource usage of the work-items of the executing kernel and the mapping of wave-fronts in the CU units. As mentioned in section 2 instructions schedulers in GPU have a constraint for the number of threads that can be created and launched for execution, called wave-front size. Any number of threads different to that value will cause idling processing cores in the GPU. Figure 3.2

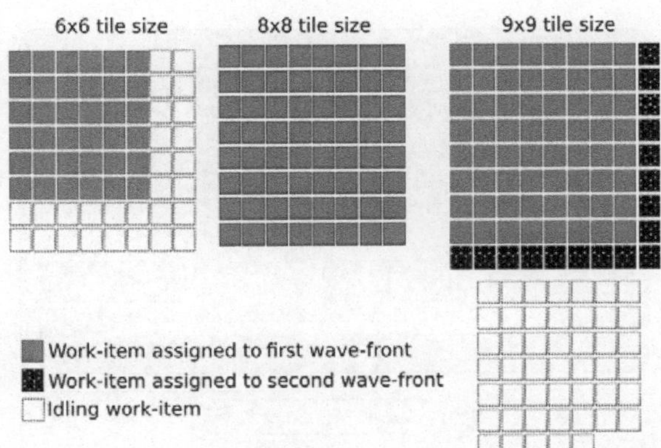

Fig. 2: wave-front scheduling in relation with the work-group size. If the number of work-items in a work-group is not a multiple of the wave-front size, some of the work-items will be idle.

shows examples for three different work-group sizes, and the resultant scheduling of wave-fronts. When the number of work-items is less than than the wave-front size (In the APU and other AMD GPUs is 64 work-items), one wave-front is enough to compute all the elements in the tile.

However, when the size increases, it is necessary to generate and schedule more than one wave-front. When the number of work-items is different to the wave-front size, the effective work that the GPU will do will be reduced since it is not possible to schedule a fewer amount of work-items for execution than the wave front size. This situation affects performance because there will be processing cores idling and also the efficiency of the data transfers is reduced.

As equation 2 shows, the total execution kernel is divided in 3 main tasks. First, the amount of time that it takes to perform the numerical computations (P_1), The data movement from global to shared memory (P_2), and from shared to private memory in the compute units (P_3). We summarize then, the total execution time (TT) into the following formula:

$$TT = \alpha_1 \cdot P_1 + \alpha_2 \cdot P_2 + \alpha_3 \cdot P_3 \quad (3)$$

Each of the P_n terms is estimated as described in the following discussion. In a sequential system, P_1 can be estimated as the number of floating-point operations necessary to finish the task. This would yield the total amount of *Time Slots* to complete the execution of an algorithm, and by multiplying the number of times slots by the execution time of a single time slot, we can have an estimate of the computation time. However, in a multi-core system such as the GPU, operations are executed with some degree of concurrency. The key is to estimate the degree of concurrency that can be achieved by taking into account the capabilities of the hardware. An important parameter is the total number of wave-fronts required to execute all the work-items in a

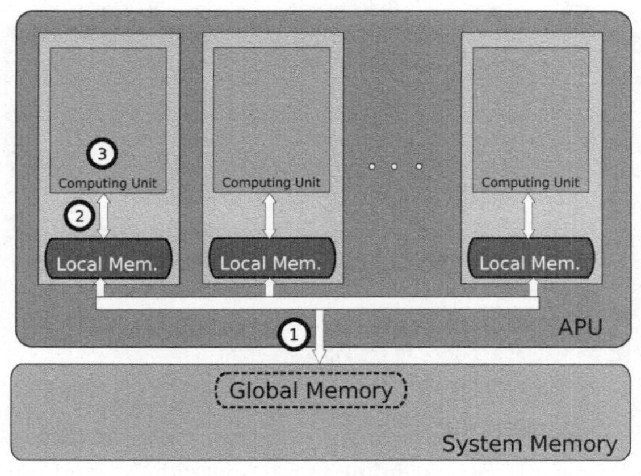

Fig. 3: Kernel execution phases. When a kernel is executed in an APU, data must be copied between global and local memory, local and private memory where the computations occur.

Table 1: Work-groups allowed to reside in a CU in function of LSD usage

Memory/Work-group	Limit of Work-groups
Less than 4kB	8
4.0kB-4.6kB	7
4.6kB-5.3kB	6

kernel launch, and in turn, the total number of wave fronts that can be executed concurrently in the GPU. There is a number of factors that affect the actual level of parallelism achievable, however the influence of such factors is not as critical as the hardware resources mentioned. Taking this into consideration will yield an estimate of the time slots required to complete a kernel execution. The maximum number of wave-fronts that can be executed concurrently in the GPU is determined by the resources needed by each work-item and those available in each CU, These resources are the number of registers and the size of the Local Data Store (LDS), a especial portion of memory inside each CU. To determine total amount of wave-fronts that can be executed at the same time across the GPU, we must know how many wave-fronts can be executed in a single CU. This is done by calculating the amount of memory from the Local Data Store that a work-item uses and then refer to the hardware specifications [5]. Table 1 summarizes the most relevant information regarding this aspect. The maximum number of concurrent wave-fronts value depends on per work-group memory needs. With that information it is possible to calculate how many work-groups can reside in a CU, then the total amount of work-group that can execute concurrently across the GPU is the obtained value multiplied by the amount of CUs in the GPU.

The term P_2 corresponds to the total amount of global memory transfers. In a simple, straight implementation of a blocked algorithm, there would be $2N^2 + N^3$ loads and stores in total, approximately the same number of arithmetical operations. Because a work-item will load an element from global memory to shared memory, and then that element will be used by t work-items in the same group, (where t is the tile width) the number of global memory transactions will be reduced as t increases. A more detailed explanation of the tile size effects regarding the reduction of global memory traffic can be found in [3]. Finally, the term P_3, that corresponds to the memory transfers from shared memory to the processing cores inside each CU. For this term, the amount of phases required to compute an output value in relation with the tile size (i.e. N/t) is an important factor. The number of phases directly affects the number of data requests from the shared memory to the global memory. The total amount of shared memory request is then the number of phases times the number of tiles in the matrix, then the resulting number multiplied by the number of required wave-fronts for a tile. This is because each row in a tile generates a memory request, and all the elements of that tile row are fetched at the same time. The memory in the GPU works in a similar way to the main system memory, where contiguous data elements are transferred in a single bus burst. Thus, by having a small tile width, more request are generated since the number of tiles to cover a matrix is larger compared to the case where the tile width increases. Summarizing, the formula is the amount of phases multiplied by the number or tiles in the matrix by the number of requests requests each tile generates. The resulting formula 5.

$$\begin{aligned} TT(t) =& \alpha_1 \cdot \frac{\lceil \frac{N^2}{WWF} \rceil}{\lceil \frac{t^2}{WWF} \rceil * MWF} + \\ & \alpha_2 \cdot \frac{N^2}{t} + \\ & \alpha_3 \cdot m * \frac{N^2}{t} * \lceil \frac{t^2}{WWF} \rceil \end{aligned} \tag{4}$$

Where WWF is the number of work-items that are grouped in a wave-front, for current AMD GPUs, it is equal to 64. The term WWF/GPU stands for Maximum number of wave-fronts that can reside in the GPU in any given moment, and as we explained at the start of the present section, , its equal to the maximum allowable work-groups per CU by the number of CUs in the GPU. To estimate the α_n parameters, statistical regression algorithms such as Kalman filter, Least Square Method (LSM) and recursive Least Square Method can be applied. We adopted LSM because it is a well-known method that used to estimate the best fit for the data set. The objective of applying the LSM consists of adjusting the parameters of our model function to best fit the data set obtained in our experiments.

The data set consists of n points (data pairs) x_i, y_i, with $i = 1, 2, \cdots, 16$, where x_i is an independent variable, tile width, and y_i is a dependent variable whose value is the execution time observed experimentally. The model function has the form $f(x, \beta)$, where the adjustable parameters are held in the vector β. The goal is to find the parameter values for the model which best fits the data. Obtaining the parameters will tell us to which extent each one of the factors contained in the formula impact the performance, which is also helpful to decide in which step of the algorithms the optimization efforts must be directed. For our experiments we use a concrete example of a matrix-matrix multiplication to obtain the data necessary to estimate the parameters and validate the model though the use of a linear regression method, in the next section, we present the experimental setup used to obtain the required experimental values needed to validate the model.

4. Performance Analysis of Tiled Matrix-Matrix Multiplication based on LPBM

In order to obtain the experimental data necessary to apply the LSM and validate the model, a program that executes the kernel function and profiles the execution time was used. The kernel code is shown in listing 1. The program was run with all the possible ranges of values for t for a matrix size of 1000. The t values range is from 1 to 16. It is not possible to create a tile of a width larger than 16 because currently OpenCL restricts the maximum size of work-groups to 256 elements.

Listing 1: MMM kernel with tiling

```
float output_value = 0;
  for(int m = 0; m < Width/TILE_WIDTH; m++) {
      local_tile_a[ty][tx] =
  input_a[Row * Width + (m*TILE_WIDTH + tx)];
      local_tile_b[ty][tx] =
  input_b[(m*TILE_WIDTH + ty) * Width + Col];
  barrier(CLK_LOCAL_MEM_FENCE);
      for(int k = 0; k < TILE_WIDTH; k++)
        output_value += local_tile_a[ty][k] * local_tile_b[k][tx];
  }
  barrier(CLK_GLOBAL_MEM_FENCE);
  output[Row * Width + Col] = output_value;
```

In our algorithm we work with single precision floating-point numbers grouped in tiles ranging from one elements to blocks of 16 by 16 elements, to store the values for our MMM kernel, we need at most $16^2 \cdot 4$ bytes of memory for one tile. Since a work-group will be composed of three tiles, each tile need 3 kB, hence the maximum allowed number of Work-groups is equal to the maximum possible amount. With this information, it is possible to calculate how many work-groups can reside in each CU and the total amount of work-group that can execute concurrently across the GPU by multiplying by the number of CUs in the GPU. To obtain the timing data, we make use of the timers provided by the OpenCL specification to inquire the total kernel execution time. The timers have a resolution of $1ns$. The program was run 1000 times and the execution time is an average of all the measured timings for each tile size. The employed APU is based in the Evergreen family of GPUs. The hardware resources and configuration of the APU hardware are shown in table 2

Table 2: Machine Characteristics

APU Model	AMD A8-3820
Clock freq.	3.0 GHz
System memory	12 GB
Compute Units	5
GPU Clock freq.	400 MHz
Global Memory	256 MB
Local Memory	32 kB

5. Experiments and Results

After running the experiments and collecting the data, the LSM is applied to estimate the α_n parameters in our model equation. The calculated performance from the experimental results as well as the values calculated from the model is shown in figure 2 As shown in figure 5, we can observe that the obtained results for the model closely match those for the experiments. The reason for the discrepancies are manifold, they can be attributed to non-uniformity in the execution of the kernel, like bank conflicts and not enough latency hiding in some cases; as well as another execution details not considered in the model like the influence of caches. Caches are relatively a new addition in the graphics hardware and were not considered in this paper for simplicity purposes. However, the accuracy achieved with the proposed model reflects that the considered parameters are those who have a major impact on the performance like the maximum number of wave-fronts that can run concurrently across the GPU and the impact of the tile size in the number of memory request that must be generated to transfer all the data elements. These factors explain the observed saw tooth pattern when the tile size is greater than 8, because in the ideal case the performance should continue scaling like the observed curve while the tile size is less than eight. The values of the parameters in the model is also useful to observe the different impact on the performance each separate component have, how much they contribute to the total time amounted for the execution of a kernel. If we breakdown the total execution times, so we can observe each term contribution, we obtain the column chart depicted in figure 3. In this figure we can observe that, as expected in a GPU device, the term P_1 that corresponds to the floating-point calculation time adds a small portion of the execution time and the major portion of the execution time is contributed by the memory transfers. Specially global memory that in the case of a tile

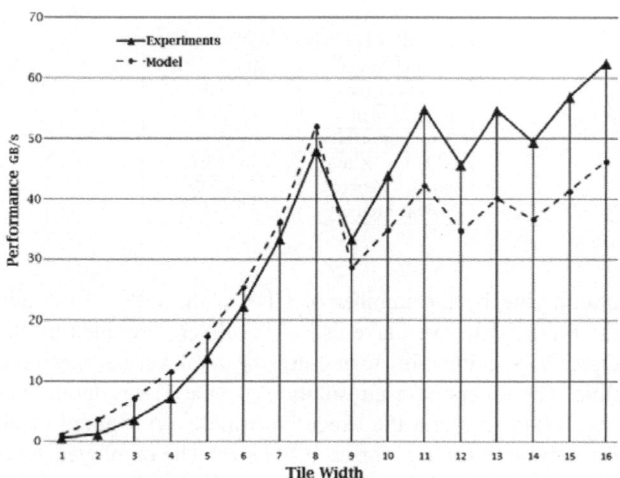

Fig. 4: APU general block diagram

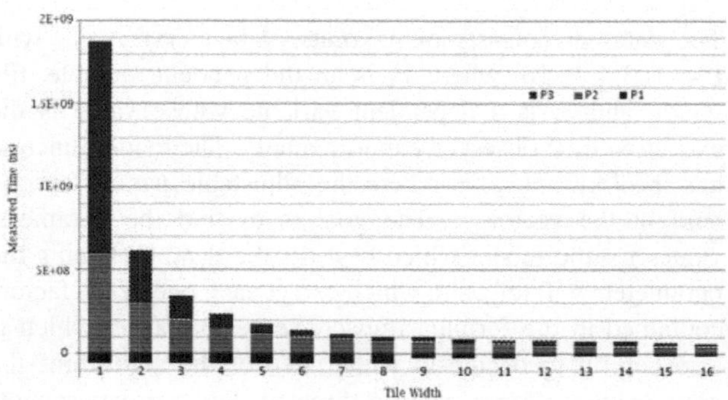

Fig. 5: Performance Breakdown

size of 1 (i.e, no tiling applied) it amends to more than 60% of the total execution time. With the increase of the tile width, the global memory transfer time is greatly reduced for the reasons explained in section 2. It is also worth observing that at some point, the reduction in execution time is not significant anymore with larger tile widths. This hints that enabling the hardware for a larger number of threads per work group will not be synonymous of an important improving in tiling algorithms. It is also worth noticing that since the global memory transfer times is reduced for large values of tile width, an important portion of the total time is attributed to the local memory transfers. This means that a improvement on the nature of this kind of memory could bear a good impact on the performance of the algorithm. As mentioned in the previous sections, another advantage of the LSM method is that it provide us with the estimation for the model parameters. This parameters can be used to produce a performance breakdown graph like the one show in figure 5. Each corresponding α_n tell to what extent each of the computation steps adds to the total computation time. This is useful because programmers can have a better understanding of where the optimization efforts can provide the best gains or to know in which steps the application is not performing as it is expected.

6. Related Work

Although a there have been much effort devoted to application development and algorithms optimization in the GPU communities, most, if not all of the available works help the designer to exploit the parallelism in the problem to take advantage of the GPU high computational throughput or provide useful techniques to improve performance by reducing memory transfer and execution times. Concerning modeling for performance on GPU architectures, there is limited reported work. in [6] the authors relate to the lack of a GPU performance model and recognize the difficulties it derives like the possibility of evaluate the suitability of the GPU to solve a particular problem. Likewise, [7] address the importance of having access to a modeling framework recognizing the fact that for GPU programs, developers should devote large amounts of time to write a program that functions correctly, yet alone utilizing the hardware to its best performance. The result of their work is a framework to generate predictive models that allows the comparison between GPU and CPU performance in a per-application base. We chose instead to focus the analysis in the GPU architecture, since we believe that at this point it is clear that if the task exhibits a good amount of parallelism, the GPU will present better performance than CPU. In 2009, Hong et al. [16] presented a study on GPU power and performance modeling. In their study, the authors demonstrate the development of an analytical model based on an abstraction of the architecture of Nvidia GPUs and then execute the related experiments to confirm the model. In the study we present in this paper, we first design and execute the set of experiments that provide us with the performance results. Then develop a model that is composed by the costs for floating-point computations and shared and global memory transfer costs, identify as the factors with major impact on performance and its relation with the tile size. In [8], the author proposes a model for execution-less performance modeling for linear algebra algorithms in CPU machines. The authors develops their model focusing on L1 cache misses, and analyze the correspondence between their model and the experimental results obtained in a Barcelona AMD CPU and a Intel Penryn. We extend the focus to systems with a fused GPU-CPU architecture and include in the analysis the cost of transfers between the various level of the GPU memory hierarchy. In our work we observe that the performance behavior due to changes in the tile size exhibits a non-uniform behavior, the first half of the experiments shows a constant increase in performance while the later half have a different behavior that forms a saw-tooth curve. The factors that influence this behavior are many-fold and we develop our model with the ones we consider are the key components. In [9] the author discuss the effects of factors such as sequential code, barriers cache coherence and scheduling in general shared memory multiprocessors. The author parts from the Amdahl's law and analyze shared memory systems (GPUs belong to this classification) to derive several models, one for each separate factor. Our approach is instead combine the most important factors into a single equation using a special case of Shared memory system and apply then the LSM method to evaluate the impact of each factor.

7. Conclusions

We developed a Lineal Performance Breakdown Model (LPBM) for the Accelerated Processing Unit (APU) and validated it with experimental data obtained from the execution of a Matrix-Matrix Multiplication (MMM) kernel optimized by tiling to observe the performance impact of work-group size. The experimental results closely matched the data obtained with the LPBM. The LPBM is also useful to estimate the time consumed by the main aspects of kernel execution: numerical computations and data transfers between the global, shared and private memory. Obtaining this breakdown of performance in the major components serves as guidance for optimizations, allowing to focus the optimization efforts in the right direction. We have confirmed that our preliminary model successfully captures the computation time cost for the execution on the APU for fixed matrix size. In our future work, we will extend the proposed model to accommodate more variables, e.g. the matrix size, so that the model can be generalized and used to predict the performance of the process for any given matrix size. Another possible application of this research is its application as a performance analyzer in an automatic optimizer framework. The LPBM provides useful feedback about the changes in time consumption for the different execution aspects that can be used for reference about the effectiveness of certain optimizations applied to the kernel code.

References

[1] *ATI Stream Profiler*, http://developer.amd.com

[2] *NVIDIA Parallel Insigth* http://developer.nvidia.com

[3] Sunpyo Hong and Hyesoon Kim. 2010. *An integrated GPU power and performance model*. SIGARCH Comput. Archit. News 38, 3 (June 2010), 280-289.

[4] David B. Kirk and Wen-mei W. Hwu. 2010. *Programming Massively Parallel Processors: A Hands-On Approach (1st ed.)*. Morgwan Kaufmann Publishers Inc., San Francisco, CA, USA.

[5] *AMD Accelerated Parallel Processing Programing Guide*, Revision 2.4, December 2012.

[6] Kothapalli, K.; Mukherjee, R.; Rehman, M.S.; Patidar, S.; Narayanan, P. J.; Srinathan, K., *A performance prediction model for the CUDA GPGPU platform*, High Performance Computing (HiPC), 2009 International Conference on , vol., no., pp.463,472, 16-19 Dec. 2009

[7] Sunpyo Hong and Hyesoon Kim. 2009. *An analytical model for a GPU architecture with memory-level and thread-level parallelism awareness*. SIGARCH Comput. Archit. News 37, 3 (June 2009), 152-163

[8] Roman Iakymchuk and Paolo Bientinesi. 2012. *Modeling performance through memory-stalls*. SIGMETRICS Perform. Eval. Rev. 40, 2 (October 2012), 86-91.

[9] Zhang, X., *Performance measurement and modeling to evaluate various effects on a shared memory multiprocessor*, Software Engineering, IEEE Transactions on , vol.17, no.1, pp.87,93, Jan 1999

[10] Andrew Kerr, Gregory Diamos, and Sudhakar Yalamanchili. 2010. *Modeling GPU-CPU workloads and systems*. In Proceedings of the 3rd Workshop on General-Purpose Computation on Graphics Processing Units (GPGPU '10)

[11] Ki-Hwan Kim, KyoungHo Kim, Q-Han Park, *Performance analysis and optimization of three-dimensional FDTD on GPU using roofline model*, Computer Physics Communications, Volume 182, Issue 6, June 2011, Pages 1201-1207, ISSN 0010-4655

[12] Yong-Kim Chong and Kai Hwang. 1995. *Performance Analysis of Four Memory Consistency Models for Multithreaded Multiprocessors*. IEEE Trans. Parallel Distrib. Syst. 6, 10 (October 1995), 1085-1099

[13] Park, Seung In and Cao, Yong and Watson, Layne T. and Quek, Francis (2012) *Performance Analysis of a Novel GPU Computation-to-core Mapping Scheme for Robust Facet Image Modeling*. Technical Report TR-12-05, Computer Science, Virginia Tech.

[14] Sara S. Baghsorkhi, Matthieu Delahaye, Sanjay J. Patel, William D. Gropp, and Wen-mei W. Hwu. 2010. *An adaptive performance modeling tool for GPU architectures*. SIGPLAN Not. 45, 5 (January 2010), 105-114

[15] Tyler Dwyer, Alexandra Fedorova, Sergey Blagodurov, Mark Roth, Fabien Gaud, and Jian Pei. 2012. *A practical method for estimating performance degradation on multicore processors*, and its application to HPC workloads. In Proceedings of the International Conference on High Performance Computing, Networking, Storage and Analysis (SC '12).

[16] Sunpyo Hong and Hyesoon Kim. 2009. *An analytical model for a GPU architecture with memory-level and thread-level parallelism awareness*. SIGARCH Comput. Archit. News 37, 3 (June 2009), 152-163.

A Framework to write Performability-Aware SPMD Applications*

Hugo Meyer[1], Ronal Muresano[1], Dolores Rexachs[2] and Emilio Luque[2]
Computer Architecture and Operating Systems Department
University Autonoma of Barcelona, Barcelona, Spain
[1] {hugo.meyer, ronal.muresano}@caos.uab.es
[2] {dolores.rexachs, emilio.luque}@uab.es

Abstract— *Optimizing the performance of HPC applications requires a great effort when writing and executing in multi-core clusters. Many variables (bandwidth of communication channels, computing cores, workload, process mapping, etc.) could affect performance, especially speedup and efficiency, when executing in these clusters. Considering that the Single Program Multiple Data (SPMD) paradigm is highly sensitive to these variables and that the failure probability increases when running applications for several hours or using many computational resources, we have designed a framework which permits us to improve performance while giving resilience to SPMD applications. The main objective is to allow programmers to write applications that automatically make better use of the available resources taking into account the trade-off relationship between speedup, efficiency and reliability. Finally, our framework analyzes the machine and the application characteristics with the aim of determining the ideal number of cores and the workload that have to be assigned to each core in order to achieve maximum speedup, while the efficiency is maintained over a threshold using a message logging protocol.*

Keywords: Performability Framework; SPMD; Efficiency; Fault Tolerance

1. Introduction

Parallel applications that are executed on High Performance Computing (HPC) clusters try to take advantage of the parallelism in order to execute more work in a short amount of time. The SPMD paradigm is one of the most used when writing parallel applications [1]. It consists of executing the same program in all processes but with a different set of tiles. Applications that belong to this paradigm have high communication rate and synchronicity through tile dependencies. These communications may seriously affect the performance and even more so when an hierarchical communication architecture is used and applications are written using an MPI library. In this sense, the current HPC clusters are composed of multicore nodes that have heterogeneous communication levels with different latencies and bandwidths (in some cases these differences are between an order of magnitude of up to one and a half in latency for a packet size [1]).

Hence, if we do not consider SPMD applications characteristics (a computation step follow by a neighbor data exchange using MPI communications) and the system characteristics (core homogeneity and different communication channels), the execution may present serious performance degradation, especially in speedup and efficiency [2]. In this sense, in a previous work [3], we have presented a method to manage the inefficiency by properly selecting the number of cores to be used and the problem size needed in order to find the maximum speedup, while the efficiency is maintained over a defined threshold for SPMD applications on multicore clusters, but without considering faults impact. The main idea of this method is to manage the communication latencies by knowing the characteristics of applications (e.g communication and computation ratio).

An example of the inefficiencies generated by executing SPMD applications on multicore clusters can be detailed in Figure 1. The figure shows how the tiles are computed in a similar time due to the homogeneity inside the cores, but the communication times can be totally different because they can be performed using different communication paths (intercore, interchip, internode, etc.). Then, our method attempts to minimize these inefficiencies adding more computation, while the communications are being performed.

Another aspect to be considered is that the mean time to failure in computer clusters has reduced due to increase of components and systems aging [4]. The fault probability when running parallel applications has increased, and so accordingly, the execution of applications without fault tolerance (FT) support may not reach their end, then the implementation of measures to deal with this is gaining importance. Current parallel applications may not only try to reach the best possible performance, but they also may need to add FT support as a new property. Managing the FT tasks in order to be the least intrusive may enable us to achieve better performability metrics than only applying them without considering their effects on performance. In this sense, when using a pessimistic message logging approach

*This research has been supported by the MICINN Spain under contract TIN2007-64974, the MINECO (MICINN) Spain under contract TIN2011-24384, the European ITEA2 project H4H, No 09011 and the Avanza Competitividad I+D+I program under contract TSI-020400-2010-120.
This paper is addressed to the PDPTA'13 conference

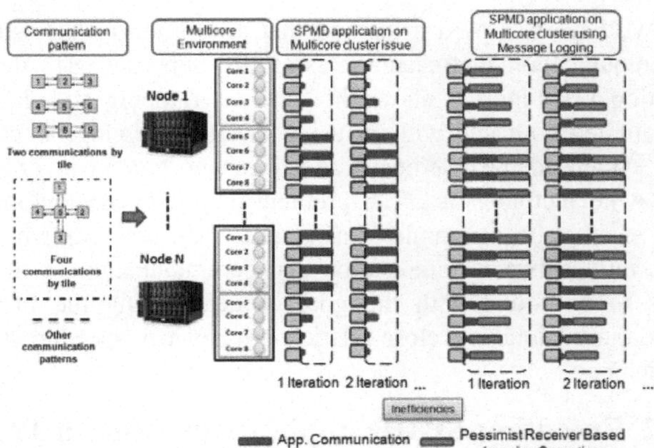

Fig. 1: Execution of SPMD application on Multicore Clusters

the inefficiencies caused by communications increase, for example, if every message is saved in a different node, all messages are forwarded using the slowest communication channel and the communication time increases (Figure 1).

Under this focus, in this paper we present the Performability Improver Methodology for Parallel Applications (PIMPA) framework that allows programmers to write SPMD applications taking advantage of an overlapping technique between computations and communications in order to avoid performance degradation. The main objective is to permit applications to achieve maximum speedup while the whilst maintaining efficiency over a threshold, using a message logging protocol as FT technique. However, the SPMD applications that we consider have to fulfill the following characteristics: static, local communication, regular and finally, they have to be N-dimensional problems.

The PIMPA framework has been adapted to use our FT solution called Redundant Array of Distributed and Independent Fault Tolerance Controllers (RADIC) [5] in order to improve the application reliability. RADIC is an application-transparent rollback/recovery based fault tolerance architecture that uses the available resources in the system and it does not rely on any central element. It also scales side by side with applications. RADIC uses an uncoordinated checkpoint strategy in combination with a pessimistic receiver based message logging protocol.

Finally, this framework allows users to include their computation function and communication pattern in the sections specified, and the framework itself handles in a transparent manner the load balancing, mapping and distribution of tiles in order to hide communication inefficiencies. The PIMPA is based in the concept of Supertile (ST). An ST is an unit which integrates a set of tiles where these tiles are divided into two types: internal and edge. The STs are assigned one per core and they deal with the communication heterogeneity and also eliminate wasted communication time of parallel execution. This method takes advantage of the communication time, assigning more computation tiles and hiding the communication effects[3]. PIMPA also, allows us to increase applications performability by hiding the overheads of a pessimistic receiver based logging approach. PIMPA can estimate execution time of an SPMD application and it may also consider the impact of a pessimistic message logging approach in its estimations. This framework is based on the methodology that has been presented in [3].

This paper is structured as follow: the related works are described in section 2. Section 3 focuses on how to increase performability in SPMD applications and introduces PIMPA. Section 4 shows the PIMPA framework. Section 5 shows example applications and finally Section 6 draws the main conclusions and refers to future works.

2. Related Work

Several tools for measuring or analyzing performance of parallel applications have been developed [6]. Performance analysis tools are usually made with the objective of finding inefficiencies during the execution of a parallel application in order to provide information on how to fix or tune applications to obtain better performance metrics. On the other hand, there are also many tools that provide fault tolerance support to parallel applications and also many MPI libraries provide their own fault tolerant mechanisms based on message logging approaches [4][7]. Nevertheless, when it comes to tools that allow development of parallel applications that consider performance and dependability features we lack options.

Liebrock [8] presented a method that allows programmers to execute applications in hybrid parallel systems with the aim of improving adaptability, scalability and fidelity. However, this work does not concern efficiency and does not consider the usage of a fault tolerant technique.

When it comes to characterizing the parallel environment where a parallel application will be executed, NetPIPE [9] performs simple ping-pong tests, bouncing messages of increasing size between processes, but it does not execute analysis with systems under full use. Considering this, PIMPA framework implements its own network characterization module which allows it to determine the communication latencies between processes.

FT-SPMD [10] is a framework that eases programming of parallel applications with fault tolerance support. In case of failure, non-failed processes may be forced to rollback because it relies on a checkpoint scheme where recovery lines are formed and it does not concern performance.

In [11] a tool has been presented that allows programmers to write SPMD applications that can be executed in a minimum time while the efficiency level is maintained over a threshold. Nevertheless, this work does not consider the effects of fault tolerance tasks on the applications.

We propose a framework that helps programmers to write code that makes an efficient use of the parallel machine allowing them to reach high speedup and that also concerns the fault probability. PIMPA tries to increase performability

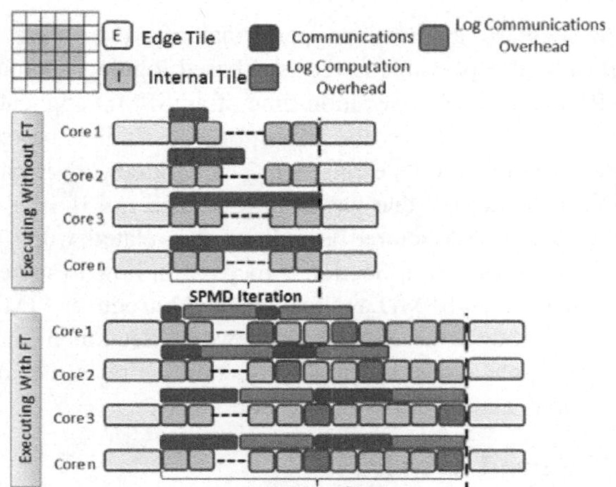

Fig. 2: Computation and Communications ST overlapping

of SPMD applications and it allows programmers to write code without considering the mapping and scheduling of the parallel execution.

3. Increasing Performability of SPMD Applications using PIMPA

Currently, the executions of parallel applications cannot be done without a previous analysis of the environment and the application itself if we hope to obtain an increment in performance metrics. In this sense, PIMPA framework has been designed taking into consideration diverse aspects: One of them is the environment and the application itself, second is the FT architecture, and finally the method for improving the performance which give us the relationship between speedup and efficiency [1].

3.1 SPMD Applications on Multicore Clusters

In this work we consider SPMD applications that have the following characteristics: *Static*: which defines the communication pattern and this cannot vary during the execution. *Local Communication*: which determines the neighboring communication and it is maintained throughout the execution. *Regular*: because communications are repeated for several iterations and finally, they also are *N-dimensional*. There are many scientific applications especially in the simulation field that accomplish all these characteristics, such as fluid dynamics, heat transfer, laplace model, wave equation, problems of finite differences, etc.

The SPMD paradigm consists of executing the same program in all parallel processes but using different set of tiles to compute and communicate. These tiles need to exchange information with neighboring tiles during a set of iterations, this can create imbalance issues that affect performance. Therefore, when SPMD applications are mapped into multicore clusters, the programmer must consider the communication heterogeneity and how this can affect the performance. The different communication patterns can vary according to the objective of the SPMD applications.

We have proposed a method that allows us to deal with communication inefficiencies using the Supertile (ST) definition [3]. Figure 2 shows how the overlapping technique is applied with and without using message logging, as can be evidenced the overheads added can be hidden in order to avoid inefficiencies. The problem of finding the optimal ST size has been formulated as an analytical problem, where the ratio between computation and communication of tiles has to be found with the goal of determining the ideal size that maintains a close relationship between speedup and efficiency.

3.2 Executing SPMD applications using a Pessimistic Receiver based Logging Protocol

In this work we use RADIC [5] in order to provide resilience to applications. RADIC is fault tolerant architecture based on a rollback-recovery protocol which uses a pessimistic receiver based message logging associated with uncoordinated checkpoints. It does not need any coordinated or centralized action or element to carry out their fault tolerance tasks and mechanisms, so application scalability depends on itself. RADIC acts as a transparent fault tolerant layer between the MPI standard and the parallel machine, providing a fault-resilient environment. RADIC middleware has been included in a message passing library, specifically Open MPI. Summarizing, RADIC provides a transparent, decentralized, scalable and flexible fault tolerance solution.

Figure 3a shows how the RADIC architecture is composed. Every message exchanged between processes pass through a component called the Observer and is saved in a component called Protector (Ti) that resides in another node. When failures occurs (Figure 3b) RADIC detection mechanism will notice this and could transfer checkpoints and message logs to a Spare Node (Figure 3c) in order to restart the failed processes and continue (Figure 3d). By using Spare nodes, initial computational capacity could be maintained and performance will be affected only during recovery, because we avoid overloading a node [5].

As every received message should be logged in a different node (even messages passed between processes on the same node), there is a considerable increase in the transmission time of each message when using RADIC (Figure 3a). Thus, when executing a tuned parallel application with message logging, the whole scenario changes, because the parallel processes will be waiting a longer time for each message and the computation will be affected by the logger threads, then the application efficiency will decrease considerably.

Figure 2 shows how our framework characterizes and hides the communication effects with the computational time of the Supertile, as can be observed when using fault tolerance communications which are longer and we need more data to compute in order to hide these communications, thus, bigger Supertile size is needed and fewer cores than when executing without fault tolerance.

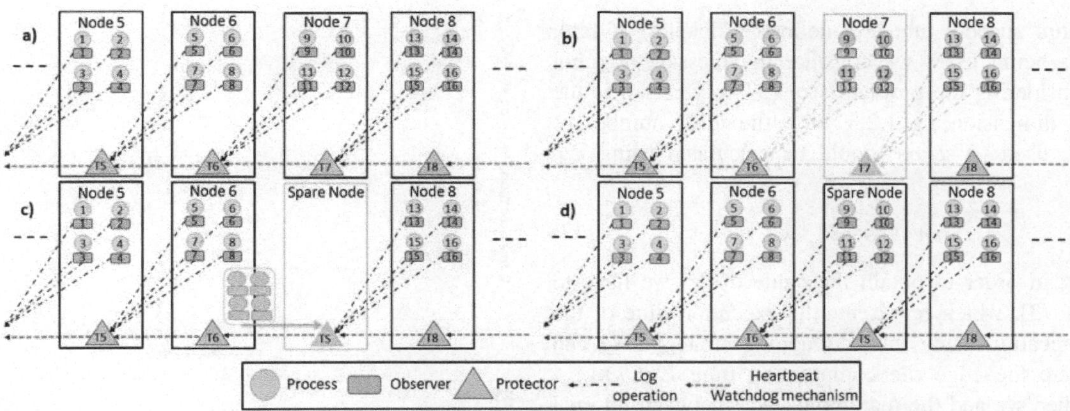

Fig. 3: RADIC Scenarios: a) Fault free execution. b) Failure in Node 7. c) Inclusion of Spare Node , transference of checkpoints, Heartbeat/watchdog restoration and assignation of a new protector to processes of Node 8. d) Restart of faulty processes in Spare Node.

3.3 Methodology to Improve Performability

In order to improve the performance metrics of an SPMD application and find the maximum speedup for an application while the CPU efficiency is maintained under a defined threshold [1], when a general purpose fault tolerant architecture such as RADIC is part of the environment, we need a previous analysis of how the application is affected by the fault tolerant tasks.

PIMPA tries to couple performance and dependability objectives by considering the environment where the SPMD application is going to be executed, then distributes the work among the processes and uses overlapping techniques in order to improve the performance metrics. PIMPA relies on 4 principal phases which are:

1. Characterization: In order to make an effective use of the parallel environment, we first characterize it. We use an application kernel or the real computation section of the SPMD program in order to obtain the communication-computation ratio ($\lambda ft(\rho)(\omega)$, where ρ indicates the communication link used, and ω indicates direction (e.g. up, right, left or down). We consider the architecture of the parallel machine (number of cores, communication levels, network topology) and then we distribute MPI processes in a subset of nodes filling up all used nodes with the processes in order to analyze the system under full use. We force a process per core (application processes and message logging processes) by using core affinity, this allows us to know what communication channels (intercore, interchip, internode) are using the processes when communication occurs. In this sense, we have to analyze both, computing and communications effects in a parallel execution. We can divide the computation in the internal tile (Cpt_{int}) and the edge tile computation (Cpt_{ed}). The internal is divided in the original computation of a tile[1] (Cpt_{tile}) plus a piece of the overhead added by the logger threads ($FTCpt_{int}$) in the protection step of the FT approach. Then the computation is measured as follow: $Cpt_{int} = Cpt_{tile} + FTCpt_{int}$.

The edge tile computation without FT (Cpt_{tile_ed}) needs to consider the time spent in packing and unpacking the sent and received tiles, plus the time of computing them ($Cpt_{tile\_ed} = Pack\_Unpack + Cpt_{tile}$). However, when calculating the edge tile computation time using FT ($Cpt_{ed} = Cpt_{tile\_ed} + FTCpt_{ed}$), we should consider the overhead caused by the logger process ($FTCpt_{ed}$).

The communication time is divided in the communication of a tile ($Comm_{tile}(\rho)(\omega)$) and the overhead of the log operation ($FTComm(\rho)(\omega)$), hence the tile communication is calculated with: $CommT(\rho,\omega) = Comm_{tile}(\rho,\omega) + FTComm(\rho,\omega)$. Then, the communication-computation ratio is estimated using Eq. (1), considering that Cpt_{ed} is not overlapped.

$$\lambda ft(\rho,\omega) = CommT(\rho,\omega)/Cpt_{int} \quad (1)$$

When characterizing, we analyze all communication links (e.g. Intercore, Interchip and Internode) for determining the channel with higher communication delay. However, Figure 4a shows the behavior of the worst communication channel (internode) with and without message logging. As can be detailed, the overhead added in a message when we apply the message logging technique has a considerable impact, which has to be considered for the model precision. As the logger threads of the protectors also consume CPU cycles, we cannot avoid that fact when characterizing the computation. Considering this, our characterization tool is designed to extract the computation time of each tile and the overhead added by the logger (an example can be observed in Figure 4b). Then, there are two overheads that have to be managed when overlapping ($FTCpt_{int}, FTComm$).

2. Distribution Model: Once the environment is characterized, we can obtain the size of the Supertile (ST) and the communication-computation ratio (Eq. (1)). The analytical model for improving performability begins by calculating the ideal Supertile size (K^n) which allows us to find

[1]The Cpt_{tile} is the original tile computation used on the method without fault tolerance approach [3].

the maximum speedup under a defined efficiency, if fault tolerance is being used, we consider the message logging effects. Considering the problem size (M^n), where n is the application dimension(e.g 1,2,3, etc), the ideal number of cores to be used $(Ncores)$ could be calculated using Eq. (2).

$$Ncores = M^n/K^n \quad (2)$$

However, in order to obtain the value of K, we have to start by Eq. (3), which represents the execution time of the SPMD application using the overlapping strategy. We can first calculate the edge tile computation time $EdComp_{(i)}$ (Eq. (4)), then we add the maximum value between internal tile computation $IntComp_{(i)}$ (Eq. 5) and edge tile communication $EdComm_{(i)}$ (Eq. 6)(applying the overlapping strategy). This process will be repeated for a set of iteration $iter$. When using message logging, all these values depend on the log effects in computation and communication that have been obtained in the characterization phase.

$$Tex_i = \sum_{i=1}^{iter}(EdComp_i + Max(IntComp_i, Edcomm_i)) \quad (3)$$

$$EdComp_i = (ST - (K-2)^n) * Cpt_{ed} \quad (4)$$

$$IntComp_i = (K-2)^n * Cpt_{int} \quad (5)$$

$$EdComm_i = K^{n-1} * Max(CommT(\rho, \omega)) \quad (6)$$

Eq.(7) represents the ideal overlapping that allows us to obtain the maximum speedup, while the efficiency $effic$ is maintained over a defined threshold. Therefore, we start from an initial condition, where the edge communication time (with or without message logging) is bigger than the internal computation time divided by the efficiency. This division represents the maximum inefficiency allowed by the model. However, Eq. (7) has to consider a constraint defined in Eq. (8) where $Edcomm_{(i)}$ can be bigger than $IntCpt_{(i)}$ over the defined efficiency (Eq. 7), but the $Edcomm_{(i)}$ has to be slower than the $IntCpt_{(i)}$ without any efficiency definition.

$$K^{n-1} * Max(CommT(\rho, \omega)) \geq \frac{(K-2)^n * Cpt_{int}}{effic} \quad (7)$$

$$K^{n-1} * Max(CommT(\rho, \omega)) \leq (K-2)^n * Cpt_{int} \quad (8)$$

However, the edge communications are in function of the $CommT$. For this reason, we need to equalize the equation in function of Cpt_{int}. This is achieved using Eq. (1). Having the internal computation and edge communication in function of Cpt_{int}, the next step is to find the value of K, replacing all the values in Eq. (7). Depending on the dimension of the SPMD application, we can obtain for example an quadratic equation, cubic equation, etc (Eq. 9).

$$k^2 - 4 * k - effic * \lambda_{ft}(\rho)(\omega) * k + 4 = 0 \quad (9)$$

The next step is to calculate the ideal number of cores (Eq. 2). The ideal ST size and number of cores will vary depending on whether or not we are using fault tolerance.

3. Mapping: The aim of this phase is to allocate the ST into each core with the aim of minimizing the communication

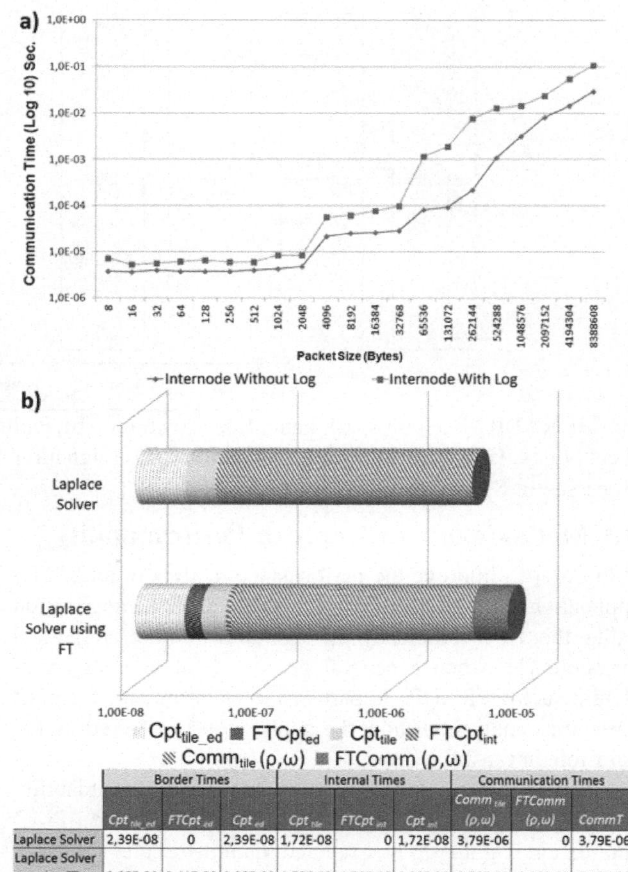

	Border Times			Internal Times			Communication Times		
	Cpt_{tile_ed}	$FTCpt_{ed}$	Cpt_{ed}	Cpt_{tile}	$FTCpt_{int}$	Cpt_{int}	$Comm_{tile}$ (ρ,ω)	$FTComm$ (ρ,ω)	$CommT$
Laplace Solver	2,39E-08	0	2,39E-08	1,72E-08	0	1,72E-08	3,79E-06	0	3,79E-06
Laplace Solver using FT	2,39E-08	8,41E-09	3,23E-08	1,72E-08	4,79E-09	2,20E-08	3,79E-06	3,36E-06	7,15E-06

Fig. 4: Characterization of the Laplace Solver App. (SZ: 1400x1400): a)Network Channel Characterization with and without Message Logging. b)Computation Time Characterization.

effects. The ST assignations are made applying a core affinity, which allows us to allocate the set of tiles according to the policy of minimizing the communications latencies. This affinity is also applied to the logger threads in order to guarantee that their overhead is distributed among all cores.

4. Scheduling: To take advantage of the overlap between internal computation and edge communications, we create two threads. One is in charge of computing the internal tiles, while the other communicates the edge tiles. Thus, we hide the logging overheads by giving more tiles to compute to a processor while edge tiles are being sent and logged.

Finally, our method allows us to obtain an ideal number of cores to execute a task with a defined efficiency threshold while the application is protected with a pessimistic receiver based logging protocol. Usually, logging approaches are combined with an uncoordinated checkpoint approach (such as the one used inside the RADIC architecture). For calculating our estimations, in this work we do not consider the added overhead that will be caused by checkpoints.

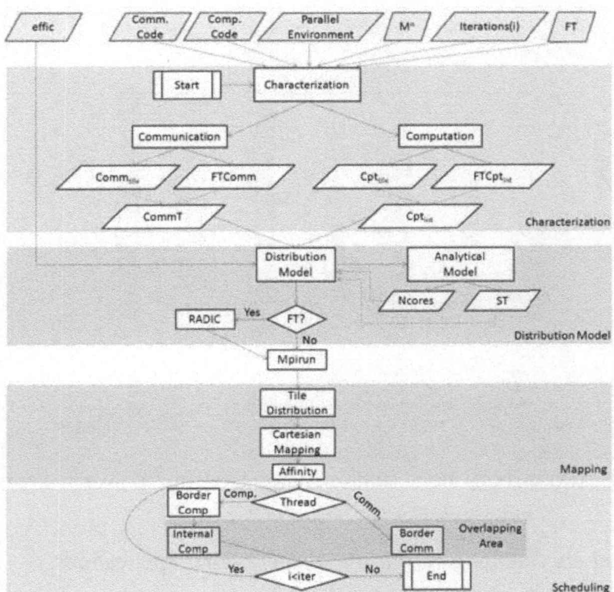
Fig. 5: Flowchart of PIMPA framework.

4. PIMPA Framework

As has been presented, PIMPA allows us to write SPMD applications that can reach maximum speedup under a CPU efficiency threshold. We now present the PIMPA framework which allows us to automatize the tuning of SPMD applications that are going to be executed on HPC clusters considering the option of a fault tolerance approach as part of the execution environment, and in this work we specifically consider the option of using the pessimistic message logging approach of RADIC. In order to ease the analysis and due to the computation homogeneity, we consider that the time spent in uncoordinated checkpoints will be added to the execution time and it will depend exclusively on the application size and number of checkpoints.

In order to use the framework with fault tolerance support, the MPI library used should be the one that has RADIC included [5]. Our framework has been written taking into consideration that the user code is written in the C language using MPI to carry out communications between processes.

Figure 5 shows the flowchart of the PIMPA framework (user's input data is highlighted in green). The user introduces the application inputs, number of iterations (i), the communication code is introduced with metadata that describes the behavior (e.g. number of neighbor communications) and the computation code that details the code that each parallel process should carry on. The user should also introduce the parallel environment, specifying number of cores that each node contains and internode configuration (cache levels, cores that share cache) obtained with HWLoc [12]. Using the input, we characterize the environment obtaining the communication and computation time with and without considering the impact of message logging.

Once characterization is over, the distribution model and the analytical model are applied, obtaining the ideal number of computational cores that can be used to obtain the requested efficiency (information about expected execution time with and without fault tolerance support will be available to the users). After confirming the execution with the obtained number of cores($Ncores$) and Supertile size (ST) the user will have the source code written.

When launching the execution, at first the mapping step takes place and all the work is divided between the number of processes (one process per core). Each process is attached to a core by using an affinity procedure and then two threads are created per process: Computing thread and Communication thread. The computing thread computes the border and then computes the internal tiles. The Communication thread is in charge of transmitting the border values to neighbors, this operation is overlapped with the internal computation. The operations of both threads are repeated for the number of iterations (i) of the problem. Also, the logging operation is hidden because of the overlap between the internal computation and communication of borders. All RADIC operations are user-transparent, the main difference between whether or not to use fault tolerance resides in the number of cores and Supertile size.

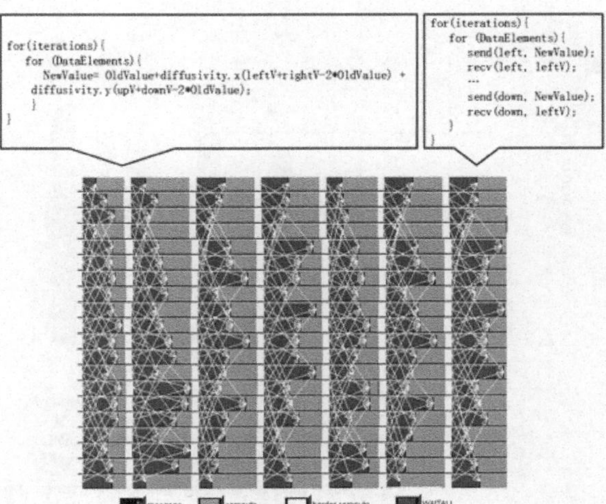
Fig. 6: Execution of a parallel Heat Transfer Application using PIMPA framework without using message logging.

5. Sample Applications

In this section we show some parallel applications that have been written using the PIMPA framework. Figure 6 shows pseudocode sections of an Heat Transfer application and a trace that shows us how the computation section of the SPMD application is overlapped with the border communications. Some communications take more time than others, but when defining the Supertile size PIMPA consider the slowest communication channel. In addition, when the message logging operation of RADIC is being used, the communications will have higher latencies and the Supertile size will increase in order to hide these inefficiencies.

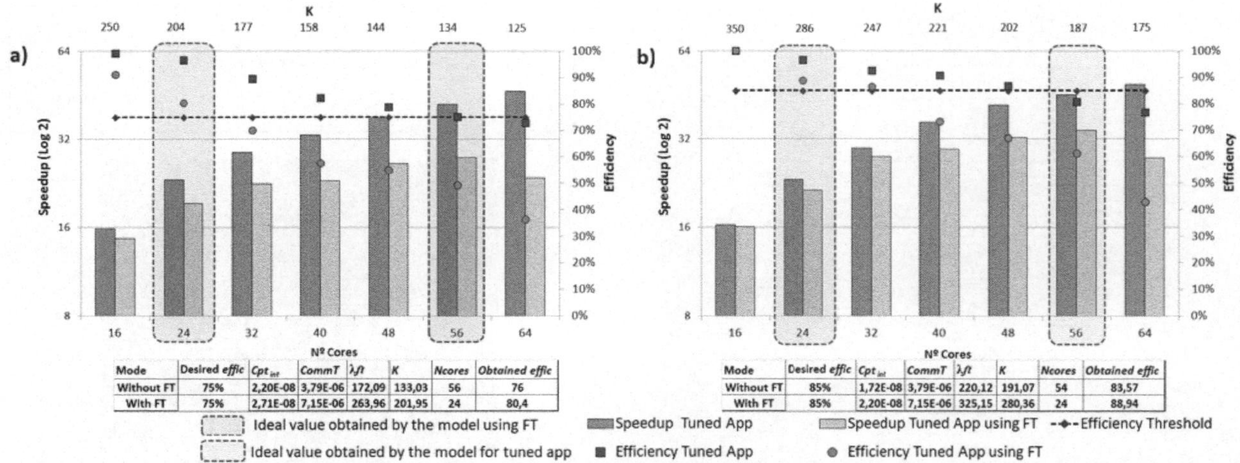

Mode	Desired effic	Cpt_{int}	CommT	$\lambda_{f}t$	K	Ncores	Obtained effic
Without FT	75%	2,20E-08	3,79E-06	172,09	133,03	56	76
With FT	75%	2,71E-08	7,15E-06	263,96	201,95	24	80,4

Mode	Desired effic	Cpt_{int}	CommT	$\lambda_{f}t$	K	Ncores	Obtained effic
Without FT	85%	1,72E-08	3,79E-06	220,12	191,07	54	83,57
With FT	85%	2,20E-08	7,15E-06	325,15	280,36	24	88,94

Fig. 7: Performance Analysis of: a) Heat Transfer App. - Size: 1000*1000, Iter: 10000. b) Laplace Eq. Solver - Size: 1400*1400, Iter: 10000

Experiments have been carried out using a Dell PowerEdge M600 with 8 nodes, each node with 2 quad-core Intel® Xeon® E5430 running at 2.66 GHz. Each node has 16 GBytes of main memory and a dual embedded Broadcom® NetXtreme IITM 5708 Gigabit Ethernet. RADIC features have been integrated into version 1.7 of Open MPI.

Figures 7a and 7b show executions of the Heat Transfer Application and Laplace Equation Solver under the PIMPA framework with different number of cores and Supertile sizes. Ideal values obtained by PIMPA with and without message logging are highlighted (the analytical values obtained by the framework are shown in the tables below each figure). In both cases PIMPA framework obtains the maximum speedup possible under an efficiency threshold (85% for Heat Transfer and 80% for Laplace Solver) with an error rate around 7% for the worst case.

6. Conclusions

This paper has presented the PIMPA framework that allows users to write performability-aware SPMD applications. PIMPA framework provides a tool to users for characterize the parallel environment where the SPMD application is going to be executed, considering the hierarchical communication levels of current HPC systems. PIMPA deals with mapping and scheduling of applications by using a distribution model that obtains the best number of cores and Supertile size to achieve maximum speedup considering an efficiency threshold. PIMPA creates threads that allow overlapping between communications (app. communication and message logging) and computations.

The sample applications written using PIMPA framework show that the ideal number of computational cores and Supertile size obtained allow more efficient executions, even when using a message logging approach as fault tolerance support. Future work will focus on extending the PIMPA framework in order to consider the effects of the checkpoints models and checkpoint interval impact on parallel applications.

References

[1] R. Muresano, D. Rexachs, and E. Luque, "Methodology for efficient execution of spmd applications on multicore environments," *10th IEEE/ACM International Conference on Cluster, Cloud and Grid Computing, CCGrid 2010, 17-20 May 2010, Melbourne, Victoria, Australia*, pp. 185–195, 2010.

[2] A. Kayi, T. El-Ghazawi, and G. B. Newby, "Performance issues in emerging homogeneous multi-core architectures," *Simulation Modelling Practice and Theory*, vol. 17, no. 9, pp. 1485–1499, 2009.

[3] R. Muresano, D. Rexachs, and E. Luque, "Combining scalability and efficiency for spmd applications on multicore clusters," *The 2011 International Conference on Parallel and Distributed Processing Techniques and Applications, Las Vegas, USA*, pp. 43–49, 2011.

[4] A. Bouteiller, T. Herault, G. Bosilca, and J. J. Dongarra, "Correlated set coordination in fault tolerant message logging protocols," pp. 51–64, 2011.

[5] H. Meyer, D. Rexachs, and E. Luque, "Radic: A fault tolerant middleware with automatic management of spare nodes," *The 2012 International Conference on Parallel and Distributed Processing Techniques and Applications, July 16-19, Las Vegas, USA*, pp. 17–23, 2012.

[6] S. Moore, D. Cronk, K. S. London, and J. Dongarra, "Review of performance analysis tools for mpi parallel programs," in *Proceedings of the 8th European PVM/MPI Users' Group Meeting on Recent Advances in Parallel Virtual Machine and Message Passing Interface*. London, UK, UK: Springer-Verlag, 2001, pp. 241–248.

[7] A. Bouteiller, G. Bosilca, and J. Dongarra, "Redesigning the message logging model for high performance," *Concurr. Comput. : Pract. Exper.*, pp. 2196–2211, 2010.

[8] L. M. Liebrock and S. P. Goudy, "Methodology for modelling spmd hybrid parallel computation," *Concurr. Comput. : Pract. Exper.*, vol. 20, no. 8, pp. 1485–1499, June 2008.

[9] Q. O. Snell, A. R. Mikler, and J. L. Gustafson, "Netpipe: A network protocol independent performance evaluator," 1996.

[10] C. Makassikis, V. Galtier, and S. Vialle, "A skeletal-based approach for the development of fault-tolerant spmd applications," pp. 239–248, 2010.

[11] R. Muresano, D. Rexachs, and E. Luque, "A tool for efficient execution of spmd applications on multicore clusters," *Proc. Computer Science*, pp. 2599 – 2608, 2010, iCCS'2010.

[12] F. Broquedis, J. Clet-Ortega, S. Moreaud, N. Furmento, B. Goglin, G. Mercier, S. Thibault, and R. Namyst, "hwloc: A generic framework for managing hardware affinities in hpc applications," pp. 180 –186, 2010.

SuperViewer: An Interactive Visual Interface to Explore the Top500 List

Leonidas Deligiannidis
Wentworth Institute of Technology
Computer Science
550 Huntington Ave.
Boston, MA
deligiannidis@wit.edu

Erik Noyes
Babson College
Entrepreneurship
231 Forest St.
Babson Park, MA
enoyes@babson.edu

Hamid R. Arabnia
University of Georgia
Computer Science
415 GSRC, UGA
Athens, GA
hra@cs.uga.edu

ABSTRACT

In this paper, we describe *SuperViewer*, an interactive visual interface which facilitates exploration of the "Top500" list, the biannual list of the world's most powerful supercomputers (1993-present). SuperViewer is both intended as a visual knowledge discovery tool for computer science students as well as a dynamic presentation tool for supercomputing experts to represent and debate points of view on critical technological and entrepreneurial developments in the industry, including the industry's past and projections for future innovation. The tool offers four ways to view and interact with historical data to explore and represent the rapid pace of innovation and competition in the industry.

Keywords: supercomputing, information visualization, education, visual knowledge discovery, visual interfaces

1. INTRODUCTION

By all accounts, the historical pace of change in the supercomputing industry has been staggering. In this paper, we describe an effort to build an interactive visual history of entrepreneurial activity in the supercomputing industry, considering computers' speeds, manufacturers, and design architectures to represent and explore broader technological disruptions shaping the industry. We present ongoing work on an interactive visual interface we name *SuperViewer*, which offers four ways to view data from the Top500 list for all the periods of the biannual list's existence (1993-2012).

SuperViewer has two intended purposes. First, it offers those teaching about supercomputing new tools to visually present and characterize historical developments (e.g., to new students of computer science). Second, it allows field experts to visually represent and debate points of view on critical entrepreneurial and technological developments in the industry, including the industry's past and projections for future innovation.

As an interdisciplinary project, our aim is to exploit domain knowledge in information visualization [1][2], interface design [3][4], and visual knowledge discovery [5] to provide windows into the concept of *creative destruction* [6][7][8]. Creative destruction is the foundational idea in entrepreneurship that technological disruption, market upheaval and specifically new venture successes and failures drive industry evolution and economic development [6]. The development of SuperViewer is part of broader effort to develop new, interactive teaching tools to highlight the dynamism of industries and entrepreneurship phenomena.

2. THE SuperViewer

We designed this application entirely in java. This enabled us to place the application on the web for researchers, educators and students to easily access it using Webstart technology. The link to the home page of the project where the application can be launch is: http://faculty.cs.wit.edu/~ldeligia/PROJECTS/Top500/index.html. The data was retrieved from top500.org as individual files; we extracted all critical fields and compiled one single data repository.

Top500.org publishes its data twice a year, once in June and once in November. The data is available from June 1993 to November 2012. The data are not consistent across all years and the format is not the same in all data files, so there was a considerable amount of data cleaning/data checking. No unique identifier is available for supercomputers listed on the site, thus we created a unique identifier as the concatenation of the "ComputerName" and the "SiteName" fields, which effectively served this function. For example, we found that the same Top500 computer name in one year could be miss-spelled, parts of it capitalized, containing or missing spaces or underscores, etc. The data is likely 97% clean at this point but additional checks are needed.

Description of what fields are provided by top500.org is given on their web site. Two of the fields that we use in all four visualization tools are the *Rmax*, which is the maximal LINPACK performance achieved by a supercomputer, and *Rpeak*, which is the theoretical peak performance. Both fields are measured in GFlops. Our application consists of four visualization methods and they are described in the sections below.

2.1. Visualizer "Ranking"

The Visualizer "Ranking", shown in figure 1, visualizes the top 500 supercomputers per year. For each year, we plot the data of all 500 supercomputers based on their Rpeak and Rmax values, which are measured in GFlops. There are two ways of plotting the data, the first is (max-per-year) and the second is (max-overall). In max-per-year mode, the maximum scale on the Y axis is the top Rpeak/Rmax value of the number 1 or fastest supercomputer for the selected year.

In max-overall mode, the maximum value on the Y scale is the maximum value of the top supercomputer of all time/all years. This way, one can compare the top 500 computers within a year (max-per-year), or one can compare the overall speed (max-overall) of the computers by keeping the scale the same for uniform comparison across all years. We also provide the ability for a user to display the Moore's law curve for the past data and make predictions for future data. The user interacts with this visualizer using a Combo box to select the type of visualization, and a slider. The Combo box, shown in figure 2, is used to select the Rpeak/Rmax variables for visualization as well as the mode (max-per-year, and max-overall) of visualization. The slider is used to select the year of the dataset to be visualized.

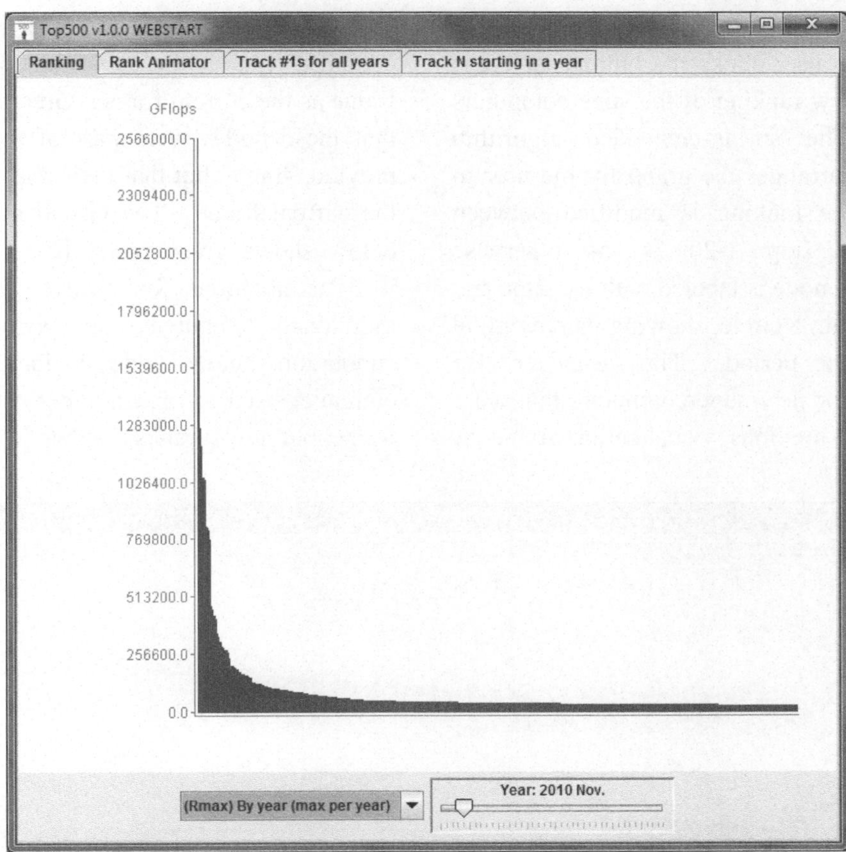

Figure 1. The Visualizer "Ranking", visualizes the top 500 supercomputers per year based on their Rpeak and Rmax values.

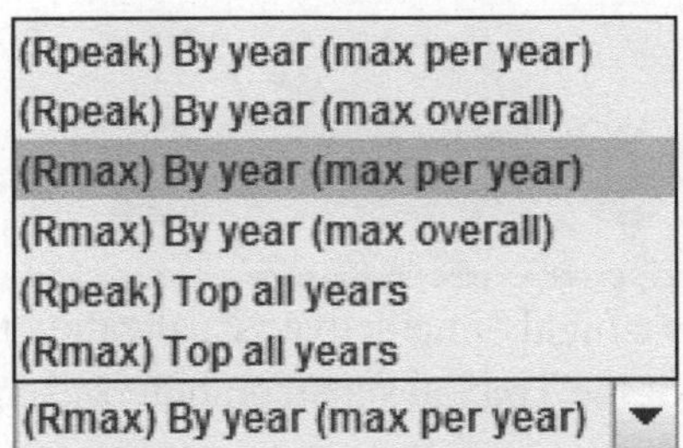

Figure 2. Variable and mode of visualization in visualizer "Ranking".

2.2. Rank Animator

The Rank Animator, shown in Figure 3, is a highly interactive visualization tool built on top of a spring-embedded algorithm that animates the Top500 ranking data as it changes over time. The user can select the top N supercomputers to visualize. Then the user can use a slider to retrieve and visualize these top N supercomputers for specific years. The left and right arrow-buttons can be used to move forward or backward one year at a time. Or the user drags the slider instead to adjust the viewed time frame.

This spring embedded visualizer automatically arranges the top N supercomputers from left to right based on their rank (Rmax value). The user can double click nodes to drill down and get more information about a particular supercomputer of interest. As the user clicks the buttons or drags the slider, the new ranking of the supercomputers is shown. The spring-embedded algorithm animates and rearranges the graph for the user to observe how the ranking is modified between different times (top 1-20 or as otherwise specified). Each node is labeled with its name and on top of it, within a circle, showing its ranking in the selected time period. The visualizer also annotates in color new supercomputers that were not part in the previous visualization frame as yellow. Bluish nodes indicate that a particular computer was at the same rank in the previous frame as the current frame. Green nodes illustrate that these nodes were part of the graph in the previous frame, but that their rank has changed in the current frame. The visualization in Figure 3 below shows green nodes (e.g., nodes 3-5), as well as notations for changes in rankings for individuals computers. For example, the "4->5" annotation below node 5 indicates that this computer used to rank number 4 in the previous frame, but now it ranks number 5.

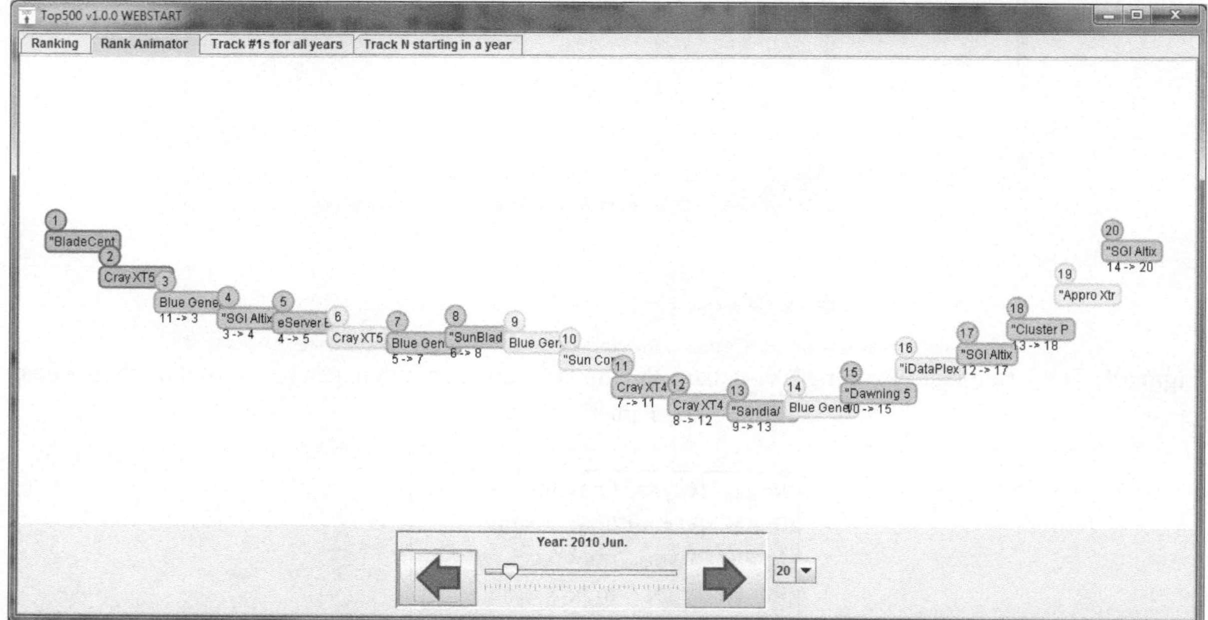

Figure 3. The "Rank Animator" is a highly interactive visualization tool that animates and arranges, in rank order, a sub-list of the Top500 supercomputers as they change over time.

2.3. Visualizer "Track #1s for all years"

This visualizer is used to visualize the history of all number-one spot supercomputers (e.g. the Top 1 in the Top500 list). It visualizes, in a single window, all number one computers and their ranking as the years progress. A number one computer in 1995 becomes number 4 the next year and number 20 the year after and so on. The green circles indicate a new super computer introduced at the specific year. Its history is a line moving downwards as the years pass by, as shown in figure 4. The zoom-factor slider is used to zoom in the data to see the history in more detail as shown in figure 5. A number above a green node indicates the number of cores/processors for this particular supercomputer.

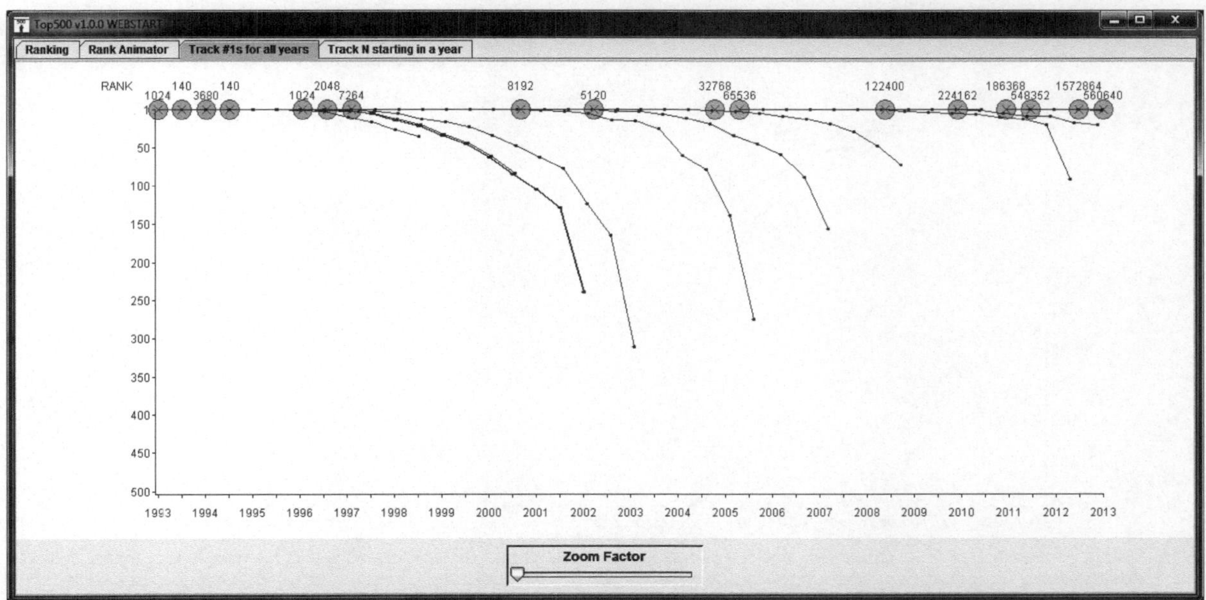

Figure 4. The visualizer "Track #1s for all years" visualizes the history of all number-one spot supercomputers; all number one computers and their ranking as the years progress.

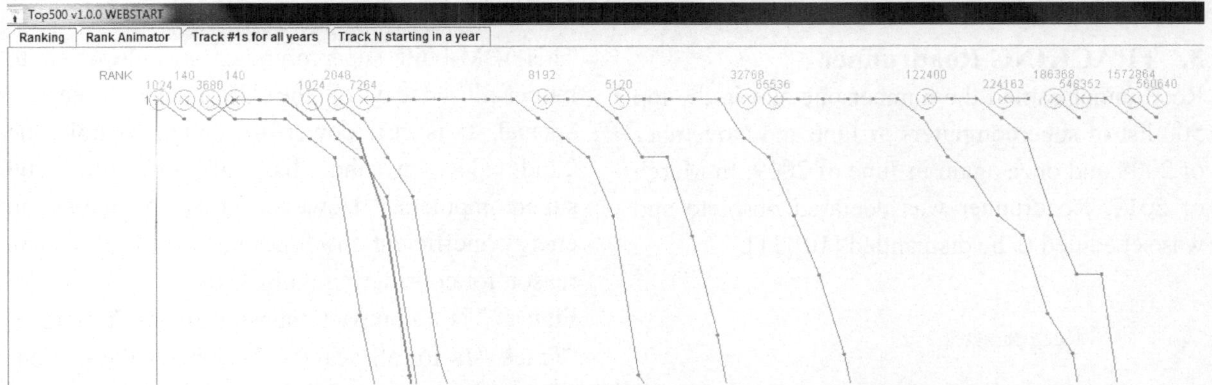

Figure 5. The zoom-factor slider is used to zoom in the data to see the history in more detail.

2.4. Visualizer "Track N starting in a year"

This visualizer is similar to the previous visualizer in regards to visualizing the downfall of top supercomputers of a specific year. In this visualizer, a user selects the top N supercomputers of a selected year. The visualizer then displays their ranking as the years progress, as shown in figure 6. The ranking of the supercomputers is based on the Rmax value. Moving forward in time, we see how fast highly-ranked supercomputers become less powerful as new faster supercomputers replace them. An alternative to this type of visualization could have been a matrix-based representation, which is suitable for large and dense graphs [9]. However, because of the simplicity of the data we found that matrix-based representation does not add any value to this tool.

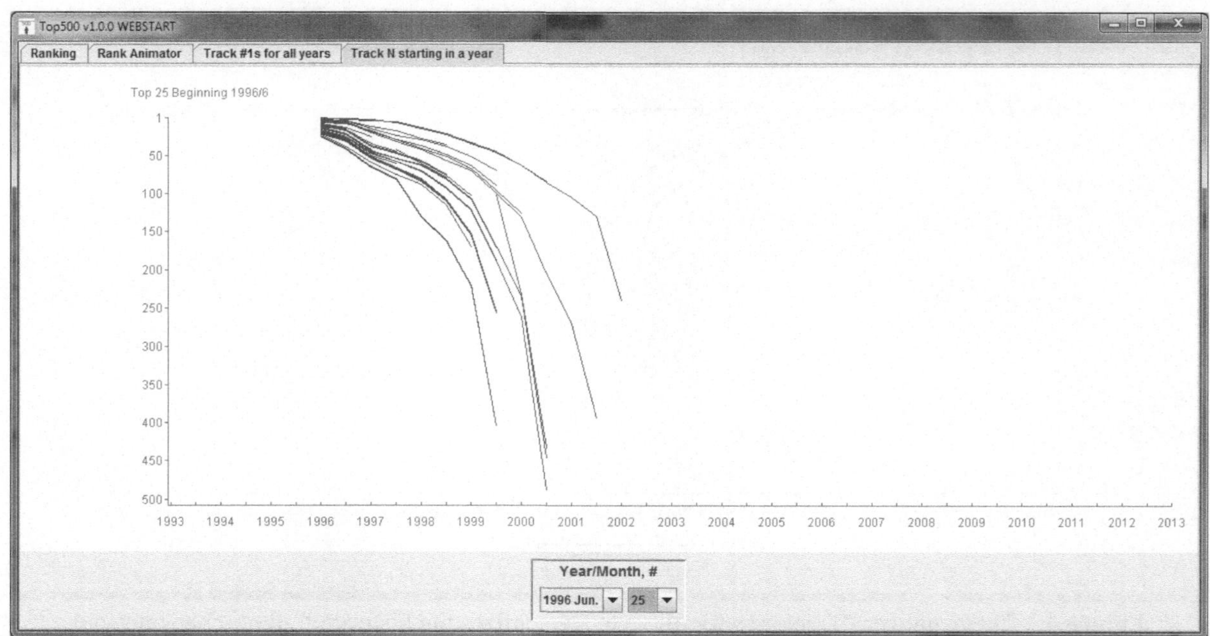

Figure 6. The visualizer "Track N starting in a year" visualizes the history of the top N supercomputers beginning at a user specified year.

3. TRACKING Roadrunner

Roadrunner earned the number one slot in the top 500 list of supercomputers in June and November of 2008 and once again in June of 2009. In March of 2013, Roadrunner was declared obsolete and was scheduled to be dismantled [10][11].

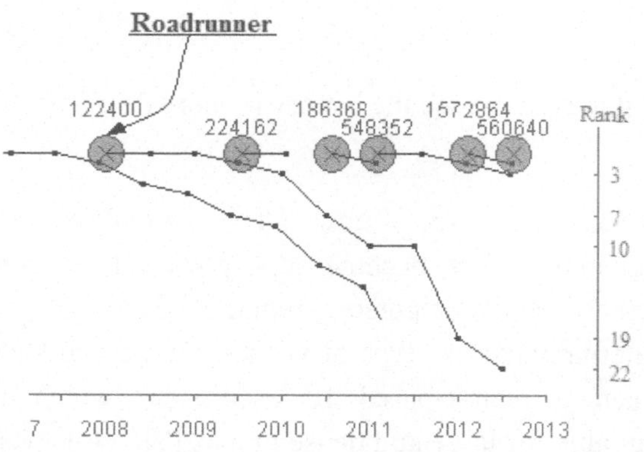

Figure 7. Visualizing the history of Roadrunner.

This IBM-built supercomputer was designed to model the decay of the US nuclear weapons arsenal. It is still powerful enough to hold the 22nd slot in the list of the top 500 supercomputers. However, it is considered an energy inefficient machine and that is the main reason for considering it obsolete.

Figure 7 is a compact snapshot of the Visualizer "Track #1s for all years". It displays the number of processors, and the decline in ranking since June 2008, from the number 1 rank down to number 22. Figure 8 consists of 10 snapshots of the Rank Animator. This figure visualizes Roadrunner from June 2008 to November 2012. We annotated (with current rank in red circles) the figure to easily track Roadrunner through history and its rank changes.

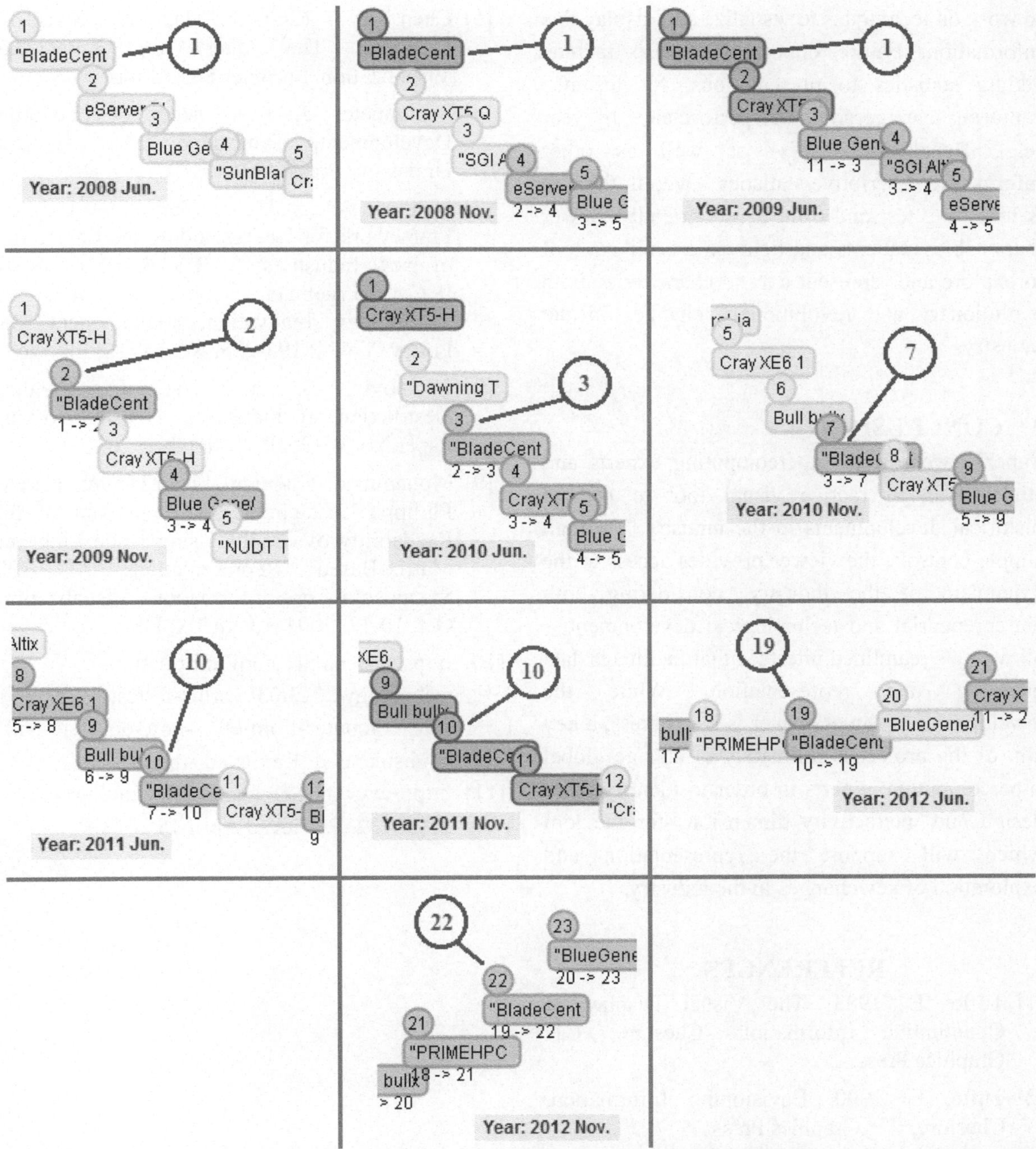

Figure 8. Ten snapshots of the Rank Animator while visualizing the history of the supercomputer Roadrunner.

4. FUTURE WORK

Future work aims to expand the range of data and views examinable in SuperViewer. We are in the process of adding other data fields and visualization possibilities to the tool, including the ability to superimpose information about computer architectures, manufacturers, international site locations, public or private ownership and other technical specifications for 1993-2012. Data has been collected but we need to work on techniques to visualize and display this information. Future opportunities also include adding statistics to presentations, for instance capturing average computer performance by year (e.g., Rpeak or RMax) as well as other informative descriptive statistics. Overall, the aim is to create, test and offer a user-friendly viewer that enables students and field experts alike a tool to explore and represent data to characterize both evolutionary and revolutionary changes in the industry.

5. CONCLUSION

SuperViewer offers supercomputing experts and students an interactive visual tool to present historical developments in the industry. Through simple controls, the viewer provides access to the dynamism of the industry, considering both entrepreneurial and technological developments--all with a streamlined interface that facilitates data querying and representation. While the development of SuperViewer is in progress, a key aim of the project is ultimately to engage global supercomputing experts in order to identify other design and interactivity dimensions for the tool which will support the representation and exploration of key changes in the industry.

REFERENCES

[1] Tufte, E. 1983. The Visual Display of Quantitative Information. Cheshire, CT: Graphics Press.

[2] Tufte, E. 1990. Envisioning Information. Cheshire, CT: Graphics Press.

[3] Schneiderman, B. (1998). Designing the User Interface: Strategies for Effective Human-Computer Interaction, third edition, Addison-Wesley.

[4] Card S. K., Mackinlay J. and Shneiderman B., Readings in Information Visualization Using Vision to Think, Morgan Kaufmann, San Francisco, CA, 1999.

[5] Chen, C. (2003). Mapping Scientific Frontiers: The Quest for Knowledge Visualization. Springer Publishing.

[6] Schumpeter, J. The Theory of Economic Development, Cambridge, MA: Harvard University Press, 1934.

[7] Van de Ven, A.H., & Garud, R. 1989. A Framework for Understanding the Emergence of New Industries. In R.S. Rosenbloom, & R.A. Burgelman (Eds.), Research on Technology Innovation, Management and Policy, Vol. 4: 195-225, New York; Elsevier.

[8] Jovanovic, B., and Tse, C. Creative Destruction in Industries, NBER Working Paper No. W12520, September, 2006.

[9] Mohammad Ghoniem, Jean-Daniel Fekete, Philippe Castagliola, “AComparison of the Readability of Graphs Using Node-Link and Matrix-Based Representations. IEEE Symposium on Information Visualization, Oct. 10-12, 2004 Austin TX, USA.

[10] http://arstechnica.com/information-technology/2013/03/worlds-fastest-supercomputer-from-09-is-now-obsolete-will-be-dismantled/ Retrieved April 15 2013.

[11] http://www.bbc.co.uk/news/technology-21993132. Retrieved April 15 2013.

Performance model for Master/Worker hybrid applications

Abel Castellanos[1], Andreu Moreno[2], and Tomàs Margalef[1]
[1]Departament Arquitectura de Computadors i Sistemes Operatius, Universitat Autonoma de Barcelona, Spain
[2]Escola Universitaria Salesiana de Sarria, Barcelona, Spain
Email: acastellanos@caos.uab.es, amoreno@euss.cat, tomas.margalef@uab.es

Abstract— *Master/worker is a commonly used parallel/distributed programming paradigm. Many applications are developed following such paradigm. This paradigm can be easily implemented using message passing programming libraries (MPI), but moreover, the multicore features of current nodes can be exploited at the node level by applying thread parallelism (OpenMP). In this way Master/Worker applications are implemented as hybrid applications. However, reaching the expected performance indexes is not so easy, because there are several parameters (number of nodes, number of threads per node, data distribution, ...) that must be tuned for each particular application or even during the execution of the application to reach a successful performance. So, a performance model for hybrid Master/Worker applications has been developed and is presented in this paper. This model can be applied during the execution of a Master/Worker application to determine dynamically the adequate configuration of the system and/or application to reach the best possible performance.*

Keywords: MPI, OpenMP, Hybrid applications, Master/Worker, Performance model.

1. Introduction

Nowadays, multicore processors are widely spread and are integrated in most computing nodes, from personal computers to supercomputer processing nodes. In this context, every computing node in a parallel/distributed system that includes several cores that can be exploited to reduce the execution time of parallel applications. One way of exploiting such features is to distribute application processes to different nodes of the system and execute different threads at the core level in each node. A commonly used programming approach for these systems is a hybrid approach with MPI processes communicated using message passing [1] and OpenMP threads exploited inside each node [2].

It is quite easy to develop applications following such hybrid approach, but reaching a successful performance index is not so easy. In this hybrid approach, there are several parameters that must be considered to determine the configuration of the application that provides the best execution time. The number of nodes that must be used, the number of threads on each node, the data distribution among processes and threads, and so on, are parameters that seriously affect the performance of the application. On one hand, the appropriate value of such parameters depends on the architectural features of the system (communication latency, communication bandwidth, cache memory size and architecture, computing capabilities, ...) and on the other hand, on the features of the application (communication pattern, computation involved). Moreover, the adequate value of the parameters depends on issues that depends on every execution of the application or even can vary dynamically during the execution of the application such as the workload being processed. So, determining the adequate value of the parameters must be determined for each execution of each application, or even tuned dynamically.

This problem is a very wide problem that cannot be tackled directly in a general way, but it is necessary to determine solutions to some particular cases to derive some general solution. So, a particular kind of application has been selected and a performance model for such kind of application has been developed to determine the value of some of the parameters and dynamically tune the performance of the application.

The master/worker programming paradigm [3] has been selected because it is a very well known paradigm for parallel/distributed applications. On the other hand, this paradigm has been deeply studied in the context of the monocore distributed systems. In particular, a performance model that determines the adequate number of workers for such applications for monocore architectures was developed in a previous work [4]. In the new context of parallel/distributed systems based on multicore nodes there are several aspects that must be taken into account and must be introduced in the performance model. One point that must be considered is the overhead introduced by the thread management and another one is the heterogeneous communication among cores and among nodes. So, this points have been introduced and a new performance model has been developed to determine the adequate values of the parameters to reach a successful performance.

The rest of this paper is organized as follow. Section 2 describes the general issues related to Master/Worker programming paradigm and analyses the involved parameters. Additionally, it's presented the mathematical expressions that represents the model. Section 3 summarizes some experimental results to demonstrate the correctness of the proposed model. Finally, section 4 concludes the paper and summarizes the ongoing work.

2. Modeling Master/Worker iteration execution time

The Master/Worker paradigm is a well-known parallel programming structure because it enables the expression, in a natural way, of the behavioral characteristics of a wide range of high-level parallel application patterns. Basically, this paradigm includes a Master process which distributes data to a set of Worker processes, then each worker makes some kind of computation on the received data and sends the results back to the Master.

Depending on the nature of the problem, the Master process might have to wait for the results from all the Workers before sending them new data, which means that the application execution is organized in iterations. In this case, if it is assumed that the load is balanced among the Worker processes, the performance of the application mainly depends on two factors: the number of Workers on the system and the number of cores dedicated to each Worker process. In this paper we will study the number of workers considering that each worker is executed given a fixed number of threads per node (4 cores in this case).

So, the first goal is to develop a performance model that determines the execution time of one iteration of the Master/Worker application. This model can be used for tuning the number of workers to gain an improvement in performance and efficiency of the applications at runtime.

One iteration of the Master process worker involves the following steps:

- The Master process makes some processing before distributing the data to the Workers.
- The Master process distributes the data to the Workers.
- All the Workers receive the corresponding data.
- The Workers manage the indicated number of threads (create, distribute data, collect data, join).
- The Threads of each Worker computes the data.
- The Workers send the results to the Master process.

So, a model for estimating the execution time of one iteration of the application must consider all these steps. Based on a proposed methodology for developing performance models for hybrid applications [5] and previous model presented in [4], a general expression to estimate the execution time of one iteration of a master-worker hybrid application including the previously mentioned issues can be derived:

$$T = \mu_m(W) + \lambda_{m-w}(W,P) + \frac{\mu_{serial}(W)}{(P*Thr)} + \Theta(W,Thr) + \lambda_{w-m}(W,P) \quad (1)$$

where W is the size of the workload, P is the number of MPI worker process, Thr is the number of threads have been used by all the workers. This equation includes the terms representing the steps mentioned above:

- μ_m is defined as the processing time spent by the master on preparation of a new set of tasks.
- λ_{m-w} is the sum of all communication times from master to all workers.
- μ_{serial} is the empirical serial time for processing the total workload which must be distributed among the total number of Workers P and threads Thr.
- Θ is the additional OpenMP overhead.
- λ_{w-m} is the time spent by the last worker to send back the result data to the master.

Note that expression $\frac{\mu_{serial}(W)}{(P*Thr)}$ is the processing time spent by the last worker to finish its task. This expression assumes a perfect scalability for the computation region.

In the next subsections, the details on how the communication time, OpenMP overhead and execution time are estimated are described.

2.1 Communication time estimation

Unlike previous models [4], our proposal considers that the cost of communication behaves non-linearly with packet size. This behavior has been studied in the literature [6] and justifies the use of bechmarks [7] to reach a more accurate characterization of MPI communication. Therefore, for the evaluation of the communication time, MPIBench [8] have been used. This benchmark is included within Level Architectural Characterization Low Benchmark Suite [9].

Figure 1 shows the characterization results of the blocking point-to-point communications obtained by running the benchmark. As was expected, the communication time is not proportional to the size of message sent. The function for obtaining the communication time for sending MPI messages is constructed through a linear interpolation of the results previously obtained with the benchmark. The

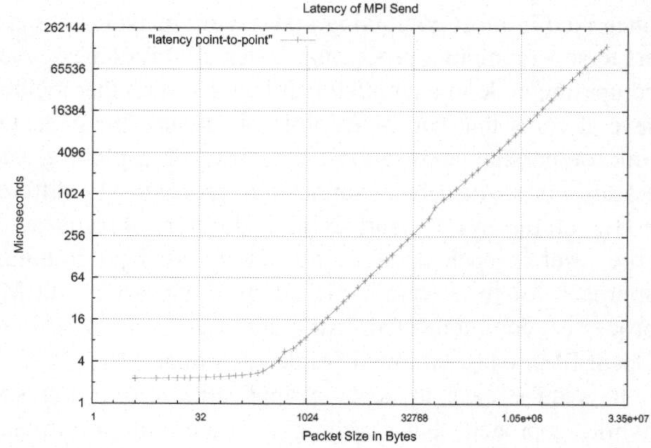

Fig. 1: Characterization of blocking communications

information obtained from this benchmark is the basic information used to evaluate the expressions $\lambda_{m-w}(W,P)$ and $\lambda_{w-m}(W,P)$. In the case of the first expression, the result is the addition of all individual communications from the master to a particular worker. Figures 2(a) and 2(b) show the errors on the communication time estimation considering 8 and 30 Workers respectively. These are the time spend in one iteration of the Master to send messages to all workers. It can be observed that the biggest error of the estimation is less than 2%. In case of the communication between the last Worker and the Master, the message size is extremely small and, therefore, the amount of time involved is negligible in the total iteration time. In this communication, the error is around 35% but it is important since it represents less than 3% of the execution time of one iteration of the application.

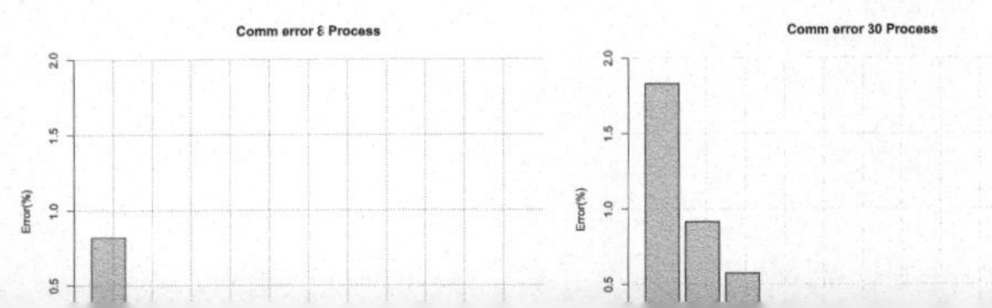

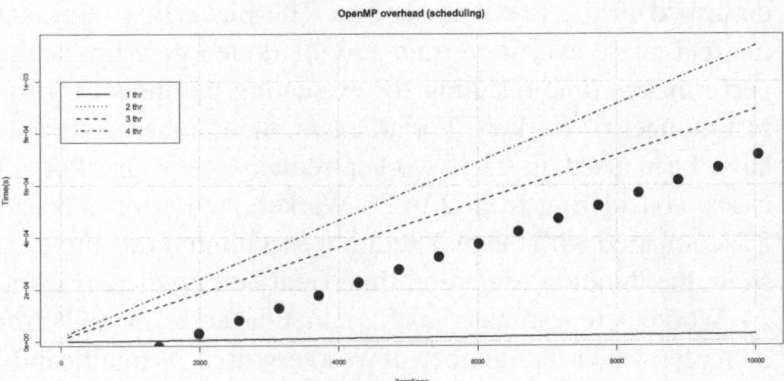

Fig. 3: OpenMP scheduling overhead for different numbers of threads.

it is necessary to measure and add the execution time of one iteration in all the nodes and then add all the values obtained. So, it is necessary to execute one iteration of the application using a certain number of nodes and cores and time for the case of multiplying matrices of 2000 x 2000 using different number of workers (from 2 to 30) and 4 cores for each worker. For this experiment the expression to be evaluated is $A(2000,2000)B(2000,2000) * C(2000,2000) *$ executed 20 times using 4 threads in the OpenMP region on each worker.

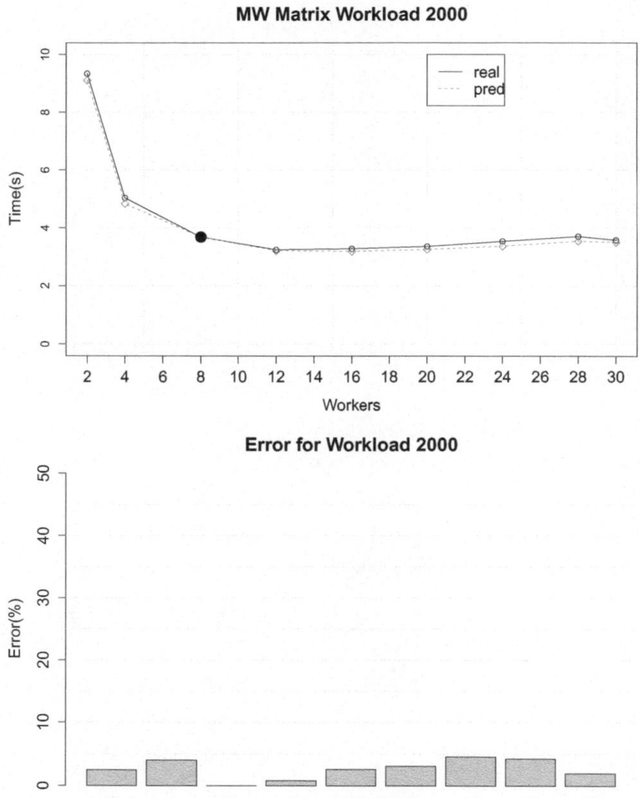

Fig. 4: (a) Real vs. Model using execution time for 8 process (b) Prediction error.

In this case μ_{serial} has been obtained using 8 workers as it is highlighted with the black circle on the figure. The predicted execution time for the rest of the number of workers is calculated applying the performance model described in the previous section. The black line represent the real phase execution time and the dotted gray line is the performance time resulting for evaluating the model for the rest number of workers. For all cases, the number of threads have been used in each worker remains constant. For all cases, considering from 2 to 30 Workers, the error is below 5% compared with the real iteration execution time. Figure 5 show the iteration execution time (real and predicted) using 24 Workers to estimate μ_{serial}. In this case, model error increases when the number of Workers used is significantly lower than that used to estimate μ_{serial} (for example 2 or 4 instead of 24). The main reason that explains the error in

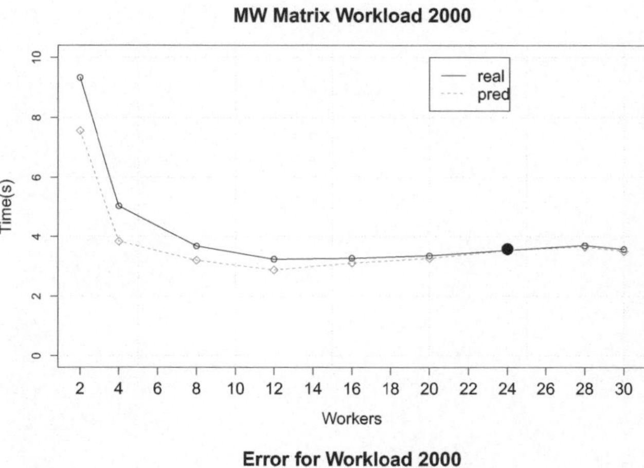

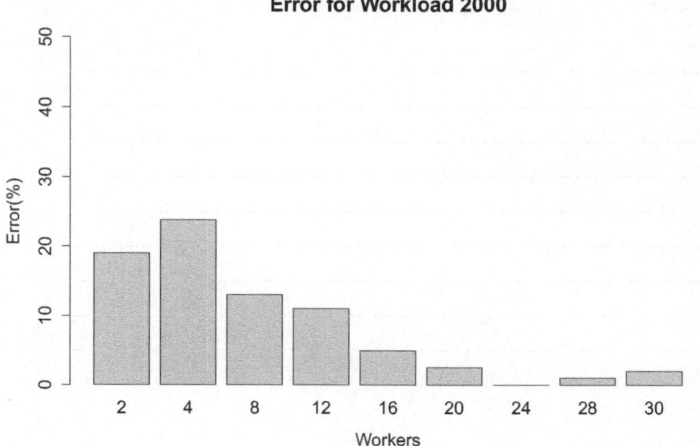

Fig. 5: (a) Real vs. Model using execution time for 24 process (b) Prediction error.

the prediction is the function that estimates the time spent by the last worker to finish its task. This function does not consider the architectural features of the system. For example, when the number of Workers is larger, the same amount of data must be divided among more Workers and therefore, the amount of data assigned to every Worker is smaller. So, it is possible that the data assigned to each Worker fits in the cache memory of one node. However, when the number of Workers is smaller, then a larger amount of data is assigned to every Worker and then it is possible that the data size assigned do not fit in the cache memory of the node provoking a high cache miss ratio.

Figure 6 shows the real and predicted iteration execution time when matrices size is 6000 x 6000, and the number of Workers used to estimate μ_{serial} was 24. In this case the predicted and real execution time fits very well from 24 to 4 Workers. In all these configurations, the error is lower than 5%. However, when the number of workers is 2 the error is around 28%. In this case the data size is larger and does not fit in the L1 cache level of the node, although it fits in the L2 level. However, when the number of Workers is 2, the

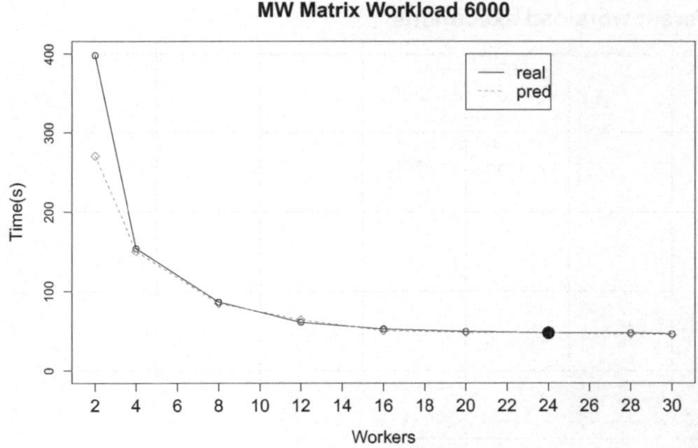

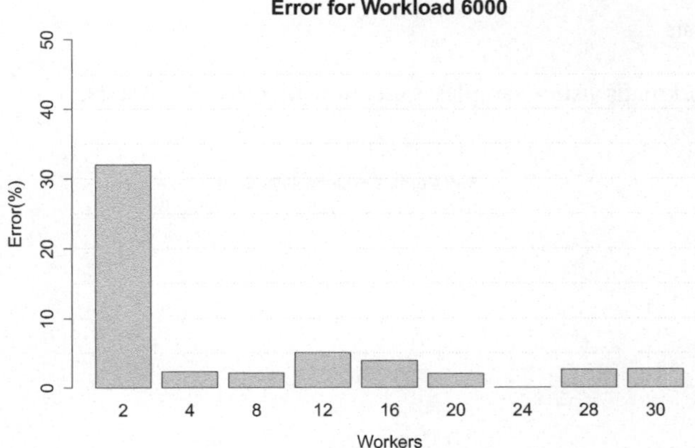

Fig. 6: (a) Real vs. Model using execution time for 24 process (b) Prediction error.

size of the data increases and then it does not fit in the L2 level and L2 misses interfere the prediction time.

So, it can be concluded that the iteration execution time prediction model fits very well the real behavior of the Master/Worker applications when the application is properly balanced and the features of the system does not affect significantly the application behavior.

The presented model can be used to determine the most adequate number of workers to execute the following iterations of the application using that number of Worker processes.

3.2 Performance prediction considering variable workload

In the previous subsection, the accuracy of the presented performance model has been analyzed showing some experimental results. In this analysis, the workload was considered fixed and the variable parameter was the number of Workers. However, in most cases, the workload is also a variable parameter and when a new execution or even a new iteration is executed the workload can be significantly different. So, it is necessary to analyze the robustness of the performance model under variable workload. Again, the most difficult parameter of the performance model to estimate is the μ_{serial}. This parameter represents the execution time of one iteration of the application on a single processor and core. It is clear that the execution time depends on the data size. It is assumed that the execution time does not depends on the data values themselves, but it only depends on the data size. So, the iteration execution time for some particular values of the workload and a certain number of Workers can be used to apply some regression technique to determine the predicted iteration execution time for a new workload value.

The main idea is using a 3-order polynomial regression using all performance time prediction for almost 4 previous iterations of the application as a input data. For each number of Workers, the regression technique is applied taking at least 4 previous values for the same number of workers. The order of the polynomial is 3 according with the complexity of the application have been used in the experiments.

Figure 7 shows the predicted iteration execution time considering different workloads (1500x1500, 3000x3000, 5000x5000 and 6000x6000) when μ_{serial} is evaluated on those particular workloads and considering 8 Workers. In the next iteration, the workload is 4500x4500 and the iteration execution time is predicted considering different numbers of workers. Figure 8 shows the predicted and real iteration execution time and the error.

Using all these performance prediction results, the performance prediction for matrix multiplication with a workload of 4500x4500 is estimated by applying the 3-order polynomial regression. The real and predicted iteration execution times are shown in figure 9.

Once again, black line represent the real execution time for this iteration and the gray one is the predicted execution time for this iteration. The biggest prediction error obtained is around 30% but there are some cases where is lower than 20%. But, the most significant point is that both curve presents the same behavior. So if we determine a suitable value for the number of Workers based on the method prediction, the number of Workers selected will provide a successful iteration execution time. At this point, the robustness of the methodology can be tested by considering that μ_{serial} for each workload has been estimated based on the execution on a different number of Workers. Figure 10 shows the prediction results for the first 4 iterations, using in each case a different number of Workers and the different workload.

For the first iteration, the application was executed with 4 worker using a workload of 1500x1500, for second iteration 12 worker have been used to process a workload of 3000x3000, in the third one the number of Workers was 20 and the workload is 5000x5000, and finally in the

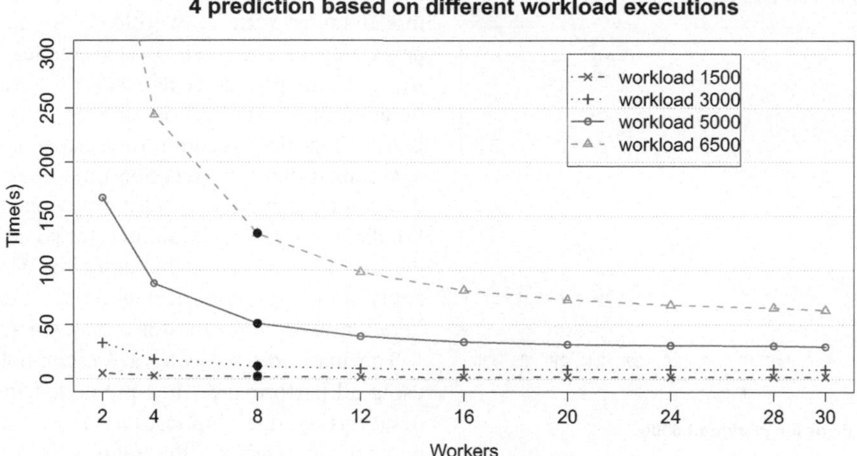

Fig. 7: (a) Performance prediction results for different workloads using samples execution time for 8 workers.

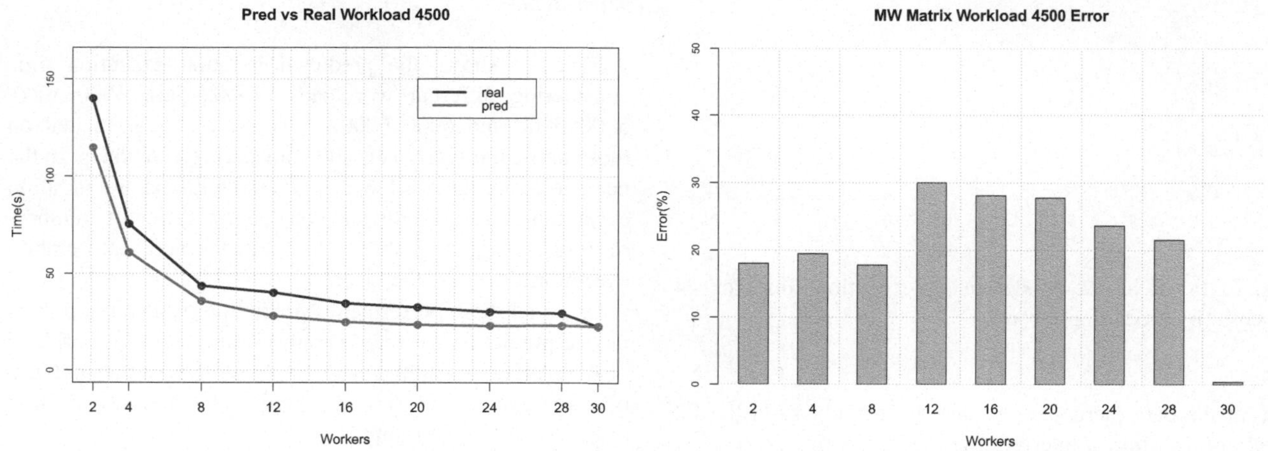

Fig. 8: (a) Prediction vs Real for matrix with 4500x4500 (b) Error.

4th iteration the number of workers is fixed to 28 and the workload is 6500x6500.

The prediction result in general are quite similar to the previous ones. In most cases, error is around 20%. But, once more, the most significant point to be considered is that the real and predicted execution times present the same behavior. This means that using the prediction value to determine the number of Workers is a quite successful approach.

4. Conclusion

We propose a performance model for hybrid MPI-OpenMP application that allows to predict the iteration execution time for Master/Worker applications when the workload is fixed. On the other hand, a technique for performance prediction when workload is varying is introduced. This technique is based on using information about previous iterations as an input data to apply polynomial regression to get prediction for the new workload.

As soon as we achieve small error in the performance prediction, we can determine dynamically the appropriate number of worker trying to reach the best possible performance. Unfortunately, the effects caused by data cache misses ratio are affecting the prediction accuracy.

In the future, we are focus on adding to the current performance model, a function to estimate additional performance penalties for memory accesses misses rate. On the other hand, a more accurate function will have to include how application is exploiting spatial and temporal locality for a different number of threads. This two factor can also impact significantly the application performance.

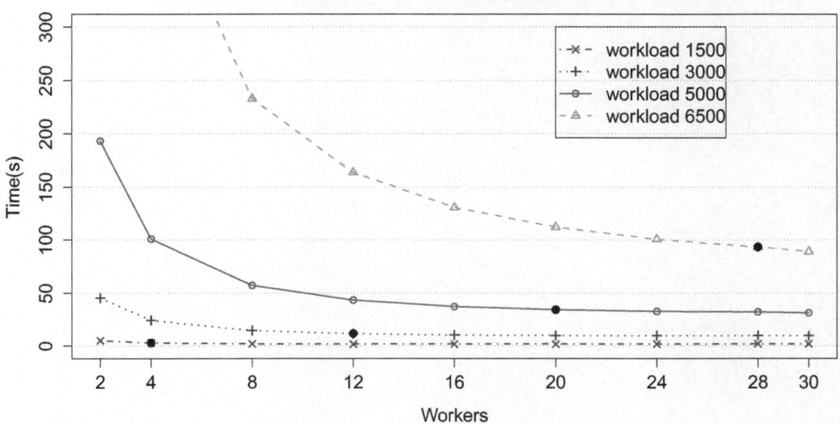

Fig. 9: (a) Performance prediction results for different workloads using samples execution time for 4,12,20 and 28 workers.

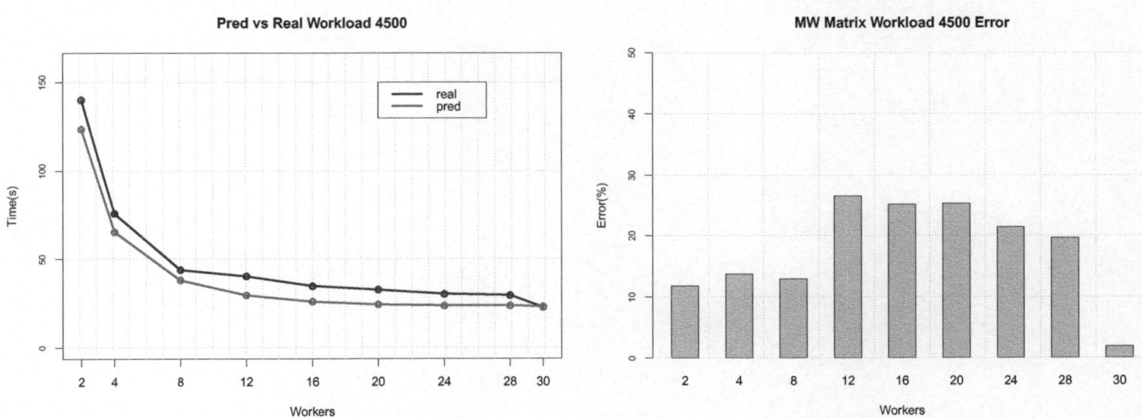

Fig. 10: (a) Prediction vs Real for matrix with 4500x4500 (b) Error.

5. Acknowledgment

This research has been supported by MICINN-Spain under contract TIN2011-28689-C02-01.

References

[1] R. Hempel, "The mpi standard for message passing," in *High-Performance Computing and Networking*, ser. Lecture Notes in Computer Science, W. Gentzsch and U. Harms, Eds. Springer Berlin / Heidelberg, 1994, vol. 797, pp. 247–252.

[2] M. Sato, "Openmp: parallel programming api for shared memory multiprocessors and on-chip multiprocessors," in *System Synthesis, 2002. 15th International Symposium on*, oct. 2002, pp. 109 –111.

[3] L. M. E. Silva and R. Buyya, "Parallel programming models and paradigms," 1998.

[4] E. Cesar, A. Moreno, J. Sorribes, and E. Luque, "Modeling master/worker applications for automatic performance tuning," *Parallel Computing*, vol. 32, no. 7-8, pp. 568–589, 2006. [Online]. Available: http://www.sciencedirect.com/science/article/pii/S0167819106000263

[5] L. M. Liebrock and S. P. Goudy, "Methodology for modelling spmd hybrid parallel computation," *Concurrency and Computation: Practice and Experience*, vol. 20, no. 8, pp. 903–940, 2008. [Online]. Available: http://dx.doi.org/10.1002/cpe.1214

[6] W. Gropp and E. Lusk, "Reproducible measurements of mpi performance characteristics," in *Recent Advances in Parallel Virtual Machine and Message Passing Interface*, ser. Lecture Notes in Computer Science, J. Dongarra, E. Luque, and T. Margalef, Eds. Springer Berlin / Heidelberg, 1999, vol. 1697, pp. 681–681.

[7] N. A. W. A. Hamid and P. Coddington, "Comparison of mpi benchmark programs on shared memory and distributed memory machines (point-to-point communication)," *International Journal of High Performance Computing Applications*, vol. 24, no. 4, pp. 469–483, 2010. [Online]. Available: http://hpc.sagepub.com/content/24/4/469.abstract

[8] D. Grove and P. Coddington, "Precise mpi performance measurement using mpibench," in *In Proceedings of HPC Asia*, 2001.

[9] P. Mucci, "Llcbench(low-level characterization benchmarks) home page," *World Wide Web, http://http://icl.cs.utk.edu/projects/llcbench (July 2000)*, 2000.

[10] J. M. Bull and D. O'Neill, "A microbenchmark suite for openmp 2.0," in *In Proceedings of the Third Workshop on OpenMP (EWOMP01)*, 2001, pp. 41–48.

SESSION

COMMUNICATION SYSTEMS + NETWORKS AND INTERCONNECTION NETWORKS + PEER-TO-PEER NETWORKS AD-HOC NETWORKS + SENSOR NETWORKS AND APPLICATIONS

Chair(s)

TBA

Real-Time Radio Wave Propagation for Mobile Ad-Hoc Network Emulation Using GPGPUs

Brian J. Henz*, David Richie†, Evens Jean‡, Song Jun Park*, James A. Ross§, Dale R. Shires*
*U.S. Army Research Laboratory, APG, MD 21005
†Brown Deer Technology, Forest Hill, MD 21050
‡Secure Mission Solutions, APG, MD 21005
§Dynamics Research Corporation, Reston, VA 20190

Abstract—**The accurate simulation and emulation of mobile radios requires the computation of RF propagation path loss in order to accurately predict connectivity and signal interference. There are many algorithms available for computing the RF propagation path loss between wireless devices including the Longley-Rice model, the transmission line matrix (TLM), ray-tracing, and the parabolic equation method. Each of these methods has advantages and disadvantages but all require a large number of floating point operations during execution. In this paper we investigate using general purpose graphics processing units (GPGPUs) to provide the computational capabilities required to perform these RF path loss calculations in real-time in order to support large scale mobile ad-hoc network emulation. Three specific methods, namely the Longley-Rice, TLM, and ray-tracing methods are explored including usage cases and performance analysis on GPUs. The Longley-Rice algorithm is solved in real-time for 1000's of transmitters and receivers, the TLM method is well suited for GPU acceleration as is ray-tracing. We will discuss the algorithm modifications required for efficient GPU use, precision issues and optimization.**

Keywords: Mobile Ad-Hoc Network, Emulation, GPGPU, RF Propagation Path loss, Longley-Rice, Transmission Line Matrix, Ray-Tracing

I. Introduction

Large scale testing, evaluation and analysis of mobile ad-hoc network (MANET) platforms is an expensive proposal with a limited parameter space and repeatability under experimental conditions. [1] Therefore, simulation and emulation tools have been developed that provide researchers with a controllable and repeatable environment for analysis of MANET platforms. In particular, emulation holds great promise for limiting the amount of live experimentation required for MANET platform development. Emulation provides for hardware-in-the-loop (HIL) testing and analysis where the physical medium is replaced by a virtual environment and a physical or simulated radio can be used with real applications. Much effort has been performed in this area to make the virtual environment as physically meaningful as possible [1]–[3] but one limitation that remains for real-time emulation is the accurate computation of the RF propagation path loss between radios.

RF propagation path loss predictions for MANET emulation has traditionally relied on either off-line link analysis using various models including high fidelity finite difference time domain (FDTD) and ray-tracing methods [2] or real-time calculations with stochastic models. [3] When calculations are performed off-line it is assumed that either the node mobility is known apriori or some large data set of node locations are computed and stored in a look-up table. Limiting the mobility apriori can be a severe limitation when experiments may involve live components or mobility is controlled by a third party application such as a force modeling simulation. One method to remove this limitation is to use interpolation between known data points but the accuracy and efficiency of this method is limited by a number of factors. These factors include the physical size of the virtual environment, machine memory for storing and accessing a look up table, signal phase, and fading affects from small obstructions are not captured because of the computed grid size. Computationally inexpensive methods such as the various free-space models are not a satisfactory solution either, as they do not capture the effect of terrain, vegetation, precipitation or man-made structures on RF propagation path loss.

RF propagation models play an essential role in the planning, analysis and optimization of radio networks [1], [4]–[7]. For instance, coverage and interference estimates of network configurations are based on field strength predictions, routing is also highly dependent upon computed path loss data. [1] The increasing fidelity of MANET emulations from packet-level to signal-level [8] analysis will require fast and accurate modeling of the physical layer. [9], [10] Using GPUs to provide the floating point performance required to compute the RF propagation path loss algorithms in real time it is possible to provide a more realistic physical layer for MANET emulations and simulations. The first algorithm discussed will be the Longley-Rice method as implemented within the irregular terrain model (ITM). The ITM is well suited for large scale emulations of 1000's of devices located in a non-urban environment. The second method investigated is the transmission line matrix or TLM which is targeted towards pico-cell scenarios within buildings or in relatively localized urban environments. The final method investigated, the ray tracing method, is used primarily for small scale to large scale urban environments.

II. Background

The scale and complexity of MANETs used by the Department of Defense (DoD) continues to increase, and is increasing particularly within the Army as a mobile fighting force. The military is rapidly becoming a network-centric force, with substantial access to sensor-derived surveillance information as well as an increasingly complicated application layer running over many different devices. Each layer introduces significant advantages to the war fighter, but also brings in new dependencies and new risks from the rapid change in configurations of the MANETs that provide network access across the battlefield. Headed by the U.S. Army Research Laboratory (ARL), the Mobile Network Modeling Institute (MNMI) was established in 2007 to exploit High Performance Computing (HPC) resources through the development of computational software. Thus enabling the DoD to design, test, and optimize networks at sufficient levels of fidelity and with sufficient speed to understand the behavior of network technologies in the full range of conditions under which they will be deployed. Operational goals of the MNMI include the development of scalable computational modeling tools for simulations and emulations, the ability to understand apriori the performance of proposed radio waveforms in the field, and to optimize the network for U.S. Army war fighters. The results of the MANET modeling effort presented here are from an effort at the ARL that is focused on the development of a framework for large scale MANET emulations, e.g. up to 5000 emulated devices. A large scale emulation environment will provide a testbed for the research, development, and evaluation of network algorithms, applications and devices in a controlled environment. [11]

III. RF Propagation Path Loss Algorithms

As previously mentioned, there are many approaches for field strength prediction and they can be roughly divided into semi-empirical, time-domain methods and ray-optical models. For example, the semi-empirical COST-Walfisch-Ikegami model [12] estimates the received power predominantly on the basis of frequency and distance to the transmitter. Ray-optical [13] approaches identify ray paths through the scene, based on wave guiding effects like reflection and diffraction. Semi-empirical algorithms usually offer fast computation times but suffer from inherent low prediction quality. Ray-optical algorithms feature a higher prediction quality at the cost of higher computation times, while time-domain methods typically increase accuracy further with even higher computational costs.

At the physical layer, the interactions between devices is governed by the RF propagation characteristics of the environment. MANET emulation with HIL capabilities further require that the RF path loss data must be computed and provided to the emulation environment in real-time. The algorithms used to compute path loss must be computed in real-time for each of the possible propagation paths. Initially assuming that all devices in a single emulation scenario are within propagation range of each other the computational complexity of the RF path loss algorithm is $O\left(n^2\right)$, where n is the number of transmitter/receiver device pairs in the scenario. Although the computational cost varies, the methods available for computing the RF path loss data all require a large number of floating point operations, necessitating a high FLOP (floating point operations) rate for real-time path loss predictions.

Recently, the use of GPUs has been identified as a solution to provide the raw floating point performance [14] required to compute the RF propagation path loss in real-time. [6], [7] Originally, GPUs were developed in order to quickly compute rasterization which requires a large number of simple floating point operations. This targeted design is the reason that the architecture has been able to exceed the performance of CPU architectures for raw FLOP rates. [15] The MANET emulation environment used here is EMANE (Extendable Mobile Ad-hoc Network Emulator) from DRS (formerly Cengen Labs) [16]. In EMANE, the GPS locations of all mobile radios are transmitted over an IP multicast group that is monitored by the emulated devices for self-location.

Although a number of path loss algorithms exist, we down-selected the methods based on various scenarios we typically encounter. For instance we have criteria for large scale non-urban environment, large scale urban environments and very localized analysis for moderate numbers of devices. In order to provide a robust path loss calculation for the non-urban environments we selected the Longley-Rice model. The Longley-Rice model is capable of predicting path loss in an area or point to point mode, with the later used here. Longley-Rice is designed for frequencies between 20 MHz and 20 GHz and for path lengths between 1 km and 2000 km [17], both within our scenario operating ranges. In point-to-point mode the model considers input parameters such as distance, antenna height, surface reflectivity, climate and the terrain profile between the transmitter and receiver. [18] The rest of the environmental parameters can be transient or fixed upon initialization. This implementation is robust in that it allows all parameters to change each time the GPU kernel is executed. The TLM method [19] is related to the FDTD method and as such discretizes space and time for computing the electromagnetic field. One advantage of the TLM method over FDTD for this application is the larger spatial discretization possible, and is well-suited for analysis of local areas or pico-cells. The final method investigated is ray tracing [13], using the shooting bouncing ray (SBR) method. The ray tracing method is computationally expensive but many of the algorithms required to compute this method translate efficiently onto GPUs, and is capable of producing results for large urban environments. In the interest of space we will give details below on the implmentation of the TLM algorithm before discussing the achieved performance for all three methods.

A. *The Transmission Line Matrix Algorithm for Real-Time Radio Wave Propagation Path Loss in Pico-Cells*

The transmission line matrix method or transmission line modeling method relies on the relationship between electromagnetic field quantities and voltage and current on transmission lines. [20] The formulation followed in this work is the three-dimensional symmetrical condensed node (SCN). [21] Although this method is more efficient that the FDTD method

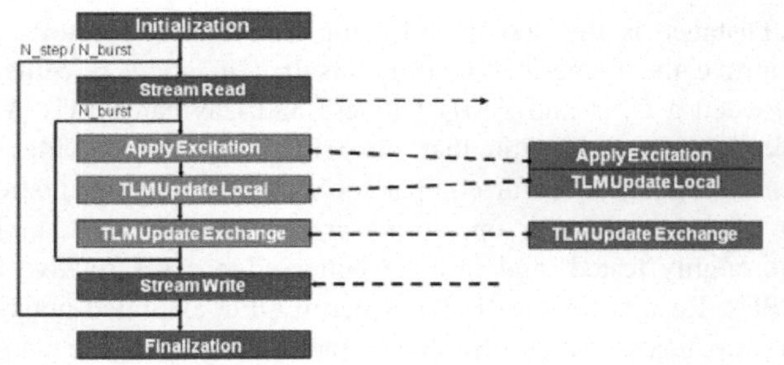

Fig. 1. TLM kernels showing those ported to GPU on the right and where communication can be limited but increasing the number of steps per burst.

that requires approximately 10 grid points per wavelength, each node in the cubic mesh requires solution of 12 values. More details of this algorithm can be found elsewhere [19]–[22].

1) TLM Implementation Details for the GPU: The TLM implementation used in this work is solved using a regular Cartesian grid and therefore memory accesses from neighboring grid points is well defined and memory efficient. This is very important for porting of an application to the GPU architecture as cache misses are much more expensive than on a general purpose CPU. In our implementation the memory access is based on a 3D stencil and calculations are mostly MADDs (Multiply-Add). The TLM code is based on a previous FDTD code optimized for GPUs using the Brook+ language. The algorithm, illustrated in Figure 1, is composed of 7 primary functions. Of these functions Initialization, Stream Read, Stream Write and Finalization are executed on the CPU. The functions within the N_burst loop, namely Apply Excitation, TLM Update Local and TLM Update Exchange are all executed on the GPU hardware. By increasing the ratio of computation to communication the transfer of data across the PCIe bus between CPU and GPU can be limited, potentially increasing performance significantly.

In the TLM implementation used here the number of time steps (N_step) for which the entire grid of Voltages is computed is predefined. This is reasonable since for a regular grid size, the maximum distance that a wave will travel before the input Voltage is insignificant can be estimated from the medium attenuation coefficient. The maximum mesh size, $\triangle l$, can be estimated from the following equation.

$$\frac{\triangle l}{\lambda} \leq 0.1 \tag{1}$$

Where $\triangle l$ is the mesh size and λ is the wavelength of interest. [20]

2) TLM algorithm optimization for GPUs: As previously discussed, the TLM method is well suited for the GPU architecture. An important optimization developed by one of the authors is called shuffled grids. Using this method it is possible to efficiently combine 4 single precision floating point operations of the TLM method into a single float4 SIMD

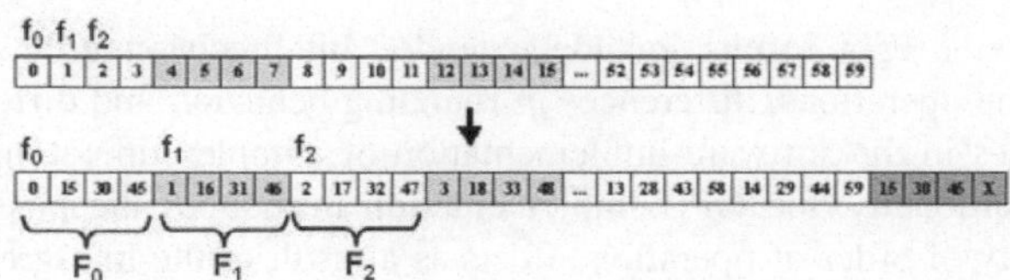

Fig. 2. The memory layout for the shuffled grid method using a 15 offset.

operation. In Figure 2 consider the simple 1D stencil.

$$g_1 = a * f_0 + b * f_1 + c * f_2 \tag{2}$$

In order to leverage float4 SIMD operations the memory is shuffled as shown in Figure 2. The calculation from Equation 2 is then rewritten using float4 SIMD operations.

$$G_1 = c_0 * F_0 + c_1 * F_1 + c_2 * F_2 \tag{3}$$

Which is equivalent to performing the following set of calculations.

$$g_1 = a * f_0 + b * f_1 + c * f_2 \tag{4a}$$
$$g_{16} = a * f_{15} + b * f_{16} + c * f_{17} \tag{4b}$$
$$g_{31} = a * f_{30} + b * f_{31} + c * f_{32} \tag{4c}$$
$$g_{46} = a * f_{45} + b * f_{46} + c * f_{47} \tag{4d}$$

Although there is a small amount of bookkeeping associated with the shuffling and unshuffling of grid points, these are performed as pre- and post-processing steps with little overhead. While the potential performance gains for the TLM algorithm are close to a 4x speedup.

IV. Numerical Stability and Consistency Across Architectures

As noted previously, single precision floating point computations are used on the GPU in order to achieve maximum performance, the trade-off being possibly decreased accuracy. Since the Longley-Rice model uses statistical estimates to compute the variability of signal path loss due to situation, time and location. The actual received signal is expected to deviate from the computed value due to these variables but the model still provides a reasonable estimate. Therefore, small variations due to single versus double precision are not expected to invalidate the computed results for its intended purpose of estimating signal loss over irregular terrain. For the Longley-Rice algorithm there are a large number of transcendental functions that do not have a double precision computation available. Algorithm development with single-precision accuracy raised concerns with numerical stability and consistency, especially, in the context of forward and inverse transcendental functions with small angles. Whereas it is possible, although not guaranteed, that reasonably precise consistency might be expected across these architectures for simple algorithms based on multiply-add operations, the complexity and reliance upon complex transcendental operations makes exact agreement here unlikely. Factors impacting the difference in results include extended bit precision used in some operations, differences in rounding behavior, and differences in the software implementation of complex operations. Additionally, the GPU implementation introduces the possibility of order-of-operation effects as a result of the fine-grain parallelism within some kernels.

An issue identified across many elements of the algorithm was the repeated use of forward and inverse transcendentals at small angles. An example of this small-angle effect is the use of great circle calculations over small areas in which the correction due to the curvature of the earth was small. A serious numerical instability was identified with the pattern of successive operations of cosine, followed by a minor calculation, and then followed by an arc cosine. Such patterns had the potential to produce an intermediate value slightly greater than 1.0 and a final result of NaN (not a number). The effects of this numerical instability can be complicated and the impact on the final path loss can range from a small error to an undefined result (NaN). In some cases a less severe numerical error results from differences in transcendental functions at limiting values. Secondary impacts were also identified, for example differences in the projected map location within the digital terrain map can introduce differences in elevation within the extracted height profile that only impact results by changing the statistical metrics calculated for these height profiles. The solution to many of these issues was to re factor the formulas found in the original reference implementation and introduce forms with greater stability at the limiting ranges found within the typical uses cases. Consider the original distance calculation, that begin by first calculating,

$$\begin{aligned} a =& \cos(90 - lat_2) * \cos(90 - lat_1) + \\ & \sin(90 - lat_2) * \sin(90 - lat_1) * \\ & \cos(lon_2 - lon_1) \end{aligned} \tag{5}$$

Where lat_1, lon_1 refer to the transmitter coordinates and lat_2, lon_2 refer to the receiver coordinates. Using the value a computed in Equation (5),

$$b = \arccos(a) \tag{6}$$

Where for the earth,

$$distance = R_{earth} * b \tag{7}$$

Here R_{earth} is the radius of the earth. For small angles this calculation can be unstable using single precision so we used the following approximation,

$$\Delta lon = lon_2 - lon_1 \tag{8a}$$

$$\Delta lat = lat_2 - lat_1 \tag{8b}$$

$$\begin{aligned} a =& (\sin(\Delta lat))^2 + \\ & \cos(lat_1) * \cos(lat_2) * \left(\sin\left(\frac{\Delta lon}{2}\right)\right)^2 \end{aligned} \tag{9}$$

$$b = 2 * \arcsin(\min(1, \sqrt{a})) \tag{10}$$

Distance is then computed using Equation (7). Efforts to improve the numerical stability resulted in good agreement between a CPU and AMD Cypress and Cayman GPUs. We take as an assumption that the CPU hardware provides a reasonable baseline for comparison since the implementation of all relevant math operations are well established, more thoroughly tested, and provide better edge cases relative to GPUs. Results for the NVIDIA Fermi GPU exhibited notable discrepancies, with a complete understanding of the cause remaining for further investigation. Numerical consistency was tested across these architectures using a simple synthetic test case involving an 8 by 8 uniform grid of radio transceivers over a DEM (digital elevation map) with 1.2M elevation points. Table I shows the percentage of the point-to-point path loss results calculated on a particular GPU architecture that agree with the results calculated on the CPU to within a tolerance of 1 dB, 2 dB, and 10 dB, respectively.

TABLE I
CONSISTENCY OF THE RESULTS CALCULATED WITH VARIOUS GPUS COMPARED TO THE BASELINE RESULTS FROM THE CPU.

Processor	<1 dB	<2 dB	<10 dB
ATI Radeon HD 5870	98 %	99 %	100 %
AMD Radeon HD 6970	98 %	99 %	100 %
NVIDIA Tesla C2070	86 %	90 %	94 %

As observed in Table I, the ATI/AMD devices provide a result more consistent with the baseline CPU. We have been unable to determine at this time the cause of the discrepancy between the two vendors but the ATI/AMD solution consistently provided results more consistent with the CPU baseline calculations.

V. PERFORMANCE AND SCALING

In this section we explore the achieved performance on each of the algorithms on several GPU platforms. In the process comparing vendor we also compare solutions from ATI/AMD and NVIDIA. Each of the algorithms has its own peculiarities that affect performance, for instance the Longley-Rice algorithm is heavily dependent upon transcendental functions and not on more typical MADD (multiply add) operations, whereas TLM has very structured memory accesses and contains almost exclusively MADD operations. This results in come interesting comparisons as the reported FLOP rates are for MADD operations, and transcendental function performance is not directly related.

A. ITM Performance

The ITM algorithm was the first method investigated and therefore this section contains a number of results and comparisons. We start by giving the overall application computation times in Table II which lists the wall clock time required for three different architectures to compute all point-to-point RF path loss values using the Longley-Rice algorithm.

As illustrated in Table II using the current ITM implementation, all of the tested GPU architectures are capable of

TABLE II
TIMING RESULTS FOR 256 TRANSMITTERS/RECEIVERS USING THE OPENCL VERSION OF THE LONGLEY-RICE ALGORITHM RUN ON AMD AND NVIDIA GPUS.

Processor	Time (s)
ATI Radeon HD 5870	0.72
AMD Radeon HD 6970	0.55
NVIDIA Tesla C2070	0.39

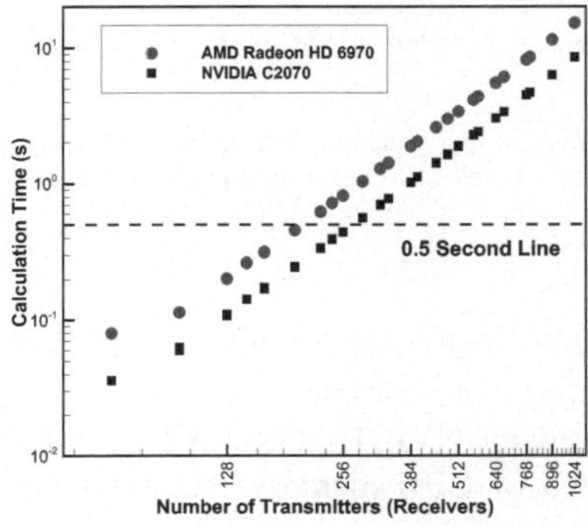

Fig. 3. Plot of total ITM (Longley-Rice) calculation time versus number of transmitters/receivers. The 0.5 second line represents the maximum time allowed for real-time computations.

providing computed RF path loss results for 256 transceivers, or 65,536 point-to-point calculations, in less than 1 second on a single GPU device. For 256 radios, the fastest time to solution is reported as 0.39 sec using an NVIDIA C2070 [23] as compared with 0.72 sec and 0.55 sec using an ATI Radeon HD 5870 and AMD Radeon HD 6970, respectively. [24] Complete performance results are plotted in Fig. 3 for a range of 32 to 1024 transceivers.

In Figure 3 a line is drawn at 0.5 seconds to show approximately the number of transceivers a particular GPU is capable of considering in real-time. It is interesting to note that the theoretical peak FLOP rate of the AMD Radeon HD 6970 is 2.703 TFLOPs and the NVIDIA C2070 is only 1.288 TFLOPs. Conversely, the number of radios supported by the Longley-Rice algorithm in less than 0.5 seconds of computation time is higher for the NVIDIA GPU. This apparent inefficiency in the AMD hardware is due to the fact that many of the floating-point operations in the Longley-Rice algorithm are transcendental functions such as cosine, sine, tangent, co secant, etc., The performance of a specific architecture on the Longley-Rice algorithm is therefore not easily predicted by theoretical peak performance. Additionally, the memory access patterns within the kernels are non-trivial, and this will also contribute to the observed performance.

Performance of complex multi-kernel algorithms can be impacted by many factors including pure computational load, memory access, host-device data transfer, and kernel launch latency. In the case of the 10 kernels in the ITM implementation, each individual kernel shows a very low execution time when directly measured in a fully blocking mode of operation. In order to investigate whether the ITM implementation is effectively using the GPU compute capability, the stripe size over which the computation is distributed was varied to observe the effect of changing the amount of work performed per kernel execution. Initially the stripe size was set at 4096 with subsequent test cases of 2048 and 1024 point-to-point calculations. The results in Table III show an improvement on the order of 10% when increasing the block size from 1024 to 4096, thus providing more work per kernel execution. This indicates that the block size of 4096 is performing only slightly better than the block size of 2048, therefore increasing the block size further would yield diminishing returns. Increasing the block size further would also decrease the efficiency of performing calculations where the number of point-to-point paths was not commensurate with block size. For example, with a workload of 65536 point-to-point calculations, increasing the block size will approach the size of the work load resulting in an efficient calculation when the work load is not a multiple of the block size.

TABLE III
PERFORMANCE FOR AMD AND NVIDIA GPUS AS A FUNCTION OF BLOCK SIZE IN TERMS OF THE NUMBER OF POINT-TO-POINT PATHS EVALUATED PER KERNEL EXECUTION.

Processor	Block Size	Time (s)
ATI Radeon HD 5870	1024	0.83
ATI Radeon HD 5870	2048	0.75
ATI Radeon HD 5870	4096	0.72
AMD Radeon HD 6970	1024	0.65
AMD Radeon HD 6970	2048	0.58
AMD Radeon HD 6970	4096	0.55
NVIDIA Tesla C2070	1024	0.42
NVIDIA Tesla C2070	2048	0.40
NVIDIA Tesla C2070	4096	0.39

B. TLM Performance

As noted previously, the TLM algorithm, much like FDTD, is well suited for the GPU architecture. In this case the biggest bottleneck is expected to be data transfer across the PCIe bus which is known to be a bottle neck for applications executing on GPUs. By limiting the number of times results are transported across the PCIe bus in the TLM algorithm we were able to optimize the calculation time by an order of magnitude, Figure 4.

Notice in Figure 4 that the time per step for CPUs remains fairly constant from 10 to 1000 steps, whereas the GPU results show an order of magnitude decrease in time per step. This illustrates the importance of increasing the computation to communication ratio when using GPUs as a co-processor. In Figure 4 the cpu-opt and gpu-opt lines refer to the use of the shuffled grid method discussed previously. The gpu-opt time per step line shows a nearly ideal 4x speedup over the unoptimized version, whereas the cpu-opt line shows

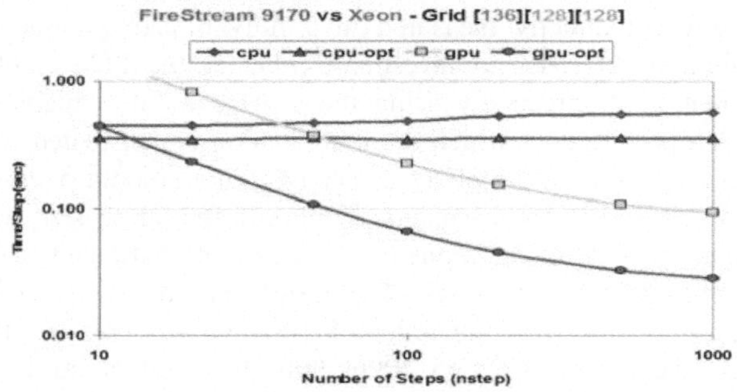

Fig. 4. Plot of time per step computed showing performance increases for GPUs with modest gains for CPUs. By increasing the nsteps parameter the ratio of computation to communication is increased. Notice the power scale on the y-axis.

Fig. 5. Side view of 3D polygon data from Tonsberg, Norway used for ray tracing algorithm development.

about a 1.2x speedup over the unoptimized CPU version. The nearly 4x speedup indicates that the algorithm is able to take advantage of the GPU ability to perform MADD functions on 4 32-bit floating point values simultaneously.

C. Ray Tracing Performance

The primary factor in determining execution time for the ray tracing algorithm is the number of rays generated and computed. The total number of rays in the system depends on the number of rays emitted by individual transmitters, the number of reflections, scattering, diffraction and refraction allowed as well as the number of planar surfaces with which the rays can interact. Note that in this experiment, we are solely focusing on emitted and reflected rays. The environment in use in our research is a polygon-based 3D representation of the town of Tonsberg, Norway, Figure 5. As noted earlier this model contains 68,356 triangle and the benchmark scenario contains two transmitters that spherically emit rays in all directions. The emission angles of individuals rays is dependent upon the user-specified n_θ and n_ϕ values. The values of n_θ and n_ϕ are equivalent over each run and vary their values between 64, 128 and 256. Each emitted ray is traced throughout the environment to generate reflected rays based on their interactions with the planar surfaces. The path of the reflected ray is computed based on the laws of reflection in light propagation.

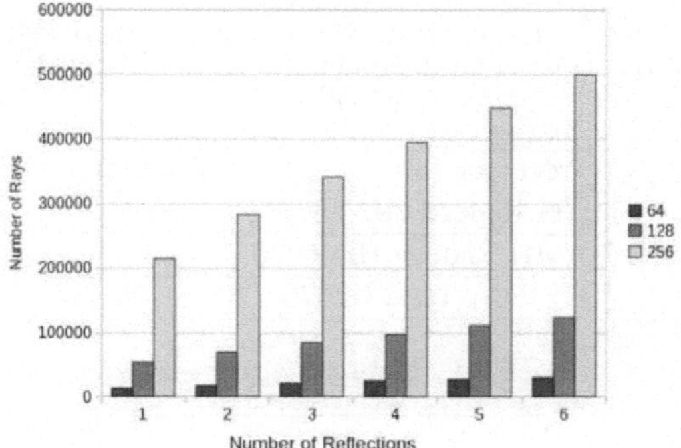

Fig. 6. The number of rays generated during the ray tracing calculation with a maximum of 1 to 6 reflections and an angular partitioning of 64, 128 or 256 partitions.

The ray tracing method is developed using OpenCL in order to take advantage of multiple platforms, although for these results we used an NVIDIA Quadro FX4800 GPGPU with 1.5GB GDDR3 of GPU memory. The total number of rays in the system is computed, and Figure 6 plots the number of rays in the system for n_θ and n_ϕ as they vary from 64 to 256. In Figure 6 the maximum number of reflections that individual rays are permitted to undergo is varied from 1 to 6. It is expected that some predetermined maximum number of reflections or unfolded ray length will be used to limit the run time while preserving accuracy.

Using the parameters from Figure 6 the run time for each configuration is collected and plotted against the number of rays generated, Figure 7. Figure 7 shows a linear relationship between run time and number of rays, but with offsets depending on the initial angular partitioning used. This is related to the cost of initial ray generation and generating new rays after intersection with a surface has occurred. The offsets are approximately equivalent to the difference between the squares of the number of angular partitions. E.g. $128^2 - 64^2 = 12288$ and $256^2 - 128^2 = 49152$. Note that for each ray, the system currently needs to analyze all of the 68,356 planar surfaces in the environment to determine its endpoint. Future performance enhancements will therefore focus on the size of the model and the number of polygons that need to be interrogated for each ray.

VI. Conclusions and Future Work

MANET emulation of large scale networks is a useful tool for network analysts but without realistic RF propagation the accuracy of the results are questionable. Using GPUs we have developed three RF propagation path loss methods that can run in real time or near real time along side a MANET emulation to provide realistic path loss data. These algorithms cover a broad range of the typical scenarios encountered by MANETs in the field, namely, non-urban large networks, large scale urban networks and pico-cells of around 20 nodes in a local area. We have investigated the use of the standard OpenCL language against vendor solutions such as Brook+ and CUDA.

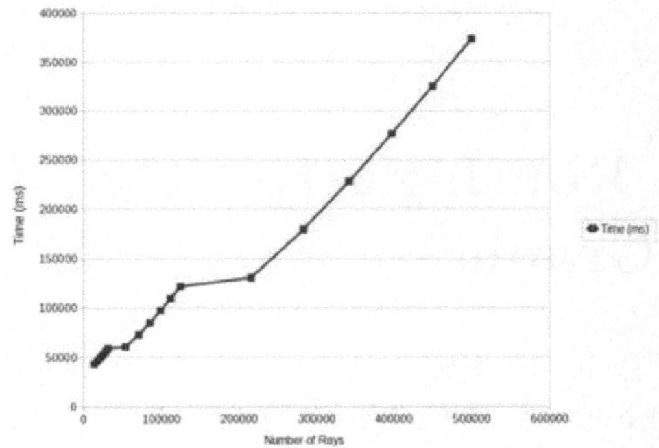

Fig. 7. Ray Tracing algorithm run time versus number of generated rays. The three different slopes correspond to the number of initial angular partitioning of 64, 128 and 256 partitions.

We have also shown how algorithm development for GPUs is very important for achieving maximum performance, such as the shuffled grid method, modifying calculations to use single precision where possible, etc. Additionally for the ITM it was possible to use reduced precision calculations, through the use of alternative calculations for edge cases to improve performance on GPUs. Load distribution and communication costs were mimed by the creation of computation blocks that limit kernel calls and minimize wasted computation cycles. These developments enable the emulation framework at ARL to provide real time situational awareness data to live field exercises and will have applicability to the integration with future modeling simulations and the fielding of upcoming devices.

Although vendor supplied languages for GPUs have shown to currently provide superior performance we have settled on using a portable standard for parallel computing systems, namely OpenCL. Using OpenCL we have developed the Longley-Rice ITM and ray tracing methods for real time RF path loss computations that supports MANET emulation. Enabled MANET emulation provides the capability to augment live exercises, integrate MANET emulation with simulations and to drive programmable attenuators for laboratory experimentation with physical devices. Prior to the development of these capabilities with GPUs, the wireless node mobility and path loss for a scenario needed to either be computed apriori or to use a large number of (i.e. 10,000) CPU cores, dedicated to path loss calculation. This was not acceptable because the CPUs cores are required to host virtual machines for MANET emulation and by using GPU co-processors it has been possible to over come this hurdle for efficient large scale MANET emulation.

VII. Acknowledgments

The authors would like to acknowledge the support received from the High Performance Computing Modernization Program Office (HPCMPO) under the Mobile Network Modeling Institute (MNMI). The authors would also like to acknowledge the support of the HPCMP PETTT (High Performance Computing Modernization Program Productivity Enhancement, Technology Transfer and Training) program.

References

[1] Arne Schmitz and Martin Wenig. The effect of the radio wave propagation model in mobile ad hoc networks. In *The 9th ACM/IEEE International Symposium on Modeling, Analysis and Simulation of Wireless and Mobile Systems (MSWiM 2006)*, October 2006.

[2] Michael A. Kaplan, Ta Chen, Mariusz A. Fecko, Provin Gurung, Ibrahim Hokelek, Sunil Samtani, Larry Wong, Mitesh Patel, Aristides Staikos, and Ben Greear. Realistic wireless emulation for performance evaluation of tactical manet protocols. In *IEEE Military Communications Conference (MILCOM)*, October 2009.

[3] Thomas Nitsche and Thomas Fuhrmann. A tool for raytracing based radio channel simulation. In *SIMUTools*, March 2010.

[4] T. Rick and R. Mathar. Fast edge-diffraction-based radio wave propagation model for graphics hardware. In *Antennas, 2007. INICA '07. 2nd International ITG Conference on*, pages 15–19, March 2007.

[5] Glenn Judd and Peter Steenkiste. Design and implementation of an rf front end for physical layer wireless network emulation. In *IEEE 65th Vehicular Technology Conference (VTC2007)*, April 2007.

[6] D. Catrein, M. Reyer, and T. Rick. Accelerating radio wave propagation predictions by implementation on graphics hardware. In *Vehicular Technology Conference, 2007. VTC2007-Spring. IEEE 65th*, pages 510 –514, april 2007.

[7] David Michéa and Dimitri Komatitsch. Accelerating a three-dimensional finite-difference wave propagation code using gpu graphics cards. *Geophysical Journal International*, 182(1):389–402, 2010.

[8] P. Andelfinger, J. Mittag, and Hartenstein. H. GPU-based Architectures and their Benefit for Accurate and Efficient Wireless Network Simulations. In *IEEE MASCOTS*, pages 421–424, July 2011.

[9] I.K. Eltahir. The impact of different radio propagation models for mobile ad hoc networks (manet) in urban area environment. In *Wireless Broadband and Ultra Wideband Communications, 2007. AusWireless 2007. The 2nd International Conference on*, page 30, aug. 2007.

[10] Illya Stepanov and Kurt Rothermel. On the impact of a more realistic physical layer on manet simulations results. *Ad Hoc Networks*, 6(1):61 – 78, 2008.

[11] Esten Ingar Grøtli and Tor Arne Johansen. Path planning for uavs under communication constraints using splat! and milp. *J. Intell. Robotics Syst.*, 65(1-4):265–282, January 2012.

[12] E. Damasso, editor. *Digital mobile radio towards future generation systems*. Office for Official Publications of the European Communities, Luxembourg, 1999.

[13] Henry L. Bertoni. *Radio Propagation for Modern Wireless Systems*. Prentice Hall Professional Technical Reference, 1999.

[14] Yang Song and Ali Akoglu. Parallel implementation of the irregular terrain model (itm) for radio transmission loss prediction using gpu and cell be processors. *IEEE Trans. Parallel Distrib. Syst.*, 22:1276–1283, August 2011.

[15] NVIDIA. *NVIDIA CUDA C Programming Guide, Version 4.0*, 2011.

[16] Various. *EMANE Developer Manual 0.7.3*. DRS CenGen, LLC, 2012.

[17] G.A. Hufford, A.G. Longley, and W.A. Kissick. A Guide to the Use of the ITS Irregular Terrain Model in the Area Prediction Mode. Technical Report 82-100, National Telecommunications and Information Administration, April 1982.

[18] G. Hufford. *The ITS Irregular Terrain Model, version 1.2.2 The Algorithm*. National Telecommunications and Information Administration Institute for Telecommunication Sciences, 1995.

[19] C. Christopoulos. *The Transmission Line Modeling Method: TLM*. IEEE Press, 1995.

[20] Sadasiva M. Rao. *Time Domain Electromagnetics*. Academic Press, 1999.

[21] P.B. Johns. A symmetrical condensed node for the tlm method. *Microwave Theory and Techniques, IEEE Transactions on*, 35(4):370 – 377, apr 1987.

[22] P. Naylor and R. A. Desai. New Three Dimensional Symmetrical Condensed Lossy Node for the Solution of Electromagnetic Wave Problems by TLM. *Electronics Letters*, 26(7):492–494, 1990.

[23] Benchmarks used the OpenCL implementation provided by the NVIDIA CUDA Toolkit v3.2.

[24] Benchmarks used the OpenCL implementation provided by the AMD ATI Stream SDK v2.3.

A Stochastic Fault-tolerant Routing Algorithm in Hyper-star Graphs

Yo Nishiyama Yuki Hirai Keiichi Kaneko
Department of Computer and Information Sciences
Graduate School of Engineering
Tokyo University of Agriculture and Technology
Koganei-shi, Tokyo 184-8588, JAPAN
50011268507@st.tuat.ac.jp yhirai@cc.tuat.ac.jp k1kaneko@cc.tuat.ac.jp

Abstract ***A hyper-star graph $HS(2n, n)$ is promising as a generic topology for interconnection networks of parallel processing systems because it has merits of a hypercube and a star graph. This paper proposes an $O(n^2 \log n)$ algorithm that constructs a fault-free path between a pair of non-faulty nodes in $HS(2n, n)$ with faulty nodes. For each node and each distance, the algorithm first calculates an estimated value of the probability of existence of a non-faulty minimal path to an arbitrary destination node with the distance from the node. Then it tries to construct a fault-free path based on the estimated values. In addition, we conduct a computer experiment to show its effectiveness.***

Keywords: interconnection network, hypercube, star graph, faulty nodes, performance evaluation

1 Introduction

Recently, research on parallel and/or distributed computation is getting more important because significant progress of performance in sequential computation cannot be expected in the future. For these two decades, studies on so-called massively parallel systems have been very active, and many new topologies for interconnection networks [3, 6, 10, 12, 18] have been proposed instead of conventional simple topologies such as rings, meshes, tori, hypercubes [19], and so on. A hyper-star graph $HS(m, n)$ is one of such topologies. It combines merits of a hypercube and a star graph, and it is promising as a generic topology for interconnection networks of parallel processing systems [13].

In a massively parallel system, it is inevitable to have faulty elements. Therefore, it is necessary to establish algorithms that assume existence of faulty elements. Hence, in this paper, we focus on a regular hyper-star graph $HS(2n, n)$ and propose an adaptive fault-tolerant routing algorithm between a pair of non-faulty nodes in an $HS(2n, n)$ with faulty nodes. If each node collects the global information of all faulty nodes, fault-free shortest paths can be found. However, this approach requires the same order of memory space as the number of nodes in the graph, and it is impractical. On the other hand, if each node collects the local information of neighbor nodes only, fault-tolerant routing with high reachability cannot be achieved. Therefore, there are some studies in which a part of global information is collected as the restricted global information to achieve high reachability [4, 5, 11, 20]. Hence, in this paper, we propose a fault-tolerant routing algorithm that attains high reachability by collecting the restricted global information.

The rest of this paper is organized as follows. We first explain related works in Section 2. Next, we introduce a definition of a hyper-star graph and other necessary definitions in Section 3. Then, in Section 4, we explain our algorithm in detail. We also conduct a computer experiment to verify effectiveness of the algorithm, which is explained in Section 5. Finally, in Section 6, we give a conclusion and future works.

2 Related works

Al-Sadi et al. have proposed a stochastic fault-tolerant routing algorithm in a hypercube [1, 2]. The time complexity of the algorithm is $O(n^2)$. On the other hand, Duong and Kaneko have proposed a stochastic fault-tolerant routing algorithm in a faulty hypercube and its improved version independently of Al-Sadi et al. [7, 8]. Their algorithms show better performance than those by Al-Sadi et al. though the time complexities of the algorithms by Duong and Kaneko are both $O(n^3)$. Myojin and Kaneko have proposed an algorithm obtained by improving the algorithm by Al-Sadi et al. [15]. Its time complexity is $O(n^2)$, and it shows better performance than the algorithm by Al-Sadi et al.

Nishiyama et al. have proposed a fault-tolerant routing algorithm in a hyper-star graph and its improved version [16, 17]. The time complexities of these algorithms are both $O(n^2)$, and they show better performance than a simple greedy fault-tolerant routing algorithm.

3 Preliminaries

In this section, we give definitions of a regular hyper-star graph, routing probability, and its estimated value.

Definition 1 (A regular hyper-star graph $HS(2n, n)$) An $HS(2n, n)$ is an undirected graph, which have ${}_{2n}C_n$ nodes. Each node $\boldsymbol{a}$ consists of $2n$ bits $(a_1, a_2, \ldots, a_{2n})$ where n bits are 1 and the remaining n bits are 0 ($\boldsymbol{a} \in \{0,1\}^{2n}$, $\sum_{i=1}^{2n} a_i = n$). For two nodes $\boldsymbol{a} = (a_1, a_2, \ldots, a_{2n})$ and $\boldsymbol{b} = (b_1, b_2, \ldots, b_{2n})$, there is an edge $(\boldsymbol{a}, \boldsymbol{b})$ between them if and only if $k (\in \{2, 3, \ldots, 2n\})$ exists such that $b_1 = \bar{a}_1$, $b_k = \bar{a}_k = a_1$, and $b_i = a_i$ $(2 \leq i \neq k \leq 2n)$. □

Figure 1 shows an example of $HS(6, 3)$. In $HS(m, n)$, sub graphs that are induced by the node sets whose right-most elements are 0 and 1 are isomorphic to $HS(m-1, n)$ and $HS(m-1, n-1)$, respectively. Table 1 shows a comparison of a hyper-star graph $HS(2n, n)$, a hypercube Q_n, and a hierarchical hypercube HHC_{2^n+n} [14], and a hierarchical cubic network $HCN(n)$ [9].

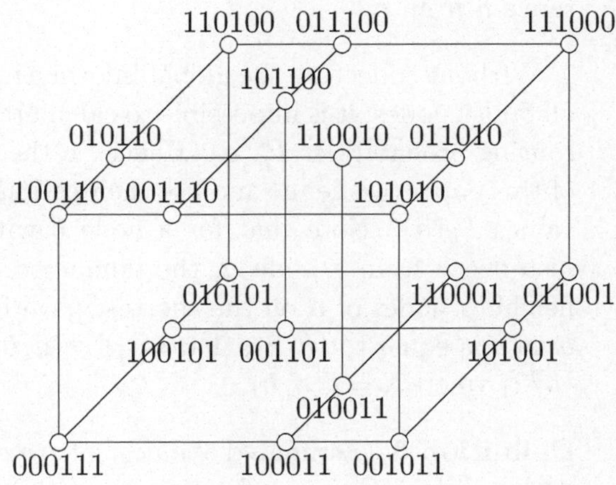

Figure 1: A hyper-star graph $HS(6, 3)$.

In $HS(2n, n)$, for two nodes $\boldsymbol{a} = (a_1, a_2, \ldots, a_{2n})$ and $\boldsymbol{b} = (b_1, b_2, \ldots, b_{2n})$, their distance $d(\boldsymbol{a}, \boldsymbol{b})$ is defined by $\sum_{i=2}^{2n} a_i \oplus b_i$. In addition, the subset of neighbor nodes of $\boldsymbol{a}$ that are on the shortest paths to $\boldsymbol{b}$ is defined by $Pre(\boldsymbol{a}, \boldsymbol{b}) = \{\boldsymbol{n} \mid \boldsymbol{n} \in N(\boldsymbol{a}), d(\boldsymbol{n}, \boldsymbol{b}) = d(\boldsymbol{a}, \boldsymbol{b}) - 1\}$, while the subset of the other neighbor nodes is defined by $Spr(\boldsymbol{a}, \boldsymbol{b}) = \{\boldsymbol{n} \mid \boldsymbol{n} \in N(\boldsymbol{a}), d(\boldsymbol{n}, \boldsymbol{b}) = d(\boldsymbol{a}, \boldsymbol{b}) + 1\}$.

We introduce the routing probability $P_h^*(\boldsymbol{a})$ of a node $\boldsymbol{a}$ with respect to a distance h in $HS(2n, n)$. It can be used as an index to show the probability of existence of fault-free minimal paths for all the non-faulty nodes with the distance h from the node $\boldsymbol{a}$.

Definition 2 (Routing probability) For an arbitrary non-faulty node $\boldsymbol{a}$ in an $HS(2n, n)$, the routing probability of $\boldsymbol{a}$ with respect to a distance h, $P_h^*(\boldsymbol{a})$, is defined to be the probability that a fault-free path of length h exists from $\boldsymbol{a}$

Table 1: Comparison of a hyper-star graph with other topologies.

	#nodes	degree	connectivity	diameter
$HS(2n,n)$	${}_{2n}C_n$	n	n	$2n-1$
Q_n	2^n	n	n	n
HHC_{2^n+n}	2^{2^n+n}	$n+1$	$n+1$	2^{n+1}
HCN_n	2^{2n}	$n+1$	$n+1$	$n+\lfloor(n+1)/3\rfloor+1$

to an arbitrary non-faulty node with the distance h from $\boldsymbol{a}$. □

Without collecting the global information of all faulty nodes, it is impossible to calculate the routing probabilities $P_h^*(\boldsymbol{a})$. Hence, in the rest of this paper, we define and use their estimated values $P_h(\boldsymbol{a})$. Note that for a node $\boldsymbol{b}$ with a distance h from a node $\boldsymbol{a}$, the number of the neighbor nodes of $\boldsymbol{a}$ on the shortest path from $\boldsymbol{a}$ to $\boldsymbol{b}$ is equal to $\lceil h/2\rceil$, that is, $|Pre(\boldsymbol{a},\boldsymbol{b})| = \lceil h/2\rceil$ where $h = d(\boldsymbol{a},\boldsymbol{b})$.

Definition 3 (Estimated values of routing probabilities) For a node $\boldsymbol{a}$ in an $HS(2n,n)$ with a faulty node set F, the estimated values of the routing probabilities of $\boldsymbol{a}$ with respect to a distance h, $P_h(\boldsymbol{a})$, is defined as follows:

$$P_h(\boldsymbol{a}) = \begin{cases} 1 & (h=0) \\ 0 & (1 \le h \le 2n-1, \boldsymbol{a} \in F) \\ \displaystyle\sum_{\substack{I \subset N(\boldsymbol{a}) \\ |I|=\lceil h/2\rceil}} \max_{\boldsymbol{n}\in I}\{P_{h-1}(\boldsymbol{n})\} \Big/ {}_nC_{\lceil h/2\rceil} & \\ & (1 \le h \le 2n-1, \boldsymbol{a} \notin F) \end{cases}$$

□

If the distance from $\boldsymbol{a}$ to the destination node $\boldsymbol{d}$ is zero, that is, $h=0$, it means that the current node $\boldsymbol{a}$ is the destination node itself. Hence, the message can be delivered with probability 1. Therefore, $P_0(\boldsymbol{a}) = 1$ holds. In case that $1 \le h \le 2n-1$ and $\boldsymbol{a} \in F$, there is no possibility that the message from the node $\boldsymbol{a}$ arrives to the destination node $\boldsymbol{d}$. Hence, $P_h(\boldsymbol{a}) = 0$ holds. Otherwise, if $1 \le h \le 2n-1$ and $\boldsymbol{a} \notin F$, the message is transferred to the node among $I = Pre(\boldsymbol{a},\boldsymbol{d})$ that has the largest estimated value of the routing probability. Then, the estimated value of the routing probability of $\boldsymbol{a}$ with respect to the distance h becomes $\max_{\boldsymbol{n}\in I}\{P_{h-1}(\boldsymbol{n})\}$. Because the estimated value of the routing probability, $P_h(\boldsymbol{a})$, is the expected value of the above values for all the nodes which have the distance h from the node $\boldsymbol{a}$, $P_h(\boldsymbol{a}) = \sum_{\substack{I\subset N(\boldsymbol{a})\\ |I|=\lceil h/2\rceil}} \max_{\boldsymbol{n}\in I}\{P_{h-1}(\boldsymbol{n})\}/{}_nC_{\lceil h/2\rceil}$ holds.

It would be very time consuming if we calculate the estimated values of the routing probabilities following the definitions. Hence, we introduce a simplified calculation method based on the following lemma.

Lemma 1 For a node $\boldsymbol{a}$ in an $HS(2n,n)$ with a faulty node set F, if $\boldsymbol{a} \notin F$, the following equation about the estimated values of the routing probabilities $P_h(\boldsymbol{a})$ with respect to a distance h $(1 \le h \le 2n-1)$:

$$P_h(\boldsymbol{a}) = \left(\sum_{k=1}^{n} {}_{k-1}C_{\lceil h/2\rceil-1}p_k\right) \Big/ {}_nC_{\lceil h/2\rceil}$$

where $p_1 \le p_2 \le \ldots \le p_n$ are obtained by sorting $\{P_{h-1}(\boldsymbol{n}) \mid \boldsymbol{n} \in N(\boldsymbol{a})\}$ in an ascending order.

(Proof) In the definition of $P_h(\boldsymbol{a})$, $p_k = \max_{\boldsymbol{n}\in I}\{P_{h-1}(\boldsymbol{n})\}$ holds if and only if both $p_k \in \cup_{\boldsymbol{n}\in I}\{P_{h-1}(\boldsymbol{n})\}$ and $\cup_{\boldsymbol{n}\in I}\{P_{h-1}(\boldsymbol{n})\} \subset \{p_1, p_2, \ldots, p_k\}$ hold. Therefore, the number of cases where p_k becomes the maximum value is equal to ${}_{k-1}C_{\lceil h/2\rceil-1}$. Hence, this lemma holds. □

Now, for a node $\boldsymbol{a}$ in an $HS(2n,n)$, we regard it faulty if its neighbor nodes are all faulty, that is, $N(\boldsymbol{a}) \subset F$. Even if the node $\boldsymbol{a}$ is non-faulty, it cannot communicate with any other node. Hence, this assumption is consistent. Then, the following lemma holds.

Lemma 2 For an arbitrary node $\boldsymbol{a}$ in an $HS(2n, n)$, $\boldsymbol{a} \in F$ holds if and only if there exists h $(1 \leq h \leq 2n-1)$ such that $P_h(\boldsymbol{a}) = 0$.
(Proof) Sufficiency is trivial since if $\boldsymbol{a} \in F$, $P_h(\boldsymbol{a}) = 0$ holds for an arbitrary h $(1 \leq h \leq 2n-1)$. For necessity, we prove the lemma based on mathematical induction on h. In case that $P_1(\boldsymbol{a}) = 0$, if $\boldsymbol{a} \notin F$, $P_1(\boldsymbol{a}) = \sum_{n \in N(\boldsymbol{a})} P_0(\boldsymbol{n})/n = 1$ from the definition of $P_1(\boldsymbol{a})$. Because this result is contradicting, $\boldsymbol{a} \in F$ must hold. For h such that $2 \leq h \leq 2n-1$, if $P_h(\boldsymbol{a}) = 0$, for an arbitrary neighbor node $\boldsymbol{n}$ of $\boldsymbol{a}$, $P_{h-1}(\boldsymbol{n}) = 0$ holds from the definition of $P_h(\boldsymbol{a})$. From the hypothesis of induction, $N(\boldsymbol{a}) \subset F$ holds, and therefore $\boldsymbol{a} \in F$ holds. □

From Lemma 2, if a node $\boldsymbol{a}$ is non-faulty, for an arbitrary distance h, $P_h(\boldsymbol{a}) > 0$ holds. Furthermore, if $\boldsymbol{a}$ is non-faulty, there exists a non-faulty neighbor node $\boldsymbol{n}$ such that $P_{h-1}(\boldsymbol{n}) > 0$ and $P_{h+1}(\boldsymbol{n}) > 0$ hold.

4 Our fault-tolerant routing algorithm

Figure 2 shows a procedure RP, which represents our fault-tolerant routing algorithm in an $HS(2n, n)$ with a faulty node set F. To send a message from a non-faulty node $\boldsymbol{s}$ to a non-faulty node $\boldsymbol{d}$, we can call the procedure by using the format RP($\boldsymbol{s}$, $\boldsymbol{d}$, F).

The procedure RP first calculates the distance h from the current node $\boldsymbol{c}$ to the destination node $\boldsymbol{d}$. Next, if $h = 0$, that is, the current node and the destination node are identical, the message is delivered to the destination node. Otherwise, the procedure finds the node $\boldsymbol{n}_p^*$ in $Pre(\boldsymbol{c}, \boldsymbol{d})$ that has the maximum estimated value of the routing probability, and the node $\boldsymbol{n}_s^*$ in $Spr(\boldsymbol{c}, \boldsymbol{d})$ that has the maximum estimated value of the routing probability. Then, if $P_h(\boldsymbol{n}_p^*) > 0$, the message is forwarded to the node $\boldsymbol{n}_p^*$. Otherwise, the message is forwarded to the node $\boldsymbol{n}_s^*$.

From Lemma 2, if the current node $\boldsymbol{c}$ is non-faulty, there always exists a non-faulty neighbor node $\boldsymbol{n}$ of $\boldsymbol{c}$. Therefore, at least either

```
procedure RP(c, d, F)
begin
  h := d(c, d);
  if h = 0 then
    delivery the message to d
  else begin
    n*_p := argmax_{n∈Pre(c,d)}{P_{h-1}(n)};
    n*_s := argmax_{n∈Spr(c,d)}{P_{h+1}(n)};
    if P_{h-1}(n*_p) > 0 then
      RP(n*_p, d, F)
    else
      RP(n*_s, d, F)
  end
end
```

Figure 2: Fault-tolerant routing algorithm based on estimated values of routing probabilities.

$P_{h-1}(\boldsymbol{n}_p^*) > 0$ or $P_{h+1}(\boldsymbol{n}_s^*) > 0$ holds. Hence, the message can be forwarded to either $\boldsymbol{n}_p^*$ or $\boldsymbol{n}_s^*$. In other words, in this procedure RP, a failure of message delivery is always caused by an infinite loop.

The next theorem estimates the time complexity of the calculation of the estimated values of routing probabilities.

Theorem 1 In each node in an $HS(2n, n)$, the time complexity to calculate the estimated values of routing probabilities with respect to all distances is $O(n^2 \log n)$.
(Proof) From Lemma 1, we calculate the numbers of cases ${}_kC_j$ for $0 \leq k, j \leq n$ in advance so as to use them to calculate the estimated values of routing probabilities. For this purpose, it takes $O(n^2)$ time complexity. On the other hand, in a node $\boldsymbol{a}$, to calculate an estimated value of a routing probability $P_h(\boldsymbol{a})$ with respect to a distance h, it is necessary to collect $P_{h-1}(\boldsymbol{n})$ from each node $\boldsymbol{n}$ in the neighbor node set $N(\boldsymbol{a})$ and sort them. For this, it takes $O(n \log n)$ time complexity. Therefore, it takes $O(n^2 \log n)$ time complexity to calculate the estimated values of routing probabilities for all h $(2 \leq h \leq 2n-1)$. From above discussion, the overall time complexity to calculate the estimated values of routing probabilities with re-

spect to all distances is $O(n^2 \log n)$. □

5 Evaluation

To evaluate performance of our algorithm, we carried out an computer experiment to compare it with the algorithm based on the directed safety levels by Nishiyama et al. [17]. The experiment is conducted based on the following procedure:

1. In an $HS(2n, n)$, for the ratio of faulty nodes $\alpha = 0, 0.1, \ldots, 0.8$, repeat Steps 2 to 4 for 10,000 times.

2. Set $\lfloor \alpha_{2n}C_n \rfloor$ faulty nodes randomly in the $HS(2n, n)$.

3. Select two distinct nodes $\boldsymbol{s}$ and $\boldsymbol{d}$ randomly such that there exists a fault-free path between them.

4. Apply our algorithm based on the estimated values of routing probabilities and the algorithm based on the directed safety levels by Nishiyama et al., and check if the message is delivered to the destination or not.

Figures 3, 4, and 5 show the results of the experiment with $HS(16, 8)$, $HS(14, 7)$, and $HS(12, 6)$, respectively.

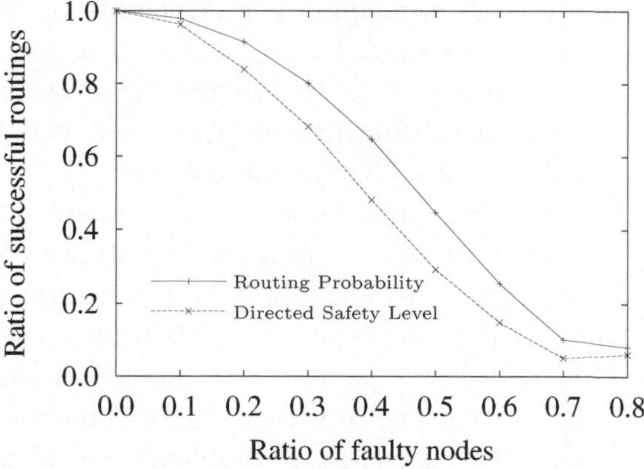

Figure 3: Ratio of successful routings by algorithms base on routing probabilities and directed safety levels in $HS(16, 8)$

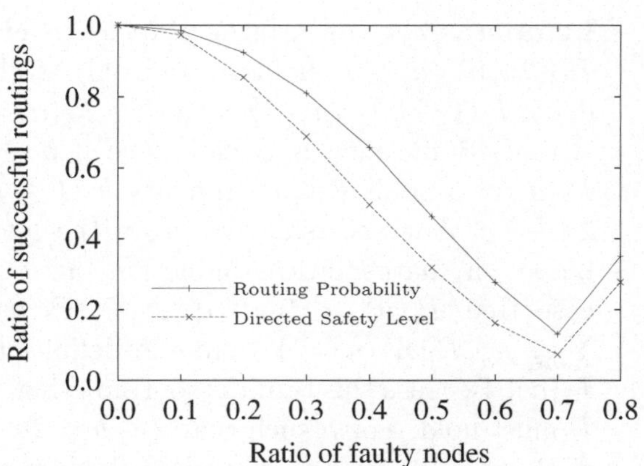

Figure 4: Ratio of successful routings by algorithms base on routing probabilities and directed safety levels in $HS(14, 7)$

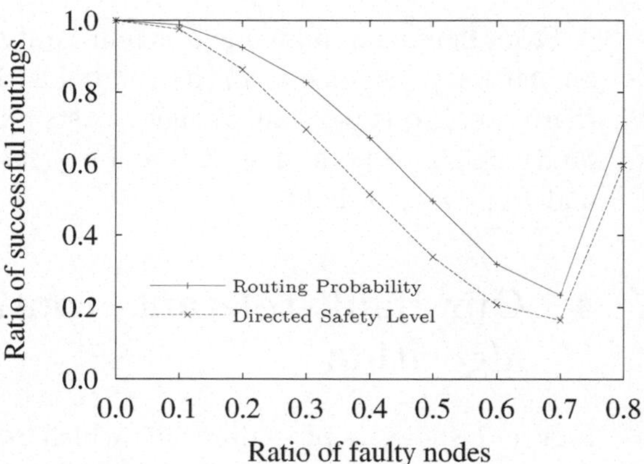

Figure 5: Ratio of successful routings by algorithms base on routing probabilities and directed safety levels in $HS(12, 6)$

According to these figures, we can see that our algorithm is superior to the algorithm by Nishiyama et al. The reason that the ratios of successful routings increased with $\alpha = 0.8$ is that the ratio of faulty nodes is so high that the pairs of $\boldsymbol{s}$ and $\boldsymbol{d}$ could be found with short distances only.

6 Conclusion

In this paper, we have proposed a fault-tolerant routing algorithm in a hyper-star graph $HS(2n, n)$. The algorithm is based on the estimated values of routing probabilities. The time complexity to calculate the estimated values is $O(n^2 \log n)$. From a computer experiment, we have compared our algorithm to the conventional algorithm and verified high reachability of our algorithm.

Future works include finding the better estimated values, and improving the algorithm so that the estimated values can be utilized more effectively. In addition, it is also interesting for us to apply our approach to other topologies.

Acknowledgement

This study was partly supported by a Grant-in-Aid for Scientific Research (C) of the Japan Society for the Promotion of Science under Grant No. 25330079.

References

[1] J. Al-Sadi, K. Day, and M. Ould-Khaoua, "Probability-based fault-tolerant routing in hypercube," *The Computer Journal*, Vol. 44, No. 5, May 2001.

[2] J. Al-Sadi, K. Day, and M. Ould-Khaoua, "Fault-tolerant routing in hypercubes using probability vectors," *Parallel Computing*, Vol. 27, No. 10, pp. 1381–1399, Sept. 2001.

[3] S. B. Akers and B. Krishnamurthy, "A group-theoretic model for symmetric interconnection networks," *IEEE Transactions on Computers*, Vol. 38, No. 4, pp. 555–566, Apr. 1989.

[4] G. M. Chiu and K. S. Chen, "Use of routing capability for fault-tolerant routing in hypercube multicomputers," *IEEE Transactions on Computers*, Vol. 46, No. 8, pp. 953–958, Aug. 1997.

[5] G. M. Chiu and S. P. Wu, "A fault-tolerant routing strategy in hypercube multicomputers," *IEEE Transactions on Computers*, Vol. 45, No. 2, pp. 143–155, Feb. 1996.

[6] P. F. Corbett, "Rotator graphs: An efficient topology for point-to-point multiprocessor networks," *IEEE Transactions on Parallel and Distributed Systems*, Vol. 3, No. 5, pp. 622–626, May 1992.

[7] D. T. Duong and K. Kaneko, "Fault-tolerant routing algorithms based on approximate routable probabilities for hypercube networks," *Proceedings of the 2011 International Conference on Parallel and Distributed Processing Techniques and Applications*, Vol. 1, pp. 116–122, July 2011.

[8] D. T. Duong and K. Kaneko, "Fault-tolerant routing algorithms based on approximate directed routable probabilities for hypercubes," *Proceedings of the 11th International Conference on Algorithms and Architectures for Parallel Processing*, pp. 106–116, Oct. 2011.

[9] K. Ghose and K. R. Desai, "Hierarchical cubic networks," *IEEE Transactions on Parallel and Distributed Systems*, Vol. 6, No. 4, pp. 427-435, Apr. 1995.

[10] J. S. Jwo, "Properties of star graph, bubble-sort graph, prefix-reversal graph and complete-transposition graph," *Journal of Information Science and Engineering*, Vol. 12, No. 4, pp. 603–617, Dec. 1996.

[11] K. Kaneko and H. Ito, "Fault-tolerant routing algorithms for hypercube interconnection networks," *IEICE Transactions on Information and Systems*, Vol. E84-D, No. 1, pp. 121–128, Jan. 2001.

[12] S. Latifi and P. K. Srimani, "A new fixed degree regular network for parallel processing," *Proceedings of the Eighth IEEE Symposium on Parallel and Distributed Processing*, pp. 152–159, Oct. 1996.

[13] H. O. Lee, J. S. Kim, E. Oh, and H. S. Lim, "Hyper-star graph: A new interconnection network improving the network cost of the hypercube," *Proceedings*

of the First EurAsian Conference on Information and Communication Technology, pp. 858–865, Oct. 2002.

[14] Q. Malluhi and M. Bayoumi, "The hierarchical hypercube: a new interconnection topology for massively parallel systems," *IEEE Transactions on Parallel and Distributed Systems*, Vol. 5, No. 1, pp. 17–30, Jan. 1994.

[15] M. Myojin and K. Kaneko, "A fault-tolerant routing algorithm using directed probabilities in hypercube networks," *Proceedings of the 2012 International Conference on Parallel and Distributed Processing Techniques and Applications*, Vol. 1, pp. 131–136, July, 2012.

[16] Y. Nishiyama, Y. Hirai, and K. Kaneko, "Fault-tolerant routing based on safety levels in a hyper-star graph," *Proceedings of the IADIS International Conference on Applied Computing 2012*, pp. 348–352, Oct. 2012.

[17] Y. Nishiyama, Y. Hirai, and K. Kaneko, "Fault-tolerant routing based on directed safety levels in a hyper-star graph," *Proceedings of the International Conference on Advanced Computer Science, Applications and Technologies*, CD-ROM, Nov. 2012.

[18] F. P. Preparata and J. Vuillemin, "The cube-connected cycles: A versatile network for parallel computation," *Communications of ACM*, Vol. 24, No. 5, pp. 300–309, May 1981.

[19] C. L. Seitz, "The cosmic cube," *Communications of the ACM*, Vol. 28, No. 1, pp. 22–33, Jan. 1985.

[20] J. Wu, "Adaptive fault-tolerant routing in cube-based multicomputers using safety vectors," *IEEE Transactions on Parallel and Distributed Systems*, Vol. 9, No. 4, pp. 322–334, Apr. 1998.

Parallel routing in exchanged hypercubes

Tsung-Han Tsai[a], Y-Chuang Chen[b], and Jimmy J.M. Tan[a*]

[a]Department of Computer Science, National Chiao Tung University, Hsinchu 300, Taiwan(R.O.C)
[b]Department of Information Management, Minghsin University of Science and Technology, Xinfeng Hsinchu 304, Taiwan(R.O.C)

Abstract. Parallel routing and diameter are two important issues in interconnection networks. The hypercube is one of the most popular interconnection networks for parallel systems due to its attractive properties such as low diameter and efficient parallel routing. The exchanged hypercube, which is a variant of the hypercube by removing some specific edges, remains several desirable properties of the hypercube. This paper discusses parallel routing in exchanged hypercubes and show the wide diameter of exchanged hypercubes.

Key words: parallel routing, exchanged hypercube, diameter, wide diameter.

1 Introduction

A graph G is a two-tuple (V, E), where V is a nonempty set, and E is a subset of $\{(u,v) \mid (u,v)$ is an unordered pair of $V\}$. We say that V is the vertex set and E is the edge set. A multi-processor system or a network can be modeled as a *graph*, in which vertices represent processors or computers, and edges represent connections or communication links. The terms *network* and *graph* can be used interchangeable throughout this paper. Two vertices, u and v, of a graph G are *adjacent* if $(u,v) \in E(G)$. A *path* P of length k from vertex u to vertex v in a graph G is a sequence of distinct vertices written as $x_0 \to x_1 \to x_2 \to \cdots \to x_k$ where $x_0 = u$, $x_k = v$, and $(x_i, x_{i+1}) \in E(G)$ for every $0 \leq i \leq k-1$ if $k \geq 1$. A path P can be written as $u \to P \to v$ to emphasize its beginning and ending vertices. A *cycle* is a path with at least three vertices such that the last vertex is adjacent to the first one. For clarity, a cycle of length k is represented by $x_1 \to x_2 \to \ldots \to x_k \to x_1$. The length of a path P, denoted by $l(P)$, is the number of edges in P. The *distance* between two distinct vertices u and v in graph G, denoted by $d_G(u,v)$, is the length of the shortest path between u and v.

The hypercube is one of the most popular interconnection networks for parallel computer/communication system due to its many attractive properties such

* Correspondence to: Professor Jimmy J.M. Tan, TEL:886-3-5712121 ext.56618 e-mail: jmtan@cs.nctu.edu.tw.

as *regularity*, *recursive structure*, *vertex and edge symmetry*, *maximum connectivity*, effective *routing* and *broadcasting algorithm*, [2, 4]. The definition of hypercubes is presented as follows. A hypercube Q_n is a graph with 2^n vertices and each vertex u is denoted by an n-bit binary string $u = u_n u_{n-1} \dots u_1$. Two vertices are adjacent if and only if their strings differ exactly in one bit position. Let $u = u_n u_{n-1} \dots u_1$ and $v = v_n v_{n-1} \dots v_1$ be two n-bit binary strings. The Hamming distance $d_H(u, v)$ between two vertices u and v is the number of different bits in the corresponding strings of both vertices. Clearly, $d_H(u, v) = d_{Q_n}(u, v)$, where $d_{Q_n}(u, v)$ denotes the distance between two vertices u and v in Q_n, i.e., the length of a shortest uv-path in Q_n. In particular, Q_n is a vertex-transitive and edge-transitive bipartite graph, and has diameter n [10].

As a variant of the hypercube, the *exchanged hypercube* proposed by Loh et al. [5] is defined by removing some edges from the hypercube. However, it maintains several desirable properties of the hypercube such as low *diameter* [5], *bipancyclicity* [7] and *super connectivity* [8]. In this paper, we shall give *internally disjoint paths* in exchanged hypercubes and show the *wide diameter* of exchanged hypercubes.

In Section 2, some definition and properties of exchanged hypercubes are given. Section 3 deals with parallel routing in exchanged hypercubes and show the wide diameter of exchanged hypercubes.

2 Exchanged hypercubes

The exchanged hypercube is defined as an undirected graph $EH(s, t) = G(V, E)$, where $s \geq 1, t \geq 1$. The set of vertices $V = \{a_{s-1} \dots a_0 b_{t-1} \dots b_0 c \mid a_i, b_j, c \in \{0, 1\}$ for $0 \leq i \leq s-1, 0 \leq j \leq t-1\}$, and the set of edges $E = E_1 \cup E_2 \cup E_3$. The edge set $E_1 = \{(v_1, v_2) \in V \times V \mid v_1[s+t : 1] = v_2[s+t : 1], v_1[0] \neq v_2[0]\}$, $E_2 = \{(v_1, v_2) \in V \times V \mid v_1[t : 1] = v_2[t : 1], H(v_1[s+t : t+1], v_2[s+t : t+1]) = 1, v_1[0] = v_2[0] = 0\}$, and $E_3 = \{(v_1, v_2) \in V \times V \mid v_1[s+t : t+1] = v_2[s+t : t+1], H(v_1[t : 1], v_2[t : 1]) = 1, v_1[0] = v_2[0] = 1\}$, where $v[x : y]$ denotes the bit pattern of v from dimension y to dimension x, and $H(u, v)$ denotes the Hamming distance between u and v.

By the definition of $EH(s, t)$, we know that the number of vertices is 2^{s+t+1} and the number of edges is $(s+t+2)2^{s+t-1}$. Since $EH(s, t)$ is a subgraph of the $(s+t+1)$-dimensional hypercube Q_{s+t+1}, it is also a bipartite graph. Loh et al. [5] state some properties of exchanged hypercubes. For example, the diameter of $EH(s, t)$ is $(s+t+2)$, $EH(s, t)$ is isomorphic to $EH(t, s)$, and $EH(s, t)$ can be decomposed into two copies of $EH(s-1, t)$ or $EH(s, t-1)$.

The subgraphs induced by the vertices of the form $\overbrace{* \cdots *}^{s} b_{t-1} \cdots b_0 0$ and $a_{s-1} \cdots a_0 \overbrace{* \cdots *}^{t} 1$ in $EH(s, t)$ are isomorphic to Q_s and Q_t, respectively, where $* \in \{0, 1\}$. The subgraphs induced by the vertex sets $V(Q_s)$ and $V(Q_t)$ are denoted by S and T, respectively. Then $S \cong Q_s$ and $T \cong Q_t$. So there are 2^t distinct induced subgraphs Q_s^i in $EH(s, t)$ for $1 \leq i \leq 2^t$, and there are 2^s

distinct induced subgraphs Q_t^i in $EH(s,t)$ for $1 \leq i \leq 2^s$. We denote that the hamming distance between u and v in the induced subgraphs Q_s of $EH(s,t)$, called $h_s(u,v)$ (simply abbreviated as h_s), is the number of bits in which labels of u and v differ from dimension $t+1$ to $s+t$. Similarly, we denote that the hamming distance between u and v in the induced subgraphs Q_t of $EH(s,t)$, called $h_t(u,v)$ (simply abbreviated as h_t) is the number of bits in which labels of u and v differ from dimension 1 to t.

3 Parallel routing and wide diameter

A vertex set $F \subseteq V(G)$ is a *separating set* or a *vertex cut* if $G-F$ is disconnected. The *connectivity* of G, written as $\kappa(G)$, is the minimum size of a vertex cut. A graph G is *k-connected* if the connectivity $\kappa(G)$ is at least k. Moreover, a graph G has connectivity k if G is k-connected but not $(k+1)$-connected. Let $\delta(G)$ be the minimum degree of G. It follows from Menger's Theorem that the connectivity of a graph is at least k if and only if there exist k internally vertex-disjoint (abbreviated as disjoint) paths between any two vertices.

Let α and β be two positive integers such that $\alpha \leq \kappa$ and $\beta \leq \kappa - 1$. Given any two distinct vertices u and v of G, let $D(u,v)$ denote the set of all α disjoint paths between u and v. Each element of $D(u,v)$ consists of α disjoint paths. The number of elements in $D(u,v)$ denoted by $|D(u,v)|$. Let $l_i(u,v)$ denote the longest length among these α path of the ith element of $D(u,v)$. We define that $d_\alpha(u,v) = \min_{1 \leq i \leq |D(u,v)|} l_i(u,v)$. The *$\alpha$-wide diameter* of G, denoted by $D_\alpha(G)$, is defined as $D_\alpha(G) = \max_{u,v \in V} \{d_\alpha(u,v)\}$. In particular, we call $D_\kappa(G)$ to be the *wide diameter* of G. Note that $D_1(G)$ is simply the diameter $D(G)$ of G.

Obviously, $D(G) \leq D_\kappa(G)$. For the hypercube Q_n, Latifi [3] proved that $D_n(Q_n) = n+1$ for $n \geq 2$. For the crossed cube CQ_n, Chang et al. [1] proved that $D_n(CQ_n) = \lceil \frac{n}{2} \rceil + 2$ for $n \geq 2$. In this section, we shall discuss the wide diameter of exchanged hypercubes, and prove that $D_{s+1}(EH(s,t)) = s+t+3$ for $3 \leq s \leq t$.

Lemma 1. *[6] The connectivity of the exchanged hypercubes $EH(s,t)$ is $s+1$ for $1 \leq s \leq t$.*

From Menger's Theorem, there exist $s+1$ internal disjoint paths between any two distinct vertices in exchanged hypercube $EH(s,t)$.

Lemma 2. *[9] Let u, v be any two vertices of the n-dimensional hypercube Q_n and assume that $d_{Q_n}(u,v) = k$. Then there are n disjoint paths between u and v such that k of them are of length k, and the remaining $n-k$ paths are of length $k+2$.*

Lemma 3. *[7] The vertices in the vertex set $V_c = \{a_s \cdots a_1 b_t \cdots b_1 c \mid a_i, b_j \in \{0,1\}$ for $1 \leq i \leq s, 1 \leq j \leq t\}$ $(c \in \{0,1\})$ are vertex-transitive.*

The following theorem gives lower bound of the wide diameter of the exchanged hypercube. For convenience of the proof of the following theorem, we abbreviate some symbols. If there are s consecutive 0's, then we denote it by 0^s, that is, $0^s = \overbrace{00\cdots0}^{s}$. If there are t consecutive 1's, then we denote it by 1^t, that is, $1^t = \overbrace{11\cdots1}^{t}$.

Theorem 1. *$D_{s+1}(EH(s,t)) \geq s+t+3$ for $1 \leq s \leq t$.*

Proof. By Lemma 1, the connectivity of the exchanged hypercubes $EH(s,t)$ is $s+1$. From Menger's Theorem, there exist $s+1$ internal disjoint paths between any two distinct vertices, denoted by u and v, in $EH(s,t)$. We consider that $u = \overbrace{00\cdots0}^{s}\overbrace{00\cdots0}^{t}0$ (simply abbreviated as 0^s0^t0) and $v = \overbrace{11\cdots1}^{s}\overbrace{11\cdots1}^{t}1$ (simply abbreviated as 1^s1^t1). Let $u' = 0^s0^t1$ be a neighbor of u and let $V' = N(u) - u'$. The shortest path P between u and v in $EH(s,t) - V'$ must pass u'. Loh et al. [5] showed that the length of the shortest path between u' and v is $H(u,v)+2 = s+t+2$. The $+2$ is because routing has to use dimension 0 twice: $1 \to 0$ and $0 \to 1$. For clarity, we write P as $< u, u', R, v >$, where R is the shortest path between u' and v in $EH(s,t) - V'$. Since $|R| = d(u',v) = s+t+2$, it follows that $d_{EH(s,t)-V'} = 1 + d(u',v) = s+t+3$. As a result, $D_{s+1}(EH(s,t)) \geq s+t+3$ for $1 \leq s \leq t$. □

The following theorem gives upper bound of the wide diameter of exchanged hypercubes.

Theorem 2. *$D_{s+1}(EH(s,t)) \leq s+t+3$ for $3 \leq s \leq t$.*

The proof of Theorem 2 can be derived from the following Lemmas 4 to 15.

Lemma 4. *Let u, v be two distinct vertices of $EH(s,t)$ for $3 \leq s \leq t$. If $u[0] = v[0] = 0$, and $h_t(u,v) = 0$, then there exist $s+1$ internally disjoint paths $P_i (1 \leq i \leq s+1)$ between u and v such that h_s of them are of length h_s, $s - h_s$ paths are of length $h_s + 2$, and one path is of length $h_s + 6$.*

Proof. By Lemma 3, without loss of generality, we consider $u = 0^s0^t0$ and $v = 0^{s-h_s}1^{h_s}0^t0$ are in the same induced subgraphs, denoted by Q_s^1. By Lemma 2, there exist s internally disjoint paths $H_i (1 \leq i \leq s)$ between u and v in the induced subgraph Q_s^1 such that h_s of them are of length h_s, and the other $s - h_s$ paths are of length $h_s + 2$. Without loss of generality, we set $|H_i| = h_s$ for $1 \leq i \leq h_s$ and $|H_i| = h_s + 2$ for $h_s + 1 \leq i \leq s$.

The following sets of $s+1$ internally disjoint paths can be set between u and v.

For $1 \leq i \leq s$,

$$P_i : u = 0^s0^t0 \to H_i \to v = 0^{s-h_s}1^{h_s}0^t0,$$

where $|P_i| = h_s$ for $1 \le i \le h_s$ and $|P_i| = h_s + 2$ for $h_s + 1 \le i \le s$.

$$P_{s+1} : u = 0^s0^t0 \to 0^s0^t1 \to 0^s0^{t-1}11 \to 0^s0^{t-1}10 \to L \to 0^{s-h_s}1^{h_s}0^{t-1}10$$
$$\to 0^{s-h_s}1^{h_s}0^{t-1}11 \to 0^{s-h_s}1^{h_s}0^t1 \to v = 0^{s-h_s}1^{h_s}0^t0,$$

where $|P_{s+1}| = h_s + 6$. Note that the path L is of length h_s in another induced subgraph, denoted by Q_s^2. □

Lemma 5. *Let u, v be two distinct vertices of $EH(s,t)$ for $3 \le s \le t$. If $u[0] = v[0] = 0$ and $h_t(u,v) \ne 0$, then there exist $s+1$ internally disjoint paths $P_i (1 \le i \le s+1)$ between u and v such that $h_s + 1$ of them are of length $h_s + h_t + 2$, and $s - h_s$ paths are of length $h_s + h_t + 4$.*

Proof. By Lemma 3, without loss of generality, we may assume that $u = 0^s0^t0$ and $v = 0^{s-h_s}1^{h_s}0^{t-h_t}1^{h_t}0$. Depending on h_s, two cases are distinguished.

Case 1: $h_s = 0$. Consider $u = 0^s0^t0$ and $v = 0^s0^{t-h_t}1^{h_t}0$ are in distinct induced subgraphs, denoted by Q_s^1 and Q_s^2, respectively. The following sets of $s+1$ internally disjoint paths can be set between u and v.

For $1 \le i \le s$,

$$P_i : u = 0^s0^t0 \to 0^{s-i}10^{i-1}0^t0 \to 0^{s-i}10^{i-1}0^t1 \to R_i \to 0^{s-i}10^{i-1}0^{t-h_t}1^{h_t}1$$
$$\to 0^{s-i}10^{i-1}0^{t-h_t}1^{h_t}0 \to v = 0^s0^{t-h_t}1^{h_t}0,$$

where $|P_i| = h_t + 4$. Note that the path R_i is of length h_t in the induced subgraph, denoted by Q_t^i.

$$P_{s+1} : u = 0^s0^t0 \to 0^s0^t1 \to R_{s+1} \to 0^s0^{t-h_t}1^{h_t}1 \to v = 0^s0^{t-h_t}1^{h_t}0,$$

where $|P_i| = h_t + 2$. Note that the path R_{s+1} is of length h_t in the induced subgraph, denoted by Q_t^{s+1}.

Case 2: $1 \le h_s \le s$. Consider $u = 0^s0^t0$ and $v = 0^{s-h_s}1^{h_s}0^{t-h_t}1^{h_t}0$ are in distinct induced subgraphs, denoted by Q_s^1 and Q_s^2, respectively. By Lemma 2, there exist s internally disjoint paths $H_i (1 \le i \le s)$ between u and $v' = 0^{s-h_s}1^{h_s}0^t0$ in the induced subgraph Q_s^1 such that h_s of them are of length h_s, and the other $s - h_s$ paths are of length $h_s + 2$. Without loss of generality, we set $|H_i| = h_s$ for $1 \le i \le h_s$ and $|H_i| = h_s + 2$ for $h_s + 1 \le i \le s$. We set $0^s0^t0 \to H_i' \to 0^{s-h_s}1^{h_s-i}01^{i-1}0^t0 \to 0^{s-h_s}1^{h_s}0^t0$ as H_i for $1 \le i \le h_s$, and $0^s0^t0 \to H_i' \to 0^{s+h_s-i}10^{i-h_s-1}1^{h_s}0^t0 \to 0^{s-h_s}1^{h_s}0^t0$ as H_i for $h_s + 1 \le i \le s$. We denote that $N_i(v) = 0^{s-h_s}1^{h_s-i}01^{i-1}0^{t-h_t}1^{h_t}0$ is the neighbor of v in Q_s^1 for $1 \le i \le h_s$, and $N_i(v) = 0^{s+h_s-i}10^{i-h_s-1}1^{h_s}0^{t-h_t}1^{h_t}0$ is the neighbor of v in Q_s^1 for $h_s + 1 \le i \le s$.

The following sets of $s+1$ internally disjoint paths can be set between u and v.

$$P_1 : u = 0^s0^t0 \rightarrow H_1 \rightarrow 0^{s-h_s}1^{h_s}0^t0 \rightarrow 0^{s-h_s}1^{h_s}0^t1 \rightarrow R_1$$
$$\rightarrow 0^{s-h_s}1^{h_s}0^{t-h_t}1^{h_t}1 \rightarrow v = 0^{s-h_s}1^{h_s}0^{t-h_t}1^{h_t}0,$$

where $|P_1| = h_s + h_t + 2$. Note that the path R_1 is of length h_t in the induced subgraph, denoted by Q_t^1.

For $2 \leq i \leq h_s$,

$$P_i : u = 0^s0^t0 \rightarrow H_i' \rightarrow 0^{s-h_s}1^{h_s-i}01^{i-1}0^t0 \rightarrow 0^{s-h_s}1^{h_s-i}01^{i-1}0^t1 \rightarrow R_i$$
$$\rightarrow 0^{s-h_s}1^{h_s-i}01^{i-1}0^{t-h_t}1^{h_t}1 \rightarrow 0^{s-h_s}1^{h_s-i}01^{i-1}0^{t-h_t}1^{h_t}0$$
$$\rightarrow v = 0^{s-h_s}1^{h_s}0^{t-h_t}1^{h_t}0,$$

where $|P_i| = h_s + h_t + 2$. Note that the path R_i is of length h_t in the induced subgraph, denoted by Q_t^i.

For $h_s + 1 \leq i \leq s$,

$$P_i : u = 0^s0^t0 \rightarrow H_i' \rightarrow 0^{s+h_s-i}10^{i-h_s-1}1^{h_s}0^t0 \rightarrow 0^{s-h_s-i}10^{i-h_s-1}1^{h_s}0^t1 \rightarrow R_i$$
$$\rightarrow 0^{s+h_s-i}10^{i-h_s-1}1^{h_s}0^{t-h_t}1^{h_t}1 \rightarrow 0^{s+h_s-i}10^{i-h_s-1}1^{h_s}0^{t-h_t}1^{h_t}0$$
$$\rightarrow v = 0^{s-h_s}1^{h_s}0^{t-h_t}1^{h_t}0,$$

where $|P_i| = h_s + h_t + 4$. Note that the path R_i is of length h_t in the induced subgraph, denoted by Q_t^i.

$$P_{s+1} : u = 0^s0^t0 \rightarrow 0^s0^t1 \rightarrow R_{s+1} \rightarrow 0^s0^{t-h_t}1^{h_t}1 \rightarrow 0^s0^{t-h_t}1^{h_t}0 \rightarrow L$$
$$\rightarrow v = 0^{s-h_s}1^{h_s}0^{t-h_t}1^{h_t}0,$$

where $|P_{s+1}| = h_s + h_t + 2$. Note that the path R_{s+1} is of length h_t in the induced subgraph, denoted by Q_t^{s+1}, and L is of length h_s in the induced subgraph Q_s^2. □

Because the proof of Lemmas 6 to 15 are long and similar to Lemmas 4 and 5, we omit the proof of Lemmas 6 to 15 here, and only state the lemmas.

Lemma 6. *Let u, v be two distinct vertices of $EH(s,t)$ for $3 \leq s \leq t$. If $u[0] = v[0] = 1$, and $h_s(u,v) = 0$, then there exist $t+1$ internally disjoint paths $P_i(1 \leq i \leq t+1)$ between u and v such that h_t of them are of length h_t, $t - h_t$ paths are of length $h_t + 2$, and one path is of length $h_t + 6$.*

Lemma 7. *Let u, v be two distinct vertices of $EH(s,t)$ for $3 \leq s \leq t$. If $u[0] = v[0] = 1$, and $h_s(u,v) \neq 0$, then there exist $t+1$ internally disjoint paths $P_i(1 \leq i \leq t+1)$ between u and v such that $h_t + 1$ of them are of length $h_s + h_t + 2$, and $t - h_t$ paths are of length $h_s + h_t + 4$.*

Lemma 8. *Let u, v be two distinct vertices of $EH(s,t)$ for $3 \leq s \leq t$. If $u[0] \neq v[0]$ and $h_s(u,v) = h_t(u,v) = 0$, then there exist $s+1$ internally disjoint paths $P_i(1 \leq i \leq s+1)$ between u and v such that s of them are of length 7, and one path is of length 1.*

Lemma 9. *Let u, v be two distinct vertices of $EH(s,t)$ for $3 \leq s \leq t$. If $u[0] \neq v[0]$, $h_s(u,v) \neq 0$ and $h_t(u,v) = 0$, then there exist $s+1$ internally disjoint paths $P_i(1 \leq i \leq s+1)$ between u and v such that h_s of them are of length $h_s + 5$, $s - h_s$ paths are of length $h_s + 7$, and one path is of length $h_s + 1$.*

Lemma 10. *Let u, v be two distinct vertices of $EH(s,t)$ for $3 \leq s \leq t$. If $u[0] \neq v[0]$, $h_s(u,v) = 0$ and $h_t(u,v) \geq s$, then there exist $s+1$ internally disjoint paths $P_i(1 \leq i \leq s+1)$ between u and v such that s of them are of length $h_t + 5$, and one path is of length $h_t + 1$.*

Lemma 11. *Let u, v be two distinct vertices of $EH(s,t)$ for $3 \leq s \leq t$. If $u[0] \neq v[0]$, $h_s(u,v) = 0$ and $1 \leq h_t(u,v) \leq s-1$, then there exist $s+1$ internally disjoint paths $P_i(1 \leq i \leq s+1)$ between u and v such that h_t of them are of length $h_t + 5$, $s - h_t$ of them are of length $h_t + 7$, and one path is of length $h_t + 1$.*

Lemma 12. *Let u, v be two distinct vertices of $EH(s,t)$ for $3 \leq s \leq t$. If $u[0] \neq v[0]$, $h_s(u,v) = s$ and $h_t(u,v) \geq s$, then there exist $s+1$ internally disjoint paths $P_i(1 \leq i \leq s+1)$ between u and v such that s of them are of length $s + h_t + 3$, and one path is of length $s + h_t + 1$.*

Lemma 13. *Let u, v be two distinct vertices of $EH(s,t)$ for $3 \leq s \leq t$. If $u[0] \neq v[0]$, $h_s(u,v) = s$, $1 \leq h_t(u,v) \leq s-1$, then there exist $s+1$ internally disjoint paths $P_i(1 \leq i \leq s+1)$ between u and v such that $h_t + 1$ of them are of length $s + h_t + 3$, $s - h_t - 1$ of them are of length $s + h_t + 5$, and one path is of length $s + h_t + 1$.*

Lemma 14. *Let u, v be two distinct vertices of $EH(s,t)$ for $3 \leq s \leq t$. If $u[0] \neq v[0]$, $1 \leq h_s(u,v) \leq s-1$ and $h_t(u,v) \geq s$, then there exist $s+1$ internally disjoint paths $P_i(1 \leq i \leq s+1)$ between u and v such that $h_s + 2$ of them are of length $h_s + h_t + 3$ and $s - h_s - 1$ paths are of length $h_s + h_t + 5$.*

Lemma 15. *Let u, v be two distinct vertices of $EH(s,t)$ for $3 \leq s \leq t$. If $u[0] \neq v[0]$, $1 \leq h_s(u,v) \leq s-1$ and $1 \leq h_t(u,v) \leq s-1$, then there exist $s+1$ internally vertex-disjoint paths $P_i(1 \leq i \leq s+1)$ between u and v such that the following two cases are distinguished.*

1. *If $h_s + h_t \geq t+1$, then $t + s - h_s - h_t - 1$ of them are of length $h_s + h_t + 5$ and $h_s + h_t - t + 2$ paths are of length $h_s + h_t + 3$.*
2. *If $s \leq h_s + h_t \leq t$, then $s-1$ of them are of length $h_s + h_t + 5$ and two paths are of length $h_s + h_t + 3$.*
3. *If $h_s + h_t \leq s-1$, then $h_s + h_t + 1$ of them are of length $h_s + h_t + 5$, $s - h_s - h_t - 1$ of them are of length $h_s + h_t + 7$ and one path is of length $h_s + h_t + 3$.*

According to Lemmas 4 to 15, the internally disjoint paths of exchanged hypercubes can be obtained. And by Theorems 1 and 2, we obtain the wide diameter of exchanged hypercubes as Theorem 3.

Theorem 3. *The wide diameter of the exchanged hypercube* $EH(s,t)$ *is* $s+t+3$ *for* $3 \leq s \leq t$.

References

1. C. P. Chang, T. Y. Sung, L. H. Hsu, Edge congestion and topological properties of crossed cubes, *IEEE Transactions on Parallel and Distributed Systems* 11, 64-80, 2000.
2. L. H. Hsu, C. K. Lin, Graph Theory and Interconnection Networks, CRC Press, 2008.
3. S. Latifi, Combinatorial analysis of fault-diameter of the n-cube, *IEEE Transactions on Computers* 42, 27-33, 1993.
4. F. T. Leighton, Introduction to Parallel Algorithms and Architectures: Arrays · Trees · Hypercubes, Morgan Kaufmann, San Mateo, 1992.
5. P. K. K. Loh, W.J. Hsu, Y. Pan, The exchanged hypercube, *IEEE Transactions on Parallel and Distributed Systems* 16, 866-874, 2005.
6. M. Ma, The connectivity of exchanged hypercubes, *Discrete Mathematics Algorithms and Applications* 2, 213-220, 2010.
7. M. Ma, B. Liu, Cycles embedding in exchanged hypercubes, *Information Processing Letters* 110, 71-76, 2009.
8. M. Ma, L. Zhu, The super connectivity of exchanged hypercubes, *Information Processing Letters* 111, 360-364, 2011.
9. Y. Saad, M. H. Schultz, Topological properties of hypercubes, *IEEE Transactions on Computers* 37, 867-872, 1988.
10. J. M. Xu, Topological Structure and Analysis of Interconnection Networks, Kluwer Academic Publishers, Dordrecht/Boston/London, 2001.

Swarm Architecture Toward P2P VoD without Playback Suspension

Yasuaki YUJI[1] **and Satoshi FUJITA**[1]
[1]Department of Information Engineering, Hiroshima University
Higashi-Hiroshima, 739-8527, Japan

Abstract— *This paper proposes a method to reduce the playback suspension in a Video-on-Demand system based on the Peer-to-Peer technology (P2P VoD). Our main contribution is twofold. The first is the proposal of a hierarchical P2P architecture with the notion of swarms. Swarm is a group of peers to have similar playback position and those swarms are connected so that requested pieces are forwarded from a swarm to another swarm in a bucket brigade manner, where the forward of pieces is regulated by the super-peer (SP) of the swarm. The second contribution is the proposal of a match making scheme between requests and uploaders. The result of simulations indicates that the proposed scheme reduces the total waiting time of a randomized scheme by 24% and the load of the media server by 76%.*

Keywords: Peer-to-Peer, video-on-demand, playback suspension, match-making.

1. Introduction

With the widespread of broadband accesses to the Internet, video streaming has attracted many users in recent years. For example, YouTube attracted more than one trillion views in 2011 and it is forecast that the streaming will occupy 55% of the global consumer traffic by 2016 [4]. In video streaming services, the playback of a video concurrently proceeds with an acquisition of the video stream from the media server. Thus, the heavy load of the media server will easily degrade the quality of streaming services, such as the delay, jitter and the temporary suspension of the playback. With such a background, video-on-demand using peer-to-peer technology (P2P VoD, for short) has recently attracted considerable attention as a way of reducing the load of the media server [3], [5], [6], [8], [9], [11].

In P2P VoDs, each video file is divided into small fragments called **pieces** and those pieces are disseminated to the client peers over a logical network called P2P overlay. Each peer acquires pieces by repeating local communication among nearby peers in the overlay, in such a way that pieces close to the playback position is acquired earlier than others. When a piece could not be acquired by the time of playback, the playback is *suspended* until the piece is acquired. Such a suspension causes considerable stress and will significantly degrade the satisfaction of users concerned with the streaming service.

In order to avoid such a playback suspension, we need to regulate the behavior of uploaders as well as the behavior of downloaders, since a requested piece could not be acquired by the deadline if the uploader does not select the downloader as the target of upload. In addition, it would also be a crucial issue for each peer that how to become adjacent with peers to have enough pieces to be downloaded. In the literature, there are several proposals such that peers requesting pieces close to their deadline are selected as the downloader [1], [13], [14]. However, if each uploader independently conducts such a selection, we could not avoid the duplicated uploads to a specific peer, which causes the waste of the upload bandwidth of the overall network and a reduction of the upload performance.

In order to overcome such issues, in this paper, we propose a hierarchical P2P architecture with the notion of swarms. **Swarm** is a group of peers to have similar playback position. In other words, peers in a swarm "share" pieces close to their playback position. With this notion, peers in the P2P system can organize a logical structure such that *requested pieces are forwarded from a swarm to another swarm in a bucket brigade manner*. The forward of pieces is regulated by the super-peer (SP) of the swarm, so that the performance degradation due to the independent selection of downloaders could be avoided. More specifically, each SP conducts a match making between sets of requests and uploaders, in such a way that the number of requests realized by an uploader is maximized. The performance of the proposed method is evaluated by simulation. The result of simulations indicates that the proposed scheme reduces the waiting time of a randomized scheme by 24% and the load of the media server by 76%.

This paper is organized as follows. Section 2 describes the model of P2P VoD. Section 3 overviews related work. Sections 4 and 5 describe the proposed swarm architecture and the scheduling algorithm, respectively. Section 6 describes the result of simulation. Finally, Section 7 concludes the paper with future work.

2. Model

2.1 P2P Network

Let $\mathcal{P}$ be a P2P network consisting of a media server, a tracker and N homogeneous peers. Peers in $\mathcal{P}$ are directly connected with the server and are mutually connected with a logical network called P2P overlay. Peers and the server can communicate with each other by sending messages over **links** connecting them. We assume that the capacity of links and the download capacity of each peer are sufficiently large. However, as for the upload capacity, we make the following assumptions:

- The server and a peer can transmit several messages to its neighbors at a time, where each message consumes a certain amount of upload bandwidth.
- The upload capacity of the server is u_s and the upload capacity of peer p is u_p for each p.

2.2 P2P VoD

Consider a P2P VoD constructed over the P2P network described above. Let F be the content file to be delivered. F is divided into several pieces of constant size by the media server, and is delivered to all peers in $\mathcal{P}$ through the overlay. Let n be the number of pieces obtained from file F. Each piece is given a unique ID (piece ID) from 1 to n, and after receiving n distinct pieces from the neighbor, each peer can restore the original file F from them. Each piece corresponds to a part of the content file, and can be played independently. Let $\eta(p)$ be a variable representing the ID of piece currently played by peer p, which is defined only for the peers which have started the playback. In the following, we call $\eta(p)$ the **playback position** (PP) of peer p. If p did not acquire a piece and $\eta(p)$ reaches the position of the missing piece, then the playback of p is "suspended" until it acquires the missing piece. If the following, we call the time period during which the playback is suspended (after starting the playback) the **waiting time** for the playback.

In order to realize a continuous playback without suspension, each peer must acquire every missing piece before its playback time. As a concrete method to be aware of the set of pieces acquired by its neighbors, we adopt **buffer map** (BM) which is commonly used in many P2P VoDs. BM for file F is a bit array of length n, and the jth element in the array represents whether it acquired the jth piece (value 1) or not (value 0). BM is periodically exchanged among neighboring peers so that each peer can learn the set of pieces acquired by each neighbor in almost real-time.

2.3 Behavior of Each Peer

Suppose that peer p newly joins the system. The behavior of p before leaving the system is described as follows.

Preparation: At first, peer p asks the tracker to send back a list of peers in the overlay. After receiving the list, p contacts each peer q in the list to become a neighbor of q. It then generates its BM and exchanges a copy of BM with its neighbors. The BM of p is updated when it acquires a new piece, and the exchange of a copy of BM is periodically conducted until it leaves the system.

Playback: Peer p acquires the first few pieces of file F from the media server. After that, it starts the playback from piece 1. In the succeeding steps, p executes the acquisition and the playback in a concurrent manner. Pieces to be acquired are determined by the **piece selection rule**. The request for a selected piece j is sent to an adjacent peer holding the piece, where p can judge whether q holds j by referring to a copy of BM received from q. A request received from a neighbor can be forwarded to another neighbor if necessary. Suppose that p holds several pieces requested by other peers. If the number of requests exceeds u_p, then p selects u_p requests using an appropriate **peer selection algorithm**.

Departure: Each peer can leave the P2P VoD at any point in time. In general, the leave of peers can be classified into two types, i.e., leave with normal procedure and leave without normal procedure. In the following, we assume that peers can leave the system without conducting normal procedure except for specific peers such as super peers.

3. Related Work

BiToS is a P2P VoD based on the following piece selection rule [10]. Each peer divides the set of un-acquired pieces into two groups by the closeness to the PP and conducts the selection of a piece in the following two steps: 1) select a group with a certain probability, and 2) select a piece from the selected group according to the rarest first rule [2]. Although the piece selection rule adopted in BiToS is widely used as a reference in the literature [16], it is pointed out in [7] that the selection of pieces from the high priority set should be conducted in such a way that both of the rareness and the closeness to the PP are taken into account.

In [13], a way of constructing an overlay such that each peer p is adjacent with peers to have as many un-acquired pieces of p as possible. More concretely, 1) for each neighbor q, p maintains the number of pieces which are held by q but are not held by p, and 2) when this number becomes less than a threshold, p asks the tracker to recommend a candidate q' for a new neighbor such that the PP of q' is close to the PP of p. An apparent drawback of this approach is that the tracker should keep track of the PP for all peers participating in the system, whose cost significantly increases as the number of peers increases.

In [14], BitTorrent is extended so that each request carries the deadline of the request and upon receiving such requests, each peer determines the target of upload in the descending order of the criticalness of deadline. A similar idea has been proposed in [1]. In this method, the set of neighbors is dynamically divided into high priority group and low priority group, and in selecting the target of upload, it first selects a group with a certain probability and then selects requests in the descending order of the criticalness of deadline.

The way of selecting appropriate uploaders by downloaders is also considered in the literature [7], [14]. In general, a peer which receives many requests could not respond to given requests appropriately. In the method proposed in [14], each peer keeps the number of un-responded requests for each neighbor, and sends a request to a neighbor to have the least un-responded requests. Such a selection of uploaders considering the load balancing could effectively avoid the concentration of requests compared with a scheme in which the downloader sends a request to all of the relevant peers.

4. Swarm Architecture

4.1 Overview

As was described previously, in order to realize a continuous playback of a video stream, each peer p must collect pieces close to its playback position (PP) as soon as possible, where the PP of p continuously goes ahead as the playback of the stream proceeds. An efficient way to realize such a continuous piece acquisition is to contact a peer q whose PP is slightly ahead of p and to ask q to upload pieces to p. In addition, if there are several possible uploaders, those uploads should be appropriately regulated so as not to cause a duplicated upload nor the missing of urgent pieces.

In order to solve such issues, in this paper, we propose a hierarchical P2P architecture such that peers to have similar PP organize a group of peers called **swarm**. In this architecture, each peer belongs to exactly one swarm which has exactly one super peer (SP) selected from the members of the swarm. Those SPs are connected with an overlay described later, and any two peers participating in the system can communicate with each other via SPs corresponding to them. Each SP manages the information on all peers in the corresponding swarm such as the residual upload capacity and the latest BM to regulate uploads conducted by the peers. Each request (for a piece) issued by a peer is sent to the SP of the same swarm, and as will be described later, it will be forwarded to other SPs and the media server if necessary.

The overlay of SPs can be used to support VCR operations as well. In fact, since each swarm consists of peers to have similar PP, if peer p could identify an SP with a PP close to the piece requested by p through the overlay of SPs, p can quickly identify a swarm associated with it after conducting a VCR operation. Concrete way for such an identification will be described later.

4.2 Construction of Swarm

In the proposed architecture, all swarms are generated by the tracker, and are given a sequence number starting from 0. For each swarm, the first peer in the swarm is selected as the (first) SP of the swarm. More concretely, the tracker keeps two variables x and y, where x indicates the sequence number of the latest swarm and y indicates the number of normal (i.e., non-super) peers in the latest swarm, and those variables are updated as follows:

- When a new peer arrives at the system, y is incremented by one in modulo γ, where γ is a parameter indicating the intended swarm size.
- When y becomes zero, x is incremented by one and the first peer in the new swarm becomes the SP of the swarm.

The succeeding $\gamma - 1$ peers automatically become the members of the swarm, where in order to establish a connection to the corresponding SP, the tracker notifies the information about the latest SP to each peer arriving at the system.

Each peer including SP is allowed to leave the swarm at any point in time. However, if an SP p wishes to leave, it should select a successor according to the following procedure, and notify the information on the successor to the tracker and all members of the swarm before leaving:

- For each peer q, let σ_q denote the piece ID such that: 1) all pieces from PP to σ_q are acquired by q and 2) the next piece of σ_q is not acquired by q or σ_q is the last piece of the given video file. In the following, we call σ_q the **acquisition position** of q. Note that σ_q indicates the status of piece acquisition by q ahead of the PP.
- Let q^* be a peer in the swarm managed by p such that "σ_{q^*} is the most ahead among all peers in the swarm." Then, p selects q^* as the successor of p.

A reason of why we use σ_p instead of PP is to take into account the status of piece acquisition rather than the status of playback. Intuitively, we expect that the new SP acquires more pieces than any other peer in the swarm.

4.3 Overlay of SPs

SPs construct an overlay such that for each swarm X, the SP of X is connected with the SP of another swarm $pre(X)$ which acquired more pieces than X. The role of the overlay is to realize a continuous upload of pieces from $pre(X)$ to X, which is completely regulated by the SP of $pre(X)$, and to notify necessary information from $pre(X)$ to X such as the list of peers and the set of latest BMs. See Figure 1 for illustration.

A key point of our proposal is that such a "*pre*" relation is defined so that there are few X's satisfying $pre(X') = X$ for each X. Let us say that X' is a "*fol*" of X if $pre(X') = X$. Suppose that the tracker keeps the time of generating each swarm in addition to variables x and y. Then, swarm $pre(X)$ is determined by the tracker when X is generated, according to the following procedure:

- if there is a (non-empty) swarm generated earlier than X by more than τ time units, then among such swarms, select a swarm Y with the least *fol* swarms as $pre(X)$, where τ is an appropriate parameter, and
- otherwise, select the oldest swarm as $pre(X)$.

In this method, the tracker determines the predecessor of swarm X (i.e., swarm $pre(X)$) by referring to the generation time and the number of successors of the existing swarms without communicating with SPs[1]. A critical point is that a swarm Y' which is generated "just before" X may not

[1]In other words, it assumes that the time after the generation precisely reflects the status of piece acquisition. However, such an assumption does not hold in general particularly when the playback is frequently suspended. How to compensate this issue is left as a future work.

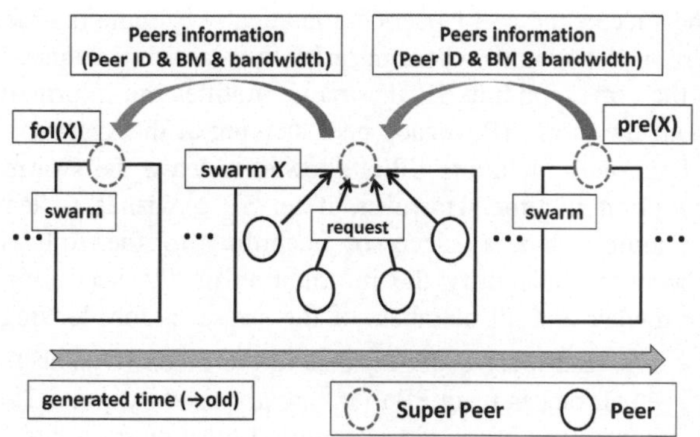

Fig. 1: Swarm architecture.

have enough pieces for X. For example, consider the case in which many peers arrive at the system almost at the same time. In such a case, swarms X and Y' have a similar status of piece acquisition. Thus, even if we construct a "pre-fol" relationship among those swarms, it is highly probable that $pre(X)$ does not have enough pieces for X, which would result in a long delay for the piece acquisition. This indicates that we should select a swarm, which stays in the system for a long time and has enough pieces for X, as the predecessor of swarm X.

In the following, we denote the set of peers in $pre(X)$ as $pre(X)$ and the set of peers in fol swarms of X as $fol(X)$.

4.4 Efficient Support of VCR Operations

This section describes how to support VCR operations in the proposed architecture. Suppose that the PP of peer p in swarm X is updated to η by conducting a VCR operation. Then, p moves to a swarm to have enough pieces ahead of η, in the following manner.

1) Starting from swarm X, p traverses predecessors as
$$pre(X), pre(pre(X)), pre(pre(pre(X))), \ldots,$$
and identifies the "first" swarm Y such that the acquisition position of the SP is ahead of η and the "last" swarm Z such that the acquisition position of the SP is behind of η. Note that Y may not exist in general.
2) Peer p moves to swarm Y if it contains a peer holding the piece with ID η and moves to Z otherwise.

If we merely consider the benefit of the moving peer p, it would be better to select the oldest swarm as the target of the move. However, as the age of the target swarm X' increases, it becomes harder for p to contribute to the other peers in $X' \cup fol(X')$ as an uploader. Thus, in the proposed method, we select a swarm to have an acquisition position sufficiently close to η (i.e. Y or Z) as the target of move.

The reader should note that since it sequentially checks swarms starting from X, in the worst case, it takes a time and communication cost proportional to the number of swarms in the system. An improvement of the method using a technique similar to DSL (Dynamic Skip List) [12] and VMesh [15] is an important open problem.

5. Assignment of Uploaders

In this section, we describe how to assign peers to the requests received from downloaders. As was described previously, each peer in swarm X can acquire pieces from peers in $X \cup pre(X)$. In the proposed scheme, it first partitions received requests into two classes, i.e., priority ones and normal ones, and conducts an assignment of uploaders for each class so as not to cause the waste of resources nor the missing of urgent pieces. The reader should recall that although each peer can simultaneously issue several requests, each uploader consumes one upload port for each request assigned to it.

5.1 Classification of Requests

In the proposed method, each peer requests pieces in the same order with the playback. However, since the acquisition of a piece generally takes a longer time than the playback in P2P environment, we assume that each peer should reserve at least α (≥ 1) pieces ahead of the playback position (PP) in its local buffer. More concretely, when the difference between the PP and the earliest lacking piece (i.e., the next of the acquisition position) is less than or equal to α, the lacking piece is directly acquired from the media server[2]. The other pieces are acquired from neighbors (as an exceptional case, it can acquire a piece from the media server if it could not meet the deadline). Requests for such pieces are classified into two types by an appropriate threshold β $(> \alpha)$, as follows:

- it is a **priority request** if the difference to the PP is smaller than or equal to β, and
- it is a **normal request**, otherwise.

5.2 Preliminaries

In the following, we assume that each request is identified by a pair of peer ID and piece ID. Let R be the set of requests received by the SP p of swarm X. The reader should note that R consists of requests issued by peers in $X \cup fol(X)$. As was described above, p is aware of the upload bandwidth and the latest BM of the peers in swarm X. The objective of the assignment algorithm is that given R and X, to calculate a matching between R and X. If such a matching is given, each peer in X can autonomously decide the target of uploads and pieces to be uploaded. More concretely, we consider the problem of maximizing the number of requests assigned to the uploader, subject to the following constraints:

- The number of requests assigned to peer p does not exceed u_p (constraint on the upload capacity).

[2]If the number of direct requests is sufficiently small, the media server can respond to all of such requests since the upload bandwidth of the media server is generally much wider than that of normal peers.

- Each request is assigned to at most one peer (avoidance of duplicated upload).
- If a peer is assigned to a normal request and it has a piece requested by a priority request, then the priority request must be assigned to some peer by the assignment (preference of priority requests).

This problem is equivalent to the problem of finding a maximum matching in bipartite graph with vertex set $R \cup X$ if we neglect the priority of requests. If the given bipartite graph has n vertices and m edges, the maximum matching problem can be solved in $\mathcal{O}(n^{1/2}m)$ time. However, in P2P VoDs considered in this paper, each SP (the scheduler) must complete an assignment of requests to the set of uploader within one second, which means that the running time of the above optimum algorithm is not satisfactory for our purpose. Hence in the proposed scheme, we will take an approach to calculate a quasi-optimal solution using heuristic method.

5.3 Algorithm

Given set R of requests and set P of peers, let us construct a bipartite graph $G = (R, P, E)$, as follows: vertices $r \in R$ and $p \in P$ are connected by edge $e \in E$, if and only if the piece requested by r is held by p. Let $d(u)$ denote the degree of vertex u in G. Then the proposed algorithm proceeds as follows:

1) Select peer $p^* \in P$ such that $d(p^*) = \max_{p \in P}\{d(p)\}$. Let $R^*(\subseteq R)$ be the set of neighbors of p^* and r^* be a request in R^* such that $d(r^*) = \min_{r \in R^*}\{d(r)\}$.
2) Add edge $\{r^*, p^*\}$ to the solution, i.e., determine that "request r^* is assigned to peer p^*."
3) Remove r^* and its all incident edges from G, and if the number of edges incident to p in the solution becomes u_p, then remove p and its all incident edges from G.
4) If E becomes empty, then terminate the algorithm. Otherwise, go to Step 1.

In the proposed scheme, we apply the above algorithm to priority requests and normal requests sequentially in this order. More concretely, we first execute the algorithm by letting R be the set of priority requests and $P := X \cup pre(X)$, and then execute the algorithm by letting R be the set of normal requests and $P := X$. The reader should note that the upload port of several peers in X are used after the first assignment, and that in the first assignment, the SP of X assigns peers in $pre(X)$ to the priority requests issued by X (a way of resolving such "conflicts" of assignments will be discussed in the next subsection). The running time of the algorithm depends on the number of vertices in graph G. More precisely, since the size of R decreases by at least one in each iteration and a minimum (or maximum) element in a set can be found in logarithmic time by implementing it using heap, the running time of the algorithm is bounded as $\mathcal{O}(|R|(\log|P| + \log|R|))$. In our swarm architecture, the number of peers in each swarm is bounded by γ on average, and the number of requests issued by the peers in a swarm can be bounded by a constant. Thus, each SP can generate a quasi-optimal solution in a short computation time.

5.4 Conflict Resolution

In the proposed scheme, such an assignment is executed by all SPs in parallel. Hence each peer in swarm X will be regarded as an uploader by several SPs, i.e., the SP of swarm X and SPs of its *fol* swarms. The conflict of assignments conducted by those SPs is resolved by the following rule:

1) Assignment of priority requests conducted by the SP of X is given the highest priority.
2) Assignment of priority requests conducted by the SP of *fol* swarms is given the second highest priority.
3) Assignment of normal requests conducted by the SP of X is given the lowest priority.

In other words, each SP tries to use resources in its own swarm X as much as possible, and resources in $pre(X)$ can be used by the peers in X only when there remains a room in $pre(X)$ after the first assignment. The reader should recall again that if there remain unassigned (urgent) requests, they are forwarded to the media server to meet the deadline, as long as the server has enough residual upload capacity.

6. Simulation

6.1 Preliminaries

We conducted simulation to evaluate the performance of the proposed scheme. In the following, we assume that all peers are synchronized to the global clock, and the time for sending requests and conducting assignments are negligible. 200 $(= N)$ peers sequentially arrive at the system according to the Poisson distribution with mean 12 sec. A new peer starts its playback after collecting the first 3 pieces and leaves the system after completing the playback of the last piece. No peer conducts VCR operation. The media server is the last resort to acquire pieces by the deadline, although if the server receives more than u_s requests, it selects u_s requests in the descending order of the piece ID.

We compare the performance of the proposed scheme with the following randomized scheme. Peer p in swarm X requests δ $(\geq \beta)$ pieces ahead of the PP $\eta(p)$ to peers in the same swarm X, where if the requested piece is within distance β from $\eta(p)$, the request is also sent to swarm $pre(X)$. Peer q receiving requests selects at most u_q requests *independently and randomly*, and uploads them to the corresponding peers. The reader should note that in the simulation, we do not use a deterministic scheme in which the target of upload is selected by the priority of requests, since it easily causes a duplicated upload and a missing of low priority pieces. Those two schemes are evaluated with respect to the following metrics.

- Startup time $W_s(p)$ and waiting time $W(p)$ of peer p, where $W(p)$ includes $W_s(p)$. Let $W_{all} \stackrel{\text{def}}{=} \sum_{i=1}^{N} W(i)$.

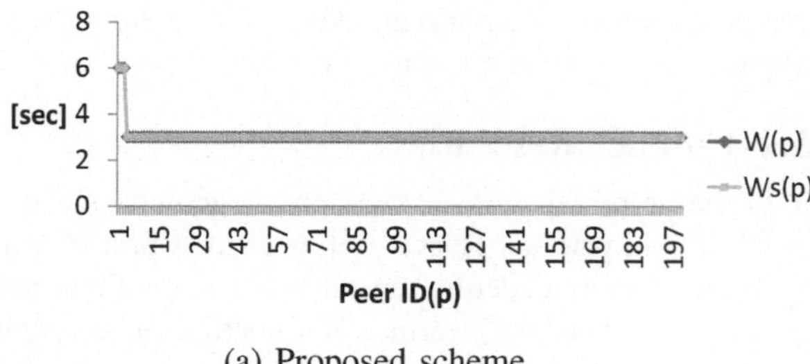

(a) Proposed scheme.

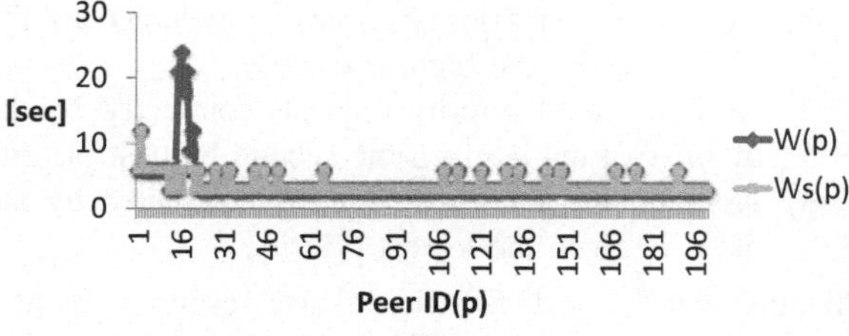

(b) Randomized scheme.

Fig. 2: Waiting time of each peer (u_s = 20).

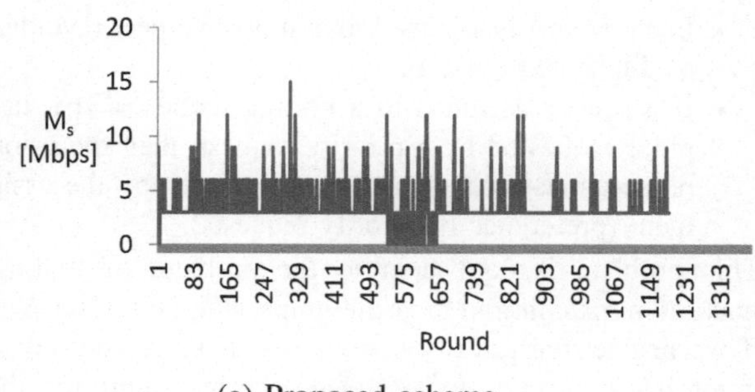

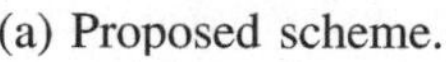

(a) Proposed scheme.

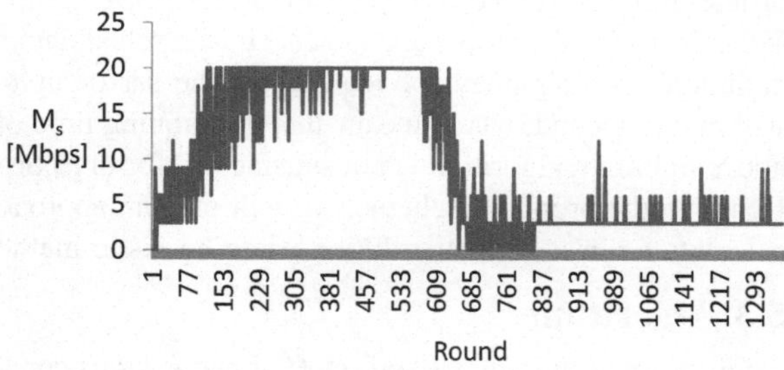

(b) Previous scheme.

Fig. 3: Upload rate M_s of the media server.

- The amount M_s of uploaded data per second and the total number of pieces U_p uploaded by the server.

Parameters are fixed as follows. We consider a video file of length 1600 sec with playback bit rate of 512 Kbps, which is divided into 534 pieces of size 192 KB each. Hence the playback of a piece takes 3 sec. The upload capacity of the server is 20 Mbps and the upload capacity of each peer is 3 Mbps. In other words, the server (resp. a peer) can upload at most 13 (resp. 2) pieces during the playback of a piece. Two thresholds used in the proposed scheme are fixed as $\alpha = 1$ and $\beta = 3$, and the threshold used in the randomized scheme is fixed as $\delta = 4$. That is, one piece ahead of the PP is acquired from the server, two pieces are acquired using priority request, and additional one piece is acquired by the randomized scheme. The size of each swarm is fixed to $\gamma = 20$ and parameter τ is fixed to 10 sec.

6.2 Waiting Time

The average waiting time of the proposed and the randomized schemes are 3.05 sec and 3.95 sec, respectively, i.e., it attains a reduction of 24%. Figure 2 illustrates the value of W and W_s for each peer. In the proposed scheme, the waiting time equals to the startup time (i.e., 3 sec) except for the first three peers, i.e., they do not encounter the playback suspension after starting the playback. This is best possible for our setting, since it needs at least 3 sec to acquire a piece, where the acquisition from the server might take longer time if the server becomes busy. In other words, the above result indicates that the server has enough residual capacity so that new peers can certainly acquire pieces from the server.

On the other hand, in the randomized scheme, the frequent playback suspension occurs in early steps of the simulation. Those peers are members of the first swarm. They should acquire pieces from the media server because they have no enough predecessors, but since the server should (continuously) upload the first few pieces to newly joined peers, the inefficiency of the randomized scheme increases the waiting time as the number of participants increases. In addition to peers in the first swarm, several peers encounter a long startup time of more than 3 sec, which indicates that the load of the server keeps high during the simulation.

6.3 Server Stress

Playback suspension occurs if a piece is not acquired from the media server by the deadline. Since newly arrived peers rely on the download from the media server, when M_s is low and there remains enough capacity at the media server, we could simultaneously reduce the frequency of playback suspension and the startup time of each peer.

Figure 3 illustrates the temporal transition of M_s. The horizontal axis is the number of rounds (one round corresponds to 3 sec in our simulation). In the proposed scheme, M_s is bounded by 15 Mbps and a peak occurs only when the server simultaneously uploads to a peer with the most ahead PP and newly joined peers. On the other hand, in the randomized scheme, many peers continuously rely on the server and after the 130th round, M_s frequently reaches the upload capacity 20 Mbps. The number of pieces U_p actually uploaded from the media server is 2577 in the proposed scheme and 8618 in the randomized scheme, which indicates that the proposed scheme reduces the load of the server by 76%.

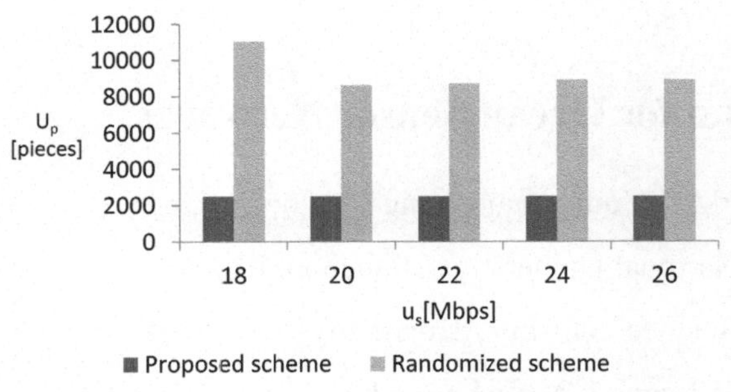

Fig. 4: Impact of u_s to the number of uploaded pieces.

6.4 Impact of Upload Bandwidth of Server

Finally, we evaluate the impact of the upload capacity to the performance of the schemes by varying it from 26 to 18 Mbps. The average waiting time of the proposed scheme is around 3.05 sec regardless of the value of u_s. However, in the randomized scheme, while it attains 3.05 sec when u_s is 26 Mbps, it significantly degrades as u_s decreases. In fact, although the difference to the proposed scheme is kept small until 20 Mbps, it rapidly increases to more than 45 sec for 18 Mbps, which is apparently because a "chain of playback suspension" violates the continuous flow of pieces from predecessors to the successors.

Similar phenomena could be observed for the number of uploaded pieces U_p. Figure 4 illustrates the result. Although U_p is stable regardless of the value of u_s in the proposed scheme, in the randomized scheme, it slightly increases by decreasing u_s from 26 to 20 Mbps and significantly increases by further decreasing it to 18 Mbps, which is because of the increase of the number of requests forwarded to the server. By the above results, we can conclude that the superiority of the proposed scheme becomes significant particularly when the upload bandwidth of the media server is not large, i.e., it would be a good choice for the designers who wish to realize a P2P VoD with low construction cost.

7. Concluding Remarks

This paper proposes a hierarchical P2P architecture with the notion of swarms for P2P VoDs without playback suspension. The result of simulations indicates that the proposed scheme reduces the total waiting time of a randomized scheme by 24% and the load of the media server by 76%. A future work is to evaluate the performance of the proposed scheme in an environment in which several peers conduct VCR operation such as pause, jump and fast forward.

References

[1] O. Abboud, K. Pussep, M. Mueller, A. Kovacevic and R. Steinmetz. "Advanced Prefetching and Upload Strategies for P2P Video-on-Demand," in *Proc. ACM Workshop on Advanced Video Streaming Techniques for Peer-to-Peer Networks and Social Networking*, 2010, pages 31–36.

[2] BitTorrent. http://www.bittorrent.co.jp/

[3] N. Carlsson, D. L. Eager and A. Mahanti. "Peer-Assisted On-Demand Video Streaming with Selfish Peers," in *Proc. the 8th Int'l IFIP-TC 6 Networking Conf.*, 2009, pages 586–599.

[4] Cisco. Cisco Visual Networking Index: Forecast and Methodology, 2011-2016, May. 2012.

[5] C. Dana, D. Li, D. Harrison, C.-N. Chuah. "BASS: BitTorrent Assisted Streaming System for Video-on-Demand," in *Proc. the Int'l Workshop on Multimedia Signal Processing*, 2005, pages 1–4.

[6] Y. Huang, T. Z. J. Fu, D.-M. Chiu, J. C. S. Lui and C. Huang. "Challenges, Design and Analysis of a Large-Scale P2P-VoD System," in *Proc. ACM Conf. on Data Communication (SIGCOMM)*, 2008, pages 375–388.

[7] S. Sakashita, T. Yoshihisa, T. Hara and S. Nishio. "A Data Reception Method to Reduce Interruption Time in P2P Streaming Environments," in *Proc. the 13th Int'l Conf. on Network-Based Information Systems*, 2010. pages 166–172.

[8] R. Uedera and S. Fujita. "Adaptive Prefetching Scheme for Peer-To-Peer Video-On-Demand Systems with a Media Server," *IEICE Trans. on Information and Systems*, E94-D(12): 2362–2369, December 2011.

[9] R. Uedera and S. Fujita. "Complementary Piece-Based Buffer Map for P2p Vods Supporting VCR Operations," In *Proc. Seventh International Conference on P2P, Parallel, Grid, Cloud and Internet Computing (3PGCIC-2012)*, 2012, pages 25–32.

[10] A. Vlavianos, M. Iliofotou and M. Faloutsos. "BiToS: Enhancing BitTorrent for supporting streaming applications," in *Proc. IEEE INFOCOM 2006*, 2006, pages 1–6.

[11] N. Vratonjic, P. Gupta, N. Knezevic, D. Kostic and A. Rowstron. "Enabling DVD-like Features in P2P Video-on-Demand Systems," in *Proc. Workshop on Peer-to-Peer Streaming and IP-TV*, 2007, pages 329–334.

[12] D. Wang and J.-C. Liu. "A dynamic skip list-based over-lay for on-demand media streaming with VCR interactions, " *IEEE Trans. Parallel and Distributed Systems*, 19(5): 503–514, 2008.

[13] X.-Y. Yang, M. Gjoka, P. Chhabra, A. Markopoulou and Pablo Rodriguez. "Kangaroo: Video Seeking in P2P Systems," in *Proc. the 8th Int'l Conf. on Peer-to-Peer Systems (IPTPS'09)*, 2009, pages 6.

[14] Y. Yang, A. L. H. Chow, L. Golubchik and D. Bragg. "Improving QoS in BitTorrent-like VoD Systems," in *Proc. IEEE INFOCOM 2010*, 2010, pages 2061–2069.

[15] W. P. K. Yiu, X. Jin and S. H. G. Chan. "VMesh: Distributed segment storage for peer-to-peer interactive video streaming, " *IEEE J. Sel. Areas Commun.*, 25(9): 1717–1731, 2007.

[16] Y.-P. Zhou, D.-M. Chiu and J. C. S. Lui. "A Simple Model for Analyzing P2P Streaming Protocols," in *Proc. ICNP 2007*, 2006, pages 226–235.

MCM Based Cluster Algorism for Ocean Sensor Networks

Hwanghyuk Lee*, Sang-Eon Park**, Young-Jun Chung*

* Computer Science Department, Kangwon National University, Chunchon, Korea

** Department of Mathematics and Computer Science, Salisbury University, MD, USA

{yhhyuk, ychung}@kangwon.ac.kr, sxpark@salisbury.edu

Abstract

OSN runs at the worst operating environments. OSN requires more reliable and more stable operating conditions to extend the network lifetime compared to other WSN. In this paper, we propose a MCM based clustering algorithm for OSN. As properly managing the number of cluster member nodes, our proposed algorithm increases the lifetime of network nodes, enhances the network efficiency, and predicts the network performance and reliability. In addition, NS-2 simulation results show that our algorithm has the better performance compared to LEACH and extends the network lifetime.

Keywords: OSN, WSN, MCM, clustering algorithm, network reliability

1. Introduction

Recent advances in wireless sensor network technology have made it possible to develop many real-time sensor networks for monitoring a marine ecosystem. The network consists of various sensor nodes, which are able to measure light, sound, motion, wind velocity, surface reflection, and salt concentration. Collected raw data acquired from these nodes can be used for ocean weather forecast enhancement and marine ecosystem understanding.

An ocean sensor network (OSN) is an ad hoc wireless networks deployed in a wide area with tiny, low-powered smart sensor nodes to monitor a marine phenomenon. A node gathers sensing data and sends it to a sink node, which aggregates the data sent from these nodes [1]. The aggregate data is then sent to a user for further data processing.

The operating conditions of OSN such as ocean surface reflection and the ocean weather is worse than any other WSN. OSN should be designed with more stable and more reliable requirements than any other WSN. In addition, OSN is once deployed and operated until the sensor battery died without node maintenance and battery recharging. The routing algorithm of OSN should be an energy-efficient routing algorithm to maintain a long network lifetime.

The clustering routing algorithm is appropriate to require a hierarchical communication structure such as OSN. One of a noble clustering algorithm is LEACH (Low Energy Adaptive Clustering Hierarchy). LEACH requires high communication overheads on cluster heads. The drawback causes to reduce the network lifetime and to make a network partitioning problem due to the unbalanced battery-consumption of nodes.

In this paper, we propose a MCM(Maximum Cluster Members) based Clustering algorithm for OSN. This algorithm aims to reduce communication loads of cluster heads, to extend the network lifetime with maintaining balanced node battery consumption, and eventually enhance the network reliability.

Section 2 describes the operating environment of OSN and LEACH as a noble cluster routing protocols and then identifies problems. Section 3 presents detailed designs of our algorithm such as basic concept, cluster composition, cluster factors (BS, cluster heads, cluster members) and network reliability. In Section 4, we will discuss the results of our simulation with comparison to LEACH and finish with our final conclusions.

2. Related Studies

2.1 Ocean Sensor Network (OSN)

The ocean sensor network (OSN) has many design considerations compared to the typical wireless sensor network (WSN). The ocean has the worst operational conditions for wireless sensor network. The reflection rate of the sea surface is bigger. The ocean weather and the wind speed changes rapidly. The probability that sensor nodes are lost is larger. Also the deployment and maintenance of OSN is difficult. In addition, as the delay time and the error rate are high, OSN requires more stable, reliable, and energy-efficient network to maintain a long lifetime [1]. The cluster structure is known to be suitable in OSN [2].

In a cluster based OSN, sensor nodes are partitioned into many clusters, which integrates data collected from sensor nodes and transmits them to the sink node of the network. A cluster has a cluster head which collects data from sensor nodes within its group. The head completes data aggregation, and sends it to the sink node of the network. Such data aggregation can reduce the consumption of node energy and the transmission delay as compared to the multi-hop routing protocol. Many clustering algorithms have been proposed. One of novel algorithm is LEACH (Low Energy Adaptive Clustering Hierarchy).

2.2 LEACH

LEACH [3][4][5] is a cluster routing protocol in which a cluster head collects data from sensor nodes belonging to the cluster and sends the data to the sink node after data aggregation. To make all sensor nodes in this network consume their node energy equally and extend the life time of the network, this algorithm randomly changes the cluster head, which in turn uses more energy than any other node belong to the cluster, every time period. To reduce overall communication costs, the cluster head performs data aggregation and then send the data to the sink node.

The cluster head is determined by the following function (1):

$$T(n) = \begin{cases} \dfrac{P_t}{1 - P_t \cdot (r \cdot \bmod \dfrac{1}{P_t})}, & if\ n \in G \\ 0, & otherwise \end{cases} \quad (1)$$

where P_t is the desired percentage of cluster heads, r is the current round number, G is the set of nodes that have not been cluster-heads in the last $1/P_t$ rounds.

A round consists of two phases; a set-up phase and a steady state phase. The former is a stage for configuration of a cluster head and a cluster, and the latter is a stage for data transfer by the TDMA schedule.

When a new round starts, each sensor node generates a random number in the range of 0 and 1, computes a threshold value by using equation (1), and compares the two numbers. If the generated number is smaller than the threshold value, the node is nominated as a cluster head; otherwise it neglects the number and remains a plain node.

The nominated cluster head broadcasts advertisement messages over neighbor nodes. The neighbor node that receives the advertisement messages selects one of broadcasting nodes that transmits the strongest broadcasting signal as its head cluster node, and sends a "Join-REQ" message to the head cluster. After receiving the "Join- REQ" message, the head cluster registers the node onto its own member node table. The cluster head makes a TDMA schedule for data transfer within the cluster network and broadcasts the schedule to its member nodes. It is at this point that the setup phase to select a cluster head is complete.

In the next steady state phase, each node in a cluster network sends information data to its cluster head by the TDMA schedule. The cluster head sends the aggregated data to the sink node, called its base station. To reduce the overhead of the cluster head selection once a cluster head has been selected, many rounds of data frame transfer are performed followed by a repeat of the cluster reconfiguration procedure.

Since LEACH uses probability in selection of cluster heads, its advantage is that all nodes have a chance of becoming a cluster head. Since LEACH periodically performs the set-up phase, it spends much battery power on cluster configuration. Also since LEACH does not have any restriction of the cluster size, the heads of a big cluster that has many member nodes spend more power and are exhausted earlier than the others.

3. MCM Clustering Algorithm

Due to LEACH's drawbacks such as unbalanced node power consumption, we have introduced a MCM clustering algorithm that extends the network lifecycle and enhances the efficiency of sensor's energy consumption. The algorithm can assign the maximum number of cluster nodes during clustering composition and reduce communication overhead of cluster heads and data processing loads. In addition, this scheme provides a metric to determine the reliability of communication between base nodes and sensor nodes.

3.1 Basic Concept

The ocean sensor node has a limited battery power. It is impractical to repair the node and to recharge the node battery. It is necessary efficiently to manage node battery-power consumption in order to extend the lifetime of the sensor network. If possible, we need to keep battery-power consumption of nodes balanced and minimize dead nodes. In our proposed algorithm, we make a formation of clusters, each of which has a cluster head and consists of a limited number of nodes. The cluster head aggregates node data in its own cluster and forwards data to the base station (BS). We can reduce the power consumption caused by communication overheads between BS and nodes.

The bigger the size of a cluster is, the larger the number of member nodes is. As a result, communication burden of cluster heads is increased and causes to shorten their lifetime.

In the next section, we show an operation procedure and cluster configuration of our proposed algorithm to reduce unbalanced power consumption of nodes. We define the maximum number of member nodes in a cluster as MCM. First, sensor nodes begin to make a clustering formation with MCM. Failed nodes during the clustering formation retry to perform new cluster configuration. Repeat these processes. Since a cluster has a limited number of nodes, we prevent the cluster head from excessive consumption of its batter power for communication and data aggregation with node members. The criterion of cluster configuration which makes the cluster size consistent enhances the reliability of collected data and the validation of ocean sensor networks.

3.2 Cluster Composition

The nodes received MSG_h reply a cluster-join message MSG_j to a cluster head candidate. When the preliminary cluster heads receive reply messages MSG_j, they build a table for their cluster member information and send a confirmation message $MSG_{confirm}$ to the cluster member node.

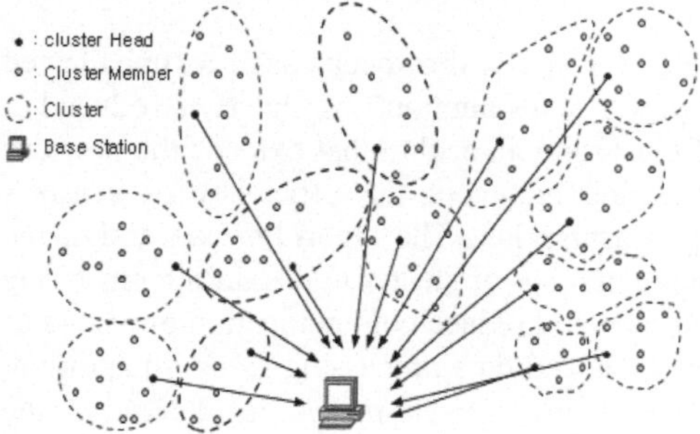

Figure 1. Overview of MCM Cluster network (MCM =10).

When sensor nodes receive $MSG_{confirm}$, the nodes finish the cluster configuration. However, sensor nodes that do not receive $MSG_{confirm}$, they, as a new cluster head candidate, try to flood a cluster head candidate message MSG_h again until the requirement for cluster configuration is satisfied. A operation flow chart for cluster configuration is shown in Figure 2.

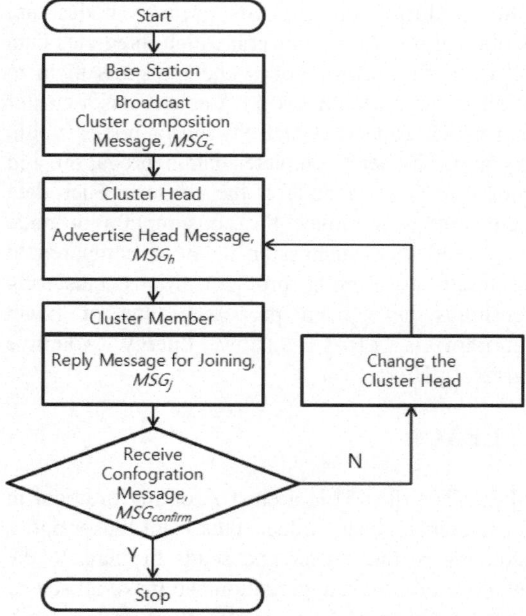

Figure 2. Flowchart of MCM cluster configuration.

3.2.1 Base Station (BS)

BS is a central data collection device that aggregates Information data received from all sensor nodes. BS commands all sensor nodes including cluster heads and manages the network operation procedures, and also sends collected data to the central data management center for further processing. BS transmits a clustering starting command MSG_c for cluster configuration. MSG_c is flooded over all nodes and some cluster heads are elected. The cluster configuration message, MSG_h, as shown in Figure 5, includes BS Identification (BID), Message types, and the maximum Cluster Members as MCM_c that indicates the maximum number of node a cluster. MCM_c can limit the number of node in a cluster and protect the cluster head from early node death due to battery power exhaustion.

3.2.2 Cluster Head (CH)

As a cluster configuration command is broadcasted from BS, a cluster head election process starts. A cluster head candidate advertises a cluster management message (MSG_h) and builds a cluster node management table with reply messages (MSG_j) of cluster node members. The table, as shown in Figure 3, includes Member ID, the cumulative renewal of cluster members, message type, and remaining batter energy information. The cluster head send the replied nodes a confirmation message that finalizes the cluster formation. The confirmation message includes a ordered list of member nodes in terms of residual battery energy and the number of cluster members.

Cumulative renewal	Member ID	Message Type	Remaining energy of members
2	#1	Detection data	###
1	#8	Composit on reply	###
…	…	…	…

Figure 3. A table for management of cluster nodes.

In our algorithm, a cluster head is elected among nodes with much battery power and when the residual energy reaches a threshold value, another cluster head election process starts in order to choose a node with more residual batter energy as a cluster head. The change of the cluster head is informed to BS. The cluster head utilizes a cumulative renewal count *($Count_{cr}$)* to determine whether the node succeeds in joining a cluster or not. If $Count_{cr}$ is less than 30% of MCM, the cluster head regards a sensor node as a failed node and excludes the node from a cluster member list.

3.2.3 Cluster Member

The cluster member (*CM*) uses two types of messages. When *CM* receives an advertise message MSG_h from a cluster head candidate, CM send a reply message for cluster joining. And CM becomes a cluster member after receiving a confirmation message, $MSG_{confirm}$, from the cluster head. CM sends the cluster head both its remaining battery information data and explored information data. Also CM has a memory buffer to store configuration messages and advertise messages for cluster formation. When CM does not get $MSG_{confirm}$ even after sending MSG_j, CM sends another cluster-join message, MSG_j', to the next cluster head candidate from an ordered list of cluster head candidates. Otherwise, CM can advertise a cluster head candidate message MSG_h to operate as a preliminary cluster head.

3.2.4 Cluster Reconfiguration for Reliable Operation

The sensor node is have a lifetime for operation due to limited battery power. Also they get in inoperable status due to other failures and bad environments. To recover such fault situations, an alarm message is used for network system reconfiguration, as shown in Figure 4. The alarm message is issued when CMs and CHs report a fault conditions to BS in order to keep on performing network functions properly. Based upon reported alarm messages, BS recognize that some of nodes are malfunctioning or performing in inoperable conditions. In that case, BS issues a cluster reconfiguration message for reliable operation. Also BS estimate numbers of operable nodes and failed nodes by counting the accumulated alarm messages. Based on the number of available and operable nodes, the validation of the ocean sensor network is determined.

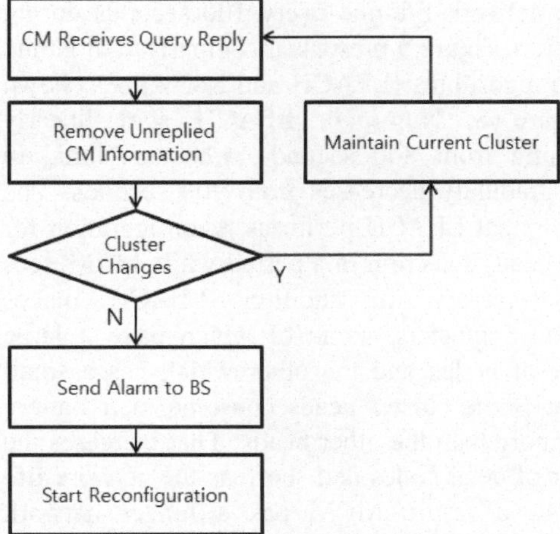

Figure 4. Flowchart of MCM cluster Reconfiguration.

4. Performance Evaluation

For performance evaluation of proposed MCM and LEACH, a simulation is performed using NS-2[6]. We use the same simulation parameters in LEACH for performance comparison and assign the maximum number of members, MCM_c, to implement our MCM algorithm. The simulation analyses the number of living nodes over time in respect with network lifetime and node energy efficiency. The validation of the ocean sensor network is evaluated based upon the number of survival nodes and the alarm message count of nodes.

4.1. Simulation Environment

Table 1. Simulation parameters.

Parameters	Values
Network Size	100 m X 100 m
The number of nodes	100
MCM(Maximum of Cluster Members)	10
Threshold for alarm occurence	Less than 5
Initial energy of a node	2J
Data Packet Size	512 bytes

Energy consumption	600 mW
Simulation Time	1300 sec

In this simulation, our experiment model consists of 100 nodes that were randomly distributed in a 100×100 square meter area. A hundred of nodes are randomly deployed. The simulation parameters are used as shown in table 1.

4.2. Network Lifetime

We observed the number of living nodes Num_{ln} for the network lifetime every 100 seconds during simulation. Figure 5 presents a comparison of Num_{ln} for two algorithms (LEACH and MCM). As shown in Figure 8, Num_{ln} in LEACH start linearly decreasing from 800 seconds, whereas Num_{ln} in MCM gradually decreases from 900 seconds. The reason is that LEACH performs reconfiguration for cluster heads selection in a period while MCM does when necessary. In addition, LEACH makes unbalanced clusters, some of which have a large number of nodes and the other which has a small number. Some cluster heads consume their battery power more than the other heads. That increases the number of dead nodes and shortens the network life time. As a result, MCM has a longer network lifetime than LEACH

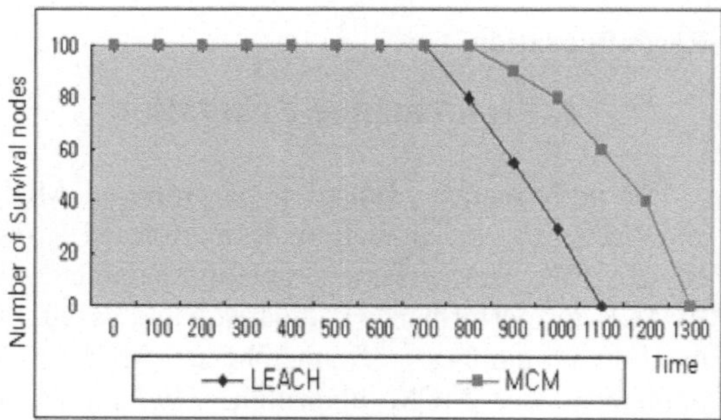

Figure 5. Comparison of Num_{ln} for LEACH and MCM.

4.3. Network Reliability

Figure 6 shows a comparison of the survival rate of nodes and the accumulate renewal rate of alarms for MCM. In MCM, the cluster head sends BS an alarm message when the size of a cluster is less than 30% of MCM. As the cumulative renewal count, $Count_{cr}$ increases, the number of survival nodes decreases. In other word, the survival rate of nodes can be estimated with $Count_{cr}$. The survival rate can be used as a metric for evaluation of network reliability and availability.

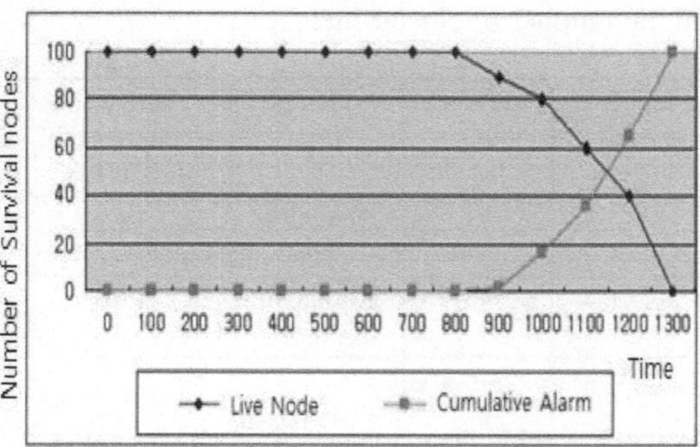

Figure 6. Comparison of the survival rate of nodes and the accumulate renewal rate of alarms for MCM.

5. Conclusions

In this work, we proposed a MCM based clustering algorithm for OSN. The algorithm restricts the number of cluster nodes with MCM. Also this algorithm avoids building such clusters that the number of cluster nodes is less than the threshold. The restriction reduces the unnecessary battery-power consumption of cluster heads and eliminates unstable clusters that cause excessive communication overheads. Our algorithm maintains that the battery-power consumption of nodes is balanced. The balanced power consumption makes the lifetime of nodes longer and eventually extends the network life time. Also since the number of survival nodes is countable, the network reliability can be predictable. Our simulation shows that our algorithm has a better performance than LEACH in terms of the network lifetime and the battery power consumption. Consequently, it is our belief that our proposed algorithm can effectively extend the network lifetime without other critical communication overheads and performance degradation.

Acknowledgement

This study has been supported by Kangwon Information and Telecommunication Institutes, Kangwon National University, Korea and Salisbury University, MD., USA.

References

[1] Sang-Keun Kim, Yi-Sok , "Comparison of Moment Method/Monte-Carlo Simulation and PO for Bistatic Coherent Reflectivity of Sea Surfaces," KIEES, Jan, 2006.

[2] Ulsang-Kim, Hyounsoo-Kim, Joongnam-Jeon, “A Routing-Tree Construction Algorithm for Energy Efficiency in Wireless Sensor Network”, Korea Information processing Society, DEC, 2009

[3] H.Jeong, J.O.Lee, J.Y.Lee, N.S.Park, G.J.Jim, B.s.Kim, “Technical Trends of Sensor Networking”, ETRI, Jun. 2007.

[4] W. Heinzelman, A. Chandrakasan and H. Balakrishnan. "Energy-Efficient Communication Protocol for Wireless Micro sensor Networks," Hawaii Conference on System Sciences, Jan, 2000..

[5] Q. Jiang and D. Manivannan, “Routing Protocols for Sensor Networks,” IEEE Consumer Communications and Networking Conference, Jan, 2004.

[6] Information Sciences Institute, "The Network Simulator ns-2" http://www.isi.edu/nanam/ns/, University of Southern California.

A Point-Based Incentive Scheme for P2P Reputation Management Systems

Takuya NISHIKAWA[1] **and Satoshi FUJITA**[1]
[1]Department of Information Engineering, Hiroshima University
Higashi-Hiroshima, 739-8527, Japan

Abstract— *This paper proposes an incentive scheme for P2P resource management systems which encourages the users to evaluate the "trustworthiness of evaluations" given by the other users. More concretely, in the proposed scheme, each user earns a reward from other users by evaluating their evaluations, and a user which acquires a large number of evaluations will be granted a right to access high quality services. To this end, we introduce the notion of evaluation points which mediates the "evaluation of services" and the "evaluation of evaluations." The performance of the proposed incentive scheme is evaluated by simulation. The simulation results indicate that: 1) the proposed scheme certainly encourages the users to conduct an evaluation of evaluations, 2) it encourages users to provide high quality evaluations of the services, and 3) a rational strategy for the users is to repeat evaluation of evaluations after conducting a certain number of evaluations of services.*

Keywords: Peer-to-Peer resource management, reputation, incentive scheme.

1. Introduction

In recent years, Peer-to-Peer systems (P2Ps) have attracted considerable attention in the field of distributed computing and network applications. A P2P consists of a large number of autonomous computers called **peers** which can play the role of a client and a service provider at the same time. P2Ps have many advantages such as the fault-tolerance and the high scalability compared with traditional client/server systems, so that they are used in many network applications such as file sharing, live streaming, and IP phone. However, due to the anonymity of participants and the openness of the underlying network, P2Ps involve several critical issues such as the lack of authenticity and the low reliability of transactions which should be conducted with anonymous clients and/or service providers.

To overcome such a weakness of P2Ps, the use of trust management systems has also attracted attention in recent years. So far, many types of trust management systems have been proposed in the literature [17], [2], [15], [6], [7]. The main objective of the trust management in P2Ps is to make assessments and decisions regarding the dependability of potential transactions, and to allow users and the system managers to increase and correctly represent the reliability of themselves and their systems [5]. It is also commonly recognized that a key challenge in designing a trust management system in P2P environment is how to overcome the lack of central authorities to conduct assessments and necessary decisions (i.e., each user must make a decision about the trust of other users on her own responsibility while she could refer to the decision of other users collected to a central server), and how to overcome the lack of prior information concerned with other participants, since they are distributed systems consisting of many anonymous users.

In general trust management systems, the "reputation" of customers is commonly used as the source of information concerned with the trustfulness of service providers. In fact, online auction systems such as eBay[1] and customer review services in shopping sites such as Amazon[2], try to increase their reliability by allowing customers to make an assessment of their past counterparty or of their product reviews, and by disclosing the result of such assessments to all users. Even in the P2P environments, the outcome of assessments on past transactions could be effectively used to identify (and sometimes to exclude) malicious users who involve potential risks, such as the upload of inauthentic files, a long delay of transactions and a sudden cancellation of ongoing transactions.

A critical issue in the reputation-based trust management in P2Ps with no central authorities, is that *the reputation given by a malicious user may not be reliable.* Although it would be possible to omit "all" reputations given by suspected users, we cannot identify a sufficient number of reliable users under such a pessimistic approach if the number of unsuspected users is not large. We need to carefully take into account the reputation given by every user (including suspected ones) to identify as large number of reliable users as possible. Another critical issue in actual reputation management systems is that it tends to lack the number of evaluations provided by the participants. For example, in KaZaA file sharing system, only 1% of shared files are evaluated by the users [8]. Too small number of evaluations would degrade the accuracy of the resultant reputation, even if we could effectively eliminate less reliable evaluations by using a scheme proposed in [11], for example.

[1]eBay: http://www.ebay.com/
[2]Amazon.com: http://www.amazon.com/

In this paper, we propose an incentive scheme which encourages the users to evaluate the trustworthiness of evaluations given by the other users. More concretely, in the proposed scheme, each user earns a reward from other users by evaluating the evaluation given by them, and a user which acquired a large number of evaluations will be granted a right to access high quality services. To this end, we introduce a formal model of the evaluation cost as well as the definition of evaluation point which mediates the "evaluation of services" and the "evaluation of evaluations." The performance of the proposed incentive scheme is evaluated by simulation. The simulation results indicate that: 1) the proposed scheme certainly encourages the participants to conduct an evaluation of evaluations, 2) it encourages to provide high quality evaluations of the services, and 3) a rational strategy for the participants is to repeat evaluation of evaluations after conducting a certain number of evaluations of services.

The remainder of this paper is organized as follows. Section 2 overviews related works. Section 3 describes a model of P2P reputation systems. Section 4 describes an incentive scheme proposed in this paper. Section 5 shows the simulation results. Finally, Section 6 concludes the paper with future works.

2. Related Work

How to give an incentive to the users to evaluate received services has been a main concern in realizing practical P2P reputation systems. Miura and Kawaura [10] focused on a knowledge-sharing community called Yahoo!Chiebukuro[3] and analyzed the motivation of users to provide answers to given queries using a questionnaire survey. In the analysis, they classified the motivation of users into four types, i.e., 1) assistance motivation, 2) reciprocal motivation, 3) social motivation and 4) reward motivation, where each type respectively means: 1) the tendency of helping a questioner, 2) repaying a kindness in the past and expecting future benefits, 3) social meaning of answering behavior and 4) rewards acquired by answering.

Different from knowledge-sharing communities, in P2P reputation systems, the assistance motivation and the reciprocal motivation do not work well, since the target of assistance is not clear in P2Ps and it has a strong anonymity in nature. In fact, existing incentive mechanisms designed for P2Ps promote the reward motivation to encourage peers to reciprocally cooperate. For example, in eMule [4], a higher priority is given to a downloader if it shares a large number of files with the other peers, and BitTorrent [1] adopts the Tit-for-Tat strategy in such a way that a peer which uploaded chunks to another peer will be granted a right to download chunks from that peer.

[3] Yahoo!Chiebukuro: http://chiebukuro.yahoo.co.jp

In this paper, we will focus on the reward motivation similar to existing works. However, unlike conventional schemes which use the provisioning of resources such as an upload bandwidth and shared files as a concrete contribution, in our scheme, we will use the "evaluation of evaluations" as the source of contributions. This enables the participants to make a contribution to the system much easier than conventional schemes which are merely based on the resource provisionings. Note that the notion of evaluation of evaluations has already been proposed in the literature in a slightly different context [13]. The main difference to our scheme is that in the previous scheme, the evaluation of evaluations called feedback reputation is linked with the evaluation of services so that the feedback reputation concerned with a service is automatically notified to all peers which evaluated the service in the past, when (and only when) a peer makes the evaluation of the service. In contrast, in our scheme, we explicitly separate the evaluation of evaluations and the evaluation of service so as to increase the chance of contributing to the system as an evaluator.

3. Model

3.1 Model of P2P

In this paper, we consider a model of P2P consisting of a tracker and a set of peers. The set of peers might contain a malicious peer, but it must follow the protocol described below (more concretely, the only parameter controlled by a malicious peer is services and evaluations). The set of peers is divided into two subsets, i.e., a set of Service Providers (SPs) and a set of Client Peers (CPs), where the intersection of those subsets is not empty in general. Each CP can receive a service from an SP, whereas each SP can provide several services to CPs. The tracker issues (virtual) points to CPs in reward for an evaluation. Such a behavior of the tracker is realized either by using a server as in hybrid P2Ps or by using a secure authentication chain proposed in the literature [3].

The quality of a service is *evaluated* by CPs by describing a survey report, where the evaluator of a service must be a recipient of the service. In the following, we call such an evaluation of services a **qualification**. Each qualification is associated with a real number in $[0, 1]$ called qualification value, where value 1 indicates that the quality of the service is absolutely high and value 0 indicates that the quality of the service is absolutely low. We use symbol $Q_{p,s}$ to denote the value of a qualification of service s evaluated by CP p.

In addition to the qualification of services, in our model, each CP can evaluate qualifications given by other CPs by designating a real number in $[0, 1]$, where similar to the case of qualifications, the evaluator of a qualification must be a recipient of the corresponding service. In the following, we call such an evaluation of qualifications a **vote**. In a vote, value 1 indicates that the evaluator completely agrees with the qualification. We use symbol $V^s_{p,q}$ to denote the value associated with a vote which is given by CP p on a qualification of service s conducted by CP q.

The reader should note that in the above framework, the target of evaluation is either a service or a qualification, and it does not directly measure up the SP who provided the service nor the CP who provided a qualification. This reflects a natural insight such that a good player might not always exhibit a good performance.

3.2 Model of Evaluation

Next, we describe the model of evaluation conducted by each node. The parameter controlled by each evaluator is the cost of evaluation as well as its opinion on the target, and the resulting quality of evaluations is determined by the cost and several parameters while we assume that the evaluator is not aware of those parameters. Let c_s be a local variable representing the cost of qualification. Before conducting a qualification, each CP sets a value in range $[c_{\min}, c_{\max}]$ to its local variable c_s, which indicates that "how much effort will be necessary to complete the qualification." The quality of qualification monotonically increases as c_s increases, and increases in proportion to the **skill** of the evaluator represented by a real number in range $(0, 1]$ (the skill of evaluator is not disclosed to any CP including the evaluator itself). More precisely, we assume that the quality of qualification is defined as follows:

$$\Psi(c_s, \sigma) := \left(\frac{c_s}{c_{\max}}\right)^k \times \sigma \quad (1)$$

where σ denotes the skill of the evaluator and k is an appropriate parameter greater than one. The reader should note that Ψ is a convex function with respect to c_s, which is intended to model a situation in which less effort leads to much worse quality. In addition, the reader should remind that the quality of qualification is independent of the qualification value $Q_{p,s}$ given by the evaluator.

Let c_r denote the cost of voting. In the following, we assume that c_r takes a fixed value smaller than or equal to $c_{\min}$. This definition reflects an intuition such that a vote simply judges whether a given qualification is useful and match its own opinion concerned with the corresponding service. More specifically, the value of $V^s_{p,q}$ is determined by the evaluation of the qualification value $Q_{p,s}$ and the evaluation of the quality of qualification given by Equation (1). A detailed model of such evaluations used in simulations is given in the Appendix. The key idea behind the model is that each user in the real world cannot be completely objective in providing a vote, since her vote on a qualification should be biased by the closeness of the qualification to her opinion.

A list of parameters used in our model is summarized in Table 1.

Table 1: Parameters used in the model of evaluations (the last three parameters are used in Appendix).

Parameter	Meaning
$Q_{p,s} \in [0, 1]$	Qualification of service s evaluated by CP p
$V^s_{p,q} \in [0, 1]$	Vote given by CP p on a qualification of service s conducted by CP q
$c_s \in [c_{\min}, c_{\max}]$	Cost of qualification
$c_r\ (\leq c_{\min})$	Cost of voting
$\sigma \in (0, 1]$	Skill of evaluator in providing a qualification
$k > 1$	Parameter used in function Ψ
t^*_p	Credibility of evaluator p
$E^s_{p,q}$	Second part of vote given by p on a qualification of service s conducted by q
$\hat{Q}_{p,s}$	Qualification on service s given by p if it *was* conducted by p.

4. Proposed Scheme

4.1 Incentive Scheme

A collection of qualifications "approximates" the actual quality of the corresponding services. However, it might contain malicious qualifications which intentionally provide wrong values to illegally control the "reputation" of the corresponding services. Although the impact of such malicious qualifications could be reduced by increasing the number of collected qualifications, it is difficult to collect many qualifications since the cost of qualification is generally large. In order to overcome such a problem, our model adopted the notion of voting. In other words, if we collected a sufficient number of votes for each qualification, we could evaluate the trustworthiness of qualifications and accurately evaluate the quality of services without increasing the number of qualifications.

In this paper, we propose a point-based scheme to encourage voting and qualification. The proposed incentive scheme, which is based on the notion of **evaluation point** and **contribution point**, is described as follows (see Figure 1 for illustration):

- By conducting a qualification, the CP receives P_s evaluation points from the tracker, and
- When CP p votes for a qualification given by CP q, 1) p receives P_r evaluation points from q and 2) q receives P_c contribution points from the tracker, where
  - if the evaluation points possessed by q are less than P_r, then any CP can not vote for the qualifications given by q,
  - P_r is fixed to satisfy inequality $P_r \leq \left(\frac{c_r}{c_{\max}}\right) \times P_s$ in order to encourage qualification rather than voting, and
  - P_c equals to $V^s_{p,q} \in [0, 1]$, i.e., as the value associated with the vote increases, the contribution point received from the tracker increases.

4.2 Service Differentiation

Service differentiation is a common technique used in many incentive schemes. In the proposed scheme, we realize

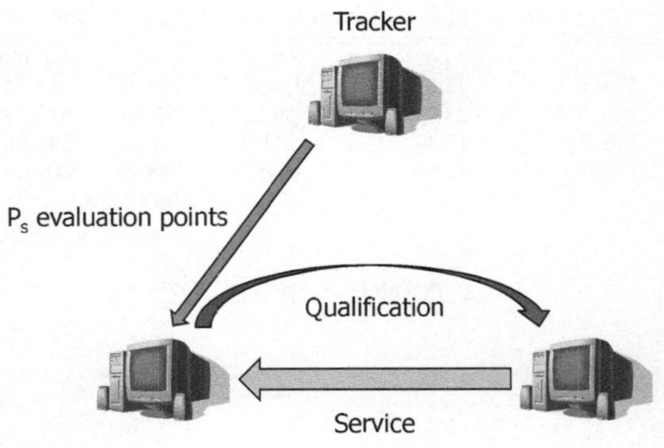

(a) Qualification.

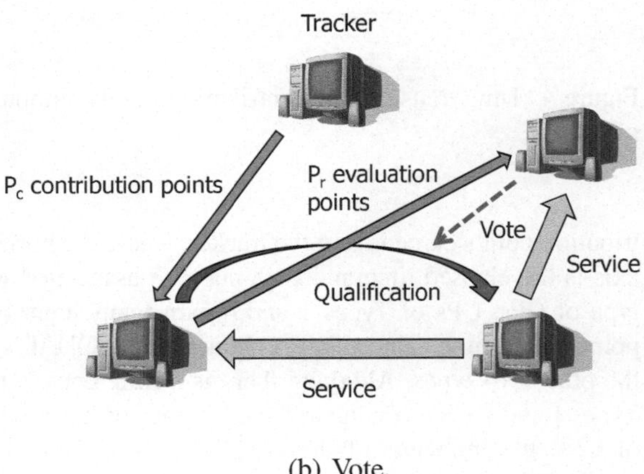

(b) Vote.

Figure 1: Flow of points in the proposed scheme.

a service differentiation using contribution points. More precisely, by paying contribution point to an SP, the CP is granted to receive a high quality service from the SP. Since it can receive contribution points from the tracker equivalent to the value associated to the acquired votes, it works as an incentive to give a high quality qualification which attracts many votes with a high evaluation value. In addition, the notion of evaluation points works as another incentive to give a vote for existing qualifications, although it is not directly connected to the service differentiation. In fact, in order to acquire many votes from evaluators, it must have enough evaluation points which can be earned only through: 1) the issue of a qualification on a service, or 2) a vote for a qualification given by another CP.

4.3 Lifetime of Evaluation Points

In the above point-based scheme, evaluation points can be infinitely provided to the system by the tracker. Thus, to avoid an "inflation" of the evaluation points which reduces the relative value of the evaluation points, we introduce the

Table 2: The probability of selecting each action.

When $P < 30$.

	QUAL	VOTE	NONE
Type1	80%	10%	10%
Type2	10%	80%	10%
Type3	10%	10%	80%
Type4	80%	10%	10%

When $P \geq 30$.

	QUAL	VOTE	NONE
Type1	40%	10%	50%
Type2	10%	80%	10%
Type3	10%	10%	80%
Type4	40%	10%	50%

notion of lifetime to the evaluation points, so that a point is expired from the system if the lifetime of the point becomes zero. The lifetime is set to L at the time of provisioning by the tracker and is linearly decreased as the elapsed time increases, while it is "reset" to L when it is transferred to another CP as a reward of voting. The notion of lifetime has an important side effect such that CPs should continuously conduct evaluations to keep a sufficient amount of evaluation points. Such an effect of lifetime will be evaluated by simulation in the next section.

5. Simulation

5.1 Setup

We conducted simulations to evaluate the performance of the proposed scheme. In the simulation, we consider a P2P consisting of a single SP and several CPs, where the number of services provided by the SP is fixed to 150. The reader should note that the SP models a collection of independent SPs, i.e., we do not consider a situation in which several SPs simultaneously provide services to a CP in a collaborative manner. The simulation time is divided into 500 intervals called **time steps**, and in each time step, each CP conducts one of the following three actions:

- QUAL : Randomly select a service and receive it. After that, conduct a qualification of the service by spending a cost selected from $[c_{\min}, c_{\max}] := [1, 5]$.
- VOTE : Randomly select a qualification of a service which has been received by the CP, and vote for it.
- NONE: Randomly select a service and receive it, but no qualification is conducted.

With respect to the way of contribution to the system, we assume that CPs are classified into the following four types: A CP is said to be of Type 1 (resp. 2 and 3), if it prefers to action QUAL (resp. VOTE and NONE) and the credibility of the CP is high (i.e., 0.9), where the credibility of each service is randomly selected from range $[0, 1]$ and a model of evaluations which takes into account the credibility of evaluations is given in the Appendix. A CP is said to be of Type 4 if it prefers to action QUAL but the credibility of the CP is low (i.e., 0.0). More detailed specification of the setting

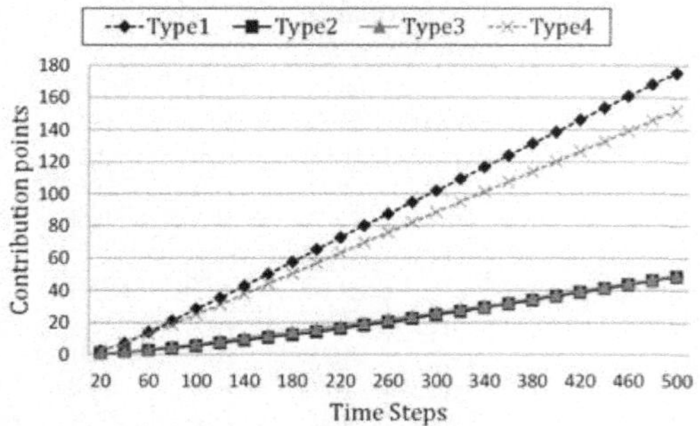

Figure 2: Time transition of contribution points earned by each CP.

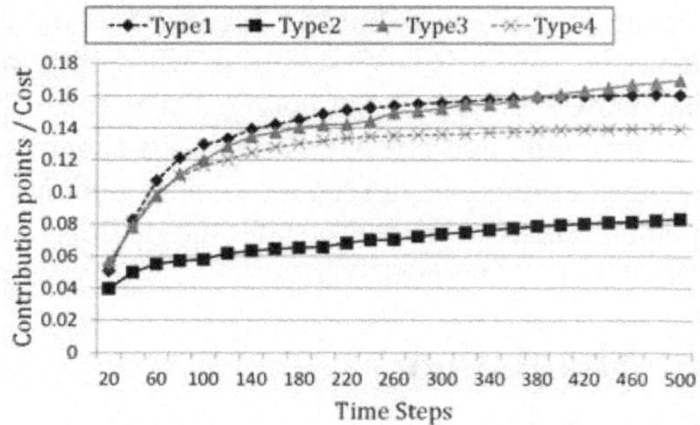

Figure 3: Time transition of contribution points per cost.

used in the simulations is summarized in Table 2. As shown in the table, we assume that the behavior of a CP depends on the evaluation points P possessed by the CP. Namely, if P is smaller than a threshold, which is fixed to 30 in the simulation, it follows probabilities shown in the left table and otherwise, it follows probabilities shown in the right table. It should be noted that the probability of choosing action QUAL by a CP of Type 1 or 4 becomes small if it possesses enough evaluation points. This reflects a natural intuition such that the incentive to conduct qualifications should become weak if it possesses enough evaluation points.

Under the above settings, we simulated the behavior of CPs and observed earned contribution points and the cost required for the evaluations. The other common parameters are fixed as follows: 1) the number of CPs is 30 for each type, 2) the amount of evaluation points earned through evaluations are $P_s = 5$ and $P_r = 1$, and 3) the lifetime of each evaluation point is 20 time steps.

5.2 Comparison by Types

At first, we evaluate the behavior of CPs by their types. Parameters used in Equation (1) are fixed as $c_s = 5$, $\sigma = 1.0$, and $k = 2.0$.

Figure 2 illustrates the time transition of the average contribution points earned from the tracker, where the horizontal axis is the elapsed time and each curve is associated with a type of CPs. CPs of Types 1 and 4 earn many contribution points over time, since they conduct more QUAL's than the other two types. Although there is a difference between Types 1 and 4 which is due to the difference of the credibility of CPs, the influence of the credibility is limited. Such a trend slightly changes if we consider the evaluation cost. Figure 3 illustrates the time transition of contribution points per cost. While CPs of Type 3 earn only few contribution points, the contribution point per cost gradually approaches to Type 1 and eventually overtakes it. Such a high efficiency of Type 3 is due to the expiration of the evaluation points. See Table 3. This table summarizes that: 1) how many points are earned (the second column), 2) how many points are paid as a reward (the third column), 3) how many points are expired (the fourth column), and 4) how many points are possessed on average (the first column). Although CPs of Type 3 earn a small amount of evaluation points, the ratio of expired points to the earned points is 78% which is smaller than 87% of Type 2. Thus, although the number of qualifications is small and they are rarely chosen as the target for a vote in an early stage of the simulation, as the number of (accumulated) qualifications increases, the low probability of selecting QUAL improves the efficiency of Type 3 with respect to the earned contribution points per cost.

The reader might think that CPs of Type 2 are "useless" since they exhibit the worst performance with respect to both of the above two metrics, but it is not true. They actually play a crucial role in the proposed scheme. Figure 4 shows the result of simulation without CPs of Type 2. The amount of contribution points earned by the CPs (of

Table 3: The stats about evaluation points

	Average possession	Receive	Pay	Expired
Type1	43.13	1045.47	189.20	813.14
Type2	24.73	593.87	55.40	513.73
Type3	12.44	311.93	56.43	243.06
Type4	42.60	1038.50	188.90	807.00

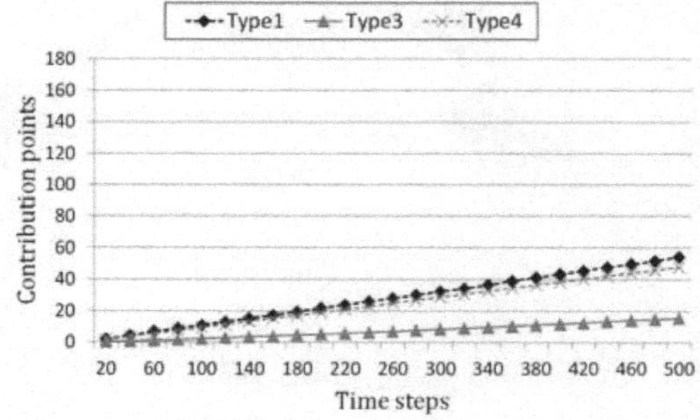

Figure 4: Time transition of contribution points without CPs of Type 2.

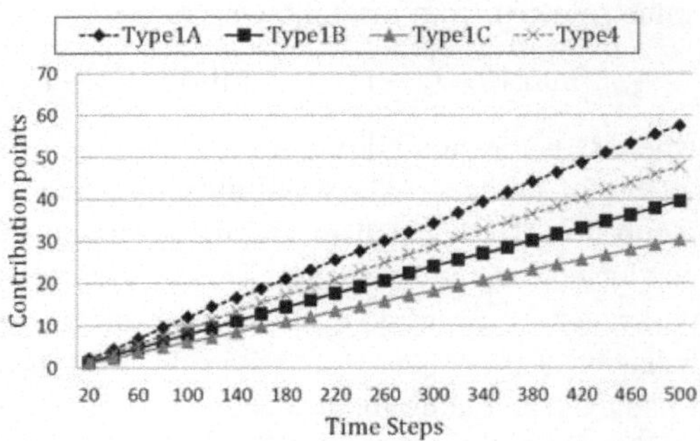

Figure 5: Impact of qualification cost c_s to the contribution points.

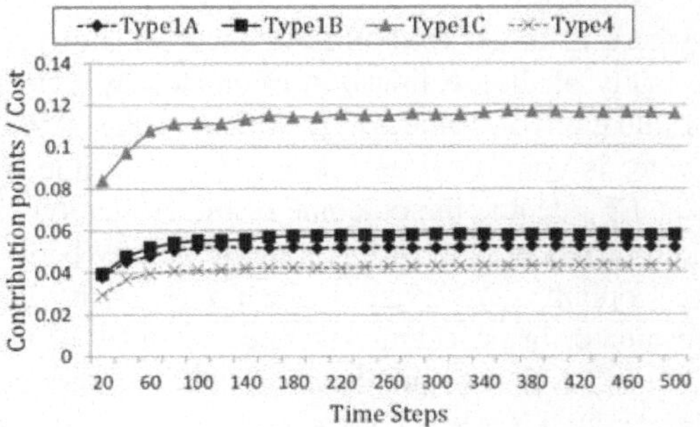

Figure 6: Impact of qualification cost c_s to the contribution points per cost.

Types 1, 3 and 4) significantly decreases compared with Figure 2, which indicates that under the proposed scheme, VOTE is necessary for all CPs to earn a sufficient amount of contribution points.

By the above observations, we can conclude that a rational strategy for CPs to quickly, efficiently earn contribution points is *to repeat voting to keep the amount of evaluation points after conducting a certain number of qualifications.* In practical situations, however, such a simple strategy is not enough since older qualification becomes less attractive to earn many votes with a high evaluation value. Thus, CPs should repeat such a strategy with an appropriate interval.

5.3 Impact of Qualification Cost

In the second simulation, we evaluated the impact of qualification cost c_s to the contribution points, by considering a P2P consisting of a single SP and CPs of Types 1 and 4. Parameters are fixed as in the first simulation except for the qualification cost of CPs of Type 1. More specifically, we partition Type 1 into three Types such that a CP is said to be of Type 1A (resp. 1B and 1C) if it sets c_s to 5 (resp. 3 and 1). We prepare 30 CPs for each of the above four types.

Figure 5 illustrates the time transition of contribution points earned by the CPs. The amount of contribution points monotonically increases as c_s increases, since we are assuming that the quality of qualifications is a monotonic function of c_s in Equation (1). In addition, CPs of Type 4 earn more contribution points than Types 1B and 1C, which indicates that the amount of contribution points is more sensitive to the spent qualification cost rather than the credibility of evaluators. This encourages CPs to provide high quality qualifications by spending more cost.

Figure 6 illustrates the time transition of the contribution points per cost. We can see that CPs of Type 1C earn contribution points much more efficiently than the other three types. The badness of Types 1A and 1B compared with Type 1C could be explained as follows. The first reason is that in the simulation, qualifications to be evaluated are randomly selected without considering the quality of qualifications. In other words, the increase of c_s does not always increase the chance to be evaluated. The second reason is that the amount of earned contribution points was a concave function of the qualification cost. In other words, although CPs of Type 1A spent qualification cost which is five times as large as the qualification cost spent by Type 1C, the amount of earned contribution points is only the twice of Type 1C. To overcome such an inefficiency for CPs which try to provide high quality qualifications, we should introduce another mechanism so that the earned contribution point increases according to a concave function of the acquired vote values. This important and interesting matter is left as a future work.

6. Concluding Remarks

In this paper, we propose an incentive scheme for P2P reputation management systems focusing on the cost of evaluations. The proposed scheme is based on the notion of evaluation points which mediates between the evaluation of services and the evaluation of evaluations, and the notion of contribution points which is used for the service differentiation. The performance of the scheme is experimentally evaluated by simulation.

The topics for future work are listed as follows:

1) We need to evaluate the effectiveness of the proposed scheme under a more practical setting. The application of the scheme to existing reputation management systems would be a perspective way to do so.
2) We need to carefully examine the influence of the anonymity to the incentive scheme, since in actual reputation systems, the opinion of a big name strongly affects the reputation given by other normal users.
3) We need to evaluate the robustness of the scheme against malicious attacks, and try to increase the robustness without incurring additional cost to the users.

References

[1] BitTorrent `http://www.bittorrent.com/`

[2] F. Cornelli, E. Damiani, S. D. C. Vimercati, S. Paraboschi and P. Samarati. "Choosing Reputable Servents in a P2P Network." In *Proc, of the 11th International World Wide Web Conference*, pp. 207–216, 2002.

[3] P. Dewan and P. Dasgupta. "P2P Reputation Management Using Distributed Identities and Decentralized Recommendation Chains." *IEEE Transactions on Knowledge and Data Engineering*, 22(7):1000-1013, July 2010.

[4] eMule-Project.net `http://www.emule-project.net/`

[5] W. M. Grudzewski, I. K. Hejduk, A. Sankowska and M. Watuchowicz. "Trust Management in Virtual Work Environments: A Human Factors Perspective." *CRC Press Taylor & Francis Group*, p. 38, 2008.

[6] Y. Ito and H. Kawano. "Evaluation of P2P Contents Distribution System with Cryptographic Trust Chains." *DBSJ Letters*, 6(1): 21–24, 2007.

[7] S. D. Kamvar, M. T. Schlosser and H. Garcia-Molina. "The EigenTrust algorithm for reputation management in P2P networks." In *Proc. of the 12th International Conference on World Wide Web*, pp. 640–651, 2003.

[8] J. Liang, R. Kumar, Y. Xi and K. W. Ross. "Pollution in P2P File Sharing Systems." In *Proc. IEEE INFOCOM*, Vol. 2, pp. 1174–1185, 2005.

[9] P. Maymounkov and D. Mazières. "Kademlia: a peer-to-peer information system based on the XOR metric." In *Proc. of International Workshop on Peer-to-Peer Systems*, pp. 53–65, 2002.

[10] A. Miura and Y. Kawaura. "Why do people join Web-based knowledge-sharing communities?: Analysis on questioning and answering behaviors." *Japanese Journal of Social Psychology*, 23(3): 233–245, 2008.

[11] T. Nishikawa and S. Fujita. "A Reputation Management Scheme in Peer-To-Peer Networks Using the EigenTrust Algorithm." *Journal of Information Processing*, 20(3), 2012 (online)

[12] S. Ratnasamy, P. Francis, M. Handley, R. Karp and S. Shenker. "A scalable content-addressable network." In *Proc. of ACM SIGCOMM*, pp. 161–172, 2001.

[13] G. Swamynathan, B. Y. Zhao, K. C. Almeroth, and H. Zheng. "Globally Decoupled Reputations for Large Distributed Networks," *Advances in Multimedia*, Hindawi Publishing Corporation, Volume 2007, Article ID 92485, 14 pages, 2007.

[14] I. Stoica, R. Morris, D. Liben-Nowell, D. Karger, M. F. Kaashoek, F. Dabek and H. Balakrishnan. "Chord: a scalable peer-to-peer lookup service for internet applications. In *Proc. of ACM SIGCOMM*, pp. 149–160, 2001.

[15] L. Xiong and L. Liu. "PeerTrust: Supporting Reputation-Based Trust for Peer-to-Peer Electronic Communities." *IEEE Trans. on Knowledge and Data Engineering*, 16(7): 843–857, 2004.

[16] N. Yoshikai. "Study on Reputation Systems for Trusty Information Network." *IPSJ SIG Technical Reports*, 108(160): 89–96, 2008.

[17] R. Zhou and K. Hwang. "PowerTrust: a robust and scalable reputation system for trusted peer-to-peer computing." *IEEE Trans. on Parallel and Distributed Systems*, 18(4): 460–473, 2007.

Appendix

Each qualification given by CP p is associated with a real number $Q_{p,s}$ representing the quality of the corresponding service s, where the criterion for determining the value of $Q_{p,s}$ depends on applications. For example, in the case of video streaming, the criteria would include download speed, interruption of playback, picture quality and others. In addition, since it is purely subjective, it differs for each evaluator, and of course, it is generally different from the actual (i.e., objective) quality of the corresponding service. To model such a variance of qualification value $Q_{p,s}$, we use the RBA model recently proposed by Nishikawa and Fujita [11]. More concretely, we assume that $Q_{p,s}$ is a random value selected from the following range:

$$\left[\max\{0, Q_s + t_p^* - 1\}, \min\{1, Q_s - t_p^* + 1\}\right]$$

where t_p^* is the credibility of evaluator p and Q_s is the actual quality of service s. The **credibility** of an evaluator is a real number in $[0, 1]$ which means the accuracy of evaluations conducted by the evaluator. The reader should note that parameter t_p^* is introduced only for the modeling of the behavior of the evaluator and the value of t_p^* is not disclosed to any CP including the evaluator.

The evaluation of the quality of qualifications, which is the first part of a vote, is conducted in a similar way. More concretely, we assume that it is a random value selected from the following range:

$$\left[\max\{0, \Psi + t_p^* - 1\}, \min\{1, \Psi - t_p^* + 1\}\right],$$

where t_p^* is the credibility of the evaluator p and Ψ is the quality of the qualification calculated by Equation (1). The evaluation of value $Q_{q,s}$, which is the second part of a vote, is conducted as follows. Let p be the evaluator and let $E_{p,q}^s$ denote the outcome of the evaluation. The key idea of our model is to focus on the proximity between $Q_{q,s}$ and p's opinion on service s. Such a proximity is used by the evaluator in providing a vote consciously or unconsciously. Let $\hat{Q}_{p,s}$ be the qualification value on service s *which is given by p if it was conducted by p*. Then, the value of $E_{p,q}^s$ is calculated as follows:

$$E_{p,q}^s := 1 - \left|Q_{q,s} - \hat{Q}_{p,s}\right|.$$

Finally, the value $V_{p,q}^s$ associated to a vote for qualification $Q_{q,s}$ is calculated by taking an average of the above two values.

Decycling hierarchical cubic networks

Antoine Bossard
Faculty of Information Systems Architecture
Advanced Institute of Industrial Technology, Tokyo Metropolitan University
Shinagawa-ku Higashiooi 1-10-40, Tokyo 140-0011, Japan

Abstract—*A hierarchical cubic network (HCN) is a topology based on hypercubes which has been introduced as interconnection network for massively parallel systems. Benefiting from interesting properties, it supersedes classic hypercubes networks on several aspects. For example, while retaining a similar diameter, the number of links per node is significantly lower than that of a hypercube of the same size. Finding a node set of minimum size such that removing these nodes from the network also eliminates all the cycles in the network is known as the decycling problem. Solving this problem is critical as it has many important applications, such as preventing resource allocation issues like deadlocks and starvations. In this paper, we describe an efficient algorithm generating in an n-dimensional HCN a decycling set of at most $2^{2n-1} - (2^{2n-2}/n + \lfloor 2^{n-1}/n \rfloor)$ nodes.*

Keywords: algorithm, parallel processing, interconnection network, feedback vertex set, HCN

1. Introduction

Modern massively parallel systems contain hundreds of thousands of computing nodes. For instance, the Fujitsu K computer, ranked no. 1 in the TOP500 list of world's supercomputers as of November 2011, includes 705,024 CPUs [1]. Considering this huge number of nodes, interconnection networks are a critical component of such systems in order to efficiently connect CPUs and thus retain high performance. Such networks have to deal with physical limitations of today's hardware. For example, there is a restriction on the number of links per node. Hence, for a network topology to be suitable as interconnection network, it must enable the connection of a large number of nodes while at the same time keeping the number of links per node low. The network diameter (i.e. density) is also a critical topological property to ensure efficient communication.

So as to address these issues, several topologies have been introduced in the literature; we can cite dual-cubes [2] and pancake graphs [3] as examples. In this paper, we focus on hierarchical cubic networks (HCN) [4]. An HCN has a two-level hierarchical structure: nodes are grouped into clusters, which are in turn connected each other. Clusters are hypercubes. So, an HCN can benefit from the hypercube topology properties inside clusters, such as a short diameter, and can also connect many nodes while retaining a low degree and a short diameter compared to a hypercube of the same size. Precisely, an n-dimensional HCN can connect 2^{2n} nodes with a degree of $n+1$, whereas a hypercube of the same size has a degree of $2n$.

Aiming at retaining performance high, several routing algorithms in an HCN have been described: optimal shortest-path routing [5], node-to-node and node-to-set disjoint-path routing [6], [7] are some examples. Closely related, we focus in this paper on the decycling problem in an HCN. This problem is about finding a node set of minimum size such that excluding these nodes from the network removes the presence of any cycle; we say that the network is acyclic. This is an important problem which has a broad range of applications, from combinatorial circuit design to artificial intelligence, and, critical for distributed computing, lock-free resource allocation, meaning that notorious resource allocations problems such as deadlocks, livelocks and starvations are guaranteed never to occur [8].

This famous problem has been largely studied. Karp showed that finding a decycling set of minimum size for an arbitrary graph is NP-complete [9]. On the other hand, there exist polynomial solutions for several graph categories, such as 3-regular graphs [10], convex bipartite graphs [11] and permutation graphs [12]. We propose in this paper an efficient algorithm finding in an n-dimensional HCN a decycling set of size at most $2^{2n-1} - (2^{2n-2}/n + \lfloor 2^{n-1}/n \rfloor)$.

2. Preliminaries

In this section we introduce notations and definitions used hereinafter. We start by defining a hypercube and an HCN.

An n-dimensional hypercube, denoted by Q_n, is made of 2^n nodes, each having a unique n-bit address. Two nodes a and b of a Q_n are adjacent if and only if their Hamming distance $H(a, b)$ is equal to 1.

An n-dimensional HCN, denoted by $HCN(n)$, is made of 2^{2n} nodes, each having a unique $2n$-bit address. Nodes are grouped into clusters, each isomorphic to a Q_n; there are 2^n such clusters. So, the first n bits of a node address identify the cluster containing the node, it is the *clusterID*. The remaining n bits of a node address distinguish nodes inside a same cluster, it is the *nodeID*. Thus a node a can be written as a pair of two n-bit sequences, say $a = (u, v)$, and the cluster of a is denoted by $Q_n(u)$. Two nodes $a = (u, v)$ and $b = (w, z)$ of an $HCN(n)$ are adjacent if and only if they satisfy one of the three following conditions:

1) $u = w$ and $H(v, z) = 1$
2) $u = z$ and $v = w$
3) $u = v$ and $w = z = \bar{u}$

where $\bar{u}$ is the complement (binary negation) of any bit sequence u. We give a different name to these three edge categories. Condition 1 induces *internal edges*, that is edges inducing clusters. Conditions 2 and 3 induce *external edges*. More precisely, we say that Condition 2 induces external edges of *type 1*, whereas Condition 3 induces external edges of *type 2*. An example is given in Figure 1. Thus, an $HCN(n)$ has a degree of $n+1$ and $2^{2n-1}(n+1)$ edges.

A cluster with a clusterID of even parity (resp. odd parity) is simply referred to as even cluster (resp. odd cluster). Similarly, a node with a nodeID of even parity (resp. odd parity) is simply referred to as even node (resp. odd node).

In a graph G, for a node $a \in G$, let $N(a)$ denote the set of the nodes of G that are adjacent to a, and let $d(a) = |N(a)|$ denote the degree of a. An edge between two nodes a, b is similarly denoted by $a \to b$ or $b \to a$.

The algorithm presented in this paper will *remove* and *revive* nodes of an HCN. Removing a node a from a graph G means that the graph $G \setminus \{a\}$ is considered, where naturally all edges incident with a are discarded. Reviving a node a happens only when a had been previously removed. It means that the

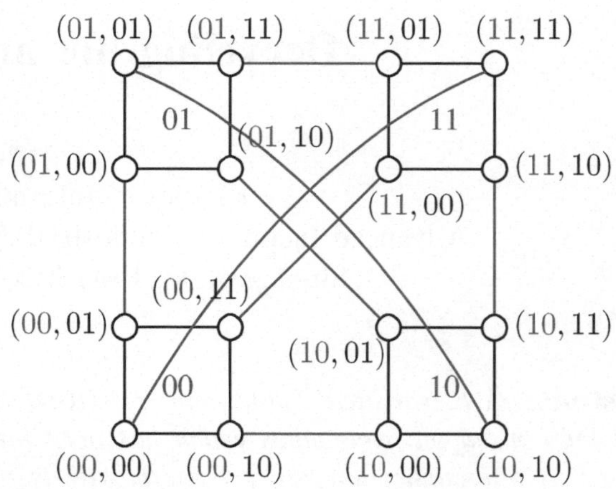

Fig. 1: A 2-dimensional HCN, $HCN(2)$. External edges of type 1 and type 2 are coloured in blue and green, respectively. ClusterIDs are also represented.

graph $(G \setminus \{a\}) \cup \{a\} = G$ is considered. Importantly, reviving a also revives the edges incident with a in the original graph G.

Regarding the size of a decycling set, Beineke and Vandell established in [13] a lower bound as detailed in the following theorem.

Theorem 1: [13] In a graph $G = (V, E)$ of maximum degree Δ, any decycling set S satisfies

$$|S| \geq \left\lceil \frac{|E| - |V| + 1}{\Delta - 1} \right\rceil$$

Lastly, the decycling problem in a hypercube has been extensively researched [13], [14], [15]. As of today, the best upper bound on the size of a decycling set for a hypercube has been established by Pike [16]. It is recalled in the following theorem.

Theorem 2: [16] In an n-dimensional hypercube, a decycling set S of minimum size satisfies

$$|S| \leq 2^{n-1} - \frac{2^{n-1}}{n}$$

In other words, in a Q_n, a decycling set of minimum size contains at most $2^{n-1} - 2^{n-1}/n$ nodes.

3. Decycling algorithm

We propose in this section an efficient algorithm producing a decycling set S of competitively small size for an $HCN(n)$. An $HCN(1)$ is isomorphic to a Q_2; in other words it is a ring. So obviously, removing one node is enough to decycle it and it is an optimal solution. Hence, we consider the case $n \geq 2$. We first give in Section 3.1 an optimal solution for the case

Table 1: A decycling set of minimum size in an $HCN(2)$.

Cluster	00	01	11	10
Node	$(00, 01)$ $(00, 10)$	$(01, 10)$	$(11, 01)$	$(10, 01)$

$n = 2$. Then, we describe in Section 3.2 the main HCN decycling algorithm of this paper.

3.1 An optimal solution for the case $n = 2$

In order to illustrate our objective and method, we present in this section an optimal solution to the decycling problem in an $HCN(2)$. We recall that an $HCN(2)$ is shown in Figure 1. This first, simple explanation will help the reader understand the main idea of the algorithm of Section 3.2. We proceed in three steps.

Step 1. We first remove all the nodes of odd nodeID. See Figure 2b. Obviously, this operation removes all cycles from an $HCN(2)$. In other words, we obtain a subgraph of an $HCN(2)$ that is acyclic. In total, $2^{2 \cdot 2}/2 = 8$ nodes have been removed in this step.

Step 2. Many nodes have been removed in Step 1, too many. So let us try to revive some of these removed nodes, aiming at finding an acyclic subgraph of an $HCN(2)$ that contains the most nodes as possible. First, we attempt to revive some nodes inside clusters of odd clusterIDs. We recall that naturally, when a node is revived so are all its incident edges as of the original HCN. See Figure 2c. We were able to revive 2 nodes in this step, $(01, 01)$ and $(10, 10)$. Note that $(01, 01)$ and $(10, 01)$, $(01, 10)$ and $(10, 01)$, and $(01, 10)$ and $(10, 10)$ are other possibilities.

Step 3. Finally, we attempt to revive some nodes inside clusters of even clusterIDs, still aiming at finding an acyclic subgraph of an $HCN(2)$ of the highest order as possible. See Figure 2d. We were able to revive 1 node in this step, $(11, 10)$. Note that $(11, 01)$, $(00, 01)$ and $(00, 10)$ are other possibilities.

Hence, we have removed a total of $8 - 2 - 1 = 5$ nodes inside an $HCN(2)$ (see Table 1). In other words, we have found a decycling set S for an $HCN(2)$ with $|S| = 5$.

Theorem 3: The proposed solution for the case $n = 2$ is optimal.

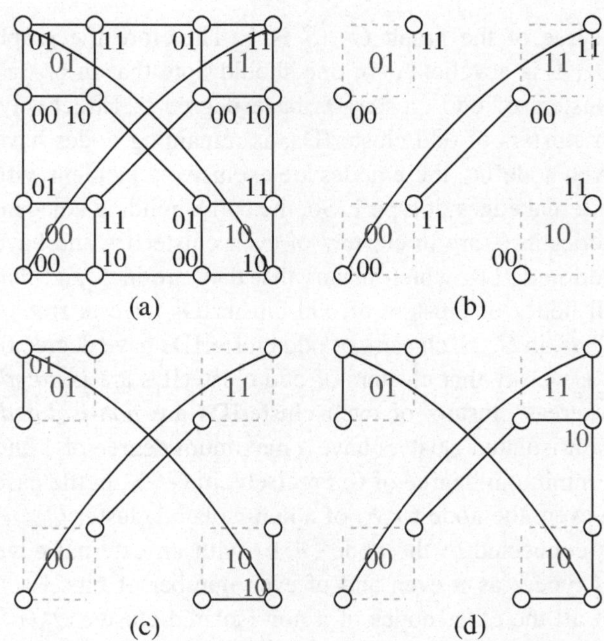

Fig. 2: Three steps leading to an optimal solution for the decycling problem in an $HCN(2)$.

Proof: The subgraph of Figure 2d is obviously acyclic. As detailed in Section 2, an $HCN(2)$ has 16 nodes, 24 edges and a degree of 3. So, from Theorem 1, the size of a decycling set for an $HCN(2)$ is at least $\lceil (24 - 16 + 1)/(3 - 1) \rceil = 5$. Therefore, the solution presented in this section is optimal as we have obtained a decycling set of size 5. ∎

3.2 An algorithm for the general case $n \geq 3$

We give in this section a decycling algorithm for the case $n \geq 3$. Note that this algorithm generates the optimal solution of the case $n = 2$ as presented in Section 3.1. For the sake of notations clarity, let G be the $HCN(n)$ considered. We distinguish three main steps, separated in different subsections.

3.2.1 Removal of nodes with an odd nodeID

Put in S all the nodes of odd nodeIDs. In other words, all the nodes of odd nodeIDs are removed from G. Since each cluster of an $HCN(n)$ is isomorphic to a Q_n, the graph $G \backslash S$ contains no internal edge. Thus, the graph $G \backslash S$ contains only external edges (type 1 and 2), not all of them though (some were incident with a node of S). Now, as each node of an HCN is incident with one single external edge, the remaining external edges are all mutually disconnected, that is the maximum degree of the graph $G \setminus S$ is 1. Therefore the graph $G \setminus S$ is acyclic. Also, one should note that in $G \setminus S$, clusters of odd clusterIDs have degree 0. Effectively, in clusters of odd clusterIDs, as remaining nodes have even nodeIDs, these nodes are exclusively incident with external edges of type 1. So, the corresponding adjacent nodes in G are in clusters of even clusterIDs and have odd nodeIDs, which means that they are in S and that all nodes of clusters of odd clusterIDs have degree 0. Thus, in $G \setminus S$, clusters of odd clusterIDs have degree 0. So, we say that clusters of odd clusterIDs are *isolated*, whereas clusters of even clusterIDs are *non-isolated*. Non-isolated clusters have a maximum degree of 1 and a minimum degree of 0. Precisely, in $G \setminus S$, in the case n even, the node (u, u) of a non-isolated cluster $Q_n(u)$ is connected to the node $(\bar{u}, \bar{u})$ with an external edge of type 2 as u even and of even number of bits. Each of all the other nodes of a non-isolated cluster $Q_n(u)$, say a node (u, v), is connected to the node (v, u) with an external edge of type 1 as u and v even. In the case n odd, the node (u, u) of a non-isolated cluster $Q_n(u)$ has degree 0 as u even and of odd number of bits. Each of all the other nodes of a non-isolated cluster $Q_n(u)$, say a node (u, v), is connected to the node (v, u) with an external edge of type 1 as u and v even. So, $G \setminus S$ contains external edges of type 2 only in the case n even.

Such decycling set S is a somehow trivial solution to the decycling problem in an HCN. So, from now on, we aim at reducing the size of S. We shall thus remove some nodes from S; in other words, as mentioned in Section 2, we shall revive some nodes of S, naturally altogether with their incident edges as of the original HCN.

3.2.2 Revival of nodes in clusters of odd clusterIDs

Inside each isolated cluster, revive nodes according to Theorem 2. As a cluster of an $HCN(n)$ is isomorphic to a Q_n, at least $2^{n-1}/n$ nodes can be revived in such cluster while retaining that cluster acyclic. We obtain a new set S' with $|S'| < |S|$. These revived nodes are connected either to a revived node of another isolated cluster, or, to a node of a non-isolated cluster. Effectively, each of all revived nodes, say (u, v), has an odd nodeID. So, if its clusterID (which is odd) is distinct from its nodeID, the revived node is incident to an external edge of type 1 and connected to a node of an isolated cluster of odd nodeID, that is, a revived node. As there is only one external edge of type 1 between any two clusters, and because there is no path connecting two revived nodes inside a cluster by Theorem 2, this situation keeps $G \setminus S'$ acyclic. Now assume $u = v$. If n is odd, (u, v) is connected to the node $(\bar{u}, \bar{u})$ of even nodeID of a non-isolated cluster with an external edge of type 2. As there is no internal edge inside a non-isolated cluster, this situation also keeps $G \setminus S'$ acyclic. If n is even, (u, v) is connected to the node $(\bar{u}, \bar{u})$ of odd nodeID of an isolated cluster with an external edge of type 2 *providing* that the node $(\bar{u}, \bar{u})$ has been revived. If $(\bar{u}, \bar{u})$ has not been revived, the revival of (u, v) induces no external edge revival, so this situation keeps $G \setminus S'$ acyclic. If $(\bar{u}, \bar{u})$ has been revived, (u, v) is connected to $(\bar{u}, \bar{u})$ with an external edge of type 2. We enunciate the following lemma.

Lemma 1: For n even, let S be the set of all nodes of odd nodeIDs, and let R be the set of revived nodes. In $(G \setminus S) \cup R$, for $(u, v), (u, w) \in R$ with $H(v, w) = n$, there is no path connecting (u, v) and (u, w) inside $Q_n(u)$.

Proof: Consider the cluster $Q_n(u)$. Nodes of $Q_n(u)$ are abbreviated to their nodeIDs only. Suppose there exists such a path, say $v, a, b, \ldots, w$. Since in a hypercube any two nodes at distance 2 are located on a same 4-cycle, there exists in $Q_n(u)$ a node $c \in N(v) \setminus \{a\}$ with v, a, b, c, v a 4-cycle. This contradicts Theorem 2 which revives nodes while keeping a cluster acyclic. ∎

We recall that between any two clusters of G, there is one external edge of type 1 and one of type 2. We are in the case both nodes $(u, v = u)$ and $(\bar{u}, \bar{u})$ have been revived; they are linked by an external edge of type 2. So, even if the external edge of type 1 $(u, \bar{u}) \to (\bar{u}, u)$ between $Q_n(u)$ and $Q_n(\bar{u})$ has also been revived, by Lemma 1 there is no path linking (u, v) to $(u, \bar{u})$ in $Q_n(u)$, and there is no path linking $(\bar{u}, \bar{u})$ to $(\bar{u}, u)$ in $Q_n(\bar{u})$. Hence, this situation also keeps $G \setminus S'$ acyclic.

3.2.3 Revival of nodes in clusters of even clusterIDs

We recall that in an $HCN(n)$, each of all clusters is isomorphic to a Q_n. So, we can assume without loss of generality that all the isolated clusters of $G \setminus S'$ have the same nodes revived by Theorem 2. In other words, for any two distinct isolated clusters $Q_n(u), Q_n(v)$, the set of the nodeIDs of the nodes revived in $Q_n(u)$ is equal to the set of the nodeIDs of the nodes revived in $Q_n(v)$.

So, in the case n even, as revived nodes have odd nodeIDs and are in clusters of odd clusterIDs, revived edges connect only nodes of (distinct) isolated clusters. In the case n odd, revived edges similarly connect nodes of (distinct) isolated clusters, but additionally, *at most one node* in each isolated cluster is connected to a node in a non-isolated cluster with an external edge of type 2. Conversely, at most one node of a non-isolated cluster is connected to a node in an isolated cluster; if such case arises, it revives the unique external edge of type 2 between these two clusters. Precisely, in an isolated cluster $Q_n(u)$, if (u, u) is revived, then it is connected with an external edge of type 2 to the node $(\bar{u}, \bar{u})$ which is in a non-isolated cluster as both n and u odd.

Proceed as follows. Initially all non-isolated clusters are unmarked. For each of all non-isolated clusters that are unmarked, say $Q_n(u)$, revive one node, say (u, v). Mark all (non-isolated) clusters linked to a neighbour node of v in $Q_n(u)$. We thus obtain a new set S'' with $|S''| < |S'|$. Assume n is even. At the end of Step 2 there is no external edge between a non-isolated cluster and an isolated cluster. So, by reviving one node inside a non-isolated cluster, a non-isolated cluster is connected to at most one isolated cluster. Now, by definition of the cluster marking process there are no two non-isolated clusters linked by two nodes of degree 2 (i.e. there is no external edge $(u, v) \to (v, u)$ with $d((u, v)) = d((v, u)) = 2$), and then $G \setminus S''$ is acyclic. Assume n is odd. A non-isolated cluster $Q_n(u)$ can be connected to an isolated cluster with two distinct external edges incident to (u, u) and (u, v) where $H(u, v) = n$. As $n \geq 3$, the revived node in $Q_n(u)$ cannot be adjacent to both (u, u) and (u, v). So, in the case there are two external edges between a non-isolated cluster $Q_n(u)$ and an isolated cluster, at least one of $\{(u, u), (u, v)\}$ is of degree 1 where $H(u, v) = n$. Thus, we are guaranteed that at least one of the two external edges between such two clusters is not in a cycle. Hence, we can assume without loss of generality that we are back in the case n even, where there is at most one external edge between a non-isolated cluster and an isolated cluster.

Finally, let us count how many nodes have been revived, and deduce how many nodes have been removed, that is $|S''|$, an upper bound on the decycling number of an *HCN*(n).

Inside each of the 2^{n-1} isolated clusters, at least $2^{n-1}/n$ nodes are revived by Theorem 2. Inside a non-isolated cluster, at most one node is revived. Also, one such revived node in a non-isolated cluster induces at most n marked (non-isolated) clusters. So, in total, at least $\lfloor 2^{(n-1)}/n \rfloor$ nodes are revived as for non-isolated clusters. Obviously, this discussion holds for both cases n even and n odd.

Hence, in total, at least

$$2^{n-1} \cdot \frac{2^{n-1}}{n} + \left\lfloor \frac{2^{n-1}}{n} \right\rfloor \qquad (= \beta)$$

nodes are revived. Adding all the nodes of even nodeIDs, we have at least $2^{2n-1} + \beta$ nodes inside the acyclic graph $G \setminus S''$. Therefore, $|S''| \leq 2^{2n-1} - \beta$, that is, a decycling set of size at most $2^{2n-1} - (2^{2n-2}/n + \lfloor 2^{n-1}/n \rfloor)$ has been found by our algorithm.

From this discussion we can state the following theorem.

Theorem 4: In an *HCN*(n), we can find a decycling set of size at most $2^{2n-1} - (2^{2n-2}/n + \lfloor 2^{n-1}/n \rfloor)$.

3.3 Complexity analysis

As a pre-processing, all clusters are initially set to an unmarked state. This requires $O(2^{2n})$ as all clusters have to be iterated. The first operation consists of removing all nodes of odd nodeIDs; it requires $O(2^{2n})$ as there are 2^{2n-1} such nodes. Then, let $O(k_n)$ be the time complexity of an algorithm producing a decycling set in a Q_n as of Theorem 2. We can assume from Theorem 2 that in a Q_n such a decycling set can be found in $\Omega(2^n)$ time. Thus, we have $O(k_n) \geq O(2^n)$. So, reviving nodes inside each of all isolated clusters aiming at finding a decycling set as of Theorem 2 takes in total $O(2^n \cdot k_n)$ as there are 2^{n-1} such clusters. Lastly, non-isolated clusters are iterated, and only unmarked ones have one of their nodes revived. This requires $O(2^{n-1})$ time as there are 2^{n-1} such clusters, and since checking whether a cluster is marked or not can be done in constant time. Hence, in total, our algorithm can find a decycling set in an *HCN*(n) as of Theorem 4 in $O(2^n \cdot k_n)$ time, where 2^{2n} is the order of an *HCN*(n).

4. Conclusions

Eliminating cycles in an interconnection network is a critical problem of parallel processing; it has important applications such as lock-free concurrent access to shared resources. Finding a decycling set of minimum size is an NP-complete problem. We have described in this paper an efficient algorithm finding a decycling set in a hierarchical cubic network $HCN(n)$. The decycling set produced contains at most $2^{2n-1} - (2^{2n-2}/n + \lfloor 2^{n-1}/n \rfloor)$ nodes.

Future works include refining this algorithm to produce a decycling set of smaller size, or showing that our algorithm produces a decycling set of minimum size.

References

[1] TOP500, "Japan's K computer tops 10 petaflop/s to stay atop TOP500 list," http://top500.org/lists/2011/11/, last accessed February 2013.

[2] Y. Li, S. Peng, and W. Chu, "Efficient collective communications in dual-cube," *The Journal of Supercomputing*, vol. 28, no. 1, pp. 71–90, 2004.

[3] L. Gargano, U. Vaccaro, and A. Vozella, "Fault-tolerant routing in the star and pancake interconnection networks," *Information Processing Letters*, vol. 45, no. 6, pp. 315–320, 1993.

[4] K. Ghose and K. R. Desai, "Hierarchical cubic network," *IEEE Transactions on Parallel and Distributed Systems*, vol. 6, no. 4, pp. 427–435, 1995.

[5] S. K. Yun and K. H. Park, "Comments on "hierarchical cubic networks"," *IEEE Transactions on Parallel and Distributed Systems*, vol. 9, no. 4, pp. 410–414, 1998.

[6] J.-S. Fu, G.-H. Chen, and D.-R. Duh, "Node-disjoint paths and related problems on hierarchical cubic networks," *Networks*, vol. 40, no. 3, pp. 142–154, 2002.

[7] A. Bossard and K. Kaneko, "Node-to-set disjoint-path routing in hierarchical cubic networks," *The Computer Journal*, vol. 55, no. 12, pp. 1440–1446, 2012.

[8] P. Festa, P. M. Pardalos, and M. G. C. Resende, "Feedback set problems," *Handbook of Combinatorial Optimization*, vol. A, pp. 209–258, 1999.

[9] R. Karp, "Reducibility among combinatorial problems," in *Complexity of computer computations*, R. Miller and J. Thatcher, Eds. Plenum Press, 1972, pp. 85–103.

[10] D.-M. Li and Y.-P. Liu, "A polynomial algorithm for finding the minimum feedback vertex set of a 3-regular simple graph," *Acta Mathematica Scientia (English Ed.)*, vol. 19, no. 4, pp. 375–381, 1999.

[11] Y. D. Liang and M.-S. Chang, "Minimum feedback vertex sets in cocomparability graphs and convex bipartite graphs," *Acta Informatica*, vol. 34, no. 5, pp. 337–346, 1997.

[12] Y. D. Liang, "On the feedback vertex set problem in permutation graphs," *Information Processing Letters*, vol. 52, no. 3, pp. 123–129, 1994.

[13] L. W. Beineke and R. C. Vandell, "Decycling graphs," *Journal of Graph Theory*, vol. 25, no. 1, pp. 59–77, 1997.

[14] S. Bau, L. W. Beineke, Z. Liu, G. Du, and R. C. Vandell, "Decycling cubes and grids," *Utilitas Mathematica*, vol. 59, pp. 129–137, 2001.

[15] S. Bau and L. W. Beineke, "The decycling number of graphs," *Australasian Journal of Combinatorics*, vol. 25, pp. 285–298, 2002.

[16] D. A. Pike, "Decycling hypercubes," *Graphs and Combinatorics*, vol. 19, no. 4, pp. 547–550, 2003.

Heuristics for Reconfigurable Three Dimensional Free Space Optical Networks

Johan Kosumo[1], Danny Luong[1], C.S. James Wong[2], and G. Young[1]
1. Computer Science Department, California State Polytechnic University, Pomona, CA 91768
2. Computer Science Department, San Francisco State University, San Francisco, CA 94132

Abstract

Free space optic (FSO) is line-of-sight technology that uses beams of light to provide optical bandwidth connections that can transmit images, videos, voice, and data. Due to the increasing popularity of FSO network and its advantages over traditional optic fiber cable network and radio frequency wireless network, the technology of FSO has become more prevalent. However, one of the major limitations of FSO is line of sight maintenance. To ensure uninterrupted data flow, auto-aligning transmitter and receiver modules are necessary.

In this paper, we propose a three dimensional (3D) FSO network model and define types of diagonal links that can be inserted to reconfigure the network. We propose several heuristics to handle link reconfigurations to improve efficiency and reliability of such networks after link failures. Finally, we present analytical and simulation results to evaluate the proposed heuristics on the overall performance in terms of average node distance and network diameter.

Keywords: *3D Mesh Network, Routing, Reconfigurable Network, Free Space Optics, Wireless Network.*

1. Introduction

The telecommunications world is evolving dramatically toward challenging scenarios where the fast and efficient transportation of information is becoming a key element in today's society. The size and complexity of telecommunications networks and the speed of information exchange have increased at an unprecedented rate over the last decades. Living in this new era of information superhighway era, people are using a number of devices with advanced multimedia applications to obtain and exchange information. The current trends in multimedia communications include voice, video, data, and images. These trends are creating a demand for flexible networks with extremely high capacities that can accommodate the expected vast growth in the network traffic volume [18].

Over the last few decades, optical fiber with its enormous potential has established the ability to satisfy the demand for these networks. Telecommunications companies have been increasing the reach of their fiber optic networks to their customers. Optical fiber is highly reliable and it has unlimited growth potential. Single mode fiber offers a transmission medium with Tbps bandwidth, which has enough capacity to deliver a channel of 100 Mbps to hundreds of thousands of users. However, even with all these potentials, optical fiber has been costly in its installations. Laying in-ground cable would require dealing with government bodies, digging trenches, lots of manpower, and time. Due to these reasons alone, a new optical communication technology has emerged.

A fiber optic communication link uses light sources and detectors to send and receive information through fiber optic cable. Similarly, Free Space Optics (FSO) uses light sources and detectors to send and receive information, but through the atmosphere instead of a cable. The motivation for FSO is to eliminate the cost, time, and effort of installing fiber optic cable, yet retain the benefit of high data rates, up to 1 Gbps and beyond. Furthermore, FSO technology does not require any RF spectrum licensing making it easier from a political/ bureaucratic perspective to install. It also can be removed and installed elsewhere, thus, allowing recycling of equipment. FSO technology may become prominent in next generation broadband networks. Multi-gigabit potential data rates, unlicensed spectrum, excellent security and quick and inexpensive setup are among its most attractive features [22].

2. Free Space Optic (FSO)

FSO is a line-of-sight technology that uses beams of light to provide optical bandwidth connections that can transmit images, videos, voice, and data. Commercially available systems offer capacities in the range of 100 Mbps to 2.5 Gbps, and demonstration systems report data rates as high as 160 Gbps. Free space optic systems can function over distances of several kilometers. As long as there is a clear line of sight between the source and the destination, and enough transmitter power, FSO communication is possible. Over the last few decades, this new technology has been studied extensively [6, 11, 13, 15-17, 19, 20, 24]

Ranging from hospitals, banks and telecommunications companies to municipal and military installations, Free-Space optics systems are filling a variety of wireless data communication needs. For private corporate networks, wireless optics systems provide a very high bandwidth link between sites without the recurring costs of leased lines. For high bandwidth applications such as video conferencing, Free-Space optics provides new alternatives to installing fiber optic cable between sites where it is very expensive or impossible to lay. For temporary network connectivity needs, such as at exhibitions, conventions, sporting events, or disaster recovery, high bandwidth links can be easily and quickly provided using portable FSO systems. In addition, wireless optics systems are also used as high-speed wireless backup for fiber optic cable and as "Last Mile" solutions, connecting customer sites to fiber backbones [1, 18].

Despite these strengths, FSO also has some weaknesses. Free Space Optic is essentially a line-of-sight (LOS) technology using air as its medium. Because of this reason alone, before employing FSO, we have to consider potential disturbances that could happen such as rain, fog, physical obstructions, scintillation, beam wander, and building's movement/seismic activities [6, 19, 24].

In summary, the applications of FSO technology seems most suited to is clear weather short distance link establishment, such as last-mile connections to broadband network backbones and backbone links between buildings in metropolitan area network (MAN) or campus area network (CAN) environment. There is also significant potential for use of this technology in temporary networks, where the advantages of being able to establish area network quickly or being able to relocate network in a relatively short time frame outweigh the network unreliability issues.

3. The 3D FSO Network Model

3.1. Assumptions

We design our model based on the well-studied mesh network topology model [4, 5, 10]. For the purpose of our study, we are going to present a new model of the FSO network. We assume that our network model would only be comprised of the FSO devices. Therefore, our network model would be *homogenous n* x *n* x *n* mesh network topology.

Our FSO network would have these characteristics:

- The network would be an *n* x *n* x *n* mesh 3D network
- Each node would have connectivity of 6.
- Maximum degree of connectivity of each node is six (6), including the boundary nodes.

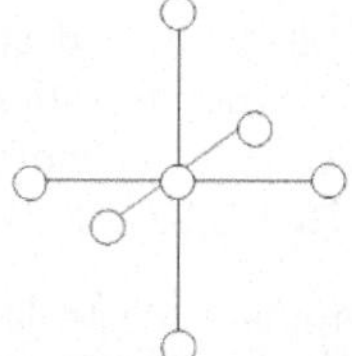

Figure 3.1 Each Node has 6 connectivity

Since our network model is a *n* x *n* x *n* 3D mesh network, we have to modify or apply different strategies in reconfiguring the network in case of link failures. The link reconfiguration strategy of a n x n mesh network have been studied by Lee and Young in 2004 [16, 17]. To study our *n* x *n* x *n* 3D network model, we are going to break down our network model into three planes *xy, yz,* and *xz* plane

3.2. Types of Links/Connections

Since we are introducing diagonal links to reconfigure the network, we are going to define different types of diagonal links that we can use. For our network model, we are going to define three types of connections or links.

3.2.1. Type I Link

Type I link is the regular link between two transceivers or nodes. Figure 3.2 shows all possible Type I links for the black node. Type I links connect all the transceivers in our FSO network before any reconfigurations. A node can connect with another node 1 hop movement away on one of its axes through Type 1 link.

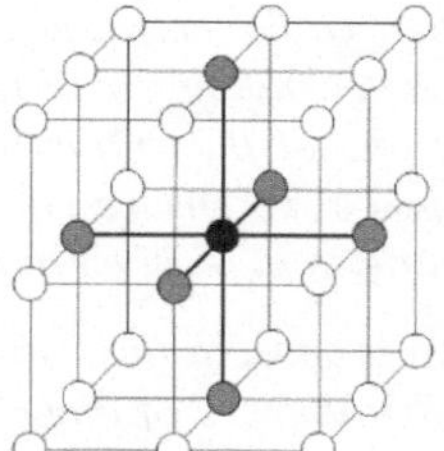

Figure 3.2 Type I link

In summary, a node with coordinates (x, y, z) can connect up to 6 nodes by using Type I link, as shown below:

(x, y, z) --- (x + 1, y, z) (x, y + 1, z) (x, y, z +1)
(x – 1, y, z) (x, y – 1, z) (x, y, z – 1)

3.2.2. Type II Link

Type II link, is a resulting diagonal link formed by two regular length links or edges. Figure 3.3 illustrates a connected free space optic network with some Type II diagonal links showed as dashed lines. Type II link can also be described as a link that connects a node with another node one hop movement away on two of its axes.

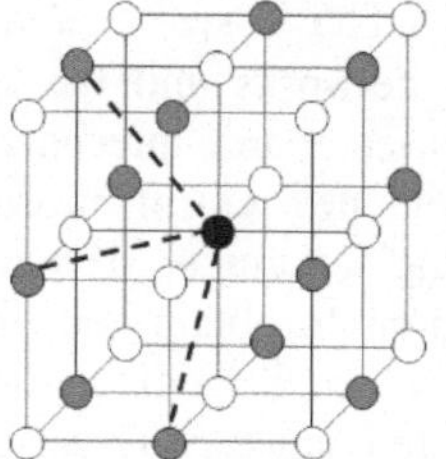

Figure 3.3 Type II link, a diagonal link

In summary, a node with coordinates (x, y, z) can connect up to 12 nodes by using Type II link, as shown below:

(x, y, z) --- (x + 1, y + 1, z) (x + 1, y, z + 1)
(x, y + 1, z +1) (x – 1, y - 1, z)
(x, y – 1, z - 1) (x - 1, y, z – 1)
(x + 1, y – 1, z) (x – 1, y + 1, z)
(x + 1, y, z – 1) (x – 1, y, z + 1)
(x, y – 1, z + 1) (x, y + 1, z - 1)

3.2.3. Type III Link

The second type of diagonal link, Type III link, is a resulting diagonal link formed with a Type I link and a Type II diagonal link. Shown in Figure 3.4, the Type III diagonal link is the dashed line between the gray nodes and the black node in the center of the network. Type II link connects two nodes diagonally on the same plane. On the other hand, the Type III link connects two nodes that are located on different planes diagonally. Type III link connects a node with another node 1 hop movement away on all of its three axes.

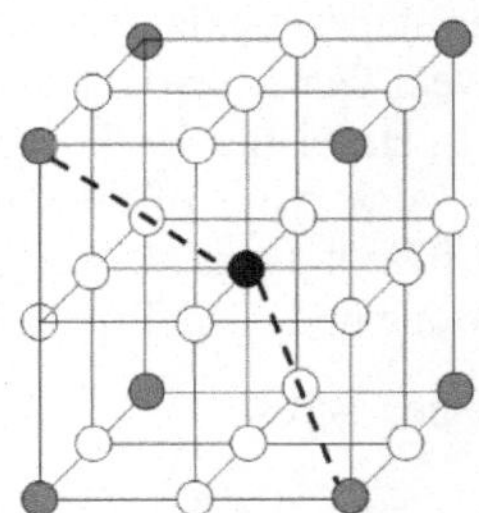

Figure 3.4 Type III link

In summary, a node with coordinates (x, y, z) can connect up to 8 nodes by using Type III link, as shown below:

(x, y, z) --- (x + 1, y + 1, z + 1) (x + 1, y + 1, z - 1)
(x - 1, y + 1, z +1) (x – 1, y + 1, z - 1)
(x + 1, y – 1, z + 1) (x + 1, y - 1, z – 1)
(x - 1, y – 1, z + 1) (x – 1, y - 1, z - 1)

3.3. Possible Connections for Each Node

Each node has a maximum degree of connectivity of 6 connections. However, each of the transceiver can also rotate to make a diagonal link connection to another transceiver provided both transceivers themselves still have not used up all their available 6 connections. Figure 3.5 illustrates possible connections. The black-colored node has 6 solid line links which illustrates the maximum degree of connectivity of the transceiver. The dashed line links illustrates the possible diagonal link connections that can be made by a transceiver.

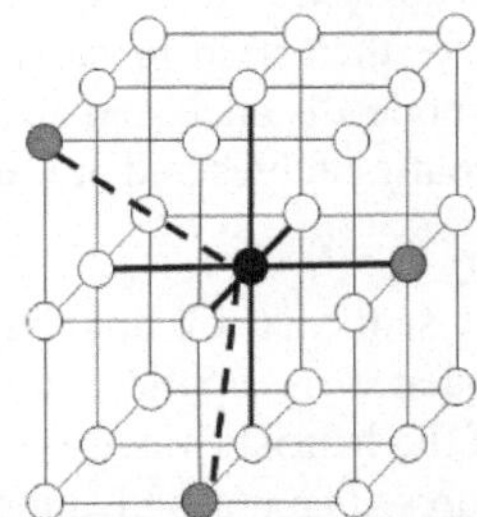

Figure 3.5 Possible Connections for each node

In a fully connected *n* x *n* x *n* 3D network, such as in Figure 3.6, all available connections are used. Depending on the locations, not all of the nodes have the maximum degree of connectivity of 6. The black node at the center of the network has the maximum 6 connections, while the gray node on the left can only connect to a maximum of 5 other nodes. The gray node on the right, which located at the corner edge of the network, has a maximum of only 3 connections.

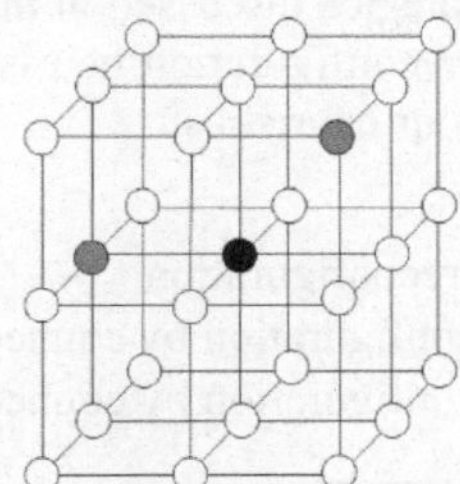

Figure 3.6 Fully connected *n* x *n* x *n* network

Boundary Nodes

Boundary nodes are the nodes that are located at the corners of the 3D mesh network, along the edge between corners, and on the faces of the 3D mesh network. Boundary nodes share one property that they all start with less than the maximum degree of connection before reconfiguration.

Initial connection 3:

These are the corners nodes. Total number of such nodes is 8, since there are 8 corners in our 3D mesh network.

Initial connection 4:

These are nodes that are located along the edge between the corners. There are total of 12 such edges. Each edge has two corner nodes. Therefore, total number of such node is (n-2)12.

Initial connection 5:

These are the nodes that are located at the faces of the 3D mesh network, excluding edge. There are six faces in total, so the total number of such nodes is $(n-2)^2 6$.

4. Reconfiguration Algorithms

In this paper, we extend the work of Lee and Young research in 2004 [16, 17]. They introduced the possibility of reconfiguring FSO network after links failures, focused on a 2 dimensional *n* x *n* mesh network. Our research focuses on a new network model, the *n* x *n* x *n* mesh 3D network. Inspired by various shortest path algorithms and reconfigurable network models [2-5, 7-9, 12, 14, 21, 23], we come up with several reconfiguration heuristics for our 3D mesh network.

Our reconfiguration algorithm scans the pair of nodes whose link is failed or broken for its neighboring diagonal nodes. Each node or transceiver has a maximum connectivity of 6. If any of the neighboring diagonal transceiver has not used all of its connections, we connect a diagonal link from the transceiver to the diagonal transceiver. If any of the target transceivers has already maxed out all its connections, then a new link will not be formed.

```
begin
check the neighboring diagonal nodes of each node
  if the neighboring diagonal nodes' connectivity < 6 then
     establish a diagonal link for each node
  end if
end
```

4.1. Reconfiguration Heuristics

Based on the strategies discussed in the previous sections, we propose several reconfiguration heuristics. The following are the properties of our heuristics:

Pattern:

- 0: No links reconfiguration
- 1: Links reconfiguration by connecting only one node
- 2: Links reconfiguration by connecting two nodes

Descriptions of the heuristics:

- H0: No reconnection after link failures
- H1: Try to reconnect by connecting only one node with a Type II link
- H2: Try to reconnect by connecting each node with a Type II link.
- H3: Try to reconnect by connecting only one node with a Type III link.
- H4: Try to reconnect by connecting each node with a Type III link.
- H5: Try to reconnect by connecting only one node with a Type II or Type III link.
- H6: Try to reconnect by connecting each node with a Type II or Type III link.
- H7: Try to reconnect by connecting one node with a Type II link, and the other node with a Type III link.

We use H_0, which does not reconfigure after link failure, as a control model to be compared with the other heuristics, which reconfigure after link failures. H_0 will almost certainly provide the worst results among all the proposed heuristics, since it does not reconfigure the network after link failures. For H_0, we can predict that the network will have isolated nodes or network sections the fastest. As for our heuristics, H_1 to H_7, we expect that they will yield better performance in terms of average node distance and network diameter. We classify our heuristics into two separate groups:

- Links reconfiguration using 1 node
- Links reconfiguration using 2 nodes

4.2. Links Reconfiguration Using 1 Node

Since a link is a connection between two nodes, a broken link will always involve two nodes. Our heuristics under this group try to reconnect by connecting only one of the nodes involved to an available diagonal neighboring node. The idea is to replace one broken link with one new diagonal link. Our heuristics that belong to this group are H_1, H_3, and H_5.

Pseudo codes for the heuristics:

```
procedure
begin
check the neighboring diagonal nodes of the first node of the pair of
                    nodes
  if its neighboring diagonal nodes have free transceivers then
    establish a diagonal link
  else if check the second node that shares the link for its diagonal
                    nodes then
    if its neighboring diagonal nodes have free transceivers then
      establish a diagonal link
    end if
  end if
end
```

4.3. Links Reconfiguration Using 2 Nodes

Our heuristics under this group try to reconnect by connecting each of the two nodes involved to its own available diagonal neighboring node, maximize reconnection by using the two nodes involved. Our heuristics belonged to this group are H_2, H_4, H_6 and H_7. Heuristics H_2, H_4, and H_6 reconnect the two nodes by using same types of diagonal links. However, heuristic H_7 uses different types of diagonal links for each node, i.e. Type II for one node and Type III link for the other.

Pseudo codes for the heuristics:

```
procedure
begin
check the neighboring diagonal nodes of each node
  if the neighboring nodes have free transceivers then
    establish a diagonal link for each node
  end if
end
```

5. Simulation

5.1. Simulation Setup

Operating System:	MS Windows 7 Professional
Computer Model:	Dell Latitude E6400 Notebook
Processor:	Intel Core 2 Duo 2.4GHz
Development Tool:	MS Visual Studio 2010
Programming:	C Sharp
Network Parameters:	Average node distance, Network diameter

Each node maintains a routing table for the purpose of computing the statistical results. Initially, the 3D mesh is created with all regular vertical and horizontal links, or with Type I links. Then, links are randomly chosen and broken. Different heuristics are then used to handle the link failures. Then, both average node distance and network diameter are calculated from the routing tables and are recorded.

Number of link failures

In this simulation, a sequence of link failures is generated. Then the same sequence is applied to the original mesh network and each of the heuristics is used to handle the same sequence of link failures. The reason behind this is to compare the heuristics under the exact same situation.

The following are the settings for our simulation:

- Size of 3D mesh network: 17 x 17 x 17 3D mesh
- Number of nodes: 4913
- Initial number of links: 13872
- Statistical interval: 500 links failures
- Sequence length: 13872 failures

Our study focus on *permanent* link failures. Failed link will not recover. Also, new links added to network through reconfiguration will not be subjected to failures. In the end, the network will be only connected through reconfigured links. The number of links throughout the simulation is consistently decreasing and never increasing.

5.2. Simulation Results

Some data in the following results are omitted due to disconnected nodes. Once there is a disconnected node in the network, the average node distance and network diameter become infinity. Data for experiments is show in tables and corresponding graphs are plotted.

5.2.1. Average Node Distance Vs. Number of Link Failures

Table 5.1 Average Node Distance vs. Link Failures

Failure	H_0	H_1	H_2	H_3	H_4	H_5	H_6	H_7
0	24.004	24.004	24.004	24.004	24.004	24.004	24.004	24.004
500	24.005	19.682	19.114	20.403	20.910	19.685	19.200	18.726
1000	24.007	18.099	17.899	19.584	19.262	18.410	17.935	17.249
1500	24.159	18.150	17.586	18.255	18.587	17.555	17.173	16.694
2000	24.166	17.630	17.199	17.552	18.109	16.862	16.916	16.311
2500	24.202	17.186	16.965	17.109	18.020	16.472	16.659	15.958
3000	∞	16.842	16.758	16.211	17.465	16.170	15.952	15.752
3500	∞	16.400	16.661	16.048	∞	15.919	15.742	15.175
4000	∞	16.108	16.367	∞	∞	15.729	∞	14.965
4500	∞	15.957	∞	∞	∞	15.508	∞	14.874
5000	∞	15.664	∞	∞	∞	15.481	∞	14.562
5500	∞	15.502	∞	∞	∞	∞	∞	14.445
6000	∞	15.459	16.112	∞	∞	∞	∞	14.243
6500	∞	15.308	15.914	∞	∞	∞	∞	14.129
7000	∞	15.274	15.846	∞	∞	∞	∞	14.003
7500	∞	14.999	15.722	∞	∞	∞	∞	13.734
8000	∞	14.989	15.677	∞	∞	∞	∞	13.592
8500	∞	14.899	15.739	∞	∞	∞	∞	13.548
9000	∞	14.816	15.721	∞	∞	∞	∞	13.473
9500	∞	14.720	15.693	∞	∞	∞	∞	13.373
10000	∞	14.643	15.576	∞	∞	∞	∞	13.355
10500	∞	14.677	15.575	∞	∞	∞	∞	13.317
11000	∞	14.628	15.473	∞	∞	∞	∞	13.277
11500	∞	14.619	15.459	∞	∞	∞	∞	13.191
12000	∞	14.560	15.479	∞	∞	∞	∞	13.176
12500	∞	14.546	15.457	∞	∞	∞	∞	13.154
13000	∞	14.381	15.484	∞	∞	∞	∞	13.120
13500	∞	14.381	15.272	∞	∞	∞	∞	13.042
13872	∞	∞	∞	∞	∞	∞	∞	13.011

We simulated each heuristic and computed the average node distance of the network. The result is tabulated in Table 5.1 and Figure 5.1. As expected, H_0 became disconnected soon after, and without reconfiguration, the average node distance increased as number of link failures increased. The network became disconnected after about 3000 link failures. We predicted that reconfiguration heuristics would yield smaller average node distance, and the simulations proved that to be true. However, some of the heuristics did not perform well at all. For instance, although H_3 decreased the network's average node distance, the network also became disconnected quite early. Heuristic H_4, however, became disconnected after about 3000 link failures, the same time as H_0. While the average node distance for H_0 was increasing before the network became disconnected; the average node distance for H_3 was actually decreasing to about 70% of the initial average. H_1 and H_2 performed similarly, although H_2's average node distance is smaller than H_1's. Heuristics H_1 and H_2 eventually became disconnected when all the Type I links were broken. In other words, when the network totally collapsed, even with reconfigurations of heuristics H_1 and H_2, the network was not be able to transmit anything at all.

Heuristic H_2 was interesting because the network became disconnected at about 4500 links failures, then became connected again at about 6000 links failures. This was due to more reconnections as more broken links were introduced into the network. Heuristic H_7 was a hybrid heuristic which combined of H_1 and H_3, and we expected better result than those two heuristics. The simulation proved that to be true as H_7 was the only heuristic that kept the whole network connected the whole time and yielded the smallest average node distance, about 54% smaller.

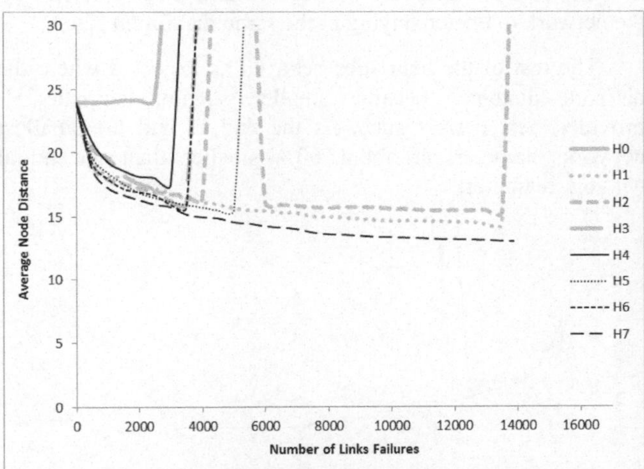

Figure 5.1 Average Node Distance vs. Link Failures Graph

5.2.2. Network Diameter Vs. Number of Link Failures

Table 5.2 Network Diameter vs. Links Failures

#	H_0	H_1	H_2	H_3	H_4	H_5	H_6	H_7
0	48	48	48	48	48	48	48	48
500	48	38	36	40	40	38	37	35
1000	48	34	34	35	34	35	34	33
1500	48	34	33	32	32	31	31	31
2000	48	32	33	29	31	30	31	30
2500	48	32	31	28	31	29	31	29
3000	∞	31	31	28	30	28	29	28
3500	∞	30	31	26	∞	28	29	27
4000	∞	30	30	∞	∞	27	∞	27
4500	∞	29	∞	∞	∞	27	∞	27
5000	∞	28	∞	∞	∞	27	∞	26
5500	∞	27	∞	∞	∞	∞	∞	25
6000	∞	27	28	∞	∞	∞	∞	24

6500	∞	27	28	∞	∞	∞	∞	24
7000	∞	27	28	∞	∞	∞	∞	24
7500	∞	27	27	∞	∞	∞	∞	23
8000	∞	27	27	∞	∞	∞	∞	22
8500	∞	26	27	∞	∞	∞	∞	22
9000	∞	26	27	∞	∞	∞	∞	22
9500	∞	26	27	∞	∞	∞	∞	22
10000	∞	26	27	∞	∞	∞	∞	22
10500	∞	26	27	∞	∞	∞	∞	22
11000	∞	26	27	∞	∞	∞	∞	22
11500	∞	26	27	∞	∞	∞	∞	22
12000	∞	25	27	∞	∞	∞	∞	21
12500	∞	25	27	∞	∞	∞	∞	21
13000	∞	25	26	∞	∞	∞	∞	21
13500	∞	25	26	∞	∞	∞	∞	21
13872	∞	∞	∞	∞	∞	∞	∞	20

In terms of network diameter, the results are similar to the results from the average node distance simulation, as we can observe from the lines in the graphs from Figure 5.1 and 5.2. We simulated each heuristic, and computed the diameter of the network in Table 5.2. Then, we plotted the results in Figure 5.2. Without reconfiguration, H_0, had the maximum network diameter until the network became disconnected with the network diameter staying at the same maximum size.

The rest of the heuristics behaved as expected where the network diameter became smaller. Again, heuristic H_7 provided best performance. At the end, it had the smallest network diameter, at about 60% smaller than the initial network diameter.

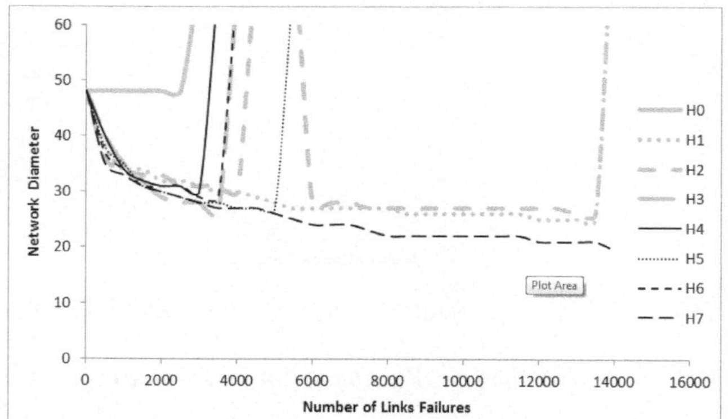

Figure 5.2 Network Diameter vs. Links Failures Graph

5.3. Summary of Results

One main conclusion can be drawn from the above result is that by inserting diagonal links to replace broken links decreases the average node distance and the network diameter. However, the types of diagonal link used does matter. As we can see from the graphs, heuristics using Type II links only, i.e. H_1 and H_2, outperformed the other heuristics, except H_7 which uses both links at the same time. The following are some factors that contribute to the performance of each heuristics:

- Types of link used
- Degree of connectivity of each node

Type of Link Used

As mentioned before, Type II link has the possibility to connect up to 12 nodes in total. A node will not connect to 12 nodes by using Type II link since each node can only make 6 connections in total. However, having these possible connections certainly gives Type II link more flexibility. On the other hand, Type III link can only connect up to 8 nodes in maximum. It has less flexibility than Type II link.

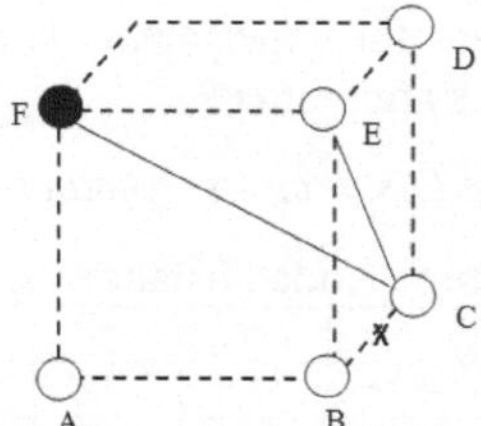

Figure 5.3 Links needed to maintain connection

Our reconfiguration heuristics insert diagonal links replacing broken links to keep the nodes connected. It is obvious that they still require Type I links in addition to the diagonal links to maintain connection. In this regard, Type II link also has the advantage because it only requires one Type I link to maintain connection. Figure 5.3 shows a section of a 3D FSO network. When the link between B and C is broken, heuristic H_1 is going insert Type II link between C and E. We only require 1 connection between E and B to maintain the connection between B and C. However, if we use heuristic H_3, a Type III link is established between C and F. Now, to maintain the connection between B and C, we have to use at least 2 Type I links, such as F-A and A-B. As more Type I links are broken, heuristics using Type III link will be more susceptible to isolated networks or network disconnection. Our simulation results showed that heuristics H_3 and H_4 performed poorly. Both heuristics managed to decrease the average node distance and network diameter, but the network became disconnected very early.

Degree of Connectivity of Each Node

Due to broken links and reconfigurations, each node's degree of connectivity and the performance could change, especially when reconnections cannot be established because the diagonal nodes already have 6 connections. Heuristic H_2 is a good example for this. H_2 reconnects a broken link by connecting 2 Type II links. We believed this happened because it could not reconnect with the diagonal nodes due to maximum degree of connectivity. It performed as expected until 4000 broken links when the network became disconnected. As more broken links were introduced, more nodes opened up their slots for reconnections, and H_2 was able to reconnect the network again after 2000 more broken links.

6. Conclusion

Our research introduces the possibility of reconfiguring a 3D FSO mesh network after link failures. Due to the increasing popularity of FSO network and its advantage over traditional optic fiber cable network and radio frequency wireless network, FSO has become more prevalent. We study the failure handling mechanism in order to improve reliability and efficiency of such networks. We propose several heuristics to handle link reconfigurations to improve efficiency and reliability of such networks after link failures.

We studied and computed the impact of reconfiguration on the overall network performance in terms of average node distance and network diameter. Theoretically, reconfigurations by reconnecting two nodes with diagonal links offer better performance in average node distance and network diameter then reconfigurations by using one node. Types of diagonal links also contribute to the overall network performance. Our simulation confirms the result and therefore, we proposed a hybrid reconfiguration heuristic that make use of both types of diagonal links. Future work could be done on developing more intelligent heuristics while still utilizing both types of diagonal links, especially Type III link. The assumption of reconfigurations are always successful could be removed. Heuristics that follow some patterns could also be considered.

REFERENCES

[1] J. S. Beasley, *Networking, 2nd Editon*. Upper Saddle River, NJ: Pearson Education, Inc. 2009.

[2] Y. Ben-Asher, D. Peleg, and A. Schuster, The complexity of reconfiguring networks models, *Information and Computation, 121,* pp. 41-58, 1992.

[3] Y. Ben-Asher, D. Peleg, R. Ramaswami, and A. Schuster, The Power of Reconfiguration, *Journal of Parallel and Distributed Computing*, *13*(2), pp.139-153, 1991.

[4] V. Bokka, H. Gurla, S. Olariu, and J. L. Schwing, Constant-Time Convexity Problems on Reconfigurable Meshes, *Journal of Parallel and Distributed Computing, 27*(1), pp. 86-99, 1995.

[5] K. Bondalapati and V. Prasanna, Reconfigurable Meshes: Theory and Practice, *Reconfigurable Architectures Workshop, International Paralllel Processing Symposium, 76*, pp.50-53, 1997.

[6] V. Brazda, V. Schejbal, and O. Fiser, "Rain impact on FSO link attenuation based on theory and measurement," *Antennas and Propagation (EUCAP), 2012 6th European Conference on,* pp.1239, 1243, 26-30, March 2012.

[7] J. D΄ıaz, J. Petit, and M. Serna, A random graph model for optical networks of sensors, *IEEE Transactionson Mobile Computing, 2*(3), pp.86-196, 2003.

[8] E. W. Dijkstra, A note on two problems in connection with graphs, *Numerische Mathematik*, vol.1, pp.269-271, 1959.

[9] S. E. Dreyfus, An appraisal of some shortest-path algorithms, *Operations Research*, vol.17, no.3, pp.395-412, 1969.

[10] G. Ellinas, Routing and Restoration Architectures in Mesh Optical Networks. *SPIE Optical Networks Magazine,* vol.4, no.1, pp.91-106, 2003.

[11] J. M. Kahn, R. H. Katz, and K. S. J. Pister, Next century challenges: Mobile networking for "smartdust", *Proc.ACM/IEEE International Conference on Mobile Computing and Networking,* pp.271-278, 1999.

[12] E. L. Lawler, A procedure for computing the K best solutions to discrete optimization problems and its application to the shortest path problem, *Management Science,* vol.18, no.7, pp.401-405, 1972.

[13] J. Llorca, A. Desai, U. Vishkin, C. Davis, and S. Milner, Reconfigurable optical wireless sensor networks. *Optics in Atmospheric Propagation and Adaptive Systems VI, 5237, pp.*136-146, 2004.

[14] M. H. Macgregor and W. D. Grover, Optimized k-shortest-paths algorithm for facility restoration. *Software–Practice and Experience,* vol.24, no.9, pp.823-834, 1994.

[15] W. Mao and J. M. Kahn, Free-space Heterchronous Imaging Reception of Multiple Optical Signals. *IEEE Transactions on Communications,* vol.52, pp.269-279, 2004.

[16] T. Lee and G. Young, "Multipath Routing in Reconfigurable Free Space Optics Networks," Proceedings of the 2007 International Conference on Parallel and Distributed Processing Techniques and Applications, pp.817-821, June 2007.

[17] T. Lee and G. Young, "Routing in Reconfigurable Free Space Optics Network," Proceedings of the 2004 International Conference on Parallel and Distributed Processing Techniques and Applications, pp.946-952, 2004.

[18] A. S. Tanenbaum, *Computer Networks, 4th Edition*, Upper Saddle River, NJ: Prentice Hall, 2003.

[19] M. Tatarko, L. Ovsenik, and J. Turan, "Availability and reliability of FSO links estimation from measured fog parameters," *MIPRO, 2012 Proceedings of the 35th International Convention* , pp.192, 195, 21-25, May 2012.

[20] A. Vavoulas, H. G. Sandalidis, and D. Varoutas, "Weather effects on FSO network connectivity," *Optical Communications and Networking, IEEE/OSA Journal of*, vol.4, no.10, pp.734, 740, Oct. 2012.

[21] B. A. Warneke, M. D. Scott, B. S. Leibowitz, L. Zhou, C. L. Bellew, J. A. Chediak, J. M. Kahn, B. E. Boser, and K. S. J. Pister, Autonomous 16mm3 Solar-powered Node for distributed wireless sensor networks, *Proc. IEEE Sensors*, pp.1510-1515, 2002.

[22] S. G. Wilson, M. Brandt-Pearce, Q. Cao, and J. Leveque, Free-space optical MIMO transmission with Q-ary PPM. *IEEE Trans. Communication,* vol.53, no.8, pp.1402-1412, 2005

[23] D. Xu, Y. Chen, Y. Xiong, C. Qiao, and X. He, "On finding disjoint paths in single and dual link cost networks," *In Proc. IEEE Infocom*, pp.53-54, 2004.

[24] S. A. Zabidi, W. A. Khateeb, M. R. Islam, A. W. Naji, "The effect of weather on free space optics communication (FSO) under tropical weather conditions and a proposed setup for measurement," *Computer and Communication Engineering (ICCCE), 2010 International Conference on* , pp.1,5, 11-12, May 2010.

GPU-based Multi-stream Analyzer on Application Layer for Service-oriented Router

Kazumasa Ikeuchi, Janaka Wijekoon, Shinichi Ishida, Hiroaki Nishi
Nishi Laboratory, Graduate School of Science and Technology, Keio University, Japan
{ikeuchi, janaka, sin}@west.sd.keio.ac.jp, west@sd.keio.ac.jp

***Abstract*—Service-oriented router (SoR) is a new router architecture for providing rich services to Internet users by utilizing useful information extracted from network traffic. In SoR, stream reconstruction and selection is a fundamental process for providing the services in the application layer. After real-time reconstruction of stream data, SoR used a software character string analyzer to extract important required information. One of the promised services is a router-level network intrusion detection system. Because a network consists of hundreds of thousands of data streams, achieving an intended throughput while analyzing these stream data is a critical problem. We propose an acceleration method of string matching based on a heterogeneous system consisting of a CPU and a graphics processing unit. In addition, we designed and implemented a task controller that improves the distribution of POSIX-thread-based processes so that string matching can be performed concurrently depending on the status of the string matching system.**

Keywords—Service-oriented router; string matching; GPU; application layer analysis

I. Introduction

A router forwards a packet to another router after receiving it from an end-host. This process is repeated until the packet arrives at a destination end-host. This forwarding process is performed on the basis of both the destination IP address indicated in the packet header and a router forwarding table. A typical router checks only the packet header for seeking the next hop. A security attack is mainly hidden in the packet body as contents of the packet. If a router can control or refuse the forwarding process of a malicious packet to targeted clients autonomously, the risk of clients being intruded over the Internet can be reduced. To achieve this level of network security services, a stream reconstruction function is crucial because TCP/IP divides the original data stream into multiple packets. That is, the router providing the services has to reconstruct data streams from fragmented packets. After that, to find the security attacks from original data streams, a high-throughput string matching function is required. Without these reconstruction and string matching functions, routers cannot obtain the data stream or analyze information from the data stream.

To realize new services including router-level security, we propose a service-oriented router (SoR) [1] as a new router architecture. The SoR reconstructs stream data to extract application layer information and decides the forwarding route of a packet according to the contents of the packet. In the SoR, upon arrival at the SoR, packets are stored in an in-memory database (DB) after pre-processing of TCP/IP stream reconstruction in a network processor (NP). A stream processing engine (SPE), as a software-based string matching function, extracts desired information from stream data stored in the in-memory DB.

To provide a network intrusion detection system (NIDS) as a router-level security application, the SoR should search signatures of malicious packets. When the SoR detects a stream that is trying to attack any other clients, it suspends the forwarding process of the malicious stream, and it can notify the clients that they are the targets of an attack. After the notification, the SoR stores information about the attack in the DB. In addition to the SoR-based NIDS, the SoR can provide more flexible services that can be accomplished only by the SoR, such as a recommendation service that is based on cross-sectional behavioral analysis and efficient content delivery networking that is based on requested content [2].

One of the problems to be overcome in contents-based services on the SoR is that an efficient processing method is needed to handle a large amount of string information, which is not required in typical Layer-3 routing based on the IP address of a packet. The SPE has to handle a number of string data extracted from reconstructed streams. To achieve this, a typical router with an ASIC-based stream processing co-processer can accelerate the string matching function with reduced processing flexibility.

In this study, we present a software-based string analysis system that has both sufficient throughput for string searching and flexibility for providing services. To accomplish flexible and high-throughput processing, we used a graphics processing unit (GPU) as a high-performance processor that has highly parallelized architecture and data structures for achieving effective calculation power. A GPU is typically used for image processing such as image rendering and vertex calculation to create 3D images. However, recently, the opportunities to use the processer for general applications have increased because the requirements of flexible processing and low-cost computation are increasing. NVIDIA, a major provider of GPUs, also provides a flexible GPU-based program development environment called Compute Unified Device Architecture (CUDA) [3] as the development application programming interface (API) of general-purpose GPUs (GPGPUs). In the near future, a high-performance router with conventional PC parts such as the GPGPU will be introduced to the market.

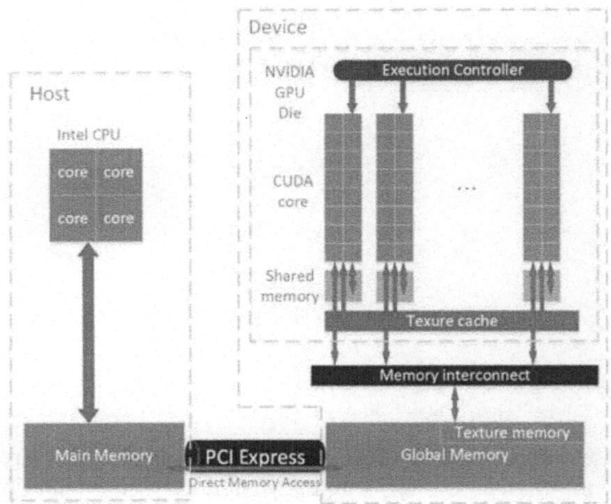

Fig. 1. A typical unified system consists of a CPU and a GPU.

According to the advancement of commoditization of routers, Maxeler Technologies released a new router named MaxNode 10G [4], which can be attached GPUs to its main system to accelerate processing. Moreover, Intel is developing the Intel Data Plane Development Kit [5], which realizes effective packet processing on a commonly used single Intel architecture CPU. In addition, Juniper Networks is developing the JunosV App Engine [6], which enables customization and optimization of network services by virtualizing network applications and providing services on general devices. With the advancement of GPUs and commoditization of router architecture, the possibility is very high that highly functional routers will use GPU-based technology to accelerate application layer information analysis.

Several studies attempted to solve the string matching problem on GPUs, and several new GPU-based string matching methods were recently proposed [11] [12]. According to related works and our preliminary study about GPU-based string matching, we proved that the GPU could achieve high-performance string matching by tuning the algorithm of parallel string matching. However, real-time and high-throughput processing for multiple-stream data of traffic has not been proposed but is indispensable for the Layer-7 analysis on the router. Our aim is to propose a multiple-stream processing algorithm of string matching on a GPGPU, which is also indispensable to the future SoR with conventional devices.

The main contribution of this paper is to provide a software solution using a GPU for string matching with multiple streams and multiple sets of queries extracted from NIDS software. We designed and implemented a GPU-based string matching program on CUDA, and the architecture of a task controller that monitors the status of the stream buffer and GPU resources and schedules processes depending on the status. The task controller uses a POSIX threads (pthreads) library to issue tasks concurrently and an effective asynchronous process scheduling method. POSIX thread, usually referred to as pthread, is a POSIX standard for threads [13]. We tested the combination string matching and task control system in an offline experimental environment and evaluated its performance.

TABLE I. FEATURES OF GPU MEMORIES

Memory	Location	Speed	Cache	Accessibility	Capacity
Register	on die	fast	n/a	read/write	16 KB/block
Shared	on die	fast	n/a	read/write	48 KB/block
Texture	off	fast (cache hit)	spatial cache	read only	n/a
Global	off	slow	yes	read/write	2,024 MB

This paper is arranged as follows. We explain features of the GPU and the parallel computing platform on CUDA in Section 2. We present related works about multiple string matching and adaptation of the string matching to the GPU architecture in Section 3 and describe the problem, goal, setup, design of the task controller, and implementation in Section 4. We evaluate our experimental results in Section 5 and finally conclude the paper with possible future works in Section 6.

II. Architecture of Graphics Processing Unit

A GPU has more than 100 of cores and several types of memories that have different access speeds and cache mechanisms. A GPU typically performs well when processing highly parallelized datasets such as in image rendering. In addition, the software design using GPU technology becomes more general in parallel processing, such as in financial simulation and genetic analysis. This design paradigm is called GPGPU. NVIDIA has provided a unified development environment named CUDA, which is a programming language used to design and program parallel processing for both the CPU and the GPU. CUDA uses general C/C++ code and the NVCC compiler, which is provided by NVIDIA to compile CUDA code. NVCC compiles the unified code and generates two types of executable code: one is host code that is executed on the CPU and the other code is kernel, which is executed on the GPU. After the host transfers the compiled kernel codes to the GPU via a PCI Express I/O serial interface, multiple GPU cores run the parallel program written in the kernel. All I/O data required in the process have to be transferred via PCI Express.

Figure 1 shows an example of a unified system that mainly consists of a CPU, a PCI Express bus, and a GPU. The GPU has more than 100 processing cores called CUDA cores, and it manages the CUDA cores as units of a streaming processor (SM), which consists of 32 CUDA cores. The CUDA architecture is based on the single-instruction, multiple-thread model, which executes a single instruction with multiple logical threads simultaneously. CUDA executes a parallelized kernel program with 3D threads and blocks that are hierarchically constructed in the grain of execution. A thread is the smallest unit of a logical processing unit. A kernel can employ a number of threads, and management of the threads strongly affects the processing performance. Although this processing strategy is suitable for effective parallel processing, warp divergence, namely fatal performance degradation, occurs when part of a thread in a single warp diverges by executing an "if" branch instruction. Hence, it is better to avoid warp divergence whenever possible.

A GPU has several kinds of memory, and Table I summarizes features of those memories. Global memory, also called device memory, has the largest capacity, approximately 2–6 GB among the GPU memories. However, the access speed to global memory is extremely slow, which consumes about 400–600 clock cycles. Shared memory has approximately 48 KB of capacity and is located on each block. This memory can be accessed only in a few clock cycles, because it is located on the GPU die. Texture memory shares the memory space of global memory, and the memory has a hardware cache mechanism to accelerate the accesses by using a spatial locality. Effective use of both the hierarchically structured threads and various memories is vital to high-performance processing on a GPU.

III. Multi-Pattern String Matching Algorithm

A string matching algorithm is used for searching multiple text patterns from other text data. String matching algorithms can be classified into two types: 1) string matching for a single pattern and 2) string matching for a pattern set consisting of multiple patterns simultaneously. Single-pattern string matching can be classified into prefix matching and suffix matching. One well-known prefix matching algorithm is the Knuth-Morris-Pratt (KMP) algorithm [7]. In the suffix matching algorithm, the matching process is started from the suffix of a pattern. The Boyer-Moore (BM) algorithm [8] is an effective string matching algorithm that consists of two processes, namely, a process to construct failure transition and a process of matching that is started from the suffix of a pattern.

Finding a pattern set that consists of multiple patterns requires some advanced techniques. A potentially possible solution to effective string matching with multiple patterns is the Aho-Corasick (AC) algorithm [10]. We thus used the AC algorithm as the basis of our GPU-based string matching algorithm for the SoR. In the next subsection, we explain how it works, why the AC algorithm can potentially satisfy our purpose, and how it can be applied to the GPU-based string matching system on the SoR.

A. Aho-Corasick algorithm

Many studies have recently been conducted around string matching algorithms. Alfred V. Aho proposed the AC algorithm, which uses a deterministic finite automaton (DFA) constructed by using a pattern set to find desired patterns [10]. The AC algorithm searches all patterns in a single path with $O(N)$ of time complexity, where N indicates the number of text data.

The DFA traverses its transition state to search patterns over a state transition table (STT) depending on the stream of input text. A STT is represented as a 3D table in which rows are indexed by a state and columns are indexed by a possible input character. The AC algorithm uses the STT to define the behavior of the DFA by using the following branches on condition. The first branch is the "goto" function, which defines transition to the next state corresponding to the combination of the current state and an input character. The second branch is the "output" function, which determines whether the next state matches the state of any patterns. When the "output" function returns a matched state, the program outputs the combination of the matched pattern and the position in the input text where the matched pattern exists. The third branch is the "failure" function, which defines the state transition corresponding to the current state, regardless of input character whenever the "goto" function reports a failure of state transition to the automaton. Figure 2 shows an example of DFA associated with five patterns {"he," "his," "she," "her," "hers"}. The solid lines in Figure 2 indicate transition of the "goto" function, the dashed lines indicate transition defined as a failure transition on the "failure" function, and at double-circled nodes, the "output" function has reported a match of a specific pattern.

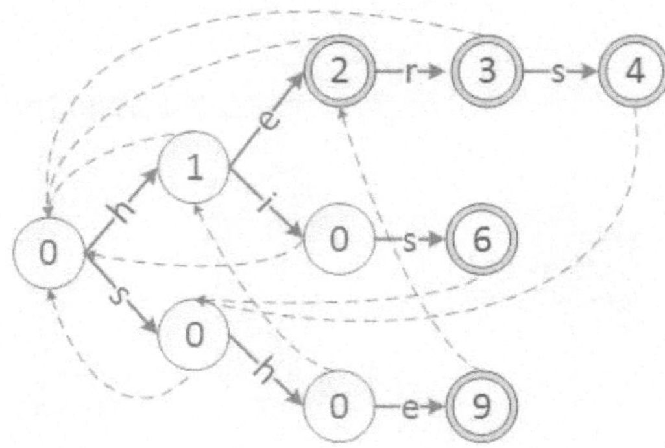

Fig. 2. An example behavior of DFA associated with five patterns {"he," "his," "she," "her," "hers"} in AC algorithm.

When implementing the AC algorithm to a GPU program written in CUDA directly, a couple of problems interfere with effective matching. The first problem is that the branch on condition leads to significant degradation of throughput. Because processing performance is highly dependent on the divergence of threads, we should manage our GPU program to minimize the number of "if" branches. In addition, because the "goto," "failure," and "output" functions cause performance degradation, these functions should be eliminated. The second problem is management of memory allocation and memory accesses. The AC algorithm requires many kinds of memory accesses, such as reading the character from an input stream and next transition from the STT and writing the matching result account for those memory accesses. Optimization of these memory accesses is required to exploit resources of the GPU and to improve performance.

B. Adaptation of the Aho-Corasick algorithm for a GPU

To address the problems of warp divergence and memory access described above, Lin et al. proposed the Parallel Failureless Aho-Corasick (PFAC) algorithm as a GPU-based multiple-string matching algorithm [11]. In the PFAC algorithm, the string matching process is performed with a pre-constructed PFAC automaton, which traverses the STT only by the "goto" function. This method eliminates the warp divergence caused by branch instructions of failure transitions.

The PFAC automaton can be represented only by two branches: one is a state transition defined by the "goto" function, and the other is the "output" function. In this method, however, another problem occurs because the "failure" function lacks a "backtrack" function. Figure 3 shows behavior of the DFA associated with the five patterns in the PFAC algorithm. The PFAC automaton cannot detect patterns that appear in the middle of a matching process of a thread, and this is a fatal problem. To compensate for the lack of a "backtrack" function, every thread begins the matching process from every character of the text data as a starting point correspondingly. A searching process of each thread is terminated when the thread fails to match patterns. This matching method uses each character in every position of text data as a starting point. Thus, the method eliminates any misdetection of pattern that is caused by the lack of a "backtrack" function.

It is important to optimize memory accesses, especially in the PFAC algorithm. Memory accesses in the PFAC algorithm are classified into three parts. The first part entails reading a byte of character from an input stream. The second part consists of reading the number of next states corresponding to the combination of current state and an input character, and the third entails writing a matching result after the matching process is terminated. In the PFAC method, the STT is allocated in texture memory, which has a cache mechanism to accelerate accesses by using a spatial locality. HTTP traffic shows strong spatial locality because the traffic data information is represented in structured languages, such as XML and HTML. Threads frequently access columns associated with specific characters of the STT. Furthermore, the frequent access to rows of the STT associated with the characters is also dominant.

IV. Design of Task Controller and Implementation

A. *Design of task controller*

For a string matching function on a SoR, throughput and latency are the most important factors to be considered in order to provide a better user experience. Another requirement of the string matching on a SoR is fault avoidance. The faults in the string matching process are situations where some of the matching processes in the device terminate in failure. The faults can occur when there is not enough memory in the device. To improve the actual throughput of the string matching process, and to avoid faults, we propose a task controller that handles multiple-string matching tasks depending on the status of the host and the device.

When designing the task controller, we found it imperative to consider the reasonable architecture and parameterization of the status of the system: CPU memory usage, cache hit ratio, etc. The total performance of the proposed PFAC automaton strongly depends on this architecture. The statuses of the system that possibly affect the throughput of the process are a construction of the PFAC automaton, data transfer between host and device, and kernel execution on device. Every single process of the PFAC method has already been optimized sufficiently at the algorithmic level. On the other hand, actual use of the PFAC method for a string matching function on a router requires optimization of the task handling method.

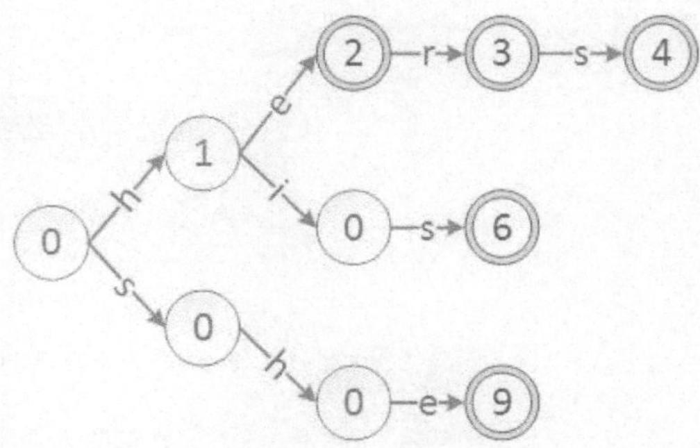

Fig. 3. An example behavior of the DFA associated with five patterns {"he," "his," "she," "her," "hers"} in the PFAC algorithm.

As a first step toward improving the task handling method, the task controller distributes multiple-string matching processes to multiple pthreads in order to process the multiple tasks effectively. The task assigned to a pthread is executed by the same single pthread, and the task controller is issued the multiple pthreads asynchronously. The task controller improves the overall throughput of the string matching processes by processing the multiple tasks concurrently in the method. As a second step to improve throughput, we set a threshold for the amount of accumulated data in the stream buffer. The string matching process consists of kernel execution and data transfer between host and device. The processing throughput can be maximized when enough stream data are stored in the buffer. The amount of accumulated stream data in a single request of the string matching process significantly affects the throughput of the execution of the string matching. Therefore, the task controller issues the ignition request of the string matching process to a pthread only when the amount of data in the stream buffer exceeds the threshold. In this method, each pthread can exploit the resources of the device.

In order to reduce the processing latency of the string matching process, we also set a threshold of waiting time for completing input stream data. If possible, the task controller waits until the stream buffer is filled with input stream data up

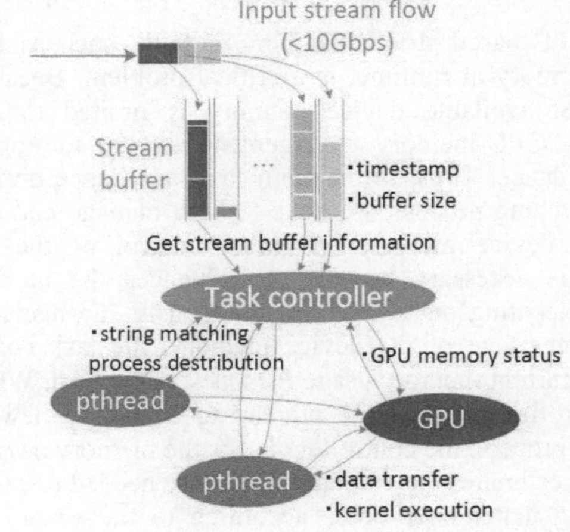

Fig. 4. Implementation of process destribution and monitoring mechanisms.

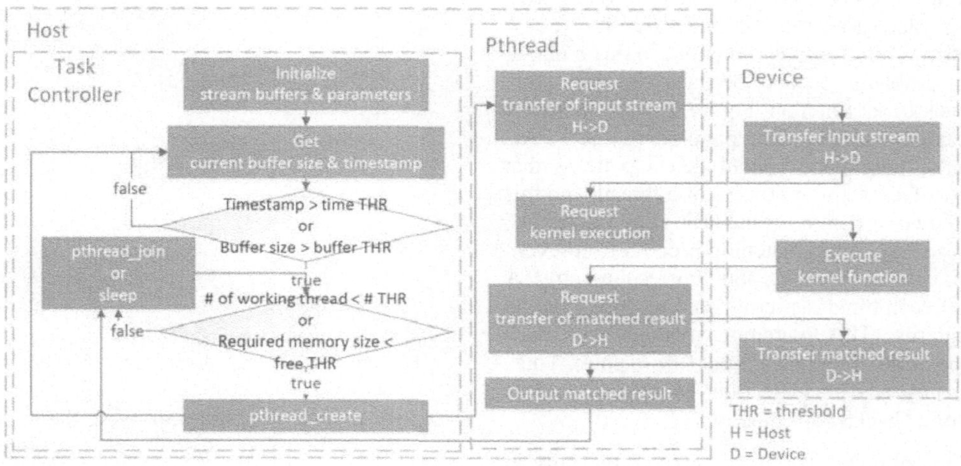

Fig. 5. Flowchart of process destribution and monitoring mechanisms of overall systems.

TABLE II. BASIC INFORMATION OF EXPERIMENTAL COMPONENTS

Component		Details
Host	CPU	Intel Core i7-3930K CPU @ 3.2 GHz
	Memory	32 GB DDR3 @ 1,600 MHz
Device	GPU	NVIDIA GeForce GTX 680
	Memory	2,048 MB 256-bit-GDDR5 memory

to a timeout. However, in terms of delay, the task controller should not wait for a long time because the waiting time for the completion of input stream data is added to the total delay of packet forwarding and occasionally causes degradation in user experience. When the waiting time exceeds a timeout, the task controller requests the string matching process to a pthread, and the device executes the process regardless of the amount of accumulated data in the buffer. On the other hand, waiting time timeouts that are too short may also cause deterioration of throughput and exhaustion of both GPU resources and the PCI Express bandwidth. One of our purposes is to decide the optimal value of the threshold practically through experiments.

On GPU-based string matching, a fault, such as lack of device memory at runtime, is a critical problem. Because the amount of available device memory is limited to several gigabytes, GPU-memory management is vital to improving fault avoidance. Thus, to maintain fault avoidance during the string matching process, we have to both manage and control usage of device memory. Accurate control of the device memory is necessary because it influences the number of kernels executing on a GPU simultaneously. To manage and control the usage of the device memory, the task controller provides current memory usage feedback to the host. When the task controller launches the pthread to execute a new string matching process, the controller checks the memory usage. The controller estimates the amount of memory needed to execute a new string matching process according to the stream buffer size. Moreover, the controller compares the amount of available memory with the amount of memory required to execute the new process. If the amount of available memory does not meet the requirement, a new pthread is not launched until enough memory is released by the finishing pthreads.

The task controller operations for managing throughput, latency, and scalability are presented in Figure 4 as an architecture and in Figure 5 as a flowchart. After initializing stream buffers and pthreads, the controller obtains the states of the buffers and a timestamp. When a timeout occurs or the amount of the stream buffer exceeds the threshold, a condition flag becomes true, which indicates whether the stream data should be processed or not. If the task controller detects a stream whose condition is true, the controller checks the status of device memory. If all conditions are satisfied, the task controller calls the "pthread_create" API to create a new pthread to request a string matching process of accumulated stream data. If the conditions are not satisfied, the task controller waits for a timeout. Finally, the controller calls the "pthread_join" API to terminate a pthread.

B. Implementation

Table II shows specifications of our implemented experimental environment. The host components have an Intel i7-3930K CPU and 32 GB of Double-Data-Rate 3 (DDR3) main memory. The device consists of an NVIDIA GeForce GTX 680 GPU. The host and the device are connected via a PCI Express 2.0 x16 interface, which has 16 GBps of bidirectional bandwidth. Our experimental software environment included a task manager program written in C/C++ language with a pthreads library, and an NVCC compiler that compiles the program. We used the CUDA toolkit to develop an application that provides a comprehensive development environment for C/C++ developers to use to build GPU-accelerated applications. The toolkit and compiler run on CentOS 6.3 on a 64-bit Linux system. In addition, we used Snort Rules [14] as a desired pattern set. Snort is open-source signature matching NIDS software. We extracted signatures specified by a "content" statement and used the signatures as malicious patterns to be searched. As input text streams for the experiment, we used traffic data captured from December 5 to 12, 2011, by the gateway that connects the Nishi Laboratory to the Internet.

TABLE III. RATIO OF STREAM SIZE IN TRAFFIC

Data size	Percentage
>16 MB	62.1
>8 MB	66.1
>4 MB	72.1
>2 MB	76.8

V. EVALUATION

We first evaluated the throughput of the string matching process in terms of the number of concurrent pthreads. Figure 6 shows the throughput of each kernel on a device when the stream size and concurrent numbers of pthreads are varied. In Figure 6, the horizontal axis corresponds to the amount of stream buffer to be processed, and the vertical axis corresponds to the throughput. In this case, the controller issues up to eight pthreads concurrently. The processing throughput for small-sized stream data is poor regardless of the number of concurrent streams. This is because the constant overhead to launch a kernel is relatively large. On the other hand, the string matching process for the stream buffer that stores more than 16 MB of data achieved a throughput of up to 108 Gbps, and this throughput is 3.4 times faster than the performance achieved in a previously published study [11]. On the other hand, the processes with four and eight concurrent pthreads show poor performance, at 49.8 Gbps and 14.2 Gbps, respectively, in the best case because of the congestion in the execution engine. From the evaluation, we found that well-managed assignment of multiple processes may improve the performance of the kernel function of application layer analysis.

We also evaluated the relationship between the waiting time for the stream buffers and the throughput of the overall task in a pthread (Figure 7). The horizontal axis corresponds to the timeout, and the vertical axis corresponds to the throughput. The processes in a pthread include transferring stream data to a device from a host, kernel execution, and transferring matching results to a host from a device. Each line in Figure 7 shows the throughput of a single process that works with different numbers of concurrent pthreads. The single pthread with longer waiting time showed better throughput, at most 8.0 Gbps under the condition of 12,800 ms of waiting time. In this case, approximately 16 MB of traffic data was accumulated in the stream buffer. The stream buffer with longer waiting time can accumulate more traffic data in the stream buffer. The performance of string matching depends significantly on the amount of stream size, as shown in Figure 7. Table III shows the ratio of the total amount of stream data communicated in streams of 2, 4, 8, and 16 MB. According to the table, streams communicating more than 4 MB occupy 72.1% of the amount of all traffic data communicated in the network. If it is assumed that the task controller performs the process only for streams that communicate more than 4 MB of data, approximately 7.21 Gbps of throughput on average is a requirement. In this experiment, the throughput of the processes with 6,400 ms of waiting time fully meets the requirement except concurrent execution with eight pthreads.

As mentioned above, fault avoidance is an important factor; thus, we implemented three methods memory management and evaluated both the number of errors and the memory usage at runtime. Figure 8 shows the amount of memory used by two

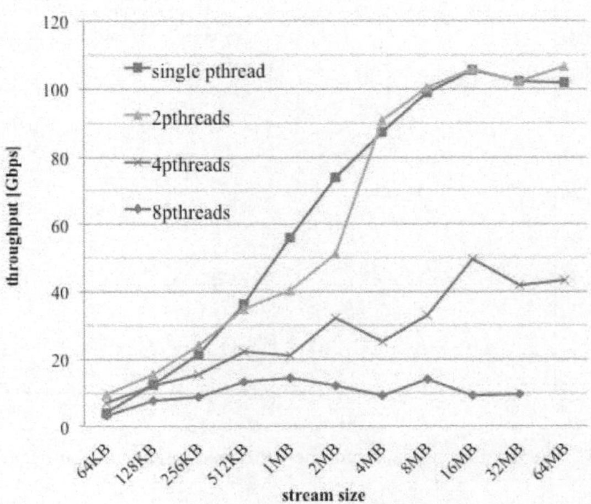

Fig. 6. Comparison of throughputs of processing in the GPU kernel with different numbers of concurrent pthreads.

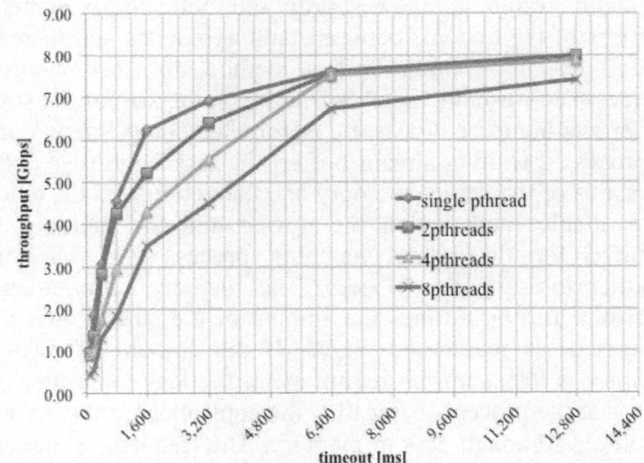

Fig. 7. Relationships between the length of timeout of stream buffer and the throughput of overall processing in each pthread.

pthreads executing different string matching processes concurrently in each management method. The timeout of the stream buffer is set to 400 ms because the evaluation of the relationship between waiting time of the stream buffer and throughput of the string matching process implied that a waiting time of over 400 ms can meet the throughput requirement. The three management methods are titled "no threshold," "constant threshold," and "dynamic threshold" in Figure 8. In the "no threshold" results, the task controller issues string matching processes to pthreads regardless of the status of the device memory. When the task controller detects that a stream buffer is filled with enough stream data or that a timeout of the stream buffer has occurred, the controller issues a new process to handle the string matching. The pthreads processing string matching is issued up to the maximum number of pthreads. In this experiment, the memory usage results with the "no threshold" method in Figure 8 indicate that 12 of 829 processes aborted because of an out-of-memory error.

We also tested the "constant threshold" method, in which the task controller can issue new processes only when there is enough available memory in the device. The amount of available memory is constant throughout the whole processes. We set the constant threshold of memory size to 800 MB of free memory. Although doing this eliminated all runtime errors,

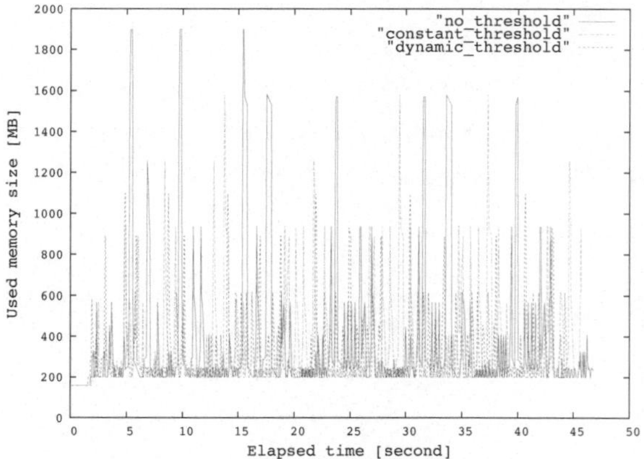

Fig. 8. The memory usage at runtime with three management methods.

the overall execution time increased by 8.3% compared with that of the "no threshold" method.

The third implementation method named "dynamic threshold" resulted in the best proposed fault avoidance method in terms of the tradeoff between fault avoidance and increased overall execution time. In this method, the task controller decides the threshold value depending on the size of the stream buffer waiting to be processed. Before launching a new pthread to process a waiting stream buffer, the task controller obtains the status of the device memory and then compares the amount of available memory on the device and the memory size required for the string matching process and determines whether to issue the process. The memory requirement is determined to be 5 times the amount of the stream data to be processed, as mentioned above. If the amount of available memory is less than the requirement, the task controller does not issue the process. After that, the controller waits 100 ms to accumulate enough data in memory. The frequent reference to the device status deteriorates the throughput of the string matching process because the reference places a burden on the device. With these techniques, we also eliminated all runtime errors and improved the performance reduction to only a 0.8% increase of overall execution time, which is less than one-tenth of an increase with the "constant threshold" method.

VI. Conclusion

We proposed and implemented a GPU-based application layer analyzer for an SoR. This study is the first proposal and implementation that enables the parallel and multiple-stream analysis that is an essential requirement to use the router. The analyzer accelerated a string matching function that is required to analyze application layer information extracted from reconstructed streams on the SoR. The main contribution of the analyzer is a task controller, which is designed to optimize the workload of GPU tasks for the string matching process. The task controller on a host system distributes the string matching processes to multiple pthreads optimally and concurrently by monitoring GPU memory usage, the amount of stream data stored in stream buffers, and timestamp of a stream. The task controller improves overall throughput and latency of the string matching process and fault avoidance.

In our experiment using actual traffic data captured in Nishi Laboratory and NIDS rules extracted from the filtering database used in Snort, we found that the proposed GPU-based string matching achieved up to 108 Gbps of kernel-level throughput when processing 16 MB of stream data. We concluded that 4 MB is an optimal stream buffer threshold size to process the stream data effectively. From an evaluation of the waiting time of the stream buffer, we concluded that 6,400 ms of waiting time is sufficient to achieve at least 7.41 Gbps of throughput required for processing data streams that communicate more than 4 MB of data. To realize fault avoidance of the analyzer, we evaluated GPU memory management methods in three ways. We confirmed that the "dynamic threshold" method shows most stable memory usage without causing fatal errors. In addition, the method suppressed the degradation of overall execution time of the string matching process to only 0.8%.

Acknowledgment

This work was partially supported by Funds for integrated promotion of social system reform and research and development, Ministry of the environment and Grant-in-Aid for Scientific Research (B) (25280033).

References

[1] Inoue, K., Akashi, D., Koibuchi, M., Kawashima, H., and Nishi, H., "Semantic router using data stream to enrich services," Proc. International Conference on Future Internet Technologies (CFI08) Seoul, Korea, June 18–20, 2008, pp. 20–23.

[2] Wijekoon, J., Harahap, E., and Nishi, H., "SoR based request routing for future CDN," 6th International Conference on Application of Information and Communication Technologies (AICT) 2012, October 17–19, 2012, pp. 1–5.

[3] NVIDIA, Developer Zone, https://developer.nvidia.com/category/zone/cuda-zone.

[4] MAXELER Technologies, http://www.maxeler.com/.

[5] Intel Data Plane Development Kit Video, http://www.intel.com/content/www/us/en/communications/embedded-data-plane-development-kit-video.html?wapkw=data+plane+development+kit.

[6] JunosV App Engine - Network Virtualization Software Platform - Juniper Networks, http://www.juniper.net/us/en/products-services/software/junosv-app-engine/.

[7] Weiner, P., "Linear pattern matching algorithms," IEEE Conference Record of 14th Annual Symposium on Switching and Automata Theory, 1973. SWAT '08, October 15–17, 1973, pp. 1–11.

[8] Moore, J.S., "Introducing iteration into the Pure Lisp theorem prover," IEEE Transactions on Software Engineering, vol. SE-1, no. 3, pp. 328–338, September 1975.

[9] Karp, R.M., and Rabin, M.O., "Efficient randomized pattern-matching algorithms," IBM J. Res. Dev., vol. 31, no. 2, pp. 249–260, March 1987.

[10] Aho, A.V., and Corasick, M.J., "Efficient string matching: an aid to bibliographic search," Commun. ACM, vol. 18, pp. 333–340, June 1975.

[11] Peng, J., Chen, H., and Shi, S. "The GPU-based string matching system in advanced AC algorithm," 2010 IEEE 10th International Conference on Computer and Information Technology (CIT), June 29–July 10, 2010, 1158–1163.

[12] Zha, Xinyan; Sahni, Sartaj, "GPU-to-GPU and Host-to-Host Multipattern String Matching on a GPU," *Computers, IEEE Transactions on* , vol.62, no.6, pp.1156,1169, June 2013

[13] Information technology -- Portable Operating System Interface (POSIX) -- Part 1: System Application Program Interface, http://www.iso.org/iso/catalogue_detail.htm?csnumber=24426.

[14] Snort, Home Page, http://www.snort.org/.

Minimum Spanning Tree For Energy Saving in Interconnection Networks

Hai Nguyen, Daniel Franco and Emilio Luque
Computer Architecture & Operating Systems Department
Universitat Autònoma de Barcelona, 08193 Bellaterra, Spain
hai.nguyen@caos.uab.es, daniel.franco@uab.es, emilio.luque@uab.es

Abstract— *While processing nodes are completely connected only with a minimum spanning tree, over provisioning network resource is necessary to deal with fault tolerance and load balancing. However, in low traffic load situation those network resources consume a substantial unproductive energy. Network components contribute an increasing amount of energy consumption of an interconnected system. Many energy saving mechanisms have been proposed to have a better use of the network resources in term of energy consumption. Dynamic Link Width mechanism judiciously adjusts the link width as the function of traffic and thus reduces the power consumed when the traffic load is low. However, this mechanism incurs an additional serialization latency when packets are carried in thinner links. In this paper, we present a mechanism where a minimum tree with maximum link width is maintained. This mechanism saves energy while minimizes the serialization latency incurred.*

Keywords: minimum spanning tree, energy saving, dynamic link width, interconnection networks

1. Introduction

With the ever-increasing in link speed and consequently its energy consumption, network performance is no longer the only priority in interconnection network systems. Link component contributes a substantial portion of the energy consumed by the network, with about 58% [1]. However, the energy burned in the link component is insensitive to the fluctuation of the trafffic on them. Thus a better link power management is received more attention.

Link energy consumption saving has been addressing by many proposals with different approaches. The Dynamic Voltage Scaling approach [1] adjusts the link frequency as a function of traffic. This approach has a potential of save a substantial amount of energy but it faces a complexity in hardware design. Another approach, Dynamic Link Shutdown mechanism takes the Dynamic Voltage Scaling to an extreem. This mechanism turns off underutilized links and maintains only a subset of network resources that are adequate for a given traffic [2], [3], [4], [5]. This mechanism has to deal with the complication in the changes of topology and deadlock avoidance. The Dynamic Link Width approach judiciously tunes the link width according to the bandwidth required [6], [7], [8]. With the emerging bit-serial technology, every link consists of several physical lanes. For example, Infiniband offers the link configuration with up to 12 lanes (denoted as $12x$), similarly links in PCI-Express comes with varied width level up to $16x$. With this technology, the Dynamic Link Width approach comes naturally. Our work focuses on that approach leveraging the dynamic link width variance.

The 2013 International Conference on Parallel and Distributed Processing Techniques and Applications (PDPTA'13)

With Dynamic Link Width mechanism, in low load situation links are adjusted to be thinner and therefore they have low bandwidth. The average packet latency suffers from the increase in serialization latency. When performance is the first priority for many systems this increase in latency is sometimes not tolerable. To address this problem, we propose a mechanism that expands the Dynamic Link Width approach, where a Minimum Spanning Tree (MST) serves as a minimum subset of network resources. It guarantees the connectivity of the system and it is maintained at maximum bandwidth. Coupling with a routing policy that gives preference to the link belonging to the MST, in low load situation the mechanism saves energy with less additional serialization latency introduced by thin links. This paper also gives the analysis about the low bound of link energy consumption for different size of the network, when using MST.

In this paper, the Minimum Spanning Tree configuration for the main family of network topology (Fat-tree) and the low bound for link energy consumption when applying the mechanism is presented in section 2. Next, we explains the Monitoring & Decision process in section 3. Section 4 describes our proposed routing algorithm that takes into account the fact that all links in MST are always at maximum speed. Our experiments in section 5 show that there is a significant improvement in latency when maintaining a MST with full network capacity when applying the saving mechanism. Finally, in section 6 we draw some conclusions about our work.

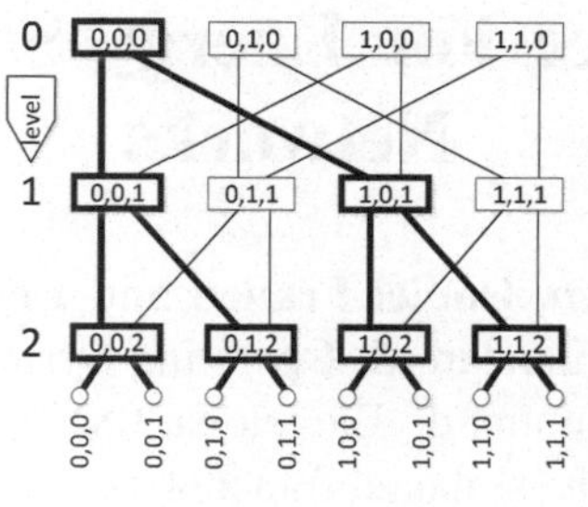

(a) 2-ary 3-tree

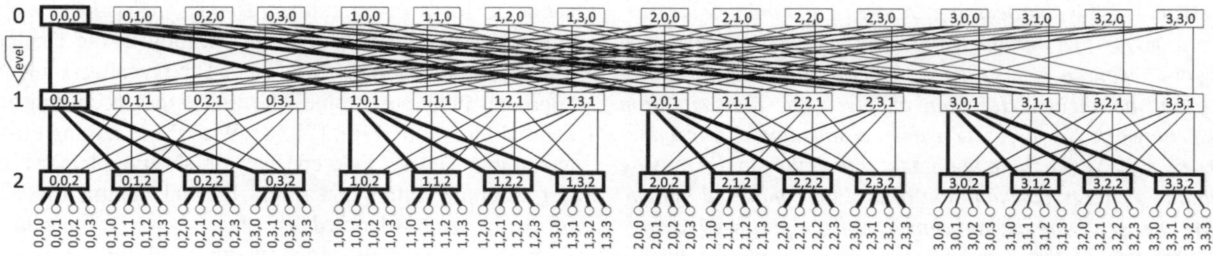

(b) 4-ary 3-tree

Fig. 1: MST for k-ary n-tree

2. Minimum Spanning Tree Configuration

For an interconnection network system, the resource over-provisioning provides path redundancy and facilitates load balancing and fault tolerance. In general a minimum spanning tree (MST) with bidirectional links is enough to keep the whole network connected. In low load situation this subset of the network is enough to deliver the demanded traffic. k-ary n-tree is one of the most popular network topology, it offers a low hop count and it makes use of the high radix of modern routers. We will describe the MST configuration for this topology in more detail.

A k-ary n-tree [9] provides the connectivity for $N = k^n$ processing nodes and $S = nk^{n-1}$ intermediate routers. The routers are arranged in n stages labeled from level 0 to $n-1$, level 0 is the root level. Every router is connected with k outputs and k inputs. Processing nodes are identified by n digits radix k. Thus a node is addressed by $(p_0, p_1, ..., p_{n-1})$ where $p_i \in \{0, 1, ..., k-1\}$. Routers are identified by $n-1$ digits radix k combined with their level. A router is addressed by $(w_0, w_1, ..., w_{n-2}, l)$, where $w_i \in \{0, 1, ..., k-1\}$ and $l \in \{0, 1, ..., n-1\}$, l is the level of the stage where the router belongs to.

Two routers $(w_0, w_1, ..., w_{n-2}, l)$ and $(w'_0, w'_1, ..., w'_{n-2}, l')$ are connected if they are belong to 2 consecutive stages $l' = l+1$ and $w_i = w'_i$ with all $i \neq l$. Processing nodes are only connected to the routers at the $n-1$ level, and a node $(p_0, p_1, ..., p_{n-1})$ is connected with a router $(w_0, w_1, ..., w_{n-2}, n-1)$ if $p_i = w_i$ with all $0 \leq i \leq n-2$.

A minimum spanning tree for for a k-ary n-tree is a subset of the tree that connects all the processing nodes. It consists of all processing nodes, a number of routers and bidirectional channels between them. A router $(w_0, w_1, ..., w_{n-2}, l)$ belongs to the MST if has one of these two properties:

1) $l = n-1$ (all the routers that in the $l-1$ level belongs to the tree
2) $l < n-1$ and $w_i = 0$ with $\forall i \in \{l, ..., n-2\}$

An MST corresponds to the rules above for 2-ary 3-tree is shown in Fig. 1(a), for 4-ary 3-tree is illustrated in Fig. 1(b). In those figures the MST is highlighted in bold.

The number of routers in every stage is k^{n-1}, with n stages makes the total number of routers $|R|$ is nk^{n-1}. The total number of uni-directional links in k-ary n-tree is $L_{total} = 2k|R| = 2nk^n$.

The number of routers that participate in MST is: $|MST_R| = k^{n-1} + k^{n-2} + ... + k + 1 = \frac{k^n - 1}{k-1}$

The number of processing nodes $|P|$ is: k^n. Thus the total of nodes is:

$|MST| = |MST_R| + |P| = \frac{k^{n+1} - 1}{k-1}$

The number of unidirectional links in MST is $L_{MST} = 2(|MST| - 1) = \frac{2k(k^n - 1)}{k-1}$

Assuming that a link consumes the energy proportionally with its width level and a link consists of M lanes corresponding to M link width level. In the lowest energy consumption situation when only links belonging to MST are at maximum link width level, and others are at minimum width level (level 1). It sets the minimum bound ρ_{min} of energy consumed by links:

$$\rho_{min} = \frac{L_{MST} * M + (L_{total} - L_{MST}) * 1}{ML_{total}} = \frac{(M-1)k(k^n - 1) + nk^n(k-1)}{Mnk^n(k-1)}$$

The low bound of energy consumption for k-ary n-tree topology with different size and number of lanes is described in Table 1.

Table 1: Low bound of energy consumption of k-ary n-tree

k	n	Processing nodes	M	ρ_{min}
4	3	64	4	57.81%
8	3	512	4	53.52%
16	3	4096	4	51.66%
32	3	32768	4	50.81%
4	3	64	12	48.44%
8	3	512	12	43.19%
16	3	4096	12	40.92%
32	3	32768	12	39.87%

3. Monitoring & Decision Making

If a link belongs to MST, it is always maintained at maximum width level and thus maximum speed. Otherwise, if it does not belong to MST, its utilization is monitored to prescribe whether to adjust its width according to the traffic carried on it. At a given time t, if there is a $phit$ being carried by the link then the link is marked as being used at that time. The usage history of the link is recorded for the last H cycles as the sliding window as described in equation 1.

$$LU = \frac{\sum_{t=1}^{H} A(t)}{H} \quad (1)$$

Where A(t) = $\begin{cases} 1 \text{ if traffic passes in cycle } t \\ 0 \text{ if no traffic passes in cycle } t \end{cases}$ and H is a sliding history window size.

Every certain period of time T the mechanism is triggered to check whether the link is under-utilized or over-utilized. The value of link utilization (LU) of the most recent sliding window denoted as $LU\_current$, while the LU of the earlier sliding window is shown as LU_past. Then the predicted LU is calculated as:

$$LU\_prediction = \alpha * LU\_past + (1-\alpha) * LU\_current \quad (2)$$

Where α is the weighed value for the past. The higher the value α the more weight the mechanism put on the past. If $\alpha = 0$ the mechanism only considers the value of $LU_{current}$.

The predicted LU has the value ranged from 0 to 1. It reflects how busy the link is. If the value of $LU\_prediction$ exceeds the high utilization threshold th_high and the link is not at its maximum width level then the mechanism triggers the link to increase its width. On the other hand, if $LU\_prediction$ is lower than the low utilization threshold th_low and the link is not operating at its minimum width then its width is adjusted to the lower level. The link is never completely turned off to avoid the complication with the dynamic topology changes.

4. MST-Channel-Considered-First Routing Algorithm

With the MST configured with all channels at maximum link speed, in low load situation it is preferred to move traffic only on MST and leave the lower speed links idle and being put at their minimum width. By doing so, we can avoid the serialization latency incurred by spreading packets in low bandwidth links. This behavior is achieved by an adaptive routing algorithm that prioritizes high speed links when there are more than one option to deliver a packet.

Taking an example in k-ary n-tree topology, a packet is routed in 2 phases. The first phase is the ascending phase when a packet go up to the $Nearest\ Common\ Ancestor$. After that, the descending phase takes place where the packet is delivered to its desired destination. The routing path in descending phase for the packet is deterministic. However, in the ascending phase, at every intermediate router the packet has k productive options to choose. Even though all these k options take the packet toward its desired destination, the decision about which port to take is related to the load balancing problem where packets are preferred to be carried in a less congested paths. Similar situation for k-ary n-cube topology, for minimum routing algorithm at every intermediate router the packet has n productive ports towards the destination.

In low load traffic, only a small fraction of network resource is enough to deliver packets. Thus the congestion and traffic load balancing are not an issue in that situation. Our objective is to deliver packets so that they incur a minimum serialization latency while maximizing the number of links being put in low speed mode for energy saving purpose.

We propose a routing policy that takes into account this information about the high speed of MST-channel to give preference for those channels. With a set of several compatible output ports, there are 2 cases:

1) There is not a MST-channel in the compatible output set. In this case normal routing algorithm is applied to select output port.
2) There is a MST-channel in the output port set. The routing algorithm takes the outport coupled with this channel as the selected output port, unless there is a strong evidence not to do so (using a normal routing

algorithm instead). The routing algorithm does not take that outport if one of these conditions holds:

- Other channels are also at maximum speed
- The input buffer at the far end of the channel is higher than a threshold $buffer\_occupancy\_threshold$. It is a signal indicating that this channel is over-utilized and packets should take another port.

Because the topology remains unchanged, there is no special care needed for deadlock avoidance issue. The routing decision is summarized in Algorithm 1.

Algorithm 1 MST-Channel-Considered-First Routing Algorithm

```
Getting the set of compatible ports
if There is not a MST-channel is in that set then
    best_outport = Normal_Routing_Alg()
else
    if Other links are at maximum speed or buffer occupancy exceeds the threshold then
        best_outport = Normal_Routing_Alg()
    else
        best_outport = the port of the MST-channel
    end if
end if
Exporting the best_outport
```

5. Experimental Results

Experiments were conducted using the modified version of $booksim$ framework [10]. The interconnection network consists of 64 processing nodes, arranged in 4-ary 3-tree networks. The router architecture is configured with virtual channel flow control, there are 16 virtual channels, each has 16 flits in the input buffer length. Packets have the same size with 4 flits.

For synthetic traffic patterns, 2 patterns were generated are $transpose$ and $uniform$. The th_low and th_high value were configured with 0.2 and 0.6 respectively. Every channels consists of 12 lanes. The weighed value for the past α is 0.1. The energy consumption of the link is assumed to be proportional to the number of active lanes. The relative link energy consumption is the percentage of the power consumed by the link component when the energy saving mechanism is applied versus the default system (with no energy saving mechanism).

To see the effects of the mechanism, simulations were carried out with different level of traffic load. There is a clear trend in how much energy the link component consumes as shown in Fig. 2. When the traffic load is low, the relative link energy consumption has the value around 52.5%, which is very close to the theoretical value of 48.44% which was pointed in Table 1. With the load increases, the mechanism triggers more links to increase their width to increase the link bandwidth. As the consequence, the relative link energy consumption increases steadily with the traffic load. And the mechanism gains no energy saving with the normalized traffic load higher than 0.6.

The energy saving comes with the expense of latency increase. For both traffic patterns, when the relative energy consumption is equal to the value of the default system (no energy saving achieved) the latency in our mechanism with the routing algorithm described in 4 is less than or equal to the latency of the default system with Adaptive Routing Nearest Common Ancestor [11]. With the normalized load less than 0.6 there is a typical tradeoff with a slight increase in average packet latency for energy saving, as can be seen from Fig. 3.

Other experiments were conducted with traffic load imported from a trace file. The traffic is traced from the application Fluid Animate Particle Simulation using Smoothed Particle Hydrodynamics [12] using the Netrace framework [13] with the network configured as described above.

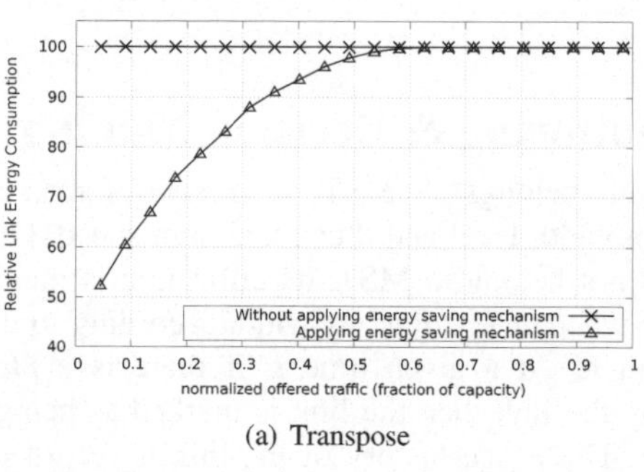

(a) Transpose

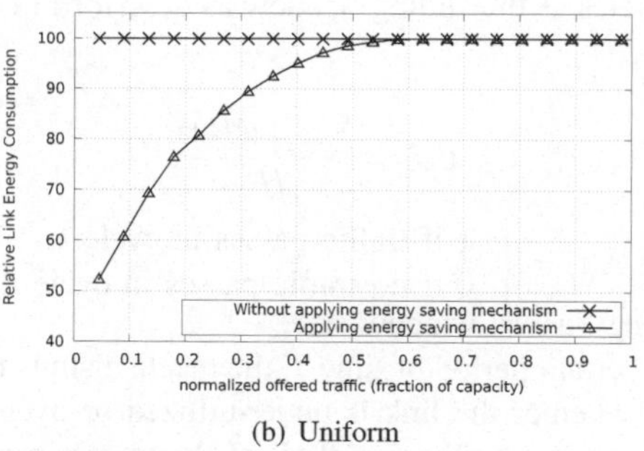

(b) Uniform

Fig. 2: Relative Link Energy Consumption

To verify the effectiveness of the mechanism in reducing average serialization latency, 3 set of experiments were set up. The first case is no energy saving mechanism is applied, the second is the saving mechanism is applied but no MST is taken into account with the Adaptive Routing Nearest Common Ancestor routing algorithm [11]. And the third is when the mechanism considers the MST with our proposed routing algorithm described in 4.

The average packet latency and the relative link energy

Table 2: MST For Energy Saving Analysis

	No saving applied	Applied without MST	Applied with MST
Average Packet Latency	37.81 cycles	59.26 cycles	40.19 cycles
Percentage Latency Increase	0%	56.73%	6.29%
Relative Link Energy Consumption	100%	39.52%	48.55%

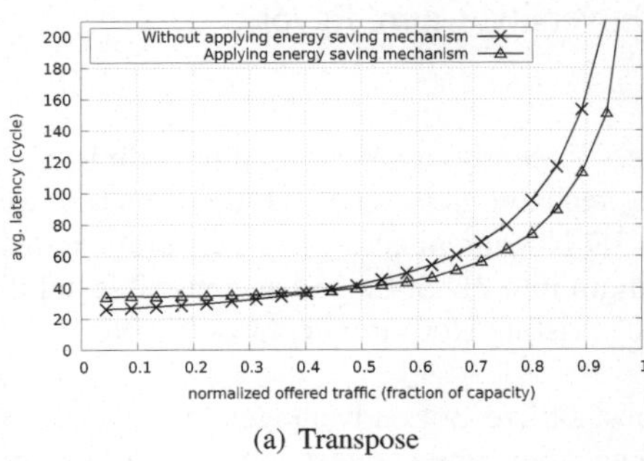

(a) Transpose

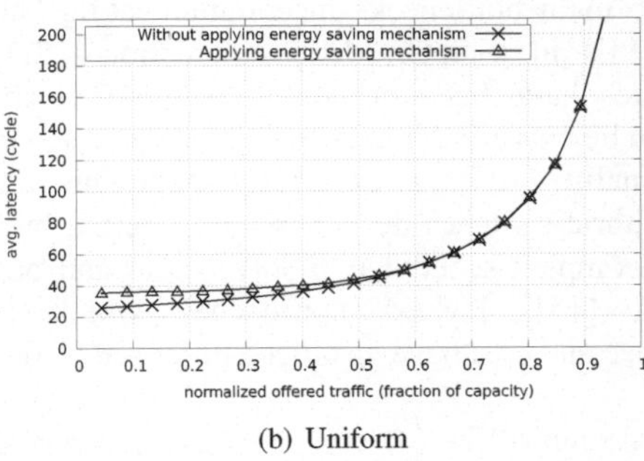

(b) Uniform

Fig. 3: Latency behavior comparison

consumption are described in Table 2. As we can see the average packet latency of the default system is 37.81 cycles. When applying the Dynamic Link Width mechanism without considering the MST we break the theoretical bound of relative link energy consumption described in Table 1, but with the expense of 56.73% increase in the average latency. With the MST maintaining at maximum speed the latency increase is much lower with only 6.29%, it comes with 48.55% energy compared with the default system.

6. Conclusions

We have proposed and analyzed the Minimum Spanning Tree for energy saving in interconnection networks. With this subset of the network resources kept in maximum speed, the additional serialization latency when applying the saving mechanism is greatly reduced. Our future work concerns about reducing more energy consumed by putting idle links in deep sleeping state.

Acknowledgments

This research has been supported by the MEC-Spain under contract TIN2011-24384.

References

[1] L. Shang, L.-S. Peh, and N. Jha, "Dynamic voltage scaling with links for power optimization of interconnection networks," in *International Symposium on High-Performance Computer Architecture (HPCA-9 2003)*, feb. 2003, pp. 91 – 102.

[2] B. Heller, S. Seetharaman, P. Mahadevan, Y. Yiakoumis, P. Sharma, S. Banerjee, and N. McKeown, "Elastictree: saving energy in data center networks," in *Proceedings of the 7th USENIX conference on Networked systems design and implementation*, ser. NSDI'10. Berkeley, CA, USA: USENIX Association, 2010, pp. 17–17. [Online]. Available: http://dl.acm.org/citation.cfm?id=1855711.1855728

[3] M. Alonso, S. Coll, V. Santonja, J.-M. Martínez, P. López, and J. Duato, "Power-aware fat-tree networks using on/off links," in *Proceedings of the Third international conference on High Performance Computing and Communications*, ser. HPCC'07. Berlin, Heidelberg: Springer-Verlag, 2007, pp. 472–483. [Online]. Available: http://dl.acm.org/citation.cfm?id=2401945.2402000

[4] A. G. Savva, T. Theocharides, and V. Soteriou, "Intelligent on/off dynamic link management for on-chip networks," *JECE*, vol. 2012, pp. 6:6–6:6, Jan. 2012. [Online]. Available: http://dx.doi.org/10.1155/2012/107821

[5] J. Yin, P. Zhou, A. Holey, S. S. Sapatnekar, and A. Zhai, "Energy-efficient non-minimal path on-chip interconnection network for heterogeneous systems," in *Proceedings of the 2012 ACM/IEEE international symposium on Low power electronics and design*, ser. ISLPED '12. New York, NY, USA: ACM, 2012, pp. 57–62. [Online]. Available: http://doi.acm.org/10.1145/2333660.2333675

[6] K. Kant, "Power control of high speed network interconnects in data centers," in *Proceedings of the 28th IEEE international conference on Computer Communications Workshops*, ser. INFOCOM'09. Piscataway, NJ, USA: IEEE Press, 2009, pp. 145–150. [Online]. Available: http://dl.acm.org/citation.cfm?id=1719850.1719875

[7] ——, "Multi-state power management of communication links," in *Communication Systems and Networks (COMSNETS), 2011 Third International Conference on*, 2011, pp. 1–10.

[8] D. Abts, M. R. Marty, P. M. Wells, P. Klausler, and H. Liu, "Energy proportional datacenter networks," *SIGARCH Comput. Archit. News*, vol. 38, no. 3, pp. 338–347, June 2010. [Online]. Available: http://doi.acm.org/10.1145/1816038.1816004

[9] C. E. Leiserson, "Fat-trees: universal networks for hardware-efficient supercomputing," *IEEE Trans. Comput.*, vol. 34, no. 10, pp. 892–901, Oct. 1985. [Online]. Available: http://dl.acm.org/citation.cfm?id=4492.4495

[10] G. M. J. B. B. T. J. K. Nan Jiang, Daniel U. Becker and W. J. Dally, "A detailed and flexible cycle-accurate network-on-chip simulator," in *Proceedings of the 2013 IEEE International Symposium on Performance Analysis of Systems and Software*, 2013.

[11] W. Dally and B. Towles, *Principles and Practices of Interconnection Networks*. San Francisco, CA, USA: Morgan Kaufmann Publishers Inc., 2003.

[12] C. Bienia, "Benchmarking modern multiprocessors," Ph.D. dissertation, Princeton University, January 2011.

[13] J. Hestness, B. Grot, and S. W. Keckler, "Netrace: dependency-driven trace-based network-on-chip simulation," in *Proceedings of the Third International Workshop on Network on Chip Architectures*, ser. NoCArc '10. New York, NY, USA: ACM, 2010, pp. 31–36. [Online]. Available: http://doi.acm.org/10.1145/1921249.1921258

Optimization of TSV-based Crossbars for a 3D Memory-Centric Network-on-Chip

Hossam H. Sarhan[1] **and Amr G. Wassal**[2]
[1]School of ICT, Nile University, Cairo, Egypt
[2] Computer Engineering Department, Cairo University, Cairo, Egypt

Abstract - *Large and complex system-on-chip devices are becoming common in the semiconductor industry nowadays. To communicate, these processing elements need to have a network-on-chip (NoC) that is scalable enough to support a large number of elements. Many NoC topologies have been examined in the literature, including 3D NoC architectures. In particular, the 3D memory-centric NoC topology utilizes the memory-shared NoC topology and the 3D technology. The crossbar is the central communication component in most 3D NoC architectures. This paper proposes efficient architectures and topologies for the 3D crossbar. Different cross-point implementations, which vary in their use of pass-logic and buffer insertion, are examined and compared. The architecture scalability is evaluated. An analytical model for the power and delay of the crossbar has been developed and validated.*

Keywords: 3-D IC, Crossbar fabrics, network-on-chip, interconnection architectures, switching circuits.

1 Introduction

The recent trend to use more on-die processor cores rather than trying to increase the clock frequency, is driven by several factors. The most important factors are power densities in the new technologies, low return on investment in terms of performance for a single core, and widening the productivity gap for design and verification in the newer technologies [1] and [2].

The straight-forward approach to tackle these problems is to reuse mature single-core designs and mature IP blocks, and tile them onto a homogenous chip. However, in modern system-on-chip (SoC) designs, the complexity of this approach lies in efficiently designing the interconnect between such tiled processing elements (PEs). This interconnect is often referred to as a network-on-chip (NoC). The NoC should be physically routable in a small area with minimal routing congestion. It also needs to support non-blocking low-power high-bandwidth communication between the PEs.

Many NoC topologies have been proposed to satisfy these NoC requirements for a single-die SoC [3]-[5]. Such proposals are facing scalability and power density issues on a single die. Recently work on three dimensional (3D) integration technologies, such as die stacking [6], raised interest in 3D NoC architectures as a natural extension to the NoC paradigm into 3D SoCs and as a possible solution to the problems of existing NoC architectures [7]-[9].

To best utilize SoC advantages, an efficient design of the communication interconnect is required. The crossbar is one of the main bottlenecks in communicating between the different PEs in a SoC. Many conventional 2D crossbar architectures have been proposed [10]-[14]. Such crossbar fabrics can be classified into two main categories; un-buffered and internally buffered crossbars. Although un-buffered crossbar fabric switches do not require internal buffers, they require a complex scheduler to solve input and output ports contention [15]. Hybrid approaches which trade off performance and cost have also been proposed [16].

The design of the 3D crossbar has been investigated in [17]. Several architectures have been proposed for both CMOS, and for optical and beyond CMOS 3D crossbar architectures [18]-[20]. This paper investigates architectures for the 3D crossbar optimized for power and delay. It also examines several crosspoint circuit implementations. An analytical model of the system is presented and used to evaluate its performance and analyze the power-delay trends of different topologies and circuit implementations.

This paper is organized as follows. Section 2 briefly introduces the relevant background for NOC and the 3D memory-centric NoC architecture. Section 3 presents the proposed 3D crossbar architecture, as well as the various cross-point implementations. The delay and power analytical models are presented in Section 4. Section 5 presents the performance evaluation results. The conclusion is given in Section 6.

2 Background

2.1 Networks-on-chip (NoC)

Interconnects between PEs in many-cores chips have become one of the bottlenecks in chip design. The NoC concept has been developed to deliver data between PEs.

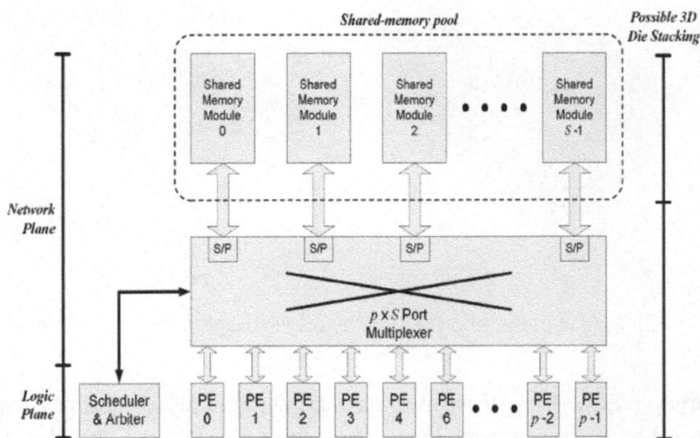

Fig. 1. 3D Memory-Centric NoC topology [23].

Several NoC topologies have been proposed to achieve the optimum communication architecture in terms of area, power, delay, scalability, and routing schemes [3]-[5]. The most common topologies are the mesh, torus, ring, and binary tree. Comparisons between some of these topologies have been reported in [4], [21] and [22].

The memory-centric NoC topology overcomes many of the issues of the conventional topologies, such as NoC scalability and high transactional applications [22] and [23].

2.2 3D Memory-Centric NoC

The memory-centric NoC (McNoC) topology contains memory modules, a crossbar and an arbiter. The McNoC is structured such that the centralized memory modules are connected to the PEs through a global switching crossbar. The PEs exchange data by writing to, and reading from, memory locations. The arbiter controls this communication theme by granting the source PE access to write to a specific memory location, and informing the destination PE to read from that memory location.

The McNoC concept was described in [22], [23], and [29]. A detailed performance comparison between the 2D McNoC and the traditional 2D mesh NoC is given in [23]. The comparison indicates that the McNoC architecture can tolerate high transactional implementations better than the traditional mesh topology.

Using the advantages of the 3D die-stacking technology [24]-[27], the expansion of the conventional mesh NoC topology into a 3D stacked mesh NoC topology has been proposed in [7], [9], and [28]. A novel 3D McNoC architecture is proposed in [23]. The new architecture overcomes the shortcomings of previous conventional 3D NoC topologies by combining the advantages of the 3D technology and the McNoC architecture, as shown in [23].

The topology of this 3D McNoC is shown in Fig. 1. It consists of two planes; a logic plane and a network plane. The logic plane contains the PEs, while the network plane contains the shared memory modules that act as the central hub of the network. Each plane may be distributed on more than one die. A central crossbar is used as a port multiplexer to connect the memory module ports to a larger number of PE ports.

3 3D Crossbar Architecture

3.1 Previous Work

Conventional 2D crossbars have been widely studied in the literature [10]-[14]. The crossbar fabrics can be classified into two main categories; un-buffered and internally buffered crossbars. Un-buffered crossbar fabric switches have the advantage of using no internal buffers. However, they require a complex scheduler to solve input and output ports contention [15]. Approaches that compromise between the performance and cost of the buffered crossbar have been proposed, e.g., [16]. This work focuses on the unbuffered crossbar design. However, the same concepts can be used for internally buffered crossbars.

Different architectures have been proposed for 3D crossbars, including CMOS crossbars [17], and optical and beyond CMOS crossbars [18]-[20]. Lewis [17] proposed modifying the 2D crossbar through column-, or row-, splitting and multiplexing to obtain a 3D crossbar. Fig. 2(a) illustrates the column-split multiplexed 3D crossbar.

Some issues of the multiplexed stacked crossbar have been outlined in [17]. The first issue is the scalability: as the number of stacked dies increases, the number of TSVs needed from each layer increases, which will increase the total area of the crossbar. Increasing the number of TSVs also increases the capacitance, which increases the power and delay across the crossbar.

Moreover, this design will lead to non-identical dies, since the number of the TSVs passing through a die from the top die to the bottom die differs from die to die. In other words, the top die will connect with only the TSVs needed by this die, while the second die will pass the TSVs of the previous die and introduce new TSVs, and so on, as illustrated in Fig. 2(a).

3.2 The Proposed Compact 3D Crossbar

The proposed optimized 3D crossbar architecture stacks the TSVs of the different dies, as illustrated in Fig. 2(b). Arbitration is accomplished using local arbiters at each die. One of the arbiters will be the master arbiter, which will arbitrate between requests from the different dies to determine the output of the whole crossbar.

The main advantage of the proposed stacked TSVs is the compact design, which will reduce both power and delay. The design scales well with increasing number of dies, since the number of TSVs per die will not depend on the number of the

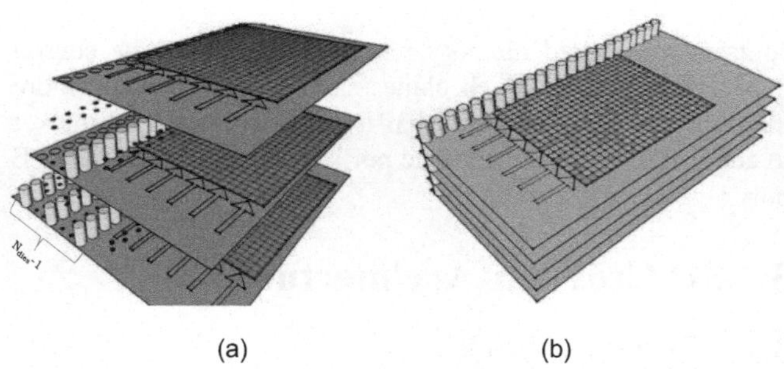

(a) (b)

Fig. 2. (a) The multiplexed crossbar [17], and (b) The proposed stacked TSVs 3D crossbar architecture.

dies, i.e., each die will not pass TSVs from the previous dies. Moreover, this design guarantees identical die structure, which is particularly useful for many cores applications where all dies contain the same PEs.

Since this is a 3D structure, there is no need to get the output from the edge of the crossbar. Moreover, to decrease the length of the average and the critical signal paths, the TSVs can be placed inside the crossbar. Therefore, the output will be obtained from the middle of the crossbar, as shown in Fig. 3(a). Using this topology, power consumption is reduced by reducing the average signal path length from the input port to the output TSV. This topology will also reduce the critical signal path length from the input port to the output TSV, which in turn will decrease the critical path delay.

Since the diameter and pitch of TSVs are relatively large compared to the crossbar size [26], a strip of TSVs will be much longer than the crossbar which will highly increase the spacing between the crosspoints. To overcome this problem, TSVs are placed in a zigzag topology to reduce the total length of the TSV strip. Fig. 3 illustrates both linear and zigzag internal TSVs crossbar topologies. The zigzagged TSVs topology can be achieved using two or more zigzagged

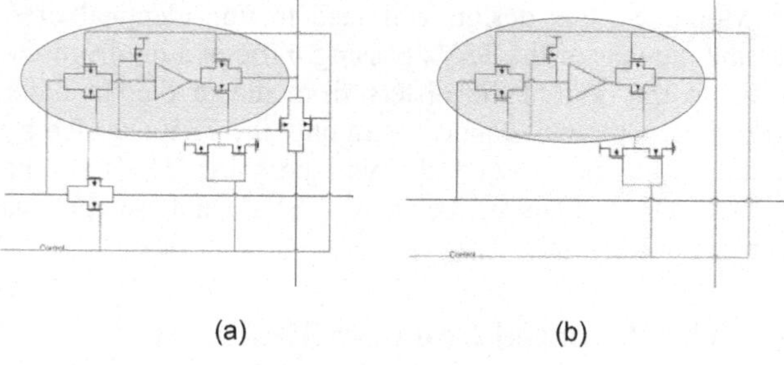

(a) (b)

Fig. 4. (a) Case 1, and (b) Case 2 crosspoint implementations.

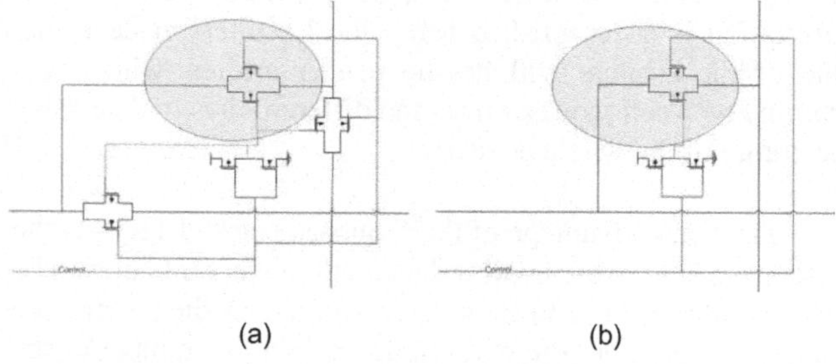

(a) (b)

Fig. 5. (a) Case 3, and (b) Case 4 crosspoint implementations.

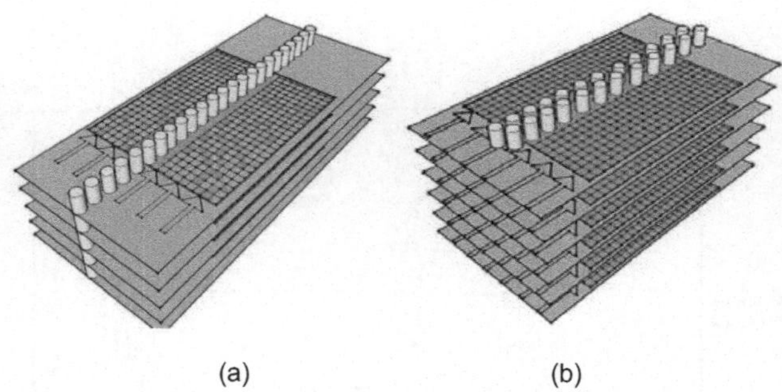

(a) (b)

Fig. 3. (a) Linear, and (b) Two-layers zigzagged, internal TSVs 3D crossbar topologies.

layers. Fig. 3(b) illustrates two zigzagged layers. Increasing number of zigzagged layers will better optimize the delay, power, and size of the crossbar.

To summarize, this optimized 3D crossbar architecture achieves:

1. A compact design that is scalable with number of stacked dies.
2. Identical dies.
3. A shorter average path length from input to TSV, i.e., less power.
4. A shorter critical-path length from input to TSV, i.e., less critical-path delay.

3.3 Crosspoint Implementation

There are several options for implementing the crosspoint switches using pass-transistors to connect and disconnect crossing wires, and buffer insertion to reduce the path delay [12]-[14], [17], and [30]. Pass-transistor logic suffers from the voltage drop (V_{out_max}=V_{DD}-V_{Tn}) [30]. Therefore, in the proposed design, transmission gates (TGs) are used instead control the crosspoints in the crossbar.

In this work, four different combinations of TGs and buffer insertion in both signal direct-path (horizontal/vertical) and turn-path (highlighted) are proposed and compared, as shown in figures 4 & 5. Power and delay trade-offs are examined in all four cases.

4 Analytical Model

4.1 Analytical Model Concept

Analytical models are used to early estimate the performance of a system in the design process, e.g., [31]-[42]. In our system, the crossbar consists of three components; the driving buffers, the TGs, and the wire interconnecting the crosspoints, as illustrated in Fig. 6(a). The proposed analytical model employs several design input factors and technology parameters to estimate both power and delay. The objective of the model is to determine an RC chain equivalent to the crossbar components.

The simplest way to model a TG is a lumped resistor and capacitor. A more accurate model, proposed by Eisele [35], models the TG as a π-RC network, Fig. 6(b). The resistor (R_{TG}) is the equivalent average on-resistor of the PMOS parallel to the NMOS across different input voltages (from 0V to V_{DD}). The two capacitances, C_{DT} and C_{ST}, are the parasitic capacitance at the drain and source nodes. These parameters can be obtained either from the technology files, or by using characterization simulations on SPICE.

The wiring interconnect is modeled as distributed RC-sections. Rabaey [30] showed that Elmore delay for a very large number of identical RC-sections equals (RC/2), where R and C are the total lumped resistance and capacitance, respectively.

4.2 Crossbar Delay Model

Using the concepts presented above, the model used to estimate the worst-case delay is developed as follows. The total critical-path delay of the 3D crossbar can be decomposed into two components: the delay due to the planar crossbar (one die), and the delay due to the vertical TSVs. First, the delay of a single planar crossbar is estimated for the four crosspoint implementations. Then, the delay due to the TSVs will be considered. According to Elmore delay [32], for a general RC chain, the 50% propagation delay at node 'i' is given by:

$$t_{delay_i} = \sum_{k=1}^{N} C_k R_{ik} \qquad (1)$$

By examining the equivalent RC tree of a signal path between two buffers for Case 1 crosspoint implementation, Fig. 4(a), the TG resistance (~5KΩ) is much larger than the wire resistance (~17.9Ω). So the effect of wiring resistance can thus be neglected. Therefore, the critical path delay can be expressed as in equation (2).

The architecture of Case 2 implementation, Fig. 4(b), is similar to that of Case 1, except for the removal of the direct-path TGs. From a modeling point of view, this is equivalent to the exclusion of the resistance and the capacitance of the TGs. So the estimated delay between two buffers in one crossbar plane is expressed as in equation (3).

$$t_{d_{Case1}} = (C_{ST} + 2C_{DT} + C_{W_H})R_{TG} * \frac{O(O-1)}{2} + O(C_{ST} + C_B)R_{TG} + R_B[O(C_{ST} + 2 * C_{DT}) + OC_{W_H} + C_B] + (C_{ST} + 2 * C_{DT} + C_{W_V})R_{TG} * \frac{I_{prt}(I_{prt}-1)}{2} + I_{prt}(C_{ST} + C_B)R_{TG} + R_B[I_{prt}(C_{ST} + 2 * C_{DT}) + I_{prt}C_W + C_B] \qquad (2)$$

$$t_{d_{Case2}} = R_B * [OC_W + (O + 1)C_{DT} + C_{ST} + C_B] + 0.5(OC_W)(OR_W) + OR_W[C_{ST} + (O + 1)C_{DT} + C_B] + R_{TG}(C_{ST} + C_B) \qquad (3)$$

Where I_{prt} is the number of input ports per layer (die), O is the total number of output ports, R_{TG}, C_{DT}, and C_{ST} are the TG parameters, R_B and C_B are the driving buffer output resistance and input capacitance, respectively, and R_{WH}, C_{WH}, R_{WV}, and C_{WV} are the horizontal and vertical wire

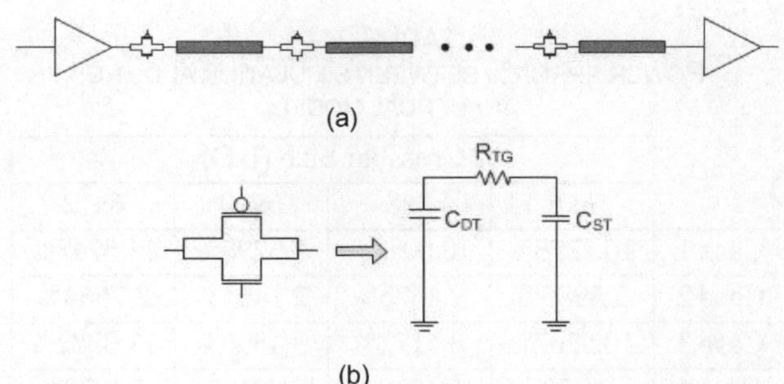

Fig. 6. (a) Interconnection between two driving buffers, and (b) Transmission gate modeling as π-RC network.

interconnect parasitics. These parasitics are either extracted from the technology files, or determined using characterization SPICE simulations. TSV parameters are extracted similar to the model used in [31].

Case 3 implementation, Fig. 5(a), differs from the previous two cases in the removal of the intermediate buffer (on the turn-path), while the direct-path TGs are preserved, similar to Case 1. So the model of Case 3 can be expressed by equation (4). Case 4, Fig. 5(b), combines both of the concepts of Case 2 and Case 3, i.e., both the intermediate buffer and the direct-path TGs are removed. The delay can be estimated using equation (5).

$$t_{d_{Case3}} = (C_{ST} + 2C_{DT} + C_{W_H})R_{TG} * \frac{O(O-1)}{2} + (C_{ST} + 2C_{DT} + C_{W_V})\left[(O - 1)R_{TG} + \frac{I_{prt}(I_{prt}+1)}{2}R_{TG}\right] + (C_{ST} + C_B)(O + I_{prt})R_{TG} + R_B[(O + I_{prt})(C_{ST} + 2C_{DT} + (O - 1)C_{W_H} + I_{prt}C_{W_V} + C_B)] \qquad (4)$$

$$t_{d_{Case4}} = R_B(OC_{W_H} + 2C_{ST} + 2C_{DT} + I_{prt}C_{W_V} + C_B) + 0.5[R_{W_H}O(OC_{W_H} + I_{prt}C_{W_V}) + (I_{prt}R_{W_V})(I_{prt}C_{W_V})] + O * R_{W_H}(C_{DT} + C_{ST} + C_B) + R_{TG}(C_{DT} + 2C_{ST} + C_B + I_{prt}C_{W_V}) + I_{prt}R_{W_V}C_B \qquad (5)$$

Equations (1) through (5) were derived for the outside TSV crossbar topology, shown in Fig. 2(b). For the inside TSV topology, shown in Fig. 3(a), the number of input ports will decrease, i.e., Iprt will be replaced by Iprt/2. For the zigzagged internal TSV topology, the spacing between the crosspoints will decrease as the number of the zigzagged layers, ZL, is increased. Therefore, the values of the horizontal wire resistance and capacitance will be R_{WH}*0.707/(ZL-1) and C_{WH}*0.707/(ZL-1), respectively.

TABLE 1
The percentage error in delay between the SPICE simulation and the analytical model

	Crossbar Size (IxO)			
	6x6	6x8	6x10	6x12
Case 1	-2.768%	-13.06%	-9.383%	-5.226%
Case 2	6.731%	3.0673%	0.1458%	-1.451%
Case 3	7.1063%	-9.653%	7.926%	1.103%
Case 4	4.9914%	2.2017%	-0.448%	-1.479%

TABLE 2
POWER ERROR% BETWEEN SIMULATION AND THE ANALYTICAL MODEL

	Crossbar Size (IxO)			
	6x6	6x8	6x10	6x12
Case 1	10.7775%	10.0057%	7.5298%	11.5747%
Case 2	2.5986%	2.4575%	2.1451%	2.7664%
Case 3	10.5267%	8.7172%	3.4590%	11.3382%
Case 4	6.82%	6.4635%	5.8213%	6.4078%

4.3 Delay Model Validation

To validate the proposed models, SPICE simulations were performed for TSMC 65nm technology, for crossbars of different sizes. The percentage error is estimated using equation (6).

$$\text{Error\%} = \frac{\text{Sim}_{\text{value}} - \text{Model}_{\text{value}}}{\text{Sim}_{\text{value}}} * 100 \quad (6)$$

Table 1 shows error values between the model delay and SPICE delay. The error shown is comparable to the figures reported in literature [36]-[38]. The main contributor to this error is the use of first order Elmore delay, which gives 10-20% error against SPICE simulations [42]. Higher order models, such as those proposed in [39] can be more accurate but come at the expense of increasing the model complexity.

4.4 Crossbar Power Model

The analytical power modeling concept used in the proposed model is similar to that used in [33]-[38]. In the proposed model, leakage power is neglected, compared to the dynamic power. Power validation is performed to estimate the error due to this assumption. Generally, the average power of the crossbar per port is given by:

$$\text{Power} = \alpha f V_{DD}^2 W C_t \,. \quad (7)$$

where α is the switching activity factor of the input data, f is the input frequency, V_{DD} is the supply voltage, W is the port width (in bits), and C_t is the total capacitance seen on the signal path. The estimated total average power of the crossbar is computed as the product of the estimated power per port and the total number of input ports. The actual difference between the four implementation cases is the different total capacitance seen on the signal path, C_t.

4.5 Power Model Validation

Table 2 shows the power model error for different crossbar sizes using the four crosspoint implementation cases. The maximum error is about 11.5%. The error between the power model and SPICE simulations is mainly due to neglecting the leakage and short-circuit power. This error is comparable to the figures reported in the literature. For example, Wassal and Hasan report an error of 8.4% [29], and Kahng et al., report 6.5-11% error in their power models [34].

5 Performance Results

This section presents performance results for the different crossbar topologies and the different crosspoint implementations. The estimated delay and power depend on the different design parameters. In our study, the TSV's diameter, pitch, and length are chosen from the ITRS roadmap [26], and the interconnect model is taken from TSMC's 65nm technology for specific sizing and wire length and width.

5.1 Adding More Ports

To examine the effect of increasing the number of ports, the number of the output ports (for a certain input port number, i.e. I=6, and a certain width for each port, i.e. W=30) is swept. In a McNoC architecture, the number of the output ports (O) affects the number of shared memory modules, while the numbers of the input ports (I) affects the number of input PEs with port width (W) [23].

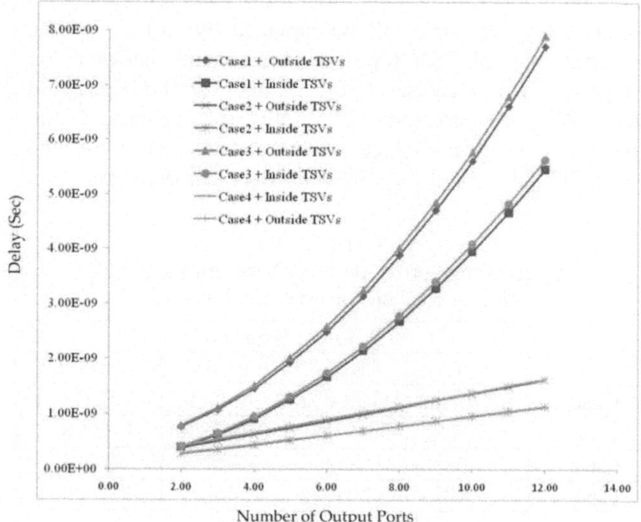

Fig. 7. Critical path delay variation versus the number of output ports for different crossbar topologies.

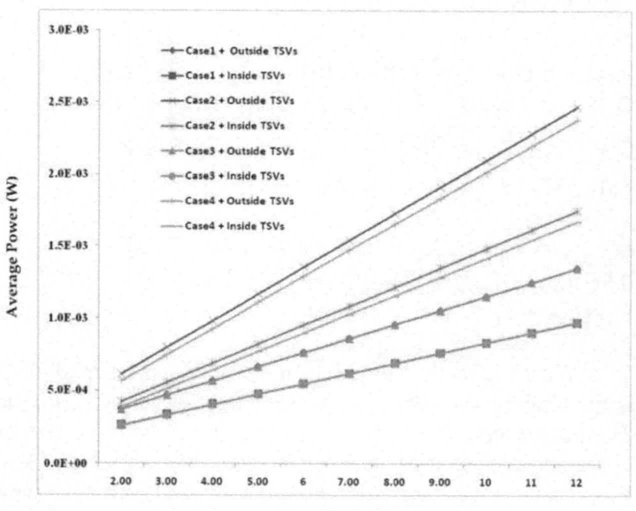

Fig. 8. Average power dissipation versus the number of output ports for different crossbar topologies.

Fig. 7 plots the critical path delay versus the number of output ports for the four crosspoint implementations. Each crosspoint case is demonstrated in two topologies, the outside TSVs and the inside (2-layer zigzagged) TSVs. Fig. 7 indicates that Case 3 exhibits the largest delay, followed by Case 1. This is because in both cases, the direct-path TGs have large resistances which increase the delay significantly.

Moreover, the outside TSVs topology has higher delay than that of the internal zigzagged TSVs. The reduction in delay between the outside TSVs and the internal zigzagged TSVs is about 29% using cases 1 and 3, and 29.7% using cases 2 and 4, for the 6x12 crossbar (W=30).

Fig. 8 plots the average power per port consumed by the crossbar versus the number of output ports. The figure indicates that Case 2 consumes the largest average power, followed by Case 4. Cases 2 and 4 consume more power than cases 1 and 3 because the capacitance of the long wiring is higher than that of the direct-path TGs. Case 2 consumes more power than Case 4 due to the additional direct-path TGs and buffer. Cases 1 and 3 exhibit very similar power consumption values, since the capacitance of the additional buffer in Case 1 is negligible, compared to the total path capacitance.

Fig. 8 also indicates that the power consumed by the outside TSVs topology is higher than that of the inside zig-zagged TSVs topology. The power reduction between the outside TSVs and the internal zigzagged TSVs is about 29.2% using cases 2 and 4, and 27.7% using cases 1 and 3, for the 6x12 crossbar (W=30).

6 Conclusion

This paper discusses a novel 3D memory-centric NoC architecture which combines the shared memory concept with the 3D integration technology to address the issues of the previous conventional 3D NoC architectures. The main focus was the design of the 3D switching crossbar, which is the main center of communication between the processing elements and the memory modules. The paper proposed optimized topologies (internal and zigzagged TSVs) which reduce both the power and delay of the crossbar significantly. However choosing a certain topology should be also associated with the whole system floor-planning. Four different crosspoint implementations were analyzed and recommended for either delay or power optimized designs.

7 References

[1] S. Borkar, "Thousand Core Chips—A Technology Perspective," in Proceedings of the 44th ACM/IEEE Design Automation Conference, 2007.

[2] R F. J. Pollack, "New Microarchitecture Challenges in the Coming Generations of CMOS Process Technologies," in Proceedings of the 32nd Annual IEEE/ACM International Symposium on Microarchitecture, 1999.

[3] L. Benini and G. De Micheli, "Networks on Chips: A New SoC Paradigm," IEEE Computer, vol. 35, no. 1, pp. 70-78, Jan. 2002.

[4] P. Pande, C. Grecu, M. Jones, A. Ivanov, and R. Saleh, "Performance Evaluation and Design Trade-Offs for Network-on-Chip Interconnect Architectures," IEEE Transactions on Computers, August 2005.

[5] T. Bjerregaard and S. Mahadevan, "A Survey of Research and Practices of Network-on-Chip," ACM Computing Surveys, June 2006.

[6] K. Bernstein, et al., "Interconnects in the Third Dimension: Design Challenges for 3D ICs," in Proceedings of the 44th ACM/IEEE Design Automation Conference, 2007.

[7] V. F. Pavlidis and E. G. Friedman, "3-D Topologies for Networks-on-Chip," IEEE Transactions on Very Large Scale Integration Systems, 2007.

[8] B. S. Feero and P. P. Pande, "Networks-on-Chip in a Three-Dimensional Environment: A Performance Evaluation," IEEE Transactions on Computers, vol. 58, no. 1, pp. 32-45, Jan. 2009.

[9] A. Bartzas, K. Siozios, and D. Soudris, Networks-on-Chips: Theory and Practice, Chapter 1: Three-Dimensional Networks-on-Chip Architectures, Taylor & Francis Group, LLC, 2009.

[10] N. McKeown, "A Fast Switched Backplane for a Gigabit Switched Router," Business Communication Review, vol. 27, no. 12, 1997.

[11] N. McKeown, M. Izzard, A. Mekkittikul, B. Ellersick, and M. Horowitz, "The Tiny Tera: A Packet Switch Core," IEEE Micro, 1997.

[12] V. Betz and J. Rose, "Circuit Design, Transistor Sizing and Wire Layout of FPGA Interconnect", in Proceedings of the IEEE Custom Integrated Circuits Conerence, pp. 171-174, May 1999.

[13] M. Sheng and J. Rose, "Mixing Buffers and Pass Transistors in FPGA Routing Architectures", in Proceedings of the 2001 ACM/SIGDA ninth international symposium on Field programmable gate arrays, Feb. 2001.

[14] K. Lee, S.-J. Lee, S.-E. Kim, H.-M. Choi, D. Kim, S. Kim, M.-W. Lee, and H.-J. Yoo, "A 51mW 1.6 GHz On-Chip Network for Low-Power Heterogeneous SoC Platform", in Proceedings of the International Solid-State Circuits Conference (ISSCC), pp. 152-158, Feb. 2004.

[15] M. Katevenis, G. Passas, D. Simos, I. Papaefstathiou, and N. Chrysos, "Variable Packet Size Buffered Crossbar (CICQ) Switches", International Conference on Communications, in Proceedings of the IEEE Conference on Communications, vol. 2, pp. 1090-1096, Jun. 2004.

[16] L. Mhamdi, "PCB: A Partially Buffered Crossbar Packet Switch", IEEE Transactions on Computers, vol. 58, Nov. 2009.

[17] D. Lewis, S. Yalamanchili, and H. Lee, "High Performance Non-blocking Switch Design in 3D Die-Stacking Technology," in Proceedings of the IEEE Computer Society Annual Symposium on VLSI, May 2009.

[18] C. Dong, D. Chen, S. Haruehanroengra, and W. Wang, "3D nFPGA: A Reconfigurable Architecture for 3D CMOS Nano-material Hybrid Digital Circuits", IEEE Transactions on Circuits and Systems I, Nov. 2007.

[19] S. Fujita, K. Nomura, K. Abe, and T. H. Lee, "3D Nano-architecture with carbon nano-tubes mechanical switches for future on-chip network beyond CMOS Architecture", IEEE Transactions on Circuits and Systems I, Nov. 2007.

[20] K. Nomura, K. Abe, S. Fujita, and A. Detion, "Novel design of Three-Dimensional Crossbar for Future Network on Chip based on Post-Silicon Devices", in Proceedings of the IEEE 1st International Conference on Nano-Networks and workshops (NanoNet '06), pp. 1-5, Sep. 2006.

[21] S. Mubeen, Evaluation of Source Routing for Mesh Topology Network on Chip Platforms, M.Sc. Thesis, Jönköping University, Sweden, 2009.

[22] D. Kim, K. Kim, J. Kim, S. Lee, and H. Yoo, "Solutions for Real Chip Implementation Issues of NoC and Their Application to Memory-Centric NoC," in Proceedings of the First International Symposium on Networks-on-Chip (NOCS '07), May 2007.

[23] A. Wassal, H. Sarhan and A. ElSherief, "Novel 3D Memory-Centric NoCArchitecture for Transaction-Based SoC Applications", in Proceedings of the 2011 Saudi International Electronics, Communications and Photonics Conference (SIECPC), pp. 1-5, Apr. 2011.

[24] S. Das, A. Chandrakasan, and R. Reif , "Three-Dimensional Integrated Circuits: Performance, Design Methodology, and CAD Tools", IEEE Computer Society Annual Symposium on VLSI, 2003.

[25] K. Banerjee, S. J. Souri, P. Kapur, and K. C. Saraswat, "3-D ICs: A Novel Chip Design for Improving Deep-Submicrometer Interconnect Performance and Systems-on-Chip Integration", Proceedings of the IEEE, vol. 89, no. 5, pp. 602-633, May 2001.

[26] International Technology Roadmap for Semiconductors, ITRS, Interconnect Edition, 2009.

[27] Tezzaron Semiconductor, www.tezzaron.com.

[28] Brett Feero and ParthaPratimPande, "Performance Evaluation for Three-Dimensional Networks-On-Chip", IEEE Computer Society Annual Symposium on VLSI, pp. 305-310, Mar. 2007.

[29] A. G. Wassal and M. A. Hasan, "Low-Power System-Level Design of VLSI Packet Switching Fabrics," IEEE Transactions on Computer-Aided Design of Integrated Circuits and Systems, vol. 20, no. 6, Jun. 2001.

[30] J. Rabaey, Digital Integrated Circuits, 2nd ed., Prentice Hall, 2003.

[31] I. Savidis and E. Friedman, "Closed-Form Expression of 3-D Via Resistance, Inductance, and Capacitance", IEEE Transactions on electron devices, vol. 56, no. 9, pp. 1873-1881, Sep. 2009.

[32] W. C. Elmore, "The Transient Response of Damped Linear Networks with Particular Regard to Wideband Amplifiers", Journal of Applied Physics, vol. 19, no. 1, pp. 55-63, Jan. 1948.

[33] H.-S. Wang, X. Zhu, L.-S. Peh, and S. Malik, "Orion: A Power-Performance Simulator for Interconnection Networks", in Proceedings of IEEE/ACM International Symposium on Microarchitecture, 2002.

[34] A. B. Kahng, B. Li, L.-S. Peh, and K. Samadi, "Orion 2.0: A Fast and Accurate NoC Power and Area Model for Early-Stage Design Space Exploration", in Proceedings of the Conference on Design, Automation and Test in Europe (DATE '09), pp. 1530-1591, Apr. 2009.

[35] V. Eisele, B. Hoppe, and O. Kiehl, "Transmission Gate Delay Models for Circuit Optimization", in Proceedings of the European Design Automation Conference, pp. 558-562, Mar. 1990.

[36] N. Muralimanohar, R. Balasubramonian, and N. Jouppi, "CACTI 6.0: A Tool to Model Large Caches", HP Laboratories, 2007.

[37] S. Wilton and N. Jouppi, "An Enhanced Access and Cycle Time Model for On-Chip Caches", Western Research Laboratory, 1994.

[38] M. Lin, A. El Gammal, Y. Lu, and S. Wong, "Performance Benefits of Monolithically Stacked 3D-FPGA", IEEE Transactions on Computer-Aided Design of Integrated Circuits and Systems, vol. 26, Feb. 2007.

[39] J. Rubinstein, P. Penfield, and M. Horowitz, "Signal Delay in RC Tree Networks", IEEE Transactions on Computer Aided Design, Jul. 1983.

[40] M. Horowitz, Timing model for MOS circuits, PhD dissertation, Stanford University, Jan. 1984.

[41] Stephen Tarzia, "A Survey of 3D Circuit Integration", Mar. 2008.

[42] N. Nassif, M. Desai, and D. Hall, "Robust Elmore Delay Models Suitable for Full Chip Timing Verification of a 600Mhz CMOS Microprocessor", in Proceedings of the 35th Design Automation Conference, 1998.

A Methodology to characterize the parallel I/O of the message-passing scientific applications

Sandra Méndez, Dolores Rexachs and Emilio Luque
Computer Architecture and Operating Systems Department (CAOS)
Universitat Autònoma de Barcelona, Barcelona, Spain

Abstract— *The increase in computational power of processing units and the complexity of scientific applications which use high performance computing require more efficient Input/Output (I/O) systems. To use the I/O subsystems efficiently it is necessary to know its performance capacity to determine if it fulfills applications I/O requirements. Evaluating the performance capacity of the I/O subsystem is difficult due to the diversity of architectures and the complexity of its software stack.*

Furthermore, parallel scientific applications have different behavior depending on their access patterns. Then, it is necessary to have some method to evaluate the I/O subsystem capacity taking into account the applications access patterns that can be used in different I/O subsystems.

We propose a methodology to characterize the parallel I/O of scientific applications, including the I/O subsystem at library and devices levels. We represent the message-passing applications through an I/O model. The model allows us to evaluate the I/O subsystem taking into account the I/O phases of the application.

Keywords: Parallel I/O System, Access Pattern, I/O Configuration, I/O Modeling, I/O phases

1. Introduction

Due to the historical "gap" between the computing and Input/Output (I/O) performance, the I/O system is, in many cases, the bottleneck in parallel systems. Increasing computational power of processing units and the complexity of scientific applications that use high performance computing require more efficient Input/Output systems. In order to hide the "gap" and to efficiently use the I/O, it is necessary to identify the I/O factors with the biggest effect on performance. The I/O factors depend on the I/O architecture and I/O software stack, however the application performance will depend on its access pattern.

Computer clusters are built to provide parallel computing to several applications. These applications have different I/O requirements and the same I/O system is not always appropriate for all applications. Programmers can modify their programs to efficiently manage I/O operations, but they need to know the I/O system, especially the I/O software stack.

Users need information to answer questions like: Is the I/O subsystem a problem for the access patterns of the application? How much I/O subsystem capacity is being used by the application? How the application access patterns are done in a target subsystem?

We use an I/O model of the scientific applications to support the evaluation of I/O performance of computer clusters. We have implemented a tracing tool (PAS2P library extension [1]) for extracting "I/O patterns" in message-passing applications, and based on these patterns, we have defined the concept of "I/O phase" of parallel scientific applications. These I/O phases are the key elements to define an I/O behavior model of the parallel scientific applications. This model allows us to evaluate an I/O subsystem taking into account the parallel application.

In a previous paper [2], we have proposed a methodology for performance evaluation of the I/O system which was focused in I/O path. In the present paper, we extend our methodology focused in the I/O characterization of the application. We have refined the stages of characterization and analysis of the I/O subsystem. We explain the process to performance evaluate of the I/O subsystem focused in the I/O model.

We have applied our methodology in three computer clusters where we have used parallel filesystem OrangeFS, Lustre and network filesystem NFS. We have evaluated the performance on three I/O systems taking into account the I/O model of the application. The methodology is applied to MadBench2 [3] and Flash-IO [4]. The characteristics of the I/O subsystem are evaluated, as well as their usage by the different I/O phases of the I/O model.

The rest of this article is organized as follows: in Section II we review the related work, Section III introduces our proposed methodology. In Section IV we review the experimental validation. Finally, we present our conclusions and future work.

2. Related Work

There are several papers [5] [6] [7] [8] that present the characterization of I/O of parallel applications in specific computers clusters or supercomputers. Due to the diversity of I/O architectures and the complexity of stack software, each researcher try to evaluate the I/O components with the biggest impact in their subsystems. Usually the evaluation is done for I/O benchmarking and the results are used to evaluate the performance of an specific I/O system.

Other important point in the evaluation of I/O subsystem is the tracing tool to identify the I/O access pattern.

Byna et. al. [9] presented a classification of I/O patterns for parallel applications, I/O signatures at local process level and an applying of signatures to prefetching technicals. We use their proposed to identify access patterns. However, we have identified the global access pattern because we need the I/O for the parallel application. From local access patterns and by similarity, we have defined the global access pattern, then global access patterns are divided in the I/O phases.

H. Shan and J. Shalf [10] have used IOR to mimic the I/O pattern of parallel scientific applications. Also, they used this mimic to predict the performance for the application. We have used IOR to represent the I/O model of the application. The I/O model is represented by an I/O phases sequence and IOR is applied to each I/O phases. In this way, we only focus in time where the application does I/O operations.

Carns [11] presented the Darshan tracing tool for the I/O workloads characterization of the petascale. Darshan is designed to capture an accurate picture of the application I/O behavior, including properties such as patterns of access within files, with minimum overhead. It is a tools available to download and it is free.

Most of these researches are aimed at supercomputers, while our strategy is focused on computer clusters. However, the main difference is that our methodology is focused to evaluate the performance capacity of I/O subsystem from an I/O model. We use the model to describe the I/O requirements of the application and to compare qualitatively the I/O subsystems. We have expressed the access patterns of the application in an I/O model and this can be used on different I/O subsystems.

3. Proposed Methodology

The proposed methodology is composed of three stages: Characterization, I/O Analysis and Evaluation. Next, we explain each stage.

3.1 Characterization

The characterization is applied to the I/O subsystem and parallel scientific application. This stage has two objectives: i) Extracting the I/O model of the application; and ii) Identifying and obtaining of performance basic characteristics of the different configurations in the I/O subsystem. These activities are independent.

3.1.1 Scientific Application

The I/O model of an application is represented by three major characteristics: i) meta-data, ii) the temporal global I/O pattern; and iii) the spatial global I/O pattern.

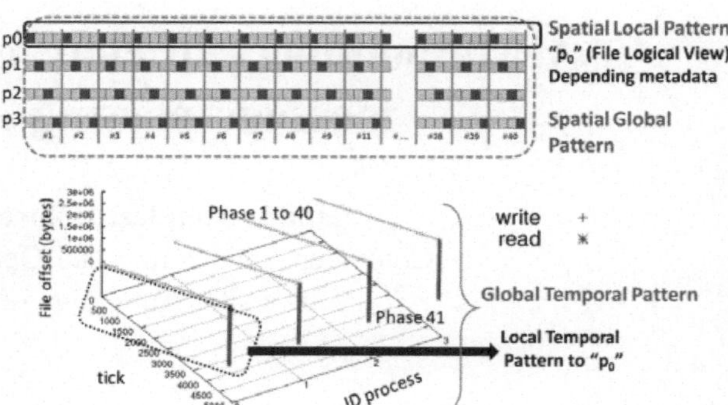

Fig. 1: I/O model example for 4 processes with request size 2MB, 40 I/O phases of a writing operation and weight 40MB, 1 phase of 40 reading operations with weight 1600MB

We characterize the application off-line and once at I/O library level because this allows us to obtain a model of the application's I/O independent from the execution environment, i.e. the computer cluster.

The I/O model of application is expressed by I/O phases, where an I/O phase is a repetitive sequence of same pattern on a file for a number of processes of the parallel application. The process to extract the I/O model is described in [12].

In order to consider the order of occurrence of the events of message-passing parallel applications we use the concept of tick. A tick is defined as a logical unit time, and it is incremented by each communication event and I/O event. An I/O event is a segment of application where the I/O operation is called. The I/O event is composed of an ID file, mpi-io operation, offset, displacement, size of etype, size of filetype, name of file, number of event, size of request, logical time, duration, count of datatype, and size of datatype.

The algorithm to identify the I/O patterns is based on type of operation, request size, displacement, and distance. Where, distance is the number of tick between two I/O operations and the displacement is the difference between the offset of two consecutive I/O operations. The similarity of pattern is determined by the relation between the pattern and the new value. If the relation is > 0.8 and < 1.2 then we consider the new value how a new occurrence of the pattern analyzed. This criteria is used to the displacement and the distance. The new value must be equal to the type of operation and the request size of the pattern analyzed to be considered a new occurrence.

The weight of a phase depends on the number of processes, request size and repetitions of each access pattern that is part of a phase. The weight is expressed in Megabytes and it is used to determine transferred data in each I/O phase. The I/O model depends on I/O phases and weight, allowing us to know "when" and "how" the I/O subsystem will be used.

Figure 1 shows an example of I/O model, where the global access pattern is shown through its spatial local pattern, spatial global pattern, temporal local pattern, and temporal global pattern. Also, we show the global access pattern in three dimensional space, where for each operation the *file Offset* indicates the position where the *process* "p" is accessing in the *tick* "t".

3.1.2 I/O System

The I/O subsystem characterization has as objective to development of adequate yardsticks for measuring and comparing such configurations in a appropriate manner taking into account the application access patterns. To do this, we apply the following steps:

i) Identifying I/O configurations: In this step, we identify the I/O subsystem configurations. An I/O configuration depends on number and type of filesystem (local, distributed and parallel), number and type of network (dedicated use and shared with the computing), number of I/O devices, I/O devices organization (RAID level, JBOD), and number and placement of I/O node.

ii) Setting input parameters for the Benchmarks: IOR [13] is applied at I/O library level and Global Filesystem level. IOzone [14] is applied at I/O devices level on local filesystem. Parameters values are selected according to the characteristics of the configurations identified. We consider that minimum size of file to test must be $= 2 * RAMsize$, where the RAM size is of the node where the benchmark will be executed. This is necessary to guarantee the access to disk. The access mode to a file can be sequential, strided, and random. The access type can be shared or unique, where shared is one file for all processes and unique is one file per process. Also, it is necessary to select the type of operations (write, read) and the request size (KBytes, MBytes, Gbytes) of the operations.

We have executed the benchmarks in each I/O subsystem with different I/O patterns and we have generated a data base by I/O subsystem configuration with performance measures (bandwidth, latency, iops).

3.2 Input/Output Analysis

To compare the I/O pattern of the application with benchmarks, we define the similar data structure for the access pattern of each I/O phase.

We analyze the I/O phases of the application and its weight to select the candidate I/O system. We search the I/O patterns of phases on performance databases. Then, we calculate the I/O time for the I/O phases and we select the I/O systems with less I/O time.

When there is not a characterization of I/O subsystem for similar patterns to the most significant phases of I/O model we use the I/O model to mimic the I/O model of the application. The I/O model is used to set up the input parameters of the benchmark IOR [13]. We only execute the benchmark for the phases with higher weight of the I/O model.

The following setting of input parameters are applied on IOR for each I/O phase:

- Strided Access: $s = Iter$; $b = RS_{(IdPh)}$; $t = RS_{(IdPh)}$; $NP = np_{(IdPh)}$; $-F$ if there is 1 file per process; $-c$ if there is collective I/O.
- Sequential Access: $s = 1$; $b = weight(IdPh)$; $t = RS_{(IdPh)}$; $NP = np_{(IdPh)}$; $-F$ if there is 1 file per process; $-c$ if there is collective I/O.

Then IOR is run in the subsystem target. I/O time and transfer rate obtained from IOR running are named $Time_{io(CH)}$ and $BW_{(CH)}$. The estimated I/O time is calculated by expression (1).

$$Time_{io} = \sum_{i=1}^{n} Time_{io}(phase[i]) \tag{1}$$

Where the $Time_{io}(phase[i])$ is I/O time for each I/O phase that is calculated by expression (2).

$$Time_{io}(phase[i]) = \frac{weight_{(phase[i])}}{BW_{(CH)}(phase[i])} \tag{2}$$

$BW_{(CH)}(phase[i])$ is the characterized transfer rate at I/O library level for a similar access pattern.

3.3 Evaluation

We evaluate the utilization of I/O subsystem by the relation between the bandwidth characterized $BW_{(PK)}$ at I/O devices level and measured $BW_{(MD)}$ when the application is executed, expressed in equation 3.

$$SystemUsage(phase[i]) = \frac{BW_{(MD)}(phase[i])}{BW_{PK(IOP(phase[i]))}} * 100 \tag{3}$$

The I/O model is used to determine what system can provide the best I/O performance for the I/O phase with more impact in the I/O of the application. To evaluate the estimation's accuracy of the I/O time estimated we evaluate the relative error produced by the I/O time estimation. Relative error is calculated by expression (4); where $Time_{io(MD)}$ and $BW_{(MD)}$ are the I/O time and transfer rate obtained from running of application.

$$error_{rel} = 100 * \left(\frac{error_{abs}}{Time_{io(MD)}(phase[i])}\right) \tag{4}$$

Where absolute error is calculated by the expression (5).

$$error_{abs} = |Time_{io(CH)}(phase[i]) - Time_{io(MD)}(phase[i])| \tag{5}$$

4. Experimentation

We present the experiments in two part: 1) We extract the I/O model of MadBench2 [3] and we used it to evaluate the utilization of the two I/O subsystems. This approach is adequate when there is an exhaustive characterization of the I/O subsystem. 2) We extract the I/O model of Flash-IO

Table 1: Description of the I/O subsystems of systems A and B

I/O Element	System A	System B
I/O library	mpich2	OpenMPI
Communication Network	1 Gbps Ethernet	1 Gbps Ethernet
Storage Network	1 Gbps Ethernet	1 Gbps Ethernet
Filesystem Global	OrangeFS	NFS Ver 3
I/O nodes	10	32 DAS and 1 NAS
Metadata Server	1	1
Filesystem Local	Linux ext3	Linux ext4
Level Redundancy	-	RAID 5
Number of I/O Devices	11 disks	5 disks
Capacity of I/O Devices	500 GB	1.8 TB
Mounting Point	/mnt/orengafs	/home

benchmark [4] and we used it to tune parameters of IOR benchmark in order to evaluate the I/O performance for the I/O model. This approach is adequate when there is not an exhaustive characterization of the I/O subsystem. Table 1 shows the I/O subsystems of the System A and B.

System A is composed of 14 computing nodes:

- 4 cores of AMD Phenom™ II (8MB cache) or Athlon™ II (2MB cache), 4 DIMM slots for up to 16GB DDR3

System B is composed of 32 IBM x3550 Nodes:

- 2 x Dual-Core Intel(R) Xeon(R) CPU 5160 @ 3.00GHz 4MB L2 (2x2), 12 GB Fully Buffered DIMM 667 MHz

4.1 I/O subsystem Characterization

Figure 2 shows performance measured with IOR at I/O library level for the I/O system of A and B.

The I/O subsystem A (Figure 2(a)) shows a increasing I/O performance with the increment of request sizes for the writing operations and reading operations. For the request sizes upper to 16 MB we can observe a performance drop for reading operations. For the writing operations we can observe a drop in performance for the request sizes upper to 64MB. The I/O subsystem B (Figure 2(b)) shows a regular behavior for the reading operations regardless of the file size and request sizes. However, for the writing operations the request size is the I/O factor with the highest impact in performance. We can observe greater transfer rates for bigger request sizes ($> 256MB$), we also can observe a drop in performance for request size of 32 MB.

Peak values for the I/O subsystems are: Write=1120 MB/sec, Read=1260MB/sec for the system A and Write=165 MB/sec, Read=180MB/sec for the system B. These values allows us to limit the performance waited, because usually these are not possible to achieve due to the overhead of I/O software stack. However, the peak value allows us to know: How much performance capacity can provide I/O hardware?,

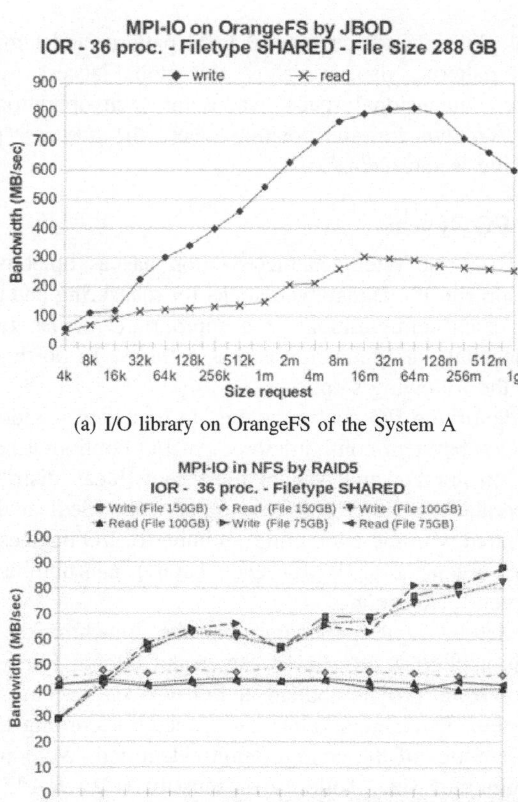

(a) I/O library on OrangeFS of the System A

(b) I/O library on NFS of the System B

Fig. 2: Performance characterized at I/O library on global filesystem

and How much I/O subsystem capacity are applications really using?

We can observe that the I/O subsystem performance of the system A is higher to I/O subsystem performance of the system B. Also, when we have evaluated the I/O performance for the I/O subsystem B we have observed that this I/O system is not adequate to I/O intensive applications with small request size. Also, we have observed in I/O characterization of the system A that is not adequate to application with request size upper to 1GB. The I/O subsystem A has been configured to applications that will use parallel HDF5 and parallel NetCDF on MPI-IO through a parallel filesystem. However, the I/O subsystem B is configured to parallel applications that can use MPI-IO without support of a parallel filesystem.

4.2 I/O subsystem utilization

To evaluate the system usage we analyze the I/O phases to MADBench2 in the I/O subsystems of system A and B. MADbench2 is a tool for testing the overall integrated performance of the I/O, communication and calculation subsystems of massively parallel architectures under the stress of a real scientific application. MADbench2 is based

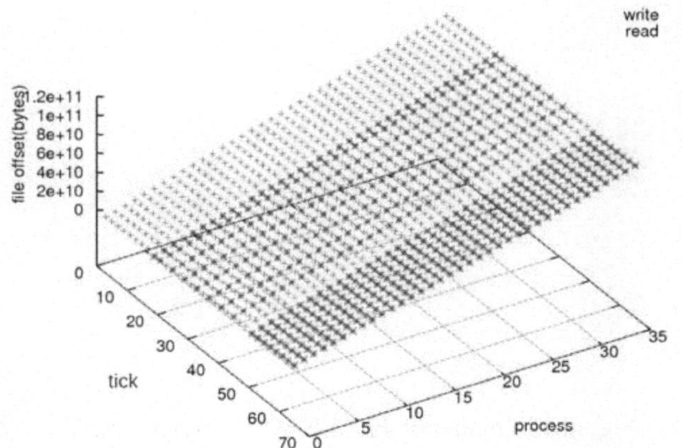

Fig. 3: I/O model of MADBench2 for 36 processes, 40KPIX, and file type SHARED

Table 2: I/O phases description of MADBench2 for $np = 36$ processes with request size $rs = 352$ in MB

Phase	#Oper.	rep	$weight$
1	$(np * rep)$ write	8	102GB
2	$(np * rep)$ read	2	25GB
3	$(np * rep)$ write	6	75GB
	$(np * rep)$ read	6	75GB
4	$(np * rep)$ write	2	25GB
5	$(np * rep)$ read	8	102GB

on the MADspec code, which calculates the maximum likelihood angular power spectrum of the Cosmic Microwave Background radiation from a noisy pixelated map of the sky and its pixel-pixel noise correlation matrix.

MADbench2 can be run on IO mode, in which all calculations/communications are replaced with busy-work.

MADbench2 reports the mean, minimum and maximum time spent by each function during calculation/communication, busy-work, reading and writing in each function. Running MADbench2 requires a n^2 number of processors.

We have obtained the I/O model of MADBench2 for 36 processes. Figure 3 shows I/O model of MADBench2 for 36 processes, 40KPIX, and file type SHARED.

Table 2 shows the five phases identified.

By tracing MADBench2 with our tool we have obtained its metadata: Individual file pointers, Non-collective I/O operations, Blocking I/O operations; sequential access mode, Shared access type; and a file shared by all processes.

The I/O subsystem utilization is analyzed for 36 processes in the I/O subsystems of the systems A and B.

Table 4 shows the utilization of the I/O subsystem B. We also show the amount of data transferred in each I/O phase ($weight$), the number and type of I/O operation (W=write, R=read, W-R=write-read), $BW_{(MD)}$ and $BW_{(PK)}$ in MB/second.

Table 3 shows the utilization of the I/O subsystem A

Table 3: I/O system utilization, $BW_{(PK)}$ and $BW_{(MD)}$ in MB/second for MADBench2 with 36 processes, file size 102 GB, RS=352MB and a shared file on System A

Phase	#Oper.	weight	$BW_{(PK)}$	$BW_{(MD)}$	System Usage(%)
1	288 W	102GB	1120	802	72
2	72 R	25GB	1260	254	20
3	432 W+R	150GB	1190	363	31
4	72 W	25GB	1120	636	57
5	288 R	102GB	1260	296	24

Table 4: I/O system utilization, $BW_{(PK)}$ and $BW_{(MD)}$ in MB/second for MADBench2 with 36 processes, file size 102 GB, RS=352MB and a shared file on System B

Phase	#Oper.	weight	$BW_{(PK)}$	$BW_{(MD)}$	System Usage (%)
1	288 W	102GB	204	76	37
2	72 R	25GB	300	44	15
3	432 W+R	150GB	252	41	16
4	72 W	25GB	204	60	30
5	288 R	102GB	300	41	14

for the MADBench2 to 40KPIX and 36 processes. We can observe that the I/O phases 1 and 4 (with writing operations) have utilized greater performance capacity than phases 2, 3 and 5 (phases with reading operations or composed). The third phase has used at about 31% of the performance capacity, a percentage similar to phases with reading operations that have used at about 20%.

Table 4 shows the utilization of the I/O subsystem for the MADBench2 to 40KPIX and 36 processes. We can observe that the I/O phases 1 and 4 (with writing operations) have utilized higher I/O performance capacity than phases 2, 3 and 5 (phases with reading operations or composed). The third phase has used at about 16% of the performance capacity, a percentage similar to phases with reading operations that have used at about 15%.

We can observe that the first phase has more impact in the I/O subsystem because need used more capacity of the I/O subsystem. The other phases with more impact are the fourth and the fifth. The second and the third phase have low impact in the I/O subsystem because the I/O operations are not consecutive, in fact, the I/O operations are done at interval of time sufficient to finish the I/O operations before that data are used.

4.3 FLASH-IO Benchmark

The aim of this experimentation is to extract the I/O model and select I/O phases with more weight to evaluate in other I/O subsystem. We have extracted the I/O model in I/O subsystem A and we have applied the I/O model in Finisterrae [15].

Finisterrae is composed of 143 computing nodes:

- 142 HP Integrity rx7640 nodes with 16 Itanium Montvale cores and 128 GB of memory each.
- 1 HP Integrity Superdome node with 128 Itanium Montvale cores and 1,024 GB of memory.

The I/O subsystem of Finisterrae used in this experiment is composed by: mpich2 and HDF5, 1 interconnection network Infinibad 20 Gbps, 1 storage Network Infinibad 20 Gbps, Filesystem Global Lustre (HP SFS), 18 OSS, 2 Metadata Server with 72 cabins SFS20, Filesystem Local Linux ext3, Level Redundancy RAID 6, 866 disks with a capacity of I/O Devices 866*250GB and a mounting point $HOMESFS.

FLASH-IO Benchmark simulates the I/O employed by FLASH for the purposes of benchmarking the code. FLASH is a block-structured adaptive mesh hydrodynamics code. The computational domain is divided into blocks which are distributed across the processors. Typically a block contains 8 zones in each coordinate direction (x,y,z) and a perimeter of guard-cells (presently 4 zones deep) to hold information from the neighbors. The code will produce a checkpoint file (containing all variables in 8-byte precision) and two plot files (4 variables, 4-byte precision, one containing corner data, the other containing cell-centered data). The checkpoint and plot file routines are identical to those used in the FLASH Code.

4.3.1 Extracting the I/O model

We have obtained the following meta-data of FLASH-IO in the parallel HDF5 version with our tool:

- Explicit offset, Blocking I/O operations, Collective operations and Non-collective.
- Strided access mode, Shared access type for three files.
- MPI-IO routine MPI_Set_view with etype of with different etype and filetype for collective and non-collective operations.

FLASH-IO performs only I/O operations and there are no communication events. I/O operations of parallel HDF5 are converted into MPI primitives. Table 5 shows the description of the I/O phases. Where IdPh. is the Identifier of the Phase, Oper. is the Type of operation, RS is the Size of request, Iter. is the number of iterations, Dist. is the Distance, OI is the initial offset, Disp. is the Displacement, and 1°Tick is the first tick (1°Tick) of the phase. Distance is the number of events of communication or events of I/O between two phases. The first tick represents the tic's number from the first pattern of one phase. Displacement defines the location where a view begins, this is the file displacement.

We can observe five phases for the first file. In this case the are several MPI_File_set_view to achieve strided access. There are two types of writing operations: MPI_File_write_at and MPI_File_write_at_all. We show the phases for the collective operations because they represent the 90% of I/O. The I/O model of flash is shown in Figure 4.

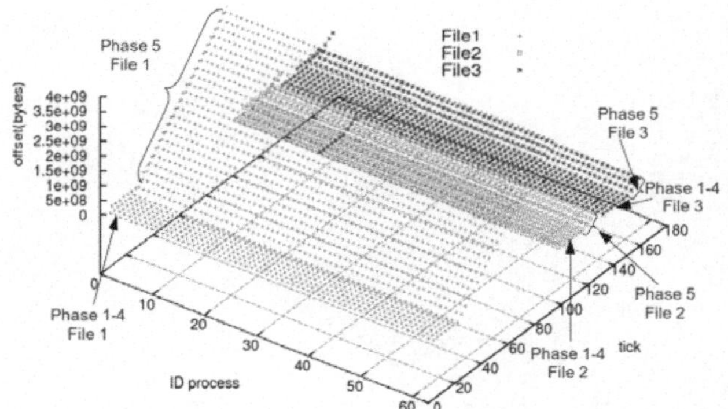

Fig. 4: I/O model of FLASH-IO for 64 processes

Table 5: I/O model of FLASH-IO Write_at_all

IdPh.	RS	Iter.	Dist.	OI	Disp.	1°Tick
1° F.						
1	320	2	3	6288	20732	9
2	4800	1	3	47752	310980	15
3	1920	2	3	358732	124392	18
4	3840	1	3	609564	439012	24
5	2621440	24	3	1048576	169869312	27
2° F.						
1	320	2	3	6288	20732	109
2	4800	1	3	47752	310980	115
3	960	2	3	358732	62196	118
4	1920	1	3	485172	301260	124
5	1310720	4	3	786432	84934656	127
3° F.						
1	320	2	3	6288	20732	149
2	4800	1	3	47752	310980	155
3	960	2	3	358732	62196	158
4	1920	1	3	485172	301260	164
5	1572160	4	3	786432	101974016	167

The I/O model shows three file used during the run of the application. Files are enumerated taking into account the order in which they were opened. Table 5 shows the description of phases for the first file (1° F.), second file (2° F.), and the third file (3° F.). We can observe small request size for the phases 1 to 4 for the three files and 2MB for first file and 1MB for the second and third file in the fifth phase.

4.3.2 Applying the I/O model

We use the I/O model of FLASH-IO to set the parameters of IOR. We select phase 5 to mimic with IOR because it is the most weighted phase. The parameters are set as follows and we run IOR in the same order:

- File 1: -np 64 -a MPIIO -c -s 24 -b 2621440 -t 2621440
- File 2: -np 64 -a MPIIO -c -s 4 -b 1310720 -t 1310720
- File 3: -np 64 -a MPIIO -c -s 4 -b 1572160 -t 1572160

We have evaluated the I/O time of IOR and I/O time of flash in the cluster Finisterrae. Table 6 shows the I/O time obtained with IOR $Time_{io(CH)}$, I/O time for FLASH-IO $Time_{io(MD)}$, and relative error $error_{rel}$. We observe higher

Table 6: Error of I/O time estimation on Finisterrae for 64 and 128 processes for phase 5 of FLASH-IO

Phase	$Time_{io(CH)}$	$Time_{io(MD)}$	$error_{rel}$
64p			
File 1	47.73	51.02	6%
File 2	3.07	4.62	33%
File 3	3.80	4.83	21%
128p			
File 1	98.88	102.25	3%
File 2	8.74	8.44	3%
File 3	10.02	11.14	10%

errors for 64 processes in the File 2 and File 3, this is due to the size of Files (400MB). However, we can observe that the error is decreased in 128 processes for the File 1. This is the file with the highest size.

Flash increases its I/O requirements when the number of processes is increased. For example, the weight of the fifth phase of the File 1 is $2621440*24*512$ to 512 processes and $2621440 * 24 * 256$ to 256 processes. We have analyzed the I/O model for 256 and 512 processes and we have observed that the I/O phases have the same request size, therefore, the I/O requirements are increased in function of the number of processes for each I/O phases. For this application the I/O system have more impact when the number of processes is increased.

5. Conclusions

We have applied a methodology to characterize the parallel I/O of scientific applications. We have represented the message-passing applications through an I/O model. The model allows us to evaluate the I/O subsystems taking into account the I/O phases of the application. We have used an exhaustive performance characterization of I/O subsystem for different access patterns with the benchmark IOR at I/O library level and IOzone at I/O devices level.

Furthermore, we have used the I/O model to set the IOR benchmark input parameters for the access patterns of each I/O phase of Flash-IO. This approach is adequate when the I/O subsystem does not allows us an exhaustive I/O performance characterization. We have evaluated this approach to FLASH-IO. We have used the I/O model to estimate the I/O time. Relative errors have shown that the I/O time estimation is more accurate when the I/O is representative of the application.

The I/O model can be used to evaluate the performance of the application without executing it. This is very useful particularly for the real applications that usually need several libraries in order to be executed.

Currently, we are extending the I/O phases identification to different applications in order to show others I/O behaviors. Also, we are analyzing the relationship between the I/O model and number of I/O and stripe size. We plan to provide an useful configuration method to users and administrators. We expect that by using our tool they will be able to configure the number of I/O node and the stripe size, by considering only the most relevant phases of one application.

Acknowledgment

This research has been supported by the MICINN Spain under contract TIN2007-64974, the MINECO (MICINN) Spain under contract TIN2011-24384, the European ITEA2 project H4H, No 09011 and the Avanza Competitividad I+D+I program under contract TSI-020400-2010-120.

Appreciation to The Centre of Supercomputing of Galicia (CESGA), Science and Technology Infrastructures (in spanish ICTS).

References

[1] A. Wong, D. Rexachs, and E. Luque, "Extraction of parallel application signatures for performance prediction," in *HPCC, 2010 12th IEEE Int. Conf. on*, sept. 2010, pp. 223–230.

[2] S. Mendez, D. Rexachs, and E. Luque, "Methodology for performance evaluation of the input/output system on computer clusters," in *Workshop IASDS on Cluster Computing (CLUSTER), 2011 IEEE International Conference on*, sept. 2011, pp. 474 –483.

[3] J. Carter, J. Borrill, and L. Oliker, "Performance characteristics of a cosmology package on leading hpc architectures," in *High Performance Computing - HiPC 2004*, ser. Lecture Notes in Computer Science, L. Bougé and V. Prasanna, Eds., vol. 3296. Springer Berlin / Heidelberg, 2005, pp. 21–34.

[4] A. Laboratory. (2013) Flash io benchmark. [Online]. Available: http://www.mcs.anl.gov/research/projects/pio-benchmark/

[5] J. M. Kunkel and T. Ludwig, "Performance evaluation of the pvfs2 architecture," in *Parallel, Distributed and Network-Based Processing, 2007. PDP '07. 15th EUROMICRO International Conference on*, feb. 2007, pp. 509 –516.

[6] J. H. Laros *et al.*, "Red storm io performance analysis," in *CLUSTER '07: Procs of the 2007 IEEE Int. Conf. on Cluster Computing*. USA: IEEE Computer Society, 2007, pp. 50–57.

[7] S. Lang, P. Carns, R. Latham, R. Ross, K. Harms, and W. Allcock, "I/O performance challenges at leadership scale," in *Proceedings of SC2009: High Performance Networking and Computing*, November 2009.

[8] P. Carns, K. Harms, W. Allcock, C. Bacon, R. Latham, S. Lang, and R. Ross, "Understanding and improving computational science storage access through continuous characterization," in *27th IEEE Conference on Mass Storage Systems and Technologies (MSST 2011)*, 2011.

[9] S. Byna, Y. Chen, X.-H. Sun, R. Thakur, and W. Gropp, "Parallel i/o prefetching using mpi file caching and i/o signatures," in *High Performance Computing, Networking, Storage and Analysis, 2008. SC 2008. International Conference for*, nov. 2008, pp. 1–12.

[10] H. Shan and J. Shalf, "Using IOR to analyze the I/O performance of HPC platforms," in *Cray Users Group Meeting (CUG) 2007*, Seattle, Washington, May 7-10, 2007.

[11] P. Carns, R. Latham, R. Ross, K. Iskra, S. Lang, and K. Riley, "24/7 Characterization of Petascale I/O Workloads," in *Proceedings of 2009 Workshop on Interfaces and Architectures for Scientific Data Storage*, September 2009.

[12] S. Mendez, D. Rexachs, and E. Luque, "Modeling parallel scientific applications through their input/output phases," in *CLUSTER Workshops'12*, 2012, pp. 7–15.

[13] H. . S. J. Shan, "Using ior to analyze the i/o performance for hpc platforms," LBNL Paper LBNL-62647, Tech. Rep., 2007. [Online]. Available: www.osti.gov/bridge/servlets/purl/923356-15FxGK/

[14] W. D. Norcott, "Iozone filesystem benchmark," Tech. Rep., 2006. [Online]. Available: http://www.iozone.org/

[15] C. Finisterrae, "Centre of supercomputing of galicia (cesga)," Science and Technology Infrastructures (in spanish ICTS), Tech. Rep., 2012. [Online]. Available: https://www.cesga.es/

Control and Marking Data Flows

A. HENNI Djamel-Eddine[1], B. MEKKAKIA Zoulikha [2], and C. GHOMARI Abdelghani[3]
[1]Post-Graduation Department, INTTIC, Oran, Algeria
[2]IT Department, USTOMB, Oran, Algeria
[3]IT Department, University of Oran, Oran, Algeria

Abstract— *This document focuses on DiffServ Quality of Service approach and in particular on marking data flows in IP networks. One of the congestion causes in these networks is the burst size of IP packets. Marking these packets is to give them priority depending on their criticality so that routers and switches can process them according to their importance. Traffic shaping and congestion control are very important mainly when VBR (Variable Bit Rate) and CBR (Constant Bit Rate) are present in the network. Many methods were proposed to solve this hardness. The target of these methods is to maximise the quantity of transmitted data flows when maintained the required QoS and to reduce congestion in the network. We have studied the impact of traffic shaping on CBR and VBR flows in a DiffServ network. Simulations were done on NS-2 using CBR and VBR traffic shaped by token buckets and marked by different kind of markers such as simple, two rate and Time Sliding Window Three Color Marker. Application of these markers with and without the presence of the shaper leads to different results.*

Keywords: DiffServ, Marking, QoS, PHB, Shaping

1. Introduction

To support the quality of service (QoS) [1] on IP based networks, the Internet Engineering Task Force (IETF) has proposed the Differentiated Services (DiffServ) [2]. DiffServ provides simple and predefined per-hop behavior (PHB) level service differentiation. The IETF has defined one class for Expedited Forwarding (EF) PHB and four classes for Assured Forwarding (AF) PHB [3] [4]. AF PHB allows an Internet service provider (ISP) to provide different levels of forwarding assurances according to the user profile. The major benefit of the DiffServ (DS) approach is its practicality and scalability, due to aggregation of different packet streams (data flows) with the same required service. The main consequence of this concept is that traffic signalling can be almost completely cut off if the communication end-points are in the same DiffServ Domain, otherwise it has to be performed only at the inter-domain links. This can be achieved because in this approach Quality of Service provision is guaranteed aggregating different data flows with the same quality requirements, thus achieving scalability especially in the core network, where it is difficult to maintain separate information because of the large amount of different data flows.

1.1 Related Works

Several studies have been conducted on data flows so that interconnection equipments can differentiate IP packets according to their priorities. In [5] the authors introduce a new packets marking algorithm which will be used in the AF (Assured Forwording) of the DiffServ model. This new algorithm was proposed to overcome the problem of equity occurred in other marking algorithms. In [6] a new algorithm of MPEG4 flows marking was proposed, the authors were interested to QoS interactions between MPEG4 video applications and DiffServ IP networks. These interactions result by associating an elementary MPEG flow (Video, audio, indication, ODs) to a PHB of DiffServ, AF/EF. The objectif of this study focuses on two idea, the first one, the establishment of an encapsulation protocol for MPEG4 packets through RTP/IP (Real Time Protocol/Internet Protocol). The second one, the proposition of marking mechanism for DiffServ routers (DVMA algorithm). Other flows markers had been studied, in [7] the researchers prposed the AFM (Aggregate Fairness Marker) which is an intermediate marker associated to the uf-TCM (User Flow Three Color Marker) in order to overcome the problem of fairness experienced by IP packets during the congestion control and offering a differentiation service throughout the communication chain when it comes to cross several diffserv areas.

1.2 DiffServ Network Organization

The DiffServ architecture distinguishes the border from the inside of un administration domain. This architecture is composed of a number of functional elements implemented in network nodes, including a small set of per-hop forwarding behaviors, packet classification functions, and traffic conditioning functions including metering, marking, shaping, and policing. This architecture achieves scalability by implementing complex classification and conditioning functions only at network boundary nodes, and by applying per-hop behaviors to aggregates of traffic which have been appropriately marked using the DS field in the ipv4 or ipv6 headers [1]. Per-hop behaviors are defined to permit a rea-

[1] the ipv4 header TOS octet or the ipv6 traffic Class octet when interpreted in conformance with the definition given in [8]. The bits of the DSCP field encode the DS codepoint, while the remaining bits are currently unused.

sonably granular means of allocating buffer and bandwidth resources at each node among competing traffic streams. Per-application flow or per-customer forwarding state need not be maintained within the core of the network.

1.3 Standardized Per-Hop-Behavior

1.3.1 The Expedited Forwording PHB

Network nodes that implement the differentiated services enhancements to IP use a codepoint in the IP header to select a per-hop behavior (PHB) as the specific forwarding treatment for that packet [8]. We describe here brievely a particular PHB called expedited forwarding (EF) PHB which can be used to build a low loss, low latency, low jitter, assured bandwidth, end-to-end service through DiffServ domains. Loss, latency and jitter are all due to the queues traffic experiences while transiting the network. Therefore providing low loss, latency and jitter for some traffic aggregate means ensuring that the aggregate sees no (or very small) queues. Queues arise when (short-term) traffic arrival rate exceeds departure rate at some node. Thus a service that ensures no queues for some aggregate is equivalent to bounding rates such that, at every transit node, the aggregate's maximum arrival rate is less than that aggregate's minimum departure rate. The EF PHB is defined as a forwarding treatment for a particular diffserv aggregate where the departure rate of the aggregate's packets from any diffserv node must equal or exceed a configurable rate [3]. The EF traffic should receive this rate independent of the intensity of any other traffic attempting to transit the node. It should average at least the configured rate when measured over any time interval equal to or longer than the time it takes to send an output link MTU sized packet at the configured rate. (Behavior at time scales shorter than a packet time at the configured rate is deliberately not specified.) The configured minimum rate must be settable by a network administrator (using whatever mechanism the node supports for non-volatile configuration).

1.3.2 The Assured Forwording PHB

The AF PHB group provides delivery of IP packets in four independently forwarded AF classes. Within each AF class, an IP packet can be assigned one of three different levels of drop precedence. A DiffServ node does not reorder IP packets of the same microflow if they belong to the same AF class. In a DS node, the level of forwarding assurance of an IP packet thus depends on how much forwarding resources has been allocated to the AF class that the packet belongs to, and what is the current load of the AF class, and, in case of congestion within the class, what is the drop precedence of the packet [4]. For example, if traffic conditioning actions at the ingress of the provider DS domain make sure that an AF class in the DS nodes is only moderately loaded by packets with the lowest drop precedence value and is not overloaded by packets with the two lowest drop precedence values, then the AF class can offer a high level of forwarding assurance for packets that are within the subscribed profile (i.e., marked with the lowest drop precedence value) and offer up to two lower levels of forwarding assurance for the excess traffic. The table below summarizes the recommended AF codepoint values.

Table1: AF Codepoint Values.

PHBs AF_{ij}	class 1	class 2	class 3	class 4
Low Drop Prec	001010	010010	011010	100010
Medium Drop Prec	001100	010100	011100	100100
High Drop Prec	001110	010110	011110	100110

1.4 QoS Parameters

The quality of service (QoS) refers to several related aspects of telephony and computer networks that allow the transport of traffic with special requirements. In particular, much technology has been developed to allow computer networks to become as useful as telephone networks for audio conversations, as well as supporting new applications with even stricter service demands. It is a concept based on the statement that not all applications need the same performance from the system/network over which they run. Thus, applications may indicate their specific requirements to the network, including cost, before they actually start transmitting data.

1.4.1 Major Parameters Defining QoS

- **Throughput**: the total amount of work completed during a specific time interval.
- **Delay**: the elapsed time from when a request is first submitted to when the desired result is produced.
- **Jitter**: the delays that occur during playback of a stream.
- **Reliability**: how errors are handled during transmission and processing of continuous media.

1.5 Marking and Coloring IP Packets

IP packets coloration is a way to mark them modifing the DSCP field of the IP header. In a DS domain, marking process take place near the flow classification mechanism or after the transition in the supervision module of an edge router of a DS domain. Packets can be colored into green, yellow, or red. In case of multimedia application, attention will be focused on the AF classes. Three packets coloration algorithms had been studied by the IETF (Internet Engineering Task Force):

1- Single Rate Three Color Marker (srTCM).
2- Two Rate Three Color Marker (trTCM).
3- Time Sliding Window Three Color Marker (TSWTCM).

1.5.1 Single Rate Three Color Marker

The Single Rate Three Color Marker (srTCM) meters an IP packet stream and marks its packets either green, yellow, or red. Marking is based on a Committed Information Rate (CIR) and two associated burst sizes, a Committed Burst

Size (CBS) and an Excess Burst Size (EBS). A packet is marked green if it doesn't exceed the CBS, yellow if it does exceed the CBS, but not the EBS, and red otherwise. The srTCM is useful, for example, for ingress policing of a service, where only the length, not the peak rate, of the burst determines service eligibility. The Meter meters each packet and passes the packet and the metering result to the Marker [9]. The Meter operates in one of two modes. In the Color-Blind mode, the Meter assumes that the packet stream is uncolored. In the Color-Aware mode the Meter assumes that some preceding entity has precolored the incoming packet stream so that each packet is either green, yellow, or red. The Marker (re)colors an IP packet according to the results of the Meter. The color is coded in the DS field [8] of the packet in a PHB specific manner (see section 4 for an example).

1.5.2 Two Rate Three Color Marker

The Two Rate Three Color Marker (trTCM) meters an IP packet stream and marks its packets either green, yellow, or red. A packet is marked red if it exceeds the Peak Information Rate (PIR) [10], otherwise it is marked either yellow or green depending on whether it exceeds or doesn't exceed the Committed Information Rate (CIR). The trTCM is useful, for example, for ingress policing of a service, where a peak rate needs to be enforced separately from a committed rate. The Meter meters each packet and passes the packet and the metering result to the Marker. The Meter operates in one of two modes. In the Color-Blind mode, the Meter assumes that the packet stream is uncolored. In the Color-Aware mode the Meter assumes that some preceding entity has precolored the incoming packet stream so that each packet is either green, yellow, or red. The Marker (re)colors an IP packet according to the results of the Meter. The color is coded in the DS field of the packet in a PHB specific manner.

1.5.3 Time Sliding Window Three Color Marker

The Time Sliding Window Three Colour Marker (TSWTCM) is designed to mark packets of an IP traffic stream with colour of red, yellow or green. The marking is performed based on the measured throughput of the traffic stream as compared against the Committed Target Rate (CTR) and the Peak Target Rate (PTR). The TSWTCM is designed to mark packets contributing to sending rate below or equal to the CTR with green colour. Packets contributing to the portion of the rate between the CTR and PTR are marked yellow. Packets causing the rate to exceed PTR are marked with red colour. The TSWTCM has been primarily designed for traffic streams that will be forwarded based on the AF PHB in core routers [11].The TSWTCM consists of two independent components: a rate estimator, and a marker to associate a colour (drop precedence) with each packet. If the marker is used with the AF PHB, each colour would correspond to a level of drop precedence. The marker uses an estimated rate module to probabilistically associate packets with one of the three colours. Using a probabilistic function in the marker is beneficial to TCP flows as it reduces the likelihood of dropping multiple packets within a TCP window. The marker also works correctly with UDP traffic, i.e., it associates the appropriate portion of the UDP packets with yellow or red colour marking if such flows transmit at a sustained level above the contracted rate. The colour of the packet is translated into a DS field packet marking. The colours red, yellow and green translate into DS codepoints representing drop precedence 2, 1 and 0 of a single AF class respectively. Based on feedback from four different implementations, the TSWTCM is simple and straightforward to implement. It can be implemented in either software or hardware depending on the nature of the forwarding engine.

2. Main Results

In what follows, we present contribution of markers on VBR (Variable Bit Rate) and CBR (Constant Bit Rate) flows. We hold out the study of the three main markers (srTCM, trTCM and TSWTCM) with a flow shaping. The target of this study is to assign a green marking to priority flows (real-time flows), so to do this, we have done our study on VBR and CBR flows, with and without the presence of the shaper.

2.1 Experimentation Environnement

The test platform is a virtual machine in which the operating system is LINUX Ubuntu with NS2(Network Simulator2) installed in. The topologies used in our simulations are composed of sources and destinations connected across to a DiffServ network consisting of three routers (one CORE router and two EDGE routers), simulation parameters (flows configuration, simulation time, markers type...etc) are described thereafter.

Table 2: Simulation Parameters.

Parametres	Values
DiffServ Architecture	Six Nodes
Markers	srTCM trTCM TSW3CM
Flows	FTP VBR CBR
Packets Size	200 octets 250 octets
Transport	TCP UDP
Simulation Time	150s
Shaper	Token Bucket

Table 3: Flows Parameters.

Flows Rate	Values
VBR	900 Kbit/s
VBR burst_time	150 ms
VBR idle_time	20 ms
CBR	900 Kbit/s
TCP	1 Mbit/s

Table 4: TCM rates and sizes.

TCM Parameters	Values
CIR	600000 bit/s
CBS	2000 octets
EBS	3000 octets
PIR	800000 bit/s
CBS	2000 octets
PBS	4000 octets

In the first script, the topology is composed of one source and two destinations separated through a DiffServ network as shown in the following figure. The source S1 generate two identical VBR flows towards two destinations D1 and D2. First, the two streams are subjected to a single rate TCM marker at the input of the network. We mesure for the two streams their instantaneous flowrate received by destinations D1 and D2, their packets loss rate, their average delay and jitter. we also measure the number of packets marked in green, yellow and red. Next, we take the same parameters of the simulation above but this time a flow shaping is applied on the flow generated from S1 towards D1 then we mesure the instantaneous flowrate received by the two destinations D1 and D2, their packets loss rate, their average delay and jitter. we also measure the number of packets marked in green, yellow and red. We repeate the two previous tests with double rate and time sliding window TCM.

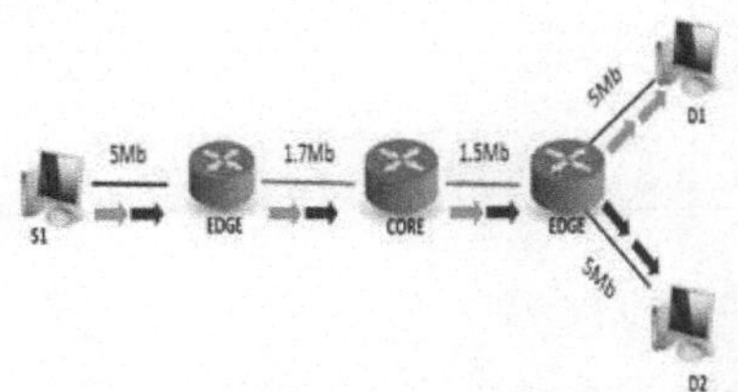

Fig. 1: Simulation Topology with VBR flows

2.2 Simulation Results

2.2.1 VBR flow

After running the simulation on the topology described above, we obtain different results of QoS parameters depending on the use or not of traffic shaping. The following table contains the QoS parameters results without the use of stream shaping with different markers (Single Rate Three Color Marker, Two Rate Three Color Marker and Time Sliding Three Color Marker).

Table 5: Simulation Results for VBR flows without shaping.

Marker	VBR1		VBR2	
srTCM	Sent Packets	291132	Sent Packets	288207
	Packets Loss	7200	Packets Loss	6966
	Delay(ms)	19.355	Delay(ms)	19.378
	Jitter(ms)	$540 * 10^{-3}$	Jitter(ms)	$554 * 10^{-3}$
trTCM	Sent Packets	289769	Sent Packets	293080
	Packets Loss	5656	Packets Loss	5999
	Delay(ms)	27.556	Delay(ms)	27.451
	Jitter(ms)	$38 * 10^{-3}$	Jitter(ms)	$40 * 10^{-3}$
TSWTCM	Sent Packets	289664	Sent Packets	290839
	Packets Loss	5642	Packets Loss	5630
	Delay(ms)	29.384	Delay(ms)	29.342
	Jitter(ms)	$45 * 10^{-3}$	Jitter(ms)	$46 * 10^{-3}$

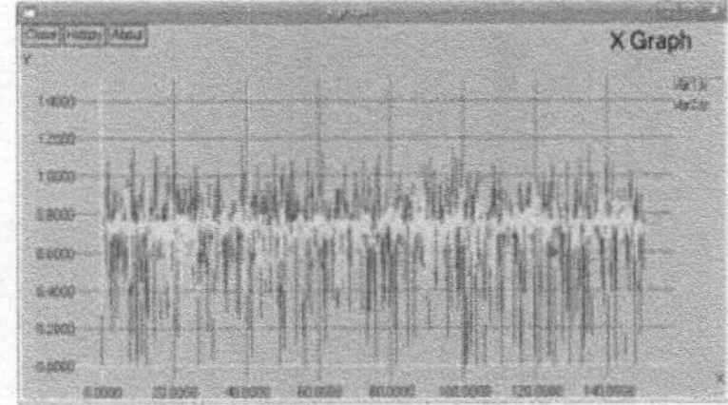

Fig. 2: Received flowrate by destinations D1 and D2 without traffic shaping

The following table contains the QoS parameters results with the use of stream shaping:

Table 6: Simulation Results for VBR flows with shaping.

Marker	VBR1		VBR2	
srTCM	Sent Packets	298388	Sent Packets	281218
	Packets Loss	4	Packets Loss	12951
	Delay(ms)	22.641	Delay(ms)	21.971
	Jitter(ms)	$21 * 10^{-3}$	Jitter(ms)	$65 * 10^{-3}$
trTCM	Sent Packets	297148	Sent Packets	287873
	Packets Loss	12	Packets Loss	11880
	Delay(ms)	33.658	Delay(ms)	32.562
	Jitter(ms)	$6 * 10^{-6}$	Jitter(ms)	$63 * 10^{-6}$
TSWTCM	Sent Packets	295907	Sent Packets	285314
	Packets Loss	85	Packets Loss	10555
	Delay(ms)	35.355	Delay(ms)	34.278
	Jitter(ms)	$16 * 10^{-3}$	Jitter(ms)	$76 * 10^{-3}$

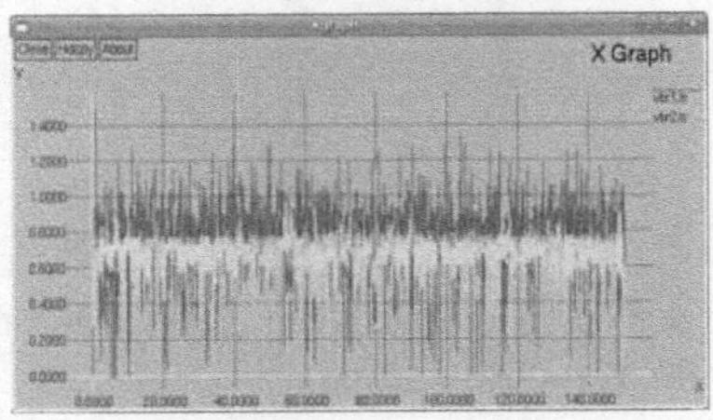

Fig. 3: Received flowrate by destinations D1 and D2 after traffic shaping

Now, we are going to see the imapact of markers changement on CBR flows. To do so, we modified the network topology adding an other source S2 to have two flows generators. The first one will generate CBR stream towards D1 while the seconde one will generate a TCP stream towards D2 which would obstruct the CBR stream on which we apply QoS when changing the DSCP code of the IP header with

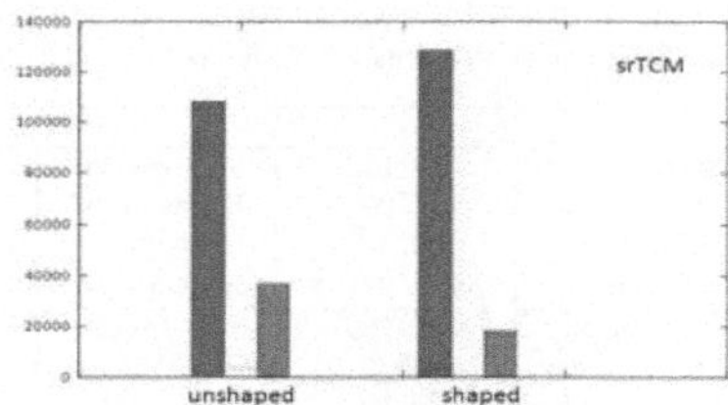

Fig. 4: Number of generated green, yellow and red packets with and without traffic shaping

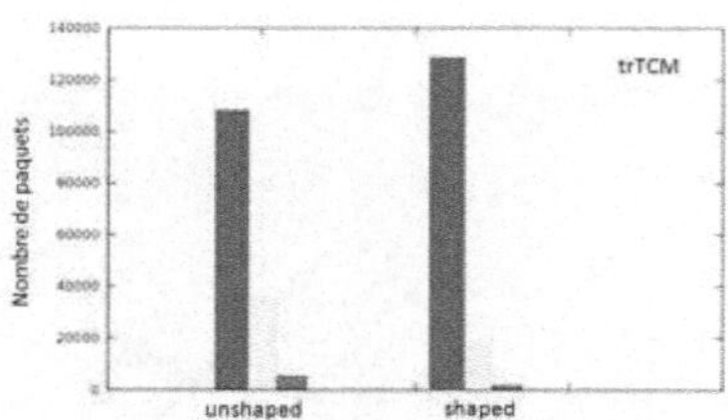

Fig. 5: Number of generated green, yellow and red packets with and without traffic shaping

different markers. First, we don't apply flow shaping and we mesure for the two streams their instantaneous flowrate received by destinations D1 and D2, their packets loss rate, their average delay and jitter. we also measure the number of packets marked in green, yellow and red. Next, we apply a stream shaping on the CBR flow whiwh passes between S1 and D1 then we take the same measures as above. We repeate the two previous tests with double rate and time sliding window TCM.

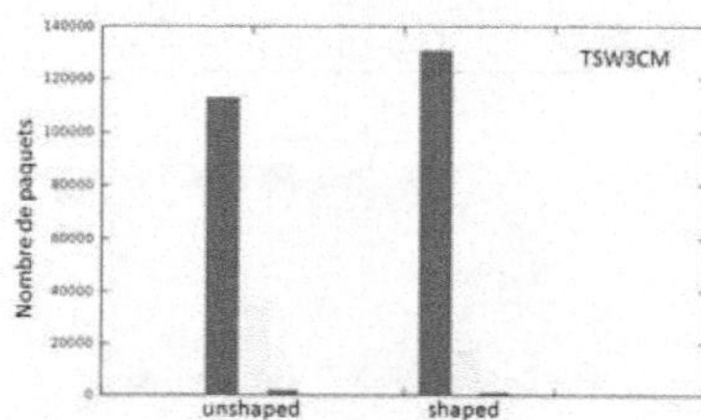

Fig. 6: Number of generated green, yellow and red packets with and without traffic shaping

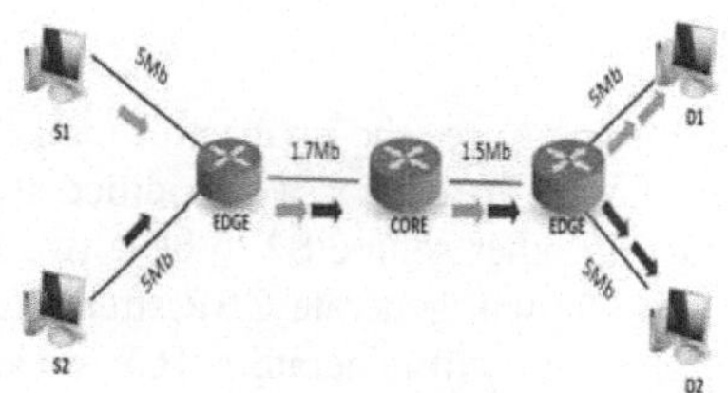

Fig. 7: Simulation Topology with CBR and TCP flows

2.2.2 CBR and TCP flows

The following table contains the QoS parameters results without the use of stream shaping with different markers:

Table 7: Simulation Results for CBR flows without shaping.

Marker	CBR		FTP	
srTCM	Sent Packets	309934	Sent Packets	318555
	Packets Loss	11493	Packets Loss	1153
	Delay(ms)	19.248	Delay(ms)	12.434
	Jitter(ms)	$72 * 10^{-3}$	Jitter(ms)	2.4
trTCM	Sent Packets	309960	Sent Packets	325621
	Loss Packet	11471	Loss Packet	647
	Delay(ms)	27.6	Delay(ms)	16.458
	Jitter(ms)	$76{*}10^{-3}$	Jitter(ms)	2.7
TSWTCM	Sent Packets	308599	Sent Packets	325951
	Loss Packet	12831	Loss Packet	573
	Delay(ms)	30.88	Delay(ms)	18.418
	Jitter(ms)	96^{-3}	Jitter(ms)	2.7

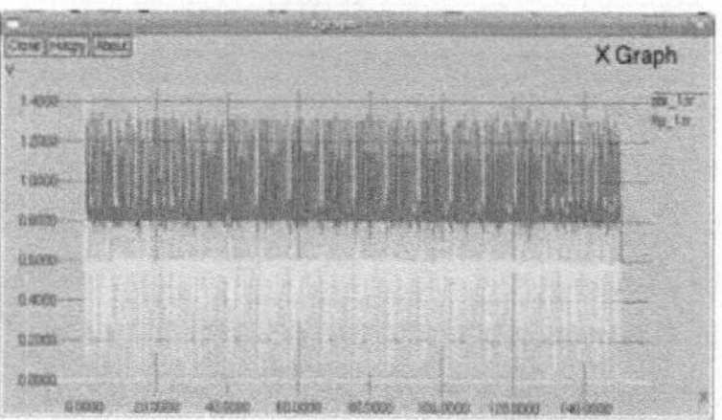

Fig. 8: Received flowrate by destinations D1 and D2 without traffic shaping

The following table contains the QoS parameters results with the use of stream shaping:

Table 8: Simulation Results for CBR flows with shaping.

Marker	VBR1		VBR2	
srTCM	Sent Packets	320905	Sent Packets	262605
	Packets Loss	527	Packets Loss	247
	Delay(ms)	42.995	Delay(ms)	24.312
	Jitter(ms)	$2 * 10^{-3}$	Jitter(ms)	3.34
trTCM	Sent Packets	320915	Sent Packets	262590
	Packets Loss	517	Packets Loss	274
	Delay(ms)	42.964	Delay(ms)	24.292
	Jitter(ms)	$3 * 10^{-3}$	Jitter(ms)	3.35
TSWTCM	Sent Packets	320005	Sent Packets	267625
	Packets Loss	1427	Packets Loss	179
	Delay(ms)	57.253	Delay(ms)	31.534
	Jitter(ms)	$7 * 10^{-3}$	Jitter(ms)	3.3

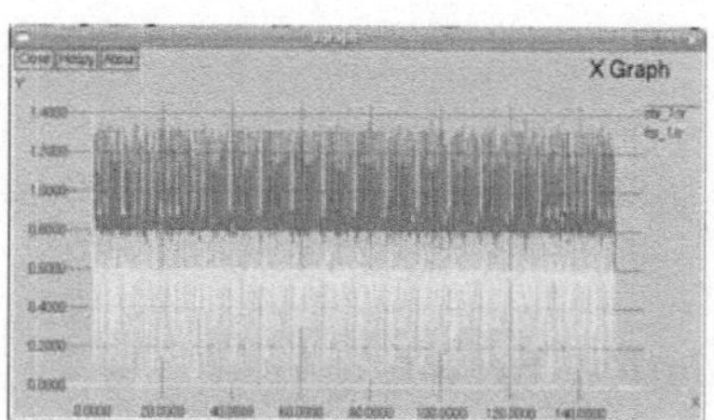

Fig. 9: Received flowrate by destinations D1 and D2 after traffic shaping

2.3 Results Discussion

2.3.1 VBR Flows

When Analysing obtained results when changing the marker with and without traffic shaping, we note that when-

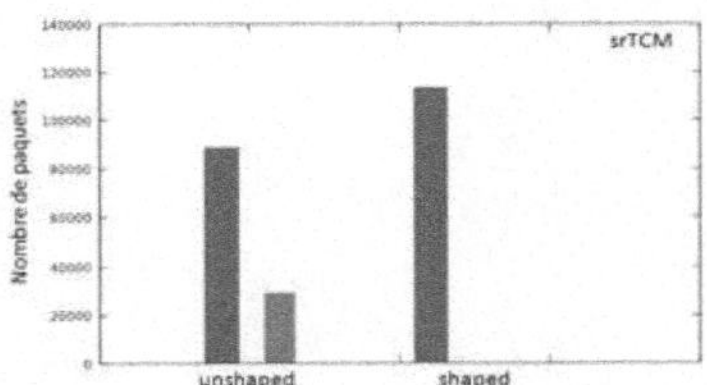

Fig. 10: Number of generated green, yellow and red packets with and without traffic shaping

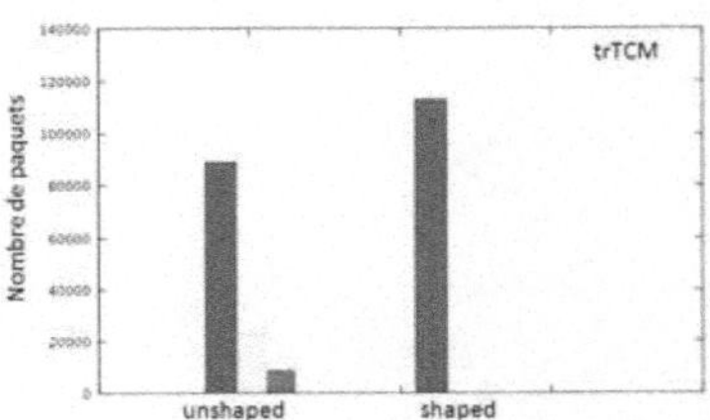

Fig. 11: Number of generated green, yellow and red packets with and without traffic shaping

ever we apply a traffic shaping, the number of green packets increases in a remarkable way regardless of the marker type. The percentage of this increase differs from a marker to another as show in the table bellow.

Table 9: Improvement Percentage of Green Packets.

Marker	Improvement Percentage
srTCM	18,90%
trTCM	19,21%
TSW3CM	15,87%

We note that green packets generated by the EDGE router increases when changing the marker even without the use of traffic shaping. The marker which generates more packets is the TSWTCM followed by the srTCM, but when we apply a traffic shaping we note the marker which generates more packets is the trTCM followed by the srTCM. So if we have a network in which a traffic shaping is used, we choose the trTCM in order to promote VBR flows but if the network is devoided of traffic shaping, we use the TSWTCM.

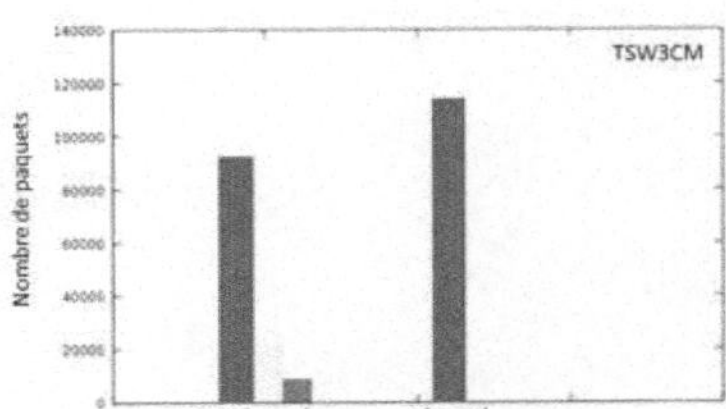

Fig. 12: Number of generated green, yellow and red packets with and without traffic shaping

Packets Loss

For the Packets Loss , and when we don't use a traffic shaping, the marker having the lowest loss rate is the TSWTCM. The use of traffic shaping greatly reduces the packets loss rate for all markers (more than 95%). During simulations, the marker which reduces packets loss rate more then the others is the TSWTCM (96.01%) versus 95.33% for trTCM and 95.15% for srTCM.

End to End Delay

It is quite clear that adding another element in the network will increase the end to end delay, except that it differs from a marker to an other. When we don't use a traffic shaping, the marker with which we obtain the best end to end delay is the srTCM since its simplicity of design. When we apply the traffic shaping, the end to end delay increases (up to 30%). The marker which have the lowest end to end delay is the srTCM.

Jitter

Jitter is the measure of the variability over time of the packet latency across a network. When we don't apply a traffic shaping, marker having the best jitter is the trTCM. When using traffic shaping, jitter is greatly reduced for all markers, especially with trTCM.

2.3.2 CBR and TCP Flows

As seen previously with VBR flows, we note that whenever we use a traffic shaping, number of green packets greatly increases regardless the marker kind. Increase percentage differs from a marker to another. The following table summarizes this increase.

Table 10: Improvement Percentage of Green Packets.

Marker	Improvement Percentage
srTCM	27,45%
trTCM	27,32%
TSW3CM	23,32%

Packets Loss

The Transmission Control Protocol (TCP) is one of the two original core protocols of the Internet protocol suite (IP), it provides reliable, ordered, error-checked delivery of a stream of octets between programs running on computers connected to the network. But for CBR flows, they are sent on UDP which doesn't ensure error-checked delivery and packets loss control. Analysing previous results, we note that packets loss rate for CBR flows is greater compared to TCP flows when we don't apply a traffic shaping, but once, it's applied, packets loss rate of CBR flow reduces greatly.

End to End Delay

As seen previously with VBR flows, adding another element

in the network will increase the end to end delay. The marker with which we obtain the best end to end delay is the srTCM since its simplicity of design either with or without using traffic shaping.

Jitter

When we don't apply a traffic shaping, the marker with which we obtain the best jitter is the trTCM. When using traffic shaping, jitter is greatly reduced for all markers especially for srTCM.

3. Conclusion

We have studied the impact of traffic shaping before marking data flows in DiffServ network, we have done our studies on a DiffServ network composed of three nodes but we can generalize it on another one composed of many nodes but still based on CORE and EDGE routers. The use of markers in DiffServ networks is primordial to implement QoS, the heterogeneity of data flows leads to use different types of markers. We have seen the effect of traffic shaping and marking on VBR and CBR flows in a DiffServ network, traffic shaping allows to increase green packets and QoS parameters (packets loss and jitter). The choice of marker when implementing DiffServ QoS is very important to optimize the results.

References

[1] J. Ferguson and G. Huston. Quality of service. Technical report, Willey, New York, 1998.

[2] S. Blake, D. Blake, M. Carlos, E. Davies, Z. Wang, and W. Weiss. An Architecture for Differentiated Services. IETF, RFC 2475, 1998.

[3] V. Jacobson, K. Nichols, and K. Poduri. An Expedited Forwarding PHB. IETF, RFC 2598, June 1999.

[4] J. Heinhanen, F. Baker, W. Weiss, and J. Wroclawski. Assured Forwarding PHB group. IETF, RFC 2597, 1999.

[5] Mohammed A. El Gendy and Kang G. Shin. Equation-Based Packet Marking for Assured Forwarding Services, Decembre 1999.

[6] T.Ahmed, G.Buridant, A.Mehaoua, and J.Claude. Un Algorithme de Marquage pour les Flux MPEG4 dans un Reseau DiffServ, Decembre 2001.

[7] J. Park, K. Hur, S. Jun, C. Cho, N. Park, and D. Eom. An Aggregate Flow Marker for Improving TCP Fairness in Multiple Domain Diffserv Networks, Janvier 2003.

[8] K. Nichols, S. Blake, F. Baker, and D. Black. Definition of the Differentiated Services Field (DSField) in the IPv4 and IPv6 Headers, RFC 2474, December 1998.

[9] J. Heinanen and R. Guerin. A Single Rate Three Color Marker, RFC 2697, September 1999.

[10] J. Heinanen and R. Guerin. A Two Rate Three Color Marker, RFC 2698, September 1999.

[11] W. Fang, N. Seddigh, and B. Nandy. A Two Rate Three Color Marker, RFC 2698, June 2000.

History-Aware Adaptive Routing Algorithm For Energy Saving in Interconnection Networks

Hai Nguyen, Gonzalo Zarza, Daniel Franco and Emilio Luque
Computer Architecture & Operating Systems Department
Universitat Autònoma de Barcelona,08193 Bellaterra, Spain
hai.nguyen@caos.uab.es, gonzalo.zarza@uab.es, daniel.franco@uab.es, emilio.luque@uab.es

Abstract— *The increase of link speeds in the interconnection networks is evident both inside and outside of a datacenter. Thus it contributes an increasing portion of the power budget of the interconnection system. Link power management has been receiving more attention and many mechanisms were proposed. The emerging bit-serial link technology allows the links to work with different numbers of lanes & speeds. When the traffic load is slight, links are put in low-speed mode and consume less energy. However, links working in the low speed mode result in the increase in serialization latency. We propose a routing algorithm that takes into account the history usage of the links to focus network traffic in a small subset of high-speed links. It keeps high-speed links busier and leaves low-speed links with more idle time. Thus the mechanism saves energy and reduces the incurred serialization latency.*

Keywords: energy saving, history-aware, routing algorithm, interconnection networks

1. Introduction

Network components consume 10-20% of the total power of an interconnected system [1]. The energy consumption and heat dissipation problem for interconnection systems make the need for a more efficient networking become more evident. Network links contribute a major portion of the energy required for the network, around 58% [2]. However the link utilization in the interconnection system is low. We have conducted simulations with 64 processing nodes arranged in fat tree topology [3]. The traffic patterns are imported from two benchmarks modeling Black-Scholes partial differential equation and Fluid Animate Particle Simulation using Smoothed Particle Hydrodynamics [4]. For both applications the average link utilization is lower than 5%. The energy consumption for links is almost insensitive to the fluctuation of the traffic intensity, thus they burn the same amount of energy while working very little. The average link utilization will be less in the future with the ever-increasing link speed [5]. Besides, for a particular traffic pattern, the link utilization is not spatially uniform. There are some links that are almost idle and others that are much busier. Less energy consumption for those almost idle links is a desired behavior. Many studies have been focusing on a better link power management. Researchers have proposed many mechanisms for the better use of links with different approaches.

The 2013 International Conference on Parallel and Distributed Processing Techniques and Applications (PDPTA'13)

The first approach is dynamically turning a number of links on and off as the function of traffic [6], [7], [8], [9], [10]. In this approach, a link activation request can be sent from a sending node by inherent system events to reduce the link re-activation time overhead [11]. When applying this approach the path diversity is greatly reduced and the deadlock avoidance becomes an issue. Another approach is the Dynamic Voltage Scaling (DVS) mechanism to dynamically adjust link frequency and voltage with the history-based policy of the link utilization [2]. This approach has the potential to save a significant amount of energy in the link components even though it introduces more complexity in the hardware design. Another approach for the link power management control is to judiciously adjust the width of the link [5], [12], [13]. With the use of bit-serial link technology, where every link consists of multiple lanes, the link width control mechanism works naturally. Links in PCI-Express are available in up to 16-lane configuration (denoted as $x16$). Similarly, Infiniband has made available the multi-lane links with $x4$ and $x12$. Our work focuses on the last approach.

To date, the dynamic link width mechanism is applied with a history-oblivious routing algorithm. Traffic is spreaded through many links to prevent and alleviate congestion situation. However, in light traffic load scenarios, some fraction of the traffic is routed through low-speed links while other high-speed links still do not work at full capacity. Thus the mechanism incurs an additional serialization latency. To solve this issue, we propose a history-aware adaptive routing algorithm that prioritizes the route of traffic on a small subset of links and focuses the traffic on that subset. This subset of links has a high value of link utilization and thus will be kept at high speed, consequently the serialization latency is reduced. Moreover, as a side effect the routing algorithm at the same time leaves more links idle and thus gives them more opportunity to be adjusted to the low-speed mode and save more energy.

This paper makes a contribution in proposing a history-aware adaptive routing algorithm. It makes the comparison about the latency behavior and the energy consumption between history-aware and history-oblivious routing algorithms. It also conducts experiments, analyzes results for both synthetic traffic and traffic imported from trace files.

The paper is organized as follows: In section 2, the basics of the dynamic link speed mechanism based on dynamic link width is presented. It involves the Monitoring & Decision Making phase. Section 3 describes the history-aware adaptive routing algorithm. Section 4 illustrates and explains the experimental results. Finally, we draw conclusions in section 5.

2. Dynamic Link Speed Mechanism Basics

The dynamic speed behavior of a link is achieved by varying its width according to the fluctuation of traffic on it. The main process of the mechanism is *Monitoring & Decision Making*, where the link activities are monitored to decide whether to change the link width.

The monitoring and decision making process involves detecting when to change the link speed. Link Utilization (LU) is monitored at the port basis. The mathematical definition of LU is presented in the equation 1.

$$\mathbf{LU} = \frac{\sum_{t=1}^{H} A(t)}{H} \tag{1}$$

Where $A(t) = \begin{cases} 1 \text{ if traffic passes in cycle } t \\ 0 \text{ if no traffic passes in cycle } t \end{cases}$ and H is a sliding history window size.

The value of LU is less than 1, and it directly reflects how frequent a link was used. The larger the value of LU, the busier the link is. When the value of LU drops below the threshold value th_low and the link is not at its minimum width, the mechanism triggers the link to reduce its width one level. To simplify the routing algorithm, avoid deadlock avoidance issue and reduce the re-activation time overhead, a link is never turned off and it never has the width of 0. In contrast, when LU exceeds the threshold th_high and the link is not at its maximum width, the mechanism increases the link width one level.

Another criterion for the mechanism is the input buffer occupancy of the next router. This information is available for the mechanism based on the credit-based flow control of the router. If the input buffer occupancy at the far end of the link is higher than the threshold $th\_buffer\_occupancy$, it is the signal indicating that the network is congested at the far end of the link. The movement of packets in that situation is restricted by the availability of the buffer space, not the link bandwidth. Thus the mechanism can reduce the link width more aggressively without sacrificing the serialization latency.

Algorithm 1 Changing Link Speed Decision

```
Monitoring the next input buffer occupancy
if buffer_occupancy > th_buffer_occupancy then
    th_low= th_low for congestion
    th_high=th_high for congestion
else
    th_low=th_low for non − congestion
    th_high=th_high for non − congestion
end if
Monitoring the LU value of the link
if (LU of the link < th_low) and (The link is not at minimum width) then
    Decreasing The Link Width
end if
if (LU of the link > th_high) and (The link is not at maximum width) then
    Increasing The Link Width
end if
```

The decision making process is made every period of time T. The pseudo code for this mechanism is described in Algorithm 1.

The values of the thresholds are configurable and they are configured depending on the objective of the network. The higher the values of th_low and th_high the more agressive the mechanism triggers links to reduce their width to save more energy. The difference between th_low and th_high also should be carefully selected to avoid the link flip flop when traffic fluctuates often.

3. History-Aware Adaptive Routing Algorithm

With the typical path redundancy of network configurations (to facilitate the load balancing and fault tolerance), at every intermediate router, there might be several output ports a packet can take to make the progress towards its destination. For example, for k-ary n-cube network topology, every router has n productive ports for packets to come closer their destination.

For a network applied the Dynamic Link Width mechanism, any given router connects with its set of links that are at different speeds. Any port p_i couples with a link with the link width value of W_i, the input buffer occupancy at the far end of the link has the value of $Buffer\_Occupancy(p_i)$ as illustrated in Fig. 1. In this figure, the link couples with port p_1 is at a high link width level and thus has a higher bandwidth compared with the links coupled with the other ports p_2,...,p_k. It is preferred that packets move on the link connected with port p_1 to have less serialization latency.

However, if the routing policy is oblivious about the history usage of the links and spreads packets through many links then all the links have a low average utilization values

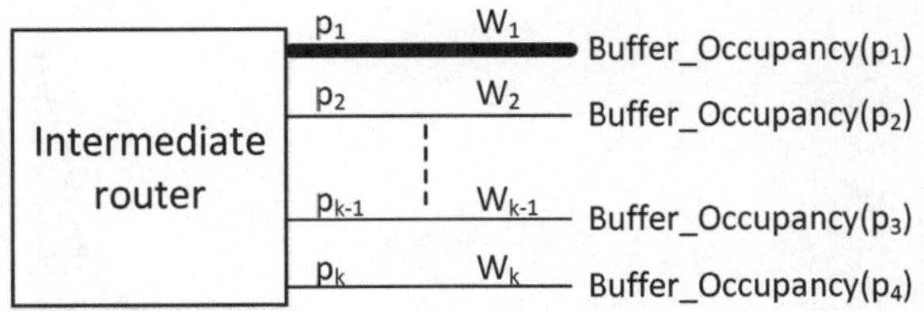

Fig. 1: Multi-port with different link speeds

and thus being put at a low speed. Consequently the average packet latency increases due to the serialization latency by moving in thin links. In the low load situation, a better routing policy that focuses traffic in a subset of high speed links while leaves other links idle is a desired behaviours.

At every router, with a set of compatible output ports, the history-aware routing policy gives the decision about which output to take with the preference for the most-recently-used port, unless there are a strong evidence not to do so but using a normal adaptive routing instead. A normal adaptive routing algorithm will be used if one of the following conditions hold:

- All the links of the router are at maximum speed. This is the situation when high traffic load is present in the network and the routing policy should balance the traffic by spreading packets to many links.
- The input buffer occupancy at the far end of the link coupled with the most-recently-used port is higher than the threshold value of $buffer\_threshold$. This is the signal that the link is over-utilized and the continuity of traffic injection to them can lead to congestion.

The proposed routing algorithm takes advantage of high bandwidth links in the case of low traffic load. In high traffic load situation when all links are in high utilization and thus in high-speed status, normal adaptive routing algorithm takes place. The routing decision is summarized in Algorithm 2.

Algorithm 2 History-Aware Adaptive Routing Algorithm

```
Getting the set of compatible output ports
Choosing the most recently used port as the outport
if All links are at maximum special or The buffer occupancy higher than buffer_threshold then
    outport=Normal_Routing_Algorithm()
end if
Exporting the outport
```

Since the topology of the network does not change, no special care for deadlock avoidance techniques is required. When taking into account the link history usage, it results in having some maximum-speed links carry a large fraction of the traffic load, while others links are mostly idle and put in low-speed mode. It is preferred to have a small fraction of links to work at full capacity and deliver the majority of traffic. With packets moving in a subset of high-speed links according to the proposed routing algorithm, the serialization latency is reduced. Besides, when the majority of traffic moves in the small fraction of high-speed links, the other fraction of links is almost idle and being put in a low-speed status, the energy consumption is further reduced.

4. Experimental Results

In this section, we evaluate the History-Aware Adaptive Routing Algorithm versus a History-Oblivious Routing Algorithm, both of them are applied in the interconnection networks with the dynamic link width mechanism to save energy.

The framework for the simulation is the modified version of $booksim$ [14]. The interconnection network is configured with 64 processing nodes, arranged in the 4-ary 3-stage fat tree topology with virtual channel flow control. There is 16 virtual channel for each link, the virtual channel buffer size is 16 flits, a packet consists of 4 flits. To minimize the impact of the mechanism to the average packet latency, only links between routers are considered to adjust the width. Thus the communication between a processing node and its immediate connected router is performed with maximum speed.

Traffic patterns directly impact to the efficiency of the energy saving mechanism and the history-aware routing algorithms. We have conducted the experiments with both synthetic traffic and traffic imported from trace files.

The synthetic traffic patterns generated are the $bit\ complement$ and $uniform$ patterns. The th_low, th_high in non-congested situation are 0.2 and 0.6, in congested situation are 0.35 and 0.75 accordingly. The $th\_buffer\_occupancy$ to detect congestion for the next immediate input buffer is 0.5. The number of lanes for every link is 12. Energy consumption for the link is assumed to be proportional to the number of active lanes. The relative link energy consumption in the results is the percentage of energy consumed for the link component of the network when they work with and without dynamic link width mechanism.

To see the impact of the history-aware adaptive routing algorithm in action, simulations were conducted with two different routing algorithms. We have used Nearest Common Ancestor (NCA)[15] and History-Aware Nearest Common Ancestor (HA-NCA) as specified in section 3.

As we can see from Fig. 2 for both traffic patterns, when applying the dynamic link width mechanism the relative link energy consumption is proportional to the traffic load. With low traffic load a large fraction of links is put in low-speed mode and consume less energy. In contrast, in the high traffic situation almost all the links are at maximum width and speed, then the energy consumption is equal to the energy consumption when no saving mechanism is applied. The history-aware adaptive routing algorithm gains more energy

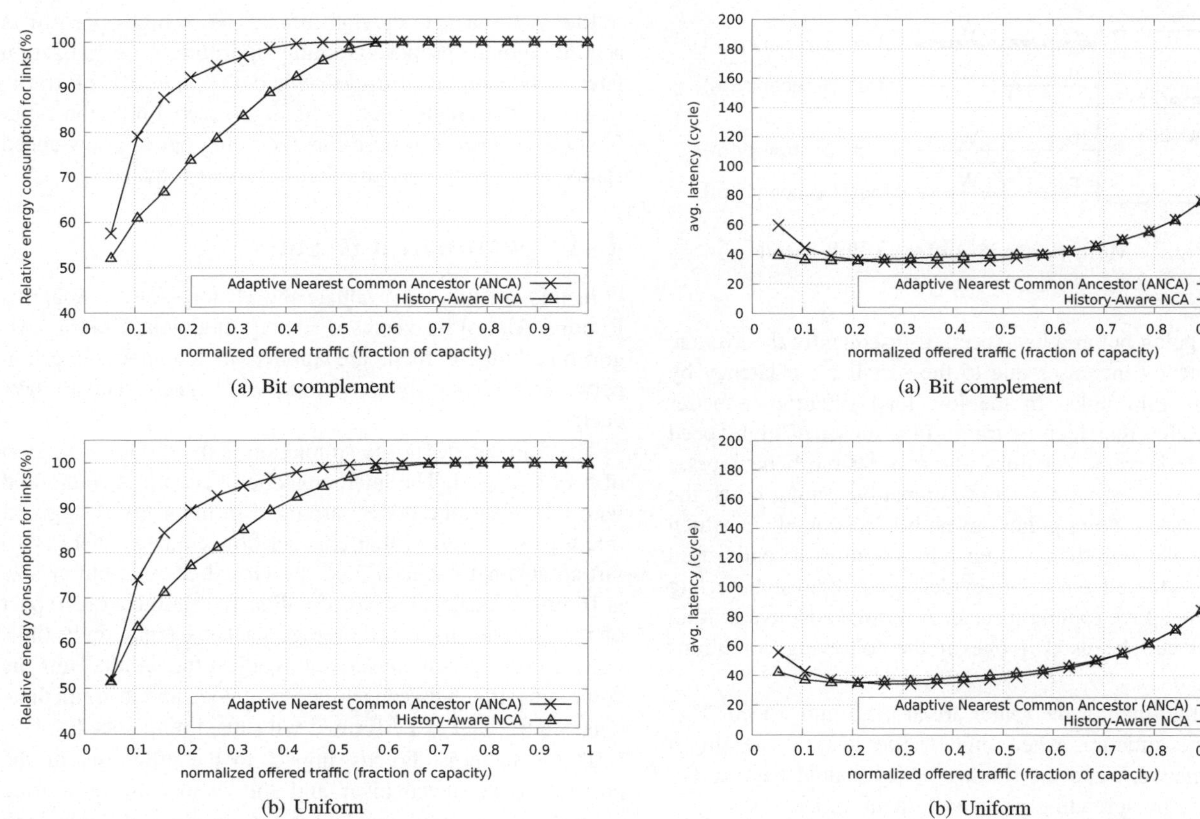

(a) Bit complement

(b) Uniform

Fig. 2: Relative Link Energy Consumption

(a) Bit complement

(b) Uniform

Fig. 3: Latency behavior comparison

saving because it makes a better use of a small fraction of links carrying the traffic and leave the others links idle.

Fig. 3 shows the latency behavior when applying the two routing algorithms. Even though the history-aware adaptive routing algorithm gains more energy saving, the latency behaviors for both of them are similar. Thus the proposed routing algorithm saves more energy without sacrificing the average packet latency.

As aforementioned, when applying dynamic link width mechanism the network incurs an additional serialization latency. Fig. 4 depicts the relationship between the latency behavior of the network with and without applying the saving mechanism. In both situations the history-aware routing algorithm was deployed. As we can see there is only a slight increase in average packet latency as opposed to a larger percentage of energy consuming reduction in Fig. 2.

To compare the impact of two routing algorithms with traffic imported from trace files. The traffic for the application Fluid Animate Particle Simulation using Smoothed Particle Hydrodynamics [4] was imported into the network with the same aforementioned network configuration using the Netrace framework [16]. Two routing algorithms are again put into comparison.

Without the energy saving mechanism the average packet latency is 37.81 cycles. The latency behaviors and the the relative link energy consumption when applying the dynamic link width mechanism with different routing algorithms is described in Table 1.

For this particular traffic pattern the relative link energy consumption is around 39.55% compared with the energy consumed by the links of the default system (without applying the mechanism). There is a typical trade-off where the energy consumption reduction comes with an increase in average packet latency. The energy saving gained by the dynamic link width mechanism is almost the same when applying History-Aware (HA-NCA) or History-Oblivious (NCA) Routing Algorithms. However with HA-NCA the increase in latency is lower than the NCA (29.60% as opposed to 56.75%).

5. Conclusions

We have proposed a history-aware adaptive routing algorithm to take the link history usage into account when making the routing decision. Our algorithm focuses traffic on a subset of high-speed links and put more links into the low-speed mode in the low load situation. The result is more energy saving is achieved with less additional average

Table 1: History Oblivious & Aware Routing Algorithm Comparison

	No saving mechanism applied	Applied with NCA	Applied with HA-NCA
Average Packet Latency	37.81 cycles	59.26 cycles	48.99 cycles
Percentage Latency Increase	0%	56.75%	29.60%
Relative Link Energy Consumption	100%	39.52%	39.58%

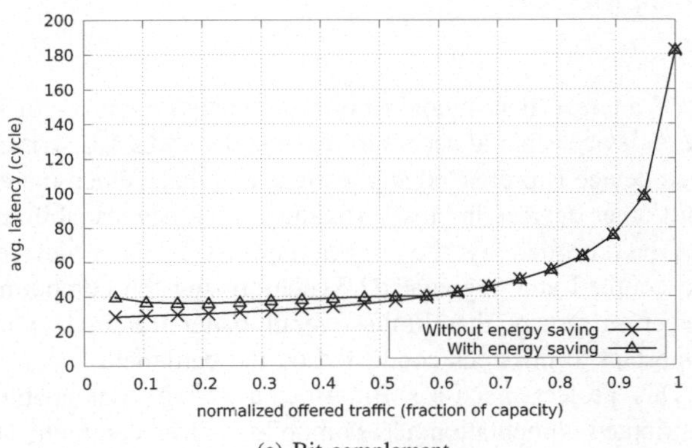

(a) Bit complement

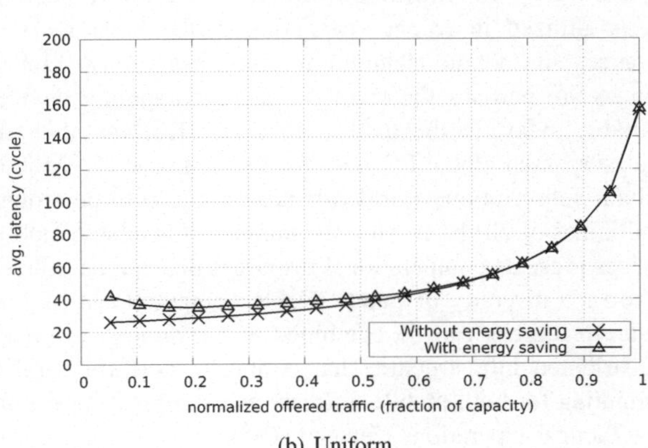

(b) Uniform

Fig. 4: Latency behavior with/ without mechanism

packet latency. Our future work includes further applying this adaptive routing algorithm to the dynamic link width mechanism for energy saving.

Acknowledgments

This research has been supported by the MEC-Spain under contract TIN2011-24384.

References

[1] A. Greenberg, J. Hamilton, D. A. Maltz, and P. Patel, "The cost of a cloud: research problems in data center networks," *SIGCOMM Comput. Commun. Rev.*, vol. 39, no. 1, pp. 68–73, Dec. 2008. [Online]. Available: http://doi.acm.org/10.1145/1496091.1496103

[2] L. Shang, L.-S. Peh, and N. Jha, "Dynamic voltage scaling with links for power optimization of interconnection networks," in *International Symposium on High-Performance Computer Architecture (HPCA-9 2003)*, feb. 2003, pp. 91 – 102.

[3] C. E. Leiserson, "Fat-trees: universal networks for hardware-efficient supercomputing," *IEEE Trans. Comput.*, vol. 34, no. 10, pp. 892–901, Oct. 1985. [Online]. Available: http://dl.acm.org/citation.cfm?id=4492.4495

[4] C. Bienia, "Benchmarking modern multiprocessors," Ph.D. dissertation, Princeton University, January 2011.

[5] K. Kant, "Power control of high speed network interconnects in data centers," in *Proceedings of the 28th IEEE international conference on Computer Communications Workshops*, ser. INFOCOM'09. Piscataway, NJ, USA: IEEE Press, 2009, pp. 145–150. [Online]. Available: http://dl.acm.org/citation.cfm?id=1719850.1719875

[6] V. Soteriou and L.-S. Peh, "Design-space exploration of power-aware on/off interconnection networks," in *IEEE International Conference on Computer Design: VLSI in Computers and Processors (ICCD 2004)*, oct. 2004, pp. 510 – 517.

[7] M. Alonso, S. Coll, J. Martinez, V. Santonja, P. Lopez, and J. Duato, "Dynamic power saving in fat-tree interconnection networks using on/off links," in *International Parallel and Distributed Processing Symposium (IPDPS 2006)*, april 2006, p. 8 pp.

[8] B. Heller, S. Seetharaman, P. Mahadevan, Y. Yiakoumis, P. Sharma, S. Banerjee, and N. McKeown, "Elastictree: saving energy in data center networks," in *Proceedings of the 7th USENIX conference on Networked systems design and implementation*, ser. NSDI'10. Berkeley, CA, USA: USENIX Association, 2010, pp. 17–17. [Online]. Available: http://dl.acm.org/citation.cfm?id=1855711.1855728

[9] A. G. Savva, T. Theocharides, and V. Soteriou, "Intelligent on/off dynamic link management for on-chip networks," *JECE*, vol. 2012, pp. 6:6–6:6, Jan. 2012. [Online]. Available: http://dx.doi.org/10.1155/2012/107821

[10] J. Yin, P. Zhou, A. Holey, S. S. Sapatnekar, and A. Zhai, "Energy-efficient non-minimal path on-chip interconnection network for heterogeneous systems," in *Proceedings of the 2012 ACM/IEEE international symposium on Low power electronics and design*, ser. ISLPED '12. New York, NY, USA: ACM, 2012, pp. 57–62. [Online]. Available: http://doi.acm.org/10.1145/2333660.2333675

[11] J. Li, W. Huang, C. Lefurgy, L. Zhang, W. E. Denzel, R. R. Treumann, and K. Wang, "Power shifting in thrifty interconnection network," in *Proceedings of the 2011 IEEE 17th International Symposium on High Performance Computer Architecture*, ser. HPCA '11. Washington, DC, USA: IEEE Computer Society, 2011, pp. 156–167. [Online]. Available: http://dl.acm.org/citation.cfm?id=2014698.2014904

[12] K. Kant, "Multi-state power management of communication links," in *Communication Systems and Networks (COMSNETS), 2011 Third International Conference on*, 2011, pp. 1–10.

[13] D. Abts, M. R. Marty, P. M. Wells, P. Klausler, and H. Liu, "Energy proportional datacenter networks," *SIGARCH Comput. Archit. News*, vol. 38, no. 3, pp. 338–347, June 2010. [Online]. Available: http://doi.acm.org/10.1145/1816038.1816004

[14] G. M. J. B. B. T. J. K. Nan Jiang, Daniel U. Becker and W. J. Dally, "A detailed and flexible cycle-accurate network-on-chip simulator," in *Proceedings of the 2013 IEEE International Symposium on Performance Analysis of Systems and Software*, 2013.

[15] W. Dally and B. Towles, *Principles and Practices of Interconnection Networks*. San Francisco, CA, USA: Morgan Kaufmann Publishers Inc., 2003.

[16] J. Hestness, B. Grot, and S. W. Keckler, "Netrace: dependency-driven trace-based network-on-chip simulation," in *Proceedings of the Third International Workshop on Network on Chip Architectures*, ser. NoCArc '10. New York, NY, USA: ACM, 2010, pp. 31–36. [Online]. Available: http://doi.acm.org/10.1145/1921249.1921258

BlueHoc: Bluetooth Ad-Hoc Network Android Distributed Computing

G. Hinojos, C. Tade, S. Park, D. Shires, and D. Bruno
Computational Sciences Division
U. S. Army Research Laboratory
Aberdeen Proving Ground, MD, USA

Abstract—*Mobile devices are ubiquitous in everyday life and are becoming valuable devices for today's Soldiers as part of a larger battlefield network. Due to the open nature of the development platform, Android was recently selected to be a supported operating system within this evolving and maturing technology delivery paradigm. The Army's networks must operate in often hostile environments and are mobile and* ad hoc *in nature; thus often rendering communication links tenuous at best. Common, however, on handheld device are low-power network capabilities such as WiFi and Bluetooth. This work analyzes the use of Bluetooth as a low-power network protocol for coupling handhelds operating in a deployed setting. By aggregating the capabilities of distributed handhelds through Bluetooth, task and data parallelism can be achieved, thus providing potentially faster solutions and reduced battery drain. This paper discusses the performance of a preliminary scalable boss-worker paradigm known as "BlueHoc" in the context of a simplified test case with proposed extensions that will provide greater capabilities to Soldiers operating at the tactical edge.*

Keywords: Mobile ad hoc networks, Bluetooth, distributed computing, Android

1. Introduction

Computer networks are common in modern society and span a wide range of wired (DSL, Ethernet) and wireless (3G, 4G, WiFi) services. Military missions, particularly those of the Army, do not have the luxury of a fixed infrastructure with high capacity and low latency. Working in hostile environments is common, and mobile *ad hoc* networks (MANETs) will form the backbone of the deployed forces. These networks can be hierarchical and complex with widely varying data rates at all levels.

Typically the last hop to an edge node, such as a handheld device, is the most costly of all. Cloud-based services in well-covered network areas have extended capabilities to streaming data rather than just guaranteed access to data. Rapid processing of requests coming from handhelds, such as that offered by Apple's Siri service, is handled by offloading from handhelds to high capacity servers. Planning is underway in Army MANET delivery to provide the required bandwidth to the deployed network, but processing and data delivery at deployed edge nodes will remain a critical need.

Of interest then is how to exploit capabilities inherent in these devices should access to existing networks fail. Within each device is preloaded applications and data. When paired with other devices in close proximity, what new capabilities can be afforded by the higher capacity if these devices are coupled and aggregated? Synchronizing the computing power in a way that limits overall battery drain is very important to missions conducted on the battlefield.

This project discusses BlueHoc, a system that enables distributed computation across mobile devices communicating wirelessly via Bluetooth. Mobile devices have become highly utilized in recent years; due to the high demand, advances in mobile technology occur every day. Mobile devices are perhaps the most pervasive computing devices available today. In the final quarter of 2010, smarthphone sales surpassed global PC sales for the first time [1]. Mobile cellular subscriptions worldwide are estimated to be around 6 billion as of 2011 [2]. The vast number of available mobile devices presents computational resources that can be utilized to solve a diversity of parallelizable computations. Mobile device resources can be combined and leveraged to create a distributed infrastructure that is able to perform parallel computing for both mobile Soldiers and stationary operators in a Tactical Operations Center (TOC).

By aggregating computing power, important questions, such as "what computing capacity can I achieve from many Army connected devices?" and "what new capabilities can they bring to the Army operational domain?", can be answered. These questions are nontrivial and extremely valuable for the Army as it is not always feasible to build a single node High Performance Computing (HPC) system in the field or ensure its connectivity at all times. Furthermore, traditional cloud-based services will not always be available at the tactical edge where Soldiers operate. High throughput networks will not be available to off-load computing requests, and methods to overcome this limitation are only beginning to be explored [3]. This project attempts to bring HPC closer to the Soldiers and make it possible to build a HPC system from resources that are available and underutilized.

In the following, Section 2 summarizes related work in distributed computing using Bluetooth. Section 3 describes the operational and testing environments that were selected for this architecture and implementation. Preliminary results of the performance of the system are given in Section 4. Finally, conclusions and possible future extensions are briefly discussed in Section 5.

2. Related Work

The use of mobile phones to form small clusters of shared resources has not been well researched. Proposed architectures, built on the Bluetooth standard, would enable small mobile computers such as those found in robotics to communicate. The DynaMP architecture achieves scalability to larger networks through the formation of scatternets; larger networks formed by dedicating one node per subnet to communicate with another link node in another subnet [4]. The BlueHoc design roughly mirrors the architecture described in DynaMP and attempts to test the design in an actual hardware and software system. Issues with the communication protocols suggested in DynaMP are identified and differing methods are employed in BlueHoc to perform actual communication between nodes.

Gartrell et al. describe another architecture for Bluetooth device communication known as BlueHydra [5]. BlueHydra proposes methods for remote method invocation and uses the Marge framework for remote device discovery. The architecture is evaluated in terms of the Java Wireless Toolkit emulation framework and hence does not use an actual hardware and software device pairing. BlueHoc leverages built-in Bluetooth chat clients to implement the network and handle device communication under an Android operating system. This allows for testing of performance on physical ARM-based processors that would be commonly found in handhelds. Rather than evaluate the system in emulation, data rate tests of the Bluetooth network were performed using PandaBoard platforms.

3. Operational and Testing Environment

Bluetooth technology provides for dynamically linked mobile devices that can exploit the potential of wireless networks used in parallel computing. Bluetooth provides a low power transmission mechanism that is commonly embedded in most mobile devices nowadays. The widespread nature of Bluetooth makes it an ideal technology for building *ad hoc* networks to create a multiprocessor distributed infrastructure from mobile devices. Bluetooth offers a great means of wireless communication for mobile devices: it offers low power consumption, low cost, robustness, and *ad hoc* networking protocol capabilities [6]. Bluetooth v4.0 was the most recent version of the standard as this research was being conducted and it significantly reduces energy consumption over prior versions [7].

The target platform for this project is Android. Android is an open source project and is the most popular mobile platform in the market; 68.1% of mobile devices shipped during the second quarter of 2012 use Android as their operating system [8]. The prevalent and sophisticated nature of Android allows for the creation of countless applications with endless possibilities. Additionally, the Army is moving towards utilizing Android as their main operating system for mobile devices [9].

3.1 Android Parallel Computing Support

In the world of HPC, message passing (and the Message Passing Interface [MPI]) is a widely used and tested paradigm for parallelism. Following the Single Program-Multiple Data (SPMD) paradigm, it can be useful for both task and data parallelism. It has also been shown to be effective in distributed memory systems [10]. MPI is a library of routines for portable message passing programs in parallel systems and thus the project's initial investigation evaluated MPI support for Android. Due to the fact that Android deviates from the Linux kernel, Android does not fully support common Linux applications and libraries. Consequently, MPI was not successfully ported to Android. As a result, an alternate approach to MPI was developed using the radio frequency communication (RFCOMM) protocol embedded in Bluetooth and fully supported by Android.

The difficulty of porting Linux applications to Android lies in the two significant differences between the operating systems. First, the Android operating system does not utilize the standard Linux kernel. For example, Google chose to branch off from the GNU kernel to create their own kernel which gave them the flexibility to make changes that they felt were necessary to increase efficiency on a low power device. The Android kernel replaces the GNU libc with Bionic, a lightweight libc library developed by Google to target low power devices. The first of many differences between the two libraries is that Bionic does not support the full C/C++ standard. It does not handle, throw, or pass C++ exceptions. Since Android's primary programming language is Java, Google made the decision that all exceptions would be handled at the Java run-time level. Additionally, Bionic does not have the C++ Standard Template Library (STL). While missing a few C++ libraries may not inhibit the porting of many Linux libraries, additional differences between Android and Linux certainly increases the difficulty.

The second difference between the Linux and Android operating system is the degree to which they have implemented additional libraries. When Google has a need for certain functionality in the Android operating system that another Linux library already provides, they choose, like most programmers, to utilize the tried and tested Linux library. That being said, Google forks their own version, just like their kernel, and may only choose to support a couple of functions in that library while leaving the others undefined or unimplemented. In particular, the libpthread library utilized by the Dalvik JVM has been stripped of a few functions required by many of the libraries. Most of the pthread library and functionality are still there, but it is missing functions like pthread_cancel(); Google decided not to support pthread_cancel() because doing this would involve making the C library significantly larger for very little benefit [11]. While many may argue that pthread_cancel() may be required in certain scenarios and cannot or should not be replaced by other pthread calls, ultimately, Google has the choice of whether or not certain functionality is included in its forked libraries. As such, the developer usually has to build all required dependencies themselves should they wish to port a Linux library to Android.

3.2 Bluetooth Technology Networks

The context of field operations assumes a zero network infrastructure where dependence shifts to *ad hoc* networks. An example MANET at the tactical edge could be a collection of wireless mobile devices that can configure to form a network without any preexisting infrastructure. MANETs are robust, dynamic networks that can be rapidly deployed and reconfigured, making them ideal for military applications. Since they are extremely important parameters, the Bluetooth standard is adopted to address the challenges related to power consumption and battery life. Bluetooth operates within the 2.4 GHz ISM band and hops over 79 channels (2 through 80) at a rate of 1600 hops per second using the Time Division Duplex (TDD) scheme [12].

The BlueHoc system architecture is boss-worker, where the boss can connect with a maximum of seven workers in a piconet. A piconet is an *ad hoc* network connecting wireless devices using the Bluetooth protocol. Because piconets have a 3-bit address space notation, the maximum number of devices is limited to $2^3 = 8$, or eight devices composed of one boss and seven workers. To expand the physical size of the piconet network, two or more piconets can share a common Bluetooth device acting as a bridge between piconets to form a larger network known as scatternet. A scatternet is formed in an *ad hoc* fashion when two or more independent piconets overlap where a member of one piconet, either a boss or a worker, elects to participate in a scatternet. In a scatternet, a Bluetooth device can participate as a worker in several piconets, but can only be a boss in one piconet [13]. Figure 1 depicts an example configuration of a scatternet consisting of three piconets.

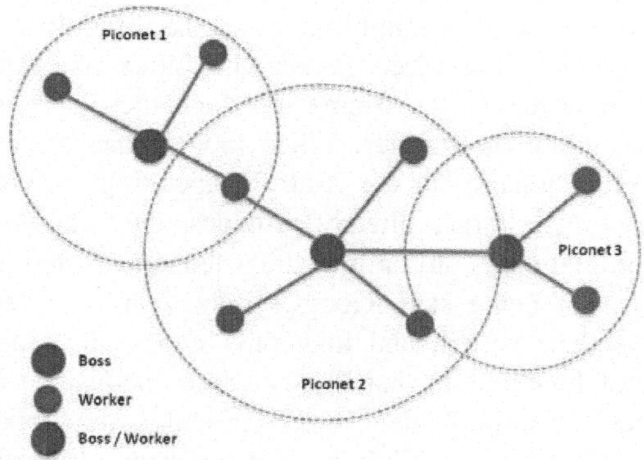

Fig. 1: A scatternet configuration composed of three piconets.

The current architecture of BlueHoc is static, meaning that the workers are required to join the network and remain connected throughout the work interval. For this preliminary implementation, the boss waits for the workers to connect to the network. After all the workers have completed the join process, the boss is able to issue job requests. Job requests are distributed among the workers as tasks by the boss and the computed results are sent back by the workers to the boss for the final result calculation. More elaborate protocols for scatter-gather-broadcast could also be substituted into this basic communication configuration. Figure 2 illustrates the data flow of job requests and computed results of the BlueHoc system architecture.

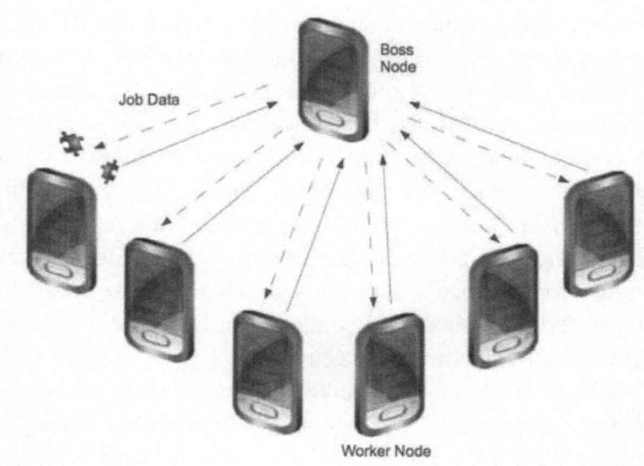

Fig. 2: BlueHoc architecture data exchange.

3.3 Network Performance

Latency and throughput tests are executed within an Android application developed for the project. BlueHoc is built upon an existing Bluetooth chat client provided as an example for Bluetooth connectivity by the Android SDK. The application delivers a very basic user interface (UI) that provides the user with a text entry box and button to send streams of text between boss and worker devices. There is an option menu that allows for device connection and enabling device discovery as well as a browser to select from files to send. Device names are added and removed from a "connected devices" list as each device enters/exits the network. A series of performance tests were conducted to determine the overall speed of transmission throughput and latency of the network. The tests were performed between two PandaBoards in close proximity running BlueHoc.

The ping utility (l2ping for Bluetooth devices) was not functional for the Ice Cream Sandwich Android OS build for PandaBoard. Therefore, the latency tests were conducted programmatically. The latency was determined by transmitting a small stream of data (44 bytes) and recording the round trip time (RTT). The clock times were taken from a single device to avoid synchronization between device clocks. The latency was found to be about 37.8 ms taken from an average of 500 recorded RTTs. As seen in Figure 3 the latency tends to stay between the 30 ms to 50 ms range. Values were recorded periodically throughout a 30 minute time window.

Next, the throughput tests were conducted for this Bluetooth network setup. An increasing range of file sizes was transferred via data stream buffers over open Bluetooth sockets between two PandaBoards. The process was repeated

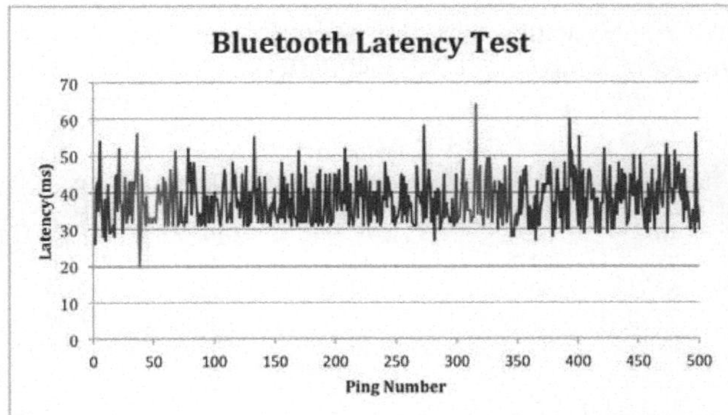

Fig. 3: PandaBoard Bluetooth latency test results.

for multiple iterations to develop an average transfer time. The ratio of file sizes to transmission time was recorded and plotted. As seen in Figure 4, the throughput is very low for less-than-one kilobyte of data. This speed steadily increases until the file size exceeds five kilobytes at which point transfer rate levels off at around 0.9 mbps. Considering the bandwidth of the Bluetooth module on the PandaBoard ES is rated at 2.1 mbps, the results suggest an achieved throughput of roughly half the theoretical data rate. Performance reduction can be justified by the application and network overhead (e.g. broadcast traffic, packet collisions, routing protocols, OS jitter).

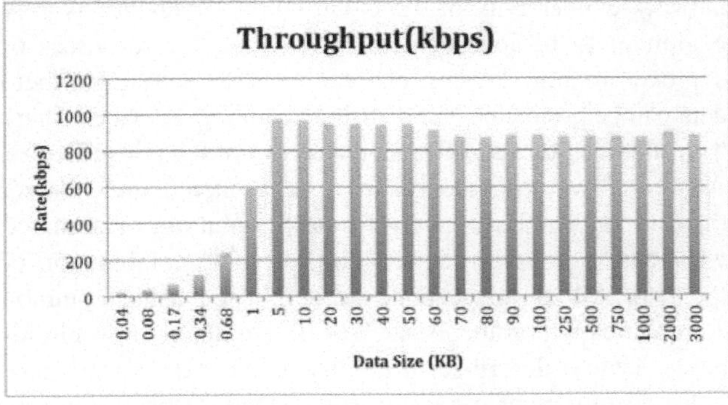

Fig. 4: PandaBoard Bluetooth throughput test results.

4. Application and Performance

The Monte Carlo method for π estimation served as a experimental application for distributed computing with Android devices. Leveraging Bluetooth wireless technology to establish a low power *ad hoc* network, multiple mobile systems can collaborate in performing a collective computation. The method used to estimate π followed the implementation of the popular random darts method [14]. This method allows for an approximation of π to be calculated by throwing darts randomly at a hypothetical dart board. Imagine a unit circle circumscribed by a square. By randomly throwing darts, hits inside the circle and square will be proportional to the respective area of each part, which can be written as

$$\frac{ndc}{nds} = \frac{ac}{as} = \frac{\pi r^2}{4r^2}, \tag{1}$$

where ndc is the number of darts in the circle, nds is the number of darts in the square, ac is the area of the circle, as is the area of the square, and r is the radius of the circle.

After substituting the number of darts in the square with the total number of throws, solving for π leads to the following equation:

$$\pi = 4 \times \frac{ndc}{nt}, \tag{2}$$

where nt is the number of dart throws. For this Monte Carlo method, the value of π becomes more precise as the iteration count increases.

A simple block scheduling algorithm handled the workload distribution across the multiple devices. The total number of iterations is evenly divided by the number of available devices for computation. For the cases where the number of devices fails to evenly divide the number of iterations, the ceiling value of the division is issued to workers. Each device is then initialized to compute their assigned number of iterations for the problem. At this beginning stage of Android distributed computing evaluation, the scheduling technique ignores differences in performance characteristics of a heterogeneous network of mobile devices. For example, given twenty million iterations and five worker devices, each device would compute four million iterations individually. In the current implementation, the designated boss node does not perform any dart throws, but gathers the results from the connected nodes and performs the final calculation from collected data.

Table 1: Specifications of Android devices.

Android Device	Processor	Android OS version
PandaBoard ES	Cortex-A9 1.2 GHz	Ice Cream Sandwich
Nexus 7	Tegra 3 1.3 GHz	Jelly Bean
Samsung Galaxy SII	Cortex-A9 1.2 GHz	Ice Cream Sandwich
Asus Transformer	Tegra 3 1.2 GHz	Jelly Bean
Motorola Xoom	Tegra 2 1 GHZ	Honeycomb

The π application was analyzed on five different Android platforms. Details regarding hardware specification and operating system setup are organized in Table 1. Non-distributed, base performance measurements of a single device for different Android devices are summarized in Figure 5. Regarding the unexpected result of the Samsung Galaxy SII, running background user applications adversely affected its execution time (being an actively utilized smartphone). Consequently, compared to the other Android devices under examination, the Galaxy SII had a multitude of user applications installed and loaded, taking a noticeable toll on the algorithm's performance.

The experimental test setup analyzed both homogeneous and heterogeneous Bluetooth device networks. For this exercise with block scheduling, the results obtained for uniform device networks outperformed the mixed Android

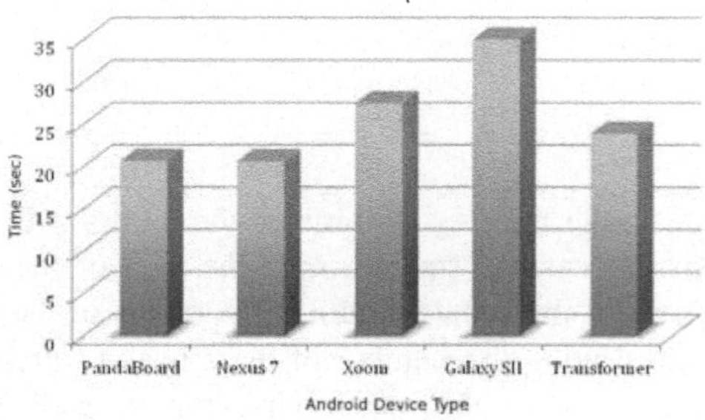

Fig. 5: Single device execution times for various Android platforms.

device network since the workload distribution was optimal. Recorded execution times for PandaBoard networks are presented in Table 2. To test a non-uniform Android devices network, a heterogeneous network was formed by using PandaBoard, Nexus 7, Samsung Galaxy, and Asus Transformer. This simulates a scenario where Soldiers have different types of mobile devices with different characteristics at their disposal. Table 3 provides the execution times for a Bluetooth network setup composed of different Android devices as the number of iterations is increased to 10^8. A graphical representation of the performance measurements achieved is presented in Figure 6.

For the π estimation algorithm, parallel computing via work distribution across multiple Android devices unequivocally reduces overall time to solution. As expected, a network with a homogeneous makeup of devices shows superior scalability as the overall time to result is bounded by the slowest device (and hence inefficiencies for processors that are spinning idle). Regardless of iterations or network type, leveraging four Android devices for this computationally intensive task decreased execution time to less than one third of its original time in the worst case. The execution time reduction exhibits the potential advantage of distributed computing with Bluetooth networked Android devices.

Table 2: Execution times for homogeneous networks consisting of PandaBoards.

	PandaBoards (sec)			
Iterations (millions)	1	2	3	4
10	8.11	4.15	3.09	2.12
25	20.21	10.16	7.39	5.20
50	40.08	20.14	15.18	10.33
75	65.00	30.52	22.59	15.47
100	84.34	41.74	33.00	20.83

Table 3: Execution times for heterogeneous networks consisting of a mixture of Android devices.

Iterations (millions)	PandaBoard (sec)	PandaBoard Nexus 7 (sec)	PandaBoard Nexus 7 Asus Trans (sec)	PandaBoard Nexus 7 Asus Trans Galaxy SII (sec)
10	8.11	4.75	3.19	2.49
25	20.21	11.16	7.49	6.22
50	40.08	22.14	17.28	12.06
75	65.00	33.52	24.39	18.30
100	84.34	43.74	34.05	24.09

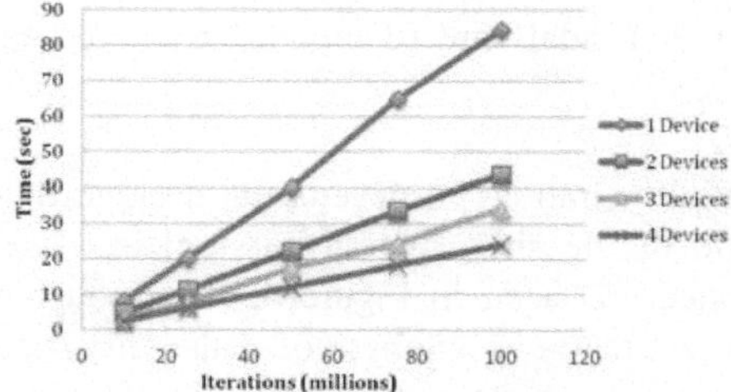

Fig. 6: Mixed Android devices networks execution times.

5. Conclusion and Future Work

The capacity and capabilities of handheld devices continue to improve with processing power and the creativity of application developers. One of the biggest advances of these devices is how they allow for geospatial awareness; the user's location can bring a wealth of information and be an important filter to the vast number of queries these devices process daily. By subscribing to the larger cloud, these handhelds also become important sensors in the field. From reporting weather, restaurant reviews, or traffic speeds, important and often temporal data can be broadcast to a wider user community.

However, making data and processing available when the network connectivity of the cloud is not guaranteed is only beginning to be investigated. By pooling the resources of deployed mobile devices, one can envision scenarios where data can be preloaded and distributed amongst devices where the internal storage of one device would be insufficient. Additionally, these devices can be brokered and shared, thus providing either a faster time to solution, or a shared workload to conserve battery life, or some combination of the two. All of this can be accomplished using common communication protocols, such as Bluetooth on the Android-based devices described in this paper. This framework provides an important capability for a small group of friendly forces geospatially co-located, and has been evidenced in the small test study described in this paper.

As with other past research being conducted on mobile networks using Bluetooth, BlueHoc is at its infancy. Further advances are being planned, such as improvements in scheduling to allow for device drop-out and drop-in along with better load balancing. Discovery protocols will need to incorporate host processor types and expected performance, possibly coupled with scheduling approaches such as guided self scheduling, to achieve optimal workload distribution.

6. Acknowledgments

This work was supported in part by the Army High Performance Computing Research Center (AHPCRC) cooperative agreement.

References

[1] "Industry first: Smartphones pass PCs in sales," http://tech.fortune.cnn.com/2011/02/07/idc-smartphone-shipment-numbers-passed-pc-in-q4-2010/, 2011.

[2] "Measuring the information society," http://www.itu.int/dms_pub/itu-d/opb/ind/D-IND-ICTOI-2012-SUM-PDF-E.pdf, 2012, international Telecommunication Union.

[3] D. Shires, B. Henz, S. Park, and J. Clarke, "Cloudlet seeding: Spatial deployment for high performance tactical clouds." Parallel and Distributed Processing Techniques and Applications, 2012.

[4] R. Shepherd, J. Story, and S. Mansoor, "Parallel computation in mobile systems using bluetooth scatternets and java," in *Parallel and Distributed Computing and Networks*, 2004, pp. 159–164.

[5] M. Gartrell, J. Kelly, and S. Razgulin, "Bluehydra: Distributed computing on mobile bluetooth-enabled devices," University of Colorado at Boulder, Tech. Rep., 2008.

[6] "About the bluetooth sig: Overview," http://www.bluetooth.org/About/bluetooth_sig.htm.

[7] "Specification of the bluetooth system," Bluetooth Special Interest Group, Tech. Rep., June 2010, covered Core Package version: 4.0.

[8] D. Reisinger, "Android smartphone share quadruples iOS in Q2," http://news.cnet.com/8301-1035_3-57488926-94/android-smartphone-share-quadruples-ios-in-q2/, August 2012.

[9] E. Montalbano, "Army selects android for mobile battlefield network," http://www.informationweek.com/government/mobile/army-selects-android-for-mobile-battlefi/229402123, April 2011.

[10] P. S. Pacheco, *Parallel programming with MPI.* San Francisco, CA, USA: Morgan Kaufmann Publishers Inc., 1996.

[11] "Bionic C library overview," http://github.com/android/platform_bionic/blob/master/libc/docs/OVERVIEW.TXT, 2009.

[12] T. Rappaport, *Wireless Communications: Principles and Practice*, 2nd ed. Upper Saddle River, NJ, USA: Prentice Hall PTR, 2001.

[13] "Scatternet - part 1," Ericsson, Tech. Rep., June 2004, baseband vs. Host Stack Implementation.

[14] "Monte carlo methods," in *Statistics Applied to Clinical Trials*, T. Cleophas, A. Zwinderman, T. Cleophas, and E. Cleophas, Eds. Springer Netherlands, 2009, pp. 479–486. [Online]. Available: http://dx.doi.org/10.1007/978-1-4020-9523-8_41

Comparison of NoC Routing Algorithms Using Formal Methods

Z. Sharifi[1], S. Mohammadi[1], and M. Sirjani[2]
[1] School of Electrical and computer engineering, University of Tehran, Tehran, Iran
[2] School of Computer Science, Reykjavik University, Reykjavik, Iceland

Abstract - *Network on Chip (NoC) has emerged as a promising interconnection paradigm for complex on-chip communications. As fabrication cost is high, model based design of NoC and early exploration to make proper design decisions are important challenges in NoCs. To tackle these challenges, we use formal methods and utilize their expressivity and flexibility to model different behaviors of a NoC and their abstraction to support early analysis of the design. We propose a formal approach for selection of the best routing algorithm in a NoC, according to its performance requirements. We present a model for two-dimensional mesh NoC using actor based modeling language Rebeca. Both functional and timing behaviors are modeled. The model is then used to compare three routing algorithms XY, Odd-Even and DyAD with respect to the maximum end-to-end packet latency in different scenarios.*

Keywords: Network on Chip (NoC), model checking, Rebeca, routing algorithm

1 Introduction

Asynchronous paradigm has become conspicuous in Network on Chip (NoC) design to overcome problems of clock skew and clock tree distribution of fully synchronous design. Thereby Globally Asynchronous Locally Synchronous (GALS) NoC has gained attention in design of such systems [1]. Functional verification is a major challenge in these systems to avoid increase in design errors; but a functionally verified GALS NoC may not meet all its desired performance. Thus, performance prediction in the various stages of the design is another necessity that should be performed to help the designer make proper design decisions according to the parameters of the system and also performance requirements. One important design decision for systems where end-to-end latency is a concern is to select a routing algorithm that results in the least end-to-end latency.

As fabrication cost is high, it is desirable to perform analysis on NoC design before having the first prototype and even in the early stages of design process. For model-based analysis we need to capture the crucial details in the model. However, to the best of our knowledge existing models of GALS NoC do not present the required details for modeling adaptive, dynamic and deterministic routings.

One important point in asynchronous systems is that lack of a reference clock leads in an interleaved execution of processes. Therefore, in GALS NoCs, a sent packet might be delayed by different number of disrupting packets and may have various end-to-end latencies. Thus, for analysis of such systems it is essential to consider all possible behaviors of the system and generate the whole state space. However, existing work based on simulation techniques cannot be applied for exhaustive verification. Also, ensuring correctness to a certain degree using simulation is highly time-consuming.

In this paper, we use model checking for performance prediction on two-dimensional mesh GALS NoC. Model checking is a promising approach that can be used for both performance evaluation and correctness checking and allow us to perform exhaustive search in the state space [2]. Important advantages of using model checking for performance prediction, in the case of this work are:

- Expressiveness: by using a suitable modeling language we can simply model both functional and timing behavior of GALS NoC, and also consider asynchronous paradigm and nondeterministic behavior of the system.
- Abstraction: for higher efficiency and for verifying more complicated properties we can model only the necessary details with respect to the property and abstract away the irrelevant parts. Abstraction enables us to perform analysis in the various stages of the design flow.
- Exhaustive verification: given the model of the system and the targeted properties, model checker explores the whole state space to check for property satisfaction rather than a set of traces.
- Finding the violating execution path: Model checker can return the execution path in which the property is violated (in contrast to mathematical and analytical approaches), and thus can help the designer for improving the design.

We used Timed Rebeca (Reactive Objects Language) [3, 4, 5] as the modeling language. Timed Rebeca is an actor-based modeling language capable of modeling functionalities and timing behaviors of asynchronous systems. In an actor model there are numbers of actors which are communicating via message passing. Consistency between the computational model of Rebeca and GALS NoC, enables us to model a GALS NoC naturally and simply. Each router in a GALS NoC is modeled as an actor and the communication between routers are modeled as message passing between actors.

To estimate the maximum end-to-end packet latency, the delay for read/write from/to a buffer, and delays of links and routing are considered in the model. Four-phase handshake communication protocol is also modeled for communication through channels. To model different kinds of routing algorithms, especially adaptive and dynamic algorithms, we capture buffer statuses (number of elements in the buffers). Subsequently, the model is used for comparison of some routing algorithms, namely XY, Odd-Even and DyAD. Results of comparison can be further used by designers to take proper decision about routing algorithms in the early phases of design.

The remainder of the paper is organized as follows. In Section 2 related work is introduced, Section 3 contains preliminaries. Section 4 presents GALS NoC model in Rebeca. Three routing algorithms are introduced and modeled in Section 5. Results are shown in Section 6, and finally conclusion and future work are presented.

2 Related work

There exist many simulation based works on analysis of different aspects of NoCs. Various arbitration and routing algorithms, router switches, and traffic patterns have been modeled using simulators. Nirgam [6] and gem5 [7] are two simulators for analyzing NoCs. In [8] a simulation based method for deadlock detection in a multiprocessor system with many running processes is proposed. As discussed before, simulation based methods are non-exhaustive and cannot be applied for early exploration because they do not have the adequate level of abstraction.

Formal and mathematical approaches are able to perform exhaustive verification at the expense of losing some precision. There are some works based on mathematical approaches; such as [9], which uses deductive method to prove that a routing algorithm is deadlock free. Although mathematical techniques are powerful, they cannot show how a violation occurred in the system. Formal methods are able to address this challenge.

There exist formal tools used for functional verification and performance prediction of the same model simultaneously. Formal techniques have been widely used for analysis of different aspects of multiprocessor systems that are in close relation with NoCs. A Petri net model is presented in [10] for performance modeling of asynchronous circuits. In [11] and [12] multiprocessor systems have been modeled by Timed Automata considering bus based methodology as interconnect network. In none of the above works GALS NoC was analyzed; GALS NoC has many special timing details and complex modules.

In [13] a NoC is modeled in Extended Timed Automata, and its router is verified against some functional properties. Authors in [14] applied Interactive Markov Chain (IMC) and Interactive Probabilistic Chain (IPC) to model a buffer used in NoC design. However, details of hardware timing and link model are not mentioned. In [15] an analytical method based on Markov chain stochastic processes is proposed for computation of mean latency of the end-to-end communications via a 2-dimensional mesh NoC. Using probabilities reduces the state space at the expense of losing the buffer analysis.

In this paper, we use formal methods to model different kinds of routing algorithms. The comparison is performed with respect to the maximum end-to-end packet latencies. In contrast to existing works based on formal methods, our model considers hardware details like link and buffer (read and write) delays and buffer statuses and thus can model adaptive and dynamic routing algorithms. Also, the model could be easily extended to contain more details in various stages of design flow and can help the designer to make better architectural choices.

3 Preliminaries

Here, Timed Rebeca is introduced as the modeling language used for our analysis.

3.1 Timed Rebeca

Timed Rebeca is an extension to Rebeca, capable of modeling functional and timing behaviors of distributed reactive systems.

Rebeca is an actor based modeling language [16] with a Java-like syntax. Actors can be considered as a reference model for concurrent computation. A Rebeca model consists of reactive classes and a main part that contains instantiation of reactive objects (rebecs) from reactive classes. Rebecs have encapsulated states and their own execution thread. Each rebec contains a set of state variables, methods and a set of known rebecs with which it can communicate. Communication is asynchronously established through message passing. Message passing is fair and implemented by method calls; calling a method of a rebec results in sending a message to the actor that invokes corresponding message server. Each rebec has a buffer, called a queue, for arriving messages. In each step a rebec is executed by removing a message from the top of its queue and executing its corresponding message server.

Model ::= *Class** *Main*
Main ::= **main** { *InstanceDcl** }
InstanceDcl ::= *className rebecName*(⟨*rebecName*⟩*) : (⟨*literal*⟩*);
Class ::= **reactiveclass** *className* { *KnownRebecs Vars MsgSrv** }
KnownRebecs ::= **knownrebecs** { *VarDcl** }
Vars ::= **statevars** { *VarDcl** }
VarDcl ::= *type* ⟨*v*⟩⁺;
MsgSrv ::= **msgsrv** *methodName*(⟨*type v*⟩*) { *Stmt** }
Stmt ::= *v* = *e*; | *Call*; | *if* (*e*) { *Stmt** } [*else* { *Stmt** }] | **delay**(*t*);
Call ::= *rebecName*.*methodName*(⟨*e*⟩*) [**after**(*t*)] [**deadline**(*t*)]

Fig. 1: Syntax for Timed Rebeca

To model timing behaviors of a system, three constructs are provided as follows:

- *delay (t)*: causes a delay of *t* time units.
- *after (t)*: this construct is paired with an invocation of a message server (method call), and causes a message to be sent with a delay of *t* units of time.
- *deadline (t)*: this construct is paired with a method call, and the corresponding message will be deleted from the queue after t time units.

Abstract syntax of Timed Rebeca is illustrated in Fig. 1.

4 GALS NoC model

If the model is too abstract, results may become imprecise; on the other hand very low level of abstraction may intensively increase complexity and leads analysis to state explosion. Using the proper abstraction level is the key for model based analysis of NoC. To this end one should define the constituent of the model with respect to the properties that the model is verified against.

In this paper we target maximum end-to-end packet latency for comparison of different routing algorithms. Network topology, router buffers, routing algorithm, communication policy, storage strategy and channels are modeled. Timing behaviors like link delay and the delay for writing and reading to/from buffers are also considered in the model.

Using an actor based modeling language we can efficiently map the constituents of GALS NoC, to actor model. Different elements of a GALS NoC can be modeled as follows,

- Router: each router can be modeled as an actor which communicates with other routers through message passing. Delay for scheduling or routing algorithms can be modeled by "*after*" construct. As each router has four ports we made this decision such that the delay of routing in one port does not affect the latency of other packets in other ports.

```
reactiveclass Router{
knownrebecs{
  Router[4] neighbor; //0:North, 1:East, 2:South, 3:West
 }
 statevars{
  int[4] buffer;
  boolean[4] bufferFull, inEnable, outEnable
  int Xid, Yid, bufferSize, packetSent, packetReceived;
 }
 Router(int X, int Y){
  Xid = X; Yid = Y;
  bufferSize = 2;
  for(i == 0; i<4; i++){
    buffer[i] = 0;
    bufferFull[i]=false;
    inEnable[i]= true;
    outEnable[i] = true;
  }
  if(Xid==0 && Yid ==0) self.reqSend(3,3,1,0) after(t1);
  if(Xid==2 && Yid ==0) self.reqSend(3,0,1,0) after(t2);

 msgsrv reqSend(int dstX, int dstY, int srcPort, int packId){
   if( inEnable[srcPort]==true){
    int outPort = XY_routing (dstX, dstY);
    if(outEnable[outPort]==true){
     outEnable[outPort] = false;
     InEnable[srcPort] = false;
     neighbor[outPort].
                  giveAck(dstX,dstY,srcPort, packId) after(t3);
    buffer[srcPort]++;
    if(buffer[srcPort]==bufferSize)
      bufferFull[srcPort]=true;
    if(packId==predefinedNum )
      packetSent = true;
   }else wait;
 } else wait; }
 msgsrv getAck(int srcPort){
   buffer[srcPort]--;
   bufferFull[srcPort]= false;
   outEnable[sender] = true;
   inEnable[srcPort] = true;
 }
 msgsrv giveAck(int dstX, int dstY, int srcPort, int packId){
   int port = sender.portNumber;
   if(dstX==Xid && dstY ==Yid) { //packet reached its destination
    if(packId==predefinedNum )
      packetReceived = true;
    sender.getAck(srcPort) after(t4);
   }else if(! bufferFull[port]){
     sender. getAck(srcPort) after(t4);
     self.reqSend(dstX,dstY,srcPort,packId);
   }else wait; }}
main(){
 Router r00(r03,r10,r01,r30):(0,0);
}
```

Fig. 2: Pseudo code for GALS NoC model

- Routing algorithm: we can define some message servers to model routing algorithms. An actor in Rebeca model is able to recognize who has invoked its message server, thus the router can understand from which port a packet entered and then decide to which router the packet should be sent.

- Buffer: router buffers can be seen as an array of elements (packets). We can use Rebec queues to model buffers, and then keep track of the number of packets in the buffer by defining a state variable as a counter for the number of elements in the buffer. Doing so, we always have the number of packets in the buffer, thus being able to model adaptive and dynamic routings. Delay of writing and reading to/from buffers can be modeled by "*after*" constructs.

- Packet: we model a packet only with its identifier and its destination.

- Channel (link): channels can be simply modeled by message passing. Delay of passing through a channel can be modeled using "*after*" construct.

- Communication protocol: by defining appropriate message servers, we can model communication protocols of a GALS NoC.

Fig. 2 shows a pseudo code for our model for GALS NoC 4×4 in Rebeca. The code is not limited to 4×4 NoCs and can be used for larger ones provided that we take into consideration the problem of state space explosion. The code is available in [17]. According to the pseudo code the model consists of one reactive class Router, and sixteen instantiated rebecs namely r00, r01, r02 to r33.

Packets are generated in initial message server of routers. Each packet only contains its destination address and no data are modeled, because only analysis of communication part of a NoC is of interest. Packets transfer through channels, using four-phase handshake communication protocol. We modeled channel functionalities by means of message passing capability of Rebeca. Four-phase handshake protocol is modeled using three message servers *reqSend*, *giveAck* and *getAck*. A router calls its *reqSend* message server to send a request to its neighbors; *reqSend* requires as parameter, a direction that determines in which input buffer the packet is stored and a destination address that shows the destination of the packet. Routing algorithm selects which neighbor router the packet should be sent to, and then *giveAck* message server of the selected neighbor router is called. *giveAck* first checks if the corresponding input buffer have enough capacity to store the packet, if it does, the packet will be stored and an acknowledgement is sent to the sender by calling its *getAck* message server. Then, it will be either consumed or sent to other neighboring routers using *reqSend* message server. While the buffer is full the packet will not be stored and should wait until the buffer has an empty place.

In two *reqSend* and *giveAck* message servers the length of the buffer can change. when a packet is inserted or deleted from the buffer. Writing and reading delays are also considered for buffers.

5 Model for routing algorithm

Routing algorithms can be classified into *deterministic* and *adaptive* routings. In a deterministic routing there can only be one path between a source and a destination, whereas in adaptive routing more than one possible path may exist and the algorithm considers dynamic network condition to decide in which direction a packet should be transferred.

In the following sub-sections we present a formal model for XY and Odd-Even routing algorithms as instances for deterministic and adaptive routings respectively. Dynamic Adaptive Deterministic (DyAD) is also modeled.

5.1 XY routing

In this algorithm, first packets move along X direction to get to the column of the destination, and then along Y direction to reach their destination.

To model this algorithm, a router (X,Y) compares its X location to that of the packet destination, if it is greater/smaller, it calls the *giveAck* method of west/east neighbor. The same approach is done for the Y coordinate.

5.2 Odd-Even routing

Odd-Even routing is an adaptive routing algorithm based on Odd-Even turn model [18]. Odd-Even turn model restricts the turns in the packet path to ensure about the deadlock freedom. According to Odd-Even turn model *north-to-west* and *south-to-west* turns are prohibited in routers located in an odd column and *east-to-south* and *east-to-north* turns are prohibited in routers located in an even column.

Among possible directions where an Odd-Even router can send packet, the direction in which the downstream router has less empty slots in its corresponding input buffer is selected.

In this algorithm each router keeps track of the number of packets in input buffer of each of its neighbors. In our model whenever the size of an input buffer of a router changes, it informs its corresponding upstream neighbor by sending a message.

5.3 DYAD routing

DyAD routing dynamically uses a deterministic or an adaptive routing exploiting both of them in different network congestion conditions.

Each router monitors the occupation ratio of its input buffers (except for the local buffer). Whenever one of the buffers reaches a predefined *congestion threshold* a *mode* flag is set to inform the corresponding neighboring router about the congestion. On the other hand, each router continuously

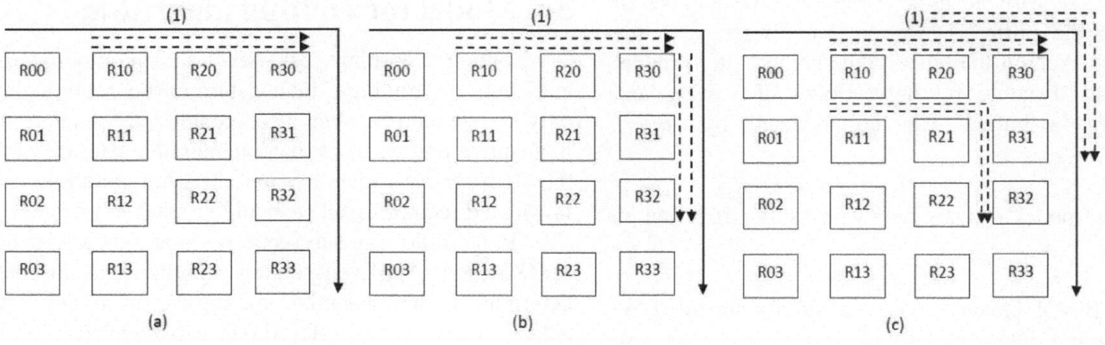

Fig. 3: Scenarios 1, 2 and 3.

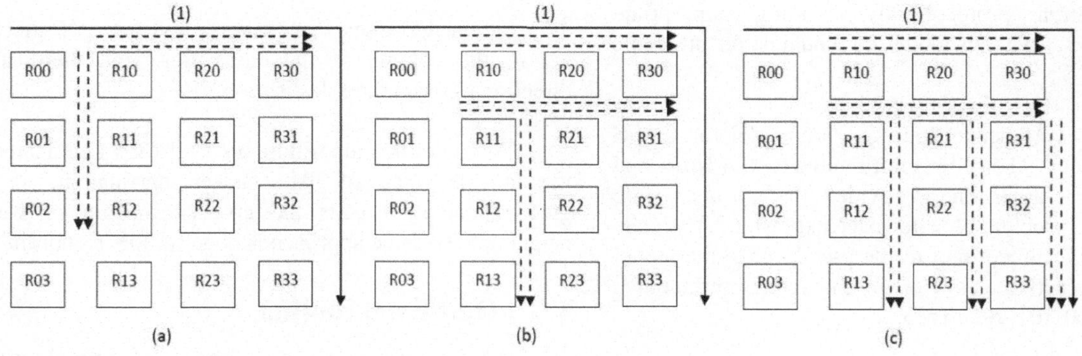

Fig. 4: Scenarios 4, 5 and 6.

checks mode flag of its neighbors to decide whether to work with deterministic or adaptive routing. According to [19] if at least one of the neighboring routers were congested the router would decide to work with adaptive routing; otherwise it would work with deterministic routing.

To model a DyAD router we add a mode flag to our model. The mode flag becomes true if the size of the corresponding input buffer reaches the congestion threshold.

6 Results

We use Afra [20] tool for model checking of XY, Odd-Even and DyAD Rebeca models, and compare them with respect to the maximum latency of the target packet. The NoC size in these comparisons is 4×4. All input buffers are of size 3 packets and %33 congestion threshold.

To compare the three algorithms we introduce six different scenarios describing different network conditions. In all scenarios the target packet is packet (1). We call the path of a packet to its destination *R-path*, when it is routed by the routing algorithm *R*. The scenarios are as follows:

Scenario 1. Router R10 generates two packets[1] as soon as it receives packet (1). The two packets may cause disruption for packet (1) (Fig. 3. a).

Scenario 2. Each of the routers R10 and R30 sends two packets to R30 and R33. This may cause disruption to any packet transferring from their paths (Fig. 3. b).

Scenario 3. Three routers R10, R20 and R21 send packets in XY-path of packet (1) in a way that they disrupt packet(1) (Fig. 3. c).

Scenario 4. R10 sends two packets to each of the routers R30 and R21 as soon as it receives the packet (1); hence, they will cause disruption to packet (1) in all directions (Fig. 4. a).

Scenario 5. R10 sends two packets to R30 causing DyAD and Odd-Even to rout packets in south direction of R10 to avoid being delayed. On the other hand, R11 sends two packets to each of its south and east neighboring routers that would cause delay for packet(1) if DyAD or Odd-Even was used(Fig. 4. b).

[1] We mean two packets are sent with negligible delay between their generation time.

Scenario 6. As illustrated in Fig. 4. c routers R10, R11, R21 and R31 send some packets to their neighbors making delay for packet (1) while it passes through them.

These scenarios can be divided into two categories. In the first three ones most of the network traffic is directed in XY-path of packet (1). As illustrated in Fig.5 in these scenarios, DyAD and Odd-Even avoid congestion by monitoring their neighbors and thus have less end to end packet latency. Also, DyAD has better results than Odd-Even because it exploits the low latency of deterministic routings in low traffics. The second three scenarios show distributed traffic in which disrupting packets exist in all possible directions, by which the target packet can get to its destination. These scenarios investigate the impact of low latency of deterministic routings which is the result of their simplicity in contrast to adaptive ones. As shown in Fig. 6, XY works as the best in these cases; as stated in [19] because XY has a global and long term knowledge about the traffic, it exhibits better results than the others.

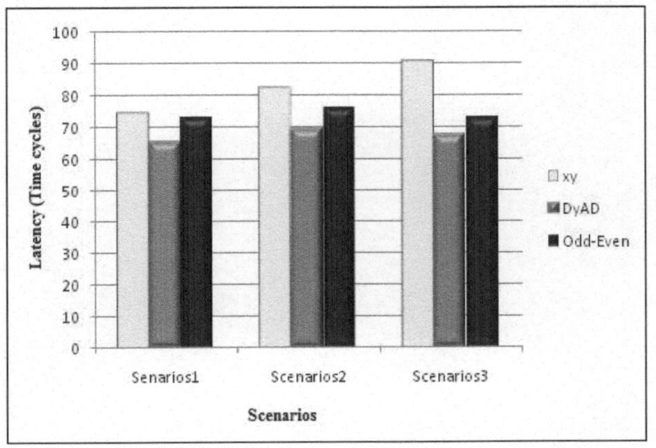

Fig. 5: Results for comparison of XY, DyAD and Odd-Even under 1-3 scenarios.

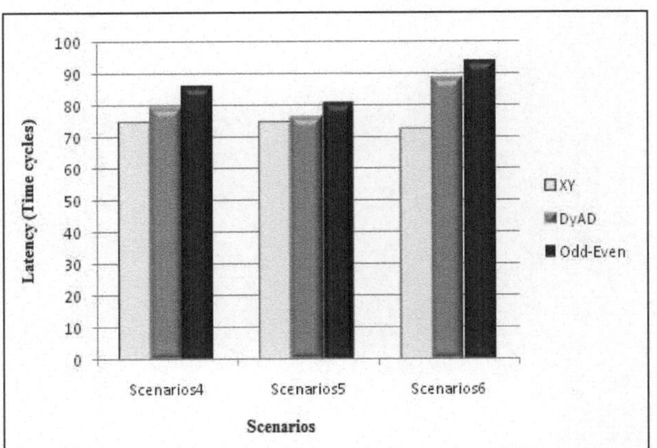

Fig. 6: Results for comparison of XY, DyAD and Odd-Even under 4-6 scenarios.

7 Conclusion and future work

This paper used formal methods that are able to perform exhaustive verification to performance prediction on GALS NoC in the early phase of design flow. To this end, a formal model for GALS NoC was presented using high level modeling language Rebeca. The model was then used for comparison between three routing algorithms, namely XY (deterministic), Odd-Even (adaptive) and DyAD (dynamically adaptive and deterministic) with respect to the maximum end-to-end packet latency. Results of comparison are presented under two different traffic patterns and show that under distributed traffic a deterministic routing could better work. However, in a directed traffic -that is of more interest in real applications- adaptive routing algorithms are better. The routing performance results obtained through Rebeca model checking confirm the same previously published results in simulations.

Results of such comparisons can help designers to make early decision about the parameters of the system based on the performance parameters. To have more realistic model and more precise analysis, our model can be extended by inserting more details of the system along with progress in the design flow, which we leave as future work.

Acknowledgments The work of the third author has been partially supported by the project "Timed Asynchronous Reactive Objects in Distributed Systems: TARO" (nr. 110020021) of the Icelandic Research Fund.

8 References

[1] *International Technology Roadmap for Semiconductors-* ITRS 2011, http://www.itrs.net/Links/2011ITRS/Home2011.htm

[2] Christel Baier, Boudewijn R. Haverkort, Holger Hermanns, and Joost-Pieter Katoen. "Performance Evaluation and Model Checking Join Forces"; Commun. ACM, vol. 53, Issue 9, 76—85, Sep 2010.

[3] Ehsan Khamespanah, Zeinab Sabahi Kaviani, Ramtin Khosravi, Marjan Sirjani, and Mohammad Javad Izadi. "Timed Rebeca Schedulability and Deadlock-Freedom Analysis Using Floating-Time Transition System"; Proc. AGERE!, 23—34, 2012.

[4] Marjan Sirjani, Ali Movaghar, Amin Shali and Frank S. De Boer. "Modeling and Verification of Reactive Systems using Rebeca"; Fundemental Information, vol. 63, Issue 4, 385—410, Jun 2004.

[5] Marjan Sirjani and Mohammad Mahdi Jaghoori. "Ten Years of Analyzing Actors: Rebeca Experience"; Formal Modeling: Actors, Open Systems, Biological Systems, 20—56, 2011.

[6] NIRGAM, http://nirgam.ecs.soton.ac.uk/.

[7] The gem5 simulator, dx.doi.org/10.1145/2024716.2024718, 2011.

[8] Alper Sen, Vinit Ogale and Magdy S. Abadir. "Predictive Runtime Verification of Multi-Processor SoCs in SystemC"; Design Automation Conference, 948—953, 2008.

[9] William J. Dally, and Charles L. Seitz. "Deadlock-Free Message Routing in Multi-processor Interconnection Networks"; IEEE Trns. Computers, vol. 36, Issue 5, 547—553, May 1987.

[10] Mehrdad Najibi, and Peter A. Beerel. "Performance Bounds of Asynchronous Circuits with Mode-Based Conditional Behavior"; IEEE Asynchronous Circuits and Systems Conference, 9—16, 2012.

[11] Gabor Madl. "Model-based Analysis of Event-driven Distributed Real-time Embedded Systems"; PhD. dissertation, University of California, 2009.

[12] Aske Brekling. "Modelling and Verification of MPSoC"; M.Sc. dissertation, Technical University of Denmark, 2006.

[13] Yean-Ru Chenl, Wan-Ting SU, Pao-Ann Hsiungt, Ying-Cherng Lan, Yu-Hen Hu, and Sao-Jie Chen. "Formal modeling and verification for network-on-chip"; Green Circuits and Systems (ICGCS), 299—304, 2010.

[14] Nicolas Coste, Holger Hermanns, Etienne Lantreibecq and Wendelin Serwe. "Towards Performance Prediction of Compositional Models in GALS Designs"; Proc. Computer Aided Verification Conference, 204—218, 2009.

[15] Sahar Foroutan, Yvain Thonnart, Richard Hersemeule, and Ahmed Jerraya. "Analytical Computation of Packet Latency in 2D-Mesh NoC"; Proc. Circuits and Systems and TAISA Conference, 1 — 4, 2009.

[16] Carl Hewitt. "Description and Theoretical Analysis (Using Schemata) of PLANNER: A Language for Proving Theorems and Manipulating Models in a Robot"; National Technical Information, 1971.

[17] Rebeca Homepage, http://www.rebeca-lang.org/wiki/pmwiki.php/Examples/NOC4x4

[18] Ge-Ming Chiu. "The odd-even turn model for adaptive routing"; IEEE Transactions on Parallel and Distributed Systems, vol. 11, Issue 7, 729—738, Jul. 2000.

[19] Jingcao Hu and Radu Marculescu. "DyAD – Smart Routing for Networks-on-Chip"; Proc. Design Automation Conference, 260—263, 2004.

[20] Rebeca Formal Modeling Language, http://www.rebeca-lang.org

SESSION

CLUSTER COMPUTING + MULTI-CORE, GPU, FPGA PROCESSING AND APPLICATIONS

Chair(s)

TBA

Cluster-SkePU: A Multi-Backend Skeleton Programming Library for GPU Clusters

Mudassar Majeed, Usman Dastgeer, and Christoph Kessler
Department of Computer and Information Sciences (IDA), Linköping University, Sweden
{mudassar.majeed, usman.dastgeer, christoph.kessler}@liu.se

Abstract— *SkePU is a C++ template library with a simple and unified interface for expressing data parallel computations in terms of generic components, called skeletons, on multi-GPU systems using CUDA and OpenCL. The* smart containers *in SkePU, such as Matrix and Vector, perform data management with a lazy memory copying mechanism that reduces redundant data communication. SkePU provides programmability, portability and even performance portability, but up to now application written using SkePU could only run on a single multi-GPU node. We present the extension of SkePU for GPU clusters without the need to modify the SkePU application source code. With our prototype implementation, we performed two experiments. The first experiment demonstrates the scalability with regular algorithms for N-body simulation and electric field calculation over multiple GPU nodes. The results for the second experiment show the benefit of lazy memory copying in terms of speedup gained for one level of Strassen's algorithm and another synthetic matrix sum application.*

Keywords: Structured parallel programming, Skeleton Programming, GPU Cluster, SkePU, Scalability, Scientific Applications

1. Introduction

Many supercomputers in the Top500 list contain Graphics Processing Units (GPUs) for accelerating data parallel computations in large-scale parallel applications. For example, Titan, a Cray XK7 system installed at Oak Ridge, contains 560,640 processors, plus 261,632 NVIDIA K20x accelerator cores [1].

These recent developments in multi- and many-core based, multi-GPU systems and GPU clusters and increasing demands for performance in scientific computing have pushed the change in programming paradigms. In order to exploit the processing power of the aforementioned architectures, legacy serial codes for scientific applications have to be rewritten using parallel programming paradigms. For instance, many scientific applications with computationally intensive data parallel computations have been ported to CUDA and OpenCL for performance reasons. However, CUDA and OpenCL are at relatively low level of abstraction, requiring the explicit offloading of the computationally intensive tasks by transfering their operand data to/from the accelerators, invoking kernels etc. GPU performance tuning requires that programmers are experts in the specific languages and architectural features. Several other programming models such as distributed memory and bulk synchronous parallelism exist that require the knowledge of task and data partitioning, orchestration, communication and synchronization from the application programmer. Furthermore, debugging, maintaining and porting a parallel application to other (and future) architectures requires code modification, leading scientific application programmers to focus more on development details instead of domain specific issues.

We have taken initiative towards a structured approach for writing massively parallel applications with multiple backends. The aim is to develop a rich skeleton library for heterogeneous multi-node architectures with a number of accelerators like GPUs for writing structured and non-trivial large-scale massively parallel applications. Writing large-scale parallel applications in different domains may require different kinds of distributed sparse or regular data structures, like graphs, trees, vectors, matrices, meshes etc [2] and high level computation and communication patterns or *algorithmic skeletons*. In this prototype, we provide the regular data structures with smartness of data management (we refer to such data structures as *smart containers*). Similarly we provide simple high-level *algorithmic skeletons* for expressing relatively regular algorithms in terms of the provided skeletons. In on-going work, we are extending the design and implementation of SkePU so that it can be used for (certain kinds of) irregular applications as well.

Those applications may also require several optimizations at different points, like the communication of data at different levels of granularity, data caching, prefetching and data locality etc. So the library has to be equipped with certain flexibilities for making better (online or offline) choices, like the data partitioning granularity, communication and computation patterns and other important parameters. Initially, for that purpose, we have implemented several real scientific applications with the provided simple *algorithmic skeletons*.

In earlier work [3] we started with the structured parallel programming approach using skeletons as a solution for the portability, programmability and even performance portability problems in GPU-based systems. Skeleton programming frameworks provide generic constructs, so-called *skeletons*, that are based on higher order functions parameterizable in problem-specific sequential code, that express frequently occurring patterns of control and data dependence, and for which efficient (also parallel and platform specific) expert-provided implementations may exist [4], [5], [6]. The application programmer expresses the scientific computation in terms of the given skeletons. The programming interface remains sequential, all parallelism, data transfer, synchronization and other platform specific details are encapsulated in the skeleton implementations. A number of skeleton programming systems have been developed in the last 20 years, in particular in the form of libraries such as Muesli [7], a C++ skeleton library for clusters, SkelCL [8], a skeleton library for GPU systems, BlockLib [9], a C skeleton library for IBM Cell/B.E., and the C++ based SkePU [3] for multi-GPU systems. Most of these skeleton libraries are specific to a particular backend like BlockLib is for the IBM Cell/B.E. and work for simple kernels.

Muesli [7] was initially designed for MPI/OpenMP clusters and has recently evolved to CUDA and GPU computing. On the contrary, SkePU was initially designed for single-node GPU-based system (OpenMP/CUDA/OpenCL) and is evolving towards MPI based clusters. This difference in approach results in several key programming differences. SkePU supports OpenCL which makes it much more applicable to other GPU and accelerator (FPGA etc.) platforms not supporting CUDA. Although Muesli supports task parallel skeletons for MPI/OpenMP, only a data parallel skeleton (*Map*) for CUDA with few communication variations is supported which limits program portability. SkePU supports a wide range of data parallel skeletons (*Map*, *Reduce*, *MapOverlap*, *MapArray*, *Scan* etc.) uniformly across all backends. There exists no equivalents of the *MapArray*, *MapOverlap* skeletons in Muesli which allow to implement applications ranging from N-body simulation to Conjugate Gradient solver.

In this work, we extend SkePU for providing scalability across multiple nodes of GPU clusters, such that the same SkePU application can now run on several nodes for the provided simple and regular skeletons. Each node, being a complete multi-GPU system, runs one instance of SkePU and the given computation is partitioned among the nodes. By a simple compiler switch, the application programmer can run the code on a GPU cluster e.g. for running the application for larger problem sizes that may not fit in one or two GPUs' device memory space. We perform experiments for four scientific applications and one synthetic matrix sum application by expressing their computation intensive parts in terms of SkePU skeletons. We explain one application in details. Initially, we see that simple algorithms like the brute force implementation of N-body simulation and the calculation of electric field on a 3D grid scale across multiple nodes. We also show that extending the lazy memory copying mechanism across multiple nodes gives benefit in terms of speedup.

The rest of this paper is outlined in the following way. In Section 2, we provide some background knowledge about the SkePU skeleton library. Section 3 presents the extension of SkePU, in our current prototype for all its dataparallel skeletons and the vector container. Section 4 explains one of the four scientific applications rewritten in SkePU and how the extended version of SkePU works for it with respect to data communication, synchronizations and other details. Section 5 gives the experimental results and discussion. Finally, Section 6 concludes the paper.

2. The SkePU Library

SkePU is a C++ template library that provides a simple and unified interface for specifying data- and task-parallel computations with the help of skeletons on GPUs using CUDA and OpenCL [3]. The interface is also general enough to support other architectures, and SkePU implements both a sequential CPU and a parallel OpenMP backend. SkePU provides six data parallel skeletons including *Map*, *MapArray*, *MapOverlap*, *Scan*, *Reduce* and *MapReduce* and one Generate skeleton for data initialization. These skeletons can operate on vector and matrix containers, which encapsulate the skeleton operand data and keep track of copies and thus allow to optimize memory transfers.

An example code written in SkePU using the *MapOverlap* skeleton is shown in Figure 1. The SkePU library provides a way to generate user functions using macros. The user function *over* is written using the *OVERLAP_FUNC* macro, where *over* is the name of the user function, *float* is the return type, *3* is passed as the overlap size parameter, *a* is a reference to an element in the used container. The last parameter is the actual user code that is translated into the selected backend. Notice that the semantics of the *MapOverlap* skeleton requires that here only *3* elements (before and after) the element pointed by *a* can be accessed in the user function *over* in the example SkePU code (Figure 1). The computation in the user function is expressed in terms of these seven values. During execution, the SkePU container transfers the required data according to the same semantics.

During compilation, the macro is converted into actual code based on the compilation flags set for backend selection. The set of SkePU user function variants generated from a macro based specification are placed in a struct *over* with member functions for CUDA and CPU, and strings for OpenCL. An instance of the struct *over* is passed to create an instance of the *MapOverlap* skeleton named *conv* in the *main* function in Figure 1. A vector *v0* is initialized with 40 elements and the user function *over* is applied on every element of *v0* using the skeleton *MapOverlap*. The code in the *main* function looks pretty sequential, but it is executed in parallel according to the selected backend.

The SkePU containers (Vector and Matrix) are implemented using the *STL vector*. These containers are smart and perform the necessary data transfers using a lazy memory copying mechanism. This means that the data is transferred

```
OVERLAP_FUNC(over, float, 3, a,
        return a[-3]*0.8f + a[-2]*0.4f + a[-1]*0.2f +
        a[0]*0.1f + a[1]*0.2f + a[2]*0.4f + a[3]*0.8f;
)
int main()
{
        skepu::Init(NULL,NULL);
        skepu::MapOverlap<over> conv(new over);
        skepu::Vector<float> v0(40, (float)10);
        skepu::Vector<float> r;
        skepu::cout << "v0: " << v0 << "\n";
        conv(v0, r, skepu::CONSTANT, (float)0);
        skepu::cout << "r: " << r << "\n";
        skepu::Finalize();
        return 0;
}
```

Fig. 1: SkePU code for a 1D convolution using the MapOverlap skeleton

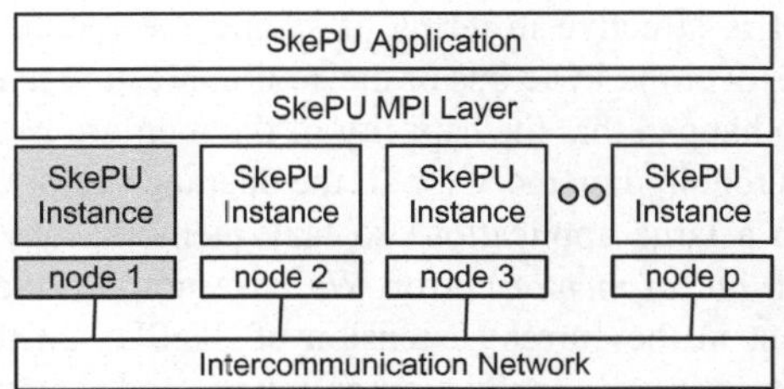

Fig. 2: SkePU instances with MPI layer

only when it is needed for performing computation or saving output data. If the input data is used for some other computation (kernel), it is not copied again. Furthermore, the data for intermediate results remains available for further computation (on GPU memory, with the CUDA/OpenCL backend) and transferred back to the host memory once it is required. The SkePU skeleton library is an on-going work with addition of more containers like sparse matrices for implementing irregular computations and dynamically changing data distributions. Furthermore, auto-tuning for selecting the execution plan has been addressed in [10]. In the current version of SkePU, the code is run on a single multi-GPU node and in the rest of the paper, we present the extension of SkePU for multiple nodes.

3. Extending SkePU by a MPI Layer

In this work we consider the extension of SkePU for the vector container only. On a single multi-GPU system (i.e., one cluster node), the skeletons can execute on one or more GPUs and upload their data to the device memory according to the selected number of GPUs or cores. The data access patterns for the vector container for different skeletons are shown in the upper portion of Figure 3. For example, in case of the *Map* skeleton, the user function f_2 is applied on the ith element of the input vector(s) and the result is stored in the corresponding i^{th} index of the output vector. In the *MapOverlap* skeleton, the neighbouring $overlap$ elements are also used in the calculation of ith output element.

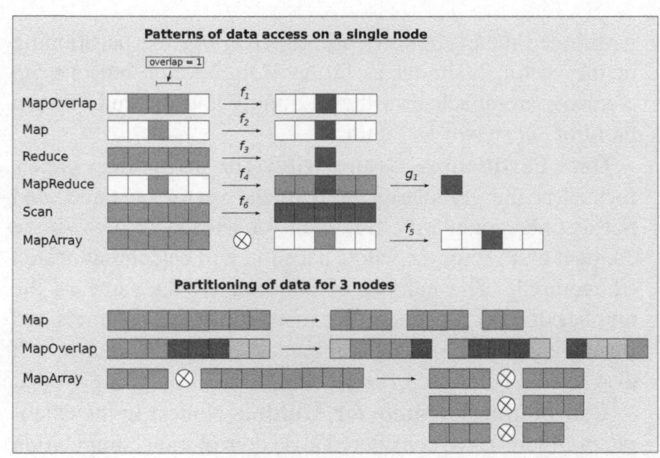

Fig. 3: Data access patterns for single node and data partitioning for 3 nodes.

The MPI Layer: In order to run skeletons on several nodes, each SkePU instance on a node runs the same code but the data is internally partitioned according to the semantics of the selected skeleton. For the necessary communication we add an MPI layer connecting the SkePU instances running on the nodes. The block diagram for the SkePU extension is given in Figure 2. The grey colored box shows the root node that runs the MPI process with rank 0. For broadcasting, scattering and gathering data over several nodes, we use the collective MPI calls, *MPI_BCast*, *MPI_Scatterv* and *MPI_Gatherv* respectively. There can be any number of nodes (and SkePU instances) over the MPI layer that is actually determined by the number of MPI processes selected while executing the parallel application. The MPI layer remains transparent to the user but the same SkePU code for the application will internally use the MPI layer to partition the data and computations.

Data Partitioning over Multiple GPU Nodes: The data partitioning is performed when a skeleton on the vector inputs is called. For example, in case of a *Map* skeleton and 3 nodes, a vector of length 8 is partitioned into 3 parts as shown in the lower portion of Figure 3. The output vector is also initialized on each node with the same lengths (as the lengths of the partitions of input vector). Then each instance of SkePU on each node computes the smaller computation with the same semantics of the *Map* skeleton. Notice that the *MapArray* skeleton has two vector inputs, when the ith element of the output vector is calculated (with the user function f_5, in Figure 3) by using the ith element of the second input vector and all the elements of first input vector. So, while partitioning, the second vector is partitioned in a similar way as in the *Map* skeleton case, but the first vector is broadcasted to each node. In this way, the *MapArray* computation is subdivided into smaller computations (that are performed according to *MapArray* semantics) on the partitioned data. Similarly, in *MapOverlap*, the partitioning of the vector is similar as in the *Map* skeleton but *overlap* elements are attached in the beginning and the end of each partition as shown in Figure 3.

Data Partitioning Granularity: The partitioning is performed at the granularity level of the vector container and not at finer granularity. So, even for an update of a single element of a vector the whole partition will be communicated (if required). The number of partitions is the same as the number of MPI processes. For more complex containers and finer granularities of data communication, the container will also handle coherency (being addressed in on-going work).

Convolution Example for Multiple Nodes: In the example of Figure 1, we considered a 1D convolution computation using the *MapOverlap* skeleton. The SkePU code for the *MapOverlap* instance (conv), when executed on the GPU cluster, runs on all the nodes. The root process (MPI process with rank 0) initializes the vector *v0* with data and all the other processes (running on other nodes) keep the vector empty. When every process calls the *conv* skeleton, the root process partitions $v0$ in p parts where p is the number of MPI processes (or nodes used), and scatters the parts to p MPI processes. In each part, additional d elements, on both sides, are appended where d is the overlap size (here d = 3), which is a (statically known) parameter of the skeleton. Every MPI process (running one instance of SkePU) fills its $v0$ vector with the part it receives and performs the *over* kernel on the respective part (on CPU or GPU, according to the preselection made by the programmer). The results are gathered on the root process when they are required.

Lazy Memory Copying on Multiple Nodes: The lazy memory copying mechanism of the vector container is also extended for the cluster implementation of SkePU. In case the SkePU application is executed on a single node with CUDA or OpenCL backend, the input vector containers are uploaded on the device from the host memory and the references of those vectors are maintained in a hash table. Maintaining the hash table adds an extra overhead in the lazy memory copying mechanism but access to the hash table is an expected O(1) operation. If any of these input vectors is required again for another skeleton call, the reference of that vector already resides in the hash table so the vector is not uploaded again.

When the data in the vector is changed on the GPU and then accessed on the CPU the reference is removed from the hash table and the updated vector is downloaded. The lazy memory copying involves only the data uploading and downloading to/from the device memory. Whereas, in case of multiple nodes, data communication over the network is also involved besides the data uploading/downloading on device. As mentioned earlier the computation carried out for a skeleton on multiple nodes is actually done by the same skeleton calls on the different partitions of the operand data (vector) so the hash tables are also maintained on all the nodes including the root node. The root process performs the check whether the data is already distributed or not. It performs this check by finding the reference of the (partitioned) vector in the hash table. Then it either scatters the vector or does nothing depending upon absence or availability of the partitioned vector's reference in the hash table. On all the other nodes, similar checks are performed and the vector data is either gathered or nothing is done depending upon the absence or availability of vector data on the nodes' GPU devices.

In case of a backend not requiring a GPU device, there is no data uploading or downloading but the lazy memory copying is still useful in saving redundant communications over the network. This intelligent mechanism of data management is effective in terms of saving the redundant data transfers over the PCIe bus or the communication network. It can also happen that the capacity of the memory is less than the total required memory for all the operand vector elements used (in a large application) so lazy memory copying will cause an *out of memory* error. We have not considered this constraint in the current extension of SkePU. On the other hand, executing the application on several nodes may resolve this problem because the accumulated storage capacity of multiple GPUs will be larger than for a single GPU device memory and the data will be partitioned (requiring less memory on each GPU device). We will see in the results that the benefit of lazy memory copying depends upon the nature of the computations and data dependencies.

Implicit Barriers: As we are using the blocking collective calls of MPI, like *MPI_BCast* etc, there will be an implicit barrier in each collective call. There is no overlapping of data communications and computations. The semantics of SkePU as suggested by the sequential programming interface requires barrier synchronization where multiple nodes execute the code in an SPMD fashion. Certain applications may require barriers for correct computations so these implicit barriers are helpful. We will discuss possible benefits of these implicit barriers in the discussion of the N-body problem in Section 4.

Utilization of CPU Cores: The SkePU code follows the serial execution semantics between calls and for computation intensive data parallel kernels, it uses the selected backend for parallel execution. So at least one core is used for data uploading, downloading (on one node) and for data distribution (in case of multiple nodes). On each node, only one MPI process executes (irrespective of the number of CPU cores or GPUs) and based on backend selection, like the OpenCL, CUDA or OpenMP, the GPU and CPU cores are used (on each node).

The programmer needs not modify the code for running on the cluster, and in case the code is executed on the cluster, the distribution and synthesis of data is hidden from the programmer. The programmability of SkePU code is not affected, but scalability is achieved. We will discuss the scalability in the Section 5. For all the other skeletons, the partitioning of the data is performed in the similar way.

4. N-body Simulation

The N-body simulation is a well known problem for understanding the interaction of N bodies (e.g. electric particles or galactic bodies). The time complexity of the naive serial algorithm is $O(KN^2)$ where N is the number of particles and K is the number of timesteps of the whole simulation.

The simple algorithm for N-body simulation in SkePU is shown in Figure 4. The application starts the serial execution and initializes the skeleton instances *nbody_init* and *nbody_simul-ate_step* using the user functions *init_kernel* and *move_kernel* respectively. Then two vectors of size N are created. The skeleton instance *nbody_init* is used to initialize the particles' initial positions, velocities, accelerations and masses. The particles are positioned in a 3D space with some initial velocities and accelerations. *ARRAY_FUNC* and *GENERATE_FUNC* are macros like *OVERLAP_FUNC* as explained in Section 2. After initialization of all the particles, the actual simulation starts in a *for-loop* using the *nbody_simulate_step* skeleton instance of *MapArray*. After every time step, the user function *move_kernel* is called using the *nbody_simulate_step* skeleton instance. The SkePU vector *all_particles* contains the positions, velocities and accelerations of all particles in the previous time step, and *ith_particle* points to the ith particle in *all_particles*. The *move_kernel* updates the ith particle as shown in Figure 4. The nature of the application is such that the output data is updated on the host (or root node in case of multiple nodes) so that the next skeleton call is made on the current state of the system. The skeletons are called *time_steps* times, with the first argument as the updated vector.

Execution using Multiple Nodes: In case the application is executed on a cluster (with multiple nodes), the first vector is internally broadcasted and the second vector is distributed/scattered to every MPI process in each iteration. In this way, the large problem is divided into smaller problem of the same nature. But due to the large computations the partitioning still gives benefit even there is communication overhead.

Synchronizations and Barriers: In each iteration, the skeleton call *nbody_simulate_step* is made two times. This is because the first argument requires the current state of the system of particles. The implicit barriers make it possible that the current state of the system is used after it is computed completely. This synchronization is inherently present in the nature of the computation of the N-body problem but using the current implementation (Cluster-SkePU) this synchronization is also enforced for any other application and overlapping of computation and communication cannot be exploited (we are addressing this in on-going work).

```
GENERATE_FUNC( init_kernel, Particle, index, seed,
  Particle p;
  // initialize location, velocity etc
  return p;
)
ARRAY_FUNC( move_kernel, Particle, all_particles, ith_particle,
  // calculate the force exerted on ith_particle from
  // all the other particles given in all_particles
  // update acceleration, velocity and position of ith_particle
  return ith_particle;
)
int main()
{
  skepu::Generate<init_kernel> nbody_init(new init_kernel);
  skepu::MapArray<move_kernel> nbody_simulate_step(new move_kernel);
  skepu::Vector<Particle> particles(n);
  skepu::Vector<Particle> latest(n);
  nbody_init(n, particles);
  nbody_init(n, latest);
  for(t=0;t<time_steps/2; t=t+1)
  {
    nbody_simulate_step(particles, latest, latest);
    // Update vectors on the host
    nbody_simulate_step(latest, particles, particles);
    // Update vectors on the host
  }
}
```

Fig. 4: SkePU code for N-body Simulation

Ratio of Computations and Communications: In this application, the parallel computations performed by the threads (either CUDA, OpenMP) are $O(N^2)$ in each update of the system of particles whereas the amount of data communicated is $O(N)$.

Effect of Lazy Memory Copying: The nature of computation of N-body simulation does not exploit the benefit of lazy memory copying.

The code for N-body simulation is simply written as serial code in C++ in terms of skeletons but executes on several SkePU backends including the GPU cluster backend.

All the other selected scientific applications are expressed in SkePU in a similar way in terms of *MapArray*, *Generate* and *Map* skeletons by following their semantics. The code looks serial but, following the semantics of the given skeletons, the expressed code can be executed on all backends implemented in SkePU.

5. Experimental Results

We have implemented several scientific applications (expressing their data parallel computations in terms of SkePU skeletons) including, N-body simulation, electric field calculation, smoothed particles hydrodynamics, one-level of Strassen's recursive matrix multiplication algorithm, and a synthetic matrix sum application. We performed experiments on two machines M1 and M2 and used OpenMP/MPI and CUDA/MPI backends respectively. Machine M1 has 805 nodes (for checking the scalability, we use up to 16 nodes only as more than 16 nodes were not accessible to us), each with two 2.33 GHz Xeon quad core chips and at least 16 GiB RAM, running under CentOS5. The nodes are interconnected by Infiniband. Machine M2 has 6 nodes each with 2 Intel Xeon E5620 CPUs, 3 NVIDIA Tesla M2090 GPUs with NVIDIA CUDA Toolkit V.4.0, and nodes are interconnected by Infiniband. We could use up to 3 accessible nodes with single GPU (with CUDA only) on each node for experiments.

Scalability over Multiple Nodes: In the first experiment, the results show the scalability for the first three scientific applications with CUDA/MPI and/or OpenMP/MPI backends as shown in Figure 5. The horizontal axis in Figure 5 shows the number of particles for N-body simulation, smoothed hydrodynamics and electric field applications. The vertical axis shows the speedup for the three applications. The graphs mentioned with 1C/2C show the speedup for 2 CUDA nodes against a single CUDA node on M2 for each application in Figure 5. We also found that the CUDA/MPI backend with three nodes on M2 gives at most 4X performance than the OpenMP/MPI backend with 16 nodes on M1 for two scientific applications (shown by 16P/3C in Figure 5) besides the performance portability across different parallel architectures without code modification. These three scientific applications are computation intensive such that each node gets considerably large computations to perform for the given amount of communicated data among the nodes. For example, (considering the CUDA/MPI backend), in case of N-body simulation, $O(N)$ parallel tasks (each containing $O(N)$ operations) are performed by P nodes and data communication per iteration of N-body simulation will be $O(N)$. In this case, distributing the computation will have more benefit than the communication overhead. Note also that these computations are quite regular and use brute force algorithms, whereas better $O(N \log N)$ work algorithms exist that we considered in on-going extension work of SkePU.

For the SkePU implementation of other scientific applications with $O(N)$ parallel tasks each of asymptotically less than $O(N)$ work (e.g. $O(\log N)$ operations), we experienced increased communication cost outweighing the benefit of distributing the computation among several GPU nodes. This is because of the regular patterns of (blocking) communication (at the granularity level of containers) hidden in the simple skeletons in which the data parallel computations of the applications are expressed. Here we experience that finer granularity levels of communications are required for optimizing the communication as in [11] and [12]. The authors in [11] and [12] demonstrate the scalability of scientific applications like fluid dynamics, Strassen's algorithm and conjugate gradient method using CUDA and MPI over multiple nodes by using non-blocking (optimized) communication among the nodes. Hence, more complex skeletons and *smart containers* are required to express non-trivial and irregular scientific applications with varying granularity of data partitioning, prefetching and data caching. As we noted above certain computation intensive scientific applications can still get benefits from scaling over multiple nodes with ease of writing the parallel code (we demonstrated three).

Lazy Memory Copying over Multiple Nodes: In the second experiment, we implemented a one-level recursive variant of Strassen's algorithm for matrix muliplication and another synthetic matrix sum application that simply adds 12 $N \times N$ matrices. The results are shown in Figure 6. In the one-level Strassen's algorithm, two matrices A and B with dimensions $N \times N$ are partitioned into submatrices A_{11}, A_{12}, A_{21}, A_{22} and B_{11}, B_{12}, B_{21}, B_{22} respectively. These submatrices are used (more than once, but communicated only once with lazy memory copying) in the computations of intermediate product submatrices $P_1, ..., P_7$. Similarly, the intermediate product submatrices $P_1, ..., P_7$ stay distributed (not communicated) and the final result's submatrices $C_{11}, C_{12}, C_{21}, C_{22}$ are computed (see Figure 7). We see that lazy memory copying reduces the communication and gives speedup against the application that does not use lazy memory copying. Similarly, in our synthetic matrix sum application, the intermediate result matrix R is not communicated until the last addition is done (see Figure 7). Here, we see even more benefit than with Strassen's algorithm. This is because most of this synthetic matrix sum application benefits from lazy memory copying.

We further observe that the benefit of lazy memory copying decreases for the two applications when multiple nodes are used (as shown in Figure 6). For example, we see that the speedup decreases for both the applications when two nodes are used. Whereas, when 3 nodes are used, the benefit decreases even more in the synthetic matrix sum application but increases in case of Strassen's algorithm. This is because of the following reasons. In case of a single node, more data is transferred to the device memory using the PCIe bus (without partitioning of data). Whereas, in case of 2 nodes, first the data is partitioned in to 2 parts (scattered over the network) and then smaller partitions are transferred to device memories (on each node) in parallel. This decreases the overall transfer time on PCIe bus. So if we save these data transfers, we save less data transfer time (on 2 nodes) and hence speedup decreases as compared to a single node. A further increase in the number of nodes (and partitions) decreases the benefit even more in the case of the synthetic matrix sum application because the data is scattered over the network and even more smaller (three) partitions are transferred on three device memories in parallel. But in Strassen's algorithm we are using the *MapArray* skeleton (in several skeleton calls with broadcasts of several matrices) that increases the communication over the network with increasing number of nodes. So saving the communication with lazy memory copying gives more benefit. Although we get a benefit by lazy memory copying on multiple nodes, the nature of the application affects the speedup. The benefit achieved using the lazy memory copying also suggests to explore more smartness in future work on regular and irregular distributed containers.

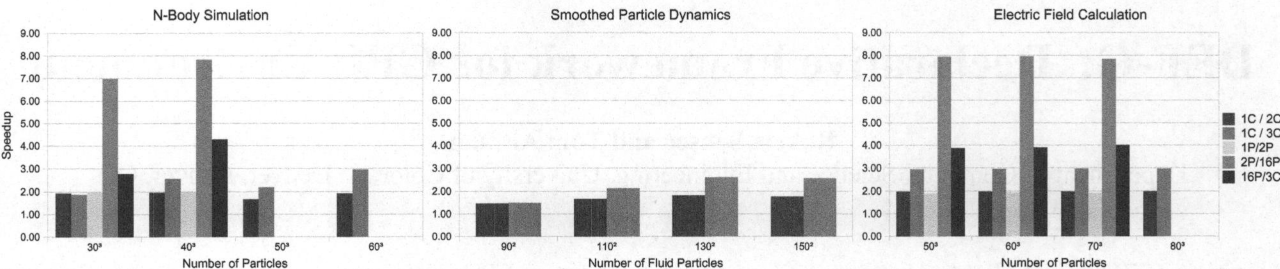

Fig. 5: Speedup of three scientific applications. xC: x nodes are used each with 512 CUDA threads. xP: x nodes are used each with 8 OpenMP threads.

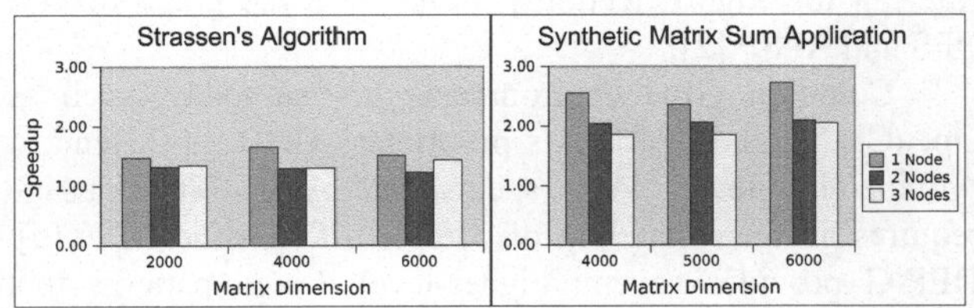

Fig. 6: Speedup gained by using lazy memory copying for one level Strassen's algorithm and a synthetic matrix sum application

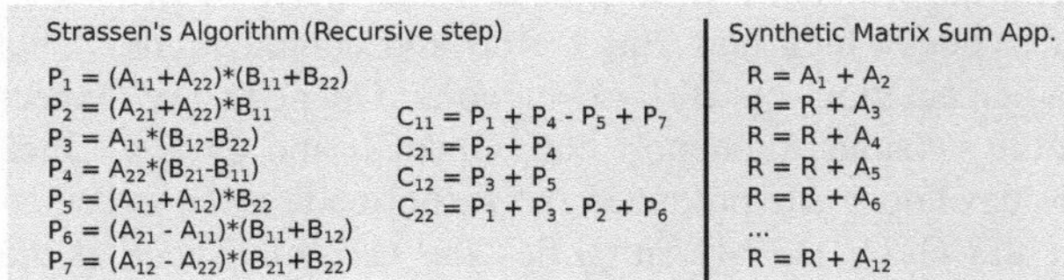

Fig. 7: Possibilities of lazy memory copying in one-level Strassen's algorithm and synthetic matrix sum application

6. Conclusions and Future Work

We have provided the principles and a first prototype for the extension of SkePU for GPU clusters and implemented four scientific and one synthetic matrix sum application. To the best of our knowledge, this is the first skeleton library implementation for GPU clusters that is also evaluated on a GPU cluster (note that the recent framework by Ernsting et al. [7] is evaluated with multiple MPI processes running either on a single GPU node or on a non-GPU cluster). We performed two experiments where the results show scalability, portability and programmability. SkePU code looks serial (easy to maintain and debug) and can be compiled and executed using a number of backends without code modification. We found that certain computation intensive applications (expressed in SkePU skeletons) can scale over multiple nodes even with the current extension of SkePU. The smartness of the containers can give speedup (depending upon the nature of computations). Future work will address improvements in the containers and skeletons in order to make Cluster-SkePU more useful in different domains of scientific computing.

Acknowledgments

This work was partly funded by Higher Education Commission Pakistan (HEC), Swedish e-Science Research Center (SeRC), and EU FP7 project PEPPHER (www.peppher.eu). We are also thankful to Supercomputing Centers NSC (www.nsc.liu.se) and PDC (www.pdc.kth.se) for providing us with the computing resources and technical support.

References

[1] Top500 supercomputer sites. www.top500.org, Nov. 2012.

[2] K. A. Yelick, S. Chakrabarti, E. Deprit, J. Jones, A. Krishnamurthy, and C. po Wen. *Data structures for irregular applications,* DIMACS Workshop on Parallel Algorithms for Unstructured and Dynamic Problems, 1993.

[3] J. Enmyren and C. W. Kessler. *SkePU: a multi-backend skeleton programming library for multi-GPU systems,* Proceedings of the fourth international workshop on High-level parallel programming and applications, pages 5-14, New York, NY, USA, 2010.

[4] M. Cole. *Recursive splitting as a general purpose skeleton for parallel computation,* Proceedings of the Second International Conference on Supercomputing, pages 133-140. 1987

[5] M. Cole. *Algorithmic skeletons: structured management of parallel computation,* MIT Press, Cambridge, MA, USA, 1991.

[6] M. Cole. *A skeletal approach to the exploitation of parallelism,* Proceedings of the conference on CONPAR, pages 667-675, 1988 New York, NY, USA, 1989.

[7] S. Ernsting and H. Kuchen. *Algorithmic skeletons for multicore, multi-GPU systems and clusters,* International Journal of High Performance Computing and Networking, pages 129-138, 2012.

[8] M. Steuwer, P. Kegel, and S. Gorlatch, *SkelCL - A portable skeleton library for high-level gpu programming,* Parallel and Distributed Processing Workshops (IPDPSW-11), pp. 1176-1182. 2011.

[9] M. Alind, M. V. Eriksson, and C. W. Kessler. *Blocklib: a skeleton library for Cell broadband engine,* 1st Int. Workshop on Multicore Software Engineering (IWMSE-08) , pages 7-14, Leipzig, Germany 2008.

[10] U. Dastgeer , J. Enmyren , C. W. Kessler, *Auto-tuning SkePU: a multi-backend skeleton programming framework for multi-GPU systems,* Fourth Int. Workshop on Multicore Software Engineering (IWMSE-11) USA, p.25-32, May 2011.

[11] D. Jacobsen, J. C. Thibault, and I. Senocak. *An MPI-CUDA implementation for massively parallel incompressible flow computations on multi-GPU clusters,* Aerospace Sciences Meeting and Exhibit (AIAA-10), 2010.

[12] N. Karunadasa and D. N. Ranasinghe. *Accelerating high performance applications with CUDA and MPI,* ICIIS'09, pages 28-31.

DEF-G: Declarative Framework for GPU Environment

Robert Senser and Tom Altman
Department of Computer Science and Engineering, University of Colorado Denver, Denver, CO

Abstract - *DEF-G is a declarative language and framework for the efficient generation of OpenCL GPU applications. Using our proof-of-concept DEF-G implementation, run-time and lines-of-code comparisons are provided for three well-known algorithms (Sobel image filtering, breadth-first search and all-pairs shortest path), each evaluated on three different platforms. The DEF-G declarative language and corresponding OpenCL kernels generated complete OpenCL applications in C/C++. Initial lines-of-code comparison demonstrates that the DEF-G applications require significantly less coding than hand-written CPU-side OpenCL applications. The run-time results demonstrate very similar performance characteristics compared to the hand-written applications. We also provide useful observations, which we found to be noteworthy for practitioners, concerning the effectiveness of certain OpenCL API options.*

Keywords: OpenCL, graph algorithms, declarative language

1 Introduction

Producing high performance computing (HPC) software for use on graphical processing units (GPUs) is often a difficult and daunting task. This type of software tends to require the use of specialized, parallel algorithms and requires the use of low-level application programming interfaces (APIs), in the context of a thorough understanding of the GPU architecture. The *Declarative Framework for GPUs* (DEF-G) provides a domain-specific computer language (DSL) to assist the software developer. It mitigates the need for a deep understanding of the full CPU-side API used with technologies such as OpenCL, while allowing the user to focus on the algorithms being used and on the most efficient usage of the overall GPU architecture.

Our research in processing large, sparse graphs on GPUs has, out of necessity, led to the direct development of DEF-G. As these large graphs tend to lack locality of reference, the parallel algorithms needed to process them efficiently tend to be complex. Sample problem domains range from graph problems such as the Breadth-First Search (BFS), Single-Source Shortest Path (SSSP), and All-Points Shortest Path (APSP) to iterative matrix inversion, parallel prefix computation, and parallel sorting. Using DEF-G permits us to focus on the algorithms, which were coded mainly in the GPU kernels, and to spend less time focusing on the CPU-side code. In this proof-of-concept implementation of DEF-G, we have implemented and measured, in terms of lines-of-code and run-time performance, three well-known algorithms: Sobel image filtering for edge detection [1] and from the graph theory: BFS and APSP [2].

Common GPU environments in use today, such as OpenCL [3] and NVIDIA's proprietary CUDA [4], tend to provide low-level, very specialized APIs. Their usage requires an understanding of complex, CPU-side APIs [5]. DEF-G provides several higher-level design patterns that abstract the CPU-side coding to a declarative level. Much as the now-ubiquitous relational databases accept database requests as declarative SQL statements and quickly return the requested data, DEF-G uses design patterns and declarative statements to produce high performance CPU-side code, which performs the desired computations. This implementation of DEF-G supports OpenCL; we expect future versions to support both OpenCL and CUDA. Once the developer has produced the kernel code to be executed on the GPU, DEF-G simplifies the task of executing the kernel code. Complex CPU-side operations outside the context of the DEF-G design patterns can be utilized by DEF-G as callable functions.

The current DEF-G implementation consists of a parser written in Java, using ANTLR 3 [6], and our code generator, which is written in C++. The parser handles syntax checking and results in an abstract syntax tree, expressed as an XML document. This abstract syntax tree is then processed by our code generator, which uses the TinyXML2 library [7] to accept the syntax tree. For example, the twelve lines of DEF-G code shown in Figure 1 result in approximately 200 lines of C/C++ code, a snippet of which is shown in Figure 2. The OpenCL kernel executed by this code is shown in Figure 3. Note that this generated OpenCL code is intended to execute on any supported OpenCL device, including the CPU.

OpenCL is an open and cross-platform standard for developing high performance applications on parallel hardware. This standard is supported by major vendors including NVIDIA, AMD, and Intel. There are two major components defined by the standard: the OpenCL C programming language used on the parallel device and the CPU-side APIs for C/C++ that provide access to the device's OpenCL kernels. The CPU manages the execution of the kernels on the OpenCL parallel device.

```
declare application  sobel
  declare integer Xdim (0)
  declare integer Ydim (0)
  declare integer BUF_SIZE (0)
  declare gpu gpuone ( any )
  declare kernel  sobel_filter SobelFilter_Kernels  ( [[ 2D,Xdim,Ydim ]] )
  declare integer buffer image1 ( $BUF_SIZE )
        integer buffer image2 ( $BUF_SIZE )
  call init_input (image1(in) $Xdim (out) $Ydim (out) $BUF_SIZE(out))
  execute run1 sobel_filter ( image1(in) image2(out) )
  call disp_output (image2(in) $Xdim (in) $Ydim (in) )
end
```

Figure 1: Sample DEF-G Code

```
// *** buffers in
cl_mem    buffer_image1    =    clCreateBuffer(context,    CL_MEM_READ_ONLY|CL_MEM_COPY_HOST_PTR,    (BUF_SIZE    *
sizeof(int)),(void *) image1, &status);
if (status != CL_SUCCESS) { handle error }
status = clSetKernelArg(sobel_filter, 0, sizeof(cl_mem), (void *)&buffer_image1);
if (status != CL_SUCCESS) { handle error }
cl_mem buffer_image2 = clCreateBuffer(context, CL_MEM_WRITE_ONLY, (BUF_SIZE * sizeof(int)),(void *) NULL, &status);
if (status != CL_SUCCESS) { handle error }
status = clSetKernelArg(sobel_filter, 1, sizeof(cl_mem), (void *)&buffer_image2);
if (status != CL_SUCCESS) { handle error }
// *** execution
size_t global_work_size[2]; global_work_size[0] = Xdim ; global_work_size[1] = Ydim ;
status = clEnqueueNDRangeKernel(commandQueue, sobel_filter, 2, NULL, global_work_size, NULL, 0, NULL, NULL);
if (status != CL_SUCCESS) { handle error }
// *** result buffers
status = clEnqueueReadBuffer(commandQueue, buffer_image2, CL_TRUE, 0, BUF_SIZE * sizeof(int), image2, 0, NULL, NULL);
if (status != CL_SUCCESS) { handle error }
```

Figure 2: Snippet of Generated OpenCL Code

```
__kernel void sobel_filter(__global uchar4* inputImage, __global uchar4* outputImage) {
        uint x = get_global_id(0);  uint y = get_global_id(1);
        uint width = get_global_size(0);  uint height = get_global_size(1);
        float4 Gx = (float4)(0);  float4 Gy = Gx;
        int c = x + y * width;
        /* Read each texel component and calculate ..*/
        if( x >= 1 && x < (width-1) && y >= 1 && y < height - 1)
        {
                float4 i00 = convert_float4(inputImage[c - 1 - width]);
                // similar lines omitted
                float4 i22 = convert_float4(inputImage[c + 1 + width]);
                Gx =  i00 + (float4)(2) * i10 + i20 - i02  - (float4)(2) * i12 - i22;
                Gy =  i00 - i20  + (float4)(2)*i01 - (float4)(2)*i21 + i02  -  i22;
                /* taking root of sums of squares of Gx and Gy */
                outputImage[c] = convert_uchar4(hypot(Gx, Gy)/(float4)(2));
        }
}
```

Figure 3: Snippet of Sobel OpenCL Kernel Code (from AMD APP SDK 2.8) [18]

The OpenCL C/C++ CPU-side code is required to obtain the kernel source code and call appropriate OpenCL APIs to compile the kernel code. In addition, the OpenCL CPU-side code is required to acquire and manage the low-level buffers accessed by the device kernel. These two requirements tend to make the CPU-side code verbose and often complex; additional complexity is added by the OpenCL requirement to support many different types of parallel platforms and devices, examples being CPUs, GPUs, and even specialized FPGA [8] and DSP [9] hardware. This requirement adds numerous specialized API parameters to the OpenCL API. It can be argued that the OpenCL API is unnecessarily complex, not easily learned, and somewhat hard to use and debug. DEF-G takes over much of the burden of writing the OpenCL CPU-side code, permitting the developer more focus on the device kernels and parallel algorithms proper.

We approached our work as follows: using three existing OpenCL applications and using the existing OpenCL kernels without any changes, we replaced the existing CPU-side code with the DEF-G generated code. The DEF-G source modules needed on average about 90% fewer lines of code. We then compared the computational performance of the three applications over three different OpenCL platforms. Performance variations between the DEF-G results and the reference results were identified and analyzed.

The next sections describe related work, followed by the three existing OpenCL applications that were used as reference/benchmark applications and converted to DEF-G. We then present our experimental results in terms of lines of code and run times, and make some observations for GPU practitioners. A summary of ongoing and future work is presented in the last section.

2 Related Work

Numerous attempts have been made to construct languages, compilers, and tools to make the production of high performance parallel solutions easier. In 2005, Shen et al. [10] talked about the "holy grail" of parallelization, which is the automated parallelization of serial programs, being out of reach. However, progress is being made. One approach towards the efficient production of GPU-based parallel solutions is the use of domain-specific languages (DSL). DEF-G is a DSL, a language and associated tools that facilitate the production of OpenCL applications. Martin Fowler defines a DSL as a "computer programming language of limited expressiveness focused on a particular domain," and suggests that DSLs can be broken into two categories: *internal* DSLs and *external* DSLs [11]. DSLs of both varieties have been produced for GPU-based HPC.

Internal DSLs for GPU-based HPC include extensions to Python such as: PyGPU [12], PyCUDA [13], and PyOpenCL [14]. These DSLs tend to consist of Python wrappers placed around a particular GPU API. There are also C/C++ extensions such as Bacon [15]. Aside from DEF-G, other GPU external DSLs include the SPL digital signal processing language [16] and the MATLAB Parallel Computing Toolbox (which supports CUDA and permits passing some MATLAB functions to the GPU and permits GPU kernel execution [17]). Both MATLAB and DEF-G require that the GPU kernel be provided.

The BFS and APSP implementations we chose for our DEF-G testing were existing implementations, easily obtained from software development kits (SDKs) and benchmarks [18-19]. There exists many other published algorithms and implementations that may provide better overall run-time performances. We anticipate implementing a subset of these in DEF-G. For example, Merrill, et al. suggest a much faster BFS solution which uses *prefix sum* to help distribute the work among GPU threads without locking [20]. We intend to apply the prefix sum lock-avoidance approach to graph-oriented algorithms, which were not addressed in this study. For APSP, Katz and Kider provide a method for using *tiling* with the Floyd-Warshall APSP algorithm to minimize GPU global memory access times [21].

3 DEF-G Framework Language

The DEF-G *declarative language* consists of a number of `declare`, `execute` and `call` statements, and some *optional statements* such as `sequence/times` and `loop/while`. An example DEF-G source file is shown in Figure 1. The `declare` statement is used to name the DEF-G application, define and name the GPU kernels to be executed, define any required scalar variables such as a graph's node count, and define the buffers to be given to the GPU. Lines 1 to 8, in the DEF-G sample, show `declare` statements. The syntax on line 6 enclosed in "[["and"]]" brackets is our method for setting the global grid size. The `call` statement is used to invoke C/C++ functions, e.g., to obtain the input data; the sample has `call` statements on lines 9 and 11. The `execute` statement on line 10 is used to execute the kernel. The flow of control is a design pattern built into DEF-G.

The optional statements are used to provide support for more complex design patterns where the kernels may have to be executed a variable number of times. Figure 4 contains a DEF-G example which executes the kernel once for each graph node. Figure 4, line 9, shows the `sequence` statement application. DEF-G contains statements to process scalar values returned by kernels. This capability was used in the DEF-G BFS solution to conditionally stop the parallel device processing. DEF-G generates OpenCL 1.1 code.

4 Discussion of Results

To test the viability of DEF-G, we selected three existing OpenCL solutions based on well-known algorithms: Sobel image filtering and Floyd-Warshall APSP, both from the AMD APP SDK [16], and breadth-first search from the OpenDwarfs benchmark [17]. We will refer to these solutions as SOBEL, FW, and BFS, respectively. SOBEL was chosen because it represents the class of simpler GPU problems, where a single kernel is called once and because it has significant RAM locality of reference.

```
declare application floydwarshall
declare integer NODE_CNT (0)
declare integer BUF_SIZE (0)
declare gpu gpuone ( any )
declare kernel floydWarshallPass FloydWarshall_Kernels ( [[ 2D,NODE_CNT ]] )
declare integer buffer buffer1 ( $BUF_SIZE )
        integer buffer buffer2 ( $BUF_SIZE )
call init_input (buffer1(in) buffer2(in) $NODE_CNT(out) $BUF_SIZE(out))
sequence $NODE_CNT times
  execute run1 floydWarshallPass ( buffer1(inout) buffer2(out) $NODE_CNT(in) $CNT(in) )
call disp_output (buffer1(in) buffer2(in) $NODE_CNT(in))
end
```

Figure 4: Sample DEF-G Code Showing a Sequence

In future implementations of DEF-G, we expect to support several concurrent GPU devices in a declarative manner and SOBEL provides a good test case for this added support.

FW and BFS were selected because they represent two different classes of graph-oriented GPU problems, with BFS being the more complex. The FW algorithm requires the same operation to be repeated for each graph node; in this implementation, the FW kernel is called once for each node. This call-for-each-node behavior must be managed from the CPU-side. The OpenDwarfs BFS implementation is based on the work by Harish [22] and uses a version of Dijkstra's algorithm [2]. The actual OpenDwarfs code is a port of the BFS CUDA code from the Rodinia benchmark [23]. This BFS implementation requires that a pair of kernels be repeated until success is indicated by the second kernel. This repetition is managed by the CPU-side code.

All three of these were converted to DEF-G, keeping the unmodified OpenCL kernels. The conversions to DEF-G produce exactly the same results as the corresponding reference version. Before discussing the performance results, we summarize the hardware and software used. The tests were run on three different configurations, which we call CPU, GPU-GT 430, and GPU-Tesla T20, which are listed in order of increasing power, as shown in Table 1.

In terms of module line count results, the three DEF-G versions were much smaller than their reference counterparts. Table 2 shows the line counts for SOBEL, BFS, and FW. Shown are the number of lines of DEF-G declarative code, the number of lines of generated code, and the estimated number of non-comment lines in the reference version. This data is shown graphically in Plot 1. On average, the DEF-G code is 7.7 percent of the generated code, and 4.4 percent of the reference code. It should be noted that the reference code tended to include additional functionality; therefore, the comparison with the generated code is likely to be more indicative of the DEF-G's effectiveness.

The run-time performance comparison turned out to be very interesting. The raw run times, in milliseconds, are presented in Table 3. Plot 2 shows this data presented in 3D form. The results shown are the average of ten runs done for each case. Where we encountered unexpected results, we often reran the tests with manual code changes to isolate the underlying technical causes. We made these code changes to both the DEF-G and reference OpenCL code. However, the numbers shown here are only the original times, i.e., those prior to any manual code modifications.

SOBEL is the simplest application and the run-time performance results between DEF-G and the reference cases are comparable. The SOBEL results are shown on the graph in purple. The DEF-G performance was slightly faster on the CPU and GPU-GT 430 runs, and was slightly slower on the GPU-Tesla T20. This similarity of results is not surprising as the CPU-side support needed for SOBEL is not complex.

The run-time results of the FW tests, which are shown in green, were a surprise to us. We saw no obvious explanation for why DEF-G should be consistently faster. We reviewed the OpenCL code for both DEF-G and the AMD SDK-supplied reference case, and did not find any significant differences in buffer usage or the OpenCL API functions used. We did notice that the reference case was using asynchronous events when not required and we temporarily disabled them and reran the reference case. The FW reference case run

Table 1: Test Configurations

Name	Configuration Data
CPU	Windows 7, Intel I3 Processor, 1.33 GHz, 4 GB RAM, using AMD OpenCL SDK 2.8 (no GPU)
GPU-GT 430	Windows 7, Intel Pentium 4 Processor, 3.2 GHz, 1.5 GB RAM, using NVIDIA OpenCL SDK 4.2, NVIDIA GT 430 GPU with 2 Compute Units, 1400 MHz and 1024M RAM
GPU-Tesla T20	Penguin Computing Cluster, Linux Cent OS 5.3, AMD Opteron 2427 Processor, 2.2 GHz, 24 GB RAM, using NVIDIA OpenCL SDK 4.0, NVIDIA Tesla T20 with 14 Compute Units, 1147 MHz and 2687M RAM

Table 2: Lines of Code

	DEF-G Declarative	DEF-G Generated	Reference
BFS	33	291	364
FW	12	238	478
SOBEL	12	208	442

times dropped three-fold from an average 51.2 ms to 17 ms. This difference was later traced to what we identified as an error in the OpenCL event handling. We feel the DEF-G Tesla time of 11.3 ms and the reference case time of 17 ms are reasonably close and this test tends to show that, for this implementation of the Floyd-Warshall algorithm, both implementations' run times were comparable.

The BFS run-time comparisons used two different graphs. The first graph has 4,096 nodes, shown in blue on the graph, and the second has 65,536 nodes, shown in red. It is clear that the reference case runs significantly faster than DEF-G. For example, on the Tesla, the reference case ran in an average of 11.3 ms and DEF-G in an average of 59.4 ms. As we had done with the FW tests, we analyzed the performance difference. We found that DEF-G was moving buffers to the OpenCL device when not required. After manually adjusting the code to eliminate the movement of these buffers in the generated OpenCL code, the 59.4 ms run time dropped to an average of 28.6 ms. This performance can be improved even more by enhancing the DEF-G language to distinguish between buffers that are moved on each kernel execution and those that are initialized only once, and by the addition of buffer-use optimization to the DEF-G OpenCL code generator. The current code generator contains very little optimization functionality, but we are optimistic DEF-G can come close to the reference-case performance with these, and perhaps additional, enhancements.

We cannot leave the BFS performance topic without noting that the OpenCL CPU configuration's performance was better than either of the GPU performances, except for the Tesla 65,536 node case. We postulate that this is explained by the BFS implementation being used. This graph algorithm implementation is based on the work by Harish [22], which does not compensate for the lack of memory caching on many GPUs. The CPU version most likely fared so well due to the multiple levels of memory caching provided by the Intel I3; it is also likely that the 65,536 node case did not fit entirely in the Intel I3's cache.

In summary, these four comparison tests have shown that, at least in these three cases, the declarative approach used in DEF-G can be used to produce OpenCL applications with fewer lines of code and comparable performance levels.

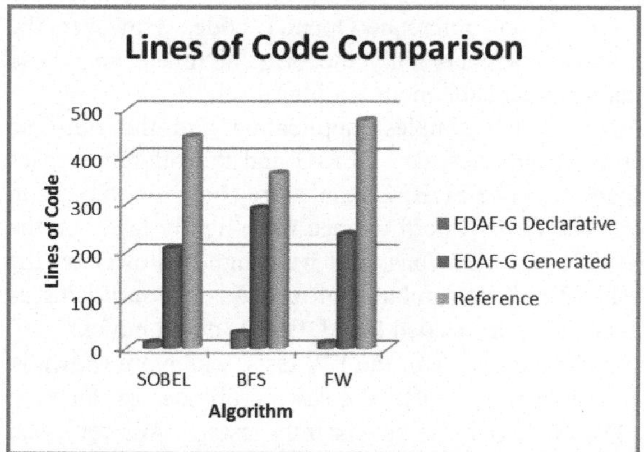

Plot 1: Size Comparison of Module Sizes

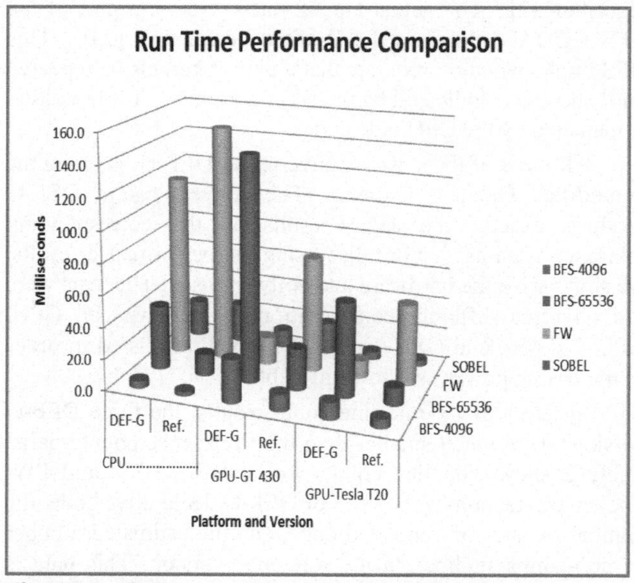

Plot 2: Performance Comparison of Run Times

Table 3: Run-time Performance, in milliseconds

	CPU		GPU-GT 430		GPU-Tesla T20	
	DEF-G	Ref.	DEF-G	Ref.	DEF-G	Ref.
BFS-4096	4.7	2.6	27.2	10.7	10.6	5.8
BFS-65536	40.9	14.2	143.9	26.5	59.4	11.3
FW	115.6	152.0	17.9	73.5	11.3	51.2
SOBEL	23.0	24.8	11.1	20.0	5.3	4.1

5 Observations for Practitioners

Although our performance tests were limited to three platforms and four tests cases, we have two important observations for OpenCL HPC developers.

Observation One: The OpenCL "implicit model" worked well. The OpenCL clEnqueueNDRangeKernel() API call is used to execute kernels and its sixth parameter describes the number of work items that make up a work group. This can be hard to calculate and optimize. There is an option to set this parameter to NULL and allow OpenCL to set this internally. This is referred to as the "implicit model," by Munshi, et al. [24]. The proof-of-concept version of DEF-G uses this implicit model; much to our surprise the implicit model performance was equal in many cases to the tuned setting. We suggest that practitioners may want to try using the implicit mode as part of their performance testing to help verify that their explicitly-set values are superior.

Observation Two: The clCreateBuffer() CL_MEM_COPY_HOST_PTR option gave inconsistent performance. This option permits the clCreateBuffer() call to provide the address of the host buffer and avoid later calls to clEnqueueReadBuffer()/clEngueueWriteBuffer(). Use of this option appeared to introduce performance issues in a limited number of our tests; we encountered cases where using this option and avoiding the associated clEnqueueReadBuffer()/clEngueueWriteBuffer() calls did add significantly to the run time. We suspect the performance of this option could vary by GPU vendor and device; we suggest trying both approaches with your specific OpenCL device.

6 Ongoing and Future Work

This proof-of-concept DEF-G implementation has shown that our declarative approach is able to produce results with less code written and still maintain similar run-time performance, at least for this family of test cases. The addition of buffer optimization to DEF-G would greatly benefit its buffer management performance and, hence, the overall run times. DEF-G also needs the addition of high-performance data loaders and result displays, as well as simple debugging aids such as logging and formatted buffer dumps. We anticipate expanding the DEF-G toolkit to support the use of multiple GPUs, to have optional automatic tuning of various GPU parameters, and to have callable modules generated by DEF-G. Once we have automatic tuning capabilities, we will consider producing a code generator for NVIDIA's CUDA. We also expect to implement the generation of human-readable OpenCL C/C++ code that is a starting point for customized GPU applications and to implement other higher-performance approaches to BFS and APSP.

DEF-G was developed as a result of a specific need; that need being the rapid and efficient production of CPU-side code for use in GPU-based parallel algorithms research. Our DEF-G results look very promising. DEF-G provides a tool to achieve the quick performance analysis of new OpenCL kernels and algorithms. Given this success, we anticipate enhancing DEF-G and making this tool publicly available. The DEF-G toolkit should be a useful asset in future GPU high-performance algorithms research.

7 References

[1] Vincent, O. R., and O. Folorunso. "A descriptive algorithm for sobel image edge detection." In Proceedings of Informing Science & IT Education Conference (InSITE), pp. 97-107. 2009.

[2] Cormen, Thomas H.; Leiserson, Charles E., Rivest, Ronald L., Stein, Clifford. Introduction to Algorithms (3rd ed.). MIT Press and McGraw-Hill. 2009.

[3] "The OpenCL Specification 1.1," [Online]. Available: http://www.khronos.org/opencl/

[4] "CUDA 5 Programing Guide," [Online]. Available: http://docs.nvidia.com/cuda/cuda-c-programming-guide

[5] OpenCL Reference Pages, [Online]. Available: http://www.khronos.org/registry/cl/sdk/1.1/docs/man/xhtml/

[6] ANTLR 3, [Online]. Available: http://www.antlr3.org/

[7] Tiny XML2, [Online]. Available: http://www.grinninglizard.com/tinyxml2/index.html

[8] Altera Corporation OpenCL, [Online]. Available: http: www.altera.com/opencl

[9] Texas Instruments OpenCL, [Online]. Available: http://e2e.ti.com/support/dsp/omap_applications_processors/f/447/t/132798.aspx

[10] Shen, John Paul, and Mikko H Lipasti. Modern Processor Design : Fundamentals of Superscalar Processors. Boston: McGraw-Hill Higher Education, 2005.

[11] Fowler, Martin. Domain-specific languages, Addison-Wesley Professional, 2010.

[12] PyGPU, [Online]. Available: http://fileadmin.cs.lth.se/cs/Personal/Calle_Lejdfors/pygpu/

[13] PyCUDA, [Online]. Available: http://mathema.tician.de/software/pycuda

[14] PyOpenCL, [Online]. Available: http://mathema.tician.de/software/pyopencl

[15] Tuck, Nat. "Bacon: A GPU Programming Language With Just in Time Specialization (Draft)." University of Massachusetts Lowel, Lowel MA 01854.

[16] Jianxin Xiong, Jeremy Johnson, Robert Johnson, and David Padua.. SPL: a language and compiler for DSP algorithms. In Proceedings of the ACM SIGPLAN 2001 conference on Programming language design and implementation (PLDI '01). ACM, New York, NY, USA, 298-308, 2001.

[17] Matlab Parallel Computing Toolbox, [Online]. Available: http://www.mathworks.com/products/parallel-computing/

[18] AMD APP SDK 2.8, [Online]. Available: http://developer.amd.com/tools/heterogeneous-computing/amd-accelerated-parallel-processing-app-sdk/

[19] OpenDwarfs Benchmark, [Online]. Available: https://github.com/opendwarfs/OpenDwarfs

[20] Duane Merrill, Michael Garland, and Andrew Grimshaw. 2012."Scalable GPU graph traversal." In Proceedings of the 17th ACM SIGPLAN symposium on Principles and Practice of Parallel Programming (PPoPP '12). ACM, New York, NY, USA, 117-128.

[21] Katz, Gary J., and Joseph T. Kider Jr. "All-pairs shortest-paths for large graphs on the GPU." In Proceedings of the 23rd ACM SIGGRAPH/EUROGRAPHICS symposium on Graphics hardware, pp. 47-55. Eurographics Association, 2008.

[22] Harish, Pawan, and P. Narayanan. "Accelerating large graph algorithms on the GPU using CUDA." High Performance Computing–HiPC 2007 (2007): 197-208.

[23] Rodinia GPU Benchmark, [Online]. Available: http://lava.cs.virginia.edu/Rodinia/

[24] Munshi, Aaftab, Benedict Gaster, and Timothy G. Mattson. OpenCL programming guide. Addison-Wesley Professional, 2011.

Workstation Footprint Tactical Computing

S. Park[1], **D. Shires**[1], **J. Ross**[2], **D. Richie**[3], **J. Ruloff**[2], **and B. Henz**[1]
[1]Computational Sciences Division, U. S. Army Research Laboratory, APG, MD, USA
[2]Dynamics Research Corp., Andover, MA, USA
[3]Brown Deer Technology, Forest Hill, MD, USA

Abstract— *In terms of computing hardware, heterogeneous processor types have now become an integral part in a number of modern devices. In particular, graphics processing units (GPUs) are complementing central processing units from portable smartphones to large scale supercomputers. By having a mixture of resources available, optimally mapping algorithms to computing architectures improves performance and saves power. With the advances in raw theoretical floating-point processing power of massively parallel graphics processors, mobile high-performance GPU-populated workstations are now a feasible option for advancing compute-intensive tactical computations on-board. This compact form of computing system is evaluated and leveraged for enhancing a tactical operation scenario consisting of determining a ballistic threat field in a three-dimensional urban environment. The core algorithm performs ray-plane intersection tests on a triangular mesh input data using kernels developed in the OpenCL framework to exploit the parallel processing elements of AMD and NVIDIA products. To deliver an intuitive interface to the end user, serving as a layer of abstraction to GPU computing, the interactive world viewer named World Wind was employed for the static optimization ballistic threat demonstration. The World Wind package provides a display and interaction functionality for the workstation with multiple consumer-grade graphics cards installed. Opportunities of hybrid core deployable systems as tactical computing assets are investigated in respect to performance and programming development.*

Keywords: Parallel computing, GPGPU, tactical computing, high performance computing

1. Introduction

The U.S. Army Research Laboratory (ARL) Computational Sciences Division (CSD) hosts one of the Defense Supercomputing Resource Centers within the DoD High Performance Computing Modernization Program, and in this role maintains several high performance systems to support Army and DoD research, development, testing, and evaluation in numerous scientific disciplines. One of the unclassified systems, Pershing, equipped with Intel 8-core Sandy Bridge processors, has a theoretical peak performance of 420 trillion floating-point operations per second (TFLOPS), which places this system in 62nd place on the TOP500 ranking [1]. In addition to supporting Soldiers through the supercomputing facility, advanced tactical computing research being done in CSD attempts to push supercomputing out into the field and closer to dismounted Soldiers. Due to bandwidth restrictions and proximity of supercomputing centers, supporting the lower levels of the Army hierarchy in a battlefield via a U.S. located computational facility is not feasible. Securing bandwidth to a supercomputing center might be the correct solution for theater-wide operations under high command, but this computational resource connectivity for squad units would require a different approach. Addressing this issue, the tactical computing concept is to provide as much high performance computing (HPC) capacity to under-served small Soldier teams.

Apart from the commercial space, unique challenges exist within operating environments for the Army. First, a dependable network infrastructure cannot be assumed in a battlefield scenario. Network connectivity is going to be characterized by frequent disconnections and oversubscribed bandwidth (or a complete lack thereof). Second, data explosion related to collected sensor data approaches intractability. With the expanding flow of data, time to decision and extracting actionable intelligence require higher processing power. Third, the lack of a common standard across fielded systems thwarts the ability to share data and work in cooperation. Mitigating these issues will aid toward enhancing situational awareness and building a common operational picture.

The popularity of heterogeneous computing architectures, such as coupling central processing units (CPUs) with graphics processing units (GPUs), is spreading from personal computers and laptops to mobile devices and HPC facilities. The use of graphics accelerators can be observed in ARM-based PowerVR incorporated processors in smartphones and in AMD or NVIDIA video card augmented supercomputers [2] [3] [4] [5]. Similarly, the hybrid computing concept is being leveraged by select Intel Sandy Bridge processors, iPhone's A5 processors, and AMD's Fusion processors. Undoubtedly, the collaborative technology of CPU and GPU is being utilized in many different fields. This multitude of market-driven forces, along with traditional purposes such as driving displays and gaming, continues to push the demand for video processing forward. Note that, unlike specialized and custom designed processors, a popular consumer demand exists for GPU products. Furthermore, pervasive characteristic of GPU products typically leads to continual advances in hardware and software that increase performance as a function of time. Hence, the risk of technology fading away over time is mitigated for the GPU technology. The low cost entry point of GPU general-purpose computing is another resulting aspect of mass marketed GPUs. For example, the recently announced "Ouya" gaming system will retail for ≈$100 and also contain a dedicated NVIDIA Tegra 3 chip [6].

In addition to being ubiquitous, GPUs pack a large number of math function processing units since the parallel nature of graphics applications calls for a massively multithreaded architecture. For instance, a single GPU chip from AMD's Radeon HD 7970 contains 2,048 stream processors leading to a peak performance of 3.7 TFLOPS for single-precision operation [7]. As indicated by the theoretical performance, discrete graphics cards have become quite powerful in recent years, ideal for applications with high levels of data parallelism. For this project, the main objective was to leverage a GPU's floating-point capabilities for advancing military applications (that is, using graphics hardware for the purpose of number crunching rather than rendering images on a screen).

2. Mobile High Performance Computing

One of the visions behind this research was to investigate new compute capabilities for Soldiers that would be possible if they have ready access to supercomputing power. The tricky part is striking a balance between portability and performance. Imposing a limitation of physical dimension of a system to a size of a workstation, the project attempted to pack as much processing power as possible in this small form factor. Designed to support massive amounts of parallelism, graphics cards were the preferred hardware of choice to ramp up the raw floating-point compute capability in a workstation footprint system.

At the high-end of the spectrum, dual GPU consumer cards from AMD rated at 1.2 TFLOPS in double-precision are available. Just a few years ago, stacking four of these cards would equate to a theoretical peak performance of 4.8 TFLOPS and would place the system in the TOP500 list [8]. This system would need only a single outlet for power and no specialized room or space requirement for dedicated colling infrastracture. In other words, a five-year-old supercomputer can be constructed using off-the-shelf consumer products within a workstation form factor. Moreover, the cost associated with GPU general-purpose computing falls in the dollar range to where it can be personally financed. Thus, redundant placement of these resources is possible to alleviate frequently disconnected users in the field as described in [9]. Instead of a single point of failure, mobile high-performance computing systems can be distributed in a network.

The HPC workstation "box" represents a portable computational power in the field that allows for the possibility of on-board processing of complex computations. With enhanced computing resources, time-sensitive information can be extracted in near real-time, the fidelity of certain calculations can be improved, and greater amounts of data can be processed. For the mobile HPC study, three different hardware configurations of GPU-equipped workstations were procured for evaluations. All machines contain dual Intel Xeon X5675 CPUs and 24 GB of memory as a base configuration. The first machine has four AMD Radeon HD 6770 cards, the second machine has four NVIDIA GeForce GTX 580 boards, and the last machine has one NVIDIA GeForce GTX 590 model installed. Figure 1 illustrates the workstation from SuperMicro populated with four NVIDIA GPUs.

Fig. 1: Four NVIDIA GPUs installed in a workstation.

Unfortunately, improving performance costs power. The typical thermal design power (TDP) for high-end graphics cards is around 250 W for single GPU cards and 375 W for dual-GPU chip cards. TDP is a value calculated by the manufacturer that describes an average maximum power under normal and realistic use of hardware. It does not, however, indicate an absolute maximum, where TDP is typically 20 to 30 percent less than the maximum. With four single graphics chip boards, a 1.4 kW power supply handles the power requirement of the quad GPU workstation. To identify power source availability in a mobile setting, a literature search was performed on vehicle power system options and found that heavy-duty inverters can output 2 kW [10], and advanced custom-engineered power solutions can produce up to 30 kW at higher engine speeds for military vehicles integrated with a 45 kW generator [11]. The on-board vehicle power supply requirement manual by the U.S. Marine Corps specifies minimum output of 1.8 kW for inverters and 10 kW for the on-the-move High Mobility Multi-purpose Wheeled Vehicle (HMMWV)-based systems [12]. Therefore, a cursory look at these vehicle power specifications insinuates that the electrical power requirement of a multi-GPU workstation in a mobile platform is within attainable scope.

3. Ballistic Threat Surveillance Optimization Algorithm

The core computation in the ballistic threat surveillance optimization algorithm is the calculation of line-of-sight ballistic hit probability in an urban environment. Figure 2 displays the three-dimensional visualization of the input triangle mesh representing building structures and terrain information. As a variant of the ray-tracing algorithm, the first-hit ray-casting algorithm was designed and implemented to compute ballistic threat. To accelerate the calculations of ray-plane intersection, the quad-tree spatial decomposition was adopted to minimize the total number of triangle tests. In computing ray-plane intersections, a series of rays are cast out from an ememy's position (red forces) and propagated until the first intersection with a polygon is detected. In addition to computing the line-of-sight, a ballistic hit probability formula is applied to the calculation to model ballistic characteristics as a function of distance. Figure 3 illustrates an output result for the ground plane line-of-sight ballistic threat calculation, watermarked in red, for a single hostile position on the building's roof.

Fig. 2: Three-dimensional model representing an urban town, color coded by height.

Fig. 3: Single enemy soldier line-of-sight ballistic hit probability shaded in red.

The total floating-point operations of the ray-triangle intersection were calculated for the implementation to illustrate the computational intensity of the ballistic threat algorithm. The implemented ballistic application's input scenario has 480,000 rays (800 by 600) and 65,000 triangles as the input setup. Assuming roughly 91 floating-point operations for a ray-triangle calculation, a naive floating-point operation requirement equates to 2.8 trillion floating-point operations for a single enemy soldier's position. As the floating-point operation requirement reveals, the ray casting algorithm is a computationally expensive task exhibiting a challenge for achieving near real-time execution.

The algorithm supports a number of flexible scenarios by using an extensible XML format as scenario inputs that enables arbitrary multiplicity in entities and computations. The construction of scenarios for execution would be specified by the XML file. The technical objective was to support arbitrary numbers of simulation elements. The basic elements of a scenario are captured by the object types categorized as map, view, entity, and evaluator. As the name implies, the map field would contain terrain input information, which could be LIDAR or 3D polygon representation. The type view can represent the rendering engine, camera perspective, or window size. The type entity can specify enemy dismounted soldiers, observers, vehicles, or sensors. Once the functionality part of the ballistic threat field calculation was successfully implemented, the application was extended and augmented to solve for surveillance situations calling for a mathematical optimization.

The objective of the static optimization was to position reconnaissance Soldiers (friendly forces or "blue" forces) such that the ballistic threat is minimized while maximizing the line-of-sight observation to a point of interest. The goal is to determine the optimum locations of one or more Soldiers while minimizing their risk of being observed by the enemy (red forces). A Markov Chain Monte Carlo sampling technique was employed to obtain the optimal locations in a high-dimensional space generated by multiple entities. Markov Chain Monte Carlo provides a means to generate a sequence of random samples that explores the space of high probability [13].

The surveillance optimization application was interfaced with the World Wind software allowing for users to interactively place hostile soldiers and watch points interactively. World Wind is Java-based and an open-source, cross platform virtual globe software developed by NASA. World Wind's graphical user interface is shown in Figure 4. From the end user's perspective, World Wind Java provides an intuitive functionality and access to the compute intensive, OpenCL derived STDCL code. STDCL is a simplified interface to OpenCL [14] that reduces the verbosity of OpenCL setup process [15] [16] [17]. STDCL library eases the OpenCL programming burden and improves source code readability without adversely affecting performance.

Fig. 4: A screenshot of World Wind Java interface.

Figure 5 is the ballistic threat surveillance demonstration output for the case of two dismounted enemy soldiers and two watch points. The Monte Carlo optimization method computes the two optimal locations for the friend Soldiers (blue dots). For this example, watch points were placed on the entry points of the buildings and hostile guards were separately located; one on the building's roof and one in the open field. Using World Wind as the user interface, red and green dots were placed within the three-dimensional urban terrain map. Figure 6 shows extending the previous scenario by adding additional hostile forces and points of interest resulting in a total of four enemy forces and four observation points. The server-client model acts as a glue for the interface between the World Wind and the STDCL ballistic threat surveillance algorithm.

Fig. 5: Ballistic threat surveillance optimization demonstration. Red dots represents hostile forces, green dots denote watch points, and blue dots are optimal locations for surveillance.

Fig. 6: Output view for the scenario with four enemy forces (red) and four points of interest (green).

4. Timing Results

Since the ballistic threat surveillance application was constructed in OpenCL, it was quickly ported across Intel, NVIDIA, and AMD processors for benchmarking. In addition to portability, the OpenCL approach generates an efficient parallelized execution model for targeting architectures. The OpenCL development begins with a parallel paradigm perspective and targets higher throughput. Thereby addressing parallel computing from the very start. The application was tested on two different workstations; a standard workstation, equipped with 3 GHz Xeon dual-core 5160 processor and a Tesla C2050 graphics card, and a developmental workstation footprint high-performance system configured with dual 3.06 GHz Xeon hexa-core X5675 and four Radeon HD 6970 cards. Performance measurements were collected for CPUs and for GPU-augmented configurations. The execution runtime measurements for the four enemy soldiers and four watch points case are summarized in Figure 7.

The x86 implementation of OpenCL optimizes for execution on all available logical cores and enables SSE operations for mainstream CPUs. On a dual-core Intel processor, the execution time exceeded six minutes, which fails in creating a quick and responsive interactive user experience. Even dual

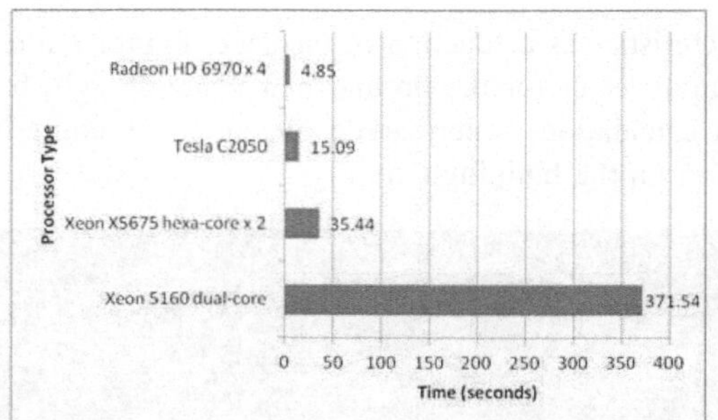

Fig. 7: Runtime measurements of four enemy soldiers and four watch points scenario showing the advantage of parallel computing.

hexa-core from Intel, equivalent to 24 logical cores, requires over half a minute to complete the ballistic threat surveillance optimization calculation. A single Tesla graphics card still requires over fifteen seconds to complete the four and four scenario computation. It is with four concurrent discrete GPU operation that the wait time falls within a reasonable window for an interactive experience for an operator. The timing results across different processor types convey how the architecture's throughput parallelism is greatly leveraged to accelerate the algorithm.

Running multiple GPUs in parallel presented unforeseen challenges during the development stage. Linux support for single node concurrent multiple GPU execution failed to work correctly depending on the version of the graphics drivers. The workload was divided and distributed across separate graphics cards, but the actual execution on each GPU was serialized, failing to achieve concurrent execution in all GPUs. Rolling back to the previous generation of driver fixed the multi-GPU issue. However, odd system behaviors were observed when reverting back to a previous graphics driver version, requiring a fresh installation. These types of behaviors highlight the relative immaturity of the GPU developmental tool chains compared to a stable and mature x86 environment.

5. Conclusion

Driven by the commercial market demand, theoretical computational power has become affordable to the general public. In terms of peak performance, previous generations of supercomputing capability are attainable in a smaller form factor with lower power. This project intended to evaluate the transfer of computational capacity into a workstation footprint to assist in tactical computing. However, optimally leveraging the underlying compute resources rests on software development. Regardless of processor type, embracing parallelism is the key for achieving higher performance. Even the mainstream processors from Intel and AMD require parallel programming to take advantage of their multiple cores. The allure of OpenCL is the code portability across different architectures. Once an algorithm is developed in OpenCL framework, it can run on AMD graphics cards,

NVIDIA boards, and Intel processors. The OpenCL approach, although low-level, allows developers to circumvent being restricted to a particular vendor or architecture.

This research explored a deployable HPC system in a workstation footprint. With the goal of supporting a realistic tactical application, the ballistic threat surveillance optimization algorithm was developed and implemented for assessment. The amount of parallelism and the computational requirement of line-of-sight hit probability calculations make the algorithm a good candidate for justifying tactical HPC. The combination of mobile HPC and an intuitive software interface delivers enhanced capability out in the field for information and processing superiority. This demonstration manifests the feasibility of solving what was once considered computationally expensive tasks requiring a conventional HPC facility in a workstation dimension.

6. Future Work

Moving forward, plans include testing the application in a different set of detailed three-dimensional polygon representations of urban environments and assessing the effects and limitations of map input sizes. Work is currently underway for implementing an extension to support ray-tracing by taking reflections and refractions into account. Here, secondary rays further increase the computational intensity calling for innovative hardware and software solutions to achieve interactive tactical computing.

Another natural continuation of this project is to add realism by supporting dynamic entities where red forces are not stationary but able to move around the map. As a single entity multiplies into many points in space to represent this dynamic scenario, the processing requirement of the application is anticipated to increase dramatically.

References

[1] "Top500 list - november 2012," http://www.top500.org/list/2012/11.

[2] "Powervr graphics driving mass market smartphone graphics adoption," http://www.imgtec.com/corporate/newsdetail.asp?NewsID=669, February 2012.

[3] E. Guizzo, "China builds world's fastest supercomputer," November 2010. [Online]. Available: http://spectrum.ieee.org/tech-talk/computing/hardware/china-builds-worlds-fastest-supercomputer

[4] "Tsubame2 system architecture," http://tsubame.gsic.titech.ac.jp/en/tsubame2-system-architecture.

[5] R. Vuduc and K. Czechowski, "What gpu computing means for high-end systems," *Micro, IEEE*, vol. 31, no. 4, pp. 74–78, July-Aug.

[6] D. Gross. (2013, March) Here comes Ouya, the $99 gaming console. [Online]. Available: http://www.cnn.com/2013/03/12/tech/gaming-gadgets/ouya-julie-uhrman-sxsw/

[7] "Amd radeon hd 7970 graphics," http://www.amd.com/us/products/desktop/graphics/7000/7970/Pages/radeon-7970.aspx.

[8] "Top500 list - november 2006 (401-500)," http://www.top500.org/list/2006/11/500.

[9] M. Flynn, "Memo to the department of defense," August 2009.

[10] "Power conversion solutions guide," Analytic Systems, Tech. Rep., August 2009.

[11] "Advanced power management for military vehicles," BAE Systems, Tech. Rep., 2007.

[12] "On-board vehicle power systems for legacy miltary vehicles," 2007.

[13] W. K. Hastings, "Monte Carlo sampling methods using Markov chains and their applications," *Biometrika*, vol. 57, no. 1, pp. 97–109, Apr. 1970. [Online]. Available: http://dx.doi.org/10.2307/2334940

[14] *STDCL: A Simplified C Interface for OpenCL*, Brown Deer Technology, 2011, hypertext at http://www.browndeertechnology.com/docs/stdcl-manual.html.

[15] "Opencl - the open standard for parallel programming of heterogeneous systems," http://www.khronos.org/opencl, accessed: 11/12/2012.

[16] A. Munshi, B. R. Gaster, T. G. Mattson, J. Fung, and D. Ginsburg, *OpenCL Programming Guide*. Addison-Wesley Professional, 2011.

[17] J. Stone, D. Gohara, and G. Shi, "Opencl: A parallel programming standard for heterogeneous computing systems," *Computing in Science Engineering*, vol. 12, no. 3, pp. 66 –73, may-june 2010.

Exploiting Heterogeneous Systems: Keccak on OpenCL

Allan Mariano de Souza [1], Fábio Dacêncio Pereira [1], and Edward David Moreno [2]
[1] Department of Computer Science/ COMPSI,University Center Euripides of Marília, Marília, Brazil
[2]Department of Computer Science/DCOMP, Federal University of Sergipe, Aracaju, Brazil

Abstract - *Using graphics processing units (GPUs) in high-performance parallel computing continues to become more prevalent, often as part of a heterogeneous system. CUDA and OpenCL are APIs and enables programmers to developer GPGPU applications and softwares to massively parallel processors. In October 2, 2012, NIST announced the winner of its five-year competition to select a new cryptographic hash algorithm, one of the fundamental tools of modern information security. This work is proposed to explore the winner algorithm of the SHA-3 competition, the Keccak, and subsequently implement the propose heterogeneous platform architecture on OpenCL with intuit to obtain performance data. Finally, will be compared OpenCL implementation of keccak with CPU and GPU execution.*

Keywords: GPGPU; OpenCL; Heterogeneous Systems; SHA-3 Keccak;

1 Introduction

In recent years, more and more multi-core/many-core processors are superseding sequential ones. Increasing parallelism, rather than increasing clock rate, has become the primary engine of processor performance growth, and this trends likely to continue [1]. Particularly, today's GPUs (Graphic Processing Units), greatly outperforming CPUs in arithmetic throughput and memory bandwidth, can use hundreds of parallel processor cores to execute tens of thousands of parallel threads [2]. Researchers and developers are becoming increasingly interested in harnessing this power for general purpose computing, an effort known collectively as GPGPU (General-Purpose computing on the GPU)[3], to rapidly solve large problems with substantial inherent parallelism.

CUDA (Compute Unified Device Architecture) and OpenCL (Open Computing Language) are APIs and enables programmers to developer GPGPU applications and softwares to massively parallel processors.

One of the methods to ensure information integrity is the use of hash functions, which generates a stream of bytes (hash) which must be unique. But most functions can no longer prevent malicious attacks and ensure that the information have just a hash. In order to solve this problem, the National Institute of Standards and Technology (NIST) convened the scientific community through a competition to create a new hash function standard, called SHA-3.

NIST received significant feedback from the cryptographic community. Based on the public feedback and internal reviews of the second-round candidates, NIST selected five SHA-3 finalists - BLAKE, Grøstl, JH, Keccak, and Skein to advance to the final round of the competition on December 9, 2010, which ended the second round of the competition[6].

In October 2, 2012, NIST announced the winner of the SHA-3 competition and the winner was Keccak and now will become official NIST's SHA-3 hash algorithm.

In this context, this work aims to study the winner SHA-3 algorithm, The keccak and then propose an implementation for heterogeneous systems using OpenCL to obtain performance data and comparison with CPU and GPU execution.

2 CUDA vs OpenCL

CUDA and OpenCL are fast, and on GPU devices they are much faster than the CPU for data-parallel codes, with 10X speedups commonly seen on data-parallel problems. Both CUDA and OpenCL can fully utilize the hardware. They are both entirely sufficient to extract all the performance available in whatever hardware device

Both CUDA and OpenCL can fully utilize the hardware. They are both entirely sufficient to extract all the performance available in whatever hardware device. Both OpenCL and CUDA provide a general-purpose model for data parallelism as well as low-level access to hardware, but only OpenCL provides an open, industry-standard framework. As such, it has garnered support from nearly all processor manufacturers including AMD, Intel, and NVIDIA, as well as others that serve the mobile and embedded computing markets. As a result, applications developed in OpenCL are now portable across a variety of GPUs and CPUs.

Spafford's ran ORNL's Scalable Heterogeneous Computing Benchmark Suite (SHOC) that has been optimized for both CUDA and OpenCL, and found that OpenCL can match CUDA performance on most of the basic math kernels[15].

GPU software maker AccelerEyes has seen CUDA and OpenCL performance equalize. The company, which recently released OpenCL-powered beta versions of their two flagship software products, ArrayFire and Jacket, has found that for most kernel codes, the two technologies now exhibit similar performance[15].

The Future Technology Group at Oak Ridge National Lab (ORNL), has been benchmarking the two technologies for some time and is now convinced that OpenCL performance is now on par with that of CUDA. The figure 2.1 shows the results of the benchmarking.

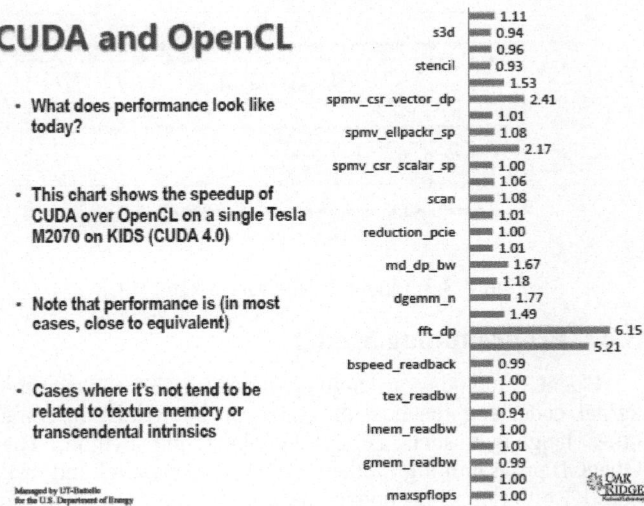

Figure 2.1: Benchmarking of performance CUDA and OpenCL [15]

Due to the high portability across a variety of GPUs and CPUs, the high performance power and your growing of OpenCL. This paper present an proposed implementation of keccak's algorithm for a heterogeneous systems using OpenCL.

3 OpenCL

OpenCL is an industry standard cross-platform and parallel-computing for programming heterogeneous applications that can be formed collection of CPUs, GPUs and other computing devices organized into a single platform. It's more than a language, OpenCL is an framework for parallel programming and includes a language, API, libraries an runtime system to support software development [4].

Single programs written on OpenCL can run on a wide range of systems, from cell phones, to laptops, to nodes in massive super-computers. No other parallel programming standard has such a wide reach [5].

The core idea behind OpenCL can be describe using follow hierarchy models. Platform model(3.1), execution model(3.2), memory model(3.3) and programming model(3.4).

3.1 Platform Model

The platform model consists of a host that are connected to one or more OpenCL devices (CPUs, GPUs, PDAs), The OpenCL devices are divided into one ore more compute units (CUs) which are further divided into one or more processing elements (PEs). The computations that are executed on OpenCL devices occur within the processing elements [4].

The figure 3.1 illustrate the OpenCL platform model that was described.

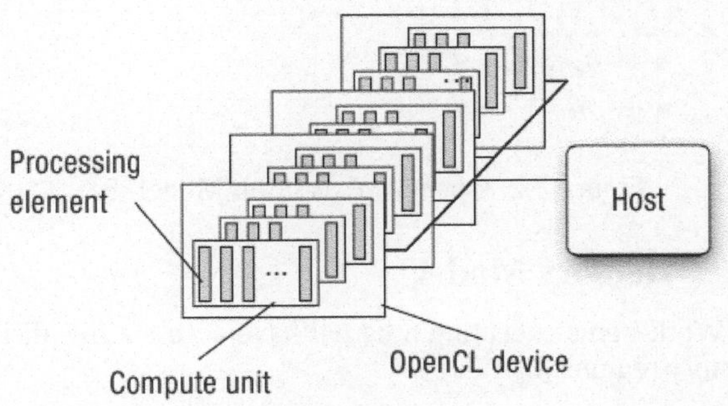

Figure 3.1: OpenCL Platform Model [5].

3.2 Platform Model

Execution of an OpenCL program occurs in two parts: kernels that are parallel parts or functions executed on one or more OpenCL devices and a host program serial parts executed on the host. The host program defines the context and parameters for kernels and manages their execution [4].

The core of the OpenCL execution is defined by how kernels are executed. When the host program submits a kernel for execution an index space are defined called NDRange, where these index can be one dimensional (1D), tow dimensional (2D) or three dimensional (3D). Each point in these index space are called work-item and each work-item are an instance of the kernel and each work-item has index (global ID) to compute memory addresses and make control decisions.

Work-items are organized into work-groups. The work-groups provide a more coarse-grained decomposition of the index space. Work-groups are assigned a unique work-group ID with the same dimensionality as the index space used for the work-items. Work-items are assigned a unique local ID within a work-group so that a single work-item can be uniquely identified by its global ID or by a combination of its local ID and work-group ID. The work-items in a given work-group execute concurrently on the processing elements of a single compute unit [4].

The figure 3.2 are an example of how the global IDs, local IDs, and work-groups indices are related for a two-dimensional NDRange. Other parameters of the index space are defined in the figure. The shaded block has a global ID of (gx, g y) = (6, 5) and a work-group plus local ID of (wx, w y) = (1, 1) and (lx, ly) =(2, 1).

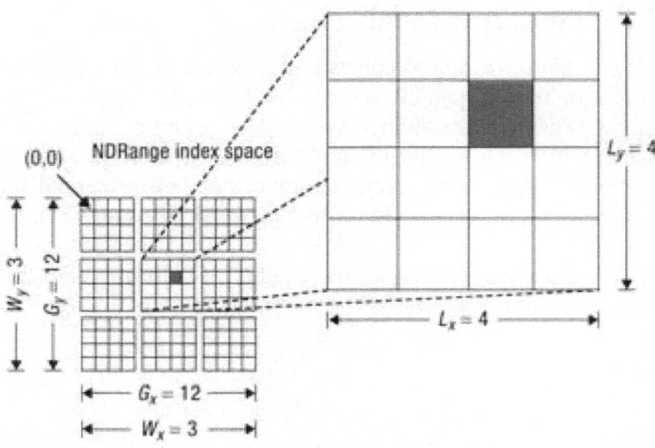

Figure 3.2: OpenCL Execution Model [5].

3.3 Memory Model

Work-items executing a kernel have access a five distinct memory regions [5].

- **Host memory:** This memory region is visible only to the host. As with most details concerning the host, OpenCL defines only how the host memory interacts with OpenCL objects and constructs.
- **Global Memory:** This memory region permits read/write access to all work-items in all work-groups. Work-items can read from or write to any element of a memory object. Reads and writes to global memory may be cached depending on the capabilities of the device.
- **Constant memory:** This memory region of global memory remains constant during the execution of a kernel. The host allocates and initializes memory objects placed into constant memory. Work-items have read-only access to these objects.
- **Local memory:** This memory region is local to a work-group. This memory region can be used to allocate variables that are shared by all work-items in that work-group. It may be implemented as dedicated regions of memory on the OpenCL device. Alternatively, the local memory region may be mapped onto sections of the global memory.
- **Private memory:** This region of memory is private to a work-item. Variables defined in one work-item's private memory are not visible to other work-items.

The figure 3.3 shows a summary of the memory model in OpenCL and how the different memory regions interact with the platform model.

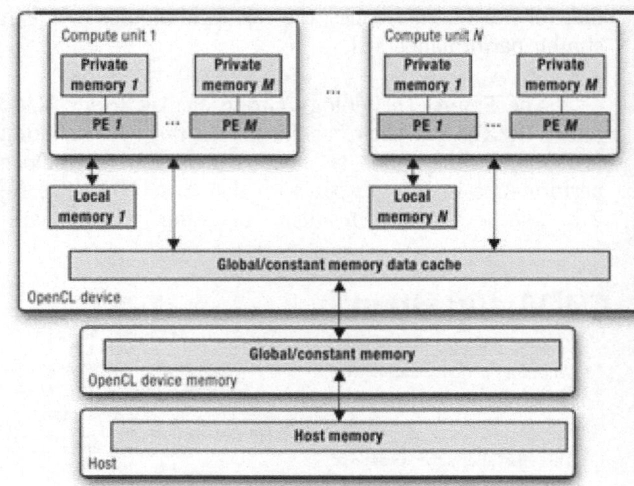

Figure 3.3: OpenCL Memory Model [5].

3.4 Programming Model

OpenCL includes an language based on C99 to write the kernel code, and the host program can be written in some other languages such as: C/C++, Java and Python. The OpenCL programming model supports data parallel and task parallel programming models, as well as supporting hybrids of these tow models.

4 Keccak Algorithm

The design philosophy of Keccak is the hermetic sponge strategy [7]. It uses the sponge construction for having provable security against all generic attacks. It calls a permutation that should not have structural properties with the exception of a compact description[8].

Keccak is a family of hash functions that is based on the sponge construction, and hence is a sponge function family. In Keccak, the underlying function is a permutation chosen in a set of seven Keccak-f permutations, denoted Keccak-f[b], where $b \in \{25, 50, 100, 200, 400, 800, 1600\}$ is the width of the permutation. The width of the permutation is also the width of the state in the sponge construction[9].

The state is organized as an array of 5×5 lanes, each of length $w \in \{1, 2, 4, 8, 16, 32, 64\}$ (b=25w). When implemented on a 64-bit processor, a lane of Keccak-f[1600] can be represented as a 64-bit CPU word. For obtain the Keccak[r,c] sponge function, with parameters capacity c and bitrate r, if we apply the sponge construction to Keccak-f[r+c] and by applying a specific padding to the message input.

All the operations on the indices are done modulo 5. A denotes the complete permutation state array, and A[x,y] denotes a particular lane in that state. B[x,y], C[x],D[x] are intermediate variables. The constants *r*[*x*,*y*] are the rotation offsets, while RC[i] are the round constants. rot(W,r) is the usual bitwise cyclic shift operation, moving bit at position I into position i+r (modulo the lane size). The constants r[x, y] are the cyclic shift offsets and are specified in the table I.

TABLE I - CONSTANTS R[X,Y] – KECCAK ALGORITHM

	$x=3$	$x=4$	$x=0$	$x=1$	$x=2$
$y=2$	25	39	3	10	43
$y=1$	55	20	36	44	6
$y=0$	28	27	0	1	62
$y=4$	56	14	18	2	61
$y=3$	21	8	41	45	15

The constants RC[i] (see Table II) are the round constants. The following table specifies their values in hexadecimal notation for lane size 64. For smaller sizes they must be truncated.

TABLE II - CONSTANTS RC[I]- – KECCAK ALGORITHM

RC[0]	0x0000000000000001	RC[12]	0x000000008000808B
RC[1]	0x0000000000008082	RC[13]	0x800000000000008B
RC[2]	0x800000000000808A	RC[14]	0x8000000000008089
RC[3]	0x8000000080008000	RC[15]	0x8000000000008003
RC[4]	0x000000000000808B	RC[16]	0x8000000000008002
RC[5]	0x0000000080000001	RC[17]	0x8000000000000080
RC[6]	0x8000000080008081	RC[18]	0x000000000000800A
RC[7]	0x8000000000008009	RC[19]	0x800000008000000A
RC[8]	0x000000000000008A	RC[20]	0x8000000080008081
RC[9]	0x0000000000000088	RC[21]	0x8000000000008080
RC[10]	0x0000000080008009	RC[22]	0x0000000080000001
RC[11]	0x000000008000000A	RC[23]	0x8000000080008008

The keccak first start with the description of Keccak-f in the pseudo-code below. The number of rounds nr depends on the permutation width, and is given by nr = 12+2l, where 2l = w. This gives 24 rounds for Keccak-f[1600].

```
Round[b](A,RC) {
θ step
C[x] = A[x,0] xor A[x,1] xor A[x,2]
       xor A[x,3] xor A[x,4],
D[x] = C[x-1] xor rot(C[x+1],1),
A[x,y] = A[x,y] xor D[x],
ρ and π steps
B[y,2*x+3*y] = rot(A[x,y], r[x,y]),
χ step
  A[x,y] = B[x,y] xor ((not B[x+1,y])
and B[x+2,y]),
ι step
A[0,0] = A[0,0] xor RC
return A
}
```

The four steps (Θ,ρπ,χ,ι) of hash function keccak have data dependency of first level, ie, the current step depends only of the outcome of the previous step. This feature allows exploring techniques of parallelism in heterogeneous systems. In this context, this paper presents a proposed architecture that exploits the parallelism using OpenCL.

5 Keccak Implementations

Pierre-Louis Cayrel[11] present an implementation of the Keccak hash function family on graphics cards, using NVIDIA's CUDA framework. That implementation allows to choose one function out of the hash function family and hash arbitrary documents. In addition he presents the first ready-to-use implementation of the tree mode of Keccak which is even more suitable for parallelization.

Guillaume Sevestre[12] presents a Graphics Processing Unit implementation of Keccak cryptographic hash function, in a parallel tree hash mode to exploit the parallel compute capacity of the graphics cards using CUDA.

In your work Xu Guo[10] describe a consistent and systematic approach to move a SHA-3 hardware benchmark process from FPGA prototyping to ASIC implementation, and we present our latest results for ASIC evaluation of the 14 second round SHA-3 candidates.

Perreira [13] present an keccak's implementation on FPGA using pipeline architecture with intuit to obtain performance data.

TABLE III. KECCAK'S IMPLEMENTATIONS

Authors	Title	Implementation
[11]	GPU Implementation of the Keccak Hash Function Family	NVIDIA GTX 295 GPU
[12]	Implementation of Keccak hash function in Tree mode on Nvidia GPU	Core i5-750 2.6 Ghz Nvidia GTS 250
[13]	Pipeline architecture	Virtex 5
[10]	Fair and Comprehensive Performance Evaluation of 14 Second Round SHA-3 ASIC implementation	FPGA implementation
		ASIC implementation

6 Keccak on OpenCL

In this section the approach to the parallelization of Keccak will be presented. We made two implementations to try to reduce the time needed to the hash computation by simultaneously execution the keccak's algorithm. The first implementation, the host program was written in python and to execute the kernel we utilized a unique work-group with the same size of NDRange specified where all work-items in the NDRange space computate the keccak's algorithm. The second implementation we written the host program in C language to make some tests with AMD CodeXL, and the NDRange space was divided in work-groups of 256 work-items, than we compare if has any difference between C and python's implementation.

The original Keccak structure have been almost completely maintained in this solution, even thought some adjustments have been made to maximize the performance on GPU.

The OpenCL architecture supports thousands of work-items in hardware. The host program of our implementation was written in python and kernel function on OpenCL. We utilize different sizes of NDRange and use all work-items in the NDRange to execute the four steps (Θ,ρπ,χ,ι) of keccak algorithm. To execute the tests we started with 25 work-items executed se same round of keccak and ended with 1 bilion of work-items executing the algorithm. The tests on GPU was made in an AMD/ATI Radeon HD 6400M series that has 160 Stream Processing Units, and the CPU's tests was made in a Intel Core I5. To calculate the time of the execution's kernel we got the time before the submission of the kernel to execution (T1) and the time after to kernel's execution (T2) and the result of time is the difference of T2 and T1 (T2 – T1).

The figure 6.1 shows an OpenCL kernel pseudo-code to demonstrate the execution of the first test with 25 work-items. Each work-item will instantiate the kernel function and execute completely the code.

```
1  __kernel void Keccak(__global __constant uint64_t *data,
2                       __global __constant uint64_t *out)
3  {
4      int id = get_global_id(0);
5
6      if(id < 25){
7          for(int i=0; i< ROUNDS; i++){
8              Keccak_f(data);
9          }
10         out[id] = data[id];
11     }
12 }
```

Figure 6.1: OpenCL keccak's kernel

Lines one and two shows the definition and parameters of the kernel that will be executed per all work-items. The first parameter is the input state (matrix A 5x5), and the second parameter is the out of state after keccak-f permutation. The variable id defined in line four receive the global_ID of each work-item.

Line 6 to 8 indicates the core execution of keccak but just will be executed per work-items that have id less than 25. Finally line 10 represents the attribution of the variable out that will receive the result of keccak permutation and will be transfered to the host program.

Table IV shows the python's implementation with the numbers of work-items and the time that all work-items led to execute the algorithm. The results was compared with GPU and CPU execution.

TABLE IV. KECCAK'S IMPLEMENTATION IN PYTHON + OPENCL

No. Work-items	**Time in seconds**	
	CPU Intel core I5	GPU AMD Radeon HD 6400M
25	0.0001890659332	0.0013608932495
50	0.0002439022064	0.0007479190826
100	0.0002799034118	0.0017559528350
500	0.0008549690259	0.0007867813110
1000	0.0019378662110	0.0018019676208
50000	0.0698390007019	0.0070748329163
100000	0.130648136139	0.0138649940491
500000	0.6393702030	0.06292104721
1000000	1.29261088371	0.123764038086
50000000	62.931710	6.18758797
100000000	125.824690104	12.0365948677
500000000	628.15016818	60.4733588
1000000000	1258.75649595	119.857429981

The results of this first implementation shows that GPU execution is approximately 10 times faster than CPU execution.

AMD CodeXL is a comprehensive tool suite that enables developers to harness the benefits of AMD CPUs, GPUs and APUs. It includes powerful GPU debugging, comprehensive GPU and CPU profiling, and static OpenCL kernel analysis capabilities, enhancing accessibility for software developers to enter the era of heterogeneous computing. AMD CodeXL is available both as a Visual Studio extension and a standalone user interface application for Windows and Linux[14].

To make some tests with CodeXL we have to written the host program to C language and we make some changes in the kernel to collect more informations of the execution.

Figure 6.2 shows details of the kernel execution, and some additional information such as, duration of kernel's execution, global size and local size, kernel occupancy and others. the results were collected with AMD CodeXL.

Name	=	keccak_f
Device	=	Caicos
Command Type	=	CL_COMMAND_NDRANGE_KERNEL
Queued Time	=	192.946 millisecond
Submit Time	=	193.000 millisecond
Start Time	=	194.044 millisecond
End Time	=	223.261 millisecond
Duration	=	29.217 milliseconds
clEnqueue API Name	=	clEnqueueNDRangeKernel
clEnqueue API Start Time	=	192.909 millisecond
clEnqueue API End Time	=	192.985 millisecond
clEnqueue API Duration	=	75.401 microseconds
clEnqueue Call Index	=	27
Global Work Size	=	{256000}
Local Work Size	=	{256}
Kernel Occupancy	=	12.50%

Figure 6.2: Results colected with CodeXL.

The C implementation shows the same results of the python's implementation, the GPU execution is approximately 10 times faster than CPU execution. The table V shows some results of C implementation.

TABLE V. KECCAK'S IMPLEMENTATION IN C + OPENCL

No. work-items	Time in seconds	
	CPU Intel core I5	GPU AMD Radeon HD 6400M
2560	0.00544497	0.00247133
256000	0.343549	0.0292091
256000000	295.781	29.3051

7 Conclusions

This article presented an overview on the use of GPU to accelerate processing algorithms dedicated as keccak. Were presented CUDA and OpenCL platforms and a study showing that OpenCL is improving with each generation.

In the sequence was described the main module of architecture OpenCL and structure of the keccak algorithm. Keccak implementations on different technologies were presented. This algorithm is in evidence, as was recently selected as the new standard SHA-3 hash functions.

The objective of this work was not to develop the best implementation of keccak in GPU, but the use of OpenCL as an alternative for high performance applications.

For this, two implementations were coded. The first implementation, the host program was written in python and the second in C language to make some tests with AMD CodeXL: a comprehensive tool suite that enables developers to harness the benefits of AMD CPUs, GPUs and APUs.

The results shows a speedup of approximately 10 times between the CPU and GPU implementation. This gain can be further enhanced with other techniques of parallelism, such as pipeline and distribution of items running on tree model. However the aim was achieved showing that a basic implementation can achieve good level of performance.

8 References

[1] M. Garland, S. Le Grand, J. Nickolls, J. Anderson, J. Hardwick, S. Morton, E. Phillips, Y. Zhang, and V. Volkov, “Parallel Computing Experiences with CUDA,” IEEE Micro, vol. 28, pp. 13–27, July 2008.

[2] J. Nickolls and W. J. Dally, “The GPU Computing Era,” IEEE Micro, vol. 30, pp. 56–69, March 2010. 2. Oxford: Clarendon, 1892, pp.68-73.

[3] Jianbin Fang, Ana Lucia Varbanescu and Henk Sips, “A Comprehensive Performance Comparison of CUDA and OpenCL”, International Conference on Parallel Processing , 2011

[4] Khronos OpenCL Working Group, The OpenCL Specification, 2011.

[5] Aaftab Munshi, et al. OpenCL Programming Guide, 2011.

[6]FIPS 180-3, Secure Hash Standard, Cryptographic Hash Algorithm Competition, , available from http://csrc.nist.gov/groups/ST/ hash/sha-3/index.html, 2011

[7] Daemen, J. et al. “Sponge Functions”. 2011, available from http://sponge.noekeon.org/Sponge Functions.pdf

[8] G. Bertoni, J. Daemen, M. Peeters and G. Van Assche, The Keccak reference, 2011.

[9] G. Bertoni, J. Daemen, M. Peeters and G. Van Assche, The Keccak SHA-3 submission, 2011.

[10]X. Guo, S. Huang, L. Nazhandali and P. Schaumont, Fair and Comprehensive Performance Evaluation of 14 Second Round SHA-3 ASIC Implementations, Second SHA-3 Candidate Conference, 2010

[11]Pierre-Louis Cayrel, Gerhard Hoffmann, Michael Schneider, GPU Implementation of the Keccak Hash Function Family, SERSC International Journal of Security and Its Applications Vol. 5 No 4, October, 2011.

[12]Guillaune Sevestre, Implementation of Keccak hash function in Tree mode on Nvidia GPU, 2011

[13]Pereira, F. D. ; Ordonez, E. D. M.; Sakai, I. D. Hash function keccak: exploring parallelism with pipeline. In: PDCS- Parallel and Distributed Computing and Systems, 2011.

[14]AMD Developer Central, AMD CodeXL: comprehensive debugging profiling and analysis tool for CPU, GPU and APU. Available from http://developer.amd.com/tools/heterogeneous-computing/codexl, 2012

[15] Michael Feldman, OpenCL Gains Ground On CUDA, available from: http://www.hpcwire.com/hpcwire/2012-02-28/opencl_gains_ground_on_cuda.html

GPU Acceleration of a Genetic Algorithm for the Synthesis of FSM-based Bimodal Predictors

Martin Burtscher[1] **and Hassan Rabeti**[2]
[1]Department of Computer Science, Texas State University, San Marcos, TX, USA
[2]Department of Mathematics, Texas State University, San Marcos, TX, USA

Abstract - *This paper presents a fast GPU implementation of a genetic algorithm for synthesizing bimodal predictor FSMs of a given size. Bimodal predictors, i.e., predictors that make binary yes/no predictions, are ubiquitous in microprocessors. Many of these predictors are based on finite-state machines (FSMs). However, there are countless possible FSMs and even heuristic searches for finding good FSMs can be slow when billions of predictions need to be assessed. We designed such a search heuristic that maps well onto GPU hardware. It is based on a multi-start genetic algorithm. On our six traces, the resulting FSMs are 1% to 29% more accurate than saturating up/down counters. On a Kepler-based GTX 680, the CUDA implementation evaluates 18 to 73 billion predictions per second, which is 14 to 18 times faster than a multicore version running on a hex-core Xeon X5690 with hyper-threading.*

Keywords: GPGPU, genetic algorithm, automated design, finite-state machines, bimodal predictors

1. Introduction

Modern processors contain large numbers of finite-state machines (FSMs), many of which are used as bimodal predictors. Such FSMs can be found in branch predictors [13, 15, 19], memory-disambiguation hardware [20], cache way predictors [2], confidence estimators [9], and selectors in hybrid predictors [14]. Their purpose is to improve performance and/or reduce power consumption [17]. We use FSMs to compress program execution traces in real time [16]. In nearly all of these applications, the FSM has to repeatedly make a 1-bit prediction, *i.e.*, a bimodal prediction, and is then updated with the true 1-bit outcome. *E.g.*, for every branch instruction, an FSM might predict whether it will be taken or not. After the branch has executed, the FSM is updated with the true direction the branch took. The goal is to make as many correct predictions as possible. However, there are countless choices of FSMs and it is generally unknown which FSM is the best for a given task.

An n-bit FSM holds n bits of internal state, which serves as its 'memory'. The 1-bit prediction is a function of the current state, such as choosing one of the n bits. During an update, the FSM transitions from the current state to a new state based on the input (true outcome) bit. Conceptually, a bimodal n-bit FSM implements a transition table like the one shown in Figure 1, where the n bits of current state are concatenated with the input bit to form an address (index) to select a row in the table, which holds the next n-bit state. As the boxed-in letters in Figure 1 illustrate, the transition table consists of $n \times 2^{n+1}$ independent bits, yielding 2 ^ ($n \times 2^{n+1}$) possible n-bit FSMs. Whereas not all bit assignments result in meaningful FSMs (*e.g.*, there are redundancies and not every FSM can reach all states), the number of possibilities grows super-exponentially with n. There are 16 possible 1-bit FSMs but 65,536 possible 2-bit and 281.5 trillion possible 3-bit bimodal FSMs. Hence, using an exhaustive search to determine the best n-bit FSM is not computationally tractable on current workstations for $n > 2$.

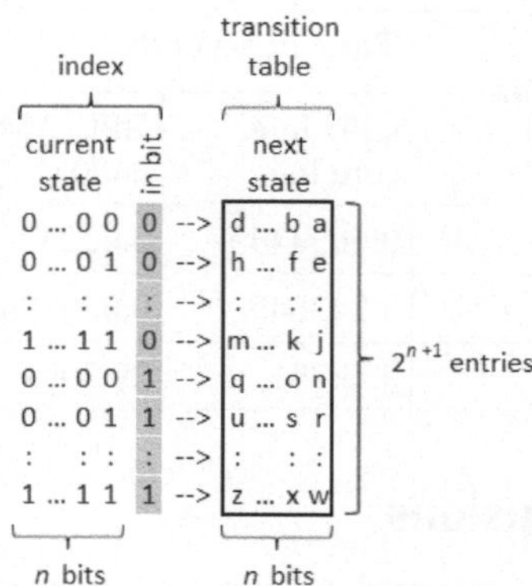

Figure 1. State transition table of an n-bit bimodal FSM

A saturating up/down counter is a specific bimodal FSM that works as follows. Its n-bit state is interpreted as an n-bit value. When updated, the value is incremented if the input bit is 1 and decremented otherwise. However, the value is never incremented above 2^n-1 and never decremented below 0, *i.e.*, it saturates at the minimum and maximum. The prediction is the most significant bit (MSB). The saturating up/down counter is so called because it counts the number of 0 and 1 outcomes that were encountered in the recent past. If there were many zeros, the count is low and the MSB a '0'. Conversely, if there were many ones, the count is high and the MSB a '1'. Hence, this FSM essentially makes a majority prediction over the recently seen events. The saturating up/down counter works well in practice, which is why it is widely used. However, it has known weaknesses. For example, it performs poorly on sequences of alternating zeroes and ones. Also, it tends to make the same prediction after a '1 1 0 1' sequence as it does after a '1 0 1 1' sequence.

Whereas there is generally only one piece of logic that implements the FSM in hardware, the *n*-bit state itself is often replicated, resulting in an array of states, to improve the prediction accuracy by retaining separate state for different instructions, cache lines, *etc*. Some of the lower bits of the program counter (PC) of the executing instruction are typically used to select an entry in the state array.

Since performing an exhaustive search for finding the best FSM is computationally intractable for all but the smallest problem sizes, heuristic approaches for finding near-optimal solutions need to be used. Examples include simulated annealing [1], genetic algorithms [8], ant colony optimization [3], and multi-start search algorithms [5]. We use a combination of a genetic and a multi-start algorithm because it maps particularly well to current GPUs.

Our algorithm generates multiple sets of random transition tables (*i.e.*, FSMs) and then attempts to improve each set independently using a genetic algorithm (GA) until a locally optimal solution is reached. In each GA step, the FSMs of the current 'population' are evaluated to determine how many correct predictions they make on a given input. (The input is a trace of 1-bit events and their corresponding PC values to index the state array.) Then, the next generation of FSMs is created using mutation and crossover operations. A quarter of the new population is generated by mutating random bits of the best-performing FSM from the previous generation, that is, each bit in the state-transition table is randomly flipped with 25% probability. The remaining three quarters of the new population is generated by combining the best FSM with a randomly selected FSM from the previous generation (we chose these values because they result in a simple implementation and good performance). Each of these crossovers uses a different random bit mask to select which bits should be taken from the best FSM. Each bit has a 75% chance of coming from the better 'parent' FSMs. The best FSM is copied over into the new generation to ensure that the performance never drops.

This paper makes the following contributions.

- It presents the first GPUGA for optimizing predictor FSMs.
- It describes how to efficiently map this algorithm to GPUs and compares its performance to multicore CPU code.
- It provides results for Fermi- and Kepler-based GPUs.
- It analyzes, visualizes, and discusses the best FSMs.
- The CUDA source code is publicly available at http://cs.txstate.edu/~burtscher/research/FSM_GA/.

The rest of this paper is organized as follows. Section 2 explains the CUDA implementation in detail. Section 3 summarizes related work. Section 4 presents the evaluation methodology. Section 5 evaluates the parameter space and discusses the performance results. Section 6 concludes the paper with a summary.

2. CUDA implementation

The combination of a multi-start search with a genetic algorithm for determining well-performing FSMs was chosen because it is particularly well suited for GPU acceleration. It avoids potential performance hurdles such as uncoalesced memory accesses, thread divergence, and inter-block dependencies. Moreover, it naturally maps to the GPU's block and thread hierarchy and takes advantage of the block scheduler for load balancing.

Each population of FSMs is evaluated in its own block. This makes the blocks independent except for a single atomicMax operation to determine the globally best FSM. Each GA-based search terminates when the performance of the best FSM has not improved over the previous generation. This means that some blocks have to evaluate more generations than other blocks do, resulting in load imbalance. However, the GPU's block scheduler automatically launches another block as soon as one block has finished executing, thus keeping all SMs busy until the scheduler runs out of new blocks towards the end.

For all but very short inputs, the innermost loop that evaluates the prediction accuracy is the most time consuming code section. It iterates over the trace entries, contains no control transfers in its body and is therefore thread divergence-free, reads the trace data in a fully coalesced manner from global memory and also performs fully coalesced reads and writes of the state arrays in local memory. The code exclusively uses integer data and operations.

Users can parameterize the implementation along four dimensions: (1) the population count, which determines the number of blocks, (2) the population size, which determines the number of threads per block, (3) the number of entries per state array, and (4) the size of the FSM. For clarity, we only focus on 3-bit FSMs in this paper.

Given the above assignments and current GPU specifications, the population count has to be between 1 and 65,535 on Fermi and between 1 and 2^{31}-1 on Kepler, the population size needs to be between 1 and 1024, and the number of entries in the state arrays has to be a power of two (for efficiency) between 1 and 32,768 due to local-memory size limitations. All FSM state arrays are initialized to zero. The LSB of the FSM's state is used for making predictions.

To maximally exploit the GPU hardware, it is advisable to select a population count that is substantially larger than the number of blocks the SMs can execute concurrently (to fully load the GPU and to allow the scheduler to balance the load). The population size should be a multiple of 32 (to fill warps entirely) and at least 192 on Fermi (because it can run up to 8 blocks per SM) and 128 on Kepler (because it can run up to 16 blocks per SM) to reach 1536 and 2048 threads per SM, respectively. Larger population counts and sizes result in longer runtimes but potentially also better results. The number of entries in the state arrays is likely problem dependent, but shorter arrays result in better data-cache performance and therefore better overall throughput.

The input trace consists of a sequence of 2-byte values, one value per event, where the least significant bit is the true outcome and the remaining 15 bits represent the bottom 15 bits of the PC (that are not always zero). The only constraint is that the trace has to fit into the GPU's main memory. For example, a GPU with 2 GB of DRAM can process traces with up to one billion events.

Even though the GA is orders of magnitude faster for large FSMs than an exhaustive search, it still needs to evaluate

state transitions. Assuming a trace with one million events, 128 populations, a population size of 512, and an average of 5 generations, this amounts to 328 billion state transitions to be evaluated. At 30 billion state transitions per second on a fast GPU, this takes about 11 seconds to execute. The same parameters but with a one-billion-event trace result in a runtime of 3 hours, highlighting the importance of accelerating even genetic algorithms. Note that many and/or long traces are necessary to improve the generality of the FSM. Large population sizes and large population counts in particular are needed to improve the prediction accuracy by allowing the GA to diversify, *i.e.*, not get stuck in a local maximum.

The code uses random numbers to initialize the transition tables of the first generation of FSM, to determine the mask values for the crossover operations, and to select bits to flip for the mutation operations. We use the XORWOW pseudo-random number generator from the cuRAND library that is included with CUDA 5.0.

For comparison purposes, we also wrote a multicore CPU version of our code. It is largely the same as the CUDA implementation. In particular, the most time-consuming loop that iterates over the trace entries is identical. The CPU code parallelizes the loops that iterate over the FSMs of a population using OpenMP *parallel for* directives with a dynamic schedule. Since the code uses the *rand_r* function from the standard C library to generate the random numbers, the results between the C and the CUDA implementations are not directly comparable, which is why we only compare the throughputs.

3. Related work

Fogel *et al.* first developed evolutionary programming [6] and considered using it to evolve FSMs for time-series predictions [7]. Similar to their approach, we evolve FSMs using mutations and crossovers of state transition tables to find better machines. Holland furthered the application of evolutionary techniques by creating Genetic Algorithms (GAs), *i.e.*, a framework of genetic operations on populations of individuals [10].

Since the introduction of CUDA, many genetic algorithms have been accelerated using GPUs, in particular the fitness evaluation, which generally represents the overwhelming majority of the computation (also indicated by our results) [12]. However, to the best of our knowledge, there is no prior work on GPU acceleration of a genetic algorithm for determining good FSMs. The following three projects are the most similar to our work in that their goal is also to automatically generate well-performing FSMs.

Emer and Gloy introduced an algebraic-style notation to express state identification and feedback processes [4]. In their genetic programming search, they represent individuals by a tree that consists of predictor, function, and terminal nodes. The predictors contain dedicated memory (used in dynamic predictions), size and index information as well as conditions for updating the state of the predictor (feedback process). Functions are internal relation operations such as XOR or SATUR (saturating add). Terminals handle the input and updates for each prediction problem. These nodes can be modified in the genetic programming process to evolve more sophisticated predictors. *E.g.*, by performing a crossover they might combine one predictor's function with another predictor (with some constraints) or modify the size of memory allotted for that predictor. The result of the genetic programming search is the most successful predictors with the smallest misprediction ratio (fitness measure) as well as their configurations. Note that Emer and Gloy employ genetic programming to search for (arbitrarily complex) candidate predictors whereas we explore candidate transition tables of fixed-size bimodal FSMs.

Sherwood and Calder introduced an approach that automatically builds FSM predictors designed to find efficient n^{th}-order Markov model FSMs for small design areas by analyzing profile information [18]. They do not use a genetic algorithm. Rather, they express sets of compact strings in form of regular expressions. By mapping these regular expressions to FSMs, the FSMs can identify the input strings of their corresponding language. A key difference between their work and ours is the use of an nth-order Markov model compared to our genetic search. This results in the cost of having to maintain a Markov table for the history of probabilities. Moreover, much of their work is not directed towards performance, which is one of our key objectives.

Jackson and one of us proposed a pure hardware implementation of a genetically evolving set of bimodal FSMs for confidence estimation that does not require intervention from the user or profiling [11]. Confining the method to hardware allows for dynamic adaptation but restricts the population count and size to very small values compared to the software solution presented here.

4. Experimental methodology

4.1 Systems and compilers

We evaluate the CUDA code on two GPUs, a Fermi-based GeForce GTX 480 and a Kepler-based GeForce GTX 680. The GTX 480 has 15 SMs with 480 CUDA cores in total, 1.5 GB of global memory, is clocked at 1.4 GHz, and supports compute capability 2.0. The GTX 680 has 8 SMXs with 1536 CUDA cores in total, 2 GB of global memory, is clocked at 1.05 GHz, and supports compute capability 3.0. The compiler is nvcc version 5.0. The CUDA source code is the same for both GPUs, but the compiler flags are '-O3 -arch=sm_20' for the Fermi and '-O3 -arch=sm_30' for the Kepler. The code uses 48 kB of L1 data cache and 16 kB of shared memory per SM.

The CPU code is written in C, parallelized with OpenMP,

and run on two hex-core Xeon X5690 CPUs with hyper-threading, *i.e.*, 24 threads in total. The two processors are clocked at 3.47 GHz, have a 12 MB L3 cache each, and share 24 GB of main memory. Each CPU core has dual 32 kB L1 caches and a 256 kB L2 cache. We use gcc version 4.4.6 with the '-O3 -msse4.2 -fopenmp' switches. The operating system is 64-bit CentOS version 6.3.

To maximize the performance, we hardcode the user selectable parameters, *i.e.*, the population count, the population size, the number of elements in the state arrays, and the FSM size in both the C and CUDA codes. This requires a recompilation after every parameter change but results in faster program execution. Since each of our experiments takes several minutes or longer to run, the approximately one second of compilation time is easily amortized.

4.2 Measurements

All timing and throughput measurements are performed by instrumenting the source code, *i.e.*, by adding code to count the number of generations and to read a timer before and after the measured code section. We measure the wall time of the CUDA kernel or the C function that evaluates the FSMs and performs the genetic algorithms – which, on our traces, represents essentially all of the total runtime. Each experiment is conducted once because tests showed the runtimes to be quite stable between multiple runs with identical parameters.

4.3 Trace datasets

We use six datasets for our evaluation. They were extracted from two SPEC programs running on a 64-bit RISC machine. One program is gcc compiling a 638-line C program that implements the Barnes-Hut *n*-body simulation algorithm. The other program is mcf, a combinatorial optimization code running the provided train input. We extracted three traces from the user and library code of both programs (*i.e.*, we did not capture the operating system code, which is negligible in SPEC programs). The first trace records, for all executed branch instructions, whether they were taken or not. The second trace records, for all executed load instructions, whether their effective addresses are stride prefetchable. The third trace records, for all executed load and store instructions that hit in a 2-way associative data cache, whether the first or the second set holds the accessed data.

Table 1. Trace information

Program	Trace type	Length [entries]	Length [MB]	Ones [%]	Unique PCs	$2^{H(PC)}$
gcc	branch outcome	60,666,667	115.7	27.0	14,881	2754.7
gcc	prefetchability	97,155,132	185.3	48.6	22,631	4476.8
gcc	way selection	144,637,560	275.9	50.4	26,420	4900.5
mcf	branch outcome	29,474,825	56.2	45.1	943	89.8
mcf	prefetchability	38,047,003	72.6	40.0	1,698	142.3
mcf	way selection	61,234,883	116.8	51.7	2,562	119.3

Table 1 summarizes pertinent information about each dataset. The 'ones' column indicates the percentage of the trace entries with a true outcome of '1', that is, how biased the entries are. The unique PCs reflect how many of the 32,768 possible PC values occur in the trace. This determines the maximum number of state-array entries that will be used. However, some PCs occur rarely whereas others are very frequent. To account for this variability, we also computed the entropy of the PCs: *H(PC)*. Raising 2 to the power of this entropy yields a 'weighted' number of PCs and therefore state-array entries, *i.e.*, a measure of the working-set size below which significant aliasing is likely to occur.

5. Results

Unless otherwise stated, the default parameters for our genetic algorithm are a population count of 128, a population size of 512, and 1024 entries in the state arrays. These population counts and sizes result in good 3-bit FSMs and in high throughputs on the GPUs, as they map well to the given architectures. We picked 1024-entry state arrays because that is a reasonable size for hardware tables.

5.1 FSM quality

We first evaluate the quality of the best 3-bit bimodal FSMs that the genetic algorithm finds by comparing them to the 3-bit saturating up/down counter as well as to the optimal bimodal 1-bit and 2-bit FSMs, which were determined with an exhaustive search. Figure 2 plots the misprediction ratio in percent against the state-array size for the four types of FSMs. The left panels refer to gcc and the right panels to mcf. The top pair of panels shows the results for the branch outcome traces, the middle pair for the stride prefetchability traces, and the bottom pair for the cache way traces. Note that the y-axes are different for each panel and are not zero based to improve readability.

The optimal 1-bit FSM performs relatively poorly, especially on the two branch outcome traces, because it retains the least amount of state. Nevertheless, it occasionally outperforms the 3-bit saturating up/down counter on the non-branch traces, particularly with large state arrays. On mcf's cache way trace, the optimal 1-bit FSM is consistently and significantly better than the 3-bit counter, which is the worst FSM on that trace. This highlights that saturating counters are not always good choices, particularly when predicting non-branch events.

On both branch traces, the optimal 2-bit FSM is, in fact, the 2-bit saturating up/down counter (with large state arrays). Interestingly the 3-bit saturating up/down counter always outperforms the 2-bit counter on gcc, but on mcf the 3-bit counter is sometimes worse than the 2-bit counter. The optimal 2-bit FSM always outperforms the optimal 1-bit FSM because the 2-bit FSMs are a superset of all possible 1-bit FSMs. The optimal 2-bit FSM often beats the 3-bit counter except on the gcc branch trace. Yet, the optimal 2-bit FSM never outperforms the best 3-bit FSM produced by the GA, indicating that the genetic algorithm works well.

In fact, on our traces, the GA always yields the best FSM for all state-array sizes tested. These FSMs perform 1% to 90% better than the optimal 1-bit FSM, 1% to 29% better than the optimal 2-bit FSM, and 1% to 41% better than the

3-bit saturating counter. Importantly, on all six traces, the best 3-bit FSM often outperforms (by up to 26%) the optimal 2-bit FSM with twice the state-array entries, making the 3-bit FSM the more state-efficient solution. Similarly, the best 3-bit FSM often outperforms (by up to 52%) the optimal 1-bit FSM with four times as many state-array entries, again making the 3-bit FSM more size efficient.

Interestingly, on five of the six traces, the best FSMs sometimes perform worse with larger state arrays. This generally happens at the low end, where the aliasing in the state array is high. Apparently, increased aliasing does not always hurt the prediction accuracy. In fact, the mcf cache-way trace is best predicted by all four FSM types when they are only given one entry in the state array. Clearly, there is a substantial amount of correlation between the selected cache way in this trace, which, overall, is the most difficult-to-predict of our six traces.

Notwithstanding the constructive aliasing in very small state arrays with 16 or fewer entries, we find that the entropy-based minimal number of needed entries (*cf.* the last column in Table 1) accurately indicate the state-array size above which the performance improvement flattens out in all six panels of Figure 2.

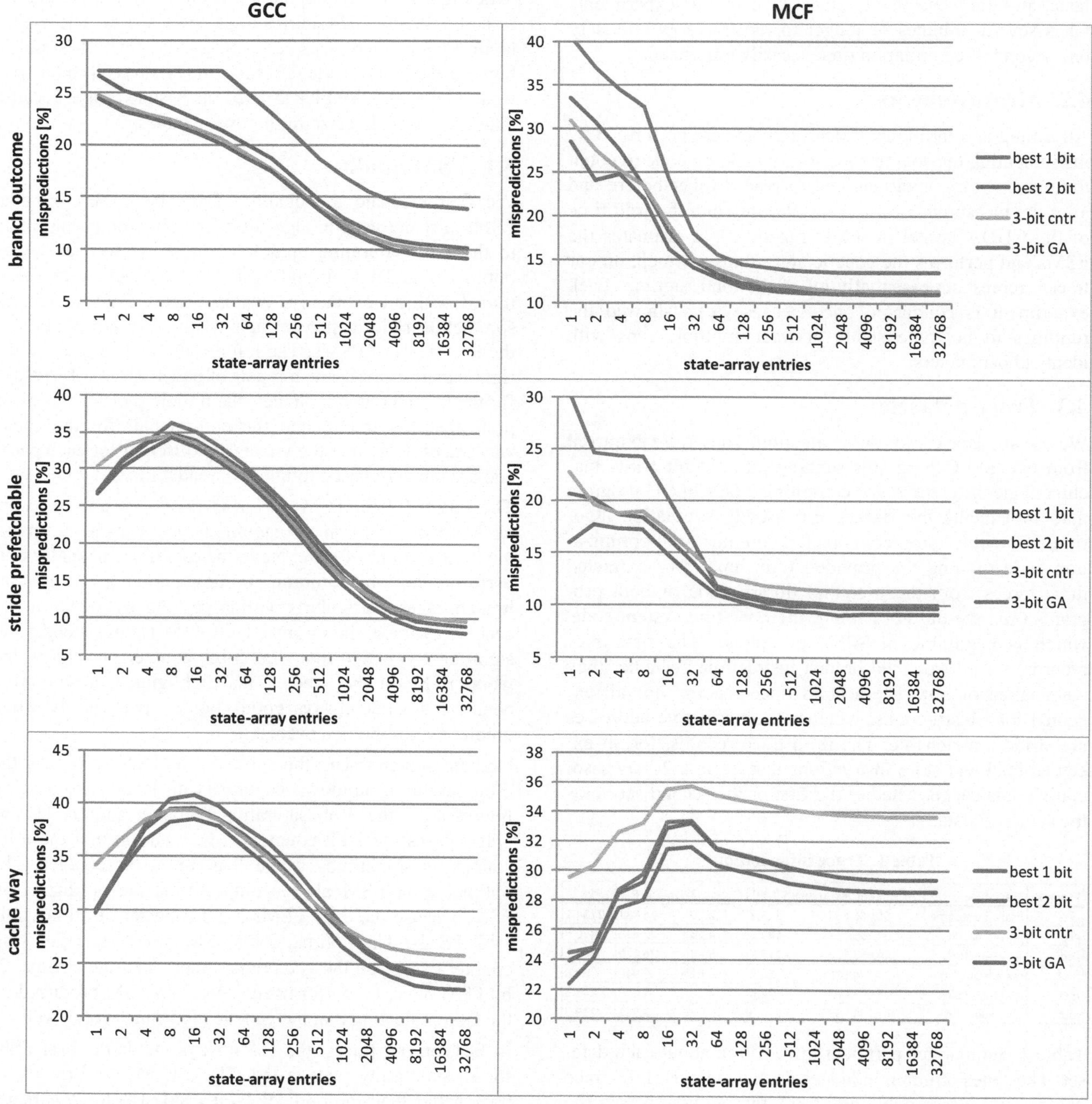

Figure 2. Percent misses (y-axes) for different state-array sizes (x-axes) of four bimodal FSMs on the six traces

5.2 Throughput comparison

This subsection compares the throughput (in billion state transitions evaluated per second) of the CUDA code running on two different GPUs and the OpenMP code running on a system with dual hex-core X5690 CPUs and hyper-threading. For clarity, we only show results for the stride prefetchability trace from mcf.

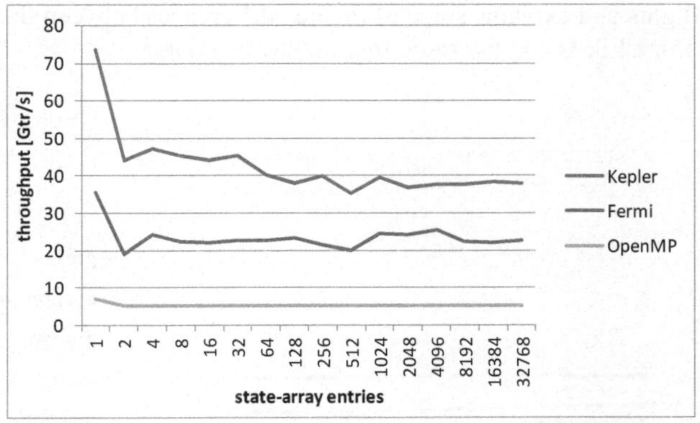

Figure 3. Throughput as a function of the number of state-array entries

Figure 3 shows the throughput for different state-array sizes. On all three processors, a single state yields the highest throughput because the compilers scalarize the 1-entry arrays. The Kepler evaluates 73.6 billion state transitions per second (Gtr/s) in this configuration, the Fermi reaches 35.5 billion, and the two CPUs together peak at 6.9 billion. All larger state-array sizes result in lower but relatively stable throughputs. The Kepler's throughput drops to under 40 Gtr/s for larger array sizes. The Fermi's throughput hovers around 23 Gtr/s. The CPUs' throughput is very stable at 5.3 Gtr/s. Thus, the Kepler outperforms the Fermi by about a factor of 1.5 to 2 and the CPUs by a factor of 7 to 9 or, in a chip-to-chip comparison, one CPU by a factor of 14 to 18.

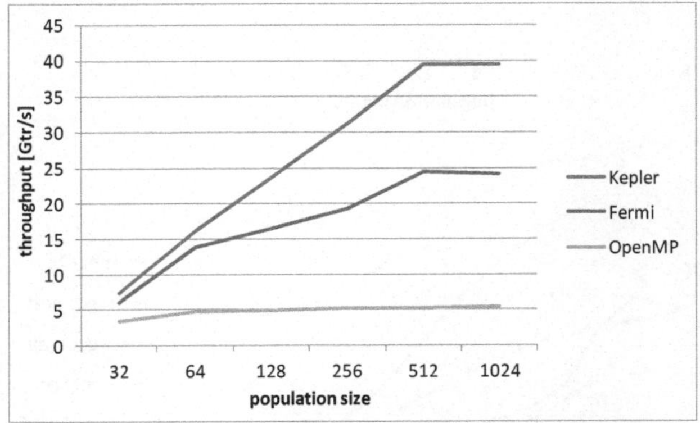

Figure 4. Throughput as a function of the population size

Figure 4 compares the throughputs for different population sizes. Beyond a population size of 32, the CPUs' throughput is almost constant, but the GPUs need a population size of at least 512 to reach their full potential. Since the population size equals the number of threads in a block, it appears that a block size under 512 threads results in inefficient utilization of the GPU hardware.

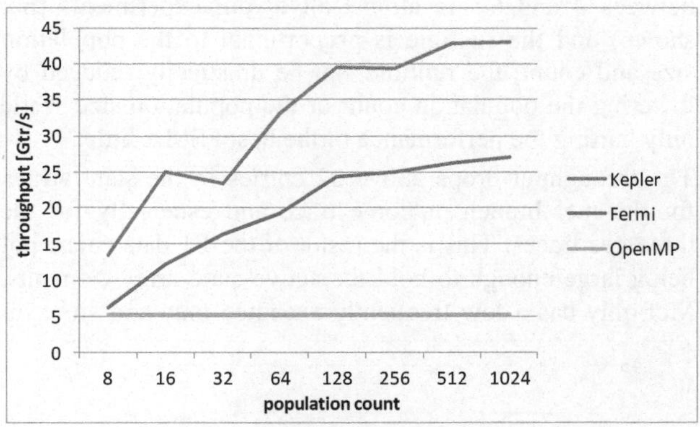

Figure 5. Throughput as a function of the population count

Figure 5 shows the throughputs for different population counts. Because the OpenMP code is parallelized over the FSMs within a population, there is no difference in its throughput when varying the number of populations. However, the CUDA code uses a hierarchical parallelization approach to match the GPU hardware. At least 128 populations (*i.e.*, thread blocks) are necessary to saturate the GPUs. Their performance keeps increasing beyond 128 blocks because larger numbers of blocks result in relatively less load imbalance towards the end when the scheduler runs out of blocks to allocate to the SMs. Note that the Fermi has 15 SMs, which means that a population count of 8 leaves almost half of the SMs with no work. Because SMs can run multiple blocks simultaneously, the Fermi needs at least 45 blocks with 512 threads each to fully load its SMs and the Kepler needs at least 32 blocks. However, at these numbers of blocks, no load balancing is possible as all blocks immediately start running. This is why the throughput only starts to flatten out at about 128 blocks.

In summary, the number of entries in the state arrays does not affect the throughput much, but the population count and size do. On both of our GPUs, the population size should be at least 512 and the population count 128 to fully exploit the hardware. At these sizes, the Kepler GPU is roughly nine times faster than our two high-end CPUs.

5.3 Parameter-space exploration

Figure 6 illustrates how the throughput on the Kepler and the misprediction ratio of the best 3-bit bimodal FSM depend on the population size, the population count, and the number of entries in the state arrays for the six traces.

Increasing the population size or count greatly improves the throughput but only minimally reduces the misprediction ratio. This is expected as genetic algorithms generally already produce a good solution on a single population. The purpose of the multiple populations (*i.e.*, the random restarts) is to provide variability to escape local maxima. For instance, going from 8 to 1024 populations improves the best FSM by 1.3% to 3.8%, and going from a population size of 32 to a population size of 1024 improves the best FSM by 1.7% to 3.7%.

Since the average number of generations is consistently between 4 and 6.5 in almost all of our experiments (not shown) and the runtime is proportional to the population size and count, the runtime can be drastically reduced by lowering the population count or the population size while only hurting the performance of the best FSM a little.

The throughput drops above 32 entries in the state arrays for the mcf branch outcome trace and especially for the three gcc traces. This is the result of the L1 data cache not being large enough to hold the active state-array elements. Mcf only has a few frequently executed load and store instructions, which is why its prefetchability and cache-way traces do not suffer from a similar drop in throughput.

5.4 Best FSMs

Due to space limitations, we refer the reader to our technical report at http://cs.txstate.edu/~mb92/papers/pdpta13.pdf for a visualization and discussion of three of the FSMs that our genetic algorithm generated. This technical report highlights and explains some of the key differences between the three FSMs and the saturating up/down counter.

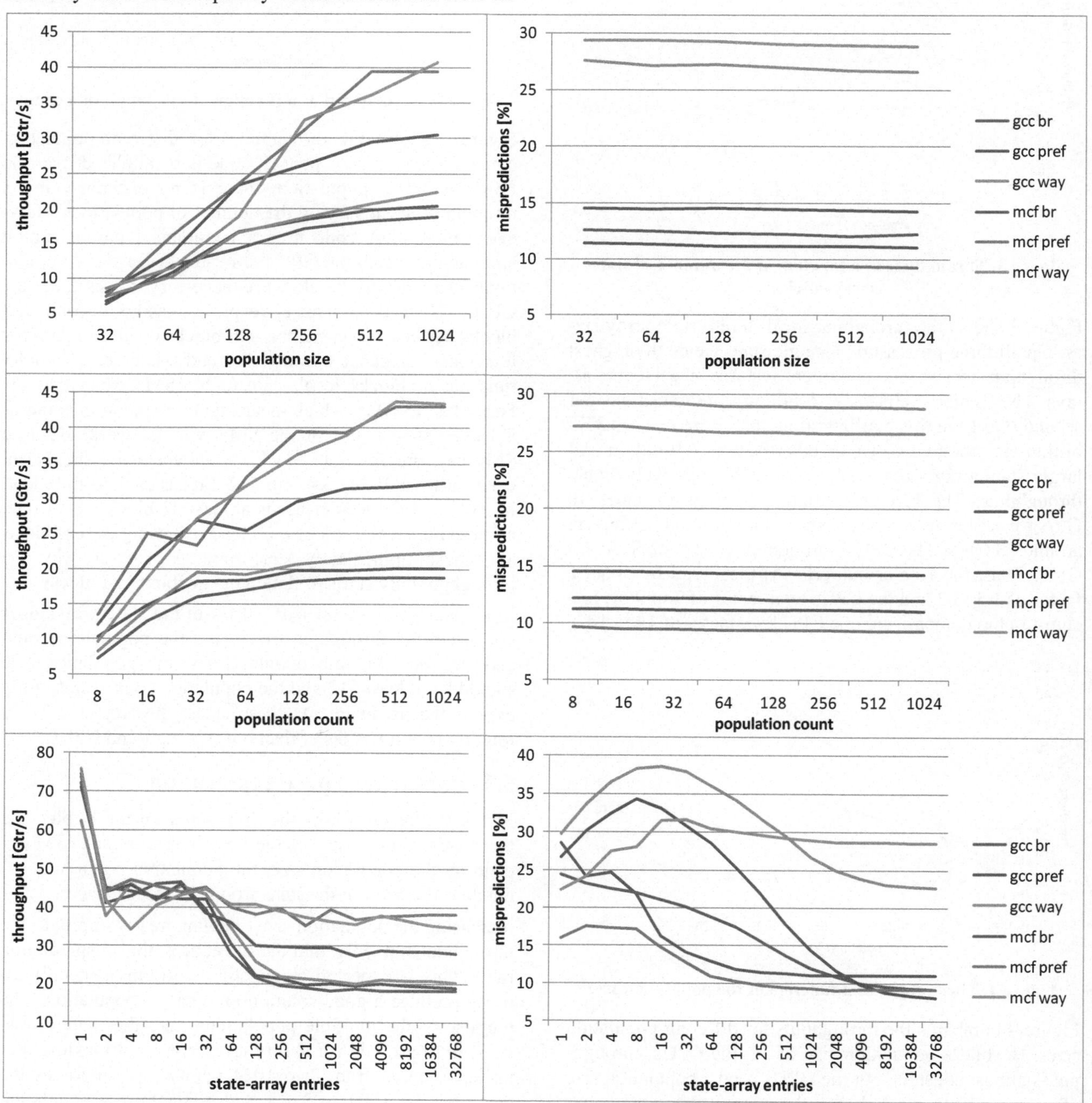

Figure 6. Throughput and misprediction ratio on the six traces as a function of different parameters

6. Summary and conclusions

This paper describes a multi-start genetic algorithm for the synthesis of well-performing bimodal FSMs for designing hardware predictors. The implementation of this algorithm is GPU friendly in that it avoids potential performance bottlenecks and exploits the GPU's capabilities well.

It takes about a dozen cycles per GPU core to evaluate a state transition, *i.e.*, to make a prediction, check its correctness, and update the FSM's state based on the true outcome. On a GTX 680, our code assesses up to 73 billion state transitions per second. On our six traces with tens to hundreds of millions of entries, it takes just seconds to generate FSMs that outperform the saturating up/down counter, a widely-used FSM, in many cases by a large margin. Compared to OpenMP code running on a high-end hex-core Xeon X5690 with hyper-threading, the GPU code is 14 to 18 times faster.

We conclude that GPU acceleration is very useful in this domain and that our implementation exploits the GPU hardware well. Moreover, studying the resulting FSMs can provide insight into the structure of the traces, *i.e.*, the nature of the events being predicted, that explains why saturating up/down counters sometimes do not perform well.

7. Acknowledgments

This work was supported by NSF grants 1141022 and 1217231 and as well as donations from Nvidia Corporation.

8. References

[1] Aarts, E. and Korst, J. 1988. *Simulated annealing and boltzmann machines*. New York, NY; John Wiley and Sons.

[2] Bellas, N. *et al.* 1999. Using dynamic cache management techniques to reduce energy in a high-performance processor. *Low Power Electronics and Design, 1999. Proceedings. 1999 International Symposium on* (1999), 64–69.

[3] Dorigo, M. *et al.* 1996. Ant system: optimization by a colony of cooperating agents. *Systems, Man, and Cybernetics, Part B: Cybernetics, IEEE Transactions on*. 26, 1 (1996), 29–41.

[4] Emer, J. and Gloy, N. 1997. A language for describing predictors and its application to automatic synthesis. *24th Annual International Symposium on Computer Architecture* (1997), 304–314.

[5] Feo, T.A. and Resende, M.G.C. 1995. Greedy randomized adaptive search procedures. *Journal of global optimization*. 6, 2 (1995), 109–133.

[6] Fogel, L. *et al.* 1966. *Artificial Intelligence through Simulated Evolution*. John Wiley.

[7] Fogel, L.J. *et al.* 1995. Approach to Self-Adaptation on Finite State Machines. *Evolutionary Programming IV: Proceedings of the Fourth Annual Conference on Evolutionary Programming* (1995), 355.

[8] Goldberg, D.E. 1989. Genetic algorithms in search, optimization, and machine learning. *Addison Wesley*. (1989).

[9] Grunwald, D. *et al.* 1998. Confidence estimation for speculation control. *25th Annual International Symposium on Computer Architecture* (1998), 122–131.

[10] Holland, J.H. 1975. Adaptation in natural and artificial systems, University of Michigan press. *Ann Arbor, MI*. 1, 97 (1975), 5.

[11] Jackson, S.J. and Burtscher, M. 2006. Self-optimizing Finite State Machines for Confidence Estimators. *Workshop on Introspective Architecture*. (2006).

[12] Langdon, W.B. 2011. Graphics processing units and genetic programming: An overview. *Soft Computing-A Fusion of Foundations, Methodologies and Applications*. 15, 8 (2011), 1657–1669.

[13] Lee, C.C. et al. 1997. The bi-mode branch predictor. *Microarchitecture, 1997. Proceedings., Thirtieth Annual IEEE/ACM International Symposium on* (1997), 4–13.

[14] Loh, G.H. and Henry, D.S. 2002. Predicting conditional branches with fusion-based hybrid predictors. *Parallel Architectures and Compilation Techniques, 2002. Proceedings. 2002 International Conference on* (2002), 165–176.

[15] McFarling, S. 1993. *Combining branch predictors*. Technical Report TN-36, Digital Western Research Laboratory.

[16] Milenkovic, A. *et al.* 2011. Caches and predictors for real-time, unobtrusive, and cost-effective program tracing in embedded systems. *Computers, IEEE Transactions on*. 60, 7 (2011), 992–1005.

[17] Peress, Y. *et al.* Re-Defining the Tournament Predictor for Embedded Systems. *Workshop on Optimizations for DSP and Embedded Systems* (2010), 53–61.

[18] Sherwood, T. and Calder, B. 2001. Automated design of finite state machine predictors for customized processors. *Computer Architecture, 2001. Proceedings. 28th Annual International Symposium on* (2001), 86–97.

[19] Yeh, T.-Y. and Patt, Y.N. 1993. A comparison of dynamic branch predictors that use two levels of branch history. *Proceedings of the 20th annual international symposium on computer architecture* (1993), 257–266.

[20] Yoaz, A. *et al.* 1999. Speculation techniques for improving load related instruction scheduling. *Computer Architecture, 1999. Proceedings of the 26th International Symposium on* (1999), 42–53.

A Fast Implementation of Parallel Discrete-Event Simulation on GPGPU

Janche Sang[1], Che-Rung Lee[2], Vernon Rego[3], and Chung-Ta King[2]
[1]Dept. of Computer and Info. Science, Cleveland State University, OH 44115, USA
[2]Dept. of Computer Science, National Tsing Hua University, HsinChu, Taiwan, ROC
[3]Dept. of Computer Science, Purdue University, West Lafayette, IN 47907, USA

Abstract—*Modern General Purpose Graphics Processing Units(GPGPUs) offer much more computational power than recent CPUs by providing a vast number of simple, data parallel, multithreaded cores. In this study, we focus on the use of a GPGPU to perform parallel discrete-event simulation. Our approach is to use a modified service time distribution function to allow more independent events to be processed in parallel. The implementation issues and alternative strategies will be discussed in detail. We use Thrust, an open-source parallel algorithms library which resembles the C++ Standard Template Library (STL), to build our tool. The experimental results show that our implementation can be more than 60 times faster than the sequential simulation. Furthermore, the speedup curve scales well which indicates that our implementation is suitable for large-scale discrete-event simulation models.*

Keywords: Parallel Simulation, Discrete-Event Simulation, GPGPU, CUDA, Thrust Library

1. Introduction

Discrete Event Simulation (DES) is a widely-used technique that allows an analyst to study the dynamic behavior of a complex system. DES exploits a computer to model a system stochastically at discrete points in simulated time. A simulation program operates on a model's state variables during each of a sequence of time-ordered events and schedules future events during such processing. However, simulation is usually computationally intensive and time-consuming. Typical simulation applications often execute for hours or even days. Therefore, exploiting the availability and the power of multiprocessors to speed up the simulation execution is of considerable interest.

Parallel discrete event simulation (PDES) attempts to speed up a simulation's execution by partitioning the simulation model into components, each of which has its own event set and is executed by a *Logical Process*(LP) on a different processor. To guarantee the distributed events will be executed in an appropriate order, two main types of synchronization mechanisms among LPs have been proposed: conservative and optimistic [1]. Conservative mechanisms do not allow an LP to process an event until it is certain that causality violation will not occur. This means that an LP will not receive an event with a smaller timestamp than its current clock from another LP. However, An LP may wait for events that never arrive. Therefore, LPs may send null messages to other LPs to avoid deadlocks [2]. Optimistic mechanisms ignore inter-process synchronization issues, but make compensations by performing rollbacks to a check-pointed consistent state when a causality error occurs [3]. This requires periodic state-saving of the simulator.

With the advance of graphics hardware technology, programming and executing general applications on GPGPUs is more feasible. Nowadays, a single GPGPU with hundreds or even thousands of processing cores has great potential for improving the performance of various computational intensive applications. In this paper, we focus on the use of a GPGPU to perform parallel discrete-event simulation. Note that the architecture of GPGPU can be classified as Single Instruction, Multiple Data(SIMD). To allow more events to be processed in parallel based on SIMD, our approach is to use a modified service time distribution function which guarantees that the events clustered to be executed simultaneously are independent of each other and hence causality errors will not occur. In other words, our method can be treated as a conservative approach from certain viewpoint.

Our implementation is done with the Thrust [4] on the NVIDIA Compute Unified Device Architecture(CUDA) platform. Thrust is a CUDA library of parallel algorithms with a user-friendly interface resembling the C++ Standard Template Library (STL). It hides the details of low-level CUDA function calls and provides highly-optimized implementation of standard algorithms, such as searching, sorting, reduction, compaction, etc., which greatly enhances developer productivity. Therefore, GPGPU-based applications implemented with Thrust are readable, concise, and efficient.

The organization of this paper is as follows. Section 2 describes related work. In Section 3, an old algorithm which we borrow some ideas from is investigated. Section 4 presents our implementation strategies. In Section 5, the experiments and the results for performance evaluation are presented. We give a short conclusion in Section 6.

2. Related Work

In the area of practical parallel simulation, two apparently orthogonal streams of effort have developed over the past decades. The *replication*-based effort entails natural parallelism and is able to utilize massive data-parallel computational power. The *EcliPSe* toolkit described in [5], [6] has proven to be a very successful system for replication-based simulations. The *distribution*-based effort emphasizes functional decomposition of a model across processors. Examples of systems supporting distributed simulation include ModSim[7], Sim++[8], $ParaSi$[9], and $ParaSol$[10]. An inherent difference between the two approaches is that replication exploits statistical sampling to speed up the generation of multiple (typically, but not necessarily independent) sample paths, while distribution exploits model partitioning to speed up the generation of a single sample path.

Because of its massively data parallel computing power, GPGPU has been used by more and more researchers for simulating large-scale models over the past few years. For example, a discrete-event simulation of heat diffusion performed on GPGPU can be found in [11]. The algorithm selects the minimum among all update times and uses it as a timestep to perform a synchronous update of state across all elements in the grid. Another work reported in [12] focuses on a high-fidelity network modeling and uses the GPU as a co-processor to distribute computation-intensive workloads. Our approach is similar to the work in [13] and [14] which develop an event clustering and execution scheme based on the concept of approximation time. In these two papers, the former illustrates practical implementation strategies, while the latter presents an analysis of the approximation error in their algorithm. Our algorithm borrows some ideas from their algorithm for updating service facilities. The old algorithm will be studied in detail in the next section.

3. The Old Algorithm

The work in [13] and [14] introduced a time-synchronous/event algorithm using a time interval instead of a precise time. Figure 1 shows the pseudo code of the hybrid algorithm. To achieve more parallel processing, their algorithm clusters events within a time interval. That is, the simulation time is divided into many fixed-sized time slots which is similar to the time-based simulation, a methodology usually used for continuous physics/dynamics simulation [15]. However, unlike the pure time-based simulation which advances the time slot by slot, the old algorithm directly moves the clock to the slot which contains the event with the minimum timestamp in the future event set. This could reduce the execution time if a slot doesn't have any events to be processed. Therefore, as shown in Figure 1, all of the events whose timestamps are less than or equal to the time slot boundary (i.e. the smallest multiple of time interval greater than or equal to the minimum timestamp) can be extracted from the future event set and then be executed.

```
while ( current_time  <  simulation_time )
   min_timestamp = find_min(future_event_set);
   current_step = the smallest multiple of time
                  interval greater than or
                  equal to min_timestamp;
   parallel for each event e in future_event_set
       if (the timestamp of e <= current_step)
          extract e from future_event_set;
          process e and generate new events
              into future_event_set;
       end if
   end for
   current_time = current_step;
end while
```

Fig. 1: The pseudo code of the old algorithm

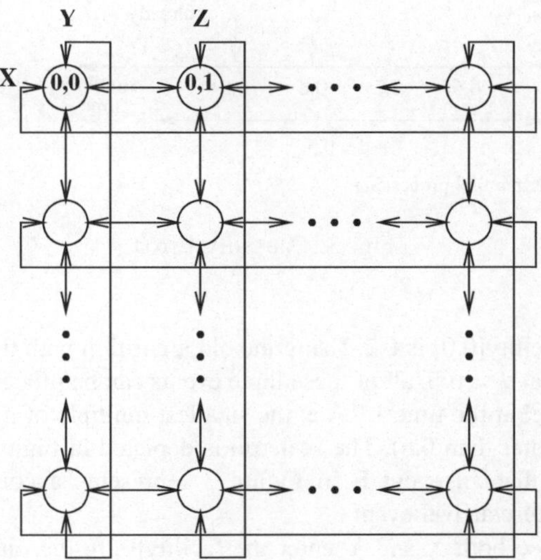

Fig. 2: Torus Queuing Network

However, the old algorithm cannot be directly used in the precise-time PDES. Note that the PDES should handle the events in a causal consistent way exactly as the sequential DES does. Let's use the simulation of a torus queueing network as an example. As shown in Figure 2, a torus consists of service facilities arranged in a two dimensional mesh. Each facility has four outgoing and four incoming channels. When a token arrives at a service facility, it gets the service for some random amount of time if the server is idle. Otherwise, the token has to wait in the server's waiting queue. After being served, the token moves to one of the four neighbors. For simplicity, we assume that the probabilities of a token leaving a facility on any given outgoing channel are equal (i.e. 0.25).

Assume that there are three tokens X, Y, and Z in the torus network (see Figure 2). The token X and the token Y enter the service facility[0,0] at time 0.6 and 0.7, respectively. The token Z will arrive at the facility[0,1] at time 0.9. Also assume that the service time for the token X being served at

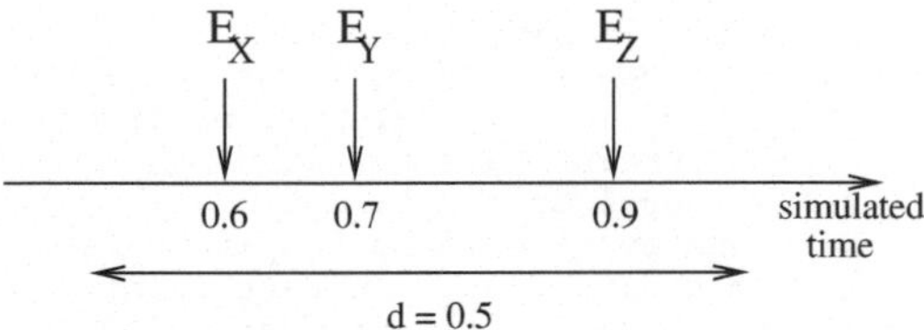

(a) before parallel processing

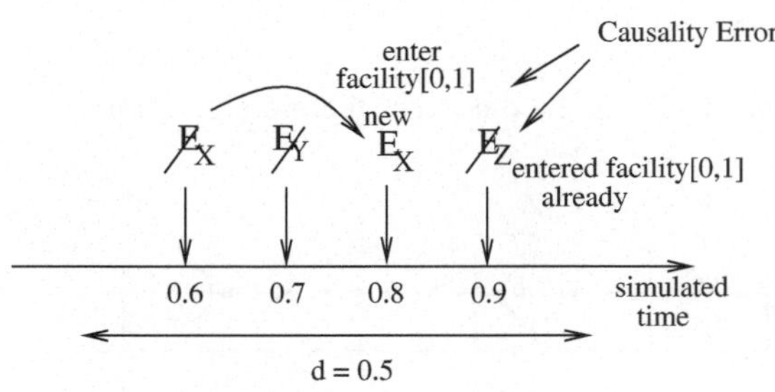

(b) after parallel processing

Fig. 3: Causality Error

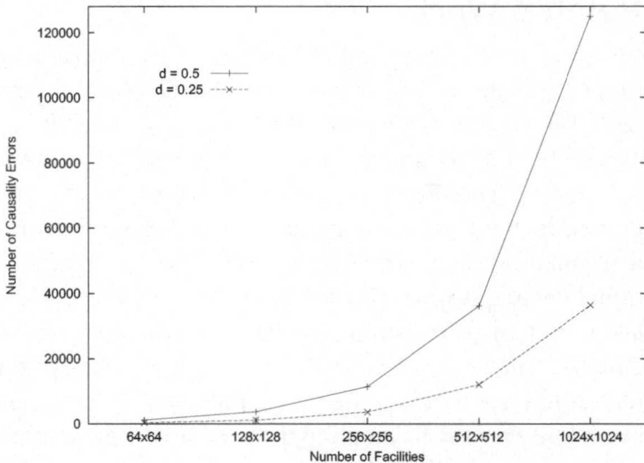

Fig. 4: Causality Errors with varying the number of facilities

the facility[0,0] is 0.2. Using the old algorithm with the time interval $d = 0.5$, all of these three events can be processed in parallel at the time 1.0 (i.e. the smallest multiple of d which is greater than 0.6). The scenario is depicted in Figure 3(a). Note that an event E in Figure 3 represents a combined departure/arrival event.

Since both X and Y enter the facility[0,0], the old algorithm uses the original timestamps to keep the causal order. That is, the token X will get the service immediately, while the token Y will stay in the waiting queue. However, if we use the original timestamp for the token X to calculate its departure/arrival time, the token X should enter the facility[0,1] at time 0.8. As shown in Figure 3(b), a causality error occurs because the token Z, with the arrival time at 0.9, has been served in the facility[0,1] already. Therefore, the old algorithm cannot process the events exactly as the causal order in the sequential DES. We also conducted an experiment to verify this. We recorded the last arrival time for each service facility. If the timestamp of a new arrival is smaller than the last arrival time, a causality error is detected. Figure 4 shows that the larger the interval, the more causality errors occurred in the simulation.

4. The Improved Implementation

Our algorithm for PDES is based on the precise time, not the approximation time as in [13], [14]. The first issue we need to deal with is the potential causality error as discussed in the previous section. To solve the problem, we let the service time for each token contain the constant time interval d and subtract the constant d from the mean service time in the invocation of the service time distribution function. More precisely, if the service time is exponentially distributed, we change the expression of calling exponential distribution function from

```
expon(M)
```

to

```
expon(M-d) + d
```

where M is the mean service time. Note that in the modified formula, the mean service time is still M, but the service time for any token is always greater than d. Therefore, the aforementioned causality error will not occur. For example, the timestamp of the new departure/arrival event for the token X in Figure 3 will be at least $0.6 + d = 1.1$ which is after the token Z enters the facility[0,1].

Another advantage of using the modified formula for the service time is that the full time interval can be used to cluster events for parallel processing. Our algorithm extracts any event which has the timestamp less than or equal to

```
minimum_timestamp + d
```

and hence will include more events than the old algorithm. The more parallel events be executed, the faster program runs. For example, assume that $d = 0.5$ and the minimum timestamp in the future event set is 1.42, the events with the timestamp between 1.42 and 1.50 can be processed concurrently in the old algorithm. The effective range size is only 0.08. Using our algorithm, the range is between 1.42 and 1.92. In general, giving the same interval d, the average effective range size of the old algorithm is half of the range size in our algorithm. However, our method still has its disadvantage. The biased distribution function will yield a small difference as compared with the result of using the original distribution function. The empirical evaluation of the difference will be reported in the next section.

Figure 5 shows our implementation on the host using the Thrust library. As mentioned before, Thrust is a CUDA library of parallel algorithms with an interface resembling the C++ Standard Template Library (STL). One of the

```
thrust::device_ptr<FACTYPE> all_fac = thrust::device_malloc<FACTYPE>(N*N);
FACTYPE *facp = thrust::raw_pointer_cast(all_fac);

thrust::device_ptr<TOKENTYPE> all_tkn = thrust::device_malloc<TOKENTYPE>(1);
TOKENTYPE *tknp = thrust::raw_pointer_cast(all_tkn);

thrust::device_ptr<float> events = thrust::device_malloc<float>(N*N);
float *ep = thrust::raw_pointer_cast(events);

thrust::device_ptr<int> chzn = thrust::device_malloc<int>(N*N);
int  *cp = thrust::raw_pointer_cast(chzn);

thrust::device_ptr<bool> rdndnt = thrust::device_malloc<bool>(N*N);
bool *rp = thrust::raw_pointer_cast(rdndnt);


...

while (clock < SIMTIME ) {
   thrust::device_ptr<float> mptr =  thrust::min_element(events, events + N*N);

   clock = *mptr + d;

   thrust::device_ptr<int> chzn_last =thrust::copy_if(key,key+N*N,events,chzn,leq(clock));

   int chzn_num = chzn_last - chzn;

   int gridSize = (chozen_num+blocksize-1)/blocksize;

   process_departure<<<gridSize,blocksize>>> (facp,tknp,ep,cp,chzn_num);

   chk_redundant<<<gridSize,blocksize>>> (facp,tknp,ep,cp,rp,chzn_num);

   process_arrival<<<gridSize,blocksize>>> (facp,tknp,ep,cp,rp,chzn_num);
}
```

Fig. 5: The improved implementation using the Thrust library

reasons we use Thrust is that it abstracts away the details of low-level CUDA function calls, such as cudaMalloc, cudaMemcpy, kernel launch, etc. For example, it provides the device pointer which allows programmers access the device memory without calling cudaMemcpy explicitly. The `*mptr` in Figure 5 is such a case. For interoperability with C, the device pointer can be converted into a raw pointer and then the users can use it as a parameter to launch a CUDA C kernel.

Another reason we use the Thrust library is that it provides the `min_element` and the `copy_if` functions. So we don't need to write our own and hence the programming effort can be saved greatly. Furthermore, both functions have been tuned and optimized particularly for the NVIDIA GPGPU architecture. For example, the code used in the old algorithm to find the minimum element based on the parallel reduction method is out-of-date and inefficient. Figure 6 shows the general ideas of how the parallel reduction steps are performed in the old algorithm and in the Thrust library, respectively. The former uses the interleaved addressing approach, in which the distance between the two elements to be compared in the array is doubled for each reduction step. The latter adopts the sequential addressing approach, in which the distance is reduced half in every step. In theory, there is no difference between these two methods because both need $O(\log n)$ steps to find the minimum value among n elements. In practice, the latter is bank conflict free and takes advantage of the CUDA memory coalescing within a warp to improve performance [16].

Another important thing is how to extract the aggregated events from the future event set. It is straightforward that the comparison of each event's timestamp with the interval's upper bound can be done in parallel on each thread. The issue here is the management of the chozen events to run after the comparison. The way how this is implemented is not discussed in [13]. The simplest approach is to let the thread discontinue to run if the selection criteria is not met, while the thread which gets TRUE in the comparison will continue to execute the event, i.e., handling the departure/arrival, updating the facility, generating new events, etc.

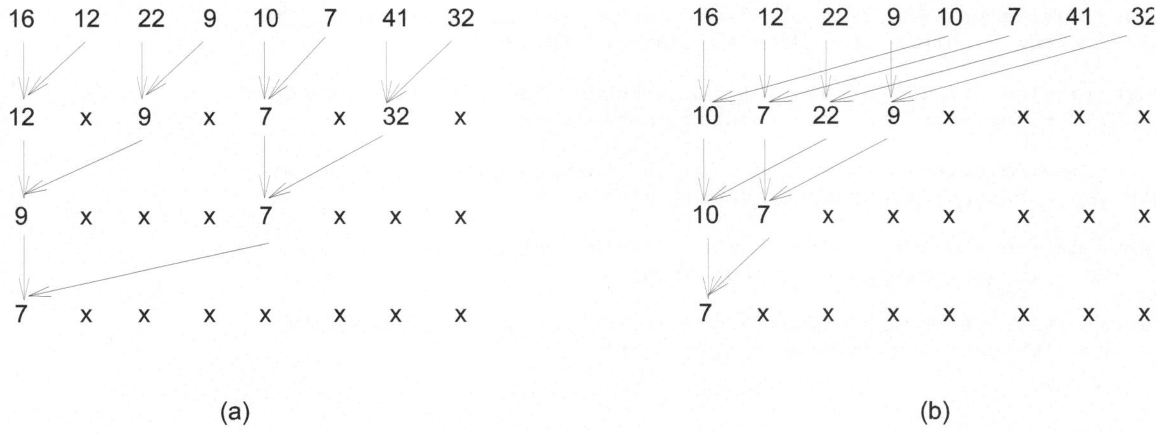

Fig. 6: Parallel Reduction Steps using (a) Interleaved Addressing (b) Sequential Addressing

However, based on our experience, only a small portion of events will be selected in a large-scale simulation. Hence, this approach will cause many threads idle and only two or three threads in a warp can run.

The better approach is to use two phases of processing. In the first phase, the parallel events are collected into an array which stores the identifiers of the selected events. Therefore, the number of the chozen events can be known and then we can run that many of threads to execute the events in the second phase. For collecting the chozen events into an array, each thread needs to figure out the correct position to be stored in the array. There are two implementation methods for this. One method is that we can use an index counter which will be incremented by one for each newly selected event. Since the index counter is shared by many threads, the addition has to be an atomic operation. This can be done by using the CUDA `atomicAdd()` function. Another method, which is used in the Thrust `copy_if` function, adopts the list ranking algorithm with the parallel prefix sum operation[17] to obtain the position of each selected event. Currently, we use the latter because of its availability. However, the choice of which method depends on how many items satisfy the condition. Basically, if the number of items that satisfy the condition is small, using `atomicAdd()` could be better. The empirical comparison of these two methods is worth further investigation.

Figure 7 shows the pseudo code of event execution in the second phase of processing. When a token leaves a facility, the first token, if any, in the waiting will get its service and a departure event will be scheduled for it. For the leaving token, an uniform random variable will be generated to determine its destination and its token identifier and timestamp will be put into the next service facility's corresponding incoming port. Note that it is possible there are more than one token arrived at the same facility. This will cause more than one thread handling of the same facility and mess up the computation. To solve the problem, we use the pre-defined port order, east → south → west → north, to determine which thread has to process the arrivals at the facility. As shown in the Figure 5 and Figure 7, the decision making is a separated kernel launch of the function `chk_redundant()`. For processing the arrivals at a facility, we append all of the incoming tokens to the waiting queue if the service facility is busy. Otherwise, the newly arrived token with the smallest timestamp can start the service, while the rest of incoming tokens will be put in the waiting queue based on their timestamp order.

Note that the processing of the departures, the checking of the redundant threads, and the processing of the arrivals should be launched from the kernel respectively. This is because we have to wait until all of the threads finishes one kernel launch and then start running the next kernel function. Otherwise, the incoming port data will not be consistent due to the clean up at the end of the function `process_arrival()`. Furthermore, the CUDA function `__syncthreads()` cannot be used here as a barrier because it can only synchronize the threads within a warp, not all of the threads.

5. Experimental Results

In this section, we compare our PDES implementation on the GPGPU with a sequential heap-based DES on the CPU. The experimental platform, supported by Ohio Supercomputing Center, has one HP ProLiant SL390s G7 Node with two Intel Xeon x5650 CPUs (2.67GHz, 48GB memory). The OS is 64-bit Linux, kernel version 2.6.32. The GPGPU used in the experiments is a NVIDIA Tesla M2070, which contains 14 multiprocessors (448 CUDA cores in total) and 6GB GDDR5 memory. A warp, the scheduling unit in CUDA, has 32 threads and these 32 threads perform SIMD computation on a multiprocessor. The device programs use CUDA compiler driver 5.0. The parallel algorithm runs on

```
__global__ void process_departure( parameters )
{
   calculate the statistics;
   If the facility's waiting queue is empty
      set the state of the facility to be idle;
   else
      remove the front token from the waiting
         queue and put it in service.;
      schedule a departure event for the token;
   determine destination for the leaving token;
}

__global__ void chk_redundant( parameters)
{
  check the four incoming ports of the facility;
  if there are more than one arrival, use the
     predefined port order to determine which
     arrival's corresponding thread can run.
}

__global__ void process_arrival( parameters )
{
   if the thread is marked as redundant
      return;
   sort the incoming tokens by their timestamps;
   if the state of the facility is idle
      let the first incoming token get the service
           and schedule a departure event for it;
      put the rest of incoming tokens into the
           waiting Q;
   else
      append the incoming tokens to the waiting Q;
   clean up the data in the four incoming ports.
}
```

Fig. 7: Pseudo code for event processing

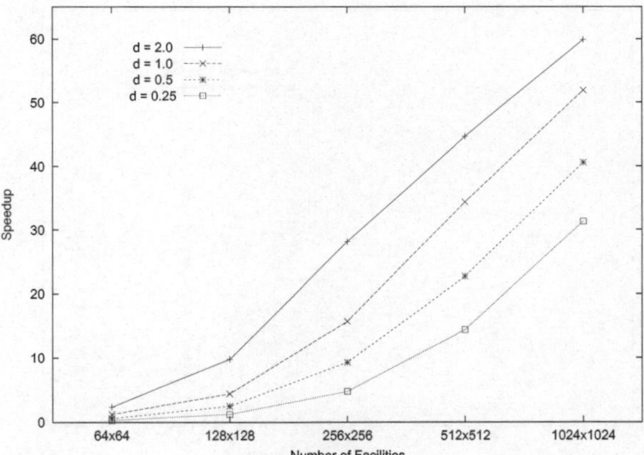

Fig. 8: Speedups

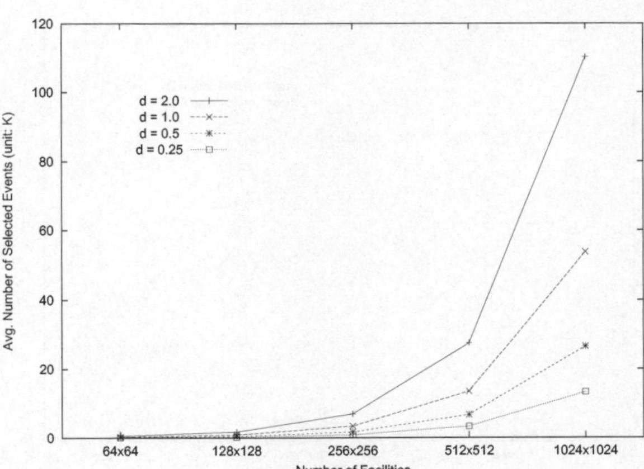

Fig. 9: Average number of parallel events

the host and the device, while the sequential algorithm runs on the host.

The torus queueing network model mentioned in the earlier section was used for the simulation. In the first experiment, we measured the simulation execution times by varying the number of facilities and the interval sizes. The mean service time (i.e. the parameter M in calling the function `expon()`) of the service facility is set to 10. Figure 8 shows the performance improvement in the GPGPU experiments compared to sequential simulation on the CPU. The speedups grow when the number of facilities increases. In particular, our PDES implementation outperforms the sequential DES by 60x speedup for 1024x1024 facilities with $d = 2.0$. The curve also scales well which implies that the speedup could be increased further for simulating a larger scale torus network. It can also be seen in Figure 8 that the larger the interval value d, the larger the speedup obtained. This is because a larger interval allows more parallel events to run. To verify this, we also measured the average number of parallel events for different number of facilities and different interval sizes. The result can be found in Figure 9.

In another experiments, we evaluated the difference in simulation summary statistics due to the use of the modified service time distribution function. Figure 10 shows the difference in the facility server utilization for varied intervals. The simulation with smaller time interval behaves closer to running the simulation with the original service distribution function. As the interval d increases, the utilization also increases because the service time is at least large as d. Figure 11 shows similar effect on the system waiting time, which is the average time of a token staying in a service facility, including the service time and the waiting time in the queue. Unlike utilization, the system waiting time drops as interval increases. For the purpose of comparison, we also used two mean service times: 10 and 20. For the same interval d, the larger mean service time has smaller difference in utilization and system waiting time because the interval d occupies a smaller portion in the service time.

6. Conclusion and Future Work

We presented a fast implementation of PDES on GPGPU by using the productivity-oriented Thrust library. Our scheme exploits a modified service distribution function to allow clustered events to be processed in parallel, while

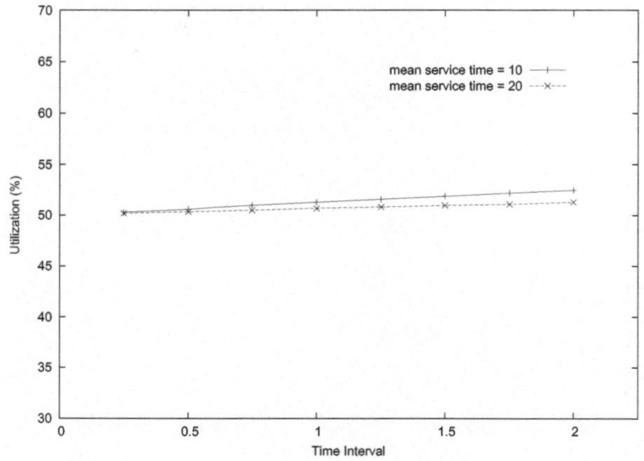

Fig. 10: Utilization with with different time interval d

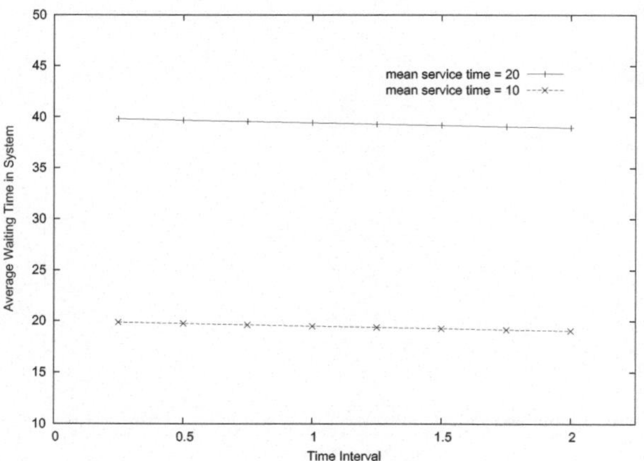

Fig. 11: System Waiting Time with different time interval d

preserving timestamp ordering and causal relationships of events. Thrust, which provides a collection of optimized data parallel primitives such as reduce, stream compaction, prefix sums, etc., makes our implementation more efficient. The experimental results are encouraging. We were able to achieve 60x speedup using our implementation at the expense of accuracy in the results. The speedup curve scales well which indicates that our implementation utilizes the massively data parallel processing power of GPGPU and is suitable for large-scale simulation models.

In the future, we plan to investigate various optimization techniques, such as using shared memory and/or register file, to improve the program performance. Moreover, the performance comparison of Thrust's `copy_if()` and the implementation using `atomicAdd()` in our simulation tool is worth of further studies.

Acknowledgments

This research was supported by a Fulbright Senior Research Grant, facilitated by the Foundation for Scholarly Exchange in Taiwan, and by an allocation of computing time from the Ohio Supercomputer Center.

References

[1] R. Fujimoto, "Parallel discrete event simulation," *CACM*, vol. 33(10), pp. 30–53, 1990.

[2] K. M. Chandy and J. Misra, "Distributed simulation: A case study in design and verification of distributed programs," *IEEE Trans. on Software Engineering*, vol. 5, no. 5, pp. 440–452, May 1979.

[3] D. Jefferson, "Virtual time," *ACM Trans. on Programming Languages and Systems*, vol. 7, pp. 404–425, July 1985.

[4] J. Hoberock and N. Bell, "Thrust: A parallel template library," 2010. [Online]. Available: http://code.google.com/p/thrust/

[5] V. S. Sunderam and V. J. Rego, "Eclipse: A system for High Performance Concurrent Simulation," *Software-Practice and Experience*, vol. 21(11), pp. 1189–1219, 1991.

[6] V. J. Rego and V. S. Sunderam, "Experiments in Concurrent Stochastic Simulation: The Eclipse Paradigm," *Journal of Parallel and Distributed Computing*, vol. 14(1), pp. 66–84, January 1992.

[7] J. West and A. Mullarney, "ModSim: a language for distributed simulation," in *Proceedings of SCS Multiconference on Distributed Simulation*, 1988.

[8] D. Baezner, G. Lomow, and B. W. Unger, "Sim++: The transition to distributed simulation," in *Proceedings of the SCS Multiconference on Distributed Simulatio*, 1990, pp. 211–218.

[9] J. Sang, E. Mascarenhas, and V. Rego, "Mobile-Process Based Parallel Simulation," *Journal of Parallel and Distributed Computing*, February 1996.

[10] E. Mascarenhas, F. Knop, R. Pasquini, and V. Rego, "Minimum cost adaptive synchronization: experiments with the parasol system," *ACM Trans. on Modelingand Computer Simulation*, vol. 8, no. 4, pp. 401–430, 1998.

[11] K. S. Perumalla, "Discrete-event execution alternatives on general purpose graphical processing units (gpgpus)," in *Proceedings of the 20th Workshop on Principles of Advanced and Distributed Simulation*, ser. PADS '06, Washington, DC, USA, 2006, pp. 74–81.

[12] Z. Xu and R. Bagrodia, "Gpu-accelerated evaluation platform for high fidelity network modeling," in *PADS*, 2007, pp. 131–140.

[13] H. Park and P. A. Fishwick, "A gpu-based application framework supporting fast discrete-event simulation," *Simulation*, vol. 86, no. 10, pp. 613–628, 2010.

[14] H. Park and P. A. Fishwick, "An analysis of queuing network simulation using gpu-based hardware acceleration," *ACM Trans. Model. Comput. Simul.*, vol. 21, no. 3, p. 18, 2011.

[15] R. L. Woods and K. L. Lawrence, *Modeling and simulation of dynamic systems*. Upper Saddle River, NJ: Prentice-Hall, 1997.

[16] D. B. Kirk and W.-m. W. Hwu, *Programming Massively Parallel Processors: A Hands-on Approach*, 1st ed. San Francisco, CA, USA: Morgan Kaufmann Publishers Inc., 2010.

[17] J. C. Wyllie, "The complexity of parallel computations," PhD thesis, Cornell University, Ithaca, NY, USA, Tech. Rep., 1979.

A GPU-based Multiresolution Pipeline for Compressed Volume Rendering

Julián Lamas-Rodríguez[1], Francisco Argüello[1], and Dora B. Heras[1]
[1]CITIUS, University of Santiago de Compostela, Spain

Abstract— *The recent improvements in data-acquisition methods have resulted in the emergence of increasingly larger volumetric datasets. The design of GPU volume rendering solutions must have into account this trend while dealing with the limited available memory in a graphics card. In this work, we present a pipeline for volume rendering that stores a compressed version of the dataset in the GPU memory. During visualization, the volume is divided in bricks, which are decompressed and rendered with a specific level of resolution depending on their distance to the camera. As the main tasks of our pipeline are executed entirely on the GPU, we minimize the communication between the CPU and the graphics hardware. We obtain competitive results with other GPU implementations of compressed volume rendering, with a refresh rate between 30 and 60 FPS for volumes of size in the range between* 256^3 *and* 512^3.

Keywords: compressed volume rendering, multiresolution, wavelet transform, GPU, CUDA

1. Introduction

The evolution from graphics-specific accelerators to programmable vector processors has made of GPUs a standard platform for rendering volumetric datasets. However, recent years have witnessed significant improvements in the data-acquisition methods, and, as a result, the size of datasets has increased. This poses a challenge given the limited memory resources available in current graphics hardware, and although each new GPU generation expands its memory capacity, the current trend shows that this problem will continue to exist in the future [1]. In this context, compression stands as an effective solution for processing increasingly larger datasets in the GPU.

A wide variety of approaches have been developed to build a compact representation of the data. In volume rendering, these solutions are usually assimetric, i.e., the original dataset is decomposed in an offline process which is executed only once, while the decompression and visualization processes are executed in real time. Common methods for data decomposition may involve applying a wavelet transform [2], [3], a vector quantization [4], [5], [6], or a multiscale tensor approximation [7]. For a more comprehensive survey on compressed GPU-based volume rendering, we refer the reader to [8].

In this work, we have used a wavelet transform to compress the volume into a compact hierarchical form. Although there is a wide collection of wavelet transforms, we have selected the Haar wavelet, as it is computationally simple and very effective for fast reconstruction. Most of the coefficients of this transform are computed as sample-to-sample differences of the original volume data. This means that these coefficients will be of a small magnitude, or even zero, and therefore can be neglected without any significant loss of information. Our encoding scheme, a generalization of [2], benefits from this characteristic to obtain a more compact format of the compressed volume.

In the context of volume rendering, bricking is a common divide-and-conquer approach that consists in subdividing the volume in several blocks (or bricks) so a single brick fits into the memory of the GPU. Bricks are loaded and rendered one at a time. In our implementation, we use a single OpenGL 3D texture buffer to store the contents of a brick of data, and this buffer is reused every time a new brick is processed. The final visualization is achieved through texture mapping (also known as texture slicing) [9], which, along with ray casting, is one of the most popular methods to render volume data. In this rendering technique, the 3D texture is mapped onto a proxy geometry composed of planar polygons that constitute camera-oriented translucent slices, i.e., the volumetric object is cut into slices that are rendered always parallel to the image plane [10], [11].

Several techniques of compressed volume rendering that can be found in the literature rely on storing the compressed volume data in a memory space different from the GPU (as the CPU main memory or a hard disk) [12], [13]. These out-of-core techniques require to transfer decompressed portions of the volume to the GPU memory before they can be rendered. Their performance is limited, at least, by the transfer rate of the PCI bus (e.g., 8 GB/s for PCIe 2.0).

In this paper, we present a solution that stores the volume in the GPU memory in its compressed form. We couple decompression and rendering by dividing the volume in bricks which are processed one at a time, benefiting from the higher transfer rate of the GPU memory bus (192.4 GB/s in an NVIDIA GTX 580). Additionally, as our encoding scheme uses a wavelet transform, it supports decompressing bricks at different levels of resolution. The final rendering is executed using the texture mapping technique. We have obtained high speedups for the CUDA implementation of the steps of the algorithm. The complete pipeline performs at an interactive and stable frame rate independent of the viewport size, while keeping a good compression ratio with a high visualization quality.

The rest of this paper is organized as follows. Section 2 describes the GPU architecture. Section 3 examines the design of our GPU-based pipeline for compressed volume rendering. Section 4 analyzes the experimental results, and compares our implementation with other similar works. Finally, section 5 concludes discussing our main contributions and future work.

2. GPU architecture

GPUs are nowadays programmable architectures consisting of several many-core processors capable of running hundreds of thousands of threads concurrently. In this section we present a brief overview on the Fermi GPU architecture [14], which we have used to test our implementation of a GPU volume-rendering pipeline.

NVIDIA's CUDA architecture [15] provides a high computational power by combining a huge number of cores (or streaming processors, SPs), distributed in a set of streaming multiprocessors (SMs), with a very high memory bandwidth. As an example of this architecture, the GeForce GTX 580 has 16 SMs with 32 SPs each, resulting in 512 cores.

The programming model encourages a fine-grained level of parallelism within the single program multiple data (SPMD) paradigm [16]. Hence, a CUDA program (or *kernel*) is run by a *grid of threads*, which are grouped in *thread blocks*. Programmers can configure the size and distribution of the grid to their convenience and according to the requirements of the tasks to compute.

The architecture features several memory spaces. The *global memory* and *texture memory* spaces are accessible by the GPU, and also by the CPU through the PCI bus. Other memory spaces are located inside the chip, and provide a much lower latency: a read-only *constant memory*, a *shared memory* (which is private for each SM), a *texture cache* and, finally, a two-level cache that is used to speed up accesses to the global memory.

Coordination between threads within a kernel is achieved through *synchronization barriers*. However, as thread blocks run independently from all others, their scope is limited to the threads within the thread block.

3. GPU-based rendering pipeline

Our solution involves two different stages: preprocessing and visualization. The preprocessing is executed on the CPU to generate the compressed volume from the original dataset. The visualization stage runs on the GPU, and shows on the screen a reconstruction of the volume with different resolution levels depending on the distance to the camera.

Figure 1 shows the different data structures used in this implementation. The original volume data is divided into

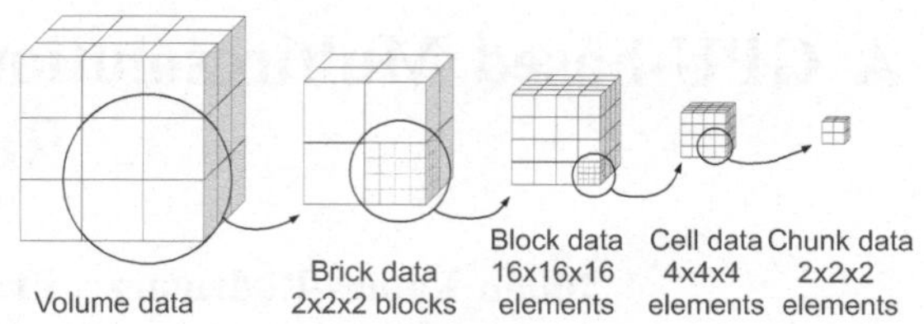

Fig. 1: Data structures used in this work.

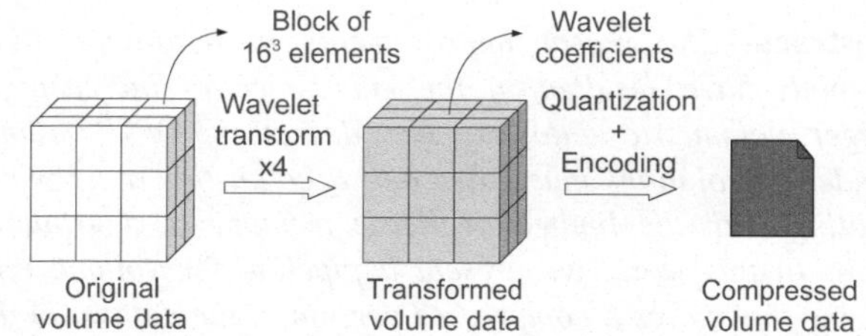

Fig. 2: Preprocessing pipeline for the compression of the original volume data.

blocks of $16\times16\times16$ elements. These blocks are grouped in bricks. The figure shows an example where a brick contains $2 \times 2 \times 2$ blocks. Elements in blocks are grouped in cells, each cell containing $4 \times 4 \times 4$ elements. Finally, a chunk contains a group of $2 \times 2 \times 2$ elements.

Our compression algorithm splits the volume data in blocks and cells. Moreover, the wavelet transform that is applied to blocks processes data in a chunk basis. During the visualization stage, the volume is considered to be divided in bricks, which are processed individually.

The different steps of the preprocessing and visualization stages will be described in the next subsections.

3.1 Preprocessing

The preprocessing stage takes place whenever the user selects a volumetric dataset to be compressed. Figure 2 shows the different steps performed during this stage, and the data generated at each step. First, a wavelet transform is applied to the volumetric data. Then, a quantization step scales down the coefficients obtained in the wavelet transform, nullifying those with a close-to-zero value. Finally, the encoding step generates the compressed volume data, which is later stored in the hard disk. All these steps are executed on the CPU.

3.1.1 Wavelet transform

This step applies a wavelet-transform operator to blocks of $16 \times 16 \times 16$ elements using a Haar filter. Our CPU implementation is similar to other solutions that can be found in the literature [2]. The transform is recursively applied to each block, generating bands of coefficients.

Figure 3 shows how the wavelet transform generates the coefficients for a $16\times16\times16$ block, which are then grouped in eight bands. These bands are labeled from LLL to HHH.

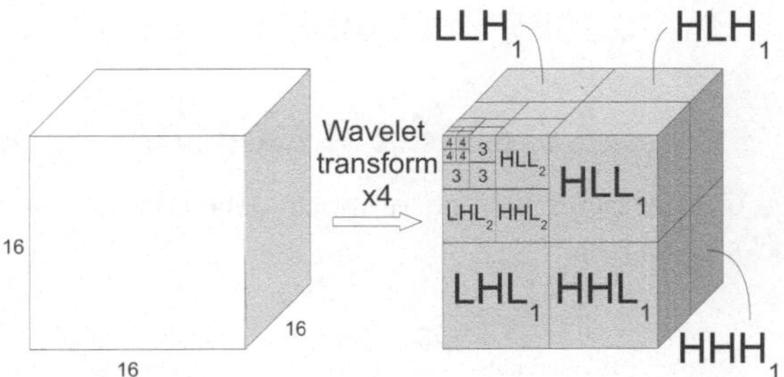

Fig. 3: The result of applying a 4-level wavelet transform to a $16 \times 16 \times 16$ block of data.

The LLL band contains the average coefficients, and the detail coefficients are stored in the remaining bands. The transform is recursively applied to the LLL band, generating new levels of subbands until we get four levels of transform. These levels are the basis of our multiresolution pipeline.

To avoid any data loss during this step the wavelet coefficients are not normalized. This means that the magnitude of the coefficients (specially the low-frequency ones) grows each time the transform is applied. However, this approach guarantees that the only source of data loss is in the quantization step.

3.1.2 Quantization

Quantization is a lossy compression technique that reduces the range of the values of the compressed dataset [17]. In our implementation we have chosen a scalar quantization solution with fixed-rate coding that removes the least significant bits of the coefficients obtained from the previous wavelet transform. This quantization reduces the magnitude of the coefficients, and nullifies those with a close-to-zero value.

3.1.3 Encoding

This step converts the resulting volumetric data from the wavelet-transform and quantization steps into its final compressed form.

Figure 4 shows the main data structures used in this step and their relations with the decompressed volume. The cell-tag–table array stores a cell-tag table for each block in the volume. A cell-tag table contains two-byte tags labeling each cell in a block. The most significant byte stores the width in bytes of the coefficients in the cell (or zero for a null cell), and the less significant byte stores the index of the significance map for the cell. The significance-map array contains a bitmap for each non-null cell in the volume. This bitmap is used to flag coefficients in the cells as zero or non-zero. Finally, four arrays store all the non-zero coefficients from the transformed volume data. Each coefficient is stored in an array depending on its width in bytes. This encoding supports coefficients of up to four bytes.

Our encoding solution increases the flexibility of the implementation presented in [2], that was limited to $4\times4\times4$-cell blocks. Two-byte cell tags enable using bigger blocks, so more resolution levels could be supported, as the maximum number or recursive wavelet transforms that can be applied is restricted by the size of the block.

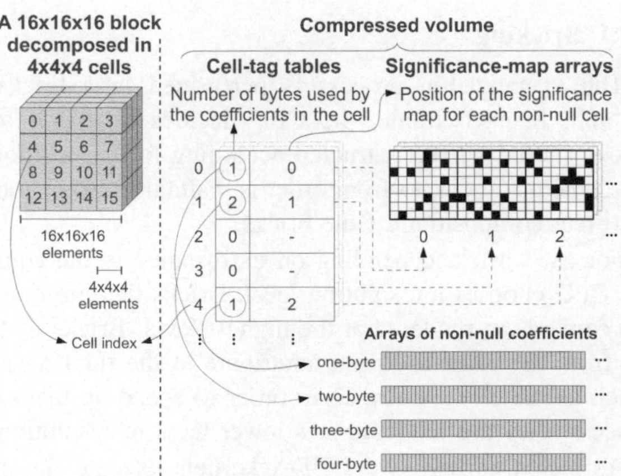

Fig. 4: Structure of the compressed data.

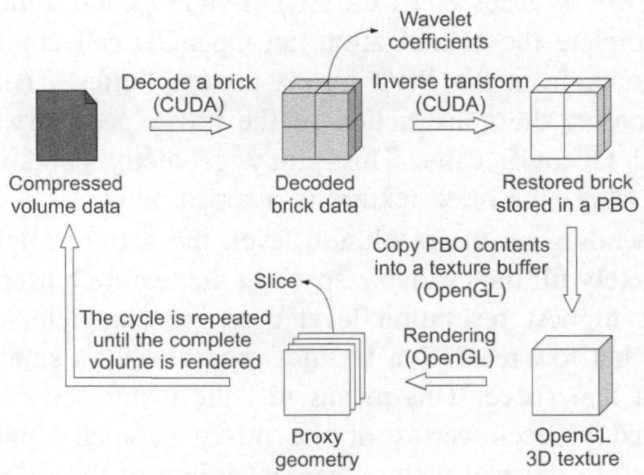

Fig. 5: Visualization pipeline for decompressing and rendering the volume data.

3.2 Visualization

The visualization stage is responsible of reconstructing the compressed volume on the GPU and rendering it on the screen. Figure 5 shows the different steps that take place in this stage. The volume is processed in a brickwise fashion. First, a brick is selected from the compressed volume and reconstructed at a specific level of resolution. This reconstruction involves the steps of decoding and inverse transform, which have been implemented in CUDA kernels, and hence, run on the GPU. The restored brick data are stored in an OpenGL Pixel Buffer Object (PBO), and then copied into a texture buffer to be mapped onto a proxy geometry. These operations, including the final rasterization, are implemented using the OpenGL API. The process continues with another brick until the complete volume has been rendered.

3.2.1 Bricking

The visualization process is performed in a brickwise fashion. In each frame, the CPU decides in which order bricks should be reconstructed according to the position of the camera. A back-to-front order is maintained to guarantee a correct composition of the bricks.

For each brick, depending on its distance to the camera, the CPU chooses a resolution level. Bricks that are close to the camera are rendered at the highest level. Bricks that are far from the camera do not contribute to the final result as much as the closer ones, so in order to speed up the whole process, they are rendered at a lower level of resolution.

As stated earlier, two CUDA kernels execute the steps of decoding and inverse transform required to decompress the brick data. The decompressed data are stored in a PBO, which can be accessed by the CUDA and OpenGL functions. To complete the visualization, an OpenGL call copies the brick data from the PBO into a texture buffer. Then, the CPU orders the construction of the proxy geometry using several OpenGL calls. This proxy geometry contains the slices where the brick texture is mapped onto.

Depending on the resolution level, the texture might not completely fill the available space in the texture buffer. That is, the highest resolution level uses the complete texture space, but low-resolution textures require only a small portion of that space. This means that the texture coordinates assigned to each vertex of the proxy geometry must be adjusted to the real texture size according to the resolution level chosen for the current brick.

3.2.2 Decoding

The process of decoding is performed in a kernel on the GPU. This kernel reads the compressed data of the brick from the compressed volume stored in the GPU global memory and writes the decoded data in a previously allocated buffer (to be later processed by the inverse wavelet transform). Each data block in the brick is assigned to a thread block, where each thread processes a cell (whose size is $4 \times 4 \times 4$ in our implementation).

The decoding process is as follows. Each thread starts by determining if its cell is non-null or not, as indicated by the cell tag associated to the cell. If the cell is non-null, the data reconstruction begins. The thread loops through the elements of the cell, and tries to load them from the arrays of non-zero coefficients in the compressed volume (see Figure 4). If the cell's significance map identifies a coefficient as non-zero, its value is stored as is in the preallocated buffer in global memory, otherwise a zero is written.

To increase the spatial locality of memory accesses, the decoded data are contiguously stored in global memory in a blockwise fashion. Figure 6 illustrates this process for a brick composed of two data blocks. The top of the figure shows how data from different blocks are interleaved when they are stored in global memory attending solely to their absolute position in the brick. Instead, our algorithm arranges the data of each block together, as it is shown in the bottom of the figure, to increase the spatial locality, and, as a result, to improve the performance of the memory accesses.

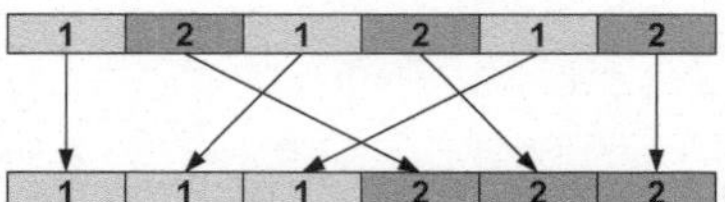

Fig. 6: Blockwise storage of brick data considering two blocks (1 and 2).

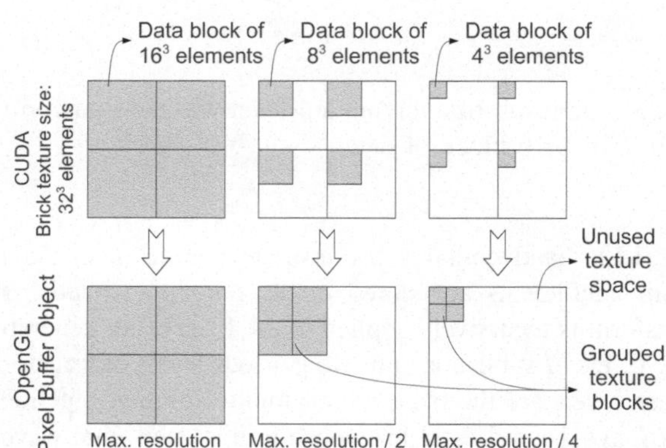

Fig. 7: Storing data from shared memory into the PBO for different resolutions.

3.2.3 Inverse wavelet transform

Once the decoding kernel has restored the coefficients of the transformed brick in global memory, another kernel performs an inverse wavelet transform on the GPU to restore the brick contents. Each data block in the brick is assigned to a thread block depending on its identifier, and each thread processes a chunk of $2 \times 2 \times 2$ voxels.

The inverse transform is also a recursive process, and it is applied until the desired level of resolution is achieved (in the lowest level of resolution, no processing is needed). The resulting coefficients of processing a level of resolution are stored in shared memory, where this data will be available to compute the next level of resolution. When the desired level is reached, these coefficients are copied from shared memory into the OpenGL PBO. In the case of processing the highest level of resolution, the coefficients are directly stored in the PBO, bypassing the shared memory and consequently reducing its impact on the memory load.

When storing data in the PBO, the positions where data are placed are determined by the identifiers of the thread block and the current resolution level. For low resolution levels, the data generated by each thread block are grouped in order to avoid chunks of data scattered in the PBO. Figure 7 shows how a $32 \times 32 \times 32$ restored brick is stored

Table 1: Datasets used in this work

Name	Size	Bytes/voxel	File size
BrainWeb	$256 \times 256 \times 181$	2	23 MB
ModelHead	$512 \times 512 \times 348$	2	174 MB
RealHead	$160 \times 512 \times 512$	2	80 MB

Table 2: Compression quality for different levels of quantization

# bits	Compressed volume size	Compression ratio	MSE	PSNR
		BrainWeb		
0	25.52 MB	1 : 0.89	0.00	∞
1	25.10 MB	1 : 0.90	0.45	99.77
2	18.92 MB	1 : 1.20	0.72	97.75
3	16.81 MB	1 : 1.35	2.28	92.76
4	14.85 MB	1 : 1.52	8.84	86.86
5	13.25 MB	1 : 1.71	35.34	80.85
6	11.41 MB	1 : 1.98	137.92	74.93
7	8.63 MB	1 : 2.62	509.06	69.26
8	5.57 MB	1 : 4.06	1614.11	64.25
9	2.89 MB	1 : 7.83	3488.04	60.90
10	1.81 MB	1 : 12.50	6628.75	58.12
11	1.15 MB	1 : 19.67	12135.79	55.49
		ModelHead		
0	111.82 MB	1 : 1.56	0.00	∞
1	89.08 MB	1 : 1.95	0.45	99.79
2	64.35 MB	1 : 2.70	0.63	98.31
3	45.87 MB	1 : 3.79	1.34	95.05
4	33.02 MB	1 : 5.27	3.25	91.21
5	23.95 MB	1 : 7.27	8.58	87.00
6	17.74 MB	1 : 9.81	23.81	82.56
7	13.09 MB	1 : 13.29	66.71	78.09
8	9.57 MB	1 : 18.18	187.64	73.60
9	7.08 MB	1 : 24.58	504.59	69.30
10	5.29 MB	1 : 32.89	1320.25	65.12
11	3.82 MB	1 : 45.55	3117.75	61.39

in the PBO for different levels of resolution.

4. Results

We performed our tests on an NVIDIA GeForce GTX 580 with 512 processor cores grouped into 16 SMs of 32 SPs each, at a clock rate of 1.544 GHz, and with 1.5 GB of global memory. Each SM has 64 kB of RAM with a configurable partitioning of shared memory and L1 cache (16 kB of shared memory and 48 kB of L1 cache, or vice versa). Additionally, a unified L2 cache of 768 kB is available for all SMs [15]. This GPU was mounted in a machine with an Intel Core 2 Quad Q9450 with four cores at 2.66 GHz and 6 GB of RAM. We compiled our code using the NVIDIA `nvcc` compiler provided within the CUDA 4.0 toolkit and `gcc` version 4.4.3 under Linux.

Table 1 details the different datasets used in this work. The *BrainWeb* dataset was obtained at the BrainWeb Simulated Brain Database [18]. *ModelHead* corresponds with a volumetric CT of a synthetic model of the human head, whereas *RealHead* is volumetric dataset of a real human head obtained with an MRI technique. Figure 8 shows renderings from the three datasets using our solution.

4.1 Quality analysis

We have measured the quality of our decoding implementation with the *BrainWeb* and *ModelHead* datasets. These two datasets can be considered as representative instances of volumes obtained from organic tissues and synthetic materials, respectively.

Quality is measured in terms of compression ratio, mean squared error (MSE) and peak signal-to-noise ratio (PSNR). Table 2 shows the values obtained for the two aforementioned datasets with different levels of quantization. At each quantization level we remove a specific number of least significant bits from the coefficients of the wavelet transform (see Section 3.1.2), as indicated in the table.

Generally, a value of PSNR above 60 is considered good, so we have chosen a quantization level of 8 bits in our tests to measure performance of the complete GPU volume-rendering pipeline (see below). We noticed that changing the number of bits removed during quantization did not significantly affect the performance.

4.2 Performance analysis

In order to evaluate the performance we focus on the GPU implementation of the different steps of our rendering pipeline. First, we measured the speedup of the decoding and inverse-transform kernels compared to the CPU implementations. Second, we executed the complete pipeline on the GPU and took measures of execution time for each step and of FPS for the whole pipeline.

Regarding the speedup measurements, we focus on the implementations of the decoding and the inverse-transform steps on the GPU. Table 3 shows the results we have obtained for different volumes that were constructed from the *RealHead* dataset. For both algorithms, the value of speedup increases with the volume size, as the computational capabilities of the GPU are better exploited when the dataset to process is larger [16].

We also evaluate the performance of the whole rendering process on GPU showing the results for each step. Table 4 shows the performance for each dataset using different brick sizes. Once again, our solution offers a better performance with large brick sizes (except for *BrainWeb*, where using a brick size much larger than the dataset results in poor results). Generally, incrementing the brick size increases the time required to process a brick, but reduces the number of bricks, resulting in a lower time to complete a frame.

4.3 Comparison with other works

To the best of our knowledge, this is the first GPU implementation of a decompression scheme based on [2]. The authors reported their solution required, at best, nearly

 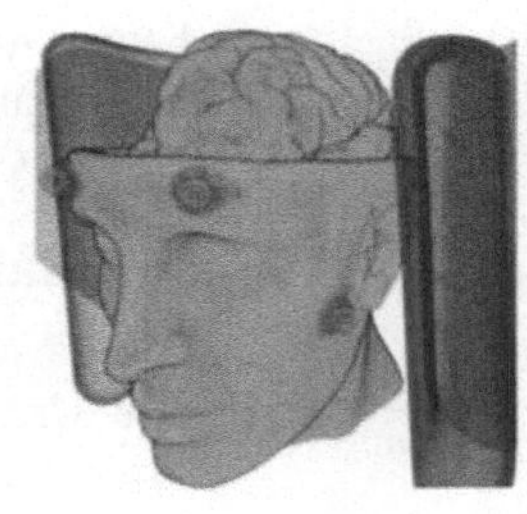 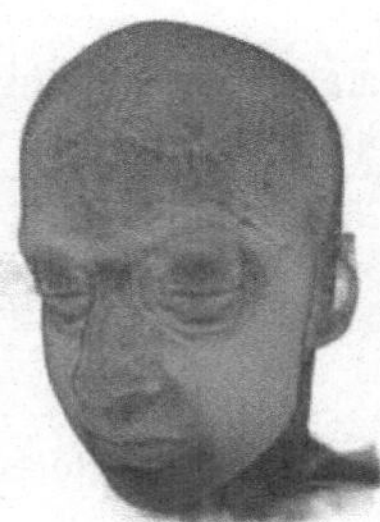

Fig. 8: Volume rendering of the datasets. From left to right: *BrainWeb*, *ModelHead*, and *RealHead*.

Table 3: Execution times in seconds and speedups respect to the CPU implementation of the decoding and inverse-transform kernels for different volume sizes

		64 × 64 × 64	128 × 128 × 128	256 × 256 × 256	512 × 512 × 512
Decoding	GPU	0.000076	0.000296	0.002153	0.013647
	CPU	0.003173	0.024237	0.207878	1.626087
	Speedup	41.6x	81.9x	96.5x	119.2x
Inv. transf.	GPU	0.000033	0.000204	0.001459	0.011550
	CPU	0.009205	0.069018	0.557935	4.434827
	Speedup	280.3x	338.9x	382.5x	384.0x

Table 4: Execution times in seconds and FPS for the steps of the GPU rendering pipeline using different datasets

Dataset	Brick size	# bricks	Decode (CUDA)	Inv. Transf. (CUDA)	Copy (OpenGL)	Render (OpenGL)	**Total per brick**	**Total per frame**	**FPS**
BrainWeb	64 × 64 × 64	48	0.000081	0.000027	0.000016	0.000726	**0.000850**	**0.041**	**15**
	128 × 128 × 128	8	0.000226	0.000191	0.000023	0.001188	**0.001628**	**0.013**	**30**
	256 × 256 × 256	1	0.001571	0.001534	0.000038	0.002282	**0.005425**	**0.005**	**60**
	512 × 512 × 512	1	0.003169	0.012279	0.000070	0.002337	**0.017855**	**0.018**	**30**
ModelHead	64 × 64 × 64	384	0.000075	0.000027	0.000016	0.000529	**0.000647**	**0.248**	**2**
	128 × 128 × 128	48	0.000215	0.000192	0.000023	0.000940	**0.001369**	**0.066**	**10**
	256 × 256 × 256	8	0.001206	0.001524	0.000037	0.001559	**0.004326**	**0.035**	**20**
	512 × 512 × 512	1	0.007975	0.012277	0.000068	0.002965	**0.023286**	**0.023**	**28**
RealHead	64 × 64 × 64	192	0.000077	0.000027	0.000016	0.000382	**0.000502**	**0.096**	**5**
	128 × 128 × 128	32	0.000196	0.000192	0.000023	0.000699	**0.001110**	**0.036**	**15**
	256 × 256 × 256	4	0.001205	0.001526	0.000038	0.001546	**0.004315**	**0.017**	**30**
	512 × 512 × 512	1	0.005388	0.012280	0.000069	0.002314	**0.020052**	**0.020**	**30**

10 seconds to reconstruct a volume of $512 \times 512 \times 512$ elements on CPU. This includes both the decoding step and the inverse transform step. For a brick of the same size, Table 4 shows a performance between 15 and 20 milliseconds for both steps on the GPU.

Our inverse wavelet transform compares favorably with other GPU implementations in the literature. In a recent work [19], the performance of a 3D fast wavelet transform was measured on a GPU processing 64 frames of a video at different resolutions, requiring 6.8 ms for a 512×512 video, and 13.4 ms for a 1024×1024 video. This implementation performed a one-level transform using a Daubechies D^4 wavelet [20]. To compare these results, we have measured the performance of our inverse-transform kernel for a single level instead of four. Processing a brick of size $256 \times 256 \times 256$, which is exactly the same size as the former video, requires 1 ms in our solution. A $512 \times 512 \times 512$ brick, which is twice the size of the latter video, requires 7 ms.

The performance of the GPU decompression and rendering pipeline is also competitive with similar solutions in the literature. A scheme based on the Karhunen-Loève transform [21] is presented in [1]. Compression is performed on CPU using a vector quantization approach that preserves the coefficients from blocks containing the most relevant edges. Visualization is achieved in a two-pass render, the first one devoted to decompress several slices of data, and the second one to the actual rendering. A $512 \times 512 \times 512$ is rendered at a rate between 6 and 11 FPS, depending on the size of the viewport. For a volume with a similar size (*ModelHead*), our solution achieves 28 FPS without the size of the viewport affecting significantly.

Finally, a solution based on the S3 texture compression

algorithm (also known as DXT) [22] was introduced in [23] for time-varying 3D datasets. The reconstruction of the compressed volume data is embedded into a programmable shader, and up to three frames are compressed into the RGB channels of a texture. The authors show results for a volume of size $400 \times 600 \times 400$ visualized at 35 FPS. Although this performance is slightly higher than our solution's, our compression scheme provides better results in terms of quality, with a greater PSNR for a similar compression ratio.

5. Conclusions and future work

In this work we have presented a GPU solution for decompressing and visualizing volumetric compressed datasets using a bricking approach with multiresolution rendering.

The GPU stores a compressed hierarchical version of the original volume. Our pipeline processes the compressed volume in a brickwise fashion. For each brick a level of resolution is selected depending on its distance to the camera, and the brick data are decompressed up to that level. The decompression involves decoding and computing the inverse wavelet transform of the data. We have implemented both steps as CUDA kernels, so they are executed within the GPU. Unlike other out-of-core techniques, communication between CPU and GPU is minimal, avoiding the bottleneck that the PCI bus between both is. As we apply four levels of wavelet, our approach supports up to four different levels of resolution (five including the original one).

The visualization is carried out using the texture mapping technique. The decompressed brick data is copied into an OpenGL texture buffer and mapped onto a proxy geometry composed of several parallel polygonal slices. The GPU rasterizes the geometry by blending the slices to produce the final image.

We have tested our solution with three datasets. We have obtained competitive results compared to other recent GPU implementations of compressed volume rendering, with a refresh rate between 30 and 60 FPS, a PSNR value greater than 60, and a compression ratio between 1:4 and 1:18 for volume sizes in the range between 256^3 and 512^3.

As future work, we plan to extend our solution to larger datasets, including datasets that do not fit inside the GPU memory. For these cases, empty-space–skipping techniques are essential to identify bricks in the volume that do not add essential information to the final rendering in order to keep an interactive refresh rate.

Acknowledgments

This work was supported in part by the Ministry of Science and Innovation, Government of Spain, and FEDER funds under contract TIN 2010-17541, and by the Xunta de Galicia under contracts 08TIC001206PR and 2010/28. Julián Lamas-Rodríguez acknowledges financial support from the Ministry of Science and Innovation, Government of Spain, under a MICINN-FPI grant.

References

[1] N. Fout and K.-L. Ma, "Transform coding for hardware-accelerated volume rendering," *IEEE Transactions on Visualization and Computer Graphics*, vol. 13, no. 6, pp. 1600–1607, Nov.–Dec. 2007.

[2] I. Ihm and S. Park, "Wavelet-based 3D compression scheme for interactive visualization of very large volume data," *Computer Graphics Forum*, vol. 18, no. 1, pp. 3–15, March 1999.

[3] S. Guthe, M. Wand, J. Gonser, and W. Straßer, "Interactive rendering of large volume data sets," in *Proc. Vis'02*, 2002.

[4] J. Schneider and R. Westermann, "Compression domain volume rendering," in *Proc. Vis'03*, 2003.

[5] R. Parys and G. Knittel, "Giga-voxel rendering from compressed data on a display wall," *Journal of WSCG*, vol. 17, no. 1–3, pp. 73–80, 2009.

[6] E. Gobbetti, J. A. Iglesias Guitián, and F. Marton, "COVRA: A compression-domain output-sensitive volume rendering architecture based on a sparse representation of voxel blocks," *Computer Graphics Forum*, vol. 31, no. 3pt4, pp. 1315–1324, 2012.

[7] S. K. Suter, J. A. Iglesias Guitian, F. Marton, M. Agus, A. Elsener, C. P. Zollikofer, M. Gopi, E. Gobbetti, and R. Pajarola, "Interactive multiscale tensor reconstruction for multiresolution volume visualization," *IEEE Transactions on Visualization and Computer Graphics*, vol. 17, no. 12, pp. 2135–2143, 2011.

[8] M. B. Rodríguez, E. Gobbetti, J. I. Guitián, M. Makhinya, F. Marton, R. Pajarola, and S. Suter, "A survey of compressed GPU-based direct volume rendering," in *Proc. Eurographics'13*, 2013, preprint.

[9] A. V. Gelder and K. Kim, "Direct volume rendering with shading via three-dimensional textures," in *Proc. 1996 Symposium on Volume Visualization*, 1996, pp. 23–30, 98.

[10] K. Engel, M. Hadwiger, J. M. Kniss, C. Rezk-Salama, and D. Weiskopf, *Real-time volume graphics*. A K Peters, Ltd., 2006.

[11] Q. Zhang, R. Eagleson, and T. M. Peters, "Volume visualization: a technical overview with a focus on medical applications," *Journal of Digital Imaging*, vol. 24, no. 4, pp. 640–664, Aug. 2011.

[12] E. Gobbetti, F. Marton, and J. A. I. Guitián, "A single-pass GPU ray casting framework for interactive out-of-core rendering of massive volumetric datasets," *The Visual Computer*, vol. 24, no. 7–9, pp. 797–806, July 2008.

[13] B. Liu, G. J. Clapworthy, F. Dong, and E. C. Prakash, "Octree rasterization: accelerating high-quality out-of-core GPU volume rendering," *IEEE Transactions on Visualization and Computer Graphics*, vol. (preprint), July 2013.

[14] J. Nickolls and W. J. Dally, "The GPU computing era," *IEEE Micro*, vol. 30, no. 2, pp. 56–69, March–April 2010.

[15] *CUDA C programming guide (version 4.0)*, NVIDIA, 2011.

[16] D. B. Kirk and W.-m. W. Hwu, *Programming massively parallel processors: a hands-on approach*. Burlington, Massachusetts, USA: Elsevier, 2010.

[17] R. M. Gray and D. L. Neuhoff, "Quantization," *IEEE Transactions on Information Theory*, vol. 44, no. 6, pp. 2325–2383, Oct. 1998.

[18] C. Cocosco, V. Kollokian, R.-S. Kwan, and A. Evans, "BrainWeb: online interface to a 3D MRI simulated brain database," *NeuroImage*, vol. 5, no. 4, p. S425, May 1997.

[19] G. Bernabe, G. D. Guerrero, and J. Fernandez, "CUDA and OpenCL implementations of 3D fast wavelet transform," in *Proc. LASCAS'12*, March 2012, pp. 1–4.

[20] I. Daubechies, *Ten Lectures on Wavelets*. Philadelphia, Pennsylvania, USA: Society for Industrial and Applied Mathematics, 1992.

[21] R. D. Dony, "Karhunen-Loève transform," in *The Transform and Data Compression Handbook*. Boca Raton, Florida, USA: CRC Press, 2004.

[22] K. I. Iourcha, K. S. Nayak, and Z. Hong, "System and method for fixed-rate block-based image compression with inferred pixel values," US Patent 5 956 431, Sept. 21, 1999.

[23] Y. Cao, L. Xiao, and H. Wang, "Hardware-accelerated volume rendering based on DXT compressed datasets," in *Proc. ICALIP'10*, 2010, pp. 523–527.

Data-flow Concurrency on Distributed Multi-core Systems

George Michael[1], Samer Arandi[2] and Paraskevas Evripidou[1]
[1]Department of Computer Science, University of Cyprus, Nicosia, Cyprus
[2]Department of Computer Engineering, An-Najah National University, Nablus, Palestine

Abstract— *The Dynamic Data-Flow model of execution has many inherit properties, such as tolerance to latencies and distributed concurrency, which make it suitable for distributed execution. Data-Driven Multithreading (DDM) is a hybrid Data-flow/Control-flow model that implements the Data-Flow principles at the Thread level on sequential processors. In this paper we demonstrated that the Data-Driven Multithreading Virtual Machine (DDM-VM), can achieve high performance in Distributed Nodes (multi-core systems). A shared Global Address Space is supported across all the Nodes in the system to facilitate data movement. We have evaluated our work on both Homogeneous and Heterogeneous systems. The performance evaluation shows that the distributed execution achieves 80-84% of the maximum possible speedup using off-the-shelf networking.*

Keywords: multi-core, data-driven multithreading, heterogeneous, homogeneous, distributed

1. Introduction

Data-Driven Multithreading (DDM) has demonstrated that Data-Flow concurrency can be implemented in commercial control-flow processors in an efficient manner [16]. The Data-Driven Multithreading Virtual Machine (DDM-vm) is a parallel software platform that supports Data-Flow concurrency on conventional control-flow multi-core systems. The DDM model combines the latency tolerance and distributed concurrency of the dynamic data-flow model of execution with the efficient execution of the control-flow model. The DDM-vm targets both homogeneous and heterogeneous multi-core architectures.

In this work we advance the state-of-the-art by supporting DDM execution across Distributed multi-core systems. Previous implementation either supported distributed DDM execution across single-processor Nodes [16] or DDM execution within a multi-core Node [21]. The results of this work further demonstrates that data-flow concurrency can be utilized to tolerate synchronization and network latency efficiently.

First, we present the DDM-vm that is executing on symmetric multi-core architectures. Then we highlight the extensions and modifications of the DDM-vm design to support distributed DDM execution across multiple computers. Concluding, with the evaluation of single- and distributed-Node DDM-vm using a suite of benchmark applications and multiple, different clusters.

This work was supported in part by the EU FP7 TERAFLUX (249013) project

The evaluation of the single-Node DDM-vm shows that it achieves an overall average speedup of 9.6 out of 11. The evaluation of the distributed execution shows that it achieves an average of 80% to 84% of the maximum possible speedup when utilizing various number of cores per Node. The results are stable across different cluster configurations. These results demonstrate the efficiency and scalability of the DDM-vm.

The rest of the paper is organized as follows: An overview of Data-driven Multithreading is presented in Section 2. Section 3 describes the DDM-vm. Section 4 presents the support for distributed DDM-vm execution. The evaluation is presented in Section 4. The related work is presented in Section 5 and Section 6 concludes this paper.

2. Data-Driven Multithreading

DDM [16] is a multithreaded model that applies dynamic Data-flow principles for the communication among threads and exploits highly efficient control-flow execution within a thread. Programming constructs such as loops and functions are mapped into DDM threads (D-Threads).

DDM decouples the synchronization part of a program from the execution part and allows them to execute asynchronously, thus shortening the critical path. At the core of the DDM model is the Thread Scheduling Unit (TSU) [11] which schedules threads at run-time based on data-availability. DDM utilizes data-driven caching policies, called Cacheflow, to implement deterministic data prefetching which can substantially improve the locality of sequential processing [15].

DDM has shown that it can exploit efficiently Data-flow concurrency on commercially available multi-core systems [1], [2]. DDM does not need traditional memory coherence because it enforces the single-assignment semantics for data exchange among threads.

In DDM all D-Threads that are ready for execution are held in the Firing queue of each core. Thus, DDM prefetching [15] is deterministic and can be very near to optimal. The ability of DDM to deterministically prefetch data allows high performance without the need for complex and expensive modules such as Out of Order Execution (OOE). Thus, DDM inspired processors had the potential to have simple and low power designs and at the same time achieve high performance.

DDM programs are partitioned at compile time into a number of threads. Each thread is associated with its meta-data: Instruction Frame pointer (IFP), Data-Frame Pointers (DFP), Consumer threads and the Ready Count (RC) which is the number of producer threads.

DDM supports dynamic Data-flow concurrency based on the U-Interpreter [3] principles. It uses the tagging system of the U-Interpreter to distinguish between different instantiations of a static code template. It maps the tag of the U-Interpreter into a unique integer, called the *context* in DDM. Consequently it maps the entire unravelled Data-flow graph into the virtual space of the machine.

3. The Data-Driven Multithreading Virtual Machine

The Data-Driven Multithreading Virtual Machine (DDM-vm) software model is composed of the:

- Thread Scheduling Unit (TSU), that is implemented as a software module executing on one of the cores
- Network Interface Unit (NIU) is implemented as a software module that is executing on the same core as the TSU
- Runtime support system that (with the help of the TSU) handles the tasks of thread scheduling, execution instantiation and data management implicitly on the rest of the cores

The DDM-vm can be used both on heterogeneous multi-cores with software-managed memory (the Cell B.E. Processor [12]), and on symmetric multi-cores. DDM-vm support for symmetric multi-cores is described in the following sections. A detailed description and performance results of the DDM-vm on the Cell B.E. Processor can be found in [1].

The *synchronization graph* contains the *meta-data* of the threads which mainly convey the consumer/producer dependency relationships of each thread. The virtual machine uses the *meta-data* to schedule threads based on data-availability; a thread is scheduled for execution when all its producers finish execution. The scheduling of threads is interleaved with their execution, thus shortening the critical path of the application. In the case of architectures with a software-managed memory hierarchy the DDM-vm prefetches the thread data from the main memory to the cache of the processor before starting its execution.

The overall architecture of DDM-vm is depicted in Figure 2. The support of Data-Driven execution on control-flow processors communication is achieved by changing the state of the TSU structures allocated in main memory.

Next, we describe the structures and operations of the TSU and the TSU-Processor interface for symmetric multi-cores.

3.1 The Thread Scheduling Unit (TSU)

a) The TSU Memory Structures: are allocated in main memory. Some of the structures are common for all the cores: Synchronization Memory (SM) and and Graph Memory (GM) and the rest: (1) Acknowledge Queue (AQ), (2) Waiting queue and (3) Firing Queue (FQ)are local in each core. The common TSU structures are:

The **Graph Memory (GM)**: holds the *synchronization template* of each thread:

- **Thread identifier** (ThreadId),
- **Instruction Frame Pointer** (IFP),
- **Consumers List** number of Data Frame Pointers,
- **Ready Count** (RC): number of producer threads
- **Data Frame Pointers** (DFPs) which are retrieved at runtime by calling a helper-function.
- **Thread attributes**: (i) Scheduling policy , (ii) Type of Synchronization Memory (More information can be found in [1]), and the (iii) *Arity* of the specifying the loop nesting level.
- **Consumer List** (CL): contains two fields, *Cons1* and *Cons2*, which can hold the thread identifier for one or two consumers. If the thread has more than two consumers, a CL entry is created that holds the list of consumer threads. In that case, the GM entry is modified so that *Cons1* is set to zero and *Cons2* is set to point to the entry in the CL.

The Synchronization Memory (SM): holds the Ready Count (RC) values for each invocation of a DDM thread. The SM entries are uniquely indexed using the *context* of the invocations. The RC value in the GM entry is used to initialize the RC entries in the Synchronization Memory. As the performance of the SM is critical to the overall system performance, we have utilized three different implementations of the SM. Details of the implementations and their performance is presented in [1].

b) The per-core TSU structures: are also allocated in main memory:

The Acknowledgement Queue (AQ): holds requests to decrement the RC of one or more invocations of consumer threads. The AQ requests are enqueued when a producer thread finishes execution. The request include the consumer identifier, *context* and the decrement value by which the consumer(s) RC is decremented. A sample of this request can be seen on figure 1 as the command Dec.

The Waiting Queue (WQ): holds the information of threads which with RC=0 and are waiting for prefetching to be completed.

The Firing Queue (FQ): holds the information of threads that are ready to execute. This includes the IFP, *context* and the DFP list. The latter is needed for supporting distributed DDM execution, in which part of the thread data could be allocated dynamically by the TSU (described in the

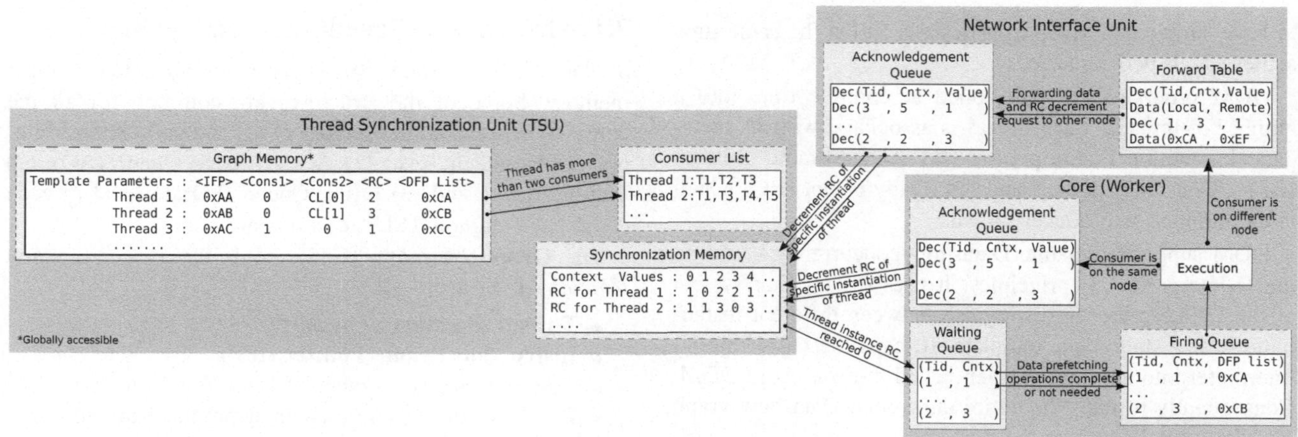

Fig. 1: TSU organization and transitions

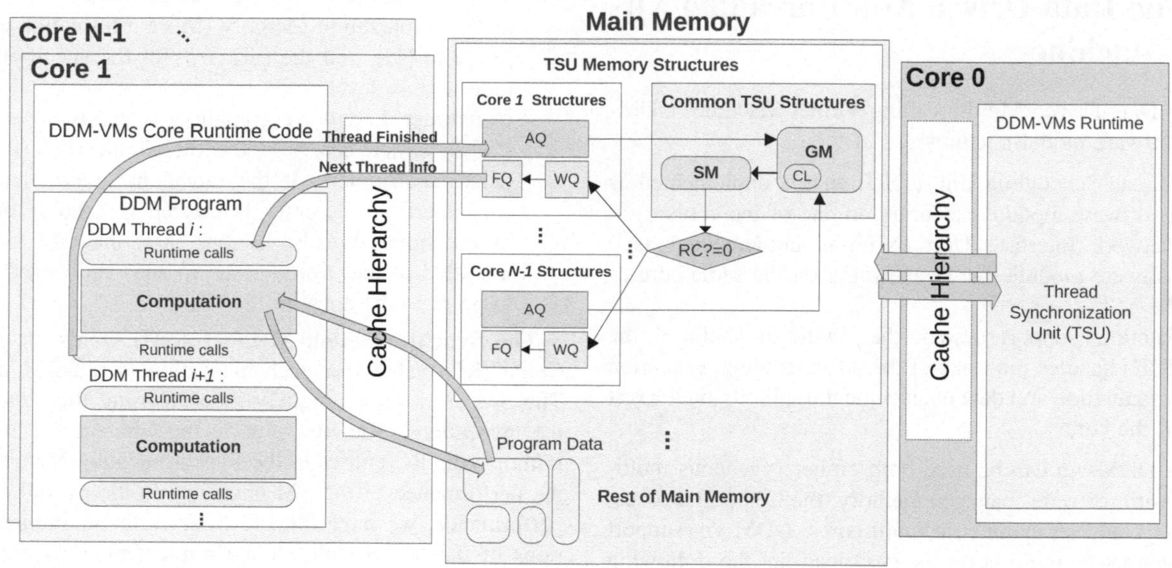

Fig. 2: The architecture of the DDM-vm

following section).

Figure 2 depicts the structures of the TSU.

3.2 Thread Execution and the TSU-Processor interface

The DDM thread execution takes place on the cores and consists of two types of operations or phases: computation and synchronization. The synchronization operations are performed by the runtime, which communicates with the TSU via the TSU-Processor interface. The purpose of the communication is to:

1) Inform the TSU to decrement the RC of the consumers of the thread that has just completed execution by inserting requests in the AQ
2) Providing the execution cores with the information of the next ready thread to execute. This is achieved by accessing the meta-data of ready threads in the FQ.

The two tasks are implemented by accessing the related TSU structures in main memory directly: The AQ in the first task and the FQ in the second task.

The TSU operations:

1) The TSU running on one of the cores processes the AQ requests to decrement the RC of consumer threads.
2) If any RC reaches zero, the corresponding thread invocation is scheduled for execution on a core that is selected by a scheduling policy. This is done by inserting the thread information into the Waiting Queue (WQ) were it waits from Data prefetching.
3) Finally the metadata of the threads are then moved

from the WQ into the Fire Queue (FQ) indicating they are ready for execution.

Figure 2 depicts the various operations performed by the TSU and the runtime.

4. Distributed DDM-vm Execution

Tolerating the Network and Synchronization latencies is the key for the efficiency of Distributed systems. The Data-Flow model provides tolerance to such latencies; an operation starts only after all it s data has been produced. Furthermore, Data-flow concurrency enforces the minimal ordering of objects as dictated by the true data-dependencies. Constructs like critical session and barriers do not exists in Data-Flow systems. Cache coherence is also a major challenge of the distributed systems. This is also not needed in Data-Flow inspired systems such as DDM.

The main difference between single-Node and distributed/multi-Node DDM execution is the introduction of remote memory accesses resulting from producer and consumer threads running on different Nodes. To this end, we employ data *forwarding* [19], [13], to the Node where the consumer is scheduled to run. We facilitate this by supporting a shared Global Address Space (GAS) across all the Nodes. A Network Interface Unit (NIU) has been implemented in the TSU to handle the low-level communication operations.

In terms of the distribution of threads across the cores of the system Nodes, this work explores a *static* scheme, in which the mapping is determined at compile time and does not change during the execution. This simplifies the scheduling and data management tasks and, in the presence of an accurate knowledge of the threads execution loads, can lead to a very efficient and balanced parallel execution. It is important to note that a static distribution only specifies *where* the thread will be scheduled once its ready, however, *when* the thread is ready is decided based on data-availability. The benefit of this approach extends to programmability. *Distributed* DDM-vm programs are fundamentally the same as *single-Node* ones. Aside from the distribution of program data in the GAS across the Nodes at startup and gathering the results after the program execution.

Next, we highlight the additions and modifications to the TSU structures & operations that are required for supporting distributed execution.

4.1 Modifications to the Thread Scheduling Unit

The DDM-vm runtime adopts a distributed organization consisting of multiple TSU units (one per Node[1]) communicating across the network to coordinate the overall DDM execution. As shown in Figure 3.

[1]Node: multi-core processor

4.1.1 The TSU structures

In the Graph Memory (GM) of each Node, we only load the *metadata* of the threads that are expected to execute on that Node. The rest of the TSU structures remain unchanged. Two new structures to support distributed execution have been added:

1) **The Distributed Acknowledgement Queue (AQ)** This queue holds the decrement RC requests coming from the TSUs on the remote Nodes.
2) **Forward Table (FT)** This table holds the address and size of the data that will be forwarded to remote Nodes.

4.1.2 The TSU operations

When the TSU is notified that a thread finished execution, it determines by the scheduling policy (ThreadId,*context*) weather it will on the producer Node or at a remote Node. If the core is on the same Node, an entry is inserted in the AQ of the local Node TSU. However, if the core belongs to a remote Node, a message containing the invocation (ThreadId,*context*) is sent to that Node. When the message is received, a request to decrement the RC of that invocation is enqueued in the *distributed* AQ on that Node. In addition to the request message, the data produced by the thread is also forwarded to the remote Node.

The TSU on each Node continuously checks the local AQ(s) and the distributed AQ in order to decrement the RC of threads invocations.

Once the RC of a specific thread invocation reaches zero, its metadata is moved into the Waiting Queue (WQ). The rest of the activities proceed as described in 3.1. The additional steps required for managing the forwarding of produced data to consumers running on remote Nodes,are described in Section 4.3.

4.2 The Network Interface Unit (NIU)

The NIU, is responsible for the handling the inter-Node communication. NIU was used in a previous DDM implementation [16] to support communication among distributed single-processor Nodes, however it was implemented as a hardware module. In this work the NIU is implemented as a software module that relies on the underlying network hardware interface. Initially, we have consider using MPI [9] for handling the low-level network connectivity in the NIU. However, our evaluation has shown that the expected overheads of invoking an external library were very high. This combined and our need for customized communication, we decided to develop our own optimized connectivity layer using non-blocking TCP sockets.

The NIU is responsible for managing the network initialization, establishing connections with the other Nodes in the system and providing communication services to the TSUs during the execution. The NIU also supports

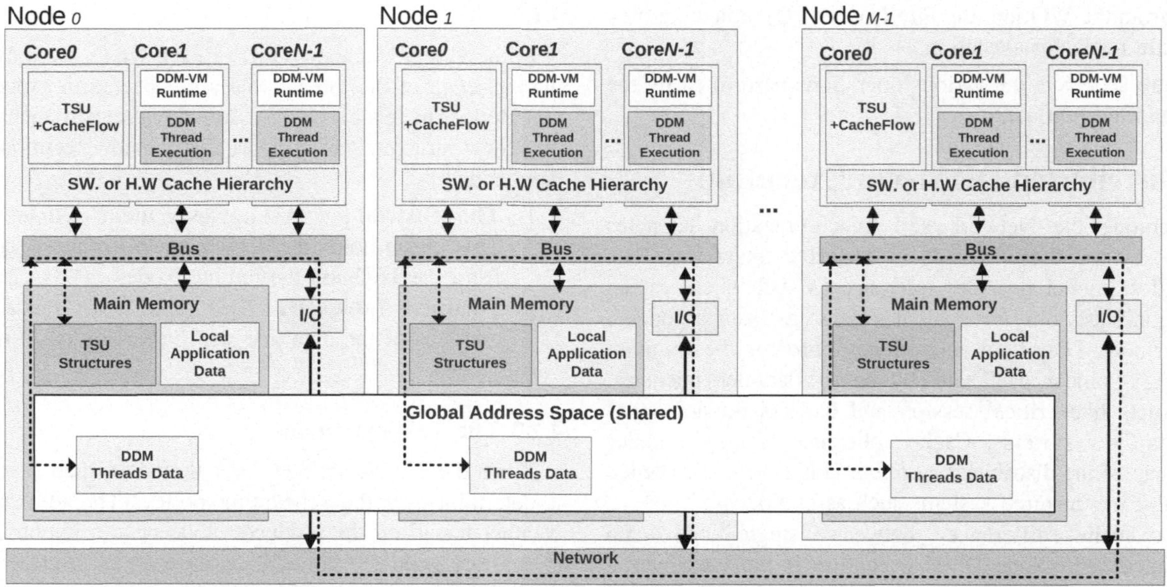

Fig. 3: The Distributed DDM-vm architecture

distributing/gathering data across the global address space in the system at start-up and post-execution of the DDM-vm program.

In the initialization stage the NIU on each Node establishes connections with all the other Nodes. For each Node two non-blocking sockets are allocated, one for sending (*outgoing* socket) and one for receiving (*incoming* socket). Once the connections are established through the sockets, the NIUs exchange information related on the number of cores utilized for DDM execution on each Node. This information is maintained in a table, which used later by the TSU to determine on which Node each core is located.

The NIU abstracts the underlying network and provides the TSU with a simple communication interface. The TSU uses this interface to exchange:

- **Synchronization commands or messages**: the most important one is the request to decrement the *RC* of a specific consumer invocation.
- **Data *forwarding***: when a thread produces data that is needed by a consumer on a remote Node, the TSU passes the data to the NIU to *forward* it to the remote Node.

The NIU tolerates the latencies of network communication by overlapping its work and data transfers with threads execution and the rest of the TSU work. The NIU module is naturally split into two main independent sub-units:

- **The *send* sub-unit**: responsible for sending commands and forwarding data to remote Nodes. Both commands and data are first encapsulated in a simple message with a header describing the content, before they are sent to the remote Node. The sending operation returns when the messages have been stored in the O.S. network layer buffers.
- **The *receive* sub-unit**: responsible for receiving and processing the messages sent from remote Nodes. It continuously polls the *incoming* network connections in a round-robin fashion. The received messages are processed according to their type. In the case of decrement RC request commands, the metadata of the message is inserted as an entry in the *distributed* AQ.

On symmetric multi-cores the *receive* sub-unit is launched in an auxiliary thread (that is pinned to the same core running the TSU), taking advantage of the fact that the processor is an SMT supporting two hardware threads [12]. Furthermore, we further distribute the work of the *send* sub-unit across the cores. This is possible because the services of the *send* sub-unit are invoked by the DDM-vm runtime threads on the cores. Thus, removing the tasks of the *send* sub-unit from the critical path of the TSU.

4.3 Distributed Shared Memory

The DDM-vm supports a Distributed Shared Memory (DSM) [20] abstraction in which part or all of the main memory address space on each Node is mapped to the Global Address Space (GAS) of the DSM. The GAS is a collection of ordered pairs **(Node_id, local_address)** that is shared among all Nodes. The first component refers to the Node identifier and the second refers to a conventional main memory address on that Node. Figure 3 illustrates the GAS across the system Nodes.

Coherence-management operations typically associated with DSM systems [20] are not required between the Nodes, because produced data is *forwarded* to consumers running on remote Nodes. Coherence operations are only required within each Node's memory hierarchy and so it is managed by the hardware on symmetric multi-cores.

The mapping of the program data into the GAS depends on the assignment of the program threads. The data of each specific invocations of a thread is mapped to the part of the GAS belonging to the Node where this invocations is scheduled to run. The movement of data between producers and consumers running on different Nodes during the execution is managed automatically by the DDM-vm without the Need for programmer intervention of the.

A number of runtime calls facilitate the allocation and release of the data in the GAS. The calls also abstracts the distribution and gathering of data among the Nodes. These calls invoke the services of the NIU to move the data between the main memories of the Nodes.

Data forwarding: DDM-vm employs *Data Forwarding* [19], [13] for tolerating data communication latency across the Nodes. When a *producer* thread executes *Data forward command* the produced data is send immediately to the remote Node where the *consumer* thread is scheduled to execute. This increases the chances of tolerating the communication latency and eliminates the need for remote read operations. Thus, resulting in reducing the total communication cost since remote read operations are usually more costly that remote write operations [14].This also eliminates coherence management operations as previously mentioned.

The forwarding of data completes before decrementing the RC of the consumer thread. Consequently, when a thread RC reaches zero, its data is **guaranteed** to reside in the main memory of remote Node.

The DDM-vm supports threads that produce data consumed by multiple remote consumers running on different Nodes. In this case a *list* of output addresses is provided (instead of only one) and the DDM-vm *forwards* the data to all the locations in the list by creating an FT entry for each remote address.

5. Evaluation

In this section we present the evaluation of the single-Node execution on symmetric multi-cores and the distributed/multi-Node execution both for symmetric multi-cores and the Cell processor. The evaluation of the single-Node execution on the Cell processor is presented in [1].

5.1 Experimental Setup

For the evaluation of the distributed execution we used three clusters each connected using an off-the-shelf Gigabit Ethernet switch. Technical information are listed in Table 1.

The characteristics of the benchmark suite are shown in Tables 2 and 3. The applications used for evaluating the two implementations are the same, However, some of their characteristics differ, such as the granularity (the average dynamic execution time of the application threads) due to the vectorization of the computational kernels in the case of the Cell and the fact that the code is compiled with different compilers. Moreover, the symmetric multi-core system has more main memory compared to that on the PS3, which enables us to use larger input sizes.

5.2 The symmetric multi-core single-Node evaluation

We executed the benchmarks for the *large* input size and the 64x64 granularity. Figure 4 depicts the speedup results. The baseline for the speedup is the best sequential (non-DDM) execution among all the granularities. Note that the maximum possible speedup is 11, since we reserve one core out of the 12 cores for the execution of the TSU.

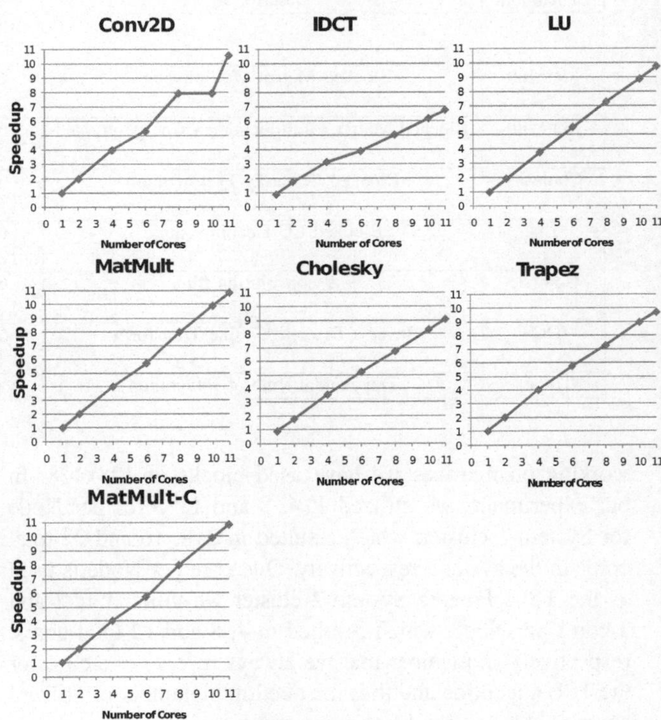

Fig. 4: Symmetric multi-core single-Node speedup

The results demonstrate that overall, the system scales well over the range of the benchmarks and achieves - when utilizing all the cores - an average speedup of 9.6 out of 11, which indicates the efficiency and scalability of the system.

5.3 Distributed symmetric multi-core execution

The benchmarks we executed contains applications with little communication during the execution (Conv2D, IDCT and MatMult, Trapez), and ones with heavy inter-Node communication (LU and Cholesky). For all the benchmarks

Table 1: Experimental setup

Configuration	Nodes	Processors per Node	Memory per Node	O.S.	Network
Homogeneous System 1	2	2 x Six-Core AMD Opteron(tm) Processor 2427	32 GB	Ubuntu Linux 2.6.31	Giga-bit Ethernet
Homogeneous System 2	4	Four-Core AMD Phenom(tm) II X4 B95 Processor	4 GB	Ubuntu Linux 2.6.31	Giga-bit Ethernet
Heterogenous Sony PS3	4	One+Six-Core Cell Broadband Engine	256MB	Fedora Linux 2.6.23-r1	Giga-bit Ethernet

Table 2: The benchmarks suite characteristics - DDM-vm on Cell

Benchmark	Description	Average Granularity of Benchmark Threads		Problem Size		
		Granularity	Execution Time	Large	XLarge	XXLarge
MatMult	Blocked Matrix Multiplication	64x64 block	22.1μs	2048x2048	3072x3072	-
Cholesky	Blocked Cholesky Factorization (vectorized)	64x64 block	22μs	2048x2048	3072x3072	-
Cholesky-S	Blocked Cholesky Factorization (scalar)	64x64 block	8.2ms	2048x2048	3072x3072	-
LU	Blocked LU Decomposition	64x64 block	1.82ms	2048x2048	3072x3072	-
Conv2D	9x9 convolution filter	64x64 block	48.11μs	2048x2048	3072x3072	4096x4096
		96x96 block	107μs			
IDCT	Inverse Discrete Cosine Transform	64x64 block	98.8μs	2048x2048	3072x3072	4096x4096
Trapez	Trapezoidal rule for integration	variable	variable	675K steps	5400K steps	10800K steps

Table 3: The benchmarks suite characteristics - DDM-vm AMD processor

Benchmark	Description	Average Granularity of Benchmark Threads			Problem Size	
		Granularity	Execution Time		XLarge	XXLarge
			System-2	System-1		
MatMult	Blocked Matrix Multiplication	64x64	387 μs	528 μs	4096x4096	8192x8192
		128x128	3333 μs	4540 μs		
MatMult	Blocked Matrix Multiplication - Coarge-grained	64x64	7250 μs	8436 μs	4096x4096	8192x8192
		128x128	28500 μs	36350 μs		
Cholesky	Blocked Cholesky Factorization	64x64	134 μs	182 μs	4096x4096	8192x8192
		128x128	916 μs	1240 μs		
LU	Blocked LU Decomposition	64x64	380 μs	520 μs	4096x4096	8192x8192
		128x128	2918 μs	3975 μs		
Conv2D	9x9 convolution filter	64x64	626 μs	855 μs	4096x4096	8192x8192
		128x128	2500 μs	3416 μs		
IDCT	Inverse Discrete Cosine Transform	64x64	12 μs	17 μs	8192x8192	16384x18384
		128x128	49 μs	68 μs		
Trapez	Trapezoidal Rule of Integration	variable	variable	variable	675M steps	1350M steps

working on matrices we have used blocks of 128x128. In our experiments we utilized 1, 4, 8 and 11 cores per Node for System-1 cluster, which resulted in 2, 8, 16 and 22 total cores in the system, respectively. One core per Node is used as the TSU. For the System-2 cluster we utilized 1, 2 and 3 cores per Node, which resulted in 4, 8 and 12 total cores, respectively (remember that we always reserve one core for the TSU execution and thus the maximum number of utilized cores is 11 on the 12-core machine and 3 on the 4-core machine). We have used two input sizes per benchmark. Figure 5 illustrates the speedup results for both clusters.

The results show that for the largest input size the system achieves an average of 80% and 84% of the maximum possible speedup for the System-1 and System-2 clusters, respectively, which is a very good result. Analysing the results further, it is clear that as the input size increases the system scales better. The average speed-up utilizing all the cores is 13.1 out of 22 for the smaller input size and 16 out of 22 for the larger input size for the System-1 cluster. The average speedup on the System-2 cluster is 8.9 out of 12 for the smaller input size and 9.5 out of 12 for the larger

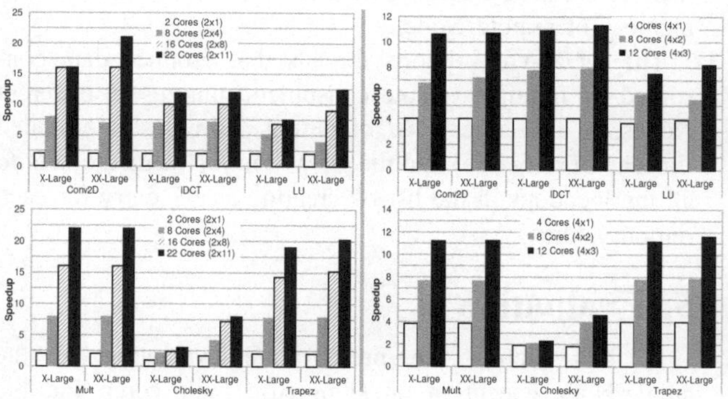

Fig. 5: Distributed symmetric multi-core execution (System-1 left, System-2 right) - Speedup

input size. This is expected as larger problem sizes allow for amortizing the overheads of the parallelization. The results are summarized in Table 4.

Input sizes and granularities (compared to single-Node execution) need to scale as the distributed system scales.

Table 4: Distributed symmetric multi-core execution results - Summary

	System-1 Cluster		System-2 Cluster	
	Smaller Input Size	Larger Input Size	Smaller Input Size	Larger Input Size
Average Speedup Percentage	74%	80%	79%	84%
Average Speedup (utilizing all cores)	13.1/22	16/22	8.9/12	9.5/12

The Cholesky benchmark yields the least performance as its threads exchange data heavily across the Nodes and so it is affected to a great extent by the large latency of the the network. The LU benchmark similarly has a heavy inter-Node data exchange, however, because its threads have a larger granularity compared to Cholesky's (for the same block size), the TSU has a better chance of overlapping the network latencies, thus yielding better performance.

5.4 Distributed execution on the Cell processor

For the evaluation of distributed on the Cell processor execution we used a cluster of four PS3 Nodes. We used the same benchmarks as in 5.3. For all the benchmarks working on matrices we have used blocks of 64x64 except for the Conv2D benchmark in which we used 96x96 blocks. For the Cholesky benchmark we used scalar computational kernels instead of the vectorized ones as the latter proved too fine-grained for the application to scale. We denote the version using the scalar kernels as Cholesky-S. In our experiments we have utilized 1, 2, 4 and 6 SPEs per Node, which resulted in 4, 8, 16 and 24 total SPEs in the system, respectively. Moreover, we have used two input sizes per benchmark. Figure 6 illustrates the speedup results.

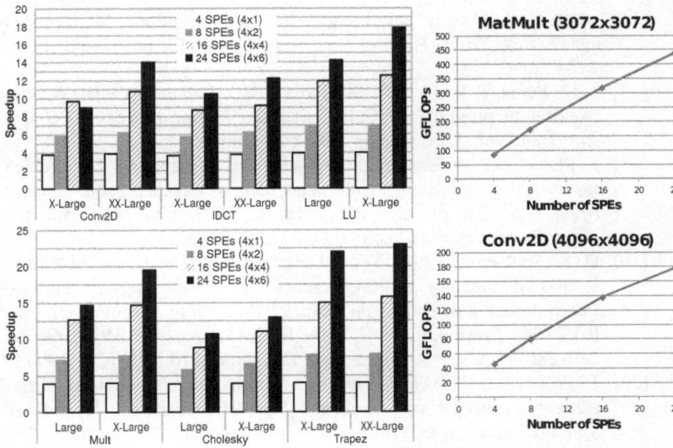

Fig. 6: Distributed execution on the Cell processor - Speedup (left), GFLOPs performance results for MatMult and Conv2D (right)

The results show that for the largest input size the system achieves an average of 80% of the maximum possible speedup for all the benchmarks, which is a very good result. Similar to the results in 5.3, the system scales better as the input size increases as this allows for amortizing the overheads of the parallelization. The average speedup (on all the benchmarks) utilizing all the SPEs is 13.4 out of 24 for the smaller input size and 16.54 out of 24 for the larger input size.

As noted in 5.3, compared to single-Node execution, larger input sizes (on all the benchmarks) and larger granularities (on Conv2D and Trapez) are needed for the system to scale due to the additional latencies introduced by the network data and synchronization messages transfer.

Figure 6 reports the GFLOPs performance results for the two computationally intensive benchmarks MatMult and Conv2D.

The results illustrate that utilizing all the SPEs on the four Nodes the system delivers an impressive 0.44 TFLOPs for the MatMult benchmark and 178 GFLOPs for the Conv2D benchmark, which demonstrates the efficiency of the distributed execution on the Cell.

6. Related Work

Star Superscalar (StarSs) [4], [17], [18] is a parallel programming platform that targets symmetric multiprocessors and multi-cores, the Cell processor and GPUs. It schedules annotated tasks at run-time based on data-dependencies. StarSs focuses on the ease of programmability and portability and utilizes a source-to-source compiler and a number of runtime libraries. Unlike the approach adopted by our work, where we build the dependency graph statically if possible, StarSs always builds its task dependency graph at run-time which incurs extra overheads. Performance comparison between the DDM-vm and the Cell implementation of the StarSs platform can be found in [2].

Open Multi-Processing (OpenMP) [5] is a widely-utilized parallel programming API that supports shared-memory programming. OpenMP traditionally targets loop-based parallelism, but the standard was recently extended with the concept of tasks to accommodate irregular applications.

OmpSs [6] is a variant of OpenMP that incorporates ideas from StarSs to support asynchronous task parallelism on clusters of heterogeneous architectures. It emphasizes programming productivity and uses a compiler/runtime approach to move data across a disjoint address space. The programmer annotates the sequential code with compiler directives that are translated into calls to a runtime system that manages the parallelism extraction and data coherence and movement. The information provided by the programmer is used by the runtime to distribute the work across the cluster while optimizes communications using affinity scheduling and caching of data.

The Message Passing Interface (MPI) [9] has been traditionally the *de facto* for programming clusters and distributed systems. MPI allows achieving high-performance but sacrifices the ease of programmability. As the programmer has to handle all the low-level tasks of parallelism (partitioning of data and computations, movement of data during program execution, coherence, etc.). This is in contrast with our approach which automates most of these tasks.

A number of programming models have emerged, which try to facilitate the programmability of distributed systems by providing a global address space view of the aggregated memories of all the Nodes in the system. Such a view facilitates porting sequential applications and reduces the complexity of distributed programs. Examples of such models include UPC [10], Chapel [7] and X10 [8]. Although such systems ease the burden of the programmer, achieving good performance still requires a non-trivial effort from the programmer especially that the distribution of data and the coherency are still handled by the programmer. Moreover, such systems require the support of special compilers and libraries.

7. Conclusion and Future Work

In this paper we have demonstrated that Data-flow concurrency can be efficiently implemented on distributed multi-core systems. We have implemented DDM in heterogeneous and homogeneous systems utilizing off-the-shelf networking (Gigabit Ethernet). The evaluation analysis have shown that the achieved results are consistent across multiple different platforms and configurations. This further confirms that the hybrid Data-Flow models, such as DDM, are very promising alternative to the sequential model for distributed systems.

We believe that the DDM model can inspire the evolution of the micro-architecture of the next generation multi-core systems with the addition of a hardware TSU on-chip and the use of a data-driven hierarchy of scratch-pad memories that can replace the traditional multi-level cache hierarchy. Such memory hierarchies will be deterministic and smaller in size than current cache hierarchies. We have built and evaluated a software implementation of such a system for the Cell processor. We are currently developing an FPGA-based distributed multi-core system in which we are introducing these micro-architectural changes.

References

[1] S. Arandi and P. Evripidou, "Programming multi-core architectures using data-flow techniques," in *SAMOS '10: Proceedings of the 10th International Conference on Embedded Computer Systems: Architectures, Modeling and Simulation*, Samos, Greece, July 2010.

[2] ——, "DDM-VMc: the data-driven multithreading virtual machine for the cell processor," in *Proceedings of the 6th International Conference on High Performance and Embedded Architectures and Compilers*, ser. HiPEAC '11. New York, NY, USA: ACM, 2011, pp. 25–34.

[3] Arvind and K. P. Gostelow, "The u-interpreter," *Computer*, vol. 15, no. 2, pp. 42–49, 1982.

[4] P. Bellens, J. M. Pérez, R. M. Badia, and J. Labarta, "CellSs: a Programming Model for the Cell BE Architecture," in *SC '06: Proceedings of the 2006 ACM/IEEE conference on Supercomputing*. New York, NY, USA: ACM, 2006, p. 86.

[5] O. A. R. Board, "Openmp 3.0 specification," May 2008, http://www.openmp.org.

[6] J. Bueno, L. Martinell, A. Duran, M. Farreras, X. Martorell, R. M. Badia, E. Ayguade, and J. Labarta, "Productive cluster programming with ompss," in *Proceedings of the 17th international conference on Parallel processing - Volume Part I*, ser. Euro-Par'11. Berlin, Heidelberg: Springer-Verlag, 2011, pp. 555–566.

[7] B. Chamberlain, D. Callahan, and H. Zima, "Parallel programmability and the chapel language," *Int. J. High Perform. Comput. Appl.*, vol. 21, no. 3, pp. 291–312, Aug. 2007.

[8] P. Charles, C. Grothoff, V. Saraswat, C. Donawa, A. Kielstra, K. Ebcioglu, C. von Praun, and V. Sarkar, "X10: an object-oriented approach to non-uniform cluster computing," *SIGPLAN Not.*, vol. 40, no. 10, pp. 519–538, Oct. 2005.

[9] J. J. Dongarra, R. Hempel, A. J. Hey, and D. W. Walker, "A proposal for a user-level, message-passing interface in a distributed memory environment," Knoxville, TN, USA, 1993.

[10] C. W. W. et al, "Introduction to upc and language specification," University of California-Berkeley, Tech. Rep., 1999.

[11] P. Evripidou, "Thread Synchronization Unit (TSU): A Building Block for High Performance Computers," *In: Proceedings of the International Symposium on High Perfomance Computing, Fukuoka, Japan.*, 1997.

[12] J. A. Kahle, M. N. Day, H. P. Hofstee, C. R. Johns, T. R. Maeurer, and D. Shippy, "Introduction to the cell multiprocessor," *IBM J. Res. Dev.*, vol. 49, no. 4/5, pp. 589–604, 2005.

[13] D. A. Koufaty, X. Chen, D. K. Poulsen, and J. Torrellas, "Data forwarding in scalable shared-memory multiprocessors," *IEEE Trans. Parallel Distrib. Syst.*, vol. 7, pp. 1250–1264, December 1996. [Online]. Available: http://portal.acm.org/citation.cfm?id=245565.245581

[14] C. Kyriacou, "Data driven multithreading using conventional control flow microprocessors," Ph.D. dissertation, Dept. of Computer Science, University of Cyprus, 2005.

[15] C. Kyriacou, P. Evripidou, and P. Trancoso, "Cacheflow: A Short-Term Optimal Cache Management Policy for Data Driven Multithreading,," *Proc. EuroPar-04*, pp. 561–570, Aug. 2004.

[16] ——, "Data-Driven Multithreading Using Conventional Microprocessors," *IEEE Trans. Parallel Distrib. Syst.*, vol. 17, no. 10, pp. 1176–1188, 2006.

[17] J. M. Pérez, P. Bellens, R. M. Badia, and J. Labarta, "Cellss: Making it easier to program the Cell Broadband Engine processor," *IBM J. Res. Dev.*, vol. 51, no. 5, pp. 593–604, 2007.

[18] J. Planas, R. M. Badia, E. Ayguadé, and J. Labarta, "Hierarchical task-based programming with starss," *Int. J. High Perform. Comput. Appl.*, vol. 23, pp. 284–299, August 2009. [Online]. Available: http://dl.acm.org/citation.cfm?id=1572226.1572233

[19] D. K. Poulsen and P.-C. Yew, "Data prefetching and data forwarding in shared memory multiprocessors," in *Proceedings of the 1994 International Conference on Parallel Processing - Volume 02*, ser. ICPP '94. Washington, DC, USA: IEEE Computer Society, 1994, pp. 280–280. [Online]. Available: http://dx.doi.org/10.1109/ICPP.1994.81

[20] J. Protic, M. Tomasevic, and V. Milutinovic, "Distributed shared memory: concepts and systems," *Parallel Distributed Technology: Systems Applications, IEEE*, vol. 4, no. 2, pp. 63 –71, summer 1996.

[21] K. Stavrou, M. Nikolaides, D. Pavlou, S. Arandi, P. Evripidou, and P. Trancoso, "TFlux: A Portable Platform for Data-Driven Multithreading on Commodity Multicore Systems," in *ICPP '08: Proceedings of the 2008 37th International Conference on Parallel Processing*. Washington, DC, USA: IEEE Computer Society, 2008, pp. 25–34.

A Highly Extensible Framework for Molecule Dynamic Simulation on GPUs

Xiao Zhang[1], Wan Guo[1], Xiao Qin[2] and Xiaonan Zhao[1]
[1]School of Computer Science Northwestern Polytechnical University 127 Youyi xi Road, Xi'an Shaanxi China
[2]Department of Computer Science and Software Engineering Auburn University, AL 36849-5347
E-mail: zhangxiao@nwpu.edu.cn;xilouyouki@163.com;xqin@auburn.edu;zhaoxn@nwpu.edu.cn

Abstract—*Molecular dynamics (MD) was widely used in chemistry and bio molecules. Numerous attempts have been made to accelerate MD simulations. CUDA enabled NVIDIA Graphics processing units (GPUs) use as a general purpose parallel computer chips as CPU. But it is not easy to port a program to GPU. We present a highly extensible framework for molecular dynamics simulation. And we discuss how to accelerate the process of port to GPU. We introduce how to find the performance battle and how to port the time costly procedure to GPU. We discuss about how to decrease the memory usage in GPU and how to improve the maintenance of molecular dynamics simulation. At last, we present the performance of linear and parallel simulation with different number of molecules. Source codes can be found at https://github.com/orlandoacevedo/MCGPU.*

Keywords: Molecular dynamics; Maintainability; Reproducible

1. Introduction

Graphics processing units(GPU) originated as specialized hardware to accelerate graphical operations. GPUs typically handle computation for graphics, such as 3D rendering and ray tracing. General-purpose computing on graphics processing units (GPGPU) is to perform computation in applications traditionally handled by the central processing unit (CPU). OpenCL is currently the dominant open general-purpose GPU computing language. The dominant proprietary framework is Nvidia's CUDA.

The CUDA architecture is built around a scalable array of multi-threaded Streaming Multiprocessors (SMs). It generates multiple threads on multiple processors. It uses Single Instruction Multiple Thread (SIMT) architecture. In contrast with SIMD vector machines, SIMT enables programmers to write thread-level parallel codes for independent, scalar threads, as well as data-parallel codes for coordinated threads.[1]

Molecular dynamic(MD) is widely used in chemistry and biomolecules. It is a compute intensive application. This kind of application can be accelerated by GPUs. There are several different algorithms used in MD. Several previous studies have implemented special algorithms on GPUs. Stone *et al.* introduce GPU-accelerated applications of electrostatics, molecular dynamics, and quantum chemistry[2]. ACEMD is a commercially licensed biomolecular dynamics software package; it is designed for execution on a single workstation with multiple GPUs. It appears to be most effective for system sizes of 10K to 100K atoms[3]. Folding@home is an early project developed on GPUs for molecular dynamics. They worked with ATI since 2005, and they have ported and optimized with CUDA for NVIDIA hardware. These kernels are also deployed in OPENMM software library. [4]. NAMD is a parallel molecular dynamics code designed for high-performance simulation of large biomolecular systems. It scales to hundreds of processors on high-end parallel platforms[5]. HOOMD is a freely available software designed for GPU execution [6]. It speeds up of over a factor of 30 compared to LAMMPS[7]. Elsen *et al.*, implemented a simple implicit solvent model (distance dependent dielectric) [8]. Stone *et al.* have examined a GPU implementation for molecular modeling[9]. Anderson *et al.* have implemented several algorithms, including integrators, neighbor lists, Lennard-Jones, and bond forces[10].

The BOSS program is a general purpose molecular modeling system that performs molecular mechanics (MM) calculations, Metropolis Monte Carlo (MC) statistical mechanics simulations. The MC simulations can be carried out for pure liquids, solutions, clusters, or gas-phase systems; typical applications include computing properties of a pure liquid, free energies of solvation, effects of solvation on relative energies of conformers, changes in free energies of solvation along reaction paths, and structures and relative free energies of binding for host-guest complexes.[1].

2. Challenges of Porting to GPU

GPUs offer high performance parallel computing capacities. There are several difficulties in applying GPU on big scale MD simulations.[11]. Some of the challenges are still present after four years.

2.1 Integration with Original System

There are many MD simulation systems running on CPU. MD simulation systems are compute-intensive systems. GPUs have a huge advantage for these kinds of systems. Many simulation systems have migrated to run

[1]http://zarbi.chem.yale.edu/software.html#boss

on GPU. There are several methods to migrate current systems on GPUs (e.g, plugin, rewrite). Porting a current system allows a legacy code to take advantage of accelerators without rewriting the entire thing. In some cases, the effect of GPU performance improvements will be decreased by too many data transmission between CPU and GPUs. AMBER 11 begins to use NVIDIA GPU to massively accelerate PMEMD for both explicit solvent PME and implicit solvent GB simulations[2]. NAMD is a parallel molecular dynamics code designed for high-performance simulation of large biomolecular systems based on Charm++ parallel objects[12]. GROMACS uses OpenMM acceleration library and plugins to run simulations on GPU[13]. LAMMPS use Geryon library to support GPU. It also allows portability to AMD accelerators, CPUs, and any future chips with OPENCL support[2].

2.2 Scale

Algorithms used for MD are traditionally evaluated based on how they scale with the number of atoms being simulated. GPUs have enough compute units to handle small or medium sized proteins.

One problem is how to increase the number of atoms that a GPU can simulate. It needs lots of memory to store atom states before computing. In order to compute in GPU, it needs another copy of data. These halve the maximum computable number of atoms in theory. In a big simulation process, the target can be divided into smaller areas and simulate by serial. But status of all atoms should be generated and stored at the beginning. Virtual memory can help avoid the shortage of memory; it stores big arrays in disk instead of physical memory. But it delays the transfer between memories to CPU.

Another problem is how to make several GPUs work together in one simulation process. GPU could not communicate with other GPUs directly before 2010. For example, If GPU in node A(GPU-A) need to communicate with GPU in node B(GPU-B). GPU-A needed to pass the data to a CPU in the same node(CPU-A). The CPU-A send the data to a CPU in another node(CPU-B). Then the CPU-B would transfer the data to GPU-B in node B. Most popular method divides the computing to several tasks run on different CPU. Communication between GPU and CPU should be kept to a minimum. NVIDIA provide GPUDirect; it adds support for peer-to-peer communication between GPUs through InfiniBand cards. Using GPUDirect, 3rd party network adapters, solid-state drives (SSDs), and other devices can directly read and write CUDA host and device memory, eliminating unnecessary system memory copies and CPU overhead.

MGPU is a C++ programming library targeted at single-node multi-GPU systems[14]. Such systems combine disproportionate floating point performance with high data locality

[2]http://ambermd.org/gpus/

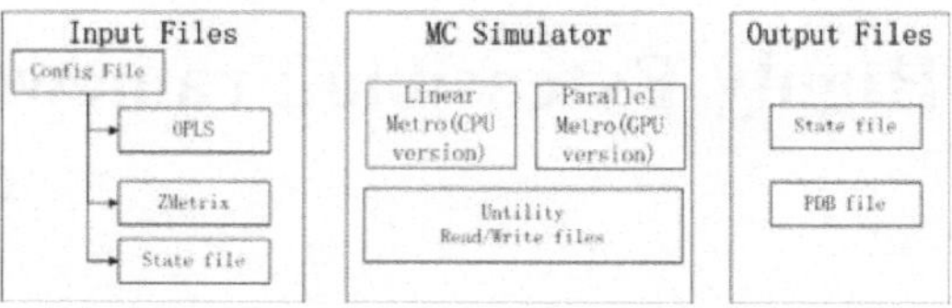

Fig. 1: Input/Output of MC Simulator

and are thus well suited to implement real-time algorithms. They have a speed-up of about 1.7 using 2 GPUs and reach a final speed-up of 2.1 with 4 GPUs.

3. Design

The simulator is used to find a stable state of molecules in solvation box. The core theory of the simulation about solvation is that the energy will keep decreasing until a stable state during the movement of molecules. The process is shown below:

1) Initialization of simulator: This step places a given number of molecules in a box. The position and angle of molecules are generated at random.
2) Calculate energy of all molecules: This step calculates the energy of all molecules.
3) Random movement of molecule: This step chooses one molecule at random. Then it moves and rotates the selected molecule.
4) Calculate new energy after movement: This step calculates the energy of new state.
5) Judgment of movement: If the new energy is less than the old energy, then the movement is acceptable, use the new state to continue. If the new energy is larger than old energy, then it has a little possibility to accept it.
6) If the simulation step is less than given step number, go to step 2.

The first step is to find which part is most time costly. GNU gprof is a profiler tool on Linux. It can find where the program spent its time and called times of each functions. It inserts code at the beginning and end of each function to collect timing information. After the program is complied with special option (-pg), the program will generate information needed for gprof. Simply run the program as usual; it will generate the performance data and write it into a file called 'gmon.out'. gprof can interpret the data and output a table listing the function name, call times and time used. From these, we can find that the calculation of energy is a compute intensive task.

3.1 Object Oriented

With compiler nvcc provided by NVIDIA, we can compile source codes including the host code and device code. For the host code, nvcc supports full features of object oriented designs. But for the source code that runs on device, nvcc supports features of data aggregation class and derived class. It does not support run time type information (RTTI) and the C++ standard library. Seiller *et al.* present an object oriented framework for GPGPU-based image processing[15]. They created an interface for classes used in GPU and implemented different classes on CUDA and GLSL. MinGPU proposed a general purpose computation library based on object oriented framework[16]. But they do not support object oriented.

To compare simulation results and performance improvement, we implement serial and parallel methods to simulate the random movement of molecules. These two methods share most source codes runs on CPU, and the parallel simulation runs on GPU to calculate the energy of molecules. We want to apply the object oriented design during development. We implement GPU acceleration in C++ and CUDA. We have more experience in C++ than CUDA. So we implement a C++ version simulator without parallel. Then we add CUDA code to implement parallel compute on GPU. To make it easy to maintain and develop, we wanted to

1) minimize the amount of coding required
2) simplify the methods to port different algorithm to parallel
3) use same input files and get same results with two versions.

As shown in Figure 2, we use class BoxState to store all states of atoms including atom position, angles, and bonds. Class Calculator computes the free energy of a given state. Class generator moves molecules in the box and decides if the movement is acceptable. Simulator initiate the state of BoxState and calls Generator repeatedly by the given steps. All of these classes work together to simulate molecule solution in the box on CPU. We reuse class BoxState and Generator in the GPU version. Class used in GPU cannot be derived from class used in CPU. So class GPUBoxState is not the subclass of BoxState; it depends on BoxState. The class allocates memory in GPU and stores states in it. It creates a BoxState object to save states in CPU and synchronizes the data to GPU. The class GPUBoxState is just a wrapper of BoxState; all states of atoms are saved in BoxState. Many functions are reused just like the linear method, such as save/load atom state from disks and move molecules.

3.2 Memory model

There are 6.02*10^{23} molecules in 1 mol of water. The maximum system size that can be treated with the GPU is limited by the memory size. The CUDA programming model assumes that both the host and the device maintain their own separate memory spaces in DRAM. In particular, Langevin temperature regulation and the use of larger cotoffs for the effective Born radii calculations increase the memory requirements. By using AMBER, Tesla C2070 with 6.0 GB GPU memory can treat 54,000 atoms[17].

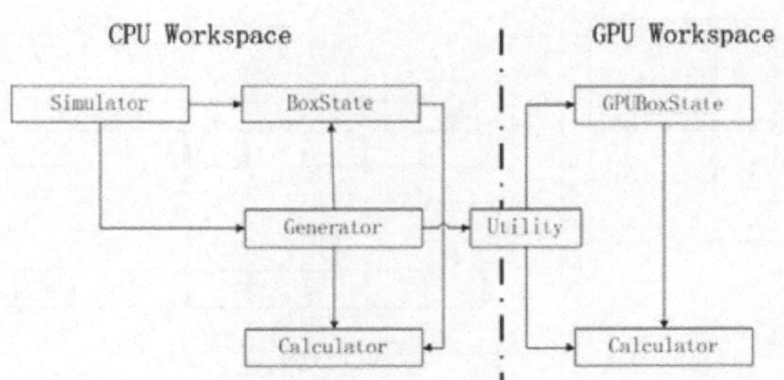

Fig. 2: Class structure of the Simulator

Name	Description	size
molecule	state of molecule, pointers to atoms and other structure	72
atoms	position and type of atoms in molecules	56
bonds	bond between 2 atoms	24
angles	angle of 2 adjacent atoms	24
dihedrals	the angle created by two planes	24
hops	atom pairs and their node distance(hops) away from each other	12

Table 1: Data Structure size

In our simulation, we need store molecule state, including atoms, bonds, angles, dihedral, and hops. We list the size of each structure in Table 1. As for a water molecule, it needs 5 atoms (2 are dummy), 4 bonds, 3 angels, 2 dihedrals, and 2 hops. The memory usage can be calculated by Formula 1.

$$\begin{aligned} Mem_{molecule} &= \sum(size_{items} * num_{items}) + size_{molecule} \\ &= 5 * 56 + 4 * 24 + 3 * 24 + 2 * 24 + 2 * 12 \\ &+ 72 \\ &= 592 \\ Mem_{simulator} &= Mem_{molecule} \times num_{molecules} \end{aligned} \tag{1}$$

To simulate 10,000 molecules (50,000 atoms), it needs 5,920,000 bytes. In our simulation, the atom is the most important element during computing. It stored the 3-dimension position, sigma and epsilon used in LJ calculations. The angles and hops between atoms may change in the real world, but in a simplified model, we can assume the molecules move as a whole, which means bond, angle, dihedral, and hop are equal within all molecules of the same kind. By merging all of these items into one block and having all molecules point to it, we can get a simplified memory usage formula 2. To simulate 10,000 molecules (50,000 atoms), it needs 3,520,000 bytes, about 3.36GB. It decreases 40% of the memory usage. This optimization does not affect the compute efficiency. Because the relative position of atoms in one molecule is same, we can also save position information in the molecule instead of atoms. To simulate 10,000 molecules (50,000 atoms), it needs 2,560,000 bytes, about 2.44GB. This optimization has bad influence on compute speed, because it needs to calculate the position of each atom before use them.

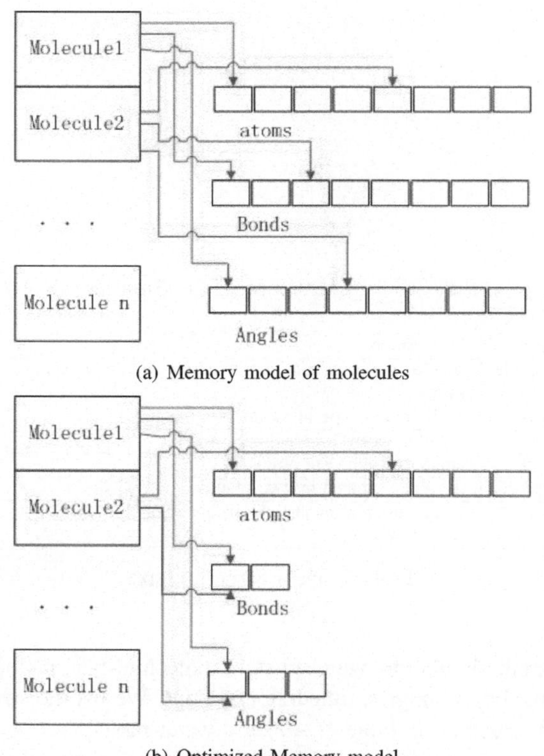

(a) Memory model of molecules

(b) Optimized Memory model

Fig. 3: Memory Model for Simulation

$$\begin{aligned} Mem_{molecule} &= \sum(size_{atom} * num_{atom}) + size_{molecule} \\ &= 5 * 56 + 72 = 352 \\ Mem_{simulator} &= Mem_{molecule} \times num_{molecules} + size_{items} \end{aligned} \quad (2)$$

The CPU and GPU memories are in different address spaces. This means data must be synchronized between different address spaces. CUDA provides APIs to copy memory between CPU and GPU, but it is a big performance penalty for these synchronizations. Applications should strive to minimize data transfer between the host and the device. To avoid performance penalty, we identified the changed data during the computation in GPU, and synchronized the changed part. In each procedure of the energy computation, only one atom changed, so what we need is to copy single atom information to GPU, and copy energy results back to CPU memory. Because of the overhead associated with each transfer, many small transmissions are combined into a single large transfer.

In the inner calculating of MD, it uses a molecule i and loops over all molecules j to calculate the minimum image separations. If molecules are separated by distances greater than the potential cutoff, the program skips to the end of the loop. One method is to create a neighbor list for each atom. The list is quite large, and it consists of dimensions

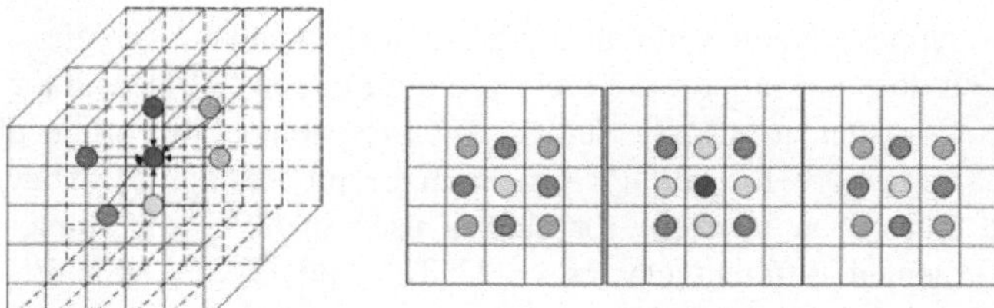

Fig. 4: Neighbor searching in Rubik's Cube structure

roughly $4\pi r\ 3\rho N/6$. Meanwhile it spends lots of time on computing the distance of each pair. We use a cube structure to store the neighbor relations between different atoms. We divided the box into small cubes according to the cutoff size. We can judge which cube hte atoms are in simply by their positions. As shown in Figure 4, if an atom in the central cube(red), we only need to check the atoms in the adjacent ones(yellow) and catercorner ones(blue and green). Assume the molecules distribute equably in the box, the number of atoms in each cube is roughly equal. We can use a list to store the atoms in each cube and map the 3-D cube into a linear data structure. The cube structure can be set up and used rapidly. The search operation allows the programmer to find neighboring atoms within 26 other cubes. The GPU is not used to speed up the search for an individual atom, but instead it is used to run multiple searches in parallel.

3.3 Improvement of Maintainability

The MD simulation tries to find the most probable distribution of molecules. This means an outcome will occur in a proportion of the time it occurs over the long run - this is the relative frequency with which that outcome occurs. Successful simulation using the same model will get similar results after long run. But it is difficult to verify the modification of the algorithm by a long run. It takes too much time to run a whole simulation. On the other hand, it's difficult to say which result is better especially since the difference is so small.

We try to find a way to make the simulation process repeatable. There are two steps using random process. During the initialization of the simulation environment, we use random numbers to place the molecules well-distributed among the volent box. Then we use random numbers to choose which molecule should move and how it will move (position and rotation). We must generate the same random sequence to get the same simulation result. For the initialization of molecule position, we can write the state of each molecule into a state file which is used to initialize the state of other simulation. This makes all the simulations begin with same states. A random seed is a long integer used to initialize a pseudo random number generator. Random seeds are often generated from the state of the computer system (such as the time). If we initialize a pseudo random number generator by a constant seed, the random generator will generate

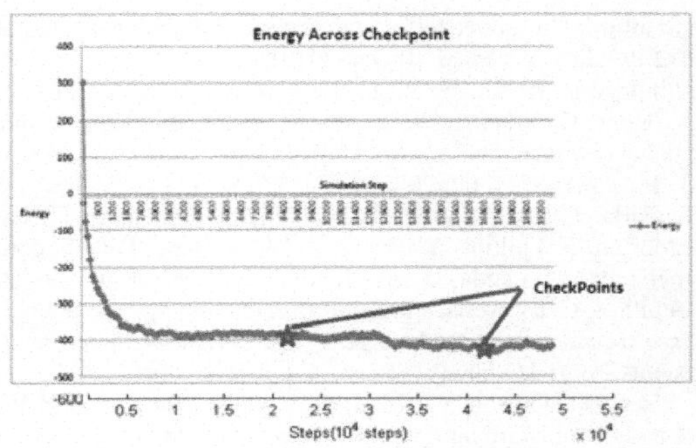

Fig. 5: Illustrate of Checkpoints

the same random sequence. For the random number used in movement, we can use the same random seed used in the previous simulation. And in linear version and parallel version simulators, we use the same generator class to make sure it uses the random sequence in the same method. We output random seeds on screen and the log file. If we want to repeat the simulation process, then we write the state file and random seed in the configuration file, which will get the exact same result as the previous simulation.

4. Performance

We use dense memory cluster (DMC) in Alabama supercomputer center[18]. The DMC has 1800 CPU cores and 10 terabytes of distributed memory. The DMC has sixteen GPU (Graphic Processing Unit) chips. These are a combination of two Tesla S1070 units (external GPUs connected in pairs to four DMC nodes) and four DMC nodes configured with a pair of Tesla M2070 cards each. These multi-core GPU chips are similar to those in video cards, but there are installed as math coprocessors. This can give significant performance advantages for software that has been adapted to use these processors. Thus the processing capacity of the DMC cluster is: single precision GPU capacity is 18.6 TFLOPS and double precision GPU capacity is 4.8TFLOPS. The job that runs on GPU can use a max of 120GB memory in large serial mode.

4.1 Memory usage

We moved all memory allocation and free memory into BoxState class and GPUBoxState to manage all memory used in GPU. Before the modification, the memory increases with atom number and simulation steps. After the modification, the memory only depends on the number of atoms as shown in Figure 6.

4.2 Development productivity

Unfortunately, it is hard to find a metric to measure the Eventual Efficiency of the design. One metric is how many codes one developer can produce per hour. But for this project, most source codes can be reused. Function

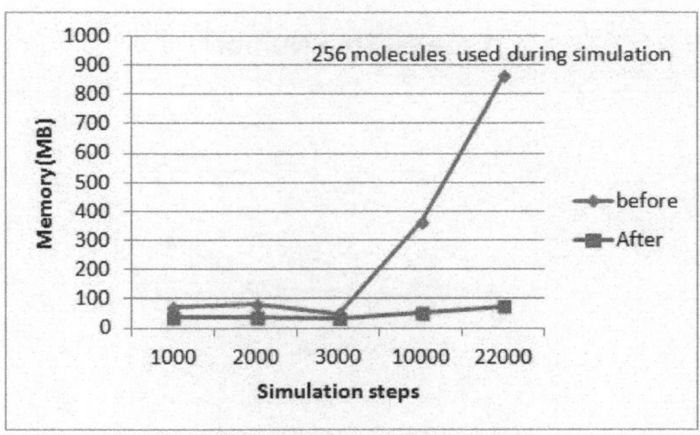

(a) constant molecule numbers

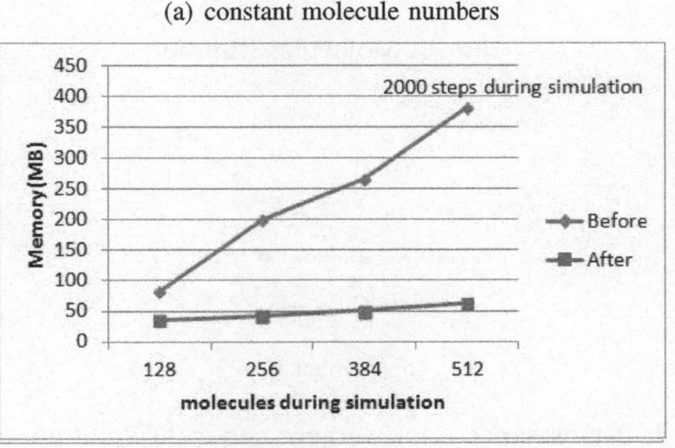

(b) constant steps

Fig. 6: Memory usage under different conditions

oriented designs may create more source codes than object-oriented. It saves succeeding developer work hours because the solution is easy to comprehend and reuse. With the improvement of maintainability, the correctness of extension and modification can be verified in a few minutes with previous input and output files. It saved many times in the test.

4.3 Performance Improvement

After modifying the search method for neighbor, the time complexity of search algorithm was optimized from exponential growth to linear growth. It is 90% faster after modification as shown in Figure 7.

5. Conclusion

In the paper, we present a framework to accelerate the developing process of porting MC simulation to graphical processing units. The implementation runs on single NVIDA GPU using CUDA program model. In this contribution, we described how to distinguish which part is time-costly. And we discussed how to port these codes to GPU with less program work. We also improved the memory model to make it capable of simulating large systems. Another contribution is that we found a way to make the simulation process repeatable. This modification makes it easy to verify future extension and enhancement.

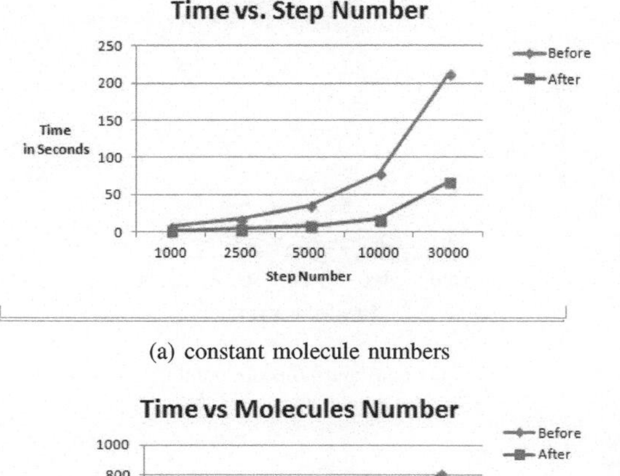

(a) constant molecule numbers

(b) constant steps

Fig. 7: Performance improvement under different conditions

Limited by the memory size, it can only simulate 54,000 atoms in one GPU. By using MPI, it can simulate large systems by running on different GPUs. There are some limits in our simulation; we did not change the related distance and angle of atoms in one molecule.

Acknowledgments

This work was made possible thanks to the NPU Fundamental Research Foundation under Grant No. JC20110227, the National Science and Technology Ministry No.2011BAH04B05, National High-tech R&D Program of China (863) under Grant No.2013AA01A215, and the National Natural Science Foundation of China under Grant No.61033007. And this work was supported by China Scholarship Council. Xiao Qin's research was supported by the U.S. National Science Foundation under Grants CCF-0845257 (CAREER), CNS-0917137 (CSR), CNS-0757778 (CSR), CCF-0742187 (CPA), CNS-0831502 (CyberTrust), CNS-0855251 (CRI), OCI-0753305 (CI-TEAM), DUE-0837341(CCLI), and DUE-0830831 (SFS).

References

[1] N. Corporation, "Nvidia cuda c programming guide," http://docs.nvidia.com/cuda/cuda-c-programming-guide/index.html, 2012, [Online; accessed 19-Sep-2012].

[2] J. Stone, D. Hardy, I. Ufimtsev, and K. Schulten, "Gpu-accelerated molecular modeling coming of age," *Journal of molecular graphics & modelling*, vol. 29, no. 2, p. 116, 2010.

[3] M. Harvey, G. Giupponi, and G. Fabritiis, "Acemd: accelerating biomolecular dynamics in the microsecond time scale," *Journal of Chemical Theory and Computation*, vol. 5, no. 6, pp. 1632–1639, 2009.

[4] F. Stanford, "Introduce to folding@home," http://folding.stanford.edu, 2012, [Online; accessed 10-Dec-2012].

[5] J. Phillips, R. Braun, W. Wang, J. Gumbart, E. Tajkhorshid, E. Villa, C. Chipot, R. Skeel, L. Kale, and K. Schulten, "Scalable molecular dynamics with namd," *Journal of computational chemistry*, vol. 26, no. 16, pp. 1781–1802, 2005.

[6] M. Garland, S. Le Grand, J. Nickolls, J. Anderson, J. Hardwick, S. Morton, E. Phillips, Y. Zhang, and V. Volkov, "Parallel computing experiences with cuda," *Micro, IEEE*, vol. 28, no. 4, pp. 13–27, 2008.

[7] C. Phillips, C. Iacovella, and S. Glotzer, "Stability of the double gyroid phase to nanoparticle polydispersity in polymer-tethered nanosphere systems," *Soft Matter*, vol. 6, no. 8, pp. 1693–1703, 2010.

[8] E. Elsen, M. Houston, V. Vishal, E. Darve, P. Hanrahan, and V. Pande, "N-body simulation on gpus," in *Proceedings of the 2006 ACM/IEEE conference on Supercomputing*. ACM, 2006, p. 188.

[9] J. Stone, J. Phillips, P. Freddolino, D. Hardy, L. Trabuco, and K. Schulten, "Accelerating molecular modeling applications with graphics processors," *Journal of computational chemistry*, vol. 28, no. 16, pp. 2618–2640, 2007.

[10] J. Anderson, C. Lorenz, and A. Travesset, "General purpose molecular dynamics simulations fully implemented on graphics processing units," *Journal of Computational Physics*, vol. 227, no. 10, pp. 5342–5359, 2008.

[11] M. Friedrichs, P. Eastman, V. Vaidyanathan, M. Houston, S. Legrand, A. Beberg, D. Ensign, C. Bruns, and V. Pande, "Accelerating molecular dynamic simulation on graphics processing units," *Journal of computational chemistry*, vol. 30, no. 6, pp. 864–872, 2009.

[12] U. of Illinois, "Namd," http://www.ks.uiuc.edu/Research/namd/, 2013.

[13] GROMACS, "Gromacs openmm," http://www.gromacs.org/Documentation/Installation_Instructions_4.5/GROMACS-OpenMM, 2013.

[14] S. Schaetz and M. Uecker, "A multi-gpu programming library for real-time applications," *Algorithms and Architectures for Parallel Processing*, pp. 114–128, 2012.

[15] N. Seiller, N. Singhal, and I. Park, "Object oriented framework for real-time image processing on gpu," in *Image Processing (ICIP), 2010 17th IEEE International Conference on*. IEEE, 2010, pp. 4477–4480.

[16] P. Babenko and M. Shah, "Mingpu: a minimum gpu library for computer vision," *Journal of Real-Time Image Processing*, vol. 3, no. 4, pp. 255–268, 2008.

[17] A. Gotz, M. Williamson, D. Xu, D. Poole, S. Le Grand, and R. Walker, "Routine microsecond molecular dynamics simulations with amber on gpus. 1. generalized born," *Journal of Chemical Theory and Computation*, vol. 8, no. 5, p. 1542, 2012.

[18] ASC, "Alabama supercomputer center," http://www.asc.edu/, 2012.

Adding semi-coordinated checkpoints to RADIC in Multicore clusters

Marcela Castro[1], **Dolores Rexachs**[1], **and Emilio Luque**[1]
[1]Computer Architecture and Operating Systems Department, Universitat Autònoma de Barcelona, Barcelona, Spain

Abstract— *Fault tolerance strategies should be adapted to current High Performance Computing with a growing number of processors.*

RADIC is a fault tolerance architecture based on pessimistic protocol based on receiver that follows a distributed behavior for protection and recovery. This protocol is effective in recovery, however, it introduces more overhead than others in protection.

In multicore clusters, the latency added to protect messages between processes executing on a node, is increased due to the differences between intra-node network bandwidth and the inter-node one. When Coordinated checkpointing is used to save the state of the processes in a node, the overhead is reduced in not logging the those internal communications.

A semi-coordinate checkpoint protocol is proposed in this paper. It combines the received-based pessimistic protocol with coordinated checkpoint. An overhead description is exposed to find out which message passing parallel applications are benefited using this alternative protocol. Experimental results using SPMD and MW compare the behavior of both protocols.

Keywords: Fault-tolerance; High-Availability; RADIC; message passing; socket

1. Introduction

High Performance Computing systems are evolving by adding multicores to their nodes. As a consequence, the probability of having node failures increases and fault tolerance solutions are used to assure the parallel application ends successfully in spite of such failures. However, the demand of more performance and availability drives to adapt fault tolerance strategies to multicore and manycores architectures.

Fault tolerance rollbackrecovery protocols were explained and classified by Elnozahy [1]. One of the most used approaches is the coordinated checkpointing, although it is not advisable to scale to a large number of processes because it usually has a high coordination cost and whole processes would have to rollback in case of failure.

RADIC [2] [3], a fault tolerance architecture for parallel applications, was designed to be distributed to not interfere with the scalability of the application being protected. As a general rule, a centralized component might add more than a proportional overhead when the number of processors increases reducing then the speedup and the scalability.

The receiver-based pessimistic rollback-recovery protocol combined with uncoordinated checkpoint was adopted by RADIC because it accomplishes the distributed requirement during *protection* as well as in *recovery* phases. This design was made for cases that use one process by node [2].

The guaranty of successfully ending an execution in spite of failures has a performance cost or overhead. This cost has two parts. On the one hand, the overhead added during *protection*, also known as *failure-free* operations, and on the other hand, the overhead of the tasks of *recovery* phase.

The analysis of the cost of recovery done in [4] concludes that receiver-based pessimistic protocol presents the lowest overheads in recovery time, however, it is expensive in *failure-free* operation.

The overhead added by receiver-based pessimistic protocols in *protection* is caused by the time of logging each received message in stable storage. Consequently, the latency of *send* is theoretically duplicated since at least two hops are needed, one, to arrive to the receiver and the second to reach the stable storage located on a different node.

Moreover, when the sender and the receiver are hosted on the same multicore node, the latency added to protect the message is dramatically increased due to the differences between intra-node network bandwidth and the inter-node one. As a consequence, the performance drawback of received-based pessimistic message logging is even more noticeable in multicore systems.

Processes executing on the same node, which we named **group**, are related by failure probability [5]. Using coordinated checkpointing among the members of the **group** would save the cost of logging the received messages interchanged among them. Nevertheless, a coordination is required to avoid *in-transit* for obtaining a consistent recovering line free of *orphan* messages.

This paper presents a semi-coordinated protocol which minimizes the overhead added by the receiver-based pessimistic protocol during *protection* but keeping the distributed behavior. It consists in using coordinated checkpoints among the members of the **groups** combined with receiver-based pessimistic message log for communications done between processes hosted by different nodes. The content of this paper is organized as follows. In Section II we mention the related works. Section III describes the fully uncoordinated rollback recovery protocol currently used in RADIC designed at socket level [3] [6].

The Section IV explains how the semi-coordination protocol is added to RADIC obtaining a new model for *protection* and for *recovery*. The experimental evaluation is presented in Section V, and lastly, we state the conclusions and the future work in Section VI.

2. Related Works

The combination of using coordinated checkpointing together with message logging has been already used in previous researches. A correlated set coordination among processes executing on the same multicore node combined with pessimistic message logging is presented in [5]. In this work a coordinating among processes in a node is done and also it is combined with a pessimist message log but based on sender. A different coordination protocol and the validation and experiments were done using Open-MPI while we are using RADIC at socket level [3] [6].

The research work [7] proposes a hybrid protocol combining coordinated with uncoordinated checkpoint. As it is targeted to grid environment, the criteria used to group processes is based on the network and the communication pattern to determine the kind of checkpoint that would be done. To obtain a global consistent state for the group, Communication Induced checkpoint (CIC) combinated with a pessimistic message logging. Using CIC for coordination might be not scalable for highly coupled processes since the number of forced checkpoints grows uncontrollably.

Group-based coordinated checkpoint is stated in [8]. In this case, not message-log is used thus, a complete coordination is needed for recovery. It is applied to MVAPICH2.

A combination of coordinated checkpoint with message log is proposed in [9], as a way to scale the most extended strategy of coordination of the whole processes. However, the criteria for grouping the processes is based on the communication behavior. A trace is done to give support on the creation of groups. Our approach uses the location of the processes to coordinate them as a unique set of processes but the user can also configure a different frequency of checkpoint for each process. In that case, the groups are formed with processes on the same node and with the same of frequency of checkpoint. Using this configuration, the user would give a more accurate checkpoint interval for each group according to the communication pattern of the parallel application.

3. Fully Uncoordinated RADIC Model

This section explains the receiver-based pessimistic message log followed by RADIC. We begin with a brief of the architecture and how it works at socket level. Then, the protocol is described by separating the procedure done in *protection* from the followed in *recovery*. On both cases we focus on describing the overheads of each step.

3.1 RADIC-based Message Passing Fault Tolerance System

RADIC has a distributed behavior in *protection, detection* and *recovery* phases. It uses uncoordinated checkpointing and receiver-based pessimist message log. Critical data like checkpoints and received messages of each parallel process are stored on a different node from the one in which it is running. This selection assures the execution completion if a minimum of three nodes are left operational after **n** non-simultaneous faults. RADIC applied at socket layer would let fault tolerance parallel applications using different kind of message-passing libraries, which usually use the standard Socket API [10] for interconnection of the processes. There are two components also depicted in Figure 1:

- **Observer (Oi):** this entity is responsible for monitoring the application's communications and masks possible errors generated by communication failures. In RADIC at socket level, the observer intercepts *send* and *recv* functions to follow the message log protocol. The state is saved periodically by checkpointing. Critical data for recovering formed by received messages and checkpoints are sent to the protector **Ti-1**. There is an observer **Oi** attached to each parallel process **Pi**.
- **Protector: (Ti)** There is one on each node protecting the processes running on node **Ni+1.** It stores the critical data sent by the observers. In case of failure, the protector restarts the failed process using the last checkpoint. Protector detects node failures by sending heartbeats to its neighbors and by the detection of sockets errors.

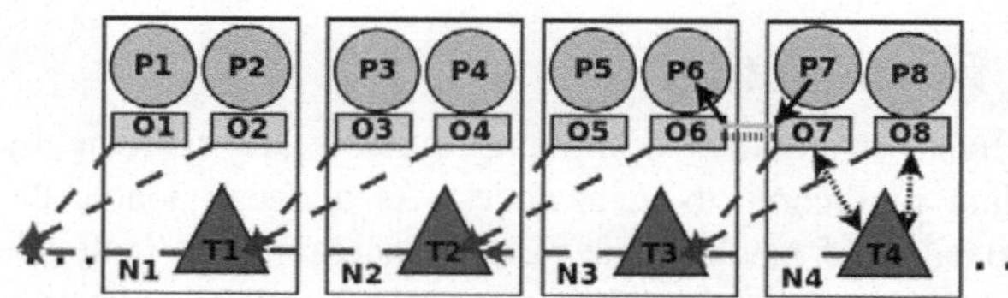

Fig. 1: RADIC diagram shows each observer **Oi** sends the critical data to its protector **Ti-1**. Each protector **Ti** sends heartbeat signal to **Ti-1**

The observers use five types of sockets to keep the control and reliability of their communications which are depicted in Figure 1. First, the **virtual socket** is the id known by the process to communicate with a remote peer, are the solid black arrows that connects **P6** and **P7** with its observer. Second, the **real socket** represented by a solid yellow line is the one that is actually connected with the peer, since the original connection could be broken after a checkpoint or a failure. Third, the **control-ft socket**, depicted using a blue dotted line, it is an internal socket opened by two observers involved in a communication to interchange control information during re-connections and message logging. Then, dashed lines are **RADIC-sockets** used between **Oi** with **Ti-1** and lastly, dotted black lines are used by each protector **Ti** to answer **Oi** the state of **Ti-1** in case of failure.

3.2 Receiver-based pessimistic Protocol in Protection Phase

A receiver-based pessimistic rollback recovery protocol let recover the state of each process until the point of failure. It adds more overhead than others like optimistic or causal approaches during the *protection* tasks but simplifies the recovery procedure because the effects of a failure are confined only to the restarting processes [4] [1]. Usually, it is used with uncoordinated checkpoint to decrease the rollback time in case of failure.

Receiver-based pessimistic rollback recovery protocol assumes that all nondeterministic events are identified and their corresponding determinants are logged to stable storage. Receiving a packet is considered a nondeterministic event to log. Thus, this is solved interposing *recv* socket function and sending the received message to the protector afterwards. But pessimistic logging protocols are designed under the assumption that a failure can occur after any nondeterministic event in the computation. This assumption is "pessimistic" since in reality, failures are rare [1] and stipulates that if an event has not been logged on stable storage, then no process can depend on it. Because of that, a sender of a message waits until the complete sent message is saved in stable storage to validate it before continuing the operation. Once a received message is completely saved on stable storage, an acknowledgment is sent to the sender.

The Figure 2 shows how a message is treated since it is generated from the sender process. Each step adds an overhead which is named prefixing it with **Ts-** or with **Tr-** depending on if they are related to the *send* or with *recv* respectively.

1) The *send(X)* operation is interposed by the sender observer **Os**, which sends a numerated ack requirement to the **Or** using the **control-ft** socket. **X** is the length of the message. The overhead is named **Ts-ack-req.** The time used for sending the message **Ts-msg** it is not considered overhead because it corresponds with operation time performed by the process.
2) A *recv(X1)* operation is interposed by the receiver observer **Or**. **X1** is the length of the expected message. According to the standard of *recv* socket function, when **X1** is greater than the **X** actually available, a maximum of **X** would be delivered. Therefore, we consider that the length **X1** is less or equal than the **X** sent. **Or** receives the acknowledgement requirement on a **Tr-ack-req** time.
3) **Or** receives the **X** bytes from the **real-socket**. The time used to receive the message **Tr-msg** is not an overhead due to it corresponds to the *read* operation performed by the process. The message is sent to the protector to save it in a **Tr-save-msg(X)** time.
4) **Or** sends the acknowledgment to the **Os** using the **control-ft** socket. **Tr-send-ack** is added. On the other peer, **Os** receives the acknowledgment and the *send(X)* finishes. **Ts-wait-ack** is the overhead of this wait.
5) Lastly, only if **X1** is less than **X**, a set of *recv(Xi)* is performed until **X** is completely read. In such cases, **Or** copies the next bytes from the X bytes received previously. The time is considered in **Tr-msg(Xi)**.

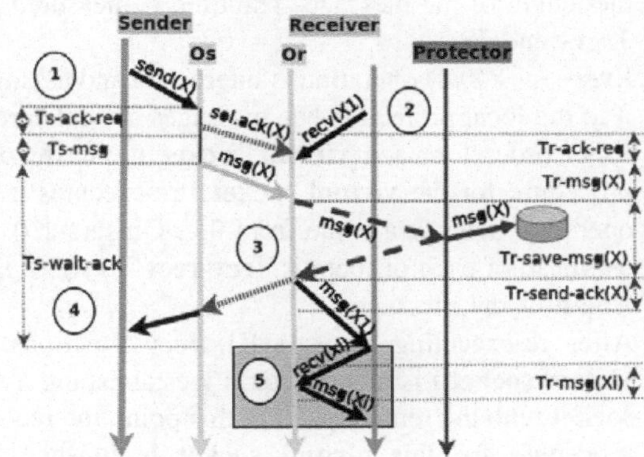

Fig. 2: Receiver-based Pessimistic Protocol in Protection Phase: Virtual/Real sockets: Solid lines - Control-Ft sockets: dotted lines - RADIC sockets: dashed lines

3.3 Receiver-based Pessimistic Protocol in Recovery

When one of the nodes fails down, the failure is detected by the protector which restarts the processes that were running in failed node using the last checkpoint. BLCR [11] library is used to do uncoordinated checkpointing and restarting each parallel process.

The recovery procedure is carried out by the observer by rolling forward the previous execution from the checkpoint until the point of failure. The saved messages are using in each re-execution of *recv* functions since those messages are not going to send them again. By the other hand, the *send* operations are skipped because they were done before the failure. However, as each *send* has associated a numerated acknowledgment requirement, the observers are able to detect and to skip a duplicated message if it is re-sent. This functionality is useful because this protocol considers that the recovery procedure finishes when the last message in stable storage is processed by a *recv*, but if the failure happened after a *send*, it would be re-sent as it is not considered part of the recovery.

The Figure 3 depicts the recovery procedure and the overheads prefixed with **Trcv-** related to one of the **virtual**

sockets named **i**. The same procedure is repeated for socket used by the parallel process.

1) Immediately after restarting from checkpoint, the state of recovering is detected by obtaining it from BLCR library. Then, a connection with the local protector is established to query how many messages are pending to re-process for the **virtual socket i**. The value of **Qmsg(sv[i])** is returned. The overhead of this step is measured with **Trcv-qmsg**.
2) Every send(X)(j) operation is interposed and skipped to avoid re-send messages, **j** is an integer greater or equal to 0 representing the amount of *sends* function being rolling forward in this **virtual socket i.** X is the length of the message. The time is measured with **Trcv-send(X)(j)**.
3) Every *recv(Y)(k)* operation is interposed and asking for it to the local protector. The messages are delivered in FIFO order for each **virtual socket i**. The recovery procedure for the **virtual socket i** re-executes **k** *recv* operation being **k** a value from 0 to Qmsg(sv[i]). The overhead of each of them is **Trcv-recv(Y)(k)**. Y is the length of the message.
4) After re-executing **Qmsg(sv[i])** *recv* functions, the **virtual socket i** is reconnected by establishing a **real-socket** with the remote peer. In this point, the recovery procedure for this **virtual socket** is finished. The overhead is **Trcv-re-conn**.

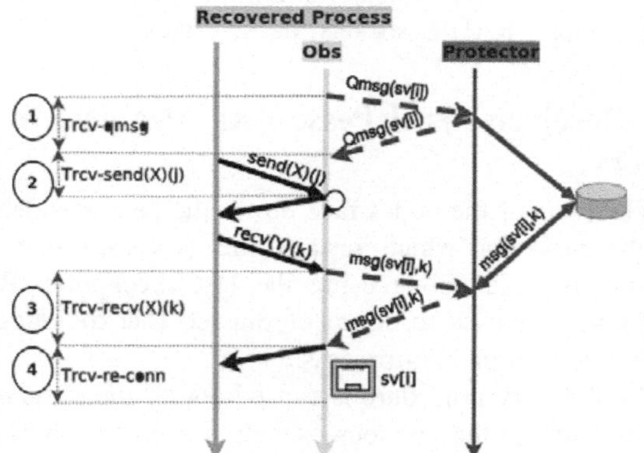

Fig. 3: Receiver-based Pessimistic Protocol in Recovery Phase

4. Semi-Coordinated RADIC Model

Semi-coordinated checkpointing allows to RADIC to provide an alternative rollback recovery protocol to reduce overheads in multicore clusters.

The performance drawback of received-based pessimist rollback recovery protocol becomes even worst during failure-free operations for communication between members of a group. The latency added to log the message is dramatically increased due to the differences in intra-node network bandwidth and inter-node one. However, a coordination among the members of the group, introduces an overhead. Several algorithms have been proposed to coordinate checkpoint like the Chandy-Lamport algorithm [12] or the blocking coordinated [13]. The communications have to be silenced before checkpointing to avoid *in-transit* messages.

When multicore clusters are used to execute parallel application, the processes running on the same node are related in case of a failure since they must be restarted and re-executed until the same point in time. As they are being located on the same node, they are likely to having or needing an intensive or fasting communication among them. Therefore, a coordination checkpoint protocol is useful because it avoids logging messages for communications between members of the group.

RADIC protectors known which processes are executing in its node and the observers also can identified if the peer process is located or not at the same node. This section explains the whole strategy used for coordinating checkpoints among the members of **groups** combined with receiver-based pessimistic protocols for communications done between processes hosted by different nodes. First, the changes in current RADIC model are stated. Second, the coordination protocol used among the processes running on the same node before checkpointing is exposed. Lastly, the semi-coordinated checkpoint protocol is described both in *protection* and in *recovery*.

4.1 RADIC Model changes

The proper component to carry out the coordination task among the members of **groups** for not adding additional tasks to observers is RADIC local protector. Actually, a connection between each observer with its local protector is established but until now it was just used just in case of a failure. Now, it is used also for perform the coordination. The Figure 4 represents a parallel application running on N nodes of a Multicore cluster. Each node i has a group of M_{Ni} members.

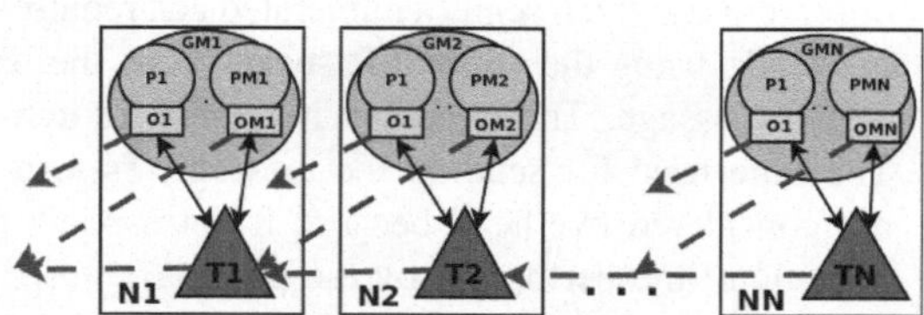

Fig. 4: Coordinated Groups in Multicore Cluster

Each **group** is coordinated by its local protector **Tx** to silence internal communication. The received-based pessimist protocol is kept for communications between members of different groups. By default, RADIC would consider that processes running on a node have the same checkpoint interval but, since this is a configuration value for each process, when different intervals are configured, the groups are formed with the processes on the same node and with the same interval. In such cases, received-based pessimist protocol is used for communication between processes in the same node but with different checkpoint interval. This configuration would be useful for cases with processes that having different communication pattern are running on the same node but the optimal checkpoint interval is too much different. Moreover, as an extreme case, this functionality let turn again to a fully uncoordinated checkpointing by configuring different checkpoint interval for each parallel process. In order to facilitate the explanation, it is considered that each group in a node has the same checkpoint interval.

In addition, when a node fails, and no spare node is available, RADIC recovery model establishes that the failed processes are recovered in the previous node where critical-data was saved. In such cases, the Protector **Tx-1** has to be able to recognize automatically at least two groups, the first that is still running on node **x-1**, and the second one being recovered. Although after node failure the groups are in the same node, RADIC keeps the groups uncoordinated until the end of execution to let move them if an spare node is available later.

4.2 Coordinated Checkpointing Protocol

The protocol for coordinating the processes is shown in Figure 5. Two entities are involved in this procedure. The first is the protector T_n running in one of N nodes depicted in Figure 4. In this node **n**, there are 1 to M_n parallel processes to coordinate. The second entity is observer O_{nm} attached to each of member of the group. When T_n detects it is time for checkpointing, sends a message to each. After receiving that message, the observer stops the communication activity in the beginning of the next *send* or *recv* function. In this state, the coordination requirement of no *in-transit* messages between processes of the **group** is accomplished because all send operations are completely finished and acknowledged. Each observer replies to its local protector **Tn** that it is ready for the checkpoint. Once all the members are ready, the **Tn** calls to BLCR for checkpointing each process. BLCR executes the callback function provided by each O_{nm} and the checkpoint is performed. After finishing, checkpoint files are sent to **Tn-1** by **Tn**.

4.3 Semi-Coordinated Protocol in Protection

RADIC at socket level keeps an identification of the remote process for each **virtual socket**. This information is interchanged when the **control-ft socket** is established. The identification is formed by node-id, process-id and virtual-socket. **Group-id** is now incorporated to support this new model. Using this data, the observer is able to know if the remote peer belongs to its group or not. The group-id is assigned in the beginning by the local protector **Tx** when the

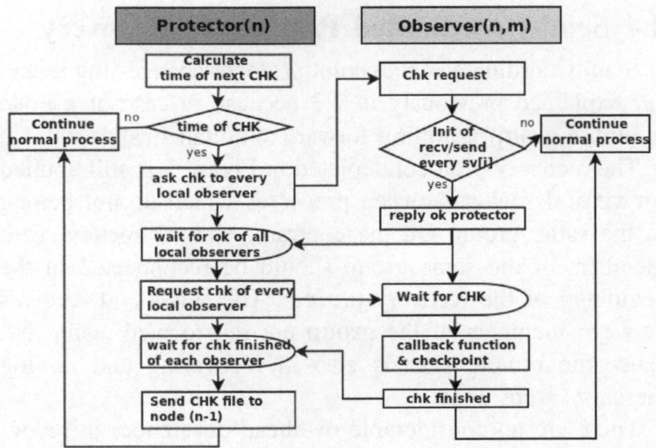

Fig. 5: Coordinated Checkpointing Protocol

first communication is established between them. By default, the value is 0.

The Figure 6 represents the procedure used by the observers when sender and receiver belong to the same group. It is different from the explained in 2 in that the saving of the received message in stable storage is skipped. Consequently, both sender and receiver overheads are reduced in the time needed to log messages, due to **Or** returns the acknowledge immediately after reading the message.

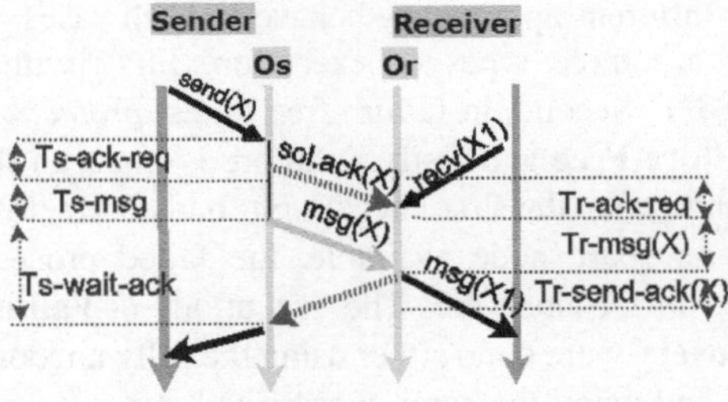

Fig. 6: Protection protocol for Intra-Group Communications

Instead, when the two peers belong to different **groups**, the observers still follow the protocol displayed in Figure 2.

Although the overheads are reduced by avoiding logging messages done among groups, the execution time would not be reduced when:

- The amount of data interchanged by each group is not considerable.
- The application is computation bounded and most of the time the processes are executing and not waiting for communications results. As the communication is overlapped with the computations, less communication overhead does not mean less execution time.
- The overhead added by coordination protocol is more considerable than the saving time on eliminating the group message logging.

4.4 Semi-Coordinated Protocol in Recovery

Semi-Coordinated checkpoint protocol changes the *recovery* explained previously in 3.3 because in case of a node failure, a **group** is rolling forward simultaneously.

The recovery protocol depicted in Figure 3 is still applied for **virtual socket** between processes which do not belong to the same group. On the contrary, **virtual sockets** with members of the same group should be reconnected in the beginning of the recovery process. The sends and receives between members of the **group** are re-executed again, because the remote peer is also in recovering and no log messages were done.

There are no considerable overhead differences in recovery. The sends and receive operations for **group** communications now are performed instead of skipping and looking for in storage respectively.

5. Experimental Results

We test the fault tolerance system to compare the fully uncoordinated RADIC model with semi-coordinated one.

The experiments were executed on a cluster formed by 4 nodes Intel® Core™ i5-650 Processor 6GB RAM, Network Gigabit Ethernet. The OS used is Ubuntu 10.04 Kernel 2.6.32-33-server.

We use heat-transfer SPMD application and a sum of matrices Master/Worker based on TCP sockets, which follow different communication patterns. This allows us to observe how the different approaches behave in both cases.

There are three types of execution. First, without FT, label **No FT**. Second, in failure-free to test *protection* phase label **Failure-Free** and lastly, a failure is inject in the node **N3** seconds after the first checkpoint, named **Recovery**. As there is no spare node available, the failed processes are recovered in the node **N2**. The executions in **Failure Free** and **Recovery** were done either using the fully uncoordinated protocol and using the semi-coordinated one.

Checkpoints were done only on processes executing in **N3**. As each checkpoint closes and then reconnects the communications, using checkpoints in other processes would disturb current experiments by adding additional overheads not related to log messages protocols and coordination.

The diagram used for comparing both protocols are the throughput by seconds. This metric let observe how the overheads introduced by fault tolerance impacts in the work effectively done by each of the processes.

The Figure 7 compares the different executions No FT, failure-free and recovery of SPMD P5 process located on node **N3**. When fully uncoordinated is used the throughput falls down more than in semi-coordinated protocol. This advantage makes the process to only need 2.37% more time than the execution without FT. Instead, when fully uncoordinated adds 9.48% in execution time. Recovery using semi-coordinated shows a better performance as well, adding 27.49% against to 52.13% of uncoordinated case.

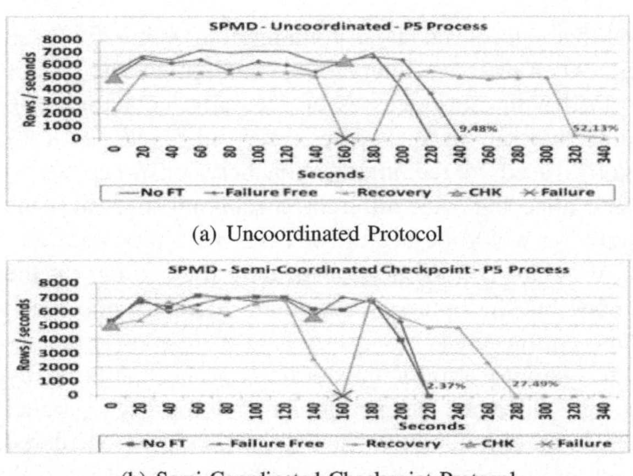

(a) Uncoordinated Protocol

(b) Semi-Coordinated Checkpoint Protocol

Fig. 7: SPMD Process P5 executions

In MW application, a sum of a 1000x1000 float matrix is done. The master sends 11k to each worker to sum and 11 bytes are returned to master. Executions of a worker hosted by failed node **N3** are graphed in Figure 8. shows that using uncoordinated protocol is slightly better than semi-coordinated one, adding 4.49% and 33.23% in failure-free and recovery respectively to executions without FT. It can be seen that the overhead added by coordination increases the execution time in semi-coordinated protocol while no overhead is saving in messages log because only node **N1** executing master and two workers have group communication.

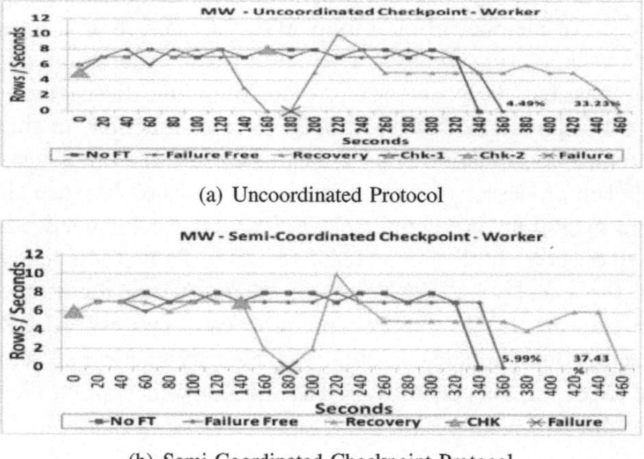

(a) Uncoordinated Protocol

(b) Semi-Coordinated Checkpoint Protocol

Fig. 8: MW Worker Executions

To evaluate how the comparing results are related to the package size in use, executions using different workloads are done. Table 9 shows SPMD execution time in failure-free and recovery. The heat transfer application in this experiment is configured to make more intensive communications. It is observed that uncoordinated protocol is better for small packet size. Usually, in those cases, the communication is overlapped with computation and the overhead of logging does not increase the execution times. Moreover, the coordination of checkpointing of each group impacts on it. In the same way, MW executions follow the same behavior. The results are displayed in table 10. As the package size increase, the semi-coordinated protocol is a better option for both communication patterns tested.

SPMD Workload	PAQ.	NOFT	Protection			
			Uncoord.		Semi-Coordinated	
			Sec.	Ov.	Sec.	Ov.
1000x600	2K	168	186	10,7%	199	18,5%
1000x1000	4K	263	304	15,6%	295	12,2%
1000x1500	6K	370	435	17,6%	394	6,5%

(a) Uncoordinated Protocol

SPMD Workload	PAQ.	NOFT	Recovery			
			Uncoord.		Semi-Coordinated	
			Sec.	Ov.	Sec.	Ov.
1000x600	2K	168	217	29,2%	208	23,8%
1000x1000	4K	263	324	23,2%	319	21,3%
1000x1500	6K	370	473	27,8%	483	30,5%

(b) Semi-Coordinated Checkpoint Protocol

Fig. 9: SPMD using different package size

MW WORKLOAD	PAQ.	NOFT	Protection			
			Uncoord.		Semi-Coordinated	
			Sec.	Ov.	Sec.	Ov.
10000X5000	55K	241	265	10,0%	269	11,6%
10000X6000	66K	283	325	14,8%	316	11,7%
10000X7000	77K	322	355	10,2%	354	9,9%

(a) Uncoordinated Protocol

MW WORKLOAD	PAQ.	NOFT	Recovery			
			Uncoord.		Semi-Coordinated	
			Sec.	Ov.	Sec.	Ov.
10000X5000	55K	241	301	24,9%	306	27,0%
10000X6000	66K	283	363	28,3%	359	26,9%
10000X7000	77K	322	401	24,5%	398	23,6%

(b) Semi-Coordinated Checkpoint Protocol

Fig. 10: MW using different package size

6. Conclusions and Future Work

A semi-coordinating checkpoint protocol is added to RADIC model as an alternative fault tolerance algorithm to be used with parallel applications running on a multicore clusters. The experiments show that this protocol allows to decrease the overhead of fault tolerance. Applications using intensive or larger group communications are the target since they are likely to obtain a better execution time by avoiding the logging of their intra-node messages.

This implementation is an early stage and has several instrumentations for taking times. We plan to do several optimizations and extending this work to standard MPI. We are working on a set of experiments to do a deeper comparative analysis between semi-coordinated and uncoordinated checkpointing protocol using a varied packet sizes and communication patterns.

Acknowledgments

This research has been supported by the MICINN Spain under contract TIN2007-64974, the MINECO (MICINN) Spain contract TIN2011-24384, the European ITEA2 project H4H, No 09011 and the Avanza Competitividad I+D+I contract TSI-020400-2010-120.

References

[1] E. N. Elnozahy, L. Alvisi, Y.-M. Wang, and D. B. Johnson, "A survey of rollback-recovery protocols in message-passing systems," *ACM Comput.Surv.*, vol. 34, no. 3, pp. 375–408, September 2002.

[2] G. Santos, A. Duarte, D. Rexachs, and E. Luque, "Providing non-stop service for message-passing based parallel applications with radic," ser. Lecture Notes in Computer Science, vol. 5168 LNCS, 2008, pp. 58–67.

[3] M. Castro, D. Rexachs, and E. Luque, "Transparent fault tolerance middleware at user level," in *HPCS'12*, 2012, pp. 566–572.

[4] S. Rao, L. Alvisi, and H. M. Vin, "The cost of recovery in message logging protocols," *IEEE Trans.on Knowl.and Data Eng.*, vol. 12, no. 2, pp. 160–173, mar 2000. [Online]. Available: http://dx.doi.org/10.1109/69.842260

[5] A. Bouteiller, T. Herault, G. Bosilca, and J. J. Dongarra, "Correlated set coordination in fault tolerant message logging protocols," in *Proceedings of the 17th international conference on Parallel processing - Volume Part II*, ser. Euro-Par'11. Berlin, Heidelberg: Springer-Verlag, 2011, pp. 51–64. [Online]. Available: http://dl.acm.org/citation.cfm?id=2033408.2033415

[6] M. Castro, D. Rexachs, and E. Luque, "Radic-based message passing fault tolerance system," in *ADVCOMP 2012, The Sixth International Conference on Advanced Engineering Computing and Applications in Sciences*, 2012, pp. 59–64.

[7] Y. Luo and D. Manivannan, "Hope: A hybrid optimistic checkpointing and selective pessimistic message logging protocol for large scale distributed systems," *Future Generation Computer Systems*, vol. 28, no. 8, pp. 1217–1235, 10 2012.

[8] Q. Gao, W. Huang, M. J. Koop, and D. K. Panda, "Group-based coordinated checkpointing for mpi: A case study on infiniband," in *Parallel Processing, 2007. ICPP 2007. International Conference on*, 2007, pp. 47–47, iD: 1.

[9] J. C. Y. Ho, C.-L. Wang, and F. C. M. Lau, "Scalable group-based checkpoint/restart for large-scale message-passing systems," in *Parallel and Distributed Processing, 2008. IPDPS 2008. IEEE International Symposium on*, 2008, pp. 1–12.

[10] M. K. McKusick, K. Bostic, M. J. Karels, and J. S. Quarterman, *The design and implementation of the 4.4BSD operating system.* Redwood City, CA, USA: Addison Wesley Longman Publishing Co., Inc., 1996.

[11] P. H. Hargrove and J. C. Duell, "Berkeley lab checkpoint/restart (blcr) for linux clusters," *Journal of Physics: Conference Series*, vol. 46, no. 1, p. 494, 2006.

[12] K. M. Chandy, "Distributed snapshots: Determining global states of distributed systems," *ACM Transactions on Computer Systems*, vol. 3, pp. 63–75, 1985.

[13] C. Coti, T. Herault, P. Lemarinier, L. Pilard, A. Rezmerita, E. Rodriguez, and F. Cappello, "Blocking vs. non-blocking coordinated checkpointing for large-scale fault tolerant mpi," in *Proceedings of the 2006 ACM/IEEE conference on Supercomputing*, ser. SC '06. New York, NY, USA: ACM, 2006. [Online]. Available: http://doi.acm.org/10.1145/1188455.1188587

Comparative Study of High Performance Computing Using Multi-core Parallel Systems

Hyo Jong Lee[1,2], **Hyeon Kyu Kim**[1]
[1] Division of Computer Science and Engineering
[2] Center for Advanced Image & Information Technology
Chonbuk National University, Jeonju Korea
hlee@jbnu.ac.kr, hkskyp@gmail.com

Abstract - Multi-core based high performance computing systems are available with a reasonable price. Parallel programming paradigm needs to be adjusted to an individual system. Parallel computing systems were compared in this paper. Electroencephalography signals were collected in order to measure performance of parallel computing for CPU and GPU based systems. A CPU based system showed better performance for smaller data set, while a GPU system showed better performance for larger data set. GTX580 processor, which has 512 CUDA cores, showed consistent speedup as input data was increased continuously. However, CPU has a limited speedup due to the lack of parallelism. For the FIR filter computation, GPU showed a good scalability, while a CPU system did not. The performance of GPU was better than CPU system slightly.

Keywords: CPU; GPU; multi-core; High Performance Computing; parallel FIR filter;

1 Introduction

Recently the high performance computing systems are taking a direction to multi-core based microprocessor since the power demands of increased clock speeds cannot be managed efficiently. Owing to the advanced VLSI and CPU design technology, multi-core systems are becoming popular satisfying customers' needs. Some scientists expect the core counts per chip would rise as the number of transistor increase according to Moore's law [1]. It is experienced that high performance computing (HPC) system is easy to build up by using basic building block of multi-core chips sharing memory in a single node. Clustering those basic computing blocks with a high speed network would be a convenient way to construct more powerful computing systems.

Programming models for parallel systems require different approaches. Traditionally it was common to develop parallel programming models for heterogeneous systems equipped with hybrid memory systems. Parallel library developers take advantage of the shared memory within a single node, but tried to optimize the inter-connected communications. Thus, a user may get good performance for his parallel applications using a single standardized programming model. A programming model for shared memory system is easy to control, but must overcome increased memory bandwidth for a large scale problem. Jin et al. [1] proposed a hybrid method to program multi-core based HPC systems combining standardized programming models. They also extended the OpenMP model with new data locality extensions to better match the more complex memory system.

GPU (Graphics Processing Units) system is a typical many-core system. In the beginning they were used for graphics processing only. Since NVIDIA released CUDA, the GPU becomes GPGPU (general-purpose computing on graphics processing units) and more applications became much accessible on it. Although programming on GPU requires optimization to utilize the maximum potential of the CPU, its performance was proved to be worth to pay the cost for optimization. For example, 2D Discrete Cosine Transform (DCT) problem for a 256x256 grey image took 10 seconds on a CPU, but just 48 milliseconds on a CPU using an optimized implementation [2].

There are other criteria besides performance to evaluate parallel programming models, such as scalability and the cost to performance ratio. The scale of some problems is not big to require an expensive supercomputer, although parallel programming approach would help users. Thus, it is important to investigate performance characteristics considering the cost to performance ratio. The low priced parallel computing system may be beneficial to a small scale parallel computing.

In this study we compare the performance of four different systems, a common desktop PC with a quad-core, a medium level work station, a low and a high priced GPU system. They are all easy to purchase depending on a user's various circumstance. A target problem was selected from a bioinformatics area called analysis of electroencephalography (EEG) signals. The same problem was implemented for each system for performance measurement. Each implementation did not require any special skill or serious programming time. That is, the cost for implementation would be considered as similar level.

2 Background

2.1 Electroencephalography signal

A target problem adopted in this study is to select correct bandwidth from electroencephalography (EEG). It is required to understand the concept of EEG. EEG is the recording of electrical activity along the scalp. Electrical recordings from the surface of the brain or even from the outer surface of the head demonstrate that there are continuous electrical activities in the brain. Both the intensity and the patterns of this electrical activity depend on the level of excitation of different parts of the brain resulting from sleep, wakefulness, or brain diseases such as epilepsy or even psychoses. The undulations in the recorded electrical potentials are known as brain waves, and the entire record is called an EEG [3]. Intensity of EEG recording range from 0 to 200 microvolt on the surface of the scalp, and their frequency ranges from once every few seconds to 50 or more per second. The characteristics of the waves are dependent on the degree of activity in respective parts of the cerebral cortex. The waves change markedly between the states of emotions. Much of the time, the brain waves are irregular, and no specific pattern can be discerned in the EEG.

There are mainly five types of Brain waves: Delta waves (0.5-4 Hz) which are considered to be related to the deep sleep [4] in the adults or premature babies. It is usually found in the frontal region of brain in adults and posterior region in children. A common Theta wave (4-8 Hz) which occurs in children and adults when they are in emotional stress or they have deep midline disorders. It is found in parietal and occipital region. Another type of theta waves is named frontal midline theta. The theta waves exist during the various tasks which need the correlation of the increased mental effort and sustained concentration [5]. Alpha wave (8-13 Hz), which occurs in quiet resting state but not sleep, is found in the occipital region. Alpha waves can reflect the relaxation level a person is having. They are also believed to be responsible for the movement related brain activity. Another role of Alpha rhythms is to handle a perceptual processing, memory tasks, and emotions [4]. Beta wave (13-30 Hz) occurs in active and busy concentration or anxious thinking state. It is found in the frontal and parietal region and is related to the concentration level of people [6]. An increase in a beta power may reflect the increase of the arousal level of an emotional state [5]. Gamma wave (30-100 Hz) which occurs in certain cognitive or motor functions. It is often used for diagnosis of the certain brain illness [4].

2.2 Finite Impulse Response filter

A finite impulse response (FIR) is a digital filter whose impulse response is of finite duration in signal processing. This is in contrast to infinite impulse filters, which may have internal feedback and may continue to respond indefinitely. The output y of a linear time invariant system is determined by convolving its input signal x with its impulse response h. Figure 1 displays a discrete-time FIR filter of order M. For a discrete-time FIR filter, the output is a weighted sum of the current and a finite number of previous values of the input marked as h in Figure 1.

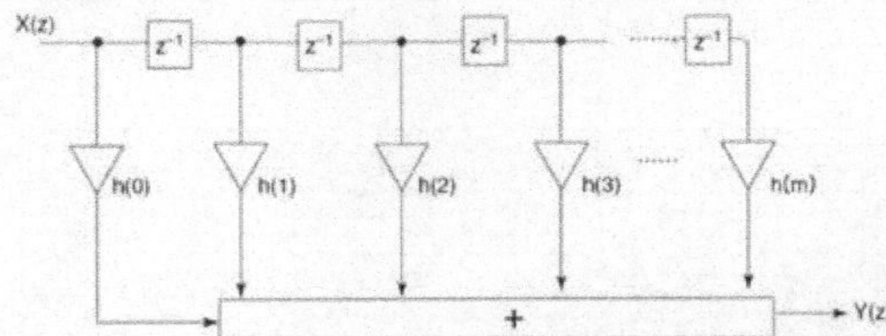

Fig 1. Diagram of discrete-time FIR filter design

The operation of FIR filter is described by Equation (1), which defines the output sequence Y(z) in terms of its input sequence X(z).

$$y[z] = \sum_{i=0}^{M} b_i x[z-i] \tag{1}$$

One property of the FIR filter is not to require feedback. That is, any rounding errors are not compounded by summed iterations. The same relative error occurs in each calculation. Another property is that the filter is inherently stable. This is due to the fact that all the poles are located at the origin and thus are located within the unit circle. Generally speaking, it is easy to design to be linear phase by making the coefficient sequence symmetric. Selection of coefficients is a key step in designing of filters. Most of the time filter specifications refer to the frequency response of the filter.

Applying the FIR filter to EEG signals, desired bandwidth of brain waves may be selected. First of all, FIR filter can eliminate unwanted artifact signals from the raw EEG signals. Figure 2 shows the original EEG signals for each channel. Each channel is affected by electrical noises or eye blinking noise. Since the magnitude of EEG signal is very low compared to those artifact signals, those unwanted signal must be removed.

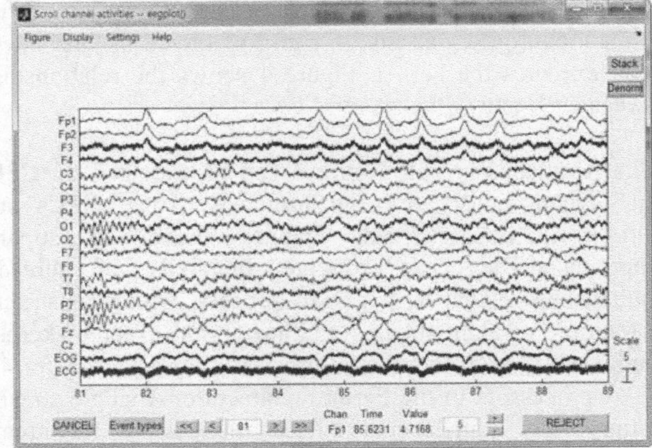

Fig 2. Example of original raw EEG signals

Figure 3 shows the result signals after applying FIR filter to eliminate electrical noise. The part of artifact signals were cleanly removed by selecting band of 4~50Hz. The electrical noise is distributed around 60Hz, the FIR filter was able to remove noise components.

Fig 3. Result signals of Fig. 2 after applying FIR filter of 4~50HZ

2.3 CUDA

Since NVIDIA introduced CUDA, a general purpose parallel computing and programming model became available to developers as an ideal tool to solve many complex computational problems in a more efficient way than a traditional model on a CPU. CUDA comes with a programming environment that developers can use C programming language as a native to a GPU system. The proposed programming model exploits the maximum power of multi-core CPU or GPU system by deploying parallel technique. The challenge of multi-core system is to develop application software that transparently scales its parallelism to leverage the increasing number of processor cores. The CUDA programming model is designed to overcome this problem.

In CUDA programming tasks are handled by kernel function call. A kernel function is the function being executed in GPU and consists with blocks and grids. The computational grid consists of a grid of thread blocks. Each thread executes the kernel. Figure 4 shows the relationship between CPU and GPU.

The parallel kernel in Figure 4 can be executed on CPU either synchronously or asynchronously. Thus, GPUs are multi-thread computational engines based on stream computing. They can execute hundreds of threads simultaneously. That is, a CUDA process, which constructs the multiple of eight streams multiprocessor, executes kernel functions. A single stream multiprocessor consists of 32 or 48 CUDA processors in the Fermi architecture. A single stream multiprocessor can execute 1,536 threads at maximum concurrently [7]. The construction of threads in a unit block is critical to the performance of CUDA programming. It is important to make sure the optimal construction for the best performance.

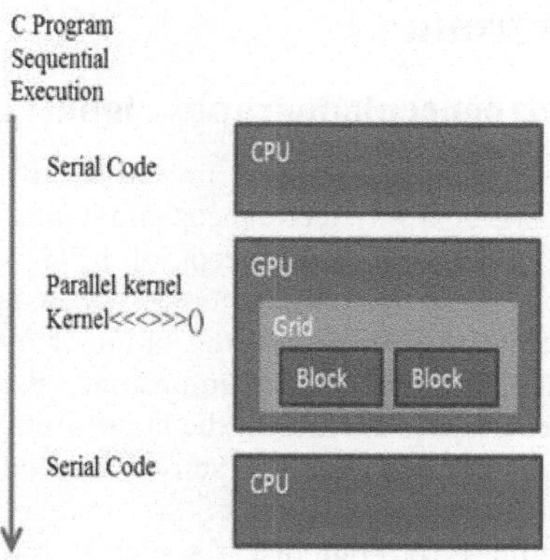

Fig 4. Relationship between CUDA and CPU

3 Experiment

Data processing time of EEG data is obviously proportional to the number of channels and experimental duration. The size of data is 17Mbytes (for double precision) approximately for one hour collection from a single channel. In this experiment the international standard 10-20 system was used to measure EEG signals using19 channels. The international 10-10 system has 71 electrodes to cover a whole brain. Assuming one hour of experiment duration, data size would be 260Mbytes and 973Mbyes approximately for 10-20 and 10-10 system, respectively. In this paper data collection time was controlled so that 24.7Mbytes, 49.4Mbytes, 98.8Mbytes, and 197.6Mbytes of data were collected.

The FIR filter function has been implemented for both CPU and GPU system. Two main systems were used for this experiment. The first system is a desktop PC equipped with Intel Core i5-2500 3.30GHz, which has a quad-core. This system also has NVIDIA GeForce GTX550 Ti 1GiB installed. This system runs on Window7 Enterprise 64-bit. The other system is a middle class server, which has a Dual Intel Xeon X5650 2.67GHz. The system has total 12 physical CPUs or 24 logical CPUs permitting the Hyper Threading technology. This system also has a NVIDIA GeForce GTX 580 3GiB installed. The system runs on CentOS 6.3 64-bit. Both system installed Version 5.0 of CUDA driver.

Different parallel approaches were applied for a CPU system based on multicores and GPU system based on many cores. Total number of electrodes were distributed to each core similarly (or equally) for a CPU system. In this case a single core processed all data distributed to the core by deploying FIR filter. In the case of a GPU system data collected by a single channel is processed on to a single kernel function. That is, a single thread handled a single input data stream. For example, a single core of a quad-core CPU system will process data collected from 5 channels, while a single thread processes a single channel data by calling a kernel function 20-times.

Firstly, the coefficient *b* from Equation 1 was implemented based on EEGLab [9] implementation. Then, FIR filter was parallelized separately for both of CPU system and GPU system. A loop unrolling technique has been used for optimization for both CPU and CUDA. OpenMP 2.0 was used for CPU parallel implementation, which required minimal code changes for a shared memory system. A SSE (Streaming SIMD Extensions) 2.0 operations were also used for CPU parallelism. The pseudo code of FIR filter for a CPU system is depicted in Figure 5. The usage of directive was prohibited in order to minimize variable spaces, which increases due to the directives under loop unrolling. At line 07 from Figure 5 (0:6) means that seven variables from zero to six were used. (0:2:120 represents that variable 0 to 12 were used for only even numbered variables. Since the data was double type, two SSE instructions were processed at lines between 07 and 12 from Figure 5.

The FIR filter was translated to CUDA version of C language. . In the CUDA, add and multiply operators called in a FIR filter were translated into a single MAD (multiply / add) operator. Figure 6 shows a pseudo code of FIR filter for CUDA. The function fir_filter was executed on a CPU system and a kernel function was executed on a GPU system. The bandwidth of data communication between GPU and GPU was efficiently reduced by using OpenMP. The line 07 was optimized by substitution of MAD instructions after CUDA compilation options.

The source codes were compiled with Visual Studio 2010 SP1 with an O3 option for code optimization. For CentOS system, GCC 4.6.3 was used for compilation. A binary code was created with the same level of optimization – O3. The CUDA compiler nvcc was used for both systems with the same compiler option level.

```
01   #pragma omp parallel for
02   for( size_t i = 0; i < eeg_data.size(); ++i ) {
03     size_t j = 0;
04     size_t size = (Y.size()/14)*14;
05     for( ; j < size; j+=14 ) {
06      for( size_t k = 0; k < b.size(); ++k ) {
07       __m128d sb = _mm_set_pd(b[k], b[k]);
08       __m128d sY(0:6) = _mm_load_pd(&Y[j+(0:2:12)]);
09       __m128d sX(0:6) = _mm_load_pd(&X[j+(0:2:12)+k]);
10       sX(0:6) = _mm_mul_pd(sb, sX(0:6));
11       sY(0:6) = _mm_add_pd(sY(0:6), sX(0:6));
12       _mm_store_pd(&Y[j+(0:2:12)], sY(0:6));
13      }
14     }
15     for( ; j < Y.size(); ++j ) {
16      for( size_t k = 0; k < b.size(); ++k ) {
17       Y[j] += b[k]*X[j+k];
18      }
19     }
20   }
```

Fig 5. Pseudocode of FIR filter for CPU parallelism

```
01      __global__ void kernel(b, X, Y) {
02       int gid = blockDim.x*blockIdx.x + threadIdx.x;
03       if( gid < Y_size ) {
04        double sum = 0.0;
05        #pragma unroll 8
06        for( size_t i = 0; i < b_size; ++i ) {
07         sum = b[i]*X[gid+i]+sum;
08        }
09        Y[gid] = sum;
10       }
11      }
12      function fir_filter(b, X, Y) {
13       #pragma omp parallel for
14       for( size_t i = 0; i < eeg_data.size(); ++i ) {
15        memcpy host to device;
16        kernel<<<blocks, threads>>>(b, X[i], Y[i]);
17        memcpy device to host;
18       }
19      }
```

Fig 6. Pseudocode of FIR filter for CUDA

4 Result And Discussion

The FIR filter function has been successfully implemented and compiled as described in Section III. In order to measure correct execution times, four different executable files were created for a desktop PC, a server, and two GPU programs for both systems. Table I and II summarized execution times for both systems.

Table 1. Performance measurement of CPU and GPU for FIR filter for a desktop (unit: milli-second)

Data length x Multiples	**CPU(Intel i5-2500)**			**GPU**
	Thread 1	***Thread 4***	***Thread 8***	***GTX 550 Ti***
161,890x1	1,405	379	533	351
161,890x2	2,189	617	753	531
161,890x4	4,021	1,133	1264	976
161,890x8	7,429	2,175	2262	1,517

Table 2. Performance Measure of CPU and GPU In FIR filter for a server (unit: milli-second)

Data length x Multiples	**CPU(Dual Xeon X5650)**					**GPU**
	Thread 1	***Thread 4***	***Thread 8***	***Thread12***	***Thread24***	***GTX 580***
161,890x1	1,632	423	280	208	270	339
161,890x2	2,747	713	470	357	429	393
161,890x4	5,058	1301	851	625	759	522
161,890x8	9,431	2446	1601	1,197	1,422	820

The desktop PC supported up to four cores. Table I shows the execution time decreased as the number of cores increased linearly. The GTX 550 Ti supports 192 CUDA cores. According to Table I the execution on the GPU system is slightly better than quad-core system. Table II summarized the result from a server processor, which provides 24 HT cores including 12 physical cores. The execution time of a server processor showed decreased linearly as the number of threads increased until 12-thread. However, the execution time of 24-thread is longer than the 12-thread due to the limited ALU functionality. The HT technique allows two logical cores for a single physical core; however, those two logical cores must share a single ALU. This restriction becomes speedup bottle neck for computing intensive problems. Since a FIR filter is belongs to a computing intensive problem, it experienced slow-down for more logical cores. GPU system installed on a server was GTX 580, which has 512 CUDA cores. Its performance was slightly better than the GPU installed on a desktop PC. It also shows slightly better than six-core case, but 60% slower than 12-core for small problem cases (161,890x1x20 and 161,890x2x20). This delay was caused by the same reason as shown in a desktop PC. However, as the problem size gets larger, GPU upbeats the server system.

Figure 7 displays the speedups of each system based on the Xeon X5650 single-thread, which showed the slowest processing time. In the case of CPU parallel implementation, a speedup reached up to 8-fold. However, both systems did not demonstrate that their performances would be better than the 8-fold. A GPU system on a server showed about 11-fold faster speedup. As the size of problem is increased, the speedup is also increased because more computing available threads are available. The speedups of GTX are higher compared to CPU for larger problem domains. The reason for this better performance is caused by wider memory bandwidth in a GPU processor. In the case of GTX 580, the speedup is worse than CPU due to the increased communication overhead.

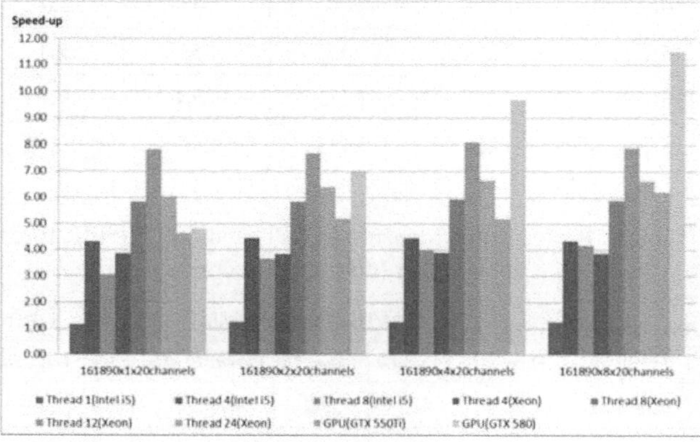

Fig 7. Speedups for GPU and CPU based on Xeon CPU

5 Conclusions

In this paper the performances of FIR filter execution were compared on various machines. The input data were collected through EEG system, of which sample rate was 500Hz. The EEG signals were assumed to be collected for 5min, 10min, 20min and 40 minutes. CPU showed better performance for smaller data set, which were collected for 5 min and 10 min, while GPU showed better performance for larger data set, which were collected for 20 min and 40 min. GTX580 processor, which has 512 CUDA cores, shows consistent speedup as input data is increased continuously. However, CPU has a limited speedup due to lack of parallelism. For the FIR filter computation, GPU showed a good scalability, while CPU did not. The performance of GPU was better than CPU, however, the difference was not significant due to small problem size of a FIR filter.

Acknowledgment

This work was supported by the National Research Foundation of Korea (NRF) grant funded by the Korea government (MEST) (No. 2012R1A2A2A03).

References

[1] H. Jin, D. Jespersen, P. Mehrotra, R. Biswas, L. Huang, B. Chapman, "High performance computing using MPI and OpenMP on multi-core parallel systems", Parallel Computing Vol 37, pp. 562-575, 2011.

[2] M. Nixon and A. Aguado, Feature Extraction & Image Processing, Newnes, 2002.

[3] Guyton,A.C.,Hall J.E, Textbook Of Medical Physiology, Elsevier Inc., Philadelphia, 2005.

[4] S. Sanei and J. Chambers, EEG signal processing. Chichester, England; Hoboken, NJ: John Wiley & Sons, 2007.

[5] D. Sammler, M. Grigutsch, T. Fritz, and S. Koelsch, "Music and emotion: Electrophysiological correlates of the processing of pleasant and unpleasant music," Psychophysiology, vol. 44, pp. 293-304, 2007.

[6] Larsen, R. J., & Buss, D. M. Personality psychology. NewYork: McGraw-Hill, 2002

[7] NVIDIA. (2009). FERMI Compute Architecture White Paper (v1.1ed.). http://www.nvidia.com/

[8] Kennett R. Modern electroencephalography. J Neurol 2012;259: 783-9

[9] D. A and M. S., "EEGLAB: an open source toolbox for analysis of single-trial EEG dynamics including independent component analysis," Journal of Neurosci Methods, vol. 134, pp. 9-21, 2004.

A Numerical Modeling MATLAB Approach to Memory Behavior on a Multi-core Architecture on a Beowulf Cluster Single-Node

Damian Valles
Computer Science, Montana Tech of the University of Montana, Butte, Montana, USA

Abstract - *This paper studies a numerical modeling approach to memory behavior by using bandwidth performance of a single compute-node on a Scyld Beowulf cluster. The CacheBench benchmark is used to obtain memory bandwidth values as it is implemented in simulated single and multi-process execution on the Scyld cluster. The polynomial curve-fitting linear regression is the modeling approach to represent the memory behavior using MATLAB polyfit() function. The models show bandwidth performance for each process for single-instance and distinct bandwidth models for multi-instance and special cases of CacheBench. Model accuracy at large problem sizes in all scenarios depict actual values from CacheBench programs; however, improvement on modeling approach in using polyfit() function is necessary to better represent lower problem sizes for all scenarios.*

Keywords: cluster, performance, memory, modeling

1 Introduction

The Beowulf cluster is a parallel computer system conforming to the Beowulf architecture, which consists of a collection of commodity off-the-shelf (COTS) computers (referred to as "nodes"), connected via a private network running an open-source operating system [1]. A Beowulf cluster consists of a front-end machine that communicates with the outside world, and manages and distributes jobs to identical compute-nodes. The compute-nodes are connected to the front-end via a private network that normally uses a commonly available communication protocol such as Ethernet and/or InfiniBand for communication. Together, the compute-nodes and associated private network form a homogenous environment that make-up the structure of the cluster. The compute-nodes are servers that are always listening for incoming requests and provide the necessary processing computational power to the assigned tasks coming from the front-end machine [2].

Scyld is a Penguin Computing Scyld ClusterWare6 cluster system that consists of a front-end machine, twenty compute-nodes and one storage node. Throughout Scyld, the processing architecture is constant in all compute-nodes that consist of two Intel eight-core Sandy Bridge Xeon processors as shown in Figure 1. Both processors communicate with each other through the two QuickPath Interconnect (QPI) channels, and each processor has four Double Data-Rate 3 (DDR3) channels in where each channel handles up to three Dual-In Memory Model (DIMM) memory cards. The focus is to analyze the memory behavior within a compute-node in this type of cluster environment in order to forecast memory performance for different single and multi-process jobs and memory sizes.

The CacheBench benchmark was utilized to measure the memory performance found on Scyld's compute-nodes. CacheBench is a benchmark designed to evaluate the performance of the memory hierarchy of computer system and establish peak computation rate given optimal cache reuse and to verify the effectiveness of high level of compiler optimization on tuned and unturned codes [3]. CacheBench was launched on all compute-nodes and spawned the desired job size instances to the processing cores. It consists of eight different benchmarks in where each computes the total amount of data accessed in bytes over its time of completion to obtain bandwidth value. This bandwidth metric is use to numerically model the memory behavior for each of the compute-nodes.

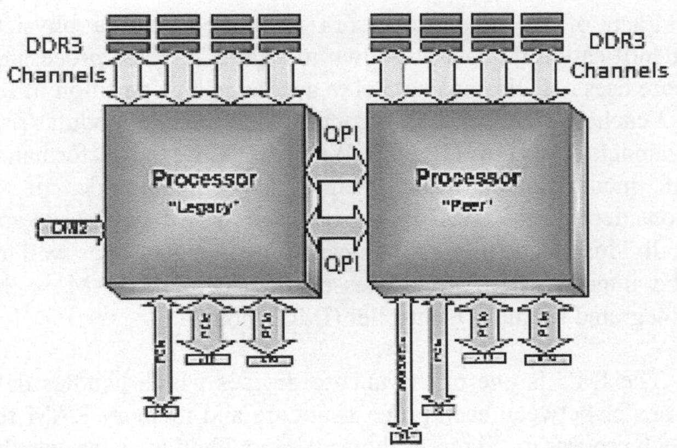

Figure 1. Intel Xeon Sandy Bridge Configuration at each compute-node [4]

The approach to model memory behavior is to simulate identical job scenarios on the Scyld cluster. Most of the jobs submitted consist of data-intensive, high memory load through MPI (Message Passing Interface) programs. The considered scenarios using CacheBench are: 1) single-instance of benchmark program with different load sizes, 2) multiple-instances with same load sizes, and 3) special case in where the first two scenarios are present at the same time. It is hypothesized that by using the CacheBench benchmark through the many combinational scenarios, memory behavior representation can be obtain to better understand and forecast memory performance at the single-node level by using polynomial curve-fitting linear regression as the numerical model approach for the bandwidth values representation using linear MATLAB function *polyfit()*.

2 Hardware Overview

The Scyld cluster system consists of a front-end machine, twenty dedicated compute-nodes and one storage-node. Where all compute-nodes consist of homogenous architecture parts which include two Intel eight-core Sandy Bridge processors with hyper-threading capabilities. In effect, the cluster can have up to six hundred and forty processing workers on a single application not including the front-end machine. The homogenous configuration yields the opportunity to study and model the Scyld memory behavior to further understand and predict its memory performance.

The two Sandy Bridge processors is the architecture implemented on each compute-node with a total of thirty-two hyper-threaded processing cores. Each core has its own Level-1 (L1) and Level-2 (L2) cache memory. The shared Level-3 (L3) cache has a total of 20MB and divided in eight ways to allocate to each processing core. At the compute-node level, each unit had a total of 64GB of DDR3 RAM between the two processors. This represents the memory hierarchy in which the bandwidth values will be obtained from the different programs of the CacheBench benchmark.

Each of the two processors is labeled with a physical identification number as shown in Figure 2. Each processing core uses a dedicated channel to access its own partition of the L3 cache which is also interconnected to the two modular ring channels as seen in Figure 2. When modeling the performance of memory bandwidth within a compute-node, it is considering the data path between RAM memory and individual cache hierarchy in each processing core; as well as, the interface between processor and memory RAM is the Integrated Memory Controller (IMC) module.

The IMC is one of the uncore devices which handles data transfer between each processing core and memory RAM for each processor. Figure 3 shows the module that constructs the IMC and its interfaces with the Home Agent (HA) module, Physical Box (PBOX) module and other uncore internal devices in the processor. The IMC device uses four dedicated channels to receive/transmit data to RAM through the PBOX module. Each channel is connected to one of the dedicated memory counters (MC-0 to MC-3) within the IMC to capture memory events at each channel.

The PBOX layer is a physical interconnect module that interfaces the DIMM channels outside the processor to the IMC's memory counters. The HA contains the processor target address configuration and monitoring registers for the memory controller. Regardless of the memory technology, the HA receives memory reads and write request from the modular rings. It checks the memory transaction type, detects and resolves the coherent conflict, and finally schedules a corresponding transaction to the memory controller. It is also responsible for returning the response and completion of all requests [6].

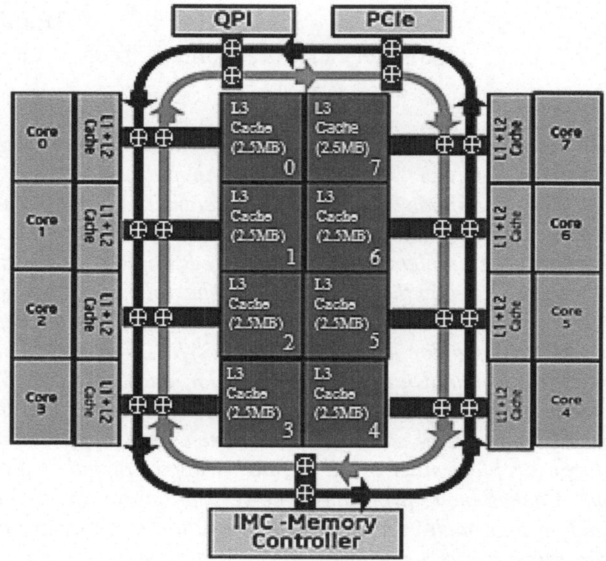

Figure 2. Ring architecture in the Intel Xeon processor E5-2600 product family [5]

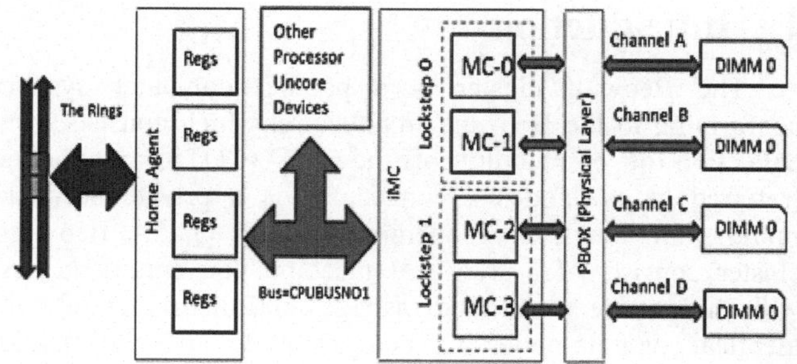

Figure 3. The internal Memory Controller module and its interfaces

The memory controller and HA devices communicate through a shared CPU bus that is shared between all uncore devices as seen in Figure 3. Other uncore devices in the processor include the QPI and Peripheral Component Interconnect Express (PCIe) device from Figure 2. As mentioned before, the QPI channels are the communication between the two processors on each node, and the PCIe is where the Infiniband communication is established between the front-end machine and each of the compute-nodes. It is important in how the uncore devices interact since two of the devices are part of the data path between RAM and processing core, as well as, benefits to explain in how the architecture effects the memory behavior. As the programs of the CacheBench are executed, the data will travel between the hierarchy of caches and DIMMs from each IMC channels. The bandwidth values will indicate not only the performance of cache-level paths and DIMMs, but it will include in how the uncore devices will react to the different scenarios used to model the memory behavior.

3 Hardware Modeling

To find the numerical models that could help explain the memory behavior, we looked at previous research that had been done in modeling hardware. Fedorova et al. [7] provided a useful approach that partially explained how to obtain some of the modeling functions and numerical linear approaches that were used to determine compute-node related functions. This approach was then implemented on [8] to model processor performance for scheduling modifications.

The general approach of [7] is based on the number of Instructions per Cycle (IPC) defined in the equation (1). The model consists of a function of three variables when executing threads in the virtual processors: The number of concurrent threads, N, the Miss Rate at L2 cache while executing *N* concurrent threads, L2_*MR(N)*, and the number of perfect Cycles per Instruction (CPI) that hit L2 cache, with no misses, from *N* of concurrent threads, *perf_cache_CPI(N)*.

$$\text{IPC} = f(\text{N}, \text{L2\_}MR(N), perf\_cache\_CPI(N)) \quad (1)$$

The IPC function determines the number of instruction per cycle which describes the performance of the hardware for each task executing in a single virtual processor. Since the model only describes a single thread executing in a virtual processor, it does not accurately model a multi-core compute-node executing many processes. For this situation, [7] describes a multithreaded modeling approach that considers "probability of virtual processors being busy or stalled and a linear regression model obtained through benchmark runs". The multithreaded model is described as:

$$\text{IPC} = \sum_{\text{N}=0}^{\text{V}} P(\text{N}) * R\_IPC(\text{N}) \quad (2)$$

, where *P*(N) is the probability of a processor is in state N. A linear regression function is then applied that is a function of *N-number* of concurrent threads and the perfect-L2-cache IPC achieved by V threads. The linear regression function is represented as:

$$R\_IPC(\text{N}) = f(\text{N}, \text{perf\_cache\_IPC(N)}) \quad (3)$$

The model evaluation consists of determining the highest degree of concurrency in IPC units. This approach is used to model Scyld's memory behavior in a compute-node by the bandwidth performance values from CacheBench programs. Knowledge of the bandwidth model can help understand and forecast the compute-node's availability of memory bandwidth in respect to the job size and the number of processes running in parallel.

3.1 Modeling Scyld's Memory Behavior

To begin modeling memory behavior from Scyld compute-nodes, the CacheBench benchmark was used in order to determine bandwidth values. As mentioned before, CacheBench consists of eight benchmark programs: *Cache Read, Cache Write, Cache Read-Modify-Write, Hand-tuned Read, Hand-tuned Write, Hand-tuned Read-Modify-Write (RMW), memcpy() and memset()* from C library [3]. Each of the programs are used in different scenarios that simulate job program execution to the Scyld cluster: 1) single-instance of CacheBench with different load sizes, 2) multiple-instances with same load sizes, and 3) special cases of combinations of scenarios one and two. For all instances of CacheBench, the benchmark was executed on all the compute-nodes of the cluster to run all eight programs. The parameters of each instance in all case scenarios are:

- DOUBLE as the data type for all test runs.
- Five seconds per iteration
- Once the number of times each test is run.
- Log base 2 of the maximum problem size tested in bytes: CB_Memsize = between 31 and 36
- The number of test sizes measured between powers of two. CB_Resolution = 2

3.1.1 Single-Instance Memory Behavior

The single-instance case consists of only one process running at each compute-node executing all eight programs of the benchmark and obtaining bandwidth values from each program run. Each compute-node was tested with different maximum problem sizes from 2^{31} (M=31) to the maximum amount of RAM at each node 2^{36} (M=36). As bandwidth values were obtained, each test run showed identical values to the different problem sizes throughout all the nodes. Since the architecture of the nodes is homogeneous and each process owns all the resources, it can then be assumed that the bandwidth values from each of the program runs are closely identical throughout all the nodes. Therefore, the values were averaged for each program run from all of the nodes from problem sizes M=31 to M=36. Then for each problem size, the average approach to each program run is:

$$f\text{avg}_\alpha = \frac{1}{j}\sum_{i=0}^{j} f_\alpha^i \quad (4)$$

, in where *j* is the total number of compute-nodes, *i* is the node number, and each program as *α :{ Cache Read, Cache Write, Cache RMW, Hand-tuned Read, Hand-tuned Write, Hand-tuned RMW, memset(), memcpy()}*.

Figure 4 shows the average values obtained from all the nodes for *memcpy()* and *memset()* for problem size M = 31. For the *memcpy()* program, the high bandwidth peak represents the high availability bandwidth within the cache levels as data is being fetch in order to be copied back to memory. As the program size increases to maximum setting, both programs show a bandwidth convergence as the problem size reaches 100Mbytes. Data size at this point becomes too large that occupies all of the caching and bottleneck increases through the IMC channels and modular rings.

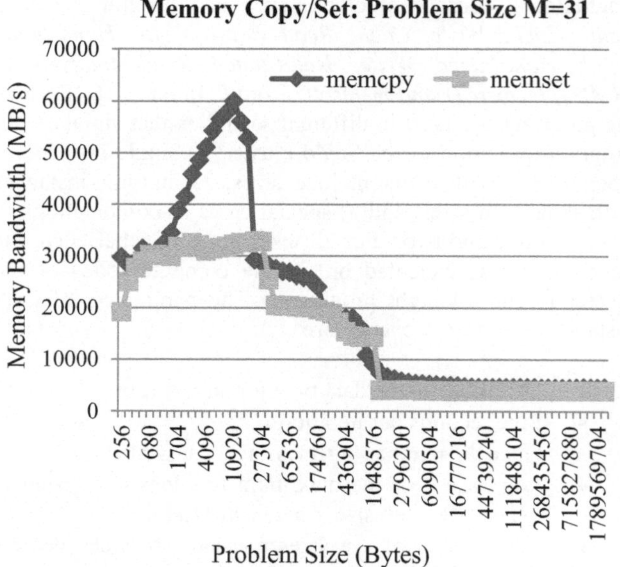

Figure 4. Single-Instance average values for *memcpy()* and *memset()* at problem size M=31

To represent a numerical model from the results from Figure 4, the polynomial curve-fitting regression is used for each of the programs from CacheBench. In using the linear MATLAB function *polyfit()* generates a desired n[th]-order polynomial that can fit X-Y (Problem Size-Bandwidth) parameters. It was found the polynomial models best fit of orders between 15 and 17. Then from the coefficients obtained from the *polyfit()* function, each of the programs can be represented as:

$$f_\alpha = k_1x^n + k_2x^{n-1} + \cdots + k_{n+1}x^0 \quad (5)$$

, in where n is the nth-order parameter between 15 and 17, k is the coefficients obtained from *polyfit()*, and as α describe for (4).

3.1.2 Multiple-Instances Memory Behavior

The multiple-instances case consists of launching two or more processes running at each compute-node. Each of the processes executing on the node is configured to the same problem size and executing its own CacheBench instance. For each of the problem size value, the number of process is increased by one after each run until reaching full utilization of RAM. Since more instances of the benchmark are launched, it can be assumed that the bandwidth values and models will be lower from the single-instance cases. This type of scenarios to multiple-instances simulates multi-process programs that are designed to run on cluster systems using MPI.

Figure 5 shows the values obtained from using four instances of the *Cache Write* program for problem size M=34 of each process. For all of the processes, it can be seen that the bandwidth performance is identical from small to medium problem sizes. However, the processes break into two different bandwidth groups when the problem size increases from 8MB. This type of behavior is seen throughout all other multiple-instance cases where roughly half of the processes are split into two bandwidth groups.

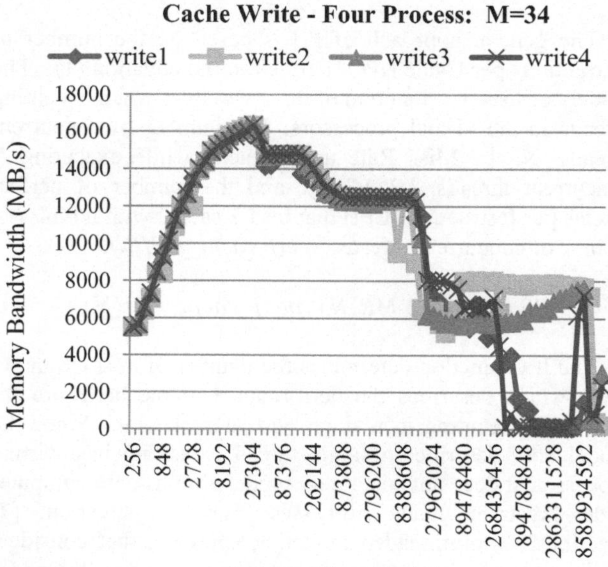

Figure 5. Four-Process values for *Cache Write* program at problem size M=34

To obtain a numerical model from the results from Figure 5, the polynomial curve-fitting regression will follow the trend of the process in splitting into two groups. The approach is to obtain a model from the higher-valued bandwidth process and a lower-valued bandwidth process. The rest of the processes will be placed to either at the high-end or lower-end bandwidth group since any process can either yield high-end or low-end bandwidth values. Therefore, the trend of the two groups is:

$$f\alpha_i = \begin{cases} h_1x^n + h_2x^{n-1} + \cdots + h_{n+1}x^0 & ; P(i) \geq 0.5 \\ l_1x^n + l_2x^{n-1} + \cdots + l_{n+1}x^0 & ; 1 - P(i) \geq 0.5 \end{cases} \quad (6)$$

, in where n is the nth-order parameter between 15 and 17, h is the coefficients for higher-valued bandwidth, l is the coefficients for lower-valued bandwidth, the *P(i)* is the probability of the process on higher bandwidth, and α_i represents each individual process at each program in α. The *P(i)* probably refers to the same probability described (2). In this case, the *P(i)* refers to the probability a process-*i* is in state of high-end bandwidth (*probHB*), and probability of low-end bandwidth (*probLB)*. Then from [6], it is derived that:

$$P(i) = \binom{i}{x}(probLB)^x(probHB)^{i-x} \quad (7)$$

3.1.3 Special Cases: Multi-Instance, Multi-problem Size

In the special cases, it was designed to launch multiple processes grouped with same problem sizes to other multiple processes grouped with different problem sizes of other groups. The total number of problem sizes of all process had to equal the maximum RAM size of the node. Each of the processes executing on the node is configured to the same problem size in its group and executing its own CacheBench instance. In all of the special cases, the one requirement was that the entire test runs added to maximum RAM size at each node. Since the entire RAM is utilized in all of the scenarios of special cases, swapping occurred during execution of all of the programs.

Figure 6 shows the values obtained from using eight instances of the *Hand-tuned Read* program for problem size M=31 of each process while running another eight-process group at problem size at M=32 and a single-process at problem size M=33. The data shows in how variant each of the process becomes when increasing problem size for each process. However, the processes continue to break into many grouping as the problem size increases. This type of behavior is seen throughout all other multiple-instance-multi-problem-size cases where some processes show zero bandwidth because of swapping state in the node.

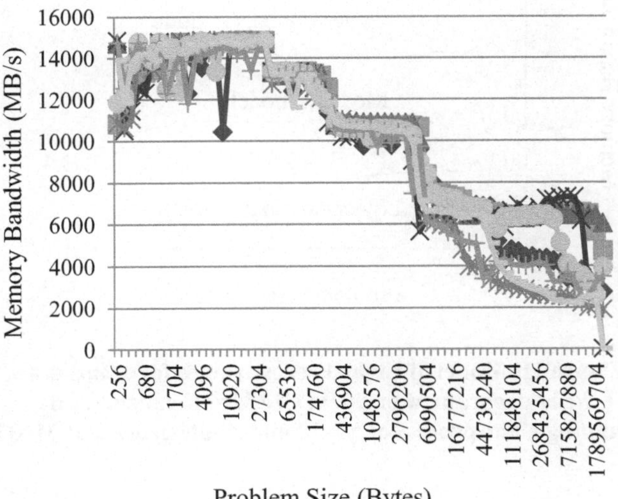

Figure 6. Eight-Process values for *Hand-tuned Read* program at problem size M=31, concurrently running eight-process at M=32 and single process at M=33

To obtain a numerical model from the results from Figure 6, the polynomial curve-fitting regression cannot follow the trend of the process in splitting into individual tail-ends. The approach is to obtain a model from the upper and lower boundaries. The rest of the processes exist between the boundaries where the model is the area between the two. Therefore, the upper-bound is defined as:

$$f_{upper} = u_1x^n + u_2x^{n-1} + \cdots + u_{n+1}x^0 \quad (8)$$

, where u_i are the coefficients of the upper-boundary polynomial and n is the nth-order parameter between 15 and 17. The lower-bound as:

$$f_{lower} = w_1x^n + w_2x^{n-1} + \cdots + w_{n+1}x^0 \quad (9)$$

, where w_i are the coefficients of the lower-boundary polynomial and n is the nth-order parameter between 15 and 17 then the medium-model between the two is:

$$f_{medium} = \sum_{i=1}^{n}\left(\frac{u_{i-1}-w_{i-1}}{2} + w_{i-1}\right)x^i \quad (10)$$

4 Results

For the single-instance case, an example of one of the results is showed in Figure 7 from programs *Cache Read/Write/RMW* at problem size M=31. The resultant models using (5) for the results of the three programs in Figure 7 are showed on Figure 8. The model for the *Cache Read* is highly precise since the bandwidth stayed constant throughout all problem sizes. However, the models for *Cache Write & RMW* lose precision for the low to medium problem sizes until both converge to the same convergences that are in Figure 7.

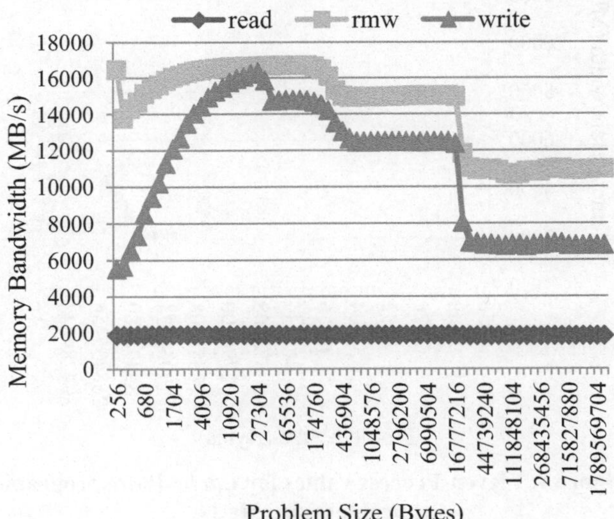

Figure 7. Single-Instance average values for *Cache Read/Write/RMW* at problem size M=31

For the multiple-instance case, an example of one of the results is showed in Figure 9 from programs *Cache Write* at problem size M=31. The resultant models using (6) for the results of the processes in Figure 9 and including its single-instance model are showed on Figure 10. The model for the *Cache Write* is divided to its high-end and low-end polynomials. Each of the processes both exists on the high or low-ends of bandwidth values of the program and converges to the same point as in Figure 9. However, the models continue to lose precision for the low to medium problem sizes.

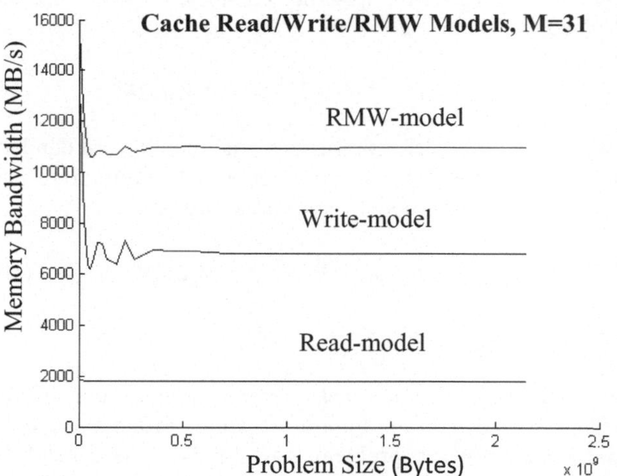

Figure 8. Model of single-instance average values for *Cache Read/Write/RMW* at problem size M=31

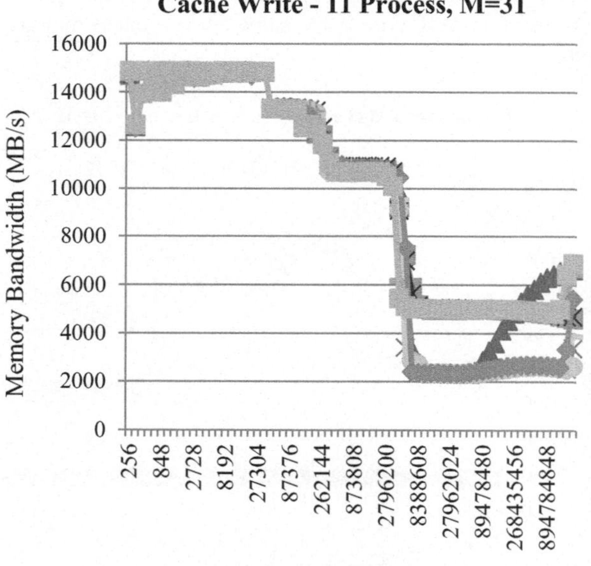

Figure 9. Eleven-Process values for *Cache Write* program at problem size M=34

The resultant model using (10) for the results of the processes in Figure 6 are showed on Figure 10 for Eight-Process values for *Hand-tuned Read* program at problem size M=31, while concurrently running eight-process at M=32 and single process at M=33. The model in (10) is showed as the polynomial between the upper and lower-boundaries found on Figure 6. The area model can be a representation for all of the process between the two boundaries, especially when the number of processes increases between the boundaries. However, the model trend to converge to the lower-boundary model as the problem size increases. The reason for this behavior can be due to bottlenecks on the architecture and as the number of processes increases, the rate of bandwidth per process lowers as problem sizes increases.

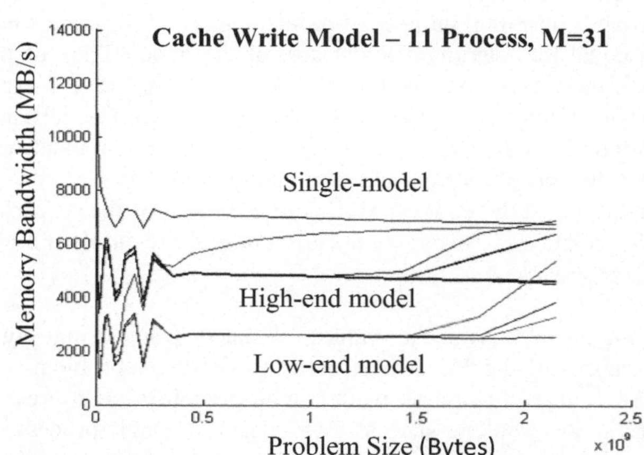

Figure 10. Model of Eleven-Process values for *Cache Write* program at problem size M=34

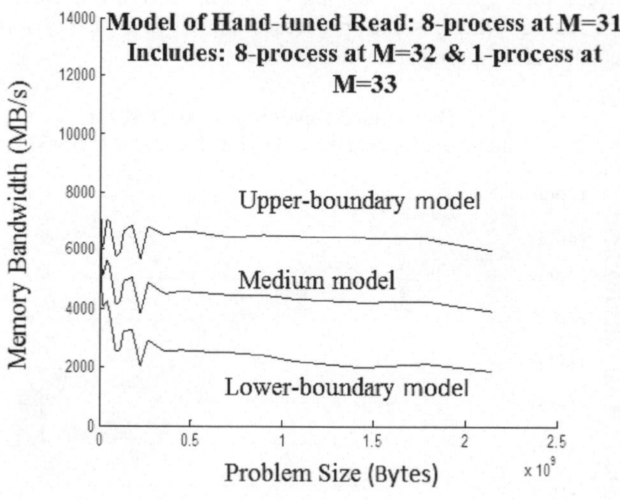

Figure 11. Model of Eight-Process values for *Hand-tuned Read* program at problem size M=31, concurrently running eight-process at M=32 and single process at M=33

5 Conclusions

The CacheBench benchmark was utilized to obtain bandwidth values as a memory performance metric from each compute-node in order to model memory behavior on the Scyld cluster. Each of the CacheBench programs were configured to execute to maximum problem sizes from 2^{31} to compute-node's total RAM 2^{36}. Three scenarios were introduced to simulated MPI execution programs: 1) single-instance of benchmark to all nodes, 2) multi-instances of benchmark with equal problem size, and 3) special cases of instances of the benchmark from the first two cases.

The numerical model approach to the bandwidth values obtained from the benchmark was the polynomial curve-fitting linear regression method. The MATLAB linear function *polyfit()* was utilized to model the data obtained from each of the program runs at different problems sizes on all cases. The nth-orders between 15 to 17 of the *polyfit()* function gave the best fitting polynomials of the memory behavior.

For the single-instance case, all of the values of each node were averaged for each of the programs that represent the single process model defined in (5). For the multiple-instance case, the processes of equal problem size showed separation of two bandwidth groups as seen in (6). The models for such case were defined into the high and low-end given the probability of each process being on either bandwidth state. For the special cases, the processes do not follow a discrete trend but use bandwidth rates between upper and lower boundaries of processes defined in (8) and (9) respectively. The area between the processes is used as the model in (10) to describe the memory behavior of the group of processes at different problem sizes on the same node.

The results show that for the models presented for all cases do show great accuracy for large problem sizes. The models also display the different behaviors of each of the processes when dealing with multi-instances of the CacheBench at a single node. However, the models can be improved in order to increase precision for the lower problem size values by developing a better polynomial curve-fitting algorithm from the MATLAB's function *polyfit()*.

6 References

[1] Penguin Computing, Inc., "User's Guide: Scyld ClusterWare Release 6.3.3-633g0000" *Scyld ClusterWare Overview*, October 2012.

[2] D. Valles, D. Williams, P. Nava, "Load Balancing Approach Based on Limitations and Bottlenecks of Multi-core Architectures on a Beowulf Cluster Compute-Node," in *Proc. PDPTA'12*, Las Vegas, NV, 2012.

[3] Mucci, Philip J., London, K.., Thurman, J., "The CacheBench Report", Department of Computer Science, University of Tennessee at Knoxville, November 1998.

[4] Intel, "Intel Xeon Processor E5-1600/E5-2600/E5-4600 Product Families" Datasheet – Volume One, May 2012.

[5] Farrel, Kathy (2012). Intel Xeon Processor E5-2600/E5-4600 Product Family Technical Overview Article. *http://software.intel.com/en-us/articles/intel-xeon-processor-e5-26004600-product-family-technical-overview*. [Accessed: January 2013]

[6] Intel, "Intel Xeon Processor E5-1600/E5-2600/E5-4600 Product Families" Datasheet – Volume Two, May 2012.

[7] Alexandra Fedorova, Margo Seltzer and Michael D. Smith, "A Non-Work-Conserving Operating System Scheduler for SMT Processors," In Proceedings of the Workshop on the Interaction between Operating Systems and Computer Architecture (WIOSCA), in conjunction with ISCA-33, June 2006.

[8] D. Valles, D. Williams, P. Nava, "Scheduling Modifications for Improvement Performance on a Beowulf Cluster Single-Node," in *Proc. CAINE'12*, New Orleans, LA, 2012.

[9] Intel, "Intel Xeon Processor E5-2600 Product Family Uncore Performance Monitoring Guide" Datasheet – Reference No. 327043-001, March 2012.

Applying the Parallel GPU Model to Radiation Therapy Treatment PDPTA '13

J. Steven Kirtzic*, David Allen, Ovidiu Daescu**
Department of Computer Science
University of Texas at Dallas
Richardson, TX USA
{jsk061000, dallen, daescu}@utdallas.edu

Abstract— *With current advances in high performance computing, particularly the applications of GPUs, it is easy to see the need for a model for GPU algorithm development. We developed a model which offers a multi-grained approach intended to accommodate nearly any GPU.*

Radiation therapy is one of the most effective forms of cancer treatment available. In order to minimize the risk to the patient, physicians design treatment plans that expose the tumor to the prescribed levels of radiation while minimizing the exposure to the surrounding tissues. Our system allows users to quickly and easily visualize and compare treatment plans in order to identify the best one, with the most critical aspect of the simulation being implemented on the GPU using our parallel algorithm design model. In this paper, we show how the application of our model results in significant increases in algorithm performance, particularly in radiation therapy treatment simulation.

Keywords: GPU algorithm design, parallel processing, radiation therapy, cancer treatment

1. Introduction

The rapid advancement of the Graphics Processing Unit, or *GPU*, over the last few years has opened up a new world of possibilities for high-speed computation, ranging from biomedical to computer vision applications. Recent examples include [1], [2], and [3]. However, the GPU architecture is unlike that of any other, and designing algorithms to fully harness the capabilities of a GPU is not an easy task, especially when one considers the advantages and disadvantages of the various resources that a GPU has available to it.

Radiation therapy is a technique commonly used to eradicate malignant cancerous tumors. The therapy works by applying a controlled dosage of radiation to the tumor tissue in an attempt to damage the cancerous cells. Healthy tissue can also be damaged by the radiation, which raises the importance of optimizing the treatment in such a way that the tumor receives as much radiation as possible while the surrounding tissues receive as little as possible. We have developed a visualization system which provides treatment planners several different viewpoints to aid in choosing the best radiation treatment plan. The primary component of our system is an intensity mapping algorithm which utilizes a simple yet novel mapping scheme combined with a color-based representation of accumulated dosages to simulate the total amount of radiation delivered to a given target and the surrounding tissue. The result is an accurate, multi-view, navigable 3D representation of a given treatment plan that is beneficial for both practical clinical situations as well as educational environments.

The initial version of our system suffered from lag issues and was not capable of displaying multiple treatments with their accumulated dosages in real-time. Therefore, we utilized this as an opportunity to apply our Parallel GPU Model (PGM) to this system, more specifically to the mapping algorithm, as a validation of our model. The results were that our PGM version of the intensity mapping algorithm was able to not only perform in real-time, but also at a higher frame-rate, regardless of the granularity the various treatments were displayed at.

In this paper we present this application of our parallel algorithm design model for the GPU architecture, which demonstrates its effectiveness when applied to highly parallelizable tasks such as radiation treatment computation and simulation. In Section 2 we discuss the GPU architecture and the PGM; in Section 3 we present a brief overview of radiation therapy; in Section 4 we discuss the methods and materials used in the development of our simulation; in Section 5 we show the application of our PGM to the simulation itself, particularly to the intensity mapping algorithm; in Section 6 we discuss the results of the application of our model as compared to other implementations; and finally in Section 7 we conclude and remark on future work.

1.1 Contribution

We believe that our main contribution with this paper is to demonstrate the potential advantages of utilizing the high-performance computing power of the GPU. In this case we have chosen to apply our Parallel GPU Model to the task of simulating radiation therapy treatments for cancer patients.

*Kirtzic's research was supported by NSF award 0742477
**Daescu's research has been supported by NSF award CNS-1035460

With the application of our PGM, we are able to develop a version of our simulation which allows highly detailed simulations of treatments as they are delivered in real-time. We hope that this example of the benefit of utilizing GPUs will not only demonstrate the validity of our model, but will also encourage other researchers to take advantage of all that the GPU architectures has to offer.

1.2 Related Work

Borfield and Webb [4] have done work in the field of dosage calculation algorithms, as did Otto [5] and Vassilev [6]. Hamza-Lup et al [7] discuss the need for 3D treatment plan representation systems which allow both the clinician and the patient the ability to visually understand the advantages as well as the disadvantages of a given treatment plan. They present a system which allows the modeling of a plan in a 3D environment given a variety of input parameters. While producing fairly accurate results, their system does suffer from certain limitations, including the fact that it is web-based which makes its performance unpredictable due to bandwidth changes, as well as the lack of ability to view multiple treatments side by side, and the lack of a visual representation of accumulated dosage over a multi-beam treatment. While these methods have contributed considerably to the field of radiation therapy, they are limited when addressing the real-time, fine-grained needs of advancing current clinical treatment capabilities.

While there were several influences in the development of our Parallel GPU Model, the most noteworthy was the work of Leslie Valiant and his BSP model. The BSP, or bulk-synchronous parallel model, was proposed to overcome the limitations of the PRAM model [9], while maintaining its simplicity. In the BSP model, a BSP computer consists of a set of n processor/memory pairs (nodes) that are interconnected by a communication network. The BPS model is *Multiple Instruction Multiple Data* (MIMD) in nature, and uses the concept of a *superstep*, which is comprised of a computation step, a communication step, and a synchronization step. The BSP model is also variable grained, loosely synchronous, has non-zero overhead, and uses message passing or shared variables for communication.

The program executes as a strict sequence of supersteps. In each superstep, a process executes the computation operations in at most w cycles, a communication operation that takes gh cycles, and a barrier synchronization that takes l cycles. Note that in the communication overhead gh, g is the proportional coefficient for realizing a h relation. The value of g is platform-dependent, but independent of the communication pattern. In other words, gh is the time that it takes to execute the most time-consuming h relation.

Within a superstep, each computation operation uses only data in its local memory. This data is put into the local memory, either at the program start-up time or by the communication operations of previous supersteps. Therefore,

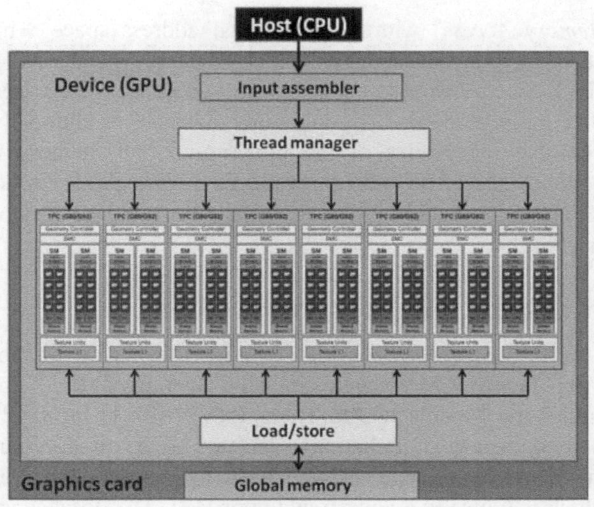

Fig. 1: NVIDIA GeForce 8800 architecture

the communication operations of a process are independent of other processes.

The BSP model is more realistic than the PRAM model because it accounts for all overheads except for the parallelism overhead for process management. The time for a superstep is estimated by the sum

$$w + gh + l \tag{1}$$

This model is highly regarded and has formed the basis for other parallel models, such as the parallel phase model [9]. However, its generality is its shortcoming when one attempts to apply it to more specific architectures, such as that of the GPU. Valiant recently extended his model to include multi-core CPUs [10]. While this model is much more akin to the architectural nature of the GPU, it still does not take into consideration the complexities of the typical GPU architecture. Thus we developed a parallel algorithm design model for the GPU architecture which addresses these issues, which we first presented here [11].

2. The GPU architecture and the Parallel GPU Model

In this paper we will often refer to the machine containing the GPU as the "host" and the GPU itself as the "device". The NVIDIA GeForce 8800 series is an example of a typical GPGPU (General Purpose GPU) device, which utilizes NVIDIA's CUDA (*Compute Unified Device Architecture* GPU design. The GeForce 8800 contains 16 multiprocessors, each containing 8 semi-independent cores for a total of 128 processing units (see Figure 1). Each of the 128 processors can run as many as 96 threads concurrently, for a maximum of 12,288 threads executing in parallel.

The computing model is SIMD (*Single Instruction Multiple Data*), and the memory model is NUMA (*Non-Uniform*

Memory Access) with a semi-shared address space. This stands in contrast to a modern CPU, which is typically either SISD (*Single Instruction Single Data*) or MIMD, in the case of a multi-processor or multi-core machine. Additionally, from the perspective of the programmer, all memory is explicitly shared (in multi-threading environments) or explicitly separate (in multi-processing environments) on a desktop machine.

3. Radiation Therapy

In this paper we consider two main radiation therapy types: Intensity Modulated Radiation Therapy (IMRT), and Volumetric Modulated Arc Therapy (VMAT). In the IMRT method, beams of radiation calculated to be of a certain shape and intensity are administered to a particular *target*, which is typically a cancerous tumor [12]. The dosages are delivered in a discrete step-wise succession, a "step and shoot" method, with the typical treatment averaging around 6 - 9 beam dosages [13].

The VMAT method is similar to the IMRT method, however VMAT is a smoother, more contiguous method of delivery [14]. VMAT allows for the same dosage amounts as IMRT, but provides dosages in a pre-calculated arc of delivery. This results in the dosages being delivered in a continuous manner over a shorter span of time. Further discussion of the details of these methods can be found in [15], [16], and [17].

In both of these methods, a *multi-leaf collimator* or MLC is used to shape the beam of radiation. The "leaves" of the collimator can be moved back and forth to block parts of the source beam. Effective treatment plans adjust the leaf positions in such a way that they shield as much healthy tissue as possible from radiation exposure while the source beam is active.

4. Methods and Materials

We have developed a system which allows the visualization of a given treatment plan from a variety of viewpoints, allowing the physician to compare different treatment plans and determine which is the best suited to a given patient. Our system has the potential to simulate multi-beam IMRT treatments as well as VMAT treatments. The intended users of our software are medical students and physicians, with the aim of providing training in developing higher quality treatment plans as well as educating patients about the benefits and risks of individual plans.

The simulation work-flow is as follows: the user is presented with an interface which allows the user to load, edit, add, or remove a patient's treatment record from a treatment database. This database contains all of the necessary patient treatment information and could be made available online, allowing anyone with the proper permissions to access patients' treatment records.

Once a particular patient's treatment file is identified, our system can simulate potential treatments, allowing the physician to select the best of all possible treatments available. This is primarily accomplished by simulating an *intensity map* that maps levels of radiation absorbed by a section of tissue to its physical location. Our system can provide real-time simulations of a given treatment plan and present it in a variety of granularities. The interface allows the user to visualize a treatment from a variety of viewpoints, including a MLC view, a beam's-eye view of the target tumor, and a general 3rd-person view of the intensity map. In addition, the interface allows the user to switch between multiple views within the individual quadrants while the simulation is running. Perhaps the most useful feature of our system is the ability to have all four quadrants display four different treatment plans as intensity maps as they are running in real-time, allowing the user to compare the plans in high detail.

4.1 Mapping Algorithm

The input of our mapping algorithm consists of CT scans of the target at various time steps. We also require a data file representing the list of all MLC leaf movements (in mm) between times t_i and $t_i + 1$ for all t_i of a specific treatment plan *X*. We denote this file as the *input array*. We assume that the MLC leaves begin in a closed position at t_0.

The region represented by the CT scan is discretized into a grid of cells (Figure 2(a)). We equate each column on the grid to a millimeter of leaf movement and each row to a pair of opposing leaves in the MLC. The number of rows and columns represents the granularity of the system, as increasing the number of either rows or columns will increase the detail of the resulting intensity map with respect to the region in the CT scan image. Often these values are restricted by the physical characteristics of the MLC to be used, as different collimators may have different numbers and sizes of leaves, as well as different leaf motion parameters. In the examples below, we assume each leaf is 1 mm in width and moves 1 mm per unit of time to simplify the grid representation. In practice, the width of the leaves will be higher due to current manufacturing limitations.

Each cell in the grid is associated with a bar that represents the total amount of radiation that has accumulated in the area of the cell. The *input array* is parsed for every time step *t* of the simulation, and the position of each leaf in the MLC is updated by the appropriate amount. As each leaf moves it either exposes or covers cells on the grid, affecting the amount of radiation the cells receive and thus the growth rate of the associated bars.

Every cell that is exposed receives one unit of radiation intensity for every time step that the cell is exposed, increasing the corresponding bar height by one as well as changing the bar color based on the total amount of radiation received. An example of this process is shown in Figure 3, with numbers representing different intensity levels on the

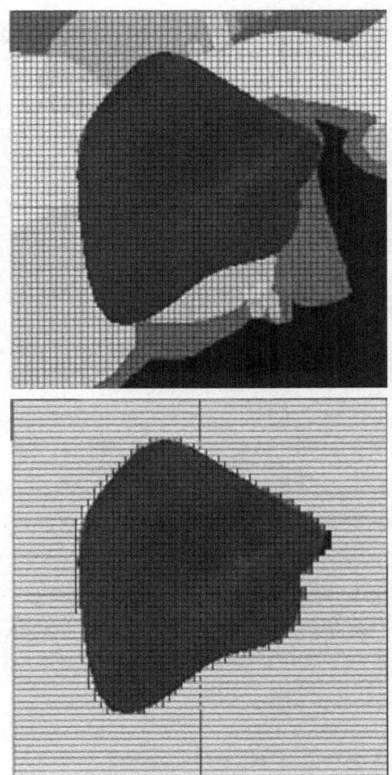

Fig. 2: (a) The intensity map bar grid overlaid on the CT scan of the target at t_0. (b) The leaves positioned around the target tumor to shield the surrounding tissue from the radiation beam

grid cells. After the simulation has completed, the resulting bar heights represent the total amount of dosage received by each cell grid. Different colors provide an extra means of visually processing the total dosage received at a cell. Blue indicates little or no radiation, red and orange indicates moderate amounts and bright yellow/white indicates a high amount. The example shown assumes a constant rate of radiation absorption, but in practice the dosage is not constant due to the differences in density and radiation absorption properties of different tissue types. We currently use density as the only factor affecting radiation absorption rates. The implementation identifies tissue density by the average lightness value of the grayscale colors in the CT scan image slice corresponding to a given grid cell. Brighter colors are assumed to be more dense and more resilient to radiation absorption, while darker colors are less dense and absorb radiation quickly.

From a time-space complexity perspective, given m number of time steps, n number of leaves, and d number of millimeters each leaf moves per time step, the run-time can be expressed as O(mnd) for a serial implementation of the algorithm.

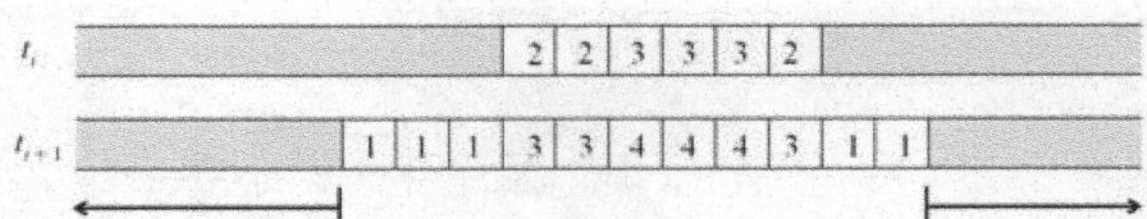

Fig. 3: A depiction of how the intensity values for each exposed bar increase from time t_i to time t_{i+1}.

4.2 Simulation Design Considerations

The basic flow of the system is the following: it first obtains from the list of leaf positions which bar sections are exposed to the beam, and which are not. Next it computes the dosage values received at each cell, and adjusts the height and color of the associated bar accordingly. The final radiation dosage values can be concatenated to a string and saved in a database, to be retrieved for later comparison or use. As discussed above, each kind of tissue absorbs radiation at a different rate, and so regions of the same tissue will have similar intensity values.

The colors and heights of the bars at the conclusion of the beam represent the total amount of radiation delivered to the corresponding area on the target or surrounding tissue. The user is able to toggle whether the bar heights are shown. With the heights disabled, the bars are simply squares of different colors overlaid onto the CT scan image and represent a heat map corresponding to the radiation delivered at each grid cell. The bars can also be made translucent, allowing the CT scan below to be seen and permitting the user to spatially visualize which tissue sections are receiving the most radiation.

We implemented our algorithm on the following hardware: we used a Dell desktop with a 2.99GH Intel Core 2 Duo with 3GB of RAM. We also used an NVIDIA 9800 GTX+ graphics card with 512 MB of memory and 128 streaming multiprocessors for the graphics duties. The fact that we implemented and ran our algorithm using commodity or "off the shelf" hardware indicates that our algorithm may be employed by practically anyone in a related field.

5. Application of the Parallel GPU Model

While the simulation that we have presented above can provide much in the way of designing and implementing highly effective radiation therapy treatments, the initial implementation of this system in a serial, CPU-based manner had its limitations. Particularly, the most critical part of our system (the intensity mapping algorithm visualization), suffered considerable lag when we attempted to apply it to higher detailed images. Specifically, we wanted the ability to view a given treatment in real-time, at various levels of detail, all the way to the millimeter level. Our experimentation proved that this was not possible with a serial implementation of our algorithm, given the hardware we had

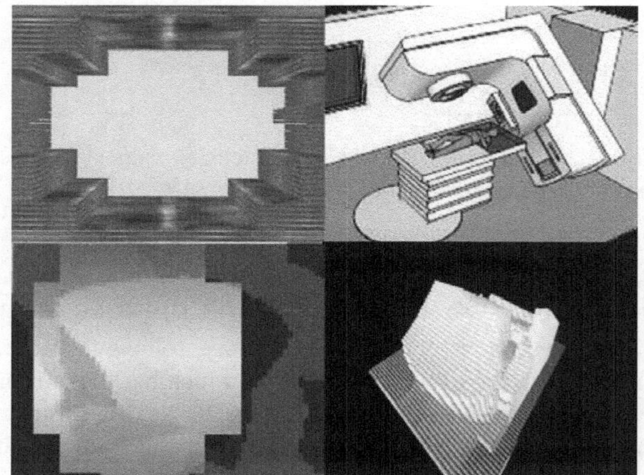

Fig. 4: This is the main interface of our visualization system as implemented strictly on the CPU in serial. Note that the various quadrants display differing views of a given treatment. Clockwise from the top-left: the first quadrant displays the position MLC leaves at time t_i; the second quadrant provides a view of the position of the gantry about the patient at t_i; the third quadrant displays accumulation of radiation dosages as a height map (before implementation on the GPU); and finally the fourth quadrant displays dosage accumulation as a heat map from a beam's eye view.

available. Consequently, this algorithm seemed to be a prime candidate for the application of our PGM.

We began applying our PGM to this problem by first developing the serial, CPU, brute-force version of our algorithm. This is the version that we had been using initially, which resulted in the performance lag identified earlier. Following the recommendations of the model, we then implemented an optimized version of this algorithm using OpenMP.

Again following the PGM model, we implemented a näive version of the intensity mapping algorithm by simply porting the algorithm to the GPU architecture, meaning we sent all of the data to the GPU and let the GPU kernels operate on the data, allowing the GPU thread scheduler to handle data distribution and thread allocation and management. We then went a step further in the model and considered data dependencies and preprocessing. This led to the optimized version of our algorithm, which includes preprocessing steps in which we import all of the necessary data from the database and convert it into simple arrays and image files before sending it to the GPU for computation and rendering. We have also off-loaded other preprocessing calculations to the CPU, including initial dosage calculations for each bar per each beam step, and total overall growth for each bar per each beam step. These results are temporarily stored in the host's RAM until this data is transferred to the device for real-time calculation and rendering.

Following with another aspect of our model, we considered the various types of GPU memory that we had access to, and distributed our data accordingly. It is not difficult to see that certain data elements of our system are read only (i.e. the treatment planning input, including the MLC movements and the CT scans), which according to the PGM should be loaded into the GPU's texture memory.

Finally, in following with the final step of the PGM, we fine-tuned our GPU-accelerated intensity mapping algorithm by adjusting it to suit the physical nature of our particular GPU. Knowing that our GPU (NVIDIA's 9800 GTX+) had 128 cores, with 512 MB global memory and 16K shared local memory for each SM, we broke down all computations so that they were allocated in groups of 32, aligning with the GPU's preferred warp format. However, considering that there were more available cores than there were calculations to be performed, even the use of memory coalescing and warp-filling does not result in a truly optimal use of the GPU structure, as a GPU operates the most efficiently when all of its threads are occupied.

6. Results and Discussion

By initializing the radiation levels at each cell to zero and applying our mapping algorithm and the leaf motions from the *input array*, we can generate the quad-view simulation of a given treatment plan as shown in Figure 4. This allows the user to select any quad and examine it in great detail. Each bar in the intensity map accumulates the dosage delivered over each beam in the treatment plan giving the physician or student a clear indication of how much radiation has been delivered to a given area of a target or the surrounding tissue.

This allows medical professionals to plan treatments of higher quality that minimize the exposure of healthy tissue to radiation while maximizing the dosage delivered to the target. Medical students studying radiology can use our system to simulate and visualize hypothetical treatment plans. Students receive feedback by comparing the resulting intensity maps of plans of their own design by observing the total amount of radiation delivered to the tumor versus the amount delivered to healthy tissues. This feedback assists in fostering an intuitive sense of what goes into planning an optimal treatment and therefore has the potential to improve the quality of the future real world treatment plans designed by the student. Moreover, the student or teacher may design example plans or exercises that highlight specific treatment complications and special situations. This has the effect of revealing to the student the best techniques for optimizing the plan under specific constraints.

As mentioned previously, patient education is another potential application. Doctors and radiologists can use our simulation to visually demonstrate the treatment process and explain exactly what the patient should expect. Treatment plans can be compared and contrasted for the patient using the multi-view interface mode, and the potential risks and benefits of each can be explained and visualized in greater detail. This has the potential to increase patient understanding of and comfort with the therapy procedure.

In Table 1 we list the overall averaged run times and memory copy times for the different versions of our intensity mapping algorithm that were employed, including the näive CPU version, the optimal CPU version, the näive GPU version, and the optimal GPU version over 100 trials.

Table 1: Run time and data copy time for the Intensity Mapping algorithm, as represented for a näive CPU implementation, an optimized CPU implementation, a näive GPU implementation, and an optimized GPU implementation. All times are in milliseconds.

	Run Time	Copy Time
Näive CPU Intensity Mapping	192173.96	N/A
Optimized CPU Intensity Mapping	82186.34	N/A
Näive GPU Intensity Mapping	2007.12	197.78
Optimized GPU Intensity Mapping	199.94	2.04

As the table shows, optimizing the serial version of our algorithm using OpenMP did not show a significant increase in performance (approximately 2x speedup). This is due to the fact that we were using a dual core CPU, so considering the data transfer required between the two cores along with the synchronization step, the performance increase was fairly minimal (see Table 1).

When we simply ported our algorithm to the GPU architecture, our näive implementation resulted in a significant speedup (greater than an order of magnitude).

Regarding the optimized GPU version of the algorithm, we were able to reduce the overall runtime of the algorithm significantly by off-loading all of the necessarily serial work onto the CPU and only employing the GPU to do the parallel computation, specifically that of computing the values of each bar, as well as the overall accumulated values for each bar, at each cycle. This allows for optimal access speed as well as making this data available for the largest number of threads possible, resulting in a speedup of approximately an order of magnitude over the näive GPU implementation.

Regarding the visual performance of the Intensity Map (the calculations described above combined with the rendering), all implementations of the algorithm except the original näive CPU implementation allow the mapping to run in real-time. The GPU versions, however, allow the visualization to run in "hyper" real-time, at a variety of speeds, which should insure that the overall simulation can run in real-time or better regardless of the tasks it is performing, as shown in in Figure 5.

As shown above, we were able to provide a significant speedup in performance of our Intensity Mapping algorithm utilizing the high performance computing power of the GPU. Furthermore, we did so by applying our PGM to the problem of optimizing our Intensity Mapping algorithm, resulting in a significant speedup (a couple of orders of magnitude) over the original serial implementation.

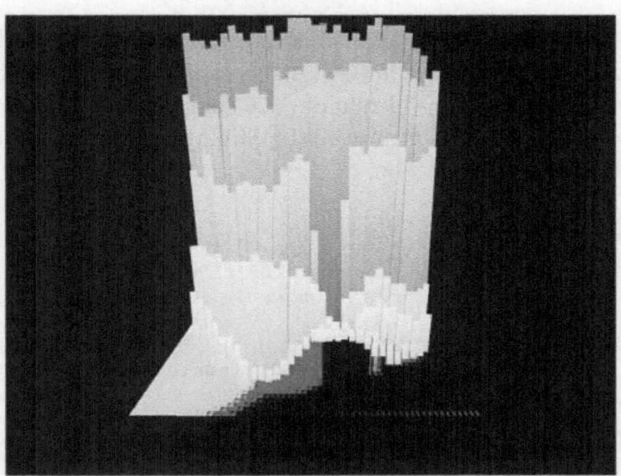

Fig. 5: The 3D rendering which shows the GPU implementation of how the radiation dosage will be delivered to the various areas of the target at time t_n, along with the total accumulated dosage (represented by the "heat scale" color gradation), according to this particular treatment plan.

7. Conclusion and Future Work

As presented in the previous sections, our visualization system offers a fast and inexpensive option for simulating radiation treatment plans in a real-time, multi-grained manner. This allows physicians and students the ability to quickly and easily compare multiple treatment plans to determine the optimal plan with considerable accuracy. We have then augmented this ability by applying our Parallel GPU Model to parallelize the computation being done on the intensity mapping aspect of our simulation, making it possible to now display a given treatment at a very fine-grained level of detail, in a fully navigable environment and in real-time, making it possible to view and compare multiple treatments as they would actually be delivered.

Based upon the the success of this application of our PGM, our future work with this system involves applying our model to the other aspects of the simulation to see which may also benefit from parallelization on the GPU. We will also be mindful to apply the same to any additional functionalities which we may include in future versions of our software.

In addition, the current version of our simulation handles single beam IMRT treatments. Future implementations will be able to handle multi-beam treatments as well as the continuous motion of the MLC during VMAT treatments. Another addition planned is to implement a module that *automatically* computes a radiation treatment plan. Although this treatment plan may not be optimal it can be made as close to optimal as possible with computational methods. Such a module would allow users to easily obtain a baseline treatment plan to which they can compare the treatment plans they develop themselves, providing an extra mode of feedback and evaluation.

References

[1] D. Qiu, S. May, and A. Nüchter, "GPU-accelerated nearest neighbor search for 3d registration," *Computer Vision Systems*, pp. 194–203, 2009.

[2] P. Noël, A. Walczak, K. Hoffmann, J. Xu, J. Corso, and S. Schafer, "Clinical evaluation of GPU-based cone beam computed tomography," *Proc. of High-Performance Medical Image Computing and Computer-Aided Intervention (HP-MICCAI)*, 2008.

[3] J. Huang, S. Ponce, S. Park, Y. Cao, and F. Quek, "GPU-accelerated computation for robust motion tracking using the CUDA framework," in *Visual Information Engineering, 2008. VIE 2008. 5th International Conference on.* IET, 2008, pp. 437–442.

[4] T. Bortfeld and S. Webb, "Single-arc IMRT," *Physics in medicine and biology*, vol. 54, p. N9, 2009.

[5] K. Otto, "Letter to the editor on 'Single-Arc IMRT'," *Physics in medicine and biology*, vol. 54, p. L37, 2009.

[6] O. N. Vassiliev, T. A. Wareing, J. McGhee, G. Failla, M. R. Salehpour, and F. Mourtada, "Validation of a new grid-based Boltzmann equation solver for dose calculation in radiotherapy with photon beams," *Physics in Medicine and Biology*, vol. 55, no. 3, p. 581, 2010. [Online]. Available: http://stacks.iop.org/0031-9155/55/i=3/a=002

[7] F. Hamza-Lup, I. Sopin, and O. Zeidan, "Online external beam radiation treatment simulator," *International Journal of Computer Assisted Radiology and Surgery*, vol. 3, no. 3, pp. 275–281, 2008.

[8] L. G. Valiant, "A bridging model for parallel computation," *Commun. ACM*, vol. 33, no. 8, pp. 103–111, 1990. [Online]. Available: http://portal.acm.org/citation.cfm?id=79181

[9] K. Hwang and Z. Xu, *Scalable parallel computing: technology, architecture, programming*. WCB/McGraw-Hill, 1998.

[10] L. Valiant, "A bridging model for multi-core computing," *Journal of Computer and System Sciences*, vol. 77, no. 1, pp. 154–166, 2011.

[11] J. S. Kirtzic and O. Daescu, "A parallel algorithm development model for the GPU architecture," *International Conference on Parallel and Distributed Processing Techniques and Applications (accepted for publication)*, 2012.

[12] R. McMahon, R. Berbeco, S. Nishioka, M. Ishikawa, and L. Papiez, "A real-time dynamic-MLC control algorithm for delivering IMRT to targets undergoing 2D rigid motion in the beamâĂŹs eye view," *Medical physics*, vol. 35, p. 3875, 2008.

[13] X. Wu and J. Abraham, "The intensity level reduction in radiation therapy," in *Proceedings of the 2005 ACM symposium on Applied computing*. ACM, 2005, pp. 242–246.

[14] D. Rangaraj, S. Oddiraju, B. Sun, L. Santanam, D. Yang, S. Goddu, and L. Papiez, "Fundamental properties of the delivery of volumetric modulated arc therapy (VMAT) to static patient anatomy," *Medical physics*, vol. 37, p. 4056, 2010.

[15] D. Rangaraj, G. Palaniswaamy, and L. Papiez, "DMLC IMRT delivery to targets moving in 2D in beamâĂŹs eye view," *Medical physics*, vol. 35, p. 3765, 2008.

[16] M. Langer, V. Thai, and L. Papiez, "Improved leaf sequencing reduces segments or monitor units needed to deliver IMRT using multileaf collimators," *Medical Physics*, vol. 28, p. 2450, 2001.

[17] L. Papież, "DMLC leaf-pair optimal control of IMRT delivery for a moving rigid target," *Medical physics*, vol. 31, p. 2742, 2004.

A Benchmark-Driven Modelling Approach for Evaluating Deployment Choices on a Multicore Architecture

A. Osprey[1,2], G. D. Riley[3], M. Manjunathaiah[4], and B. N. Lawrence[1,2]
[1]Department of Meteorology, University of Reading, UK
[2]National Centre for Atmospheric Science (NCAS), Natural Environment Research Council, UK
[3]School of Computer Science, University of Manchester, UK
[4]School of Systems Engineering, University of Reading, UK

Abstract— *The complexity of current and emerging high performance architectures provides users with options about how best to use the available resources, but makes predicting performance challenging. In this work a benchmark-driven performance modelling approach is outlined that is appropriate for modern multicore architectures. The approach is demonstrated by constructing a model of a simple shallow water code on a Cray XE6 system, from application-specific benchmarks that illustrate precisely how architectural characteristics impact performance. The model is found to recreate observed scaling behaviour up to 16K cores, and used to predict optimal rank-core affinity strategies, exemplifying the type of problem such a model can be used for.*

Keywords: Performance modelling, shallow water model, Cray XE6, multicore

1. Introduction

Climate modelling is one of the grand challenge problems of current times. To gain a greater understanding of the climate system, scientists are adding complexity to their models through increased resolution, modelling of additional physical processes, and increasing numbers of ensemble experiments to quantify uncertainty, all requiring vast computational resources [1]. Thus climate modelling is one of the application areas making use of the top high performance systems across the globe, and to make best use of these expensive resources means adapting to the new architectures that are emerging.

Current supercomputing trends are for multicore processors and the use of co-processor accelerators, both of which have lead to increased levels of heterogeneity within high performance systems. Apart from the different types of processor that might coexist, for example CPUs and GPUs, modern multicore architectures often have several hierarchies inherent within the system. For the processor this may include cache-sharing, non-uniform memory access times and floating point unit sharing as with the AMD Bulldozer [2], and for the network this may be due to full connectivity between groups of nodes and then point to point connections between the groups, as in the IBM Power 7 Host Fabric Interface (HFI). This means that the user has many choices about how best to use the system in order to maximise floating point throughput and minimise data transfer costs. For example, it has been found that under-populating nodes, altering the domain decomposition or changing the rank-core affinity can all alter performance [3], [4], [5].

Currently, finding the best way to run an application on a given architecture, especially for highly complex scientific code such as the UK Met Office climate model, is often a lengthy process of trial and error [4]. Recent work has been done with automated optimisation techniques, such as simulated annealing, to guide the search for optimal performance tuning parameter values [6].

In this paper, we introduce a benchmark-driven predictive modelling approach that allows the rapid evaluation of different deployment choices, without the execution of costly full-model runs. The model is based on commonly used analytical modelling techniques, but driven solely by data from a series of application-specific benchmarks designed to capture the effects of various resource sharing scenarios. The use of benchmark data over analytical models of the architecture leads to a shorter model development cycle. Since both the application and architecture are complex, building accurate performance models may be time-consuming, and in many cases, unnecessary. Often it is sufficient to know that one choice performs better than another. The method is outlined in Section 3.

The approach is demonstrated on a complex modern architecture, the Cray XE6, that exhibits many of the heterogeneous features mentioned. A simple shallow water code is chosen as it displays one of the main patterns of behaviour seen in atmosphere and ocean models: the calculation of regular grids of data using a finite difference scheme requiring periodic boundary exchanges. The code uses an MPI parallelisation and straightforward rectangular 2-dimensional domain decomposition. The simplicity of the application means that effort can be focused on understanding the complexity of the architecture. The methodology could, however, be extended to explore application issues, such as parallelisation strategies and communication patterns.

The resulting model is described in Section 4 and used to predict run times for a series of scaling experiments. These predictions are then evaluated against measured results to quantify the model accuracy. The usefulness of the model is tested by exploring rank-core affinity strategies in Section 5. It is known that assigning approximately square domains to each rank minimises costly off-node communications [7], and this is reproduced by the model and confirmed by measured results.

2. Performance modelling

A performance model combines information about an application and underlying architecture to make an estimation of the expected wallclock run time. The application part of the model describes the amount and type of work that needs to be performed, at any granularity from subroutines to low-level operations, and the machine part supplies the times to complete each portion of work, which may be from benchmark measurements or a mathematical representation of features of the hardware. Typically for a scientific application, the work to be performed can be split into two broad categories: i) computations, the bulk of which will be loops of floating point calculations, and ii) communications, the MPI operations that transfer data between ranks. This requires machine models of the processor and network respectively.

There are many different means of building performance models [8]. Logically the process begins with the creation of the application model, which can be done automatically by a tool, or written by hand with expert knowledge and analysis of the code, each of which are discussed in the following sections.

2.1 Automated methods

Application models can be generated automatically by profiling tools which log the operations a program performs as it executes. The resulting trace file can then be replayed by a machine simulator which has the ability to emulate a different architecture to the one on which the application was originally run. An example of this is the PMaC prediction framework described by Snavely et al [9] and Carrington, Snavely and Walter [10]. The process cannot however predict changes to the number of processors or other application inputs. A similar but more flexible method (the WARPP toolkit) is described by Hammond et al [11].

Although automated tools require minimal human effort and limited knowledge of the code, fundamentally the code must exist and be executable. Often it is treated as a black box, therefore such methods are limited in their ability to explore deployment choices, as this involves parameterisation in terms of application inputs such as problem size.

2.2 Analytical methods

Analytical application models are generally constructed by hand, based on an abstract view of the program code. Typically for scientific applications, the processor and network are modelled with a mixture of analytical and empirical techniques. Performance models have been developed in this way for many applications including, in the climate science domain, the POP ocean code (Kerbyson and Jones [12]), HYCOM ocean code (Barker and Kerbyson [13]) and WRF weather prediction code (Kerbyson et al [14]). A systematic description is given by Hoefler et al [15]. First, the application input parameters, code kernels, communication patterns, and any overlap with computations are identified. These are used to compose the analytical application model. Next, empirical steps are taken to provide run times for the model. For computations, an expression of the sequential time for each of the kernels is derived by measuring the code for different problem sizes. Communication times are expressed as a LogGP model of point-to-point messages [16], with the parameters derived from benchmark experiments [17].

One of the main criticisms of detailed analytical application models is the human effort required to build them. Ultimately, the purpose of the modelling procedure should be to improve performance by aiding understanding, highlighting areas for optimisation, informing the tuning process and so forth. For these purposes a fully accurate model may not be required, and so automatic tool-based methods or simple coarse analytical models may be preferred. An example of this is the work of Dennis, Jessup and Waite [18] who use a prototyping tool (SLAMM) to compare the memory usage of several algorithmic implementations within POP. Although far more simplistic than the Kerbyson and Jones model [12], theirs is sufficient to substantially optimise the code.

3. Benchmark-driven modelling approach

Here we propose an updated analytical and empirical modelling approach that is suited to a complex and heterogeneous architecture such as the Cray XE6. There are three main differences to the methodology described by Hoefler et al [15].

Firstly, for modern architectures simple models of data transfers can become highly complicated. The number of parameters involved can quickly rise with the different communication protocols in use (large and small messages), links along which data can travel (on-node and off-node) and contention due to multiple cores per node accessing the same network interface. This can be seen in the work of Mudalige, Vernon and Jarvis [19] for a Cray XT4 system which is somewhat more simplistic than the Cary XE6 considered here. Since collecting benchmark data is a necessary part of the creation of these models, we propose skipping the modelling phase and simply interpolating from the data.

Secondly, part of the time spent in MPI transfers includes accessing the data from it's location in cache or memory. Although packing the data into a buffer may be done as a separate stage, Fortran 90 compilers are able to do this automatically, even with non-contiguous subsections of data. For data stored as a 2-dimensional array, retrieving subsections in one of the directions will lead to non-contiguous accesses. In this benchmarking approach, both contiguous and non-contiguous accesses are included in the transfer time, without having to be explicitly modelled.

Thirdly, it is insufficient to provide only the sequential computation time, as the model needs to account for the effects of resource-sharing such as multiple cores accessing the same cache. Therefore here, multiple benchmarks are run to account for each of these cases.

As in Hoefler et al [15] the first steps of this approach are to express the application analytically in terms of code kernels and communication patterns. The empirical steps, however, involve an additional stage which is to identify the resource sharing scenarios to be measured. Compute benchmarks are based on an instrumented version of the application. The communications benchmarks are bespoke versions of standard tools. Data from the benchmarks are then organised in a database which is accessed by a deployment model. This translates a given runtime scenario into a performance prediction interpolating from the measured results as necessary. Assuming applications follow the shared memory program multiple data (SPMD) paradigm, all cores execute the same code but over different data domains. Here it is also assumed that all cores are synchronised, thus only the maximum time per core is needed.

4. Performance model of a shallow water code

Using the benchmark-driven approach described, a model is constructed for a version of the NCAR shallow water code [20], [21] on the HECToR supercomputer, a Cray XE6 system based at the University of Edinburgh [22]. The following sections describe the shallow code (Section 4.1) and HECToR system (Section 4.2), after which the performance model is outlined (Section 4.3) and evaluated (Section 4.4).

4.1 The NCAR shallow water code

The NCAR shallow water code (herein 'shallow') uses a second-order finite-difference solver to evaluate the shallow water equations. Calculations are performed over a rectangular domain of size M by N with periodic boundary conditions in both directions to replicate the behaviour on a sphere whilst avoiding the use of poles. The version of shallow used here is a Fortran 90 implementation with a 2-d parallel domain decomposition. Local domains are sized m by n with arrays dimensioned as $m+1$ by $n+1$ to allow for a single halo row and column. There are 13 local array fields and at each timestep the code performs 10 array update loops, 3 array copies, and 7 exchanges of halo data.

Halo exchanges update the values at boundary cells from the domains held by neighbouring ranks, and in this version these are implemented with `MPI_Sendrecv` operations. As shallow uses double-precision real numbers, the total data volume sent and received each halo update will be $(m + n + 2) \times 8$ bytes. This data volume only depends on the local data size and will not vary with the global data size or total number of ranks. Thus, under ideal conditions the wallclock communication time should remain constant for the same local array size (weak scaling). In reality however, the physical mapping of ranks to cores will affect the run time and, as the total size of the communicator increases, interference and load imbalance may increase.

As well as the transfer time between cores, additional time will be spent on overheads associated with initialising the exchange and loading the data from its location in cache or memory. Since the data is stored in 2-dimensional arrays, halos sent in the M-direction will require loading $n + 1$ cachelines as the data in this dimension will be held non-contiguously in memory. Conversely, the halos in the N-direction will require only $(m+1)/8$ cachelines as this data will be contiguous.

4.2 HECToR

HECToR is the national UK supercomputing facility based at the University of Edinburgh and funded by the UK research councils. It is currently in Phase 3 of its lifespan which is a Cray XE6 system, consisting of 2816 compute nodes for a total of 90,112 cores.

Each compute node on HECToR comprises two sixteen-core AMD Opteron Interlagos chips, part of the Bulldozer family. The Interlagos chips are made up of two 8-core dies, each directly connected to their own 8 GB memory and consisting of four 'compute modules'. A module contains two integer cores that share a single floating point execution unit and 2 MB of L2 cache. Additionally, integer cores have their own 16 KB L1 data cache and all cores on the die share 6 MB of L3 cache with an extra 2 MB given over to maintaining cache coherency. Caches in the AMD Opteron series are exclusive with lower levels acting as victim caches for the higher levels. Cores operate at a frequency of 2.3 GHz and are capable of processing 8 double precision floating point operations per cycle. The nature of the shared floating point unit means that codes can obtain double the cache and memory space per task by running with only one of the integer cores and still have access to the full floating point capability. Diagrams representing the hardware can be found on the HECToR website [23].

All four dies on a node are connected to each other via HyperTransport (HT) links forming a non-uniform memory access (NUMA) node meaning that all dies can access the total 32 GB of memory. The links between dies vary, with 24-bits between dies on the same chip, 16 bits between opposite dies, and 8-bits between diagonally opposite dies.

In addition, each node has a single link to a Gemini Network Interface Controller (NIC) that connects nodes into a 3-dimensional torus [24].

4.3 Performance model

From the information in Sections 4.1 and 4.2, a performance model of shallow can be constructed. The application model consists of a series of identical timesteps, each comprising i) some volume of floating point compute work dependent on the local array size, and ii) several halo-exchanges with a single row and column transferred per rank. Array copies are not considered, as they only account for around 10% of the runtime. If needed they could be benchmarked in a similar way to the compute loops. The next step is to design and run the benchmark experiments to generate data with which to populate the model. The computation and communication models are described in the following sections.

Computation model

To benchmark the computations, an instrumented version of shallow is run over a set of 23 problem sizes ranging from L1 resident to memory resident. Timers are inserted around each block of compute loops with an MPI barrier before the timer call so that all cores are synchronised. This means that times are consistent from run to run with full resource sharing. In real application runs however, it is unlikely that cores would be synchronised, leading to less resource-sharing (increasing performance), but also more waiting time in the halo exchanges (decreasing performance).

The benchmark is run over a variety of cases that illustrate each resource-sharing scenario. These are: i) core pair mode, where only one of the integer cores in each module is in use, with no floating-point unit or L2 cache sharing, and ii) compact mode, where both integer cores are used, causing floating point and L2 cache sharing. Both cases are measured on a single die, with one to four modules to account for L3 cache sharing as well. In reality, the achieved performance may be reduced slightly by communication overheads, although this may be offset by increased performance due to the lack of interruption by timer and barrier calls.

Each experiment is repeated a total of 5 times to provide a mean flop rate, with the number of flops taken from the source code. The benchmark results are shown in Figure 1, with features of the architecture clearly identifiable. The per-core performance drops when both integer cores are in use, from a peak of 3.3 GF to 2.6 GF. This does, however, increase the per-module performance to 5.2 GF, showing the benefits of two feeds to the floating point pipelines. Performance differs little with the number of modules when the problem size fits in each module's L2 cache, with only a slight degradation when all modules are in use. As the problem size increases further, the performance decreases for each additional module due to contention for L3 cache, memory bandwidth and the translation lookaside buffer (TLB).

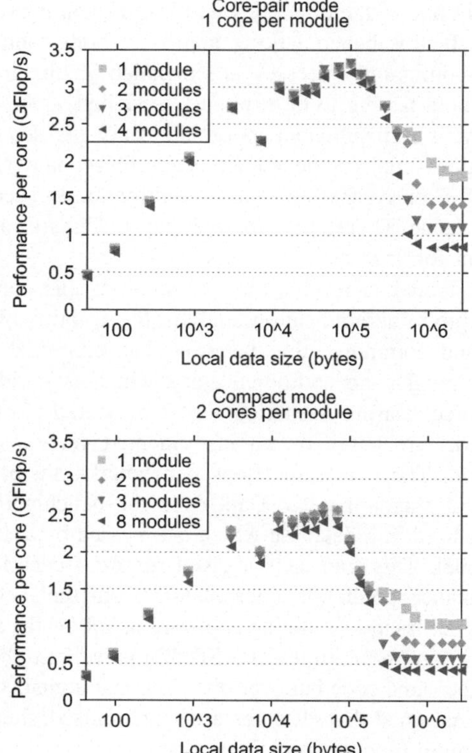

Fig. 1: Computational performance per core as measured by benchmark experiments. The local data size is based on storing 13 array fields.

Communication model

A bespoke benchmark code is used to measure the halo-exchanges. It is based on the Intel MPI Benchmarks (IMB) [25], but with greater control over the pairs of cores to transfer between, contiguous and non-contiguous memory access and location of data in cache or memory.

The benchmark takes as input a series of message lengths spaced roughly exponentially, with extra values around the boundaries between different MPI message protocols (for small and large messages). To ensure messages are accessed from the correct cache level, the benchmark takes two other inputs: the size of the cache to operate from ('the operating cache'), and the total size of all caches that are closer to the core ('the higher cache'). Message buffers are taken from an array of size roughly equal to the size of the operating cache. This is initially loaded into the processor, then pushed into the operating cache by loading a dummy array which is the same size as the higher cache. Several message transfers are performed and a mean value taken to reduce timer overhead and effects of timer granularity. To ensure that each message is actually taken from the operating cache, a different slice of the buffer is extracted each time, similar to the approach taken by the IMB. In this way both contiguous messages and non-contiguous messages are measured. It should be noted that these memory assumptions do not account for copies of data made by subroutines or held in MPI buffers, therefore data may be located further from the processor. The same assumptions are made for the application code, although the benchmark does not replicate all behaviour. Furthermore, as the benchmark performs multiple consecutive communications, any overheads associated with initialising MPI buffers will be lost, whereas in the application these costs may be more significant.

Experiments are performed over all types of connection along which data may be transferred. On the XE6, these can be categorised as between i) cores on the same module (shared L2 cache), ii) cores on the same die (shared L3 cache), iii) dies on a node (HT links), or iv) nodes in the torus (Gemini interconnect). To minimise complexity, means are taken over the different bandwidths between dies on a node and different numbers of hops between two nodes on the torus. This can be justified since, unless a very large communication volume is taking place, little difference is observed in the achieved bandwidths between dies. Furthermore, on the XE6 it is not known in advance which group of nodes the scheduler will select, thus the number of hops cannot be predicted. In most cases the scheduler selected nodes on the same or neighbouring NICs, yet frequently the nodes were as many as 13 hops away.

Along with the message lengths, cache usage, contiguous and non-contiguous accesses and connections to measure, it is also necessary to quantify the contention due to different numbers of cores communicating along the same link concurrently. Experiments are therefore run with 1 to 8 cores per die for transfers within and between dies, and from 1 to 32 cores for transfers between nodes. Selected results for off-node transfers and off-die transfers are shown in Figure 2, showing the per-transfer slow down when all cores communicate along the same link simultaneously. Non-contiguous transfers achieve approximately a factor of 8 lower bandwidth than contiguous transfers (as expected), and off-die transfers generally achieve a higher bandwidth than off-node transfers, except where only a single core per node is used.

4.4 Evaluation

The performance model of shallow combines the data from the computation and communication benchmarks to make a prediction about the total application runtime. The model was evaluated by comparing predictions to measured times for several examples. Three global problem sizes were used initially: 256×256, 512×512 and 1024×1024. Each of these was run with 4, 8, 16 and 32 cores per node on 1 to 16 nodes, up to a total of 512 cores. It should be noted that, up to 32 cores per node, only one integer core

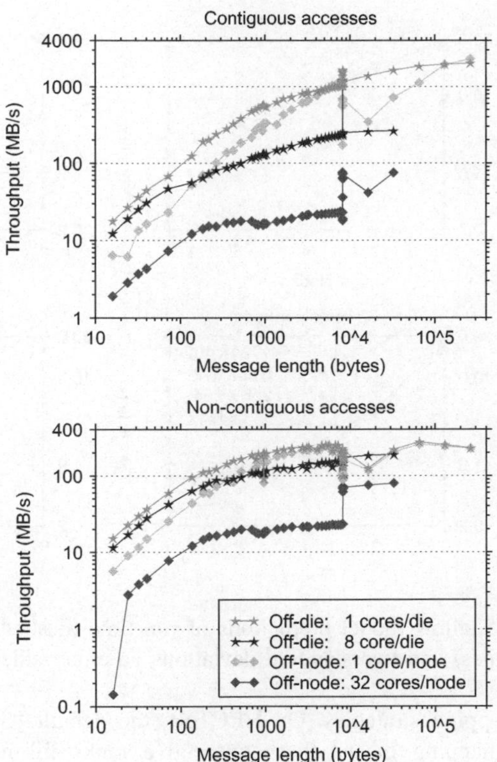

Fig. 2: Bandwidths as observed by halo-exchange benchmarks. Off-node values are means over 10 runs with pairs of nodes selected by the scheduler. Off-die values are means of two runs over each pair of dies within a node.

per module is used to make best use of the floating point units. These examples test how well the model captures the interactions within a node. It is also useful to look at larger problem sizes that scale out to thousands of cores. A second set of examples therefore takes two larger problem sizes, 2048×2048 and 4096×4096, and scales these out to 512 nodes with 16 or 32 cores per node, up to a total of 16,384 cores.

Model predictions and measured run times are shown in Figure 3. Shallow runs were performed 5 times, with the mean and two standard deviations either side shown, which assumes a normal distribution of run times. The modelled run times can be seen to accurately reproduce the measured behaviour. Model errors are defined as the difference between the predictions and mean run times for each set of problem sizes and number of cores per node. The median percentage errors, the form often quoted in the literature, range from 0.8% to 25%. Up to 20% is generally considered reasonable.

5. Rank-core mapping strategies

The usefulness of the model is further tested by predicting performance under various MPI rank to physical

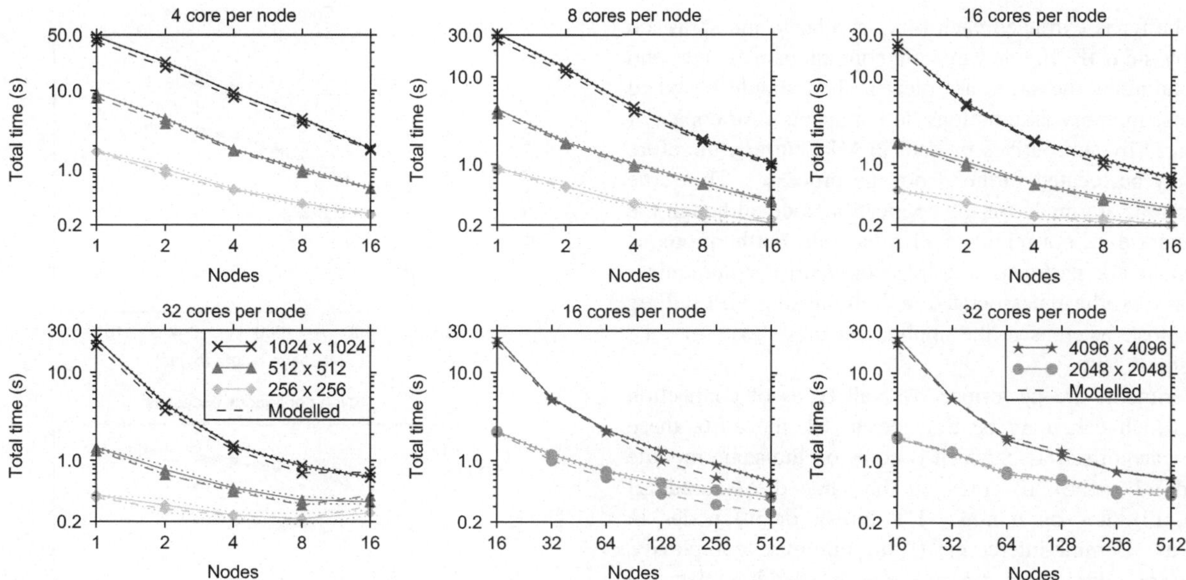

Fig. 3: Shallow model predictions of run time (dashed lines) versus measured times for a series of 5 runs, with the mean (solid lines) and two standard deviations on either side of the mean (dotted lines).

core mapping strategies. On HECToR, the default "SMP-style" mapping means that consecutive ranks fill nodes one at a time. For shallow, this corresponds to rows (or portions of a row) of the subdomain being mapped to each node. Intuitively, for nearest-neighbour communications it is better to assign rectangular subdomains to each node in order to minimise the off-node data transfer volume. Such a "custom" mapping can be generated automatically on HECToR with the `grid_order` tool. An alternative mapping strategy, "round-robin", assigns subsequent ranks to each different node in turn. For a small number of ranks this leads to columns of the subdomain being assigned to each node, however for large numbers of ranks each neighbour will reside on a different node, maximising the off-node transfer volume. These three options should produce distinct performance behaviour, and this hypothesis was tested using the predictive model and measured runs.

To test the hypothesis, the larger problem sizes from the evaluation runs were used (2048×2048 and 4096×4096 up to 512 nodes). As the computational work per rank remains the same, only the communication model is used. Shallow runs were repeated 5 times as before to quantify the variability in run time. Figure 4 shows the model predictions and the mean measured run time and two standard deviations either side. The model successfully predicts the order of performance in all cases, although the run times themselves are reproduced with varying degrees of accuracy. The custom mapping shows least variability and the best prediction. This is likely to be since it has the smalled volume of off-node transfers which are affected by network traffic. For a real climate model application the communication dependencies are more complex than just nearest neighbour and so a more sophisticated model would be required to evaluate the optimal mapping.

6. Conclusion

In this paper we have presented a benchmark-driven performance modelling approach, based on existing work but designed specifically to quickly evaluate application performance on complex architectures. Communication and computation work are both expressed as functions of benchmarked results rather than detailed analytical models, yet predict performance well enough to replicate scaling behaviour and identify the best of three different rank-core affinity strategies. The assumptions inherent to the model are discussed, along with potential sources of error which will be analysed further in upcoming work. In addition, similar models of shallow will be constructed for the IBM Power 7 and BlueGene/Q systems which display substantially different performance behaviour.

A similar approach to that defined here could also be applied to more complex kernels of climate science applications, to aid directly in performance optimisation. In such cases, the compute kernels may be larger, reducing inaccuracies due to timer overheads, and the communication may extend to other patterns beyond halo-exchanges.

References

[1] J. Shukla, T. N. Palmer, R. Hagedorn, B. Hoskins, J. Kinter, J. Marotzke, M. Miller, and J. Slingo, "Towards a new generation of world climate research and computing facilities," *Bulletin of the American Meteorological Society*, vol. 91, no. 10, pp. 1407–1412, 2010.

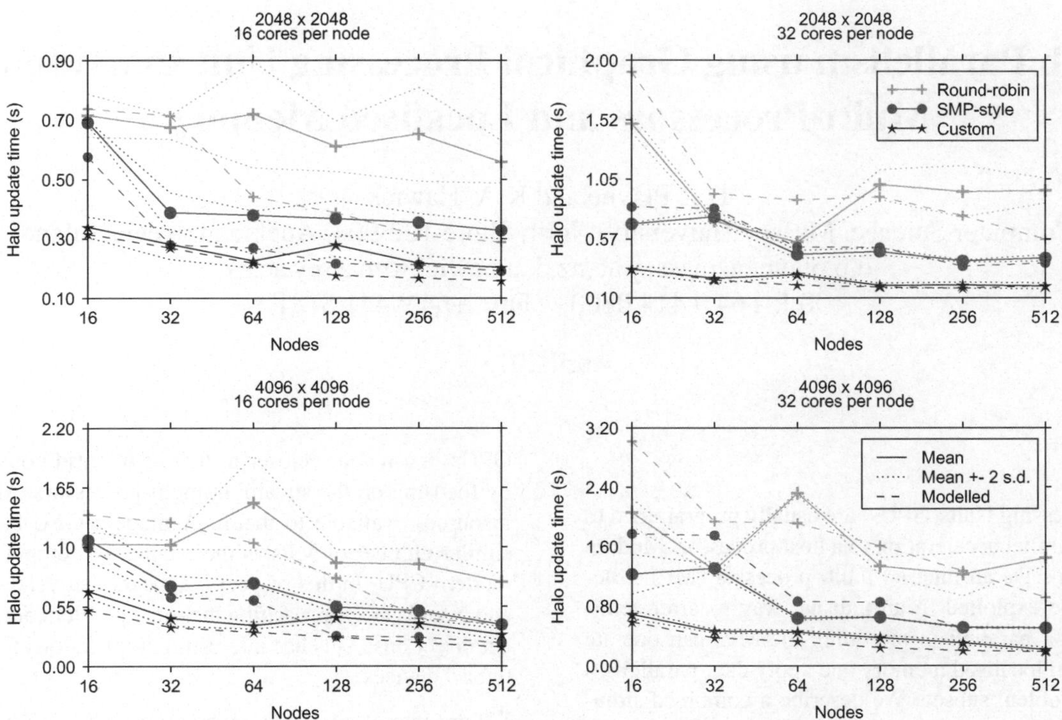

Fig. 4: Shallow model predictions of run time (dashed lines) versus measured times for a series of 3 runs, with the mean (solid lines) and two standard deviations on either side of the mean (dotted lines).

[2] D. Kanter, "AMD's Bulldozer microarchitecture," Real World Tech online article, August 2010, http://www.realworldtech.com/bulldozer/.

[3] I. Bermous, J. Henrichs, and M. Naughton, "Application performance improvement by use of partial nodes to reduce memory contention," *CAWCR Research Letters*, vol. 9, pp. 19–22, December 2012.

[4] T. Edwards, "Optimising UPSCALE on HERMIT," Cray CoE for HECToR, Report, May 2012.

[5] D. Whitaker, "Case study: AWP-ODC and MPI re-ordering," Part of presentation at the Cray XE6 performance workshop entitiled "Optimising Communication on the Cray XE6", November 2012, available: http://www.hector.ac.uk/coe/cray-xe6-workshop-2012-Nov/pdf/comms.pdf.

[6] T. Edwards, "Applying automated optimisation techniques to HPC applications," in *Geoengineering the future: Online proceedings of the 2013 Cray User Group*, May 2013.

[7] R. Rabenseifner, G. Hager, and G. Jost, "Hybrid MPI/OpenMP parallel programming on clusters of multi-core SMP nodes," ser. PDP '09, 2009, pp. 427–436.

[8] S. Pllana, I. Brandic, and S. Benkner, "A survey of the state of the art in performance modeling and prediction of parallel and distributed computing systems," *International Journal of Computational Intelligence Research*, vol. 4, no. 1, January 2008.

[9] A. Snavely, L. Carrington, N. Wolter, J. Labarta, R. Badia, and A. Purkayastha, "A framework for performance modeling and prediction," in *Proceedings of the 2002 ACM/IEEE conference on Supercomputing*, 2002, pp. 1–17.

[10] L. Carrington, A. Snavely, and N. Wolter, "A performance prediction framework for scientific applications," *Future Gener. Comput. Syst.*, vol. 22, no. 3, pp. 336–346, 2006.

[11] S. D. Hammond, G. R. Mudalige, J. A. Smith, S. A. Jarvis, J. A. Herdman, and A. Vadgama, "WARPP: a toolkit for simulating high-performance parallel scientific codes," in *Simutools '09*, 2009, pp. 1–10.

[12] D. J. Kerbyson and P. W. Jones, "A performance model of the parallel ocean program," *Int. J. High Perform. Comput. Appl.*, vol. 19, no. 3, pp. 261–276, 2005.

[13] K. J. Barker and D. J. Kerbyson, "A performance model and scalability analysis of the HYCOM ocean simulation application," in *IASTED PDCS 2005*, November 2005.

[14] D. J. Kerbyson, K. J. Barker, and K. Davis, "Analysis of the weather research and forecasting (WRF) model on large-scale systems," in *ParCo 2007*, vol. 15, 2007, pp. 89–98.

[15] T. Hoefler, W. Gropp, W. Kramer, and M. Snir, "Performance modeling for systematic performance tuning," in *State of the Practice Reports*, ser. SC '11, 2011, pp. 6:1–6:12.

[16] A. Alexandrov, M. F. Ionescu, K. E. Schauser, and C. Scheiman, "LogGP: incorporating long messages into the LogP model for parallel computation," *J. Parallel Distrib. Comput.*, vol. 44, no. 1, pp. 71–79, 1997.

[17] T. Hoefler, T. Mehlan, A. Lumsdaine, and W. Rehm, "Netgauge: A Network Performance Measurement Framework," in *HPCC'07*, vol. 4782, Sep. 2007, pp. 659–671.

[18] J. M. Dennis, E. R. Jessup, and W. M. Waite, "SLAMM - automating memory analysis for numerical algorithms," *Electron. Notes Theor. Comput. Sci.*, vol. 253, no. 7, pp. 89–104, Sep. 2010.

[19] G. Mudalige, M. Vernon, and S. Jarvis, "A plug-and-play model for evaluating wavefront computations on parallel architectures," in *IPDPS 08*, April 2008, pp. 1–14.

[20] *NCAR HPC shallow water model tutorial*, UCAR, October 2006, http://www.cisl.ucar.edu/docs/hpc_modeling/.

[21] R. Sadourny, "The dynamics of finite-difference models of the shallow-water equations," *Journal of the Atmospheric Sciences*, vol. 32, pp. 680–689, 1975.

[22] *HECToR - UK National supercomputing service*, UoE HPCX Ltd, The University of Edinburgh, 2013, http://www.hector.ac.uk/.

[23] *Good Practice Guide: HECToR Phase 3 (32-core)*, UoE HPCX Ltd, The University of Edinburgh, 2012, http://www.hector.ac.uk/cse/documentation/Phase3/.

[24] *Gemini Network Whitepaper*, Revision 1.1 ed., Cray Inc., August 2010.

[25] *Intel MPI benchmarks: User guide and methodology description*, Document number 320714-007en ed., Intel Corporation, August 2011.

Job Parallelism using Graphical Processing Unit Individual Multi-Processors and Localised Memory

D.P. Playne and K.A. Hawick
Computer Science, Massey University, North Shore 102-904, Auckland, New Zealand
d.p.playne@massey.ac.nz, k.a.hawick@massey.ac.nz
Tel: +64 9 414 0800 Fax: +64 9 441 8181

April 2013

Abstract

Graphical Processing Units(GPUs) are usually programmed to provide data-parallel acceleration to a host processor. Modern GPUs typically have an internal multi-processor (MP) structure that can be exploited in an unusual way to offer semi-independent task parallelism providing the MPs can operate within their own localised memory and apply data-parallelism to their own problem subset. We describe a combined simulation and statistical analysis application using component labelling and benchmark it on a range of modern GPU and CPU devices with various numbers of cores. As well as demonstrating a high degree of job parallelism and throughput we find a typical GPU MP outperforms a conventional CPU core.

Keywords: GPU; task parallelism; data parallelism; hybrid parallelism; multi-processor.

1 Introduction

A great deal of the present research and developmental effort going into processor development is in increasing the number of cores that can be used concurrently on a single processor chip package. At the time of writing there are two complementary approaches being adopted. The first is addition of high capability central processing unit (CPU) cores, where each core presents computational capabilities to the applications programmer that individually appear very much the same as a traditional single core CPU. This approach is very much linked to the processor product development approach taken by Intel and AMD and at the time of writing is typified by devices with 4, 6, 8 core with recent devices announced fielding 16 and 32 such cores. The other approach is that typified by the GPU devices fielded by companies like NVidia. To a large extent the recent success of GPUs for general purpose (non graphical) programming has been due to the data parallelism possibilities offered by the large and rapidly growing number of simpler compute cores available. Recent GPUs have fielded 512 and 1536 such cores.

In this paper we explore the idea that one can also program GPUs in a manner closer to that of the traditional CPU core by focusing on the streaming multi-processors (MPs) and the resources available to them. A modern GPU has a broadly similar number of MPs as the number of compute cores on a modern CPU. In this respect it appears that vendors like Intel and NVidia are approaching the same problem but from different directions. This has interesting implications for future and hybrid devices.

We are interested in how one can use GPU MPs using a job parallelism approach. In separate work we have explored how jobs can be placed on completely separate GPU accelerators run by the same CPU host program, but in this present paper we explore independent jobs running on the MPs of a single GPU. There are a number of appropriate simulation models for which this is a powerful paradigm for enhancing throughput.

We present performance analysis based on an example such as simulating the 2D Game of Life (GoL) cellular automaton (CA) model [5, 7], but we also incorporate a sophisticated model analysis algorithm using cluster component labelling and histogramming [11].

Component labelling [6, 22] is a long standing problem of interest on parallel computers with a range of parallel approaches reported in the literature [19]. We have reported prior work of our own in achieving fast component labelling on a single GPU [8] where memory was not at a premium. In this present paper we include a report of our new work in achieving component labelling performed within the memory resources of a single MP.

Using bit-wise programming instructions and data structures we are able to cram a combined simulation model and its statistical component analysis software into the memory of individual MPs. The hosting CPU is thus able to manage independent jobs across all the MPs of its accelerating GPU device, and furthermore this can be extended if more than one GPU device is available.

The problem of managing job parallelism on modern multicore devices is not a new one and much has been shown to depend of the efficiency and ease of programming using multiple threads of control [2, 3, 9, 10, 17]. These technologies are typically needed to manage parallelism within a multi-cored CPU, with a language and environment such as NVidia's Compute Unified Device Architecture (CUDA) [13, 14] being used to program the GPU accelerator code. A coarser grain parallelism is also available across different host nodes altogether using hybrids of message passing and GPU accelerator techniques [23].

Our article is structured as follows: In Section 2 we summarise the simulation model and component analysis ideas that are central to this paper and which we aim to run independently upon the individual MPs of one or more GPUs. In Section 3 we review the various relevant technical characteristic GPU models which allow us to device various compact and bit-packing programming implementations which we describe in Section 4. We present a selection of performance results achieved with different GPU models in Section 5 and discuss the implications for this job parallelism paradigm in Section 6. We offer some concluding ideas and areas for further work in Section 7.

2 Model and Analysis Background

In this paper we focus on bit-wise models where there is a well-defined time-stepping procedure to update the bit-field based on a some localised calculation. A bit-field in d-dimensions can be analysed into its individual component clusters, which can be categorised by size and histogrammed appropriately. This is a particularly interesting analysis to incorporate into our performance testing since component labelling is no longer a localised calculation but must propagate information – about which site is connected to which cluster component – across the whole of the memory structure used for the bit-field. Although this approach applied to a wide class of complex systems simulation models, cellular automaton models are particular useful as concise benchmarks to discuss n this paper.

Cellular Automata (CA) models [1, 18] have long played an important role in exploring and understanding of the fundamentals of complex systems [21]. One classic CAs that provide a basis for much other work is Conway's Game of Life(GoL) [5]. There is a space of similarly formulated automaton rules [15] in the same family as GoL [12] but the Conway precise specification turns out to be particularly special in the rule set space of the family, having highly complex behaviour.

Much work has been done on studying the coherent structures that occur in GoL and its variants [4]. It is possible to implant specific patterns such as gliders, glider guns and so forth to obtain specific sequences of GoL automata configurations. However, in this present paper we investigate GoL automata systems that have been randomly initialised with an initial fraction of live cells. Providing we simulate a large enough sample of large enough automata systems, many different individual patterns can occur by chance, will interact and the system will eventually arrive a static or dynamical equilibrium.

The Game of Live is implemented using the Moore neighbourhood on a $d = 2$ dimensional array of cells, where the number of (Moore) Neighbouring sites $N_M = 8$, for $d = 2$. We define the (square) lattice Length as L and hence the number of sites N, typically $N = L^d$. We define the number of live sites N_L, and so the metric fraction $f_l = N_L/N$ and similarly the number of dead sites N_D, and fraction $f_D = N_D/N$.

Algorithm 1 Synchronous **automaton update** algorithm.

for all i, j in (L, L) **do**
    gather Moore Neighbour-hood $\mathcal{M}_{i,j}$
    apply rule $b[i][j] \leftarrow \{s[i][j], \mathcal{M}_{i,j}\}$
end for
for all i, j in (L, L) **do**
    copy $b[i][j] \rightarrow s[i][j]$
end for

In prior work [7] we have explored various simple metrics that can be applied to the GoL bit-field, but in this paper we focus on the size distribution of components of live cells as a function of time after random initialisation. Our long term interest is in building up histograms of this size distribution averaged over many independent configurations so we can track the time dependent behaviour to explore theoretical predictions such as Becker Doring [16].

We do not discuss the computational science and statistical mechanics aspects further in this present paper, but focus on the GPU and performance aspects using this applications model as a representative benchmark. The key aspects of the model as we employ it here are that although we only need a bit-field of $N = L^2$ elements for the simulation, we need an integer field to hold the working site labels when we perform the component analysis. This gives rise to various memory and size tradeoffs as described in Section 4 and the tradeoff space is different for different combinations of MPs and non-shared memory in the different GPU models described below.

3 GPU Architectural Background

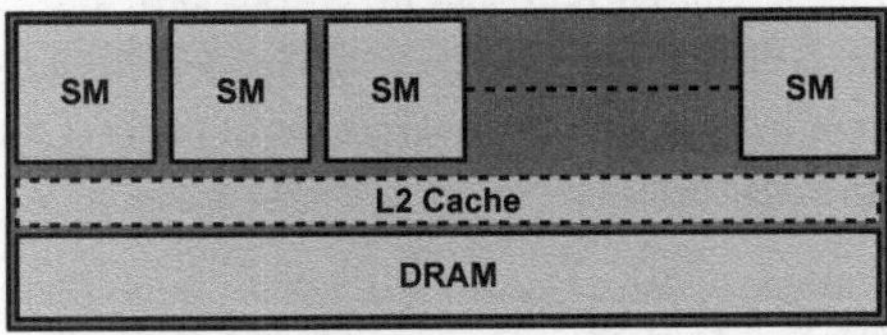

Figure 1: Overview of the GPU Architecture showing the role of the Streaming Multi-Processors (MPs). This scalable model easily allows additional MPs to be added to the GPU.

Graphical Processing Units have proved themselves as powerful and effective for large scale computational simulations. Acceptance of the GPU is shown by the number of GPU accelerated machines in the June 2012 TOP500 list [20]. Of the top 100 machines from this list, 15% are GPU accelerated, given the relatively recent rise of GPU computing this is a significant percentage.

GPUs can achieve a high computational throughput by provid-

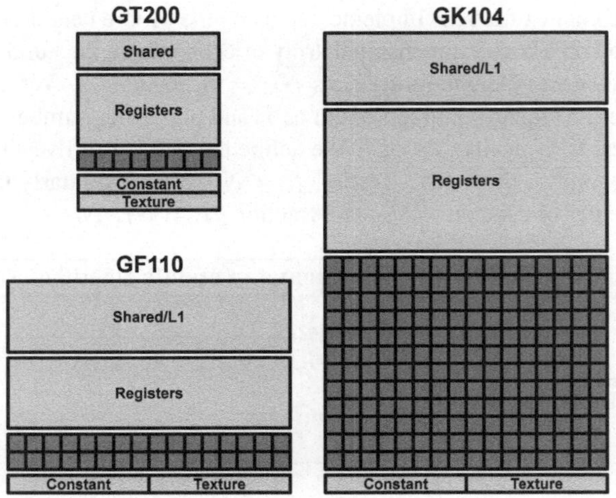

Figure 2: Streaming Multi-Processor Architecture showing three generations - Tesla (GT200), Fermi (GF110) and Kepler (GK104). It can be seen that although the number of cores on each MP has grown significantly in each generation

ing a large number of simple cores and small cache structures. This approach contrasts with modern CPU design which instead contains a small number of powerful cores that are kept busy by large cache hierarchies. GPUs also control thread management and scheduling in hardware which allows them to manage a large number of threads running at a time. Various thread scheduling techniques can be used to hide memory latencies and allow GPUs to perform efficiently when executing a large number of threads.

NVIDIA GPUs each contain a number of Streaming Multiprocessors (MPs), each of which contains a number of cores as well as registers and shared memory. The main memory area of a GPU is global memory which can be accessed by both the MPs of the GPU and also by the host through the PCIe bus. The Fermi and Kepler architecture GPUs also have an area of L2 cache that is shared between all of the MPs on the device The general GPU architecture can be seen in Figure 1. The main difference between the generations of GPU is the configuration of the MPs themselves.

Tesla generation (G80, GT200) MPs each contained 8 cores, either 32KB or 64KB of registers and 16KB of shared memory. The Fermi architecture (GF110) improved on this with 32 cores per MP with 128KB of registers and 48KB of shared memory. It also introduced an L1/L2 cache which automatically cached read/write transactions to global memory (the main device memory). The recently release Kepler architecture (GK104) GPUs contain SMX units (next generation MPs) with 192 cores, 256KB of registers and 48KB of shared memory. A illustration of the different MP configurations is shown in Figure 2.

At this point in most GPU articles, a detailed description of global memory accesses and the various caches for accessing global memory (constant, texture, L1/L2) would be described. However, this research takes a different approach to GPU-based computation. Instead of achieving high computational throughput by creating a large number of threads and processing a large data set like most GPU simulations, we instead investigate how GPU MPs can be used to process **small** data sets.

Traditionally GPUs struggle with small data sets because it limits the number of threads that can be active at once and the memory transactions to global memory cannot be hidden effectively. In this article we investigate how simulations with small data sets can be computed entirely on a single MP. This means the data set must fit into shared memory and the simulation computed entirely by a single block of threads. This obviously places strict restrictions on the maximum size of the system and presents a set of challenges not normally faced by GPU developers. The advantage of this approach is that the only slow global memory transactions are the writes to output the results of the simulation. All other memory transactions are through either the very fast registers or relatively fast shared memory.

Device Model (NVidia)	Multi Procs	CUDA Cores	Global Mem per GPU (MBytes)	GPU Clock (GHz)
GTX 260+	24	216	896	1.40
GTX 580	16	512	1,536	1.59
GTX 590	2x16	2x512	1,536	1.22
GTX 680	8	1536	2,048	0.71
M2075	14	448	5,375	1.15

Table 1: Configurations and relevant properties of the GPU devices.

In Table 1 we list the relevant memory and core configurations and clock speeds of the various GPUs we used. The GTX "Gamer" devices were hosted with Intel CPUs in conventional desktop computers and the M2075 was hosted in a blade unit with Xeon CPU host.

CPU Model (Intel)	CPU Cores	Cache (MBytes)	CPU Clock (GHz)
Q8200 Core2	4	4	2.33
X5675 Xeon	6	12	3.06
2600K Core-i7	4	8	3.40

Table 2: CPU relevant Properties.

Table 2 lists the relevant core numbers, cache sizes and clock speeds of the conventional CPU devices we experimented with.

4 Implementation Method

There are a number of important aspects to implementing the simulation and component labelling code on GPUs. In this section we discuss storage issues; the update algorithm; CUDA aspects; and the component labelling algorithm.

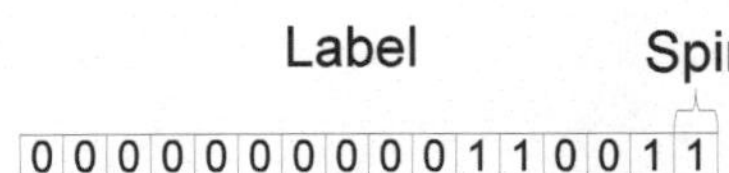

Figure 3: Bit-packing used to store a cell's spin and label in the same 16-bit unsigned short int. This cell is 'alive' and has the label 25.

4.1 Storage Requirements

The storage requirements for the Game of Life are relatively small, each cell has only two possible state - alive or dead. Thus a single bit per cell is sufficient to represent the system. For the different threads in the kernel to be able to access this system, it must be stored in shared memory - 16KB on a Tesla or 48KB on a Fermi/Kepler GPU. To make full use of this shared memory area to store for the state of the system, the state of the cells must be packed into an unsigned char, unsigned int or a similar data type. This means the maximum system size that can be stored in shared memory is $\approx 360^2$ on a Tesla and $\approx 620^2$ on a Fermi/Kepler GPU.

However, for this application there are additional storage requirement. Not only does the storage for the Game of Life need to fit into shared memory but also the space required for the component labeling. In order to support the number of labels required, an unsigned short int is used for each label. This data type gives a maximum of 2^{16} or 65536 labels. This limits the maximum system size to $\approx 150^2$ which gives a maximum of $22,500$ cells. In turn this means only 15 of the 16 bits in the short integer are required for the label. The extra bit can be used to store the spin for the Game of Life system. This is shown in Figure 3.

This allows both the labels and the Game of Life system to be stored in a lattice of unsigned short ints and give a maximum size of $\approx 150^2$ for a Fermi/Kepler device or $\approx 90^2$ for a Tesla device.

4.2 Update Method

Unfortunately this maximum storage size only takes the memory to store a single system into account. As the Game of Life uses a synchronous update method, two system states are usually used to compute the model. One is used to store the current state and to calculate the next state of each cell, this new state is written to the second system. However, this method immediately doubles the memory required to store a Game of Life system. For most implementations this would not cause a major problem, however in this case there is a very limited amount of memory available and another method must be used.

In this method only one full system is stored and two buffers are used to store rows of previous states. The system is updated one row at a time and writes the new value of each row directly updates the system. However, before each new row is written to memory the old value is copied to a buffer. The values from this buffer can then be used to calculate the update for the next row. Because this simulation uses periodic boundaries, another buffer is also required to store the original value of the first row as it is required for the calculation of the final row. This update method is illustrated in Figure 4.

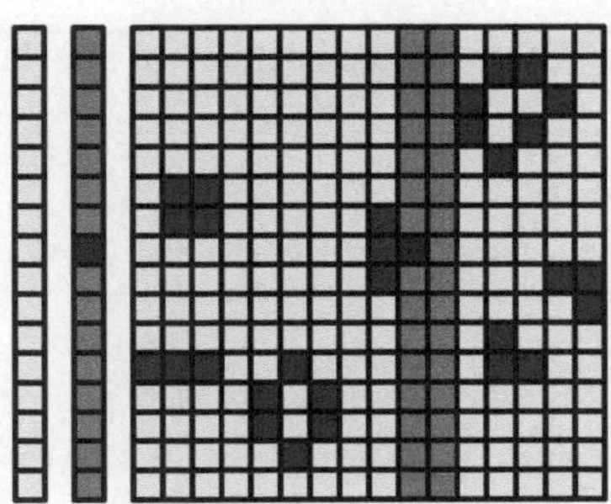

Figure 4: Update of a Game of Life system using buffers. The highlighted green rows are the rows currently being using in the update. This example shows how a blinker can be correctly updated by using the buffer to store the previous row.

4.3 CUDA implementation

Normally CUDA kernels create one thread for each cell, but unfortunately in this case it would also overrun the available registers. The easiest way to implement this update method in CUDA is to create one row of threads, each of which is responsible for update one column of cells. Before the update of the system begins, the first row and last rows are copied into the buffers. The buffer containing the first row will remain untouched until the last stage of the update while the other buffer will be continually updated. Each thread then reads three values from the buffer (representing the previous row) and the other six values from the system. Using these values it will calculate the new value of the cell. Once the new value has been calculated it will write the old value to the buffer and the new value to memory. All the threads must synchronize after each row has been updated to ensure that the buffer contains the correct values. This implementation is given in Algorithm 2.

However, this implementation will limit the number of threads to a maximum of L. This will limit the maximum performance of the implementation as the MPs use thread scheduling to hide memory latency. A better approach is to create a block of threads that process the field several rows at a time. In this implementation only the first row of the block will read from the buffer and only the last row will write to it. This allows a greater number of threads to run at once and makes better use of the MPs. The optimal number of rows updated by the block will depend on the total size of the system.

4.4 Connected Component Labelling

The other stage of the kernel is to label the connected components of the system. The same method of iterating through the cells used by the simulation can be used by the labeling phase. The labeling method used by this implementation is based on previous implementations and is outlined in algorithm 3.

This algorithm is used by both the GPU and CPU implementations albeit with some minor implementation modifications.

Algorithm 2 CUDA implementation of the buffer update method.

```
declare __shared__ s[L][L]
declare __shared__ b0[L]
declare __shared__ b1[L]
declare xm1=(threadIdx.x == 0) ? L-1 : threadIdx.x-1
declare xp1=(threadIdx.x == L-1) ? 0 : threadIdx.x+1
for t = 0 to t_e do
    copy s[0][threadIdx.x] to b1[threadIdx.x]
    copy s[L-1][threadIdx.x] to b0[threadIdx.x]
    for y = 0 to L do
        declare sum = 0
        sum += b0[xm1] + b0[threadIdx.x] + b1[xp1]
        sum += s[y][xm1] + s[y][xp1]
        if y == L-1 then
            sum += b0[xm1] + b0[threadIdx.x] + b0[xp1]
        else
            sum += s[y+1][xm1] + s[y+1][threadIdx.x] + s[y+1][xp1]
        end if
        syncthreads
        copy s[y][threadIdx.x] to b0[threadIdx.x]
        if sum == 3 then
            s[y][threadIdx.x] = 1
        else if sum < 2 or sum > 3 then
            s[y]threadIdx.x] = 0
        end if
    end for
end for
```

Algorithm 3 Component labelling algorithm outline.

```
declare change = true
for y = 0 to L do
    label[y][threadIdx.x] = y*L + threadIdx.x
end for
while changed == true do
    changed = false
    for y = 0 to L do
        ln = find lowest connected label in neighbours
        if ln < label[y][threadIdx.x] then
            label[y][threadIdx.x] = ln
            changed = true
        end if
    end for
    for y = 0 to L do
        declare l0 = label[y][threadIdx.x]
        while l0 != label[l0/L][l0 % L] do
            l0 = labe[l0];
        end while
        label[y][threadIdx.x] = l0
    end for
end while
```

Because the GPU implementation still has a degree of parallelism to it some synchronizations are required in order to ensure that the connected components are correctly labelled.

4.5 CPU Threading Implementation

In order to make a fair comparison and assessment of our approach on GPUs we also implemented the simulation and component labelling using a threading system across the (conventional) high capability cores of various CPU models. Intel's Threading Building Blocks [9] has been used to implement this multi-threading for the CPU implementations. Effectively the Game of Life simulations are distributed as jobs to the available cores on the CPU. This allows each simulation to remain as local as possible to the core and make best use of the available cache while still making use of the CPU cores.

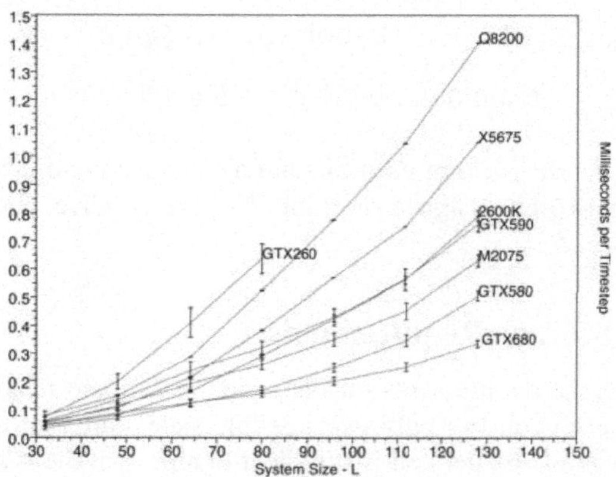

Figure 5: Comparison of CPU cores and GPU MPs computing a single Game of Life simulation with Connected Component Labelling.

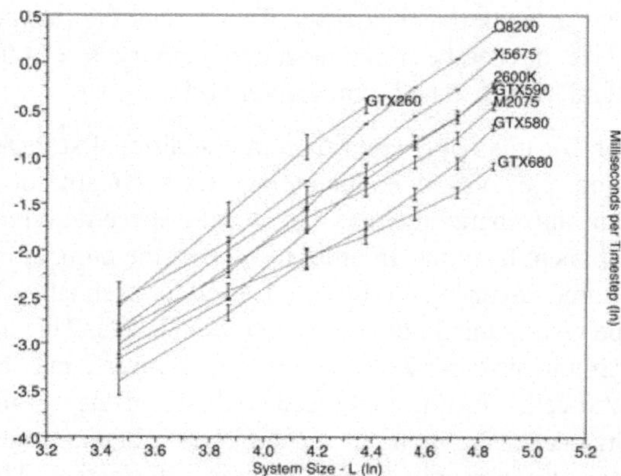

Figure 6: ln-ln scale comparison of CPU cores and GPU MPs computing a single Game of Life simulation with Connected Component Labelling, with least-squares fitted slopes between 1.8 and 2.1.

5 Performance Results

The performance of the GPUs described in Table 1 and CPUs from Table 2 have been compared for two different situations - computing a single Game of Life simulation and computing 100 simulations. The error-bars shown in the plots were obtained from standard deviations obtained by averaging time measurements over multiple runs with independently seeded initial conditions for the model.

The first comparison allows the performance of a single CPU core to be compared with a single MP of a GPU. This comparison is shown in Figure 5 both of which show the time taken by a single core of the CPUs and and single MP of the GPUs to compute a step of a Game of Life simulation with connected component labelling across various system sizes. This is also shown in log-log scale in Figure 6

The second compares the CPUs and GPUs as an entire processing architecture. It is expected that the GPUs will be able to provide higher performance when computing many simula-

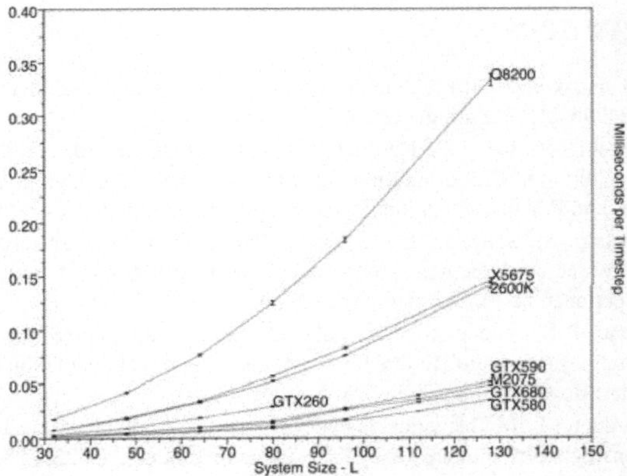

Figure 7: Comparison of CPUs and GPUs computing one hundred Game of Life simulations with Connected Component Labelling.

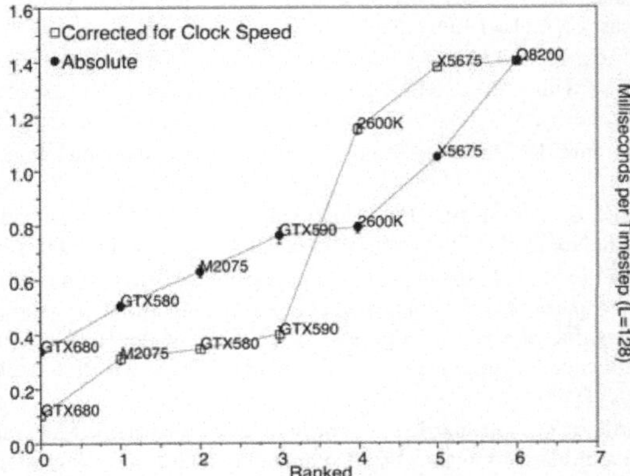

Figure 8: Comparison of CPUs computing one hundred Game of Life simulations with Connected Component Labelling.

tions as they generally contain many MPs compared to CPUs which generally contain 2-6 cores. This can be seen in Figure 7 which shows the time taken by all the available cores of the CPUs and all available MPs of the GPUs to compute a step of a Game of Life and label the connected components. Results are shown across a range of system sizes $L = 32...128$.

6 Discussion

The software architectural model we adopt is essentially a CPU master program that controls as many slave programs as practically possible given the available CPU cores, GPU devices and MPS available on the GPUs. Our outer loop therefore tries to schedule M_j slave jobs across N_{mp} multiprocessors or N_T threads across N_D devices on each of N_N individual nodes. There is therefore a significant choice in which level of parallelism to exploit to maximum the number of jobs that can be executed at once. In this paper we limit our investigation to a single GPU device, driven by a single hosting node, but there is obviously scope for deploying multiple nodes with multiple devices.

Figure 8 shows the mean timing result for the model system size $L = 128$ ranked in ascending time and shows how the various single CPU cores and single GPU MPs compared. The solid points plotted are the absolute times and show a steady increase in time from the fastest device we tested (the Kepler architecture GTX 680 GPU MP) up to the slowest (the Core2 CPU). As one might expect faster clock speeds in the CPU devices lead to a improved times. There is approximately a ratio of 3.5 between the times for slowest and fastest. Averaged over a larger number of jobs that can be scheduled across many CPU cores or many GPU MPs, improves this ratio even further to a factor of approximately 8.

If we attempt to normalise the times by clock speed, we see a marked separation of the data in Figure 8 into two very definite clusters - one for the GPU MP and one for the CPU core. This is plotted as the open data points, which again, we have ranked in order to highlight the changes. Obviously this approach only gives a very broad brush comparison between individual GPU MP and CPU core but within the two categories it does highlight some interesting effects.

One might expect the improved Kepler architecture GPU (680) with it greater number of cores to outperform the Tesla architecture devices (2075, 590 and 580 models). The M2075 has error-checked memory (which is why it needs a slower clock speed than the other Fermi devices - 580 and 590) and the M2075 generally outperforms the GTX devices on floating point calculations. Our benchmark application however primarily uses bit-wise, integer and memory manipulations, but the M2050 is still the best Fermi GPU architecture when clock speed is factored out.

Analysing the slopes from Figure 6 also shows some interesting results. Plotting the log of the time versus the log of the problem size L normally indicates the computational complexity exponent ν from the slope and the relationship $t \approx \mathcal{O}(L^\nu)$. We obtain values for the exponent ν from inverse error-weighted least-squares fitting to the whole curves.

The slope of the CPU performance plots are all similar at ≈ 2.1. This is expected as the complexity of computing the Game of Life should increase with $\approx L^2$ but the connected component labeling should be slightly greater than L^2. However, the Fermi architecture GPUs all show a similar slope of $\approx 1.8 - 1.9$. This suggests that the computational power of the MPs is still being under utilized and that the GPU would be able to provide more efficient computation if a larger system size could be fit into shared memory. This is even more pronounced in the Kepler GPU which had a slope of ≈ 1.4.

While the GPU architectures provide very efficient computation they are still severely limited by the available memory and especially by the available cache. Unfortunately this problem appears to be amplified in the latest GPU architecture which has increase the number of cores per MP from 32 to 192 with no increase in shared memory.

7 Conclusion

We have described our use of streaming multi-processors of various NVidia GPU device models to implement independent job parallelism for accelerating complex systems simulations. We have showed that even quite sophisticated applications can be fit into the memory of an MP and that both the simulation itself as well as a more elaborate component analysis calculation can use this approach. We have also implemented the same application algorithm for individual single CPU cores scheduling across the multiple cores in Intel CPUs.

We have discussed the tradeoff space offered by the particular memory and MP mix available on current GPUs. We anticipate this space offering even more memory per MP on future devices and therefore this paradigm is likely to become viable for other application problems and algorithms. This approach is in contrast to the high successful data-parallel approach often used by applications programmers on GPU accelerators. We observe the broadly similar numbers of conventional CPU cores available from 2012 Intel chip offers and the number of MPs available on NVidia GPUs available in 2012. We postulate some convergence and continued growth of these numbers as hardware and production capabilities improve.

We observe that generally the present trend is still towards multi-core CPUs being somewhat easier to program than are GPUs using CUDA even when we have to use multi-threading code and a library like Intel TBB. However with appropriate parallel programming and bit-packing we obtained higher performance using the GPU MPs than from the CPU cores.

In this paper, we have focused on the MP parallelism with a single GPU. However, combining all sources of parallelism: from multiple host nodes in a cluster; where each node is itself a multi-cored CPU being accelerated by multiple GPUs; and where each GPU has multiple MPs; and each MP is capable of data-parallelism across its cores and threads, offers great potential for job thoughput speedup in the applications context we have described. Not all applications nor applications programmers will be able to or have the time and inclination to exploit all these levels of parallelism however. There is therefore scope for code generation and compiler directives and other tools to help achieve this. We expect to be able to deploy this approach for many of the complex systems applications of interest to us, extending the work to higher dimensional model systems and other forms of statistical measurements including time correlation analyses.

We expect vendors will continue to announce higher numbers of CPU cores and MPs in the course of the next few years and that the arena of programming language and associated software environment will be of growing importance for the continued exploitation of hybrid combinations of multi-core CPU and multi-processor GPUs by applications programmers. Finally, this work emphasises the current need to fit key data structures of applications into local uncontended fast memory wherever possible. GPU memory architecture appears to allow more opportunity for this with this application category.

References

[1] Adamatzky, A. (ed.): Game of Life Cellular Automata. No. ISBN 978-1-84996-216-2, Springer (2010)

[2] Blumofe, R., Joerg, C., Kuszmaul, B., Leiserson, C., Randall, K., Zhou, Y.: Cilk: An efficient multithreaded runtime system. In: Symp. Principles and Practice of Parallel Programming. pp. 207–216. ACM (1995)

[3] Bokhari, S., Saltz, J.: Exploring the Performance of Massively Multithreaded Architectures. Concurrency and Computation: Practice and Experience 22(5), 588–616 (April 2010)

[4] Evans, K.M.: Game of Life Cellular Automata, chap. Larger than Life's Extremes: Rigorous Results for Simplified Rules and Speculation on the Phase Boundaries, pp. 179–221. Springer (2010)

[5] Gardner, M.: Mathematical Games: The fantastic combinations of John Conway's new solitaire game "Life". Scientific American 223, 120–123 (October 1970)

[6] Hambrusch, S.E., Winkel, L.E.T.: A Study of Connected Component Labeling Algorithms on the MPP. In: Proceedings of 3rd Int. Conference on Supercomputing. vol. 1, pp. 477–483 (May 1988)

[7] Hawick, K.A.: Static and dynamical equilibrium properties to categorise generalised game-of-life related cellular automata. In: Int. Conf. on Foundations of Computer Science (FCS'12). pp. 51–57. CSREA, Las Vegas, USA (16-19 July 2012)

[8] Hawick, K.A., Leist, A., Playne, D.P.: Parallel Graph Component Labelling with GPUs and CUDA. Parallel Computing 36(12), 655–678 (December 2010), www.elsevier.com/locate/parco

[9] Intel: Intel(R) Threading Building Blocks Reference Manual. Intel (May 2010)

[10] Lamie, E.L.: Real-Time Embedded Multithreading - Using ThreadX and MIPS. No. ISBN 978-1-85617-631-6, Newnes - Elsevier (2009)

[11] Lumetta, S.S., Krishnamurthy, A., Culler, D.E.: Towards modeling the performance of a fast connected components algorithm on parallel machines. In: Supercomputing '95: Proceedings of the 1995 ACM/IEEE conference on Supercomputing (CDROM). p. 32. ACM, New York, NY, USA (1995)

[12] Martinez, G., Adamatzky, A., Morita, K., Margenstern, M.: Game of Life Cellular Automata, chap. Computation with Competing patterns in Life-Like Automaton, pp. 547–572. Springer (2010)

[13] Nickolls, J., Buck, I., Garland, M., Skadron, K.: Scalable parallel programming with CUDA. ACM Queue 6(2), 40–53 (March/April 2008)

[14] NVIDIA® Corporation: NVIDIA CUDA C Programming Guide Version 4.1 (2011), http://www.nvidia.com/ (last accessed April 2012)

[15] de Oliveira, G.M.B., Siqueira, S.R.C.: Parameter characterization of two-dimensional cellular automata rule space. Physica D: Nonlinear Phenomena 217, 1–6 (2006)

[16] R.Becker, W.Doring: Droplet Theory. Ann.Phys. 24, 719 (1935)

[17] Reinders, J.: Intel Threading Building Blocks: outfitting C++ for multi-core processor parallelism. No. ISBN 978-0596514808, O'Reilly, 1st edn. (2007)

[18] Sarkar, P.: A Brief History of Cellular Automata. ACM Computing Surveys 32, 80–107 (2000)

[19] Suzuki, K., Horiba, I., Sugie, N.: Fast Connected-Component Labeling Based on Sequential Local Operations in the Course of Forward Raster Scan Followed by Backward Raster Scan. In: Proc. 15th International Conference on Pattern Recognition (ICPR'00). vol. 2, pp. 434–437 (2000)

[20] TOP500.org: TOP 500 Supercomputer Sites. http://www.top500.org/, last accessed August 2012

[21] Wolfram, S.: Complex Systems theory. Tech. rep., Institute for Advanced Study, Princton, NJ 08540 (6-7 October 1984 1985), presented at Santa Fe Workshop on "A response to the challenge of emerging synthesis in science"

[22] Wu, K., Otoo, E., Suzuki, K.: Optimizing Two-Pass Connected-Component Labeling Algorithms. Pattern Anal. Applic. 12, 117–135 (2009)

[23] Yang, C.T., Huang, C.L., Lin, C.F.: Hybrid CUDA, OpenMP, and MPI parallel programming on multicore GPU clusters. Computer Physics Communications 182, 266–269 (2011)

SESSION

DATA-DRIVEN NETWORKING SYSTEMS WITH HIGH TOLERANCE FOR DISASTER, FAULT AND CONGESTION

Chair(s)

Prof. Hiroaki Nishikawa

Effective Flooding over Disaster Tolerant Ad Hoc Network based on exchange of Neighbor Information

Naoya Imaizumi, , Keisuke Utsu, Hiroshi Sano, and Hiroshi Ishii
Department of Communication and Network Engineering,
School of Information and Telecommunication Engineering, Tokai University, Minato, Tokyo, Japan

Abstract – *Mobile Ad Hoc Networks (MANET) is a useful means instead of network infrastructure when disaster happens. In this situation, information distribution without addresses of nodes is able to be realized by the existing Simple Flooding (SF). But SF causes redundant message transmission, performance degradation and waist of finite battery resources. Making network lifetime without external energy source as long as possible is one of the main goals in case of any disasters or emergency situations. We propose a new broadcasting method that allows reducing power consumption by decreasing a number of redundant re-broadcastings, "Effective Flooding based on Neighbor information Exchange-Revised (EFNEX-R)". Through computer simulation, we showed the effectiveness of our method compared with existing Simple Flooding.*

Keywords: Mobile Ad hoc Network, flooding, Disaster

1 Introduction

The Mobile Ad Hoc Networks (MANET) [1] is considered to be a useful communication means alternative to the infrastructure that might be out of service in case of big disaster such as earthquake and tsunami. MANET has been studied from the various perspectives. Among them, we have focused on the layer 3 message forwarding functionalities. Major study issues in MANET layer 3 are mainly on the routing protocols. The objective of the routing is transfer of information from a specific source to another specific destination or destinations, based on unicasting or multicasting technologies, respectively.

Supposing the situation just after disaster happens, communication infrastructure becomes out of order and MANET is to be organized urgently. In this situation, address assigned to each MANET node is often private so that a global address must be newly assigned. Since DNS server seems not available, the assignment is not easy (time consuming). Each node in the MANET has little knowledge about other members' addresses, names, or positions. That means MANET is not useful just like broken infrastructure in a context of poin-to-(multi)point communication requiring IP addresses. Then, how should we do? Instead of unicasting, collection of information existing over the network such as about asylus, your friends, home, and family, and at the same time, distribution of those information over the network are needed. Fortunately, this kind of communication does not necessarily require specific addresses but just broadcast address.

Communication without specific addresses can be executed by "Flodding" by use of repetition of "Broadcasting" over MANET[2] [3]. Flooding, however, requires every node in the MANET re-broadcast the message that results in redundant packet generation. MANET must suffer from heavy load caused by flooding. Since every MANET node is driven by finite battery, redundancy of traffic will accerelate the consumption of battery energy and shorten the network life time. In the initial stage of MANET, broadcast-based flooding is only applicable message transfer mechanism but the the redundancy must be resolved.

There have been several studies that achieve high "packet reachability (the ratio of nodes successfully receiving the packet to all the nodes)" and reduce redundant packets[4-11]. We have also proposed a new method named Load-aware Dynamic Counter-based Flooding (LDCF) [12-14] that can reduce re-broadcasting without any message exchange among neighbor nodes. However, these existing methods require some complex processing and judge re-broadcasting based on state transition using internal variables.

To realize more simplified but efficient braodcasdting, we have proposed a procedure named EFNEX that can reduce the number of transmitting nodes and make only small number of nodes execute the procedure [15-16]. This paper proposes a revised EFNEX and shows the efficiency of the revision by use of network simulation.

Chapter 2 shows existing procedures, Chapter 3 explainns the EFNEX and its revision, Chapter 4 evaluates our proposal by network simulation, and CHapter 5 concludes our discussion.

2 Existing studies

2.1 Simple Flooding

Simple Flooding [3] is the simplest way of transferring information over the network. A node that receives a message broadcasted by the information generating node will do as follows:

(1) if the message is received at the first time, the node must re-broadcast it, or
(2) if the message has been already received by the node, the node discards it.

Simple Flooding can tranfer messages effectively in case nodes are distributed sparsely (low node density). But in case node density is high, nodes must suffer from multiple reception of the same message and result in inefficiency of message transfer. And packet loss and buffer overflow will also be likely to happen. Such situation causes execcive battery consumption. Hence, number of redundant rebroadcasting must be reduced.

2.2 Counter-based scheme

Counter based scheme [5-7] determines whether a packet is to be rebroadcasted or not based on the number of receipts of the same packet. Upon the receipt of the first packet, the counter is reset. During the random time period after the first receipt, at every time when the node receives the same packet (with same ID of the first one), counter value is added by "1". If the counter value reaches the threshold during the time period mentioned above, the rebroadcast is cancelled. It means that many packets exist around the node and that the necessity of rebroadcast is low. Otherwise (the counter value does not reach the threshold after the time period), the node rebroadcasts the packet.

The problem of this scheme is that the threshold is fixed and how to determine the optimum value is not clear. It is because the threshold value must be affected by the traffic condition around the node. And this scheme must make every node manage the status of each packet with the same packet ID so that the process must be complicated.

2.3 Load-aware Dynamic Counter-based Flooding (LDCF)

LDCF solves the problem of counter-based scheme shown in 2.2 by enabling dynamic adaptation of threshold value sependent on the load [12-14]. It estimates load of the node by observing the length of Layer 2 transmission buffer. If the load is estimated being high, the counter threshold value is set small. On the contrary, if low, it is set big. We have already shown LDCF can much improve the packet penetration rate and reduce redundant packets compared with Simple Flooding and Counter-based scheme.

This scheme is very much superior to the existing schemes in the context of improvement in inefficiency of flooding. It, however, requires management of every packet status and variables to be managed such as dynamic threshold values is added to existing other methods. This fact may cause complexity of the system.

2.4 Effective Flooding based on Neighbor Information Exchange (EFNEX)

As stated in the previous sections, existing flooding schemes have several problems to be solved from the perspectives of redundancy, penetration rate, battery consumption, and complexity in state management. Hence the requirements for the new scheme are:

(R1) Reducing redundant packets and suppressing battery consumption
(R2) Simplification of node processing

Simple Flooding cannot satisfy the requirement (R1). Counter-based scheme and LDCF cannot satisfy the requirement (R2).

To meet the requirements, we proposed "Effective Flooding based on Neighbor Information Exchange (EFNEX)" [15-16]. In EFNEX, the broadcaster selects the next broadcasting node with the maximum number of neighbors by collecting neighbor node information within a radio area. EFNEX satisfies (R1) by eliminating the number of rebroadcasting nodes and (R2) by simple adding and sustraction instead of complex status management.

Simulation study shows EFNEX can reduce the number of packets received to 1/4 of the Simple Flooding scheme. But the packet penetration rate is 65% which not sufficiently high. So, the revision of EFNEX is required to realize higher penetration rate.

3 Proposed scheme (EFNEX-R)

In order to improve the packet penetration rate of EFNEX, we propose "Effective Flooding based on Neighbor Information Exchange-Revised (EFNEX-R)".

This procedure has two phases: Initializing and Transfer ones. Initializing phase is one before the user message communication and Transfer phase is one during user message communication is executed. The procedure is shown below.

3.1 Initializing phase

This phase of EFNEX-R has the same procedure as EFNEX.

We assume that
- only one node initiates the procedure and the others do not;
- Within a time duration, all the hello exchanges terminate;
- No collision occurs (all the messages can reach one hop destination without loss); and
- No node has any mobility.

The detailed procedure of Initializing phase is as follows;

(i1) Each node broadcasts a hello message with its name within a radio range. See Fig.1

(i2) Each node that receives a hello message from a neighbor node records the name of the neighbor node.

(i3) After some time duration, each node counts the number of names collected from all the hello messages and makes own neighbor list (NL). NL includes NL creator node name, list of neighbor names and the number of the neighbors.

(i4) Each NL is broadcasted.

(i5) Each NL is revised upon receipt of NLs broadcasted in procedure (i4). See Fig.2.

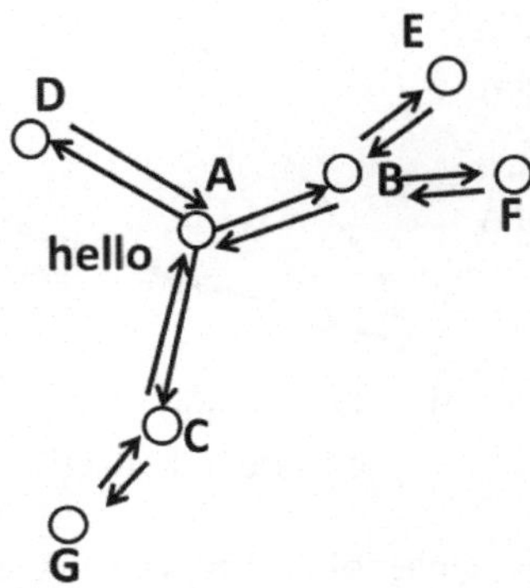

Fig. 1 Hello message exchange

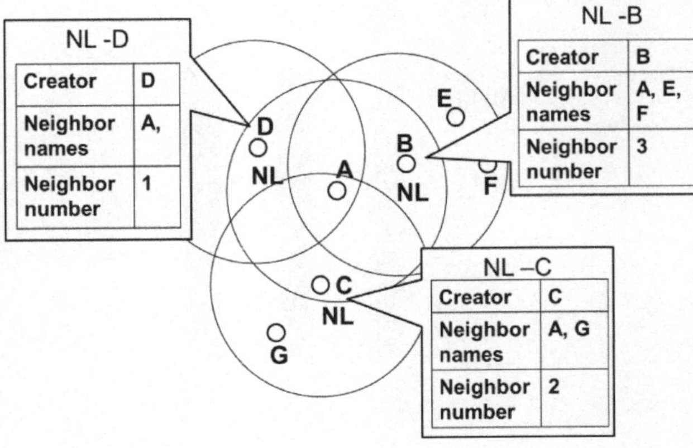

Fig.2 NL collection

3.2 Transfer phase

(t1) The message originator is the first broadcaster. Before a packet is broadcasted by a broadcaster, the node compares all the neighbors' NLs and selects a specific node as a next broadcaster that has the biggest number of neighbors who are not in the broadcaster's own neighbor list. If there are multiple neighbors who have same number of neighbors who are not in the broadcaster's own neighbor list, one of them is selected randomly by the broadcaster as a next broad caster.

(t2) The broadcaster broadcasts a data packet, which contains data, a packet ID, a name of next broadcaster selected in (t1), and its own NL.

(t3) The selected next broadcaster merges the NL sent by prior broadcaster and its own NL. Nodes not selected as a next broadcaster receives the packet if it is the first time reception and otherwise the packet is discarded.

(t4) Procedures (t1) through (t3) are repeated until the next broadcaster cannot be selected.

The existing EFNEX does not consider the name of neighbors but just counts the number only. This is the difference between EFNEX and EFNEX-R.

4 Evaluation

4.1 Simulation conditions

Proposed procedure, EFNEX-R, is evaluated by comparing with existing Simple Flooding and EFNEX by use of network simulator, OPNET [17].

Table 1 shows the simulation conditions.

Table 1. Simulation Condition.

number of nodes	50
Network area	1,000m*600m
Radio area (radius)	200m
Packet size	512B
Frame rate	15frames/s
Mobility	none

This phase of EFNEX-R has the same procedure as EFNEX.

We assume that
-This procedure is initiated by a node;
- A message is transferred in a packet;
- The message is video-type for One-seg broadcasting;
- No mobility is considered;
- Information is assumed as several minute motion picture; and
- The number of generated packets is less than 10 thousand.

4.2 Evaluation items

Next two items are evaluated.

(1) Total number of packets transmitted and received (NT)

A packet is generated by the originator and it is penetrated in the network. It means that the packet is received by nodes within a radio area and re-broadcasted by those nodes in Simple Flooding case and by a selected node in EFNEX and EFNEX-R cases, and the procedure is repeated.

Here, Nsi is the number of packets sent by the node I, Nri is that received by node i.

Then,

$$\mathrm{NT} = \sum_i Nsi + Nri$$

In EFNEX and EFNEX-R, NT includes both initializing and transfer phases.

(2) Packet penetration rate (P)

First, for a packet whose ID is "i", the ratio of the number of nodes who receive the packet "i" to the total number of nodes in the network is calculated. Then, the ratio is averaged for all the generated packets, which is the penetration rate.

$$P = \frac{\sum_{i=1}^{M} \frac{r_i}{N}}{M}$$

where

M: total number of packets generated
N: total number of nodes
i: packet ID (i=1,2,…..,M)
r_i: number of node receiving the packet "i".

dithe neighbors' NLs and selects a specific node as a next broadcaster that has the biggest number of neighbors who are

4.3 Evaluation results

Fig.3 and Fig.4 shows the simulation results .

(1) Total number of packets transmitted and received (NT)

Fig.3 shows that EFNEX and EFNEX-R can reduce total number of packets sent and received drastically compared with Simple Flooding. The effect is 1/4 of Simple Flooding. EFNEX-R and EFNEX has no big difference but from the average value EFNEX-R can reduce about 7% of packets to EFNEX.

(2) Packet penetration rate (P)

FIg.4 shows that packet penetration rate of Simple Flooding is about 90% and ones of EFNEX and EFNEX-R are 65% and 70%, respectively. Here, EFNEX-R improves P by about 5% compared with EFNEX.

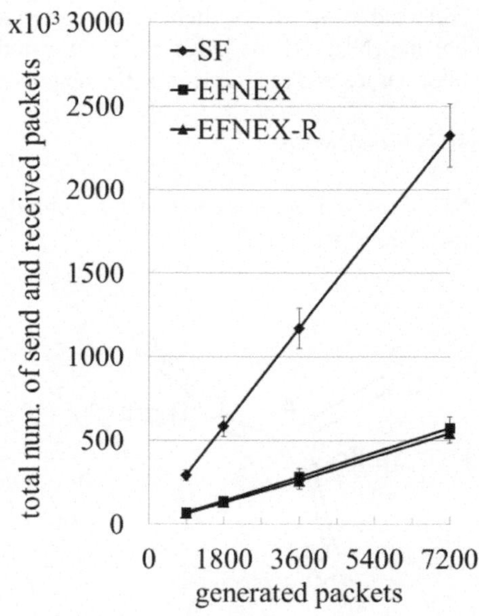

Fig.3 Total number of packets sent and received

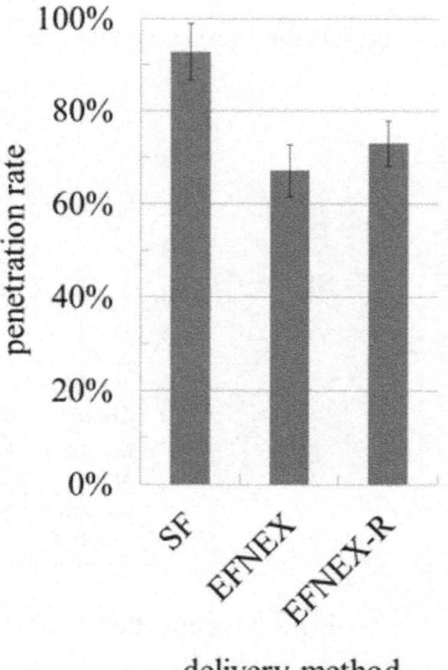

Fig.4 Packet penetration rate

5 Conclusion

This paper proposes EFNEX-R that aims at improvement of packet penetration rate of EFNEX. It evaluates the proposed procedure by use of network simulation.

As a result, proposed EFNEX-R realizes very small total number of sent and received packets (1/4) compared with Simple Flooding and also 7% less number than that of EFNEX.

EFNEX-R also improves packet penetration rate compared with EFNEX by 5%.

Further study is necessary for improvement of the procedure to achieve higher penetration rate and quantitative evaluation of processing load.

Acknowledgment

The ULP-DDNS project are partially supported by Core Research for Evolutional Science and Technology (CREST), Japan Science and Technology Agency.

Reference

[1] C. Siva Ram Murthy, B. S. Manoj : "Ad Hoc Wireless Networks – Architectures and Protocols", PRENTICE HALL, Professional Technical Reference (2004)

[2] T. Sato, K. Mase, K. Nakano, M. Sengoku, " Flooding Protocol for Mobile Ad Hoc Networks", IEICE Technical Report on Radio Communication Systems, RCS2001-21, CQ-2001-21, pp.31-38, (2001) [in Japanese]

[3] Jorjeta G. Jetcheva, David A. Malts, : "A Simple protocol for Multicast and Broadcast in Mobile Ad Hoc Networks," IETF MANET Working Group Internet-Draft, <draft-ietfmanet- simple-mbcast.txt>, (2001)

[4] Amir Qayyum, Laurent Viennot, Anis Laouiti, : "Multipoint Relaing for Flooding Broadcast Messages in Mobile Wireless Networks," Proceedings of the 35th Hawaii International Conference on System Sciences, IEEE Computer Society, (2002)

[5] Brad Williams, Tracy Camp, : "Comparison of Broadcasting Technics for Mobile Ad Hoc Networks," Proceedings of the 3rd ACM International Symposium on Mobile Ad HocNetworking and Computing, pp.194-205, (2002)

[6] YU-CHEE TSENG, SZE-YAO NI, YUH-SHYAN CHEN, JANG-PINIG-SHEU, : "The Broadcast Problem in a Mobile Ad Hoc Network," Wireless Networks Volume 8, Springer, pp.153-167, Kluwer Academic Publishers, (2002)

[7] Yu-Chee Tseng, Sze-Yao Ni, En-Yu Shih, : "Adaptive Approaches to Relieving Broadcast Storm in a Wireless Multihop Mobile Ad Hoc Network," IEEE Transactions on Computers, Vol. 52, No. 5, pp. 545-556, (2003)

[8] Abdalla M. Hanashi, Aamir Siddique, Irfan Awan, Mike Woodward,: "Performance evaluation of dynamic probabilistic broadcasting for flooding in mobile ad hoc networks," Simuation Moddeling Practice and Theory 17, pp. 364-375, Elsevier, (2009)

[9] Yu-Chee Tseng, Sze-Yao Ni, En-Yu Shih, : "Adaptive Approaches to Relieving Broadcast Storm in a Wireless Multihop Mobile Ad Hoc Network," IECE Transactions on Computers, Vol. 52, No. 5, pp. 545-556, (2003)

[10] M. Noto, J. Arikawa, M. Matsuda, "Low-Power Flooding Method in Ad-Hoc Networks", IEICE Trans. on Information and Systems, J91-D(5), 1252-1260, (2008)

[11] D. Kasamatsu, N. Shinomiya, T. Ohta, " A Broadcasting Method Considering Battery Lifetime and Distance between Nodes in MANET", IEICE Transaction on Communication, J91-B(4), 364-372, (2008)

[12] K. Utsu, H. Ishii, "Load-aware Flooding for Streaming over Ad Hoc Networks", The transactions of the Institute of Electrical Engineers of Japan. C, A publication of Electronics, Information and System Society 130(8), 1367-1378, (2010)

[13] Keisuke Utsu, Hiroaki Nishikawa, Hiroshi Ishii, : "Load-aware Flooding over Ad Hoc Networks achieving a Reduction in Traffic and Power Consumption," the 2010 International Conference on Parallel and Distributed Processing Techniques and Applications (PDPTA'10), Las Vegas, USA, Jul. (2010)

[14] K. Utsu, H. Ishii, " Load and Battery Charge oriented Flooding for Broadcast Streaming over Ad Hoc Networks", The transactions of the Institute of Electrical Engineers of Japan. C, A publication of Electronics, Information and System Society 132(5), 640-648, (2012)

[15] Turganzhan Kassymov, Keisuke Utsu, Hiroshi Sano, Naoki Morita, Hiroshi Ishii, "Effective Flooding based on neighbor list exchange over Ad Hoc Networks, 2011 IEICE Society Conference, B-7-65, (2011)

[16] Naoya Imaizumi, Keisuke Utsu, Hiroaki Nishikawa, Hiroshi Ishii, "Effective Flooding Over Ad Hoc Network Based on Neighbor Information Exchange", APSITT '12

[17] The network simulator "OPNET," http://www.opnet.com

Video Streaming Performance of Load and Battery Charge Oriented Flooding over Disaster Tolerant Ad Hoc Network

Keisuke UTSU[1], Hiroaki NISHIKAWA[2], and Hiroshi ISHII[1]
[1]Department of Communication and Network Engineering,
School of Information and Telecommunication Engineering, Tokai University, Minato, Tokyo, Japan
[2]Department of Computer Science, Graduate School of Systems and Information Engineering,
University of Tsukuba, Tsukuba, Ibaraki, Japan

Abstract – *Large-scale disasters often disable existing communication infrastructures. At the times of the disasters, one can assume reporting of damage conditions or evacuation instructions by real-time streaming of video and audio from designated nodes throughout the network. To achieve this, we have proposed Load and Battery Charge oriented Flooding (LBF). In this study, the video streaming performance for the method is evaluated through network simulations. The simulation result concludes that the method can prolong the running time for nodes without degradations of delivery quality.*

Keywords: Broadcast, Streaming, Ad hoc communication

1 Introduction

Large-scale disasters often disable existing communications infrastructures or render stable power supply to communications terminals or base stations difficult. At the time of a disaster, one can assume reporting of damage conditions or evacuation instructions by real-time streaming of video and audio from designated nodes throughout the network.

Ad hoc networks are being studied as being resilient in a disaster situation [1]. Most previous research on ad hoc networks has dealt with client-server streaming by unicast or multicast. In particular, many studies dealt with video streaming. However, communications using the current unicast routing protocols are not suitable for delivery throughout a network composed of many nodes. In addition, IP addresses must be assigned appropriately to all nodes prior to communications, which is not necessarily possible at the time of a disaster.

One may consider flooding to broadcast information without using routing protocols. However, when existing simple flooding algorithms are used to deliver packets generated at a high rate, as in the case of video and audio streaming, redundant rebroadcasts frequently occur, thus causing data frame collisions and buffer overflows, which strongly degrades communication quality. Therefore, improvement of packet reachability must be considered. There have also been attempts to modify simple flooding so as to reduce redundant rebroadcasts [2-5].

It is also difficult to assure a steady power supply to communication terminals and base stations at the time of a disaster. In case of ad hoc networks, control by base stations is not used, but communication terminals are powered by batteries with limited life. Thus, when delivering packets generated at a high rate, as in the case of video and audio streaming, batteries are discharged quickly, which may lead to node failures because of battery depletion and to deterioration of the communication performance of the entire network. Therefore, depletion of node batteries must be limited and power consumption must be reduced as much as possible by elimination of redundant communications. In addition, node failures caused by low battery levels must be prevented.

From the above we may conclude that in broadcast streaming of video and audio, packet reachability must be improved, and deterioration must be suppressed. In addition one should consider efficient use of remaining battery charge by lower power consumption at network nodes, and prevention of failures caused by battery depletion. However, we are not aware of any existing research aimed at meeting all these requirements.

To tackle with the above mentioned issues, we have proposed a broadcast streaming method named *Load and Battery charge oriented Flooding (LBF)* [6], which is a part of our research *the Infrastructure-less Broadcast-based Information Delivery Architecture*, as shown in Fig.1. This paper evaluates the video performance of the proposed method through network simulations, and compares it to existing methods. Below we overview existing methods and their problems in Section 2. Then we present the proposed method in Section 3 and demonstrate its efficiency through network simulations in Section 4. We give a summary of the study in Section 5.

2 Existing methods and their problems

As mentioned in Section 1, simple flooding is used as a scheme for broadcast information dissemination. In this scheme, on receiving a packet, a node rebroadcasts the packet

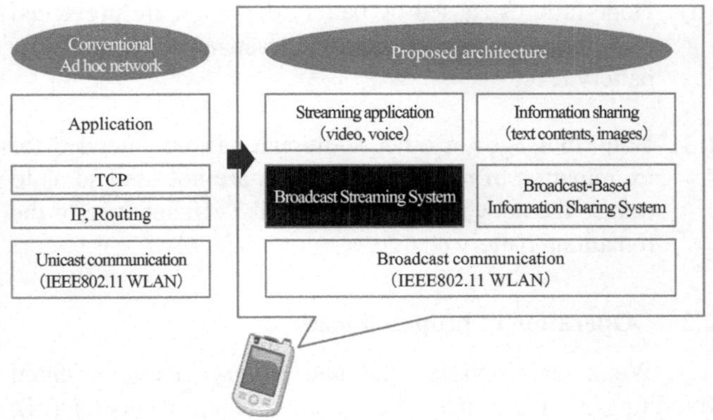

Fig.1 Infrastructure-less Broadcast-based information delivery Architecture

if it was never received before (non-identical packets). Packets that were received earlier (identical packets) are rejected. Every packet contains the ID of the generating node and the packet sequence number; the combination of these parameters provides unique identification. In this scheme, any non-identical packet is rebroadcast, which causes redundant rebroadcasts. Thus, a number of methods have been proposed to reduce redundant rebroadcasts [3-5]. Typical examples are described below.

2.1 Assumed network environment and requirements

The counter-based scheme is a well-known modification of simple flooding for broadcast information delivery not dependent on GPS (Global Positioning System) or other particular devices. In this method, performance or non-performance of rebroadcasting is determined by how many times an identical packet has been received. The basic procedure is explained below.

1. On receiving a packet, a node sets its counter at 1 if the packet is non-identical. Identical packets are rejected.

2. The counter value is incremented by 1 if an identical packet has been received during an arbitrary period of time (*decision_time*).

3. If the counter reaches a threshold value (*c_threshold*) after expiration of *decision_time*, rebroadcasting is canceled.

In this scheme, the setting of *c_threshold* affects performance [4]. If *c_threshold* is small (e.g., 2) in a network with low node density (sparse network), rebroadcasting is strongly suppressed but packet reachability declines. On the other hand, the setting of *c_threshold* has no major effect on packet reachability in networks with high node density (dense networks). *c_threshold* should be set at 3 to 4; with settings of 6 or more, redundant rebroadcasts cannot be reduced and the network behaves in the same way as with simple flooding [5].

An adaptive counter-based scheme has been proposed to set *c_threshold* dynamically [5]. Specifically, every node sends Hello messages periodically, and nodes receiving these messages can recognize the number of neighboring nodes. Based on this information, rebroadcasting is performed or not performed.

In the two schemes described above, redundant rebroadcasts of identical packets are eliminated, thus preventing collisions and improving packet reachability. However, the node load is not taken into account. As a result, avoidance of collisions and buffer overflows cannot be guaranteed when packets are generated at a high rate, as in the case of video and audio. In addition, the remaining battery charge is ignored. Hence there is a high probability that rebroadcasting will not be suppressed at nodes with depleted batteries, and that such nodes will shut down.

2.2 Assumed network environment and requirements

Some methods taking account of the node battery level have been proposed [7], [8]. Koide et al. [7] proposed a flooding scheme implemented on a routing protocol; in particular, the delay time is set according to the remaining battery charge, and duplicate packets received within this time are rejected. In addition, in a method proposed by Kasamatsu et al. [8], the delay time is set according to the node distance acquired by GPS and the remaining battery charge, and duplicate packets received within this time are rejected. As a result, nodes with low battery level are less likely to be chosen for rebroadcasting.

The former method [7] is intended for transmission of routing protocol messages, and delivery of packets generated at a high rate such as video or audio is not assumed and not evaluated. The latter method [8] assumes that nodes are GPS-enabled so that information on the nodes' position and distance is available. However, considering response to disasters, accurate information is not necessarily available via GPS. Thus, these two methods are obviously unsuitable under the circumstances described in Section 1.

3 Proposed method

3.1 Assumed network environment and requirements

In this study we assume unidirectional live streaming. In addition, we assume that a network is composed of portable communication terminals not provided with GPS or other special instruments, and that communications can be implemented by an IEEE 802.11 wireless LAN. Best-effort communication without QoS (Quality of Service) control is provided.

Below we consider a method to meet the following requirements (i) to (iii) in the presence of the circumstances described in Section 1.

Variables and parameters

```
○Variable: Integer queue
// The num. of packets at the MAC transmission queue.
○Variable: Real remain_battery
// The remaining battery level at the node.
○Variable: Real max_battery
// The maximum battery level at the node.
○Variable: Integer c_threshold
// The threshold value of the counter.
○Variable: Integer max_c_threshold
// The maximum value of c_threshold
○Variable: Integer counter
// The number of times that the same packet has been received.
○Parameter: Integer get_interval
// The time interval for getting the num. of packets at the MAC
transmission queue and the remaining battery level.
○Procedure: getQueue()
// The function to get the num. of packets at the MAC transmission queue.
○Procedure: getBattery()
// The function to get the remaining battery level.
```

(a) The method of getting data on the remaining battery level
Executed at certain intervals (*get_interval*)

```
queue ← getQueue()
if (queue > 0)
  then   (b) is not executed (all re-broadcast is canceled)
  else   remain_battery ← getBattery()
         c_threshold
           ← ceil(max_c_threshold*(remain_battery /max_battery)).
end if
End.
```

(b) The receiving and rebroadcast procedure

```
Receiving a packet.
if (The same packet as one that the node has already received)
  then  END.
  else  counter ← 1.
        decision_time ← Random() * 2^(max_c_threshold - c_threshold).
        while (decision_time)
                  if (Receiving the same packet again)
                    then   counter++.
                  end if
        end while
        if (counter >= c_threshold)
          then     Rebroadcast is cancelled.
          else     Rebroadcast the packet.
        end if
end if
End.
```

Fig.2 The operation of a node for LBF

(i) In case of delivery of packets generated at a high rate such as video or audio, deterioration of communication quality caused by collisions and other troubles is limited and power consumption is reduced by suppression of superfluous packet transmission.

(ii) Node failures caused by battery depletion are prevented by active suppression of rebroadcasts at nodes with low battery level

(iii) Hello messages or other additional packets intended for examination of network conditions are not used so as to reduce the network load and to make efficient use of the remaining battery charge.

3.2 Operation of proposed method

We have proposed load and battery charge oriented flooding (LBF) as a method of meeting requirements (i)–(iii). As regards (i), the conventional counter-based scheme eliminating redundancy of identical packets by means of a counter is supplemented consideration of node load. Specifically, when there are packets in the MAC transmission queue, the node load is considered heavy and rebroadcasting is canceled. As regards (ii), each node checks its battery level periodically and sets the counter threshold (*c_threshold*) accordingly. Specifically, *c_threshold* is set small at nodes with a low battery level to suppress rebroadcasting. As regards (iii), communications can be performed without using Hello messages.

Below we explain the proposed method in detail. A pseudo-language description is given in Fig. 2. First, the maximum counter threshold (*max_c_threshold*) and range of definition of the random value function (Random()) are assumed to be preset by the user. The procedure shown in Fig. 2(a) is applied to every node at a certain interval (*get_interval*). If there are packets in the MAC transmission queue, packets are not rebroadcast when received (that is, the procedure in Fig. 2(b) is not executed). On the other hand, if there are no packets in the MAC transmission queue, the remaining battery charge is examined and is substituted into the variable *remain_battery*. Then *c_threshold* is determined as follows:

$$c\_threshold = \mathbf{ceil}\,(max\_c\_threshold *(remain\_battery\,/\,max\_battery)) \quad (1)$$

Here **ceil** (real x) returns the real-valued variable x rounded up to the nearest integer. As indicated by Eq. (1), *c_threshold* is set smaller for nodes with lower remaining battery charge, thus suppressing rebroadcasting. This aims at preferential suppression of rebroadcasting at nodes with low battery level.

Then the procedure in Fig. 2(b) is performed when a message is received from a generating node (initiator node). Specifically, the following operations are executed.

1. If a node receives a non-identical packet, the counter is set to 1. Identical packets are rejected.

2. The wait time until decision whether to rebroadcast (*decision_time*) is chosen as follows:

Table 1 Parameters for each delivery method

	c_threshold	*max_c_threshold*
SF	-	-
C4	4 (fixed)	-
C3	3 (fixed)	-
C2	2 (fixed)	-
LB4	Determined by Eq.(1)	4
LB3	Determined by Eq.(1)	3
LB2	Determined by Eq.(1)	2
LB4 w. MDC	Determined by Eq.(1)	4
LB3 w. MDC	Determined by Eq.(1)	3
LB2 w. MDC	Determined by Eq.(1)	2

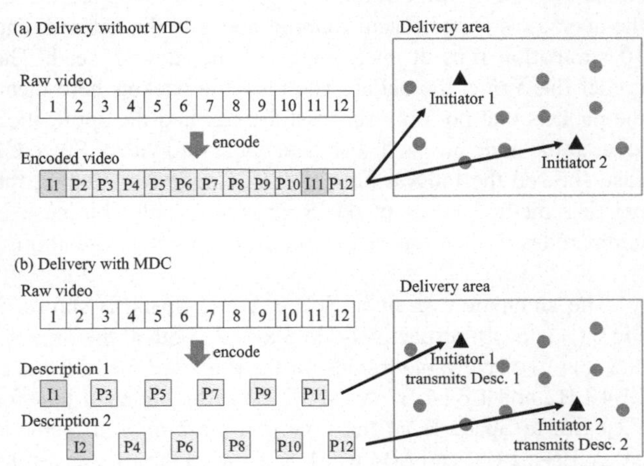

Fig.3 Delivery without/with MDC

$$decision\_time = \text{Random}() * 2^{(max\_c\_threshold\ -\ c\_threshold)} \quad (2)$$

As can be seen from Eq. (2), the lower the remaining battery charge, the longer the wait time is set. Like Eq. (1), this produces preferential suppression of rebroadcasting at nodes with low battery level.

3. If the same packet is received again during *decision_time*, then the counter is incremented by 1.

4. After the expiration of *decision_time*, rebroadcast is canceled if the counter value exceeds *c_threshold*. Otherwise, the packet is rebroadcast.

4 Evaluation by simulations

Our previous researches have shown the performance of the proposed method [6][9]. They reported that the proposed method can prolong the node running time in the video and the voice streaming without degradation of the packet level delivery performance. The objectives of the evaluation in this section is to evaluate the video frame level delivery performance in the video streams, node running time, and to consider the application of Multiple Description Coding (MDC). In the evaluation, we compare the node running time and delivery quality for the proposed method LBF and the conventional scheme by using the OPNET network simulator [9].

4.1 Simulation assumptions

The simulation conditions are described below. We assume a network with 100 nodes, a IEEE802.11b node MAC layer, and a data rate of 2 Mbps. The transmitted power is 0.005 W, and the received power threshold is -85 dBm. The initial positions of the nodes are assumed to be random. All nodes move at a speed of [0.00, 4.00] according to the random waypoint model. This model is based on the human walking and running speed. Two simulation areas are defined: 1000m×600m (space A) and 2000m×1200m (space B). Dense and sparse networks are considered in each case. The number of initiator nodes was 2.

A node's remaining battery charge is modeled as follows. The maximum battery capacity (*max_battery*) is 500 W-s. At the initial stage of simulation, the remaining battery charge is set to 500 W-s (100%) for initiator nodes and to [100, 400] W*s (20%-80%) for other nodes. With reference to the study of Feeney et al. [10], the transmitting power *tp* [μW*s] and receiving power *rp* [μW*s] per packet are assumed as follows:

$$tp = 2.000 * frame\ length\ [\text{byte}] + 270 \quad (3)$$
$$rp = 0.500 * frame\ length\ [\text{byte}] + 60 \quad (4)$$

In this evaluation we assume that the energy consumption at every node is described by the above equations. However, power consumption during non-communication periods is ignored. A node shuts down when its remaining battery charge drops to 0.

The values obtained by Random () are set to [0, 33] ms at every node with reference to the packet generation rate. We consider nodes receiving messages from initiator nodes to compare conventional simple flooding (SF), the fixed *c_threshold* scheme (corresponds to counter-based scheme), and the proposed LBF scheme. As shown in Table 1, three thresholds C4–C2 are set for fixed *c_threshold* scheme; and three values *max_c_threshold* LB4–LB2 are set for the proposed scheme LBF. These settings govern rebroadcasting. The threshold settings were selected with reference to the previous study [5] suggesting that the values should be from 3 to 4. The battery level check interval (*get_interval*) is set to 1 s.

4.2 Application of MDC

The evaluation also examines the cases of the proposed method LBF using MDC. The details of MDC are explained in [13]. MDC in the existing studies aim to improve the packet reachability using multiple path transmission. On the other hand, the main purpose of MDC application in this study is to reduce number of transmitted and received packets

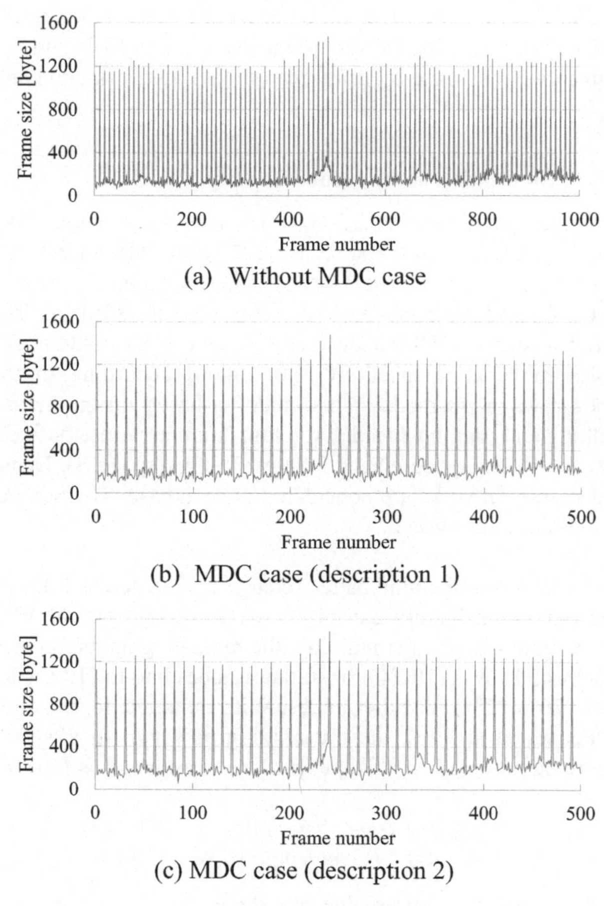

(a) Without MDC case

(b) MDC case (description 1)

(c) MDC case (description 2)

Fig.4 Packet size distribution

in the network, as shown in Fig.3 (b). In the simulation, the delivery parameters for MDC applied cases were described as LB4-LB2 w. MDC in Table 2.

4.3 Video configurations

Suppose that there are 2 initiator nodes, and the initiator nodes are streaming video using the H.264 codec [11]. 1000 frames of QCIF (Quarter Common Intermediate Format) highway [12] are encoded using jml4.2 [11]. We assume a frame rate of 30 fps (that is, a packet generation rate of 33 ms). The frames are composed of I frames and P frames, and the GoP (Group of Pictures) is set to 10. These 1000 frames are generated repeatedly. The frame size distribution was shown in Fig. 4.

4.4 Evaluation of node running time

Evaluation is performed by the time at 5% of nodes stop in the network; the average was found for 10 simulation runs at every value of the random seed. The larger this value, the better.

The simulation result in Space A and Space B shows in Fig.5 (i) and (ii), respectively. In the both spaces A and B, the proposed method cases show the longer time than the existing method cases. This means that the proposed method can reduce the energy consumption at the node and prolong the node running time. In addition, in the proposed method with MDC cases show the longer time than the case without MDC cases. This means that MDC application can prolong the node running time.

4.5 Evaluation of delivery performance

Evaluation is performed by the percentage of playable packets at the time when (b) the initial period of the video streaming and the time when (c) 5% of nodes stopped in C2; the average is found for all running nodes in the network and 10 simulation runs at every value of the random seed. The higher this value, the better. The playable packets here mean the packets that not only successfully reached the application layer at the node but were also decodable into video. Since C2 case showed the longest time at 5% of node stop among the existing method cases in the Section 4.4, only this case is compared with the proposed method cases in this evaluation.

The simulation result in Space A and Space B shows in Fig.6 (i) and (ii), respectively. In Space A, both at the time (b) and (c) , % of viewable frames for the proposed method cases, LB4-LB2 and LB4-LB2 w. MDC, were higher than that for C2 case. In Space B, at the time (b), the proposed methods cases, LB4, LB3, and LB4 w. MDC showed the similar results to the C2 case. Among the proposed method cases, the % for with MDC cases showed the lower % than that for without MDC cases. This means that MDC may not contribute to maintain the delivery performance in the sparsely distributed network.

5 Conclusions

This paper has considered the infrastructure-less broadcast streaming methods which can achieve to maintain delivery quality and long node running time. For this purpose, we have already proposed Load and Battery Charge Oriented Flooding (LBF). In this paper, the performance of the proposed methods has been evaluated through the network simulations.

The time at 5% of node stop in the network was evaluated in Section 4.4. The evaluation result showed that the proposed method LBF can reduce the energy at the node and prolong the node running time. In addition, in the proposed method cases, the cases with MDC show the longer time than the case without MDC cases. The results concluded that MDC application can prolong the node running time.

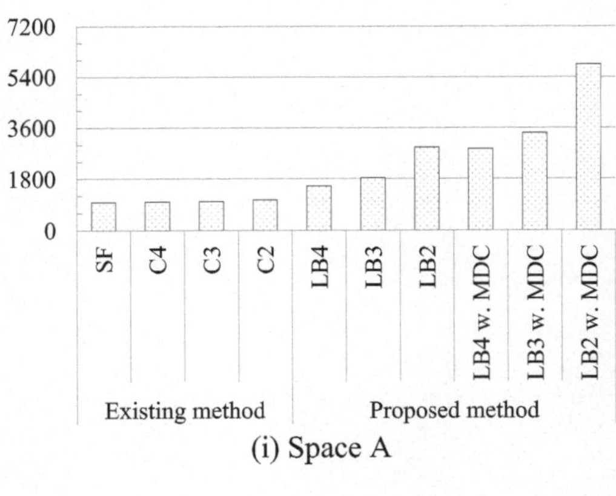

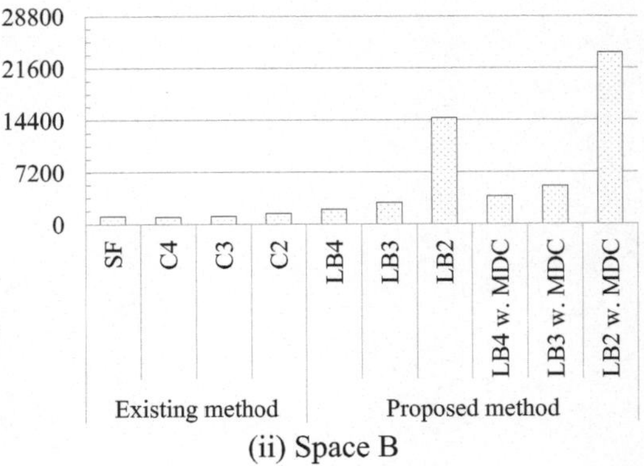

Fig.5 time at 5% of nodes stop, simulation result

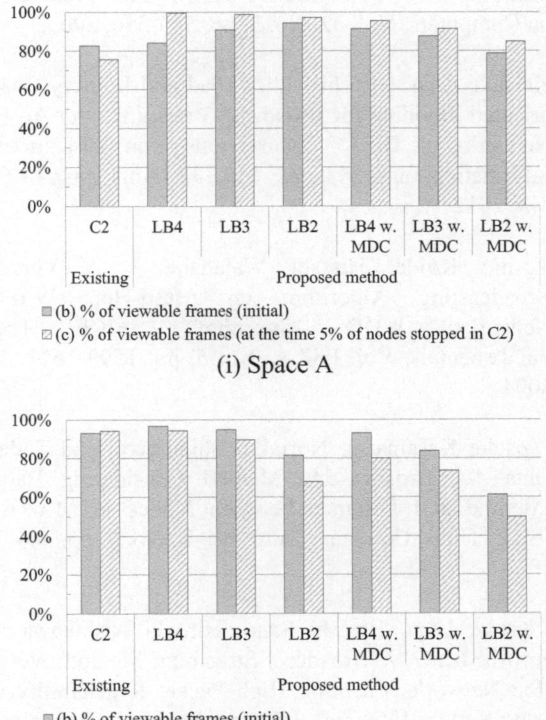

Fig.6 average % of playable frames, simulation result

The percentage of playable packets at the time when 5% of nodes stopped for C2 case was evaluated in Section 4.5. The evaluation result showed that the proposed method cases showed the better delivery quality than C2 case both at the time when the initial period of the video streaming. In the sparsely distributed network, the some cases of the proposed method (LB4, LB3, and LB4 w. MDC) shows the similar results to C2 case. On the other hand, in the sparsely distributed network, the other cases of the proposed methods showed the worse delivery performance than C2 case.

Considering both node running time and delivery quality, the better parameter choices of the proposed method were LB4, LB3, and LB4 w. MDC. From the above results, we can conclude that the proposed method can prolong the network running time without degradation of delivery quality with the above parameters. The future issue is to improve the delivery performance for the proposed method in the sparsely distributed network.

6 Acknowledgments

This research has been supported by The Nakajima Foundation, Japan.

7 References

[1] C. Siva Ram Murthy and B. S. Manoj, "Ad Hoc Wireless Networks - Architectures and Protocols," Prentice Hall, Professional Technical Reference

[2] Jorjeta G. Jetcheva, David A. Malts, "A Simple protocol for Multicast and Broadcast in Mobile Ad Hoc Networks", IETF MANET Working Group Internet-Draft, <draft-ietf-manet-simple-mbcast. txt>, 2001

[3] Brad Williams, Tracy Camp, "Comparison of Broadcasting Techniques for Mobile Ad Hoc Networks", Proceedings of the 3rd ACM International Symposium on Mobile Ad Hoc Networking and Computing, pp. 194-205, 2002

[4] Yu-Chee Tseng, Sze-Yao Ni, Yuh-Shyan Chen, Jang-Pinig-Sheu, "The Broadcast Problem in a Mobile Ad Hoc Network", Wireless Networks Volume 8, Springer, pp. 153-167, Kluwer Academic Publishers, 2002

[5] Yu-Chee Tseng, Sze-Yao Ni, En-Yu Shih, "Adaptive Approaches to Relieving Broadcast Storm in a Wireless

Multihop Mobile Ad Hoc Network", IEEE Transactions on Computers, Vol. 52, No. 5, pp. 545-556, 2003.

[6] Keisuke Utsu, Hiroshi Ishii, "Load and Batttery Charge oriented Flooding for Broadcast Streaming over Ad Hoc Networks", IEEJ Transactions on Electronics, Informations and Systems, Vol.132, No.5, pp.640-648, Mar 2012

[7] Toshio Koide, Hitoshi Watanabe, "A Versatile Broadcasting Algorithm on Multi-Hop Wireless Networks: WDD Algorithm", IEICE Trans. Fundamentals, Vol. E87-A, No. 6, pp. 1599-1611, Jun. 2004

[8] Daisuke Kasamatsu, Norihiko Shinomiya, and Tadashi Ohta, "A Broadcasting Method Considering Battery Lifetime and Distance between Nodes in MANET", IEICE Trans. Commun. , Vol. J91-B, No. 4, pp. 364-372, 2008

[9] Keisuke Utsu, Hiroshi Sano, Hiroaki Nishikawa and Hiroshi Ishii, "A Broadcast Streaming Method over Ad Hoc Networks Enabling High Packet Reachability and Long Battery Lifetime", 9th Asia-Pacific Symposium on Information and Telecommunication Technologies (APSITT2012), Nov. 2012

[10] The network simulator "OPNET", http://www.opnet.com

[11] Feeney L. M., Nilsson M., "Investigating the Energy Consumption of a Wireless Network Interface in an Ad Hoc Networking Environment", INFOCOM 2001, Twentieth Annual Joint Conference of the IEEE Computer and Communications Societies, Vol. 3, pp. 1548-1557, IEEE, 2001

[12] H. 264/AVC Reference Software (jm14. 2), http://iphome. hhi. de/suehring/tml/download/old_jm/

[13] Patrick Seeling, Frank H. P. Firzek and Martin Reosslein, "Video Traces for Network Performance Evaluation," Springer, 2007

A Proposal on Broadcast based Information Sharing System over Disaster and Congestion Tolerant Ad Hoc Network

Keisuke UTSU[1], Hiroaki NISHIKAWA[2], and Hiroshi ISHII[1]
[1]Department of Communication and Network Engineering,
School of Information and Telecommunication Engineering, Tokai University, Minato, Tokyo, Japan
[2]Department of Computer Science, Graduate School of Systems and Information Engineering,
University of Tsukuba, Tsukuba, Ibaraki, Japan

Abstract – *In a disaster situation, since existing communication infrastructure will be unavailable, it is difficult to share information such as text, image, and audio data with neighboring mobile communication devices. To enable information sharing without using existing communication infrastructure in communication infrastructure unavailable areas, we propose a novel method Broadcast-Based Information Sharing System (BBISS) in this paper. In addition, the paper shows the preliminary performance evaluation of the proposed method.*

Keywords: information sharing, broadcast, ad hoc communication

1 Introduction

Owing to the growth in the number of smart phones and tablet PCs, our lives depend on the information stronger than before. On the other hand, large-scale disasters often happen and disable existing telephone networks and mobile networks for many hours. Such disasters cause not only physical destruction of communication infrastructures but also serious traffic congestions. Since many people wish to access the existing network, the traffic congestions become more and more serious. Once the situation happens, our mobile communication devices do not work as usual. Although communication techniques in the infrastructure unavailable situations has been required and studied for a long time, no major techniques exist today.

An example of assumed applications in the infrastructure unavailable situations is shown in Fig.1. In the infrastructure unavailable area, people with wireless communication devices collect disaster information and broadcast evacuation instructions. In addition, cars and emergency vehicles with the wireless communication devices will disseminate information which is collected at the infrastructure available area to the unavailable area. The application will enable to collaborate with the Internet, social media, and mass media. Therefore, it will contribute to the information collection and dissemination by polices, fire-fighting, and local governments.

This paper is concerned with the realization of the above application. In fact, existing ad hoc network architecture [1], cannot be applied in the infrastructure unavailable situations because IP addresses and servers are not available. To realize the application, we propose a novel method, Broadcast-Based Information Sharing System (BBISS), a part of our research *Infrastructure-less Broadcast Information Delivery Architecture*. In this paper, the preliminary performance evaluation of the proposed method is demonstrated through network simulation to show the effectiveness of the method.

Below Section 2 introduces related works of the ad hoc network which has been expected to apply as a networking technique in the infrastructure unavailable situations. Section 3 describes a detailed methodology of the proposed method BBISS. Section 4 shows the preliminary performance evaluation of the proposed method through the network simulation. Lastly, Section 5 concludes this paper.

2 Existing studies and their problems

The existing ad hoc network architecture has been studied as the networking technique in the infrastructure unavailable situations, and many routing protocols have been proposed. In general, available IP addresses must be assigned at nodes in the network to communicate using routing protocols. However, the IP addresses cannot be available in the infrastructure unavailable situations owing to the large-scale disaster. Moreover, some servers must be required to collect and disseminate the information to adopt the existing client-server applications. Considering the above problems, the existing ad hoc network architecture cannot be applied to the applications discussed in the Section 1.

Related studies of the ad hoc network architecture are introduced below. Epidemic routing has been proposed in [2]. In this method, a contents holder copies the contents to its neighboring nodes. Although the methods have been proposed to deliver the information to the destination node, method cannot be applied to disseminate the information to whole the area.

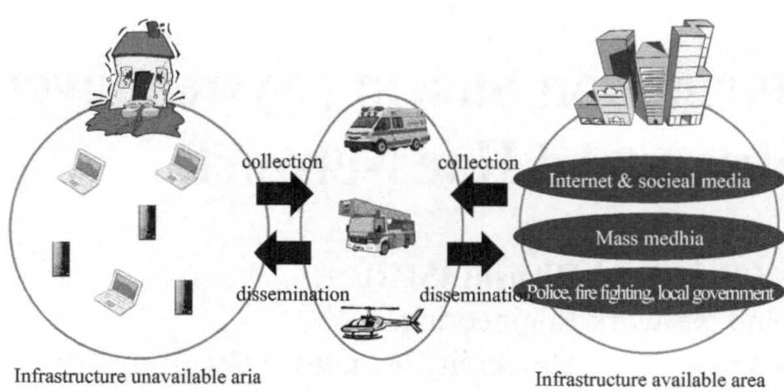

Fig.1 An assumed application

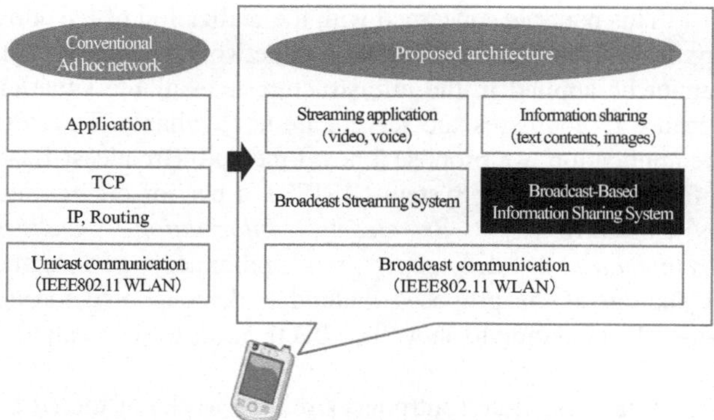

Fig.2 Infrastructure-less broadcast-based information delivery architecture

The Simple Flooding (SF) has been implemented in ad hoc network routing protocols to deliver routing messages in the broadcasting manner [3]. Although, Simple Flooding is one solution to disseminate the information to the whole network, it has problems below. In this method, when a node receives a packet, the packet is re-broadcast if the packet was never received before (non-identical packet). Therefore, many nodes re-broadcast the packet in the network, and data frame collisions are occur, the packet reachability is degraded. Probabilistic scheme and Counter-based scheme has been proposed as the methods without HELLO packet exchanges and dedicated devices such as GPS (Global Positioning System) [4][5]. Since the above methods do not assume to deliver the information consisting of multiple packets such as data files, they do not consider the communication reliability. In other words, the packet reachability is not assured in the methods.

Considering the above, the proposed method in this paper, BBISS, is in the area where has not been studied yet.

3 Proposed method

3.1 Assumed environment

This paper assumes the following environment. The large-scale disaster happens, and public telephone networks and mobile networks are unavailable. Although users in the disaster area have mobile phones and tablet PCs, the devices cannot be assigned available IP addresses and cannot obtain gateway information. At the time, the devices support the broadcast communication by the IEEE802.11 wireless LAN on ad hoc mode. Therefore, this paper studies the information sharing system by the broadcast communication. The information sharing system assumes to deliver text data (several kBytes – hundreds kBytes) and image data (hundreds kBytes). Developments of dedicated applications and implementations to the devices are our future issues to be tackled.

3.2 Requirements and solutions

The requirements of the proposed method are as follows.

(Requirement #1) The IP addresses and the routing protocols are not needed:

Since IP addresses and gateway information are not available, and it is difficult to develop servers to configure that information. Therefore, the proposed method uses only broadcast transmission without routing protocol.

(Requirement #2) TCP and unicast transmission are not used to assure the reliability:

To deliver the information consisting of the multiple packets, the packet reachability must be assured. In general, in the Internet and LAN (Local Area Network), the communication reliability is assured by TCP. However, in the ad hoc communication environment, the communication using TCP cause many retransmission requests and its reply, then many packets are lost due to collisions.

To assure the information reachability (i.e. reliability), the proposed method does not use the transmission using TCP and does not require retransmission request and its reply by the unicast transmission, but assures the reachability using only the broadcast transmission.

(Requirement #3) The energy consumption of node should be reduced.

Since the users' communication devices are usually battery driven, it is quite difficult to assure the stable power supply for many hours. Therefore, the power consumption at the nodes should be reduced as much as possible.

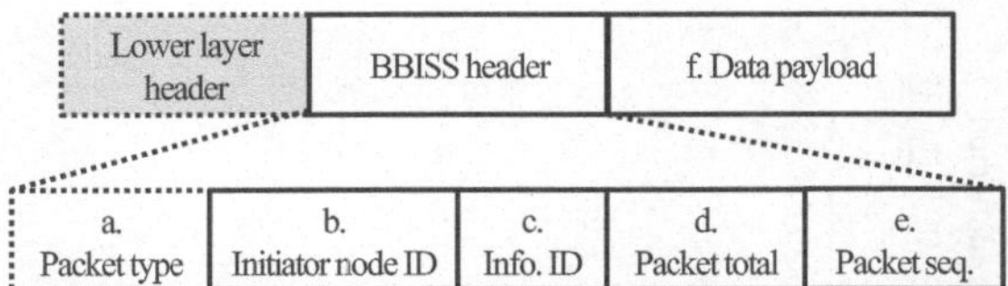

a.Normal packet and Retransmission packet

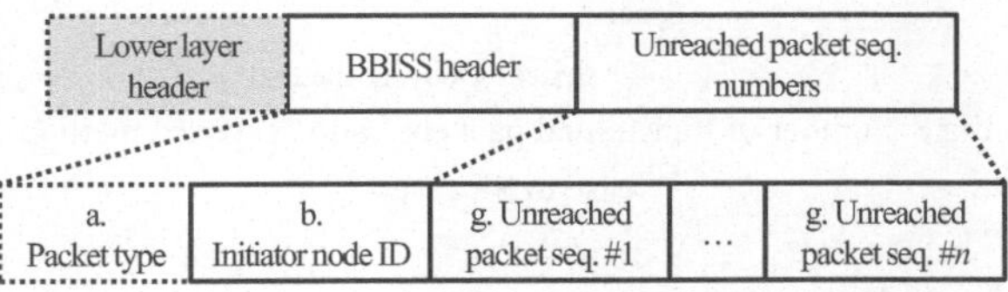

b. Retransmission request packet

Fig.3 packet format

To reduce the power consumption, the proposed method reduces redundant relay transmission in the proposed method.

3.3 Design of the proposed method

3.3.1 Packet format

Three types of packet formats: Normal packet, Retransmission packet, Retransmission request packet are defined in this method as shown in Fig.3. The roles of the each field are explained below:

a. Packet type: The packet type (Normal pakcet, Retransmission packet, Retransmission request packet) is recognized by this field.

b. Initiator node ID: The ID of the information initiator is recognized by this field.

c. Information ID: The field shows the ID of the information.

d. Packet Total: The number of packets that consists of the information is recognized by the field.

e. Packet sequence number: The sequence number of the packet in the information is recognized by the field

f. Data: Divided data is contained in the field. The size of the field is determined by the parameter *payload_size*.

In addition, Retransmission request packets contain the following.

g. Unreached packet sequence numbers: If the node receives information but it has any unreached packets,

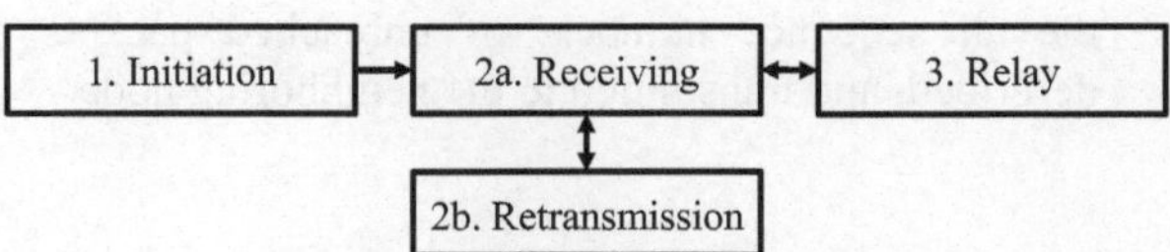

Fig.4 Processes of the proposed method

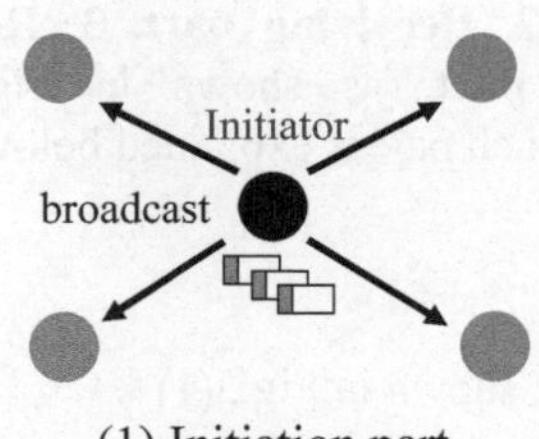

(1) Initiation part

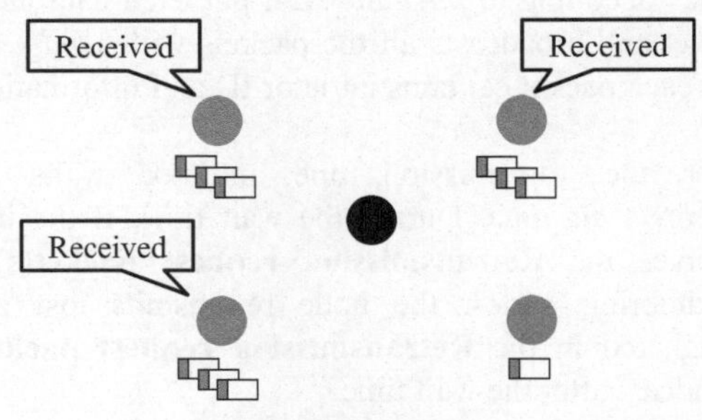

(2a) Receiving part

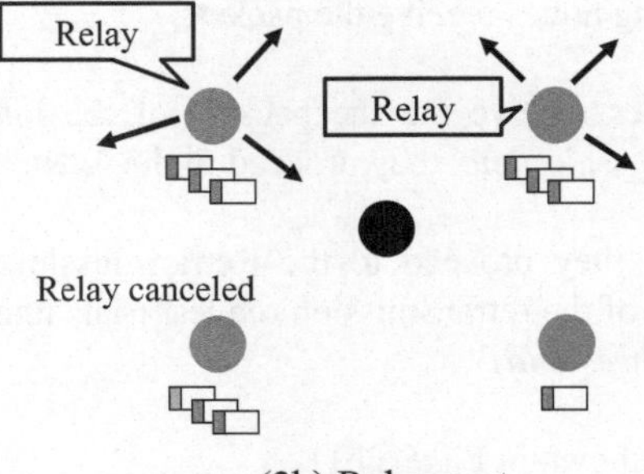

(2b) Relay part

(3) Retransmission part

Fig.5 Outline of the proposed method

the all sequence numbers of unreached packets are described, and transmitted to the neighboring node.

3.3.2 Operation of the proposed method

This subsection explains the operation of the proposed method. The proposed method consists of 4 parts: 1. **Initiation part**, 2. **Receiving part**, 3. **Relay part**, and 4. **Retransmission part**, as shown in Fig.4. The detailed procedure in the each part is explained below.

1. **Initiation part:** shown in Fig.5(1)

1.1. The initiator node divides an information into several "data" accoding to *payload_size*, put each data into each packet and broadcasts all the packets with *send_interval*. The each packet contains initiator ID and Information ID.

1.2. After the transmission, the initiator waits during *retrans_wait_time*. During the wait time, if the initiator receives the **Retransmission request packet**(s) from neighboring nodes, the node retransmits lost packets designated in the **Retransmission request packet**(s)by broadcast after the wait time

2. **Receiving part:** shown in Fig.5(2a)

2.1. Neighboring nodes receive the packets.

2.2. If the nodes receive the the packets of the information during *req_wait_time*, they proceed to the 3. **Relay part.**

2.3. Otherwise, they proceed to the Retransmission process. (The num. of the retransmission request trials must be less than *req_threshold*)

3. **Relay part:** shown in Fig.5(2b)

3.1. The nodes wait during *relay_wait_time*.

3.2. During this wait time, the nodes count the num. of the relaying nodes.

3.3. After the wait time, If the num. of relaying nodes is less than relay_threshold, the information is rebroadcast. Otherwise, the relay transmission is canceled

3.4. After the relaying, retransmission requests are accepted with the same manner in 1.**Initiation part**

4. **Retransmission part**: shown in Fig.5(3)

4.1. The node transmits the **Retransmission request packet**(s).

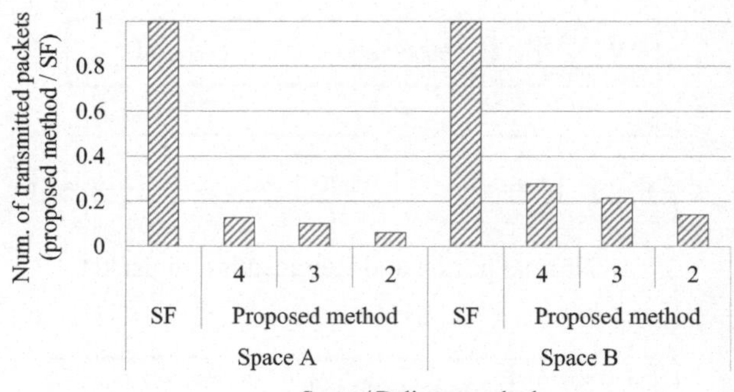

Fig.8 Number of transmitted packets (ratio proposed method case to SF case)

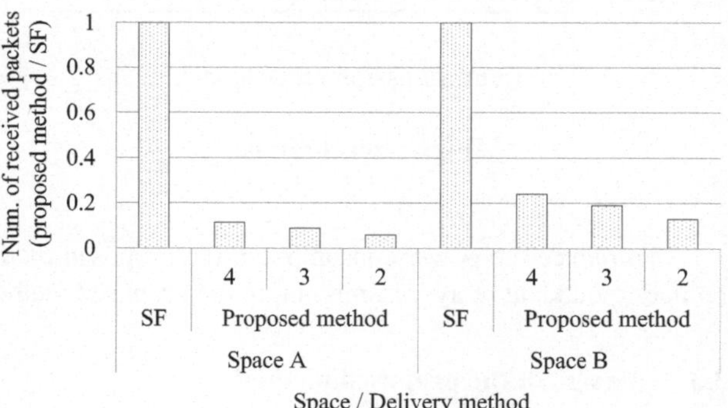

Fig.9 Number of received packets (ratio proposed method case to SF case)

4.2. Then, the sender broadcasts the lost packets. The receiving node receives the packets with the same manner in 2.**Receiving part**.

4.3. If the node receives all packets, proceeds the 3.**Relay part**.

4 Preliminary evaluation

To show the effectiveness of the proposed method, the preliminary evaluation is demonstrated through the network simulator OPNET[6] in this paper. The evaluation compare the number of transmitted packets and received packets for the existing method SF with the proposed method BBISS. Then we confirm that the proposed method can contribute to the reduction of the transmitted and received packets. The simulation condition is really simple: the number of initiator nodes is 1, and the number of initiated packets at the initiator node is 1. In the condition, since the generated packet was delivered in whole network in a short time, the node mobility is negligible.

We assume a network with 100 nodes (this includes 1 initiator node), a IEEE802.11b node MAC layer, and a data rate of 11 Mbps. The transmitted power is 0.005 W, and the received power threshold is -85 dBm. The initial positions of the nodes are assumed to be random. Two simulation areas are defined: 1000m×600m (space A) and 2000m×1200m (space B). Dense and sparse networks are considered in each case. The initial positions of the nodes are assumed to be random. The average is found for 10 simulation runs at every initial node positions. We consider nodes receiving packet from initiator nodes to compare SF and BBISS. Three values of *relay_threshold*, 4, 3, 2 are set for the proposed method. The waiting time for information retransmission in both methods is 1s to simplify the evaluation.

The simulation result is described as follows. Figure 8 and Fig.9 show the number of transmitted packets and received packets, respectively. The result showed that BBISS reduces 72%-94% of the transmitted packets and 76%-94% of the received packets.

5 Conclusions

This paper proposed a novel infrastructure-less broadcast information delivery system, BBISS, to share the information such as text contents and image contents. Then the number of transmitted and received packets for the proposed method was compared with that for the SF through the network simulation. The simulation result can conclude that the propose method can contribute to the reduction of transmitted packets and received packets. The reduction will contribute the congestion avoidance.

In future, we plan to evaluate the delivery performance through the network simulation. In addition, we plan to develop applications and implement it in existing PCs, cell phones, and Tablet PCs.

6 Acknowledgments

This research has been supported by The Nakajima Foundation, Japan.

7 References

[1] C. Siva Ram Murthy and B. S. Manoj, “Ad Hoc Wireless Networks - Architectures and Protocols,” Prentice Hall, Professional Technical Reference

[2] Vahdat Amin, and David Becker “Epidemic routing for partially connected ad hoc networks.” Technical Report CS-200006, Duke University, 2000.

[3] Jorjeta G. Jetcheva, David A. Malts, "A Simple protocol for Multicast and Broadcast in Mobile Ad Hoc Networks", IETF MANET Working Group Internet-Draft, <draft-ietf-manet-simple-mbcast. txt>, 2001

[4] Brad Williams, Tracy Camp, "Comparison of Broadcasting Techniques for Mobile Ad Hoc Networks", Proceedings of the 3rd ACM International Symposium on Mobile Ad Hoc Networking and Computing, pp. 194-205, 2002

[5] Yu-Chee Tseng, Sze-Yao Ni, Yuh-Shyan Chen, Jang-Pinig-Sheu, "The Broadcast Problem in a Mobile Ad Hoc Network", Wireless Networks Volume 8, Springer, pp. 153-167, Kluwer Academic Publishers, 2002

[6] The network simulator “OPNET”, http://www.opnet.com

An Overload-Free Data-Driven Ultra-Low-Power Networking Platform Architecture

Shuji SANNOMIYA[1], Yukikuni NISHIDA[2], Makoto IWATA[3], and Hiroaki NISHIKAWA[1]
[1]Faculty of Engineering, Information and Systems, University of Tsukuba,
Tsukuba Science City, Ibaraki, 305-8573 Japan
[2]Graduate School of Systems and Information Engineering, University of Tsukuba,
Tsukuba Science City, Ibaraki, 305-8573 Japan
[3]School of Information, Kochi University of Technology,
Kami, Kochi, 782-8502 Japan

Abstract—*In order to enhance the sustainability of communication especially in times of disaster, both low-power consumption and the tolerance for traffic increased due to the emergency communication should be realized urgently. Already our previous study has presented ULP-DDNS (Ultra-Low-Power Data-Driven Networking System) extending the lifetime of battery-operated devices to form an ad-hoc network which can provide a communication environment in the area where fixed and wired networks are disabled due to the disaster. In this paper, a networking platform architecture with a runtime overload-avoidance mechanism to dynamically maintain the processing load within the design target is revealed to provide the ULP-DDNS with the tolerance for the increased traffic. The runtime overload-avoidance mechanism exploits the unique positive correlation between the processing load and consumption current in the data-driven processors realized by self-timed pipeline, and it enhances the throughput for reducing the processing load by runtime voltage scaling when the current increases.*

Keywords: data-driven processor, protocol handling, real-time multiprocessing, self-timed pipeline

1. Introduction

To enhance the sustainability of communication is one of the urgent issues in emergent situations especially in times of disaster. We have already proposed ULP-DDNS (Ultra-Low-Power Data-Driven Networking System) [1] to achieve ultra-low-power consumption indispensable to extend the lifetime of the battery-operated mobile devices to form an ad-hoc network which can provide a communication environment in the area where fixed and wired networks are disabled due to the disaster. To ensure the connectivity over the ULP-DDNS, it is indispensable to provide tolerance for traffic increased due to emergency communication for safety confirmation, information gathering, and so forth. Concretely, protocol processing should be guaranteed on every platform (network node) even when traffic increases.

However, the platform may become inoperative when incoming traffic increases. This is because the increased traffic may increase the number of packets concurrently processed in the platform beyond the design target, i.e., the pipeline occupancy which is the ratio of the number of valid data to the number of pipeline stages may exceed the design target. To make the platforms free from such overload situation, both observability and controllability on the pipeline occupancy are indispensable. Unfortunately, the pipeline occupancy of currently mainstream processors cannot be observed accurately because the number of valid data may change at runtime depending on the unpredictable branches or/and interrupts.

In contrast, data-driven processors realized by self-timed pipeline can provide direct observability on their pipeline occupancy because the localized data transfer of the self-timed pipeline drives only pipeline stages with valid data and thus the consumption current of the self-timed pipeline is in proportion to the runtime pipeline occupancy, i.e. the pipeline occupancy can be externally observed by the amount of the consumption current. Moreover, the throughput of the self-timed pipeline can be controlled in real-time by changing the supplied voltage based on a DVS (Dynamic Voltage Scaling) technique [2]. Consequently, the pipeline occupancy can be kept within the design target by increasing the pipeline throughput by the DVS when the consumption current is increased due to the increased traffic.

In this paper, an overload-free data-driven networking platform architecture is proposed based on the direct observability and controllability on the pipeline occupancy of the self-timed pipeline. The changing of the throughput based on the DVS technique takes time because of both the signal propagation in the control circuit and the parasitic capacitance on the circuit, and thus the fluctuation of the pipeline occupancy should be temporally smoothed and reduced in order to keep the pipeline occupancy within the design target until the throughput becomes a target value. The key idea of the proposed architecture is to temporally smooth and lower the pipeline occupancy at runtime by changing the parallelism of target protocol handling based on the real-time multiprocessing capability of the data-driven processor realized by the self-timed pipeline. The feasibility of the

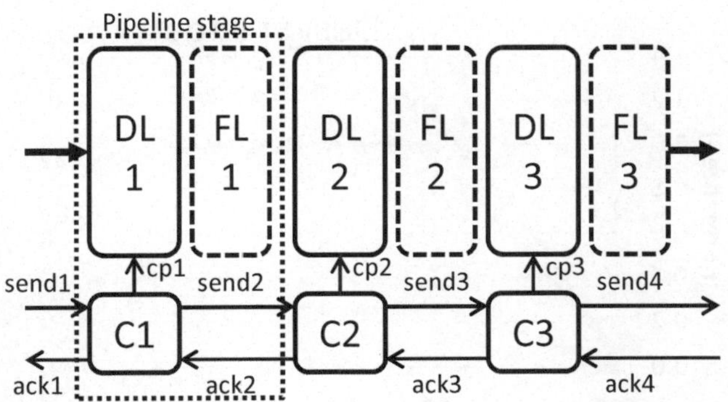

Fig. 1: Self-timed (clockless) pipeline.

proposed architecture is discussed based on the measurement of the latest version of the data-driven processors realized by self-timed pipeline [3].

2. ULP-DDNS platform

To realize the overload-free networking platform, both the observability and controllability on the pipeline occupancy are indispensable. Fortunately, they can be provided in the data-driven networking platform of the ULP-DDNS.

In this section, how these indispensable features are provided is explained, and a basic technique to exploit this unique feature for achieving an overload-free networking platform is discussed.

2.1 Ultra-low-power data-driven networking processor

The platform of the proposed ULP-DDNS is realized by both an ad-hoc networking scheme for reducing the redundant traffic and a data-driven processor for handling communication protocols with low-power.

The proposed ad-hoc networking scheme realizes an ad-hoc network over mobile devices in the area where existing fixed- and wired-network infrastructure becomes inoperative due to fault or disaster, and it reduces the redundant traffic caused by existing simple flooding (broadcasting) to deliver urgent information all over the ad-hoc network [4]. As a result of our evaluation, it is revealed that the proposed ad-hoc networking scheme reduces the traffic to 1/10 [1]. This reduction of the traffic directly decreases the number of sending and receiving packets in every node (platform) in the ad-hoc network, and thus it contributes to the lowering power consumption of every platform.

In addition to the ad-hoc networking scheme, a data-driven networking processor is proposed to lower the power consumption required to handle the protocol for both sending and receiving each packet. The proposed data-driven networking processor, named ULP-DDCMP (Ultra-Low-Power Data-Driven Chip MultiProcessor), is realized by using an optimized circular pipeline which makes it possible to bypass the pipeline stages for firing control to detect the arrival of a pair of operands when unary operations are executed [3]. Each processor core of the ULP-DDCMP is named ULP-CUE (Ultra-Low-Power CUE) as a successor of the CUE series data-driven processors [3].

The ultra-low-power consumption as a result of the synergistic effect between the traffic reduction by the ad-hoc networking scheme and the low-power protocol handling by the ULP-DDCMP is demonstrated by using simulators and a prototype VLSI chip of the ULP-DDCMP, and it is revealed that the ULP-DDNS can reduce power consumption to a several-hundredth in comparison with an existing network system [1].

2.2 Real-time observability and controllability

One of the main contributors to the ultra-low-power consumption is the localized data transfer of the self-timed pipeline (STP) which is used to realize the ULP-DDCMP. The localized data transfer also provides both a strong positive correlation between the pipeline occupancy and consumption current and the real-time adaptability for dynamic voltage scaling.

In the STP, only pipeline stages with valid data are driven exclusively as a consequence of the localized data transfer called handshake. Figure 1 shows the basic structure of the STP in which each stage consists of a data-latch (DL), functional logic (FL) and transfer control unit (C). The STP is a kind of asynchronous bundled data pipelines, and it employs four-phased handshake [5]. Based on the four-phased handshake, the valid data in the STP are transferred between adjacent stages, as follows.

- Reset: After the assertion of the reset signal, the C negates both its send signal representing transfer request and ack signal representing acknowledge.
- The C asserts its ack signal after its send signal is asserted.
- After the assertion of the ack signal, the preceding C negates its send signal.
- After the negation of the send signal, the C asserts both its gate open signal (cp) and its send signal and it negates concurrently its ack signal, only if the ack signal is negated. As a result, the data is latched in the stage to which the C belongs.
- The succeeding C repeats the above steps similarly to the C.

This handshake not only concentrates dynamic consumption current into the pipeline stages with valid data but also eliminates global clocks. Generally, clock-synchronized circuit requires PLL (Phase-Locked Loop) circuit to change the clock-frequency according to the supplied voltage, and it takes several tens of μ seconds to change the clock-frequency by the PLL. That is, the supplied voltage should be kept at constant within several tens of μ seconds.

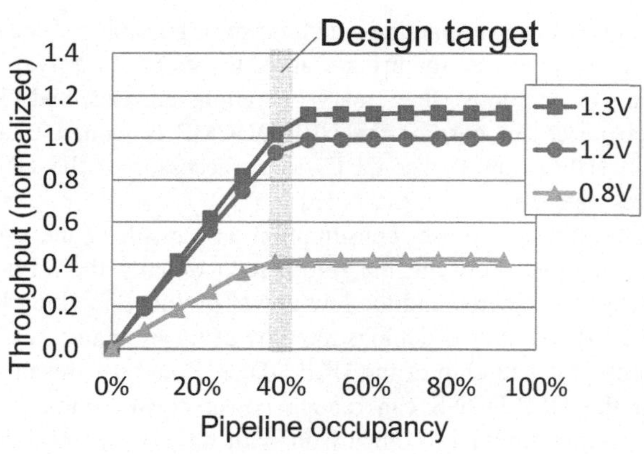

(a) Correlation between pipeline occupancy and throughput

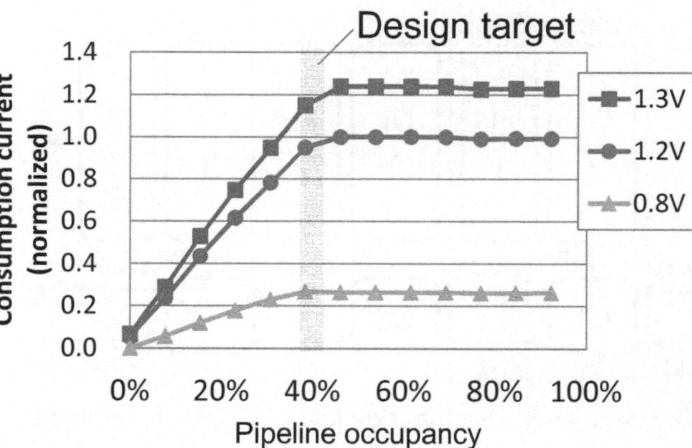

(b) Correlation between pipeline occupancy and consumption current

Fig. 2: Direct observability on pipeline occupancy.

In contrast, no PLL is required in the STP, and the delay times of the DL, FL and C are changed at equal rate according to the supplied voltage. Therefore, the supplied voltage of the STP can be scaled at runtime while the rate of change of the voltage is moderate enough to guarantee the transistor switching, i.e., the throughput of the ULP-DDCMP can be changed while target protocols are handled.

In the ULP-DDCMP, both the occupancy and throughput increase when the number of packets processed concurrently increases. Figure 2 shows the characteristics which are measured by using the existing ULP-DDCMP chip. As shown in this figure 2(a), the throughput is kept at a maximum value regardless of the pipeline occupancy while the pipeline occupancy exceeds the design target value, therefore, the ULP-DDCMP may become inoperative due to the overflow of the STP if the input traffic continues to exceed the design target. That is, the pipeline occupancy should be kept within the design target to realize the overload-free networking platform.

As shown in the figure 2(b), the pipeline occupancy correlate with the consumption current of the STP, i.e., the statically unpredictable pipeline occupancy can be observed at runtime based on the consumption current.

Consequently, the overload situation can be avoided by increasing the pipeline throughput to keep the pipeline occupancy within the design target value when the pipeline occupancy increases.

3. Runtime overload-avoidance mechanism

Based on the direct observability and controllability, the throughput of the protocol handling in the DDCMP can be changed when input traffic increases. To realize this runtime load control for overload-avoidance, the platform architecture is discussed in this section.

3.1 Networking platform architecture

As already described, the observation of the pipeline occupancy by the consumption current and the control of the effective throughput by the DVS can be realized at runtime. Unfortunately, some delay time is introduced until the effective throughput becomes a target value after the pipeline occupancy changes because of the signal propagation delay through control circuits and their parasitic capacitance. Therefore, the fluctuation of the pipeline occupancy should be temporally moderate to provide enough time for changing the effective throughput.

To make the pipeline occupancy fluctuation temporally smooth without any runtime overhead, the data-driven programs of target protocols are modified to reduce the variety of the numbers of operations executed concurrently.

As illustrated in figure 3, the programs are defined by data-flow graph (DFG) in the data-driven processors. The DFG consists of nodes and arcs, and each node describes an operation while each arc represents the data-dependency between two successive operations. The data-dependencies between operations represent naturally the ILP (Instruction Level Parallelism) inherent in the programs, and thus describing target program by using DFG results in extracting the ILP in the target programs.

In the data-driven processors, each operand is executed independently from the other operands and the execution time of each operand is also independent from that of the other operands as a result of the real-time multiprocessing [6]. Based on this feature, the number of operations executed concurrently can be changed by postponing the execution timing of the operations on non-critical paths, as shown in figure 3. This program modification can temporally smooth

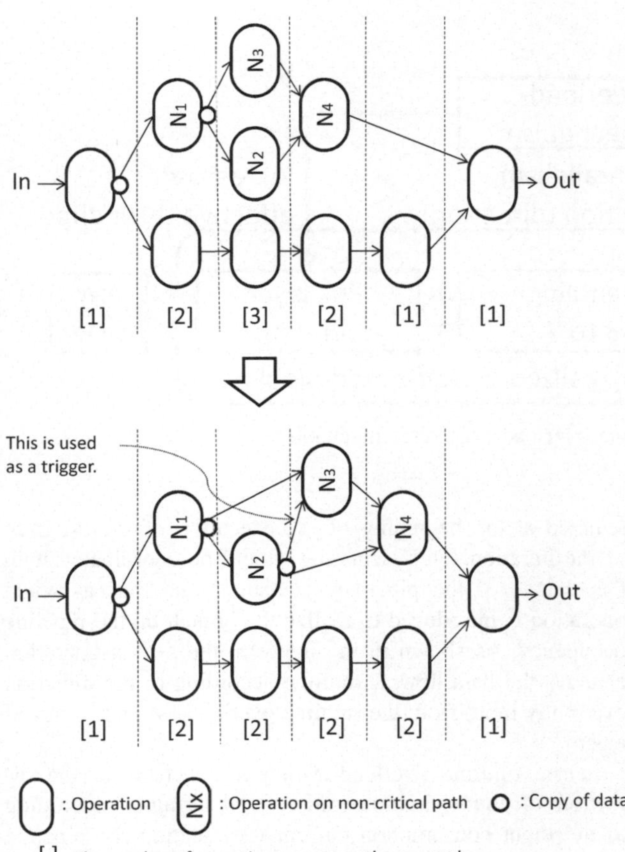

Fig. 3: Temporally-smoothing the number of operations executed concurrently.

the number of operations executed concurrently without any overhead on the execution time of the operations on the critical path of target programs.

Figure 4 shows the basic architecture to realize an overload-free networking platform based on the techniques discussed. To enhance the throughput of the protocol handling when the input traffic increases, a runtime overload avoidance mechanism is introduced to increase the supplied voltage according to the increased consumption current. This runtime overload avoidance mechanism can be implemented by using runtime voltage scaling technique [2] for the self-timed pipeline.

This kind of load control in the platform should not increase the traffic in the ad hoc network because the increasing traffic leads to the network congestion. From this standpoint, the throughput of the protocol handling for receiving packets should be kept at constant to guarantee the receiving packets because the retransmission due to the denial of packet reception increases the traffic in the ad hoc network. Therefore, the receiving protocol handling at link layer is out of the throughput control as shown in the figure 4. On the other hand, the throughput of the protocol handling for sending packets is enhanced by increasing the supplied voltage in order to reduce the pipeline occupancy for the increased traffic. Based on this basic architecture, the pipeline occupancy derived from the protocol handling up to network layer can be reduced for the increased traffic. However, the pipeline occupancy depends on not only the protocol handling up to the network layer but also the internal processing including the upper layer protocol handling and the application processing.

3.2 Runtime parallelism transformation

As for the internal processing, the enhancement of the throughput may not necessarily result in the reduction of the pipeline occupancy because some of the internal processing may be resident. For example, a GUI (Graphical User Interface) manager continues to run while the display device is lit.

To reduce the pipeline occupancy derived from such internal processing, the number of data (tokens in the data-driven processors) flowing through the STP should be reduced. However, tokens derived from different programs are concurrently processed at the different stages of the STP without any distinction on the types of processing, and thus it is difficult to selectively remove the flowing tokens of a particular processing type.

Fortunately, the processing time constraint of the upper layer protocol handling and the application processing is often lazy in comparison with that of the link level protocol handling. For instance, the response time of the MAC (Media Access Control) protocol handling is strictly and tightly determined on the μ second time scale depending on the specification of the physical layer hardware while the several seconds delay time of a mailer application can be accepted or ignored. By utilizing such slack time of some internal processing, the pipeline occupancy can be temporally smoothed and reduced in the data-driven processors.

By utilizing the real-time multiprocessing feature, the number of operations executed simultaneously can be reduced as already shown in the figure 3. As for the internal processing with the slack time, the number of the concurrently executing operations can be more reduced at the expense of the increase in the processing time. In an extreme case, it can be 1 as shown in figure 5 while the increased time is acceptable. Consequently, the pipeline occupancy derived from the internal processing with the slack time can be reduced by transforming the parallelism of the programs.

To realize such transformation of the parallelism, any overhead on the processing time of the running programs should be avoided in order to satisfy the processing time constraints required. In this paper, a runtime parallelism transformation with no overhead on the processing time is introduced by exploiting the real-time multiprocessing capability of the data-driven processor realized by the STP. The runtime parallelism transformation is realized by switch-

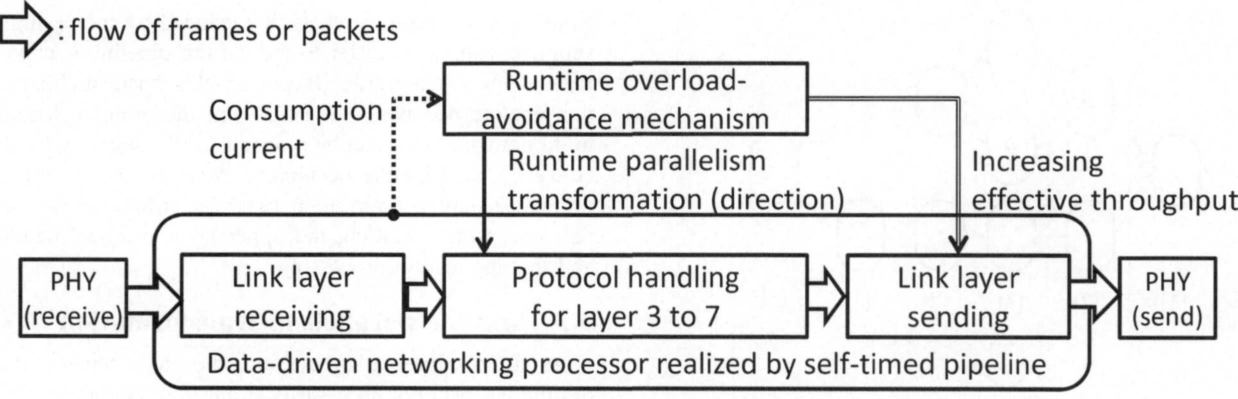

Fig. 4: Networking platform with runtime overload-avoidance mechanism.

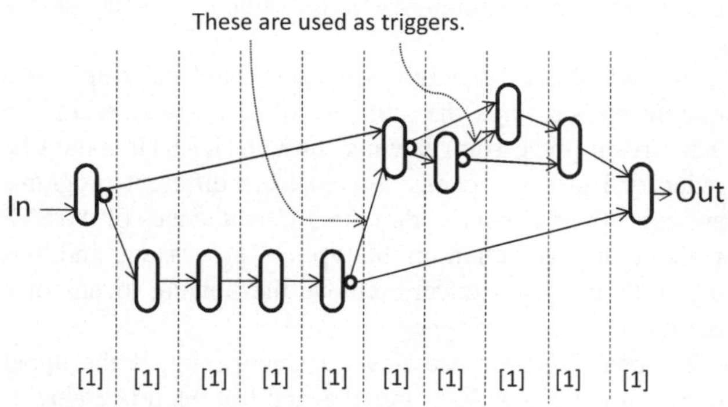

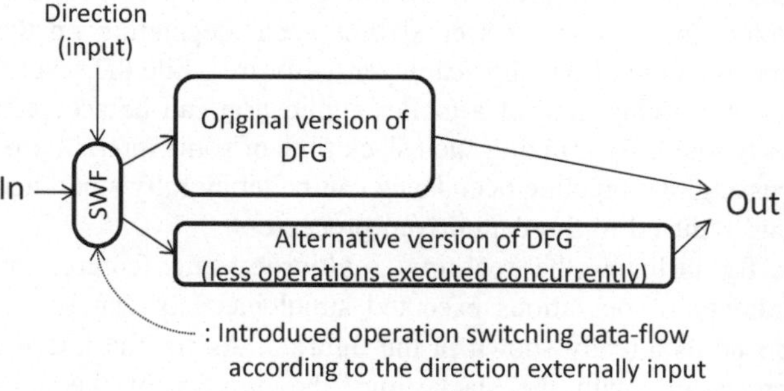

Fig. 5: Runtime parallelism transformation by switching DFG.

ing the program at runtime, i.e. an internal processing program with high throughput (parallelism) is switched to its alternative version with low parallelism when the pipeline occupancy increases.

It is difficult to switch the running program to the alternative version because the tokens of the running program are spread over the STP. Therefore, the switching should be realized at the beginning of the execution of the program or the iteration. This switching should be coordinated with the change of the pipeline occupancy, and thus a switch operation is introduced to realize the branch on the pipeline occupancy. As shown in the figure 5, the switch operation changes the data-flow at runtime according to the direction externally input from the runtime overload-avoidance mechanism.

In the runtime overload-avoidance mechanism, the direction of the switch operation is determined according to the input consumption current representing the pipeline occupancy. As a result of the control by the runtime overload-avoidance mechanism, the pipeline occupancy can be reduced by both enhancing the throughput of the protocol handling for sending packets and decreasing the number of operations executed concurrently when the input traffic increases.

3.3 Preliminary evaluation

The proposed architecture completely depends on not only the already proposed runtime DVS technique [2] but also both the parallelism transformation of the target protocol handling program and the real-time processing capability of the data-driven processors realized by the STP. As a preliminary evaluation of the feasibility of the proposed architecture, both the parallelism transformation and the real-time multiprocessing are verified by using the ULP-DDCMP chip which is the latest data-driven processor realized by the STP.

As a concrete protocol, UDP/IP is focused on because its connection-less packet transfer results in low-power consumption indispensable in ad-hoc networking, i.e., it is one of the protocols expected to be used in ad hoc networking.

As shown in figure 6(a), the ULP-DDCMP chip houses four ULP-CUE's interconnected by a multi-stage token router realized by the STP. In the design of this chip, the circular STP realizing each ULP-CUE is divided finely in order to eliminate the pipeline bottleneck. As a result of this

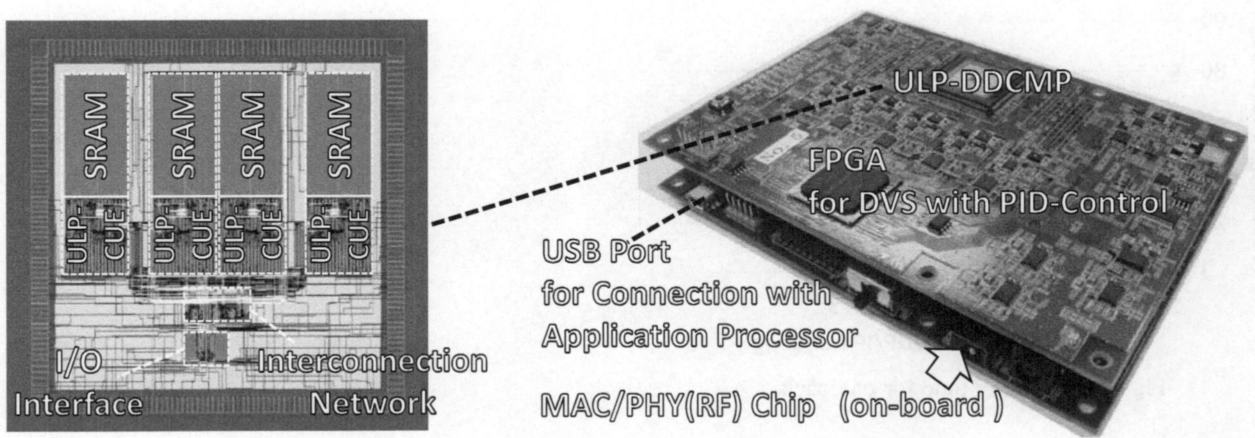

Fig. 6: ULP-DDCMP chip and its evaluation board.

pipeline division, the number of stages of each ULP-CUE is 13. The chip is fabricated by 65nm CMOS 7-metal-layer process technology. The ULP-DDCMP is implemented on an evaluation board which mounts two FPGA's; one FPGA is used to realize the runtime DVS with PID (Proportional Integral Derivative) control to stabilize the supplied voltage at a target value and the other FPGA realizes logging of the performance and power consumption. The evaluation board is shown in the figure 6(b).

The ULP-DDCMP provides an instruction set enough to describe the UDP/IP handling program. Actually, the data-driven program of the UDP/IP handling is described by using the instruction set. The described UDP/IP handling program realizes the checksum calculation and the generation of the UDP/IP header, and the packets containing pseudo header and payload are input to the program and the program outputs IP datagrams. The number of the operations executed simultaneously in the originally described program varies from 1 to 5, and thus the maximum pipeline occupancy becomes approximately 38% (= 5/13). This means that one UDP/IP handling can be executed in one ULP-CUE within the design target because the design target of each ULP-CUE is 40% as shown in the figure 2.

To verify the temporally-smoothing of the number of concurrently executed operations, an alternative version of the UDP/IP handling is derived from the original version by using the introduced scheme as shown in the figure 5. In the derived alternative version, the number of operations executed concurrently is reduced to almost 1. That is, it is verified that the parallelism can be changed by modifying the program.

By using the alternative version, the real-time processing capability is verified. The processing time required to process one packet is measured by using the logging function on the evaluation board while the number of input packet is increased, i.e. the multiplicity is increased. Figure 7 shows the measured result. In the sequential processing, the processing time per one packet is in proportion to the multiplicity. In contrast, the real-time processing capability of the ULP-DDCMP can keep the processing time per packet at approximately constant regardless of the multiplicity, as shown in the result. In addition, the processing time per one packet is measured for the different input timing of the packets, and the same results are obtained. That is, the processing time of a program is independent from that of the other programs.

It is true that the processing time per packet experiences approximately a 10% increase when the multiplicity is 4 in comparison with the other results. The cause of this increase is the elastic capability of the STP. The STP can maintain its maximum throughput even when the pipeline occupancy exceeds the design target, as shown in the figure 2. The number of the operations executed concurrently in the alternative version is not exactly 1 and it temporarily becomes 2, therefore, the pipeline occupancy exceeds the design target temporarily when the multiplicity is 4. In other words, the STP provides a tolerance for temporal overload naturally. If the increased processing time is not acceptable, the processing time can be kept at constant by limiting the multiplicity to be within 3 or by pipelining the STP more deeply.

4. Conclusion

In this paper, a data-driven networking platform architecture with a runtime overload-avoidance mechanism is revealed in order to realize an overload-free networking platform indispensable to realize sustainable networking environment. Based on the direct observability and controllability on the pipeline occupancy which is the processing load of the platform, the overload-avoidance mechanism makes it possible to dynamically keep the pipeline occupancy within the design target. Concretely, the pipeline occupancy is

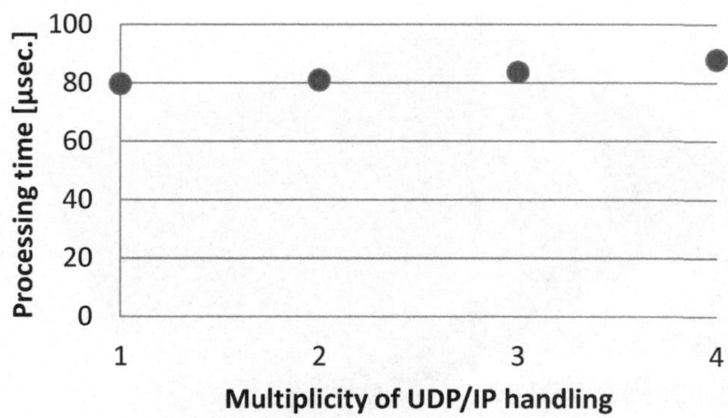

Fig. 7: Processing time for one packet.

observed by the consumption current, and it is reduced by increasing the pipeline throughput with the runtime DVS when the input traffic increases. Moreover, a runtime parallelism transformation is proposed to make the control delay time inherent in the DVS circuit ignorable. As a preliminary evaluation, the feasibility of the newly proposed runtime parallelism transformation is verified through the measurement of the latest version of data-driven processors.

Now we are developing a simulator [7] realizing the comprehensive evaluation on the ad hoc network environment realized by the proposed architecture, and the evaluation result will be reported soon.

Acknowledgement

Although it is impossible to give credit individually to all those who organized and supported our project, the authors would like to express their sincere appreciation to all the colleagues in the project.

This research work was supported in part by Core Research for Evolutional Science and Technology (CREST), Japan Science and Technology Agency (JST).

References

[1] Kazuhiro Aoki, Hiroshi Ishii, Makoto Iwata, and Hiroaki Nishikawa, "A Comprehensive Evaluation of ULP-DDNS by Platform Simulator," in Proc. of PDPTA, pp.445-451, July 2012.

[2] Kei Miyagi, Shuji Sannomiya, Makoto Iwata, and Hiroaki Nishikawa, "Low-Powered Self-Timed Pipeline with Runtime Fine-Grain Power Supply," in Proc. of PDPTA, pp.472-478, July 2012.

[3] Shuji Sannomiya, Kazuhiro Aoki, Makoto Iwata, and Hiroaki Nishikawa, "Power-Performance Verification of Ultra-Low-Power Data-Driven Networking Processor: ULP-CUE," in Proc. of PDPTA, pp.465-471, July 2012.

[4] Hiroshi Ishii, Keisuke Utsu, and Hiroaki Nishikawa, "Integrated Evaluation on Effectiveness of ULP-DDNS Networking Layer," in Proc. of PDPTA, pp.452-457, July 2012.

[5] C. J. Myers, "Asynchronous circuit design," Univ. of Utah John Wiley & Sons, Inc., 2001.

[6] Hiroaki Nishikawa, "Design Philosophy of a Networking-Oriented Data-Driven Processor: CUE," IEICE Transactions on Electronics, Vol.E89-C No.3, pp.221-229, Mar. 2006.

[7] Kazuhiro Aoki, Shuji Sannomiya, Makoto Iwata, Hiroshi Ishii and Hiroaki Nishikawa, "An Implementation of Platform Simulator for Congestion-Free Ultra-Low-Power Data-Driven Networking System," in Proc. of PDPTA, PDP2081, July 2013.

An Implementation of Platform Simulator for Congestion-Free Ultra-Low-Power Data-Driven Networking System

Kazuhiro Aoki[1], **Shuji Sannomiya**[2], **Makoto Iwata**[3], **Hiroshi Ishii**[4] **and Hiroaki Nishikawa**[2]
[1]Information Infrastructure Laboratory, Inc., Tsukuba Science City, Ibaraki, JAPAN
[2]Faculty of Engineering, Information and Systems, University of Tsukuba, Tsukuba Science City, Ibaraki, JAPAN
[3]School of Information, Kochi University of Technology, Kami, Kochi, JAPAN
[4]School of Information and Telecommunication Engineering, Tokai University, Minato, Tokyo, JAPAN

Abstract— *This paper describes implementation of platform simulator which is essential to realize ultra-low-power data-driven networking system (ULP-DDNS) supplying congestion-free network. For keeping networking system available, it is crucial issue to avoid congestion when traffic increases not only in an emergency but also in an ordinary time. The authors propose information sharing scheme and overload avoiding scheme on ultra-low-power data-driven networking scheme for congestion-free. This paper firstly introduces their schemes. It is necessary to verify effect of their schemes to various traffic pattern. This paper then explains the objective of our platform simulator as a verification tool of congestion-free ULP-DDNS. Furthermore, this paper reports how to implement platform simulator for congestion-free ULP-DDNS. Finally, this paper shows current status of this study and discusses data-driven platform for congestion-free ULP-DDNS.*

Keywords: congestion-free, low-power, networking, data-driven, simulator

1. Introduction

In Japan, earthquakes whose magnitude are more than 7 have been occurred many times in this century. Therefore, buildings and communication infrastructure are designed to resist earthquakes. However, wired telecommunication which had been main communication infrastructure at that time was interrupted by Han - Shin Awaji Earthquake disaster and Mid Niigata Prefecture Earthquake. And mobile communication which had been then main communication infrastructure as well as wired telecommunication was also suspended by the Great East Japan Earthquake. These interruption were great obstacles for rapid evacuation, relief activities and inquiries.

When traffic increases in emergency, telecommunication carrier usually restricts the number of call and suspends some services to avoid congestion. The restriction as a scheme to avoid congestion then causes interruption of communication infrastructure because it doesn't consider that communication environment is kept available. It is necessary to realize robust communication environment whose services are available in an emergency. Although there are some study about congestion-free network [1],[2], it is essential to study robust communication environment from several point of view such as congestion, power consumption and networking architecture.

Furthermore, It is important to keep communication environment available not only in emergency but also in an ordinary time because data traffic increases rapidly by smartphones. Infrastructureless communication environment can be then supposed to avoid interruptions of services. And power consumption is also crucial issue to keep communication environment available for a long time as possible in emergency [3]-[5].

The authors have been studying an implementation of ultra-low-power data-driven networking system (ULP-DDNS) [6]. ULP-DDNS project has been aiming at development of data-driven networking system which can achieve ultra-low-power consumption. And we have evaluated that ULP-DDNS can achieve about 1/200 power consumption less than the present system.

ULP-DDNS project have applied mobile ad hoc network [7] to ULP-DDNS. Ad hoc network is an infrastructureless network and is a group of wireless devices that organize themselves in a mesh topology to find routes and relay packets from the hardware platform through the network layer to application. The authors have proposed flooding scheme to reduce traffic for ultra-low-power. And our data-driven chip multiprocessor has been applied to networking platform in order to reduce power consumption. The authors have started research about congestion-free networking system based on ULP-DDNS. This paper describes implementation of platform simulator which is essential to realize ultra-low-power data-driven networking system (ULP-DDNS) supplying congestion-free network.

This paper firstly introduces information sharing scheme which is proposed to congestion-free on mobile ad hoc network. This paper also refers to overload avoiding scheme on ultra-low-power data-driven chip multiprocessor (ULP-DDCMP) in order to avoid congestion. For verifications of these scheme, the authors have been studying to enhance functions in platform simulator.This paper then explains the objective of our platform simulator as a verification tool of congestion-free ULP-DDNS. Furthermore, this paper reports how to implement platform simulator for congestion-free ULP-DDNS. Finally, this paper shows current status of this study and discusses data-driven platform for congestion-free ULP-DDNS.

2. Congestion-Free Ultra-Low-Power Data-Driven Networking System

This section reports schemes to avoid congestion in each layer of congestion-free ULP-DDNS. Fig. 1 shows layer of ULP-DDNS. A node of ULP-DDNS is a platform which is used data-driven chip multiprocessor(UDP-DDCMP) and self-timed elastic pipeline(ULP-STP). Runtime voltage scaling and power gating function are implemented on the platform for ultra low power consumption. For realizing congestion-free network, the authors have been studying overload avoiding scheme as an additional function on the platform.

Ad hoc networking Application and UDP/IP handling is also implemented on the platform. Furthermore, load-aware dynamic counter based flooding (LDCF) is applied as a traffic reducing scheme on a mobile adhoc network. Then, the authors have proposed broad-band information sharing scheme (BBISS) as an additional traffic reducing scheme to avoid congestion. We have been studying BBISS over layers from link layer to application layer.

These schemes for realizing congestion-free ULP-DDNS introduce in following subsections of this section.

2.1 Information Sharing Scheme of Ad hoc Networking Architecture

The authors have studied mobile ad hoc network as an applicable network architecture to disaster situation. In disaster situation, effective information discovery is firstly important.

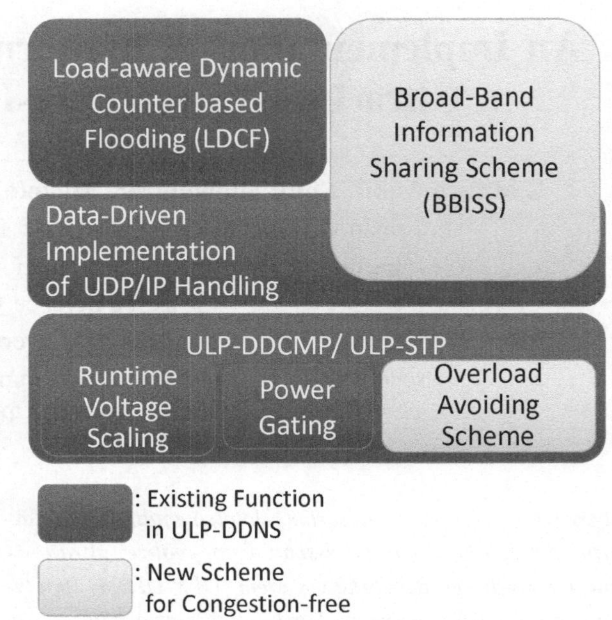

Fig. 1: Layer on Congestion-free Data-Driven Networking Platform

At a same time, effective secure communication is needed. They should be realized under the effective data transfer on ad hoc network. We have proposed these schemes in ultra low power consumption and we have evaluated effects of these schemes in reducing traffic and power consumption [8], [9].

To keep communication environment available, broad-band information sharing scheme (BBISS) has been proposed to avoid congestion. Fig. 2 shows summary of BBISS. When source node which is shown in Fig. 2 broadcast a data which is composed of several packets, nodes which received packets relay a data by rebroadcast as the occasion demands. If a node which lost a packet which is a part of the complete data, the other node which has a lost packet provide just a packet to the node which lost the packet. This scheme can reduce traffic because rebroadcast is not necessary to complement the data.

The authors have studied load-aware dynamic counter-based flooding (LDCF) for streaming data. LDCF can achieve very low traffic and high reachability for streaming. However, it isn't very important to complement data because streaming data can keep the value of information without a part of data. BBISS is aiming to be applied for non-streaming data such as text messages and static pictures. It is essential to complement data because an incomplete message can't keep the value of information. It is then important to reduce

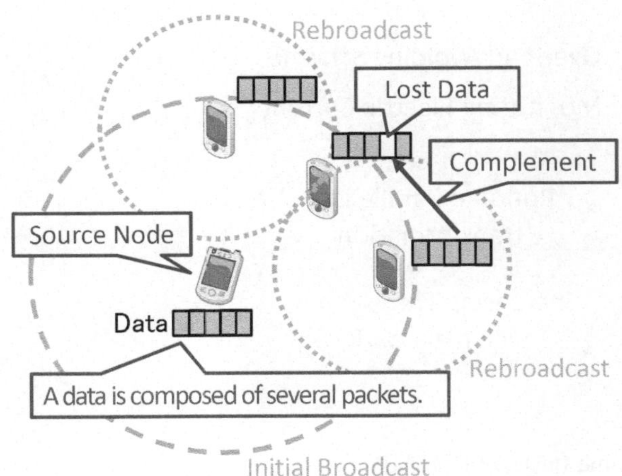

Fig. 2: Broad-Band Information Sharing Scheme (BBISS)

traffic in order to share information for realizing congestion-free network. BBISS is described in [10], and refer [11], [12] about related works.

2.2 Overload Avoiding Scheme on Data-Driven Networking Platform

This section refers to overload avoiding scheme on data-driven chip multiprocessor as a part of data-driven networking platform. Congestion is caused by rapid increase of traffic on the network and overload in a platform. The authors have proposed overload avoiding scheme in order to realize congestion-free networking system. The study of overload avoiding scheme is based on the study of ultra-low-power data-driven chip multiprocessor (ULP-DDCMP). The authors have studied data-driven chip multiprocessor based on self-timed elastic pipeline for ultra-low-power in realtime multiprocessing.

In data-driven chip multiprocessor, both the dynamic and static power dissipations are minimized by distributing the processing load over multiple processing cores which is slowed down by using runtime/dynamic voltage scaling (DVS) technique as long as the required processing speed is satisfied [13]. In addition, the voltage-supply to idle circuit blocks or cores is cut by using fine-grained power gating (PG) technique [14] as shown in Fig. 1. It is therefore intended that ULP-DDCMP would be implemented by self-timed power-aware elastic pipeline named ultra-low-power self-timed pipeline (ULP-STP)[15], [16]. Because of self-timed elastic data-transfer mechanism of the original STP, it can work well under variable voltage without adjusting clock frequency even if the altered voltage could transiently fluctuate at individual pipeline stage. Since the pipeline throughput can be adaptive to its processing load only by altering supply-voltage appropriately, a power-aware pipeline scheme can be realized naturally in terms of dynamic power saving. For instance, proportional-integral differential (PID) control method can be applied to such voltage control by monitoring consumption current of a target power domain within the chip. The STP is also suitable for gating power-supply to fine grain circuits since its stage-by-stage data-transfer control independently activates only pipeline stages with valid data. We therefore proposed a stage-by-stage power gating scheme adopted in the STP. This scheme provides natural signal gating, i.e., it stops the unnecessary signal propagation and transistor-switching at pipeline stage level without any global control mechanisms resulting in both power dissipation and processing speed degradation. Moreover, it makes it possible to scale the voltage even when the stages are activated because it can be realized without any global oscillator such as phase-locked loop (PLL) circuit, which forces pipeline flush ahead of the frequency and voltage change. In order to analyze the low-power characteristics of the ULP-STP and to estimate power-performance of various ULP-STP based systems, an experimental LSI chip has been fabricated by using 65 nm CMOS process. We have implemented ULP-DDCMP based on evaluation of the experimental LSI.

Overload avoiding scheme is realized by enhancing power consumption reducing scheme with DVS technique and PG technique. Fig. 3 shows mechanism of overload avoiding scheme. ULP-DDCMP based on ULP-STP handles receiving data inputted from physical layer on link layer. And protocols from layer 3 to layer 7 are also handled on ULP-DDCMP. Furthermore, ULP-DDCMP handles sending data to physical layer on link layer. Overload avoiding scheme then monitors electric current which is consumed by ULP-DDCMP. Because consumption current is proportion to processing load on the ULP-DDCMP, the increase of load can be detected by monitoring consumption current. If load on the ULP-DDCMP is higher than the target load, overload avoiding scheme control load in protocol handling among layer3-7 with runtime parallelism transformation in order to avoid overload on the ULP-DDCMP. Runtime parallelism transformation is realized by changing alternative program whose parallelism is lower than the original program. Rightfully, the alternative program provide same output of the original program. Then, ULP-DDCMP handles sending process of link layer rapidly in high voltage because of reducing load on ULP-DDCMP. The authors will utilize DVS technique and PG technique as a runtime parallelism transformation mechanism and rapid handling mechanism of protocol handling.

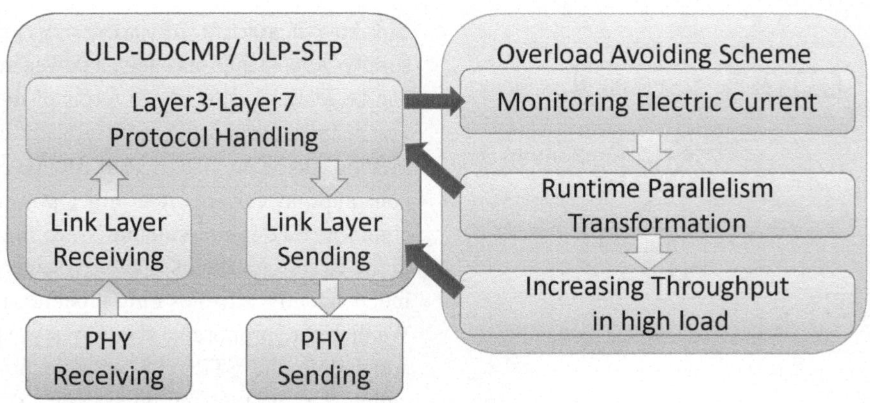

Fig. 3: Overload Avoiding Scheme on ULP-DDCMP

Furthermore, the authors will utilize overload tolerance of ULP-DDCMP as additional function of overload avoiding scheme. ULP-DDCMP is chip multiprocessor which has 4 cores. A core whose name is ULP-CUE has optimized circular pipeline [17]. Circular pipeline of ULP-CUE has 2-way to bypass matching memory which consumes high power. Furthermore, the matching memory has PG mechanism to reduce power consumption. 2-way circular pipeline and matching memory may be utilize as a buffer to avoid overload. Refer [18] about the description of overload avoiding scheme.

3. An Implementation of Platform Simulator for Congestion-free ULP-DDNS

3.1 Platform Simulator to Evaluate Overload Avoiding Scheme

This subsection describes an implementation of platform simulator to evaluate overload avoiding scheme. Then, this section also reports coordination between network simulator which evaluate BBISS and platform simulator for comprehensive evaluation of congestion-free ULP-DDNS.

Platform simulator have been developed to evaluate power consumption of platform in ULP-DDNS [19]. The authors will add functions for evaluating overload avoiding function to platform simulator. Fig. 4 shows image of summation of power consumption and summation of the number of tokens as the load on a platform. Network simulator have already used evaluation in ad hoc networking application. As comprehensive evaluation, we proposes using logs as a network simulation result to input of the platform simulator. Platform simulator can evaluate power consumption and turn-around time of program on data-driven chip multiprocessor. The authors will enhance platform simulator to be able to evaluate load on data-driven chip multiprocessor.

Platform simulator is necessary to evaluate energy and load of platform in UDP/IP handling, process on link layer, and so on because analog electronic circuit simulator which is SPICE is too complicated to measure power and turn-around time in UDP/IP handling according to network simulation log. In execution program, logs which has input time and data length can be used as input for the platform. Summation power consumption, turn-around time and the number of tokens as the load in each platform is a total energy and load of ULP-DDNS.

Platform simulator has hierarchy among self-timed elastic pipeline (e.g. ULP-STP), cores (e.g. ULP-CUE), and platform (e.g. ULP-DDCMP) as shown in Fig. 4. Firstly, platform simulator evaluates power consumption and switching time of stages of ULP-STP. In addition, platform simulator checks existence of a token in each stage as the load of stage. Power in each stage and send/ack time between stages are then derived from ULP-DDNS node, prototype of ULP-STP and gate simulation. In overload avoiding scheme, time in change supply voltage and target Vdd is simulated by platform simulator. Value of supply voltage used by platform simulator is tuned by result of gate simulation. Platform simulator sums up energy/load of stages in each module. Then, energy is the product of power and send/ack time. Module is a part of circular pipeline. For example, ULP-CUE consists of some module such as firing control (FC), function processor (FP), instruction decode (ID), instruction fetch (IF), merge (M), branch (B) and memory processor (MEM). All modules of which ULP-CUE consists is connected as a circular pipeline. Topology of a circular pipeline can be designed on the platform simulator freely as shown in following subsection. Platform simulator also sums up

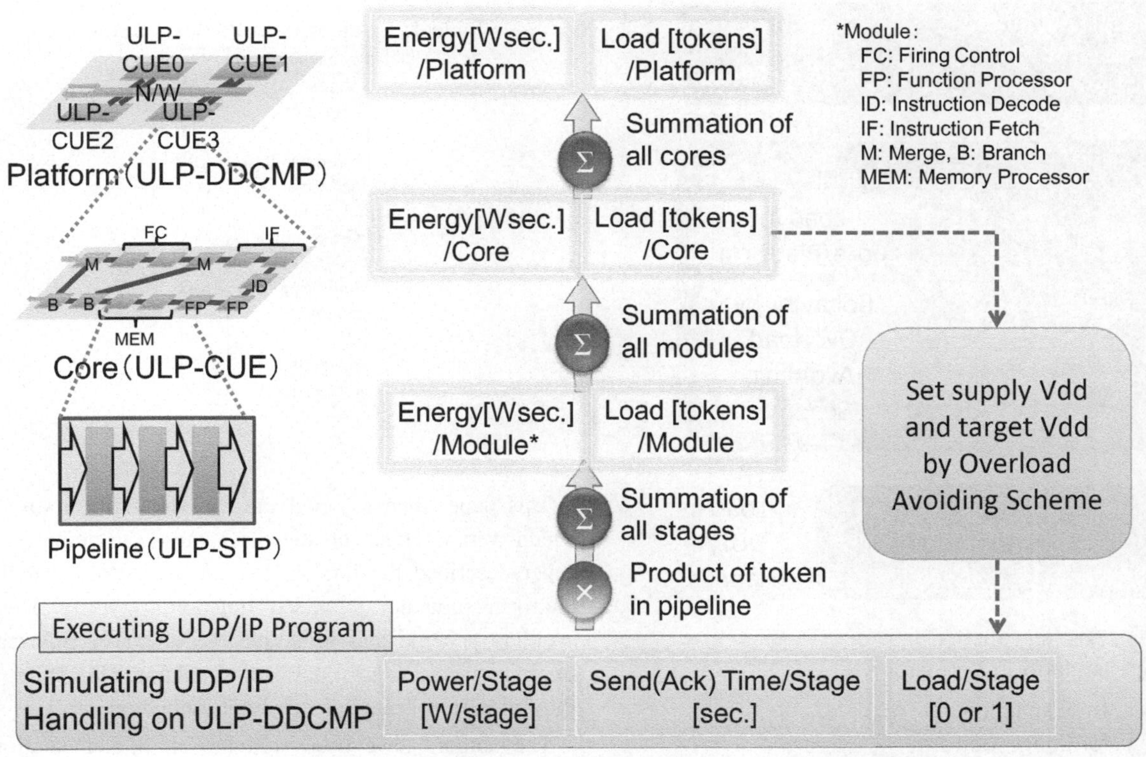

Fig. 4: Comprehensive Evaluation of Congestion-free ULP-DDNS

energy/load of all stages of a circular pipeline which is elements of an core such as ULP-CUE. Furthermore, the simulator sums up energy/load of all cores on an platform. For example, ULP-DDCMP has 4 cores (ULP-CUE0, ULP-CUE1, ULP-CUE2 and ULP-CUE3) and switches among cores as an inter-core network(N/W). Power consumption and load of a platform can be get from platform simulator by these process.

3.2 Coordinating Platform Simulator and Ad hoc Network Simulator

This subsection discusses coordinating network simulator to evaluate BBISS and platform simulator which is added functions to verify the effects of overload avoiding scheme.

This subsection firstly describes specification of platform simulator and its interface. Fig. 5 shows input to platform simulator and output from it. Platform simulator requires schedule of token stream as an input. This schedule is generated from network simulation logs. Platform simulator also demands UDP/IP program to evaluate power consumption and load in UDP/IP handling. Platform simulator has a topology of platform and a topology of core. These topologies can be designed freely using edit function of platform simulator. Parameters which indicate specification in each stage such as power and switching time in order to calculate power consumption of platform. Table 1 shows parameters prepared for tuning in platform simulator. Voltage is initial voltage in the simulation. Temperature is set because speed of electric circuit can be changed by temperature. Power(active) is wattage which is consumed when a token exist on the stage. Power(standby) is wattage with no token in the stage. Send/Ack time is time spent hand-shaking. PG-Send time is time to resume from power gating. And Ack-PG time is time to switch off of the stage. Monitoring interval is a cycle to monitor consumption currency. ΔV is voltage which can be increased or decreased by DVS controller. Voltage(max.) and Voltage(min.) are maximum/minimum value of voltage in DVS. In addition, platform simulator calculates load in core and platform. Load is the number of token in a platform to judge whether a platform is overload state or not. Platform simulator also imitates the behavior of protocol handling controlled by overload avoiding scheme to evaluate the effects of overload avoiding scheme. Platform simulator then outputs energy and turn-around time in UDP/IP handling. Furthermore, platform simulator also outputs load of an platform in UDP/IP handling.

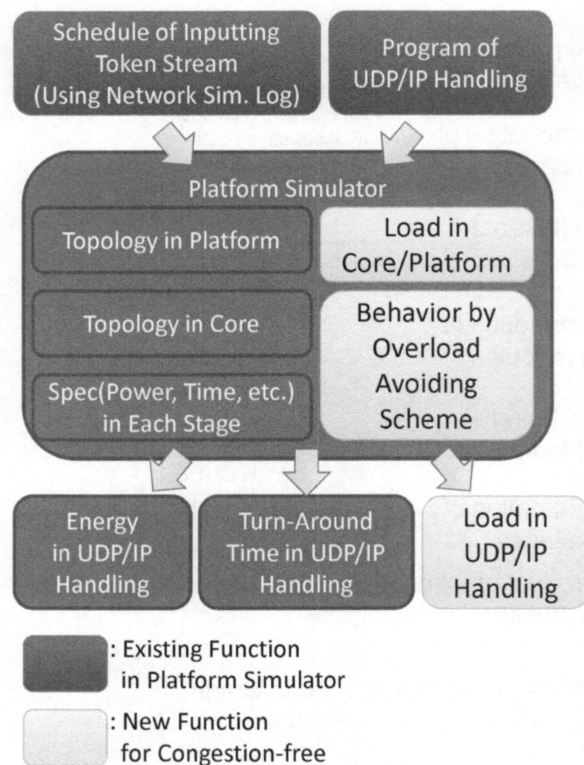

Fig. 5: Specification of Platform Simulator for Congestion-free ULP-DDNS

The authors have been studying how to evaluate schemes which are BBISS and overload avoiding scheme comprehensively. Network simulator would be able to imitate traffic pattern which is quite capable of congestion. BBISS can be evaluated reducing effect of non-streaming traffic by the network simulator. The authors think that traffic pattern and the effect applying BBISS can be included in the evaluation by platform simulator using network simulation log and so on. However, it may be difficult to reflect the effect of overload avoiding scheme to the evaluation by network simulator. It is essential because the effect of overload avoiding scheme influences the amount of traffic all over the network. We may implement functions which are a part of network simulator in platform simulator to solve this problem.

4. Conclusion

This paper firstly introduced information sharing scheme and overload avoiding scheme on ultra-low-power data-driven networking scheme which were proposed for realizing congestion-free ULP-DDNS.

Table 1: Parameters in Platform Simulator

Parameter	*Unit*
Voltage	V
Temperature	°C
Power(active)	μW
Power(standby)	μW
Send time	psec.
Ack time	psec.
PG-Send time	psec.
Ack-PG time	psec.
Monitoring interval	μsec.
ΔV	V
Voltage(max.)	V
Voltage(min.)	V

This paper then reported the role of platform simulator which verify effect of their schemes. Furthermore, this paper described the implementation of platform simulator. Platform simulator is added function to verify overload avoiding scheme and to derive the effect of information sharing scheme from a network simulator. This paper then showed current status of this implementation.

The authors have been studying an implementation of data-driven chip multiprocessor as a platform of congestion-free ULP-DDNS. We think that realizing interface which generate tokens from signal is essential to achieve veritable congestion-free ULP-DDNS. As a future works, the authors will realize data-driven chip multiprocessor as a VLSI to demonstrate the performance in congestion-free and ultra-low-power.

Acknowledgments

Although it is impossible to give credit individually to all those who organized and supported the CUE project and the ULP-DDNS project, the authors would like to express their sincere appreciation to all the colleagues in the project.

The CUE project and the ULP-DDNS project are partially supported by Core Research for Evolutional Science and Technology (CREST), Japan Science and Technology Agency, Strategic Information and Communications R&D Promotion Programme (SCOPE), Ministry of Internal Affairs and Communications, Japan, the Grants-in-Aid for Scientific Research of Japan Society for the Promotion of Science and Semiconductor Technology Academic Research Center (STARC). And, this work is supported by VLSI Design and Education Center(VDEC), the University of Tokyo in collaboration with Synopsys, Inc. and Cadence Design Systems, Inc.

References

[1] Kumaran, T.S. and V. Sankaranarayanan, "Congestion free routing in adhoc networks," Journal of Computer Science, Vol. 8, No. 6, pp. 971–977, June 2012.

[2] Gavalda, Arnau and Duch, Jordi and Gómez-Gardeñes, Jesús, "Reciprocal interactions out of congestion-free adaptive networks," Journal of Physical Review E, Vol. 85, No. 2, pp. 026112-1–026112-6, Feb. 2012.

[3] T. Inagaki and S. Ishihara, "HGAF: A Power Saving Scheme for Wireless Sensor Networks," IPSJ Journal Vol.50, No.10, pp. 2520–2531, Oct. 2009.

[4] A. Keshavarz-Haddad and R. Riedi, "Bounds on the benefit of network coding: Throughput and energy saving in wireless networks," IEEE INFOCOM 2008, Phoenix, Arizona, USA, pp. 376–384, April 2008.

[5] L. Sukyoung, K. Laeyoung and K. Hojin, "MIPv6-Based Power Saving Scheme in Integrated WLAN and Cellular Networks," IEICE transactions on communications Vol. E90-B, No. 10, pp. 2780–2783, Oct. 2007.

[6] Hiroaki Nishikawa, Hiroshi Ishii, and Makoto Iwata, "Collaborative Research Project on Ultra-Low-Power Data-Driven Networking System," Proc. of the 2008 Int'l Conf. on Parallel and Distributed Processing Techniques and Applications, pp. 697–703, July 2008.

[7] Jie Wu, Ivan Stojmenovic, "Ad Hoc Networks," IEEE Computer, Vol.37, No.2, pp.29–31, Feb. 2004.

[8] Hiroshi Ishii, Keisuke Utsu and Hiroaki Nishikawa "Integrated Evaluation on Effectiveness of ULP-DDNS Networking Layer," Proc. of the 2012 Int'l Conf. on Parallel and Distributed Processing Techniques and Applications, pp.452–457, July 2012.

[9] Keisuke Utsu, Hiroaki Nishikawa, and Hiroshi Ishii, "Performance Evaluation of Load and Battery Charge Oriented Broadcast Streaming Method over Ad Hoc Networks," Proc. of the 2012 Int'l Conf. on Parallel and Distributed Processing Techniques and Applications, pp.458–464, July 2012.

[10] Keisuke Utsu, Hiroaki Nishikawa and Hiroshi Ishii, "A Proposal on Broadcast based Information Sharing System over Disaster and Congestion Tolerant Ad Hoc Network," Proc. of the 2013 Int'l Conf. on Parallel and Distributed Processing Techniques and Applications, PDP2079, July 2013.

[11] Naoya Imaizumi, Keisuke Utsu, Hiroshi Sano, Hiroshi Ishii, "Effective Flooding over Disaster Tolerant Ad Hoc Network based on Exchange of Neighbor Information," Proc. of the 2013 Int'l Conf. on Parallel and Distributed Processing Techniques and Applications, PDP2077, July 2013.

[12] Keisuke Utsu, Hiroaki Nishikawa and Hiroshi Ishii, Video Streaming Performance of Load and Battery Charge Oriented Flooding over Disaster Tolerant Ad Hoc Network," Proc. of the 2013 Int'l Conf. on Parallel and Distributed Processing Techniques and Applications, PDP2078, July 2013.

[13] Anantha P. Chandrakasan, Samuel Sheng, and Robert W. Brodersen, "Low Power CMOS Digital Design," IEEE Trans. on Solid-state Circuits., vol. 27, No. 4, pp.473–483, Apr. 1992.

[14] Shin-ichiro Mutoh, Satoshi Shigematsu, Yoshinori Gotoh, Shinsuke Konaka, "Design Method of MTCMOS Power Switch for Low-Voltage High-Speed LSIs," Proc. of Asia and South Pacific Design Automation Conference, Hong Kong, pp.113–116, Jan. 1999.

[15] Kei Miyagi, Shuji Sannomiya, Makoto Iwata, and Hiroaki Nishikawa, "Low-Powered Self-Timed Pipeline with Variable-Grain Power Gating and Suspend-Free Voltage Scaling," Proc. of the 2013 Int'l Conf. on Parallel and Distributed Processing Techniques and Applications, PDP2082, July 2013.

[16] Ryuichi Taguchi, Hajime Ohiso, Keizo Mendori, Kei Miyagi, and Makoto Iwata, "Self-Timed Single Circular Pipeline for Multiple FFTs," Proc. of the 2013 Int'l Conf. on Parallel and Distributed Processing Techniques and Applications, PDP2083, July 2013.

[17] Shuji Sannomiya, Kazuhiro Aoki, Makoto Iwata and Hiroaki Nishikawa, "Power-Performance Verification of Ultra-Low-Power Data-Driven Networking Processor: ULP-CUE," Proc. of the 2012 Int'l Conf. on Parallel and Distributed Processing Techniques and Applications, pp.465–471, July 2012.

[18] Shuji Sannomiya, Yukikuni Nishida, Makoto Iwata, Hiroaki Nishikawa, "An Overload-Free Data-Driven Ultra-Low-Power Networking Platform Architecture, " Proc. of the 2013 Int'l Conf. on Parallel and Distributed Processing Techniques and Applications, PDP2080, July 2013.

[19] Kazuhiro Aoki, Hiroshi Ishii, Makoto Iwata, and Hiroaki Nishikawa, "A Comprehensive Evaluation of ULP-DDNS by Platform Simulator," Proc. of the 2012 Int'l Conf. on Parallel and Distributed Processing Techniques and Applications, pp. 445–451, July 2012.

Low-Powered Self-Timed Pipeline with Variable-Grain Power Gating and Suspend-Free Voltage Scaling

Kei MIYAGI[1], **Shuji SANNOMIYA**[2], **Makoto IWATA**[1], **and Hiroaki NISHIKAWA**[2]
[1]School of Information, Kochi University of Technology, Kami, Kochi, Japan
[2]Department of Computer Science, Graduate School of Systems and Information Engineering, University of Tsukuba, Tsukuba Science City, Ibaraki, Japan

Abstract— *This paper describes a variable-grain power gating and suspend-free voltage scaling scheme based on the self-timed pipeline (STP) circuits. The STP operates with its local hand-shake signal so that it does not require the global clock distribution, i.e., centralized control. Therefore, various power supply control for the STP can be naturally localized in both spatial and temporal domains without stopping its effective data transfer, e.g., program execution in case of microprocessors. As a result, the power supply scheme proposed in this paper can efficiently incorporate both commonly used voltage scaling (VS) and power gating (PG) techniques and it can further produce synergetic effects on its total amount of power saving. This paper reports evaluation results of the proposed scheme through actual power measurement of our fabricated STP-based data-driven processor.*

Keywords: self-timed pipeline, power gating, voltage scaling

1. Introduction

With the advancement of modern semiconductor integration technology, higher power-performance efficiency of LSI systems is required more and more. For example, power efficient LSI systems contribute to help wireless ad hoc networks more tolerant and dependable, especially in case of emergent conditions such as natural or artificial disasters.

As for static (leakage) power consumption of LSI systems, power gating (PG) technique is usually employed to power-off idle part of LSI and cut off leakage current [1]. As for dynamic (switching) power consumption, voltage scaling (VS) technique is commonly used to lower both power supply voltage and clock frequency to reduce switching power of transistors [2].

However, conventional PG schemes coping with coarse grain power domain such as processor core or whole die has some performance overhead derived from longer wakeup time [3], and they cannot cut off leakage power of a finer part of LSI. In case of applying conventional VS to clock synchronous LSI systems, there is some performance overhead since the LSI circuit has to be suspended during the transition time when both voltage and clock frequency are scaled. Furthermore, combinations of voltage level and frequency are predetermined at the design phase so that flexibility of power supply is limited.

In order to overcome those problems, the authors have been studying a runtime fine-grain power supply scheme [4], [5] in a collaborative research project on ultra-low-power LSIs. By the runtime fine-grain power supply scheme, voltage scaling operation adaptive to processing load saves switching power, and fine-grain power gating operation within short idle time reduces leakage power even in run-time. To realize both operations, we are focusing on the self-timed pipeline (STP) circuit. The STP can operate under different supply voltages without changing the clock frequency and thus throughput performance of the STP autonomously alters depending on the scaled voltage. Furthermore, data transfer control signals between adjacent pipeline stages can be utilized to control the power switch for PG and the wakeup time of the stage can be enclosed in hand-shake time with its preceded stage. However, the performance and power overheads will increase in the condition where the processing load changes frequently or drastically.

This paper therefore focuses on realizing adaptive control of power supply according to processing load. The proposed scheme provides multiple policies to control PG and VS operations and adjusts the tradeoff point of power supply control depending on various conditions. The paper reports evaluation results of the proposed scheme through actual power measurement of our STP-based data-driven processor fabricated by 65 nm CMOS process.

2. Runtime fine-grain power supply

In general, processing load within a parallel processor momentarily alters depending on the parallelism of the programs and frequency of processing requests from outside of the processor. The runtime fine-grain power supply scheme aims to realize PG and VS adaptive to such processing load fluctuations with as small performance overhead as possible. To maximize performance per power, it is important to consider balance between the size of power domain and energy overhead as follows. Figure 1 illustrates the spectrum of power supply control.

1) Spatially fine-grained power-domain and temporally fine-grained control for minimizing power supply

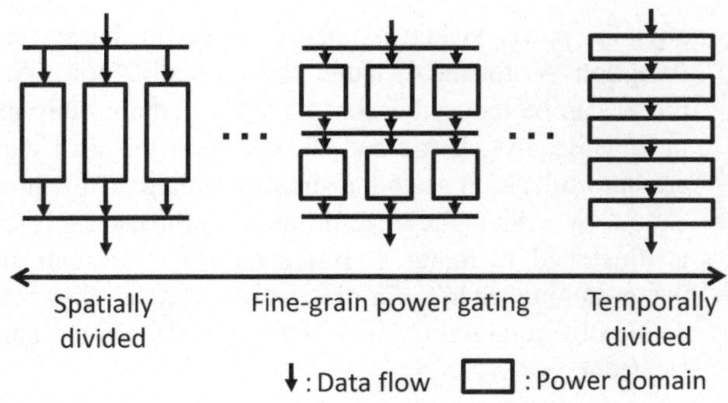

Fig. 1: Fine-grain power supply.

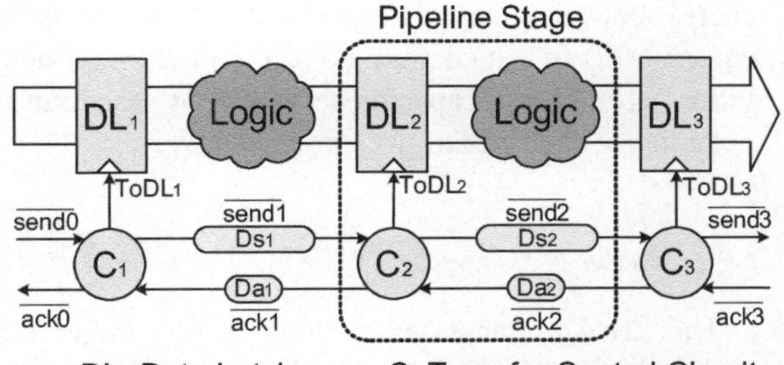

Fig. 2: Basic structure of self-timed pipeline.

2) Suspend-free control for avoiding performance degradation
3) Adaptive power supply control to processing load

The authors have already proposed a fine-grain (stage-by-stage) PG and a suspend-free VS based on STP. In this paper, more rich information for adaptive power supply control is extracted from the circuit and it is utilized to change the control policy of the target grain.

This section briefly introduces the autonomous behavior of STP and the runtime fine-grain power supply scheme [6] utilizing the STP behavior.

2.1 Self-Timed Pipeline

Basic STP circuit is configured as shown in Figure 2. Each pipeline stage is composed of a data latch DL_i operating as a pipeline resister, a functional logic, and a coincidence flip-flop C_i controlling data transfer between its neighbor pipeline stages. A set of data transferred in the pipeline is packed in a form of packet with a set of tags. Every packet is transferred at stage-by-stage based on localized control signals (send and ack signals) between adjacent pipeline stages as follows.

1) **(Beginning of packet transfer)** In C_{i-1} at stage $(i-1)$, $send_{i-1}$ signal is asserted for its succeeded stage (i). At the same time, data latch D_{i-1} sends a packet to the stage (i).
2) **(Handshake)** C_i opens the data latch DL_i when both $send_{i-1}$ and ack_i signals are asserted.
3) **(Acknowledge signal)** At the same time, ack_{i-1} signal is asserted at C_i to allow next packet transfer from its preceded stage.
4) **(Send signal)** C_i asserts $send_i$ signal and begins to send the packet to its succeeded stage $(i+1)$.
5) The above steps are iterated as long as there are packets in the pipeline.

By virtue of this localized data transfer control among pipeline stages, STP provides (a) power saving feature that the switching power is consumed only when the stage transfers and processes packets and (b) autonomous buffering (elastic) capability against fluctuated packet flow in the pipeline.

2.2 Runtime fine-grain power supply with STP

The send and ack signals of a pipeline stage represents whether the valid data is processed in the pipeline stage or not. By utilizing these signals for power control, the power can be concentrated to only pipeline stages with valid data. To realize such localized power gating, a power switch is inserted between the power line and each pipeline stage and it is switched off only when the corresponding pipeline stage has no valid data. This fine-grain power gating can deeply reduce the leakage current in comparison with the widely-used processor-core level power gating. Figure 3 shows the circuit diagram of the self-timed pipeline with the fine-grain power gating. To reduce the leakage current through the power switch itself, a high-threshold NMOS transistor is used as the power switch between the ground-line VSS and both the DL and Logic. To control the power switch, a control circuit called PC is introduced. The PC observes the send and ack signals, and it closes and opens the power switch. Generally, isolation cells are inserted between the powered-on and powered-off circuits to stop the propagation of the unstable signals from the powered-off circuit to the powered-on circuit. Fortunately, a part of the DL circuit can behave as the isolation cell in the self-timed pipeline, and thus the isolation cells are no longer required. Moreover, the absence of the isolation cells makes it possible to dynamically adjust the size of a target cluster in which the pipeline stages are powered-off at a time.

As for the dynamic voltage scaling, the self-timed pipeline is suitable because of its clock-less principle. The data transfer timing is determined by the C as already described, and it can be changed by scaling the supplied voltage to the C. The self-timed pipeline can continues to run even in the transition period when the supplied voltage changes as long as the difference among the potentials in the VDD lines is within a certain value enough to guarantee the switching of every transistor. Moreover, the whole consumption current

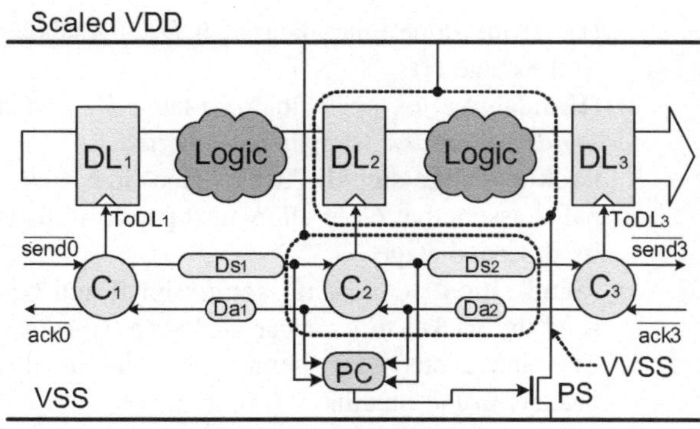

Fig. 3: Runtime fine-grain power-supply control of STP.

through the self-timed pipeline is in proportion to the number of valid data flowing in the self-timed pipeline because only the pipeline stages with valid data are driven as a result of the handshake. This graceful feature is preserved as long as any interlocking or forwarding mechanisms are not introduced, and it cannot be realized by using clock-synchronized circuit in which power is consumed independently from the number of valid data. By exploiting the graceful feature, the number of valid data flowing in the self-timed pipeline can be observed by the whole consumption current of the self-timed pipeline. Consequently, the power consumption can be reduced by setting the supplied voltage to a minimum value enough to achieve the throughput (the number of valid data flowing the self-timed pipeline) observed by the consumption current. This is because the power consumption generally is in proportion to the square of the supplied voltage

On the other hand, the clock-synchronized circuit should introduce a PLL (Phase-Locked Loop) circuit providing several clock-frequencies according to the supplied voltage in order to change the supplied voltage. Unfortunately, the PLL takes several tens of μ seconds to switch the clock-frequency [7], and thus the supplied voltage cannot be changed during the several tens of μ seconds. In contrast, the absence of the PLL in the self-timed pipeline makes it possible to realize truly runtime voltage scaling as long as the amount of change of the supplied voltage is moderate enough to guarantee the switching of transistors.

As explained above, both the power gating and the dynamic voltage scaling can be deeply exploited to reduce the power consumption by focusing on the unique features of the self-timed pipeline.

2.3 Break even model

The power gating reduces the leakage current through the powered-off circuit while the switching of the power switch consumes power. In addition, the rush current which flows after the power switch is opened results in the power consumption. As for the dynamic voltage scaling, the switching power can be reduced according to the required throughput, meanwhile, the charge and discharge of the load capacity are unavoidable to scale the supplied voltage. An equivalent circuit by which these gains and overheads are modeled is illustrated in figure 4. Based on the equivalent circuit, the switching energy for the power switch, E_{PS}, can be defined by equation (1) in which C_{PS} denotes the parasitic capacitance.

$$E_{PS} = C_{PS} \times VDD^2 \tag{1}$$

Based on both the equivalent circuit and a paper [8], the energy consumed by the rush current can be defined by equation (2) in which C_{VVSS}, C_L and Δ_{VVSS} denote the virtual ground, the capacitance of the target circuit and the potential of the virtual ground, respectively.

$$E_{rush} = (C_{VVSS} + \frac{1}{2}C_L) \times VDD \times \Delta_{VVSS} \tag{2}$$

The Δ_{VVSS} increases as long as the target circuit is powered-off, and it asymptotically reaches to the VDD. This fact indicates that the amount of the reduced leakage current increases along with the sleep time while the short sleep time exposes the overhead energy. That is, the sleep time is the break-even point to determine the gain of the power gating. Based on the equation (1) and (2), the break-even sleep time can be defined by an approximate expression (3) in which P_{active} and P_{sleep} denote the energy consumed by the isolation parts, the power consumed by the leakage current during powered-on and the power consumed by the leakage current during powered-off, respectively.

$$BET = \frac{E_{PS} + E_{rush}}{P_{active} - P_{sleep}} \tag{3}$$

The gain of the power gating can be obtained by satisfying the equation (3), and it can be defined by an approximate expression (4) which calculates the difference between the gain and loss based on the equation (3).

$$E_{PG\_gain} = \sum_{i=1}^{N} (T_{sleep}(P_{active} - P_{sleep}) - E_{rush} - E_{PS}) \tag{4}$$

In the equation (4), the i and T_{sleep} denote the number of pipeline stages and the sleep time of the target circuit, respectively.

As for the dynamic voltage scaling, the break-even point can be modeled. The energy is reduced after the supplied voltage decreases, and the charge and discharge due to the increase and decrease of the supplied voltage results in the power overhead. Based on these facts, a break-even processing load (BEPL) is introduced to explain how many

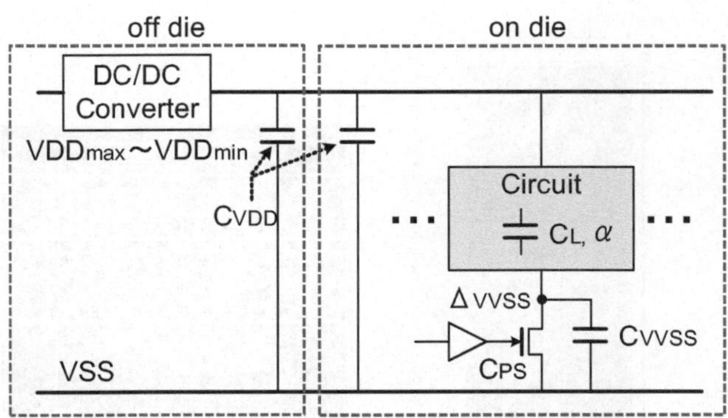

Fig. 4: Runtime fine-grain power-supply control of STP.

times the target circuit should be driven after a decrease of the supplied voltage to obtain the gain. The BEPL can be defined by an approximate expression (5) in which C_{VDD}, C_L and α denote the capacitance of power line, the capacitance of both the DL and Logic, the switching probability of the transistors of both the DL and Logic, respectively.

$$BEPL = \frac{C_{VDD}}{C_L \times \alpha} \quad (5)$$

The gain of the dynamic voltage scaling can be obtained by satisfying the equation (5), and it can be defined by an approximate expression (6) which calculates the product of the ratio of actually-measured parameters and the difference between the gain and loss based on the equation (5).

$$E_{VS\_gain} = (VDD^2 - VDD_{min}^2)(C_L \times \alpha \times PL - C_{VDD}) \quad (6)$$

In the equation (6), VDD_{min} and PL denote the minimum value of the supplied voltage and the processing load fo the target circuit, respectively. The concrete values of the equations can be calculated by measuring the parameters by using the prototype VLSI chip.

3. Variable-grain power gating

In the variable-grain power gating, several pipeline stages are clustered and powered-off at a time. The size of the cluster is changed dynamically between 1 (stage-by-stage) to a certain number to keep the sleep time of the cluster longer than the BET defined by the equation (3). In this section, the circuit implementation of the variable-grain power gating is discussed.

The PG enable signal which is the output of the PC should be asserted when the sleep time of the cluster is longer than the BET. The sleep time is determined by the time interval between the sets of data transferred in the self-timed pipeline. To detect whether the time interval is longer

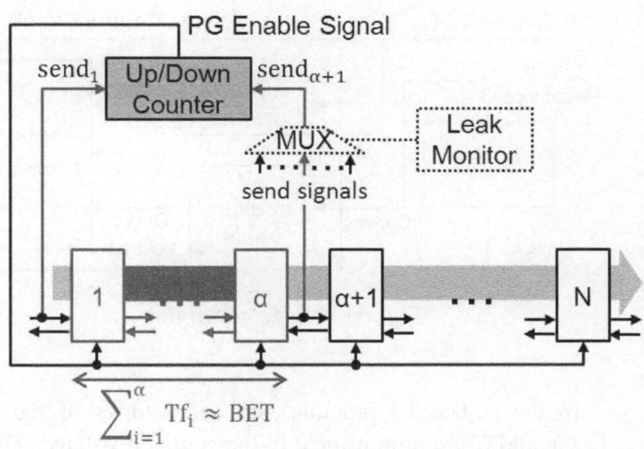

Fig. 5: Realization method for variable-grain power gating.

than the BET or not, a counter-based detection scheme is introduced.

The counter-based detection scheme is shown in figure 5, and it counts how many sets of data are transferred during the BET by focusing on the processing time of the self-timed pipeline. The processing time of the self-timed pipeline is determined by the sum of the forwarding delays of the successive pipeline stages. The forwarding delay of the i-th stage is denoted by Tf_i in the figure 5. In the counter-based detection scheme, several successive pipeline stages are selected so that the processing time of them becomes nearly equal to the BET, and the number of the sets of data transferred during the BET is counted by using a up/down counter which increases when the send (transfer request) signal to the first pipeline stage is asserted and decreases when the send signal of the last pipeline stage is asserted. As a result of this counting, if the count is 0 or 1, it is indicated that the time interval between the sets of data transferred is longer than the BET, i.e., the PG enable signal should be asserted. On the other hand, if the count is greater than 1, it is indicated that the BET is not met and thus the number of the pipeline stages in a cluster should be increased.

In runtime, the BET may change according to the change of temperature of the circuit. To reconfigure the number of the successive pipeline stages according to the BET dynamically, a MUX is introduced to select the appropriate last stage. The MUX also makes it possible to select an arbitrary successive pipeline stages over non-liner self-timed pipelines such as a circular pipeline indispensable to realize the data-driven processors.

4. Suspend-free voltage scaling

The suspend-free voltage scaling makes it possible to change the throughput of the running self-timed pipeline by scaling the supplied voltage without any suspend operation.

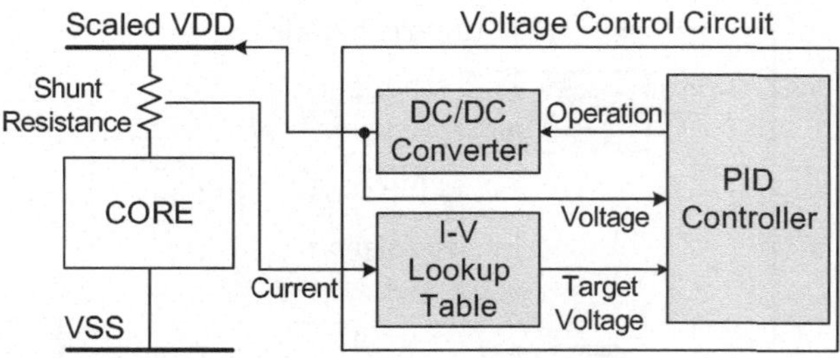

Fig. 6: Voltage controller.

In the self-timed pipeline, the delay times of the DL, Logic and C are proportional to the supplied voltage. Therefore, the supplied voltage of the self-timed pipeline can be scaled at runtime without any suspension. By exploiting this nature, the power consumption can be reduced by keeping the supplied voltage at minimum value enough to achieve the throughput required by a target application even when the required throughput changes at runtime. The required throughput can be directly known based on the whole consumption current of the self-timed pipeline. This is because the localized data transfer of the self-timed pipeline drives only pipeline stages with valid data and thus the consumption current of the self-timed pipeline is in proportion to the number of valid data processed at a time, that is, the throughput.

However, a temporally-sharp magnitude of the fluctuation of the supplied voltage exposes the effects of the overshoots and undershoots, and thus it may result in both the false operation of circuit and the noise on the power lines. Therefore, the rate of change of the supplied voltage should be moderate enough to ignore the effects of the overshoots and undershoots.

To realize such moderate scaling of the supplied voltage, PID (Proportional Integral Derivative) control is introduced in the circuit implementation. The suspend-free voltage scaling circuit is illustrated in figure 6, and it consists of PID controller, I-V mapping table and DC/DC converter. The I-V mapping table is used to lookup the target supplied voltage according to the consumption current, and each supplied voltage value in the table is set to maximize the throughput-power efficiency. Based on both the target supplied voltage value and the currently supplied voltage, the PID controller calculates the amount of change of the supplied voltage. Finally, the DC/DC converter actually changes the supplied voltage according to the calculated amount of change.

5. Power-performance estimation

In order to evaluate power performance characteristic, a data-driven processor ULP-CUE based on the self-timed pipeline has been implemented by using 65 nm CMOS process. In this section, the ULP-CUE is briefly introduced and then the basic power-performance characteristics are evaluated by integrating actual measurement results of the ULP-CUE chip and SPICE simulation results. Finally, total power reduction effects of the proposed variable-grain power gating and suspended-free voltage scaling are revealed in the case of the ULP-CUE.

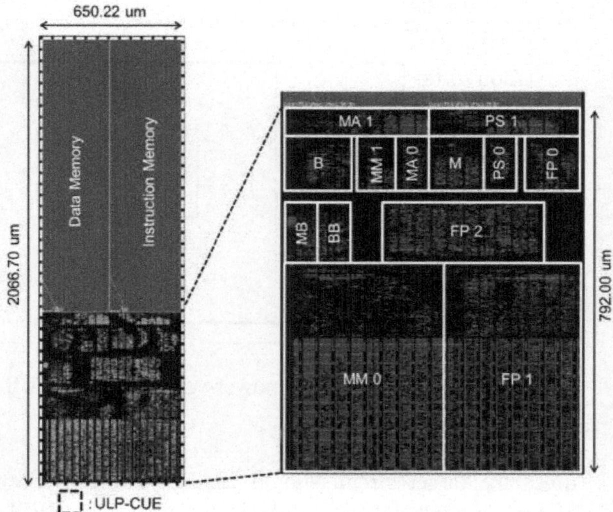

Fig. 7: Layout of ULP-CUE.

5.1 Circuit configuration of ULP-CUE

The ULP-CUE is a 32 bit dynamic data-driven processor composed of the 13-stages ring-shaped STP.Each STP stage is designed to perform the following elemental function.

- MB: merging function of input tokens and internally circulated tokens.
- MM: firing control function to detect a pair of operand tokens for its instruction execution. It is divided into two STP stages, MM0 and MM1.
- M: merging function for tokens bypassing the MM stages.
- PS: instruction fetching function. It is divided into two stages, PS0 and PS1.
- FP: instruction decoding function (FP0) and execution function, i.e., ALU. It is divided into two stages, FP1 and FP2.
- MA: data-memory access function. It is divided into two stages, MA0 and MA1.
- B: branch function to bypass the MM stages or not.
- BB: branch function to ether output port or the circular STP.

Those stages are placed and routed on a die shown in figure 7. As shown in the figure, area of each stage is different from others so that the load capacitance of each stage is different. This means its break-even condition is different.

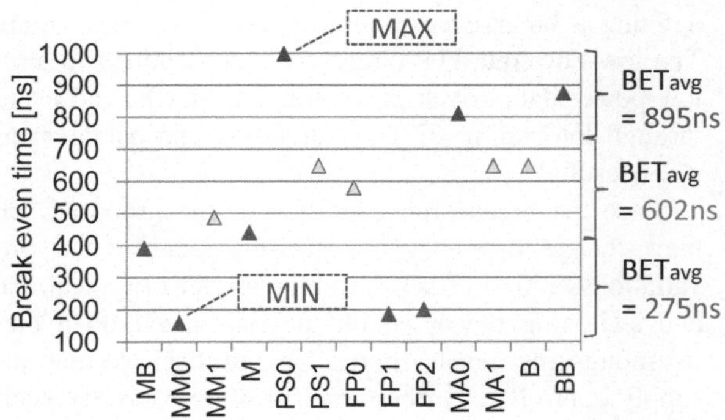

Fig. 8: Break even time of each STP stage (0.8 V, 25°C).

5.2 Estimation of power gating

Because each STP stage of the ULP-CUE is implemented as different circuits, the break-even time is different. For each stage, it is difficult to measure every parameter in equation (3). Thus, in this evaluation, PS switching energy E_{PS}, energy consumption caused by rush current E_{rush}, and leakage power Pleak are evaluated by SPICE simulation of each stage. This is because the detailed breakdown of each stage's power consumption cannot be measured on the fabricated ULP-CUE chip. Since the voltage of the VVSS depends on sleep time, the SPICE simulation is conducted in many times in the case of different sleep time.

Figure 8 shows the break-even time and power reduction effect of each STP stage composing the ULP-CUE at 0.8 V, 25°C. The triangulate plot shows the break-even time. The MM0 stage has the shortest BET, 159 ns. This is because its area is the largest in all stages. Furthermore, the gate width of the PS0 can be shortened because the switching probability of transistors composing the MM0 is not so high compared with other stages. The PS0 has the longest BET, 998 ns. It is about 5 times longer than the shortest one.

Based on those analyses, power saving effect of the proposed variable grain PG is roughly estimated. In this estimation, the stages of ULP-CUE is categorized into three classes; a small-area stage (BET = 895 ns), a middle-area stage (BET = 602 ns), and large-area stage (BET = 275 ns), and an evaluated processor is configured by 12 STP stages including four stages per stage class. Figure 9 shows estimated power depending on the interval time between flowing tokens in the pipeline at 0.8 V, 80°C. This result shows that the variable grain PG is more power efficient in shorter interval time rather than the stage-by-stage PG, e.g., 17 ns shorter in the case of interval time 85 ns.

5.3 Estimation of voltage scaling

As for the voltage scaling, total power of the ULP-CUE processor can be measured on the fabricated chip as shown in figure 10. This measured wave shows an example of consumption current of the ULP-CUE in the case the supply voltage VDD is changed from 0.8 V to 1.2 V by using the PID controller. This consumption current includes charge current to both C_{VDD} and C_L. If electric current when the voltage of VDD is raised from 0.8 V to 1.2 V is measured without operating a program, only the electric current concerning C_{VDD} (overhead cost) can be observed. Moreover, it becomes possible to calculate C_L as difference with the consumption current of figure 10. As a result, the break-even processing load can be calculated based on the equation (5).

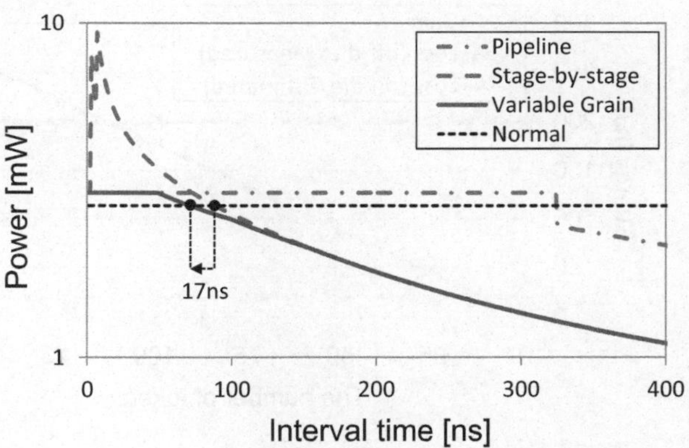

Fig. 9: Evaluation of variable grain power gating.

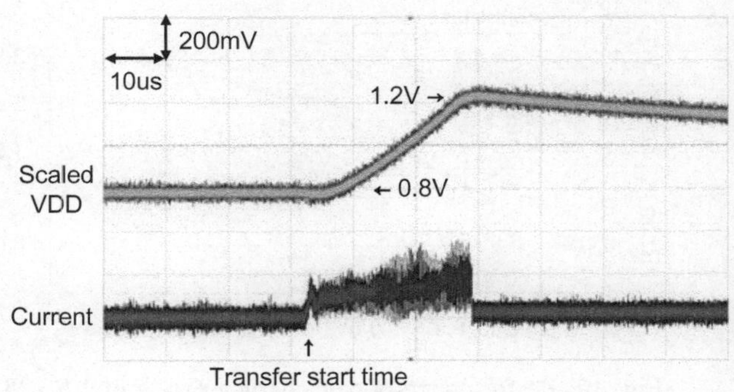

Fig. 10: An example measurement result of suspend-free voltage scaling.

As for the voltage scaling, the break-even processing load is evaluated based on the equation (6). Figure 11 shows the break-even processing load of the ULP-CUE based on the measurement current of the chip when the supply voltage is changed from 0.8 V to 1.2 V. The diamond-shape plots indicate C_L, i.e., the denominator part of the equation (5), and the square-shape plots indicate C_{VDD}, i.e., the numerator part of that. From this result, the BEPL is about 113 tokens.

The measured chip is not equipped with the on-die DC/DC convertor. If a DC/DC convertor can be implemented on a die, the load capacitance of the power line, C_{VDD}, can be

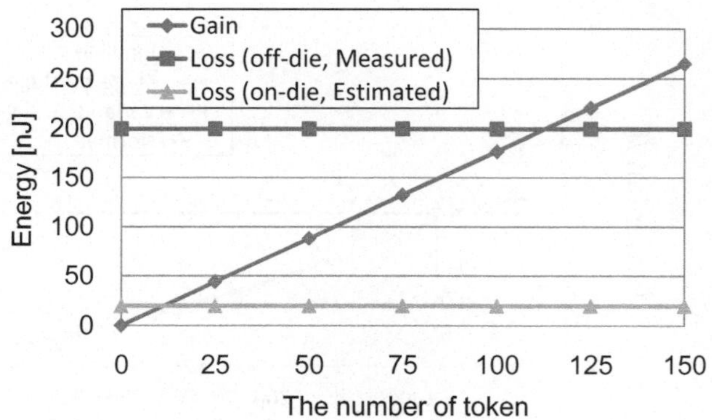

Fig. 11: Break even processing load of ULP-CUE.

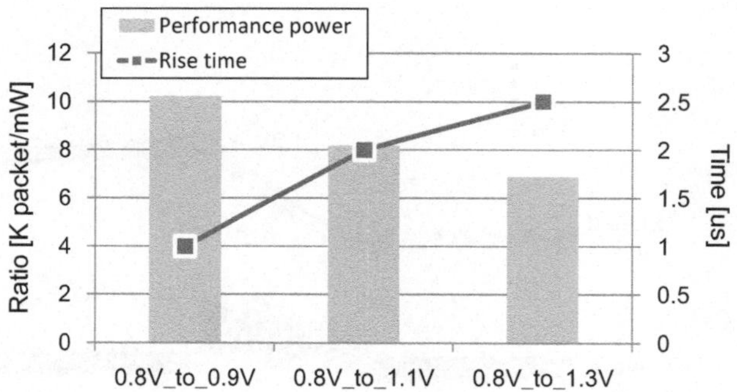

Fig. 12: Performance-power characteristics of VS (25°C).

reduced to one-tenth of that [9]. In this case, the break-even processing load can be reduced to 11 tokens.

Figure 12 shows the measured transient power-performance ratios and voltage rise times when the supply-voltage is altered from 0.8 V to 0.9 V, 1.1 V, and 1.3 V. Even during such transient time of supply-voltage, the ULP-CUE can work at reasonable power-performance ratio. Therefore, total performance-power ratio could be improved as well as better dependability against hard real-time constraints can be obtained. On condition of 0.8 V to 0.9 V, it was the throughput performance of 5 [M token/sec]. And on condition of 0.8 V to 1.3 V, the maximum throughput performance of 5.5 [M token/sec] was able to be maintained. Be subject to frequent work load changes application, it is shown that continuation of processing can be performed by the minimum performance overhead. In addition, it is important parameters for considering applicability to real applications.

6. Conclusion

In this paper, a variable-grain power gating and suspend-free voltage scaling mechanism based on the self-timed elastic pipeline (STP) was proposed to realize lower-power LSI circuits and then its effectiveness was analyzed by defining a break-even model in terms of energy trade-off. The low-powered STP circuit was then applied to an ultra-low-power data-driven processor, ULP-CUE, and evaluated through integrating SPICE simulation and actual measurement results.

Since the break-even condition of the proposed scheme may change depending on the temperature and process variations, a kind of self-checking circuit of typical leakage and switching power should be introduced on a die and its monitoring result should be fed back to the power-supply controller. Furthermore, in order to verify such on-die mechanism in terms of power performance efficiency, a microarchitecture simulator must be developed which can simulate not only architectural behavior but also transient power consumption. We are now developing such a platform simulator and then we will report the comprehensive evaluation results using this simulator in near future.

Acknowledgement

This research work was supported in part by Core Research for Evolutional Science and Technology (CREST), Japan Science and Technology Agency (JST). The circuit design work was supported by VLSI Design and Education Center (VDEC), the University of Tokyo in collaboration with Synopsys, Inc. and Cadence Design Systems, Inc.

References

[1] S. Mutoh, S. Shigematsu, Y. Gotoh, and S. Konaka, "Design method of MTCMOS power switch for low-voltage high-speed LSIs," Proceedings of the Asia and South Pacific Design Automation Conference (ASP-DAC'99), pp. 113–116, July 1999.

[2] P. Pillai, and K. Shin, "Real-Time Dynamic Voltage Scaling for Low-Power Embedded Operating Systems," Proceedings of the 18th ACM Symposium on Operating Systems Principles (SOSP'01), pp. 89–102, October 2001.

[3] K. Kawasaki, T. Shiota, K. Nakayama, and A. Inoue, "A Sub-us Wake-Up Time Power Gating Technique with Bypass Power Line for Rush Current Support," Proceedings of the IEEE Symposium on VLSI Circuits (VLSIC'08), pp. 146–147, June 2008.

[4] K. Miyagi, S. Sannomiya, M. Iwata and H. Nisikawa, "Self-Timed Power-Aware Pipeline Chip and Its Evaluation," Proceedings of the 2011 International Conference on Parallel and Distributed Processing Techniques and Applications (PDPTA'11), pp. 442–448, July 2011.

[5] K. Miyagi, M. Iwata, S. Sannomiya, and H. Nishikawa, "Low-powered self-timed pipeline with runtime fine-grain power supply," Proceedings of The 2012 International Conference on Parallel and Distributed Processing Techniques and Applications (PDPTA'12), pp. 472–478, July 2012.

[6] H. Terada, S. Miyata, and M. Iwata, "DDMP's: Self-Timed Super-Pipelined Data-Driven Processors," Proceedings of the IEEE, vol. 87, no. 2, pp. 282–296, February 1999.

[7] S. Lee, and T. Sakurai, "Run-Time Voltage Hopping for Low-Power Real-Time Systems," Proceedings of the Design Automation Conference (DAC'00), pp. 806–809, June 2000.

[8] Z. Hu, A. Buyuktosunoglu, V. Srinivasan, V. Zyuban, H. Jacobson, and P. Bose, "Microarchitectural Techniques for Power Gating of Execution Units," Proceedings of the 2004 International Symposium on Low Power Electronics and Design (ISLPED'04), pp. 32–37, August 2004.

[9] A. Inoue, "Design constraint of fine grain supply voltage control LSI," Proceedings of the Asia and South Pacific Design Automation Conference (ASP-DAC'11), pp. 760–765, January 2011.

Self-Timed Single Circular Pipeline for Multiple FFTs

Ryuichi TAGUCHI, Hajime OHISO, Keizo MENDORI, Kei MIYAGI, Makoto IWATA
Graduate School of Engineering, Kochi University of Technology,
Kami, Kochi, 782-8502 Japan

Abstract— *Future wireless ad hoc network should accommodate different types of mobile terminals equipped with different wireless communication schemes. Especially when disaster will happen, to guarantee dependable connectivity among mobile terminals will be indispensable for delivering emergent information by using available wireless links. In order to realize such heterogeneous wireless communication systems, one of the key technologies is adaptive fast Fourier transform (FFT) engine to accept multiple wireless signal sequences with different sampling rate and different FFT point.*

This paper discusses a basic idea of novel FFT engine based on the self-timed (clockless) pipeline circuit to compute multiple FFT's in parallel. After that, the potential performance of the proposed circuit is evaluated through its FPGA implementation. Preliminary results indicate the proposed circuit could process two 4096-point FFT's at 276 M sample/s per each FFT.

Keywords: heterogeneous wireless communication, ad hoc network, FFT, self-tiemd pipeline

1. Introduction

Diverse wireless communication devices have permeated throughout our daily lives in modern information society. Therefore, wireless networks supporting higher throughput and wider coverage area are increasingly demanded. Since the modern homogeneous wireless networks are facing severe limitation of transmit power level affecting coverage range and the amount of interference, heterogeneous wireless networks are becoming part of the mainstream wireless communication infrastructures [1], [2], [3]. Those heterogeneous wireless communication devices can be utilized to configure more dependable and flexible ad hoc networks, especially in emergent conditions such as natural or artificial disasters.

Heterogeneous wireless communication devices should be equipped with a multimode and multiband receiver module so as to select optimum modulation, channel, and network dynamically depending on its individual wireless communication condition. To realize such intelligent multimode devices, sophisticated radio link management decision among available wireless connections is required. Frequency domain equalizer (FDE) [4] with channel estimation is one of the most important functions for the intelligently dependable mobile terminal, because its channel estimation result can be utilized to decide an appropriate radio link and FDE itself improves the bit error rate (BER) to mitigate interference within both air and RF devices.

In our prior research project, ultra-low power data-driven networking system for ad hoc wireless network has been investigated. The final results of the project demonstrated that our ultra-low-power data-driven chip-multiprocessor LSI fabricated in 65 nm CMOS process can perform at less than a few-tenth of power of conventional embedded microprocessors [5], [6]. Since the target protocols in the project were over layer 3, for further investigation of low-power wireless networking technologies, it is necessary to study layer 2 and baseband process.

Our research project therefore aims to establish a self-timed pipeline (STP) implementation for the dependable wireless systems (DWS) supporting multimode and multi-band interfaces. Since the STP circuit inherently has clock-less passive operation mode [7], [8], it can flexibly process any combination of signal sequences even if they are sampled at different frequencies. In this paper, fast Fourier transform (FFT), one of the heaviest functions in the DWS, is focused on and its STP design is proposed. Finally, its feasibility is discussed through a preliminary field programmable gate array (FPGA) design of STP-based FFT circuit.

2. Pipeline Parallelism of Multichannel FFT

The single carrier FDE module performs on the receiver side after the FFT calculation to combat frequency-selective fading and phase distortion [4]. To equalize the transmitted data in frequency domain, a pilot signal is used for estimating the transfer function and the noise power in the air channel. Therefore, after the received data are transformed from time domain to frequency domain by FFT, they are equalized based on estimated results and then retransformed to time domain by IFFT.

In case of orthogonal frequency division multiplexing (OFDM), FFT is also used for modulating data onto each subcarrier and IFFT is for demodulating data on each subcarrier. Furthermore, in multiple-input multiple-output (MIMO) antenna configuration, a multichannel FFT/IFFT processor is necessary in a transmitter/receiver.

Therefore, we aim to implement a multichannel FFT processor in which multiple FFT operations of variable sizes are simultaneously performed for multiple input signal sequences sampled in variable frequencies.

Originally FFT is a fast version of discrete Fourier transform (DFT). N point DFT is defined by the equation (1).

$$X(k) = \sum_{n=0}^{N-1} x(n) W_N^{kn}$$
$$W_N^{kn} = e^{-j2\pi kn/N}, \quad k = 0, 1, ..., N-1 \tag{1}$$

where the input sequence of N complex data $x(0)$, $x(1)$, $\cdots$, $x(N-1)$ is transformed into an N-periodic sequence of complex data. In the Cooley-Tukey FFT algorithm, radix-r butterfly operations are recursively applied to N input signals, and the depth of recursion is $log_r N$. In each recursion, the number of butterfly operations (i.e., r-point FFT) is N/r and they can be calculated in parallel, because there is no data dependency among them. An example of a decimation-in-time FFT (N=8, r=2) is shown in Figure 1. As seen in this dataflow diagram, four butterfly operations can be concurrently executed in each recursion step.

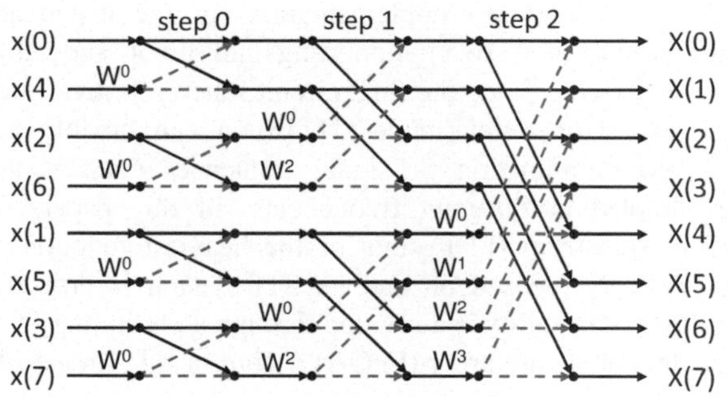

Fig. 1: Dataflow diagram of radix-2 decimation-in-time FFT (N=8).

If the dataflow diagram of FFT shown in Figure 1 is interpreted based on the dynamic dataflow model [7], multiple instances of the same FFT diagram can be allowed to be executed by introducing a channel identifier, which differentiates between them. In the same way, the dataflow diagram of a butterfly operation can be interpreted for multiprocessing of the butterfly if every data flowing the diagram have a set of identifiers ID, which is composed of channel identifier ch, step identifier $step$, and butterfly instance identifier within the step btf. In this case, it is necessary to provide a function supplying appropriate set of operands with those identifiers and storing intermediate data in the memory buffer. This parallel execution scheme in case of radix-2 butterfly is illustrated in Figure 2. In the figure, every operand and result of butterfly are identified by $ID(ch, step, btf)$ and multiple sets of operands are issued from the commutator consecutively. The commutator manages the number of operand sets for butterfly instances, which represents the degree of parallelism P_{ch}. At the same time, the commutator attaches appropriate identifiers to those issued operands.

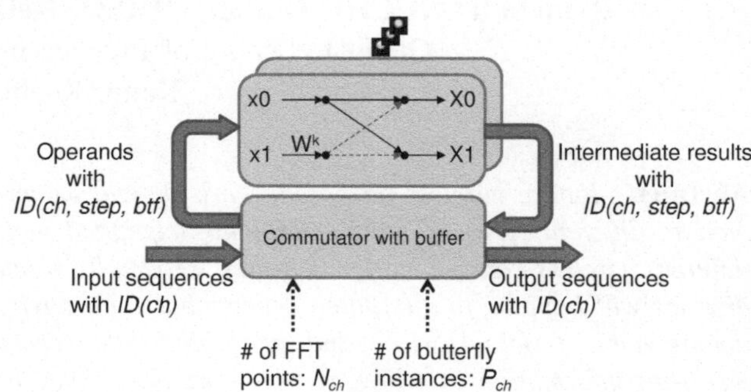

Fig. 2: Parallel execution scheme of multiple butterfly instances.

As long as the butterfly operation with a correct set of identifiers is executed under dynamic dataflow model, valid execution of multiple FFT calculations is guaranteed even if the size of an FFT N_{ch} and the sampling frequency of its input data sequence are different from others.

However, the connectivity in each step is different from that in others, as seen in Figure 1 so that commutator might be complex. Therefore, in our design, the original FFT structure is modified to uniform FFT structure shown in Figure 3. By adopting this FFT structure, the ID handling function in the commutator is simply defined as shown in Figure 4.

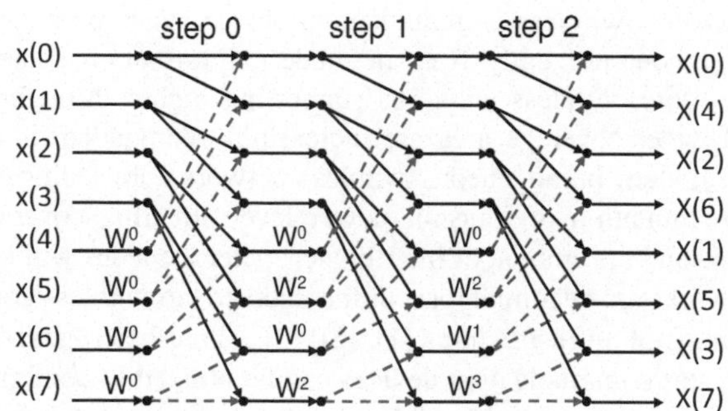

Fig. 3: Uniformity in radix-2 FFT structure (N=8).

Furthermore, this uniform type of FFT structure allows the comutator to fetch r operands from the buffer memory in parallel. Because the memory access pattern is invariant at all steps, the buffer memory can be composed of r single-port memory banks.

Figure 5 shows a dataflow graph representation of the proposed parallel execution scheme of multichannel FFT. Firstly, the input complex data is stored in multi-bank buffer memory consecutively. If a set of operands for the first

```
do {
        btf += P_ch;
        if (btf >= (N_ch/r)) {
                step++;
                btf %= (N_ch/r);
        }
} while ( step < log_r N_ch);
```

Fig. 4: ID handling function in commutator.

butterfly is ready to be computed, an instance of FFT is initiated and P_{ch} sets of identifiers IDs are issued at ID handling module according to input data arrival. After that, r operands are read from the buffer memory in parallel based on the issued ID. Similarly, twiddle factors are read from TF lookup table in parallel and radix-r butterfly is calculated. The r resultant data from the butterfly are written into the buffer memory in parallel. Then, preparation of a continuous butterfly operation is conducted as defined in Figure 4. After executing the last butterfly in the FFT instance, the output data read from the buffer memory are reordered.

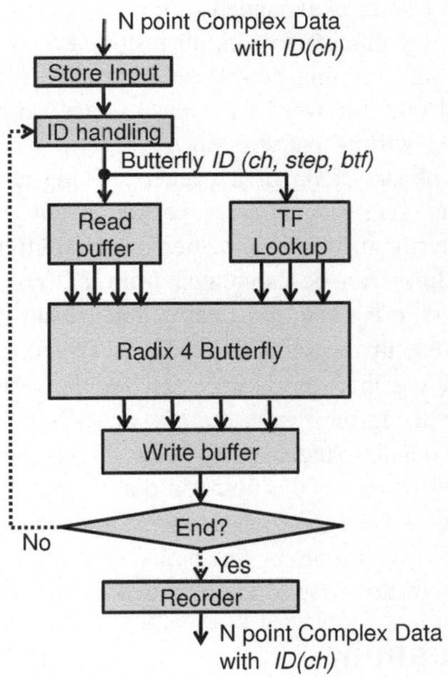

Fig. 5: Dataflow diagram of the proposed scheme.

3. STP Implementation of Multichannel FFT

The parallel execution scheme proposed in the previous section is an abstract model and that does not deal with temporal information such as sampling frequency. In order to process multiple input sequences with different frequencies, its circuit implementation should have a passive operation mode enabling to accept input data adaptively along with outside conditions. Therefore the self-timed pipeline (STP) circuit is employed for implementing multichannel FFT.

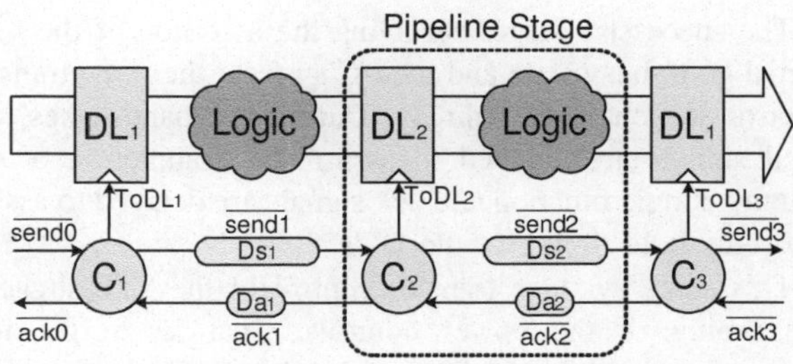

Fig. 6: Self-timed pipeline.

In this section, the passive and autonomous behavior of the STP is briefly introduced and then its natural contribution to multichannel FFT implementation is discussed.

3.1 Self-Timed Pipeline

Each pipeline stage of the STP consists of a data latch as a pipeline register, function logic, and transfer control unit named C-element. The basic structure of the STP is shown in Figure 6. The data latch, function logic, and C-element are denoted by DL, Logic, and C, respectively. The data is packed with tag into packet form, and the packet is transferred between the pipeline stages as a result of the communication between the C's in the adjacent stages. The communication is performed stage-by-stage according to the 4-phase handshake protocol [9] by using transfer request and acknowledge signals which are called send signal and ack signal respectively. The stage-by-stage transfer control changes the states of each pipeline stage independently, and the states of the stages are defined below according to the handshake protocol. Here, the C-element in the i-th stage is denoted by C_i.

- Reset state: The send and ack signals are negated after the assertion of the reset signal.
- Idle state: The C_i waits until the $send_{i-1}$ is asserted.
- Busy state: The $send_{i-1}$ is asserted at the beginning of the transfer of the packet from the precedent $(i-1)$-th stage. After the assertion of the $send_{i-1}$, the C_i asserts its ack signal (ack_{i-1}). In response to the assertion, the C_{i-1} negates the $send_{i-1}$. After that, if and only when both the $send_{i-1}$ and ack_i are negated, the C_i asserts the $ToDL_i$ to open the DL_i and it asserts $send_i$ at the same time. As a consequence, the packet is latched in the i-th stage, and the i-th stage goes to idle state. Otherwise, the C_i waits until the ack_i is negated while it keeps its send and ack signals.

The successive stages receiving the assertion of the send signal go to busy state and their C's repeat the same transfer control sequence individually. During the handshakes, the send signals are delayed to assure the completion of the primitive logic function and ack signals are delayed to assure the setup-hold timing of the DL's.

This stage-by-stage transfer control of the STP suggests the timing of the power controls. That is, in the idle stages, the circuit of the DL and combinational logic can be powered-off, i.e., the supply-voltage can be cut, while that of the C and sequential logic can be powered-down, i.e., the supply voltage can be lowered enough to keep the circuit's states [10]. Moreover, in the busy stages, those circuits should be powered-down enough to assure the switching of the transistors, i.e., the supply-voltage can be lowered as long as the required switching speed is achieved [11].

3.2 Multichannel FFT Implementation

In order to realize the dataflow shown in Figure 5, it is essential to maintain stable dataflow in the STP without any pipeline bottleneck as well as to guarantee atomic (i.e., read-after-write) accesses of intermediate data stored in the buffer memory during execution. Therefore, the buffer memory accesses must be integrated at the single STP stage. Moreover, intermediate resultant data of radix-r butterfly are written in different buffer addresses from that of operands when the uniform type of FFT structure is employed. Thus, in our design, we adopt dual buffer memory modules each of which is used for butterfly operations in either even step or odd step of the FFT. It requires $2N_{ch}$ words SRAM for N_{ch}-point FFT. As a result, multichannel FFT engine is designed as shown in Figure 7 to utilize the passive operation mode of STP. This FFT engine operates as follows.

All data flowing in the pipeline has an operation code *op* as well as $ID(ch, step, btf)$. The *op* is assigned one of operations, i.e., in, $read$, $write$, or *out*. Every stage in the STP-based FFT engine changes its operation depending on *op* of the packet.

- **input phase**: N_{ch} input data from a channel ch consecutively arrive at one of input ports of the merge stage. At that time, each input data is composed as a packet form including a complex number, ch identifier, index i(=0,...,N_{ch}-1) and *op*($= in$). The input data reaching to the buffer memory stage is written in a place associated with index i of the packet.
- **instantiation phase**: If *op* of a packet arriving at the ID handler stage is in, an FFT for the channel ch may be instantiated. Only when r operands necessary for the first butterfly are stored in the buffer memory, an FFT instance for the channel ch is initiated. ID(ch, 0, 0) for the first butterfly is issued with *op*($= read$). After that, succeeded butterfly instances are instantiated with ID(ch, 0, 1),..., ID(ch, 0, P_{ch}-1) within the allowable degree of parallelism P_{ch}.
- **read phase**: If *op* of a packet arriving at the buffer memory stage is $read$, r operands for the btf-th butterfly instance are read out from the buffer memory in parallel. Their addresses can be calculated from $ID(ch, step, btf)$. To allow those parallel accesses, the buffer memory is composed of dual r-way memory banks. If the $step$ is even, the operands are read from the first set of r-way memory banks. If odd, the second one is accessed for operand fetches. At the same time, $(r-1)$ twiddle factors necessary for the butterfly are fetched from the twiddle factor lookup table in parallel. Since the lookup table holds twiddle factors only in the fourth quadrant, each lookup data needs the change of quadrant by swapping the real and imaginary number, or changing on one(or both) sign(s) of the number(s).
- **butterfly phase**: If *op* of a packet arriving at the butterfly stage is $read$, a butterfly instance is executed using r operands and $r-1$ twiddle factors.
- **prerelease ID phase**: If *op* of a packet arriving at the ID handler stage is $read$, this stage prepares to write r resultant data to the buffer memory. In the uniform type of FFT, all results of a butterfly should be stored to one of memory banks. Therefore, word length of each memory bank is expanded to $r \times$ (*length of a complex word*). By this expansion, all results are written at the same time. In this prerelease ID phase, r results are packed into one word with *op*($= write$) to prepare for the next writing phase.
- **write phase**: If *op* of a packet arriving at the buffer memory stage is $write$, a packed result of the btf-th butterfly instance is written in the buffer memory. Its address can be calculated from $ID(ch, step, btf)$. If the $step$ is even, the intermediate result of the FFT is written in the second set of r-way memory banks. If odd, the first one is accessed for the result storing. After writing the result, the ID packet is transferred to the ID handler stage. In this stage, $ID(ch, step, btf)$ is updated based on the function defined in Figure 7 and then *op* is changed to $read$. If $step$ exceeds $log_r N_{ch}$, the FFT operation is finished and buffered data are output. In this case, *op* is changed to *out*.

4. Evaluation

In order to evaluate the performance of the stream-driven FFT processing, its STP circuit is designed and implemented on FPGA (Stratix II, Altera Corp.). Table 1 shows the specifications of the implemented self-timed FFT circuit on the FPGA. This FPGA design was conducted for confirming that parallel butterfly instances works well in pipelined parallel processing of the single circular STP circuit. In the preliminary result of non-optimized circuit, the processing time of 1024-point FFT was 424 us. This means that the acceptable sampling rate is 2.4 M sample/s. In this case, the maximum pipeline tact in 13 pipeline stages was 20.6

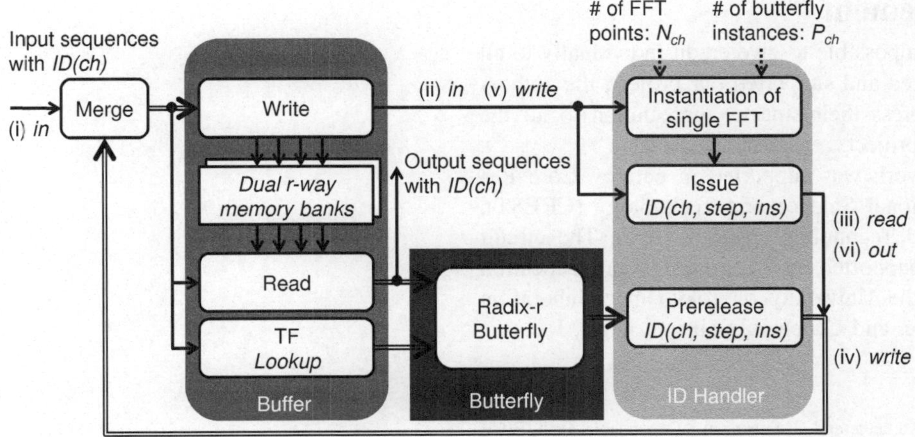

Fig. 7: STP implementation of multichannel FFT.

ns. The number of logic cell (LC) Combinationals, LC Registers, block memory bits, and DSP slices required for the designed FFT circuit are 1200, 2008, 40062, and 12 respectively.

Table 1: Specifications of the self-timed FFT circuit on FPGA

# of FFT points N_{ch}	$16 \sim 1024$
Radix r	4
Degree of parallelism P_{ch}	2
Complex data (real, imaginary)	32 bit, fixed point integer (16bit, 16bit)
# of STP stages	13

The processing time T_{FFT} of the implemented STP circuit can be approximated by the equation (1).

$$T_{FFT} = \left(\frac{r-1}{r}N_{ch} + 2\frac{N_{ch}log_r N_{ch}}{rP_{ch}}S\right) * T_{fmax} \quad (2)$$

where T_{fmax} denotes the maximum pipeline tact in the STP, S denotes the number of pipeline stages, and P_{ch} denotes the number of parallel instances of butterfly. The first term in this equation expresses the initiation delay to wait the arrival of a set of operands for the first butterfly. The second term expresses the parallel exectuion time of all butterfly instances. As understood from this equation, r and P_{ch} should be increased and T_{fmax} should be decreased in order to shorten the FFT processing time T_{FFT}.

Based on our ASIC design experiences for the STP, T_{fmax} can be reduced to about 1 ns if 65 nm CMOS process will be used to implement the proposed FFT circuit. Through those considerations, the performance of the proposed self-timed FFT circuit can be estimated as shown in Figure 8. For example, two 4096-point radix-8 FFTs will be performed at 276 M samples/s in case of 8 parallel instances, i.e., the degree of pipeline parallelism for radix-8 butterfly operations.

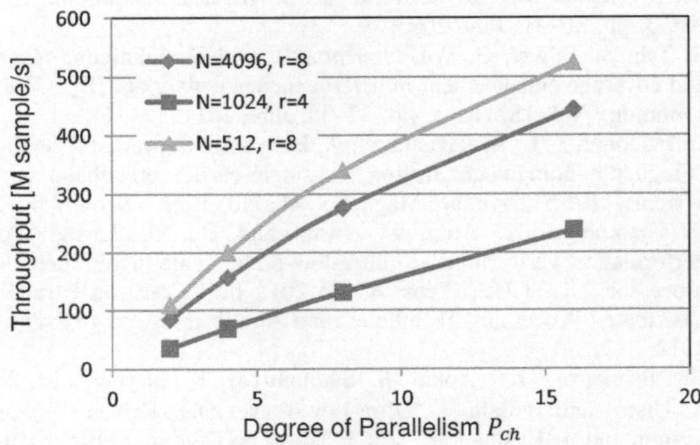

Fig. 8: Performance estimation of the self-timed FFT circuit.

5. Conclusion

In order to establish low-power and dependable wireless networks, mobile devices should be equipped with a multimode and multiband transceiver/receiver module for both cellular networks and ad hoc networks. Such mobile terminals would be useful and sustainable in case of emergent situation as well as normal situation.

This paper focuses on a multichannel FFT engine used for MIMO OFDM and SC-FDE and proposes a basic idea of its self-timed pipeline implementation based on the dynamic data-driven multiprocessing model. The preliminary results indicated that the proposed STP implementation will be feasible to the required performance for heterogeneous wireless communication environment involving mobile broadband wireless access (MBWA), wireless local area network (WLAN), wireless personal area network (WPAN).

Acknowledgement

Although it is impossible to give credit individually to all those who organized and supported our project, the authors would like to express their sincere appreciation to all the colleagues in the project.

This research work was supported in part by Core Research for Evolutional Science and Technology (CREST), Japan Science and Technology Agency (JST). The circuit design work was supported by VLSI Design and Education Center (VDEC), the University of Tokyo in collaboration with Synopsys, Inc. and Cadence Design Systems, Inc.

References

[1] K. Tsubouchi, S. Kameda, and N. Suematsu, "Dependable Air," IEICE Trans. Electron., Vol. J95-C, No. 12, pp. 450–459, Dec. 2012 (in Japanese).

[2] D. Cavalcanti, D. Agrawal, C. Cordeiro, B. Xie, and A. Kumar, "Issues in integrating cellular networks, WLAN, and MANETS: a futuristic heterogeneous wireless network," IEEE Wireless Commun., Vol. 12, No. 3, pp. 30–41, June 2005.

[3] S. Yeh, S. Talwar, G. Wu, N. Himayat, and K. Johnsson, "Capacity and coverage enhancement in heterogeneous networks," IEEE Wireless Commun., Vol. 18, No. 3, pp. 32–38, June 2011.

[4] D. Falconer, S. L. Ariyavisitakul, A. Benyamin-Seeyar, and B. Eidson, "Frequency-domainequalization for single-carrier broadband wireless systems," IEEE Commun. Mag., Vol. 40, No, 4, pp. 58–66, Apr. 2002.

[5] S. Sannomiya, K. Aoki, M. Iwata and H. Nishikawa, "Power-performance verification of ultra-low-power data-driven networking processor: ULP-CUE," Proc. of the 2012 Int'l Conf. on Parallel and Distributed Processing Techniques and Applications, pp.465–471, July 2012.

[6] H. Nishikawa, K. Aoki, S. Sannomiya, K. Miyagi, M. Iwata, K. Utsu, and H. Ishii, "Ultra-Low-Power Data-Driven Networking System and its Evaluation," IEICE Trans. on Communication, Vol.J96-B, No.6, Jun. 2013. (to be published)

[7] H. Terada, M. Iwata, and S. Miyatta, "DDMP's: self-timed super-pipelined data-driven multimedia processors," Proc. of the IEEE, Vol. 87, No. 2, pp. 282–296, Feb. 1999.

[8] K. Komatsu, S. Sannomiya, M. Iwata, H. Terada, S. Kameda, and K. Tsubouchi, "Interacting self-timed pipelines and elementary coupling control modules," IEICE Trans. Fundamantals, Vol. E92-A, No. 7, pp. 1642–1651, Jul. 2009.

[9] C. J. Myers, "Asynchronous circuit design," John Wiley & Sons, Inc., July 2001.

[10] K. Miyagi, S. Sannomiya, M. Iwata, and H. Nishikawa, "Autonomous power-supply control for ultra-low-power self-timed pipeline," Proc. of The 2008 Int'l Conf. on Parallel and Distributed Processing Techniques and Applications, pp. 704–709, July 2008.

[11] K. Miyagi, M. Iwata, S. Sannomiya, and H. Nishikawa, "Low-powered self-timed pipeline with runtime fine-grain power supply," Proc. of The 2012 Int'l Conf. on Parallel and Distributed Processing Techniques and Applications, pp. 472-478, July 2012.

SESSION

POSTERS AND SHORT RESEARCH PAPERS

Chair(s)

TBA

Perfect Difference Networks and Graphs and Their Applications

Mikhail Rakov and John R. Mackall
Mackall and Rakov
Santa Barbara, California

Keywords: Graph theory; Network topology, Perfect difference network; Graph search; Perfect difference graph; PDN

The new topological structure known as a Perfect Difference Network (PDN) has numerous applications in both hardware and software. Two specific applications are noted below, but we begin with a description of the PDN topology. The PDN structure is the optimal method of connecting a number of nodes into a network with diameter 2, so that any node is reachable from any other node in no more than two hops.

The PDN interconnection scheme is based on the mathematical notions of projective geometry, finite fields and perfect difference sets, which form the basis for a new topology previously unknown in graph theory or network topology. The PDN topology can accommodate an asymptotically maximal number of nodes with the smallest possible node degree, fashioned in a network with a diameter of 2. It has a highly desirable mix of power (ability to interconnect many nodes), simplicity (fewer connecting lines), symmetry and other properties.

Because of the general character of this topology, the PDN concept applies to both hardware and software structures, including CPUs, supercomputers, database organization, optical interconnection systems and other challenges. Introduced via scholarly papers published in 2005, PDNs constitute an important addition to the repertoire of computer and communications systems designers and offer additional design points that can be exploited by new and emerging technologies, in software or in hardware. Various PDN derivatives, such as multidimensional, hierarchical and hybrid PDNs, most of which remain unpublished, offer many further advantages in designing complex networks. The high degree of symmetry makes it possible to add a logic system, so the network can be "intelligent" as well as efficient.

In software, consider the new "Graph Search" initiative underway at Facebook, which seeks to find and harvest the hidden information originating in its own network in the billions of interconnections among more than a billion nodes. The PDN topology and its various derivatives are well suited to meet the Graph Search challenge and other problems posed by extremely large networks, such as Facebook, Google +, and LinkedIn. The PDN topology is by far the most efficient system for mapping the connections within any large system of nodes (the "Graph," as Facebook calls it) which in turn will identify information that was otherwise unknown and unknowable (the "Search"). The challenge of finding useful information within extremely large social networks is an entirely new challenge for which there is no solution. The PDN topology offers a flexible mathematical platform to conceptualize the graph and a variety of general and special tools, including logic, that function efficiently on such a platform and facilitate searches within the graph.

For the same reasons, Facebook's EdgeRank algorithm can be optimally implemented by using the PDN topology, specifically by its variant with functional nodes. The PDN topological structure can organically accommodate such parameters of social networks as frequency and times of contacts between customers, relative ranks of nodes and so on. There is almost an endless list of potential logical functions that can be optimally implemented in a PDN topology. This flexibility will be highly attractive in social networks with millions of participants.

In hardware, the "network on chip" and "system on chip" sectors create opportunities to apply PDN design tools. More and more IP cores (nodes) need to be interconnected on densely packed chips. The interconnection problems grow exponentially, leading to blocking problems as the proliferating wires intersect, and undesirable energy consumption due to the same proliferation of wires. The PDN design is the optimal method for interconnecting the nodes. As NoC and SoC designs grow in complexity, presenting difficult interconnection requirements, the PDN design will be the only practical solution. Other network topologies require exponential growth in the number of interconnecting lines (N), whereas the PDN topology can achieve the same interconnection results using far fewer lines, requiring only the square root of N lines. Thus, 100 lines can be replaced by 10 lines.

These two examples (graph search in software, and system-on-chip requirements in hardware) illustrate that the PDN topology has the potential to become a dominant interconnection topology, providing optimal solutions for many complex interconnection challenges. The PDN topology can be the new language of network design.

REFERENCES

1. Rakov, M., Method of Interconnecting Nodes and a Hyperstar Interconnection Structure - Patent #5,734,580, March 1998.

2. Rakov, M. and Mackall, J., Method of Interconnecting Functional Nodes and a Hyperstar Interconnection Structure - Patent #6,330,706, December 2001.

3. Rakov. M., Hyperstar: A New Interconnection Topology, Journal of China Universities of Posts and Telecommunications, vol. 5, #2, pp. 10-18, December 1998.

4. Rakov, M., Parhami, B., Application of Perfect Difference Sets to the Design of Efficient and Robust Interconnection Networks, Communication in Computing, pp. 207-216, 2005.

5. Parhami, B., Rakov, M., Perfect Difference Networks and Related Interconnection Structures for Parallel and Distributed Systems, IEEE Transactions on Parallel and Distributed Systems, vol. 16, issue 8, pp. 714-724, August 2005.

6. Parhami, B., Rakov, M., Performance Algorithmic, and Robustness Attributes of Perfect Difference Networks, IEEE Transactions on Parallel and Distributed Systems, vol. 16, issue 8, pp. 725-736, August 2005.

7. Gaikwad, M. and Patrikar R., Perfect Difference Network for Network-on-Chip Architecture, International Journal on Computer Science and Network Security, vol. 9, #12, pp. 286-290, December 2009.

8. R. Venkadeshan, M. Jegatha, Super peer deployment in unstructured peer-to-peer networks, Advances in Intelligent Systems and Computing, vol. 176, pp. 661-669, 2012

Parallelization of Initial Thread-level Work in Depth-First-Search Tree-Search on GPUs

Mark Fienup
Computer Science Department, University of Northern Iowa, Cedar Falls, Iowa, USA

Abstract - *Depth-first search (DFS) tree searching algorithms are a common implementation approach for many NP-complete optimization algorithms (traveling salesperson problem (TSP), 0-1 Knapsack problem, etc.). In a GPU environment the host computer typically performs a breadth-first expansion of the top of the search tree to determine subtrees that can be assigned to GPU threads, then these subtrees are transferred from the host memory to the GPU-device global memory before the GPU threads can start their search. This paper describes a parallel algorithm that allows the GPU threads to determine their initial subtrees.*

Keywords: Backtracking Algorithm, GPU computing

1 Introduction

Depth-first search (DFS) tree searching algorithms are a common implementation approach for many NP-complete optimization algorithms [1]. Consider the traveling salesperson problem (TSP) for the graph in Figure 1, a salesperson starting at her hometown (say v_1) and wants to visit every other city exactly once before return to her hometown (called a *tour*) using a minimum total cost. For this toy example, the minimum tour is $[v_1, v_3, v_4, v_2, v_1]$ with a total cost of 21.

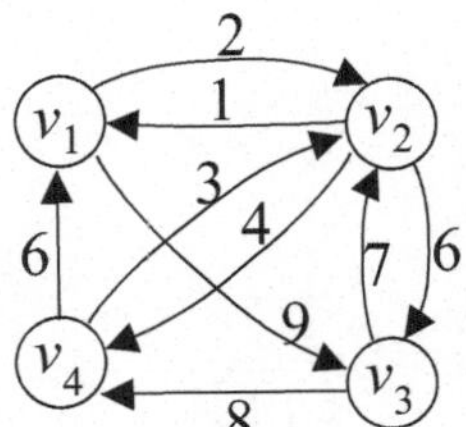

Figure 1. TSP Graph

In a GPU environment the host computer typically performs a serial breadth-first expansion of the top of the search tree to determine subtrees that can be assigned to GPU threads. Figure 2 shows the expansion for the TSP graph in Figure 1. These subtrees are transferred from the host memory to the GPU-device global memory before the GPU threads can start their search on the subtrees.

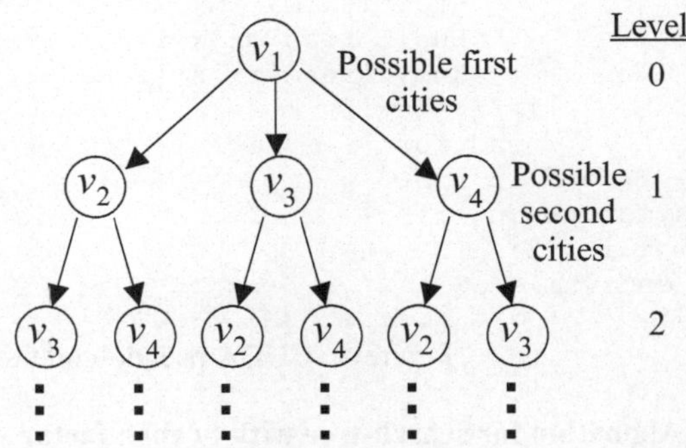

Figure 2. Top of Search-Tree for the TSP Graph

2 Parallelization algorithms

2.1 Algorithm for search-tree branching factor > 2

The following parallel algorithm allows *t* (a power of 2) GPU threads to determine their initial subtrees. Thus, avoid host computer's serial breadth-first expansion. Consider a search tree with a branching factor of n at each level, we can visualize the total work of the search tree using two arrays Start and End as in Figure 3 (a). To split the work into two halves, half of level 1's values can be split off as in Figure 3 (b) by thread 0.

Level	Start	End
0	0	0
1	1	n
2	1	n
3	1	n
	⋮	⋮
n-1	1	n

(a) Work for complete tree

Level	Start	End
0	0	0
1	1	n/2
2	1	n
3	1	n
	⋮	⋮
n-1	1	n

Level	Start	End
0	0	0
1	(n/2)+1	n
2	1	n
3	1	n
	⋮	⋮
n-1	1	n

(b) Work split into two halves

Figure 3. Two views of Search-Tree Work

Each of the two halves can be split in parallel by two threads (0 and *t*/2) into four quarters with level 1 values in the ranges: 1..(n/4), (n/4)+1..(n/2), (n/2)+1..(3n/2), (3n/4)+1..n. When a thread's Start value at level i equals its End value at level i, it splits its work by splitting its level i+1 values in half. Four threads can split the four quarters of work into eighths, etc.

The CUDA pseudo-code for this binary-tree scattering of search-tree work among the threads is shown in Figure 4.

```
// binary-tree scatter of work, threadsPerBlock must be a power of 2
i = blockDim.x;
while (i > 1) {
    if (threadIdx.x % i == 0) {
        for (level = 2; level < n; level++) {
            if (Start[threadIdx.x][level-2] == End[threadIdx.x][level-2] || included) {
                Start[threadIdx.x+i/2][level-2] = Start[threadIdx.x][level-2];
                End[threadIdx.x+i/2][level-2] = End[threadIdx.x][level-2];
            } else {
                mid = (Start[threadIdx.x][level-2] + End[threadIdx.x][level-2])/2;
                Start[threadIdx.x+i/2][level-2] = mid+1;
                End[threadIdx.x+i/2][level-2] = End[threadIdx.x][level-2];
                End[threadIdx.x][level-2] = mid;
            } // end if
        } // end for
    } // end if
    syncthreads();
    i = i / 2;
} // end while
```

Figure 4. CUDA pseudo-code for binary-tree scattering of search-tree work

2.2 Algorithm for search-tree with branch factor = 2

Some NP-complete problems search for optimal subsets of items from a set of size n (e.g., 0-1 Knapsack problem, subset-sum problem, etc.). In these cases the above binary-tree scattering of work is not even needed. Each of the t (a power of $2 = 2^k$) GPU thread Id's can be thought of as a k-bit binary number. Each k-bit binary number of the GPU thread Id represents a unique starting subtree at level k in the search tree. Figure 5 illustrates a small example of $t = 8 = 2^3$ with binary thread Ids: 000, 001, 010, 011, 100, 101, 110, 111.

2.3 Continuation of DFS tree-search

After a GPU thread is assigned an initial subtree (regardless of the search-tree's branching factor), its initial state and feasibility must be evaluated if a promising function is being used to prune branches of the search tree.

3 Future work

The above algorithms to assign initial subtrees to GPU threads for the TSP and 0-1 Knapsack problems have been implemented. However, threads completing their subtrees currently sit idle until the search completes. Future work will focus on dynamically load-balancing as described in [2].

4 References

[1] P.S. Pacheco, "An Introduction to Parallel Programming". p. 299. Morgan Kaufmann Publishers, 2011.

[2] A. Grama, A. Gupta, G. Karypis, and V. Kumar. "Introduction to Parallel Computing". Second Edition, pp. 482-485. Pearson Education Limited, 2003.

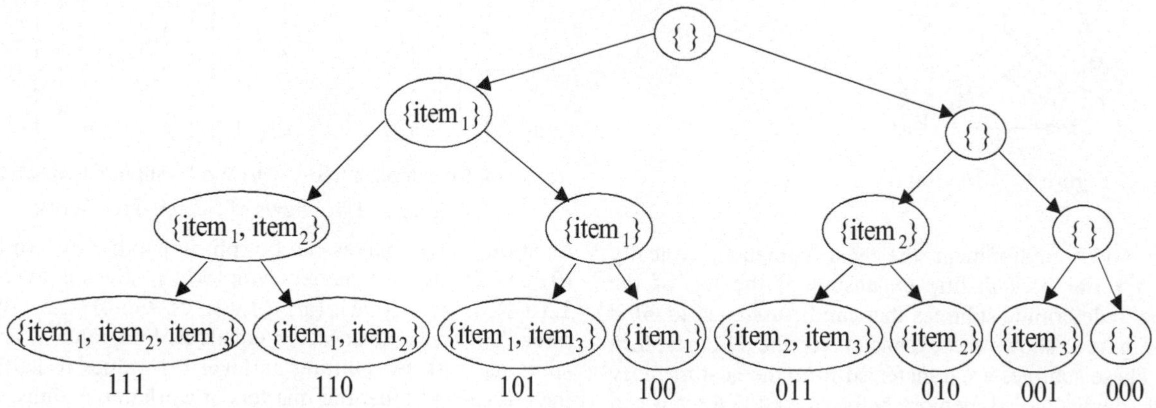

Figure 5. Level-3 Subtrees Corresponding to Binary Thread Ids

Runtime Performance Evaluation of GPU and CPU using a Genetic Algorithm Based on Neighborhood Model

Vincent W. A. Tadaiesky[1], Ádamo L. de Santana[1], Lilian de J. C. Dias[1], Ivan de I. de Oliveira[1], Antonio F. L. Jacob Junior[2], and Fábio M. F. Lobato[1]

[1]Laboratory of Computational Intelligence and Operational Research, Federal University of Pará, Belém, Pará, Brazil

[2]Center of Technological Sciences, Uniersity of Amazon, Belém, Pará, Brazil

Abstract— *Bio-inspired techniques like Genetic Algorithms have a comprehensive applicability to optimization problems. Given the ease of parallelism implementation inherent of these techniques several researches have been developed in such area making use of parallel platforms, especially the CUDA platform. However, the majority of these works are focused on strategies to improve the algorithms convergence without concern for the performance against their runtime. In this context, the present research introduces a runtime comparison of a Genetic Algorithm implementation in CUDA and traditional CPU aiming to investigate the performance difference between them. The results showed that although the Genetic Algorithm has a native parallelism, the CPU overcomes the GPU implemetation due to a hardware limitation.*

Keywords: Genetic Algorithms; CUDA; Performance Evaluation; GPGPU; CPU;

1. Introduction

Genetic Algorithms (GA) has demonstrated to be a powerful tool to find solutions for optimization problems [1]. Nevertheless, this technique demands a high computational cost as a result of the evaluation of all possible solution in each generation [2]. Aiming to attenuate such problem, parallel processing systems like the General Purpose Graphical Processing Unit (GPGPU) are being utilized [2] [3] [4].

GPGPU are graphic processors used not only to image rendering, but to any problem requiring massive data parallel processing. To facilitate its use, the NVIDIA® corporation provides an API that uses C/C++ languages to program in their graphics cards, called CUDA.

Concerning the efficiency of the CUDA platform, several works have been conducted in order to evaluate its performance, including problems which involve the use of GA. These problems, generally, are aimed to evaluate the comparison with the corresponding CPU implementation.

In this context, the present work proposes a performance comparison of Genetic Algorithms in CPU and GPU, focusing on their runtime and not in their solution convergence in order to verify the best emviroment for its implementation.

This paper is organized as follows. Related Work are showed in Section 2 where some similar works using GA or CUDA are described; Test configuration are presented in Section 3, describing how the benchmark was performed; The Section 4 presents the results obtained. Finally, the Section 5 presents an analysis of the results and future works.

2. Related Works

Many researches involving genetic algorithms and CUDA have been developed, in general, in the pursue of GA implementation strategies capable of taking advantage of the parallelism inherent to the platform. There are also researches which aim to benchmark the performance of CUDA in various hardware configurations and operating systems.

Regarding the design of GA, [3] presents a island-based GA, which the individuals are allocated in islands. The population in each island evolves independently from each other. This implementation proves to be effective when each island is allocated in a CUDA core, since each CUDA core can work isolatedly, requiring the synchronization only at the end of the GA process.

In [2], the GA strategy is presented using stationary state selection. This implementation defines that the two individuals with best fitness are selected for crossover while the two worst individuals are replaced by their descendants. Given the execution independence between cores, this strategy is proved efficient because it does not need to syncronize the population.

Concerning the performance evaluation of CUDA, [4] develops a benchmark of the CUDA plataform used in various hardware configurations and Microsoft Windows® operating system versions. It was verified that, apart from the configuration used, the GPU load is always superior when the problem can be processed in parallel.

It is important to notice that the benchmarking process can change dogmas of some areas, as in [5]. There the authors compared the most used programming languages in bioinformatics. The parameter measured was the runtime of recurrent algorithms in the area, running on two operating systems: Windows® and Linux. The results defeated the most commonly used programming language, Perl, while Java was, surprisingly, as efficient as C and C++.

In tis context, the directions of this area of research, and how it has been approached, motivated this study, denoting the comparison of CUDA and CPU performances running a GA; as shown in the next section.

3. Experiment Configuration

This research reports the performance comparison of a GA based on neighborhood model in the CUDA and CPU enviroment. For such, the following computer configuration was used: GNU/Linux operating system with Intel® Core™ i5-2310 CPU @ 2.90GHz x 4 with GPU NVIDIA GeForce 8400GS with the CUDA 5.0 enabled.

The objective of the implemented GA is the optimization of the following three benchmark functions obtained from [6]: g01, g04 and g07. They were chosen due to their wide number of variables and restrictions, which collaborate to the CUDA performance, ensuring a massive parallel processing of the data. The GA codification for each benchmark function is identical, except for the fitness calculation that are adapted for each one.

At this point, the GA project for the CUDA platform was coded according to the hardware limitation. In the neighborhood model, each individual is allocated in one core of the GPU. Given the 16 cores available in the graphic card, the model was adapted to allocate each individual in one thread, being the population composed of 500 individuals. The individuals would then compete to be executed in one of the GPU cores.

There were performed 10 iterations of the GA for each function, both in CPU and GPU, with elitism of 25%. The stop criteria used was the number of 100,000 generations so they do not contaminate the test results due to the difference between their convergence solution. It is noteworthy that the object of this study was the runtime comparison, not the GA performance related to its convergence.

4. Results

The results obtained from the experiment's execution are summarized in Table 1 for the CPU and GPU runtime. Each column represents one of the optimization functions chosen, and each row is the corresponding to architecture for GA implementation.

From the results a significant difference could be noticed between the runtimes, where the GPU are more than 60 times higher than the CPU for every function. These values are the opposite of the results described in [4], where the GPU outperforms the CPU regardless of the enviroment configuration on both operational system and hardware.

Taking into consideration the project utilized to exploit the CUDA platform parallelism, the gap between the results indicate a hardware limitation found in the graphic card used,

Table 1: Linux CPU and GPU runtime

Architecture \ Functions	g01	g04	g07
CPU	31.1s	21.2s	34.7s
GPU	36min 29s	22min 9s	35min 50s

caused by the number of precessors core and mostly by the available memomy space in them, i.e. the memory was the limiting factor to the GA chromossome encoding.

5. Conclusions and future work

Several researches involving GAs in the CUDA platform are currently being developed, especially on new strategies to take complete advantage of the parallelism offered by the platform. In this scope, this work implemented a GA based on neighborhood model, using benchmarking functions, in order to evaluate the performance of the CUDA platform in relation to CPU.

The experiments indicated that there are a substantial difference between the implemetations, possibly caused by a hardware limitation of the CUDA hardware utilized - CUDA platform performance is directely related to the number of cores in the processor and the available amount of memory. Thus, despite the inherent parallelism present in some bio-inspired techniques, its implemetation in a multiprocessor enviroment, such as GPU, do not guarantee an expected improve in performance.

Considering a memory limitation observed during the experiments, it is intended to verify, in future works, algorithms that require the comunication CPU/GPU, specially in the cache memory of the graphic processors, e.g. problems that occurs when the encoded GA chromossome exceeds the cache memory available in the GPU processors.

References

[1] P. Bajpai and M. Kumar, "Genetic algorithm - an approach to solve global optimization problems," *Indian Journal of Computer Science and Engineering*, vol. 1, no. 3, pp. 199–206, 2010.

[2] M. Oiso, T. Yasuda, K. Ohkura, and Y. Matsumura, "Accelerating steady-state genetic algorithms based on cuda architecture," in *IEEE Congress on Evolutionary Computation*, 2011, pp. 687–692.

[3] M. C. Feier, C. Lemnaru, and R. Potolea, "Solving np-complete problems on the cuda architecture using genetic algorithms," in *Proceedings of the 2011 10th International Symposium on Parallel and Distributed Computing*, ser. ISPDC '11. Washington, DC, USA: IEEE Computer Society, 2011, pp. 278–281. [Online]. Available: http://dx.doi.org/10.1109/ISPDC.2011.50

[4] N. N. D. Zlotrg and A. Huseinovic, "Utilizing cuda architecture for improving application performance," in *Telecommunications forum TELFOR*, 2011.

[5] M. Fourment and M. R. Gillings, "A comparison of common programming languages used in bioinformatics," *BMC Bioinformatics*, vol. 9, no. 1, p. 82, 2008. [Online]. Available: http://www.ncbi.nlm.nih.gov/pubmed/18251993

[6] A. Aguirre, A. Muñoz Zavala, E. Villa Diharce, and S. Botello Rionda, "Copso: Constrained optimization via PSO algorithm," no. I-07-04, 2007.

Key Management Schemes Roadmap for Body Sensor Networks Based on Physiological Signals

H. Zhao[1,3], M. Shu[2,3], and J. Qin[4]

[1]School of Compute Science & Technology, Shandong University of Finance and Economics, Jinan, China

[2]School of Information Science and Engineering, Shandong University, Jinan, China

[3]Shandong Computer Science Center, Jinan, China

[4]School of Mathematics, Shandong University, Jinan, China

Abstract - *Recently, the deployment of body sensor networks in the human bodies has attracted much attention in intelligent healthcare. To secure the messages exchanged in body sensor networks, many researches develop efficient physiological-signals-based key management schemes. However these existing research results have security and practicality problems when they are used to body sensor networks. To address these problems, this paper presents a research roadmap to improve physiological-signals-based key management schemes.*

Keywords: key management scheme; physiological signals; sensor network security; body sensor networks

1 Introduction

Although network security has been extensively investigated [1][2][3][4][5][6][7], security of body sensor network has yet attracted more attention. Body sensor networks (BSNs) are composed of a number of biosensors that can be deployed on/into the human bodies to collect and deliver physiological signals in real time, which will have great application values in intelligent healthcare. Because physiological signals collected by BSNs contain privacy information, they must be protected as biometrics [8][9][10][11][12][13].

The first step for building security mechanisms is designing efficient key management schemes. Due to stringent resources in biosensors, traditional key management schemes for wireless sensor networks [14][15][16]] are not suitable for BSNs. Recently, researchers find some physiological signals such as ECG and SpO2 having good randomness and can be gathered from different parts of the human body. These signals can be good candidates for negotiating shared keys in BSNs. Thus, many researches try to make use of these physiological signals to design low-resource-cost key management schemes. Fuzzy commitment based schemes assume that physiological signals collected from the human body are kept secret from the adversary [16]. In [18], it is reported that Ultra Wide Band (UWB) technology can remotely capture some physiological signals and break these security meachnisms.

2 A research roadmap for physiological signals based key management

In order to improve the security and practicality of physiological-based key management schemes, we plan to design a new key management scheme using fuzzy extractor technology [19]. The research roadmap is described below.

2.1 Designing a new key negotiation scheme

We first investigate the formal definition of key negotiation based on fuzzy extractor. The definition will include two parts: One is feasibility definition that requires that two parts could negotiate a shared key if the difference of physiological signals collected by two parts is in the tolerance of a pointed error-correcting code. Another one is security definition where we will design two attack games: adaptive chosen physiological signals attack games and the adaptive chosen commitments attack game. The former requires that any adversary cannot find the relationship between the physiological signals and corresponding commitment even if it can launch UWB attack; the latter requires that any adversary cannot find the relationship between the public commitment and the shared key.

And then, according to the formal definition of key negotiation, we plan to use predistributed keys and random functions to optimize key negotiation in two aspects: one is to resist UWB attack; another one is to remove the dependence of high-entropy physiological signals.

2.2 Designing an efficient physiological signals encryption scheme

Reference [17] proposed a linear interpolation encryption for physiological. Yet it did not describe how to produce the interpolation factors.

To solve the problem, we plan to design a method to use the shared key to produce interpolation factors. However, the interpolation encryption only includes add and multiplication operation which makes the ciphertext weak. To solve the problem, we plan to use linear equations to secure plaintext.

2.3 Design a series lightweight protocols

In the research, we mainly consider the security design and lightweight design of key negotiation protocols. In the former design, we will take the following measures: (1) adopting the right security mechanisms to provide secure services, for instance, we will use the keyed pseudo-functions to provide integrity service; (2) explicitly presenting original part and destination part in the protocol messages; (3) avoiding different messages having the same construction. In the latter design, we will reduce the steps of protocol as far as possible, and merger more messages in one transmission, which helps to use one integrity verification code to protect more messages.

3 Conclusions

Physiological-signals-based key negotiation schemes have higher efficiency than traditional key negotiation schemes, and are suitable for BSNs. In the paper, we give a research roadmap to improve their security and practicality.

Acknowledgement

This work was supported by Shandong Provincial Natural Science Foundation (ZR2011FL027, ZR2012FM005), National Natural Science Foundation (61101162; 61101085;60873041;61272091), Jinan Independent Innovation Foundation of Universities and Institutes (201202009).

4 References

[1] J. Hu, I. Khalil, S. Han, A. Mahmood, “Seamless integration of dependability and security concepts in SOA: A feedback control system based framework and taxonomy,” *Journal of Network and Computer Applications*, vol. 34, Issue 4, pp.1150-1159, 2011.

[2] B. Tian, S. Han, S. Parvin, J. Hu, S. Das, “Self-healing key distribution schemes for wireless networks: A survey,” *Computer Journal*, vol. 54, Issue 4, pp.549-569, 2011.

[3] J. Hu, Y. Tang, K. Xi, “Correlation keystroke verification scheme for user access control in cloud computing environment,” *Computer Journal*, vol. 54, Issue 10, pp.1632-1644, 2011.

[4] S. Wang, and J. Hu, "Alignment-Free Cancellable Fingerprint Template Design: A Densely Infinite-to-One Mapping (DITOM) Approach," *Pattern Recognition*, Elsevier, 2012, Volume 45, Issue 12, pp. 4129-4137, 2012.

[5] A.N. Mahmood, J. Hu, Z. Tari, C. Leckie, "Critical infrastructure protection: Resource efficient sampling to improve detection of less frequent patterns in network traffic, " *Journal of Network and Computer Applications*, vol. 33, Issue 4, pp. 491-502, 2010.

[6] F. Han, X. Yu, Y. Feng, and J. Hu, "On multiscroll chaotic attractors in hysteresis-based piecewise-linear systems, " *IEEE Transactions on Circuits and Systems II: Express Briefs*, vol. 54, Issue 11, pp.1004-1008, 2007.

[7] J.K. Hu, H.H. Chen, T.W. Hou, “A hybrid public key infrastructure solution (HPKI) for HIPAA privacy/security regulations,” *Computer Standards and Interface*,vol.32,no.5-6, pp. 274-280.(2010).

[8] T. Ahmad, J. Hu, and S. Wang, "Pair-polar coordinate-based cancelable fingerprint templates," *Pattern Recognition*, vol. 44, issues 10, pp. 2555-2564, 2011.

[9] K. Xi, T. Ahmad, F. Han, and J. Hu, "A fingerprint based bio-cryptographic security protocol designed for client/server authentication in mobile computing environment," *Security and Communication Networks*, vol. 4, no. 5, pp. 487-499, 2011.

[10] J. Hu, D. Gingrich, and A. Sentosa, "A k-nearest neighbor approach for user authentication through biometric keystroke dynamics," *Proc. of IEEE International Conference on Communications,* pp.1556-1560, 2008.

[11] J.Hu, "Mobile fingerprint template protection: Progress and open issues," *Proc. IEEE Conference on Industrial Electronics and Applications*, pp. 2133-2138, 2008.

[12] P. Zhang, J. Hu, C. Li, M. Bennamoun, and V. Bhagavatula, "A pitfall in fingerprint bio-cryptographic key generation, " *Computers and Security*, vol. 30, Issue 5, pp. 311-319, 2011.

[13] B. Tian, S. Han, J.Hu, T. Dillon, "A mutual-healing key distribution scheme in wireless sensor networks, " *Journal of Network and Computer Applications,* vol. 34, Issue 1, pp. 80-88, 2011.

[14] H.W. Zhao, J. Hu, J. Qin, V. Varadharajan, "Hashed random key pre-distrbution scheme for large heterogenerous sensor networks," *Proc. the 11th IEEE International Conference on Trust, Security and Privacy in Computing and Communications,* pp. 706-713, 2012.

[15] H.W. Zhao, J. Qin, M.L. Shu, J. Hu, “A hash chains based key management scheme for wireless sensor networks,” *Lecture Notes in Computer Science, LNCS Vol. 7672, pp.296-308, 2012.*

[16] H.W. Zhao, J. Qin, J. Hu, “Energy efficient key management scheme for body sensor networks,” *IEEE Transactions on Parallel and Distributed Systems,* 2013, DOI : http://doi.ieeecomputersociety.org/10.1109/TPDS.2012.320.

[17] F.M. Bui, D. Hatzinakos, “Biometric methods for secure communications in body sensor networks resource-efficient key management and signal-level data scrambling,” *EURASIP J. Adavances in Signal Processing*, pp.1-16, 2008.

[18] S.D. Bao, L.F. Shen, and Y.T. Zhang, “A novel key distribution of body area networks for telemedicine,” *Proc. IEEE Int. Workshop on Biomedical Circuits and Systems,* pp. 1–11, 2004.

[19] Y. Dodis, L. Reyzin, A. Smith, “Fuzzy extractors: How to generate strong keys from biometrics and other noisy data,” *Proc. Advances in Cryptology- Eurocrypt' 04*, pp. 523-540. 2004.

ANALYZE THE EFFECT OF CONTEXTUAL BASED FUZZY MRF MODELS IN SATELLITE IMAGES

Rakesh Dwivedi[a]
[a]Indian Institute of Technology Roorkee, India

S. K. Ghosh[a] and Anil Kumar[b]
[a]Indian Institute of Technology Roorkee, India
[b]Indian Institute of Remote Sensing, Dehradun, India

***Abstract*— Since, the advent of remote sensing technology it has become an attractive option to capture the information about land cover classes at a global scale in less time in form of digital images. Image classification is one of the important image analysis methods. The accuracy of image classification is to map the real world scenario is restricted by the presence of mixed pixels. To some extent fuzzy based classification methods such as Fuzzy-c-Means(FCM), can handle the problem of mixed pixels. FCM gives the membership value of the pixel to various classes. In the comparative analysis, the accuracy of this approach is found to be less than that of Possibilistic c-Means (PCM).The membership value generated by PCM is interpreted as the degree of belongingness instead of degree of sharing. The PCM approach exploits the information present only in spectral domain, whereas, it has been observed that including the information from spatial domain increases the accuracy of the classifier. This spatial domain information or spatial contextual information can be integrated with PCM to provide more accurate results. In this paper, PCM and spatial contextual information based soft classification method has been developed. Also, two different MRF prior models have been used. It has been observed that using Discontinuity Adaptive prior models preserve the edges and also, increase the overall accuracy of the classifier. It has been found with the experiments performed, that not all soft accuracy assessment techniques are suitable in case of PCM classifier such as PCM-MRF, as it doesn't follow the hyperline constraint. For generating the reference data set, a finer resolution image was used. It has also been discussed with results, that same classifier is more appropriate to use for generating the reference data set.**

Keywords—Possibilistic -c-Means, Markov Random Fields, DA models, edge preservation.

I. INTRODUCTION

The determination of optimum number of parameters and their values for each hybrid classifier is critical and have to be investigated (Aziz, 2004). The main motivation behind Possibilistic c-Means (PCM) relates to the relaxaction of the constraint on membership value of Fuzzy *c*-Mean (FCM) and gives absolute membership value.The objective function, which satisfies this requirement, may be formulated as mentioned in Eq. (1);

$$J_m(U,V) = \sum_{i=1}^{N}\sum_{j=1}^{c} \mu_{ij}^{\ m} \left\| X_i - v_j \right\|_A^2 + \sum_{j=1}^{c}\eta_j \sum_{i=1}^{N} 1-\mu_{ij}^{\ m} \qquad (1)$$

Subject to constraints;

$\max_j u_{ij} > 0$ *for all i*

$\sum_{i=1}^{N}\mu_{ij} > 0$ *for all j*

$0 \le \mu_{ij} \le 1$ *for all i, j*

In case of PCM, this membership value represents the "degree of belongingness or compatibility or typicality", contrary to that represented by FCM, where it is, "degree of sharing. Markov Random Field (MRF) use smoothness priors to include spatial contextual information and to avoid over smoothening, Regularizes and Discontinuity Adaptive (DA) Models have been introduced.

(Li, 1995), gave DA models to be used as prior models in MRF, which are said to take into account the discontinuities and avoid over smoothening. In (Li, 1995),it was shown that solution to DA models can be obtained by using gradient descent method, but its direct use may cause getting trapped into local minima. Further details are also, provided in (Li, 2009).

II. CLASSIFIERS AND ACCURACY ASSESSMENT APPROACHES

A. *Possibilistic c- Mean with Contextual Algorithm*

The basic objective function of PCM is given in Eq. (1), includes the information about the distance of the feature vector from the cluster mean in the feature space but it does not include information on spatial context. The spatial context here includes the influence of the neighbouring pixel on the target pixel in the image space.

The MAP-MRF (Maximum A Posterior Solution-Markov Random Field) framework works by maximizing the posterior probability which is related to prior and conditional energy. Eq.(2) states the PCM objective function formulated using smoothness prior. From now onwards the objective function in Eq.(2) will be referred as NC-S.

$$U(u_{ij}/d) = (1-\lambda)\left[\sum_{i=1}^{n}\sum_{j=1}^{c} u_{ij}^{\ m}\left\|X_i - v_j\right\|_A^2 + \sum_{j=1}^{c}\eta_j\sum_{i=1}^{n} 1-u_{ij}^{\ m}\right] + \lambda\left[\sum_{i=1}^{n}\sum_{j=1}^{c}\sum_{j'\in n_i}\beta\, u_{ij}-u_{ij'}^{\ 2}\right] \qquad (2)$$

where $U(u_{ij}/d)$ = Posterior energy of image μ, given image d.

λ=Weight for spectral and contextual information (smoothness strength).

u_{ij} = Membership value of pixel of class.

n = Number of pixels.

m = weighting exponent.

$$(d_{ij})^2 = (x_j - v_i)^T A_i (x_j - v_i)$$

β= weight for neighbors.

n_i= Neighborhood window around pixel i.

B. *Soft accuracy assessment methods*

For the uncertainty visualization and evaluation of the classification results, the entropy criterion is proposed (Dehghan.,2006. This measure expresses by the following Eq.(3)

$$Entropy(x) = \sum_{i=1}^{m} -\mu(w_i/x)\log_2(\mu(w_i/x)) \qquad (3)$$

III. STUDY AREA AND DATA USED

The study area for the present research work belongs to Sitarganj Tehsil, Udham Singh Nagar District, Uttarkhand, India. It is located in the southern part of the state. In terms of Geographic lat/long, the area extends from 28°52'29"N to 28°54'20"N and 79°34'25"E to 79°36'34"E. The images for this research work have been taken from three different sensors namely AWiFS, LISS-III and LISS-IV belonging to satellite IRS-P6.

IV. METHODOLOGY

All three datasets (AWiFS, LISS-III, and LISS-IV) were geometrically corrected with RMSE less than 1/3 of a pixel and resampled using nearest neighbor resample method at 60 meter,20 meter, and 5 meter spatial resolution respectively. The flow chart of the methodology adopted is shown in Fig. 1

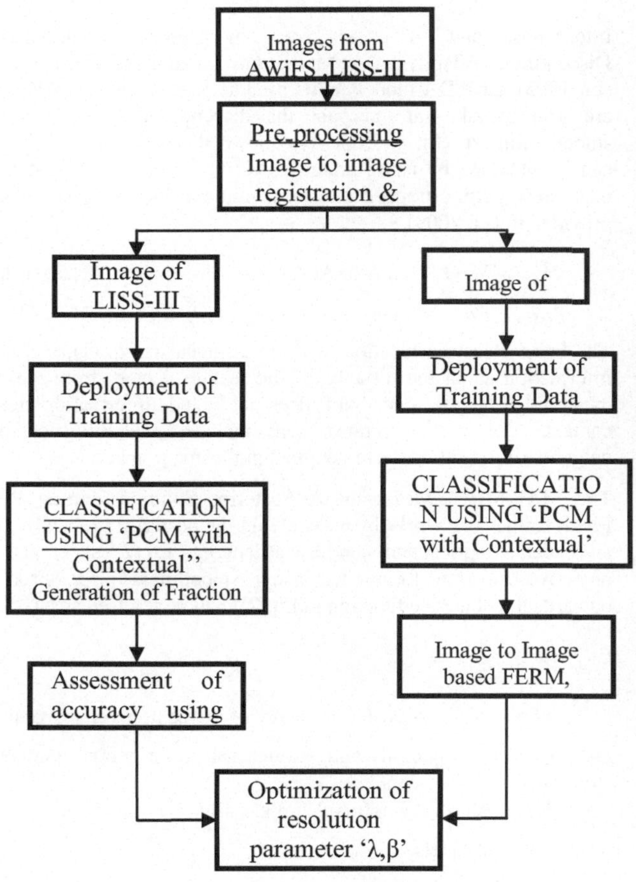

Fig.1 Methodology Adopted

V. RESULTS AND DISCUSSIONS

Due to the remoteness of the area field visit is not always possible and realistic. So it is necessary to adobe an effective way to generate soft reference data from available fine resolution dataset(Kumar and Ghosh , 2007). In this study LISS-IV data was used to generate soft reference data.

A. Accuracy assessment via Entropy of PCM with Contextual Classifier

The uncertainty estimation of the classification results is important and necessary to evaluate the classifier performance. This study addresses the evaluation of entropy, based on PCM with Contextual classifier which estimates uncertainty in classification results. The uncertainty criteria have been estimated from computed entropy based on actual output of classifier. For setting the optimized value of weighting exponent 'm', smoothness controller 'β', and Weight for spectral and contextual information (smoothness strength) 'λ', a number of experiments have been conducted individually for this classifier by varying 'm' from 1.0 to 4.0, while values of smoothness controller 'β' is varying from 1 to 10 and contextual information (smoothness strength) 'λ' is varying from 0 to 1. It has been observed from the result that for homogenous classes like Agricultural crop land, Agriculture non crop land, Agriculture moist land without crop, and Water Body for PCM with Contextual classifier the optimized value of 'm' is 2.6. Similarly for heterogeneous classes like Sal forest and Eucalyptus plantation, the optimized value of 'm' is also 2.7 for PCM with Contextual classifier. It has also been observed that for fixed weighting exponent (m), β=3.0, and λ=0.7.These findings suggest that using these optimized values of for PCM with Contextual classifier on homogenous and heterogeneous land cover classes the range of the computed entropy varies between the range of [0,3]. This in turn states that the information uncertainty is not exceeding more than 3%. In this research entropy has been used to measure the accuracy in terms of uncertainty without using any kind of ground reference data. This classification accuracy is directly measured by entropy. Measuring the spatial statistics of a satellite image using an entropy, of six land cover classes can be measured using Eq. (3) i.e. 6*(-1/6*log21/6)=2.585(Stein and Gorte., 2002). The fraction images are shown Fig 2

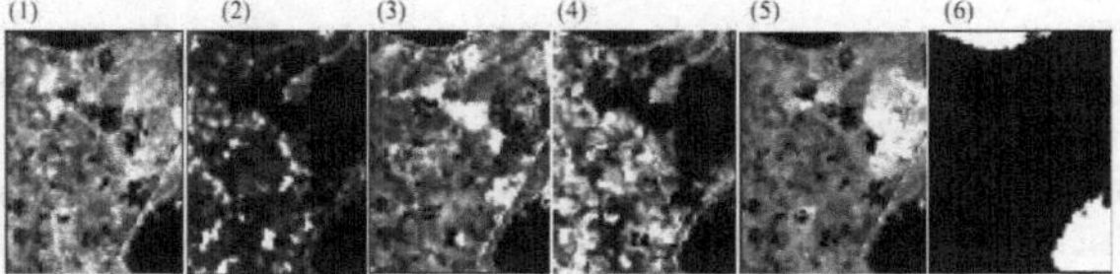

Fig .2 Fraction Images Generated with PCM with Contextual

VI. CONCLUSION

In this research work it has been tried to generate fraction outputs from PCM with Contextual classifier. These outputs have been generated from AWIFS, LISS-III and LISS-IV images of IRS-P6 data. Assessment of entropy and identification of membership values is being done with the help of fraction images. The objective of this research on spatial data to is to investigate, how uncertainties arise, and propagated in the spatial data. It has been shown in result that the entropy value, with minimum uncertainty in it, for the optimized values of these parameters. The entropy and membership verifications are taken as an indirect measure to check the accuracy of classified image. From this work it can be concluded that fuzzy based hybrid approach using PCM with Contextual generates classified output with minimum uncertainty.

References

[1] Aziz,M. A. Evaluation of soft classifiers for remote sensing data, unpublished Ph.D thesis, IIT Roorkee, Roorkee, India, 2004.

Dehghan and Ghassemian, "Measurement of uncertainty by the entropy: application to the classification of MSS data," *International journal of remote sensing*, vol. 27, no. 18, pp. 4005–4014, 2006..

[2] Kumar, A., Ghosh, S. K., and Dadhwal V. K. (2007). A comparison of the performance of fuzzy algorithm versus statistical algorithm based sub-pixel classifier for remote sensing data. Proceedings of mid-term symposium ISPRS, 8–11th May 2006, ITC-The Netherlands.

[3] Li, S. Z. Markov random fields modeling in image analysis□ : e-book, Third edition. London: Springer, 2009.

[4] Stein, A., Meer, F. V. D. and Gorte B. 2002. "Spatial Statistics for Remote Sensing," 1st edition, Kluwer Academic Publishers, Netherlands

This paper is being submitted as a poster

Practical Simulatable Adaptive Oblivious Transfer Protocol

J. Qin[1], **H. Zhao**[2,3], **and J. Cai**[1]
[1]School of Mathematics Shandong University, Jinan, China
[2]School of Compute Science & Technology, Shandong University of Finance and Economics, Jinan, China
[3]Shandong Computer Science Center, Jinan, China

Abstract - *Oblivious Transfer protocol (OTP) is a primitive and also a paramount important tool in modern cryptography. An adaptive version of OTP named* $\mathrm{OT}_{k\times 1}^{N}$ *is useful when a large database should be queried in an adaptive version. Due to its importance, the task of constructing efficient and secure* $\mathrm{OT}_{k\times 1}^{N}$ *has attracted a lot interests. This paper presents a research roadmap to construct a practical adaptive fully-simulatable* $\mathrm{OT}_{k\times 1}^{N}$ *based on Chaum's blind signature.*

Keywords: Adaptive oblivious transfer; blind signature; one-more-RSA-inversion problem; full-simulation

1 Introduction

Data privacy and access control have attracted a wide spectrum of research activities from many aspects [1][2][3][4][5][6][7][8][9][10][11]. OTPs *(oblivious transfer protocols)* are one of the most basic and widely used primitives in cryptography. It can be used as stand-alone protocols, e.g., for trading digital information, or as a building block for more complex protocols, e.g., for privacy-preserving auctions. It is a fundamental theory on multi-party computation and also plays an important role to a variety of practical problems such as keyword search in cloud computing, oblivious search database, treasure hunting, location-based services and etc.. Due to its general importance, OTP has attracted a lot of interests since it was introduced by Rabin [12].

1.1 Security notions of oblivious transfer protocol

There are three security notions for OTP presented in the previous literatures as the *semi-honest* or *honest-but-curious* model, the notion of *half-simulatable* model and *fully-simulatable* model. The notion of *fully-simulatable* model was introduced and formalized by Camenisch, Neven and Shelat [13]. In this model, the security property employs the real/ideal world paradigm for both the receiver and the sender. The efficient OTPs that achieve fully-simulatable security level are of great interests.

1.2 Adaptive Version of $OT_{k\times 1}^{N}$

An adaptive version of $\mathrm{OT}_{k\times 1}^{N}$ in this paper contains two phases, initialization and transfer. The sender and the receiver run the initialization phase during which they first agree on a hash function $H(\cdot)$ and a block cipher *Enc* =(*E*, *D*), then the sender who owns the *N* private messages encrypts the messages by using *Enc* and puts the cipher-texts on a public network. During the transfer phase, the receiver will send *k* queries to the sender. The *i*-th query is determined by the sender's responses to the previous *i*-1 queries. So the *k* queries are not pre-determined. In this sense, the protocol is adaptive.

2. Fully-Simulatable Adaptive Oblivious Transfer Protocol

2.1 Initialization phase

The protocol operates over Z_n^*, where n is a RSA modulo. Sender S knows both the public and the private keys of a RSA signature scheme namely (*n*, *e*, *d*). Sender S and receiver R agree on a hash function H($\cdot$). Let *Enc* =(*E*, *D*) be a secure block cipher and open to both S and R, and we suppose that decryption keys of *Enc* is identical to its encryption keys. S makes use of *Enc* to encrypt his/her private messages and puts the corresponding cipher-texts on a public network. R can get these cipher-texts freely.

Input S inputs his/her messages $m_1,\mathrm{L}\ ,m_N$ and computes $E_{k_1}(m_1),\mathrm{L}\ ,E_{k_n}(m_N)$, where $k_1,k_2,\cdots,k_N$ are the corresponding keys. From R's view, these cipher-texts are random elements in Z_n^*, we denote them as $U_1,U_2,\mathrm{L}\ ,U_N$ respectively. R inputs his/her choices $\sigma_1,\cdots,\sigma_k$, where $\sigma_1,\mathrm{L}\ ,\sigma_k \in \{1,2,\mathrm{L}\ ,N\}$.

Output R gets $m_{\sigma_1},\mathrm{L}\ ,m_{\sigma_k}$ indicating that R gets the information at his/her choices $\sigma_1,\mathrm{L}\ ,\sigma_k$.

2.2 Transfer phase

Procedure 1 For $j=1,2,\mathrm{L}\ ,k$, R picks U_{σ_j} in accordance with his/her choice σ_j and computes $H(U_{\sigma_j})$. In order to blind $H(U_{\sigma_j})$, R picks a random number $b_j \xleftarrow{R} Z_n^*$ and computes $SP\left(U_{\sigma_j}\right)b_j^e$. Then R sends it to S. On receiving $SP\left(U_{\sigma_j}\right)b_j^e$, S randomly picks his/her own blinding factor $r_j \in_R Z_n^*$, signs and blinds $Y_j = \left(SP\left(U_{\sigma_j}\right)b_j^e\right)^d r_j = \left(SP\left(U_{\sigma_j}\right)\right)^d b_j r_j$. Meanwhile, S calculates a set of hash values $\left\{K_i = H\left(SP(U_i)^d r_j, i\right)\right\}_{i=1,2,\cdots,N.}$, which are used to encrypt k_i by the following equations $C_i = K_i \oplus k_i$, $i = 1,2,L\ ,N$. Then S sends Y_j together with C_i $(i = 1,2,L\ ,N)$ to R.

Procedure 2 Upon receiving Y_j, R removes his/her blinding factor by calculating $Y_j b_j^{-1} = SP\left(U_{\sigma_j}\right)^d r_j$. Then R calculates $K_{\sigma_j} = H\left(SP\left(U_{\sigma_j}\right)^d r_j, \sigma_j\right)$ to decrypt $k_{\sigma_j} = C_{\sigma_j} \oplus K_{\sigma_j}$. In the end, R outputs $m_{\sigma_j} = D_{k_{\sigma_j}}\left(U_{\sigma_j}\right)$, $j = 1, 2, L\ , k$.

Remark 1 : S should update the encryption key k_i periodically to enhance the security of the scheme. The blinding factors of both S and R must be chosen from a large enough domain, such that the probability that the same blinding factors is used more than once is negligible.

Remark 2 : The only computation that S must perform on-line is the calculation of Y_j. The rest of computations can be done off-line, as soon as S chooses his/her blinding factor.

Remark 3 : There are two remarkable differences of our protocol comparing to the protocol of [14]. First, $U_i = E_{k_i}(m_i)\,(i = 1,2,\cdots,N)$ is the cipher-text and it looks like random in Z_n^* because *Enc* is a secure block cipher. U_i can be pre-calculated by the sender. Second, the sender uses K_i to encrypt the encrypted key k_i of *Enc* and sends it to the receiver. It reduces the communication complexity and bandwidth in the transfer phase. It also reduces the on-line computations.

3 Conclusions

In this paper we have proposed a roadmap of fully-simulatable adaptive security $\mathrm{OT}_{k\times 1}^N$. Our scheme modifies the secure model in full-simulation instead of semi-simulation in [14] and it has an adaptive property.

Acknowledgement

This work is supported by the National Nature Science Foundation of China (60873041, 61272091) and National Nature Science Foundation of Shandong (ZR2012FM005).

4 References

[1] J. Hu, Y. Tang, K. Xi, “Correlation keystroke verification scheme for user access control in cloud computing environment,” *Computer Journal*, vol. 54, Issue 10, pp.1632-1644, 2011.

[2] J. Hu, I. Khalil, S. Han, A. Mahmood, “Seamless integration of dependability and security concepts in SOA: A feedback control system based framework and taxonomy,” *Journal of Network and Computer Applications*, vol. 34, Issue 4, pp.1150-1159, 2011.

[3] B. Tian, S. Han, S. Parvin, J. Hu, S. Das, “Self-healing key distribution schemes for wireless networks: A survey,” *Computer Journal*, vol. 54, Issue 4, pp.549-569, 2011.

[4] T. Ahmad, J. Hu, and S. Wang, "Pair-polar coordinate-based cancelable fingerprint templates, " Pattern Recognition, vol. 44, issues 10, pp. 2555-2564, 2011.

[5] K. Xi, T. Ahmad, F. Han, and J. Hu, "A fingerprint based bio-cryptographic security protocol designed for client/server authentication in mobile computing environment," *Security and Communication Networks*, Volume 4, no. 5, pp. 487-499, 2011.

[6] A.N. Mahmood, J. Hu, Z. Tari, C. Leckie, "Critical infrastructure protection: Resource efficient sampling to improve detection of less frequent patterns in network traffic, " *Journal of Network and Computer Applications*, vol. 33, Issue 4, pp. 491-502, 2010.

[7] J. Hu, D. Gingrich, and A. Sentosa, "A k-nearest neighbor approach for user authentication through biometric keystroke dynamics," *Proc. of IEEE International Conference on Communications*, pp.1556-1560, 2008.

[8] F. Han, X. Yu, Y. Feng, and J. Hu, "On multiscroll chaotic attractors in hysteresis-based piecewise-linear systems, " *IEEE Transactions on Circuits and Systems II: Express Briefs*, Vol. 54, Issue 11, pp.1004-1008, 2007.

[9] B. Tian, S. Han, J.Hu, T. Dillon, "A mutual-healing key distribution scheme in wireless sensor networks, " *Journal of Network and Computer Applications*, vol. 34, Issue 1, pp.80-88, 2011.

[10] J.Hu, "Mobile fingerprint template protection: Progress and open issues, " *The 3rd IEEE Conference on Industrial Electronics and Applications* Singapore, pp. 2133-2138, 2008.

[11] P. Zhang, J. Hu, C. Li, M. Bennamoun, and V. Bhagavatula, "A pitfall in fingerprint bio-cryptographic key generation, " *Computers and Security*, vol. 30, Issue 5, pp. 311-319, 2011.

[12] M. Rabin, "How to exchange secrets by oblivious transfer," Technical Report TR-81, Aiken Computation Laboratory, Harvard University, 1981.

[13] J. Camenisch, G. Neven and A. Shelat, "Simulatable adaptive oblivious transfer," *In Advances in Cryptology-Eurcrypt'2007*, pp.590-614, 2007.

[14] D. Malkhi and Y. Sella, "Oblivious Transfer based on the blind signatures," Technical Report 2003-31, Leibniz Center, Hebrew, University 2003.

[15] W. Ogata, K. Kurosawa, “Oblivious keyword search”. *Journal of Complexity*, 20(2-3):356-371, 2004.

A Simulation Platform for SRAM-TCAM Based Memory Architectures

Oluleye Olorode, Mehrdad Nourani
Department of Electrical Engineering
University of Texas at Dallas
Richardson, Texas, USA
{olorode,nourani}@utdallas.edu

Abstract **– The increasing demand for high speed and low power memory systems has led to the introduction of Ternary Content Addressable Memories to cache architectures, because of their ability to store the don't care value in addition to 1's and 0's. However, existing simulator platforms have been built to support SRAM and DRAM based memory models. In this paper, we present a platform that enables the simulation of these emerging cache architectures used in memory systems. We also describe the handling of cache replacement because of their vital role in cache performance. For experimentation and evaluation of the new simulator platform, we ran simulations on SPEC 2006 benchmarks and compared results against an equally configured conventional cache to confirm no loss in cache performance.**

Keywords – aggregation; cache; replacement; hit ratio; simplescalar; tag; ternary content addressable memory (TCAM).

I. INTRODUCTION

Processors have become increasingly complex and require large memory systems for improved performance. Using larger caches in memory systems promise increased access hit rates, which in turn improves processor performance. The cost of this improved performance is usually increased power consumption. Current memory systems are usually implemented with SRAMs, DRAMs and/or CAMs [1,2] which are only capable of storing 1's and 0's. But these incur significant area and power overhead as memory sizes increase.

Studies have been conducted with the aim of reducing the tag area of an on-chip cache, Hong Wang et al. [3] took a closer look at the locality property of memory references and after extensive simulation experiments, observed that address tags of cached data are usually clustered/identical at a given time frame during program execution. This causes many tags to be identical during a period of time, effectively making the working set of unique tags much smaller than the working set of data references. This suggests that tag area can be significantly reduced without compromising cache performance. Therefore, an architecture that allows multiple similar entries to be grouped into a single one makes it possible to significantly reduce hardware and power overhead with some performance tradeoff. One approach used to achieve this is the use of ternary Content Addressable Memories (TCAMs) which are capable of storing Don't Care (*) value, in addition to 1's and 0's. For example, suppose two cache tag entries differ only in their least significant bit - LSB, these two entries could be combined into a single entry as shown in Fig. 1. This can be extended to more entries; for example, four entries which differ only in the two LSBs (e.g. 00, 01, 10, and 11) can be aggregated into two entries (0* and 1*), if a single TCAM is used per tag entry, or aggregated to a single entry (**) if two TCAM cells are used to implement the two LSBs of the entries. This process of combining multiple entries to a single one by using TCAMs is referred to as *aggregation* [4] throughout this paper.

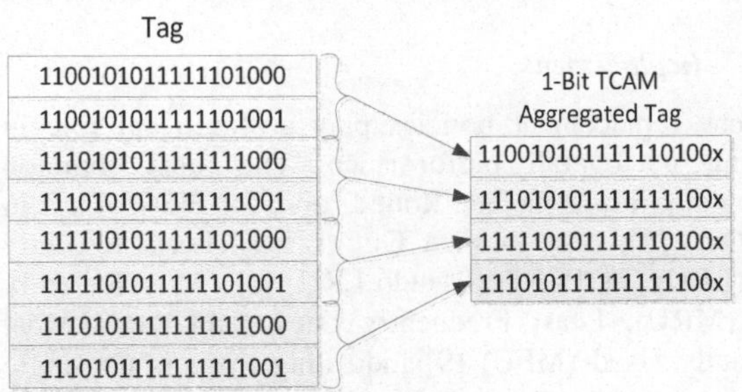

Fig.1: 1-Bit TCAM Aggregation of Cache Tag

The major contribution of this work is the implementation of a simulator platform that allows for the seamless simulation of different SRAM-TCAM based cache configurations.

II. TCAM BASED SIMULATOR

Our TCAM simulation platform leverages existing simplescalar code to mimic the TCAM behavior. We specifically modified the *simoutorder.c* code to accept a new configuration variable known as the *degree of aggregation,* to control the number of TCAM cells used per entry. For example, an architecture that targets tag compression/aggregation may choose to use one TCAM cell per tag entry which implies only two entries can be compressed to a single one. Alternatively, two TCAM cells could be used per tag entry, allowing storage of four entries in a single tag. In what follows, we describe the process of aggregation, followed by the replacement process in our simulator platform.

PDPTA: ABSTRACT/POSTER PAPER. Contact: Olorode

A. Aggregation

Aggregation is achieved in our simulator, by allowing normal conventional cache lookup/allocation to take place, then using the TCAM configuration variable passed into *simoutorder.c*, we generate a mask value which is the same bit-width as the cache entry using a few TCAM cells. All bits of the mask are set to 1's except the TCAM cell bit locations which are all set to 0's. For example, an 8-bit entry with 1-bit aggregation in the LSB will use 1 TCAM per entry and a mask of 11111110. This ensures all similar entries differing in LSB yield the same result after masking. This masking process achieves the desired aggregation by yielding the same number of logical entries expected in the hardware implementation. When aggregation is desired across *cache ways* in associative caches, we modify the cache configuration in the *cache.c* file according to (1) to give a new associativity which is a function of the degree of aggregation. Where A_ω is the new configured associativity, μ is the conventional associativity desired and α is the degree of aggregation. For example, a 4-way cache with 2-bit aggregation will be set up as a 16-Way set associative cache. The masking process then reduces it to four logical ways since the 2 LSBs of the mask are zeros, effectively aggregating 4 entries into a single one.

$$A_\omega = \mu * 2^\alpha \quad (1)$$

B. Replacement

Cache replacement policies play a significant role in dictating its overall performance. The most common caching algorithms include Round-robin (or FIFO - First In First Out) [6], Last In First Out (LIFO), Least Recently Used (LRU) [7], PLRU (Pseudo LRU) [8], Most Recently Used (MRU), Least Frequently Used (LFU) and Most Frequently Used (MFU) [9] indicating there is no single optimal cache replacement policy. Of the several replacement policies available, LRU is often regarded as the most efficient one [10] while PLRU is considered the best for ease of hardware implementation [13]. For the purpose of simulating these policies in SRAM-TCAM based architectures, the multiple entries aggregated together are evicted as a group using the same mask previously described. This masked eviction occurs after any existing policy selects a single entry to be evicted. We also added logic for improved performance by retaining some of the aggregated entries that are aggregatable with a new one on a replacement. This was implemented as an additional configurable option in the modified simulator.

Finally we ran simulations on SPEC2006 benchmarks to verify our simulator gives comparable results for SRAM-TCAM (hybrid) caches when compared with an equivalently configured conventional cache. Fig. 6 shows that most of the benchmarks gave similar performance in both the hybrid and equivalent conventional cache. The NAMD benchmark shows a slight degradation possibly due to aggregate replacements by a single entry.

III. CONCLUSION

The use of TCAM cells in cache architectures allows the use of fewer cells to store the same data as a conventional cache. The aggregation of multiple entries also necessitates the eviction of multiple entries which may not necessarily give the same performance results as an equivalently configured conventional cache with no TCAMs. The simulation platform presented in this paper, allows the seamless simulation of these SRAM-TCAM based cache architectures, which enables cache designers to make informed architectural decisions early in the design phase.

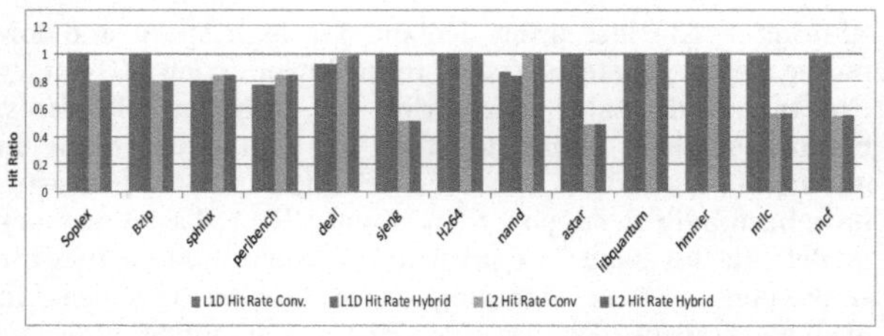

Fig. 2: Cache Hit Rate for Conventional and Hybrid Caches

REFERENCES

[1] Hao Wang , Haiquan (Chuck) Zhao, Bill Lin and Jun (Jim) Xu, "Design and Analysis of a Robust Pipelined Memory System," IFOCOM, IEEE Proceedings, March 2010.

[2] Jorge Garc´ıa, Jes´us Corbal, "Design and Implementation of High-Performance Memory Systems for Future Packet Buffers," In 36th Annual IEEE/ACM International Symposium on Microarchitecture, (MICRO-42) 2003.

[3] Hong Wang,Tong Sun and Qing Yang, "Minimizing Area Cost of On-Chip Cache Memories by Caching Address Tags," IEEE Transactions on Computers, vol. 46, no. 11, Nov. 1997.

[4] Rupak Samanta, Surprise, Jason and Mahapatra, R, "Dynamic Aggregation of Virtual Addresses in TLBs using TCAMs," 21st International Conference on VLSI Design, 2008.

[5] Todd M. Austin, and Doug Burger, "The SimpleScalar Tool Set, Version 2.0," University of Wisconsin-Madison Computer Sciences Technical Report #1342, June 1997.

[6] Intel ®□Xscale ™□Core – Developer's Manual, December 2000, http://developer.intel.com.

[7] Ackland B. et al., "A Single-Chip, 1.6 Billion, 16-b MAC/s Multiprocessor DSP," IEEE Journal of Solid-state circuits, vol. 35, no. 3, pp. 412-423, 2000

[8] Intel ®□Pentium ®□4 and Intel ®□Xeon Processor Optimization – Reference Manual ™□- Reference Manual, http://developer.intel.com.

[9] Heiko Sparenberg, Matthias Martin, Siegfried Foessel, "Introduction of Eviction Strategies for caching Scalable Media Files," Seventh International Conference on Digital Information Management (ICDIM), August 2012.

[10] Hussein Al-Zoubi, Aleksandar Milenkovic, Milena Milenkovic, "Performance Evaluation of Cache Replacement Policies for the SPEC CPU2000 Benchmark Suite," in Proc. of 42nd ACM Southeast Conf., April 2004.

[11] W. A. Wong and J.L. Baer, "Modified LRU policies for improving second-level cache behavior," in HPCA-6, 2000.

SESSION

POSITION AND REGULAR - COMMUNICATION SYSTEMS, CLOUD COMPUTING, RECONFIGURABLE SYSTEMS, PARALLEL AND DISTRIBUTED COMPUTING, SCHEDULING, ARCHITECTURES, AND APPLICATIONS

Chair(s)

Prof. Hamid Arabnia
University of Georgia

Study of Link Utilization of Perfect Difference Network and Hypercube

Rakesh Kumar Katare
Department of Computer Science
A.P.S. University,
Rewa (M.P.), India - 486003
katare_rakesh@yahoo.com

N.S. Chaudhari
Department of CSE,
IIT,
Indore, (M.P.), India - 452017
narendra@iiti.ac.in

Shazad Ahmed Mughal
Department of Computer Science
A.P.S. University,
Rewa (M.P.), India - 486003
Shazadmughal47@gmail.com

Shah Imran
Department of Computer Science
A.P.S. University,
Rewa (M.P.), India - 486003
shahimran21@gmail.com

Rajesh Roshan Raina
Department of Computer Science
A.P.S. University,
Rewa (M.P.), India - 486003
luckyrajmn@gmail.com

Shashi Kant Verma
Department of MCA
ITM Universe,
Gwalior (M.P.), India – 474001
skv.shashi@gmail.com

Abstract- In this paper, the comparision of perfect difference network and hypercube shows the performance and robustness of the two architectures. The topological properties of the two architectures are presented in the form of lemmas. We have made attempts to study the circuits to show the robustness of these architectures. In these architectures, the diameter remains same during normal course and during link failure.

The comparison between these two architectures and their diameters can be shown on their adjacency matrices as well. In the lemmas, we have shown that the degree of a node of these architectures can be changed while changing in the architectural design.

Keywords – ***Perfect Difference Set (PDS), Perfect Difference Network (PDN), Hypercube, Circuits, Adjacency Matrix.***

I. Introduction

This paper presents study of link utilization of the Perfect Difference Network (PDN) architecture. When data is distributed in an interconnected network it passes through certain nodes and takes certain paths. The PDN architecture is presented in the form of circuits to study the utilization of nodes, its properties and performance. To prove all these properties and characteristics the lemmas are presented. It is shown that the diameter of this architecture remains the same during removing one node and during the link failure; the degree of a node may be changed while a change is brought in the architecture design

A. Perfect Difference Set

1) Formulation of Perfect Difference Set: As we know from remainder theorem that

Numerator=Remainder+ Denominator * Quotient.

The Perfect Difference Set (PDS) can be formulated from remainder theorem as [1] an integer (numerator) is equal to the addition of remainder and denominator where quotient is one. Now integer is a member of set of $(1, 2, ..., \delta^2 + \delta)$, where δ is a prime or power of prime and the remainder is the difference $S_i - S_j$,

where $i \neq j,\ 0 \leq i, j \leq \delta$.

So we can write that

$$(\delta^2 + \delta) = (S_i - S_j) + (\delta^2 + \delta + 1) * Q$$

or

$$(S_i - S_j) = (\delta^2 + \delta) - (\delta^2 + \delta + 1) * Q$$

2) Definition of Perfect Difference Set: A set {s0, s1, ..., sδ} of $\delta + 1$ integers having the property that their $\delta^2 + \delta$ differences, $0 \leq i \neq j \leq \delta$, are congruent modulo $\delta^2 + \delta + 1$, to the integers 1, 2, ..., $\delta^2 + \delta$ in some order is a perfect difference set of order δ. Perfect Difference sets [13] are sometimes called simple difference sets, given that they correspond to the special $\delta = 1$ case of difference sets for which each of the possible differences is formed in exactly δ ways, where δ is a prime or power of prime and

$$n = \delta^2 + \delta + 1 \text{ and } (S_i - S_j) = (\delta^2 + \delta) \bmod n$$

3) Evaluation of PDS: The Perfect Difference Set of each node of the PDN can be evaluated by the remainder theorem i.e.,

N = R + D * Q,

Where N = Numerator, R = Remainder, D = Denominator and Q = Quotient

The above equation can be written as

$$\text{Integer} = (S_i - S_j) + (\delta^2 + \delta + 1) * 1$$

Where integer is a member of the set $(1, 2, ..., \delta^2 + \delta)$ and $S_i - S_j$ is numerator or the difference set.

So we can write as -

$$(S_i - S_j) = (\text{Integer}) \bmod (\delta^2 + \delta + 1) \quad (1)$$

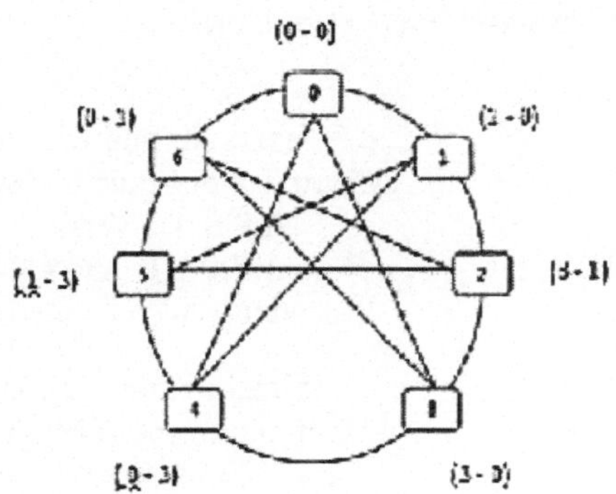

Fig. 1: PDN with n = 7, δ = 2 and PDS = {0, 1, 3}

Example 1 : Let $S_i - S_j = 1 - 0$, $\delta = 2$, $n = \delta^2 + \delta + 1 = 7$ and integer = 1 as shown in the Fig. 1.1

Therefore, eq(1) can be written as:

$(1 - 0) = 1 \bmod 7$

$\Rightarrow \quad 1 = (1 - 0) + 7$

$\Rightarrow \quad 1 = 1 + 7$

$\Rightarrow \quad 1 = 8$

But 8 mod 7 = 1

Hence (1 – 0) is the Perfect Difference Set for node 1.

Example 2 : Let $S_i - S_j = 3 - 1$, $\delta = 2$, $n = \delta^2 + \delta + 1 = 7$ and integer = 2 as shown in the Fig. 1.1

Therefore, eq(1) can be written as:

$(3 - 1) = 2 \bmod 7$

$\Rightarrow \quad 2 = (3 - 1) + 7$

$\Rightarrow \quad 2 = 2 + 7$

$\Rightarrow \quad 2 = 9$

But 9 mod 7 =2

Hence (3 – 1) is the Perfect Difference Set for node 2.

Example 3 : Let $S_i - S_j = 3 - 0$, $\delta = 2$, $n = \delta^2 + \delta + 1 = 7$ and integer = 3 as shown in the Fig. 1.1

Therefore, eq(1) can be written as:

$(3 - 0) = 3 \bmod 7$

$\Rightarrow \quad 3 = (3 - 0) + 7$

$\Rightarrow \quad 3 = 3 + 7$

$\Rightarrow \quad 3 = 10$

But 10 mod 7 = 3

Hence (3 – 0) is the Perfect Difference Set for node 3.

Example 4 : Let $S_i - S_j = 0 - 3$, $\delta = 2$, $n = \delta^2 + \delta + 1 = 7$ and integer = 4 as shown in the Fig. 1.1

Therefore, eq(1) can be written as:

$(0 - 3) = 4 \bmod 7$

$\Rightarrow \quad 4 = (0 - 3) + 7$

$\Rightarrow \quad 4 = -3 + 7$

$\Rightarrow \quad 4 = 4$

Hence (0 – 3) is the Perfect Difference Set for node 4.

Example 5 : Let $S_i - S_j = 1 - 3$, $\delta = 2$, $n = \delta^2 + \delta + 1 = 7$ and integer = 5 as shown in the Fig. 1.1

Therefore, eq(1) can be written as:

$(1 - 3) = 5 \bmod 7$

$\Rightarrow \quad 5 = (1 - 3) + 7$

$\Rightarrow \quad 5 = -2 + 7$

$\Rightarrow \quad 5 = 5$

Hence (1 – 3) is the Perfect Difference Set for node 5.

Example 6 : Let $S_i - S_j = 0 - 1$, $\delta = 2$, $n = \delta^2 + \delta + 1 = 7$ and integer = 6 as shown in the Fig. 1.1

Therefore, eq(1) can be written as:

$(0 - 1) = 6 \bmod 7$

$\Rightarrow \quad 6 = (0 - 1) + 7$

$\Rightarrow \quad 6 = -1 + 7$

$\Rightarrow \quad 6 = 6$

Hence (0 – 1) is the Perfect Difference Set for node 6.

Example 7 : Let $S_i - S_j = 0 - 0$, $\delta = 2$, $n = \delta^2 + \delta + 1 = 7$ and integer = 0 as shown in the Fig. 1.1

Therefore, eq(1) can be written as:

$(0 - 0) = 0 \bmod 7$

$\Rightarrow \quad 0 = 0$

Hence (0 – 0) is the Perfect Difference Set for node 0.

This way we can find out any PDS appropriate to which node number in the Perfect Difference Network architecture.

4)Perfect Difference Network: Perfect Difference Network [1][8][9][11] is the network architecture, in which the diameter is always 2, i.e., every node ith needs to visit only two links to communicate with other nodes $i \pm 1$ & $i \pm s_j \pmod n$, for $2 \leq j \leq \delta$. In a Perfect Difference Network, the total number of nodes is $\delta^2 + \delta + 1$, i.e., if $\delta = 2$ then the total number of nodes in PDN is 7 and if $\delta = 3$, then number of nodes in PDN is 13. Also the degree of every node in a PDN is 2δ i.e., if $\delta = 2$ then degree of every node in a PDN is 4 and similarly for other prime or power of prime numbers.

The design of Perfect difference network is done in such a way where each node is connected via directed links to every other node. The links in PDN architecture are bidirectional in nature and the connectivity leads to a chordal ring of degree 2δ i.e., δ in-degree and δ out-degree and diameter D = 2 [3][9].

δ	n	PDS of order δ in normal form
2	7	{0, 1, 3}
3	13	{0, 1, 3, 9}
4	21	{0, 1, 4, 14, 16}
5	31	{0, 1, 3, 8, 12, 18}
7	57	{0, 1, 3, 13, 32, 36, 43, 52}
8	73	{0, 1, 3, 7, 15, 31, 36, 54, 63}
9	91	{0, 1, 3, 9, 27, 49, 56, 61, 77, 81}
11	133	{0, 1, 3, 12, 20, 34, 38, 81, 88, 94, 104, 109}
13	183	{0, 1, 3, 16, 23, 28, 42, 76, 82, 86, 119, 137, 154, 175}
16	273	{0, 1, 3, 7, 15, 31, 63, 90, 116, 127, 136, 181, 194, 204, 233, 238, 255}

Fig. 2: PDS of order δ in normal form

5) Topological properties of PDN: Some of the topological properties of PDN [2][5][6] are as under:

- Average inter-node distance: - Each node has distance of 0 to itself, 1 to its 2δ neighbors and 2 to the other $\delta^2 - \delta$ nodes. Hence, $D = [2\delta + 2(\delta^2 - \delta)]/n = 2\delta^2/n$. If we did not count the distance of a node to itself, the average inter-node distance would become $2\delta^2/(n - 1) = 2\delta /(\delta + 1)$. Hence the average inter-node distance of PDN of order δ is D = 252/n.
- The upper bound of the PDN is $\min(2S_{all}, nM_{odd} - S_{odd} + S_{even})$, where M_{odd} is the number of odd elements in the PDS, S_{even} and S_{odd} represent the sum of all PDS elements that are even and odd respectively, and S_{all} is the sum of all s_i values for the PDS. For an element s_i of a specific PDS of order define s_i as s_i if $s_i < n/2$ and as $n - s_i > n/2$.
- The total number of links going between odd and even nodes is:

$$\sum (n - s_j) + \sum S_j = nM_{odd} - S_{odd} + S_{even}$$

- Oddskips and Evenskips
- The lower bound on the bisection width of PDN is $((\delta+1)(n+1)/4)$ [7].
- The calculation of bisection width for an arbitrary graph is an NP-Complete problem.

6) Hypercube: Hypercube are loosely coupled parallel processors based on binary n. The hypercube network n-cube parallel processor consists of 2^n identical processors. In hypercube architecture the degree and diameter of the graph is same i.e. 3, because of this equality they achieve a good balance between the communication speed and complexity of the topologic network [1].

The hypercube architecture has many other limitations. Primarily k-dimensional hypercube have N=2n vertices, so their structures are restricted to having exactly 2k nodes. Because structures size must be 2, there are large gaps in the size of systems that can be built with the hypercube. This restricts the number of possible nodes. The perfect difference set establishes the structure that can be constructed for every prime power n=pr. This provides a large advantage over the hypercube architecture, where structures exist only for the powers of 2 [6][12].

The hypercube is well known as one of the most efficient network topologies, especially for interconnection in parallel computers. The configuration of a three-dimensional (3D) hypercube (the familiar cube) network is shown in Figure-3 as an example. A 3D hypercube has 8 vertices and 12 edges, which correspond to network nodes and links, respectively. We define an n-dimensional hypercube network as follows. It consists of N=2n nodes, each of which is labeled by a unique binary node number. Nodes whose nodes numbers differ by only one bit from each other are interconnected by a bidirectional link. As shown in Figure-3, Node (000) is link-connected to Node (001), (010), and (100) since their numbers differ by only one bit from Node (000), in accordance with the definition. The total number of bidirectional links for an n-dimensional hypercube is (N/2) Log2N. This characteristic makes the hypercube scalable since the number of links in this network is proportional to O (NLog2N), which for large-scale networks is much smaller than O (N2), the number of links in a full mesh network, which is the richest network topology. The hypercube network subsumes lower-order network topologies such as mesh, tree, and ring, and thus exhibits the features of these network topologies [6][10].

A unique feature of the hypercube with three or more dimensions is that it can form at least three disjoint paths between any arbitrary pair of nodes, which makes the hypercube robust and reliable enough to secure the network against multiple failures, these features make the hypercube network attractive.

7) Topological properties of Hypercube: A hypercube is a multidimensional mesh of nodes with exactly two nodes in each dimension. A d-dimensional hypercube consists of k nodes, where k=2n [13].

- A hypercube has n dimensions; where n can be any positive integer (including zero).
- The n cube is a connected graph of diameter n.

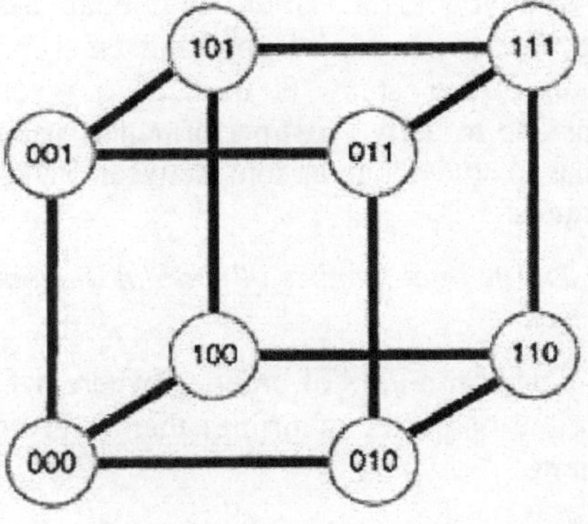

Fig. 3: Configuration of a 3D hypercube network.

- A hypercube has 2n vertices.
- There are n connections (line) that meet at each vertex of a hypercube.
- All connections at a hypercube vertex meet at right angles with respect to each other.
- The hypercube can be constructed recursively from lower dimensional cubes.
- An architecture where the degree and diameter of a graph is the same then they will achieve a good balance between, the communication speed and complexity of the topology network [7].
- An n-cube graph is an undirected graph of $k=2^n$ vertices labeled from 0 to $2^n - 1$ and such that there is an edge between any two vertices if and only if the binary representations of their labels differ by one and only one bit [8].
- Any two adjacent nodes A and B of an N cube are such that the nodes adjacent to A and those adjacent to B are connected in one-to-one fashion.
- There are *n* different ways of tearing an n-cube, i.e., of splitting it into two (n – 1) sub cubes so that their respective vertices are connected in a one-to-one way [4].
- There are $n!\,2^n$ different ways in which the 2^n nodes of an n-cube can be numbered.
- A graph G=(V,E) is an n-cube if and only if
  - V has 2^n vertices;
  - Every vertex has degree n;
  - G is connected;
  - Any two adjacent nodes A and B are such that the nodes adjacent to A and those adjacent to B are linked one-to-one fashion.

II LINK UTILIZATION OF PDN AND HYPERCUBE

Network topologies offer additional design points to accommodate the needs of new and emerging technologies. Therefore, further study is needed to resolve some open questions and to derive cost/performance, robustness in terms of lemmas to study comparisons between PDN and Hypercube architectures.

Lemma 1: *The total number of chordal diagonals in a PDN is always even.*

Proof – Consider a PDS of order n, (where $n = \delta^2 + \delta + 1$ and δ is a prime or power of prime) then it gives the following conclusions.

In PDN, we have total degree of a node = 2δ vertices and since each node is connected to two ring links, therefore, we have total number of chordal diagonals = $2\delta - 2$.

Case 1: if δ is even then $2 * \delta$ result an even integer and therefore $(2*\delta - 2)$ also result an even integer.

Case 2: if δ is odd then $2 * \delta$ again result an even integer and therefore $(2*\delta - 2)$ also result an even integer.

As, we know that subtracting 2 in even integer always turns an even integer.

So, the total number of chordal diagonals in PDN is always even.

Lemma 2: *The 'diameter of the PDN' remains always same while removing one node of the PDN.*

Proof: We know that $\delta = 2$, $n = \delta^2 + \delta + 1$, then on removing one node of the PDN will loses its properties and n becomes n – 1 nodes i.e., $n = \delta^2 + \delta$.

The other properties becomes as:

- Total number of edges '$n.\delta$' becomes '$n.\delta - 2\delta$'.
- Total degree $2n.\delta$ of PDN architecture becomes $2\delta(n - 1)$. These changes can be reflected in chordal diagonals also.

But the only property of the PDN i.e., diameter of the PDN remains always same as shown in the Fig. 4. Hence the remaining network works as a normal network with maximum diameter 2.

From the Fig. 4 if we have to visit node 6 from node 4, we have to visit only two edges to reach to the destination node i.e., 4-5-6 or 4-3-6.similarly, if the source node is 4 and destination node is 2 then paths can be 4-3-2, 4-5-2 and 4-1-2. It shows that paths can be more than 2 but the maximum diameter is always 2. In other words, PDN is robust.

Lemma 3: The 'diameter of the PDN' remains always same while removing one edge of the PDN.

Proof: As we know $\delta = 2$, $n = \delta^2 + \delta + 1$, then on removing one edge from the PDN, its properties becomes as:

- Total number of edges '$n.\delta$' becomes '$n.\delta - 1$'.
- Total degree of PDN is equal to $2n\delta - 2$ as one edge is removed.
- The chordal ring property is also lost.

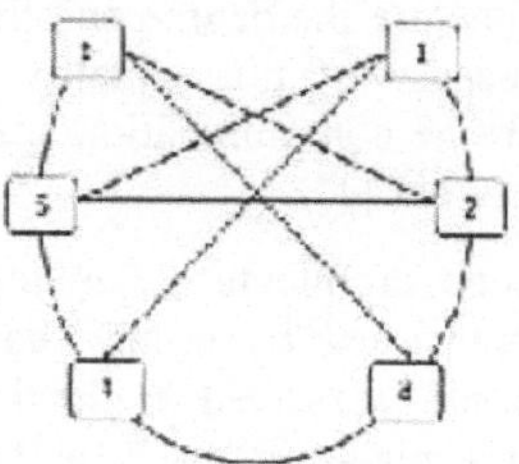

Fig. 4: PDN without one node

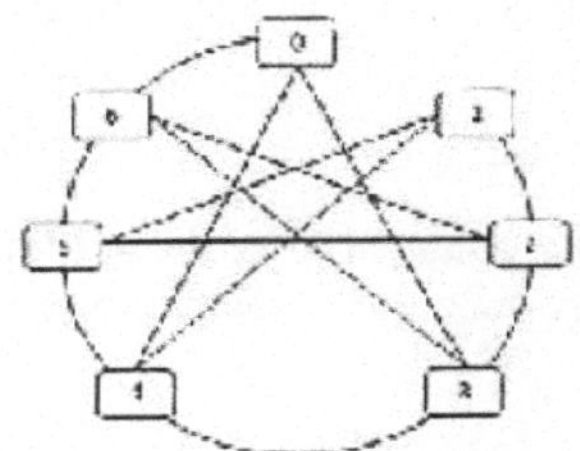

Fig. 5: PDN without one edge

- Lesser number of circuits are formed.

The only property of the PDN i.e., diameter of the PDN remains always same as shown in the Fig. 5. Hence the remaining network works as a normal network with maximum diameter 2.

From the figure if we have to visit node 1 from node 6, we have to visit only two edges to reach to the destination node i.e., 6-2-1 or 6-5-1. Similarly, if the source node is 0 and destination node is 1 then path can be 0-4-1. It shows that there is change is path formation circuits but the maximum diameter is always 2. So it is clear from the figure that PDN loses its properties except the 'diameter' and the remaining network will be used as a normal network with maximum diameter 2. It also shows that PDN is robust in nature.

Lemma 4: *The 'chordal ring property of the PDN' remains same while removing more than one chordal diagonals of the PDN. The remaining network will work as ring topology.*

Proof: As we know $\delta = 2$, $n = \delta^2 + \delta + 1$, then on removing more than one chordal diagonal from the PDN, its properties becomes as:

- Total number of edges 'n.δ' becomes 'n.δ – number of edges to be removed'.
- Total degree of PDN is not equal to 2nδ as more than one diagonal edge is removed.
- The diameter property in this situation is also lost.

The only chordal ring property of the PDN remains same as shown in the Fig. 6. Hence the remaining network works as a normal ring topology network.

In the Fig. 6, given above, it is clear that the chordal ring property of the PDN is not lost by removing the chordal diagonals. It is also clear from the figure that the diameter

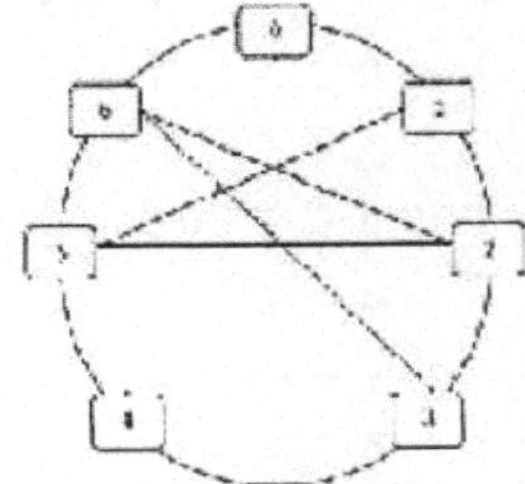

Fig. 6: PDN without More than One Chordal Diagonal

property is not no more exist. For example, if we have to move from the node 0 to node 4, there are different ways to reach to the destination node, like 0 – 6 – 5 – 4 or 0 – 6 – 2 – 3 – 4 or 0 – 6 – 3 – 4 or 0 – 1 – 2 – 3 – 4. So it is clear that the diameter of the PDN is lost by removing the chordal diagonals (more than one).

Lemma 5: *Diameter of Perfect Difference Network (PDN) is equal to total degree of node/Prime number or power of prime.*

Proof: To prove that diameter of a PDN = 2

Let, Prime or power of prime = δ

Then, Total degree of a node = 2δ

Therefore,

Diameter = 2δ/δ

= 2 Hence it is proved.

Lemma 6: *Total number of vertices in a PDN is always odd. Each vertex of PDN has always even number of edges.*

Proof: Consider a PDS is of order n, (where $n = \delta^2 + \delta + 1$ and δ is a prime or power of prime) then it gives the following conclusions.

Since, a PDN has $n = \delta^2 + \delta + 1$ vertices.

Case 1: if δ is even then $\delta^2 + \delta$ result in an even integer

Case 2: if δ is odd then $\delta^2 + \delta$ again result an even integer

As, we know that adding 1 in even integer always turns an odd integer.

So, the total number of vertices in PDN is always odd.

Again, since each ith node of PDN is connected to $(i \pm 1)$ mod n and $(i \pm s_j)$ mod n node, where $2 \le j \le \delta$ and any two vertex having one edge between them.

Therefore d (v) = 2.δ, where δ is also equal to total number of non-zero elements in a PDS.

So each node of PDN has even number of edges.

Lemma 7: *The degree of a node is increased by 2 in case of PDN of PDNs. In this case the diameter also changes while traversing from one PDN to another PDN.*

Proof: Since each ith node of PDN is connected to $(i\pm1)$ node of other PDN, and any two vertexes having one edge between them. Therefore, each node requires 2 more edges to connect to the 2 nodes of the PDN in a PDN of PDN's.

The given below Figure-7 depicts the above assumption. Similarly if we want to traverse from one node of a PDN to another node of another PDN in a PDN of PDNs, the diameter can be changed as shown in the figure given below:

In this case the diameter changes from one PDN to another PDN and can be equal to 2 + shortest distance between two concerned PDN's.

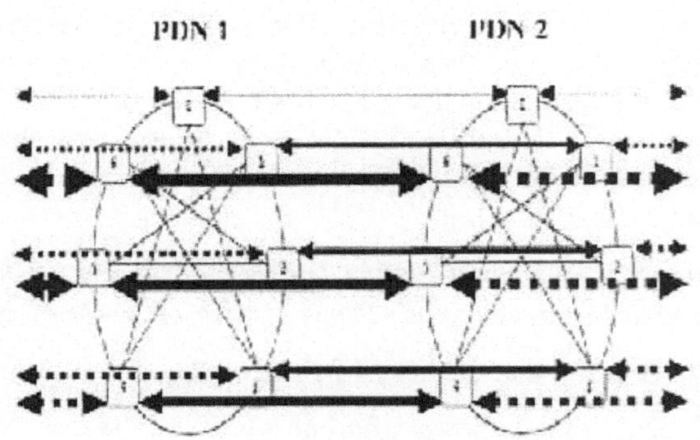

Fig. 7: PDN of PDN's

Lemma 8: *The circuits formed in a PDN are a combination of odd and even length. And the smallest circuit in a PDN is of length 3.*

Proof: The circuits formed from the PDN with 7 nodes are shown below:

Circuit	Length
$0 \to 4 \to 3 \to 0$	(Odd Length)
$0 \to 4 \to 1 \to 0$	(Odd Length)
$0 \to 3 \to 6 \to 0$	(Odd Length)
$0 \to 6 \to 5 \to 1 \to 0$	(Even Length)
$0 \to 6 \to 5 \to 2 \to 1 \to 0$	(Odd Length)
$0 \to 6 \to 5 \to 4 \to 1 \to 0$	(Odd Length)
$0 \to 6 \to 5 \to 4 \to 0$	(Even Length)
$0 \to 6 \to 5 \to 4 \to 3 \to 0$	(Odd Length)
$0 \to 6 \to 5 \to 4 \to 3 \to 2 \to 1 \to 0$	(Odd Length)
$0 \to 1 \to 2 \to 6 \to 0$	(Even Length)
$0 \to 1 \to 2 \to 3 \to 0$	(Even Length)
$0 \to 1 \to 2 \to 3 \to 6 \to 0$	(Odd Length)
$0 \to 1 \to 2 \to 3 \to 4 \to 0$	(Odd Length)
$1 \to 5 \to 4 \to 1$	(Odd Length)
$1 \to 5 \to 2 \to 1$	(Odd Length)
$1 \to 5 \to 4 \to 3 \to 2 \to 1$	(Odd Length)
$1 \to 4 \to 3 \to 2 \to 1$	(Even Length)
$2 \to 6 \to 5 \to 2$	(Odd Length)
$2 \to 3 \to 6 \to 2$	(Odd Length)
$2 \to 5 \to 4 \to 3 \to 2$	(Even Length)
$2 \to 6 \to 5 \to 4 \to 3 \to 2$	(Odd Length)
$3 \to 6 \to 5 \to 4 \to 3$	(Even Length)

From the circuit calculations given above, it is clear that the circuits formed in PDN are a combination of odd and even lengths.

Lemma 9: *The matrix of PDN is always $n \times n$. In a PDN matrix, the row i is formed from row (i±1) by shifting i number of bits.*

Proof: The adjacency matrix of the PDN is shown below:

From the adjacency matrix of the Perfect Difference Network, the second row of the PDN is obtained by shifting the bits of first row towards right as given below:

First row:

0 1 0 1 1 0 1

Now shift the bits of first row by one towards right, then the row will be:

1 0 1 0 1 1 0

The row that we obtained after the shifting of bits of first row towards right is same as the second row:

1 0 1 0 1 1 0

Now we will do this for the third row of the adjacency matrix. For this we have to shift the bits of second row by one towards right, already obtained from first row by shifting of bits by one, as given below:

Second row:

1 0 1 0 1 1 0

Now shift the bits towards right by one, the row will be:

0 1 0 1 01 1

The row that is obtained from the second row is same as third row of the adjacency matrix of the Perfect Difference Network. If we do it for the remaining rows, we can easily get the next rows of adjacency matrix of the Perfect Difference Network.

Lemma 10: *Diameter of a Perfect Difference Network and Hypercube can be calculated from their adjacency matrices.*

Proof: The adjacency matrix of the PDN having 7 nodes is shown in Fig. 9. It shows dotted lines between rows/columns for Diameter of PDN when n=7.

	0	1	2	3	4	5	6
0	0	1	0	1	1	0	1
1	1	0	1	0	1	1	0
2	0	1	0	1	0	1	1
3	1	0	1	0	1	0	1
4	1	1	0	1	0	1	0
5	0	1	1	0	1	0	1
6	1	0	1	1	0	1	0

Fig. 8: Adjacency Matrix of PDN Having 7 Nodes

	0	1	2	3	4	5	6
0	0	1	0	1 –	– 1	0	1
1	1	0	1	0	1 –	– 1	0
2	0	1	0	1	0	1 –	– 1
3	–1–	0	1	0	1	0	–1–
4	1 –	– 1	0	1	0	1	0
5	0	1 –	– 1	0	1	0	1
6	1	0	1 –	– 1	0	1	0

Fig. 9: Diameter of PDN when n=7

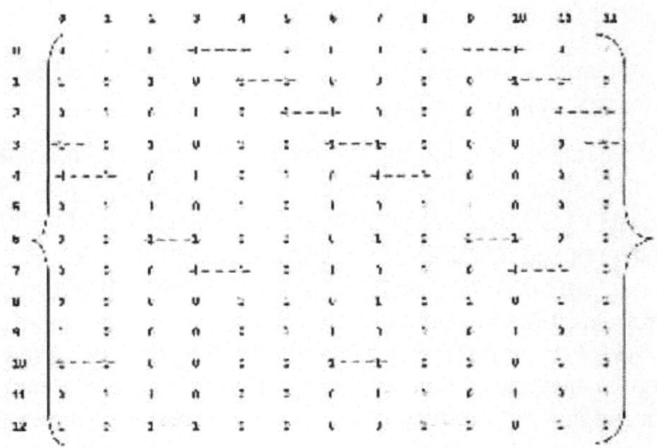

Fig. 10: Diameter of PDN when n=13

The adjacency matrix of the PDN having 13 nodes is shown in Fig. 10.

From the matrices Fig.10 & Fig.11, the consecutive two 1's represented as dotted lines in each matrices shows the diameter of these two architecture i.e., the maximum length from any source node to the destination node in Perfect Difference Network is 2 while as it is 3 in case of Hypercube. It shows dotted lines between rows/columns for Diameter of PDN when n=13.

Similarly the diameter of Hypercube can be calculated as shown below in the Fig.11. It shows dotted lines between two rows/columns as diameter of Hypercube.

Lemma 11: *The number of circuits formed in hypercube is of even length.*

Proof: 3D hypercube and its circuits whose source and destination node is '0' is shown below as:

Circuits	Length
0 → 1 → 2 → 3→0	(Even Length)
0 → 1 → 2 → 3→4→7→0	(Even Length)
0 → 1 → 2 → 3→4→5→6→7→0	(Even Length)
0 → 1 → 2 → 5 →4→3→ 0	(Even Length)
0 → 1 → 2 → 5 → 4 → 7→ 0	(Even Length)
0 → 1 → 2 → 5 → 6 → 7→0	(Even Length)
0 → 1 → 2 → 5 → 6→7→4→3→0	(Even Length)
0 → 1 → 6 → 5 → 4 → 7→0	(Even Length)
0 → 1→6 → 7 → 0	(Even Length)
0 → 1 → 6 → 7 → 4→ 3→ 0	(Even Length)
0 → 1 → 6 → 5 → 2→ 3→ 0	(Even Length)
0 → 1 → 6 → 5 → 2 → 3→4→7→0	(Even Length)
0 → 1 → 6 → 7 → 4 → 5→ 2→3→0	(Even Length)
0→3→2→5→4→7→0	(Even Length)
0→3→2→5→4→7→6→1→0	(Even Length)
0→3→2→5→6→7→0	(Even Length)
0→3→2→5→6→1→0	(Even Length)
0→3→2→1→6→7→0	(Even Length)
0→3→2→1→6→5→4→7→0	(Even Length)
0→3→4→7→0	(Even Length)
0→3→4→7→6→0	(Even Length)
0→3→4→5→6→7→0	(Even Length)
0→3→4→7→6→5→2→1→0	(Even Length)
0→3→4→5→6→1→0	(Even Length)
0→3→4→5→2→1→0	(Even Length)
0→3→4→5→2→1→6→7→0	(Even Length)
0→7→4→3→2→5→6→1→0	(Even Length)
0→7→4→5→2→1→0	(Even Length)
0→7→4→5→2→3→0	(Even Length)
0→7→4→5→6→1→2→3→0	(Even Length)
0→7→4→5→6→1→0	(Even Length)
0→7→6→5→4→3→0	(Even Length)
0→7→6→5→2→3→0	(Even Length)
0→7→6→5→2→1→0	(Even Length)
0→7→6→5→4→3→2→1→0	(Even Length)
0→7→6→1→2→3→0	(Even Length)
0→7→6→1→2→5→4→3→0	(Even Length)
⋮	⋮

From the above circuit calculations it is shown that the length of each circuit is even. Therefore, number of nodes in hypercube is 2^n, if the nodes are even then the associated adjacent edges are also even, hence proved.

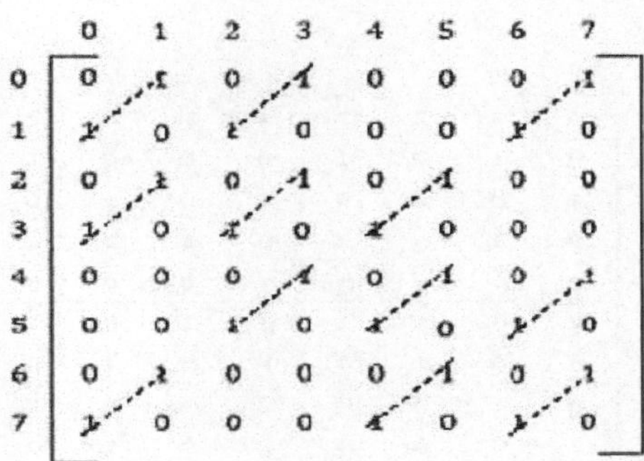

Fig. 11: Diameter of Hypercube.

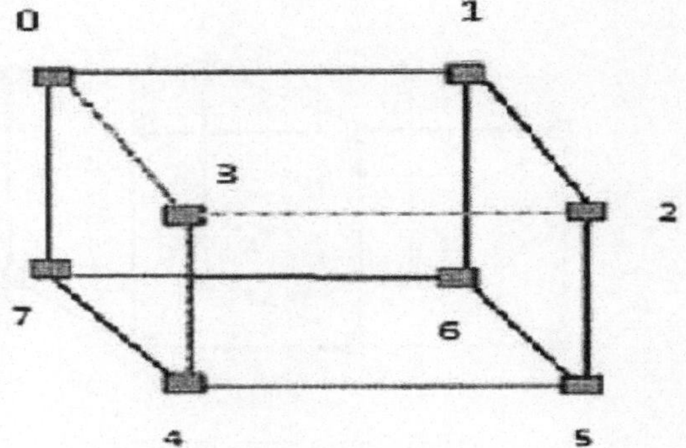

Fig. 12: 3D Hypercube

Lemma 12: *The minimum cycle length of the circuits formedin Hypercube is 4 and maximum is 8.*

Proof: As shown in the Lemma 11, it is clear that the minimum length of the circuit is 4 and its maximum length is 8, hence proved.

Lemma 13: *All the rows and columns of sub-graph of matrix of hypercube is a circuit if the sub-graph matrix of matrix of hypercube is minimum 4×4 matrix.*

Proof: From the Lemma 11, it is clear that each face of the hypercube is a combination of 4 vertices; therefore each face of the hypercube is a sub graph of the 3D hypercube graph. It is also shown in the above matrix (Fig. 13) that sub-graph matrix of matrix of hypercube is minimum of 4×4 matrix, hence proved.

Lemma 14: *When two Hypercubes are connected then the degree of middle vertices are increased by one and the degree or corner vertices remains same.*

Proof: As we know that the degree of the hypercube is n i.e., 3 , but it can be seen from the Fig. 14 that node '1', '4', '7', and '10' has degree n+1 i.e. 4 and the remaining nodes have the same degree. Hence when two hypercubes are connected then the degree of middle vertices are increased by one and the degree or corner vertices remains same.

	0	1	2	3	4	5	6	7
0	0	1	0	1	0	0	0	1
1	1	0	1	0	0	0	1	0
2	0	1	0	1	0	1	0	0
3	1	0	1	0	1	0	0	0
4	0	0	0	1	0	1	0	1
5	0	0	1	0	1	0	1	0
6	0	1	0	0	0	1	0	1
7	1	0	0	0	1	0	1	0

Fig. 13: Matrix of hypercube is 4 sub-matrices of 4x4

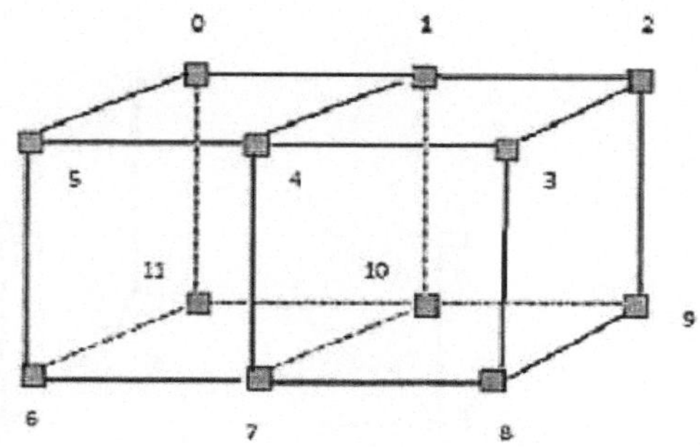

Fig. 14: Two connected hypercubes.

III Conclusion

A comparative study of hypercube and perfect difference network is done on the basis of topological properties.

Hypercubes are loosely coupled parallel processors based on the binary n-cube network; n-cube parallel processor consists of 2^n identical processors. In hypercube architecture, the degree and diameter of the graph is same i.e. n. So because of this equality they achieve a good balance between the communication speed and the complexity of the topology network. Perfect difference networks (PDNs) that are based on the mathematical notion of perfect difference sets to comprise an asymptotically optimal method for connecting a number of nodes into a network with diameter 2 and its performance lies between hypercube and complete graph.

In this paper, we have derived the properties of hypercube and perfect difference network in the form of lemmas for comparing these two architectures. The comparison between these architectures has been shown with the help of circuits. The circuits formed in hypercube are of even length while as in PDN, it is a combination of odd and even lengths. We have derived that the minimum length of circuits formed in hypercube is 4 and maximum 2^n while as in PDN, minimum length is 3 and maximum length is the total number of nodes formed in PDN. We have studied that the adjacency matrix of hypercube is a combination of 4 sub-matrices of order 4x4, while as in PDN, there is only nxn matrix. We have explored that the degree of middle vertices of two connected hypercubes is increased by one while as in PDN of PDNs, the degree of a node is increased by 2. We have studied that the number of vertices in PDN is odd and has even number of edges while as, it is not the case in Hypercube. We have made attempts to study the circuits to show the robustness of these architectures. In these architectures, the diameter remains same during normal course and during link failure.

The comparison between these two architectures and their diameters can be shown on their adjacency matrices as well.

REFERENCES

[1] Ammon, J., **Hypercube Conncetivity within cc NUMA architecture** Silicon Graphics , 201LN. Shoreline Blvd. Ms 565, Mountain View, CA 91343.

[2] Behrooz Parhami, Fellow, IEEE, and Mikhail Rakov, **Perfect Difference Networks and related Interconnection Structures for Parallel and Distributed Systems**, IEEE transactions on parallel and distributed systems, vol. 16, no. 8, August 2005.

[3] Jó Ágila Bitsch Link, Christoph Wollgarten, Stefan Schupp, Klaus Wehrle **Communication and Distributed Systems** (Informatik 4), RWTH Aachen University Aachen, Germany {jo.bitsch, christoph.wollgarten, stefan.schupp, klaus.wehrle} @rwth-aachen.de.

[4] Katare , R.K., Chaudhari, N.S., **Some P-RAM Algorithms for Sparse Linear Systems**, Journal of Computer Science, USA 2008.

[5] Katare, R.K ., Chaudhari, N.S., **A Comparative Study of Hypercube and Perfect Difference Network for Parallel and Distributed System and its Application to Sparse Linear System**, Vol . 2 Sandipani Academic, Ujjain [M.P.] pp. 13-30, 2007.

[6] Katare, R.K., Chaudhari, N.S., **Study Of Topological Property Of Interconnection Networks And Its Mapping To Sparse Matrix Model** International Journal of Computer Science and Applications, Technomathematics Research Foundation Vol. 6, No. 1. Oct. 2009.

[7] P. Guerrier and A. Grenier, **A Generic Architecture for on Chip Packetswitched Interconnections**, In Proc. Design Automation and Test in Europe Conf. (DATE), pp. 250-256, 2000.

[8] Parhami , B., and D.- M. Kwai, **Challenges in Interconnection Network Design in the Era of Multiprocessor and Massively Parallel Microchips,** Proc. Int'l Conf. Communications in Computing , June 2000.

[9] Parhami Behrooz, Rakov Mikhail, **"Application of Perfect Difference Sets to the Design of Efficient and Robust Interconnection Networks"**.

[10] Parhami, B., Fellow, IEEE, and Rakov, M., **Performance, Algorithmic, and Robustness Attributes of Perfect Difference Networks**, IEEE transactions on parallel and distributed systems, vol. 16, no. 8, August 2005.

[11] Parhami, B., **Swapped Interconnection Networks: Topological, Performance, and Robustness Attributes**, J.Parallel and Distributed Computing, to appear.

[12] Rakov, M., **Multidimensional Hyperstar and Hypercube Interconnection Methods and Structure**, US Patent Application No. 09/140 175, filed September 1999. www.wikipedia.com

[13] Singer J. **A Theorem in Finite Projective Geometry and Some Applications to Number Theory.** Trans. American Mathematical Society, Vol. 43, pp. 377-385, 1938.

Scalable Software Practice Environments Featuring Automatic Provision and Configuration in the Cloud

Germán Moltó, Miguel Caballer

Instituto de Instrumentación para Imagen Molecular (I3M).
Centro mixto CSIC - Universitat Politècnica de València - CIEMAT
Camino de Vera s/n, 46022 Valencia, España
Email: gmolto@dsic.upv.es,micafer1@upv.es

***Abstract*—This paper describes an architecture to deploy scalable Software Practice Environments (SPE) to support the practice lessons that require computer resources that can be remotely accessed. The architecture enables (i) to dynamically and on-demand provision the required computing resources from different IaaS Cloud providers, (ii) to perform the automatic software configuration to satisfy the requirements of the practical lesson, (iii) to suspend and resume the virtual infrastructure in order to cut down costs during a course and (iv) to support different elasticity approaches in order to create scalable virtual infrastructures. The paper describes the proposed architecture and details a case study that involves deploying the virtual infrastructure of an online course on Cloud Computing with Amazon Web Services (AWS) on top of AWS itself. It also describes scalability approaches that can be employed to provide infrastructure access to SPEs for larger audiences, such as those found in MOOCs.**

Keywords: Cloud computing, virtual infrastructures, automated deployment, elasticity

I. INTRODUCTION

The students of Computer Science, specially those of Distributed Computing subjects, require access to different computing infrastructures in order to develop the appropriate skills required to efficiently use them. For example, when developing distributed algorithms, the students require access to a set of computers with the appropriate software tools (i.e., compilers, libraries, debuggers, etc.) that allow them to efficiently program those algorithms during the practice lessons. In the context of this paper, a Software Practice Environment (SPE) includes:

- A hardware configuration that satisfies the requirements of the practice lesson. This includes the CPU architecture, the disk size available for students and also special devices (as an example, a practical lesson on programming GPUs requires access to a GPU on which to run the developed codes).
- A software configuration that satisfies the requirements of the practice lesson. This includes the Operating System (OS), the required software, libraries and utilities required for the students to develop the practice lesson. It also includes the user accounts and the configuration of each account.
- Supporting Data. This includes all the data required to perform the practice lesson. For example, the developed algorithms might require certain input data files to perform some benchmarks.

However, deploying and configuring SPEs is far from being a trivial task. Traditionally, many organizations prepare Golden Images that encapsulate the software and data configuration to perform the duties of some (or all of the) subjects. These disk images are then deployed on the PCs of a physical laboratory. However, these approach exhibits many problems. First of all, it hinders extensibility, since including a new application implies modifying the golden image and redeploy it on all the PCs of the laboratory. Second, using a physical laboratory sets an upper bound to the scalability of the computational resources configured to perform the practice lessons (typically no more than two students per PC).

Nowadays, there are two trends that coexist and which enable to surpass the limitations of traditional approaches when it comes to providing a customized software experience for students. On the one hand, Cloud computing is a model that provides network access to a pool of configurable computing resources which can be rapidly provisioned with minimal effort, typically on a pay-per-use basis in the case of public Clouds [1]. On the other hand, the Bring Your Own Device (BYOD) [2] approach enables students to use their own computers and devices in order to access the subject materials. Specially in the case of online courses, where users are not required to attend a physical laboratory, these two trends can be combined in order to offer the users a remote Software Practice Environment (SPE).

This way, the professor can automatically deploy in a Cloud provider (which involves provisioning the virtual infrastructure and configuring it) right before the course starts the required virtual infrastructure that the students require. In the case of using a public Cloud provider, the cost is proportional to the computational and storage resources consumed (mainly hours of Virtual Machine and GBytes of data stored and transferred). Once the course has finished, the infrastructure is relinquished in order to avoid additional costs. In addition, we propose to suspend the deployed infrastructure during unused hours (for example at night) in order to cut down costs. For online courses with different editions through an academic year, this approach is very beneficial, since a new edition of the course simply involves deploying an instance of the virtual infrastructure, which represents a fresh and new install for the new users (without any potentially malicious modifications by the previous students).

The remainder of the paper is structured as follows. First, section II describes related work in this area. Next, section III introduces the main architecture of the proposed system and describes its main components. Later, section IV describes a case study that involves deploying the virtual infrastructure required to support an online course on Cloud Computing with AWS. Next, section V extends the proposed architecture to consider the case of MOOCs, where a scalable virtual infrastructure is required for a large number of students. Finally, section VI summarises the paper and points to future work.

II. Related Work

This paper focuses on the automatic deployment of a virtual infrastructure in a Cloud back-end to support a Software Practice Environment (SPE) that can be remotely accessed by students.

There are different tools that enable to deploy virtual infrastructures in a Cloud. If we focus on open-source tools, Nimbus [3] is project that provides Nimbus Infrastructure, which enables to create Infrastructure as a Service (IaaS) Clouds. It also deals with application contextualization, enabling to deploy virtual clusters on the Cloud. StarCluster [4] also enables to create and manage distributed computing clusters hosted on Amazon EC2. This is also the case of ViteraaS [5], a tool that provides on-demand high performance computing, in the shape of virtual clusters, for research projects, e-learning and teaching within a private Cloud.

All the aforementioned previous works focuses on clusters of PCs deployed on the Cloud. However, our proposed architecture does not focus exclusively on virtual clusters (although it is also able to deploy virtual clusters in a Cloud). In addition, this work extends previous works with two contributions: i) it leverages dynamic configuration without requiring pre-configuration of the Virtual Machine Images, and ii) it focuses on scalability approaches in order to accommodate a large number of users.

There are also commercial tools that automate application deployment and software configuration. For example, rPath, before it was acquired by SAS in November 2012, provided methods to automate the process of packaging, deploying and updating software stacks across physical, virtual and cloud-based environments. Tools such as Kace or BMC Application Automation provide software deployment tools together with automated solutions in order to deploy and manage software throughout an organization.

In our case, we combine application provisioning from a Cloud provider and application deployment and configuration, relying on open-source *DevOps* tools. This enables to have high level recipes to specify the desired infrastructure and enact them on different Clouds.

III. Proposed Architecture

The proposed architecture enables to dynamically provision and configure virtual infrastructures. It features both horizontal and vertical elasticity capabilities to enable scaling the virtual infrastructure, composed of multiple replicated Software Practice Environments (SPEs), to accommodate an increased or reduced number of students. The students can remotely access them using their own devices, typically via SSH, in order to perform a practice lesson.

The proposed architecture builds on some previous developments which, for the sake of completeness, are summarised here:

- The Resource Application Description Language (RADL) [6] is a high level declarative language that includes the hardware, software and configuration requirements of the virtual infrastructure to be deployed. For example, one could describe the requirements for 10 VMs with GNU/Linux Ubuntu 12.04, JDK 1.7+, the installation of the ImageMagick software and 15 user accounts with a set of pre-defined passwords.
- The Infrastructure Manager (IM) [6] is a service-oriented component that takes as input a RADL description of a virtual infrastructure and it provisions the required resources and configures them in order to satisfy the requirements imposed by the RADL description. The IM supports different IaaS Cloud backends, such as OpenNebula [7], OpenStack [8] and Amazon EC2 [9]. As such, it provides a uniform layer to deploy virtual infrastructures on multiple Clouds with the same RADL document. Provisioning resources from multiple Cloud providers is typically known as Sky Computing [10].
- The Configuration Manager. This component is part of the IM and is in charge of performing the deployment and configuration of software, together with the customization of the Virtual Machines (VM). It automates the creation of user accounts, downloading software packages, modifying files, etc. The Configuration Manager currently supports Puppet [11] and Ansible [12]. Both software packages belong to the *DevOps* category and they allow to create recipes in order to automate software deployment and configuration, thus guaranteeing determinism. Puppet uses a pull approach, where agents installed in the VMs of the virtual infrastructure contact a server for instructions on how to configure the VMs. However, Ansible uses a push approach, where configuration is pushed into the VMs from a central server. In our case, we currently rely on Ansible which has proved to be highly scalable.
- The Virtual Machine image Repository & Catalog (VMRC) [13] enables to index and store Virtual Machine Images (VMIs). A VMI is an encapsulation of a virtual hardware configuration together with an Operating System (OS), a set of applications and data. VMs can then be created as instances of a VMI, thus exposing the configuration specified by the VMI. Unlike other catalogs

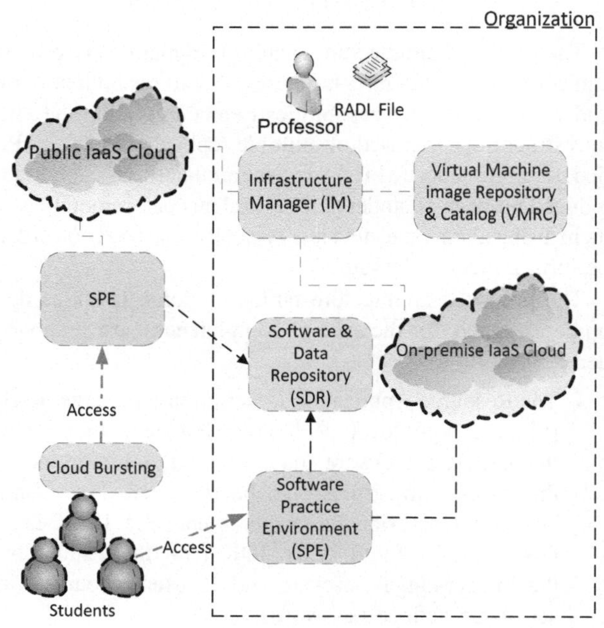

Fig. 1. Simplified architecture to deploy a multi-node Software Practice Environment in a hybrid Cloud scenario.

of VMIs, VMRC stores metadata of the VMIs (such as the OS, the hypervisor employed to create it, the applications installed, etc.). This metadata can be employed using a query language in order to obtain a ranked list of VMIs that satisfy a given set of requirements (the rank is user-dependent according to the satisfaction of the requirements imposed by the user). For example, one could query the catalog for a suitable list of VMIs based on GNU/Linux Ubuntu greater than 12.04 (hard requirement) and it would be desirable that it had SciLab 4.2+ (this is an example of a soft requirement, where this software can be installed at runtime to satisfy the requirement of the user).

Figure 1 summarises a simplified version of the architecture employed to provision and configure a Software Practice Environment (SPE). The figure assumes an scenario in which the organization (an education center) has an on-premise IaaS Cloud deployment (these are also known as private Clouds, supported by tools such as OpenNebula [7], OpenStack [8] or Eucalyptus [14]). It has also access to a public IaaS Cloud provider such as Amazon Web Services [15], or Rackspace [16], among many others.

The idea is to deploy the SPE in the on-premise Cloud and in the public Cloud. This could be performed simultaneously or using a Cloud bursting approach [17], where the public Cloud is only employed when the on-premise Cloud cannot cope with the workload (an increase in the number of SPE instances due to a large number of users). Regardless of the scenario, using a hybrid approach composed of an on-premise and a public Cloud where the same precise configuration exists on both instances of the SPE, introduces fault-tolerance and better ability to workload distribution (different students can connect to different SPE instances).

We summarize the steps required for the professor (or sysadmin) to deploy a SPE using the proposed architecture. First of all, the professor describes the requirements of the infrastructure in a RADL document. This description is submitted to the Infrastructure Manager (IM) which queries the VMRC system to obtain a list of the most appropriate VMIs that satisfy the requirements imposed by the user (the professor in our case). The IM provisions the VMs with the credentials supplied by the professor to access each Cloud infrastructure. Notice that the very same RADL document serves to deploy similar virtual infrastructures with the same configuration. Then, the IM delegates on Ansible to perform all the software installation and configuration. In particular this means:

- To download and install software and required data from both the Software & Data Repository (SDR) or from other external repositories (such as the Ubuntu software repositories). The SDR stores course-dependent data files such as practice guides, input data sets, specific software versions, etc.
- To configure system services. For example, to provide a specific configuration for the SSH server.
- To create user accounts. Using a pre-defined list of account names and passwords, this enables to provide SSH-based access to the SPE for the students.

Once the SPE is up and running, the students connect to it via SSH (or using a graphical desktop via tools such as FreeNX). The ability to define the virtual infrastructure only once in a high-level declarative recipe (using RADL) to deploy a similar virtual infrastructure on different Cloud providers represents a huge step forward when compared to the manual installation and configuration of software. First of all, the professor is now able to perform multiple, deterministic deployments of a similar virtual infrastructure regardless of the Cloud back-end. Secondly, software updates become automatic, since new deployments of the virtual infrastructure, if accompanied by on-demand installation of software, results in an updated virtual infrastructure. Finally, it is possible to deploy new SPE instances on-demand (either in the on-premise Cloud or in the public Cloud) in order to accommodate a larger number of students.

IV. Case Study: The Online Course of Cloud Computing and AWS

The Institute for Molecular Imaging Technologies (I3M) at the Universitat Politècnica de València in Spain offers a three-week online course on Cloud Computing with Amazon Web Services (AWS)[1]. The course involves theoretical concepts about the Cloud and hands-on practice lessons that demonstrate the usage of the AWS services to create scalable Cloud applications that efficiently access data in the Cloud. The *aws*

[1]Further information available at http://www.grycap.upv.es/cursocloud

command-line tool [18] is used to manage AWS services such as Amazon EC2 (Elastic Compute Cloud), Amazon S3 (Simple Storage Service), Amazon SQS (Simple Queue Service) and Amazon SimpleDB. In addition, the official command-line tools to interact with Amazon CloudWatch and Auto Scaling are used. Other services such as Amazon RDS (Relational Database Service) are accessed via a web browser and a database client.

The students connect to a GNU/Linux machine (the SPE) on which they find a pre-configured environment (user accounts, AWS credentials, required tools to interact with AWS). There can be many replicas of this machine since the user state during the practice lessons is always stored in AWS and not in the SPE and, thus, students can connect to whichever instance of the SPE is available. Therefore, students need access to a SPE with the following configuration:

- A VM with GNU/Linux Ubuntu 12.04+, 512+ MB, outbound and inbound connectivity.
- A set of user accounts, each one with the following configuration:
  - A specific username and password pre-allocated by the professor.
  - The Access Key ID and the Secret Access Key to authenticate the student to use the AWS services.
- The following software packages installed:
  - The *aws* tool, described earlier.
  - The Auto Scaling and CloudWatch tools to access those services.
  - A MySQL client (to access databases created with Amazon RDS).
  - OpenJDK JRE 7. This is a requirement for the Auto Scaling and CloudWatch tools.
- The following services configuration:
  - Enable password-based SSH access to the instance (which is disabled by default in Amazon EC2's instances).
- The following data:
  - A package containing the practice guides, sample scripts that demonstrate some AWS services, scripts to populate databases, sample files to be uploaded to Amazon S3, etc.

All this information is specified in an RADL document, which is summarized in Figure 2. The syntax and data has been slightly modified to accommodate the formatting of the paper. Notice that the RADL specifies: i) the physical requirements (such as network with outbound connectivity or a minimum number of RAM), ii) the OS requirements (a minimum version of Ubuntu) and iii) the software and services configuration required in the SPE. Notice that software is automatically downloaded from the SDR and installed. If files are updated in the SDR, the next deployment of the virtual infrastructure will have updated software. The SSH is automatically configured (not shown in RADL) and restarted to allow password-based connections, which is by default disabled in Amazon EC2.

```
network public (outbound = 'yes')
system cursoaws (
cpu.arch='x86_64' and
cpu.count>=1 and
memory.size>=512m and
net_interfaces.count = 1 and
net_interface.0.connection = 'public' and
net_interface.0.dns_name = 'cursoaws' and
disk.0.os.name='linux' and
disk.0.os.flavour='ubuntu' and
disk.0.os.version>='12.04'
)
configure cursoaws (
@begin
- vars:
  - pw_00: O3Je2QxgM0w
  - ak_00: AKIAJAIPMN42O7ADSC5A
  - sk_00: ft0ftS7FD0M5L5Tu3V/
 tasks:
    - user: name=alucloud00 password=$pw_00
     - copy: dest=/home/alucloud00/.awssecret
                content="$ak_00 $sk_00"
  - get_url: url=<sdr_url>/${item} dest=/tmp/${item}
     with_items:
       - cursoaws_1.0_all.deb
       - autoscaling_1.0.61.2_all.deb
       - cloudwatch_1.0.13.4_all.deb
   - command: dpkg -i /tmp/${item}
     with_items:
       - cursoaws_1.0_all.deb
       - autoscaling_1.0.61.2_all.deb
       - cloudwatch_1.0.13.4_all.deb
  - apt: pkg=openjdk-7-jre state=latest
  - get_url: url=<location>/aws
                 dest=/usr/local/bin/aws
   - apt: pkg=mysql-client-5.5 state=installed
   - service: name=ssh state=restarted
@end
)
deploy cursoaws 1
```

Fig. 2. An excerpt of the RADL document to deploy the SPE for the course on Cloud Computing with AWS.

In this online course, the SPE is deployed on Amazon EC2, although in past courses we also deployed the SPE in an on-premise Cloud based on OpenNebula. Using an on-premise Cloud enables to reduce the costs and offer the same SPE for the students. The number of SPE instances depends on the number of users enrolled in each edition. In order to cut down costs it is convenient to schedule the practice lessons (or at least to have available the infrastructure only during the day, and suspend it at night) in a suspend-resume approach that will be described in the next section.

With the developed system it is possible to deploy, for example, two SPE instances in an average of 7 minutes, involving resource provisioning, software and data downloading and installation and customization (user accounts, ssh configuration, etc.). Notice that multiple instances of SPE are submitted and configured in parallel.

V. Scalable Virtual Infrastructures for MOOCs

With the advent of Massively Open Online Courses (MOOC), we wanted to explore the feasibility of providing a scalable cost-effective access to a Software Practice Environment (SPE) for remote users. Popular courses enroll tens of thousands of students. At the moment, the most common approach to provide a SPE for MOOC students is to prepare a Virtual Machine Image (VMI) with a predefined configuration of the OS, tools and data required to perform the course activities. However, if online services have to be employed (as in the case of the online course on Cloud Computing and AWS), there is no other alternative than providing students with remote access to a GNU/Linux-based SPE so that the student can perform the practice lessons. Some of these courses distribute the cost of using Cloud resources by encouraging students to sign up with a public Cloud provider. In this section, we wanted to explore the possibility that the educational center pays for the infrastructure costs.

Figure 3 describes an architecture to offer scalable SPEs, by leveraging different services from Amazon Web Services (AWS). The proposed architecture is generic enough to be deployed in other public Cloud provider (such as Windows Azure) using the corresponding services.

AWS consists of geographically distributed *regions* across the world which consist of several isolated locations called *availability zones*. The Amazon EC2 service provisions Virtual Machines (called *instances*) from Amazon Machine Images (AMIs). AWS includes many services that fit in the proposed architecture:

- AWS Identity and Access Management (IAM). The professor creates one user credential per student from a single AWS account. These accounts can be temporarily suspended (useful to prevent AWS usage when an edition of the course has finished) and reused by the students of the new edition (since those are not personal accounts).
- Amazon CloudFront. It enables to distribute content at a scale by distributing replicas to different edge locations in the world. Users that request the content will access the nearest replica. This is useful when starting a MOOC with expected peaks in data access (for example, an introductory video accessed by 70k students).
- Auto Scaling. It enables to increase (scale out) and decrease (scale in) the size of the virtual infrastructure. The next subsection focuses specifically on scaling approaches.

A. On Scaling the Virtual Infrastructure

When considering a variable number of users requiring access to a SPE, elasticity, or the ability to increase and decrease the number of instances and the capacities of a SPE, is a key feature. AWS supports different elasticity schemes:

1) Horizontal Elasticity: Within a region, the Auto Scaling service enables to create fleets of instances (an *auto scaling group* (ASG)) that can shrink and grow according to some elasticity rules based mainly on workload or schedule. The ASG includes an Elastic Load Balancer (ELB) that distributes incoming requests for the ELB to the instances of the ASG. The elasticity rules can indicate for example that if the average CPU usage of the instances of the ASG exceeds a 70% during the last 3 periods of 5 minutes, then increase the ASG with 4 additional instances (there are similar rules to scale in).

This approach can accommodate new online students that are performing the practice lessons. If workload is increased, the ASG is increased, and new students that connect to the ELB will be forwarded to an instance of the SPE. Since all the SPE instances are clones and provide the same environment, it does not matter which instance fulfills the request. However, if shared state among the different instances of SPEs is mandatory, these data can be stored in Amazon S3 and pulled by the user to the local instance upon login in the SPE.

Notice that ELB at the moment only supports HTTP(S). Therefore, if access via SSH is required to the SPE then another load balancer such as HAProxy [19], or specific solutions for SSH load balancing such as Ballast [20] should be employed.

In fact Figure 3 depicts an scenario with a two-level load balancing scheme. The students connect to an instance of HAProxy (there could be several of them) which distributes the requests among different ASG in different regions. As such, this provides an scalable approach to perform access to a SPE for multiple students.

Notice that horizontal elasticity automatically manages the number of SPE instances to accommodate an increased or decreased number of students accessing to perform the practice lessons.

2) Vertical Elasticity: In the right lower side of Figure 3, a vertical elasticity approach to scalability is shown. Vertical elasticity is the ability to modify the performance features of a Virtual Machine in order to accommodate an increased (scale up) or reduced (scale down) workload.

Many hypervisors support the ability of dynamically increasing the memory of a running VM without downtime (see for example [21] for a case study with the KVM hypervisor). However, in the case of Amazon EC2, the performance features of an instance cannot be modified without downtime.

Amazon EC2 offers different instance types that range from *m1.small* (1.7 GB of RAM, 160 GB of disk, 32-bit or 64-bit CPU architecture) to *cr1.8xlarge* (244 GB of RAM, 32 virtual CPUs, 240 GB of SSD disk).

AMIs in Amazon EC2 can be of two types: (i) instance-store, where changes in the filesystem are lost when the instance is terminated and (ii) EBS-backed, where an EBS volume (block-based storage) is attached to the instance to store the filesystem changes. An EBS-backed instance can be started (where a per-hour cost for the running instance and a per GB-month for the allocated EBS volume is charged). These instances can be stopped and thus, only the per GB-month cost applies (which is in the order of $0.10 per GB-month in the region on Virginia as of June 2013).

Therefore, vertical elasticity can be achieved by stopping the instance, modifying the instance type for an increased or reduced performance and start the instance again, to be able to accommodate a larger workload (a larger number of users). However, the resumed instance changes its IP, a problem that can be circumvented by using Amazon's Elastic IP, an IP

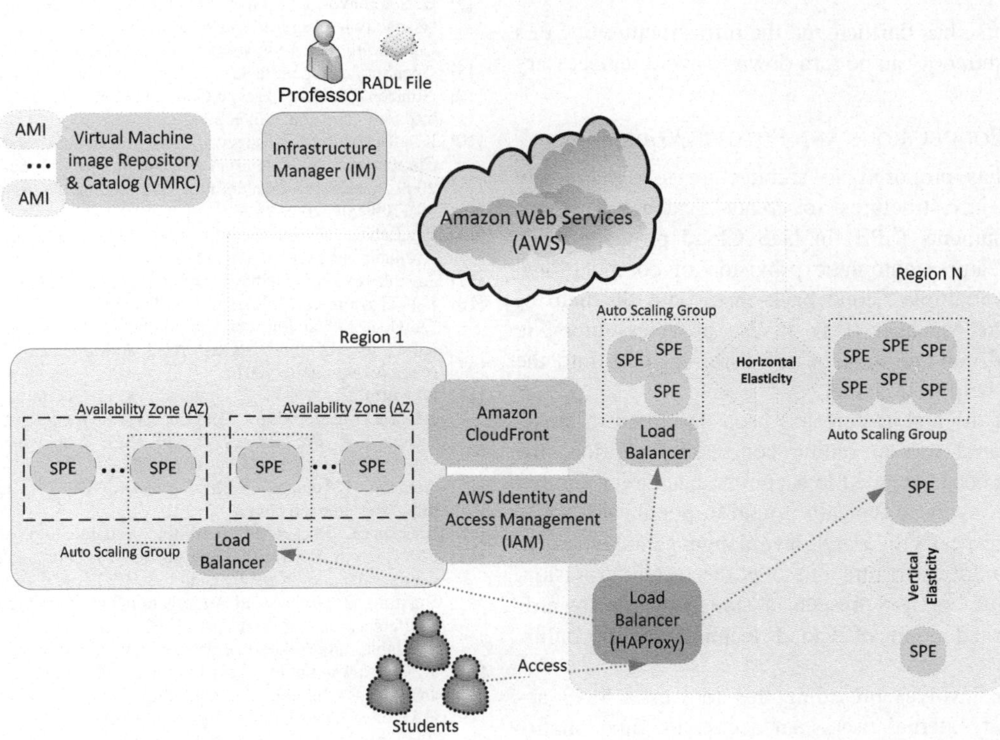

Fig. 3. An architecture to provide scalable Software Practice Environments for MOOCs in Amazon Web Services.

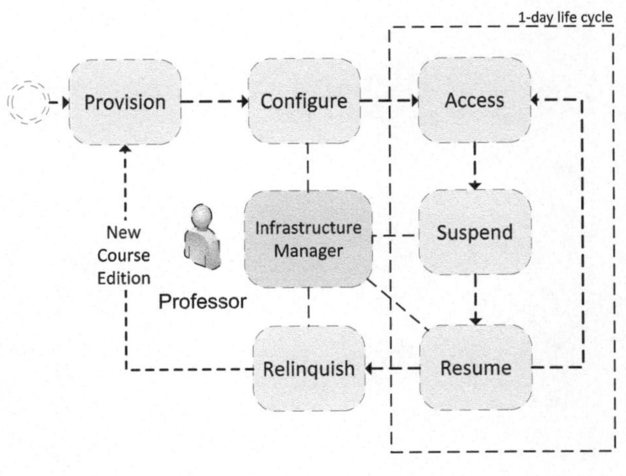

Fig. 4. Flow diagram with the life cycle of a virtual infrastructure.

address that can be dynamically allocated to different instances (by making the resumed instance to attach itself to the Elastic IP).

B. Virtual Infrastructure Life Cycle

Depending on each course, the SPE might be available 24x7 for students to perform the practice lessons at anytime (probably because there are students from different time zones, as in the case of MOOCs). However, consider an scenario in which practice lessons are performed at scheduled intervals (or only during the day). Then it is possible to suspend the virtual infrastructure so that only storage costs (of the EBS volume) are charged. This assumes a suspend-resume approach of the virtual infrastructure, like the one depicted in Figure 4.

When an edition of the course starts, the professor automatically provisions and configures the virtual infrastructure (composed by the SPEs) so that they are ready for users to access them via SSH.

To have an idea of the costs, consider the following scenario of a 3-week course with 400 enrolled students and 10 SPEs to accommodate 40 students per SPE (a GNU/Linux box to which students connect via SSH to use some online services). Deploying a virtual infrastructure 24x7 with 10 *m1.medium* instances on the Virginia region, and 10 EBS volumes with 80 GB each, costs $955 per month. If you implement a suspend-and-resume approach to maintain the SPEs only accessible for 8-hours a day the cost can be cut down to $369.80, thus achieving a reduction of 61%.

Having the infrastructure suspended enables to have the virtual infrastructure ready for service much faster (in the order of a minute) than dynamically deploying and configuring the virtual infrastructure from scratch (which can be performed in the order of 7-10 minutes depending on the complexity of the recipe).

Once the course has finished and the infrastructure of SPEs is no longer required it can be torn down to avoid unnecessary costs.

VI. Conclusions and Future Work

This paper has proposed an architecture to dynamically deploy virtual infrastructures to create Scalable Software Practice Environments (SPE) in IaaS Cloud providers. The infrastructure features automatic provision of computational resources from multiple Cloud back-ends, with the help of the Infrastructure Manager (IM). It also provides automatic deployment and configuration of software and data into the SPEs, with the help of Ansible.

The usage of the architecture has been described to create the SPEs required for an online course. In addition, the architecture has been extended to accommodate larger number of students such as those typically found in popular MOOCs.

The ability to specify in a high level language a declarative description of an infrastructure and to let the system provision, deploy and configure it represents a step forwards towards the widespread adoption of Cloud technologies in online education.

Future works involves providing this tool as a SaaS application so that external users can access its functionality to deploy on other Clouds on behalf of the user. We also plan to extend the tool in order to coordinate the deployment of complex virtual infrastructures (hybrid clusters, Grids, etc.) on the computational resources of an education center. These technologies can greatly simplify the administration of computing resources in an educational center, dealing with the multiple configurations required by the different subjects or courses.

Acknowledgements

The authors would like to thank the financial support received from the Generalitat Valenciana for the project GV/2012/076 and to the Ministerio de Economía y Competitividad for the project CodeCloud (TIN2010-17804)

References

[1] P. Mell and T. Grance, "The NIST Definition of Cloud Computing. NIST Special Publication 800-145 (Final)," Tech. Rep., 2011. [Online]. Available: http://csrc.nist.gov/publications/nistpubs/800-145/SP800-145.pdf

[2] M. R. Rafael Ballagas, "BYOD: Bring Your Own Device," in *Proceedings of the Workshop on Ubiquitous Display Environments, Ubicomp*, 2004. [Online]. Available: http://citeseerx.ist.psu.edu/viewdoc/summary?doi=10.1.1.58.9939

[3] K. Keahey and T. Freeman, "Contextualization: Providing One-Click Virtual Clusters," in *Fourth IEEE International Conference on eScience*, 2008, pp. 301–308.

[4] MIT, "StarCluster." [Online]. Available: http://web.mit.edu/stardev/cluster/

[5] F. Doelitzscher, M. Held, A. Sulistio, and C. Reich, "ViteraaS: Virtual Cluster as a Service," *wolke.hs-furtwangen.de*. [Online]. Available: http://www.wolke.hs-furtwangen.de/assets/downloads/CRL-2010-03.pdf

[6] C. de Alfonso, M. Caballer, F. Alvarruiz, G. Molto, and V. Hernández, "Infrastructure Deployment Over the Cloud," in *2011 IEEE Third International Conference on Cloud Computing Technology and Science*. IEEE, Nov. 2011, pp. 517–521. [Online]. Available: http://ieeexplore.ieee.org/lpdocs/epic03/wrapper.htm?arnumber=6133186

[7] B. Sotomayor, R. Montero, I. Llorente, I. Foster, and F. de Informatica, "Capacity leasing in cloud systems using the opennebula engine," *Cloud Computing and Applications*, vol. 2008, pp. 1–5, 2008.

[8] OpenStack, "OpenStack." [Online]. Available: http://openstack.org

[9] Amazon, "Amazon Elastic Compute Cloud (EC2)." [Online]. Available: http://aws.amazon.com/ec2

[10] K. Keahey, M. Tsugawa, A. Matsunaga, and J. Fortes, "Sky Computing," *IEEE Internet Computing*, vol. 13, no. 5, pp. 43–51, Sep. 2009. [Online]. Available: http://www.computer.org/portal/web/csdl/doi/10.1109/MIC.2009.94

[11] P. Labs, "Puppet," http://www.puppetlabs.com, 2010. [Online]. Available: http://www.puppetlabs.com

[12] AnsibleWorks, "Ansible." [Online]. Available: http://ansible.cc

[13] J. V. Carrión, G. Moltó, C. De Alfonso, M. Caballer, and V. Hernández, "A Generic Catalog and Repository Service for Virtual Machine Images," in *2nd International ICST Conference on Cloud Computing (CloudComp 2010)*, 2010.

[14] D. Nurmi, R. Wolski, C. Grzegorczyk, G. Obertelli, S. Soman, L. Youseff, and D. Zagorodnov, "The Eucalyptus Open-source Cloud-computing System," in *Proceedings of 9th IEEE International Symposium on Cluster Computing and the Grid*, 2009.

[15] Amazon, "Amazon Web Services (AWS)." [Online]. Available: http://aws.amazon.com

[16] Rackspace, "Rackspace." [Online]. Available: http://www.rackspace.com

[17] S. K. Nair, S. Porwal, T. Dimitrakos, A. J. Ferrer, J. Tordsson, T. Sharif, C. Sheridan, M. Rajarajan, and A. U. Khan, "Towards Secure Cloud Bursting, Brokerage and Aggregation," in *2010 Eighth IEEE European Conference on Web Services*. IEEE, Dec. 2010, pp. 189–196. [Online]. Available: http://dl.acm.org/citation.cfm?id=1932685.1932867

[18] T. Kay, "aws-simple access to Amazon EC2 and S3 and SQS and SDB and ELB." [Online]. Available: http://timkay.com/aws/

[19] HAProxy, "The Reliable, High Performance TCP/HTTP Load Balancer." [Online]. Available: http://haproxy.1wt.eu

[20] NASA, "Ballast." [Online]. Available: http://ti.arc.nasa.gov/opensource/ballast/

[21] G. Moltó, M. Caballer, E. Romero, and C. de Alfonso, "Elastic Memory Management of Virtualized Infrastructures for Applications with Dynamic Memory Requirements," in *International Conference on Computational Science (ICCS 2013)*, 2013.

PARTIAL RECONFIGURATION OF A LINEAR RECURSIVE PROCESS AND APPLICATION ON [Q,R]-DECOMPOSITION

Etienne Aubin Mbe Mbock
Mathematics and Computer Science
University of Heidelberg
Applied University of Furtwangen
Robert Gerwig Platz 1, 78120
Furtwangen, Schwarzwald, Germany
email:mbe@hs-furtwangen.de

ABSTRACT

This research article provides a new approach to the standard [Q, R]-decomposition algorithm. The decomposition demonstrations has now been deduced using the concept of partial reconfiguration. The analysis of reconfiguration will develop a method to solve linear systems using the hardware partial reconfiguration concept. With this research article, we present a new matrix decomposition methodology that will be of great importance in matrix related problems. We develop and efficiently apply the algorithm to classical problems. In addition to this analysis, we propose an implementation of the algorithm in pseudo codes and its FPGA implementation.

KEY WORDS

Partial, Reconfiguration, Linear, Process, Recursion, [Q,R]-Decomposition.

1 Introduction

Dynamic reconfigurability is essential when it comes to modifying a system during runtime. For an FPGA device, partial reconfiguration means modifying a subset of logic in an operating FPGA design by downloading a partial configuration file [1–5]. In general, a system that is change sensitive will be reconfigurable. In addition, the following conditions are valid for FPGA dynamic reconfigurability: the resources of the FPGA are must be time-multiplexed, the FPGA must be able to switch tasks, the FPGA must have the capacity to be reused, and the FPGA must have a reconfiguration portion optimization ability [6–8]. For this research article we suppose that these premises are valid when it comes to reconfiguration of algorithms. The experiment that we conduct in this research article supposes that, given a general recursive linear process, this process is specified by a starting state q_1 and the states q_j, $j \in \{2, 3 \cdots, N\}$ related to each other. This state dynamic is a linear recursive process given by the following equation:

$$q_j = \sum_{i=1}^{j-1} \alpha_{ji}\, q_i.$$

This will be denoted by:

$$\left\{q_1, \quad q_j = \textstyle\sum_{i=1}^{j-1} \alpha_{ji} q_i, \quad j \in \{2, 3, \cdots, N\}\right\}.$$

This research article will focus on the presentation of the dynamic and deduce the [Q, R]-decomposition from the dynamic. A descriptive comparison of the results will be provided. In addition to this description, we propose an algorithm that can solve the [Q,R]-decomposition problem with the partial reconfiguration based analysis. Although this research article is concerned with the recursive dynamic process, it assumes some matrix analysis and computation basics [9–14]. We suppose that the dynamic of this research article takes place in a vector space denoted VectSpace of dimension N. Computations that are valid with this research article include scalar-vector multiplication and addition, matrix-vector multiplication and addition, matrix-matrix multiplication and addition and the inverse of a matrix M denoted M^{-1}. We suppose that any dynamic state is an element of VectSpace. A linear combination of N several states of the same size, is given by

$$\sum_{i=1}^{N} \alpha_i A_i,$$

where $\alpha_i \in \mathbb{R}$, $i \in \{1, 2, \cdots N\}$. A linear transformation that operates on the state vector space VectSpace is denoted by $\mathbb{L}$. To this experimentation we join the least square estimator that finds the norm minimality under [Q, R]-decompostion. That is,

$$\text{optimize Norm}^2 = \|Aq - Z\|^2 = Aqq^tA^t - 2AqZ^t + ZZ^t$$

set to $[Q, R]$-decomposition for finding the optimum $\hat{q} = q$,

where A and Z satisfy the normal equation $q^tA^tA = Z^tA$. We suppose further that the product qq^t is the square of the 2-norm of q and the sum of two states q1 and q2 is $\{q := q1 + q2\}$. The aim of this research article is to analyse the linear recursive process that leads to the [Q,R]-decomposition computational algorithm and the presentation of the PR-[Q,R] algorithm that implements its computations. In addition to the proposed algorithm, we construct the hardware for the recursive linear scheme using references [16–18].

2 Method: Recursive Linear Process

2.1 Principles and Theorems

The development and construction of the [Q,R]-decomposition based on any recursive linear process assumes some principles and theorems for a better understanding of this dynamic. We postulate the following three principles. The first principle states that the recursive dynamic process is stable by adding. The second principle states that, given a linear transformation $\mathbb{L}$, there exists a [Q,R]-decomposition that minimises the square of the 2-Norm. The third is the mapping of a linear transformation $\mathbb{L}$ on a recursive linear process is still a recursive linear process.

The following equation describes the fact that addition of two linear processes results in a recursive linear process

$$\left\{s_1,\ s_j = \sum_{i=1}^{j-1} \alpha_{ji} s_i,\ j \in \{2,3,\cdots,N\}\right\}.$$

Principle 2.1. Recursive Linear Process Stability

Optimize $A\mathbb{L}\{q\}\mathbb{L}\left\{q^t\right\}A^t - 2A\mathbb{L}\{q\}\mathbb{L}\left\{Z^t\right\} + \mathbb{L}\{Z\}\mathbb{L}\left\{Z^t\right\}$

and use [Q, R]-decomposition to find the optimum.

$$\mathbb{L}\{\hat{q}\} = \mathbb{L}\{q\}$$

Principle 2.2. [Q, R]-Decomposition under Linear Transformation $\mathbb{L}$

The mapping of a linear transformation $\mathbb{L}$ on a recursive linear process is given by

$$\left\{q_1,\ q_j = \sum_{i=1}^{j-1} \alpha_{ji} q_i,\ j \in \{2,3,\cdots,N\}\right\}.$$

Theorem 2.3. Linear Recursive Process Mapping Theorem

In theorem 2.3 we assume that $\mathbb{L}\{q_1\} = l_1$ and $\mathbb{L}\left\{q_j\right\} = l_j,\ j \in \{2,\cdots,N\}$. We suppose further that any state vector is q_j. The following four steps perform the proof.

Proof. Because $\mathbb{L}$ is a linear transformation,

1. $\mathbb{L}\left\{q_j\right\} = \mathbb{L}\left\{\sum_{i=2}^{j-1} \alpha_{ji} q_i\right\}$ per definition of $\mathbb{L}$
2. $\mathbb{L}\left\{q_j\right\} = \sum_{i=1}^{j-1} \alpha_{ji} \mathbb{L}\{q_i\}$ per linearity of $\mathbb{L}$
3. $\mathbb{L}\left\{q_j\right\} = \sum_{i=2}^{j-1} \alpha_{ji} l_i$
4. $\left\{l_1,\ l_j = \sum_{i=2}^{j-1} \alpha_{ji} l_i,\ j \in \{2,3,\cdots,N\}\right\}$ is the recursive linear process under the linear transformation $\mathbb{L}$.

□

2.2 The Dynamic Equations and Partial Reconfiguration Analysis

Let's consider the general recursive process

$$\left\{q_1,\ q_j = \sum_{i=1}^{j-1} \alpha_{ji} q_i,\ j \in \{2,3,\cdots,N\}\right\}.$$

A dynamic system is represented by the following state configurations:

$$\begin{pmatrix} q_2 \\ q_3 \\ \vdots \\ q_N \end{pmatrix} = q_1 \begin{pmatrix} \alpha_{21} \\ \alpha_{31} \\ \vdots \\ \alpha_{N1} \end{pmatrix} + q_2 \begin{pmatrix} 0 \\ \alpha_{32} \\ \vdots \\ \alpha_{N2} \end{pmatrix} + \cdots \quad (1)$$

We assume that 1 is satisfied for any recursive dynamic process. For the partial reconfiguration, we consider the following objects: the coefficients of the recursive dynamic system represented by the $m \times n$ matrix Alpha, the initial state matrix represented by Beta that contains all possible initial states of the recursive process. Beta will be of the same size as the matrix Alpha and Gama, which represents all state $q_j,\ j \in \{1,2,\cdots,N\}$. Further we assume that the following classes apply: operation, addition, multiplication, and transpose. The analysis of these operations gives the $\theta\left(N^2\right)$ for the addition class and $\theta\left(N^2\right)$ for the multiplication class. In oder to implement the recursive linear process we need the exact number of additions and multiplications and set the number of transpose operations to zero. If the state index j is set to 2, then the exact number of additions and multiplications is 1. If we iterate this process by setting j equals N, then the number of additions and multiplications is equal to N-1. This gives a total number of addition operations and multiplication operations by

$$\frac{N(N-1)}{2}.$$

3 Construction of the Algorithm

The analysis conducted in the previous section gives the following algorithm, which constructs the recursive linear dynamic process

$$\left\{q_1,\ q_j = \sum_{i=1}^{j-1} \alpha_{ji} q_i,\ j \in \{2,3,\cdots,N\}\right\}.$$

We assume, that the matrices Alpha, Beta, and Gama exist and satisfy the specifications given in the previous section

Algorithm 3.1.

```
function PROBLEM(Alpha, Beta)
    [m, n] ← size(Alpha)
    if size(Alpha) = size(Beta) then
        Gama[1] ← Beta[k],
        k ∈ {1, 2, ··· , m}
        for j = 2, 3, ··· , n do
            Gama[j] = 0
            for i = 1 : j − 1 do
                Rr(i, j) ← Alpha(i, j)
                Gama[j] ← Gama[j]+
                Rr(i, j) * Gama[i]
            end for
        end for
        Gama[j] = Gama[j]
    end if
end function
```

4 Partial Reconfiguration and Simulation of the Recursive Dynamic Process

In the recursive dynamic process in equation 1, parts of the process are reconfigurable. For these we partially transform the process in the following way:

1. The coefficient matrix Alpha will be set to any $m \times n$ matrix A.
2. The dynamic is reconfigured as

$$\left\{ \begin{array}{ll} p_1 - q_1 = 0, & p_j - q_j = \sum_{i=1}^{j-1} \alpha_{ji} q_i, \\ j \in \{2, 3, \cdots, N\} & \end{array} \right\}.$$

3. The coefficients of the matrix Alpha see (1) are reconfigured according to the following table.

q_1	q_2	q_3	$\cdots$	$\cdots$	q_{N-1}
$p_2 \cdot q_1$	0	0	0	$\vdots$	0
$p_3 \cdot q_1$	$p_3 \cdot q_2$	0	0	$\vdots$	$\vdots$
$p_4 \cdot q_1$	$p_4 \cdot q_2$	$p_4 \cdot q_3$	0	0	$\vdots$
$\vdots$	$\vdots$	$\vdots$	$\ddots$	0	0
$\vdots$	$\vdots$	$\vdots$		$\ddots$	0
$p_N \cdot q_1$	$p_N \cdot q_2$	$p_N \cdot q_3$	$\cdots$	$\cdots$	$p_N \cdot q_{N-1}$

The simulation shown in the following figures construct the recursive dynamic system by providing the matrix R_r and the recursive linear process states Gama considering a pascal matrix and the identity matrix of size 5. We consider a 5×5 dimensional positive integer matrix. A pascal matrix of order 5, represents the matrix Alpha, while the matrix Beta is the 5×5 dimensional identity matrix. All matrix entries in the simulation are positive integers, as algorithm 3.1 anticipated. The first column of the matrix R_r is reduced to zero; and cancelling that column results in an upper triangular matrix with positive matrix entries as expected in algorithm 3.1,(see figure 2). The state matrix Gama is made of column vectors that represent

$$q_j = \sum_{i=1}^{j-1} \alpha_{ji} q_i, \; j \in \{2, 3, \cdots, N\}.$$

See the construction in figure 2 right. For this simulation we suppose further, that the starting state q_1 is Beta (2)

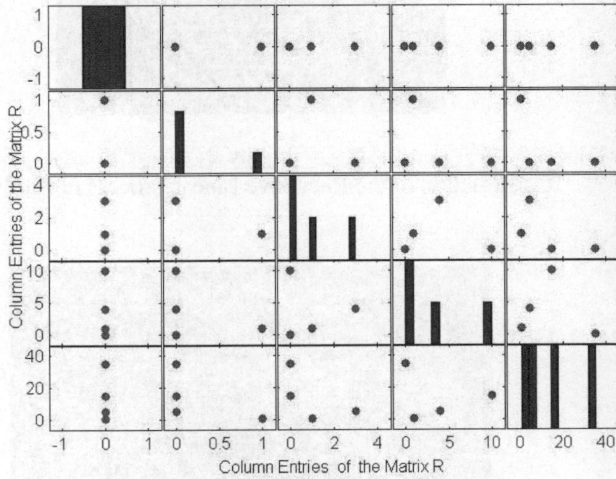

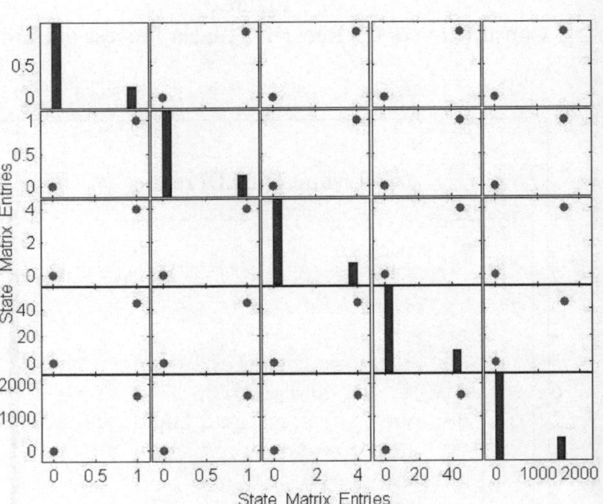

Figure 1
Construction of the Recursive Linear Process

The diagonals of the constructed recursive linear process, represent the columns of R_r and Gama respectively as a histogram. The first histogram represents the first column of R_r and a last histogram representing the last state q_5.

5 Results and FPGA Realization of the Dynamic Recursive Process

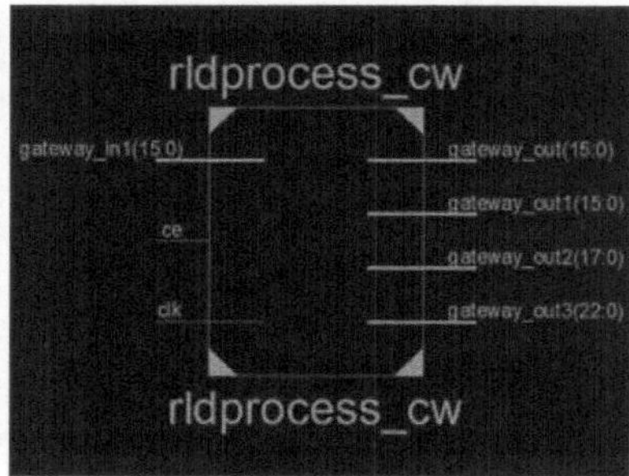

Figure 2
Construction of the Recursive Linear Process in Hardware

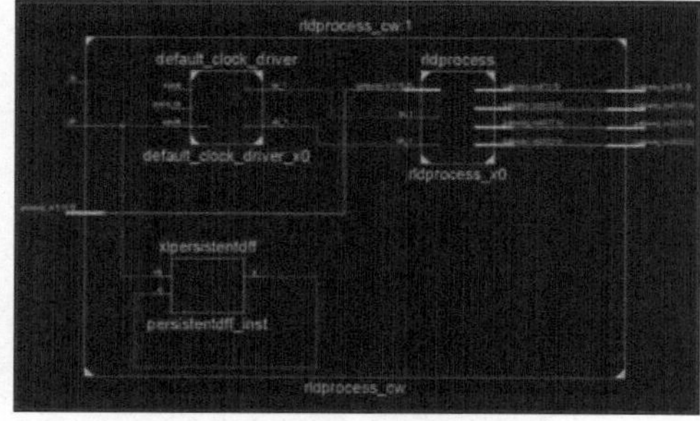

Figure 3
Construction of the Recursive Linear Process in Hardware

Listing 1: RLDProcess

```
Generated from Simulink block RLDProcess

entity rldprocess is
  port (
    ce_1: in std_logic;
    clk_1: in std_logic;
    gateway_in1: in std_logic_vector(15 downto 0);
    gateway_out: out std_logic_vector(15 downto 0);
    gateway_out1: out std_logic_vector(15 downto 0);
    gateway_out2: out std_logic_vector(17 downto 0);
    gateway_out3: out std_logic_vector(22 downto 0)
  );
end rldprocess;

architecture structural of rldprocess is
  attribute core_generation_info: string;
  attribute core_generation_info of structural : architecture is "RLDProcess,sysgen_core,{clock_period=10.00000000,clocking=Clock_Enables,compilation=HDL_Netlist,sample_periods=1.00000000000,testbench=0,total_blocks=51,xilinx_adder_subtracter_block=3,xilinx_gateway_in_block=1,xilinx_gateway_out_block=4,xilinx_input_scaler_block=7,xilinx_system_generator_block=1,}";

  signal ce_1_sg_x1: std_logic;
  signal clk_1_sg_x1: std_logic;
  signal gateway_in1_net: std_logic_vector(15 downto 0);
  signal gateway_out1_net: std_logic_vector(15 downto 0);
  signal gateway_out2_net: std_logic_vector(17 downto 0);
  signal gateway_out3_net: std_logic_vector(22 downto 0);
  signal gateway_out_net: std_logic_vector(15 downto 0);

begin
  ce_1_sg_x1 <= ce_1;
  clk_1_sg_x1 <= clk_1;
  gateway_in1_net <= gateway_in1;
  gateway_out <= gateway_out_net;
  gateway_out1 <= gateway_out1_net;
  gateway_out2 <= gateway_out2_net;
  gateway_out3 <= gateway_out3_net;

  rdpsg_4c3d9f806b: entity work.rdpsg_entity_4c3d9f806b
    port map (
      ce_1 => ce_1_sg_x1,
      clk_1 => clk_1_sg_x1,
      in1 => gateway_in1_net,
      addsub1_x0 => gateway_out2_net,
      addsub2_x0 => gateway_out3_net,
```

```
      scale1_x0 => gateway_out_net,
      scale2_x0 => gateway_out1_net
    );

end structural;
```

The constructed hardware is an instance of the linear recursive process. A 4×4 matrix is considered with pascal entries. The hardware will generate the four states that are predicted by the algorithm 3.1. The harware were created by the Ise Design Tools and System Generator [15–17]. In the figure that follows, the predicted input vector is a unit vector. This vector corresponds to Gama[1] in the 3.1 algorithm. The hardware in figure 2 shows the gateway input In[15:0]. Because the integer matrix is a pascal matrix of order 4, applying the algorithm 3.1 to this matrix generates four output states labeled gate outputs: Out[15:0], Out[15:0], Out[17:0], and Out[22:0], (see figure 2). Figure 3 constructs the extended hardware of the linear recursive process. This hardware will represent the register transfer level graphical representation of the linear recursive process, as described in [15, 18, 19]. Figure 4 gives a model of the constructed hardware. This model will

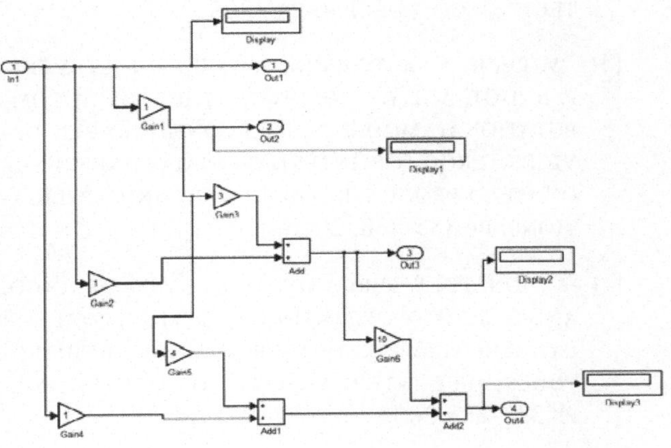

Figure 4
Model of the Recursive Linear Process Construction in Hardware

be viewed as an upper triangular matrix and the output will give the four states of the system. This is a reduced matrix that will not have zero entries in row 2. This is true provided that Beta (k) in algorithm 3.1 is set to Beta(2). This method allows us reduce all integer matrices of all size. In the special case of the pascal integer matrix, the model will be made of an upper triangular 3×3 matrix with the first row consisting of 1s, the second containing a 3 and a 4 and the third row containing 10. When the system is on, the display will show the sequence of integers $\begin{bmatrix} 1 & 1 & 4 & 45 \end{bmatrix}$ on Matlab and Simulink programming environments [20–25]

Listing 2: RLDProcess Architecture

```
architecture structural of rldprocess_cw is
  component xlpersistentdff
    port (
      clk: in std_logic;
      d: in std_logic;
      q: out std_logic
    );
  end component;
  attribute syn_black_box: boolean;
  attribute syn_black_box of xlpersistentdff: component is true;
  attribute box_type: string;
  attribute box_type of xlpersistentdff: component is "black_box";
  attribute syn_noprune: boolean;
  attribute optimize_primitives: boolean;
  attribute dont_touch: boolean;
  attribute syn_noprune of xlpersistentdff: component is true;
  attribute optimize_primitives of xlpersistentdff: component is false;
  attribute dont_touch of xlpersistentdff: component is true;

  signal ce_1_sg_x1: std_logic;
  attribute MAX_FANOUT: string;
  attribute MAX_FANOUT of ce_1_sg_x1 : signal is "REDUCE";
  signal clkNet: std_logic;
  signal clk_1_sg_x1: std_logic;
  signal gateway_in1_net: std_logic_vector(15 downto 0);
  signal gateway_out1_net: std_logic_vector(15 downto 0);
  signal gateway_out2_net: std_logic_vector(17 downto 0);
  signal gateway_out3_net: std_logic_vector(22 downto 0);
  signal gateway_out_net: std_logic_vector(15 downto 0);
  signal persistentdff_inst_q: std_logic;
  attribute syn_keep: boolean;
  attribute syn_keep of persistentdff_inst_q: signal is true;
  attribute keep: boolean;
  attribute keep of persistentdff_inst_q: signal is true;
  attribute preserve_signal: boolean
```

```
    ;
  attribute preserve_signal of
      persistentdff_inst_q: signal
      is true;

begin
  clkNet <= clk;
  gateway_in1_net <= gateway_in1;
  gateway_out <= gateway_out_net;
  gateway_out1 <= gateway_out1_net;
  gateway_out2 <= gateway_out2_net;
  gateway_out3 <= gateway_out3_net;

  default_clock_driver_x0: entity
      work.default_clock_driver
    port map (
      sysce => '1',
      sysce_clr => '0',
      sysclk => clkNet,
      ce_1 => ce_1_sg_x1,
      clk_1 => clk_1_sg_x1
    );

  persistentdff_inst:
      xlpersistentdff
    port map (
      clk => clkNet,
      d => persistentdff_inst_q,
      q => persistentdff_inst_q
    );

  rldprocess_x0: entity work.
      rldprocess
    port map (
      ce_1 => ce_1_sg_x1,
      clk_1 => clk_1_sg_x1,
      gateway_in1 => gateway_in1_net
      ,
      gateway_out => gateway_out_net
      ,
      gateway_out1 =>
          gateway_out1_net,
      gateway_out2 =>
          gateway_out2_net,
      gateway_out3 =>
          gateway_out3_net
    );

end structural;
```

6 Conclusion

This research article focuses on the partial reconfiguration of the linear recursive process. The analysis in this paper prepares the linear recursive to be implemented within hardware. This method allows us to program the linear recursive process on an FPGA. The approach in this paper is new, from the invention of the linear recursive process to its construction in hardware using the "Xilinx and System Generator". The use of partial reconfiguration will have the following consequences: It will modify the [Q,R]-decomposition, it will create novel matrix inverse computation method, it will solve of linear systems of equations. The hardware will construct two matrices that are inverse to each other, from any given integer matrix. The approach of reconfiguration in this article is new. The linear recursive process is analysed as a new mathematical concept. The resulting research, algorithms, and the hardware constructions will serve computer scientists, computer engineers, and mathematicians.

References

[1] OSTERLOH, MICHALIK, HABINC, AND FIETHE, DYNAMIC PARTIAL RECONFIGURATION IN SPACE APPLICATIONS, CONFERENCE PUBLICATION, PP336-343, 2009.

[2] E. CHEN, D. SABAZ, W. A. GRUVER, AND L. SHANNON, REPLACEMENT OF THE FIXED MULTI-PR REGION MODEL WITH A FLEXIBLE, DYNAMIC PR DOMAIN FOR DPR SYSTEMS, PROC OF INTERNATIONAL CONFERENCE ON FIELD PROGRAMMABLE TECHNOLOGY, DECEMBER 2008.

[3] W. PECK, E. ANDERSON, J. AGRON, J. STEVENS, F. BAIJOT, AND D. ANDREWS, HTHREADS: A COMPUTATIONAL MODEL FOR RECONFIGURABLE DEVICES, PROC. OF INTERNATIONAL CONFERENCE ON FIELD PROGRAMMABLE LOGIC AND APPLICATIONS, PP 885-888, 2006.

[4] A. DONATO, F. FERRANDI, M. D. SANTAMBROGIO, AND D. SCIUTO, OPERATING SYSTEM SUPPORT FOR DYNAMICALLY RECONFIGURABLE SOC ARCHITECTURES, IEEE INTERNATIONAL SOC CONFERENCE, PP 233-238,2005.

[5] E. LBBERS AND M. PLATZNER, RECONOS: MULTITHREADED PROGRAMMING FOR RECONFIGURABLE COMPUTERS, ACM TRANSACTIONS ON EMBEDDED COMPUTING SYSTEMS, PP 1-33, 2009.

[6] J. WILLIAMS AND N. BERGMANN, EMBEDDED LINUX AS A PLATFORM FOR DYNAMICALLY SELF-RECONFIGURING SYSTEMS-ON-CHIP,PROC. OF INTERNATIONAL CONFERENCE ON ENGINEERING OF RECONFIGURABLE SYSTEMS AND ALGORITHMS, PP 163-169, 2004.

[7] C. KAO, BENEFITS OF PARTIAL RECONFIGURATION XCELL JOURNAL, FOURTH QUARTER, PP 65-68, 2005.

[8] R. KSHIRSAGAR AND R. PATRIKAR, DESIGN OF A RECONFIGURABLE MULTIPROCESSOR CORE FOR

HIGHER PERFORMANCE AND RELIABILITY OF EMBEDDED SYSTEMS, IFIP INTERNATIONAL CONFERENCE ON VLSI, PP 251- 254, 2006.

[9] B.N. DATTA, NUMERICAL LINEAR ALGEBRA AND APPLICATIONS, BROOKS/COLE PUBLISHING COMPANY, PACIFIC GROVE, CA, 1995.

[10] J.W. DEMMEL, APPLIED NUMERICAL LINEAR ALGEBRA, SIAM, PHILADELPHIA, PA, 1997.

[11] G.H. GOLUB AND C.F. VAN LOAN, MATRIX COMPUTATIONS, SECOND EDITION, JOHNS HOPKINS UNIVERSITY PRESS, BALTIMORE, MD, 1989.

[12] M.T. HEATH, SCIENTIFIC COMPUTING: AN INTRODUCTORY SURVEY, MCGRAW-HILL, BOSTON, MA, 1997.

[13] N.J. HIGHAM, ACCURACY AND STABILITY OF NUMERICAL ALGORITHMS, SIAM, PHILADELPHIA, PA, 1996.

[14] R.D. SKEEL AND J.B. KEIPER, ELEMENTARY NUMERICAL COMPUTING WITH MATHEMATICA, MCGRAW-HILL, NEW YORK, NY, 1993.

[15] XILINX EARLY ACCESS PARTIAL RECONFIGURATION WITH PLANAHEAD 9.2 USERS GUIDE, XILINX INC., 2008.

[16] UPEGUI, HTTP://LSLWWW.EPFL.CH/ UPEGUI/DOCS/DPR.PDF .

[17] XILINX, INC, HTTP://WWW.XILINX.COM/SUPPORT/DOCUMENTATION/ WHITE-PAPERS/374-PARTIAL-RECONFIG-XILINX-FPGAS.PDF,2012.

[18] J.OU, AND PRASANNA, A MATLAB=SIMULINK BASED TOOL FOR SYNTHESIZING PARAMETERIZED AND ENERGY EFFICIENT DESIGNS USING FPGAS, PROC. INT. SYMP. ON FIELD-PROGRAMMABLE CUSTOM COMPUTING, 2005.

[19] XILINX, INC, TWO FLOW OF PARTIAL RECONFIGURATION: MODULE-BASED AND DIFFERENCE-BASED TECHNICAL REPORT XAPP290, XILINX INC.,2003.

[20] B.D. HAHN, ESSENTIAL MATLAB FOR SCIENTISTS AND ENGINEERS, JOHN WILEY SONS, NEW YORK, NY, 1997.

[21] D.R. HILL AND D.E. ZITARELLI, LINEAR ALGEBRA LABS WITH MATLAB, SECOND EDITION, PRENTICE HALL, UPPER SADDLE RIVER, NJ, 1996.

[22] B. KOLMAN, INTRODUCTORY LINEAR ALGEBRA WITH APPLICATIONS, SIXTH EDITION, PRENTICE HALL, UPPER SADDLE RIVER, NJ, 1997.

[23] R.E. LARSON AND B.H. EDWARDS, ELEMENTARY LINEAR ALGEBRA, THIRD EDITION, D.C. HEATH AND COMPANY, LEXINGTON, MA, 1996.

[24] S.J. LEON, LINEAR ALGEBRA WITH APPLICATIONS, FIFTH EDITION, PRENTICE HALL, UPPER SADDLE RIVER, NJ, 1998.

[25] G. STRANG, LINEAR ALGEBRA AND ITS APPLICATIONS, SECOND EDITION, ACADEMIC PRESS, ORLANDO, FL, 1980.

A Graphical Language for Development of Parallel Applications

J. L. Quiroz-Fabián[1], G. Román-Alonso[1], M. A. Castro-García[1], M. Aguilar-Cornejo[1] and J. Buenabad-Chávez[2]
[1]Departamento de Ing. Eléctrica, UAM-I, México City, D.F, 09340 México
Emails: {jlqf, grac, mcas, mac}@xanum.uam.mx
[2]Departamento de Computación, CINVESTAV-IPN, México City, D.F, 07360 México
Email: jbuenabad@cs.cinvestav.mx

Abstract—*The complexity of parallel programming for hybrid architectures composed of multicores, GPUs and clusters of these, either private or in the cloud, calls for flexible programming environments wherein users can better concentrate at the programming task at hand. We are developing GDEC, a* Graphical Development Environment of parallel applications in the Cloud. *GDEC will provide a GUI for program development, and allow users to develop applications from any computer with a web browser and to run their applications on private or cloud-based platforms.*

The focus of this paper is the GDEC graphical language and its grammar based on hyperedge replacement grammars. *Programmers must select adequate GDEC icons to compose their application and configure them to specify particular input/output data and* sequential code *for processing. However, users do not need to specify low-level communication based on shared variables or message passing. GDEC may run sequential code in parallel if specified for an icon representing a parallel computing model such as SPMD. A comparison of GDEC to other graphical platforms for developing parallel applications is also presented.*

Keywords: Parallel Computing, Graphical Language, Graph Grammars

1. Introduction

The use of parallel computing for the solution of demanding applications in science and business intelligence is widening thanks to the increasing availability of parallel architectures. Multicores, Graphics Processing Units (GPUs) and clusters of these are now readily available at institutions and in the cloud, offering unprecedented processing capacity at a very reasonable price. However, the development of *efficient* parallel applications for these architectures is a real challenge, despite the many software tools available [survey], if made using basic communication primitives, such as shared variables (e.g., locks and barriers) for multicores and GPUs and message passing for clusters of these. The challenge lies not only on specifying communication for processing elements to share data and code and to synchronise their tasks; a load balancing mechanism must also be developed in order to ensure good performance since the response time of a parallel application corresponds to the response time of the slowest processing element.

To hide the complexity of parallel programming, various middlewares for parallel computing have been developed that provide programmers with a simpler interface than that provided by the Message Passing Interface (MPI) [1] [2], Pthreads [3] and OpenMP [4] [5]. Examples of these middlewares included Skeletons [6], the Data List Management Library (DLML) [7] and Mapreduce [8]. Mapreduce, for example, is a programming model and environment developed by Google that requires from programmers only sequential functions. The Mapreduce environment runs multiple instances of these sequential functions in parallel, taking care both of synchronising them and of load balancing and fault tolerance throughout the computation.

Graphical user interface (GUI) platforms have also been developed for the purpose of hiding the complexity of parallel and distributed programming. They support graphical design of workflows through interconnecting icons (graphical elements) that represent web/grid services [9], [10]. Users basically need to drag, drop and interconnect relevant icons, and thus can concentrate better on the conceptual solution of their problems. Kepler [11], Taverna [12] and Triana [13] are open free software examples of these GUI platforms. They all were initially targeted to assist a particular area of science (biology, biology and astronomy, respectively). But being organised around web/grid services, they can be used in other areas simply by developing the relevant web/grid services framework.

We are designing GDEC, a *Graphical Development Environment of parallel applications in the Cloud*. Like other GUI platforms, GDEC offers a GUI for program development through interconnecting icons that represent data or some form of processing. Being based on the cloud, GDEC will allow users to access their applications and resources from any computer with a web browser. In contrast, the GUI platforms mentioned above require the GUI module to be installed in a client computer. GDEC will also allow users to choose different computing platforms to run their applications, through configuring their account with the specification of available computing platforms which may be private or cloud-based.

The focus of this paper is the design of GDEC graphical language. The GDEC language offers programmers various different icons that represent input data, various forms of processing (e.g., SPMD, MPMD, etc.) and output data. Programmers must select adequate icons for their application and configure them to specify particular input/output data or files and sequential code for processing but, as in Mapreduce, do not need to specify low-level communication based on shared variables or message passing. GDEC icons represent software modules that include such communication and thus only need to be configured as just described. The grammar of the GDEC language is based on *hyperedge replacement grammars*, a formalism that facilitates the visualisation of graphical representations and their functioning. For GDEC, it will facilitate the implementation of debugging and monitoring functions.

The paper continues as follows. In Section 2 we present the main icons of the GDEC language. In Section 3 we describe the grammar of the GDEC language. A comparison of GDEC and other graphical languages is presented in Section 4. We conclude and present future work in Section 5.

2. GDEC Model

The GDEC language supports an icon-based composition model for the development of parallel applications. The programmer selects GDEC icons that represent the data and the processing of an application. GDEC icons are classified into three main types:

- Input Data
- Processing / Computation
- Output Data / Results

Each icon, when selected by the programmer, requires information from the programmer in order for the icon to be configured for a particular way of functioning or accessing particular resources.

2.1 Data Icons

2.1.1 Input Data Icons

Input data icons refer to data to be processed. When the icon shown in Figure 1.(a) is used, the programmer must type in the data to be processed. When the icon shown in Figure 1.(b) is used, the programmer must type the name of the file that contains the data to be processed.

Fig. 1: Input Data Icons

2.1.2 Output Data Icons

Output data icons are used to specify how the final results of a GDEC application should be managed. When the icon shown in Figure 2.*(a)* is used, results are displayed on the screen. When the icon shown in Figure 2.*(b)* is used, results are written to a file whose name must be specified. The results of a computation icon can both be displayed on the screen and written to a file.

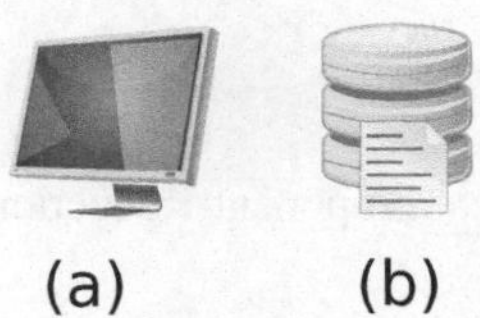

Fig. 2: Output Icons

2.2 Processing/Computation Icons

Processing (computation) icons correspond to parallel computation patterns commonly used [14] [15] [16]. The most representative patterns include:

- Reduction
- Sequential Processing
- Grid (Embarrassingly Parallel)
- Master / Slave
- Work Pool (or Independent Data)
- Pipeline

The behaviour of these patterns is considered by the proposed graphical processing icons, which can be interconnected following the GDEC language grammar. Below we briefly describe each processing icon.

2.2.1 Reduction

Reduction refers to combining multiple results produced by multiple tasks into a single result. GDEC supports two types of reduction icons. The first icon, called *Task-Reduction* (Figure 3), allows the parallel execution of N tasks, where N is a default value that can be modified by the programmer. Each receives an input data set. The programmer must specify the sequential code for each task, which can be the same for all tasks (SPMD model), or different (MPMD model). The reduction operator combines (reduces) the partial results generated by all tasks into a single global result.

Fig. 3: Task-Reduction Icon

The second reduction icon of GDEC is called *Component-Reduction* (Figure 4). This icon receives a set of partial results coming from other distinct processing icons (not necessarily parallel processing icons), and combines all the partial into a single global result.

Fig. 4: Component-Reduction Icon

2.2.2 Sequential Processing

The Sequential-Processing icon, shown in Figure 5, is a particular Task-Reduction icon where N=1. This icon receives a data set as input and generates a data set as output.

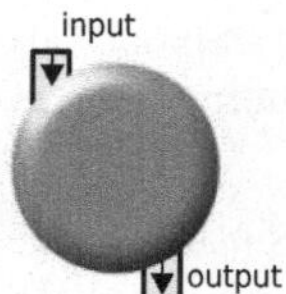

Fig. 5: Sequential Processing Icon

2.2.3 Grid

The Grid icon, shown in Figure 6, performs the processing of a data set using *NxN* tasks, where N has a default value that can be modified by the programmer. The tasks generate *NxN* results, one from each task.

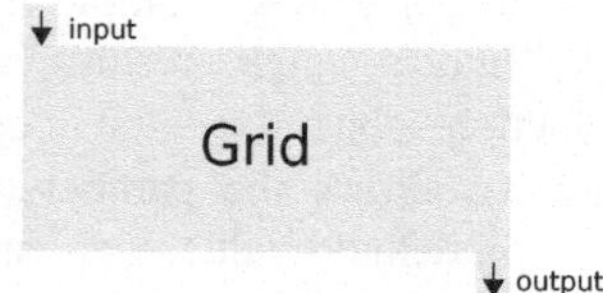

Fig. 6: Grid Icon

2.2.4 Master/Slave

This icon represents a Master/*N*-Slave processing, where *N* establishes the total number of slave tasks; *N* has a default value that can modified by the programmer. The master task receives an input data set to be processed by the slaves as assigned by the master. The code of the slave tasks may be the same or different. The processing ends when the whole data collection has been processed and each slave has transferred its results to the master task.

Fig. 7: Master-Slave Icon

2.2.5 Work Pools

The Work Pool icon, shown in Figure 8, processes a non-determined number of data items with no dependency between them for processing. A data container is linked to this icon, representing the data (work pool) to be processed. Initially, this icon requires at least one data item in the container; more new data items can be generated dynamically and placed in the container. The sequential code specified by the programmer to process each data item may run in parallel. The processing finishes when the container becomes empty. The container may actually be distributed among the multiple instances running the sequential code. In this case, the Work Pool icon underlying structure (not the sequential code specified by the programmer) will implement work stealing of data items between the various containers, thus balancing the workload. Work Pools can be used to implement Peer-to-Peer computations.

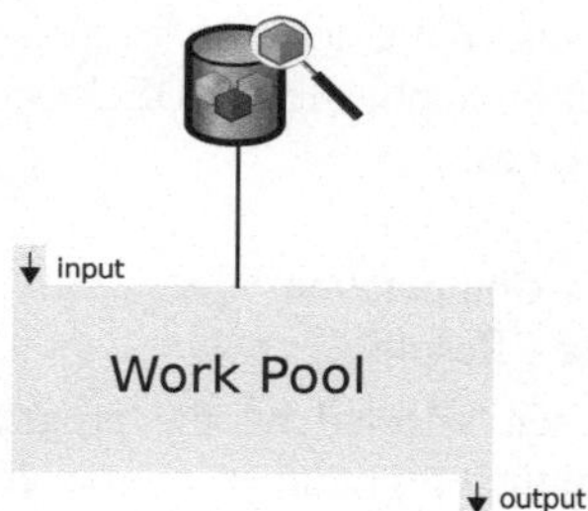

Fig. 8: Work Pool Icon

2.2.6 Pipeline

This icon is shown in Figure 9. It represents an *N*-tasks pipeline, where *N* has a default value that can modified by the programmer. The programmer must specify the sequential code of all the *N* tasks. The initial task receives an input data set, and the final tasks produces the results data set. Another property of this icon is the *repetition* behaviour, shown in Figure 10, wherein the data from the last task is fed to first task of the pipeline. The stop condition of the repetition must be entered by the programmer when applying this property.

3. GDEC Language

The set of programs that can be composed with the GDEC language are specified by the formalism of *Hyperedge Re-*

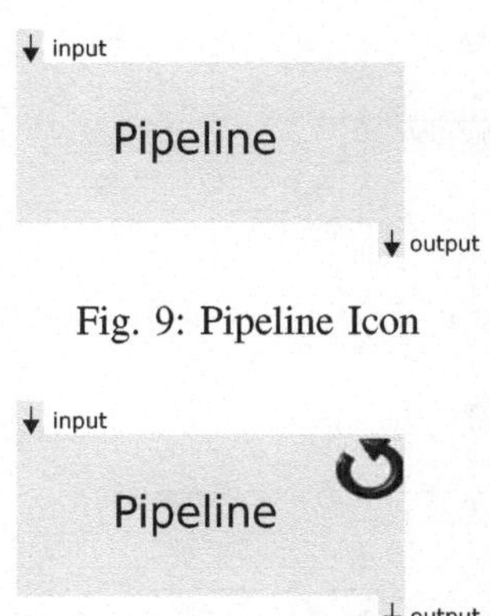

Fig. 9: Pipeline Icon

Fig. 10: Pipeline Icon using Repetition

placement Grammars. A brief introduction to this theory is presented in Section 3.1. Section 3.2 then describes our proposed GDEC grammar.

3.1 Hyperedge Replacement Grammars

In computer science it is often easier and more natural to represent things as graphs as opposed to strings. This was the main reason for the development of graph grammars, which started in the late 1960's, as an extension to the concept of formal grammars on strings. Hyperedge replacement grammars were introduced early in the 1970s, to simplify the visualisation of graphical components and their functions. They have found useful applications in pattern recognition, database systems, semantics of programming languages, etc. [17] [18]. This section presents the main concepts of Hyperedge replacement grammars, which are the basis for our GDEC language definition.

Definition (Hyperedge) The hyperedge is an atomic item that has an ordered set of tentacles. A hyperedge *e* has a type, denoted *type(e)*, which is the same as the number of tentacles of *e*. Figure 11 shows a hyperedge with *k* tentacles.

Fig. 11: Hyperedge with k tentacles; type(e)=k.

A collection of hyperedges and set of nodes form a *hypergraph* if each tentacle is attached to a node. A hypergraph is equipped with a set of especial nodes called *external nodes*, which are used to perform the replacement of hyperedges by hypergraphs.

Definition (Hypergraph) Let C be an arbitrary but fixed set of labels. A hypergraph H over C is a tuple *(V, E, lab, att, ext)*, where:

- V and E are disjoint finite sets of nodes and hyperedges, respectively.
- $lab : E \rightarrow C$ is a mapping that labels each hyperedge such that $type(lab(e)) = |att(e)|$.
- $att : E \rightarrow V^*$ is a mapping assigning a set of pairwise distinct *attachment nodes* $att(e)$ to each $e \in E$.
- $ext \in V^*$ is a set of pairwise distinct external nodes.

If H is a hypergraph, its components can be denoted by V_H , E_H , att_H , lab_H and ext_H respectively. We use the expression $type_H(e)$ to mean $e \in E_H$. The type of a hypergraph H is $|ext_H|$, and is denoted *type(H)*.

Figure 12 shows an example of a hypergraph. In order to emphasise the external node in that hypergraph, its background color is black; and is identified with number 1.

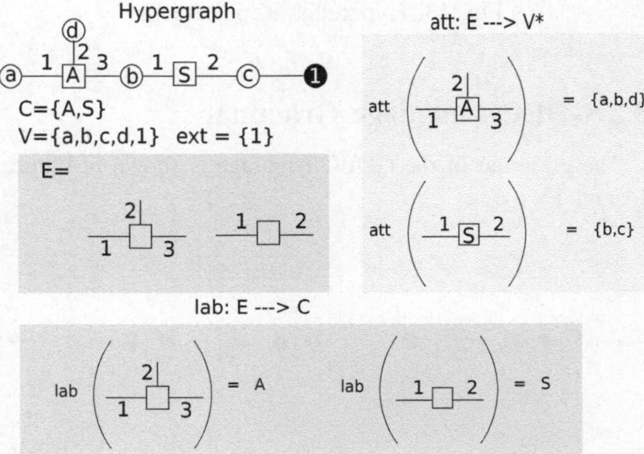

Fig. 12: Hypergraph

Definition (Hyperedge replacement) Let H and H' be two hypergraphs, so that $e \in E_H$ with $type_H(e) = type(H')$. Then the replacement of *e* by H' in H is obtained as follows:

- Build H - e by removing e from H.
- Take the disjoint union of H - e and H'.
- For all i $\in$ $\{1, ..., type_H(e)\}$, identify and replace the i-th attached node of e with the i-th external node of H'.

Figure 13 shows an example of hyperedge replacement, where the *S* hyperedge is replaced by the hypergraph *B*. Note that this replacement is possible because *type(Hypergraph B)* = *2* = *type(S)*.

Definition (Hyperedge replacement grammar) A hyperedge replacement grammar is a tuple $G = (N, \Sigma, R, S)$, where

- $N, \Sigma \subseteq C$ are finite and disjoint sets of nonterminal and terminal labels, respectively.
- R is a set of rules of the form $A \rightarrow H$ with $A \subseteq N$ and H is a hypergraph such that $type(A) = type(H)$.
- $S \in N$ is the initial nonterminal.

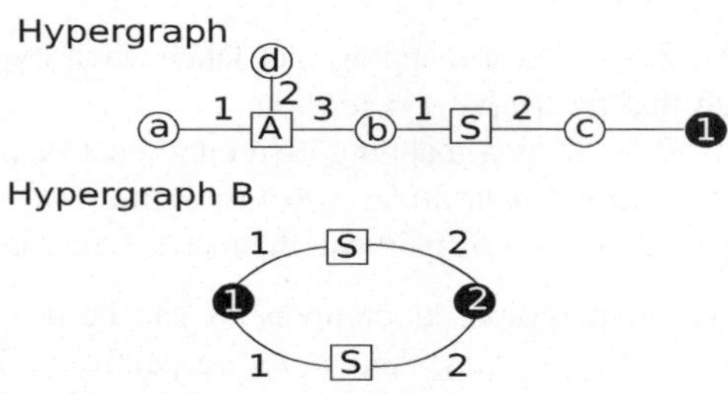

Replacement of S in Hypergraph

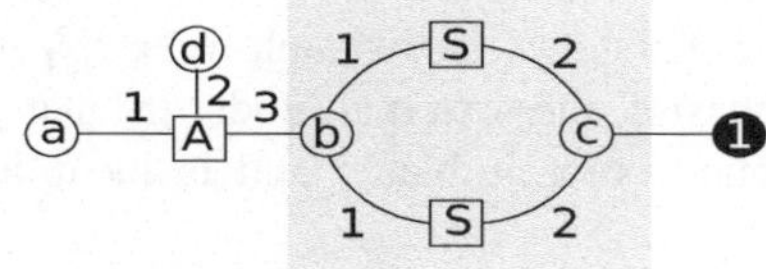

Fig. 13: Hyperedge Replacement

3.2 GDEC Language Grammar

The grammar of the GDEC language is shown in Figures 14 and 15.

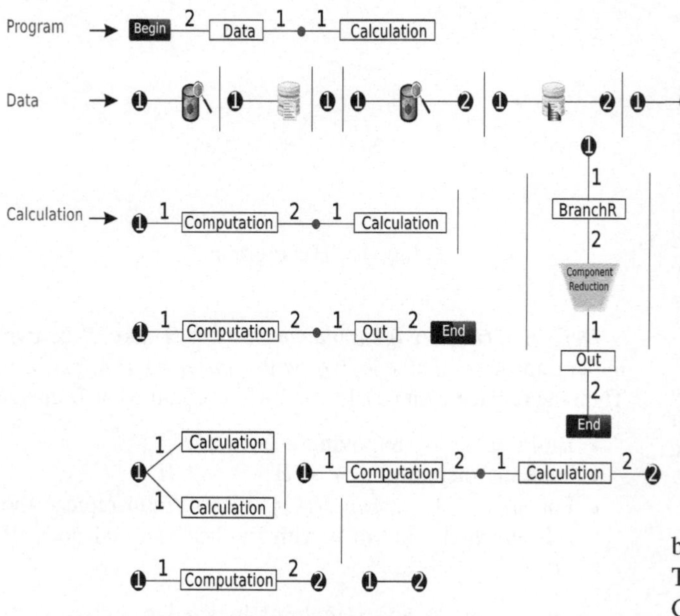

Fig. 14: GDEC Grammar, Part 1.

The set of graphs generated by the GDEC grammar are the set of programs that can be developed in GDEC. The GDEC grammar is defined by the tuple (N, Σ, R, S), whose components are initialized as follows.

- N = { Program, Computation, Data, Calculation, BranchR y Out }
- Σ = GDEC icons
- R Corresponds to:
  - *Program*: Initial rule (initial nonterminal).

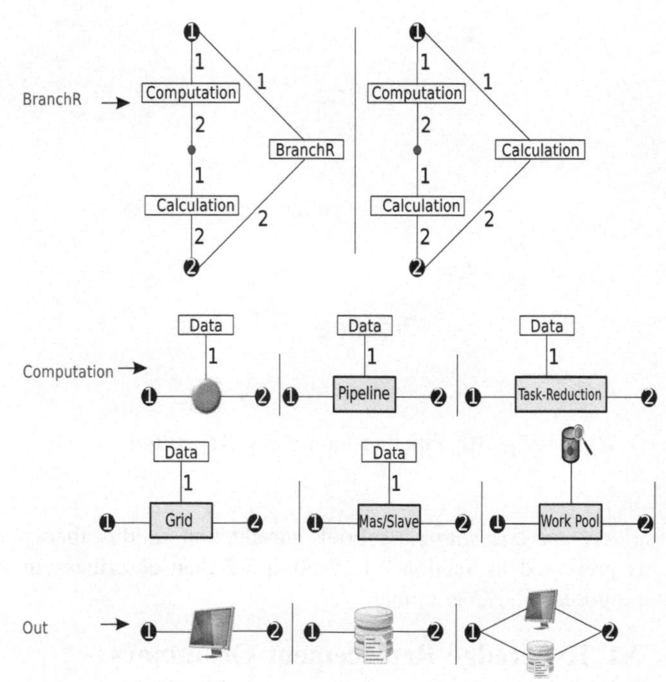

Fig. 15: GDEC Grammar, Part 2.

  - *Computation*: Defines the types of computation icons that can be used in GDEC.
  - *Data*: Define data containers, which as shown in the grammar, may or may not be the beginning of a program, and may or may not connect to a computation icon.
  - *Calculation*: Rule to connect (to define) sequences of computation icons.
  - *BranchR*: Rule for reducing a set of partial results generated by a set of computation icons.
  - *Out*: Rule that defines the different ways to manage the results in GDEC.
- S = *Program*

Any application developed through the GDEC language begins and ends with the labelling icons *Begin* and *End*. The example in Figure 16 shows the derived structure of a GDEC application that uses a pipeline and gets data both from a file and from a container; both data sources must be declared and initialized by the programmer. The result of the pipeline is passed on to a sequential processing, which finally shows the result on the screen.

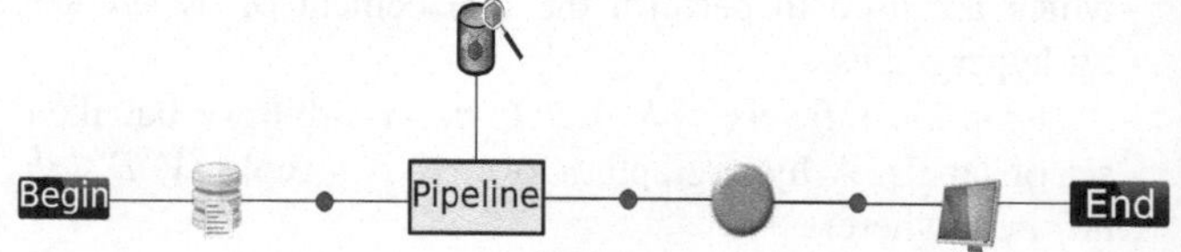

Fig. 16: Using the Pipeline Icon

Figure 17 presents another example of a GDEC program. It consists of three tasks that perform sequential processing on an input data set. A reduction operator is applied to the results of three tasks to obtain a global result, which is displayed on the screen.

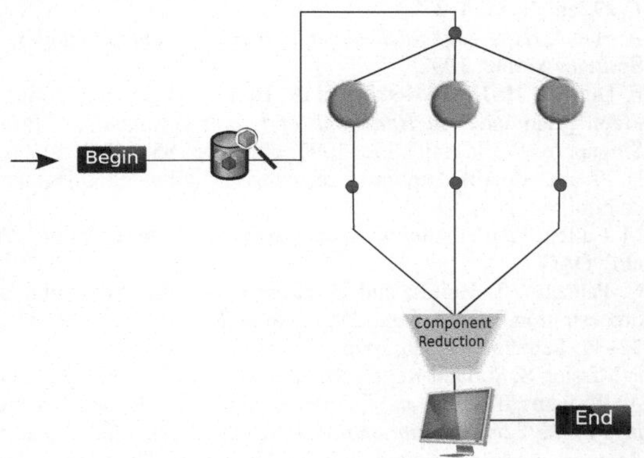

Fig. 17: Using Component-Reduction

4. Other Graphical programming languages

There is a variety of graphical languages to develop parallel and distributed applications. Some of these languages are focused on representing applications as workflows, like Condor DAGMan *(Condor Directed Acyclic Graph Manager), JOpera, Taverna* and *P-GRADE*. Other languages are focused on specifying the implementation of the applications (*VisualGOP*, *PNPL* and *PNVPL*), i.e. how the applications are structured, how are synchronized, the flow of information between applications, and how applications can be monitored.

In more detail, Condor DAGMan [19] is a tool to *High Throughput Computing (HTC)*[1]. Condor DAGMan allows applications to run and to be monitored on different infrastructures such as Globus, Amazon EC2, PBS and LSF. Applications executed by this tool must define pre- and post-conditions (e.g., a file to read the input data or to write the results). These applications are sent to Condor DAGMan through a graphical interface called PyDAG [20].

JOpera [21] provides users with a GUI where icons represent web services. Users can create applications as workflows to run, debug and monitor through the *Eclipse* development environment. JOpera offers a few basic web services for data management, and remote connections. User are responsible to develop the web services relevant to their application area.

Taverna [22] provides a graphical interface to generate applications as workflows and it must run from a client machine. Taverna is focused mainly on applications of Biology and Bioinformatics, and it offers a variety of implemented services (components) to researchers from these areas. Like Taverna, Kepler [23] provides a graphical interface to generate workflows and must also run in a client machine. Kepler is focused mainly on ecological applications. These platforms platforms are organised around web/grid services, and thus can be used in other areas simply by developing the relevant web/grid services framework. However, designing, implementing and deploying web services is not a trivial task. End user may thus be hindered to develop new applications.

[1]Parallel computing where applications require long processing time.

GDEC icons only require from the programmer sequential code which GDEC may run in parallel. They are already deployed and only need to be configured for a particular function.

P-GRADE [24] is a web portal that provides users with a graphical editor to create workflows to run on different *Middlewares* such as *Globus* or *Glite*. The workflows correspond to sequential applications or parallel MPI applications. The editor runs on the client machine but there is no need to install it therein. P-GRADE internally uses Condor DAGMan as engine to execute the workflows.

VisualGOP [25] allows programmers to compose their applications as graphs. However, programmers must specify communication and synchronization among application components based on message passing.

PNPL [26] [27] is a parallel programming language based on Petri nets. Concurrent applications developed with PNPL can run on multiprocessor machines. However, as in VisualGOP, programmers in PNPL must specify communication and synchronisation based on message passing.

We note that the graphical components offered by P-GRADE, VisualGOP and PNPL, require from the programmer the specification of communication for synchronisation and for sharing data between the graphical components. GDEC icons only require from the programmer sequential code which GDEC may run in parallel. GDEC icons are designed and implemented with internal communication and synchronisation to combine them according the grammar of the GDEC language. Basically, this communication is based on the standard input and output of each computation icon, and thus can be implemented through pipes.

5. Conclusions and Future Work

The graphical programming language GDEC was designed using Hyperedge Replacement Grammar theory. Its purpose is to simplify the development of general purpose parallel applications by eliminating the complexity of specifying the communication for data sharing and synchronization. The computation icons of GDEC correspond to widely used parallel programming patterns which must configured with sequential code provided by the programmer. GDEC may run sequential code in parallel, providing the necessary synchronisation among the multiple copies of the running code.

We are currently implementing a beta version of our GDEC programming language, and designing new computation icons components. Our beta version of GDEC runs through a web browser and is based on HTML 5, JavaScript, and PHP. We are currently evaluating the suitability of using MPI and OpenMP primitives to generate the code for GDEC icons communication.

Acknowledgment

José Luis Quiroz F. gratefully acknowledges the scholarship from CONACyT (The National Council on Science and Technology of Mexico) to pursue his postgraduate studies.

References

[1] E. Gabriel, G. E. Fagg, G. Bosilca, T. Angskun, J. J. Dongarra, J. M. Squyres, V. Sahay, P. Kambadur, B. Barrett, A. Lumsdaine, R. H. Castain, D. J. Daniel, R. L. Graham, and T. S. Woodall, "Open MPI: Goals, concept, and design of a next generation MPI implementation," in *Proceedings, 11th European PVM/MPI Users' Group Meeting*, Budapest, Hungary, September 2004, pp. 97–104.

[2] W. Gropp, E. Lusk, and A. Skjellum, *Using MPI (2nd ed.): portable parallel programming with the message-passing interface*. Cambridge, MA, USA: MIT Press, 1999.

[3] D. R. Butenhof, *Programming with POSIX threads*. Boston, MA, USA: Addison-Wesley Longman Publishing Co., Inc., 1997.

[4] B. Chapman, G. Jost, and R. v. d. Pas, *Using OpenMP: Portable Shared Memory Parallel Programming (Scientific and Engineering Computation)*. The MIT Press, 2007.

[5] T. Mattson, "An introduction to openmp," in *Cluster Computing and the Grid, 2001. Proceedings. First IEEE/ACM International Symposium on*, 2001, pp. 3–3.

[6] M. Cole, "Bringing skeletons out of the closet: a pragmatic manifesto for skeletal parallel programming," *Parallel Computing*, vol. 30, no. 3, pp. 389–406, 2004.

[7] M. A. Castro-García, "Programación con listas de datos para cómputo paralelo en clusters," Ph.D. dissertation, CINVESTAV-IPN, México 07360, D.F., 2007.

[8] J. Dean and S. Ghemawat, "Mapreduce: Simplified data processing on large clusters," in *Operating Systems Design and Implementation*, 2004, pp. 137–149.

[9] J. Yu and R. Buyya, "A taxonomy of scientific workflow systems for grid computing," *SIGMOD Record*, vol. 34, no. 3, pp. 44–49, 2005. [Online]. Available: http://doi.acm.org/10.1145/1084805.1084814

[10] G. C. Fox and D. Gannon, "Special issue: Workflow in grid systems," *Concurrency and Computation: Practice and Experience*, vol. 18, no. 10, pp. 1009–1019, Aug. 2006.

[11] B. Ludascher, I. Altintas, C. Berkley, D. Higgins, E. Jaeger, M. Jones, E. A. Lee, J. Tao, and Y. Zhao, "Scientific workflow management and the kepler system," *Concurrency and Computation: Practice and Experience*, vol. 18, no. 10, pp. 1039–1065, Aug. 2006.

[12] T. M. Oinn, R. M. Greenwood, M. Addis, M. N. Alpdemir, J. Ferris, K. Glover, C. A. Goble, A. Goderis, D. Hull, D. Marvin, P. Li, P. W. Lord, M. R. Pocock, M. Senger, R. Stevens, A. Wipat, and C. Wroe, "Taverna: lessons in creating a workflow environment for the life sciences," *Concurrency and Computation: Practice and Experience*, vol. 18, no. 10, pp. 1067–1100, Aug. 2006.

[13] S. Majithia, M. S. Shields, I. J. Taylor, and I. Wang, "Triana: A graphical web service composition and execution toolkit," in *International Conference on Web Services (ICWS)*. IEEE Computer Society, 2004, p. 514. [Online]. Available: http://doi.ieeecomputersociety.org/10.1109/ICWS.2004.118

[14] T. Mattson, B. Sanders, and B. Massingill, *Patterns for parallel programming*. USA: Addison-Wesley Professional, 2004.

[15] B. Wilkinson, J. Villalobos, and C. Ferner, "Pattern programming approach for teaching parallel and distributed computing," in *Proceeding of the 44th ACM technical symposium on Computer science education*, ser. SIGCSE '13. New York, USA: ACM, 2013, pp. 409–414.

[16] L. Moura E Silva and R. Buyyaz, "Parallel programming models and paradigms," in *High Performance Cluster Computing: Programming and Applications*. Upper Saddle River, NJ, USA: Prentice Hall PTR, 1999, ch. 1, pp. 4–27.

[17] A. Habel, *Hyperedge Replacement: Grammars and Languages*. USA: Springer Verlag, 1992.

[18] F. Drewes, H.-J. Kreowski, and A. Habel, "Hyperedge replacement, graph grammars," in *Handbook of Graph Grammars*. Printed in Singapore: World Scientific, 1997, ch. 2, pp. 95–162.

[19] H. Team. (2012) http://research.cs.wisc.edu/htcondor/dagman/dagman.html.

[20] M. Calleja. (2012) http://www.ucs.cam.ac.uk/scientific/camgrid/technical/PyDAG.

[21] C. Pautasso, T. Heinis, and G. Alonso, "Jopera: Autonomic service orchestration," *IEEE Data Engineering Bulletin*, vol. 29, no. 3, pp. 32–39, September 2006 2006.

[22] P. Missier, S. Soiland-Reyes, S. Owen, W. Tan, A. Nenadic, I. Dunlop, A. Williams, T. Oinn, and C. Goble, "Taverna, reloaded," in *Proceedings of the 22nd international conference on Scientific and statistical database management*, ser. SSDBM'10. Berlin, Heidelberg: Springer-Verlag, 2010, pp. 471–481.

[23] B. Ludäscher, I. Altintas, C. Berkley, D. Higgins, E. Jaeger, M. Jones, E. A. Lee, J. Tao, and Y. Zhao, "Scientific workflow management and the kepler system: Research articles," *Concurr. Comput. : Pract. Exper.*, vol. 18, no. 10, pp. 1039–1065, Aug. 2006.

[24] Z. Farkas and P. Kacsuk, "P-grade portal: A generic workflow system to support user communities," *Future Generation Comp. Syst.*, vol. 27, no. 5, pp. 454–465, May 2011.

[25] F. Chan, J. Cao, A. T. S. Chan, and K. Zhang, "Visual programming support for graph-oriented parallel-distributed processing: Research articles," *Softw. Pract. Exper.*, vol. 35, no. 15, pp. 1409–1439, Dec. 2005.

[26] Y. Nakamura, T. Taniguchi, H. Murakoshi, and Y. Dohi, "Implementation of a petri net based parallel programming language pnpl on workstation," in *Proceedings of the International Conference on Industrial Electronics, Control, and Instrumentation*, ser. IECON'93. Hawaii, USA: IEEE, 1993, pp. 127–132.

[27] M. Usher and D. Jackson, "A petri net based visual programming language," in *IEEE International Conference on Systems, Man, and Cybernetics*, ser. SMC'98. California, USA: IEEE, 1998, pp. 107–112.

A Proposal for an Efficient Integral Multi-Agent Sensor Network Simulation Architecture Design

A. Filippou[1], D.A. Karras[2]
[1]University of Bolton, UK, alexfilippoy@yahoo.gr
[2] Sterea Hellas Institute of Technology, Greece, Automation Dept., Psachna, Evoia, Hellas (Greece) P.C. 34400, dakarras@ieee.org, dimitrios.karras@gmail.com

Abstract- *During this research we spot several key issues concerning WSN design process. Due to the nature of these networks, debugging after deployment is unrealistic, thus an efficient testing method is required. WSN simulators perform the task, but still code implementing mote sensing and RF behaviour consists of layered and/or interacting protocols that for the sake of designing accuracy are tested working as a whole, running on specific hardware. Simulators that provide cross layer simulation and hardware emulation options may be regarded as the last milestone of the WSN design process. The herein proposed multi-agent simulation architecture aims at designing a novel WSN simulation system independent of specific hardware platforms but taking into account all hardware entities and events for testing and analysing the behaviour of a realistic WSN system.*

Keywords- *Wireless Sensor Networks; Simulation; MCU Emulation; CUDA; OpenCL; GPGPU.*

1 Introduction

A WSN is a distributed system. It consists of a usually large number of autonomous devices that form a network. The diversity of missions and environments deployed in, introduces issues and parameters of paramount importance during design process. Success of this process is considered delivering **specific code running on specific hardware**, both meeting mission and production cost requirements.

In general, a mote is a device that consists of a medium access hardware interface, a processing module and a sensor array. In case of WSN, the medium is the RF channel, and the hardware interface is a RF transceiver. In case of submerged SNs the medium is water (acoustic signals) and the hardware interface is a microphone and a loudspeaker. The trivial case scenario is a Wireless Sensor Network, running on batteries, with limited computational ability and memory, operating in a harsh and hostile environment. By using simulation tools we gain pre-deployment knowledge estimating the network's behavior. In most cases, the design and implementation of application and protocol stack code, running on specific hardware setup, are viewed through energy consumption, security and production cost prisms.

The first task of a WSN after deployment is to configure itself. Every mote uses its transceiver to establish connections with its neighbors, in order to construct a topology. The mote acquires its location which is unknown at the beginning, through collaboration with other motes, starting from a few motes with known locations. The Localization protocol responsible for the above task uses physical quantities such as RSS AoA, ToA, to calculate the mote's location. After identifying its neighbors, and being identified, the mote is part of the network, able to produce sensor data, propagate data to sink, collaborate with neighboring motes to perform a computational or sensing task, create cluster, and so on. The total activity of a mote extends to multiple levels – or layers – each having its own procedure and parameters to calculate QoS. The overall performance is derived from the combination and cross layer code collaboration [1], and as stated in [2] does not necessarily means optimal performance in every layer.

In the next part of this paper, we highlight topology, simulation and hardware design issues that back up our choices in design of our optimal simulator. We spot the parameters taken in consideration in order to calculate the simulation metrics in each case. Our goal is to design a sensor simulator able to perform cross layer code , communication medium and environmental simulation, while keeping an inside view in every aspect of this process, giving every detail needed in order to extract conclusions about network behavior, in mote, local (an area containing a number of motes) or global (entire network) level.

2 A Critical Overview of WSN Field

From our point of view, WSN coding may be categorized in two main categories. **Application Code** and **Network / Maintenance Code**. Application code is responsible for the collection and interpretation / processing of sensor data, or for actions in case of collaborating actuators. Application code operates on the platform provided by Network / maintenance code, which implements the WSN backbone. The backbone includes network protocol stack, topology, security, and configuring protocols, and provides services to the application code clear of such issues. All above share in most cases limited resources, eg memory, and processing time.

Simulating a protocol spans from a single protocol testing to testing the entire MCU code. The simulator runs protocol models or emulates the processing unit of the mote running the actual code to be uploaded. Modelling protocol is prone to errors of inaccuracy, for there is a gap between model and final code, in terms of behaviour and interactions with the rest of the code in the MCU memory. In addition modelling requires additional work.

Any mote after deployment completes tasks related to network configuration. Starting from authentication of neighbours, proceeding to synchronization and localization.

A. Authentication

After deployment, a mote searches for neighbours. This is done by transmitting its presence at maximum power, waiting for replies. Any protocol that uses the network leaves traces in the mote's transmissions. Keeping this in mind and in the case of authentication, in order to gain access, an adversary's mote presents itself as a trusted one, becoming part of the network, by being included in neighbouring mote's list of motes that have faulty authenticated it. Authentication protocols have thein own front of attack, thus security issues, starting from their transmission traces. This is an attack on topology, varying from communication disturbing, gaining access to cryptographic keys and routing tables in order to launch fake messages to sink [3][4]

B. Synchronization

Due to the nature of oscillators, every mote's clock function differs from the ideal (c(t)=t) and is modelled[5] as :

$$Ci(t) = \phi\iota + \omega it + e$$

The parameters φi and ωi, are called the clock offset (phase difference) and clock skew (frequency difference), in relation to the reference clock respectively, and e stands for random noise. The goal of synchronization is to provide to each mote the reference clock, by calculating these parameters for every mote i.[6]: Other tasks depend on the accuracy of the synchronization protocol :

1) Data Fusion:The interpretation of collected data in most cases requires that the data is time stamped. For example in target tracking, if the target if k covered, k event packets will be created for the same target. In network processing by neighboring motes according to event time, will determine the report packet sent to sink.

***2) Power Management*:** Using redundant motes organized in groups, a network of sensor motes creates a reduced topology by switching off groups in turns. Accurate synchronization is required for the sleep-wake-up circle of topology maintenance[7].

***3) Slotted transmission schemes*:** Slotted ALOHA, TDMA use time synchronization in order to determine the slot time boundaries. Accurate synchronization avoids collisions, reduces retransmissions thus saves energy.

4) Protocols: Localization protocols, routing protocols (eg LEACH) require synchronization or time stamped messages.

It is clear that evaluation of a synchronization protocol is related to cross layer simulation, due to dependency among protocols. The LEACH protocol uses TDMA scheme for in-cluster communication, thus its performance is proportional to synchronization protocol accuracy. Also, simulation of the synchronization protocol without assumptions requires a **hardware aware simulator able to emulate e.g. clock drift**.

C. Localization

After identifying neighbors, every mote estimates its position by activating the **Localization Protocol.** The Localization Protocol uses hardware input parameters related to physical quantities such as received signal strength (RSS), time of arrival (ToA, TDoA), angle of arrival (AoA) or sound[11] , to calculate the mote's location. This process begins from motes with known locations (anchors) and gradually is spread throughout the entire network.

Some localization schemes rely on additional hardware to operate, or their simulation is somehow hardware related:

1) Time Difference of Arrival, is used in two ways: difference between two signals of different nature e.g. RF and ultrasonic, and difference between RF signals of different motes of known location. The former scheme requires additional hardware, increasing complexity and mote cost. In addition, ultrasonic pulse reception suffers from severe multipath effects. The distance between the motes is derived obviously **without the need of synchronization**. But due to multipath effects, this method provides fairly accurate distance estimation.

2) Roundtrip propagation time measurements measure the difference between the time when a signal is sent by a sensor and the time when the signal returned by a second sensor comes back to the original sensor. Since the same local clock is used to compute the roundtrip propagation time, there is no synchronization problem[8]. The response of the second mote must include the processing time of the reply, which is sent to the first sensor to be subtracted. It is clear that processing time in the second mote depends on its clock, and on the number of machine cycles needed to execute code that handles and transmits the reply. The above properties depend on the chosen MCU or MCUs in case of an heterogeneous WSN. In addition, in some energy saving strategies, one solution is adjusting the clock to lower frequencies through software during runtime. This spots the need for simulation tool that **can handle different MCUs, clocks and clock adjustments** and able to **calculate processing time of a subroutine**.

3) Beacons using directional antennas, transmit their location and angle of transmission, or motes use their directional antenna to calculate transmissions of anchors. In general, protocols using AoA require a channel simulator that can handle sector type transmissions e.g. Opnet[9] .

***4) Underwater*:** In [10] a localization protocol is proposed for underwater sensor networks using the DNR (dive end rise) of anchors equipped with GPS, in order to update their location, and then using sound waves to transmit their locations. Besides that a pressure sensor in every mote helps in estimating the depth underwater. The whole scenario takes place not on a 2d plane but in 3d space. The localization is constant, considering the fact that the simulated UWSN may operate in a area with strong currents.

An imaginary scenario[11] where localization is not needed goes as follows: The electrical company connects every flat of a district with its network through a consumption accumulator device. Once every two months a company's clerk visits every accumulator device and records its reading of consumption. In case of a WSN, the reading is transmitted to a local sink along with the accumulator device serial number. In this scenario, as in many other cases of data acquisition e.g. industrial plants, the question "where" does not need an answer containing geographical coordinates.

In every case, simulation of localization protocols require **(a)**. Hardware aware simulator, able to emulate behavior of components such as antennas, MCUs for accurate time measurement **(b)**. An accurate medium simulator (RF spectrum, sound) able to represent the nature of signal propagation (multipath fading, reflection, diffraction, attenuation). **(c)**. An environmental simulator, in case that environmental properties or phenomena (obstacles, sea currents, water pressure, forest fires[2]) should be taken in consideration.

Authentication. Synchronization and Localization protocols are activated during **topology construction phase** and during **every topology maintenance phase[12]**. The topology construction phase provides the initial (full) topology, where motes have authenticated all their neighbors, and are synchronized. The topology maintenance phase updates neighbor motes tables by deleting energy depleted, deactivated or destroyed motes, or by inserting new ones, in case of a redeployment over a blind hole. Topology protocols such as [7] provide the reduced (logical) topology, the platform on which routing operates. However, in [13] authors introduce a rooting protocol under the concept of virtual coordinates, which are randomly initialized in each mote, and updated each time the mote relays a packet. This updating process consists of the sending mote retrieving the virtual coordinates of its neighbors and updating its virtual coordinates by using a centroid transformation. In this case, localization and routing are processes that run concurrently.

Concluding, all the above three types of protocols have their own trace in motes transmissions, and share processing time. The fact that sensing ability looses MCU focus is taken in consideration during design process, with solutions on both software and hardware level.

D. Routing

In [15] the routing protocol Directed Diffusion [21] is examined, using a **diagnostic tool**, plugged in Tossim[14]. The case study is the fact that despite good communication, the protocol fails to deliver packets of interest to the sink. As stated "The diagnostic simulator is motivated by the idea that, in a distributed computing environment, nodes have to interact with each other in some manner defined by their distributed protocols in order to perform tasks correctly. These interaction patterns are the concatenation of distributed sequences of events on multiple nodes. In a correctly functioning system, these sequences of events follow a path that the protocol is designed to handle. Occasionally, design flaws or omissions lead to sequences that the protocol designer did not envision, potentially causing the protocol to fail or manifest a bug. The challenge is to identify this special sequence of events which is responsible for the failure among hundreds of other common sequences that are logged during the execution but are unrelated to the failure. [15]". In this fine work the need for **fine grained debugging** is pointed out, providing also a solution as a plug in tool. However, Tossim **lacks** ability of simulating different code in every mote and using a different hardware platform eg a PIC or a Freescale MCU based mote.

In [2], The EMA routing protocol is introduced, in which main concept is the environmental awareness of the protocol. The low consumption orientation of routing protocols such as LEACH [16], PEGASIS [17] TEEN [18], is not the optimal solution when a mote is facing destruction threat from e.g. forest fire. The protocol estimates also the probability of that threat in order to use resources of motes that are about to fail.

The Greedy-Face-Greedy (GFG) and Greedy Perimeter Stateless Routing (GPSR) protocols are the most widely adopted geographic routing protocols for WSN.[19]. Every node applies Gabriel Graph Transformation to the connectivity graph, for the protocol to perform over its planar version the left hand rule. In this way, protocol recovers from geographical dead ends caused by blind holes. The assumption that communication regions are perfectly circular disks does not hold in real-world propagation conditions, causing the protocols to fail, in case [13] of obstacles. In addition Gabriel Graph Transformation does not function with limited positioning accuracy [20].

Concluding, protocol relies on topology to operate. Topology protocols or topology related protocols provide the platform whose accuracy routing protocol QoS depends on. In [2] is shown that even efficient protocols do not operate well in all situations. The goal is the overall performance of protocol code and this is tested by cross layer simulation, provided the ability to monitor protocol interactions.

E. Sensing

The sensor array of a mote is consisted of at least one sensor or sensor device. They are mostly analog, and connected to MCU through an Analog to Digital converter, which is built-in or external. In most cases, the MCU-ADC channel is shared among all sensors of the mote, using a time slot mechanism. Sensors as electronic parts, function according to their physical properties, such as range, energy consumption, response delay, drifting over time etc. Their performance characteristics introduce problems that span from coding to security and life expectancy of the sensor itself, and as a consequence, life expectancy of the network [22]:

Transfer Function: Is the function that shows the relationship between physical stimulus and the electrical signal. The signal is processed (eg amplified, converted to digital) and transferred to the MCU for interpretation by the application level. **The problems that arise** in order select the suitable sensor is the **computational load** of the interpretation, and the **energy consumption** of the in-circuit processing of the signal. The above spot the need of modeling the sensor itself, and for simulator tools that have the ability to switch between sensor devices and able to model the hardware specs of these devices, including energy consumption of the circuitry that supports the sensor.

Sensitivity: Is the factor between variation of stimulus and consequent variation of electrical signal. A sensor is sensitive, if a small change of stimulus results in a large change of the electrical signal. Is sensitivity of the selected sensor devices adequate for the desired detect ability of the entire network? Is it safe to assume detect ability modeled by an deterministic (binary) sensing model? What computational load would contribute a process that detects events in a continuously streaming sensor data in case of a stochastic sensing model? (e.g. correlating sound) [23].The answer lies on the ability of the simulator to model real world phenomena or scenarios. A crack on the concrete construction of a bridge lasts for milliseconds and has to be identified among sounds and noises of various amplitudes and frequencies e.g. car tires, engines, contraction – expansion of metal skeleton etc. Simulating

WSN for sniper detection through identifying sound source position of multiple sensor readings requires modeling of the environment e.g buildings, echoes, sound attenuation etc.

Dynamic Range or Span: The range of physical signal that can be converted to electrical according to specs, is the dynamic range of the sensor device. The response of the sensor outside of this range is faulty. In real life, it is impossible to detect inaccurate reading coming from the sensor array, unless we use a variety of sensor types to measure the same physical quantity. During design process it is essential to know the probability of an inaccurate reading coming from sensor array, and the impact on the network. To cope with this task, we need simulation tools that **(a)** model the sensor, the environmental phenomena of which we collect readings, and **(b)** provide the ability to implement metrics over the accuracy of these readings.

Noise and Resolution: The output signal of a sensor, is contaminated with noise, which is usually distributed across the frequency spectrum. In case that noise is similar to minimum detectable signal fluctuation (**resolution**), the performance of the system is limited, thus during the design process, the selections in hardware are examined on how they contribute to noise.

Sensing Range: A sensor's sensing area is a disc or sector, sphere or cone. The sensitivity of a sensor may depend on the distance of the stimulus. The binary sensing model is not always a wise choice without taking in consideration the sensor specifications related to stimulus distance from the device. When referring to network lifetime, the dominant issue is energy consumption. Main resource is considered to be the battery, and main consumer the transceiver. Active sensors e.g. accelerometers, require energy to provide output electrical signal. Thus the volume of measurements affect network lifetime, and along with communication management and MCU sleep-wake up cycle, sensor activation management needs to be included in the total energy consumption policy. Chemical sensors, sensors used in contamination spread scenarios, detection of explosives, toxics etc. employ substances, e.g. electrolytes, which quantity decrease in every measurement. Draining a sensor of that resource makes the mote useless in terms of coverage. In addition, the sensor is exposed to unlimited numbers of chemical combinations [26], able to alter the sensor's behavior.

In conclusion, sensors as electronic devices have properties that may have a major impact on sensor network behavior. Modeling of sensors, along with the environmental properties or phenomena that provide data as sensor measurements, contributes to the fact that it is feasible to obtain a fine grained detail of the environment – WSN interaction, revealing possible failures or bug prone design choices during simulation.

Coverage and Connectivity : Every sensor has a sensing range. Range varies from type to type, spanning from a single point e.g. temperature sensor to an area usually of circular shape. A point of an area or space is covered if it is in range of at least one sensor. Coverage is the QoS that quantifies the ability of a deployed sensor network to report an event or a reading in the deployment area. Sensor readings and their processing produce data to be routed to sink. The Sink is aware of the events spotted or data produced by motes if routing protocol succeeds in delivering data. Thus apart from being in range of at least one sensor, a point in the area of interest is covered, if there is a routing path available to deliver consequent data to sink. If there is no available path, then from the sink's view point, there is no response from the motes of the disconnected area, and even though an event is tracked by a sensor, this area is regarded as a blind hole.

Every mote has a sensing range (coverage) for each type of sensor it carries and a communication range (connectivity). Assuming that a WSN is static and isotropic [25], and modeling a network as such, reduces our ability to test the protocol performance (of any layer) over a transmission power – energy management or mobility scheme [24]. Finding neighbors by transmitting In full power or in permitted power according to battery power level, is one of choices in reacting to a connectivity loss scenario. In general a mote has the ability to adjust its transmission power during runtime, if the total resource management strategy contains the ability. That includes the **hardware choice of including a battery level indicator on the mote**.

In [27], the model of Trap Coverage is introduced. From our point of view this model is a realistic one, for it allows lack of coverage over bounded areas, in other words, the WSN continues to operate when in real life blind holes appear due to node energy depletion. The same model generalizes full coverage, when the diameter of the permitted blind hole is near 0.

Apart from managing transmission power, mobility [24] is among choices, where mobile motes are moving to a position that restores connectivity. From obviously expensive motes, we move to motes that we are able to use in large quantities: Deploying redundant motes, organizing them to operate in turns in order to prolong network lifetime. In Cover Sets [7][28][29] motes are organized in sets that cover the same area, and scheduled in a way that one set is active at the time. In many schemes, like [7][28][29] a cross layer simulation is needed, for deriving in this case the appropriate MAC layer, considering the flood in transmissions.

Event detection in most cases requires multiple readings from different sensors. Processing of sensor data in mote clusters or at the sink, produces the report message. Even though simulated models of mote collaboration, successful routing at most circumstances and hard conditions, data fusion at the sink may conclude to success in event tracking thus coverage, after deployment, hardware details may prove the protocols inadequate. The assumption that sensors of a mote can sense at the same time is not valid in case of a single MCU ADC channel. Sensors are triggered in turns, and in case of a **time bounded** event (a crack of concrete) some sensors of the sensor array of the mote will miss the event. Dealing with the problem in [30] authors introduce the concept of **logical sensor** , in which sensors are distributed over different motes, kept active and the cluster of motes that provide all types of sensors is considered as a logical sensor. In the cluster the fusion of data occurs, creating the necessary report to be routed to sink. The problem of **sensor cost** is dealt also. In the same concept, the problem of minimizing expensive sensors while maintaining coverage is dealt with logical sensors. In the past, one of the assumptions made, was the disk model of a sensor, usually binary. Technology has to offer a variety of products, in this case sensors, with properties to be taken into consideration in the design process of a WSN. There are directional sensors (e.g. ultrasonic, cameras, etc), thus simulating a WSN equipped with these sensors requires simulator with the ability to model in every extension the nature of sensors used. In [31] authors propose **Maximum Coverage with Rotatable Angles (MCRA)**, in which the goal of the protocol is to increase coverage by turning the orientation of directional sensors, while minimizing the angles of rotation. Minimizing angle of rotation concludes to low energy consumption, minimum movement detection of the deployed WSN, and positioning of motes in adequate manner to cover a given area (surveillance applications)

Concluding, coverage is not only a matter of sensing radius and routing backbone. Details that affect coverage are spread across layers, and cross layer simulation is needed to obtain precise evaluation of code – protocol performance, in terms of reducing mote cost, increasing network lifetime, and of course coverage itself.

3 The Proposed Simulator Architecture

In the previous part, we spotted details taken into consideration while designing a protocol or the entire protocol collection running on mote's MCU. Hardware specific simulators like Tossim and Atemu lack flexibility concerning hardware for they are bounded with a specific platform. Avrora emulates every mote in its own thread, and thus performs and scales according to thread ability of the computer it runs on. None of the above takes advantage of GPGPU abilities (CUDA, OpenCL)

We propose an architecture, able of scaling, providing fine grain detail of the simulation, and configuring all the parameters of RF channel, Environment and Hardware. Our goal is to provide a multi agent simulation tool, to serve among others as a WSN Simulator.

A. Architecture

Our proposal consists of four basic elements: (a) Agents (b) The Controller (c) Interfaces (d) Services.

Agents: There are two types of agents. (a) Built in agents. They are commonly used components such as plotters, visualizers, or emulators. They are at the disposal of the user and not necessarily part of every simulation. (b) User defined agents. User writes code to define the agent behaviour. These are implemented by an interpreter, whose functionality is described later.

The Controller: The controller activates or deactivates agents according to simulation clock and/or event handling instructions written in user defined code. In case of a simulation clock, the controller uses a basic time step which is the greatest common divisor GCD of all time steps of the clocks of time dependant agents. In case of time independent agents, their code is activated at every pace of the controller.

Interfaces: The interfaces of agents are implemented with a byte array. Two agents communicate through a set of bytes eg from index a to index b in this array, using b-a bytes. These two integers (a and b), describe the interface. All interchanged data (numerical quantities, text, fluctuation of a quantity for a period of time eg a waveform from t=k to t=k+10, signals or combinations) is described in bytes. Every interface may be used by two or more agents putting interchanged data in wide scope. An event handling mechanism notifies every agent using the interface (eg form a to b) that contents are changed. An agent may use as many interfaces as user requires. By using interfaces the user may project data from inside the agent to defined scope. Below is an example of a mote built up using four agents and the interface array. The parts of the interface array that are used by this mote are coloured with grey.

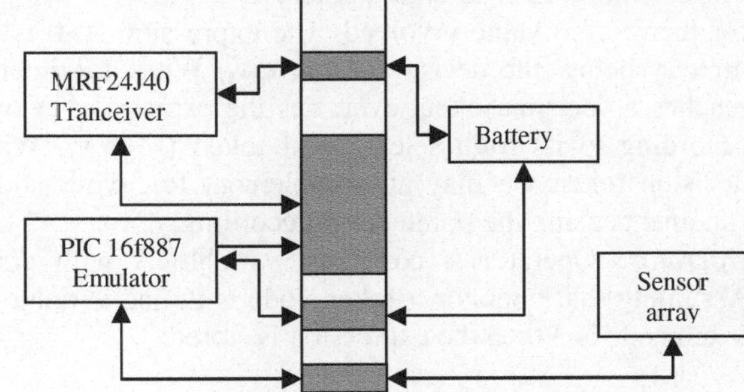

Fig. 1 A Mote Example

In the above example the PIC emulator uses 3 interfaces, of different width. The pace of the emulator is one machine cycle, (usually for MCUs execution of one instruction). In the lab we may measure the exact energy consumption of one cycle. This emulator uses as input the compiled program to be uploaded to the real device. The battery agent subtracts from a starting quantity energy consumption of MCU and radio, sending a shutdown signal to MCU emulator in case of energy depletion deactivating the virtual mote. Sensor array agent sends analog data to MCU emulator. The interface is as wide as needed to describe the possible value range of data. Due to ADC conversion latency, the ADC may be modelled separately using a fifth agent.

Services: There are two types of services: (a) built in library. They are functions and procedures widely used in fields of engineering or science. (b) User defined: user writes code to describe the functionality of their procedure or function. Services are sets of procedures and/or functions in scope of any agent. They are activated when called by agents and their data is valid even when they are inactive. An implementation example is the RF medium. When a mote transmits, sends to RF medium service its coordinates, time, and transmission power along with data. RF medium service stores these values in a table. When a mote listens, the service calculates the signal at his location, according to all active signals above a given SNR. In case of an CSMA-CD MAC layer, both services (transmitting, listening) are active at the same time.

B. Interpreter

The interpreter consists of three main parts: (a) A 4XN integer array (b) The actual code that executes user programs (c) A byte array where data is stored.

1) 4XN Integer Array The simple program is:

1. If (A>0) 2. B← B+1 3. else 4.C←C+5 5. Endif 6. D←B+C

Ends up translated in tokens and stored in the 4XN

integer array. There are 4 basic types of token supported: (a) decision (b) operator (c) assignment (d) variable or value. At the first column contains the token code. Columns 2 and 3 contain pointers pointing at the next token to execute in the token (4XN) array. Column 4 contains pointer pointing to data memory. In detail :

Decision: if A>0 is true then the next token to execute is the assignment token in line 2, else executes assignment token in line 4. Assuming that decision token code is number 1, and x and y are the indexes that tokens in lines 2 and 4 are stored respectively, then the line in which the decision token is stored in the 4XN would be like:

1	x	Y	

There is no pointer to data memory for there is no value involved. The expression A>0 is stored directly below the decision token row. When the interpreter reaches a decision token, evaluates the expression below and according to its truth selects next token (x or y). With the decision token we may also implement for, while, do until statements using the pointers x,y accordingly.

Operator: Operator > compares variable A with value 0. Assuming that operator > token code is 2, and variable-value token code is 3 then the expression is stored:

Indx	1	2	3	4
10	1	x	y	
11	2	12	13	
12	3	0	0	m
13	3	0	0	n

Memory
<A>
0

Fig 2. 4XN Token Array and Memory Array

The algorithm that evaluates expressions is

```
Evaluate (x)
{ y=Token(x,2); z=Token(x,3)
IF z=0 and y=0 THEN return mem(Token(x,4));
ELSEIF z=0 THEN return op(Token(x,1),evaluate(y))
ELSEIF y=0 THEN Return op(Token(x,1),evaluate(z))
ELSE Return op(Token(x,1),evaluate(y),evaluate(z))
ENDIF },
```

where x,y,z are indexes in the 4XN array of tokens, and m,n are indexes in the data memory (array of type byte).

Assignment: The assignment token evaluates the expression on its right, stores the result in memory, and proceeds to next token execution. From assignment token in line 2, next to be executed is the assignment token in line 6. The same for assignment token in line 4. The token code for the assignment is 4 and for the + is 5. The memory pointer in column 4 in an assignment row, points the location to store the results. Completing the arrays:

Memory

indx	
m	<A>
n	0
o	<B>
p	1
q	<C>
r	5
s	<D>

Index	1	2	3	4
10	1	14	18	0
11	2	12	13	0
12	3	0	0	m
13	3	0	0	n
14	4	22		o
15	5	16	17	0
16	3	0	0	o
17	3	0	0	p
18	4	22		q
19	5	20	21	0
20	3	0	0	q
21	3	0	0	r
22	4			s
23	5	24	25	0
24	3	0	0	o
25	3	0	0	q

Fig 3. The representation of the program in the two arrays.

Data Types: The interpreter engine uses its own set of basic data types: Char, string, int, real, bool, byte, binary and their combinations (structs). Binary is used for binary numbers bigger than 255. From the user's point of view, data memory and interfaces are transparent. From inside the agent, interface is seen and used as a simple variable or a struct. The interpreter's engine is responsible for any transformation needed, relieving user from the task.

The basic advantage of this interpreter implementation is that is simple and can be used also:

MCUs: The interpreter is uploaded in the MCU EEPROM. Application and protocol coding now becomes data. Sink transmits code along with data altering WSN mission at runtime.

In the 4XN array we may store 1 or more programs. Each program starts at a specific index of this array. The interpreter using a priority mechanism may execute these programs concurrently, by executing a number of tokens of each, in every pace. This feature makes the interpreter able to serve as a base of a WSN OS.

GPGPU: The function evaluate(x) is the part of the interpreter that calculates expressions. The other part is a simple switch (x) statement where x is the token code. Using a non recursive version of evaluate(x) we eliminate external dependencies and calls. One would expect difficulty in handling the sum of data involved due to variety of data types. In our case all data and code are contained in two arrays. Code and data can fit in a CUDA thread. In other words, one agent in every thread. The amount of data is constant (arrays). Both are copied to GPU memory using:

```
#define X 100; #define Y 4;  #define Z 1000 ;
Int      Tkn      [X]      [Y];      Byte      mem      [Z];
cudaMemcpy(dTkn,Tkn,X*Y*sizeof(int),cudaMemcpyHostTo
Device);
cudaMemcpy(devicemem,mem,z,cudaMemcpyHostToDevice);
```

4 Other Simulators and prospects for the Proposed Design

The proposed architecture is similar with the architecture of SENSE[32]. SENSE is built on top of COST. A simulation is dealt as a composition of components. Each component is implemented in C++, and communicates with other components via inports and outports. Inports and outports are used to reduce interdependencies between components and allow code reuse. The universal interface mechanism in our architecture provides the ability of interchanging any type of data and of any size and organization (structs). An interface may serve as a private channel used by two agents, or as a group channel, only by the use of two indexes that specify the channel width and location on the byte array.

Avrora, AvroraZ, tossim and Atemu, are AVR emulators, with AvroraZ[33] giving the ability of emulating the cc2420 chip. All are limited to AVR MCU's implementations, and they do no support network-communication level simulation[34]. SensorMaker [34] is written in C, provides network information in fine grain, (packet collisions, packet path, cluster layout) along with mote information mainly energy level. However, modelling – coding gap still remains for the designer to fill. Collecting ideas and implementations, we conclude the set of desired features of a simulating tool: (1) Easy to use [34] (2) code reuse [32] (3) Hardware emulation [14][33] (4) Visualization and interpretation of data [34] (5) Network toolbox[34] (6) precise timing [14][33].

Our proposal is a multi agent simulator. Using agents and services the user may implement hardware emulation, channel – medium (RF sound) modelling, environmental phenomena modelling, event monitors and handlers, data visualisation interpretation and storage. All the components of the simulator are connected directly, or via the multi type interface structure. The simulation controller activates each agent (a) according to a time interval (time dependant agents), (b) at every pace (continually), (c) or according to an event (a change in an interface, a memory location, a variation of an environmental parameter etc). Agent or service behaviour is implemented in code which is executed by the interpreter or the simulator. The interpreter's back end is en array of tokens in which the user's code is translated. The interpreter's front end is a C like language, but in the future others will be supported (Delphi, Basic). Controller may control channel (RF or sound) simulation, Environmental (temperature variations over an area) simulation and device simulation/emulation (model/real code)

References

[1] Masri W.,Mammeri Z. "***On QoS Mapping in TDMA Based Wireless Sensor Networks***" Wireless and Mobile Networking IFIP Joint Conference on Mobile Wireless Communications Networks MWCN 2008.

[2] Bernd-Ludwig Wenning et al. "***Environmental Monitoring Aware Routing in Wireless Sensor Networks***" Wireless and Mobile Networking IFIP Joint Conference on Mobile Wireless Communications Networks MWCN 2008

[3] S. Dziembowski, A. Mei, A Panconesi "***On Active Attacks on Sensor Network Key Distribution Schemes***" Algorithmic Aspects of Wireless Sensor Networks 5th International Workshop ALGOSENSORS 2009 Rhodes Greece July 10,11 2009

[4] Karlof, C., Wagner, D.: "***Secure routing in wireless sensor networks: attacks and countermeasures***." Ad Hoc Networks 1(2-3), 293–315 2003.

[5] Serpedin E. Chaudhari Q. "***Synchronization in Wireless Sensor Networks Parameter Estimation Peformance Benchmarks and Protocols***" Cambridge University Press 2009

[6] Giridhar A., Kumar P.R. "***The Spatial Smoothing Method of Clock Synchronization in Wireless Networks***" Theoretical Aspects of Distributed Computing in Sensor Networks Springer 2011

[7] Slijepcevic, S., Potkonjak, M.:" ***Power efficient organization of wireless sensor networks***." Proceedings of IEEE International Conference on Communications, vol. 2, pp. 472–447 2001

[8] Guoqiang Mao Barış Fidan "***Localization Algorithms and Strategies for Wireless Sensor Networks***" Premier Reference Source – information Science Reference 2009

[9] www.opnet.com

[10] He, T., Stoleru, R., Stankovic John, A." ***Range free localization. Technical report***" , University of Virginia (2006)

[11] Timo Ojala et al "***UBI-AMI: Real-Time Metering of Energy Consumption at Homes Using Multi-Hop IP-based Wireless Sensor Networks***" Advances In Grid and Pervasive Computing GPC Oulu Finland 2011 pp 274-284

[12] M.A Labrador, P.M. Wightman "***Topology Control in Wireless Sensor Networks***" Springer 2009

[13] Watteyne T. et al " ***Centroid Virtual Coordinates – A novel Near – Shortest Path Routing Paradigm***" Computer Networks 17 October 2008

[14] Levis, P., Lee, N., Welsh, M., Culler, D.: "***Tossim: Accurate and scalable simulation of entire tinyos applications.***" First International Conference on Embedded Networked Sensor Systems (SenSys 2003) (November 2003)

[15] Khan M, Abdelzaher T.,Gupta K.K "***Towards Diagnostic Simulation in Sensor Networks***" Distributed Computing in Sensor Systems 4th IEEE International Conference DCOSS 2008 Santorini Island Greece June 11-14 2008

[16] W.B. Heinzelman, A.P. Chandrakasan, H. Balakrishnan," ***An application-specific protocol architecture for wireless microsensor networks***", IEEE Transactions on Wireless Communications , 1(4): 660-670, October 2002.

[17] S. Lindsey, C.S. Raghavendra, "***PEGASIS: power efficient gathering in sensor information systems***", in: Proc. IEEE Aerospace Conference, Big Sky, Montana, March 2002.

[18] A. Manjeshwar and D.P. Agrawal," ***TEEN: A Protocol For Enhanced Eficiency in Wireless Sensor Networks***", in Proceedings of the 1International Workshop on Parallel and Distributed Computing Issues in Wireless Networks and Mobile Computing, San Francisco, CA April 2001.

[19] H. Frey and I. Stojmenovic "***On delivery guarantees of face and combined greedy-face routing algorithms in ad hoc and sensor networks***" in twelfth ACM Annual International Conference on Mobile Computing and Networking (MOBICOM) Los Angeles CA USA ACM September 23-29 2006 pp 390-401

[20] T Watteyne, et al. "***On using virtual coordinates for routing in the context of wireless sensor networks***" in 18th Annual International Symposium on Personal Indoor and Mobile Radio Communications (PIMRC) Athens Greece IEEE, September 3-7 2007.

[21] Inatanagonwiwat, C., Govindan, R., Estrin, D.: "***Directed diffusion: A scalable and robust communication paradigm for sensor networks***." Mobicom 2000, Boston, MA, USA (2000)

[22] Jon S. Wilson ed. "***Sensor Technology Handbook***" Elsevier 2005.

[23] Patrick Kuckertz et all "***Sniper fire localization using Wireless sensor networks and genetic algorithm based data fusion***" Military Communications Conference 2007 MILCOM 2007 IEEE (2007)

[24] Muhammad Imran et al "***Application-Centric Connectivity Restoration Algorithm for Wireless Sensor and Actor Networks***" Advances in Grip and Pervasive Computing GPC 2011 pp 243-253

[25] Habib M. Ammari "***Challenges and Opportunities of Connected k Covered Wireless Sensor Networks - From Sensor Deployment to Data Gathering***" Springer 2009

[26] Fraden J. "***Handbook of Modern Sensors – Physics Designs and Applications***" Springer Verlag 2004.

[27] Balister P., Kumar S., Zheng Z., Sinsha P., "***Trap Coverage : Allowing Coverage Holes of Bounded Diameter in Wireless Sensor Networks***" Infocom/IEEE 2009

[28] Cardei, M., Thai, M.T., Li, Y., Wu, W.: "***Energy-efficient target coverage in wireless sensor networks***". In: IEEE INFOCOM (2005)

[29] Cheng, M.X., Ruan, L., Wu, W.: "***Achieving minimum coverage breach under bandwidth constraints in wireless sensor networks***." IEEE INFOCOM (2005)

[30] Saukh O., Sauter R, Marron P.J. "***Time-Bounded and Space-Bounded Sensing in Wireless Sensor Networks***" Distributed Computing in Sensor Systems DCOSS 2008, LNCS 5067, pp. 357–371

[31] Liang C.K Chen Y.T " ***The Target Coverage Problem in Directional Sensor Networks with Rotatable Angles***". Distributed Computing in Sensor Systems DCOSS 2008, LNCS 5067 pp. 264–273

[32] Chen, Gilbert, et al. "**SENSE: a wireless sensor network simulator**." *Advances in Pervasive Computing and Networking* (2005): 249-267

[33] de Paz Alberola, Rodolfo, and Dirk Pesch. "**AvroraZ: extending Avrora with an IEEE 802.15. 4 compliant radio chip model**." *Proceedings of the 3nd ACM workshop on Performance monitoring and measurement of heterogeneous wireless and wired networks*. ACM, 2008

[34] Yi, Sangho, et al. "**SensorMaker: A wireless sensor network simulator for scalable and fine-grained instrumentation**." *Computational Science and Its Applications–ICCSA 2008* (2008): 800-810.

Automatic run-time mapping of polyhedral computations to heterogeneous devices with memory-size restrictions

Yuri Torres, Arturo Gonzalez-Escribano, and Diego R. Llanos
Departamento de Informática
Edif. Tecn. de la Información, Universidad de Valladolid,
Campus Miguel Delibes, 47011 Valladolid, Spain
E-mail: {yuri.torres, arturo, diego}@infor.uva.es

***Abstract*—Tools that aim to automatically map parallel computations to heterogeneous and hierarchical systems try to divide the whole computation in parts with computational loads adjusted to the capabilities of the target devices. Some parts are executed in node cores, while others are executed in accelerator devices. Each part requires one or more data-structure pieces that should be allocated in the device memory during the computation.**

In this paper we present a model that allows such automatic mapping tools to transparently assign computations to heterogeneous devices with different memory size restrictions. The model requires the programmer to specify the access patterns of the computation threads in a simple abstract form. This information is used at run-time to determine the second-level partition of the computation assigned to a device, ensuring that the data pieces required by each sub-part fit in the target device memory, and that the number of kernels launched is minimal. We present experimental results with a prototype implementation of the model that works for regular polyhedral expressions. We show how it works for different example applications and access patterns, transparently executing big computations in devices with different memory size restrictions.

***Keywords*—Heterogeneous devices, Polyhedral model, Memory-size restrictions, Automatic mapping tools**

I. Introduction

Heterogeneous systems can be built with very different hardware devices (CPU-cores, accelerators) grouped in several nodes and interconnected in a distributed environment. Portable codes for such systems should implement parallel algorithms, while abstracting them from the mapping activities that adapt the computation to the platform. Thus, the programming model should encapsulate the mapping techniques and the CPU/accelerator synchronization with appropriate abstractions.

Taking into account the memory size limitations of heterogeneous target devices is an additional challenge. Currently, many approaches do not focus in this problem, working with fixed sized middle-grain tasks [1], or assuming that the tasks fit, or are generated to fit into the devices [2], [3]. Other approaches simply advise to add more computation devices to allow finer partitions [4]. A simple way to tackle the problem is to generate more distributed processes than system nodes, mapping several of them to the same device [5]. In this way, each process is responsible for a smaller part of the computation. When enough processes are launched, the parts are small enough to fit in any target device. However, this leads to more costly inter-process communications and scalability problems. A more sophisticated approach is to consider the device memory limitations while creating the high-level partition [6]. This approach highly complicates the whole partitioning activity.

An associated problem for memory-restrictions-aware systems is to find a proper representation of the parallel computation that allows the system to locate, and measure the size, of the data portions required by a generic part of the computation. This information is needed for both generating a balanced partition, and mapping the parts adequately [6], even for libraries that make transparent the node to device communication [7].

In this work we propose a solution to allow a hidden layer to: (1) Split an arbitrarily large computation in parts that fit the memory limitations of an assigned target device; (2) transparently launch the partial kernels generated; and (3) move the required pieces of the data structures between the main node memory and the target device memory when needed. We present a model of parallel applications that allows to express access patterns to data structures in terms of the thread index domains. These expressions allow the system to automatically compute the memory requirements of a computation part (a block of threads). We introduce a generic algorithm for regular polyhedral computations to compute at run-time an appropriate partitioning of the thread space that minimizes the number of kernels launched, ensuring that the pieces of the data structures needed by each kernel fit into the target device memory.

We also present examples of how to represent with this model parallel kernels and applications. Experimental results obtained with a prototype implementation of the model show its feasibility.

The rest of the paper is organized as follows: Section II describes the proposed approach and how it integrates in a previous run-time mapping framework. Section III describes the model for parallel computations and access patterns. Section IV presents an algorithm for computing a partition with memory size limitations. Section V shows experimental results with a prototype implementation, while Sect. VI presents our conclusions.

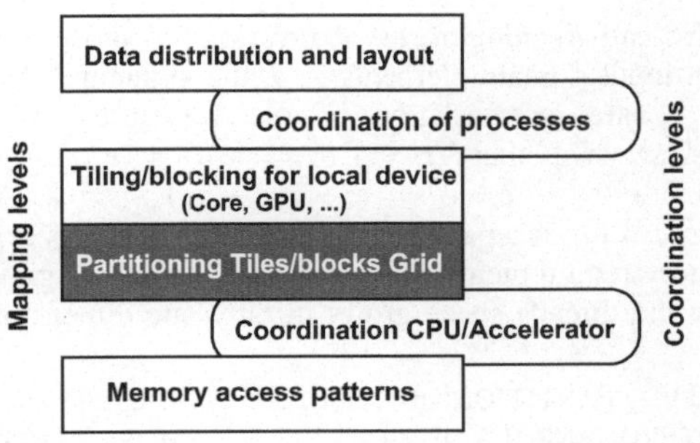

Fig. 1. Mapping/Coordination levels. The new level of automatic partitioning is highlighted with a dark-grey shadowed box.

II. Run-time approach for mapping

A. Hitmap run-time mapping framework

In a previous work [5] we proposed a programming approach and framework based on: (1) Several layers of plug-in modules that encapsulate mapping functions; and (2) functionalities to build the coordination (synchronization and communication) structures of an algorithms, which are transparently adapted at run-time in terms of the results of the mapping functions. The approach was incorporated into Hitmap [8], [9], a parallel programming library where partition policies are implemented through a set of plug-ins with a common interface.

Figure 1 shows the original mapping and coordination layers (white boxes). There are two levels of partition. The first one is designed to encapsulate coarse-grain mapping techniques, appropriate for distributed-memory nodes. At this level logical processes are assigned to processing nodes, or accelerator devices. Coordination patterns are built with high-level point-to-point, or collective communications, using the results automatically generated at run-time by the partition strategies. Thus, if partition or distributed topology details change, the communication structure will reflect the changes automatically.

Given the computation part in a logical process, assigned to a target device, the second mapping level allows to compute a proper middle-grain blocking partition. The mapping plug-ins at this level encapsulate heterogeneous policies to generate appropriate tiling sizes for CPU cores, thread-block geometry for GPU devices, etc. The coordination, data movement between the CPU and accelerators, and kernel launch, is automatized by a run-time system, using the second-level partition results.

The programmer naturally introduces a third level of mapping inside the kernel code by implementing specific, thread-level memory access patterns.

B. Integration approach

In the previous mapping approach, the computation partitioning is done top-down. The whole computation is first split and coordinated among logical processes in a distributed-memory environment. Load balancing techniques can be used at this level to adapt the amount of computation of each part to the computation power and characteristics of each device assigned to a process.

As we mentioned in the previous section, although device memory restrictions can be considered at this level in the partition policies, these policies would become much more complicated. For huge computations, they will lead to the creation of a higher number of logical processes, with the associated penalties for coordination and communication.

Our solution is to keep using simple partition policies at the highest level, that do not take into account the memory restrictions of heterogeneous accelerator devices attached to the system nodes. Then, we introduce a hidden abstraction layer that splits the computation in several parts which memory requirements fit the device limits. This layer is applied after determining the appropriate tile or block geometry (see the dark shaded box in Fig. 1). To keep the optimizations obtained by the tiling/blocking techniques of the upper layer, this new internal partition uses as basic mapping elements the tiles or blocks. Sections of the grid of tiles/blocks are going to be sequentially launched to the device as separate kernels.

In general, due to communication costs between the main node and the device memories, the partition of a computation should be minimal. Besides this, when launching a subpart of a computation, the exact pieces of data structures accessed by each part are determined by the application algorithm, and the design details of the parallel solution. In our approach, we introduce a simple abstraction to help the programmer express the access patterns of the threads to any data structure involved. Thus, the system can automatically derive expressions to compute at run-time the exact memory requirements, and the exact locations of data pieces needed for a given computation subpart (a section of the tiles/blocks grid).

III. Model for parallel computations and accesses patterns

A. Polyhedral domain spaces

We define a *domain* D as a collection of n-tuples of integer numbers that define a space of n-dimensional indexes. For dense arrays, the index domain is a subspace of Z^n, defined by a rectangular parallelotope. In this work we also allow *strided* domains, where the parallelotopes are defined by its dimensional limits, and a stride value for each dimension. A *Signature* is a 3-tuple of integer numbers $S = (b, e, s) : b, e, s \in \mathbb{Z}$ representing a subset of integer numbers where the begin or lower limit is b, the end or upper limit is e, and the elements are selected using the stride value s. We denote this subset of integer numbers as the *range* of the signature $\breve{S}$.

$$S = (b, e, s);\ \breve{S} = \{x \in \mathbb{Z} : x \geq b,\ x \leq e,\ (x - b) \mod s = 0\}$$
$$D < S_0, \ldots, S_n >= \{(p_0, \ldots, p_n) : p_i \in \breve{S}_i\}$$

Domains are used in this work to represent the index space of a data structure, a set of indexed threads, the geometry of a tile/block of threads, a grid of tiles/blocks, or a superblock geometry (a subdomain of a grid of tiles/blocks).

B. Parallel computations

A data structure or tile T is a map between elements of a domain and data elements of a given type: $T : D \to dataType$. We denote with $d(T)$ the Domain of a tile.

We define a *Parallel Computation* $P < D, f, T_0, \ldots, T_m >$ as a collection of threads manipulating data in one or more data structures or tiles $T_0, \ldots, T_m$. The domain of the computation D defines the number and indexes of the threads to be executed. The computation is the application of the function f (or collection of statements) by each thread on data elements. A *Polyhedral Computation* is a parallel computation where its domain D can be expressed as a parallelotope, and where the function f uses affine expressions on the thread indexes to locate and access data elements in any data structure T_i.

C. Access patterns

An *Access Pattern* AP is a set of access expressions. An *Access Expression* represents a domain transformation $A : D, \mathbb{Z}^n \rightarrow D$. It is a tuple of n *Signature Functions* $A = (A_0, \ldots, A_n)$. Each signature function maps a signature, and one domain element, to another signature: $A_i : S, \mathbb{Z}^n \rightarrow S$.

Affine Access Expressions are those whose signature functions determine the resulting signatures using affine expressions in terms of the input domain element $\vec{x} \in D$, to compute the begin and end elements of the new signature and the resulting stride is proportional to the original one.

$$A_i < \vec{a}_b, b_b, \vec{a}_e, b_e, c > (S, \vec{x}) = (b', e', s') : \\ b' = \vec{a}_b \cdot \vec{x} + b_b, \\ e' = \vec{a}_e \cdot \vec{x} + b_e, \\ s' = c \times s$$

In some real parallel computations one dimension of a data structure is fully traversed by any thread. We model this special behavior using infinity values in the signature function to refer to the limits of the input signature. If $b_b = -\infty$, then $b' = b$. If $b_e = \infty$, then $e' = e$.

D. Union of domains

The union of generic domains expressed by signatures, cannot always be expressed themselves by signatures. As an example, consider the situation where there is a gap between their extremes, such in $S = (2, 100, 2), S' = (250, 300, 2)$, or when the strides are not compatible, such in $S = (2, 100, 2), S' = (2, 100, 3)$.

We define the *Signature coarse union* operator $\sqcup$ as: $S \sqcup S' = (b'', e'', s'') : b'' = \min(b, b'), e'' = \max(e, e'), s'' =$ m.c.d.(s, s'). We can also extent the operator definition to n-dimensional domains. The *Domain coarse union* of two domains is calculated applying the signature coarse operator to each pair of signatures with the same index: $D \sqcup D' = (S_0 \sqcup S'_0, \ldots, S_n \sqcup S'_n)$. The application of this operator to merge two strided parallelotope domains generates another strided parallelotope that can be expressed with signatures, with minimal number of extra added elements.

E. Domain transformations

We define a *Domain transformation* $\Gamma : D, AP, D \rightarrow D$ as the coarse union of the domains obtained applying each access pattern to each element of the second domain, using as reference the first domain, or data-structure domain.

$$\Gamma(D, AP, D') = \sqcup\{A(D, \vec{x})\} \ \forall \vec{x} \in D' \wedge \forall A \in AP$$

We call *Regular access expressions* to those that for two given input domain elements $\vec{x}, \vec{y}$, the signatures $A_i(D, \vec{x}) = (b, e, s)$ are a translation of the signatures $A_i(D, \vec{y}) = (b', e', s')$ such that $\forall i$: (1) $b' = b, e' = e, s' = s$, or (2) $b' = b + (y_i - x_i), e' = e + (y_i - x_i), s' = s$. A *Regular access pattern* is a pattern with only regular access expressions. Memory requirements of regular access patterns grow linearly when the threads space grows in only one dimension.

IV. Partition of Regular Computations for Heterogeneous Devices with Memory Limitations

This section presents a general algorithm that, given a polyhedral parallel computation with regular access patterns, determines how to split in regular parts the grid of tiles/blocks of threads, in such a way that the number of parts is minimal, and the memory requirements of each part does not exceed an arbitrary memory limit. To introduce the basic concept we present first the special case for 1-dimensional domains. Then, we present the solution for 2-dimensional domains. Algorithms for higher dimensions can be deduced from these ones.

To simplify the presentation, in the following algorithms we assume that the thread index space has stride 1, and starts at 1, for all dimensions. It is straightforward to extend the algorithm to use generic thread index domains with any stride or starting positions.

A. Inputs/Outputs

The algorithms have the following parameters:

Input: The device memory limit $devLim \in \mathbb{N}$.
Input: The dimensional sizes of the grid of tiles/blocks $\vec{g} \in \mathbb{N}^n$.
Input: The dimensional sizes of the tile/block $\vec{b} \in \mathbb{N}^n$.
Input: A collection of data structures or tiles $T_0, \ldots, T_m$.
Input: A collection of access patterns, one for each tile $AP_0, \ldots AP_m$.
Output: The number of blocks in each dimension that will form a subpart $\vec{r} \in \mathbb{N}^n$.

B. Algorithm for 1-dimensional spaces

The algorithm is based on determining the linear increasing rate of memory requirements when more blocks are grouped together, and represent it with a line equation. Substituting the device memory limit into the equation, we can obtain the higher number of blocks which memory requirements fits in the available space.

1. $B_1 = ((1, b, 1)), B_2 = ((1, 2 \times b, 1))$
2. $s_1 = \sum_i |\Gamma(d(T_i), AP_i, B_1)|$, $s_2 = \sum_i |\Gamma(d(T_i), AP_i, B_2)|$
3. Compute $\alpha, \beta, \gamma : 0 = \alpha x + \beta y + \gamma$ is the line equation that contains both $(1, s_1)$ and $(2, s_2)$.
4. Return $r = \lfloor -(\beta \cdot devLim + \gamma)/\alpha \rfloor$

C. Algorithm for 2-dimensional spaces and beyond

For two dimensional spaces we obtain a plane equation for the memory requirements of three samples of block groups. Substituting the device memory limit into the equation, we obtain a line equation. The points of this equation determine

Vector addition

1. $\forall i \in d(\vec{z})$
1.1. $z_i = x_i + y_i$
2. Return $\vec{z}$

Cellular automata

1. for i=1...t
1.1. $A' = A$
1.2. $\forall (i,j) \in d(A)$
1.2.1. $A(i,j) = (A'(i-1,j) + A'(i+1,j) + A'(i,j-1) + A'(i,j+1))/4$
2. Return A

Matrix-matrix multiplication

1. $C = 0$
1. $\forall (i,j) \in d(C)$
1.1. $\forall\ k \in [0, m-1]$
1.1.1. $C(i,j) = C(i,j) + A(i,k) \times B(k,i)$
2. Return C

Fig. 2. Algorithms for the three study cases.

the best candidates for the solution. These candidates are checked to determine which one leads to less number of parts due to better alignment of multiples of the new superblock sizes with the grid dimensions.

1. $B_1 = ((1,b_0,1),(1,b_1,1)), B_2 = ((1,b_0,1),(1,2\times b_1,1)), B_3 = ((1,2\times b_0,1),(1,b_1,1))$
2. $s_1 = \sum_i |\Gamma(d(T_i), AP_i, B_1)|$,
$s_2 = \sum_i |\Gamma(d(T_i), AP_i, B_2)|$,
$s_3 = \sum_i |\Gamma(d(T_i), AP_i, B_3)|$,
3. Compute $\alpha, \beta, \gamma, \delta : 0 = \alpha x + \beta y + \gamma z + \delta$ is the plane equation that contains $(1,1,s_1)$, $(1,2,s_2)$, and $(2,1,s_3)$.
4. Substitute $z = devLim$ to obtain a line equation $0 = \alpha x + \beta y + \delta'$.
5. $\forall\ \vec{r} = (r_0, r_1) : r_0 = \lfloor q_0 \rfloor, r_1 = \lfloor q_1 \rfloor : 0 = \alpha q_0 + \beta q_1 + \delta'$
5.1. Compute $k(\vec{r}) = \lceil g_0/r_0 \rceil \times \lceil g_1/r_1 \rceil$
6. Return $\vec{r}$ with the minimum value of $k(\vec{r})$.

D. Study cases

In this section we present some examples of regular kernels and applications to show how our model can be used to express different access patterns. The base algorithms for the study cases are presented in Fig. 2.

1) Vector addition: This simple kernel computes $\vec{z} = \vec{y} + \vec{x}$ using one thread to compute the result of each z_i element. It uses a 1-dimensional thread space of as many threads as elements in the arrays. The access pattern for this kernel have a single access expression:

$$A_0 < 1, 0, 1, 0, 1 >$$

Thus, the resulting signature

$$S' = A_0(S, \vec{x}) = (1 \times x_0 + 0, 1 \times x_0 + 0, 1) = (x_0, x_0, 1)$$

contains only one point in its range $\breve{S}' = \vec{x}$.

2) Stencil program: Cellular automata: This is an example of an stencil application in a two dimensional array space. It implements a PDE solver to compute the heat distribution is a 2-dimensional discretized space using the Jacobi method. The application has a step loop that applies a stencil computation, computing the new value of a matrix position using the old values of its four neighbors. There is only one input/output parameter, a matrix A.

The thread domain is the same as the matrix index domain. Each thread compute one matrix position. All threads synchronize on each i loop step.

The access pattern for this kernel can be expressed with one access expression for each matrix access, or in a compact form with only one expression:

$$A = (A_0 < 1, -1, 1, 1, 1 >, A_1 < 1, -1, 1, 1, 1 >)$$

Thus, the resulting signatures are

$$S'_0 = A_0(S_0, \vec{x}) = (x_0 - 1, x_0 + 1, 1)$$
$$S'_1 = A_1(S_1, \vec{x}) = (x_1 - 1, x_1 + 1, 1)$$

This compact form directly includes in the access pattern result the four *corner* elements that are not really accessed. However, the resulting domain is a parallelotope. When the pattern is applied to a subset of the thread index space, the amount of added data is negligible, and the parallelotope shape conveniently simplifies the movement of data between node and device memories.

Note that, for threads in the limits of the thread domain, the resulting accessed pattern exceeds the limits of the original matrix. To avoid the use of costly conditional evaluations in the fine-grain threads, the A matrix should be extended with *ghost borders*, or the thread index space should be reduced by one element on each border.

3) Matrix multiplication: In all the previous examples the resulting domains do not need to take into account the domain description of the data structures. Thus, the input signatures on the access expressions are simply ignored.

This study case is a direct implementation of the classical matrix-matrix multiplication $C_{n,n} = A_{n,m} \times B_{m.n}$, with three loops. It implements a fine-grain parallelization of the first two loops. Each thread executes the third loop to compute one position of the resulting matrix.

There are three different access patterns for this application, one for each matrix. Each pattern has a single access expression:

For matrix A: $(A_0 < 0, -\infty, 0, +\infty, 1 >, A_1 < 1, 0, 1, 0, 1 >)$
For matrix B: $(A_0 < 1, 0, 1, 0, 1 >, A_1 < 0, -\infty, 0, +\infty, 1 >)$
For matrix C: $(A_0 < 1, 0, 1, 0, 1 >, A_1 < 1, 0, 1, 0, 1 >)$

This access patterns indicate that each thread accesses to a full row of the A matrix, a full column of the B matrix, and one element of the C matrix, with the same indexes as the thread.

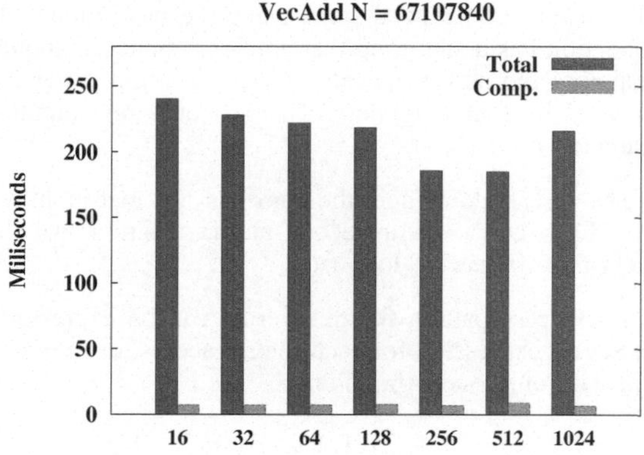

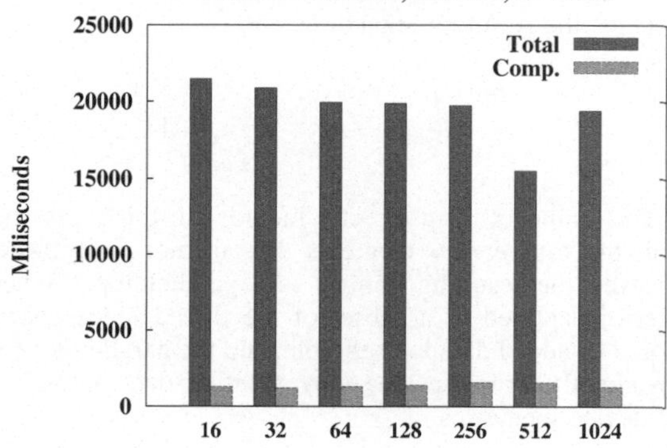

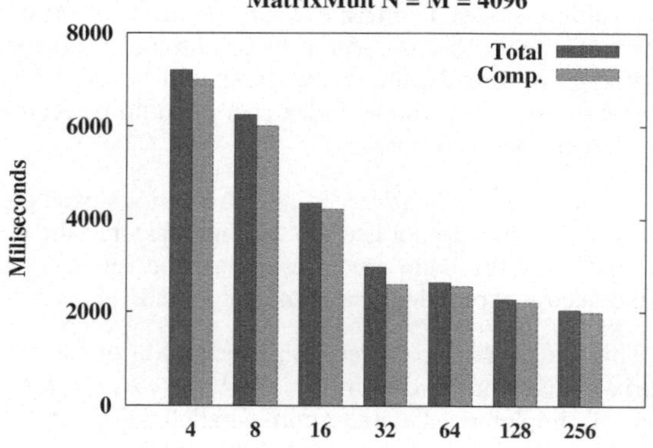

Vector Addition

Memory limit MBs	1	2	4	8	16	32	64	128	256	512	1024
#Kernels	.	.	.	.	49	25	13	7	3	2	1
Kernel size	.	.	.	.	16	32	64	128	256	512	767

Cellular Automata

Memory limit MBs	1	2	4	8	16	32	64	128	256	512	1024
#Kernels	.	.	.	.	48	24	13	7	4	2	1
Kernel size	.	.	.	.	11	21	43	85	170	241	512

MM Multiplication

Memory limit MBs	1	2	4	8	16	32	64	128	256	512	1024
#Kernels	.	.	1103	433	128	43	19	9	1	.	.
Kernel size	.	.	0.4	1.2	4	12	28	60	192	.	.

Fig. 3. Execution times for: (a) Vector addition; (c) Stencil computation; (d) Matrix-matrix multiplication. The tics in the x-axis indicate the value of the memory-size-limit parameter. The table shows for each program and each memory-size-limit value, the number of sub-kernels generated by our system for this case, and the memory size actually used.

V. Experimental study

We have developed a prototype implementation of the algorithms presented in Sect. IV. The implementation uses Hitmap, a library for automatic partition and mapping of parallel applications using hierarchical tiling arrays, that was briefly described in Sect. II. Our prototype layer implements the automatic computation of the best partition, the transparent movement of the required portions of the data structures to/from the target device memory, and the sequential execution of each part as a different kernel. The hidden layer is integrated in a new kernel launching function, that receives one access pattern specification along with each tile parameter.

We have implemented the three study cases presented above using the new tools. The codes are similar to the original ones, with expressions of the access patterns for each data structure involved in the computation. We have tested the prototype with a GPU target device, manually changing the memory-size-limit parameter to simulate different scenarios.

Our experimental platform is a GForce GTX 680 (Kepler, 2048 MB GDDR5) NVIDIA GPU device. The host machine is a 64-bits Intel(R) Core(TM) i7 CPU 960 3.20GHz, with a global memory of 6 GB DDR3. It runs an UBUNTU desktop 10.10 (64 bits) operating system. The applications have been developed using CUDA 4.2 toolkit and the 295.41 64-bit driver.

The use of integer or float data element lead to practically the same execution time in CUDA. Thus, we select integer as data type. The data structures size chosen for each benchmarks are different, in order to obtain stable execution time values. The number of items are the following: (1) Vector addition: $n = 67\,107\,840$; (2) cellular automata: $n = m = 8\,192$, and (3) matrix multiplication $n = m = 4\,096$. These sizes are multiple of the selected threadBlock size to avoid any padding operation.

To simulate results for different kinds of devices, we decided to manually change the memory-size-limit parameter. We have selected values that are powers of two in the range of 1 to 1024 Mbytes. For each kernel there is a different range of this parameter that leads to a feasible number of sub-kernels with a reasonable kernel size. Figure 3 shows the execution times (in milliseconds) obtained for some memory-size-limit parameter values. The first bar indicates the total execution time, while the second bar indicates the time devoted to real computation. The rest of the time is spent in node-device communications.

The results show that, as expected, for the kernels with low computational load per thread (vector addition and cellular automata), the ratio of communication vs. computation is very high, being very small in the remaining cases. When communication times dominate the total execution time, we observe a trend to reduced communication times for particular memory restrictions. This effect can be explained by the fact that the PCI Express bus works faster for memory transactions of particular sizes. Thus, when the subkernels generated require memory sizes that fit well in the PCI bus, the communication times are reduced. This information can be exploited by a library to split the communication in proper block sizes [10].

For the unidimensional example, vector addition, we can

see that the algorithm generates kernels that fit the memory limit almost perfectly. However, this is not the case for 2-dimensional problems. In the current implementation, the stage 5 of the 2-dimensional algorithm has not been yet implemented, leading to suboptimal partition results. However, the performance results show the same trends when manually selecting the best candidate.

The intensive reutilization of caches by the concurrent dot products in matrix multiplication application, leads to reduced total execution times when the kernels have bigger sizes.

The results show that the hidden layer does not impose a substantial overhead on the execution of the whole computation, and it can take away the burden of considering memory-size restrictions from upper mapping layers. Moreover, a deeper research on the information provided by the access patterns may also leads to detect situations where the system can get profit of the artificial automatic partition of the kernels to improve performance results.

VI. Conclusions

In this paper we present a model of parallel computations that allows to build a transparent mapping layer that divides and executes a computation taking into account the memory restrictions of the assigned device. The model requires the programmer to specify the access patterns of the computation threads in a simple abstract form. This information is used at run-time to compute the pieces of data-structures required by a generic partition, and to determine the best partition that ensures that each subpart fits in the device memory.

We discuss an implementation of this concept into an automatic mapping tool that allows to apply high-level distributions in heterogeneous devices without the need to take into account the memory limitations of the target devices. Our experimental results show that feasibility of the solution proposed.

Future work includes a further study of the opportunities to deal with more irregular access patterns at run-time, adding to the model considerations about optimal kernel sizes, and analyzing memory transactions cost between node and target devices.

Acknowledgments

The authors would like to thank Prof. Murray Cole for many fruitful discussions. This research is partly supported by the Castilla-Leon Regional Government (VA172A12-2); Ministerio de Industria, Spain (CENIT OCEANLIDER); MICINN (Spain) and the European Union FEDER (Mogecopp project TIN2011-25639, CAPAP-H3 network TIN2010-12011-E, CAPAP-H4 network TIN2011-15734-E); and the HPC-EUROPA2 project (project number: 228398) with the support of the European Commission - Capacities Area - Research Infrastructures Initiative.

References

[1] C. de la Lama, P. Toharia, J. Bosque, and O. Robles, "Static multi-device load balancing for opencl," in *Parallel and Distributed Processing with Applications (ISPA), 2012 IEEE 10th International Symposium on*, july 2012, pp. 675 –682.

[2] A. Binotto, C. Pereira, and D. Fellner, "Towards dynamic reconfigurable load-balancing for hybrid desktop platforms," in *Parallel Distributed Processing, Workshops and Phd Forum (IPDPSW), 2010 IEEE International Symposium*, April 2010, pp. 1 –4.

[3] E. Burrows and M. Haveraaen, "A hardware independent parallel programming model," *Journal of Logic and Algebraic Programming*, vol. 78, pp. 519–538, 2009.

[4] J. Barnat, P. Bauch, L. Brim, and M. Ceska, "Employing multiple cuda devices to accelerate ltl model checking," in *Proc. ICPADS'2010*, dec. 2010, pp. 259 –266.

[5] Y. Torres, A. Gonzalez-Escribano, and D. Llanos, "Encapsulated synchronization and load-balance in heterogeneous programming," in *Euro-Par 2012 Parallel Processing*, ser. LNCS. Springer Berlin Heidelberg, 2012, vol. 7484, pp. 502–513.

[6] M. M. Baskaran, U. Bondhugula, S. Krishnamoorthy, J. Ramanujam, A. Rountev, and P. Sadayappan, "Automatic data movement and computation mapping for multi-level parallel architectures with explicitly managed memories," in *Proc. ACM PPoPP'08*. New York, NY, USA: ACM, 2008, pp. 1–10.

[7] A. Aji, J. Dinan, D. Buntinas, P. Balaji, W. chun Feng, K. Bisset, and R. Thakur, "Mpi-acc: An integrated and extensible approach to data movement in accelerator-based systems," in *Proc. HPCC-ICESS'2012*, june 2012, pp. 647 –654.

[8] C. de Blas Cartón, A. Gonzalez-Escribano, and D. R. Llanos, "Effortless and Efficient Distributed Data-Partitioning in Linear Algebra," in *Proc. HPCC'2011*. IEEE, Sep. 2010, pp. 89–97.

[9] J. Fresno, A. Gonzalez-Escribano, and D. R. Llanos, "Automatic Data Partitioning Applied to Multigrid PDE Solvers," in *PDP'2011*. IEEE, Feb. 2011, pp. 239–246.

[10] F. Song and J. Dongarra, "A scalable framework for heterogeneous gpu-based clusters," in *Proc. ACM SPAA'2012*. New York, NY, USA: ACM, 2012, pp. 91–100.

Optimizing Data Locality for Iterative Matrix Solvers on CUDA

Raymond Flagg, Jason Monk, Yifeng Zhu PhD., Bruce Segee PhD.
Department of Electrical and Computer Engineering, University of Maine, Orono, ME, USA

Abstract—*Solving systems of linear equations is an important problem that spans almost all fields of science and mathematics. When these systems grow in size, iterative methods are used to solve these problems. This paper looks at optimizing these methods for CUDA Architectures. It discusses a multi-threaded CPU implementation, a GPU implementation, and a data optimized GPU implementation. The optimized version uses an extra kernel to rearrange the problem data so that there are a minimal number of memory access and minimum thread divergence. The normal GPU implementation achieved a total speedup of 1.60X over the CPU version whereas the optimized version was able to achieve a total speedup of 1.78X. This paper demonstrates the importance of pre-organizing the data in iterative methods and its impact.*

Keywords: Block Jacobi, CUDA, Multi-GPU, Iterative Methods, GPGPU

1. Introduction

Systems of linear equations are ubiquitous in computer engineering, as well as throughout all of science. They are used to solve problems from linear circuits all the way to discretization of more complex problems such as Finite Element Methods. The fact that they are deeply imbedded in so much of the work done in these areas means that there has always been a scientific advantage in being able to solve these systems faster.

Generally these systems are solved through algorithms that are referred to as direct approaches. They are called direct approaches because they involve a series of steps that can be followed and, when completed, the matrix has been solved. These direct approaches generally have two drawbacks; they are inherently sequential and are often extremely slow for large numbers of variables. This is where indirect or iterative solvers take the stage. Iterative methods involve performing a step or series of steps over and over again. There is no direct way of knowing how many steps are required; instead they converge towards a solution. There are a variety of ways of telling if the solution is close to convergence, and therefore close to correct.

This paper focuses on the implementation of the Jacobi Algorithm, which is used mostly for simplicity. This modification to the algorithm should be easily adaptable to use a variety of iterative methods. This algorithm has been implemented for a single and multiple CPUs using C++ and the pthreads library. This implementation will serve as a baseline for the tests performed on a single GPU. The addition of GPU support will be a CUDA-based solver.

2. Related Work

The natural parallel nature of iterative linear solvers are generally very attractive to the GPGPU environment [1]. Iterative linear solvers have been implemented on GPUs for a variety of problems in several areas of science. Both CUDA and OpenGL implementations were tested by Amorim et al in 2009 [2]. CUDA based systems were successfully tested by Wang et al 2009 [3], Zhang et al 2009 [4], and Amador and Gomes 2009 [5] to mention a few examples. In most cases there was a noticeable benefit for iterative solvers running on the GPU.

Amorim et al 2009 performed a comparison of OpenGL and CUDA implementations with a single threaded SSE-enabled CPU baseline. The OpenGL code was implemented by writing a shader that would read the current iteration from one texture and write the next iteration into another. The CUDA implementation showed to be noticeably better than OpenGL, with a maximum speedup of 31x vs only 17x achieved through OpenGL. This was a good comparison of the two approaches however it was only tested on fairly small problems ($n < 10$). [2]

Wang et al 2009 performed some testing up to much larger sizes ($n < 4000$). This implementation was, however, a much less efficient implementation that was only able to reach speedups between 1.5x and 3x. It did show that to utilize the full potential of the GTX280 being tested (240 Processors) that the n must be greater than or equal to 512. The performance showed the most computational power at $n = 512$, decreasing slightly for $n > 512$. [3]

Zhang et al 2009 created an implementation that performed well and was tested on matrix sizes up to 10,000. This implementation had support for both single and double precision, which both performed significantly better than the CPU. The single precision had a peak speedup of 59x, while the double had a peak speedup of 19x. [4]

Amador and Gomes 2009 did a comparison of three different iterative solvers. They were the Jacobi Method, Gauss-Seidel (A Derivative of Jacobi), and Conjugate Gradient. Their results showed significantly greater speedup of Jacobi and Gauss-Seidel implementations. This suggested that Jacobi-based methods are significantly more parallelizable, and a better candidate for multi-GPU applications. [5]

Iterative methods have been implemented on a GPU cluster at least once before by Ali Cevahir 2010. [6] It was an implementation of a conjugate gradient method. It had 15x more processing power by using 2 GPUs/node rather than 2 CPUs/node. This method required a significant amount of preconditioning to the matrix.

3. Iterative Solvers

There are many types of iterative methods that are used commonly in solving large linear systems. Many of them are arguably better at producing solutions than the Jacobi Method. What the Jacobi Method lacks in convergence rate it makes up for in how parallelizable it is as well as the simplicity in implementing it.

3.1 Jacobi

For a brief explanation of the Jacobi Method let us examine the matrix equation below. Where A is a matrix of size n by n, b is a column vector of size n, and x is a column vector of unknowns of size n.

$$A * x = b \tag{1}$$

The simplest explanation of the Jacobi Method can be described by splitting the system into a series of rows. Each row can represent a single linear equation. The following would be a single equation representing row i, in a system of size n.

$$A_{i,0} * x_0 + A_{i,1} * x_1 + ... + A_{i,n} * x_n = b_i \tag{2}$$

The basis of the Jacobi Method is to solve the ith equation for the ith unknown for all i.

$$x_i = \frac{b_i - \sum_{j!=i} A_{i,j} * x_j}{A_{i,i}} \tag{3}$$

By inserting the current values of x into the right hand side of the above equation, the Jacobi method produces the next iteration for x. The equation below shows how x moves from one iteration to the next.

$$x_i^{k+1} = \frac{b_i - \sum_{j!=i} A_{i,j} * x_j^k}{A_{i,i}} \tag{4}$$

Now the benefit of the Jacobi Method is clear because each of the unknowns can be solved for completely independently within each iteration, making this a very parallelizable algorithm.

3.2 Block-based Jacobi

The Block Jacobi Algorithm takes this already parallel method and lends itself even more so to the CUDA architecture. The modification of the algorithm is a small one. It divides the matrix into blocks of unknowns and each block is iterated separately; the results are only communicated after several iterations have passed.

If the block algorithm was being applied with two groupings then each of the blocks B1 and B2 could be $[x_0, x_{n/2}]$ and $[x_{n/2+1}, x_n]$. Both B1 and B2 are iterated separately without updating any values outside their respective blocks; this is referred to as an inner iteration. Several inner iterations are completed before values outside a block are updated. When all of the values are updated this is referred to as an outer iteration.

The division of the unknowns cuts down on the communication bandwidth that is needed. It also allows for some computational optimization that is discussed in the Reorganization section.

4. Parallel Block Jacobi

This section describes how the version of the Block Jacobi Algorithm was implemented. First it describes the CPU version and how the block algorithm applies to multithreading. Then this section discusses the CUDA structuring and applications related to the architecture.

4.1 CPU Structure

To focus on the calculation of the solution the process is divided into three different stages. The program reads from input, then calculates the solution in parallel, and finally writes the output. Figure 1 shows this flow for three processing threads.

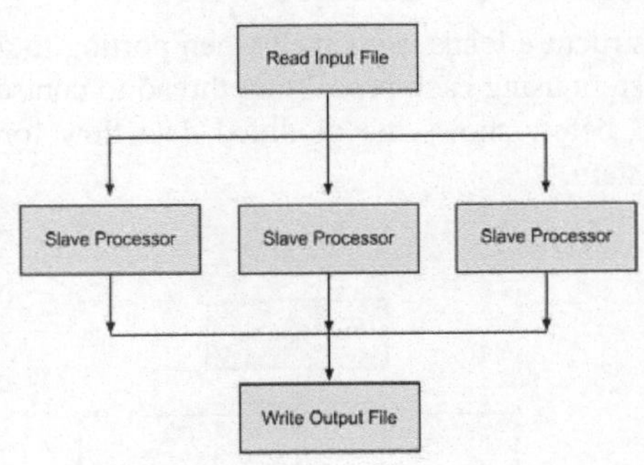

Fig. 1: Program Flow for 3 Threads

While in the processing stage there are a number of processing threads that handle inner iterations and a master thread that tracks convergence of the group. When an outer iteration occurs, each of the slave processors transmits updates to each of the other slave processors and sends information about its convergence state to the master thread. Figure 2 shows the flow between threads during an outer iteration.

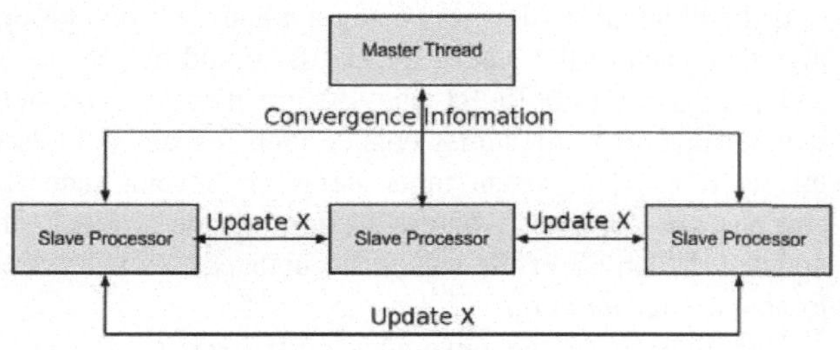

Fig. 2: Outer Iteration Communication

Given that on the CPU each of the threads controls a block, the size of the blocks being used in the algorithm can be controlled by the number of threads being used.

4.2 GPU Structure

The Block GPU Algorithm lends itself extremely well to the CUDA kernel structures. A CUDA Block can share memory and fits well to hold a single block of the Block Jacobi algorithm. This allows each CUDA thread to update the values of a single variable, unlike the CPU where each thread controls an entire Jacobi Block.

Each group of inner iterations is contained within a single kernel, and between each kernel an outer iteration is performed by doing a Device-to-Device memory copy.

4.3 Multi-GPU Structure

This structure lends itself well when porting to a multiple GPU system using each processing thread to control a GPU. Figure 3 below shows the modified data flow for a multi-GPU system.

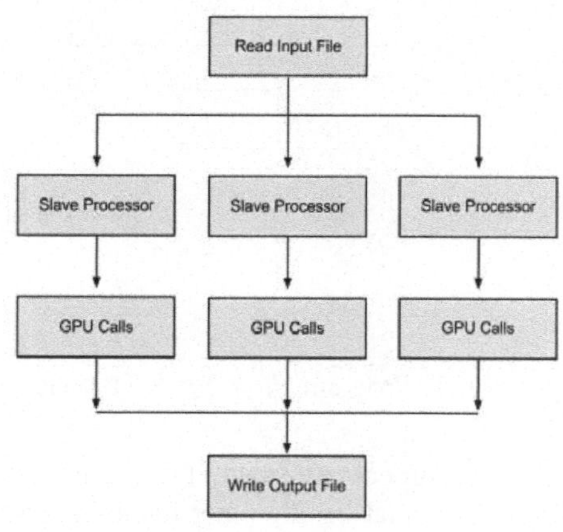

Fig. 3: Program Flow for 3 GPUs

The kernel requires little modification because inner iterations are isolated to occur on a single GPU. Outer iterations require that the updated X values are shared between each of the GPUs using a similar structure to the CPU Implementation.

4.4 Sparse Storage

A **sparse matrix** is a matrix that is composed mostly of zeros. These kinds of matrices are very common in some types of modeling (e.g., FEM). Figure 4 shows an example of a matrix generated by a 2-D FEM problem, where black pixels represent non-zero elements.

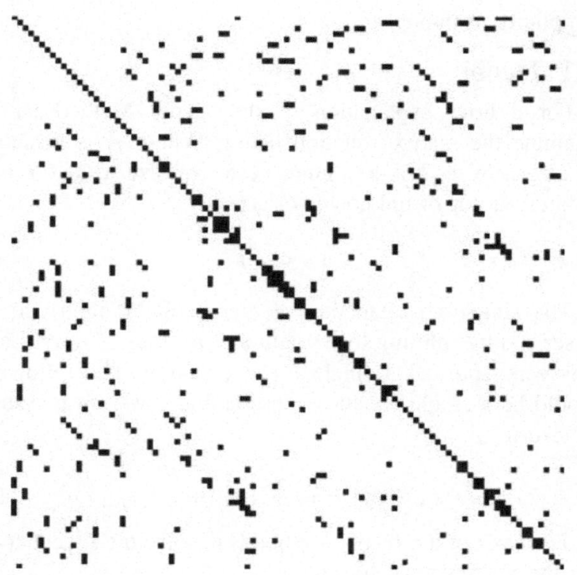

Fig. 4: Non-zero Elements in Sparse Matrix

When a matrix is composed mostly of zeros it becomes more efficient to only store the non-zero elements rather than the entire array in memory. The linear equations solver implements a simple form of sparse storage. Each row of the matrix is stored as a list of indices and a list of coefficients. A pair consisting of an index and a coefficient represent one value in the row and the index into the row where the value should reside.

4.5 Reorganization

To handle large systems the data passed to the GPU is sparsely stored to save space. Each CUDA thread loops across the summation shown in Equation 4. This is not a good structure for CUDA because for each time through the summation there are two categories it can fall into. A variable can be within the Jacobi block so the value must be pulled from an updated list in shared memory, or it can be outside of the Jacobi block meaning a static value should be pulled from global memory. Since CUDA has 32-thread groups operating in an SIMD nature, having divergent threads in each loop is bad for performance.

To make the code more optimized for CUDA, a second kernel was added. This second kernel was run once at the beginning of operation and would reorganize the data to remove conditional situation within the main loop. To do this the kernel takes the lists describing the coefficients in a specific equation and divides them into the groups for static coefficients (coefficients multiplied by values outside the Jacobi block) and dynamic coefficients (coefficients multiplied by values within the jacobi block). Figure 5 shows an example of this division, where static coefficients are indicated by an S. Global indices are represented by I and local indices (within a Jacobi block) are represented by L.

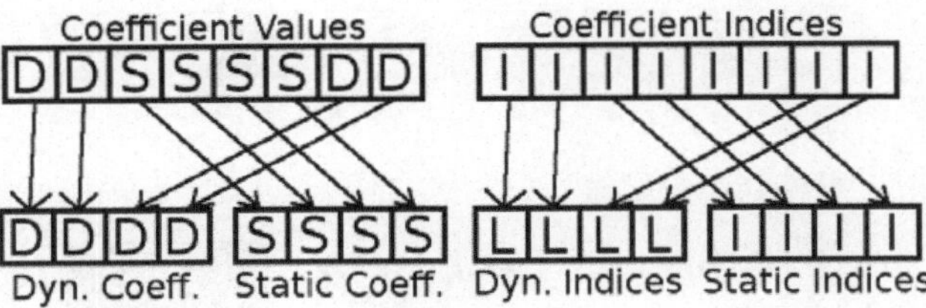

Fig. 5: Reorganization of Sparse Matrix Row

Figure 5 also shows that when storing the indices for the dynamic list the problem converts the indices from global indices to local indices. These lists are created for each of the threads. When stored in memory the array is transposed to ensure that each thread read happens within a single cache line to minimize memory accesses.

5. Performance Analysis

The code was tested on both a small and large linear system for analysis. The inputs were generated using Finite Element Models. The small test was generated with a simple 1-D heat flow finite element model with 100 nodes (unknowns). The larger test case is one generated using the University of Maine Ice Sheet Model, a 2-D problem with 168,861 nodes (unknowns).

5.1 Hardware Configuration

Having insufficient supporting hardware can be detrimental to performance of the GPU. The configuration used was built for GPU computing at the University of Maine. Table 1 shows an overview of the hardware for the machine.

Table 1: GPGPU Machine Configuration

CPU:	Intel Core i7 990X
GPU:	2 x NVIDIA GTX 580 1 x NVIDIA GTX 680
Memory:	24 GB DDR 1600
Motherboard:	ASUS Rampage III Extreme
Storage:	50 GB SSD 500 GB HDD

5.2 CPU Tests

The CPU implementation was tested on each of the inputs described above. The number of processing threads was varied from one to eleven. Figure 6 shows the runtime averaged over three runs for each of the numbers of threads for the smaller test data.

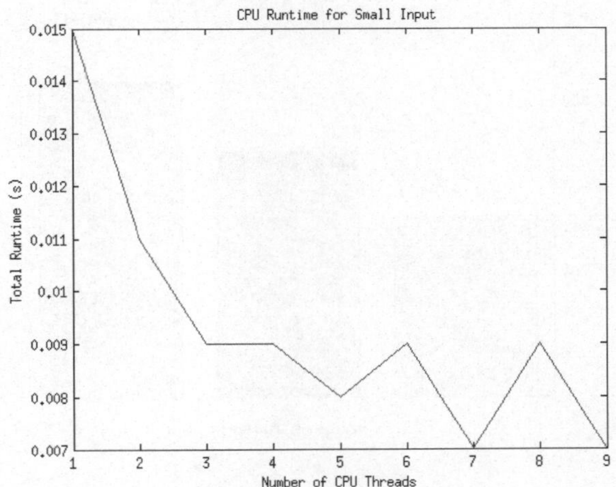

Fig. 6: CPU Runtime for Small Test Data

The results clearly show the total runtime starting to level off around six threads, the number of physical cores the processor being used for testing. Figure 7 below is the results for the same tests with the larger input set.

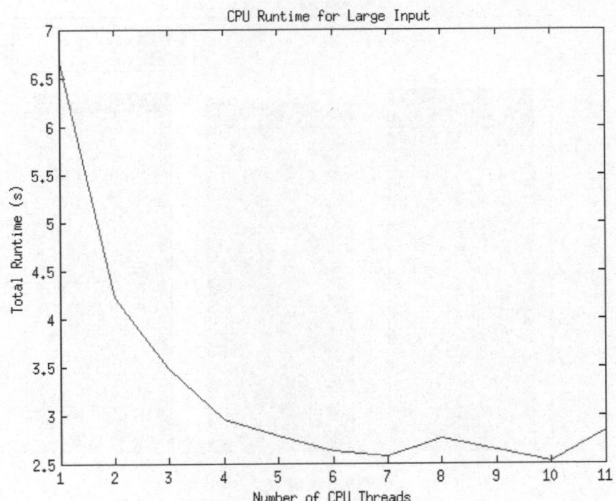

Fig. 7: CPU Runtime for Large Test Data

5.3 GPU Tests

The same data was tested on 1-3 GPUs. All single GPU tests use the NVIDIA GTX 680. All multi-GPU tests use one NVIDIA GTX 680 and all additional GPUs are NVIDIA

GTX 580s. Figure 8 shows the runtimes for these tests. It shows that the runtime increased as the GPUs were added. This was a fairly small test set (only 100 unknowns), so the lack of performance is expected.

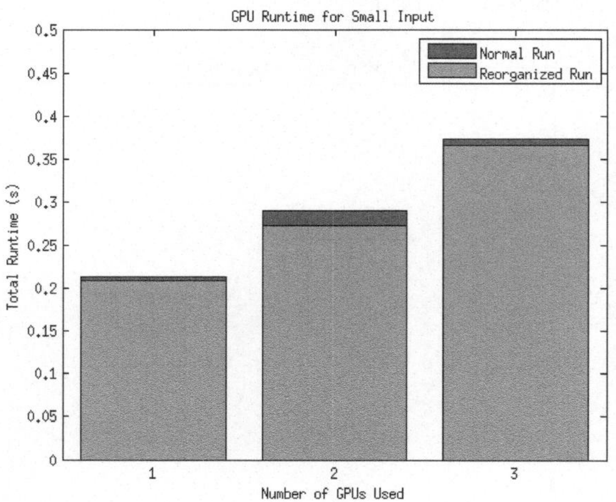

Fig. 8: GPU Runtime for Small Test Data

Figure 9 shows the GPU performance on the larger dataset. With the larger dataset there was a very slight decrease in runtime from one to two GPUs being used (not existent in the reorganized version).

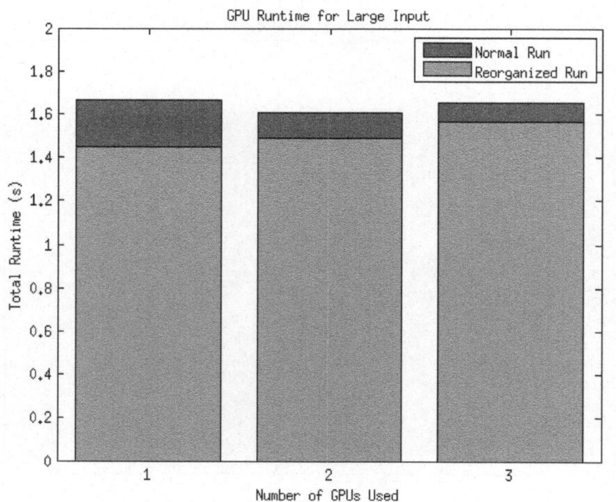

Fig. 9: GPU Runtime for Large Test Data

Table 2 shows the total speedup for the large dataset with one, two, and three GPUs for both normal and reorganized runs. For this dataset, two GPUs offered the best speedup, 1.60X.

Table 2: Table of Large Dataset Total Speedup

Number of GPUs	Normal Speedup	Reorganized Speedup
1	1.55X	1.78X
2	1.60X	1.73X
3	1.56X	1.65X

Given the lack of significant increase in performance from the addition of GPUs, the processing time (excluding setup and shutdown of program) was examined. Figures 10 and 11 show the processing time for each of the datasets.

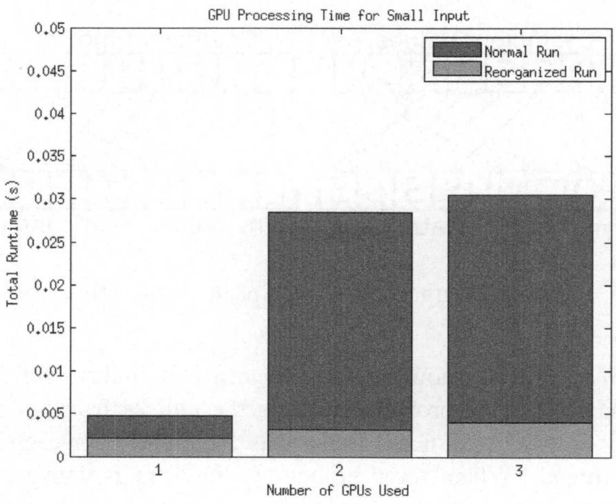

Fig. 10: GPU Processing Time for Small Test Data

The small dataset shows a noticable increase in processing time taken from adding GPUs. This indicates that the communication overhead of the GPUs is not worth the extra computational power given.

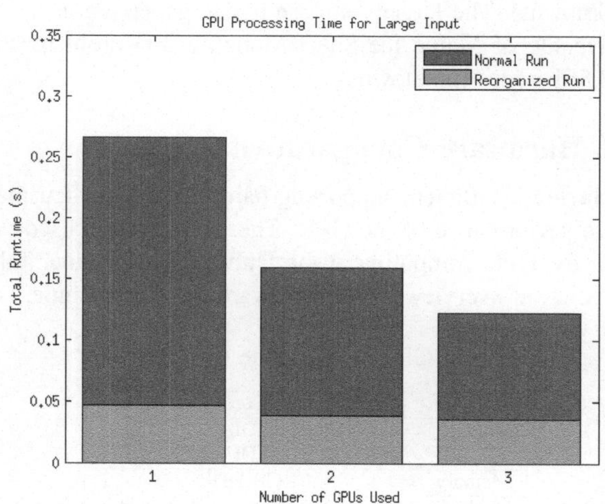

Fig. 11: GPU Processing Time for Large Test Data

Table 3 shows the processing speedup for the large dataset with one, two, and three GPUs for both normal and reorganized runs. For this dataset, one GPU offered the best speedup for the reorganized data, 6.72X, while two GPUs offered the best speedup for normal data, 3.86X.

Table 3: Table of Large Dataset Processing Speedup

Number of GPUs	Normal Speedup	Reorganized Speedup
1	3.30X	6.72X
2	3.86X	5.77X
3	3.82X	4.78X

The larger dataset shows much better results for adding GPUs. The processing time decreased for GPUs being added for both the normal and reorganized versions of the code. Analysis of the rest of the code showed that there was an increase in the setup time for the GPUs as more were added. This setup time was used to transfer the problem data to all of the GPUs. Figures 12 and 13 show the setup times for each of the tests.

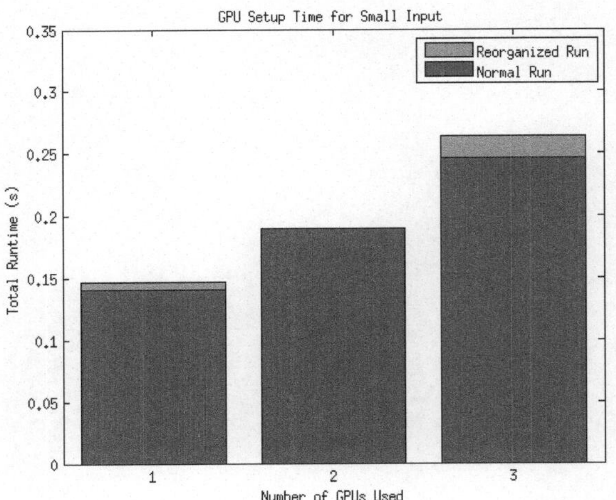

Fig. 12: GPU Setup Time for Small Test Data

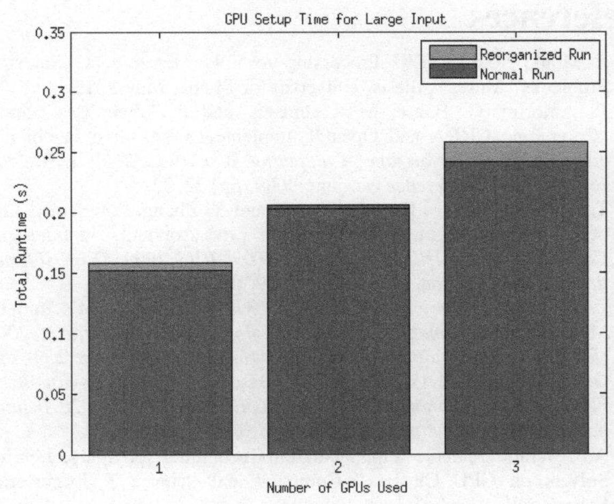

Fig. 13: GPU Setup Time for Large Test Data

The increase in setup time is nearly linear for both cases. This is easily explained by the limited bandwidth of the PCI-E bus. As the number of GPUs increases the amount of data that must be transferred increases almost linearly as each of the GPUs requires the full initial state of most of the values.

6. Conclusion

The Linear Equations Solver described in this paper had good results when ported to the GPU. Including the complete runtime, the GPU had a maximum speedup of 1.78X over the CPU. Looking at only the processing time, the GPU had a speedup of 6.72X over the CPU. The processing went 6.72X faster on a data set significantly larger than the related work described in Section 2. The reorganization of the data for CUDA had a significant impact on the runtime in all tests.

7. Acknowledgements

This work was partially funded by NFS grants EAR 1027809, OIA 0619430, DRL 0737583, CCF 0754951, EPS 0918018, EPS 0904155, and NIH grant R01 HL092926.

References

[1] J. Monk, "Using GPU Processing to Solve Large-Scale Scientific Problems," Master's thesis, University of Maine, May 2013.

[2] R. Amorim, G. Haase, M. Liebmann, and R. Weber dos Santos, "Comparing CUDA and OpenGL implementations for a Jacobi iteration," in *High Performance Computing Simulation, 2009. HPCS '09. International Conference on*, june 2009, pp. 22–32.

[3] T. Wang, Y. Yao, L. Han, D. Zhang, and Y. Zhang, "Implementation of Jacobi iterative method on graphics processor unit," in *Intelligent Computing and Intelligent Systems, 2009. ICIS 2009. IEEE International Conference on*, vol. 3, nov. 2009, pp. 324–327.

[4] Z. Zhang, Q. Miao, and Y. Wang, "CUDA-Based Jacobi's Iterative Method," in *Computer Science-Technology and Applications, 2009. IFCSTA '09. International Forum on*, vol. 1, dec. 2009, pp. 259–262.

[5] G. Amador and A. Gomes, "CUDA-Based Linear Solvers for Stable Fluids," in *Information Science and Applications (ICISA), 2010 International Conference on*, april 2010, pp. 1–8.

[6] A. Cevahir, "Scalable Implementation Techniques for Sparse Iterative Solvers on GPU Clusters," Computational Science & Engineering Laboratory.

DLML-IO: a library for processing large data volumes

Luis A. Pérez-Suárez[1], Miguel A. Castro-García[1], Graciela Román-Alonso[1], Manuel Aguilar-Cornejo[1] and Jorge Buenabad-Chávez[2]
[1]Depto. de Ing. Eléctrica, UAM-I, México, DF., A.P. 55-534 MÉXICO.
[2]Depto. de Computación, CINVESTAV-IPN, México, DF., A.P. 14-740 MÉXICO.
luis.lwr@gmail.com, {mcas,grac,mac}@xanum.uam.mx, jbuenabad@cs.cinvestav.mx

Abstract— *The analysis of large volumes of data is common nowadays and MapReduce applications are widely used for this task. The Data List Management Library (DLML) has some similarities with MapReduce in that it processes data lists in parallel and balances the workload dynamically and transparently to the programmer. Unlike MapReduce, DLML was initially designed to process data lists resident in main memory.*

This paper presents DLML-IO, a new design of DLML extended to process large volumes of data in files. The design of DLML-IO borrows from the design of MapReduce, particularly the partitioning of data in files for the purpose of IO to proceed in parallel in order to improve performance. We present experimental results comparing the performance of DLML-IO and MapReduce using four applications. DLML-IO performs better than MapReduce running two of those applications, but worse than MapReduce running the other two applications.

Keywords: Parallel Computing, MapReduce, Load Balancing, Message Passing

1. Introduction

Processing large data volumes is common in many areas including scientific analysis in nuclear physics, decision-making for designing new products, and simulations of large-scale visualizations [1], [2], [3]. A popular tool to process large amounts of data is MapReduce, a programming model and runtime environment developed by Google. Sorting data, data mining and machine learning are some of the tasks that Google carries out with MapReduce [4]. MapReduce has been widely adopted by the academia and enterprises in general. Hadoop [5] is a free open source version of MapReduce that can run on a private commodity cluster or in the Cloud, e.g., through Amazon web services [6]. Hadoop is currently a core part of the computing infrastructure of Yahoo, Facebook, LinkedIn, and Twitter.

MapReduce has been widely adopted for a number of reasons. It can be used to process both structured and unstructured data and is thus more flexible than database systems. It runs in parallel on clusters of commodity processors and network hardware. Yet the programming is sequential. It supports both fault tolerance and load balancing transparently to the programmer. A number of open free projects are currently enhancing the MapReduce applicability and its ease of use. For example, CGL-MapReduce [7] is a MapReduce implementation that uses streaming for all communications and it enables iterative MapReduce computations. In [8] a MapReduce implementation is described that uses MPI to exploit the high bandwidth to send intermediate data. Another MapReduce version described in [9] allows setting data access semantics to improve performance by reducing the number of phases in applications.

The Data List Management Library (DLML) processes data lists in parallel. DLML users only need to organise their data into items to *insert* into and *get* from a list using DLML functions; the programming looks sequential. DLML applications run under the Single Program Multiple Data (SPMD) model: all processors run the same program but operate on distinct data lists. When a list becomes empty, it is refilled (by DLML) through *stealing* data items from another list transparently to the programmer. Thus the workload gets balanced according to the processing capacity of each processor.

The first version of DLML was a design based on multi-process parallelism and message passing, with MPI. It runs an application process and a DLML process for each processing element (processor or core) running an application. The DLML process is in charge of making and serving data requests to/from remote nodes, using a global auction policy which is not scalable as it involves all compute nodes running an application. In [10], a design based on partial information was presented to improve the scalability of the auction policy. Multicore-DLML was presented in [11], a design aimed at improving intra-node parallelism in clusters of multicore nodes, performing twice as fast as DLML in such platforms. The hierarchical design of DLML reported in [12] was targeted at Grid environments. However, in all these DLML designs, data lists are restricted to be resident in main memory prior to being processed.

This paper presents DLML-IO, an extension to DLML that allows processing data in files, creating data items to process as such data is read into memory. This mechanism allows DLML to process large amounts of data much larger than the available memory. We compare DLML-IO to MapReduce (including programming models) using four applications. DLML-IO performs better than MapReduce running two of those applications, but worse than MapReduce running the other two applications.

The paper continues as follows. Section 2 presents MapReduce and a sample MapReduce application used in our experiments. Section 3 presents background material to the operation of DLML, the design of DLML-IO, and the same sample application coded for DLML-IO. Section 4 presents our experimental platform, applications and results on the performance of DLML-IO and of MapReduce. We conclude in Section 5.

2. MapReduce

MapReduce is a programming model and a runtime environment. A MapReduce application consists of one or more pairs of map-reduce functions. Each function is a sequential program that reads from its standard input, carries out some processing for each record it reads, and writes a result to the standard output. Map and reduce functions can be written in Java, Python and a few other languages.

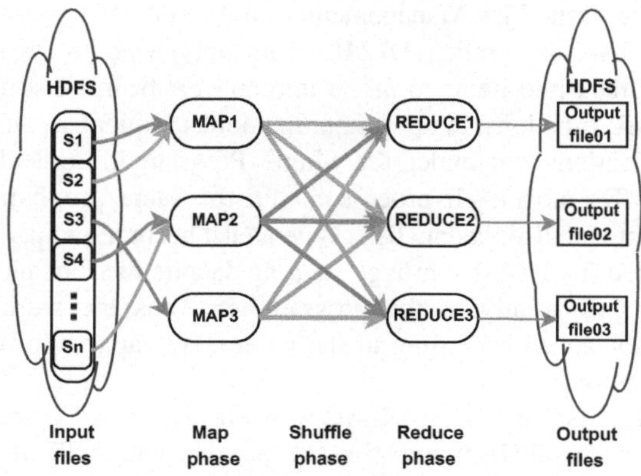

Fig. 1: MapReduce runtime environment.

2.1 MapReduce Environment

Figure 1 shows the MapReduce Hadoop runtime environment. It replicates and runs in parallel each map function and reduce function, in various nodes of a cluster. The number of copies of the map function is determined by the number of blocks in disks to be processed. The input data to the map phase reside in a parallel distributed file system, generally of the kind of HDFS (Hadoop Distributed File System). HDFS is fault tolerant (this feature is based on replicating data blocks in various distinct nodes) and allows to process in parallel distinct data by distinct copies of the map function (see Figure 1).

The reduce function also runs in parallel after all instances of the (pair) map function have finished. The user can specify how many instances of the reduce function should run (the reduce phase). Note the *shuffle* phase between the map phase and the reduce phase in the figure. This phase collects the data produced by all the replicas of a map function, partitions that data according to a user-specified key, and then passes one or more *entire* partitions as input to each of the replicas of the (pair) reduce function. That is, each instance of a reduce function receives all the data items with the same key. Note that the reduce phase writes to HDFS. In contrast, the shuffle phase uses local files in each node running the map function.

When a map phase is running, the MapReduce environment waits for all the map (function) replicas to finish. If one replica is late after a threshold, the environment launches another copy of the map function to run in a different process, possibly in a different node, and waits for either the new copy or the old copy to finish; whichever finishes first, the other one is discarded.

2.2 Matrix Addition in MapReduce

Suppose we have two matrices B and C of size 2×2 stored each in a different file. In each file, each record contains the values of a row but the first value corresponds to the row number, as shown in Figure 2.a. With this setting, Figure 2.b and Figure 2.c show a possible implementation of a *map* function and a *reduce* function to carry out the matrix addition $A = B + C$.

```
Row  Data



  0  1 2
  1  3 4

B: file1

  0  5 6
  1  7 8

C: file2
        a)
```

```
map( key, values ) {
  first_element = 0;
  column = 0;
  for each element in values {
    if ( first_element == 0 ) {
      row = element;
      first_element = 1;
    } else {
      key2 = new_key( row, column );
      EmitIntermediate(key2, element);
      column++;
    }
  } // end for
}
        b)
```

```
reduce( key2, List_of_values ) {
  sum = 0;
  for each element in List_of_values
    sum = sum + element;
  EmitIntermediate(key2, new_element);
}
        c)
```

Fig. 2: Example of matrix addition in MapReduce: (a) data layout in input matrix files B and C; (b) map function code; (c) reduce function code.

The map function receives two parameters: 1) the offset of a record, a row, within file B or C, and 2) the values in that row. The offset of each record is not shown in the figure and in our matrix addition is not used.

The purpose of the map function is to generate and emit, for each matrix element, a record consisting of the position of the element in a matrix and the value of the element. The position, generated by the function `new_key( row, column)`, is a string consisting of the row and column numbers separated by one space, .e.g.: "0 0" for the first element in the first row, in either file B or C.

The reduce function (Figure 2.c) receives two parameters (iteratively): a *key2* value (generated by the map function) and the list of values associated with the value of the key. As each copy of a reduce function receives all the values associated with a particular key value, the reduce function simply adds those values and emits both the position and final value of the corresponding element in the results matrix. The output of the reduce function is written onto HDFS.

3. DLML-IO

The Data List Management Library (DLML) processes data lists in parallel. DLML users only need to organise their data into items to *insert* and *get* from a list using DLML functions `DLML_get()` and `DLML_insert`. Internally, DLML uses one list for each processing element, and when a list becomes empty, DLML *refills* it through stealing data items from another list transparently to the programmer, thus balancing the workload according to the processing capacity of each processor. Only when `DLML_get()` does not return a data item the processing in all nodes is over. DLML functions hide synchronization communication from users, while automatic list refilling tends to balance the workload, which is essential for good performance. DLML is written in C and uses MPI.

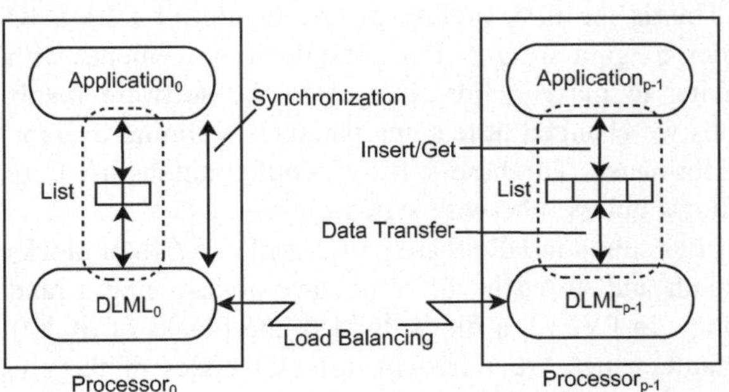

Fig. 3: DLML Architecture.

3.1 DLML Environment

Figure 3 shows the architecture of DLML. An application process and a DLML process are run for each processor or for each core within a multicore node. The application process runs the application code: inserting, getting and processing data items from its list. When an application process finds its list empty, it sends a message to its sibling DLML process indicating it to request data items from remote nodes; the application process then locks waiting for a message from its sibling DLML process. The response message will indicate either the number of (new) data items to be received or to terminate execution because no data was found in remote nodes. DLML processes also serve data requests from remote nodes whose lists have become empty, if possible. DLML was first designed to use data lists resident entirely in main memory.

3.2 DLML-IO Design

DLML-IO is an extension to DLML for the purpose of processing large amounts of data in files. The main extensions added to DLML are the following functions:

- *DLML_distributeOffsets*: partitions the input files to be processed into logical data segments, and informs each DLML application process as to the data segment(s) it will process.
- *DLML_Load*: receives the data segments to process, out of which creates data items to insert into the DLML list of the DLML application process that called *DLML_Load*. For that purpose, it receives information about the data layout in data segments and the *operation* to carry out with the data in order to create the data items accordingly. The operations currently supported are: "+", "*", and "w", each operator determines how data in one or two files are to be read and how to create the relevant data item. For example, with the operators "+" and "*", the data in input files are considered a matrix data, and for both options, a data item to create and insert into a DLML list will contain: 1) the position of the element in the results matrix to be computed, and 2) the values of the elements in the input matrices to use in the computation. For the "w" option, each element created from the file contains only the word (string) that was read. See Figure 4.

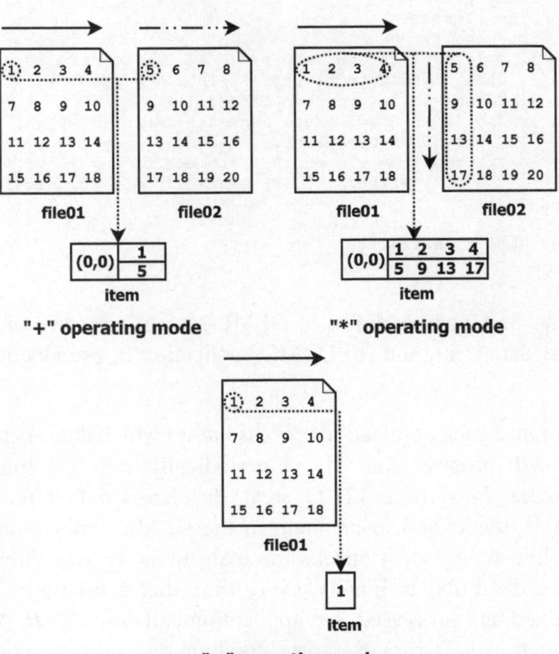

Fig. 4: Operations of function DLML_Load.

During the creation of data items, *DLML_Load* uses a threshold of free available main memory. If creating a new data item reduces main memory below that threshold, no more items are created and the processing of the items (already created and inserted) in the list of the relevant application process is started or continued. As data items are processed, memory is freed and more data items are created from data segments in files.

- *DLML_Write* allows the writing of partial results in files. This function takes as input parameters the file id to write in, the position (offset) where the write should take place (optional), and the result to write.

3.3 Matrix Addition in DLML-IO

Suppose we have the same input files for the matrix addition example in MapReduce (Figure 2.a). Their data will be loaded as data items into lists with the operator "+". Figure 5 shows the structure of each list item and the DLML application for matrix addition in pseudocode. First, each application process in each node initialises the DLML environment which involves creating the sibling DLML process (line 6). Then, only the application process with id 0 is responsible for executing the *DLML_distributeOffsets* function (line 9-10), in order for the input files to be logically partitioned among the application processes available.

```
1  typedef struct DLML_item item;
2  struct DLML_item{
3     int  a, b, position;
4     item *next;
5  };
             a)

6  DLML_Init();
7  item element;
8  int result;
9  if ( id_application == 0 )
10    DLML_distributeOffsets( "file01", "file02");
11  info_segments = receive_offsets();
12  while( DLML_Load( &info_segments, &List, "+") ){
13     while(DLML_Get(&List, &element)){
14        result = element.a + element.b;
15        DLML_Write( "file", element.position, result );
16     }
17  }
18  DLML_Finalize();

             b)
```

Fig. 5: Matrix addition in DLML-IO: (a) structure of each list data item, and (b) DLML application in pseudocode.

Once each application process knows which data segments it will process (line 11), it periodically calls the function *DLML_Load* (line 12) to create list items out of the data in segments and insert them in the DLML application list. While doing so, it checks the main memory size threshold described above. Finally, every time that a list item is obtained and processed, the application calls the *DLML_Write* function to write the corresponding result in its position (lines 13-16). Once no data is found in file segments nor in lists, the DLML environment finishes (line 18).

Note that the partitioning of data segments among DLML application processes remains fixed once it takes place, i.e.: each DLML application process will load in memory the data in segments assigned to it and will create the relevant list items. However, load balancing (through list refilling/work stealing as described earlier) remains dynamic throughout computation. This is possible in our implementation because, as shown in Figure 4, each list item contains all the values to compute an element in the results matrix.

4. Experimental Evaluation

This section presents our experimental platform, applications and results to compare the performance of DLML-IO and MapReduce. We first describe the hardware and software used with all our applications, then for each application we give a brief description of it and present the results.

Our hardware platform is a cluster with 5 nodes, where 1 acts as a server and the remaining 4 as slave nodes. The server node has an Intel Core2 Quad processor at 2.4 GHz, 4G RAM, and each slave node has 2 Intel Dual Core processors at 3GHz, 2GB RAM, all running CentOS 5.4. All nodes are connected through a Gigabit Ethernet switch.

For the MapReduce runs, we use Hadoop and HDFS v. 0.20.2. For the DLML-IO runs, we use the MPI library LAM/MPI v. 7.1.4., and PVFS2 [13]. PVFS2 is a parallel file system that partitions and stores files throughout the nodes in a cluster for parallel access.

This is the first, preliminary evaluation of DLML-IO in order to gain insight into possible improvements without having to make major changes to the software involved. Thus we changed little some parameters aiming to improve performance. The base software configurations used are as follows unless otherwise stated.

Files stored in HDFS are partitioned into 64MB blocks by default and stored in different slave nodes using a random policy. In PVFS2, a file is divided into blocks of 64 KB by default, which are stored in different nodes of the cluster using a round-robin policy [14].

Our applications are the WordCount (WC) typical application to describe the workings of MapReduce, a Matrix Addition (MA) algorithm, a Matrix Multiplication (MM) algorithm, and the Non-Attacking Queens (NAQs) [15].

4.1 Word Count

WC consists of counting the number of occurrences of each work in a collection of documents. It is the kind of application where MapReduce performs well.

WC for MapReduce uses a map function that prints 1 for each occurrence of a word, and a reduce function that, for each word, adds the number 1's and prints the sum (see Figure 6). In WC for DLML-IO, the use of the DLML_distributeOffsets and DLML_Load functions allows reading words from files and building a list item for each word until the memory threshold is reached or until no

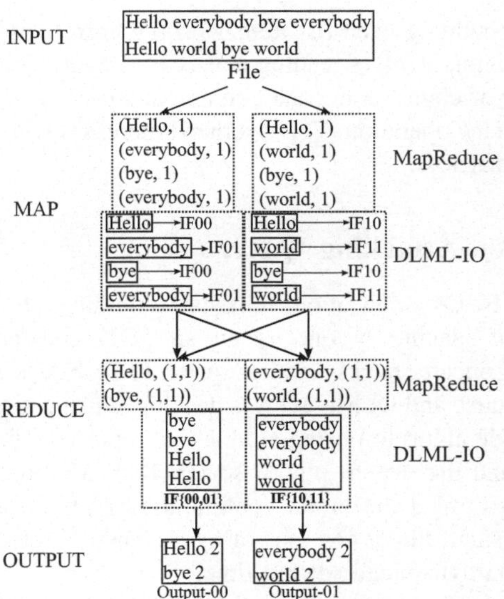

Fig. 6: WordCount flow for MapReduce and DLML-IO.

more words are found. Later, they get a list item and by using a hash function, the word is saved in an specific local intermediate file (*IF*). Note that each application manages a total amount of *IF* files equal to the total number of application process in the system. After all the words are stored, the files are transferred to the application process taking into account the last digit of file ID. As Figure 6 shows, the *IF* files with IDs 00 and 01 are transferred to the application process with ID 0, and the *IF* files with IDs 10 and 11 are transferred to the application process with ID 1. The process of creating the IF files and transferring for their processing corresponds to the shuffle of MapReduce as described in Section 2. Finally the counting of occurrences of each word is made with the UNIX commands: sort and uniq.

Our experiments process data files from Freebase [16]. Particularly we used files of size 300, 400, 500, 600 and 700 MB, which were grouped into folders. For MapReduce, we are showing results using two map processes and two reduce processes per node. (We also tried with one map process and one reduce process per node, and with 4 map processes and 4 reduce processes per node, but performance deteriorated — we think this was because the relatively small memory of the slave nodes, 2GB.) For DLML, we are showing results with four application processes and four DLML processes per node.

Figure 7 shows the response time of MapReduce and DLML-IO for WC, for different data volumes in GB (2 to 16 GB). DLML-IO with PVFS2 performs worse than MapReduce with HDFS. WC is an I/O intensive application, i.e., the cost of IO is relatively high compared to the cost of processing each of the data fetched from secondary storage to main memory. Therefore it is convenient to read into memory as much data as possible every time secondary storage is accessed. The larger disk block used by HDFS, 64MB, compared to that of PVFS2, 64KB, means a smaller number of accesses to disk by MapReduce than by DLML-IO, and hence better performance.

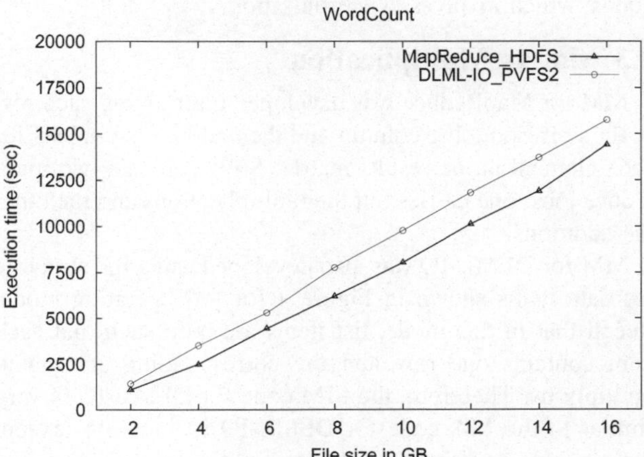

Fig. 7: WordCount response time.

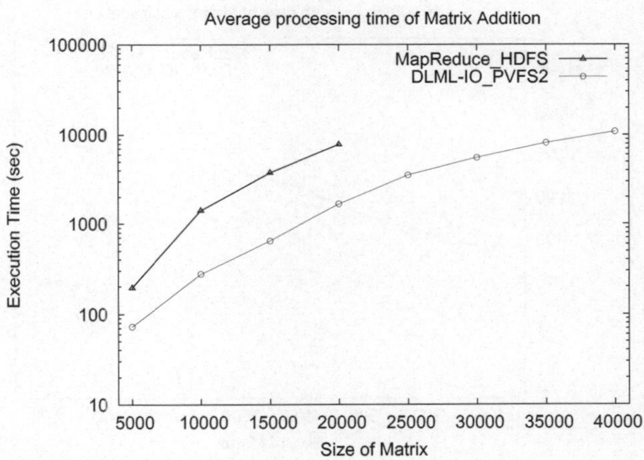

Fig. 8: Matrix Addition response time.

4.2 Matrix Addition

MA for MapReduce and DLML-IO was implemented as shown in Figures 2 and 5, respectively.

Figure 8 shows the response time of MapReduce and DLML-IO for MA for different sizes of matrices. DLML-IO performs much better than MapReduce consistently, generally over twice better. Note that the scale is logarithmic.

The main factor for DLML-IO to perform better than MapReduce with MA is that DLML-IO has no shuffle phase, and thus no local IO operations are incurred. As shown in Figure 5, MA for DLML-IO builds list items that contain all the information to compute the value of an element in the results matrix. Once the parallel phase begins, the processing of each item does not involve communication. In contrast, MapReduce does involve a shuffle phase and, in addition, MA for MapReduce partitions the data in both input matrices with the id row-column, and this means that reducers need to wait for the two values to add probably from different nodes, which involves synchronisation.

4.3 Matrix Multiplication

MM for MapReduce was developed multiplying each row × the corresponding column and then adding the values for each element in the results matrix. So we created two map-reduce jobs: one carries out the multiplications and the other the additions.

MM for DLML-IO was also developed using the structure for data items shown in Figure 4 for "*" operating mode. Recall that in this mode, list items are built such that each item contains one row and the corresponding column to multiply by. Therefore, the MM code for DLML-IO is very similar to the MA code for DLML-IO in Figure 5, except that the MM code involves the multiplication of the row and column and then the addition of the multiplication results, as opposed to only the addition of two values.

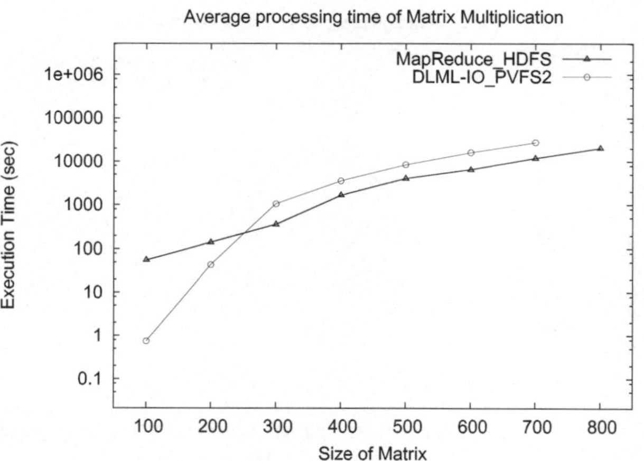

Fig. 9: Matrix Multiplication response time.

Figure 9 shows the response time of MapReduce and DLML-IO for MM for different sizes of matrices. DLML-IO performs better than MapReduce for the two smallest sizes of matrices, while MapReduce performs better than DLML-IO for all other runs.

As in MA, in MM there is no shuffle phase. Hence DLML-IO has in principle a performance advantage over MapReduce, which shows itself for the two smallest sizes of matrices. However, as the size of matrices increases, another factor comes into play which is that MM for DLML-IO incurs more accesses to disk in order to build the list items shown in Figure 4. Both input matrices, say A and B, are stored in disk by rows: a file record corresponds to a row. Hence, building each list item with the corresponding row and column, involves reading matrix B as many times as the number of elements in each column, and each *read* is made after a *seek* operation. This overhead increases with the size of the matrices.

4.4 Non-Attacking Queens

The NAQs application consists of finding all possible ways of placing N queens on an NxN chessboard, so that no queen attacks another queen [15]. NAQs for both MapReduce and DLML-IO was developed using a search on amplitude algorithm using a table that represents the chess-board and the queens placed so far. Both MapReduce and DLML-IO read the initial configuration of the chessboard from a small file, a few tens of bytes. Then NAQs generate new data dynamically at run time.

For MapReduce, we launched as many map phases (to compute the solutions) as the number queens-1. If a solution is found a map process emits a number 1 (much the same as in the WC problem); otherwise nothing is emitted. There is only one reduce process which adds all the 1's and prints the result.

For DLML-IO, we do not need to use the functions DLML_Load and DLML_distributteOffsets (unlike the other applications) because, as mentioned above, the bulk of the data processed by NAQs is dynamically generated at runtime. We only use DLML_Write function to write the final result.

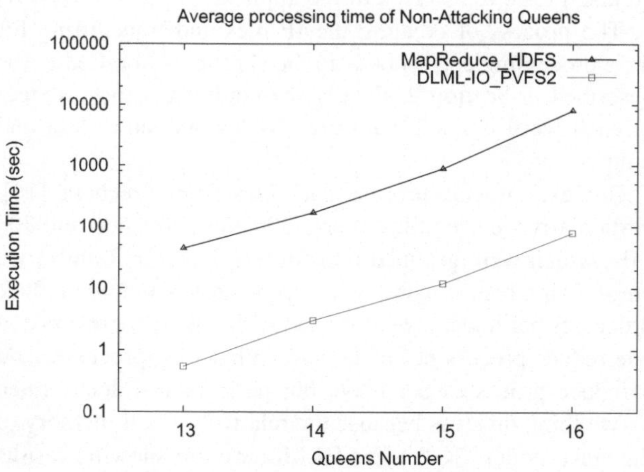

Fig. 10: Non-Attacking Queens response time.

Figure 10 shows the response time for various numbers of Non-Attacking Queens. DLML-IO with PVFS2 performs much better than MapReduce consistently. This is because of the cost of the shuffle phase of MapReduce, which involves local writes — even though there is only one reduce process. This overhead is not present in DLML-IO.

5. Conclusions and Future Work

We have presented DLML-IO, an extension to DLML that allows processing large volumes of data in files with typical list operations. Our extension was compared with MapReduce using static and dynamic applications, four in total. DLML-IO performs better than MapReduce for two applications, while MapReduce performs better for the other applications. Overall, our preliminary evaluation has let us understand better the issues in involved in processing in parallel large data sets stored in disk. We plan to extend DLML-IO with HDFS and improve it in various ways to make its use more intuitive.

Acknowledgment

Luis A. Pérez Suárez wishes to acknowledge the scholarship of CONACyT (Consejo Nacional de Ciencia y Tecnología) for his postgraduate studies.

References

[1] E. L. Lusk, S. C. Pieper, and R. M. Butler, "More scalability, less pain: A simple programming model and its implementation for extreme computing," *Scientific Discovery through Advanced Computing (SciDAC) Review*, vol. 17, pp. 30–37, 2009.

[2] J. F. Gantz, C. Chute, A. Manfrediz, S. Minton, D. Reinsel, W. Schlichting, and A. Toncheva, "The diverse and exploding digital universe," International Data Corporation, Tech. Rep., 2008.

[3] C. Mitchell, J. P. Ahrens, and J. Wang, "Visio: Enabling interactive visualization of ultra-scale, time series data via high-bandwidth distributed i/o systems," in *25th IEEE International Symposium on Parallel and Distributed Processing, IPDPS 2011*, Alaska, USA, 2011, pp. 68–79.

[4] J. Dean and S. Ghemawat, "MapReduce: Simplified data processing on large clusters," in *6th Symposium on Operating System Design and Implementation, OSDI 2004*, California, USA, 2004, pp. 137–150.

[5] "Hadoop," http://hadoop.apache.org, December 2011.

[6] "Amazon elastic compute cloud," http://aws.amazon.com/ec2, July 2012.

[7] J. Ekanayake, S. Pallickara, and G. Fox, "Mapreduce for data intensive scientific analyses," in *Fourth International Conference on e-Science, e-Science 2008*, Indiana, USA, 2008, pp. 277–284.

[8] Y.-F. Ho, S.-W. Chen, C.-Y. Chen, Y.-C. Hsu, and P. Liu, "A MapReduce Programming Framework Using Message Passing," in *International Computer Symposium, ICS 2010*, Tainan, Taiwan, 2010, pp. 883–888.

[9] S. Sehrish, G. Mackey, J. Wang, and J. Bent, "MRAP: A Novel MapReduce-based Framework to Support HPC Analytics Applications with Access Patterns," in *Proceedings of the 19th ACM International Symposium on High Performance Distributed Computing, HPDC 2010*, Illinois, USA, 2010, pp. 107–118.

[10] J. Santana-Santana, M. A. Castro-García, M. A. Cornejo, and G. Román-Alonso, "Load balancing algorithms with partial information management for the dlml library," in *Proceedings of the 18th Euromicro Conference on Parallel, Distributed and Network-based Processing, PDP 2010*, Pisa, Italy, 2010, pp. 64–68.

[11] J. Buenabad-Chávez, M. A. Castro-García, J. L. Quiroz-Fabián, E. F. Hernández-Ventura, G. Román-Alonso, D. M. Yellin, and M. Aguilar-Cornejo, "Reducing communication overhead under parallel list processing in multicore clusters," in *Electrical Engineering Computing Science and Automatic Control (CCE), 2011 8th International Conference on*, Yucatán, México, 2011, pp. 780–785.

[12] A. H. Hernández, G. Román-Alonso, M. A. Castro-García, M. Aguilar-Cornejo, S. Domínguez-Domínguez, and J. Buenabad-Chávez, "A software architecture for parallel list processing on grids," in *Parallel Processing and Applied Mathematics - 9th International Conference, PPAM 2011*, Torun, Poland, 2011, pp. 720–729.

[13] "Parallel virtual file system, version 2," http://www.pvfs.org, November 2012.

[14] W. Tantisiriroj, S. W. Son, S. Patil, S. Lang, G. Gibson, and R. B. Ross, "On the duality of data-intensive file system design: reconciling HDFS and PVFS," in *Conference on High Performance Computing Networking, Storage and Analysis, SC 2011*, Washington, USA, 2011, pp. 67–78.

[15] A. Bruen and R. Dixon, "The n-queens problem," *Discrete Mathematics*, vol. 12, pp. 393–395, 1975.

[16] "Freebase," http://download.freebase.com/wex/2012-07-14, November 2012.

Dynamic Scheduling Scheme for Linearly Extensible Multiprocessor Systems

A. Samad[1], M.Q. Rafiq SMIEEE[2], O. Farooq[3]
[1]University Women's Polytechnic, AMU, Aligarh, India
[2]Department of Computer Engineering, AMU, Aligarh, India
[3]Department of Electronics Engineering, AMU, Aligarh, India

Abstract— *The key advantage of massively parallel systems is to allow concurrent execution of workload characterized by computation units known as processes or tasks, which can be independent programs or partitioned modules of a single program. The scheduling problem is to maintain a balanced execution of all the tasks among the various available processors (nodes) in a multiprocessor network. In this paper a novel dynamic scheduling scheme named as Multi Round Scheduling (MRS) scheme has been proposed for scheduling the load on various multiprocessor interconnection networks. In particular, the performance of the proposed scheme is evaluated for linearly extensible multiprocessor systems, however, a comparison is also made with other standard existing multiprocessor systems. The MRS operates in multiple steps to make the network fully balanced with minimum overhead. The comparative simulation study shows that the proposed MRS scheme gives better performance in terms of task scheduling on various linearly extensible multiprocessor networks.*

Keywords: Dynamic Scheduling, Multiprocessor, Interconnection Network, Tasks, Muli Round Scheme.

1. Introduction

The idea of a single-processor computer is fast becoming ancient and it is almost impossible to improve computer performance using a single processor system due to several reasons. The possible reasons may be high power consumption, conflicting performance indices, like the minimization of communication and parallel overheads. It is more practical to use many simple processors (nodes) to attain the desired performance at low cost. The benefits of parallel computing need to take into consideration the number of nodes in the systems as well as the communication cost overhead incurred in the uniform distribution of load among the nodes. In such a system optimizing the system performance will spin on good parallel programming at all level. The main objective is how to distribute the tasks evenly and run them concurrently among different nodes while utilizing these nodes efficiently.

A fundamental problem is that the conventional parallel schedulers are static in nature. Once a job is allocated to various nodes, the nodes remain busy until the completion of job. A more flexible approach may be the dynamic allocation of load, where the set of nodes allocated to jobs can be expanded or contracted at run time. The dynamic algorithm makes its decision on fly according to the status of the system [1], [2], [3].

The processes of implementing scheduling algorithms in hardware or in software for parallel machines are more related. We can not think of parallel algorithm without thinking of the parallel architectures. Therefore, considering the efficient and scalable configuration of the interconnection network is also an important issue in evaluating the performance of such systems. The parallel system generally uses a regular point-to-point interconnection network, instead of a random network configuration. Over the last decade, many different interconnection networks have been used commercially. Some examples are found in ring network, hypercube, folded hypercube, debruijn network, Linearly Extensible Tree (LET) network, Linearly Extensible Cube (LEC) network, star graphs etc. [4], [5], [6], [7], [8]. In this paper two linearly extensible multiprocessor interconnection networks having similar topological properties [9], [10] are considered for the purpose of simulation (Figure 1 to Figure 2). In addition the performance is also evaluated for a modified hypercube architecture known as Folded Hypercube (FH) [11] shown in figure 3 and a comparative study is made. The important properties of these interconnection networks are given in Table 1.

Table 1: Summary of some Interconnection Network Characteristics

Type	Size (N) (Nodes)	Degree (d)	Diameter (D)	Bisection Width (B)	Extensibility
Folded Hypercube	$N = 2^n$	N+1	n/2	2^n	Exponential
LET	$\sum_{k=1}^{n} k$	4	$\sqrt{N}$	$2\log_2(n+2)$	Linear
LEC	N=2*n	4	O([N])	N	Linear

The rest of the paper is organised into five sections. Section 1 is the introduction. Section 2 is an overview of the given scheduling problem, while section 3 describes the proposed Multi Round Scheduling scheme. The simulation results of the proposed scheme is discussed in section 4. Section 5 concludes the paper.

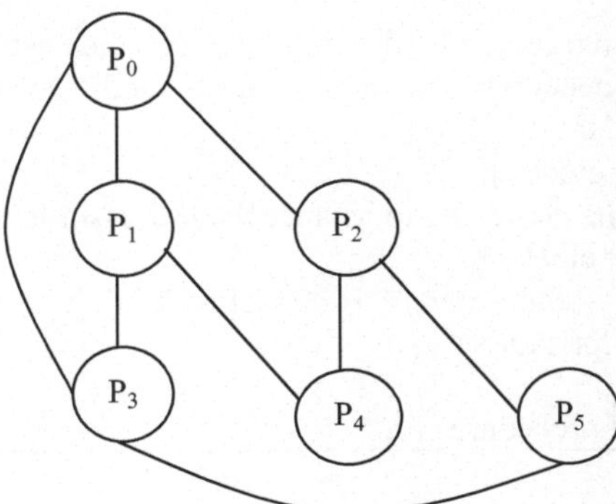

Figure 1. A six processor LET network

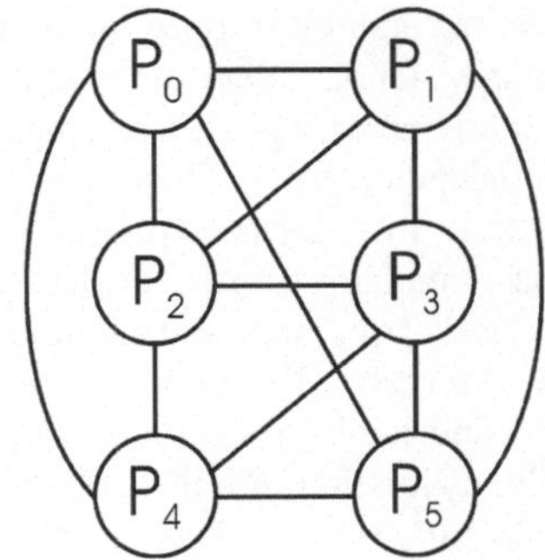

Figure 2. A six processor LEC network

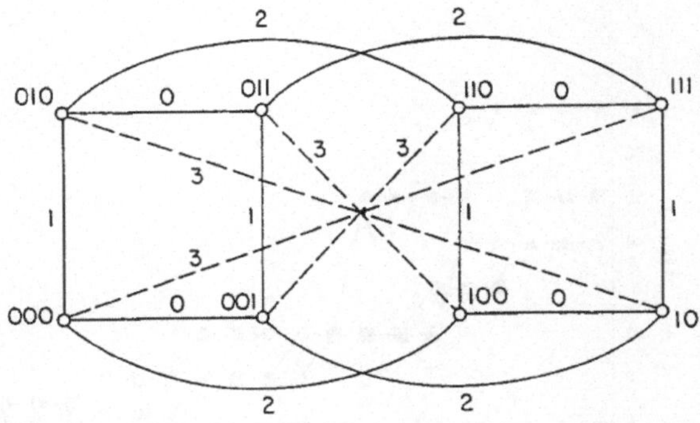

Figure 3. An eight processor folded hypercube network

2. Dynamic Task Scheduling Model

Designing an efficient task scheduling algorithm is more difficult since multiple tasks may cooperate with each other to achieve the common goal. Many algorithms attempt to design strategic algorithms which can provide an automatic way of communicating with each other and to follow the optimal network structure [9], [10]. The performance of a parallel system can be characterized by communication delay, distribution of load among the processors and scheduling overhead. The important issues in dynamic schemes are:

- When to invoke a balancing operation.
- Who makes load balancing decision according to what information and,
- How to manage load migration between processors.

Besides, there are two important parameters when dynamic scheduling algorithms are implemented on parallel systems. The first is that, parallel systems generally use a regular point-to-point interconnection network, instead of random network configuration. Similarly, the load imbalance occurs mainly, because of the un-even and unpredictable nature of tasks. There are many schemes which are based on the principle of minimum distance feature [12] [13]. Minimum distance is the property which assures the minimization of the communication in distributing subtasks and collecting partial results. A scheduling scheme operates with this property such as Minimum Distance Scheduling (MDS) minimizes overhead and ensures the maximum possible speedup. Similarly a Two Round Scheduling Scheme has been reported which consider only one intermediate node of the network to perform task migration [13], [14], [15].

For the purpose of simulation we assume a simple problem characterization in which the load is partitioned into a number of tasks. All tasks are independent and may be executed on any processor in any sequence. The scheduling performance of the strategy has been tested on the three different networks by simulating artificial dynamic load. In order to simulate the load on the proposed network, it is characterized as a group of task structures i.e. uniform load. The primary inputs needed by the algorithm are the number of tasks, structure of the tasks and the nature of the interconnection networks.

Using the above pattern of task structure (load), the performance of the networks has been tested for various scheduling schemes as well as with a new scheduling scheme. The performance is measured in terms of Load Imbalance Factor (LIF) i.e. the load imbalance left after a balancing action at each stage of the load. The above simulation has been performed on various similar multiprocessor networks using IBM server X series 226 having Intel Xeon 3.0 GHz processor.

3. MUTI Round Scheduling (MRS) Scheme

The scheme has been developed for a tree type problem structure. It is dynamic in the sense that no priory knowledge of problem tree is assumed except that the problem can be represented as a tree. The proposed algorithm works as a logical extension of MDS and TRS. It takes into consideration those destination nodes which are not connected directly to source node. There may be more than one path between the donor and acceptor processors which require multi-hop. However, large number of hopes are there greater will be the communication cost. There is a trade-off between the number of hopes and the communication cost when mapping parallel applications on the systems. To perform the load balancing, the algorithm calculates ideal load (IL) value for each iteration, which is used by load balancer as a threshold to detect load imbalances and make load migration decisions. The load imbalance factor for k^{th} iteration, denoted as LIF_k, is defined as

$LIF_k = [\max\{load_k(P_i)\} - (ideal\_load)_k] / (ideal\_load)_k$

Where,

$(ideal\_load)_k = [load_k(P_0) + loadk(P_1) + \ldots + load_k(P_{N-1})] / N$,

and $\max(load_k(P_i))$ denotes the maximum load pertaining to iteration k on a processor P_i ,$0 \leq I \leq N-1$,and $Load_k(P_i)$ stands for the load on processor P_i due to k^{th} iteration. Based on the IL value, the donor (overloaded) processors and acceptors (underloaded) processors are identified. Migration of task, if any can take place between donor and acceptor processors only. The scheme may be define in the following three steps:

i) Calculate IL and identify the donors and acceptors processors.
ii) Check the connectivity of donor and acceptors with the help of adjacency matrix and migrate tasks.
iii) If no direct connection is there between donor and acceptor, then find the alternative path by considering intermediate nodes in successive manner, and perform migrations.

The whole algorithm is implemented in 'C' language. A pseudo code of the algorithm is shown in Table 2.

Table 2 : The MRS Algorithm

```
proposed_dynamic_schedulinng
{
lif, prev = 0, n_donr = 0, n_accr = 0;
   Let level of connectivity = 1;
 Identify the donors and set n_donr.
 Identify the acceptors and set n_accr
. while (lifac > LIF)
   {
    for (i = 0; i < n_donor; i++)
   {
    while (donr[i] is overloaded)
   {
   { for (j = 0; j < n_accr; j++)
   {
     if (donr[i] is connected to accr [j])
       migrate load;
   }
     donr (i) is exhausted or balanced;
s(n) = tp(i) tp(N)
   }}
if desired level of Lif is not achieved then set the level of connectivity to higher level and repeat above procedure
start = clock ();
 call the procedure to balance the processor load.
 end = clock ();
 time = (end – start) * 1000 / CLK_TCK
s(n) = tp(i) tp(N)
    }
End of procedure
```

4. Comparative Study of Results

In this section, we show the different results obtained while scheduling the tasks on various multiprocessor systems. Let us assume we have a parallel algorithm of N independent tasks that can be mapped on an interconnection network of n-nodes. Under ideal circumstances it is also assumed that there is no interprocessor communication due to the task independence. Therefore, the cost of interprocessor and interthread communication is not considered. The simulation run consists of generating various types of task structures and mapping them on the six processors Linearly Extensible Tree (LET), six processors LEC and eight processors folded hypercube architectures. The estimation of LIF is obtained for various levels of the tasks structures and the curves are plotted as the average percent LIF against the load for different stages shown in Figure 4.

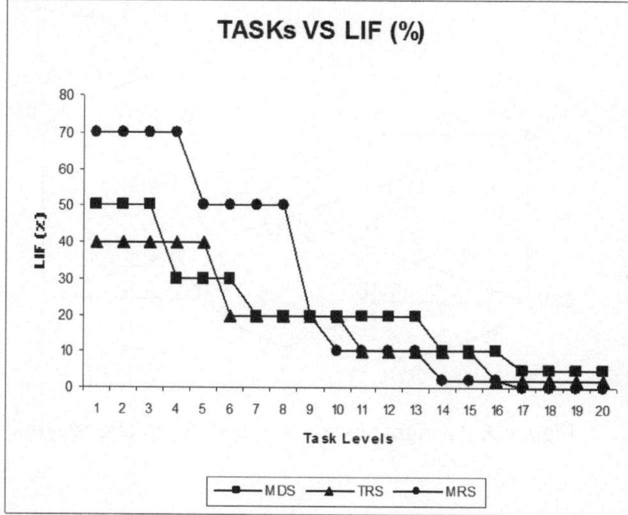

Figure 4. Performance of MRS scheme on LEC network

The trends of curves obtained in figure 4 indicate the behaviors of the load imbalance factor with respect to the number of task on LEC network. The P_0 is considered as a root processor which has a direct connectivity to n-1 nodes in the network. Initially, when the tasks are lesser the value of LIF is greater and shows a similar pattern in all the scheduling schemes. However, when the tasks are increasing the LIF also start reducing. The curve clearly shows the behavior of reducing the value of LIF. At level 14 of the task structure the LIF is approximately tend to zero in case of the proposed scheduling scheme. The other schemes i.e. MDS and TRS are also producing similar results but at greater levels of task structures. Therefore, a good balancing could be obtained when sufficient number numbers of tasks are available. The experimental results show that the optimal results of MRS scheme are obtained with larger of nodes in the system.

Similarly, the estimation of average percentage of LIF is obtained and the curves are plotted against the various levels of task structure on LET network, shown in Figure 5. The results indicate that MDS scheme initially having a higher imbalance as there is lesser number of nodes which are directly connected. It is also observed that both TRS and MRS producing similar results at lesser level of tasks. However, the MRS scheme shows the lesser imbalance with negligible average value of LIF as we tend to higher load stages. The value of LIF becomes almost zero, when the network receives good amount of number of tasks. Therefore, it can be argued that MDS scheme is not performing better for tree types of architectures.

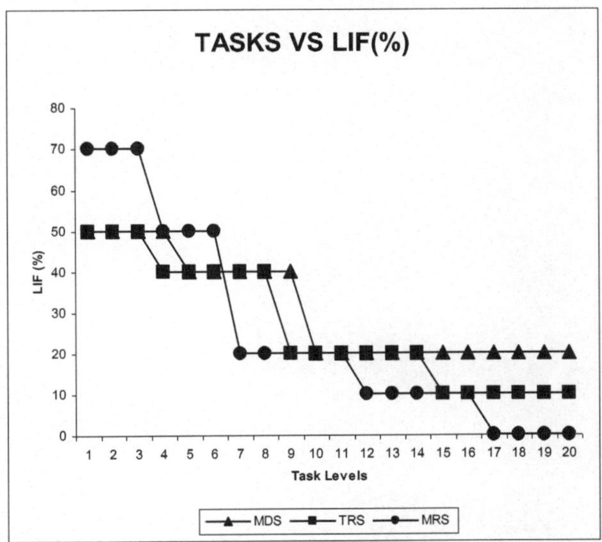

Figure 5. Performance of MRS scheme on LET network

To further analyze the results all the three scheduling schemes are also implemented on a cube type of architecture. The folded hypercube with eight processors has taken into consideration and the results are obtained as shown in Figure 6.

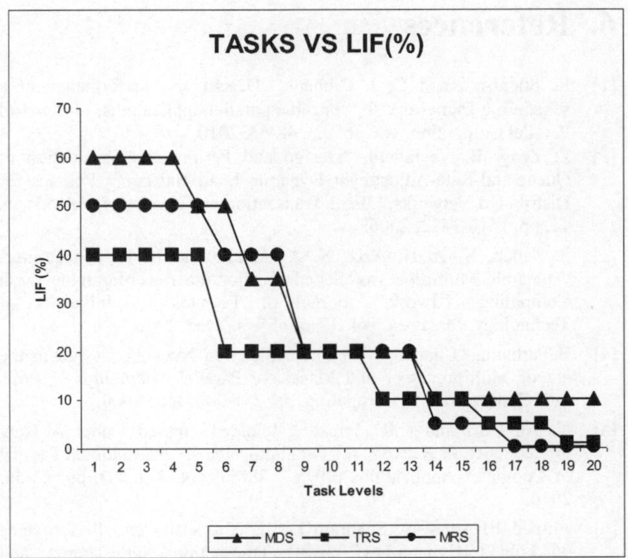

Figure 6. Performance of MRS scheme on FH network

Observing the results in figure 6 we can analyze that the pattern of balancing action exhausted in case of both MDS and TRS after certain level of task structures. Though TRS is making the value of LIF approximately to zero but at higher levels of task structure. It may cause a lengthy balancing operation which ultimately increases the cost. On the other hand MRS scheme is making the network fully balanced at lower level of task structures with lesser overhead. Therefore, it can be concluded that MRS scheme is equally good for cube type of architectures.

5. Conclusion

The model discussed here determines the performance of a new dynamic scheduling scheme over multiprocessor systems. We have considered a simple class of system known as linearly extensible multiprocessor systems for evaluating the performance of the proposed algorithm. However, its performance is also evaluated on cube based architecture. The comparison study shows that the proposed scheme is performing better on various classes of multiprocessor architectures. All nodes available in the system are performing computations evenly which results proper utilization of the system. It reduces the response time of tasks running in parallel by proper mapping of tasks among different nodes. Similarly, it is also reducing the Load Imbalance Factor (LIF) at a very fast rate as compared to other scheduling schemes.

The experimental results obtained show that the MRS scheme producing optimal results with larger number of nodes and with higher level of task structure. Therefore, it can be concluded that proposed scheme is performing better by monitoring the task pattern and help to reduce under-utilization of nodes in the system. The proposed MRS scheme may be applied to other similar multiprocessor networks for better network utilization.

6. References

[1] R. Sudarsan, and C. J. Ribbens, "Design and performance of a scheduling framework for resizable parallel applications," Journal of Parallel Computing, vol. 36, p.p. 48-64, 2010.

[2] Z. Zeng, B. Veeravalli, "Design and Performance Evaluation of Queue-and-Rate-Adjustment Dynamic Load Balancing Policies for Distributed Networks," IEEE Transaction on Computers, vol. 55, no. 11, pp. 1410-1422, 2006.

[3] S. Salleh, N. A. B. Aziz, N. A. Azmee and N. H. Mohammed, "Dynamic Multiprocessor Scheduling for the Reconfigurable mesh Computing Network," Journal of Technology, University of Technology, Malaysia, vol. 37, pp. 55-66, Dec. 2002.

[4] B Parhami, "Challenges in Interconnection Network Design in the era of Multiprocessor and Massively Parallel Microchips," Proc. Int'l Conf. comm. in Computing, pp. 241-246, June 2000.

[5] N. Adhikari and C.R. Tripathy, "Folded crossed Cube: A New Interconnection Network for Parallel Systems," International Journal of Computer Applications (0975 – 8887), vol. 4, no. 3, pp. 43-50, 2010.

[6] Ahmed EI-Amaway, Shahram Latifi, "Properties and Performance of Folded Hypercubes," IEEE Transactions on Parallel and Distributed Systems, vol. 2, no. 1, Jan-1991.

[7] M. Q. Rafiq, P. Kumar and J. P. Gupta, "A Novel Tree-Structured Multiprocessor Network," In Proceedings of International Conference of on Robotics Vision and Parallel Processing for Automation, Malaysia, vol. 2, pp. 576-585.

[8] P. Rajput and V. Kumari, "Modelling and Evaluation of Multiprocessor Architecture" International Journal of Computer Applications (0975 – 8887) Vol. 51, No. 22, 2012.

[9] A. Samad, M. Q. Rafiq and O. Farooq, "A Novel Algorithm for Fast Retrieval of Information from A Multiprocessor Server," In Proceedings of 7th WSEAS International Conference on Software Engineering, Parallel and Distributed Systems (SEPADS '08), University of Cambridge, UK, pp. 68-73.

[10] L. Peng, B.Yang, L. Zhang, and Y. Chen, "A parallel evolving algorithm for flexible neural tree," Journal of parallel computing, vol. 37, pp. 653-666, 2011.

[11] Y. Q. Zhang, "Folded-Crossed Hypercube: A Complete Interconnection Network," journal of System architecture, Elsevier Science, vol. 47, pp. 917-922, 2002.

[12] A. Samad and M. Q. Rafiq, "A Novel Server Architecture for Networking. In Proc. Int'l Conf. on Robotics, Vision Information and Signal Processing, Malaysia, pp. 1029-1032, July 2005.

[13] B. Towles and W. Dally, "Principles and Practices of Interconnection Network," Morgan Kaufmann Press, san Francisco.

[14] A. Samad, M. Q. Rafiq and O. Farooq, "Two Round Scheduling (TRS) Scheme for Linearly Extensible Multiprocessor Systems" International Journal of Computer Applications (0975 – 8887) Vol. 38, No. 10, pp. 34-40, 2012.

[15] N. Kumar, "Simulation Study for Performance and Prediction of Parallel Computations," International Journal of IT (BIJIT), vol. 4, no. 2, ISSN 0973-5655.

Pathfinding on a Specialized Vector Processor*

M.M. Tatur[1], Y.N. Seitkulov[2], N.L. Verenik[1], A.I. Girel[1]
[1]Department of Computer Systems and Networks,
Belarusian State University of Informatics and Radioelectronics, Minsk, Republic of Belarus
E-mail: tatur@bsuir.by, nick.verenik@gmail.com, alexey.girel@gmail.com
[2]Department of Information Technology,
L.N. Gumilyov Eurasian National University, Astana, Republic of Kazakhstan
E-mail: seitkulov_y@enu.kz

Abstract - *The article describes the algorithm of the shortest path search in the specific graph structure of self-developed architecture of semantic processor. A simulation model of the processor was developed for using in research, model also discussed in the article. Described basic principles used for development of GDM. Also it's given a short description of the processor architecture, data format, instruction set and basic operation principles. Formal solution algorithm which includes processor computer code is constructed.*

Keywords: information processing; semantic network; vector processor; parallel computing.

1 Introduction

At the heart of any "intelligent" information processing it can be identified a number of topical basic tasks such as the presentation of information in the form of semantic networks, semantic analysis of the information and associative search of information on some key. Semantic net is understood to be the graph structure, vertices and arcs which, in accordance with certain rules are endowed with some meaning.

Semantic networks there is still nothing as a model of knowledge representation, generally accepted theory that determines the methods of coding and processing of information in semantic networks. According to several undertaken studies [1], theoretical foundation for necessary unification can be the concept of platform independence. Created methods and algorithms of semantic information processing top-level intelligent system developed independently of their hardware and software implementation at a lower level. This is possible only under the condition that the semantic network can be formally converted (recoded) into a graph. Then the information processing in the lower level of intelligent system will represent graph-dynamic process, i.e. the process of transforming the graph structure of the semantic web, in which not only the state of the structure elements changes, but also its configuration.

Figure 1 shows the general scheme of intelligent system based on the principle of platform independence. For mathematical notation (algorithmic) of lower level semantic processing apparatus the successful (according to the opinions of authors) term - an abstract graph-dynamic machine (GDM) is suggested.

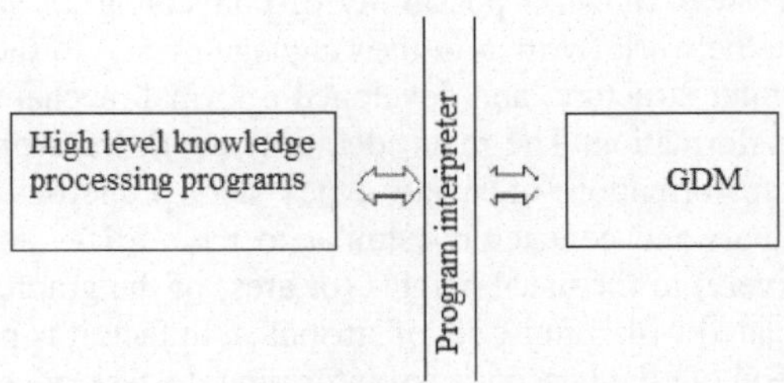

Fig. 1. General scheme of intelligent system, illustrating the principle of platform independence

It is believed that systems built on this principle, can have the flexibility to evolve in an upward direction – designing ontologies in different areas, developing methods and algorithms of semantic representation and knowledge analysis, and in a downward direction - software and hardware implementation. Platform independence is implemented by software interpreter that translates (encoding) programs of high level semantic processing into format of specific GDM commands.

Researchers mostly use GPU as a kind of affordable hardware platform with a parallel architecture. Indeed, using universal multi-processor systems can improve the efficiency of solving problems of certain class, but ultimately leads to a number of other different fundamental difficulties. The division of tasks between processors, data between memory blocks, interaction between processors, high computational complexity and irregularity of computing pose intractable

* Supported by a grant of Kazakhstan, Project: Mapping of semantic information processing algorithms on massive parallelism computers architecture.

problems during parallelizing algorithms. Ultimately, this leads to the effect of slowdown in productivity growth by increasing the number of processing elements, formulated in the form of laws of Gustafson-Barsis's [2] and Amdahl-Ware [3]. According to the experience of using parallel systems in the case of irregular structure of graph computations, the computational efficiency is maximized when working four or five processors, and connecting a larger number of processors, it begins to drop because of the rapidly increasing costs of providing interaction between the processors.

A kind of "golden mean" between universal systems and special processors oriented on knowledge processing, are problem-oriented processors [4, 5, 6]. The basic idea of using them is to provide processor unification within "some" limits, while maintaining a sufficient level of performance. At the same time, achievable technical specifications and cost of providing original architecture versatility must be competitive in comparison with special and serial parallel processors (multi-core CPU, GPU, DSP).

The article gives a brief description of original architecture of developed problem-based SIMD-processor, and then discusses a simulation model of such processor. Simulation of architecture on typical tasks of semantic processing and associative search is a key step in the development of software and hardware platform. In the work [7] there was shown a possibility of conversing an arbitrary semantic network (written in the language of SC) to the graph of a regular structure, and developed a formal mechanism for this transformation. The main idea of network transformation is a transformation of many types and properties of its components and connectors (similar to the vertices and arcs, respectively) to the usual heights (or arcs) of the graph, which is associated with a finite set of attributes. In fact, it is possible to judge about the possibility of informing the task of semantic analysis to a set of classical graph tasks, the solution of which, however, is often not a trivial.

For example (and further detailed architecture) there was chosen as one of the most widely-known problems of graph theory - finding the shortest path in the graph. In the course of solving a test problem has been validated simulation model developed by the vector processor.

2 Graph-dynamic machine model

As the typical architecture of GDM is encouraged to use SIMD-architecture of the main type with the local random access memory. Fig. 2 shows a scheme of the proposed GDM SIMD-architecture.

The system can allocate the total control unit and a plurality of processing elements (PE), parallel to the performing team overall. Each PE has its own independent (local) memory and is responsible for interaction with it. For a hardware implementation PE is maximally simplified (functionally comparable to a simple comparator), and this, in turn, allows for a great number of them on the same chip. By changing the amount of memory per one PE, you can adjust various features of the system, such as volume of processed knowledge base, cost, etc., to achieve the best compliance with the technical specifications. At the same time, the property of variable graph structure regularity and hence executable algorithms enables to provide the effective parallelism of computational process.

The first rapid assessment of processor effectiveness can be made during the operation of associative search by the key. In our case, the search is the simultaneous (parallel) poll device control all the connected to it PE, which is equivalent to an exhaustive search of knowledge of the system in one standard unit of time. On the other hand, the sequential architecture would require to sort out all memory cells, having spent N standard units of time. Obviously, increasing the number of PE in the present system leads to a linear increase of overall system performance.

Fig. 3 presents the scheme of processor data output, allowing to read the contents of table cells consistently. In general, priority is given to the cell connected to the data bus above the rest. This means that if the search command "answered" has more than one table element, then when you try reading the highest priority cell contents is given to the data bus. In this case, all elements below it will be broadcasted signal that disables them from the data bus. This scheme has the property of scalability, which is consistent with the overall architectural concept of the processor.

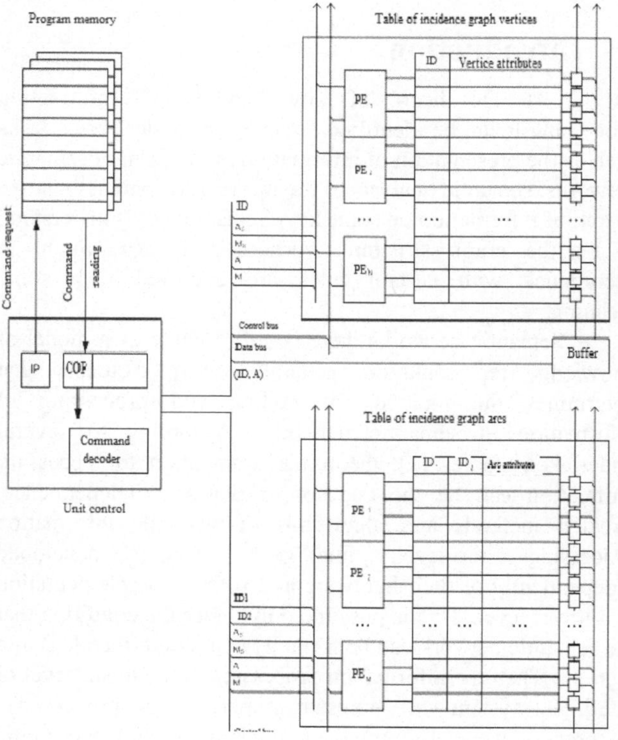

Fig. 2. Scheme of GDM architecture

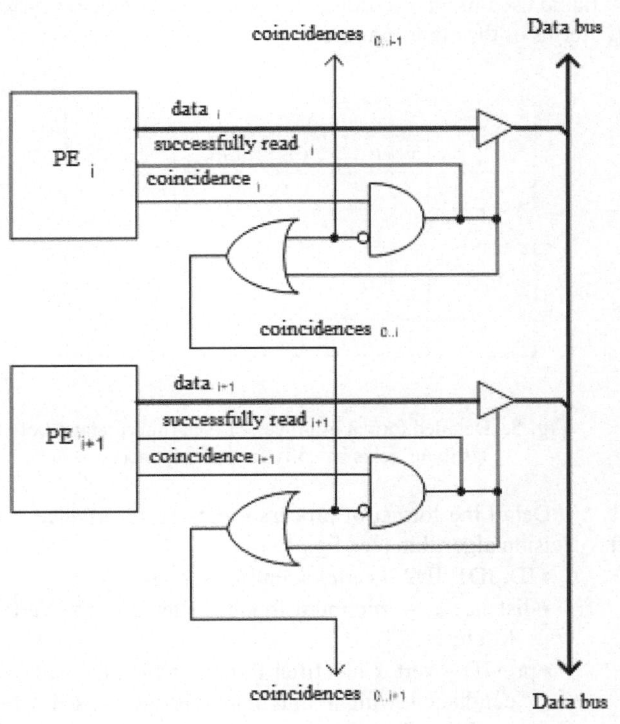

Fig. 3. Scheme of output from the cell memory of the processor (an element of the graph).

3 Instruction system of the processor

Consider the general principle of the command processor building. For this enter the following notations:

- COP – code of operation, used in decoding commands;
- ID – vertex identifier field;
- A – field of incidence graph vertices (arc) attributes;
- M – bit mask field for attributes.

Fig. 4 shows a scheme according to which processor commands construct. Conditionally command format can be divided into 3 parts: code of operation, the address of the target element and arguments of the operation. Code of operation is used in decoding commands.

Under the target element cell table is understood (or multiple cells) that will be targeted by the operation. Address of the target command element can be one of two ways: specific identifier vertex (or two identifiers in the case of referring to an arc) or search query. Search query is described with the fields of A_S and M_S, which corresponds to the address to all the cells in which the bits of field attributes A highlighted by mask M_S, are equal to A_S bits. In fact, the search is a bitwise comparison of each element of the graph followed by a reaction according to the type of operation. When working with a table of arcs a variant of treatment to all arcs is also possible entering the definite vertex or going out of it, which is fixed one of the corresponding identifiers (ID1 or ID2).

By analogy, the data for recording in the element is also represented by two fields: the attributes of A and M mask that defines the bits of the field A, which will be recorded in the target cell.

Consider the implementation of a search query processor more closely. First of all recording operation is performed for graph elements which correspond to a condition. For example, those elements which have a value of "5" in the first byte field attribute record unit in i-th bit attribute field (not included in the byte value). Marked in this way vertices form a set of not read results of the initial search query (elements with a value of "5").

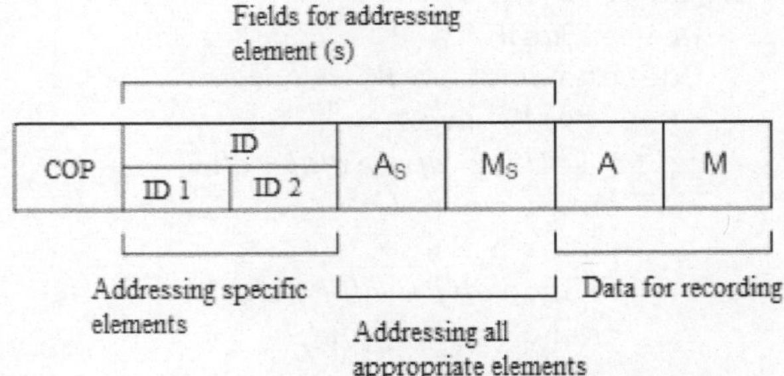

Fig. 4. Construction scheme of command processor format

In a second step we have to consider all the results for which read operation for all elements having a value "1" in i-th bit of the attribute field with simultaneous reset to "0» i-th bit is performed. Eventually only one memory cell will be read (according to the above scheme of priorities), which will also be excluded from the set of unread search query results (due to reset of i-bit). Consequently, the next analogous read command will return next not repeat element from the result of the initial search query. Thus, consistently performing a read operation as long as at least one cell of data table works, we are able to read the entire search result.

It should be noted that the provision of bit access to attributes of graph elements allows removing the dependence of processor data format from task in hand. In fact, the responsibility for how to interpret the attributes of elements lies on the programmer. However, it is possible to implement some complex commands (obviously, being a superposition of base) at the level of the unit control that allows to "tune" the processor for more effectively solving a wide range of problems.

4 Problem of finding the shortest path in the graph

Given a weighted graph *G (V, A)* without loops and arcs of negative weight. Need to find the shortest path from a vertex of a graph G to all other vertices of the graph.

We enter the following notations:

- V – set of graph vertices;
- A –set of graph arcs;
- $c[ij]$– cost (weight, length) of arc ij;
- a – vertex, the distance from which sought;
- U –set of graph vertices;
- W – set of vertices containing the wave front;
- $d[u]$ – at the end of algorithm it is equal to the distance of the shortest path from a vertex to u vertex;
- $p[u]$ – at the end of algorithm it contains the shortest path from a vertex to u vertex.

Pseudo-code of the proposed algorithm can be written as the following:

```
Label d[a] ← 0, p[a] ← a
Enter a in W
While ∃u∈W
 delete u from W
 For ∀v∈V, uv∈A
   If v∉U or d[v] > d[u] + c[uv]
     enter v in U
     enter v in W
     change d[v] ← d[u] + c[uv]
     change p[v] ← p[u], v
```

At the beginning of the algorithm the distance for the initial vertex is set equal to zero and all other distances can be ignored, because it is believed that if the vertex $v \notin U$ then $d[v]=\infty$. Further so called wave front forms initially comprising only one vertex a. Then main cycle starts.

At each step of the cycle the wave is spread from vertices that make up wave front to all vertices connected to their outgoing arcs. The distance to the vertex is calculated as the distance to the previous vertex plus the arc value between them. In contrast to the classical wave algorithm, we consider each vertex not one single time when it achieving the wave. In fact, each vertex v is considered for all possible paths of wave in the graph, but changes its state (shortest path), only if the distance in it (in v) is bigger than the sum of the distances to the current vertex u and arc length uv. All vertices that changed its state in the current cycle iteration comprise the wave front for the next iteration. Thus, the cycle is complete when at all vertices it will be set the minimum possible value of the distance $d[u]$, which would correspond to the iteration, at which there will not be changed any vertex, i.e. wave would damp.

5 Implementation of decision algorithm

Consider the implementation of decision algorithm described above based on the architecture developed by the vector processor. First of all, perform "tuning" of processor under the task. To do this, we will specify processor data format (for each bit the attribute fields are according to certain variable used in the solution), and extend the command system (in terms of the algorithm used).

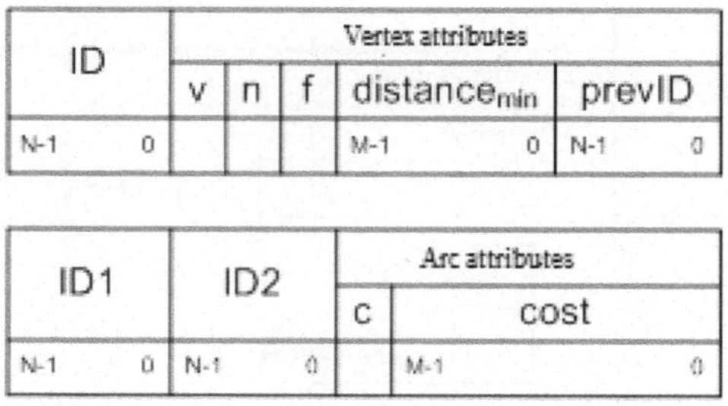

ID	Vertex attributes				
	v	n	f	$distance_{min}$	prevID
N-1 0				M-1 0	N-1 0

ID1	ID2	Arc attributes	
		c	cost
N-1 0	N-1 0		M-1 0

Fig. 5. Detailed format of processor data (interpretation of attribute fields by software programmers)

Detail the format of processor data in accordance with the decision algorithm (see fig.5):

- ID, ID1, ID2 – vertex identifiers, N bit;
- $distance_{min}$ – minimum found distance to the vertex, M bit;
- prevID – vertex identifier through which the path was conducted with a minimum distance (used while road-building solutions after the end of the main algorithm), N bit;
- v – (visited) flag, defining whether the wave reaches the vertex (in case that the flag is set «0», minimum found distance to vertex is accepted equal to infinity), 1 bit;
- f – (wave front) vertices labeled with this flag contain the front wave for the current algorithm iteration, 1 bit;
- n – (next wave front) vertices labeled with this flag contain the front wave for the next algorithm iteration, 1 bit;
- c – (connected) flag used while searching for all arcs going from the vertex, 1 bit.

Thus the size of one cell vertex table is (N+2M+3) bit. Size of one cell arc table – (2N+M+1) bit.

Entering additional processor commands focused on a specific algorithm solution, enables to avoid working directly with the bits of element graph attribute field, thus simplifying the final solution of the problem by programmer. List of commands thus obtained is shown in Table 1.

Table 1. Extensive system of processor commands

Commands for working with vertex table		
createVertex(ID)		Creates vertex in processor graph.
ID	identifier of new vertex	

Init		For all vertices a processor graph resets flags v, n, f and variables $distance_{min}$, prevID into zero.
setMinDistance(ID, distance, prevID)		Records value distance and prevID in vertex ID.
ID	identifier of target vertex	
distance	minimum distance to vertex	
prevID	identifier of previous vertex in the path	
setWaveStartVertex(ID)		Adds vertex ID into wave front (sets bit f in «1»).
ID	identifier of target vertex	
readNextVertexFromWave front		Reads next vertex from many vertices containing wave front (bit f is set to «1»), simultaneously resetting bit into «0».
readVertex		Reads vertex ID
ID	identifier of target vertex	
moveWavefront		For all vertices labeled with bit n, makes resetting bit n into «0» and setting bit f into «1».
Commands for working with arc table		
createArc		Creates arc (going out from the vertex ID1, going into vertex ID2, with cost cost) into processor graph.
ID1	vertex identifier that is incident to the arc	
ID2	vertex identifier that is incident to the arc	
cost	arc cost (weight, length)	
findAllOutputArcs		Finds all output arcs from vertex ID, by flag c
ID	identifier of target vertex	
readNextOutputArc		Reads next arc from many arcs labeled with bit c, simultaneously resetting bit into «0».

Hereafter a fragment of program is presented that implements considered algorithm on the basis of constructed simulation model of the processor. The function input receives objects vertexTable and arcTable, that provide an interface for the access to processor data (to vertex table and arc table respectively), as well as additional methods for decoding the attribute fields. The variables ID1 and ID2 represent the vertex identifiers the path between them must be found. The output function returns a Boolean value indicating whether the path is found.

```
bool findPath(MVertexTable&vertexTable,
MArcTable&arcTable, uint ID1, uint ID2){
vertexTable.init();
vertexTable.setWaveStartVertex(ID1);

while (true) {
while (vertexTable.readNextVertexFromWavefront() == true)
{
MVertexsrcVertex = vertexTable.getBuffer();
arcTable.findAllOutputArcs(srcVertex.m_ID);
while (arcTable.readNextOutputArc() == true) {
MArc arc = arcTable.getBuffer();
uint distance =
vertexTable.getMinDistance(srcVertex.m_attributes) +
arcTable.getCost(arc.m_attributes);
vertexTable.readVertex(arc.m_ID2);
MVertexdstVertex = vertexTable.getBuffer();
if ((vertexTable.isVertexVisited(dstVertex.m_attributes) ==
false) || (distance
<vertexTable.getMinDistance(dstVertex.m_attributes))) {
vertexTable.setMinDistance(dstVertex.m_ID, distance,
srcVertex.m_ID);
} } }
if (vertexTable.moveWavefront() == false) break;
}
if (vertexTable.readVertex(ID2) == true) {
MVertex vertex = vertexTable.getBuffer();
returnvertexTable.isVertexVisited(vertex.m_attributes); }
return false;
}
```

6 Conclusions

This paper describes an approach to create applied intelligent systems (systems-oriented on intelligent information processing), based on the principle of platform independence. As a hardware implementation of GDM (graph-dynamic machine) vector task-oriented processor was used with the original architecture.

To verify and evaluate the effectiveness of the proposed architecture software simulation processor model has been built which allowed detailing data format and commanding system, testing the basic principles of processor operation as a whole. As the target purpose one of the typical problems of semantic information processing was chosen, in particular, the problem of finding the shortest path in the graph. To solve it, parallel decision algorithm was built.

In the future we plan to continue detailing the possibilities of the processor through simulation of other typical tasks of semantic processing. It is planned to formalize and automate the process of carrying out of tests that will systematize obtained results of the research of productivity growth with various configurations of the original graph. The ultimate goal of the study is to build a hardware prototype of the semantic processor with SIMD-architecture.

7 References

[1] V. V. Golenkov, N. A. Guliakina. “Graphodynamical models of parallel knowledge processing” / Open Semantic Technologies for Intelligent Systems (OSTIS-2013). pp. 23–52, Feb 2013.

[2] John L. Gustafson. “Reevaluating Amdahl's Law” Communications of the ACM 31(5). – pp. 532–533, May 1988.

[3] Gene M. Amdahl. “Validity of the Single Processor Approach to Achieving Large-Scale Computing Capabilities” / AFIPS Conference Proceedings (30). – pp. 483–485, April 1967.

[4] S. A. Bairak, D. N.Adzinets, M. M. Tatur, P. Philipoff, M. Munoz. “Parallel processors for intelligent systems development” / Open Semantic Technologies for Intelligent Systems (OSTIS-2013). pp. 135–140, 2012.

[5] Ye. N. Seitkulov “New Methods of secure outsourcing of scientific computations” / The Journal of Supercomputing, V. 65, Issue 1, pp 469-482, July 2013.

[6] M. M. Tatur, D. N.Adzinets, M. M. Lukashevich, S. A. Bairak. “Synthesis and analysis of classifiers based on generalized model of identification” / Advances in intelligent and soft computing. Vol. 71. – pp. 529–536, 2010.

[7] Nick L. Verenik, Yerzhan N. Seitkulov, Mikhail M. Tatur. “Development of ASIP for semantic information processing” / Electronics info. № 8. – pp. 95–98, 2012.

Control Synthesis of For-Loops in a Pipeline System

Heung Sun Yoon, Jae Young Park, and Jong Tae Kim
Department of electrical and computer engineering,
Sungkyunkwan University, Suwon, Gyeonggi-Do, South Korea

Abstract - *Pipelining has been a basic technology for high performance digital system, but handling loops in pipeline system is very difficult problem to be solved. In this paper we discuss how to model nested loops in pipeline scheduling and perform automated control synthesis. In our work loops are unrolled partially and treated as conditional branches. We propose a global controller that consists of an FSM controller for each cluster and the FSM activation control part. And we also discuss how to generate control specifications for each FSM.*

Keywords: Control synthesis, Loop, Pipeline architecture

1 Introduction

Pipelining is the key implementation technique used to make fast digital systems for many DSP algorithms. In pipelining, each input computation task (e.g. an instruction) is subdivided into a sequence of subtasks and each of these subtasks is executed during the clock cycle by a specialized hardware stage that operates concurrently with other stages in the pipeline. Every clock cycle has the same time period. Successive tasks are initiated at some fixed or variable intervals, which are integer multiples of a clock cycle and are bounded by the execution time of a task. In this fashion, execution of subtasks of consecutive tasks may overlap in time on different parts of the pipeline circuits. If a task is initiated every clock cycle, i.e., the initiation interval is 1, this is the fastest pipeline design and there is no resource sharing between the executions of subtasks. However, if the design is constrained on the cost, i.e., there are not enough functional modules to be allocated, some resources must be shared by more than one subtask. Since operators are shared between stages of the pipe and within a stage, handling loop in pipeline system is very difficult problem to be solved. There are several loop pipelining algorithms used in high level synthesis or optimizing compiler [1][2][3]. The loop folding is to achieve pipelining effect by initiating the next iteration of a loop before the current iteration is finished. Thus this transformation achieves speedups. However, if there are data dependency between successive loop iterations, i.e., the data produced at the last operation of the current iteration is consumed at the first operation of the next iteration, the loop folding has no advantages. For-loop is deterministic loop construct which uses an index variable. This index specifies the range of loop iteration and is assumed to be known prior to entering the loop body. Loops are either unrolled completely or treated as conditional branches. Figure 1 shows a general model for a nested loop. The nested loops are numbered 1 through *n* from the inner most nested loop to the outer most one. The number of time steps in a loop body *i* can be calculated using the following recursive formula.

$$TS_1^i = s_1^i \times k_1^i,$$

$$TS_n^i = \left(b_n^i + TS_{n-1}^i + a_n^i\right) \times k_n^i,$$

where s_1^i is the size of the inner most loop, k_n^i denotes the number of iterations for the nth nested loop, b_n^i and a_n^i are the number of time steps before, and after the (n - 1)th nested loop. TS_n^i denotes the number of time steps in the loop upto the nth nested loop from the inner most nested loop and TS_n^i means the number of time steps for the inner most nested loops of the loop body *i*.

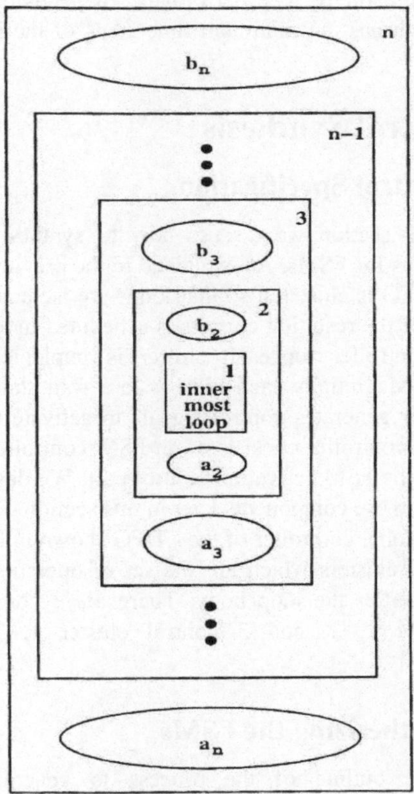

Figure 1 A model of nested loop body

Let's also assume that there are m different loop bodies in a DFG and each loop body i is nested n_i times as shown in Figure 2, where i = 1, 2 , ⋯, m. The total number of time steps P for the input CDFG is given by $P = \sum_{i=1}^{m} TS^{i}_{n_i} + \sum_{j=1}^{m+1} p_j$, where TS^{i}_{ni}. is the total number of the time steps in the ith loop body which has n_i nested loops, p_j is the number of time steps between loop bodies, p_1 is the time steps before the first loop body, and p_{m+1} is the number of time steps after the last loop body.In our model loop capacity $LC_i = [TS^{i}_{1}/L]$, where TS^{i}_{1} is the number of time steps in the inner most nested loop of the loop body i. The loop capacity LCi is defined as the maximum number of different jobs that can be executed concurrently by a loop body.

2 Pipeline Scheduling

If loop unrolling is not practical, we schedule the DFG as follows. First, the input DFG is partitioned with the intention of clustering the loops separately from the rest of the DFG. For example, in Figure 3, this method would result in 3 clusters: Cluster 1 (nodes before the loop body), Cluster 2 (the loop body), and Cluster 3 (the nodes after the loop body). Loops are detected easily during syntax analysis of structured languages so that the CDFG can be marked accordingly. Loops are transformed into a DAG by breaking the feedback edge and adding the node vL after the last operation of the loop body as in the Figure 3(a). Next, each cluster is scheduled separately. The performance depends on the loop body i which has the minimum time steps of the inner most loop.

3 Control Synthesis

3.1 Control Specification

In this section we discuss how to synthesize control specifications for FSMs. As explained in the previous section, the input DFG is clustered so that loops are isolated from the rest. Each of the resulting clusters is scheduled independently and the controller for each cluster is implemented as a separate FSM. Initially each FSM is in a wait state until the loop handler generates control signals to activate the FSMs. The Global controller consists of an FSM controller for each cluster and the FSM activation control part. We describe how to construct these components later in this section. Figure 3.11 shows the global controller of the CDFG shown in Figure 3.9. There are 3 clusters which are the set of operations before, within, and after the loop body. There are 3 corresponding FSMs: FSM 1, 2, and 3 control cluster 1, 2, and 3, respectively.

3.2 Synthesizing the FSMs

The outline of the process to generate control specifications for each FSM is as follows:

1. Find MESs and PEMs for each time step.
2. Attain the patterns of the overlapping time steps for each FSM from the scheduling and allocation phases.
3. Decide the states for each pattern.
4. For each FSM determine the state transition.

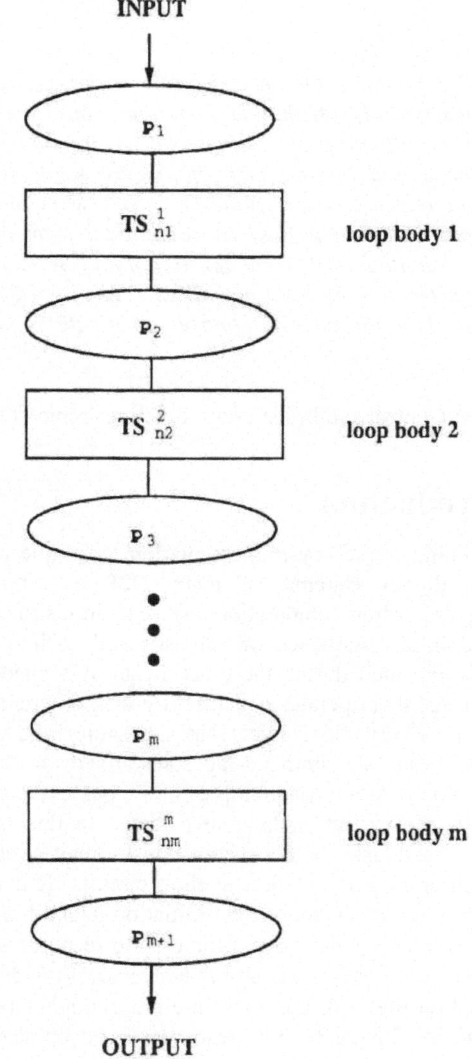

Figure 2 A generalized DFG with loops

Initially each FSM is in a wait state and will be activated as soon as the necessary conditions are met and these conditions are provided by initiation control and the loop control part. Looking at Figure 4 as an example, the initiation, loop enter, and loop exit control signals activate the FSM for Cluster 1, the FSM for cluster 2, and the FSM for cluster 3, respectively. The FSM for cluster 1 in Figure 4 is in a wait state until the loop enter signal from the control counter is received, it will then be activated at time step 1, and goes back to the wait state at time step 4.

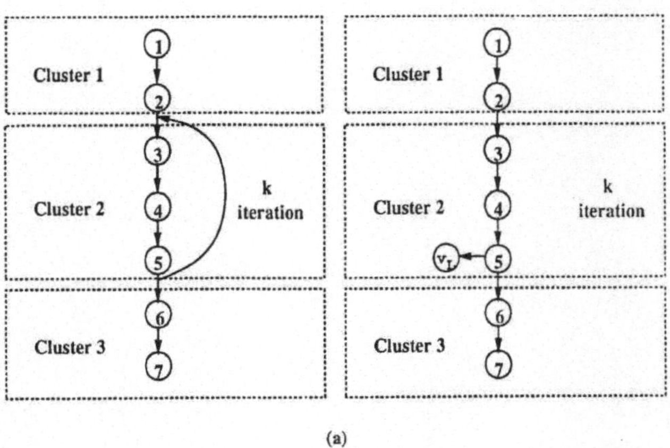

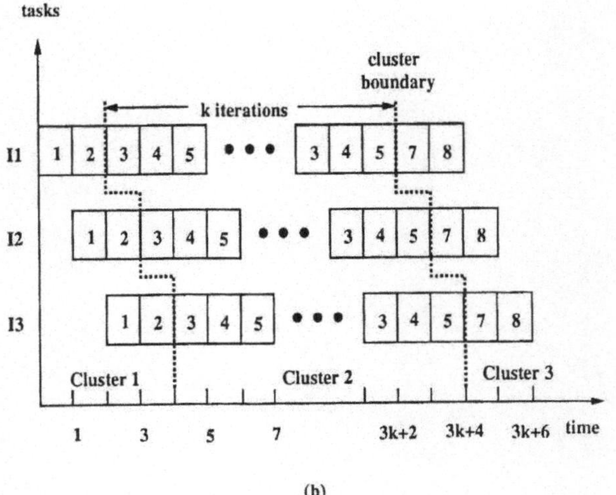

Figure 3 Clustering and Loop transformation

3.3 FSM Activation Control

FSM activation control provides the initiation, loop enter, loop exit control signals. A simple way to construct the initiation controller is by using an Lt-bit vector whose ith bit is 1 if a new initiation is started at the ith time unit of each cycle. For example for the cycle $L_t = 10, L = 2,\ and\ LC = 3$, the 10-bit initiation vector is 1010100000. Then a shift register controller takes this vector and cyclically rotates it once every clock cycle. If at the start of any clock the left-most bit is 1, a new initiation signal is sent to the necessary FSM. This is very simple method, but if L_t is very large (especially if loops are involved) this is not practical. Instead of using this method we can build the initiation controller using a counter and the supporting combinational circuits. Counter counts up to L_t and is reset at L_t. The combinational circuit provides the initiation control and reset signals.

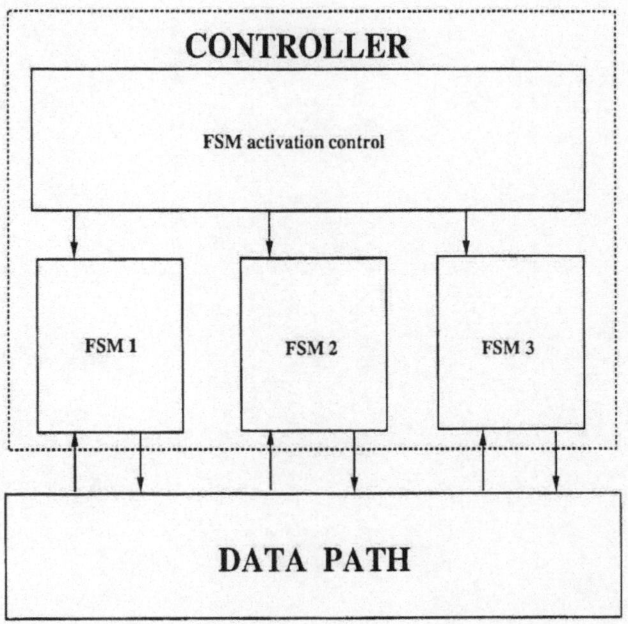

Figure 4 Global Controller for CDFG with loops

4 Conclusions

Pipelining has been a good methodology for designing fast digital system, but pipeline architectures become quite complex to design if loops are involved. Automated controller design tools in high level for pipeline system are necessary to cope with such complexity and explore the design space efficiently. In this paper we discuss how to model nested loops in pipeline scheduling and how to synthesize of controllers for pipelined data paths. We use the general nested loop model and loops are unrolled partially and treated as conditional branches in our work. We propose a global controller that consists of an FSM controller for each cluster and the FSM activation control part. And we also discuss how to generate control specifications for each FSM.

5 References

[1] E. Girczyc, Loop winding – a data flow approa-ch to functional pipelining. In proceedings of ISCAS, IEEE, May 1987.

[2] M. Hatto, et. al., An automatic code modification and optimization system for high-level synthesis. In Bulletin of Networking, Computing, Systems, and Software, Vol. 2, No. 1, pp 12-17, January 2013.

[3] B. Goldberg, Translation Validation of Loop Optimizations and Software Pipelining in the TVOC Framework, SAS 2010, LNCS 6337, pp. 6-21, 2010.

SESSION

LATE BREAKING PAPER - cloud computing, optimization, sensor networks, scheduling, and applications

Chair(s)

Prof. Hamid Arabnia

Deployment of Customized Virtual Machine on Cloud Platform

Gaochao Xu[1,2], Yushuang Dong[1], Kun Yang[3], Xiaodong Fu[1], and Jia Zhao[1,*]
[1]College of Computer Science and Technology, JiLin University, Changchun, China
[2]Symbol Computation and Knowledge Engineer of Ministry of Education, JiLin University, Changchun, China
[3]School of Computer Science & Electronic Engineering, University of Essex, United Kingdom
*Corresponding author

Abstract— *The cloud platform has abundant resources for users to choose. To reduce communication overhead of virtual machine (VM) deployment, this paper proposes a Deployment of Customized Virtual Machine (DCVM) strategy. This algorithm utilizes Linux From Scratch (LFS) to customize VM image. LFS can reduce the size of VM image efficiently and user can customize the VM image flexibility. This algorithm also applies a rapid deployment method for customized VM. It is a mixed approach for enhancing the speed of deployment validly and efficiently. It uses multicast to transmit data to reduce the communication overhead. It also achieves running sub-VMs independent of parent-VM by synchronizing the VM disk data. The experimental results have shown that LFS reduces the size of customized VM image efficiently and the proposed VM deployment algorithm is more effectiveness and efficiency in terms of deployment time and boot time than traditional VM deployment strategy.*

Keywords: Cloud computing, Linux From Scratch, Customized Virtual Machine, Virtual Machine Deployment

1. Introduction

Cloud computing is forefront technology of the information field. To provide a better infrastructure service [1] and improve the utilization rate of resources, virtualization technology has been applied to the cloud computing. The underlying hardware provides more and more support to virtualization [2]. The results of Nathan Regola and Jean-Christophe Docum [3] show that under the conditions of hardware virtualization technology and InfiniBand high-performance network, a typical MPI program in the virtual cluster system only has a slight performance loss. Studies [4,5] have shown the typical applications running on high performance system are also suitable for running in the cloud computing environment.

Deployment of virtual machine (VM) has attracted much more attention and quickly became a research hotspot of industrial circles. The traditional VM deployment strategy is mainly composed of dispatch center, host, and image template library. To provide better service and reduce the user waiting time, a strategy to improve the efficiency of VM deployment is necessary. Our research focuses on reducing the size of VM image and optimizing the deployment strategy. It will take a long time to transfer a big size VM image and reduces deployment efficiency. This paper analyses to reduce the size of VM image through Linux From Scratch (LFS) [6]. The traditional VM deployment strategy needs frequently hangs the source VM during the deployment process then leading to long downtime of the source VM. It also transfers many memory pages during the deployment process. This paper proposes a Deployment of Customized VM (DCVM) method. It is a mixed approach combines pre-copy [7,8] algorithm and post-copy [9,10] algorithm to reduce the downtime of deployment process. It uses the incremental compressed mechanism [11,12,13] to compress the data of memory pages and use the multicast to transmit the data in order to reduce the communication overhead. It also achieves running sub-VMs independent of parent-VM through synchronizing the VM disk data.

2. Relevant work

The traditional VM image is so large that has a profound impact on the VM deployment and system operation. Linux kernel cutting methods are usually used to customize the Linux kernel for embedded system [14,15] and many specific field [16]. These methods are not appropriate for cloud computing and micro-kernel technology is not yet universally applied to the cloud computing. With cloud computing application development on mobile platforms and others, the micro-kernel technology will be more demanded under cloud computing environment. This paper analysis to get customized VM image through LFS. The process of LFS is as follow: (1) Temporary tool chain compiled by source code of the tool set on the host system. (2) Get an independent glibc library by compile the glibc source code using the temporary toolchain. (3) Use the independent glibc library in the host system environment to build independent toolchain, independent build environment completed. (4) Compile the Linux source code package in the independent build environment and build the Linux kernel for the operating system. (5) Remove the source package, temporary toolchain, and independent build environment.

VM deployment is always performed in conjunction with VM migration [17]. Many idea of VM migration can be applied to VM deployment. Pre-copy [7,8] algorithm is a dynamic migration of virtual machine mechanism. Many optimized solutions for pre-copy algorithm have been proposed. Some solutions [11,12,13] use memory compression to reduce the communication data size. Paper [18] tries to change the order of transferring dirty memory pages for many pages modified frequently should be transferred at last to reduce retransfers. CPU scheduling mechanism [19] adjusts the CPU time slices allocated to the VM being migrated to reduce the rate of dirty memory pages.

In contrast to the classic pre-copy algorithm, post-copy [9,10] dynamic migration algorithm postponed memory synchronization process to run the VM on the destination host. Incremental compression [11,12,13] is a way that saves the memory page before the changes of the memory state to gain incremental data through XOR the current memory page with prior saved memory pages.

Schmidt Matthias [17] compared multiple data transmission methods include unicast, binary tree, bit torrent and multicast in VM deployment process. As the result that multicast is significantly faster than all other methods. Reference [20] compared bittorrent and multicast for different VM size in VM deployment process and compared multicast file transfer tools UDPcast and UFTP. As the result that multicast is faster than other transfer methods if deploy a certain amount of VMs.

So far, there is a series of projects devoted to the study of virtual machine cloning technology. SnowFlock mentioned in [21,22] is the first project that solves the low-latency problem of virtual machine cloning under a cluster or cloud computing environment. Potemkin project [23] implements a honeypot spanning a large IP address range. Reference [24] defined cloud deployment time and application running time as cloud time. It designed an efficient cloud deployment scheme for large-scale cloud applications called Jump-start cloud to minimize cloud time. The proposed method DCVM references current VM deployment method and combine the optimized live migration method to achieve better deployment efficiency. It also synchronizes the VM disk data when multicast the VM memory data to achieve running sub-VMs independent of parent-VM.

3. LFS technology achieves customized VM image

According to user needs, there are many applications and components need to install on user customized VM image. To achieve incremental installation of customized VM image and provide interface for management process, this paper analysis to realize automatically generate customized VM image with our own shell scripts.

(1) User interface. It's easy to access and operate by using the interactive interface of traditional web, and gives a list of applications and components in a platform. User can select their needs through a user interactive interface, and sent the request information to management process. The applications and components provided by the management side of the cloud platform also can be dynamically updated when new applications or components need to be updated to the cloud platform. Administrators of cloud platform can dynamically update the existing applications and components.

(2) Configuration file. The user selects their needs through user interface and sends the request information to the management process. Then the management process receives the request information and extracts it to form a customized XML configuration file.

(3) Customize VM image. The management process extracts the information Iconf from the configuration file. The information of Iconf includes the user request. According to Iconf, user needs K VM nodes. There are N exist VM image copies stored on cloud platform. The VM image copy is used to generate VM image which users customized previously. The match degree is calculated by matching configuration file information of VM image copy with Iconf. The customized VM image generation process is as follows:

```
P_0 ← initial VM image copy
S_0 ← size of P_0
I_0 ← configuration file information of P_0
M_0 ← match degree of P_0
P_target ← target VM image copy
S_target ← size of P_target
M_target ← match degree of P_target
P_target = P_0, S_target = S_0, M_target = M_0
c = 0
While c < N do
    If I_c exactly matches with I_conf
        P_target = P_c
        Break
    Else
        If I_c exist other information beyond I_conf
            S_c = 0, M_c = -1
        Else
            If M_c > M_target
                P_target = P_c, S_target = S_c, M_target = M_c.
            End if
            If M_c = M_target and S_target < S_c
                P_target = P_c, S_target = S_c, M_target = M_c
            End if
        End if
    End if
    c = c + 1
End while
If c == N
    P_temp ← According to I_conf, complete the P_target installing
    P_target = P_temp
End if
store the P_target and I_target on cloud platform, set the host as target host
generate customize VM image through P_target, create K VM nodes
```

4. Deployment of Customized VM (DCVM)

In this paper, we use LFS to customize VM image. The customized VM image process generates the customized VM image and selects the target host and the parent-VM instantiates it. At the same time, the deployment process is deploying the sub-VMs. This paper introduces a strategy of deployment of customized VM combining with the advantage of pre-copy and post-copy as well as using incremental compression technology to reduce network load. In order to transfer data to all sub-VMs effectively, multicast subsystem is being built to the daemon on the host.We assume that network environment is good enough and dirty page transfer speed is faster than dirty page growth speed. The process of Deployment of Customized VM as showed in Fig.1.

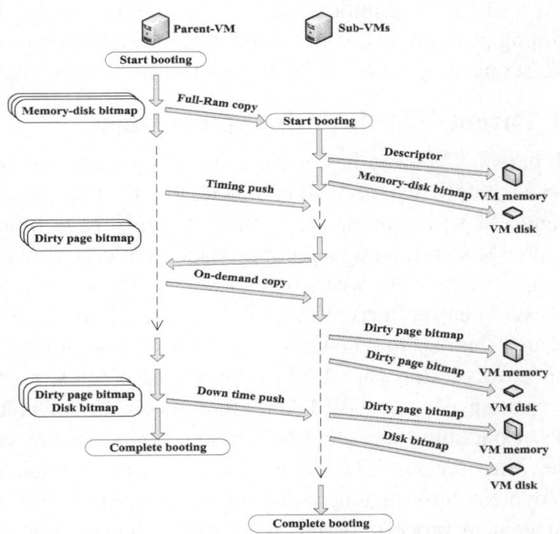

Fig. 1: Deployment of Customized VM Process

4.1 Full-Ram copy stage

The purpose of Full-Ram copy is synchronizing the most pages for just one transporting. Create a disk bitmap for recording the VM disk address has been read or written. According to disk bitmap, transfer the VM disk in Parent-VM downtime push stage and it can avoid the data retransfer.

In the whole booting process, when parent-VM reading or writing the VM disk data, records the VM disk address and marks the flag as read or write in disk bitmap. One VM disk address only has one disk bitmap record at most. If the VM disk has been written, the flag of this VM disk address record will always be marked as write. The process of recording disk bitmap is as follows: 1) If read VM disk data, go to 2). 2) $DA \leftarrow$ the VM disk address. If no record of DA in disk bitmap, go to 3). 3) $DB \leftarrow$ new disk bitmap record, DB->$DA = DA$, DB->$flag \leftarrow$ mark as read. Go to 4). 4) If write VM disk data, go to 5). 5) $DA \leftarrow$ the VM disk address. If no record of DA in disk bitmap, go to 6), else go to 7). 6) $DB \leftarrow$ new disk bitmap record, DB->$DA \leftarrow DA$, DB->$flag \leftarrow$ mark as write. 7) $DBE \leftarrow$ the exist record of DA in disk bitmap. If DBE->$flag$ marked as read, DBE->$flag \leftarrow$ mark as write.

Create a memory-disk bitmap for recording the VM memory data written by the VM disk data and restore the VM disk data in sub-VMs. It can ensure the VM memory data is exactly the VM disk data and avoid the data retransfer.When parent-VM writes the VM memory, update memory-disk bitmap and disk bitmap. One VM memory address only has one memory-disk bitmap record at most. The process of writing VM memory in the full-Ram copy stage is as follows: 1) Write VM memory, $MA \leftarrow$ the VM memory address, If VM memory data read from VM disk, go to 2), else go to 8). 2) $DA \leftarrow$ the VM disk address. If no record of MA in memory-disk bitmap, go to 3), else go to 4). 3) $MDB \leftarrow$ new memory-disk bitmap record, MDB->$MA \leftarrow MA$, MDB->$DA \leftarrow DA$. 4) $MDBE \leftarrow$ the exists record of MA in memory-disk bitmap. If $MDBE$->DA != DA, go to 5). 5) $DBE \leftarrow$ the record of $MDBE$->DA in disk bitmap. If DBE->$flag$ marked as read, go to 6), else go to 7). 6)Delete DBE in disk bitmap, go to 7). 7) $MDBE$->$DA = DA$. 8) If there is exist record of MA in memory-disk bitmap, go to 9). 9) $MDBE \leftarrow$ the exists record of MA in memory-disk bitmap, $DBE \leftarrow$ the record of $MDBE$->DA in disk bitmap. If DBE->$flag$ marked as read, go to 10), else go to 11). 10) Delete DBE in disk bitmap, go to 11). 11) Delete $MDEB$ in memory-disk bitmap.

When the parent-VM reaches a certain booting status, VM kernel of the parent-VM quiesces its I/O devices, and issues a hypercall suspending the VM's execution. When the hypercall succeeds, a privileged process maps the suspended VM memory to populate the descriptor [21]. A VM Descriptor is a condensed VM image contains: (1) metadata describing the VM and its virtual devices, (2) memory pages of parent-VM current booting status, (3) a few memory pages shared between the VM and the Xen hypervisor, (4) the registers of the main VCPU, (5) the Global Descriptor Tables, (6) the page tables of the VM.

After populating the descriptor, multicast the descriptor and memory-disk bitmap to the sub-VMs, and continuing the parent-VM booting process. When sub-VMs receive the descriptor and memory-disk bitmap, sub-VMs load the descriptor and set the memory address mapping status. According to memory-disk bitmap, save the data on VM disk in sub-VMs when sub-VMs load the memory data, and then resume the sub-VMs booting process.

4.2 Parent-VM timing push stage

After the Full-Ram copy stage, parent-VM starts the timing push process. After resuming the parent-VM booting process, create an improved dirty page bitmap.

If the parent-VM memory is rewritten, use dirty page bitmap record the information of VM dirty memory page. One VM memory address only has one dirty page bitmap record at most. Maybe the same memory page can be rewritten for many times, so we record the timestamp in the dirty page bitmap. It can make sure the memory page only has one incremental compressed data relative to current memory page in parent-VM and reduce frequency of restoring the same memory page in sub-VMs. The process of rewriting the memory in parent-VM timing push stage is as follows: 1) $B \leftarrow$ new dirty page bitmap record, B->MA $\leftarrow$ VM memory address. If VM memory is new VM memory, go to 2), else go to 3). 2) $T \leftarrow$ all memory page data is 0, go to 4). 3) $T \leftarrow$ memory page data before rewrite, go to 4). 4) Rewrite memory page, $R \leftarrow$ VM memory data after rewrite. If no record of B->MA in dirty page bitmap, go to 5), else go to 7). 5) B->IC = XBRLE(T XOR R), B->TS $\leftarrow$ timestamp. If VM memory rewrite data read from VM disk, go to 6). 6) B->DA $\leftarrow$ VM disk address. 7) $BE \leftarrow$ the exists record of B->MA in dirty page bitmap, B->IC = XBRLE((XBRLE(BE->IC) XOR T) XOR R), B->TS $\leftarrow$ timestamp. If VM memory rewrite data read from VM disk, go to 8), else go to 9). 8) B->DA $\leftarrow$ VM disk address, go to 9). 9) If BE->DA != null and BE->DA != B->DA, go to 10), else go to 12). 10) $DB \leftarrow$ the exists record of BE->DA in disk bitmap. If DB->$flag$ marked as read, go to 11), else go to 12). 11) Delete DB in disk bitmap, go to 12). 12) Delete BE in dirty page bitmap.

After the Full-Ram copy stage, parent-VM continuing booting process and timing push the dirty page bitmap generated by rewriting VM memory pages. Set up a pushing timer in parent-VM and then set the preset time of pushing timer and the preset length of dirty page bitmap. If pushing timer reaches the preset time and no dirty page record in dirty page bitmap, stop the timing push process. If pushing timer reaches the preset time or the length of dirty page bitmap reaches preset length, multicast dirty page bitmap to sub-VMs if dirty page bitmap has the record of dirty page, then reset pushing timer and clear dirty page bitmap, continue the timing push process.

4.3 On-demand copy stage

After sub-VMs received the dirty page bitmap from parent-VM, set the VM memory address mapping status immediately. Tag the VM memory page mapping to the "missing page". When sub-VMs reading the "missing page" status memory page in sub-VMs booting process, start On-demand copy process of sub-VMs. On-demand process of sub-VMs is as follows: 1) If VM memory page is actually ąřmissing pageąś, go to 2), else go to 3). 2) $T \leftarrow$ all VM memory page data is 0, go to 4). 3) $T \leftarrow$ VM memory page data, go to 4). 4) $MA \leftarrow$ VM memory address. If there is no record of MA in dirty page bitmap, go to 5), else go to 6). 5) Send memory request of MA to parent-VM, wait sub-VMs receive the record of MA in dirty page bitmap, go to 6). 6) $Blist \leftarrow$ record list of MA in dirty page bitmap with timestamp in ascending order, go to 7). 7) For each B in $Blist$, T = T XOR XBRLE(B->IC), if B->DA not null, store T to VM disk address B->DA. go to 8). 8) Rewrite VM memory of MA with T, delete all record of MA in dirty page bitmap.

When parent-VM receives the missing page request from sub-VMs, notify On-demand copy process of parent-VM to handle the request. In this process, we achieve the page prefetching. On-demand process of parent-VM is as follows: 1) $MA \leftarrow$ VM memory address of missing page request. If parent-VM is handling the request of MA, go to 2), else go to 3). 2) Delete this request. 3) If there is no record of MA in dirty page bitmap, go to 4), else go to 5). 4) Send hang-up order to sub-VMs, wait parent-VM rewrite VM memory of MA, go to 5). 5) Multicast dirty page bitmap to sub-VMs. If timing push process is not stopped, go to 6), else go to 7). 6) Reset pushing timer, go to 7). 7) Clear dirty page bitmap.

4.4 Parent-VM downtime push stage

If parent-VM meet the condition that stops the timing push process before parent-VM complete the booting process, parent-VM will continue generating the dirty page bitmap. Parent-VM stop running temporarily and multicast dirty page bitmap to sub-VMs when parent-VM completed the boot process. Then multicast VM disk data that do not record in VM disk bitmap to sub-VMs. After parent-VM down time push process, stop parent-VM deployment process, resume the running of parent-VM, and start receiving calculating tasks. Continuing the sub-VM booting process at the same time, when the sub-VM booting finished, clear the sub-VM deployment information, notify cloud computing platform management process to start receiving assigned computing task. So far deployment processes accomplished initial status creation of virtual cluster in the cloud computing platform.

5. Evaluation

To establish a customized LFS system requires about 1.3GB of the partition so as to have enough space to store and compile all the source packages. The LFS system itself does not occupy so much space and most of the space required used to provide adequate temporary space for the software compiler. The kernel uses swap space to store the data in order to free up memory space for running processes. The swap partition that LFS system uses can be the same with the one that the host system uses. So we do not have to create a new one for the LFS system when the host system already has a swap partition.

In our experimental configuration, hosts with the same type are selected. We use HP proLiant ML350 as hosts in cloud platform. These hosts are configured with Xeon E5506 2.13GHz four core processor, 8GB DDRIII RAM, 4TB 7.2K 6Gbps hard disk and NC326i PCI Express 1000Mbit/s

NIC. In order to simplify the process of customized VM image generation, we install LFS Live CD 6.2-3 with kernel 2.6.16.26 on all hosts as host system. Virtual Tool is Xen 4.1.1. We configure all VMs with single core, 40GB VM hard disk. To ensure parent-VM boot successfully, we configure VM memory size with 128M, 512M and 1G respectively in experiments. We respectively customize VM image with 38.6M, 405M and 1021M for deployment experiments. We use the Linux traffic shaping interface to limit network bandwidth for deployment process. We limit bandwidth to 500Mbit/sec, 400Mbit/sec, 300Mbit/sec, 200Mbit/sec, 100Mbit/sec, 50Mbit/sec and 5Mbit/sec. We deploy VMs ten times in each experiment and take average data of the ten tests as results. We compare DCVM with the following method: 1) Full State Copy (FSC). This method completes the parent-VM boot process with loading customized VM image first. Then multicast the full parent-VM state to target hosts. After target hosts receive the VM state, sub-VMs on target hosts load the VM state. 2) SnowFlock. This method boots the parent-VM with loading customized VM image. After parent-VM complete the boot process, clone the parent-VM to sub-VMs with VM fork.

5.1 VM image size

To reduce system resource occupation and fundamentally solve the problem of too long virtual machine downtime in the deployment process, the VM image size should be as small as possible. We compare the customized VM image generated by LFS with current lite release version of Linux.

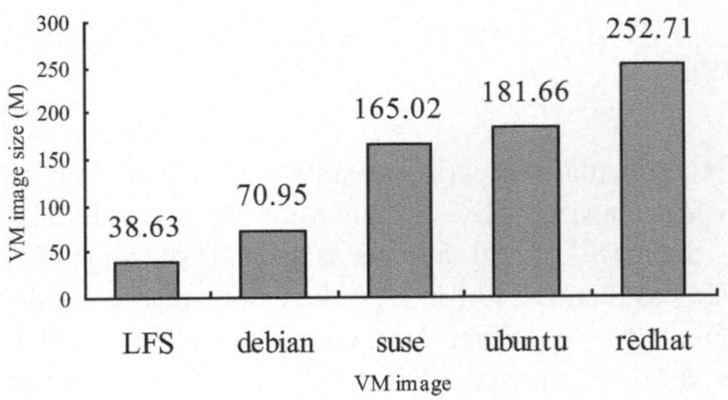

Fig. 2: VM image size

We customize VM image as web servers. Each VM image installs Apache 2.2.22 and network components. Comparison result as showed in Fig.2. We can limit the size of customized VM image generated by LFS at 38.63M. We install Apache on other lite version of Linux, size of Debian is 70.95M, size of suse is 165.02M, size of ubuntu is 181.66M and size of Redhat is 252.71M. LFS visibly reduce the system consumption. LFS is much easier in the minimizing process comparing with others. By LFS, it also has much advantage in booting speed and system consumption, comparison result as showed in Fig.3, we configure VM memory size with 512M. LFS only take 6.76s

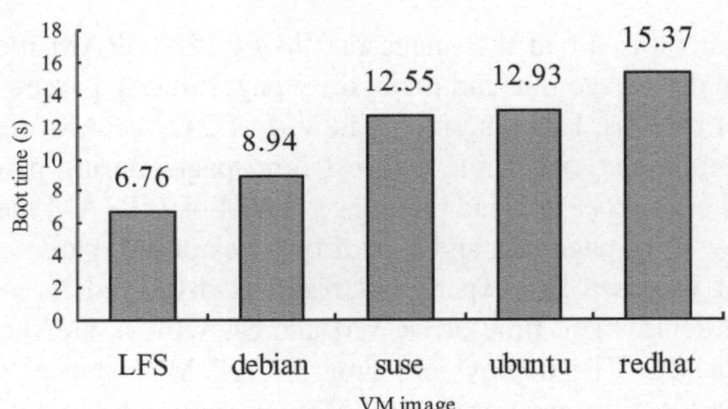

Fig. 3: VM Boot time of every VM image

to complete the booting process. Debian boot time is 8.94s, suse boot time is 12.55s, ubuntu boot time is 12.93s and Redhat boot time is 15.37s. The boot speed of VM that load customized VM image generated by LFS is faster than others. By the reduction of VM image size, we effectively reduce the VMs communication consumption and optimize the VM deployment speed between virtual nodes.

5.2 VM image deployment time

To provide better cloud service for users, deployment time should be as short as possible. We customize three VM images with different size and set all installed services as daemon. We deploy 8 VMs compare the deployment time of DCVM with Full state copy and SnowFlock in different network bandwidth.

We customize a small VM image with size of 38.6M, load the image in parent-VM configure with 128M RAM, 512M RAM and 1024M RAM respectively in different bandwidths. It means a low dirty page rate and less dirty pages during parent-VM boot process. The experiment result is displayed in Fig.4. The deployment time of DCVM and SnowFlock are shorter than FSC. The deployment time of DCVM is close to SnowFlock, but we also can see the deployment time of DCVM is weakly shorter than SnowFlock.

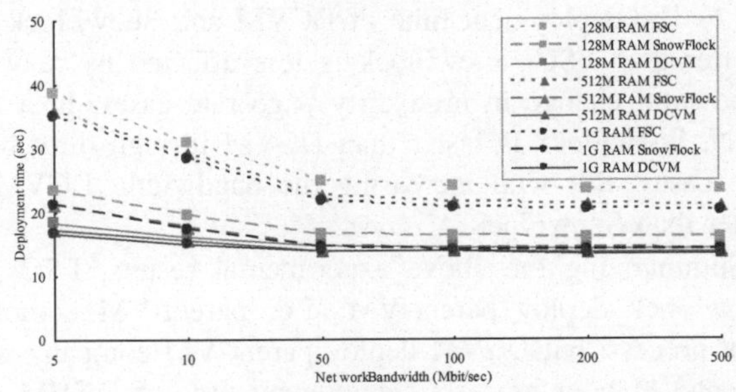

Fig. 4: VM deployment time with loading 38.6M customized VM image in different bandwidths

We customize a VM image with middle size of 405M, load the image in parent-VM configure with 128M RAM, 512M RAM and 1024M RAM respectively in different bandwidths. Load the image in VM of 128M RAM means high dirty page rate and many dirty pages during parent-VM boot process. Load the image in VM of 512M RAM means common dirty page rate and less dirty pages during parent-VM boot process. Load the image in VM of 1G RAM means a low dirty page rate and less dirty pages during parent-VM boot process. The experiment result is displayed in Fig.5. The deployment time of DCVM and SnowFlock are shorter than FSC. The deployment time of DCVM is shorter than SnowFlock in most cases. In 5Mbit/sec network bandwidth, deploy 128M RAM VM with SnowFlock will take about 80s and DCVM will take 89s which represents SnowFlock is a little faster than DCVM when generate many dirty pages in a low LAN.

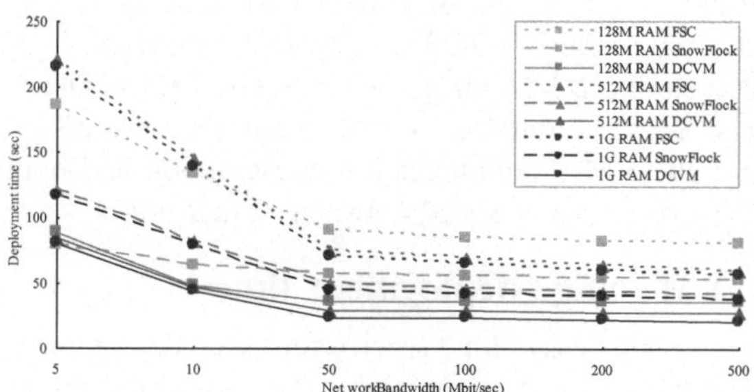

Fig. 5: VM deployment time with loading 405M customized VM image in different bandwidths

We customize big VM image with size of 1021M, load the image in parent-VM configure with 128M RAM, 512M RAM and 1024M RAM respectively in different bandwidths. Load the image in VM of 128M RAM means fairly high dirty page rate and a lot of dirty pages during parent-VM boot process. Load the image in VM of 512M RAM means high dirty page rate and many dirty pages during parent-VM boot process. Load the image in VM of 1G RAM means less dirty page rate and many dirty pages during parent-VM boot process. The experiment result is displayed in Fig.6. The deployment time of DCVM and SnowFlock are shorter than FSC. SnowFlock is less affected by network bandwidth change in high dirty page rate cases. In a low LAN, SnowFlock is faster than DCVM in high dirty page rate cases. But with increasing the bandwidth, DCVM is faster than SnowFlock.

Summarizing the above experimental results, FSC and SnowFlock deploy parent-VM after parent-VM complete boot process, but DCVM deploy parent-VM company with parent-VM boot process. Deployment time of DCVM and SnowFlock are shorter than FSC. FSC is not affected by dirty page rate and the amount of dirty pages. Network bandwidth and RAM size determine the efficiency of FSC. SnowFlock is faster than DCVM in high dirty page rate and low LAN cases, but SnowFlock does not synchronize the VM disk data. In most cases, DCVM is faster than SnowFlock and it

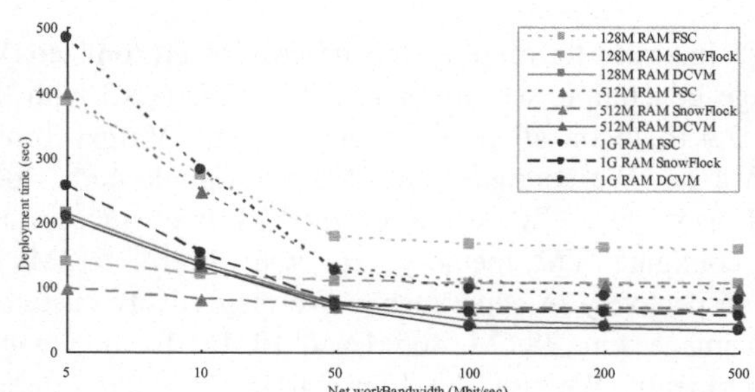

Fig. 6: VM deployment time with loading 1021M customized VM image in different bandwidths

synchronizes the VM disk data.

5.3 Total transfer data size of deployment process

To decrease the network overhead, transfer data during deployment process should be as little as possible. We set the bandwidth to 100Mbit/sec for above experiments and compare the total transfer data size of DCVM with FSC and SnowFlock.

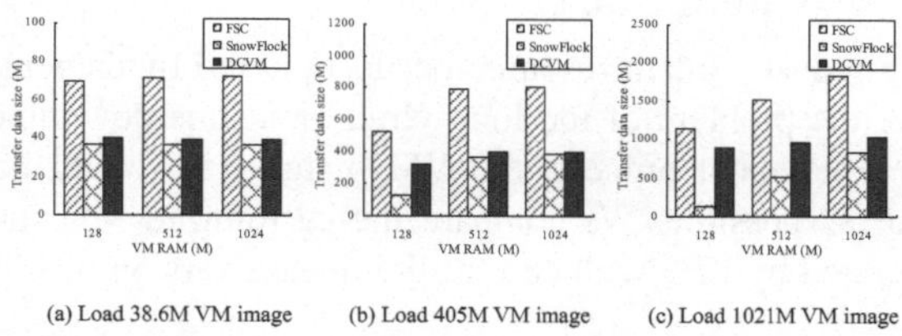

(a) Load 38.6M VM image (b) Load 405M VM image (c) Load 1021M VM image

Fig. 7: Total transfer data size of FSC, SnowFlock and DCVM

Experimental comparison results as showed in Fig.7. Total transfer data size of DCVM and SnowFlock are significantly less than FSC. Total transfer data size of SnowFlock is much less than DCVM in high dirty page rate cases showed in Fig.7 (b), (c). When VM configure with a small RAM relative to customized VM image, SnowFlock will transfer less data. Total transfer data size of DCVM will close to SnowFlock with increase of memory size. When VM configure with an enough RAM size relative to image, DCVM transfer a little more data than SnowFlock, but DCVM synchronize the VM disk data with less extra data transfer. DCVM achieves sub-VMs independent of parent-VM by synchronizing VM disk data.

6. Conclusion

In this paper, we presented the design, implementation and evaluation of a rapid deployment method for customized VM in the cloud platform. We customize the VM image with LFS to reduce the VM image size. The customized VM satisfy the user request and consume less space. It also speeds up the VM deployment process and decreases the amount of transfer data. To improve the efficiency of VM deployment we use a rapid deployment method combines pre-copy algorithm and post-copy algorithm. To decrease the transfer data and reduce the communication overhead in deployment process, we use the incremental compressed mechanism to compress the data of memory pages and use the multicast to transfer the data. In order to achieve running sub-VMs independent of parent-VM, we synchronize the VM disk data during the deployment process. The experimental results show that our approach is efficient for VM deployment.

To further improve the performance of VM deployment, there are also many problems need to be solved in the future. In customized VM image generation process, we find the target host only considers the match degree. In a cloud platform with workload or in a heterogeneous cloud platform, it is not enough to only consider the match degree and the target host we find may be not the best one. We plan to add the performance parameter for finding the target host. It usually selects the hosts for deploying the VMs with simple methods. It is unreasonable in a cloud platform with workload or in a heterogeneous cloud platform. To select reasonable hosts for VM deployment, we plan to abstraction hosts selection problem for a packing problem and consider the performance and power consumption as parameters. In our approach, trigger condition of Full-Ram copy process is VM memory page rewritten. In a few cases, it is too late to rewrite VM memory page firstly and it causes the Full-Ram copy process starts too late in boot process. In these cases, advantage of our approach cannot be expressed. Assign the time of trigger Full-Ram copy process is an open question. Our approach uses the multicast to transfer the data in a LAN, but multicast is not appropriate for WAN. We plan to use multicast in LAN and bit torrent in WAN in order to extend our approach to a wide area network.

References

[1] WANG Li-zhe, TAO Jie, KUNZE M, "Scientific cloud computing: early definition and experience [C]," Proc of the 10th IEEE International Conference on High Performance Computing and Communications. 825-830, 2008.

[2] Nakajima J, Lin Q, Yang S, et al, "Optimizing Virtual Machines Using Hybrid Virtualization," Proc. Of the 2011 ACM Symposium on Applied Computing (SACąŕ11). 573-578, 2011.

[3] Nathan Regola, Jean-Christophe Ducom, "Recommendations for Virtualization Technologies in High Performance Computing," 2010 IEEE second International Conference on Cloud Computing Technology and Science. 409-416, 2010.

[4] Hao Sun, Kento Aida, "AHybrid and secure Mechanism to Execute Parameter Survey Applications on Local and Public Cloud Resources," 2010 IEEE Second International Conference on Cloud Computing Technology and Science. 118-126, 2010.

[5] Kim Hyunjoo,El-Khamra Yaakoub, Jha Shantenu, Parashar Manish, "Exploring application and infrastructure adaptation on hybrid grid-cloud infrastructure," HPDC 2010 Proceedings of the 19th ACM International Symposium on High Performance Distributed Computing. 402-412, 2010.

[6] Gerard Beekmans, "Linux From Scratch," http://www.linuxfromscratch.org/lfs/view/stable/, 2012.

[7] Clark C, Fraser K, Hand S, et al, "Live migration of virtual machines [C]," Proceedings of the Second Symposium on Networked Systems Design and Implementation (NSDIąŕ 05). Boston: USENIX ASSOC. 273-286, 2005.

[8] Nelson M, Lim B, Hutchins G, "Fast transparent migration for virtual machines[C]," Proceedings of the USENIX Annual Technical Conference (USENIXąŕ 05). Anaheim: USENIX ASSOC. 391-394, 2005.

[9] Michael R Hines, Umesh Deshpande, Kartik Gopalan, "Post-copy live migration of virtual machines," ACM SIGOPS Operating Systems Review. 14-26, 2009.

[10] Michael R Hines, Kartik Gopalan, "Post-Copy Based Live Virtual Machine Migration Using Adaptive Pre-Paging and Dynamic Self-Ballooning," Proc. of the 2009 ACM SIGPLAN/SIGOPS International Conf. on Virtual Execution Environments. 51-60, 2009.

[11] Ori Ben-Yitzhak, Irit Goft, et al, "An algorithm for parallel incremental compaction," ACM SIGPLAN Notices - MSP 2002 and ISMM 2002(Proceedings of the 3rd international symposium on Memory management). 100-105, 2003.

[12] H Jin, L Deng, S Wu, X Shi and X Pan, "Live Virtual Machine Migration with Adaptive Memory Compression," Proc. of International Conf. on Cluster Computing and Workshops(CLUSTER '09). 1-10, 2009.

[13] P Svärd, B Hudzia, J Tordsson, "Evaluation of Delta Compression Techniques for Efficient Live Migration of Large Virtual Machine," Proc. of the 2011 ACM SIGPLAN/SIGOPS International Conf. on Virtual Execution Environments. 111-120, 2011.

[14] AA Fröhlich, W Schröder-Preikschat, "Tailor-made operating systems for embedded parallel applications," Lecture Notes in Computer Science. 1361-1373, 1999.

[15] Hasan MZ, Sotirios SG, "Customized kernel execution on reconfigurable hardware for embedded applications," Microprocessors and Microsystems. 211-220, 2008.

[16] Montgomery J, Brewster GB, Yee WG, "A customized Linux Kernel for Providing Notification of Pending Financial Transaction Information," 7th IEEE Consumer Communications and Networking Conference. 1021-1022, 2010.

[17] Schmidt Matthias, Fallenbeck Niels, Smith Matthew, Freisleben Bernd, "Efficient distribution of virtual machines for cloud computing," Proceedings of the 18th Euromicro Conference on Parallel, Distributed and Network-Based Processing. 567-574, 2010.

[18] P Svärd, J Tordsson, B Hudzia, E Elmroth, "High performance live migration through dynamic page transfer reordering and compression," Proc. of the 3rd IEEE International Conf. on Cloud Computing Technology and Science. 542-548, 2011.

[19] H Jin, W Gao, S Wu, X Shi, X Wu, F Zhou. Optimizing the live migration of virtual machine by CPU scheduling. Journal of Network and Computer Applications. Vol. 34, No. 4, 1088-1096 (2011).

[20] Laurikainen R, Laitinen J, Lehtovuori P, Nurminen JK, "Improving the Efficiency of Deploying Virtual Machines in a Cloud Environment," 2012 INTERNATIONAL CONFERENCE ON CLOUD AND SERVICE COMPUTING (CSC). 232-239, 2012.

[21] H. Andres Lagar-Cavilla, Joseph A. Whitney, Adin Scannell, Philip Patchin, Stephen M. Rumble, Eyal de Lara, Michael Brudno, M. Satyanarayanan, "SnowFlock: Rapid Virtual Machine Cloning for Cloud Computing," EuroSys 09 Proceedings of the 4th ACM European conference on Computer systems. 2009.

[22] Lagar-Cavilla HA, Whitney JA, Bryant R, et al, "SnowFlock: Virtual Machine Cloning as a First-Class Cloud Primitive," ACM Transactions on Computer Systems (TOCS). Vol. 29, No. 2, 1-45, 2011.

[23] Vrable M, Ma J, Chen J, et al, "Scalability, fidelity and containment in the Potemkin virtual honeyfarm," Proc 20th Symposium on Operating Systems Principles (SOSP). 148-162, 2005.

[24] Wu XX, Shen ZM, Wu R, Lin YF, "Jump-start Cloud: Efficient Deployment Framework for Large-scale Cloud Applications," CONCURRENCY AND COMPUTATION-PRACTICE & EXPERIENCE. 2120-2137, 2012.

Optimizing Performance for Coalition Structure Generation Problems' IDP Algorithm

Francisco Cruz-Mencía
Computer Architecture Department.
Universitat Autònoma de Barcelona. Spain
Institut d'Investigació en
Intel·ligència Artificial
IIIA-CSIC. Spain

Jesús Cerquides
Institut d'Investigació en
Intel·ligència Artificial
IIIA-CSIC. Spain

Antonio Espinosa
Computer Architecture Department.
Universitat Autònoma de Barcelona.
Spain

Juan Carlos Moure
Computer Architecture Department.
Universitat Autònoma de Barcelona.
Spain

Juan Antonio Rodriguez-Aguilar
Institut d'Investigació en
Intel·ligència Artificial
IIIA-CSIC. Spain

Abstract—**The Coalition Structure Generation (CSG) problem is well-known in the area of Multi-Agent Systems. Its goal is establishing coalitions between agents while maximizing the global welfare. Between the existing different algorithms designed to solve the CSG problem, DP and IDP are the ones with smaller temporal complexity. After analyzing the performance of the DP and IDP algorithms, we identify which is the most frequent operation and propose an optimized method. Then, we analyze the memory access pattern and find that its irregular behavior represents a potential performance bottleneck. In addition, we study and implement a method for dividing the work in different threads. We show that selecting the best algorithmic options can improve performance by 10x or more. Furthermore, the execution in a dual-socket, six-core processor computer may increase performance by an additional 5x-6x.**

I. Introduction

In the multi-agent systems area, coalition formation is one of the central types of collaboration. It involves the creation of disjoint groups of autonomous agents that collaborate in order to satisfy their individual or collective goals. One of the major research challenges in the field is the search for an effective set of coalitions that maximises the global satisfaction [1] of the agents.

Coalition formation is applied to many actual-world problems such as distributed vehicle route planning [2], task allocation [1], and airport slots allocation [3]. More recently, it has been considered in the realm of social networks [4].

According to [2], the coalition formation process is divided into three activities. In this paper we focus on the first one, namely coalition structure generation (CSG). Notice that finding the optimal coalition structure is $\mathcal{NP}$-complete [2]. The search space handled by CSG is very large since the number of possible coalition structures grows exponentially with the number of agents.

Several algorithms in the literature tackle the CSG problem. In particular, we distinguish three approaches: (i) optimal algorithms based on dynamic programming (e.g. DP [5], IDP [6]), which offer guaranteed run-times over arbitrary coalition value distributions; their complexity is $\Theta(3^n)$, where n is the number of agents; (ii) optimal algorithms with anytime properties whose convergence time to a solution largely depends on the coalition value distribution, which present a complexity $\Theta(n^n)$; and (iii) heuristic approximate algorithms (e.g. [1]), which aim at computing solutions faster than optimal algorithms without offering quality guarantees. Unfortunately, as widely noticed in the literature, the computational costs of optimal algorithms are highly demanding even for a moderate number of agents.

Against this background, in this paper we propose to optimize the algorithms based on dynamic programing. The implementation can be used as a building block for heuristic algorithms as a means to explore complete subspaces in an effective way.

As proposed in D-IP [7], where a distributed anytime algorithm is presented, in this paper we present an algorithm able to exploit the power of distribution but using a different paradigm. Our proposal is building a IDP based algorithm able to run in a shared memory scenario, which is common in nowadays computers [8]. Using a shared memory paradigm simplifies the communication between computation nodes, since there is no need to send messages between them, but it requires a data dependence study, because of possible synchronization.

As far as we are concerned, no reference implementation neither of DP nor IDP algorithms has been published. When studying and evaluating different implementation alternatives, we have found, though, non-negligible issues on the algorithmic details that have a considerable impact on the overall performance. The contributions of this work can be summarized as:

- We analyze and evaluate fast methods for generating splittings, the most critical operation, establishing that a bad choice can degrade performance by $10x$ or more.

- We parallelize the generation of splittings and execute the problem on a shared-memory, multi-core, multi-thread and multi-processor system.
- We identify the main performance bottleneck: both the sequential and parallel execution are limited by the lack of temporal and spatial locality of the memory access pattern, and by the weak support for irregular and scattered accesses provided by current memory hierarchies.
- We find out that the performance advantage of IDP versus DP is only realized for large problems, when reducing memory bandwidth requirements pay off.
- We make our code publicly available at the following URL: https://github.com/CoalitionStructureGeneration/DPIDP.

The paper is organized as follows. Section 2 introduces the CSG problem and describes the state of the art on dynamic programming techniques. Section 3 analyzes implementation issues such as data representation, most frequent operations and bottlenecks in a single core environment and proposes solutions to reduce execution time. Section 4 studies how to parallelize the IDP algorithm and Section 5 evaluates the performance of single and multi-threaded implementations. The paper ends summarizing the conclusions and presenting future work in Section 6.

II. The Coalition Structure Generation (CSG) Problem

In this section we describe what a Coalition Structure Generation (CSG) problem is and how dynamic programming algorithms have addressed it to find an optimal solution. To do so, we will use the following terminology:

- **Agent** (a_x): A single agent. E.g. Ann or Bob.
- **Agent Set** (A): The set of all available agents. $A = \{a_1, a_2, \ldots, a_n\}$.
  E.g. A= {Ann, Bob, Chris, Dave}.
- **Coalition** (C): $C \subseteq A$. C is a subset of A that contains the agents participating in a coalition.
  E.g. C= {Ann, Chris, Dave}.
- **Split** : Is the operation performing a binary partition of a coalition.
  E.g. {Ann,Chris,Dave} $\rightarrow$ ({Ann},{Chris,Dave}).
- **Splitting** : Is the result of the split operation. A splitting is a 2-tuple represented by (C_1, C_2). C=$C_1 \cup C_2$ where $|C_1|$,$|C_2|$ >0, $C_1 \cap C_2$=$\emptyset$.
  E.g. ({Ann},{Chris,Dave}) or ({Ann,Chris},{Dave}).
- **Coalition Structure** (CS): Is a collection of disjoint Coalitions such that their union constitute the Agent Set.
  E.g. ({Ann},{Bob},{Chris,Dave}).

Consider a group of n agents A=$\{a_1$,a_2,..., $a_n\}$. Agents can establish coalitions with other agents in order to perform a task. Each agent has its own preferences, meaning that some coalitions are preferred. These preferences are expressed by a value assigned to each possible coalition, denoted $value[C]$. It can be predefined or can be computed by every agent on the basis of its view of the world. In any case, coalition values are inputs known before solving the CSG problem. They can be represented by a table of size 2^n, one per coalition. Table I shows an example of the input data for a CSG Problem of size 4.

The goal of the CSG problem is to find the coalition structure providing maximum global satisfaction. From Table I one can notice that the coalition formed by $\{a_2$,$a_3\}$ has lower value than the sum of $value[\{a_2\}]$ and $value[\{a_3\}]$, meaning that agents a_2 and a_3 prefer to work alone rather than collaborate.

C	$value[C]$	C	$value[C]$	C	$value[C]$
$\{a_1\}$	33	$\{a_1,a_3\}$	87	$\{a_1,a_2,a_3\}$	97
$\{a_2\}$	39	$\{a_1,a_4\}$	70	$\{a_1,a_2,a_4\}$	111
$\{a_3\}$	13	$\{a_2,a_3\}$	36	$\{a_1,a_3,a_4\}$	100
$\{a_4\}$	40	$\{a_2,a_4\}$	52	$\{a_2,a_3,a_4\}$	132
$\{a_1,a_2\}$	87	$\{a_3,a_4\}$	67	$\{a_1,a_2,a_3,a_4\}$	151

TABLE I: Coalition values for a CSG problem of size 4.

A. DP Algorithm

The DP[5] algorithm uses Dynamic Programming to find the optimal solution of the problem. For a given input data, DP first evaluates all the possible coalitions of size 2. For each possible pair of agents a_x and a_y, DP evaluates if it is better to form a coalition or not. This is done by comparing $value[\{a_x$,$a_y\}]$ with $value[\{a_x\}]$+ $value[\{a_y\}]$. The maximum value represents the preferred formation and substitutes the previous $value[\{a_x, a_y\}]$.

After evaluating all coalitions of size 2, DP starts evaluating all possible coalitions of size 3, saving the maximum between $value[\{a_x, a_y, a_z\}]$ and all its possible splittings. There are three ways to split the coalition: $\{a_x, a_y\}$+$\{a_z\}$, $\{a_x, a_z\}$+$\{a_y\}$ and $\{a_x\}$+$\{a_y, a_z\}$. Note that all the splittings for coalitions of size 3 have at most 2 elements. Since DP evaluates the coalitions of size 3 after evaluating and finding optimal values for coalitions of size 2, the new coalition values computed for size 3 will also be optimal. This process is repeated incrementing the size of the coalitions (m).

Algorithm 1 Pseudo-code of the DP Algorithm

```
1: for m = 2 → n do
2:     for C ← coalitionsOfSize(m) do            ▷ (n choose m) iterations
3:         max_value ← value[C]
4:         C1 ← getFirstSplit(C)
5:         while (C1) do                         ▷ 2^(n-1) - 1 iterations
6:             C2 ← C - C1
7:             if (max_value < value[C1] + value[C2]) then
8:                 max_value ← value[C1] + value[C2]
9:             end if
10:            C1 ← getNextSplit(C1)
11:        end while
12:        value[C] ← max_value
13:    end for
14: end for
```

The DP algorithm (see Algorithm 1) is composed of three nested loops: (i) the outer loop (line 1), where coalition size

(m) grows from 2 to the total number of agents (n), (ii) the intermediate loop (line 2), where all coalitions of size m are generated, a total of $\binom{n}{m}$, and (iii) the inner loop (line 5), where each coalition is split and evaluated, a total of $2^{m-1}-1$ splittings. The temporal complexity of the DP algorithm is determined by these three loops: $\Theta(3^n)$.

B. IDP Algorithm

While DP generates all the possible splittings of each coalition, IDP [6] introduces conditions to avoid the generation and evaluation of a large amount of splittings. The performance advantage of IDP is a reduction in the total number of operations and memory accesses. Overall, IDP explores only between 38% and 40% of the splittings explored by DP for problems from 22 to 28 agents. Algorithm 2 presents the pseudo-code of IDP, where the main changes are the filters introduced on lines 4 and 6.

Algorithm 2 Pseudo-code of the IDP Algorithm

```
1: for m = 2 → n do
2:    for C ← coalitionsOfSize(m) do            ▷ (n choose m) iterations
3:       max_value ← value[C]
4:       (lower_bound, high_bound) ← IDPBounds(n, m)
5:       C1 ← getFirstSplit(C, lower_bound)
6:       while (sizeOf(C1) ≤ high_bound do
7:          C2 ← C − C1
8:          if (max_value < value[C1] + value[C2] then
9:             max_value ← value[C1] + value[C2]
10:         end if
11:         C1 ← getNextSplit(C1, C)
12:      end while
13:      value[C] ← max_value
14:   end for
15: end for
```

III. Single-Thread Implementation

In this section we analyze the operations of generating and evaluating splittings inside the inner loop, which consumes $\approx$ 99 % of the execution time. We compare two suitable options and analyze their performance and the impact of the memory access pattern.

A. Data representation

The coalitions and their associated values are stored in a vector. A coalition is represented using an integer index where the bit at position x of the index indicates that agent x is a member of the coalition. The index determines the vector element containing the coalition value. Using this representation, the input of the CSG problem fits into a vector of $2^n - 1$ positions. With coalitions represented by 4-byte words, we can run problems up to 32 agents.

B. Splitting generation

The splitting generation problem can be reduced to the subset enumeration problem, since each coalition splitting is composed by a subset, C_1, and its complementary, C_2. Generating all the subsets C_1 from a coalition C and then calculating the complementary $C_2 = C - C_1$, though, would produce the same splitting twice: once for each of the splitting subsets.

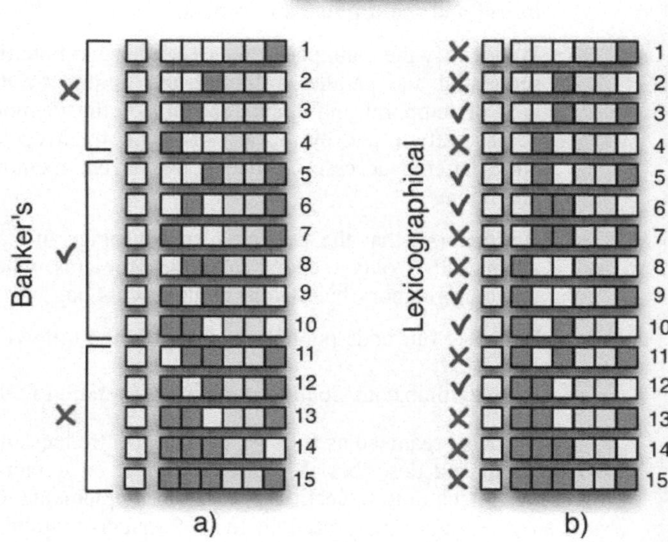

Fig. 1: a) Banker's sequence versus b) lexicographical order.

We remove one element from the coalition (the agent with the highest rank) when performing the subset enumeration, so that the removed element is never part of the enumerated subset and always belongs to its complementary.

There exist several ways of enumerating subsets [9], like banker's sequence, lexicographical order, and gray codes. The banker's sequence seems a suitable option for IDP, since it generates the splittings in growing order of $|C_1|$, and then simplifies the filtering of splittings by its size. Figure 1a shows a scheme of the banker's sequence operation for C=$\{a_1,a_4,a_5,a_6,a_7\}$, and assuming that only coalitions with $|C_1|$=2 need to be evaluated. Note that element a_7 is always assigned to the complementary subset (lighted colour). The generation starts directly from the first splitting of size $|C_1| = 2$, follows with the remaining $\binom{4}{2} - 1$ subsets of the same size, and stops before generating the first subset of size 3. The code does not waste instructions generating useless subsets.

When generating splittings in lexicographical order (see Fig. 1b), some filtering code is required to check that the size of the splitting ranges between a given pair of bounds. Execution resources are wasted to generate splittings that are then discarded, and to perform the filter check. In Fig. 1, only 6 out of 14 splittings are actually needed (note the check and discard crossed signs).

Both methods were implemented using recurrent functions that calculate the next splitting from the previous one. The lexicographical order was implemented with a few number of very simple operations: $C_1 \leftarrow (C_1 + C^{**})$ AND C, where C^{**} is the two's complement of C, that can be precalculated for all the splittings of a given coalition. The whole splitting code requires only 7 machine code instructions in a current x86 ISA. On the other hand, our implementation of banker's sequence, an improved version of the algorithm published in [9], required, on average, 6 times more instructions. More details about the implementation, like the usage of a special population count instruction for computing $|C_1|$, can be found in the published code.

C. Memory accesses

All memory accesses correspond to reads from the vector of coalition values performed in the inner loop of the algorithm, and a few writes on the intermediate loop. The total number of data read operations done by the DP algorithm is around 2×3^n. As explained above, IDP evaluates only a subset of the splittings, corresponding to 38%-40% of the read operations performed by DP.

The memory-level parallelism of the algorithm is moderate. The inner loop recurrence can generate multiple independent read requests, without having to wait for data, subject to storage availability for pending requests and for the window of instructions blocked on those data.

The data-reuse degree of the algorithm is high. There are 2^n elements in the $value$ vector, and so the average number of reads to the same data item is $\approx 2\times(3/2)^n$ ($\approx$100,000 for $n = 27$). However, accesses to the same item are scattered in time, specially when the algorithm analyzes medium- or large-size coalitions. The combinatorial nature of the problem involves a pseudo-random read access pattern, where reads that are consecutive in time refer to data from distant positions in memory.

The bad performance behavior of the memory access pattern arises for vectors that do not fit into the processor's cache. The vector size is 2^{n+2} bytes, which is 16 MBytes for n=22. For larger n's an important amount of vector accesses will miss the cache and will request a full 64-Byte cache block to DRAM. This creates both latency and bandwidth problems. The moderate memory-level parallelism helps hiding part of the DRAM latency but, as we will show later, an important amount of this latency is exposed in the execution time. Also, given the lack of spatial locality, most of the 64-Byte block read from DRAM will be unused. In the worst situation, only 4 Bytes out of 64 will be used, giving a bandwidth efficiency of $1/16$= 0.0625.

IV. Multi-thread Implementation

This section analyzes the algorithm's data workflow in order to find its potential thread-level parallelism (TLP). Exploiting concurrency efficiently is not straightforward, and a new method to generate coalitions is devised. Finally, potential performance problems are described.

A. Identifying sources of TLP

The simplest and most efficient approach is always to parallelize the outer loop of a program. DP and IDP, though, exhibit loop-carried dependencies on the outer loop: the optimal values for coalitions of size m must be generated before using them for generating the optimal values for coalitions of size $m+1$.

The intermediate loop generates all the coalitions of a given size, and for each coalition it analyzes all the splittings of certain sizes. Tasks corresponding to coalitions are independent: they only modify the value associated to the coalition, and only read values corresponding to coalitions of lower size. Therefore, there cannot exist read-after-write (RAW) dependencies nor any other false data dependence among the tasks. However, the single-thread code was designed to accelerate coalition generation by using an inherently sequential algorithm that uses the previous coalition to generate the next one in lexicographical order. The next subsection describes a method for breaking this artificial dependence.

B. Speeding up Work distribution among threads

Assume we have t threads and we want each thread to evaluate a disjoint set of coalitions. We must distribute work to assure good load balance, and do it in a fast and efficient way. Table II illustrates the generation of all the possible coalitions of size m=3 from a set of n=6 agents. The single-thread code implements a sequential algorithm to generate in lexicographical order all $\binom{6}{3}$=20 coalitions, represented as bitmaps in the binary encoding columns of Table II. In practice, we must calculate cnt=$\binom{n}{m}$ and then assign cnt/t coalitions to each thread. Once a thread obtains its starting position in the coalition series, say k, it can generate the whole range with the fast sequential method. But we need an efficient strategy to generate the kth coalition without having to compute all the previous coalitions from the beginning.

Order (k)	Encoding Bin	Dec	Coalitions	Order (k)	Encoding Bin	Dec	Coalitions
1	...111	7	$\{a_1, a_2, a_3\}$	11	..111.	14	$\{a_2, a_3, a_4\}$
2	..1.11	11	$\{a_1, a_2, a_4\}$	12	.1.11.	22	$\{a_2, a_3, a_5\}$
3	.1..11	19	$\{a_1, a_2, a_5\}$	13	1..11.	38	$\{a_2, a_3, a_6\}$
4	1...11	35	$\{a_1, a_2, a_6\}$	14	.11.1.	26	$\{a_2, a_4, a_5\}$
5	..11.1	13	$\{a_1, a_3, a_4\}$	15	1.1.1.	42	$\{a_2, a_4, a_6\}$
6	.1.1.1	21	$\{a_1, a_3, a_5\}$	16	11..1.	50	$\{a_2, a_5, a_6\}$
7	1..1.1	37	$\{a_1, a_3, a_6\}$	17	.111..	28	$\{a_3, a_4, a_5\}$
8	.11..1	25	$\{a_1, a_4, a_5\}$	18	1.11..	44	$\{a_3, a_4, a_6\}$
9	1.1..1	41	$\{a_1, a_4, a_6\}$	19	11.1..	52	$\{a_3, a_5, a_6\}$
10	11...1	49	$\{a_1, a_5, a_6\}$	20	111...	56	$\{a_4, a_5, a_6\}$

TABLE II: Coalitions generated using lexicographical order.

Algorithm 3 describes $getCoalition(n, m, k)$, a function that generates the kth coalition in lexicographical order of m elements from a set of n. The description is done recursively to help understand how it works, although the actual implementation is iterative in order to improve its performance. The coalition is created recursively, bit by bit, starting from the least significant bit and considering $\binom{n}{m}$ possibilities. The first half of the possible coalitions have the less significant bit set to 1. If the requested rank, k, is lower than or equal to h=$1/2\times\binom{n}{m}$, then the bit is set to 1, and m is decremented by one. Otherwise, the bit is set to zero, and the rank k is reduced to $k-h$. Each recursive call decrements the number of bits to consider to $(n-1)$.

C. Potential Parallel Performance Hazards

The first and last iterations of the outer loop exhibit few TLP, compromising the efficiency of the parallel execution. We tuned the implementation so that threads are launched in parallel only for iterations that have a minimum amount of work. A minor problem is the need for a few number of synchronization barriers at the end of every iteration of the outer loop. They can be neglected, except for very small problem sizes.

Algorithm 3 pseudocode of $getCoalition(n, m, k)$

if $((m == 0)$ OR $(k == 0))$ **then**
  return 0
end if
$h \leftarrow \binom{n-1}{m-1}$
if $(k \leq h)$ **then**
  return 1 + $2 \times getCoalition(n-1, m-1, k)$
end if
return $2 \times getCoalition(n-1, m, k-h)$

An important performance issue is the occurrence of false cache sharing misses. They occur when different threads update different positions in the vector of values that happen to be mapped to the same cache line.

Finally, there is also the issue of true cache sharing. Threads generate values for coalitions of size m that are stored into local caches. When all the threads need to access those values for handling larger coalitions, data has to be moved from local storage to all the execution cores.

V. Experimental Results

The computer system used in our experiments is a dual-socket Intel Xeon E5645, each socket containing 6 Westmere cores at 2.4 GHz, and each core executing up to 2 H/W threads using hyperthreading (it can simultaneously execute up to 24 threads by H/W). The Last Level Cache (LLC) provides 12 MiB of shared storage for all the cores in the same socket. 96 GiB of 1333-MHz DDR3 RAM is shared by the 2 sockets, providing a total bandwidth of 2×32 GB/sec. The Quickpath interconnection (QPI) between the two sockets provides a peak bandwidth of 11.72 GB/sec per link direction.

Input data was created using a uniform distribution as described by [10] for problem sizes $n = 18 \ldots 27$.

A. Single-thread Execution

DP and IDP were executed using both the banker's and lexicographical splitting generation methods. Figure 2a plots the execution time in logarithmic scale for the four algorithmic variants. Lexicographic order is around $7x$ to $11x$ faster than banker's and, therefore, in the remaining of the paper we will use the first splitting method.

Figure 2b represents the execution time of DP and IDP divided by 3^n (algorithmic complexity). This metric evaluates the average time taken by the program to execute a basic algorithmic operation, in this case a splitting evaluation. It is similar to the CPI (Cycles Per Instruction) metric, but at a higher level. The metric helps identifying performance problems at the architecture level. Figure 2b shows two different problem size regions: those that fit into the LLC (n<22), and those that do not. A small problem size determines a computation-bound scenario, where DP slightly outperforms IDP, even when it executes around 20% more instructions. The reason is that IDP is penalized by a moderate number of branch mispredictions.

Large problem sizes determine a memory-bound scenario, where IDP amortizes its effort on saving expensive memory

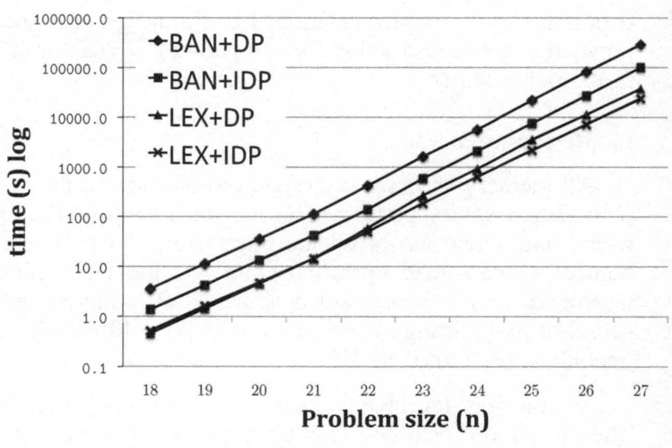

(a) Execution time (log).

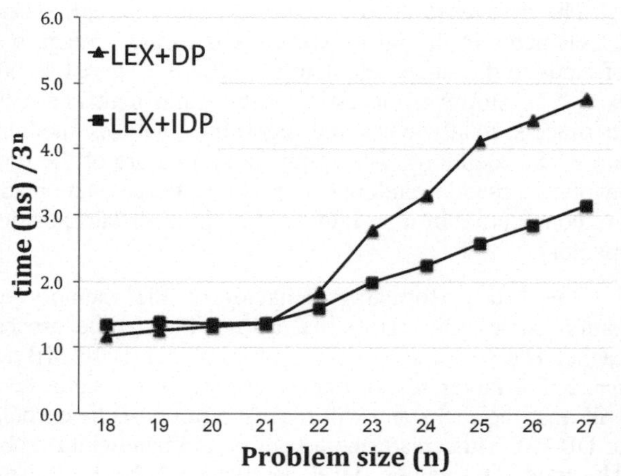

(b) Time / Complexity $\Theta(3^n)$.

accesses to outperform DP by 40-50%. Figure 2c shows the effective memory bandwidth consumption seen by the programs. The shape of the curves can be deduced from Figure 2b, but we are interested on the actual values. The effective bandwith ranges between 0.5 and 1.0 GB/sec. A small fraction of this bandwidth comes from the LLC and lower-level caches, and the remaining fraction comes from DRAM. Even considering the worst case described in section 3.3, that only 4 bytes out of the 64-Byte cache block are effectively used, it is still a very small value compared to the peak 32 GB/sec. The conclusion is that DRAM latency is the primary performance limiter. Results on the next subsection corroborate this conclusion.

B. Multi-thread Execution

We focus our multi-thread analysis on IDP, which outperforms DP for interesting problem sizes. We run IDP using t= 6, 12, and 24 threads. The case t=6 corresponds with using a single processor socket. The case t=12 uses only one socket but also exploits its hyperthreading capability. Finally, t= 24 is an scenario where all 2 sockets have their 6 cores running 2 threads each, using hyperthreading. Figure 3 shows

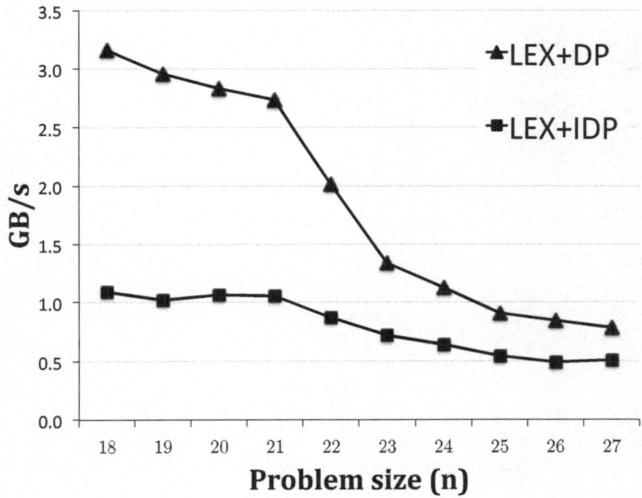

(c) Effective Memory Bandwidth (GB/s).

Fig. 2: Experimental data (BAN: Banker's sequence; LEX: Lexicographical order).

the speedup compared to the single-thread execution. Again, distinguishing between small and big problem sizes is useful.

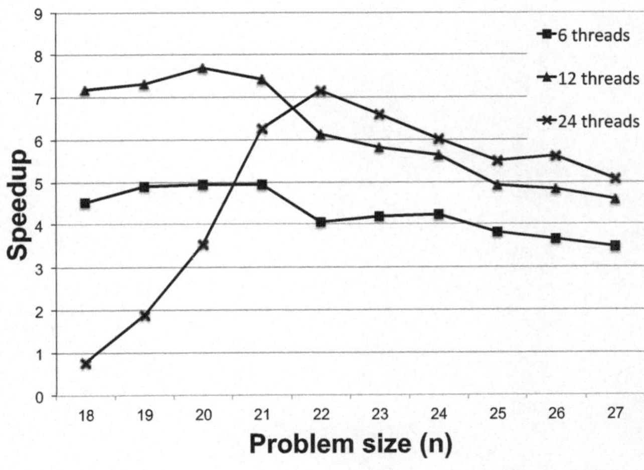

Fig. 3: Single-thread IDP versus 6-, 12- and 24-thread IDP execution

The t=6 configuration provides a speedup of 5 for small problems, and lower than 4 for large problems. The t=12 configuration further increases performance around 60% for small problems, and 30% for bigger problems. The fact that executing two threads per core do improves performance corroborates previous latency limitations, since hyperthreading is a latency-hiding mechanism. It also indicates that 6 threads do not generate enough LLC and DRAM requests to fully exploit the available LLC and DRAM bandwidth.

The effective memory bandwidth achieved with 12 threads is around 2.5 GB/sec for the bigger problem sizes, or around 13 times lower than the peak achievable bandwidth. Given the lack of spatial locality of DRAM accesses, we are probably reaching the maximum bandwidth available for the pseudo-random memory access pattern of the problem.

The t=24 configuration checks the benefit of using a second socket. Performance is highly penalized for small problems, due to the overhead of communication traffic along the QPI links for both false and true cache sharing coherence. On average, half of the data accessed by a thread is fetched from the other socket. Compared to the single-socket scenario, where all data is provided from local caches, performance drops up to 7 times for very small problems.

Large problems benefit very little from a second socket, with improvements near to 10%. The advantage of the 2-socket configuration is that the available DRAM bandwidth is duplicated, and the overhead due to coherence traffic is not so important, given that most of the data is obtained from DRAM. Anyway, the small performance gain does not justify using a second socket. Again, the symmetric, scattered memory access pattern does not fit well with the NUMA hierarchy. We are currently working on a way to partition data that reduces communication between sockets.

VI. Conclusions and Future Work

This paper presents an optimized implementation of the DP and IDP algorithm and a novel contribution describing the first parallel version of DP and IDP.

Our implementations clearly outperform the results found in the literature. According to [11], they need 2.5 days to solve a CSG problem with 27 agents, in some unspecified computer, and using a code implementation that is not provided. Our best single-thread implementation solves a same sized CSG problem in 5.8 hours. The multi-core implementation reduces execution time to 1.2 hours. Therefore, we claim that our implementation is the fast implementation of IDP published so far. We have made available to the community our source code.

We have analyzed the bottlenecks of DP and IDP. The pseudo-random memory access pattern lacks locality, and exploits the memory system capabilities very inefficiently. The latency tolerance ability of multi-threading improves performance on a multi-core processor. However, a dual-socket NUMA system is not appropriate for solving neither small nor big problems. The use of GPUs or accelerators with massive thread parallelism will be analyzed in the future.

We also want to study alternatives for coalition indexing and storage that provide higher locality, even at the expense of increasing instruction count, which is not a performance limiter for large problems.

Acknowledgment

This research has been supported by MICINN-Spain under contracts TIN2011-28689-C02-01, TIN2012-38876-C02-01 and the Generalitat of Catalunya (2009-SGR-1434).

REFERENCES

[1] O. Shehory and S. Kraus, "Methods for task allocation via agent coalition formation," *Artif. Intell.*, vol. 101, no. 1-2, pp. 165–200, 1998.

[2] T. W. Sandholm and V. R. Lesser, "Coalitions among computationally bounded agents," *Artificial Intelligence*, vol. 94, pp. 99–137, 1997.

[3] S. Rassenti, V. Smith, and R. Bulfin, "A combinatorial auction mechanism for airport time slot allocation," *The Bell Journal of Economics*, pp. 402–417, 1982.

[4] T. Voice, S. D. Ramchurn, and N. R. Jennings, "On coalition formation with sparse synergies," in *AAMAS*, 2012, pp. 223–230.

[5] D. Yun Yeh, "A dynamic programming approach to the complete set partitioning problem," *BIT Numerical Mathematics*, vol. 26, pp. 467–474, 1986, 10.1007/BF01935053. [Online]. Available: http://dx.doi.org/10.1007/BF01935053

[6] T. Rahwan and N. R. Jennings, "An improved dynamic programming algorithm for coalition structure generation," in *AAMAS (3)*, 2008, pp. 1417–1420.

[7] T. Michalak, J. Sroka, T. Rahwan, M. Wooldridge, P. McBurney, and N. Jennings, "A distributed algorithm for anytime coalition structure generation," in *Proceedings of the 9th International Conference on Autonomous Agents and Multiagent Systems: volume 1-Volume 1*. International Foundation for Autonomous Agents and Multiagent Systems, 2010, pp. 1007–1014.

[8] H. Sutter, "The free lunch is over: A fundamental turn toward concurrency in software," *Dr. Dobb's Journal*, vol. 30, no. 3, pp. 202–210, 2005.

[9] J. Loughry, J. van Hemert, and L. Schoofs, "Efficiently enumerating the subsets of a set," http://www.applied-math.org/subset.pdf, 2000. [Online]. Available: http://www.applied-math.org/subset.pdf

[10] K. S. Larson and T. W. Sandholm, "Anytime coalition structure generation: an average case study," *J. of Experimental & Theoretical Artificial Intelligence*, vol. 12, no. 1, pp. 23–42, 2000. [Online]. Available: http://www.tandfonline.com/doi/abs/10.1080/095281300146290

[11] T. Rahwan, S. D. Ramchurn, V. D. Dang, A. Giovannucci, and N. R. Jennings, "Anytime optimal coalition structure generation," in *AAAI*, 2007, pp. 1184–1190.

Partial Parallelization of the Successive Projections Algorithm using Compute Unified Device Architecture

Lauro Cássio Martins de Paula, Anderson da Silva Soares, Telma Woerle de Lima, Wellington Santos Martins
Institute of Informatics
Federal University of Goiás
Goiânia, Brazil

Arlindo Rodrigues Galvão Filho
Department of System and Control
Technological Institute of Aeronautics
São José dos Campos, Brazil

Clarimar José Coelho
Computer Science Departament
Pontifical University Catholic of Goiás
Goiânia, Brazil

***Abstract*—This paper proposes a partial parallelization for the Successive Projections Algorithm (SPA), which is a variable selection technique designed for use with Multiple Linear Regression. This implementation is aimed at improving the computational efficiency of SPA, without changing the outcome of the algorithm. For this purpose, a new strategy of inverse matrix calculation is employed. The advantage of the proposed implementation is demonstrated in an example involving large matrixes. In this example, gains of speedup were obtained.**

Keywords: Successive Projections Algorithm, parallelization, Multiple Linear Regression, CUDA.

I. Introduction

The Successive Projections Algorithm (SPA) is a technique that aims at selecting variables to minimize collinearity problems in Multiple Linear Regression (MLR). Originally proposed in [9], the SPA has the restriction that the variable incorporated in each iteration must be as less multicolinear possible with the previously selected variables [11], [16], [18]. Through the use of SPA, it is possible to obtain good results in various problems of multivariate analysis, such as determining sulfur in diesel samples [2], determining the quality parameters in vegetable oils [15], determining the levels of moisture and protein in wheat samples [12], among others. The SPA is composed of three stages. In phase 1 are generated chains of minimally redundant variables. Phase 2 evaluates the subsets of variables with higher predictive potential from the variable chains obtained in stage 1. Such assessment is measured by the prediction error in the multiple linear regression models. The equation 1 shows how regression coefficients are calculated, and the equation 2 shows how the predictive ability of a particular subset of variables is measured by calculating the error $RMSEP$ (Root Mean Square Error).

$$\beta = (\mathbf{X}^T\mathbf{X})^{-1}\mathbf{X}^T\mathbf{y}, \quad (1)$$

where $\mathbf{X}$ is the matrix of variables and samples, $\mathbf{y}$ is the vector of dependent variables and β is the vector of regression coefficients.

$$RMSEP = \sqrt{\frac{\sum_{i=0}^{N}(y_i - \hat{y}_i)^2}{N}}, \quad (2)$$

where $\hat{y}$ is the estimated value and y is the actual value of the property of interest.

Regarding the computational cost, phase 2 represents the highest cost compared to the other phases, because this stage involves the calculation of an inverse matrix as shown in equation 1. In [7] was proposed to reduce the cost of Phase 2 of the SPA through sequential regressions. This idea is based on updating the calculation of the inverse of the linear regression when adding a new variable instead of performing any inverse calculation. The benefit of the proposed implementation was shown through an example involving a data set near-infrared (NIR) of wheat samples. In such example, computational gains were achieved compared with the traditional SPA implementation. Despite the results obtained, such technique does not exploit the recent advances in computing power of computers, in particular the possibility of performing tasks in parallel, since sequential regressions have a sequential formulation.

In [17] was proposed the SPA parallelization in order to explore the ability of multiple processing cores (multicore) on new computer architectures. The results obtained showed that it was possible to reduce the computational cost of the algorithm as more than one processing core becomes available. However, this processing architecture currently is limited to using a maximum of eight cores.

Despite the use of sequential regressions and multicore parallelization reducing the computational time, both strategies do not make use of the latest advances in terms of processing capacity in architecture computers $Intel^{®}$. Calculating the inverse matrices using parallel programming can be more interesting due to the fact of using the parallel computing resources provided by GPUs (Graphics Processing Unit) [3], [1], [10], [20].

In this work, a new strategy for reducing the computational

cost of the SPA is proposed. In particular a partial parallelizing of phase 2 of the algorithm is proposed, involving calculation of matrix inversion by using the Compute Unified Device Architecture (CUDA) on GPUs. While the current multi-core architectures have two, four or eight cores, GPUs have hundreds or even thousands of processing cores. However, unlike the parallelization on CPUs (Central Processing Unit) multicore, the organization and number of threads, which are executed independently on the GPU cores, are managed manually by the programmer.

This article is organized as follows. Section 2 details the Successive Projections Algorithm. The proposed parallelization on phase 2 of the SPA is detailed in section 3. Section 4 describes the materials and methods used. The results are discussed in section 5. Section 6 shows the conclusions.

II. Successive Projections Algorithm Review

The multivariate calibration refers to obtaining a mathematical model that allows to provide the value of a quantity y based on values measured from a set of explanatory variables x_1, x_2, ..., x_k [12]. Thus, it is possible to obtain a suitable model

$$y = \beta_0 + \beta_1 x_1 + ... + \beta_k x_k + \varepsilon, \quad (3)$$

where β_0, β_1, ..., β_k, $k = 1, 2, ..., K$, are the coefficients to be determined, and ε is a portion of random error. The process for obtaining coefficients is also known as MLR, typically being performed by the least squares method [8]. The Multiple Linear Regression is a statistical technique used to build models that describe reasonably relationships between several explanatory variables of a given process [14], [4].

The goal of SPA is to select a subset of variables with low collinearity that allows the construction of a MLR model with a capacity of adequate prediction. Data modeling for the SPA implementation are divided into two sets: calibration, containing N_c observations, and validation containing N_v observations, where $N_c + N_v = N$. The data calibration and validation are arranged respectively in matrixes X_c ($N_c \times K$) and X_v ($N_v \times K$). In SPA's phase 1 are generated K chains with M variables each, being

$$M = min(N_c - 1, K). \quad (4)$$

In step 2, the SPA uses the validation set to evaluate subsets of variables extracted from the chains generated in stage 1. As a result of phase 2, the best subset of variables is the one that leads to the smallest value of $RMSEP$ among subsets tested. The algorithm of phase 2 is shown in the algorithm 1.

Obtaining $RMSEP$ can be performed in two ways:

- If validation is used to test series, a set of validation samples must be defined. Soon after, the best subset is determined by the lowest root value of mean squared error on a validation set calculated by the equation 2 for all subsets of variables;

Algorithm 1: Step 2 of the SPA

1) Do $k = 1$
2) While $k < K$
3) Do $m = 1$
4) While $m < M$
5) Let $\mathcal{X}_{km}$ be a subset of varibles formed by m first elements of k-th chain generated on phase 1.
6) Let $\mathbf{S}_{km}^{-1}$ be the inverse of the equation 1.
7) Using the variables contained in $\mathcal{X}_{km}$, calculate the inverse $\mathbf{S}_{km}^{-1}$ and subsequently the remainder of the equation 1.
8) Calculate the error $RMSEP$ of k-th chain with m variables, according to equation 2.
9) Do $m = m + 1$
10) End While $m < M$
11) Do $k = k + 1$
12) End While $k < K$

- If the cross-validation is used, the best subset is determined by the lowest root value of mean squared error of cross validation in the calibration set, which can be obtained by an equation similar to equation 2.

The third and last phase consists of eliminating variables that do not contribute significantly to the predictive capacity of the resulting MLR model. For such, each variable selected in phase 2 is associated with a "relevancy index" given by the product of the sample standard deviation and the regression coefficient modulus of this variable [18].

III. Proposed Parallelization

A square matrix A is said to be invertible if there exists another matrix A^{-1} such that $A^{-1}A = I$ and $AA^{-1} = I$, where I is called identity matrix. According to the literature, A matrix has an inverse if and only if $det(A) \neq 0$.

Calculating the inverse of a matrix can require significant computational effort, especially when A is large. Therefore, using the parallel computing resources provided by a GPU can be viable. The GPU was initially developed as a driven-flow technology, optimized for calculations of intensive data use, where many identical operations can be accomplished in parallel on different data. Unlike a multicore CPU, which normally executes some threads in parallel, the GPU was designed to run thousands of threads in parallel [5].

Programming models such as CUDA [5] and OpenCL [19], allows that applications can be run more easily on the GPU. CUDA was the first architecture and interface for programming application (API), created by $NVIDIA^{®}$ in 2006 to allow the GPU could be used for a wide variety of applications. Like any technology, the GPU has its limitations. Depending on the data volume, GPU's computational performance may prove inferior when compared to CPU performance. In this case, the data amount to be transferred to the GPU memory must be taken into account, because there is an overhead associated with the parallelization of tasks on the GPU [13]. Factors regarding the access time to memory can also influence the computational performance. In other words, access to GPU global memory usually has a high latency and it is subject to a coalesced access to data in memory [6].

In this paper, a strategy for the parallelization at step of the calculation of inverse matrix used in phase 2 of the Successive Projections Algorithm is presented.

Let $A_{n \times n}$ and $I_{n \times n}$ be the matrix to be calculated the inverse and identity matrix, respectively. Recursively, i = 0, 1, ..., $n-1$, through the use of two kernel functions ($kernel1$ and $kernel2$), each thread performs an operation on each element of the matrix . In the first kernel function are set $\sqrt{n}$ blocks with $\sqrt{n}$ threads each, where each thread accesses a single element and divide it by the pivot of row i of the matrix A. In the second function are created n blocks with n threads each. Each block of threads handles a line of matrices, and only threads whose its global identifier (id) divided by the number of columns ($\frac{id}{n}$) is different from index i implementing operations. For example, in the first iteration (i = 0), threads with id = 0, 1, ..., $n-1$ do not satisfy the condition $\frac{id}{n}$ $\neq i$. Only the threads that satisfy this condition continue its execution and, after all threads have been executed, the elements below the pivot of the first column are zeroed.

Figure 1 shows the strategy used. Each arrow in the figure represents an iteration of the algorithm. Initially, there are the matrixes $A_{3 \times 3}$ and $I_{3 \times 3}$. All operations applied to the matrix elements A are also applied in parallel to the elements of the matrix I. After the last iteration, the matrix A becomes the identity matrix, and the matrix I becomes A^{-1}.

$$A = \begin{vmatrix} 5 & 6 & 9 \\ 4 & 1 & 7 \\ 1 & 7 & 6 \end{vmatrix} \Rightarrow \begin{vmatrix} 1 & 1.2 & 1.8 \\ 0 & -3.8 & -0.2 \\ 0 & 5.8 & 4.2 \end{vmatrix} \Rightarrow \begin{vmatrix} 1 & 0 & 1.73 \\ 0 & 1 & 0.05 \\ 0 & 0 & 3.89 \end{vmatrix} \Rightarrow \begin{vmatrix} 1 & 0 & 0 \\ 0 & 1 & 0 \\ 0 & 0 & 1 \end{vmatrix}$$

$$I = \begin{vmatrix} 1 & 0 & 0 \\ 0 & 1 & 0 \\ 0 & 0 & 1 \end{vmatrix} \Rightarrow \begin{vmatrix} 0.2 & 0 & 0 \\ -0.8 & 1 & 0 \\ -0.2 & 0 & 1 \end{vmatrix} \Rightarrow \begin{vmatrix} -0.05 & 0.31 & 0 \\ 0.21 & -0.26 & 0 \\ -1.42 & 1.52 & 1 \end{vmatrix} \Rightarrow \begin{vmatrix} 0.58 & -0.36 & -0.44 \\ 0.22 & -0.28 & -0.01 \\ -0.36 & 0.39 & 0.25 \end{vmatrix}$$

Fig. 1. Parallelization strategy used in the calculation of the inverse of a 3x3 matrix.

Algorithms 2 and 3 respectively show the implementation of the functions $kernel1$ and $kernel2$.

Algorithm 2: $kernel1$ implementation.

---

begin
  Parameters: A, I, $index$, $size$ = number of columns;

  $id \leftarrow$ thread global identification
  if $id < size$ **then**
    $pivo \leftarrow$ A(index, index)

    A(index, id) $\leftarrow \frac{A(index,id)}{pivo}$

    I(index, id) $\leftarrow \frac{I(index,id)}{pivo}$
  end if
end

Algorithm 3: $kernel2$ implementation.

---

begin
  Parameters: A, I, $index$, n = number of columns, $size$ = number of rows $\times$ number of columns;

  $id \leftarrow$ thread global identification
  $idBlock \leftarrow$ block identification
  $idThread \leftarrow$ thread local identification
  if $id < size$ **then**
    if $(\frac{id}{n}) \neq index$ **then**
      $m \leftarrow A(\frac{id}{n}, index)$

      $A(idBlock, idThread) \leftarrow A(idBlock, idThread)$ - $(m \times A(index, idThread))$

      $I(idBlock, idThread) \leftarrow I(idBlock, idThread)$ - $(m \times I(index, idThread))$
    end if
  end if
end

IV. Experimental

The dataset employed in this work consists of 775 NIR spectra of whole-kernel wheat, which were used as shoot-out data in the 2008 International Diffuse Reflectance Conference (http://www.idrc-chambersburg.org/shootout.html). Each spectrum comprises 1050 variables in the range 400-2500 nm. Protein content (%) was used as the y-property in the regression calculations.

A. Computational setup

All calculations were carried out by using a desktop computer with an Intel Core i7 2600 (3.40 GHz), 8 GB of RAM memory and a $NVIDIA^{®}$ GeForce GTX 550Ti graphics card with 192 CUDA cores and 2 GB of memory config. The Matlab 7.12.0 (R2011a) software platform was employed throughout. All the matrices used in this paper were generated by using $randn()$, which is a built-in function of Matlab.

V. Results and Discussion

Figure 2 presents the time required for completion of Phase 2 depending on the maximum number M of variables to be selected. For M = 100, for instance, regressions involving one up to 100 variables are carried out and matrix inversion in the same order (100x100). As can be observed, the computational time increases with the matrix size, but the increase is less pronounced if the parallel regression procedure is used. For M = 1000, for example, this procedure reduces the time by a factor of two. Although the computational gains obtained for the sizes of small matrices time required for execution of Phase 2 is lower by using CPU. This case can be observed in Figure 3. The implementation using GPU is more efficient for matrices from 300x300. Although the proposal is feasible for matrices larger than 300x300, we believe that the proposal is important once the devices used in this type of problem have generated data with ever larger. Until five years ago the appliances generated matrixes with few hundreds of variables, while recently it is in the thousands. In this sense, the development of computational algorithms used in this type of problem is important to computational not to become unviable.

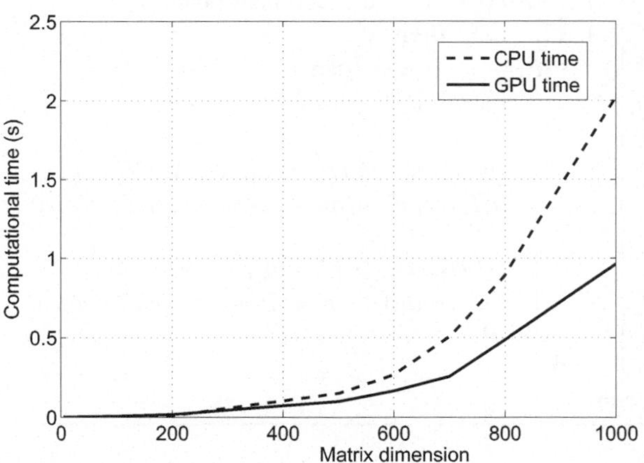

Fig. 2. Comparison of computational performance between CPU and GPU.

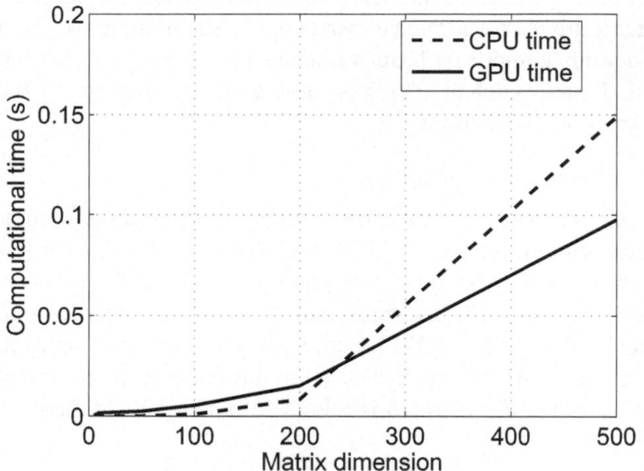

Fig. 3. Detail of Figure 2, showing a comparison of computational performance between CPU and GPU for matrix size up to 500x500.

VI. Conclusion

This paper proposed a partial parallelization of the Successive Projections Algorithm based on Compute Unified Device Architecture. This procedure was employed in Phase 2 of SPA, which is the computational bottleneck of the overall algorithm. The results obtained by using a large dataset of NIR spectra (775 samples and 1050 variables) revealed that substantial gains in computational efficiency can be obtained by using the proposed implementation.

Acknowledgment

The authors thank the research agencies CAPES and FAPEG for the support provided to this research.

References

[1] Nesrin Aydin Atasoy, Baha Sen, and Burhan Selcuk, *Using gauss - jordan elimination method with {CUDA} for linear circuit equation systems*, Procedia Technology **1** (2012), no. 0, 31 – 35.

[2] Mrcia C. Breitkreitz, Ivo M. Raimundo, Jr., Jarbas J. R. Rohwedder, Celio Pasquini, Heronides A. Dantas Filho, and Mrio C. U. Jos, Gledson E.and Arajo, *Determination of total sulfur in diesel fuel employing nir spectroscopy and multivariate calibration*, The Analyst **128** (2003), 1204–1207.

[3] Lau Mai Chan and Rajagopalan Srinivasan, *A graphic processing unit (gpu) algorithm for improved variable selection in multivariate process monitoring*, 11th International Symposium on Process Systems Engineering (Iftekhar A. Karimi and Rajagopalan Srinivasan, eds.), Computer Aided Chemical Engineering, vol. 31, Elsevier, 2012, pp. 1532 – 1536.

[4] J. Cortina, *Interaction, nonlinearity, and multicollinearity: Implications for multiple regression*, Journal of Management **19** (1993), no. 4, 915–922.

[5] NVIDIA CUDA, *Nvidia cuda c programming guide*, 4.0 ed., NVIDIA Corporation, 2701 San Tomas Expressway Santa Clara, CA 95050, 2011.

[6] NVIDIA $CUDA^{TM}$, *Nvidia cuda c programming best practices guide*, NVIDIA Corporation, 2701 San Tomas Expressway Santa Clara, CA 95050, 2009.

[7] Anderson da Silva Soares, Arlindo Rodrigues Galv ao Filho, Roberto Kawakami Harrop Galv ao, and Mário César Ugulino Araújo, *Improving the computational efficiency of the successive projections algorithm by using a sequential regression implementation: A case study involving nir spectrometric analysis of wheat samples*, Journal of the Brazilian Chemical Society **21** (2010), 760–763.

[8] Norman Richard Draper and Harry Smith, *Applied regression analysis*, 1998.

[9] Mario C. U. Araújo et al, *The successive projections algorithm for variable selection in spectroscopic multicomponent analysis*, Chemometrics and Intelligent Laboratory Systems (2001), 57–65.

[10] Fabio Fabris and Renato A. Krohling, *A co-evolutionary differential evolution algorithm for solving minmax optimization problems implemented on {GPU} using c-cuda*, Expert Systems with Applications **39** (2012), no. 12, 10324 – 10333.

[11] Roberto Kawakami Harrop Galvao, Mario Cesar Ugulino Araujo, Wallace Duarte Fragoso, Edvan Cirino Silva, Gledson Emidio Jose, Sofacles Figueredo Carreiro Soares, and Henrique Mohallem Paiva, *A variable elimination method to improve the parsimony of {MLR} models using the successive projections algorithm*, Chemometrics and Intelligent Laboratory Systems **92** (2008), no. 1, 83 – 91.

[12] Arlindo R. Galvao Filho, Roberto K. H. Galvao, and Mario Cesar U. Araujo, *Effect of the subsampling ratio in the application of subagging for multivariate calibration with the successive projections algorithm*, Journal of the Brazilian Chemical Society (en).

[13] David B. Kirk, *Nvidia cuda software and gpu parallel computing architecture*, NVIDIA Corporation, 2008.

[14] T. Naes and B. H. Mevik, *Understanding the collinearity problem in regression and discriminant analysis*, Journal of Chemometrics **15** (2001), no. 4, 413–426.

[15] Alessandra Félix Costa Pereira, Márcio Jose Coelho Pontes, Francisco Fernandes Gambarra Neto, Sergio Ricardo Bezerra Santos, Roberto Kawakami Harrop Galvao, and Mario Cesar Ugulino Araujo, *Nir spectrometric determination of quality parameters in vegetable oils using ipls and variable selection*, Food Research International **41** (2008), 341–348.

[16] Marcio Jose Coelho Pontes, Roberto Kawakami Harrop Galvao, Mario Cesar Ugulino Araujo, Pablo Nogueira Teles Moreira, Osmundo Dantas Pessoa Neto, Gledson Emidio Jose, and Teresa Cristina Bezerra Saldanha, *The successive projections algorithm for spectral variable selection in classification problems*, Chemometrics and Intelligent Laboratory Systems **78** (2005), no. 1, 11 – 18.

[17] Anderson da Silva Soares, Roberto K. H Galvao, Mario C. U. Araujo, S. F. C Soares, and Luiz Alberto Pinto, *Multi-core computation in chemometrics: case studies of voltammetric and NIR spectrometric analyses*, Journal of the Brazilian Chemical Society **21** (2010), 1626 – 1634 (en).

[18] Sófacles F. Soares, Adriano A. Gomes, Mario C. Araujo, Arlindo R. Filho, and Roberto K. Galvo, *The successive projections algorithm*, TrAC Trends in Analytical Chemistry **42** (2012), 94–98.

[19] Ryoji Tsuchiyama, Takashi Nakamura, Takuro Iizuka, Akihiro Asahara, Jeongdo Son, and Satoshi Miki, *The opencl programming book*, Fixstars, 2010.

[20] Ahmet Artu Yldirim and Cem Ozdogan, *Parallel wavelet-based clustering algorithm on {GPUs} using {CUDA}*, Procedia Computer Science **3** (2011), no. 0, 396 – 400.

A New Key Negotiation Method Based on Fuzzy Extractor Technology for Body Sensor Networks

H. Zhao[1,2], M. Shu[2], and J. Qin[3]
[1]School of Compute Science & Technology, Shandong University of Finance and Economics, Jinan, China
[2]School Shandong Computer Science Center, Jinan, China
[3]Department School of Mathematics, Shandong University, Jinan, China

Abstract - *Privacy issue is an important security problem in body sensor networks, and key negotiation method is the foundation to address the problem. In the paper, we first present a formal definition of key negotiation method which includes two aspects, correction and security. And then, according to the definition, we further give a concrete structure of a new fuzzy-extractor-based key negotiation method that not only enlarges the option of physiological signals to produce shared keys, but also can resist a new attack based on ultra wide band technology. Analyses show the new key negotiation method is suitable to body sensor networks.*

Keywords: Key Management; Physiological Signals; Security; Body Sensor Networks; Fuzzy Extractor

1 Introduction

Compared with enormous research efforts made on the cyber security of critical infrastructure [1][2][3][4][5][6][7][8], security of body sensor network is virtually an unchartered territory.

Body sensor networks (BSNs) is an important branch of wireless sensor networks (WSNs) [9]. A BSN is a medical information system in the field of e-health, and consists of some biosensor nodes that form a wireless micro-network on the human body. These biosensor nodes are micro-scale equipment integrated with biosensors and transceivers [15], and can provide a capability of automated, continuous human monitoring when they are worn on or implanted in the human body. At present, various biosensors has been designed to measure diverse physiological values, such as Blood Pressure (systolic and diastolic), Electrocardiogram (ECG), Blood Oxygen level (SpO2) etc., and are available in many different forms including wrist wearable, ambulatory devices and as part of biomedical smart clothes [16][17]. Based on the functions of biosensors, BSNs can not only monitor people's health, but also execute intelligent treatment, such as accurate drug delivery. Applications of BSNs will greatly improve the society's medical conditions and promote living qualities of people.

Data exchanged in a BSN contain sensitive medical information which should be protected [18]. For example, the leaked medical data will divulge personal privacy, and the tampered medical data will cause serious medical accidents which could threaten a patient's life. National regulations are being established to ensure the privacy and security of healthcare data from data generation, transmission, storage and usage where the HIPAA (The Health Insurance Portability and Accountability Act USA) has set a benchmark [19]. However, the computational and bandwidth limitations of BSNs are on par with those found in the so-called micro-sensor network, which makes traditional security paradigms [19][20] designed for conventional WSNs not directly applicable to BSNs. So, there are great challenges in designing security schemes for BSNs. One of the core problems is how to establish shared keys among biosensor nodes. Note that biometric data coming from physiological signals themselves have an advantage over conventional cryptography in authenticating genuine users [19], a natural solution of protecting biometric data will be the combination of conventional cryptography and biometric data, i.e., bio-cryptography [22].

In this paper, to design a key negotiation method suitable to body sensor networks, we make the following contributions: (1) we design two attack games to simulate the practical attacks launched by the adversary, and then according to the two attacks, we give a formal definition of key negotiation method based on fuzzy extractor. (2) By the definition we build a concrete key negotiation method that not only can enlarge the option of physiological signals, but also can resist the developing ultra wide band technology.

The rest of the paper is organized as follows: Section 2 presents current research work related to key negotiation schemes for body sensor networks and fuzzy extractor technology. Section 3 proposes a formal definition of key negotiation based on fuzzy extractor. A new key negotiation method and its correctness and security analyses are given in Section 4. Finally, in Section 5 conclusions are drawn.

2 Related work

2.1 Key Management Methods Based on Fuzzy Commitment

In a human body, some physiological signals have high level randomness, and can be encoded as pseudo-random numbers, so biometric data coming from these signals can be used in biometric security. Reference [25] proposed to use a group of similar random numbers generated from these physiological signals at different sites of the human body to encrypt and decrypt a symmetric key. Since the same biometric value captured at different locations of the body have slight differences, they employed a fuzzy commitment scheme [26] to ensure that errors in a recovered encryption key can be removed by a certain error-correcting code *C*. At the transmission terminal, a biometric value coming from a high-entropy physiological signal, *x*, is used to commit the key k_{shared} that is a secret code word of *C*: $F(k_{shared}, x) = h(k_{shared}) \| (x \oplus k_{shared})$, where $\oplus$ is the bitwise XOR operation and $\|$ means concatenation. At the receiving terminal, if the same kind of collected biometric value *x*' is similar to *x*, and the difference between them is tolerable to *C*, the receiving terminal can use *x*' and *C* to decommit the key k_{shared}. Compared with traditional key negotiation schemes, the non-interactive fuzzy commitment scheme has less energy consumption in messages transmission, and is suitable for BSNs. A number of algorithms have been developed following the work of [25]. The method proposed in [27] only transfers commitments to complete keys negotiation. The method is conductive in reducing messages transferred in negotiation of shared keys, and is suitable to establish shared keys among biosensor more than two nodes. Reference [28] used a hybrid topology that combines two topologies, star and mesh, to establish shared keys. In the scheme, identities of biosensor nodes are used to authenticate shared keys, and a mechanism of changing cluster heads according to energy is proposed to maximize the lifetime of BSNs. Reference [29] proposed a method that uses time slots to solve synchronization problem of high-entropy biometric data between biosensors. Reference [30] pointed out by experiment that the timing information of heartbeats has high entropy characteristic, and can be used to negotiate shared keys in BSNs. Reference [30] further brought forward that a developing technology, UWB (Ultra Wideband Radar), can remotely capture some biometric data (such as heart rate), and could post a new attack, called as RCB (remotely capturing biometric data) attack, to key negotiation methods based on biometric methods.

Though many achievements have been made on this topic, several challenging problems remain: (1) Only high-entropy physiological signals are considered to negotiate keys. Up to now, only the timing information of heartbeats is proved by experiment in [30] to be high-entropy signals, which greatly limits applications of the technology in key negotiation. (2) Shared keys are only generated from the set of error-correcting codes, which restrict the choice space of keys. (3) Shared keys are vulnerable to the developing RCB attack, that is, when an adversary remotely captures a physiological signal *x* that is used to negotiate shared keys, and eavesdrops the corresponding commitment: $p = x \oplus k_{shared}$, he can easily get the shared key by : $p \oplus x = x \oplus k_{shared} \oplus x = k_{shared}$.

2.2 Fuzzy extractor technology

Following the development of the fuzzy commitment technology, another biometric cryptography, fuzzy extractor technology, was proposed in [31]. The technology includes two procedures: one is called secure sketch, and can help two parts to negotiate the same biometric value using the same kind of physiological signal; another is called extractor, and is used to extract a secret value from biometric value. Since fuzzy extractor technology can help two parts produce a shared key from the same kind of physiological signals, and the key space does not depend on error-correcting codes, which makes it be superior to fuzzy commitment technology in negotiating shared keys in body sensor networks.

However, recently, many researchers have found out that the construction of fuzzy extractor is not adequate for multiple uses of the same secret biometric value. Reference [32] pointed out that an improper sketch construction and a biased error correction code are both the source of leaking secret biometric data. Reference [33] pointed out that fuzzy extractor cannot resist active attack, and when commitments are tampered, the authentication service provided by fuzzy extractor will be invalid. Reference [34] showed that some of more popular constructions that have been shown to have serious security weaknesses in presence of even very weak adversaries. Reference [35] explained the root of vulnerability of fuzzy extractor, that is, because the key derived from biometric data must be indistinguishable to uniform random distribution, the leakage of information associated with the biometric data is unavoidable. According to above results, reference [36] proposed a series of robust key management methods that decrease the leakage of entropies, however the methods also depend on high-entropy physiological signals, and also cannot resist RCB attack.

3 Formal definition of key negotiation based on fuzzy extractor

In this section, we propose a new key negotiation method called as fuzzy negotiation that is based on fuzzy extractor technology and is superior to fuzzy extractor technology in terms of practicality and security.

Like fuzzy commitment and fuzzy extractor, fuzzy negotiation makes use of error-correcting codes to negotiate shared keys. Let *M* be a space of messages with distance function $dist(\cdot)$, more formally an error-correcting code *C* is a subset of *K* number of distinct code words $\{c_0, ..., c_{k-1}\}$ of *M* . The minimized distance of *C* is the smallest *d* such that $dist(c_i, c_j) \geq d$ for all $i \neq j$, which means that *C* can detect up to $d-1$ errors, and the error-correcting distance is $t = \lfloor (d-1)/2 \rfloor$.

As our work is in the computational setting, we use κ to denote the security parameter. All algorithms are assumed to be a polynomial time in κ. Then a function $\varepsilon(\kappa)$ is negligible if for all positive polynomial $p(\cdot)$ and sufficiently large κ, $\varepsilon(\kappa) \le 1/p(\kappa)$.

In a BSNs, let K denote the preloaded secret of all biosensor nodes, W is a variable of M with length $|W|=l$, w and w' are values of W, r is a random value with length l, and t is the error-correcting distance of a selected public error-collecting code C where the length of each code word c is l. Then, we give a formal definition of fuzzy negotiation as follows:

Definition1:
A structure of fuzzy negotiation is a pair of randomized procedures, "Trans" and "Rec", with the following properties:

On input w, K, r and c, the generation procedure "Trans" outputs an extracted secure string $R \in \{0,1\}^l$ and a public string $P \in \{0,1\}^*$ to commit R.

Correction: The reproduction production "Rec" takes an element w' and a public string $P \in \{0,1\}^*$ as inputs. The correctness property of fuzzy negotiation guarantees that if $dist(w,w') \le t$, and R, P are generated by $(R,P) \leftarrow Trans(K,w,r,c)$, then $Rec(K,w',P,C)=R$. If $dist(w,w')>t$, then no guarantee is provided about the output of "Rec".

Security: Any adversary wins the adaptive chosen biometric data attack game and adaptive chosen commitment attack game defined as follows with negligible possibilities.

3.1 Adaptive chosen biometric data attack game

We define an adaptive chosen biometric data attack game against fuzzy negotiation as the following game between a challenger and an adversary. In the initialization, the challenger is assigned with a secret K.

Preparation: The adversary chooses a kind of physiological signal, and describes it as a biometric variable $W \in M$. And then, the adversary gives the specification of W (such as the kind of the physiological signal) to the challenger.

Queries: The adversary makes up to q possibly adaptive queries: To form adaptive query i, the adversary produces a value w_i of W, a random value r, and a code word c from C, and then sends all of them to the challenger. The challenger produces $(P_i,R_i) \leftarrow Trans(K,w_i,r,c)$, and sends P_i to the adversary.

Challenge: The adversary produces a value w of W, a random value w' with length $|w|$, a random value r and selects a code word c from C, and then sends all of them to the challenger. The challenger randomly produces a bit b, if $b=1$, the challenger computes $(P^*,R^*) \leftarrow Trans(K,w,r,c)$, and if $b=0$, the challenger computes $(P^*,R^*) \leftarrow Trans(K,w',r,c)$ instead. Finally, the challenger sends P^* to the adversary.

More Queries: The adversary runs additional queries as described in step "Queries".

Response: The adversary eventually produces a bit b', and wins if $b'=b$.

Let *adversary*(P^*) be the output of the adversary when it gets P^*, and $w \mid w'$ be an alternative choice with a probability of 1/2. Then, the adversary's advantage in this game is defined as:

$$adv^{Acb}(\kappa) = | Pr[b \leftarrow adversary(P^*) \mid P^* = Trans(K,w \mid w',r,c)] - 1/2 |.$$

3.2 Adaptive chosen commitments attack game

Let Δ be the set of perturbation functions over a messages space M, i.e., $\Delta = \{\delta : M \to M\}$ where $dist(w,\delta(w))$ can be greater than t. We define an adaptive chosen commitments attack game against a fuzzy negotiation as the following game between a challenger and an adversary. In the initialization, the challenger is assigned with an error-correcting code C and a secret K.

Preparation: The adversary points a kind of physiological signal as a biometric variable $W \in M$. And then, the adversary gives the specification of W (such as the kind of the physiological signal) to the challenger.

Public queries: The adversary makes up to q possibly adaptive queries: to form adaptive query i, the adversary produces a value w_i of W, a random value r, and chooses a code word c from C, and then sends all of them to the challenger. The challenger produces $(P_i,R_i) \leftarrow Trans(K,w_i,r,c)$, and sends P_i to the adversary.

Keys queries: The adversary makes up to q' possible adaptive reproduction queries that can be interspersed with public queries as follows: To form query i, the adversary chooses $\delta_i' \in \Delta$, a biometric value w' and P' that is generated from w' in the "public queries" step, and then sends them to the challenger. The challenger computes $R_i' = Rec(K,\delta_i'(w'),P_i',C)$ and returns R_i' to the adversary. In order to let the adversary do enough exercises, the procedure "Rec" will return the adversary a value, such as a fault R_i' even δ_i' satisfies $dist(w',\delta_i'(w'))>t$.

Challenge: The adversary chooses $P^* \in \{P_1,\ldots,P_q\}$ from strings returned by the challenger in a public query and in any key query (δ_i',w',P^*) the distance has $dist(w',\delta_i'(w'))>t$. The adversary sends P^* to the challenger. The challenger randomly produces a bit b, if $b=1$, the challenger computes $R'=Rec(K,w',P^*,C)$ with unperturbed w', and gives it to the adversary. Otherwise, if $b=0$, it chooses a random string with length of $|R'|$ and gives it to the adversary instead.

More Queries: The adversary runs additional queries as described in step "Public queries".

Response: the adversary eventually produces a bit b' and wins if $b'=b$.

The adversary's advantage in this game is defined as: $adv^{Acc}(\kappa)=|Pr[b \leftarrow adversary(key) \,|\, R=Rec(K,w',P^*,C)] -1/2|$.□

Theorem 1: We say that the fuzzy negotiation can be against adaptive chosen biometric data attack, if for any PPT (Probability Polynomial Time) adversary, it holds that $adv^{Acb}(\kappa) \le \varepsilon(\kappa)$ for a negligible small $\varepsilon(\kappa)$.

The adaptive chosen biometric data attack game simulates adaptive attack to the "Trans" procedure of fuzzy negotiation in practice: an adversary can adaptively capture some kind of biometric value w (such as timing information of heartbeats) by RCB (remote capturing biometric data) attack, and get the corresponding commitment P by eavesdropping. In such way, the adversary can do enough adaptive exercises to analyze the relationships between biometric data and corresponding commitments. If in such attacks, the adversary's advantage is negligible in step "challenge", it means that the adversary cannot find the relationships between them, and then, he cannot make use of commitments to compute biometric data which he cannot capture remotely.

Theorem 2: We say that the fuzzy negotiation can be against adaptive chosen commitments attack in Δ, if for any PPT adversary, it holds that $adv^{Acc}(\kappa) \le \varepsilon(\kappa)$ for a negligible small $\varepsilon(\kappa)$.

The attack simulates the adaptive chosen commitments attack to the "Rec" procedure of fuzzy negotiation in practice: Before a user uses a BSN product, an adversary can get the BSN product by some means (e.g. the adversary unpacks the BSN product unauthorizedly in the transportation) to launch adaptive chosen commitments attack where, for a pair of biometric value and commitment adaptively chosen, the adversary can get corresponding shared key. So, the adversary can do enough adaptive exercises to analyze the relationships between commitments and corresponding shared keys.

4 The concrete structure of fuzzy negotiation and its correction and security analyses

4.1 The Concrete Structure of Fuzzy Negotiation

According to the above definition in section III we design a fuzzy negotiation structure as follows: The structure consists of a pair of procedures:" Trans" and "Rec". In the initialization of the structure, each biosensor node is preloaded a secret K that is divided into two keys, k_0 and k_1, with $|k_0|=|k_1|=l$. In addition, each biosensor node is assigned with a keyed one-way pseudo-random function $F_k(\cdot):\{0,1\}^l \rightarrow \{0,1\}^l$ with $|k|=l$, an error-correcting function $Dec(\cdot)$ belonging to a selected error-correcting code C and a function $f(\cdot):\{0,1\}^l \times \{0,1\}^l \rightarrow \{0,1\}^l$ that satisfies $z=f(x,y) \Rightarrow y=f(x,z) \Rightarrow x=f(z,y)$.

Procedure "Trans"

Collecting a biometric value from a pointed physiological signal, and encoding it into a binary value w with $|w|=l$;

Selecting a code word c from the error-correcting code C, and computing the relationship between c and w: $v=f(w,c)$;

Generating an open random value r with $|r|=l$, and then using $F(\cdot)$ to hide v: $u=v \oplus F_{k_0}(r)$;

Finally, deriving the shared key: $k_{shared}=F_{k_0}(F_{k_1}(w \oplus r))$ ($\oplus$ is bitwise XOR operation), and outputting the commitment corresponding w : $P=<u,r,F_{k_0}(u \| r \| c)>$ ("$\|$" denotes concatenation operation).

Procedure "Rec"

Collecting the same kind of biometric value, and encoding it into a binary value w' with $|w'|=l$;

Using the pre-deployed key k_0 to recover the relationship v: $v=u \oplus F_{k_0}(r)$;

Encoding w' and v into c^*: $c^*=f(w',v)$ that is a fuzzy version of c;

Using $Dec(\cdot)$ to correct c^* : $c'=Dec(c^*)$. If $F_{k_0}(u \| r \| c)=F_{k_0}(u \| r \| c')$, the correction is successful, and w can be recovered as: $w=f(v,c)$. And then, the shared key can be reproduced as: $k_{shared}=F_{k_0}(F_{k_1}(w \oplus r))$. Otherwise, if $F_{k_0}(u \| r \| c) \neq F_{k_0}(u \| r \| c')$, it means the failure of shared keys' negotiation.

The structure of fuzzy negotiation is shown by Fig.1.

4.2 Correctness of Fuzzy Negotiation

For simplicity, we define $f(\cdot)$ as bitwise XOR operation $\oplus$, and then in procedure "Trans" v and u can be defined as $v=w \oplus c$ and $u=w \oplus c \oplus F_{k_0}(r)$ respectively.

Accordingly, P can be defined as: $< w \oplus c \oplus F_{k_0}(r), r, F_{k_0}(w \oplus c \oplus F_{k_0}(r) \| r \| c) >$, and the shared key can be defined as: $k_{shared} = F_{k_0}(F_{k_1}(w \oplus r))$.

In procedure "Rec", c^* can be defined as $c^* = f(v, w') = u \oplus F_{k_0}(r) \oplus w' = w \oplus c \oplus w' = e \oplus c$, where e is the difference between w and w'. If $e \le t$, procedure "Rec" can recover c by the error-correcting function $Dec(\cdot)$ which causes $F_{k_0}(u \| r \| c) = F_{k_0}(u \| r \| c')$. And then, procedure "Rec" can recover w by $w = f(v, c)$ to generate $k_{shared} = F_{k_0}(F_{k_1}(w \oplus r))$ that is shared with procedure "Trans". If $e > t$, procedure "Rec" cannot recover c effectively, and the key negotiation fails.

4.3 Security of fuzzy negotiation

Here we also define $f(\cdot)$ as bitwise XOR operation $\oplus$ .Let $l = 128$ bits, $f(\cdot): \{0,1\}^{128} \times \{0,1\}^{128} \to \{0,1\}^{128}$, and $F_{k_0}(\cdot): \{0,1\}^{128} \to \{0,1\}^{128}$. In the following, we analyze security of fuzzy negotiation according to the two attack games: adaptive chosen biometric data attack game and adaptive chosen commitments attack game. Firstly, we suppose that a 128-bit value is secure to the exhaustive attack, the adversary can get biometric value w by RCB attack, and the error-correcting code C is open.

In the former attack game, when the adversary gets commitment $P = < w \oplus c \oplus F_{k_0}(r), r, F_{k_0}(w \oplus c \oplus F_{k_0}(r) \| r \| c) >$, it can compute $F_{k_0}(r)$. Since $F_{k_0}(\cdot)$ is a keyed one-way function, the adversary only can guess the right k_0 from $F_{k_0}(r)$ and r with a negligible probability. Then, we can say that though the adversary can get a biometric value by RCB attack and its commitment by eavesdropping, it only finds the relationship between them with a negligible probability. In other words, the adversary wins the former attack game with a negligible probability. In the situation, the adversary cannot launch RCB attack to a biometric value which he cannot capture remotely, as he cannot deduce the biometric value by its public commitment. This can protect these biometric data from being known by the adversary.

In the latter attack game, the adversary can get enough pairs of w and $Rec(K, \delta(w), P, C) = F_{k_0}(F_{k_1}(w \oplus r))$. Though w, r and $F_{k_0}(F_{k_1}(w \oplus r))$ are known to the adversary, it will search the key space of $2^{128} \times 2^{128}$ before getting the right k_0 and k_1, which is an infeasible task. Then, without k_0 and k_1, the adversary can hardly compute the relationship between the commitment of w and the shared key k_{shared}, even given w, $\delta(w)$ and C. So, we can say that the adversary wins the latter attack game with a negligible probability.

It is worthy to note that, in fuzzy negotiation we don't require w must be a high-entropy biometric value. The reason is that in the equation $k_{shared} = F_{k_0}(F_{k1}(w \oplus r))$, r is a random value and $F_k(\cdot)$ is a keyed pseudo-random function, which causes the input of $F_{k_0}(\cdot)$ is a secret value that is computing-indistinguishable from a uniformly random value even w is a constant value. Thus, in the "key queries" step of the adaptive chosen commitments attack game, the adversary cannot obtain any knowledge of k_{shared} from w. So, in our fuzzy negotiation structure, biometric values with any entropy can be used to establish shared keys.

5 Conclusions

Up to now, many researches have been made to design key negotiation methods based on physiological signals, however they come up short in respects of practicality and security. In the paper, we merge fuzzy extractor technology with technology of predistributed keys and pseudo-function to design a new key negotiation method called as fuzzy negotiation. Fuzzy negotiation not only can use physiological signals with any entropy to negotiate shared keys, but also can use predistributed keys to resist the new RCB attack, which make the method is superior to existing key negotiation methods based on fuzzy commitment and fuzzy extractor in terms of practicality and security.

Acknowledgement

This work was supported in part by Shandong Provincial Natural Science Foundation (ZR2011FL027, ZR2012FM005), National Natural Science Foundation (61101162\61101085\61272091), Jinan Independent Innovation Foundation of Universities and Institutes (201202009)

References

[1] J. Zhang, Y. Xiang, Y. Wang, W. Zhou, Y. Xiang, and Y. Guan, "Network traffic classification using correlation information", *IEEE Transactions on Parallel and Distributed Systems*, vol. 24, no. 1, pp.104-117, 2013.

[2] S. Cesare, Y. Xiang, and W. Zhou, "Malwise - An effective and efficient classification system for packed and polymorphic malware", *IEEE Transactions on Computers*, vol. 62, no. 6, pp. 1193-1206, 2013.

[3] J. Zhang, C. Chen, Y. Xiang, W. Zhou, and Y. Xiang, "Internet traffic classification by aggregating correlated Naive Bayes predictions", *IEEE Transactions on Information Forensics and Security*, vol. 8, no. 1, pp. 5-15, 2013.

[4] Y. Xiang, D. Peng, Y. Xiang, and S. Guo, "A novel Z-domain precoding method for blind separation of spatially

correlated signals", *IEEE Transactions on Neural Networks and Learning Systems*, vol. 24, no. 1, pp. 94-105, 2013.

[5] W. Khan, Y. Xiang, M. Aalsalem, and Q. Arshad, "Mobile phone sensing systems: A survey", *IEEE Communications Surveys and Tutorials*, vol. 15, no. 1, pp. 402-407, 2013.

[6] J. Zhang, Y. Xiang, W. Zhou, and Y. Wang, "Unsupervised traffic classification using flow statistical properties and IP packet payload", *Journal of Computer and System Sciences*, vol. 79, no. 5, pp. 573-585, 2013.

[7] J. Hu, Y. Tang, K. Xi, "Correlation keystroke verification scheme for user access control in cloud computing environment," *Computer Journal*, vol. 54, Issue 10, pp.1632-1644, 2011.

[8] J. Hu, I. Khalil, S. Han, A. Mahmood, "Seamless integration of dependability and security concepts in SOA: A feedback control system based framework and taxonomy," *Journal of Network and Computer Applications*, vol. 34, Issue 4, pp.1150-1159, 2011.

[9] B. Tian, S. Han, S. Parvin, J. Hu, S. Das, "Self-healing key distribution schemes for wireless networks: A survey," *Computer Journal*, vol. 54, Issue 4, pp.549-569, 2011.

[10] A.N. Mahmood, J. Hu, Z. Tari, C. Leckie, "Critical infrastructure protection: Resource efficient sampling to improve detection of less frequent patterns in network traffic," *Journal of Network and Computer Applications*, vol. 33, Issue 4, pp. 491-502, 2010.

[11] J. Hu, D. Gingrich, and A. Sentosa, "A k-nearest neighbor approach for user authentication through biometric keystroke dynamics," *Proc. of IEEE International Conference on Communications*, pp.1556-1560, 2008.

[12] F. Han, X. Yu, Y. Feng, and J. Hu, "On multiscroll chaotic attractors in hysteresis-based piecewise-linear systems, " *IEEE Transactions on Circuits and Systems II: Express Briefs*, Vol. 54, Issue 11, pp.1004-1008, 2007.

[13] J.Hu, "Mobile fingerprint template protection: Progress and open issues, " *The 3rd IEEE Conference on Industrial Electronics and Applications* Singapore, pp. 2133-2138, 2008.

[14] P. Zhang, J. Hu, C. Li, M. Bennamoun, and V. Bhagavatula, "A pitfall in fingerprint bio-cryptographic key generation, " *Computers and Security*, vol. 30, Issue 5, pp. 311-319, 2011.

[15] T. Gu, L. Wang, H.H. Chen, X.P. Tao, J. Lu, "Recongnizing multiuser activities using wireless body sensor networks," *IEEE Trans. Mobile Computing*, vol. 10, no. 11, pp. 1618-1631, Nov. 2011, doi:10.1109/TMC.2011.43.

[16] C. Otto, A. Milenkovic, C. Sanders and E. Jovanov, "System architecture of a wireless body area sensor network for ubiquitous health monitoring," *J. Mobile Multimedia*, vol.1, no. 4, pp.307-326, Jan. 2005.

[17] F. Axisa, P. M. Schmitt, C. Gehin, G. Delhomme, E. McAdams, and A. Dittmar, "Flexible technologies and smart clothing for citizen medicine, home healthcare, and disease prevention," *IEEE Trans. Information Technologies in Biomedicine*, vol. 9, no. 3,pp.325-336, Setp. 2005,doi: 10.1109/TITB.2005.854505

[18] P. Lukowicz, U. Anliker, J. Ward, G. Troster, E. Hirt, and C. Neufelt,"AMON: A wearable computer for high risk patients," *Proc. 6th International Symposium on Wearable Computers*, Washington, pp. 133-134, 2002.

[19] J. Hu, H.H. Chen, T.W. Hou,"A hybrid public key infrastructure solution(HPKI) for HIPAA privacy/security regulations," *Computer Standards and Interface*,vol.32,no.5-6, pp. 274-280, 2010.

[20] Y. Wang, J.Hu and D. Philip, "A fingerprint orientation model based on 2D Fourier Expansion (FOMFE) and its application to singular-point detection and fingerprint Indexing," *Special Issue on Biometrics: Progress and Directions, IEEE Transactions on Pattern Analysis and Machine Intelligence*, April 2007, pp.573-585.

[21] H.W. Zhao, J.K. Hu, J. Qin, V. Varadharajan, "Hashed random key pre-distrbution scheme for large heterogenerous sensor networks," *Proc. IEEE 11th International Conference on Trust, Security and Privacy in Computing and Communications*, pp. 706-713,2012.

[22] H.W. Zhao, J. Qin, M.L. Shu, J.K. Hu, "A hash chains based key management scheme for wireless sensor networks," *Lecture Notes in Computer Science, LNCS Vol. 7672, pp.296-308, 2012..*

[23] K. Xi, T. Ahmad, F.Han, and J. Hu, "A fingerprint based bio-cryptographic security protocol designed for client/server authentication in mobile computing environment," *Special Issue on Biometric Security for Mobile Computing, Journal of Security and Communication Networks*, John Wiley, vol. 4, issue 5, 2011, pp. 487-499.

[24] S. Cherukuri, K. K. Venkatasubramanian, and S. K. S. Gupta, "Biosec: A biometric based approach for securing communication in wireless networks of biosensors implanted in the Human body," *Proc. 32nd International Conference on Parallel Processing (ICPP '03)*, pp. 432–439, Oct. 2003.

[25] A. Juels and M. Wattenberg, "A fuzzy commitment scheme," *Proc. 6th ACM Conf. Computer and Communication Security(CSS'99)*, pp. 28–36, Nov.1999.

[26] F.M. Bui, D. Hatzinakos, "Biometric methods for secure communications in body sensor networks resource-efficient key management and signal-level data scrambling," *EURASIP J. Adavances in Signal Processing*, vol. 2008,pp.1-16, Jan. 2008, doi:10.1155/2008/529879.

[27] S. Mesmoudi, M. Feham, "BSK-WBSN-Biometric symmetric keys to secure wireless body sensors networks," *Int.J. Network Security& Its Applications*, vol.3, no.5, pp.155-166, Oct. 2011, doi: 10.5121/ijnsa.2011.3512.

[28] K. K. Venkatasubramanian and S.K.S. Gupta, "Security for pervasive health monitoring sensor applications," *Proc. 4th Int. Conf. Intelligent Sensing and Information Processing*, pp. 197-202, Dec. 2006, doi: 10.1109/ICISIP.2006.4286096.

[29] S.D. Bao, L.F. Shen, and Y.T. Zhang, "A novel key distribution of body area networks for telemedicine," *Proc. IEEE Int. Workshop on Biomedical Circuits and Systems*, pp. 1–11,20a, Dec. 2004,doi: 10.1109/BIOCAS.2004.1454091.

[30] Y. Dodis, L. Reyzin, A. Smith, "Fuzzy extractors: How to generate strong keys from biometrics and other noisy data," *Proc. Advances in Cryptology- Eurocrypt' 04*, pp. 523-540, 2004.

[31] X. Boyen, "Reusable cryptographic fuzzy extractors," *The 11th ACM Conf. Computer and Communications Security*, pp.82-91, Oct. 2004, doi: 10.1145/1030083.1030096.

[32] Y.Dodis, L. Reyzin, A. Smith, " Fuzzy extractor, A brief survey of results from 2004 to 2006," Security with Noisy Data. Heidelberg: Springer, 2007, ch5.

[33] K. Simoens,P. Tuyls and B. Preneel, "Privacy weaknesses of biometric sketches," *IEEE Symp. Security and Privacy*, pp. 188–203, Aug. 2009, doi: 10.1109/SP.2009.24.

[34] M. Blanton, M. Aliasgari, "On the (Non-) reusability of fuzzy sketches and extractors and security in the computational setting," *Proc. Int. Conf. Security and Cryptography*, pp.68-77, Jul.2011.

[35] Y.Dodis, B. Kanukurthi, J.Katz, L. Reyzin, A. Smith "Robust fuzzy extractors and authenticated key agreement from close secrets," *IEEE Trans. Information Theory*, vol.59,no.9, pp.6207-6222, 2012.

Performance Evaluation of Two-Dimensional Distributed Factoring Self-Scheduling Scheme for Heterogeneous Computer Systems

Satish Penmatsa and Abel Oji

Department of Mathematics and Computer Science
University of Maryland Eastern Shore
Princess Anne, MD 21853, USA

Abstract - *A major characteristic of distributed computing systems is their heterogeneity. In practical computing, the computers or processing elements that make up any given distributed system may have varying processing speeds. Efficient loop scheduling schemes for concurrent processing of computational tasks on such systems need to take into consideration, the varying speeds of the component processors. In this paper we evaluate the performance of a two-dimensional distributed factoring self-scheduling scheme for parallel loops by comparing with its one-dimensional counterpart. The schemes are implemented on the Ranger Computer Cluster at the Texas Advanced Computing Center with varying number of processors and problem sizes.*

Key words: Load balancing, scheduling, parallel loops, heterogeneity, distributed systems.

1. Introduction

Distributed computing systems are often used to solve computation intensive scientific problems. These computation intensive problems or applications often consist of parallel code which when scheduled for concurrent execution can reduce the total execution of the application significantly. Parallel code can be in the form of loops with or without any dependencies between the loop iterations. Parallel loops without dependencies are commonly known as DOALL loops [1] and loops with dependencies among the iterations are known as DOACROSS loops [2].

However, scheduling in large-scale distributed systems for achieving a load balanced execution that minimizes the loop completion time is not straightforward. Factors such as the non-uniformity of iterate execution times and geographic distribution of the computing and communication resources lead to application performance degradation. Hence, efficient loop scheduling schemes are invaluable for improving the performance of applications on distributed systems. Also, the computing resources (processors) of distributed systems are usually heterogeneous (*e.g.* have different speeds). Hence, efficient loop scheduling schemes should consider the heterogeneity into account in making allocation decisions.

Loop scheduling schemes which do not take the heterogeneity of a distributed system into account are called 'simple' schemes whereas the schemes that take the heterogeneity of the system into account are called 'distributed' schemes. Also, depending on when the scheduling decisions are made, loop scheduling can be categorized into 'static' and 'dynamic'. Static scheduling schemes determine the task allocation to the processors prior to the execution of the application. Dynamic scheduling (or self-scheduling) is an automatic loop scheduling method in which idle processors request new loop iterations to be assigned to them during run time.

2. Related Work and Contribution

Various simple and distributed loop scheduling schemes have been proposed and analyzed in the past. For example, please see [3 - 10] and references therein. Some loop scheduling schemes partition only the outermost loop of a program loop structure and assign tasks (chunks of iterations) to the processors. This may not be efficient for multi-dimensional nested loops. Studies on two-dimensional (2D) loop scheduling can be found in [4, 9, 10] and references therein.

In this paper we evaluate the performance of a two-dimensional distributed factoring self-scheduling scheme (DFSS-2D) for parallel loops by comparing with its one-dimensional counterpart (DFSS-1D). The schemes are implemented on the Ranger Computer Cluster at the Texas Advanced Computing Center with varying number of processors and problem sizes. Preliminary results related to the above can be found in [10].

3. Two-Dimensional Distributed Factoring Self-Scheduling

Self-scheduling is an automatic loop scheduling method in which idle computers (or processors) (PEs) request new loop iterations to be assigned to them [2, 9, 10]. These self-scheduling schemes are based on the Master-Slave (Master-Worker) architecture model. In a generic self-scheduling scheme, at the *i*-th scheduling step, the master computes the chunk-size (a few consecutive iterations) C_i, a starting (iteration) index *istart*, and the remaining number of tasks (iterations) R_i as follows:

Initially, $R_0 = I$, *istart* = J (lower loop bound). The Master PE computes the chunk-size for the *i*-th scheduling step as:

$$C_i = f(R_{i-1}, p)$$

where *p* is the number of processors. The function f( ) can possibly have more inputs than just R_{i-1} and p. Then the master assigns to a slave PE C_i tasks and a starting (iteration) index *istart*. Then the *istart* and R_i for the next scheduling step are updated as:

$$istart = istart + C_i \qquad R_i = R_{i-1} - C_i$$

Factoring Self –Scheduling (FSS): FSS consists of rounds of p scheduling steps. In each round i_r the master distributes $\lceil R_{i_r-1}/2 \rceil$ iterations to the p workers. Thus, $C_{p \times i_r + n} = \lceil R_{i_r-1}/2p \rceil$ for $n = 1, \dots, p$ and the remaining iterations are $R_{i_r} = R_{i_r-1} / 2$.

One dimensional self-scheduling schemes partition only the outermost loop of a nested loop construct. Two dimensional self-scheduling schemes partition both the outer loop and the inner loop of a two-level nested loop construct.

To offer load balancing in heterogeneous distributed systems, loop scheduling schemes must take into account the processing speeds of the computers forming the system. Here, the relative computing powers of the processors in the system are used as weights that scale the size of the sub-problem each processor is assigned to compute [9, 10]. This can significantly reduce the total execution time when a heterogeneous computing environment is used.

The methodology for computing the two-dimensional chunks is described in [9]. The two-dimensional chunks will be allocated to the worker processors by the master PE based on the worker available powers. A worker with higher available power will be allocated more chunks than compared to a worker with lower available power.

The algorithm for Two-Dimensional Distributed Factoring Self-Scheduling (DFSS-2D) is similar to the Two-Dimensional Distributed Trapezoid Self-Scheduling (DTSS-2D) presented in [9] with Two-Dimensional Trapezoid Self-Scheduling (TSS-2D) replaced by Two-Dimensional Factoring Self-Scheduling (FSS-2D).

4. Implementation and Results

The scheduling schemes are implemented in C++ using the distributed programming framework offered by the Message Passing Interface (MPI) [11]. The Sun Constellation Linux Cluster named Ranger at the Texas Advanced Computing Center (TACC) [12] at the University of Texas at Austin is used for the experiments.

The schemes are evaluated with the number of slave (worker) PEs ranging from 4 to 12. The test problem used is the Mandelbrot computation [13]. The Mandelbrot computation is a doubly nested loop without any dependencies. The schemes are evaluated with the problem sizes ranging from 8000 x 8000 to 32000 x 32000. To simulate a heterogeneous system (processing elements with varying speeds), we added loads (continuously running matrix multiplication process) in the background on half of the slave processors considered to reduce their available power.

In the following, we present the experimental results for various problem sizes and number of slave processors. T_p denotes the total execution time (for a given problem size) measured on the master processor. The times presented for the worker processors are their total compute times for the iterations assigned to them by the master processor. All timings are in seconds (s) and milliseconds (ms).

Table's 1 - 11 present the T_p of DFSS-1D and DFSS-2D with varying number of slave PEs and problem sizes. It can be observed that DFSS-2D shows substantial performance improvement compared to DFSS-1D. It can also be observed that the slave computation times in the case of DFSS-2D are very well load balanced compared to DFSS-1D.

Table 1. Slave PEs: 4, Problem Size: 8000x8000

PE	DFSS-1D	DFSS-2D
1	35s 954ms	10s 515ms
2	42s 635ms	12s 471ms
3	41s 924ms	10s 512ms
4	45s 910ms	10s 835ms
Tp	45s 913ms	12s 474ms

Table 2. Slave PEs: 4, Problem Size: 16000x16000

PE	DFSS-1D	DFSS-2D
1	143s 784ms	47s 907ms
2	170s 424ms	52s 559ms
3	169s 910ms	61s 739ms
4	185s 830ms	52s 140ms
Tp	185s 830ms	61s 739ms

Table 3. Slave PEs: 4, Problem Size: 32000x32000

PE	DFSS-1D	DFSS-2D
1	574s 919ms	207s 4ms
2	681s 869ms	174s 635ms
3	681s 867ms	230s 141ms
4	739s 343ms	212s 307ms
Tp	739s 344ms	230s 144ms

Table 4. Slave PEs: 6, Problem Size: 8000x8000

PE	DFSS-1D	DFSS-2D
1	26s 25ms	8s 206ms
2	24s 580ms	8s 526ms
3	29s 107ms	7s 532ms
4	28s 288ms	7s 959ms
5	24s 123ms	7s 529ms
6	32s 855ms	8s 631ms
Tp	32s 855ms	8s 631ms

Table 5. Slave PEs: 6, Problem Size: 16000x16000

PE	DFSS-1D	DFSS-2D
1	103s 933ms	31s 95ms
2	98s 240ms	31s 850ms
3	116s 569ms	32s 724ms
4	114s 148ms	33s 552ms
5	97s 955ms	31s 111ms
6	132s 703ms	32s 814ms
Tp	132s 704ms	33s 553ms

Table 6. Slave PEs: 6, Problem Size: 32000x32000

PE	DFSS-1D	DFSS-2D
1	415s 792ms	124s 513ms
2	393s 5ms	127s 307ms
3	466s 243ms	130s 786ms
4	458s 797ms	135s 54ms
5	393s 680ms	125s 938ms
6	533s 782ms	131s 643ms
Tp	533s 783ms	135s 54ms

Table 7. Slave PEs: 8, Problem Size: 32000x32000

PE	DFSS-1D	DFSS-2D
1	288s 278ms	104s 214ms
2	291s 212ms	102s 416ms
3	294s 968ms	104s 127ms
4	364s 486ms	102s 416ms
5	356s 768ms	121s 566ms
6	368s 260ms	102s 413ms
7	334s 648ms	111s 421ms
8	404s 822ms	102s 615ms
Tp	404s 823ms	121s 567ms

Table 8. Slave PEs: 10, Problem Size: 8000x8000

PE	DFSS-1D	DFSS-2D
1	15s 309ms	4s 987ms
2	15s 44ms	4s 987ms
3	14s 980ms	4s 987ms
4	15s 846ms	5s 13ms
5	18s 924ms	5s 10ms
6	17s 207ms	5s 504ms
7	16s 163ms	5s 849ms
8	14s 988ms	5s 41ms
9	19s 499ms	5s 199ms
10	20s 930ms	5s 401ms
Tp	20s 930ms	5s 850ms

Table 9. Slave PEs: 10, Problem Size: 16000x16000

PE	DFSS-1D	DFSS-2D
1	61s 141ms	19s 991ms
2	60s 136ms	20s 413ms
3	59s 852ns	19s 992ms
4	63s 231ms	19s 991ms
5	73s 903ms	19s 991ms
6	71s 858ms	20s 685ms
7	64s 137ms	21s 982ms
8	79s 836ms	21s 414ms
9	56s 162ms	22s 458ms
10	74s 74ms	20s 115ms
Tp	79s 837ms	22s 459ms

Table 10. Slave PEs: 10, Problem Size: 32000x32000

PE	DFSS-1D	DFSS-2D
1	246s 466ms	82s 46ms
2	240s 546ms	81s 240ms
3	239s 118ms	79s 760ms
4	253s 925ms	79s 760ms
5	295s 925ms	79s 760ms
6	288s 75ms	79s 756ms
7	258s 662ms	87s 809ms
8	226s 661ms	92s 604ms
9	298s 9ms	77s 993ms
10	321s 653ms	88s 532ms
Tp	322s 62ms	92s 605ms

Table 11. Slave PEs: 12, Problem Size: 32000x32000

PE	DFSS-1D	DFSS-2D
1	194s 2ms	68s 790ms
2	197s 305ms	69s 500ms
3	183s 542ms	67s 59ms
4	195s 921ms	67s 59ms
5	224s 86ms	67s 121ms
6	246s 1ms	67s 59ms
7	241s 670ms	68s 438ms
8	209s 829ms	66s 992ms
9	261s 984ms	70s 972ms
10	206s 643ms	67s 96ms
11	264s 979ms	69s 696ms
12	266s 553ms	71s 854ms
Tp	266s 554ms	72s 106ms

5. Conclusions

In this paper, we compared the performance of Two-Dimensional Distributed Factoring Self-Scheduling scheme (DFSS-2D) with its One-Dimensional counterpart (DFSS-1D). The schemes are implemented and their performance compared using the Ranger high performance computing cluster. Results showed that DFSS-2D performs substantially better compared to DFSS-1D and also present a more balanced load distribution of the workload among the computers in the system.

References

[1] A. Kejariwal, A. Nicolau, and C. Polychronopoulos, History-aware self-scheduling, *International Conference on Parallel Processing*, pp. 185–192, Aug 2006, Columbus, OH.

[2] F. M. Ciorba, I. Riakiotakis, T. Andronikos, G. Papakonstantinou, and A. T. Chronopoulos, Enhancing self-scheduling algorithms via synchronization and weighting, *Journal of Parallel and Distributed Computing*, vol. 68, no. 2, pp. 246–264, 2008.

[3] I. Banicescu, F. M. Ciorba, and R. L. Carino, Towards the robustness of dynamic loop scheduling on large-scale heterogeneous distributed systems, *The 8th International Symposium on Parallel and Distributed Computing*, Page(s): 129 - 132, June 30 - July 4, 2009, Lisbon.

[4] R. L. Carino and I. Banicescu, A dynamic load balancing tool for one and two dimensional parallel loops, *The 5th International Symposium on Parallel and Distributed Computing*, Page(s): 107 - 114, 6-9 July 2006, Timisoara.

[5] F. M. Ciorba, T. Hansen, S. Srivastava, I. Banicescu, A. A. Maciejewski, and H. J. Siegel, A Combined Dual-stage Framework for Robust Scheduling of Scientific Applications in Heterogeneous Environments with Uncertain Availability, *26th IEEE International Parallel and Distributed Processing Symposium Workshops & PhD Forum*, Page(s): 193 - 207, 21-25 May 2012, Shanghai.

[6] J. Herrera, E. Huedo, R. S. Montero, and I. M. Llorente, Loosely-coupled loop scheduling in computational grids, *Proc. of the 20th IEEE Intl. Parallel and Distributed Processing Symp.*, Rhodes Island, Greece, 25 - 29 April 2006.

[7] J. Diaz, S. Reyes, A. Nino, and C. Munoz-Caro, Derivation of self-scheduling algorithms for heterogeneous distributed computer systems: Application to internet-based grids of computers, *Future Generation Computer Systems, Elsevier Publishers*, vol. 25, no. 6, pp. 617-626, 2009.

[8] C. T. Yang, C. C. Wu, and J. H. Chang, Performance-based parallel loop self-scheduling using hybrid openMP and MPI programming on multicore SMP clusters, *Concurrency and Computation: Practice and Experience*, vol. 23, no. 8, pp. 721-744, 2011.

[9] A. T. Chronopoulos, L. M. Ni, and S. Penmatsa, Multidimensional dynamic loop scheduling algorithms, *IEEE International Conference on Cluster Computing*, Austin, TX, 17-20 Sept. 2007, pp. 241 – 248.

[10] A. T. Chronopoulos, S. Penmatsa, N. Jayakumar, and E. Ogharandukun, Two-Dimensional Dynamic Loop Scheduling Schemes for Computer Clusters, *Proceedings of the 11th IEEE International Symposium on Network Computing and Applications*, Cambridge, MA, USA, August 23-25, 2012.

[11] P. Pachecho, Parallel Programming with MPI. *Morgan Kauffman*, 1997.

[12] http://www.tacc.utexas.edu.

[13] M. F. Bransley, R. L. Devaney, B. B. Mandelbrot, H. O. Peitgen, D. Saupe, R. F. Voss, Y. Fisher, and M. McGuire, The Science of Fractal Images, NY: Springer-Verlag, 1988.

A Method for Eliminating Abnormal Values of Received Signal Strength Indicator (RSSI) in WLAN

Yanfang Jing[1,2], Minglei Shu[2],Ming Yang[2],Huawei Zhao[3,2], Jiankun Hu[4,2]
[1]School of Computer Science, Liaocheng University, Liaocheng , China
[2]Shandong Provincial Key Laboratory of Computer Network, Shandong Computer Science Center, Ji'nan , China
[3]School of Computer Science and Technology, Shandong University of Finance and Economics, Ji'nan,China
[4]School of Engineering and Information Technology,University of New South Wales, Canberra, Australia

Abstract - *Received signal strength indicator plays a very important role in many WLAN applications. However wireless signal strength will be greatly affected by noise and disturbance. It is critical to remove the abnormal data in order to provide a reliable estimation of the received signal strength indicator. Conventional mean value based approaches require large amount of data which would lead to unreliable results for applications with small amount of data. This paper proposes a practical method of capturing the received signal strength indicator in WLAN, and gives the improved Grubbs rule for effectively eliminating abnormal value of measuring signal strength.*

Keywords: WLAN; RSSI; abnormal value; Grubbs criterion

1 Introduction

Wireless communication signal propagates in the electromagnetic wave form in the atmospheric environment, and the signal strength will decrease with the increase of the propagation distance [1]. Measuring the RSSI (received signal strength indicator) is important for many applications, such as mobile device location [2], wireless channel estimation and transmission scheduling [3][4].

However, the measured values are different at each time. Even with the same measuring instruments and environments, some large abnormal values may appear during measurement, due to the external disturbance such as obstacles and people walking. Theoretically, we can obtain more accurate mathematical expectation value by calculating the average of infinitely measured values. But in the experiments especially in actual applications, we usually have limited measurements, so these abnormal values will greatly reduce the quality of measurement data, which leads to the significant variation in the result of statistical analysis. The skewed estimation can lead to incorrect overall reasoning, prediction and control actions. Therefore, identifying and eliminating abnormal data is very important.

2 A practical method for capturing packets in wlan

Most of Windows network applications achieve the network communication by the Winsock API of operating system, a kind of high-level programming interface which can access the TCP/IP protocol stack. The normal transmission path of data packet is via NIC card, device driver layer, data link layer, IP layer, transport layer, and application, respectively [5]. Through the third party capture components or libraries, such as WinPcap, network program can bypass the TCP/IP protocol stack of the operating system, add a bypass process in data link layer, filter and buffer the transmitted and received data packets, and finally passed directly to the application program. This packet capture mechanism can achieve some lower, more flexible network function than ordinary method, and do not influence the data packets process of operating system in network stack.

The conventional method of wireless packet capture is data sniffer based on LibPcap/WinPcap. But the loss rate of packets will increase rapidly with the network throughput increases, and the CPU occupancy rate is relatively large. In order to improve the performance of packet capture, this paper improves the method in the following aspects:

1) Using a special wireless network card. In the Linux platform, the common wireless NIC can be set to monitor mode. But most of the Windows driver does not support this function. This paper provides improved driver which can combine with a special network adapter to realize the mode conversion, whose core chip is Atheros AR9170 and can be applied to Windows platform and support RF monitoring mode.

2) Removing the step of filtering packages in the conventional acquisition process. The wireless network card cooperates with Winpcap to capture 802.11 a/b/g/n control, management and data frames. It can realize the multi-channel data acquisition by using the multichannel composite technology.

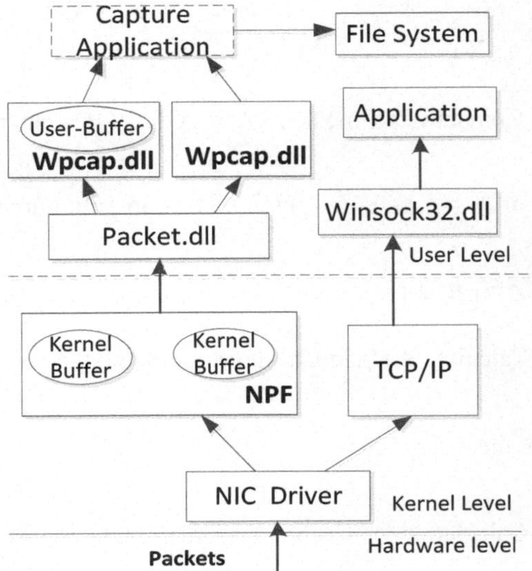

Figure 1. Architecture of Winpcap data packet capture

3) Using the improved packet process algorithm, we can directly read data package from the kernel buffer provided for application solution. By which we can reduce the CPU occupancy rate and packet loss rate, and can solve the packet loss problems when the network data packet is large (such as large file transfer). Fig 1 shows the process diagram about data packet capture using Winpcap.

3 Analysis of packet capture

In this paper, the network packet capture and analysis are implemented in Visual Studio 2012 under Windows 8. In order to improve the stability and efficiency of the whole system, a new thread is created from the main thread to complete the packet capture and analysis. The process of obtaining and processing RSSI by capturing and analyzing network packets from the wireless network card is illustrated in Fig 2.

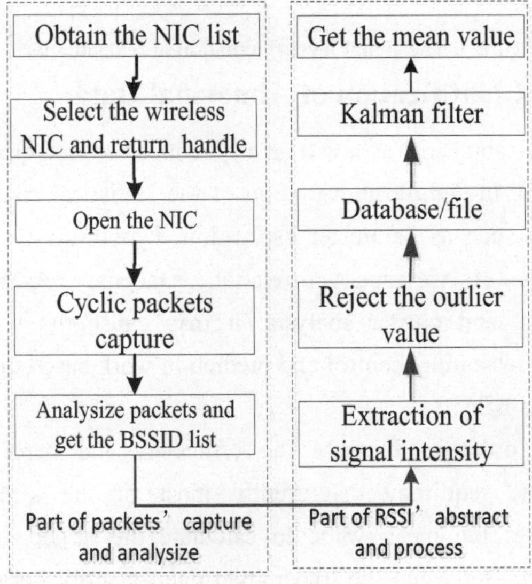

Figure 2. The procedure of packets capture and RSSI' process

The process module achieves real-time analysis of the captured data packets by defining a packet processing class. First it extracts the packet head, and obtains the information of channel, RSSI, receiving time etc, then according to the frame header structure defined in the 802.11 protocol it obtains the name and MAC address of each AP and STA, and subsequently establishes the AP list. Because each AP MAC address is different, so we can judge different AP's RSSI according to the MAC address.

4 Process of RSSI

RSSI plays a very important role in many applications. But the signal strength is highly sensitive to the environment [6]. Hence all kinds of interferences caused by uncertain external factors will affect the measurement accuracy. It can be seen from Fig 3 that the original data acquisition will show a great fluctuation. So recognition and elimination of RSSI singular value is an important step after extraction of signal intensity.

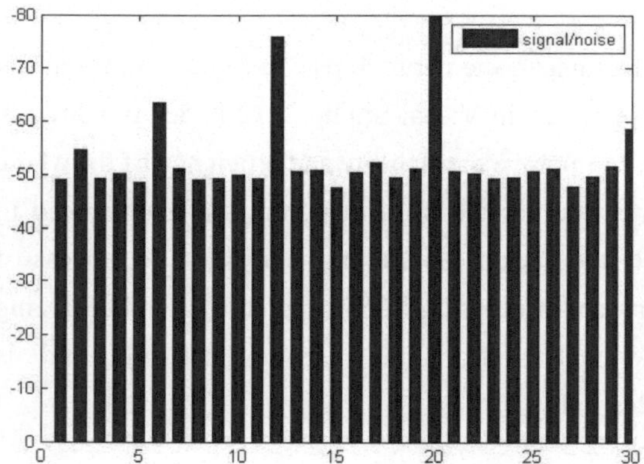

Figure 3. The signal level fluctuation in real situation

4.1 Identification of Abnormal Data

The abnormal data will greatly reduce the data quality, resulting in significant variation of the statistical analysis results, such as parameter estimation, hypothesis testing, analysis of variance, correlation analysis, regression analysis, and cluster analysis. It may cause the wrong overall reasoning, control and prediction work based on the noisy sample.

In order to improve the efficiency and meet the real-time requirement, currently most of the systems computes the mean value to calculate the target signal strength. But when the transmitted data quantity between the sending and receiving node is not enough, abnormal values of signal strength will produce large interference on the estimation results.

For repeated measurement data, these methods, such as Pauta criterion method, Chauvenet criterion method, Dixon criterion method, Grubbs criterion method, are commonly used to identify and eliminate outliers. In the case of small sample data size, Grubbs criterion method is internationally recommended. The working of the Grubbs is as follows extracting signal data, calculating the mean value and standard deviation, comparing the original data to the mean, identifying outlier and eliminating it. Grubbs' test detects one outlier at a time. This outlier is expunged from the dataset and the test is iterated until no outliers are detected.

In practical applications, the outliers in the collected signal strength data are significantly smaller in number than that of true values. When the data are few and the outliers are highly singular, the calculation of mean value and standard deviation will be influenced greatly by these abnormal data. In this case, the Grubbs' algorithm may not produce accurate and reliable results.

4.2 The Modified Grubbs Criterion

When RSSI data collected from some APs are few, the mean will be influenced greatly by these abnormal values. To address this problem, this paper proposes to use the median instead of the mean, as the Grubbs criterion. The median of a finite list of numbers can be found by arranging all the observations from lowest value to highest value and picking the middle one or the mean of the two middle values if there is an even number of observations. The median is obtained by sorting, and it is not affected by large or small data. Therefore, the median is more appropriate than mean in the Grubbs criterion method. It can effectively eliminate the shielding effect of the ipsilateral abnormal data, and getting the more robust result.

Suppose the number of repeated measurements is n and repeated measurement values are $X_i (i = 1, 2, ..., n)$, the modified Grubbs criterion method used for testing whether X_i is an abnormal value is given as below:

1) Sort X_i in an ascending order, i.e., X1≤X2≤…≤Xn.

2) Compute the median $\tilde{X} = X_{r+1}$ (n is an odd number) or $\tilde{X} = (X_r + X_{r+1})/2$ (n is an even number), in which $r = \lfloor n/2 \rfloor$;

3) Calculate the standard deviation using the median instead of the mean. $S = \sqrt{\frac{1}{n}\sum_{i=1}^{n}(X_i - \tilde{X})^2}$.

4) Calculation of Grubbs statistics, including lower Grubbs number $g(1)$ and upper Grubbs number $g(n)$.

$$g(1) = \frac{\tilde{X} - X_1}{S} \quad , \quad g(n) = \frac{X_n - \tilde{X}}{S}$$

In the formula: $\tilde{X}, s$ is the median and standard

deviation of n repeated measurement data;

5) For the significant level α (usually 0.05 or 0.01), according to α and n (n is the number of samples), select the Grubbs criterion number $T(n,\alpha)$ in table;

6) If $g(1) \geq T(n, \alpha)$, then X_1 is an abnormal data, remove it;

If $g(n) \geq T(n, \alpha)$, then X_n is an abnormal data, remove it;

7) Repeat the above steps and reject the abnormal values until all the abnormal values are eliminated.

It can be seen from Fig 4: we can get rid of 4 abnormal data in 30 sample data if the mean is used as the calculation factor in Grubbs criterion, while 6 abnormal values can be removed if the median based Grubbs criterion is adopted. The experimental results show that the improved Grubbs criterion can better reject the abnormal data.

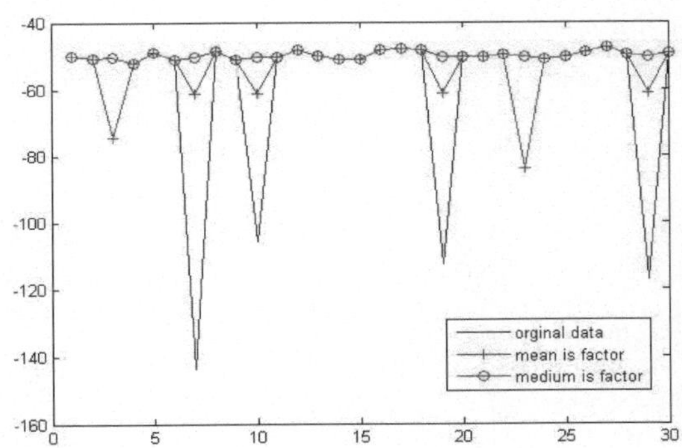

Figure 4. the impression drawing of rejecting the outlier

Because the Grubbs criterion is suitable for small sample data, when the number of data between the send and receive nodes is very large, we can take advantage of modified Grubbs criterion based on data grouping calculation. In the process of realization, we store the collected signal strength of AP in memory as an array. Before these data are written into a file or database, we use the modified Grubbs criterion to reject the abnormal data.

4.3 Filtering the White Noise

Because wireless networks have wide coverage range, high transmission rate and short access time, it is susceptible to interference from channel. In the process of communication, due to the influence of various factors, wireless signal may produce diffraction, reflection or scattering, so there are many invalid redundant data in the collected signal strength. These data do not deviate obviously but fluctuate around a mean value, and we call them the white noise. In order to further improve the accuracy of data, we read all data from the database in which the outlier have been rejected, and filter the white noise by Kalman filter, then we can get a relatively stable signal strength range. The parameter of Kalman filter can be obtained by literature [7]. Finally, by calculating the mean we can get an expected value closer to the real value.

The original data and the processed data by the Grubbs criterion and Kalman filter are shown in Fig 5. From the results we can see that the method proposed is suitable for removing the white noise and singular values, and the mean of data accurately reflects the real value of signal strength.

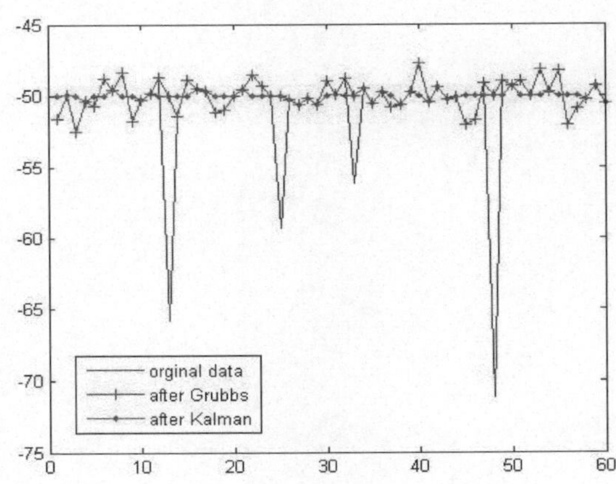

Figure 5. Comparison of original and processed data

5 Conclusion

This paper proposed an improved Grubbs criterion for processing RSSI data that contain significant singular abnormal data. The advantage is that it can deal with small sample data size A practical method of wireless transmission packet capturing has also been proposed. Numberic experiments have been conducted to validate the proposed scheme.

6 References

[1] Wang Xiaoying, Chen Yingge, Mine Location Algorithm Based on Multiple Linear Regression, Applied Mechanics and Materials, Pages 1830-1835,June 2011.

[2] Cui Huanqing, Wang yinglong, Multi-mobile-beacon assisted distributed node localization scheme, Journal on Communications, Pages 103-111, Mar 2012.

[3] Li, P., Guo, S., Hu, J. and Sarker, R. (2012), Lifetime optimization for reliable broadcast and multicast in wireless ad hoc networks. Wireless Communication and Mobile Computing, doi: 10.1002/wcm.1247.

[4] S. Wang, and J. Hu, Blind channel estimation for single-input multiple-output OFDM systems: Zero padding based or cyclic prefix based? Wireless Communication and Mobile Computting, Volume 13, Issue 2, Pages 204-210, Feb 2013.

[5] Zhang Panyong, Wang Dawei, Network packet capture oriented INIC design and implementation, Journal on Communication, Pages 125-130 , Feb 2006.

[6] Liu Ruiqiang, Detection of RSSI anomalies in CDMA Network, Modern Science & Technology of Telecommunications, Pages 93-96,Feb 2012.

[7] R.K.k，V.Apte, Y.A Powar. Improving the accuracy of wireless Lan based location Determination system using Kalman Filter and Multiple Observes, proceedings of wireless Communications and Networking Conference, Las Vegas, 2006.